INTERNATIONAL FISHING

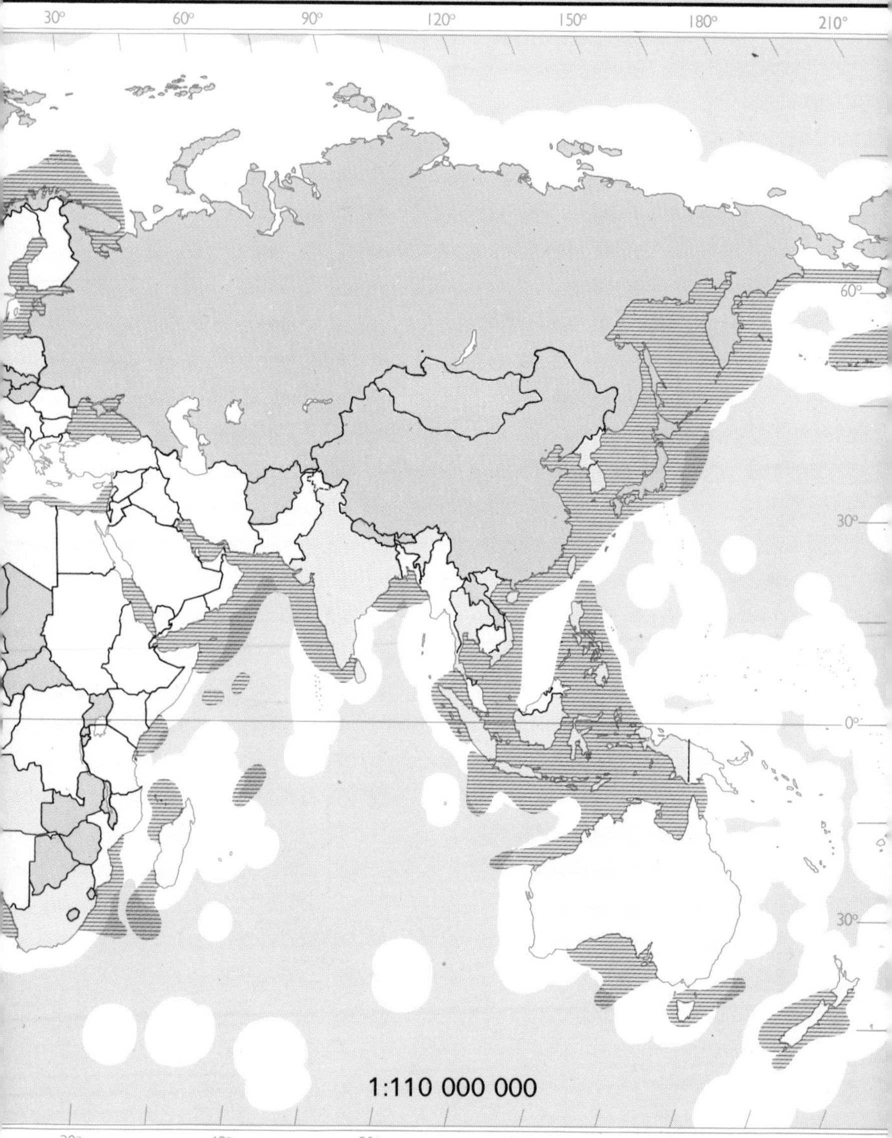
30°
60°
90°
120°
150°
180°
210°
60°
30°
0°
30°
1:110 000 000
30°
60°
90°
120°
150°
180°

THE STATESMAN'S YEAR-BOOK

1981–1982

Man hat behauptet, die Welt werde durch Zahlen regiert:
das aber weiss ich, dass die Zahlen uns belehren, ob sie gut
oder schlecht regiert werde.   GOETHE

Editors

THE
STATESMAN'S
YEAR-BOOK

STATISTICAL AND HISTORICAL ANNUAL
OF THE STATES OF THE WORLD
FOR THE YEAR

1981–1982

EDITED BY

JOHN PAXTON

ST. MARTIN'S PRESS
NEW YORK

First published in 1864
118th edition 1981

For information, write:
ST. MARTIN'S PRESS, INC.
175 Fifth Ave., New York, N.Y. 10010

Printed in Great Britain by
RICHARD CLAY (THE CHAUCER PRESS) LTD.
Bungay, Suffolk

Library of Congress Catalog Card Number 4–3776

ISBN 0–312–76094–9

This edition published United States of America 1981

PREFACE

When THE STATESMAN'S YEAR-BOOK was computer-set in 1978 the editor brought about some fundamental changes to the format and these were well received. In this the 118th edition there are further improvements. Great emphasis has been placed on the French overseas departments and territories and French-speaking countries. The former Condominium of New Hebrides is now Vanuatu and specially prepared maps show 'World Islam' and 'International Fishing'. The editor regrets that, at the time of going to press, many of the US Ambassadors to be appointed under the new administration were not known.

Again the editor would like to thank all his correspondents for superb help during the year and would like to reiterate that he is always pleased to receive constructive and informed criticism. Sometimes it is not possible to bring about change immediately but all suggestions are considered.

The second edition of THE STATESMAN'S YEAR-BOOK WORLD GAZETTEER is available for those who need more detailed information about individual towns.

J.P.

THE STATESMAN'S YEAR-BOOK OFFICE,
THE MACMILLAN PRESS LTD,
LITTLE ESSEX STREET,
LONDON, WC2R 3LF

WEIGHTS AND MEASURES

On 1 Jan. 1960 following an agreement between the standards laboratories of Great Britain, Canada, Australia, New Zealand, South Africa and the USA, an international yard and an international pound (avoirdupois) came into existence. 1 yard = 91·44 centimetres; 1 lb. = 453·59237 grammes.

The abbreviation 'm.' signifies 'million(s)' and tonnes implies metric tons.

LENGTH		DRY MEASURE	
Centimetre	0·394 inch	Litre	0·91 quart
Metre	1·094 yards	Hectolitre	2·75 bushels
Kilometre	0·621 mile		

WEIGHT—AVOIRDUPOIS

LIQUID MEASURE		WEIGHT—AVOIRDUPOIS	
		Gramme	15·42 grains
		Kilogramme	2·205 pounds
Litre	1·75 pints	Quintal (= 100 kg)	220·46 pounds
Hectolitre	22 gallons	Tonne (= 1,000 kg)	{ 0·984 long ton { 1·102 short tons

SURFACE MEASURE		WEIGHT—TROY	
Square metre	10·76 sq. feet	Gramme	15·43 grains
Hectare	2·47 acres	Kilogramme	{ 32·15 ounces { 2·68 pounds
Square kilometre	0·386 sq. mile		

BRITISH WEIGHTS AND MEASURES

LENGTH		WEIGHT	
1 foot	0·305 metre	1 ounce (= 437·2 grains)	28·350 grammes
1 yard	0·914 metre	1 lb. (= 7,000 grains)	453·6 grammes
1 mile (= 1,760 yds)	1·609 kilometres	1 cwt. (= 112 lb.)	50·802 kilogrammes
		1 long ton (= 2,240 lb.)	1·016 tonnes
		1 short ton (= 2,000 lb.)	0·907 tonne

SURFACE MEASURE		LIQUID MEASURE	
1 sq. foot	9·290 sq. decimetres	1 pint	0·568 litre
1 sq. yard	0·836 sq. metre	1 gallon	4·546 litres
1 acre	0·405 hectare	1 quarter	2·909 hectolitres
1 sq. mile	2·590 sq. kilometres		

CONTENTS

Part I: International Organizations

Part II: Countries of the World A–Z

CONTENTS

CONTENTS

xii   CONTENTS

MAPS

World Islam

International Fishing

WHEAT

Countries	Area (1,000 hectares)					Production (1,000 tonnes)				
	Average 1969–71	1976	1977	1978	1979	Average 1969–71	1976	1977	1978	1979
Algeria	2,214	2,295	1,907	1,864	1,700	1,359	1,630	827	1,083	1,200
Argentina	4,402	6,428	3,910	4,685	4,564*	5,873	11,000	5,300	8,100	7,800
Australia[1]	7,695	8,956	9,955	10,189	11,580	9,014	11,667	9,370	18,250	16,100
Bulgaria[1,2]	1,023	793	774	935	770	2,899	3,152	3,028	3,466	3,000
Canada	7,669	11,252	10,114	10,584	10,500	13,901	23,587	19,862	21,146	17,746
Chile[1]	737	698	628	580	560	1,296	866	1,219	893	995
China[1]	28,336	31,001	35,001	36,001	40,001	31,005	45,001	45,001	52,002	60,003
Czechoslovakia[2]	1,076	1,276	1,281	1,270	1,100	3,436	4,807	5,214	5,601	4,400
Egypt[1]	551	590	509	584	584	1,509	1,962	1,699	1,942	1,856
France	3,892	4,275	4,109	4,166	4,063	14,112	16,126	17,350	20,970	13,393
Germany, Fed. Rep. of[2]	1,511	1,632	1,599	1,619	1,609	6,268	6,702	7,235	8,118	7,971
Greece	1,010	934	939	994	960*	1,867	2,450	1,766	2,734	2,411*
Hungary[1,3]	1,289	1,325	1,312	1,326*	1,135	3,410	5,148	5,319	5,677	3,706
India	16,941	20,454	20,922	21,456	22,220	20,859	28,846	29,010	31,749	34,982
Iran	5,370	5,631	5,000*	5,000*	4,550*	3,946	6,044	5,517	5,700*	5,000*
Iraq	1,216	1,499	858	1,496	1,750	1,080	1,312	696	910	1,492*
Italy	4,089	3,544	2,796	3,472	3,400	9,756	9,516	6,347	9,332	9,140
Japan[1]	227	89	86	112	144*	557	222	236	367	440*
Morocco	1,952	1,922	1,929	1,754	1,656	1,819	2,135	1,288	1,876	1,796
Pakistan[1]	6,122	6,111	6,390	6,360	6,696	6,796	8,691	9,144	8,367	9,944
Poland[1]	2,004	1,832	1,834	1,852	1,549	4,924	5,745	5,308	6,029	4,220
Portugal	498	537	263	360	316	614	694	229	255	233
Romania[1]	2,527	2,389	2,269	2,284	2,155*	4,433	6,724	6,463	6,243	4,684
S. Africa, Republic of	1,330	1,867	1,705	1,792	1,900	1,461	2,239	1,860	1,690	2,220
Spain[2]	3,727	2,772	2,715	2,752	2,548	4,734	4,436	4,064	4,806	4,118
Tunisia[2]	908	1,182	1,043	1,131	1,134	520	880	570	750	680
Turkey[2]	8,732	9,308	9,375	9,346	9,300	11,423	16,578	16,720	16,769	17,631
USSR[1]	65,230	59,467	62,140	62,898	57,682	92,804	96,882	92,165	120,824	90,100
UK	980	1,231	1,076	1,257	1,370	4,140	4,740	5,274	6,613	7,140
USA	18,669	28,640	26,895	23,043	25,333	40,034	58,307	55,420	48,922	58,289
Yugoslavia[2]	1,928	1,723	1,604	1,712	1,524	4,760	5,979	5,595	5,355	4,512
World total	215,911	236,571	234,650	236,207	238,723	329,030	419,661	390,697	450,059	425,478

* Unofficial figures.   [1] Sown area.   [2] Includes spelt.   [3] Field crops and other crops.

xiv

RYE

Countries	Area (1,000 hectares)					Production (1,000 tonnes)				
	Average 1969–71	1976	1977	1978	1979	Average 1969–71	1976	1977	1978	1979
Argentina	440	340	240	260	241	271	330	170	210	209
Austria	143	120	119	109	106	417	410	351	410	278
Belgium [1]	23	15	20	17	14*	82	53	69	64*	54*
Bulgaria [1]	22	13	13	13	20	27	15	15	19	20
Canada	356	250	250	319	330	474	440	407	605	525
Czechoslovakia [2]	243	187	210	185	166	586	561	641	630	500
Denmark	42	72	89	84	70	137	213	324	315	245
Finland	67	65	47	38	37	130	178	80	74	77
France	139	114	135	139	123	297	310	389	432	360
German Demo. Rep.	679	600	619	652	640*	1,594	1,455	1,644	1,895	1,720*
Germany, Fed. Rep. of	868	663	702	651	561	2,862	2,100	2,540	2,457	2,105
Hungary [1,3]	155	93	92	78	69	193	157	144	138	95
Italy	34	16	15	15	15	65	35	32	36	37
Netherlands	60	21	21	17	12	196	65	74	68	49
Poland [1]	3,766	2,934	3,116	3,030	2,868	7,143	6,922	6,249	7,434	5,233
Portugal	227	219	190	213	208	164	165	103	123	113
Romania [1]	45	40*	40*	40*	35*	52	49*	50	57	40
Spain	320	224	236	228	212	292	214	228	251	215
Sweden	78	123	111	81	57	239	427	338	298	198
Turkey	663	530	520	473	500*	781	740	690	620	620
USSR [1]	9,588	9,035	6,697	7,719	6,476	12,235	13,991	8,480	13,607	8,100
USA	603	292	285	403	384	984	380	440	664	624
Yugoslavia	115	76	69	63	59	132	105	87	81	81
World total	20,246	17,584	15,338	16,400	14,798	31,049	31,303	25,443	32,495	23,705

* Unofficial figures. [1] Sown area. [2] Includes mixture of wheat and rye. [3] Field crops and other crops.

BARLEY

Countries	Area (1,000 hectares)					Production (1,000 tonnes)				
	Average 1969–71	1976	1977	1978	1979	Average 1969–71	1976	1977	1978	1979
Algeria	773	932	741	666	800	470	589	260	397	400
Argentina	431	476	310	355	270*	497	760	353	554	329
Australia[1]	2,024	2,321	2,803	2,777	2,605	2,372	2,847	2,383	3,995	3,657
Bulgaria[1]	416	524	529	473	520	1,108	1,781	1,481	1,488	1,600
Canada	4,483	4,353	4,751	4,263	3,723	10,024	10,513	11,798	10,387	8,460
Czechoslovakia	810	854	851	906	1,042	2,543	2,901	3,207	3,642	3,300
Denmark	1,342	1,479	1,528	1,570	1,624	5,175	4,801	6,142	6,301	6,680
France	2,825	2,780	2,911	2,813	2,816	8,865	8,530	10,262	11,321	11,238
German Demo. Rep.	646	960	997	1,035	1,030*	2,093	3,456	3,681	4,135	3,635*
Germany, Fed. Rep. of	1,456	1,735	1,811	1,951	1,982	5,219	6,487	7,582	8,608	8,157
Hungary[1,2]	322	228	224	225	262	749	749	708	763	710
India	2,693	2,802	2,241	2,001	1,836	2,642	3,192	2,344	2,311	2,121
Iran	1,532	1,481	1,350	1,300*	1,200*	1,042	1,487	1,230	1,000*	900
Iraq	582	576	536	714	920	692	579	458	617	872*
Japan[1]	224	80	78	96	117	629	210	206	326	375*
Korea, South[1]	723	711	516	554	473*	1,589	1,759	814	1,348	1,508
Mexico	230	364	248	296	326	240	549	418	505	505
Morocco	2,003	2,142	2,341	2,415	2,193	2,190	2,862	1,347	2,328	1,888
Peru[1]	184	163	180*	180*	185*	164	150	170*	175*	175*
Poland[1]	861	1,210	1,235	1,203	1,470	2,182	3,617	3,396	3,635	3,785
Romania[1]	309	410	595	722	771*	615	1,231	1,859	2,307	2,037
Spain	2,235	3,240	3,348	3,519	3,421	3,922	5,473	6,766	8,068	6,150
Syria	520	1,172	1,021	1,033	1,102	328	1,059	337	729	395
Tunisia	333	451	376	497	642	126	270	100	200	270
Turkey	2,611	2,635	2,620	2,577	2,750*	3,720	4,900	4,750	4,750	5,217
USSR[1]	21,782	34,261	34,514	32,690	37,005	35,132	69,539	52,687	62,077	46,000
UK[1]	2,317	2,182	2,400	2,348	2,340	8,257	7,648	10,531	9,848	9,550
USA	3,963	3,358	3,871	3,744	3,024	9,476	8,111	9,150	9,783	8,238
Yugoslavia	287	293	306	273	291	442	653	650	560	631
World total	77,061	93,975	95,532	93,744	97,746	138,482	188,020	176,280	193,852	172,175

* Unofficial figures.   [1] Sown areas.   [2] Field crops and other crops.

OATS

Countries	Area (1,000 hectares)					Production (1,000 tonnes)				
	Average 1969–71	1976	1977	1978	1979	Average 1969–71	1976	1977	1978	1979
Argentina	328	383	430	500	416	420	530	570	676	536
Australia	1,390	995	1,076	1,355	1,330	1,378	1,072	990	1,756	1,492
Austria	101	95	90	89	95	281	283	279	304	273
Belgium	89	59	48	40	37*	331	174	165	161*	146*
Canada	2,834	2,409	2,131	1,828	1,540	5,508	4,831	4,303	3,620	2,978
China	1,133	950	900	900	900	1,100	1,000	1,000	1,000	1,100
Czechoslovakia ²	372	169	166	132	149	882	379	454	454	400
Denmark	191	98	78	61	61	699	263	270	206	144
Finland	516	551	417	446	451	1,297	1,573	1,022	1,082	1,283
France	829	652	624	608	558	2,317	1,431	1,901	2,194	1,675
German Demo. Rep.	237	190	153	153	140*	735	506	411	595	400*
Germany, Fed. Rep. of	840	856	793	749	729	2,832	2,497	2,714	3,202	2,999
Hungary ¹, ²	49	39	32	27	44	79	92	69	82	94
Irish Republic	68	40	35	31	28	222	130	135	124	103*
Italy	297	236	225	228	222	488	439	354	468	438
Netherlands	61	25	21	25	21	243	103	94	140	109
Poland ¹	1,409	1,115	1,097	1,030	1,094	3,156	2,695	2,552	2,491	2,199
Portugal	164	215	145	177	164	92	127	60	64	66
Romania ¹	130	45	54	48	40*	138	55	61	57	59*
Spain	481	455	405	442	410	504	528	418	553	443
Sweden	505	450	458	453	456	1,561	1,251	1,416	1,550	1,646
Turkey	326	241	230	225	220*	446	415	370	370	371
USSR ¹	9,394	11,269	13,026	12,097	12,239	13,974	18,113	18,407	18,507	14,000
UK	375	235	195	180	136	1,300	764	790	706	535
USA	7,051	4,834	5,442	4,624	3,979	13,350	7,930	10,899	8,650	7,757
World total	30,499	27,906	29,557	27,700	26,759	54,766	48,735	51,254	50,556	42,909

* Unofficial figures.   ¹ Sown area.   ² Includes mixture of oats and barley.   ³ Field crops and other crops.

MAIZE

Countries	Area (1,000 hectares)					Production (1,000 tonnes)				
	Average 1969–71	1976	1977	1978	1979	Average 1969–71	1976	1977	1978	1979
Argentina	3,880	2,766	2,532	2,660	2,800	8,717	5,855	8,300	9,700	8,700
Brazil	10,021	11,176	11,797	11,084	11,314	13,680	17,845	19,256	13,533	16,309
Bulgaria	623	731	702	601	730	2,436	3,031	2,513	2,236	3,300
China	10,521	11,041	11,036	11,037	13,050	27,820	33,114	27,595	31,607	40,620
Colombia	684	648	581	671	615	856	884	753	862	870
Egypt	634	795	742	797	791	2,370	3,048	2,725	3,117	2,938
France	1,436	1,396	1,624	1,803	2,003	7,394	5,625	8,505	9,531	10,293
Ghana	387	273	291	330*	340*	417	286	309	340*	380*
Greece	162	128	123	113	130*	498	505	496	513	627
Hungary	1,272	1,351	1,295	1,321	1,372*	4,542	5,141	6,007	6,655	7,400*
India	5,794	6,000	5,683	5,779	5,500	6,087	6,361	5,973	6,219	5,000
Indonesia	2,667	2,095	2,567	3,025	2,600	2,575	2,572	3,143	4,029	3,200
Italy	986	889	983	928	936	4,601	5,321	6,455	6,221	6,260
Mexico	7,412	6,783	7,470	7,184	7,148	9,025	8,017	10,138	10,909	9,255
Morocco	474	433	425	394	415	380	493	184	390	312
Pakistan	640	624	656	650	656	697	764	821	798	846
Peru	373	385	415*	300*	360*	605	726	749	623	600*
Philippines	2,356	3,257	3,445	3,332	3,276	1,915	2,767	3,037	2,860	3,300
Portugal	432	368	380	386	357	599	429	491	500	456
Rhodesia	403	475*	475*	475*	450	966	1,400*	1,300*	1,400*	1,000
Romania	3,170	3,378	3,318	3,179	3,330*	7,354	11,583	10,114	10,208	12,380
S. Africa, Republic of	5,290	5,700	5,700	6,000	6,000	6,691	7,312	9,630	9,930	8,240
Spain	526	432	442	443	461	1,804	1,545	1,892	1,969	2,237
Turkey	646	597	580	580	600*	1,058	1,310	1,265	1,300	1,358
USSR¹	3,617	3,303	3,362	2,535	2,667	9,993	10,138	10,979	8,951	8,400
USA	23,749	28,854	28,680	28,439	28,726	122,649	159,172	163,213	180,008	197,208
Venezuela	606	489	496	506	519	698	532	774	804	848
Yugoslavia	2,391	2,374	2,321	2,146	2,251	7,399	9,106	9,870	7,585	10,082
World total	108,841	116,903	118,796	118,059	120,540	278,389	334,626	346,227	363,927	394,231

* Unofficial figures.   ¹ For dry grain only.

RICE (Paddy)

Countries	Area (1,000 hectares)					Production (1,000 tonnes)				
	Average 1969–71	1976	1977	1978	1979	Average 1969–71	1976	1977	1978	1979
Bangladesh	9,842	9,882	10,028	10,083	10,000	16,540	17,628	19,441	19,273	19,355
Brazil	4,788	6,583	5,992	5,551	5,439	6,847	9,560	8,994	7,242	7,589
Burma	4,748	5,180*	4,864	5,011	5,013	8,107	9,320	9,462	10,500	10,000
China	34,622	36,686	37,078	37,552	38,575	111,599	129,054	129,470	138,202	143,400
Egypt	487	453	437	433	436*	2,567	2,300	2,275	2,351	2,507
India	37,677	38,511	40,283	40,196	38,500	62,861	63,052	79,006	80,743	69,000*
Indonesia	8,158	8,369	8,360	8,929	8,850	19,136	23,301	23,356	25,781	26,350
Iran	362	460	460	315*	300*	1,041	1,566	1,400	1,280*	1,212*
Iraq	97	52	63	55	80	268	163	199	172	284*
Italy	172	182	186	191	181	858	907	693	979	1,014
Japan	2,966	2,779	2,757	2,548	2,500*	16,281	15,292	17,000	16,354	15,600*
Kampuchea, Democratic	2,074	1,400	1,500	1,400	1,300	3,016	1,800	1,800	1,500	1,000
Korea, South	1,204	1,215	1,208	1,233	1,228	5,573	7,249	8,291	8,342	8,051
Madagascar	992	1,064	1,096	1,037	1,216	1,894	2,043	2,154	1,914	2,327
Malaysia	708	730	730	593	757	1,696	1,995	1,922	1,527	2,161*
Mexico	152	159	180	121	151	390	463	567	397	489
Pakistan	1,527	1,749	1,899	2,026	1,975	3,431	4,106	4,424	4,908	4,953
Philippines	3,157	3,548	3,509	3,524	3,500	5,225	6,461	6,895	7,318	7,000
Sierra Leone	331	390*	410	425	400	474	580*	600	620	480*
Spain	63	64	68	68	69	384	406	379	401	427
Sri Lanka	579	635	782	839	899	1,463	1,253	1,677	1,890	1,806
Thailand	6,919	8,463	7,947	8,288	8,300	13,475	15,068	13,921	17,530	15,640
USSR	356	524	546	580	610	1,272	2,001	2,217	2,096	2,400
USA	777	1,004	910	1,202	1,206	3,953	5,246	4,501	6,040	6,199
Vietnam	4,916	5,350	5,409	4,889*	5,618	9,752	12,076	10,885	10,040	10,500
World total	134,295	143,108	144,481	145,133	145,268	311,506	350,365	369,729	386,303	379,814

* Unofficial figures.

MILLET

Countries	Area (1,000 hectares)					Production (1,000 tonnes)				
	Average 1969–71	1976	1977	1978	1979	Average 1969–71	1976	1977	1978	1979
Argentina	160	231	255	244	238	168	294	340	330	310
Australia	39	28	24	50	33	37	27	19	33	25
Cameroon	477	430	423	490	440	343	390	326	409	390
Chad	925	1,075*	1,133*	1,140	1,140	615	507*	574*	580	580
Egypt	206	199	172	182	171	847	758	649	681	635
Ghana	218	243	223*	238*	240*	120	144*	133*	125*	130*
India	19,618	17,927	18,277	18,417	17,500	10,182	9,650	9,666	10,486	8,500
Korea, South	59	26	14	6	3	47	27	17	7	3
Mali	953	1,244	1,417	1,400	1,400	784	832*	751	1,035*	744*
Niger	2,313	2,527	2,729	2,747	2,800	974	1,019	1,130	1,123	1,246
Nigeria	5,022	4,800	4,920*	5,000*	5,000*	2,792	2,865*	2,950*	3,060*	3,100*
Pakistan	713	648	641	659	629	339	311	318	317	310
Poland	21	10*	8	7	...	26	8*	5	5	...
Rhodesia¹	390	390	390	390	390	230	220	220	220	140
Senegal	1,006	955	899	950*	900	543	555	420	803	500*
Sri Lanka	23	44	38	35	35	17	24	22	21	21
Sudan	750	1,111	1,256	1,327	1,200	424	430	515	557	370
Syria	25	20	25	19	30	18	16	24	17	25
Togo	190	200	154	210	200	121	120*	113	130*	120
Turkey	39	23	20	20	19*	54	34	29	29	13
Uganda	739	498	527	550	550	737	449	475	480	450
USSR	2,821	2,998	3,048	2,924	2,784	2,477	3,198	2,012	2,196	1,800
Upper Volta	843	911	900	910	900	352	370	350	403*	400
Zaire	31	35	35	35	30	22	26	26	26	20
World total	52,945	52,699	53,031	54,524	53,207	32,658	35,946	33,203	36,091	32,962

* Unofficial figures.

¹ On farms and estates.

SORGHUM

Countries	Area (1,000 hectares)					Production (1,000 tonnes)				
	Average 1969–71	1976	1977	1978	1979	Average 1969–71	1976	1977	1978	1979
Argentina	1,979	1,903	2,461	2,254	2,044	3,823	5,167	6,730	7,200	6,200
Australia	374	504	532	394	468	759	1,124	956	714	1,127
El Salvador	121	125	132	137	144*	144	156	151	162	177*
Ethiopia¹,²	950	718	747	763	726	827	803	756	708	680
Ghana	209	249	188*	238*	240*	147	189*	140*	180*	200*
Honduras	36	57*	66	62*	54*	46	47	49	44	36*
India	17,585	15,772	16,318	16,125	15,500	8,516	10,524	12,064	11,563	10,000
Mexico	934	1,251	1,413	1,397	1,456	2,584	4,027	4,325	4,185	3,902
Morocco	67	49	41	32	63	70	19	5	36	23
Niger	589	615	733	796	810	262	286	342	364	346
Nigeria	5,572	5,940	6,000*	6,000*	6,000*	3,632	3,680*	3,750*	3,770*	3,785*
Pakistan	518	447	519	470	477	308	261	284	253	280
Rwanda	132	138	145	153	140	141	155	164	172	150
Saudi Arabia	174	192	273	125	150	185	153	139	90	100
Sudan	1,828	2,617	2,781	3,081	2,700	1,525	1,762	2,200	2,400	1,970
Uganda	299	327	280	350	350	337	490	420	520	400
USA	5,820	5,958	5,703	5,488	5,240	19,314	18,284	20,143	18,995	20,684
Upper Volta	1,054	1,138	1,000	1,100	1,000	528	717	610	620*	600
World total	51,043	51,735	52,306	52,319	50,879	56,294	64,948	69,493	68,514	67,268

* Unofficial figures.　　¹ Includes teff.　　² Unspecified millet and sorghum.

CENTRIFUGAL RAW SUGAR

(in 1,000 tonnes)

Countries	Average 1969–71	1974	1975	1976	1977	1978	1979
Argentina	985	1,530	1,353	1,599	1,666	1,397	1,381*
Australia [1]	2,511	2,849	2,854	3,296	3,318	2,902	2,963
Barbados [2]	146	113*	101*	106	124*	104*	117*
Brazil	5,161	6,986*	6,186*	7,598*	8,760*	7,770*	7,000*
Canada	130	101	133	163	149	129	112
China	2,478	4,327	4,347	4,652	3,076	3,213	3,582
Cuba	6,388	6,044*	6,432	6,279*	6,607*	7,457*	7,992*
Czechoslovakia	731	750*	800*	620*	939*	885*	930*
Dominican Rep.	1,010	1,230	1,234*	1,287*	1,258	1,199*	1,220*
Egypt	564	611*	550*	668	668	634*	678*
France	2,873	2,947	3,240	2,974	4,268	4,065	4,240
Fiji [1]	329	273	272	296	362	347	474
German Demo. Rep.	487	655*	665*	560*	780*	780*	720*
Germany, Fed. Rep. of	2,158	2,439	2,540	2,733	3,075	2,997	3,333*
Guyana	361	345	311	343	253*	342*	316*
India [3]	4,188	4,292	5,211	4,632	5,261	7,018	6,400
Indonesia [4]	760	1,137*	1,030	1,033	1,106	1,105	1,325
Italy	1,271	1,012	1,442	1,675	1,359	1,619	1,685*
Jamaica	383	372	361	369	295	307*	306*
Mauritius [4]	659	697	496	731	705	705	759
Mexico	2,486	2,834	2,727	2,720*	2,728	3,072	3,060*
Pakistan [3]	557	661	542	631	800	936	662*
Peru	782	1,021	990	959	926	856	695
Philippines	1,859	2,534	2,396	2,514	2,688	2,335	2,355
Poland	1,581	1,589	1,840*	1,801	1,850*	1,763*	1,581*
Puerto Rico	383	261	274	279	239	183	174
S. Africa, Rep. of	1,629	1,883	1,801	2,042	2,084	2,082	2,079
Spain	882	597	937	1,491	1,213	1,132	774*
Sweden	233	302	277	302*	343	337	346*
Trinidad	229	186	167	207	179	148*	144*
USSR	8,722	7,800*	7,702*	7,350*	8,825*	9,100*	7,600*
UK	1,033	622	701	746	1,015	1,111*	1,196*
USA [5]	5,258	4,924	6,308	6,257	5,254	5,353	5,059
World total	70,850	77,409	80,870	85,342	89,747	90,524	88,910

[1] 94° net titre.
[2] Includes the sugar equivalent of fancy molasses.
[3] Includes sugar (raw value) refined from gur.
[4] Tel quel.
[5] Includes Hawaii.
* Unofficial figures.

WORLD ESTIMATED CRUDE OIL PRODUCTION
(in 1,000 tonnes)

	1960	1970	1979	1980
North America				
USA	384,080	533,677	478,590	485,000
Canada	27,480	69,954	83,255	82,000
Caribbean Area				
Venezuela	148,690	193,209	122,755	113,000
Trinidad	6,075	7,225	11,073	11,300
Colombia	8,100	11,071	6,425	5,765
Other Latin America				
Mexico	14,125	21,877	80,815	110,000
Argentina	9,160	19,969	23,905	25,000
Brazil	390	8,009	8,520	9,300
Ecuador	2,680	191	10,515	10,000
Peru	450	3,450	9,360	9,800
Bolivia	990	1,128	1,355	1,150
Chile		1,620	970	1,530
Middle East				
Saudi Arabia	61,090	176,851	475,200	495,000
Iran	52,065	191,663	151,390	74,000
Iraq	47,480	76,600	168,025	138,000
Kuwait	81,860	137,397	127,205	86,000
Abu Dhabi	—	33,288	71,060	65,000
Qatar	8,210	17,257	24,404	22,800
Oman	—	17,169	14,594	14,200
Dubai	—	4,306	17,720	17,500
Egypt	3,600	16,404	25,983	30,000
Syria	—	4,350	8,500	8,500
Turkey	350	3,461	2,884	2,600
Bahrain	2,250	3,834	2,497	2,500
Sharjah	—	—	646	480
Africa				
Nigeria	880	53,420	113,479	101,000
Libya	—	159,201	98,943	85,600
Algeria	8,630	47,253	53,175	44,850
Gabon	850	5,460	10,300	10,100
Angola	70	5,066	6,700	8,000
Tunisia	—	4,151	5,507	5,200
Congo	—	—	2,604	3,000
Zaire	—	—	1,027	1,000

[1] Excluding small scale production in Afghánistan, Bangladesh, Cuba, Guatemala, Israel, Mongolia, Morocco, New Zealand, Taiwan and Thailand.

WORLD ESTIMATED CRUDE OIL PRODUCTION
(*contd.*)

(in 1,000 tonnes)

	1960	1970	1979	1980
Western Europe				
UK	90	84	77,854	80,000
Norway	—	—	18,288	23,700
Germany, Fed. Rep. of	5,560	7,536	4,772	4,685
Austria	2,440	2,798	1,728	1,550
Spain	—	156	1,165	1,500
Netherlands	1,920	1,919	1,582	1,600
France	2,260	2,308	1,241	1,330
Italy	1,990	1,408	1,826	1,950
Denmark	—	—	431	350
Far East				
Indonesia	20,560	42,102	79,137	77,500
Australia	—	8,292	20,522	18,750
Brunei	4,690	6,916	12,010	11,500
India	440	6,809	12,840	10,000
Malaysia	—	—	13,435	13,100
Burma	530	750	2,000	2,500
Japan	510	750	483	450
Pakistan	360	486	525	510
USSR and Eastern Europe				
USSR	148,000	352,667	586,000	603,000
Romania	11,500	13,377	12,323	12,000
Yugoslavia	1,040	2,854	4,143	4,200
Albania	600	1,199	3,000	3,500
Hungary	1,215	1,937	2,030	2,050
Poland	195	424	330	300
German Dem. Rep.	—	60	55	55
Bulgaria	200	334	260	260
Czechoslovakia	140	203	110	100
China	5,000	20,000	106,150	106,000
World Total	1,090,080	2,336,153	3,189,054	3,065,625

ENERGY

Oil Import Targets

	1980 (in 1,000 tonnes)	1985 (in 1,000 tonnes)
Australia	13,500	17,000
Austria	11,500	13,500
Belgium	30,000	31,000
Canada	7,400	29,400
Denmark	16,500	11,000
Germany, Fed. Rep. of	143,000	141,000
Greece	14,800	16,500
Irish Republic	6,500	8,000
Italy	103,500	124,000
Japan	265,300	308,700
Luxembourg	1,500	2,000
Netherlands	42,000	49,000
New Zealand	4,200	4,400
Norway	−15,500	−18,300
Spain	51,000	52,900
Sweden	29,900	29,000
Switzerland	14,000	14,500
Turkey	17,000	25,000
UK	12,000	−5,000
USA	437,200	436,000
Total	1,205,300	1,289,600

World Primary Energy Consumption[1]

(1,000 tonnes oil equivalent)

	1970	1978	1979	1980
Oil	1,939,000	2,478,000	2,510,000	2,500,000
Natural Gas	733,000	853,000	870,000	890,000
Coal[2]	833,000	826,000	850,000	850,000
Water power	264,000	344,000	350,000	370,000
Nuclear power	19,000	137,000	145,000	180,000
Total	3,788,000	4,638,000	4,725,000	4,790,000

[1] Excluding USSR, Eastern Europe and China.
[2] Peat, wood, animal wastes etc. could add a further 300m. tonnes of oil equivalent a year to the total.

TERRITORIAL SEA LIMITS (IN MILES)

State	Territorial Sea	Jurisdiction over fisheries (measured from the baseline of the territorial sea)
Albania	15 (1976)	—
Algeria	12 (1963)	—
Angola	20 (1976)	200 (1976)
Argentina	200 (1967)	—
Australia	3 (1878)	200 (1979)
Bahamas	3 (1878)	200 (1977)
Bahrain	3	—
Bangladesh	12 (1974)	200 (1974)[1]
Barbados	12 (1977)	200 (1978)[1]
Belgium	3	up to median line (1978)
Benin	200 (1976)	—
Brazil	200 (1970)	—
Bulgaria	12 (1951)	—
Burma	12 (1968)	200 (1977)[1]
Cameroon	50 (1974)	—
Canada	12 (1970)	200 (1977)
Cape Verde	12 (1978)	200 (1978)[1]
Chile	3	200 (1952)
China	12 (1958)	—
Colombia	12 (1970)	200 (1978)[1]
Comoros	12 (1976)	200 (1976)[1]
Congo	200 (1977)	—
Costa Rica	12 (1972)	200 (1975)[1]
Cuba	12 (1977)	200 (1977)[1]
Cyprus	12 (1964)	—
Denmark (including Faroe Islands and Greenland)	3 (1966)	200 (1977)
Dominica	3 (1878)	200 (1977)[1]
Dominican Republic	6 (1967)	—
Ecuador	200 (1966)	—
Egypt	12 (1958)	—
El Salvador	200 (1950)	—
Equatorial Guinea	12 (1970)	—
Ethiopia	12 (1953)	—
Fiji	12 (1976)	200 [1,2]
Finland	4 (1956)	12 (1975)
France	12 (1971)	200 (1977)[1] (except Mediterranean)
Gabon	100 (1972)	—
Gambia	12 (1969)	200 (1978)
German Democratic Republic	3	up to median line (1978)
Germany, Federal Republic of	In accordance with international law	200 (1977)
Ghana	200 (1977)	—
Greece	6 (1936)	—
Grenada	12 (1978)	200 (1978)[1]
Guatemala	12 (1934)	200 (1976)[1]
Guinea	200 (1965)	—
Guinea-Bissau	12 (1978)	200 (1978)[1]
Guyana	12 (1977)	200 (1977)
Haiti	12 (1972)	200 (1977)[1]
Honduras	12 (1965)	200 (1951)[1]
Iceland	12 (1979)	200 (1979)[1]

[1] Economic zone.
[2] Legislation enacted but not in force (1980).

TERRITORIAL SEA LIMITS (IN MILES)—*contd.*

State	Territorial Sea	Jurisdiction over fisheries (measured from the baseline of the territorial sea)
India	12 (1967)	200 (1977) [1]
Indonesia	12 (1957) [2]	200 (1980) [1]
Iran	12 (1959)	[3]
Iraq	12 (1958)	—
Irish Republic	3 (1959)	200 (1977)
Israel	6 (1956)	—
Italy	12 (1974)	—
Ivory Coast	12 (1977)	200 (1977) [1]
Jamaica	12 (1971)	—
Japan	12 (1977)	200 (1977)
Jibuti	12 (1971)	200 (1979) [1]
Jordan	3 (1943)	—
Kampuchea, Democratic	12 (1969)	200 (1978) [1]
Kenya	12 (1969)	200 (1979) [1]
Kiribati	3 (1878)	200 (1978)
Korea (North)	12 (1967)	200 (1977) [1]
Korea (South)	12 (1978)	20–200 (1952–54)
Kuwait	12 (1967)	—
Lebanon	—	6 (1921)
Liberia	200 (1976)	—
Libya	12 (1959)	—
Madagascar	50 (1973)	—
Malaysia	12 (1969)	200 (1980) [1]
Maldive, Republic of	3–55 [3]	(1976) [1,4]
Malta	12 (1978)	24 (1978)
Mauritania	70 (1978)	200 (1978) [1]
Mauritius	12 (1970)	200 (1977) [1]
Mexico	12 (1969)	200 (1976) [1]
Monaco	12	—
Morocco	12 (1973)	200 [5,6]
Mozambique	12 (1976)	200 (1976) [1]
Namibia	3	12 (1964)
Nauru	12 (1971)	200 (1978) [1]
Netherlands	12	200 (1977)
New Zealand	12 (1977)	200 (1978) [1]
Nicaragua	3	200 (1980) [1]
Nigeria	12 (1967)	200 (1978) [1]
Norway	4 (1812)	200 (1977) [1]
Oman	12 (1977)	200 (1977)
Pakistan	12 (1966)	200 (1976) [1]
Panama	200 (1967)	—
Papua New Guinea	12 (1978)	200 (1978) (offshore waters)
Peru	200 (1947) [7]	200 [7]
Philippines	[8]	200 (1979) [1]

[1] Economic zone.

[2] The territorial sea of Indonesia is measured by straight lines surrounding the archipelago.

[3] Outer limits of the superjacent waters of the continental shelf. Median line in the Sea of Oman (1973).

[4] Territorial limits and economic zone defined by geographical co-ordinates.

[5] Legislation enacted but not yet in force (1980).

[6] Six miles for Strait of Gibraltar.

[7] Sovereignty and jurisdiction over the sea, its soil and subsoil up to 200 miles (1947).

[8] The territorial sea of the Philippines is determined by straight base-lines joining appropriate points of the outermost islands forming the Philippine archipelago in accordance with Treaties of 1898, 1900 and 1930 (1961).

TERRITORIAL SEA LIMITS (IN MILES)—*contd.*

State	Territorial Sea	Jurisdiction over fisheries (measured from the baseline of the territorial sea)
Poland	12 (1977)	up to median line (1978)
Portugal	12 (1977)	200 (1977) [2]
Qatar	3	[1]
Romania	12 (1951)	—
St Lucia	3 (1878)	—
St Vincent	3 (1878)	—
São Tomé	12 (1978)	200 (1978) [2]
Saudi Arabia	12 (1958)	[1]
Senegal	150 (1976)	200 (1976)
Seychelles	12 (1977)	200 (1977) [2]
Sierra Leone	200 (1971)	—
Singapore	3 (1878)	
Solomon Islands	12 (1978)	200 (1978)
Somalia	200 (1972)	—
South Africa, Republic of	12 (1977)	200 (1977)
Spain	12 (1977)	200 (1978) [2] (except Mediterranean)
Sri Lanka	12 (1971)	200 (1977) [2]
Sudan	12 (1960)	—
Suriname	12 (1978)	200 (1978) [2]
Sweden	4 (1779)	200 (1978)
Syria	12 (1964)	—
Tanzania	50 (1973)	—
Thailand	12 (1966)	—
Togo	30 (1977)	200 (1977) [2]
Tonga	3	—
Trinidad and Tobago	12 (1969)	—
Tunisia	12 (1973)	—
Turkey	6 (1964)	12 (1964)
Tuvalu	—	200 (1978)
USSR	12 (1909)	200 (1977)
United Arab Emirates	3 [4]	—
UK	3 (1878)	200 (1977)
USA	3 (1793)	200 (1977)
Uruguay	200 (1969)	—
Vanuatu	3	200 (1980) [2]
Venezuela	12 (1956)	200 (1978) [2]
Vietnam	12 (1977)	200 (1977) [2]
Western Samoa	12 (1977)	200 [5]
Yemen, Peoples Dem. Rep. of	12 (1970)	200 (1978) [2]
Yemen, Republic of	12 (1967)	—
Yugoslavia	12 (1979)	—
Zaïre	12 (1974)	—

[1] Outer limits of the superjacent waters of the continental shelf (1974).

[2] Economic zone.

[3] Territorial limits defined by geographical co-ordinates (173–177° W. and 15–23° 30′ S.) (1887).

[4] Sharjah, 12 miles.

[5] Legislation enacted but not in force (1980).

The table above, reproduced from a survey prepared by the FAO of the UN shows: (*a*) the territorial sea limit, and (*b*) jurisdiction over fisheries.

Books of Reference

Buzan, B., *Seabed Politics*. New York, 1976
Janis, M. W., *Sea Power and the Law of the Sea*. Lexington, 1977
Luard, E., *The Control of the Sea-Bed*. London, 1974
Moore, G., *Legislation on Coastal State Requirements for Foreign Fishing. FAO Legislative Study No. 21*. Rome, 1981

ADDENDA

ANGOLA. *UK Ambassador:* Francis Kennedy.

AUSTRALIA. On 16 Feb. 1981, Robert Elliott resigned as Minister of Home Affairs and the Environment and his portfolios were assumed by Michael Mackellar and on 15 April the Minister for Industrial Affairs, Andrew Peacock, resigned.

BELGIUM. On 6 April 1981, Mark Eyskens was appointed Prime Minister following the resignation of Wilfred Martens. Robert Vandeputte became Finance Minister.

CENTRAL AFRICAN REPUBLIC. On 3 April 1981, David Dacko was sworn in as the first democratically elected President.

ECUADOR. *UK Ambassador:* A. C. Buxton.

POLAND. *UK Ambassador:* C. M. James.

THAILAND. An attempted *coup* against Gen. Prem was mounted on 1 April 1981 by Gen. Sant but failed.

ZAÏRE. The Prime Minister, Nzuza Karl I Bond resigned on 17 April 1981.

PART I

INTERNATIONAL ORGANIZATIONS

THE UNITED NATIONS

The United Nations is an association of states which have pledged themselves, through signing the Charter, to maintain international peace and security and to co-operate in establishing political, economic and social conditions under which this task can be securely achieved. Nothing contained in the Charter authorizes the organization to intervene in matters which are essentially within the domestic jurisdiction of any state.

The United Nations Charter originated from proposals agreed upon at discussions held at Dumbarton Oaks (Washington, D.C.) between the USSR, US and UK from 21 Aug. to 28 Sept., and between US, UK and China from 29 Sept. to 7 Oct. 1944. These proposals were laid before the United Nations Conference on International Organization, held at San Francisco from 25 April to 26 June 1945, and (after amendments had been made to the original proposals) the Charter of the United Nations was signed on 26 June 1945 by the delegates of 50 countries. Ratification of all the signatures had been received by 31 Dec. 1945. (For the complete text of the Charter see THE STATESMAN'S YEAR-BOOK, 1946, pp. xxi–xxxii.)

The United Nations formally came into existence on 24 Oct. 1945, with the deposit of the requisite number of ratifications of the Charter with the US Department of State. The official languages of the United Nations are Arabic, Chinese, English, French, Russian and Spanish; the working languages are English, French and (in the General Assembly) Arabic, Chinese, Spanish and Russian.

The headquarters of the United Nations is in New York City, USA.

Flag: United Nations blue with UN emblem in white in the centre.

Membership. Membership is open to all peace-loving states whose admission will be effected by the General Assembly upon recommendation of the Security Council.

The table on pp. 12–15 shows the member states of the United Nations and their participation in the Related Agencies, and those non-member states which have been admitted to certain Related Agencies.

The Principal Organs of the United Nations are: 1. The General Assembly. 2. The Security Council. 3. The Economic and Social Council. 4. The Trusteeship Council. 5. The International Court of Justice. 6. The Secretariat.

1. **The General Assembly** consists of all the members of the United Nations. Each member is entitled to be represented at its meetings by 5 delegates and 5 alternate delegates, but has only 1 vote. The General Assembly meets regularly once a year, commencing on the third Tuesday in Sept.; the session normally lasts until mid-December and is resumed for some weeks in the new year if this is required. Special sessions may be convoked by the Secretary-General if requested by the Security Council, by a majority of the members of the United Nations or by 1 member concurred with by the majority of the members. The General Assembly elects its President for each session.

The first regular session was held in London from 10 Jan. to 14 Feb. and in New York from 23 Oct. to 16 Dec. 1946.

Special sessions have been held on Palestine (1947, 1948), Tunisia (1961), Financial Situation of UN (1963), South West Africa, Peace-Keeping, Postponement of Outer Space Conference (1967), Raw Materials and Development (1974), New International Economic Order (1975), Peace-keeping force in the Lebanon, Namibia, Disarmament (1978), Economic Issues (1980); Emergency Special sessions were held on

Suez, Hungary (1956), Lebanon-Jordan-United Arab Republic dispute (1958), Congo (1960), Middle East (1967), Afghanistan, Palestine (1980).

The work of the General Assembly is divided between 6 Main Committees and the Special Political Committee, on each of which every member has the right to be represented by 1 delegate. I. Political Security. II. Economic and Financial. III. Social, Humanitarian and Cultural. IV. Trust and Non-Self-Governing Territories. V. Administrative and Budgetary. VI. Legal.

In addition there is a General Committee charged with the task of co-ordinating the proceedings of the Assembly and its Committees; and a Credentials Committee which verifies the credentials of the delegates. The General Committee consists of 25 members, comprising the President of the General Assembly, its 17 Vice-Presidents and the Chairmen of the 7 Main Committees. The Credentials Committee consists of 9 members, elected at the beginning of each session of the General Assembly. The Assembly has 2 standing committees—an Advisory Committee on Administrative and Budgetary Questions, and a Committee on Contributions. The General Assembly establishes subsidiary and *ad hoc* bodies when necessary to deal with specific matters. These include: Special Committee on Peace-keeping Operations (33 members), Commission on Human Rights (32 members), Commission for the unification and rehabilitation of Korea (7 members), Committee on the peaceful uses of outer space (28 members), Conciliation Commission for Palestine (3 members), Committee on Disarmament (40 members), International Law Commission (25 members), Scientific Committee on the effects of atomic radiation (15 members), Special Committee on the implementation of the declaration on the granting of independence to colonial countries and peoples (24 members), Special Committee on the policies of Apartheid of the Government of the Republic of South Africa (11 members), UN High Commissioner for Refugees, UN Relief and Works Agency for Palestine Refugees in the Near East, Peace Observation Commission (14 members), UN Commission on International Trade Law (29 members) and Committee on the Peaceful Uses of Sea-bed and Ocean Floor Beyond the Limits of National Jurisdiction (91 members), Governing Council for Environmental Programmes (54 members).

The General Assembly may discuss any matters within the scope of the Charter, and, with the exception of any situation or dispute on the agenda of the Security Council, may make recommendations on any such questions or matters. For decisions on important questions a two-thirds majority is required, on other questions a simple majority of members present and voting. In addition, the Assembly at its fifth session, in 1950, decided that if the Security Council, because of lack of unanimity of the permanent members, fails to exercise its primary responsibility for the maintenance of international peace and security in any case where there appears to be a threat to the peace, breach of the peace or act of aggression, the General Assembly shall consider the matter immediately with a view to making appropriate recommendations to members for collective measures, including in the case of a breach of the peace or act of aggression the use of armed force when necessary, to maintain or restore international peace and security.

The General Assembly receives and considers reports from the other organs of the United Nations, including the Security Council. The Secretary-General makes an annual report to it on the work of the Organization.

2. **The Security Council** consists of 15 members, each of which has 1 representative and 1 vote. There are 5 permanent and 10 non-permanent members elected for a 2-year term by a two-thirds majority of the General Assembly.

Retiring members are not eligible for immediate re-election. Any other member of the United Nations will be invited to participate without vote in the discussion of questions specially affecting its interests.

The Security Council bears the primary responsibility for the maintenance of peace and security. It is also responsible for the functions of the UN in trust territories classed as 'strategic areas'. Decisions on procedural questions are made by an affirmative vote of 9 members. On all other matters the affirmative vote of 9 members must include the concurring votes of all permanent members (in practice, however, an abstention by a permanent member is not considered a veto), subject to the provision that when the Security Council is considering methods for the peaceful settlement of a dispute, parties to the dispute abstain from voting.

For the maintenance of international peace and security the Security Council can, in accordance with special agreements to be concluded, call on armed forces, assistance and facilities of the member states. It is assisted by a Military Staff Committee consisting of the Chiefs of Staff of the permanent members of the Security Council or their representatives.

The Presidency of the Security Council is held for 1 month in rotation by the member states in the English alphabetical order of their names.

The Security Council functions continuously. Its members are permanently represented at the seat of the organization, but it may meet at any place that will best facilitate its work.

The Council has 2 standing committees, of Experts and on the Admission of New Members. In addition, from time to time, it establishes *ad hoc* committees and commissions such as the Truce Supervision Organization in Palestine. It has also appointed a Representative for India and Pakistan.

Permanent Members: China, France, USSR, UK, USA.
Non-Permanent Members: Ireland, Japan, Spain, Uganda (the fifth to be decided) (until 31 Dec. 1982); German Democratic Republic, Mexico (1981), Niger, the Philippines, Tunisia (until 31 Dec. 1981).

3. **The Economic and Social Council** is responsible under the General Assembly for carrying out the functions of the United Nations with regard to international economic, social, cultural, educational, health and related matters.

By Nov. 1977, 15 'specialized' inter-governmental agencies working in these fields had been brought into relationship with the United Nations. The Economic and Social Council may also make arrangements for consultation with international non-governmental organizations and, after consultation with the member concerned, with national organizations; by Sept. 1978, 231 non-governmental organizations had been granted consultative status and a further 534 were on the register.

The Economic and Social Council consists of 1 delegate each of 54 Member States elected by a two-thirds majority of the General Assembly. Nine are elected each year for a 3-year term. Retiring members are eligible for immediate re-election. Each member has 1 vote. Decisions are made by a majority of the members present and voting.

The Council nominally holds 2 sessions a year, and special sessions may be held if required. The President is elected for 1 year and is eligible for immediate re-election.

The Economic and Social Council has the following commissions:

Regional Economic Commissions: ECE (Economic Commission for Europe. Geneva); ESCAP (Economic and Social Commission for Asia and the Pacific. Bangkok); ECLA (Economic Commission for Latin America. Santiago, Chile); ECA (Economic Commission for Africa. Addis Ababa). ECWA (Economic Commission for Western Asia. Beirut). These Commissions have been established to enable the nations of the major regions of the world to co-operate on common problems and also to produce economic information.

(1) Six functional Statistical Commissions; with subcommission on Statistical Sampling. (2) Commission on Human Rights; with subcommission on Prevention of Discrimination and Protection of Minorities; (3) Social Development Commission; (4) Commission on the Status of Women; (5) Commission on Narcotic Drugs; (6) Population Commission.

The Economic and Social Council has the following standing committees: The Economic Committee, Social Committee, Co-ordination Committee, Committee on Non-Governmental Organizations, Interim Committee on Programme of Conferences, Committee for Industrial Development, Advisory Committee on the Application of Science and Technology to Development, Committee on Housing, Building and Planning.

Other special bodies are the Permanent Central Opium Board, the Drug Supervisory Body, the Interim Co-ordinating Committee for International

Commodity Arrangements and the Administrative Committee on Co-ordination to ensure (1) the most effective implementation of the agreements entered into between the United Nations and the specialized agencies and (2) co-ordination of activities.

Membership: Argentina, Bangladesh, Burundi, Byelorussia, Cameroon, Canada, China, Denmark, Fiji, India, Kenya, Nicaragua, Norway, Peru, Poland, Sudan, USSR, UK (until 31 Dec. 1983): Australia, Bahamas, Belgium, Bulgaria, Chile, Ethiopia, Iraq, Italy, Jordan, Libya, Malawi, Mexico, Nepál, Nigeria, Thailand, USA, Yugoslavia, Zaïre (until 31 Dec. 1982); Algeria, Barbados, Brazil, Cyprus, Ecuador, France, German Democratic Republic, Federal Republic of Germany, Ghana, Indonesia, Irish Republic, Morocco, Pakistan, Senegal, Spain, Turkey, Venezuela, Zambia (until 31 Dec. 1981).

4. The Trusteeship Council. The Charter provides for an international trusteeship system to safeguard the interests of the inhabitants of territories which are not yet fully self-governing and which may be placed thereunder by individual trusteeship agreements. These are called trust territories.

All of the original 11 trust territories except one, the Pacific Islands (Micronesia), administered by the USA, have become independent or joined independent countries.

The Trusteeship Council consists of the 1 member administering trust territories: USA; the permanent members of the Security Council that are not administering trust territories: China, France, USSR and UK. Decisions of the Council are made by a majority of the members present and voting, each member having 1 vote. The Council holds one regular session each year, and special sessions if required.

5. The International Court of Justice was created by an international treaty, the Statute of the Court, which forms an integral part of the United Nations Charter. All members of the United Nations are *ipso facto* parties to the Statute of the Court.

The Court is composed of independent judges, elected regardless of their nationality, who possess the qualifications required in their countries for appointment to the highest judicial offices, or are jurisconsuls of recognized competence in international law. There are 15 judges, no 2 of whom may be nationals of the same state. They are elected by the Security Council and the General Assembly of the United Nations sitting independently. Candidates are chosen from a list of persons nominated by the national groups in the Permanent Court of Arbitration established by the Hague Conventions of 1899 and 1907. In the case of members of the United Nations not represented in the Permanent Court of Arbitration, candidates are nominated by national groups appointed for the purpose by their governments. The judges are elected for a 9-year term and are eligible for immediate re-election. When engaged on business of the Court, they enjoy diplomatic privileges and immunities.

The Court elects its own President and Vice-Presidents for 3 years and remains permanently in session, except for judicial vacations. The full court of 15 judges normally sits, but a quorum of 9 judges is sufficient to constitute the Court. It may form chambers of 3 or more judges for dealing with particular categories of cases, and forms annually a chamber of 5 judges to hear and determine, at the request of the parties, cases by summary procedures.

Competence and Jurisdiction. Only states may be parties in cases before the Court, which is open to the states parties to its Statute. The conditions under which the Court will be open to other states are laid down by the Security Council. The Court exercises its jurisdiction in all cases which the parties refer to it and in all matters provided for in the Charter, or in treaties and conventions in force. Disputes concerning the jurisdiction of the Court are settled by the Court's own decision.

The Court may apply in its decision: (*a*) international conventions; (*b*) international custom; (*c*) the general principles of law recognized by civilized nations; and (*d*) as subsidiary means for the determination of the rules of law, judicial decisions and the teachings of highly qualified publicists. If the parties agree, the Court may decide a case *ex aequo et bono.* The Court may also give an advisory opinion on any legal question to any organ of the United Nations or its agencies.

Procedure. The official languages of the Court are French and English. At the request of any party the Court will authorize the use of another language by this party. All questions are decided by a majority of the judges present. If the votes are equal, the President has a casting vote. The judgment is final and without appeal, but a revision may be applied for within 10 years from the date of the judgment on the ground of a new decisive factor. Unless otherwise decided by the Court, each party bears its own costs.

Judges. The judges of the Court, elected by the Security Council and the General Assembly, are as follows: (1) To serve until 5 Feb. 1982: André Gros (France), Isaac Forster (Senegal), Sir Humphrey Waldock (UK), Nagendra Singh (India), José Maria Ruda (Argentina). (2) To serve until 5 Feb. 1985: Manfred Lachs (Poland), Taslim Olawale Elias (Nigeria), Hermann Mosler (Federal Republic of Germany), Shigeru Oda (Japan), Abdallah Fikri El-Khani (Syria). (3) To serve until 5 Feb. 1988: Platon D. Morozov (USSR), Roberto Ago (Italy), A. El. Erian (Egypt), J. Sette-Camara (Brazil), Stephen Schwebel (USA).

'National' Judges. If there is no judge on the bench of the nationality of the parties to the dispute, each party has the right to choose a judge. Such judges shall take part in the decision on terms of complete equality with their colleagues.

The Court has its seat at The Hague, but may sit elsewhere whenever it considers this desirable. The expenses of the Court are borne by the UN.

Registrar: Santiago Torres Bernárdez (Spain).

Year-Book of the International Court of Justice. The Hague, 1950 ff.

6. **The Secretariat** is composed of the Secretary-General, who is the chief administrative officer of the organization, and an international staff appointed by him under regulations established by the General Assembly. However, the Secretary-General, the High Commissioner for Refugees and the Managing Director of the Fund are appointed by the General Assembly. The first Secretary-General was Trygve Lie (Norway), 1946–53; the second, Dag Hammarskjöld (Sweden), 1953–61; the third, U. Thant (Burma), 1961–71.

The Secretary-General acts as chief administrative officer in all meetings of the General Assembly, the Security Council, the Economic and Social Council and the Trusteeship Council.

Secretary-General: Kurt Waldheim (Austria), appointed 1 Jan. 1972.

The Secretary-General is assisted by about 20 Under-Secretaries-General and nearly 20 Assistant Secretaries-General.

The *UN Development Programme*, created on 22 Nov. 1965, is an amalgamation of the programme of Technical Assistance and the Special Fund. *Administrator:* Bradford Morse (USA).

The *UN Conference on Trade and Development* was established in 1964. It comprises those states which are members of the UN, its specialized agencies or the International Atomic Energy Agency. Its permanent organ, the Trade and Development Board (55 members), meets twice a year. Its 4 subsidiary organs meet annually: these are the Committees on Commodities, Manufactures, Shipping, and Invisibles and Financing Related to Trade. The first UNCTAD was held in Geneva in 1964, the second in New Delhi in 1968, the third in Santiago (Chile) 1972, the fourth in Nairobi (Kenya) 1976 and the fifth in Manila (Philippines) 1979. *Secretary-General:* Gamani Corea (Sri Lanka, appointed May 1974). *Headquarters:* Geneva, Switzerland.

The *UN Industrial Organization* (UNIDO) has worked as an autonomous body with the UN to promote industrialization and co-ordinate activities undertaken by the UN family in this field since 1967. Principal body is the 45-member Industrial Development Board, which formulates UNIDO's policy and its programme of activities. UNIDO tries to help the urgent need of developing countries to accelerate their promotional and operational activities and supports them by relevant studies and research. *Executive Director:* Abderraham Khane (Algeria). *Headquarters:* Wagramerstrasse 5, Vienna XXII, Austria.

Office of the United Nations High Commissioner for Refugees (UNHCR) was established by the UN General Assembly with effect from 1 Jan. 1951, originally for 3 years. Since 1954, its mandate has been renewed for 5-year periods. Under General Assembly resolution 32/67 adopted in Nov. 1977 the Office was prolonged until 31 Dec. 1983.

The task of UNHCR is of a purely humanitarian and non-political character.

The main functions of the Office of the High Commissioner are to provide international protection for refugees, to seek permanent solutions to their problems through voluntary repatriation, resettlement in other countries or integration into the country of present residence. UNHCR may also be called upon to provide emergency relief and supplementary aid where necessary.

UNHCR concerns itself with refugees who have been determined to come within its mandate under the Statute, and with persons in analogous circumstances whom it assists under the terms of the good offices resolutions adopted by the General Assembly.

The High Commissioner is elected by the General Assembly and follows policy directives given him by the General Assembly or the Economic and Social Council. He reports to the Third Committee of the General Assembly (Social and Humanitarian Affairs), through the Economic and Social Council. The Executive Committee of the High Commissioner's Programme gives the High Commissioner guidance in respect of material assistance programmes and advises him at his request in the exercise of his functions under the Statute. It meets normally once a year at Geneva. It includes representatives of 31 states, members and non-members of the UN. Its annual sessions are normally held in October in Geneva. In recent years it has been customary for the High Commissioner to invite representatives of member states to meet with him informally at least once between sessions to keep them abreast of important developments.

International protection is the primary function of UNHCR. Its main objective is to promote and safeguard the rights and interests of refugees. In so doing UNHCR devotes special attention to promoting a generous policy of asylum on the part of governments and seeks to improve the status of refugees in their country of residence. It also helps them to cease to be refugees through the acquisition of the nationality of their country of residence when voluntary repatriation is not applicable. UNHCR pursues its objectives in the field of protection by encouraging the conclusion of intergovernmental legal instruments in favour of refugees, by supervising the implementation of their provisions and by encouraging governments to adopt legislation and administrative procedures for the benefit of refugees. The main instrument in this field is the 1951 Convention Relating to the Status of Refugees. It prescribes a minimum standard of treatment for refugees in such important matters as employment, social security and freedom of movement, and provides for the issuance, by contracting states, of travel documents in lieu of national passports. The most important provision of the Convention is embodied in Article 33 which forbids the return of a refugee to a country where his life or liberty would be in danger because of persecution for reasons of race, religion, nationality or political opinion (*refoulement*).

A protocol relating to the status of refugees came into force in 1967 and had the effect of extending the provisions of the 1951 Convention (which applies to persons who have become refugees as a result of events prior to that date) to new groups of refugees.

On 1 Oct. 1980, 83 member states had acceded to the 1951 Convention and/or the 1967 Protocol.

The Sub-Committee of the Whole on International Protection took up at its 1980 session the questions of extradition of refugees, voluntary repatriation, temporary refuge and the protection of asylum-seekers, particularly at sea. The sub-committee requested that the High Commissioner convene a group of experts to study the question of temporary refuge, particularly in cases of large-scale influxes. Abuses in the treatment of refugees, including violations of the internationally-recognized principle of *non-refoulement*, continued to be brought to the attention of the High Commissioner and were a cause of great concern to his Office. The thirty-first session of the Executive Committee of the High Commissioner's Programme acknowledged that, despite progress in the field of protection, serious problems still remained. It also urged wider dissemination of information on refugee law.

Throughout 1979 the two areas of the world of greatest concern to UNHCR were Asia and Africa. In May, a Conference on the Situation of Refugees in Africa, sponsored jointly by UNHCR, the OAU and the Economic Commission for Africa, met in Arusha, United Republic of Tanzania. The Conference, noting that the African continent harboured the greatest concentration of refugees in the world, sought to promote an increased effort on the part of the international community to provide assistance. UNHCR's involvement is primarily directed at local integration, in rural settlements or in an urban environment, and includes counselling services and educational and training programmes.

In Dec. 1979 the Lancaster House Constitutional Conference in London provided for free elections in Southern Rhodesia leading to an independent Zimbabwe. At the request of the UK Government, UNHCR undertook to co-ordinate the repatriation of some 220,000 Zimbabwean refugees from Botswana, Mozambique and Zambia. At the request of the new Government, the Secretary-General appointed the High Commissioner to co-ordinate, for an initial period, the reinstallation and rehabilitation of the returnees and displaced persons. programme aimed at resettling some 650,000 persons was put into effect at an estimated cost of $140m. which was met chiefly through the response to a special appeal launched by the High Commissioner to the international community.

Events in the Horn of Africa compounded the effects of severe drought and caused more than 1m. persons to flee their homelands by mid-1980. Resolutions of the Economic and Social Council called upon UNHCR and other relevant UN bodies to provide assistance and a Special Co-ordinator for the region was appointed by the High Commissioner in Feb. 1980. Some $55m. were earmarked, under general programmes, for humanitarian assistance and local integration of refugees in Jibuti, Ethiopia, Somalia and the Sudan in 1980.

In the light of world-wide publicity for the plight of the 'boat people', the Secretary-General of the UN convened, in July 1979, a meeting on Refugees and Displaced Persons in South-East Asia. Following the meeting, UNHCR announced that pledges amounting to $160m. in cash and in kind as well as 260,000 resettlement places had been offered by participating countries. The governments of Indonesia and the Philippines offered to host Refugee Processing Centres to accommodate refugees for whom resettlement guarantees had been secured. Just prior to the meeting, on 30 May 1979, a memorandum of understanding between the Government of Vietnam and UNHCR was concluded to permit the orderly departure of family reunion and other humanitarian cases.

In 1979, a total of 270,882 Indo-Chinese refugees, 205,489 of whom were 'boat people', arrived in countries of temporary asylum. During the same period, some 192,115 persons were resettled with UNHCR assistance in third countries. Monthly arrivals had decreased to fewer than 4,000 persons by Dec. 1979 after having reached a peak of almost 70,000 the previous June. Numbers rose in 1980 to over 17,000 in May but averaged only 9,700 per month in the first 9 months of 1980 against an average departure rate of 23,400 per month. As of 30 Sept. 1980, 186,437 Indo-Chinese refugees were still awaiting permanent solutions in the camps of South-East Asia, not including Kampucheans who arrived in Thailand in 1979 who received UNHCR assistance in holding centres near the Kampuchean border.

Also in Asia, some 932,000 refugees from Afghanistan were registered by the Pakistani authorities as of June 1980. UNHCR initially responded with $190,000 from the Emergency Fund for shelter, food and clothing, followed by the implementation of an assistance programme which included establishment of basic health units and income-generating agricultural and handicraft projects.

In its on-going capacity as co-ordinator of UN humanitarian assistance in Cyprus, UNHCR in 1979 channelled some $6m. in aid for displaced persons throughout Cyprus for shelter, rafforestation and agriculture, health care and medical supplies.

In Oct. 1980, the Executive Committee of the High Commissioner's Programme approved a revised target figure for 1980 General Programmes of $299m., including some $165m. for assistance programmes in Asia and $98m. for African refugees; a 1981 General Programmes target of $335m. was also approved. It was thought that, with the greatly expanded number of persons of concern to the High Commissioner, UNHCR's overall financial requirements would be in the region of $500m. in 1980, with approximately the same amount needed for 1981.

Headquarters: Palais des Nations 1211, Geneva 10, Switzerland.
UK Office: 36 Westminster Palace Gardens, London, SW1P 1RR.
High Commissioner: Poul Hartling (Denmark).
Deputy High Commissioner: D. S. de Haan (USA).

UNHCR reports. Geneva, 1966 ff.
UNHCR Bulletin. Geneva, 1968–74
UNHCR Tabloids. Geneva, 1974 ff.
UNHCR *Refugee Update* Geneva 1979 ff.
UNHCR *The Last Ten Years.* Geneva 1980
Forty Years of International Assistance to Refugees. Geneva, 1962
The Red Cross and the Refugees. Geneva, 1963
A Mandate to Protect and Assist Refugees. Geneva, 1971
The Refugee Problem Isn't Hopeless Unless You Think So. Geneva, 1975
Habitat: Refugees in Human Settlements. Geneva, 1976

The United Nations Relief and Works Agency for Palestine Refugees in the Near East (UNRWA) was established by the General Assembly in Dec. 1949. It is supported by private contributions and by governmental pledges made each year at the General Assembly. UNRWA's operations, direct relief, long-term rehabilitation and vocational training, cover the Gaza Strip, Jordan, Lebanon and Syria, where over 1m. refugees were living before the war of June 1967.

Headquarters: Storchengasse 1, A-1150 Vienna, Austria.
Commissioner-General: Thomas W. McElhiney (USA).

The Children's Fund (UNICEF), established by the General Assembly on 11 Dec. 1946, functions under the supervision of the Economic and Social Council. It assists child health, nutrition and welfare programmes in 116 countries and territories. Its work is financed through voluntary contributions from governments and donations from the public.

Estimated income 1973 (including contributions for special emergencies), $95·8m.

Headquarters: United Nations Headquarters, New York City.
Executive Director: Henry R. Labouisse (USA).

The Budget of the United Nations. The financial year coincides with the calendar year; accountancy is in US$. Budget for 1978–79, $1,090,113,500.
Membership and percentage scale of contributions to UN budget, 1980–82:

Afghánistán	0·01	Burma	0·01	Dominica	0·01
Albania	0·01	Burundi	0·01	Dominican Republic	0·03
Algeria	0·12	Byelorussia	0·39	Ecuador	0·02
Angola	0·01	Cameroon	0·01	Egypt	0·07
Argentina	0·78	Canada	3·28	El Salvador	0·01
Australia	1·83	Cape Verde	0·01	Equatorial Guinea	0·01
Austria	0·71	Central African Rep.	0·01	Ethiopia	0·01
Bahamas	0·01	Chad	0·01	Fiji	0·01
Bahrain	0·01	Chile	0·07	Finland	0·48
Bangladesh	0·04	China	1·62	France	6·26
Barbados	0·01	Colombia	0·11	Gabon	0·02
Belgium	1·22	Comoros	0·01	Gambia	0·01
Benin	0·01	Congo	0·01	German Demo. Rep.	1·39
Bhután	0·01	Costa Rica	0·02	Germany, Federal Rep.	8·31
Bolivia	0·01	Cuba	0·11	Ghana	0·03
Botswana	0·01	Cyprus	0·01	Greece	0·35
Brazil	1·27	Czechoslovakia	0·83	Grenada	0·01
Bulgaria	0·16	Denmark	0·74	Guatemala	0·02

Guinea	0.01	Mauritania	0·01	Somalia	0·01
Guinea-Bissau	0·01	Mauritius	0·01	South Africa, Rep. of	0·42
Guyana	0·01	Mexico	0·76	Spain	1·70
Haiti	0·01	Mongolia	0·01	Sri Lanka	0·02
Honduras	0·01	Morocco	0·05	Sudan	0·01
Hungary	0·33	Mozambique	0·01	Surinam	0·01
Iceland	0·03	Nepál	0·01	Swaziland	0·01
India	0·60	Netherlands	1·63	Sweden	1·31
Indonesia	0·16	New Zealand	0·27	Syria	0·03
Iran	0·65	Nicaragua	0·01	Tanzania	0·01
Iraq	0·12	Niger	0·01	Thailand	0·10
Irish Republic	0·16	Nigeria	0·16	Togo	0·01
Israel	0·25	Norway	0·50	Trinidad and Tobago	0·03
Italy	3·45	Oman	0·01	Tunisia	0·03
Ivory Coast	0·03	Pakistan	0·07	Turkey	0·30
Jamaica	0·02	Panama	0·02	Uganda	0·01
Japan	9·58	Papua New Guinea	0·01	Ukraine	1·46
Jibuti	0·01	Paraguay	0·01	USSR	11·10
Jordan	0·01	Peru	0·06	United Arab Emirates	0·10
Kampuchea, Demo.	0·01	Philippines	0·10	UK	4·46
Kenya	0·01	Poland	1·24	USA	25·00
Kuwait	0·20	Portugal	0·19	Upper Volta	0·01
Laos	0·01	Qatar	0·03	Uruguay	0·04
Lebanon	0·03	Romania	0·21	Venezuela	0·50
Lesotho	0·01	Rwanda	0·01	Vietnam	0·03
Liberia	0·01	St Lucia	0·01	Western Samoa	0·01
Libya	0·23	St Vincent	0·01	Yemen Arab Republic	0·01
Luxembourg	0·05	São Tomé	0·01	Yemen, People's Dem.	
Madagascar	0·01	Saudi Arabia	0·58	Rep.	0·01
Malawi	0·01	Senegal	0·01	Yugoslavia	0·42
Malaysia	0·09	Seychelles	0·01	Zaïre	0·02
Maldive, Republic of	0·01	Sierra Leone	0·01	Zambia	0·02
Mali	0·01	Singapore	0·08	Zimbabwe	0·02
Malta	0·01	Solomon Islands	0·01		

Books of Reference

Yearbook of the United Nations, New York, 1947 ff. Annual
United Nations Chronicle. Quarterly
Monthly Bulletin of Statistics
General Assembly: Official Records: Resolutions
Reports of the Secretary-General of the United Nations on the work of the Organization. 1946 ff.
Documents of the United Nations Conference on International Organization, San Francisco, 1945. 16 vols.
Charter of the United Nations and Statute of the International Court of Justice. Text in English, French, Chinese, Russian and Spanish.
Repertory of Practice of UN's Organs. 5 vols. New York, 1955
Official Records of the Security Council, the Economic and Social Council, Trusteeship Council and the Disarmament Commission
Demographic Yearbook, 1948 ff. New York, 1969
Everyman's United Nations. 7th ed. New York, 1958 ff. Annual
Statistical Yearbook. New York, 1947 ff.
Yearbook of International Statistics. New York, 1950 ff.
World Economic Survey. New York, 1947 ff.
Economic Survey of Asia and the Far East. New York, 1946 ff.
Economic Survey of Latin America. New York, 1948 ff.
Economic Survey of Europe. New York, 1948 ff.
Economic Survey of Africa. New York, 1960 ff.
Bailey, S. D., *The General Assembly.* London, 1960
Boyd, A., *Fifteen Men and a Powder Keg.* London, 1971
Foote, W., *Dag Hammarskjöld—Servant of Peace.* London, 1962
Forsythe, D., *United Nations Peacemaking: The Conciliation Commission for Palestine.* Johns Hopkins Univ. Press, 1973
Hiscocks, R., *The Security Council: A Study in Adolescence.* New York, 1974
Lie, Trygve, *In the Cause of Peace.* London, 1954

Luard, E., *The United Nations in a New Era*. London, 1972
Meron, T., *The United Nations Secretariat*. Lexington, 1977
Nicholas, H. G., *The United Nations as a Political Institution*. OUP, 1959
Ogley, R., *The United Nations and East–West Relations*. Univ. of Sussex, 1972
Richards, J. H., *International Economic Institutions*. London, 1970
Rikhye, I. J., Harbottle, M., Egge, B., *The Thin Blue Line*. London, 1974
Symonds, R., and Carder, M., *The United Nations and the Population Question*. London, 1973
Thant, U., *Towards World Peace*. New York, 1964
Urquhart, B., *Hammarskjöld*. London, 1973
Walters, F. P., *A History of the League of Nations*. 2 vols. London, 1952
Winton, H. N. M. (comp. and ed.), *Man and the Environment. A Bibliography of Selected Publications of the United Nations System 1946–1971*. New York, 1972
Witthauer, K., *Die Bevölkerung der Erde: Verteilung und Dynamik*. Gotha, 1958.—*Distribution and Dynamics Relating to World Population*. Gotha, 1969
Her Majesty's Stationery Office. *Sectional List 23* (currently revised) and *International Organizations Publications* contain a full list of publications on UN and Specialized Agencies, issued by HMSO.

London Information Centre. 14–15 Stratford Place, W1N 9AF

AGENCIES IN RELATIONSHIP WITH THE UN

(as in 1980)

	IAEA	ILO	FAO	UNESCO	WHO	BANK & FUND	ICAO	UPU	ITU	WMO	IFC	IMCO	GATT
Afghánistán	*	*	*	*	*	*	*	*	*	*	*	—	—
Albania	*	—	*	*	*	—	—	*	*	*	—	—	—
Algeria	*	*	*	*	*	*	*	*	*	*	—	*	—
Angola	—	*	*	*	*	—	*	*	*	*	—	*	—
Argentina	*	*	*	*	*	*	*	*	*	*	*	*	*
Australia	*	*	*	*	*	*	*	*	*	*	*	*	*
Austria	*	*	*	*	*	*	*	*	*	*	*	*	*
Bahamas	—	*	*	—	*	*	*	*	*	—	—	*	—
Bahrain	—	*	*	*	*	*	*	*	*	—	—	*	—
Bangladesh	*	*	*	*	*	*	*	*	*	*	*	*	*
Barbados	—	*	*	*	*	*	*	*	*	*	—	*	*
Belgium	*	*	*	*	*	*	*	*	*	*	*	*	*
Benin	—	*	*	*	*	*	*	*	*	*	*	—	—
Bhután	—	—	—	—	—	—	*	—	—	—	—	—	—
Bolivia	*	*	*	*	*	*	*	*	*	*	*	—	—
Botswana	—	*	*	—	*	*	*	*	*	*	*	—	—
Brazil	*	*	*	*	*	*	*	*	*	*	*	*	*
Bulgaria	*	*	*	*	*	—	*	*	*	*	—	*	—
Burma	*	*	*	*	*	*	*	*	*	*	*	*	—
Burundi	—	*	*	*	*	*	*	*	*	*	*	—	*
Byelorussia	*	*	—	*	*	—	—	*	*	*	—	—	—
Cameroon	*	*	*	*	*	*	*	*	*	*	*	*	*
Canada	*	*	*	*	*	*	*	*	*	*	*	*	*
Cape Verde	—	*	*	*	*	*	*	*	*	*	—	—	—
Central African Rep.	—	*	*	*	*	*	*	*	*	*	—	—	*
Chad	—	*	*	*	*	*	*	*	*	*	—	—	*
Chile	*	*	*	*	*	*	*	*	*	*	*	*	*
China	—	—	*	*	*	*	*	*	*	*	*	*	—
Columbia	*	*	*	*	*	*	*	*	*	*	*	*	*
Comoros	—	*	*	*	*	—	*	*	*	*	—	—	—
Congo	—	*	*	*	*	*	*	*	*	*	—	*	*
Costa Rica	*	*	*	*	*	—	*	*	*	*	*	—	—
Cuba	*	*	*	*	*	—	*	*	*	*	—	*	*

See notes on pp. 14–15.

	IAEA	ILO	FAO	UNESCO	WHO	BANK & FUND	ICAO	UPU	ITU	WMO	IFC	IMCO	GATT
Cyprus	*	*	*	*	*	*	*	*	*	*	*	*	*
Czechoslovakia	*	*	*	*	*	—	*	*	*	*	*	*	*
Denmark	*	*	*	*	*	*	*	*	*	*	*	*	*
Dominican Rep.	*	*	*	*	*	*	*	*	*	*	*	*	*
Ecuador	*	*	*	*	*	*	*	*	*	*	*	*	—
Egypt	*	*	*	*	*	*	*	*	*	*	*	*	*
El Salvador	*	*	*	*	*	*	*	*	*	*	*	—	—
Equatorial Guinea	—	—	—	*	—	*	*	*	*	*	—	*	—
Ethiopia	*	*	*	*	*	*	*	*	*	*	*	*	—
Fiji	—	*	*	—	*	*	*	*	*	*	—	*	—
Finland	*	*	*	*	*	*	*	*	*	*	*	*	*
France	*	*	*	*	*	*	*	*	*	*	*	*	*
Gabon	*	*	*	*	*	*	*	*	*	*	*	*	*
Gambia	—	—	*	*	*	*	*	*	*	*	—	*	*
German Democratic Republic	*	*	—	*	*	—	—	*	*	*	—	*	—
Germany, Federal Republic of	*	*	*	*	*	*	*	*	*	*	*	*	*
Ghana	*	*	*	*	*	*	*	*	*	*	*	*	*
Greece	*	*	*	*	*	*	*	*	*	*	*	*	*
Grenada	—	*	*	*	*	*	—	*	—	*	*	—	—
Guatemala	*	*	*	*	*	*	*	*	*	*	*	—	—
Guinea	—	*	*	*	*	*	*	*	*	*	—	*	—
Guinea-Bissau	—	*	*	*	*	*	*	*	*	*	*	*	—
Guyana	—	*	*	*	*	*	*	*	*	*	*	*	*
Haiti	*	*	*	*	*	*	*	*	*	*	*	*	*
Holy See	*	—	—	—	—	—	—	*	*	*	—	—	—
Honduras	—	*	*	*	*	*	*	*	*	*	*	*	—
Hungary	*	*	*	*	*	—	*	*	*	*	—	*	*
Iceland	*	*	*	*	*	*	*	*	*	*	*	*	*
India	*	*	*	*	*	*	*	*	*	*	*	*	*
Indonesia	*	*	*	*	*	*	*	*	*	*	*	*	*
Iran	*	*	*	*	*	*	*	*	*	*	*	*	—
Iraq	*	*	*	*	*	*	*	*	*	*	*	*	—
Irish Republic	*	*	*	*	*	*	*	*	*	*	*	*	*
Israel	*	*	*	*	*	*	*	*	*	*	*	*	*
Italy	*	*	*	*	*	*	*	*	*	*	*	*	*
Ivory Coast	*	*	*	*	*	*	*	*	*	*	*	*	*
Jamaica	*	*	*	*	*	*	*	*	*	*	*	*	*
Japan	*	*	*	*	*	*	*	*	*	*	*	*	*
Jibuti	—	*	*	—	*	—	*	*	*	*	—	*	—
Jordan	*	*	*	*	*	*	*	*	*	*	*	*	—
Kampuchea, Demo.	*	*	*	*	*	*	*	*	*	*	—	*	—
Kenya	*	*	*	*	*	*	*	*	*	*	*	*	*
Korea, North	*	—	*	*	*	—	*	*	*	*	—	—	—
Korea, Rep. of	*	—	*	*	*	*	*	*	*	*	*	*	*
Kuwait	*	*	*	*	*	*	*	*	*	*	*	*	—
Laos	—	*	*	*	*	*	*	*	*	*	—	—	—
Lebanon	*	*	*	*	*	*	*	*	*	*	*	*	—
Lesotho	—	*	*	*	*	*	*	*	*	*	*	—	—
Liberia	*	*	*	*	*	*	*	*	*	*	*	*	—
Libya	*	*	*	*	*	*	*	*	*	*	*	*	—
Liechtenstein	*	—	—	—	—	—	—	*	*	*	—	—	—
Luxembourg	*	*	*	*	*	*	*	*	*	*	*	—	*
Madagascar	*	*	*	*	*	*	*	*	*	*	*	*	*
Malawi	—	*	*	*	*	*	*	*	*	*	*	—	*
Malaysia	*	*	*	*	*	*	*	*	*	*	*	*	*
Maldive Is.	—	—	*	—	*	*	*	*	*	*	—	*	—
Mali	*	*	*	*	*	*	*	*	*	*	*	—	—
Malta	—	*	*	*	*	—	*	*	*	*	—	*	*
Mauritania	—	*	*	*	*	*	*	*	*	*	*	*	*
Mauritius	*	*	*	*	*	*	*	*	*	*	*	*	*
Mexico	*	*	*	*	*	*	*	*	*	*	*	*	—
Monaco	*	—	—	*	*	—	—	*	*	*	—	—	—
Mongolia	*	*	*	*	*	—	—	*	*	*	—	—	—

	IAEA	ILO	FAO	UNESCO	WHO	BANK & FUND	ICAO	UPU	ITU	WMO	IFC	IMCO	GATT
Morocco	*	*	*	*	*	*	*	*	*	*	*	*	—
Mozambique	—	*	*	*	*	—	*	*	*	*	—	*	—
Namibia	—	*	*	*	*	—	—	—	—	—	—	—	—
Nauru	—	—	—	—	—	—	*	*	*	—	—	—	—
Nepál	—	*	*	*	*	*	*	*	*	*	*	*	—
Netherlands	*	*	*	*	*	*	*	*	*	*	*	*	*
New Zealand	*	*	*	*	*	*	*	*	*	*	*	*	*
Nicaragua	*	*	*	*	*	*	*	*	*	*	*	—	*
Niger	*	*	*	*	*	*	*	*	*	*	—	*	*
Nigeria	*	*	*	*	*	*	*	*	*	*	*	*	*
Norway	*	*	*	*	*	*	*	*	*	*	*	*	*
Oman	—	—	*	*	*	*	*	*	*	*	*	*	—
Pakistan	*	*	*	*	*	*	*	*	*	*	*	*	*
Panama	*	*	*	*	*	*	*	*	*	*	*	*	—
Papua New Guinea	—	*	*	*	*	*	*	*	*	*	*	*	—
Paraguay	*	*	*	*	*	*	*	*	*	*	*	—	—
Peru	*	*	*	*	*	*	*	*	*	*	*	*	*
Philippines	*	*	*	*	*	*	*	*	*	*	*	*	*
Poland	*	*	*	*	*	—	*	*	*	*	*	*	*
Portugal	*	*	*	*	*	*	*	*	*	*	*	*	*
Qatar	*	*	*	*	*	*	*	*	*	*	—	*	*
Romania	*	*	*	*	*	*	*	*	*	*	*	*	*
Rwanda	—	*	*	*	*	*	*	*	*	*	*	*	*
St Lucia	—	*	*	—	—	—	*	—	—	—	—	*	—
San Marino	—	—	*	*	*	—	—	*	*	—	—	—	—
São Tomé	—	—	—	*	*	*	*	*	*	—	—	—	—
Saudi Arabia	*	*	*	*	*	*	*	*	*	*	*	*	*
Senegal	*	*	*	*	*	*	*	*	*	*	*	*	*
Seychelles	—	*	*	*	*	*	*	*	—	*	—	*	*
Sierra Leone	*	*	*	*	*	*	*	*	*	*	*	*	*
Singapore	*	*	—	*	*	*	*	*	*	*	*	*	*
Solomon Islands	—	—	—	—	—	*	—	—	—	—	—	—	—
Somalia	—	*	*	*	*	*	*	*	*	*	*	*	—
South Africa, Rep. of	*	—	—	—	*	*	*	*	*	*	*	—	*
Spain	*	*	*	*	*	*	*	*	*	*	*	*	*
Sri Lanka	*	*	*	*	*	*	*	*	*	*	*	*	*
Sudan	*	*	*	*	*	*	*	*	*	*	*	*	*
Suriname	—	*	*	*	*	*	*	*	*	*	—	*	*
Swaziland	—	*	*	*	*	*	*	*	*	—	*	—	—
Sweden	*	*	*	*	*	*	*	*	*	*	*	*	*
Switzerland	*	*	*	*	*	—	*	*	*	*	—	*	*
Syria	*	*	*	*	*	*	*	*	*	*	*	*	—
Tanzania	*	*	*	*	*	*	*	*	*	*	*	*	*
Thailand	*	*	*	*	*	*	*	*	*	*	*	—	—
Togo	—	*	*	*	*	*	*	*	*	*	*	—	*
Tonga	—	—	—	—	*	—	—	*	*	—	—	—	—
Trinidad	—	*	*	*	*	*	*	*	*	*	*	*	*
Tunisia	*	*	*	*	*	*	*	*	*	*	*	*	—
Turkey	*	*	*	*	*	*	*	*	*	*	*	*	*
Uganda	*	*	*	*	*	*	*	*	*	*	—	—	—
Ukraine	*	*	—	*	*	—	—	*	*	*	—	*	—
USSR	*	*	—	*	*	—	*	*	*	*	—	*	—
United Arab Emir.	*	*	*	*	*	*	*	*	*	—	*	*	—
UK	*	*	*	*	*	*	*	*	*	*	*	*	*
USA	*	*	*	*	*	*	*	*	*	*	*	*	*
Upper Volta	—	*	*	*	*	*	*	*	*	*	*	—	—
Uruguay	*	*	*	*	*	*	*	*	*	*	*	*	—
Venezuela	*	*	*	*	*	*	*	*	*	*	*	*	—
Vietnam	*	*	*	*	*	*	*	*	*	*	—	—	—
Western Samoa	—	—	*	—	*	*	—	—	—	—	*	—	—
Yemen Arab Republic	—	*	*	*	*	*	*	*	*	*	—	*	—
Yemen, People's Dem. Rep.	—	*	*	*	*	*	*	*	*	*	—	*	—
Yugoslavia	*	*	*	*	*	*	*	*	*	*	*	*	*
Zaire	*	*	*	*	*	*	*	*	*	*	*	*	—
Zambia	*	*	*	*	*	*	*	*	*	*	*	—	—

UNESCO has 1 associate member: the British Eastern Caribbean Group.
WHO has 2 associate members: Zimbabwe and Namibia.

The 158 members of UPU include the following not listed in the table: Netherlands Antilles, Overseas Territories for the international relations of which the Government of the United Kingdom of Great Britain and Northern Ireland is responsible.

The 150 members of WMO include the following 6 members not listed in the table which maintain their own meteorological service: British Caribbean Territories, French Polynesia, Hong Kong, Netherlands Antilles, New Caledonia, and Rhodesia.

The 118 members of IMCO include 1 associate member: Hong Kong.

GATT: The 86 contracting parties to GATT include Rhodesia. In addition there are 3 countries—Colombia, Tunisia and the Philippines—which have provisionally acceded to the Agreement, and 24 countries—to whose territories GATT had been applied before independence and which now as independent states maintain a *de facto* application of the GATT pending final decisions as to their future commercial policy.

In ICAO, USSR membership includes Byelorussia and the Ukraine.

INTERNATIONAL ATOMIC ENERGY AGENCY (IAEA)

Origin. The International Atomic Energy Agency came into existence on 29 July 1957. Its statute had been approved on 26 Oct. 1956, at an international conference held at UN Headquarters, New York. A relationship agreement links it with the United Nations. The IAEA had 110 member states in 1980.

Functions. (1) To accelerate and enlarge the contribution of atomic energy to peace, health and prosperity throughout the world, and (2) to ensure that assistance provided by it or at its request or under its supervision or control is not used in such a way as to further any military purpose.

The IAEA gives advice and technical assistance to developing countries on nuclear power development (provides a series of training courses on nuclear power project planning), on health and safety, on radioactive waste management, on legal aspects of the use of atomic energy, and on prospecting for and exploiting nuclear raw materials; in addition it promotes the use of radiation and isotopes in agriculture, industry, medicine and hydrology through expert services, training courses and fellowships, grants of equipment and supplies, research contracts, scientific meetings and publications. Since 1958 the Agency has provided technical assistance totalling $108m., consisting of the services of 3,742 experts and lecturers, 7,739 fellowships, equipment worth $37m. not including research contracts. The IAEA has research laboratories in Austria and Monaco. At Trieste, the International Centre for Theoretical Physics was established in 1964 which is now operated jointly by UNESCO and IAEA.

The IAEA applies safeguards in 29 States pursuant to NPT and in 21 States under other agreements to 117 power reactors, 4 conversion plants, 33 fabrication plants, 4 enrichment plants, 5 reprocessing plants, 171 research reactors and critical assemblies, 19 separate storage facilities, 40 locations containing more than 1 effective kg of nuclear material, 307 locations containing 1 or less than 1 effective kg of nuclear material. The above figures include facilities safeguarded under agreement with the European Atomic Energy Community and its non-nuclear-weapon States.

Organization. The Statute provides for an annual General Conference, a Board of Governors of 34 members and a staff headed by a Director-General.

Headquarters: Vienna International Centre, PO Box 100, A-1400 Vienna, Austria.
Director-General: Sigvard Eklund (Sweden).

INTERNATIONAL LABOUR ORGANISATION (ILO)

Origin. The ILO, established in 1919 as an autonomous part of the League of Nations, is an intergovernmental agency with a tripartite structure, in which representatives of governments, employers and workers participate. It seeks through international action to improve labour conditions, raise living standards and promote productive employment. In 1946 the ILO was recognized by the United Nations as a specialized agency. In 1969 it was awarded the Nobel Peace Prize. In 1980 it numbered 144 members.

Functions. One of the ILO's principal functions is the formulation of international standards in the form of International Labour Conventions and Recommendations. Member countries are required to submit Conventions to their competent national authorities with a view to ratification. If a country ratifies a Convention it agrees to bring its laws into line with its terms and to report periodically how these regulations are being applied. More than 4,800 ratifications of 153 Conventions had been deposited by mid-1980. Machinery is available to ascertain whether Conventions thus ratified are effectively applied.

Recommendations do not require ratification, but member states are obliged to consider them with a view to giving effect to their provisions by legislation or other action. By the end of 1980 the International Labour Conference had adopted 162 recommendations.

Organization. The ILO consists of the International Labour Conference, the Governing Body and the International Labour Office.

The Conference is the supreme deliberative organ of the ILO; it meets annually at Geneva. National delegations are composed of 2 government delegates, 1 employers' delegate and 1 workers' delegate.

The Governing Body, elected by the Conference, is the executive council. It is composed of 28 government members, 14 workers' members and 14 employers' members.

Ten governments hold permanent seats on the Governing Body because of their industrial importance, namely, Brazil, Canada, China, Federal Republic of Germany, France, India, Italy, Japan, USSR and UK, with the addition in 1980 of US. The remaining 18 government seats were, at the end of 1980, held by Bangladesh, Cameroon, Colombia, Ivory Coast, Spain, Guyana, Honduras, Iran, Lebanon, Niger, Peru, Romania, Sierra Leone, Czechoslovakia, Thailand, Tunisia, Venezuela and Zambia.

The Office serves as secretariat, operational headquarters, research centre and publishing house.

The ILO budget for 1980–81 amounted to US$203m.

Activities. In addition to its research and advisory activities, the ILO extends technical co-operation to governments under its regular budget and under the UN Development Programme and Funds-in-Trust in the fields of employment promotion, human resources development (including vocational and management training), development of social institutions, small-scale industries, rural development, social security, industrial safety and hygiene, productivity, etc. Technical co-operation also includes expert missions and a fellowship programme. Some $79m. was spent on technical co-operation in 1979. Projects were in progress in over 100 countries and nearly 1,000 experts involved.

Major emphasis is being given to the ILO's World Employment Programme, launched in 1969 with the purpose of stimulating national and international efforts to increase the volume of productive employment, and so to counter the problem of rising unemployment in developing countries. Employment strategy missions were carried out under the Programme in Colombia, Iran, Kenya, Sri Lanka, the Philippines and the Dominican Republic. The work of these missions was complemented by an ILO programme of research designed to provide policy-makers with the information to promote employment. A World Employment Conference was held in June 1976. The International Labour Conference (Geneva, June 1980) adopted a Recommendation on older workers and prepared the way for new instruments on collective bargaining, equality of treatment for workers with family responsibilities and safety and health.

In 1960 the ILO established in Geneva the International Institute for Labour Studies. The Institute specializes in advanced education and research on social and labour policy. It brings together for group study experienced persons from all parts of the world—government administrators, trade-union officials, industrial experts, management, university and other specialists.

A training institution was opened by the ILO in Turin, Italy, in 1965—the International Centre for Advanced Technical and Vocational Training. The Centre provides opportunities for technical, vocational and management training for individuals who have advanced beyond the facilities available in their own countries. Courses are geared particularly to the needs of developing countries.

Headquarters: International Labour Office, CH-1211 Geneva 22, Switzerland.
Director-General: Francis Blanchard (France).

Chairman of the Governing Body: Vijit Sangtong (Thailand).
London Branch Office: 96/98 Marsham St., SW1.

The ILO has regional offices in Addis Ababa (for Africa), Bangkok (for Asia and the Pacific) and Lima (for Latin America and the Caribbean). It has other offices in Abidjan, Algiers, Ankara, Beirut, Belgrade, Bonn, Brasilia, Brussels, Budapest, Buenos Aires, Cairo, Dacca, Dakar, Dar es Salaam, Dresden, Islamabad, Jakarta, Kinshasa, Kuwait, Lagos, London, Lusaka, Manila, Mexico City, Moscow, New Delhi, New York, Ottawa, Paris, Port-of-Spain, Rome, San José (Costa Rica), Santiago (Chile), Sofia, Suva (Fiji), Tananarive, Tehrán, Tōkyō, Warsaw, Washington and Yaoundé.

Publications. Regular periodicals in English, French and Spanish include the *International Labour Review* (bi-monthly); *Legislative Series* (bi-monthly); *Bulletin of Labour Statistics* (quarterly); *Official Bulletin* (quarterly); the *Year Book of Labour Statistics*; a number of research studies and manuals including: *International Migration and Development in the Arab Region. Basic Needs, Poverty and Government Policies in Sri Lanka. Managing and Developing New Forms of Work Organisation. Case Method in Management Development. Conciliation and Arbitration Procedures in Labour Disputes: A Comparative Study. Labour Administration: A General Introduction. Standards and Policy Statements of Special Interest to Women Workers. The Impact of Micro-Electronics: A Tentative Appraisal of Information Technology.* All 1980.

FOOD AND AGRICULTURE ORGANIZATION OF THE UNITED NATIONS (FAO)

Origin. The UN Conference on Food and Agriculture in May 1943, at Hot Springs, Virginia, set up an Interim Commission in Washington in July 1943 to plan the Organization, which came into being on 16 Oct. 1945.

Functions. FAO gives international support to national programmes to increase the efficiency of agriculture, forestry and fisheries, and to improve the conditions of the people engaged in relevant activities.

FAO keeps world food and agricultural conditions under continuous review and supplies member governments with facts and figures, appraisals and forecasts relating to trends in the world agricultural situation and on production, trade and consumption.

The FAO Conference meets every 2 years. At its 20th session held in Nov. 1979, it admitted 3 new States: Dominica, Western Samoa and Saint Lucia.

Reporting to the 78th session of the FAO Council in Nov. 1980, the Director-General warned of the deteriorating state of world food and agriculture. Increases in production had been only marginal, while per caput output had declined for the second consecutive year. The situation was extremely grave in Africa, where more than 150m. people were affected by abnormal food shortages mainly due to drought conditions. Difficulties were compounded in many instances by the presence of large numbers of refugees and displaced persons.

The world cereal situation was precarious as a result of bad weather in several major grain producing and exporting countries. Since import needs of developing countries were expected to increase, cereal stocks would have to be drawn down to levels considerably below the margin of safety needed for world food security. Prices, especially for maize, continued to rise.

Food production in some developing regions was not keeping pace with growing population. The consequences would be increased dependence of food-importing developing countries on world markets. Food production in the Far East was expected to increase by over 3% in 1980, but food and agricultural production in the developed countries as a whole was likely to be more than 1% lower than 1979.

The international food aid goals, such as that of the International Emergency Food Reserve, had not been met and the lack of an internationally co-ordinated system of national cereal stocks was making the world more prone to a food crisis.

The value of world exports of agricultural, forestry and fishery products increased by over 14% in 1979 and continued to rise in early 1980. The greater part of the increase benefited developed countries. Only about one-third of the increased value of agricultural exports was due to increased volume of products, the rest was predominantly price-based.

FAO provides secretariat services for the exchange of information and for co-operative action in its field of concern. More than 2,000 experts are assigned to field projects in developing countries. Through co-operative arrangements with private and public lending institutions, such as the World Bank, it helps to mobilize capital backing to programmes of development. With the UN, FAO sponsors the World Food Programme, which uses food and cash pledged by member countries for economic and social development projects and for alleviating distress during emergencies. Through the Freedom from Hunger/Action for Development Programme, which is conducted by some 100 national committees, FAO arouses concern over the gravity and extent of the world food situation and mobilizes public support for programmes to improve the quality of life of rural communities.

Organization. FAO's programme and overall policy are approved by a Conference (composed of one representative of each of the 147 member nations) and interim supervision is given by a Council (consisting of 49 nations elected by the Conference). The work of the Organization is carried out by an international staff led by a Director-General.

Budget for 1980–81: $278·74m.

Headquarters: Viale delle Terme di Caracalla, Rome, Italy.
Director-General: Dr Edouard Saouma (Lebanon).

FAO publications include: FAO Books in Print 1978: The State of Food and Agriculture (annual), 1974 ff.; *Animal Health Yearbook* (annual), 1957 ff.; *Production Yearbook* (annual), 1947 ff.; *Trade Yearbook* (annual), 1947 ff.; *FAO Commodity Review* (annual), 1961 ff.; *Yearbook of Forest Products Statistics* (annual), 1947 ff.; *Yearbook of Fishery Statistics* (in two volumes). *Ceres* (bimonthly). *Food and Nutrition* (bi-annual), *FAO Fertilizer Yearbook, FAO Plant Protection Bulletin* (quarterly), *World Animal Review* (quarterly).

UNITED NATIONS EDUCATIONAL, SCIENTIFIC AND CULTURAL ORGANIZATION (UNESCO)

Origin. A Conference for the establishment of an Educational, Scientific and Cultural Organization of the United Nations was convened by the Government of the UK in association with the Government of France, and met in London, 1–16 Nov. 1945. UNESCO came into being on 4 Nov. 1946.

Functions. The purpose of UNESCO is to contribute to peace and security by promoting collaboration among the nations through education, science and culture in order to further universal respect for justice, for the rule of law and for the human rights and fundamental freedoms which are affirmed for the peoples of the world, without distinction of race, sex, language or religion, by the Charter of the United Nations. The UNESCO budget for 1980 was $115·5m.

Activities. The education programme has four main objectives: the extension of education; the improvement of education; and life-long education for living in a world community.

To train teachers specialized in the techniques of fundamental education UNESCO is helping to establish regional and national training centres. A centre for Latin America was opened in Mexico in 1951, one for the Arab States was set up in Egypt in 1953. UNESCO seeks to promote the progressive application of the right to free and compulsory education for all and to improve the quality of education everywhere.

In the natural sciences, UNESCO seeks to promote international scientific co-operation, such as the International Hydrological Programme which began in 1966. It encourages scientific research designed to improve the living conditions of mankind. Science co-operation offices have been set up in Montevideo, Cairo, New Delhi, Nairobi and Jakarta.

In the field of communication, UNESCO endeavours, by disseminating information, carrying out research and providing advice, to increase the scope and quality of press, film and radio services throughout the world.

Organization. The organs of UNESCO are a General Conference (composed of representatives from each member state), an Executive Board (consisting of 45 government representatives elected by the General Conference) and a Secretariat. UNESCO had 153 members and 1 associate member in 1980.

National commissions act as liaison groups between UNESCO and the educational, scientific and cultural life of their own countries.

Budget for 1981: $200,133,700.

Headquarters: UNESCO House, 9 Place de Fontenoy, Paris (7eme).
Director-General: Amadou Mahtar M'Bow (Senegal).

Periodicals. Museum (quarterly, English and French); *International Social Science Journal* (quarterly, English and French); *Impact of Science on Society* (quarterly, English and French); *Unesco Courier* (monthly, English, French and Spanish); *Fundamental and Adult Education Bulletin* (quarterly, English, French and Spanish); *Copyright Bulletin* (twice-yearly, English and French); *Unesco News* (English, French and Spanish); *Unesco Bulletin for Libraries* (monthly, English, French and Spanish).

WORLD HEALTH ORGANIZATION (WHO)

Origin. An International Conference, convened by the UN Economic and Social Council, to consider a single health organization resulted in the adoption on 22 July 1946 of the constitution of the World Health Organization. This constitution came into force on 7 April 1948.

Structure. The principal organs of WHO are the World Health Assembly, the Executive Board and the Secretariat. Each of the 155 member states and 1 Associate Member (1980) has the right to be represented at the Assembly, which meets annually usually in Geneva, Switzerland. The 30-member Executive Board is composed of technically qualified health experts designated by as many member states elected by the Assembly. The Secretariat consists of technical and administrative staff headed by a Director-General. Health activities in member countries are carried out through regional organizations which have been established in Africa (regional office, Brazzaville), South-East Asia (New Delhi), Europe (Copenhagen), Eastern Mediterranean (Alexandria) and Western Pacific (Manila). The Pan American Sanitary Bureau in Washington serves as the Regional Office of WHO for the Americas.

Functions. WHO's objective, as stated in the first article of the Constitution is 'the attainment by all peoples of the highest possible level of health'. As the directing and co-ordinating authority on international health it establishes and maintains collaboration with the UN, specialized agencies, government health administrations, professional and other groups concerned with health. The Constitution also directs WHO to assist governments to strengthen their health services, to stimulate and advance work to eradicate diseases, to promote maternal and child health, mental health, medical research and the prevention of accidents; to improve standards of teaching and training in the health professions, and of nutrition, housing, sanitation, working conditions and other aspects of environmental health. The Organization also is empowered to propose conventions, agreements and regulations and make recommendations about international health matters; to revise the international nomenclature of diseases, causes of death and public health practices; to develop, establish and promote international standards concerning foods, biological, pharmaceutical and similar substances.

Methods of work. Co-operation in country projects is undertaken only on the request of the government concerned, through the 6 regional offices of the Organization. Worldwide technical services are made available by headquarters. Expert committees whose members are chosen from the 47 advisory panels of experts meet to advise the Director-General on a given subject. Scientific groups and consultative meetings are called for similar purposes. To further the education of health personnel of all categories, seminars, technical conferences and training courses are organized and advisors, consultants and lecturers are provided. WHO awards fellowships for study to nationals of member countries.

Activities. WHO's main activities in 1980 were towards promoting national, regional and global strategies for the attainment of the main social target of the member states for the next two decades, 'Health for all by the year 2000'.

Water supply and sanitation needs of more than 100 countries were assessed in preparation for the International Drinking Water Supply and Sanitation Decade launched by the UN General Assembly on 10 Nov. Several interregional, regional and national workshops were conducted to develop national strategies for the Decade. Co-operation was given to Member Governments in planning their water supply and sanitation programmes.

An expert group reviewed the progress of the Priority Programme for the Control of Diarrhoeal Diseases, and recommended launching of national programmes based on oral dehydration therapy (ORT) and better feeding and hygienic practices. ORT is a simple method of preventing dehydration – the main cause of death in acute diarrhoea – by giving the patient a solution made up of table salt, baking powder, potassium chloride, and sugar dissolved in water.

Co-operation was given to more than 100 countries under the Expanded Programme on Immunization (EPI) against childhood diseases – diphtheria, pertussis, tetanus, poliomyelitis, measles and tuberculosis. An essential requirement of the programme is the 'cold chain' refrigerators and cold boxes suitable for storage and transportation of vaccines in tropical climates. A number of the new cold chain products were developed and introduced during the year and training manuals published.

The 33rd World Health Assembly meeting in May proclaimed at a special ceremony the global eradication of smallpox. It recommended that vaccination against smallpox be discontinued in every country except for investigators at special risk, and no certificates of vaccination against the disease be required from international travellers.

The 32nd World Health Assembly met in May 1979 and adopted an effective working budget of $427·29m. for the work of WHO in 1980–81.

In programmes relating to non-communicable diseases, such as cardiovascular diseases and cancer, research figures prominently. Work in cancer is carried out both at the International Agency for Research on Cancer at Lyons in the field of environmental biology, and in a number of WHO collaborating centres which are concerned with clinical studies, classification and cancer control services. The medical research programme of WHO is based on a world-wide network of collaborating centres and on advisory committees on medical research established in its 6 regions. Six tropical diseases, malaria, schistosomiasis, trypanosomiasis, filariasis, leishmaniasis and leprosy, are the target of a special research programme to develop new tools, strengthen research institutions and train workers in the countries affected. In mental health the focus is on research and on development of service delivery models suitable for countries with limited resources. In pharmacology and toxicology work is geared to ensuring the availability of effective and safe drugs to developing countries at prices that they can afford.

Headquarters: 1211 Geneva 27. *Regional Offices:* Alexandria, Brazzaville, Copenhagen, Manila, New Delhi, Washington.

Director-General: Dr Halfdan T. Mahler (Denmark).

Basic Documents. 30th ed., 1980 (English, French, Russian, Spanish)
Handbook of Resolutions and Decisions. Vol. I, 1973 and Vol. II, 1979 (Arabic, English, French, Russian, Spanish).
WHO Chronicle (monthly from 1947; English, French, Russian and Spanish)
Bulletin of WHO (quarterly, 1947–51; 6 issues a year from 1978; English and French)
International Digest of Health Legislation (quarterly, from 1948; English)
World Health, the Magazine of WHO. 1957 ff. (10 issues a year; Arabic, English, French, German, Italian, Persian, Portuguese, Russian and Spanish)
WHO Technical Report Series, 1950 ff. (English, French, Russian, Spanish)
WHO Monograph Series, 1951 ff. (English, French, Russian, Spanish)

Public Health Papers, 1959 ff. (English, French, Russian, Spanish)
World Health Statistics Annual (from 1939; English, French and Russian)
World Health Statistics Quarterly (monthly, 1947–76 then quarterly; English and French)
Weekly Epidemiological Record (from 1926; English and French)
Publications of the WHO, 1947–57; a bibliography (1958).—*1958–62* (1965).—*1963–67* (1969).— *1968–72* (1974)
World Directories:
    Dental Schools, 1963 (1967); *Medical Schools, 1979*; *Post-Basic and Post-Graduate Schools of Nursing* (1965); *Schools of Pharmacy, 1963* (1966); *Schools of Public Health, 1971* (1972); *Venereal Disease Treatment Centres at Ports* (1972); *Veterinary Schools, 1971* (1973). *Schools for Medical Assistants, 1973* (1976); *Auxiliary Sanitarians 1973* (1978); *Dental Auxiliaries 1973* (1977); *Medical Lab. Technicians and Assistants, 1973* (1977)
The International Pharmacopoeia. 3rd. ed., 1979 (English, French and Spanish)
Manual of the International Statistical Classification of Diseases, Injuries and Causes of Death. 9th rev. (1977; English, French, Russian, Spanish)
IARC Monographs on the Evaluation of Carcinogenic Risk of Chemicals to Humans. 1967 ff. (English)
International Histological Classification of Tumours. Books and slides, from 1967, No. 25 1980. (English, French, Russian and Spanish)
Report on the World Health Situation. 1959 ff. (English, French, Russian, Spanish); Sixth report 1973–77 (1979)

INTERNATIONAL MONETARY FUND (IMF)

The International Monetary Fund was established on 27 Dec. 1945 as an independent international organization; its relationship with the UN is defined in an agreement of mutual co-operation which came into force on 15 Nov. 1947. The first amendment to the Fund's articles creating the special drawing right (SDR) took effect on 28 July 1969 and the second amendment took effect on 1 April 1978.

The Fund is authorized under its Articles of Agreement to supplement its resources by borrowing. In Jan. 1962, a 4-year agreement was concluded with 10 industrial members (Belgium, Canada, France, Federal Republic of Germany, Italy, Japan, Netherlands, Sweden, UK, USA) who undertook to lend the Fund up to $6,000m. in their own currencies, if this should be needed to forestall or cope with an impairment of the international monetary system. These agreements, which have now been extended until 1985, were used to finance drawings made by the UK in 1964, 1965, 1968, 1969 and 1977, by France in 1969 and 1970 and by USA in 1978.

Purposes: To promote international monetary co-operation, the expansion of international trade and exchange stability; to assist in the removal of exchange restrictions and the establishment of a multilateral system of payments; and to alleviate any serious disequilibrium in members' international balance of payments by making the resources of the Fund available to them under adequate safeguards.

Activities. Each member of the Fund undertakes a broad obligation to collaborate with the Fund and other members to ensure the existence of orderly exchange arrangements and to promote a system of stable exchange rates. In addition, members are subject to certain obligations relating to domestic and external policies that can effect the balance of payments and the exchange rate. The Fund makes its resources available, under proper safeguards, to its members to meet short-term or medium-term payments difficulties. The Fund also supplements, as and when needed, the existing reserve assets of participants in the Special Drawing Account. The first allocation of special drawing rights was made on 1 Jan. 1970. Total allocations amounted to SDR 9,300m. On 24 Sept. 1978 the Fund agreed on a 50% increase in quotas under the 7th general review of quotas which would raise the Fund's general resources to SDR 59,900m. To further enhance its balance of payments assistance to its members the Fund established a compulsory financing facility on 23 Feb. 1963, an oil facility on 12 June 1974, an extended facility for medium term assistance to members with special balance of payments problems on 13 Sept. 1974, an oil facility on 4 April 1975, and a trust fund on 5 May 1976. The Board of Governors approved a resolution, on 24 Sept. 1978, authorizing the allocation of SDR 4,000m. in each of the 3 years 1979, 1980 and 1981.

A Report on Reform of the International Monetary System was submitted to the

Board of Governors at the 1972 annual meeting. During the meeting the Committee on Reform of the International Monetary System and Related Issues, generally known as the Committee of Twenty, held its first session, with the mandate to advise and report to the Board on all aspects of the international monetary system, including proposals for any amendments of the Articles of Agreement. The Committee of Twenty ceased to exist after submitting its final report in 1974. An Interim Committee of the Board of Governors on the International Monetary System and a Joint Ministerial Committee of the Boards of Governors of the World Bank and the Fund on the Transfer of Real Resources to Developing Countries (Development Committee) were established and held their initial meetings in Jan. 1975 and since then have met on a semi-annual basis.

Organization. The highest authority in the Fund is exercised by the Board of Governors on which each member government is represented. Normally the Governors meet once a year, although the Governors may take votes by mail or other means between annual meetings. The Board of Governors has delegated many of its powers to the executive directors in Washington, of whom there are 22, of which 6 are appointed by individual members and the other 16 elected by groups of countries. Each appointed director has voting power proportionate to the quota of the government he represents, while each elected director casts all the votes of the countries which elected him. The 6 appointed executive directors represent the US, UK, France, Federal Republic of Germany, Saudi Arabia and Japan.

The managing director is selected by the executive directors; he presides as chairman at their meetings, but may not vote except in case of a tie. His term is for 5 years, but may be extended or terminated at the discretion of the executive directors. He is responsible for the ordinary business of the Fund, under general control of the executive directors, and supervises a staff of about 1,400.

Headquarters: 19th & H St. NW, Washington, D.C., 20431. Offices in Paris and Geneva.

Managing Director: Jacques de Larosière (France).

Publications. Summary Proceedings of Annual Meetings of the Board of Governors.—Annual Report of the Executive Directors.—Financial Statement (quarterly).—*International Financial Statistics* (monthly).—*IMF Survey* (bi-monthly).—*Balance of Payments Statistics.* Washington, monthly.—*IMF Staff Papers* (three times a year). Washington, from Feb. 1950.—*Annual Report on Exchange Restrictions.* Washington, 1950 ff.—*Finance and Development.* Washington, from June 1964 (quarterly).—*Direction of Trade.* Washington (monthly). *World Economic Outlook.* Washington (annual).

de Vries, M. G., *The International Monetary Fund 1966–1971.* Washington D.C., 1976

INTERNATIONAL BANK FOR RECONSTRUCTION AND DEVELOPMENT

Conceived at the Bretton Woods Conference, July 1944, the Bank began operations in June 1946. Its purpose is to provide funds and technical assistance to facilitate economic development in its poorer member countries.

The Bank obtains its funds from the following sources: Capital subscribed by member countries; sales of its own securities; sales of parts of its loans; repayments; and net earnings. The subscribed capital of the Bank amounted to $34,429m. at 30 June 1980. On 4 Jan. 1980, the Board of Governors adopted a resolution that increased the authorized capital stock of the Bank by 331,500 shares. This represented an increase of approximately $40,000m. The resolution provides that the paid-in portion of the shares authorized to be subscribed under it will be 7·5%, compared with the 10% paid-in portion of existing capital stock. Borrowing in the market had reached $45,932m. by 30 June 1980, of which $29,667m. was outstanding, and sales of portions of Bank loans from portfolio had totalled $2,980m. The Bank is self-supporting. Its net earnings for year ending 30 June 1980 amounted to $588m.; in addition, the Bank had reserves of $3,995m.

By 30 June 1980 the Bank had made 1,875 loans totalling $59,341·4m. in 100 of its 139 member countries. Lending was for the following purposes: Agriculture and rural development, $12,102m.; Development Finance Companies, $5,981m.; education, $2,098m.; energy, $12,688m.; industry, $4,680m.; non-project, $2,516m.; population, health and nutrition, $227m.; power, $12,902m.; telecommunications, $1,264m.; tourism, $364m.; transportation, $12,902m.; urban development, $1,137m.; water supply and sewerage, $2,658m., and technical assistance, $42m.

In order to eliminate wasteful overlapping of development assistance and to ensure that the funds available are used to the best possible effect, the Bank has organized consortia or consultative groups of aid-giving nations for the following countries: Bangladesh, Colombia, Egypt, Korea, Nepál, Pakistan, the Philippines, Sudan, Uganda, Zaïre and the Caribbean Group for Co-operation in Economic Development. The Bank furnishes a wide variety of technical assistance. It acts as executing agency for a number of pre-investment surveys financed by the UN Development Programme. Resident missions have been established in 23 developing member countries as well as 3 regional missions in East and West Africa and Thailand primarily to assist in the preparation of projects. The Bank helps member countries to identify and prepare projects for the development of agriculture, education and water supply by drawing on the expertise of the FAO, WHO, UNIDO and UNESCO through its co-operative agreements with these organizations. The Bank maintains a staff college, the Economic Development Institute in Washington, D.C., for senior officials of the member countries.

To help the poorest member countries the INTERNATIONAL DEVELOPMENT ASSOCIATION (IDA) was established in 1960. IDA grants development credits on a long-term, interest-free basis. By 30 June 1980 IDA had extended 973 credits to 72 countries, totalling $20,570m. for the same general purpose as bank loans. IDA's primary lending resources have been the subscriptions and supplementary contributions of member countries, chiefly its 21 wealthiest. The World Bank has made grants to IDA out of its net income; the Association also has a small flow of net income of its own.

Headquarters: 1818 H St., NW, Washington, D.C., 20433, USA. *European office:* 66 avenue d'Iéna, 75116 Paris, France. *London office:* New Zealand House, Haymarket, SW1Y 4TE, England. *Tōkyō office:* Kokusai Building, 1–1, Marunouchi 3-chome, Chiyoda-ku, Tōkyō 100, Japan.

President: Alden W. (Tom) Clausen.

Publications. Annual Reports. 1946 ff.—Summary Proceedings of Annual Meetings. 1947 ff.—The World Bank Group. 1971.—The World Bank Atlas. 1967 ff.—The World Bank, Group Policies and Operations. 1974.—Catalog of Publications, 1979.—IDA, 1979.—World Development Report. 1978 ff.

INTERNATIONAL FINANCE CORPORATION (IFC)

The Corporation, an affiliate of the World Bank, was established in July 1956. Paid-in capital at 30 June 1980 was $307m., subscribed by 113 member countries. In addition, it has accumulated earnings of $140m. IFC supplements the activities of the World Bank by encouraging the growth of productive private enterprises in less developed member countries. Chiefly, IFC makes investments in the form of subscriptions to the share capital of privately owned companies, or long-term loans, or both. The Corporation will help finance new ventures, and it will also assist established enterprises to expand, improve or diversify their operations.

At 30 June 1980 IFC had approved investments amounting to $3,209m., in 73 countries. The total amount of loans and equity which IFC had sold or agreed to sell to other investors as of that date was $1,157·7m.

President: Alden W. (Tom) Clausen.

Executive Vice-President: Moeen A. Qureshi (Pakistan).

Publications. Annual Reports. 1956 ff.—General Policies. 1979.

INTERNATIONAL CIVIL AVIATION ORGANIZATION (ICAO)

Origin. The Convention providing for the establishment of the International Civil Aviation Organization was drawn up by the International Civil Aviation Conference held in Chicago from 1 Nov. to 7 Dec. 1944. A Provisional International Civil Aviation Organization (PICAO) operated for 20 months until the formal establishment of ICAO on 4 April 1947.

The Convention on International Civil Aviation superseded the provisions of the Paris Convention of 1919, which established the International Commission for Air Navigation (ICAN), and the Pan American Convention on Air Navigation drawn up at Havana in 1928.

Functions. It assists international civil aviation by establishing technical standards for safety and efficiency of air navigation and promoting simpler procedures at borders; develops regional plans for ground facilities and services needed for international flying; disseminates air-transport statistics and prepares studies on aviation economics; fosters the development of air law conventions. As part of the UN Development Programme it provides technical assistance to States in developing civil aviation programmes.

Organization. The principal organs of ICAO are an Assembly, consisting of all members of the Organization, and a Council, which is comprised of 33 states elected by the Assembly, for 3 years, and meets in virtually continuous session. In electing these states, the Assembly must give adequate representation to: (1) member states of major importance in air transport; (2) those member states not otherwise included which make the largest contribution to the provision of facilities for the international civil air navigation; (3) those member states not otherwise included whose election will ensure that all major geographical areas of the world are represented. The main subsidiary bodies are: the Air Navigation Commission, composed of 15 members appointed by the Council; Air Transport Committee, open to council members; and the Legal Committee, on which all members of ICAO may be represented. There are 146 members. Budget for 1979: $25,436,000.

Headquarters: International Aviation Building, 1000 Sherbrooke St West, Montreal, Quebec, Canada H3A 2R2.
President: Dr Assad Kotaite (Lebanon).
Secretary-General: Yves Lambert (France).

Annual Report of the Council. 1980 (English, French, Russian, Spanish).

UNIVERSAL POSTAL UNION (UPU)

Origin. The UPU was established on 1 July 1875, when the Universal Postal Convention adopted by the Postal Congress of Berne on 9 Oct. 1874 came into force. The UPU was known at first as the General Postal Union, its name being changed at the Congress of Paris in 1878. In 1980 there were 158 member countries.

Functions. The aim of the UPU is to assure the organization and perfection of the various postal services and to promote, in this field, the development of international collaboration. To this end, the members of UPU are united in a single postal territory for the reciprocal exchange of correspondence.

Organization. The UPU is composed of a Universal Postal Congress, which usually meets every 5 years, a permanent Executive Council consisting of 40 members, a consultative Committee, which consists of 35 members elected on a geographical basis by each Congress, and an International Bureau, which functions as the permanent secretariat.

Since 1 July 1948 the Union has been governed by the revised Convention adopted by the twelfth Congress in Paris on 5 July 1947.
Budget for 1976: $4·26m.

Headquarters: Weltpoststrasse 4, 3000, Berne 15, Switzerland.
Director-General: Mohamed Ibrahim Sobhi (Egypt).

Publications. Documents of the Lausanne Congress 1974. Bern, 1975.—*Universal Postal Convention: Paris, 5 July, 1948.* (Cmd. 7435).—*The Postal Union* (monthly, Arabic, Chinese, English, French, German, Spanish, Russian).—*The UPU: Its Foundation and Development.* Bern, 1959.

INTERNATIONAL TELECOMMUNICATION UNION (ITU)

Origin. The International Telegraph Union, founded in Paris in 1865, and the International Radiotelegraph Union, founded in Berlin in 1906, were merged by the

Madrid Convention of 1932 to form the International Telecommunication Union. ITU came into being on 1 Jan. 1934. The ITU has been governed since 1 Jan. 1975 by the revised International Telecommunication Convention adopted on 23 Oct. 1973.

Functions. The ITU: (1) allocates radio frequencies and registers radio-frequency assignments; (2) seeks to establish the lowest rates possible, consistent with efficient service and taking into account the necessity for keeping the independent financial administration of telecommunication on a sound basis; (3) promotes the adoption of measures for ensuring the safety of life through telecommunication; and (4) makes studies and recommendations and collects and publishes information for the benefit of its members.

Organization. The ITU consists of the Plenipotentiary Conference, Administrative Conferences, the Administrative Council of 36 members, the General Secretariat, the International Frequency Registration Board, and 2 international consultative committees (radio, telephone and telegraph).

Budget for 1975: $62·32m.

Headquarters: Place des Nations, Geneva, Switzerland.
Secretary-General: Mohamed Mili (Tunisia).
Deputy Secretary-General: Richard E. Butler (Australia).

Publications. *International Convention on Telecommunications, Malaga-Torremolinos,* 1973.— *Yearbook of Common Carrier Telecommunication Statistics (1964–73),* 1975.—*Telecommunication Journal* (monthly).—*Radio Regulations.* 1971.

WORLD METEOROLOGICAL ORGANIZATION (WMO)

Origin. A Conference of Directors of the International Meteorological Organization (set up in 1873), meeting in Washington in 1947, adopted a Convention creating the World Meteorological Organization. The WMO Convention became effective on 23 March 1950, and WMO was formally established on 19 March 1951, when the first session of its Congress was convened in Paris. An agreement to bring WMO into relationship with the United Nations was approved by this Congress and came into force on 21 Dec. 1951 with its approval by the General Assembly of the United Nations.

Functions. (1) To facilitate world-wide co-operation in the establishment of networks of stations for the making of meteorological observations as well as hydrological or other geophysical observations related to meteorology, and to promote the establishment and maintenance of meteorological centres charged with the provision of meteorological and related services; (2) to promote the establishment and maintenance of systems for the rapid exchange of meteorological and related information; (3) to promote standardization of meteorological and related observations and to ensure the uniform publication of observations and statistics; (4) to further the application of meteorology to aviation, shipping, water problems, agriculture and other human activities; (5) to promote activities in operational hydrology and to further close co-operation between meteorological and hydrological services; and (6) to encourage research and training in meteorology and, as appropriate, to assist in co-ordinating the international aspects of such research and training.

Organization. WMO is an inter-governmental organization of 147 member states and 5 member territories responsible for the operation of their own meteorological services. Constituent bodies of WMO are the World Meteorological Congress which meets every 4 years, the executive commitee composed of 29 members elected in their personal capacity and including the President and 3 Vice-Presidents of the Organization, 6 regional associations of members and 8 technical commissions established by the Congress. A permanent secretariat is maintained in Geneva.

Budget for 1980: $17,495,000.

Headquarters: Case postale 5, CH-1211, Geneva 20, Switzerland.
Secretary-General: A. C. Wiin-Nielsen (Denmark).

Publications. WMO Bulletin. 1952 ff.—*Meteorological Services of the World.* 1971.— *Publications of the World Meteorological Organization, 1951–1979.*

INTER-GOVERNMENTAL MARITIME CONSULTATIVE ORGANIZATION (IMCO)

Origin. IMCO was established as a specialized agency of the UN by a convention drawn up at the UN Maritime Conference held at Geneva in Feb./March 1948. The Convention became effective on 17 March 1958 when it had been ratified by 21 countries, including 7 with at least 1m. gross tons of shipping each. IMCO started operations in Jan. 1959.

Functions. To facilitate co-operation among governments on technical matters affecting merchant shipping, especially concerning safety at sea; to prevent and control marine pollution caused by ships; to encourage abolition of discriminatory and restrictive practices affecting merchant shipping. IMCO is responsible for convening international maritime conferences and for drafting international maritime conventions.

Organization. IMCO had 118 members (and 1 associate member) in 1980. The Assembly, composed of all member states, normally meets every 2 years. The Council of 24 member states acts as governing body between Assembly sessions. The Maritime Safety Committee deals with all technical questions. It can establish specialized sub-committees to deal with specific problems and like the Marine Environment Protection Committee, Legal Committee, Facilitation Committee and Committee on Technical Co-operation is open to all IMCO members. The Secretariat is composed of international civil servants.

IMCO is depositary authority for the International Convention for the Safety of Life at Sea, 1960, and the Regulations for Preventing Collisions at Sea, 1948 and 1960; the International Convention for the Prevention of Pollution of the Sea by Oil, 1954, as amended in 1962 and 1969; the Convention on Facilitation of International Maritime Traffic, 1965; the International Convention on Load Lines, 1966; the International Convention on Tonnage Measurement of Ships, 1969; the International Convention relating to Intervention on the High Seas in cases of Oil Pollution Casualties 1969; the International Convention on Civil Liability for Oil Pollution Damage, 1969; Convention on International Compensation Fund for Oil Pollution Damage, 1971; Special Trade Passenger Ships Agreement, 1971; Convention on International Regulations for Preventing Collisions at Sea, 1972; the International Convention for Safe Containers, 1972; the International Convention on Prevention of Pollution from Ships, 1973; the International Convention for the Safety of Life at Sea, 1974; Athens Convention relating to the Carriage of Passengers and their Luggage by Sea, 1974; Convention on the International Maritime Satellite Organization, 1976; Convention on Limitation of Maritime Claims, 1976; Torremolinos International Convention for the Safety of Fishing Vessels, 1977; International Convention on Standards of Training, Certification and Watchkeeping for Seafarers, 1978; International Convention on Maritime Search and Rescue, 1979.

Headquarters: 101 Piccadilly, London, W1V 0AE.
Secretary-General: C. P. Srivastava (India).
Secretary, Maritime Safety Committee: Capt. G. Kostylev (USSR).

IMCO and its Activities. 1979
Imco News

GENERAL AGREEMENT ON TARIFFS AND TRADE (GATT)

Origin. The General Agreement on Tariffs and Trade was negotiated in 1947 and entered into force on 1 Jan. 1948. Its 23 original signatories were members of a Preparatory Committee appointed by the UN Economic and Social Council to draft the charter for a proposed International Trade Organization. Since this charter was never ratified, the General Agreement, intended as an interim arrangement, has instead remained as the only international instrument laying down trade rules accepted by countries responsible for most of the world's trade. In Nov. 1980 there were 85 contracting parties, with a further 32 countries participating under special arrangements.

Functions. GATT functions both as a multilateral treaty that lays down a common code of conduct in international trade and trade relations and as a forum for negotiation and consultation to overcome trade problems and reduce trade barriers. Key provisions of the Agreement guarantee most-favoured-nation treatment (exceptions being granted to customs unions and free trade areas, and for certain preferences in favour of developing countries); require that protection be given to domestic industry only through tariffs (apart from specified exceptions); provide for negotiations to reduce tariffs (which are then 'bound' against subsequent increase) and other trade distortions; and lay down principles (particularly in Part IV of the Agreement, added in 1965) to assist the trade of developing countries. The Agreement also provides for consultation on, and settlement of, disputes, for 'waivers' (the grant of authorization, when warranted, to derogate from specific GATT obligations) and for emergency action in defined circumstances.

Seven 'rounds' of multilateral trade negotiations, including the Kennedy Round of 1964–67, took place in GATT up to 1979. The latest in this series, the Tōkyō Round, although held in Geneva, was so called because it was launched at a Ministerial meeting in the Japanese capital in Sept. 1973.

Ninety-nine countries participated in the Tōkyō Round. In Nov. 1979, the negotiations were successfully concluded with agreements covering: An improved legal framework for the conduct of world trade (which includes recognition of tariff and non-tariff treatment in favour of and among developing countries as a permanent legal feature of the world trading system); non-tariff measures (subsidies and countervailing duties; technical barriers to trade; government procurement; customs valuation; import licensing procedures; and a revision of the 1967 GATT anti-dumping code); bovine meat; dairy products; tropical products; and an agreement on free trade in civil aircraft. The agreements contain provisions for special and more favourable treatment for developing countries.

Participating countries also agreed to reduce tariffs on thousands of industrial and agricultural products, for the most part over a period of 7 years beginning on 1 Jan. 1980. As a result of these concessions, industrialized countries will reduce the average level of their import duties on manufactures by about 34%, a cut comparable to that achieved in the Kennedy Round of 1964–67.

The agreements providing an improved framework for the conduct of world trade took effect in Nov. 1979. The other agreements took effect on 1 Jan. 1980, except for those covering government procurement and customs valuation, which will take effect on 1 Jan. 1981, and the concessions on tropical products which began as early as 1977. Committees were established in 1980 to supervise implementation of the agreements which entered into force that year. Negotiations continued in 1980 on the 1 major unresolved Tōkyō Round issue of whether to revise GATT rules on emergency safeguard action against imports.

A new GATT work programme, established in Nov. 1979, gave priority to full implementation of the Tōkyō Round agreements, future trade liberalization and further efforts to assist the trade of developing countries; the rôle of the Committee on Trade and Development, which is largely responsible for these efforts, was strengthened in the work programme, and a sub-committee was established in March 1980 to examine protective measures taken against imports from developing countries.

To assist the trade of developing countries, GATT established in 1964 the International Trade Centre (since 1968 operated jointly with the UN Conference on Trade and Development) to provide information and training on export markets and marketing techniques. Other GATT action in favour of developing countries includes training courses on trade policy questions.

Budget for 1981: Sw. Frs. 41·86m.

Headquarters: Centre William Rappard, 154 rue de Lausanne, 1211 Geneva 21, Switzerland.

Director-General: Arthur Dunkel (Switzerland).

Publications. Basic Instruments and Selected Documents. 4 vols and 26 supplements 1952–79.—*International Trade* [i.e., annual review], 1952 ff. Annually from 1953.—*GATT, What It Is, What It Does* (1980).—*GATT Activities,* 1960 ff. Annually from 1972.—*GATT Studies in International Trade.* 1971 ff. (irregular series).—*The Tokyo Round of Multilateral Trade Negotiations.* Report of the Director-General, 2 vols., 1979

Casadio, G. P., *Transatlantic Trade: USA–EEC Confrontation in the GATT Negotiations.* Farnborough, 1973
Dam, K. W., *The GATT: Law and International Economic Organization.* Chicago and London, 1970
Golt, S., *The GATT Negotiations, 1973–75: A Guide to the Issues.* London, 1974
Hudec, R. E., *The GATT Legal System and World Trade Diplomacy.* New York, 1975
Jackson, J. H. *World Trade and the Law of GATT: A Legal Analysis of the General Agreement on Tariffs and Trade.* New York, 1969

THE INTERNATIONAL NARCOTICS CONTROL BOARD (INCB)

Origin. The INCB was established by the Single Convention on Narcotic Drugs, 1961, and assumed the functions of the Permanent Central Board and the Drug Supervisory Body, which were themselves treaty organs created by the narcotics Conventions of 1925 and 1931 respectively. The 1961 Convention came into force on 13 Dec. 1964. The INCB entered upon its duties on 2 March 1968. Its functions and membership were enlarged by the 1972 Protocol amending the 1961 Convention.

Functions. The functions of the Board under the Treaties are to work with governments to ensure that the aims of the drug control treaties are not seriously endangered by reason of the failure of any country or territory to carry out the provisions of such treaties; to limit the cultivation, production, manufacture and use of drugs to an adequate amount required for medical and scientific purposes; to prevent the illicit cultivation, production and manufacture of, and illicit trafficking in and use of, drugs; to ensure the availability of drugs for medical and scientific purposes; to encourage universal co-operation in the field of drug control. The 1971 Convention on Psychotropic Substances broadens the scope of the Board's activities to include the supervision of national control over these substances.

Organization. The INCB is composed of 13 members, elected by the Economic and Social Council in their individual capacities and not as representatives of governments, who, by their competence, impartiality and disinterestedness, will command general confidence. During its sessions held at least twice a year, the Board reviews the drug situation throughout the world and supervises the implementation of the various drug control treaties. The INCB is assisted by a permanent secretariat which is in continuous dialogue with national authorities. Information received from over 170 governments is analysed by the secretariat and submitted for the Board's attention during its sessions.

Headquarters: Vienna International Centre, Vienna, Austria.
President: Professor Paul Reuter.
Secretary: Abdelaziz Bahi.

Publications. Report of the International Narcotics Control Board. 1968 ff.—*Estimated World Requirements of Narcotic Drugs.* With supplements. 1969 ff.—*Statistics on Narcotic Drugs and Maximum Levels of Opium Stocks.* 1967 ff.—*Comparative Statement of Estimates and Statistics on Narcotic Drugs.* 1967 ff.—*List of Narcotic Drugs under International Control.* 1968 ff.—*Statistics on Psychotropic Substances.* 1977 ff.—*List of Psychotropic Substances under International Control.* 1980 ff.

WORLD INTELLECTUAL PROPERTY ORGANIZATION (WIPO)

Origin. The Convention establishing WIPO was signed at Stockholm in 1967 by 51 countries, and entered into force in April 1970. In Dec. 1974 WIPO became a specialized agency of the UNO.

Objectives. The objectives of WIPO are to promote the protection of intellectual property throughout the world through co-operation among States and, where appropriate, in collaboration with any other international organization, and to ensure administrative co-operation among the Unions established by various treaties for the protection of intellectual property. The Convention provides expressly for the encouragement of the conclusion of international agreements designed to promote the protection of intellectual property, and for the provision of legal-technical assistance at the request of States.

Intellectual property includes the rights relating to: literary, artistic and scientific works; performances of performing artists, phonograms and broadcasts; inventions in all fields of human endeavour; scientific discoveries; industrial designs; trademarks, service marks and commercial names and designations; protection against unfair competition and all other rights resulting from intellectual activity in the industrial, scientific, literary or artistic fields.

Functions. Among its other functions, WIPO performs the administrative tasks of certain international treaties dealing with various subjects of intellectual property, assembles and disseminates information concerning the protection of intellectual property, carries out and promotes studies in this field, publishes the results of such studies, and maintains services, including registration and publication services, facilitating the international protection of intellectual property.

WIPO performs the administrative tasks conferred by the Paris Convention for the Protection of Industrial Property, by various Special Agreements made within the framework of the Paris Convention and by the Berne Convention for the Protection of Literary and Artistic Works. The Special Agreements referred to, and currently in force, are: Madrid Agreement for the Repression of False or Deceptive Indications of Source on Goods, Madrid Agreement concerning the International Registration of Marks, Patent Co-operation Treaty, The Hague Agreement concerning the International Deposit of Industrial Designs, Nice Agreement concerning the International Classification of Goods and Services for the Purposes of the Registration of Marks, Lisbon Agreement for the Protection of Appellations of Origin and their International Registration, Locarno Agreement Establishing an International Classification for Industrial Designs, Strasbourg Agreement concerning the International Patent Classification Trademark Registration Treaty, Budapest Treaty on the International Recognition of the Deposit of Micro-organisms for the Purposes of Patent Procedure. Other special agreements to be administered by WIPO when they come into force, are: Vienna Agreement for the Protection of Type Faces and their International Deposit and the Protocol to that Agreement, Vienna Agreement Establishing an International Classification of the Figurative Elements of Marks and Geneva Treaty on the International Recording of Scientific Discoveries. In the field of neighbouring rights, the International Convention for the Protection of Performers, Producers of Phonograms and Broadcasting Organizations administered by WIPO, the International Labour Organization and Unesco. There are also the Convention for the Protection of Producers of Phonograms Against Unauthorized Duplication of their Phonograms, which is administered by WIPO and the Convention Relating to the Distribution of Programmes carrying Signals Transmitted by Satellite.

Technical Assistance. The legal-technical assistance programme of WIPO is intended to assist developing countries in the improvement of their intellectual property systems in order to support their national and regional plans for economic development. The methods used include expert advice on the modernization of laws and on the building of appropriate governmental institutions, including the training of staff, together with the stimulation of industrial research and development activities by assisting in the flow of scientific and technical information.

Two Permanent Programs for Development Co-operation have been established, one in the field of industrial property, the other in the field of copyright and neighbouring rights. Their objective is to promote and encourage inventive and innovative activity in developing countries, as well as to facilitate the dissemination of intellectual creations.

Membership in WIPO is open to any State which is a member of at least one of the Unions and to other States which are members of the organizations of the United

Nations system, are party to the Statute of the International Court of Justice, or are invited to join by the General Assembly of WIPO. Membership of the Unions is open to any State. The total combined membership of WIPO and of the Unions on 10 Dec. 1980, was 116 states.

WIPO member States: Algeria, Argentina, Australia, Austria, Bahamas, Barbados, Belgium, Benin, Brazil, Bulgaria, Burundi, Byelorussian SSR, Cameroon, Canada, Central African Republic, Chad, Chile, China, Colombia, Congo, Cuba, Czechoslovakia, Denmark, Egypt, El Salvador, Fiji, Finland, France, Gabon, Gambia, German Democratic Republic, Federal Republic of Germany, Ghana, Greece, Guinea, Hungary, India, Indonesia, Iraq, Irish Republic, Israel, Italy, Ivory Coast, Jamaica, Japan, Jordan, Kenya, Republic of Korea, Korea (North), Libya, Liechtenstein, Luxembourg, Malawi, Malta, Mauritania, Mauritius, Mexico, Monaco, Mongolia, Morocco, Netherlands, Niger, Norway, Pakistan, Peru, Philippines, Poland, Portugal, Qatar, Romania, Senegal, Republic of South Africa, Spain, Sri Lanka, Sudan, Surinam, Sweden, Switzerland, Togo, Tunisia, Turkey, Uganda, Ukrainian SSR, USSR, United Arab Emirates, UK, USA, Upper Volta, Uruguay, Vatican, Vietnam, Yemen Arab Republic, Yugoslavia, Zaïre, Zambia. (95 States.)

Paris Union: Algeria, Argentina, Australia, Austria, Bahamas, Belgium, Benin, Brazil, Bulgaria, Burundi, Cameroon, Canada, Central African Republic, Chad, Congo, Cuba, Cyprus, Czechoslovakia, Democratic People's Republic of Korea, Denmark, Dominican Republic, Egypt, Federal Republic of Germany, Finland, France, Gabon, German Democratic Republic, Ghana, Greece, Haiti, Hungary, Iceland, Indonesia, Iran, Iraq, Irish Republic, Israel, Italy, Ivory Coast, Japan, Jordan, Kenya, Republic of Korea, Lebanon, Libya, Liechtenstein, Luxembourg, Madagascar, Malawi, Malta, Mauritania, Mauritius, Mexico, Monaco, Morocco, Netherlands, New Zealand, Niger, Nigeria, Norway, Philippines, Poland, Portugal, Romania, San Marino, Senegal, Republic of South Africa, Spain, Sri Lanka, Surinam, Sweden, Switzerland, Syria, Tanzania, Togo, Trinidad and Tobago, Tunisia, Turkey, Uganda, USSR, UK, USA, Upper Volta, Uruguay, Vatican, Vietnam, Yugoslavia, Zaïre, Zambia. (89 States.)

Berne Union: Argentina, Australia, Austria, Bahamas, Belgium, Benin, Brazil, Bulgaria, Cameroon, Canada, Central African Republic, Chad, Chile, Congo, Costa Rica, Cyprus, Czechoslovakia, Denmark, Egypt, Fiji, Finland, France, Gabon, German Democratic Republic, Federal Republic of Germany, Greece, Guinea, Hungary, Iceland, India, Irish Republic, Israel, Italy, Ivory Coast, Japan, Lebanon, Libya, Liechtenstein, Luxembourg, Madagascar, Mali, Malta, Mauritania, Mexico, Monaco, Morocco, Netherlands, New Zealand, Niger, Norway, Pakistan, Philippines, Poland, Portugal, Romania, Senegal, Republic of South Africa, Spain, Sri Lanka, Surinam, Sweden, Switzerland, Thailand, Togo, Tunisia, Turkey, UK, Upper Volta, Uruguay, Vatican, Yugoslavia, Zaïre. (72 States.)

Organization. The bodies of WIPO are: The *General Assembly*, consisting of all States members of WIPO which are members of any of the Unions. Among its other functions, the General Assembly appoints and gives instructions to the Director General, reviews and approves his reports and adopts the biennial budget of expenses common to the Unions. The *Conference*, consisting of all States members of WIPO whether or not they are members of any of the Unions. Among its other functions, the Conference adopts its biennial budget and establishes the biennial programme of legal-technical assistance. The *Co-ordination Committee*, consisting of the States members of WIPO which are members of the Executive Committees of the Paris or Berne Unions.

In addition, the Paris and Berne Unions have Assemblies and Executive Committees, with functions similar to those of the WIPO bodies in respect of the biennial and annual budgets and programmes of the Unions.

Headquarters: 34, chemin des Colombettes, 1211 Geneva 20, Switzerland.
Director General: Arpad Bogsch (USA).

Principal publications. Industrial Property (monthly, in English and French).—*Copyright* (monthly, in English and French).—*Les Marques internationales* (monthly, in French).—

Manuals and Brochures of Conventions and Agreements.—Collections of Laws and Treaties.— Model Laws for Developing Countries on Inventions, on Marks Trade Names and Acts of Unfair Competition on Designs on Copyright and on Neighbouring Rights (in English, French and Spanish).—*Licensing Guide for Developing Countries* (in Arabic, Chinese, English, French and Spanish).

INTERNATIONAL UNION FOR THE PROTECTION OF NEW VARIETIES OF PLANTS (UPOV)

The Director General of WIPO is also the Secretary-General of the International Union for the Protection of New Varieties of Plants (UPOV) whose headquarters are at the same address. The Secretary-General is assisted by a Vice-Secretary-General.

Origin. The Convention establishing UPOV was signed in Paris in 1961 and revised in 1972 and 1978. The revised text of 1978 was not in force in 1980.

Functions. The purpose of the Convention for the Protection of New Varieties of Plants is to recognize and secure to the breeder of a new plant variety an intellectual property right (plant breeder's right) in the member states, in particular to ensure that he receives a fair remuneration for his work. The effect of the right of the breeder is that his prior authorization shall be necessary for the production of propagating material of his protected variety for the purpose of sale, and for the offering for sale and sale of such material. Before protection is granted the new variety is subject to examination for novelty, distinctness from other varieties, stability and homogeneity and must have received an acceptable denomination. UPOV assists member states in the introduction of plant variety protection legislation and in the promotion of international co-operation in the examination of varieties.

Member States: Belgium, Denmark, France, Federal Republic of Germany, Israel, Italy, Netherlands, Republic of South Africa, Spain, Sweden, Switzerland, UK. (12 states.)

Signatory states of the revised text of the UPOV Convention (1978): Belgium, Canada, Denmark, France, Federal Republic of Germany, Irish Republic, Italy, Japan, Mexico, Netherlands, New Zealand, Republic of South Africa, Sweden, Switzerland, UK, USA. (16 states.)

Principal publications: UPOV Newsletter (normally 4 issues a year, in English). *General Information Brochure* (in English, French, German, Japanese and Spanish). *Guidelines for the Conduct of Tests for Distinctness, Homogeneity and Stability* (a *General Introduction* and individual guidelines dealing with some 80 species, in English, French and German).

THE COMMONWEALTH

Constitution. The Commonwealth is a free association of sovereign independent nations, numbering 44 at the end of 1980. There is no charter, treaty or constitution; the association is expressed in co-operation, consultation and mutual assistance for which the Commonwealth Secretariat is the central co-ordinating organization.

The Commonwealth was first defined by the Imperial Conference of 1926 as a group of 'autonomous communities within the British Empire, equal in status, in no way subordinate one to another in any aspect of their domestic or foreign affairs, though united by a common allegiance to the Crown, and freely associated as members of the British Commonwealth of Nations'. The basis of the association changed from one owing allegiance to a common Crown, and the modern Commonwealth was born, in 1949 when the member countries accepted India's intention of becoming a republic at the same time continuing 'her full membership of the Commonwealth of Nations and her acceptance of the King as the symbol of the free association of its independent member nations and as such the Head of the Commonwealth'. There are now (1980) 15 Queen's realms, 25 republics, and 4 other monarchies in the Commonwealth. All acknowledge the Queen symbolically as Head of the Commonwealth.

The Queen's legal title rests on the statute of 12 and 13 Will. III, c. 3, by which the succession to the Crown of Great Britain and Ireland was settled on the Princess Sophia of Hanover and the 'heirs of her body being Protestants'. By proclamation of 17 July 1917 the royal family became known as the House and Family of Windsor. On 8 Feb. 1960 the Queen issued a declaration varying her confirmatory declaration of 9 April 1952 to the effect that while the Queen and her children should continue to be known as the House of Windsor, her descendants, other than descendants entitled to the style of Royal Highness and the title of Prince or Princess, and female descendants who marry and their descendants should bear the name of Mountbatten-Windsor. The Royal Style and Titles of Queen Elizabeth are: In *Australia*: 'Elizabeth the Second, by the Grace of God Queen of Australia and Her other Realms and Territories, Head of the Commonwealth'. In the *Bahamas*: 'Elizabeth the Second, by the Grace of God, Queen of the Commonwealth of the Bahamas and of Her other Realms and Territories, Head of the Commonwealth'. In *Barbados*: 'Elizabeth the Second, by the Grace of God, Queen of Barbados and of Her other Realms and Territories, Head of the Commonwealth'. In *Canada*: 'Elizabeth the Second, by the Grace of God of the United Kingdom, Canada and Her other Realms and Territories Queen, Head of the Commonwealth, Defender of the Faith'. In *Fiji*: 'Elizabeth the Second, by the Grace of God, Queen of Fiji and of Her other Realms and Territories, Head of the Commonwealth'. In *Grenada*: 'Elizabeth the Second, by the Grace of God, Queen of the United Kingdom of Great Britain and Northern Ireland and of Grenada and Her other Realms and Territories, Head of the Commonwealth'. In *Jamaica*: 'Elizabeth the Second, by the Grace of God of Jamaica and of Her other Realms and Territories Queen, Head of the Commonwealth'. In *Mauritius*: 'Elizabeth the Second, Queen of Mauritius and of Her other Realms and Territories, Head of the Commonwealth'. In *New Zealand*: 'Elizabeth the Second, by the Grace of God Queen of New Zealand and Her Other Realms and Territories, Head of the Commonwealth, Defender of the Faith'. In *Papua New Guinea*: 'Elizabeth the Second, Queen of Papua New Guinea and Her other Realms and Territories, Head of the Commonwealth'. In *Saint Lucia*: 'Elizabeth the Second, by the Grace of God, Queen of Saint Lucia and of Her other Realms and Territories, Head of Commonwealth'. In *Saint Vincent and the Grenadines:* 'Elizabeth the Second, by the Grace of God, Queen of Saint Vincent and the Grenadines and of Her other Realms and Territories, Head of the Commonwealth'. In *Solomon Islands*: 'Elizabeth the Second by the Grace of God Queen of Solomon Islands and of Her other Realms and Territories, Head of the Commonwealth'. In *Tuvalu*: 'Elizabeth the Second by the Grace of God, Queen of Tuvalu and of Her other Realms and Territories, Head of the Commonwealth'. In the *United Kingdom*: 'Elizabeth the Second, by the Grace of God of the United Kingdom of Great Britain and Northern Ireland and of Her other Realms and Territories Queen, Head of the Commonwealth, Defender of the Faith'.

A number of territories, formerly under British jurisdiction or mandate did not join the Commonwealth on independence: Egypt, Iraq, Transjordan, Burma, Palestine, Sudan, British Somaliland, South Cameroons, the Maldive Islands and Aden. Two countries, the Republic of South Africa in 1961 and Pakistan in 1972, have left the Commonwealth.

Nauru, Tuvalu and Saint Vincent and the Grenadines are special members, with the right to participate in all functional Commonwealth meetings and activities but not to attend meetings of Commonwealth Heads of Government.

Member States. The following are the member countries, with their dates of independence, and, where appropriate, the date on which they became republics: *United Kingdom*; *Canada* 1 July 1867; *Australia* 1 Jan. 1901; *New Zealand* 26 Sept. 1907; *India* 15 Aug. 1947 and became a Republic on 26 Jan. 1950; *Sri Lanka* 4 Feb. 1948 (Republic on 22 May 1972); *Ghana* 6 March 1957 (Republic on 1 July 1960); *Malaysia* 31 Aug. 1957 as Federation of Malaya, 16 Sept. 1963 as Federation of Malaysia; *Cyprus* 16 Aug. 1960 (Republic on independence); *Nigeria* 1 Oct. 1960 (Republic on 1 Oct. 1963); *Sierra Leone* 27 April 1961 (Republic 19 April 1971);

Tanzania—Tanganyika 9 Dec. 1961 (Republic 9 Dec. 1962), Zanzibar 10 Dec. 1963 (Republic on independence), United Republic of Tanganyika and Zanzibar 26 April 1964; renamed Tanzania 29 Oct. 1964; *Western Samoa* 1 Jan. 1962; *Jamaica* 6 Aug. 1962; *Trinidad and Tobago* 31 Aug. 1962 (Republic on 1 Aug. 1976); *Uganda* 9 Oct. 1962 (Republic 8 Sept. 1967, second republic 25 Jan. 1971); *Kenya* 12 Dec. 1963 (Republic on 12 Dec. 1964); *Malawi* 6 July 1964 (Republic on 6 July 1966); *Malta* 21 Sept. 1964 (Republic on 13 Dec. 1974); *Zambia* 24 Oct. 1964 (Republic on independence); *The Gambia* 18 Feb. 1965 (Republic on 24 April 1970); *Singapore* 16 Sept. 1963 as a state in the Federation of Malaysia, 9 Aug. 1965 as an independent state and republic not part of Malaysia; *Guyana* 26 May 1966 (Republic on 23 Feb. 1970); *Botswana* 30 Sept. 1966 (Republic on independence); *Lesotho* 4 Oct. 1966; *Barbados* 30 Nov. 1966; *Nauru* 31 Jan. 1968 (Republic on independence); *Mauritius* 12 March 1968; *Swaziland* 6 Sept. 1968; *Tonga* 4 June 1970; *Fiji* 10 Oct. 1970; *Bangladesh* seceded from Pakistan 16 Dec. 1971, recognized by United Kingdom 4 Feb. 1972; *Bahamas* 10 July 1973; *Grenada* 7 Feb. 1974; *Papua New Guinea* 16 Sept. 1975; *Seychelles* 29 June 1976 (Republic on independence); *Solomon Islands* 7 July 1978; *Tuvalu* 1 Oct. 1978; *Dominica* 3 Nov. 1978 (Republic on independence); *Saint Lucia* 22 Feb. 1979; *Kiribati* 12 July 1979 (Republic on independence); *Saint Vincent and the Grenadines* 27 Oct 1979; *Zimbabwe* 18 April 1980 (Republic on independence); *Vanuatu* 30 July 1980 (Republic on independence).

Associated States. The Caribbean islands of Antigua, St Christopher–Nevis–Anguilla, Dominica, Grenada and Saint Lucia entered into a new form of association with Britain in Feb. 1967. St Vincent became an associated state on 27 Oct. 1969. Each has control of its internal affairs, with the right to amend its own constitution (including the power to end the associated status and declare itself independent). Britain continues to be responsible for external affairs and defence. Grenada became independent, within the Commonwealth, on 7 Feb. 1974, Dominica on 3 Nov. 1978, Saint Lucia on 22 Feb. 1979, Saint Vincent and the Grenadines on 27 Oct. 1979, which means that there are (Dec. 1980) 2 associated states, *viz.* Antigua and St Christopher–Nevis. The Cook Islands and Niue are similarly associated with New Zealand.

An Act of the UK Parliament, the Anguilla Act (which came into effect on 19 Dec. 1980, formally separated Anguilla from the Associated State of St Christopher–Nevis–Anguilla, Anguilla thus now has *de jure* the status of a separate dependency which it has enjoyed *de facto* since 1969.

Dependent Territories. There are 14 British dependent territories, 6 Australian dependent territories and 2 New Zealand dependent territories. A dependent territory is a territory belonging by settlement, conquest or annexation to the British, Australian or New Zealand Crown.

United Kingdom dependent territories administered through the Foreign and Commonwealth Office comprise, in the Far East: Hong Kong; in the Indian Ocean: British Indian Ocean Territory; in the Mediterranean: Gibraltar; in the Atlantic Ocean: Bermuda, Falkland Islands and dependencies South Georgia and South Sandwich Islands, British Antarctic Territory, St Helena and dependencies of Ascension and Tristan da Cunha; in the Caribbean: Belize, Montserrat, British Virgin Islands, Cayman Islands, Turks and Caicos Islands, Anguilla (*see above*); in the Western Pacific: Pitcairn. The Australian dependent territories are: Coral Sea Islands Territory, Cocos (Keeling) Islands, Christmas Island, Heard and McDonald Islands, Norfolk Island and the Australian Antarctic Territory. The New Zealand dependent territories are: Tokelau Islands and Ross Dependency.

While constitutional responsibility to Parliament for the government of the British dependent territories rests with the Secretary of State for Foreign and Commonwealth Affairs, the administration of the territories is carried out by the Governments of the territories themselves.

Brunei is a sovereign state in treaty relationship with Great Britain, whereby Great Britain is responsible for the conduct of external affairs and has a consultative responsibility for defence. It has never been a dependent territory, and in 1971 ceased to be a protected state. A Treaty of Friendship and Co-operation was signed on 7 Jan. 1979, becoming effective on 31 Dec. 1983 when Brunei will assume her full international responsibilities and Britain will give up her consultative commitment over defence matters.

British Government Department. With effect from 17 Oct. 1968, the Secretary of State for Foreign and Commonwealth Affairs is responsible for the conduct of relations with members of the Commonwealth as well as with foreign countries, and for the administration of British dependent territories.

Commonwealth Secretariat. The Commonwealth Secretariat is an international body at the service of all 44 member countries. It provides the central organization for joint consultation and co-operation in many fields. It was established in 1965 by Commonwealth Heads of Government and has observer status at the UN General Assembly.

The Secretariat disseminates information on matters of common concern, organizes and services meetings and conferences, co-ordinates many Commonwealth activities, and provides expert technical assistance for economic and social development through the multilateral Commonwealth Fund for Technical Co-operation. The Secretariat is organized in divisions and sections which correspond to its main areas of operation: International affairs, economic affairs, food production and rural development, youth education, information, applied studies in government, science and technology, law and health. Within this structure the Secretariat organizes the biennial meetings of Commonwealth Heads of Government, annual meetings of Finance Ministers of member countries, and regular meetings of Ministers of Education, Law, Health, and others as appropriate.

To emphasize the multilateral nature of the association, meetings are held in different cities and regions within the Commonwealth. Heads of Government decided that the Secretariat should work from London as it has the widest range of communications of any Commonwealth city, as well as the largest assembly of diplomatic missions.

The Commonwealth Secretary-General, who has access to Heads of Government, is the head of the Secretariat which is staffed by officers from member countries and financed by contributions from member governments.

Headquarters: Marlborough House, Pall Mall, London, SW1Y 5HX.
Secretary-General: Shridath S. Ramphal (Guyana).

Books of Reference

Year-Book of the Commonwealth. HMSO, 1980
The Cambridge History of the British Empire. 8 vols. CUP, 1929 ff.
Economic Survey of the Colonial Territories. 7 vols. HMSO. 1952 ff.
Ball, M., *The Open Commonwealth.* Duke Univ. Press, 1971
Bradley, K. (ed.), *The Living Commonwealth.* London, 1961
Burns, Sir Alan, *In Defence of Colonies.* London, 1957
Garner, J., *The Commonwealth Office, 1925–1968.* London, 1978
Grierson, E., *The Imperial Dream.* London, 1972
Griffiths, Sir P., *Empire into Commonwealth.* London, 1969
Hailey, Lord, *An African Survey.* Rev. ed. Oxford, 1957.—*Native Administration in the British African Territories.* 5 vols. HMSO, 1951 ff.
Hall, H. D., *Commonwealth: A History of the British Commonwealth.* London and New York, 1971
Ingram, D. T., *The Commonwealth at Work.* London, 1969.—*The Imperfect Commonwealth.* London, 1977
Jeffries, Sir C., *The Colonial Office.* London, 1956
Keeton, G. W. (ed.), *The British Commonwealth: Its Laws and Constitutions.* 9 vols. London, 1951 ff.
Kuczynski, R. R., *Demographic Survey of the British Colonial Empire.* 3 vols. London, New York, Toronto, 1948–53
McIntyre, W. D., *The Commonwealth of Nations: Origins and Impact 1869–1971.* Univ. of Minnesota Press and OUP, 1978
Mansergh, N., *The Commonwealth Experience.* London, 1969
Maxwell, W. H. and L. F., *A Legal Bibliography of the British Commonwealth of Nations.* 2nd ed. London, 1956
Miller, J. D. B., *Survey of Commonwealth Affairs.* London, 1974
Morris, J., *Heaven's Command: An Imperial Progress.* London, 1973

Roberts-Wray, K., *Commonwealth and Colonial Law*. London, 1966
Wade, E. C. S., and Phillips, G. G., *Constitutional Law: An Outline of the Law and Practice of the Constitution, Including Central and Local Government and the Constitutional Relations of the British Commonwealth and Empire*. 8th ed. London, 1970
Walker, A., *The Modern Commonwealth*. London, 1976.—*A New Look at the Commonwealth*. Oxford, 1977
Wheare, K. C., *The Statute of Westminster and Dominion Status*. 5th ed. Oxford, 1953.—*Constitutional Structure of the Commonwealth*. Oxford, 1960

WORLD COUNCIL OF CHURCHES

The World Council of Churches was formally constituted on 23 Aug. 1948, at Amsterdam, by an assembly representing 147 churches from 44 countries. By 1980 the member churches numbered nearly 300, from over 100 countries.

The basis of membership (1975) states: 'The World Council of Churches is a fellowship of Churches which confess the Lord Jesus Christ as God and Saviour according to the Scriptures and therefore seek to fulfil together their common calling to the glory of the one God, Father, Son and Holy Spirit.' Membership is open to Churches which express their agreement with this basis and satisfy such criteria as the Assembly or Central Committee may prescribe. Today 271 Churches of Protestant, Anglican, Orthodox, Old Catholic and Pentecostal confessions belong to this fellowship.

The World Council was founded by the coming together of several diverse Christian movements. These included the overseas mission groups gathered from 1921 in the International Missionary Council, the Faith and Order Movement founded by American Episcopal Bishop Charles Brent, and the Life and Work Movement led by Swedish Lutheran Archbishop Nathan Söderblom.

On 13 May 1938 at Utrecht a provisional committee was appointed to prepare for the formation of a World Council of Churches. It was under the chairmanship of William Temple, then Archbishop of York.

Assembly. The governing body of the World Council, consisting of delegates specially appointed by the member Churches. It meets every 6 or 7 years to frame policy and to consider some main theme. The Assembly has no legislative powers and depends for the implementation of its decisions upon the action of the member Churches. Assemblies have been held in Amsterdam (1948), Evanston (1954), New Delhi (1961), Uppsala (1968), and Nairobi (1975). The next is to be held in Vancouver, Canada in 1983 under the theme 'Jesus Christ: the Life of the World'. In between assemblies, a 134 member Central Committee meets annually to carry out the assembly mandate, with a smaller 26 member Executive Committee meeting twice a year.

Presidents. Hon. President: The Rev. Dr W. A. Visser't Hooft. *Presidium:* Mrs Justice A. R. Jiagge (Ghana), Prof. José Miguez-Bonino (Argentina), Dr T. B. Simatupang (Indonesia), Most Rev. Olof Sundby (Sweden), Dr Cynthia Wedel (USA), His Holiness Ilyia II (USSR).

WCC programmes are organized from headquarters in Geneva, Switzerland by a staff of 300 and a range of supervisory committees drawn from member churches. The 3 programme units are:

(*i*) Justice and Service which includes Inter-Church Aid, Refugee and World Service (channelling over $30m. from member churches to areas of need); the Commission on the Churches' Participation in Development; the Commission of the Churches on International Affairs, the Programme to Combat Racism and the Christian Medical Commission.

(*ii*) Education and Renewal includes sections dealing with renewal and congregational life, women, youth, church-related education, biblical studies, family ministry and the Programme on Theological Education.

(*iii*) Faith and Witness includes the Commission on World Mission and Evangelism, Church and Society and the sub-unit on Dialogue with People of Living Faiths and Ideologies.

A General Secretariat with a Communication Department, finance and central services co-ordinates the work of these 3 units.

Since 1975 the WCC has held several major world conferences on such diverse themes as 'Faith, Science and the Future', 'Your Kingdom Come', 'Family Power and Social Change', 'Strategies for Churches Combating Racism in the 1980's', 'The Community of Women and Men in the Church' and 'Giving an Account of the Hope that is in Us'.

Officers of the Central and Executive Committees: *Moderator:* The Most Rev. Edward W. Scott (Canada). *Vice-Moderators:* His Holiness. Karekin II (Lebanon); Jean Skuse (Australia). *General Secretary:* The Rev. Dr Philip A. Potter.

Office: PO Box 66, 150 route de Ferney, 1211 Geneva 20, Switzerland.

The British Council of Churches, which is an associated national council of the World Council, acts as agent for the WCC in the UK.

Books of Reference

Official Reports: The First [. . . etc.] *Assembly* (London, 1948, 1955, 1962, Geneva, 1968)
New Delhi to Uppsala 1961–68. Geneva, 1968
Uppsala to Nairobi 1968–75. Geneva, 1975
Official Reports of the Faith and Order Conferences at Lausanne 1927, Edinburgh 1937, Lund 1952, Montreal 1963, Meeting of Faith and Order Commission, Louvain 1971, Accra 1974, Bangalore 1978.
Official Reports of the Life and Work Conferences at Stockholm 1925 and Oxford 1937; World Conference on Church and Society 1966
Minutes of the Central Committee. Geneva, 1949 to date
Goodall, N., *The Ecumenical Movement.* 3rd ed. OUP, 1966.—*Ecumenical Progress, 1961–1971,* OUP, 1972
Hudson, D., *The World Council of Churches in International Affairs.* Leighton Buzzard, 1977
Paton, D. M., *Breaking Barriers—Nairobi 1975.* London, 1976
van der Bent, A. J., *What in the World is the World Council of Churches?* Geneva, 1978

INTERNATIONAL TRADE UNIONISM

International trade-union co-operation is organized through the three major 'Internationals', the democratic International Confederation of Free Trade Unions (ICFTU), the Communist-directed World Federation of Trade Unions (WFTU) and the World Confederation of Labour (WCL). In addition, federations of specific trades or industries protect their special interests by organizing on an international level and are associated to a varying degree with their corresponding 'Internationals'. The International Trade Secretariats (ITS) are completely autonomous but seek to co-ordinate their policies and activities with those of the ICFTU; the International Trade Federations (ITFs) are very closely integrated with the WCL; the Trade Union Internationals (TUIs) are completely subservient to WFTU.

Coldrick, A. P., and Jones, P., *International Directory of the Trade Union Movement.* London, 1979

History. The first general trade-union International, the International Federation of Trade Unions (IFTU), was set up in 1913, but no real achievement was possible until its post-war reconstitution in 1919. Some trade-union movements, seeking to implement the social precepts of the Christian faith, established the International Federation of Christian Trade Unions (IFCTU) in 1920. The name was changed to the World Confederation of Labour in 1968.

During the Second World War moves to establish universal trade unionism resulted in the formation of the World Federation of Trade Unions (WFTU) in 1945. The Christian trade unions refused to join the new association and reconstituted the IFCTU. Attempts by the Communists to impose their own ideology within the WFTU led to the eventual secession of the democratic elements, which reconstituted themselves in the ICFTU in 1949.

EUROPEAN TRADE UNION CONFEDERATION. In Feb. 1973 the European Trade Union Confederation was formed by trade unionists in 15 Western European countries to deal with questions of interest to European working people arising inside and outside the EEC. All the founding organizations were ICFTU affiliates but subsequently they accepted into membership European WCL affiliates, the Irish Congress of Trade Unions and the Italian Communist trade union centre (CGIL) and other national organizations. The ETUC Congress meets every 3 years and the Executive Committee 6 times a year. The membership is now about 40m. from 31 centres in 18 countries.

General Secretary: Mathias Hinterscheid.
Headquarters: Rue Montagne aux Herbes Potagères 37, 1000 Brussels.

INTERNATIONAL CONFEDERATION OF FREE TRADE UNIONS. The first congress of ICFTU was held in London in Dec. 1949. The constitution as amended provides for co-operation with the United Nations and the International Labour Organization and for regional organizations to promote free trade unionism, especially in less-developed countries.

Organization. The Congress meets every 3 years. It elects the Executive Board of 29 members nominated on an area basis for a 3-year period; the Board meets at least twice a year. Various committees cover policy *vis-à-vis* such problems as those connected with Atomic Energy and also the administration of the International Solidarity Fund. There are joint ICFTU–ITS Committees for co-ordinating activities and also for women workers' problems. Headquarters: 37–41, rue Montagne aux Herbes Potagères, Brussels 1000, Belgium.

General Secretary: Otto Kersten.

Regional organizations exist in America, office in Mexico City; Asia, office in New Delhi.

Membership. The ICFTU has 126 affiliated organizations in 90 countries, which together represent about 70m. workers. The biggest groups were the British Trades Union Congress (11m.), the Federal German Deutscher Gewerkschaftsbund (7·4m.), the Confederazione Italiana Sindacati Lavoratori (2·1m.), the Swedish Landsorganisationen (1·9m.), the Canadian Labour Congress (1·3m.), the Österreichischer Gewerkschaftsbund (1·6m.), the Belgian General Federation of Labour (900,000), the Indian National Trade Union Congress (3·3m.), the French Confédération Générale du Travail Force Ouvrière (900,000), Brazilian Confederacao Nacional dos Trabalhadores no Comercio (2·5m.), Australian Council of Trade Unions (1·3m.), Japanese Confederation of Labour, Domei (1·3m.).

The American Federation of Labor and Congress of Industrial Organizations disaffiliated in Feb. 1969.

Publications (in 4 languages). *Free Labour World* (monthly); *ICFTU Bulletin* (bi-monthly); *Press and Radio Service* (weekly); *International Trade Union News* (fortnightly).

THE WORLD FEDERATION OF TRADE UNIONS. The WFTU formally came into existence on 3 Oct. 1945, representing trade-union organizations in more than 50 countries of the world, both Communist and non-Communist, excluding Federal Republic of Germany and Japan, as well as a number of lesser and colonial territories. Representation from the USA was limited to the Congress of Industrial Organizations, as the American Federation of Labor declined to participate.

In Jan. 1949 the British, USA and Netherlands trade unions withdrew from WFTU, which had come under complete Communist control; and by June 1951 all non-Communist trade-unions, including the Yugoslavian Federation, had left WFTU.

Organization. The Congress meets every 4 years. In between, the General Council, of 134 members (including deputies), is the governing body, meeting (in theory) at least once a year. The Bureau controls the activities of WFTU between meetings of the General Council; it consists of the President, the General Secretary and members from different continents, the total number being decided at each Congress. The Bureau is elected by the General Council.

General Secretary: Enrique Pastorino (Uruguay).

Membership. A total membership of 190m. from 73 national centres is claimed. The biggest groups are the Soviet All-Union Central Council of Trade Unions (90m.), the German Democratic Republic Free German Trade Union Federation (7·5m.), the Polish Central Council of Trade Unions (7m.), the Czechoslovak Central Council of Trade Unions (5·5m.), the Italian General Confederation of Labour (GCIL, 3·5m.), the Romanian General Confederation of Labour (3·5m.), the Hungarian Central Council of Trade Unions (3m.) and the French Confederation of Labour (CGT, 2·5m.).

Publications. World Trade Union Movement (monthly, in 9 languages); *Trade Union Press* (fortnightly, in 6 languages).

WORLD CONFEDERATION OF LABOUR. The first congress of the International Federation of Christian Trade Unions (IFCTU), as the WCL was then called, met in 1920; but a large proportion of its 3·4m. members were in Italy and Germany, where affiliated unions were suppressed by the Fascist and Nazi régimes, and in 1940 IFCTU went out of existence. It was reconstituted in 1945, and declined to merge with WFTU and, later, with ICFTU. The policy of IFCTU was based on the papal encyclicals *Rerum novarum* (1891) and *Quadragesimo anno* (1931), but in 1968, when the Federation became the WCL, it was broadened to include other concepts. The WCL now has Protestant, Buddhist and Moslem members as well as its mainly Roman Catholic members.

Organization. The WCL is organized on a federative basis which leaves wide discretion to its autonomous constituent unions. Its governing body is the Congress, which meets every 4 years. The Congress appoints (or re-appoints) the Secretary-General at each 4-yearly meeting. The General Council which meets at least once a year, is composed of the members of the Confederal Board (at least 22 members, elected by the Congress) and representatives of national confederations, international trade federations, and trade union organizations where there is no confederation affiliated to the WCL. The Confederal Board is responsible for the general leadership of the WCL, in accordance with the decisions and directives of the Council and Congress. Headquarters: 50 rue Joseph II, Brussels 1040, Belgium.

Secretary-General: Jan Kulakowski.

There are regional organizations in Latin America (office in Caracas), Africa (office in Banjul, Gambia) and Asia (office in Manila). There is also a liaison centre in Montreal.

Membership. A total membership of 15m. in about 90 countries is claimed. The biggest groups are the French Democratic Confederation of Labour (800,000), the Confederation of Christian Trade Unions of Belgium (1·1m.), the Netherlands Catholic Workers' Movement (340,000).

Publication. Labour Press and Information (11 each year, in 5 languages).

ORGANISATION FOR ECONOMIC CO-OPERATION AND DEVELOPMENT (OECD)

History and Membership. On 30 Sept. 1961 the Organisation for European Economic Co-operation (OEEC), after a history of 14 years (*see* THE STATESMAN'S

YEAR-BOOK, 1961, p. 32), was replaced by the Organisation for Economic Co-operation and Development. The change of title marks the Organisation's altered status and functions: with the accession of Canada and USA as full members it ceased to be a purely European body; while at the same time it added development aid to the list of its other activities. The member countries are now Australia, Austria, Belgium, Canada, Denmark, Federal Republic of Germany, Finland, France, Greece, Iceland, Irish Republic, Italy, Japan, Luxembourg, the Netherlands, New Zealand, Norway, Portugal, Spain, Sweden, Switzerland, Turkey, UK and USA. Yugoslavia participates in the Organisation's activities with a special status. The Commission of the European Communities generally takes part in OECD's work.

Objectives. To promote economic and social welfare throughout the OECD area by assisting its member governments in the formulation of policies designed to this end and by co-ordinating these policies; and to stimulate and harmonize its members' efforts in favour of developing countries.

Organs. The supreme body of the Organisation is the Council composed of one representative for each member country. It meets either at Permanent Representative level (about once a week) under the Chairmanship of the Secretary-General, or at Ministerial level (usually once a year) under the Chairmanship of a Minister elected annually. Decisions and Recommendations are adopted by mutual agreement of all members of the Council.

The Council is assisted by an Executive Committee composed of 14 members of the Council designated annually by the latter. The major part of the Organisation's work is, however, prepared and carried out in numerous specialized committees and working parties and sub-groups, of which there exist over 200. Thus, the Organisation comprises Committees for Economic Policy; Economic and Development Review; Development Assistance (DAC); Trade; Invisible Transactions; Financial Markets; Fiscal Affairs; Restrictive Business Practices; Maritime Transport; International Investment and Multinational Enterprises; Energy Policy; Industry; Steel; Scientific and Technological Policy; Education; Manpower and Social Affairs; Environment; Agriculture; Fisheries, etc. Moreover there exists a High-Level Group–Commodities.

Four autonomous or semi-autonomous bodies also belong to the Organisation: the International Energy Agency (IEA); the Nuclear Energy Agency (NEA); the Development Centre and the Centre for Educational Research and Innovation (CERI).

The Council, the committees and the other bodies are serviced by an international Secretariat headed by the Secretary-General of the Organisation.

Chairman of the Council (ministerial): Elected annually.
Chairman of the Council (official level): The Secretary-General.
Chairman of the Executive Committee: A. F. Maddocks (UK).
Secretary-General: Emile van Lennep (Netherlands).
Deputy Secretaries-General: Jacob M. Myerson (USA), Paul Lemerle (France).
Headquarters: Château de la Muette, 2, rue André Pascal, 75775 Paris Cedex 16, France.

Publications of the OECD include:
Activities of OECD. Annual, from 1972
News from OECD. Monthly
Main Economic Indicators. Monthly, from 1965
The OECD Observer. Bi-monthly, from 1962
The OECD Economic Outlook. 1966 ff.
OEEC/OECD Economic Surveys of Member Countries. 1954 ff.
European Nuclear Energy Agency, Activity Report. 1959 ff.
The Flow of Financial Resources to Countries in Course of Economic Development. 1960 ff.
Development Assistance Efforts and Policies. 1962 ff.
Tourism Policy and International Tourism in OECD Member Countries. 1955 ff.
Energy Policies and Programmes of the IEA Member Countries. 1977 ff.

NORTH ATLANTIC TREATY ORGANIZATION (NATO)

On 28 April 1948 the Canadian Secretary of State for External Affairs broached the idea of a 'security league' of the free nations, in extension of the Brussels Treaty of 17 March 1948. The United States Senate, on 11 June, recommended 'the association of the United States with such regional and other collective arrangements as are based on continuous self-help and mutual aid, and as affect its national security'. Detailed proposals were subsequently worked out between the Brussels Treaty powers, the USA and Canada.

On 4 April 1949 the foreign ministers of Belgium, Canada, Denmark, France, Iceland, Italy, Luxembourg, the Netherlands, Norway, Portugal, the UK and the USA met in Washington and signed a treaty, the main clauses of which read as follows:

Article 1. The parties undertake, as set forth in the Charter of the United Nations, to settle any international disputes in which they may be involved by peaceful means in such a manner that international peace and security and justice are not endangered, and to refrain in their international relations from the threat or use of force in any manner inconsistent with the purposes of the United Nations.

Article 2. The parties will contribute toward the further development of peaceful and friendly international relations by strengthening their free institutions, by bringing about a better understanding of the principles upon which these institutions are founded, and by promoting conditions of stability and well-being. They will seek to eliminate conflict in their international economic policies and will encourage economic collaboration between any or all of them.

Article 3. In order more effectively to achieve the objectives of this treaty, the parties, separately and jointly by means of continuous and effective self-help and mutual aid, will maintain and develop their individual and collective capacity to resist armed attack.

Article 4. The parties will consult together whenever, in the opinion of any of them, the territorial integrity, political independence or security of any of the parties is threatened.

Article 5. The parties agree that an armed attack against one or more of them in Europe or North America shall be considered an attack against them all and consequently they agree that, if such an armed attack occurs, each of them, in exercise of the right of individual or collective self-defence recognized by article 51 of the Charter of the United Nations, will assist the party or parties so attacked by taking forthwith, individually and in concert with the other parties, such action as it deems necessary, including the use of armed force, to restore and maintain the security of the North Atlantic area. Any such armed attack and all measures taken as a result thereof shall immediately be reported to the Security Council. Such measures shall be terminated when the Security Council has taken the measures necessary to restore and maintain international peace and security.

Article 6. For the purpose of Article 5 an armed attack on one or more of the parties is deemed to include an armed attack (*i*) on the territory of any of the parties in Europe or North America, on the Algerian Departments of France,[1] on the territory of Turkey or on the islands under the jurisdiction of any of the parties in the North Atlantic area north of the Tropic of Cancer; (*ii*) on the forces, vessels or aircraft of any of the parties, when in or over these territories or any other area in Europe in which occupation forces of any of the parties were stationed on the date when the treaty entered into force or the Mediterranean Sea or the North Atlantic area north of the Tropic of Cancer.[2]

Article 8. Each party declares that none of the international engagements now in force between it and any other of the parties or any third state is in conflict with the provisions of this treaty, and undertakes not to enter into any international engagement in conflict with this treaty.

Article 10. The parties may, by unanimous agreement, invite any other European state in a position to further the principles of this treaty and to contribute to the security of the North Atlantic area to accede to this treaty. Any state so invited may become a party to the treaty by depositing its instrument of accession with the government of the United States of America. The government of the United States of America will inform each of the parties of the deposit of each such instrument of accession.

Article 12. After the treaty has been in force for 10 years, or at any time thereafter, the parties shall, if any of them so requests, consult together for the purpose of reviewing the treaty, having regard for the factors then affecting peace and security in the North Atlantic area, including the development of universal as well as regional arrangements under the Charter of the United Nations for the maintenance of international peace and security.

Article 13. After the treaty has been in force for 20 years, any party may cease to be a party one year after its notice of denunciation has been given to the government of the United States of America, which will inform the governments of the other parties of the deposit of each notice of denunciation.

[1] The relevant clauses of the treaty have become inapplicable to the Republic of Algeria as from 3 July 1962.

[2] This Article was modified as a result of the accession of Greece and Turkey to the treaty.

The treaty came into force on 24 Aug. 1949. Greece and Turkey were admitted as parties to the treaty in 1951 (effective Feb. 1952), the Federal Republic of Germany in Oct. 1954 (effective 5 May 1955).

NATO is an organization of sovereign states equal in status. Decisions taken are expressions of the collective will of member governments arrived at by common consent.

The North Atlantic Council is composed of representatives of the 15 member countries. At Ministerial Meetings of the Council, member nations are represented by Ministers of Foreign Affairs. These meetings are held twice a year. The Council also meets on occasion at the level of Heads of State and Government. In permanent session, at the level of Ambassadors, the Council meets at least once a week.

The Defence Planning Committee is composed of representatives of the 14 member countries taking part in NATO's integrated military structure. Like the Council, it meets both in permanent session at the level of Ambassadors and twice a year at Ministerial level. At Ministerial Meetings member nations are represented by Defence Ministers.

The Council and Defence Planning Committee are chaired by the Secretary General of NATO at whatever level they meet. Opening sessions of Ministerial Meetings of the Council are presided over by the President, an honorary position held annually by the Foreign Minister of one of the member nations.

Nuclear matters are discussed by the Nuclear Planning Group in which 13 countries now participate. It meets regularly at the level of Permanent Representatives (Ambassadors) and twice a year at the level of Ministers of Defence.

The Permanent Representatives of member countries are supported by the National Delegations located at NATO Headquarters. The Delegations are composed of advisors and officials qualified to represent their countries on the various committees created by the Council. The Committees are supported by the International Staff responsible to the Secretary General.

The International Staff comprises the Office of the Secretary General, the Executive Secretariat, 5 major Divisions (Political Affairs; Defence Planning and Policy; Defence Support; Infrastructure, Logistics and Council Operations; and Scientific Affairs), the Office of Management and the Office of the Financial Controller. Through their structure of Directorates and Services, the Divisions support the work of the Committees in numerous fields including Political Affairs; Economic Affairs; Information; Force Planning and Policy; Nuclear Planning; Civil Emergency Planning; Armaments and Defence Research; Command, Control and Communications; Air Defence; Infrastructure and Logistics; Environmental Problems; Administration and Personnel; and Civil and Military Budgetary Affairs.

Headquarters: 1110 Brussels, Belgium.
Secretary-General: Joseph Luns (Netherlands), appointed Oct. 1971.
Flag: Dark blue with a white compass rose of 4 points in the centre.

The Secretary-General takes the chair at all Council meetings, except at the opening and closing of Ministerial sessions, when he gives way to the Council President. The office of President is held annually by the Foreign Minister of one of the Treaty countries.

The *Military Committee* is responsible for making recommendations to the Council/Defence Planning Committee on military matters and for supplying guidance to the Allied Commanders. Composed of the Chiefs-of-Staff of all member countries except France and Iceland (which has no military forces), the Committee is assisted by an integrated International Military Staff. It meets at Chiefs-of-Staff level at least twice a year but remains in permanent session at the level of national military representatives. Liaison between the Military Committee and the French

High Command is effected through the French Mission to the Military Committee. The permanent chairman of the Military Committee is elected by the Chiefs-of-Staff for a period of 2–3 years. The present chairman is Admiral Robert H. Falls (Canada), appointed July 1980.

The area covered by the North Atlantic Treaty is divided among three commands: The Atlantic Ocean Command, the European Command and the Channel Command. Defence plans for the North American area are developed by the Canada–US Regional Planning Group.

The NATO commanders are responsible for the development of defence plans for their respective areas, for the determination of force requirements and for the deployment and exercise of the forces under their command.

The *Allied Command Europe* (ACE) covers the area extending from the North Cape to the Mediterranean and from the Atlantic to the eastern border of Turkey, excluding the UK and Portugal, the defence of which does not fall under any one major NATO Command. The European area, which is subdivided into a number of subordinate commands, is under the Supreme Allied Commander Europe (SACEUR) whose Headquarters, near Mons in Belgium, are known as SHAPE (Supreme Headquarters Allied Powers Europe).

SACEUR has also under his orders the ACE Mobile Force, composed of both land and air force units from different member countries, which can be ready for action at very short notice in any threatened area. The present SACEUR is Gen. Bernard W. Rogers (USA).

Under the Supreme Allied Commander Atlantic (SACLANT) the *Atlantic Command* extends from the North Pole to the Tropic of Cancer and from the coastal waters of North America to those of Europe and Africa, but excludes the Channel and the British Isles. SACLANT, who would have the primary task in wartime of ensuring the security of the sea lanes in the whole Atlantic area, is an operational rather than an administrative commander. Under his direct command is the Standing Naval Force Atlantic (STANAVFORLANT) which is a permanent international squadron of ships drawn from NATO Navies which normally operate in the Atlantic.

The present SACLANT, whose Headquarters are in Norfolk (USA), is Admiral Harry D. Train (US), appointed Oct. 1978.

The *Channel Command* covers the English Channel and the southern North Sea. Under the Allied Commander-in-Chief Channel (CINCHAN) its mission is to control and protect merchant shipping in the area, co-operating with SACEUR in the air defence of the Channel. The forces earmarked to the Command in emergency are predominantly naval but include maritime air forces. CINCHAN has also under his command the NATO Standing Naval Force Channel (STANAVFORCHAN) a permanent mine counter measures force comprising ships drawn from the navies of Belgium, the Netherlands and the UK. The present CINCHAN, with Headquarters at Northwood (UK), is Admiral Sir James Eberle (UK), appointed May. 1979.

The *Canada–US Regional Planning Group*, which covers the North American area, develops and recommends to the Military Committee plans for the defence of this area. It meets alternately in Washington and Ottawa.

The NATO Handbook.—NATO: Facts and Figures.—The NATO Review (bi-monthly).— Aspects of NATO.—NATO Pocket Guide.—NATO Folder.—NATO and the Warsaw Pact.—Economic and Scientific Publications.

WESTERN EUROPEAN UNION

On 17 March 1948 a 50-year treaty 'for collaboration in economic, social and cultural matters and for collective self-defence' was signed in Brussels by the Foreign Ministers of the UK, France, the Netherlands, Belgium and Luxembourg. (*See* THE STATESMAN'S YEAR-BOOK, 1954, pp. 32 f.)

On 20 Dec. 1950 the functions of the Western Union defence organization were transferred to the North Atlantic Treaty command, but it was decided that the reorganization of the military machinery should not affect the right of the Western Union Defence Ministers and the Chiefs of Staff to meet as they please to consider matters of mutual concern to the Brussels Treaty powers.

After the breakdown of the European Defence Community on 30 Aug. 1954 a conference was held in London from 28 Sept. to 3 Oct. 1954, attended by Belgium, Canada, France, the Federal Republic of Germany, Italy, Luxembourg, the Netherlands, the UK and the USA, at which it was decided to invite the Federal Republic of Germany and Italy to accede to the Brussels Treaty, to end the occupation of Western Germany and to invite the latter to accede to the North Atlantic Treaty; the Federal Republic agreed that it would voluntarily limit its arms production, and provision was made for the setting up of an agency to control the armaments of the 7 Brussels Treaty powers; the UK undertook not to withdraw from the Continent her 4 divisions and the Tactical Air Force assigned to the Supreme Allied Commander against the wishes of a majority, *i.e.*, 4 of the Brussels Treaty powers, except in the event of an acute overseas emergency.

At a Conference of Ministers held in Paris from 20 to 23 Oct. 1954 these decisions were embodied in 4 Protocols modifying the Brussels Treaty which were signed in Paris on 23 Oct. 1954 and came into force on 6 May 1955.

The *Council of WEU* consists of the Foreign Ministers of the 7 powers or their representatives; it is so organized as to be able to exercise its functions continuously. An *Assembly*, composed of representatives of the Brussels Treaty powers to the Consultative Assembly of the Council of Europe, meets twice a year, usually in Paris. An *Agency for the Control of Armaments* and a *Standing Armaments Committee* have been set up in Paris. The social and cultural activities were transferred to the Council of Europe on 1 June 1960.

After the breakdown of the negotiations for Britain's entry into the Common Market in 1963 the 6 EEC countries proposed to the UK that the WEU Council (the Six and the UK) should meet every 3 months 'to take stock of the political and economic situation in Europe'. The UK welcomed this proposal, and regular meetings took place. Following the re-opening of negotiations in 1970 which led to the signing of the Treaty of Accession in Jan. 1972 this arrangement has been discontinued.

Headquarters: 9 Grosvenor Place, London, SW1.
Secretary-General: Edouard F. T. Longerstaey.

COUNCIL OF EUROPE

In 1948 the 'Congress of Europe', bringing together at The Hague nearly 1,000 influential Europeans from 26 countries, called for the creation of a united Europe, including a European Assembly. This proposal, examined first by the Ministerial Council of the Brussels Treaty Organization, then by a conference of ambassadors, was at the origin of the Council of Europe. The Statute of the Council was signed at London on 5 May 1949 and came into force 2 months later. The founder members were Belgium, Denmark, France, the Irish Republic, Italy, Luxembourg, the Netherlands, Norway, Sweden and the UK. Turkey and Greece joined in 1949, Iceland in 1950, the Federal Republic of Germany in 1951 (having been an associate since 1950), Austria in 1956, Cyprus in 1961, Switzerland in 1963, Malta in 1965, Portugal in 1976, Spain in 1977 and Liechtenstein in 1978.

Membership is limited to European States which 'accept the principles of the rule of law and of the enjoyment by all persons within [their] jurisdiction of human rights and fundamental freedoms'. The Statute provides for both withdrawal (Art. 7) and suspension (Arts. 8 and 9). Greece withdrew from the Council in Dec. 1969 and rejoined in Nov. 1974.

Structure. Under the Statute two organs were set up: an inter-governmental *Committee of [Foreign] Ministers* with powers of decision and of recommendation to governments, and an inter-parliamentary deliberative body, the *Parliamentary Assembly* (referred to in the Statute as the *Consultative Assembly*)—both of which are served by the Secretariat. In addition, a large number of committees of experts have been established, two of them, the Council for Cultural Co-operation and the Committee on Legal Co-operation, having a measure of autonomy; on municipal matters the Committee of Ministers receives recommendations from the Conference of Local and Regional Authorities of Europe.

The Committee of Ministers meets usually twice a year, their deputies 10 times a year.

The Parliamentary Assembly normally consists of 170 parliamentarians elected or appointed by their national parliaments (Austria 6, Belgium 7, Cyprus 3, Denmark 5, France 18, Federal Republic of Germany 18, Greece 7, Iceland 3, Irish Republic 4, Italy 18, Liechtenstein 2, Luxembourg 3, Malta 3, Netherlands 7, Norway 5, Portugal 7, Spain 12, Sweden 6, Switzerland 6, Turkey 12, UK 18); it meets 3 times a year for approximately a week. For domestic reasons Cyprus is not at present represented in the Assembly. The work of the Assembly is prepared by parliamentary committees.

The *Joint Committee*, which acts as an organ of co-ordination and liaison between representatives of the Committee of Ministers and members of the Parliamentary Assembly and gives members an opportunity to exchange views on matters of important European interest.

The European Convention on Human Rights, signed in 1950, set up special machinery to guarantee internationally fundamental rights and freedoms. A *European Commission* investigates alleged violations of the Convention submitted to it either by States or, in most cases, by individuals. Its findings can then be examined by the *European Court of Human Rights* (set up in 1959), whose obligatory jurisdiction has been recognized by 18 States, or by the Committee of Ministers, empowered to take binding decisions by two-thirds majority vote.

For questions of national refugees and over-population, a Special Representative has been appointed, responsible to the governments collectively. In 1956 the Resettlement Fund for National Refugees and Over-Population was created on the initiative of the special representative. With 19 member countries, the main purpose of the Fund is to give financial aid, particularly in the spheres of housing, vocational training, regional planning and regional development. Since its foundation, the total amount of loans thus granted comes to over US$1,000m.

In 1970 the Council set up a European Youth Centre where young people can discuss their own approach to international co-operation. More recently, a European Youth Foundation was created, administered by the Secretary-General, and which provides money to subsidize activities by European Youth Organizations.

Aims and Achievements. Art. 1 of the Statute states that the Council's aim is 'to achieve a greater unity between its members for the purpose of safeguarding and realising the ideals and principles which are their common heritage and facilitating their economic and social progress'; 'this aim shall be pursued . . . by discussion of questions of common concern and by agreements and common action'. The only limitation is provided by Art. 1 (*d*), which excludes 'matters relating to national defence'.

Although without legislative powers, the Assembly acts as the power-house of the Council initiating European action in key areas by making recommendations to the Committee of Ministers. As the widest parliamentary forum in Western Europe, the Assembly also acts as the conscience of the area by voicing its opinions on important current issues. These are embodied in resolutions. The Ministers' role is to translate the Assembly's recommendations into action, particularly as regards lowering the barriers between the European countries, harmonizing their legislation or introducing where possible common European laws, abolishing discrimination on grounds of nationality and undertaking certain tasks on a joint European basis.

In May 1976 the Committee of Ministers adopted the first 5-year plan (1976–80) of intergovernmental co-operation to be undertaken by the Council of Europe. The plan, which is reviewed every 2 years, takes account of political developments and progress achieved, and covers 8 key areas: human rights, social and socio-economic questions, education and culture, youth, public health, environment and regional planning, local and regional government, and legal co-operation. The first revision was undertaken in 1978.

More than 100 Conventions and Agreements have been concluded covering such matters as social security, patents, extradition, medical treatment, training of nurses, equivalence of degrees and diplomas, innkeepers' liability, compulsory motor insurance, the protection of television broadcasts, adoption of children, transportation of animals and *au pair* placement. In the legal field, of particular significance in 1977, was the adoption of the European Convention on the Suppression of Terrorism, as well as the European Convention on the Legal Status of Migrant Workers. In 1980 the Committee of Ministers adopted a European Convention for the protection of individuals with regard to the automatic processing of personal data. A Social Charter which came into force in 1965 sets out the social and economic rights which all member governments agree to guarantee to their citizens.

The official languages are English and French.

Chairman of the Committee of Ministers: (held in rotation).

President of the Parliamentary Assembly: Hans J. de Koster (Netherlands).

President of the European Court of Human Rights: Prof. Giorgio Balladore Pallieri (Italy).

President of the European Commission of Human Rights: James E. S. Fawcett (UK).

Secretary-General: Franz Karasek (Austria).

Headquarters: Palais de l'Europe, 67006, Strasbourg, CEDEX, France.

Flag: Dark blue with a ring of 12 gold stars in the centre.

European Yearbook. The Hague, from 1955

Forum. Strasbourg, from 1978, 4 times a year

Guide to the Council of Europe. Strasbourg, 1979

Manual of the Council of Europe. London, 1970

Yearbook on the Convention on Human Rights. Strasbourg, from 1958

Nova, F., *Contemporary European Governments*. Dublin, 1965

P.E.P., *European Organisations*. 2nd ed. London, 1966

Cook, C., and Paxton, J., *European Political Facts, 1918–73*. London, 1975

Robertson, A. H., *The Council of Europe*. 2nd ed. London, 1961.—*European Institutions*. 2nd ed. London, 1966

EUROPEAN COMMUNITIES

In May 1950 Belgium, France, the Federal Republic of Germany, Italy, Luxembourg and the Netherlands started negotiations with the aim of ensuring continual peace by a merging of their essential interests. The negotiations culminated with the signing of the Treaty of Paris creating the European Coal and Steel Community (ECSC). After it was found impossible to create European Communities covering Defence and Foreign Affairs, two more communities with the aims of gradually integrating the economies of the 6 nations and of moving towards closer political unity. The European Economic Community (EEC) and the European Atomic Energy Community (EAEC or Euratom) were created in 1957 by the signing of the Treaties of Rome.

Until 1 July 1967 the 3 Communities, though legally separate under their constituent treaties, had some institutions in common. On that day they merged their 3 executives in one Commission of the European Communities and also their 3 councils. Although each of the 3 communities still retains its distinct legal personality. The Court of Auditors of the European Communities was created by the Treaty of Brussels which came into force on 1 June 1977.

On 30 June 1970 membership negotiations began between the Six and UK, Denmark, Irish Republic and Norway. On 22 Jan. 1972 those 4 countries signed the Treaty of Accession to the Community. In Nov. 1972 a Norwegian referendum rejected entry, but on 1 Jan. 1973 UK, Irish Republic and Denmark became full members.

On 28 May 1979 the Treaty concerning the accession of Greece to the Community was signed. The Treaty, which entered into force on 1 Jan. 1981, was ratified by the Greek Parliament on 28 June 1979.

The *Commission* consists of 13 members appointed by the member states to serve for 4 years; the President and 5 Vice-Presidents serve for 2 years. The Commission acts independently in the interests of the Community as a whole. Its task is the implementation of the Treaties, and in this it has the right of both initiative and execution: it proposes to the Council of Ministers the methods by which the aims of the Treaties can be achieved, and is then responsible for carrying them through.

President: Gaston Thorn.
Address: 200 rue de la Loi, 1049, Brussels.

The *Council of Ministers* consists of ministers from the 10 national governments and represents the national as opposed to the Community interests. It is the body which has the power of decision in the Community. Under the Treaties many of its decisions are taken to be by qualified majority vote; since the 'Luxembourg Compromise' of 1966 majority voting has been used for minor matters only. In addition, at a meeting held in Dec. 1974, the Heads of Government decided to meet 3 times a year as the *European Council* to discuss Community and foreign policy topics. The presidency of the Council is held for a 6 month term in the following order of member states: Belgium, Denmark, Federal Republic of Germany, Greece, France, Irish Republic, Italy, Luxembourg, Netherlands, UK. From 1 July—31 Dec. 1981 (Denmark).

Address: 170 rue de la Loi, 1048, Brussels.

The *European Parliament* consists of 434 members of whom all but the 24 Greek members were elected by direct universal suffrage on 7 and 10 June 1979. France, Federal Germany, Italy and the UK each returned 81 members, the Netherlands 25, Belgium 24, Denmark 16, Ireland 15 and Luxembourg 6. Party representation in the new Parliament was as follows: Socialist 112, European People's Party—Christian Democratic Group 108, European Democratic Group (formerly European Conservative Group) 64, Communists and Allies 44, Liberal and Democratic Group 40, European Progressive Democratic Group 22, Others 20. Prior to these elections the Parliament consisted of 198 members delegated by the 9 national Parliaments. The Parliament has to be consulted over the annual budgets of the 3 Communities and a wide range of other matters. It can dismiss the Commission on a motion of censure approved by a two-thirds majority. As part of the decision in 1970 to provide the Community with its own independent financial resources, the Parliament has been given more control over the administrative budget consisting of non-mandatory expenditure, *i.e.*, expenditure not arising directly from the Treaty or from regulations made under it. The budgetary power of the Parliament was reviewed in 1973 and was enlarged in 1975 and was first used in Dec. 1979.

President: Simone Veil.
Address: Centre Européan du Kirchberg, Luxembourg.

Annuaire—Manuel de l'Assemblée Parlementaire Européenne. Annual, from 1959

The *Court of Justice* is composed of 10 judges and 4 advocates-general, is responsible for the adjudication of disputes arising out of the application of the treaties, and its findings are enforceable in all member countries.

President: Josse Mertens de Wilmars.
Address: Palais de la Cour de Justice, Kirchberg, Luxembourg.

The *Economic and Social Committee* has an advisory role and consists of 156 representatives, employers, trade unions, consumers, etc. The *Consultative Committee*, of 84 members, performs a similar role for the ECSC.

Community Law. Provisions of the Treaties and secondary legislation may be either directly applicable in Member States or only applicable after Member States have enacted their own implementing legislation. Secondary legislation consists of: regulations, which are of general application and binding in their entirety and directly applicable in all member states; directives which are binding as to the result to be achieved within a given time, upon each Member State but leave the national authority the choice of form and method of achieving this result; decisions, which are binding in their entirety on their addressees. In addition the Council and Commission can issue recommendations and opinions, which have no binding force.

The Community's Legislative Process starts with a proposal from the Commission (either at the suggestion of its services or in pursuit of its declared political aims) to the Council. The Council seeks the views of the European Parliament on the proposal, and the Parliament adopts a formal Opinion, after consideration of the matter by its specialist Committees. The Council may also (and in some cases is obliged to) consult the Economic and Social Committee, which similarly delivers an opinion. When these opinions have been received, the Council will decide. Most decisions are taken on a majority basis, but will take account of reserves expressed by individual member states. The text eventually approved may differ substantially from the original Commission proposal.

Community Finances. The general budget of the European Communities for 1980 was (in ECUm.; 1EUA = US$1·31 or £0·55 on 31 Dec. 1980):

Receipts		*Expenditure*	
Own resources		Agriculture	11,878
Agricultural levies	2,223	Social	374
Import duties	5,668	Regional	403
VAT	7,164	Industry, energy,	
		research	380
	15,055	Administration and	
Miscellaneous	628	miscellaneous	2,648
	15,683		15,683

In addition the European Development Fund spent ECU 544m.

The *European Investment Bank* (EIB) was created by the EEC Treaty to which its statute is annexed. Its governing body is the Board of Governors consisting of ministers designated by member states. Its main task is to contribute to the balanced development of the common market in the interest of the Community by financing projects: developing less-developed regions, for modernizing or converting undertakings or developing new activities, or of common interest to several member states.

Address: 100, Boulevard Konrad Adenhauer, Plateau du Kirchberg, Luxembourg.

EUROPEAN ECONOMIC COMMUNITY or COMMON MARKET.
The EEC came into being on 1 Jan. 1958, based on the treaty signed in Rome on 25 March 1957, by Belgium, France, Federal Republic of Germany, Luxembourg, Italy and the Netherlands. UK, the Irish Republic and Denmark became members on 1 Jan. 1973; Greece became a member on 1 Jan. 1981.

The Customs Union. A complete customs union between the 6 original member states was acheived on 1 July 1968 when they ceased to apply to each other any customs duties, charge having equivalent effect, or quantitative restrictions and commenced applying a common basic customs legislation and a Common Customs Tariff to non-Member Countries. The UK, Ireland and Denmark had phased out customs tariffs between each other and between themselves and the original 6 members states by 1 July 1977. Greece is to end its customs tariffs with the existing 9 member states by 1 Jan. 1986.

Freedom of movement for persons, services and capital. Under the Treaty individuals, companies and firms from one member state may establish themselves in another Member State for the purposes of pursuing an economic activity under the same conditions as are applied to nationals of that state. With a few exceptions restrictions have been ended on the transfer of capital between one Member State and another.

The Common Agricultural Policy (CAP). The objectives as set out in the Treaty are to increase agricultural productivity, to ensure a fair standard of living for the agricultural community, to stabilize markets, to assure the availability of supplies, and to ensure reasonable consumer prices. In Dec. 1960 the Council laid down the fundamental principles on which the CAP is based: a single market, which calls for common prices, stable currency parities and the harmonizing of administrative, health and veterinary legislation; Community preference, which protects the EEC single market from imports and world market fluctuations; common financing of the European Agricultural Guidance and Guarantee Fund (EAGGF) which seeks to improve agriculture through its Guidance secton, and, through its Guarantee section, to stabilize markets through a system of intervention measures, and levies and refunds on imports and exports. By 1980 common market organisations covered 96% of Community agricultural production. Greece will bring its agricultural prices into line with Community prices over a period depending on the product of up to 7 years.

The European Monetary System (EMS), whose immediate objective is to create a zone of monetary stability in Europe by closer monetary cooperation, began operating in March 1979. All member states (expect the UK, 1981) limit fluctuations in the exchange rates of their currencies against a central rate denominated in ECU (European Currency Unit), a basket of the currencies of all the member states. The Greek drachma will join the ECU by 31 Dec. 1986.

External Relations are mainly dealt with as a joint Community matter when they concern trade (as a result of the Customs Union and the Common Agricultural Policy) and Aid (as a result of the European Development Fund). Following the accession of UK, Ireland and Denmark in 1973, the Community formed a free trade zone for industrial goods with the European Free Trade Association; reciprocal arrangements were made for some agricultural goods. Association agreements which could lead to accession or customs union have been made with Turkey, Cyprus and Malta. An agreement was concluded in 1976 with Canada for economic and commercial agreement in the fields of industrial trade, science and natural resources. Algeria, Morocco, Tunisia, Egypt, Israel, Jordan, Lebanon and Syria have commercial, industrial, technical and financial aid agreements with the Community. Some 60 African, Caribbean and Pacific countries (mainly former colonies of member states) have concluded the Lomé Convention, first signed in 1975 and renewed in 1979, which removes customs duties without reciprocal obligations for most of their exports to the Community, and under which ECU 5,600m. of financial and technical aid will be granted between 1980–84. An economic and commercial co-operation agreement was signed in 1980 with ASEAN.

General Report on the Activities of the Community (annual, from 1958).—*Bulletin of the EEC* (monthly).—*Bulletin Général de Statistiques* (monthly).—*Statistique Mensuelle du Commerce Extérieur* (monthly).—*The Agricultural Situation in the Community*. 1980.—*Ninth Report of Competition Policy*. 1980.—*The European Community Today and Tommorrow*. 1978

European Community (monthly), obtainable from the UK office of the Commission of the European Communities, 20 Kensington Palace Gdns, London, W8 4QQ
Arbuthnott, H. and Edwards, G., (eds) *A Common Man's Guide to the Common Market*. London, 1979
Bellamy, C., and Child, G. D., *Common Market Law of Competition*. London, 1973
Böhning, W. R., *The Migration of Workers in the United Kingdom and the European Community*. New York, OUP, 1972
Butler, D., and Kitzinger, U., *The 1975 Referendum*. London, 1976
Calmann, J. (ed.), *The Rome Treaty: The Common Market Explained*. London, 1967
Cocks, Sir Barnett, *The European Parliament*. HMSO, 1973
Coffey, P., *The External Economic Relations of the E.E.C.* London, 1976
Cook, C., and Francis, M., *The First European Elections*. London, 1979
Drew, J., *Doing Business with the European Community*. London, 1979
Dyas, G. P., and Thanheiser, H. T., *The Emerging European Enterprise*. London, 1976
Fennell, R., *The Common Agricultural Policy of the European Community*. London, 1979
Goodhart, P., *Full-hearted Consent*. London, 1976
Hallstein, W., *Europe in the Making*. London, 1973
Herman, V., and Lodge, J., *The European Parliament and the European Community*. London, 1978
Kitzinger, U., *Diplomacy and Persuasion: How Britain Joined the Common Market*. London, 1972
Korah, V., *An Introductory Guide to EEC Competition Law and Practice*. Oxford, 1979
Love, J., *Jane's Major Companies of Europe 1976*. London, 1976
Mally, G., *The European Community in Perspective*. Lexington, Mass., 1973
Marx, E., and Kendall, W., *Unions in Europe: A Guide to Organised Labour in the Six*. Univ. of Sussex, 1971
Mathijsen, P. S. R. F., *A Guide to European Community Law*. London, New York, 1972
Mayne, R., *The Recovery of Europe*. London, 1970
Mowat, R. C., *Creating the European Community*. London, 1973
Palmer, D. M., *Sources of Information on the European Communities*. London, 1979
Parry, A., and Hardy, S., *EEC Law*. London, 1973

Paxton, J., *The Developing Common Market*. London, 1976.—*A Dictionary of the European Economic Community*. London, 1977
Pryce, R., *The Politics of the European Community*. London, 1973
Shanks, M., *European Social Policy, Today and Tomorrow*. Oxford, 1977
Spinelli, A., *The European Adventure*. London, 1972
Swann, D., *The Economies of the Common Market*. 4th ed. Harmondsworth, 1978
Taylor, P., *When Europe Speaks with One Voice*. London, 1979
Thomas, H., *Europe: The Radical Challenge*. New York, 1973
Wallace, H., *National Governments and the European Communities*. London, 1973
Wallace, W., and Herreman, I. (eds.), *A Community of Twelve?* Bruges, 1978
Walsh, A. E., and Paxton, J., *Trade in the Common Market Countries*. London, 1965.—*Trade and Industrial Resources of the Common Market and EFTA Countries*. London, 1970.—*Competition Policy*. London, 1975

EUROPEAN COAL AND STEEL COMMUNITY. The ECSC came into being on 10 Aug. 1952 following the ratification of a treaty signed in Paris on 18 April 1951. The original suggestion for it was made in the Schuman Plan on 9 May 1950, which proposed the pooling of Franco-German coal and steel production in a Community open to other western European countries as a first step towards a United States of Europe. (*See* map in THE STATESMAN'S YEAR-BOOK, 1958.) UK, the Irish Republic and Denmark joined the ECSC as full members on 1 Jan. 1973 and Greece on 1 Jan. 1981.

Until 1 July 1967 the *High Authority* was the executive body of the ECSC and consisted of 8 members appointed by the 6 governments plus one co-opted member. After the merger of the Executives its power passed to the single European Commission which is now responsible for the execution of the ECSC Treaty.

The Common Market for Coal and Steel. A common market for coal, iron ore and scrap was established on 10 Feb. 1953, for steel on 1 May 1953 and for special steels on 1 Aug. 1954. A harmonized external tariff on steel is between 4–8% on most products. Rules for fair competition have been established; currency restrictions, the dual-pricing system (under which prices for export and home-consumed coal and steel varied) and discriminatory transport rates based upon nationality have been abolished within the Community.

To meet the changing circumstances in the two industries, and especially to ensure that the contraction of the coal industry occurs without social or economic dislocation, there are ECSC readaption, retraining and other schemes to which the Commission makes grants. In 1979 the Commission contributed ECU67m. to the redevelopment of 34,000 workers throughout the Community.

A Common Energy Policy. Of the various forms of energy, coal falls within the competence of the ECSC, nuclear energy within that of Euratom, and all others within that of the EEC. The 1972 Paris summit set up the goal of a common energy policy; the post-1974 energy crisis has intensified the need for ensuring supplies.

The ECSC operating budget was (1979) ECU 143m.

General Report of the High Authority (annual, from 1953).—*Bulletin Statistique* (bi-monthly from 1952).—*Investment Report* (annual, from 1956).—*Financial Report* (annual, from 1956).—*Journal Officiel de la CECA* (1952–58).—*Journal Officiel des Communautés Européennes* (from 1958).—*European Community* (monthly, from 1963)

EUROPEAN ATOMIC ENERGY COMMUNITY (EURATOM). Euratom came into being on 1 Jan. 1958 following the ratification of a treaty signed in Rome on 25 March 1957. Its task is to promote a common effort between its members in the development of nuclear energy for peaceful purposes. It is in no way concerned with the military uses of nuclear energy; indeed, the member governments are forbidden under the treaty to use nuclear materials obtained from or through the Community in national military programmes.

The execution of the treaty now rests with the *European Commission*, which is advised by a *Scientific and Technical Committee* (28 members) and the *Economic and Social Committee*. Major decisions are taken by the *Council of Ministers*.

Euratom supplements and co-ordinates research undertaken by the member states, pools scientific information and promotes the training of scientists and technicians. It promotes research (a) through its own research centres at Ispra, Italy (concentrating on the Orgel heavy-water reactor), at Geel, Belgium (the Central Nuclear Measurements Bureau), at Karlsruhe, Germany (the European Transuranium Institute) at Culham, Oxfordshire, UK (Joint European Torus) and at Petten, Netherlands (a general-purpose research establishment); (b) by contracting specific tasks to national centres or firms, and by 'association contracts' under which it contributes finance and personnel to joint teams; (c) by joining international projects such as the European Nuclear Energy Agency project at Winfrith Heath, England (the Dragon reactor).

Euratom has its own large Information and Documentation Centre, has set up a radioisotope information bureau and has worked out a Community policy on ownership of patents resulting from nuclear research. It has laid down basic standards for health protection throughout the Community, and worked out an insurance convention for large-scale atomic risks.

A common market for all nuclear materials and equipment came into force, and external tariffs were suspended, on 1 Jan. 1959. Since 1966 Euratom has been growing steadily less effective though attempts are still made to rationalize the research centres' operations, and co-ordinate them with national efforts.

International Links. An agreement was signed with the US Atomic Energy Commission in Nov. 1958 and widened in 1964. UK, the Irish Republic and Denmark joined Euratom on 1 Jan. 1973.

General Report on the Activities of the Community (annual, from 1958).—*Euratom Bulletin* (quarterly, from Jan. 1962)

EUROPEAN FREE TRADE ASSOCIATION (EFTA)

The European Free Trade Association has 6 member countries: Austria, Iceland, Norway, Portugal, Sweden and Switzerland. A seventh country, Finland, is an associate member. The Stockholm Convention establishing the Association entered into force on 3 May 1960 and Finland became associated on 27 March 1961. Iceland joined EFTA on 1 March 1970 and was immediately granted duty-free entry for industrial goods exported to EFTA countries, while being given 10 years to abolish her own existing protective duties. Two founder members of EFTA, the UK and Denmark, left EFTA on 31 Dec. 1972 to join the EEC.

When the Association was created it had three objectives: to achieve free trade in industrial products between member countries, to assist in the creation of a single market embracing the countries of Western Europe, and to contribute to the expansion of world trade in general.

The first objective was achieved on 31 Dec. 1966, when virtually all inter-EFTA tariffs were removed. This was 3 years earlier than originally planned. Finland removed her remaining EFTA tariffs a year later on 31 Dec. 1967 and Iceland removed her tariffs on 31 Dec. 1979.

The fulfilment of the second aim was secured in 1972. On 22 Jan. 1972 the UK and Denmark signed the Treaty of Accession to the EEC whereby they became members of the enlarged Community from 1 Jan. 1973. On 22 July 1972, 5 other EFTA countries, Austria, Iceland, Portugal, Sweden and Switzerland signed Free Trade Agreements with the enlarged EEC. A similar agreement negotiated with Finland was signed on 5 Oct. 1973. Norway, whose intention of joining the EEC was reversed following a referendum, signed a similar agreement on 14 May 1973. Through these agreements virtually complete free trade in industrial goods was achieved in 16 Western European countries from 1 July 1977. The free trade agreements apply also to Greece since its accession to the EEC on 1 Jan. 1981. A multilateral free trade agreement between EFTA countries and Spain, a candidate for EEC membership, came into force on 1 May 1980 and the first tariff cuts were applied on 1 June 1980.

The third objective was to contribute to the expansion of world trade. In 1959 trade between the countries then in EFTA amounted to US$759m. and total exports were US$6,852m. In 1979 the respective figures were US$15,105m. and US$98,315m. More than half EFTA trade is with the EEC.

EFTA tariff treatment applies to those industrial products which are of EFTA origin, and these are traded freely between member countries. Each EFTA country remains free, however, to impose its own rates of duty on products entering from outside EFTA or the EEC.

Generally, agricultural products do not come under the provisions for free trade, but bilateral agreements have been negotiated to increase trade in these products.

The operation of the Convention is the responsibility of a Council assisted by a small secretariat. Each EFTA country holds the chairmanship of the Council for 6 months.

Secretary-General: Charles Müller (Switzerland).
Headquarters: 9–11 Rue de Varembé, 1211 Geneva 20, Switzerland.

Convention Establishing the European Free Trade Association (new ed. 1979)
EFTA Bulletin (Six issues a year)
EFTA What it is, What it does
The European Free Trade Association. 1980

COUNCIL FOR MUTUAL ECONOMIC ASSISTANCE [1]

Membership. Founder members were USSR, Bulgaria, Czechoslovakia, Hungary, Poland and Romania. Later admissions were Albania (1949; ceased participation 1961), German Democratic Republic (1950), Mongolia (1962), Cuba (1972), Vietnam (1978). In 1964 Yugoslavia concluded an agreement with CMEA whereby Yugoslavia would participate in the work of some CMEA bodies (at present 21). Afghánistán, Angola, Ethiopia, Laos, Mozambique and the People's Democratic Republic of Yemen attend CMEA sessions as observers.

External relations. There are co-operation agreements with Finland, Iraq and Mexico. Talks with the EEC at expert level on possible commercial co-operation were resumed in July 1980.

The Charter. The charter consists of a preamble and 18 articles. Extracts (in the language of the official English version) are as follows:

Article 1. Aims and Principles: 1 'The purpose of the Council is to promote, by uniting and co-ordinating the efforts of the member countries, the further extension and improvement of co-operation and the development of socialist economic integration, the planned development of their national economies, the acceleration of economic and technical progress in these countries, higher level of industrialization of the less industrialized countries, a continuous increase in labour productivity, a gradual approximation and equalization of economic development levels and a steady improvement in the wellbeing of the peoples. 2 The Council is based on the principles of the sovereign equality of all member countries.'

Article 2. Membership 'open to other countries which subscribe to the purposes and principles of the Council'.

Article 3. Functions and Powers to (a) 'organize all-round . . . co-operation of member countries in the most rational use of natural resources and acceleration of the development of their productive forces'; (b) 'foster the improvement of the international socialist division of labour by co-ordinating national economic development plans, and the specialization and co-operation of production in member countries'; (c) to assist in . . . carrying out joint measures for the development of industry and agriculture . . . transport . . . principal capital investments . . . [and] trade'.

[1] *Abbreviations and Foreign Names.* CMEA is the official abbreviation. Other unofficial abbreviations are Comecon and CEMA. The working language of the organization is Russian. The Russian form is *Sovet Ekonomicheskoi Vzaimopomoshchi* (SEV).

Article 4. Recommendations and Decisions '. . . shall be adopted only with the consent of the interested member countries.'

The Structure. The supreme authority is the 'Session' of all members held (usually annually) in members' capitals in rotation under the chairmanship of the head of the delegation of the host country; all members must be present, and decisions must be unanimous. Delegations are usually led by prime ministers.

The *Executive Committee* is made up of 1 representative from each member state of deputy premier rank. It meets at least once every 3 months.

The administrative organ is the *Secretariat*.

Headquarters: Prospekt Kalinina, 56, Moscow, G-205.
Secretary: N. V. Faddeev (appointed 1958).

There is a *Committee for Co-operation in the Field of Planning* and a *Committee for Scientific and Technical Co-operation* set up in 1971 and a *Committee for Material and Technical Supply* set up in 1974. There are *Permanent Commissions* on: Statistics, Foreign Trade, Currency and Finance, Electricity, Peaceful Uses of Atomic Energy, Geology, Coal Industry, Oil and Gas Industry, Chemical Industry, Iron and Steel Industry, Non-Ferrous Metals Industry, Engineering Industry, Radio Engineering and Electronics Industries, Light Industry, Food Industry, Agriculture, Construction, Transport, Posts and Telecommunications, Standardization, Civil Aviation, Public Health.

There are 7 *Standing Conferences:* for Legal Problems; of Ministers of Internal Trade; of Chiefs of Water Resources Authorities; of Chiefs of Patent Authorities; of Chiefs of Pricing Authorities; of Chiefs of Labour Authorities, and of Representatives of Freight and Shipping Organizations.

There are 3 semi-autonomous bodies within CMEA: The Institute of Standardization, The Bureau for the Co-ordination of Ship Freighting and The International Institute of Economic Problems of World Socialist System.

In 1980 there were 20 technical and economic agencies associated with CMEA.

Also associated with CMEA are:

The **International Bank for Economic Co-operation** was founded in 1963 with a capital of 300m. roubles and started operating on 1 Jan. 1964. It undertakes multilateral settlements in 'transferable roubles' (*i.e.*, used for intra-CMEA clearing accounts only) and advances credits to finance trading and other operations. The transferable *rouble* is a unit of account: gold content 0·987412 gramme.

The **International Investments Bank** was founded in 1970 and went into operation on 1 Jan. 1971 with a capital of 1,000m. roubles (70% transferable and 30% convertible or in gold).

Banking and Sources of Finance in Comecon. London, 1978
Charter of the Council for Mutual Economic Assistance. Moscow, 1980
Council for Mutual Economic Assistance: Thirty Years. Moscow, 1979
Comprehensive Programme for the Further Extension and Improvement of Co-operation and the Development of Socialist Economic Integration by the CMEA-member Countries. Moscow, 1971 (The official English-language version. This document also frequently referred to as the *Complex Programme*, etc.)
Ekonomicheskoe Sotrudnichestvo Stran-Chlenov SEV. Moscow, 6 a year
Multilateral Economic Co-operation of Socialist States: A Collection of Documents. Moscow, 1977
Statistical Year Book of CMEA Member Countries. Moscow, annual
Survey of CMEA Activities. Moscow, annual
Bautina, N. V., *CMEA Today: from Economic Co-operation to Economic Integration.* Moscow, 1975
Bystrický, R., *Le Droit de l'Intégration Économique Socialiste.* Geneva, 1979
Shaeffer, H. W., *Comecon and the Politics of Integration.* New York and London, 1972
Szawlowski, R., *The System of the International Organizations of the Communist Countries.* Leyden, 1976
van Brabant, J. M. P., *Essays on Planning, Trade and Integration in Eastern Europe.* Rotterdam Univ. Press, 1974
Wilcox, H., *Comecon and the Politics of Integration.* New York and London, 1972
Wilczynski, J., *Technology in Comecon.* London, 1974

COLOMBO PLAN

The Colombo Plan was established for co-operative economic development in south and south-east Asia in 1951 as a result of a meeting of Commonwealth foreign ministers held in 1950. It seeks to improve the living standards of the people of the area by reviewing development plans and co-ordinating development assistance. Aid to member countries is negotiated and administered bilaterally. Membership comprises 20 developing countries within the region: Afghánistán, Bangladesh, Bhután, Burma, Fiji, India, Indonesia, Iran, Kampuchea, Republic of Korea, Laos, Malaysia, Republic of the Maldives, Nepál, Pakistan, Papua New Guinea, Philippines, Singapore, Sri Lanka and Thailand; and 6 non-regional members: Australia, Canada, Japan, New Zealand, UK and USA.

The annual meetings of the Consultative Committee are also attended by observers from major international and regional organizations concerned with development. There was no Consultative Committee meeting in 1979; instead there was a meeting of Senior Officials of Colombo Plan countries held in Colombo to discuss the 'Future role of the Colombo Plan'.

Technical Co-operation. The Colombo Plan has no permanent secretariat. A small Bureau, set up in Colombo in 1951, operates under the supervision of a Council for Technical Co-operation in South and South-East Asia, representing member governments. An information unit has been attached to the Bureau since 1953. The Colombo Plan Staff College for Technician Education was established at Singapore in 1974. The Council publishes its own annual report.

During 1979, 2,054 experts were assigned to countries of the region, and 3,787 student and training places were provided. Most training is given outside the region, but the Bureau has increasingly urged members to make more use of training facilities available within the region, by adequate arrangements for the exchange of students.

External Aid. Total Colombo Plan assistance to regional member countries in 1979 exceeded US$56·7m. In addition there is substantial private investment from countries outside the region. In 1979 UK net bilateral aid amounted to US$490·4m., bringing the total since 1950 to US$4,446m. Of the total expenditure in 1979, US$58m. was on technical co-operation, bringing the total of such expenditure since 1950 to US$413m.

The Colombo Plan (Cmd. 8080). HMSO, 1950; reprinted 1952.—*Annual Report.* HMSO, 1952 to 1971 followed by Colombo Plan Bureaux, Sri Lanka, 1972 to date
Reports of the Council for Technical Co-operation. HMSO annually until 1966–67 followed by the Colombo Plan Bureau, Sri Lanka, 1967–68 to date

ASSOCIATION OF SOUTH EAST ASIAN NATIONS (ASEAN)

History and Membership. The Association of South East Asian Nations is a regional organization formed by the governments of Indonesia, Malaysia, the Philippines, Singapore and Thailand through the Bangkok Declaration which was signed by the Foreign Ministers of ASEAN countries on 8 Aug. 1967.

Objectives. The main objectives are to accelerate economic growth, social progress and cultural development, to promote active collaboration and mutual assistance in matters of common interest, to ensure the stability of the South East Asian region and to maintain close co-operation with existing international and regional organizations with similar aims. Principal projects concern economic co-operation and development, with the intensification of Intra-ASEAN trade and trade between the region and the rest of the world; joint research and technological programmes; co-operation in transportation and communications; promotion of tourism and south-east Asian studies; including cultural, scientific, educational and administrative exchanges.

Organs. The highest authority in ASEAN are the Heads of Government of the Member Countries who meet as and when necessary to give directions to ASEAN.

The highest policy-making body is the Meeting of Foreign Ministers, commonly known as the Annual Ministerial Meeting, which convenes in each of the ASEAN members countries on a rotational basis in alphabetical order. The Standing Committee, comprising the Foreign Minister of the country hosting the Ministerial Meeting in that particular year and the accredited ambassadors of the other member countries, carries out the work of the Association in between the Ministerial Meetings and handles the routine matters to ensure continuity and to make decisions which can not wait for the Ministerial Meetings and submit for the consideration of the Foreign Ministers all reports and recommendations of the various ASEAN committees. There are 4 specialized committees under the Standing Committee and five others under the ASEAN Economic Ministers that recommend and draw up programmes of ASEAN co-operation. These committees are responsible for the operation and implementation of ASEAN projects in their respective fields. Each ASEAN capital has an ASEAN National Secretariat. The central secretariat for ASEAN is located in Jakarta, Indonesia, and is headed by the ASEAN Secretary General, a post that revolves among the member states in alphabetical order every 2 years. Bureau directors and other officers of the ASEAN Secretariat remain in office for 3 years.

Secretary-General: Narciso G. Reyes (Philippines).

Book of Reference

Wong, J., *ASEAN Economics in Perspective*. London, 1979

ORGANIZATION OF AMERICAN STATES

On 14 April 1890 representatives of the American republics, meeting in Washington at the First International Conference of American States, established an 'International Union of American Republics' and, as its central office, a 'Commercial Bureau of American Republics', which later became the Pan American Union. This international organization's object was to foster mutual understanding and co-operation among the nations of the western hemisphere. Since that time, successive inter-American conferences have greatly broadened the scope of work of the organization.

This led to the adoption on 30 April 1948 by the Ninth International Conference of American States, at Bogotá, Colombia, of the Charter of the Organization of American States. This co-ordinated the work of all the former independent official entities in the inter-American system and defined their mutual relationships. The purposes of the OAS are to achieve an order of peace and justice, promote American solidarity, strengthen collaboration among the member states and defend their sovereignty, territorial integrity and independence. The OAS is a regional organization of the United Nations for the maintenance of peace and security.

Membership is on a basis of absolute equality. Each country has one vote in the Council of the Organization and its organs. The member countries were (1980): Argentina, Barbados, Bolivia, Brazil, Chile, Colombia, Costa Rica, Cuba, Commonwealth of Dominica, Dominican Republic, Ecuador, El Salvador, Grenada, Guatemala, Haiti, Honduras, Jamaica, Mexico, Nicaragua, Panama, Paraguay, Peru, Saint Lucia, Suriname, Trinidad and Tobago, USA, Uruguay, Venezuela.

The OAS has been concerned increasingly in recent years with programmes to promote Latin American economic and social development. The OAS provides specialized training for thousands of Latin Americans each year in a wide variety of development-related fields. It also carries out several missions projects each year in response to requests from member governments.

On 27 Feb. 1967 the Third Special Inter-American Conference in Buenos Aires approved the Protocol of Amendment to the Charter of the OAS, which contained new standards for inter-American co-operation and a number of structural changes in the Organization.

On 14 April 1967 the Declaration of the Presidents of America, signed in Punta del Este, Uruguay, expressed the commitment of the American chiefs of state to promote Latin American economic integration; to join in efforts to increase substantially Latin American foreign-trade earnings; to modernize the living conditions of the rural population and raise agricultural productivity; and to expand programmes in education, science, technology and health.

On 22 Feb. 1968, in the Resolution of Maracay, the Inter-American Cultural Council launched new regional programmes for educational development and for scientific and technological development.

On 27 Feb. 1970, by ratification of more than the mandatory two-thirds of the OAS member states, the Protocol of Buenos Aires, modifying the 1948 Charter, entered into effect.

Under the amended Charter, the OAS accomplishes its purposes by means of:

(a) The *General Assembly*, which meets annually in various countries of the member states.

(b) The *Meeting of Consultation of Ministers of Foreign Affairs*, held to consider problems of an urgent nature and of common interest.

(c) Three councils of equal rank: the *Permanent Council*, which replaces the old OAS Council; the *Inter-American Economic and Social Council*; and the *Inter-American Council for Education, Science and Culture*. Functions are to direct and co-ordinate work in the areas of their competence and render the governments such specialized services as they may request. Each council is composed of 1 representative from each member state, appointed by his government.

(d) The *Inter-American Juridical Committee* which acts as an advisory body to the OAS on juridical matters and promotes the development and codification of international law. Eleven jurists, elected every 4 years by the General Assembly, represent all the American States.

(e) The *Inter-American Commission on Human Rights* which oversees the observance and protection of human rights. Seven members represent all the OAS member states.

(f) The *General Secretariat* is the central and permanent organ of the OAS.

(g) The *Specialized Conferences*, meeting to deal with special technical matters or to develop specific aspects of inter-American co-operation.

(h) The *Specialized Organizations*, intergovernmental organizations established by multilateral agreements to discharge specific functions in their respective fields of action, such as women's affairs, agriculture, child welfare, Indian affairs, geography and history, and health.

Secretary-General: Alejandro Orfila (Argentina).
Assistant Secretary-General: Valerie McComie (Barbados).

The Secretary-General and the Assistant Secretary-General are elected by the General Assembly for 5-year terms. The General Assembly approves the annual budget for the Organization, which is financed by quotas contributed by the member governments.

General Secretariat: Washington, D.C., 20006, USA.
Flag: Light blue with the OAS seal in colour in the centre.

Books of Reference

Publications of the OAS General Secretariat include:

Charter of the Organization of American States. 1948.—*As Amended by the Protocol of Buenos Aires in 1967*
Americas. Illustrated monthly, from 1949. (Spanish, Portuguese and English edition)
Organization of American States, a Handbook. Rev. ed. 1977
Organization of American States. Directory. Quarterly, from 1951
Report on the Tenth Inter-American Conference, Caracas 1954. 1955
Inter-American Review of Bibliography. Quarterly, from 1951
Annual Report of the Secretary-General
Status of Inter-American Treaties and Conventions. Annual
The Alliance for Progress: The Charter of Punta del Este. 1962
Human Rights in the American States. 1960
Report of Inter-American Commission on Human Rights. From 1970

Publications on Latin America (*see also* the bibliographical notes appended to each country):

Revenue, Expenditure and Public Debts of the Latin American Republics. Division of Financial Information, US Department of Commerce. Annual

Fortnightly [from July 1960 also *Quarterly*] *Review of Business and Economic Conditions in South and Central America.* Bank of London and South America. London, 1935–66; restyled *B.O.L.S.A. Review,* from Jan. 1967

Boundaries of the Latin American Republics: An Annotated List of Documents, 1493–1943. Department of State, Office of the Geographer. Washington, 1944

Latin America: An Introduction to the Basic Books in English. 2nd. ed. Hispanic & Luso-Brazilian Councils, London, 1966

Baerresen, D. W., and others, *Latin American Trade Patterns.* Washington, D.C., 1965

Bailey, H. M., and Nasatir, A. P., *Latin America: The Development of its Civilization.* London, 1960

Burgin, M. (ed.), *Handbook of Latin American Studies.* Gainesville, Fla., 1935 ff.

Calvert, P., *Latin America: Internal Conflict and International Peace.* London, 1969

Davies, H. (ed.), *The South American Handbook.* London, 1924 to date

Ferguson, J. M., *Latin America: The Balance of Race Redressed.* OUP, 1961

Hirschman, Albert O., *Latin American Issues:* [11] *Essays and Comments.* New York, 1961

Humphreys, R. A., *Latin American History: A Guide to the Literature in English.* London, 1958

James, P. E., *Latin America.* 3rd ed. New York, 1959

Karnes, T. L., *The Future of Union: Central America 1824–1960.* Univ. of N. Carolina, Chapel Hill, 1961

Munro, D. G., *The Latin American Republics; A History.* London, 1961

Nehemkis, P., *Latin America: Myth and Reality.* New York, 1964

Pendle, G., *A History of Latin America.* Rev. ed. Harmondsworth, 1967

Plaza, G., *The Organization of American States: Instrument for Hemispheric Development.* Washington, 1969.—*Latin America Today and Tomorrow.* Washington, 1971

Steward, J. H. (ed.), *Handbook of the South American Indian.* 7 vols. Washington, 1946–59

Szulc, T., *Winds of Revolution.* New York, 1965

Thomas, A. V. W. and A. J., *The Organization of American States.* Southern Methodist Univ. Press, 1963

Ureña, P. H., *A Concise History of Latin American Culture.* London, 1966

Worcester, D. E., and Schaeffer, W. G., *The Growth and Culture of Latin America.* OUP, 1956

LATIN AMERICAN ECONOMIC GROUPINGS

The Economic Commission for Latin America, an organ of the United Nations, with headquarters in Santiago, Chile, has facilitated the co-operation of two groups of countries concerning production, tariffs and trade.

Latin American Free Trade Association was concluded in Montevideo on 18 Feb. 1961 by Argentina, Bolivia, Brazil, Chile, Mexico, Paraguay, Peru and Uruguay. Colombia (3 Oct. 1961), Ecuador (20 Oct. 1961) and Venezuela (1 Sept. 1966) have joined the ALALC/LAFTA Treaty. The permanent secretariat is at Montevideo. The 11 signatories held the 19th Extraordinary Conference at Acapulco, 16–27 June 1980. A Constitution was drawn up for a new Latin American Integration Association (LAIA) to take over after LAFTA expired on 31 Dec. 1980.

Central American Common Market (ODECA). On 13 Dec. 1960, at Managua, El Salvador, Guatemala, Honduras and Nicaragua concluded a general treaty on Central American integration; a protocol on the equalization of import duties and charges; and an agreement establishing the Central American Bank for Economic Integration. Costa Rica acceded in 1962 and in Sept. 1963 ratified the charter of the Banco Centroamericano de Integración Económica (in Tegucigalpa), whose capital was thereupon increased to US$20m.

The San Salvador Charter, signed on 14 Dec. 1962, expanded these provisions, envisaging permanent political, economic, educational, defence, etc., councils. The permanent secretariat is at Guatemala City.

Total intra-ODECA trade increased from US$8·6m. in 1960 to US$176m. in 1966. Total USA investments in the area are about $400m.

The Andean Group (*Grupo Andino*). On 26 May 1969 an agreement was signed by Bolivia, Chile, Colombia, Ecuador and Peru creating the Andean Group. Venezuela was initially actively involved but did not sign the agreement. The Group signed a further agreement on 31 Dec. 1970 on common regulations controlling foreign investments. Under the Cartagena Agreement of 1975 the development of an integrated petrochemical industry in each of the member countries was established.

Sistema Económico Latinoamericano (SELA) was created by 25 countries (not including USA) meeting at Panama, 17 Oct. 1975. Its Permanent Secretary is Jaime Moncayo, former Finance Minister of Ecuador. It held an 'extraordinary' technical meeting at Caracas, 5 Jan. 1976, to prepare for other activities, such as UNCTAD, at Nairobi in May 1976.

Britain and Latin America. Latin America Bureau, London (annual)
British Bulletin of Publications on Latin America, the Caribbean, Portugal and Spain. London, from June 1949 (half-yearly)
Hispanic and Luso-Brazilian Councils, Portuguese and Spanish Dictionaries. London, 1971
Instruments of Economic Integration in Latin America and the Caribbean. New York, 1975
Libre Comercio. Revista oficial de la Associación de Empresarios participantes de la ALALC. Montevideo, from June 1964 (monthly)
Committee on Latin America (COLA), *Latin American Economic and Social Serials.* London, 1969
Brooks, J. (ed.), *The South American Handbook.* Bath (Annual)
Einaudi, L., R. (ed.), *Beyond Cuba: Latin America Takes Charge of its Future.* New York, 1974
Furtado, C., *Economic Development of Latin America.* London, 1970
Griffin, K., *Financing Development of Latin America.* London, 1971
Jaguaribe, H., *Political Development: A General Theory and a Latin American Case Study.* New York, 1973
Loveman, B., and Davies, T. M., *The Politics of Antipolitics: The Military in Latin America.* Univ. Nebraska Press, 1978
Milenky, E. S., *The Politics of Regional Organization in Latin America. The Latin American Free Trade Association.* New York, 1973
Morawetz, D., *The Andean Group: A Case Study in Economic Integration Among Developing Countries.* MIT Press, 1974
Sánchez-Albornoz, N., *The Population of Latin America: A History.* Univ. of Calif. Press, 1974
UN Economic Commission for Latin America. *The Latin America Economy.* Washington (annual)
van Niekerk, A. E., *Populism and Political Development in Latin America.* Rotterdam Univ. Press, 1974
Wellman, F. W., *Dictionary of Tropical American Crops and Their Diseases.* Metuchen, 1977

CARIBBEAN COMMUNITY (CARICOM)

Establishment and Functions. The Treaty establishing the Caribbean Community, including the Caribbean Common Market, and the Agreement establishing the Common External Tariff for the Caribbean Common Market, was signed by the Prime Ministers of Barbados, Guyana, Jamaica and Trinidad and Tobago at Chaguaramas, Trinidad, on 4 July 1973, and entered into force on 1 Aug. 1973. Six less developed countries of CARIFTA signed the Treaty of Chaguaramas on 17 April 1974. They were Belize, Dominica, Grenada, St Lucia, St Vincent and Montserrat, and the Treaty came into effect for those countries on 1 May 1974. Antigua acceded to Membership on 4 July 1974 and on 26 July the Associated State of St Kitts–Nevis–Anguilla signed the Treaty of Chaguaramas in Kingston, Jamaica, and became a member of the Caribbean Community.

The Caribbean Community has 3 areas of activity: economic integration (that is, the Caribbean Common Market which replaces CARIFTA); co-operation in non-economic areas and the operation of certain common services; and co-ordination of foreign policies of independent member states.

The Caribbean Common Market provides for the establishment of a Common External Tariff, a common protective policy and the progressive co-ordination of external trade policies; the adoption of a scheme for the harmonization of fiscal incentives to industry; double taxation arrangements among member countries; the co-ordination of economic policies and development planning; and a special regime for the less developed countries of the community.

Membership: Antigua, Barbados, Belize, the Commonwealth of Dominica, Grenada, Guyana, Jamaica, Montserrat, St Kitts–Nevis–Anguilla, Saint Lucia, St Vincent and Trinidad and Tobago.

Structure: The *Heads of Government Conference* is the principal organ of the Community, and its primary responsibility is to determine the policy of the Community. It is the final authority of the Community and the Common Market, and for the conclusion of treaties and relationships between the Community and international organizations and States. It is responsible for financial arrangements for meeting the expenses of the Community.

The *Common Market Council* is the principal organ of the Common Market and consists of a Minister of Government designated by each member state. Decisions in both the Conference and the Council are in the main taken on the basis of unanimity.

The *Secretariat*, successor to the Commonwealth Caribbean Regional Secretariat, is the principal administrative organ of the Community and of the Common Market. The Secretary-General is appointed by the Conference on the recommendation of the Council for a term not exceeding 5 years and may be reappointed. The Secretary-General shall act in that capacity in all meetings of the Conference, the Council, and of the institutions of the Community.

Institutions of the Community, established by the Heads of Government Conference, are: Conference of Ministers responsible for Health; Standing Committees of Ministers responsible for Education, Industry, Labour, Foreign Affairs, Finance, Agriculture, Mines and Transport, and the Meteorological Council.

Associate Institutions: East Caribbean Common Market Council of Ministers; West Indies Associated States Council of Ministers; Caribbean Development Bank; Caribbean Examinations Council; Caribbean Investment Corporation; Council of Legal Education; Regional Transport Council; University of the West Indies; University of Guyana.

Field Projects: Caribbean Agricultural and Rural Development Advisory and Training Service; Caribbean Agricultural Research and Development Institute; Caribbean Food Corporation; Caribbean Tourism Research Centre; West Indies Shipping Corporation; Small Vessel Shipping Project; LIAT 1974 Ltd. and Caribbean Aviation Training Institute.

Secretary-General: Dr Kurleigh King.
Deputy Secretary-General: Roderick Rainford.
Headquarters: Bank of Guyana Building, PO Box 10827, Georgetown, Guyana.

The language of the Community is English.

Books of Reference

CARICOM Perspective. (Bi-monthly). *CARICOM Bibliography* (Bi-annual)

THE LEAGUE OF ARAB STATES

Origin. The formation of the League of Arab States in 1945 was largely inspired by the Arab awakening of the 19th century. This movement sought to re-create and reintegrate the Arab community which, though for 400 years a part of the Ottoman Empire, had preserved its identity as a separate national group held together by memories of a common past, a common religion and a common language, as well as by the consciousness of being part of a common cultural heritage. The leaders of the Arab movement in the 19th century and of the Arab revolt against Turkey in the First World War sought to achieve these aims through secession from the Ottoman Empire into a united and independent Arab state comprising all the Arab countries in Asia. However the 1919 peace settlement divided the Arab world in Asia (with the exception of Saudi Arabia and the Yemen) into British and French spheres of influence and established in them a number of separate states and administrations (Syria, Lebanon, Iraq, Jordan and Palestine) under temporary mandatory control.

By 1943, however, 7 of these countries had substantially achieved their independence. An Arab conference therefore met in Alexandria in the autumn of 1944; it formulated the 'Alexandria Protocol', which delineated the outlines of the Arab League. It was found that neither a unitary state nor a federation could be achieved, but only a league of sovereign states. A covenant, establishing such a league, was signed in Cairo on 22 March 1945 by the representatives of Egypt, Iraq, Saudi Arabia, Syria, Lebanon, Jordan and Yemen. There were (1980) 21 members of the League: Algeria, Bahrain, Iraq, Jibuti, Jordan, Kuwait, Lebanon, Libya, Mauritania, Morocco, Oman, Palestine L.O., Qatar, Saudi Arabia, Somalia, Sudan, Syria, Tunisia, United Arab Emirates, P.D.R. of Yemen and Yemen Arab Republic

Egypt's membership of the League was suspended, in accordance with a resolution passed at the Baghdad summit, in March 1979, at which time it was also agreed that the League secretariat should be moved from Cairo to Tunis. This action was taken in response to the signing of a bilateral peace treaty between Egypt and Israel.

Organization. The machinery of the League consists of a Council, a number of Special Committees and a Permanent Secretariat. On the Council each state has one vote. The Council may meet in any of the Arab capitals. Its functions include mediation in any dispute between any of the League states or a League state and a country outside the League. The Council has a Political Committee consisting of the Foreign Ministers of the Arab states.

The Permanent Secretariat of the League, under a Secretary-General (who enjoys, along with his senior colleagues, full diplomatic status), has its seat in Tunisia.

The League considers itself a regional organization within the framework of the United Nations at which its secretary-general is an observer.

Secretary-General: Chazli Klibi (Tunisia).

Flag: Dark green with the seal of the Arab League in white in the centre.

Arab Common Market. The Arab Common Market came into operation on 1 Jan. 1965. The agreement, reached on 13 Aug. 1964 and open to all the Arab League states, has been signed by Iraq, Jordan, Syria and Egypt. The agreement provides for the abolition of customs duties on agricultural products and natural resources within 5 years, by reducing tariffs at an annual rate of 20%. Customs duties on industrial products are to be reduced by 10% annually. The agreement also provides for the free movement of capital and labour between member countries, the establishment of common external tariffs, the co-ordination of economical development and the framing of a common foreign economic policy.

Books of Reference

Arab Maritime Data, 1979–80. London, 1979
Atlas of the Arab World and the Middle East. London and New York, 1960
Oxford Regional Economic Atlas: The Middle East and North Africa. OUP, 1960
Glubb, Sir John, *Britain and the Arabs.* London, 1956
Gomaa, A. M., *The Foundation of the League of Arab States.* London, 1977

ORGANIZATION OF THE PETROLEUM EXPORTING COUNTRIES

Aims. The Organization was founded in Iraq in 1960 with the following founder members, Iran, Iraq, Kuwait, Saudi Arabia and Venezuela, with the aims of unifying and co-ordinating members' petroleum policies and to safeguard their interests generally.

Membership (1979). Algeria, Ecuador, Gabon, Indonesia, Iran, Iraq, Kuwait, Libya, Nigeria, Qatar, Saudi Arabia, United Arab Emirates and Venezuela.

OPEC Fund. The Fund was established in 1976 to provide financial aid to developing countries, other than OPEC members, on advantageous terms.

Secretary-General: Rene G. Ortiz.

Headquarters: Obere Donaustrasse 93, 1020 Vienna, Austria.

Books of Reference

OPEC publications include: *Annual Statistical Bulletin. Annual Report. Proceedings of the OPEC Seminar 1977. OPEC Bulletin* (monthly). *OPEC Review* (quarterly). *OPEC Papers* (bi-monthly).
Al-Chalabi, Dr F., *OPEC and the International Oil Industry: A Changing Structure.* OUP, 1980
Abolfathi, F., *The OPEC Market to 1985.* Lexington, 1977
Ghadar, F., *The Evolution of OPEC Strategy.* Lexington, 1977

ORGANIZATION OF AFRICAN UNITY

On 25 May 1963 the heads of state or government of 32 African countries, at a conference in Addis Ababa, signed a charter establishing an 'Organization of African Unity' (*Organisation de l'Unité Africaine*).

Its chief objects are the furtherance of African unity and solidarity; the co-ordination of the political, economic, cultural, health, scientific and defence policies and the elimination of colonialism in Africa.

The organs of the Organization are: (1) the conference of the heads of state or government; (2) the council of foreign ministers; (3) the general secretariat; (4) a commission of mediation, conciliation and arbitration. Arabic, French and English are recognized as working languages.

Chairman: President Siaka Stevens (Sierra Leone).

Headquarters: Addis Ababa.

Flag: Horizontally green, white, green, with the white fimbriated yellow, and the seal of the OAU in the centre.

DANUBE COMMISSION

The Danube Commission was constituted in 1949 based on the Convention regarding the regime of navigation on the Danube, which was signed in Belgrade on 18 Aug. 1948. The Belgrade Convention reaffirmed that navigation on the Danube from Ulm to the Black Sea, with access to the sea through the Sulina arm and the Sulina Canal, is equally free and open to the nationals, merchant shipping and merchandise of all states as to harbour and navigation fees as well as conditions of merchant navigation.

The Danube Commission is composed of representatives from the countries on the Danube (1 for each of these countries), namely, Austria, Bulgaria, Hungary, Romania, Czechoslovakia, USSR and Yugoslavia. Since 1957, representatives of the Ministry of Transport from the Federal Republic of Germany have attended the meetings of the Commission as guests of the Secretariat.

The functions of the Danube Commission are to check that the provisions of the Convention are carried out, to establish a uniform buoying system on all the Danube's navigable waterways and to establish the basic regulations for navigation on the river. The Commission co-ordinates the regulations for river, customs and sanitation control as well as the hydrometeorological service and collects statistical data concerning navigation on the Danube.

The Danube Commission enjoys legal status. It has its own seal and flag. The members of the Commission and elected officers enjoy diplomatic immunity. The

Commission's official buildings, archives and documents are inviolable. French and Russian are the official languages of the Commission.

Since 1954 the headquarters of the Commission have been in Budapest.

Flag: Blue, with a red strip fimbriated white along the bottom edge, and the initials of the Commission within a wreath in the canton—Latin letters on obverse Cyrillic on reverse.

Books of Reference

Danube Commission's publications include: *Summary Records and Documents Adopted by the Sessions of the Danube Commission. Rules of Procedure of the Danube Commission. Basic Regulations for Navigation on the Danube. Reports on the Maintenance of the Navigability of the Danube. Guidebook for Sailors. Hydrological Yearbooks. Statistical Yearbooks. Mileage Chart of the Danube. Ice Control on the Danube. Collection of Internal Laws Concerning Navigation on the Danube. Collection of International Agreements Relating to Navigation on the Danube. Radio-Codes for Navigation on the Danube.*

PART II

COUNTRIES OF THE WORLD
WORLD

A—Z

AFGHÁNISTÁN

Capital: Kábul
Population: 17·05m. (1976)
GNP per capita: US$240 (1978)

Democratic Republic of Afghánistán

HISTORY. A military *coup* on 17 July 1973 overthrew the monarchy of King Záhir Shàh. The *coup* was led by the King's cousin and brother-in-law Mohammad Daoud who declared a Republic. King Záhir abdicated on 24 Aug. 1973. President Daoud was killed in a military *coup* in April 1978 which led to the establishment of a pro-Soviet government of the People's Democratic Party of Afghánistán.

AREA AND POPULATION. Afghánistán is situated between parallels 29° and 38° 35′ N. lat., and 60° 50′ and 71° 50′ E. long., with a long narrow strip extending to 75° E. long. (Wákhán). For the boundaries, *see* THE STATESMAN'S YEAR-BOOK, 1925, pp. 654–55.

A new boundary agreement with the Soviet Union was signed in Moscow in June 1946; a joint commission completed the demarcation in Sept. 1948.

A border treaty with China was signed in 1963; the frontier was demarcated in 1964.

The area is 245,664 sq. miles (636,266 sq. km). Population, according to the (1976) Afghan estimate, is 17·05m., of which some 2·4m. are nomadic tribes. Birth rate (1970) 39 per 1,000 live births; death rate 16 per 1,000.

Estimate (1975), Kábul 749,000. Estimates of population of other towns (1975) were: Kandahár, 209,000; Herát, 157,000; Kunduz, 108,000; Charikar, 98,000; Mazár-i-Sharif, 97,000; Pulialam, 88,000; Baghlan, 85,000; Cheghcheran, 82,000; Faizabad, 77,000; Meterlam, 76,000; Qala-i-nau, 70,000; Taluqan, 67,000; Uiback, 63,000; Sherberghan, 59,000; Jalálábád, 58,000; Gardez, 54,000.

The main ethnic group are the Pashtuns. Other ethnic groups include the Tajiks, the Hazaras, the Turkomans and the Uzbeks.

CONSTITUTION AND GOVERNMENT. The 1964 Constitution was abolished by Presidential decree in 1973 and on 14 Feb. 1977 a new Constitution was adopted by the *Loya-Jirgah* (Grand Assembly). The 1977 Constitution was abrogated in April 1978 by the new Head of State, Noor Mohammad Taraki. On 16 Sept. 1979 President Taraki was ousted in a *coup* and replaced by Hafizullah Amin. In Dec. 1979 Soviet troops invaded Afghánistán and Hafizullah Amin was deposed. The pretext for the airlift of combat troops to Kábul was the Treaty of Friendship signed in Dec. 1978 between USSR and Afghánistán. In March 1981 there were up to 95,000 Soviet troops in Afghánistán.

President: Babrak Karmal.
National flag: Three equal horizontal stripes of red, black and green, with the national arms in the canton.

The official languages are Pushtu and Dari (Persian).

DEFENCE

Army. The Army is based on selective conscription with a regular cadre of officers and n.c.o.s. An agreed figure of conscripts is chosen in each province under local arrangements. A proportion of conscripts is drafted into the Labour Corps (employed mainly on public works). Call-up begins at the age of 20, and is for 2 years (1 year for conscript officers). Reserve liability is up to the age of 42. There is a reserve of officers.

The peace-time strength of the Army was about 80,000. Reserves, 150,000. It was organized in 3 armoured and 10 infantry divisions, 3 mountain infantry brigades and 1 artillery brigade. Equipment is almost entirely Russian and includes T-62, T-54 and T-34 tanks and surface-to-air missiles. Transport is mainly mechanized.

The Army had the following training establishments: a military academy (formed 1932), a school for each principal arm, a technical school, an n.c.o.s' school and a military high school (Kábul), which takes boys from the age of 10, and from which the regular element in the armed forces is mainly drawn. Selected officers receive training abroad, chiefly in USSR. In early 1981 it was impossible to give strength or deployment of the Army.

Air Force. The Air Force, which is Russian-equipped, has about 260 aircraft and 10,000 officers and men. There are 2 squadrons of Su-7 attack aircraft, 3 squadrons of supersonic MiG-21 interceptors (about 40 aircraft), 4 squadrons of MiG-17s (about 50 aircraft), 2 bomber squadrons each with about 10 twin-jet Il-28s, a helicopter attack force of about 30 Mi-24s, a transport wing with 10 twin-turboprop An-26s, about 20 piston-engined An-2s and Il-14s, 30 Mi-8 and Mi-4 helicopters and 1 or 2 turboprop Il-18s, and Yak-11, Yak-18, Aero L-39 and MiG-15UTI trainers. The main fighter station is Bagram, with facilities for the largest jet airliners and bombers. A Russian-built bomber station was completed at Shindand in 1963. There is a training station at Mazár-i-Sharif and an air academy at Sherpur with about 400 cadets. Large numbers of 'Guideline' and 'Goa' surface-to-air missiles are operational in Afghánistán. Strong Soviet forces in Afghánistán in 1980 included large numbers of Mi-8 assault helicopters and Mi-24 helicopter gunships, some of which may have been transferred to the Afghán Air Force.

Gendarmerie. The *gendarmerie*, about 30,000 strong, is administered by the Ministry of the Interior.

INTERNATIONAL RELATIONS

Membership. Afghánistán is a member of UN and of the Colombo Plan.

ECONOMY

Planning. The first two 5-year plans ran 1956–61 and 1962–67. The third plan (1967–72) envisaged expenditures of Afs. 33,000m. (compared with actual expenditures of 25,000m. during the second plan), but was never approved by Parliament. It was later tacitly abandoned, although some of the projects mentioned in the plan were implemented. The Minister of Planning then prepared a series of 1-year rolling plans but abandoned these in favour of a third 7-year plan which was in preparation in 1976. A 5-year plan for 1980–85 is in preparation.

Budget. In 1980–81 the budget envisaged expenditure of Afs. 33,759m. and revenue of Afs. 33,759m.

Currency. The monetary system is on the silver standard. The unit is the *afgháni*, weighing 10 grammes of silver 0·900 fine, which is subdivided into 100 *puls*. Rates of exchange fluctuate round Afs. 110 = £1; Afs. 44 = US$1.

Banking. The Afghan State Bank (*Da Afghánistán Bánk*) is the largest of the 3 main banks and also undertakes the functions of a central bank, holding the exclusive right of note issue. Total assets of the 3 main banks were: Da Afghánistán Bánk (1967), Afs. 28,074·4m.; Pashtany Tejaraty Bánk (1980), Afs. 5,682m.; Bánk-i-Milli (1967), Afs. 1,410·29m.

Weights and Measures. Weights and measures used in Kábul are: Weights: 1 *khurd* = 0·244 lb.; 1 *pao* = 0·974 lb.; 1 *charak* = 3·896 lb.; 1 *sere* = 16 lb.; 1 *kharwár* = 1,280 lb. or 16 maunds of 80 lb. each. Long measure: 1 yard or *gaz* = 40 in. The metric system is in common use by the bigger cloth merchants in Kábul. Square measures: 1 *jaríb* = 60 × 60 kábuli yd or ½ acre; 1 *kulbá* = 40 jaríbs (area in which 2½ kharwárs of seed can be sown); 1 jaríb yd = 29 in.

Local weights and measures are in use at Kandahár, Herát and Jalálábád.

ENERGY AND NATURAL RESOURCES

Minerals. Mineral resources are scattered and little developed. Coal is mined at Karkar in Pul-i-Khumri, Ishpushta near Doshi, north of Kábul and Dara-i-Suf south of Mazar (total production, 1975–76, 150,000 tonnes). Natural gas is found in northern Afghánistán around Shiberghan and Sar-i-Pol; this is now being piped to the USSR, and 57,700m. cu. metres are to be supplied by 1985. Rich, but as yet unexploited, deposits of iron ore exist in the Hajigak hills about 100 miles west of Kábul; beryllium has been found in the Kunar valley and barite in Bamian province. Other deposits include gold; silver (now unexploited, in the Panjshir valley); lapis lazuli (in Badakhshán); asbestos; mica; sulphur (near Maimana); chrome (in the Logar valley and near Herát); and copper (in the north).

Agriculture. Although the greater part of Afghánistán is more or less mountainous and a good deal of the country is too dry and rocky for successful cultivation, there are many fertile plains and valleys, which, with the assistance of irrigation from small rivers or wells, yield very satisfactory crops of fruit, vegetables and cereals. It is estimated that there are 14m. hectares of cultivable land in the country, of which 7,844,000 hectares are being cultivated (5·34m. hectares of this being irrigated land). Afghánistán is virtually self-supporting in foodstuffs (including wheat in 1973), apart from sugar.

In 1980 USSR signed an agreement to supply 130,000 tonnes of wheat.

The castor-oil plant, madder and the asafœtida plant abound.

Fruit forms a staple food (with bread) of many people throughout the year, both in the fresh and preserved state, and in the latter condition is exported in great quantities. The fat-tailed sheep furnish the principal meat diet, and the grease of the tail is a substitute for butter. Wool (annual production, about 10,000 tonnes, of which about 7,000 tonnes are exported) and skins provide material for warm apparel and one of the more important articles of export. Persian lambskins (Karakuls) are one of the chief exports.

Seed cotton production, 1979, was estimated at 108,000 tonnes; wheat, 2·2m.; barley, 400,000; maize, 750,000; rice, 450,000.

Livestock (1979): Cattle, 3·98m.; horses, 400,000; sheep, 23m.; goats, 3m.; poultry, 20·1m.

INDUSTRY AND TRADE

Industry. At Kábul there are factories for the manufacture of cotton and woollen textiles, leather, boots, marble-ware, furniture, glass, bicycles, prefabricated houses and plastics. A large machine shop has been constructed and equipped by the Russians, with a capability of manufacturing motor spares. There is a wool factory and there are several cotton-ginning plants; a small cotton factory at Jabal-us-Seráj and a larger one at Pul-i-Khumri. A cotton-seed oil extraction plant has been built in Lashkargah by a British firm which also has a contract for the construction of 4 factories in the north which became operative in 1972. Germans have built and equipped a large modern cotton textile factory at Gulbahar, and another has been built and equipped by the Chinese at Bagram. A large cotton plant has recently been completed in the north at Balkh.

An ordnance factory manufactures arms and ammunition, boots and clothing, etc. for the Army. There is a beet sugar plant at Baghlan (equipped with Russian machinery) and a fruit-canning factory in Kandahár. Hydro-electric plants have been constructed at Sarobi, Nangarhár, Naghlu, Mahipár, Pul-i-Khumri and Kandahár; more hydro and thermal plants are under construction.

Industries include hydro-electric projects, cement, coalmining, cotton textiles, small vehicle assembly plants, fruit canning, carpet making, leather tanning, footwear manufacture, sugar manufacture, preparation of hides and skins, and building. Most of these are relatively small and, with the exception of hides and skins, carpets and fruits, do not meet domestic requirements.

Commerce. Trade is supervised by the Government through the Ministries of Commerce and Finance and the Da Afghánistán Bánk. The Association of Afghan Chambers of Commerce works in close liaison with the Ministry of Commerce.

The Government monopoly controls the import of petrol and oil, sugar, cigarettes and tobacco, motor vehicles and consignment goods from bilateral trading countries. Transit agreements have been reached with Pakistan (Karachi being the most important port for the transit of Afghan imports and exports) and the USSR.

In the year ended 20 March 1977–78 Afghan imports (c.i.f.), totalled US$319·2m. and exports (f.o.b.) US$313·4m.

Main export commodities were karakul skins (US$20·8m.), raw cotton (US$ 61·4m.), dried fruit and nuts (US$35·2m.), fresh fruit (US$23·5m.) and natural gas (US$39·5m.). Main items imported were petroleum products (US$34·4m.), textiles (US$67m.).

Total trade between Afghánistán and UK (in £1,000 sterling, British Department of Trade returns):

	1976	1977	1978	1979	1980
Imports to UK	18,508	21,865	17,927	20,276	20,174
Exports and re-exports from UK	7,577	11,427	17,524	9,567	6,818

Tourism. Owing to internal political instability there was negligible tourism in 1980.

COMMUNICATIONS

Roads. There were in 1978 over 2,500 km of asphalted road. The Americans have asphalted the Kandahár–Chaman and Kábul–Torkham roads. The Russians have constructed a road and tunnel through the Salang pass (over 11,000 ft) which was opened in Sept. 1964 and cuts 120 miles off the old road from Kábul to the north; they have continued this road to Kunduz and Sherkhan Bandar (Qizil Qala) on the Oxus. In addition, the Americans in 1966 completed the road between Kábul and Kandahár and the Russians have constructed a concrete road between Kandahár and Herát. In 1968 the Americans completed an asphalt road from Herát to the Iranian frontier at Islam Qala. With Soviet assistance a metalled road from Pul-i-Khumri to Mazár-i-Sharif was completed in 1969 and Mazár-i-Sharif to Shiberghán in 1971.

Railways. There are no railways in the country.

Aviation. On 29 June 1956 Afghánistán signed an agreement with the USA for the development of civil aviation, including the construction of the international airport at Kandahár, comprising a loan of $5m. and a grant of $9·56m. Kábul airport has been expanded with Russian assistance. New runways at Kábul and Kandahár airports have been completed. Provincial all-weather airports have been constructed at Herát, Qunduz, Jalálábád and Mazár-i-Sharif.

Ariana Afghan Airlines (a national airline) operates regular services to Tehrán, Istanbul, Amsterdam, Frankfurt, Rome, London, New Delhi, Tashkent and Moscow.

Bakhtar Afghan Airlines (the domestic national airline) began operations on 8 Feb. 1968 and regularly served the main internal airfields and the remoter airfields at Bamian, Chakcharan, Lashkargah, Faizabad, Khost, Maimana, Neemroz and Taleqan before 1979.

Shipping. There are practically no navigable rivers in Afghánistán, and timber is the only article of commerce conveyed by water, floated down the Kunar and Kábul rivers from Chitral on rafts. A port has been built at Qizil Qala on the Oxus; barge traffic is increasing on the Oxus. Three river ports on the Amu Darya have been built at Sherkhan Bandar, Tashguzar and Hayratan, linked by road to Kábul.

Post and Broadcasting. Telephones, installed in most of the large towns, numbered 31,200 in 1978. There is telegraphic communication between all the larger towns and between Kábul and Kandahár and Peshawar and Chaman. A wireless installation connects Kábul with Europe, Bombay, the Far East, America and other parts of the world. Kábul Radio broadcasts in Pushtu, Persian, Urdu, English, French, Russian and German. The first TV colour transmissions in Kábul began in mid-1978. The telecommunication system is being expanded slowly, mainly with German assistance.

JUSTICE, RELIGION, EDUCATION AND WELFARE

Justice. A Supreme Court was established in June 1978. If no provision exists in the Constitution or in the general laws of the State, the courts follow the Hanafi jurisprudence of Islamic law.

Religion. The predominant religion is Islam, mostly of the Sunni sect, though there is a minority of about 1m. Shiah Moslems.

Education. The number of elementary schools is rapidly increasing, but secondary schools exist only in Kábul and provincial capitals. Both elementary and secondary education are free. In 1975 there were 694,240 pupils (19,158 teachers) in primary schools and 172,263 pupils (7,835 teachers) in secondary schools. There are several teacher-training institutions in Kábul and a few elsewhere; UNESCO is supporting a 30-year expansion programme. Technical, art, commercial and medical schools exist for higher education. The Kábul University was founded in 1932 and has 9 faculties (medicine, science, agriculture, engineering, law and political science, letters, economics, theology, pharmacology). The University of Nangarhar in Jalálábád was founded in 1963. A Polytechnic in Kábul was completed in 1968. In 1974 there were 10,956 students in higher education, 7,173 in teacher-training schools and 4,516 in technical schools.

Health. In 1978 there were 1,027 doctors and 3,600 hospital beds.

DIPLOMATIC REPRESENTATIVES

OF AFGHÁNISTÁN IN GREAT BRITAIN
(31 Prince's Gate, London, SW7 1QQ)

Chargé d'Affaires: Mohammad Gul Jahangiri.

OF GREAT BRITAIN IN AFGHÁNISTÁN
(Karte Parwan, Kábul)

Chargé d'Affaires: M. E. Howell, OBE.

OF AFGHÁNISTÁN IN THE USA (2341 Wyoming Ave., NW, Washington, D.C., 20008)

Chargé d'Affaires: Abdul Ghaffar Farahi.

OF THE USA IN AFGHÁNISTÁN
(Wazir Akbar Khan Mina, Kábul)

Chargé d'Affaires: Hawthorne O. Mills.

OF AFGHÁNISTÁN TO THE UNITED NATIONS

Ambassador: Dr Bismellah Sahak.

Books of Reference

Afghanistan Republic Annual, 1976
Adamec, L., *Afghanistan's Foreign Affairs to the Mid-Twentieth Century.* Tuscon, 1974
Dupree, L., *Afghanistan.* Princeton Univ. Press, 1974
Fraser-Tytler, Sir W. K., *Afghanistan.* Rev. ed. OUP, 1967
Gilbertson, G. W., *Pakkhto Idiom Dictionary.* 2 vols. London, 1932
Gregorian, V., *The Emergence of Modern Afghanistan.* Stamford, 1970
Griffiths, J. C., *Afghanistan.* New York, 1967
Hanifi, M. J., *Historical and Cultural Dictionary of Afghanistan.* Metuchen, 1976
Humlum, J., *La Géographie de l'Afghanistan.* Copenhagen, 1959
Klimburg, M., *Afghanistan.* Vienna, 1966
Mele, P. F., *Afghanistan.* Florence, 1966
Newell, R. S., *The Politics of Afghanistan.* Cornell Univ. Press, 1972

Sykes, P. M., *A History of Afghanistan.* 2 vols. New York, 1975
Watkins, M. B., *Land in Transition*, London, 1964
Wilber, D. N. (ed), *Afghanistan.* 2nd ed. New Haven, 1962.—(ed.), *Afghanistan, A Bibliography.* 2nd ed. New Haven, 1963

ALBANIA

Capital: Tirana
Population: 2·59m. (1979)
GNP per capita: US$740 (1978)

Republika Popullore
Socialiste e Shqipërisë

HISTORY. After the death of Gjergj Kastrioti Skënderbeu (Skanderbeg), Albania's national hero, in 1468 Albania passed under Turkish suzerainty until 1912. Independence was proclaimed at Vlonë on 28 Nov. 1912, and the London conference of ambassadors decided upon its frontiers and nominated as its ruler Prince William of Wied, who arrived at Durrës on 7 March 1914, but on 3 Sept. 1914 left the country, which fell into a state of anarchy. By the secret Pact of London of 26 April 1915 provision was made for the partition of Albania; but this arrangement was repudiated on 3 June 1917, when the Italian C.-in-C. in Albania proclaimed at Gjirokastër the independence of Albania. In Jan. 1925 a republic was proclaimed and on 1 Sept. 1928 a monarchy. Ahmed Beg Zogu, President since 31 Jan. 1925, reigned as King Zog till April 1939, when, on the occupation of the country by the Italians, he fled to England. After the liberation he was deposed *in absentia* on 2 Jan. 1946. During the years 1939–44 the country was overrun by Italians and Germans. The official Albanian date of the liberation is 29 Nov. 1944.

On 10 Nov. 1945 the British, US and USSR Governments recognized the Provisional Government under Gen. Enver Hoxha, on the understanding that it would hold free elections. The elections of 2 Dec. 1945 resulted in a Communist-controlled assembly, which on 11 Jan. 1946 proclaimed Albania a republic.

In 1946 Great Britain and the USA broke off relations with Albania and vetoed its admission to the United Nations. Albania was finally admitted on 15 Dec. 1955, the USA abstaining from voting.

Because of Albania's Stalinist and pro-Chinese attitudes diplomatic relations with USSR were broken off in 1961. In 1977 Albania terminated its special relationship with China by making ideological attacks on the post-Mao Chinese leadership's foreign policy, and in July 1978 China cut off all aid to Albania.

AREA AND POPULATION. The area of the country is 28,748 sq. km (11,101 sq. miles). By the peace treaty Italy restored the island of Sazan (Saseno) to Albania. At the census of Jan. 1979 the population was, 2,590,600 (34% urban; density, 90 per sq. km). The capital is Tirana (1978 population (in 1,000), 198); other large towns are Shkodër (Shkodra, Scutari) (62·5), Durrës (Durrsi, Durazzo) (61), Vlorë (Vlona, Vlonë, Vlora, Valona) (58·4), Korçë (Korça, Koritza) (50·9), Elbasan (50·7). Other towns (1975): Berat (30), Fier (28), Gjirokastër (Argyrocastro) (22), Lushnjë (21), Kavajë, 1971 (18), Qytet Stalin (formerly Kuçovë) (14).

There is a small Greek minority (1977 estimate, 50,000).

Vital statistics, 1975 (per 1,000): Births, 29·4; deaths, 6·7; marriages (1974), 7·9; divorces (1969), 0·8. Natural increase, 22·6. Life expectancy in 1979 was 69 years.

The country is administratively divided into 26 districts (*rreth*, pl. *rrethët*) (*see* map in THE STATESMAN'S YEAR-BOOK, 1962. N.B. The district of Ersekë has been renamed Kolonjë). Districts are subdivided into *lokaliteteve*.

Districts	Area (sq. km)	Population (in 1,000) (1973)	Districts	Area (sq. km)	Population (in 1,000) (1973)
Berat	1,026	124·3	Gramsh	695	29·4
Dibrë	1,569	106·8	Gjirokastër	1,137	53·5
Durrës	859	182·4	Kolonjë	805	19·2
Elbasan	1,466	154·7	Korçë	2,181	175·4
Fier	1,191	171·5	Krujë	607	75·6

Districts	Area (sq. km)	Population (in 1,000) (1973)	Districts	Area (sq. km)	Population (in 1,000) (1973)
Kukës	1,564	71·4	Pukë	969	32·8
Lezhë	479	40·5	Sarandë	1,097	66·5
Librazhd	1,013	48·5	Skrapar	775	30·8
Lushnjë	712	94·1	Shkodër	2,528	178·5
Mat	1,028	53·5	Tepelenë	817	37·8
Mirditë	698	29·4	Tirana	1,222	272·0
Përmet	930	31·7	Tropojë	1,043	30·5
Pogradec	725	49·3	Vlorë	1,609	133·5

The districts are for the greater part named after their capitals; exceptions: Tropojë, chief town, Bajram Curri; Mat, Burrel; Mirditë, Rrëshen; Skrapar, C'orovodë.

The Albanian language is divided into two dialects—Gheg, north of the river Shkumbi, and Tosk in the south. Many places therefore have two forms of name: Vlonë (Gheg), Vlorë (Tosk), etc., and many are known also by an Italian name, *e.g.*, Valona. Since 1945 the official language has been based on Tosk.

CONSTITUTION AND GOVERNMENT. The political structure derived from the Constitution of 14 March 1946 as amended in 1950, 1955, 1960 and 1963. In Dec. 1976 a new Constitution was adopted, by which Albania became a 'Socialist People's Republic'. The supreme legislative body is the single-chamber People's Assembly of 250 deputies, which meets twice a year, and delegates its day-to-day functions to a Presidium composed of a chairman, 3 deputy chairmen, a secretary and 10 members. Election to the People's Assembly is by universal suffrage (at 18) every 4 years.

In the elections of 12 Nov. 1978 it was claimed that 1,436,287 of the electorate of 1,436,288 voted for the 250 candidates on the single list of the Albanian Democratic Front. (There were 3 spoiled papers.)

The Government consists of a prime minister (Chairman of the Council of Ministers), 4 deputy prime ministers, 13 ministers and the chairman of the State Planning Commission. Effective rule is exercised by the Albanian Labour (*i.e.*, Communist) Party, founded 8 Nov. 1941, whose governing body is the Politburo.

In 1971 the Party had 68,858 full and 18,127 candidate members (women, 22%; workers, 36%; peasants, 30%; professional and managerial, 34%). In 1979 the Party had 88,000 full members and 13,500 candidates (37·5% workers, 29% farmers, 27% women).

Titular Head of State: Chairman of the Presidium of the People's Assembly: Haxhi Lleshi, elected July 1953. In March 1981 the chief Party and Government posts were filled as follows: Full members of the Politburo:

First Secretary of the Central Committee of the Party: Enver Hoxha. *Chairman of the Council of Ministers:* Mehmet Shehu. Adil Çarçani,[1] Spiro Koleka, Kadri Hazbiu (*Minister of Defence*), Hekuran Isai, Pali Miska,[2] Haki Toska (*Minister of Finance*); Manush Myftiu, Mrs Rita Marko. *Secretaries of the Central Committee:* Ramiz Alia, Prokop Muran. Candidate members: Lenka Çuko; Simon Stefani (*Chairman, People's Assembly*); Pilo Peristeri; Llambi Gegprifti; Qirjako Mihali. Not in the Politburo: *Foreign Minister:* Nesti Nase. *Minister of Foreign Trade:* Nedin Hoxha. *Minister of Agriculture:* Mrs Themi Thomal. *Chairman, State Planning Commission:* Petro Dode. *Minister of the Interior:* Fekor Shehu.

[1] First Deputy Chairman, Council of Ministers.   [2] Deputy Chairman, Council of Ministers.

Local Government is carried out by People's Councils at village, *lokalitet*, town and district level. Councillors are elected for 3 years.

National flag: Red, with a black double-headed eagle and a red, gold-edged 5-pointed star above it. *Mercantile flag:* red, black, red (horizontal) with a red yellow-edged star in the centre.

National anthem: Rreth Flamurit te per bashkuar (The flag that united us in the struggle).

DEFENCE. Albania withdrew from the Warsaw Pact in 1968 in protest against the invasion of Czechoslovakia. Albania's military equipment has been largely supplied by China. Chinese military aid ceased in July 1978.

Ranks were abolished in March 1966 and political commissars re-introduced.

Army. Army service is 2 years. Strength in 1980, 30,000 in 8 infantry and 1 armoured brigade, with about 100 T-34, T-54 and T-59 tanks. Security police ('SSSh') had a strength of 13,000, divided into 4 security battalions, and 5 battalions of frontier-guards.

Navy. The Navy consists of 3 submarines, 2 fleet minesweepers, 4 patrol vessels, 4 fast missile ships, 4 inshore minesweepers, 44 torpedo boats, 6 fast gunboats, 11 minesweeping boats, 1 degaussing ship, 4 oilers, 2 diving tenders, 5 tugs and 20 small auxiliaries and service tenders. Navy personnel (1981) 3,000 officers and ratings, including 300 coastal frontier guards. Service for ratings is 3 years. There are naval bases at Durrës and Vlorë.

Air Force. The Air Force, controlled by the Army, has about 100 combat aircraft and 8,000 officers and men. Service is 3 years. There are about 4 fighter squadrons of Chinese-built MiG-21s and MiG-19s, some Il-28 twin-jet light bombers and 2 ground attack squadrons of MiG-15s and MiG-17s. Transport and training types include 3 Il-14s, 10 An-2s, Mi-4 helicopters, Yak-11s, Yak-18s and MiG-15UTIs.

INTERNATIONAL RELATIONS

Membership. Albania is a member of UN.

ECONOMY

Planning. For the first four 5-year plans *see* THE STATESMAN'S YEAR-BOOK, 1976–77. The fifth covered 1971–75, during which it is claimed that national income increased by 38%, industrial production by 52% and agricultural production by 33%. The sixth 5-year plan ran from 1976 to 1980. The seventh 5-year plan covers 1981–85. Target increases: agricultural production, 41%, industrial, 40%. Emphasis is laid on industrial expansion, especially in the oil, mining and chemical industries. It is now stated that economic policy is founded on 'the revolutionary principle of self-reliance'.

Budget. Budget figures for 1979: Revenue, 7,800m. leks (7,200m. leks from enterprises and agricultural co-operatives); expenditure, 7,750m. leks (industry, 4,800m. leks; social, 1,800m. leks; defence, 885m. leks).

Currency. The monetary unit is the *lek* of 100 *qintars*. It replaced the gold franc (*franc ar*) in July 1947. In Aug. 1965 a new *lek* was introduced: 10 old *leks* = 1 new *lek*. Exchange rates, 1981: (official) US$1 = 4·66 *leks*; £1 = 7·12 *leks*; (tourist) US$1 = 9·75 *leks*; £1 = 16·94 *leks*.

Banking. The Albanian State Bank was founded in 1925 with Italian aid. In 1970 savings deposits amounted to 572m. leks. In 1970 the Agricultural Bank was set up as a credit institution for agricultural co-operatives.

Weights and Measures. The metric system is in force.

ENERGY AND NATURAL RESOURCES

Electricity. There are 6 hydro-electric power plants operational and one under construction. Electric power production in 1973 was 1,603m. kwh., of which 1,127m. was hydro-electric.

Oil. The oil industry is being rapidly expanded. Output in 1973: Crude, 2,107,000 tonnes; refined, 1,596,000 tonnes. Refining capacity in 1970 was over 1m. tonnes. Oil is produced chiefly at Qytet Stalin which a pipeline connects to the port of Vlorë. Natural gas is extracted.

Minerals. The mineral wealth of Albania is considerable but is only recently being developed. In 1971 there were 8 coal, 7 chromium (1977 output 900,000 tonnes) and 6 copper mines. Ferro-nickel ores are mined and output is increasing. In 1969 extensive coal deposits were discovered at Valias, near Tirana. There is no bituminous coal. Salt is extracted near Vlorë and bitumen mined at Selenicë. Production in tonnes (1973): Chrome ore, 611,000; copper ore, 435,000; ferro-nickel ore, 384,000; brown coal, 811,000; phosphate, 110,000; nitrogenous fertilizer, 106,000; bitumen (1964), 242,000; cement (1965), 133,600.

Agriculture. The country for the greater part is rugged, wild and mountainous, the exceptions being along the Adriatic littoral and the Korçë (Koritza) Basin, which are fertile. In 1973 a programme of land reclamation and anti-erosion measures was instituted. In 1970 arable land comprised 599,000 hectares and pasture 623,000 hectares. 283,200 hectares were irrigated.

Land is held by the State (largely forests and non-agricultural), state farms (33 in 1970 holding 100,700 hectares of arable land) and co-operatives (459 in 1973 holding 500,900 hectares). Co-operatives are divided into 'advanced' and 'ordinary'. A pension plan for collective farmers was enacted in 1972. Tractors in 1980 numbered 17,300 (in 15-h.p. units).

The yield of the main crops in 1979 was (in 1,000 tonnes): Wheat, 420; cotton, 20; tobacco, 14; potatoes, 132; sugar-beet, 260; maize, 320; fruit, 125; rice, 17; beans, 16; sunflower seeds, 26; grapes, 62.

Livestock, 1979: Cattle, 474,000; sheep, 1,163,000; goats, 665,000; pigs, 120,000; horses and mules, 65,000; poultry, 2·38m.

Forestry. 47% of the territory of Albania is forest land, of which 38% is oak forest, 26% elm and 18% pine and birch. Timber reserves reach 44·5m. cu. metres. In 1967 forests covered 1,242,100 hectares; 6,784 hectares were afforested, 10,000 hectares improved in 1967.

Fisheries. The catch in 1964 was 3,600 tonnes.

INDUSTRY AND TRADE

Industry. All industry is nationalized down to the smallest workshop. Output is small, and the principal industries are agricultural product processing, textiles, oil products and cement. Chemical and engineering industries are being built up. The metallurgical combine at Elbasan is being extended.

Labour. In 1973, 462,900 persons worked in the socialist sector of the national economy, of whom 34·7% were employed in industry. In 1976, 46% of wage-earners were women.

Minimum wages may not fall below one-third of maximum. A new labour code was introduced in 1980 normalising an 8-hour 6-day week and 12 days yearly paid holiday.

Commerce. Between 1954 and 1978 Chinese aid amounted to US$5,000m., but economic relations have now been broken off. In July 1980 trade agreements were signed with Yugoslavia; and Albania also trades with Italy, France, Czechoslovakia and India. The establishment of joint companies with, and the acceptance of credits from, capitalist firms is forbidden by the Albanian constitution. In 1980 indebtedness to the West was US$100m.

Exports include crude oil, bitumen, chrome, nickel, copper, tobacco, fruit and vegetables.

Total trade between Albania and UK (British Department of Trade returns, in £1,000 sterling):

	1975	1976	1977	1978	1979	1980
Imports to UK	117	40	61	52	62	107
Exports and re-exports from UK	644	127	222	255	701	1,478

COMMUNICATIONS

Roads. There were, in 1960, 3,100 km of roads suitable for motor traffic. The mountain districts of the north are still mostly inaccessible for wheeled vehicles, and communications are still by means of pack ponies or donkeys. Registered motor vehicles in 1960: Cars, 1,900; lorries and buses, 3,400. Road traffic carried 8·6m. passengers in 1970; goods carried, 34m. tonnes.

Railways. Total length, in 1980, was 228 km. They comprise the lines Durrës–Tirana, Durrës–Kavajë–Pegin–Elbasan, Vlorë–Memaliaj, Vlorë–Milot, Durrës–Tirana/Laç. In 1974 a railway was opened from Elbasan to the iron mines at Pishkash and a line is under construction from Fier to Balkh. Work started in 1979 on a 35 km extension from Laç to Shkoder, close to the Yugoslav frontier. Goods carried in 1970 amounted to 2,324,000 tonnes; passengers (1971), 6·4m.

Aviation. There are regular scheduled flights from Tirana (Rinas Airport) to Belgrade, Bucharest, Budapest and East Berlin. Olympic Airways operate a weekly flight from Athens to Tirana.

Shipping. The ports are Shëngjin (San Giovanni di Medua), Durrës (Durazzo), Vlorë (Valona) and Sarandë (Santi Quaranta). 567,000 tonnes of freight were carried in 1970. The Sino-Albanian Joint Shipping Company, formed in 1961, was annulled by Albania in Sept. 1978.

Post and Broadcasting. Number of post and telegraph offices (1970), 292; telephones (1963), 10,150. There are 17 broadcasting stations, including Tirana and Korçë. Radio Tirana operates a foreign service in 18 languages. Radio receiving sets (1978), 200,000; television sets, 5,000. Regular television broadcasting began in 1971.

Cinemas and Theatres (1973). There were 105 cinemas with an attendance of 7·9m. and 27 theatres with an attendance of 1·6m.

Newspapers. In 1976 there were 25 newspapers with an annual circulation of 47m. The Party paper is *Zëri i Popullit* (Voice of the People) (daily circulation, 105,000).

JUSTICE, RELIGION, EDUCATION AND WELFARE

Justice is administered by People's Courts. Judges of the Supreme Court are elected by the People's Assembly for 4-year terms. The Office of the Procurator-General oversees the administration of justice. In 1966 the Ministry of Justice was incorporated into the Ministry of the Interior. In 1968 tribunals were set up in towns and villages to try minor crimes which had previously been dealt with by courts.

Religion. Albania is constitutionally an atheist state. In 1967 the Government closed all mosques and churches. For details of the situation before 1967 *see* THE STATESMAN'S YEAR-BOOK, 1969–70. The population had been mainly Moslem.

Education. Primary education is free and compulsory in 8-year schools from 7 to 15 years. Secondary education is available in 12-year (general), technical–professional or lower vocational schools. Periods of productive work and military service are intermingled with full-time education. There were, in 1973–74, 1,615 kindergartens with 52,899 pupils and 2,790 teachers; 1,470 primary schools with 569,600 pupils and 22,686 teachers; 39 secondary schools with 32,900 pupils; 116 technical–professional schools with 69,700 pupils (the last two categories had 3,990 teachers taken together); and (in 1969–70) 36 institutes of higher education with 36,525 students and 941 teachers, including a university in Tirana (founded 1957), a polytechnic, an agricultural college, a medical school, 5 teachers' training colleges and an institute of science. In 1969–70 there were 382 teachers and 12,783 full-time students at Tirana University. An Albanian Academy was founded in 1973.

Health. Medical services are free. In 1970 there were 15,100 hospital beds. In 1976 there was 1 doctor per 780 inhabitants.

DIPLOMATIC REPRESENTATIVE
OF ALBANIA TO THE UNITED NATIONS

Ambassador: Abdi Baleta.

Books of Reference

Vjetari Statistikor (Statistical Yearbook). Tirana, irregular, from 1959
30 vjet Shqipëri socialiste (statistical handbook). Tirana, 1974

History of the Labor Party of Albania. Tirana, 1971

Bertolino, J., *Albanie: la Citadelle de Staline.* Paris, 1979

Hoxha, E., *Réflexions sur la Chine.* Paris, 1979.—*Speeches, Conversations and Articles, 1969–1970.* Tirana, 1980.—*The Khrushchevites: Memoirs.* Tirana, 1980

Logoreci, A., *The Albanians: Europe's Forgotten Survivors.* London, 1977

Mann, S. E., *An Historical Albanian–English Dictionary.* London 1948.—*An English–Albanian Dictionary.* CUP, 1957

Marmullaku, R., *Albania and the Albanians.* London, 1975

Martin, N., *La Forteresse Albanaise: un Communisme National.* Paris, 1979

Pano, N. C., *The People's Republic of Albania.* Baltimore, 1968

Pollo, S. *et. al., Histoire de l'Albanie des Origines à Nos Jours.* Roanne, 1974

Prifti, P. R., *Socialist Albania since 1944.* Cambridge, Mass., 1978

Russ, W., *Der Entwicklungsweg Albaniens.* Meisenheim-am-Glan, 1979

ALGERIA

Capital: Algiers
Population: 18·25m. (1979)
GNP per capita: US$1,260 (1978)

El Djemhouria El Djazaïria
Eddemokratia Echaabia—
République Algérienne
Démocratique et Populaire

HISTORY. On 1 Nov. 1954 the National Liberation Front (FLN) went over to open warfare against the French administration and armed forces.

On 19 Sept. 1958 a free Algerian government was formed in Cairo with Ferhat Abbas as provisional President of the National Assembly.

A referendum was held in Metropolitan France and Algeria on 6–8 Jan. 1961 to decide on Algerian self-determination as proposed by President de Gaulle. His proposals were approved by 15,200,073 against 4,996,474 votes in Metropolitan France, and by 1,749,969 against 767,546 votes in Algeria. In Metropolitan France 20·2m. out of 27·2m registered voters went to the polls; in Algeria 2·5m. out of 4·5m. registered voters.

Long delayed by the terrorism, in Metropolitan France as well as Algeria, of a secret organization (OAS) led by anti-Gaullist officers, a cease-fire agreement was concluded between the French Government and the representatives of the Algerian Nationalists on 18 March 1962; but OAS terror acts continued for some months.

On 7 April a provisional executive of 12 members was set up, under the chairmanship of Abderrhaman Farès.

On 8 April 1962 a referendum in Metropolitan France approved the Algerian settlement with 17,505,473 (90·7%) against 1,794,553 (9·3%) and 1,102,477 invalid votes; 6,580,772 voters abstained. On 1 July 1962, 5,975,581 Algerians voted in favour of, 16,534 against the settlement.

AREA AND POPULATION. Algeria (2,381,745 sq. km). Population (census 1977) 17,273,000; estimate (1979) 18·25m.

The 31 departments are as follows:

Departments	Area (sq. km)	Population (1978)	Departments	Area (sq. km)	Population (1978)
Adrar	422,498	142,046	Médéa	8,704	482,183
Alger (Algiers)	786	1,988,000	Mostaganem	7,024	766,167
Annaba	3,489	507,806	M'Sila	19,825	438,317
Batna	14,882	589,146	Ouahran (Oran)	1,820	761,507
Béchar	306,000	148,101	Ouargla	559,234	199,691
Béjaia	3,444	554,876	Oum el Bouaghi	8,123	400,182
Biskra	109,728	544,798	Saida	106,177	373,366
Blida	3,704	909,930	Sétif	10,350	990,157
Bouira	4,517	385,452	Sidi-Bel-Abbès	11,648	531,694
Constantine	3,562	686,671	Skikda	4,748	493,929
Djelfa	22,905	330,406	Tamanrasset	556,000	45,622
El Asnam	8,677	885,200	Tébessa	16,575	372,479
Guelma	8,624	552,455	Tiaret	23,456	619,826
Jijel	3,704	506,488	Tizi-Ouzou	3,756	875,075
Laghouat	112,052	307,977	Tlemcen	9,284	596,677
Mascara	5,846	435,776			

The chief towns (estimates, 1974) are as follows: Algiers, 1,503,720; Oran, 485,139; Constantine, 350,183; Annaba, 313,174; Tizi-Ouzou, 223,702; Blida, 158,947; Sétif, 157,065; Sidi-Bel-Abbès, 151,148; Skikda, 127,968; Batna, 115,138; Tlemcen, 115,054; Al Asnam, 114,327; Bejaia, 103,996; Médéa, 102,336; Mostaganem, 101,780.

CONSTITUTION AND GOVERNMENT. On 3 July 1962 President de Gaulle proclaimed Algeria independent and handed over sovereign power.

On 25 Sept. the National Assembly met and elected Ferhat Abbas President of the Assembly and Ben Bella President of the Council of Ministers.

A national referendum held on 15 Sept. 1963 elected Ben Bella, the only candidate, as President of the new Democratic People's Republic of Algeria.

The Government was overthrown by a junta of army officers which, on 19 June 1965, established a Revolutionary Council under Col. Houari Boumédienne.

Elections to the National People's Assembly took place on 25 Feb. 1977. This was the first election since the *coup* of 1965. The 261 members of the Assembly were elected for a 5-year term and 78·5% of the electorate voted.

President of the Republic, General Secretary of the FLN and Minister of Defence: Col. Bendjedid Chadli (sworn in 9 Feb. 1979).

Prime Minister: Col. Mohamed Benahmed Abdelghani.
Foreign Affairs: Mohamed Seddik Benyahia.

National flag: Vertically green and white, a red crescent and star over all in centre.

The official language is Arabic, French being the principal foreign language.

DEFENCE

Army. The Army in 1980 had a strength of 90,000 men, organized in 1 armoured, 1 mechanized and 4 motorized brigades, 3 tank battalions, 2 parachute, 11 air defence, 4 engineer and 63 independent battalions. Equipment includes Soviet T-54 and T-55 tanks.

Navy. The Navy consists of 2 fleet minesweepers, 6 patrol vessels, 17 fast missile boats, 4 torpedo boats acquired from the USSR, 18 coastguard fast gunboats, 1 landing vessel, 1 diving tender, 2 training craft, 1 torpedo recovery vessel, 1 survey ship, 6 fishery protection craft and 18 coastguard cutters. Naval personnel, 1981: 300 officers and cadets and 3,500 ratings.

The French naval base of Mers el Kebir was taken over by the Algerian army and navy in Feb. 1968.

Air Force. Five MiG-15 jet-fighters were delivered in 1962 as the nucleus of an Algerian Air Force. Since then many more aircraft of Soviet design have followed, and the Air Force now has about 250 combat aircraft and 7,000 personnel. Training and technical assistance have been given by Egypt and the Soviet Union. There are 3 squadrons of MiG-21s, 2 squadrons of MiG-23 variable-geometry fighters, 2 squadrons of MiG-17 fighter-bombers, 2 squadrons of Su-7 and Su-20 variable-geometry attack aircraft, 2 squadrons (each nominally 10 aircraft) of Il-28 twin-jet bombers, some MiG-25 fighter and reconnaissance aircraft, 20 Mi-24 helicopter gunships, 1 squadron of 4 turboprop An-12 and Il-18 transports, 5 An-24, 10 F.27 Friendship and 3 Beech King Air twin-turboprop transports, a wing of 4 Mi-6, 12 Mi-8, about 10 Mi-4, 5 Puma and 6 Hughes 269 helicopters, and training units equipped with Yak-11s, CM.170 Magister armed jet counter-insurgency/trainers (26), 3 Beech Queen Air twin-engine/instrument trainers, and MiG-15s and -15UTIs. Surface-to-air missile units have Soviet-built 'Guidelines', 'Gainfuls' and 'Gaskins'.

INTERNATIONAL RELATIONS

Membership. Algeria is a member of UN, OAU, the Arab League, OAPEC, OPEC and the Maghreb Organization.

ECONOMY

Planning. The second 4-year development plan (1974–77) envisaged investment of DA 110,000m. The third development plan (1980–84) gives priority to education and agriculture.

Currency. The Algerian currency is the *dinar* (DA). There are in circulation bank-notes of DA 5, 10, 50, 100 and 500 and coins of 1, 2, 5, 20 and 50 centimes and DA 1. Money in circulation in Dec. 1977, DA 47,634m.

Budget. The budget (including extraordinary budget) was as follows in calendar years (in DA 1m.):

	1974	1975	1976	1977	1978
Revenue	23,438	25,093	26,215	28,000	36,788
Expenditure	13,498	13,068	20,118	27,472	29,946

Banking. The Banque Centrale d'Algérie is the government emission bank. Other banks operating in Algeria are Banque National d'Algérie, Crédit Populaire d'Algérie, Banque Extérieure d'Algérie, Caisse Algérienne de Développement, Banque Algérienne de Développement.

Weights and Measures. The metric system is in use.

ENERGY AND NATURAL RESOURCES

Electricity. Production of energy in 1978 totalled 52,120m. gwh.

Oil. Two large oilfields went into production in 1957 around Edjélé and Hassi Messaoud and in 1959 at El Gassi. In 1960 about 200 wells were productive. Natural gas was discovered at Djebel Berga in 1954 and at Hassi-R'Mel in 1956. Oil pipelines from Edjélé to Skirra (Tunisia) and from Hassi Messaoud to Bougie, and a gas pipeline from Hassi Messaoud via Hassi-R'Mel to Mostaganem–Oran–Algiers, have been completed. Oil production in 1978, 57·2m. tonnes. Oil revenue in 1972, DA 3,200m. Production of natural gas in 1977 was 81,286m. cu. metres.

Minerals. Algeria possesses deposits of iron, zinc, lead, mercury, copper and antimony. Kaolin, marble and onyx, salt (110,000 tonnes in 1957) and coal are also found. Mineral output in 1977 (1,000 tonnes): Ferrous metals, 3,183; zinc, 5·7; copper, 1·5; lead, 1·4; phosphates, 1,173.

Agriculture. There exists a small area of highly fertile plains and valleys near the coast, mainly owned by self-management committees and some Europeans, which is cultivated scientifically, and where profitable returns are obtained from vineyards, cereals, etc. Self-management groups supplied 60% of revenue from agriculture in 1970, and held 80% of cultivated land. The greater part of Algeria is of limited value for agricultural purposes. In the northern portion the mountains are generally better adapted to grazing and forestry than agriculture, and a large portion of the native population is quite poor. In spite of the many excellent roads built by the Government, a considerable area of the mountainous region is without adequate means of communication and is accessible only with difficulty. There were an estimated 16·3m. hectares of agricultural land in 1970–71, of which 6·4m. hectares were arable; 292,000 hectares under vine and 35·3m. hectares pastures and brushlands.

The chief crops in 1979 were (in 1,000 tonnes): Wheat, 1,200; barley, 400; dates 208; wine, 200; olive oil, 16.

Livestock, 1979: 150,000 horses, 695,000 mules and asses, 1,313,000 cattle, 10·9m. sheep, 2·6m. goats and 140,000 camels.

Forestry. The greater part of the state forests are mere brushwood, but there are very large areas covered with cork-oak trees, Aleppo pine, evergreen oak and cedar. The dwarf-palm is grown on the plains, alfa on the table-land. Timber is cut for firewood, also for industrial purposes, for railway sleepers, telegraph poles, etc., and for bark for tanning. Considerable portions of the forest area are also leased for tillage, or for pasturage for cattle and sheep.

Fisheries. There are extensive fisheries for sardines, anchovies, sprats, tunny fish, etc., and also shellfish. In 1977, 692 boats were employed in fishing. Fish taken in 1977 amounted to 43,475 tonnes, value DA179,952,000.

INDUSTRY AND TRADE

Industry. The main industries are iron and steel, plastics and fertilizers.

Commerce. The foreign trade of Algeria was as follows (in DA 1m.):

	1975	1976	1977	1978
Imports	23,755	22,227	29,534	34,439
Exports	18,563	22,205	25,356	25,037

Crude oil and refined products accounted for 90% of exports in 1979. In 1972, 61·4% of imports and 57·8% of exports were with EEC, of which 30·2% and 23·3% were with France.

Total trade between Algeria and UK (British Department of Trade returns, in £1,000 sterling):

	1975	1976	1977	1978	1979	1980
Imports to UK	87,490	80,228	49,762	37,930	87,526	114,054
Exports and re-exports from UK	78,681	101,834	98,655	120,642	115,016	142,552

Tourism. In 1976, 184,800 tourists visited Algeria.

COMMUNICATIONS

Roads. There were in 1978, 19,157 km of national highway. Motor vehicles in 1977 included 347,462 passenger cars and 226,060 commercial vehicles.

Railways. In 1981 there were 3,890 km of which 2,632 km is of standard gauge (256 km electrified) and 1,258 km of narrow gauge railway open for traffic. In 1979 the railways carried 1,900m. passengers-km and 2,500 tonne-km of freight.

Aviation. There are 65 airfields controlled by government and 135 owned by petroleum companies. Air Algeria serves the main Algerian cities, and an international network. Algeria is also served by Swissair, Royal Air Maroc, United Arab Airline, Tunis Air, SABENA, Aeroflot, Interflug, Alitalia and Air France. In 1977 the airports handled 1·9m. passengers and 10·4m. tonnes of freight.

Shipping. In 1977, 58m. tonnes of goods were handled at Algerian ports.

A state shipping line, Compagnie Nationale Algérienne de Navigation, was formed in Jan. 1964 and possesses 7 vessels and also charters others.

Post and Broadcasting. There were, in 1969, 862 post offices; number of telephones (1978), 297,689, of which 111,682 were in Algiers and 28,425 in Oran. In 1974 there were some 3·5m. radio receivers and 500,000 TV licences issued.

Post office savings accounts on 31 Dec. 1971 numbered 314,807, with a total balance of DA 12,000m.

Newspapers (1980). There were 4 daily newspapers, 1 in French and 3 in Arabic, with a combined circulation of 350,000.

JUSTICE, RELIGION, EDUCATION AND WELFARE

Justice. There are appeal courts at Algiers, Constantine and Oran; and in the *arrondissements* are 17 courts of first instance. There are also commercial courts and justices of the peace with extensive powers. Criminal justice is organized as in France.

The Supreme Court is at the same time Council of State and High Court of Appeal.

Religion. The overwhelming part of the population are Moslems. The Roman Catholic Church has an archbishop and 2 bishops, with some 400 officiating clergymen. Jews number about 150,000.

There are 13 Protestant pastors and 6 Jewish rabbis sharing in government grants.

Education. About 57% of children attended school in 1970. Primary schools had 3,614,000 pupils in 1977; secondary schools had 332,318 pupils including 105,239 girls. The University of Algiers had 60,000 students in 1977. A university in Oran opened in 1967 and others are now open at Constantine and Annaba. There are also university centres at Tlemcen, Tizi-Ouzou, Sétif, Batna and Tiaret.

Health. There were in 1978, 183 general and specialized hospitals with together 45,029 beds; there were 2,726 doctors, 713 dentists, 666 pharmacists. There were (1969) 1,225 dispensaries and consulting rooms, 308 health centres and 49 specializing centres for tuberculosis, venereal disease and trachoma. There were 18 hospitals built between 1965 and 1969. National disease prevention campaigns are carried out mainly against tuberculosis (by BCG vaccination), trachoma, malnutrition and malaria.

DIPLOMATIC REPRESENTATIVES

OF ALGERIA IN GREAT BRITAIN
(54 Holland Park, London, W11 3RS)

Ambassador: Abdelkrim Benmahmoud.

OF GREAT BRITAIN IN ALGERIA (Résidence Cassiopée,
7 Chemin des Glycines, Algiers)

Ambassador: R. S. Faber, CMG.

OF ALGERIA IN THE USA (2118 Kalorama Rd., NW,
Washington, D.C., 20008)

Ambassador: Redha Malek.

OF THE USA IN ALGERIA (4 Chemin Cheikh Bachir Brahimi,
Algiers)

Ambassador: Ulric St. Clair Haynes, Jr.

OF ALGERIA TO THE UNITED NATIONS

Ambassador: Mohamed Bedjaoui.

Books of Reference

Statistical Information: The Service de Statistique Générale (12, rue Bab-Azoun, Alger) publishes the annual *Statistique Générale de l'Algérie, Documents statistiques sur le commerce de l'Algérie* (from 1902). *Tableaux de l'économie algérienne* (1960).

Gordon, D. C., *The Passing of French Algeria.* OUP, 1965
Horne, A., *A Savage War of Peace: Algeria 1954–1962.* London, 1977
Ministère de l'Information et de la Culture, *La Révolution Algérienne: Réalités et Perspectives,* Algiers, 1972.—*Dix années de réalisations 19 juin 1965–19 juin 1975.* Algiers, 1976.—*Statistiques 1967–78.* Algiers, 1980
L'Algérie en Chiffres. Algiers, 1972
Ottaway, D., *Algeria: The Politics of a Socialist Revolution.* Berkeley, 1970
Thé, B. de, *Essai de bibliographie du Sahara Français.* Paris, 1961
Verlaque, C., *Le Sahara pétrolier.* Paris, 1964
Verlet, B., *Sahara.* Paris, 1960
Verneuil, H., *Sahara.* Paris, 1960

ANDORRA

Capital: Andorra-la-Vieille
Population: 32,700 (1980)

Les Vallées d'Andorre— Valls d'Andorra

HISTORY AND CONSTITUTION. The political status of Andorra was regulated by the *Paréage* of 1278 which placed Andorra under the joint suzerainty of the Comte de Foix and of the Bishop of Urgel. The rights vested in the house of Foix passed by marriage to that of Béarn and, on the accession of Henri IV, to the French crown. The sovereignty is exercised jointly by the President of the French Republic and the Bishop of Urgel.

The co-princes are represented in Andorra by the '*Viguier français*' and the '*Viguier Episcopal*'. Each co-prince has set up a Permanent Delegation for Andorran affairs; the Prefect of the Eastern Pyrenees is the French Permanent Delegate.

The valleys pay every second year a due of 960 francs to France and 460 pesetas to the bishop.

A 'General Council of the Valleys' submits motions and proposals to the Permanent Delegations. Its 28 members are elected for 4 years; half of the council is renewed every 2 years.

The council nominates a First Syndic (*Syndic Procureur Général*) and a Second Syndic from outside its members.

First Syndic: Estanislau Sangra Font.

National flag: Three vertical strips of blue, yellow, red, with the arms of Andorra in the centre.

AREA AND POPULATION. The co-principality of Andorra is situated in the eastern Pyrenees on the French–Spanish border. The country consists of gorges, narrow valleys and defiles, surrounded by high mountain peaks varying between 1,880 and 3,000 metres. Its maximum length is 30 km and its width 20 km; it has an area of 465 sq. km (190 sq. miles) and a population of (1980) 32,700, scattered in 7 villages.

Catalan is the spoken language.

ECONOMY

Currency. French and Spanish currency are both in use.

Tourism. Tourism is the main industry, and over 6·4m. people visited Andorra in 1978.

COMMUNICATIONS

Roads. A good road connects the Spanish and French frontiers by way of Sant Julià, Andorre-la-Vieille, les Escaldes, Encamp, Canillo and Soldeu: it crosses the Col d'Envalira (2,400 metres). Another road connects Andorre-la-Vieille with La Massana and Ordino. Motor vehicles (1980) 28,630.

Aviation. The nearest airports are at Barcelona and Perpignan.

Post and Broadcasting. Number of telephones (1978) 10,366. Radio Andorra and Sud Radio are private commercial broadcasting companies. Number of receivers (1973), 6,000.

JUSTICE, RELIGION AND EDUCATION

Justice. Judicial power is exercised in civil matters in the first instance, according to the plaintiff's choice, by either the *Bayle Français* or the *Bayle Episcopal*, who are nominated by the respective co-princes. The judge of appeal is nominated alternately for 5 years by each co-prince; the third instance (*Tercera Sala*) is either the supreme court of Andorra at Perpignan or the ecclesiastical court of the Bishop at Urgel.

Criminal justice is administered by the *Corts* consisting of the 2 Viguiers, the judge of appeal, 2 *rahonadors* elected by the general council of the valleys, a general attorney and a deputy attorney nominated for 5 years alternatively by each of the co-principalities, adjudicating several times a year. The accused may be assisted by a barrister.

Religion. The prevailing religious denomination is Roman Catholic.

Education. In 1979–80 there were 1,694 pupils at infant schools, 3,017 at primary schools and 2,005 at secondary schools.

Books of Reference

Brutails, *La Coutume d'Andorre*. Paris, 1904
Corts Peyret, *J., Geografia e Historia de Andorra*. Barcelona, 1945
Llobet, S., *El medio y la vida en Andorra*. Barcelona, 1947
Vidally Guitart, J. M., *Institutiones politicas y sociales de Andorra*. Madrid, 1949

ANGOLA

Capital: Luanda
Population: 7m. (1979)
GNP per capita: US$300 (1978)

HISTORY. Angola, with a coastline of over 1,000 miles, is separated from the Congo by the boundaries assigned by the convention of 12 May 1886; from Zaïre by those fixed by the convention of 22 July 1927; from Rhodesia in accordance with the convention of 11 June 1891, and from South West Africa in accordance with that of 30 Dec. 1886. The Congo region was discovered by the Portuguese in 1482, and the first settlers arrived there in 1491. Luanda was founded in 1575. It was taken by the Dutch in 1641 and occupied by them until 1648.

AREA AND POPULATION. Angola is bounded by Congo on the north, Zaïre on the north and north-east, Zambia on the east, South West Africa/Namibia on the south and the Atlantic ocean on the west. The area is 1,246,700 sq. km (481,351 sq. miles). Angola is divided into 18 provinces: Cabinda, Zaïre, Uíge, Luanda, Bengo, Cuanza Norte, Cuanza Sul, Malange, Lunda-Norte, Lunda-Sul, Benguela, Huambo, Bié, Moxico, Cuando-Cubango, Moçâmedes, Huíla and Cunene. The important towns are S. Paulo de Luanda (capital), Benguela, Moçâmedes, Lobito, Lubango, Malange and Huambo. The population at census, 1970, was 5,673,046, of whom 300,000 were white. Estimate (1979) 7m., of whom 38% speak Umbundu, 27% Kimbundu, 13% Lunda and 11% Kikongo. Portuguese remains the official language. There were (1978) about 40,000 whites in Angola.

CONSTITUTION AND GOVERNMENT. On 15 Jan. 1975 the 3 Angolan liberation groups signed an agreement under which Angola became independent on 11 Nov. 1975. Following the capture of most of the strategic towns in the north and south of Angola by the liberation movement, *Movimento Popular de Libertação de Angola* (MPLA), which was supported by the USSR, assumed effective military control of Angola by Feb. 1976. The People's Republic of Angola was proclaimed in Nov. 1975. In Dec. 1978 the post of Prime Minister was abolished.

The Cabinet in Aug. 1980 was as follows:

President: Jose Eduardo dos Santos.
Planning: Roberto Antonio Victor Francisco de Almeida. *Defence:* Col. Pedra Maria Tonha. *Foreign Affairs:* Paulo Teixeira Jorge. *Justice:* Dr Diogenes de Assis Boavida. *State Security:* Kundi Payama. *Power:* Pedro Van-Dunem. *Health:* Agostinho Mendes de Carvalho. *Interior:* Lieut.-Col. Manuel Rodrigues. *Education:* Ambrosio Lukoki. *Culture:* Antonio Jacinto do Amaral Martins. *Finance:* Ismael Gaspar Martins. *Labour and Social Security:* Horacio Braz da Silva. *Domestic Trade:* Carlos Alberto Van-Dunem. *Foreign Trade:* Roberto Antonio Lopo do Nascimento. *Construction and Housing:* Manuel Barros Mangueira. *Industry:* Maj. Alberto do Carmo Bento Ribeiro. *Transport:* Fernando Faustino Muteka. *Fisheries:* Emilio Guerra. *Agriculture:* Manuel Pedro Pacavira. *Petroleum:* Jorge Morais. *Provincial Co-ordination:* Evaristo Domingos. *Social Affairs:* Maria da Assuncao Vahekeni.

In addition there are 15 deputy ministers and all provincial governors are *ex-officio* members of the Government.

Flag: Horizontally red over black, with a star and an arc of cogwheel crossed by a machete, all yellow over all in the centre.

DEFENCE

Army. The Army has 2 armoured, 17 infantry, and 4 air defence brigades. Total strength (1980): 30,000.

Navy. Twenty Portuguese naval craft were transferred on independence in 1975 and at least 8 vessels were acquired from the Soviet Navy in 1976–77 when 8 merchant ships were taken over from local trade for naval use. There are 4 fast torpedo boats,

2 fast gunboats, 5 patrol craft, 9 coastal patrol boats, 17 landing craft and 8 auxiliary vessels. Naval personnel in 1981 totalled 1,500.

Air Force. The Angolan People's Air Force (FAPA) was formed in 1976. Combat equipment is mainly of Soviet origin, comprising about 11 MiG-21 and 15 MiG-17 fighters and 3 MiG-15UTI two-seat trainers, supplemented by 2 Fiat G.91R-4 fighter-bombers donated by Portugal at the time of 1975 withdrawal. FAPA also has 1 F.27 Maritime overwater reconnaissance aircraft, 6 Noratlas, 1 F.27 Friendship, 1 L-100-20 Hercules, 7 An-26 and 3 C-47 transports, 6 Islander twin-engined light transports, 4 Turbo-Porter liaison aircraft and 13 Alouette III, 10 Mi-4 and 15 Mi-8 helicopters.

INTERNATIONAL RELATIONS

Membership. Angola is a member of UN and OAU.

ECONOMY

Budget. In 1974 the budget envisaged an expenditure of 19,475,000 contos, and public debt, 9,066,000 contos.

Currency. The currency is the *kwanza* divided into 100 *lwei*. In March 1981, £1 = 70 *kwanza*; US$1 = 27.6 *kwanza*.

Banking. Banking is under state control and the main bank is Banco National de Angola.

Weights and Measures. The metric system is in force.

NATURAL RESOURCES

Oil. Total production (1979) 130,000 bbls a day.

Minerals. The country possesses valuable diamond deposits. Production of diamonds during 1980 totalled 1·4m. carats (1978, 650,000). Production (1973) of salt, 96,717 tonnes. There has been no production of iron ore since 1975, but the mines at Kassinga were restarted in 1980 and a second project near Dondo was about to start production in early 1981.

Agriculture. The principal crops are coffee, maize, sugar, palm-oil and palm kernels. Other products are cotton, wheat, tobacco, cacao, sisal and wax.

Livestock (1979): 3·1m. cattle, 220,000 sheep, 930,000 goats, 380,000 pigs.

COMMERCE. Imports 1978, US$780m.; exports, 1978, US$1,060m. The chief imports are textiles, transport equipment, foodstuffs, pig-iron and steel; chief exports are crude oil, coffee, diamonds, sisal, fish, maize, palm-oil. Oil represents 70% of exports.

Total trade between Angola and UK for calendar years (British Department of Trade returns, in £1,000 sterling):

	1977	1978	1979	1980
Imports to UK	5,506	44,818	49,469	83,125
Exports and re-exports from UK	10,501	20,326	30,561	27,811

COMMUNICATIONS

Roads. There were, in 1973, 72,323 km of roads.

Railways. The length of railways open for traffic in 1979 was 3,810 km. The Benguela Railway runs from Lobito to the Zaïre border at Dilolo where it connects with the National Railways of Zaïre. Other lines link Luanda with Malange; Gunza with Gabela; and Moçâmedes with Menongue. In 1972 Angola's railways carried 2,495,000 passengers and 7,878,000 tonnes of freight.

Aviation. Luanda has international air links to Lisbon, Rome, Paris, Moscow, Budapest, Brazzaville, Saõ Tomé, Lusaka, Maputo, Sal (Cape Verde Islands), Havana, Kinshasa, Libreville, Berlin, Tripoli, Lagos, Algiers, Niamey, and Sofia.

Shipping. In 1973, 6,500 vessels of 16,256,322 net tons entered Angolan ports.

Post and Broadcasting. Angola is connected by cable with east, west and south African telegraph systems. There were, in 1973, 1,808 km of telegraph lines, 77 telephone stations (with 29,796 instruments in 1978), 162 telegraph stations and 31 wireless stations.

Emissora Oficial de Angola is the largest of the 18 stations operating on medium- and short-waves. *Emissora Oficial* transmits 3 programmes as well as operating 2 regional stations.

Four regional stations are under construction. Number of receivers (1974): 110,000.

Cinemas. There were, in 1972, 47 cinemas with a seating capacity of 35,142.

Newspaper. The national daily newspaper is *Jornal de Angola.*

RELIGION, EDUCATION AND WELFARE

Religion. Article 7 of the Constitution of the People's Republic of Angola states that: 'The People's Republic of Angola is a lay state, where there is a complete separation of religious institutions from the state. All religions will be respected and the State will give protection to churches and religious places and objects so long as they accept the laws of the State'.

There are considerable numbers of Christians, both Catholic and Protestant, but the majority of the population is animist.

Education. For primary education there were (1977) 25,000 primary school teachers with 1,026,291 pupils. There were 105,363 pupils at secondary level and 1,109 uni- versity students.

Health. In 1971 there were 523 doctors and 15,000 hospital beds.

DIPLOMATIC REPRESENTATIVES

OF GREAT BRITAIN IN ANGOLA (Rua Diogo Cao, Luanda)
Ambassador: H. C. Byatt, CMG.

OF ANGOLA TO THE UNITED NATIONS
Ambassador: Elisio de Figueiredo.

Books of Reference

Anuário Estatístico de Angola. Luanda, from 1897
Araújo, A. Correia de, *Aspectos do desenvolvimento económico e social de Angola.* Lisbon, 1964
Bahia dos Santos, F., *Angola.* Lisbon, 1954
Bender, G. J., *Angola under the Portuguese.* London, 1979
Davidson, B., *In the Eye of the Storm.* London, 1972
Dias, G. de Sousa, *Os portugueses em Angola.* Lisbon, 1959
Pelissier, R., *Les guerres grises.* Montamets, 1980—*La Colonie du Minotaure.* Montamets,
    1980.—*Le naufrage des coravelles.* Montamets, 1980
Wheeler, D. L., and Pélissier, R., *Angola.* London, 1971
Zirka, A. K., *Angola Libre?* Paris, 1975

ARGENTINA

República Argentina

Capital: Buenos Aires
Population: 27·86m. (1980)
GNP per capita: US$2,042 (1979)

HISTORY. In 1515 Juan Díaz de Solís discovered the Río de La Plata. In 1534 Pedro de Mendoza was sent by the King of Spain to take charge of the 'Gobernación y Capitanía de las tierras del Río de La Plata', and in Feb. 1536 he founded the city of the 'Puerto de Santa María del Buen Aire'. In 1810 the population rose against Spanish rule, and in 1816 Argentina proclaimed its independence. Civil wars and anarchy followed until, in 1853, stable government was established.

AREA AND POPULATION. The Argentine Republic is bounded in the north by Bolivia, in the north-east by Paraguay, in the east by Brazil, Uruguay and the Atlantic Ocean and the west by Chile. The republic consists of 22 provinces, 1 federal district, and the National Territories of Tierra del Fuego, the Antarctic and the South Atlantic Islands (census of 1960 and census of 1970) as follows:

Provinces	Area: sq. km. 1960	Population: census, 1960 (1,000)	Population: census, 1970 (1,000)	Pop. per sq. km, 1965
Litoral				
Federal Capital (Buenos Aires)	200	3,040	2,906	17,061·0
Buenos Aires (La Plata)	307,804	7,139	8,788	24·2
Corrientes	88,199	559	574	6·75
Entre Ríos (Paraná)	76,216	825	821	11·7
Chaco (Resistencia)	99,633	559	562	6·3
Santa Fé	133,007	1,928	2,122	15·7
Formosa	72,066	189	232	2·8
Misiones (Posadas)	29,801	415	447	14·9
Norte				
Jujuy	53,219	253	306	5·1
Salta	154,775	435	507	3·0
Santiago del Estero	135,254	489	507	3·9
Tucumán	22,524	818	781	39·2
Centro				
Córdoba	168,766	1,829	2,087	11·8
La Pampa (Santa Rosa)	143,440	161	169	1·2
San Luis	76,748	180	183	2·5
Andina				
Catamarca	99,818	179	172	1·9
La Rioja	92,331	133	137	1·6
Mendoza	150,839	869	979	6·25
San Juan	86,137	370	391	4·65
Neuquén	94,078	116	164	1·4
Patagonia				
Chubut (Rawson)	224,686	151	195	0·73
Río Negro (Viedma)	203,013	203	263	1·1
Santa Cruz (R. Gallegos)	243,943	55	83	0·16
Tierra del Fuego (Ushuaia)	20,912	7	14	0·38
Grand total	2,777,815 [1]	20,900 [2]	23,390	8·3

[1] Total area claimed was 2,808,602 sq. km (1,084,120 sq. miles).
[2] The official census including the 'Antarctic Sector', and stated to comprise the 'Malvinas' (Falklands), South Orcadas (Orkneys), South Georgias, South Sandwich Islands and the 'sovereign territories of Argentina in the Antarctic': population, 3,300.

Estimated registered voters, 31 Dec. 1966, were 6·37m. men and 6·31m. women; total, 12·68m. (1973 total, 14m.). In 1970 the urban population, *i.e.*, in communities of 2,000 or more inhabitants, was 72% of the total; 36% of the inhabitants lived in greater Buenos Aires; of the national total, 11,617,000 were men and 11,773,000 women; foreign born, 2,180,918. Preliminary population, census 1980, 27·86m.

The population is overwhelmingly European in origin (principally from Italy and Spain) with little mixture with the aborigines. The dwindling Indian population is estimated at from 20,000 to 30,000. Immigration was, under the Perón Constitution, restricted to white persons, exception being made for the relatives of non-white persons (Japanese, etc.) already resident. An agreement signed in Buenos Aires on 19 Oct. 1964 provided for immigration of French subjects formerly resident in North Africa.

Movement of population:

	Births	Deaths	Immigrants	Emigrants
1964	496,256	193,141	905,644	878,385
1965	481,814	196,467	966,081	939,571
1966	479,396	194,450	967,700	959,200
1967	480,459	195,224	1,038,000	1,008,900
1968	...	...	1,136,900	1,116,400

In 1970 births were 20·9 (per 1,000 population); deaths, 8·4; migrations, 1·2.

The population of the capital, Buenos Aires (census 1970), was 2,972,453; and, in 1,000: Rosario, 807; Córdoba, 791; Mendoza, 471; La Plata, 391; Tucumán, 366; Santa Fé, 245; Bahía Blanca, 182; Paraná, 128.

Canals, S., *Poblaciones Indígenas de la Argentina*. Buenos Aires, 1953
Serrano, A., *Los Aborígenes Argentinos*. Buenos Aires, 1947
Censo nacional de poblacion, familias y viviendas—1970. National Institute of Statistics and Census. Buenos Aires, 1970

CONSTITUTION AND GOVERNMENT. Until 16 March 1949 the Constitution of the Argentine Republic was that of 1853, with modifications of 1860, 1866 and 1898. On the date mentioned a new constitution drafted by the Perón government and passed by the Constitutional Convention elected 5 Dec. 1948 came into force giving the Government great powers over the national economy. At a National Constituent Assembly held in Santa Fé Sept.–Nov. 1957 it was decided to revert to the 1853 constitution as amended up to 1898; thereafter the President and Vice-President were to be elected through electoral colleges by popular vote for 6-year terms. The President was not to be immediately re-elected. The Vice-President was to preside over the Senate. The President would be Commander-in-Chief of the Armed Services and would make appointments to all civil services and Judicial Offices. The President would be responsible with the Cabinet for the Executive. Both President and Vice-President must be Roman Catholic and of Argentine birth.

A law of 11 July 1975 provided that, should the Presidency become vacant, the president of the Senate should assume the office, but Congress should meet within 48 hours to choose a new president from among senators, deputies and provincial governors; he would serve the remainder of the interrupted term.

The National Congress consisted of a Senate and House of Deputies: the Senate with 2 representatives from the capital and each province (with a total of 46 seats), elected by popular vote for 9 years (one-third retiring every 3 years). The House of Deputies was to have 192 seats, each deputy being elected for 4 years and half the seats renewable each 2 years. The 2 Chambers meet annually from 30 Sept. to 2 May. Since 1912 voting has been free, secret and obligatory. Women were enfranchised on 9 Sept. 1947; beginning with the presidential election on 11 Nov. 1951, all women 18 years of age or older must vote. Equal suffrage was confirmed by a revisionary law of Aug. 1961.

The military leaders supported by the Navy and Air Force staged a *coup d'état* on 27 June 1966, and the temporary Revolutionary Junta of the Commanders-in-Chief of the three Armed Services deposed Dr Illia and his Government elected in 1963. A former Commander-in-Chief of the Army, Lieut.-Gen. Onganía, was appointed President and the Junta dissolved. The previous Constitution remained in force in so far as it was consistent with the statutes and objectives of the Revolution.

In Aug. 1967 a law was promulgated decreeing the registration of communists and excluding them from holding any public office, any position in employers' and workers' trade unions, and any teaching post in state and private schools.

The following is a list of Presidents from 1946 onwards:

Gen. Juan Domingo Perón. 4 June 1946–22 Sept. 1955. (Deposed.)

Gen. Eduardo Lonardi. 23 Sept.–13 Nov. 1955. (Deposed.)

Gen. Pedro Aramburu. 13 Nov. 1955–30 April 1958.

Dr Arturo Frondizi. 23 Feb. 1958–29 March 1962. (Deposed.)

Dr José Maria Guido. 29 March 1962–12 Oct. 1963.

Dr Arturo Illia. 12 Oct. 1963–June 1966. (Deposed.)

Gen. Juan Carlos Onganía. 29 June 1966–8 June 1970. (Deposed.)

Brig.-Gen. Robert Marcelo Levingston. 18 June 1970–22 March 1971. (Deposed.)

Gen. Alejandro Agustin Lanusse. 26 March 1971–May 1973.

Dr Hector Cámpora. 27 May 1973–13 July 1973.

Gen. Juan Domingo Perón. 12 Oct. 1973–1 July 1974.

Maria Estela (Isabel) Martinez Perón. 1 July 1974 (*a.i.* from 29 June 1974)–23 March 1976. (Deposed.)

Gen. Jorge Rafael Videla. 29 March 1976– March 1981.

On 24 March 1976 President Maria Estela Perón was deposed by a military junta consisting of Gen. Leopoldo Galtieri, Adm. Emilio Massera and Brig. Orlando Agosti.

President of the Republic: Gen. Roberto Viola (appointed March 1981).

After the general election of 11 March 1973 the distribution of seats in the National Congress was: Frente Justicialista de Liberación (Fréjuli), 145; Union Civica Radical (UCR), 51; Alianza Popular Federalista, 20; Alianza Popular Revolucionaria, 12; others, 15.

On 19 Dec. 1979 the military junta published plans for the return to normal political life and the gradual transfer of power to civilians.

National flag: Three horizontal stripes of light blue, white and light blue, with the gold Sun of May in the centre.

National anthem: Oid, mortales, el grito sagrado Libertad (words by V. López y Planes, 1813; tune by J. Blas Parera).

Local Government. From 1958 until the June 1966 Revolution, apart from the period March 1962 to Oct. 1963, the governors were elected for terms of either 3 or 4 years. The Provinces elected their own Legislature and have control over their own internal affairs. After the Revolution of June 1966 the governors were appointed by the President and are responsible to him.

Ravignani, Emilio, *Asambleas Constituyentes Argentinas.* 6 vols. Buenos Aires, 1939

DEFENCE

Army. The Army is a National Militia, service in which is compulsory for all citizens from their 20th to their 45th year. Naturalized citizens are exempt for a period of 10 years. For the first 10 years the men belong to the 'active' Army, or first line. After completing 10 years in the first line the men pass to the National Guard, and serve in it for another 10 years, finishing their service with 5 years in the Territorial Guard; the latter is mobilized only in case of war. The period of continuous service, or training in the ranks with the permanent forces, is for 1 year for the Army or Air Force, and 14 months for the Navy. The reservists can be called out for training periodically.

The territory of the republic is divided into 5 military districts for administrative purposes. The Army is organized in 4 army corps; it consists of 2 armoured and 6 infantry brigades, 3 mountain brigades, 1 airborne brigade, 1 aviation and 6 air defence battalions.

In 1980 the Army was 85,000 strong, of whom 65,000 were National Service men and the remainder, an officer corps of 5,000 and 15,000 n.c.o.s, all of whom were career regulars.

The trained reserve numbers about 250,000, of whom 200,000 belong to the National Guard and 50,000 to the Territorial Guard.

Navy. Principal ships of the Argentine Navy:

Com- pleted	Name	Standard displace- ment Tons	Armour Belt In.	Armour Guns In.	Principal armament	Tor- pedo tubes	Shaft horse- power	Speed Knots
			Aircraft Carrier [1]					
1945	Veinicinco de Mayo [2]	15,892	—	—	21 aircraft (capacity): light A.A.	—	40,000	24·0

[1] The aircraft carrier *Independence*, ex-*Warrior*, purchased from the UK in 1958 was withdrawn from service in 1971.

[2] Ex-*Karel Doorman*, purchased from the Netherlands in 1968, ex-*Venerable*, purchased from UK in 1948.

					Cruisers			
1939	General Belgrano [3]	10,800	4	3–5	15·6-in., 8·5-in.	—	100,000	32·5

[3] Ex-*Phoenix*, purchased from the USA in 1951. Sister ship *Nueve de Julio* (ex-USS *Bloise*) was withdrawn from service in 1980. The cruiser *La Argentina* was stricken from the list in 1975.

There are also 2 new German-built submarines, 2 old *ex*-US submarines, 2 new British-built destroyers (Type 42), 7 old *ex*-US destroyers, 2 new small frigates, 2 old training frigates, 1 corvette (*ex*-fleet minesweeper), 4 coastal minesweepers, 2 minehunters, 6 patrol vessels (armed ocean tugs), 4 missile boats, 2 fast patrol vessels, 2 torpedo boats, 6 patrol craft, 3 survey ships, 2 survey launches, 1 training ship, 5 transports, 3 oilers, 1 dock landing ship, 5 landing ships, 23 minor landing craft, 2 icebreakers, 20 auxiliary vessels and service craft and 16 tugs.

The new construction programme includes 6 diesel-powered patrol submarines, 4 destroyers and 6 fast frigates.

The active personnel of the Navy in 1981 comprised 31,000 (2,900 officers and 28,100 men, including 12,000 conscripts, who serve 14 months). The Marine Corps numbered 6,000 including coast artillery. There is a naval school and an engineering school.

The Naval Aviation Service, formed on 17 Oct. 1919, has some 125 fixed-wing aircraft and helicopters with 2,000 personnel, in 4 wings. Aircraft include 14 A-4Q Skyhawk attack bombers, 10 Aermacchi M.B.326 light jet armed trainers, 5 P-2H Neptune and 10 S-2A/S-2E ship-based Tracker anti-submarine aircraft, navalized Harvard trainers, and North American armed T-28s bought from France, and a variety (a dozen types) of training, transport and general purpose aircraft, plus 7 types of helicopters. Skyhawks, Trackers and Sea King and Alouette helicopters are operated from the aircraft carrier.

Air Force. The Air Force, founded on 10 Aug. 1912 and autonomous since 4 Jan. 1945, is organized into Air Operations, Air Regions, Materiel and Personnel Commands. Air Operations Command, responsible for all operational flying, is made up of 8 air brigades, each with 1 to 4 squadrons, usually operating from a single base. No. I Air Brigade is a military air transport service, with responsibility also for LADE (state airline) operations into areas of Argentina not served by civilian companies. Its equipment includes 7 C-130E/H Hercules and 9 F.27 Friendship/Troopship turboprop transports, 2 KC-130H Hercules tanker/transports, 5 twin-turbofan F.28 Fellowship freighters, 6 C-47s, 5 Twin Otters, 15 Guarani IIs, the Presidential Boeing 707-320B, twin-turboprop HS 748, and many older or smaller types. No. II Air Brigade has 7 Canberra twin-jet bombers and 2 Canberra trainers; a photographic squadron with Guarani IIs. No.III Air Brigade has 2 squadrons of IA 58 Pucara twin-turboprop COIN aircraft. No. IV Air Brigade comprises 2 ground attack squadrons equipped with about 20 A-4P Skyhawks and 25 Paris light jet combat and liaison aircraft. No. V Air Brigade comprises 2 squadrons with a total of about 40 A-4P Skyhawk strike aircraft. No. VI Air Brigade received 26 Dagger (Israeli-built Mirage III) fighters to equip 2 squadrons in 1978–79. No. VII Air Brigade has 1 squadron with 14 armed Hughes 500M, 6 Lama, 5 Sikorsky S-58T/S-61, 8 Bell 212 and 9 Bell UH-1 helicopters; a search and rescue squadron with 3 HU-16B Albatross amphibians; and a COIN/training squadron of T-34 Mentors. No. VIII Air Brigade has 1 squadron with 16 Mirage IIIE fighter-bombers and 2 Mirage IIID trainers. There is a flying school at Córdoba, equipped with piston-engined T-34 Mentors and Paris jets. Total strength of the Air Force is about 20,000 personnel and 375 aircraft.

INTERNATIONAL RELATIONS

Membership. Argentina is a member of UN, OAS and LAIA (formerly LAFTA).

ECONOMY

Budget. The financial year commences on 1 Nov. Budget receipts in 1980 33,400,000m. pesos and expenditure 37,200,000m. pesos.

Currency. The monetary system is on a gold-exchange standard, the unit for foreign transactions being, nominally, the *peso oro* (gold peso) and for domestic transactions, the *peso moneda nacional* (paper peso), legal tender for all domestic debts.

The gold peso weighs 1·6129 grammes of gold 0·900 fine; it is divided into 100 *centavos*, but gold is not in circulation. Circulation consists chiefly of paper notes (issued since 1897) ranging from 100,000 down to 50 pesos. The coins actually circulating, 1968, were steel–nickel, 25, 10, 5, 1 peso and 50 centavos. The government in 1970 introduced a 'new peso', equivalent to 100 of the present units of currency.

Due to constant inflation, the international value of the peso has fallen steadily. In Oct. 1955 it was 18 to US$1; in March 1981 it was officially 1,240 to US$1. The buying and selling of foreign exchange is now controlled, and with certain minor exceptions may only be through authorized institutions.

Monetary circulation 592,495m. pesos on 31 Dec. 1976. Gold and foreign-exchange reserves were equal to US$7,900m. in May 1979.

Banking. A law promulgated 25 March 1946 nationalized the Central Bank (established in 1935), originally as an autonomous institution, but later, in Oct. 1949, placed under the Minister of Finance, who became president. Six decree-laws of Oct. 1957 have brought back a greater elasticity to the structure, especially as regards the deposits and loans of the private banks, which have regained their autonomy. The Central Bank continues the normal functions of a national institution.

On 31 July 1948 there were 44 banks, each with capital of 1m. paper pesos or over (including the Banco de la Nación, with 36% of the total assets of the banking system), consisting of 9 provincial banks, 25 domestic banks and 10 foreign banks, all of which are shareholders in the Central Bank. The Banco de la Nación (founded in 1891) has 306 branches and agencies, including one at Asunción, Paraguay. In March 1974 the Government nationalized 7 foreign banks, including subsidiaries of the Citibank and the Banco de Santander. There are 5 Stock Exchanges.

Weights and Measures. Since 1 Jan. 1887 the use of the metric system has been compulsory.

ENERGY AND NATURAL RESOURCES

Electricity. Electric power production (1972) was 25,319 kwh.

Oil. Crude oil production (1979) 27·47m. cu. metres. Investment of US$10,000m. is envisaged by 1985 in the oil industry with the aim of achieving self-sufficiency.

Minerals. Mining is of mainly local importance. Since 1954 it has been under state control. Argentina produced 472,300 tonnes of washed coal in 1968 (Río Turbio, with reserves of 300m. tonnes). Gold, silver and copper are worked in Catamarca, where there are also 2 tin-mines, and gold and copper in San Juan, La Rioja and the south-western territories. Iron ore (102,000 tonnes in 1972), tungsten, beryllium, mica, uranium (25 tonnes in 1972), lead (39,900 tonnes in 1972), barites, zinc (43,500 tonnes in 1972), tin (1·8m. tonnes in 1972), manganese and limestone are produced.

Agriculture. Argentina has an area of about 670,251,000 acres, of which about 41% is pasture land, 32% woodland and 11% (73·73m. acres) cultivated. It was estimated (1966) that 30m. hectares were cultivated by the country's 110,600 tractors.

Argentina's wealth is based on agriculture and livestock. She has long led the world (pre-war average, 662,000 tonnes). In 1972 production amounted to 2·58m. tonnes carcase weight.

The livestock estimate (1979) showed: Cattle, 60·17m.; sheep, 35·4m.; pigs, 3·7m.; horses, 3m. The Province of Buenos Aires has 38% of the cattle. Wool production, 1972, was 194,000 tonnes.

Wheat production usually exceeds 6m. tonnes (1973, provisional, 7·6m.), ahead of Australia but behind Canada and US. Other cereals and linseed are also important.

Crop statistics with area (in 1,000 hectares) and production (in 1,000 tonnes) are shown as follows:

| | 1976–77 | | 1977–78[1] | | 1978–79[1] | |
	Area	Output	Area	Output	Area	Output
Wheat	7,192	11,000	4,600	5,300	5,230	7,800
Linseed	722	617	950	810	900	630
Maize	2,980	8,300	3,100	9,700	3,300	9,000
Oats	1,471	530	1,480	570	1,545	676
Barley	962	650	890	353	761	554
Rye	2,300	330	2,140	170	1,722	210
Sunflower seed	1,460	900	2,200	1,600	1,745	1,270
Sugar-cane	360	16,000	356	13,600	...	...

[1] Provisional.

The total grain and meat exports, in tonnes:

	Wheat	Maize	Barley	Meat
1976	3,154,590	3,079,965	16,297	364,424
1977	5,634,436	5,430,261	36,675	389,613
1978	1,607,567	5,894,663	7,365	435,228

Argentina's meat exports are calculated in terms of actual weight; not 'carcase weight', as is the international practice.

Cotton, potatoes, vine, tobacco, citrus fruit, olives, rice, soya, and yerba maté (Paraguayan tea) are also cultivated. There are 36 cane-sugar mills and 1 beet-sugar factory; production, 1979, about 14·12m. tonnes. Potato harvest, 1979, amounted to 1,694,000 tonnes. The area under tobacco, 1979, was 76,000 hectares; output 68,000 tonnes.

Before the Second World War the country was the largest grower and shipper of linseed (flaxseed), but, preferring to convert it into oil, exported virtually none from 1946 until April 1950, when export was resumed. Sunflower seed, first grown by Russian immigrants in 1900, now furnishes the country's most popular edible oil. There are more than 10m. olive trees, of which 48% are in Mendoza. 672,000 tonnes of groundnuts were produced in 1979 (mainly in Córdoba). Argentina is the world's largest source of tannin.

Flour-milling ranks second to refrigeration. In 1972 Argentine mills produced 427,000 tonnes of flour.

Fisheries. Fish landings in 1976 amounted to 250,400 tonnes. On 5 Jan. 1968 a government decree extended Argentina's territorial waters to 200 miles offshore. Fishing by foreign vessels inside this limit up to 12 miles from the coast would be granted.

INDUSTRY AND TRADE

Industry. Cotton yarn produced in 1972 amounted to 88,800 tonnes; mixed cotton yarn, 75,900; rayon, acetate and man-made fibre yarns, 52,150; wood pulp (1971), 206,000; paper and board (1971), 678,000; sulphuric acid, 242,000; caustic soda, 123,000; nitrogenous fertilizers, 38,000; plastics and resins, 146,000; fuel oils, 14·68m.; motor spirit, 4·5m. Cement output, 1972, was 5·5m. tonnes; pig-iron and ferro-alloys was 849,000 tonnes; crude steel, 2·15m. tonnes.

In Aug. 1974 the Government nationalized all distribution outlets of fuel and gas.

Trade Unions. According to the 1965 national census of workers' associations there are 502 trade unions with a total of nearly 1,764,700 paying members. Of these unions 240 are connected with manufacturing industries, 5 with construction, 36 with gas, water, electricity and sanitary services, 70 with commerce, 62 with transport, storage and communications and 117 with other services. The majority of these unions are affiliated to the General Confederation of Labour. The economically active population was estimated at the end of 1964 to total 8,422,700, of which 6,623,700 were males and 1,799,000 females. The main groups are agriculture and fishing (19%), manufacturing industries (20%), commerce (12%) and other services (28%).

Legal status which confers authority to negotiate wage agreements and other privileges is granted by the Secretary of Labour (Ministry of Economy and Labour) to one union in each industry or activity. The minimum wage law provides for a twice-yearly adjustment of the minimum wage to take account of cost-of-living changes. On 1 May 1966 the minimum monthly wage for a family consisting of a man, wife and 2 children was fixed at 22,500 pesos and that for a single man at 15,750 pesos.

The Trade Union Law was revised by decree in 1966. Political activity within the unions is prohibited, finances are placed under government supervision and all strikes must be decided by a two-thirds majority obtained by secret ballot.

Commerce. Import values include charges for carriage, insurance and freight; export values are on a f.o.b. basis. Real values of foreign trade (in US$1m.), exclusive of coin and bullion:

	1972	1973	1974	1975	1976	1977	1978	1979
Imports	1,905	2,235	3,216	3,510	2,766	4,162	3,834	6,300
Exports	1,941	3,266	3,930	2,961	3,916	5,652	6,400	7,750

Principal imports, 1976	US$1m.	Principal exports, 1976	US$1m.
Mineral products	651	Animals and animal products	478
Chemical products	645	Vegetable products	1,465
Iron and steel products	395	Machinery and transport	
Other metals and metal		equipment	418
manufactures	110	Food, drink, tobacco	574
Machinery and transport		Metal products	131
equipment	807	Chemical products	143
		Textiles and leather	440

Total trade between Argentina and UK (British Department of Trade returns, in £1,000 sterling):

	1975	1976	1977	1978	1979	1980
Imports to UK	53,461	90,113	120,040	153,191	145,064	114,286
Exports and re-exports from UK	67,796	63,356	130,271	113,826	128,278	172,830

Tourism. In 1974, 955,000 tourists visited Argentina, contributing about US$110m. to the economy.

COMMUNICATIONS

Roads. In 1974 there were 309,086 km of national and provincial highways. The 4 main roads constituting Argentina's portion of the Pan-American Highway were opened to traffic in 1942. In 1976 there were 2·59m. cars and 1·1m. lorries and buses.

Railways. The system, based on the 1949 amalgamation of 18 government, British and French-owned railways, comprises 6 railways with a total route-km of 34,079 km (122 km electrified) on metre, 1,435 mm and 1,676 mm gauges. In 1980, Argentine Railways was mid-way through a 5-year modernization plan aimed at expanding its role as a bulk freight haulier and improving inter-city passenger services between principal cities. Over 10,000 km of uneconomic route has been closed under the plan.

Aviation. Commercial airlines flew a total of 26m. km in 1972, carrying 607,000 passengers. Lines operating international flights to and from Buenos Aires include BUA, Aerolíneas Argentinas, Air France, Iberia, Alitalia, KLM, Swissair, SAS, Canadian Pacific Airlines, Lufthansa and PANAM.

Shipping. The merchant fleet, 31 Dec. 1973 (registered with Lloyd's), consisted of 1,453,000 GRT; traffic during 1971: vessels of 13·27m. GRT entered ports; 14m. tonnes of goods were unloaded and 10·6m. tonnes were loaded.

The state-owned ocean and river fleet (1963) included 216 vessels of over 1,000 GRT which totalled 1,200,061 GRT.

Post and Broadcasting. In 1949 the telephone service was nationalized; instruments numbered 2,584,801 in 1978. Privately owned exchanges operated 213,494 instruments. There were, in 1945, 4,382 post offices. There are (1964) 90 broadcasting stations and 10 television stations with 5·2m. viewers. Cable service to other Latin-American countries and US is provided by All-America Cables.

Cinemas (1972). Cinemas number 1,650, with seating capacity of 611,400.

Newspapers (1972). Daily newspapers numbered 162 with an aggregate daily circulation of 3,677,000. The largest circulation daily and 9 other newspapers have been closed since May 1974.

JUSTICE, RELIGION, EDUCATION AND WELFARE

Justice. Justice is administered by federal and provincial courts. The former deal only with cases of a national character, or in which different provinces or inhabitants of different provinces are parties. The chief federal court is the Supreme Court, with 5 judges at Buenos Aires. Other federal courts are the appeal courts, at Buenos Aires, Bahía Blanca, La Plata, Córdoba, Mendoza, Tucumán and Resistencia. Each province has its own judicial system, with a Supreme Court (generally so designated) and several minor chambers. Trial by jury is established by the Constitution for criminal cases, but never practised, except occasionally in the provinces of Buenos Aires and Córdoba.

The death penalty was re-introduced in 1976 for the killing of government, military police and judicial officials, and for participation in terrorist activities.

The police force is centralized under the Federal Security Council.

Religion. The Roman Catholic religion is supported by the State.

In 1888, civil marriage was established in the republic. Divorce was made legal in Dec. 1954 but ceased to be so by a decree of 1 March 1956.

The Department of Worship is under the Ministry of Foreign Affairs. The tax exemption enjoyed by some religious establishments has been derogated. There are at present 2 Cardinal-Archbishops, 11 Archbishops and 46 bishops. The clergy has 10 seminaries. On 10 Oct. 1966 Argentina returned to the Vatican the right to appoint bishops and archbishops, who had been nominated by the Argentine Government since 1853.

Education. Education is free (subsidized by the central and provincial governments), secular and compulsory for children from 6 to 14 years of age. In 1970 the pre-primary schools had 11,639 teachers and 223,251 pupils; primary schools had 175,929 teachers and 3,385,790 pupils; secondary schools had 132,721 teachers and 974,826 pupils; higher schools had 22,477 teachers and 274,634 pupils. Recurring expenditure on education for the year was 1·6m. pesos, capital expenditure 166,820 pesos. This represented 14% of public expenditure, and 61% of that was spent in salaries.

There are national universities at Córdoba (founded 1613), with, 1966, 47,000 students; Buenos Aires (1821), with 81,000 students; La Plata (1897), with 57,000 students; Tucumán (1914), with 8,000 students; the National University of the Litoral, in Santa Fé, with branches in Rosario (1920), and in Corrientes (1920), with 15,000 students; the National University of Cuyo, with 14,700 students, and that of the North-East, with 4,300 students. In 1956 the Technological Institute in Bahía Blanca was raised to the status of 'Universidad del Sur'; (1968) 7,000 students. Since 29 July 1966 these formerly autonomous institutions are under the authority of the Ministry of Education.

Health. Free medical attention is obtainable from public hospitals. Many trade unions provide medical, dental and maternity services for their members and dependants. Welfare services are scanty in places distant from urban centres. A

Ministry of Social Welfare was set up in 1966. In 1971 there were 2,864 hospitals with 133,847 beds.

DIPLOMATIC REPRESENTATIVES

OF ARGENTINA IN GREAT BRITAIN (9 Wilton Crescent, London, SW1X 8RP)

Ambassador: Dr Carlos Ortiz de Rozas (accredited 15 Feb. 1980).

OF GREAT BRITAIN IN ARGENTINA (Luis Agote 2412/52, Buenos Aires)

Ambassador: A. J. Williams, CMG.

OF ARGENTINA IN THE USA (1600 New Hampshire Ave., NW, Washington, DC., 20009)

Ambassador: Jorge A. Aja Espil.

OF THE USA IN ARGENTINA (4300 Colombia, Palermo, Buenos Aires)

Chargé d'Affaires: Claus W. Ruser.

OF ARGENTINA TO THE UNITED NATIONS

Ambassador: Dr Enrique Jorge Ros.

Books of Reference

Boletín del comercio exterio Argentino y estadísticas económicas retrospectivas. Annual
Anuario de comercio exterior de la República Argentina. Annual
Economic Review, Banco de la Nación. Buenos Aires
Síntesis Estadística Mensual. Dirección General de Estadistica. Buenos Aires, 1947 ff.
Boletín Internacional de Bibliografía Argentina. Ministry of Foreign Relations. Buenos Aires. Monthly
Geografía de la República Argentino. Ed. by the Sociedad Argentina de Estudios Geográficos. 7 vols. Buenos Aires, 1945–53
Bridges, E. L., *Uttermost Part of the Earth* [*Tierra del Fuego*]. New York, 1949
Daus, F. A., *Geografía de la Argentina.* 2 vols. Buenos Aires, 1946–53
Ferns, H. S., *Britain and Argentina in the 19th Century.* OUP, 1960.—*The Argentine Republic 1516–1971.* Newton Abbot, 1973
Ferrer. A., *Argentina.* New York, 1969
Romero, José Luis, *A History of Argentine Political Thought.* Stanford and OUP, 1963
Santillán, Diego A. de (ed.), *Gran Enciclopedia Argentina.* 9 vols. 1956–64
Snow, P. G., *Political Forces in Argentina.* Rev. ed. New York and London, 1979
Tornquist, Ernesto, & Co. Ltd., *Business Conditions in Argentina.* Buenos Aires, from 1916; monthly from Jan. 1968

AUSTRALIA

Capital: Canberra
Population: 14·42m. (1979)
GNP per capita: US$7,920 (1978)

HISTORY. On 1 Jan. 1901 New South Wales, Victoria, Queensland, South Australia, Western Australia and Tasmania were federated under the name of the 'Commonwealth of Australia', the designation of 'colonies' being at the same time changed into that of 'states'—except in the case of Northern Territory, which was transferred from South Australia to the Commonwealth as a 'territory' on 1 Jan. 1911.

In 1911 the Commonwealth acquired from the State of New South Wales the Canberra site for the Australian capital. Building operations were begun in 1923 and Parliament was opened at Canberra on 9 May 1927 by HRH the Duke of York (afterwards King George VI). A further area at Jervis Bay was acquired in 1915.

Territories under the administration of Australia in Jan. 1977, but not included in it, comprise Norfolk Island, the territory of Ashmore and Cartier Islands, and the Australian Antarctic Territory (24 Aug. 1936), comprising all the islands and territory other than Adélie Land, situated south of 60° S. lat. and between 160° and 45° E. long.

The British Government transferred sovereignty in the Heard Island and McDonald Islands to the Australian Government on 26 Dec. 1947. Cocos (Keeling) Islands on 23 Nov. 1955 and Christmas Island on 1 Oct. 1958 were also transferred to Australian jurisdiction.

AREA AND POPULATION. Area and population, estimate 30 June 1979:

States and Territories (capitals in brackets)	Area (sq. km)	Males	Females	Total	Per 100 sq. km
New South Wales (Sydney)	801,600	2,534,900	2,543,600	5,078,500	634
Victoria (Melbourne)	227,600	1,921,300	1,932,200	3,853,500	1,693
Queensland (Brisbane)	1,727,200	1,104,900	1,092,500	2,197,400	127
South Australia (Adelaide)	984,000	645,000	648,800	1,293,800	131
Western Australia (Perth)	2,525,500	632,500	610,400	1,242,800	49
Tasmania (Hobart)	67,800	208,900	208,800	417,700	616
Northern Territory (Darwin)	1,346,200	63,500	52,400	115,900	9
Aust. Cap. Terr. (Canberra)	2,400	112,900	109,400	222,300	9,263
Total	7,682,300	7,223,900	7,198,100	14,421,900	188

Population in State capitals and other major cities, estimate 30 June 1979:

Statistical division	State	Persons
Sydney	NSW	3,193,300
Melbourne	Vic.	2,739,700
Brisbane	Qld	1,015,200
Adelaide	SA	933,300
Perth	WA	883,600
Newcastle [1]	NSW	379,800
Canberra [1,2]	ACT	241,300
Wollongong [1]	NSW	224,000
Hobart	Tas.	168,500
Gold Coast [1,3]	Qld	143,300
Geelong [1]	Vic.	141,100

[1] Statistical District of 100,000 persons or more.
[2] Includes Queanbeyan.
[3] Includes Tweed Heads.

The number of occupied dwellings in Australia (at 1976 census) was 4,166,437, distributed as follows: New South Wales, 1,500,017; Victoria, 1,127,262; Queensland, 603,586; South Australia, 392,761; Western Australia, 339,448; Tasmania, 122,764; Northern Territory, 23,553; Australian Capital Territory,

57,046. There were also 429,418 unoccupied dwellings. Total completed new dwellings numbered 117,134 in 1978–79.

Vital statistics for 1978:

States and Territories	Marriages	Divorces[1]	Births	Deaths	Infant deaths
New South Wales	35,904	13,806	77,773	40,394	1,004
Victoria	27,178	10,830	58,861	29,096	616
Queensland	15,431	6,110	34,465	16,619	444
South Australia	9,800	3,806	18,558	9,763	227
Western Australia	9,404	3,387	20,611	7,794	230
Tasmania	3,148	1,132	6,788	3,311	97
Northern Territory	576	291	2,692	536	53
Aust. Cap. Terr.	1,517	1,271	4,433	912	62
Total	102,958	40,633	224,181	108,425	2,733
Rate[2]	7·23	2·87	15·73	7·61	12·19

[1] Includes nullities of marriages and judicial separations.
[2] Rate per 1,000 mean population.

Overseas arrivals during 1979 numbered 2,104,807 and departures 2,026,316. Of these 167,127 were long-term and permanent arrivals and 98,107 were long-term and permanent departures. Of these 72,236 came to Australia intending to settle. There were 23,420 Australian residents departing permanently.

Australian Bureau of Statistics, *Demography Bulletin*. Canberra, 1911–71

National Population Inquiry, Population and Australia, A Demographic Analysis and Projection. Canberra, 1975

National Population Inquiry, Population and Australia: Recent Demographic Trends and their Implications. Canberra, 1978

CONSTITUTION AND GOVERNMENT. *Federal Government:* Under the Australian Constitution legislative power in Australia is vested in a Federal Parliament, consisting of the Queen, represented by a Governor-General, a Senate and a House of Representatives. Under the terms of the constitution there must be a session of parliament at least once a year.

The Senate comprises 64 Senators (10 for each State voting as one electorate and as from Aug. 1974, 2 Senators respectively for the Australian Capital Territory and the Northern Territory). Senators representing the States are chosen for 6 years. The terms of Senators representing the Territories expire at the close of the day next preceding the polling day for the general elections of the House of Representatives. In general, the Senate is renewed to the extent of one-half every 3 years, but in case of disagreement with the House of Representatives, it, together with the House of Representatives, may be dissolved, and an entirely new Senate elected. The House of Representatives consists, as nearly as practicable, of twice as many Members as there are Senators, the numbers chosen in the several States being in proportion to population as shown by the latest statistics, but not less than 5 for any original State. The numerical size of the House after the election in 1980 was 125, including the Members for Northern Territory and the Australian Capital Territory. The Northern Territory has been represented by 1 Member in the House of Representatives since 1922, and the Australian Capital Territory by 1 Member since 1949 and 2 Members since May 1974. The Member for the Australian Capital Territory was given full voting rights as from the Parliament elected in Nov. 1966. The Member for the Northern Territory was given full voting rights in 1968. The House of Representatives continues for 3 years from the date of its first meeting, unless sooner dissolved. Every Senator or Member of the House of Representatives must be a British subject, be of full age, possess electoral qualifications and have resided for 3 years within Australia. The franchise for both Houses is the same and is based on universal (males and females aged 18 years) suffrage. Compulsory voting was introduced in 1925. If a Member of a State Parliament wishes to be a candidate in a federal election, he must first resign his State seat.

Executive power in Australia is vested in the Governor-General, who is advised by an Executive Council. This is presided over by the Governor-General, and its members hold office at his pleasure. All Ministers of State, who are members of the party or parties commanding a majority in the lower House, are members of the Executive Council under summons. A record of proceedings of meetings is kept by the Secretary to the Council. At Executive Council meetings the decisions of the Cabinet are (where necessary) given legal form, appointments made, resignations accepted, proclamations, regulations and the like made.

The policy of a ministry is, in practice, determined by the Ministers of State meeting without the Governor-General under the chairmanship of the Prime Minister. This group is known as the Cabinet. The Cabinet of the Liberal–National Country Party Coalition Government comprises the 14 senior Ministers. Other Ministers attend meetings of Cabinet only when required. Meetings of the full Ministry are held when necessary. There are 7 Standing Committees of the Cabinet comprising varying numbers of Cabinet and non-Cabinet Ministers. In Labor Governments all Ministers have been members of Cabinet. Cabinet meetings are private and deliberative and records of meetings are not made public. The Cabinet does not form part of the legal mechanisms of Government; the decisions it takes have, in themselves, no legal effect. The Cabinet substantially controls, in ordinary circumstances, not only the general legislative programme of Parliament but the whole course of Parliamentary proceedings. In effect, though not in form, the Cabinet, by reason of the fact that all Ministers are members of the Executive Council, is also the dominant element in the executive government of the country.

The legislative powers of the Federal Parliament embrace trade and commerce, shipping, etc.; taxation, finance, banking, currency, bills of exchange, bankruptcy, insurance; defence; external affairs, naturalization and aliens, quarantine, immigration and emigration; the people of any race for whom it is deemed necessary to make special laws; postal, telegraph and like services; census and statistics; weights and measures; astronomical and meteorological observations; copyrights; railways; conciliation and arbitration in disputes extending beyond the limits of any one State; social services; marriage, divorce etc.; service and execution of the civil and criminal process; recognition of the laws, Acts and records, and judicial proceedings of the States. The Senate may not originate or amend money bills; and disagreement with the House of Representatives may result in dissolution or, in the last resort, a joint sitting of the two Houses. No religion may be established by the Commonwealth. The Federal Parliament has limited and enumerated powers, the several State parliaments retaining the residuary power of government over their respective territories. If a State law is inconsistent with a Commonwealth law, the latter prevails.

The Constitution also provides for the admission or creation of new States. Proposed laws for the alteration of the Constitution must be submitted to the electors, and they can be enacted only if approved by a majority of the States and by a majority of all the electors voting.

The 32nd Parliament was elected on 18 Oct. 1980.

House of Representatives (as at 25 Nov. 1980): Liberal Party, 54; National Country Party of Australia, 20; Australian Labor Party, 51; total 125.

Senate (as at 1 July 1981): Liberal Party, 28; National Country Party of Australia, 3; Australian Labor Party, 27; Australian Democrats, 5; Independent, 1; total, 64.

Governor-General: Sir Zelman Cowen, GCMG (sworn in 8 Dec. 1977).

The following is a list of Governors-General of the Commonwealth:

Earl of Hopetoun	1901–02	HRH the Duke of Gloucester	1945–47
Lord Tennyson	1902–04	Sir William McKell	1947–53
Lord Northcote	1904–08	Viscount Slim	1953–60
Earl of Dudley	1908–11	Viscount Dunrossil	1960–61
Lord Denman	1911–14	Viscount De L'Isle	1961–65
Viscount Novar	1914–20	Lord Casey	1965–69
Lord Forster	1920–25	Sir Paul Hasluck	1969–74
Lord Stonehaven	1925–31	Sir John Kerr	1974–77
Sir Isaac Isaacs	1931–36	Sir Zelman Cowen	1977–
Earl Gowrie	1936–45		

National flag: The British Blue Ensign with a large star of 7 points beneath the Union Flag, and in the fly 5 stars of the Southern Cross, all in white.

The Liberal–National Country Party Coalition (constituted Dec. 1975) was in Dec. 1980:

Prime Minister: Rt. Hon. Malcolm Fraser, CH (L).
Deputy Prime Minister, Trade and Resources: J. Douglas Anthony (NCP).
Industry and Commerce: Phillip Lynch (L).
Communications and Leader of the House: Ian Sinclair (NCP).
National Development and Energy, Vice President of the Executive Council and Leader of the Government in the Senate: J. L. Carrick (L).
Foreign Affairs: A. A. Street (L).
Primary Industry: P. J. Nixon (NCP).
Treasurer: John Howard (L).
Industrial Relations: Andrew Peacock (L).
Defence: D. J. Killen (L).
Finance: Margaret Guilfoyle (L).
Employment and Youth Affairs, Minister Assisting the Prime Minister: Ian Viner (L).
Attorney-General: Peter Durack (L).
Social Security: F. M. Chaney (L).
Home Affairs and Environment: R. J. Ellicott (L).
Transport: Ralph J. Hunt (NCP).
Health: M. J. R. MacKellar (L).
Education and Minister Assisting the Prime Minister in Federal Affairs: Wal Fife (L).
Immigration and Ethnic Affairs: Ian MacPhee (L).
Science and Technology: David Thomson (NCP).
Administrative Services and Minister Assisting the Minister for Defence: Kevin Newman (L).
Business and Consumer Affairs: John Moore (L).
Capital Territory and Minister Assisting the Minister for Industry and Commerce: Michael Hodgman (L).
Veteran's Affairs and Minister Assisting the Treasurer: Tony Messner (L).
Aboriginal Affairs and Minister Assisting the Minister for National Development and Energy: Peter Baume (L).
Housing and Construction and Minister Assisting the Minister for Trade and Resources: D. T. McVeigh (NCP).

The Acts of the Parliament of the Commonwealth of Australia Passed from 1901 to 1973. 12 vols. Annual volumes, 1974 to date

Parliamentary Handbook of the Commonwealth of Australia. Canberra, 1915 to date

Commonwealth of Australia Directory [1921–1958 The Federal Guide; 1961–72 *Commonwealth Directory;* 1973–75 *Australian Government Directory*]. *Prime Minister's Department.* Canberra, 1924 to date

Butler, D., *The Canberra Model: Essays on Australian Government.* Melbourne and London, 1974

Crisp, L. F., *Australian National Government.* 3rd ed. Melbourne and London, 1975

Davis, S. R., *The Government of the Australian States.* London, 1960

Else-Mitchell, R., *Essays on the Australian Constitution.* 2nd ed. Sydney, 1961

Hughes, C. A., and Graham, B. D., *A Handbook of Australian Government and Politics.* Canberra, 1968

Odgers, J. R., *Australian Senate Practice.* 4th ed. Canberra, 1971

Paton, Sir George (ed.), *The Commonwealth of Australia: its Laws and Constitution.* London, 1952

Sawer, G., *Australian Federal Politics and Law 1901–1929, 1929–1949.* 2 vols. Melbourne, 1974.—*Australian Government To-day.* 11th ed. Melbourne, 1973

Spann, R. N. (ed.), *Public Administration in Australia.* 3rd ed. Sydney, 1973

Wynes, W. A., *Executive and Judicial Powers in Australia.* 5th ed. Sydney, 1976

State Government: In each of the 6 States (New South Wales, Victoria, Queensland, South Australia, Western Australia, Tasmania) there is a State government whose constitution, powers and laws continue, subject to changes embodied in the Australian Constitution and subsequent alterations and agreements, as they were before federation. The system of government is basically the same as that described above for the Commonwealth—*i.e.*, the Sovereign, her representative (in this case a Governor), an upper and lower house of Parliament (except in Queensland, where the upper house was abolished in 1922), a cabinet led by the Premier and an Executive Council. Among the more important functions of the State governments are those relating to education, health, hospitals and charities, law, order and public safety, business undertakings such as railways and tramways, and public utilities such as water supply and sewerage. In the domains of education, hospitals, justice, the police, penal establishments, and railway and tramway operation, State government activity predominates. Care of the public health and recreative activities are shared with local government authorities and the Federal Government, social services other than those referred to above are now primarily the concern of the Federal Government, and the operation of public utilities is shared with local and semi-government authorities.

Administration of Territories. Since 1911, responsibility for administration and development of the Australian Capital Territory has been vested in Federal Ministers and Departments. In 1930, the ACT Advisory Council was established, with both elected and appointed Members, to advise the Minister on administration of the Territory.

Late in 1974 the Government replaced the ACT Advisory Council with a Legislative Assembly of eighteen Members all of whom are elected and on 29 June 1979 the Legislative Assembly became the House of Assembly. While the Assembly has been accorded the forms of a legislature, it continues to perform an advisory function for the Minister for the Capital Territory.

On 1 July 1978 the Northern Territory of Australia became a self-governing Territory with expenditure responsibilities and revenue-raising powers broadly approximating those of a State, although the Territory is not a State under the Constitution.

Under self-government the Legislative Assembly and Ministers of the Northern Territory have responsibility in the areas of insurance, banking, taxation, provision of credit and assistance; Public Service of the Territory; maintenance of law and order and the administration of Justice etc.; civil liberties; markets and marketing; inquiries and administrative reviews; consumer affairs; sales and leases of goods and supply of services etc.; prices and rent control; industry and regulation of businesses and professions; tourism; printing and publishing; labour relations and industrial safety; mining and minerals; land and land use; transport; environment protection and conservation; fire prevention; water resources; energy planning, public utilities and public works; local government; housing, education, health, welfare etc.; censorship; Supreme Court, agreements between the Territory and the Commonwealth, State or States.

Local Government. The system of municipal government is broadly the same throughout Australia, although local government legislation is a State matter.

Each State is sub-divided into areas known variously as municipalities, cities, boroughs, towns, shires or district councils, totalling about 900. Within these areas the management of road, street and bridge construction, health, sanitary and garbage services, water supply and sewerage, and electric light and gas undertakings, hospitals, fire brigades, tramways and omnibus services and harbours is generally part of the functions of elected aldermen and councillors. The scope of their duties, however, differs considerably, for in all States the State Government, either directly or through semi-government authorities, also carries out some or all of these types of services.

In some instances, *e.g.*, in New South Wales, a number of local government authorities combine to conduct a public undertaking such as the supply of water or electricity.

DEFENCE. The Minister for Defence has responsibility under legislation for the control and administration of the Defence Force. The Chief of Defence Force Staff is vested with command of the Defence Force. He is the principal military adviser to the Minister. The Secretary, Department of Defence is the Permanent Head of the Department. He is the principal civilian adviser to the Minister. The Chief of Defence Force Staff and the Secretary are jointly responsible for the administration of the Defence Force except with respect to matters falling within the command of the

Defence Force or any other matter specified by the Minister.

The Chief of Naval Staff, the Chief of the General Staff and the Chief of the Air Staff command the Navy, Army and Air Force respectively. They have delegated authority from the Chief of Defence Force Staff and the Secretary to administer matters relating to their particular Service.

The structure of Defence is characterized by 3 organizational types: (*i*) A Central Office comprising 5 groups of functional orientated Divisions: Strategic Policy and Force Development; Supply and Support; Manpower and Financial Services; Management and Infrastructure Services; and, Defence Science and Technology; (*ii*) the 3 Armed Services of the Defence Force, each having a Service Office element in addition to the command structure; and (*iii*) a small number of outrider organizations concerned with such specialist fields as intelligence and natural disasters.

Army. Overall organization and financial control of the Australian Army is vested in the Chief of General Staff. Under the Defence Force Re-organisation Act, which received the Royal Assent on 9 Sept. 1975, the Military Board, which was previously the controlling body of the Army, was abolished. The Act became effective on 1 Feb. 1976. A functional command structure, Headquarters Field Force Command, Headquarters Logistic Command, and Headquarters Training Command, with Headquarters in military districts, was introduced in 1973.

The strength of the Army was 32,298 in 1980. There is emphasis in the field force organization on the combat element and high-priority logistic units to meet the requirements for limited war and tropical warfare with light air-portable formations. The Field Force is organized on the divisional structure, on the basis of 6 battalions organized in 3 task forces each with combat and logistic support.

There is a volunteer Regular Army Emergency Reserve of 103 former members of the Regular Army, and the effective strength of the Army Reserve in 1980 was 22,718.

Training for commissioned rank is carried out at the Royal Military College and the Officer Cadet School. The Royal Military College was established in Canberra in 1911, to train young men from Australia and New Zealand for the Regular Armies of those two countries. The college, which is affiliated with the University of New South Wales, accepts young men between the ages of 17 and 20 who are qualified to enter university. The course covers 4 years and leads to the award of the university's degrees of Bachelor of Arts and Bachelor of Science.

The Officer Cadet School was established at Portsea, Victoria, in 1952. The course there takes 11 months.

Staff and command training is, in the main, carried out at the Australian Staff College, Queenscliff, Victoria and the Land Warfare Centre, Canungra, Queensland.

Expenditure on Army capital equipment was $A74·22m. in 1978–79, $A63·35m. in 1979–80.

Navy. The overall control of the Royal Australian Navy is vested in the Chief of Naval Staff assisted by the Deputy Chief of Naval Staff with the Chief of Naval Personnel, the Chief of Naval Technical Services and the Chief of Naval Material. Under the Defence Re-organisation Act effective from 1 Feb. 1976 the Naval Board was abolished. The command, operation and administration of the Fleet is the responsibility of the Flag Officer Commanding HM Australian Fleet. The Naval Support Commander, formerly the Flag Officer Commanding East Australia area, is responsible for the material support for the fleet.

Aircraft carrier of the Royal Australian Navy:

Completed	Name	Standard displacement, tons	Principal armament	Shaft horse-power	Speed, knots
1955	Melbourne (*ex*-Majestic)[1]	20,000	12 40-mm AA	42,000	23

[1] Sister ship *Sydney* (ex-*Terrible*), completed as an aircraft carrier in 1949, converted to a fast military transport in 1961, officially announced for disposal on 20 July 1973, left Sydney for shipbreakers on 23 Dec. 1975.

There are also 6 British-built 'Oberon' class submarines, *Onslow*, *Otway*, *Ovens* and *Oxley* (completed in 1967–69) and *Orion* and *Otama* (completed in 1977–78), 3 US-built guided-missile destroyers, *Brisbane*, *Hobart* and *Perth* (completed in 1965–68), 1 'Daring' class destroyer, *Vampire* now used as a training ship (sister ship *Vendetta* paid off 1979), 6 destroyer escorts or 'Type 12' fast anti-submarine frigates, 3 oceanographic research and survey ships, 2 minehunters, 1 minesweeper, a destroyer tender, 12 attack class patrol craft, 6 landing craft, 1 fleet oiler, 14 auxiliary vessels, 8 service craft and 55 workboats, etc. An oceanographic research ship (*Cook*) was commissioned in Oct. 1980. HMAS *Jervis Bay* (formerly the ANL ro-ro vessel *Australian Trader*) was commissioned in 1977 as the RAN's training ship. In 1980 it was announced a fourth frigate, *Darwin*, will be delivered in 1984. In Aug. 1974 the Minister for Defence signed for the purchase of 2 'patrol frigates' of 3,500 tons with a length of 445 ft to be completed in US shipyards in 1981–82. This order was later increased to 3, the ships to be named *Adelaide*, *Canberra* and *Sydney*. In Aug. 1975 the Minister for Defence announced plans to provide a replacement fleet tanker for HMAS *Supply* in 1985. The vessel will be similar to the French 'Durance' class design and will be built by Vickers Cockatoo Dockyard in Sydney. A second 'Durance' class ship will also be built. The first was named *Success*. Fifteen patrol boats to replace the 'Attack' class are to be built over a 6-year period. The first, HMAS *Fremantle*, was built by Brooke Marine Ltd at Lowestoft, England, arrived in Australia in Aug. 1980. The remaining 14 are to be built by North Queensland Engineers and Agents at Cairns with the last due to be launched in 1985. A further 10 patrol boats will be built after the completion of the 'Fremantle' class projects. A new amphibious ship (LSH), HMAS *Tobruk*, based on an update of the British 'Sir Bedivere' class is nearing completion at Carrington slipways, Newcastle. She is due to be commissioned in mid-1980 and the acquisition of replacement patrol craft towards the end of the decade.

Naval dockyards are at Garden Island, Sydney, and Williamstown, Victoria. Naval shipbuilding is carried out at Williamstown, at Cockatoo Dock and Engineering Company, Sydney, or by private contract. The main repair base and store depots are at Sydney.

The main training establishments are HMAS *Cerberus* in Victoria, HMAS *Watson*, HMAS *Penguin* and HMAS *Nirimba* at Sydney, HMAS *Albatross* (Naval Air Station) at Nowra, NSW, and HMAS *Creswell* (Royal Australian Naval College) at Jervis Bay, ACT. Training for junior recruits is carried out at HMAS *Leeuwin* in Fremantle, WA, and Reserve training in naval establishments in all major seaboard capital cities.

The Fleet Air Arm was established in 1948. At 30 June 1980 it had 74 aircraft and consisted of 6 squadrons the operational elements of which were 1 Skyhawk, 1 Tracker and 1 Sea King squadrons embarked in HMAS *Melbourne*. The Wessex, Iroquois and Bell 206B helicopters are used in the utility/search and rescue role. The 2 HS 748 aircraft are now employed in the electronic warfare training role.

The serving strength at 30 June 1980 totalled 16,961 personnel including 967 WRANS.

Navy estimates 1977–78, $A565,172,000; 1978–79, $A676,347,000; 1979–80, $A851,849,000; 1980–81, $A1,048,782,000.

Air Force. Command of the Royal Australian Air Force is vested in the Chief of the Air Staff (CAS) assisted by the Deputy Chief of the Air Staff, Chief of Air Force Personnel, Chief of Air Force Technical Services, Director-General Supply—Air Force and Assistant Secretary Resources Planning.

The CAS administers and controls RAAF units through two commands: Operational Command and Support Command. Operational Command is responsible to the CAS for the command of operational units and the conduct of their operations within Australia and overseas. Support Command is responsible to the CAS for training of personnel, and the supply and maintenance of service equipment.

Flying establishment comprises 16 squadrons, of which 2 are equipped with 20 F-111C/RF 111-C strike/reconnaissance aircraft. Of the others, 1 is equipped with Canberras for target flying and photographic duties, 3 with missile-armed Mirage III-O Mach-2 fighters, 2 with Orion maritime reconnaissance aircraft. There are eight transport squadrons, two with Hercules turboprop transports, 1 of the squadrons also operates Boeing 707 aircraft, 1 with Caribou STOL transports, 1 with a mix of fixed-wing Caribou and Iroquois helicopters, 1 with Boeing Vertol CH-47C medium lift helicopters, 2 with Iroquois helicopters, and a special transport squadron equipped with BAC One-Eleven, Mystère 20 and HS 748 aircraft. Training aircraft include piston-engined Airtrainers, built in New Zealand, Aermacchi MB 326H jets for pilot training, and HS 748 aircraft for navigator training.

Training for commissioned rank is carried out at the RAAF Academy and Officers' Training School, both located at Point Cook, Victoria. Other major training activities which lead to commissioned rank include basic aircrew training and technical and commercial cadet schemes. Basic ground training to tradesman level is conducted at RAAF technical training schools. Higher command and staff training is, in the main, carried out at the RAAF Staff College, Fairbairn, A.C.T.

The authorized service manpower ceiling for the Permanent Air Force was 22,071 at 30 June 1980. Combat aircraft totalled about 100.

Long, G. (ed.), *Australia in the War of 1939–45.* 22 vols. Canberra, 1952 ff.
Millar, T. B., *Australia's Defence.* Melbourne Univ. Press, 1965

INTERNATIONAL RELATIONS

Membership. Australia is a member of the UN, the Commonwealth, OECD, Colombo Plan and SEATO.

ECONOMY

Budget. In 1929, under a financial agreement between the Federal Government and States, approved by a referendum, the Federal Government took over all State debts existing on 30 June 1927 and agreed to pay $A15–17m. a year for 58 years towards the interest charges thereon, and to make substantial contributions towards a sinking fund to extinguish existing debts in 58 years and future debts in 53 years. The Federal Government arranges or must approve all borrowing for both Federal Government and States through a loan council consisting of representatives of Federal Government and State governments. Since 1942 the Federal Government alone has levied taxes on incomes. In return for vacating this field of taxation, the States are reimbursed by a grant from the Federal Government out of revenue received.

Receipts, Financing Transactions and Outlays of the Federal Government for years ending 30 June (in $A1m.):

Receipts:	1975–76	1976–77	1977–78	1978–79
Income taxes	11,813	13,946	15,313	15,913
Estate duty	76	76	96	82
Gift duty	10	11	7	1
Customs duties	1,044	1,273	1,232	1,457
Excise duties	2,331	2,485	2,733	3,845
Sales tax	1,408	1,650	1,758	1,770
Primary production taxes	116	189	179	283
Stevedoring industry charge	37	47	29	19
Payroll tax	17	19	20	13
Other taxes, fees, fines, etc.	85	109	135	151
Total taxes, fees, fines	16,937	19,806	21,501	23,533
Income from public enterprises	434	657	820	1,007
Property income	119	156	200	182
Total receipts	17,490	20,619	22,521	24,723
Financing Transactions:	3,951	3,492	4,360	4,187
Total funds available	21,442	24,111	26,882	28,911
Outlay:				
General public services	1,482	1,618	1,810	1,909
Defence	1,852	2,181	2,377	2,606
Education:				
University	598	719	781	810
Primary and Secondary	616	709	788	830
Other	675	784	819	883
Total education	1,889	2,212	2,388	2,522

Outlay (*cont*):	1975–76	1976–77	1977–78	1978–79
Health				
Hospital and clinical services	1,659	1,446	1,761	1,805
Other	1,285	1,094	933	1,097
Total health	2,944	2,540	2,694	2,901
Social security and welfare				
Care of and assistance to				
Aged persons	2,247	2,576	3,042	3,343
Incapacitated and				
handicapped persons	474	590	689	795
Unemployed and sick	776	746	942	1,061
Ex-servicemen	599	694	835	893
Families and children	296	1,056	1,077	1,038
Other	637	713	849	971
Total social security, etc.	5,029	6,375	7,434	8,102
Housing and community amenities	941	748	641	427
Recreation and culture	252	256	263	277
Economic services				
Agriculture, forestry and fishing	209	256	375	308
Mining, manufacturing and construction	193	122	52	138
Transport and communication	1,699	1,804	1,940	1,804
Other	399	468	489	560
Total economic services	2,500	2,650	2,856	2,810
Other purposes	4,553	5,531	6,420	7,357
Total outlay	21,442	24,111	26,882	28,911

The following table shows Government securities on issue on account of the Commonwealth Government and States, at 30 June 1980:

Currency in which repayable	Australian Government	States	Total
Australian Dollar ($A1,000)	13,160,783	14,225,370	27,386,152
Sterling (£1,000)	23,898	22,845	46,743
United States Dollar (US$1,000)	1,942,606	19,189	1,961,795
Canadian Dollar (Can.$1,000)	1,264	6,554	7,818
Swiss Francs (SW.F.1,000)	1,433,761	—	1,433,761
Netherlands Guilders (fl.1,000)	980,949	4,384	985,333
Deutsche Marks (DM 1,000)	2,775,174	—	2,775,174
European Units of Account (EUA1,000)	—	—	—
Japanese Yen (Yen 1m.)	257,418	—	257,418
Total ($A1,000 equivalents)[1]	20,575,853	14,278,342	34,854,194

[1] Converted at rate of exchange ruling at 30 June 1980.

Debt per head of population at 30 June 1979 was $A2,156, while the annual interest charge amounted to $A164 per head.

States: The following table presents a summary of the receipts and outlay of State and local authorities during 1978–79 (in $A1m).

	NSW	Vic.	Qld	SA	WA	Tas.	NT	All States
Receipts and Financing Transactions								
Taxes, fees, fines, etc.	2,335	1,753	725	482	469	147	23	5,934
Income from public enterprises	110	233	160	47	28	58	−15	621
Grants from Commonwealth								
Government	3,024	2,287	1,561	1,015	1,054	408	290	9,639
Advances from Commonwealth								
Government (net)	361	284	137	162	112	73	−2	1,127
All other	1,087	1,045	532	212	346	77	2	3,301
Total funds available	6,917	5,603	3,115	1,918	2,009	763	298	20,622

	NSW	Vic.	Qld	SA	WA	Tas.	NT	All States
Outlay								
Final consumption expenditure	3,714	2,977	1,571	1,112	1,119	398	142	11,033
Interest paid	701	631	383	213	180	102	1	2,209
Gross fixed capital expenditure on								
new assets	2,214	1,745	1,085	485	672	246	142	6,589
All other	288	250	76	108	38	17	13	791
Total outlay	6,917	5,603	3,115	1,918	2,009	763	298	20,622

Finance (5 parts), Australian Bureau of Statistics, Canberra, 1907–1962/63
Australian National Accounts. Australian Bureau of Statistics. 1953–54 to date
Public Authority Finance, No. 1. Australian Bureau of Statistics, 1972
Public Authority Finance: Commonwealth Finance, Australia. Australian Bureau of Statistics, 1962–63 to date
Public Authority Finance: State and Local Government Finance, Australia. Australian Bureau of Statistics, 1971–72 to date.
Public Authority Finance: Public Authority Estimates 1977–78. Australian Bureau of Statistics, 1976
National Income and Expenditure. Australian Bureau of Statistics. Canberra, 1946 to date
Australia's *Committee of Economic Enquiry.* Report. Canberra, 1965
Treasury Information Bulletin (and Supplements). Canberra Treasury Dept., 1956 to date (quarterly)
Arndt, H. W. (ed.), *The Australian Economy.* Melbourne, 1963
Campbell, W. J., *Australian State Public Finance.* Sydney, 1954
Karmel, P. H., *The Structure of the Australian Economy.* Melbourne, 1962
Maxwell, J. A., *Commonwealth–State Financial Arrangements in Australia.* Melbourne Univ. Press
Ratchford, B. U., *Public Expenditure in Australia.* Durham, N.C., 1959

Currency. On 14 Feb. 1966 Australia adopted a system of decimal currency. The currency unit, the *dollar* ($) is divided into 100 *cents*. The transition period ended on 31 July 1967. Decimal system notes have been issued in denominations of $1, 2, 5, 10, 20 and 50. Coins have been issued in denominations of 50, 20, 10, 5 and 2 cents and 1 cent.

Australian notes, issued by the note-issue department of the Reserve Bank, are legal tender throughout Australia. The total value of notes in circulation on 25 June 1980 was $A4,586·1m., of which $A4,085·2m. were held by the public. Coins are minted by the Royal Australian Mint and distributed by the Reserve Bank.

Banking. The banking system in Australia comprises:

(*a*) The Reserve Bank of Australia. This is the central bank which in addition to its central banking business (including the note-issue department) provides special financing facilities through the rural credits department for the processing, manufacture and marketing of primary produce.

(*b*) Seven major trading banks: (i) The Commonwealth Trading Bank of Australia; (ii) 6 private trading banks: The Australia and New Zealand Banking Group Ltd, The Bank of Adelaide, the Bank of New South Wales, The Commercial Bank of Australia Ltd, The Commercial Banking Company of Sydney Ltd and The National Bank of Australasia Ltd.

(*c*) Other trading banks: (i) 3 State Government banks—The Rural Bank of New South Wales, the State Bank of South Australia, and the Rural and Industries Bank of Western Australia; (ii) one joint stock bank—The Bank of Queensland Ltd, formerly The Brisbane Permanent Building and Banking Co. Ltd, which has specialized business in one district only; (iii) branches of 2 overseas banks—the Bank of New Zealand and the Banque Nationale de Paris, which are mainly concerned with financing trade, etc., between Australia and overseas countries.

(*d*) The Commonwealth Development Bank of Australia.

(*e*) Savings Banks.

(*f*) The Australian Resources Development Bank Ltd opened on 29 March 1968. Its main objective is to assist Australian enterprises in the development of Australia's natural resources, through direct loans and equity investment or by refinancing loans made by trading banks. The bank is jointly owned by the 7 major Australian trading banks.

(g) The Primary Industry Bank of Australia Ltd commenced operations on 22 Sept. 1978. The initial equity capital of the bank consists of nine shares of $A625,000 each. Eight shares are held by the Australian Government and the 7 major trading banks while the ninth share is held equally by the 4 State banks. The main objective of the bank is to facilitate the provision of loans to primary producers on longer terms than are otherwise generally available. The role of the bank is restricted to re-financing loans made by banks and other financial institutions.

The Reserve Bank's functions and responsibilities derive from the Reserve Bank Act 1959 and the Banking Act 1959, which came into effect in 1960. They had their origins, however, in the development of the central banking role of the Commonwealth Bank, which was established in 1911 as a Government savings and trading bank.

Control of the Australian note issue was transferred from the Commonwealth Treasury to a Notes Board in 1920 and, in 1924, to the Bank. The Commonwealth Bank Act 1945 formally constituted the Bank as a central bank, and these powers were carried through into the 1959 Act establishing the Reserve Bank.

The Acts of 1959 provided for: (i) the separation of the central bank from the Commonwealth group of banking institutions and its reconstitution as the Reserve Bank of Australia; (ii) the establishment of an entirely separate Commonwealth Banking Corporation, with responsibilities for the non-central-banking elements that had developed from within the original Commonwealth Bank—namely the Commonwealth Trading Bank, the Commonwealth Savings Bank and the Commonwealth Development Bank, the latter being basically an amalgamation of the Mortgage Bank and Industrial Finance Department of the Commonwealth Bank.

At 30 June 1980 the capital of the Reserve Bank totalled $A49·4m. and reserve funds (including a special reserve for IMF special drawing rights) $A4,402m. The capital was distributed as follows: Central banking business, $A40m.; rural credits department, $2,058m. Reserve funds held were: Central banking business, $A9m.; rural credits department, $A64m.; rate issue department, $A2,280. Profits for the year ended 30 June 1980 (including all departments) amounted to $A251m.

Particulars as at 30 June 1979 for the banks under the control of the Commonwealth Banking Corporation: Commonwealth Trading Bank, capital, $A14·9m.; reserve fund, $A48m.; profits for the year, $A27m. Commonwealth Development Bank, capital, $A61·7m.; reserve fund, $A109m.; profits for the year, $A5m. Commonwealth Savings Bank, reserve fund, $A262m.; profits for the year, $A45m.

At 30 June 1980 the 13 trading banks operating in Australia provided full banking facilities at 5,088 branches and 1,009 agencies all over Australia.

The weekly average of deposits in Australia with all trading banks (under (b) and (c) above) during June 1980 amounted to $A25,647m.; the average of advances made by the banks was $A20,402m.; the average of total assets was $A34,076m.

At 30 June 1980, 13 savings banks were operating in Australia. These are the 7 major savings banks being wholly owned subsidiaries of the trading banks; the Bank of New Zealand Saving Bank Ltd; and operating, with certain exceptions, in all States and Territories; the State Savings Banks in Victoria and South Australia; the Rural and Industries Bank of Western Australia, and 2 Trustee Savings Banks in Tasmania. At 30 June 1980 these savings banks provided savings facilities at 5,677 branches and 11,921 agencies throughout Australia. At end of June 1980 they held deposits in Australia amounting to $A21,261m.

In 1979 there were 47 companies registered under the Life Insurance Act, 1945, transacting life insurance business in Australia; in addition there were 2 State government institutions. During 1978–79 premiums received were $A1,808m. and claims, etc., paid were $A1,199m.

The following table is a summary of banking and insurance business (in $A1m.) in the several States of the Commonwealth:

Particulars	NSW	Vic.	Q'ld	SA	WA	Tas.	Australia (including A.C.T. and N.T.)
All trading banks: [1]							
Fixed deposits	6,829·3	3,175·6	2,343·1	1,046·3	958·5	209·8	14,755·5
Current deposits	4,838·0	2,631·3	1,591·7	605·7	788·7	198·7	10,891·5
Advances	8,777·3	4,524·9	2,509·2	1,938·3	1,826·5	373·7	20,402·0
Savings bank deposits [2]	6,124·4	7,838·7	2,884·6	2,276·9	1,216·2	642·1	21,260·9
Life insurance: [3]							
New policies issued (sum insured)							
Ordinary	2,380·2	3,172·8	1,892·6	969·1	1,129·3	275·7	12,505·4
Superannuation	359·8	2,143·5	814·8	385·9	458·1	127·0	9,442·8
Industrial	61·4	61·1	43·1	25·3	11·7	1·6	207·4
Policies existing [2] (sum insured)							
Ordinary	11,652·2	15,718·1	9,660·6	5,225·7	5,477·8	1,503·2	60,421·4
Superannuation	1,888·5	9,344·9	2,746·5	1,907·2	1,916·4	588·4	36,656·3
Industrial	546·8	414·1	283·2	156·0	106·0	23·7	1,556·9

[1] Weekly averages for June 1980.   [2] At June 1980.   [3] Year ended 30 June 1979.

Treasury Information Bulletin. Department of the Treasury. Canberra, 1956 to date (quarterly)
Reserve Bank of Australia. *Statistical Bulletin.* Sydney, 1937 to date (monthly)
Arndt, H. W., and Harris, C. P., *The Australian Trading Banks.* 3rd ed. Melbourne, 1965
Gifford, J. L. K., Wood, J. V., and Reitsma, A. J., *Australian Banking.* 4th ed. Brisbane, 1960

Weights and Measures. Conversion to the metric system is in progress.

ENERGY AND NATURAL RESOURCES

Electricity. Total production 1978–79, 90,851m. kwh. (of which hydro, 16,173m.).

Minerals. The mineral output was valued at the mine as follows (in $A1,000) [1]:

Mineral	1977–78	1978–79	Mineral	1977–78	1978–79
Copper [2]	155,279	261,173	Brown coal [3]	64,925	79,630
Gold [2]	82,340	102,351	Petroleum	671,233	919,793
Iron ore	769,408	801,636			
Lead [2]	225,162	357,472	Total (value of		
Rutile	50,631	51,267	minerals and		
Tungsten	...	43,253	construction		
Zinc [2]	120,579	138,464	materials)	4,902,640	5,670,941
Black coal	1,576,914	1,670,553			

[1] The values in this table include the value of materials used in process of production, whereas those in preceding and subsequent tables exclude these values to show net value.
[2] Value of all minerals containing the metal shown as the principal content.
[3] Excludes value of brown coal used in making briquettes.

Gold production (1,000 grammes), in 1974–75, 15,153; 1975–76, 16,901; 1976–77, 15,608; 1977–78, 21,127; 1978–79, 18,765.

Black coal (1,000 tonnes) mined in 1974–75, 70,142; 1975–76, 69,269; 1976–77, 75,982; 1977–78, 79,338; 1978–79, 81,197.

Agriculture. In 1979, of a total Australian area of 768m. hectares, 417m. hectares (54·2%) were leased or licenced Crown lands, 249m. hectares (32·4%) were occupied by the Crown or reserved, unreserved or unoccupied; private lands formed the remainder, of which 79m. hectares (10·3%) were alienated and 24m. hectares (3·1%) were in the process of alienation.

Area and production of the principal crops in 1978–79:

Crops	Total area (1,000 hectares)	Total production (1,000 tonnes)
Wheat (grain)	10,249	18,090
Oats (grain)	1,359	1,763
Barley (grain)	2,785	4,006
Maize (grain)	50	169
Hay (cereal)	293	955
Potatoes (ordinary)	35	795
Sugar-cane (for crushing)	252	21,457
Vineyards	71	716
		(1,000 litres)
Wine made (1977–78)	...	345,392
Orchards and fruit gardens	97	...

The following summary shows the production and gross value of the most important items or classes of production, classified by States:

1978–79	NSW	Vic.	Q'ld	SA	WA	Tas.	Aust.[1]
Area of crops (1,000 hectares)	5,020	2,209	2,307	2,827	4,993	80	17,438
Production of wheat (1,000 tonnes)	6,640	2,998	1,962	2,086	4,400	3	18,090

1979–80	NSW	Vic.	Q'ld	SA	WA	Tas.	Aust.[1]
Total wool production (1,000m. tons)	242·2	142·4	61·2	95·8	157·7	20·2	720·0
Factory butter (1,000 kg)	3,189	68,647	3,522	...	...	5,461	84,314
Non-processed cheese (1,000 kg)	11,766	94,829	11,328	18,000	2,866	15,431	154,221
All meat (tonnes, carcase weight)							
1977–78	874,151	806,845	662,907	203,142	231,802	83,004	2,896,540
1978–79	806,863	660,427	731,709	188,411	217,389	66,971	2,707,939
1979–80[2]	664,442	553,373	593,568	184,866	211,590	57,939	2,312,872
Total Agriculture (value $A1m.)							
1978–79	3,074·2	2,148·6	2,207·4	1,084·1	1,339·3	262·3	10,232·7

[1] Includes Northern Territory and Australian Capital Territory.
[2] Preliminary, subject to revision.

Livestock (in 1,000) at 31 March 1980 (preliminary):

	NSW	Vic.	Q'ld	SA	WA	Tas.	N. Terr.	ACT	Australia
Cattle	6,013	4,279	10,515	1,115	1,967	646	1,772	13	26,321
Sheep	48,200	24,435	12,443	16,300	29,966	4,255	...	112	135,711
Pigs	792	423	522	381	298	67	4	...	2,488

Forestry. At 31st March 1979 there were 655,000 hectares of coniferous plantations. Roundwood production is more than 3·0m. cu. metres per annum.

INDUSTRY AND TRADE

Industry. Statistics of the manufacturing industries in Australia in 1978–79: Number of establishments, 26,312; workers employed, 1,143,891; salaries and wages paid, $A11,966m.; value-added, $A22,230m. (excludes small single-establishment enterprises employing less than 4 persons).

Estimated gross value (in $A1,000) of the products of Australia:

Products	1974–75	1975–76	1976–77	1977–78	1978–79
Crops	3,203,767	3,247,485	3,189,799	3,058,173	4,931,199
Livestock slaughtering and other disposals	1,019,213	1,246,393	1,685,739	1,966,516	3,081,600
Livestock products	1,650,709	1,676,322	1,881,187	1,966,054	2,219,910
Forestry, fishing and hunting	334,110	391,737	481,530	523,925	594,626
Mining and quarrying	3,304,012	3,841,444	4,491,445	4,902,640	5,670,941

Labour. The majority of wage and salary earners in Australia have their minimum wages and conditions of work prescribed in awards of industrial arbitration authorities established under federal and State legislation. However, in some States, some conditions of work (*e.g.*, normal weekly hours of work, long-service leave, annual leave) are set down in State legislation. Practically all employees in Australia have a standard working week of 40 hours or less; paid annual leave of at least 4 weeks; and paid long-service leave (*i.e.*, leave granted to workers who remain with one employer over an extended period of time and in certain other areas) of at least 13 weeks after 15 years' continuous service. For most occupations equal pay for males and females has been granted.

In addition to the minimum rates of pay for a standard working week prescribed in awards of industrial arbitration authorities, many wage-earners are in receipt of over-award pay and payments for overtime. At the end of Oct. 1979 it was estimated that the average weekly earnings of adult males (other than managerial, professional and higher supervisory staff) in full-time private and government employment was $A242·60 and average weekly hours 40·9.

Employees in all States are covered by workers' compensation legislation and by certain industrial award provisions relating to work injuries.

During 1979 industrial disputes involving stoppages of work of 10 man-days or more accounted for 3,964,400 working days lost. In these disputes 1,862,900 workers were involved.

The following table shows estimates (in 1,000) of the civilian population, by employment status. The estimates are derived by the ABS from the population survey which is based on a sample of dwellings, carried out by personal interview, covering about two-thirds of 1% of the population of Australia. Prior to Feb. 1978, when monthly surveys were introduced, the surveys were conducted quarterly. The labour force estimates for Feb. 1978 and subsequent months are based on population estimates derived from the 1976 Population Census, adjusted for under-enumeration and were obtained using a new sample and revised questionnaire. Estimates for earlier periods have been revised to make them comparable with current surveys.

	May 1976	May 1977	May 1978	May 1979	May 1980
In the labour force	6,258·2	6,378·0	6,394·0	6,439·9	6,651·4
Employed	5,982·3	6,024·2	5,998·7	6,043·3	6,237·8
Unemployed	275·9	353·8	395·3	396·6	413·6
Not in the labour force	3,808·0	3,864·2	4,051·7	4,193·6	4,167·7
Civilian population aged 15 years and over	10,066·2	10,242·2	10,445·7	10,633·5	10,819·1

The following table shows estimates (in 1,000) of the civilian wage and salary earners in Australia classified by industry (excluding defence forces, and employees in agriculture and private domestic service):

Industry[1]	June 1976	June 1977	June 1978	June 1979
Forestry, fishing and hunting[2]	15·5	15·5	15·2	15·5
Mining	78·3	78·9	74·7	76·7
Manufacturing	1,217·1	1,184·2	1,152·4	1,164·8
Electricity, gas and water	101·3	102·9	105·7	107·6
Construction	376·4	367·5	357·2	346·1
Wholesale and retail trade	988·2	989·8	984·3	997·6

[1] Australian Standard Industrial Classification. Some Division totals include industries not specified separately.
[2] Excludes ASIC Sub-divisions 01 (Agriculture) and 02 (Services to agriculture).

Industry[1]	June 1976	June 1977	June 1978	June 1979
Transport and storage	273·4	272·4	271·3	274·7
Communication	125·9	124·6	125·1	124·9
Finance, insurance, real estate and business services	405·7	412·1	413·6	424·2
Public administration and defence[2]	243·4	246·0	251·4	255·3
Community services	816·3	851·9	879·8	897·0
Health	344·3	362·0	374·0	380·8
Education, libraries, museums, and galleries	318·7	334·8	346·8	356·0

Industry[1]	June 1976	June 1977	June 1978	June 1979
Entertainment, recreation, restaurants, hotels and personal services[3]	291·3	291·0	291·1	296·8
Total	4,932·8	4,936·9	4,921·8	4,981·0

[1] Australian Standard Industrial Classification. Some Division totals include industries not specified separately.   [2] Excludes members of the permanent defence forces.
[3] Excludes ASIC Sub-division 94 Private households employing staff.

The following table shows the number of unemployed persons and job vacancies registered with the Commonwealth Employment Service and the number of persons in receipt of unemployment benefit:

	June 1975	June 1976	June 1977	June 1978	June 1980[2]
Registered unemployed	245,975	265,251	332,793	393,842	427,429
Registered job vacancies	25,517	19,194	19,129	17,203	17,612
Unemployment benefit recipients	160,748	188,423	253,809[1]	286,091	311,232

[1] July 1977.   [2] No data compiled 1979.

Trade Unions. At the end of 1979 there were 315 trade unions reporting in Australia with an estimated membership of 2,855,100. About 55% of wage and salary earners were estimated to be members of unions. In 1979 there were 32 unions with fewer than 100 members and 7 unions with 80,000 or more members. Many of the larger trade unions are affiliated with central labour organizations, the oldest being the Australian Council of Trade Unions formed in 1927. Other central labour organizations have as affiliates Public Service associations, and salaried and professional associations.

Labour Statistics. Australian Bureau of Statistics. Canberra, 1980
Foenander, O. de R., *Industrial Conciliation and Arbitration in Australia.* Sydney, 1959.—*Trade Unionism in Australia.* Sydney, 1962.—*Shop Stewards and Shop Committees.* Melbourne Univ. Press, 1965
Huntly, P., *Inside Australia's Top 100 Trade Unions.* Sydney, 1976
Isaac, J. E. and Ford, G. W., *Australian Industrial Relations.* Melbourne, 1971
O'Dea, R., *A Guide to Industrial Relations in Australia.* Sydney, 1967
Portus, J. H., *The Development of Australian Trade Union Law.* Melbourne, 1958
Rawson, D. W., *A Handbook of Australian Trade Unions and Employees' Associations.* Canberra, 1977
Sykes, E. I., *Strike Law in Australia.* Sydney, 1960
Walker, K. F., *Australian Industrial Relations Systems.* Cambridge, Mass., 1970

Commerce. Throughout Australia there are uniform customs duties, and trade between the States is free. For 1979–80[1] the gross revenue collected from customs duties amounted to $A1,576·2m. and from excise $A4,848·2m.

Value of the total imports and exports for years ending 30 June, in $A1,000:

	Imports	Exports (excluding ships' and aircraft stores)		
		Australian produce	Re-exports	Total
1977–78	11,166,553	11,922,219	347,311	12,269,530
1978–79	13,751,845	13,784,489	458,258	14,242,747
1979–80[1]	16,216,390	18,221,213	665,954	18,887,167

[1] Preliminary, subject to revision.

The Australian customs tariff provides for preferences to goods produced in and shipped from certain specified countries such as UK, Canada, New Zealand and Ireland. Preferences occur as a result of reciprocal trade agreements between Australia and these countries.

Australia also has bilateral agreements with a number of other countries guaranteeing reciprocal treatment in matters of trade.

The Australia–New Zealand free-trade agreement came into force on 1 Jan. 1966 in certain scheduled goods.

In addition, Australia is a signatory to the multilateral General Agreement on Tariffs and Trade (GATT).

Principal commodities exported and imported from Australia (in $A1,000) in 1979-80[1]:

	Exports	Imports		Exports	Imports
Live animals	209,716	25,496	Power generating machinery and equipment	38,620	504,033
Meat	1,740,406	9,076	Machinery specialized for particular industries	156,341	889,882
Dairy products	264,013	33,200	Metalworking machinery	20,444	128,648
Fish	242,142	154,310	General industrial machinery and equipment, n.e.s. and machine parts, n.e.s.	126,629	784,540
Cereals	2,893,438	16,583			
Fruit and vegetables	210,843	114,505			
Sugar, etc., and honey	700,433	9,631			
Coffee, tea, etc.	22,444	242,998			
Food for animals	25,742	26,491	Office machines and automatic data processing equipment	46,354	499,110
Miscellaneous food	14,177	23,172			
Beverages	28,077	74,402			
Tobacco	13,299	67,628	Telecommunications and sound recording and reproducing apparatus and equipment	27,184	416,905
Hides, skins, etc.	377,503	2,602			
Oil-seeds, nuts, kernels	35,584	7,264			
Crude rubber	2,904	77,560			
Wood, timber and cork	169,141	195,029	Electrical machinery, apparatus and appliances, n.e.s. and electrical parts thereof (including non-electrical counterparts n.e.s., of electrical household type equipment)	86,556	708,352
Pulp and waste paper	1,417	92,292			
Textile fibres and their waste	1,606,534	89,841			
Crude fertilizers and minerals	83,064	162,336			
Metalliferous ores and metal scrap	3,244,042	32,410			
Crude animal & vegetable materials, n.e.s.	47,261	40,825			
Coal, coke & briquettes	1,690,165	4,060	Road vehicles (including air cushion vehicles)	159,840	1,409,008
Petroleum and products	426,541	2,092,459			
Petroleum gases	...	274	Other transport equipment	196,033	314,278
Animal oils and fats	91,351	553			
Fixed vegetable oils and fats	1,504	62,933	Sanitary, plumbing, heating and lighting fixtures and fittings, n.e.s.	4,849	37,753
Animal and vegetable oils and fats	6,890	17,725	Furniture and parts thereof	7,759	78,316
Organic chemicals	46,104	486,360			
Inorganic chemicals	74,206	152,708	Travel goods, handbags and similar containers	1,090	50,648
Dyeing, tanning and colouring materials	21,649	84,355	Articles of apparel and clothing accessories	22,531	290,539
Medicinal and pharmaceutical products	70,188	152,371	Footwear	3,867	106,050
Essential oils and perfumes, etc.	28,788	83,326	Professional, scientific and controlling instruments and apparatus, n.e.s.	75,790	290,624
Fertilizers, manufactured	5,491	32,125			
Explosives and pyrotechnic products	5,865	10,619			
Plastic materials	59,195	372,021	Photographic apparatus, equipment and supplies and optical goods, n.e.s.; watches and clocks	83,070	311,544
Chemical materials and products, n.e.s.	68,252	20,433			
Leather manufactures, n.e.s.	42,826	42,547	Miscellaneous manufactured articles, n.e.s.	117,319	840,079
Rubber manufactures, n.e.s.	11,806	200,065	Commodities and transactions of merchandise trade, not elsewhere classified [2]	562,751	214,985
Wood and cork manufactures (except furniture)	7,386	78,548			
Paper and paperboard	50,566	420,014			
Textile yarn, fabrics, etc.	108,722	953,948	Total merchandise trade	18,628,155	16,029,816
Non-metallic mineral manufactures, n.e.s.	124,697	336,219	Commodities and transactions not included in merchandise trade	259,013	186,572
Iron and steel	606,844	337,378			
Non-ferrous metals	1,250,606	95,590			
Manufactures of metal, n.e.s.	159,306	436,342	Total recorded trade	18,887,168	16,216,388

[1] Preliminary.   [2] Industrial petroleum gases.

Total trade (in $A1,000) with the more important countries, according to origin (imports) and consignment (exports):

| | 1978–79 | | 1979–80[1] | |
From or to	Imports	Exports	Imports	Exports
Belgium–Luxembourg	100,457	147,276	120,719	200,571
Canada	383,486	274,362	446,057	338,641
China—excl. Taiwan Province	141,638	437,570	199,708	845,456
Egypt, Arab Republic of	92	193,971	79	327,403
France	249,666	296,429	306,889	337,810
Germany, Fed. Republic of	1,031,278	434,103	1,021,416	495,322
Hong Kong	331,559	318,227	380,522	279,376
India	104,019	112,581	119,299	173,449
Indonesia	99,239	217,582	241,793	293,145
Iran	38,932	115,904	83,688	251,815
Italy	372,739	358,933	420,499	427,074
Japan	2,426,240	4,108,961	2,526,638	5,071,828
Kuwait	159,569	75,848	311,065	97,165
Malaysia	152,549	330,736	185,820	427,855
Netherlands	174,915	182,786	190,330	234,596
New Zealand	424,850	747,377	546,698	864,772
Pakistan	10,797	66,358	17,065	69,690
Papua New Guinea	69,608	293,691	86,459	369,064
Saudi Arabia	359,497	125,956	625,607	220,501
Singapore, Republic of	277,683	264,060	442,259	393,401
Sri Lanka	13,561	26,474	15,930	34,972
Sweden	232,944	58,584	307,920	71,994
Switzerland	178,648	11,927	160,360	14,035
USSR	7,597	264,902	66,406	979,255
UK	1,492,376	571,310	1,647,638	951,531
USA	3,225,597	1,781,653	3,576,250	2,055,833

[1] Preliminary.

Imports and exports for particular State ($A1,000):

| | 1978–79 | | 1979–80[1] | |
States, etc.	Imports	Exports	Imports	Exports
New South Wales	5,760,063	3,766,173	6,703,818	4,464,579
Victoria	4,693,631	2,708,165	5,506,573	3,784,020
Queensland	1,027,709	3,285,778	1,321,214	4,265,101
South Australia	865,554	922,754	882,389	1,603,141
Western Australia	1,161,057	2,821,715	1,449,756	3,853,797
Tasmania	140,652	516,495	179,780	660,526
Northern Territory	96,644	217,721	164,282	252,119
Aust. Cap. Terr.	6,536	3,945	8,578	3,885
Total	13,751,845	14,242,747	16,216,390	18,887,167

In this table the value of goods sent from one state to another for transhipment abroad has been included in the State from which the goods were finally dispatched.

[1] Preliminary, subject to revision.

Overseas Trade. Australian Bureau of Statistics. Canberra, 1906 to date

Total trade between UK and Australia (British Department of Trade returns, in £1,000 sterling):

	1976	1977	1978	1979	1980
Imports to UK	394,300	343,054	349,068	474,902	484,112
Exports and re-exports from UK	687,756	761,009	856,317	839,871	815,652

Tourism. During 1979, 793,345 overseas visitors arrived in Australia intending to stay for less than 12 months, and international tourism receipts were $A474m.

Australian Bureau of Statistics, Canberra: *Rural Industries.* 1962–63 to date.—*Manufacturing Establishments: Details of Operations.* 1968–69 to date.—*Non-rural Primary Industries.* 1967–68 and 1968–69.—*Value of Production.* 1964–65 to 1968–69.—*Manufacturing Industry.* 1963–64 to 1967–68.—*Manufacturing Commodities.* 1963–64 and 1964–65.—*Building and Construction.* 1964–65 to date

Quarterly Review of Agricultural Economics. Bureau of Agricultural Economics. Canberra, 1948 to date

Atlas of Australian Resources. Department of National Development. Canberra, 1953–60

Developments in Australian Manufacturing Industry. Department of Trade. Melbourne, 1954–55 to date (annual)

The Australian Mineral Industry Review. Department of National Development—Bureau of Mineral Resources, Geology and Geophysics. Canberra, 1948 to date

Australian Economy. Department of the Treasury. Canberra, 1956 to date

Australasian Institute of Mining and Metallurgy. *Proceedings: New Series.* Melbourne, 1912 to date

Barnard, J. A. (ed.), *The Simple Fleece: Studies in the Australian Wool Industry.* Melbourne, 1962

Beattie, W. A., *A Survey of the Beef-cattle Industry of Australia.* Melbourne, 1956

James, W., *Wine in Australia.* 3rd ed. Melbourne, 1962

Roughley, T. C., *Fish and Fisheries of Australia.* Rev. ed. Sydney, 1961

Shann, E. O. G., *An Economic History of Australia.* London, 1948

Shaw, A. G. L., *Economic Development of Australia.* 4th ed. Melbourne, 1960

Wadham, Sir Samuel, Kent Wilson, R., and Wood, J., *Land Utilisation in Australia.* 3rd ed. Melbourne, 1957

COMMUNICATIONS

Roads. The length of roads in Australia for general traffic is about 817,000 km, of which approximately 238,000 is sealed, 211,000 of gravel, crushed stone or other improved surface, and 368,000 of cleared or formed surface only.

At 30 June 1979, 7,358,300 motor vehicles, including 5,657,200 cars and station wagons, 879,700 utilities and panel-vans, 533,100 truck type vehicles and buses and 288,200 motor cycles, were registered in Australia. The revenue derived from registration fees and motor tax for the year 1978–79 was $A506·3m., drivers' and riders' licences, $A75·4m., and miscellaneous, $A213·8m. Preliminary new motor vehicle registration figures for 1979–80 include 451,961 cars and station wagons, 73,991 utilities and panel-vans, 42,479 truck type vehicles and buses and 53,945 motor cycles.

Railways. Government railways for the year ended 30 June 1979:

System	Route-km open	Revenue train-km run, 1,000	Passenger journeys, 1,000	Goods and livestock, carried, 1,000 tonnes	Gross earnings, $A1,000	Working expenses, $A1,000
State:						
New South Wales	9,763[3]	56,860[3]	182,750	33,482	391,700[3]	638,100[3]
Victoria	6,304	30,855	93,891	11,190	188,816	348,640
Queensland	9,789	32,100	27,275	36,542	310,418	365,070
Western Australia	5,770	12,068	9,088	19,721	155,966	163,107
Australian National[1,2]	6,838	11,217	710	8,773	131,829	204,244
Tasmanian Region	851	1,276	...	1,850	...	...

[1] The Australian National Railways operates services of the former Commonwealth Railways, the non-metropolitan South Australian Railways and the Tasmanian Railways.

[2] Excludes Adelaide metropolitan rail passenger services and the Tasmanian Region.

[3] Figures for 1978.

The State railway gauges are: New South Wales, 1,435 mm; Victoria, 1,600 mm (325 km 1,435 mm); Queensland, 1,067 mm (111 km 1,435 mm); South Australia, 1,600 mm for 2,533 km, 1,824 km 1,435 mm and the rest 1,067 mm; West Australia, 137 km, 1,435 mm and the rest 1,067 mm, and Tasmania, 1,067 mm. Of the Australian National Railways, the gauge of the Trans-Australian and Australian Capital Territory is 1,435 mm, for the Central Australia 1,067 mm for 869 km and 1,435 mm for 350 km and for North Australia, 1,067 mm. Under various Commonwealth–State standardization agreements Brisbane, Sydney and Melbourne are linked by a standard 1,435 mm gauge line and Sydney is linked with Perth, *via* Broken Hill to Port Pirie (South Australia), from Port Pirie to Kalgoorlie (Western Australia) and from Kalgoorlie to Perth. The overall length of the Sydney–Perth railway is 3,961 km. The Central Australia railway extends as far north as Alice Springs (1,067 mm gauge from Marree to Alice Springs).

Aviation. Civil flying in Australia and Territories is subject to legislative control by the Australian Government. The administration of the Air Navigation Act and

Regulations is a function of the Commonwealth Department of Transport under the Minister of Transport.

Operations of regular internal air services in Australia include flights of all Australian-owned airlines, except Qantas Airways. During 1979–80 hours flown numbered 285,898. The total distance flown was 138m. km. Paying passengers carried numbered 11,533,317; weight of goods carried was 129,885 tonnes, and gross weight of mail was 15,069 tonnes.

During 1979–80 hours flown by Australian regular overseas services numbered 74,879; km flown, 59m.; paying passengers, 1,933,580; freight, 51,159 tonnes; mail, 3,878 tonnes.

Expenditure by the Australian Government on air transport for the year 1979–80 was $A273·1m. (including $A7·86m. on capital works).

At 30 June 1980 there were 355 licensed aerodromes and 80 governmental aerodromes in Australia.

Shipping. As at 30 June 1980 the Australian merchant marine (vessels of 150 tons gross and over) consisted of 84 coastal vessels of 1,264,220 tons gross and 20 overseas vessels of 592,159 tons gross.

Entrances and clearances of vessels (with cargo and in ballast) engaged in overseas trade:

	Entrances		Clearances	
	No.	Net tons	No.	Net tons
1976–77	5,830	79,666,000	5,823	79,985,000
1977–78	5,615	80,154,378	5,668	80,443,256
1978–79	5,677	82,754,869	5,655	82,509,498

The following summary shows shipping activity by States, 1978–79:

Particulars	NSW	Vic.	Q'ld	SA	WA	Tas.	NT	Aust.
Entrances of overseas vessels direct								
Number	1,302	545	1,121	275	2,040	168	226	5,677
Net tonnage (1,000 tonnes)	16,564	5,546	14,328	2,709	38,537	2,764	2,308	82,755
Overseas cargo:								
Discharged { 1,000 tonnes	6,204	2,972	2,259	2,854	6,176	371	1,047	21,884
{ 1,000 cu. metres	3,003	2,239	710	366	376	40	20	6,753
Loaded { 1,000 tonnes	24,767	5,967	30,786	3,844	90,897	4,735	4,098	165,094
{ 1,000 cu. metres	602	579	99	472	380	34	44	2,210

Post and Broadcasting. Business, year ended 30 June 1980. Number of post offices, 5,169. Earnings: Postal, $A690·2m. Working expenses: $A678·5m.

At 30 June 1980, there were 7,152,990 telephone instruments, 4,742,662 telephone services and 5,513 telephone exchanges.

Wireless broadcasting stations are in operation in all State capitals and in other areas throughout Australia. The National Broadcasting Service is provided by the Australian Broadcasting Commission, which at 30 June 1980 operated 91 medium-wave, 9 frequency modulation and 6 high-frequency stations, and 14 high-frequency stations for overseas services. In addition, 118 medium-wave, and 6 frequency modulation, commercial broadcasting stations plus 26 public radio stations (both MW and FM) were operating.

Television services are conducted in each State and the Australian Capital Territory by the National Television Service and by the Commercial Television Service. There were 170 national stations (including translators) and 50 commercial television stations in operation at 30 June 1980.

The Overseas Telecommunications Commission (OTC), established by the Overseas Telecommunications Act 1946, is responsible for the establishment, maintenance, operation and development of all public telecommunications' services between Australia and other countries, between Australia and its external territories and with ships at sea. In co-operation with Telecom and communications carriers in other countries, OTC provides ISD, other international telephone, telegram, facsimile, phototelegram, telex, leased circuit, audio broadcast and data transmission services to countries throughout the world by means of submarine cables, communications satellites and, in a decreasing number of cases, short wave radio.

Television relay is provided to and from countries with access to satellite communications' facilities.

Cinemas (1971). There were 976 cinemas including 241 drive-in cinemas, with a total seating capacity of about 478,000.

Newspapers (1979). There was 1 national newspaper (average daily circulation 126,000) and 14 metropolitan daily newspapers in Australia with a combined daily circulation of 3·6m. Of these, 3 papers published in Melbourne accounted for 1·3m. and 4 published in Sydney for 1·2m.

Australian Transport 1974–75. Annual Report. Department of Transport, Canberra
Australian Transport. Sydney, Institute of Transport, 1937 to date (quarterly)
Brogden, S., *The History of Australian Aviation.* Melbourne, 1960

JUSTICE, RELIGION, EDUCATION AND WELFARE

Justice. The judicial power of the Commonwealth of Australia is vested in the High Court of Australia (the Federal Supreme Court), in the Federal courts created by the Federal Parliament (the Federal Court of Australia, the Family Court of Australia, the Federal Court of Bankruptcy and the Australian Industrial Court) and in the State courts invested by Parliament with Federal jurisdiction.

High Court. The High Court consists of a Chief Justice and 6 other Justices, appointed by the Governor-General in Council. The Constitution confers on the High Court original jurisdiction, *inter alia*, in all matters arising under treaties or affecting consuls or other foreign representatives, matters between the States or the Commonwealth, matters to which the Commonwealth is a party and matters between residents of different States. Federal Parliament may make laws conferring original jurisdiction on the High Court, *inter alia*, in matters arising under the Constitution or under any laws made by the Parliament. It has in fact conferred jurisdiction on the High Court in matters arising under the Constitution and in matters arising under certain laws made by Parliament.

The High Court may hear and determine appeals from its own Justices exercising original jurisdiction, from any other Federal Court, from a Court exercising Federal jurisdiction and from the Supreme Courts of the States. It also has jurisdiction to hear and determine appeals from the Supreme Courts of the Territories. No appeal from the High Court to the Privy Council is permitted on questions as to the limits *inter se* of the constitutional powers of the States or the Commonwealth and the States except on the certificate of the High Court. No appeal to the Privy Council, whether special or otherwise, is permitted from a decision of Federal Courts (not being the High Court) or of the Supreme Court of a Territory. Appeal from the High Court to the Privy Council by special leave of the Privy Council is possible only in a matter in which the decision of the High Court was a decision that (*a*) was given on appeal from a decision of a Supreme Court of a State given otherwise than in the exercise of Federal jurisdiction and (*b*) did not involve the interpretation of the Constitution, a law made by the Federal Parliament or an instrument (including an ordinance, rule, regulation or by-law) made under a law made by the Parliament.

Other Federal Courts. Since 1924, 4 other Federal courts have been created to exercise special Federal jurisdiction. These are the Federal Court of Australia, the Family Court of Australia, the Australian Industrial Court (*see below*) and the Federal Court of Bankruptcy. The Federal Court of Australia, which was established in 1977 to exercise jurisdiction in a number of matters that were previously invested in either the High Court, the Australian Industrial Court, the Federal Court of Bankruptcy or State and Territory Supreme Courts, exercises both original and appellate jurisdiction. The Federal Court will ultimately take over all the original jurisdiction now conferred on the Australian Industrial Court and the Federal Court of Bankruptcy, as well as exercising jurisdiction under other Acts, and will also act as a court of appeal from State and Territory courts in relation to Federal matters. Appeal from the Federal Court to the High Court will be by way of special leave only. The State Supreme Courts have also been invested with Federal jurisdiction in bankruptcy.

State Courts. The general Federal jurisdiction of the State courts extends, subject to certain restrictions and exceptions, to all matters in which the High Court has jurisdiction or in which jurisdiction may be conferred upon it. In matters of non-Federal jurisdiction a right of appeal is still possible, as a matter of law, from the State courts direct to the Privy Council.

Industrial Tribunals. The 2 major Federal industrial tribunals of Australia are at present the Australian Industrial Court, constituted by judges, and the Australian Conciliation and Arbitration Commission, constituted by presidential members (with the status of judges) and commissioners. The Australian Industrial Court deals with questions of law, the judicial interpretation of awards, imposition of penalties, etc. Whereas the Commission's functions include settling industrial disputes, making awards, determining the standard hours of work, wage fixation, etc.

Australian Digest of Reported Decisions of the Australian Courts and of Australian Appeals to the Privy Council. 2nd ed. Sydney, Law Book Co. 1963—Supplements 1964 ff.

Baalman, J., *Outline of Law in Australia.* 3rd ed. Sydney, 1969

Benjafield, D. G., and Whitmore, H., *Principles of Australian Administrative Law.* 3rd ed. Sydney, 1966

Cowen, Z., *Federal Jurisdiction in Australia.* 2nd ed. Melbourne, 1978

Fleming, J. G., *The Law of Torts.* 5th ed. Sydney, 1977

Gunn, J. A. L., *Australian Income Tax Law and Practice.* 9th ed. by F. C. Bock and E. F. Mannix, Sydney, 1969, and *Butterworth's Taxation Service* to date

Howard, C., *Criminal Law.* 3rd ed. Sydney, 1975

Joske, P. E., *Matrimonial Causes and Marriage and Practice of in Australia and New Zealand.* 2 vols. 5th ed. Sydney, 1969

Mills, C. P., and Sorrell, G. H., *Federal Industrial Law.* (*Nolan and Cohen.*) 5th ed. Sydney, 1975

O'Connell, D. P. (ed.), *International Law in Australia.* Sydney, 1966

Paterson, W. E., and Ednie, H. H., *Australian Company Law.* 2nd ed. Sydney, 1976, and *Butterworth's Company Service* to date

Wynes, A., *Legislative, Executive and Judicial Powers in Australia.* 5th ed. Sydney, 1976

Yorston, R. K., and Fortescue, E. E., *Australian Mercantile Law.* 14th ed. Sydney, 1971

Religion. Under the Constitution the Commonwealth cannot make any law to establish any religion, to impose any religious observance or to prohibit the free exercise of any religion, nor can it require a religious test as qualification for office or public trust under the Commonwealth. The figures in the table refer to those religions with the largest number of adherents at the census of 1976. The census question on religion was not obligatory, however.

Religion	Persons	Religion	Persons
Christian		Non-Christian	
Baptist	17,415	Hebrew	53,441
Brethren	20,719	Muslim	45,205
Catholic, Roman [1]	1,520,011	Other	30,422
Catholic [1]	1,962,836		
Churches of Christ	86,850	Total Non-Christian	129,096
Church of England	3,752,222		
Congregational	53,444	Indefinite	51,271
Jehovah's Witness	41,359	No religion	1,130,300
Orthodox	372,234	No reply	1,592,959
Lutheran	191,548		
Methodist	983,240	Grand Total	13,548,448
Presbyterian	899,950		
Salvation Army	63,336		
Seventh-day Adventist	41,471		
Protestant (undefined)	206,160		
Other (including Christian undefined)	236,928		
Total Christian	10,644,851		

[1] As stated in individual census schedules.

Education. Under the Federal Constitution education is a responsibility of the six State Governments, which administer their own systems of primary, secondary and technical education through government departments responsible to State Ministers. In each State, except New South Wales and South Australia, a single Education Department is responsible for these three levels of education. In New South Wales and South Australia the Education Department concentrates on primary and secondary education and a separate department is responsible solely for technical and further education.

The Australian Government provides education services in the Australian Capital Territory, Norfolk Island, Christmas Island and the Cocos (Keeling) Islands. From 1 July 1979 education in the Northern Territory became the responsibility of the Northern Territory Government. The Australian Government also has special responsibilities for student assistance, international relations in education and for supplementing the general educational provisions to meet the special needs of the Aboriginal people and migrants.

The Australian Constitution empowers the Australian Government to make grants to the States and to place conditions upon such grants. This power has been used to provide financial assistance to the States specifically for educational purposes. There are two national Education Commissions which advise the Australian Government on the needs of educational institutions throughout Australia for the purpose of financial assistance. The Schools Commission, established in 1973, advises on the provision of financial assistance to the States for government and non-government schools. The Tertiary Education Commission, which was established in 1977 to replace three former commissions (the Universities Commission, the Commission on Advanced Education and the Technical and Further Education Commission), advises on the provision to the States of total funding for universities and colleges of advanced education and of supplementary financial assistance for their institutions of technical and further education.

School attendance is compulsory throughout Australia between the ages of 6 and 15 years (16 years in Tasmania), at either a government school or a recognized non-government educational institution. In all States and Territories the opportunity for 4-year-olds to attend pre-schools, either government or voluntary organizations, is becoming more widely available. Government schools are usually co-educational and comprehensive. Non-government schools are usually single-sex and associated with religious denominations. Tuition is free at government schools, but fees are normally charged at non-government schools.

The following is a summary for 1979 of primary and secondary school education:

States and Territories	Schools		Teachers[1]		Pupils[2]	
	Government	Non-government	Government schools	Non-government schools	Government schools	Non-government schools
New South Wales	2,221	794	46,243	11,435	807,761	224,941
Victoria	2,155	617	40,779	11,344	614,419	211,141
Queensland	1,249	335	19,481	4,595	349,182	94,863
South Australia	632	155	14,603	2,295	224,525	39,972
Western Australia	674	196	11,495	2,569	207,029	45,581
Tasmania	254	60	4,751	793	73,046	14,401
Northern Territory	119	13	1,360	185	21,410	3,746
Aust. Cap. Terr.	89	30	2,497	770	39,346	15,568
	7,393	2,200	141,210	33,986	2,336,718	650,213

[1] Full-time teachers plus the full-time equivalent of part-time teaching. Pre-school teachers in primary schools in Western Australia, Tasmania and Northern Territory were excluded for the first time in 1979.
[2] School census August. Students enrolled in pre-primary education undertaken on a sessional basis or in a recognized pre-school class of a primary/secondary school in Western Australia, Tasmania and Northern Territory have been excluded for the first time in 1979.

Post-secondary education takes place at institutions of technical and further education, colleges of advanced education and universities. Education in post-secondary institutions has been free since 1974. The majority of institutions of technical and further education are operated by State authorities and offer vocational and personal-interest courses to students, most of whom are part-time and employed. Universities and colleges of advanced education are autonomous institutions, the colleges tending to offer courses which have a more applied emphasis and are more vocationally oriented than university courses.

Universities and colleges of advanced education at 30 April 1978:

		Universities		Colleges of advanced education		
States and Territory	Number	Students	Staff[1]	Number	Students	Staff[1]
New South Wales	6	61,748	5,003	24	35,260	2,328
Victoria	4	41,958	3,362	23	52,232	3,592
Queensland	3	21,958	1,690	10	20,138	1,333
South Australia	2	12,904	1,170	8	15,996	1,085
Western Australia	2	12,099	1,023	6	18,465	1,073
Tasmania	1	3,517	326	1	2,796	248
Aust. Cap. Terr.	1	5,851	1,261	1	5,035	303
	19	160,035	13,834	73	149,922	9,962

[1] Full-time academic staff plus the full-time equivalent of part-time academic staff.

The major part of technical and further education (TAFE) in Australia is provided in a network of government-administered institutions. In addition, TAFE vocational courses are conducted by certain colleges of advanced education and by agricultural colleges in New South Wales and Victoria, and a large number of bodies, both statutory and voluntary, participate in the provision of adult education programmes. Enrolments in 1979 numbered 888,228 (48,703 full-time, 780,276 part-time and 59,249 external enrolments).

Teacher education usually takes place in colleges of advanced education, though a substantial number of secondary teachers and a few primary teachers receive their pre-service education in a university. Government school teachers are recruited by the State departments of education, and in the Australian Capital Territory and the Northern Territory by the Commonwealth Teaching Service. Non-government schools recruit their own teachers.

The Australian Government provides a number of schemes of assistance for students to facilitate access to education. The Secondary Allowances Scheme aims to help parents with a limited income to keep their children at school for the final 2 years of secondary education. The Assistance for Isolated Children Scheme provides special support to families whose children are isolated from schooling or are handicapped. The Adult Secondary Education Assistance Scheme provides assistance for mature-age students undertaking full-time the final year of matriculation studies. The Tertiary Education Assistance Scheme is a means-tested scheme to assist students enrolled for full-time study in approved courses at post-secondary institutions. Allowances are also available for post-graduate study and overseas study. Aboriginal students are eligible for assistance under the Aboriginal Secondary Grants Scheme and the Aboriginal Study Grants Scheme. The States also offer various schemes of assistance, principally at the primary and secondary levels.

There are a number of bodies at the national level which have an important coordinating, planning or funding role. These include: the Australian Education Council, comprising the Federal and State Ministers of Education, the Conference of Directors-General of Education, the Education Research and Development Committee and the Curriculum Development Centre.

Total expenditure on education in Australia in 1978–79 was estimated at $A6,172m.

Austin, A. G., *Australian Education 1788–1900*. Melbourne, 1961
Commonwealth Education Directory. Canberra, 1978
Directory of Higher Education Courses 1979. Canberra, 1978
Education in Australia. Canberra, 1977
Jones, P. E., *Education in Australia*. Melbourne, 1974
Primary and Secondary Schooling in Australia. Canberra, 1977
Schools Commission, *Triennium 1979–81. Report for 1980*. Canberra, 1979
Tertiary Education Commission, *Report for 1979–81, Triennium Vol. 3: Recommendations for 1980*. Canberra, 1979

Social Security. The National Welfare Fund finances all Federal Government social and health benefits except Medibank, repatriation and certain other payments primarily of a capital nature. Total expenditure from the Fund during 1977–78 was $A7,691m.

The following summarizes the rates and conditions of the major benefits provided at June 1979. For expenditure on these benefits during 1978–79, *see* table on p. 104.

Age and invalid pensions—men 65 years of age or more and women 60 years of age or more may receive an age pension. Persons 16 years of age or more who are permanently blind or permanently incapacitated for work to the extent of at least 85% may receive an invalid pension. To be paid a pension, a person must have lived in Australia for a specified period and, unless permanently blind or over 70 years of age, also satisfy an income test. The maximum rates are $A57.90 a week in the case of the 'standard' rate pension, and in the case of the 'married' rate pension, $A96.50 a week ($A48.25 each). These amounts are subject to income tax. Additional amounts, subject to an income test, are paid to pensioners with dependent children. Pensions, free of the income test, are paid to permanently blind persons and to persons 70 years of age and over. Supplementary assistance of up to $A5 a week may be paid to a pensioner paying rent or for lodging. Supplementary assistance and additional pension for children are not taxable.

Widows' pensions—widows, divorcees, certain deserted wives, women who have been the dependant of a man for 3 years immediately prior to his death and women whose husbands are in mental hospitals or prison may, if they satisfy a residence requirement and a means test, receive a widow's pension. Such women with at least one dependent child may be paid a pension of up to $A57.90 a week plus a mother's allowance of $A4 a week ($A6 if she has an invalid child requiring full-time care or a child under 6 years) plus $A7.50 a week for each child. Persons who pay rent may also receive supplementary assistance of up to $A5 a week. Pensions, but not mothers' allowances, additional pension for children or supplementary assistance, are subject to income tax.

Supporting parents benefit—unmarried mothers or fathers and parents who are deserted *de facto* partners, *de facto* wives of prisoners and separated spouses ineligible for widow's pension may, if they satisfy a residence requirement and a means test, receive supporting parents benefit. It is payable at the same rate as the widow's pension payable to a widow with one or more children in her care and is subject to the same income test.

Family allowance—is paid without income test to families with children under 16 years or eligible student children aged 16 years or more but under 25 years. It is not subject to income tax. Weekly rates payable are: 1 child, $A3.50; 2 children, $A8.50; 3 children, $A14.50; 4 children, $A20.50; an additional $A7 for each additional child after the fourth. For each child or eligible student in an approved institution, the rate is $A5 per week.

Handicapped child's allowance—payable to parents or guardians of severely physically or mentally handicapped children in the family home and needing constant care and attention. The allowance is $A15 per week and is free of income test.

Double orphan's pension—the guardian of a child under 16 years of age or of a full-time student under 21, both of whose parents are dead, or one of whose parents is dead and the whereabouts of the other parent unknown, may receive double orphan's pension of $A11 a week. The payment is not subject to an income test.

Unemployment and sickness benefits—are paid, subject to an income test, to persons between the ages of 16 and 65 (males) and 16 and 60 (females) who are temporarily unemployed, or temporarily incapacitated and thereby suffer loss of income. The maximum rates of benefit are $A51.45 (single) and $A96.50 (married). To be granted benefit a person must have resided in Australia for at least 12 months preceding his claim or intend to reside permanently in Australia. For unemployment benefit purposes unemployment must not be due to direct participation in a strike.

Medical legislation was passed in 1973 authorizing the Commonwealth Government to pay medical benefits and to enter into agreements with State Governments for the provision of free hospital services. The medical side of this scheme commenced on 1 July 1975 in all States and Territories, and provided a benefit of 85% of the schedule fee for medical services and certain other services, with a maximum patient contribution of $A5 for any one service where the schedule fee was charged. The hospital side of the programme was introduced in the States and Territories at varying times between 1 July 1975 and 1 Oct. 1975. Patients could elect to be admitted to recognized public hospitals as private patients if they so wished; private patients were treated by the medical practitioner of their choice and were required to pay for their hospital accommodation.

From 1 Oct. 1976 free medical and hospital cover applied only to persons below a certain income level. Persons above that level contributed through a taxation levy or through payments for membership of a private health insurance fund.

From 1 July 1978 medical benefits were reduced to 75% of the schedule fee with a maximum patient payment of $A10 for any one service. Benefits for pensioners with Pensioner Health Benefit entitlements remained at 85% of the schedule fee or the schedule fee less $A5, whichever was the greater.

From 1 Nov. 1978, Commonwealth medical benefits were reduced to cover 40% of schedule medical fees with a maximum patient contribution of $A20 for any one service where the schedule fee was charged. The arrangements existing for pensioners with Pensioner Health Benefit cards and their dependants were unchanged. Doctors were able to bill the Government direct for services provided to patients indentified by them as being disadvantaged and received 75% of the schedule fee as payment for the service. On 1 Sept. 1979 the 40% Commonwealth benefit was deleted, but benefits were payable for the anmount (if any) by which the schedule fee exceeds $A20. The special arrangements for eligible pensioners and disadvantaged persons remained unchanged.

Hospital. The system of standard hospital coverage, by which everyone without private insurance for hospital benefits is entitled to free standard ward accommodation in recognized hospitals with treatment by doctors engaged by the hospital continued without alteration. In Queensland those with private insurance for hospital benefits are also eligible for free standard ward coverage if they so choose.

Nursing Home Benefits. Basic nursing home benefits, which are reviewed annually, are available to qualified patients in approved nursing homes. A supplementary benefit of $A6 a day is paid in respect of patients who require and receive extensive nursing home care. Patients who are insured with a registered hospital benefits organization receive the benefits, basic and supplementary, from the organization. Patients who are not insured are covered for benefit entitlements by the Commonwealth.

Nursing Home Type Patients in Hospitals. During 1980 some States and Territories introduced new arrangements whereby after 60 days of hospitalization non-acute, nursing home type patients are required to make a personal, uninsurable contribution towards their care and accommodation in the same manner as similar patients in nursing homes. It is anticipated that other States/Territories will follow early in 1981.

Domiciliary Nursing Care Benefit. A domiciliary nursing care benefit is payable at the rate of $A42 a fortnight to persons who are willing and able to care, in their own homes, for aged parents or immediate relatives who would otherwise qualify for nursing home benefits. The basic criteria for the payment of the benefit are that the patient must be aged 16 years or over and be in need of continuing nursing care and receiving regular visits by a registered nurse. This benefit is not subject to a means test and is payable, under the National Health Act, in addition to any entitlements that persons may have under the Social Services Act or the Repatriation Act for pensions or other supplementary allowances.

Pharmaceutical Benefits. A comprehge of drugs and medicinal preparations is available. In general, a fee of $A2.75 is charged for each prescription.

Service pensions—are paid, subject to a means test, to veterans on the grounds of: (*a*) age and (*b*) permanent unemployability. Wives of service pensioners are also eligible provided that they do not receive pensions from the Department of Social Security.

Disability pensions—are not subject to an income test and may be paid to veterans who have incurred incapacity as a result of service, and a separate allowance may be paid to their dependants.

Department of Territories, *Progress Towards Assimilation*. Canberra, 1958
Bilton, J., *The Royal Flying Doctor Service of Australia*. Sydney, 1961
Henderson, R., *People in Poverty*. Melbourne, 1970
Kewley, T. H., *Social Security in Australia*. Sydney University Press, 1965
Scott, D., *Leisure: A Social Enquiry into Leisure Activities and Needs in an Australian Housing Estate*. Melbourne, 1962
Stoller, A. (ed.), *The Family Today*. Melbourne, 1962.—*Growing Old: Problems of Old Age in the Australian Community*. Melbourne, 1960

DIPLOMATIC REPRESENTATIVES

OF AUSTRALIA IN GREAT BRITAIN (Australia House, Strand, London, WC2B 4LA)
Deputy High Commissioner: F. C. Murray.

OF GREAT BRITAIN IN AUSTRALIA (Commonwealth Ave., Canberra)
High Commissioner: Sir John Mason, KCMG.

OF AUSTRALIA IN THE USA (1601 Massachusetts Ave., NW, Washington, D.C., 20036)
Chargé d'Affaires: Robert N. Birch.

OF THE USA IN AUSTRALIA (Moonah Pl., Canberra)
Ambassador: Philip H. Alston, Jr.

OF AUSTRALIA TO THE UNITED NATIONS
Ambassador: H. D. Anderson, OBE.

Books of Reference

Statistical Information: The Australian Bureau of Statistics (Cameron Offices, Belconnen, A.C.T., 2616) was established in 1906. All the activities of the Bureau are covered by the Census and Statistics Act, which confers authority to collect information and contains secrecy provisions to ensure that individual particulars obtained are not divulged. Under the provisions of the Statistics (Arrangements with States) Act which became law on 12 May 1956, the statistical services of all the States have been integrated with the Australian Bureau. An outline of the development of statistics in Australia is published in the *Official Year Book*, No. 51, 1965. *Australian Statistician:* Dr R. J. Cameron.

The principal publications of the Bureau are:

Official Year Book of Australia. 1907 to date
Pocket Year Book Australia. 1913 to date
Monthly Summary of Statistics Australia. Oct. 1937 to date
Digest of Current Economic Statistics Australia. Aug. 1959 to date
Catalogue of Publications, 1976 to date

Other Official Publications

Atlas of Australian Resources. Dept. of National Development, Melbourne, 1955 ff.
Climatological Atlas of Australia. Bureau of Meteorology. Melbourne, 1940
Norfolk Island—Annual Report. Government of New South Wales and Commonwealth of Australia. From 1896
Cocos (Keeling) Islands—Annual Report. Dept. of Administrative Services, Canberra
Christmas Island—Annual Report. Dept. of Administrative Services, Canberra. From 1958

Australian Books: Select List of Works About or Published in Australia. National Library of Australia, Canberra, 1934 to date
Australian National Bibliography. Canberra, 1936 to date
Historical Records of Australia. 34 vols. National Library, Canberra, 1914–25
Australia: Official Handbook. Dept. of the Capital Territory, Canberra, 1961 to date
Annual Report. Dept. of Foreign Affairs, Canberra, 1932 to date
Australian Foreign Affairs Record. Dept. of Foreign Affairs, Canberra, 1936 to date
Australian Treaty List. Dept. of Foreign Affairs, Canberra, consolidated volume from Federation to 1970 with supplements to date
Coxon, H., *Australian Official Publications.* Oxford, 1981
Documents on Australian Foreign Policy 1937–49. Vol. 1: 1937–38, Vol. 2: 1939, Vol. 3 in preparation. Dept. of Foreign Affairs, Canberra
Diplomatic List. Dept. of Foreign Affairs, Canberra. 1949 to date
Consular and Trade Representatives. Dept. of Foreign Affairs, Canberra. 1936 to date

Non-Official Publications

Australian Quarterly: A Quarterly Review of Australian Affairs. Sydney, 1929 to date
Australian National Travel Association. *Australian Tourist Guide.* Melbourne, 1960
Barnes, V. S. (ed.), *The Modern Encyclopædia of Australia and New Zealand.* Sydney, 1965
Bechervaise, J., *Science: Men on Ice in Australia.* Melbourne, 1978
Butler, D., *The Canberra Model: Essays on Australian Government.* London, 1974
Chipman, E., *Australians in the Frozen South.* Melbourne, 1978
Chisholm, A. H. (ed.), *Australian Encyclopædia.* 10 vols. Sydney, 1962
Clark, C. M. H. (ed.), *Select Documents in Australian History, 1788–1900.* 2 vols. Sydney, 1950–55
Ferguson, Sir John, *Bibliography of Australia, 1784–1850.* 4 vols. Sydney, 1941–55; vol. 5 (1851–1900), Part 1, 1963. Parts 2 and 3 in preparation
Grant, B., *The Crisis of Loyalty: A Study of Australian Foreign Policy.* Sydney, 1972
Greenwood, G. (ed.), *Australia, A Political and Social History.* 3rd ed. Sydney, 1960.—(ed.), *Australia in World Affairs, 1950–55.* Melbourne, 1957
Hancock, Sir Keith, *Australia.* Brisbane, 1961
Horne, D., *The Australian People.* Sydney, 1972
Menzies, Sir Robert, *Speech is of Time.* London, 1958
Noble, N. S. (ed.), *The Australian Environment.* 3rd ed. Melbourne, 1960
Serle, P., *Dictionary of Australian Biography.* 2 vols. Sydney, 1949
Taylor, T. G., *Australia: A Study of Warm Environments and their Effect on British Settlement.* 7th ed. London, 1959
Who's Who in Australia. Melbourne, 1906 to date

National Library: The National Library, Canberra, A.C.T. *Director-General:* Dr G. Chandler.

AUSTRALIAN TERRITORIES

AUSTRALIAN CAPITAL TERRITORY

HISTORY. The area, now the Australian Capital Territory, was first visited by white men in 1820 and settlement commenced in 1824. Until its selection as the seat of government it was a quiet pastoral and agricultural community.

AREA AND POPULATION. The area of the Australian Capital Territory is 2,432 sq. km (including Jervis Bay area). The population at 30 June 1979 was 222,300. Previous census population:

	Males	Females	Total		Males	Females	Total
1911	992	722	1,714	1961	30,858	27,970	58,828
1921	1,567	1,005	2,572	1966	49,991	46,041	96,032
1933	4,805	4,142	8,947	1971	73,945	71,629	145,574
1947	9,092	7,813	16,905	1976	103,236	100,113	203,349
1954	16,229	14,086	30,315				

(Figures before 1961 exclude particulars of full-blood Aborigines.)

CONSTITUTION AND GOVERNMENT. The Constitution of Australia provided (Sec. 125) that the seat of government should be selected by parliament and that it should be within New South Wales but at least 161 km from Sydney. The present area was surrendered by New South Wales and accepted by the Australian Government from 1 Jan. 1911. In 1915 an additional 73 sq. km at Jervis Bay was transferred from New South Wales to the Commonwealth. In 1911 an international competition was held for the city plan. The plan chosen was that of W. Burley Griffin, of Chicago. Construction was delayed by the First World War, and it was not until 1927 that, with the transfer of parliament and certain departments, Canberra became in fact the seat of government. Most Australian Government departments now have their headquarters in Canberra.

The general administration of the Territory is in the hands of the Minister for the Capital Territory, but certain specific services are undertaken by other Federal Government Departments and Authorities. Since Sept. 1974 the Minister has been advised on matters of local concern by the ACT Legislative Assembly consisting of 18 elected members. Prior to that date this function was performed by an Advisory Council consisting of both nominated and elected members.

The Australian Capital Territory Representation (House of Representatives) Act, 1973, provided for the representation of residents of the Territory by 2 elected members in the House of Representatives. The Senate (Representation of Territories) Act 1973 provided for the election of 2 Senators from the Territory. Elections took place in Dec. 1975.

FINANCE. The receipts and outlay of the Australian Capital Territory cover the transactions of the Australian Government in the Consolidated Revenue and other funds. They also include details of the ACT public corporations.

Receipts and outlay ($A1,000) for years ended 30 June:

	Receipts	Capital	Outlay Current	Total
1976	56,645	201,029	159,300	369,928
1977	80,286	198,288	187,335	396,577
1978	106,005	219,339	206,651	435,220
1979	98,170	163,019	222,330	392,937

The chief sources of receipts in 1978–79 were taxes, fees and fines, $A48m.; and interest and rent, $A29m. Capital outlay comprised gross capital formation, $A168m., and advances to other sectors, $A8m.

PRODUCTION. The Territory is predominantly pastoral. Livestock, 31 March 1979: 14,236 cattle, 117,294 sheep. A considerable amount of reafforestation (mostly pine) has been undertaken, the total area of commercial plantations at 30 June 1980 being 14,700 hectares. There is no secondary industry of any importance.

EDUCATION. In 1974 education in government schools became the direct responsibility of the Commonwealth Government. A School's Authority has been established to administer the Australian Capital Territory government school system. There are 66 government primary and infants schools, including 1 in the Jervis Bay area, with a total enrolment (Aug. 1979) of 24,862 pupils. Secondary education is provided at 16 secondary schools and 6 secondary colleges with an enrolment, at Aug. 1979, of 14,484 pupils. Pre-school education is provided at 71 centres with a total enrolment of 4,812 (Aug. 1979). There are also 30 non-government schools, 11 of which provide secondary education; total enrolment (Aug. 1979) 15,568. The Canberra Technical College and Bruce College of Technical and Further Education with a total enrolment of about 15,000 in 1979 provide training for apprentices and journeymen and also offer commercial and special courses.

The Canberra School of Music, opened in 1965, had 307 students in 1979.

The Canberra College of Advanced Education commenced operation in 1970. Courses are available in the schools of administrative studies, applied science, computing studies, liberal studies and teacher education. Enrolments (1979) 5,190.

The Australian National University is situated in Canberra.

AUSTRALIA

Books of Reference

A.C.T. Statistical Summary. Australian Bureau of Statistics. From 1960
Annual Report. National Capital Development Commission. From 1958
Tomorrow's Canberra. National Capital Development Commission, 1970
Wigmore, L., *Canberra: A History of Australia's National Capital.* 2nd ed. Canberra, 1971

NORTHERN TERRITORY

HISTORY. The Northern Territory, after forming part of New South Wales, was annexed on 6 July 1863 to South Australia and in 1901 entered the Commonwealth as a corporate part of South Australia. The Commonwealth Constitution Act of 1900 made provision for the surrender to the Commonwealth of any territory by any state, and under this provision an agreement was entered into on 7 Dec. 1907 for the transfer of the Northern Territory to the Commonwealth, and it formally passed under the control of the Commonwealth Government on 1 Jan. 1911. For details of Constitutional development until 1978 *see* THE STATESMAN'S YEAR-BOOK 1980–81 pp. 123–24. The Commonwealth Government retained responsibility until Self-Government was granted on 1 July 1978.

AREA AND POPULATION. The Northern Territory is bounded by the 26th parallel of S. lat. and 129° and 138° E. long. Its total area is 1,346,200 sq. km. The coastline is about 6,200 km in length, the principal port being Darwin. The greater part of the interior consists of a tableland rising gradually from the coast to a height of about 700 metres. On this tableland there are large areas of excellent pasturage. The southern part of the Territory is generally sandy and has a small rainfall, but water may be obtained by means of sub-artesian bores. The climate is tropical, but varies considerably over the whole Territory.

In the coastal region, there are two main climatic divisions—the wet season, Nov. to April, and the dry season, May to Oct. Farther south the climate is of a continental type, showing a great variation between the hottest and coldest months.

The capital and seat of Government, Darwin is situated on the north coast. Darwin had an annual population of 50,612 in July 1979. The total population of the Territory is about 118,700. Other main centres include Katherine (4,500), 330 km south of Darwin; Alice Springs (16,500), in Central Australia; Tennant Creek (4,000), a rich mining centre 500 km north of Alice Springs; Nhulunbuy (3,500), a bauxite mining centre on the Gove Peninsula in eastern Arnhem Land; and Jabiru, a model town being built to serve the rich Uranium Province in eastern Arnhem Land with a planned population of 6,000. There also are a number of large selfcontained Aboriginal communities.

Vital statistics for 1976: Births, 2,607; deaths, 567; marriages, 541; divorces, 423.

CONSTITUTION AND GOVERNMENT. The Northern Territory (Self-Government) Act 1978 established the Northern Territory as a body politic as from 1 July 1978, with Ministers having control over and responsibility for Territory finances and the administration of the functions of government as specified by the Federal Government by regulations made pursuant to the Act. Regulations have been made conferring executive authority for the bulk of administrative functions. Responsibility for health services was transferred on 1 Jan. 1979, and for education on 1 July 1979. Proposed laws passed by the Legislative Assembly in relation to a transferred function require the assent of the Administrator. Proposed laws in all other cases may be assented to by the Administrator or reserved by the Administrator for the Governor-General's pleasure. The Governor-General may disallow any law assented to by the Administrator within 6 months of the Administrator's assent.

The Northern Territory has federal representation electing 1 member to the House of Representatives and 2 members to the Senate.

FINANCE. The revenue and expenditure (in $A1,000) for years ended 30 June cover the transactions the Department of the Northern Territory to 1977–78 and then for Northern Territory Government:

	1975–76	1976–77	1977–78	1978–79	1979–80
Revenue	22,290	30,383	44,234	349,400	530,000
Expenditure	302,687	56,298	66,735	348,400	528,900

The chief sources of revenue for 1975–76 were: Electricity supply, $A5·2m.; rents and rates, $A4·8m. Capital expenditure (excluding business undertakings) amounted to $A55·3m.

NATURAL RESOURCES, INDUSTRY AND TRADE

Oil. In 1979–80, 7 new offshore permits were granted and applications were invited for a further 6 in the Arafura Sea. On 30 June 1980 there were 14 offshore permits covering 2,698 blocks and 7 onshore oil permits totalling 111,150 sq. km. There are 12 onshore oil permits and three oil leases under application.

Minerals. The mining industry is the Northern Territory's main industry. The main minerals produced are bauxite ore, manganese ore, copper, gold and bismuth ore. The value of all mineral production in 1979–80 was $A369·6m.

In the Gove area of Arnhem Land a bauxite/alumina project has been completed. Development costs were in excess of $A310m. Exports of bauxite commenced in June 1971 and in 1979–80, 4·9m. tonnes of bauxite were mined (2·3m. exported). Exports of alumina totalled 1·1m. tonnes.

Manganese ore is produced on Groote Eylandt. Northern Territory production in 1979–80 was 3·7m. tonnes. The ore is shipped to Tasmania, Japan, Europe and the USA.

Shipments of iron ore from Frances Creek through the port of Darwin ceased in Dec. 1975, after the bulk loading facilities at the wharf had been badly damaged by cyclone 'Tracy'.

Mines in the Tennant Creek area are the principal producers of gold, copper and bismuth in the Northern Territory. In 1977–78 the Northern Territory production of these minerals was bismuth concentrate, 5,650 tonnes; copper, 14,911 tonnes; silver (1974–75), 1,876,974 grammes; and gold, 4,263 kg.

In the Alligator River region 250 km east of Darwin, rich deposits of uranium have been discovered at Nabarlek, Jabiru (Ranger), Koongarra and Jabiluka. This area is considered to be a uranium province of world importance.

Agriculture. General agriculture is conducted on a small scale in the Northern Territory. Small quantities of fruit, vegetables, eggs, dairy produce, poultry and pasture are produced. Seeds were produced in areas adjacent to the principal population centres. The total gross value of agricultural production for 1978–79 was $A2,372,246. However the beef cattle industry is the main rural activity in the Northern Territory, and production depends almost entirely on exprt markets. Due to comparatively low production costs, the value of beef production for the year 1978–79 was $A76,773,437. Buffalo production realized $A500,000 (1975–76). A recent development has been an increase in the export of live cattle and buffalo to overseas countries which has provided alternative markets to producers.

Despite the depressed state of the industry, the accelerated eradication programme for tuberculosis and brucellosis is progressing satisfactorily and compensation payments are now extended to include cattle slaughtered as brucellosis reactors.

Livestock (31 March 1977): 1·7m. cattle; 1,000 sheep; 2,700 breeding sows.

Forestry. A forest development programme which commenced in 1970 has continued the multiple use management of Northern Territory forested areas; this programme included a softwood programme of 400 hectares per year, the introduction of additional suitable tree species in both arid and higher rainfall areas, conservation and management of native forests for production and recreational purposes, survey and assessment of resources, fire control activities and the creation of training opportunities for Aboriginals in forestry and allied saw-milling activities.

Local production of sawn timber, mainly Cypress pine, amounted to 870 cu.

metres of pine in 1975–76. This was supplemented by 35,500 cu. metres of timber imported from interstate and overseas.

Local production of treated poles and rails amounted to 115 cu. metres. Only 280 hectares of plantation were established during the year because of complications arising from cyclone 'Tracy'.

During 1975–76 the Forestry Section of the Department of the Northern Territory redeveloped parks and open-space areas on behalf of the Darwin Reconstruction Commission.

Fisheries. The fishing industry is second only to beef cattle in Northern Territory primary industries. During 1977–78 the industry employed over 1,200 people and used vessels and equipment worth in excess of $A58m. The major fishery is prawning, and for 1977–78 over 900 tonnes (processed weight) of prawns were exported. This represented 12% of the total Australian prawn exports and was valued at $A8m.

The other main fishery in the Territory is scale fish, particularly Barramundi (Giant Perch). Total scale fish production for 1977–78 was 1,450 tonnes live weight, valued at $A2m.

A major review of Northern Territory fisheries was carried out between 1973 and 1975 with assistance of a consultant resource economist and the final report contains several specific recommendations designed to increase the economic stability of fisheries.

INDUSTRY AND TRADE. In 1975–76 value added in the manufacturing industry, from 69 factories (with 4 or more persons employed) was $A45·8m. 2,036 persons were employed in these factories. In 1977, 65 trade unions had 15,700 members.

Tourism. In 1979–80, there were 267,969 tourists contributing about $A85m. to the economy.

National Parks and Reserves. About 43,000 sq. km have been set aside as wildlife sanctuaries under the Wildlife Conservation and Control Ordinance. They are controlled by the Chief Inspector of Wildlife who is an officer of the Department of the Northern Territory. 236,000 sq. km of Aboriginal reserves are also wild-life protected areas.

The Northern Territory Reserves Board administers some 37 national parks and reserves covering an area of over 249,926 hectares. The Board is responsible under the National Parks and Gardens Ordinance for the care, control and management of these reserves, and its functions include the preservation and protection of natural and historical features and the encouragement of public use and enjoyment of land set aside in such reserves.

COMMUNICATIONS

Roads. There are now 4,999 km of sealed road within the Northern Territory. They include three major interstate links: the Stuart Highway from Darwin to the South Australian border, the Barkly Highway, Tennant Creek to Mt. Isa, 447 km of which is in the Northern Territory, and the Victoria Highway, Katherine to the Western Australian border, a distance of 452 km. In addition to this there are 2,119 km of gravel roads, 6,464 km of formed roads and 6,715 km of unformed roads or tracks, totalling approximately 20,297 km of roads within the Northern Territory. In 1976–77 registrations of new motor vehicles included 1,451 cars, 2,784 utilities etc., 432 trucks, 38 buses and 925 motor cycles.

Railways. Services ceased from 20 June 1976 on the narrow-gauge railway from Darwin to Larrimah (510 km).

Alice Springs is connected by a narrow-gauge (869 km) and standard-gauge railway (342 km) through Port Augusta to the Australian rail network. Alice Springs is linked to the Trans-continental network by a new standard (1,435 mm) gauge railway to Tarcoola (831 km), opened in 1980. This replaced the largely narrow gauge line to Port Augusta.

Aviation. Darwin is the first port of arrival in Australia for some aircraft from Europe and Asia. In 1976–77, 237,411 passengers were carried and 6,389 tonnes of freight. There are regular inland services connecting Darwin with all the State capitals and many inland towns.

Shipping. Regular freight shipping services connect Darwin with Western Australia, the eastern States and overseas. Passenger vessels also call at Darwin at irregular intervals.

The ports of Melville Bay (Gove) and Milner Bay (Groote Eylandt) are connected with Darwin, the eastern States and overseas by regular shipping freight services.

The island and coastal communities around the coast are provided with regular freight barge services from Darwin. Some of these communities also receive a barge freight-transhipment service out of a Brisbane vessel which calls at Melville and Milner Bays, where the transhipment is effected.

EDUCATION AND WELFARE

Education. In 1977 there were 121 schools (of which 11 were private). Teachers totalled 1,513 and pupils 26,360.

Health. In 1980 there were 6 hospitals with 756 beds. Community health services are provided from 9 urban Health Centres and 62 rural Health Centres including mobile units.

AUSTRALIAN EXTERNAL TERRITORIES

AUSTRALIAN ANTARCTIC TERRITORY. An Imperial Order in Council of 7 Feb. 1933 placed under Australian authority all the islands and territories other than Adélie Land situated south of 60° S. lat. and lying between 160° E. long. and 45° E. long. The Order came into force with a Proclamation issued by the Governor-General on 24 Aug. 1936 after the passage of the Australian Antarctic Territory Acceptance Act 1933. The boundaries of Adélie Land were definitively fixed by a French Decree of 1 April 1938 as the islands and territories south of 60° S. lat. lying between 136° E. long. and 142° E. long. The Australian Antarctic Territory Act 1954 declared that the laws in force in the Australian Capital Territory are, so far as they are applicable and are not inconsistent with any ordinance made under the Act, in force in the Australian Antarctic Territory.

In 1968 responsibility for the administration of this Act was transferred from the Minister for External Affairs to the Minister for Supply; in 1972 responsibility was transferred to the Minister for Science.

On 13 Feb. 1954 the Australian National Antarctic Research Expeditions (ANARE) established a station on Mac-Robertson Land at lat. 67° 36′ S. and long. 62° 52′ E. The station was named Mawson in honour of the late Sir Douglas Mawson. Meteorological and other scientific research is conducted at Mawson, which is the centre for coastal and inland survey expeditions.

A second Australian scientific research station was established on the coast of Princess Elizabeth Land on 13 Jan. 1957 at lat. 68° 34′ 36″ S. and long. 77° 58′ 36″ E. The station was named Davis in honour of Capt. John King Davis, Mawson's second-in-command on 2 expeditions. The station was temporarily closed down in Jan. 1965 and re-opened in Feb. 1969.

In Feb. 1959 the Federal Government accepted from the US Government custody of Wilkes Station, which was established by the US on 16 Jan. 1957 on the Budd Coast of Wilkes Land, at lat. 66° 15′ S. and long. 110° 32′ E. The station was named in honour of Lieut. Charles Wilkes, who commanded the 1838–40 US expedition to the area, and was closed in Feb. 1969. Operations were then transferred to the new station, Casey. Construction commenced on Casey station in Jan. 1965 and was continued, mainly during summer visits, until Feb. 1969, when it was opened. The station, specially designed to withstand blizzard winds and prevent inundation by snow, is situated 2·4 km south of Wilkes at lat. 66° 17′ S. and long. 110° 32′ E. It was named after Lord Casey, Governor-General of Australia 1965–69. The Antarctic Division has also operated a station, since March 1948, at Macquarie Island, about 1,370 km south-east of Hobart. Macquarie Island is a dependency of the State of Tasmania.

On 1 Dec. 1959 Australia signed the Antarctic Treaty with Argentina, Belgium, Chile, France, Japan, New Zealand, Norway, South Africa, the USSR, the UK and the USA. Poland, Czechoslovakia, German Democratic Republic, Netherlands, Romania, Brazil and Denmark have subsequently acceded to the Treaty. Poland became a full member of the Antarctic Treaty in 1977. The Treaty reserves the Antarctic area south of 60° S. lat. for peaceful purposes, provides for international co-operation in scientific investigation and research, and preserves, for the duration of the Treaty, the *status quo* with regard to territorial sovereignty, rights and claims. The Treaty entered into force on 23 June 1961. Since then the Antarctic Treaty powers have held 10 consultative meetings.

COCOS (KEELING) ISLANDS. The Cocos (Keeling) Islands are 2 separate atolls comprising some 27 small coral islands with a total area of about 14·2 sq. km, are situated in the Indian Ocean at 12° 05′S. lat. and 96° 53′E. long. They lie 2,768 km north-west of Perth and 3,685 km west of Darwin, while Colombo is 2,255 km to the north-west of the group.

The main islands in this Australian Territory are West Island (the largest, about 10 km from north to south) on which is an airport and most of the European community; Home Island, occupied by the Cocos Malay community; Direction, South and Horsburgh Islands, and North Keeling Island, 24 km to the north of the group.

Although the islands were discovered in 1609 by Capt. William Keeling of the East India Company, they remained uninhabited until 1826, when the first settlement was established on the main atoll by an Englishman, Alexander Hare. Hare left the islands in 1831, by which time a second settlement had been formed on the main atoll by John Clunies-Ross, a Scottish seaman and adventurer, who landed with several boat-loads of Malay seamen to begin commercial development of the islands' coconut palms.

In 1857 the islands were annexed to the Crown; in 1878 responsibility was transferred from the Colonial Office to the Government of Ceylon, and in 1886 to the Government of the Straits Settlement. By indenture in 1886 Queen Victoria granted all land in the islands to George Clunies-Ross and his heirs in perpetuity (with certain rights reserved to the Crown). The head of the family had semi-official status as resident magistrate and representative of the Government. In 1903 the islands were incorporated in the Settlement of Singapore and in 1942–46 temporarily placed under the Governor of Ceylon. In 1946 a Resident Administrator, responsible to the Governor of Singapore, was appointed.

On 23 Nov. 1955 the Cocos Islands were placed under the authority of the Australian Government as the Territory of Cocos (Keeling) Islands. The Cocos (Keeling) Islands Act 1955 is the basis of the Territory's administrative, legislative and judicial systems. The laws of the Colony of Singapore which were in force in the islands immediately before the transfer have, with certain exceptions, been continued in force. They can be amended, repealed or substituted by ordinances made by the Governor-General. An Administrator, appointed by the Governor-General, is the Government's representative in the Territory and is responsible to the Minister for Home Affairs. The Cocos (Keeling) Islands Council, established as the elected body of the Cocos Malay community in July 1979, advises the Administrator on all issues affecting the Territory.

In 1978 the Australian Government purchased the Clunies-Ross family's entire interests in the islands, except for the family residence. A Cocos Malay co-operative has been established to take over the running of the Clunies-Ross copra plantation (323 tonnes of copra were exported in 1979) and to engage in other business with the Commonwealth in the Territory, including construction projects.

The population of the Territory at 30 June 1980 was 487, distributed between Home Island (294) and West Island (193).

The group of atolls is low-lying, flat and thickly covered by coconut palms, and surrounds a lagoon in which ships drawing up to 7 metres may be anchored, but which is extremely difficult for navigation.

The climate is equable and pleasant, being usually under the influence of the south-east trade winds for about three-quarters of the year. However, the winds vary at times, and meteorological reports from the Territory are particularly valuable for those engaged in forecasting for the eastern Indian Ocean. The temperature varies between 21° and 32° C., the rainfall is moderate and there are occasional violent storms.

The Cocos (Keeling) Islands Act 1955–1975 is the basis of the Territory's administrative, legislative and judicial systems. The laws of the Colony of Singapore which were in force in the islands immediately before the transfer have, with certain exceptions, been continued in force. They can be amended, repealed or substituted by ordinances made by the Governor-General.

The *Singapore Ordinances Application Ordinance* 1979 had the effect of repealing all Singapore Ordinances in force in the Territory and applying the provisions of 95 selected Singapore Ordinances only to be laws of the Territory.

Administrator: C. I. Buffett, MBE.

CHRISTMAS ISLAND is in the Indian Ocean, lat. 10° 25′ 22″ S., long. 105° 39′ 59″ E. It lies 360 km S., 8° E. of Java Head, and 417 km N. 79° E. from Cocos Islands, 1,310 km from Singapore and 2,623 km from Fremantle. Area about 135 sq. km. The climate is moderate. The island was formally annexed on 6 June 1888, placed under the administration of the Governor of the Straits Settlements in 1889, and incorporated with the Settlement of Singapore in 1900. Sovereignty was transferred to the Australian Government on 1 Oct. 1958. The population (estimate, 1980), 3,184 (Europeans, 382; Chinese, 1,834; Malays, 847 and 121 others).

The legislative, judicial and administrative systems are regulated by the Christmas Island Act, 1958–73, which is administered by the Minister for Home Affairs with an Administrator, responsible for the local administration. The laws of Singapore which were in force before the transfer have been continued but can be amended, repealed or substituted by ordinances made by the Governor-General.

Extraction and export of rock phosphate and phosphate dust is the island's only industry. In Dec. 1948 Australia and New Zealand bought the lease rights of the Christmas Island Phosphate Co. and set up the Christmas Island Phosphate Commission, for which the British Phosphate Commissioners act as managing agents. The export of phosphate rock during 1979–80 was 1,430,950 tonnes, which is shipped to Australia and New Zealand; in addition, 110,227 tonnes of phosphate dust was shipped to Singapore, Malaysia and Australia and 3,000 tonnes of citraphos and calciphos was shipped to New Zealand.

There is direct radio communication with Australia and Singapore. Regular air charter flights commenced in 1974 to Australia.

At 30 June 1980 there were 575 primary and secondary pupils at the Christmas Island Area School. There is a technical school which provides commercial, apprenticeship and adult education courses, with (1979) some 587 students.

Medical, dental and hospital services are provided free of charge by the British Phosphate Commission.

Administrator: R. McN. Holten, CMG.

NORFOLK ISLAND. 29° 04′ S. lat, 167° 57′ E. long., area 3,455 hectares, population, approximately 1,700. The island was formerly part of the colony of New South Wales and then of Van Diemen's Land. It has been a distinct settlement since 1856, under the jurisdiction of the state of New South Wales; and finally by the passage of the Norfolk Island Act 1913, it was accepted as a Territory of the Australian Government. The Norfolk Island Act 1957 is the basis of the Territory's legislative, administrative and judicial systems. An Administrator, appointed by the Governor-General and responsible to the Minister for Home Affairs, is the senior government representative in the Territory.

The Norfolk Island Act 1979 equips Norfolk Island with responsible legislative and executive government to enable it to run its own affairs to the greatest practicable extent. Wide powers are exercised by the Norfolk Island Legislative Assembly and by an Executive Council, comprising the executive members of the Legislative Assembly who have ministerial-type responsibilities. The Act preserves the Commonwealth's responsibility for Norfolk Island as a Territory under its authority, with the Minister for Home Affairs being the responsible Minister, and indicates the Parliament's intention that consideration will be given to an extension of the powers of the Legislative Assembly and the political and administrative institutions of Norfolk Island within 5 years.

The Assembly has legislative and executive powers over a specified range of matters. The Government will consider increasing these powers no later than 5 years after the Assembly is incorporated.

The island's Supreme Court sits as required and a Court of Petty Sessions exercises both civil and criminal jurisdiction.

The Territory Administration is financed from an annual Commonwealth grant which in 1977–78 amounted to $A126,000 and from local revenue which for the same period totalled $A2,020,732. A further $A288,214 was provided by the Commonwealth during the year for the restoration and maintenance of historic structures.

Public revenue is derived mainly from the sale of postage stamps, customs duties, liquor sales and company registration and licence fees. Residents are not liable for income tax on earnings within the Territory, nor are death and personal stamp duties levied. In 1979–80 imports totalled $A10·8m. and exports $A1·6m.

An estimated 20,000 visitors a year travel to Norfolk. Descendants of the *Bounty* mutineer families constitute the 'original' settlers and are known locally as 'Islanders', while later settlers, mostly from Australia, New Zealand and UK, are identified as 'mainlanders'. Over the years the Islanders have preserved their own lifestyle and customs, and their language remains a mixture of West Country English and Tahitian.

The Administration subsidises a public hospital and dispensary, and health services, together with free dental services for children, are provided by qualified government officers.

Norfolk Island's public school is staffed by the New South Wales Department of Education and follows the State's education system. A bursary scheme is available to provide students with secondary education on the mainland.

A radio telephone service between the island and Sydney is maintained by the Overseas Telecommunications Commission, and there is a local automatic telephone service.

Administrator: W. P. Coleman.

HEARD AND McDONALD ISLANDS. These islands, about 2,500 miles south-west of Fremantle, were transferred from UK to Australian control as from 26 Dec. 1947. Heard Island is about 43 km long and 21 km wide; Shag Island is about 8 km north of Heard. The total area is 412 sq. km (159 sq. miles). The McDonald Islands are 42 km to the west of Heard.

TERRITORY OF ASHMORE AND CARTIER ISLANDS. By Imperial Order in Council of 23 July 1931, Ashmore Islands (known as Middle, East and West Islands) and Cartier Island, situated in the Indian Ocean, some 320 km off the north-west coast of Australia, were placed under the authority of the Commonwealth.

Under the Ashmore and Cartier Islands Acceptance Act, 1933, the islands were accepted by the Commonwealth under the name of the Territory of Ashmore and Cartier Islands, and the effective date was proclaimed by the Governor-General to be 10 May 1934. It was the intention that the Territory should be administered by the State of Western Australia, but owing to administrative difficulties the Territory was annexed to and deemed to form part of the Northern Territory of Australia (by amendment to the Act in 1938) with relevant laws of the Northern Territory, applying to the Territory of Ashmore and Cartier Islands. From 1 July 1978, responsibility for the administration of Ashmore and Cartier Islands passed to the Commonwealth portfolio of the Minister for Home Affairs.

The islands are uninhabited but Indonesian fishing boats, which have traditionally plied the area, fish within the Territory and land to collect water in accordance with an agreement between the governments of Australia and Indonesia. An automatic weather station on West Ashmore Island (completed in Sept. 1962) supplies the Commonwealth Meteorological Bureau with regular reports.

Periodic visits are made to the islands by ships of the Royal Australian Navy, and aircraft of the Royal Australian Air Force make aerial surveys of the islands and neighbouring waters.

TERRITORY OF CORAL SEA ISLANDS. The Territory was created on 30 Sept. 1969 and consists of several small islands and reefs in the Pacific ocean, off the coast of Queensland. The sole inhabitants are 3 meteorologists on Willis Island. There is an unmanned automatic weather station on Cato Island.

Books of Reference

The Northern Territory: Annual Report. Dept. of Territories, Canberra, from 1911. Dept. of the Interior, Canberra, from 1966–67. Dept. of Northern Territory, from 1972
Australian Territories, Dept. of Territories, Canberra, 1960 to 1973. Dept. of Special Minister of State, Canberra, 1973–75. Department of Administrative Services, 1976
Northern Territory Statistical Summary. Australian Bureau of Statistics, Canberra, from 1960
Prospects of Agriculture in the Northern Territory. Dept. of Territories, Canberra, 1961
Northern Territory Scientific Liaison Conference, Darwin, 1961, *Conference Papers.* Melbourne, 1961
Holmes, J. M., *Australia's Open North.* Sydney, 1963
Lockwood, D. W., *Fair Dinkum.* London, 1960
Polisheck, N., *Life on the Daly River.* London, 1961

NEW SOUTH WALES

HISTORY. New South Wales became a British possession in 1770; the first settlement was established at Port Jackson in 1788; a partially elective Council was established in 1843, and responsible government in 1856. New South Wales federated with the other Australian states to form the Commonwealth of Australia in 1901.

AREA AND POPULATION. New South Wales is situated between the 28th and 38th parallels of S. lat. and 141st and 154th meridians of E. long., and comprises 309,433 sq. miles (801,428 sq. km), inclusive of Lord Howe Island, 6 sq. miles (17 sq. km), but exclusive of the Australian Capital Territory (911 sq. miles, 2,359 sq. km) at Canberra and 28 sq. miles (73 sq. km), at Jervis Bay.

Lord Howe Island, 31° 33′ 4″ S., 159° 4′ 26″ E., a dependency of New South Wales, situated about 702 km north-east of Sydney; area, 1,656 hectares, of which only about 120 hectares are arable; population (30 June 1979), 250. The island, which was discovered in 1788, is of volcanic origin. Mount Gower, the highest point, reaches a height of 866 metres.

A Board at Sydney and an elected Island Advisory Committee manage the affairs of the island and supervise the Kentia palm-seed industry.

Census population of New South Wales (includes full-blood Aboriginals from 1966):

	Males	Females	Persons	Population per sq. km	Average annual increase % since previous census
1881	410,211	339,614	749,825	1	4·07
1891	609,666	517,471	1,127,137	1	4·16
1901	710,264	645,091	1,355,355	2	1·86
1911	857,698	789,036	1,646,734	2	1·97
1921	1,071,501	1,028,870	2,100,371	3	2·46
1933	1,318,471	1,282,376	2,600,847	3	1·76

	Males	Females	Persons	Population per sq. km	Average annual increase % since previous census
1947	1,492,211	1,492,627	2,984,838	4	0·99
1954	1,720,860	1,702,669	3,423,529	4	1·98
1961	1,972,909	1,944,104	3,917,013	5	1·94
1966	2,126,652	2,111,249	4,237,901	5	1·58
1971	2,349,600	2,329,800	4,679,400	6	...
1976	2,455,800	2,458,400	4,914,300	6	0·98

At 30 June 1976 the census population (adjusted for under-enumeration) of New South Wales was 4,914,300 (1979, estimate, 5,078,500). Sydney (Statistical Division), 3,094,750 (3,193,300); Newcastle (Statistical District), 370,450 (379,800); Wollongong (Statistical District), 218,850 (223,950). Population of principal country municipalities: Albury, 34,100 (36,600); Armidale, 20,550 (21,150; Bathurst,[1] 19,300 (22,600); Broken Hill, 28,850 (28,600); Casino, 10,250 (10,600); Dubbo, 21,050 (22,850); Goulburn, 22,650 (23,100); Grafton, 17,250 (17,450); Lismore,[1] 23,050 (31,900); Lithgow, Greater,[1] 12,900 (19,850); Orange,[1] 26,500 (30,650); Port Macquarie, 14,100 (16,000); Queanbeyan, 19,750 (20,100); Tamworth, 30,700 (32,650); Taree, 13,450 (14,400); Wagga Wagga, 35,600 (38,150).

[1] As a result of boundary changes proclaimed since 1976 these areas are not comparable.

Vital statistics for calendar years:

	Live births	Marriages	Divorces	Deaths (excluding still-births)	Infantile mortality per 1,000 live births	Estimated net migration
1976	78,492	38,487	22,147	42,122	14·7	800
1977	77,996	36,159	15,781	40,380	12·2	8,700
1978	77,773	35,904	13,797	40,394	12·9	26,600
1979	77,134	36,906	12,606	38,817	11·4	29,400

The annual rates per 1,000 of mean population in 1979 were: Births, 15·19; deaths, 7·65; marriages, 7·27

CONSTITUTION AND GOVERNMENT. Within the State there are three levels of government: the Commonwealth Government, with authority derived from a written constitution; the State Government with residual powers; the local government authorities with powers based upon a State Act of Parliament, operating within incorporated areas extending over seven-eighths of the State.

The Constitution of New South Wales is drawn from several diverse sources; certain Imperial statutes such as the Colonial Laws Validity Act (1865) and the Commonwealth of Australia Constitution Act (1900); the Australian States Constitution Act (1907); the Letters Patent and the Instructions to the Governor; an element of inherited English law; amendments to the Commonwealth of Australia Constitution Act; the State Constitution Act and certain other State Statutes; numerous legal decisions; and a large amount of English and local convention.

The Parliament of New South Wales may legislate for the peace, welfare and good government of the State in all matters not specifically reserved to the Commonwealth Government.

The State Legislature consists of the Sovereign, represented by the Governor, and two Houses of Parliament, the Legislative Council (upper house) and the Legislative Assembly (lower house).

Under legislation passed in 1978, the Legislative Council is to consist of 45 members elected by popular vote for a term of 9 years, with 15 members retiring every 3 years at the same time as the Legislative Assembly elections.

The President has an annual salary (1980) of $A31,407; the Leader of the Opposition, $A31,135; the Chairman of Committees, the Deputy Leader of the Government (if not a Minister) and the Deputy Leader of the Opposition (when a leader of a party), $A19,210 each; the Deputy Leader of the Opposition (when not a leader of a party) and Government and Opposition Whips, $A17,435 each. The President is paid an annual expense allowance of $A3,866; the Leader of the Opposition,

$A3,541; the Chairman of Committees, the Deputy Leader of the Government (if not a Minister) and the Deputy Leader of the Opposition (when a leader of a party), $A2,125 each; the Deputy Leader of the Opposition (when not a leader of a party) and Government and Opposition Whips, $A1,003 each. Other members who are not Ministers receive an annual salary of $A14,985. All members receive an annual electoral allowance of $A5,159. Special expenses allowances (ranging from $A2,871 to $A3,587) are paid to members who are not Ministers and reside in outlying electorates.

The Legislative Assembly has 99 members elected by popular vote for a period of 3 years. Voting is compulsory. British subjects above 18 years of age, having resided 6 months in Australia, 3 months in the State and 1 month in any one electoral district, are eligible for enrolment as electors. Women were enfranchised in 1902. Salaries are adjusted annually, and those given are for 1980.

The Speaker of the Legislative Assembly and the Leader of the Opposition receive a salary of $A42,964 each; the Chairman of Committees and the Deputy Leader of the Opposition, $A31,135 each; Government and Opposition Whips, $A29,059 each. The Speaker and the Leader of the Opposition also receive an expense allowance of $A6,444 each; the Chairman of Committees and the Deputy Leader of the Opposition, $A3,541 each; Government and Opposition Whips, $A1,672 each. Members who are not Ministers receive an annual salary of $A24,975. All members receive an annual electoral allowance ranging from $A8,599 to $A13,538 according to the location of their constituencies.

The Legislative Assembly, elected on 7 Oct. 1978, consisted in Oct. 1980 of the following parties: Labor, 62; Liberal and Country Party, 32; Independent, 1.

The executive is in the hands of a Governor, appointed by the Crown, and an Executive Council consisting of members of the Cabinet. Ministers receive the following annual salaries: Premier, $A54,546; Deputy Premier, $A48,877; the Leader of the Government in the Legislative Council, $A49,465; other Ministers, $A45,968. Ministers also receive an expense allowance (Premier, $A13,793; Deputy Premier, $A6,896; other Ministers, $A6,444 each). Ministers also receive an electoral allowance ranging from $A8,599 to $A13,538 to members of the Legislative Assembly, according to the location of their electorate; and $A5,159 to each member of the Legislative Council.

Governor: Sir Roden Cutler, VC, KCMG, KCVO, CBE, KStJ (sworn in 20 Jan. 1966).

The Labor Party Cabinet, in Oct. 1980, was as follows:

Premier and Treasurer: The Hon. N. K. Wran, QC, MP.
Deputy Premier, Minister for Public Works and Minister for Ports: The Hon. L. J. Ferguson, MP. *Minister for Transport:* The Hon. P. F. Cox, MP. *Attorney-General and Minister of Justice:* The Hon. F. J. Walker, LLM, MP. *Minister for Industrial Relations and Minister for Energy:* The Hon. P. D. Hills, MP. *Minister for Planning and Environment:* The Hon. E. L. Bedford, BA, MP. *Minister for Agriculture:* The Hon. J. R. Hallam, MLC. *Minister for Education and Vice-President of the Executive Council:* The Hon. D. P. Landa, LLB, MLC. *Minister for Local Government and Minister for Roads:* The Hon H. F. Jensen, MP. *Minister for Lands, Minister for Forests and Minister for Water Resources:* The Hon. A. R. L. Gordon, MP. *Minister for Health:* The Hon. K. J. Stewart, MP. *Minister for Consumer Affairs:* The Hon. S. D. Einfeld, MP. *Minister for Mineral Resources and Minister for Technology:* The Hon. R. J. Mulock, LLB, MP. *Minister for Sport and Recreation, Minister for Tourism and Assistant Treasurer:* The Hon. K. G. Booth, MP. *Minister for Youth and Community Services:* The Hon. R. F. Jackson, MP. *Minister for Corrective Services:* The Hon. W. H. Haigh, MP. *Minister for Industrial Development and Minister for Decentralization:* The Hon. Donald Day, MP. *Minister for Police and Minister for Services:* The Hon. W. F. Crabtree, MP. *Minister for Housing, Minister for Co-operative Societies and Assistant Minister for Transport:* The Hon. T. W. Sheahan, BA, LLB, MP.

Agent-General in London: Hon. J. B. Renshaw (66 Strand, WC2N 5LZ).

Local Government. A system of local government extends over most of the State, including the whole of the Eastern and Central land divisions and more than two-thirds of the sparsely populated Western division. At 30 June 1980 there were 80 municipalities, and 119 corporate bodies called shires. A number of the municipalities and shires have combined to form 43 county councils, which administer electricity or water supply undertakings or render other services of common benefit.

ECONOMY

Budget. State Consolidated Revenue Fund: statement of receipts and payments (in $A1,000) for financial years ending 30 June:

	1976–77	1977–78	1978–79	1979–80
Revenue	2,941,923	3,296,072	3,569,625	4,089,282
Working Expenditure	2,714,484	3,033,827	3,293,933	3,791,995
Debt Charges	224,535	260,367	275,388	301,746
Total	2,939,020	3,294,195	3,569,321	4,093,740
Surplus/deficit	+2,903	+1,877	+304	−4,458

State Government revenue in 1979–80 included (in $A1,000) receipts from the Commonwealth Government of 1,858,644; namely, towards public debt charges, 5,835; general financial assistance, 1,663,466; health, etc., 23,773; education, 141,022; other purposes, 24,548. State Government expenditure in 1979–80 included (in $A1,000) expenditure on education, 1,434,839; health etc., 615,233; law, order and public safety, 424,621; state resources, 277,350, and social amelioration, 244,950.

Public Debt. In terms of the financial agreement between the Commonwealth and State Governments, the Commonwealth Government has assumed responsibility for debts of the Australian States, and contributes towards the interest thereon and sinking funds established for redemption of the debts. Loans for the States are raised by the Commonwealth Government in accordance with decisions of the Australian Loan Council.

The public debt of New South Wales at 30 June 1980 (overseas loans converted to Australian currency equivalent at current rates of exchange) comprised the following (in $A1,000): Repayable in Australia, 4,630,824; in London, 26,548; in New York, 7,299; in Canada, 1,549; in Netherlands, 622. Interest liability for 1979–80 amounted (in $A1,000) to 385,743, of which 2,088 was in respect of the external debt. Contributions to the sinking fund for New South Wales debt, 65,566, include 12,580 contributed by the Commonwealth Government. The net cost of securities redeemed in the year was 69,530.

Banking. There were 10 trading banks operating in New South Wales at 30 June 1980, including the Commonwealth Trading Bank and Rural Bank (Government banks) and 1 New Zealand bank. The trading bank business is transacted chiefly by the Commonwealth Trading Bank and 6 private banks, all of which have their head offices in Australia. At 30 June 1980 the 10 banks operated 1,843 branches and 316 agencies in New South Wales.

The weekly average amount of deposits held in New South Wales by the 10 banks was $A11,667·3m. in June 1980, consisting of $A7,428·8m. bearing interest and $A4,238·5m. not bearing interest. Bank advances, overdrafts, bills discounted, etc., amounted to $A8,777·3m. A statement of other assets and liabilities of the banks in New South Wales is of little significance, as banking business is conducted on an Australia-wide basis.

Savings bank deposits at the end of June 1980 amounted to $A6,124m., representing $A1,194 per head of population.

ENERGY AND NATURAL RESOURCES

Minerals. New South Wales contains extensive mineral deposits. The most important minerals mined are: Coal (which accounts for 65% of the value of the State's mineral production); silver–lead–zinc (17%); construction materials (sand, gravel, stone, etc., 9%); and mineral sands (rutile, zircon etc., 3%). At 30 June 1979, there were 527 mining establishments with an average employment of 25,293. During 1978–79, wages and salaries paid were \$A424m., and value added was \$A1,050m. Mine production of coal and metallic minerals (gross content) is shown below:

	1976–77	1977–78	1978–79	1979–80
Antimony (tonnes)	1,572	1,486	1,588	1,413
Cadmium (tonnes)	975	953	1,053	1,208
Coal (tonnes)	45,985,838	49,534,333	50,517,079	48,973,309
Cobalt (tonnes)	109	108	86	87
Copper (tonnes)	10,788	12,285	17,675	19,078
Gold (grammes)	473,897	380,281	468,783	511,042
Lead (tonnes)	225,134	232,029	244,665	235,361
Silver (grammes)	269,337,390	278,613,775	314,924,620	288,961,969
Sulphur (tonnes)	210,512	211,609	223,952	242,706
Tin (tonnes)	1,413	2,209	2,588	2,557
Titanium dioxide (tonnes)	180,270	144,779	142,192	108,477
Zinc (tonnes)	282,722	282,252	297,454	320,617
Zircon (tonnes)	171,900	131,337	141,275	111,084

The value of output in mining and quarrying in 1978–79 was \$A1,407,535,529.

Land settlement. The total area of land alienated, virtually alienated or in process of alienation from the Crown on 30 June 1979 was 28,790,584 hectares, exclusive of the Australian Capital Territory; 40,031,284 hectares (including 30,424,904 hectares of the Western Division) were held under perpetual lease from the Crown; 2,644,269 hectares under the Crown leasehold tenures, and the total area of land neither alienated nor leased (including roads, reserves for public purposes, etc.) was 8,676,642 hectares.

Agriculture. The area under cultivation in New South Wales during 3 years (ended 31 March) and the principal crops (in tonnes) produced were as follows:

	1977	1978	1979
Hectares under cultivation	4,743,278	5,142,211	5,253,281
Value (farm) of all crops	\$A762m.	\$A717m.	\$A1,231m.

	1977		1978		1979	
Principal crops	Hectares	Produce	Hectares	Produce	Hectares	Produce
Wheat { Grain	3,115,757	5,141,000	3,377,413	3,846,187	3,162,108	6,640,401
Wheat { Hay	18,605	51,588	20,007	42,156	11,989	38,350
Maize Grain	19,659	65,387	15,964	48,392	15,216	55,398
Barley { Grain	417,066	571,279	485,576	445,993	467,638	675,937
Barley { Hay	1,973	4,521	1,478	3,158	1,438	3,382
Oats { Grain	249,558	307,112	288,407	241,815	431,466	594,251
Oats { Hay	25,874	70,892	27,044	60,081	28,474	84,300
Potatoes	8,399	111,861	8,694	114,777	8,256	124,156
Lucerne (hay)	101,641	394,628	69,280	241,550	51,090	227,213
Tobacco	937	1,622	780	1,280	768	1,366
Rice	89,201	518,960	88,397	476,312	105,864	674,440
Cotton	24,982	61,173	30,600	101,075	35,400	115,664

In 1978–79, 14,052 hectares of sugar-cane were cut for crushing, the yield being 1,321,537 tonnes. The total area under grapes was 14,604 (including 972 not bearing) hectares; the production of table grapes was 5,352 tonnes; of wine, 78,503,000 litres; of dried vine fruits, 9,747 tonnes.

In 1978–79, 5,301 hectares of banana plantations; yield from 4,698 hectares, 62,530 tonnes; there were 25,199 hectares of orchard fruit.

At 31 March 1979 the State had 48·4m. sheep and lambs, 6,484,204 cattle and 758,625 pigs. The production of wool in 1978–79 was 219·4m. kg (greasy). In the year ended 30 June 1980 production of butter was 3,194,177 kg; cheese, 13,024,151 kg, and bacon and ham, 24,147,027 kg.

Forestry. The estimated area of Crown and private lands is 16·3m. hectares. The total area of State forests amounts to 3·3m hectares, and 353,761 hectares have been set apart as timber reserves.

The revenue from royalties, licences, etc., amounted in the year ended June 1979 to $A17,435,000. At 30 June 1979 there were 657 saw-mills, employing 6,867 persons. The value of forestry production for 1978–79 was $A81·4m.

INDUSTRY AND TRADE

Industry. Approximately 25% of the civilian work force in New South Wales is employed in manufacturing industries.

A very wide range of manufacturing activities is undertaken in the Sydney area, and there are large iron and steel works and associated metal fabrication works in operation in proximity to the coalfields at Newcastle and Port Kembla.

The following table shows a summary of manufacturing industries' statistics for 1978–79:

Industry	Estab- lishments[1] (No.)	Employment[2] Males (No.)	Females (No.)	Wages and salaries[3] ($A1m.)	Value added ($A1m.)
Food, beverages and tobacco	955	44,909	16,391	663·2	1,336·1
Textiles	224	6,094	4,848	108·8	212·4
Clothing and footwear	774	5,576	20,820	215·4	348·6
Wood, wood products and furniture	1,280	21,469	3,980	230·9	432·8
Paper, paper products, printing and publishing	1,102	25,822	10,995	414·5	748·6
Chemical, petroleum and coal products	404	20,545	9,376	375·3	959·1
Non-metallic mineral products	548	14,450	1,873	199·4	390·3
Basic metal products	206	49,324	3,430	681·4	1,248·2
Fabricated metal products	1,537	31,705	7,905	398·0	702·8
Transport equipment	397	34,025	3,595	408·4	597·3
Other machinery and equipment	1,577	51,645	19,463	742·5	1,232·7
Miscellaneous manufacturing	799	15,790	9,197	250·8	465·7
Total manufacturing	9,803	321,354	111,873	4,688·6	8,674·6

[1] Operating at 30 June 1979. Excludes single-establishment manufacturing enterprises with less than 4 persons employed.
[2] Persons employed—average over whole year, including working proprietors.
[3] Excludes drawings of working proprietors.

Some of the principal articles manufactured in 1979–80 were:

Article	Quantity	Article	Quantity
Flour (1,000 tonnes)	484	Raw steel (1,000 tonnes)	6,615
Footwear (1,000 prs)	4,947	Electric motors (1,000)	1,937
Cloth: cotton, wool, rayon, syn- thetic (1,000 sq. metres)	73,434	Claybricks (1m.)	887
		Electricity (1m. kwh.)	37,865
Pig-iron (1,000 tonnes)	5,564		

During 1979–80 the value of all building jobs commenced in New South Wales was $A2,556m. (of which jobs valued at $A357m. were being built for government ownership), jobs completed were valued at $A2,531m. ($A484m. for government ownership), and jobs under construction at the end of the period were valued at $A2,047m. ($A630m. for government ownership).

Labour. Two systems of industrial arbitration and conciliation for the adjustment of industrial relations between employers and employees are in operation—the State system which operates within the territorial limits of the State, and the Commonwealth system, which applies to industrial disputes extending beyond State borders.

The industrial tribunals are authorized to fix minimum rates of wages and other conditions of employment. Their awards may be enforced by law, as may be industrial agreements between employers and organizations of employees, when registered.

The principal State tribunal is the Industrial Commission of New South Wales, composed of judges. The Commission is empowered to exercise all the arbitration and conciliation powers conferred on subsidiary tribunals, and has in addition authority to determine any widely defined 'industrial matter', to adjudicate in case of illegal strikes and lockouts, etc., to investigate union ballots when irregularities are alleged and to hear appeals from subsidiary tribunals. Subsidiary tribunals are Conciliation Committees for various industries, each having an equal number representing employers and employees and a Conciliation Commissioner as chairman.

The chief industrial tribunals of the Commonwealth are the Industrial Division of the Federal Court of Australia, composed of judges, and the Australian Conciliation and Arbitration Commission, composed of presidential members, and commissioners.

Most State awards and agreements prescribe a basic wage and, for each industry, margins assessed on skill, etc. Since May 1974, the State Industrial Commission has also specified a minimum wage in line with Commonwealth awards. In July 1980, the minimum wage payable in Sydney for a full week's work by an adult male or female was $A136 under both State and Commonwealth awards.

A standard working week of 40 hours is prescribed for employees in most industries. Overtime is permitted under prescribed conditions.

Trade Unions. Registration of trade unions is effected under the New South Wales Trade Union Act, 1881, which follows substantially the Trade Union Acts of 1871 and 1876 of England. Registration confers a quasi-corporate existence with power to hold property, to sue and be sued, etc., and the various classes of employees covered by the union are required to be prescribed by the constitution of the union. For the purpose of bringing an industry under the review of the State industrial tribunals, or participating in proceedings relating to disputes before Commonwealth tribunals, employees and employers must be registered as industrial unions, under State or Commonwealth industrial legislation respectively.

Commerce. The external commerce of New South Wales, exclusive of interstate trade, is included in the statement of the commerce of Australia (*see* pp. 110–12). The overseas commerce of the State is given in $A1,000 ending 30 June:

	Imports	Exports[1]		Imports	Exports[1]
1974–75	3,494,781	1,979,005	1977–78	4,634,833	3,107,347
1975–76	3,451,189	2,253,660	1978–79	5,763,757	3,758,382
1976–77	4,278,450	2,718,362	1979–80	6,703,818	4,556,353

[1] Includes non-Australian produce ($A352m. in 1979–80).

The main exports from New South Wales of Australian produce in 1979–80 were coal (17%), cereal grains (13·4%), wool (9·1%), iron and steel (9·1%), meat (9%), machinery (5·5%), non-ferrous metals (4·4%). Principal imports were machinery and transport equipment (34·7%), chemicals (11·2%), petroleum and petroleum products (7·3%), textiles (5·7%), paper and paperboard (3%), photographic apparatus and optical goods (2·5%), precision instruments and apparatus (2·2%).

Principal destinations of all exports from New South Wales in 1979–80 were Japan (22%), EEC countries (14·2%), New Zealand (7·9%), USA (5%), Papua New Guinea (4·3%), China (3·6%). Major sources of supply were EEC countries (24·6%), USA (24·1%), Japan (16%), Saudi Arabia (4·2%) and New Zealand (3·7%).

COMMUNICATIONS

Roads. There are 204,571 km of roads and streets in New South Wales, comprising 424 km cement concrete, 7,462 km bituminous concrete, 62,595 km other bitumen surface, 66,413 km gravel, 39,188 km earth formed and 28,490 km natural surface. The bridge across Sydney Harbour is one of the largest arch bridges in the world.

The principal bus services in Sydney and Newcastle are operated by the State Government.

The number of registered motor vehicles (excluding tractors and trailers) on 30 June 1980 was 2,510,600, including 1,945,500 cars and station wagons, 150,700 utilities, 134,800 panel vans, 165,900 trucks, 13,500 buses and 100,200 motor cycles.

Railways. On 30 June 1979, 9,773 km of government railway were open. The revenue in 1979–80 was \$A507m.; the expenditure from revenue, \$A835m.; the number of passengers carried, 183m. Also open for traffic are 324 km of Victorian Government railways which extend over the border; 68 km of private railways (mainly in mining districts) and 47 km of Commonwealth Government-owned track.

Aviation. Sydney is the major airport in New South Wales and Australia's principal international air terminal. During the year ended 31 Dec. 1978 aircraft movement at Sydney totalled 108,390. Passengers totalled 5,401,223 on domestic services and 1,919,631 on international services. Freight handled on domestic and international services was 53,440 tonnes and 73,093 tonnes respectively.

Shipping. The vessels engaged in the overseas trade which entered the ports of New South Wales in 1978–79 numbered 2,501; net tonnage, 25,853,492; the clearances were 2,517 vessels, 25,988,245 tons. Sydney Harbour is the principal port of Australia. The number of overseas vessels which entered in 1978–79 was 1,558; net tonnage, 13·2m.

JUSTICE, RELIGION, EDUCATION AND WELFARE

Justice. Legal processes may be carried on in Lower or Magistrates' Courts, or in the Higher Courts presided over by judges. There is also an appellate jurisdiction. Persons charged with the more serious crimes must be tried before the Higher Courts.

Children's Courts have been established with the object of removing children as far as possible from the atmosphere of a public court. There are also a number of tribunals exercising special jurisdiction, e.g., the Industrial Commission and the Workers' Compensation Commission.

In 1978 there were 3,069 distinct persons convicted at the Higher Courts. At 30 June 1978 there were 3,437 persons (including 100 females) held under sentence in prison.

Religion. There is no established church in New South Wales, and freedom of worship is accorded to all.

The following table shows the statistics of the religious denominations in New South Wales at the census, and of ministers of religion registered for the celebration of marriages, in 1976:

Denomination	Ministers	Adherents	Denomination	Ministers	Adherents
Church of England	888	1,538,786	Hebrew	24	21,700
Roman Catholic	1,719	1,314,374	Moslem	1	22,206
Presbyterian	353	310,200	Other Non-Christian	9	10,055
Methodist	360	271,814	Others	...	852,206[1]
Baptist	285	57,866			
Lutheran	44	30,535	Total	4,721	4,777,105
Other Christian	1,038	347,365			

[1] Includes 309,195 'no religion' and 528,634 'religion not stated' (this is not a compulsory question in the census schedule).

Education. The State maintains a system of primary and secondary education, and attendance at school is compulsory from 6 to 15 years of age. In all state schools education is free. Private schools are subject to State inspection.

In Aug. 1979 there were 2,221 state schools, comprising 1,689 primary and infant schools, 67 combined primary and secondary schools, 353 secondary schools and 112 special-purpose schools. In Aug. 1979 the effective enrolment was 807,761 children, comprising 516,675 receiving primary instruction and 291,086 receiving secondary instruction. There were, in 1979, 45,626 full-time teachers.

In Aug. 1979 there were 794 private schools with 10,602 full-time teachers and an effective enrolment of 224,941 pupils, of which 611 were Roman Catholic schools, having 8,282 teachers and 187,587 scholars. Church of England schools numbered 33 with 903 teachers and 15,454 scholars; other denominational schools, 48; teachers, 738; pupils, 12,749; non-denominational schools, 102; teachers, 679, and scholars, 9,151.

The University of Sydney, founded in 1850, in 1979 had 17,345 students (including

7,179 women). There are 6 colleges providing residential facilities at the university.

The University of New England at Armidale, previously affiliated with the University of Sydney, was incorporated on 1 Feb. 1954, and in 1979 had 8,383 students (including 3,720 women).

The University of New South Wales was established by the State Government in 1949. Enrolments in 1979 numbered 18,466 (including 5,571 women). There are 7 colleges providing residential facilities at the university. The University of Newcastle, previously affiliated with the University of New South Wales, was granted autonomy from 1 Jan. 1965, and in 1979 had 4,364 students (including 1,629 women). The University of Wollongong, also previously associated with the University of New South Wales, became autonomous on 1 Jan. 1975, and in 1979 had 2,797 students (including 916 women). The Macquarie University in Sydney, established on 12 June 1964, in 1979 had 10,493 students (including 4,994 women).

Colleges of Advanced Education were first established in 1971 to provide tertiary training with a vocational emphasis. In 1979 there were 36,741 students (including 16,309 part-time students) enrolled at 24 colleges.

Post-school technical and further education is provided at State technical colleges, principally in the evening. Students enrolled in 1979 totalled 275,644 (including 17,779 correspondence students).

State Government expenditure (including loan expenditure) on education in 1978–79 was \$A1,246·2m.

Social Welfare. The Commonwealth Government makes provision for social benefits, such as age and invalid pensions, widows' pensions, family allowances, health benefits, and unemployment and sickness benefits.

The number of age and invalid pensions (including wives' pensions) current in New South Wales on 30 June 1980 was: Age, 495,944 (males, 160,227; females, 335,717; invalid, 111,948 (males, 61,209; females, 50,739). Expenditure for the year ended 30 June 1980 was \$A1,309·17m. for age pensions and \$A314,725,000 for invalid pensions.

Commonwealth Government widows' pensions current in New South Wales at 30 June 1980 numbered 63,240, the expenditure for 1979–80, \$A219,261,000.

Under the Family Allowance scheme, which commenced on 15 June 1976, payments to families and approved institutions for children under 16 years and full-time students under 25 years (1,445,415 such children or students) during 1979–80 amounted to \$A372·1m.

Unemployment, sickness and special benefits commenced on 1 July 1945. During the year 1979–80 claims totalling \$A419m. were paid in New South Wales. At 30 June 1980 unemployment benefit was being paid to 106,256 persons, and sickness and special benefits to 24,574 persons.

Direct State social welfare services are limited, for the most part, to the assistance of persons not eligible for Commonwealth Government benefit and the provision of certain forms of assistance not available from the Commonwealth Government. The State also subsidizes many approved services for indigent persons. During 1979–80, expenditure on social amelioration and war obligations was \$A247,022,000.

Books of Reference

Statistical Information: The NSW Government Statistician's Office was established in 1886, and in 1957 was integrated with the Commonwealth Bureau of Census and Statistics (now called the Australian Bureau of Statistics). *Deputy Commonwealth Statistician*: J. E. Dulley. Its principal publications are:

Official Year Book of New South Wales (1886/87–1900/01 under the title *Wealth and Progress of NSW*): latest issue, 1979

New South Wales Handbook of Local Statistics: latest issue, 1980

New South Wales Principal Subject Bulletins (previously published under the title *Statistical Register* (since 1858); latest issue of separate bulletins, 1978–79 and 1979

New South Wales Pocket Year Book. Published since 1913; latest issue, 1980

Monthly Summary of Statistics. Published since May 1931

New South Wales in Brief. 1980

New South Wales Dept. of Tourism, *New South Wales—Australia*. Sydney, 1977

New South Wales Dept. of Decentralization and Development, *New South Wales Handbook for Industrialists.* 1977
State Planning Authority, *Sydney Region, 1970–2000: Outline Plan.* Sydney, 1968
State Planning Authority, *Hunter Region, Growth and Change: Prelude to a Plan.* Sydney, 1972
New South Wales Planning and Environment Commission, *Gosford-Wyong: Structure Plan.* Sydney, 1975
State Planning Authority, *The New Cities of Campbelltown, Camden, Appin: Structure Plan.* Sydney, 1973

State Library: The State Library of NSW, Macquarie St., Sydney. *State Librarian:* R. F. Doust, BA, M.Lib, FLAA.

QUEENSLAND

AREA AND POPULATION. Queensland comprises the whole north-eastern portion of the Australian continent, including the adjacent islands in the Pacific Ocean and in the Gulf of Carpentaria. Estimated area 1,727,000 sq. km.

The increase in the population as shown by the censuses since 1901 has been as follows:

	Population at census date			Intercensal increase	
Year	Males	Females	Total	Numerical	Rate per annum %
1901	277,003	221,126	498,129	—	—
1911	329,506	276,307	605,813	107,684	1·98
1921	398,969	357,003	755,972	150,159	2·24
1933	497,217	450,317	947,534	191,562	1·86
1947	567,471	538,944	1,106,415	158,881	1·11
1954	676,252	642,007	1,318,259	211,844	2·53
1961	774,579	744,249	1,518,828	200,569	2·04
1966	849,390[1]	824,934[1]	1,674,324[1]	144,857	1·84
1971	921,665[1]	905,400[1]	1,827,065[1]	152,741[1]	1·76[1]
1976	1,024,611[1]	1,012,586[1]	2,037,197[1]	210,132[1]	2·20[1]

[1] Including Aboriginals.

Statistics on birthplaces from the 1976 census are as follows: Australia, 1,771,120 (86·9%); UK, 135,436 (6·6%); other countries, 130,641 (6·4%).
Vital statistics (including Aboriginals) for calendar years:

	Total births	Marriages	Divorces	Deaths
1977	34,935	15,737	7,302	16,415
1978	34,465	15,431	6,111	16,619
1979	35,195	16,082	5,826	16,391

The annual rates per 1,000 population in 1979 were: Marriages, 7·3; births, 16; deaths, 7·5. The infant death rate was 10·9 per 1,000 births.

Brisbane, the capital, had on 30 June 1979 a population of 1,015,200 (Statistical Division). The populations of the other chief towns at the same date were: Gold Coast, 102,500; Townsville, 84,900; Toowoomba, 72,500; Rockhampton, 53,900; Cairns, 36,200; Bundaberg, 32,500; Mount Isa, 26,800; Maryborough, 22,000; Mackay, 21,800; Gladstone, 20,500; Hervey Bay, 12,700; Gympie, 11,300.

CONSTITUTION AND GOVERNMENT. Queensland, formerly a portion of New South Wales, was formed into a separate colony in 1859, and responsible government was conferred. The power of making laws and imposing taxes is vested in a Parliament of one House—the Legislative Assembly, which comprises 82 members, returned from 4 electoral zones for 3 years, elected for single-member constituencies at compulsory ballot. Members are entitled to $A29,630 per annum, with individual electorate allowances for travelling, postage, etc., of from $A7,360 to $A18,990.

At the general election of 12 Nov. 1977 there were 1,209,494 persons registered as qualified to vote under the Elections Act 1915–1976. This Act provides franchise for all males and females, 18 years of age and over, qualified by 6 months' residence in Australia and 3 months in the electoral district.

The Legislative Assembly, following the elections of 12 Nov. 1977, was composed of the following parties: National, 35; Liberal, 24; Australian Labor, 23; total, 82.

Governor of Queensland: Cde Sir James Maxwell Ramsay, KCMG, CBE, DSC (assumed office April 1977).

The Executive Council of Ministers, at 29 July 1980, consists of the following members:

Premier: Johannes Bjelke-Petersen (National). *Treasurer and Deputy Premier:* Llewellyn Roy Edwards (Liberal). *Mines and Energy:* Victor Bruce Sullivan (National). *Labour Relations:* Frederick Alexander Campbell (Liberal). *Health:* Sir William Knox (Liberal). *Lands, Forestry and Water Resources:* Neville Thomas Eric Hewitt (National). *Local Government, Main Roads and Police:* Russell James Hinze (National). *Transport:* Kenneth Burgoyne Tomkins (National). *Education:* Valmond James Bird (National). *Industry and Administrative Services:* Norman Edward Lee (Liberal). *Works and Housing:* Claude Alfred Wharton (National). *Justice and Attorney-General:* William Daniel Lickiss (Liberal). *Survey and Valuation:* John Ward Greenwood (Liberal). *Aboriginal and Island Affairs:* Charles Robert Porter (Liberal). *Welfare:* Samuel Sydney Doumany (Liberal). *Maritime Services and Tourism:* Maxwell David Hooper (National). *Culture, National Parks and Recreation:* Ivan James Gibbs (National). *Primary Industries:* Michael John Ahern (National).

Each Minister has a salary of $A48,700, the Premier receives $A61,880, the Deputy Premier, $A53,070, and the Leader of the Opposition, $A42,030.

Acting Agent-General in London: G. W. Swan (392 Strand, WC2).

Local Government. Provision is made for local government by the subdivision of the State into cities, towns and shires. These are under the management of aldermen or councillors, who are elected by all persons 18 years and over. Local Authorities are charged with the control of all matters of a parochial nature, such as sewerage, cleansing and sanitary services, health services, domestic water supplies, and roads and bridges within their allotted areas. In addition to Government grants and subsidies, Local Authority revenue is derived from general rates, paid by landowners on the unimproved capital value of land, and by charging for some specific services. Loans for most capital works are raised subject to the provisions of the Loan Council.

Shires are mostly rural districts although most contain some urban centres not classed officially as towns.

The number and area of these subdivisions, together with the receipts and expenditure (including receipts and expenditure from loans) for the year ended 30 June 1979, were:

	No.	Area in sq. km	Receipts,[1] $A1,000	Expenditure,[1] $A1,000	Rateable values, $A1,000
City of Brisbane	1	1,220	233,616	234,383	1,645,752
Other Cities	15	43,609	192,887	188,863	1,354,160
Towns	4	1,751	10,453	10,222	61,686
Shires	113	1,680,638	334,619	331,846	1,770,435
Total	133	1,727,218	771,575	765,312	4,832,033

[1] These columns include receipts from loans and loan subsidies of $A164·8m.; expenditures from loans and loan subsidies of $A164·6m.; and the receipts and expenditures of business undertakings (principally water supply, sewerage and transport) which were $A217·3m. and $A214·9m. respectively.

ECONOMY

Budget. Revenue and expenditure of the Consolidated Revenue Fund of Queensland during 5 years ending 30 June (in $A1,000):

	1976–77	1977–78	1978–79	1979–80	1980–81[1]
Revenue	1,610,538	1,815,953	1,947,444	2,206,954	2,511,066
Expenditure	1,611,555	1,816,863	1,946,867	2,207,893	2,511,265

[1] Estimates.

Total funds available to the Queensland Government in 1978–79 were $A2,318·9m., of which Taxation and Federal Government grants amounted to $A2,101·8m. Expenditure from these funds included: Education, $A760·8m.; economic services (roads, electricity, etc.), $A493·4m.; health, $A378·9m.

Revenue and expenditure of Commonwealth Government departments on account of Queensland are not included.

Debt. The gross public debt of the State at par rates of exchange amounted, on 30 June 1980, to $A1,930m. The debt was domiciled as follows (in $A1,000): Australia, 1,924,689; UK, 3,232; USA, 450; Canada, 342; Netherlands, 94; other European countries, 954. The annual interest charge on the public debt at 30 June 1980 was $A148·3m.

Banking. There were 10 trading banks operating in Queensland at 30 June 1980, including the Commonwealth Trading Bank of Australia, the 6 larger Australian trading banks, a Queensland bank with head office in Brisbane, the Bank of New Zealand and the Banque Nationale de Paris. The Commonwealth Trading Bank had 151 branches and 63 agencies; the other banks had 653 branches and 109 agencies in the State. Queensland deposits of all trading banks, including the Commonwealth Trading Bank of Australia, amounted to $A3,934·8m.; and loans, advances and bills discounted in Queensland were $A2,509·2m. At 30 June 1980 savings bank business was conducted in Queensland by 8 banks, the Commonwealth Savings Bank with 165 branches and 1,202 agencies, and 7 other banks with 639 branches and 995 agencies. Depositors' balances amounted to $A2,884·6m. in 3·03m. accounts.

ENERGY AND NATURAL RESOURCES

Electricity. The State Electricity Commission, established in 1938 and under a single Commissioner since 1948, co-ordinates the electricity industry in Queensland.

Electricity generated by the principal stations in the year ended 30 June 1980 was 11,355m. kwh. Natural gas is being used for electric generation at Roma. Black coal was used to generate 94% of the power; hydro-electric stations generated 5%.

Minerals. Principal minerals produced during 1978–79 were: Copper, 173,839 tonnes; coal, 26,507,000 tonnes; lead, 158,000 tonnes; zinc, 128,000 tonnes; silver, 476,217 kg; tin, 2,030 tonnes; gold, 635 kg; bauxite, 8,095,000 tonnes; mineral sands concentrates, 128,000 tonnes; uranium, 680 tonnes. Value of output, at the mine, was $A1,405m. The chief mines are Mount Isa (copper, silver, lead, zinc), Weipa (bauxite), Mount Morgan (copper, gold), Moreton and Bowen Basin (coal), Greenvale (nickel) and Mary Kathleen (uranium).

Land Settlement. Of the total area of the State, 12·8m. hectares had been alienated at 31 Dec. 1978; in process of alienation, under deferred payment system, were 19·22m. hectares, leaving 140·7m. hectares, still the property of the Crown, or 81·5% of the total area. A large proportion of the area is leased for pastoral purposes (97·4m. hectares at 31 Dec. 1978).

In the western portion of the State water is comparatively easily found by sinking artesian bores. At 30 June 1979, 3,388 such bores had been drilled, of which 2,304 were flowing.

Agriculture. Livestock on farms and stations at 31 March 1979 numbered 10·86m. cattle, 13,592,000 sheep and 487,000 pigs. The wool production (greasy) was, in 1978–79, 63·8m. kg, valued at $A127·4m. The total area under crops during 1978–79 was 2,370,039 hectares, 209,216 hectares were irrigated in 1978–79, the principal crops so watered being sugar-cane, fodder crops, vegetables, cereals, tobacco, cotton and fruit.

Crop	Area (hectares)		Yield (tonnes)[1]	
	1977–78	1978–79	1977–78	1978–79
Sugar-cane, crushed	280,449	237,680	22,330,767	20,135,471
Wheat	606,791	746,956	569,234	1,962,235
Maize	28,733	34,122	79,594	111,101
Sorghum	293,145	279,961	503,992	712,908
Barley	200,235	232,462	216,305	583,321
Oats	9,625	30,171	4,820	43,221
Potatoes	5,973	5,857	103,724	114,519
Pumpkins	4,240	4,054	28,185	31,057
Tomatoes	2,852	3,046	37,981	41,094
Peanuts	29,959	36,601	38,295	61,464
Tobacco	4,133	3,792	7,987	8,075
Apples[1]	3,773	3,655	25,225	39,245
Grapes[1]	1,357	1,399	5,618	6,057
Citrus[1]	2,178	2,032	41,484	46,801
Bananas[1]	1,761	1,986	32,194	44,245
Pineapples[1]	3,703	3,885	98,230	104,881
Green fodder[2]	289,200	305,081	...	...
Hay (all kinds)	34,058	32,046	146,060	163,159
Cotton (raw)	10,977	14,442	10,871	14,110

[1] Bearing area only.   [2] Excluding lucerne.

Forestry. A considerable area consists of natural forest, eucalyptus, pine and cabinet woods being the timbers mostly in evidence; a large quantity of ornamental woods are utilized by cabinet makers. The amount of native timber processed in 1978–79 was (in cu. metres): Conifers, 514,000; hardwoods, structural timbers and cabinet woods, 755,000. Forest and timber reservations total 4·2m. hectares (30 June 1979); areas for national parks, 2·7m. hectares. The State Forest Service had planted 120,000 hectares for reforestation and had treated 470,000 hectares for natural regeneration by June 1979. Thinnings from State reforestation areas are used for hardboard and paper pulp.

INDUSTRY AND TRADE

Industry. Approximately one-third of the secondary production of the State is from works processing primary products, the most important being sugar-mills, meat works, butter factories and saw-mills. There are 30 cane-crushing mills, 3 oil refineries, 1 alumina refinery, 2 sugar refineries, 47 meat works (including bacon factories) producing largely for export, 13 butter factories and many saw-mills and plywood and veneer mills. Other industries include engineering works, railway workshops, copper and nickel refining, cement, cardboard and building board manufacture, ammonia and fertilizer works and the production of various items of food, clothing and vehicles, chiefly for local use. In 1978–79 there were 2,886 establishments, with 4 or more workers, employing 91,200 males and 21,759 females, and providing goods and services worth $A6,591m. The value of production (value added in manufacture) was $A2,322m.

The gross value of Queensland primary production, excluding mining (in $A1,000) during 1978–79 amounted to 2,307,411, which included crops, 1,097,281; livestock disposals, 868,396; livestock products, 241,704; forestry, 35,738; fishing, 61,268; hunting, 3,024.

Labour. Of the total population of 2·2m., 927,300 were in employment in Aug. 1980, 138,900 in manufacturing. Industrial wages and conditions are controlled partly by Federal and State authorities. A State Industrial Commission is empowered to determine all industrial matters in relation to employers and employees, to fix minimum wage-rates and other conditions of employment. An Industrial Court hears appeals and decides points of industrial law. The Australian Industrial Court, Conciliation and Arbitration Commission are superior within their jurisdictions. In Queensland most employees (62%) work under State awards; 26% under Federal awards.

Rates of wages for each occupation are prescribed by these courts. The minimum weighted average award wage for adult males was $A180.68 and for adult females $A163.26, at 30 June 1980, while average weekly earnings (including overtime, etc.) were $A240.90 per employed male unit. (Average earnings are calculated on a unit basis, as earnings are not available separately for males and females.) A standard working week of 40 hours is prescribed for most awards.

Trade Unions. Unions both of employees and employers must be registered with the State or Australian Commission. There were 75 employees' and 39 employers' unions registered with the State Commission at 31 Dec. 1979, the former comprising 349,373 and the latter 36,457 members.

Commerce. The overseas commerce of Queensland is included in the statement of the commerce of Australia (*see* pp. 110–12).

Total value of the direct overseas imports and exports of Queensland (in $A1,000) f.o.b. port of shipment for both imports and exports:

	1974–75	1975–76	1976–77	1977–78	1978–79	1979–80
Imports	580,051	634,250	835,771	887,179	1,028,010	1,321,214
Exports	2,007,775	2,322,021	2,815,608	2,821,362	3,285,778 [1]	4,265,101 [1]

[1] State of origin.

In 1979–80 interstate exports totalled $A1,589·6m. and imports $A3,282m. The chief exports overseas are minerals including alumina, coal, meat (preserved or frozen), sugar, wool, cereal grains, copper and lead, and manufactured goods. Principal overseas imports are machinery, motor vehicles, mineral fuels (including lubricants, etc.), chemicals and manufactured goods classified by material. Chief sources of imports in 1979–80 were Japan ($A278·1m.), USA ($A277·9m.), Singapore ($A104·4m.); exports went chiefly to Japan ($A1,493·9m.), USA ($A631·7m.), UK ($A444·3m.), EEC, excluding UK ($A407·7m.).

COMMUNICATIONS

Roads. At 30 June 1979 there were 160,327 km of roads; of these, 134,586 km were formed roads, of which 45,348 km were surfaced with concrete sealed pavement.

At 30 June 1979 motor vehicles registered in Queensland totalled 1,183,400, comprising 835,200 cars and station wagons, 153,400 utilities, 55,500 panel vans, 4,800 buses, 55,500 trucks and 75,600 motor cycles.

Railways. Practically all the railways are owned by the State Government. Total length of line at 30 June 1979 was 9,789 km. In 1978–79, 27,275,000 passengers and 36·5m. tonnes of goods and livestock were carried.

Aviation. Queensland is well served with a network of air services, with overseas and interstate connexions. Subsidiary companies provide planes for taxi and charter work, and the Flying Doctor Service operates throughout western Queensland.

Shipping. In 1978–79, 2,029 vessels totalling 21·7m. net tons entered Queensland ports. Cargo discharged was 2·26m. tonnes and 0·71m. cu. metres, and cargo shipped was 30·8m. tonnes and 0·1m. cu. metres.

Broadcasting. At 30 June 1979, 52 broadcasting and 43 television stations were in operation throughout Queensland.

JUSTICE, RELIGION, EDUCATION AND WELFARE

Justice. Justice is administered by a Supreme Court, District Courts, Magistrates' Courts and Children's Courts. The Supreme Court comprises a Chief Justice, a senior puisne judge and 13 puisne judges; the District Court, 17 district court judges. Stipendiary magistrates preside over the Lower Courts, except in the smaller centres, where justices of the peace officiate. A parole board may recommend prisoners for release.

The total number of persons convicted of serious offences by the superior courts in 1978–79 was 946; the summary convictions in lower courts (including cases of bail estreated and committals to higher courts for sentence or trial) numbered 120,664. There were, at 30 June 1979, 5 prisons, 2 gaols for short-term prisoners, 2 prison farms conducted on the honour system and 1 prison for mentally-ill prisoners, with 1,697 male and 43 female prisoners. The total police force, including policewomen and 3 native trackers, was 4,135 at 30 June 1979.

Religion. There is no State Church. Membership, census 1976: Church of England, 560,874; Roman Catholic and Catholic (not further defined), 494,345; Methodist, 179,345; Presbyterian, 179,076; Lutheran, 46,214; Baptist, 29,919; other Christian, 135,989; Muslim, 1,717; Hebrew, 1,530; all others (including not stated and no religion), 408,188.

Education. Education is compulsory between the ages of 6 and 15 years. Education is free in State primary and high schools. Expenditure on education, including Loan Fund for 1978–79, net of certain receipts, was $A761m. At Aug. 1979 there were 1,114 state primary schools (including 12 schools administered by the Department of Aboriginal and Islanders Advancement, 55 special schools and 1 correspondence school), with 11,859 teachers and enrolment of 243,849 scholars. Secondary education was provided during 1979 by 134 state high schools, 1 correspondence school and 85 primary schools with secondary students, with 7,613 teachers, the enrolment being 105,333 scholars, and by 8 subsidized grammar schools (3 for boys, 3 for girls, 2 mixed), with 304 teachers and an enrolment of 4,736 secondary and 41 primary pupils. There were, in addition, 327 other, mostly church, schools with 4,700 teachers and an enrolment of 90,086 children.

In 1978, tertiary level course enrolments at colleges of advanced education, including teachers' colleges, and technical colleges were 11,951 full-time and 9,344 part-time. Non-tertiary (vocational, post-secondary) level course enrolments at these establishments and rural training schools numbered 3,595 full-time and 34,268 part-time, including correspondence and apprenticeship students. Full-time teaching staff at the Queensland University and Griffith University at Brisbane and the James Cook University at Townsville comprised, at 30 April 1978, 294 professors, associate professors and readers, 807 senior lecturers, lecturers and teaching registrars; 412 assistant lecturers, demonstrators, tutors and teaching fellows. Students enrolled numbered 21,958. There are 7 denominational and 3 undenominational residential colleges attached to the Queensland University in Brisbane with 4 denominational residential colleges and 1 undenominational hall of residence at the University in Townsville.

Social Welfare. Public hospitals are maintained by State and Federal Government endowment, supplemented by fees from patients not in public wards. Welfare institutions providing shelter and social care for the aged, the handicapped, and children, are maintained or assisted by the State. A maternal and child welfare service is provided throughout the State. Age, invalid, widows', disability and war service pensions, maternity allowances, family allowances, and unemployment and sickness benefits are paid by the Federal Government. Age pensioners in the State at 30 June 1979 numbered 198,017; invalid pensioners, 34,706; disability pensioners, 114,741 (including dependants). Maternity allowance was paid to 34,493 mothers during 1978–79.

There were 21,004 widows' pensions current at 30 June 1979, and at the same date family allowances were being paid to 307,287 families in respect of 646,642 children under 16 years or students aged 16 or more but under 25. In addition, family allowances were paid to 1,672 children and students in institutions.

Housing. In 1979–80, 29,183 new dwellings were completed and 8,955 were being built at 30 June 1980. The Queensland Housing Commission, financed by Federal and State Government loans, builds dwellings for sale and for rental. Building and co-operative housing societies are assisted by Federal and State Government loans.

Books of Reference

Statistical Information: The Statistical Office (345 Ann St., Brisbane) was set up in 1859. *Deputy Commonwealth Statistician:* O. M. May. A *Queensland Official Year Book* was issued in 1901, the annual *ABC of Queensland Statistics* from 1905 to 1936 with exception of 1918 and 1922. Present publications include: *Queensland Year Book*. Annual, from 1937 (omitting 1942, 1943, 1944).—*Queensland Pocket Year Book*. Annual from 1950.—*Monthly Summary of Queensland Statistics*. From Jan. 1961.

Australian and New Zealand Association for the Advancement of Science, *Introducing Queensland*. Brisbane, 1961

Queensland Department of Agriculture and Stock, *The Queensland Agricultural and Pastoral Handbook*. 2 vols. Brisbane, 1962

Australian Sugar Year Book. Brisbane, from 1941

Bolton, G. C., *A Thousand Miles Away! A History of North Queensland to 1920*. Brisbane, 1963

Cilento, R., and Lack, C., *Triumph in the Tropics*. Brisbane, 1959

Greenwood, G., and Laverty, J., *Brisbane 1859–1959*. Sydney, 1959

Greenwood, R. H., *Queensland, City, Coast and Country*. London, 1959

Lack, C., *Queensland, Daughter of the Sun*. Brisbane, 1959.—*Three Decades of Queensland Political History*. Brisbane, 1962

State Library: The State Library of Queensland, William St., Brisbane. *State Librarian:* S. L. Ryan.

SOUTH AUSTRALIA

AREA AND POPULATION. The total area of South Australia is 380,070 sq. miles (984,377 sq. km). The settled part is divided into counties and hundreds. There are 49 counties proclaimed, covering 23m. hectares, of which 19m. hectares are occupied. Outside this area there are extensive pastoral districts, covering 76m. hectares, 46m. of which are under pastoral leases.

Census population (exclusive of full-blood Aboriginals before 1966):

	Males	Females	Total		Males	Females	Total
1891	161,920	153,292	315,212	1947	320,031	326,042	646,073
1901	180,485	177,861	358,346	1961	490,225	479,115	969,340
1911	207,358	201,200	408,558	1966	550,196	544,788	1,094,984
1921	248,267	246,893	495,160	1971	586,051	587,656	1,173,707
1933	290,962	289,987	580,949	1976	620,162	624,594	1,244,756

The number of Aboriginals (as reported on Census schedules) in the State at the Census of 30 June 1976 was 10,174.

Vital statistics for calendar years:

	Births	Marriages	Divorces	Deaths
1977	19,260	10,126	4,422	9,784
1978	18,558	9,800	3,806	9,763
1979	18,478	9,778	3,797	9,661

The infant mortality rate in 1979 was 9 per 1,000 live births.

CONSTITUTION AND GOVERNMENT. South Australia was formed into a British province by letters patent of Feb. 1836, and a partially elective Legislative Council was established in 1851. The present Constitution bears date 24 Oct. 1856. It vests the legislative power in an elected Parliament, consisting of a Legislative Council and a House of Assembly. The former is composed of 22 members. Every 3 years half the members retire, and the resulting vacancies are filled at a general election on the basis of proportional representation with the State as one multi-member electorate. The qualifications of an elector are, to be a natural born or naturalized British subject of at least 18 years of age and to have lived continuously in Australia for at least 6 months, in South Australia for at least 3 months and in the sub-division for which he is enrolled for at least 1 month. War service may substitute for residential qualifications in some cases. By the Constitution Act Amendment Act, 1894, the franchise was extended to women, who voted for the first time at the general election of 25 April 1896. The qualifications for election as a member of both Houses are the same as for an elector. Certain persons are ineligible for election to either House.

The House of Assembly consists of 47 members elected for 3 years, representing single electorates. Election of members of both Houses takes place by preferential secret ballot. Voting is compulsory for those on the Electoral Roll.

The House of Assembly, elected on 15 Sept. 1979, consists of the following members: Liberal Party of Australia, 25; Australian Labor Party, 19; Australian Democrats, 1; National Country Party, 1; Independent, 1. The Legislative Council consists of 11 Liberal Party of Australia, 10 Labor and 1 Australian Democrat members.

Each member of Parliament receives $A25,025 per annum with allowances of $A5,000–18,500 according to location of electorate, a free pass over government railways and superannuation rights. Electors enrolled (Sept. 1979) numbered 825,586.

The executive power is vested in a Governor appointed by the Crown and an Executive Council, consisting of the Governor and the Ministers of the Crown. The Governor has the power to dissolve the House of Assembly but not the Legislative Council unless that Chamber has twice consecutively with an election intervening defeated the same or substantially the same Bill passed in the House of Assembly by an absolute majority.

Governor: Keith D. Seaman, OBE (sworn in 1 Sept. 1977).

The South Australian Liberal Ministry, in Sept. 1979 was as follows:

Premier, Treasurer, Minister of State Development and Minister of Ethnic Affairs: David Oliver Tonkin, MP.

Deputy Premier and Minister of Mines and Energy: Eric Roger Goldsworthy, MP. *Attorney-General and Minister of Corporate Affairs:* Kenneth Trevor Griffin, MLC. *Minister of Industrial Affairs and Minister of Public Works:* Dean Craig Brown, MP. *Minister of Education and Minister of Aboriginal Affairs:* Harold Allison, MP. *Chief Secretary, Minister of Fisheries and Minister of Marine:* William Allan Rodda, MP. *Minister of Local Government, Minister of Housing, Minister of Arts and Minister Assisting the Premier in Ethnic Affairs:* Charles Murray Hill, MLC. *Minister of Agriculture and Minister of Forests:* William Edwin Chapman, MP. *Minister of Environment and Minister of Planning:* David Charles Wotton, MP. *Minister of Transport and Minister of Recreation and Sport:* Michael Minell Wilson, MP. *Minister of Community Welfare and Minister of Consumer Affairs:* John Charles Burdett, MLC. *Minister of Health and Minister of Tourism:* Jennifer Lillian Adamson, MP. *Minister of Water Resources, Minister of Irrigation, Minister of Lands and Minister of Repatriation:* Peter Bruce Arnold, MP.

Ministers are jointly and individually responsible to the legislature for all their official acts, as in the UK.

Agent-General in London: J. L. Rundle (50 Strand, WC2).

Local Government. The closely settled part of the State (mainly near the sea-coast and the river Murray) is incorporated into local government areas, and sub-divided into district councils (rural areas only), municipal corporations (mainly metropolitan, but including larger country towns) and cities (more densely populated areas with a qualification of 15,000 residents in the Adelaide metropolitan area, and 10,000 in the country). The main functions of councils are the construction and maintenance of roads and bridges. Other functions include health, welfare, recreation and garbage disposal.

The number and area of the sub-divisions, together with revenue expenditure (in $A1,000) for the year ended 30 June 1978, were:

	No.	Area (1,000 hectares)	Roads and bridges	Health and recreation	All other	Total expenditure
Adelaide statistical division	32	185·2	26,196	23,967	54,280	104,443
Other municipal corporations and district councils	98	14,967·2	20,326	9,018	29,444	58,788
Total	130	15,152·4	46,522	32,985	83,724	163,231

ECONOMY

Budget. Revenue and expenditure (in $A1,000) for years ended 30 June:

	1975	1976	1977	1978	1979	1980
Revenue	828,985	1,036,985	1,174,025	1,167,196	1,264,705	1,384,589
Expenditure	820,601	1,034,698	1,183,180	1,192,063	1,258,252	1,384,589

The public debt of the State amounted, on 30 June 1980, to $A1,781·6m.

Banking. There were 9 trading banks at 30 June 1980, including the Federal and State Government Banks. In June 1980 their average deposits were $A1,652m. and average loans and advances $A1,938·3m.

The 8 savings banks on 30 June 1980 had deposits amounting to $A2,276·9m. or $A1,758 per head of population.

NATURAL RESOURCES

Minerals. The value of minerals produced in 1978–79 was $A174·4m. The principal minerals produced are opals, natural gas, iron ore, copper, gypsum, salt, talc, clays, limestone, dolomite and sub-bituminous coal.

Agriculture. Of the total area of South Australia (984,377 sq. km), 67,982 sq. km were alienated, 597,471 sq. km were held under lease and 318,923 sq. km were unoccupied. Area under cultivation, at 31 March 1979, was 61,027 sq. km.

Soil Conservation. Under the direction of special officers in the Department of Agriculture and Fisheries, determined efforts are made to deal with the problems of erosion and soil conservation. Included in the programme are the planting of cereal rye, perennial rye and other grasses to check sand drifts; contour-furrowing and contour banking; contour planting with vines and fruit trees and several water-diversion schemes.

Irrigation. For the year ended 31 March 1979, 78,386 hectares were under irrigated culture, being used as follows: Vineyards, 18,892; orchards, 12,338; vegetables, 6,409; and other crops and pasture, 40,747. Most of these areas are along the river Murray.

Gross value of production (in $A1,000), 1978–79: Crops, 609,613; livestock slaughtering, 253,376; livestock products, 221,153; forestry, fishing and hunting, 50,976. Total gross value, 1,135,118; local value (*i.e.*, less marketing costs), 1,027,672.

	1977–78		1978–79	
Chief crops	Hectares	Tonnes	Hectares	Tonnes
Wheat	1,089,975	510,818	1,295,296	2,085,729
Barley	1,073,353	591,771	1,091,115	1,422,672
Oats	129,990	55,362	170,507	176,772
Hay	138,087	326,064	219,612	665,837
Vines	...	203,219,000 [1]	...	202,050,000 [1]

[1] Litres of wine.

Fruit culture is extensively carried on, and in 1978–79, 230,406 tonnes of fresh fruit were produced. Other products, in addition to all kinds of root crops and vegetables, are grass seeds and oil seeds. Livestock, March 1979: 1,085,887 cattle, 14,939,960 sheep and 330,416 pigs. In 1978–79, 87,354 tonnes of wool and 321·2m. litres of milk were produced.

INDUSTRY AND TRADE

Industry. The turnover for manufacturing industries for 1978–79 was $A4,536m. The following statistics for 1978–79 are not comparable with factory statistics for years prior to 1968–69.

Industry sub-division	Establish-ments (No.)	Persons employed (No.)	Wages and salaries ($A1m.)	Turnover ($A1m.)	Value added ($A1m.)
Food, beverages and tobacco	372	16,977	156	943	333
Textiles, clothing and footwear	106	3,856	55	212	97
Wood, wood products and furniture	311	7,932	68	282	115

Industry sub-division	Establish- ments (No.)	Persons employed (No.)	Wages and salaries ($A1m.)	Turnover ($A1m.)	Value added ($A1m.)
Paper, paper products, printing and publishing	188	7,284	72	256	137
Chemical, petroleum and coal products	48	2,819	33	177	76
Non-metallic mineral products	140	3,634	42	200	86
Basic metal products	36	9,084	108	590	207
Fabricated metal products	348	8,990	80	338	142
Transport equipment	112	20,245	214	747	301
Other machinery and equipment	283	17,030	166	566	258
Miscellaneous manufacturing	175	6,022	58	225	100
Total	2,119	106,302	1,052	4,536	1,851

Practically all forms of secondary industry are to be found, the most important being smelting, motor vehicle manufacture, saw-milling and the manufacture of household appliances, basic iron and steel, meat and meat products, and wine and brandy.

Labour. Two systems of industrial arbitration and conciliation for the adjustment of industrial relations between employers and employees are in operation—the State system, which operates when industrial disputes are confined to the territorial limits of the State, and the Federal system, which applies when disputes involve other parts of Australia as well as South Australia.

The industrial tribunals are authorized to fix minimum rates of wages and other conditions of employment, and their awards may be enforced by law. Industrial agreements between employers and organizations of employees, when registered, may be enforced in the same manner as awards. The Commission fixed the minimum wage in July 1980 at $A134.40.

Commerce. The commerce of South Australia, exclusive of inter-state trade, is comprised in the statement of the commerce of Australia given under the heading of the Commonwealth, see pp. 110–12.

Overseas imports and exports in $A1,000 (year ending 30 June):

	1974–75	1975–76	1976–77	1977–78	1978–79	1979–80
Imports	482,077	501,476	629,309	628,568	865,554	882,389
Exports[1]	764,410	685,029	789,872	661,887	922,754	1,603,141

[1] From 1978–79 exports are recorded by 'State of Origin', whereas details prior to this are by 'State of Lodgment of Documents'.

Principal exports in 1979–80 were (in $A1,000): Wheat, 376,918 (2,471,101 tonnes); barley, 191,806 (1,590,723 tonnes); wool, 183,745 (79·5m. kg); lead, 180,458 (174,681 tonnes); meat, 98,633 (60,657 tonnes); live sheep and lambs, 49,370 (1,820,988 head).

Principal imports in 1979–80 were (in $A1,000): Transport equipment, 112,502; petrol and products, 310,346; machinery, 145,244.

In 1979–80 the leading suppliers of imports were (in $A1m.): Saudi Arabia (293), Japan (152·2), USA (115·5), UK (63·3); main exports went to USSR (233·1), Japan (176), China (104·3), USA (103·2), Iraq (72·1), New Zealand (70·3), and Saudi Arabia (60·2).

Tourism. In June 1980 there were 256 hotels and guest houses with 6,537 rooms; 153 caravan parks had a total of 17,815 sites.

COMMUNICATIONS

Roads. At 30 June 1979, of the roads customarily used by the public, there were 2,616 km of national roads, 10,959 km of arterial roads and 86,905 km of local roads, totalling 100,480 km. Lengths of road classified by surface were as follows: Sealed, 18,150 km; unsealed, 21,093 km; formed, 24,213 km; natural, 37,024 km. Costs of construction and maintenance are shared by the State and Federal governments and by the councils of the local areas. Motor vehicles registered at 30 Sept. 1979 include 467,358 cars, 76,431 station wagons, 117,665 commercial vehicles and 30,380 cycles.

Railways. There were (1978) 6,034 km of railway, including the South Australian portion of the Transcontinental Railway from Port Pirie in South Australia to Kalgoorlie in Western Australia, which, in connexion with various State lines, completes a through rail connexion between Brisbane on the north-east coast and Fremantle on the west coast. It also includes the South Australian portion of the Australian National Railways from Port Augusta to the Northern Territory and private railways from Iron Knob to Whyalla and Coffin Bay to Port Lincoln. In the year ending 30 June 1979 12m. tonnes of freight and livestock were carried on non-urban railways.

Aviation. For the year ended 30 June 1979 there were 1,801,084 passengers and 21,539 tonnes of freight handled at Adelaide, South Australia's principal airport. On 30 June 1979 there were 9 government and 20 licensed aerodromes.

Shipping. There are several good harbours, of which Port Adelaide is the principal one. In 1978–79, 889 vessels (exceeding 200 NRT) of 6,963,571 net tonnage entered South Australian ports direct from interstate or overseas.

Post and Broadcasting. At 30 June 1979, there were 701 post offices. Telephone services connected totalled 420,871 on 30 June 1979; on 30 June 1979 there were 21 radio and 13 television stations.

JUSTICE, RELIGION, EDUCATION AND WELFARE

Justice. There is a Supreme Court, which incorporates admiralty, civil, criminal, land and valuation, and testamentary jurisdiction; district criminal courts, which have jurisdiction in many indictable offences; local courts and courts of summary jurisdiction. Circuit courts are held at several places. Bankruptcy jurisdiction is administered by the State Court of Insolvency at Adelaide which is invested with jurisdiction by the Federal Bankruptcy Act. During the year ending 30 June 1979 there were 847 sequestrations and schemes under the Bankruptcy Act; 1,258 adults convicted in the higher courts in 1978 and 105,413 in the courts of summary jurisdiction in 1977–78. The total number of convicted prisoners on 30 June 1979 was 768.

Religion. At the Census of 1976 the religious distribution of the population (as reported on Census schedules) was as follows: Church of England, 275,338; Roman Catholic and Catholic (so described), 247,572; Methodist, 195,890; Lutheran, 62,344; Presbyterian, 34,778; Baptist, 22,004; other Christians, 136,454; non-Christian, 4,849; indefinite, 5,528; no religion, 140,070; no reply, 119,930.

Education. Education is secular and is compulsory for children 6–15 years of age. Primary and secondary education at government schools is free. In 1979 there were 632 government schools, comprising 448 primary, 62 primary and secondary, 100 secondary schools and 22 special schools. There were 224,525 full-time students. The Department of Further Education is responsible for technical, adult and vocational education. In 1980 there were 13 metropolitan and 15 country colleges of further education, and 1 college of external studies. Tertiary education, including teacher education, is provided by the 2 universities and 6 colleges of advanced education. There were 155 non-government schools and colleges, most of which are associated with religious denominations (39,972 students) and 487 day care and pre-school centres with a total enrolment of 28,723 pre-school children.

Social Welfare. Age, invalidity, war, etc., pensions are paid by the Federal Government. The number of pensioners in South Australia at 30 June 1979 was: Disability and service, 62,505; age, 126,691; invalid, 20,169. There are schemes for maternity allowances, family allowances, widows, unemployment and sickness and hospital and pharmaceutical benefits.

Books of Reference

Statistical Information: The State branch of the Australian Bureau of Statistics is in Prudential Building, 195 North Terrace, Adelaide (GPO Box 2272). *Deputy Commonwealth Statistician:* B. E. Leonard. Although the first printed statistical publication was the *Statistics of South Australia, 1854* with the title altered to *Statistical Register* in 1859, there is a written volume for each year back to 1838. These contain simple records of trade, demography, production, etc. and were prepared only for the use of the Colonial Office; one copy was retained in the State.

The publications of the State branch include the *South Australian Year Book*, the *Pocket Year Book of South Australia* and a *Monthly Summary of Statistics*, a quarterly bulletin of building constructions, quarterly bulletin of trade statistics and approximately 55 special bulletins issued each year as particulars of various sections of statistics become available.

South Australia: Development. Dept. of Industry and Commerce, Adelaide, 1977
Best, R. J. (ed.), *Introducing South Australia.* Cambridge, 1959
Crowley, F. K., *South Australian History: A Survey for Research Students.* Adelaide, 1965
Douglas, J., *South Australia from Space.* Adelaide, 1980
Finlayson, H. H., *The Red Centre: Man and Beast in the Heart of Australia.* 2nd ed. Sydney, 1952
Gibbs, R. M., *A History of South Australia.* Adelaide, 1969
Whitelock, D., *Adelaide, 1836–1976: A History of Difference.* Univ. of Queensland Press, 1977

State Library: The State Library of S.A., North Terrace, Adelaide. *State Librarian:* R. K. Olding, BEc., FLAA.

TASMANIA

HISTORY. Abel Janzoon Tasman discovered Van Diemen's Land (Tasmania) on 24 Nov. 1642. The island became a British settlement in 1803 as a dependency of New South Wales; in 1825 its connexion with New South Wales was terminated; in 1851 a partially elective Legislative Council was established, and in 1856 responsible government came into operation. On 1 Jan. 1901 Tasmania was federated with the other Australian states into the Commonwealth of Australia.

AREA AND POPULATION. Tasmania is an island separated from the mainland by the Bass Strait with an area (including islands) of 68,330 sq. km, or 6·83m. hectares, of which 6,441,000 hectares form the area of the main island. The population at 10 consecutive censuses was:

	Population	Increase % per annum		Population	Increase % per annum
1901	172,475	1·64	1954	308,752	2·65
1911	191,211	1·04	1961	350,340	1·82
1921	213,780	1·12	1966	371,436	1·18
1933	227,599	0·52	1971	390,220	0·99
1947	257,078	0·87	1976	407,363 [1]	0·86

[1] Adjusted for under-enumeration.

The census population on 30 June 1976 consisted of 204,118 males and 203,245 females. At the census of 30 June 1976, 5·7% were natives of the British Isles, 3·3% natives of other European countries and 90·3% natives of Australia and New Zealand, almost exclusively of European ancestry. The last Tasmanian Aboriginal died in 1876.

Vital statistics for calendar years:

	Marriages	Divorces[1]	Births	Deaths	Natural increase
1975	3,206	591	6,981	3,340	3,641
1976	3,477	1,761	6,702	3,389	3,313
1977	3,166	1,134	6,735	3,269	3,466
1978	3,148	1,132[2]	6,788	3,311	3,477

[1] Family Court came into operation during 1976.   [2] Preliminary.

CONSTITUTION AND GOVERNMENT. Parliament consists of the Governor, the Legislative Council and the House of Assembly. The Council has 19 members, elected by adults with 6 months' residence. Members sit for 6 years, 3 retiring annually and 4 every sixth year. There is no power to dissolve the Council. Vacancies are filled by by-elections. The House of Assembly has 35 members; the maximum term for the House of Assembly is 4 years. Members of both Houses are paid a basic salary of $A25,949 (1980–81), plus an electorate allowance, according to the division represented. The annual allowance payable is calculated as a percentage of basic salary. The amounts vary from $A2,854 (11%) to $A9,082 (35%). Women received the right to vote in 1903. Proportional representation was adopted in 1907, the method now being the single transferable vote in 7-member constituencies. Casual vacancies in the House of Assembly are determined by a transfer of the preference of the vacating member's ballot papers to consenting candidates who were unsuccessful at the last general election.

A Minister must have a seat in one of the two Houses; only one of the present Ministers is a member of the Legislative Council.

In addition to the salary paid to Ministers as members of either House, the following allowances are payable: Premier, in conjunction with a ministerial office, $A32,436; Deputy Premier, in conjunction with a ministerial office, $A22,056; other Ministers, $A18,164. The Leader of the Opposition in the House of Assembly receives an allowance of $A18,164. The holders of some other offices receive allowances ranging from $A1,556 to $A8,650.

An election held in July 1979 saw the return of the Labor Government. A by-election was held in Feb. 1980 after the election results of the Denison Division were declared void. The resultant composition of the House of Assembly was Labor, 19 seats; Liberal, 15 and Australian Democrats, 1.

The Legislative Council is predominantly independent without formal party allegiance; 3 members are Labor-endorsed.

Governor: Sir Stanley Burbury, KCVO, KBE.

The Labor Party Cabinet is composed as follows:

Premier, Treasurer, Minister for Energy: D. A. Lowe.

Deputy Premier, Economic Planning and Development, Tourism, Licensing: M. T. C. Barnard. *Attorney-General, Health Services, Immigration and Ethnic Affairs:* B. K. Miller. *Education, Racing and Gaming, Police and Emergency Services:* H. N. Holgate. *Construction, Industrial Relations and Manpower Planning, the Arts:* T. G. Aulich. *Main Roads and Transport, Local Government:* M. W. Field. *Primary Industry, Environment, Forests, Water Resources:* J. J. Amos. *Lands, National Parks and Wildlife, Community Welfare and Child Care, Handicapped Persons' Services:* B. K. Lohrey. *Housing, Mines, Recreation:* D. J. Baldock. *Public Health, Consumer Affairs, Administrative Services:* G. H. James.

Agent-General in London: W. A. Neilson.
Official Secretary: C. Langbant (485/9 Strand, WC2).

Local Government. For the purposes of local government, the State is divided into 49 municipal areas comprising the cities of Hobart, Launceston and Glenorchy and 46 municipalities. The cities and municipalities are managed by elected aldermen and councillors, respectively, with reference to local matters such as sanitation and health services, domestic water supplies and roads and bridges within each particular area. The chief source of revenue is rates (based on improved values) levied on owners of property.

Tasmanian Islands. Three inhabited Tasmanian islands (Bruny, King and Flinders) are organized as municipalities. Nearly 1,600 km south-east lies Macquarie Island, part of the State, and used only as an Australian research base and meteorological station.

ECONOMY

Budget. The revenue is derived chiefly from taxation (payroll tax, motor, land, stamp and death duties), and from grants and reimbursements from the Federal Government. Customs, excise, sales and income tax are levied by the Federal Government, which makes grants to Tasmania for both revenue and capital purposes. Federal Government grants to Tasmania in 1979–80 totalled $A466m. These included Financial Assistance Grants, $A273m.; specific purpose payments, $A164m.; and Capital Grants, $A29m.

Specific purpose payments are mainly used to provide essential services such as housing, roads and schools, while Financial Assistance Grants have been paid since 1942 to compensate the State for the loss of income tax to the federal government.

Consolidated Revenue Fund receipts and expenditure, in $A1,000, for financial years ending 30 June:

	1974–75	1975–76	1976–77	1977–78	1978–79	1979–80
Revenue	268,522	322,091	396,617	444,263	495,822	560,192
Expenditure	282,065	317,947	395,033	450,706	492,961	563,917

The public debt at current exchange rates amounted to $A970m. at 30 June 1980.

In 1979–80 State taxation receipts amounted to $A113·4m., of which pay-roll tax provided $A45·9m.; motor vehicles, $A16m.; death duties, $A3·9m.; land tax, $A5·1m., and stamp duties, $A24·6m.

Banking. Trading bank activity in Tasmania is divided between 6 private banks and the Commonwealth Bank of Australia. For the month of June 1980 liabilities represented by depositors' balances averaged $A409m. and assets represented by advances, $A374m. The 9 savings banks operating in Tasmania are the Commonwealth Savings Bank, 2 trustee savings banks and 6 private savings banks operated by trading banks. At 30 June 1980 total savings bank deposits were $A642m.

ENERGY AND NATURAL RESOURCES

Electricity. Tasmania has good supplies of hydro-electric power because of assured rainfall and high level water storages (natural and artificial). The Hydro-Electric Commission, Tasmania's sole commercial supplier of electricity, has been surveying water power resources of the State for many years and it is estimated that about 3m. kw. can be economically developed. By mid-1980, 1,780,400 kw. of generating plant was in commission. In 1979 the peak loading was 1,151,000 kw. A major construction project, completed in 1978, was the Gordon River scheme involving the construction of Australia's largest artificial water storage (combined area of the 2 lakes created is over 500 sq. km) and one of the nation's largest dams. Water is carried from the Lake Gordon storage by a near vertical shaft to the power station 186 metres underground, which is operated by remote control from Hobart, 160 km away. Generator capacity of the Gordon River (Stage 1) scheme is 288,000 kw. The major project under construction is the $A530m. Pieman River Power Development, comprising 3 power stations, which is scheduled for completion in 1986.

Minerals. The assayed content of principal metallic minerals contained in locally produced concentrates for 1978–79 was (in tonnes): Zinc, 73,074; iron, 1,569,946; copper, 24,471; lead, 21,172; tin, 6,960; gold, 1,764 kg; silver, 80,918 kg. Coal production (1978–79), 252,800 tonnes.

Primary Industries. The estimated gross value of recorded production from agriculture in 1978–79 was (in $A1,000): Livestock products, 90,518; livestock slaughterings and other disposals, 91,737; crops, 80,053; total gross value, 262,308. Estimated gross value of production in forestry, fisheries and hunting was $A82m.

Agriculture. The area occupied by the 6,142 holdings in 1978–79 totalled 2,231,718 hectares, of which 984,700 were devoted to crops and sown pasture. The following table shows the area and production, in tonnes, of the principal crops:

	1976–77		1977–78		1978–79	
	Hectares	Production	Hectares	Production	Hectares	Production
Wheat	1,980	3,929	1,257	1,545	1,366	2,867
Barley	11,644	24,571	11,444	19,403	11,938	26,971
Oats	6,387	8,801	4,616	4,279	8,564	11,826
Green peas, ex-shell	6,374	31,640	6,228	27,230	6,483	30,179
Potatoes	3,705	112,269	3,592	107,240	3,646	124,385
Hay	72,001	344,549	48,601	172,348	68,035	304,847
Hops (bearing) (dry)	587	1,330	565	1,201	578	1,457

Livestock at 31 March 1979: Sheep, 4m.; cattle, 657,000; pigs, 61,000.

Wool produced during 1978–79 was 19m. kg, valued at $A42m. In 1978–79 butter production was 7,075 tonnes; cheese, 17,494 tonnes.

Forestry. Indigenous forests cover a considerable part of the State, and the saw-milling industry is very important. Production of sawn timber in 1979–80 was 349,700 cu. metres. 928,100 cu. metres of logs were used for milling in 1979–80 and a further 3·6m. cu. metres were used for chipping, grinding or flaking. Newsprint and paper are produced from native hardwoods, principally eucalypts.

INDUSTRY AND TRADE

Industry. The most important manufactures for export are refined metals, newsprint and other paper manufactures, pigments, woollen goods, fruit pulp, confectionery, butter, cheese, preserved and dried vegetables, sawn timber, iron ore pellets and processed fish products. The electrolytic-zinc works at Risdon near Hobart treat large quantities of local and imported ore, and produce zinc, sulphuric acid, super-phosphate, sulphate of ammonia, cadmium and other by-products. At George Town, large-scale plants produce refined aluminium and manganese alloys. During 1979–80, 3·7m. tonnes (green weight) of woodchips were produced. In 1978–79 the average employment in manufacturing establishments employing 4 or more persons was 26,066; wages and salaries (excluding proprietors drawings), $A266m.; turn-over, $A1,401m.; value added, $A549m.; and number operating at 30 June, 552.

Labour. The Commonwealth Industrial Court (judicial powers) and Commonwealth Conciliation and Arbitration Commission (arbitral powers) have jurisdiction over federal unions, *i.e.*, with interstate membership. The Arbitration Commission abolished the concept of the basic wage in June 1967 and made an award in terms of total wage; in June 1969 it adopted the principle of equal pay for equal work for females. The Commission adopted wage indexation in principle in May 1975 as a result of the national wage case. The Commission decided to sit quarterly to consider the national wage pending a firm decision on wage indexation. Quarterly percentage wage increases were subsequently granted in line with the increase in the consumer price index during the March, June, Sept. and Dec. quarters, 1975, the Sept. quarter, 1976 and the March quarter, 1978. Increases, based on the consumer price index, were granted for the March, June and Dec. quarters, 1976, and for all quarters, 1977, but not to the full extent of the increase in the index. In Sept. 1978 the Commission decided to adjust award wages and salaries every 6 months in relation to the last two quarterly movements of the consumer price index. The Commission sits in Oct. and April each year.

Most Tasmanian employees not covered by federal awards operate under State Industrial Boards established for the various trades by resolution of Parliament or proclamation of the Governor. Each Board consists of a Chairman appointed by the Governor with equal representation of employers and employees. The Boards have authority over minimum rates for wages or piece work, number of working hours for which the wage is payable, conditions of apprenticeship, annual leave and adjustment of wage and piece-work rates. Industrial Boards follow to a large extent the wage rates fixed by the Conciliation and Arbitration Commission; from Oct. 1968 to June 1978 they followed the quantum of increase in the minimum wage fixed by the Australian Commission but did not abolish the basic wage concept.

Commerce. Trade by sea and air in $A1m. for years ending 30 June:

	1972–73	1973–74	1974–75	1975–76	1976–77
Imports	356·1	451·8	529·5	607·6	689·8
Exports	570·2	698·7	637·8	728·3	859·7

In 1977–78 exports by sea and air totalled $A1,027m.; comprising $A645m. to other Australian states and $A382m. to overseas countries. The principal countries of destination (with values in $A1m.) for overseas exports were: Japan, 155; USA, 48; Indonesia, 18; Malaysia, 30; and Singapore, 16. Imports totalled $A750m.; comprising $A634m. from other Australian states and $A116m. from overseas countries. The principal countries of origin (with values in $A1m.) for overseas imports were: Japan, 18; USA, 18; New Zealand, 13; UK, 13; and Canada, 12.

The main commodities by value (with values in $A1m.) exported during 1977–78 were: Ores and concentrates (iron, copper, lead, tin, wolfram and scheelite), 163; refined zinc, 87; timber, 38; and textiles, 33. Other main exports, for which details are not available for separate publication were newsprint, printing and writing papers, refined aluminium, ferro-alloys and chocolate confectionery. The main imports (with values in $A1m.) were: Petroleum products, 110; new motor vehicles, 88; machinery, 78; ores and concentrates, 44, and clothing, cocoa beans, alumina and wood-pulp.

Tourism. In 1977–78 a total of 550,000 persons entered Tasmania. It is estimated that of this total 330,000 were visitors to the State and 264,000 were tourists.

COMMUNICATIONS

Roads. The total road length at 30 June 1978 was 22,228 km, consisting of a classi-fied road system of 3,696 km maintained by the State Department of Main Roads, and the remainder maintained by local government authorities, the Forestry Commission and the Hydro-Electric Commission. Motor vehicles registered at 31 Dec. 1978 comprised 174,800 cars, 41,800 commercial vehicles and 4,700 motor cycles.

Railways. There is an 851-km network of 1,067-mm gauge lines linking Hobart and Launceston with coastal and country areas, formerly operated by Tasmanian Government Railways, but since 1 July 1975 worked by the Australian National Railways Commission. Earnings in 1976–77 were $A8·8m. and expenditure $A23·3m.

Aviation. Regular daily passenger and freight air services connect the south, north and north-west of the State with the mainland of Australia. In 1978 there was a total of 29,700 scheduled aircraft movements at Tasmanian airports; a total of 997,000 passengers and 27,300 tonnes of freight, including mail, was carried.

Shipping. In 1977–78 a total of 1,528 vessels (6,992,000 net tons), from overseas and other Australian states, arrived at ports in Tasmania. These vessels discharged 2·13m. tonnes and 1,731,000 cu. metres of cargo and shipped 5,328,000 tonnes and 1,513,000 cu. metres.

For posts and telegraphs, see p. 114.

JUSTICE, RELIGION, EDUCATION AND WELFARE

Justice. The Supreme Court of Tasmania, with civil, criminal, ecclesiastical, ad-miralty and matrimonial jurisdiction, established by Royal Charter on 13 Oct. 1823, is a superior court of record, with both original and appellate jurisdiction, and consists of a Chief Justice and 5 puisne judges. There are also inferior civil courts with limited jurisdiction, licensing courts, mining courts, courts of petty sessions and coroners' courts.

During the year 1978, 36,703 persons were summarily convicted in lower courts (25,017 for traffic offences) and 235 persons were convicted in the Supreme Court. The total police force on 30 June 1978 was 1,030. There was 1 gaol, with 273 inmates at the end of June 1978.

Religion. There is no State Church. At the census of 1976 the following numbers of adherents of the principal religions were recorded:

Church of England	158,748	Congregational	3,266
Roman Catholic	75,092	Other religions	23,985
Methodist	37,107	No religion	27,624
Presbyterian	14,899	Not stated [1]	50,221
Baptist	7,940		
Brethren	3,986	Total [1]	402,868

[1] 'As counted' Census results.

Education. Education is controlled by the State and is free, secular and compulsory between the ages of 6 and 16. At 1 Aug. 1979 government schools had a total enrolment of 73,046 pupils, including 28,193 at secondary level; private schools had a total enrolment of 14,401 pupils, including 6,312 at secondary level.

The University of Tasmania, established 1890, had 301 full-time teachers with 3,435 students in 1979.

Social Welfare. Old Age, Invalid, War Service and Widows' Pensions are paid by the Federal Government. The number of pensioners in Tasmania (including wives' pensions) on 30 June 1979 was: Age, 38,885; invalid, 6,427; war (disability), 18,127; widows, 5,229. Benefit payments totalled $A152·8m.

Books of Reference

Statistical Information: The State Government Statistical Office (Commonwealth Government Centre, Hobart), established in 1877, became in 1924 the Tasmanian Office of the Australian Bureau of Statistics, but continues to serve State statistical needs as required. *Deputy Commonwealth Statistician and Government Statistician:* R. Lakin.

Main publications: *Annual Statistical Bulletins (e.g., Demography, Agricultural Industry, Finance, Manufacturing Establishments* etc.).—*Pocket Year Book of Tasmania.* Annual (from 1913).—*Tasmanian Year Book.* Annual (from 1967).—*Monthly Summary of Statistics* (from July 1945).

Department of Planning and Development, *Tasmanian Manufacturers Directory.* Hobart. Annual.—*Establishing a Business.* Hobart, 1979
Premier's Dept., *Tasmania—Australia.* Hobart, 1979
Angus, M., *The World of Olegas Truchanas.* Hobart, 1975
Clark, C. I., *The Parliament of Tasmania.* Hobart, 1947
Davies, J. L. (ed.), *Atlas of Tasmania.* Hobart, 1965
Green, F. C. (ed.), *A Century of Responsible Government.* Hobart, 1956
Mercury-Walch Pty. Ltd, *The Tasmanian Almanac.* Hobart. Annual
Townsley, W. A., *The Government of Tasmania.* Univ. of Queensland Press, 1976
Wettenhall, R. L., *A Guide to Tasmanian Government Administration.* Hobart, 1968

State Library: The State Library of Tasmania, Hobart. *Librarian:* W. L. Brown, FLA, ALAA.

VICTORIA

AREA AND POPULATION. The State has an area of 227,600 sq. km, and a census population of 3,746,000 at 30 June 1976. Estimate (1979) 3,853,500.

The population of the Melbourne Statistical Division at 30 June 1979 was 2,739,700 or 71·1% of the population of the State. The population of each Statistical District in Victoria was: Ballarat, 73,190; Bendigo, 59,590; Geelong, 141,130; Morwell, 16,540; Shepparton-Mooroopna, 34,110.

The census population (exclusive of full-blood aboriginals prior to 1961) was:

Date of census enumeration	Males	Population Females	Total	On previous census Numerical increase	Increase %
3 April 1881	451,623	409,943	861,566	131,368	17·99
5 April 1891	598,222	541,866	1,140,088	278,522	32·33
31 March 1901	603,720	597,350	1,201,070	60,982	5·35
3 April 1911	655,591	659,960	1,315,551	114,481	9·53
4 April 1921	754,724	776,556	1,531,280	215,729	16·40
30 June 1933	903,244	917,017	1,820,261	288,981	18·87
30 June 1947	1,013,867	1,040,834	2,054,701	234,440	12·88
30 June 1954	1,231,099	1,221,242	2,452,341	397,640	19·35
30 June 1961	1,474,536	1,455,830	2,930,366	478,025	19·49
30 June 1966	1,614,240	1,605,977	3,220,217	289,851	9·89
30 June 1971	1,760,651	1,759,706	3,520,357	300,140	9·32
30 June 1976	1,870,097	1,875,884	3,745,981	225,625	6·41

The population of urban Melbourne (capital city) on 30 June 1976 was 2,480,670. The population of urban Geelong was 122,080; urban Ballarat, 60,737; urban Bendigo, 50,169. Other urban centres: Shepparton-Mooroopna, 25,848; Warrnambool, 20,195; Moe-Yallourn, 18,804; Wangaratta, 16,157; Morwell, 16,094; Traralgon, 15,089; Mildura, 14,417; Sale, 12,111; Horsham, 11,647; Colac, 10,431; Hamilton, 9,504; Bairnsdale, 9,130; Benalla, 8,300; Portland, 8,298; Ararat, 8,288; Swan Hill, 7,857; Castlemaine, 7,583; Maryborough, 7,569; Warragul, 7,442.

Vital statistics for calendar years:

	Births	Marriages	Divorces	Deaths
1976	60,667	28,760	16,633	30,753
1977	59,518	27,558	10,851	29,478
1978	58,861	27,178	10,821	29,096
1979	57,767	27,019	9,471	29,078

The annual rates per 1,000 of the population in 1979 were: Marriages, 7·01; births, 14·99; deaths, 7·55; divorces, 2·42.

CONSTITUTION AND GOVERNMENT. Victoria, formerly a portion of New South Wales, was, in 1851, proclaimed a separate colony, with a partially elective Legislative Council. In 1855 responsible government was conferred, the legislative power being vested in a parliament of two Houses, the Legislative Council and the Legislative Assembly. At present the Council consists of 44 members who are elected for 6 years, one-half retiring every third year. The Assembly consists of 81 members, elected for 3 years from the date of its first meeting unless sooner dissolved by the Governor. Members and electors of both Houses must be aged 18 years and natural born or naturalized British subjects. Women are fully enfranchised. No property qualification is required, but judges, members of the Commonwealth Parliament and undischarged bankrupts may not be members of either House. Single voting (one elector one vote) and compulsory preferential voting apply to Council and Assembly elections. Enrolment for Council and Assembly electors is compulsory. The Council may not initiate or amend money bills, but may suggest amendments in such bills other than amendments which would increase any charge. Any Minister, with the consent of the House of which he is not a member, may sit and speak in that House to explain a bill relating to the department administered by him, but may not vote in that House. A bill shall not become law unless passed by both Houses, except that, in the event of a continued disagreement between the two Houses as to a bill passed by the Assembly, other than certain constitutional bills, the Governor having dissolved the Assembly may subsequently dissolve the Council, and if the disagreement still continues he may convene a joint sitting of the members of the Council and the Assembly; if at such joint sitting the bill in dispute is passed by an absolute majority of all members it shall become law.

Private members of both Houses receive salaries of $A29,526 per annum, additional allowances rising from $A6,785 to $A9,120 (outer electorates), and a living-away-from-home allowance of $A35 for each day of attendance for each member (not being a responsible Minister or a metropolitan member).

Members holding the following offices receive the salaries and allowances specified: The President of the Council, $A51,671 salary and $A3,248 expense allowance; the Speaker of the Assembly, $A51,671 salary and $A3,248 expense allowance; the Chairman of Committees of the Council, $A38,974 salary and $A1,181 expense allowance; the Chairman of Committees of the Assembly, $A38,974 salary and $A1,181 expense allowance; the Leader of the Opposition in the Assembly, $A51,671 salary and $A5,315 expense allowance; the Deputy Leader of the Opposition in the Assembly, $A38,974 salary and $A1,772 expense allowance; the Leader of the Third Party, $A38,974 salary and $A1,772 expense allowance; a member of either House who is the Parliamentary Secretary of the Cabinet, $A38,974 salary and $A1,772 expense allowance; the Government Whip in the Assembly, $A34,841 salary; the Whip of any recognized Party which consists of at least 12 members of Parliament, of which Party no member is a responsible Minister, $A32,774 salary. All members have free passes over the Victorian Railways; country members are also entitled to certain allowances for air travel.

The Legislative Assembly, elected on 5 May 1979, is composed as follows: Liberal Party, 41; Labor Party, 32; National Party, 8.

Governor: Sir Henry Winneke, KCMG, KCVO, OBE, KStJ, QC.

In the exercise of the executive power the Governor is advised by a Cabinet of responsible Ministers. Section 50 of the Constitution Act 1975 provides that the number of responsible Ministers shall not at any one time exceed 18, of whom not more than 6 may sit in the Legislative Council. No responsible Minister may hold office for more than 3 months unless he is or becomes a member of the Council or the Assembly.

Responsible Ministers receive the following amounts: The Premier, $A59,052 salary and $A12,401 expense allowance; the Deputy Premier, $A54,623 salary and $A6,200 expense allowance; 16 other responsible Ministers, $A51,671 salary and $A5,315 expense allowance. Each responsible Minister also receives an electorate allowance, an electorate office allowance, a residential allowance (where applicable) and, when travelling on business of the State, a travelling allowance. The President, Speaker, Chairman of Committees in the Assembly and in the Council, Parliamentary Secretary of the Cabinet, Leader and Deputy Leader of the Opposition in the Assembly, Leader of the Opposition in the Council and Leader in the Assembly of the Third Party, also receive a travelling allowance when travelling on official business. Members of Committees receive attendance fees and certain travelling expenses when on Committee duties.

The Liberal Party Government (first appointed 7 June 1955) is as follows:

Premier, Minister for State Development, Decentralization and Tourism: R. J. Hamer, ED, MP.

Deputy Premier, Treasurer and Minister for Police and Emergency Services: L. H. S. Thompson, CMG, MP. *Education:* A. J. Hunt, MLC. *Attorney-General, Federal Affairs:* Haddon Storey, QC, MLC. *Local Government:* D. G. Crozier, MLC. *Minerals and Energy:* J. C. M. Balfour, MP. *Health:* W. A. Borthwick, MP. *Agriculture:* I. W. Smith, MP. *Conservation, Lands and Soldier Settlement:* W. V. Houghton, MLC. *Housing, Youth, Sport and Recreation:* B. J. Dixon, MP. *Water Supply and Forests:* F. J. Granter, MLC. *Transport:* R. R. C. Maclellan, MP. *Community Welfare Services:* Walter Jona, MP. *Labour, Industry and Consumer Affairs:* J. H. Ramsey, MP. *Public Works and Property and Services:* T. L. Austin, MP. *Planning and Assistant Minister of Health:* L. S. Lieberman, MP. *Immigration and Ethnic Affairs and Assistant Minister for State Development, Decentralization and Tourism:* A. R. Wood, MP. *Arts and Assistant Minister of Education:* N. Lacy, MP. *Parliamentary Secretary of the Cabinet:* G. Jenkins, MLC.

Agent-General in London: The Hon. J. A. Rafferty (Victoria House, Melbourne Place, Strand, London, WC28 4LG).

Local Government. With the exception of Yallourn Works area (26·9 sq. km) and the unincorporated areas—French Island (154 sq. km), Lady Julia Percy Island (1·3 sq. km), the Bass Strait Islands and part of Gippsland Lakes (313 sq. km) and Tower Hill Lake Reserve (5 sq. km), the State is divided (at 30 June 1978) into 211 municipal districts, namely 65 cities, 6 towns, 7 boroughs and 133 shires. The constitution of cities, towns, boroughs and shires is based on statutory requirements concerning population, rate revenue and net annual value of rateable property.

ECONOMY

Budget. The receipts and payments (in $A1,000) of the Consolidated Fund in the years shown (ended 30 June) were:

	1976–77	1977–78	1978–79	1979–80	1980–81[1]
Receipts	2,955,620	3,294,891	3,543,598	3,985,502	4,442,795
Payments	2,955,620	3,294,891	3,543,598	3,953,106	4,475,191

[1] Estimates.

The principal receipt items (in $A1,000) during 1978–79 were: Taxation, 2,261,558 (including Federal Government reimbursement, 1,090,025, but excluding 224,218 paid to special funds); railways, 188,837; other Federal Government payments, 319,030, and mining royalties, 88,142. The principal heads of expenditure were: Interest and public debt charges (including railways), 294,839; railways, 348,642; education, 1,038,563; health, hospitals and charities, 435,277.

The amount raised by taxation (exclusive of taxes collected by the Federal Government or paid to special funds but inclusive of the Federal Government reimbursements under the uniform taxation scheme), as shown in the above paragraph, was approximately $A589.50 per head of population.

The public debt of Victoria (in $A1m.) on 30 June 1979 was 3,428. During the year ending 30 June 1979, an amount of 432 was expended on capital works. Of this amount, 164 was spent on education, 51 on railways, 36 on water supply, irrigation and drainage, 10 on protection of the environment (including sewerage), 14 on forestry, 65 on health services, 5 on agricultural, pastoral, etc., services, 26 on culture and recreation, 21 on law, order and public safety, 11 on legislature and general administration, development and decentralization, and 29 on all other purposes. In addition to the public debt noted above, Victoria had other liabilities due to the Federal Government at 30 June 1979. These included 1,046·6 advances for housing, 11·5 special assistance loans for soldier settlement, 73·7 advance for sewerage, 65·9 for rural and dairy reconstruction, 80 for growth centres and 37·1 for land acquisition.

Banking. On 30 June 1980 there were 7·15m. operative accounts (excluding school bank accounts) in savings banks in Victoria. The total credit due to depositors amounted to $A7,839m., made up of State Savings Bank, $A3,872m.; Commonwealth Savings Bank, $A1,577m.; private savings banks, $A2,389m.

The weekly average of deposits and advances of trading banks operating in Victoria during June 1980 were as follows: Deposits, not bearing interest, $A2,294m.; deposits, bearing interest, $A3,512m.; total deposits, $A5,806m.; loans, advances, and bills discounted, $A4,524m. The weekly average of debits to customers' accounts (excluding debits to Federal and State Government accounts at City branches in State capitals) for the same period totalled $A7,855m.

ENERGY AND NATURAL RESOURCES

Electricity. All electricity in this State for public supply is generated by the largest electricity supply authority in Australia—the State Electricity Commission of Victoria. Its supply network serves over 99% of the entire Victorian population and some New South Wales municipalities as well as irrigation settlements bordering the Murray River.

The major base load generating stations are located in the Latrobe Valley on top of a large brown coal field with estimated geological reserves of 107,847m. tonnes. Burning raw brown coal on site and with an installed generating capacity of 2,991,000 kw., these stations produce over 80% of Victoria's electricity. The chief one is Hazelwood, which was completed in 1971 with a capacity of 1·6m. kw. The total installed generating capacity of all thermal stations in Victoria is 3,542,000 kw. including the base load stations in the Latrobe Valley and smaller ones in Melbourne, and some provincial cities.

The total installed capacity of the Commission's system at 30 June 1979 was 4,945,000 kw.; it includes Victoria's share of about one-third (1,059,000 kw. at 30 June 1979) of the Snowy Mountains hydro-electric scheme in New South Wales and its half share (25,000 kw.) of the Hume hydro-electric station, shared with New South Wales. Excluding the Snowy and Hume schemes in New South Wales the installed hydro-electric capacity totalled 316,500 kw. at 30 June 1979, with Kiewa (3 stations totalling 183,600 kw.) being the chief undertaking.

Total power generated and purchased in 1978–79 was 21,276 gwh.

Oil and Natural Gas. Crude oil in commercially recoverable quantities was first discovered by the Esso/BHP partnership in 1967 in 2 large fields offshore in East Gippsland in Bass Strait between 65 and 80 km from land. These fields, Halibut and Kingfish, with 5 smaller fields since discovered—Barracouta, Mackerel, Tuna, Cobia and Flounder, have been assessed as containing initial recoverable reserves of more than 2,917m. bbls of treated crude oil. Total production since 1969 from the 4 producing fields to the end of Sept. 1979 has amounted to 1,158m. bbls, leaving a balance of recoverable reserves of 1,759m. bbls.

Gippsland crude now supplies approximately 71% of Australia's refinery requirements, and during 1979 a total of 146m. bbls were produced from the 4 fields, Mackeral, Halibut, Kingfish and Barracouta. Depletion of production from the 2 major fields, Kingfish and Halibut and the smaller Barracouta field, is now expected to occur in the late-1980s.

Natural gas was discovered offshore in East Gippsland in 1965. The initial recoverable reserves of treated gas are 7,621,000m. cu. ft. Reserves are sufficient for 30 years. Following an extensive development and distribution programme, natural gas was first connected to homes and industry in Victoria in April 1969. All gas consumers in Melbourne, Geelong, Ballarat, Bendigo, Shepparton, Euroa, Benalla, Wangaratta, Wodonga, Albury and a number of towns near Melbourne, in the Latrobe Valley and in East Gippsland, are now using natural gas. At 30 June 1979 a total of 771,203 consumers were being supplied with it. During the period 1 July 1978 to 30 June 1979 a total volume of 3,715m. cu. metres of gas was consumed in Victoria, including commercial sales and plant usage.

Natural gas and crude oil are conveyed from the producing fields to a large treatment plant at Longford in East Gippsland from where both hydrocarbons are distributed by a network of transmission lines to tank farms and city gate distribution points.

The crude oil is then distributed to refineries in Victoria by pipeline and to other States by seagoing tankers. Natural gas is distributed to residential and industrial consumers through pipelines comprising some 1,684 km of high-pressure lines and over 13,700 km of transfer, direct high-pressure and reticulation lines.

Liquefied petroleum gas is now being produced after extraction of the propane and butane fractions from the untreated oil and gas; about 1·7m. tonnes a year is exported by Esso and BHP, mainly to Japan.

Brown Coal. Major deposits of brown coal are located in the Central Gippsland region and comprise approximately 94% of the total reserves in Victoria. In the Latrobe Valley section of this region the thick brown coal seams underlie an area from 10–30 km wide and extend over a length of approximately 70 km from Yallourn in the west to the south of Sale in the east. Small fields have also been found at Stradbroke in the ranges on the southern flank of the Valley and in the Gelliondale–Welshpool area near the coast. On a geological basis the brown coal reserves in Central Gippsland are estimated to be in the order of 108,000 megatonnes, of which about 65,000 megatonnes are proven and the remaining 43,000 megatonnes are inferred.

About 54% of the reserves occur in areas where the overburden over the uppermost seam is less than 30·5 metres while 95% is in areas with less than 91·4 metres of overburden. The current primary use of these reserves is to fuel the major base load electricity generating stations located at Morwell and Yallourn, and larger cuts have been opened for this purpose at these localities.

Land Settlement. Of the total area of Victoria (22·76m. hectares), 13,857,000 hectares on 30 June 1980 were either alienated or in process of alienation. The remainder (8,773,000) constituted Crown land as follows: Perpetual leases, grazing and other leases and licences, 2,378,000; reservations including forest and timber reserves, water, catchment and drainage purposes, national parks, wildlife reserves, water frontages and other reserves, plus unoccupied and unreserved including areas set aside for roads, 6,395,000. Rural establishments at 31 March 1979 numbered 48,855.

Agriculture. The following table shows the area under the principal crops and the produce of each for 3 seasons (in 1,000 units):

	Total crop area	Wheat		Oats		Barley		Potatoes		Hay	
	Hec-	Hec-		Hec-		Hec-		Hec-		Hec-	
Season	tares	tares	Tonnes	tares	Tonnes	tares	Tonnes	tares	Tonnes	tares	Tonnes
1976–77	1,948	1,103	1,780	241	309	366	402	10	244	518	2,004
1977–78	2,174	1,270	1,497	228	269	418	359	12	303	380	1,252
1978–79	2,215	1,337	2,998	291	446	365	519	11	280	510	2,012

In 1978–79 there were 20,558 hectares of vines, yielding 65,201 tonnes of grapes for wine-making and 177,623 tonnes of grapes for drying or for table use. Green fodder covered 54,593 hectares, and orchards and vegetables, including potatoes and onions, occupied 44,495 hectares.

At March 1979 there were in the State 4·1m. head of cattle, 22,750,116 sheep and 389,976 pigs. In 1978–79, 553,373 tonnes of fresh meat was produced. The wool produced in the season 1979–80 amounted to 139m. kg, valued at $A271m. The quantity of butter produced in 1978–79 was 80·7m. kg.

The gross value of Victorian primary production in (rural and non-rural) 1978–79 was $A2,223m.

Minerals. The recorded production of certain metals and minerals raised in Victoria for the year 1978–79 was: Gold, 26,000 grammes, value $A129,000; coal, brown, 32·1m. tonnes, value $A79·6m.

INDUSTRY AND TRADE

Industry. From the 1975–76 Census of Manufacturing Establishments onwards only a limited range of data—employment and wages and salaries—has been collected from single-establishment manufacturing enterprises with less than 4 persons employed. This procedure significantly reduces the statistical reporting obligations of small businesses. Data in respect of the larger manufacturers provides reliable information for the evaluation of trends in the manufacturing sector of the economy. From the 1977–78 census, the classification of census units to industry is based on the 1978 edition of the Australian Standard Industrial Classification. The following data relates to manufacturing establishments owned by multi-establishment enterprises, and single-establishment manufacturing enterprises with 4 or more persons employed.

The total number of manufacturing establishments in Victoria in 1978–79 (figures for 1977–78 in brackets) was 8,550 (8,571). Persons employed, including working proprietors, on the last pay day in June were males 279,270 (280,708) and females 115,613 (116,014). Salaries and wages paid were $A4,102m. ($A3,831m.), excluding drawings of working proprietors. The cost of purchases, transfers in, and selected expenses was $A11,142m. ($A9,638m.) and sales, transfers out and other operating revenue were $A18,229m. ($A16,175m.).

The preceding figures exclude gas and electricity producing and distributing establishments. In terms of persons employed the most important manufacturing activities were: Basic and fabricated metal products including transport equipment, other machinery and equipment, 151,186 (149,448); textiles, clothing and footwear, 64,029 (64,472); food, beverages and tobacco, 55,227 (58,234).

Trade Unions. There were 166 trade unions with a total membership of 747,100 operating in Victoria in Dec. 1979.

Commerce. The commerce of Victoria, exclusive of inter-state trade, is included in the statement of the commerce of Australia, *see* pp. 110–12.

The total value of the overseas imports and exports of Victoria, including bullion and specie but excluding inter-state trade, was as follows (in $A1,000):

	1974–75	1975–76	1976–77	1977–78	1978–79	1979–80 [1]
Imports	2,793,411	2,875,772	3,665,914	3,855,619	4,694,481	5,506,573
Exports	1,696,828	1,820,081	2,216,237	2,505,768	2,702,452	3,779,152

[1] Preliminary.

The chief exports[1] in 1979–80 were: Textile fibres and their wastes, meat, cereals, petroleum products and gases, dairy products, hides and skins, fruit and vegetables, road vehicles, non-ferrous metals.

[1] From 1 July 1978 state export figures changed from 'State of Lodgement of documents with the Bureau of Customs' to 'State of Origin'.

COMMUNICATIONS

Roads. At 30 June 1978 there were 156,701 km of road open for general traffic consisting of 58,691 km of bituminous seal, etc., 45,353 km of waterbound macadam, gravel, etc., 27,380 km formed, but not paved, and 25,277 km not formed. The number of registered motor vehicles (other than tractors) at 31 Dec. 1978 was 1,931,000.

Railways. All the railways are the property of the State and are under the management of a 9-member governing board, appointed by, and responsible to, the Victorian Government.

At 30 June 1978, 6,364 km of government railway were open. During the year 1977–78 the gross revenue amounted to $A176,522,363 and the total working expenses to $A332,508,410. 97,033,418 passengers, 10,843,866 tonnes of freight and 276,506 tonnes of livestock were carried.

Aviation. During the year ended 31 Dec. 1978 there were 81,793 aircraft movements at Melbourne (Tullamarine) airport. Passengers totalled 4·7m. on domestic flights (international, 893,210). Freight handled, 72,680 tonnes, domestic flights (24,384 international).

JUSTICE, RELIGION, EDUCATION AND WELFARE

Justice. There is a Supreme Court with a Chief Justice and 20 puisne judges. There are magistrates' courts, county courts, a court of licensing, and a bankruptcy court.

Criminal statistics for 1976: 353,352 convictions (in addition approximately for 209,349 driving and traffic offences) in magistrates' courts; 1,259 convicted persons in higher (judges') courts.

There are 11 gaols in Victoria. At 30 June 1979 there were confined in these prisons, 1,470 males and 28 females.

Religion. There is no State Church in Victoria, and no State assistance has been given to religion since 1875. At the date of the 1976 census the following were the enumerated numbers of each of the principal religions: Catholic, Roman,[1] 384,305; Catholic,[1] 606,152; Church of England, 791,852; Methodist, 209,138; Presbyterian, 303,498; Protestant (undefined), 98,204; other Christian, 374,917; Hebrew, 25,756; other non-Christians, 24,310; indefinite, 14,846; no religion, 341,932; no reply, 472,065.

[1] So described on individual census schedules.

Education. Education establishments in Victoria consist of 4 universities, established under special Acts and opened in 1855, 1961, 1967 and 1977; Colleges of Advanced Education; government schools (primary, primary-secondary, high and secondary technical, and further education colleges), and non-government schools.

The University of Melbourne, founded in 1853, had, in 1979, 15,943 students (including 6,189 females) and 1,490 teaching and research staff.

Monash University, founded in 1958 in an eastern suburb of Melbourne, had, in 1979, 13,910 students (including 5,800 females) and 1,108 teaching and research staff.

La Trobe University, founded in 1964 in a northern suburb of Melbourne, had 8,709 students (including 4,108 females) and 554 teaching and research staff in 1979.

Deakin University (1974) near Melbourne had 4,403 students and 239 staff in 1979.

Primary education of children of the ages of 6 to 15 years inclusive is free, secular and compulsory. At 1 Aug. 1979 there were 1,683 government primary schools and 63 special schools with 19,351 full-time and 759 part-time teachers and an enrolment of 376,988 pupils; 20 government primary-secondary schools had 502 full-time and 70 part-time teachers and an enrolment of 6,862 pupils. There were also 389 government secondary schools, including junior technical schools and high schools with 18,243 full-time and 3,838 part-time teachers and an enrolment of 230,566 pupils. In 1979 there were 174,708 students enrolled in technical and further education schools and colleges.

Non-government Schools. There were at 1 Aug. 1979, 617 non-government schools, excluding commercial colleges, with 10,330 full-time and 2,326 part-time teachers and 211,141 pupils enrolled. Of these schools, 480 were Roman Catholic.

Social Services. Victoria was the first State of Australia to make a statutory provision for the payment of Age Pensions. The Act providing for the payment of such pensions came into operation on 18 Jan. 1901, and continued until 1 July 1909, when the Australian Invalid and Old Age Pension Act came into force. The Social Services Consolidation Act, which came into operation on 1 July 1947, repealed the various legislative enactments relating to age (previously old-age) and invalid pensions, maternity allowances, child endowment, and unemployment, and sickness benefits and while following in general the Acts repealed, considerably liberalized many of their provisions: it has since been amended. On 31 Oct. 1979 there were 356,933 aged and 54,305 invalid pensioners in Victoria, and the amount paid in pensions, including payments to wives of invalid pensioners, during 1978–79 was $A1,023·5m.

The number of disability pensions (members of the forces and their dependants) payable in Victoria on 30 June 1979 was 113,819, and the number of service pensions was 53,182. The amount paid in war and service pensions by the Federal Government during 1978–79 was $A214·7m.

During the year ended 30 June 1979 maternity allowances were granted to 26,137 mothers in the State, the total amount paid in allowances during the year being $A900,000. Payments of this allowance ceased on 1 Nov. 1978.

Under the Australian Unemployment and Sickness Benefit Act 1944, there were 78,536 persons receiving benefits at June 1979 (excluding migrants in accommodation centres) and the amount paid in benefits totalled $A243·5m. in the year ended 30 June 1979.

The number of widows' pensions in force in Victoria at 30 June 1979 was 43,928, and the total amount paid in allowances during the year was $A133·6m.

The number of family allowances in force in Victoria at 30 June 1979 was 1,155,540 (including students). In addition (in 1979), endowment was being paid in respect of 3,026 children who were being maintained in approved institutions. The total amount paid in endowment in Victoria during the year ended 30 June 1979 was $A267·3m.

State Housing. The various State housing authorities were consolidated under the control of the Ministry of Housing early in 1973. The authorities include the Housing Commission, the Teacher Housing Authority, the Co-operative Housing Registry, and the Decentralised Industry Housing Authority which was established in April 1973 to provide housing for key personnel of industries in the country. The Co-operative Housing Registry administers distribution of finance to the co-operative building societies from loan moneys advanced by the Federal Government.

On the coming into operation of amending legislation on 24 Jan. 1979, the Housing Commission, as it was constituted, ceased to exist and was replaced by a Commission consisting of a full-time Chairman and 3 part-time members. The Director of Housing (the Permanent Head of the Ministry of Housing) is, *ex officio*, Chairman of the Commission. The Housing Advisory Council was also created under that legislation, its functions being to advise on and investigate matters affecting housing and to consult with all sections of the housing industry. The Council consists of the Director and 6 part-time members appointed by the Minister of Housing.

Since its inception in 1938, the Housing Commission had built, to 30 June 1980, 89,908 housing units, of which 49,512 had been sold. Approximately 39·7% of all construction since 1938 is located outside the Melbourne metropolitan area.

Rental charges for the year ended 30 June 1980 were $A68,818,824, against which $A12,766,179 was allowed in rent rebates to tenants on low incomes, including pensioners.

Books of Reference

Statistical Information: Australian Bureau of Statistics (Commonwealth Banks Building, corner of Elizabeth and Flinders Streets, Melbourne, 3000). *Deputy Commonwealth Statistician:* I. M. Cowie, B.Com.

    Victorian Year Book. (Annually since 1873)
    Victorian Pocket Year Book. (Annually since 1956)
    Victorian Statistical Register. (Annually from 1854 to 1916)
    Monthly Summary of Statistics (from Jan. 1960)

Victoria: The First Century. Official History of Victoria. Melbourne, 1934
Victoria Municipal Directory. Melbourne, From 1866
Grant, J., and Serle, G. *The Melbourne Scene 1803–1956.* Melbourne Univ. Press, 1956
Pratt, A., *The Centenary History of Victoria.* Melbourne, 1934

State Library: The State Library of Victoria, Swanston St., Melbourne, 3000. *State Librarian:* K. A. R. Horn, BA, Mus.B(NZ), ANZLA.

WESTERN AUSTRALIA

HISTORY. In 1791 Vancouver, in the *Discovery*, took formal possession of the country about King George Sound. In 1826 the Government of New South Wales sent 20 convicts and a detachment of soldiers to King George Sound and formed a settlement then called Frederickstown. In 1827 Captain (afterwards Sir) James Stirling surveyed the coast from King George Sound to the Swan River, and in May 1829 Captain (afterwards Sir) Charles Fremantle took possession of the territory. In June 1829 Captain Stirling, newly appointed Lieut.-Governor, founded the colony now known as the State of Western Australia. On 1 Jan. 1901 Western Australia became one of the 6 federated States within the Commonwealth of Australia.

AREA AND POPULATION. Western Australia lies between 113° 09′ and 129° E. long. and 13° 44′ and 35° 08′ S. lat.; its area is 2,525,500 sq. km.

The enumerated population at each census from 1921 was as follows[1]:

	Males	Females	Total		Males	Females	Total
1921	177,278	155,454	332,732	1961	375,452	361,177	736,629
1933	233,937	204,915	438,852	1966	432,569	415,531	848,100
1947	258,076	244,404	502,480	1971	534,100	509,000	1,043,100
1954	330,358	309,413	639,771	1976	596,800	573,100	1,169,800

[1] 1961 and earlier exclude full-blood Aboriginals; from 1966 figures refer to total population (*i.e.*, including Aboriginals).

Of the census population in 1976, 832,419 were born in Australia. Married persons numbered 518,407 (260,797 males and 257,610 females); widowers, 8,776; widows, 39,610; divorced, 8,819 males and 10,167 females; never married, 291,841 males and 243,604 females. The number of males under 21 was 231,444 and of females 219,699.

Perth, the capital, had an estimated population of 883,600 at June 1979. Of this, the area administered by the City of Perth had a population of 88,850 while the population in the area for which the City of Fremantle is responsible (which includes the chief port of the State) was 23,480.

Principal towns outside the metropolitan area, with population at the census of 30 June 1976: Bunbury, 19,513; Kalgoorlie–Boulder, 19,041; Geraldton, 18,773; Albany, 13,696; Port Hedland, 11,144; Mandurah, 7,050; Northam, 6,866; Collie, 6,771; Busselton, 5,550; Carnarvon, 5,341; Esperance, 5,262; Narrogin, 4,812.

Vital statistics for calendar years[1]:

	Births	Ex-nuptial births	Marriages	Divorces	Deaths
1977	20,651	2,528	10,063	3,975	7,899
1978	20,611	2,654	9,404	3,387	7,794
1979	20,469	2,783	9,239	3,397	8,022

[1] Including Aboriginals.

CONSTITUTION AND GOVERNMENT. In 1870 partially representative government was instituted, and in 1890 the administration was vested in the Governor, a Legislative Council and a Legislative Assembly. The Legislative Council was, in the first instance, nominated by the Governor, but it was provided that in the event of the population of the colony reaching 60,000, it should be elective. In 1893 this limit of population being reached, the Colonial Parliament amended the Constitution accordingly.

The Legislative Council consists of 32 members, 2 members representing each of the 16 electoral provinces. Each member is elected for a term of 6 years, one-half of the members retiring every 3 years.

There are 55 members of the Legislative Assembly, each member representing one of the 55 electoral districts of the State. Members are elected for the duration of the Parliament, normally 3 years. The qualifications applying to candidates and electors are identical for the Legislative Council and the Legislative Assembly. A candidate must have resided in Western Australia for a minimum of 12 months, be at least 18 years of age and free from legal incapacity, be a British subject, and be enrolled, or qualified for enrolment, as an elector. A judge of the Supreme Court, the Sheriff of Western Australia, an undischarged bankrupt or a debtor against whose estate there is a subsisting order in bankruptcy may not be elected to Parliament. No person may hold office as a member of the Legislative Assembly and the Legislative Council at the same time. An elector must be at least 18 years of age, be a British subject free from legal incapacity, must have resided in the Commonwealth of Australia for 6 and in Western Australia for 3 months continuously and in the electoral district for which he claims enrolment for a continuous period of 1 month immediately preceding the date of his claim. Enrolment is compulsory for all qualified persons except Aboriginal natives of Australia, who are entitled but not required to enrol. Voting at elections is on the preferential system and is compulsory for all enrolled persons.

Ordinary members of the legislature are paid a salary of $A26,041 a year, with an additional electorate allowance, ranging from $A7,560 to $A16,110 according to location of electorate. Members are entitled to free travel on Western Australian government railways and on the Metropolitan (Perth) Passenger Transport Trust omnibus and ferry services, and, by arrangement, once every year on government railways in other States. All members of Parliament contribute to superannuation benefits.

The Premier receives a salary, including an electorate allowance, of $A62,304, the Deputy Premier $A55,443, the Leader of the Government in the Legislative Council $A53,694, and all other Ministers $A49,824–56,294 according to location of electorate.

The Legislative Assembly, elected on 23 Feb. 1980, is composed as follows: Liberal Party, 26; Australian Labor Party, 23; National Country Party, 3; National Party, 3. The Legislative Council, one-half of which was elected on the same day, is composed of 19 Liberal Party, 9 Australian Labor Party, 3 National Country Party, 1 National Party.

Governor: Rear-Admiral Sir Richard Trowbridge, KCVO.

The Liberal–National Country Party coalition Cabinet was, at 30 June 1980:

Premier, Treasurer, and Minister Co-ordinating Economic and Regional Development: Hon. Sir Charles Walter Michael Court, KCMG, OBE, MLA.

Deputy Premier, Minister for Labour and Industry, Consumer Affairs, Immigration, Regional Administration and the North West, and Tourism: Hon. Raymond James O'Connor, MLA. *Minister for Agriculture:* Hon. Richard Charles Old, MLA. *Attorney-General and Minister for Federal Affairs, and Leader of the Government in the Legislative Council:* Hon. Ian George Medcalf, ED, QC, MLC. *Minister for Works, Water Resources, Minister Assisting the Minister Co-ordinating Economic and Regional Development, and Housing:* Hon. Andrew Mensaros, MLA. *Minister for Resources Development, Mines, Fuel and Energy, and Industrial Development and Commerce:* Hon. Peter Vernon Jones, MLA. *Minister for Transport:* Hon. Edgar Cyril Rushton, MLA. *Minister for Health:* Hon. Raymond Laurence Young, FCA, MLA. *Minister for Education, Cultural Affairs, and Recreation:* Hon. William Leonard Grayden, MLA. *Minister for Lands and Forests:* Hon. David John Wordsworth, MLC. *Minister for Local Government, and Urban Development and Town Planning:* Hon. Margaret June Craig, MLA. *Chief Secretary, Minister for Police and Traffic, and Community Welfare:* Hon. William Ralph Hassell, LLB, MA, MLA. *Minister for Fisheries and Wildlife, and Conservation and the Environment:* Hon. Gordon Edgar Masters, MLC. *Honorary Minister assisting the Ministers in the portfolios of Housing, Regional Administration and the North West, and Tourism:* Hon. Ian James Laurance, MLA. *Honorary Minister assisting the Minister in the portfolio of Industrial Development and Commerce:* Hon. Barry John MacKinnon, MLA.

Agent-General in London: L. W. Slade (Western Australia House, 115 Strand, WC2R 0AJ).

Local Government. The only unincorporated area in mainland Western Australia is King's Park, a public reserve of about 403 hectares in Perth. Including the lord-mayoralty of Perth there were 12 cities, 12 towns and 114 shires at 30 June 1980. The executive body in each of these districts is normally an elective council, presided over by a mayor (city and town) or a president (shire), but in certain circumstances it may be a commissioner appointed by the Governor. Their functions include road construction and repair, the provision of parks and recreation grounds, the administration of building controls and local services such as health and, in some country districts, traffic. Finance is derived largely from rates levied on property owners as well as charges for services and government grants (mainly for road construction).

ECONOMY

Budget. The revenue and expenditure (in $A) of Western Australia in years ended 30 June, are given as follows:

	1978	1979	1980	1981[1]
Revenue	1,311,204,538	1,443,334,252	1,641,191,281	1,857,330,000
Expenditure	1,311,204,538	1,443,334,252	1,641,191,281	1,857,330,000

[1] Estimates.

Main items of revenue in 1979–80: Railways ($A156,470,202), taxation ($A326,529,625), lands, timber and mining ($A85,429,600), public utilities other than railways ($A32,707,007), from Federal Funds ($A853,442,655). Western Australia had a net loan liability of $A1,359,650,722 on 30 June 1980, the charge for the year being $A121,874,165.

Banking. There are 9 trading banks in Western Australia including the Commonwealth Trading Bank and The Rural and Industries Bank of Western Australia. In June quarter, 1980, the average of customers' balances was $A1,776·4m. and average advances $A1,804·8m.

At 30 June 1980, the 8 savings banks held deposits of $A1,216·2m., in 1,579,722 accounts.

ENERGY AND NATURAL RESOURCES

Minerals. The mining industry has been for many years of considerable significance in the Western Australian economy. Until the mid-1960s the major mineral produced was gold. However, in recent years gold has been displaced by iron ore, crude oil, bauxite and nickel concentrates in terms of value.

The total ex-mine value of minerals from mining and quarrying in the State in 1978–79 was $A1,369·4m. Principal minerals produced in 1978–79 were: Iron ore, 79m. tonnes, value $A823·8m.; crude oil, 1·7m. cu. metres, value $A73·3m.; gold bullion, 15·1m. grammes, value $A78·7m.; construction materials (excluding sand and gravel), value $A25·5m.; mineral sands, 1·53m. tonnes, value, $A59·4m.; black coal, 2·41m. tonnes, value $A34·5m.; salt, 4·49m. tonnes, value $A31·6m.; tin concentrates, 604 tonnes, value $A5·49m.; nickel concentrates, 353,000 tonnes; bauxite, 12·9m. tonnes, and natural gas, 835m. cu. metres.

Land Settlement. Up to 31 Dec. 1979, of the entire area of the State (252·55m. hectares) 16,519,170 hectares had been alienated; on that date 2,386,203 hectares were in process of alienation; the area alienated and in process of alienation thus amounting to 18,905,373 hectares. There were in force leases comprising an area of 97,073,525 hectares, of which 93,865,488 hectares were pastoral, 832,970 hectares were timber, 129,134 hectares mining leases, 12,810 hectares miners' homestead leases and 2,233,123 hectares for reserves, residential lots, special and perpetual leases.

Agriculture.

Crop	1977–78		1978–79	
	Hectares	Production	Hectares	Production
Wheat (tonnes)	3,608,871	2,945,461	3,705,610	4,399,520
Oats (tonnes)	414,978	415,645	427,494	490,884
Barley (tonnes)	613,623	751,265	616,348	778,443
Hay (tonnes)	191,106	596,594	183,842	585,819
Potatoes (tonnes)	2,066	53,289	2,039	62,572
Apples (cases)	3,639	1,781,249	3,295	2,372,603
Pears (cases)	372	237,078	348	258,974
Oranges (cases)	1,083	399,994	1,142	288,076
Currants, raisins and sultanas (tonnes, dried)	—	916	—	821

Irrigation has been established by the Government along the south-western coastal plain and in the north of the State. Reservoirs with an aggregate capacity of 6,137m. cu. metres provided irrigation water for 21,393 hectares in 6 districts during 1978–79.

The livestock at 31 March 1979 consisted of 2,091,940 cattle, 30,264,660 sheep and 271,490 pigs.

The wool clip in 1978–79 was 148,960 tonnes; the exports for 1978–79, greasy wool, 136,136 tonnes; degreased wool, 14,049 tonnes.

Forestry. The area of State forests and timber reserves at 30 June 1979 was 2,219,000 hectares; 1978–79 production of sawn timber was 349,126 cu. metres, principally Jarrah and Karri hardwoods.

Fisheries. The catch of fish, crustaceans and molluscs in Western Australia in 1978–79 totalled 25,505 tonnes for a gross value of $A80·2m. Of this, rock lobsters, with a total catch of 11,461 tonnes accounted for $A56·8m. As at 31 Dec. 1979, 1,960 boats, with a value of $A103,169,000 and employing 4,305 persons, were licensed to fish in the State.

Value of Primary Commodities Produced. The estimated gross value of Western Australian primary commodities (excluding mining) during 1978–79 was as follows: Crops, $A765·39m.; livestock slaughterings and other disposals, $A227·24m.; livestock products, $A347·19m.; forestry, fishing and hunting, $A128·51m.

INDUSTRY AND TRADE

Industry. Up to the early 1950s most of the factories in Western Australia were small and medium sized establishments supplying the local market and carrying out some processing of the State's primary products for export. Development of heavy industry and large-scale operations since the early 1950s has been associated with the establishment of a large oil refinery at Kwinana in 1954 which provided the basis for an integrated industrial complex adjacent to Perth; more recent developments have been associated with the processing of the State's vast deposits of iron ore, nickel, bauxite and mineral sands.

The following table shows manufacturing industry statistics for 1978–79 [1]:

Industry sub-division	Number of establishments operating at 30 June	Persons employed [2]	Wages and salaries $A1,000	Turnover $A1,000	Value added $A1,000
Food, beverages and tobacco	333	12,960	129,789	883,276	266,814
Textiles	29	801	7,494	30,672	12,550
Clothing and footwear	49	1,428	9,790	22,456	13,259
Wood, wood products and furniture	411	7,381	62,241	242,513	115,275
Paper, paper products, printing and publishing	169	6,133	60,589	193,217	106,462
Chemical, petroleum and coal products	65	3,191	42,436	260,095	105,001
Non-metallic mineral products	194	5,059	58,384	266,161	120,762
Basic metal products	35	5,548	75,749	782,339	214,431
Fabricated metal products	375	8,383	81,616	340,313	138,796
Transport equipment	151	5,448	53,317	134,343	73,114
Other machinery and equipment	240	6,857	71,259	255,293	119,407
Miscellaneous manufacturing	151	2,043	18,107	88,149	35,812
Total	2,202	65,232	670,772	3,498,828	1,321,683

[1] Excludes single establishment enterprises with less than 4 persons employed.
[2] Annual average. Includes working proprietors.

Labour. The Industrial Arbitration Act Amendment Act (No. 2), 1963 which came into operation on 1 Feb. 1964, abolished the Court of Arbitration and established The Western Australian Industrial Commission and the Western Australian Industrial Appeal Court.

The Western Australian Industrial Commission consists of a President, a Chief Industrial Commissioner, a Senior Commissioner, and 'such number of other Commissioners as may, from time to time, be necessary'. There were 5 'other Commissioners' at 1 March 1980. A person shall not be appointed as President unless he is qualified to be a Judge, and on appointment he is entitled to the status of a Puisne Judge. The President or a Commissioner sitting or acting alone constitutes the Commission and may exercise the appropriate powers of the Commission.

The Commission can inquire into any industrial matter and make an award, order or declaration relating to such matter. 'Industrial matter' means any matter affecting or relating to the work, privileges, rights, or duties of employers or employees in any industry and includes any matter relating to the wages, salaries, allowances, or other remuneration of employees or the prices to be paid in respect of their employment; the hours of employment, sex, age, qualification or status of employees and the mode, terms and conditions of employment including conditions which are to take effect after the termination of employment. The Commission may also make inquiries where industrial action has occurred or is likely to occur.

The Commission in Court Session is constituted by not less than 3 Commissioners sitting or acting together, and may make General Orders, hear matters referred by the Commission, and hear appeals from decisions of Boards of Reference.

The Full Bench is constituted by not less than 3 members of the Commission, 1 of whom is the President, and may hear matters referred by the Commission on questions of law, and appeals from decisions of the Commission.

The following table shows particulars relating to The Western Australian Industrial Commission.

At 30 June	1975	1976	1977	1978	1979
Awards in force	393	402	414	393	355
Industrial agreements in force[1]	150	184	180	205	135
Unions of workers:					
Number	85	85	80	77	77
Membership	178,171	180,137	185,186	184,578	192,056
Unions of employers:					
Number	14	15	15	15	14
Membership	2,181	2,026	2,021	2,156	2,102

[1] Consent awards under the *Industrial Arbitration Act, 1979.*

The Western Australian Industrial Appeal Court consists of 3 judges, one of whom is the Presiding Judge. An appeal lies to the Court from any decision of the President, the Full Bench, or the Commission in Court Session on the ground that the decision is erroneous in law or is in excess of jurisdiction.

Commerce. The external commerce of Western Australia, exclusive of interstate trade, is comprised in the statement of the commerce of Australia, *see* pp. 110–12.

The total value of the imports and exports, including interstate trade in 5 years (30 June) is, in $A, as follows:

	1974–75	1975–76[2]	1976–77[2]	1977–78[2]	1978–79[2]
Imports	1,711,926,586	2,056,164,777	2,470,955,480	2,765,860,023	3,210,787,251
Exports[1]	2,133,505,924	2,408,630,977	2,901,942,796	2,944,104,696	3,266,342,542

[1] Excluding ships' stores.   [2] Excludes interstate value of horses.

Selected exports (in $A) for 1978–79 (excluding ships' stores): Iron ore, 978,315,371; wool and other animal hair, 327,117,742; wheat, 257,414,134[1]; petroleum and petroleum products, 135,000,566; gold, processed, 99,933,077; beef and veal, 90,215,748; machinery, 79,217,699; iron and steel, 72,590,542; rock lobster tails, 51,064,472; live sheep and lambs, 45,915,419; barley, 40,829,821[1]; salt, 31,242,333[1]; mutton and lamb, 31,059,386; hides, skins and furskins, raw, 29,280,355; prawns, 20,005,438; transport equipment, 18,083,741; ilmenite and leucoxene, 15,894,917[1,2]; tallow, 15,102,542; furniture, 11,919,562; rock lobsters, whole, 11,521,979; timber,10,507,775; oats, 10,217,676[1]; clothing and clothing accessories, 9,942,965; paper and paperboard, etc. and articles thereof, 5,694,045; apples, 5,266,053; tin ore and concentrates, 5,074,167.

[1] Overseas exports only.   [2] Excluding beneficiated ilmenite.

Selected imports (in $A) for 1978–79: Machinery, 584,311,904; transport equipment, 581,055,225; petroleum and petroleum products, 425,567,397; textiles and apparel, 249,139,143; food, 224,310,819; chemicals, 223,836,353[1]; iron and steel,

[1] Excluding inorganic chemicals.

149,876,342; beverages and tobacco, 71,434,865; paper and paperboard, etc. and articles thereof, 63,834,907; rubber and rubber manufactures, 55,480,089.

The chief countries exporting to Western Australia in 1978–79 were (in $A): USA, 217,671,647; Japan, 124,171,112; Iraq, 94,524,670; Kuwait, 89,597,292; UK, 81,236,626; Federal Republic of Germany, 73,440,904. Western Australian exports in 1978–79 (in $A) went chiefly to: Japan, 1,118,297,892; USA, 374,161,598; People's Republic of China, 186,279,021; Federal Republic of Germany, 105,319,876; USSR, 67,160,750; Hong Kong, 60,085,784; Indonesia, 58,307,239.

Tourism. In 1979 425,000 (estimate) tourists contributed about $A136m. to the economy.

COMMUNICATIONS

Roads. At 30 June 1979 there were 120,684 km of prepared and formed roads in Western Australia, namely, 35,344 km of bituminous surface, 39,214 other constructed surfaces and 46,126 formed but not metalled or otherwise prepared. In addition, there are approximately 40,788 km unprepared except for clearing which are used for general traffic.

New motor vehicles registered in Western Australia during the year ended 30 June 1980 were 58,548.

Railways. At 30 June 1979 the State had 5,764 km of State government railway and 732 km of Federal line, the latter being the western portion of the Trans-Australian line (Kalgoorlie–Port Pirie), which links the State railway system to those of the other States of the Commonwealth. At 30 June 1979, mining companies operated 1,155 km of private railways for the transport of ore to ports on the north-west coast.

Aviation. An extensive system of regular air services operates in Western Australia for the transport of passengers, freight and mail. During the year ended 30 June 1978, Perth Airport handled a total of 16,342 aircraft movements, 17,213 tonnes of freight and 1,006,432 passengers on domestic and international services.

Shipping. In 1978–79, the number, net tonnage of vessels entering and cargo shipped at major ports were as follows: Port of Fremantle, 1,055 vessels of 9·6m. net tonnage, shipped 5·2m. tonnes plus 220,108 cu. metres of cargo; Dampier, 489 vessels of 12·4m. net tonnage, shipped 33·3m. tonnes, plus 36,538 cu. metres of cargo; Port Hedland, 460 vessels of 12m. net tonnage, shipped 31·9m. tonnes plus 1,214 cu. metres of cargo; Port Walcott, 121 vessels of 4·7m. net tonnage, shipped 11·9m. tonnes of cargo.

Post and Broadcasting. Postal, telephone and telegraph facilities are afforded at 525 offices. An additional 42 offices provide only telephone and telegraph facilities. Telephones connected totalled 514,460 at 30 June 1979.

There were 38 wireless broadcasting and 39 television stations, including translator stations, in operation at 30 June 1979.

JUSTICE, RELIGION, EDUCATION AND WELFARE

Justice. In Western Australia justice is administered by a Supreme Court, consisting of a Chief Justice and 6 puisne judges at 31 Dec. 1979, a District Court comprising a chairman of judges and 5 district court judges and Magistrates' Courts exercising both civil and criminal jurisdiction. The lower courts are presided over by justices of the peace, except in the more important centres, where the court is constituted by a stipendiary magistrate. There are special Magistrates' Courts for juvenile offenders.

Offences against law	1975	1976	1977	1978	1979
Charges [1]	127,813	116,347	108,756	117,408	124,196
Lower Court convictions [2]	111,478	102,557	94,823	105,136	111,864
Higher Court convictions	880	818	1,154	1,204	1,584

[1] In the case of concurrent offences each offence is included.
[2] Includes convictions for traffic offences: 59,852 in 1975; 50,932 in 1976; 44,176 in 1977; 50,235 in 1978; 56,310 in 1979. In addition, small fines were imposed for minor traffic offences as follows: 1975, 265,096; 1976, 315,953; 1977, 306,885; 1978, 307,396; 1979, 333,545.

The total number of admissions to prison for penal imprisonment in the year ended 30 June 1979 was 4,503. Inmates at 30 June 1980 numbered 1,310 males and 59 females.

Religion. There is no State Church, and freedom of worship is accorded to all. At the census, 30 June 1976, the principal denominations were: Church of England, 360,337; Roman Catholic and Catholic, 283,241; Methodist, 77,011; Presbyterian, 42,630; Baptist, 14,450; Lutheran, 7,123; other Christian, 90,437; Hebrew, 2,886; all other, including not stated and no religion, 266,745.

Education. School attendance is compulsory from the age of 6 until the end of the year in which the child attains 15 years. Pre-school education is provided by a kindergarten system partly financed from government subsidy. In 1980 there were 690 government primary and secondary schools providing free education to 220,820 pupils and 198 non-government primary and secondary schools providing education, for which fees are charged, to 46,655 pupils.

Technical education is available at a number of technical colleges, schools and centres, which are staffed and controlled by the Education Department.

In 1980 the full-time teaching and research staff of the University of Western Australia was 731 and the number of students enrolled was 9,791. Murdoch University enrolled 2,485 students in 1980. Full-time teaching and research staff numbered 176.

Tertiary education is also offered by the Western Australian Institute of Technology and 5 colleges of advanced education.

State Government expenditure from consolidated revenue on education, including financial assistance to the Universities, during the year ended 30 June 1980, amounted to $A403,954,080.

Social Welfare. At 30 June 1980 there were 48 general hospitals and 8 nursing homes maintained wholly by public funds and 50 general hospitals and 9 nursing homes partly assisted therefrom. In addition, there are numerous private hospitals. Government mental health services comprise 4 approved hospitals, 17 clinics, 4 rehabilitation units, 32 units concerned with the intellectually handicapped, 1 after-care hostel and 1 in-patient unit for children.

The Department for Community Welfare is responsible for the provision of welfare services throughout the State. There are 34 district offices, 6 country divisional offices, 7 metropolitan divisional offices and 3 metropolitan sub-offices.

The Department runs 9 facilities for the care, assessment, training and support of children who have behavioural problems or are emotionally disturbed. It also provides accommodation at 29 hostels, mainly for Aboriginal children.

There are specialized units working in the areas of child abuse, drug abuse, adoptions and youth activities, and the Department offers help for parents having difficulties looking after their families and supervises all day care centres in the State. There is a homemaker service, a psychological service and a counselling and welfare service attached to the Family Court.

The Department administers the Children's Courts and the Children's (Suspended Proceedings) Panels.

Through the Department, the State Government makes financial assistance available to people in necessitous circumstances.

At 30 June 1980, 1,958 families were receiving assistance.

Age, invalid, widows' and war and service pensions are paid by the Federal Government. The number of pensioners in Western Australia at 30 June 1978 was: Age, 96,558, invalid, 15,045; widows, 12,232; and repatriation benefits, veterans, 27,341.

Housing. The State Housing Commission was established in Jan. 1947 to replace the Workers' Homes Board created in 1912. The objects of the Commission are 'the improvement of existing housing conditions' and 'the provision of adequate and suitable housing accommodation for persons of limited means and certain other persons not otherwise adequately housed'. The Commission provided 791 new dwelling units for sale and for rental in 1978–79. During the same period 11,148 new houses and 3,507 new other dwellings were completed throughout the State.

Books of Reference

Statistical Information: The State Government Statistician's Office was established in 1897 and now functions as the Western Australian Office of the Australian Bureau of Statistics (1–3 St George's Tce, Perth). *Deputy Commonwealth Statistician and Government Statistician:* W. M. Bartlett. Its principal publications are: *Statistical Register of Western Australia* (annual, from 1896 to 1967–68). *Statistics of Western Australia* (annual from 1968–69). *Western Australian Year Book* (new series, from 1957). *Western Australian Pocket Year Book* (from 1919). *Quarterly Statistical Abstract* (from 1917).

Battye, J. S., *Western Australia: A History from its Discovery to the Inauguration of the Commonwealth.* Oxford, 1924.—*The Cyclopedia of Western Australia.* Adelaide, Vol. 1 (1912), Vol. 2 (1913)

Crowley, F. K., *A Short History of Western Australia.* Melbourne, 1959.—*Australia's Western Third.* London, 1960

Crowley, F. K., and De Garis, B. K., *A Short History of Western Australia.* Melbourne, 1969

Gentilli, J., *Atlas of Western Australian Agriculture.* Perth, 1941

Kerr, Alex, *The South-West Region of Western Australia.* Perth, 1965.—*Australia's North-West.* Perth, 1967

Kimberley, W. B., *History of Western Australia: A Narrative of Her Past.* Melbourne, 1978

Metropolitan Region Planning Authority, *The Corridor Plan for Perth.* Perth, 1970

Stephenson, G., and Hepburn, J. A., *Plan for the Metropolitan Region: Perth and Fremantle.* Perth, 1955

State Library: The State Library of Western Australia, Perth. *State Librarian:* R. C. Sharman, BA, FLAA.

AUSTRIA

Republik Österreich

Capital: Vienna
Population: 7·46m. (1971)
GNP per capita: US$7,030 (1978)

HISTORY. On 27 April 1945 a provisional government restored the Republic of Austria and was recognized by the Allied Control Council on 20 Oct. 1945.

AREA AND POPULATION. For the boundaries of Austria according to the Treaty of St Germain, signed in Sept. 1919, *see* THE STATESMAN'S YEAR-BOOK, 1920, pp. 674–75.

Federal States	Area, sq. km	Population (census 12 May 1971)	Percentage of population	Population per sq. km
Vienna (Wien)	415	1,614,841	21·7	3,892
Lower Austria (Niederösterreich)	19,171	1,414,161	19·0	74
Burgenland	3,966	272,119	3·6	69
Upper Austria (Oberösterreich)	11,979	1,223,444	16·4	102
Salzburg	7,154	401,766	5·4	56
Styria (Steiermark)	16,387	1,192,100	16·0	73
Carinthia (Kärnten)	9,533	525,728	7·0	55
Tirol	12,647	540,771	7·3	43
Vorarlberg	2,601	271,473	3·6	104
Total	83,853 [1]	7,456,403	100·0	89

[1] 32,375 sq. miles.

Vital statistics for calendar years:

	Live births	Still births	Deaths [1]	Marriages	Divorces	Emigration Austrians	Others
1976	87,446	683	95,140	45,767	11,168	29	1,186
1977	85,595	673	92,402	45,378	11,668	23	1,335
1978	85,402	562	94,617	44,573	12,400	10	2,071
1979	86,388	561	92,012	45,445	13,042	11	2,597

[1] Excluding still births.

The population of the principal towns (excluding Vienna), according to the census of 12 May 1971 (area, 1 Jan. 1980) was as follows:

Graz	248,500	Steyr	40,578	Bregenz	22,839	Braunau	
Linz	202,874	Leoben	35,153	Baden	22,631	am Inn	16,432
Salzburg	128,845	Wiener		Klosterneu-		Bruck an	
Innsbruck	115,197	Neustadt	34,774	burg	21,912	der Mur	16,359
Klagenfurt	82,512	Dornbirn	33,810	Amstetten	21,692	Ternitz	16,343
Villach	50,993	Wolfsberg	29,002	Feldkirch	21,214	Lustenau	15,239
St Pölten	50,144	Kapfenberg	26,001	Traun	20,843		
Wels	47,279	Krems a.d.D.	23,409	Mödling	18,712		

CONSTITUTION AND GOVERNMENT. Austria recovered its sovereignty and independence on 27 July 1955 by the coming into force of the Austrian State Treaty between the UK, the USA, the USSR and France on the one part and the Republic of Austria on the other part (signed on 15 May).

On 12 March 1938 Austria was forcibly absorbed in the German Reich until it was liberated by the American, British, French and Soviet armies in spring 1945. Already in the Moscow Declaration of Oct. 1943, UK, the USA and the USSR had resolved upon the re-establishment of a free and independent Austria.

On 27 April 1945 Dr Karl Renner set up a provisional government which restored the Republic of Austria in the spirit of the Constitution of 1920/29, and was recognized by the Four-Power Allied Control Council on 20 Oct. 1945. The last occupation forces left Austria in Oct. 1955.

President of the Republic: Dr Rudolf Kirchschläger, former Minister of Foreign Affairs, elected on 23 June 1974 and re-elected on 18 May 1980.

On 6 March 1979 the elections were held for the National Assembly, which returned 95 Socialists, 77 People's Party, 11 Freedom Party.

The government of the Socialist Party which was formed in Oct. 1971 was composed March 1981 as follows:

Chancellor: Dr Bruno Kreisky.

Vice-Chancellor and Education and the Arts: Dr Fred Sinowatz. *Finance:* Dr Herbert Salcher; Elfriede Karl (*Minister of State*). *Social Welfare:* Alfred Dallinger; Franziska Fast (*Minister of State*). *Foreign Affairs:* Dr Willibald Pahr. *Interior:* Erich Lanc. *Agriculture and Forestry:* Günther Haiden; Albin Schober (*Minister of State*). *Transport:* Karl Lausecker. *Justice:* Dr Christian Broda. *Trade, Commerce and Industry:* Dr Josef Staribacher; Anneliese Albricht (*Minister of State*). *Defence:* Otto Rösch. *Construction and Technology:* Karl Sekanina; Dr Beatrix Eypeltourer (*Minister of State*). *Science and Research:* Dr Hertha Firnberg. *Health and Environment:* Dr Kurt Steyrer. *Federal Chancellory:* Dr Adolf Nussbaumer (*Minister of State*). *Family Policy:* Elfriede Karl (*Minister of State*); Franz Löschnak (*Minister of State*); Johanna Dolmal (*Minister of State*).

The *Federal Council* (*Bundesrat*) which represents the federal provinces has 58 members and (1980) the Socialist Party had 29 members and the People's Party 29. The *Nationalrat* and *Bundesrat* together form the National Assembly.

National flag: Three horizontal stripes of red, white, red.

National anthem: Land der Berge, Land am Strome (words by Paula Preradovic; tune by W. A. Mozart).

The official language is German.

Local Government. The Republic of Austria comprises 9 Federal States (Vienna, Lower Austria, Upper Austria, Salzburg, Styria, Carinthia, Tirol, Vorarlberg, Burgenland). There is in every province an elected Provincial Assembly.

Every commune has a Council, which chooses one of its number to be head of the Commune (burgomaster) and a committee for the administration and execution of its resolutions.

Adamovich, L., *Grundriss des österreichischen Verfassungsrechts.* 8th ed. Vienna, 1953

DEFENCE. The supreme command is vested in the Federal President; operational control is exercised by the Minister of Defence.

Army. The Army consists of an alert force (*Bereitschaftruppe*) of 15,000 regulars and a militia (*Landwehr*) of 6-month conscripts and reservists (186,000). The country is divided into 2 corps areas, I (Graz) and II (Salzburg). The aim is to deploy 1 mechanized division, 3 ordnance regiments and 28 *Landwehrregimenter* of local defence battalions and companies. Strength (1980) 46,000 (conscripts, 32,000).

Air Force. The Air Force is an integral part of army command and comprises 15 squadrons with (1981) about 4,300 personnel and 160 aircraft, divided among 3 Flight Regiments each of which includes air defence battalions of anti-aircraft guns. About 34 Saab-105Oe jet light attack aircraft equip a surveillance wing of 2 squadrons with responsibilty for defence of Austrian airspace; a fighter-bomber wing of 2 squadrons, 1 of which is also responsible for weapon training of jet pilots; and a jet training squadron which undertakes basic training of pilots after primary training on Saab Safir piston-engined aircraft. Helicopters equip 8 squadrons for transport/support, communications, observation and search and rescue duties, in addition to training units; types in service include Alouette III, armed Kiowa, JetRanger, heavy-lift Sikorsky S-65Oe, and Agusta-Bell 212. Fixed-wing transports comprise 2 Skyvans and 12 Turbo-Porters.

INTERNATIONAL RELATIONS

Membership. Austria is a member of UN and EFTA.

External debt. The external debt was (1977) 120·9m. schilling.

ECONOMY

Budget. The budget for calendar years provided revenue and expenditure (ordinary and extraordinary) as follows (in 1m. schilling):

	1973	1974	1975	1976	1977[1]	1978[1]	1979
Revenue	128,315	148,598	159,533	177,904	197,213	227,065	244,595
Expenditure	141,151	167,133	196,697	221,901	240,767	267,491	243,038

[1] Provisional.

Currency. The Austrian unit of currency is the *schilling* of 100 *groschen*. The rate of exchange in March 1981, £1 = 33·25 *schilling*, US$1 = 15·01 *schilling*. Exchange rates since 24 Aug. 1971 have been floating.

Banking. The National Bank of Austria, opened on 2 Jan. 1923, was taken over by the German Reichsbank on 17 March 1938. It was re-established on 3 July 1945. At 31 Dec. 1979 foreign exchange amounted to 44,133m. and note circulation to 71,985m. schilling. The balance-sheet showed assets and liabilities of 148,310m. schilling.

Weights and Measures. The metric system of weights and measures is in use.

ENERGY AND NATURAL RESOURCES

Electricity. Electric energy produced (1m. kwh.): 1978, 38,069; 1979, 40,645.

Oil. The commercial production of petroleum began in the early 1930s. Production of crude oil (in tonnes): 1960, 2,448,391; 1965, 2,854,544; 1971, 2,798,237; 1976, 1,930,848; 1978, 1,790,312; 1979, 1,728,306.

Minerals. The mineral production (in tonnes) was as follows:

	1978	1979		1978	1979
Lignite	3,075,680	2,740,742	Pig-iron	3,077,167	3,702,440
Iron ore	2,788,435	3,200,000	Raw steel	4,335,016	4,917,179
Lead and zinc ore[1]	476,340	504,019	Rolled steel	3,557,592	3,843,525
Raw magnesite[1]	982,320	1,103,649			

[1] Including recovery from slag.

Austria is one of the world's largest sources of high-grade graphite. Production, which averaged 20,000 tonnes yearly from 1929 to 1944, dropped to 246 in 1946, but rose to 102,237 in 1964, and fell again to 23,992 in 1970, 33,057 in 1976, 35,488 in 1977, 40,501 in 1978 and 40,519 in 1979.

Agriculture. In 1978 the total area sown amounted to 1,498,247 hectares.
The chief products (area in hectares, yield in tonnes) were as follows:

	1977		1978		1979	
	Area	Yield	Area	Yield	Area	Yield
Wheat	285,158	1,071,848	286,038	1,194,808	270,188	849,921
Rye	118,749	351,344	108,912	409,525	105,542	277,974
Barley	328,477	1,211,734	355,485	1,423,602	373,205	1,128,714
Oats	89,628	279,189	89,271	304,273	95,032	272,732
Potatoes	60,198	1,352,246	56,902	1,400,892	58,048	1,493,706

Production of raw sugar in 1949, 66,700; 1955, 219,300; 1960, 308,000; refined sugar: 1970, 298,000; 1978, 328,000; 1979, 327,000 tonnes.
Livestock (1979): Cattle, 2,594,000; pigs, 4,007,000; sheep, 192,000; goats, 36,000; horses, 45,000; poultry, 14·94m.

Forestry. Felled timber, in cu. metres: 1960, 10,015,925; 1970, 11,122,896; 1972, 10,153,360; 1973, 9,713,886; 1974, 10,023,540; 1975, 9,598,917; 1976, 11,579,586; 1977, 10,706,588; 1978, 10,547,662; 1979, 12,752,442.

INDUSTRY AND TRADE

Industry. On 26 July 1946 the Austrian parliament passed a government bill, nationalizing some 70 industrial concerns. As from 17 Sept. 1946 ownership of the 3 largest commercial banks, most oil-producing and refining companies and the principal firms in the following industries devolved upon the Austrian state: River navigation; coal extraction; non-ferrous mining and refining; iron-ore mining; pig-iron and steel production; manufacture of iron and steel products, including structural material, machinery, railroad equipment and repairs, and shipbuilding; electrical machinery and appliances. Six companies supplying electric power were nationalized in accordance with a law of 26 March 1947.

According to the Census of Industrial Establishments 1977 (average), there were 6,709 establishments employing 633,970 persons, producing a gross output of 383m. schillings. In 1979, 6,757 industrial establishments employed 622,714 persons.

GDP *per capita* (1976) US$5,407.

Commerce. Imports and exports are as follows (excluding coined gold):

	Imports			Exports		
	1977	1978	1979	1977	1978	1979
Quantity (1,000 tonnes)	30,638	32,068	36,090	11,730	12,819	14,564
Value (1m. sch.)	234,841	231,888	269,862	161,781	176,112	206,253

The total trade between Austria and UK (British Department of Trade returns, in £1,000 sterling):

	1976	1977	1978	1979	1980
Imports to UK	232,436	268,630	324,132	345,446	307,267
Exports and re-exports from UK	212,352	251,923	240,127	259,251	279,681

Statistik des Aussenhandels [from 1964: *Der Aussenhandel*] *Österreichs*. Vienna, Statistisches Zentralamt. Annually 1949–50; quarterly from 1951

Tourism. Tourism is an important industry. In 1979, 22,331 hotels and boarding-houses had a total of 666,307 beds available; 12,875,292 foreigners visited Austria; of these 366,512 came from the UK and 409,815 from the USA.

COMMUNICATIONS

Roads. On 1 Jan. 1980 federal roads had a total length of 10,140 km, 743·2 km autobahn; provincial roads, 22,996 km. On 31 Dec. 1979 there were registered 3,319,766 motor vehicles, including 2,138,678 passenger cars, 172,464 lorries, 323,535 tractors and 179,179 trailers.

Railways. Austrian railways have been nationalized since before the First World War. Length of track (Dec. 1979), 5,857 km, of which 2,895 km were electrified. Twenty private railways have a total length of 605 km. Passengers in 1979 numbered 169m. and 45m. tonnes of freight.

Aviation. Austria has 6 airports in Vienna (Schwechat), Linz, Salzburg, Graz, Klagenfurt and Innsbruck. In 1979, 64,506 aircraft arrived and departed at Austrian airports on scheduled flights.

Shipping. Austria has no sea frontiers, but the Danube is an important waterway. Goods traffic (in tonnes): 5,436,735 in 1976; 5,550,925 in 1977; 5,883,596 in 1978; 6,583,433 in 1979. Coal and coke, mineral oil products and iron ore comprise in bulk more than two-thirds of these cargoes. The Danube Steamship Co. (DDSG) is the main Austrian shipping company.

Post and Broadcasting. All postal, telegraph and telephone services are run by the State. On 1 Jan. 1979 there were 2,617,600 telephones.

Österreichischer Rundfunk transmits 4 programmes, including a 24 hours overseas service. There is also regional and local broadcasting. All broadcasting is financed by licence payments and advertisements. There were 2·3m. registered listeners in Oct. 1980. Television was inaugurated in autumn 1955 and 2 programmes are transmitted, both in colour.

Cinemas (1979). There were 534 cinemas.

Newspapers (1979). There were 32 daily newspapers (6 of them in Vienna) with a combined circulation of 2,633,719.

JUSTICE, RELIGION, EDUCATION AND WELFARE

Justice. The Supreme Court of Justice (*Oberster Gerichtshof*) in Vienna is the highest court in the land. Besides there are 4 higher provincial courts (*Oberlandesgerichte*), 20 provincial and district courts (*Landes- und Kreisgerichte*) and 205 local courts (*Bezirksgerichte*).

Religion. In 1971 there were 6,540,294 Roman Catholics (87·7%), 446,307 Protestants (6%), 111,558 others (1·5%), 320,031 without religious allegiance (4·3%) and 38,213 (0·5%) unknown. The Roman Catholic Church has 2 archbishoprics and 7 bishoprics.

Education (1978–79). There were in Austria 5,235 elementary and special schools with 59,773 teachers and 904,082 pupils. Of all kinds of secondary schools there were 1,449 with 548,880 pupils.

There were also 99 commercial academies with 25,236 students and 3,515 teachers. There were 173 schools of technical and industrial training (including schools of hotel management and catering) with 4,527 teachers and 43,209 pupils; 33 schools of women's professions (secondary level) with 9,230 pupils; 8 training colleges of social workers with 614 pupils. 138 trade schools had 27,394 pupils.

Austria has 12 universities and 6 colleges of arts maintained by the State: Universities at Vienna (3,108 teachers, 40,710 students), Graz (1,260 teachers, 14,565 students), Innsbruck (1,247 teachers, 14,203 students) and Salzburg (1,086 teachers, 7,766 students). There are also technical universities at Vienna (1,311 teachers, 8,738 students) and Graz (570 teachers, 4,604 students), a mining university at Leoben (212 teachers, 1,019 students), an agricultural university at Vienna (250 teachers, 2,297 students), a veterinary university at Vienna (223 teachers, 1,260 students), a commercial university at Vienna (298 teachers, 6,898 students), a university for social and economic sciences at Linz (308 teachers, 4,356 students) and a university for educational sciences at Klagenfurt (205 teachers, 1,296 students). There is an academy of fine arts at Vienna (133 teachers, 628 students), a college of applied arts at Vienna (153 teachers, 765 students), 3 colleges of music and dramatic art at Vienna (376 teachers, 2,252 students), Salzburg (208 teachers, 1,192 students) and Graz (208 teachers, 863 students); the college for industrial design at Linz (86 teachers, 351 students).

Health. In 1978 there were 17,712 doctors, 320 hospitals and 84,959 hospital beds.

DIPLOMATIC REPRESENTATIVES

OF AUSTRIA IN GREAT BRITAIN (18 Belgrave Mews West, London, SW1X 8HU)

Ambassador: Dr Heinrich Gleissner (accredited 12 Feb. 1979).

OF GREAT BRITAIN IN AUSTRIA (Reisnerstrasse 40, 1030 Vienna)
Ambassador: D. Mc D. Gordon, CMG.

OF AUSTRIA IN THE USA (2343 Massachusetts Ave., NW, Washington, D.C., 20008)

Ambassador: Karl Herbert Schober.

OF THE USA IN AUSTRIA (IX Boltzmangasse, 16, A-1091 Vienna)
Ambassador: Philip M. Kaiser.

OF AUSTRIA TO THE UNITED NATIONS
Ambassador: Thomas Klestil.

Books of Reference

Statistical Information: The Austrian Central Statistical Office was founded in 1863. *Address:* Neue Burg, Heldenplatz, A-1014 Vienna. *President:* Dr Lothar Bosse. Main publications:

Statistisches Handbuch für die Republik Österreich. New Series from 1950. Annually
Statistische Nachrichten. Monthly
Beiträge zur österreichischen Statistik (585 vols.)
Ergebnisse der nichtlandwirtschaftlichen Betriebszählung, 1964. 1971
Ergebnisse der Volkszählung vom 12 Mai 1971
Ergebnisse der Häuser- und Wohnungszählung vom 12 Mai 1971
HA-Taschenbuch 75. Annually from 1971
Republic of Austria 1945–1975. Vienna, 1976

Barker, E., *Austria 1918–1972.* London, 1973
Bobek, H. (ed.), *Atlas der Republik Österreich.* 3 vols. Vienna, 1961 ff.
Österreich Lexikon. Wien-München, 1966
Scheidl, L. G., and Lechleitner, H., *Österreich—Land, Volk, Wirtschaft.* Vienna, 1967
Steiner, K., *Politics in Austria.* Boston, 1972

National Library: Österreichische Nationalbibliothek, Vienna. *Librarian:* Dr Zessner-Spitzenberg.

THE COMMONWEALTH OF THE BAHAMAS

Capital: Nassau
Population: 234,000 (1979)
GNP per capita: US$2,620 (1978)

HISTORY. The Bahamas were discovered by Colombus in 1492 but the Spanish did not make a permanent settlement. British settlers arrived in the 17th century and it was occupied by Britain, except for a short period in the 18th century, until it gained independence.

AREA AND POPULATION. The Commonwealth of the Bahamas consists of 700 islands and more than 1,000 cays off the south-east coast of Florida. They are the surface protuberances of two oceanic banks, the Little Bahama Bank and the Great Bahama Bank. Land area, 5,353 sq. miles (13,864 sq. km). The total rainfall (New Providence) in 1972 was 48·57 in.; highest in July (10·01 in.). Average winter temperature, 69·9° F. (21·1° C.); average summer temperature, 82·8° F. (28·2° C.).

Principal islands with census population in 1970: New Providence (101,503, containing capital, Nassau; estimate, 1979, 138,500), Abaco (6,501), Harbour Island and Spanish Wells (3,221), Grand Bahama (25,859), Cat Island (2,657), Long Island (3,861), Mayaguana (581), Eleuthera (6,247), Exuma (3,767), San Salvador or Watling's Island (776), Acklin's Island (936), Crooked Island (689), Inagua (1,109), Andros (8,845), Bimini (1,503), Ragged Island (208).

Census population, 1970, 168,812. Estimate (1979) 234,000. Vital statistics, 1977: Births, 4,871; deaths, 1,067 (excluding still-births); marriages, 1,297.

CONSTITUTION AND GOVERNMENT. Internal self-government with cabinet responsibility was introduced 7 Jan. 1964.

Qualification for membership of the House of Assembly, under the 1973 Independence Constitution requires that a member shall be a citizen of the Bahamas of the age of 21 years or upwards, and shall have been ordinarily resident in the Bahamas for a period of not less than 1 year immediately before the date of his nomination for election. The Representation of the People's Act provides for adult suffrage. Women are eligible for election to the House of Assembly.

The Constitution of the Commonwealth of the Bahamas (1973) establishes the Bahamas as a free and democratic sovereign state. The constitution is the supreme law of the Bahamas and where any other law is inconsistent with it, the Constitution shall prevail and the other law shall, to the extent of the inconsistency be void.

The Constitution created the office of Governor-General, the holder of which is appointed by Her Majesty. There is a Senate of 16 members, 9 appointed by the Governor-General on the advice of the Prime Minister, 4 appointed by the Governor-General on the advice of the Leader of the Opposition and 3 appointed by the Governor-General on advice of the Prime Minister after consultation with the Leader of the Opposition. The House of Assembly consists of 38 members. The life of a Parliament is 5 years, but it may be prorogued or dissolved at any time by the Governor-General on the advice of the Prime Minister.

At the elections of 19 July 1977 the Progressive Liberal Party obtained 30 seats, the Bahamas Democratic Party 6 seats and the Free National Movement 2 seats.

Independence from Britain took place on 10 July 1973.

Governor-General: Sir Gerald Cash, GCMG, KCVO, OBE.

The Cabinet in Jan. 1981 was composed as follows:

Prime Minister and Minister of Economic Affairs: Rt. Hon. Lynden O. Pindling. *Deputy Prime Minister and Minister of Finance:* Arthur D. Hanna. *Tourism:* Livingston

N. Coakley. *Education and Culture:* Darrell E. Rolle. *Works and Utilities:* A. Loftus Roker. *Labour and Home Affairs:* Clement T. Maynard. *External Affairs and Attorney-General:* Paul L. Adderley. *Agriculture, Fisheries and Local Government:* George A. Smith. *Minister of State:* Alfred T. Maycock. *Health and National Insurance:* Perry G. Christie. *Transport:* Philip M. Bethel. *Youth, Sports and Community Affairs:* Kendal W. Nottage.

National flag: Three horizontal stripes of aquamarine, gold, aquamarine, with a black triangle on the hoist.

INTERNATIONAL RELATIONS

Membership. The Commonwealth of the Bahamas is a member of UN, the Commonwealth and an ACP state of EEC.

ECONOMY

Budget (in B$):	*1978*[1]	*1979*[1]	*1980*[1]
Revenue	173,000,000	208,600,000	234,438,200
Expenditure	172,000,000	198,600,000	233,432,447

[1] Estimate.

The main sources of revenue were customs duties and receipts from fees, post office and public utilities.

Currency. A decimal system of currency was introduced in 1966. Bahamian $2.18 = £1 sterling (March 1981). Notes: $0.50, 1, 3, 5, 10, 20, 50, 100; coins: 1, 5, 10, 15, 25, 50 cents, $1, 2, 5. Sterling currency has been withdrawn. American currency is generally accepted.

Bank of England and Canadian notes are not accepted, except at the banks from travellers from the UK.

Banking. The Central Bank of the Bahamas was established in June 1974 with assets (Dec. 1976) B$68·69m. and capital and reserves of B$12·38m. The Royal Bank of Canada, the Bank of Nova Scotia, Barclays Bank International, Canadian Imperial Bank of Commerce, the Bank of London and Montreal, Chase Manhattan Bank, Citibank, E. D. Sassoon Banking Co., Butlers Bank, Commonwealth Industrial Bank, International Bank of Washington and the Mercantile Bank of the Bahamas have branches in Nassau. The Royal Bank of Canada, Bank of Nova Scotia, Chase Manhattan Bank and Barclays Bank International have branches on several other islands.

On 10 Aug. 1978 there were 275 institutions licensed to carry on banking and/or trust business under the Banks and Trust Companies Regulations Act. There were 7 trust companies designated by the Exchange Control Department to act as custodians and dealers in foreign securities.

Post office savings bank, 30 June 1972, depositors, 34,831; balance due (30 June 1971), B$2,633,711.

Weights and Measures. The UK (Imperial) system is in force.

ENERGY AND NATURAL RESOURCES

Electricity. Electricity for lighting and power is available in New Providence, Grand Bahama and the Family Islands. Total units generated in New Providence/Paradise Island in 1976–77, 345,446,000 kwh. Total number of consumers 1976–77, 33,545.

Agriculture. There are about 200,000 acres of agricultural land mainly on Abaco, Andros and Grand Bahama. During 1976 various programmes designed to stimulate the production of food for both domestic and export markets were continued. These measures included the clearing and allocation of Crown Land on Abaco, Andros and Eleuthera; the land improvement subsidy; short-term credit for farming and fishery supplies; the expansion of the marketing system; and the promotion of co-operatives.

Total agricultural production was valued at about B$20m. in 1978.

Livestock (1979): Cattle, 4,000; sheep, 33,000; goats, 17,000; poultry, 785,000.

Forestry. Production of cascarilla bark and pulp-wood in 1976 was B$1·8m., all of which was exported.

Fisheries. Total production was valued at B$10·5m. in 1976.

INDUSTRY AND TRADE

Industry. Tourism is the major industry. Several light industries have been established on Grand Bahama and New Providence in response to special encouragement legislation, these include garment manufacturing, ice, furniture, purified water, plastic containers, perfumes, industrial gases, jewellery and others. Larger industrial activities in the Bahamas include oil refining, oil transhipment, manufacture of alcoholic beverages, pharmaceuticals, aragonite mining, solar salt production and manufacture of steel piping. Two industrial sites, one in New Providence and the other in Grand Bahama, have been developed as part of the industrialization programme.

Commerce. The principal exports in 1976 were hormones, rum, salt, crawfish, cement, aragonite and pulpwood.

The principal imports in 1974 were: Food, drink and tobacco, raw materials and articles mainly unmanufactured, articles wholly or mainly manufactured, animals not for food.

Imports and exports (excluding bullion and specie) for 6 calendar years in B$:

	Imports	*Exports*		*Imports*	*Exports*
1972	484,867,873	301,401,104	1975	2,696,903,595	2,508,332,684
1973	764,260,752	529,743,304	1976	2,992,329,236	3,124,469,061
1974	1,908,377,389	1,443,585,764	1977	3,568,210,461	3,260,671,673

The Bahamas became affiliated with CARIFTA (now CARICOM) in 1968.

Total trade between Bahamas and UK, in £1,000 sterling (British Department of Trade returns):

	1975	*1976*	*1977*	*1978*	*1979*	*1980*
Imports to UK	9,851	15,094	13,960	12,650	21,758	59,123
Exports and re-exports from UK	7,698	7,801	21,995	104,204	79,851	77,366

Tourism. Tourism is the most important industry in the Bahamas. It accounts for approximately 58% of government revenue and 66% of employment. In 1979 there were 1·8m. foreign arrivals in the Bahamas.

COMMUNICATIONS

Roads. There are 240 miles of paved roads in New Providence, and 426 miles in Grand Bahama. The other major islands have 400 miles of motorable roads. In 1978, 51,290 motor vehicles were registered. There are no railroads.

Aviation. Nassau international airport is located on the island of New Providence, about 10 miles from the city of Nassau. There is another international airport at Freeport. Scheduled flights—Air Canada: 3 times weekly from Toronto and once weekly from Montreal to Nassau; twice weekly from Toronto and once weekly from Montreal to Freeport. Air Jamaica: once daily from Chicago, Kingston and Montego Bay to Nassau. British Airways: 4 times weekly from London and Bermuda, twice weekly from Kingston and Panama and once weekly from Mexico City to Nassau; once weekly from London, Bermuda, Kingston and Panama to Freeport. Delta: twice daily from New York, once daily from Boston and Newark to Nassau. American Airlines: once daily from New York to Nassau. Eastern Airlines: 3 flights daily from Miami, once daily from Fort Lauderdale, twice weekly from Baltimore, Washington and Philadelphia, once daily from Newark, twice daily from New York *via* Miami and Fort Lauderdale to Nassau; 3 times daily from Miami, once daily from Baltimore and Philadelphia to Freeport: International Air Bahama: once weekly from Luxembourg to Nassau; once weekly from Luxembourg to Freeport. Lufthansa: 3 times weekly from Frankfurt and Mexico and once weekly from Merida to Nassau. There are numerous domestic schedules to the Family Islands. Bahamasair provides commercial and charter services to the Family Islands and Florida. There are 53 airstrips on the various Family Islands and numerous water alighting areas. During 1977, 494,263 passengers landed at Nassau and 38,840 aircraft arrivals. At Freeport in 1977, 407,772 passengers landed from 41,799 aircraft arrivals.

Shipping. In 1979, 606 cruise liners cleared Nassau carrying 419,845 passengers; 593 cargo vessels discharged 257,534 tons of cargo at Nassau. There are cargo services with UK, USA and Canada and passenger services with UK, USA, the West Indies and South America.

Telecommunications. New Providence and all the major islands have automatic telephone systems of the latest type in operation, together with an extensive system of underground cables. The total number of telephones in use at 1 Jan. 1978 was 61,756; 170 radio-telephone channels provide service *via* the USA to any part of the world. In 1971 direct dialling was introduced to the USA and in 1973 to Canada. All the important islands are connected with Nassau by means of radio-telegraphy, and in most cases radio-telephony is also available. Connexion through Nassau to the UK, the USA, Canada and Central America can be provided. Radio-teletype to Bermuda and Florida and ship-shore radio-telephone services are also available. Radio-teletype service is provided from Nassau to Freeport and West End in Grand Bahama. In 1976 a fully automated Telex exchange came into service. The Bahamas broadcasting station operates on 1,540, 1,240 and 810 kc.

Cinemas (1977). There are 16 cinemas and 3 drive-ins.

Newspapers (1977). There are 2 daily and 1 weekly newspapers in Nassau.

JUSTICE, EDUCATION AND WELFARE

Justice (1977). 9,655 cases (traffic, 3,550; criminal, 3,218; civil, 1,880; domestic, 1,007) were dealt with in the magistrates' court, and civil, 816; divorce, 256 in the Supreme Court. The strength of the police force (1973) was 932 officers and other ranks.

Education. Education is under the jurisdiction of the Ministry of Education and Culture. In 1979–80 there were 227 schools, and of these, 187 (with 48,510 pupils and 2,299 staff) are fully maintained by Government and 40 (with 13,066 pupils and 664 staff) are independent schools. There are 38 government-owned schools in New Providence and 149 on the Family Islands. 24 independent schools are located on New Providence and 12 on the Family Islands. 181 students attended 4 special schools, 3 on New Providence and 1 on Grand Bahama; total staff, 38. Free education is available in ministry schools in New Providence and the Family Islands. Courses lead to the Bahamas Junior Certificate and the General Certificate of Education (GCE).

Independent schools provide education at primary, secondary and higher levels. Several schools of continuing education offer secretarial and academic courses. The Government-operated Princess Margaret Hospital offers a nursing course at two levels. The College of the Bahamas was established in 1974. It provides a 2- or 3-year programme leading to an associate degree in any of the 7 academic divisions. Several college degree programmes are offered in conjunction with the University of the West Indies and the University of Miami. The Hotel Training College offers a wide range of subjects up to middle management level in aspects of hotel work. Enrolment in this institution includes Bahamian as well as regional and international students.

Health. In 1980 there was a government general hospital in Nassau (460 beds) and 1 in Freeport (50). Grand Bahama has 4 clinics, 3 staffed by district medical officers and 1 by a nurse and the Family Islands have about 50 health centres. There are 2 private hospitals. Dental treatment is provided for smaller islands by a flying dentist service. There are 122 doctors, 387 nurses, 8 midwives and 5 dentists in the government service. There are many private doctors, dentists, nurses and midwives providing health care on a fee basis.

DIPLOMATIC REPRESENTATIVES

OF THE BAHAMAS IN GREAT BRITAIN (39 Pall Mall,
London, SW1Y 5JG)

High Commissioner: R. F. Anthony Roberts.

OF GREAT BRITAIN IN THE BAHAMAS (Bitco Bldg., East St., Nassau)
High Commissioner: J. A. S. Papadopoulos, MVO, MBE.

OF THE BAHAMAS IN THE USA (600 New Hampshire Ave., NW,
Washington, D.C., 20037)
Chargé d'Affaires: Dr P. E. J. Rodgers.

OF THE USA IN THE BAHAMAS (Queen St., Nassau)
Ambassador: William B. Schwartz, Jr.

OF THE BAHAMAS TO THE UNITED NATIONS
Ambassador: Dr. Davidson L. Hepburn.

Books of Reference

Bahamas Handbook and Businessman's Annual (Annual)
Albury, P., *The Story of the Bahamas.* London, 1975
Craton, M. A., *A History of the Bahamas.* London, 1962
Hunte, G., *The Bahamas.* London, 1975

Library: Nassau Public Library.

BAHRAIN

Capital: Manama
Population: 350,000 (1980)
GNP per capita: US$2,410 (1976)

HISTORY. Treaties with Britain of 1882 and 1892 were replaced by a treaty of friendship which was signed on 15 Aug. 1971. Under the earlier treaties Britain had been responsible for Bahrain's defence and foreign relations. On the same day Bahrain declared its independence.

AREA AND POPULATION. The Bahrain islands form an archipelago in the Arabian Gulf, between the Qatar peninsula and the mainland of Saudi Arabia. The total area is about 255 sq. miles. Bahrain ('Two Seas'), largest island, is 30 miles long and 10 miles wide. Muharraq, to the north-east, 4 miles long and 1 mile wide, is connected with Bahrain by a causeway, nearly 1·5 miles long, carrying a motor road. Other islands are Sitra, to the east, 3 miles long and 1 mile wide; Umm An-Nassan, to the west, 3 miles by 2 miles; Jidda, also to the west, 1 mile by 0·5 mile, the Hawar group off Qatar and several islets, some uninhabited. From Sitra oil pipelines and a causeway carrying a road extend out to sea for 3 miles to a deep-water anchorage. The islands are low lying, the highest ground being a hill in the centre of Bahrain, 450 ft high.

The population in 1971 (census) was 216,815. Estimate (1980) 350,000. The majority of the people are Moslem Arabs.

Manama, the capital of the state and the commercial centre, is situated at the northern end of the largest island and extends for 1·5 miles along the shore. It has a population of 82,345 (1971 census). Estimate (1978) 114,030. Electricity from the government power-station in Manama supplies light and power in Manama, Muharraq (48,161, 1978 estimate), Hidd (6,725), Rifa'a (13,696) and Isa Town (9,573) and the villages. Water is obtained from artesian wells, and there is a piped supply in Manama, Muharraq, Isa Town, Rifa'a and most villages.

CONSTITUTION AND GOVERNMENT. A Constituent Assembly met in Dec. 1972 to draft a Constitution and this was published in 1973. A National Assembly with a proposed 4-year life met for the first time in 1973 but was dissolved at the end of 1975. Bahrain is administered by a cabinet, which was formed in 1971 to succeed the Council of State.

Reigning Amir: The ruling family, the Al Khalifa, an Arab dynasty, who have been in power since 1782. The present Amir, HH Shaikh Isa bin Sulman Al-Khalifa (born 1933) succeeded on 2 Nov. 1961. *Heir Apparent and Minister of Defence:* Shaikh Hamed bin Isa Al-Khalifa.

Prime Minister: Shaikh Khalifa bin Sulman Al-Khalifa.

Defence: Shaikh Hamed bin Isa Al-Khalifa. *Transport:* Ibrahim Mohammed Hassan Homaidan. *Housing:* Shaikh Khalid bin Abdulla Al-Khalifa. *Information:* Tariq Abdulrahman Almoayyed. *Education:* Shaikh Abdul Aziz bin Mohammed Al-Khalifa. *Justice:* Shaikh Abdullah bin Khalid Al-Khalifa. *Health:* Dr Ali Fakhro. *Labour and Social Affairs:* Shaikh Khalifa bin Salman Al-Khalifa. *Works, Power and Water:* Majid Jawad Al Jishi. *Interior:* Shaikh Mohammed bin Khalifa Al-Khalifa. *Foreign Affairs:* Shaikh Mohammed bin Mubarak Al-Khalifa. *Finance:* Ebrahim Abdul-Karim. *Development and Industry:* Yusuf Ahmed Al-Shirawi. *Commerce and Agriculture:* Habib Kassem. *Minister of State for Cabinet Affairs:* Jawad Salim Al-Arrayed. *Minister of State for Legal Affairs:* Dr Hussain Al Baharna.

Flag: Red, with white serrated vertical strip on hoist.

DEFENCE

Army. The Army consists of 1 infantry battalion and 1 armoured car squadron with a personnel strength of 2,300 (1980).

Air Wing. Equipment comprises 3 MBB BO 105 twin-engined light helicopters to support the Defence Force.

INTERNATIONAL RELATIONS

Membership. Bahrain is a member of UN, the Arab League and OAPEC.

ECONOMY

Budget. The revenue of the State is derived from oil royalties and from customs duties, which are 10% *ad valorem* for luxury goods and 5% for essential goods. The exceptions are liquor (75%) and tobacco (15%). Total revenues in 1974, BD 53m.; 1975, BD 134m.; 1976, BD 181m.; 1977, BD 249m.; 1978, BD 280m.

On 2 Jan. 1958 Manama was declared a free transit port and the former 2% transit duty was abolished, but storage charges are levied.

Reserves were BD 200m. in Dec. 1977.

Currency. The Bahrain *dinar* is divided into 1,000 *fils*. The Bahrain currency board issues notes of 10, 5, 1 and $\frac{1}{2}$ *dinars*, and coins of 100, 50, 25 and 5 *fils*. £1 = BD 0·818 in March 1981; US$1 = BD 0·037.

Banking. Banking facilities are provided by the National Bank of Bahrain, the Bank of Bahrain and Kuwait and branches of the Chartered Bank, the British Bank of the Middle East, the Arab Bank, Habib Bank (Overseas), United Bank, Citibank, Banque du Caire, Chase Manhattan, National & Grindlays Bank, Bank Melli, Algemene Bank, Bank Saderet, Continental Bank of Chicago, Bank of Paris, National Bank of Abu Dhabi, Rafidain Bank, Barclays International, Al-Ahli Commercial Bank.

Weights and Measures. The metric system of weights and measures is officially in use.

NATURAL RESOURCES

Oil. In 1931 oil was discovered. Operations are being conducted by the Bahrain Petroleum Co., registered in Canada but owned by US interests, under a concession granted by the Shaikh. Production of crude oil in 1979 was 18.74m. bbls. A large oil refinery on Bahrain Island, besides treating crude oil produced locally, also processes oil from Saudi Arabia transported by pipeline.

In 1975 the Bahrain Government assumed a direct 60% interest in the Bahrain oilfield and related crude oil facilities of BAPCO. Bahrain's gas reserves are 100% government-owned.

Under the terms of the agreement signed between Bahrain and Saudi Arabia in 1958, Bahrain will receive 25% of the profits on any oil produced in the Abu Saafa area of sea between Bahrain and Saudi Arabia. Aramco, which is responsible for the development of this field, began production in 1966.

Gas. There is an abundant supply of natural gas with known reserves of 9,000,000m. cu. ft.

INDUSTRY AND TRADE

Industry. Bahrain is being developed as a major manufacturing state, the first important enterprise being the Aluminium Bahrain Smelter, a company whose original shareholders included the Bahrain Government and British, Swedish, Federal German and US interests. In 1975, the government acquired a majority shareholding in the enterprise. The aluminium operation is the largest non-oil industry in the Gulf. Ancillary industries developed around aluminium smelting include the production of aluminium powder. Other projects at present under consideration include the further development of marine industries. The Arab Shipbuilding and Repair Yard (ASRY), commissioned in 1977, is now in service. The dry dock can handle up to 50 tankers (550,000 DWT each) annually. A US$400m. petrochemical complex will go on stream in 1984.

In addition to the traditional minor industries such as boat-building, weaving, pottery, etc., other modern industries have developed, which include the manufacture of building materials, soft drinks, drinking straws, paper bags, woollen garments, plastic and other consumer goods. There is also an important fishing industry and a fairly large farming community. The most important crops are dates and vegetables, and there is also poultry farming.

Livestock (1979): Cattle, 5,000; sheep, 3,000; goats, 13,000; poultry, 504,000.

The pearling industry for which Bahrain used to be famous has considerably declined. Only about 10 boats visit the pearl banks each year, as compared with the 600–1,000 that were employed 30 years ago.

Commerce. In 1979 imports totalled BD 916m.; exports and re-exports, non-oil, BD 912m. Chief imports were manufactured goods, machinery and transport equipment, food and live animals, chemicals.

Import of arms and ammunition and telecommunication equipment is subject to special permission; the sale of alcoholic liquor is restricted and the import of cultured pearls is forbidden.

Total trade between Bahrain and UK (British Department of Trade returns, in £1,000 sterling):

	1976	1977	1978	1979	1980
Imports to UK	30,146	13,673	34,704	23,780	25,063
Exports and re-exports from UK	89,628	113,777	119,855	123,467	115,569

COMMUNICATIONS

Aviation. The airport, situated at Muharraq, can take the largest aircraft. British Airways, Gulf Air, Middle East Airlines, Pakistan International Airways, Qantas, Kuwait Airways, Air India International, Singapore Airlines, UTA, Saudi Arabian Airlines, KLM, Iran Airways, Egyptair, Alia, Cyprus Airways, Ethiopian Airlines and Sudan Airways also operate to and from Bahrain. Bahrain International Airport is the Arabian Gulf's main air communication centre.

Shipping. Bahrain's traditional position as the entrepôt of the Southern Gulf has been supplemented by the development of Mina Sulman—the new modern harbour—as a free transit and industrial area. Local and international companies have developed industries in this area, which is also used as a storage centre for firms selling elsewhere in the Gulf. The facilities offered by Mina Sulman include engineering and ship repairing yards; the Basrec slipway is probably the largest between Rotterdam and Hong Kong.

Post and Broadcasting. There were, at 1 Jan. 1978, 38,284 telephones. There is a state-operated radio and television station.

EDUCATION. There were, in 1976, 112 state schools for boys and girls with 2,826 teachers and 61,201 pupils. Four boys' secondary schools have a commercial studies section. There are 2 boys' technical schools at secondary level, with 718 pupils. In addition there are 7 private schools. The Men's Teacher Training College (established 1966) and the Women's Teacher Training College (established 1967) give 2-year courses. Approximately 1,000 Bahrainis have graduated from universities abroad. The Gulf Technical College opened in Bahrain in Sept. 1968. Adult literacy centres have been opened throughout Bahrain.

HEALTH. There is a free medical service for all residents of Bahrain. There are 19 government hospitals and health centres with 1,124 beds, an American mission hospital, an oil company hospital, a military hospital and an international hospital.

DIPLOMATIC REPRESENTATIVES

OF BAHRAIN IN GREAT BRITAIN (98 Gloucester Rd.,
London, SW7 4AU)

Ambassador: Shaikh Abdul-Rahman Faris Al-Khalifa (accredited 17 Dec. 1980).

OF GREAT BRITAIN IN BAHRAIN (Government Rd., North, Manama)
Ambassador: H. B. Walker, CMG.

OF BAHRAIN IN THE USA (2600 Virginia Ave., NW, Washington D.C., 20037)

Ambassador: Abdulaziz Abdulrahman Buali.

OF THE USA IN BAHRAIN (Shaikh Isa Road, Manama)

Ambassador: Peter A. Sutherland.

OF BAHRAIN TO THE UNITED NATIONS

Ambassador: Dr Salman Mohamed Al Saffar.

Books of Reference

Statistical and General Information: Ministry of Information, PO Box 253, Manama.

Belgrave, J. H. D., *Welcome to Bahrain.* 9th ed. Manama, 1975
Rumaihi, M. G., *Bahrain: Social and Political Change since the First World War.* New York and London, 1976

BANGLADESH

People's Republic
of Bangladesh

Capital: Dacca
Population: 88·7m. (1980)
GNP per capita: US$90 (1978)

HISTORY. The state was formerly the Eastern Province of Pakistan. In Dec. 1970 Sheikh Mujibur Rahman's Awami League Party gained 167 seats out of 300 at the Pakistan general election and immediately made known their wish for greater independence for the then Eastern Province. Martial law was imposed following disturbances in Dacca, and civil war developed in March 1971. The war ended in Dec. 1971 and Bangladesh was proclaimed an independent state.

AREA AND POPULATION. Bangladesh is bounded west and north-west by West Bengal (India), north by Assam and Meghalaya (India), east by Assam, Tripura (India) and Burma, south by the Bay of Bengal. The area is 55,598 sq. miles (144,020 sq. km); population (1974 census), 71,316,517 (36,949,033 male, 34,367,484 female), an increase of 40·27% since 1961. Population estimate, 1977, 80·56m. (41m. male, 39·5m. female). Birth rate (1970–75), 49·5 per 1,000; death rate (1970–75), 28·1 per 1,000. The capital is Dacca (population, 1,310,972 in 1974; estimate (1976), 2m.) and its ports are Chittagong (416,733) and Khulna (437,304). Other large cities are Narayanganj (176,459), Rajshahi (132,909) and Barisal (98,127). There are 20 districts:

	Area (sq. km)	Population 1980		Area (sq. km)	Population 1980
Dinajpur	6,757	3,228,000	Kushtia	3,551	2,403,000
Rangpur	9,593	6,739,000	Jessore	6,597	4,212,000
Bogra	3,890	2,785,000	Khulna	12,049	4,514,000
Rajshahi	9,464	5,383,000	Barisal	6,757	4,673,000
Pabna	4,861	3,485,000	Patuakhali	4,224	1,809,000
Rajshahi division	*34,565*	*21,620,000*	Khulna division	*33,178*	*17,611,000*
Tangail	3,370	2,527,000	Sylhet	12,393	5,808,000
Mymensingh	13,105	6,732,000	Comilla	6,718	7,041,000
Jamalpur	3,405	2,464,000	Noakhali	4,804	3,928,000
Dacca	7,464	9,853,000	Chittagong	7,006	5,658,000
Faridpur	6,977	4,859,000	Chittagong Hill Tracts	13,191	603,000
Dacca division	*30,916*	*26,435,000*	Chittagong division	*44,112*	*23,038,000*

The language is Bengali.

GOVERNMENT AND CONSTITUTION. Bangladesh is a republic. The Constitution came into force on 16 Dec. 1972 and provided for a parliamentary democracy. On 25 Jan. 1975 Sheikh Mujibur Rahman took on the office of President, with an advisory Parliament. All political parties were abolished, and replaced by the new Bangladesh Krishak Sramik Awami League. On 15 Aug. 1975 Sheikh Mujibur Rahman and his family were killed; martial law was introduced on 20 Aug. and political parties were banned (including the new BKSAL) on 30 Aug. K. M. Ahmed was installed as President on 15 Aug. and replaced on 7 Nov. by former Chief Justice A. M. Sayem. Elections to parliament were promised for Feb. 1977 but postponed indefinitely in 1976. Political parties were made legal once again and requested to apply for registration in Aug. 1976.

On 29 Nov. 1976 Maj.-Gen. Ziaur Rahman became Chief Martial Law Administrator, with the Chiefs of Naval and Air Staff as his deputies. On 21 April 1977 President Sayem resigned and Maj.-Gen. Ziaur Rahman was sworn in as President.

On 22 April 1977 the constitution of 1972 was amended to establish 'absolute trust and faith in Allah' as the first fundamental principle of state and to provide for a Supreme Judicial Council which would prescribe a code of conduct for judges and advise the President. Three political parties (JSD, Bangladesh Communist Party (pro-Soviet) and Democratic League) were dissolved in Oct. 1977. The President was confirmed in office by general election. Martial law ended in April 1979.

Parliament has one chamber of 300 members directly elected every 5 years by citizens over 18. There are 30 seats reserved for women members elected by Parliament. The judiciary is independent of the executive.

A general election was held on 18 Feb. 1979, resulting in a victory for President Ziaur Rahman's Bangladesh National Party which won 207 seats in the 300-member Parliament. The Government was in autumn 1980 composed as follows:

President, Defence, Cabinet Affairs, Science and Technology: Mr. Ziaur Rahman.
Vice-President: Mr Justice Abdus Sattar.
Prime Minister and Education: Shah Azizur Rahman.
Law and Parliamentary Affairs, Youth Development: Abdus Sattar. *Finance:* M. S. Rahman. *Foreign Affairs:* M. Shamsul Huq. *Food:* A. M. Khan. *Establishment:* M. Majedul Huq. *Local Government, Rural Development and Co-operatives:* A. Halim Chowdhury. *Home Affairs:* A. S. M. Mustafizur Rahman. *Industries and Deputy Prime Minister:* J. Ahmed. *Ports, Shipping and Inland Water Transport:* N. Huq. *Agriculture and Forests:* Nurul Islam. *Civil Aviation and Tourism:* K. M. Obaidur Rahman. *Fisheries and Livestock, Deputy Prime Minister:* S. A. Bari. *Railways, Roads, Highways and Road Transport:* Abdul Alim. *Information and Broadcasting:* S. H. Chowdhury. *Religious Affairs:* A. Rahman. *Petroleum and Mineral Resources:* Akbar Hussain. *Planning:* F. Mahtab. *Relief and Rehabilitation:* E. A. Sarker. *Labour and Industrial Welfare:* R. Ahmed. *Textiles:* M. Ali. *Posts, Telegraph and Telephones:* M. Islam. *Jute:* H. Khan. *Health and Population Control:* M. A. Matin. *Water Resources and Flood Control:* K. A. Haque.

National flag: Bottle green with a red disc in the centre.
National anthem: Amar Sonar Bangla, ami tomay bhalobashi (My golden Bengal, I love you). Words by Rabindranath Tagore.

DEFENCE

Army. There are 5 infantry divisions with 27 battalions and 2 tank regiments, 9 artillery regiments, 3 engineer battalions and supporting arms. Strength, 65,000. There are 66,000 paramilitary militia volunteers. By ordinance, 5 Oct. 1975 the Rakkhi Bahini militiamen were incorporated into the Army and the body disbanded.

Navy. The Navy was organized on 10 Dec. 1971. Naval bases are at Chittagong (handed over by India on 14 Feb. 1972) Kaptai, Khulna and Dacca.

The fleet strength in 1980 comprised 2 former British frigates (*Ali Hyder*, *ex*-HMS *Jaguar*, 2,520 tons full load, transferred in July 1978; and *Umar Farooq*, *ex*-HMS *Llandaff*, 2,408 tons full load, transferred in Dec 1976); 2 *ex*-Yugoslav 200-ton patrol vessels, 2 *ex*-Indian 150-ton patrol craft, 1 British-built 140-ton patrol craft, 5 indigenously built 70-ton river gunboats, 1 repair vessel and 1 training ship of 710 tons.

The manpower of the Navy in 1981 was 5,250, comprising 250 officers and 5,000 ratings.

Air Force. Initial combat equipment of the Air Wing of the Defence Force comprised a few Sabre 6 jet fighters salvaged from former Pakistan Air Force units. Subsequent deliveries, from the Soviet Union and China successively, have built up the current strength of about 36 F-6 (MiG-19) fighter-bombers; 3 MiG-21MF fighters; 2 F.27 Friendship, 3 An-12, 1 An-24 and 2 An-26 turboprop transports; 1 DC-6 piston-engined transport; about 16 Mi-8, Bell 212 and Alouette III helicopters; a few Chinese BT-6 piston-engined primary trainers, 8 Magister armed jet trainers and some light aircraft, including Otters. Personnel strength, 3,000.

INTERNATIONAL RELATIONS

Membership. Bangladesh is a member of the UN and all its related agencies and of the Colombo Plan.

External Debt. In Aug. 1979 the IMF agreed that Bangladesh might purchase currencies up to 85m. Special Drawing Rights. By previous agreements with the World Bank SDR62·5m. were granted in 1975, SDR62·5m. in 1972, SDR31·2m. in 1974 and SDR51·5m. under an 'oil-facility' scheme.

Treaties. Bangladesh signed an economic and technical co-operation agreement with China on 4 Jan. 1977. The amended constitution of 1977 states that Bangladesh seeks fraternal relations with Moslem countries based on Islamic solidarity.

ECONOMY

Planning. The development budget for 1979–80 was Tk.20,700m., of which the highest proportion is for agriculture, irrigation, flood control and rural development.

The second 5-year plan was launched in 1980, as part of a 20-year perspective plan. There was a 2-year interim plan 1978–80, with an envisaged investment of Tk.36,700m. mainly for rural development.

Budget. Details were as follows for two financial years (Tk.1m.):

	1978–79 (Revised)	1979–80		1978–79 (Revised)	1979–80
Expenditure	11,290·3	11,939·6	Receipts	15,026·8	18,120·7
Defence	2,069·4	2,200·0	Tax Receipts	11,556·3	14,242·7
Education	1,541·9	1,651·6	Non-tax Receipts	3,470·8	3,878·0
Health	549·0	628·5			

Money supply (June 1979) stood at Tk.15,150·6m. and foreign exchange reserves (June 1977) at Tk.4,561·6m.

Currency. A new currency, the *Taka*, was floated in 1976 (Tk.36·90 = £1 and Tk.15·9 = US$1 in March 1981).

Banking. The former private banking system, except for foreign banks, has been nationalized. In June 1978 there were 2,756 bank branches (1,594 rural).

Weights and Measures. Imperial measures are in use. Weight is in the *seer* (1 *seer* = 2 lb.); the *maund* (1 *maund* = 40 *seers*) and the ton.

ENERGY AND NATURAL RESOURCES

Electricity. There is a hydro-electric power station at Kaptai on Karnafulli and other power stations at Siddhirganj (80 mw), Ashuganj (120), Ghorasal (110), Shahjibazar (1,000), Khulna (60) and Bheramara (40). Installed capacity for electric power (1976) 755,000 kw (of which 80,000 kw are from hydro-electric plants). Production (1975), 1,378m. kwh., of which 355m. kwh. are hydro-electricity.

Water. On 5 Nov. 1977 India and Bangladesh signed an agreement on sharing the water of the river Ganges. The flow will be monitored daily at the Farakka barrage and two other points. A joint rivers commission is studying how to increase the flow.

Oil. Supplies have been located in the Bay of Bengal.

Gas. Natural gas from Titas is piped to Dacca; drilling is in progress at other sites. Production (1974) 850m. cu. metres.

Minerals. Coal has been found at Jamalpur (about 700m. tons). Other minerals include salt (750,000 tonnes in 1975), limestone, white clay, glass sand. The Rajshahi area has known reserves of deep-lying coal. In 1979 the Saudi fund for Development invested US$30m. for a limestone and cement project at Jaipurhat.

Agriculture. Agriculture contributes about 55% of GDP and employs about 80% of the economically active population; 64% of the total area is under cultivation; 80% of that is under rice and 9% under jute. Cultivable waste is about 1·5m. acres. About 3·6m. acres (1977–78) is irrigated. Rice is the most important food crop, production in 1978–79, 12·6m. tonnes. Other crops in 1979 (1,000 tonnes): Sugar-cane, 6,900; wheat, 486; tobacco, 49; tea, 84m. lb. There were 2,250 tractors in use in 1974.

Livestock in 1977–78 (1,000): Poultry, 85,663; cattle, 30,520; goats, 12,339; sheep, 1,001; buffalo, 1,429; horses, 43.

Bangladesh produces about 50% of the world production of raw jute which is the principal foreign exchange earner. Production, 1978–79 (estimate), 5·3m. bales.

Forestry. The total area under forests (1977) is 9,283 sq. miles, of which 5,105 sq. miles are Reserved Forests. The output of timber in 1975 was 15·9m. cu. metres of roundwood (broad-leaved timber) and 410,000 cu. metres of sawn wood. Among minor forest products are 76·5m. stems of bamboos, 415,000 canes, 6,500 maunds of honey annually.

Fisheries. Being bounded on the south by the Bay of Bengal and having numerous rivers, streams, khals and bils, the state is pre-eminently a fish-producing area and possesses great possibilities for the manufacture of various oils and fish products. Fish production, 1977–78, 835,000 tonnes.

INDUSTRY AND TRADE

Industry. Out of the existing industries, the textile-mills, sugar factories, match factories, glass works, hosiery factories, a paper-mill, jute-mills, aluminium works and a cement factory, with a capacity of 2m. tons per annum, are the most prominent. Refinery distillation capacity, 1·68m. tonnes. There is a steel mill at Chittagong with a capacity of 250,000 ingot-tons per annum. There is also a newsprint factory, a fertilizer factory, a shipyard and a dockyard. Production in 1978–79 (1,000 tons): Jute textiles, 510; steel ingots, 122; fertilizer, 338; woven cotton fabric, 85m. yd.; cotton yarn, 97m. lb; sugar, 131. Industry employs about 7% of the active population and provides 8·5% of the GNP.

Labour. In 1974–75, 1,417 firms (employing more than 10 people) had 293,200 paid employees earning Tk.1,298·7m.; value added, Tk.3,781m.

Commerce. The main export commodities are jute, hide, skins, leather and tea. Bangladesh has resumed trade with Pakistan. In 1978–79 exports were valued at Tk.8,251m., of which 71% was from jute and jute products. Principal imports (Tk.23,337m.) are machinery, transport equipment, food grains, mineral fuels, chemicals, drugs, medicines and consumer goods.

Value of trade (1978–79 April–March) in Tk.1m.: Exports, 9,632; imports, 21,727.

Total trade between Bangladesh and UK (British Department of Trade returns, in £1,000 sterling):

	1977	1978	1979	1980
Imports to UK	25,001	40,712	60,421	73,084
Exports and re-exports from UK	30,627	68,054	90,071	110,408

Tourism. In 1975 there were 63,847 visitors to Bangladesh. They spent the equivalent of US$3m.

COMMUNICATIONS

Roads. The State is backward in the matter of road communications, but there are some 2,500 miles of paved and 2,000 miles of unpaved road. In 1976 there were 66m. motor vehicles.

Railways. In 1980 there were 2,874 km of railways, comprising 981 km of 1,676 mm gauge and 1,893 km of metre gauge. In 1978–79 the railways carried 3·2m. tonnes and 89·8m. passengers.

Aviation. Bangladesh Biman (Bangladesh Airways) has domestic flights from Dacca and international services to Calcutta, Kathmandu, Bombay, Dubai, Abu Dhabi, Jeddah, Bangkok, Singapore and London.

Shipping. Bangladesh possesses important natural advantages in her navigable channels which give valuable service in carrying produce by 5,000 miles of cheap water routes. There are 3 principal waterways, the Padma, Brahmaputra and Meghna. These are freely used by inland steam vessels, which serve areas where railways cannot be economically constructed. The Bangladesh Shipping Corporation owns 25 ships including a 93,000-ton oil tanker (*Banglar Noor*) and a passenger vessel (*Hizbul Bahar*). The Corporation has the capacity to carry 20% of imports and 12% of exports.

Post and Broadcasting. There were 89,211 telephones in 1978. Dacca and Islamabad were linked by telephone in Oct. 1976 and a second telephone circuit was agreed on 11 April 1977. International communications are by satellite, Chittagong being linked to the Indian Ocean Intelsat IV satellite.

Newspapers. In Nov. 1980 there were 42 daily newspapers, 128 weeklies, 19 fortnightlies, 142 monthlies and 80 quarterly periodicals. Most papers are published in Dacca. The Government has set up a paper (*Dainik Barta-at Rajshahi*) to stimulate a regional press. Most papers are privately owned. Press censorship and restrictions of 1975 were removed by the Newspaper (Annulment of Declaration) Repeal Ordinance of June 1976. There is a Press Institute.

JUSTICE, RELIGION, EDUCATION AND WELFARE

Justice. The amended constitution in 1977 set up a Supreme Judicial Council to establish a code of conduct for Supreme Court and High Court judges, who may be removed from office by the President on the Council's recommendation.

Religion. Islam is the official religion, about 80% of the people being Muslim and the rest Hindus, Buddhists and Christians.

Education. In 1977 (estimate) under 23% of the population was literate. The compulsory primary education scheme has been replaced by model primary education. The Government has dissolved the District School Boards and taken over school administration.

In 1977 there were 40,165 primary schools, 8,080 secondary schools and about 600 intermediate and degree colleges. Primary schools had 8m. students, secondary schools about 2m. and technical colleges about 16,000. There were 6 universities including those at Dacca, Rajshahi, Mymensingh and Chittagong (founded 1964); one university is for engineering and one for agriculture. Universities had about 28,000 students in 1977. There are 12 teacher-training colleges, 47 primary training institutes, 22 polytechnics and 35 vocational institutes.

Health. In 1978 there were 134 government hospitals, 1 mental and 2 tuberculosis hospitals, 8 medical colleges and nursing training centres which train about 1,200 nurses annually. In 1977 the number of beds was 18,233.

DIPLOMATIC REPRESENTATIVES

OF BANGLADESH IN GREAT BRITAIN
(28 Queen's Gate, London, SW7)
High Commissioner: A. R. S. Doha (accredited 15 Feb. 1978)

OF GREAT BRITAIN IN BANGLADESH
(D.I.T. Bldgs., Dilkhusha, Dacca, 2)
High Commissioner: Sir Michael Scott, KCVO, CMG.

OF BANGLADESH IN THE USA
(3421 Massachusetts Ave., NW, Washington, D.C., 20007)
Ambassador: Tabarak Hossein.

OF THE USA IN BANGLADESH
(Adamjee Court, Motijheel, Dacca)
Ambassador: David T. Schneider.

OF BANGLADESH TO THE UNITED NATIONS
Ambassador: Khwaja Mohammed Kaiser.

Books of Reference

Bangladesh Bureau of Statistics, *Statistical Digests.—Statistical Pocket Book of Bangladesh.* 1979

Bangladesh Planning Commission, *The First Five Year Plan.—The Second Five Year Plan.*

Ministry of Finance. *Bangladesh Economic Survey.* 1979–80

Chen, L. C. (ed.), *Disaster in Bangladesh. Health Crisis in a Developing Nation.* OUP, 1973

Chowdhury, R., *The Genesis of Bangladesh.* London, 1972

Dutt, K., *Bangladesh Economy: An Analytical Study.* New Delhi, 1973

Kamal, K. A., *Sheikh Mujibur Rahman.* 2nd ed. Dacca, 1970

Kashyap, S. C. (ed.), *Bangla Desh: Background and Perspectives.* New Delhi, 1971

Khan, A. R., *The Economy of Bangladesh.* London, 1972

Oliver, T. W., *The United Nations in Bangladesh.* Princeton Univ. Press, 1978

Rahman, M., *Bangladesh Today: An Indictment and a Lament.* London, 1978

Robinson, E. A. G., and Griffin, K. (ed.), *The Economic Development of Bangladesh.* London, 1974

BARBADOS

Capital: Bridgetown
Population: 258,000 (1976)
GNP per capita: US$1,940 (1978)

HISTORY. Barbados was occupied by the British in 1627 and during its colonial history never changed hands. Full internal self-government was attained in 1961. Barbados became an independent sovereign state within the Commonwealth on 30 Nov. 1966.

AREA AND POPULATION. Barbados lies to the east of the Windward Islands. Area 166 sq. miles (430 sq. km). The hot and rainy seasons last from June to December, and the average rainfall is 56 in. per year. In 1976 the estimated population was 258,500. Births, 4,593; deaths 2,266. Bridgetown is the principal city: population, 8,789, and its suburbs, 88,097.

CONSTITUTION AND GOVERNMENT. The Legislature consists of the Governor-General, a Senate and a House of Assembly. The Senate comprises 21 members appointed by the Governor-General, 12 being appointed on the advice of the Prime Minister, 2 on the advice of the leader of the opposition and 7 in the Governor-General's discretion. The House of Assembly comprises 24 members elected every 5 years. In 1963 the voting age was reduced to 18.

The Privy Council is appointed by the Governor-General after consultation with the Prime Minister. It consists of 12 members and the Governor-General as chairman. It advises the Governor-General in the exercise of the royal prerogative of mercy and in the exercise of his disciplinary powers over members of the public and police services.

In the general election of Sept. 1976 the Barbados Labour Party held 17 seats and the Democratic Labour Party 7 seats.

Governor-General: Sir Deighton Ward, GCMG, CVO.

The Cabinet, appointed in March 1980, was:

Prime Minister, Finance and Planning: Rt Hon. J. M. G. M. Adams, PC.

Trade, Industry and Tourism: Bernard St John. *Labour and Community Service:* Dr Donald Blackman. *Attorney-General and External Affairs:* Henry Forde. *Agriculture, Food and Consumer Affairs:* Lloyd Brathwaite. *Health and National Insurance:* Billie Miller. *Housing and Environment:* Lionel Craig. *Communications and Works:* Lindsay Bolden. *Education and Culture:* Louis Tull. *Broadcasting, Press Public Relations:* Nigel Barrow.

National flag: Three vertical strips of blue, gold, blue, with a black trident in the centre.

INTERNATIONAL RELATIONS

Membership. Barbados is a member of UN, OAS, CARICOM, the Commonwealth and an ACP state of EEC.

ECONOMY

Budget. The fiscal year runs from 1 April to 31 March; accounts in BD$:

	1975–76	1976–77	1977–78	1978–79
Revenue	203,041,202	216,804,579	246,372,000	315,664,759
Expenditure	189,929,820	225,082,713	252,657,000	357,434,970
Public debt	213,700,000	271,200,000	...	...

Currency. The monetary unit is the *Barbados dollar* (BD$) divided into 100 *cents*. In March 1981, £1 = BD$4.36; US$1 = 2.18.

Banking. Ten main banks operate in Barbados including Barclays Bank International, the Royal Bank of Canada, Canadian Imperial Bank of Commerce, the Bank of Nova Scotia, the Bank of America, Chase Manhattan Bank, First National Bank of Chicago and Citibank, The Barbados National Bank.

Barbados is headquarters for the Caribbean Development Bank. It is a member of the Caribbean Common Market (CARICOM). The Barbados Development Bank opened on 15 April 1969 and Barbados became a member of the Inter-American Development Bank on 19 March 1969.

NATURAL RESOURCES

Agriculture. Of the total area of 106,240 acres, about 54,932 acres are arable land. The land is intensely cultivated, and sugar-cane occupies 64,000 acres, 39,178 were reaped in 1977. The agricultural sector accounted for 14·4% of GDP in 1970 (1946, 45%; 1967, 24%). In 1976, 4,342 persons were employed on sugar estates and 498 in sugar factories. In 1977, 117,911 tons of sugar were produced. There are 12 sugar factories, 1 syrup plant and a rum distillery in production.

Livestock (1979): Cattle, 19,000; sheep, 51,000; goats, 28,000; pigs, 38,000; poultry, 420,000.

Fisheries. There are about 544 powered boats and many men and women are employed during the flying-fish season. Large numbers of these boats are laid up from July to Oct. The annual catch is about 2,240 tons.

INDUSTRY AND TRADE

Industry. Industries operating in Barbados in 1977 numbered 178 and ranged from the manufacture of processed food to small specialized products such as garment manufacturing, furniture and household appliances, electrical components, plastic products and electronic parts.

Commerce. Total trade for calendar years in BD$:

	1975	1976	1977	1978	1979
Imports[1]	437,240,000	473,314,000	547,046,000	630,700,000	415,300,000
Exports[1]	178,218,000	133,442,000	147,077,000	261,200,000	132,200,000

[1] Exclusive of bullion and specie.

In 1977 the principal imports (provisional) were: Machinery and transport equipment, $105,649,000; food, $104,763,000; manufactured goods, $102,225,000; lubricants, mineral fuels, etc., $72,266,000; chemicals, $50,924,000; crude materials inedible, except fuel, $14,337,000; beverages and tobacco, $11,249,000; animal and vegetable oils, $8,098,000. In 1977 the principal domestic exports (provisional) were: Sugar, $48,065,000; clothing, $37,787,000; electrical parts, $15,053,000; molasses and syrup, $5,841,000; rum, $5,709,000; lard and margarine, $3,742,000; crustacea and molluscs, $1,979,000; biscuits, $1,777,000.

Total trade between Barbados and UK (British Department of Trade returns, in £1,000 sterling):

	1976	1977	1978	1979	1980
Imports from UK	1,639	5,239	11,765	8,414	7,630
Exports and re-exports to UK	19,141	24,713	24,367	27,253	29,860

Tourism. In 1979, 370,916 visitors came to Barbados, spending BD$332m. The industry employs over 10,000 people.

COMMUNICATIONS

Roads. There are 1,020 miles of road open to traffic, of which 840 miles are all-weather roads. In 1977 there were 22,000 private cars, 2,000 taxis, 266 buses and 4,000 other vehicles.

Aviation. There is an international airport at Seawell, Christ Church, Barbados, served by British Airways, BWIA, Leeward Islands Air Transport, PANAM, Air Canada, SAS, Caribbean Airways and Eastern Airlines, Cubana Airlines, Venezuelan Airlines. In 1976, 360,170 passengers arrived by air; 217,729 were in transit.

Shipping. A deep-water harbour opened in 1961 at Bridgetown provides 8 berths for ships 500–600 ft in length, including one specially designed for bulk sugar loading. The number of merchant vessels entering in 1972 was 1,381 of 4,067,500 net tons.

Post and Telephone. There is a general post office in Bridgetown and 13 branches on the island. In Jan. 1978 there were 47,266 telephones and, in 1974, 39,445 stations in service.

Cinemas. There were (1977) 6 cinemas with a seating capacity of 5,040, and 2 drive-in cinemas for 600 cars.

Newspapers. In 1979 there was 1 daily newspaper (average daily circulation 20,463 and 32,685 on Sundays) and 1 bi-weekly (circulation 48,287).

JUSTICE, RELIGION, EDUCATION AND WELFARE

Justice. Justice is administered by the Supreme Court and by magistrates' courts. All have both civil and criminal jurisdiction. There is a Chief Justice and 3 puisne judges of the Supreme Court and 8 magistrates.

Religion. The majority (about 70%) of the population are Anglicans, the remainder mainly Methodists, Moravians and Roman Catholics.

Education. In 1976 children in primary schools numbered 36,000; in 21 secondary schools, 22,629; in 18 approved secondary schools, 6,904. There are 19 government-aided independent schools with 7,506 pupils and a number of independent schools for which no accurate figures are available. As from Jan. 1962 tuition fees were abolished for children at all government secondary schools.

In 1963 Erdiston College became one of the constituent Colleges of the University of the West Indies Institute of Education. The College of Arts and Sciences of the University of the West Indies in Barbados was opened in Sept. 1963 and Cave Hill campus in 1967. In 1973–74, 942 students attended. Education at this College is free for Barbadians. However, students in the Faculty of Law are required to pay a fee. A Community College for higher education at pre-university level was opened in 1969. In 1973–74, 1,517 students attended the S. J. Prescod Polytechnic which was opened in Nov. 1969 to give training in, among other things, construction, electrical and engineering trades. In 1972–73, 74 government scholars, bursars and exhibitioners were attending universities overseas. Government expenditure on education during 1979–80 is estimated at BD$68,948,197.

Health. In 1972 there were 2,220 hospital beds and (1973) 160 doctors.

DIPLOMATIC REPRESENTATIVES

OF BARBADOS IN GREAT BRITAIN
(6 Upper Belgrave St., London, SW1X 8AZ)

High Commissioner: A. W. Symmonds.

OF GREAT BRITAIN IN BARBADOS
(147/9 Roebuck St., Bridgetown)

High Commissioner: J. S. Arthur, CMG.

OF BARBADOS IN THE USA
(2144 Wyoming Ave., NW, Washington, D.C. 20008)

Ambassador: Oliver H. Jackman.

OF THE USA IN BARBADOS (PO Box 302, Bridgetown)

Ambassador: Sally A. Shelton.

OF BARBADOS TO THE UNITED NATIONS

Ambassador: Ronald G. Mapp.

Books of Reference

Statistical Information: The Barbados Statistical Service (NIS Bldg, Fairchild St, St Michael) produces selected monthly statistics and annual abstracts. *Government Statistician:* Keith Padmore.

Barbados Economic Survey, 1978
Barbados Development Plan, 1979–83
Chandler, M. J., *A Guide to Records in Barbados*. University of the West Indies, 1965
Hoyos, F. A., *Barbados, Our Island Home*. London, 1970.—*Barbados: A History from the Amerindians to Independence*. London, 1978
Starkey, O. P., *Commercial Geography of Barbados*. Indiana Univ. Press, 1961

Library: The Barbados Public Library, Bridgetown. *Acting Chief Librarian:* Betty Carrillo.

BELGIUM

Royaume de Belgique—
Koninkrijk België

Capital: Brussels
Population: 9·8m. (1979)
GNP per capita: US$9,070 (1978)

HISTORY. The kingdom of Belgium formed itself into an independent state in 1830, having from 1815 been part of the Netherlands. The secession was decreed on 4 Oct. 1830 by a provisional government, established in consequence of a revolution which broke out at Brussels, on 25 Aug. 1830. A National Congress elected Prince Leopold of Saxe-Coburg King of the Belgians on 4 June 1831; he ascended the throne 21 July 1831.

By the Treaty of London, 15 Nov. 1831, the neutrality of Belgium was guaranteed by Austria, Russia, Great Britain and Prussia. It was not until after the signing of the Treaty of London, 19 April 1839, which established peace between King Leopold I and the King of the Netherlands, that all the states of Europe recognized the kingdom of Belgium. In the Treaty of Versailles (28 June 1919) it is stated that as the treaties of 1839 'no longer conform to the requirements of the situation', these are abrogated and will be replaced by other treaties.

AREA AND POPULATION. Belgium is bounded north by the Netherlands, north-west by the North Sea, west and south by France, east by Federal Republic of Germany and Luxembourg. Belgium has an area of 30,519 sq. km (11,778 sq. miles). The Belgium exclave of Baarle–Hertog in the Netherlands has an area of 7 sq. km, and a population (1 Jan. 1980) of 1,108 males and 1,036 females.

By an agreement, 23 Sept. 1956, the frontier with Germany was slightly readjusted.

Census	Population	Increase % per annum	Census	Population	Increase % per annum
1900	6,693,548	1·03	1947	8,512,195	0·36
1910	7,423,784	1·09	1961	9,189,741	0·52
1920	7,465,782	0·06	1970	9,650,944	0·55
1930	8,092,004	0·84			

Provinces	Provincial capitals	Area (hectares)	1970[1]	Estimated population (31 Dec.) 1977	1978	1979
Antwerp(Anvers)	Antwerp	286,725	1,533,249	1,568,949	1,571,023	1,573,647
Brabant	Brussels	335,811	2,176,373	2,218,649	2,216,938	2,220,699
Flanders { West	Bruges	313,439	1,054,429	1,075,807	1,076,236	1,078,239
Flanders { East	Ghent	298,167	1,310,117	1,326,723	1,328,070	1,330,134
Hainaut	Mons	378,669	1,317,453	1,318,015	1,313,294	1,308,931
Liège	Liège	386,213	1,008,905	1,009,681	1,007,490	1,005,947
Limbourg	Hasselt	242,231	652,547	698,519	704,741	710,715
Luxembourg	Arlon	444,114	217,310	220,759	221,374	222,317
Namur	Namur	366,501	380,561	400,311	402,488	404,481
Total		3,051,871	9,650,944	9,837,413	9,841,654	9,855,110

[1] Census.

In 1979 there were 4,818,944 males and 5,036,166 females.
Foreigners numbered 890,038 on 1 Jan. 1980.
Vital statistics for calendar years:

	Births	Deaths	Marriages	Divorces	Immigration	Emigration
1975	119,273	119,273	72,869	11,245	69,886	40,151
1976	120,472	118,765	71,093	12,925	58,724	56,921
1977	121,523	112,208	69,109	13,031	55,298	55,076
1978	121,983	115,060	67,206	13,645	52,594	58,495
1979	123,658	112,156	65,476	13,499	54,854	59,552

	1977	1978	1979
Illegitimate births	3,766	...	...
Of the total births			
including still-born	122,894	123,658	121,983
Boys	62,992	63,905	62,429
Girls	59,902	59,753	59,554

The most important towns, with estimated population on 1 Jan. 1980:

Brussels and suburbs[1]	1,008,715	Hasselt	64,439
Ghent (Gand)	241,695	Genk	61,512
Charleroi	221,911	Verviers	56,209
Liège (Luik)	220,183	Mouscron (Moeskroen)	54,553
Antwerp (Anvers)	194,073	Roeselare (Roulers)	51,752
Brugge (Bruges)	118,243	Berchem	46,368
Namur (Namen)	100,712	Borgerhout	44,369
Mons (Bergen)	96,784	Wilruyck	43,161
Leuven (Louvain)	85,632	Merksem	41,202
Aalst (Alost)	79,340	Herstal	39,190
Deurne	78,646	Turnhout	37,652
Mechelen (Malines)	77,667	Hoboken	34,640
Kortrijk (Courtrai)	76,424	Vilvoorde (Vilvorde)	33,644
Oostende (Ostende)	70,125	Lokeren	33,126
Tournai (Doornik)	69,862	Lier (Lierre)	31,319
St Niklaas (St Nicolas)	68,080	Ronse (Renaix)	24,463
Seraing	65,371		

[1] The suburbs comprise 18 distinct communes, viz., Anderlecht, Etterbeek, Forest Ixelles, Jette, Koekelberg, Molenbeek St Jean, St Gilles, St Josse-ten-Noode, Schaerbeek, Uccle, Woluwe-St Lambert, Auderghem, Watermael-Boitsfort, Woluwe-St Pierre, Berchem, Ste Agathe, Evere and Ganshoren.

KING. Baudouin, born 7 Sept. 1930, succeeded his father, Leopold III, on 17 July 1951, when he took the oath on the constitution before the two Chambers: married on 15 Dec. 1960 to Fabiola de Mora y Aragón, daughter of the Conde de Mora and Marqués de Casa Riera.

Father of the King. Leopold III, born 3 Nov. 1901, son of the late King Albert (died 17 Feb. 1934) and of Queen Elisabeth, Duchess of Bavaria (died 23 Nov. 1965); married (1) on 4 Nov. 1926 to Princess Astrid of Sweden, died 29 Aug. 1935, and (2) on 11 Sept. (civil marriage, 6 Dec.) 1941, to Mlle Mary Lilian Baels, Princess de Rethy, daughter of Hendrik Baels, formerly Minister of Agriculture. Leopold III succeeded to the throne on 23 Feb. 1934; on 20 Sept. 1944 parliament elected Prince Charles, Count of Flanders, Leopold's brother as Regent of the Kingdom. The Regency ended on 22 July 1950; but King Leopold delegated his powers to Prince Baudouin on 11 Aug. 1950, and abdicated on 16 July 1951.

Brother and Sister of the King. (1) Josephine Charlotte, Princess of Belgium, born 11 Oct. 1927; married to Prince Jean of Luxembourg, 9 April 1953; (2) Albert, Prince of Liège, born 6 June 1934; married to Paola Ruffo di Calabria, 2 July 1959; *offspring:* Prince Philippe, born 15 April 1960; Princess Astrid, born 5 June 1962; Prince Laurent, born 19 Oct. 1963. *Half-brother and half-sisters of the King.* Prince Alexandre, born 18 July 1942; Princess Marie Christine, born 6 Feb. 1951; Princess Maria-Esmeralda, born 30 Sept. 1956.

Uncle and Aunt of the King. (1) Prince Charles, Count of Flanders, born 10 Oct. 1903. (2) Princess Marie-José, born 4 Aug. 1906, married to Prince Umberto (King Umberto II of Italy in 1946) on 8 Jan. 1930.

BELGIAN SOVEREIGNS

Leopold I	1831–65	Leopold III	1934–44, 1950–51
Leopold II	1865–1909	Regency	1944–50
Albert	1909–34	Baudouin	1951–

CONSTITUTION AND GOVERNMENT. According to the constitution of 1831, Belgium is a constitutional, representative and hereditary monarchy. The legislative power is vested in the King, the Senate and the Chamber of Representatives. The royal succession is in direct male line in the order of primogeniture.

By marriage without the King's consent, however, the right of succession is for-feited, but may be restored by the King with the consent of the two Chambers. No act of the King can have effect unless countersigned by one of his Ministers, who thus becomes responsible for it. The King convokes, prorogues and dissolves the Chambers. In default of male heirs, the King may nominate his successor with the consent of the Chambers. If the successor be under 18 years of age the two Chambers meet together for the purpose of nominating a regent during the minority.

National flag: Three vertical strips of black, yellow, red.

National anthem: Après des siècles d'esclavage (La Brabançonne; words by Jenneval, 1830; tune by F. van Campenhout, 1930).

French, Dutch and German are official languages.

Those sections of the Belgian Constitution which regulate the organization of the legislative power were revised in Oct. 1921. For both Senate and Chamber all elec-tions are held on the principle of universal suffrage.

The Senate consists of members elected for 4 years, partly directly and partly indirectly. The number elected directly is equal to half the number of members of the Chamber of Representatives. The constituent body is similar to that which elects deputies to the Chamber; the minimum age of electors is 21 years, and the minimum length of residence required is 6 months. Women were given the suffrage at parlia-mentary elections on 24 March 1948. In the direct elections of members both the Senate and Chamber of Representatives the principle of proportional representation was introduced by law of 29 Dec. 1899.

Senators are elected indirectly by the provincial councils, on the basis of 1 for 200,000 inhabitants. Every addition of 125,000 inhabitants gives the right to 1 sena-tor more. Each provincial council elects at least 3 senators. There are at present 50 provincial senators. No one, during 2 years preceding the election, must have been a member of the council appointing him. Senators are elected by the Senate itself in the proportion of half the preceding category. The senators belonging to these two latter categories are also elected by the method of proportional repre-sentation. All senators must be at least 40 years of age. They receive 900,000 francs per annum. Sons of the King, or failing these, Belgian princes of the reigning branch of the royal family, are by right senators at the age of 18, but have no voice in the deliberations till the age of 25 years; this prerogative is hardly ever used.

The members of the Chamber of Representatives are elected by the electoral body. Their number, at present 212 (law of 3 April 1965), is proportional to the population, and cannot exceed one for every 40,000 inhabitants. They sit for 4 years. Deputies must be not less than 25 years of age, and resident in Belgium.

Each deputy has an annual allowance of 900,000 francs. Senators and deputies have also free railway passes.

The Senate and Chamber meet annually in October and must sit for at least 40 days; but the King has the power of convoking extraordinary sessions and of dis-solving them either simultaneously or separately. In the latter case a new election must take place within 40 days and a meeting of the chambers within 2 months.

An adjournment cannot be made for a period exceeding 1 month without the consent of the Chambers.

After the revision of the Constitution by the laws of 24 Dec. 1970 and 28 July 1971 establishing three regions and two cultural councils, legislation on 'preparatory regionalization' was enacted in July 1974.

Parliament was dissolved on 15 Nov. 1978 and general elections were held on 17 Dec. 1978.

Parties in the Senate after the election: *Christelijke Volkspartij,* 29; *Parti social chrétien,* 12; *Socialistische Partij,* 13; *Parti Socialiste Belge,* 18; *Partij voor Vrijheid en Vooruitgang,* 11; Other parties, 23.

Parties in the Chamber of Representatives after the election: *Christelijke Volks-partij,* 57; *Parti social chrétien,* 25; *Parti Socialiste,* 32; *Socialistische Partij,* 26; *Partij voor Vrijheid en Vooruitgang,* 22; Other parties, 50.

A 4-party coalition government was formed in Oct. 1980 and in March 1981 was composed as follows:

Prime Minister: Dr Wilfried Martens (CVP).

Deputy Prime Ministers: Guy Spitaels, PS (*Transport*); Willy Claes, SP (*Economic Affairs*); José Desmarets, PSC (*Planning and Middle Classes*). *Public Works and Institutional Reform* (*Flemish Section*): Jos Chabert (CVP). *Foreign Affairs:* Charles-Ferdinand Nothomb (PSC). *Agriculture:* Albert Lavens (CVP). *Social Security and Public Health:* Luc Dhoore (CVP). *Interior and Budget:* Guy Mathot (PS). *Foreign Trade:* Robert Urbain (PS). *Finance:* Mark Eyskens (CVP). *Employment and Labour:* Roger de Wulf (SP). *Justice and Institutional Reform* (*French-speaking Section*): Philippe Moureaux (PS). *Development Co-operation:* Daviel Coens (CVP). *Public Service, Scientific Policy and Environment:* Philippe Maystadt (PSC). *Pensions:* Pierre Mainil (PSC). *Posts and Telecommunications:* Freddy Willockx (SP). *Defence:* Dr Frank Swaelen (CVP). *Ministers with Community and Regional Responsibilities:* Dr Mark Galle (SP), Gaston Geens (CVP), Dr Willy Calewaert (SP), Dr Michel Hansenne (PSC), Jean-Maurice Dehousse (PS), Dr André Degroeve (PS), Philippe Busquin (PS).

Local Government. Belgium has 9 provinces and since the so-called 'Amalgamation Law' of 30 Dec. 1975, 589 communes (instead of 2,359). They have a large measure of autonomous government. According to the law of 15 April 1920, changed by law, 1 July 1969, all Belgians over 18 years of age without distinction of sex, who have been domiciled for at least 6 months, have the right to vote in communal elections. Proportional representation is applied to the communal elections, and communal councils are to be renewed every 6 years. In each commune there is a college composed of the burgomaster as the president and a certain number of aldermen.

DEFENCE. Belgium is a full member of NATO since 1949 and of the Eurogroup since 1968. The need to extend European armaments co-operation led to the formation of the Independent European Program Group (IEPG) in 1976. Its members include Belgium.

According to the Military Law of 30 April 1962, the Belgian Army is recruited by annual calls to the colours and by voluntary enlistments.

Compulsory service lasts 8 or 10 months for private soldiers, 13 months for voluntary reserve officers and 15 for the paracommando regiment. Duration of military obligation is 8 years for most soldiers called for compulsory service.

Army. The Army comprises as major units 1 armoured and 3 mechanized brigades (2 of which are deployed as the Belgian divisions in the Belgian corps area in the Federal Republic of Germany) and 1 paracommando regiment. There are also 3 reconnaissance and 2 motorized battalions. Total strength about 63,500 (including medical services). *Gendarmerie,* 16,300.

Equipment includes nearly 330 LEOPARD Main Battle Tanks, 135 SCORPION Light Tanks, 150 SCIMITAR Armoured Fighting Vehicles, 1,150 Armoured Personnel Carriers and 80 JPK 90mm Self-Propelled Anti-Tank Guns; Artillery Battalions are equipped with 105mm, 155mm and 203mm Self-Propelled Howitzers, LANCE Surface-to-Surface Missiles, HAWK Surface-to-Air Missiles and GEPARD Armoured Vehicles with 35mm Anti-Aircraft Guns.

Other equipment in use: MILAN Anti-Tank Guided Weapon, STRIKER Armoured Fighting Vehicle with SWINGFIRE Anti-Tank Guided Weapon, Islander aircrafts, Alouette II helicopters, Epervier Remotely Piloted Vehicle.

Navy. The naval forces include 4 new frigates (the first fully designed by the Belgian Navy and built in Belgian yards) of 2,430 tons full load (and armed with guided missiles as well as guns, torpedoes, anti-submarine mortars and rocket launchers) built in 1974–78, 7 ocean minehunters, 2 command and logistic support ships, 2 coastal minehunters, 3 coastal minesweepers, 14 inshore minesweepers, 2 research ships, 8 river patrol boats, 5 tugs and 7 miscellaneous craft. Naval personnel in 1981 totalled 4,600 officers and ratings.

The naval air arm comprises 3 Alouette III general utility helicopters.

Air Force. The Air Force has a strength of about 20,000 personnel and more than

270 aircraft in 14 operational squadrons and support units. There is 1 all-weather fighter wing (2 squadrons), of F-16s; 1 fighter-bomber wing (2 squadrons) of F-104G Starfighters, which will convert to F-16s in 1982–83; 2 tactical wings with 3 squadrons of Mirage 5Bs, including Mirage 5BD two-seat trainers, and 1 squadron of Mirage 5BR photo-reconnaissance aircraft; and 1 wing (2 squadrons) equipped with 12 C-130H Hercules turboprop transports, 2 light twin-jet Falcons, 3 HS 748 twin-turboprop transports, 5 Swearingen Merlin III light turboprop transports and 2 Boeing 727. Two wings, based in Germany, have Nike surface-to-air missiles. Other types in service include Sea King Mk 48 search and rescue helicopters, Puma transport helicopters, and SIAI-Marchetti SF.260M and Alpha Jet training aircraft. 12 twin-engined Islanders and light helicopters are operated by the Army.

INTERNATIONAL RELATIONS

Membership. Belgium is a member of UN, EEC, Benelux Economic Union, Council of Europe, NATO, OECD and WEU.

ECONOMY

Budget. Revenue and expenditure for calendar years (in 1m. francs):

	1975	1976	1977	1978	1979	1980[1]
Receipts						
Current	581,251	656,913	747,509	877,324	941,484	1,022,163
Capital	102,183	118,586	159,515	167,769	175,687	14,001
Total	683,434	775,499	907,024	1,045,093	1,171,171	1,036,164
Expenditure						
Current	656,403	758,789	865,733	1,012,521	1,092,766	1,168,997
Capital	72,653	77,114	85,225	113,351	119,212	150,612
Total	729,056	835,903	950,958	1,125,872	1,211,978	1,319,609

[1] Budget estimates.

On 31 Aug. 1980 the Belgian public debt consisted of (in 1m. francs): Internal debt consolidated, 1,307,387; short and middle terms, 359,050; at sight, 87,371. External debt, 139,193.

Currency. The *franc*, containing 0·01826 gramme of fine gold, is the unit of currency.

No gold has been minted since 1882 (save only 5m. francs struck in 1914). New silver coins of 100 francs have been issued since 15 Oct. 1948 and new silver coins of 250 francs since 16 March 1976. Note circulation 31 Dec. 1980, 371,796m. francs.

The official rate of exchange in March 1981 was US$1 = 35 francs; £1 = 77 francs.

Banking. The bank of issue in Belgium is the National Bank, instituted in 1850. It is the cashier of the State, and is authorized to carry on the usual banking operations. The note circulation on 31 Dec. 1979 amounted to 371,796m. francs. The articles of association of the National Bank of Belgium were modified on 13 Sept. 1948 so as to strengthen public control.

The savings banks are mainly operated by the Caisse Générale d'Epargne et de Retraite and by the private savings banks. The Caisse Générale d'Epargne et de Retraite is an autonomous institution with legally regulated functions; operating under the supervision of the Minister of Finance. It co-operates with the Belgian postal service, thus obviating any need of a postal-savings system. The savings deposits and savings bonds of the Caisse d'Epargne amounted to 504,421m. francs on 31 Dec. 1979. The private savings banks, whose liabilities expressed in savings accounts and bonds amounted to 495,156m. francs on 31 Dec. 1978, are controlled by the 'Commission bancaire'.

Weights and Measures. The metric system is in force.

Evalenko, R., *Régime économique de la Belgique*. Brussels, 1968

ENERGY AND NATURAL RESOURCES

Electricity. The production of electricity (1m. kwh.) amounted to 45,001 in 1976; 44,774 in 1977; 48,357 in 1978; 49,648 in 1979.

Gas. Production of gas (in 1m. cu. metres): 1,729 in 1976; 667 in 1977; 703 in 1978; 730 in 1979.

Minerals. Output (in tonnes) for 5 calendar years:

	1975	1976	1977	1978	1979
Coal	7,478,703	7,237,738	7,068,041	6,590,268	6,124,503
Briquettes	268,730	165,930	126,080	124,496	152,492
Coke	5,727,825	6,216,084	5,568,703	5,747,192	6,450,354
Cast iron	9,068,719	9,864,755	8,910,532	10,127,996	10,775,843
Wrought steel	11,587,172	12,149,321	11,261,005	12,604,240	13,444,799
Finished steel	7,909,684	8,470,509	8,631,802	9,696,177	10,364,011

Agriculture. Of the total area of 3,050,708 hectares, there were, in 1979, 1,432,287 hectares under cultivation, of which 398,397 were under cereals, 17,047 vegetables, 125,578 industrial plants, 115,716 root crops, 710,182 pastures and meadows.

Chief crops	Area in hectares			Produce in tonnes		
	1977	1978	1979	1977	1978	1979
Wheat	176,942	178,352	182,478	741,707	956,476	953,429
Barley	151,678	153,239	155,670	675,557	764,884	766,675
Oats	38,670	32,331	28,091	114,849	136,114	118,826
Rye	17,485	15,112	12,236	60,849	57,123	46,742
Potatoes	41,002	35,360	36,263	1,370,367	1,261,821	1,178,830
Beet (sugar)	93,603	109,799	115,716	4,343,189	5,224,217	5,867,937
Beet (fodder)	22,807	20,359	18,248	2,211,552	1,953,685	1,710,063
Tobacco	469	475	524	1,566	1,587	1,796

In 1979 there were 36,598 horses, 2,893,922 cattle, 84,097 sheep, 6,086 goats and 4,987,212 pigs.

Forestry. In 1970 the forest area covered 19·7% of the land surface. In 1970, 2·85 cu. metres of timber were felled.

Fisheries. The total quantity of fish landed amounted to 32,157 tons valued at 1,578m. francs in 1979. The fishing fleet had a total tonnage of 20,036 gross tons at 31 Dec. 1979.

INDUSTRY AND TRADE

Industry. In 1979 there were 16 sugar factories, output 243,073 tonnes of raw sugar; 3 sugar refineries, output 243,868 tonnes; 10 distilleries, output 395,684 hectolitres of potable and industrial alcohol; 147 breweries, output 13,680,511 hectolitres of beer; margarine factories, output 149,660 tonnes; match factories, output (1973) 43,631m. matches.

Six trusts control the greater part of Belgian industry: the Société Générale (founded in 1822) owns about 40% of coal, 50% of steel, 65% of non-ferrous metals and 35% of electricity; Brufina-Confinindus operates in steel, coal, electricity and heavy engineering; the Groupe Solvay rules the chemical industry; the Groupe Copée has interests in steel and coal; Empain controls tramways and electrical equipment; the Banque Lambert owns petroleum firms and their accessories.

Commerce. By the convention concluded at Brussels on 25 July 1921 between Belgium and Luxembourg and ratified on 5 March 1922 an economic union was formed by the two countries, and the customs frontier between them was abolished on 1 May 1922. Dissolved in Aug. 1940, the union was re-established on 1 May 1945. On 14 March 1947, in execution of an agreement signed in London on 5 Sept. 1944, there was concluded a customs union between Belgium and Luxembourg, on the one hand, and the Netherlands, on the other. The union came into force on 1 Jan. 1948, and is now known as the Benelux Economic Union. A joint tariff has been adopted and import duties are no longer levied at the Netherlands frontier, but import licences may still be required. A full economic union of the three countries came into operation on 1 Nov. 1960.

Benelux information is supplied by the Secrétariat Général de l'Union Douanière Néerlando-Belgo-Luxembourgeoise, Rue de la Régence, 39, 1000 Brussels. It publishes *Benelux. Bulletin Trimestriel de Statistique; Statistisch Kwartaalbericht* (1955 ff.).

Trade by selected countries (in 1,000 Belgian francs):

	Imports from			Exports to		
	1977	1978	1979[1]	1977	1978	1979[1]
France	230,210,614	249,721,868	278,358,781	256,714,865	268,428,093	316,135,750
USA	87,192,432	88,121,739	116,854,647	56,582,701	58,229,966	61,656,460
UK	112,781,992	127,829,099	140,937,862	92,047,687	101,709,590	132,963,610
Netherlands	245,285,418	249,998,413	293,640,282	225,998,054	231,811,668	266,200,565
German Dem. Rep.	3,226,498	3,457,158	3,907,476	2,923,571	2,181,039	2,810,508
Germany, Fed. Rep.	321,724,839	350,757,138	389,166,374	301,609,151	321,946,172	371,215,379
Argentina	4,990,666	5,404,244	5,101,347	1,441,905	1,925,534	3,416,840
Italy	57,424,765	61,201,460	71,869,075	58,874,261	64,526,931	87,517,658
Switzerland	20,633,682	28,384,857	35,248,572	26,688,647	32,748,581	47,027,696
Zaïre	22,639,326	24,134,337	28,072,792	6,464,987	5,606,154	5,633,809
Denmark	6,703,733	7,319,739	8,116,143	18,760,551	16,568,266	19,721,520
USSR	14,535,229	14,764,621	17,368,641	9,798,501	10,992,736	13,696,683
India	7,461,474	9,702,653	7,045,428	9,370,028	14,285,312	11,504,743
Rep. of S. Africa	10,584,708	10,394,745	12,410,201	4,808,623	4,578,206	5,036,955
Canada	11,890,041	12,043,189	14,238,517	4,612,284	4,846,105	5,258,118
Brazil	7,064,321	6,911,810	8,177,834	3,678,440	3,528,360	4,323,469
Australia	6,774,864	4,511,986	6,048,463	3,836,419	3,419,572	3,319,165

[1] Provisional.

Imports and exports for 6 calendar years (in 1,000 Belgian francs):

	Imports	Exports		Imports	Exports
1974	1,160,684,663	1,099,824,920	1977	1,447,981,180	1,344,704,149
1975	1,130,944,557	1,056,879,476	1978	1,526,044,142	1,410,257,630
1976	1,368,961,214	1,266,457,241	1979[1]	1,769,488,987	1,648,128,948

[1] Provisional.

The total trade between Belgium and Luxembourg and UK was as follows (British Department of Trade returns, in £1,000 sterling):

	1976	1977	1978	1979	1980
Imports to UK	1,300,229	1,682,511	1,831,278	2,324,561	2,596,962
Exports and re-exports from UK	1,401,243	1,837,119	2,201,820	2,467,631	2,624,108

Principal Belgian–Luxembourg exports to UK in 1979[1] (tonnes; francs): Textiles (63,013; 9,021m.); metals (551,572; 12,465m.); chemical and pharmaceutical products (569,971; 12,288m.); precious stones and manufactures thereof (199; 26,377m.).

Principal Belgian–Luxembourg imports from the UK in 1979[1] (tonnes; francs): Machinery and electrical apparatus (71,492; 15,320m.); vehicles, chiefly motor cars, and aircraft (175,157; 18,949m.); textiles (38,719; 5,737m.); precious stones (60; 46,367m.); base metals and manufactures thereof (223,021; 6,755m.).

[1] Provisional.

COMMUNICATIONS

Roads. The total length of the roads in Belgium on 31 Dec. 1978 was as follows: State roads (including 1,110 km of motorway), 12,774 km; provincial roads, 1,372 km; communal roads, 111,815 km. The majority of roads are metalled. Number of motor vehicles in Belgium, 1 Aug. 1980, 3,753,745, including 3,158,737 passenger cars, 19,560 buses, 267,669 lorries, 31,415 non-agricultural tractors, 127,449 agricultural tractors, 113,057 motor cycles and 35,858 special vehicles.

Railways. The main Belgian lines were a State enterprise from their inception in 1834. In 1926 the Société Nationale des Chemins de Fer Belges (SNCB) was formed to take over the railways. The State is sole holder of the ordinary shares of SNCB, which carry the majority vote at General Meetings. The length of railway operated on 31 Dec. 1979 was 3,998 km. Revenue (1979), 44,001m. francs; expenditure, 44,155m. francs. SNCB is to absorb the Belgian National Light Railway (SNCV has 205 km of electrified, metre gauge) under a plan announced in 1980.

Aviation. The national Belgian airline SABENA (*Société anonyme belge d'exploitation de la navigation aérienne*) was set up in 1923. Its capital is 750m. francs. In addition to its European network, SABENA operates different routes to North and South America, to North, Central and South Africa and to the Near, the Middle and the Far East. In 1979 its airfleet comprised 25 aircraft. In 1979 SABENA flew 53m. km, carrying 2,032,912 revenue passengers, 406·82m. ton-km of freight and 10,992,000 ton-km of mail.

Shipping.[1] On 1 Jan. 1980 the Belgian merchant fleet was composed of 80 vessels of 1,719,355 tons. There were 48 shipping companies, of which the most important were the Compagnie Maritime Belge, with 24 ships, and the Belgian Fruit Lines, SA, with 3 ships.

[1] Belgian shipping returns are given in the official 'Moorsom tons', which may be converted into net tons by deducting 19·85% from the Moorsom total.

The navigation at the port of Antwerp in 1979 was as follows: Number of vessels entered, 17,425; tonnage, 103,541,922. Number of vessels cleared, 17,378; tonnage, 103,735,970.

The total length of navigable waterways (rivers and canals) was 1,573·7 km in 1979.

Post and Broadcasting. On 31 Dec. 1978 there were 1,864 post offices. The gross revenue of the post office in the year 1978 amounted to 14,012m. francs.

A régie of telegraphs and telephones for running the services on business lines was created in 1930. Telegraph offices for dispatching and receiving wires numbered 106; for dispatching only, 26. Receipts for 1978 were 3,719,452,919 francs; expenditure, 3,072,470,808 francs.

In 1978 the telephone service comprised 635 exchanges, connecting 6,170 public telephone stations and 2,159,065 subscribers. Number of telephones, 1 Jan. 1978, 3,270,882. Receipts in 1978, 28,628,194m. francs; expenditure, 27,840,201m. francs.

Radiodiffusion-Télévision Belge de la Communauté Culturelle Française (RTBF)–Belgische Radio en Televisie (BRT) is a public service broadcasting on medium-and short-waves and on FM. There are 3 programmes in each network including regional broadcasts. The short-wave service is mainly intended for Africa and it is broadcast in French (RTBF), Dutch, English and Spanish (BRT) languages. RTBF broadcasts TV programmes in French and BRT in Dutch. The programmes are financed by state grants in aids. Colour programmes are broadcast by PAL system. Number of receivers (1979), radio, 4,450,944; TV, 2,924,846 (including 1,593,059 colour sets).

Cinemas (1978). There were 516 cinemas, with a seating capacity of 197,906.

Newspapers (1980). There are 36 daily newspapers (some of them only regional or local editions of larger dailies), of which 22 are in French, 13 in Dutch and 1 in German.

JUSTICE, RELIGION, EDUCATION AND WELFARE

Justice. Judges are appointed for life. There is a court of cassation, 5 courts of appeal, and assize courts for political and criminal cases. There are 26 judicial districts, each with a court of first instance. In each of the 222 cantons is a justice and judge of the peace. There are, besides, various special tribunals. There is trial by jury in assize courts.

Religion. Of the inhabitants professing a religion the majority are Roman Catholic, but no inquiry as to the profession of faith is now made at the censuses. There are, however, statistics concerning the clergy, and according to these there were in 1979: Roman Catholic higher clergy, 128; inferior clergy, 6,958; Protestant pastors, 80; Anglican Church, 10 chaplains; Jews (rabbis and ministers), 26. The State does not interfere in any way with the internal affairs of any church. There is full religious liberty, and part of the income of the ministers of all denominations is paid by the State.

There are 8 Roman Catholic dioceses subdivided into 261 deaneries.

Estimated number of Protestants, 24,000; of Jews, 35,000.

The Protestant (Evangelical) Church is under a synod. There is also a Central Jewish Consistory, a Central Committee of the Anglican Church and a Free Protestant Church.

Education. On 8 Nov. 1962/2 Aug. 1963 a linguistic frontier was fixed between the Dutch-speaking, French-speaking and German-speaking parts of Belgium. In the north, Dutch is recognized as the official language, in the south, French, and along the eastern border, German. The city and *arrondissement* of Brussels are bilingual. The percentage of the population in the Flemish, French, German and bilingual regions was 57, 32·1, 0·7, 10·2 on 1 Jan. 1980. (*See* map in THE STATESMAN'S YEAR-BOOK, 1967–68.)

Higher Education (1978–79). Higher education is given in state universities: Ghent (12,034 students), Liège (9,245 students), Mons (1,326 students), the Polytechnic Faculty in Mons (503 students), the Antwerp State University Centre (1,372 students), the Gembloux Faculty of Agronomical Sciences (631 students), the Royal Military School in Brussels (694 students) and in the private universities: Catholic University of Louvain (36,436 students), the Free University of Brussels (18,036), University Institution Antwerp (1,323 students), St Ignatius Antwerp (2,487 students), Our Lady of Peace in Namur (2,877 students), Catholic University Faculty in Mons (416 students), St Lewis in Brussels (1,306 students), the Limbourg University Centre (827 students) and the Protestant Faculty of Theology in Brussels (125 students). The total number of students in university colleges, faculties and institutes was 89,638.

There are 5 royal academies of fine arts and 5 royal conservatoires at Brussels, Liège, Ghent, Antwerp and Mons.

Secondary Education. 1,145 (1973–74) middle schools, 3,506 (1973–74) technical schools and 545 (1973–74) schools of the new system had a total of 224,009 (1979–80) pupils in the general classes and 288,248 in the technical classes in the traditional system and 338,601 pupils in the new system.

Elementary Education. There were 7,773 (1974–75) primary schools, with 877,138 pupils in 1979–80 and 5,382 (1974–75) infant schools, with 384,901 pupils in 1979–80.

Normal Schools. There were 57 (1974–75) schools for training secondary teachers (10,972 students) in 1979–80; 93 for training elementary teachers (7,590 students), 63 technical normal schools in 1974–75 with (1979–80) 3,093 students and 46 normal infant schools with 2,118 students.

Health. In 1979 there were 23,415 physicians (including 541 dentists), 3,491 other dentists, 9,389 pharmacists and (1978) 3,593 midwives. Hospital beds numbered 90,442 in 1978.

Social Security. Social security is based on the law of Dec. 1944. It applies to all workers subject to an employment contract, and is administered by the Central National Office of Social Security (ONSS), which collects from employers and employees all contributions referring to family allowances, health insurance, old age insurance, holidays and unemployment. These sums are distributed by the Central Office to the various institutions concerned with these benefits. Insurance against unemployment is organized through a common fund, which also undertakes to retrain the unemployed for another employment while providing for their families. Since 1944 further laws have increased allowances, made fresh provisions for housing (1945), injuries while working, professional illnesses, etc. (1948).

Apart from private charity, the poor are assisted by the communes through the agency of the *Centre Public d'Aide Sociale* in French-speaking parts of the country and *Openbaar Centrum voor Maatschappelijk Welzijn* in Dutch-speaking areas. Provisions of a national character have been made for looking after war orphans and men disabled in the war. Certain other establishments, either state or provincial, provide for the needs of the deaf-mutes and the blind, and of children who are placed under the control of the courts. Provision is also made for repressing begging and providing shelter for the homeless.

DIPLOMATIC REPRESENTATIVES

OF BELGIUM IN GREAT BRITAIN (103 Eaton Sq., London, SW1W 9AB)

Ambassador: Robert Vaes, KCMG (accredited 17 Feb. 1977).

OF GREAT BRITAIN IN BELGIUM (Britannia Hse., rue Joseph II 28, 1040 Brussels)

Ambassador: Sir Peter Wakefield, KBE, CMG.

OF BELGIUM IN THE USA (3330 Garfield St., NW, Washington, D.C., 20008)

Chargé d'Affaires: Count Francis de la Barrre d'Erquellinnes.

OF THE USA IN BELGIUM (Blvd. du Régent 27, 1000 Brussels)

Ambassador: Anne Cox Chambers.

OF BELGIUM TO THE UNITED NATIONS

Ambassador: André Ernemann.

Books of Reference

Statistical Information: The Institut National de Statistique (44 rue de Louvain, Brussels) was set up on 24 Jan. 1831, under the designation of Bureau de Statistique Générale; after several changes, it received its present name on 2 May 1946. *Director-General:* Dr P. van Landeghem. *Main publications:*

Bulletin du Commerce Extérieur
Bulletin de Statistique. Monthly
Annuaire Statistique de la Belgique (from 1870).—*Annuaire statistique de poche* (from 1965)
Statistiques Agricoles. Monthly
Recensement général de la population au 31 déc. 1970. 13 vols.
Recensement de l'agriculture au 15 mai 1970. 3 vols.
Recensement de l'industrie et du commerce au 31 déc. 1970. 10 vols.

Annuaire administratif et judiciaire de Belgique. Annual. Brussels
L'économie belge. Ministère des Affaires Economiques. Annual (from 1947)
Belgium, Investment Guide. Ministère des Affaires Economique, 1974
Guide des Ministères: Revue de l'Administration Belge. Brussels, Annual
Belgique: Un Panorama. Institut Belge d'Information et de documentation, Brussels, 1969
Molitor, A., *L'Administration de la Belgique.* Brussels, 1974

BELIZE

Capital: Belmopan
Population: 151,607 (1978)
GNP per capita: US$840 (1978)

HISTORY. The early settlement of the territory was probably effected by British woodcutters about 1638; from that date to 1798, in spite of armed opposition from the Spaniards, settlers held their own and prospered. In 1780 the Home Government appointed a superintendent, and in 1862 the settlement was declared a colony, subordinate to Jamaica. It became an independent colony in 1884. Self-government was attained in 1964.

AREA AND POPULATION. Belize is bounded north by Mexico, west by Guatemala and south and east by the Caribbean sea. Area, 22,963 sq. km. There are 6 districts:

	Sq. km	Population census, 1970		Sq. km	Population census 1970
Corozal	1,860	15,504	Cayo	5,338	16,034
Belize	4,204	49,661	Stann Creek	2,176	13,044
Orange Walk	4,737	16,666	Toledo	4,649	8,954

Total population (census, 1970) 119,863. Estimate, 1978, 151,607. Voters on the roll numbered 33,737 in 1974. In 1977 the birth rate per 1,000 was 43·9 and the death rate 6·1; infantile mortality 40 per 1,000 births; there were 871 marriages and (1974) 19 divorces.

Main city, Belize City; population, census 1970, 39,050. Estimate, 1978, 49,749. Following the severe hurricane which struck the territory on 31 Oct. 1961 the capital Belmopan (population, 1978, 4,000) has been moved to a new site 50 miles inland; construction began in Jan. 1967 and it became the seat of government on 3 Aug. 1970. See map in the 1978–79 edition of THE STATESMAN'S YEAR-BOOK.

CONSTITUTION AND GOVERNMENT. Under the constitution, which came into force on 1 Jan. 1964, Belize, formerly British Honduras has a 2-chamber legislature, with a ministerial system and cabinet responsibility. The House of Representatives consists of 18 members elected by universal suffrage. The Senate consists of 8 members, 5 of whom are appointed on the advice of the Premier, 2 on the advice of the Leader of the Opposition and 1 by the Governor.

At the general elections held in Nov. 1979 the Peoples' United Party held 13 of the 18 parliamentary seats and the United Democratic Party 5 seats.

The Governor retains responsibility for defence, external affairs, internal security, the safeguarding of conditions of service of public officers, and over finance 'so long as the Government of Belize is in receipt of budgetary aid from the UK'.

In Nov. 1980 the UN called for an independent Belize. In March 1981 Britain and Guatemala agreed a formula for the resolution of the 32-year old territorial dispute over Belize. It was hoped that this will lead to a constitutional conference later in 1981.

Governor and C.-in-C.: James Patrick Ivan Hennessy, CMG, OBE.
Premier and Minister of Finance: George Price.
Flag: Blue with the arms of the Colony surrounded by a green garland on a white disc in the centre; flown in conjunction with the Union Flag.

ECONOMY

Budget. Revenue and expenditure (in $B) for calendar years:

	1974	1975	1976	1977	1978	1979
Revenue	40,164,477	49,500,000	68,911,795	42,461,090	53,309,995	62,624,655
Expenditure	40,164,477	29,094,428	36,370,823	42,798,120	44,303,753	53,121,227

Public debt, 31 Dec. 1978, $B21,933,683; sinking fund, $B829,253.

Currency. There was (29 April 1980) a paper currency of $B17,695,000 in government notes of $B20, 10, 5, 2 and 1, and a subsidiary mixed metal coinage of 1-, 5-, 10-, 25- and 50-cent pieces whose issues amount to $B3,026,000.

Banking. The Royal Bank of Canada took over the business of the local bank in 1912; it has 8 branches. There are 7 government savings banks; depositors, about 10,000; deposits, $B60·2m. on 31 Dec. 1975.

Barclays Bank International have 7 branches, Bank of Nova Scotia have 5 branches and Atlantic Bank 3 branches.

NATURAL RESOURCES

Agriculture. The main agricultural export is sugar, followed by citrus fruit, chiefly grapefruit and oranges, whole, canned, juice and concentrates. Citrus production, 1977–78, 987,452 boxes. Sugar production in 1979 was 98,599 tons. Banana production began in 1973, and first shipments began in 1974; exports, 1979, 732,755 boxes. [Ed. note: Box of grapefruit, 80 lb., oranges, 90 lb., bananas, 42 lb.]

Livestock (1979): Cattle, 57,000; sheep, 3,000; pigs, 26,000; poultry, 346,000.

Forestry. 2,964 sq. miles, 49% of the total land area, are under forests which include mahogany, cedar, Santa Maria, pine and rosewood, and many secondary hardwoods of known or probable market value, as well as woods suitable for pulp production. Exports of forest produce in 1978 amounted to $B2·1m.

Fisheries. Food and game fish are plentiful, and domestic consumption is heavy. The total exported in 1979 was valued at $B7·9m. Turtles—Hawksbill, Loggerhead and Green—are plentiful but as yet are not exported.

LABOUR. The labour market alternates between full employment, often accompanied by local shortages in the citrus and sugar-cane harvesting (Jan.–July), and under-employment during the wet season (Aug.–Dec.), aggravated by the seasonal nature of the major industries.

COMMERCE. In 1978 total imports amounted to US$103m. Total domestic exports, US$67·1m. The principal domestic exports were timber, sugar, fish products and citrus fruit.

Total trade between Belize and UK (British Department of Trade returns, in £1,000 sterling):

	1975	1976	1977	1978	1979	1980
Imports to UK	11,154	9,156	13,300	13,120	13,515	13,168
Exports and re-exports from UK	6,469	7,346	8,129	10,807	10,347	11,824

COMMUNICATIONS

Aviation. In 1979, 132,122 passengers and 2,948 tonnes of freight arrived and departed on international flights.

Shipping (1974). Registered shipping, 15 sailing vessels, 1,340 net tons, and 397 motor vessels, 446,234 net tons.

Post. Telephone lines connect Belize City with Corozal Town and Consejo on the coast, Orange Walk Town on New River, San Antonio on the Rio Hondo and other stations in the north, San Ignacio and Benque Viejo Towns in the west, Dangriga and Punta Gorda Town and other points in the south. Number of telephones (1978), 5,787. The government-operated telecommunication services were taken over by Cable and Wireless Ltd in 1962, which installed an automatic telephone service in 1963 and also operates a radio-telephone service. The Belize Telecommunication Authority has instituted a country-wide fully automatic telephone dialling facility. There are 6 post offices and 45 rural sub-post offices.

Cinemas (1979). There were 13 cinemas with seating capacity of 10,000.

Newspapers. There were 4 weekly newspapers and 4 monthly magazines in 1979.

JUSTICE, EDUCATION AND WELFARE

Justice. There are 3 magistrates' courts in Belize and 1 in each district town. The police force contained (1978) 29 officers and 455 n.c.o.s and constables.

Education. In 1979, 15 government, 179 grant-aided and 15 private primary schools had a total enrolment of 34,149 pupils; 23 secondary schools, 5,913 pupils; a government technical high school, 477 pupils; 2 government junior colleges, 588 pupils. All aided schools, except the government technical high school, are under the management of Christian bodies. Three colleges for post-secondary education had 580 students. In Sept. 1979 the Belize College of Arts, Science and Technology was opened for post-sixth form courses. There is also a Teachers' College offering courses for primary school teachers. The 3-year course leads to a teachers' diploma granted by the University of the West Indies.

Health. In 1979 there were 2 general hospitals and 2 private hospitals with 45 doctors and 545 hospital beds.

Books of Reference

Annual Report, 1972. Government Printer, Belize City, 1974
Abstract of Statistics 1975. Government Printer, Belize City, 1976
Anderson, A. H., *Brief Sketch of the British Honduras.* 7th ed. Belize, 1958
Bianchi, W. J., *Belize: The Controversy Between Guatemala and Great Britain.* New York, 1959
Dobson, D., *A History of Belize.* Belize, 1973
Floyd, B., *Focus on Honduras.* Univ. of West Indies, Jamaica, 1970
Grant, C. H., *The Making of Modern Belize.* CUP, 1976
Romney, D. H., (ed.), *Land in British Honduras.* HMSO, 1959

BENIN

République Populaire du Benin

Capital: Porto Novo
Population: 3·47m. (1979)
GNP per capita: US$230 (1978)

HISTORY. The territory of the present State was occupied by France in 1892 and was constituted a division of French West Africa in 1904 under the name of Dahomey. It became an independent republic within the French Community on 4 Dec. 1958, and acquired full independence on 1 Aug. 1960.

In the sixth *coup* since independence, Maj. Mathieu Kerekou came to power on 26 Oct. 1972 and proclaimed a Marxist–Leninist state, whose name was altered from Dahomey to Benin in Dec. 1975.

AREA AND POPULATION. The People's Republic of Benin is bounded east by Nigeria, north by Niger and Upper Volta and west by Togo. The area is 112,622 sq. km, and the population, in 1979, 3,470,000. The seat of government is Porto Novo (104,000 inhabitants in 1975); the chief port and business centre is Cotonou (178,000); other important towns are Natitingou (50,800), Abomey (41,000), Kandi, Ouidah and Parakou. There are 6 administrative provinces: Atakora, Borgou, Zou, Ouémé, Atlantique and Mono.

French is the official language, while 47% of the people speak Fon, 12% Adja, 10% Bariba and 9% Yoruba.

CONSTITUTION AND GOVERNMENT. The ruling political party is the Benin People's Revolutionary Party. In Aug. 1977 under a new Constitution there is a unicameral legislature, the National Revolutionary Assembly of 336 People's Commissioners. Elections were held on 20 Nov. 1979.

President, Prime Minister, Minister of Planning and Defence: Lieut.-Col. Ahmed (Mathieu) Kerekou.

National flag: Green with a red star in the canton.

DEFENCE

Army. The Army consists of 1 engineer and 2 infantry battalions and support units; strength (1980), 2,100. There is a paramilitary *gendarmerie* of about 1,100.

Navy. A naval force was formed in 1979 with 4 fast attack craft and 2 coastal patrol craft transferred from the USSR. Personnel (1980) 150.

Air Force. The Air Force has a strength of about 60 officers and men, 2 twin-turboprop An-26, 2 F.27 Friendship and 2 C-47 transports, 1 Cessna Skymaster, 1 Aero Commander 500, 3 Broussard communications aircraft, an Agusta-Bell 47G and an Alouette II helicopter. A twin-turboprop Corvette is operated by the Air Force on VIP missions for government agencies.

INTERNATIONAL RELATIONS

Membership. Benin is a member of UN, OAU and is an ACP country of EEC.

ECONOMY

Planning. A 3-year development plan began in Oct. 1977 with the aim of developing agriculturally based industries so that imports could be reduced.

Budget. The ordinary budget for 1978 balanced at 23,210m. francs CFA.

Currency. The monetary unit is the *franc CFA* (*Communauté financière africaine*), which is divided into 100 *centimes*.

ENERGY AND NATURAL RESOURCES

Oil. The Semé oilfield, located 10 miles offshore, was discovered in 1968. Production is expected to commence in 1981–82 and should reach 150,000 bbls a day.

Agriculture. The population is mainly agricultural, production in 1977 amounting to 610,000 tonnes of cassava, 564,000 of yams, 235,000 of maize, 76,000 of sorghum and 70,000 of palm kernels. In 1979 there were 800,000 cattle, 1·9m. sheep and goats, 470,000 pigs, 6,000 horses, 1,000 donkeys. The forests contain oil palms, which have been profitably utilized. These furnish the chief exports—kernels and oil. Cotton cultivation has been successfully introduced in the north; coffee cultivation has given good results in the southern districts.

TRADE. Imports in 1977, 60,354m. francs CFA; exports, 7,642m. francs CFA. The principal imports in 1975 (in 1m. francs CFA): Textiles, 5,744; machinery, 5,415; motor vehicles and parts, 3,852; clothing and footwear, 2,877. The principal exports were: Cotton lint, 1,542; palm-oil, 828; cocoa beans, 642; cement, 556.

Total trade between Benin and UK (British Department of Trade returns, in £1,000 sterling):

	1976	1977	1978	1979	1980
Imports to UK	2,814	3,057	566	2,558	2,856
Exports and re-exports from UK	6,860	10,045	11,463	12,480	13,119

COMMUNICATIONS

Roads. There were 6,937 km of roads in 1972. There were 14,000 motor cars and 8,600 goods vehicles in 1974.

Railways. Railways (metre-gauge) connect Cotonou with Parakou (438 km); Pahou–Segboroué on Lake Aheme (34 km); Cotonou–Pobé (107 km).

Aviation. In 1976, 45,113 passengers used Cotonou airport. There are other airports at Abomey, Natitingou, Kandi and Parakou.

Shipping. In 1976, 1,079 vessels of 2,797,000 net tons entered the port of Cotonou. There were (1979) 8 vessels of 1,074 GRT registered in Benin.

Post and Broadcasting. There were, in 1975, 9,624 telephones. A telegraph line connects Cotonou with Abomey, Togo, Niger and Senegal. In 1972 there were 150,000 radios and 100 television receivers.

Newspapers. In 1978 there were 2 daily newspapers with a circulation of 2,000.

RELIGION, EDUCATION AND WELFARE

Religion. 65% of the population follow animist beliefs, 17% are Christian and 13% Moslem.

Education. There were, in 1976, 279,673 pupils in primary schools, 45,572 in secondary schools, 1,687 students in technical schools and (1972) 2,553 in teaching-training. The University of Benin (Cotonou) had 2,578 students in 1972.

Health. In 1976 there were 361 hospitals and dispensaries with 4,394 beds, 93 doctors, 10 dentists, 34 pharmacists and 243 midwives.

DIPLOMATIC REPRESENTATIVES

OF BENIN IN GREAT BRITAIN

Ambassador: Yaya Mede-Moussa (resides in Paris).

OF GREAT BRITAIN IN BENIN

Ambassador: M. Brown, CMG, OBE (resides in Lagos).

OF THE USA IN BENIN (Rue Caporal Anami Bernard, Cotonou)
Chargé d'Affaires: James R. Bullington.

OF BENIN TO THE UNITED NATIONS
Ambassador: Thomas Setondji Boya.

Book of Reference

Ronen, D., *Dahomey: Between Tradition and Modernity.* Cornell Univ. Press, 1975

BERMUDA

Capital: Hamilton
Population: 54,893 (1980)
GNP per capita: US$9,260 (1978)

HISTORY. The Spaniards visited the islands in 1515, but, according to a 17th-century French cartographer, they were discovered in 1503 by Juan Bermudez, after whom they were named. No settlement was made, and they were uninhabited until a party of colonists under Sir George Somers was wrecked there in 1609. A company was formed for the 'Plantation of the Somers' Islands', as they were called at first, and in 1684 the Crown took over the government.

AREA AND POPULATION. Bermuda consists of a group of some 150 small islands (about 20 inhabited), situated in the western Atlantic (32° 18′ N. lat., 64° 46′ W. long.); the nearest point of the mainland, about 570 miles distant, is Cape Hatteras, N.C., and 690 miles from New York; noted for its climate and scenery; a favourite resort for Americans.

The area is 20·59 sq. miles (53·3 sq. km), of which 2·3 sq. miles were leased in 1941 for 99 years to the US Government for naval and air bases. The civil population (*i.e.*, excluding British and American military, naval and air force personnel) in 1980 was estimated at 54,893.

Chief town, Hamilton; population, about 3,000.

In 1979 there were 779 live births, 517 marriages and 357 deaths; infantile mortality rate (1978) was 15·4 per 1,000 live births.

CONSTITUTION AND GOVERNMENT. Bermuda is a colony with representative government. Under the constitution of 8 June 1968 the Governor, appointed by the Crown, is normally bound to accept the advice of the Cabinet in matters other than external affairs, defence, internal security and the police, for which he retains special responsibility. The Cabinet is appointed from among members of the bicameral legislature, on the recommendation of the Premier. The Legislative Council, of whom one or two members may serve on Cabinet, consists of 11 members; 5 are appointed in the discretion of the Governor, 4 on the recommendation of the Premier and 2 on the recommendation of the Opposition Leader. The 40 members of the House of Assembly are elected 2 from each of 20 constituencies under full universal, adult suffrage. The general election on 18 May 1976 resulted in the return of 26 members of the United Bermuda Party and 14 members of the Progressive Labour Party. A by-election was held on 21 Sept. 1976 resulting in a total of 25 members of the United Bermuda Party and 15 members of the Progressive Labour Party.

Governor: Sir Richard Posnett, KCMG, OBE.
Premier: John David Gibbons.
Flag: The British Red Ensign with the badge of the Colony in the fly.

DEFENCE. The Bermuda Regiment had 650 men and women in 1980.

ECONOMY

Budget. Revenue and expenditure in $B for years ending 31 March:

	1976–77	1977–78	1978–79	1979–80	1980–81[1]
Revenue	77,130,526	81,832,869	91,392,263	105,207,166	111,702,260
Expenditure	64,772,621	78,334,832	85,901,549	101,224,172	115,797,500

Expenditure in $B1,000 (excluding capital items) was earmarked as follows:

	1976–77	1977–78	1978–79	1979–80	1980–81[1]
Agriculture and fisheries	2,223	2,633	3,112	3,874	3,906
Tourism and trade development	5,051	5,996	6,234	7,136	7,791
Education	11,832	15,362	15,862	19,189	22,838

[1] Estimate.

213

	1976–77	1977–78	1978–79	1979–80	1980–81[1]
Police	5,738	6,646	7,034	8,003	8,821
Post Office	2,209	2,398	2,923	2,806	3,223
Health and social services	12,853	13,751	15,619	18,189	20,460
Public transportation	2,899	3,482	3,430	4,214	4,133
Public works	6,042	7,625	11,303	12,105	14,198
Marine and air services	2,861	3,473	3,301	4,539	7,070
All other expenditure	13,065	16,969	17,084	21,169	23,358

[1] Estimate.

Chief sources of revenue in 1979–80 were: Customs duties, $45,694,000; employment tax, $8,671,000; land tax, $6,445,000; companies tax, $5,226,000; hospital tax, $4,506,000; passenger tax, $3·58m.; hotel occupancy tax, $4,459,000; vehicle licences, $3,551,000; stamp duties, $3,708,000.

Public debt, as at 31 March 1980, was $13m.

Currency. Decimal currency based on a *Bermuda dollar* of 100 *cents* was introduced on 6 Feb. 1970. In March 1981 £1 = 2.18 Bermuda dollars and US$1 = 1 Bermuda dollar. The Bermuda Monetary Authority issues notes in denominations of $50, $20, $10, $5 and $1, and coins in values of 50c, 25c, 10c, 5c and 1c.

Banking. There are 4 banks, the Bank of Bermuda, Ltd, the Bank of N. T. Butterfield and Son, Ltd, the Bermuda National Bank, Ltd, and the Bermuda Provident Bank, Ltd.

Weights and Measures. British, except that US instead of Imperial fluid measures are used.

AGRICULTURE. The chief products are fresh vegetables, bananas and citrus fruit. In 1979, 689 acres were under cultivation. In 1978 1·3% of the work force were engaged in agriculture, fishing and horticulture.

In 1979, total value of agricultural products was $B5m.

Livestock (1979): Cattle, 1,000; pigs, 2,000; poultry, 48,000.

TRADE UNIONS. Legislation providing for trade unions was enacted in Oct. 1946, and there are 10 trade unions with a total membership (1980) of 8,806.

COMMERCE. Imports and exports in $B:

	1976	1977	1978	1979
Imports	165,445,000	185,575,000	211,622,000	234,000,000
Exports	47,049,000	39,128,000	41,177,000	31,290,000

The visible adverse balance of trade is more than compensated for by invisible exports, including tourism.

Imports in 1979 from USA, $114·4m.; Netherlands West Indies, $37·5m.; UK, $27·4m.; Canada, $14·9m.; Japan, $7·5m.; France, $3·7m.; Federal Republic of Germany, $3·7m.; Hong Kong, $3·3m.; Italy, $2·6m.; all other countries, $19m. Exports in 1977 to Jamaica, $6·9m.; USA, $4·2m.; Spain, $3·9m; UK, $1·2m.

In 1979 the principal imports were finished manufactures ($89m.), food, drink and tobacco ($57·5m.), chemicals ($45m.), mineral fuels ($39·9m.), raw materials ($2·5m.); the principal local exports, beauty preparations ($144,817) and liquor ($12,303).

Total trade between Bermuda and UK, in £1,000 sterling (British Department of Trade returns):

	1975	1976	1977	1978	1979	1980
Imports to UK	3,179	3,065	5,780	11,259	3,794	2,900
Exports and re-exports from UK	17,927	14,396	19,686	22,200	17,209	24,499

TOURISM. In 1979, 599,145 tourists visited Bermuda including 140,364 cruise ship visitors. Tourism represents 40·9% of GDP.

COMMUNICATIONS

Roads. In 1948 the railway service was discontinued and a government-operated bus service introduced.

Between 1908 and Aug. 1946 the use of motor vehicles, with the exception of ambulances, fire engines and other essential services, was prohibited. With the passing of the Motor Car Act in 1946, the use of motor vehicles, subject to certain limitations on size and horse-power, became lawful. In 1978, out of 35,000 registered vehicles 12,741 were private cars.

Aviation. American Airlines, Delta Airlines and Eastern Airlines maintain regular services between Bermuda and the USA. British Airways also have regular flights through Bermuda linking London with Mexico and the Caribbean. Air Canada Airlines call at Bermuda on their service between Canada, Barbados, Antigua and Trinidad; they also operate services between Canada, Toronto, Montreal and Halifax.

Shipping. The registered shipping consisted (1979) of 6 steam vessels, 48 sailing vessels and 254 motor vessels with a total gross tonnage of 1,852,164. In 1979 the gross tonnage of 699 vessels entered and cleared was 6,234,851 tons.

Post and Broadcasting (1980). There are 15 post offices. The telephone company is privately owned and operated 44,569 telephones in 1980. Cables connect the islands with the USA, Halifax (N.S.) and Tortola, providing connexion with the world.

Radio and television broadcasting is commercial.

Cinemas. There were (1980) 2 cinemas with a seating capacity of 1,054.

JUSTICE, EDUCATION AND WELFARE

Justice. There are 4 magistrates' courts, a Supreme Court and a court of appeal. The police had a strength of 397 men and women in 1979.

Education. Education is compulsory between the ages of 5 and 16, and government assistance is given by the payment of grants, and, where necessary, of school fees. Free elementary education was introduced on 1 May 1949 and free secondary education in Sept. 1965. In 1979, there were 11 government nurseries (442 pupils), 6 special units for the handicapped (227 pupils), 18 government primary schools (4,878 pupils), 9 government secondary schools (3,707 pupils), the Bermuda College (509 full-time and about 1,500 part-time students). Four private, fee-paying schools accommodated an additional 1,994 pupils of all ages. Total enrolment was 11,757 pupils.

Health. In 1980 there were 65 doctors.

Books of Reference

Annual Report, 1971. HMSO, 1972
Bermuda Historical Quarterly. 1944 ff.
Baron, S., *Your Guide to Bermuda.* London, 1965
Bell, E. Y., *Beautiful Bermuda.* 10th ed. New York and Bermuda, 1947
Dyer, H. T., *The Next 20 Years: A Report on the Development Plans for Bermuda.* Hamilton, 1963
Wilkinson H. C., *Bermuda from Sail to Steam.* OUP, 1973
Zuill, W. S., *The Story of Bermuda and Her People.* London, 1973

National Library: The Bermuda Library, Hamilton. *Head Librarian:* Mrs M. Skiffington.

BHUTÁN

Druk-yul

Capital: Thimphu
Population: 1·1m. (1979)
GNP per capita: US$100 (1978)

HISTORY. In 1774 the East India Company concluded a treaty with the ruler of Bhután. Under a treaty signed in Nov. 1865 the Bhután Government was granted an annual subsidy. By an amending treaty concluded in Jan. 1910 the British Government undertook to exercise no interference in the internal affairs of Bhután, and the Bhután Government agreed to be guided by the advice of the British Government in regard to its external relations.

The Government of India concluded a fresh treaty with Bhután on 8 Aug. 1949. Under this treaty the Government of Bhután continues to be guided by the Government of India in regard to its external relations, and the Government of India have undertaken not to interfere in the internal administration of Bhután. The subsidy paid to Bhután has been increased to Rs 500,000, and the Government of India agreed to retrocede to Bhután an area of about 32 sq. miles in the territory known as Dewangiri, which was annexed in 1865.

AREA AND POPULATION. Bhután is situated in the eastern Himalayas, between 26° 45′ and 28° N. lat. and between 89° and 92° E. long., bordered on the north and east by Tibet and India, on the west by Sikkim and on the south by India. Extreme length from east to west 190 miles: extreme breadth 90 miles. Area about 18,000 sq. miles (46,600 sq. km); population estimated at approximately 1·1m. (1979). Life expectancy (1977) was 46 years. The capital is at Thimphu. There are 17 districts.

KING. Jigme Singye Wangchuck, succeeded his father Jigme Dorji Wangchuck who died 21 July 1972.

GOVERNMENT. In 1907 the Tongsa Penlop (the governor of the province of Tongsa in eastern Bhután), Sir Ugyen Wangchuk, GCIE, KCSI, was elected as the first hereditary Maharaja of Bhután. The Bhutánese title is Druk Gyalpo, but his successor is now addressed as King of Bhután. From Oct. 1969 the absolute monarchy was changed to a form of 'democratic monarchy'. The National Assembly (*Tshogdu*) was reinstituted in 1953. It has approximately 150 members and meet twice a year. Two-thirds are representatives of the people and are elected for a 3-year term. All Bhutánese over 25 years may be candidates. Ten monastic representatives are elected by regional ecclesiastical bodies, while the remaining members are nominated by the King, and include members of the Council of Ministers and the Royal Advisory Council.

The official languages are Dzongkha, Nepali and English.

National flag: Diagonally orange over dark red, over all in the centre a white dragon.

DEFENCE. Bhután has an army of about 4,000 men.

ECONOMY

Planning. The Government of Bhután has drawn up four 5-year development plans (1961–65, 1966–70, 1971–76, 1976–81), with the active co-operation and financial support of the Government of India. Educational facilities are being expanded and medical facilities are being provided. Forest and mineral wealth is to be exploited. About 1,300 km of new roads have been built.

Budget. The budget for 1979–80 envisaged expenditure of N250m. and revenue of N106m.

Currency. Paper currency has been introduced, known as the *Ngultrum*. Silver currency is known as *Tikchung*. Indian currency is also legal tender.

Banking. The Bank of Bhután was established in 1968. The headquarters are at Phuntsholing with branches at Thimphu, Chirang, Samchi, Tashigang. Chimakothi, Samdrup Jongkhar and Geylegphug.

ENERGY AND NATURAL RESOURCES

Electricity. In 1974 construction work began on the Chukha hydro-electric project at a cost of US$92m. and in 1979, 15 towns and 97 villages had electricity.

Minerals. Large deposits of limestone, marble, dolomite, graphite, lead, copper, slate, coal, talc, gypsum, beryl, mica, pyrites and tufa have beidfound.

Agriculture. The area under cultivation in 1978 was 5,534 sq. km. The chief products are rice, millet, wheat, barley, maize, cardomom, potatoes, oranges, apples, handloom cloth, timber and yaks. Extensive and valuable forests abound.

Livestock (1979): Horses, 20,000; asses, 17,000; cattle, 207,000; pigs, 59,000; sheep, 41,000; poultry, 107,000.

INDUSTRY AND TRADE

Industry. In 1980 there were about 40 small-scale industrial units and also a cement plant, a fruit processing factory, a teachest ply veneer factory, a resin and turpentine factory and 3 distilleries.

Commerce. Trade with India is considerable but timber, cardomom and liquor are also exported to the Middle East, Singapore and Western Europe. Bhután imported from the UK in 1980 goods valued at £93,000.

Tourism. The country has been opened for tourism since 1974 and it is the largest source of foreign exchange. In 1979–80, 1,500 tourists visited Bhután.

COMMUNICATIONS

Roads. In 1978 there were about 1,775 km of roads. In 1979, there were 2,179 vehicles, of which 1,432 were private cars and 747 buses and trucks.

Post. A modern postal system was introduced in 1962. There are 53 general post offices and 28 branch post offices. In 1979 there were 1,086 km of telephone lines, 15 automatic exchanges and (1978) 1,355 telephones.

Newspapers. There is a government weekly newspaper published in 3 languages (English, Dzongkha and Nepali). Total circulation (1979) about 5,000.

RELIGION, EDUCATION AND WELFARE

Religion. The majority of the people are Mahayana Buddhists of the Drukpa subsect of the Karyud School which was first introduced from Tibet during the 12th century.

Education. In 1980 there were 144 state schools, 1 college and 2 technical schools with 31,892 pupils. There were 1,206 teachers. Many students were receiving training under the Colombo Plan in Australia, New Zealand, Japan, Singapore and UK in 1979.

Health. There were (1980) 12 general hospitals, 39 dispensaries, 43 basic health units, 4 indigenous dispensaries, 3 leprosy hospitals, 1 mobile hospital, 1 health school and 15 malaria eradication centres. In 1979 beds totalled 536 and there were 52 doctors.

DIPLOMATIC REPRESENTATIVE

OF BHUTÁN TO THE UNITED NATIONS

Ambassador: Om. Pradhan.

The Government of Bhután is in diplomatic relations with Bangladesh and India at ambassadorial level.

Books of Reference

Bhutan, Himalayan Kingdom. Bhutan Government, Thimphu. 1979
Das, N., *The Dragon Country*. New Delhi, 1973
Labh, K., *India and Bhutan*. New Delhi, 1974
Mehra, G. N., *Bhutan: Land of the Peaceful Dragon*. New Delhi, 1974
Olschak, B. C., *Bhutan: Land of Hidden Treasures*. New Delhi, 1971
Rahul, R., *Modern Bhutan*. New Delhi, 1971
Rathore, L. S., *The Changing Bhutan*. New Delhi, 1974
Ronaldshay, the Earl of, *Lands of the Thunderbolt*. 2nd ed. London, 1931
Rose, L. E., *The Politics of Bhutan*. Cornell Univ. Press, 1977
Rustomji, N., *Bhutan: The Dragon Kingdom in Crisis*. OUP, 1978
Singh, N., *Bhutan*. New Delhi, 1972

BOLIVIA

República de Bolivia

Capital: La Paz
Population: 5·15m. (1980)
GNP per capita: US$510 (1978)

HISTORY. Until 1884, when Bolivia was defeated by Chile, she had a strip bordering on the Pacific which contains extensive nitrate beds and at that time the port of Cobija (which no longer exists). She lost this area to Chile; but in Sept. 1953 Chile declared Arica a free port and, although it is no longer a free port for Bolivian imports, Bolivia still has certain privileges.

AREA AND POPULATION. Bolivia is a landlocked state with an area of some 424,160 sq. miles (1,098,580 sq. km). In the series of disastrous wars in the 19th and early 20th centuries its territorial losses to each of 5 neighbouring nations reduced its area from an estimated 1·16m. sq. miles.

The following table shows the area and population of the departments (the capitals of each are given in brackets):

Departments	Area (sq. km)	Census Aug.– Sept. 1950	Census 1976	Per sq. km 1975
La Paz (La Paz)	133,985	948,446	1,456,078	12·50
Cochabamba (Cochabamba)	55,631	490,475	720,952	15·57
Potosí (Potosí)	118,218	534,399	657,743	7·98
Santa Cruz (Santa Cruz)	370,621	286,145	710,724	1·36
Chuquisaca (Sucre)	51,524	282,980	358,516	9·69
Tarija (Tarija)	37,623	126,752	186,704	5·95
Oruro (Oruro)	53,588	210,260	310,409	6·93
Beni (Trinidad)	213,564	119,770	168,367	0·99
Pando (Cobija)	63,827	19,804	34,493	0·55
Total	1,098,581	3,019,031 [1]	4,687,718	4·85

[1] An official estimate allowing for under-enumeration; the total actually recorded was 2,704,165.

Total population (census 1976) 4,687,718.
Population (census 1976) of the principal towns: La Paz, 654,713; Santa Cruz, 255,568; Cochabamba, 204,414; Oruro, 124,414; Potosí, 77,233; Sucre, 63,259; Tarija, 38,500.
Crude birth rate, 1968, 42 per 1,000 population; crude death rate (1978), 17·4; crude marriage rate (1958); 4; infantile mortality, 140 (1978) per 1,000 live births.
The language of the educated classes is Spanish, that of the majority of Indians, Aymará (25·2%) or Quechua (34·4%).

CONSTITUTION AND GOVERNMENT. The Republic of Bolivia was proclaimed on 6 Aug. 1825; its first constitution was adopted on 19 Nov. 1826.
La Paz is the actual capital and seat of the Government, but Sucre is the legal capital and the seat of the judiciary.

National flag: Three horizontal stripes of red, yellow, green, with the arms of Bolivia in the centre.
National anthem: Bolivianos, el hado propicio (words by I. de Sanjinés; tune by B. Vincenti).

The following is a list of presidents since 1931 and the date on which they took office:

Dr Daniel Salamanca, 5 March 1931 (resigned Nov. 1934).

Luis Tejada Sorzano, 27 Nov. 1934 (deposed 17 May 1936).

Col. José David Toro, 17 May 1936 (deposed 13 July 1937).

Lieut.-Gen. German Busch, 13 July 1937 (committed suicide 23 Aug. 1939).

Gen. Carlos Quintanilla (provisional), 23 Aug. 1939–12 March 1940.

Gen. Enrique Peñaranda, 12 March 1940 (deposed 20 Dec. 1943).

Maj. Gualberto Villaroel, 20 Dec. 1943 (deposed and lynched 21 July 1946).

Dr Néstor Guillén (provisional) 27 July–1 Aug. 1946.

Chief Justice Monje Gutiérrez (15 Aug. 1946–9 March 1947).

Dr Enrique Hertzog (10 March 1947–23 Oct. 1949).

Dr Mamerto Urriolangoitia (24 Oct. 1949–15 May 1951).

Gen. Hugo Ballivián Rojas (15 May 1951–8 April 1952).

Dr Victor Paz Estenssoro (16 April 1952–6 Aug. 1956).

Dr Hernán Siles Zuazo (6 Aug. 1956–6 Aug. 1960).

Dr Victor Paz Estenssoro, (deposed) 6 Aug. 1960–4 Nov. 1964.

Gen. René Barrientos Ortuño, 4 Nov. 1964–26 May 1965 (Head of Military Junta).

Gen. René Barrientos Ortuño and Gen. Alfredo Ovando Candia (joint Presidents), 26 May 1965–Jan. 1966.

Gen. Alfredo Ovando Candia, Jan. 1966–6 Aug. 1966.

Gen. René Barrientos Ortuño (Constitutional President killed in air accident), 6 Aug. 1966–27 April 1969.

Dr Luis Adolfo Siles Salinas (deposed), 27 April 1969–26 Sept. 1969.

Gen. Alfredo Ovando Candia, 26 Sept. 1969–6 Oct. 1970.

Gen. Juan José Torres, 7 Oct. 1970–21 Aug. 1971.

Gen. Hugo Banzer Suarez, 21 Aug. 1971–21 July 1978.

Gen. Juan Pereda Asbun, 21 July 1978–24 Nov. 1978.

Gen. David Padilla A, 24 Nov. 1978–8 Aug. 1979.

Dr Walter Guevara A, 8 Aug. 1979–1 Nov. 1979.

Lidia Gueiler, 20 Nov. 1979–17 July 1980.

Gen. Luis García Meza, 18 July 1980.

Following elections in July 1979 which were inconclusive an interim President was chosen with the agreement of the three parties who had polled most votes. For details of political history 1970–78 *see* THE STATESMAN'S YEAR-BOOK, 1980–81. On 1 Nov. 1979, Dr Guevara was overthrown by Col. Alberto Natusch Busch who failed to become President and Congress named Lidia Gueiler as the first woman president and was sworn in on 20 Nov. 1979. Presidential and congressional elections took place in June 1980. Dr Siles Zuazo won about one-third of the votes but on 17 July Lidia Gueiler was overthrown by a military junta led by Gen. García Meza.

The Cabinet consists of the President and 15 Ministers of State.

President: Gen. Luis García Meza.
Minister of Foreign Affairs: Mario Rolon Anaya.

The republic is divided into 9 departments, established in Jan. 1826, with 98 provinces administered by sub-prefects, and 1,272 cantons administered by corregidores. The supreme authority in each department is vested in a prefect appointed by the President.

DEFENCE. Bolivia is divided into 8 military districts, with divisional headquarters in Viacha, Oruro, Villa Montes, Camiri, Roboré, Riberalta, Santa Cruz, Cochabamba; regional HQ are located at La Paz, Sucre, Tarija, Potosí, Trinidad and Cobija.

Army. The law of 1943 provided for a permanent force of 15,000 men, including the police force and the frontier carabineers, but the standing army in 1981 numbered 20,000 men. Military service is compulsory for all males from the 19th to the 49th year. The Army consists of 13 infantry regiments, 1 motorized regiment, 1 mechanized and 4 cavalry regiments, 3 artillery regiments, a paratroop battalion (CITE) and 2 ranger regiments specially trained in anti-guerrilla warfare.

Air Force. The Air Force, established in 1923, has 3 ground attack/operational training squadrons, equipped with 13 Canadian-built T-33 armed jet trainers, about 4 F-86F Sabre fighter-bombers, and 30 T-6G armed piston-engined trainers for counter-insurgency operations. Other types in service include Brazilian T-23 Uirapuru and American T-41 primary trainers, Italian SF.260M and Swiss turboprop-powered Pilatus PC-7 basic trainers, 1 Electra four-turboprop transport, 5 Fokker F.27 and 5 Israeli-built Arava twin-turboprop light transports, 4 Convair

580 twin-turboprop transports, 2 C-130H/L-100-30 Hercules, 2 C-54, 7 C-47 and 6 Convair 440 piston-engined transports with which a military airline service is operated, and some light aircraft and helicopters. Personnel strength is about 4,000.

Navy. A small Navy exists for river and lake patrol. Strength (1980) 2,300 officers and men.

INTERNATIONAL RELATIONS

Membership. Bolivia is a member of UN, OAS, LAIA (formerly LAFTA), the Andean Group and the Amazon Pact.

External Debt. The contracted external debt was US$3,000m., Dec. 1979.

ECONOMY

Budget. The foreign-exchange revenue is derived mainly from sales of tin and other non-ferrous metals (furnishing about 70% of export revenue in 1979), but oil and gas produced 19% of export revenue in 1979. Revenue and expenditures in 1m. *pesos bolivianos* balanced as follows: 1967, 860·4; 1968, 1,224·7; 1969, 1,265·3. In 1975 expenditure exceeded income by 142·6. Aid from USA in 1971 was about US$20·2m.

Currency. On 1 Jan. 1963 the *peso boliviano* ($b.) was introduced. Exchange rates were $b.25 = US$1 and $b.54 = £1 in March 1981.

Banking. The Banco Central de Bolivia was established in 1911 as Banco de la Nacion Boliviana and re-organized in 1928. The Bank was nationalized in 1939. In 1945 the Banco Central de Bolivia was divided into two independent departments, the Banking Department and the Monetary Department. The latter has the sole power of note issue and must maintain a legal reserve equal to the amount of notes in circulation; 50% of such reserve must be in gold and foreign exchange and 50% in securities. At 30 June 1980 the Bank's gross gold and foreign exchange reserves amounted to US$222·43m. and Bolivia's net reserves stood at US$83·3m. The country also has a stand-by agreement of US$115m. with the International Monetary Fund.

There are Argentine, Brazilian, Peruvian, US and domestic banks.

Weights and Measures. The metric system of weights and measures is used by the administration and prescribed by law, but the old Spanish system is also employed.

ENERGY AND NATURAL RESOURCES

Electricity. Electric power production is expanding. Installed capacity was estimated at 428,595 kw. at the end of 1978. Estimated production from all sources (1978), 1,340,996 Mwh.

Oil and Gas. There are petroleum and natural gas deposits in the Santa Cruz–Camiri areas. A pipeline for crude oil connects Caranda (Santa Cruz) with the Pacific coast at Arica (Chile) and a natural gas pipeline to Argentina was inaugurated in May 1972. Bolivia is self-sufficient in most petroleum products. All production, refining and internal distribution is now in the hands of *Yacimientos Petroliferos Fiscales Bolivianos* (the State Petroleum Organization), the Bolivian Gulf Oil Co. having been nationalized on 17 Oct. 1969. Total production of petroleum and condensates in 1979 was estimated at 10·25m. bbls. Production of natural gas in 1979 was estimated at 1,942m. cu. metres.

Minerals. Mining is the most important industry, accounting for about 69% of the foreign-exchange earnings. About half the mineral mined is tin. Tin mines are at altitudes of from 12,000 to 18,000 ft, where few except native Indians can stand the conditions; transport is costly. Bolivian tin is extracted by shaft-mining, frequently very deep; the ore yields only 0·7% or less of tin and is very refractory; tin is exported in concentrates called *barrilla*, through Pacific ports for refining. A twin dredger has been installed by Grace & Co. to exploit alluvial deposits and another dredger is operated by COMSUR. Smelting capacity was increased in 1980 and it is planned to smelt all the ores from the State Mining Co. by 1981. Tin production in 1979 was estimated at 27,300 tonnes.

A decree of 31 Oct. 1952 nationalized the mining companies of the Patiño, Hochschild and Aramayo groups, which were responsible for about 60% of Bolivia's mineral output. Provisional compensation proposed was: Patiño, US$7·5m.; Hochschild, US$9·25m.; Aramayo, US$4,976,324. Agreements were concluded during 1953 for the gradual payment of compensation on a sliding scale based on prices received for Bolivian tin abroad, but a final settlement has still to be negotiated. The state industry is being run by the *Corporación Minera de Bolivia* (COMIBOL) employing about 23,000 in mining and administrative capacities.

Alluvial gold deposits in the Alto Beni region are being exploited. Co-operative mines at Tipuani produced 770 kg in 1978.

Foreign firms are seeking exploration rights for uranium and a small uranium processing plant was opened in Oct. 1980 at Cotaje (Potosí province). Large deposits of salt are found near Lake Poopó and in the south of Bolivia.

Agriculture. The extensive and still largely undeveloped region east of the Andes comprises about three-quarters of the entire area of the country, and since the agrarian reform of 1952 sugar-cane, rice and cotton have been grown in this *Oriente* in increasing abundance, reaching self-sufficiency in all these products. Output in tonnes in 1978 was: Sugar-cane, 3,246,620; rice, 88,580; coffee, 22,250; maize, 132,454; fodder maize, 198,681; potatoes, 793,000; wheat, 59,925, and cotton (lint), 17,335.

The public lands of the State have an area of about 245,000 sq. miles, of which 104,000 sq. miles are reserved for special colonization. The National Agrarian Reform Service reported in Nov. 1969 that since May 1965 it had distributed 5·5m. hectares of land in 323,046 properties.

A colony of Jewish refugees was established in 1940 at Buena Tierra, 60 miles east of La Paz and, more recently, Japanese and Okinawan settlements in the region of Santa Cruz. The Bolivian Development Corporation has a programme for relief of over-population on the barren altiplano and in 1964 resettled 1,217 families in tropical areas.

Livestock: In 1979 there were some 3·99m. head of cattle, mostly in the Santa Cruz and Beni departments; some are exported to Peru; horses, 393,000; asses, 784,000; pigs, 1·41m.; sheep, 8·7m.; goats, 3m.; poultry, 8·45m.

Forestry. Tropical forests with woods ranging from the 'iron tree' to the light *palo de balsa* are beginning to be exploited. In 1962 the Forestry Service announced proved reserves of 46·3m. hectares, plus a similar amount available for immediate development.

INDUSTRY AND TRADE

Industry. There are few industrial establishments and the country relies on imports for the supply of many consumer goods. However a new investment law passed in 1971 provides incentives and protection for new investment, both foreign and domestic, and for reinvestment in various fields including manufacturing industry, mining, agriculture, construction and tourism. The new law of hydrocarbons encourages foreign participation in developing the petroleum and natural gas resources of the State.

GDP *per capita* (1978) US$510.

Labour. The Ministry of Planning estimated economically active population in 1970 at 1·48m., of whom 1m. were employed in agriculture, 118,300 in industrial manufacture, 35,100 in construction, 74,000 in commerce and finance, 65,000 in central and local government, 47,800 in mining and 41,900 in transport. The ban on trade unions, imposed in 1974, was lifted in 1978.

Commerce. The value of imports and exports in US$1,000 has been as follows:

	1974	1975	1976	1977	1978	1979
Imports	471,200	510,000	536,000	552,000	848,200	928,000
Exports	627,500	449,000	545,000	556,000	640,300	793,000

Tin ore remains the principal export. Total exports, 1979, of all minerals, in concentrates, ingots or solder, were valued at US$546m.

Bolivia having no seaport, imports and exports pass chiefly through the ports of Arica and Antofagasta in Chile, Mollendo-Matarani in Peru, through La Quiaca on the Bolivian–Argentine border and through river-ports on the rivers flowing into the Amazon. The chief imports are lard, flour, cooking oil, iron and steel products, mining machinery, pharmaceuticals, paper products and textiles.

Total trade between Bolivia and UK for 5 years (British Department of Trade returns, in £1,000 sterling):

	1976	1977	1978	1979	1980
Imports to UK	24,510	37,333	32,202	37,619	33,179
Exports and re-exports from UK	9,995	12,049	16,493	9,594	8,684

COMMUNICATIONS

Roads. A highway, in poor condition, 497 km long, runs from Cochabamba to the lowland farming region of Santa Cruz. La Paz and Oruro are also connected by a metalled road. Of other main highways (unmetalled) there is one from La Paz through Guaqui into Peru, another from La Paz, *via* Oruro, Potosí, Tarija and Bermejo, into Argentina, with branches to Cochabamba, Sucre and Camiri, passable throughout the year except at the height of the rainy season, and others from Villazón to Villa Montes *via* Tarija, passable during the dry season. The total length of the road system is 37,708 km (1977). Motor vehicles registered in 1979, 89,445, including 38,140 cars, 50,255 heavy goods vehicles and buses and 1,050 agricultural tractors.

Railways. In 1964 Bolivian National Railways (ENFE) was formed by the amalgamation of the Bolivian Government Railways, Bolivian Railway Co. and the Bolivian section of the Antofagasta (Chili) & Bolivia Railway. The Guaqui-La Paz Railway, formerly operated by Peru, became part of ENFE in 1973. Access to the Pacific is by 3 routes: to Antofagasta and Arica in Chile, and to Mollendo in Peru via Guaqui, the Lake Titicaca train ferry to Puno (Peru), then rail to the coast. Construction began in 1978 of a 150 km line linking Puno with Desaguadero on the Bolivian border which would by-pass the train ferry, though gauge difference would still prevent through running to Peru. Current network totals 3,538 km of metre gauge, comprising unconnected Eastern (1,386 km) and Western (2,152 km—65 km electrified) systems.

Aviation. The national airline is Lloyd Aéreo Boliviano; in 1978 a total of 20,620 hours were flown, carrying 1,060,044 passengers. The airline runs regular services between La Paz and Lima, São Paulo, Buenos Aires, Miami, Caracas, Salta and Arica as well as many internal services. Braniff International Airways runs regular flights between La Paz, Lima, Buenos Aires, Santiago and Asunción, linking Bolivia (*via* Lima) to the USA. Lufthansa links Bolivia with Europe. Other airlines serving Bolivia are Aerolineas Argentinas, Cruzeiro, Aero Peru, Lan Chile and Avianca.

Shipping. Traffic on Lake Titicaca between Guaqui and Puno is carried on by the steamers of the Peruvian Corporation. About 12,000 miles of rivers, in 4 main systems (Beni, Pilcomayo, Titicaca–Desaguadero, Mamoré), are open to navigation by light-draught vessels.

Post and Broadcasting. In Bolivia there were, in 1978, 458 post offices, of these, 205 provided telegraph and telephone services together with a further 245 offices for telegraph and telephone service only. There is telephone service in the cities of La Paz, Cochabamba, Oruro, Sucre, Potosí, Santa Cruz, Tarija, Camiri, Tupiza, Villazon, Riberalta and Trinidad with (1978), 101,500 telephones. There are about 119 broadcasting stations, of which 7 are state-owned. There is a commercial government television service.

Newspapers. There are 7 daily newspapers in La Paz, and 2 in Cochabamba. Several other towns have regular newspapers devoted to local news, but most of them appear only a few times a week. An economic monthly journal *Revista Economica* and 4 daily newspapers are produced in Santa Cruz. Oruro has 2 dailies.

JUSTICE, RELIGION, EDUCATION AND WELFARE

Justice. Justice is administered by the Supreme Court, superior district courts (of 5 or 7 judges) and courts of local justice. The Supreme Court, with headquarters at Sucre, is divided into two sections, civil and criminal, of 5 justices each, with the

Chief Justice presiding over both. Members of the Supreme Court are chosen on a two-thirds vote of Congress.

Religion. The Roman Catholic is the recognized religion of the state; the free exercise of other forms of worship is permitted. The Catholic Church is under a cardinal (in Sucre), an archbishop (in La Paz), 6 bishops (Cochabamba, Santa Cruz, Oruro, Potosí, Riberalta and Tarija) and vicars apostolic (titular bishops resident in Cueva, Trinidad, San Ignacio de Velasco, Riberalta and Rurrenabaque).

By a law of 11 Oct. 1911 all marriages must be celebrated by the civil authorities. Divorce is permitted by a law enacted on 15 April 1932.

Education. Primary instruction is free and obligatory between the ages of 6 and 14 years. Estimates for 1974 show that 989,858 children between 6 and 14 years attended school. All illiterates between 15 and 50 years are obliged to attend literacy classes and in 1977 this represented 40% of the population.

At Sucre, Oruro, Potosí, Cochabamba, Santa Cruz, Tarija, Trinidad and La Paz are universities; La Paz is the most important of them while the San Francisco Xavier University at Sucre is one of the oldest in America, having been founded in 1624. The universities were closed on 17 July 1980, following the *coup d'état*.

Health. In 1972 there were 2,143 doctors.

DIPLOMATIC REPRESENTATIVES

OF BOLIVIA IN GREAT BRITAIN (106 Eaton Sq., London, SW1W 9AD)
Chargé d'Affaires: Humberto Zannier.

OF GREAT BRITAIN IN BOLIVIA (Avenida Arce 2732–2754, La Paz)
Ambassador: A. C. Buxton, CMG.

OF BOLIVIA IN THE USA (3014 Massachusetts Ave, NW,
Washington, D.C. 20008)
Ambassador: (Vacant).

OF THE USA IN BOLIVIA (Banco Popular Del Peru Bldg, La Paz)
Ambassador: Marvin Weissman.

OF BOLIVIA TO THE UNITED NATIONS
Ambassador: Fernando Ortiz Sanz.

Books of Reference

There is a weekly official gazette.

Anuario Geográfico y Estadístico de la República de Bolivia
Anuario del Comercio Exterior de Bolivia
Boletín Mensual de Información Estadística
Constitución Política del Estado. La Paz, 1961
Baptista Gumucio, M., *Cultural Policy in Bolivia.* UNESCO, 1978
Fifer, J. V., *Bolivia: Land, Location and Politics Since 1825.* CUP, 1972
Guillermo, L., *A History of the Bolivian Labour Movement 1848–1971.* CUP, 1977
Mitchell, C., *The Legacy of Populism in Bolivia.* New York, 1977
Osborne, H., *Bolivia: A Land Divided.* R. Inst. of Int. Affairs, 3rd ed. 1964.—*Indians of the Andes,* London, 1952
Pardo Valle, N., *Poligrafía de Bolivia.* La Paz, 1966

BOTSWANA

Capital: Gaborone
Population: 831,000 (1979)
GNP per capita: US$620 (1978)

HISTORY. In 1885 the territory was declared to be within the British sphere; in 1889 it was included in the sphere of the British South Africa Company, but was never administered by the company; in 1890 a Resident Commissioner was appointed, and in 1895, on the annexation of the Crown Colony of British Bechuanaland to the Cape of Good Hope, the British Government was in favour of transferring the Protectorate to the BSA Company, but the three major chiefs of the Bakwena, the Bangwaketse and the Bamangwato went to England to protest against this proposal, and agreement was reached that their country should remain a British Protectorate if they ceded a strip of land on the eastern side of the country for railway construction. This railway was built in 1896–97.

On 30 Sept. 1966 the Bechuanaland Protectorate became an independent and sovereign member of the Commonwealth under the name of the Republic of Botswana.

AREA AND POPULATION. Botswana comprises the territory lying between the Molopo River on the south and the Zambezi on the north, and extending from the Transvaal Province and Rhodesia on the east to South-West Africa on the west. The climate is on the whole sub-tropical and the atmosphere throughout the year is very dry. Area about 222,000 sq. miles (575,000 sq. km); population, according to the census of 1971, was 630,379 (estimate, 1979, 831,000). The most important tribes are the Bamangwato (216,058), under Chief Ian Khama; the Bakgatla (31,150), under Chief Linchwe II; the Bakwena (62,251), under Chief Bonewamang P. Sechele; the Bangwaketse (71,289), under Chief Seepapitso IV; the Batawana (42,347), under Chief Letsholathebe; the Bamalete (13,861), under Regent Kelemogile Mokgosi (brother of the late Chief Mokgosi, who died in 1966); the Batlokwa (3,711), under Acting Chief Kema Gaborone; the Barolong (10,662), under Chief Besele.

The main business centres (with estimated population, 1980) are Gaborone (54,000), Francistown (32,000), Selebi-Phikwe (29,000), Kanye (22,000), Lobatse (20,000), Mochudi (20,000), Molepolole (19,000), Mahalapye (19,000), Maun (16,000).

The seat of government is at Gaborone.

The official language is English; the national language is Setswana.

CONSTITUTION AND GOVERNMENT. The Constitution of the republic is based on the Constitution which came into effect in March 1965, with some minor alterations.

The executive rests with the President of the Republic who is responsible to the National Assembly.

The National Assembly consists of 36 members (32 elected by universal suffrage, 4 nominated by the President, the Attorney-General and the Speaker *ex-officio*). The fourth general election, held in Oct. 1978, returned 30 members of the Botswana Democratic Party, 1 Botswana People's Party and 1 Botswana National Front.

The President is an *ex-officio* member of the Assembly. If the President is already a member of the National Assembly, a by-election will be held in the constituency of that member.

There is also a House of Chiefs to advise the Government. It consists of the Chiefs of the 8 principal tribes and 4 members elected by and from among the sub-chiefs in 4 districts.

The first President of Botswana, who was re-elected 3 times, was Sir Seretse Khama, KBE, who died 13 July 1980.

President of the Republic: Dr Quett Ketumile Joni Masire.

On 18 July 1980 the Cabinet was as follows:

Vice President and Minister of Local Government and Lands: L. M. Seretse. *Finance and Development Planning:* P. S. Mmusi. *Public Service and Information:* D. K. Kwelagobe. *External Affairs:* A. M. Mogwe. *Health:* L. Makgekgenene. *Agriculture:* W. Meswele. *Works and Communications:* C. Blackbeard. *Commerce and Industry:* M. P. K. Nwako. *Mineral Resources and Water Affairs:* Dr G. K. T. Chiepe. *Education:* K. P. Morake. *Home Affairs:* K. L. Disele. *Assistant for Finance and Development Planning:* J. L. T. Mothibamele. *Assistant for Local Government and Lands:* D. Kwele. *Assistant for Agriculture:* G. U. S. Matlhabaphiri. *Attorney-General:* Moleleki Mokama. *Speaker of the National Assembly:* J. G. Haskins.

National flag: Light blue with a horizontal black stripe, edged white, across the centre.

Local Government. Local government is carried out by 9 district councils and 4 town councils. Revenue is obtained mainly from local income tax, levied on all inhabitants in the area; from rates in the towns and from central government subventions in the districts.

DEFENCE

Army. A defence force has been created for border control and comprises 2 infantry battalions; strength, total armed forces (1980) 2,000. Paramilitary forces number 1,260.

Air Force. Equipment includes 5 Britten-Norman Defender armed light transports for border patrol, counter-insurgency and casualty evacuation duties, 6 Bulldog piston-engined basic trainers, 2 Skyvan turboprop passenger/cargo transports and a Cessna 150 light aircraft.

INTERNATIONAL RELATIONS

Membership. Botswana is a member of UN, OAU, the Commonwealth and is an ACP state of EEC.

ECONOMY

Planning. The National Development Plan 1979–85 envisages a total capital expenditure of P530m., GDP growth of 10·1% per annum, employment growth of 7% and a strong balance of payments.

Budget. Revenue and expenditure (in 1m. Pula) for financial years ending 31 March:

	1977–78	1978–79	1979–80
Revenues and grants	118	167	220
Expenditure and net lending	123	172	227

Chief items of revenue, 1978–79: Minerals, P38·8m.; customs pool, P49·8m.; non-mineral, income tax, P20·9m.

Chief items of expenditure, 1978–79: Education, P21·9m.; works and communications development projects, P22·9m.

Public debt, on 31 March 1980, amounted to P112·8m.

Currency. The currency was formerly the South African Rand but in Oct. 1976 a new currency, the *pula*, was introduced (P1·688 = £1 sterling in March 1981).

Banking. The Standard Bank Ltd and Barclays Bank International have branches in Francistown, Lobatse, Mahalapye, Maun and Gaborone and about 46 agencies throughout the country.

A government-financed National Development Bank was founded in 1964 and had assets of P3·65m. on 31 Dec. 1977.

The post office savings bank has deposits of about P1·6m. from 11,000 depositors in mid-1976.

NATURAL RESOURCES

Minerals. An important part of government revenue comes from the diamond mine at Orapa (production started in 1971, 821,914 carats; 1979, P181m.) and the nickel–copper complex at Selebi-Phikwe (production started in 1974) with production (1978) 40,000 tonnes valued at P51m. An open-pit coalmine has been developed at

Morupule, and produced (1978) 315,000 tonnes valued at P4·3m. A new diamond mine at Jwaneng is expected to come into production in 1982.

Mineral resources in north-east Botswana are being investigated, including salt and soda ash on the Sua Pan of the Makgadikgadi Salt Pans, nickel–copper at Selkirk and Phoenix, copper south of Maun and close to Ghanzi, and coal at Mmamabula.

Agriculture. Cattle-rearing is the chief industry, but the country is more a pastoral than an agricultural one, crops depending entirely upon the rainfall. Increasing numbers of boreholes are being established where underground supply is adequate. However the rural economy is particularly vulnerable to drought and foot and mouth disease. In 1975 a reform of land ownership, which allows for more modern land use, was announced.

The abattoir at Lobatse, opened in Oct. 1954, is of great importance to the country's economy. In 1979 the number of cattle was 3·3m.; goats, 1·2m.; sheep, 450,000; poultry, 620,000.

LABOUR. In 1977, 68·8% of the labour force were engaged in agriculture, 12% was employed outside Botswana, mainly in the Republic of South Africa in the mining industry and 2·9% was engaged in domestic service. Total labour force was 384,000. In 1978 employment in Botswana was 63,000 of which 25,000, government employees, 10,000 in commerce and 4,000 in manufacturing.

COMMERCE. In 1978 imports were valued at P258·5m. including (1977): Food, beverages and tobacco, P45,996,000; machinery and electrical equipment, P30·33m.; textiles and footwear, P24,759,000; fuels, P24,523,000; vehicles and transport equipment, P23,415,000; metal and metal products, P22,119,000. Exports (1978) were P186·7m. including: Diamonds, P75m.; meat and meat products, P27m. (a large decrease owing to foot and mouth disease); copper–nickel matte, P49m.

Botswana is a member of the South African customs union with Lesotho, the Republic of South Africa and Swaziland.

Total trade between Botswana and UK (British Department of Trade returns, in £1,000 sterling):

	1976	1977	1978	1979	1980
Imports to UK	24,935	39,843	5,378	26,264	4,044
Exports and re-exports from UK	1,333	3,017	3,256	3,845	2,644

TOURISM. The infrastructure for tourism is being developed and there were 58,100 tourists from 1979.

COMMUNICATIONS

Roads. On 31 Dec. 1979, 998 km of road were bitumen-surfaced, 1,540 km gravel and 4,901 km earth. In 1979 there were 21,800 registered motor vehicles.

Railways. 640 km of the Cape Town to Zimbabwe railway line lie within Botswana. The railway is owned and operated by the National Railways of Zimbabwe but the Government of Botswana is preparing to take over the line of rail in Botswana and has formed the Botswana Railway Corporation.

In addition there are 2 Government owned branch lines which serve the coalmine at Morupule and the copper and nickel mining complex at Selibe Pikwe.

Aviation. There are 3 airports and many airstrips. Regular international flights are flown by Zambia Airways, Air Botswana and SAA into Gaborone.

Post and Broadcasting. The telegraph, telephone and railway lines from Cape Town to Zimbabwe traverse Botswana. Wireless communication has been established between headquarters at Gaborone and various district offices and police stations. There are 39 post offices and 42 agencies. There were 10,833 telephones installed in 1978. A new earth station giving independent access to the international telecommunications system, was completed in 1980.

Newspapers. In 1980 there was 1 daily newspaper.

JUSTICE, EDUCATION AND WELFARE

Justice. The Botswana Court of Appeal succeeded the Court of Appeal for Basutoland, Bechuanaland and Swaziland, which was established in 1954. It has jurisdiction in respect of criminal and civil appeals emanating from the High Court of Botswana. Further appeal lies in certain circumstances to the Judicial Committee of the Privy Council.

The High Court for Botswana succeeded the High Court for Bechuanaland, which was established in 1938. It has jurisdiction in all criminal and civil causes and proceedings. Subordinate courts and African courts are in each of the 12 administrative districts.

Police. The police force consisted of 286 officers and subordinate officers, 234 n.c.o.s and 1,434 other ranks in 1980.

Education (1978). There were 336 primary, 15 secondary, 15 governmental aided, 14 private secondary and continuation, 26 vocational training schools and 3 teacher-training colleges. The great majority of the primary schools and the junior secondary schools are controlled, under the Chief Education Officer, by school committees with district-council and mission representatives. Three secondary schools and the homecraft centre are run by missions with Government support; Moeng College by a governing council; the remaining schools by the Government. District-council schools are financed by district-council treasuries and assisted with grants from the Central Government. Enrolment in primary schools in 1979 was 156,664; government secondary, 12,175; private secondary, 4,561; vocational, 2,150; in teacher-training colleges, 690. University students on the Botswana campus of the University of Botswana and Swaziland 860 and university students abroad numbered 718. Total recurrent expenditure on education was P21·9m. for 1978–79.

In 1971, an estimated 20% of the total population were literate. In 1975, 71% of children of primary school age were receiving instruction.

Welfare (1978). There were 13 general hospitals, 21 maternity centres, a mental home, 7 health centres, 94 clinics and 381 health posts. Total number of beds, 1,871 (1977). There were 89 registered medical practitioners, 6 dentists, 335 practising registered nurses and 345 enrolled nurses. The health facilities are the concern of central and local government, medical missions, mining companies and voluntary organizations. Government expenditure on medical services was P6·5m. for the year ended 31 March 1977.

DIPLOMATIC REPRESENTATIVES

OF BOTSWANA IN GREAT BRITAIN
(162 Buckingham Palace Rd., London, SW1)
High Commissioner: Aloysius William Kgarebe (accredited 21 March 1978).

OF GREAT BRITAIN IN BOTSWANA (Private Bag 0023, Gaborone)
High Commissioner: W. Turner, CMG, CVO.

OF BOTSWANA IN THE USA
(4301 Connecticut Ave., NW, Washington, D.C., 20008)
Ambassador: Dr M. J. Melamu.

OF THE USA IN BOTSWANA (PO Box 90, Gaborone)
Ambassador: Horace G. Dawson, Jr.

OF BOTSWANA TO THE UNITED NATIONS
Ambassador: Joseph Legwaila.

Books of Reference

Statistical Information: The Director of Information and Broadcasting, PO Box 0060, Gaborone, Botswana publishes *Facts About Botswana*, the monthly *Kutlwano, The Botswana Daily News* and *Botswana Magazine*.

Statistical Bulletins Quarterly. Central Statistical Office, Gaborone
Report on the Population Census, 1971. Government Printer, Gaborone, 1972
Colclough, C. and McCarthy, S., *The Political Economy of Botswana.* OUP, 1980
Jones, D., *Aid and Development in Southern Africa.* London, 1979
Selwyn, P., *Industries in the Southern African Periphery.* London, 1975
Sillery, A., *Botswana: A Short Political History.* London, 1974
Stevens, C., *Food Aid and the Developing World.* London, 1979

BRAZIL

República Federativa do Brasil

Capital: Brasília
Population: 123m. (1980)
GNP per capita: US$1,570 (1978)

HISTORY. Brazil was discovered on 22 April 1500 by the Portuguese Admiral Pedro Alvares Cabral, and thus became a Portuguese settlement; in 1815 the colony was declared 'a kingdom', and on 13 May 1822 Dom Pedro, eldest surviving son of King João VI of Portugal, was chosen 'Perpetual Defender' of Brazil by a National Congress. He proclaimed the independence of the country on 7 Sept. 1822, and was chosen 'Constitutional Emperor and Perpetual Defender' on 12 Oct. 1822. He resigned in 1831 and 9 years later, his 14-year-old son Pedro, became the second Emperor of Brazil.

AREA AND POPULATION. Brazil is bounded east by the Atlantic and on its north-west and southern borders by all the South American countries except Chile and Ecuador. Population as at 1 Sept. 1970 (census) and July 1979 (estimate):

State and Capital	Area (sq. km)	Census 1970	Estimate 1980
North	3,581,180	3,603,860	4,923,400
Rondônia [1] (Porto Velho [2])	243,044	111,064	172,200
Acre (Rio Branco)	152,589	215,299	288,100
Amazonas [3] (Manaus)	1,564,445	955,235	1,251,700
Roraima (Boa Vista [2])	230,104	40,885	56,400
Pará (Bélem) [3]	1,250,722	2,167,018	2,980,800
Amapá (Macapá [2])	140,276	114,359	174,200
North-east	1,548,672	28,111,927	36,251,400
Maranhão (São Luis)	328,663	2,992,686	3,698,200
Piauí (Teresina)	250,934	1,680,573	2,306,800
Ceará (Fortaleza) [4]	150,630	4,361,603	5,891,000
Rio Grande do Norte (Natal)	53,015	1,550,244	2,162,700
Paraíba (João Pessoa)	56,372	2,382,617	2,963,800
Pernambuco (Recife)	98,281	5,160,640	6,607,100 [5]
Alagoas (Maceió)	27,731	1,588,109	2,012,600
Fernando de Noronha [6]	26	1,241	...
Sergipe (Aracajú)	21,994	900,744	1,094,400
Bahia (Salvador)	561,026	7,493,470	9,514,800
South-east:	924,934	39,853,498	51,574,500
Minas Gerais (Belo Horizonte)	587,172	11,487,415	13,688,900
Espírito Santo [7] (Vitória)	45,597	1,599,333	1,859,800
Rio de Janeiro (Rio de Janeiro) [8]	{ 42,912	4,742,884	—
	{ 1,356	4,251,918	12,021,900
São Paulo (São Paulo)	247,898	17,771,948	24,003,900
South	577,723	16,496,493	22,495,200
Paranã (Curitiba)	199,554	6,929,868	10,274,200
Santa Catarina (Florianópolis)	95,985	2,901,734	3,880,700
Rio Grande do Sul (Pórto Alegre)	282,184	6,664,891	8,340,300
Central West	1,879,455	5,073,259	7,787,600
Mato Grosso (Cuiabá) [9]	881,001	1,597,090	955,400
Mato Grosso do Sul (Campo Grande) [9]	350,548		1,533,500
Goiás (Goiânia)	642,092	2,938,677	5,298,700 [10]
Distrito Federal (Brasília)	5,814	537,492	...
Total	8,511,965 [11]	93,139,037	123,032,100

For notes *see* p. 231.

Density of census population, 1970, was about 11 per sq. km.

The 1970 census showed 46,331,343 males and 46,807,694 females. The urban and suburban population comprised 36·2% in 1950, 45·1% in 1960 and 55·9% in 1970.

The language is Portuguese.

The new capital, Brasília, was inaugurated 21 April 1960. The federal district (5,814 sq. km) was detached from the west-central state of Goiás, about 1,000 km north-west of Rio de Janeiro.

Population of principal cities (1979 estimates):

São Paulo	8,407,500	Goiânia	646,000
Rio de Janeiro	5,394,900	Duque de Caxias	639,100
Belo Horizonte	1,856,800	São Gonçalo	633,200
Salvador	1,445,700	Santo Andre	608,800
Recife	1,391,800	Manaus	562,400
Fortaleza	1,255,600	Campinas	467,400
Porto Alegre	1,183,500	Osasco	462,800
Nova Iguaçu	1,130,300	São João de Meriti	425,800
Brasília	978,600	São Luis	389,400
Curitiba	905,800	Maceió	375,600
Belém	899,700	Campos	352,500

The number of immigrants, between 1820 and 1953 was over 5m.; it is estimated that only one-half remained. Immigrants, by country, in recent years have numbered:

	1972	1973	1974	1975
United States	1,068	874	1,014	1,414
Portugal	1,095	581	426	959
Japan	472	25	75	111
Spain	470	225	244	410
Italy	535	402	478	1,356
Others	5,127	3,824	4,529	7,316
Total	8,767	5,931	6,766	11,566

CONSTITUTION AND GOVERNMENT. On 15 Nov. 1889 Dom Pedro II (1825–91) was dethroned by a revolution, and Brazil declared a republic.

Presidents since the establishment of the republic:

Marshal Manuel Deodoro da Fonseca, 15 Nov. 1889–23 Nov. 1891 (resigned).

Marshal Floriano Peixoto (Acting), 23 Nov. 1891–15 Nov. 1894.

Dr Prudente José de Moraes Barros, 15 Nov. 1894–15 Nov. 1898.

Dr Manuel Ferraz de Campos Salles, 15 Nov. 1898–15 Nov. 1902.

Dr Francisco da Paula Rodrigues Alves, 15 Nov. 1902–15 Nov. 1906.

Dr Affonso Augusto Moreira Penna, 15 Nov. 1906–14 June 1909 (died).

Dr Nilo Peçanha (Acting), 14 June 1909–15 Nov. 1910.

Marshal Hermes Rodrigues da Fonseca, 15 Nov. 1910–15 Nov. 1914.

Dr Wenceslau Braz Pereira Gomes, 15 Nov. 1914–15 Nov. 1918.

Dr Francisco da Paula Rodrigues Alves.[1]

Dr Delphim Moreira da Costa Ribeiro (Acting), 15 Nov. 1918–28 July 1919.

[1] Owing to illness did not take office; died 10 Jan. 1919.

[1] The name 'Território Federal do Guaporé' was changed to 'Território Federal de Rondônia' on 17 Feb. 1956.

[2] Raised to the status of territorial capitals in 1943; previously, Pôrto Velho and Boa Vista belonged to the state of Amazonas and Macapá to the state of Pará.

[3] Excluding 2,680 sq. km in dispute with the state of Pará.

[4] Includes an area of 2,614 sq. km to be demarcated between states of Piauí and Ceará.

[5] Including Fernando de Noronha territory data.

[6] Territory created in 1942 includes 8 sq. km of islets.

[7] Including the islands of Trindade and Martim Vaz.

[8] According to Complementary Law no. 20 of 1 July 1974, the States of Rio de Janeiro and Guanabara were consolidated, since 15 March 1975, into a single political unit, the State of Rio de Janeiro with the City of Rio de Janeiro as its capital city.

[9] On 1 Jan. 1979, the former state of Mato Grosso was divided into Mato Grosso (capital, Cuiabá) and Mato Grosso do Sol (capital, Campo Grande).

[10] Including federal district data.

[11] 3,286,000 sq. miles.

Dr Epitácio da Silva Pessoa, 28 July 1919–15 Nov. 1922.
Dr Arthur Bernardes, 15 Nov. 1922–15 Nov. 1926.
Dr Washington Luiz Pereira de Souza, 15 Nov. 1926–25 Oct. 1930 (deposed).
Dr Getúlio Dornelles Vargas, 26 Oct. 1930–29 Oct. 1945 (resigned).
Dr José Linhares (Provisional President), 30 Oct. 1945–31 Jan. 1946.
Gen. Eurico Gaspar Dutra, 31 Jan. 1946–31 Jan. 1951.
Dr Getúlio Dornelles Vargas, 31 Jan. 1951–died 24 Aug. 1954.
Dr João Café Filho, 24 Aug. 1954–8 Nov. 1955 (resigned).
Carlos Coimbra da Luz (Acting), 8 Nov. 1955–11 Nov. 1955 (deposed).

Nereu de Oliveira Ramos (Acting), 11 Nov. 1955–31 Jan. 1956.
Juscelino Kubitschek de Oliveira, 31 Jan. 1956–31 Jan. 1961.
Jânio da Silva Quadros, 31 Jan. 1961–25 Aug. 1961 (resigned).
João Belchior Marques Goulart, 7 Sept. 1961–31 March 1964 (deposed).
Marshal Humberto de A. Castelo Branco, 15 April 1964–15 March 1967.
Marshal Artur da Costa e Silva, 15 March 1967–31 Aug. 1969 (resigned).
Gen. Emilio Garrastazu Medici, 30 Oct. 1969–15 March 1974.
Gen. Ernesto Geisel, 15 March 1974–15 March 1979.
Gen. João Baptista de Oliveira Figueiredo, 15 March 1979–

On 24 Jan. 1967 both houses of Congress in joint session approved the new Constitution and press law which came into force on 15 March. An amendment to the Constitution, which came into force on 30 Oct. 1969, was issued on 17 Oct. The present Constitution provides for the indirect election of the President and Vice-President by an electoral college, comprising the members of Congress and delegates from the state legislatures; it grants powers to the President to issue decree-laws on matters connected with the economy and national security; it gives the President authority to intervene in any of the 22 states without consultation with Congress and the right to declare a state of siege and to rule by decree. President and Vice-President are elected for a 6-year term and are not immediately re-eligible. The Senate is elected for 8 years, the Chamber of Deputies for 4 years.

Under the 1969 Constitution, Congress consists of a 67-member Senate and a 420-member Chamber of Deputies. The Senate is two-thirds directly elected (50% of these elected for 8 years in rotation) and one-third indirectly elected. The Chamber of Deputies is elected by universal franchise (with a literacy qualification) for 4 years.

The name of the country was changed from 'Estados Unidos do Brasil' to 'Brasil' and later to 'República Federativa do Brasil'.

Freedom of speech and press are not absolute: war propaganda, the teaching of 'subversive doctrines' and the dissemination of race or class prejudices are banned, as also are political parties opposed to democracy, the existing multi-party system or to 'fundamental human rights' which include the right to own private property. The Supreme Electoral Court on 7 May 1947 declared the Communist Party illegal and on 20 Dec. 1979 the Political Parties Statute of 1965 was amended to allow for the formation of new political parties.

The Institutional Act No. 5 issued on 13 Dec. 1968 was incorporated into the new Constitution through an amendment on 17 Oct. 1969. It was repealed by the Constitutional Amendment Number 11 of 13 Oct. 1978. The Congress renewed its session on 22 Oct. 1969 and elections were held on 15 Nov. 1970, 1974 and 1978.

Voting is compulsory for men and women between the ages of 18 and 65 and optional for persons over 65. Enlisted men and illiterates (who comprise about 40% of the adult population) may not vote.

President of the Republic: Gen. João Baptista de Oliveira Figueiredo, assumed office 15 March 1979.

Minister of Foreign Affairs: Ramiro Elysio Saraiva Guerreiro.

There are Secretaries of State at the head of the following Ministries: Finance; Justice; Interior; Foreign Affairs; Transport; Communications; Agriculture; Labour; Education and Culture; Health; Industry and Commerce; Mines and Power; Welfare and Social Security; and the Ministries of Army, Marine and Air. There is a Secretariat of Planning and General Co-ordination established in 1974 as an agency of the Presidency of the Republic and equivalent to a Ministry in charge of general co-ordination of planning in the country.

National flag: Green, with yellow lozenge on which is placed a blue sphere, containing 22 white stars and crossed with a band bearing the motto *Ordem e Progresso.*

National anthem: Ouviram do Ipiranga . . . (words by J. O. Duque Estrada; tune by F. M. da Silva).

Local Government. Brazil consists of 22 states, 4 federal territories (Rondônia, Roraima, Amapá, Fernando de Noronha) and 1 federal district. Each state has its distinct administrative, legislative and judicial authorities, its own constitution and laws, which must, however, agree with the constitutional principles of the Union. The states may unite or split or form new states. Taxes on interstate commerce, levied by individual states, are prohibited. The governors and members of the legislatures are elected, but magistrates are appointed and are not removable from office save by judicial sentence. Rio de Janeiro and Guanabara became one state in 1975.

The National Congress issued a decree and, in Oct. 1977, the President of Republic enacted the law by which the State of Mato Grosso was divided in 2 distinct states: the State of Mato Grosso do Sul was established on 1 Jan. 1979, when its first governor took office, and the State of Mato Grosso.

DEFENCE

Army. Under the constitution military service is compulsory for every Brazilian man from 21 years of age to 45. The terms of service are 9 years (from the 21st to the 30th years of age) in the Army 'first line' (1 in the ranks, the rest in the reserve) and 14 years (from the 30th to the 45th years of age) in the Army 'second line' (7 in the 'second line' and 7 in the reserve of the same). The men in the Territorial Army also have an annual training of 2 to 4 weeks. The Army is organized in 8 divisions, each with up to 6 armoured, 4 mechanized or motorized infantry brigades; in addition there are 5 light 'jungle' infantry battalions, 2 independent infantry and 1 independent parachute brigades; total strength (1980) 182,750.

Navy. The principal ships [2] of the Brazilian Navy are as follows:

Completed	Name	Standard displacement Tons	Armour Belt In.	Guns In.	Principal armament	Torpedo tubes	Shaft horsepower	Speed Knots
			Aircraft Carrier					
1945	Minas Gerais [1]	15,890	—	—	10 40-mm. AA	—	40,000	24

[1] Ex-*Vengeance*, purchased from Great Britain in 1956.
[2] The 10,000-ton cruiser *Tamandaré* (ex-*St Louis*), of the 'St Louis' class purchased from USA in 1951 was offered for sale in 1975. The cruiser *Barroso* (ex-*Philadelphia*) of the 'Brooklyn' class, also transferred in 1951, was listed for disposal in 1973.

There are also 8 diesel-powered submarines (3 modern built in Britain and 5 old *ex*-US), 6 new destroyer leaders (or large frigates), the *Constituição, Defensoza, Liberal* and *Niteroi*, built in Britain, and the *Independencia* and *Uniao*, built in Brazil, 12 old *ex*-US destroyers, 10 fleet tug type corvettes, 6 coastal minesweepers, 1 river monitor, 5 river patrol ships, 6 coastal gunboats, 1 submarine rescue ship, 2 tank landing ships, 4 transports, 18 local transports, 3 oilers, 1 repair ship, 8 survey ships, 6 survey launches, 35 minor landing craft, 4 buoy tenders, 20 auxiliaries and 13 tugs. There are also 3 floating docks.

The new construction programme is being revised to replace old US submarines and destroyers. A training ship (frigate) and a river support ship are projected.

Projected ships were to have included 1 helicopter carrier, 3 anti-aircraft frigates, 6 to 12 corvettes, 4 coastal patrol craft, 1 replenishment oiler, 18 minor landing craft, 1 survey ship and 3 tugs.

Naval bases are at Rio de Janeiro, Aratu (Bahia), Belém, Natal, Recife, Salvador, with a river base at Ladario.

The Fleet Air Arm was formed on 26 Jan. 1965. Aircraft obtained from the USA for service on the carrier include 6 Sikorsky SH-3D and 5-SH-34J helicopters and 5 S-2A Tracker anti-submarine aircraft, the latter being operated by the Air Force (to be replaced by Navy S-2E Grumman Trackers). Three Wasp light anti-submarine helicopters were obtained from Britain in 1965, and were followed by 7 turbine-powered Whirlwind UH5 and 6 American-built Fairchild Hiller FH 1100 light observation helicopters. Nine Westland Lynx WC 13 helicopters were provided for the destroyer leader/frigates of the 'Niteroi' class.

The active personnel in 1981 approached 45,500 (3,900 officers and 41,600 men), including 12,000 marines and auxiliary corps.

Air Force. The Air Force, formed in 1918, has been independent of the Army and Navy since 1941. It is organized in 6 zones, centred on Belém, Recife, Rio de Janeiro, São Paulo, Porto Alegre and Brasília. The 1a ALADA (air defence wing) has 13 Mirage IIIE fighters and 3 Mirage IIID trainers, integrated with Roland mobile short-range surface-to-air missile systems deployed by the Army, and a radar/communications/computer network. One fighter group has 2 squadrons of F-5E Tiger II supersonic fighter-bombers and two-seat F-5Bs; 2 others operate AT-26 (Aermacchi MB 326G) Xavante light jet attack/trainers. Counter-insurgency squadrons are equipped with AT-26 Xavantes for reconnaissance and attack, and with Neiva Regente lightplanes, Universal armed piston-engined trainers, and UH-1D/H Iroquois and armed JetRanger helicopters for liaison and observation. There is an ASW group of S-2A/E Trackers for shore-based and carrier-based operations; a maritime patrol squadron of EMB-111 twin-turbo-prop aircraft developed from the Brazilian-designed Bandeirante transport; and 3 air-sea rescue units with RC-130E Hercules reconnaissance transports, HU-16 Albatross amphibians and UH-1D Iroquois helicopters respectively. Equipment of transport units includes 1 group of C-130E/H Hercules transports and KC-130H Hercules tankers; 1 group made up of a squadron of HS 748 and C-95 Bandeirante turboprop transports and a second squadron of HS 748s with large freight doors; 1 troop-carrier group with DHC-5 Buffaloes; and 6 independent squadrons with Bandeirantes and Buffaloes. The VIP transport group has 2 Boeing 737s, 13 HS 125 twin-jet light transports, some Bandeirantes, 5 Embraer Xingu twin-turboprop pressurized transports and 6 JetRanger helicopters. Training is performed primarily on locally-built Aerotec T-23 Uirapuru *ab initio* trainers, T-25 Universal basic trainers, and AT-26 Xavante armed jet basic trainers.

Personnel strength (1981) about 42,800, with more than 600 aircraft of all types.

INTERNATIONAL RELATIONS

Membership. Brazil is a member of UN, OAS and LAIA (formerly LAFTA).

ECONOMY

Budget. Receipts and expenditures for the federal government (excluding states, federal district and municipalities) for calendar years have been as follows in 1m. Cr$:

	1976	1977	1978	1979
Revenue	172,372	252,605	357,705	470,830
Expenditure	168,181	247,467	356,000	470,830

Chief items of revenue were in 1978 as follows (in Cr$1m.): Taxes, 309,624; government property, 5,983. Principal items of expenditure: Transport, 18,361; education, 23,740; army, 17,589; aviation and navy, 23,289; welfare and security, 11,947; finance, 7,273.

The foreign debt (including states and municipalities) of Brazil on 31 Dec. 1980 amounted to US$54,400m. Internal funded federal and states debt, 31 Dec. 1974, was Cr$32,949m. and 1975, was Cr$60,100m.

Currency. On 15 May 1970 the *cruzeiro* (Cr$) became the monetary unit, equivalent to 1 *new cruzeiro*; it is divided into 100 *centavos*. The exchange rate was in March 1981 US$1 = Cr$71.69; £1 = Cr$156.10.

Banking. The Bank of Brazil (founded in 1808 and reorganized in 1906, with an authorized capital of NCr$60m. from 1967) is not a central bank of issue but a closely controlled commercial bank; it had 1,235 branches in 1978 throughout the republic. On 31 Dec. 1978 deposits were Cr$125,997m.

On 31 Dec. 1964 the Banco Central da República do Brasil was founded.

The country's currency held by the public on 31 Dec. 1979 was Cr$167,315m. Since Sept. 1939 gold and dollar supply has risen from US$40m. to US$420m., of which the government's gold was US$288m. in May 1961.

Banking institutions numbered 107, with 10,222 agencies in Dec. 1978. All banks had on 31 Dec. 1979 deposits of Cr$1,024,609m. and loans of Cr$2,065,955m. Foreign banks had total assets of Cr$5,294,966m. in 1976.

Weights and Measures. The metric system has been in use in all official departments since 1862. It was made compulsory in 1872, but the ancient measures are still partly employed in remote districts. They are: *libra* = 1·012 lb. avoirdupois; *arroba* = 32·98 lb.; *quintal* = 129·54 lb.; *alqueire* (of Roi) = 1 Imperial bushel, or 40 litres; *oitava* = 55·34 grains.

ENERGY AND NATURAL RESOURCES

Electricity. Brazil's hydraulic potential capacity for electric power production is estimated at 104,450 mw., one of the largest in the world. Installed electric power in 1978 was 25,229 mw.; gross production, 112,575 gwh.; consumption, 97m. gwh. Of the total capital invested in industrial concerns (US$1,779,786,350), 49% was foreign-owned.

Oil. There are 13 oil refineries, of which 11 are state owned. Crude oil output was 8,160,667 tonnes in 1979, of which 33% was from the continental shelf. Promising results have been obtained with the exploration of that area which in 1974 represented only 9% of all the national oil production.

The country imported substantial amounts of oil in 1979: 50,158,455 tonnes (value US$1m: 6,721) representing 34% of total value of all Brazilian imports. Imports come mainly from Iraq and Saudi Arabia.

The government created the National Alcohol Program in 1975 with the aim of a gradual replacement of the consumption of petroleum by combustible alcohol specially from sugar-cane and cassava. About US$5,000m. will be invested by 1985. By May 1980, 281 sugar-cane alcohol distillery projects had been approved and their authorized capacity represents 61% of the national aim for 1985 (about 11m. cu. metres). An agreement between the automotive industry and the government was signed in Sept. 1979 and it is hoped that by 1982 about 900,000 vehicles utilizing 100% alcohol-combustive will be produced.

Minerals. Brazil is the only source of high-grade quartz crystal in commercial quantities; output, 1978, 95,720 tonnes; exports in 1979, 4,727 tonnes. It is an important source of industrial diamonds (exports, 1977, 215 grammes); the second largest western producer of chrome ore (reserves of 4m. tonnes; output, 1978, 957,778 tonnes); fifth in the output of mica (370 tonnes in 1977); third in zirconium, 4,301 tonnes in 1978; she is the largest producer of beryllium, output (1974) 43 tonnes; graphite (1978), 53,603 tonnes; titanium ore (1978), 20,077 tonnes, and magnesite (1978), 409,936 tonnes. Along the coasts of the states of Rio de Janeiro, Espírito Santo and Bahia are found monazite sands containing thorium; output, 1977, 2,441 tonnes; reserves are estimated at 100,000 tons. Manganese ores of high content are important (reserves in the Amapá region alone are estimated at 10m. tonnes); output, 1978, 2,744,392 tonnes. Output of tungsten ore, 1978, totalled 430,016 tonnes, unrough, 1,937 tonnes. Mine production of lead (1978), 273,931 tonnes. Asbestos production, 1978, 2,080,371 tonnes. Coal deposits exist in Rio Grande do Sul, Santa Catarina, Paraná and São Paulo. Total reserves are estimated at 5,000m. tonnes; output (1978), 11,816,259 tonnes.

Iron is found chiefly in Minas Gerais, notably the Cauê Peak at Itabira. The Government is now opening up what is believed to be one of the richest iron-ore deposits in the world, situated in Carajás, in the northern state of Pará, with estimated reserves of 18,000m. tonnes, representing the largest concentration of high-grade (66%) iron ore in the world. Total output of iron ore, 1978, mainly from the Cia. Vale do Rio Doce mine at Itabira, was 103,896,097 tonnes. The National Iron and Steel Co. at Volta Redonda, State of Rio de Janeiro, furnishes a substantial part of Brazil's steel. Brazil's total output, 1978: Pig-iron, 10,043,047 tonnes; ingots castings, 12,107,281 tonnes.

Production of aluminium was started in Minas Gerais in 1945; output of bauxite, 1978, 1,401,101 tonnes. Production of tin ore (cassiterite, processed) was 10,569 tonnes in 1978. Output of barytes (processed) in 1978, 238,257 tonnes; exports of barytes, 1979, was 43,520 tonnes. Cement output, 1979, was 23,683 tonnes. Output of phosphate rock (processed), 1977, was 650,486 tonnes.

Gold in large-scale mining is confined to a single mine in Minas Gerais; the production in 1978, was 9,459 kg. Silver output, 1978, 15,723 tonnes. Salt output (1977), 2,472,638 tonnes. Diamond districts are Diamantina Grão Mogol, Chapada Diamantina, Bagagem, Goiás and Mato Grosso; output in 1978 was 85,803 carats.

Agriculture. 44·07% of Brazil's population is rural, and 75% of her foreign exchange derives from agricultural exports. Production (in tonnes):

	1978	1979[1]		1978	1979[1]
Bananas			Cocoa	284,490	304,802
(1,000 bunches)	416,025	409,298	Coffee	2,535,323	2,589,343
Beans	2,193,977	2,186,960	Cotton, raw	1,570,177	1,635,601
Cassava	25,459,408	24,934,982	Jute	16,954	28,505
Castor beans	317,083	327,095	Maize	13,569,401	16,308,950
Oranges	7,826,336	9,881,543	Soya	9,540,577	9,958,606
Potatoes	2,013,882	2,148,959	Sugar-cane	129,144,950	138,325,014
Rice	7,296,142	7,589,282	Tobacco	405,191	422,891
Sisal	201,786	228,203	Wheat	2,690,888	2,923,522
Grapes	666,594	703,980			

[1] Preliminary.

The 4 states of São Paulo, Paraná, Espírito Santo and Minas Gerais are the principal districts for coffee-growing. Large plantations or fazendas with more than 100,000 trees are the rule. Output, 1975, from 2,216,921 hectares, 2,544,596 tonnes; exports (1979), 562,196 tonnes.

Export of cocoa was nationalized in May 1943, but in 1952 reverted to private enterprise. Bahia furnishes 95% of the output; in 1975 total output was 281,887 tonnes from 451,145 hectares; exports (1979), 156,932 tonnes. Two crops a year are grown. The US takes one-half of the crop. Castor-bean output usually exceeds 250,000 tonnes; output, 1975, 353,904 tonnes from 398,709 hectares.

Tobacco output was 356,999 tonnes in 1977. In 1978, 126,325 tonnes were exported.

Brazil now ranks second only to the US in production of oranges, output 1976, 7,334,042 tonnes; 1977, 7,164,351. Output of bananas (1,000 bunches), 1976, 381,763; 1977, 427,660. Output of cotton, raw, 1976, 904,841 tonnes; 1977, 1,462,571. Exports of cotton wool (raw), 1979, 308 tonnes; 1978, 44,515. Brazil formerly furnished only 10% of her own requirements in wheat (average output, 1934–38, 144,000 tonnes); output, 1976, 3,215,745 tonnes; 1977, 2,066,039; imports, 3,650,791 tonnes in 1979. Rice is important; output (rough rice), 1976, was 9,757,079 tonnes; 1977, 8,993,696.

Rubber is another natural product of the country, chiefly in the states of Acre, Amazonas and Pará. Output, 1979, 248,756 tonnes (natural and synthetic); peak reached in 1912 (when rubber realized US$3 a lb.) was 42,510 gross tons. Output of tyres in local factories has risen from 421,765 units (tyres and tubes) in 1940 to 57,147,392 in 1979. Brazilian consumption of rubber in 1979, was 301,400 tonnes. Brazil is the chief source of carnaúba wax, used for electric insulation and gramophone records, exporting 10,861,943 kg in 1979. Caroá fibre is grown as a substitute for Indian jute; production, 1977, 515 tonnes. Jute output, 1979, 28,505 tonnes. Plantations of tung trees established in 1930 (4m. trees in 1946) are beginning to yield tung oils in commercial quantities; output of tung, 1978, 8,863 tonnes.

Livestock (in 1,000): 1979, 90,000 cattle, 36,000 swine, 18,000 sheep, 7,400 goats, 6,000 horses, 1,750 asses and 1,700 mules. In 1979, 10m. cattle, 12·7m. swine, 1·8m. sheep and lambs, 2m. goats, 394·5m. (1978) poultry and rabbits were slaughtered for meat.

Fisheries. The fishing industry totalled a fleet of 154,695 vessels in 1968; the catch in 1977 was 752,607 tonnes.

In 1971 the sovereignty over territorial waters, including fishing rights, was extended to 200 miles.

INDUSTRY AND TRADE

Industry. The total number of persons engaged in industry (1974) was 3,396,769 and the value of production Cr$526,663·5m. Food products employed 412,080 producing (in Cr$1m.) 83,058·3; chemicals, 138,963 (77,247·9); metallurgy, 405,347 (74,611·9); transport equipment, 204,434 (46,827·4); textiles, 354,304 (41,038·7).

A paper-mill, reported to be the largest pulp-and-paper mill in South America, is at Monte Alegre, Paraná. Brazil's output of paper, 1978, was 2,534,407 tonnes.

Foreign investment is encouraged by special tax holidays for companies locating in certain regions.

Commerce. In 1957 Brazil modernized her 20-year-old tariff (at present duties are levied mainly on volume and not on values) in order to protect her infant industries and to increase government revenue. She ratified the Treaty of Montevideo on 3 Feb. 1961 (see LAIA).

Imports and exports for calendar years in Cr$1,000:

	1975	1976	1977	1978	1979
Imports	107,671,765	141,842,263	181,479,538	264,988,521	500,134,047
Exports	68,773,057	107,105,989	167,101,643	224,114,456	393,531,168

Converted into US$1m., these trade figures were:

	1975	1976	1977	1978	1979
Imports	13,592	13,726	13,257	15,054	19,804
Exports	8,670	10,128	12,130	12,659	...

Exports in 1979, 98m. tonnes; 1978, 87·5m. Imports in 1979, 75·3m. tonnes; 1978, 69·8m. tonnes.

Principal imports in 1979 were (in US$1m.): Crude petroleum, 6,720; machinery, 3,542; wheat, 630; fertilizers, 527; vehicles, 498; coal and anthracite, 319.

Principal exports in 1979 were (in US$1m.): Coffee (beans), 1,918; machinery, 1,315; soybeans (seeds and cakes), 1,257; vehicles, 1,094; cocoa beans, 487.

Of exports (in US$1m.) in 1979, USA took 2,941; Germany (Fed. Rep.), 1,115; Netherlands, 993; Japan, 887; Argentina, 718; UK, 708; Italy, 700; France, 598; Poland, 434. Of 1979 imports, USA furnished 3,629; Iraq, 2,824; Saudi Arabia, 1,947; Germany (Fed. Rep.), 1,485; Japan, 1,180; Argentina, 990; Iran, 884; France, 635; UK, 504.

Total trade between Brazil and UK (according to British Department of Trade returns, in £1,000 sterling):

	1975	1976	1977	1978	1979	1980
Imports to UK	174,883	239,491	300,576	282,574	400,378	269,340
Exports and re-exports from UK	160,890	174,286	245,405	221,423	286,481	218,159

Tourism. In 1978, 764,152 tourists visited Brazil, spending US$107·7m.

COMMUNICATIONS

Roads. There were (1978) 1,544,519 km of highways. In 1978 Brazil had 8,961,315 motor vehicles, including 4,792,344 passenger cars, 2,907,731 commercial vehicles, 873,025 lorries and tractors, 108,304 buses and minibuses. 1,173,813 motor vehicles of all types were produced in 1979.

Railways. Public railways are operated by two administrations, the Federal Railways (RFFSA) formed in 1957 and São Paulo Railways (FEPASA) formed in 1971, which is confined to the state of São Paulo. RFFSA had a route-length of 23,897 km in 1979 and FEPASA 5,107 km. Principal gauges are metre and 1,600 mm. The share of the freight market declined to a low of 15% in 1967, but subsequent heavy government investment in reconstruction and new lines, coupled with a policy of forcing bulk commodities on to rail, had raised the share to over 20% in 1974. Continued investment in new wagons, electrification, gauge-conversion, and 'export corridor' routes to the ports will further improve this figure, and some new lines are planned up to the year 2000. Except in the urban areas of

Rio de Janeiro and São Paulo, passenger traffic moving by rail is negligible. Traffic moved by RFFSA in 1979–80 amounted to 61m. tonnes. of freight and 246m. passengers. FEPASA also has a substantial investment programme underway.

There are several important independent freight railways, including the Vitoria à Minas (773 km and (1979) 39,882 ton-km of freight) and the Amapa (194 km). São Paulo has a rapid transit railway, and a similar system opened in Rio de Janeiro in 1979.

Aviation. There are 38 regular airlines (25 foreign) operating. The 4 largest Brazilian companies cover the whole territory and in 1978 they carried 10,201,000 passengers (8,771 in domestic traffic) and 1,789m. tonne-km of freight. Their commercial fleet consisted of 99 aircraft on 31 Dec. 1978. There are more than 100 taxiplane companies. The chief airline is Viação Aérea Rio Grande do Sul, (VARIG).

Shipping. Inland waterways, mostly rivers, are open to navigation over some 21,944 miles; number of vessels in 1978, 719. Rio de Janeiro and Santos are the 2 leading ports; there are 18 other large ports. Bolivia and Paraguay have been given free ports at Santos. During 1978, 34,589 vessels entered and cleared the Brazilian ports.

The Lloyd Brasileiro is owned and operated by the Government; its fleet comprised (1978), 44 vessels of 537,813 DWT. Brazilian shipping, 1978 (registered with Lloyds) amounted to 1,013 vessels of 6,175,915 DWT. Petrobrás, the government oil monopoly, took over the government tanker fleet of 26 vessels in 1958; total tanker fleet in 1978 was 165 vessels of 3,386,142 DWT.

Post and Broadcasting. Of the telegraph system of the country, about half, including all interstate lines, is under control of the Government. There were 4,323 post and telegraph offices in 1978. Telephone instruments in use, 1977, were 4,708,000. In 1976 there were 971 broadcasting and 74 television stations.

Cinemas (1977). Cinemas numbered 2,356 with a seating capacity of 1,505,620.

Newspapers (1977). There were 318 daily newspapers with a daily circulation of 1,321,000. Foreigners and corporations (except political parties) are not allowed to own or control newspapers or wireless stations. The press law of 1967 prohibits anonymous journalism and the publication of material defamatory to the armed forces and other public institutions.

JUSTICE, RELIGION, EDUCATION AND HEALTH

Justice. There is a supreme federal Court of Justice at Brasília. It has 11 judges; all are appointed by the President with the approval of the Senate. There are also federal courts in each state and the federal district and in the Territories, as well as 'electoral courts' to protect the elections, and labour tribunals. Justice is administered in the states in accordance with state law, by state courts, but in Brasília federal justice is administered. Judges are appointed for life. There are also 3,074 magistrates and 5,634 justices of the peace. In Dec. 1977 the Senate approved laws for allowing marriages to be dissolved. Brazilian citizens can apply for one divorce only during their lifetime. In the case of a marriage partner becoming mentally ill, divorce proceedings cannot begin until 5 years after the illness has been proved. The death penalty was re-introduced in Sept. 1969.

Religion. The population is overwhelmingly Roman Catholic (91% at the census, 1970). In 1889 connexion between Church and State was abolished; it was restored by the 1934 constitution, but again abolished in 1946.

In 1970 (census) Catholics numbered 85,472,022; Protestants, 4,814,728, and Spiritualists, 1,178,293.

Education. Elementary education is compulsory. In 1970 (census) there were 47,864,531 persons 5 years of age or over who could read and write; this was 60·33% of that age group; 50·9% of the literates were men.

There were, in 1977, 174,403 first degree school units, with 20,368,436 pupils and 893,138 teachers; 30,631 second degree units, with 2,437,701 pupils and 168,366 teachers; 4,072 third degree units, with 1,159,046 pupils and 95,758 teachers.

The Government undertakes to provide, in part, for higher or university instruction, but some institutions are maintained by the states, and some by private associations, while primary schools are chiefly maintained and supervised, either by the states or by the municipalities and private initiative. There were, in 1977, 62 official universities and 867 faculties not belonging to universities, including the University of Rio de Janeiro (founded on 7 Sept. 1920), the University of Bahia (founded in 1946), the University of Recife (1946), the University of Paraná (1946), the Rural University (1948, State of Rio de Janeiro), the University of São Paulo (1934), the University of Minas Garais (1927), the University of Rio Grande do Sul (1934), the University of Brasília (1960) and the University of Mato Grosso (1971). There are also 11 Catholic universities in Rio de Janeiro (1946), São Paulo (1946), Rio Grande do Sul (1948), Pernambuco (1951), Minas Gerais (1958), Bahia, Paraná, Campinas, Petrópolis and Pelotas. Students in 1976 totalled 1,096,727.

Health. In 1978 there were 15,369 health establishments of which 5,703 were for inpatients; total number of beds, 447,591 (352,785 in private institutions).

DIPLOMATIC REPRESENTATIVES

OF BRAZIL IN GREAT BRITAIN (32 Green St., London, W1Y 4AT)
Ambassador: Roberto de Oliveira Campos, GCVO (accredited 6 March 1975).

OF GREAT BRITAIN IN BRAZIL (Setor de Embaixadas Sul, Quadra 801, Conjunto K, Brasília, D.F.)
Ambassador: G. W. Harding.

OF BRAZIL IN THE USA (3006 Massachusetts Ave., NW, Washington, D.C., 20008)
Ambassador: Antonio Francisco Azeredo da Silveira.

OF THE USA IN BRAZIL (Ave das Noções, Lote 3, Brasília, D.F.)
Ambassador: Robert M. Sayre.

OF BRAZIL TO THE UNITED NATIONS
Ambassador: Sérgio Corrêa Da Costa

Books of Reference

Amazônia Mineração. *Projeto Carajás.* Belém
Anuário do Transporte Aéreo. Departamento de Aviação Civil. Rio de Janeiro, 1978
Anuário Estatístico do Brasil. Instituto Brasileiro de Geografia e Estatística, Rio de Janeiro
Anuário Estatístico das Ferrovias do Brasil. Vol. 4. Rede Ferroviária Federal. Rio de Janeiro, 1980
Anuário Estatístico dos Transportes. Vol. 9. Empresa Brasileira de Planejamento de Transportes. Brasília, 1979
Anuário Estatístico Embratur. Vol. 10. Empresa Brasileira de Turismo. Rio de Janeiro, 1979
Anuário Mineral Brasileiro. Departamento Nacional da Produção Mineral. Brasília, 1978
Atlas do Brasil. Instituto Brasileiro de Geografia. 2nd ed. Rio de Janeiro, 1959
Boletim do Banco Central do Brasil. Banco Central do Brasil. Brasília. Monthly
Bulletin of the British Chamber of Commerce in Brazil. Rio de Janeiro. Monthly
Sinopse Estatística do Brasil. Vol. 6. Instituto Brasileiro de Geografia e Estatística. Rio de Janeiro, 1979
Azevedo, Aroldo de. *Geografia do Brazil.* 2 vols. Rio de Janeiro, 1960
Banco do Brasil, *Boletim Trimestral.* Brasília, D.F. From 1966
Burns, E. B., *A History of Brazil.* New York, 1971
Calogeras, João Pandiá, *A History of Brazil.* Chapel Hill, North Carolina, 1939
Camacho, J. A., *Brazil.* R. Inst. of Int. Affairs. 2nd ed. 1954
Campbell, G., *Brazil Struggles for Development.* London, 1973
Castro, J. de, *Géographie de la faim.* Paris, 1949
Cowell, A., *The Tribe that Hides from Man.* London, 1973
Delgado de Carvalho, C. M., *Historia Diplomatica do Brazil.* Rio de Janeiro, 1961
Dickenson, J. P., *Brazil.* Folkestone, 1978
Fiechter, G.-A., *Brazil Since 1964: Modernisation Under a Military Regime.* London, 1975

Furtado, C., *The Economic Growth of Brazil*. Univ. of California Press and CUP, 1963

Garnero, Mario. *Energia: O Futuro é Hoje*. São Paulo, 1980

Hanbury-Tenison, R., *A Question of Survival for the Indians of Brazil*. London, 1973

Moraes, R. Borba de. *Bibliographia Brasiliana (1504–1900)*. 2 vols. 1958

Pierson, D., *Negroes in Brazil*. Chicago, 1942.—*Survey of Literature on Brazil of Sociological Significance*. Cambridge, Mass., 1945

Raine, P. *Brazil: Awakening Giant*. Washington, 1974

Ramos, A., *The Negro in Brazil*. Washington, 1939.—*Las Poblaciones del Brazil*. Mexico City, 1945

Roiter, F., *Brazil*. London, 1971

Saunders, J., *Modern Brazil: New Patterns and Developments*. Univ. of Florida Press, 1971

Schuh, G. E., and Alves, E. R., *The Agricultural Development of Brazil*. New York, 1970

Skidmore, T. E., *Politics in Brazil, 1930–1964*. OUP, 1967.—*Black Into White: Race and Nationality in Brazilian Thought*. OUP, 1975

Smith, P. B., *Oil and Politics in Modern Brazil*. Toronto, 1975

Smith, T. Lynn, *Brazil; People and Institutions*. Rev. ed. Baton Rouge, 1954.—(Ed.) *Brasil: Portrait of Half a Continent*. Gainesville, Fla., 1951.—*Brazilian Society*. Univ. of New Mexico Press, 1975

Wellington, R. A., *The Brazilians*. Newton Abbot, 1974

National Library: Biblioteca Nacional Avenida Rio Branco 219–39, Rio de Janeiro, G.B. *Director:* Dr Plínio Doyle Silva.

BRUNEI

Capital: Bandar Seri Begawan
Population: 212,840 (1980)
GNP per capita: US$10,640 (1978)

HISTORY. The Sultanate of Brunei was a powerful state in the early 16th century, with authority over the whole of the island of Borneo and some parts of the Sulu Islands and the Philippines. At the end of the 16th century its power had begun to decline and various cessions were made to Great Britain, the Rajah of Sarawak and the British North Borneo Company in the 19th century to combat piracy and anarchy. By the middle of the 19th century the State had been reduced to its present limits.

In 1847 the Sultan of Brunei entered into a treaty with Great Britain for the furtherance of commercial relations and the suppression of piracy, and in 1888, by a further treaty, the State was placed under the protection of Great Britain. Brunei was the only former British dependency inhabited by a Malay people that did not join the Federation of Malaysia in 1963.

AREA AND POPULATION. Brunei, on the north-west coast of Borneo, is bounded on all sides by Sarawak territory, which splits the State into two separate parts. Area, about 2,226 sq. miles (5,800 sq. km), with a coastline of about 100 miles. Estimated population in 1980 was 212,840. The 4 districts are Brunei/ Muara (114,410), Seria/Kuala Belait (70,520), Tutong (20,350), Temburong (7,560). The population comprised Malays (113,590), Chinese (50,310), other indigenous (23,930) and others (13,430). The capital is Bandar Seri Begawan, 9 miles from the mouth of Brunei River. The climate is of tropical marine type, hot and moist, with cool nights.

CONSTITUTION AND GOVERNMENT. On 29 Sept. 1959 the Sultan promulgated a constitution. There is a Privy Council, an Executive and a Legislative Council. On 6 Jan. 1965 the constitution was amended to provide for general elections to the Legislative Council; at the same time the Executive Council was renamed Council of Ministers. The Legislative Council consists of 20 members and a Speaker appointed by the Sultan. The Council of Ministers is presided over by the Sultan and consists of 6 *ex-officio* members and 4 other members, all of whom except one are members of the Legislative Council. The Mentri Besar, who is one of the *ex-officio* members of the Legislative Council and the Council of Ministers, is responsible to the Sultan for the exercise of executive authority in the State. As a result of negotiations in June 1978, the Sultan and the British Government signed a new treaty on 7 Jan. 1979 under which Brunei will become a fully sovereign and independent State at the end of 1983.

The official language is Malay, but English may be used for all official purposes.

Sultan of Brunei: Sultan and Yang di-Pertuan Sir Muda Hassanal Bolkiah Mu'izzaddin Waddaulah ibni Kebawah Duli Yang Teramat Mulia Paduka Seri Begawan Sultan Sir Muda Omar Ali Saifuddin Sa'adul Khairi Waddin, DK, PSSUB, DPKG, DPKT, PSPNB, PSNB, PSLJ, SPMB, PANB, GCMG, DK (Kelantan), DK (Johore). The Sultan was crowned on 1 Aug. 1968.

General Adviser to HH The Sultan: The Most Honourable, Pehin Orang Kaya Laila Setia Bakti Di-Raja Dato Laila Utama Haji Isa bin Pehin Datu Perdana Mentri Dato Laila Utama Haji Ibrahim, DK, SPMB, DSNB, CVO, OBE, PHBS, PJK.

Flag: Yellow, with 2 diagonal strips of white over black with the national arms in red placed over all in the centre.

DEFENCE

Army. The Royal Brunei Malay Regiment, whose strength as at 31 Dec. 1975 was approximately 200 officers and 2,750 other ranks is expanding and being provided with modern sophisticated weapons and equipment. A second battalion was formed in May 1975. All members of the regiment are now armed with the modern automatic rifles M16, while the 7·62 SLR are held in reserve and form the main equipment of the 7 platoons of the Brunei Cadet Corps from the 7 colleges in Brunei. A battalion of the British Brigade of Gurkhas is stationed in Brunei and financed by the Sultan. Strength of army (1980), 2,400.

Navy. The First Flotilla of the Royal Brunei Malay Regiment comprises 3 new fast missile-armed attack craft of 150 tons (built by Vosper-Thornycroft (Singapore) in 1978–79), 3 coastal patrol boats (built by Vosper-Thornycroft (Singapore)), 3 riverine patrol launches, 2 landing craft and 3 small patrol boats. Special Boat Squadron operates 32 fast assault boats. Personnel in 1981 numbered 333 (33 officers and 300 ratings) in the First Flotilla (for offshore work) plus 100 (5 officers and 95 men) in the Special Boat Squadron (for riverine affairs), all under a Commander, Royal Navy.

Two coastal patrol craft of 60 tons built by Vosper, Singapore, were supplied for the Brunei Police.

Air Wing. The Air Wing of the Royal Brunei Malay Regiment was formed in 1965 with 3 helicopters for communications and casualty evacuation duties. Current equipment includes up to 6 MBB BO 105, 3 Bell 205A Iroquois, 3 Bell 206B Jet-Ranger and 7 Bell 212 helicopters, a twin-turboprop HS 748 transport used also for VIP passenger and search and rescue duties, and 2 Cherokee piston-engined trainers. On order are 7 Sikorsky S-76 transport helicopters. In 1981 there were about 100 personnel.

Police. Establishment provides over 1,750 officers and men (1980). In addition, there is a small auxiliary force mostly employed on static guard duties.

ECONOMY

Planning. A fourth Five-Year National Development Plan was announced in 1979 to further improve the economic, social and cultural life of the people.

Budget. In mid-1979 the actual revenue was B$1,882m. and expenditure was B$1,048m. The main sources of revenue in 1979 were: Taxes, B$1,350m.; royalties, B$282m.; interest on investments, B$250m. The main heads of expenditure in 1979 were: Defence, B$372m.; education, B$92m.; public works, B$83m.; medical, B$40m.; police, B$39m.; other current expenditure, B$297m.; transfer to development fund, B$100m.

Currency. The currency is the *Brunei dollar* with a par value of 0·290 299 gramme of gold.

ENERGY AND NATURAL RESOURCES

Oil. The Seria oilfield, discovered in 1929, has passed its peak production. The high level of crude oil production is maintained through the increase of offshore oilfields production, which exceeds onshore oilfields production. Production is about 240,000 bbls a day. The crude oil is exported directly, and only a small amount is refined at Seria for domestic uses. Natural gas is also produced at one of the biggest liquefied natural gas plants of its kind in the world.

Forestry. Most of the interior is under forest, containing large potential supplies of serviceable timber.

INDUSTRY AND TRADE

Industry. Brunei depends primarily on its oil industry, which employs more than 7% of the entire working population. Crude oil accounts for 62% of the total value of the exports and re-exports. The second main export is liquefied natural gas, which contributes 32% and petroleum products 4%.

Other minor products are rubber, pepper, sawn timber and animal hides. Local industries include boat-building, cloth weaving and the manufacture of brass- and silverware.

Commerce. In 1979 imports totalled B$862m.; exports, B$5,796m.

Total trade between Brunei and UK (British Department of Trade returns, in £1,000 sterling):

	1975	1976	1977	1978	1979	1980
Imports to UK	618	343	454	408	419	889
Exports and re-exports from UK	9,642	14,640	17,429	16,265	22,763	23,118

COMMUNICATIONS

Roads. The State has about 828 miles of road, of which 438 miles are bituminous surfaced. The main road connects Bandar Seri Begawan with Kuala Belait and Seria. Considerable work is being undertaken for development of secondary roads. The number of motor vehicles (1978) was 43,844.

Aviation. Royal Brunei Airlines (RBA) and Singapore Airlines provide daily services linking Brunei and Singapore. RBA also operates services to Bangkok, Manila and Hong Kong. Cathay Pacific Airways also operates to Brunei and on to Western Australia from Hong Kong. British Airways provides a weekly service between Brunei and UK.

Shipping. Regular shipping services operate from Singapore, Hong Kong, and from ports in Sarawak and Sabah to Bandar Seri Begawan. The Government of Brunei operates a passenger ferry service between Bandar Seri Begawan and Labuan, Sabah, 6 days a week.

Post and Broadcasting. There were 7 post offices (1975) and a telephone network (12,388 telephones in 1978) linking the main centres. Radio Brunei is operated by the Department of Radio and Television and operates on medium- and short-waves in Malay, Iban, Dusun, English and Chinese. Number of radio receivers, 38,000 and television sets, 32,000.

A satellite communications earth station primarily to improve long-distance external communication was commissioned in Sept. 1979.

RELIGION AND EDUCATION

Religion. The official religion is Islam.

Education (1977). Free education in the Malay language is provided in government primary schools (33,053 pupils) and 5 government secondary Malay schools (1,543 pupils). Free education in English was provided in 25 government preparatory schools (8,139 pupils) and 7 government secondary schools (7,824 pupils). Teacher-training was provided in 2 government teachers' colleges, in both Malay and English for 527 students. Eight unassisted Mission schools provided education in English at kindergarten, primary and secondary level for a total of 6,074 pupils; 8 unassisted Chinese schools provided education in Chinese at the same levels for a total of 5,608 pupils. One private kindergarten and primary school, administered by the Brunei Shell Petroleum Co., provided education in either English or Dutch for a total of 986 pupils, and there was also 1 private vocational school administered by the Brunei Shell Petroleum Co. (140 artisan-trainees). Two government vocational schools provided full training courses to 274 students in the engineering and building trades.

Recurrent expenditure on education in 1979 was B$93m.

DIPLOMATIC REPRESENTATIVE

OF GREAT BRITAIN IN BRUNEI (Jalan Residency, Bandar Seri Begawan)

High Commissioner: A. C. Watson, CMG.

BULGARIA

Capital: Sofia
Population: 8·88m. (1980)
GNP per capita: US$3,200 (1978)

Narodna Republika Bulgaria

HISTORY. The Bulgarian state was founded in 681, but fell under Turkish rule in 1396. By the Treaty of Berlin, which followed the Russo-Turkish war of 1878, the Principality of Bulgaria and the Autonomous Province of Eastern Rumelia, both under Turkish suzerainty, were constituted. In 1885 Rumelia was reunited with Bulgaria. On 5 Oct. 1908 Bulgaria declared her independence of Turkey. *Rulers:* Prince Alexander I of Battenberg, 1879–86; Prince (after 1908, Tsar) Ferdinand, 1887–1918 (abdicated); Tsar Boris III, 1918–43; Tsar Simeon II, lost his throne as a result of a referendum held on 8 Sept. 1946 (3,801,160 votes for a republic, 197,176 for the monarchy, 119,168 invalid).

In 1941 Bulgaria signed the Three Power Pact and the Anti-Comintern Pact. In 1944 Bulgaria asked the UK and the USA for an armistice. The USSR declared war on Bulgaria on 5 Sept. 1944. The Fatherland Front government (established 9 Sept.) asked the USSR for an armistice, which was signed on 28 Oct. 1944 by the USSR, the UK and the USA. The peace treaty was signed in Paris on 10 Feb. 1947.

AREA AND POPULATION. On 8 Sept. 1940 by the treaty of Craiova, Romania ceded to Bulgaria the Southern Dobrudja, fixing the new frontier on the 1912 line.

In April 1941 Bulgaria occupied the Yugoslav part of Macedonia, and the Greek districts of Western Thrace, Eastern Macedonia, Florina and Castoria. The peace treaty of 1947 restored the frontiers as on 1 Jan. 1941.

The area of Bulgaria is 110,911·5 sq. km (42,823 sq. miles) and is bounded in the north by Romania, east by the Black Sea, south by Turkey and Greece and west by Yugoslavia.

The country is divided into 28 provinces (*okrŭg*, plur. *okrŭzi*). Area and population in 1978:

Province	Area (sq. km)	Pop. 1,000	Province	Area (sq. km)	Pop. 1,000	Province	Area (sq. km)	Pop. 1,000
Blagoevgrad	6,464	330	Pleven	4,184	365	Sofia (City)	1,038	1,109
Burgas	7,605	428	Plovdiv	5,591	734	Stara Zagora	4,902	399
Gabrovo	2,068	178	Razgrad	2,646	197	Tolbukhin	4,689	252
Khaskovo	4,029	295	Ruse	2,624	295	Tŭrgovishte	2,754	175
Kŭrdzhali	4,020	282	Shumen	3,374	252	Varna	3,820	452
Kyustendil	3,002	199	Silistra	2,876	175	Veliko Tŭrnovo	4,690	349
Lovech	4,129	215	Sliven	3,729	236	Vidin	3,110	174
Mikhailovgrad	3,585	235	Smolyan	3,518	169	Vratsa	4,186	302
Pazardzhik	4,379	317	Sofia	7,385	317	Yambol	4,162	207
Pernik	2,355	175						

The population at the census of 2 Dec. 1975 was 8,727,771 (males, 4,357,820; urban, 5,061,087). Population on 31 Dec. 1980 was 8·88m. (4·4m. males; 5·5m. urban). Population density 79·5 per sq. km.

Ethnic minorities are estimated to total 1·2m. The language estimates are: Bulgarian 88%, Turkish 8·6%. The remainder include Gipsies, Jews, Romanians and Armenians. Some Turks have been repatriated.

Population of principal towns (1978): Sofia, 1,031,597; Plovdiv, 332,899; Varna, 278,827; Ruse, 168,701; Burgas, 163,649; Stara Zagora, 130,768; Pleven, 118,426; Sliven, 94,803; Gabrovo, 77,742; Pernik, 90,841; Tolbukhin, 92,716; Shumen, 90,579; Yambol, 80,232; Khaskovo, 81,184; Pazardzhik, 70,740.

Vital statistics, 1980: Live births, 126,577; deaths, 95,000; marriages, 68,592; divorces, 12,756; crude birth rate, 15·5 per 1,000 population; crude death rate, 10·5; infant mortality, 22·2 per 1,000; growth rate, 5.

Expectation of life in 1980 was 71 years.

CONSTITUTION AND GOVERNMENT. A People's Republic was proclaimed by the National Assembly on 15 Sept. 1946, and the existing 'Tŭrnovo' Constitution of 1879 was replaced by the 'Dimitrov' Constitution in 1947. This was in turn replaced by a new constitution on 18 May 1971. This provides for a single-chamber National Assembly (*Narodno Sŭbranie*). The highest permanently operating organ of the state is the Council of State which consists of a chairman, 2 first vice-chairmen, 4 vice-chairmen, a secretary and 17 members; it is elected by the National Assembly from its members. Supreme power is vested in the National Assembly, which consists of 400 deputies elected from areas of equal population by direct, secret and universal suffrage (everybody at age of 18 being eligible to vote and hold office) for a term of 5 years; it is to meet at least three times every year. The National Assembly also elects the Council of State and the ministers who are responsible to it.

A general election was held on 27 Oct. 1946. The Fatherland Front, composed of the Workers (Communist), Agrarian, Socialist and Zveno Parties, and non-party independents, obtained 364 seats (277 of which went to the Communists) and the opposition 101. On 26 Aug. 1947 the oppositional Agrarian Union was dissolved; its leader, Nikola Petkov, was sentenced to death and hanged on 23 Sept. The Socialist Party was merged with the Workers' Party in Aug. 1948, and the Zveno Party dissolved itself.

The Fatherland Front became, in 1948, a unified mass organization with individual memberships. Inside the Fatherland Front, there remain two political parties, the Bulgarian Communist Party and the Bulgarian People's Agrarian Union. Petŭr Tanchev (*1st Vice-Chairman, Council of State*) is Secretary of the Agrarian Union and Pencho Kubadinski Chairman of the Fatherland Front's National Council.

In 1976 the membership of the Communist Party was 788,221 (41% workers, 23% peasants); Young Communist League, 1·3m.; Agrarian Union, 120,000; Fatherland Front, 3,770,080.

At the elections of 30 June 1976, 99·99% of the electorate voted, and 99·92% of the votes were cast for the 400 candidates (78 women) of the Fatherland Front; there were no other candidates. The list comprised 272 Communists, 100 Agrarians and 28 independents. The President of the National Assembly is Vladimir Bonev.

There is no constitutional single Head of State, but Todor Zhivkov (*Chairman of the Council of State, 1st Secretary of the Communist Party*), performs some of the functions of a Head of State.

The highest policy-making and executive body of the Bulgarian Communist Party is its Politburo, consisting of 12 full members and 4 candidate members. The Politburo is elected by and from the Central Committee.

The Politburo was in March 1981 composed as follows: FULL MEMBERS: Todor Zhivkov, Gen. Ivan Mihailov, Stanko Todorov (*Chairman, Council of Ministers, i.e., Prime Minister*), Pencho Kubadinski (*Deputy Chairman, Council of Ministers*), Tano Tsolov (*1st Deputy Chairman, Council of Ministers*), Tsola Dragoicheva, Grisha Filipov (*Secretary, Central Committee*), Aleksandŭr Lilov (*Secretary, Central Committee*); Gen. Dobri Dzhurov (*Defence Minister*), Petŭr Mladenov (*Foreign Minister*), Ognian Doinov. CANDIDATE MEMBERS: Krustiŭ Trichkov (*1st Deputy Chairman, Council of Ministers, Chairman, Committee of State Control*), Peko Takov (*Deputy Chairman, Council of State*), Todor Stoichev, Drazha Vŭlcheva (*Deputy Chairman, Council of Ministers*).

Ministers not in the Politburo include: Kiril Zarev (*Deputy Chairman, Council of Ministers, Chairman, State Planning Committee*), Khristo Khristov (*Foreign Trade*), Dimitŭr Stoyanov (*Internal Affairs*), Belcho Belchev (*Finance*).

In May 1967 a second 20-year treaty of friendship, co-operation and mutual assistance with the Soviet Union was signed.

National flag: Three horizontal stripes of white, green, red, with the national emblem in the canton.

National anthem: An arrangement of Mila Rodino (Dear Fatherland), a popular patriotic song, was declared the national anthem in 1964.

Local Government. People's Councils at province and commune level are elected for terms of 30 months, to deal with all economic, social and cultural problems of their area. They also supervise the management of state and publicly owned enterprises. The Council's executive organs are Permanent Committees. 57,188 councillors and mayors were elected on 25 March 1979.

DEFENCE. There is a compulsory service of 2 years in the Army and Air Force (3 years in the Navy).

Army. In 1980 the Army had a strength of 105,000 men, organized in 8 motorized divisions and 5 tank brigades. There are 3 Army Commands (Military Regions), Sofia, Plovdiv, Sliven. Tanks, mainly T-34s and some T-54s and T-55s, numbered 1,900. Security police numbered 27,000 (5 brigades of border guards, 8 regiments of security forces).

Navy. The Navy consists of 2 *ex*-Soviet 'R' class submarines, 2 *ex*-Soviet 'Riga' class frigates, 3 *ex*-Soviet 'Poti' class corvettes, 4 *ex*-Soviet 'Osa' class missile boats, 6 *ex*-Soviet patrol vessels, 10 *ex*-Soviet torpedo boats, 2 fleet minesweepers, 4 coastal minesweepers, 12 minesweeping boats, 30 landing craft, 3 oilers, 3 survey ships, 2 salvage craft, 8 tugs and 30 auxiliaries and service craft. Personnel, 1981, was 10,000 officers and ratings.

Air Force. The large tactical Air Force has about 200 Soviet-built combat aircraft and 34,000 personnel. There are 4 squadrons of MiG-21s; about 6 squadrons of fighter/ground attack MiG-23s and MiG-17s; 2 reconnaissance squadrons of MiG-17s; some Mi-24 helicopter gunships; a total of about 20 Tu-134, Il-18, Il-14 and An-24/26 transport aircraft; 40 Mi-4, 30 Mi-2 and a few Mi-6 and Mi-8 helicopters; and L-29 Delfin, MiG-15UTI and MiG-21UTI trainers. Soviet-built 'Guideline', 'Goa' and 'Gainful' surface-to-air missiles have also been supplied to Bulgaria.

INTERNATIONAL RELATIONS

Membership. Bulgaria is a member of UN, Comecon and the Warsaw Pact.

External Debt. Agreements of 1955 and 1963 settled outstanding financial claims by the UK and USA respectively.

ECONOMY

Planning. State economic planning started in 1947. After 1964 there was a limited decentralization in planning, culminating in the economic reform of 1 Jan. 1969. Some local planning, profitability and consumer demand have been admitted, although central price regulation has been retained. The economy has been reconstructed into large trusts for each industry, each responsible for its own foreign trade.

For the first six 5-year plans *see* THE STATESMAN'S YEAR-BOOK for 1980–81. The seventh 5-year plan (1976–80) envisaged a rise in national income of 9%, and in industrial production of 55%. The eighth 5-year plan is running from 1981 to 1985.

There are also 2-year plans and a long-term perspective plan up to 1990.

Prices of consumer goods rose by 25–30% in 1979.

Budget. The revenue and expenditure of Bulgaria for calendar years were as follows (in 1m. leva):

	1971	1972	1973	1974	1975	1976	1977	1980	1981[1]
Revenue	6,184	6,355	7,055	8,060	9,321	8,778	9,498	13,187	15,385
Expenditure	6,063	6,261	7,036	8,044	9,223	8,758	9,477	13,167	15,370

[1] Estimate.

Of the 1980 revenue 91% leva came from national economy. 1980 expenditure was: National economy, 5,777m. leva; social and education, 5,265m.; administration, 291m.

Currency. The unit of currency is the *lev* (pl. *leva*) divided into 100 *stotinki* (sing. *stotinka*). It has been linked to the Soviet rouble since May 1952. A new *lev*, equalling 10 old leva, was introduced on 1 Jan. 1962. The parity (clearing value) is 1 rouble = 1·30 leva. Official rate of exchange (March 1981) was £1 = 2·13 leva;

US$1 = 0·879 leva. Rate of exchange for non-commercial transactions: £1 = 2·40 leva; US$1 = 1·65 leva.

Banking. In 1947 banks were nationalized and the National Bank gained autonomy, freeing it from responsibility for state debts. In 1969 the banking system was reorganized. The National Bank became the central bank and was made responsible for issuing currency. It also plays an important part in the management of the economy: its chairman has ministerial rank. There is also a Foreign Trade Bank and a State Savings Bank. In 1978, 8·3m. depositors had savings totalling 7,130m. leva. The State Savings Bank has advanced personal loans up to 500 leva at 3·5% interest to some 500,000 users. Interest on deposits is from 1% to 3%.

Weights and Measures. The metric system is in general use. On 1 April 1916 the Gregorian calendar came into force in Bulgaria.

ENERGY AND NATURAL RESOURCES

Energy. Bulgaria has little oil, gas or high-grade coal and energy policy is based on the exploitation of its low-grade coal and limited water resources. Local fuels account for 32% of the power balance and water resources for 10%. The first nuclear power plant went into action in 1974 and nuclear power accounts for 20% of electric power generation. Geothermal and solar energy sources are being developed.

Electricity. A joint Romanian–Bulgarian hydroelectric station is being built on the Danube at Turnu-Magurele-Nikopol.

Oil and Natural Gas. Oil is extracted in the Balchik district on the Black Sea, in an area 100 km north of Varna and at Dolni Dubnik near Pleven. Crude oil production was 129,000 tonnes in 1977. There are refineries at Burgas (annual capacity 5m. tonnes) and Dolni Dubnik (7m. tonnes). 32m. cu. metres of natural gas were produced in 1978.

Minerals. Ore production 1978: Manganese, 11,500 tonnes; iron, 762,000 tonnes. 27·1m. tonnes of coal including 19·7m. tonnes of lignite were mined in 1978. 87 tonnes of salt were extracted in 1978.

Agriculture. In 1979 the National Agro-Industrial Union was formed, replacing the Ministry of Agriculture. It comprises state and collective organizations, and is responsible for agriculture, the food industry and agricultural machine building. In 1978 cultivated agricultural land covered 6,214,900 hectares, of which 4,733,200 hectares are arable.

Size of private plots (maximum, 1 hectare) is based on the number of members of a household. Total area of private plots in 1978 was 601,100 hectares. In 1978 these accounted for 23% of all agricultural production. There were, in 1978, 47 co-operative farms and 34 state farms. There were 54 machine-tractor stations. 151,951 tractors (in 15-h.p. units) were in use and 23,055 combine harvesters. Collective and state farms are being incorporated into 'agricultural-industrial complexes'. There were 170 of these in 1978 with 7,738,406 hectares.

In 1978, 26 irrigation systems and 139 dams irrigated 1,168,400 hectares.

Yield in 1978 (in 1,000 tonnes): Wheat, 3,466; rye, 18; maize 2,236; barley, 1,488; oats, 76; rice, 61; sunflower seed, 369; unginned cotton, 16; tobacco, 136; tomatoes, 900; potatoes 391; grapes, 1,100. Bulgaria is the world's principal supplier of attar of roses; annual production, 1,200 kg.

Other products (in 1,000 tonnes) in 1978: Meat, 1,042; wool, 34; sugar, 360; 2,221m. eggs were produced and 1,943m. litres of milk.

Livestock (1979): 123,719 horses, 1,762,509 cattle, including 684,849 milch cows, 10,104,847 sheep, 3,772,270 pigs, 40,294,503 poultry and 652,746 beehives.

Forestry. The forest area, 1978, was 3,833,000 hectares, of which 1,206,000 were coniferous. 58,593 hectares were afforested in 1978. 8·7m. cu. metres of timber were cut in 1978.

Fisheries. The catch of sea fish was 160,400 tonnes in 1976.

INDUSTRY AND TRADE

Industry. All industry was nationalized in 1947.

Industrial production	1973	1974	1975	1976	1977	1978
Electricity (1m. kwh.)	21,952	22,800	25,232	27,742	29,707	31,486
Crude steel (1,000 tonnes)	2,246	2,188	2,265	2,460	2,589	2,470
Pig-iron (1,000 tonnes)	1,610	1,528	1,560	1,612	1,664	1,538
Cement (1,000 tonnes)	4,178	4,298	4,358	4,362	4,665	5,149
Sulphuric acid (1,000 tonnes)	561	761	853	857	860	974

In 1978 there were also produced (in 1,000 tonnes): Coke, 1,441; rolled steel, 3,050; artificial fertilizers, 1,662; calcinated soda, 1,294; cotton fabrics, 355m. sq. metres; silk fabrics, 32m. metres.

Labour. Trade unions had 3,323,600 members in 1976. There is 42½-hour 5-day working week. The average wage (excluding peasantry) was 200 leva per month in 1980. Retiring age is 60 for men and 55 for women. The labour force (excluding peasantry) in 1978 was 3,895,642 (1,955,273 female), of whom 1,336,416 worked in industry, 338,827 in building and 896,553 in agriculture and forestry.

Commerce. Foreign trade is controlled by the Ministry of Foreign Trade. Bulgarian trade has developed as follows (in 1m. leva):

	1973	1974	1975	1976	1977	1978
Imports	3,171·7	4,154	5,155	5,436	6,022	6,650
Exports	3,200·7	3,723	4,467	5,200	6,061	6,801

Structure of imports and exports in 1978: Producers' goods, 87%, 69%; consumer goods, 13%, 31%; industrial products, 98%, 73%; agricultural products, 2%, 27%.

Main exports are food products, tobacco, non-ferrous metals, cast iron, leather articles, textiles and (to Communist countries) machinery; main imports are machinery, oil, natural gas, steel, cellulose and timber.

80% of Bulgaria's trade is with the Communist countries (57% with USSR). Agreements with USSR envisage the co-ordination of the Soviet and Bulgarian 5-year plans in the spirit of 'socialist internationalism'. In 1979 a 10-year plan of economic specialization and co-operation was signed with the USSR. Libya is Bulgaria's biggest non-Communist export market, Federal Republic of Germany her major non-Communist supplier.

Trade deficit with the West was some US$3,237m. in 1979.

Total trade between Bulgaria and UK (British Department of Trade returns, in £1,000 sterling):

	1976	1977	1978	1979	1980
Imports to UK	11,210	11,863	15,096	12,082	14,425
Exports and re-exports from UK	23,048	24,961	26,636	27,324	35,242

Joint Western–Bulgarian industrial ventures are permitted under laws of June 1974 and Mar. 1980. In 1979 there were 40 in operation. Western share participation may exceed 50%.

The first Anglo-Bulgarian long-term trade agreement was signed in 1970. The Anglo-Bulgarian Joint Commission held its first meeting in March 1973. On 13 May 1974 Bulgaria and the UK signed a 10-year economic, scientific and technological co-operation agreement.

COMMUNICATIONS

Roads. In 1978 there were 31,949 km of roads, including 80 km of motorways and 2,389 km of main roads. 834m. tonnes of freight and 1,774m. passengers were carried.

Railways. In 1978 Bulgaria had 4,096 km of standard gauge railway, including 1,554 km electrified. 99m. passengers and 75m. tons of freight were carried in 1978.

Aviation. BALKAN (Bulgarian Airlines) operates internal flights from Sofia (airport: Vrazhdebna) to Burgas, Khaskovo, Pleven, Plovdiv, Ruse, Silistra, Stara Zagora, Tŭrgovishte, Veliko Tŭrnovo, Varna, Vidin and Yambol and international flights to Algiers, Amsterdam, Athens, Baghdad, Bratislava, Belgrade, Benghazi, Berlin, Brussels, Bucharest, Budapest, Cairo, Casablanca, Copenhagen, Damascus, Dresden, Frankfurt, Istanbul, London, Madrid, Moscow, Nicosia, Paris, Prague, Rome,

Stockholm, Syktyvkar, Tunis, Vienna, Warsaw and Zürich. There are also flights from Burgas to Leningrad and Kiev, and from Varna to Leningrad, Kuwait, Athens and Stockholm. In 1972 BALKAN had 234 planes and in 1978 it carried 1·8m. passengers and 21,402 tonnes of freight. British Airways opened a service from London to Sofia in 1970.

Shipping. Ports, shipping and shipbuilding are controlled by the Bulgarian United Shipping and Shipbuilding Corporation. The mercantile marine in 1972 possessed 33 passenger vessels and 110 cargo vessels and tankers with a total loading capacity of 875,380 DWT. Burgas is a fishing and oil-port open to tankers of 20,000 tons. Varna is the other important port. In Nov. 1978 a rail ferry, with an initial capacity of 4·5m. tonnes of freight a year, was opened between Varna and Ilitchovsk (USSR). In 1978, 615,000 passengers and 24·4m. tonnes of cargo were carried.

Post and Broadcasting. In 1978 there were 2,798 post offices, 1,032,106 telephones, 48 broadcasting stations and 20 television stations. Radio Sofia, the government broadcasting station, transmits 2 programmes on medium- and short-waves. There is also a special tourist service, broadcast *via* the Varna II transmitter on 1,124 kHz. Advertisements are broadcast for half an hour a day. Bulgaria participates in the East European TV link 'Intervision'. Colour programmes by SECAM system. Radio receiving sets licensed in 1978, 2,208,839; television, 1,618,189.

Cinemas and Theatres (1978). There were 36 theatres, 12 puppet theatres, 7 opera houses, 1 operetta house and 3,529 cinemas. 470 films were made (30 full-length).

Newspapers and Books. In 1978 there were 14 dailies with a circulation of 2·1m. The Party newspaper is *Rabotnicheskoto Delo* ('The Workers' Cause') with a circulation of 850,000 in 1977. 4,234 book titles were published in 1978.

JUSTICE, RELIGION, EDUCATION AND WELFARE

Justice. The Constitution of 1971 provides for the election (and recall) of the judges by the people and, for the Supreme Court, by the National Assembly. The lower courts include lay assessors as well as professional judges. There are a Supreme Court, 28 provincial courts (including Sofia), 105 regional courts and 'Comrades' Courts' for minor offences.

New Family and Penal Codes were approved by the National Assembly in April 1968. The maximum term of imprisonment is now 20 years except for 'exceptionally dangerous crimes' which carry the death penalty.

The Prosecutor General, elected by the National Assembly for 5 years and subordinate to it alone, exercises supreme control over the correct observance of the law by all government bodies, officials and citizens. He appoints and discharges all Prosecutors of every grade. The powers of this office were extended and redefined by a law of 1980 to put a greater emphasis on crime prevention and the rights of citizens.

Religion. 'The traditional church of the Bulgarian people' (as it is officially described), is that of the Eastern Orthodox Church. It was disestablished under the 1947 Constitution. On 10 May 1953 the Bulgarian Patriarchate was revived and Metropolitan Kiril was elected the first Bulgarian Patriarch since 1393. Upon the death of Kiril Metropolitan Maksim of Lovech was enthroned as the new Patriarch in July 1971. The seat of the Patriarch is at Sofia. There are 11 dioceses, each under a Metropolitan, 10 bishops, 2,600 parishes and 1,500 priests. In 1976 there were 3,720 churches, 500 chapels and some 20 monasteries and nunneries.

The Constitution provides for freedom of conscience and belief but forbids propaganda against the Government. The State provides 17% of Church funds.

Churches may not maintain schools or colleges, except theological seminaries, or organize youth movements.

In 1976 there were some 50,000 Roman Catholics in 3 bishoprics with 40 priests and 30 churches, and 16,000 Protestants with 101 churches and 265 priests. There were 80,000 Moslems under a Grand Mufti and 6 regional mufti boards with 1,180 mosques.

Education. Education is free, and compulsory for children between the ages of 7 and 16. The gradual introduction of unified secondary polytechnical schools offering compulsory education for all children from the ages of 7 to 17 was begun in 1973–74. Complete literacy is claimed. Schools are classified according to which years of schooling they offer: Elementary (1–4), primary (1–7), preparatory (5–8), secondary (9–11), complete secondary (1–11).

Educational statistics for 1978–79: 6,602 kindergartens (404,001 children, 27,479 teachers); 836 elementary schools; 2,391 primary schools; 69 preparatory schools; 119 secondary schools; 198 complete secondary schools. Numbers of teachers and pupils: School years 1 to 4, 16,891 and 397,033; 5 to 8, 33,067 and 575,974; 9 to 11, 7,585 and 102,872. There were also 5 vocational-technical schools (75 teachers, 2,690 students), 221 technical colleges (9,500 teachers, 104,563 students), 34 post-secondary institutions (2,553 teachers, 23,822 students) and 25 institutes of higher education (13,025 teachers, 91,303 students). There are 3 universities: the Kliment Ohrid University in Sofia (founded 1888) had 1,195 teachers and 12,616 students (in 1977–78); the Kirill i Metodii University in Veliko Tŭrnovo (founded 1971) had 203 teachers and 5,046 students; (in 1975–76) the Paisi Hilendarski University in Plovdiv (founded 1972) had 215 teachers and 5,046 students.

The Academy of Sciences was founded in 1869.

Social Welfare. Retirement and disablement pensions and temporary sick pay are calculated as a percentage of previous wages (respectively 55–80%, 35–100%, 69–90%) and according to the nature of the employment.

Monthly family allowances for children under 16: 15 leva for 1 child, 25 leva for 2 children and 45 leva for 3 children.

In 1976, 1·92m. persons received pensions totalling 1,122m. leva including 1·06m. retirement pensions.

All medical services are free. In 1978 there were 184 hospitals (including 16 mental hospitals and addiction treatment centres) with 71,064 beds. There were 20,454 doctors and 4,496 dentists.

DIPLOMATIC REPRESENTATIVES

OF BULGARIA IN GREAT BRITAIN
(186 Queen's Gate, London, SW7 5HL)

Ambassador: Kiril Shterev (accredited 26 Nov. 1980).

OF GREAT BRITAIN IN BULGARIA
(Blvd. Marshal Tolbukhin 65–67, Sofia)

Ambassador: G. L. Bullard.

OF BULGARIA IN THE USA (2100–16th St., NW,
Washington, D.C., 20009)

Ambassador: Konstantin N. Grigorov.

OF THE USA IN BULGARIA (1 Stamboliiski Blvd., Sofia)

Ambassador: Jack R. Perry.

OF BULGARIA TO THE UNITED NATIONS

Ambassador: Dr Alexander Yankov.

Books of Reference

Kratka Bŭlgarska Entsiklopediia (Short Bulgarian Encyclopaedia), 5 vols. Sofia, 1963–69
Statisticheski Godishnik (Statistical Yearbook). Sofia from 1956
Constitution of the People's Republic of Bulgaria. Sofia, 1971
Modern Bulgaria: History, Politics, Economy, Culture. Sofia, 1981
Atanasova, T., *et al.*, *Bulgarian–English Dictionary.* Sofia, 1975
Brown, J. F., *Bulgaria under Communist Rule.* London, 1970

Dobrin, B., *Bulgarian Economic Development Since World War II*. New York, 1973
Feiwel, G. R., *Growth and Reforms in Centrally Planned Economies: the Lessons of the Bulgarian Experience*. New York, 1977
Markov, M., *System of Social Administration in Bulgaria*. Sofia, 1969
Oren, N., *Communism Administered: Agrarianism and Communism in Bulgaria*. Baltimore, 1973
Pundeff, M. V., *Bulgaria: A Bibliographic Guide*. Library of Congress, 1965
Spasov, B., *La Bulgarie*. Paris, 1973
Todorov, N., and others, *Bulgaria: Historical and Geographical Outline*. Sofia, 1965
Zhivkov, T., *Modern Bulgaria: Problems and Tasks in Building an Advanced Socialist Society*, New York, 1974

BURMA

Capital: Rangoon
Population: 33m. (1979)
GNP per capita: US$150 (1978)

Pyidaungsu Socialist Thammada Myanma Naingngandaw

HISTORY. The Union of Burma came formally into existence on 4 Jan. 1948 and became the Socialist Republic of the Union of Burma in 1974. In 1948 Sir Hubert Rance, the last British Governor, handed over authority to Sao Shwe Thaike, the first President of the Burmese Republic, and Parliament ratified the treaty with Great Britain providing for the independence of Burma as a country not within His Britannic Majesty's dominions and not entitled to His Britannic Majesty's protection. This treaty was signed in London on 17 Oct. 1947 and enacted by the British Parliament on 10 Dec. 1947.

For the history of Burma's connexion with Great Britain see THE STATESMAN'S YEAR-BOOK, 1950, p. 836.

AREA AND POPULATION. Burma is bounded east by China, Laos and Thailand, west by the Indian ocean, Bangladesh and India. The total area of the Union is 261,789 sq. miles (678,000 sq. km). Some small rectifications of the border with China were agreed upon in 1960 and with Pakistan in 1964. The population in 1973 (census) was 28,172,936. Estimate (1979) 33m. Birth rate (1977 estimate), 29·1; death rate, 10·4 per 1,000 population; infant deaths, 56·3 per 1,000 live births. The leading towns are: Rangoon, the capital (1973), 3,662,312; Mandalay, 417,266; Bassein, 355,588; Henzada, 283,658; Pegu, 254,761, Myingyan, 220,129; Moulmein, 202,967; Prome, 148,123; Akyab, 143,215; Tavoy, 101,536.

	Area in sq. km	Population 1973 census	Chief town
Kachin State	87,808	687,218	Myitkyina
Sagaing Division	99,150	3,119,054	Sagaing
Mandalay Division	34,253	3,668,493	Mandalay
Shan State	158,222	2,640,170	Taunggyi
Magwe Division	44,799	2,634,757	Magwe
Chin State	36,009	318,112	Haka
Arakan State	36,762	1,710,506	Akyab
Irrawaddy Division	35,167	4,156,673	Bassein
Pegu Division	49,787	3,177,464	Pegu
Rangoon Division	518	3,188,783	Rangoon
Kayah State	11,670	107,342	Loikaw
Karen State	28,726	660,244	Pa-an
Tenasserim Division	43,328	716,440	Tavoy
Mon State	11,831	1,387,680	Moulmein
	678,030	28,172,936	

The Burmese belong to the Tibeto-Chinese (or Tibeto-Burman) family.

CONSTITUTION. From Independence Day until 1962 Burma was a parliamentary democracy, having 2 houses, the Chamber of Deputies and the Chamber of Nationalities. The latter comprised 125 members, 62 of whom represented the central unit, 63 the states and special areas. The Chamber of Deputies had twice as many members. Both were elected for 4 years. The Head of State was the President, elected for a 5-year term, by both Chambers of Parliament in joint session.

On 29 Oct. 1958 Gen. Ne Win, the Army Chief of Staff, became prime minister of a caretaker government. The elections to the lower house, held in Feb. 1960, gave the Pyidaungsu (Union) Party, led by U Nu, 161 out of 250 seats. On 2 March 1962 Gen. Ne Win overthrew the government of U Nu and replaced it by a Revolutionary Council. Parliament and the state councils were dissolved; the latter were reformed as 'state supreme councils' under appointed chairmen.

A new Constitution was approved by referendum in Dec. 1973. On 2 March 1974 military rule ended and Burma became a one-party socialist republic. Elections to the People's Assembly took place in Jan. and Feb. 1974. U Ne Win became President under the new Constitution and in Jan. 1978 his term of office was extended for 4 years.

On 3 March 1978 the Assembly elected a Council of Ministers:

Prime Minister: U Maung Maung Kha.

Planning and Finance: U Tun Tin. *Foreign Affairs:* U Lay Maung. *Defence:* Maj.-Gen. Kyaw Htin. *Home and Religious Affairs:* Col. Sein Lwin. *Mines:* Col. Than Tin. *Construction:* Brig.-Gen. Hla Tun. *Agriculture and Forests:* U Ye Gaung. *Industry:* Col. Tint Swe; Col. Maung Cho. *Transport and Communications:* Maj.-Gen. Thuna Sau Pru. *Co-operatives:* Col. Sein Tun. *Health:* Col. Win Maung. *Education:* U Kyau Nyein. *Trade:* Col. Khin Maung Gyi. *Information and Culture:* U Aung Kyan Myint. *Labour and Social Welfare:* Rear-Adm. Chit Hlaing.

As from 22 April 1972, military ranks were dropped by most of the Revolutionary Council Members. From 15 March 1972, the entire governmental system was re-organized, with the Secretariat in Rangoon being abolished and with re-organized Security and Administrative Committees composed of officials and political representatives becoming the directing authority at central and regional levels.

National flag: Red with a blue canton bearing 2 ears of rice within a cog-wheel and a ring of 14 stars, all in white.

Language: The official language is Burmese; the use of English is permitted.

DEFENCE

Army. The strength of the Army (1980) was 159,000. The Army is organized into 9 regional commands comprising approximately 110 independent infantry battalions. Three operational divisions are directly under the Ministry of Defence and contain 30 infantry battalions. In addition there are 2 armoured and 3 artillery battalions.

Navy. The Navy includes 1 escort minesweeper (*ex*-British), 2 escort patrol vessels (*ex*-USA PCE and MSF types), 2 small indigenously built corvettes, 3 support gunboats (*ex*-landing craft), 13 coastal gunboats, 20 river gunboats, 41 small river patrol craft, 1 support ship, 2 survey vessels, 9 fishery protection cutters and 9 landing craft. Personnel in 1981: 10,000 including 800 marines.

Air Force. The Air Force is intended primarily for internal security duties. Its primary combat force comprises about 5 T-33A jet fighter/trainers supplied under MAP, supplemented by 9 SIAI-Marchetti SF.260W light piston-engined attack/trainers. Other training aircraft include 10 piston-engined SF.260Ms, 32 turboprop Pilatus PC-7s and 10 jet-powered T-37Cs. Transport and second-line units are equipped with small numbers of FH-227 and F.27 Friendship, Porter, Turbo-Porter and Cessna 180 aircraft, and Japanese-built Bell 47 (H-13) and Vertol KV-107-II, Bell UH-1, H-43B Huskie and Alouette III helicopters. Personnel about 7,500.

INTERNATIONAL RELATIONS

Membership. Burma is a member of the UN and Colombo Plan.

Aid. In Dec. 1957 Burma received a US loan of $5·4m. to reclaim land in the delta, in 1960 a £30m. loan from China to set up specified projects. In Aug. 1971 Japan extended a loan of US$10m. for offshore oil exploration. A commodity loan of 4,620m. yen was provided as well as a loan of 7,000m. yen. The International Development Association also granted a loan of US$33m. for rehabilitation of the railways and waterways.

Long-term loans amounting to K.149·2m. and short-term loans amounting to K.133·6m. were taken during 1971–72, mainly from Japan, followed by Federal Republic of Germany, USA and Czechoslovakia.

ECONOMY

Planning. The economy has been controlled since 1972 through a series of 4-year plans. The third plan began in 1978–79 and aims to increase average *per capita* output by 6·6%, and net output value by 5·9%, distributed as follows: Construction, 23·2%; financial institutions, 21·4%; power, 16·8%; mining, 13·4%; processing and manufacturing, 13·4%; transport, 8·6%; communications, 8·5%; agriculture, 5%; livestock and fish, 4·7%; forestry, 4·1%; trade, 3%; social development and administration, 2·3%.

Budget. The budget estimates (in K.1m.) for fiscal year 1 April 1980–31 March 1981 was revenue K.24,968m. and expenditure K.27,104m.

The largest items, in 1980–81, of revenue were commodities and service tax (K.2,360·1m.) and customs (K.590m.); of expenditure, processing and manufacturing (K.8,769m.); trade (K.5,222·3m.); transport and communication (K.1,736·2m.). The internal public debt was K.3,084m. at the end of March 1979.

Currency. The currency unit is now the *kyat* divided into 100 *pyas*. There are notes of *kyat* 25, 20, 10, 5 and 1, and coins of *kyat* 1; *pyas* 50, 25, 10, 5 and 1.

Currency in circulation at 31 March 1980 was valued at K.7,172m.

Banking. The Union of Burma Bank is being reconstituted into 4 banks and an insurance corporation with effect from 1 April under the 1975 Bank Law and the 1975 Insurance Law.

The banks being formed in reconstitution are the Union of Burma Bank, the Myanma Economic Bank, the Myanma Foreign Trade Bank and the Myanma Agricultural Bank and the corporation is the Myanma Insurance Corporation. Work now being carried out by the Union of Burma Bank will be continued by the 4 banks and the Corporation.

ENERGY AND NATURAL RESOURCES

Electricity. In 1979 the total installed capacity of power plants was 642,230 kw., of which 168,500 was hydro-electricity and 158,850 gas turbine; there were 264 towns and 709 villages with electricity.

Oil. Production (1979–80, provisional) of crude oil was 11·68m. bbls; natural gas, 12,846m. cu. ft.

Minerals. Production in 1977–78 (provisional): Silver, 410,000 oz.; zinc, 6,000 tons; copper matte, 90 tons; refined lead, 5,198 tons; nickel speiss, 75 tons; antimony, 1,455 tons; tin, 866 tons; tungsten, 568 tons; tin tungsten-scheelite, 500 tons; coal, 27,000 tons; gypsum, 28,000 tons; limestone, 1m. tons.

Agriculture. The area sown in 1979–80 (provisional) was 23·8m. acres; matured acreage, 22·1m. acres.

Acreage (1,000) and production (1,000 tons) of principal crops:

| | 1979–1980 | | | 1979–80 | |
	Acreage	Production		Acreage	Production
Paddy	12,395	10,493	Cotton	481	54
Maize	250	100	Groundnuts	1,494	486
Pulses	1,868	422	Tobacco	139	100
Sesamum	2,652	134	Jute	261	92
Sugar-cane	243	1,449	Wheat	206	73

Livestock (1979): Cattle, 7·6m.; buffaloes, 1·8m.

In 1979–80 the area irrigated by government-controlled irrigation works was 2,417,769 acres.

Forestry. The area of reserved forests in 1977–78 was 23,477,000 acres; other forests, 55,986,000 acres. On 1 June 1948 the Government took over one-third of the concessions held by European and indigenous lessees. On 1 Feb. 1949 the European lessees surrendered their concessions. The takeover payments amounted to K.73·45 lakhs.

Teak extracted in 1979–80 (provisional), 400,250 cu. tons; hardwood, 1,049,000 cu. tons. All the teak and about 50% of the hardwood is from the state sector.

Other forest produce (1977–78) included 13m. tons of firewood and 680,000 bamboo canes. 2,780 elephants are at work on extraction.

Fisheries. In 1977–78 (provisional) sea fishing produced almost three times as much as fresh-water fisheries. The contribution of state-owned fishing vessels (32 trawlers and 43 other craft) is about 3%.

INDUSTRY AND TRADE

Industry. In 1977–78 (provisional) there were 1,506 state-owned factories operating and 43 under construction. In the co-operative and private sector there were 35,574. Of all factories 34,574 had less than 10 workers. The main manufacturing groups (with value of production in K. lakhs): Food and beverages, 97,157; clothing, 15,066; minerals, 11,196; industrial raw materials, 7,712; construction materials, 6,583; transport vehicles, 3,303; electrical goods, 1,528; agricultural equipment, 1,423. Production (1,000 tons): Cement, 365; salt, 198; fertilizer, 131·8; sugar, 36; cotton yarn, 13·5; shirting and poplin, 17·2m. yd; bricks and tiles, 154m. units; diesel oil, 75·7m. gallons; motor spirit, 61·2m. gallons; kerosene, 51·7m. gallons; radios, 22,000 units; cars, 1,884 units; bicycles, 19,000 units; tractors, 1,300 units; cigarettes, 2,440m. units.

Labour. In 1977–78 (provisional, 1,000) the workforce numbered 12,640: Agriculture, 8,212 (state sector 73); trade, 1,206 (45); processing and manufacturing, 929 (160); administration, 483 (459); transport and communication, 420 (104); social services, 246 (174); construction, 184 (124); livestock and fisheries, 167 (8); forestry, 152 (73); mining, 67 (65); power, 15 (15).

Trade Unions. Labour disputes are dealt with by the government labour subcommittees.

Co-operatives. In 1977–78 (provisional) there were 19,477 societies with 6·7m. members; share capital, K.174·3m.; trading capital, K.1,950·7m.; turnover, K.6,604·1m.

Commerce. All foreign trade is handled by the government trading organizations.
Imports and exports (in K. lakhs) for the fiscal years 1 April–31 March:

	1974–75	1975–76	1976–77	1977–78	1978–79
Imports	6,897	14,433	16,279	20,865	30,121
Exports	8,778	13,226	17,156	17,569	18,527

In 1976–77 exports were K.17,157 lakhs: Agricultural produce (rice, maize, pulses, jute and rubber), K.8,858 lakhs; forest produce, K.3,839 lakhs; minerals and gems K.1,065 lakhs. The main customers were S.E. Asia, EEC, Japan and Sri Lanka. Imports were K.15,211 lakhs: Raw materials, K.5,440 lakhs; machinery, K.3,476 lakhs; transport equipment, K.1,514 lakhs; consumer goods, K.1,445 lakhs; building materials, K.1,397 lakhs. Main sources were Japan, S.E. Asia, EEC.

Total trade between Burma and UK (British Department of Trade returns, in £1,000 sterling):

	1975	1976	1977	1978	1979	1980
Imports to UK	2,510	2,711	3,652	5,773	6,000	5,379
Exports and re-exports from UK	6,221	7,044	12,314	26,439	18,641	20,494

Tourism. There were 21,268 tourists in 1977.

COMMUNICATIONS

Roads. There were 13,948 miles of road in 1977–78, of which 2,452 miles were union highway.

Railways. The Burma Railways were nationalized in 1948 and the present Burma Railways Corporation took over in 1972. In 1980 there were 3,137 km of route on metre gauge.
In 1977–78 the railway carried 2·29m. tons of freight and 64·2m. passengers.

Aviation. Union of Burma Airways started its internal service in Sept. 1948 and its external service in Nov. 1950. International services were in 1963 maintained between Rangoon and Bangkok and Calcutta. The routes were extended to Hong Kong in 1969 and to Dacca and Káthmándu in 1970. There were, in 1971, 43 civil aerodromes and landing grounds. In 1977–78 internal flights carried 609,000 passengers and 6,400 tons of freight; external flights, 42,000 passengers and 2,100 tons of freight.

Shipping. Burma has 60 miles of navigable canals. The Irrawaddy is navigable up to Myitkyina, 900 miles from the sea, and its tributary, the Chindwin, is navigable for 390 miles. The Irrawaddy delta has nearly 2,000 miles of navigable water. The Salween, the Attaran and the G'yne provide about 250 miles of navigable waters around Moulmein. The Inland Water Transport Board runs services from Bhamo to Myitkyina. The Burma Five Star Line Ltd operates coastal steamer services to the major ports in Burma, India, East Pakistan, Malaya, Japan, Europe and UK.

The port of Rangoon in 1974–75 handled 1·19m. tons of seaborne trade.

Post and Broadcasting. There were 1,101 post offices in 1977. Number of telephones was 32,616 in 1978, of which 22,456 are in Rangoon.

There are 287 telegraph offices, and the internal system of communication is chiefly by wireless. Radio telephone or direct wireless telegraph links exist with most Asian countries, USA, USSR, UK, Denmark, Switzerland, Australia, Canada and Italy.

Cinemas. In 1971 there were about 418 cinemas.

Newspapers. In 1978 there were 7 daily newspapers.

JUSTICE, RELIGION, EDUCATION AND WELFARE

Justice. The Chief Court has supervision over all courts in the Union. It is presided over by the Chief Justice and other judges. Its present name was revived in March 1972 having been called Chief Court since 1962. All lower courts are now replaced by People's Courts formed with ordinary citizens to preside over trials, aided by former judges and magistrates acting as law officers.

Religion. The Revolutionary Government, having repealed the amendment of 1961 which made Buddhism the state religion, recognizes 'the right of everyone freely to profess and practise his religion'.

Education. After the attainment of independence the Government has adopted a centralized system of control of schools which are graded as primary, middle and high school. The medium of instruction in all schools is Burmese; English is taught as a compulsory second language in secondary schools.

Education is free in the primary, junior secondary and vocational schools; fees are charged in senior secondary schools and universities.

In 1977–78 there were 586 state high schools with 189,146 pupils, 1,262 state middle schools with 825,195 pupils and 21,999 state primary schools with 3,841,687 pupils; the total teaching staff was 111,339, of which 80,343 were in primary schools.

The Higher Education Law 1964 has decentralized the University of Rangoon. Beside the Arts and Science University, there are independent degree-giving institutes of engineering, education, medicine, agriculture, economics and commerce, and veterinary sciences. The University of Mandalay has been similarly decentralized. A foreign-languages institute in Rangoon has about 800 students learning French, German, Russian, Japanese, Chinese and Italian.

There are intermediate colleges at Taunggyi, Magwe, Akyab and Myitkyina, and degree colleges at Moulmein and Bassein, and several technical and agricultural institutes at higher and middle level. 4,656 school teachers were being trained in 15 training colleges in 1977–78. Technical high schools had 2,488 students; agricultural schools, 1,077; other vocational colleges, 1,438, and university colleges, 63,292.

A correspondence course for universities and colleges was introduced in 1976.

Health. In 1977 there were 5,787 doctors and 512 hospitals with 22,755 beds. There were 1,459 health centres.

DIPLOMATIC REPRESENTATIVES

OF BURMA IN GREAT BRITAIN (19A Charles St., London, W1X 8ER)

Ambassador: U Kyi Maung (accredited 10 May 1978).

OF GREAT BRITAIN IN BURMA
(80 Strand Rd., Rangoon)

Ambassador: C. L. Booth, CMG, MVO.

OF BURMA IN THE USA (2300 S St., NW,
Washington, D.C., 20008)

Ambassador: U Kyau Khine.

OF THE USA IN BURMA
(581 Merchant St., Rangoon)

Ambassador: Patricia M. Byrne.

OF BURMA TO THE UNITED NATIONS

Ambassador: U Maung Maung Gyee.

Books of Reference

Statistical Information: A Central Statistical Office is organized as a department of the Ministry of National Planning.

Burma: Treaty between the Government of the United Kingdom and the Provisional Government of Burma. (Treaty Series No. 16, 1948.) HMSO, 1948
Cornyn, W. S., and Musgrave, J. K., *Burmese Glossary.* New York, 1958
Furnivall, J. S., *A Governance of Modern Burma.* New York, 1960
Lehman, F. K., *The Structure of Chin Society.* Univ. of Illinois Press, 1963
Silverstein, J., *Burma: Military Rule and the Politics of Stagnation.* Cornell Univ. Press, 1978
Smith, D. E., *Religion and Politics in Burma.* Princeton Univ. Press, 1965
Stewart, J. A., and Dunn, C. W., *Burmese–English Dictionary.* London, 1940 ff.
Tinker, H., *The Union of Burma.* OUP, 1957
Trager, F. N., *Burma: From Kingdom to Republic.* London, 1966
Woodman, D., *The Making of Burma.* London, 1962

BURUNDI

Capital: Bujumbura
Population: 4·28m. (1978)
GNP per capita: US$140 (1978)

HISTORY. Tradition recounts the establishment of a Tutsi kingdom under successive Mwamis as early as the 16th century. German military occupation in 1890 incorporated the territory into German East Africa. From 1919 Burundi formed part of Ruanda-Urundi administered by the Belgians, first as a League of Nations mandate and then as a United Nations trust territory. Elections supervised by the United Nations in Sept. 1961 resulted in a large majority for the Unité et Progrès National party (UPRONA). Internal self-government was granted on 1 Jan. 1962, followed by independence on 1 July 1962. An agreement, signed with Rwanda under United Nations auspices at Addis Ababa in April 1962, provided for a monetary and customs union. This union and all organizations operated jointly by the two governments were dissolved by 30 Sept. 1964.

On 8 July 1966 Prince Charles Ndizeye deposed his father Mwami Mwambutsa IV, suspended the constitution and made Capt. Michel Micombero Prime Minister. On 1 Sept. Prince Charles was enthroned as Mwami Ntare V. On 28 Nov., while the Mwami was attending a Head of States Conference in Kinshasa (Congo), Micombero declared Burundi a republic with himself as president.

On 31 March 1972 Prince Charles returned to Burundi from Uganda and was placed under house arrest. On 29 April 1972 President Micombero dissolved the Council of Ministers and took full power; that night heavy fighting broke out between rebels from both Burundi and neighbouring countries, and the ruling Tutsi, apparently with the intention of destroying the Tutsi hegemony. Prince Charles was killed during the fighting and it was estimated that up to 120,000 were killed. On 14 July 1972 President Micombero reinstated a Government with a Prime Minister. On 1 Nov. 1976 President Micombero was deposed by the Army. A Supreme Military Council of the Armed Forces was established which appointed Col. Jean-Baptiste Bagaza president.

AREA AND POPULATION. Burundi extends from lat. $2\frac{1}{4}°$ to $4\frac{1}{2}°$ S. and long. 29° to 31° E., and has an area of 27,834 sq. km (10,759 sq. miles). It lies astride the main Nile–Congo dividing crest (6,000–7,000 ft) bounded on the west by the narrow plain of the Ruzizi River and Lake Tanganyika (2,534 ft). The interior is a broken plateau at an average height of about 5,000 ft, sloping eastwards down to Tanzania and the valley of the Maragarazi River. The southernmost tributary of the Nile system, the Luvironza, rises in the south of the country.

The population at the last census in 1959 was 2,213,280; but was 4·28m. in 1978. There are three ethnic groups—Hutu (Bantu, forming the great majority): Tutsi (Nilotic, less than 15%); Twa (pygmoids, less than 1%). There are some 3,500 Europeans and 1,500 Asians. In 1974 some 49,000 Tutsi refugees from Rwanda were living in Burundi.

Bujumbura, the capital, had (1976 estimate) 157,100 inhabitants. Kitega (10,000 inhabitants) was formerly the royal residence.

CONSTITUTION AND GOVERNMENT. Burundi remains a republic under the new military government but the activities of the Uprona party have been suspended. The Supreme Military Council of 30 members is headed by the President as is its 11 member Executive Committee. The President is responsible to the Supreme Military Council and the government is responsible to him. The office of Prime Minister was abolished in Oct. 1978 and the President assumed the post of Head of Government.

President of the Republic: Col. Jean-Baptiste Bagaza.
Foreign Affairs: Edouard Nzambimana.

The administrative divisions are: 8 provinces, each under a military governor

(Bujumbura, Bubanza, Muramvya, Ngozi, Gitega, Muhinga, Ruyigi and Bururi); 18 arrondissements; and 78 communes.

Flag: White diagonal cross dividing triangles of red and green, in the centre a white disc bearing 3 red green-bordered 6-pointed stars.

DEFENCE. The national armed forces total (1981), 6,000 (there are also about 1,500 in paramilitary units) and include a small naval flotilla and air force flight of 4 Cessna 150 and Do 27 liaison aircraft and 4 Alouette III helicopters. The army comprises 2 infantry battalions with supporting units.

INTERNATIONAL RELATIONS
Membership. Burundi is a member of UN and OAU and is an ACP state of EEC.

ECONOMY
Budget. The revised 1976 budget envisaged receipts of 4,200m. Burundi francs, and expenditure of 3,100m. Burundi francs. Main expenditure (1976, in Burundi francs): Education, 814m.; defence, 800m.; public health, 224m.; public works, 316m.; agriculture, 147m. Development budget: Receipt, 1,492m., and expenditure, 1,890·5m.

Currency. The currency is administered by the Bank of the Republic of Burundi. The rate was 90 *Burundi francs* = £1 and 217·2 *Burundi francs* = US$1 in March 1981.

Weights and Measures. The metric system operates.

ENERGY AND NATURAL RESOURCES
Electricity. Electricity generation capacity was 6 mw in 1976.

Minerals. There is some incipient mining activity and a recent discovery of large nickel deposits as yet unexploited of some 280m. tonnes. Production (in tonnes): Basthenaesite (150, 1975), cassiterite (74, 1975), kaolin (150, 1973). Total mineral exports (1973), 29m. Burundi francs.

Agriculture. The main economic activity and the main source of employment of the country is subsistence agriculture, which accounts for well over half of the gross national product. Beans, kassava, maize, sweet potatoes, groundnuts, peas, sorghum and bananas are grown according to the climate and the region.
    The main cash crop is coffee, of which about 93% is arabica. A coffee board (OCIBU) manages the grading and export of the crop. In 1975–76, 15,000 tonnes of arabica and 2,000 tonnes of robusta were produced. The average crop 1963–73 was 21,000 tonnes. Cotton production is falling; 5,000 tonnes 1979 (7,426, 1968). Plantations of good-quality tea are being developed. Production (1979) 2,000 tonnes.
    Cattle play an important traditional role, and there were about 836,000 head in 1979. The quality is poor, but efforts are being made to improve it. There are some 921,000 goats and sheep and 51,000 pigs.

Fisheries. There is a small commercial fishing industry on Lake Tanganyika which produced 7,941 tonnes in 1973 and is undergoing further development.

Tourism. Tourism is developing and there were 13,000 visitors Jan.–June 1976.

INDUSTRY AND TRADE
Industry. Industrial development is rudimentary. In Bujumbura there are plants for the processing of coffee and by-products of cotton, a brewery, cement works, a textile factory, a soap factory, a shoe factory and small metal workshops.

Commerce. The total value of exports in 1975 was 2,513m., re-exports, 29m. Burundi francs and of imports, 4,856m. Burundi francs. Main exports in 1975 were coffee (88·8%), tea, cotton and hides (9%). Principal imports were cottons and cotton goods, motor vehicles, synthetic textiles, flour and petrol products.
    Total trade between Burundi and the UK (British Department of Trade returns, in £1,000 sterling):

	1975	1976	1977	1978	1979	1980
Imports to UK	476	993	1,817	812	710	1,881
Exports and re-exports from UK	1,003	844	1,645	1,710	1,158	583

JUSTICE, RELIGION, EDUCATION AND WELFARE

Justice. There is a Supreme Court, an appeal court and a *tribunal de première instance* at Bujumbura.

Religion. Over half the population is Roman Catholic; there is a Roman Catholic archbishop and 3 bishops. The Anglican Missions under a bishop fall within the archdiocese of Uganda.

Education. In 1970–71 the number of children in primary schools was 175,600, 7,892 pupils were receiving secondary education and 2,031 were receiving craft and technical training. The university of Bujumbura has over 400 students.

The local language is Kirundi, a Bantu language. French is also an official language. Kiswahili is spoken in the commercial centres.

Health. In 1974 there were about 70 doctors and over 4,000 hospital beds.

COMMUNICATIONS

Roads. There is a road network of 6,400 km connecting with Rwanda, Congo and Tanzania but only 300 km are macadamized.

Aviation. Bujumbura has an airport of international standard and there are regular services to Europe, Zaïre and East Africa.

Shipping. These are lake services from Bujumbura to Kigoma (Tanzania). The main route for exports and imports is *via* Kigoma, and thence by rail to Dar es Salaam.

Post and Broadcasting. Number of telephones (1978), 4,995.

DIPLOMATIC REPRESENTATIVES

OF BURUNDI IN GREAT BRITAIN

Ambassador: Cyprien Mbonimpa (resides in Brussels).

OF GREAT BRITAIN IN BURUNDI

Ambassador: J. M. O. Snodgrass, CMG (resides in Kinshasa).

OF BURUNDI IN THE USA (2717 Connecticut Ave., NW,
Washington, D.C., 20008)

Chargé d'Affaires: Clement Sambira.

OF THE USA IN BURUNDI (Chaussée Prince Louis
Rwagasore, Bujumbura)

Ambassador: Ambasssador: Frances D. Cook.

OF BURUNDI TO THE UNITED NATIONS

Ambassador: Artémon Simbananiye.

Books of Reference

Lemarchand, R., *Rwanda and Burundi*. London, 1970
Melady, T. P., *Burundi: The Tragic Years*. Maryknoll, New York, 1974
Mpozapara, G., *La République du Burundi*. Paris, 1971
Weinstein, W., *Historical Dictionary of Burundi*. Metuchen, 1976

CAMEROON

Capital: Yaoundé
Population: 8·28m. (1980)
GNP per capita: US$460 (1978)

République Unie du Cameroun

HISTORY. The former German colony of Kamerun was occupied by French and British troops in 1916. The greater portion of the territory (432,000 sq. km) was in 1919 placed under French administration, excluding the territory ceded to Germany in 1911, which reverted to French Equatorial Africa. The portion under French trusteeship was granted full internal autonomy on 1 Jan. 1959 and complete independence was proclaimed on 1 Jan. 1960.

The portion assigned to Great Britain (89,270 sq. km) consisted of 2 parts where separate plebiscites were held in Feb. 1961. The northern part decided in favour of joining the Federation of Nigeria. The Southern Cameroons held a plebiscite in Feb. 1961 and decided to join the Cameroon Republic.

On 1 Oct. 1961 the former British trusteeship territory of Southern Cameroons and the Cameroon Republic combined in the Federal Republic of Cameroon.

On 20 May 1972, as the result of a national referendum, the creation of a unitary, bilingual and pluricultural state, as The United Republic of Cameroon was overwhelmingly approved and came into force on 2 June 1972.

AREA AND POPULATION. Cameroon is bounded west by the Gulf of Guinea, north-west by Nigeria and east by Chad, with Lake Chad at its northern tip, and the Central African Republic, and south by Congo, Gabon and Equatorial Guinea.

Province	Area in sq. km.	Census 1976	Chief town	Census 1976
Centre-Sud	116,036	1,491,945	Yaoundé (capital)	313,706
Est	109,011	366,235	Bertoua	18,450
Littoral	20,239	935,166	Douala	458,426
Nord	163,513	2,233,257	Garoua	69,285
Nord-Ouest	17,810	980,531	Bamenda	67,184
Ouest	13,872	1,035,597	Bafoussam	62,239
Sud-Ouest	24,471	620,515	Buea	13,000
Total	465,054	7,663,246		

Other large towns (1975 estimate): Nkongsamba (100,000), Foumban (59,701), Kumba (50,000), Maroua (46,077) and Victoria (31,222).

CONSTITUTION AND GOVERNMENT. The 1972 Constitution, amended 1975, provides for a President as chief of state and commander of the armed forces, who is elected for a 5-year term, and a cabinet whose members must not be members of parliament.

The National Assembly, elected by universal adult suffrage for 5 years, consists of 120 representatives. Elections took place on 28 May 1978. Since 1966 the sole legal party is the *Union National Camerounaise*.

The Economic and Social Council consists of 85 members appointed for 5 years by the President of the Republic to represent various social and economic interests; its chairman, appointed by decree, is assisted by a board appointed for 1 year.

President: Ahmadou Ahidjo (re-elected for fifth 5-year term on 5 April 1980).
Prime Minister: Paul Biya.
National flag: Three vertical strips of green, red, yellow, with a gold star in the centre.

DEFENCE

Army. The Army consists of 4 infantry battalions and support units; total strength (1980), 6,600.

Navy. The Navy operates 2 fast attack craft, 1 large and 2 small patrol craft and various auxiliaries. Personnel (1981) 600.

Air Force. The Air Force has 2 C-130H Hercules turboprop transports, 2 HS.748 twin-turboprop freight transports, 2 Caribou STOL transports, 4 C-47s and 2 Dornier Do 28s for transport and communications duties, 4 Broussard liaison aircraft, 4 Magister armed jet basic trainers and 2 Alouette II helicopters. A small VIP transport fleet maintained in civil markings, comprises 1 Boeing 727 jet aircraft, 1 Alouette III helicopter and a twin-engined Puma helicopter. Personnel total about 350.

INTERNATIONAL RELATIONS

Membership. Cameroon is a member of UN, OAU and is an ACP state of EEC.

ECONOMY

Planning. The fourth 5-year development plan ran 1976–81 with envisaged expenditure of 725,232m. francs CFA.

Budget. The budget for 1979–80 balanced at 186,000m. francs CFA.

Currency. The unit of currency is the *franc CFA.*

Banking. The Banque des Etats de l'Afrique Centrale is the sole bank of issue. The main banks are Banque Internationale pour l'Afrique Occidentale, Société Camerounaise de Banque, Société Générale de Banques au Cameroun and Cameroon Bank. Most of the banks operate in all the large cities and towns throughout the United Republic.

AGRICULTURE. Production (1977, in tonnes): Bananas and plantains, 1,125,000; sugar, 467,000; cassava, 810,000; maize, 360,000; coffee (1980), 105,000; cocoa, 90,000; rubber, 18,000.
    Livestock (1979): 3·03m. cattle, 2·2m. sheep, 1·72m. goats, 806,000 pigs.

INDUSTRY AND TRADE

Industry. There are factories producing shoes, soap, oil, food products, cigarettes, aluminium. Production (1976 in tonnes): Aluminium, 54,300; cement, 210,000.

Commerce. Imports and exports in 1m. francs CFA were as follows:

	1974	1975	1976	1977	1978
Imports	104,900	128,103	145,963	192,401	237,000
Exports	114,900	102,087	122,028	172,851	182,000

In 1978 the main trade was with EEC countries, Gabon, Japan and USA.
    Total trade between Cameroon and UK (British Department of Trade returns, in £1,000 sterling):

	1976	1977	1978	1979	1980
Imports to UK	8,991	12,237	9,940	16,278	9,798
Exports and re-exports from UK	8,089	20,702	19,087	18,811	17,470

Tourism. There were an estimated 89,990 foreign visitors in 1977. There are 13 National Parks and reserves, with a total area of nearly 20,000 sq. km. There were 203 hotels in 1975 with 3,229 rooms.

COMMUNICATIONS

Roads. There were (1977) 2,155 km of tarred roads, 9,284 km earth roads and 15,482 km of secondary roads. In 1976 there were 110,700 vehicles in use.

Railways. Cameroon Railways (1,173 km in 1981) link Douala with Nkongsamba and Ngaoundére, with branches M'Banga–Kumba and Makak–M'Balmayo.

Aviation. Douala is the main international airport; other airports are at Yaoundé and Garoua. In 1976, 342,000 passengers and 20,000 tonnes of freight passed through the airports.

Shipping (1975). The major port of Douala handled 1·33m. tonnes of imports and 718,000 tonnes of exports. The second port is now Kribi (162,496 tonnes exports, of which timber amounted to 146,850 tonnes; and 10,006 tonnes imports), while another 50,000 tonnes of timber was exported through nearby Campo. The ports of Bota and Tiko (at Victoria) handled 26,305 tonnes and Garoua on the river Benue 21,041 tonnes (comprising 6,022 tonnes fertilizer imports and 15,019 tonnes cotton exports).

Post and Broadcasting. There were (1975) 150 post offices; telephone lines, 2,677 km; main telephones (1978), 14,321; radio stations, 36 with (1974) 603,000 receivers.

Cinemas. There were (1974) 40 cinemas with a capacity of 22,800 seats.

Newspapers. There were (1975) 2 daily newspapers with a circulation of 25,000.

JUSTICE, RELIGION, EDUCATION AND WELFARE

Justice. The Supreme Court sits at Yaoundé, as does the High Court of Justice (consisting of 9 titular judges and 6 surrogates, all appointed by the National Assembly). There are magistrates' courts situated in the provinces.

Religion. 21% of the population is Roman Catholic, 20% Moslem, 14% Protestant, while 45% follow traditional (animist) religions.

Education (1975–76). There were 1,122,000 pupils and 22,209 staff in primary schools, 106,266 pupils and 3,309 staff in secondary schools, 31,135 students and 1,240 staff in vocational schools and 1,115 students and 130 staff in teacher-training colleges. The University of Yaoundé had (1976–77) 8,245 students and (1975–76) 376 teachers and 4 university centres are to be opened.

Health. In 1974 there were 353 doctors and (1976) 347 hospitals with 16,734 beds.

DIPLOMATIC REPRESENTATIVES

OF THE UNITED REPUBLIC OF CAMEROON IN GREAT BRITAIN
(84 Holland Pk., London, W11 3SB)
Ambassador: Vincent Paul-Thomas Pondi (accredited 23 Feb. 1978).

OF GREAT BRITAIN IN THE UNITED REPUBLIC OF CAMEROON
(Ave. Winston Churchill, BP 547, Yaoundé)
Ambassador: Denis Edward Richards.

OF THE UNITED REPUBLIC OF CAMEROON IN THE USA
(2349 Massachusetts Ave., NW, Washington, D.C., 20008)
Ambassador: Benoit Bindzi.

OF THE USA IN THE UNITED REPUBLIC OF CAMEROON
(Rue Nachtigal, BP 817, Yaoundé)
Ambassador: Hume A. Horan.

OF THE UNITED REPUBLIC OF CAMEROON
TO THE UNITED NATIONS
Ambassador: Ferdinand Léopold Oyono.

Books of Reference

Statistical Information: The Service de la Statistique Générale, at Douala, set up in 1945, publishes a monthly bulletin (from Nov. 1950)

Debel, A., *Cameroon Today.* Paris, 1977
Le Vine, V. T., *The Cameroon Federal Republic.* Cornell Univ. Press, 1971

CANADA

Capital: Ottawa
Population: 23·9m. (1980)
GNP per capita: US$9,170 (1978)

HISTORY. The territories which now constitute Canada came under British power at various times by settlement, conquest or cession. Nova Scotia was occupied in 1628 by settlement at Port Royal, was ceded back to France in 1632 and was finally ceded by France in 1713, by the Treaty of Utrecht; the Hudson's Bay Company's charter, conferring rights over all the territory draining into Hudson Bay, was granted in 1670; Canada, with all its dependencies, including New Brunswick and Prince Edward Island, was formally ceded to Great Britain by France in 1763; Vancouver Island was acknowledged to be British by the Oregon Boundary Treaty of 1846, and British Columbia was established as a separate colony in 1858. As originally constituted, Canada was composed of Upper and Lower Canada (now Ontario and Quebec), Nova Scotia and New Brunswick. They were united under an Act of the Imperial Parliament, 'The British North America Act, 1867', which came into operation on 1 July 1867 by royal proclamation. The Act provides that the constitution of Canada shall be 'similar in principle to that of the United Kingdom'; that the executive authority shall be vested in the Sovereign, and carried on in his name by a Governor-General and Privy Council; and that the legislative power shall be exercised by a Parliament of two Houses, called the 'Senate' and the 'House of Commons'.

The present position of Canada in the British Commonwealth of Nations was defined at the Imperial Conference of 1926.

On 30 June 1931 the British House of Commons approved the enactment of the Statute of Westminster freeing the Provinces as well as the Dominion from the operation of the Colonial Laws Validity Act, and thus removing what legal limitations existed as regards Canada's legislative autonomy. A joint address of the Senate and the House of Commons was sent to the Governor-General for transmission to London on 10 July 1931. The statute received the royal assent on 12 Dec. 1931.

Provision was made in the British North America Act for the admission of British Columbia, Prince Edward Island, Newfoundland, Rupert's Land and Northwest Territory into the Union. In 1869 Rupert's Land, or the Northwest Territories, was purchased from the Hudson's Bay Company. On 15 July 1870, Rupert's Land and the Northwest Territory were annexed to Canada and named the Northwest Territories, Canada having agreed to pay the Hudson's Bay Company in cash and land for its relinquishing of claims to the territory. By the same action the Province of Manitoba was created from a small portion of this territory and they were admitted into the Confederation on 15 July 1870. On 20 July 1871 the province of British Columbia was admitted, and Prince Edward Island on 1 July 1873. The provinces of Alberta and Saskatchewan were formed from the provisional districts of Alberta, Athabaska, Assiniboia and Saskatchewan and originally parts of the Northwest Territories and admitted on 1 Sept. 1905. Newfoundland formally joined Canada as its tenth province on 31 March 1949.

In March 1981 negotiations were in progress between the Canadian government and the UK for the amendment of the British North America Act.

In Feb. 1931 Norway formally recognized the Canadian title to the Sverdrup group of Arctic islands. Canada thus holds sovereignty in the whole Arctic sector north of the Canadian mainland.

AREA AND POPULATION. Population of the area now included in Canada:

1851	2,436,297	1901	5,371,315	1951	14,009,429
1861	3,229,633	1911	7,206,643	1961	18,238,247
1871	3,689,257	1921	8,787,949	1971	21,568,311
1881	4,324,810	1931	10,376,786 [1]	1976	22,992,604
1891	4,833,239	1941	11,506,655 [1]		

[1] From 1951 figures include Newfoundland.

Population (estimated), 1 June 1980, was 23·9m.

264

Areas of the provinces, etc. (in sq. km) and population at recent censuses:

Province	Land area	Fresh water area	Total land and fresh water area	Popula-tion, 1966	Popula-tion, 1971	Popula-tion, 1976
Newfoundland	370,485	34,032	404,517	493,396	522,104	557,725
Prince Edward Island	5,657	—	5,657	108,535	111,641	118,229
Nova Scotia	52,841	2,650	55,491	756,039	788,960	828,571
New Brunswick	72,092	1,344	73,436	616,788	634,557	677,250
Quebec	1,356,791	183,889	1,540,680	5,780,845	6,027,764	6,234,445
Ontario	891,194	177,388	1,068,582	6,960,870	7,703,106	8,264,465
Manitoba	548,495	101,592	650,087	963,066	988,247	1,021,506
Saskatchewan	570,269	81,631	651,900	955,344	926,242	921,323
Alberta	644,389	16,796	661,185	1,463,203	1,627,874	1,838,037
British Columbia	930,528	18,068	948,596	1,873,674	2,184,621	2,466,608
Yukon	531,844	4,481	536,325	14,382	18,388	21,836
Northwest Territories	3,246,390	133,294	3,379,684	28,738	34,807	42,609
Total	9,220,975	755,165	9,976,140	20,014,880	21,568,311	22,992,604

Of the total population in 1971, 18,272,780 were Canadian born, 933,040 other British born and 2,362,490 foreign born, 309,640 of the latter being USA born.

The population born outside Canada in the provinces was in the following ratio (%): Newfoundland, 1·7; Prince Edward Island, 3·3; Nova Scotia, 4·7; New Brunswick, 3·7; Quebec, 7·8; Ontario, 22·2; Manitoba, 15·3; Saskatchewan, 12; Alberta, 17·3; British Columbia, 22·7.

In 1971, figures for the population, according to origin, were:

British Isles		Netherlands	425,945	Danish	75,725
English	6,245,970	Polish	316,430	Russian	64,425
Scottish	1,720,390	Indian and		Finnish	59,215
Irish	1,581,730	Eskimo	312,760	Belgian	51,135
Other	76,030	Hebrew	296,945	Austrian	42,120
		Norwegian	179,290	Japanese	37,260
Total, British	9,624,115	Hungarian	131,890	Negro	34,445
		Greek	124,475	Icelandic	27,905
French	6,180,120	Chinese	118,815	Romanian	27,375
German	1,317,200	Yugoslav	104,955	Lithuanian	24,535
Italian	730,820	Swedish	101,870	Not stated	171,645
Ukrainian	580,660	Czech and Slovak	81,870		

The native Indian registered population numbered 288,938 in 1976 and the Eskimo population was 17,550 in 1971.

Populations of Census Metropolitan Areas (CMA) and Cities (proper), 1976 census:

	CMA	City proper		CMA	City proper
Toronto	2,803,101	633,318	Halifax	267,991	117,882
Montreal	2,802,485	1,080,546	Windsor	247,582	196,526
Vancouver	1,166,348	410,188	Victoria	218,250	62,551
Ottawa	693,288	304,462	Sudbury	157,030	97,604
Winnipeg	578,217	560,874	Regina	151,191	149,593
Edmonton	554,228	461,361	St John's	143,390	86,576
Quebec	542,158	177,082	Oshawa	135,196	107,023
Hamilton	529,371	312,003	Saskatoon	133,750	133,750
Calgary	469,917	469,917	Chicoutimi-		
St Catharines-			Jonquiere	128,643	—
Niagara	301,921	—	Chicoutimi	—	57,371
St Catharines	—	123,351	Jonquiere	—	60,691
Niagara Falls	—	69,423	Thunder Bay	119,253	111,476
Kitchener	272,158	131,870	Saint John	112,974	85,956
London	270,383	240,392			

The total 'urban' population of Canada in 1976 was 17,366,970, against 16,399,920 in 1971.

While the registration of births, marriages and deaths is under provincial control, the statistics are compiled on a uniform system by Statistics Canada.

The following table gives the results for 1980, preliminary:

Province	Living births Number	Marriages Number	Deaths Number
Newfoundland	10,750	3,370	3,210
Prince Edward Island	1,960	840	1,020
Nova Scotia	12,300	6,300	6,850
New Brunswick	10,740	4,950	5,450
Quebec	93,710	45,560	43,450
Ontario	122,510	64,020	62,100
Manitoba	16,200	7,390	8,710
Saskatchewan	16,300	7,200	7,640
Alberta	36,290	17,690	12,180
British Columbia	37,590	21,380	20,320
Yukon Territory	500	200	120
N.W. Territories	1,100	280	220
	359,950	179,180	171,270

Immigrant arrivals by country of last permanent residence:

Country	1973	1974	1975	1976	1977
England	19,979	28,828	27,761	16,759	13,648
Northern Ireland	2,263	2,391	1,977	1,536	1,391
Scotland	4,038	6,259	4,182	2,343	2,284
Wales	662	931	1,031	890	659
Lesser isles	31	47	27	20	15
Total, British Isles	26,973	38,456	34,978	21,548	17,997
Australia	2,096	2,022	1,654	1,387	1,063
France	3,586	4,232	3,891	3,251	2,757
Germany, Fed. Rep. of	2,564	3,619	3,469	2,672	2,254
Greece	5,833	5,632	4,062	2,487	1,960
Hong Kong	14,662	12,704	11,132	10,725	6,371
India	9,203	12,868	10,144	6,733	5,555
Irish Republic	1,129	1,292	1,098	639	571
Italy	5,468	5,226	5,078	4,530	3,411
Japan	1,105	859	635	498	412
Lebanon	1,325	1,762	1,506	7,161	3,847
Netherlands	1,898	2,103	1,448	1,359	1,247
Pakistan	2,285	2,315	2,165	2,173	1,575
Philippines	6,757	9,564	7,364	5,939	6,232
Poland	1,261	945	809	903	902
Portugal	13,483	16,333	8,547	5,344	3,579
South Africa, Rep. of	766	1,154	1,567	1,611	2,458
Switzerland	953	1,336	1,272	1,192	944
USA	25,242	26,541	20,155	17,315	12,888
Yugoslavia	2,873	3,200	2,932	1,741	1,408
Total, all countries	184,200	218,456	187,881	149,429	114,914

Blishen, B. R. (ed.), *Canadian Society; Sociological Perspectives.* 3rd ed. Toronto, 1965

Brunet, M., *La présence anglaise et les Canadiens.* Montreal, 1958

Card, B. Y., *Trends and Change in Canadian Society: Their Challenge to Canadian Youth.* Toronto, 1968

Clark, S. D., *Urbanism and the Changing Canadian Society.* 2nd ed. Toronto, 1970.—*The Developing Canadian Community.* 2nd ed. Toronto, 1968

Cowan, H. I., *British Emigration to British North America, The First Hundred Years.* Rev. ed. Toronto, 1961

Dawe, A., *Profiles of a Nation: Canadian Themes and Styles.* Toronto, 1970

Department of the Secretary of State, *The Canadian Family Tree.* Ottawa, 1967

Garigue, P., *La Vie familiale des Canadiens français.* Montreal, 1962

Iglauer, E., *The New People: The Eskimo's Journey in Our Time.* New York, 1966

James, S., *Urban Canada.* Toronto, 1969

Jenness, D., *The Indians of Canada.* 5th ed. Ottawa, 1960

Park, J., *The Culture of Contemporary Canada.* Toronto, 1970

Porter, J., *The Vertical Mosaic.* Toronto, 1965

Rosenberg, S. E., *The Jewish Community in Canada: A History*. Toronto, 1970
Wade, M., *The French Canadians, 1760–1967*. 2 vols. 2nd ed. Toronto and London, 1968

CONSTITUTION AND GOVERNMENT. The members of the Senate are appointed until age 75 by summons of the Governor-General under the Great Seal of Canada. Members appointed before 2 June 1965 may remain in office for life. The Senate consists of 104 senators, namely, 24 from Ontario, 24 from Quebec, 10 from Nova Scotia, 10 from New Brunswick, 4 from Prince Edward Island, 6 from Manitoba, 6 from British Columbia, 6 from Alberta, 6 from Saskatchewan, 6 from Newfoundland, 1 from the Yukon Territory and 1 from the Northwest Territories. Each senator must be at least 30 years of age, a born or naturalized subject of the Queen and must reside in the province for which he is appointed and his total net worth must be at least $4,000. The House of Commons is elected by the people, for 5 years, unless sooner dissolved. Women have the vote and are eligible. From 1867 to the election of 1945 representation was based on Quebec having 65 seats and the other provinces the same proportion of 65 which their population had to the population of Quebec. In the General Election of 1949 readjustments were based on the population of all the provinces taken as a whole. Generally speaking, this format for representation has prevailed in all subsequent elections with readjustments made after each decennial census. However, on 31 Dec. 1974, the law was changed so that it has reverted somewhat to the type of system that had prevailed initially. That is to say, Quebec is to be assigned a fixed number of seats in the House of Commons and the representation of the other provinces calculated by a quotient which reflects this fact.

The thirtieth Parliament, elected on 8 July 1974, comprises 264 members and the provincial and territorial representation are: Ontario, 88; Quebec, 74; Nova Scotia, 11; New Brunswick, 10; Manitoba, 13; British Columbia, 23; Prince Edward Island, 4; Saskatchewan, 13; Alberta, 19; Newfoundland, 7; Yukon Territory, 1; Northwest Territories, 1.

State of parties in the Senate (Nov. 1978): Liberals, 71; Progressive Conservatives, 17; Independent, 2; Social Credit, 1; Independent Liberal, 1; Vacant, 12; total 104.

State of the parties in the House of Commons (Feb. 1980): Liberals, 148; Progressive Conservatives, 101; New Democratic Party, 32; total, 281. Elections took place on 19 Feb. 1980.

The following is a list of Governors-General of Canada:

Viscount Monck	1867–1868	Viscount Byng of Vimy	1921–1926
Lord Lisgar	1868–1872	Viscount Willingdon	1926–1931
Earl of Dufferin	1872–1878	Earl of Bessborough	1931–1935
Marquess of Lorne	1878–1883	Lord Tweedsmuir	1935–1940
Marquess of Lansdowne	1883–1888	Earl of Athlone	1940–1946
Lord Stanley of Preston	1888–1893	Field-Marshal Viscount Alex-	
Earl of Aberdeen	1893–1898	ander of Tunis	1946–1952
Earl of Minto	1898–1904	Vincent Massey	1952–1959
Earl Grey	1904–1911	Georges Philias Vanier	1959–1967
HRH the Duke of Connaught	1911–1916	Roland Michener	1967–1974
Duke of Devonshire	1916–1921	Jules Léger	1974–1979

Governor-General: Edward Schreyer (sworn in Jan. 1979).

National flag: Vertically red, white, red with the white of double width and bearing a stylized red maple leaf.

The office and appointment of the Governor-General are regulated by letters patent, signed by the King on 8 Sept. 1947, which came into force on 1 Oct. 1947. In 1977 the Queen approved the transfer to the Governor-General functions discharged by the Sovereign. He is assisted in his functions, under the provisions of the Act of 1867, by a Privy Council composed of Cabinet Ministers.

The following is the list of the Liberal Cabinet in March 1981, in order of precedence, which in Canada attaches generally rather to the person than to the office:

Prime Minister: Rt Hon. Pierre Elliott Trudeau.
Deputy Prime Minister and Minister of Finance: Allan MacEachen.
Transport: Jean-Luc Pépen.
Attorney-General, Justice and Minister of State for Social Development: Jean Chrétien.
Indian Affairs and Northern Development: John Munro.

Minister of State for Economic Development: Senator Bud Olson.
Industry, Trade and Commerce: Herb Gray.
Agriculture: Eugene Whelan.
Consumer and Corporate Affairs, Postmaster-General: André Ouellet.
Energy, Mines and Resources: Marc Lalonde.
Leader of the Government in the Senate: Raymond Perrault.
Fisheries and Oceans: Roméo Leblanc.
Science and Technology, Environment: John Roberts.
Health and Welfare: Monique Bégin.
Supply and Services: Jean-Jacques Blais.
Secretary of State, Communications: Francis Fox.
Defence: J. Gilles Lamontagne.
Regional and Economic Expansion: Pierre de Bane.
Minister of State Responsible for Canadian Wheat Board: Senator Hazen Argue.
Minister Responsible for Sport, Labour: Gerald Regan.
Secretary of State for External Affairs: Mark MacGuigan.
Solicitor-General: Bob Kaplan.
Minister of State Responsible for Multiculturalism: Jim Fleming.
National Revenue: Bill Rompkey.
Minister of State, Finance: Pierre Bussières.
Minister of State, Small Business: Charles Lapointe.
Minister of State, Trade: Ed Lumley.
President of the Queen's Privy Council for Canada: Yvon Pinard.
President of the Treasury Board: Donald Johnston.
Employment and Immigration, Minister of State for the Status of Women: Lloyd Axworthy.
Public Works: Paul Cosgrove.
Minister of State, Mines: Judy Erola.

The sessional allowance of members of the Senate and House of Commons is $28,600 per annum. Senators receive an additional annual tax-free expense allowance of $6,200 and members of the House of Commons $12,700. The Leader of the Government in the Senate and the Opposition Leader in the Senate receive additional remuneration of $21,200 and $9,500 respectively. The remuneration of the Prime Minister is $35,400, a cabinet minister and Leader of the Opposition $21,200, a minister without portfolio $7,500, in addition to the sessional and expense allowances they receive as members of Parliament. Each minister and the Leader of the Opposition is also entitled to a $2,000 motor vehicle allowance. The Speaker of the Senate receives a salary of $14,100 and the Speaker of the House of Commons a salary of $21,200; each is allowed $3,000 in lieu of residence. An allowance of $5,600 is given to the leader of a party with 12 or more members in the House of Commons, other than the Prime Minister and Leader of the Opposition, and to the chief Government and Opposition whips. Parliamentary Secretaries receive an additional annual allowance of $5,600.

An Act to provide retiring allowances, on a contributory basis, to members of the House of Commons was given the Royal Assent on 4 July 1952. This Act was amended in July 1963; a member can now opt for a reduced retiring allowance in favour of an additional allowance for the widow; and provision has been made for retiring allowance for former Prime Ministers and their widows.

The Canadian Parliamentary Guide. Annual. Ottawa
Report of the Royal Commission on Dominion–Provincial Relations, Canada 1867–1939. 3 vols. Ottawa, 1940
Bissonnette, B., *Essai sur constitution du Canada.* Montreal, 1963
Byers, R. B. (ed.), *Canada Challenged: The Viability of the Confederation.* Toronto, 1979
Cheffins, R. I., *The Constitutional Process in Canada.* Toronto, 1969
Corry, J. A., *Democratic Government and Politics.* 3rd ed. Toronto, 1959
Eggleston, W., *Road to Nationhood: A Chronicle of Dominion–Provincial Relations.* Toronto, 1946.—*Canada at Work.* Montreal, 1953
Henderson, G. F. (ed.), *Federal Royal Commissions in Canada, 1867–1966: A Checklist.* Toronto, 1967
Hutchinson, B., *Mr. Prime Minister, 1867–1964.* Toronto, 1964
Information Canada, *Organization of the Government of Canada.* Loose-leaf service. Ottawa, 1970

Kennedy, W. F. M., *Statutes, Treaties and Documents of the Canadian Constitution, 1713–1929*. Toronto, 1930

Kernaghan, N. (ed.), *Bureaucracy in Canadian Government, Selected Readings*. Toronto, 1969

Kunz, F. A., *The Modern Senate of Canada, 1925–63*. Toronto, 1965

Lamontagne, M., *Le Fédéralisme canadien*. Quebec, 1954

Laskin, B., *Canadian Constitution Laws*. 2nd ed. Toronto, 1960

Lower, A. R. M. (and others), *Evolving Canadian Federation*. Duke Univ. Press, Durham, NC, 1958

McWhinney, E., *Comparative Federation; States' Rights and National Power*. Toronto, 1962

Martin, C. B., *Foundations of Canadian Nationhood*. Toronto, 1955

Morton, W. L., *The Kingdom of Canada; A General History From Earliest Times*. Toronto, 1969

Olmsted, R. A., *Decisions of the Judicial Committee of the Privy Council Relating to the British North America Act, 1867, and the Canadian Constitution, 1867–1954*. Ottawa, Queens' Printer, 1954

Ricker, J. C., *How Are We Governed?* Toronto, 1961

Russell, P. H. (ed.), *Leading Constitutional Decisions; Cases on the British North America Act*. Toronto, 1968

Saywell, J. T., *The Office of Lieutenant-Governor*. Toronto, 1957

Stanley, F. G., *A Short History of the Canadian Constitution*. Toronto, 1969

Trudeau, P. E., *Federalism and the French Canadians*. London, 1968

Varcoe, F. P., *The Distribution of Legislative Power in Canada*. Toronto, 1954

Ward, N., *The Public Purse: A Study in Canadian Democracy*. Toronto, 1962

Willms, A. (ed.), *Public Administration in Canada*. Toronto, 1862

DEFENCE. The Minister of National Defence has the control and management of the Canadian Forces, the Defence Research Board and all matters relating to national defence establishments and works for the defence of Canada. He is the Minister responsible for presenting before the Cabinet, matters of major defence policy for which Cabinet direction is required. Until Oct. 1973, he was responsible for the Canada Emergency Measures Organization which was renamed the 'National Emergency Planning Establishment' effective 1 April 1974, and given wider responsibilities for the co-ordination of civil emergency planning. The new organization will remain, for administrative purposes, within the Department but will report to the Privy Council Office. The Minister will continue to be responsible for certain civil emergency powers, duties and functions. The Deputy Minister is the senior public servant in the Department and the principal civilian adviser to the Minister on all departmental affairs. He is responsible for ensuring that all policy direction emanating from the Government is reflected in the administration of the Department and in military plans and operations. The Chief of the Defence Staff is the senior military adviser to the Minister and is charged with the control and administration of the Canadian Forces. He is responsible for the effective conduct of military operations and the readiness of the Canadian Forces to meet the commitments assigned to the Department by the Government. The Defence Research Board is responsible for advice to the Minister of National Defence on scientific matters relating to defence and for evaluating the contribution of science and technology to the achievement of defence objectives. Within National Defence Headquarters, the Deputy Minister and the Chief of the Defence Staff have reporting to them, the Vice Chief of the Defence Staff, 4 assistant deputy ministers as well as the Judge Advocate General, Director General Information and Director General Departmental Administrative Services.

Command Structure. The Canadian forces are organized on a functional basis to reflect the major commitments assigned by the Government. All forces devoted to a primary mission are grouped under a single commander who is assigned sufficient resources to discharge his responsibilities. Specifically, the Canadian forces are formed into 7 major entities reporting to the Chief of the Defence Staff. These are as follows:

1. *Mobile Command* provides units trained and equipped to support the United Nations or other peacekeeping operations; provides ground forces for the protection of Canadian territory; maintains combat formations in Canada for support of overseas commitments. It is comprised of 3 airportable combat groups in Canada; the United Nations force in Cyprus; the Canadian Airborne Regiment, and 1 combat training centre. The Militia and Air Reserve components are also controlled by Mobile Command. Strength (1980), 12,675.

2. *Maritime Command.* All maritime sea forces on the Atlantic and Pacific coasts are under the Commander, Maritime Command, with headquarters in Halifax, Nova Scotia. The Maritime Commander (Pacific), who is the Deputy Commander, has his headquarters in Esquimalt, British Columbia. Maritime Command is to defend Canada against attack from the sea; provide anti-submarine defence in support of NATO; provide sea transport in support of Mobile Command. Composition of the maritime forces includes 3 submarines, 4 destroyers, 19 smaller destroyer-escorts, 3 supply ships, 6 patrol craft, 6 small support ships, 6 training vessels (*ex*-coastal minesweepers) and 34 auxiliaries and service craft. There are 16 naval reserve units in major Canadian cities which form an essential component of Maritime Command.

Active naval personnel strength in Maritime Command ships and shore establishments in 1981 was about 18% of the Regular Forces, *i.e.,* some 14,200 comprising 2,000 officers and 12,200 ratings (men and women).

3. *Air Command.* On 2 Sept. 1975, the aviation units administered by Mobile Command and Maritime Command were withdrawn and allocated to a newly-formed Air Command, which now controls all Canadian military aviation units through a single senior commander. Air Command responsibilities include maintenance of operationally-ready regular and reserve air forces to meet Canada's sovereignty requirements, participation with the USA in the air defence of North America through NORAD, and support of overseas commitments including NATO responsibilities in Europe and elsewhere. It is organized in 4 operational groups: Air Defence Group, Maritime Air Group, Air Transport Group and 10 Tactical Air Group; has reinforcement and training responsibilities to 1 Canadian Air Group (1 CAG) in Europe; and exercises command and control over Air Training Schools and the Air Reserve.

Air Defence Group, through NORAD, has entire responsibility for control of Canadian airspace. It comprises 3 squadrons of CF-101 Voodoo all-weather interceptors, armed with nuclear and conventional missiles; an electronic warfare squadron with CF-100 Mk. 5 and T-33A aircraft and 1 operational training squadron with Voodoos; eastern and western control centres and a trans-continental radar chain, integrated in NORAD through the semi-automatic ground environment (SAGE) network.

Maritime Air Group's primary responsibilities include coastal and anti-pollution patrol, fishery protection and Arctic surveillance. Its equipment includes 3 operational squadrons of Argus (being replaced with Aurora) and 1 of Tracker maritime patrol aircraft, and 2 ASW helicopter squadrons with CH-124 Sea Kings.

Air Transport Group has 2 squadrons of C-130E/H turboprop transports; 1 squadron of 5 CC-137 (Boeing 707) jet transports, of which 2 can operate as flight refuelling tankers; a VIP squadron with 2 CC-132 Dash 7 four-turboprop and 7 CC-109 Cosmopolitan twin-turboprop transports and some twin-jet Falcons; and 4 dual-role transport/search and rescue squadrons with twin-turboprop Buffalo and Twin Otter aircraft and helicopters. 10 Tactical Air Group has 2 squadrons of CF-5 fighters and 5 squadrons of CH-135 (Bell UH-1N) and CH-136 (Kiowa) helicopters.

4. *Training Command* plans and conducts all recruit and individual trades and classification training that is common to more than one command. The Command is also responsible for the Prairie Region, one of 6 military regions into which Canada is divided. The Command headquarters is in Winnipeg and the 9 bases within the Command are located in 7 provinces. A total of 24,239 students attended one or more of 1,258 courses conducted by the Command during 1973.

5. *Canadian Forces Communications Command* (*CFCC*) manages, operates and maintains strategic communications for the Canadian Forces and, in the event of emergencies, for the federal and provincial governments. The Command also provides points for interconnecting strategic and tactical networks and CFCC manages, operates and maintains the major DND automatic data processing centres.

6. *The Reserves* are composed of the Naval Reserve, the Militia and the Air Reserve.

National Defence expenditures amounted to $3·8m. in 1977–78. Estimates for 1978–79 were $4·1m. Strength of the Regular Forces in 1979 was 80,000.

7. *Canadian Forces Europe.* The Canadian Forces allocated to support NATO in Europe are part of Canadian Forces Europe. The land element is No. 4 Canadian Mechanized Brigade Group operationally responsible to the Central Army Group. The air element, No. 1 Canadian Air Group, consisting of 3 CF-104 Starfighter squadrons, is operationally assigned to No. 4 Allied Tactical Air Force. These elements are located in the Baden-Baden area of Federal Republic of Germany and are supported administratively by CFB Europe at Lahr.

Police Forces. The police forces of Canada are organized in three groups: (1) the federal force, which is the Royal Canadian Mounted Police; (2) provincial police forces—the Provinces of Ontario and Quebec have their own provincial police forces, but all other provinces engage the services of the Royal Canadian Mounted Police to perform parallel functions within their borders, and (3) municipal police forces—each urban centre of reasonable size maintains its own police force or engages the services of the provincial police, under contract, to attend to police matters.

In addition, the Canadian National Railways, the Canadian Pacific Railway Company and the National Harbours Board have their own police forces.

Royal Canadian Mounted Police. The Royal Canadian Mounted Police is a civil force maintained by the federal government. It was established in 1873, as the North-West Mounted Police for service in what was then the North-West Territories and, in recognition of its services, was granted the use of the prefix 'Royal' by King Edward VII in 1904. Its sphere of operations was expanded in 1918 to include all of Canada west of Thunder Bay. In 1920 the force absorbed the Dominion Police, and its headquarters was transferred from Regina to Ottawa, and its title was changed to Royal Canadian Mounted Police. The force is responsible to the Solicitor-General of Canada and is controlled and managed by a Commissioner who holds the rank and status of a Deputy Minister. The Commissioner is empowered under the Royal Canadian Mounted Police Act to appoint members to be peace officers in all provinces and territories of Canada.

The responsibilities of the Royal Canadian Mounted Police are national in scope. The administration of justice within the provinces, including the enforcement of the Criminal Code of Canada, is part of the power and duty delegated to the provincial governments.

All provinces except Ontario and Quebec have entered into contracts with the Royal Canadian Mounted Police to enforce criminal and provincial laws under the direction of the respective Attorneys-General. In addition, in these 8 provinces the Force is under agreement to provide police services to 194 municipalities, thereby assuming the enforcement responsibility of municipal as well as criminal and provincial laws within these communities. The Royal Canadian Mounted Police is also responsible for all police work in the Yukon and Northwest territories enforcing federal law and territorial ordinances. The 18 Operational Divisions, alphabetically designated, make up the strength of the Force across Canada; they comprise 46 sub-divisions which include 654 detachments. Headquarters Division, as well as the Office of the Commissioner, is located in Ottawa. The Force maintains liaison officers in 28 countries and represents Canada in the International Criminal Police Organization which has its headquarters in Paris.

Thorough training is emphasized for members of the Force. Recruits receive 6 months of basic training at the Royal Canadian Mounted Police Academy in Regina. This is followed by a further 6 months of supervised on-the-job training. The RCMP also operates the Canadian Police College at which its members and selected representatives of other Canadian and foreign police forces may study the latest advances in the fields of crime prevention and detection.

Many of these advances have been incorporated into the operation of the Force. A teletype system links the widespread divisional headquarters with the administrative centre at Ottawa and a network of fixed and mobile radio units operates within the provinces. The focal point of the criminal investigation work of the Force is the Directorate of Laboratories and Identification; its services, together with those of divisional and sub-divisional units, and of 6 Crime Detection Laboratories, are available to police forces throughout Canada. The Canadian Police Information Centre at RCMP Headquarters, a duplexed computer system, is staffed and operated by the Force. Law Enforcement agencies throughout Canada have access *via* a series of remote terminals to information on stolen vehicles, licences and wanted persons.

In Oct. 1979, the Force had a total strength of 19,304 including regular members, special constables, civilian members and Public Service employees. It maintained 4,874 motor vehicles, 69 police service dogs and 151 horses.

The Force has 13 divisions actively engaged in law enforcement, 1 Headquarters Division and 2 training divisions. In addition it maintains a Marine Services and Air Services with headquarters at Ottawa. The Marine Services is comprised of 13 patrol vessels and 307 smaller craft which operate on the east and west coasts, the Great Lakes and the St Lawrence River. The Air Directorate has stations throughout Canada and maintains 27 aircraft.

Dornbusch, C. E., *The Canadian Army 1855–1958; Regimental Histories.* Cornwailville, N.Y., 1959
Eayrs, J., *In Defence of Canada: Growing up Allied.* Univ. of Toronto Press, 1980
Feasby, W. R. (ed.), *Official History of the Canadian Medical Services, 1939–45.* 2 vols. Dept. of National Defence. Ottawa, 1953–56
Goodspeed, D. J., *A History of the Defence Research Board of Canada.* Defence Research Board. Ottawa, 1958
Roberts, L., *There Shall Be Wings: A History of the Royal Canadian Air Force.* Toronto, 1960
Schull, J., *The Far Distant Ships: An Official Account of Canadian Naval Operations in the Second World War.* Ottawa, Queen's Printer, 1952
Stacy, C. P., *Six Years of War: Official History of the Canadian Army.* 3 vols. Ottawa, Queen's Printer, 1955–60
Swettenham, J., *Canada and the First World War.* Toronto, 1970

INTERNATIONAL RELATIONS

Membership. Canada is a member of UN, the Commonwealth, OECD, NATO and Colombo Plan.

ECONOMY

Budget. Budgetary revenue and expenditure of the Government of Canada for years ended 31 March (in Canadian $1m.):

	1976–77	1977–78	1978–79	1979–80	1980–81
Revenue	32,721	32,866	35,215	40,159	45,200
Expenditure	39,011	42,902	46,934	51,534	59,350

Budgetary revenue, main items, 1980–81 (in Canadian $1m.):

Income tax, personal	18,425	Non-resident tax	925
Income tax, corporation	8,630	Oil export charge	755
Sales	4,975	Natural gas tax	255
Customs duties	3,150	Non-tax revenue	5,925

Details of budget estimates[1], 1980–81 (in Canadian $1m.):

Energy	3,760	External affairs	1,548
Economic development	5,883	Defence	5,067
Social affairs	24,926	Parliament	119
Justice and legal affairs	1,237	Services to government	4,020
Financial transfers	3,741		

[1] The Department of Finance now manages expenditure under a new system of broad categories (listed above) called 'envelopes'.

On 31 March 1979 the net debt was $51,341m.

Canadian Tax Foundation. *The National Finances: An Analysis of the Revenues and Expenditures of the Government of Canada.* Toronto. Annual

Currency. The denominations of money in the currency of Canada are dollars and cents. The cent is one-hundredth part of a dollar. Subsidiary coins of the denominations of 1, 5, 10, 25 and 50 cents and $1 are in use. The monetary standard is gold of 900 millesimal fineness (23·22 grains of pure gold equal to 1 gold dollar). The Currency Act provides for gold coins in the denominations of $5, $10 and $20, which are legal tender. The British and US gold coins are also legal tender, at the par rate of exchange. The legal equivalent of the British sovereign is $4.86⅔.

The Bank of Canada has the sole right to issue paper money for circulation in Canada. Restrictions introduced by the 1944 revisions of the Bank Act cancelled the right of chartered banks to issue or re-issue notes after 1 Jan. 1945; and in Jan. 1950 the chartered banks' liability for such of their notes as then remained outstanding was transferred to the Bank of Canada in return for payment of a like sum to the Bank of Canada. On 31 May 1970 the Canadian dollar which was stabilized at 92·50 US cents was allowed to fluctuate. The value of the US$ in Canadian funds was 116·39 cents and £1 sterling = Canadian $2·62 in March 1981.

The Bank of Canada issues notes, which are legal tender, in denominations of $1, $2, $5, $10, $20, $50, $100, $500 and $1,000. Under the terms of the Bank of Canada Act, the bank is required to sell gold in bars of 400 oz. to any person tendering legal tender. This obligation is at the present time suspended by Order-in-Council. The exportation of gold from Canada is prohibited except by licence issued by the Minister of Finance to the Bank of Canada or a chartered bank.

The Ottawa Mint was established in 1908 as a branch of the Royal Mint, in pursuance of the Ottawa Mint Act, 1901. In Dec. 1931 control of the Mint was passed over to the Canadian Government, and since that time has operated as the Royal Canadian Mint. The Mint issues silver, nickel, bronze and steel coins for circulation in Canada. In 1967, in celebration of Canada's Centennial of Confederation, a $20 gold piece was minted, the first gold coin struck since 1919. In 1935, on the occasion of His Majesty's Silver Jubilee, the Royal Canadian Mint issued the first Canadian silver dollars. Commemorative dollars were also issued in 1939 on the occasion of the visit of King George VI and Queen Elizabeth to Canada; in 1949, when Newfoundland became the tenth Province of Canada; in 1958, the one-hundredth anniversary of the establishment of the Colony of British Columbia; in 1964, the centennial of the Charlottetown and Quebec Conferences which paved the way to confederation. The silver dollar bearing the design of the canoe manned by an Indian and a Voyageur has been issued in the years 1935–38, 1945–48, 1950–57, 1959–63, 1965, 1966 and 1972. For centennial year the Canada goose replaced the usual canoe design on the silver dollar. Because of a world-wide shortage of silver, the Government, in Aug. 1967, authorized the Mint to change the metal content of the 25-cent and 10-cent coins. Commencing in Sept. 1968, the 10-cent, 50-cent and $1 coins were minted in pure nickel. Gold refining is one of the principal activities of the Mint. In 1978, 1,567,857 troy oz. of rough bullion were received for treatment, containing 1,277,133 oz. of fine gold and 177,565 oz. of fine silver. Coin issued: Bronze, $8,438,788; nickel, $71,339,943; silver, $744,655; gold, $18,000,900.

Banking. Commercial banks in Canada are known as chartered banks and are incorporated under the terms of the Bank Act, which imposes strict conditions as to capital, notes in circulation, returns to the Dominion Government, types of lending operations and other matters. In Sept. 1979 there were in operation 12 chartered banks incorporated under the provisions of the Bank Act, with 7,434 branches and sub-agencies in Canada and 289 branches and sub-agencies in other countries. The Bank Act is subject to revision by Parliament every 10 years. Bank charters expire every 10 years and are renewed at each decennial revision of the Bank Act. The chartered banks make detailed monthly and yearly returns to the Minister of Finance and are subject to periodic inspection by the Inspector-General of Banks, an official appointed by the Government.

The following are some particulars of the 12 chartered banks at 30 Sept. 1979: Capital paid up, $507·3m.; rest account, $4,459·4m.; Canadian currency deposits, $115,607·3m.; foreign currency deposits, $81,977·7m.; liabilities to the public, $214,602·5m.; total assets, $219,569·3m. Cheques cashed at the clearing-house centres of Canada for 1978 amounted to $3,138,384·6m.

The Bank of Canada Act, passed on 3 July 1934, provided for the establishment of a central bank for the Dominion. This bank commenced operations on 11 March 1935 with a paid-up capital of $5m. By reason of certain changes introduced into the composition of stockholders of the bank (for which see THE STATESMAN'S YEAR-BOOK, 1944, pp. 322–23), the Minister of Finance on behalf of Canada is the sole registered owner of the capital stock of the bank. The revised Bank Act, which came into force on 1 May 1967, requires the chartered banks, beginning Feb. 1968, to maintain a statutory cash ratio of 12% on demand deposits and 4% on other deposits, in the form of reserves with and notes on the Bank of Canada. A secondary reserve of 7% in treasury bills, government bonds, etc., is also required. All gold held in Canada by the chartered banks was transferred to the Bank of Canada along with the gold held by the Government as reserve against Dominion notes outstanding at the time of the commencement of operations of the Bank of Canada. The liability of the Dominion notes outstanding at the commencement of business of the Bank of Canada was assumed by the bank. The following are some of the particulars of the Bank of Canada as at 31 Oct. 1979: Notes in circulation, $9,552·3m.; chartered bank deposits, $4,614·2m.; total liabilities, $15,133·1m.; investments, $14,157·4m.

In Aug. 1944 the Industrial Development Bank, a subsidiary of the Bank of Canada, was set up for the purpose of providing credit in the post-war period to small industrial establishments. The statement of assets and liabilities of the Industrial Bank for the fiscal year ended 30 Sept. 1975 showed outstanding loans and investments of $1,175·2m. The authorized, issued and paid-up capital at this date amounted to $78m. The year ending 30 Sept. 1975 was the last year of operation of the Industrial Development Bank. During its existence from 1 Nov. 1944 to 30 Sept. 1975, the Industrial Development Bank authorized 65,000 loans for $3,000m. to more than 48,000 businesses in Canada. It is succeeded by the Crown corporation, the Federal Business Development Bank, which was proclaimed in force on 2 Oct. 1975. In the year ending 31 March 1979, the Federal Business Development Bank authorized 12,271 loans for a total of $668,593,000.

Binhammer, H. H., Money, Banking and the Canadian Financial System. Toronto, 1968
Boreham, G. F., and others, Money and Banking: Analysis and Policy in a Canadian Context. Toronto, 1969
Cairns, James P. (ed.), Canadian Banking and Monetary Policy: Recent Readings. Toronto, 1965
O'Brien, J. H., and Lerner, G., Canadian Money and Banking. 2nd ed. Toronto, 1969

Weights and Measures. The legal weights and measures are the Imperial yard, pound avoirdupois, gallon and bushel; but the hundredweight is declared to be 100 lb. and the ton 2,000 lb. avoirdupois, as in the USA. The Metric Commission, established in June 1971, advises on Canada's conversion to the metric system which will be completed in 1980.

ENERGY AND NATURAL RESOURCES

Electricity. The net generation of electricity in 1979 was 352,304,082 mwh., of which utilities accounted for 317,795,205 mwh. Of the total, 243,040,606 mwh. was from hydro-electricity 75,988,084 mwh. from conventional thermal plants and 33,275,392 mwh. from nuclear plants. Demand (1979) was 294,263 mwh.

Oil and Natural Gas. With the discovery of large oilfields in Alberta, the production of petroleum became a major Canadian industry. The Interprovincial Pipeline, Canada's longest oil pipeline, moving crude oil from Edmonton, Alberta, to Montreal, Quebec, has a length in Canada of 3,605 miles. Total pipeline mileage, including mileage of American subsidiaries, is 5,996 miles. The pipeline serves Canadian refineries from Edmonton to Montreal and many in the USA. Another pipeline, Trans-Mountain, extends from Edmonton to Vancouver with a Canadian length of 825 miles and an overall length, including American mileage, of 889 miles. Eight refineries, 4 in Canada and 4 in Washington State, are served by the pipeline. At the end of 1977 Canada's oil pipeline system had 20,824 miles (33,512 km) of line in operation. Net oil deliveries in 1977 were 885,323,199 bbls

(140,671,763 cu. metres). The Trans-Canada natural gas line is the longest in the world (5,794·7 miles in 1978). It brings natural gas from the Alberta–Saskatchewan border across the prairies, through northern Ontario to Toronto, then eastward to Montreal. Natural gas pipeline mileage totalled about 88,153·6 miles (141,189·4 km) in 1977. Net deliveries of natural gas into the pipelines in 1977 was 2,481,587m. cu. ft.

Minerals. Alberta, Ontario, British Columbia, Quebec and Saskatchewan are the chief mining provinces. Total value of minerals produced in 1979 was $26,098,267,000. Principal minerals produced in 1979 (preliminary) were as follows:

Metallics	Quantity (1,000)	Value ($1,000)
Copper (kg)	643,754	1,515,443
Nickel (kg)	131,579	826,423
Zinc (kg)	1,148,498	1,107,419
Iron ore (tonnes)	60,185	1,888,815
Gold (grammes)	49,175	543,068
Lead (kg)	315,751	414,416
Silver (kg)	1,184	451,913
Molybdenum (kg)	11,187	330,114
Total metallics	...	7,999,518
Non-metallics		
Asbestos (tonnes)	1,501	641,221
Potash (K₂O) (tonnes)	7,046	695,305
Salt (tonnes)	6,672	113,855
Sulphur, elemental (tonnes)	6,718	145,072
Gypsum (tonnes)	8,105	42,808
Total non-metallics	...	1,832,784
Fuels		
Crude petroleum (cu. metres)	89,320	7,610,953
Natural gas (cu. metres)	94,116	4,708,800
Natural gas by-products (cu. metres)	19,290	1,351,091
Coal (tonnes)	33,120	858,000
Total fuels	...	14,528,844
Structural materials		
Cement (tonnes)	11,835	736,862
Sand and gravel (tonnes)	275,127	449,030
Stone (tonnes)	114,989	346,721
Clay products (bricks, tiles, etc.)	...	125,357
Lime (tonnes)	2,0692	79,151
Total structural materials	...	1,737,121

Value (in Canadian $1,000) of mineral production by provinces:

Provinces	1978	1979	Provinces	1978	1979
Newfoundland	675,028	1,100,152	Saskatchewan	1,581,850	1,814,743
Pr. Ed. Island	2,068	2,200	Alberta	10,087,206	12,884,740
Nova Scotia	210,658	208,718	British Columbia	1,882,652	2,741,467
New Brunswick	339,610	529,926	Yukon Territory	218,804	299,564
Quebec	1,796,050	2,247,850	N.W. Territories	309,639	412,100
Ontario	2,697,852	3,271,369			
Manitoba	459,636	585,438	Total	20,261,053	26,098,267

Agriculture. Though the manufacturing industries now predominate, agriculture is still very important to the Canadian economy. It contributes between 7 and 10% of the net value of production and in 1978 accounted for about 10% of the value of commodities exported.

It is estimated that about 35% of the total land area is forested; according to the census of 1976, 259,338 sq. miles (7·2% of the total land area) is classed as occupied agricultural land.

Grain growing, dairy farming, fruit farming, ranching and fur farming are all carried on successfully. Total farm receipts (1978) $11,887m.

The following table shows the estimated value of selected agricultural production for 1979, in Canadian $1,000:

Wheat	1,910,412	Tobacco	289,790
Oats and barley	533,279	Cattle and calves	3,481,804
Rapeseed	785,495	Hogs	1,305,741
Potatoes	161,327	Sheep and lambs	17,515
Other vegetables	310,123	Dairy products	1,688,565
Fruit	223,219	Poultry and eggs	1,003,345

Number of occupied farms (census of 1976) was 300,118.

Field Crops. In 1979, 70,910,014 acres were under principal field crops. The most valuable field crops are wheat, tame hay, oats, barley, potatoes, corn for grain, flaxseed, mixed grains, rapeseed, fodder corn, soybeans and sugar-beet.

The estimated acreage and yield of the principal field crops, by provinces, 1979 were:

	Wheat		Tame hay		Oats	
	1,000	1,000	1,000	1,000	1,000	1,000
Provinces	acres	bu.	acres	tons	acres	bu.
Prince Edward Island	11	484	138	280	54	2,916
Nova Scotia	5	189	184	423	18	788
New Brunswick	9	316	178	365	40	1,940
Quebec	98	4,255	2,700	5,851	540	26,877
Ontario	515	26,179	2,820	7,849	405	23,272
Manitoba	3,000	75,000	1,350	2,600	450	20,000
Saskatchewan	17,000	374,000	2,000	3,000	1,000	41,000
Alberta	5,200	148,000	3,600	6,900	1,250	73,000
British Columbia	80	3,000	670	1,950	50	3,300
Total, Canada	25,918	631,423	13,640	29,218	3,807	193,093

	Barley		Potatoes		Corn for Grain	
	1,000	1,000	1,000	1,000	1,000	1,000
Provinces	acres	bu.	acres	cwt	acres	bu.
Prince Edward Island	41	2,276	61	2,276	—	—
Nova Scotia	6	253	4	253	—	—
New Brunswick	10	420	10	420	—	—
Quebec	78	3,826	78	3,826	200	18,738
Ontario	335	18,998	335	18,998	1,870	169,202
Manitoba	1,450	58,000	1,450	58,000	130	7,800
Saskatchewan	2,600	90,000	2,600	90,000	—	—
Alberta	4,500	209,000	4,550	209,000	—	—
British Columbia	130	5,800	130	5,800	—	—
Total, Canada	9,200	388,373	9,200	388,573	2,200	195,740

	Flaxseed		Mixed grains		Rapeseed	
	1,000	1,000	1,000	1,000	1,000	1,000
Provinces	acres	bu.	acres	bu.	acres	bu.
Prince Edward Island	—	—	68	3,638	—	—
Nova Scotia	—	—	7	293	—	—
New Brunswick	—	—	8	399	—	—
Quebec	—	—	112	5,649	—	—
Ontario	—	—	790	49,532	—	—
Manitoba	1,250	17,500	140	5,900	1,350	25,000
Saskatchewan	800	10,200	90	3,300	3,300	56,500
Alberta	250	4,400	250	13,000	3,500	63,500
British Columbia	—	—	4	200,000	270	5,400
Total, Canada	2,300	32,100	1,469	281,711	8,420	150,400

Provinces	Fodder corn 1,000 acres	Fodder corn 1,000 tons	Soybeans 1,000 acres	Soybeans 1,000 bu.	Sugar-beet 1,000 acres	Sugar-beet 1,000 tons
Prince Edward Island	10	135	—	—	—	—
Nova Scotia	11	138	—	—	—	—
New Brunswick	7	88	—	—	—	—
Quebec	263	3,890	—	—	5	116
Ontario	810	10,487	700	24,652	—	—
Manitoba	45	360	—	—	22	276
Saskatchewan	—	—	—	—	—	—
Alberta	—	—	—	—	32	550
British Columbia	27	550	—	—	—	—
Total, Canada	1,173	15,648	700	24,652	59	942

Livestock. In parts of Saskatchewan and Alberta stockraising is still carried on as a primary industry, but the livestock industry of the country at large is mainly a subsidiary of mixed farming. The following table shows the numbers of livestock (in 1,000) by provinces in Jan. 1979:

Provinces	Milch cows	Other cattle	Sheep and lambs	Swine	Poultry [1]
Newfoundland	—	—	—	—	379
Prince Edward Island	25	68	4	97	148
Nova Scotia	40	84	22	89	901
New Brunswick	30	65	8	46	474
Quebec	785	725	38	2,240	3,799
Ontario	613	2,307	128	2,600	8,802
Manitoba	85	1,025	15	745	2,513
Saskatchewan	68	2,105	56	565	1,318
Alberta	142	3,561	119	1,035	2,350
British Columbia	83	517	32	78	2,704
Total 1978	1,938	10,932	389	6,653	24,588
Total 1979	1,870	10,458	421	7,495	23,388

[1] Layers only.

Net production of farm eggs in 1963, 417·2m. doz. ($160,178,000); 1978, 459·2m. doz. ($317·6m.); 1979, 421·7m. doz.

Wool production (in tonnes), 1965, 2,048; 1967, 1,618; 1968, 1,469; 1969, 1,460; 1970, 1,483; 1971, 1,623; 1972, 1,574; 1973, 1,482; 1974, 1,410; 1975, 1,266; 1976, 1,095; 1977, 938; 1978, 885; 1979, 1,147.

Dairying. The dairy products industry has shown a marked tendency towards centralization; the number of establishments decreased between 1961 and 1977 from 1,710 to 466 (72·8%), whereas the number of employees has decreased only 16·9%. Production, 1978: Creamery butter, 102,010 tonnes; cheddar cheese, 80,978 tonnes; concentrated whole milk products, 166,830 kg; ice cream mix, 141,170 kl. Total farm production of milk in 1978 was 7,614,800 tonnes.

Fruit Farming. The value of fruit production in 1979 was (in $1,000): Ontario, 91,517; British Columbia, 79,719; Quebec, 29,911; Nova Scotia, 13,975; New Brunswick, 3,815; Prince Edward Island, 745. Total apple production in Canada in 1979 was 434,898 tonnes, value $96·9m.

Tobacco. Commercial production of tobacco is confined to Ontario and Quebec. Farm cash receipts in 1978 totalled $263m.

Forestry. The total area of land covered by forests is estimated at about 3,417,000 sq. km, of which 3,141,000 sq. km are classed as production forest land.

Lumber production (in 1,000 bd ft) 1969, 11,100,357; 1970, 10,711,645; 1971, 12,030,735; 1972, 13,279,062; 1973, 14,751,564; 1974, 12,973,302; 1975, 10,421,411; 1976, 13,989,179; 1977, 16,334,729; 1978, 17,371,986.

The volume of lumber shipments in 1978 was 17,790,274,000 bd ft valued at $3,863·5m. Pulp production was 20·15m. tonnes in 1978 and 18·2m tonnes in 1977. In 1978 mill shipments of paper amounted to 13·16m. tonnes valued at $4,729,638,000.

Fur Trade. In 1978–79 (year ended 30 June), 4,424,232 pelts valued at $125,287,217, were taken. In wild-life pelt production beaver led in total value, followed by fox, lynx, muskrat and coyote. The most important animal raised on fur farms is mink, with 99% of the total production. The value of pelts from fur farms in 1978–79 was $43,539,362, of which mink accounted for $42,392,168. There were, in 1977, 509 fur farms, of which 107 reported fox and 402 mink.

Fisheries. During 1977, landings in Canadian commercial fisheries reached 1,254,900 tonnes. The landed value was $485·3m. and the estimated market value was $1,190·8m. The landed value of principal fish in 1977 was (in $1,000): Salmon, 114,213; cod, 65,646; lobster, 56,614; herring, 56,505; scallops, 44,092; freshwater fish, 29,106; halibut, 13,539.

Canadian Mines Handbook. Annual. Toronto, from 1931
Caves, R. E., and Holton, R. H., *The Canadian Economy: Prospect and Retrospect.* Harvard Univ. Press, 1959
Innis, H. A., *The Fur Trade in Canada.* Rev. ed. Toronto Univ. Press, 1956.—*The Cod Fisheries.* Rev. ed. Toronto, 1954
LeBourdais, D. M., *Metals and Men: The Survey of Canadian Mining.* Toronto, 1957.—*Canada and the Atomic Revolution.* Toronto, 1959
Lougheed, W. F., *Secondary Manufacturing Industry in the Canadian Economy.* Toronto, 1961
Rea, K. J., *The Political Economy of the Canadian North; An Interpretation of the Course of Development in the Northern Territories of Canada.* Toronto, 1968
Robinson, J. L., *Resources of the Canadian Shield.* Toronto, 1969
Scott, Anthony, *Natural Resources: The Economics of Conservation.* Toronto, 1955
Stovel, J. A., *Canada in the World Economy.* Harvard Univ. Press, 1959
Strange, H. G. L., *A Short History of Prairie Agriculture.* Winnipeg, 1954
Wilson, G. W., and others, *Canada: An Appraisal of Its Needs and Resources.* Toronto, 1965

INDUSTRY AND TRADE

Industry. Industry groups ranked by value of shipments, 1978:

Industry	Production workers	Wages ($1,000)	Cost of materials ($1,000)	Value of shipments ($1,000)
Food and beverages	153,935	1,967,398	14,877,808	21,955,726
Transportation equipment	137,230	2,260,452	12,320,558	18,022,888
Paper and allied industries	96,882	1,653,935	4,747,011	10,197,285
Petroleum and coal products	8,852	183,611	9,060,370	10,449,426
Primary metals	93,798	1,544,412	5,241,860	10,119,542
Metal fabricating	121,329	1,673,704	4,282,792	8,464,875
Chemical and chemical prods.	45,136	675,784	3,740,837	7,591,825
Wood industries	100,491	1,481,860	3,916,497	7,476,619
Electrical products	74,683	945,124	2,609,179	5,435,292
Machinery	61,967	885,248	2,638,915	5,037,502
Printing, publishing and allied industries	56,985	790,761	1,492,158	4,089,680
Non-metallic mineral products	41,404	639,598	1,378,725	3,602,657
Textiles	53,447	579,272	1,848,932	3,403,350
Clothing	87,758	764,100	1,588,337	3,114,860
Rubber and plastics	45,808	542,202	1,533,833	3,059,906
Miscellaneous manufacturing	47,234	493,345	1,396,464	2,736,772
Furniture and fixtures	39,293	414,576	804,489	1,703,827
Tobacco products	5,716	86,703	581,850	996,429
Leather industries	21,010	194,561	456,204	848,962
Knitting mills	17,566	156,723	377,237	711,796
All industries	1,310,524	17,933,370	74,894,056	129,019,220

Labour. In Oct. 1979 the industrial distribution of the employed was estimated as follows (in 1,000): Service, 2,997; manufacturing, 2,130; trade, 1,833; transportation, communication and other utilities, 912; construction, 709; public administration, 685; finance, insurance and real estate, 544; agriculture, 479; other primary industries, 301; total employed, 10,591; unemployed, 743.

Union returns filed for 1978 in compliance with the Corporations and Returns Act (1962), show 178 labour organizations reporting on 12,333 local union branches in Canada. Union membership in 1978 was 2·9m. 32·6% of the wage and salary workers in major industry groups were members of reporting labour organizations, with about 76% of the organized workers members of unions affiliated with the Canada Labour Congress. Over 1m. of the union members were in international unions, which have branches both in Canada and the USA and in most cases belong to central labour organizations in both countries.

It is generally established by legislation, both federal and provincial, that a trade union to which the majority of employees in a unit suitable for collective bargaining belong, is given certain rights and duties. An employer is required to meet and negotiate with such a trade union to determine wage-rates and other working conditions of his employees. The employer, the trade union and the employees affected are bound by the resulting agreement. If an impasse is reached in negotiation conciliation services provided by the appropriate government board are available. Generally, work stoppages may not take place until an established conciliation procedure has been carried out and are prohibited while an agreement is in effect. Almost 28% of the workers affected by collective agreements are in the manufacturing industry.

Freedom of association is a civil right in Canada, and under common law workers are at liberty to join unions and participate in their activities. This right has also been guaranteed by statutes which make it an offence to interfere with freedom of association.

Certain specific minimum standards in regard to working conditions are set by law, for the most part by provincial labour legislation. Minimum wages, maximum hours of work or an overtime rate of pay after a specified number of hours, minimum weekly rest periods and annual vacations with pay are established for the majority of workers.

Workmen injured in the course of employment or disabled by industrial disease are required to receive compensation under workmen's compensation laws which apply to most employees except agricultural workers. Benefits during the period of disability for work are set by law at a proportion (now 75%) of the workman's average earnings, subject to a maximum established in each province. Benefits (which also include monthly allowances to dependants in the case of the death of a workman caused by an accident or disease arising out of his employment) are paid out of an accident fund administered by a government board in each province. The fund is made up of contributions from employers according to an annual assessment rate, varying from a few cents to several dollars per $100 of payroll according to the hazards of the industry.

Dept. of Labour, *Working Conditions in Canadian Industry*. Annual. Ottawa
Cameron, J. C., *The Status of Trade Unions in Canada*. Kingston, 1960
Carrothers, A. W. R., *Labour Arbitration in Canada*. Toronto, 1961
Woods, H. D., *Labour Policy and Labour Economics in Canada*. Toronto, 1962

Commerce. In the past the custom tariff of Canada has been protective, with a preferential tariff in favour of the UK, the Dominions, a number of Crown Colonies, and the Irish and South African Republics. At the Imperial Economic Conference of 1932, held in Ottawa, the UK developed further the policy of preferential tariffs to the Dominions, and on the part of the latter there was a general lowering of the existing tariffs against certain lines of UK manufacturers. Canada is one of the signatories of the General Agreement on Tariffs and Trade (GATT) and of the Kennedy Round agreements.

Imports for home consumption and domestic exports (in Canadian $1,000) for calendar years (merchandise only):

	Imports	Exports		Imports	Exports
1960	5,842,695	5,255,575	1976	37,444,389	37,575,693
1970	13,951,903	16,820,098	1977	42,155,973	43,505,799
1974	31,692,121	31,674,495	1978	49,605,912	51,681,380
1975	34,690,714	32,466,068	1979	62,724,100	65,514,400

Exports (domestic) by countries in 1979 (in Canadian $1,000):

African Commonwealth Countries		Bahrain	3,997
(not elsewhere specified)	4,074	Bangladesh	79,217
Australia	556,598	Barbados	29,674
Bahamas	31,292	Belize	5,388

Bermuda	74,119	Greece	78,145
Britain	2,588,518	Greenland	6,228
British Oceania	192	Guatemala	21,294
Cyprus	12,991	Guinea	574
Falkland Islands	15	Haiti, Republic of	30,022
Fiji	1,804	Honduras	15,822
Gambia	56	Hungary	14,083
Ghana	32,130	Iceland	6,094
Gibraltar	22	Indonesia	62,643
Guyana	12,306	Iran	22,401
Hong Kong	137,417	Iraq	104,622
India	225,784	Israel	109,839
Irish Republic	52,018	Italy	729,336
Jamaica	61,685	Ivory Coast	32,557
Kenya	18,078	Japan	4,076,925
Leeward and Windward Islands	22,307	Jordan	11,521
Malaysia	65,329	Korea, North	1,773
Malawi	2,201	Korea, South	364,300
Malta	2,209	Kuwait	66,371
Mauritius and Dependencies	2,283	Lebanon	36,108
New Zealand	90,764	Liberia	52,856
Nigeria	49,900	Libya	—
Pakistan	87,229	Madagascar	1,153
Qatar	6,007	Mauritania	7,978
Sierra Leone	612	Mexico	236,459
Singapore	114,828	Morocco	67,705
South Africa, Republic of	106,092	Mozambique	17,375
Sri Lanka	12,069	Netherlands	1,081,932
Tanzania	33,357	Netherlands Antilles	14,927
Trinidad and Tobago	126,802	Nicaragua	2,824
Uganda	1,964	Norway	279,321
Zambia	2,970	Panama	22,767
		Paraguay	2,018
Afghánistán	1,019	Peru	43,355
Albania	97	Philippines	84,751
Algeria	214,751	Poland	261,623
Angola	828	Portugal	67,812
Argentina	284,249	Portuguese Africa	173
Austria	36,744	Puerto Rico	110,235
Belgium and Luxembourg	667,642	Romania	32,153
Benin	20,474	Saudi Arabia	251,638
Bolivia	5,939	Senegal	16,833
Brazil	421,563	Somalia	1,075
Bulgaria	9,323	Spain	218,000
Burma	2,482	Spanish Africa	27,353
Cameroon Republic	9,420	St Pierre and Miquelon	18,646
Chile	92,199	Sudan	8,941
China	596,108	Suriname	4,581
Colombia	97,031	Sweden	172,808
Costa Rica	35,590	Switzerland	184,342
Cuba	257,371	Syria	11,519
Czechoslovakia	35,226	Taiwan	103,695
Denmark	83,782	Thailand	87,248
Dominican Republic	33,390	Togo	8,552
Ecuador	49,030	Tunisia	39,660
Egypt (UAR)	36,701	Turkey	45,706
El Salvador	15,603	USSR	762,953
Ethiopia	3,104	United Arab Emirates	29,183
Finland	54,553	USA	43,438,502
France	619,611	US Oceania	1,882
French Africa	10,290	US Virgin Islands	3,204
French Guiana	140	Uruguay	11,339
French Oceania	1,242	Venezuela	671,116
French West Indies	1,705	Vietnam (South)	22,421
Gabon	1,291	Yemen	16,971
German Democratic Rep.	35,858	Yugoslavia	52,702
Germany, Fed. Rep. of	1,368,290	Zaïre	4,145

Imports (for consumption) by countries in 1979 (in Canadian $1,000):

African Commonwealth Countries		German Democratic Rep.	9,776
(not elsewhere specified)	29	Germany, Fed. Rep. of	1,556,239
Australia	466,099	Greece	30,423
Bahamas	10,468	Greenland	287
Bangladesh	8,481	Guatemala	16,617
Barbados	8,567	Guinea	20,985
Belize	1,071	Haiti, Republic of	6,643
Bermuda	1,026	Honduras	30,013
Britain	1,928,516	Hungary	31,215
Cyprus	487	Iceland	5,160
Fiji	9,410	Indonesia	42,108
Ghana	2,016	Iran	351,125
Gibraltar	5	Iraq	73,752
Guyana	33,033	Israel	56,309
Hong Kong	427,084	Italy	636,003
India	93,250	Ivory Coast	6,329
Irish Republic	79,840	Japan	2,157,120
Jamaica	50,140	Korea, North	442
Kenya	15,630	Korea, South	462,864
Leeward and Windward		Kuwait	106,962
Islands	3,159	Lebanon	609
Malaysia	96,284	Liberia	2,277
Malawi	341	Libya	204
Malta	1,514	Madagascar	588
Mauritius and Dependencies	3,852	Mauritania	244
New Zealand	135,088	Mexico	208,320
Nigeria	717	Morocco	6,768
Pakistan	11,302	Mozambique	4,134
Sierra Leone	2,735	Netherlands	251,763
Singapore	164,029	Netherlands Antilles	34,661
South Africa, Republic of	240,364	Nicaragua	8,695
Sri Lanka	17,068	Norway	89,074
Tanzania	3,376	Panama	22,950
Trinidad and Tobago	19,006	Paraguay	14,501
Uganda	28	Peru	48,864
Zambia	3	Philippines	78,285
		Poland	82,778
Afghánistán	1,002	Portugal	49,550
Albania	54	Portuguese Africa	4
Algeria	87,274	Portuguese Asia	4,384
Angola	12,805	Puerto Rico	75,799
Argentina	65,463	Romania	39,488
Austria	101,799	Saudi Arabia	1,241,973
Belgium and Luxembourg	241,443	Senegal	156
Benin	2	Spain	177,395
Bolivia	16,109	Spanish Africa	7
Brazil	313,188	St Pierre and Miquelon	212
Bulgaria	6,302	Sudan	265
Burma	705	Suriname	10,422
Cameroon Republic	97	Sweden	383,457
Chile	55,355	Switzerland	323,472
China	167,451	Syria	30
Colombia	95,834	Taiwan	522,003
Costa Rica	34,801	Thailand	31,705
Cuba	106,633	Togo	48
Czechoslovakia	67,509	Tunisia	712
Denmark	117,782	Turkey	12,799
Dominican Republic	22,740	USSR	64,088
Ecuador	57,903	United Arab Emirates	905
Egypt (UAR)	89,538	USA	45,419,508
El Salvador	27,287	US Virgin Islands	375
Ethiopia	951	Uruguay	10,476
Finland	54,117	Venezuela	1,504,969
France	777,670	Vietnam, South	16
French Africa	3,155	Yemen	7
French Oceania	29	Yugoslavia	25,788
French West Indies	46	Zaïre	1,776
Gabon	1,568		

Selected imports into Canada in 1979 (in Canadian $1m.):

Motor vehicles and parts	15,021	Metal fabricated basic products	1,067
Industrial machinery	5,689	Rolling mill products	947
Crude petroleum	4,507	Apparel and accessories	884
Chemicals	3,234	Coal	865
Agricultural machinery including		Cocoa, chocolate, coffee and tea	643
tractors	2,115	Fresh fruit	505
Telecommunication and		Petroleum and coal products	391
related equipment	1,965	Fresh vegetables	339
Non-ferrous metals	1,965	Meat, fresh, chilled or frozen	339
Textile fabricated materials	1,391	Wool, cotton and man-made fibres	262
Office machines and equipment	1,347	Raw sugar	236

Selected exports (Canadian produce) in 1979 (in Canadian $1m.):

Motor vehicles and parts	11,807	Aluminium and alloys	918
Lumber, softwood	3,901	Agricultural machinery	848
Newsprint	3,222	Coal and crude bitumen	835
Pulp	3,084	Asbestos	653
Natural gas	2,889	Rolling mill products	644
Crude petroleum	2,315	Rapeseed	631
Wheat	2,180	Copper and alloys	612
Industrial machinery	1,945	Nickel and alloys	576
Iron ores and concentrates	1,354	Copper ores, concentrates and scrap	537
Fish and preparations	1,289	Nickel ores, concentrates and scrap	332
Fertilizers	987		

Total trade of Canada with UK (British Department of Trade returns, in £1,000 sterling):

	1976	1977	1978	1979	1980
Imports to UK	1,159,651	1,222,871	1,088,897	1,260,057	1,412,156
Exports and re-exports from UK	628,470	712,662	740,508	766,430	758,367

Litvak, I., and Mallen, B., *Marketing in Canada: Recent Readings*. Toronto, 1964
Mahatoo, W. H., *Marketing Research in Canada*. Toronto, 1968
Newman, D., and Newman, J. P., *Canadian Business Handbook*. Toronto, 1964
Officer, L. H. (ed.), *Canadian Economic Problems and Policies*. Toronto, 1970
Shea, A. A., *Canada 1980*. Toronto, 1960
Wilkinson, B. W., *Canada's International Trade: An Analysis of Recent Trends and Patterns*. Toronto, 1968

Tourism. The number of visitors to Canada in 1977 was 33,198,495 (1976, 33,808,232). In 1977, 31,773,811 came from USA (1976, 32,230,902).

COMMUNICATIONS

Roads. The total highway mileage in Canada in 1976 was 549,462 (884,273 km). Of this total 442,615 miles (712,319 km) were surfaced and 106,453 miles (171,336 km) improved and other earth roads. Expenditure (1976) on roads, bridges, ferries, etc., reached a total of $4,449m. Federal and provincial governments supplied $2,905m., with the remainder contributed by municipal and other sources. Federal expenditures were chiefly devoted towards the upkeep of national-park roadways and nationally owned bridges and ferries, although for the 'Mackenzie Highway' from Grimshaw, Alberta, to Hay River, Northwest Territories, the federal government paid about 68% of the total cost. In general, however, highways are provincially controlled and maintained, and the responsibility of assisting municipalities and townships falls directly on the provinces.

The Alaska Highway is part of the Canadian highway system. For the Trans-Canada Highway *see* map in THE STATESMAN'S YEAR-BOOK, 1962.

Registered motor vehicles totalled 12,975,449 in 1978; they included 9,744,994 passenger cars and taxis, 2,770,798 trucks and buses and 341,381 motor cycles.

Urban Transit. In 1979 urban transit systems (motor bus, trolley coach, street car and subway operations) carried 1,094,593,460 fare passengers 347,245,150 vehicle-miles for an operating revenue of $421,111,859. In 1978, intercity and rural bus operations carried 33,837,301 fare passengers 121,915,986 vehicle-miles, earning revenues of $ 142,770,591.

Railways. The total mileage of railways in Canada on 31 Dec. 1977 was 43,476. The total track mileage, including route duplicate, yardtrack and sidings, was 59,022.

Canada has 2 great trans-continental systems: the Canadian National Railway system (CN), a government-owned body which operates 22,244 miles of the total first maintrack, and the Canadian Pacific Limited (CP Rail), a joint-stock corporation with first maintrack totalling 15,589 miles (April 1980). From 1 April 1978, a government funded organization known as Via Rail took over passenger services formerly operated by CP and CN.

Selected statistics of Canadian railways for 1977: Passengers carried 23,862,260; revenue freight, 145,493,143 ton-miles; freight revenue, $2,935,256,583; total railway operating revenues, $3,538,093,295m.

Aviation. Civil aviation in Canada is under the jurisdiction of the federal government. The technical and administrative aspects are supervised by the Administrator of Air Transportation, while the economic functions are assigned to the Canadian Transportation Commission.

In 1979 Canadian airports handled 48,963,867 passengers, 127,066,000 kg of mail and 523·66m. kg of cargo. Operating revenue (1978) was $2,583·3m.; operating expenditure, $2,420·5m.

Shipping. The registered shipping on 31 Dec. 1978, including vessels for inland navigation, totalled 31,162 with a gross tonnage of 4,642,399. A total of 57,555 vessels (international shipping) visited Canadian ports in 1979, loading and unloading 230m. tonnes of cargo.

The major canals in Canada are those of the St Lawrence–Great Lakes waterway with their 7 locks, providing navigation for vessels of 25·75-ft draught from Montreal to Lake Ontario; the Welland Canal by-passing the Niagara River between Lake Ontario and Lake Erie with its 8 locks; and the Sault Ste Marie Canal and lock between Lake Huron and Lake Superior. These 16 locks overcome a drop of 582 ft from the head of the lakes to Montreal. The St Lawrence Seaway was opened to navigation on 1 April 1959 (*see* map in THE STATESMAN'S YEAR-BOOK, 1957). In 1978, traffic on the Montreal–Lake Ontario Section of the Seaway numbered 5,346 vessel transits carrying 56,942,680 cargo tonnes; on the Welland Canal Section, 6,626 transits with 65,670,992 gross tonnes. Value of fixed assets was $777,921,614 and investments, $34,892,056 at 31 March 1979.

Coast Guard. The Canadian Coast Guard (formed in 1962) is responsible to the Minister of Transport. In 1979 it comprised 6 heavy icebreakers; a heavy icebreaker/cable repair vessel; 8 medium icebreakers/aid tenders; 11 light ice-breakers/aid tenders; 9 aid tenders; 4 special shallow draft vessels; 2 ocean weather ships; 30 search and rescue vessels (all types and sizes); 3 hovercraft and 30 helicopters.

Post. On 31 March 1977 there were 8,392 postal facilities in operation and 5,900m. pieces of mail were processed. Gross revenue was $945·8m.; gross expenditure, $1,505m. for the fiscal year 1977–78.

There were 846,954 miles (1,363,186 km) of telegraph wire in Canada in 1977 (including external cable landed in Canada). There were 98·4m. miles (158,378,000 km) of telephone wire and 14,505,728 telephones on 1 Jan. 1978 (63·2 per 100 population).

Broadcasting. There were 622 originating stations operating in Canada at 31 March 1978, of which 91 were Canadian Broadcasting Corporation stations, 130 were CBC affiliates and 401 were privately owned and operated. Included were 379 AM radio stations, 138 FM radio stations, 102 television stations, 1 low power transmitter and 2 short-wave stations. Radio and television licence fees were abolished in 1953.

Wireless 'beam' stations are operated at Montreal for direct communications with Great Britain and Australia, and a station at Louisburg, N.S., provides a long-distance service to ships.

Cinemas (1977). There were 1,094 cinemas with a seating capacity of 642,915 and 298 drive-in theatres with a capacity of 139,689 cars.

Newspapers (1977). There were 120 daily newspapers, of which 108 were in English and 12 in French.

JUSTICE, RELIGION, EDUCATION AND WELFARE

Justice. There is a Supreme Court in Ottawa, having general appellate jurisdiction in civil and criminal cases throughout Canada. There is an Exchequer Court, which is also a Court of Admiralty. There is a Superior Court in each province and county courts, with limited jurisdiction, in most of the provinces, all the judges in these courts being appointed by the Governor-General. Police, magistrates and justices of the peace are appointed by the provincial governments.

For the year ended 31 Dec. 1977, 1,755,308 Criminal Code Offences were reported and 379,338 persons were charged.

Canadian Legal and Directory. Toronto. Annual
Anger, W. H., and Anger, H. D., *A Digest of Canadian Law.* 19th ed. Toronto, 1967
Gosse, R., *The Law on Competition in Canada.* Toronto, 1962
Houlden, L. W., *Bankruptcy Law of Canada.* Toronto, 1960
McRuer, J. D., *The Evolution of the Judicial Process.* Toronto, 1957
McWhinney, E., *Canadian Jurisprudence: Civil Law and Common Law.* Toronto, 1958
O'Connor, A. R. M., *An Analysis of and a Guide to the New Criminal Code.* Toronto, 1955

Religion. Membership of the leading denominations in 1971:

Province	Roman Catholic	United Church of Canada	Anglican Church of Canada	Presby-terian	Lutheran
Newfoundland	190,960	101,805	144,445	3,055	515
Prince Edward Island	51,215	27,830	6,905	13,050	95
Nova Scotia	286,320	162,885	135,695	40,380	11,570
New Brunswick	331,290	85,185	69,260	13,155	1,875
Quebec	5,226,150	176,825	181,875	51,785	23,845
Ontario	2,568,695	1,682,820	1,220,535	540,035	267,225
Manitoba	242,855	256,560	123,015	30,825	64,735
Saskatchewan	258,630	274,285	87,210	20,805	90,850
Alberta	391,390	456,925	170,230	57,185	133,045
British Columbia	408,330	537,565	386,670	100,940	120,335
Yukon	4,670	3,110	4,645	690	925
Northwest Territories	14,385	3,005	12,685	445	725
Total, Canada	9,974,895	3,768,805	2,543,175	872,330	715,740

Other denominations: Baptist, 667,245; Greek Orthodox, 316,605; Jewish, 276,025; Ukrainian (Greek) Catholic, 227,730; Pentecostal, 220,390; Mennonite, 168,150; other, 1,817,220.

Boon, T. C. B., *The Anglican Church from the Bay to the Rockies.* Toronto, 1962
Clark, S. D., *Church and Sect in Canada.* Toronto, 1968
Walsh, H. H., *The Christian Church in Canada.* Toronto, 1956
Wilson, D. J., *The Church Grows in Canada.* Toronto, 1966

Education. By the British North American Act each provincial government is responsible for its education system. While each system differs from the others in particulars, the general plan is similar for all provinces. Separate elementary and secondary schools for minority groups, mainly Roman Catholic, are found in most provinces. Though administration of the schools in Newfoundland has a denominational basis, they are not exclusive and a number are non-denominational. In general, education is free to the end of the secondary level. The principal sources of revenue are provincial government grants and direct taxation for school purposes. Except in Quebec the number of private schools is small; their enrolment was less than 4% of the total in elementary and secondary grades.

The federal government operates schools for Indians and Eskimos with an enrolment in 1976–77 of 33,187. An additional 38,530 attend non-federal schools.

In 1978–79, 367,968 full-time regular students were enrolled in 65 degree-granting institutions, other than purely theological institutions. In 1977–78 some 107,468 enrolled in arts and science, 28,148 in engineering, 30,230 in commercial business administration, 8,150 in medicine, 9,402 in law, 129,225 in other faculties. Another 100,529 or more students were enrolled in part-time courses.

The following statistics give information, for 1977–78, about all elementary and secondary schools, public, federal and private:

Province	Schools	Teachers	Pupils
Newfoundland	692	7,711	153,576
Prince Edward Island	73	1,426	27,225
Nova Scotia	613	11,078	196,811
New Brunswick	485	7,813	160,673
Quebec	3,021	68,494	1,297,690
Ontario	5,200	99,276	1,974,702
Manitoba	809	12,479	232,470
Saskatchewan	1,052	11,087	220,979
Alberta	1,429	22,534	448,183
British Columbia	1,866	27,955	545,062
Yukon	23	278	5,247
Northwest Territories	70	710	12,903
National Defence (overseas)	11	265	3,960
Total	15,344	271,106	5,279,481

Association of Canadian Universities & Colleges. *Canadian Universities & Colleges.* Ottawa. Annual

Craik, W. A., *History of Canadian Journalism.* 2 vols. Toronto, 1959

Harris, R. S., and Trembley, A., *A Bibliography of Higher Education in Canada.* Toronto and Quebec, 1960

Hodgetts, J. W., *Higher Education in a Changing Canada.* Toronto, 1966

Wilson, J. D., and others, *Canadian Education: A History.* Toronto, 1970

Health. Canada achieves national health insurance through a series of interlocking provincial plans which qualify the provinces for federal financial support if they meet the minimum criteria of the federal legislation with respect to comprehensiveness of coverage with regard to services, universality of coverage with regard to people, accessibility to services uninhibited by excessive user charges, portability of benefits and non-profit administration by a public agency. The federal contributions to the provinces cover about 50% of the provincial costs for the insured services of the national Hospital Insurance and Medical Care Programmes. (In the health field the federal government also furnishes the provinces with *per capita* cash contributions towards the cost of extended health care services; *e.g.*, nursing home care, certain home care services, but the provinces do not need to meet the programme criteria described above with respect to these latter contributions.)

The Canadian approach to the development of a national health programme has been to progressively provide major segments of personal health care on a publicly financed basis to virtually the whole population, and this is achieved with the co-operation of the provinces, which exercise the primary constitutional prerogative in health matters.

The insurance programmes are designed to ensure that all residents of Canada have access to needed medical and hospital care on a prepaid basis. The insured services of the Hospital Insurance Programme, which commenced in 1958, include in-patient care (including necessary drugs, diagnostic tests, etc.), as well as elective out-patient services that vary somewhat from province to province. Complementing the protection of the Hospital Insurance Programme is the Medical Care Programme, inaugurated in 1968, which covers all medically required services rendered by medical practitioners no matter where the services are rendered, and certain surgical–dental procedures undertaken by dental surgeons in hospital. All 10 provinces and the 2 northern territories are participating in both programmes, which provide health insurance coverage for over 99% of the population (or over 23m. people).

The approach taken by Canada is one of state-sponsored health insurance. Accordingly, the advent of the programmes produced little change in the ownership of hospitals, almost all of which are owned by non-governmental non-profit corporations, and the rights and privileges of private medical practice. Patients are free to choose their own general practitioners and/or specialists without losing their insured benefits (there is a minor exception in Quebec involving only a few physicians). Except for 0·5% of the population whose care is provided for under other legislation (such as serving members of the Canadian Armed Forces), all residents are eligible, regardless of whether they are in the work force. Benefits are available without upper limit so long as they are medically necessary. Benefits are also portable during any temporary absence from Canada anywhere in the world—subject to any limitation a province may impose upon treatment electively sought outside the particular province without prior approval, though such a restriction does not pertain to emergency care.

In addition to the benefits qualifying for federal contributions, provinces are free to provide additional benefits at their own discretion. Most provinces provide such benefits, which cover a variety of services (e.g., optometric care, children's dental programme, drug benefits) depending upon the province. Most provinces fund their portion of health insurance costs out of general provincial revenues. Three provinces levy premiums which meet part of the provincial costs, 1 province imposes a special income-tax surcharge and a levy on employers, and 1 province utilizes part of its sales tax revenues for this purpose. Two provinces have nominal co-charges for short-term hospital care. Three provinces have charges for long-term hospital care geared, approximately, to the room and board portion of the OAS–GIS payments mentioned under Social Welfare.

Social Welfare. The Department of Health and Welfare administers a number of social security programmes. Most notable among them, as welfare programmes, are the Family Allowances programme, introduced in 1945 and amended in 1974; the Old Age Security programme, introduced in 1952 and to which were added the Guaranteed Income Supplement in 1966 and the Spouse's Allowance in 1974; and the Canada Pension Plan which came into being in 1966. Social assistance and services programmes which are provided by the provinces and territories are cost-shared by the federal government under the Canada Assistance Plan, which was introduced in 1966.

The 1974 federal Family Allowances Act provides for the payment of a monthly Family Allowance ($23.89 in 1977) on behalf of a dependent child under the age of 18. This allowance is paid to a parent who is a resident of Canada, who wholly or substantially maintains the child and who is either a Canadian citizen, a landed immigrant or a non-immigrant admitted to Canada for a period of not less than 1 year, during which time his or her income is subject to Canadian Income Tax. Benefits are also paid under certain prescribed circumstances to Canadian citizens living abroad. A Special Allowance is paid on behalf of a child under the age of 18 who is maintained by a welfare agency, a government department or an institution. In some cases, payment is made directly to a foster parent.

The Family Allowances Act provides for the escalation of benefits, in January of each year, based on the Consumer Price Index. It also specifies that a provincial legislature may vary the monthly federal rate payable within that province subject to the fulfilment of stipulated conditions. Only the provinces of Alberta and Quebec have exercised this option.

Generally speaking, the Canada Pension Plan and the Quebec Pension Plan are an integral part of Canada's social security system, serving as the vehicle whereby millions of members of the Canadian labour force acquire and retain, during their productive years, protection for themselves and their families against loss of income due to retirement, disability or death, regardless of where their employment may take them in Canada and, under certain circumstances, outside Canada.

The Canada Pension Plan does not operate in Quebec because the province exercised its constitutional prerogative to establish a similar provincial pension plan to operate in lieu of CPP.

The Plans cover employed members of the labour force between the ages of 18 and 70, with a small number of exceptions (*e.g.*, a person working for his/her spouse, and members of certain religious sects who have opted out of the Plans). Both plans are funded through direct contributions and interest on the investment of excess funds. Contributions are deductible for income-tax purposes, while benefits are taxable and are adjusted annually to fully reflect increases in the Consumer Price Index.

The Old Age Security (OAS) pension is payable to persons 65 years of age and over who satisfy the residence requirements stipulated in the Old Age Security Act. The amount payable, whether full or partial, is also governed by stipulated conditions, as is the payment of an OAS pension to a recipient who absents himself from Canada. OAS pensioners with little or no income apart from OAS may, upon application, receive a full or partial supplement known as the Guaranteed Income Supplement (GIS). Entitlement is normally based on the pensioner's income in the preceding year, calculated in accordance with the Income Tax Act. The spouse of an OAS pensioner, aged 60 to 64, meeting the same residence requirements as those stipulated for OAS, may be eligible for a full or partial Spouse's Allowance (SA). As of July 1977, SA is payable, upon application, if the annual combined income of the couple is less than $6,816. This is subject to an income test which does not include the OAS pension, the Guaranteed Income Supplement or the Spouse's Allowance.

The OAS pension is taxable; GIS and SA are not taxable. However, they must be included in computing the net income of a dependant for income-tax purposes. OAS, GIS and SA are subject to an increase every January, April, July and October to reflect increases in the Consumer Price Index.

Under the Canada Assistance Plan, the federal government pays 50% of the cost, to the provinces, of assistance to persons in need; welfare services provided to persons who are in need or likely to become in need if they do not receive such services (welfare services means services having as their object the lessening, removal or prevention of the causes and effects of poverty, child neglect or dependence on public assistance); and work activity projects which are designed to improve the employability of persons who have unusual difficulty in finding or retaining jobs or in undertaking job training.

In addition to persons in need as defined in the Plan, federal contributions may be made towards agency costs of providing welfare services to persons who are likely to become in need, if such services are not provided. The amount of federal subsidy is dependent on the proportion of eligible persons as determined by the use of an income test or a pre-determined income level for different sized families. 'Need' is defined by each province and is determined by the 'budget deficit' method, that is, the difference between an applicant's requirements and his income and resources. The rates of assistance payable are also determined by provincial authorities and are non-taxable. No systematic indexation exists; however, provinces do adjust social assistance rates from time to time in accordance with certain economic indicators. Quebec social assistance rates are indexed at the beginning of each year by the rate of change in the Quebec Pension Index.

In 1979, the Unemployment Insurance payments totalled $4,008m. The number of beneficiaries averaged 713,426 each month for average weekly payments of $108.63.

DIPLOMATIC REPRESENTATIVES

OF CANADA IN GREAT BRITAIN
(Macdonald House., Grosvenor Sq., London, W1X 0AB)

High Commissioner: Jean Casselman Wadds.

OF GREAT BRITAIN IN CANADA
(80 Elgin St., Ottawa, K1P 5K7)

High Commissioner: Lord Moran, KCMG.

OF CANADA IN USA
(1746 Massachusetts Ave., NW, Washington, D.C., 20036)
Ambassador: Peter M. Towe.

OF THE USA IN CANADA (100 Wellington St., Ottawa)
Ambassador: Kenneth M. Curtis.

OF CANADA TO THE UNITED NATIONS
Ambassador: William H. Barton.

Books of Reference

Statistical Information: Statistics Canada, Ottawa, has been the official central statistical organization for Canada since 1918. The Bureau, which reports to Parliament through the Minister of Industry, Trade and Commerce, serves as the statistical agency for federal government departments; co-ordinates the statistics of the provincial governments along national lines; and channels all Canadian statistical data to internal organizations. *Statistician Chief of Canada:* Dr Peter G. Kirkham.

Publications of Statistics Canada are classified as periodical (issued more frequently than once a year), annual, biennial and occasional publications. The occasional publications frequently supplement the annual reports and usually contain historical information. A complete list is contained in the 1978–79 edition of the Statistics Canada catalogue and supplements, available on request. Official publications include:

The Canada Year Book. Annual, from 1905
Canada, Official Handbook. Annual, from 1930
Canadian Statistical Review. Monthly, with weekly supplements, from 1948
1966 Census of Canada. Ottawa, 1967
1976 Census of Canada. Ottawa, 1977
Tenth Decennial Census of Canada, 1961. Ottawa, 1962
Eleventh Decennial Census of Canada, 1971. Ottawa, 1972

Atlas and Gazetteer of Canada. Dept. of Energy, Mines and Resources. Ottawa, 1969
Cambridge History of the British Empire. Vol. VI. Canada and Newfoundland. Cambridge, 1930
Canadian Almanac and Directory. Toronto. Annual
Canadian Annual Review. Annual, from 1960
Canadian Dictionary: French–English. Toronto, 1970
Canadian Who's Who. 11th ed. Toronto, 1969
Canadiana; A List of Publications of Canadian Interest. National Library, Ottawa. Monthly, with annual cumulation. 1951 ff.
National Reference Book on Canadian Business Personalities. 11th ed. Montreal, 1969
Bohne, H. (ed.), *Canadian Books in Print, 1970.* Toronto, 1970
Brebner, J. B., *North Atlantic Triangle: The Interplay of Canada, the United States and Great Britain.* New York, 1958
Brown, G. W. (ed.), *Dictionary of Canadian Biography,* Vol. I. Univ. of Toronto Press, 1966
Bruchési, Jean, *L'Histoire du Canada.* 6th ed. Montreal, 1951.—*Canada, réalités d'hier et d'aujourd'hui.* Montreal, 1954.—*Le Canada.* Paris, 1952
Brunet, M., and others. *Histoire du Canada par les textes.* Montreal, 1952
Camu, P., Weeks, E. P., and Sametz, Z. W., *Economic Geography of Canada.* London, 1965
Careless, J. M. S., *Canada, A Story of Challenge.* Ref. ed. Toronto, 1963
Careless, J., and Brown, R. C. (ed.), *The Canadians, 1867–1967.* Toronto, 1967
Cook, R., *French-Canadian Nationalism; An Anthology.* Toronto, 1970.—*The Maple Leaf Forever; Essays on Nationalism and Politics in Canada.* Toronto, 1971
Creighton, Donald G., *Dominion of the North: A History of Canada.* New ed. Toronto, 1957.—*The Empire of the St Lawrence.* Toronto, 1956.—*Canada's First Century.* Toronto, 1970.—*Towards the Discovery of Canada.* Toronto, 1974
Dictionnaire Bélisle de la langue française au Canada; dictionnaire oxford. 1970
Dictionnaire canadien; français–anglais–français. Toronto, 1962
Encyclopedia Canadiana. 10 vols. Rev. ed. Ottawa, 1967
Fortin, J.-A., *Biographies canadiennes-françaises.* 16th ed. Montreal, 1952
Garneau, F. X., *Histoire du Canada.* 8th ed. Montreal, 1944–45
Glazebrook, G. P. de T., *A History of Canadian External Relations.* Toronto, 1950
Hardy, W. G., *From Sea to Sea; Canada, 1850–1920: The Road to Nationhood.* Toronto, 1960
Hawkins, F., *Canada and Immigration.* Montreal and London, 1972
Hockin, T. A., *Government in Canada.* London, 1976
Keenleyside, H. L., *Canada and the United States.* Rev. ed. New York, 1952
Kerr, D. G. G., *Historical Atlas of Canada.* Toronto, 1960

Lefebvre, F. J., *Le Canada, l'Amérique-géographique, historique, biographique, littéraire; supplément du Larousse canadien complet*. Montreal, 1954
Lower, A. R. M., *Colony to Nation: A History of Canada*. 4th ed. Toronto, 1964
Lumsden, I. (ed.), *Close the 49th Parallel, etc.; The Americanization of Canada*. Toronto, 1970
Mallory, J. R., *The Structure of Canadian Government*. Toronto, 1971
McInnis, E., *Canada: A Political and Social History*. Rev. ed. Toronto, 1959
MacLennan, Hugh, *Seven Rivers of Canada: the Mackenzie, the St Lawrence, the Ottawa, the Red, the Saskatchewan, the Fraser, the St John*. Toronto, 1961
Moir, J., and Saunders, R., *Northern Destiny: A History of Canada*. Toronto, 1970
Morton, W. L., *The Kingdom of Canada; A General History from Earliest Times*. Toronto, 1969
Putnam, D. F., *Canadian Regions. A Geography of Canada*. 2nd ed. Toronto, 1954.—*Canada: A Regional Analysis*. Toronto, 1970
Ross, M. M., *Our Sense of Identity; A Book of Canadian Essays*. Toronto, 1954
Sandwell, B. R., *La nation canadienne*. Monaco, 1954
Tanghe, R., *Bibliography of Canadian Bibliographies*. Toronto, 1962
Urquhart, M. C., and Buckley, K. A. H. (ed.), *Historical Statistics of Canada*. Toronto, 1965
Wallace, W. (ed.), *Macmillan Dictionary of Canadian Biography*. Toronto, 1963
Warkentor, J. (ed.), *Canada; A Geographical Interpretation*. Toronto, 1968
Wilson, G. W., and others, *Canada: An Appraisal of Its Need and Resources*. New York, 1965

National Library: The National Library of Canada, Ottawa, Ontario. *Librarian:* J. Guy Sylvestre.

CANADIAN PROVINCES

The 10 provinces have each a separate parliament and administration, with a Lieut.-Governor, appointed by the Governor-General in Council at the head of the executive. They have full powers to regulate their own local affairs and dispose of their revenues, provided only they do not interfere with the action and policy of the central administration. Among the subjects assigned exclusively to the provincial legislatures are: the amendment of the provincial constitution, except as regards the office of the Lieut.-Governor; property and civil rights; direct taxation for revenue purposes; borrowing; management and sale of Crown lands; provincial hospitals, reformatories, etc.; shop, saloon, tavern, auctioneer and other licences for local or provincial purposes; local works and undertakings, except lines of ships, railways, canals, telegraphs, etc., extending beyond the province or connecting with other provinces, and excepting also such works as the Dominion Parliament declares are for the general good; marriages, administration of justice within the province; education.

Local Government. Under the terms of the British North America Act the provinces are given full powers over local government. All local government institutions are, therefore, supervised by the provinces, and are incorporated and function under provincial acts.

The acts under which municipalities operate vary from province to province. A municipal corporation is usually administered by an elected council headed by a mayor or reeve, whose powers to administer affairs and to raise funds by taxation and other methods are set forth in provincial laws, as is the scope of its obligations to, and on behalf of, the citizens. Similarly, the types of municipal corporations, their official designations and the requirements for their incorporation vary between provinces. The following table sets out the classifications as at 1 Jan. 1977.

Type and size of group	Nfld.	PEI	NS	NB	Que.	Ont.	Man.
Type:							
Regional municipalities	—	—	—	—	75	39	—
Metropolitan and regional municipalities[1]	—	—	—	—	3	12	—
Counties and regional districts	—	—	—	—	72	27	—

For note see end of table.

Type and size of group	Nfld.	PEI	NS	NB	Que.	Ont.	Man.
Type (*contd.*):							
Unitary municipalities	129	36	65	112	1,500	784	185
Cities	2	1	3	6	64	45[2]	5
Towns	127[3]	8	38	21	195	144	35
Villages	—	27	—	85	242	120	40
Rural municipalities[4]	—	—	24	—	999	475	105
Quasi-municipalities[5]	171	—	—	—	—	13	17
Total	300	36	65	112	1,575	836	202
Population size group (1976 census):							
Unitary municipalities—							
Over 100,000	—	—	1	—	4	17	1
50,000 to 99,999	1	—	2	2	14	14	—
10,000 to 49,999	5	1	17	5	72	76	3
Under 10,000	123	35	45	105	1,410	677	181
Total	129	36	65	112	1,500	784	185

Type and size of group	Sask.	Alta.	BC	YT	NWT	Canada
Type:						
Regional municipalities	—	—	28	—	—	142
Metropolitan and regional municipalities[1]	—	—	—	—	—	15
Counties and regional districts	—	—	28	—	—	127
Unitary municipalities	783	327	140	3	7	4,071
Cities	11	10	33	2	1	183
Towns	135	102	10	1	4	820
Villages	344	167	59	—	2	1,086
Rural municipalities[4]	293	48	38	—	—	1,982
Quasi-municipalities[5]	7	22	—	4	10	244
Total	790	349	168	7	17	4,457
Population size group (1976 census):						
Unitary municipalities—						
Over 100,000	2	2	3	—	—	30
50,000 to 99,999	—	—	9	—	—	42
10,000 to 49,999	6	14	26	1	—	227
Under 10,000	775	311	102	2	7	3,772
Total	783	327	140	3	7	4,071

[1] Includes urban communities in Quebec; and Metropolitan Toronto, regional municipalities and the district municipality in Ontario.
[2] Includes the 5 boroughs of Metropolitan Toronto.
[3] Includes 11 rural districts.
[4] Includes municipalities in Nova Scotia; parishes, townships, united townships and municipalities in Quebec; townships in Ontario; rural municipalities in Manitoba and Saskatchewan; municipal districts and counties in Alberta; and districts in British Columbia.
[5] Includes local government communities, local improvement districts and the metropolitan area in Newfoundland; improvement districts in Ontario and Alberta; local government districts in Manitoba; local improvement districts in Saskatchewan and the Yukon Territory; and hamlets in the Northwest Territories.

ALBERTA

HISTORY. The southern half of the province of Alberta was part of Rupert's land which was granted by royal charter in 1670 to the Hudson's Bay Company. The intervention by the North West Company in the fur trade after 1783 led to the establishment of trading posts. In 1869 Rupert's land was transferred from the Hudson's Bay Company (which had absorbed its rival in 1821) to the new Dominion, and in the following year this land was combined with the former Crown land of the North Western Territories to form the Northwest Territories.

In 1882 'Alberta' first appeared as a provisional 'district', consisting of the southern half of the present province. In 1905 the Athabasca district to the north was added when provincial status was granted to Alberta.

Four parties have held office: the Liberals 1905–21; the United Farmers 1921–35; Social Credit 1935–71, and Progressive Conservative since Sept. 1971.

AREA AND POPULATION. The area of the province is 661,188 sq. km; 644,392 sq. km being land area and 16,796 sq. km water area. The population (estimate 1 June 1980) was 2,086,400; the urban population, centres of 1,000 or over, was 1,564,800 and the rural 521,600. Population of the principal cities (1 June 1979): Calgary, 560,618; Edmonton, 505,773; Lethbridge, 53,135; Red Deer, 41,371; Medicine Hat, 37,684; St Albert, 29,512, Fort McMurray, 27,784 and Grande Prairie, 22,718.

Vital statistics, *see* p. 266.

Religion, *see* p. 284.

CONSTITUTION AND GOVERNMENT. The constitution of Alberta is contained in the British North America Act of 1867, and amending Acts; also in the Alberta Act of 1905, passed by the Parliament of the Dominion of Canada, which created the province out of the then Northwest Territories. All the provisions of the British North America Act, except those with respect to school lands and the public domain, were made to apply to Alberta as they apply to the older provinces of Canada. On 1 Oct. 1930 the natural resources were transferred from the Dominion to provincial government control. The province is represented by 6 members in the Senate and 21 in the House of Commons of Canada.

The executive is vested nominally in the Lieut.-Governor, who is appointed by the federal government, but actually in the Executive Council or the Cabinet of the legislature. Legislative power is vested in the Assembly in the name of the Queen.

Members of the Legislative Assembly are elected by the universal vote of adults over the age of 18 years.

There are 79 members in the legislature (elected 14 March 1979): 74 Progressive Conservative, 4 Social Credit, 1 New Democratic Party.

Lieut.-Governor: His Hon. Frank Lynch-Staunton (sworn in 4 Oct. 1979).

Flag: Blue with the shield of the province in the centre.

The members of the Ministry (all Progressive Conservative) are as follows:

Premier, President of Executive Council: Hon. Peter Lougheed.

Provincial Treasurer: Hon. L. D. Hyndman. *Energy and Natural Resources:* Hon. C. M. Leitch. *Attorney-General and Government House Leader:* Hon. N. S. Crawford. *Hospitals and Medical Care:* Hon. D. J. Russell. *Municipal Affairs:* Hon M. E. Moore. *Agriculture:* Hon. D. W. Schmidt. *Federal and Intergovernmental Affairs:* Hon. D. Johnston. *Labour:* Hon. L. Young. *Education:* Hon. D. T. King. *Advanced Education, Manpower, Deputy Government House Leader:* Hon. J. D. Horsman. *Consumer and Corporate Affairs:* Hon. J. G. J Koziak. *Social Services and Community Health:* Hon. R. J. Bogle. *Solicitor-General:* Hon. G. L. Harle. *Housing and Public Works:* Hon. T. W. Chambers. *Environment:* Hon. J. W. Cookson. *Economic Development:* Hon H. Planche. *Transportation:* Hon. H. Kroeger. *Government Services:* Hon. S. A. McCrae. *Utilities and Telephones:* Hon. L. R. Shaben. *Tourism and Small Business:* Hon. J. A. Adair. *Recreation and Parks:* Hon. P. Trynchy. *Minister of State for Economic Development and International Trade:* Hon. H. A. Schmid. *Associate Minister of Public Lands and Wildlife:* Hon. J. E. Miller. *Associate Minister of Telephones:* Hon. Dr P. N. Webber. *Minister responsible for Native Affairs:* Hon. Dr D. J. McCrimmon. *Minister responsible for Culture:* Hon. M. J. Le Messurier. *Minister responsible for Workers' Health, Safety and Compensation:* Hon. B. W. Diachuk. *Minister responsible for Personnel Administration:* Hon. G. Stevens.

Local Government. The local government units are City, Town, New Town, Village, Summer Village, County, Municipal District and Improvement District.

There are 12 cities in Alberta, namely: Calgary, Camrose, Drumheller, Edmonton, Fort McMurray, Grande Prairie, Lethbridge, Lloydminster, Medicine Hat,

Red Deer, St Albert and Wetaskiwin. These cities operate under the Municipal Government Act. The governing body consists of a mayor and a council of from 6 to 20 members. A city can be incorporated by order of the Lieut.-Governor-in-Council. A population of 10,000 is required.

There are no limits of area specified in the statutes for any of the different local government units. The population requirement for a Town as specified in the Municipal Government Act is 1,000 people, and the area at incorporation is that of the original village.

A Village must contain 75 separate and occupied dwellings. The Municipal Government Act requires each dwelling to have been occupied continuously for a period of at least 6 months. A Summer Village must contain 50 separate dwellings.

A rural county area is an area incorporated through an order of the Lieut.-Governor-in-Council under the provisions of the County Act. One board of councillors deal with both municipal and school affairs.

A rural Municipal District is an area which has been incorporated under the Municipal Government Act. In Municipal Districts separate boards control municipal and school affairs.

Areas not incorporated as counties or Municipal Districts are termed Improvement Districts or Special Areas. Sparsely populated, such districts are administered and taxed by the Department of Municipal Affairs of the provincial government. There are no requirements as to the minimum number of residents of a County or Municipal District.

FINANCE. The budgetary revenue and expenditure (in Canadian $) for years ending 31 March were as follows:

	1976–77	1977–78	1978–79[1]	1979–80[1]	1980–81[1]
Revenue	3,226,300,000[2]	4,173,449,000[2]	4,936,000,000[2]	5,255,000,000[2]	7,158,800,000[2]
Expenditure	2,920,000,000	3,396,885,000	3,827,000,000	4,521,000,000	5,409,000,000

[1] Estimates.   [2] Excludes funds allocated to Alberta Heritage Savings Trust Fund.

Income *per capita* (1979), $9,489.

ENERGY AND NATURAL RESOURCES

Oil. In 1979, 77,079,000 cu. metres of crude oil and condensate were produced with gross sales value of $6,686·5m. Alberta produced 86% of Canada's oil output in 1979. Production of natural gas by-products was 18,755,000 cu. metres, valued at $1,313·8m.

Major deposits of oil sands are found in areas totalling 60,000 sq. km in northern and eastern Alberta. There are 4 major deposits of oil sands, the Athabasca, Cold Lake, Peace River and Wabasca deposits. A limited part of the deposits along the Athabasca River can be exploited through open-pit mining. The rest of the Athabasca, and all the deposits in the other areas, are deeper reserves which must be developed through in situ techniques. These reserves reach depths of 760 metres.

One recovery plant, situated 25 miles north of Fort McMurray, began production in 1967. The deposit being produced is sufficiently close to the surface to permit strip mining. A second plant, to produce 20,000 cu. metres per day of synthetic crude oil, began production in 1978.

Gas. Natural gas is found in abundance in numerous localities. In 1979, 81,383m. cu. metres valued at $4,265·1m. were produced.

Minerals. In 1978 the ultimate remaining recoverable coal resources of Alberta were estimated at 39,000m. tonnes; the proved remaining recoverable reserves were estimated at 12,000m. tonnes.

Value of total mineral production increased from $10,087m. in 1978 to $12,885m. in 1979.

Agriculture. Of the surveyed area of the province (about 85m. acres) approximately 70m. acres may be classed as capable of agricultural development. Up to the present, however, only 40% of this area has been brought under cultivation.

For particulars of agricultural production and livestock, *see under* CANADA, pp. 275–277. Farm cash receipts in 1979 totalled $2,835,669,000, of which crops contributed $1,214m.; livestock and products, $1,605m., and other sources, $16m.

Forestry. Alberta has an estimated net merchantable volume of 1,700m. cu. metres of timber comprised of 700m. cu. metres of hardwood and 1,000m. cu. metres of softwood. In 1979, an estimated 1,652,000 metres of lumber were produced.

Fisheries. The lakes of the province contain whitefish, pike and tullibee. Commercial catches are marketed through the Freshwater Fish Marketing Corporation which was inaugurated in May 1969 as the result of an agreement between the federal government and the provinces for the buying and exporting of freshwater fish. Marketed value of commercially caught fish in year ending 31 March 1980 was $2,818,573. This value includes fish not marketed through the corporation.

INDUSTRY. The leading manufacturing industries are food and beverages, petroleum refining, metal fabricating, wood industries, primary metal, chemical and chemical products and non-metallic mineral products industries. There were in 1978 approximately 2,050 manufacturing establishments, in which were employed about 73,669 persons, who earned in salaries and wages $1,136m.

Manufacturing shipments had a total value of $8,717·9m. in 1979. Chief among these shipments were: Food and beverages, $2,947m.; petroleum and coal products, $1,737m.; chemicals and chemical products, $696m.; metal fabricating, $511m.; primary metals $509m.; non-metallic mineral products, $503m.; wood, $418m.

Total retail sales (1979, estimate) $8,068·8m.

Tourism is of increasing importance and in 1979 contributed $1,000m. to the economy.

COMMUNICATIONS

Roads. In 1978 there were 148,148 km of roads and highways, including 97,900 km gravelled and 12,667 km paved.

At March 1980 there were 1,783,158 motor vehicles registered, including 1,025,928 passenger cars, 459,478 public and commercial vehicles, 214,752 trailers and 44,712 motor cycles.

Railways. In Dec. 1979 the length of main railway lines was 10,958 km. A rail rapid transit network (7 km) was opened in Edmonton in 1978.

Post and Telecommunications. Alberta's modern telephone system is owned and operated by the provincial government, except in the city of Edmonton and some rural lines. There were 1,542,958 telephones in service at 31 Dec. 1979.

JUSTICE AND EDUCATION

Justice. The Supreme Judicial authority of the province is the Court of Appeal. Judges of the Court of Appeal and Court of Queen's Bench are appointed by the Dominion Government and hold office until retirement at the age of 75. There are courts of lesser jurisdiction in both civil and criminal matters. District courts have full jurisdiction over civil proceedings. A Provincial Court which has jurisdiction in civil matters up to $1,000 is presided over by provincially appointed judges. Juvenile Courts have power to try boys 16 and under and girls 18 years of age and under for offences against the Juvenile Delinquents Act.

The jurisdiction of all criminal courts in Alberta is enacted in the provisions of the Criminal Code. The system of procedure in civil and criminal cases conforms as nearly as possible to the English system.

Education. Schools of all grades are included under the term of public school (including those in the separate school system which are publicly supported). The same board of trustees controls the schools from kindergarten to university entrance. In 1979–80 there were 417,291 pupils enrolled in elementary, junior high schools and high schools. The University of Alberta (in Edmonton), organized in 1907, had, in

1978–79, 18,117 full-time students. The University of Calgary, formerly part of the University of Alberta and autonomous from April 1966, had in 1979–80, 10,738 full-time students. The University of Lethbridge, organized in 1966, had in 1979–80, 1,419 full-time students. The full-time enrolment at Alberta's 10 public colleges totalled 11,098 students in 1979–80.

Books of Reference

Statistical Information: The Alberta Bureau of Statistics (Dept. of Treasury, Edmonton), which was established in 1939, collects, compiles and distributes information relative to Alberta. *Director:* Harvey W. Ford. Among its publications are: *Alberta Statistical Review* (Annual).— *Alberta Statistical Review* (Monthly).—*Alberta Economic Accounts* (Annual).—*Alberta Pay and Benefits Survey* (Annual).—*Retail and Service Trade Statistics, Alberta* (Annual).—*Alberta Fact Sheet* (Annual).—*Principal Manufacturing Statistics, Alberta* (Annual).—*Population Projections, Alberta* (Occasional).—*Quarterly Population Growth, Alberta* (Quartler).—*Alberta Spatial Price Survey* (Annual).

Dept. of Economic Development and Dept. of Federal and Intergovernmental Affairs, *Alberta Profile.* Edmonton, 1980

Hardy, W. G., *Alberta Golden Jubilee Anthology.* Toronto, 1955
Irving, J. A., *The Social Credit Movement in Alberta.* Toronto, 1959
Kroetsch, R., *Alberta.* Toronto, 1968
Macpherson, C. B., *Democracy in Alberta.* 2nd ed. Toronto, 1962
Nesbitt, L. D., *Tides in the West* [history of the Alberta Wheat Pool]. Saskatoon, 1962

BRITISH COLUMBIA

HISTORY. Vancouver Island was organized as a colony in 1849; the mainland as far as the watershed of the Rocky Mountains was organized as a colony following a gold rush on the Fraser River in 1858. The two were united as the colony of British Columbia in 1866; this became a Canadian Province in 1871.

AREA AND POPULATION. British Columbia has an area of 948,596 sq. km. The capital is Victoria. The province is bordered westerly by the Pacific ocean and Alaska Panhandle, northerly by the Yukon and Northwest Territories, easterly by the Province of Alberta and southerly by the USA along the 49th parallel. A chain of islands, the largest of which are Vancouver Island and the Queen Charlotte Islands, affords protection to the mainland coast.

The June 1976 census population was 2,466,608: estimate (July 1980) 2,642,400.

The principal cities and their populations (1976) are as follows: Greater Vancouver, 1,166,348; Greater Victoria, 218,250; Prince George, 59,929; Kamloops, 58,311; Kelowna, 51,955; Nanaimo, 40,336; Penticton, 21,344; Port Alberni, 19,585; Vernon, 17,546; Prince Rupert, 14,754; Cranbrook, 13,510; Dawson Creek, 10,528.

Vital statistics, *see* p. 266.

Religion, *see* p. 284.

CONSTITUTION AND GOVERNMENT. British Columbia (then known as New Caledonia) originally formed part of the Hudson's Bay Company's concession. In 1849 Vancouver Island and in 1858 British Columbia were constituted Crown Colonies; in 1866 the two colonies amalgamated. The British North America Act of 1867 provided for eventual admission into Canadian Confederation, and on 20 July 1871 British Columbia became the sixth province of the Dominion.

British Columbia has a unicameral legislature of 57 elected members. Government policy is determined by the Executive Council responsible to the Legislature. The Lieut.-Governor is appointed by the Governor-General of Canada, usually for a term of 5 years, and is the head of the executive government of the province.

Lieut.-Governor: The Hon. Henry P. Bell-Irving, DSO, OBE.

Flag: A banner of the arms, *i.e.*, blue and white wavy stripes charged with a setting sun in gold, across the top of a Union Flag with a gold coronet in the centre.

The Legislative Assembly is elected for a maximum term of 5 years. Every male or female Canadian citizen 18 years and over, having resided a minimum of 6 months in the province, duly registered, is entitled to vote. Representation of the parties at 10 May 1979: Social Credit Party, 31; New Democratic Party, 26; total, 57.

The province is represented in the Federal Parliament by 29 members in the House of Commons, and 6 Senators.

The Executive Council was composed as follows, Jan. 1981:

Premier and President of the Council: William Richards Bennett.

Agriculture: James J. Hewitt. *Attorney-General:* L. Allan Williams. *Consumer and Corporate Affairs:* Peter S. Hyndman. *Education:* Brian Smith. *Energy, Mines and Petroleum Resources:* Robert H. McClelland. *Environment:* C. Stephen Rogers. *Finance:* Hugh A. Curtis. *Forests:* Thomas M. Waterland. *Health:* J. A. Nielson. *Human Resources:* Grace McCarthy. *Industry and Small Business Development:* Donald M. Phillips. *Intergovernmental Relations:* Garde B. Gardom. *Labour:* John H. Heinrich. *Lands, Parks and Housing:* James R. Chabot. *Municipal Affairs:* William Vander Zalm. *Provincial Secretary and Government Services:* Evan Wolfe. *Tourism:* Patricia J. Jordan. *Transportation and Highways:* Alexander V. Fraser. *Universities, Science and Communications:* Patrick L. McGeer. *Speaker of the House:* Harvey W. Schroeder.

Agent-General in London: Lawrence James Wallace (British Columbia House, 1 Regent St., London, SW1Y 4NS).

Local Government. Vancouver City was incorporated by statute and operates under the provisions of the Vancouver Charter of 1953 and amendments. This is the only incorporated area in British Columbia not operating under the provisions of the Municipal Act. Under this Act municipalities are divided into the following classes: (*a*) a village with a population between 500 and 2,500, governed by a council consisting of a mayor and 4 aldermen; (*b*) a town with a population between 2,500 and 5,000, governed by a council consisting of a mayor and 4 aldermen; (*c*) a city where the population exceeds 5,000 governed by a council consisting of a mayor and 6 or 8 aldermen depending on population; (*d*) a district where the area exceeds 810 hectares and the average density is less than 5 persons per hectare, governed by a council consisting of a mayor and 6 or 8 aldermen depending on population.

There are two other forms of local government: the regional district covering a number of areas both incorporated and unincorporated, governed by a board of directors; and the improvement district governed by a board of 3 trustees.

Revenue for municipal services is derived mainly from real-property taxation, although additional revenue is derived from licence fees, business taxes, fines, public utility projects and grants-in-aid from the provincial government.

ECONOMY

Budget. Current provincial revenue and expenditure, including all capital expenditures, in Canadian $ for fiscal years ending 31 March:

	1977–78	1978–79	1979–80	1980–81
Revenue	4,139,742,931	4,568,926,231	5,520,000,000	5,780,000,000
Expenditure	3,999,253,953	4,429,000,000	5,270,000,000	6,153,000,000

The main sources of current revenue are the income taxes, sales and fuel taxes, contributions from the federal government, and privileges, licences and natural resources taxes and royalties.

The main items of expenditure in 1980–81 are as follows: Health and social services, $2,367·8m.; education, $1,305·3m.; highways and ferries, $668·1m.; natural resources and primary industry, $499·7m.; general government, $206·9m.;

Banking. Cheques cashed (in $1,000): 1975, 163,993,000; 1976, 194,272,000; 1977, 207,853,000; 1978, 233,387,000; 1979, 286·9m.

ENERGY AND NATURAL RESOURCES

Electricity. Generation in 1979 totalled 43,413m. kwh. of which a net 1,920m. kwh. were exported. Consumption within the province was 41,493m. kwh.

Minerals. Copper, coal, natural gas, crude oil, molybdenum and silver are the most important minerals produced. The 1979 total of mineral production was estimated at $2,824·9m. Total value of fuels produced in 1978 was estimated at $1,211m.

Agriculture. Only 3·6m. hectares or 4% of the total land area is arable or potentially arable. Farm cash receipts, in 1979, reached $635·9m.

Forestry. About 58% of British Columbia's land is forest land, with 47·8m. hectares bearing commercial forest. Over 95% of the forest area is owned or administered by the provincial government. The total cut from forests in 1979 was 76,194,000 cu. metres.

Fisheries. In 1979 the wholesale market value of fish products reached $565·6m., a 9·3% increase on the 1978 figure.

INDUSTRY AND TRADE

Industry. The selling value of factory shipments from all manufacturing industries reached an estimated $14,300m. in 1979.

Commerce. Exports through British Columbia customs ports during 1979 totalled $12,700m. in value, while imports amounted to $5,500m.

Principal export commodity groups through British Columbia customs ports (1979): Forest products, $4,186·9m.; coal, crude petroleum and natural gas, $2,915m.; metal ores, concentrates, non-ferrous metals and crude non-metallic minerals, $1,560·1m.; grain and cereal products, $1,253·4m.; fish and marine animals, $384·4m. About 40% of exports through British Columbia customs ports are products from other provinces, primarily grains, potash and fuels from the Prairie Provinces. USA is the largest market for products exported through British Columbia customs ports ($5,279·9m. in 1979) followed by Japan ($3,393·6m.) and the EEC ($1,688·1m.).

COMMUNICATIONS

Roads. At 30 Sept. 1980 there were 41,720 km of provincial roads and rights of way in the province, of which 17,163 km were paved and 24,557 km were gravelled.

Railways. The province is served by two transcontinental railways, the Canadian Pacific Railway and the Canadian National Railway. British Columbia is also served by the publicly owned British Columbia Railway, the Railway Freight Service of the B.C. Hydro and Power Authority, the Northern Alberta Railways Company and the Burlington Northern Inc. Their combined route-mileage of mainline track totals 7,891·4 km. In addition, 5 American railways interchange with Canadian railways at southern border points or connect by railway barge.

Aviation. International airports are located at Vancouver and Victoria. Daily interprovincial and intraprovincial flights serve all main population centres. Small public and private airstrips are located throughout the province.

Shipping. The major ports are Vancouver, New Westminster, Victoria, Nanaimo and Prince Rupert. The volume of international shipping handled during 1979 was 59m. tonnes.

The British Columbia Ferries connect Vancouver Island with the mainland and also provide service to other coastal points. Service by other ferry systems is also provided between Vancouver Island and the USA. The Alaska State Ferries connect Prince Rupert with centres in Alaska.

Post and Broadcasting. The British Columbia Telephone Company had (1979) 1·8m. telephones in service. There were 10 television stations and 138 radio stations operating in the province in 1979. Many of these are repeater stations.

EDUCATION AND WELFARE

Education (1979–80). Education, free up to Grade XII levels, is financed jointly from municipal and provincial government revenues. Attendance is compulsory from the age of 6 to 15. There were 511,671 pupils enrolled in public schools from kindergarten to Grade XII.

Higher education (1979–80) is provided at the University of British Columbia at Vancouver (founded 1908), 32,607 students; the University of Victoria (1963), 8,362 students; Simon Fraser University (1965), Burnaby, 9,780 students; Selkirk College (1966), Castlegar, 1,027 students; Okanagan Community College (1968), Kelowna, 2,469 students; Capilano Community College (1970), Vancouver, 3,011 students; Malaspina Community College (1969), Nanaimo, 2,018 students; New Caledonia Community College (1969), Prince George, 1,321 students; Cariboo Community College (1970), Kamloops, 1,983 students; Douglas College (1970), New Westminster, 5,646 students; Fraser Valley Community College (1974), Abbotsford, 1,530 students; East Kootenay Community College (1975), Cranbrook, 474 students; Northern Lights Community College (1975), Dawson Creek, 548 students; North Island Community College (1975), Campbell River, 1,771 students; North West Community College (1975), Terrace, 563 students; British Columbia Institute of Technology (1964), Burnaby, 14,522 students; Camosun College (1971), Victoria 2,701 students.

Health. The Government operates a hospital insurance scheme giving universal coverage after a qualifying period of 3 months' residence in the province. The province has come under a national medicare scheme which is partially subsidized by the provincial government and partially by the federal government.

Books of Reference

Statistical Information: Information Services (Ministry of Industry and Small Business Development, Hon. Don Phillips—Minister, Parliament Buildings, Victoria, B.C.), collects, compiles and distributes information relative to the Province.
    Publications include *British Columbia Business Bulletin*; *Review and Outlook*; *Manufacturers' Directory*; *External Trade Report*; *B.C. Facts and Statistics.*

Ministry of Finance, *British Columbia Financial and Economic Review.* Victoria, B.C. (annual)
Fifteenth British Columbia Natural Resources Conference, *Inventory of the Natural Resources of British Columbia*, 1964
Haig-Brown, R. L., *Living Land: An Account of the Natural Resources of British Columbia.* Toronto, 1961

MANITOBA

HISTORY. The Hudson's Bay Company formed a colony on the Red River in 1812. This being part of territory annexed to Canada in 1870. The Metis colonists (part-Indian, mostly French-speaking, Catholic) objected to the arrangements for the purchase of the Company territory by Canada and the province of Manitoba was created to accommodate them. It was extended northwards and westwards in 1881 and to Hudson Bay in 1912.

AREA AND POPULATION. The area of the province is 251,000 sq. miles (652,218 sq. km), of which 211,775 sq. miles are land and about 39,200 sq. miles water. From north to south it is 761 miles and the widest point is 493 miles.
    The population (June 1980 estimate) was 1,028,300. Population of the principal cities (census 1976): Winnipeg (capital), 578,000 (estimate, 1980); Brandon, 34,901; Thompson, 17,291; Portage la Prairie, 12,855; Flin Flon, 8,152.
    Vital statistics, *see* p. 266.
    Religion, *see* p. 284.

CONSTITUTION AND GOVERNMENT. Manitoba was known as the Red River Settlement before its entry into the Dominion in 1870. The provincial government is administered by a Lieut.-Governor and a legislative assembly of 57 members elected for 5 years. Women were enfranchised in 1916. The Electoral Division Act, 1955, created 57 single-member constituencies and abolished the transferable vote. The Electoral Divisions Act, 1979, created 27 rural electoral divisions, and 30 urban electoral divisions. The province is represented by 6 members in the Senate and 14 in the House of Commons of Canada.

Lieut.-Governor: Francis L. Jobin (sworn in 15 March 1976).
Flag: The British Red Ensign with the shield of the province in the fly.

State of parties in the Legislative Assembly (elected 11 Oct. 1977): Progressive Conservative, 32; New Democratic Party, 20; Independent, 1; Liberals, 1.

The members of the Progressive Conservative Ministry are as follows (Feb. 1981):

Premier, President of Executive Council, Minister of Dominion–Provincial Relations: Sterling R. Lyon, QC.

Deputy Premier, Energy and Mines, Minister charged with administration of Manitoba Hydro Act, Minister responsible for Manitoba Development Corporation: Donald W. Craik. *Minister without portfoilo:* Edward R. McGill. *Government Services, Minister responsible for the Manitoba Public Insurance Corporation:* Warner H. Jorgenson. *Natural Resources:* Harry J. Enns. *Economic Development and Tourism:* J. Frank Johnston. *Health:* Louis R. Sherman. *Agriculture:* James E. Downey. *Education:* Keith A. Cosens. *Attorney-General, Urban Affairs, Minister responsible for administration of Liquor Control Act:* Gerald W. J. Mercier. *Co-operative Development; Fitness, Recreation and Sport, Minister responsible for* administration of the Manitoba Lotteries Act: Robert D. Banman. *Cultural Affairs:* Norma L. Price. *Labour and Manpower, Minister responsible for Civil Service Commission:* Ken MacMaster. *Finance:* Brian Ransom. *Community Services and Corrections:* George Minaker. *Municipal Affairs, Northern Affairs, Minister responsible for the Communities Economic Development Fund:* Douglas M. Gourlay. *Highways and Transportation, Minister* responsible for the Manitoba Telephone System: Donald W. Orchard. *Consumer and Corporate Affairs and Environment, Minister responsible for Manitoba Housing and Renewal Corporation:* Gary Filmon.

Local Government. Rural Manitoba is organized into rural municipalities which vary widely in size. Some have only 4 townships (a township is 36 sq. miles), while the largest has 22 townships. The province has 105 rural municipalities, as well as 35 incorporated towns, 40 incorporated villages and 5 incorporated cities.

On 1 Jan. 1972, the cities and towns comprising the metropolitan area of Winnipeg were amalgamated to form the City of Winnipeg. A mayor and council are elected to a central government, but councillors also sit on 'community committees' which represent the areas or wards they serve. These committees are advised by non-elected residents of the area on provision of municipal services within the community committee jurisdiction. Taxing powers and overall budgeting rest with the central council. The mayor is elected at the same time as the councillors in a city-wide vote. Revisions to the City of Winnipeg Act came into effect with the municipal elections held in Oct. 1977.

Since Jan. 1945, 17 Local Government Districts have been formed in the less densely populated areas of the province. They are administered by a provincially appointed person, who acts on the advice of locally elected councils.

In the extreme north, many communities have locally elected councils, while others are administered directly by the Department of Northern Affairs. This department provides most of the funding in all these northern settlements.

FINANCE. Revenue and expenditure (current account) for fiscal years ending 31 March (in Canadian $):

	1976–77	1977–78	1978–79	1979–80[1]	1980–81[1]
Revenue	1,389,872,000	1,444,281,000	1,556,534,741	1,689,601,000	1,882,602,800
Expenditure	1,472,082,000	1,635,585,000	1,640,857,735	1,812,163,000	2,022,193,200

[1] Estimates.

ENERGY AND NATURAL RESOURCES

Electricity. The total generating capacity of Manitoba's power stations is 3·6m. kw. The Manitoba Hydro system, owned by the province, provides most of this power, while the city-owned Winnipeg Hydro provides about 190,000 kw. The systems have about 397,000 customers and consumption was 11·5m. kwh. in 1980.

Oil. Crude oil production in 1979 was valued at $48m. for the 3·7m. bbls produced.

Minerals. Total value of minerals in 1980 was about $834m. Principal minerals mined are nickel, zinc, copper, and small quantities of gold and silver. Manitoba has the world's largest deposits of caesium ore and also produces tantalite concentrates.

Agriculture. Rich farmland is the main primary resource, although the area of Manitoba in farms is only about 14% of the total land area. In 1980 the total value of agricultural production in Manitoba was $1,691m., with $1,100m. from crops, $571m. from livestock and about $20m. from the sale of other products including furs, hides and honey.

Forestry. About 40% of the land area is wooded, of which 53,700 sq. miles is productive forest land. Total sales of wood-using industries (1980) $390m.

Fur Trade. Value of fur production to the trapper was $7·9m. in 1978–79, with the value of all furs exported from the wild $18m. (1977–78).

Fisheries. From 22,000 sq. miles of rivers and lakes fisheries production was about $16·9m. in 1979–80. Whitefish, sauger, pickerel, pike, trout and perch are the principal varieties of fish caught.

INDUSTRY AND TRADE

Industry. Manufacturing, the largest industry in the province, encompasses almost every major industrial activity in Canada. Estimated shipments in 1980 totalled $4,250m. Manufacturing employed about 64,000 persons, paying $808·7m. in salaries and wages in 1980. Due to the agricultural base of the province, the food and beverage group of industries is by far the largest, accounting for about 34% of the total value. The next largest segments are machinery at about 9%, metal fabricating at 12% and transportation equipment at about 7%.

Trade. Products grown and manufactured in Manitoba find ready markets in other areas of Canada, in the USA, particularly the upper midwest region, and in other countries. Export shipments to foreign countries from Manitoba in 1979 were valued at about $998m., with about 82% going to the US. Of these, about 33% are raw materials and about 66% are processed and manufactured products.

Tourism. In 1979, Canadian, US and Manitoba tourists numbered 2·75m. contributing about $350m. to the economy.

COMMUNICATIONS

Roads. Highways and provincial roads had a total mileage of 12,300 in 1980.

Railways. At 31 Dec. 1980 the province had 4,027 miles of railway, not including industrial track, yards and sidings.

Aviation. A total of 103 licensed commercial air carriers operate from bases in Manitoba, as well as major national and international airlines.

Post. All of the province's 701,000 telephones are dial-operated.

EDUCATION. Education is controlled through locally elected school divisions, with about 80% of the financing provided through the province. There are about 204,000 children enrolled in the province's elementary and secondary schools. The University of Manitoba, founded in 1877, in Winnipeg, had a regular student enrolment of 13,300, the University of Winnipeg, 2,580, and Brandon University (1979–80), 950, during the 1980–81 year. Expenditure on education in the 1980–81 fiscal year was $399m.

Three community colleges, in Brandon, The Pas and Winnipeg, offer 2-year diploma courses in a number of fields, as well as specialized training in many trades. They also give a large number and variety of shorter courses, both at their campuses and in many communities throughout the province.

Books of Reference

General Information: Inquiries may be addressed to the Information Services Branch, Room 29, Legislative Building, Winnipeg, R3C OV8.

The Department of Agriculture publishes: *Year Book of Manitoba Agriculture*
Information Services Branch publishes: *Manitoba Facts*
Manitoba Statistical Review. Manitoba Bureau of Statistics, Quarterly
Tenth Census of Canada: Manitoba. Statistics Canada, 1971

NEW BRUNSWICK

HISTORY. Touched by Jacques Cartier in 1534, New Brunswick was first explored by Samuel de Champlain in 1604. It was ceded by the French in the Treaty of Utrecht in 1713 and became a permanent British possession in 1763. It was separated from Nova Scotia and became a province in June 1784, as a result of the great influx of United Empire Loyalists. Responsible government came into being in 1848, and consisted of an executive council, a legislative council (later abolished) and a House of Assembly.

AREA AND POPULATION. The area of the province is 28,354 sq. miles (73,000 sq. km), of which 27,633 sq. miles (71,569 sq. km) are land area. The population (census 1976) was 677,250. Of the total population (1971) about 58% are of British origin, 37% French and the remainder are principally of Netherlands, German and Scandinavian descent, and in 1979 there were about 4,775 Indians. Census population of urban centres: Saint John, 85,956; Moncton, 55,934; Fredericton (capital), 44,248; Bathurst, 16,301; Edmundston, 12,710; Campbellton, 9,282.

Vital statistics, *see* p. 266.

Religion, *see* p. 284.

CONSTITUTION AND GOVERNMENT. The government is vested in a Lieut.-Governor and a Legislative Assembly of 58 members each of whom is individually elected to represent the voters in one constituency or riding. A simultaneous translation system is used in the Assembly. Any Canadian subject of full age and 6 months' residence is entitled to vote. As a result of the provincial election held on 23 Oct. 1978 and subsequent by-elections, the Assembly is composed of 30 Progressive Conservatives and 28 Liberals. The province has 10 members in the Canadian Senate and 10 members in the federal House of Commons.

Lieut.-Governor: Hedard J. Robichaud (appointed 8 Oct. 1971).

Flag: A banner of the Arms, *i.e.*, yellow charged with a black heraldic ship on wavy lines of blue and white; across the top a red band with a gold lion.

The members of the Progressive Conservative Ministry are as follows (Oct. 1978):

Premier: Richard B. Hatfield.

Agriculture and Rural Development: Malcolm MacLeod. *Commerce and Development:* Gerald S. Merrithew. *Education:* Charles Gallagher. *Fisheries:* Jean Gauvin. *Finance:* Fernand Dubé. *Environment:* Eric Kipping. *Health:* Brenda Robertson. *Justice:* Rodman Logan. *Labour and Manpower:* Mabel DeWare. *Municipal Affairs:* Horace Smith. *Natural Resources:* J. W. Bird. *New Brunswick Electric Power Commission:* G. W. N. Cockburn. *Social Services:* Leslie Hull. *Supply and Services:* Harold Fanjoy. *Tourism:* Leland McGaw. *Transportation:* Wilfred Bishop. *Treasury Board:* Jean-Maurice Simard. *Youth, Recreation and Cultural Resources:* Jean-Pierre Ouellet. *Historical Resources:* Charles Gallagher.

Local Government. Under the reforms introduced in 1967 the province has assumed complete administrative and financial responsibility for education, health, welfare and administration of justice. Local government is now restricted to provision of services of a strictly local nature. Under the new municipal structure, units include existing and new cities, towns and villages. Counties have disappeared as municipal units. Areas with limited populations have become local service districts. The former local improvement districts have become towns, villages or local service districts depending on their size.

FINANCE. The ordinary budget (in Canadian $) is shown as follows (financial years ended 31 March):

	1976	1977	1978	1979	1980
Gross revenue	885,344,378	986,730,767	1,078,995,642	1,268,924,745	1,449,457,490
Gross expenditure[1]	866,028,571	985,877,910	1,086,747,213	1,198,129,445	1,321,661,738

[1] Excluding sinking fund instalment.

Funded debt and capital loans outstanding (exclusive of Treasury Bills) as of 31 March 1980 was $1,417·9m. Sinking funds held by the province at 31 March 1980, $342m. The ordinary budget excludes capital spending.

ENERGY AND NATURAL RESOURCES

Electricity. Hydro-electric and thermal power plants of the New Brunswick Electric Power Commission had a combined capacity of 2,526,576 kw. at 31 March 1980. This includes 6 units with a capacity of over 600,000 kw. at the Mactaquac hydro-electric development near Fredericton. Three units (1m. kw.) are in operation at Coleson Cove in the Lorneville area near Saint John. The 630,000 kw. nuclear plant at Point Lepreau will be completed in 1981. An additional 200,000 kw. of hydro and thermal capacity have been installed at Mactaquac and Dalhousie respectively. The Commission is interconnected with the neighbouring provinces of Nova Scotia, Quebec, Prince Edward Island and the New England states, USA. Hook-up permits exchange of power including large blocks from Churchill Falls in Labrador through Hydro-Quebec as well as with the state of Maine, USA.

Minerals. A considerable variety of metals, industrial minerals, fuels and structural materials occur in the province. These include zinc, lead, copper, cadmium, bismuth, nickel, gold, silver, cobalt, tungsten, tin, molybdenum, antimony, potash, salt, glauberite, limestone, dolomite, gypsum, oil, gas, coal, uranium, oil shale, sand, gravel, clay, peat, diatomite and marl. Not all have been explored sufficiently. 48% of the value of minerals produced in 1979, which totalled $530m., was attributed to zinc produced from 2 mines in the Bathurst–Newcastle area: Brunswick Mining and Smelting, Heath Steele Mines Ltd. New Brunswick is now the second largest producer of zinc in Canada. A lead smelter, fertilizer plant and port facilities have been constructed at Belledune. Numerous other discoveries have been made in the area and several deposits are now in the final stages of exploration. Canada's only primary antimony producer is located at Lake George, near Fredericton, and a large low-grade tungsten–molybdenum–bismuth deposit is being developed at Mount Pleasant. Exploration and development is also in process near Sussex and Salt Springs, where potash and salt deposits have been found. Limestone and gypsum are quarried at Havelock and Hillsborough and small quantities of oil and natural gas are produced from the Stoney Creek Field south of Moncton. Coal is mined at Grand Lake and exploration is underway for other deposits of this important energy resource.

Agriculture. The total area under crops is estimated at 312,702 acres, exclusive of improved pasture land (89,515 acres). Farms numbered 3,244 and averaged 306 acres each (census 1976). Mixed farming is common throughout the province. Dairy farming is centred around the larger urban areas, and is located mainly along the Saint John River Valley and in the south-eastern sections of the province. For particulars of agricultural production and livestock, *see under* CANADA, pp. 275–277. Farm cash receipts in 1979 were approximately $137,952,000.

Forestry. New Brunswick contains some 15·3m. acres of productive forest lands, of which 7·3m. acres is Crown-owned. The combined value of primary and secondary forest production was about $931m. in 1978, of which wood and paper and allied industries accounted for about $733m. In 1978 some 120 saw-mills shipped timber valued at about $160m. Timber-using plants employ about 14,000 men for all aspects of the forest industry, including harvesting, processing and transportation. Practically all forest products are exported from the province's numerous ports and harbours near which the mills are located or sent by road or rail to the USA.

Fisheries. Commercial fishing is one of the most important basic industries of the province. Over 35 commercial species of fish and shellfish are landed, of which lobster, herring, tuna, crabs and cod are the most valuable. Landings in 1979 amounted to $51·8m. In 1980 there were 119 fish processing plants. The gross income of fishermen in 1979 was approximately $54m., and the total market value of fish products was approximately $187m.

INDUSTRY. In 1980 there were 1,207 manufacturing and processing establishments, employing about 42,845 persons. New Brunswick's location, with deep-water harbours open throughout the year and container facilities at Saint John, makes it ideal for exporting. Industries include food and beverages, paper and allied industries, timber products. About 20% of the industrial labour force work in Saint John.

TOURISM. Tourism is a major industry. During 1979, more than 4m. tourists spent over $225m.

COMMUNICATIONS

Roads. There are about 1,400 miles of arterial highways and 1,300 miles of collector roads, 95% of which are hard-surfaced. Over 10,000 miles of local roads provide access to most areas in the province. The main highway system, including 380 miles of the Trans-Canada Highway, links the province with the principal roads in Quebec and Nova Scotia, as well as the Interstate Highway System in the eastern seaboard states of the USA. Passenger vehicles, 31 March 1979, numbered 243,301; commercial vehicles, 73,726; motor cycles, 10,903.

Railways. New Brunswick is served by main lines of both Canadian Pacific and Canadian National railways.

Post and Broadcasting. In 1979 the New Brunswick Telephone Co. Ltd had 376,514 telephones in service. The province is served by 16 radio stations. Twelve are privately owned and 4 owned by the Canadian Broadcasting Corporation. Three stations broadcast in the French language, 1 is bilingual and the CBC International Service broadcasts in several languages from its station at Sackville. The province is served by 3 television stations, 1 of which broadcasts in French.

Newspapers. New Brunswick had (1980) 6 daily newspapers, 1 in French, and 23 weekly newspapers, 7 in French or bilingual.

EDUCATION. Public education is free and non-sectarian. There are 4 universities. The University of New Brunswick at Fredericton (founded 13 Dec. 1785 by the Loyalists, elevated to university status in 1823, reorganized as the University of New Brunswick in 1859) had 5,234 students at the Fredericton campus and 626 students at the Saint John campus (Dec. 1979); Mount Allison University at Sackville had 1,446 students; the University of Moncton at Moncton, 2,779 students; St Thomas University at Fredericton, 685 students. During the period 1 July 1979 to 30 June 1980, there were 10,554 students enrolled full-time at 8 Community College campuses and at various campus training centres.

There were, in Sept. 1979, 155,819 pupils and 7,696 teachers in school buildings (Grades 1–12). Large new regional schools are absorbing numbers of small country schools; there are 35 school districts.

Books of Reference

Industrial Information: Dept. of Commerce and Development, Fredericton. *Economic Information:* Office of the Economic Advisor, Fredericton. *General Information:* NB Information Service, Fredericton.

New Brunswick and Its People. Fredericton, 1962
Department of Commerce and Development, *Annual Report.* Fredericton, 1973.—*New Brunswick in Profile.* Fredericton

NEWFOUNDLAND AND LABRADOR

HISTORY. Archaeological finds at L'Anse-au-Meadow in northern Newfoundland suggest that the Vikings had established a colony there at about A.D. 1000. Newfoundland was discovered by John Cabot 24 June 1497, and was soon frequented in the summer months by the Portuguese, Spanish and French for its fisheries. It was formally occupied in Aug. 1583 by Sir Humphrey Gilbert on behalf of the English Crown, but various attempts to colonize the island remained unsuccessful. Although British sovereignty was recognized in 1713 by the Treaty of Utrecht, disputes over fishing rights with the French were not finally settled till

1904. By the Anglo-French Convention of 1904, France renounced her exclusive fishing rights along part of the coast, granted under the Treaty of Utrecht, but retained sovereignty of the offshore islands of St Pierre and Miquelon. In 1927 the Privy Council decided the boundary between Canada and Labrador.

AREA AND POPULATION. Area, 156,185 sq. miles (383,300 sq. km). In March 1927 the Privy Council decided the boundary between Canada and New-foundland in Labrador. This area, now part of the Province of Newfoundland and Labrador, is 112,826 sq. miles. The coastline is extremely irregular. Bays, fiords and inlets are numerous and there are many good harbours with deep water close to shore. The coast is rugged with bold rocky cliffs from 200 to 400 ft high; in the Bay of Islands some of the islands rise 500 ft, with the adjacent shore 1,000 ft above tide level. The interior is a plateau of moderate elevation and the chief relief features trend north-east and south-west. Long Range, the most notable of these, begins at Cape Ray and extends north-east for 200 miles, the highest peak reaching 2,673 ft. Approximately one-third of the area is covered by water. Grand Lake, the largest body of water, has an area of about 200 sq. miles. The principal rivers flow towards the north-east. On the borders of the lakes and water-courses good land is generally found, particularly in the valleys of the Terra Nova River, the Gander River, the Exploits River and the Humber River, which are also heavily timbered.

Census population, 1976, was 557,725.

The capital of Newfoundland is the City of St John's (143,390, metropolitan area). The only other city is Corner Brook (25,198); important towns are Labrador City (12,012), Stephenville (10,284), Gander (9,301), Grand Falls (8,729), Happy Valley–Goose Bay (8,075), Windsor (6,349), Channel-Port aux Basques (6,187), Carbonear (5,026), Wabana (4,824), Bonavista (4,299), Wabush (3,769).

Vital statistics, see p. 266.

Religion, see p. 284.

CONSTITUTION AND GOVERNMENT. Until 1832 Newfoundland was ruled by the Governor under instructions from the Colonial Office. In that year a Legislature was brought into existence, but the Governor and his Executive Council were not responsible to it. Under the constitution of 1855, which lasted until its suspension in 1934, the government was administered by the Governor appointed by the Crown with an Executive Council responsible to the House of Assembly of 27 elected members and a Legislative Council of 24 members nominated for life by the Governor in Council. Women were enfranchised in 1925. At the Imperial Conference of 1917 Newfoundland was constituted as a Dominion.

In 1933 the financial situation had become so critical that the Government of Newfoundland asked the Government of the UK to appoint a Royal Commission to investigate conditions. On the strength of their recommendations, the parlia-mentary form of government was suspended and Government by Commission was inaugurated on 16 Feb. 1934.

A National Convention, elected in 1946, made, in 1948, recommendations to H.M. Government in Great Britain as to the possible forms of future government to be submitted to the people at a national referendum. Two referenda were held. In the first referendum (June 1948) the three forms of government submitted to the people were: commission of government for 5 years, confederation with Canada and responsible government as it existed in 1933. No one form of government received a clear majority of the votes polled, and commission of government, receiving the fewest votes, was eliminated. In the second referendum (July 1948) confederation with Canada received 78,408 and responsible government 71,464 votes.

In the Canadian Senate on 18 Feb. 1949 Royal assent was given to the terms of union of Newfoundland and Labrador with Canada, and on 23 March 1949, in the House of Lords, London, Royal assent was given to an amendment to the British North America Act made necessary by the inclusion of Newfoundland and Labrador as the tenth Province of Canada.

Under the terms of union of Newfoundland and Labrador with Canada, which was signed at Ottawa on 11 Dec. 1948, the constitution of the Legislature of Newfoundland and Labrador as it existed immediately prior to 16 Feb. 1934 shall, subject to the terms of the British North America Acts, 1867 to 1946, continue as the constitution of the Legislature of the Province of Newfoundland and Labrador until altered under the authority of the said Acts.

The franchise was in 1965 extended to all male and female residents who have attained the age of 19 years and are otherwise qualified as electors.

The House of Assembly (Amendment) Act, 1979, established 52 electoral districts and 52 members of the Legislature.

At 18 June 1979 there were 33 Progressive-Conservatives and 19 Liberals.

The province is represented by 6 members in the Senate and by 7 members in the House of Commons of Canada.

Lieut.-Governor: G. A. Winter (assumed office 4 July 1974).

Flag: White, in the hoist 4 solid blue triangles; in the fly 2 red triangles voided white, and between them a yellow tongue bordered in red.

The Progressive-Conservative Executive Council was, at 18 June 1979, composed as follows:

Premier and Inter-governmental Affairs: A. Brian Peckford.

Culture, Recreation and Youth and Environment: R. G. Dawe. *Development:* H. Neil Windsor. *Education:* Lynn Verge. *Finance:* Dr J. Collins. *Fisheries:* J. Morgan. *Forest Resources and Lands:* C. Power. *Health:* H. W. House. *Justice:* G. R. Otten-heimer. *Labour and Manpower:* J. Dinn. *Mines and Energy:* L. Barry. *Municipal Affairs:* H. Newhook. *Public Works and Services:* H. Young. *Rural, Agricultural and Northern Development:* J. Goudie. *Social Services:* T. Hickey. *Transportation:* C. Brett.

Agent-General in London: H. Watson Jamer (60 Trafalgar Sq., WC2).

FINANCE. Budget [1] in Canadian $1,000 for fiscal years ended 31 March:

	1975–76	1976–77	1977–78	1978–79	1979–80[2]	1980–81[3]
Gross revenue	708,955	828,258	964,235	1,084,083	1,203,565	1,340,367
Gross expenditure	708,104	823,896	955,834	1,062,244	1,183,102	1,327,858

[1] Current amount only.　　　[2] Revised estimates.　　　[3] Estimates.

Public debenture debt as at 31 March 1980 (preliminary) was $1,833·8m.; sinking fund, $290·9m.

ENERGY AND NATURAL RESOURCES

Electricity. The electrical energy requirements of the province are met mainly by hydro-electric power, with petroleum fuels being utilized to provide the balance. The total amount of energy generated in the province in 1979 was 43,516m. kwh., of which approximately 97% was derived from hydro-electric facilities. The greater part of the energy produced in 1979 came from Churchill Falls, of which 35,290m. kwh. was sold to Hydro-Quebec under the terms of a long-term contract. Energy consumed in the province during 1978 totalled 8,226m. kwh. (estimate), with approximately 6,922m. kwh., or 84%, coming from hydro-electric facilities.

At 31 Dec. 1978 total electrical generating capacity in the province was 7m. kw., with hydro-electric plants accounting for 6·4m. kw., or 91%. A 75 mw hydro project started in 1978 at Hind's Lake in central Newfoundland and should be completed in 1981. It is estimated that potential additional hydro-electric generating capacity of up to 4·5m. kw. can be developed at various sites in the Labrador part of the province.

Oil. In 1977 the province consumed refined petroleum at the rate of 44,000 bbls a day with 25% of this being refined in the province. While the refining capacity of the province is 114,000 bbls per day, there is presently only one refinery being operated, a 14,000 bbls-per-day refinery at Holyrood. Offshore exploration expenditures for oil and gas have increased substantially in recent years. The province has issued exploration permits to exploration companies, which operate for their own account or represent joint ventures, covering 168,993 sq. miles offshore on the continental shelf.

In Oct 1974, two natural-gas finds off Labrador were announced. Tests of these two wells resulted in rates of flow of 13m. and 20m. cu. ft per day respectively, with some condensate and no water present. An additional natural gas find with a flow of 9·8m. cu. ft per day and significant condensates was announced in 1976. Additional drilling is required to delineate the reserves before the significance of the finds will be known.

Minerals. The mineral resources are vast but only partially documented. Large deposits of iron ore, with an ore reserve of over 5,000m. tons at Labrador City, Wabush City and in the Knob Lake area are supplying approximately half of Canada's production. Other large deposits of iron ore are known to exist in the Julienne Lake area.

There are a variety of other minerals being produced in the province in more limited amounts.

Uranium deposits in the Kaipokak Bay area near Makkovik in Labrador are presently being studied by Brinex. The Central Mineral Belt, which extends from the Smallwood Reservoir to the Atlantic coast near Makkovik, holds uranium, copper, beryllium and molybdenite potential.

Production in 1979 (provisional): Iron ore, 33m. tons ($949·45m.); copper, 8,623 tons ($18·42m.); zinc, 112,204 tons ($49·08m.); asbestos, 86,000 tons ($41·02m.); lead, 6,460 tons ($7·7m.); silver, 364,000 troy oz. ($4·32m.); gold, 12,000 troy oz. ($4·14m.); cadmium, 147,000 lb. ($479,000); gypsum, 884,000 tons ($5·09m.); pyrophyllite ($750,000); cement ($8·18m.); clay products ($450,000); sand and gravel, 5·3m. tons ($7·95m.); stone, 750,000 tons ($2·4m.).

Agriculture. The estimated value of agricultural products sold, including livestock, 1979, was $23·8m.

Forestry. The forestry economy in the province is mainly dependent on the operation of 2 newsprint mills. In 1979 the value of newsprint exported from these 2 mills totalled $253·8m. Lumber mills, saw-log operations produced 48m. f.b.m.

Fisheries. The principal fish landings are cod, flounder, redfish, Queen crabs (in shell), lobster, salmon and herring. In 1979 a yearly average of some 9,000 persons were employed by the fish-processing industry and there were 32,352 licensed full-, part-time and casual fishermen engaged in harvesting operations. Approximately 180 processing operations were active in 1979. The production of fresh and frozen fish products was estimated at $410m. in 1979.

The total catch in 1979 was 570,666 tonnes valued at $159·3m., of which the main items were: Cod, 216,409 tonnes ($63·8m.); flounder, 81,004 ($18·7m.); herring, 51,963 tonnes ($12·2m.); redfish, 38,145 ($5·9m.); lobster, 2,592 ($9·1m.); salmon, 986 ($3·2m.).

The seal fishery in 1979 had 6 large licensed and 126 small licensed vessels with 643 men who landed 71,516 pelts. The number of pelts landed by landsmen totalled 28,313.

INDUSTRY. The total value of manufacturing shipments in 1979 was $1,031·6m. This consists largely of first-stage processing of primary resource products with two of the largest components being paper and fish products.

TRADE UNIONS. There were (1978) 395 unions representing 57,814 members of international and national unions, government employee associations as well as 16 local independent unions.

COMMUNICATIONS

Roads. In 1979 there were 8,980 km, of which 5,583 were paved.

Railways. In 1978 there were 1,457·9 km of railway, of which the Canadian National Railways operated 1,130·5 (3 ft 6 in.), the Quebec North Shore and Labrador Railway 324·8 (4 ft 8½ in.) and there were 2·4 km of private line. Car and passenger ferries operate from Port aux Basques and Argentia to North Sydney, Nova Scotia. On the island of Newfoundland, the Canadian National Railways operates a trans-island bus and rail freight service in addition to a coastal service for both passengers and freight. In the months that the Labrador coast is ice-free, usually from June to Nov., the Canadian National Railways operates a scheduled coastal steamer service every week.

Aviation. The province is linked to the rest of Canada by regular air services provided by Air Canada, Eastern Provincial Airways, Quebecair and a number of smaller air carriers.

Shipping. In 1979 there were 1,425 ships registered in Newfoundland.

Post. There were 484 post offices open in 1979, and 15 telegraph offices in the Newfoundland and Labrador postal district. Telephone connexions in the province numbered 232,343 in 1978.

EDUCATION. The number of schools in 1979–80 was 675. The enrolment was 150,661; teachers numbered 7,817. The Memorial University, offering courses in arts, science, engineering, education, nursing and medicine, had approximately 10,000 full- and part-time students. Total expenditure for education by the Government in 1979–80 was $341m.

Books of Reference

Blackburn, R. H. (ed.), *Encyclopaedia of Canada: Newfoundland Supplement*. Toronto, 1949
Bruet, E., *Le Labrador et le Nouveau-Québec*. Paris, 1949
Horwood, H., *Newfoundland*. Toronto, 1969
Loture, R. de, *Histoire de la grande pêche de Terre-Neuve*. Paris, 1949
Mercer, G. A., *The Province of Newfoundland and Labrador: Geographical Aspects*. Ottawa, 1970
Perlin, A. B., *The Story of Newfoundland, 1497–1959*. St John's, 1959
Tanner, V., *Outlines of Geography. Life and Customs of Newfoundland–Labrador*. 2 vols. Helsinki, 1944, and Toronto, 1947
Taylor, T. G., *Newfoundland: A Study of Settlement*. Toronto, 1946

NOVA SCOTIA

HISTORY. The first permanent settlement was made by the French early in the 17th century, and the province was called Acadia until finally ceded to the British by the Treaty of Utrecht in 1713.

AREA AND POPULATION. The area of the province is 21,425 sq. miles (55,000 sq. km), of which 20,401 sq. miles are land area, 1,024 sq. miles water area. The population (census 1976) was 828,571; estimate (1980) 853,100.

Population of the principal cities and towns (census 1976): Halifax, 117,882; Dartmouth, 65,341; Sydney, 30,645; Glace Bay, 21,836; Truro, 12,840; New Glasgow, 10,672; Amherst, 10,263; Sydney Mines, 8,965; North Sydney, 8,319; Yarmouth, 7,801.

Vital statistics, *see* p. 266.

Religion, *see* p. 284.

CONSTITUTION AND GOVERNMENT. Under the British North America Act of 1867 the legislature of Nova Scotia may exclusively make laws in relation to local matters, including direct taxation within the province, education and the administration of justice. The legislature of Nova Scotia consists of a Lieut.-Governor, appointed and paid by the federal government, and holding office for 5 years, and a House of Assembly of 52 members, chosen by popular vote not more than every 5 years. The province is represented in the Canadian Senate by 10 members, and in the House of Commons by 11.

The franchise and eligibility to the legislature are granted to every person, male or female, if of age (19 years), a British subject or Canadian citizen, and a resident in the province for 1 year and 2 months before the date of the writ of election in the county or electoral district of which the polling district forms part, and if not by law otherwise disqualified. State of parties in Dec. 1980: 34 Progressive Conservatives, 15 Liberals, 2 New Democrats, 1 independent.

Lieut.-Governor: John E. Shaffner.

Flag: A banner of the Arms, *i.e.*, white with a blue diagonal cross, bearing in the centre the royal shield of Scotland.

The members of the Progressive Conservatives Ministry are as follows:

Premier, President of the Executive Council and Chairman of Policy Board: John M. Buchanan, QC.

Finance: Joel Matheson. *Development and Minister in Charge of Administration of the Research Foundation Corporation Act:* Roland J. Thornhill. *Attorney-General, Provincial Secretary and Minister in Charge of Administration of Regulations Act:* Harry W. How, QC. *Education and Minister in Charge of Administration of the Advisory Council on the Status of Women Act:* Terence R. B. Donahoe. *Lands and Forests and Minister in Charge of Administration of Liquor Control Act:* George Henley. *Health, Minister in Charge of Administration of Drug Dependency Act and Registrar-General:* Gerald Sheehy. *Mines and Energy and Minister in Charge of the Nova Scotia Energy Council:* Ronald Barkhouse. *Agriculture and Marketing:* Roger S. Bacon. *Fisheries and Minister of Intergovernmental Affairs:* Edmund Morris. *Tourism:* Bruce Cochran. *Municipal Affairs:* John MacIsaac. *Manpower and Labour and Minister in Charge of Administration of the Human Rights Act:* Kenneth Streatch. *Chairman of the Management Board, Chairman of the Treasury Board and Minister in Charge of Administration of the Civil Service Act:* Ronald Giffin. *Transportation and Minister in Charge of Office of Communications Policy:* Thomas J. McInnis. *Social Services:* Laird Stirling. *Government Services and Minister in Charge of Administration of Communications and Information Act:* Gerald Lawrence. *Environment and Minister in Charge of Administration of the Nova Scotia Emergency Measures Organization Act and Regulations and the Housing Development Act:* R. Fisher Hudson. *Consumer Affairs and Minister in Charge of Administration of Residential Tenancies Act:* Ronald S. Russell. *Culture, Recreation and Fitness and Minister in Charge of the Nova Scotia Heritage Act:* J. Greg Kerr.

Agent-General in London: Donald M. Smith (14 Pall Mall, SW1Y 5LU).

Local Government. The main divisions of the province for governmental purposes are the 3 cities, the 39 towns and the 24 rural municipalities, each governed by a council and a mayor or warden. The cities have independent charters, and the various towns take their powers from and are limited by The Towns Act, and the various municipalities take their powers from and are limited by The Municipal Act as revised in 1967. The majority of municipalities comprise 1 county, but 6 counties are divided into 2 municipalities each. In no case do the boundaries of any municipality overlap county lines. The 18 counties as such have no administrative functions.

Any city (of which there are 3) or incorporated town (of which there are 39) that lies within the boundaries of a municipality is excluded from any jurisdiction by the municipal council and has its own government.

FINANCE. Revenue is derived from provincial sources, payments from the federal government under the Federal-Provincial Fiscal Arrangements and Established Programs Financing Act (the '1977 Act'). Recoveries consist generally of amounts received under various federal cost-shared programmes. Main sources of provincial revenues include income and sales taxes. Under the 1977 Act the Government of Canada makes payments designed to equalize tax revenues *per capita* available to the provinces. The 1977 Act also provides for the replacement of former cost-sharing arrangements for health and medical services and for post-secondary education with the transfer of additional personal income tax points to the provinces, plus an approximately equivalent amount in supplementary cash payments.

Provisions for debt retirement (sinking fund instalments and serial retirements) are statutorily a charge upon the revenue, money and funds of the province.

Revenue, expenditure and debt (in Canadian $1m.) for fiscal years ending 31 March:

	1977	1978	1979	1980[1]	1981[2]
Revenues and adjustments	907·4	1,146·5	1,258·5	1,428·0	1,554·8
Net expenditures	854·9	1,103·1	1,290·3	1,396·5	1,571·0
Surplus (Deficiency)	+ 52·5	+ 43·4	− 31·8	+ 31·5	− 16·2
Net capital expenditures	95·5	97·9	124·1	130·8	168·1
Direct debt	1,558·3	1,685·1	1,831·5	—	—
Net direct debt	445·2	507·0	651·4	—	—

[1] Forecast.   [2] Estimate.

NATURAL RESOURCES

Minerals. Principal minerals in 1979 were: Coal, 2·4m. tons, valued at $100·5m.; gypsum, 6·2m. tons, valued at $26·4m.; salt, 1·2m. tons, valued at $24·3m.; sand and gravel, 10m. tons, valued at $20·5m. Total value of mineral production in 1979 was about $208,718,000.

Agriculture. Dairying, poultry and egg production, livestock and fruit growing are the most important branches. Farm cash receipts for 1979 were estimated at $175·3m., with an additional $4·8m. going to persons on farms as income in kind.

Cash receipts from sale of dairy products was $48·8m., with total milk production of 372·2m. lb.

The production of poultry meat in 1979 was 37·3m. lb., of which 32·3m. lb. were chickens and 3·8m. lb. were turkeys. Egg production was 16·7m. dozen.

The main 1979 fruit crops were apples, 2·4m. bu.; blueberries, 10·9m. lb.; and strawberries, 2·5m. quarts.

Forestry. The estimated forest area of Nova Scotia is 15,555 sq. miles (40,298 sq. km), of which about 25% is owned by the province. The principal trees are spruce, balsam fir, hemlock, pine, larch, birch, oak, maple, poplar and ash. 4,151,738 cu. metres of round and sawn forest products were produced in 1979.

Fisheries. The fisheries of the province in 1979 had a landed value of $206·7m. of sea fish including scallop fishery, $71·6m., and lobster fishery, $29·1m. In 1978 there were about 5,551 employees in the fish processing industry; the value of shipment of goods was $297·9m.

INDUSTRY. The number of manufacturing establishments was 714 in 1978; the number of employees was 36,219; wages and salaries, $468·6m.; value of shipments was $2,719·9m. The value of shipments in 1979, was $3,216·9m., and the leading industries were petroleum and coal products, food and beverages, paper and allied industries and transportation equipment.

TRADE UNIONS. Total union membership during 1980 was 101,061 belonging to 92 unions comprised of 568 individual branches. The largest percentage of the total union membership was in the public administration and defence sector followed closely by the Service sector. An estimated 41,912 members in 329 branches were affiliated with the Canadian Labour Congress.

COMMUNICATIONS

Roads. In March 1980 there were 15,745 miles of highways; 1,591 miles of paved arterial highways; 2,887 miles of collector highways (of which 2,650 miles are paved); 11,267 miles of local highways (of which 2,067 miles are paved). The figures are exclusive of highways within cities and towns.

Railways. The province is covered with a network of railways, 1,223 miles in extent.

Aviation. There is a direct air service to major Canadian and USA cities, London and Bermuda.

Shipping. Ferry services connect Nova Scotia with Newfoundland, Prince Edward Island, New Brunswick and Maine. Direct service by container vessels is provided from the Port of Halifax to ports in Europe, Asia and the Caribbean.

JUSTICE AND EDUCATION

Justice. There is a Supreme Court which is a Court of common law and equity possessing original and appellate jurisdiction in civil and in criminal cases. The Supreme Court consists of an appeal division of 7 judges and a trial division of 7 judges. There are also county courts, family courts, probate courts, magistrates' courts, municipal and justices' courts. Bodies, sometimes referred to as courts, are established for the revision of assessment rolls, voters' lists and like purposes. Juvenile courts under the auspices of the family courts throughout the province have power to try boys and girls under the age of 16 years.

For the year ending 31 Dec. 1979 there were 4,364 admissions to provincial jails, of these, 2,789 were sentenced. The Adult Probation Service handled 5,730 cases during 1979.

Education. Public education in Nova Scotia is free, compulsory and undenominational through elementary and high school. Attendance is compulsory to the age of 16. In addition to over 600 public schools there are the Atlantic Inter-provincial Resource Centres for the Hearing Handicapped and for the Visually Impaired; the Nova Scotia School for Boys and the Nova Scotia School for Girls for delinquent children; and the Nova Scotia Youth Training Centre for mentally handicapped children. The province has 15 universities and colleges (including 2 junior colleges), of which the largest is Dalhousie University in Halifax. The Nova Scotia Agricultural College and the Nova Scotia Teachers' College are located at Truro. The Technical University of Nova Scotia at Halifax grants degrees in engineering and architecture.

The Adult Education programme of the Nova Scotia Department of Education administers 2 institutes of technology and a nautical institute. It also provides in-school training for the Department of Labour Apprenticeship programme.

All training arrangements for adults including those financed by the Canada Employment and Immigration Commission are the responsibility of the Adult Education Programme of the Department of Education. Short courses for fishermen and farmers are conducted by the Departments of Fisheries and Agriculture respectively.

The Continuing Education Activity of the Department of Education offers financial support and organizational assistance to local school boards for provision of weekend and evening courses in academic and avocational subjects, and citizenship for new Canadians. It also provides local authorities with specialist support services to assist them in providing community workshops and short courses in fine arts and handicrafts; and it operates a correspondence study service for children and adults.

Occupational courses at the high school level are provided by 14 regional vocational schools under the jurisdiction (except in 3 amalgamated school areas) of the Department of Education.

Total expenditure on public education for the year 1978–79 was $384,131,739, of which 70·3% was borne by the provincial government. In 1978–79, classrooms operated in 622 school houses, with 11,527 teachers and 198,650 pupils, of whom 101,606 were in elementary school grades and 97,044 in junior and senior high school grades.

Books of Reference

Atlantic Provinces Economic Council. *The Atlantic Vision, 1990.* Halifax, 1979
Nova Scotia, Today's Economy. Nova Scotia Dept. of Development. Halifax, 1980
Public Archives of Nova Scotia. *Place Names and Places of Nova Scotia.* Halifax, 1967
Beck, Murray, *The Government of Nova Scotia.* Toronto, 1957.—*Joseph Howe. The Voice of Nova Scotia.* 1964.—*The Evolution of Municipal Government in Nova Scotia, 1749–1973.* 1973
Bird, W. R., *This is Nova Scotia.* Toronto, 1955
Elliott, S. B., *Nova Scotia Book of Days: A Calendar of the Province's History.* Halifax, 1979
Fergusson, C. B., *Nova Scotia* in *Encyclopedia Canadiana*, Vol. VII. Toronto, 1968
Raddall, T. H., *Halifax, Warden of the North.* Toronto, 1972
Vaison, R., *Nova Scotia Past and Present: A Bibliography and Guide.* Halifax, 1976

ONTARIO

HISTORY. The French explorer Samuel de Champlain explored the Ottawa River from 1613. The area was governed by the French, first under a joint stock company and then as a royal province, from 1627 and was ceded to Great Britain in 1763. A constitutional act of 1791 created there the province of Upper Canada, largely to accommodate loyalists of English descent who had immigrated after the United States war of independence. Upper Canada entered the Confederation as Ontario in 1867.

AREA AND POPULATION. The total area is about 412,600 sq. miles (1,068,630 sq. km), of which some 344,100 sq. miles (891,220 sq. km) are land area and some 68,500 sq. miles (177,420 sq. km) are fresh water.

The province extends 1,000 miles from east to west and 1,050 miles from north to south.

Ontario is bounded on the north by the waters of Hudson and James Bay, on the east by Quebec, on the west by Manitoba, and on the south by the states of New York, Pennsylvania, Ohio, Michigan, Wisconsin and Minnesota.

The population of the province (census, 1 June 1976) was 8,264,465. Census population of the principal cities (1976): Toronto (provincial capital), 633,318 (city), 2,803,101 (census metropolitan area); Hamilton, 312,003 (city), 529,371 (census metropolitan area); Ottawa (federal capital), 304,462 (city), 521,341 (census metropolitan area); London, 240,392 (city); Windsor, 196,526 (city), Kitchener, 131,870 (city), 272,158 (census metropolitan area); Sudbury, 97,604 (city), 167,705 (regional municipality).

Vital statistics, *see* p. 266.
Religion, *see* p. 284.

CONSTITUTION AND GOVERNMENT. The provincial government is administered by a Lieut.-Governor, a cabinet and one chamber elected by a general franchise for a period of 5 years. Women have the vote and can be elected to the chamber. The minimum voting age is 18 years.

In Oct. 1980 the provincial legislature was composed as follows: Progressive Conservatives, 58; Liberals, 34; New Democrats, 33; total 125.

Lieut.-Governor: Hon. John B. Aird, QC, BA, LLD (appointed 15 Sept. 1980).
Flag: The British Red Ensign with the shield of Ontario in the fly.

The members of the Executive Council in Oct. 1980 were as follows (all Progressive Conservatives):

Premier and President of the Council: William G. Davis, QC.
Energy and Deputy Minister: Robert Welch, QC. *Natural Resources:* James Auld. *Provincial Secretary for Resources Development:* Rene Brunelle. *Intergovernmental Affairs:* Thomas Wells. *Northern Affairs:* Leo Bernier. *Transportation and Communications:* James Snow. *Provincial Secretary for Social Development:* Margaret Birch. *Housing:* Claude Bennett. *Treasurer and Minister of Economics:* Frank Miller. *Health:* Dennis Timbrell. *Environment:* Harry Parrott. *Education and Colleges and Universities:* Dr Bette Stephenson. *Attorney-General and Solicitor-General:* Roy McMurtry, QC. *Agriculture and Food:* Lorne Henderson. *Community and Social Services:* Keith Norton, QC. *Consumer and Commercial Relations:* Frank Drea. *Industry and Tourism:* Larry Grossman, QC. *Chairman of Management Board of Cabinet and Chairman of Cabinet:* George McCague. *Revenue:* Lorne Maeck. *Culture and Recreation:* Reuben Baetz. *Government Services:* Dr Robert Elgie. *Provincial Secretary for Justice and Minister of Correctional Services:* Gordon Walker, QC. *Without Portfolio:* Bud Gregory, Alan Pope.

Local Government. Local government in Ontario is divided into two branches, one covering municipal institutions and the other education.

The present municipal system dates from The Municipal Corporations Act enacted by The Province of Canada in 1849. It has been considerably modified in recent years with the creation of the Municipality of Metropolitan Toronto in 1954 and the launching of the Government of Ontario's local government restructuring programme in 1968. Generally, there are two levels of municipal government in Ontario. The upper level consists of 27 counties plus 12 restructured regional municipalities. The local level comprises more than 800 cities, towns and townships. Cities in the traditional county system function independently of the county in which they lie, as do 5 towns which have been separated for municipal purposes. There are no separated municipal units in regional governments.

Ontario's local municipalities are governed by councils elected by popular vote.

A city council usually consists of a mayor, aldermen and, sometimes, an executive committee known as a board of control.

Councils of towns, villages and townships usually consist of a mayor, reeve, deputy reeve, councillors and, in the case of the newer regional municipalities, one or more regional councillors who represent the area municipalities on the regional council.

County and regional government councils are federated assemblies.

A county council consists of the reeves and deputy reeves of the towns, villages and townships. The head of the county council is the warden, who is elected by the council from among its own members.

A regional council consists of the heads of council of the local municipalities, as well as a varying number of regional councillors, who are elected on the basis of representation, either directly or indirectly. The head of the regional council is the chairman who is elected by council but who, unlike a county warden, need not have been a council member.

No municipality in Ontario may incur long-term debts without the sanction of the tribunal created by the Provincial Legislature and known as the Ontario Municipal Board. Debenture obligations incurred by municipalities for utility undertakings (water-works and electric light and power systems) are discharged ordinarily out of revenues derived from the sale of utility services and do not fall upon the ratepayers.

Municipal councils have no jurisdiction for education beyond the collection of taxes for school purposes. Responsibility for providing, operating and maintaining school facilities, and for the supply of teachers, rests with local education authorities known as boards of education or school boards. These boards are now generally organized on a county or regional basis. Apart from some of the larger cities, local municipal school boards no longer exist.

Municipal institutions come under the jurisdiction of the Provincial Ministry of Intergovernmental Affairs. One of the principal functions of the Ministry is to advise and assist municipalities on such matters as accounting, reporting, auditing, budgeting and planning. Educational support and guidance at the provincial level is the responsibility of the Ministry of Education, which deals with the training of teachers and the formulation of curriculum. (At the university and community college level, education support services are provided by the Ministry of Colleges and Universities.)

There are considerable areas in the northernmost parts of Ontario where as yet there is little or no settlement of population. In such areas no municipal organization exists, and control for all purposes over such areas remains in the hands of the Provincial Government.

FINANCE. The gross revenue and expenditure and the net cash requirements (in Canadian $1,000) for years ending 31 March were as follows:

	1975–76	1976–77	1977–78	1978–79	1979–80
Gross revenue	9,520	11,148	11,782	13,233	15,246
Gross expenditure	11,319	12,467	13,544	14,413	15,830
Net cash requirement	1,799	1,319	1,762	1,180	584

Gross revenue and expenditure figures include all non-budgetary transactions, i.e., the lending and investment activity of the Government to Crown corporations, agencies and municipalities as well as the repayment of these loans or recovery of investments. Transactions on behalf of Ontario Hydro are excluded.

ENERGY AND NATURAL RESOURCES

Electricity (1979). Ontario Hydro recorded for the calendar year a dependable peak capacity of 23·9m. kw. and a net energy output generated and purchased of 106,000m. kwh.

Minerals (1979, estimate). The value of shipments (in $1m.) in the mineral products industry were: Nickel, 605; copper, 435; iron ore, 286; gold, 213. The total value of mineral production was estimated at $2,595m. in 1978. The mining industry employed about 47,000 people.

Agriculture. In 1979, 3·4m. hectares were under field crops with total farm receipts of $4,000m.

Forestry. According to the most recent inventory (1963) the total area of productive forested land is 46,644,872 hectares, comprising: Softwoods, 23,591,147; hardwoods, 5,537,313; mixed woods, 14,270,428; reproducing forests, 3,245,983. The growing stock equals 4,266,868m. cu. ft. The estimated value of shipments by the forest products industry (including logging) was (1979 census) $4,729m.

INDUSTRY AND TRADE

Industry (1979). Ontario is Canada's most highly industrialized province. About 70% of value added in commodity-producing industries is accounted for by manufacturing. Construction is next with 15%.

In 1979, the labour force was 4,289,000. Total labour income was, $53,900m. The Gross Provincial Product (GPP) was $101,200m.

The leading manufacturing industries are motor vehicles and parts, iron and steel, meat and meat preparations, dairy products, paper and paperboard, chemical products, petroleum and coal products, machinery and equipment, metal stamping and pressing and communications equipment.

Trade. In 1979 Ontario exported 41% ($26,800m.) of Canada's total foreign trade.

COMMUNICATIONS

Roads. There were, in 1979, 159,415·8 km of roads. Motor licences numbered approximately 5·4m., of which 3·6m. were passenger cars, 801,140 trucks and tractors, 21,600 buses, 587,900 trailers, 90,950 motor cycles and 195,180 snow vehicles.

Railways. The Ontario Northland Railway has about 550 miles of track and the Algoma Central Railway 325 miles and they are provincially owned. The Canadian National and Canadian Pacific Railways operate a total of about 9,500 miles in Ontario.

Post (1979). Telephone service is provided by 31 independent systems (284,288 telephones) and Bell Canada (5·53m. telephones).

EDUCATION. There is a complete provincial system of elementary and secondary schools as well as private schools. In 1979 publicly financed elementary and secondary schools had a total enrolment of 1,871,190 pupils.

In 1965 Ontario established Colleges of Applied Arts and Technology (CAATS). There are now 22 of these publicly owned colleges with full-time enrolment of over 70,430 in academic courses.

The University of Toronto, founded in 1827 (full-time enrolment, 1979, 33,270), and 14 other major universities, all receive provincial grants. The net general expenditure of the provincial ministries of education and colleges and universities for the fiscal year ending 31 March 1980 was $4,000m.

Books of Reference

Statistical Information: Annual publications of the Ontario Ministry of Treasury and Economics include: *Ontario Statistics*; *Ontario Budget*; *Public Accounts*; *Financial Report.*

PRINCE EDWARD ISLAND

HISTORY. The earliest discovery of the island is not satisfactorily known, but the first recorded visit was by Jacques Cartier in 1534, who named it Isle St Jean; it was first settled by the French, but was taken from them in 1758. It was annexed to Nova Scotia in 1763, and constituted a separate colony in 1769. Prince Edward Island entered the Confederation on 1 July 1873.

AREA AND POPULATION. The province, which is the smallest in Canada, lies in the Gulf of St Lawrence, and is separated from the mainland of New Brunswick and Nova Scotia by Northumberland Strait. The area of the island is 2,184 sq. miles (5,656 sq. km). Total population (census, 1976), 118,229. Estimate (1980) 122,500. Population of the principal cities (1980): Charlottetown (capital), 17,063; Summerside, 8,532.

Vital statistics, *see* p. 266

Religion, *see* p. 284.

CONSTITUTION AND GOVERNMENT. The provincial government is administered by a Lieut.-Governor-in-Council (Cabinet) and a Legislative Assembly of 32 members who are elected for up to 5 years. In Sept. 1980 parties in the Legislative Assembly were: Progressive Conservatives, 21; Liberals, 10; 1 vacancy.

Lieut.-Governor: Joseph Aubin Doiron (sworn in 14 Jan. 1980).

Flag: A banner of the arms, *i.e.*, a white field bearing 3 small trees and a larger tree on a compartment, all green, and at the top a red band with a golden lion; on 3 sides a border of red and white rectangles.

Premier, President of the Executive Council: J. Angus MacLean.

Fisheries and Labour: Leo F. Rossiter. *Finance:* Lloyd G. MacPhail. *Health and Social Services:* James M. Lee. *Highways and Public Works:* George R. McMahon. *Community Affairs:* Patrick G. Binns. *Justice and Attorney-General:* Horace B. Carver. *Agriculture and Forestry:* Prowse G. Chappell. *Education:* Frederick L. Driscoll. *Tourism, Industry and Energy:* Barry R. Clark.

Local Government. The Village Service Act, 1954, provides for the incorporation of villages. The city of Charlottetown and the town of Summerside have been incorporated under Special Acts. The Town Act, 1951, provides for the incorporation of all towns. The Community Improvement Act, 1968, provides for the establishment of Community Improvement Committees in the unincorporated areas of the province.

FINANCE. Revenue and expenditure (in Canadian $) for 6 financial years ending 31 March:

	1975–76	1976–77	1977–78	1978–79	1979–80	1980–81
Revenue	176,856,206	193,668,328	216,817,800	242,274,000	273,375,400	307,566,300
Expenditure	180,399,067	193,790,131	216,708,700	242,488,500	273,074,300	306,789,900

Total sinking funds on 31 March 1978 amounted to $48,620,452.

NATURAL RESOURCES

Electricity. Electric power is supplied to 98% of the population. The province's net generated and purchased consumption of electricity rose during 1979 by 7·1% to 512m. kwh. In 1977 the province completed the laying of an undersea power cable which links the island with New Brunswick and the Maritime Power Grid. In 1980, 30 miles of additional 138 kv transmission line was added to the PEI system.

Agriculture. Improved farm land occupies about 774,630 acres out of a total of 1,399,040 acres. Potatoes provided about 28% of total farm cash receipts in 1978, with dairy products, cattle, calves and hogs following in importance. Gross returns to producers in 1979 were $112m. The land in natural forest covers 920 sq. miles. For particulars of agricultural production and livestock, *see under* CANADA, pp. 275–278.

Fisheries. The fishery of the province in 1979 amounted to 110·3m. lb. with a landed value of $29·2m. Lobsters accounted for $18·1m. or 62% of the total. Landed value of all fishery products was the highest ever. The famous 'Malpeque' oyster industry had a landed value of $762,517 in 1979, an increase of 17·7% over 1978. Seaplant landings were 42·9m. lb. valued at $2·7m.; bluefin tuna landings were 282,000 lb. valued at $566,830; scallops were valued at $817,082; cod, $2,002,742, and softshell clams, $136,930.

INDUSTRY AND TRADE

Industry. Industrial establishments produced goods to a shipment value of $130·4m. in 1979.

Commerce. Average personal income rose from $4,975 in 1977 to $5,574 in 1978. The average wage rose from $196·72 per week in 1978 to $209·01 by mid-1979. The labour force grew by 4%. Total employment rose by almost 4·3% to 47,000 in 1979.

Farm cash receipts in 1979 were $112m. (1978, $96·6m.). Fisheries receipts in 1979, $29·2m. Value added in manufacturing, 1977 was $44·9m. and the value added in the construction industry was, 1977, $53·4m.

Continued growth in trade, commerce, finance and transport and other services is reflected by an increase of 16·7% (1978) in the value of retail trade.

Tourism. The value of the tourist industry was estimated at $38·6m. in 1979 with 213,403 tourist parties.

COMMUNICATIONS

Roads. The province has a total of 3,379 miles of road, including 1,896 miles of paved highway.

Railways. Rail service is provided over 283 miles of track within the province and connects with the national railways system *via* New Brunswick.

Aviation. Air service for passengers, mail and cargo is scheduled to provide 8 flights daily in each direction between the province and various points in eastern Canada. A daily bus service operates between various centres in the province as well as to Nova Scotia during the summer months.

Shipping. A ferry service provides rail and highway communication with New Brunswick by means of 4 large ferries, 2 of which are powerful ice-breakers. Another ferry service employing 2 ferries plus an additional 2 for summertime operates between the province and Nova Scotia throughout the season of open navigation. A third ferry service employing 1 ferry operates between the province and Magdalen Islands, Quebec, during the open navigation season.

Post. In 1979 there were approximately 62,639 telephones.

EDUCATION (1979–80). Under the regional school boards there are 66 schools, 1,438 teachers, 26,612 students. Two provincial vocational high schools have 415 students enrolled. There is one undergraduate university (1,332 full-time students), and a college of applied arts and technology (702 full-time students), both in Charlottetown. Total expenditure in education in the year ending 31 March 1980 is forecast to be $70,681,000.

Books of Reference

Clark, A. H., *Three Centuries and the Island.* Toronto, 1959
Hocking, A., *Prince Edward Island.* Toronto, 1978
MacKinnon, F., *The Government of Prince Edward Island.* Toronto, 1951

QUEBEC—QUÉBEC

HISTORY. Quebec was formerly known as New France or Canada from 1534 to 1763; as the province of Quebec from 1763 to 1790; as Lower Canada from 1791 to 1846; as Canada East from 1846 to 1867, and when, by the union of the four original provinces, the Confederation of the Dominion of Canada was formed, it again became known as the province of Quebec (Québec).

The Quebec Act, passed by the British Parliament in 1774, guaranteed to the people of the newly conquered French territory in North America security in their religion and language, their customs and tenures, under their own civil laws.

In the referendum held 20 May 1980, 59·5% voted against and 40·5% for 'separatism'.

AREA AND POPULATION. The area of Quebec (as amended by the Labrador Boundary Award) is 594,860 sq. miles (1,540,668 sq. km), of which 523,860 sq. miles is land area and 71,000 sq. miles water. Of this extent, 351,780 sq. miles represent the Territory of Ungava, annexed in 1912 under the Quebec Boundaries Extension Act. The population (census 1976) was 6,234,445. Estimate (1 June 1979) 6,361,900.

Principal cities (1979): Quebec (capital), 174,900; Montreal, 1,045,000; Laval, 260,500; Sherbrooke, 74,600; Verdun, 66,700; Hull, 59,600; Trois-Rivières, 50,600.

Vital statistics, see p. 266.

Religion, see p. 284.

CONSTITUTION AND GOVERNMENT. There is a Legislative Assembly consisting of 110 members, elected in 110 electoral districts for 4 years. There were, 18 Nov. 1980, 68 *Parti Québecois*, 34 Liberals, 5 Union National, 3 Independents.

Lieut.-Governor: The Hon. Jean Pierre Côté.

Flag: The Fleurdelysé flag, blue with a white cross, and in each quarter a white fleur-de-lis.

The members of the Executive Council as on 29 Oct. 1979, are as follows:

Prime Minister: René Lévesque.

Vice-Prime Minister and Minister of Education: Jacques-Yvan Morin. *Finance:* Jacques Parizeau. *Intergovernmental Affairs:* Claude Morin. *Cultural Development:* Camille Laurin. *Economic Development:* Bernard Landry. *Social Development:* Pierre Marois. *Planning:* Jacques Léonard. *Justice:* Marc-André Bédard. *Women's Affairs:* Lise Payette. *Parliamentary Leader:* Claude Charron. *Recreation and Sport:* Lucien Lessard. *Environment:* Marcel Léger. *Financial Institutions, Companies and Co-operatives:* Guy Joron. *Energy and Resources:* Yves Bérubé. *Agriculture:* Jean Garon. *Social Affairs:* Denis Lazure. *Municipal Affairs:* Guy Tardif. *Immigration:* Jacques Couture. *Industry and Commerce:* Yves Duhaime. *Transport:* Denis de Belleval. *Work and Manpower:* Pierre-Marc Johnson. *Public Works:* Jocelyne Ouellette. *Cultural Affairs:* Denis Vaugeois. *Public Functions:* François Gendron. *Revenue:* Michel Clair.

General-delegate in London: Gilles Loiselle (12 Upper Grosvenor St., W1X 9PA).

General-delegate in New York: Marcel Bergeron (17 West 50th St., Rockefeller Center, New York 10020).

General-delegate in Paris: Yves Michaud (66 Pergolèse, Paris 75116).

ECONOMY

Budget. Ordinary revenue and expenditure (in Canadian $1,000) for fiscal years ending 31 March:

	1974–75	1975–76	1976–77	1977–78	1978–79
Revenue	6,474,367	7,917,716	9,217,265	10,742,609	11,928,343
Expenditure	6,761,470	8,791,122	10,208,430	11,503,008	13,402,830

The total net debt at 31 March 1979 was $7,249·8m.

ENERGY AND NATURAL RESOURCES

Electricity. Water power is one of the most important natural resources of the province of Quebec. Its turbine installation represents about 40% of the aggregate of

Canada. At the end of 1978 the installed generating capacity was 18,543 mw. Production, 1979, was 88,988 gwh.; energy sold to final consumer, 81,005m. gwh.

Minerals (1979). The value of the mineral production (metal mines only) was $1,160,473,000. Chief minerals: Iron ore, $639,881,000; copper, $189,606,000; gold, $154·51m.; zinc, $78,765,000.

The second major iron-ore development in northern Quebec is, like the one at Knob Lake which gave birth to Schefferville, based on the Quebec–Labrador Trough which extends from Lac Jeannine to the northern tip of Ungava peninsula. The port of Sept-Iles and the railway connecting it with Schefferville allow easy shipment to the furnaces and steel mills of Canada, the USA and Europe. The setting-up of a steel industry is being explored.

Non-metallic minerals produced include: Asbestos ($532,932,000; about 80% of Canadian production), titane-dioxide ($66,595,000), industrial lime, dolomite and brucite, quartz and pyrite. Among the building materials produced were: Stone, $193,144,000; cement, $139,657,000; sand and gravel, $70·88m.; lime, $20,393,000.

Agriculture. In 1979 the total area of the principal field crops was 2,104·4 hectares. The yield of the principal crops was (in 1,000 tonnes):

Crops	Yield	Crops	Yield
Tame hay	5,308	Fodder corn	3,528
Oats for grain	414	Maize for grain	467
Potatoes	442	Barley	83
Mixed grains	115	Buckwheat	10

The farm cash receipts from farming operations in 1979 amounted to $1,925,777. The principal items being: Livestock and products, $1,578·6m.; crops, $171m.; dairy supplements payments, $120·2m., forest and maple products, $45·7m.

Forestry. Forests cover an area of 684,480 sq. km. About 490,693 sq. km are classified as productive forests, of which 611,625 sq. km are provincial crown land and 70,912 sq. km are privately owned. Quebec leads the Canadian provinces in pulpwood production, having nearly half of the Canadian estimated total.

In 1978 production of lumber was softwood and hardwood, 7,571,924 cu. metres; in 1979: woodpulp, 6,367,000 tonnes; paper and paperboard, 6,255,000 tonnes.

Fisheries. The principal fish are cod, herring, red fish, lobster and salmon. Total catch of sea fish, 1979, 72,096 tonnes, valued at $39,661,700.

INDUSTRY AND TRADE

Industry. In 1978 there were 9,701 industrial establishments in the province; employees, 386,741; salaries and wages, $4,816·6m.; cost of materials, $18,763·4m.; value of shipments, $33,272·8m. Among the leading industries are petroleum refining, pulp and paper mills, smelting and refining, dairy products, slaughtering and meat processing, motor vehicle manufacturing, women's clothing, saw-mills and planing mills, iron and steel mills, commercial printing.

Commerce. In 1979 the value of Canadian exports through Quebec custom ports was $13,420·9m.; value of imports, $12,142·3m.

COMMUNICATIONS

Roads. In 1976 there were 49,072 miles of roads and (1979) 3,825,642 registered motor vehicles.

Railways. There were (1978) 5,230 miles of railway.

Aviation. In 1977 Quebec had 2 international airports (Dorval, Montreal) with landing runway of 27,600 ft and Mirabel, Montreal with 24,000 ft.

Post and Broadcasting. Telephones numbered 3·8m. in 1978 and there were 25 television and 122 radio stations in 1980.

Newspapers (1980). There were 10 French- and 2 English-language daily newspapers.

EDUCATION. The province has 7 universities: 3 English-language universities, McGill (Montreal) founded in 1821, Bishop (Lennoxville) founded in 1845 and the Concordia University (Montreal) granted a charter in 1975; 4 French-language universities: Laval (Quebec) founded in 1852, Montreal University, opened in 1876 as a branch of Laval and became independent in 1920, Sherbrooke University founded in 1954 and University of Quebec founded in 1968.

In 1978–79 there were 81,566 full-time university students and 85,741 part-time students.

In 1978–79, in pre-kindergartens, there were 6,173 pupils; in kindergartens, 83,091; primary schools, 526,540; in secondary schools, 578,992; in colleges (post-secondary, non-university), 137,154; and in classes for children with special needs, 104,401. The school boards had a total of 71,440 teachers.

Expenditure of the Department of Education for 1978–79 (Canadian $1,000), 3,745,894 net. This included 625,491 for universities, 2,107,492 for public primary and secondary schools, 154,502 for private primary and secondary schools and 530,004 for colleges.

Books of Reference

Statistical Information: The Quebec Bureau of Statistics (Department of Industry and Commerce, Parliament Buildings, Quebec) was established in 1912. Its most important publication is the *Quebec Yearbook* (formerly *Quebec Statistical Year Book*; annually since 1914). Other annual publications include a *Directory of Manufactures* (occasional), a *Municipal Guide* (since 1914) and *Répertoire des publications gouvernementales du Québec. Revue Statistique du Québec* (a quarterly since 1963). *Quebec Economic Situation* (since 1962). *Statistiques agricoles* (since 1968).

Atlas du Québec: L'Agriculture. Ministère de l'Industrie et du Commerce, Quebec, 1966
Baudoin, L., *Le Droit civil de la province de Québec.* Montreal, 1953
Blanchard, R., *Le Canada-français.* Paris, 1959
Cook, R., *Canada and the French-Canadian Question.* Toronto, 1966
McWhinney, E., *Quebec and the Constitution.* Univ. of Toronto Press, 1979
Ouellet, F., *Histoire de la Chambre de Commerce de Québec, 1809–1959.* Québec, 1959
Raynauld, A., *Croissance et structure économiques de la province de Québec.* Québec, 1961
Trofimenkoff, S. M., *Action Française.* Univ. of Toronto Press, 1975
Wade, F. M., *The French Canadians, 1760–1967.* Toronto, 1968.—*Canadian Dualism: Studies of French-English Relations.* Quebec–Toronto, 1960

SASKATCHEWAN

HISTORY. Saskatchewan derives its name from its major river system, which the Cree Indians called 'Kis-is-ska-tche-wan', meaning 'swift flowing'. It officially became a province when it joined the Confederation on 1 Sept. 1905.

In 1670 King Charles II granted to Prince Rupert and his friends a charter covering exclusive trading rights in 'all the land drained by streams finding their outlet in the Hudson Bay'. This included all what is now Saskatchewan. The trading company was first known as The Governor and Company of Adventurers of England; later as the Hudson's Bay Company. In 1869 the Northwest Territories was formed, and this included Saskatchewan. In 1882 the District of Saskatchewan was formed. By 1885 the North-West Mounted Police had been inaugurated, with headquarters in Regina (now the capital), and the Canadian Pacific Railway's transcontinental line had been completed, bringing a stream of immigrants to southern Saskatchewan. The Hudson's Bay Company surrendered its claim to territory in return for cash and land around the existing trading posts. Legislative government was introduced.

AREA AND POPULATION. Saskatchewan is bounded on the west by Alberta, on the east by Manitoba, to the north by the Northwest Territories; to the south it is bordered by the US states of Montana and North Dakota. The area of the province is 251,700 sq. miles (652,000 sq. km), of which 220,182 sq. miles is land area and 31,518 sq. miles is water. The population (1980 estimate) was 969,200.

Population of principal cities (1979 estimate): Regina (capital), 153,848; Saskatoon, 144,269; Moose Jaw, 33,441; Prince Albert, 30,121; Yorkton, 15,077; Swift Current, 14,358; North Battleford, 13,884; Lloydminster, 12,960; Weyburn, 9,243; Estevan, 9,012; Melfort, 5,883; Melville, 5,140.

Vital statistics, *see* p. 266.

Religion, *see* p. 284.

CONSTITUTION AND GOVERNMENT. The provincial government is vested in a Lieut.-Governor, an Executive Council and a Legislative Assembly, elected for 5 years. Women were given the franchise in 1916 and are also eligible for election to the legislature. State of parties in Oct. 1980: New Democratic Party, 44; Progressive Conservative, 15; Unionist, 2.

Lieut.-Governor: C. Irwin McIntosh.

Flag: Green over gold, with the shield of the province in the canton, and a green and red prairie lily in the fly.

The NDP Ministry in Dec. 1979 was composed as follows:

Premier and President of the Executive Council: Allan Blakeney, QC.

Agriculture: Gordon MacMurchy. *Attorney-General and Intergovernmental Affairs:* Roy Romanow. *Consumer Affairs, Revenue, Supply and Services:* Wes Robbins. *Continuing Education and Education:* Doug McArthur. *Co-operation and Co-operative Development and Telephones:* Don Cody. *Culture and Youth:* Ned Shillington. *Environment:* G. R. Bowerman. *Finance:* E. Tchorzewski. *Government Services and Labour:* Gordon T. Snyder. *Health:* Herman H. Rolfes. *Highways and Transportation:* Eiling Kramer. *Industry and Commerce:* Norman Vickar. *Mineral Resources:* John R. Messer. *Municipal Affairs (Rural):* Edgar E. Kaeding. *Municipal Affairs (Urban):* Walter E. Smishek. *Northern Saskatchewan:* Jerry Hammersmith. *Provincial Secretary:* Elwood Cowley. *Social Services:* Murray Koskie. *Tourism and Renewable Resources:* Reg Gross.

Agent-General in London: W. M. Johnson, 14–16 Cockspur St., SW1 5BL.

Local Government. The organization of a city requires a minimum population of 5,000 persons; that of a town, 500; that of a village, 100 people. No requirements as to population exist for the rural municipality and the local improvement district.

Cities, towns, villages and rural municipalities are governed by elected councils, which consist of a mayor and 6–20 aldermen in a city; a mayor and 6 councillors in a town; a mayor and 2 other members in a village; a reeve and a councillor for each division in a rural municipality (usually 6). Local improvement districts are administered by the Department of Municipal Affairs.

FINANCE. Budget and net assets (years ending 31 March) in Canadian $1,000[2]:

	1976–77	1977–78	1978–79	1979–80[1]	1980–81[1]
Budgetary revenue	1,340,636	1,459,979	1,613,470	1,807,160	2,019,345
Budgetary expenditure	1,364,142	1,503,112	1,676,322	1,856,556	2,018,303
Net assets	55,919	56,871	21,424	...	...

[1] Estimate.
[2] Excludes Consolidated Fund, Community Capital Fund, Saskatchewan Heritage Fund, Energy and Resource Development Fund and The Marketing Development Fund.

NATURAL RESOURCES. Agriculture used to dominate the history and economics of Saskatchewan, but the 'prairie province' is now a rapidly developing mining and manufacturing area. It is a major supplier of oil; has the world's largest deposits of potash; is the only source of helium in the 'free world' outside the USA, which limits production to internal use; and net value of non-agricultural production account for (1979 estimate) 60% of the provincial economy.

Electricity. The Saskatchewan Power Corporation generated 8,982m. kwh. in 1979.

Minerals. The 1979 mineral production was valued at $1,835·1m., including (in $1m.): Petroleum 720; natural gas, 15·5; coal, 22; gold, 4; silver, 3; copper, 13·8; zinc, 3·5; potash, 695·3; salt, 11; uranium, 258.

Agriculture. Saskatchewan produces normally about two-thirds of Canada's wheat. Wheat production in 1979 (in 1,000 tonnes), was 10,179 (374m. bu.) from 17m. acres; oats, 632 (41m. bu.) from 1m. acres; barley, 1,960 (90m. bu.) from 2·6m. acres; rye, 203 (80m. bu.) from 360,000 acres; rapeseed, 1,281 (57m. bu.) from 3·3m. acres; flax, 259 (10m. bu.) 8m. bu. from 800,000 acres. Livestock (Jan. 1980): Cattle, 2·17m.; swine, 660,000; sheep, 60,000. Poultry in 1979: Chickens and turkeys 11·4m. Cash income from the sale of farm products in 1979 was $2,905,193,000. At the June 1976 census there were 66,258 commercial farms in the province, each being a holding having agricultural sales of $2,500 or more.

The South Saskatchewan River irrigation project, whose main feature is the Gardiner Dam, was completed in 1967. It will ultimately provide for an area of 200,000 acres of irrigated cultivation in Central Saskatchewan. In 1979–80, 32,199, acres were under development.

Forestry. Half of Saskatchewan's area is forested, but only 115,000 sq. km are of commercial value at present. Forest products valued at $162m. were produced in 1978–79. The province's first pulp-mill, at Prince Albert, went into production in 1968; its daily capacity is 1,000 tons of high-grade kraft pulp.

Fur Production. In 1978–79 wild fur production was estimated at $10,099,490. Ranch-raised fur production amounted to $410,586.

Fisheries. The lakeside value of the 1978–79 commercial fish catch of 2·6m. lb. was $538,000.

INDUSTRY. In 1979 Saskatchewan had 676 manufacturing establishments, employing 23,000 persons. The net value of non-agricultural production was $3,460m. Manufacturing accounted for $718m., construction for $1,058m.

TOURISM. An estimated 1,051,000 tourists spent $104m. in 1978.

COMMUNICATIONS

Roads. In 1979 there were 19,561 km of provincial highways, 180,647 km of municipal roads (including prairie trails). Motor vehicles registered totalled (1979) 682,821. Bus services are provided by 2 major lines.

Railways. There were (1979) approximately 12,342 km of main railway track in operation.

Aviation. Saskatchewan had 2 major airports, 176 airports and landing strips in 1976.

Post and Broadcasting. There were (1979) 716 post offices (excluding sub-post offices), 68 TV and re-broadcasting stations and 35 AM and FM radio stations. 584,456 telephones were connected to the Saskatchewan Telecommunications system.

EDUCATION. The University of Saskatchewan was established at Saskatoon on 3 April 1907. In 1978–79 it had about 10,313 (day-time) degree students, 1,116 (part-time) and 2,528 full-time and part-time teaching staff at Saskatoon and 3,342 (full-time) and 716 (part-time) students and 947 full- and part-time faculty members at the University of Regina which was established 1 July 1974. The Saskatchewan public education system in 1978–79 consisted of 120 school units and districts serving 143,456 elementary pupils, 30,629 high-school students and 3,306 students enrolled in special classes. In addition, 3 provincial technical and vocational schools provided training for approximately 14,561 technical and 2,943 trade students. There are also 17 Roman Catholic separate school districts and 2 separate high-school districts. In addition there are 15 community colleges with an enrolment of over 100,000 registrations per year.

Books of Reference

Tourist and industrial publications, descriptive of the Government's programme, are obtainable from the Department of Industry and Commerce; other government publications from Government Information Services (Legislative Building, Regina).

Saskatchewan Economic Review. Executive Council, Regina. Annual
Archer and Derby, *The Story of a Province.* Toronto, 1955
McCourt, E. A., *Saskatchewan.* Toronto, 1968
Morton, A. S., *Saskatchewan, the Making of a University.* Toronto, 1959
Richards, J. S., and Fung, K. I. (eds.), *Atlas of Saskatchewan.* Univ. of Saskatchewan, 1969
Wright, J. F. C., *Saskatchewan, the History of a Province.* Toronto, 1955

THE NORTHWEST TERRITORIES

HISTORY. The Territory was developed by the Hudson's Bay Company and the North West Company (of Montreal) from the 17th century. The Canadian Government bought out the Hudson's Bay Company in 1869 and the Territory was annexed to Canada in 1870. The Arctic Island lying north of the Canadian mainland was annexed to Canada in 1880 by Queen Victoria.

AREA AND POPULATION. The total area of the Territories is 1,304,903 sq. miles (3,379,700 sq. km), divided into 5 districts, namely, Inuvik, Fort Smith, Keewatin, Baffin and Yellowknife. The population on 1 Jan. 1978 was 46,386, about two-thirds of whom were Indians or Inuit (Eskimo). Main centres (census 1979): Inuvik (2,892), Fort Smith (2,234), Hay River (3,345), Frobisher Bay (2,454), Fort Simpson (1,001). Because of a transfer in governmental responsibility from Ottawa to the Territorial capital at Yellowknife, the population of Yellowknife was increased by the influx of civil servants from 3,741 in 1966 to 9,918 in 1979.

CONSTITUTION AND GOVERNMENT. The Northwest Territories comprises all that portion of Canada lying north of the 60th parallel of N. lat. except those portions within the Yukon Territory and the Provinces of Quebec and Newfoundland: it also includes the islands in Hudson Bay, James Bay and Ungava Bay except those within the Provinces of Manitoba, Ontario and Quebec.

The Northwest Territories is governed by a Commissioner and a Legislative Assembly. The Council is composed of 22 members elected for a 4-year term of office. The seat of government was transferred from Ottawa to Yellowknife when it was named territorial capital on 18 Jan. 1967.

Commissioner: J. H. Parker.

Flag: Vertically, blue, white, blue, with the white of double width and bearing the shield of the Territory.

Legislative powers are exercised by the Commissioner-in-Council on such matters as taxation within the Territories in order to raise revenue, maintenance of justice, licences, solemnization of marriages, education, public health, property, civil rights and generally all matters of a local nature.

The Territorial Government has now assumed responsibility for the administration of the entire Northwest Territories.

ENERGY AND NATURAL RESOURCES

Oil and Gas. As of March 1980, 2,550 permits for oil and gas exploration were held for 723,070,483 acres, of which 33 leases were on the mainland, 2,121 were on the arctic islands and 396 on the marine coast.

Crude oil, discovered in 1920, is produced and refined at Norman Wells on the Mackenzie River; value of crude oil produced was $6·2m. in 1978.

Minerals. Mineral production for the year 1979 was valued at $469,815,536, of which zinc accounted for $219,531,000; lead, $82·85m.; gold, $61,750,361; tungsten, $58,484,430; silver, $44,566,187; copper, $1,330,685 and cadmium, $1,302,873.

Yellowknife continues to be the centre of goldmining activity and Canada's Cominco Ltd is proceeding with plans for the construction of a lead-zinc mine, the Polaris Project, on Little Cornwallis Island in the central high arctic.

Trapping and Game. Fur produced during the 1978–79 season was valued at $5·7m., primarily in wolf, fox, lynx and marten. A herd of some 6,500 buffalo is protected in Wood Buffalo National Park. Barren ground caribou are increasing, due to more effective management techniques.

Forestry. The principal trees are white spruce, jack-pine, balsam, poplar and birch. In 1976, 1·52m. cu. ft measure of lumber, 153,000 cu. ft of round timber and 270,000 cu. ft of fuelwood were cut.

Fisheries. Commercial fishing, principally on Great Slave Lake, in 1979–80 produced fish valued at $1·2m., principally trout, char and whitefish.

CO-OPERATIVES. There are 40 active co-operatives in the Northwest Territories. They are active in handicrafts, furs, fisheries, retail stores, print shops, provision of housing, contracting for services, etc. Total revenue in 1979 was $16,341,549.

COMMUNICATIONS

Roads. The Mackenzie Route connects Grimshaw, Alberta, with Hay River, Pine Point, Fort Smith, Fort Providence, Rae-Edzo and Yellowknife. The Mackenzie Highway extension to Fort Simpson and a road between Pine Point and Fort Resolution have both been opened.

Clearing began in 1972 for extending the Mackenzie Highway north of Fort Simpson to the arctic coast. Highway service to Inuvik in the Mackenzie Delta was opened in spring 1980, extending north from Dawson, Yukon as the Dempster Highway.

Railways. The Great Slave Lake Railway runs from Pine Point and Hay River, on the south shore of Great Slave Lake, 435 miles south to Grimshaw, Alberta, where it connects with the CN Rail's main system.

Aviation (1979). Fourteen licensed and 1 unlicensed airports are operated by the federal Ministry of Transport and there are 17 licensed and 18 unlicensed airports operated by the Government of the Northwest Territories. Two licensed and 10 unlicensed airports are operated by private owners. Regular mail, passenger and express services are maintained throughout the Territories. A seaplane base is operated by the Ministry of Transport and there are 17 private seaplane bases. Scheduled services join major points with centres in southern Canada.

Shipping. A direct inland-water transportation route for about 1,700 miles is provided by the Mackenzie River and its tributaries, the Athabasca and Slave rivers. Subsidiary routes on Lake Athabasca, Great Slave Lake and Great Bear River and Lake total more than 800 miles.

Post and Broadcasting (1978). There were 56 post offices. The CBC northern service operated radio stations at Yellowknife, Inuvik and Frobisher Bay. Virtually all communities of 500 or over were receiving television in 1978 *via* satellite. Telephone communication has been established between southern Canada and all areas in the Mackenzie district. Several arctic communities now receive telephone service *via* satellite. High-frequency telephone service is also available throughout the eastern Northwest Territories.

EDUCATION AND WELFARE

Education. In 1978–79 the Government of the Northwest Territories operated 71 schools with 592 teachers. In addition, one public school district operated at Yellowknife, one Roman Catholic separate school district at Yellowknife, and one school society operated a school at Rae-Edzo. The total enrolment was 12,288 in March, 1980, of whom about 65% were Inuit (Eskimos) and Indians. Four large and 4 small residences accommodate 439 pupils. Free correspondence courses are available to any pupil in a settlement where appropriate instruction is not available. There is a full range of courses available in the school system: academic, industrial arts, home economics, commercial, technical and occupational training. The continuing and special education programme provides courses and financial assistance to residents who have left the school system or are taking post high school training.

Health. In 1978 there were 7 hospitals in the Territories, 3 operated by the territorial government (Yellowknife, Hay River and Fort Smith) and 4 operated by the federal government. Forty nursing stations, 6 health stations and 8 health centres were in operation.

Welfare. Welfare services are provided by professional social workers. Facilities included (1978) 5 children's receiving homes, 2 homes for the aged and 1 transit centre.

Books of Reference

Annual Report of the Department of Indian Affairs and Northern Development, 1974–75
Annual Report of the Government of the Northwest Territories, 1977
Boyle, E., and Sprudz, A., *Arctic Cooperatives, Canada 1965–68*
Dawson, C. A., *The New North-West*. Toronto, 1947
MacKay, D., *The Honorable Company*. Toronto, 1949

YUKON TERRITORY

HISTORY. Formerly part of the North-West Territory, the Yukon was joined to the Dominion as a separate territory in 1898.

AREA AND POPULATION. The Yukon Territory is situated in the extreme north-western section of Canada and comprises 482,515 sq. km. The population reached its peak in 1901 with 27,219. The census population in 1971 was 18,388; 1980 (estimate), 24,138. Principal centres are Whitehorse (capital), 16,362; Faro, 1,668; Watson Lake, 1,374; Dawson City, 1,109; Mayo-Elsa, 1,098.

Vital statistics, *see* p. 266.

Religion, *see* p. 284.

CONSTITUTION AND GOVERNMENT. The Yukon Territory was constituted a separate territory in June 1898. It is governed by a 5-member Executive Council (Cabinet) appointed from among the 16-member elected Legislative Assembly. The members are elected for a 4-year term. The seat of government is at Whitehorse. A federally appointed Commissioner has the final signing authority for all legislation passed by the Assembly.

Commissioner: Doug Bell.

Flag: Vertically green, white, blue, in the proportions 2 : 3 : 2, charged in the centre with the arms of the Territory.

The legislative authority of the Assembly includes direct taxation, education, property and civil rights, territorial civil service, municipalities and generally all matters of local or private nature. All other major administration including Crown lands, income tax, natural resources and particularly that which requires the spending of large sums of money, is federally controlled.

ECONOMY

Planning. Proposed economic development of the Yukon Territory into the 1980s envisages a total expenditure of about $5,000m. Confirmed development projects include the construction of a natural gas pipeline through the territory to deliver Alaskan natural gas from Prudhoe Bay to the continental 48 states. Another confirmed project is the reconstruction and paving of 482 km of highways through south-western Yukon. Roads subject to this are the Haines Road and the Alaska Highway. Being considered is the possible opening of 5 new mines in eastern Yukon, extension of railways from southern Canada and Alaska and a proposed aluminium smelter. The federal government and Yukon Indians are currently negotiating a land claims settlement. It is anticipated these economic projects will result in a doubling of the current Yukon population by 1985.

Finance. The territorial revenue and expenditure (in Canadian $) for fiscal years ended 31 March was:

	1974–75	1975–76	1976–77	1977–78
Revenue	46,062,417	65,368,118	73,580,104	84,483,715
Expenditure	56,481,303	69,199,232	69,516,255	78,340,311

ENERGY AND NATURAL RESOURCES

Minerals. Mining remains the main industry. Lead, zinc, copper, silver, gold and asbestos are the chief minerals. Production figures for year ending 31 Dec. 1978 were: Lead, 82,232 kg; zinc, 118,843 kg; silver, 132 kg; copper, 7,669 kg; gold, 778 grammes. The value of mining production sales in 1979 was approximately $300m.

There were 209 land use permits issued during the 1979–80 fiscal year including 93 for government projects, 62 private road construction, 20 campsite and staging areas, 17 for quarrying, 13 for woods operations and 4 for research projects.

Forestry. The forests are part of the great Boreal forest region of Canada which stretches from the east coast of Canada into Alaska and north well above the Arctic Circle. Vast areas are covered by coniferous stands in the southern portion of Yukon with white spruce and lodgepole pine forming pure stands on wet sites and in northern aspects. Deciduous species form pure stands or occur mixed with conifers throughout forest areas.

The forest industry is small with approximately 18 active saw-mills and timber operations. Most are portable 'bush' mills although a few semi-permanent mills have been established. There are also 33 commercial cutters of fuelwood the production of which ranges from 10 cords (36 cu. metres) to 200 cords (724·9 cu. metres). Production in 1979–80 was 4,083,000 cu. metres (20,440,000 bd ft) of lumber, 1,394,000 cu. ft (17,432 cords) of cordwood and (143,000 cu. ft) of round timber including poles, pilings, building logs, mine timbers and fenceposts.

Game and Furs. The country abounds with big game, such as moose, goat, caribou, mountain sheep and bear (grizzly and black). In 1978–79, 41,580 pelts were taken for a market value of $927,814. Lynx was the most valuable fur and made up 46% of the total harvest bringing in $430,613 in revenues.

TOURISM. In 1979, 362,000 tourists visited the Yukon and spent $36m.

COMMUNICATIONS

Roads. The Alaska Highway and its side roads connect Yukon's main communities with Alaska and the provinces and with adjacent mining centres. Interior roads connect the mining communities of Elsa (silver–lead–zinc–cadmium), Faro (lead–zinc), Cantung (tungsten) and mineral exploration properties (lead–zinc–iron ore–tungsten) north of Ross River. The Dempster Highway north of Dawson City connects with Inuvik, on the Arctic coast; this highway, the first public road to be built to the Arctic ocean, was opened in Aug. 1979. The Carcross–Skagway road was opened in May 1979, providing a new access to the Pacific ocean. There are 4,230 km of roads in the Territory, of which about 180 km are paved. The rest are all-weather gravel.

Railways. The 176-km White Pass and Yukon Railway connects Whitehorse with year-round ocean shipping at Skagway, Alaska. Several rail extension studies envisage the Yukon line eventually joining a transcontinental rail link.

Aviation. Commercial airlines provide services every day between Whitehorse, Watson Lake, Yellowknife, Edmonton, Winnipeg and Vancouver. Regularly scheduled air services extend from Whitehorse to Fairbanks and Juneau, Alaska; Inuvik, Northwest Territories; and interior communities of Faro, Mayo, Dawson City, Old Crow, Ross River, Haines Junction and Beaver Creek. There are several commercial bush plane operations for charter service.

Shipping. Some goods are shipped into the Territory by air or *via* the Alaska Highway, but most are containerized in Vancouver and brought up the coast by ship to Skagway, Alaska. The containers are then taken by train from Skagway to Whitehorse, and then hauled by truck to the outlying communities. Many of these trucks then return to Whitehorse hauling ore to be shipped out. Some goods are transported within the Territory by air. Although navigable, the rivers are no longer used for shipping.

Post and Broadcasting. There are 2 radio stations in Whitehorse and 14 low-power relay radio transmitters operated by CBC. There are also 5 cable-TV channels in Whitehorse, TV channels in Whitehorse and private cable operations in Faro, Dawson City and Watson Lake. Live CBC national television is provided by the Anik satellite to virtually every community in the Territory. All telephone and tele-communications in the Territory are provided by NorthwesTel, a subsidiary of Canadian National Telecommunications. Almost all pole lines have been replaced with microwave transmission.

Newspapers. In 1981 there were 1 daily, 1 weekly and 1 two-monthly newspapers in Whitehorse. Faro has a two-monthly newspaper.

EDUCATION AND WELFARE

Education. (1979–80). The Territory had 24 schools with 5,120 pupils. In addition to the courses given in the Yukon Vocational and Technical Centre, the Yukon offers a limited number of post-secondary courses through the University of Alberta. A Yukon Teacher Education Programme started in 1977 to train local residents to obtain Bachelor of Education degrees in Education and a Teaching Certificate. The course is conducted by the University of British Columbia. The Government provides financial assistance to students requiring further education elsewhere.

Health. The health care system provides all residents with the care demanded by illness or accident. The federal government operates 1 general hospital at White-horse, 3 cottage hospitals, 2 nursing stations, with a total of 150 beds, and 9 health centres. The territorial government also operates a medical evacuation programme to send patients to Edmonton or Vancouver for specialized treatment not available in the Territory.

Books of Reference

Publications of the Department of Northern Affairs and National Resources, Ottawa: *The Yukon Act, Chapter 53, Statutes of Canada, 1953*, as amended.—*Mining in the North*. 1962.— *The Yukon Today*. 1968.

Annual Report of the Commissioner. 1972–73
Yukon Territorial Government, *Statistical Review*. 1970–74
Berton, P., *Klondike*. Toronto, 1963
McCourt, E., *The Yukon and Northwest Territories*. Toronto, 1969

CAPE VERDE

República de Cabo Verde

Capital: Praia
Population: 360,000 (1976)
GNP per capita: US$160 (1978)

HISTORY. The Cape Verde Islands were discovered in 1460 by Diogo Gomes, the first settlers arriving in 1462. In 1587 its administration was unified under a Portuguese governor.

On 30 Dec. 1974 Portugal transferred power to a transitional government headed by the Portuguese High Commissioner. Full independence was granted on 5 July 1975.

AREA AND POPULATION. Cape Verde is situated in the Atlantic Ocean 350 miles WNW of Senegal and consists of 10 islands and 5 islets. Praia is the capital. The islands are divided into 2 groups, named Barlavento (windward) and Sotavento (leeward), the prevailing wind being north-east. The former is constituted by the islands of São Vicente, Santo Antão, São Nicolau, Santa Luzia, Sal and Boa Vista, and the small islands named Branco and Raso. The latter is constituted by the islands of São Tiago, Maio, Fogo and Brava, and the small islands named Rei and Rombo. São Vicente is an oiling station which supplies all navigation to South America. The total area is 4,033 sq. km (1,557 sq. miles). The population (census, 1970) was 272,071. Because of large-scale immigration from Angola the population was estimated at 360,000 in mid-1976.

The areas and populations (1975) of the islands are:

	Sq. km	Population		Sq. km	Population
Santo Antão	779	48,179	Maio	269	3,942
São Vicente [1]	227	36,433	São Tiago	991	141,866
São Nicolau	388	17,859	Fogo	476	32,342
Sal	216	6,619	Brava	67	8,659
Boa Vista	620	3,943			
			Sotavento	1,803	186,809
Barlovento	2,230	113,033			
			Total	4,033	299,842

[1] Includes Santa Luzia.

The main towns (with populations at the 1970 census) are Mindelo (28,797) and Praia, the capital (21,494).

GOVERNMENT. The National Assembly consists of 56 members all belonging to the African Party for the Independence of Cape Verde.

President: Aristides Maria Pereira.
Prime Minister: Maj. Pedro Verona Rodrigues Pires.
Foreign Minister: Abilio Duarte.

National flag: Horizontally yellow over green, with a vertical red strip in the hoist charged slightly above the centre with a black star surrounded by a wreath of maize, and beneath this a yellow clam shell.

INTERNATIONAL RELATIONS

Membership. Cape Verde is a member of UN, OAU and an ACP state of EEC.

ECONOMY

Budget. The budget (1979) balanced at 1,327m. escudos Caboverdianos.

Currency. *Escudo Caboverdianos.* In March 1981, 79·52 *Escudo* = £1.

AGRICULTURE. The chief products are bananas, salt, tunny, coffee, nuts and pozzolana. The coffee is of excellent quality; exports in 1973 were 20 tonnes. In 1979 there were 22,000 goats, 12,000 cattle, 20,000 pigs and 6,000 asses.

COMMERCE. Imports in 1976 totalled 911·4m. escudos Caboverdianos, of which 58% came from Portugal; exports in 1976 totalled 480·3m. escudos Caboverdianos, of which, 63% went to Portugal and 14% to Angola. In 1976 29% by value of exports were fish, 19% bananas and 9% salt. Total trade of Cape Verde with UK (British Department of Trade returns, in £1,000 sterling):

	1977	1978	1979	1980
Imports to UK	158	62	81	207
Exports and re-exports from UK	1,564	1,189	1,596	1,047

COMMUNICATIONS

Roads. There were 1,946 km of roads in 1972. In 1974 there were 2,500 cars and 700 commercial vehicles.

Aviation. There is an airport at Ilha do Sal.

Shipping. In 1976, 161,000 tonnes of freight were unloaded and 18,000 tonnes loaded at Mindelo and Praia.

Broadcasting. The private broadcasting stations are operating on short-waves. There were (1976) 36,000 radio receivers and (1978) 1,717 telephones.

Cinemas. In 1972 there were 6 cinemas with 2,800 seats.

RELIGION, EDUCATION AND WELFARE

Religion. The vast majority of the population are Roman Catholic (98·7% in 1965).

Education. In 1978 there were 55,406 pupils and 1,269 teachers at primary schools, 6,045 pupils and 256 teachers at secondary schools, and 782 pupils and 43 teachers at technical schools, as well as 198 students in teacher training.

Health. In 1977 there were 23 hospitals and dispensaries with 640 beds; there were also 43 doctors, 2 dentists, 6 pharmacists and 148 nursing personnel.

DIPLOMATIC REPRESENTATIVES

OF GREAT BRITAIN IN CAPE VERDE

Ambassador: C. W. Squire, CMG, MVO (resides in Dakar).

OF CAPE VERDE IN THE USA (1120 Connecticut Ave., NW, Washington, D.C., 20036)

Ambassador: Viriato de Barros.

OF THE USA IN CAPE VERDE (Rua Hoji Ya Yenda 81, Praia)

Ambassador: Peter DeVos (resides in Bissau).

OF CAPE VERDE TO THE UNITED NATIONS

Ambassador: Dr Amaro Alexandre da Luz.

Books of Reference

Annuário Estatístico de Cabo Verde. Praia. Annual
Cabo Verde. Agência-Geral do Ultramar. Lisbon, 1961

CAYMAN ISLANDS

Capital: George Town
Population: 16,677 (1979)

HISTORY. The Caymans were a dependency of Jamaica until 1959 when they became a separate dependent territory of UK.

AREA AND POPULATION. Cayman Islands consist of Grand Cayman, Little Cayman and Cayman Brac. Situated in the Caribbean Sea, about 200 miles NW of Jamaica, the islands were discovered by Columbus on 10 May 1503. Area, 100 sq. miles (260 sq. km). Census population of 1979, 16,677. Grand Cayman (population 8,932), 22 miles long, 4–8 miles broad; capital: George Town (population 3,975). Little Cayman, 10 miles long, 1 mile broad. Cayman Brac, 12 miles long and 1¼ miles wide. Total population of the lesser islands, 1,317. Vital statistics (1978): Births, 276; marriages, 102; deaths, 78.

CONSTITUTION AND GOVERNMENT. A new Constitution came into force in Aug. 1972. The Legislative Assembly consists of the Governor, not less than 2 nor more than 3 official members, and 12 elected members.

The Executive Council consists of 3 official members appointed from among the official members of the Legislative Assembly, and 4 elected members elected by the elected members of the Assembly from among the elected members of the Assembly with the Governor as Chairman.

Governor: Thomas Russell, CMG, CBE.
Flag: British Blue Ensign with the arms of the Colony on a white disc in the fly.

ECONOMY

Budget. Revenue 1979, CI$21,016,818; expenditure, CI$16,650,445. Public debt (1 Jan. 1979), CI$8,301,211; reserve fund, CI$839,696.

Banking. Fourteen commercial banks and trust companies have branches in George Town, including Barclays Bank International which also has branches at West Bay and Stake Bay, Cayman Brac.

INDUSTRY AND TRADE

Industry. Seafaring, banking and tourism are the main industries.

Commerce. Exports, 1978, totalled CI$2,860,583 (estimate) and included turtle shell, tropical fish and dried turtle meat. Imports, CI$3,569,448; principally foodstuffs, textiles, building materials, automobiles and petroleum products.

Tourism. Tourism is now the chief industry of the islands and in recent years 16 hotels have been completed. There were 159,617 visitors in 1979.

COMMUNICATIONS

Roads. There were (1979) about 110 miles of road and over 5,607 motor vehicles.

Aviation. *Lineas Aereas Costarricensus* operates regular services between Costa Rica, Grand Cayman and Miami. Cayman Airways provide regular services between Grand Cayman, Kingston and Miami. Republic Airways provide a daily service between Miami and Grand Cayman. Red Carpet Line and CAL provide a regular inter-island service.

Shipping. Motor vessels ply regularly between the Cayman Islands, Jamaica and Florida. Shipping registered at George Town, 404 vessels of 128,463 net tons (1979).

Post and Broadcasting. There were 6,263 telephones in 1980 and there are 2 broadcasting stations in the islands.

EDUCATION AND WELFARE

Education. In 1980 there were 9 government primary schools with 1,401 pupils, a government comprehensive school with 1,286 pupils, 6 private elementary schools with 879 pupils and 2 private secondary schools with 196 pupils. There was also a private institution for further education and a school for the deaf with 7 pupils. A middle school was opened by the government in Sept. 1979 with 14 teachers and 230 students.

Health. In 1980 there was a general hospital, a dental clinic, 6 district clinics and a hospital in Cayman Brac.

Book of Reference

Annual Report, 1979. Cayman Islands Government, 1980

CENTRAL AFRICAN REPUBLIC

Capital: Bangui
Population: 2·09m. (1980)
GNP per capita: US$250 (1978)

HISTORY. Central African Republic became independent on 13 Aug. 1960, after having been one of the 4 territories of French Equatorial Africa (under the name of Ubangi Shari) and from 1 Dec. 1958 a member state of the French Community. In Jan. 1959 the 4 republics formed an 'economic, technical and customs union'. A new Constitution was adopted by a special congress of the *Mouvement pour l'évolution sociale de l'Afrique noire* on 4 Dec. 1976. It provided for the country to be a parliamentary democracy and to be known as the Central African Empire. President Bokassa became Emperor Bokassa I. The Emperor was overthrown in a *coup* on 20–21 Sept. 1979 and the empire was abolished.

AREA AND POPULATION. Central African Republic is bounded north by Chad, east by Sudan, south by Zaïre and west by Cameroon. The area covers 624,977 sq. km; its population in 1980 was 2,088,000. The capital is Bangui (301,793 inhabitants in 1975): other towns, Berberati (95,000) and Bonar (51,000).

CONSTITUTION AND GOVERNMENT. Under the 1980 Constitution, there is a directly-elected President and a National Assembly elected for 5 years. The sole legal Party is the *Mouvement pour l'évolution sociale en Afrique Noire* who nominate all candidates for election. Elections were held in March 1981.

President: David Dacko.
Vice-President: Henri Maïdou.
Prime Minister: Bernard Christian Ayandho.

Central African Republic is divided into 14 prefectures, 2 'economic prefectures' and the autonomous commune of Bangui (the capital). The national language is Sango, used as a *lingua franca* throughout the country; French is also an official language. About 35% of the population is Roman Catholic and 8% Moslem.

National flag: Four horizontal stripes of blue, white, green, yellow; over all in the centre a vertical red strip, and in the canton a yellow star.

DEFENCE

Army. The Army consists of an infantry battalion of about 1,650 men.

Air Force. The Air Force has 1 twin-jet Caravelle, 1 DC-4 and 4 C-47 transports, 10 Aermacchi AL.60 and 6 Broussard liaison aircraft, 1 Alouette and 5 H-34 helicopters. It also maintains and operates the Dassault Falcon twin-jet presidential aircraft. Personnel strength (1980) about 125.

INTERNATIONAL·RELATIONS

Membership. Central African Republic is a member of UN, OAU and an ACP state of EEC.

ECONOMY

Budget. The ordinary budget in 1974 envisaged expenditure at 17,200m. francs CFA and revenue at 15,706m.

Currency. The unit of currency is the *franc CFA* divided into 100 centimes.

PRODUCTION (in tonnes), 1979: Groundnuts, 126,000; cotton, 50,000; maize, 40,000; millet, 40,000; coffee, 14,000; diamonds (1977), 297,000 carats. A record of

58,700 tonnes of cotton was produced in 1969–70. Livestock (1979): Cattle, 670,000; goats, 780,000.

TRADE. In 1978, imports amounted to 12,776m. francs CFA and exports to 16,182m. francs CFA. In 1977, France took 63% of exports and provided 55% of imports. In 1976, of all exports, coffee comprised 33·8% by value, timber 24·2%, diamonds 17·1% and cotton 16·5%.

Total trade of Central African Republic with UK (British Department of Trade returns, in £1,000 sterling):

	1975	1976	1977	1978	1979	1980
Imports to UK	287	1,635	278	798	954	1,466
Exports and re-exports from UK	342	312	868	553	808	738

COMMUNICATIONS

Roads. In Dec. 1976 there were 21,950 km. of roads and (1974) there were 9,100 passenger cars and 3,900 commercial vehicles in use.

Railways. There are no railways, but a proposal exists (1979) for an 800 km line (1,435 mm gauge) from Bangui through Cameroon and Congo to connect with the Trans-Gabon railway at Belinga.

Post and Broadcasting. There were (1976) 75,000 radio receivers and (1973) 5,000 telephones.

JUSTICE, RELIGION, EDUCATION AND WELFARE.

Justice. The Criminal Court and Supreme Court are situated in Bangui. There are 7 civil courts throughout the country.

Religion. About 57% of the population follow animist beliefs, 20% are Roman Catholic, 15% Protestant and 8% Moslem.

Education. The University of Bangui was founded in 1970 and had 555 students in 1976. In 1976 there were 221,412 pupils at primary schools and 21,509 at secondary schools; technical schools held 1,771 students, while 615 were at the 2 teacher-training establishments.

Health. In 1975 there were 3,351 hospital beds. In 1976 there were 102 doctors, 1 dentist, 5 pharmacists, 131 midwives and 510 nursing personnel.

DIPLOMATIC REPRESENTATIVES

OF CENTRAL AFRICAN REPUBLIC IN GREAT BRITAIN

Ambassador: Dr Firmin Jean-Marie Frisat (resides in Paris).

OF GREAT BRITAIN IN CENTRAL AFRICAN REPUBLIC

Ambassador: (Vacant).

OF CENTRAL AFRICAN REPUBLIC IN THE USA
(1618 22nd St., NW, Washington, D.C. 20008)

Chargé d'Affaires: Amedee Fanga-Mbourounda.

OF THE USA IN CENTRAL AFRICAN REPUBLIC
(Ave. President Dacko, Bangui)

Chargé d'Affaires: Albert E. Fairchild.

OF CENTRAL AFRICAN REPUBLIC TO THE UNITED NATIONS

Ambassador: Simon Pierre Kibanda.

CHAD

République du Tchad

Capital: N'djaména
Population: 4·41m. (1979)
GNP per capita: US$140 (1978)

HISTORY. France proclaimed a protectorate over Chad on 5 Sept. 1900, and in July 1908 the territory was incorporated into French Equatorial Africa. It became a separate colony in March 1920, and in 1946 one of the four constituent territories of French Equatorial Africa. On 1 Jan. 1959 Chad became an autonomous republic within the French Community and achieved full independence on 11 Aug. 1960, although the northern prefecture of Borkou-Ennedi-Tibesti remained under French military administration until 1965.

Conflicts between the central government of President François (later Ngarta) Tombalbaye and secessionist groups, particularly in the Moslem north and centre of Chad, began in 1965 and continued despite attempts at reconciliation. President Tombalbaye was assassinated on 13 April 1975 following an Army *coup d'état.* A Supreme Military Council of 9 members, under the Presidency of Gen. Felix Malloum, ruled until 29 Aug. 1978, when the Council was dissolved and Malloum formed a new government of 'national unity'.

Fighting continued between the differing groups and, following further peace conferences, Gen. Malloum resigned on 23 March 1979. An accord was finally signed in Lagos on 21 Aug. between representatives of 11 warring factions. A 22-member Transitional Government of National Unity (GUNT) was formed on 10 Nov., to prepare for elections within 18 months.

AREA AND POPULATION. Chad is bounded west by Cameroon, Nigeria and Niger, north by Libya, east by Sudan and south by Central African Republic. Area, 1,284,000 sq. km; its population in 1979 was estimated at 4,405,000. The capital is N'djaména, formerly Fort Lamy with 241,639 inhabitants in 1976, other large towns being Moundou (54,925), Sarh (54,047) and Abéché (43,125).

Préfecture	sq. km.	Population 1979	Capital
Borkou-Ennedi-Tibesti	600,350	88,000	Faya-Largeau
Biltine	46,850	175,000	Biltine
Ouaddaï	76,240	347,000	Abéché
Batha	88,800	354,000	Ati
Kanem	114,520	200,000	Mao
Chari-Baguirmi	82,910	676,000	N'djaména
Guéra	58,950	207,000	Mongo
Salamat	63,000	107,000	Am Timan
Moyen-Chari	45,180	524,000	Sarh
Logone Oriental	28,035	307,000	Doba
Logone Occidental	8,695	295,000	Moundou
Tandjilé	18,045	302,000	Laï
Mayo-Kabbi	30,105	684,000	Bongor

More than 100 different languages and dialects are spoken. The largest ethnic group is the Sara, forming 30% of the population, chiefly in the Chari and Logone river valleys in the tropical south. Arabic serves as a common language throughout the semi-tropical (Sahelian) centre and the Saharan north.

CONSTITUTION AND GOVERNMENT. The civil war resumed in March 1980 between the rival forces of the Defence Minister (Hissène Habré) and those of other factions within GUNT, but the forces of Habré were defeated by Dec. following the intervention of Libyan troops in support of the opposing alliance.

President: Guokouni Oueddi.
Vice-President: Wadel Abdelkader Kamougue.

The official language is French.

National flag: Three vertical strips of blue, yellow, red.

Local Government: The 14 *préfectures* are divided into 51 *sous-préfectures*.

DEFENCE

Army. Separate armed forces are maintained by most of the factions comprising the Transitional Government of National Unity following the defeat of Habré's 7000-strong *Forces Armées du Nord*, the main groups are the *Forces Armées Populaires* of President Goukouni (10,000 men), and the southern-based *Forces Armées Tchadiennes* of Vice-President Kamougue (10,000 men). About 4,000 Libyan troops remain in the country.

Air Force. The Air Force has 3 Douglas A-1D Skyraider attack aircraft, 1 Caravelle, 3 C-54 and 7 C-47 transports, 5 Reims-Cessna F337 light aircraft, 2 Turbo-Porters, 3 Broussard communications aircraft and about 14 Puma and Alouette III helicopters.

INTERNATIONAL RELATIONS

Membership. Chad is a member of UN, OAU and is an ACP state of EEC.

ECONOMY

Budget. The budget for 1978 balanced at 17,084m. francs CFA.

Currency. The unit of currency is the *franc CFA* divided into 100 centimes.

ENERGY AND NATURAL RESOURCES

Electricity. Production (1975) amounted to 56m. kwh.

Minerals. Salt (about 4,000 tonnes per annum) is mined around Lake Chad, and deposits of uranium, gold and bauxite are to be exploited.

Agriculture. In 1970, 90·1% of the 1,418,000 work force were occupied in agriculture, forestry and fishing. Cotton growing (in the south) and animal husbandry (in the central zone) are the most important industries. Production (1977, in 1,000 tonnes) was: unginned cotton, 147; millet, 574; cassava, 59; peanuts, 85.

Livestock (1979): Cattle, 4·1m.; sheep, 2·3m.; goats, 2·3m.; poultry, 2·94m.

Fisheries. Fish production from Lake Chad and the Chari and Logone rivers, was estimated at 115,000 tonnes in 1977.

TRADE (in 1m. francs CFA):

	1974	1975	1976	1977
Imports	20,859	28,325	27,593	28,111
Exports	9,053	10,103	14,861	...

In 1976 main imports: Petroleum products, textile yarn, sugar and machinery. Exports were raw cotton (80%) and meat.

The main sources of imports are France (37% in 1976) and Nigeria and main destinations of exports Nigeria (20%), France and Congo.

Total trade with UK (British Department of Trade returns, in £1,000 sterling):

	1976	1977	1978	1979	1980
Imports to UK	911	150	291	240	279
Exports and re-exports from UK	410	724	5,284	612	361

COMMUNICATIONS

Roads. In 1976 there were 30,725 km of roads, of which only 240 km are surfaced. In 1973 there were 5,800 private cars and 6,300 commercial vehicles.

Aviation. There is an international airport at N'djaména, from which UTA and Air Afrique run 4 flights per week to Paris; there are also flights to Douala, Bangui and Kinshasa. Air Tchad operates internal services to 12 secondary airports.

Post and Broadcasting. In 1978 there were 3,850 telephones and (1977), 80,000 radios in use.

JUSTICE, RELIGION, EDUCATION AND WELFARE

Justice. There are criminal courts and magistrates courts in N'djaména, Moundou, Sarh and Abéché, with a Court of Appeal situated in N'djaména.

Religion. The northern half of the country is predominantly Moslem and the southern part is mainly Christian or animist.

Education. In 1977 there were 229,191 pupils in primary schools, 18,382 in secondary schools, 649 in technical schools and 549 students in teacher-training establishments. The university at N'djaména had (1976) 547 students.

Health. There were 43 hospitals with 3,349 beds in 1976; 100 doctors, 5 dentists, 8 pharmacists, 81 midwives and 854 nursing personnel.

DIPLOMATIC REPRESENTATIVES

OF CHAD IN GREAT BRITAIN

Ambassador: (Vacant).

OF GREAT BRITAIN IN CHAD

Ambassador: (Vacant).

OF CHAD IN THE USA (2600 Virginia Ave., NW, Washington, D.C., 20037)

Chargé d'Affaires: Mahamat Ali Adoum.

OF THE USA IN CHAD (Rue du Lt. Col. Colonna D'Oranano, N'djamena)

Ambassador: Donald R. Norland (resides in Washington).

OF CHAD TO THE UNITED NATIONS

Ambassador: (Vacant).

Books of Reference

Aperçu sur le Tchad. Publication of the President. 2nd ed. N'djaména, 1973
L'essentiel sur le Tchad. Publication of the President. 2nd ed. N'djaména, 1972
Westebbe, R., *Chad: Development Potential and Constraints.* Washington, D.C., 1974

CHILE

República de Chile

Capital: Santiago
Population: 11·1m. (1980)
GNP per capita: US$1,410 (1978)

HISTORY. The Republic of Chile threw off allegiance to the crown of Spain, constituting a national government on 18 Sept. 1810, finally freeing itself from Spanish rule in 1818.

AREA AND POPULATION. Chile is bounded north by Peru, east by Bolivia and Argentina, and west by the Pacific ocean. All regions except 3 extend from the Pacific to the international boundary, while the inter-provincial boundaries in most cases now follow watersheds instead of rivers, thus confining within one province the waters of a single system and avoiding jurisdictional disputes.

Many islands to the north, west and south belong to Chile, including Easter Island (Isla de Pascua; 63·9 sq. miles), discovered in 1722. The coastline is about 2,650 miles in length; the average width of the country, 120 miles. Area, 751,626 sq. km or 292,135 sq. miles.

In 1940 Chile declared, and in each subsequent year has reaffirmed, its ownership of the sector of the Antarctic lying between 53° and 90° W. long.; and asserted that the British claim to the sector between the meridians 20° and 90° W. long. overlapped the Chilean by 27°. Five Chilean bases were established in Antarctica in 1947, 1948, 1951 and 1962. A law promulgated 21 July 1955 put the Intendente of the Province of Magallanes in charge of the 'Chilean Antarctic Territory'.

Three thinly-settled southern provinces of Magallanes, Chiloé and Aysén and the northern provinces of Arica and Iquique are known as 'free zones', which implies that all commodities imported into those areas from abroad are not subject to all national import duties.

The total population at the census of 30 June 1972 was 10,044,940. Estimate (1980) 11·1m. Density per sq. km, 1972, was 13·54.

The areas of the provinces and their census populations at 30 June 1972 were as follows:

Provinces	Area: sq. km	Population	Provinces	Area: sq. km	Population
Aconcagua	10,204	181,660	Llanquihue	18,407	225,821
Antofagasta	123,063	283,029	Magallanes	135,418	101,368
Arauco	5,756	110,401	Malleco	14,277	200,894
Atacama	79,883	174,634	Maule	5,626	92,336
Aysén	88,984	55,201	Ñuble	14,211	351,277
Bío-Bío	11,248	216,789	O'Higgins	7,112	346,258
Cautín	17,370	465,695	Osorno	9,083	179,652
Chiloé	23,446	124,442	Santiago	17,422	3,724,540
Colchagua	8,431	184,837	Talca	9,640	257,937
Concepción	5,701	723,630	Tarapacá	55,287	204,745
Coquimbo	39,889	377,372	Valdivia	20,934	304,106
Curicó	5,737	126,565	Valparaíso	4,818	820,985
Linares	9,820	210,766			

Vital statistics (1971): Revised birth rate 27·6 per 1,000 population; death rate, 8·4; marriage rate, 8·6; infantile mortality rate, 70·9 per 1,000 live births.

The great majority of the population is mixed or *mestizo*, due to the free inter-marriage between the early Spaniards and women of indigenous tribes; language and culture remain of European origin. The indigenous inhabitants are of 3 branches: The *Fuegians*, mostly nomadic, living in or near Tierra del Fuego;

the *Araucanions* in the valleys or on the western slopes of the Andes; the *Changos*, who inhabit the northern coast region and work as labourers and fishermen.

The 3 leading cities, with the estimated population at 30 June 1975, are: Santiago, 3,186,000 (Greater Santiago, 3·3m.); Valparaíso, 248,972; Concepción, 169,570. Other towns, Viña del Mar, 229,000; Talcahuano, 183,591; Antofagasta, 149,720; Temuco, 138,430; Talca, 115,130; Chillán, 102,210; Valdivia, 89,500; Osorno, 71,000; Iquique, 63,600. Punta Arenas, on the Strait of Magellan, with a population of 67,600, is the southernmost city in the world. The Antarctic Territory proper is now stated to be 484,800 sq. miles.

There are 4 geographical zones in Chile—the arid 'desert' zone in the north, which for many years furnished the world's entire supply of natural nitrate of soda, 90% of its iodine and 18% of copper consumed; the agricultural 'Mediterranean' zone in the centre; the 'forest' zone to the south; and the 'Atlantic' zone in the extreme south, barren on the Pacific side, but with rich sheltered pampa on the Atlantic side.

CONSTITUTION AND GOVERNMENT. The Marxist coalition government of President Salvador Allende Gossens was ousted on 11 Sept. 1973 by the 3 Armed Services and the *Carabineros* (para-military police). These forces formed a government headed by a Junta of the 4 Commanders-in-Chief. Gen. Augusto Pinochet Ugarte, Commander-in-Chief of the Army, took over the presidency. President Allende committed suicide on the day of the *coup*.

While the Constitution of 1925 is still nominally in force, the National Congress has been dissolved, Marxist parties outlawed and all political activities banned. The new Government assumed wide-ranging powers but the 'state of siege' ended in March 1978. A new Constitution was approved by 67·5% of the voters on 11 Sept. 1980. It provides for a return to democracy after a minimum period of 8 years. Gen. Pinochet would remain in office during this period.

For details of the 1925 Constitution and earlier political history *see* THE STATESMAN'S YEAR-BOOK, 1975–76, p. 808.

The capital is Santiago, founded on 12 Feb. 1541.

National flag: Two horizontal bands, white, red, with a white star on blue square in top sixth next to staff.

National anthem: Dulce patria, recibe los votos (words by E. Lillo, 1847; tune by Ramón Carnicer, 1828).

The following is a list of the presidents since 1927:

Gen. Carlos Ibáñez (Acting, then elected), 6 May 1927–26 July 1931 (resigned).

Pedro Opazo (Acting), 26–27 July 1931 (resigned).

Juan Esteban Montero (Acting), 27 July–18 Aug. 1931 (resigned).

Manuel Trucco (Acting), 18 Aug.–15 Nov. 1931.

Juan Esteban Montero, 15 Nov. 1931–4 June 1932 (deposed).

Socialist Junta (Carlos Dávila, Col. Marmaduke Grove, Gen. Arturo Puga), 4 June–8 July 1932.

Carlos Dávila (Acting), 8 July–13 Sept. 1932 (deposed).

Gen. Bartolomé Blanche (Acting), 13 Sept.–1 Oct. 1932 (resigned).

Abraham Oyanedel (Acting), 1 Oct.–24 Dec. 1932.

Arturo Alessandri, 24 Dec. 1932–24 Dec. 1938.

Pedro Aguirre Cerda, 24 Dec. 1938–25 Nov. 1941 (died).

Geronimo Méndez (succeeded as Vice-President), 25 Nov. 1941–1 April 1942.

Juan Antonio Rios, 1 April 1942–27 June 1946 (died).

Alfredo Duhalde (Acting), 27 June–3 Aug. 1946 (resigned).

Vice-Admiral Vicente Merino Bielech (Acting), 3 Aug.–3 Nov. 1946.

Gabriel González Videla, 3 Nov. 1946–3 Nov. 1952.

Carlos Ibáñez del Campo, 3 Nov. 1952–3 Nov. 1958.

Jorge Alessandri Rodriguez, 3 Nov. 1958–3 Nov. 1964.

Eduardo Frei Montalva, 3 Nov. 1964–3 Nov. 1970.

Salvador Allende Gossens, 3 Nov. 1970–11 Sept. 1973 (deposed).

President of the Republic: Gen. Augusto Pinochet.

Local Government. For the purposes of local government the Military Junta in pursuance of its policy of administrative decentralization, has divided the republic into 13 regions (12 and Greater Santiago). Each Region is presided over by a *Gobernador*, while the provinces (25 in all) included in it are in charge of an *Intendente* who represents the central government. The provinces are divided into municipalities under an *alcalde* (mayor). All these officials are appointed by the President.

DEFENCE. Chile on 9 April 1952 signed the Military Assistance pact with the US, promising access to raw materials and armed support in defence of the Western Hemisphere.

Army. The Chilean Army is a national militia in which all able-bodied citizens are obliged to serve. Liability extends from the 20th to the 45th year, inclusive. In many cases exemption can easily be obtained, as the supply exceeds the number that can adequately be trained. The annual intake has varied up to 20,000. Recruits are called up in their 20th year, and are trained for 24 months. After this training they pass into the reserve, which is estimated at 160,000.

Army aviation operates 6 CASA Aviocar transports.

The Army is organized in 21 infantry, 7 cavalry (3 armoured, 1 heliborne and 3 horsed), and 6 artillery regiments. Total strength (1980), about 53,000 men.

Navy. The largest ships of the Chilean Navy are as follows:

Completed	Name	Standard displacement Tons	Armour Belt In.	Armour Guns In.	Principal armament	Torpedo tubes	Shaft horsepower	Speed Knots
			Cruisers					
1943	Latorre [2]	8,200	3–4	3–5	7·6 in.	—	100,000	33·0
1938	{ Prat [1] O'Higgins }	10,000	4	3–5	15·6 in.; 8·5-in.	—	100,000	32·5

[1] Ex-*Nashville* and ex-*Brooklyn*, respectively, purchased from USA in 1951. *O'Higgins* used as an alongside accommodation ship since she was damaged by grounding in Aug. 1974 was refitted beginning 1978 and later recommissioned.
[2] Ex-*Göta Lejou*, purchased from Sweden in 1971.

There are 2 modern diesel powered patrol submarines (British 'Oberon' class), 1 old *ex*-US submarine, 6 destroyers (2 British built and 4 old *ex*-US), 5 frigates (2 modern British 'Leander' class, *Cordell* and *Lynch*, and 3 old *ex*-US destroyer escort transports), 4 torpedo boats, 6 patrol vessels, 12 coastal patrol craft, 3 landing ships, 2 repair ships (*ex*-landing ships), 13 landing craft, 1 survey ship, 6 transports, 1 training ship, 1 antarctic patrol ship, 2 oilers, 4 floating docks and 4 tugs.

Naval personnel in 1981 totalled 28,000 (1,920 officers, 23,400 ratings, 2,680 marines).

Air Force. Approximate current strength is 11,000 personnel, with 100 first-line and 150 second-line aircraft, divided among 12 groups, each comprising 1 squadron, within 4 combat and support wings. Groups 1 and 12 have twin-jet A-37Bs, from a total of 34 acquired for light strike/reconnaissance duties. Group 3 is equipped for general duties with about 22 UH-1H Iroquois, Hiller UH-12E and S-55T helicopters. Group 5 has about 15 Twin Otters for light transport and survey duties. Group 6 has some C-47 transports. Group 7 received 15 F-5E Tiger II fighter-bombers and 3 F-5F trainers. Groups 8 and 9 are also fighter-bomber units, each with a nominal strength of 10 Hunter F.71s and T.72s. Group 10 is a transport wing, with 2 C-130H Hercules, 5 DC-6Bs, about 10 C-47s, a King Air and a Puma helicopter. Group 11 has 9 twin-turboprop Beech 99A instrument/navigation trainers. Training aircraft include piston-engined Piper Dakota, T-34 and T-41D primary trainers, and T-37 jets. Sixteen Mirage 50 fighters are being delivered.

INTERNATIONAL RELATIONS

Membership. Chile is a member of the UN, OAS and LAIA (formerly LAFTA).

External Debt. Total foreign debt at 31 Dec. 1978 amounted to the estimated equivalent of US$6,462m. and hard currency reserves US$477·2m.

ECONOMY

Budget. Revenue and expenditure were as follows (1,000 escudos):

	1974	1975	1976 [1,2]	1977	1978
Revenue	1,793,555,000	4,548,919,500	34,590,300,000	56,161,900,000	100,505,500,000
Expenditure	2,379,222,000	5,298,836,002	34,182,900,000	56,100,200,000	94,534,400,000

[1] Figures shown in new currency.   [2] Estimate.

Since 1957 the estimates have consisted of a local currency budget (as above) plus a foreign-exchange budget (in US$1m.). The 1975 expenditures envisaged US$3,169m. for defence, US$3,687m. for education, US$883m. for agriculture, US$1,114m. for public works, US$1,395m. for housing and US$3,293m. for public health.

Currency. In Jan. 1960 a system came into force based on the *escudo* (equivalent of 1,000 *pesos*), the *centésimo* (10 *pesos*) and the *milésimo* (1 *peso*). On 29 Sept. 1975 the currency reverted to *pesos* with a value of 1,000 escudos to the new peso.

In March 1981 there were 84·92 *pesos* = £1 and 39 *pesos* = US$1.

Banking. Notes in circulation and deposits in currency were 56,341m. pesos at 31 Dec. 1978; total deposits in the commercial banks stood at 92,450m. pesos.

Commercial banks, since July 1979, must maintain cash reserves of 35% of all sight deposits and 10% of time deposits over 30 days.

Inflation is still high but decreasing; 31·5% in 1978.

Weights and Measures. The metric system has been legally established in Chile since 1865, but the old Spanish weights and measures are still in use to some extent.

ENERGY AND NATURAL RESOURCES

Electricity. In 1977 production of electricity was 9,683·3m. kwh.

Oil. Petroleum was discovered in 1945 in the southern area of Magallanes with an output of 998·4m. cu. metres in 1978. Production of liquefied gas amounted to 6,166·9m. cu. metres in 1978.

Minerals. The wealth of the country consists chiefly in its minerals, especially in the northern provinces of Atacama and Tarapacá.

Copper is the most important source of foreign exchange (about 48% of exports) and government revenues (over 30%). The copper industry, which is state-owned since July 1971, manages 5 large mines which in 1978 had proceeds returned to Chile amounting to US$1,006·8m. On the same basis the medium and small-sized companies recorded US$194·7m. Copper production for 1979 was 1,061,000 tonnes. Exports during 1979 were valued at US$1,800m.

Nitrate of soda is found in the Atacama deserts. Exports were US$46·8m. in 1978. Production was 535,300 tonnes in 1978. Iodine is a by-product: 1977 production totalled 1,922 tonnes. The use of solar evaporation as a means of reducing costs has developed the production of potassium salts as an additional by-product.

Iron ore, of which high-grade deposits estimated at over 1,000m. tons exist in the provinces of Atacama and Coquimbo, has overtaken nitrate as Chile's second mineral. Production in 1978 was 5,143,200 tonnes.

Coal reserves exceed 2,000m. tons, partially low in thermal unit. Net 1978 production was 1,115,381 tonnes.

In 1977 other minerals include molybdenum (10,940 tonnes, pure), zinc (2,826 tonnes), manganese (27,000 tonnes), lead (122 tonnes).

Agriculture. Agriculture and forestry contribute one-twelfth of the national product, although one-third of the population take part in it. Total area of land being exploited (census of 1968) was 52·4m. hectares; 14·9% for agriculture, 26·7% for pasture, 28·8% for forest; 29·6% is desert or unproductive.

Chile used to import annually about two-thirds of the foodstuffs needed, a quarter of the total imports, but this has now been reduced, by stimulating local production, to about 12% of total imports.

Some principal crops were as follows:

Crop	Area sown, 1,000 hectares 1978–79	Production, 1,000 tonnes 1978–79	Crop	Area sown, 1,000 hectares 1978–79	Production, 1,000 tonnes 1978–79
Wheat	561	995	Potatoes	81	771
Oats	79	150	Beans	110	116
Barley	60	112	Lentils	50	32
Maize	130	489	Peas	17	15
Rice	47	181	Sugar-beet	16	679

There were in 1955 over 300 large farms, each with more than 12,250 acres, while 500,000 peasants live on less than 4 acres per family. The military government has opted in most cases to increase the number of settlements with access to individual property. The process was completed in early 1979 with some 24,000 property titles issued, a large proportion of which were in co-operative schemes.

Production of animal products in 1976 was (in 1,000 tonnes): Cattle, 162; sheep, 32; pork, 57; poultry, 60. Eggs, 1,849m.; milk, 1,205m. litres; new wool, 35,000 tonnes.

Livestock (1979): Cattle, 3·61m.; horses, 450,000; asses, 30,000; sheep, 5·95m.; goats, 600,000; pigs, 1·03m.; poultry, 22m.

Forestry. According to the Forestry Institute, by late 1978, there were 277,944 hectares of artificial forests from Maule to Magallanes, the most important species being the pine (*pinus radiata*) which covers 640,000 hectares. Eucalyptus and poplar cover some 72,000 hectares. Native species of importance amounted to 9m. hectares in 1978.

Production during 1977 amounted to about 49m. in. of sawn timber. Exports in 1978 were valued at US$94·4m.

Paper production in 1978 was 215,000 tonnes and exports were valued at US$157m.

Fisheries. Chile's catch of fish in 1978 was 1,829,000 tonnes, including shell fish, 125,000 tonnes. Exports of seafood in 1978 were US$121·4m., of which fishmeal accounted for US$105·8m.

INDUSTRY AND TRADE

Industry. A nationally-owned steel plant operates from Huachipato, near Concepción. Output, 1977, 509,300 tonnes of steel ingots. Cellulose and wood-pulp are two industries which are rapidly developing; in 1977, 1,360·8 tonnes of cellulose were produced and exports were valued at US$90·9m.

Labour. In Sept. 1978 the 'economically active' numbered 4m. in the Santiago area. Professional and 'white-collar' workers numbered 731,900; agriculture employed 14,800; manufacturing, 334,700; mining, 5,200; construction, 83,700, and transport, 93,500.

Trade unions began in the middle 1880s.

Commerce. Imports and exports in US$1m.:

	1974	1975	1976	1977	1978	1979
Imports	2,239	1,776	1,594	2,221	2,917	4,200
Exports	2,043	1,498	2,069	2,171	2,480	3,800

In 1978 imports (in US$1m.) from USA, were valued at 810; Brazil, 253; Japan, 227; Federal Republic of Germany, 222; Argentina, 219; Iran, 160; Venezuela, 149; Ecuador, 95; France, 80; UK, 66.

In 1978 the principal imports were (in US$1m.): Fuels, 480; chemicals, 407; industrial equipment, 367; transport equipment, 283; spares, 228; live animals and foodstuffs, 116. The principal exports in 1978 were (in US$1m.): Copper, 1,202; paper and pulp, 159; timber, 94; iron ore, 80; nitrate, 47.

Total trade between Chile and UK for 5 years (British Department of Trade returns, in £1,000 sterling):

	1976	1977	1978	1979	1980
Imports to UK	80,673	76,890	82,269	131,218	126,273
Exports and re-exports from UK	36,295	39,432	37,571	45,640	55,741

Tourism. There were 296,954 foreign visitors in 1977.

COMMUNICATIONS

Roads. In 1966 there were in Chile 66,000 km of highways, of which 8,847 first-class paved, 23,290 second class and 33,863 earth. There were in 1974, 235,335 automobiles, 149,642 goods vehicles, 15,682 buses and 28,833 motor cycles and scooters.

Railways. The total length of railway lines was (1980) 6,396 km, including 890 km electrified, of broad- and metre-gauge. Further electrification is in progress between Concepción and Puerto Montt (600 km). An underground railway in Santiago was opened in Sept. 1975.

Aviation. There are 7 international airports, 16 domestic airports and about 300 landing grounds. Chile is served by 19 commercial air companies (2 Chilean). In 1978, 267,300 passengers were carried into and out of Chile on international services; 237,450 passengers were carried on internal routes.

Shipping. The mercantile marine had, in 1976, 66 ships of over 100 tons (678,556 DWT) and owned by 17 companies. Valparaíso is the chief port. The free ports of Magallanes, Chiloé and Aysén serve the southern provinces. Chilean ports handled 21·9m. tons in 1974.

There are 2,185 km of navigable rivers.

Post and Broadcasting. There are 1,486 post offices and agencies. The length of telegraph lines in 1971 was 12,870 km. In 1978 there were 483,225 (Santiago, 303,318) telephones in use.

A chain of wireless stations along the coast for shore-to-ship transmission is operated by the Navy. At the end of 1974 there were some 150 commercial broadcasting stations. Three television stations are operated by the Universities and there is a national television station using NTSC 525 line colour standards. On 9 Aug. 1968 the satellite station at Longovilo, 50 miles south-west of Santiago, was inaugurated to cover transmissions (including colour) from the USA and Europe.

Cinemas (1975). Cinemas numbered 196; 61 of them are in Santiago.

Newspapers (1975). There were 80 daily newspapers.

JUSTICE, RELIGION, EDUCATION AND WELFARE

Justice. There are a High Court of Justice in the capital, 12 courts of appeal distributed over the republic, tribunals of first instance in the departmental capitals and second-class judges in the sub-delegations. The police force had (1975) about 27,000 officers and men; it is organized and regulated by the Ministry of Defence.

Religion. The Roman Catholic religion was disestablished in 1925; it remains, however, a national Church in a state wherein 89·5% of the population are Catholics. There are 1 cardinal-archbishop, 5 archbishops, 22 bishops and 2 vicars apostolic. Latest estimates show 6·7m. Roman Catholics, 880,500 Protestants and 25,000 Jews.

Education. Education is in 3 stages: Basic (6–14 years), Middle (15–18) and University (19–23). Enrolment (1970): Pre-school (a new programme initiated in 1970), 60,360 children; primary school, 2,043,032; secondary school, 302,064.

University education is provided in the state university (founded in 1842), the Catholic University at Santiago (1888), the University of Concepción (1919), the Catholic University at Valparaíso (1928), the Universidad Técnica Federico Santa María at Valparaíso (1930), the Universidad Técnica del Estado (1952), Universidad Austral, Valdivia (1954) and Universidad del Norte, Antofagasta (1957) with a total student population of 96,000 in 1970. A decree of 30 Dec. 1980 laid down new regulations for universities including a restriction of the number of courses offered to 12. New private universities are envisaged.

Health. A national health service covered some 1·5m. employees (1977) and there are plans for an extension of the service to a further 1·5m.

DIPLOMATIC REPRESENTATIVES

OF CHILE IN GREAT BRITAIN (12 Devonshire St., London, W1N 2FS)
Ambassador: Miguel Schweitzer (accredited 26 March 1980).

OF GREAT BRITAIN IN CHILE (La Concepción 177,
Casilla 72-D, Santiago)
Ambassador: J. M. Heath, CMG.

OF CHILE IN THE USA (1732 Massachusetts Ave., NW,
Washington, D.C., 20036)
Ambassador: José Miguel Barros.

OF THE USA IN CHILE (Agustinas 1343, Santiago)
Ambassador: George W. Landau.

OF CHILE TO THE UNITED NATIONS
Ambassador: Sergio Diez Urzua.

Books of Reference

Statistical Information: The Instituto Nacional de Estadística (Santiago), was founded 17 Sept. 1847. *Director General:* Sergio Chaparro Ruíz. Principal publications: *Anuario Estadística* and the bi-monthly *Estadística Chilena.*
  Other sources are: *Geografía Económica,* by the Corporación de Fomento de la Production, and *Boletín Mensual,* by the Banco Central de Chile.

Allende, S., *Chile's Road to Socialism.* Harmondsworth, 1973
Butland, G. J., *Chile: An Outline of its Geography, Economics and Politics.* 3rd ed. R. Inst. of Int. Affairs, 1956.—*The Human Geography of Southern Chile.* London, 1957
De Vylder, S., *Allende's Chile.* CUP, 1976
Empresa Periodística, *Diccionario biográfico de Chile.* 8th ed. Santiago, 1952
Horne, A., *Small Earthquake in Chile. A Visit to Allende's South America.* London, 1972
MacEoin, G., *No Peaceful Way: Chile's Struggle for Dignity.* New York, 1974
Petras, J., and Merino, H. Z., *Peasants in Revolt: A Chilean Case Study.* Univ. of Texas Press, 1972
Pinochet de la Barra, O., *La Antártido Chilena.* Santiago de Chile, 1948

PEOPLE'S REPUBLIC OF CHINA

Capital: Peking (Beijing)
Population: 971m. (1979)
GNP per capita: US$253 (1978)

Zhonghua Renmin Gonghe Guo

HISTORY. In the course of 1949 the Communists obtained full control of the mainland of China, and in 1950 also over most islands off the coast, including Hainan.

On 1 Oct. 1949 Mao Zedong (Tse-tung) proclaimed the establishment of the People's Republic of China.

AREA AND POPULATION. China is bounded north by the USSR and Mongolia, east by Korea, the Yellow Sea and the East China Sea, with Hong Kong and Macao as enclaves on the south-east coast; south by Vietnam, Laos, Burma, India, Bhután and Nepál; west by India, Pakistan, Afghánistán and the USSR. China is composed of 22 provinces (this figure includes Taiwan), 5 autonomous regions originally entirely or largely inhabited by national minorities (owing to the immigration of Han Chinese the original nationality is sometimes outnumbered, *e.g.*, by 10 to 1 in Inner Mongolia), namely Inner Mongolia, Xinjiang–Uygur, Guangxi–Zhuang, Ningxia–Hui, Tibet and 3 centrally controlled municipalities (Peking, Shanghai, Tianjin).

The capital is Peking (Beijing).

See map in THE STATESMAN'S YEAR-BOOK, 1968–69.

The total area is estimated at 9,597,000 sq. km (3,704,400 sq. miles).

Population at the last census (1953): 601,938,035. This figure was arrived at as follows: Direct census, 574,205,940; Taiwan, 7,591,298; Chinese resident or studying abroad, 11,743,000; Chinese 'in remote border regions', 8,397,477. Urban population, 77·3m. (13·3%); rural population, 505·3m. Official population figure in 1979 (excluding Taiwan): 970·93m., of whom 110m. urban. Chinese sources put the rate of increase for 1978 at about 1·2%. In 1979 a reduction of this rate to 1%, and to 0·5% by 1985, was officially called for. To this end family planning is vigorously pursued and in 1979 penalties were imposed on families producing more than 2 children. The legal age for marriage is 20 for women and 22 for men but couples are encouraged to postpone marriage until 25 and 27 respectively. The term 'Han' is used to distinguish ethnic Chinese from other Chinese citizens. There were 55 non-Han ethnic minorities numbering 56m. in all in 1980.

Population densities vary from 10 per sq. km in the West to over 100 per sq. km in the East.

Estimates of persons of Chinese race outside China, Taiwan and Hong Kong in 1980 varied from 15m. to 20m. China permits the emigration of a limited number of persons to Hong Kong annually. There were 70,456 in 1979.

A number of widely divergent varieties of Chinese are spoken. The official 'Modern Standard Chinese' is based on the dialect of North China, and the Government is promoting its use generally. The ideographic writing system is uniform throughout the country, and has undergone systematic simplification. In 1958 a phonetic alphabet (*Pinyin*) was devised to transcribe the characters, and on 1 Jan. 1979 this was officially adopted for use in all texts in the Roman alphabet (*see also* Post and Broadcasting, p. 350). The decision of press agencies to use the *Pinyin* transcription led to the supersession of the system previously widely used in English-speaking countries (Wade). Starting with THE STATESMAN'S YEAR-BOOK,

1979–80 new names were introduced in *Pinyin*. In this edition with a few exceptions *Pinyin* forms are used for all names. *Pinyin* forms are not used in Taiwan.

From 1949 to 1955 the country was divided into 6 large administrative regions. This system was terminated in 1955, but in 1961 was revived in the form of 6 regional Party Bureaux. These ceased to function during the Cultural Revolution. The table below shows the Provinces, Autonomous Regions and Government-controlled Municipalities grouped regionally. The cities shown in brackets are the seats of the former regional Party Bureaux.

	Area (in 1,000 sq. km)	Population Census 1953 (in 1,000)	1976–80 (in 1m.)	Capital
North-Eastern Region (Shenyang)				
Heilongjiang [1]	710·0	11,897	32·00	Harbin
Jilin [1]	290·0	11,290	24·00	Changchun
Liaoning [1]	230·0	18,545	36·00	Shenyang
Northern Region (Peking)				
Hebei	202·7	35,985	50·00	Shijiazhuang
Inner Mongolia (Aut. Region) [1]	450·0	6,100	18·00	Hohhot
Peking (municipality) (Beijing)	17·8	2,768	8·70	—
Shanxi	157·1	14,314	23·00	Taiyuan
Tianjin (municipality)	4·0	2,694	7·00	—
Eastern Region (Shanghai)				
Shandong	153·3	48,877	72·00	Jinan
Jiangxi	164·8	16,773	28·00	Nanchang
Jiangsu	102·2	41,252	57·00	Nanking (Nanjing)
Shanghai (municipality)	5·8	6,204	11·00	—
Anhui	139·9	30,344	45·00	Hefei
Zhejiang	101·8	22,866	36·00	Hangzhou
Fujian	123·1	13,143	24·00	Fuzhou
Taiwan	36·0	7,591	17·00	Taibei
Central-Southern Region (Wuhan)				
Henan	167·0	44,215	70·00	Zhengzhou
Hubei	187·5	27,790	45·00	Wuhan
Hunan	210·5	33,227	50·00	Changsha
Guangdong	231·4	34,770	53·50	Canton (Guangzhou)
Guangxi–Zhuang (Aut. Region)	220·4	19,561	33·00	Nanning
South-Western Region (Chongqing)				
Sichuan	569·0	62,304	97·00	Chengdu
Guizhou	174·0	15,037	25·00	Guiyang
Yunnan	436·2	17,473	30·00	Kunming
Tibet (Aut. Region)	1,221·6	1,273	1·70	Lhasa
North-Western Region (Xian)				
Shaanxi	195·8	15,881	27·00	Xian
Gansu [1]	530·0 ⎱	12,928	⎰ 19·00	Lanzhou
Ningxia–Hui (Aut. Region) [1]	170·0 ⎰		⎱ 3·60	Yinchuan
Qinghai	721·0	1,677	3·50	Xining
Xinjiang–Uygur (Aut. Region)	1,646·8	4,874	12·00	Urumqi

[1] Boundaries restored to approximately the pre-1970 position in 1979.

Large towns, with population in 1977: Chongqing, 6m.; Canton (Guangzhou), 5m.; Shenyang, 4·4m.; Luda, 4·2m.; Wuhan, 3·5m.; Nanjing, 3m.; Harbin, 2·1m.

Manchuria, a term not used by the Chinese, is roughly identical with the 3 provinces of the N.E. Region.

Tibet. For events before the revolt of 1959 *see* THE STATESMAN'S YEAR-BOOK, 1964–65, under TIBET. After the revolt was suppressed the Preparatory Committee for the Autonomous Region of Tibet (set up 1955) took over the functions of local government, led by its Vice-Chairman, the Banqen Lama, in the absence of its Chairman, the Dalai Lama, who had fled to India in 1959. In Dec. 1964 both the Dalai and Banqen Lamas were removed from their posts and on 9 Sept. 1965 Tibet became an Autonomous Region. 301 delegates were elected to the first People's Congress, of whom 226 were Tibetans and in 1968 a Revolutionary Committee was established to administer the Region. This gave way to a People's Government in Aug. 1979. The Banqen Lama was re-elected to the Standing Committee of the Chinese

People's Political Consultative Conference in March 1978—he became one of its Vice-Chairmen in July 1979—and has made several appeals to the Dalai Lama to return to China. In 1979 the population was reported to be 1·74m. (120,000 in the capital, Lhasa) and the number of Chinese then in Tibet to be about 120,000. 4·25m. Tibetans live outside Tibet, in China, and in India and Nepál. Chinese efforts to modernize Tibet include irrigation, road-building and the establishment of light industry: more than 260 small and medium-sized factories and mines have been set up producing electric power, coal, building materials, lumber, textiles, chemicals and animal products.

In 1979, 1·6m. were engaged in agriculture, including 0·5m. nomadic herdsmen. Agricultural communes were first introduced in 1965; by 1975 it was announced that 99% of villages had formed them. In 1975 Tibet became self-sufficient in grain for the first time. There are now 16,000 km of highways, and air routes link Lhasa with Chengdu and Lanzhou.

It was officially admitted in Peking in 1980 that the administration of Tibet had been badly conducted hitherto. The borders were opened for trade with neighbouring countries, and agricultural reforms allowing for more individual autonomy within the commune system were announced.

Efforts are being made to revive Tibetan culture as part of China's new liberal policy towards minorities. Buddhist monasteries, closed in the Cultural Revolution, are now re-opening. Circulation of the Tibetan-language *Xizang Daily* now totals 38,000. By 1979 there were 6,000 primary schools, some 300 secondary schools and 4 colleges. There were more than 6,000 medical workers and nearly 500 hospitals, with a total of 4,000 beds.

The Dalai Lama, *My Land and My People* (ed. D. Howarth). London, 1962
Dawa Norbu, *Red Star Over Tibet*. London, 1974
Jäschke, H. A., *A Tibetan–English Dictionary*. London, 1934
Mele, F., *Tibet*. Paris, 1975
Richardson, H. E., *Tibet and its History*. OUP, 1962
Shakabpa, T. W. D., *Tibet: A Political History*. Yale Univ. P. 1967
Thubten, J. N., and Turnbull, C., *Tibet: Its History, Religion and People*. Harmondsworth, 1972

CONSTITUTION AND GOVERNMENT. On 21 Sept. 1949 the 'Chinese People's Political Consultative Conference' met in Peking, convened by the Chinese Communist Party. The Conference adopted a 'Common Programme' of 60 articles and the 'Organic Law of the Central People's Government' (31 articles). Both became the basis of the Constitution adopted on 20 Sept. 1954 by the 1st National People's Congress, the supreme legislative body. The Consultative Conference continued to exist after 1954 as an advisory body. Both bodies stopped functioning in the Cultural Revolution. The People's Congress was revived in 1975 and the Consultative Conference in 1978, when Deng Xiaoping was elected as its head. In 1979 it had 1,734 members.

The 1954 Constitution was both a political and an organizational document. It indicated the steps to be taken to build a 'socialist' society, defined the structure and functions of government organs and the rights and duties of citizens appropriate in the period of transition to 'socialism'.

In Jan. 1975 the 4th National People's Congress approved a constitution, under which China was defined as a 'socialist state of the dictatorship of the proletariat'. The 1975 Constitution was a simpler document than its predecessor emphasizing the role of politics in society, especially the thought of Mao, but giving fewer organizational details. In March 1978 the 5th National People's Congress adopted a new constitution of 60 articles which revives several of the provisions of the 1954 constitution dropped in the 1975 document and eliminates much of the latter's innovatory radicalism. More administrative detail is given. Provisions (Art.45) for freedom of speech and publication were withdrawn in 1980.

The National People's Congress is the highest organ of state power. It can amend the Constitution, elects and has power to remove from office the highest State dignitaries, decides on the national economic plan, etc. The Congress elects a *Standing Committee* which supervises the State Council and whose chairman is the equivalent of head of state. The present chairman (elected March 1978) is Ye Jianying.

The Constitution provides that the Congress be elected for a 5-year term and should meet once a year. It is composed of deputies elected on a constituency basis by direct secret ballot. Any voter, and certain organizations, may nominate candidates. Nominations may exceed seats by 50–100%. 3,497 deputies were elected to the 5th Congress in March 1978.

The State Council is the executive organ of the Congress, that is, the Government. In March 1981 it consisted of the Prime Minister, Zhao Ziyang, 13 Deputy Prime Ministers: Bo Yibo (*Minister in charge of Machine Building Industry Commission*), Chen Muhua (*Minister of Economic Relations with Foreign Countries*), Fang Yi (*Minister in charge of State Scientific and Technological Commission*), Geng Biao (*Defence*), Han Guang (*Minister in charge of State Capital Construction Commission*), Huang Hua (*Minister of Foreign Affairs*), Ji Pengfei, Yuan Baohua. (*Minister in charge of State Economic Commission*), Kang Shien (*Petroleum*), Wan Li (*Minister in charge of State Agricultural Commission*), Yang Jingren (*Minister in charge of State Nationalities Affairs Commission*), Yao Yilin (*Minister in charge of State Planning Commission*), Yu Qiuli (*Minister in charge of State Energy Commission*), Zhang Aiping, and 36 other Ministers including Zhao Cangbi (*Public Security*), Li Qiang (*Foreign Trade*), Lin Hujia (*Agriculture*), Wang Bingqian (*Finance*), Jiang Nanxiang (*Education*), Qian Xinzhong (*Health*), Wang Lei (*Commerce*), Wei Wenbo (*Justice*).

Since 1970 when China began to emerge from the isolation of the Cultural Revolution, her diplomatic relations have expanded considerably. On 25 Oct. 1971 the UN voted for the People's Republic to take over the China seat from the Nationalists by 76 votes to 35 with 17 abstentions. US President Nixon visited China in Feb. 1972 and in 1973 'liaison offices' were opened in the capitals of the two countries. On 1 Jan. 1979 the US recognized the Peking government as the sole legal government of China and diplomatic relations were established. In Jan.–Feb. 1979 Deng Xiaoping paid an official visit to USA. On 12 Aug. 1978 China and Japan signed a 10-year treaty of peace and friendship (ratified 22 Oct. 1978). China has announced that it will not renew its treaty of friendship with the USSR which expired in 1980.

State emblem: 5 stars above Peking's Gate of Heavenly Peace, surrounded by a border of ears of grain entwined with drapings, which form a knot in the centre of a cogwheel at the base; the colours are red and gold.

National flag: Red with a large star and 4 smaller stars all in yellow in the canton.

National anthem: 'March on, brave people of our nation' (words composed 'collectively', 1978; tune by Nie Er).

De facto power is in the hands of the Communist Party of China, which had 38m. members in 1980. There are 8 other parties, all members of the United Front headed by Deng Xiaoping. Communist Party officials hold key positions in government organs and most social, economic and cultural organizations. In mid-1966 the Party Chairman, Mao Tse-tung, launched the 'Great Proletarian Cultural Revolution' to eradicate 'revisionism' and numerous Party and State officials were dismissed. The Cultural Revolution can be taken to have terminated by April 1969 when the long-delayed 9th Party Congress was convened, although it was not officially declared to have been brought to a 'victorious conclusion' until Aug. 1977. The 9th Congress adopted a new Party Constitution which proclaimed the leading rôle of the Party in the State and designated Lin Biao as Chairman Mao's successor. A factional dispute developed, however, centred on Lin Biao (killed in an air crash in Mongolia in Sept. 1971) and in Aug. 1973 the 10th Party Congress adopted amendments to the Party Constitution, removing references to Lin Biao and the succession to Chairman Mao, and electing a new Central Committee which appointed a new Politburo and Standing Committee. In Jan. 1975 the Central Committee appointed as a vice-chairman of the Politburo Deng Xiaoping, former Party Secretary-General dismissed during the Cultural Revolution. In April 1976 a 'radical' faction in the Politburo engineered a second dismissal of Deng from all his posts, and Hua Guofeng was appointed First Party Vice-Chairman as well as Premier. On the death of Mao Tse-tung on 9 Sept. 1976 Hua became Party Chairman. In Oct. 1976 the 'radical' faction (now identified and excoriated as the 'Gang of Four': Mao's widow, Jiang

Qing, Zhang Chunqiao, Wang Hongwen and Yao Wenyuan) were placed under arrest. At the 11th Party Congress in Aug. 1977 a new Party Constitution was adopted, and a new Central Committee was elected. Changes in the leadership saw the elimination of the 'radical' faction and a second reinstatement of Deng to his Party and government posts. In Feb. 1980 Liu Shaoqi, former head of state denounced by Mao as a traitor, was posthumously reinstated, and 4 Politburo members of Maoist persuasion were dismissed. Hua Guofeng was replaced as Premier by Zhao Ziyang in Sept. 1980. The 'Gang of Four', along with Chen Boda (a former secretary of Mao), were brought to trial only on 20 Nov. 1980. At the same time the trial opened of five generals accused of complicity with Lin Biao in an attempt to seize power. All 10 accused were found guilty on 25 Jan 1981. Suspended death sentences were passed on Jiang Qing and Zhang Chungiao. The Politburo in March 1981 had 26 members, including: *Chairman and Chief of the Military Affairs Commission:* Hua Guofeng. *Vice-Chairmen:* Ye Jianying, Deng Xiaoping, Li Xiannian, Chen Yun, Hu Yaobang (*General Secretary of the Central Committee*), Zhao Ziyang (these 7 constituting the Politburo's Standing Committee); Wang Zhen, Wei Guoqing, Ulanhu, Fang Yi, Deng Yingchao, Liu Bocheng, Xu Shiyou, Li Desheng, Yu Qiuli, Zhang Tingfa, Chen Yonggui, Geng Biao, Nie Rongzhen, Ni Zhifu, Xu Xiangqian, Peng Chong, Peng Zhen; (alternate members) Chen Muhua, Seypidin.

Local Government. There are 4 administrative levels: (1) Provinces, Autonomous Regions and the municipalities directly administered by the Government; (2) prefectures and autonomous prefectures (*zhou*); (3) counties, autonomous counties and municipalities; (4) towns and rural communes. Local government after 1968 was in the hands of Revolutionary Committees. From 1 Jan. 1980 these were replaced by elected People's Congresses and People's Governments. These exist at provincial, county and commune levels and in national minority autonomous prefectures, but not in ordinary prefectures which are just agencies of the provincial government. Up to county level Congresses are elected directly.

DEFENCE. The Party Chairman is *ex officio* supreme commander of the armed forces. China is divided into 11 military regions. The military commander also commands the air, naval and civilian militia forces assigned to each region.

Conscription is compulsory but for organizational reasons selective: only some 10% of potential recruits are called up. Service is 3 years with the Army, 4 years with the Air Force and 5 years with the Navy.

Marks of rank were abolished in 1965 but uniforms distinguish officers from other ranks.

The Chinese exploded their first nuclear device in May 1964, and their twenty-fourth in Oct. 1980 and have tested guided missiles with nuclear warheads. Their first earth satellite was launched in April 1970, an eighth in Jan. 1978.

Army. The Army (PLA: 'People's Liberation Army') is divided into main and local forces. Main forces, administered by the military regions in which they are stationed but commanded by the Ministry of Defence, are available for operation anywhere and are better equipped. Local forces concentrate on the defence of their own regions. The Army consists of 185 divisions including 40 artillery, 11 armoured, 118 infantry, 3 airborne and 85 local divisions. Total strength in 1980 was 3·6m.

The security forces, including the armed police, number some 300,000.

The People's Militia consists of the Armed Militia of up to 5m. strength, the Ordinary Militia of several million, unarmed but with some basic military training, and which includes the Urban Militia, and the Civilian Production and Construction Corps of 4m.

Navy. There is a steady new construction programme of all classes of warships in modernized yards, all with advanced nuclear and missile capability. Chinese naval strength is an important element in the present and future balance of power east of Suez.

Present strength comprises 2 nuclear powered submarines, 1 submarine with ballistic missile tubes, 90 other submarines, 11 destroyers, 16 frigates, 12 patrol escorts,

170 missile boats, 20 large patrol boats, 25 fast patrol craft, 350 fast gunboats, 290 fast torpedo boats, 20 ocean minesweepers, 80 mine warfare craft, 100 coastal patrol craft, 22 survey and research ships, 40 supply ships, 18 oilers, 6 boom defence vessels, 2 repair ships, 31 landing ships, 470 landing craft, and 900 coast and river defence craft.

Active personnel in 1981 exceeded 300,000 officers and men, including 30,000 marines and 30,000 naval airmen.

Main naval bases: Qingdao (North Sea Fleet); Shanghai (East Sea Fleet); Tsamkong (Zhanjiang) (South Sea Fleet).

The largely land-based and mainly defensive naval air force of over 700 aircraft includes MiG-17, MiG-19 and MiG-21 fighters, some 150 Il-28 torpedo bombers, Madge flying boats, Hound M14 helicopters and communications and transport aircraft.

Air Force. In 1980 the Air Force was estimated at 5,200 front-line aircraft, organized in over 100 regiments of jet-fighters and about 12 regiments of tactical bombers, plus reconnaissance, transport and helicopter units. Each regiment is made up of 3 or 4 squadrons (each 12 aircraft), and 3 regiments form a division.

Equipment is predominantly Russian in design and includes about 75 F-7 (MiG-21), 1,800 F-6 (MiG-19) and 1,500 F-5 (MiG-17) home-defence interceptors, with about 450 B-5 (Il-28) jet-bombers, nearly 100 B-6 Chinese-built copies of the Soviet Tu-16 twin-jet strategic bomber, and a few piston-engined Tu-4 (Soviet copy of Boeing B-29) strategic bombers, plus several hundred obsolete MiG-15s and a growing number of A-5 twin-jet fighter-bombers, evolved from the MiG-19. Transport aircraft include about 300 An-2, An-12, An-24/26, 100 Li-2, 30 Il-14 and 10 Il-18 fixed-wing types, plus 300 Mi-4 and Mi-8 helicopters and 13 French-built Super Frelon heavy transport helicopters. The MiG fighters have been manufactured in China, initially under licence, and other types have been assembled there, including several hundred F-2 (MiG-15UTI) trainers.

Total strength (1980) about 490,000, including 220,000 in air defence organization.

INTERNATIONAL RELATIONS

Membership. The People's Republic of China is a member of UN.

ECONOMY

Planning. For planning history 1953–73 *see* THE STATESMAN'S YEAR-BOOK, 1973–74, p. 817.

The long-term aim of the present leadership is to transform China by the year 2000 into a modern developed economic power by the implementation of 'the 4 modernizations', *i.e.*, of agriculture, industry, defence and science and technology. In January 1980 Deng Xiaoping declared that China was aiming for a per capita GNP of US$1,000 by the year 2000. In 1978, as a first step to the realization of the '4 modernizations', a 10-year plan (1976–85) was introduced. However this proved in practice to be over-ambitious; many of the planned targets were too high and the scale of capital construction was too great. The pursuit of the plan caused serious imbalances in the economy. Since 1979 a policy of 'readjusting, restructuring, consolidating and improving' the economy has been followed, and is scheduled to last until 1981 when a new 10-year plan will be introduced.

The more rational approach adapted to China's material and financial limitations embodied in the readjustment programme remains the foundation of Chinese economic policy. Agriculture and light industry will receive higher priority in investment compared to heavy industry. The growth rates in 1980 were lower and the 1981 targets were twice revised downwards in an effort to balance the budget. (The total value of industrial and agricultural production in 1979 rose by 8·2%.)

Budget. 1979 revenue was 110,330m. yuan; expenditure, 127,390m. yuan. Budget deficit (1980) 17,000m. yuan.

Communes pay an agricultural tax, and this accounts for almost 10% of budgetary revenue. Since 1981 state-owned enterprises have paid a business tax instead of turning over their profits to the state. Income tax was introduced in 1980; it affects mainly foreigners. China will pay off US claims of US$80·5m. before 1 Oct. 1984, and USA will unblock Chinese assets of the same value. Registration of British claims for loss of assets in 1949 was requested by the Foreign Compensation Commission in Jan. 1981. A credit of 450m. SDF was granted by IMF in March 1981.

China's gold and foreign exchange reserves were estimated at US$6,000m. in 1978.

Currency. The currency is called Renminbi (RMB, *i.e.*, People's Currency). The unit of currency is the *yuan* which is divided into 10 *jiao*, the *jiao*, into 10 *fen*. The official rate of exchange is £1 = 3·39 *yuan*; US$1 = 1·53 *yuan*; Hong Kong $1 = 0·983 *yuan*; 1 rouble = 2·222 *yuan* (non-commercial, 1 rouble = 1·29 *yuan*).

Notes are issued for 1, 2 and 5 *jiao* and 1, 2, 5 and 10 *yuan* and coins for 1, 2 and 5 *fen*.

Banking. Banking is controlled by the People's Bank which has 30,000 branches. It is both the bank of issue and the principal commercial and domestic bank. It is also the major instrument of economic policy through which enterprises are controlled or supervised by the Government. Its president has ministerial rank.

There are 2 specialized banks: the Construction Bank and the Bank of Communications. The Bank of China, which has branches abroad (including 1 in London) is an agency of the People's Bank.

Weights and Measures. The metric system is in general use. For older units of measurement, *see* THE STATESMAN'S YEAR-BOOK, 1975–76, p. 826 and 1954, pp. 877–88.

ENERGY AND NATURAL RESOURCES

Electricity. In 1979 coal provided over 60% of China's energy, although there is a large hydro-electric potential in the centre and south. Generating is not centralized; local units range between 30 and 60 mw of output. Output in 1979: 281,950m. kwh.

Oil. China has made rapid progress in oil extraction and refining. There are probably about 100 oilfields, of which the largest are at Daqing, Shengli, Dagang and Karamai. Offshore resources in Bohai Bay are also being exploited. Refining capacity is estimated at 80m. tons per annum. Oil reserves may be as much as 10,000m. tonnes. Crude oil production was 106·15m. tonnes in 1979.

Gas. Natural gas is available from fields near Canton and Shanghai and in Sichuan province. Production was 14,510m. cu. metres in 1979, but is only used locally.

Minerals. *Coal.* Most provinces contain coal, and there are 70 major production centres, of which the largest are in Hebei, Shanxi, Shandong, Jilin and Anhui. Coal reserves are estimated at 200,000m. tonnes. Coal and lignite production was 635m. tonnes in 1979.

Iron. Iron ores are abundant in the anthracite field of Shanxi, in Hebei, in Shandong and other provinces, and iron (found in conjunction with coal) is worked in Manchuria. 300m. tons of ore are estimated to be in Shanxi; the principal iron-ore reserves total about 19,840m. tons. The Daye iron deposits, near Wuhan, are among the richest in the world. Estimated output of iron ore in 1972, 75m. tonnes. The biggest steel bases are at Anshan (in Manchuria) with a capacity of 6m. tons, Wuhan (capacity 3·5m. tonnes), Baotou and Maanshan (both 2·5m. tonnes).

Tin. Tin ore is plentiful in Yunnan, where the tin-mining industry has long existed. Tin production was 15,000 tonnes in 1978.

Tungsten. China is the world's principal producer of wolfram (tungsten ore), producing 9,000 tonnes in 1978. Mining of wolfram is carried on in Hunan, Guangdong and Yunnan.

Production of other minerals in 1978 (in tonnes): Phosphate rock, 4·5m.; aluminium, 225,000; copper, 200,000; lead, 120,000; zinc, 125,000; antimony, 9,000; manganese, 2m.; (1973) sulphur, 130,000; (1967) bauxite, 350,000; (1973) salt, 18,000; (1969) asbestos, 160,000. Other minerals produced: barite, bismuth, gold, graphite, gypsum, mercury, molybdenum, silver.

Agriculture. China remains essentially an agricultural country. Some 11% of the total land area is under cultivation. Intensive agriculture and horticulture have been practised for millennia. Present-day policy aims to avert the traditional threats from floods and droughts by soil conservancy, afforestation, irrigation and drainage projects, and to increase the 'high stable yields' areas by introducing fertilizers, pesticides and improved crops. Crop priorities: food grains; raw materials for industry (especially cotton); crops for export (especially oil seeds). Among livestock, priority is given to pig production.

In 1950 the land belonging to the feudal nobility and to monasteries and other institutions was confiscated by the State. By the end of 1952 land reform and by the end of 1958 the socialization of agriculture was declared to be complete.

By the end of 1958 the peasant population had been organized into roughly 24,000 'communes', each consisting of a number of villages and 5,000–10,000 families. The commune took over the local government function at the village (xiang) level. Centralized authority was discharged down through the production 'brigade' to the production 'team' of 10–50 families. Since 1958 modifications have been made in the commune system, size reductions. There were some 50,000 in 1977. Small private plots account for 20% or more of the peasant income which averaged 83·40 yuan in 1979.

In 1974 there were estimated to be 127m. hectares of arable land. In 1977 there were 43m. tractors (15 h.p. units).

Agricultural production (in 1m. tonnes). Total grain, 1980, 311; tea (1979), 0·28; cotton, 2·2; rice, 1976, 125·5; oilseed crops, 1979, 6·4.

Livestock, 1979: Cattle, 71·35m.; sheep and goats, 183·1m.; pigs, 319·7m. Official figures for 1978: Pigs, 301,290m.; sheep, 169,940m.; horses and cattle, 93,890m. Meat production in 1979 was 10·62m. tonnes.

Forestry. Forests cover some 12m. hectares. The chief forested areas are in Heilongjiang, Sichuan and Yunnan. The most important tree is the dong (*Jatropha Curcas* L.), from which oil is produced: it grows chiefly in Sichuan. Dong-oil production amounted to 115,000 tonnes in 1948–49. Timber output in 1978 was 51·6m. cu. metres.

The most important timber product is teak. It is estimated that some 1·3m. hectares are afforested each year.

INDUSTRY AND TRADE

Industry. 'Cottage' industry is very old in the economy and persists into the 20th century. Modern industrial development began with the manufacture of cotton textiles, and the establishment of silk filatures, steel plants, flour-mills and match factories. Expanding sectors of manufacture are: steel, chemicals, cement, agricultural implements, plastics and lorries.

1979 production (in tonnes): Chemical fertilizer, 10·65m.; chemical fibres, 326,000; pig-iron, 36·7m.; cement, 73·9m.; cotton yarn, 2·63m.; 186,000 motor vehicles were produced, 126,000 tractors and 10·09m. bicycles.

34·48m. tonnes of steel were produced in 1979. 4·4m. tonnes of paper were produced in 1978.

Labour. In 1979 the non-agricultural labour force was 95m. There were some 20m. unemployed, mainly rural youth. Factory wages in 1979 averaged 59 yuan a month. Wage increases affecting 40% of the non-agricultural workforce were introduced in Oct. 1977 and in Nov. 1979. There is a 6-day 48-hour working week.

Commerce. Foreign trade, formerly conducted exclusively through national corporations under the Ministry of Foreign Trade, is now being decentralized. Trade authorities are being established in the main cities, to date Beijing (Peking), Shanghai and Tianjin, and in selected provinces, to date Guangdong and Fujian. The quasigovernmental China International Trust and Investment Corporation also handles foreign trade. Duty-free zones have been set up in the latter. Foreign firms pay a profits tax of 15%. In 1978 China reversed its policy of not accepting foreign credit and aid. A law of July 1979 permits the establishment of joint ventures with foreign firms. There is no maximum limit on the foreign share of the holdings; the minimum limit is 25%. Foreign indebtedness was about £1,400m. in 1980.

Imports include grain, raw materials and semi-manufactured products for agriculture (primarily chemical fertilizers), light industry and textiles, advanced equipment, particularly whole plants and consumer goods. Exports include heavy industrial goods including petroleum, chemicals, minerals, machinery and equipment, light industrial goods and agricultural products.

Trade in 1979: Imports, 24,300m. yuan; exports, 21,200m. yuan.

Some 85% of China's trade is with non-Communist countries. Japan is China's biggest trading partner, and an 8-year trade agreement was signed in Feb. 1978 and extended for 5 years in March 1979. Other major trading partners are Hong Kong, Federal Republic of Germany, USA and Australia. Imports from USA totalled US$1,720m. in 1979; exports to USA were US$551m. Customs duties on imports and exports between Taiwan and the mainland were abolished in April 1980. Trade with USA is increasing rapidly.

Total trade between China and UK (British Department of Trade returns, in £1,000 sterling):

	1976	1977	1978	1979	1980
Imports to UK	86,995	104,388	110,624	137,891	153,433
Exports and re-exports from UK	68,216	62,316	91,093	213,039	169,500

In April 1978 a most-favoured-nation agreement was signed with EEC, and in 1980 the EEC extended preferential tariffs to China.

On 15 Nov. 1978 a science and technology agreement was signed by UK and China and on 4 March 1979 an agreement on economic co-operation. In July 1979 the USA and China signed a 3-year trade agreement which accords China most-favoured-nation status from 1980.

On 17 April 1980 China gained representation in the IMF, and on 15 May 1980 in the IBRD.

COMMUNICATIONS

Roads. In 1978, 35,000 km of new highway were completed, bringing the total road length to 890,000 km. 83% of communes could be reached by road in 1976. Highways are well graded but mostly unmetalled. In 1969 there were some 409,000 lorries, 60,000 cars and 30,000 buses.

In 1978, 27,900m. tonne-km of freight were transported by road.

Railways. Chinese railway history begins in 1876, when the Wusong–Shanghai line was opened. In 1976 there were some 48,000 km of railway.

The principal railways are:

(1) The great north–south trunk lines: (a) Peking–Canton Railway (over 2,300 km), via Zhengzhou–Wuhan–Zhuzhou–Hengyang.

(b) Tianjin–Shanghai Railway (1,500 km), via Pukow and Nanjing (double-tracked in July 1976).

(c) Baoji–Chongqing Railway, via Chengdu (1,174 km). Chongqing with the east–west route from Hengyang to the Vietnam border, and to Kunming, connecting there with the Yunnan Railway to the Vietnam border. Two further lines connect Baoji.

(2) Great east–west trunk lines: (a) Longhai Railway; Lianyungkang–Xuzhou–Zhengzhou (on the Peking–Canton line)–Xian–Baoji–Tianshui–Lanzhou (1,500 km). The Baoji–Lanzhou section was upgraded in 1978. (b) Lanzhou–Xinjiang Railway: Lanzhou–Yumen–Hami–Turfan–Urumqi (1,800 km); (c) Shanghai–Youyiguan (Vietnam border) via Hangzhou, Nanchang, Hengyang (on the Peking–Canton line), Guilin, Liuzhou and Nanning. (d) Peking–Lanzhou via Xining (from which a branch connects with the lines through Mongolia to the Trans-Siberian Railway), Dadong (from which a branch serves the province of Shanxi), Baotou and Yinchuan (Ningxia). (e) Zhuzhou–Guiyang (632 km). A new east–west line was opened in 1978 between Xiangfan and Chongqing.

Branches link coastal areas (e.g., Fujian province) and smaller inland centres with the main parts of the system. Surveys have been made for a new 500-km railway, linking the trunk line with the oilfield of Karamai in Xinjiang.

(3) The Manchurian system: (a) Chinese Eastern (Changchun) Railway (2,370 km), from Manzhouli on the Soviet border through northern Inner Mongolia and Manchuria via Qiqihar, Harbin and Mudanjiang to the Soviet border near Vladivostok. (b) South Manchuria Railway (705 km, 1,120 km with branches), Changchun–

Shenyang–Luda. (c) Peking–Shenyang Railway, with branches in Manchuria (854 km, 1,350 km with branches).

Branches give connexions with outlying parts of Manchuria and Inner Mongolia as well as international links with Korean railways. Chinese railways are all constructed to the standard gauge except for some 600 km of metre gauge in Yunnan. Trunk routes are being converted from single to double track. The route between Baoji and Chengdu (676 km) was electrified in 1975 and that between Yangpingguan (on the Baoji–Chengdu route) and Ankang in 1977.

Capacity is being expanded under the 1976–85 development plan: 6 new lines are to be built by 1985. Lines are planned to link Tibet with the Chinese network and to bridge gaps in the system such as Liuzhou–Canton, Kantang–Taiyuan and southern Xinjiang.

In 1978 the railways carried 1,070m. tons of freight.

Aviation. The Civil Aviation Administration of China (CAAC) flies routes to Pyongyang, Hanoi, Rangoon, Karachi, Tōkyō, Moscow, Teheran, Addis Ababa, Bucharest, Belgrade, Zürich, Paris, Frankfurt, Manila, New York, San Francisco, London and Hong Kong. It also provides services to Hong Kong. Its inventory includes 3 Boeing 747s, 10 Boeing 707s, 16 Tridents and 5 Il–62s. British Airways have a direct flight London-Beijing. Japan Airlines have a route from Tōkyō to Beijing (via Osaka and Shanghai), Air France Paris to Beijing (via Athens and Karachi), Pakistan Airlines Karachi to Beijing, Aeroflot Moscow to Beijing, Ethiopian Airlines Addis Ababa to Shanghai, Tarom (Romania) Bucharest to Beijing, Swissair Geneva to Peking and Shanghai, Iran Air Paris to Peking and PANAM Peking via Tōkyō.

In 1979 there were 160 internal routes with over 500 weekly flights.

Air services agreements have been signed with Bangladesh, Canada, the Federal Republic of Germany, Greece, Iraq, Italy, Japan, Laos, Nepal, the Netherlands, the Philippines, Spain, Sweden, Thailand, UK and USA.

Shipping. At the beginning of 1977 the ocean-going merchant fleet consisted of 400–450 vessels with a total DWT of 6·8m.

The major ports are at Tianjin, Shanghai, Qingdao, Luda and Canton. New ports are under construction at Changchiang, Huangpu, Qinhuangdao, Yantai and Lienyunkang. Ports cannot accommodate vessels over 100,000 GRT and most harbours have a draught limitation of 35 ft. 213m. tonnes of cargo was handled in 1979.

Inland waterways total about 136,000 km. Plans were announced in 1978 for a national transport waterway network.

Pipeline. A pipeline links the Daqing oilfield to the port of Luda and to refineries in Peking. There is a pipeline from Lanzhou to Lhasa.

Post and Broadcasting. Number of post offices of all kinds in 1958 was 67,000. The use of *Pinyin* transcription of place names has been requested for mail to addresses in China (e.g., 'Beijing' *not* 'Peking'; 'Tianjin' *not* 'Tientsin'; 'Guangzhou' *not* 'Canton', etc.).

In 1979 there were 99 radio broadcasting stations. In 1964 there were some 7m. radio receivers. In 1979 there were 38 television stations and in 1978 over 1m. TV receivers. Most are communally owned.

Cinemas. Cinemas numbered 1,386 in 1958.

Newspapers. In 1978 newspaper production totalled 13,080m. copies, and journals, 1,180m. copies. The Party newspaper is *Renmin Ribao* (People's Daily). In 1979 it had a daily circulation of 7m.

JUSTICE, RELIGION, EDUCATION AND WELFARE

Justice. Six new codes of law (including criminal and electoral) came into force in Jan. 1980, which, it is claimed, will regularize the legal unorthodoxy of recent years. The new codes specify a process of repentance as a precondition for a possible reduction of sentence. There is no provision for *habeas corpus*. The death penalty is prescribed for murder and treason. Courts will no longer be subject to the intervention of other state bodies, and their decisions will be reversible only by higher courts. 'People's courts' are divided into some 30 higher, 200 intermediate and 2,000 basic-level courts, and headed by the Supreme People's Court. The latter tries cases, hears appeals, and supervises the people's courts. The Ministry of Justice, abolished in 1959, was re-established in 1979.

People's courts are composed of a president, vice-presidents, judges and 'people's assessors' who are the equivalent of jurors. 'People's conciliation committees' are charged with settling minor disputes.

There are also special military courts.

Procuratorial powers and functions are exercised by the Supreme People's Procuracy and local procuracies.

Religion. Confucianism, Buddhism and Taoism have long been practised. Confucianism has no ecclesiastical organization and appears rather as a philosophy of ethics and government. Taoism—of Chinese origin—copied Buddhist ceremonial soon after the arrival of Buddhism two millennia ago. Buddhism in return adopted many Taoist beliefs and practices. It is no longer possible to estimate the number of adherents to these faiths. A more tolerant attitude towards religion had emerged by 1979, and the Government's Bureau of Religious Affairs was reactivated.

Ceremonies of reverence to ancestors have been observed by the whole population regardless of philosophical or religious beliefs.

Moslems are found in every province of China, being most numerous in the Ningxia–Hui Autonomous Region, Yunnan, Shaanxi, Gansu, Hebei, Honan, Shandong, Sichuan, Xinjiang and Shanxi. They totalled 10m. in 1980.

Roman Catholicism has had a footing in China for more than 3 centuries. In 1979 there were about 2m. Catholics who are members of the Patriotic Catholic Association, which declared its independence of Rome in 1958, and about 1,000 priests. In 1977 there were 78 bishops and 4 apostolic administrators, not all of whom were permitted to undertake religious activity. This figure included 46 'democratically elected' bishops not recognized by the Vatican. A Catholic bishop of Peking was consecrated in Dec. 1979 without the consent of the Vatican.

Protestants are members of the All-China Conference of Protestant Churches.

Education. During the Cultural Revolution and the 'Gang of Four' period the educational system was in a turmoil of radical reformation involving a reduction in the length of courses at all levels, the substitution of class background for academic achievement as a criterion for entry to higher education, a heavy emphasis on political education, and lengthy periods of manual labour sandwiched between courses. 1977 marked the beginning of a return to a more conventional system, and by 1978 3 out of every 4 children were attending school. University entry now normally follows from secondary schooling and is dependent upon entrance examinations in which political reliability tests are accompanied by tests in academic subjects. Obligatory manual labour has been reduced to 1 month per year. In 1978 a system of 'key' schools for the best-performing pupils was set up, and it was announced that new universities and colleges would be established. It was also announced that several thousand students would be sent to Western universities. In 1979 there were 633 universities and institutes of higher education, with some 1·02m. students. In 1979 there were some 146m. pupils in 1m. primary schools, and 65m. pupils in 200,000 secondary schools.

The Academy of Sciences had in 1964 some 20 provincial branches.

Among the universities are the following: People's University of China, Peking (founded 1912 by Dr Sun Yat-sen; reorganized 1950; about 3,000 students); Peking University, Peking (1898, enlarged 1945; about 10,000 students); Xiamen University, Fujian (1921 and 1937); Fudan University, Shanghai (1905); Inner Mongolia University, Hohhot; Lanzhou University, Lanzhou (Gansu Prov.); Nankai University, Tianjin (1919); Nanjing University, Nanjing (1888 and 1928); Jilin University, Changchun (Jilin Prov.); North-West University, Xian (Shanxi Prov.); Shandong University, Qingdao (1926); Sun Yat-sen University, Canton (founded 1924 by Dr Sun Yat-sen); Sichuan University, Chengdu (1931); Qinghua University, Peking; Wuhan University, Wuhan (Hubei Prov.; 1905 and 1928); Yunnan University, Kunming. In 1958 a university of science and technology was set up by the Academy of Sciences.

Health. Medical treatment is free only for certain groups of employees, but where costs are incurred they are partly borne by the patient's employing organization. In

1979 there were 830,000 Western-style doctors and 258,000 doctors of Chinese medicine. In rural areas there were also 1·8m. 'bare-foot doctors', who receive 3 months' training and remain in the community treating simple ailments and implementing public health directives.

80% of production brigades have co-operative medical services. There were 1·93m. hospital beds in 1979.

DIPLOMATIC REPRESENTATIVES

OF CHINA IN GREAT BRITAIN (31 Portland Place, London, W1N 3AG)

Ambassador: Ke Hua (accredited on 7 Nov. 1978).

OF GREAT BRITAIN IN CHINA
(11 Guang Hua Lu, Jian Guo Men Wai, Peking)

Ambassador: Sir Percy Cradock, KCMG.

OF CHINA IN THE USA (2300 Connecticut Ave., NW, Washington, D.C., 20008)

Ambassador: Chai Zemin.

OF THE USA IN CHINA (Guang Hua Lu, Peking)

Ambassador: Leonard Woodcock.

OF CHINA TO THE UNITED NATIONS

Ambassador: Ling Qing

Books of Reference

Beijing Review. Peking, weekly
The China Quarterly. London, from 1960
China Reconstructs. Peking, monthly
China's Foreign Trade. Bimonthly. Peking, from 1966
Bartke, W., *The Diplomatic Service of the People's Republic of China.* Hamburg, 1973
Bennett, G. (ed.), *China's Finance and Trade: a Policy Reader.* London, 1978
Bettelheim, C., and Burton, N. G., *China Since Mao.* New York, 1978
Boardman, R., *Britain and the People's Republic of China, 1949–1974.* London, 1976
Bonavia, D., *The Chinese.* New York, 1980
Boorman, H. L., and Howard, R. C. (eds.), *Biographical Dictionary of Republican China.* 5 vols. Columbia Univ. P. 1967 ff.
Brugger, B., (ed.) *China since the Gang of Four,* London, 1980
The Cambridge History of China. 14 vols. CUP, 1978 ff.
Chen, K. C. (ed.), *China and the Three Worlds: a Foreign Policy Reader.* London, 1979
China: A General Survey. Peking, 1979
Clubb, O. E., *20th Century China.* 2nd ed. Columbia Univ. Press., 1972
deKeijer, A. J., and Kaplan, F. M., *The China Guidebook.* London and New York, 1979
Fairbank, J. K., *The United States and China.* 4th ed. Cambridge, Mass., 1979
Gittings, J., *The World and China, 1922–1972.* London, 1974
Hermann, A., *An Historical Atlas of China.* Chicago, 1966
Hinton, H. C. (ed.), *The People's Republic of China: a Handbook.* Boulder, 1979
Houn, F. W., *A Short History of Chinese Communism.* 2nd ed. Englewood Cliffs, N.J., 1973
Howe, C., *China's Economy: A Basic Guide.* London, 1978
Hsieh, C. M., *Atlas of China.* New York, 1973
Hsü, I. C. Y., *The Rise of Modern China.* 2nd ed. New York, 1975
Hsüeh, C.-T. (ed.), *Dimensions of China's Foreign Relations.* New York, 1977
Jingrong, W., (ed.), *The Pinyin-Chinese Dictionary.* Beijing and San Francisco 1979
Kallgren, J., (ed.) *The People's Republic of China after 30 years.* Berkeley, 1979
Kaplan, F. M. (ed.), *Encyclopedia of China Today.* London, 1979
Kim, S. S., *China, the United Nations and World Order.* Princeton, 1979
Klein, D. W., and Clark, A. B., *Biographic Dictionary of Chinese Communism, 1921–1965.* Harvard U.P., 1971
Lamb, M., *Directory of Chinese Officials and Organizations, 1968–1978.* Canberra, 1978

Lardy, N. R., *Economic Growth and Distribution in China*. CUP, 1978
Mao Tse-tung, Selected works. 5 vols. Peking, 1965–77
Mathews, R. H., *Chinese–English Dictionary*. Cambridge, Mass., 1943–47
Meisner, M., *Mao's China: a History of the People's Republic*. New York, 1977
Middleton, D., *The Duel of the Giants: China and Russia in Asia*. New York, 1978
Needham, J., *Science and Civilization*. CUP, 1954 ff.—*Within the Four Seas*. London, 1969
O'Leary, G., *The Shaping of Chinese Foreign Policy*. London, 1980
Qi Wen, *China: a General Survey*. Peking, 1979
Schaller, M., *The United States and China in the Twentieth Century*. OUP, 1979
Schram, S., *The Political Thought of Mao Tse-tung*. New York, 1969
Scott, G. L., *Chinese Treaties: The Post-revolutionary Restoration of International Law and Order*. New York, 1975
Skinner, G. W. (ed.), *Modern Chinese Society: An Analytical Bibliography*. 3 vols. Stanford U.P., 1974
Szuprowicz, B. O. and M. R., *Doing Business with the People's Republic of China*. New York, 1978
The Times Atlas of China. London, 1974
US Congress Joint Economic Committee. *Chinese Economy, Post-Mao*. Washington, 1978
US Department of the Army, *Communist China: A Bibliographic Survey*. Washington, 1971
Wang, G.-W., *China and the World Since 1949*. London, 1977
Whiting, A. S., and Dernberger, R. F. *China's Future: Foreign Policy and Economic Development in the Post-Mao Era*. New York, 1977
Whitson, W. W., and Huang, C.-H., *The Chinese High Command*. London, 1973
Who's Who in Communist China. 2nd ed. Hong Kong, 1969
Yahuda, M. B. *China's Role in World Affairs*. London, 1978

TAIWAN

Republic of China

Capital: Taipei
Population: 17·48m. (1979)
GNP per capita: US$400 (1978)

HISTORY. The island of Taiwan (Formosa) was ceded to Japan by China by the Treaty of Shimonoseki on 8 May 1895. After the Second World War the island surrendered to Gen. Chiang Kai-shek in Sept. 1945 and was placed under Chinese administration on 25 Oct. 1945. USA broke off diplomatic relations with Taiwan on 1 Jan. 1979 on establishing diplomatic relations with the Peking Government. Relations between the USA and Taiwan are maintained through the American Institute on Taiwan and the Taiwan Institute for North American Affairs, set up in 1978 and accorded diplomatic status in Oct. 1980.

AREA AND POPULATION. Taiwan lies between the East and South China Seas off the coast of Fukien province. The total area of Taiwan Island and the Penghu Archipelago is 13,895 sq. miles (35,989 sq km). Population (1979), 17·48m. (9·13m. males, 8·35m. females), of whom some 2m. are mainland Chinese who came with the Nationalist Government. There are also some 260,000 aboriginals. Population density: 485·68 per sq. km.

In 1979, birth rate was 2·44%; death rate, 0·47%; rate of growth, 1·97% per annum.

Taiwan is divided into a special municipality (Taipei, the capital, population 2·16m. in 1979), 4 municipalities (Kaohsiung, Keelung, Taichung, Tainan) and 16 counties (*hsien*): Changhua, Chiayi, Hsinchu, Hualien, Ilan, Kaohsiung,

Miaoli, Nantou, Penghu, Pingtung, Taichung, Tainan, Taipei, Taitung, Taoyuan, Yunlin.

CONSTITUTION AND GOVERNMENT. Taiwan is controlled by the remnants of the Nationalist Government. On 1 March 1950, Chiang Kai-shek resumed the presidency of the 'Republic of China', and was re-elected for his fifth 6-year presidential term in March 1972. He died 5 April 1975 and was succeeded by Dr Yen Chia-kan who was replaced in the presidential elections of 21 March 1978 by Chiang Kai-shek's eldest son Chiang Ching-kuo. There are 3 political parties: the ruling Kuomintang (1·5m. members in 1976), which has a youth movement (China Youth Corps) of over 1m. members, the Young China Party and the China Democratic Socialist Party.

The National Assembly was elected in 1947. In 1978 it had 1,221 delegates. The National Assembly operates through 5 *yuan* or councils. The highest administrative organ is the Executive Yuan, headed by the premier, which includes a number of ministers. The highest legislative body is the Legislative Yuan, elected in 1948, which at the end of 1978 numbered 386 members. The National Assembly, Legislative Yuan and Control Yuan are elected bodies. Their terms of office have been extended indefinitely. As the number of original delegates dwindled, regulations introduced in 1966 and 1972 provided for the election of additional members to the National Assembly and Legislative Yuan, and elections were held in 1969, 1972 and 1975. Elections scheduled for Dec. 1978 were postponed in the wake of the US termination of diplomatic relations. Until Dec. 1980. The Kuomintang won 120 seats and independents, 26. There is also a Provincial Assembly of which the current Sixth Assembly with 77 members was elected on 19 Nov. 1977.

A political campaign by the journal *Mei-li Tao* and the Presbyterians calling on the Kuomintang to abandon its claim to represent all China and hold representative elections resulted in the sentencing of the prime movers at a court-martial in March 1980.

State emblem: A 12-pointed white sun in a blue sky.
National flag: Red with a blue first quarter bearing the state emblem in white.
National anthem: 'San Min Chu I', words by Dr Sun Yat-sen; tune by Cheng Mao-yun.

Prime Minister: Y. S. Sun.

Vice-Premier: Hsu Ching-chung. *Foreign Minister:* Shen Chang-huan. *Minister of National Defence:* Gen. Kao Kuei-yuan. *Minister of the Interior:* Chiu Chang-huan. *Minister of Finance:* Philip C. C. Chang. *Governor of Taiwan:* Lin Yang-kan.

DEFENCE. Army. The Army, which embodies the remnants of the forces which escaped to Taiwan with Chiang Kai-shek at the end of the civil war in 1949, numbered about 310,000 in 1980. It was reorganized, re-equipped and trained by the USA and now consists of 2 armoured, 12 infantry, 6 light infantry divisions, 2 armoured cavalry regiments and 2 airborne brigades. There is a conscription system for 2 years and reserve liability. Strong garrisons (about 80,000 men) are maintained on the Pescadores and the offshore islands of Quemoy and Matsu. US supplies of military equipment were resumed in 1980 after a moratorium in 1979. US forces were withdrawn by 1 May 1979.

Navy. Most of the 200 vessels in naval service are former US Navy ships now well over 30 years old and overdue for replacement. There are 2 diesel powered patrol submarines, 22 destroyers, 11 frigates, 3 escort vessels, 2 fast missile craft, 14 coastal minesweepers, 1 coastal minelayer, 8 minesweeping boats, 9 torpedo boats, 14 coastal patrol craft, 2 dock landing ships, 1 amphibious flagship, 27 landing ships, 22 landing craft, 2 repair ships, 4 surveying ships, 12 support ships, 2 transports, 7 oilers, 1 supply ship, 10 tugs, 5 floating docks and 25 service craft.

There are also 7 coastguard cutters (customs).

Active personnel in 1981 exceeded 7,100 naval officers and 28,000 ratings; 3,000 marine officers and 26,000 men.

The Navy has 12 anti-submarine torpedo helicopters and operational control of 2 squadrons of Air Force anti-submarine warfare Tracker aircraft; and the Marine Corps operates a number of observation aircraft and helicopters.

Air Force. The Nationalist Air Force is equipped mainly with aircraft of US design, including F-5E fighters built in Taiwan. It has 15 squadrons of F-104G Starfighters, F-5A/B/E supersonic fighter-bombers, and F-100 Super Sabre fighter-bombers, and 1 tactical reconnaissance squadron of RF-104G Starfighters. The transport squadrons are equipped with about 30 C-119Gs and 10 C-123 Providers. There is a naval co-operation squadron with S-2A Trackers. Search and rescue units operate Albatross amphibians and Iroquois helicopters, and there are other helicopter and large training elements. Total strength in 1980: 67,000 personnel and 385 combat aircraft.

INTERNATIONAL RELATIONS. By a treaty of 1 Dec. 1954 the USA was pledged to protect Taiwan, but this treaty lapsed 1 year after the USA established diplomatic relations with the People's Republic of China on 1 Jan. 1979. In April 1979 the US Congress approved a law to maintain privileged relations between USA and Taiwan.

The People's Republic took over the China seat in the UN from the Nationalists on 25 Oct. 1971.

ECONOMY

Planning. Taiwan is predominantly agricultural. Government policy is to 'develop industry through agriculture and expand agriculture through industry'. Regional planning was carried out through a series of 4-year plans, of which the sixth (1973–76) was terminated in 1975 because of difficulties arising from the international economic situation. The current 6-year programme (1976–81) envisages a GNP annual growth rate of 8·5% (growth in 1979, 8·03%). Emphasis is on heavy industry; there is some restriction of private spending.

Budget. The financial year ends 30 June. There are 2 budgets, the national together with a special defence budget (partly secret) and the provincial (*i.e.*, for Taiwan proper). For 1978–79 revenue was NT$275,106m. (including NT$199,345m. from taxation) and expenditure, NT$243,722m. (including NT$95,354m. on administration and defence, NT$41,828m. on education and research and NT$29,707m. on social affairs relief).

Currency. In 1945 the existing currency was converted into notes of the Bank of Taiwan. Taiwan dollars were linked to Chinese national currency at a fixed rate of exchange. When the Gold Yuan entered upon its last phase in early 1949, the Taiwan currency was detached and linked to the US$. Exchange rates (March 1980): £1 = NT$78·50; US$1 = NT$36.

Banking. The Central Bank of China (reactivated in 1961) regulates the money market, manages foreign exchange and issues currency. The former Bank of China, a foreign exchange bank with branches in New York, Chicago, Tōkyō, Osaka, Panama and Bangkok, was reorganized in 1972 as a private bank for export financing and renamed the China International Commercial Bank (capital NT$1,000m.).

The Bank of Taiwan is the largest commercial bank and the fiscal agent of the Government.

Other banking institutions include the China Development Corporation.

ENERGY AND NATURAL RESOURCES

Electricity. Output of electricity in 1979 was 37,897m. kwh.; total generating capacity was 8·1m. kw. One nuclear power-station (capacity 0·7m. kw.) came into use in 1977, two more are under construction and a fourth envisaged.

Minerals. There are reserves of coal (207m. tonnes), gold (6·7m. tonnes), copper (12·6m. tonnes), sulphur (2·4m. tonnes), oil (2·2m. kl.) and natural gas (29,132 cu. metres). In 1976 an offshore gas-field south-west of Taiwan was discovered with an annual capacity of 500m. cu. metres. Coal production was 2·72m. tonnes in 1979.

Agriculture. The cultivated area was 915,400 hectares in 1979, of which 515,300 hectares were paddy fields. Production in 1,000 tonnes, in 1978 (and 1979): Rice,

2,444 (2,450); tea, 25·8 (27·1); bananas, 182 (226·8); pineapples, 249·6 (244·8); sugar-cane, 7,914 (9,121); sweet potatoes, 1,463 (1,225); wheat, 2·4 (2·5); soybeans, 40·8 (31·8); peanuts, 91·2 (85·9); cotton, 0·3 (0·2); jute, 0·2 (0·6).

Livestock (1979): Cattle, 142,829; pigs, 5,417,706; goats, 187,687.

Forestry. Forest area, 1979: 1,865,000 hectares; forest reserves, 326,421,000 cu. metres; timber production, 654,165 cu. metres.

Fisheries. The fleet comprised 8,246 vessels over 20 GRT in 1979; the catch was 929,326 tonnes.

INDUSTRY AND TRADE

Industry. Output (in tonnes) in 1978 (and 1979): Steel, 2,656,606 (3,402,192); pig-iron, 249,384 (324,908); aluminium, 50,512 (56,218); shipbuilding, 431,130 (382,051); sugar, 727 (845); cement, 11·5m. (11·9m.); fertilizers, 2m. (2m.); paper, 660,661 (450,796); cotton fabrics, 767m. metres (754m.).

In 1979, 18,367m. litres of crude oil were refined; the main refinery at Kaohsiung has an annual capacity of 1m. tons.

Labour. In 1979 the labour force was 7·7m., of whom 2·3m. worked in agriculture, forestry and fisheries, 2·3m. in industry (including 1·9m. in manufacturing and 0·3m. in building), 0·87m. in commerce, 0·38m. in transport and communications, and 1·87m. in other services. 83,000 were registered unemployed.

Commerce. Foreign trade affairs are handled by the China External Trade Development Council (founded 1970), which operates branches in 33 countries under the name of Far East Trade Service. Principal exports: textiles, electrical machinery, foodstuffs, agricultural products, machinery, plastic products. Principal imports: minerals, oil, agricultural products, metal products, machinery. Total trade, in US$1m.:

	1972	1973	1974	1975	1976	1977	1978	1979
Imports	2,514	3,792	5,845	5,952	7,599	8,511	11,027	14,772
Exports	2,988	4,483	4,734	5,309	8,166	9,361	12,687	16,103

The Federal Republic of Germany and Hong Kong are Taiwan's major trade partners followed by Saudi Arabia and Kuwait.

Total trade between Taiwan and UK (British Department of Trade returns, in £1,000 sterling):

	1975	1976	1977	1978	1979	1980
Imports to UK	73,045	97,027	138,730	146,879	217,736	253,915
Exports and re-exports from UK	33,829	52,605	61,607	92,542	103,044	92,386

The Anglo-Taiwan Trade Committee, a private business organization, helps British businessmen engaged in trade with Taiwan.

COMMUNICATIONS

Roads. In 1979 there were 17,447 km of roads (12,137 km surfaced). 3,911,439 motor vehicles were registered in 1979 including 340,636 passenger cars, 16,565 buses, 201,302 trucks and 3,334,926 motor cycles. 1,105m. passengers and 117m. tons of freight were transported (excluding urban buses).

Railways. Total route length in 1981 was 3,403 km (914 mm gauge), of which a large proportion is owned by the Taiwan Sugar Corporation and other concerns. The state network consists of 1,008 km. Taiwan railways have various gauges, ranging from 3 ft 6 in. to 2 ft. Electrification of the west trunk line of the state network from Keelung and Kaohsiung was completed in 1979. Freight traffic in 1979 amounted to 32·7m. tons and passenger traffic to 130m.

Aviation. There are 2 international airports: Taoyuan and Kaohsiung. There are 6 domestic airlines, including China Airlines (CAL), which also operates international services to Bangkok, Hong Kong, Kuala Lumpur, Manila, Seoul, Singapore, Saudi Arabia, Japan and USA.

Shipping. The merchant marine in 1979 comprised 8,952 vessels over 20 GRT, totalling 2,558,850 GRT; it included 28 passenger ships and 387 freighters. Ocean-going freight-traffic was 22·6m. tonnes.

The 4 international ports, Kaohsiung, Keelung, Hualien and T'aichung, are being extensively redeveloped. The first two are container centres. The lesser ports of Suao and Wuchi are also being built up.

Post and Broadcasting. In 1979 there were 10,565 postal establishments. Number of telephones in 1979, 1,860,602. In 1978 there were 8m. radio receivers and 3m. TV receivers. There are 3 TV networks.

Cinemas (1976). Cinemas numbered 489.

Newspapers (1979). There were 31 daily papers and 1,772 periodicals.

RELIGION, EDUCATION AND WELFARE

Religion. The predominant faith is Confucianism, and there were 5,000 temples in 1976. There were 3·3m. Taoists in 1979 with 2,745 temples and 1,300 priests, and 7·5m. Buddhists with 2,520 temples and 7,750 priests. There are some 600,000 Christians, mainly in Hualien, of whom there were some 200,000 Presbyterians in 1978.

Education. Since 1968 there has been free compulsory education for 9 years (6–15). In that year the curriculum was modernized to give more emphasis to science while retaining the traditional basis of Confucian ethics. There were, in 1979–80, 2,394 primary schools with 68,696 teachers and 2,244,362 pupils; 995 secondary schools with 68,190 teachers and 1,585,341 pupils; 101 institutes of higher learning, including 8 universities, with 16,129 teachers and 329,603 students.

Health. In 1979 there were 87,796 registered medical personnel, including 19,401 doctors, 3,421 dentists and 3,951 'herb doctors', and 1,109 public medical institutions, including 33 general hospitals, 608 health centres and 413 mobile medical units.

Books of Reference

Statistical Yearbook of the Republic of China. Taipei, annual
China Yearbook. Taipei, annual
Taiwan Statistical Data Book. Taipei, annual
Chiu, H. (ed.), *China and the Taiwan issue.* New York, 1979
Clough, R. N., *Island China.* Cambridge, Mass., 1978
Goddard, W. G., *Formosa: A Study in Chinese History.* London, 1966
Ho, S. P. S., *Economic Development of Taiwan, 1860–1970.* Yale Univ. P., 1978
Li, V. H., *De-Recognizing Taiwan.* New York, 1977
Lin, C.-Y., *Industrialization in Taiwan, 1946–72.* New York, 1973
Mendel, D., *The Politics of Formosan Nationalism.* California Univ. P., 1970
Sih, P. (ed.), *Taiwan in Modern Times.* New York, 1973
Tierney, J. (ed.), *About Face: The China Decision and its Consequences.* New Rochelle, 1979

COLOMBIA

República de Colombia

Capital: Bogotá
Population: 26·4m. (1979)
GNP per capita: US$870 (1978)

HISTORY. The Vice-royalty of New Granada gained its independence of Spain in 1819, and was officially constituted 17 Dec. 1819, together with the present territories of Panama, Venezuela and Ecuador, as the state of 'Greater Colombia', which continued for about 12 years. It then split up into Venezuela, Ecuador and the republic of New Granada in 1830. The constitution of 22 May 1858 changed New Granada into a confederation of 8 states, under the name of Confederación Granadina. Under the constitution of 8 May 1863 the country was renamed 'Estados Unidos de Colombia', which were 9 in number. The revolution of 1885 led the National Council of Bogotá, composed of 2 delegates from each state, to promulgate the constitution of 5 Aug. 1886, forming the Republic of Colombia, which abolished the sovereignty of the states, converting them into departments, with governors appointed by the President of the Republic, though they retained some of their old rights, such as the management of their own finances. A decree of May 1928 abolished their right to borrow abroad without the sanction of the central government.

AREA AND POPULATION. Colombia is bounded north by the Caribbean sea, north-west by Panama, west by the Pacific ocean, south-west by Ecuador and Peru, north-east by Venezuela and south-east by Brazil. The estimated area of the republic as given to the United Nations is 1,138,914 sq. km (456,535 sq. miles). It lies between lat. 12° 30′ N. and 4° 30′ S., and between long. 67° and 79° W. of Greenwich. It has a coastline of about 2,900 km, of which 1,600 km are on the Caribbean sea and 1,300 km on the Pacific ocean. The area 1,138,914 sq. km (as estimated by the census bureau) and population 26·5m. according to the estimate of 24 Oct. 1978, were as follows:

Departmentos	Area (sq. km)	Population 1978	Capital	Population 1978
Antioquia	62,870	3,556,058	Medellín	1,442,244
Atlántico	3,270	1,227,319	Barranquilla	825,487
Bolívar	26,392	1,049,223	Cartagena	418,953
Boyacá	23,218	1,179,350	Tunja (M.E.)	125,700 [1]
Caldas	7,283	754,381	Manizales	246,036
Cauca	30,495	813,937	Popayán	107,800 [1]
César (El)	23,792	492,328	Valledupar	161,500 [1]
Chocó	47,205	253,968	Quibdó	48,800 [1]
Córdoba	25,175	894,279	Montería	173,100 [1]
Cundinamarca	22,373	1,219,406	—	—
Distrito Especial	1,587	3,831,098	Bogotá	3,831,098
Guajira (La)	20,180	262,056	Riohacha	56,900 [1]
Huila	19,990	545,603	Neiva	129,700 [1]
Magdalena	22,903	684,704	Santa Marta	174,200 [1]
Meta	85,770	328,077	Villavicencio	83,700 [1]
Nariño	31,045	993,050	Pasto	140,700 [1]
Norte de Santander	20,815	862,829	Cúcuta	358,240
Quindío	1,825	355,328	Armenia	196,500 [1]
Risaralda	3,962	497,122	Pereira	251,861
Santander	30,950	1,284,035	Bucaramanga	387,886
Sucre	10,523	475,637	Sincelejo	77,800 [1]
Tolima	23,325	1,024,184	Ibagué	263,669
Valle del Cauca	21,245	2,775,142	Cali	1,255,198

[1] 1973.

Intendencias	Area (sq. km)	Population 1978	Capital
Arauca	23,490	27,497 [1]	Arauca
Caquetá	90,185	88,920 [1]	Florencia
Casanare	44,532	[2]	El Yopal
Putumayo	25,570	29,137 [1]	Mocoa
San Andrés y Providencia	44	22,719 [1]	San Andrés
Comisarías			
Amazonas	121,240	12,962 [1]	Leticia
Guainía	78,065	3,602 [1]	Puerto Inírida
Vaupés	90,625	13,403 [1]	Mitú
Vichada	98,970	12,330 [1]	Puerto Carreño
Total	1,138,914	26,500,000	

[1] 1973.   [2] Included in figure for Boyacá

Of the total population in 1974, 64·3% were urban. The bulk of the population lives at altitudes of from 4,000 to 9,000 ft above sea-level. It is divided broadly into: 68% mestizo, 20% white, 7% Indio and 5% Negro.

In 1975 births were 40·6 per 1,000; deaths, 8·8.

The language spoken is Spanish.

CONSTITUTION AND GOVERNMENT. The legislative power rests with a Congress of 2 houses, the Senate, of 112 members, and the House of Representatives, of 199 members, both elected for 4 years. In 1968 a congressional committee unanimously approved a constitutional amendment providing for progressive reductions in the membership of Congress to 90 senators and 162 representatives by 1974. Congress meets annually at Bogotá on 20 July. Women were given the vote, which is now open to citizens of either sex, over 18 years of age, on 25 Aug. 1954.

The President is elected by direct vote of the people for a term of 4 years, and is not eligible for re-election until 4 years afterwards. Congress elects, for a term of 2 years, one substitute to occupy the presidency in the event of a vacancy during a presidential term. There are 13 Ministries. The Governors of Departments and the Mayor of Bogotá are nominated by the national government.

A National Economic Council, functioning since May 1935, went through several transformations, becoming in 1954 a Directorate of Planning.

National flag: Three horizontal stripes of yellow, blue, red with the yellow of double width.

National anthem: Oh! Gloria inmarcesible (words by R. Núñez; tune by O. Síndici).

The following is a list of presidents since 1945:

Dr Alberto Lleras Camargo, 7 Aug. 1945–7 Aug. 1946.

Dr Mariano Ospina Pérez, 7 Aug. 1946–7 Aug. 1950.

Dr Laureano Gómez, 7 Aug. 1950–13 June 1953.

Gen. Gustavo Rojas Pinilla, 13 June 1953–10 May 1957.

Military Junta, Maj.-Gen. Gabriel París and 4 others, 10 May 1957–7 Aug. 1958.

Dr Alberto Lleras Camargo (Lib.), 7 Aug. 1958–7 Aug. 1962.

Dr Guillermo León Valencia (Cons.), 7 Aug. 1962–7 Aug. 1966.

Dr Carlos Lleras Restrepo (Lib.), 7 Aug. 1966–7 Aug. 1970.

Dr Misael Pastrana Borrero (Cons.), 7 Aug 1970–7 Aug. 1974.

Dr Alfonso López Michelsen (Cons./Lib.), 7 Aug. 1974–7 Aug. 1978.

President: Dr Julio Cesar Turbay Ayala, heading a Liberal administration. He was elected on 4 June 1978 and took office on 7 Aug. 1978.

Minister of Foreign Affairs: Dr Diego Uribe Vargas (L.).

Gibson, W. M., *The Constitutions of Colombia.* Durham, N.C. 1948, and London, 1949

DEFENCE. On 17 April 1952 Colombia signed the Military Assistance pact with the USA.

Army. Military service is compulsory between the years of 18 and 30. Service with the colours is for 1 year. From 30 to 45 years of age the citizens are on the reserved lists, classified in 1st, 2nd and 3rd classes, with the obligation of presenting themselves on being called up. The permanent Army consists of 10 infantry and 1 training brigades, artillery, cavalry, engineer and motorized troops and the usual services. The peace effective is 53,000 men; reserves 500,000. Number of national police, about 50,000.

Colombia was the only Latin American country participating in the Korean war, with a regiment of 1,000 men (three times relieved).

Navy. Colombia has 2 new Federal German-built 1,200-ton diesel-electric powered patrol submarines, 4 Italian-built midget submarines; 2 destroyers completed in Sweden in 1958; 1 old (1944) *ex*-US destroyer; 2 old *ex*-US frigates (small DE and APD types); 3 old patrol vessels (*ex*-US fleet tugs); 4 river gunboats; 3 surveying vessels; 9 coastguard patrol vessels; 10 patrol motor launches; 1 oiler; 4 small transports, 1 training ship, 5 service craft, and 12 tugs. Personnel (1981), 700 officers and 6,500 men. The Navy has also a battalion of marines with 1,500 officers and men.

Air Force. Formed in 1922, the Air Force has been independent of the Army and Navy since 1943, when its reorganization began with US assistance. In 1980 it had about 275 aircraft, including a squadron of Mirage 5-COA fighter-bombers, 5-COR reconnaissance aircraft and 5-COD two-seat operational trainers; a squadron of 8 B-26 piston-engined bombers; a transport group equipped with 2 C-130s, 2 HS 748s, 4 Twin Otters, 19 C-47s, 5 C-54s and a small number of Arava, Otter, Beaver and Porter light transports; a presidential F-28 Fellowship jet transport; and a maritime reconnaissance and rescue unit with helicopters. Many of the transports are flown by the Air Force operated airline SATENA. Thirty Cessna T-41D primary trainer/light transports were delivered in 1968 and were followed by 10 T-37C jet advanced trainers to supplement piston-engined T-34s and T-33A armed jet trainers. Latest deliveries include 6 T-38A jet trainers for operation by the Military Air Academy. Total strength is about 3,800 personnel.

INTERNATIONAL RELATIONS

Membership. Colombia is a member of the UN, OAS, the Andean Group and LAIA (formerly LAFTA).

ECONOMY

Budget. Ordinary revenue and expenditure for calendar years in 1m. paper pesos:

	1980	1981
Revenue	192,200	196,500
Expenditure	192,200	196,500

Reserves totalled US$1,800m. in Dec. 1977.

Currency. Coins include 50, 20 and 10 *centavos* (90% steel and 10% nickel) and 5, 2 and 1 *centavos* of various combinations of copper–nickel–bronze–steel. There are also notes representing 1, 5, 10, 20, 50, 100 and 500 *gold pesos*. Exchange rate March 1981, 112·62 *pesos* = £1 sterling; 51·96 *pesos* = US$1.

Banking. On 23 July 1923 the Banco de la República was inaugurated as a semi-official central bank, with the exclusive privilege of issuing bank-notes in Colombia; its charter, in 1951, was extended to 1973. Its note issues must be covered by a reserve in gold of foreign exchange of 25% of their value.

There are 25 domestic commercial banks of importance and 5 foreign banks (English, Canadian, American, French and Franco-Italian); but a high percentage of all commercial bank deposits are with the 4 largest domestic banks, which have branches throughout the country. External debt (1979) US$4,026m.

Weights and Measures. The metric system was introduced in 1857, but in ordinary commerce Spanish weights and measures are generally used; according to new definitions by the Ministry of Development, *e.g.*, *botella* (750 grammes), *galón* (5 *botellas*), *vara* (70 cm), *arroba* (25 lb., of 500 grammes; 4 *arrobas* = 1 quintal).

ENERGY AND NATURAL RESOURCES

Electricity. Capacity of electric power (1973) is 2,795,000 kw. Electric power produced in 1976, 13,717,170 kwh. There is increasing utilization of natural gas.

In Oct. 1954 the Department of Valle del Cauca established a local power corporation closely modelled on the Tennessee Valley Authority.

Oil. Petroleum production in 1977 was 50m. bbls (of 42 gallons) and 1976, 53·4m. bbls.

Minerals. Colombia is rich in minerals; gold is found chiefly in Antioquia and moderately in Cauca, Caldas, Tolima, Nariño and Chocó; output in 1979, 265,600 troy oz., highest in South America.

Other minerals are silver (99,300 troy oz. in 1979), copper, lead, mercury, manganese, emeralds and platinum (first discovered in Colombia in 1735 and the largest deposit in the world); production of platinum, 1977, 26,000 troy oz. The working of the government-controlled emerald mines has been resumed. The chief mines are those of Muzo and Chivor.

The Government holds the monopoly, which is leased to the Banco de la República, for extracting salts from the outstanding Zipaquirá mines (several hundred feet in depth and several hundred square miles in area) and for evaporating many sea salt pans; salt production in 1977 was 180,890 tons of land salt from the Zipaquirá mines and 435,542 tons of sea salt from Manaure and Galerazamba on the Caribe coast. Colombia's coal reserves are estimated at 4,100m. tonnes; production (1975) 10m. short tons.

Agriculture. Very little of the country is under cultivation, but much of the soil is fertile and is coming into use as roads improve. The range of climate and crops is extraordinary; the agricultural colleges have different courses for 'cold-climate farming' and 'warm-climate farming'. Some 6m. acres are described as arable, 96m. pasture and 148m. forest.

Colombia is the second largest producer of coffee and ranks first in the output of mild coffee, demand for which is unaffected by over-production in Brazil. Crops are grown by smallholders, and are picked all the year round. Production (1977, in tonnes): Cotton seed, 328,198; rice, 1,417,190; barley, 101,300; maize, 1,043,141; potatoes, 1,608,600; soybean, 108,500; wheat, 55,260; bananas, 819,000; cacao, 27,888; sugar-cane, 1,060,060.

The rubber tree grows wild, and its cultivation has begun; output is a few hundred tons. Fibres are being exploited, notably the 'fique' fibre, which furnishes all the country's requirements for sacks and cordage; output about 12,000 tons. Tolú balsam is cultivated, and copaiba trees are tapped but are not cultivated. Tanning is an important industry, 12m. sq. ft of hides being exported in 1965.

Livestock (1979): 26·14m. cattle, 1·92m. pigs, 2·36m. sheep, 32·8m. poultry.

Fishery. In Sept. 1963 a *Sección de Caza y Pesca* was set up in the Ministry of Agriculture. It extended territorial waters to 200 nautical miles. The principal finance companies founded a development company with over 20m. pesos in Aug. 1966 (*Consorcio Pesquero Colombiano*).

INDUSTRY AND TRADE

Industry. Value of industrial output (located mainly in the Departments of Antioquia, Cundinamarca and Valle) by 456,188 production workers in 6,348 establishments in 1975 was 202,177m. pesos. Refined petroleum production, 1973, 58·1m. bbls (of 42 gallons). There are 69 reassembly plants, apart from the motor industry. At the end of 1965 the 101 firms with more than 50% US control equalled an investment of US$510m.; they employed over 29,000 Colombians.

GDP *per capita* (1975) 16,952 pesos.

Trade Unions. The Colombian Federation of Labour (CTC) had, in 1947, 109,000 members out of a total of 165,000 organized workers. In 1946 there was established an association of trade unions, *Unión de Trabajadores Colombianos*. In May 1963, 8·6% of the 449,000 workmen in Bogotá were unemployed.

Commerce. For the 'Charter of Quito' trading agreement in 1948 between Colombia, Ecuador, Panama and Venezuela, *see* THE STATESMAN'S YEAR-BOOK, 1956, p. 882. Colombia's entry into the Latin American Free Trade Area (ALALC) was ratified on 29 Sept. 1961. A fresh impulse to this effort was given by the Bases for an Immediate Action Programme under the 'Charter of Bogotá' signed by Colombia, Chile, Ecuador, Peru and Venezuela on 16 Aug. 1966.

Imports (c.i.f. values) and exports (f.o.b. values) (excluding export tax) for calendar years (in US$1m.):

	1977	1978	1979
Imports	2,713	3,168	4,062
Exports	1,979	2,753	3,248

Trade by principal countries, in US$1m.:

	Imports (c.i.f.)[1]		Exports (f.o.b.)[1]	
	1974	1975[2]	1974	1975[2]
Belgium–Luxembourg	13·5	12·5	17·1	25·0
Canada	42·6	43·0	19·5	13·9
France	67·0	67·2	27·0	32·0
Germany (Fed. Republic of)	144·6	131·3	170·0	217·9
Italy	31·5	37·8	31·6	38·7
Japan	135·5	128·9	20·7	27·1
Netherlands	36·9	23·7	64·4	93·5
Spain	49·5	50·3	37·9	38·6
Sweden	27·5	26·1	32·7	46·4
Switzerland	59·0	40·3	8·0	7·1
UK	59·1	53·0	22·2	41·3
USA	639·0	640·4	514·5	441·9

[1] Excluding bullion and specie.   [2] Provisional.

Important articles of export in 1973 (in US$1m.) were coffee (596·9), emeralds (79·6), cotton (79·3), meat, fresh and frozen (40·1), sugar (31·1), petroleum (26·8), fuel oil (22·5), skins and hides (20·2). The chief imports are machinery, vehicles, tractors, metals and manufactures, rubber, chemical products, wheat, fertilizers and wool.

Total trade between Colombia and UK (British Department of Trade returns, in £1,000 sterling).

	1976	1977	1978	1979	1980
Imports to UK	25,818	31,641	24,974	21,874	34,289
Exports and re-exports from UK	28,854	41,685	50,841	52,258	41,920

Tourism. Foreign visitors totalled 362,900 in 1974.

COMMUNICATIONS

Roads. Owing to the mountainous character of the country, the construction of arterial roads and railways is costly and difficult. Total length of highways, 51,253 km in 1972. Of the 2,300-mile Simón Bolívar highway, which runs from Caracas in Venezuela to Guayaquil in Ecuador, the Colombian portion is complete. Buenaventura and Cali are linked by a highway (Carreterra al Mar). Motor vehicles numbered 550,293, of which 258,526 were passenger cars and 54,730 lorries in 1977.

Railways. There are 5 divisions of the State Railway, with a total length of 2,912 km in 1978 and a gauge of 3 ft. The Pacific Railway connects Bogotá with the port of Buenaventura. The Atlantic line from Bogotá to Sta. Marta was opened in July 1961. Three connecting links are planned to improve the operating efficiency of the network. Total railway traffic, 1976, was 4m. passengers and 2,411,372 tonnes of freight.

Aviation. In civil aviation Colombia ranks perhaps second, after Brazil, among South American countries. There are 675 landing grounds of all kinds. In 1977 the national airports moved 8,071,882 passengers and 169,474 tonnes of cargo.

Shipping. Vessels entering Colombian ports in 1977 unloaded 8·07m. tonnes of imports and loaded 1·95m. tonnes of exports. The Colombian merchant fleet in 1966 owned 23 vessels of 187,906 net tons, and leased 20 of 164,360 net tons; in 1965 it carried 1·9m. tonnes.

The Magdelena River is subject to drought, and navigation is always impeded during the dry season, but it is an important artery of passenger and goods traffic. The river is navigable for 900 miles; steamers ascend to La Dorada, 592 miles from Barranquilla. In 1977 they carried 2,326,000 tonnes of cargo, of which 88·2% was manufactured goods.

Post and Broadcasting. The length of telephone lines in service is 705,852 km (Bogotá only); instruments in use, 1 Jan. 1978, 1,396,591, of which 479,000 are in Bogotá. The cable company is government-owned. There are 223 broadcasting stations. Television was established in 1954. Bogotá is now the centre of a wide repeater network.

Cinemas (1973). There were 352 cinemas.

Newspapers (1973). There were 36 daily newspapers, with daily circulation totalling 1,448,467. There were 388 periodical publications.

JUSTICE, RELIGION, EDUCATION AND WELFARE

Justice. The Supreme Court, at Bogotá, of 20 members, is divided into 3 chambers—civil cassation (6), criminal cassation (8), labour cassation (6). Each of the 61 judicial districts has a superior court with various sub-dependent tribunals of lower juridical grade.

Communism was outlawed by government decree on 5 March 1956.

Religion. The religion is Roman Catholic, with the Cardinal Archbishop of Bogotá as Primate of Colombia and 7 other archbishops in Cartagena, Manizales, Medellín, Pamplona, Popayán, Cali and Tunja, 26 bishops, 1,546 parishes and 4,020 priests. Other forms of religion are permitted so long as their exercise is 'not contrary to Christian morals or to the law'; but since 1953 the 90,000 Protestants have complained of police prosecutions and religious disorders.

Education. Primary education is free but not compulsory, and facilities are limited. Schools are both state and privately controlled. In 1974 there were 30,558 primary schools with 3,844,257 pupils and 123,139 teachers. In 4,200 secondary schools there were 1,159,996 pupils with 62,000 teachers. In the 176 industrial schools, there were 27,808 pupils with 2,855 teachers. 178 night schools had 11,504 pupils with 1,668 teachers. 81 agricultural schools catered for 7,930 pupils with 815 teachers. There were 638 commercial schools catering for 69,233 pupils with 7,844 teachers. 110 art schools had 8,681 pupils and 709 teachers. Theological institutes (all private) numbered 22 with 674 students and 180 tutors. In *normalista* schools, of which there were 239, 54,198 pupils had 5,407 teachers.

The National University in Bogotá was founded in 1867 and there are 97 other universities with 171,002 students and 17,963 lecturers.

Of the population over 7 years of age in July 1964, the National Department of Statistics estimated that 27·1% were illiterate; intensive efforts to build new schools and to reduce illiteracy are being made.

Health. In 1976 there were 670 hospitals and clinics. There were also 1,499 health centres.

DIPLOMATIC REPRESENTATIVES

OF COLOMBIA IN GREAT BRITAIN (3 Hans Crescent, London, SW1X 0LR)

Ambassador: Gustavo Bakázar-Monzón.

OF GREAT BRITAIN IN COLOMBIA (Calle 38, 13 35, Bogotá)

Ambassador: K. J. Uffen, CMG.

OF COLOMBIA IN THE USA (2118 Leroy Pl., NW, Washington, D.C., 20008)

Ambassador: Virgilio Barco.

OF THE USA IN COLOMBIA (Calle 37, 8 40, Bogotá)

Ambassador: Diego C. Asencio.

OF COLOMBIA TO THE UNITED NATIONS

Ambassador: Dr Indalecio Lievano.

Books of Reference

Anuario General de Estadistica de Colombia. Bogotá. Annual
Anuario de Comercio Exterior de Colombia. Annual
Anuario Estadístico Bogotá D.E. Annual
Boletín Mensual de Estadística. Monthly
Economía y Estadística. Occasional
Informe Financiero del Contralor General. Annual
Informe del Gerente de la Caja de Crédito Agrario, Industrial y Minero. Annual
Memorias (13) de los Ministros al Congreso Nacional. Annual
Charry Lara, Alberto, *Desarrollo histórico de la Estadística nacional en Colombia.* Nat. Dept of Statistics, Bogotá, 1954.—*El país en cifras.* 1964
Lebret, R. P. L. J., *Estudio sobre las condiciones dei desarrollo de Colombia. Informe de una Misión.* Bogotá, 1960
McGreevey, W. P., *An Economic History of Colombia, 1845–1930.* CUP, 1970
Wurfel S. W., *Foreign Enterprise in Colombia: Laws and Policies.* Univ. of N. Carolina Press, 1965

COMOROS

Etat Comorien

Capital: Moroni
Population: 297,800 (1976)
GNP per capita: US$180 (1978)

HISTORY. In the referendum held separately on each of the 4 islands on 22 Dec. 1974, 95·56% of the Comorans voted for independence, but the vote on Mayotte was 65% against independence. To avoid the expected separation of Mayotte, the Comoran Chamber of Deputies voted for an immediate unilateral declaration of independence on 6 July 1975. The next day it converted itself into the National Assembly and elected Ahmed Abdallah, President of the Executive Council since 26 Dec. 1972, as President of the new state. France retained responsibility for Mayotte, while the other 3 islands thus achieved *de facto* independence.

On 3 Aug. a *coup* mounted by the principal opposition parties, led by Ali Soilih, deposed President Abdallah. The following day a National Revolutionary Council, led by Prince Said Mohammad Jaffar, took office and abolished the National Assembly. On 10 Aug. the Revolutionary Council established a National Executive Council with Prince Said as its President. The four parties formed a coalition, the Front National Uni, which attempted unsuccessfully to persuade the Mayotte administration (the *Mouvement populaire mahouais*, led by Marcel Henry) to reunite with the other islands.

France recognized the independence of the 3 islands on 1 Jan. 1976. The next day the Executive Council and the Revolutionary Council elected Ali Soilih President.

The Revolutionary Council was superseded by a National Institutional Council to oversee the actions of the Government.

A new referendum was held on 8 Feb. 1976 on Mayotte, which resulted in a 99·4% vote for retaining the island's links with France. In another referendum on 11 April Mayotte voted against remaining an Overseas Territory of France, preferring to become an Overseas Department. France has promised to implement the electorate's wishes accordingly. The UN recognized the State of Comoro as representative of the whole group. (For history prior to independence *see* THE STATESMAN'S YEAR-BOOK, 1976–77, p. 849.) All statistics prior to 1977 include Mayotte.

AREA AND POPULATION. The Federal and Islamic Republic of the Comoros consists of 3 islands in the Indian ocean between the African mainland and Madagascar. The majority of the population throughout the islands speak Kiswahili, but a small proportion speak French or Arabic. On the 3 islands of the Comoro State, the majority of the population are Moslem, with about 2,000 Christians.

	Area sq. km	Population census 1966	Population estimate 1976	Chief town
Njazidja (Grande Comore)	1,148	126,205	150,000	Moroni
Mwali (Mohéli)	290	10,300	13,800	Fomboni
Nzwami (Anjouan)	424	80,082	134,000	Mutsamudu
	1,862	216,587	297,800	

CONSTITUTION AND GOVERNMENT. President Ali Soilih was overthrown in a *coup* in May 1978. A federal-style Constitution was adopted in Oct. 1978 and elections to the 39-member Federal Assembly were held on 8 Dec. 1978.

President: Ahmed Abdallah.
Prime Minister: Salim Ben Ali.

National flag: Green with a crescent and 4 stars all in white in the centre.

DEFENCE

Air Arm. Equipment, acquired since 1977–78, comprises 3 SIAI-Marchetti SF-260W Warrior armed light trainers built in Italy, a C-47 transport and a Cessna 402B communications aircraft.

INTERNATIONAL RELATIONS

Membership. Comoros is a member of UN and an ACP state of EEC.

ECONOMY

Budget. The ordinary budget for 1975 balanced at 2,949m. francs CFA.

Currency. The unit of currency is the *franc CFA*.

Banking. The Institut d'émission des Comores was established as the new bank of issue in 1975. The chief commercial bank is the Banque des Comores, established in 1974 by the separation of the former Comoran section of the Banque de Madagascar et des Comores.

Weights and Measures. The metric system is in force.

NATURAL RESOURCES

Agriculture. The chief product was formerly sugar-cane, but now vanilla, copra, cacao, sisal, coffee, cloves and essential oils (citronella, ylang, lemon-grass) are the most important products.

Livestock (1979): Cattle, 77,000; sheep, 8,000; goats, 86,000; asses, 3,000.

COMMERCE. Imports in 1971 amounted to 54,299 tonnes (2,834m. francs CFA), exports to 12,756 tonnes (1,572m. francs CFA). Vanilla exports were 206 tonnes (606m. francs CFA); sisal, 373 tonnes (268m. francs CFA); copra, 3,988 tonnes (206·5m. francs CFA); ylang, 67·4 tonnes (452m. francs CFA); basil, 6·5 tonnes (48·7m. francs CFA); coffee, 73 tonnes (15·4m. francs CFA). Grande Comore has a fine forest and produces timber for building.

Trade between Comoros and UK (British Department of Trade returns, in £1,000 sterling):

	1977	1978	1979	1980
Imports to UK	3	3	21	40
Exports and re-exports from UK	69	126	52	155

COMMUNICATIONS

Roads. In 1973 there were 750 km of classified roads, of which 262 km were tarmac. There were 3,600 registered vehicles.

Aviation. The new international airport at Hahaya (on Grande Comore) came into service in 1975. Air Comores have twice-weekly flights to Antanarivo, Dar es Salaam and Mombasa. Air France and Air Madagascar also have twice-weekly flights to Antanarivo. Air Comores has daily internal flights between Moroni and Anjouan, and 5 per week between Moroni and Mohéli.

In 1973 nearly 16,000 passengers landed and 900 tonnes of freight were carried.

Shipping. In 1973, 279 vessels entered Comoran ports (excluding internal traffic) to discharge 54,391 tonnes and load 8,700 tonnes.

Post and Broadcasting. There were 1,035 telephones in 1977. *Comores-Inter* broadcasts in French and Comorian on short-wave and FM for approximately 8 hours a day. Number of radios (1975): 36,000.

Cinemas. In 1973 there were 2 cinemas with a seating capacity of 800.

EDUCATION AND WELFARE

Education. In 1974, 130 primary classes had 570 teachers and 21,557 pupils, 5 secondary schools had 121 teachers and 2,920 pupils.

Health. In 1975 there were 3 hospitals and a number of clinics.

CONGO

République Populaire du Congo

Capital: Brazzaville
Population: 1·43m. (1978)
GNP per capita: US$540 (1978)

HISTORY. First occupied by France in 1882, the Congo became (as 'Middle Congo') a territory of French Equatorial Africa from 1908 until 28 Nov. 1958, when it became a member state of the French Community. It became an independent Republic on 15 Aug. 1960.

AREA AND POPULATION. The Congo Republic is bounded by Cameroon and the Central African Empire in the north, Zaïre to the east and west, the Atlantic to the south-west and Gabon to the west, and covers 342,000 sq. km; census population (1974), 1,300,120. Estimate (1978) 1,434,000. The capital is Brazzaville (310,500), and other towns include Pointe-Noire, 146,700; Jacob, 30,600; Loubomo (Dolisie), 29,600. The republic is divided into 9 regions and the capital district of Brazzaville. 50% of the population was urban in 1979.

In 1974, 45% spoke Kongo dialects, 15% Teke, 15% Sanga, 12% Ubangi; there are also about 12,000 pygmies and 12,000 Europeans (mainly French). French is the official language.

CONSTITUTION AND GOVERNMENT. In July 1979 a new Constitution was approved by referendum. Executive power was vested in the President, elected by the congress of the *Parti congolais du travail* (the sole legal party since 1969). The President is assisted by a Council of Ministers, appointed and led by him. There is a 115-member People's National Assembly.

President and Minister of Defence: Col. Denis Sassou-Nguesso.
Prime Minister: Col. Louis-Sylvain Goma.
Foreign Affairs: Pierre Nze.

National flag: Red, in the canton the national emblem of a crossed hoe and mattock, a green wreath and a gold star.

DEFENCE

Army. The Army consists of 4 battalions, 1 armoured, 1 infantry, 1 engineering, and 1 paracommando. Total personnel (1980) 5,000.

Navy. The Navy has 1 *ex*-Soviet torpedo boat, 3 gunboats, 4 river patrol craft (all *ex*-Chinese) and 12 small river patrol boats. Personnel (1981) 200 officers and men.

Air Force. The Air Force has about 325 personnel, 10 MiG-15/17 jet fighters, 1 twin-turbofan F28 Fellowship transport, 1 Frégate and 4 Antonov An-24 turboprop transports, 3 C-47 and 4 Il-14 piston-engined transports, 2 Broussard communications aircraft and 6 Alouette II and Alouette III light helicopters.

INTERNATIONAL RELATIONS

Membership. Congo is a member of UN, OAU and is an ACP state of EEC.

ECONOMY

Budget. The ordinary budget in 1978 balanced at 60,249m. francs CFA.

Currency. The unit of currency is the *franc CFA*.

ENERGY AND NATURAL RESOURCES

Oil. Oil reserves are estimated at 500–1,000m. tonnes, but production is low. Output 2·8m. tonnes in 1979 (2·4m. tonnes 1978).

Minerals. Lead, zinc and gold (15 kg in 1976) are the main minerals.

Agriculture. Production (1977, in tonnes): Cassava, 769,000; sugar-cane, 461,000; yams, 105,000.

Livestock (1979): Cattle, 71,000; pigs, 49,000; sheep, 66,000; goats, 119,000; poultry, 1m.

TRADE. Imports in 1977 totalled 49,340m. francs CFA (mainly machinery) and exports 45,560m. (of which petroleum 24,275m.). 50% of imports were from France; 36% of exports were to Italy and 14% to France.

Total trade between the Congo and UK (British Department of Trade returns, in £1,000 sterling):

	1975	1976	1977	1978	1979	1980
Imports to UK	6,765	1,683	1,822	4,520	3,339	3,416
Exports and re-exports from UK	1,460	1,784	3,478	2,072	3,391	2,943

COMMUNICATIONS

Roads. There were (1977) 11,000 km of roads. In 1976 there were 20,000 cars and 13,000 commercial vehicles.

Railways. A railway (517 km, 1,067 mm gauge) and a telegraph line connect Brazzaville with Pointe-Noire and a 200 km branch railway links Mont-Belo with Mbinda on the Gabon border.

Aviation. The principal airports are at Maya Maya and Pointe-Noire. In addition there are 22 airfields served by the local airline, Lina-Congo.

Shipping. Pointe-Noire handled (1979) 2·4m. tonnes of goods including manganese from Gabon. There were (1979) 16 vessels of 6,942 GNT registered.

Post and Broadcasting. Telephones (1978) numbered 13,376, of which 6,990 were in Brazzaville. In 1973 there were 75,000 radios and 3,800 TV sets in use.

Cinemas. In 1973 there were 7 cinemas with a seating capacity of 5,100.

RELIGION, EDUCATION AND WELFARE

Religion. 50% of the population follow animist beliefs and 48% are Christian (mainly Roman Catholic). There are about 40,000 Moslems.

Education. In 1978 there were 345,736 primary school, 127,210 secondary school and 11,123 technical school pupils. The Université Marien Ngouabi in Brazzaville had 3,642 students in 1978.

Health. There were (1976) 121 hospitals with 6,912 beds; and 190 doctors, 4 dentists, 25 pharmacists, 152 midwives and 1,734 nursing personnel.

DIPLOMATIC REPRESENTATIVES

OF THE CONGO IN GREAT BRITAIN

Ambassador: Jean-Pierre Nonault (resides in Paris).

OF GREAT BRITAIN IN THE CONGO

Ambassador: J. N. O. Snodgrass, CMG (resides in Kinshasa).

OF THE USA IN THE CONGO (PO Box 1015, Brazzaville)

Ambassador: William Lacy Swing.

OF CONGO TO THE USA AND UNITED NATIONS

Ambassador: Nicolas Mondjo.

COSTA RICA

República de Costa Rica

Capital: San José
Population: 2·19m. (1979)
GNP per capita: US$1,540 (1978)

HISTORY. The republic of Costa Rica (the 'Rich Coast') has been independent since 1821, although it formed, from 1824 to 1838, part of the Confederation of Central America.

AREA AND POPULATION. The area is estimated at 50,898 sq. km (19,652 sq. miles). The population at the census of 14 May 1973 was 1,871,780, compared with 800,875 shown in the 1950 census.

The area and official estimate of population for 1 July 1979 (2,192,410) was as follows:

Province	Population	Area (sq. km)	Capital	Population
San José	812,184	4,957·09	San José	250,079
Alajuela	378,580	9,718·10	Alajuela	38,630
Cartago	238,213	3,031·14	Cartago	25,345
Heredia	155,565	2,673·49	Heredia	26,863
Guanacaste	209,863	10,199·58	Liberia	20,408
Puntarenas	260,118	11,302·21	Puntarenas	32,028
Limón	137,887	9,218·39	Limón	48,415

Vital statistics for calendar years:

	Marriages	Births	Deaths
1975	14,683	58,140	9,685
1976	14,769	59,746	9,293
1977	15,422	63,519	8,907

Crude birth rate, 1976, was 29·7 per 1,000 population; crude death rate, 4·6; infantile death rate, 33·2 per 1,000 live births; crude marriage rate, 7·3 per 1,000 population. Males exceeded females by 14,200.

The population of European descent, many of them of pure Spanish blood, dwell mostly around the capital of the republic, San José, and in the principal towns of the provinces. Limón, on the Caribbean coast, and Puntarenas, on the Pacific coast, are the chief commercial ports. The United Fruit Co., who in 1941 abandoned their banana plantations on the Atlantic coast in favour of large new plantations on the Pacific coast, have constructed ports at Quepos and Golfito. The Standard Fruit Co. and others have cleared land since 1958 in the Atlantic coast area and now have 2,325 acres producing some 4·2m. stems a year. There are some 15,000 West Indians, mostly in Limón province. The indigenous Indian population is dwindling and is now estimated at 1,200.

Spanish is the language of the country.

CONSTITUTION AND GOVERNMENT. The Constitution, promulgated on 7 Dec. 1871, has been modified very frequently, last in 1949. The Constitution forbids the establishment or maintenance of an army. The legislative power is normally vested in a single chamber called the Legislative Assembly, which since 1962 consists of 57 deputies, 1 for every 25,214 inhabitants, elected for 4 years. The President is elected for 4 years; the candidate receiving the largest vote, provided it is over 40% of the total, is declared elected, but a second ballot is required if no candidate gets 40% of the total. By the election law of 18 Jan. 1946 all citizens who are 20 years of age are entitled to vote; married men and teachers, from the age of 18. Women over 21 were enfranchised in 1949. Elections are normally held on the first Sunday in February. Voting for President, Deputies and Municipal Councillors is secret and compulsory for all men under 70 years of age. Independent non-party candidates are barred from the ballot.

President: Rodrigo Carazo Odio, elected 5 Feb. 1978 and assumed office 8 May 1978.

Elections for the Legislative Assembly took place on 5 Feb. 1978; Opposition Party, 27; National Liberation Party, 25; People United, 3; Popular Front, 1; Cartago Agricultural Union, 1.

The administration is carried on by 13 ministers, appointed by the President. The powers of the President are limited by the constitution, which leaves him the power to appoint and remove at will members of his cabinet. All other public appointments are made jointly in the names of the President and of the minister in charge of the department concerned.

National flag: Five unequal stripes of blue, white, red, white, blue, with the national arms on a white disc near the hoist.

National anthem: Noble patria, tu hermosa bandera (words by J. M. Zeledón, 1903; tune by M. M. Gutiérrez, 1851).

DEFENCE

Army. The Army was abolished in 1948, and replaced by a Civil Guard reputed to be 5,000 strong. There has never been compulsory military service or training.

Navy. The republic has 1 fast patrol craft and 1 armed tug on the Atlantic coast and 5 small coastal patrol craft for revenue purposes and 3 smaller craft on the Pacific coast. Personnel (1981) 50 officers and men.

Air Wing. The Civil Guard operates a small air wing equipped with 3 Otter STOL utility transports, plus a few lightplanes and helicopters.

INTERNATIONAL RELATIONS

Membership. Costa Rica is a member of UN and OAS.

ECONOMY

Budget. The budget for 1980 balanced at 8,029m. colones. Of the 1980 total, 33% will be used for repayment of the public debt.

The income-tax law of 10 March 1972 raised the maximum rate to 50% for personal incomes of 350,000 colones and over, and to 40% for corporate incomes of 1m. colones and over.

Central government debt on 31 Dec. 1972 was 2,628m. colones. Debt service required 214·5m. colones in 1973.

Currency. The unit of currency is the *colone* (₡). The official rate in March 1981 was ₡8·57 = US$1; 18·75 = £1. The official rate is used for all imports on an essential list and by the Government and autonomous institutions and a free rate is for all other transactions.

The currency is chiefly notes. The Banco Central in 1951 printed and placed in circulation new notes for 5, 10, 20, 50, 100, 500 and 1,000 colones, replacing old notes previously issued by the Banco Nacional. Silver coins of 1 colone, 50 centimos and 25 centimos were in 1935 replaced by coins (2 and 1 colones and 50 and 25 centimos) made up of 3 parts copper and 1 part nickel, and given the same value as the subsidiary silver currency. There are copper coins (and chromium stainless steel coins) of 10 and 5 centimos.

Banking. By a law passed on 28 Jan. 1950 a Central Bank was established for the organization and direction of the national monetary system and of dealings in foreign exchange, the promotion of facilities for credit and the supervision of all banking operations in the country. The bank has a board of 7 directors appointed by the Government, including *ex officio* the Minister of Finance and the Planning Office Director. On 31 Dec. 1974 it had foreign exchange of US$43·3m., compared with US$61·2m. in Dec. 1973; circulating media on 31 Dec. 1969 totalled 992·7m. colones.

In June 1948 the 3 small commercial banks were compulsorily nationalized; they held deposits of 1,005·3m. colones at 31 Aug. 1970 (962·1m. at 31 Dec. 1970).

The National Insurance Institute (*Instituto Nacional de Seguros*) is a Government organization, created in 1924, which has a monopoly of new insurance business.

Weights and Measures. The metric system is legally established; but in the country districts the following old Spanish weights and measures are found: *libra* = 1·014 lb. avoirdupois; *arroba* = 25·35 lb. avoirdupois; *quintal* = 101·40 lb. avoirdupois, and *fanega* = 11 Imperial bushels.

ENERGY AND NATURAL RESOURCES

Electricity. Electricity, derived from water power in the highlands, is increasingly used as motive power. Output, 1975, was 1,263m. kwh.

Minerals. Gold output is about 3,000 troy oz. per year. Salt production from sea water is about 10,000 tonnes annually. Haematite ore was discovered on the Nicoya Peninsula late in 1960 and sulphur near San Carlos in 1966. The United Nations have offered US$1m. towards a 3-year mining survey.

Agriculture. Agriculture is the principal industry. The cultivated area is about 1m. acres; grass lands cover 1·8m. acres; forests and woodlands, 9,855,000 acres. There are thousands of square miles of public lands that have never been cleared, on which can be found quantities of rosewood, cedar, mahogany and other cabinet woods. The principal agricultural products are coffee, bananas, sugar and cattle. Coffee normally accounts for about half the country's foreign-exchange earnings. Cocoa, maize, sugar, tobacco, rice and potatoes are commonly cultivated. The distillation of spirits is a government monopoly.

Coffee production in 1978–79 was 104,941·1 tonnes. Sugar production (1978–79) 2,307,041 tonnes.

Dairy-farming and cattle-raising are substantial pursuits. In 1979 cattle numbered 2·1m. and pigs 226,000.

Costa Rica is the seat of the Inter-American Institute of Agricultural Sciences, with headquarters at Turrialba.

INDUSTRY AND TRADE

Industry. A Ministry of Industry was formed in 1961, but industry is still on a small scale, though the Industrial Development and Protection Law of 1959 affords several facilities and advantages. Main manufactured goods are foodstuffs, textiles, fertilizers, pharmaceuticals, furniture, cement, tyres, canning, clothing, plastic goods, plywood and electrical equipment.

Industrial production was valued at 16·03m. colones in 1978, compared with 1·499m. in 1972.

Labour. As Costa Rica is still essentially an agricultural country, the organization of labour has made progress only in the larger centres of population, and even there it is not a strong movement. There are two main trade unions, *Rerum Novarum* (anti-Communist) and *Confederación General de Trabajadores Costarricenses* (Communist). It is estimated that they have under 10,000 members each. In addition there were (1963) 284 other trade unions and 34 employers' organizations.

Commerce. The value of imports into and exports from Costa Rica in 5 years was as follows in US$ (8·60 colones = US$1):

	1975	1976	1977	1978	1979
Imports	693,969,367	770,412,000	1,021,430,406	1,165,730,038	1,396,812,332
Exports	455,960,193	555,405,000	828,163,886	864,906,915	934,391,357

The value (in US$1m.) of the principal imports in 1978 were: Machinery, including transport equipment, 359·2; manufactures, 381·8; chemicals, 189·6; fuel and mineral oils, 117·6; foodstuffs, 72·4.

Chief exports (in US$1m.) in 1977 were: Manufactured goods and other products, 324·4; coffee, 307·4 (mostly to Federal Republic of Germany and USA); bananas, 169·9 (to USA); sugar, 15·9; cocoa, 15·6.

Total trade between Costa Rica and UK (British Department of Trade returns, in £1,000 sterling):

	1976	1977	1978	1979	1980
Imports to UK	496	1,378	1,801	3,123	5,424
Exports and re-exports from UK	8,614	10,647	11,799	9,752	8,302

Tourism. There was a total of 340,442 visitors in 1978.

COMMUNICATIONS

Roads. In 1978 there were about 26,993 km of all-weather motor roads open. On the Costa Rica section of the Inter-American Highway it is possible to motor to Panama during the dry season. The Pan-American Highway into Nicaragua is metalled for most of the way and there is now a good highway open almost to Puntarenas. Motor vehicles, 1978, numbered 179,941.

Railways. The nationalized railway system (*Ferrocarriles de Costa Rica*), totalling 785 km (228 km electrified) of 1,067 mm gauge, connect San José with Limón, the Atlantic port, and San José with Puntarenas, the Pacific port.

Aviation. Passenger movement in and out of Costa Rica is almost entirely by air *via* the local company, LACSA, PANAM and TACA. LACSA links San José by daily services with all the more important towns. The international airport at Juan Santamaría was opened in June 1955.

Shipping. In 1978, 1,473 ships entered and cleared the ports of the republic (Puerto Limón, Puntarenas and Golfito); combined cargo, 1,918,500 tonnes.

Post and Broadcasting. A telephone service covering (1978) 145,069 subscribers operates in and between San José and 6 other provincial centres; it has been transferred to a government *Instituto Costarricense de Electricidad*, which is installing a nation-wide automatic system, and will eventually control all telecommunications.

The commercial wireless telegraph stations are operated by *Cia Radiográfica Internacional de Costa Rica*. The stations are located at Cartago, Limón, Puntarenas, Quepos and Golfito. The Government has 19 wireless telegraph stations in its local network. The principal or central station at San José also maintains international radio-telegraph circuits to Nicaragua, Honduras, San Salvador and Mexico. The Government has 202 telegraph offices and 88 official telephone stations. The official list of broadcasting stations shows 28 long-wave stations and 7 short-wave stations. Television was inaugurated in May 1960; there were 5 stations and 155,000 receivers in 1976.

Cinemas (1979). Cinemas numbered 106, with seating capacity of 105,000.

Newspapers (1979). There were 6 daily newspapers all published in San José.

JUSTICE, RELIGION, EDUCATION AND WELFARE

Justice. Justice is administered by the Supreme Court, 4 appeal courts and the Court of Cassation. There are also subordinate courts in the separate provinces and local justices throughout the republic. Capital punishment may not be inflicted.

Religion. Roman Catholicism is the religion of the State, which contributes to its maintenance but controls the Church Patronage and insists on lay instruction in history, economics and similar subjects; there is entire religious liberty under the constitution, but religious appeals are forbidden in current political discussions. The Archbishop of Costa Rica has 4 bishops at Alajuela, Limón, San Isidro el General and Tilarán.

Protestants number about 40,000.

Education. Costa Rica has a very low illiteracy rate. Elementary instruction is compulsory and free; secondary education (since 1949) is also free. Elementary schools are provided and maintained by local school councils, while the national government pays the teachers, besides making subventions in aid of local funds. In 1979 there were 3,361 public primary schools with 15,748 teachers and administrative staff and 379,925 enrolled pupils; there were 215 public and private secondary schools with 169,297 pupils. The University of Costa Rica, founded in San José in

1843, has 2,337 professors in 13 faculties and 38,629 students. A medical school was opened in 1961. The budget for 1971 provides ₡250m. for public education. Since 1944 English has been taught in all secondary schools.

Social Welfare. The labour code of 1943 provides considerable protection for the workers, while a system of social insurance against sickness covering 756,347 workers in 1968, old age and death covering 68,949, is gradually being extended throughout the country.

DIPLOMATIC REPRESENTATIVES

OF COSTA RICA IN GREAT BRITAIN
(225 Cromwell Rd., London SW5)

Chargé d'Affaires: Carlos Alberto Guardia.

OF GREAT BRITAIN IN COSTA RICA
(3202 Paseo Colon, Apartado 10056, San José)

Ambassador and Consul-General: J. M. Brown.

OF COSTA RICA IN THE USA
(2112 S St., NW, Washington D.C., 20008)

Ambassador: José Rafael Echeverria.

OF THE USA IN COSTA RICA
(Avenida 3, Calle 1, San José)

Ambassador: Francis J. McNeil.

OF COSTA RICA TO THE UNITED NATIONS

Ambassador: Rodolfo Piza Escalante.

Books of Reference

Statistical Information: Official statistics are issued by the Director General de Estadística (Ministerio de Industria y Comercio, San José) as they become available. The compilation of statistics was started in 1861.

Bell, J. P., *Crisis in Costa Rica.* London and Austin, USA, 1971
Biesanz, J. and M., *Costa Rican Life.* 3rd printing. New York, 1946
Fernández Guardia, L., *Historia de Costa Rica.* 2nd ed., 2 vols. San José, 1941
Seligson, M. A., *Peasants of Costa Rica and the Development of Agrarian Capitalism.* Univ. of Wisconsin Press, 1980
Trejos, Juan, *Geografía ilustrada de Costa Rica.* San José, 1948

CUBA

Capital: Havana
Population: 9·73m. (1978)
GNP per capita: US$810 (1978)

República de Cuba

HISTORY. Cuba, except for the brief British occupancy in 1762–63, remained a Spanish possession from its discovery by Columbus in 1492 until 10 Dec. 1898, when the sovereignty was relinquished under the terms of the Treaty of Paris, which ended the struggle of the Cubans against Spanish rule. Cuba thus became an independent republic, but the United States stipulated under the 'Platt Amendment' (abrogated by Roosevelt in 1934) that Cuba must enter into no treaty relations with a foreign power, which might endanger its independence. A convention which assembled on 5 Nov. 1900 adopted the first constitution of the republic on 21 Feb. 1901.

The revolutionary movement against the Batista dictatorship, led by Dr Fidel Castro, started on 26 July 1953 (now a national holiday). It achieved power on 1 Jan. 1959 when Batista fled the country.

An invasion force of émigrés and adventurers landed in Cuba on 17 April 1961; the main body was defeated at the Bay of Pigs (Las Villas province) and mopped up by 20 April.

The US Navy blockaded Cuba from 22 Oct. to 22 Nov. 1962.

AREA AND POPULATION. The island of Cuba forms the largest and most westerly of the Greater Antilles group and lies 135 miles south of the tip of Florida, USA. It has an area of 44,206 sq. miles (114,524 sq. km); the Isle of Youth (formerly Isle of Pines) has 1,180 sq. miles, and other islands about 1,350 sq. miles. Estimated population in 1978 was 9·73m.

The area, population and density of population of the 14 provinces and their capitals were as follows (1970 census):

	Area sq. km	Population	Capital	Population
Pinar del Rió	10,860	548,000	Pinar del Rió	73,206
La Habana	5,671	525,000	Guira de Melena	19,851
Ciudad de La Habana	740	1,735,360	La Habana	1,735,360
Isla de la Juventud	2,199	30,000	—	—
Matanzas	11,669	495,000	Matanzas	85,376
Cienfuegos	4,149	296,000	Cienfuegos	85,248
Villa Clara	8,069	701,000	Santa Clara	131,504
Sancti Spíritus	6,737	366,000	Sancti Spíritus	57,703
Ciego de Avila	6,485	273,000	Ciego de Avila	60,910
Camagüey	14,134	540,000	Camagüey	196,854
Las Tunas	6,373	386,000	Victoria de las Tunas	53,739
Holguín	9,105	772,000	Holguín	131,508
Granma	8,452	650,000	Bayamo	71,660
Santiago de Cuba	6,343	793,000	Santiago de Cuba	275,970
Guantánamo	6,366	417,000	Guantánamo	130,061
Total	110,922 [1]	8,553,395		

[1] 42,827 sq. miles, includes outlying islands and cays not within any province.

CONSTITUTION AND GOVERNMENT. The constitution has been suspended since Jan. 1959. The first socialist Constitution came into force on 24 Feb. 1976.

Since the last representative in Cuba of the King of Spain, Gen. Don Adolfo Jiménez Castellanos, handed over the island on 1 Jan. 1899 the following have been at the head of the administration:

US Military Governors	Took office		Dr Carlos Manuel de Cés-	Took office
Maj.-Gen. John R. Brooke	1 Jan. 1899		pedes	12 Aug. 1933
Maj.-Gen. Leonard Wood	23 Dec. 1899			dep. 5 Sept. 1933
			Dr Ramón Grau San Martín	10 Sept. 1933
President of the Republic				res. 15 Jan. 1934
Tomas Estrada Palma	20 May 1902		Col. Carlos Mendieta	Jan. 1934
	res. 28 Sept. 1906			res. 12 Dec. 1935
			Dr José A. Barnet	12 Dec. 1935
			Dr Miguel Mariano Gómez y	
US Provisional Governors			Arias	20 May 1936
William Howard Taft	29 Sept. 1906			impeached 23 Dec. 1936
Charles Edward Magoon	13 Oct. 1906		Dr Federico Laredo Bru	24 Dec. 1936
			Gen. Fulgencio Batista y	
Presidents of the Republic			Zaldívar	10 Oct. 1940
Gen. José Miguel Gómez	28 Jan. 1909		Dr Ramón Grau San Martín	10 Oct. 1944
Gen. Mario García Menocal	20 May 1913		Dr Carlos Prío Socarrás	10 Oct. 1948
Dr Alfredo Zayas y Alfonso	20 May 1921			dep. 10 March 1952
Gen. Gerardo Machado y			Gen. Fulgencio Batista y	
Morales	20 May 1925		Zaldívar	10 March 1952
	dep. 12 Aug. 1933			abdicated 1 Jan. 1959

President: Dr Fidel Castro Ruz became President of the Council of State on 3 Dec. 1976. He is also President of the Council of Ministers and First Secretary of the Cuban Communist Party. From Jan. 1980 he took overall charge of Defence, Interior, Health and Culture.

Dr Castro on 2 Dec. 1961 proclaimed 'a Marxist–Leninist programme adapted to the precise objective conditions existing in our country'. The provisional *Organizaciones Revolucionarias Integradas* (ORI) were established as an intermediate stage towards a single (communist) party, and gave way to the *Partido Unido de la Revolución Socialista* (PURS). This brought together the *Partido Socialista Popular*, *Movimiento de 26 Julio* and (Students') *Directorio Revolucionario*. The PURS in turn became (3 Oct. 1965) the *Partido Comunista de Cuba*. The Communist Party had been outlawed by Batista in 1954, but legally reinstated after the revolution.

National flag: 3 blue, 2 white stripes (horizontal); a white 5-pointed star in a red triangle at the hoist.

National anthem: Al combate corred bayameses (words and tune by P. Figueredo, 1868).

Local Government. The country is divided into 14 provinces and 169 municipalities. Local Government is the responsibility of the organizations of Peoples' Power. Elections were held in 1976 and 1979 for delegates to the provincial municipal assemblies and to the national assembly.

DEFENCE. The chief of the armed forces is *Comandante en Jefe* Fidel Castro, and his brother *Gen. de Ejercito* Raúl Castro Ruz, First Vice-President of the Council of State and Minister of Defence.

On 13 Nov. 1963 conscription was introduced for all men between the ages of 17 and 45 (3 years); women of the 17–35 age groups may volunteer (for 2 years).

Army. The strength was 180,000 officers and men in 1980. Reserves are estimated at 90,000.

The Army is organized in 15 infantry brigades, 3 armoured brigades and 8 independent battalions. It has over 600 Russian-built tanks. Para-military forces total 18,000 and the People's Militia, 100,000.

Navy. The Navy consists of 2 *ex*-Soviet diesel-powered submarines, 26 missile boats, 14 patrol vessels, 18 torpedo boats, 10 fast gunboats, 3 inshore minesweepers, 12 motor launches, 14 coastguard vessels, 12 survey vessels, 7 landing craft and 10 service craft. The large majority of these 128 craft are former units of the Soviet Navy. Personnel in 1981 totalled 6,000 officers and ratings. Three old patrol frigates, 1 patrol escort (PCER), an ancient gunboat and 2 auxiliary coastguard cutters were operationally discarded in 1973 although one of the frigates still exists as a harbour hulk. The USA is still in possession of the Guantánamo naval base, but the Cuban Government refuses to accept the nominal rent of US$5,000 per annum.

Air Force. The Air Force has been extensively re-equipped with aircraft supplied by USSR and in 1980 had a strength of some 16,000 officers and men and 200 combat aircraft. About 8 interceptor and 3 ground-attack squadrons fly MiG-23, MiG-21, MiG-19 and MiG-17 jet fighters. There is a squadron of An-26 twin-turboprop transports, some An-24 twin-turboprop transports, and about 30 Mi-8 and Mi-4 helicopters, Zlin 326 piston-engined trainers and MiG-15UTI and MiG-23U jet trainers. Many An-2M biplanes are operated by the Air Force, mainly on agricultural duties. Soviet-built surface-to-air ('Guideline' and 'Goa') and coastal defence and liaison ('Samlet') missiles are in service.

INTERNATIONAL RELATIONS

Membership. Cuba is a member of the UN and COMECON.

ECONOMY

Planning. The Cuban economy is now centrally planned. Since July 1972 Cuba has been a member of the Council for Mutual Economic Assistance (COMECON) and, since Jan. 1974, of the two COMECON international banks. Cuba has very large reserves of nickel and a guaranteed market in the USSR; output is currently some 36,000 tons per annum but it is to be increased to 60,000 tons after 1980. Sugar remains the mainstay of the economy. Investment in this and other agricultural sectors (rice, coffee, and dairy products) has recently been relatively high but output generally has failed to respond. Some items of food and clothing are rationed.

Budget. Revenue in 1980 was 7,584·3m. pesos and expenditure, 7,580·8m. pesos.

Currency. The Cuban *peso* has been tied to the French franc since early 1972. In March 1981, the sterling–peso rate was £1 = 1·68 *pesos*. The gold content is 0·888671 gramme of fine gold, thus 1 troy oz. of fine gold = 35 *pesos*. The law of 7 Nov. 1914, established that the monetary unit was a gold *peso* (equal to the US gold dollar) of 1·6718 grammes (1·5046 grammes fine) divided into 100 *centavos*. The old gold *pesos* and all US currency are no longer legal tender.

Copper–nickel coins of 40, 20, 5 and 1 *cent* are issued. Notes are for 100, 50, 20, 10, 5 and 1 *peso*.

Banking. On 23 Dec. 1948 the president signed the law creating a central bank (with capital of US$10m.) and which began operating on 27 April 1950.

On 14 Oct. 1960 all banks were nationalized, except the Royal Bank of Canada and the Bank of Nova Scotia, which were bought out later. All banking is now carried out by the National Bank of Cuba, through its 250 agencies. In 1964, 1·6m. small savings accounts totalled US$738m.

All insurance business was nationalized in Jan. 1964.

Weights and Measures. The metric system of weights and measures is legally compulsory, but the American and old Spanish systems are much used. The sugar industry uses the Spanish long ton (1·03 tonnes) and short ton (0·92 tonne). Cuba sugar sack = 329·59 lb. or 149·49 kg. Land is measured in *caballerías* (of 13·4 hectares or 33 acres).

ENERGY AND NATURAL RESOURCES

Electricity. Installed capacity 1979 was 2,052 mw. Production in 1979 was 8,084m. kwh.

Minerals. Iron ore abounds, with deposits estimated at 3,500m. tons, of which 90% were held as reserves by American steel interests but are now controlled by the Cuban Mining Institute; output (tonnes), wrought iron (1971), 111,107; steel (1979), 327,792.

Output of copper (1979) was 2,840 tonnes; refractory chrome (1979), 28,200 tonnes. Other minerals are nickel (1979: 32,324 tons nickel content), cobalt, silica and barytes. Gold and silver are also worked. Cuba has a small output of petroleum (1978: 6·4m. tonnes). Salt output from the solar evaporation of sea water was 122,487 tonnes in 1979.

All mineral resources were nationalized in 1960.

Agriculture. In May 1959 all land over 30 *caballerias* was nationalized and has since been turned into state farms. In Oct. 1963 private holdings were reduced to a maximum of 5 *caballerias* (approximately 67 hectares). By 1960, 764 co-operative farms had been formed, and by late 1966 almost 65% of farm land was state-owned; the balance being in private hands.

In 1979 the total cultivated land included state-owned, 3,398,200 hectares, and in the private sector, 475,400 hectares.

The staple products are tobacco and sugar, of which latter Cuba is the world's second largest producer; with its by-products it furnishes nearly 80% by value of the national exports. The 1979–80 crop (estimate) was 6·6m. tonnes. There are 150 mills, including 40 of the largest, which were taken over from US interests, and which represent 39% of total capacity. Coffee, cotton, maize, rice and potatoes are grown.

Production of other important crops in 1979 was (in tonnes): Tobacco, 30,000; rice, 500,000; maize, 95,000; coffee, 27,000.

Tobacco is grown mainly in the Vuelta–Abajo district, near Pinar del Río. Coffee is grown chiefly in the province of Oriente.

Output of henequén fibre in 1964 was 233,919 tons. A fast-growing fibre, *kenaf*, originally from India, soft in texture, is replacing jute for sacking; the tobacco industry uses *majagua*, another local fibre, while a third fibre, *yarey*, from palms is also used. 200,000 tonnes of potatoes were produced in 1978. A nitrate plant has been built at Nuevitas and a large British-built urea plant at Cienfuegos. The principal fruits exported are pineapples, citrus fruit, tomatoes and pimentos. A rice cultivation plan began in 1967 in the south of Havana province. Cultivation is highly mechanized and the area so far sown produces two crops a year.

Despite the devastation caused by hurricane Flora in Oct. 1963, citrus fruit production, 112,000 tons in 1964, was some 11·4% above 1963. In 1978 production was 280,000 tonnes.

In 1962, 2,105 *caballerias* were allocated to cotton; cotton produced, 1964, was 2,653 tons against 13,000 tons in 1962.

In 1979 the livestock included 1·85m. pigs; 847,000 horses; 356,000 sheep; 99,000 goats; 5·84m. head of cattle.

Forestry. Cuba has extensive forest lands. These forests contain valuable cabinet woods, such as mahogany and cedar, besides dye-woods, fibres, gums, resins and oils. Cedar is used locally for cigar-boxes, and mahogany is exported. During the reforestation campaign of 1959–60, 34,000 eucalyptus saplings were planted over 1,120 *caballerias*. Cedars, mahogany, *majagua*, teca, etc., are also being raised and planted out. In 1979 saplings planted included: Eucalyptus, 2,315; pine, 31,540; majagua, 4,060; mahogany, 2,269; cedar, 2,105; casuarina (1978), 10,610.

INDUSTRY AND TRADE

Industry. Production in 1979 was: Textiles, 150,467 sq. metres; cement, 2,612,800 tonnes; wheat flour, 169,524 tonnes; gasoline, 872,030 tonnes; 301,944 tyres; 193,089 tubes; shoes, 13,759,000 pairs; paint, 47,273 hectolitres; soft drinks, 1,379·2m. hectolitres; cigarettes, 17,379m.; fertilizers, 1,745,566 tonnes; cigars, 295,156,000.

Trade Unions. All workers have a right to join a trade union. The Workers' Central Union of Cuba, to which 23 unions are affiliated, had 2m. members in 1978.

Commerce. Imports and exports (including bullion and specie) for calendar years (in US$1m.):

	1975	1976	1977	1978
Imports	3,883	4,066	4,188	4,687
Exports	3,677	3,573	3,537	4,346

Cuba's principal exports are sugar, minerals, tobacco and fish, which in 1974 were planned to furnish 86%, 6·4%, 2·7% and 2·3% respectively by value. The main imports from non-Communist countries are chemicals and engineering and electrical machinery and transport equipment.

Sugar accounts for approximately 80% of the exports. In 1973 over 2m. tons were sold in free world markets, the balance going mainly to Eastern Europe under long-term guaranteed price contracts. Tobacco, fish and nickel are the other major exports. Most trade is with Eastern Europe, particularly with the USSR which supplies approximately 50% of total Cuban imports.

Total trade between Cuba and UK (British Department of Trade returns, in £1,000 sterling):

	1975	1976	1977	1978	1979	1980
Imports to UK	6,318	25,602	9,732	7,960	14,970	26,208
Exports and re-exports from UK	36,977	42,925	27,455	27,625	36,112	35,272

COMMUNICATIONS

Roads. There are 31,204 km of highways open to traffic, including the Central Highway, traversing the island for 760 miles from Pinar del Río to Santiago. On 31 Dec. 1958 passenger automobiles numbered 143,828; hire cars, 29,710; coaches and buses, 4,306; lorries, 42,480; others, 12,987.

Railways. There were (1978) 5,325 km of public railway (mainly 1,435 mm gauge) owned by the National Railways (*Ferrocarriles Nacionales de Cuba*) formed on nationalization in 1960. In addition, the large sugar estates have 9,441 km of lines on 1,435, 914 and 760 mm gauges.

Aviation. The state airline CUBANA operates all internal services, and from Havana to Mexico City, Madrid, Berlin, Montreal, Prague, Tripoli and Baghdad, and also to Lima, Panama, Kingston, Bridgetown, Port of Spain, Georgetown. The other regular foreign services are Mexican, Spanish, Soviet, Czech, East German, Canadian and Angolan. In Dec. 1977 the first charter flights since 1960 started operating between USA and Cuba.

Shipping. The coastline is over 3,500 miles long and has many fine harbours. The merchant marine, in 1980, consisted of 66 sea-going vessels of over 825,000 DWT.

Post and Broadcasting. There are 3,545 miles of public and 8,902 miles of private telegraph wires. Cuba has 103 broadcasting stations and 2 television stations. Radio receiving sets, 1974, numbered 909,000; television sets, 300,000. The national telephone system (1978) had 321,054 instruments.

Cinemas (1972). There are 439 cinemas with seating capacity of 294,300.

Newspapers (1976). The government-controlled press includes 1 morning and 1 evening newspaper in Havana.

JUSTICE, RELIGION, EDUCATION AND WELFARE

Justice. There is a Supreme Court in Havana and 7 courts of appeal (1 in each provincial capital and 1 in Holguín). The provinces are divided into judicial districts, with courts for civil and criminal actions, with municipal courts for minor offences. The civil code guaranteed aliens the same property and personal rights as are enjoyed by nationals.

The 1959 Agrarian Reform Law and the Urban Reform Law passed on 14 Oct. 1960 have placed certain restrictions on both. Revolutionary Summary Tribunals will have wide powers.

Religion. There is no state Church, though Roman Catholics predominate. There is a bishop of the American Episcopal Church in Havana; there are large congregations of Methodists in Havana and in the provinces. Protestants numbered 265,000 in 1962; they have been organized as the Cuban Council of Evangelical Churches.

Education. Education is compulsory (between the ages of 6 and 14) and free, and now available everywhere. The 1953 census showed that 22·8% of all those over 10 years of age were illiterate. It is claimed that the Year of Education (1961), in which higher-education students went out to all parts of the country, reduced this to 3·9%. In 1964 illiteracy was officially declared to have been completely eliminated.

In 1977 the 4 universities had 122,546 students and 9,934 teaching staff. There were (1977) 1,846,075 pupils and 82,250 teachers at primary schools; 642,624 pupils and 49,586 teachers at secondary schools; 187,819 students and 11,503 teaching staff at technical and specialized schools; and 118,000 students and 4,200 staff at teachers' colleges.

The Camilo Cienfuegos school city in the Sierra Maestra was designed for 12,000 boys and 8,000 girls by 1970 (1965: 4,000, total). In 1974 the V. I. Lenin vocational school opened as a forerunner of 6 such schools.

There were (1978) about 40,000 students at the 4 universities.

Health (1964). There were 4,855 posts for doctors, 154 hospitals with 47,861 beds. The 1965 health budget was $140·5m.

Free medical services are provided by the state polyclinics, though some doctors still have private practices. All serious tropical diseases are effectively kept under control, and virtually all children under the age of 15 have been vaccinated against poliomyelitis.

DIPLOMATIC REPRESENTATIVES

OF CUBA IN GREAT BRITAIN (167 High Holborn, London, WC1)

Ambassador: Jorge A. Bolaños.

OF GREAT BRITAIN IN CUBA
(Edificio Bolivar, Capdevila 101–103, Havana)

Ambassador: David C. Thomas.

OF CUBA TO THE UNITED NATIONS

Ambassador: Dr Raúl Roa Kouri.

The USA broke off diplomatic relations with Cuba on 3 Jan. 1961 but the first steps towards normal relations were taken in Sept. 1977 when missions were opened in both capitals.

Books of Reference

Anuario Estadístico de a República de Cuba. Havana, 1914, 1953, 1957, 1972, 1973, 1979
Boletín Oficial, Ministerio de Comercio. Monthly
Estadística General: Commercio Exterior. Quarterly and Annual.—*Movimiento de Población.* Monthly and Annual. Havana
Anuario azucarero de Cuba. Havana, from 1937
Aguilar, L. E., *Cuba 1933.* Cornell Univ. Press, 1972
Canet, G., and Raisz, E., *Atlas de Cuba.* Cambridge, Mass., 1949
Carpentier, A., *Reasons of State.* London, 1976
Caute, D., *¿ Cuba, Yes?* London, 1974
Chaderick, L., *A Cuban Journey.* London, 1975
Domínguez, J. I., *Cuba: Order and Revolution.* Harvard Univ. Press, 1978
Draper, T., *Castro's Revolution: Myths and Realities.* New York, 1962.—*Castroism: Theory and Practice.* New York, 1965
Guerra y Sánchez, R., and others, *Historia de la Nación Cubana.* 10 vols. Havana, 1952
Gonzalez, E., *Cuba Under Castro: The Limits of Charisma.* Boston, 1974
International Commission of Jurists, *Cuba and the Rule of Law.* Geneva, 1962
Meyer, K. E., and Szulc, T., *The Cuban Invasion.* New York, 1962
Miller, W., *The Lost Plantation.* London, 1961
Montaner, C. A., *Informe secreto sobre la revolución cubana.* Madrid, 1975
Nelson, L., *Cuba: The Measure of the Revolution.* Univ. of Minnesota Press, 1972
Núñez Jiménez, A., *Geografía de Cuba.* Havana, 1961
O'Connor, J., *The Origins of Socialism in Cuba.* London, Cornell Univ. Press, 1970
Ritter, A. R. M., *The Economic Development of Revolutionary Cuba: Strategy and Performance.* New York, 1974
Suchlicki, J. (ed.), *Cuba, Castro, and Revolution.* Univ. of Miami Press, 1972.—*Cuba: From Columbus to Castro.* New York, 1974
Thomas, H., *Cuba: Or the Pursuit of Freedom.* London, 1971

CYPRUS

Capital: Nicosia
Population: 624,600 (1979)
GNP per capita: US$2,110 (1978)

Kypriaki Dimokratia—
Kıbrıs Cumhuriyeti

HISTORY. About the middle of the 2nd millennium B.C. Greek colonies were established in Cyprus and later it formed part of the Persian, Roman and Byzantine empires. In 1193 it became a Frankish kingdom, in 1489 a Venetian dependency and in 1571 was conquered by the Turks. They retained possession of it until its cession to England for administrative purposes under a convention concluded with the Sultan at Constantinople, 4 June 1878. On 5 Nov. 1914 the island was annexed by Great Britain and on 1 May 1925 given the status of a Crown Colony.

For the history of Cyprus from 1931 to 1958 *see* THE STATESMAN'S YEAR-BOOK, 1958, pp. 237–38, and 1959, p. 236.

On 1 April 1955 the Greek Cypriots embarked on a guerrilla struggle against the British. On 19 Feb. 1959, following discussions in Zürich between the Greek and Turkish Foreign Ministers, an agreement was signed in London by the Prime Ministers of Great Britain, Greece and Turkey, and by the representatives of the Greek Cypriots and Turkish Cypriots. This agreement was implemented on 16 Aug. 1960, when Cyprus became an independent republic. By treaties between the Republic of Cyprus, Great Britain, Greece and Turkey both Enosis and partition are precluded; and Britain retains sovereignty over the areas containing her military bases in the island.

When President Makarios proposed some incisive modifications of the Zürich–London agreements, violent clashes between Greek and Turkish Cypriots broke out on 22 Dec. 1963. First, a joint force of British, Greek and Turkish troops and later a UN peace force were sent to Cyprus. A UN mediator on 26 March 1965 submitted proposals for a settlement of the Cyprus problem. These were accepted by Greece and the Greek Cypriots, but rejected by Turkey; thereupon the mediator, Dr Galo Plaza (Ecuador), resigned. The UN General Assembly on 17 Dec. 1965 called upon all states to respect the sovereignty, unity, independence and territorial integrity of Cyprus and to refrain from any intervention.

In June 1968 representatives of the Greek and Turkish Cypriots started talks in Cyprus aimed at finding a solution to the Cyprus problem but without success.

On 15 July 1974 a *coup* was staged in Cyprus by the men of the Greek ruling junta, for the overthrow of President Makarios. The President left the island and the *coup* was short-lived. On 23 July power was handed over to the President of the House of Representatives, Glafcos Clerides, in accordance with the Constitution. He acted as President until the return of President Makarios on Dec. 7.

Turkey invaded the island on 20 July, eventually landing 40,000 troops supported with heavy armament and tanks. In two military operations 20–30 July and 14–16 Aug. the Turkish troops managed to occupy 40% of the northern part of Cyprus. As a result 200,000 Greek Cypriots fled to live as refugees in the south. The Cyprus crisis was raised in the UN and the General Assembly unanimously adopted resolutions calling for the withdrawal of all foreign troops from Cyprus and the return of refugees to their homes, but without result.

On 13 Feb. 1975 at a special joint meeting of the executive council and legislative assembly of the Autonomous Turkish Cypriot Administration a Turkish Cypriot Federated State was proclaimed. Rauf Denktash was appointed President and he declared that the state would not seek international recognition. The proclamation was denounced by President Makarios and the Greek Prime Minister but welcomed by the Turkish Prime Minister.

AREA AND POPULATION. The island lies in the eastern Mediterranean, about 50 miles off the south coast of Turkey and (at the nearest points) 65 miles off the coast of Syria. Area 3,572 sq. miles (9,251 sq. km); about 150 miles is greatest length from east to west, and about 60 miles is greatest breadth from north to south. Populations by religions:

Religion	1931	1946	1956	1960	1973
Greek Orthodox	276,573	361,199	416,986	441,656	498,511
Turkish Moslem	64,238	80,548	92,642	104,942	116,000
Others	7,148	8,367	19,251	26,968	17,267
Total	347,959	450,114	528,879	573,566	631,778

Population estimate (1979) 624,600, of which 82% are Greek Cypriot (Armenian, Maronite and Latin minorities included) and 18% Turkish Cypriot. Principal towns with populations (1978 estimate): Nicosia (the capital), 121,500 (Greek Cypriots); Limassol, 102,400; Famagusta, 39,400 (1975); Larnaca, 28,900.

As a result of the Turkish invasion and the occupation of part of Cyprus, 200,000 Greek Cypriots were displaced and forced to find refuge in the south of the island. The urban centres of Famagusta, Kyrenia and Morphou were completely evacuated.

Vital statistics. The birth rate per 1,000 population in 1978 was 19·3%; death rate, 8·4%; infantile mortality per 1,000 live births, 17·1%.

CONSTITUTION AND GOVERNMENT. The legislative power is exercised by the House of Representatives of 50 members, of whom 35 were elected by the Greek community and 15 by the Turkish community. As from Dec. 1963 the Turkish members have ceased to attend.

On 13 Dec. 1959 Archbishop Makarios was elected President of the Republic, having received 144,501 votes (against 71,753 cast for the candidate sponsored by the Left). Dr Fazil Kuchuk was elected Vice-President unopposed; he resigned on 4 Jan. 1964. On 13 Feb. 1975, Rauf Denktash the Turkish-Cypriot leader announced the formation of a Turkish-Cypriot state within a federal republic.

In the presidential elections of 25 Feb. 1968 Archbishop Makarios was re-elected President of the Republic, having received 220,911 votes (against 8,577 cast for the opposition candidate and 16,215 abstentions). When he died in Aug. 1977 Spyros Kyprianou became acting President and was proclaimed President on 31 Aug. 1977 and was elected for a 5-year term on 26 Jan. 1978.

Flag: White with a copper-coloured outline of the island with 2 green olive-branches beneath.

The elections held on 5 Sept. 1976 returned 19 Democratic Front, 9 Akel Party (Communists), 4 EDEK (Socialist Party), 3 Independent. The Turks have not participated in the proceedings of the House since Dec. 1963.

On 16 Feb. 1961 the House of Representatives decided by 41 to 9 votes to apply for membership of the Commonwealth. Cyprus was admitted on 13 March.

The President reshuffled the Council of Ministers in Sept. 1980:

Foreign Affairs: Nicos A. Rolandis. *Interior and Defence:* Christodoulos Veniamin. *Finance:* Afxentis Afxentiou. *Minister to the President:* Stelios Katsellis. *Commerce and Industry:* Constantinos Kittis. *Education:* Nicolaos Konomis. *Communications and Works:* George Hadjicostas. *Agriculture and Natural Resources:* Nicos Pattichis. *Labour and Social Insurance:* George Stavrinakis. *Health:* George Tombazos. *Justice:* Andreas Demetriades. *Deputy Minister of the Interior:* Petros Stylianou.

DEFENCE

Army. Total strength (1980) 9,000 organized into 21 battalions and 15 artillery and support units. There is also a para-military force of 3,000 armed police.

The Turkish-Cypriot Security Force consisted of about 4,500 men supported by some T-34 tanks.

INTERNATIONAL RELATIONS

Membership. Cyprus is a member of UN, the Commonwealth and the Council of Europe.

ECONOMY

Planning. Under the Emergency Action Plan of 1977–78 the Government invested about £C45m. in restoring and building up manufacturing, agriculture, housing, transport and communications. The resulting budget deficit was met mainly from external aid, foreign and domestic borrowing. Private sector investment at £C127m. met 130% of its required achievement. The Plan aimed at turning output towards foreign markets.

A third plan was launched in 1979 for 3 years; expenditure, 1979, £C34·8m. Agriculture and irrigation have been emphasized (expenditure, 1977–78, £C20·3m.; 1979 (planned) £C15·2m.).

Budget. Revenue and expenditure for calendar years (in £C):

Ordinary	1975	1976	1977	1978	1979
Revenue	56,026,900	76,957,000	87,012,000	102,388,322	123,577,963
Expenditure	67,745,048	69,727,000	81,145,000	92,670,326	117,997,560
Development					
Expenditure	11,894,869	18,433,000	19,866,000	24,299,017	32,229,929

Main sources of ordinary revenue in 1979 (in £C) were: Import duties, 26,629,309; excise duties, 28,551,856; income tax, 21,282,329; rents, royalties and interest, 6,591,894; sales of goods and services, 6,951,780; other duties and taxes, 12,354,923.

Main divisions of ordinary expenditure in 1979 (in £C): Personal emoluments, 49,398,000; pensions and gratuities, 4,147,000; commodity subsidies, 7m.; subventions and contributions, 12,029,000; public debt charges, 13,982,000; refunds and drawbacks, 4,097,000.

Development expenditure for 1979 (in £C) included 8,469,000 for water development, 4·61m. for agriculture, forests and fisheries, 1,204,000 for rural development, 4,949,659 for roads, 589,492 for airports and 598,379 for tourism. (An independent Ports Authority with its own funds was set up in 1977.)

The outstanding public debt as at 31 Dec. 1979 was £C79,566,487, excluding sinking fund reserves, and accumulated sinking funds totalled £C10,932,431. Outstanding loans as at 31 Dec. 1979 totalled £C39,915,574; including £C7,884,000 to the Electricity Authority of Cyprus and £C2,956,000 to the Cyprus Telecommunications Authority.

Currency. The *Cyprus £* is divided into 1,000 *mils*. Notes of the following denominations are in circulation: £10, £5, £1, 500 *mils*, 250 *mils*. Coins in circulation: Cupronickel: 100, 50, 25 *mils*; bronze: 5 *mils*. Rate of exchange, March 1981: £1 = £C0·865; US$1 = £C2·505.

Banking. There is a Central and Issuing Bank exercising monetary functions, and the Cyprus Development Corporation created by the Government as a major source of loan funds for industrial development. Commercial banks carrying on business in Cyprus are: Bank of Cyprus Ltd, Turkish Bank Ltd, Cyprus Popular Bank Ltd, Barclays Bank International, The Chartered Bank, National Bank of Greece, Hellenic Bank Ltd, Cyprus Turkish Co-operative Central Bank Ltd, Mortgage Bank of Cyprus Ltd, Turkiye Ish Bankasi, The Co-operative Central Bank, National & Grindlays Bank and Lombard Banking (Cyprus) Ltd.

The Central Bank of Cyprus, established in 1963, is responsible for the issue of currency, the regulation of money supply and credit, administration of the exchange control law and the foreign-exchange reserves of the republic. The Bank also acts as a banker of the banks operating in Cyprus and of the Government.

At the end of March 1979 total deposits in banks were £C348m. The country's foreign exchange reserves at the end of March 1979 were £C142·9m.

Weights and Measures. Cyprus weights and measures follow the standard weights and measures of Great Britain. The metric system may also be lawfully used. In internal trade the following special Cyprus weights and measures are in use: 1

pic = ⅔ yd; 1 *oke* = 2·8 lb.; 1 *kilé* = 8 Imperial gallons. The Cyprus *donum* is approximately ⅓ acre.

ENERGY AND NATURAL RESOURCES

Water resources. Since 1960, £C33m. has been spent on water dams, water supplies, hydrological research and geophysical surveys. Existing dams have (1977) a capacity of 14,234m. gallons as against 1,358m. gallons before independence.

Minerals. The principal minerals exported during 1979 were (in long tons): Iron pyrites, 141,000; cupreous concentrates, 121,000; asbestos, 38,000; chromium ores and concentrates, 10,500. Mining provided about 6% of all exports in 1979. Total value of minerals exported in 1979 was £C7·7m. No figures for copper cement at the Xeros mines as this is the Turkish occupied area.

Agriculture. Chief agricultural products in 1979 (tonnes): Grapes, 200,000; potatoes, 170,000; milk, 65,000; barley, 63,000; grapefruit, 46,000; oranges, 35,500; meat, 32,500; water melons, 25,000; carobs, 18,200; lemons, 16,400; wheat, 13,000; olives, 10,500; carrots, 8,700; melons, 4,500; wines including commandaria, 9·2m. gallons.

Of the island's 2·3m. acres, approximately 1m. are cultivated. About 21% of the economically active population are engaged in agriculture.

Livestock in 1979 (in 1,000): Cattle, 38; sheep, 495; goats, 459; pigs, 198.

Forestry. By the end of 1977 all timber had been salvaged from forests burnt during the Turkish invasion. By Dec. 1979 9,039 hectares of burnt forests were reforested and/or cultivated. Total forest area, 1,734 sq. km.

In 1979 the chief forest products were timber, valued at £C491,937; firewood, £C16,407, figures relate to the area of Cyprus not occupied by Turkey.

INDUSTRY AND TRADE

Industry. Cyprus has no heavy industry, but a wide variety of light manufacturing industries. The establishment of a Development Bank in 1963 has given further impetus to industrial activity. Manufacturing industry in 1978 contributed about 16·7% to the GDP and gave employment to 17·6% of the economically active population. The GDP of manufacturing industries in 1978 was estimated at £C70m.

The most rapidly growing areas of the manufacturing industry in 1978 were production of cigarettes, olive oils, clothing, footwear and construction materials. Exports of manufactured products rose by 7·2% to £69·9m. in 1978.

Trade Unions and Associations. Registration of trade unions and employers' associations is compulsory and freedom of association is constitutionally and statutorily guaranteed. At the end of 1976 the trade unions were distributed as follows: Pancyprian Federation of Labour ('old' trade unions), 46,080 members in 12 unions; Cyprus Workers Confederation ('free' labour syndicates), 32,775 members in 49 unions; Pancyprian Federation of Independent Trade Unions, 654 members in 7 unions; Cyprus Turkish Trade Unions Federation, 5,668 members in 13 unions (1973); Cyprus Democratic Labour Federation, 193 members in 4 unions; Civil Service Trade Union, 9,926 members.

The 'old' trade unions are affiliated to the World Federation of Trade Unions, the 'free' labour syndicates and the Turkish Federation are affiliated to the International Confederation of Free Trade Unions.

In Dec. 1976 the total number of employers' associations was 24 with a total membership of 3,071. Some of the employers' associations are members of the Cyprus Employers' Federation, an organization with 11 trade associations consisting of 320 members.

Commerce. The commerce and the shipping, exclusive of coasting trade, for calendar years were (in £C):

	1975	1976	1977	1978	1979
Imports [1]	159,192,811	248,868,170	362,868,184	375,972,000	357,602,505
Exports [2]	78,417,357	148,865,397	185,359,554	170,732,000	161,870,504
Bullion imports	957,769	1,252,578	1,685,000	2,490,000	...

[1] Excluding Naafi imports of about £1·5m. in 1977.
[2] Including re-exports and ships stores of about £29m. in 1977.

Chief civil imports, 1979 (in £C1,000):

Fuels and lubricants	44,452	Feeding stuff for animals	5,657
Textile yarn and fabrics made up	21,972	Beverages and tobacco	4,538
Iron and steel	16,583	Meat and meat preparations	4,138
Cereals and cereal preparations	13,081	Household electrical and non-	
Transport equipment	12,243	electrical equipment	4,046
Paper, paperboard and pulp and		Medicinal and pharmaceutical	
articles thereof	10,398	products	3,890
Raw materials for plastics	10,012	Fertilizers	3,754
Road vehicles	9,660	Dairy products and eggs	3,187

Chief domestic exports, 1979 (in £C1,000):

Grapes	4,272	Minerals, mainly asbestos	7,715
Grapefruit	3,554	Cigarettes	5,705
Lemons	2,213	Paper products	5,218
Oranges	2,993	Travel goods	2,747
Fruit and vegetables, preserved	2,280	Cement	10,291
Potatoes	13,624	Clothing	22,111
Wine	6,717	Footwear	8,342

In 1979 UK supplied 16·95% of the imports; other EEC countries, 30·3%; Arab countries, 8·29%; Eastern Europe, 7·29%; others, 37·17%. Of the exports (1978), 46·7% went to Middle East; 23·4% to the UK; 7·7% to other EEC countries; 5·8% to Eastern Europe and 16·4% to other countries.

Total trade between Cyprus and UK (British Department of Trade returns, in £1,000 sterling):

	1975	1976	1977	1978	1979	1980
Imports to UK	30,365	63,315	79,749	112,014	115,636	128,386
Exports and re-exports from UK	27,155	51,009	82,906	111,183	120,101	153,754

Tourism. Foreign tourists (1979), 297,000 and 60,968 excursionists.

COMMUNICATIONS

Roads. In 1979 the total length of roads was 10,012 km, of which 4,936 km were paved and 5,076 km were earth or gravel roads. The main roads which are maintained by the Ministry of Communications and Works (Public Works Department) totalled 2,657 km, of which 2,582 km were paved. The total of urban streets was 1,616 km, of which 1,118 were paved. Village roads and streets totalled 3,832 km, of which 1,236 km were paved, the rest being of earth or gravel surface. There were also 1,906 km of unpaved forest roads.

The area controlled by the Government of the Republic and that occupied by Turkey are now served by separate transport systems, and there are no services linking the two areas.

Aviation. Nicosia airport has been closed since Aug. 1974. During 1979, 838,339 persons travelled and 28,657,000 kg of commercial air-freight was handled through Larnaca airport.

Shipping. In 1979, 3,660 ships of 5·3m. net tons entered Cyprus ports. Ships under Cyprus registry (1979) numbered 1,200 of 2·5m. tons. Famagusta has been closed to international traffic since Aug. 1974.

Post and Broadcasting. In 1979 there were 52 post offices and 535 postal agencies. There are 17 post offices and 368 postal agencies in the Turkish occupied area. Telephones (1979) 104,268. Wireless licences issued (1978) were 222,470, including television licences.

Cyprus Broadcasting Corporation broadcasts mainly in Greek, but also in Turkish, English, and Armenian on medium-waves. The corporation also broadcasts one TV programme.

Cinemas (1976). In the Greek part of Cyprus there were 66 winter cinemas (38,500 seats) and 17 open-air cinemas (9,700 seats).

Newspapers (1980). There are 9 Greek, 3 Turkish and 1 English daily newspapers and 12 Greek, 6 Turkish and 1 English weeklies.

JUSTICE, RELIGION, EDUCATION AND WELFARE

Justice. Under the Constitution and other legislation in force the following judicial institutions are established: The Supreme Court of the Republic, the Assize Courts and District Courts.

The Supreme Court is composed of 5–7 judges (at present 7), one of whom is the President. The Supreme Court adjudicates exclusively and finally: on all constitutional and administrative law matters, including any recourse that any law or decision of the House of Representatives or the budget is discriminatory against either of the two Communities; on any conflict of competence between state organs, questions of unconstitutionality of any law or decisions on any question of interpretation of the Constitution in case of ambiguity, as well as recourses for annulment of administrative acts, decisions or omissions. The Supreme Court is the highest appellate court in the republic and has jurisdiction to hear and determine all appeals from any court. It has exclusive jurisdiction to issue orders in the nature of *habeas corpus*, *mandamus*, prohibition, *quo warranto* and *certiorari* and in admiralty and matrimonial matters.

There are 6 assize courts and 6 district courts, 1 for each district. The assize courts have unlimited criminal jurisdiction and power to order compensation up to £C800. The district courts exercise original civil and criminal jurisdiction, the extent of which varies with the composition of the Bench. In civil matters (other than those within the original jurisdiction of Supreme Court) a District Court composed of not less than 2 and not more than 3 judges has unlimited jurisdiction. A President or a Senior District Judge sitting alone has jurisdiction up to £C3,000, and a District Judge sitting alone up to £C1,000, and is also empowered to deal with any action for the recovery of possession of any immovable property, and certain other specified matters. In criminal matters the jurisdiction of a District Court is exercised by its members sitting singly and is of a summary character. A President, a Senior District Judge or a District Judge sitting alone has power to try any offence punishable with imprisonment up to 3 years, or with a fine up to £C500 or with both, and may order compensation up to £C500.

Religion. *See* Area and Population, p. 381.

Education. Until 31 March 1965 each community in Cyprus managed its own schooling through its respective Communal Chamber. Intercommunal education had been placed under the Minister of the Interior, assisted by a Board of Education for Intercommunal Schools, of which the Minister was the Chairman. In 1965 the Greek Communal Chamber was dissolved and a Ministry of Education was established to take its place. Intercommunal education has been placed under this Ministry.

Greek-Cypriot Education. Elementary education is compulsory and is provided free in 6 grades to children between 6 and 13 years of age. In some towns and large villages there are separate junior schools consisting of the first three grades. Apart from schools for the deaf and blind and the Lambousa School for juvenile offenders, there are also 7 schools for handicapped children. The Ministry runs 88 kindergartens for children from low-income families; most pre-primary education is privately run. There were 439 primary schools (including privately run institutions) with 54,309 pupils and 2,260 teachers in 1978–79.

Secondary education is free for the first 3 years and is fee-paying for the rest, although senior pupils can be wholly or partially exempt from payment. The secondary school is 6 years, 3 years at the gymnasium followed by 3 years at the lykeion. There were 3 types of lykeia: classical, science, economic. There are 5- to 6-year technical schools. In 1978–79 there were 91 secondary schools with 2,770 teachers and 48,886 pupils.

Post-secondary education is provided at the Pedagogical Academy, which organizes 3-year courses for the training of pre-primary and primary school teachers, and at the Higher Technical Institute, which provides 3-year courses for technicians in civil, electrical and mechanical engineering. There is also a 2-year Forestry College (administered by the Ministry of Agriculture), a Hotel and Catering Institute and a 3-year Nurses' School and 1-year School for Health Inspectors (Ministry of

Health). Adult education is conducted through youth centres in rural areas, foreign language institutes in the towns and private institutions offering courses in business administration and secretarial work.

In 1976–77, 12,275 students were studying in universities abroad, mainly in Greece and the UK.

Turkish-Cypriot Education. The Office of Education of the Turkish Community of Cyprus caters for some 18% of the island's population and (1976) administered 10 kindergartens, 167 elementary schools (16,014 pupils), 18 secondary schools (7,190 pupils), 6 technical schools (735 pupils) and 1 teacher-training college (13 students). There were 43 evening institutes for adult education.

Greek is the language of 80% of the population and Turkish of 18%. English is widely spoken. English and French are compulsory subjects in secondary schools. Illiteracy is largely confined to older people.

Social Security. The administration of the social-security services in Cyprus is in the hands of the Ministry of Labour and Social Insurance, with the Ministry of Health providing medical services through public clinics and hospitals on a means test, except medical treatment for employment accidents, which is given free to all insured employees and financed by the Social Insurance Scheme.

Social Insurance. The island's Social Insurance Scheme, which covers compulsorily both employees and self-employed persons, provides, in the case of employees, cash benefits for sickness, unemployment, maternity, marriage (females only), old-age, widowhood and death and cash benefits with free medical treatment for employment accidents and occupational diseases as well as for invalidity cases.

Annual Holiday Scheme. An Annual Holidays with Pay Law, introduced in 1967, provides for a minimum of 9 days paid leave to all workers in the island. The law is implemented by means of regular contributions by employers into a fund administered by Government. Employers offering more than 9 days' paid leave by collective agreement or otherwise may be exempted from paying contributions into the fund.

Termination of Employment Scheme. A Termination of Employment Law also enacted in 1967 provides for the establishment of a Redundancy Fund to which all employers contribute 0·5% of their pay-roll. The law provides for a minimum period of notice to employees, from 1 to 4 weeks according to length of service; for compensation on arbitrary dismissal; for redundancy payments.

DIPLOMATIC REPRESENTATIVES

OF CYPRUS IN GREAT BRITAIN (93 Park St., London, W1Y 4ET)
High Commissioner: Tasos Panayides.

OF GREAT BRITAIN IN CYPRUS (Alexander Pallis St., Nicosia)
High Commissioner: P. A. Rhodes, CMG.

OF CYPRUS IN THE USA (2211 R. St., NW, Washington, D.C., 20008)
Ambassador: Andreas Iakovides.

OF THE USA IN CYPRUS (Therissos St., Nicosia)
Ambassador: Galen L. Stone.

OF CYPRUS TO THE UNITED NATIONS
Ambassador: Andreas Mavrommatis.

Books of Reference

Statistical Information: Statistics and Research Department, Nicosia.

Alastos, D., *Cyprus in History.* London, 1955.—*Cyprus Guerilla.* London, 1960

Bitsios, D. S., *Cyprus: The Vulnerable Republic.* Thessaloniki, 1975

Christodoulou, D., *The Evolution of the Rural Land use Pattern in Cyprus.* Bude, 1960

Crawshaw, N., *The Cyprus Revolt: An Account of the Struggle for Union with Greece.* London, 1978

Crouzet, F., *Le Conflit de Chypre 1946–1959.* Brussels, 1973

Emilianides, A., *Histoire de Chypre.* Paris, 1962.—*The Zurich and London Agreements and the Cyprus Republic.* Athens, 1962

Hill, Sir George F., *A History of Cyprus.* 4 vols. Cambridge, 1940–52

Kosut, H., *Cyprus 1946–68.* New York, 1970

Luke, Sir Harry, *Cyprus.* Rev. ed. London, 1965

Markides, K. C., *The Rise and Fall of the Cyprus Republic.* Yale Univ Press, 1977

Polyviou, P. G., *Cyprus: The Tragedy and the Challenge.* London, 1975.—*Cyprus in Search of a Constitution.* Nicosia, 1976.—*Cyprus: Conflict and Negotiation, 1960–1980.* London, 1980

Salih, H. I., *Cyprus: The Impact of Diverse Nationalism on a State.* Univ. of Alabama Press, 1979

Stavrinides, Z., *The Cyprus Conflict.* Nicosia, 1976

Vanezis, P. N., *Makarios: Faith and Power.* New York, 1972

CZECHOSLOVAKIA

Československá
Socialistická Republika

Capital: Prague
Population: 15·18m. (1979)
GNP per capita: US$4,720 (1978)

HISTORY. The Czechoslovak State came into existence on 28 Oct. 1918, when the Czech *Národní Výbor* (National Committee) took over the government of the Czech lands upon the dissolution of Austria–Hungary. Two days later the Slovak National Council manifested its desire to unite politically with the Czechs. On 14 Nov. 1918 the first Czechoslovak National Assembly declared the Czechoslovak State to be a republic with T. G. Masaryk as President (1918–35).

The Treaty of St Germain-en-Laye (1919) recognized the Czechoslovak Republic, consisting of the Czech lands (Bohemia, Moravia, part of Silesia) and Slovakia. To these lands were added as a trust the autonomous province of Subcarpathian Ruthenia.

This territory was broken up for the benefit of Germany, Poland and Hungary by the Munich agreement (29 Sept. 1938) between UK, France, Germany and Italy.

In March 1939 the German-sponsored Slovak government proclaimed Slovakia independent, and Germany incorporated the Czech lands into the Reich as the 'Protectorate of Bohemia and Moravia'. A government-in-exile, headed by Dr Beneš, was set up in London in July 1940.

Liberation by the Soviet Army and US Forces was completed by May 1945.

Territories taken by Germans, Poles and Hungarians were restored to Czechoslovak sovereignty. Subcarpathian Ruthenia was transferred to the USSR.

Elections were held in May 1946, at which the Communist Party obtained about 38% of the votes.

A coalition government under a Communist Prime Minister, Klement Gottwald, remained in power until 20 Feb. 1948, when 12 of the non-Communist ministers resigned in protest against infiltration of Communists into the police.

In Feb. a predominantly Communist government was formed by Gottwald. In May elections resulted in an 89% majority for the government and President Beneš resigned.

In the first months of 1968 mounting pressure for liberalization culminated in the overthrow of the Stalinist President and Party Secretary, Antonín Novotný, and his associates. Under a new leadership the Communist Party introduced in April 1968 an 'Action Programme' of far-reaching political and economic reforms.

Soviet pressure to abandon this programme was exerted between May and Aug. 1968, and finally, Warsaw Pact forces occupied Czechoslovakia on 21 Aug. The enforced Moscow agreement of 26 Aug. bound the Czechoslovak government to a policy of 'normalization' (*i.e.*, abandonment of most reforms) and to the stationing of Soviet forces on Czechoslovak soil. This situation was confirmed by the Czechoslovak–Soviet 'Status of Forces Agreement' of 16 Oct. In 1969–1970 Soviet pressure led to extensive changes in the Party and Government. In Oct. 1969 Czechoslovakia repudiated its condemnation of the Warsaw Pact invasion.

A Czechoslovak–Soviet 20-year Treaty of Friendship, Co-operation and Mutual Assistance was signed in May 1970. Since 1977 a dissident civil rights movement 'Charter 77' has been active despite official efforts to suppress it.

On 11 Dec. 1973 the German Federal Republic and Czechoslovakia signed a treaty normalizing relations and annulling the Munich agreement of 1938. This was ratified by both countries' parliaments in July 1974.

AREA AND POPULATION. At the census of 1 Dec. 1970 the population was 14,344,987 (4,537,290 in Slovakia; 7·4m. females; 62% urban). Population in

1979 was 15,184,323 (4,914,554 in Slovakia; 7·8m. females). There are 12 administrative regions, one of which is the capital, Prague (Praha) and one the capital of Slovakia, Bratislava.

Region	Chief city	Area in sq. km	Population 1978
Czech			
Prague	—	496	1,185,958
Středočeský	Prague (Praha)	11,004	1,142,327
Jihočeský	České Budějovice	11,347	682,578
Západočeský	Plzeň (Pilsen)	10,872	885,718
Severočeský	Ústí nad Labem	7,808	1,160,510
Východočeský	Hradec Králové	11,241	1,243,787
Jihomoravský	Brno	15,028	2,024,038
Severomoravský	Ostrava	11,067	1,921,776
Slovak			
Bratislava	—	368	362,914
Západoslovenský	Bratislava	14,491	1,665,125
Středoslovenský	Banská Bystrica	17,976	1,499,664
Východoslovenský	Košice	16,179	1,363,793

The area of Czechoslovakia is 127,877 sq. km (49,365 sq. miles) (Slovakia, 49,014 sq. km). Population density in 1978: 119 per sq. km. Growth rate in 1978, 6·9 per 1,000. Expectation of life in 1973 was 66·3 (males); 73·3 (females).

Ethnic minorities have equal political and cultural rights. In 1978 there were (in 1,000): Czechs, 9,703; Slovaks, 4,615; Hungarians, 604; Poles, 79; Germans, 75; Ukrainians and Russians, 61. There were 250,000 gipsies in 1980.

The official languages are Czech and Slovak.

The population of the principal towns in 1979 was as follows (in 1,000):

Prague (Praha)	1,189	Hradec Králové	92	Prešov	67
Brno	369	Pardubice	92	Kladno	65
Bratislava	368	České Budějovice	88	Žilina	65
Ostrava	322	Liberec	84	Banská Bystrica	62
Košice	196	Gottwaldov	82	Karlovy Vary	62
Plzeň	167	Karviná	81	Most	61
Olomouc	101	Ústi nad Labem	79	Trnava	60
Havířov	94	Nitra	71	Opava	58

Vital statistics for calendar years:

	Live births	Marriages	Divorces	Deaths
1975	289,342	141,045	32,308	169,566
1976	287,134	138,876	31,561	170,336
1977	281,722	137,488	31,163	173,006
1978	278,250	134,509	33,222	174,416

CONSTITUTION AND GOVERNMENT. For details of previous constitutions, see THE STATESMAN'S YEAR-BOOK, 1968–69, pp. 927–28.

Since 1 Jan. 1969 Czechoslovakia has been a federal socialist republic consisting of two nations of equal rights: the Czech Socialist Republic (the Czech lands, previously Bohemia, Moravia and part of Silesia), and the Slovak Socialist Republic (Slovakia). Each Republic is governed by a National Council (the Czech with 200 deputies, the Slovak with 150), which delegates to an overall Federal Assembly responsibility for constitutional and foreign affairs, defence and important economic decisions. The Federal Assembly consists of the Chamber of Nations, which has 75 Czech and 75 Slovak delegates elected by their respective National Councils, and the Chamber of the People, which has 200 deputies elected by national suffrage.

The previous constitution (1960) remains in force where not specifically superseded, but since 1971 deputies are elected for a 5-year term so as to coincide with Communist Party congresses. Minimum age of voters is 18, of deputies, 21 years. At the elections of 22–23 Oct. 1976 a single list of National Front candidates was presented. Turnout was 10,617,152 from an electorate of 10,649,621 (99·7%). 99·97% of the votes were cast for the official candidates.

President of the Republic: Gustáv Husák (born 1913), *President of the Federal Assembly:* Alois Indra.

The *de facto* primary source of power is the Communist Party of Czechoslovakia, of which the Communist Party of Slovakia (*First Secretary:* Josef Lenárt) is a constituent part. Communists head the National Front, which incorporates the remaining political parties (Czechoslovak Socialist Party, People's Party) and the trade unions and youth organizations. The Communist Party had 1·5m. members in 1979 (45% workers, 27% women). In March 1981 the Presidium consisted of Gustáv Husák (*General Secretary*); Vasil Bil'ak; Peter Colotka (*Deputy Prime Minister*); Václav Hůla (*Deputy Prime Minister and Chairman, State Planning Committee*); Alois Indra; Antonín Kapek; Josef Kempný; Josef Korčák (*Deputy Prime Minister*); Josef Lenárt; Karel Hoffman (*Chairman, Central Council of Trade Unions*); Lubomír Štrougal (*Prime Minister*).

In March 1981 members of the government not mentioned above included: (*Deputy Prime Ministers*) Karol Laco; Matej Lúčan; Rudolf Rohlíček; Josef Šimon; Jindřich Zahradník; (other ministers) Andrej Barčák (*Foreign Trade*); Martin Dzúr (*Defence*); František Ondřich (*Chairman, Czechoslovak Control Committee*); Bohuslav Chňoupek (*Foreign*); Leopold Lér (*Finance*); Michal Štancel' (*Labour*); Jaromír Obzina (*Interior*); Vlastimir Ehrenberger (*Minister of Fuel and Power*).

The Czech Prime Minister is Josef Korcák; the Slovak, Peter Colotka.

Local government is carried on by National Committees consisting of deputies elected for 5-year terms. There are 10 regional Committees, 2 City Committees with the same status for Prague and Bratislava, 108 district Committees and 7,979 town and community Committees. Elections were due in 1981.

National flag: White and red (horizontal), with a blue triangle of full depth at the hoist, point to the fly.

National anthem: Kde domov můj (words by J. K. Tyl; tune by F. J. Škroup, 1834); combined with, Nad Tatru sa blyska (words by J. Matuška, 1844).

DEFENCE. Defence is the responsibility of the Defence Council set up in Feb. 1969 and headed by the First Secretary of the Party. Army service lasts 2 years. There are 2 military districts. The security forces and frontier guards are organized in regiments and brigades repectively; total strength, 36,000.

The Warsaw Pact invasion of Aug. 1968 brought an estimated 500,000 occupation troops into the country. By early 1970 this number had been reduced to 80,000 Soviet troops, the presence of which is legalized by the Czech–Soviet 'Status of Forces' Agreement of Oct. 1968.

In Feb. 1969 the government announced an increase in defence capacity, and Czechoslovakia resumed participation in Warsaw Pact meetings.

Army. The Army is organized in 10 divisions (5 tank and 5 motorized divisions). The regular army had, in 1980, a total strength of about 140,000 men and 3,400 tanks, mainly T-55s, with some T-54s.

Air Force. The Air Force is organized as a tactical force, under overall army command, and has a strength of some 54,000 personnel and 500 combat aircraft. Service lasts 3 years. Six interceptor regiments (each 3 squadrons of 14 aircraft) are equipped with MiG-21 jets, and there are 4 regiments of Su-7, Su-20, MiG-23 and MiG-21 ground attack aircraft, as well as Mi-24 gunship helicopters. MiG-21s and adapted L-29 Delfin jet trainers are used for tactical reconnaissance. Transport units have An-24/26, Il-14 and Il-18 aircraft and Mil Mi-2 (armed), Mi-4 and Mi-8 helicopters. Training units are equipped with 2-seat MiG-21s and Czech-built aircraft, including L-29 Delfin and L-39 Albatros jet advanced trainers, totalling 300 in all. Surface-to-air ('Guideline', 'Goa', 'Gane' and 'Gainful') missile units are operational.

INTERNATIONAL RELATIONS

Membership. Czechoslovakia is a member of UN, COMECON and the Warsaw Pact.

ECONOMY

Planning. For the first five 5-year plans *see* THE STATESMAN'S YEAR-BOOK, 1978–79, p. 385. Economic reforms of the period 1965–68 were abandoned after the Soviet intervention of 1968, and the economy reverted to the traditional communist centrally planned type. In 1978 and 1980 some rationalizations in the planning system, economic levers (profits, prices, wages) and organization of labour were applied.

The sixth 5-year plan for 1976–80 envisaged an increase of 32–34% in industrial, and of 14–15% in agricultural, production but these aims were not met. The 7th 5-year plan has reduced targets and covers 1981–5.

Budget. Budgets for calendar years (in Kčs. 1m.):

	1972	1973	1974	1975	1976	1977	1978
Revenue	223,503	242,258	263,755	278,113	292,165	280,786	286,267
Expenditure	216,569	237,200	259,185	273,774	290,071	278,301	283,912

Main items of the 1978 budget were (in Kčs. 1,000m.): Revenue: from the economy, 236; direct taxes, 37. Expenditure: national economy, 127; culture, health and social services, 130; defence, 21; administration, 6.

Currency. The monetary unit in the Czechoslovak Republic is the *koruna* (Kčs.) or crown of 100 *haler*. Notes in circulation: Kčs. 10, 20, 50, 100, 500. Coin: 5, 10, 20, 50 *halers*, and Kčs. 1, 2, 5. The *koruna* is based on a gold content of 0·123426 gramme of pure gold and pegged on the rouble at Kčs. 1·80 = R.1. The International Monetary Fund did not approve this change of the par value, and Czechoslovak membership was terminated in 1954, and ceased to be a member of the International Bank. The official rates of exchange are £1 = Kčs. 9·80; US$1 = Kčs. 5·64; 1 Soviet rouble = Kčs. 8. Tourist rate: £1 = Kčs. 17·06.

It was announced in 1974 that the USA was to return gold seized by Germany (18·4 tonnes), and Czechoslovakia was to pay compensation for nationalized US property. However the Czechoslovak Federal Assembly refused to ratify this agreement. US moves in 1980 to sell the gold to obtain compensation for nationalized property were protested by the Czechoslovak government.

Banking. For previous banking history *see* THE STATESMAN'S YEAR-BOOK, 1971–72, pp. 858–59. The central bank and bank of issue is the State Bank (Statní Banka), which controls foreign exchange reserves, and is a savings bank and a commercial credit bank to enterprises, except foreign trade enterprises. These are financed by the Commercial Bank (Obchodní Banka) which carries out all foreign trade transactions. The Trade Bank (Živnostenská Banka) provides banking services for private foreign clients, and maintains branches abroad. There is also an Investment Bank (Investiční Banka), one of whose functions is to manage foreign securities. 'Foreign exchange points' (*e.g.*, hotels) have partial foreign exchange authorization.

Weights and Measures. The metric system is in force.

ENERGY AND NATURAL RESOURCES

Oil. There is an oil pipeline from the USSR with branches to Bratislava and Zaluzi and a natural gas pipeline which supplies the German Federal and Democratic Republics, Austria and Italy as well as Czechoslovakia. A second is under construction. Petrol prices were raised 50% in 1979.

Minerals. Czechoslovakia is not rich in minerals. There are hard and soft coal reserves (chief coalfields: Most, Chomutov, Kladno, Ostrava and Sokolov). There is also uranium, glass sand and salt, and small quantities of iron ore, graphite, copper and lead. Production in 1978 (in tonnes): Coal, 28m.; lignite and brown coal, 92m.

Agriculture. In 1978 there were 7m. hectares of agricultural land (4·9m. hectares arable, 0·9m. meadow, 0·8m. pasture).

Agricultural landholding units in 1978: Various state institutions with 2,124,000 hectares (including 180 state farms with 1,387,000 hectares); 1,779 collective farms (4,317,000 hectares); 960,982 collective farmers with private plots (maximum size 1 hectare) (125,000 hectares); individual farms (303,000 hectares). Crop production in 1978 (in 1,000 tonnes): Sugar-beet, 7,282; wheat, 5,601; potatoes, 3,995; barley, 3,642; maize, 619; rye, 630.

Livestock. In 1978 the number of livestock was: Cattle, 4·89m. (including 1·9m. milch cows); horses, 49,000; pigs, 7·6m.; sheep, 865,000; poultry, 46·9m. In 1978 production of meat was 1,633,079 tonnes (live weight); milk, 5,472m. litres; 4,690m. eggs. In 1979 there were 139,744 tractors.

Forestry. Czechoslovakia is a richly wooded country, and the timber industry is important. Forest area in 1979 was 4,525,391 hectares (50% spruce, 16% beech and pine, 7% oak). The area reafforested in 1978 was 65,812 hectares. The timber yield was 18·6m. cu. metres in 1978.

INDUSTRY AND TRADE

Industry. Industrialization is well developed and antedates the Communist régime. All industry is nationalized.

Output in 1978 (in 1,000 tonnes): Pig-iron, 9,944; crude steel, 15,294; coke, 10,785; rolled-steel products, 10,788; cement, 10,204; paper, 864; sulphuric acid, 1,195; nitrogenous fertilizers, 625; phosphate fertilizers, 367; plastics, 810; synthetic fibres, 163; sugar, 907; beer, 22·1m. hectolitres; cars, 175,585 (no.).

Textile production (in 1m. metres) in 1978: Cotton, 544; linen, 80; woollen, 49; shoes, 129m. pairs (61·3m. leather).

Production of electricity in 1978: 69,097m. kwh.

Labour. There were 8,641,670 persons of employable age in 1978 (i.e., males, 15–59; females 15–54), of whom 7,142,579 were employed (3·2m. women), 5·6m. in production (industry, 2·7m.; agriculture, 961,827; building, 635,017; commerce, 641,792; and 1·6m. in services.

A 5-day 42-hour week with 4 weeks annual holiday is standard. Average monthly wage in 1979: Kčs. 2,580. In 1979 the trade union movement had 6·5m. members.

Commerce. Total trade (in Kčs. 1m.) for calendar years:

	1973	1974	1975	1976	1977	1978
Imports	35,805	43,974	50,716	55,996	63,213	68,074
Exports	33,322	41,213	46,651	52,137	58,246	63,609

In 1978, trade with Communist countries amounted to 95,749m. Kčs. In 1978 Czechoslovakia imported from the USSR goods valued at Kčs. 23,844m. and exported to the USSR goods valued at Kčs. 22,018m.; followed by the German Democratic Republic (imports, 8,109m.; exports, 7,544m.) and Poland (imports, 5,720m.; exports, 5,713m.). UK is Czechoslovakia's third biggest non-Communist trade partner after the Federal German Republic and Austria. Czechoslovakia's indebtedness to the West was estimated at US$1,945,000 in 1978.

Major exports in 1978 (percentage of total): Machinery, 52·9; industrial consumer goods, 16·9; raw materials and fuel, 15·4. Imports: Machinery, 40·2; raw materials and fuel, 29·8. Oil imports in 1978, 18·6m. tonnes, 95% from USSR.

There are 11 foreign trade agencies (independent legal entities with their own capital run by state-appointed managers). Western firms are permitted to set up their own offices on Czechoslovak soil. Enterprises must obtain agreement from the Ministry of Foreign Trade before trading with foreign firms. The 5-year plans envisage a certain degree of integration with the economies of other Comecon countries.

In 1972 an Anglo-Czech Agreement on Co-operation was signed. Under this an Anglo-Czech Joint Commission was established to further the development of trade and industrial and scientific co-operation.

UK–Czechoslovak trade has been conducted since 1 Jan. 1975 on the basis of autonomous EEC measures.

Total trade between Czechoslovakia and UK for calendar years (British Department of Trade returns, in £1,000 sterling):

	1975	1976	1977	1978	1979	1980
Imports to UK	59,231	70,286	86,179	85,439	96,577	87,812
Exports and re-exports from UK	51,211	60,080	65,183	73,167	73,801	81,026

Tourism. In 1978, 14,437,893 tourists visited Czechoslovakia (611,902 from the West) and 10,174,480 Czechoslovak tourists made visits abroad (177,604 to the West).

COMMUNICATIONS

Roads. In 1978 there were 73,820 km of motorways and first-class roads and 1,982,186 passenger cars. In 1978 state road transport carried 1,959m. passengers and 327m. tonnes of freight.

Railways. In 1980 the length of railway track was 13,241 km. Of this, 2,839 km was double-tracked and 2,901 km electrified. In 1978, 423m. passengers and 278m. tonnes of freight were carried.

Aviation. Air transport is run by ČSA (Czechoslovak Airlines). The main airports are: Prague (Ruzyně), Brno (Cernovice), Bratislava (Vajnory), Olomouc (Holice), Košice (Barca). In 1978, 1·9m. passengers and 26,047 tonnes of freight were flown. There are direct flights from Prague to some 50 cities, including most European capitals, Havana, Jakarta, Conakry, New York and Montreal. British Airways operates air traffic London–Prague, Air France Paris–Prague–Bucharest.

Shipping. In 1980 Czechoslovak Maritime Shipping (*Československá námořní plavba*) (founded 1959) had 17 freighters totalling 236,135 DWT, based on Szczecin. In 1978, 1,480m. tonnes of cargo were carried. River freight transport within Czechoslovakia totalled 7·88m. tonnes. There are fleets on the Danube and Elbe.

Czechoslovak Danube Shipping (*Československá plavba dunajská*) operate 5 ships in the Mediterranean from the port of Bratislava.

Post and Broadcasting. Number of telephones in service in 1978 was 2,981,187. *Československý Rozhlas*, the governmental broadcasting station, broadcasts on 2 networks; 1 from Prague with 3 programmes in Czech and Slovak and 1 from Bratislava with 2 programmes in Slovak and additional broadcasts in Hungarian and Ukrainian. *Československá Televise* broadcast 2 television programmes nationwide, including colour broadcasts. In 1979, 3·8m. people held wireless and 4·1m. TV licences.

Cinemas and Theatres (1979). There were 3,180 cinemas and 63 theatres. 47 full-length films were made in 1979.

Newspapers (1978). There were 30 daily newspapers, including 12 in Slovak. The party daily *Rudé Právo* ('Red Justice') has a circulation of about 1m.

JUSTICE, RELIGION, EDUCATION AND WELFARE

Justice. The criminal and criminal procedure codes date from 1 Jan. 1962. Amendments of April 1973 raised the maximum penalty for 'capital' (mainly political) offences from 15 to 25 years and tightened measures for dealing with prisoners and released prisoners. The death penalty is retained for exceptionally serious crimes.

Police powers were strengthened in July 1974.

There is a Federal Supreme Court and federal military courts, with judges elected by the Federal Assembly. Both republics have Supreme Courts and a network of regional and district courts whose professional judges are elected by the republican National Councils. Lay judges are elected by regional or district local authorities. Local authorities and social organizations may participate in the decision-making of the courts.

Religion. Churches are under the control of the state Secretariat for Church Affairs, and clergymen's salaries are paid by the state. In 1977 there were 18 different faiths with 4,860 clergy and 8,228 churches. The largest single church is the Roman Catholic (11m. members, 1973): its main support is in Slovakia. Cardinal František Tomašek was installed as archbishop of Prague in 1978. The archbishopric of Olomouc was vacant in 1979. In 1979 there were 5 bishops (the remaining 8 dioceses are directed by Government-appointed capitulary vicars). In 1970 there were 3,532 Roman Catholic priests (7,040 in 1948) and, in 1967, 3,200 churches (10,473 in 1948).

The Protestant (Hussite) Community was estimated (1962) at 1·2m., including 530,000 Reformed (360,000 Czech Brethren, 150,000 Reformed Church of Slovakia), 485,000 Lutherans (435,000 in Slovakia, 50,000 in Silesia), 10,000 Methodists, 10,000 Moravians, 10,000 Unity of Czech Brethren, 5,000 Baptists.

In 1966 there were 15,000 Jews (mainly in Prague, where there is a synagogue). The Uniate Church was suppressed in 1950, when it had 305,645 adherents, 280 priests, 17 monasteries and 5 nunneries. It was permitted to revive in 1968.

Education. In 1978–79 there were 10,443 kindergartens for children from 3 to 6 years of age, with 42,501 teachers and 629,203 pupils. All children receive free education from the ages of 6 to 15, where possible remaining at a single school for the whole 9 years. In 1978–79 there were 7,398 schools with 1,877,773 pupils and 91,876 teachers.

Subsequent education is of 3 types. First, 3 final years of secondary school (in 1978–79, 339 schools with 8,481 teachers and 136,057 pupils). Secondly, technical, teachers' training and other vocational schools (1978–79, 585 schools with 324,545 students). Thirdly, higher education (1978–79, 136,312 full-time students, and 47,320 part-time and correspondence students); academic staff numbered 17,738 in 1978–79. There are 36 institutions of higher education, with 109 faculties. These include 5 universities—the Charles University in Prague (founded 1348); the Purkyně (formerly Masaryk) University in Brno (1919); the Comenius University in Bratislava (1919); the Palacký University in Olomouc (1573); the Šafárik University in Košice (1959); and 12 technical universities or institutes.

Welfare. Medical care is free. In 1977 Kčs. 3,023m. were spent on medicines and in 1978 22,039m. on health insurance benefits. There were, in 1978, 228 hospitals with a total of 116,924 beds, and 45,914 doctors and dentists. Family allowances (Kčs. per month): 1 child, 140; 2 children, 530; 3, 1,030. Old age pensions averaging 67% of salary are paid at the age of 60 (men), 53–57 (women).

DIPLOMATIC REPRESENTATIVES

OF CZECHOSLOVAKIA IN GREAT BRITAIN (25 Kensington Palace Gdns., London, W8 4QY)

Ambassador: Dr Zdeněk Černík (accredited on 16 Nov. 1977).

OF GREAT BRITAIN IN CZECHOSLOVAKIA (Thunovská 14, Prague 1)

Chargé d'Affaires: R. Thomas.

OF CZECHOSLOVAKIA IN THE USA (3900 Linnean Ave., NW, Washington, D.C., 20008)

Ambassador: Dr Jaromir Johanes.

OF THE USA IN CZECHOSLOVAKIA (Tržiste 15–12548 Praha, Prague)

Ambassador: Francis J. Meehan.

OF CZECHOSLOVAKIA TO THE UNITED NATIONS

Ambassador: Dr Ilja Hulinský.

Books of Reference

The Constitution of the Czechoslovak Socialist Republic [English ed.]. Prague, 1960
Statistical Survey of Czechoslovakia. Prague, annual since 1973
Statistická ročenka ČSSR [Statistical Yearbook]. Prague, annual since 1958
Czechoslovak Foreign Trade. Prague, monthly
Statistika. Prague, Statistical Office, monthly since 1964
Socialist Czechoslovakia. Prague, 1976
Czechoslovak Chamber of Commerce and Industry. *Facts on Czechoslovak Foreign Trade.* Prague, 1980.—*Your Trade Partners in Czechoslovakia.* Prague, 1979
Demek, J., and others, *Geography of Czechoslovakia.* Prague, 1971

Hermann, A. H., *A History of the Czechs*. London, 1975

Hejzlar, Z., and Kusin, V. V., *Czechoslovakia, 1968–1969*. New York, 1975

Korbel, J., *Twentieth-Century Czechoslovakia: The Meanings of its History*. Columbia Univ. Press, 1977

Krejči, J., *Social Change and Stratification in Postwar Czechoslovakia*. London, 1972

Kusin, V. V., *From Dubček to Charter 77*. Edinburgh, 1978

Littell, R. (ed.), *The Czech Black Book; prepared by the Institute of History of the Czechoslovak Academy of Sciences*. London, 1969

Mamatey, V. S., and Luža, R. (eds.), *A History of the Czechoslovak Republic 1918–1948*. Princeton Univ. Press, 1973

Mlynař, Z., *Night Frost in Prague: the End of Humane Socialism*. New York, 1980

Oxley, A., Pravda, A., Richie, A., *Czechoslovakia: The Party and the People*. New York, 1973

Procházka, J., *English–Czech and Czech–English Dictionary*. 16th ed. London, 1959

Šik, O., *Czechoslovakia: The Bureaucratic Economy*. New York, 1972

Teplý, J., *Économie Nationale de la Tchecoslovaquie Contemporaine*. Paris, 1977

Ulč, O., *Politics in Czechoslovakia*. San Francisco, 1974

Wallace, W. V., *Czechoslovakia*. London, 1977

DENMARK

Kongeriget Danmark

Capital: Copenhagen
Population: 5·12m. (1980)
GNP per capita: US$9,920 (1978)

HISTORY. First organized as a unified state in the 10th century, Denmark acquired approximately its present boundaries in 1815, having ceded Norway to Sweden and its north German territory to Prussia. Denmark became a constitutional monarchy in 1849.

AREA AND POPULATION. According to the census held on 9 Nov. 1970 the area of Denmark proper was 43,075 sq. km (16,631 sq. miles) and the population 4,937,579. Population, Jan. 1980: 5,122,065.

Administrative divisions		Area (sq. km) 1980	Population 1970	Population 1980	Population 1980 per sq. km
København (Copenhagen)	(city)	88	622,773	498,850	5,674
Frederiksberg	(borough)	9	101,874	88,287	10,067
Københavns	(county)	522	615,343	627,245	1,201
Frederiksborg	,,	1,347	259,442	329,141	244
Roskilde	,,	891	153,199	202,017	227
Vestsjællands	,,	2,984	259,057	277,833	93
Storstrøms	,,	3,398	252,363	260,081	77
Bornholms	,,	588	47,239	47,780	81
Fyns	,,	3,486	432,699	452,965	130
Sønderjyllands	,,	3,930	238,062	249,949	64
Ribe	,,	3,131	197,843	212,624	68
Vejle	,,	2,997	306,263	325,774	109
Ringkøbing	,,	4,853	241,327	262,751	54
Aarhus	,,	4,561	533,190	573,916	126
Viborg	,,	4,122	220,734	231,517	56
Nordjyllands	,,	6,173	456,171	481,335	78
Total		43,080	4,937,579	5,122,065	119

The population is almost entirely Scandinavian; in July 1976, of the inhabitants of Denmark proper, 97·2% were born in Denmark, including Faroe Islands and Greenland.

On 1 Jan. 1980 the population of the capital, Copenhagen (comprising Copenhagen, Frederiksberg and Gentofte municipalities), was 654,437 (including suburbs, 1,387,735); Aarhus, 244,839; Odense, 168,528; Aalborg, 153,948; Esbjerg, 79,310; Randers, 62,486; Helsingor, 56,566; Herning, 56,033; Kolding, 55,769; Horsens, 54,533.

Vital statistics for calendar years:

	Living births	Stillbirths	Marriages	Divorces	Deaths	Emigration	Immigration
1975	72,071	483	31,782	13,264	50,895	40,659	31,946
1976	65,267	431	31,192	13,064	54,001	30,000	33,320
1977	61,878	369	32,174	13,383	50,485	26,906	32,740
1978	62,036	364	28,763	13,072	52,864	26,735	32,059
1979	59,464	309	27,842	13,044	54,654	27,731	33,183

Illegitimate births: 1976, 24%; 1977, 25·9%; 1978, 27·9%; 1979, 30·7%.

REIGNING QUEEN. Margrethe II, born 16 April 1940; married 10 June 1967 to Prince Henrik, born Count de Monpezat; *offspring:* Crown Prince Frederik, born 26 May 1968; Prince Joachim, born 7 June 1969. She succeeded to the throne on the death of her father, King Frederik IX, on 14 Jan. 1972.

Mother of the Queen: Queen Ingrid, born Princess of Sweden, 28 March 1910.

Sisters of the Queen: Princess Benedikte, born 29 April 1944 (married 3 Feb. 1968 to Prince Richard of Sayn-Wittgenstein-Berleburg); Princess Anne-Marie, born 30 Aug. 1946 (married 18 Sept. 1964 to King Constantine of Greece).

The crown of Denmark was elective from the earliest times. In 1448 after the death of the last male descendant of Swein Estridsen the Danish Diet elected to the throne Christian I, Count of Oldenburg, in whose family the royal dignity remained for more than 4 centuries, although the crown was not rendered hereditary by right till 1660. The direct male line of the house of Oldenburg became extinct with King Frederik VII on 15 Nov. 1863. In view of the death of the king, without direct heirs, the Great Powers signed a treaty at London on 8 May 1852, by the terms of which the succession to the crown of Denmark was made over to Prince Christian of Schleswig-Holstein-Sonderburg-Glücksburg, and to the direct male descendants of his union with the Princess Louise of Hesse-Cassel, niece of King Christian VIII of Denmark. In accordance with this treaty, a law concerning the succession to the Danish crown was adopted by the Diet, and obtained the royal sanction 31 July 1853. Linked to the constitution of 5 June 1953, a new law of succession, dated 27 March 1953, has come into force, which restricts the right of succession to the descendants of King Christian X and Queen Alexandrine, and admits the sovereign's daughters to the line of succession, ranking after the sovereign's sons.

Subjoined is a list of the kings of Denmark, with the dates of their accession, from the time of election of Christian I of Oldenburg:

House of Oldenburg

Christian I	1448	Christian IV	1588	Frederik V	1746
Hans	1481	Frederik III	1648	Christian VII	1766
Christian II	1513	Christian V	1670	Frederik VI	1808
Frederik I	1523	Frederik IV	1699	Christian VIII	1839
Christian III	1534	Christian VI	1730	Frederik VII	1848
Frederik II	1559				

House of Schleswig-Holstein-Sonderburg-Glücksburg

Christian IX	1863	Christian X	1912	Margrethe II	1972
Frederik VIII	1906	Frederik IX	1947		

CONSTITUTION AND GOVERNMENT. The present constitution of Denmark is founded upon the 'Grundlov' (charter) of 5 June 1953.

The legislative power lies with the Queen and the *Folketing* (Diet) jointly. The executive power is vested in the Queen, who exercises her authority through the ministers. The judicial power is with the courts. The Queen must be a member of the Evangelical-Lutheran Church, the official Church of the State. The Queen cannot assume major international obligations without the consent of the *Folketing*. The *Folketing* consists of one chamber. All men and women of Danish nationality of more than 18 years of age and permanently resident in Denmark possess the franchise and are eligible for election to the *Folketing*, which is at present composed of 179 members; 135 members are elected by the method of proportional representation in 17 districts. In order to attain an equal representation of the different parties, 40 *tillægsmandater* (additional seats) are divided among such parties which have not obtained sufficient returns at the district elections. Two members are elected for the Faroe Islands and 2 for Greenland. The term of the legislature is 4 years, but a general election may be called at any time.

The *Folketing* must meet every year on the first Tuesday in October. Besides its legislative functions, it appoints every 6 years judges who, together with the ordinary members of the Supreme Court (*Højesteret*), form the *Rigsret*, a tribunal which can alone try parliamentary impeachments. The ministers have free access to the House, but can vote only if they are members.

Folketing, elected 23 Oct. 1979: 68 Social Democrats, 10 Radical Liberals, 22 Conservatives, 11 Socialist People's Party, 6 Centre Democrats, 5 Christian People's Party, 22 Liberals, 6 Left Socialists, 20 Progress Party, 5 Single-Tax Party, 2 Faroe Islands and 2 Greenland representatives.

The executive (called the State Council (*Statsraadet*) when acting with the Queen presiding) is a minority Social Democratic government, was in March 1981 as follows:

Prime Minister: Anker Jørgensen.
Foreign Affairs: Kjeld Olesen. *Finance:* Svend Jakobsen. *Economy:* Ivar Nørgaard. *Industry:* Erling Jensen. *Ecclesiastical Affairs and Greenland:* Tova Lindbo Larsen. *Social Affairs:* Ritt Bjerregaard. *Agriculture:* Bjoern Roemar Westh. *Fisheries:* Karl Hjortnaes. *Transport and Communications:* Jens Risgaard Knudsen. *Education:* Dorte Bennedsen. *Culture and Nordic Affairs:* Lise Østergaard. *Defence:* Poul Søgaard. *Labour:* Svend Auken. *Housing:* Erling Olsen. *Inland Revenue:* Mogens Lykketoft. *Energy:* Poul Nielson. *Interior:* Henning Rasmussen. *Justice:* Ole Espersen. *Environment:* Erik Holst.

The ministers are individually and collectively responsible for their acts, and if impeached and found guilty, cannot be pardoned without the consent of the *Folketing*.

In 1948 a separate legislature (*Lagting*) and executive (*Landsstyre*) were established for the Faroe Islands, to deal with specified local matters and in 1979 a separate legislature (*Landsting*) and executive (*Landsstyre*) were established for Greenland, also to deal with specified local matters.

National flag: Red with white Scandinavian cross (Dannebrog).
National anthems: Kong Kristian stod ved højen Mast (words by J. Ewald, 1778; tune by J. E. Hartmann, 1780) and Der er et yndigt land.

Local Government. For administrative purposes Denmark is divided into 275 municipalities (*kommuner*); each of them has a district council of between 5 and 25 members, headed by an elected mayor. The city of Copenhagen forms a district by itself and is governed by a city council of 55 members, elected every 4 years, and an executive (*magistraten*), consisting of the chief burgomaster (*overborgmesteren*) and 6 burgomasters, appointed by the city council for 4 years. There are 14 counties (*amtskommuner*), each of which is administered by a county council (*amstråd*) of between 13 and 31 members, headed by an elected mayor. All councils are elected directly by universal suffrage and proportional representation for 4-year terms. A third council, the Metropolitan Council, with a constitution similar to the counties was established 1 April 1974. The Metropolitan Council is responsible for overall development within Metropolitan Copenhagen.

The counties and Copenhagen are superintended by a ministry of interior affairs. The municipalities are superintended by 14 local supervision committees, headed by a County Prefect (*amtmand*) who is a civil servant appointed by the Queen.

DEFENCE. The Danish military defence is organized in accordance with the Defence Act of 1969 (amended April 1973 and prolonged March 1977) and the overall organization of the Danish Armed Forces comprises the Defence Command, the Army, the Navy, the Air Force and inter-service authorities and institutions. To this should be added the Home Guard, which is an indispensable part of Danish military defence. The Home Guard is based on the Home Guard Act of 1961 (at the latest amended May 1973).

In accordance with the Defence Act the Chief of Defence has full command of the three services: the Army, the Navy and the Air Force. The Chief of Defence, the Chief of Defence Staff and the Chiefs of the Army, the Navy and the Air Force and their staffs, are integrated in the Defence Command.

The Minister of Defence is assisted by a Defence Council consisting of the Chief of Defence, the Chief of Defence Staff, the Chief of Danish Operational Forces, and the Chiefs of the Army, the Navy and the Air Force.

The Constitution of 1849 declared it the duty of every fit man to contribute to the national defence, and this provision is still in force. According to the Personnel Act, 1969 (amended April 1973), the military personnel comprises officers, n.c.o.s and privates. Private personnel are provided by enlistment and by recruiting of volunteers. Selection of conscripts takes place at the age of 19 years, and the conscripts are normally called up for 9 months service $\frac{1}{2}$–$1\frac{1}{2}$ years later. Afterwards conscripts may be recalled for refresher training or musters.

Army. The Army comprises field army formations and the local defence forces. The field army formations are organized in an operationally balanced covering force and in reserve units. The covering force reserve numbers about 13,000 men and comprises a standing force, and a supplementary force consisting of men newly released from service. This force is part of the field army reserve which numbers 41,000. The standing force number about 21,000 men organized in standing brigade units, headquarters units and support units. The brigade units are organized in 5 mechanized infantry brigades. The field army is equipped with 200 medium battle tanks and about 650 armoured personnel carriers as well as artillery including 72 self-propelled howitzers. The local defence units consist of about 24,000 men organized in 21 infantry battalions and 7 artillery battalions. The men of the latest annual service groups form the troops of the line, while those of the previous years form the local defence, the reserve and the reserve for the Home Guard. The mobilization units of the field army and the local defence force will total about 65,000 men.

Navy. The Navy comprises the fleet and coast-defence which includes several permanent fortifications. The fleet includes 6 submarines, 5 frigates, 5 ocean escorts (for fishery protection and surveying duties), 2 corvettes, 10 fast missile craft, 6 fast torpedo boats, 4 ocean minelayers, 3 coastal minelayers, 8 coastal minesweepers, 2 torpedo recovery vessels, 23 patrol vessels, 8 coastal patrol launches, 2 oilers and the royal yacht. The Naval Air Arm comprises 8 helicopters (one is carried in each of the ocean escorts).

Naval personnel in 1981 totalled about 6,000 officers and men, and the mobilization force about 4,000 men.

Air Force. The operational units of the Air Force comprise 2 surface-to-air missile battalions and 6 flying squadrons with a total of 116 aircraft.

The air defence force consists of the 2 surface-to-air missile battalions and 2 all-weather air-defence squadrons with a unit establishment of 20 CF-104G/F-104G Starfighters.

The fighter bomber force comprises 3 squadrons with a unit establishment of 20 F-100D/F Super Sabres and F 35 Drakens, and 1 reconnaissance squadron with a unit establishment of 16 RF 35 Drakens. The F-100s are being replaced by F-16s in 1980–82.

In addition the Air Force has a number of supplementary units, including 1 transport squadron (C-130s and C-47s), 1 helicopter rescue squadron (S-61As), the control and warning system.

Total strength of the Air Force (1980) about 7,500, and the mobilization force about 8,600 men.

Home Guard. The overall Home Guard organization comprises the Home Guard Command, the Army Home Guard, the Navy Home Guard and the Air Force Home Guard.

The personnel of the Home Guard is recruited on a voluntary basis. The personnel establishment of the Home Guard is at present about 72,960 persons (56,200 in the Army Home Guard, 4,860 in the Navy Home Guard and 11,900 in the Air Force Home Guard).

INTERNATIONAL RELATIONS

Membership. Denmark is a member of UN, NATO, OECD and EEC.

ECONOMY

Budget. The budget (*Finanslovforslag*) must be laid before the Parliament (*Folketing*) not later than 4 months before the beginning of a new fiscal year.

The following shows the actual revenue and expenditure as shown in central government accounts for 1 fiscal year ending 31 March, the approved budget figures for 1 April–31 Dec. 1978 and the budgets for the calendar years 1979, 1980 and 1981 (in 1,000 kroner):

	1977–78	1978	1979	1980	1981
Revenue	81,500,159	66,368,547	98,199,458	110,493,297	120,065,511
Expenditure	87,995,703	77,603,244	111,259,378	121,144,500	136,379,894

Receipts and expenditures of special government funds and expenditures on public works are included.

The 1981 budget envisages revenue of 53,979m. kroner from income and property taxes and 66,074m. from consumer taxes.

The central government debt on 31 Dec. 1979 amounted to 85,703m. kroner.

Currency. The monetary unit is the *krone* of 100 *øre*. In 1931 Denmark went off the gold standard, as established in 1873.

Small change: 10-kroner and 5-kroner pieces of copper–nickel, 1-krone pieces of copper–nickel; 25-øre and 10-øre pieces of copper–nickel, and 5-øre pieces of copper–steel–copper clad.

Banking. On 31 Dec. 1979 the accounts of the National Bank balanced at 62,593m. kroner. The assets included 492m. kroner in gold bullion. The liabilities included 12,317m. kroner note issue, 2,531m. kroner general capital fund and reserve fund.

On 31 Dec. 1979 there were 166 savings banks, with 6·3m. accounts and deposits of 41,298m. kroner. Their advances amounted to 34,747m. kroner.

On 31 Dec. 1979 there were 74 other banks for commercial, agricultural and industrial purposes; their deposits amounted to 96,421m. kroner; advances were 76,305m. kroner.

Weights and Measures. The use of the metric system of weights and measures has been obligatory in Denmark since 1 April 1912.

ENERGY AND NATURAL RESOURCES

Electricity. Owing to the concentration of power production, the number of generating power stations has declined from 371 in 1949–50 to 23 in 1979, while the net power production (in 1m. kwh.) has risen from 1,689 in 1949–50 to 20,468 in 1979.

Agriculture. Land ownership is widely distributed. In 1979 the total number of farms was 122,722. There were 38,284 small holdings (with less than 10 hectares), 73,026 medium sized holdings (10–50 hectares) and 11,448 holdings with more than 50 hectares.

The number of agricultural workers declined from 120,442 in July 1961 to 27,193 in June 1978, while the index of production was 100 in 1975 and 114 in 1979.

In June 1979 the cultivated area was utilized as follows (in 1,000 hectares): Grain, 1,850; peas and beans, 4; root crops, 247; other crops, 138; green fodder and grass, 679; fallow, 2; total cultivated area, 2,920.

Chief crops	Area (1,000 hectares)			Production (in 1,000 tonnes)		
	1977	1978	1979	1977	1978	1979
Wheat	116	122	114	606	642	589
Rye	89	84	70	324	315	257
Barley	1,528	1,570	1,622	6,143	6,301	6,662
Oats	77	61	39	270	206	163
Mixed grain	11	8	5	35	28	19
Potatoes	38	34	32	954	932	844
Root crops	252	233	215	12,545	10,511	10,110

Livestock, 1979: Horses, 58,000; cattle, 3,034,000; pigs, 9,357,000; sheep, 55,000; poultry, 14·57m.

Production (in 1,000 tonnes) in 1979: Milk, 5,225; butter, 130; cheese, 189; beef, 274; pork and bacon, 946; eggs, 76.

In June 1979 farm tractors numbered 189,738 and harvester-threshers, 39,209.

Fisheries. The total value of the fish caught was (in 1m. kroner): 1950, 156; 1955, 252; 1960, 376; 1965, 650; 1970, 854; 1975, 1,442; 1977, 2,296. The fishing fleet in 1977 consisted of 7,340 motor boats, 182 sailing boats and 2,761 rowing boats.

INDUSTRY AND TRADE

Industry. The following table sets forth the gross factor income (in 1m. kroner) by industrial origin in 3 calendar years:

| | 1974 | | 1975 | | 1976 | |
	Current Prices	1970 Prices	Current Prices	1970 Prices	Current Prices	1970 Prices
Agriculture, fur-farming, forestry, etc.	10,279	7,881	10,151	6,936	11,009	6,804
Fishing	1,148	438	776	515	1,234	760
Total	11,427	8,319	10,927	7,451	12,243	7,564
Manufacturing	37,405	27,145	41,628	26,535	47,070	28,463
Construction	16,992	10,592	17,716	9,207	22,411	10,790
Gas, electricity and water	2,897	2,288	3,387	2,366	3,596	2,501
Total	57,294	40,025	62,731	38,108	73,077	41,754
Wholesale and retail trade	25,730	19,172	28,539	19,407	34,567	21,921
Banking and insurance	7,337	4,699	8,021	4,464	9,079	4,654
Total	33,067	23,871	36,560	23,871	43,646	26,575
Use of dwellings	13,317	9,684	15,506	10,134	19,184	11,134
Inland transport services, etc.	8,072	4,424	9,359	4,327	10,329	4,324
Maritime and air transport services	4,788	3,034	4,728	2,795	5,157	2,833
Communication services	2,363	2,143	2,632	2,214	3,076	2,455
Total	15,224	9,601	16,719	9,336	18,562	9,612
Private community services	3,126	2,017	3,457	1,955	3,680	1,896
Business services	5,150	3,462	5,902	3,929	6,926	4,222
Entertainment services, hotels, etc.	3,256	2,235	3,719	2,136	4,398	2,298
Domestic services	3,118	1,760	3,625	1,758	3,982	1,797
Total	14,650	9,474	16,703	9,778	18,986	10,213
Government services	32,703	19,391	38,961	19,862	44,895	20,414
Injected financial services	÷6,999	÷4,532	÷7,829	÷4,464	÷8,743	÷4,581
Gross domestic product at factor cost	170,683	115,833	190,278	114,076	221,850	122,685
Plus indirect taxes	30,786	—	33,495	—	40,685	—
Less subsidies	6,729	—	5,938	—	7,306	—
Gross domestic product at market prices	194,740	134,117	217,835	133,302	255,229	143,889

According to the registration of business units for VAT settlement there were in 1978 a total of 33,500 manufacturing units. In the following table 'number of wage-earners' refers to 6,904 establishments with 6 employees or more, while 'gross-output' and 'value-added' cover 3,163 kind-of-activity units of enterprises with 20 employees or more.

Branch of industry	Number of wage-earners (1,000)	Gross output in factor values (1m. kroner)	Value added in factor values (1m. kroner)
Mining and quarrying	1·1	330	261
Food products	47·0	43,727	10,051
Beverages	9·0	3,762	2,337
Tobacco	2·6	1,013	529
Textiles	11·3	3,757	1,715
Wearing apparel	10·6	1,921	1,009
Leather and products	1·2	316	147
Footwear	2·3	468	227
Wood products	7·5	2,384	1,044

Branch of industry	Number of wage-earners (1,000)	Gross output in factor values (1m. kroner)	Value added in factor values (1m. kroner)
Furniture and fixtures	10·1	2,434	1,308
Paper and products	6·7	2,788	1,342
Printing, publishing	15·8	5,732	3,858
Industrial chemicals	6·9	4,677	2,241
Other chemical products, petroleum refineries and petroleum coal products	5·9	10,765	2,999
Rubber products	2·2	641	360
Plastic products	6·2	1,803	999
Pottery, china, etc.	3·2	459	395
Glass and products	2·5	709	439
Non-metal products	12·9	4,859	2,908
Iron and steel	4·4	1,610	740
Non-ferrous metals	1·8	1,063	303
Metal products	23·3	6,847	3,513
Machinery	38·1	12,623	7,003
Electrical machinery	16·8	5,772	3,237
Transport equipment	22·3	6,642	3,375
Professional goods	4·9	1,913	1,203
Other industries	4·1	1,238	734
Total manufacturing	280·7	129,923	54,016

Labour. In 1979, 8% of the working population lived on agriculture, forestry and fishery, 24% on industries and handicrafts, 8% on construction, 15% on commerce, etc., 6% on transport and communication, and 37% on administration, professional services, etc.

Commerce. The following table shows the value, in 1,000 kroner, of general imports and exports (including trade with the Faroe Islands and Greenland) for calendar years:

	1973	1974	1975	1976	1977	1978
Imports	46,968,945	60,479,570	59,707,627	75,010,879	79,636,962	81,405,158
Exports	37,548,669	46,921,919	50,031,127	55,034,147	60,436,289	65,307,647

Imports and exports (in 1,000 kroner) for calendar years:

	1977		1978	
Leading commodities	Imports	Exports	Imports	Exports
Live animals, meat, etc.	133,442	8,601,724	144,222	9,876,717
Dairy products, eggs	135,373	3,297,719	142,066	3,837,007
Fish and fish preparations	1,012,598	2,772,808	1,188,469	3,169,464
Cereals and cereal preparation	903,790	1,198,492	770,476	1,716,491
Sugar and sugar preparations	359,809	649,979	366,412	736,987
Coffee, tea, cocoa, etc.	1,918,086	245,851	1,691,477	214,847
Feeding stuff for animals	2,241,475	1,182,616	2,094,429	1,060,044
Wood, lumber and cork	1,465,082	222,307	1,389,736	232,803
Textiles, fibres, yarns, fabrics, etc.	3,431,290	1,610,575	3,390,421	1,707,620
Fuels, lubricants, etc.	13,102,061	1,654,060	12,267,331	1,556,991
Pharmaceutical products	805,503	1,276,268	876,296	1,414,735
Fertilizers, etc.	1,073,606	216,437	1,059,608	240,759
Metals, manufactures of metals	6,771,697	2,958,098	7,257,837	3,336,528
Machinery, electric, equipment, etc.	13,491,566	12,483,725	14,761,226	13,308,102
Transport equipment	7,839,415	3,490,019	7,356,046	2,605,689

Distribution of Danish foreign trade (in 1,000 kroner) according to countries of origin and destination, for calendar years:

	Imports			Exports		
Countries	1976	1977	1978	1976	1977	1978
Belgium	2,880,170	3,081,268	2,950,093	925,621	1,067,015	1,312,570
Finland	2,140,969	2,480,886	2,836,827	1,104,640	1,137,143	1,144,597
France	2,848,524	3,352,488	3,606,893	2,299,764	2,612,554	3,008,043
Germany (Fed. Rep.)	15,635,146	15,628,258	16,936,036	7,900,424	9,162,193	11,093,746
Norway	3,513,106	3,758,268	3,423,821	3,702,203	4,468,257	4,291,569

Countries	Imports			Exports		
	1976	1977	1978	1976	1977	1978
Sweden	10,622,929	10,434,134	10,614,371	8,685,041	8,643,138	8,405,506
Switzerland	1,337,994	1,383,641	1,836,872	910,446	1,039,117	1,267,524
UK	7,665,358	8,720,647	9,327,789	9,417,899	8,468,488	9,392,054
USA	3,853,264	4,553,868	4,474,046	3,144,237	3,432,081	3,656,558
Allied forces in Fed. Rep. Germany	—	—	—	135,309	134,279	131,538

Total trade between Denmark (without the Faroe Islands) and UK (British Department of Trade returns, in £1,000 sterling):

	1976	1977	1978	1979	1980
Imports to UK	705,390	811,657	962,464	1,081,247	1,103,590
Exports and re-exports from UK	654,856	797,325	841,377	1,016,403	1,032,525

Tourism. In 1979, foreigners visiting Denmark spent some 6,914m. kroner.

Industrial Statistics. Danmarks Statistik. Copenhagen (annually)
Quarterly Statistics for the Industry: Commodity Statistics. Danmarks Statistik, Copenhagen
Statistics on Agriculture, Horticulture and Forestry. Danmarks Statistik. Copenhagen (annually)
Agriculture in Denmark. Agricultural Council of Denmark. Copenhagen, 1972
Agricultural Statistics 1900–1965. Vol. I: *Agricultural Area and Harvest and Utilization of Fertilizers.*—Vol. II: *Livestock and Livestock Products, and Consumption of Feeding Stuffs.* Danmarks Statistik. Copenhagen, 1968–69
External Trade of Denmark. Danmarks Statistik, Copenhagen
Danish Industry in Facts and Figures. Federation of Danish Industries. Copenhagen (annually)
Energy Supply of Denmark, 1900–58 and *1948–65.* Danmarks Statistik. Copenhagen, 1959, 1967. Annual Supplements 1966–75 have been published in Statistical News
Report on Fisheries. Ministry of Fisheries, Copenhagen (annually)
Eckup, C., *The Danish Chemical Industry.* Lyngby, 1971
Nash, E. F., and Attwood, E. A., *The Agricultural Policies of Britain and Denmark.* London, 1961
The 1,000 Largest Companies in Denmark. 8th ed. Copenhagen, 1975

COMMUNICATIONS

Roads. Denmark proper had (1 Jan. 1980), 464 km of motorways, 4,199 km of other state roads, 6,840 km of provincial roads and 56,691 km of commercial roads. Motor vehicles registered at 31 Dec. 1979 comprised 1,412,451 passenger cars, 263,045 lorries, 10,992 taxicabs (including 3,391 for private hire), 7,109 buses and 34,524 cycles.

Railways. There were in 1980 railways of a total length of 2,556 km open for traffic. Of this total, 2,015 km belong to the State. The revenue from 1 April to 31 Dec. 1978 amounted to 803m. kroner from passenger transport (including bus traffic) and 525m. kroner from freight.

Aviation. On 1 Oct. 1950 the 3 Scandinavian airlines, Det Danske Luftfartsselskab, ABA and DNL, combined in Scandinavian Airlines System. In 1979 SAS flew 124·4m. km and carried 8,662,061 passengers.

SAS inaugurated its transpolar routes Copenhagen–Los Angeles on 15 Nov. 1954 and Copenhagen–Tōkyō on 25 Feb. 1957, and its trans-Asian express route Copenhagen–Bangkok–Singapore *via* Tashkent on 4 Nov. 1967.

Shipping. On 31 Dec. 1979 the Danish merchant fleet consisted of 3,124 vessels (above 20 GRT) of 5,377,305 GRT.

In 1979, 44,200 vessels of 33m. NRT entered the Danish ports, unloading 47m. tonnes and loading 16m. tonnes of cargo; traffic by passenger ships and ferries is not included.

Post and Broadcasting. There were, in 1979, 1,321 post offices. On 31 Dec. 1979 the length of telephone circuits of private companies was 10,845,226 km. On 31 Dec. 1979 there were 2,176,869 telephone subscribers (including those in the Faroe Islands and Greenland). Postal revenues, 1978–79, 2,839m. kroner; expenditure, 2,803m. kroner.

Danmarks Radio is the government broadcasting station and is financed by licence fees. Television is broadcast by *Danmarks Radio* with colour programmes by

PAL system. Number of receivers: Radio, 1·9m.; television, 1,853,000, including 1·19m. colour sets.

Cinemas. In 1979 there were 466 cinemas with a seating capacity of 112,703.

Newspapers. In 1979 there were 49 daily newspapers with a combined circulation of 1·88m. on weekdays; 10 of them (896,000) appeared in Copenhagen.

JUSTICE, RELIGION, EDUCATION AND WELFARE

Justice. The lowest courts of justice are organized in 84 tribunals (*byretter*), where cases are dealt with by a single judge. The tribunals at Copenhagen have 32 judges, Aarhus 13, Odense 10, Aalborg 9, and the other tribunals have 1 to 4. Cases of greater consequence are dealt with by the superior courts (*Landsretterne*); these courts are also courts of appeal for the above-named cases. Of superior courts there are two: *Østre Landsret* in Copenhagen with 43 judges, *Vestre Landret* in Viborg with 20 judges. From these an appeal lies to the Supreme Court (*Højesteret*) in Copenhagen, composed of 15 judges. Judges under 70 years of age can be removed only by judicial sentence.

In 1978, 10,953 men and 867 women were convicted of crimes and delicts, fines not included. On 31 Dec. 1979, 1,348 men and 33 women were in the state prisons.

Religion. At the Reformation in 1536 the Danish Church ceased to exist as a legally independent unit, a part of the Roman Catholic Church, and became instead a Lutheran Church under the direction of the State. Since that time the State has, in one form or another, continued to exercise supreme authority in the affairs of the Church, and has regulated these by the passing of laws, by royal decree, or other appropriate means. The great majority of Danish citizens (about 90%) belongs to the National Church. Administratively, Denmark is divided into 10 dioceses each with a Bishop who, within the framework of the law, is the supreme diocesan authority in ecclesiastical affairs. The Bishop together with the Chief Administrative Officer of the county make up the diocesan governing body, responsible for all matters of ecclesiastical local finance and general administration. Bishops are appointed by the Crown after an election at which the clergy and parish council members of the diocese have had the opportunity of voting for the candidates nominated. Each diocese is divided into a number of deaneries (about 107 in the whole country) each with its Dean and Deanery Committee, who have certain financial powers. Local government at parish level (there are about 2,200 parishes in all) is in the hands of Parish Councils, who are elected for a 4-year period of office.

Since the Constitution of 1849 complete religious toleration is extended to every sect, and no civil disabilities attach to Dissenters.

Kjær, J. C., *History of the Church of Denmark*. Blair, Nebr., 1945
Roesen, August, *Religion in Denmark*. Copenhagen, 1963

Education. Education has been compulsory since 1814. The *folkeskole* (public primary and lower secondary school) comprises a pre-school class (*børnehaveklassen*), a 9-year compulsory basic school and 1-year voluntary tenth form. Compulsory education may be fulfilled either through attending the public *folkeskole* or private schools or through home-instruction, the only requirement being that the instruction given should be comparable to that offered in the *folkeskole*. *Folkeskolen* are mainly municipal and no fees are paid. In the year 1977–78, 2,272 primary and lower secondary schools had 807,502 pupils and employed 55,428 teachers. 13% of the total number of schools were private schools and they were attended by 6% of the total number of pupils in the primary and lower secondary schools. The 9-year compulsory basic school is in practice not streamed. However, a certain differentiation may take place in the eighth and ninth form as well as in the voluntary tenth form.

Examination after finishing the primary and lower secondary school is voluntary. After the termination of the eighth and ninth form the pupils may sit for the leaving examination of the *folkeskole* (*folkeskolens afgangsprøve*). After the termination of the tenth form the pupils may sit for either the leaving examination of the *folkeskole* (*folkeskolens afgangsprøve*) or the extended leaving examination of the *folkeskole*.

Under certain conditions the pupils may continue their education either in a 3-year gymnasium ending with *studentereksamen* or in the 2-year higher preparatory school ending with the *højere forberedelseseksamen*. There were (1977–78) 126 of these upper secondary schools with 59,290 pupils and 5,556 teachers.

Youth and leisure-time education: 254 schools (continuation schools, youth residential schools, domestic science schools, folk high schools, youth high schools and agricultural schools) with 24,313 pupils.

Vocational training, technical and commercial education: 54 vocational and technical schools with 38,543 pupils receiving vocational training as apprentices and 9,336 receiving basic vocational education. There were 61 commercial schools with 16,819 pupils receiving vocational training as apprentices, 4,468 receiving basic vocational education and 15,836 other pupils.

Teacher-training institutions: 31 teacher-training colleges with 13,373 students. 26 colleges for training of teachers for kindergartens and leisure-time activities with 6,385 students.

Degree-courses in Engineering (1977): The Technical University of Denmark had 3,405 students. The Engineering Academy of Denmark had 1,293 students and 8 engineering colleges with 2,260 students.

Universities and University Centres (1977): The University of Copenhagen (founded 1479) 29,214 students. The University of Aarhus (founded in 1928) 15,003 students. The University of Odense (founded in 1964) 4,465 students. Roskilde University Centre (founded in 1972) 1,466 students. Aalborg University Centre (founded in 1974) 2,584 students.

Other types of post-secondary education (1977): The Royal Veterinary and Agricultural College had 1,822 students. Two Colleges of Dentistry had 1,173 students. The Danish College of Pharmacy had 633 students. Eleven Colleges of Economics and Business Administration had 13,626 students. Two Schools of Architecture had 2,583 students. Five Academies of Music had 789 students. The Danish Library College had 1,269 students. The Royal Danish College of Educational Studies had 1,633 students. The Danish State Institute of Physical Education had 252 students. Four Colleges for Social Welfare Officers had 1,281 students. The Danish College of Journalism had 360 students. Six Therapeutists Colleges had 870 students. One State Midwife School had 105 students.

Schools and Education in Denmark. Copenhagen, 1972
Kirkegaard, P., *The Public Libraries in Denmark*. Copenhagen, 1950; French ed., 1960
Nellermann, A., *Schools and Education in Denmark*. Copenhagen, 1964
Rørdam, T., *The Danish Folk Schools*. Copenhagen, 1965
Skrubbeltrang, F., *The Danish Folk High Schools*. Copenhagen, 1947
Thomsen, O. B., *Some Aspects of Education in Denmark*. Toronto, 1976
Trane, E., *Education and Culture in Denmark*. Copenhagen, 1958

Social Security. The main body of Danish social welfare legislation is consolidated in 9 acts concerning (1) health insurance, (2) daily cash benefits, (3) disablement pensions, (4) old age pensions, (5) widows pensions, (6) employment injuries insurance, (7) employment services and unemployment insurance, (8) social assistance including assistance to handicapped, rehabilitation, child and juvenile guidance, care of the aged and sick, and (9) family allowances.

Health insurance, covering the entire population, provides free medical care, substantial subsidies for certain essential medicines together with some dental care and a funeral allowance. Hospitals are primarily municipal and the hospital treatment is normally free. Wage-earners are granted daily sickness allowances, others can have limited daily sickness allowances. Daily cash benefits are granted in the case of temporary incapacity for work because of illness, injury or child-birth to all persons who earn an income derived from personal work. The benefit is paid at the rate of 90% of the average weekly earnings. There is a maximum rate of 1,612 kroner a week.

Disablement and old-age pensions cover the entire population. Entitlement to benefits at the full rates is subject to the condition that the beneficiary has been ordinarily resident in Denmark for a number of years (40). For a shorter period of residence, the benefits are reduced proportionally. The basic amount of the old-age pension in 1979 was 46,248 kroner to married couples and 25,176 to single persons.

Various supplementary allowances, depending on age and income, may be payable with the basic amount. Persons over 67 years of age are entitled to the basic amount. The pensions to a married couple are calculated and paid to the husband and the wife separately. Invalidity pension is payable, having regard to the degree of disability, at a rate of up to 57,552 kroner to a single person. The rate of the widow's pension corresponds more or less to that of the old-age pension. Invalidity and widow's pensions may be subject to income regulation.

Employment injuries insurance provides for disablement or survivors' pensions and funeral allowances. The scheme covers practically all employees.

Employment services are provided by regional public employment agencies. The insurance against unemployment provides daily allowances. The unemployment insurance funds had at 1 June 1977 a membership of about 1,373,907 full-time workers.

The *Social Assistance Act* applies to the field of social legislation which rules the individually granted benefits in contrast to the other fields of social legislation which apply to fixed benefits.

Total social expenditure, including hospital and health services, amounted in the financial year 1977 to 67,901m. kroner.

Bibliography of Foreign Language Literature on Industrial Relations and Social Services in Denmark. Ministries of Labour and Social Affairs, Copenhagen, 1975
Social Conditions in Denmark. Vols. 1–8. Ministries of Labour and Social Affairs, Copenhagen
Marcussen, E., *Social Welfare in Denmark*. 4th ed. Copenhagen, 1980

THE FAROE ISLANDS
Færøerne

HISTORY. A Norwegian province 1380–1709, the islands secured the restoration of their Parliament in 1852 and full self-government in 1948.

AREA AND POPULATION. Area, 1,399 sq. km (540 sq. miles); population (1 July 1979), 43,131. Capital, Thorshavn. Population (1 July 1979) 13,534.

GOVERNMENT. The parliament (*Lagting*), elected on 8 Nov. 1980, consists of 32 members: 8 Samband Party, 7 Social Democrats, 6 Folkeflok, 2 Progressive Party, 3 Home Rule Party, 6 Republicans.

Flag: White with a red blue-edged Scandinavian cross.

From 1 Jan. 1972 the Faroe Islands were no longer members of EFTA.

COMMERCE. The main industries are fisheries and crafts. Exports, mainly fresh, frozen, filleted and salted fish, amounted to 757·7m. kroner in 1979; imports to 1,043·7m. kroner.

Total trade with UK (British Department of Trade returns, in £1,000 sterling):

	1975	1976	1977	1978	1979	1980
Imports to UK	4,180	7,637	9,791	7,342	10,669	10,559
Exports and re-exports from UK	1,845	2,061	3,277	4,357	4,189	2,434

BROADCASTING. *Utvarp Føroya* is the broadcasting station and the number of receivers 11,000.

EDUCATION. In 1979–80 there were 6,025 primary and 2,597 secondary school pupils with 484 teachers.

Books of Reference

Årbog for Færøerne. 1979
Faroes in Figures. Thorshavn, annual, from 1956
West, J. F., *Faroe*. London, 1973
Williamson, K., *The Atlantic Islands: A Study of the Faroe Life and Scene*. London, 1970

GREENLAND
Grønland

AREA AND POPULATION. Area 2,175,600 sq. km (840,000 sq. miles), made up of 1,833,900 sq. km of ice cap and 341,700 sq. km of ice-free land. The population, 1 Jan. 1980, numbered 49,773; West Greenland, 44,475; East Greenland, 3,104; North Greenland (Thule), 771, and 1,423 not belonging to any specific municipality. Of the total, 8,826 were born outside Greenland. Capital, Godthaab (1980, estimate) 9,077.

CONSTITUTION. On 5 June 1953 Greenland became an integral part of the Danish Realm with the same rights as other counties in Denmark and with a democratically elected council (*landsråd*). A referendum held in Jan. 1979 approved of home rule from 1 May 1979. At the elections held on 4 April 1979 for the new 21-member Parliament, *Landsting*, the *Siumut* gained 13 seats and the *Atassut*, the remaining 8 seats. The Premier, Jonathan Motzfeldt, formed a 5-member administration, *Landsstyre*.

INDUSTRY. Until the beginning of this century, the hunting of land and sea mammals, especially seals, was the main occupation of the population; now fishing is most important. Fish-processing industries, construction and trade are also important occupations.

Coal production ceased in 1972. A deposit of the valuable mineral cryolite has been mined at Ivigtut. The mine is now worked out, but exports from stock will continue for some years. In 1973 the Danish company Greenex A/S began producing lead and zinc concentrate near Umanak. Annual production of lead and zinc concentrates is about 45,000 tonnes and 150,000 tonnes respectively. In 1975, 6 groups of oil companies were granted 13 oil concessions off the west coast. These concessions were terminated by 31 Dec. 1978.

Public authorities are investigating uranium and coal deposits in Greenland as well as possibilities of hydro-electric power and there are other private prospectors for various minerals.

COMMERCE. Imports (c.i.f. Greenland) (in 1,000 kroner): 1973, 565,711; 1974, 633,691; 1975, 741,901; 1976, 777,911; 1977, 964,579; 1978, 980,292. Exports (f.o.b. Greenland) (in 1,000 kroner): 1973, 191,084; 1974, 551,094; 1975, 509,422; 1976, 516,519; 1977, 555,172; 1978, 559,274. Trade is mainly with Denmark.

Total trade with UK (British Department of Trade returns, in £1,000 sterling):

	1975	1976	1977	1978	1979	1980
Imports to UK	52	61	2,211	714	348	282
Exports and re-exports from UK	4,857	5,856	5,329	3,975	2,383	5,930

BROADCASTING. *Grønlands Radio* broadcasts in Greenlandic and Danish. The short wave transmitters are located at Godthaab. Number of receivers, 8,000. Several towns have local television stations.

EDUCATION. There were (1979–80) 8,066 pupils in primary schools and 3,180 in secondary schools.

Books of Reference

Greenland. R. Danish Ministry of Greenland. Copenhagen. Annual from 1968
Meddelelser om Grønland. Ed. Kommissionen for videnskabelige undersøgelser i Grønland. Copenhagen, 1897 ff.
Birket-Smith, K. (ed.), *Grønlandsbogen.* 2 vols. Copenhagen, 1950
Gad, F., *A History of Greenland.* Vol. 1. London, 1970.—Vol. 2. London, 1973
Hertling, K. (ed.), *Greenland Past and Present.* Copenhagen, 1970

DIPLOMATIC REPRESENTATIVES

OF DENMARK IN GREAT BRITAIN (55 Sloane St., London, SW1X 9SR)
Ambassador: Tyge Darlgaard (accredited 28 Feb. 1981).

OF GREAT BRITAIN IN DENMARK (36–40 Kastelsvej,
DK-2100, Copenhagen Ø)
Ambassador: Dame Anne Marion Warburton, DCVO, CMG.

OF DENMARK IN THE USA (3200 Whitehaven St., NW,
Washington, D.C., 20008)
Ambassador: Otto R. Borch.

OF THE USA IN DENMARK (Dag Hammarskjolds Alle 24,
Copenhagen)
Ambassador: Warren Demian Manshel.

OF DENMARK TO THE UNITED NATIONS
Ambassador: Wilh. Ulrichsen.

Books of Reference

Statistical Information: Danmarks Statistik (Sejrøgade 11, 2100 Copenhagen Ø.) was founded in 1849 and reorganized in 1966 as an independent institution; it is administratively placed under the Minister of Economic Affairs. *Chief:* N. V. Skak-Nielsen. Its main publications are: *Statistisk Årbog* (Statistical Yearbook). From 1896; *Statistiske Efterretninger* (Statistical News). From 1909; *Statistiske Meddelelser* (Statistical Reports). From 1852; *Handelsstatistiske Meddelelser* (Reports on Foreign Trade). From 1910; *Statistiske Tabelværker* (Statistical Tables). From 1850; *Statistiske Undersøgelser* (Statistical Inquiries).

Ministry of Foreign Affairs, *Danish Foreign Office Journal. Commercial and General Review.— Denmark.* 1961.—*Economic Survey of Denmark* (annual).—*Facts About Denmark.* 1959.— Hæstrup, J., *From Occupied to Ally: the Danish Resistance Movement.* 1963
Atlas over Danmark. R. Danish Geog. Society. Copenhagen, 1963
Bibliografi over Danmarks Offentlige Publikationer. Institut for International Udveksling, Copenhagen. Annual
Dania polyglotta. Annual Bibliography of Books . . . in Foreign Languages Printed in Denmark. State Library, Copenhagen. Annual
Kongelig Dansk Hof og Statskalender. Copenhagen. Annual
Brynildsen, F., *A Dictionary of the English and Dano-Norwegian Languages.* 2 vols. Copenhagen, 1902–07
Danstrup, J., *History of Denmark.* 2nd ed. Copenhagen, 1949
Frils, H. (ed.), *Scandinavia Between East and West.* Cornell Univ. Press, Ithaca, 1950
Gedde, K., *This is Denmark.* Copenhagen, 1948
Jones, N. G., *Denmark.* London, 1970
Krabbe, L., *Histoire de Danemark.* Copenhagen and Paris, 1950
Lauring, P., *A History of Denmark.* Copenhagen, 1960
Nielsen, B. K., *Engelsk–Dansk Ordbog.* Copenhagen, 1964
Outze, B. (ed.), *Denmark During the German Occupation.* Copenhagen, 1946
Trap, J. P., *Kongeriget Danmark.* 5th ed. 11 vols. Copenhagen, 1953 ff.
Vinterberg H., and Bodelsen, C. A., *Dansk-Engelsk Ordbog.* Copenhagen, 1966

National Library: Det Kongelige Bibliotek, Copenhagen. *Librarian:* P. Birkelund.

COMMONWEALTH OF DOMINICA

Capital: Roseau
Population: 83,000 (1978)
GNP per capita: US$440 (1978)

HISTORY. Dominica was discovered by Columbus. It was a British possession from 1805, a member of the Federation of the West Indies 1958–62, an Associated State of the UK, 1967–78 and became an independent republic as the Commonwealth of Dominica on 3 Nov. 1978.

AREA AND POPULATION. Dominica is an island in the Windward group of the West Indies situated between Martinique and Guadeloupe. 289·5 sq. miles (728 sq. km). Census population, 1970, 70,302 (males, 33,550; females, 36,752), estimate, 1978, 83,000. Chief town, Roseau (population, about 16,800). Dominica contains a Carib settlement with a population of about 500, nearly all of whom are of mixed blood.

CONSTITUTION AND GOVERNMENT. The House of Assembly has 21 elected and 9 nominated members, 1 *ex-officio* member. The Speaker is elected from among the members of the House or from outside. The Cabinet is presided over by the Prime Minister and consists of 5 other Ministers and the Attorney-General (official member). Elections were held in July 1980. The Dominica Freedom Party won 17 seats, Dominica Democratic Labour Party, 2 seats and Independents 2 seats.

President: Aurelius Marie.

The Cabinet in July 1980 was composed as follows:

Prime Minister and Minister of Finance, Foreign Affairs and Development: Mary Eugenia Charles.

Attorney-General and Minister of Legal Affairs: Roland David. *Home Affairs, Industrial Relations and Housing:* Brian G. K. Alleyne. *Agriculture, Lands, Co-operatives and Trade:* Heskeith Alexander. *Communications, Works, Tourism and Industry:* Henry Dyer. *Education, Health, Youth Affairs and Sports:* Charles Maynard.

National flag: Green with a cross over all of yellow, white, and black pieces, and in the centre a red disc charged with a Sisserou parrot in natural colours within a ring of 10 green stars.

INTERNATIONAL RELATIONS

Membership. The Commonwealth of Dominica is a member of UN, OAS, the Commonwealth and is an ACP state of EEC.

ECONOMY

Budget. Revenue, 1976, $28,517,000 and expenditure, $30,984,000.

Currency. In Jan. 1979 legislation was introduced to adopt the French *franc*, the £ sterling and the East Caribbean *dollar* as legal tender. In March 1981, EC$2·7025 = US$1 and EC$5·90 = £1.

Banking. Savings bank (1974), 2,954 depositors, with $571,794 deposits. There are branches of Barclays Bank International, Royal Bank of Canada and Dominica Co-operative Bank in Roseau, a branch of Barclays at Portsmouth and agencies of Barclays at Marigot and Grand Bay. The National Commercial and Development Bank was opened in 1977.

NATURAL RESOURCES

Agriculture. Production (1977, in tonnes): Bananas, 37,000; coconuts, 18,000.

Livestock (1979): Cattle, 4,000; pigs, 8,000; sheep, 4,000; goats, 6,000; poultry, 105,000.

INDUSTRY AND TRADE

Industry. The main industries are agriculture and tourism. A freeport is planned, to be called New Hong Kong.

Commerce (1975). Imports, $45,036,389 c.i.f.; exports, $24,646,717. Chief products: Bananas, soap, fruit juices, essential oils, cocoa, coconuts, vegetables, fruit and fruit preparations, and alcoholic drinks. Exports (1975) of cocoa, 60 long tons ($226,366); bananas, 27,917 tons ($14,407,117); coconut oil, 16,272 lb. ($172,728); essential oils, 36,284 lb. ($672,394); citrus fruits, 7,990,486 lb. ($3,154,236); soap, 404 tons ($574,628); fruit juices, 115,796 gallons ($1,017,197); vegetables, 702 tons ($487,870).

Total trade between Dominica (including St Lucia and St Vincent) and UK (British Department of Trade returns, in £1,000 sterling):

	1978	1979	1980
Imports to UK	33,025	25,126	9,146
Exports and re-exports from UK	16,763	17,112	12,868

Tourism. Tourists (1976) totalled 24,005.

COMMUNICATIONS

Roads. In 1976 there were 467 miles of road and 282 miles of track. Vehicles totalled (1976) 3,574.

Post and Broadcasting. Telephone lines, 272·5 route miles; number of telephones, 4,036 (1978). Radio receivers (1978) 9,500.

Cinemas. In 1970 there were 3 cinemas with a seating capacity of 1,500.

JUSTICE, RELIGION AND EDUCATION

Justice. There are 4 magistrates' courts. They dealt with 11 civil and 3,274 criminal cases in 1973. The police force consists of 10 officers and 247 other ranks.

Religion. 80% of the population is Roman Catholic.

Education. In 1977 there were 18,415 primary and 5,895 secondary school pupils and 3 colleges of higher education with 401 students.

DIPLOMATIC REPRESENTATIVES

OF DOMINICA IN GREAT BRITAIN (10 Kensington Ct., London, W8).
High Commissioner: Arden Shillingford, MBE (accredited 13 Dec. 1978).

OF GREAT BRITAIN IN DOMINICA
High Commissioner: J. S. Arthur, CMG (resides in Bridgetown).

Book of Reference

Commonwealth of Dominica. HMSO, 1979

Library: Public Library, Roseau. *Librarian:* Miss C. Henry.

DOMINICAN REPUBLIC

Capital: Santo Domingo
Population: 5·66m. (1978)
GNP per capita: US$910 (1978)

República Dominicana

HISTORY. On 5 Dec. 1492 Columbus discovered the island of Santo Domingo, which he called La Española; for a time it was called Hispaniola. The city of Santo Domingo, founded by his brother, Bartholomew, in 1496, is the oldest city in the Americas. The western third of the island—now the Republic of Haiti—was later occupied and colonized by the French, to whom the Spanish colony of Santo Domingo was also ceded in 1795. In 1808 the Dominican population, under the command of Gen. Juan Sánchez Ramirez, routed an important French military force commanded by Gen. Ferrand, at the famous battle of Palo Hincado. This battle was the beginning of the end for French rule in Santo Domingo and culminated in the successful siege of the capital. Eventually, with the aid of a British naval squadron, the French were forced to capitulate and the colony returned again to Spanish rule, from which it declared its independence in 1821. It was invaded and held by the Haitians from 1822 to 1844, when they were expelled, and the Dominican Republic was founded and a constitution adopted. Independence day 27 Feb. 1844. Great Britain, in 1850, was the first country to recognize the Dominican Republic. The country was occupied by American Marines from 1916 until 1924. In 1936 the name of the capital city was changed from Santo Domingo to Ciudad Trujillo; and back again in 1961.

AREA AND POPULATION. The Dominican Republic occupies the eastern portion (about two-thirds) of the island of Hispaniola, Quisqueya or Santo Domingo, the western division forming the Republic of Haiti. It consists of the National District (containing the capital, Santo Domingo; population, census 1970, 817,067), and 26 provinces.

Area is 48,442 sq. km (18,700 sq. miles) with 870 miles of coastline, 193 miles of frontier line with Haiti (marked out in 1936).

The populations of the 26 provinces at the 1970 census were:

La Altagracia	87,180	Puerto Plata	185,800
Azua	91,511	La Romana	56,995
Bahoruco	66,572	Salcedo	89,773
Barahona	112,914	Samaná	53,893
Dajabón	50,780	Sánchez Ramírez	106,177
Duarte	200,813	San Cristóbal	324,395
Espaillat	139,579	San Juan	191,065
La Estrelleta	53,228	San Pedro de Macorís	105,490
Independencia	32,580	Santiago	386,269
María Trinidad Sánchez	97,043	Santiago Rodríguez	49,958
Montecristi	69,276	El Seibo	132,795
Pedernales	12,547	Valverde	76,608
Peravia	127,587	La Vega	293,694

Census population of 1970 was 4,009,458 (2,000,824 males and 2,008,734 females) with 48% of population under 15 years and only 2% over 65. Estimate (1978) 5,658,000.

Population of the principal municipalities (1978): National District (including Santo Domingo) 1,103,425; Santiago de los Caballeros, 241,955; San Pedro de Macorís, 74,693; San Francisco de Macoris, 66,303; Barahona, 59,808.

411

The population is partly of Spanish descent, but is mainly composed of a mixed race of European and African blood.

CONSTITUTION AND GOVERNMENT. A new Constitution was promulgated on 28 Nov. 1966.

The President is elected for 4 years, by direct vote. In case of death, resignation or disability, he is succeeded by the Vice-president. There are 12 secretaries of state, a judicial adviser with secretary-of-state rank and 2 ministers without portfolio in charge of departments. Citizens are entitled to vote at the age of 18, or less when married.

Recent Presidents have been: Gen. Rafael Leonidas Trujillo Molina, 1930–38, 1942–52 (assassinated 30 May 1961); Héctor Bienvenido Trujillo Molina, 1952–60; Dr Joaquín Balaguer, 1960–62; Lic. Rafael Bonnelly, 18 Jan. 1962; Professor Juan Bosch, 27 Feb.–25 Sept. 1963 (deposed); Dr Héctor Gracia Godoy, 3 Sept. 1965–1 July 1966; Joaquín Balaguer, 1 July 1966—15 Aug. 1978.

President: Antonio Guzman (elected 26 May 1978).

The country's first free elections for nearly 40 years were held in Dec. 1962 when Juan Bosch was elected President with a clear majority, after which a new Constitution was approved on 29 April 1963. Bosch was overthrown by a military *coup d'état* in Sept. 1963 and the declared aim of the Constitutionalist side in the Civil War of April–Sept. 1965 was the restoration of Bosch as President and a return to the 1963 Constitution.

On 29 April 1965 USA landed a force of 44,000 Marine and Army, later assisted by Organization of American States contributions. The capital remained divided between these forces and various rival factions of nationals. A provisional government was eventually installed on 3 Sept. 1965.

Until elections on 1 June 1966 there was government by decree. The voting on 16 May 1974 was 924,779 votes for Dr Joaquín Balaguer (Reformist Party).

National flag: Blue, red; quartered by a white cross.

National anthem: Quisqueyanos valientes, alzemos (words by E. Prud'homme; tune by J. Reyes, 1883).

DEFENCE. The armed forces are under the command of the President of the Republic, acting through the Secretary of State for the Armed Forces.

Army. The Army has a strength (1980) of about 11,000 all ranks. It is organized in 3 infantry brigades, 1 artillery regiment and support battalions, and has some light tanks and armoured cars.

Navy. The Navy, largely comprising former US vessels, consists of 1 very old frigate, the operational flagship (former training ship, *ex*-presidential yacht), 2 escort (*ex*-fleet) minesweepers, 3 patrol vessels (*ex*-netlayers), 1 medium landing ship, 2 landing craft, 5 coastguard vessels, 8 patrol cutters, 5 motor launches, 1 training vessel, 2 oilers, 3 survey craft and 10 tugs. Personnel in 1981 totalled 4,050 officers and men.

Air Force. The Air Force, with HQ at San Isidoro, has 2 operational squadrons, each with 10 to 20 first-line aircraft. One is equipped with F-51D Mustang piston-engined interceptors; the other with jet-powered Vampire Mk. 1 and Mk. 50 fighter-bombers. Another squadron, with 6 T-28Ds, has a joint counter-insurgency/training role. There are also transport (C-47, etc.), helicopter and training units. Total strength (1980) was about 3,500 personnel and 85 aircraft.

INTERNATIONAL RELATIONS

Membership. The Dominican Republic is a member of UN and OAS.

ECONOMY

Budget. The receipts and disbursements for calendar years, in 1m. Dominican gold pesos (RD$), equal to the US$, were:

	1973	*1974*	*1975*	*1976*	*1977*[1]	*1978*[1]
Revenue	325·3	383·4	657·4	...	547·7	620·3
Expenditure	325·3	383·4	665·0	...	547·7	620·3

[1] Estimated.

Income tax, established in 1949, was replaced in 1950 by an identity-card tax, known as the 'cédula tax', but re-introduced in 1962.

Currency. In Oct. 1947 the *peso oro*, equal to the US$, was formally made the unit of currency, replacing the US gold dollar, which had been the standard since 1 July 1897. In March 1981, £1 = RD$2·1850; US$1 = RD$1.

There are silver coins for 50, 25 and 10 centavos, a copper–nickel 5-centavo piece and a copper 1-centavo piece.

Banking. On 24 Oct. 1941 a law was passed for the creation of a Dominican commercial bank (government controlled) to be known as the Banco de Reservas de la República Dominicana, with a capital of RD$1m., now increased to RD$68,877,000. This bank, starting with branches purchased from the National City Bank of New York, opened for business on 27 Oct. 1941 and now has 30 branches covering the country. It is authorized to perform all customary banking transactions. On 31 Oct. 1966 its assets and liabilities totalled RD$142,126,322. There are 4 foreign banks—the Royal Bank of Canada with 12 branches, the Bank of Nova Scotia with 11 branches, the Citibank with 6 branches, the Chase Manhattan Bank with 7 branches and the Bank of America with 4 branches. An agricultural and mortgage bank, with paid-up capital of RD$500,000, was established in 1945; in 1950 its capital was increased to RD$5m.; in 1952 steps were begun to raise it to cover a 5-year programme of agricultural expansion; it stood at RD$100m. in Nov. 1962.

In 1947 the Central Bank of the Dominican Republic was launched. Chief liability was note circulation, chiefly bank-notes of 1, 5 and 10 pesos (RD$104·5m. in 1966); total assets and liabilities were RD$215·8m. The net reserve of foreign exchange was US$32m. at 31 Aug. 1966.

A new Banco Popular Dominicano, with an authorized capital of RD$5m., opened in Jan. 1964.

Weights and Measures. The metric system was nominally adopted on 1 Aug. 1913, but English and Spanish units have remained in common use in ordinary commercial transactions; on 17 Sept. 1954 a more drastic law requiring the decimal metric system was passed.

ENERGY AND NATURAL RESOURCES

Electricity. Hurricane 'David' (Aug. 1979) damaged 3 of the hydro-electric plants which produce 30% of electricity supply. 1,943·4m. kwh. of electricity was generated in 1977.

Minerals. The Aluminium Co. of America sent its first shipment of bauxite for smelting, to Texas, on 13 Jan. 1959. Output in 1977 was 574,966 tonnes. Silver and platinum have been found, and near Neiba there are several hills of rock salt (production 1977, 48,592 tonnes). Copper production (1969) 1,200 tonnes. The Rosario Dominicana goldmines were nationalized in Oct. 1979.

Agriculture. Agriculture is the chief source of wealth, sugar cultivation being the principal industry. Of the total area, 9,900 sq. miles are cultivable, and about 3,700 are under cultivation.

Livestock in 1979: 2·15m. cattle, 700,000 pigs, 53,000 sheep.

The largest sugar estates are in the south-eastern part of the republic. Sugar production, 1980–81, was 1·25m. tonnes. Two companies produce four-fifths of the total, but in all there are 16 sugar 'centrals'.

Coffee is exported mainly to USA. Output, 1976, 31,851 tonnes. Production of rice for home consumption and export is fostered; output, 1977, 288,959 tonnes. Cocoa is the second principal crop and covers 2m. *tareas* (340,000 acres); output in 1977, 25,755 tonnes. Other principal exports are leaf tobacco and molasses (17,673 tonnes in 1977). There are useful crops of yuca (1977: 162,287 tonnes) and beans

(1977: 38,792 tonnes) for local consumption. Scientific growing of bananas (1977: 290,837 tonnes) and of tobacco (1977: 34,918 tonnes) is progressing.

INDUSTRY AND TRADE

Industry. In 1975, 1,286 industrial establishments employed 130,000 men and women, who earned RD$157·57m. Output was valued at RD$205·1m. There were 1,036 establishments in 1970. Important manufactures are sugar (1,342,000 tonnes in 1977), textiles (7m. metres of cotton fabric in 1972), cement (678,000 tonnes in 1972), glass bottles, paper and matches. Oil refining capacity was 1·5m. tonnes in 1972, and chemical plants produced 57,000 hectolitres of ethyl alcohol.

Commerce. Total imports and exports in RD$1m. (equal to US$1m.):

	1973	1974	1975	1976	1977	1978
Imports	421·9	673·0	893·4	763·6	847·6	859·2
Exports	442·1	636·8	893·8	716·4	780·5	675·5

The principal exports in 1977 were (in RD$1m.): Sugar and by-products, 247·8; coffee, 184·7; cocoa and by-products, 93; ferronickel, 92·32; bauxite, 22·09; meat, 9·3 (1974); fruit and vegetables, 8·8 (1974); tobacco, 1·05.

Total trade between the Dominican Republic and UK (British Department of Trade returns, in £1,000 sterling):

	1976	1977	1978	1979	1980
Imports to UK	4,063	2,025	971	5,174	4,788
Exports and re-exports from UK	9,537	10,501	9,660	9,627	11,514

Tourism. 395,699 tourists visited the Dominican Republic in 1977.

COMMUNICATIONS

Roads. Three main trunk highways, with branches, extend from Santo Domingo eastward to Higuey (106 miles), northward to Santiago and Montecristi and Dajabón (204 miles) and westward to San Juan (128 miles) and Elías Piña on the Haitian border (161 miles). At Elías Piña the road joins the Haitian road to Port-au-Prince. Total highway system in 1977 was 5,224 km first-, 1,538 km second- and 2,505 km third-class roads; there were 647 bridges. Road transport is the chief means of travel. There were 82,001 cars, 40,626 commercial vehicles and 34,967 motor cycles in 1977.

Railways. Some 100 km of the Dominican Government Railway remains in use between La Vega and the port of Sánchez. Other lines, including the Central Romana Railway, exist to serve the sugar industry.

Aviation. The country is reached from the American continent and the Caribbean islands by 8 international airlines. Two local aviation companies provide interior services and connect Santo Domingo with San Juan in Puerto Rico, Curaçao, Aruba and Miami.

Shipping. Santo Domingo is the leading port; Puerto Plata ranks next. In 1971, vessels of 9,833,000 tons entered the ports to discharge 3,009,000 tonnes of cargo, and vessels of 5,276,000 tons cleared the ports having loaded 1,986,000 tonnes.

Post and Broadcasting. Number of telephone instruments (1978), 139,412, of which 104,197 in Santo Domingo. The telephone system is mainly operated by an American company. The telegraph has a total length of about 500 km, privately owned; they have been leased to All-America Cables, Inc., which also controls submarine cables connecting, in the north, Puerto Plata with Puerto Rico and New York, and in the south, Santo Domingo with Puerto Rico, Cuba and Curaçao.

There are 151 broadcasting stations in Santo Domingo and other towns; this includes the 2 government stations. There are 4 television stations.

Cinemas (1978). Cinemas numbered 72, with seating capacity of about 40,000.

Newspapers (1978). There were 7 daily newspapers with a circulation of 155,000.

JUSTICE, RELIGION, EDUCATION AND WELFARE

Justice. The judicial power resides in the Supreme Court of Justice, the courts of appeal, the courts of first instance, the communal courts and other tribunals created by special laws, such as the land courts. The Supreme Court consists of a president and 8 judges chosen by the Senate, and the procurator-general, appointed by the executive; it supervises the lower courts. Each province forms a judicial district, as does the *Distrito Nacional*, and each has its own procurator fiscal and court of first instance; these districts are subdivided, in all, into 72 municipalities and 18 municipal districts, each with one or more local justices. The death penalty was abolished in 1924.

Religion. The religion of the state is Roman Catholic; other forms of religion are permitted. There is a papal nuncio as well as an archbishop, known as the Primate of the Indies.

Education. Primary instruction (5,245 schools) is free and obligatory for children between 7 and 14 years of age; there are also secondary, normal, vocational and special schools, all of which are either wholly maintained by the State or state-aided; in 1975, primary schools had 15,216 teachers and 833,439 pupils; 997 intermediate and secondary schools had 4,950 teachers and 142,501 pupils. The campaign against adult illiteracy dates from 1941, but in 1964 about 65% of the population were still illiterate.

The University of Santo Domingo (founded 1538) had (1975) 27,675 students; 5 other universities had 14,573 students.

Health. In 1978, 78 towns had complete waterworks. There were, in 1975, 1,310 doctors, 121 hospitals, health centres and polyclinics with 8,389 beds.

DIPLOMATIC REPRESENTATIVES

OF THE DOMINICAN REPUBLIC IN GREAT BRITAIN
(4 Braemar Mansions, London, SW7 4AG)

Ambassador: Alfredo A. Ricart.

OF GREAT BRITAIN IN THE DOMINICAN REPUBLIC
(Ave. Independencia 506, Santo Domingo)

Ambassador: M. A. Cafferty.

OF THE DOMINICAN REPUBLIC IN THE USA
(1715–22nd St., NW, Washington, D.C., 20008)

Ambassador: Francisco Augusto Lora.

OF THE USA IN THE DOMINICAN REPUBLIC
(Calle Cesar Nicolas Penson, Santo Domingo)

Ambassador: Robert L. Yost.

OF THE DOMINICAN REPUBLIC TO THE UNITED NATIONS

*Ambassador:*Ana Esther de la Maza Vasquez.

Books of Reference

Anuario estadístico de la República Dominicana, 1944–45. Ciudad Trujillo. 1949. This has been succeeded by separate annual reports covering foreign trade, vital statistics, banking, insurance, housing and communications.
Dirección General de Estadística. *21 años de estadísticas dominicanas 1936–1956.* Ciudad Trujillo, 1957.—*Republica Dominicana en Cifras 1978.* Ciudad Trujillo, 1979
Bell, I., *The Dominican Republic.* London, 1980
Diederich, B., *Trujillo: The Death of the Goat.* London, 1978

ECUADOR

Capital: Quito
Population: 7·81m. (1979)
GNP per capita: US$910 (1978)

República del Ecuador

HISTORY. The Spaniards under Francisco Pizarro founded a colony after their victory at Cajamarca (16 Nov. 1532). Their rule was first challenged by the rising of 10 Aug. 1809. Marshal Sucre defeated the Spaniards at Pichincha in 1821, and in 1822 Bolívar persuaded the new republic to join the federation of Gran Colombia. The Presidency of Quito became the Republic of Ecuador by amicable secession 13 May 1830.

AREA AND POPULATION. Ecuador is bounded on the north by Colombia, on the east and south by Peru, on the west by the Pacific ocean. The frontier with Peru has long been a source of dispute between the two countries. The latest delimitation of it was in the treaty of Rio, 29 Jan. 1942, when, after being invaded by Peru, Ecuador ceded the latter over half her Amazonian territories. Ecuador unilaterally denounced this treaty in Sept. 1961. *See* map in THE STATESMAN'S YEAR-BOOK, 1942. Fighting between Peru and Ecuador began again in Jan. 1981 over this border issue but a ceasefire was agreed in early Feb.

No definite figure of the area of the country can yet be given, as a portion of the frontier has not been delimited. One estimate of the area of Ecuador is 270,670 sq. km, excluding the litigation zone between Peru and Ecuador, which is 190,807 sq. km.

Ecuador has 3 distinct zones: the *Sierra* or uplands of the Andes, consisting of high mountain ridges with valleys, with 2·57m. of the population and high-priced farming land; the *Costa*, the coastal plain between the Andes and the Pacific, with 2·02m., whose permanent plantations furnish bananas, cacao, coffee, sugar-cane and many other crops; the *Oriente*, the upper Amazon basin on the east, consisting of tropical jungles threaded by large rivers.

The population is predominantly of Amerindians, with small proportions of people of European or African descent.

The official language is Spanish. The Amerindians of the highlands speak mainly the Quechua language; in the Oriental Region various tribes have languages of their own.

Ecuador's first census of population was taken on 29 Nov. 1950; it showed a total of 3,202,757 (1,594,803 males and 1,607,954 females). The census was hampered by strong opposition from the Indian villages. The working population was given as 1,940,628. Census population in 1974, 6,521,710.

The population (census at 8 April 1974) was distributed by provinces (capitals in brackets):

Provinces	Area (sq. km)	Population 1974
Azuay (Cuenca)	7,799	367,324
Bolívar (Guaranda)	3,216	144,593
Cañar (Azogues)	2,677	146,570
Carchi (Tulcán)	3,582	120,857
Chimborazo (Riobamba)	6,161	304,316
Cotopaxi (Latacunga)	4,614	236,313
El Oro (Machala)	7,451	262,564
Esmeraldas (Esmeraldas)	15,866	203,151
Guayas (Guayaquil)	21,259	1,512,333
Imbabura (Ibarra)	4,903	216,027
Loja (Loja)	28,900	342,339
Los Ríos (Babahoyo)	5,937	383,432

Provinces	Area (sq. km)	Population 1974
Manabí (Portoviejo)	18,963	817,966
Pichincha (Quito)	16,438	988,306
Tungurahua (Ambato)	3,204	279,920
Napo (Tena)	⎫	⎧ 62,186
Pastaza (Puyo)	⎪	⎪ 23,465
Morona-Santiago (Macas)	⎬ 296,390	⎨ 53,325
Zamora-Chinchipe (Zamora)	⎭	⎩ 34,493
Colon (Galápagos)	7,844	4,037
Total	455,454	6,521,710

There are 115 cantons, 212 urban parishes and 715 rural parishes. The chief towns (population census, 1974) are the capital, Quito (559,828), Guayaquil (823,219), Cuenca (104,470), Ambato (77,955), Machala (69,170), Esmeraldas (60,364), Portoviejo (59,550), Riobamba (58,087).

Vital statistics for calendar years: Births, (1964) 219,137, (1965) 226,436, (1966) 220,930; deaths, (1964) 58,989, (1965) 60,202, (1966) 59,618.

CONSTITUTION AND GOVERNMENT. On 22 June 1970 President José Maria Velasco Ibarra assumed dictatorial powers, following months of strife between student and security forces. For details of governments 1963–70, *see* THE STATESMAN'S YEAR-BOOK, 1974–75, pp. 875–76. On 15 Feb. 1972 President Velasco Ibarra was deposed. A National Military Government under Brig.-Gen. Guillermo Rodriguez Lara was formed and the 1945 Constitution reintroduced. President Rodriguez Lara resigned in Jan. 1976 and a military Junta assumed power until the 1979 elections. A new Constitution came into force on 10 Aug. 1979.

National flag: Three horizontal stripes of yellow, blue, red, with the yellow of double width, and in the centre over all the national arms.

National anthem: Salve, oh patria! (words by J. L. Mera; tune by A. Neumann, 1866).

The following is a list of the presidents and provisional executives since 1940:

Carlos Alberto Arroyo del Rio, elected 12 Jan. 1940; resigned 30 May 1944.

Dr José María Velasco Ibarra, elected by Constituent Assembly, Aug. 1944; re-elected 11 Aug. 1946, but deposed 24 Aug. 1947.

Col. Carlos Mancheno, seized power 24 Aug. 1947; deposed 3 Sept. 1947.

Mariano Suárez Veintimilla (Vice-President), 3–15 Sept. 1947.

Carlos Julio Arosemena Tola (provisional), 15 Sept. 1947–31 Aug. 1948.

Galo Plaza Lasso, 1 Sept. 1948–31 Aug. 1952.

Dr José María Velasco Ibarra, 1 Sept. 1952–31 Aug. 1956.

Dr Camilo Ponce Enríquez, 1 Sept. 1956–31 Aug. 1960.

Dr José María Velasco Ibarra, 1 Sept. 1960–8 Nov. 1961 (withdrew).

Dr Carlos Julio Arosemena Monroy, 8 Nov. 1961–11 July 1963 (deposed).

Military Junta, 11 July 1963–31 March 1966.

Clemente Yerovi Indaburu, 31 March–16 Nov. 1966 (interim).

Dr Otto Arosemena Gómez, 17 Nov. 1966–1 Sept. 1968.

Dr José María Velasco Ibarra, 1 Sept. 1968–15 Feb. 1972 (deposed).

Gen. Guillermo Rodriguez Lara, 16 Feb. 1972–11 Jan. 1976 (resigned).

Adm. Alfredo Povedo Burbano, 11 Jan. 1976–10 Aug. 1979.

President: Jaime Roldós Aguilera (sworn in on 10 Aug. 1979).

The Cabinet in Dec. 1980 was as follows:

Minister of Interior: Dr Carlos Feraud Blum. *Foreign Affairs:* Dr Alfonso Barrera Valverde. *Finance:* Rodrigo Paz Delgado. *Industry, Trade and Integration:* Dr Germánico Salgado P. *Agriculture and Livestock:* Dr Antonio Andrade Fajardo. *Natural Resources and Energy:* César Robalino Gonzaga. *Labour and Human Resources:* Dr Aquiles Rigail Santistevan. *Education and Sport:* Dr Galo García Feraud. *Defence:* Marco Subía Martínez. *Health:* Dr Humberto Guillén Murillo. *Social Welfare:* Alfredo Mancero Saman. *Public Works and Communications:* Francisco Saa Chacón. *Chamber of Representatives President:* Raúl Vaca Carbo.

Local Government. The country is divided politically into 20 provinces; 4 of them comprise the 'Región Oriental' and one the Archipelago of Galápagos, officially called 'Colón', situated in the Pacific ocean about 600 miles to the west of Ecuador and comprising 15 islands. The provinces are administered by governors, appointed by the Government; their sub-divisions, or cantons, by political chiefs and elected cantonal councillors; and the parishes by political lieutenants. The Galápagos Archipelago is administered by the Ministry of National Defence.

DEFENCE. Military service is selective, with a 2-year period of conscription. The country is divided into 4 military zones, with headquarters at Quito, Guayaquil, Cuenca and Pastaza.

Army. The Army consists of 12 infantry brigades, 6 armoured brigades, 1 parachute battalion, 3 artillery battalions, 1 horsed regiment, 3 reconnaissance squadrons, 2 engineer battalions, 1 anti-aircraft battalion and 10 independent infantry companies. A military academy for cadets and a war academy for officers are maintained at Quito. Total strength (1980) 30,000.

Navy. The Navy consists of 2 new Federal Republic of Germany-built diesel-electric powered patrol submarines; 1 old *ex*-US destroyer; 1 frigate (*ex*-US destroyer escort transport), 3 fast missile boats, 3 fast torpedo boats, 2 gunboats, 5 patrol boats, 1 landing ship, 2 medium landing ships, 1 supply ship, 1 water carrier, 3 survey vessels, 2 coastguard service craft, 2 coastal patrol launches, 1 repair vessel, 2 training ships, 1 floating dock and 6 tugs. Six corvettes have been ordered from Italy. The two old *ex*-US PCE type escort vessels are now used one as a survey ship and the other as an harbour training ship. Naval personnel in 1981 totalled 300 officers and 3,500 men.

Air Force. The Air Force, formed with Italian assistance in 1920, was reorganized and re-equipped with US aircraft after Ecuador signed the Rio Pact of Mutual Defence in 1947 but latest equipment acquired from Europe. Current strength of about 4,800 personnel and 55 combat aircraft includes a strike squadron equipped with 10 single-seat and 2 two-seat Jaguars; an interceptor squadron of 16 single-seat and 2 two-seat Mirage F.1s; a bomber squadron with 5 Canberra B.6s; 2 counter-insurgency units equipped with 10 Cessna A-37B and 12 Strikemaster light jet attack and training aircraft, 1 squadron of DC-6B and C-47 piston-engined transports, 1 C-130, 4 Electra, 2 Buffalo, 4 HS 748, 3 Twin Otter and 6 Arava turboprop transports, Alouette III, SA 330 Puma and SA 315B Lama helicopters, and Cessna 150, SIAI-Marchetti SF-260, T-28, T-33, T-34C and T-41A/D trainers.

INTERNATIONAL RELATIONS

Membership. Ecuador is a member of UN, OAS and LAIA (formerly LAFTA).

ECONOMY

Budget. Estimated revenue and expenditure for 1981 was 53,600m. sucres.

The division of the budget under main heads was, for 1976 (in 1m. sucres): Education and social development, 4,487; defence, 2,592; public works, 1,834; economic development including agriculture, 2,050.

Net international reserves, 31 Dec. 1980, were US$857m.

Currency. The monetary unit is the *sucre*, divided into 100 *centavos*. In circulation are a pure nickel 1-sucre and copper–nickel and copper–zinc 50-, 20-, 10- and 5-centavo pieces. The currency consists mainly of the notes of the Central Bank in denominations of 5, 10, 20, 50, 100, 500 and 1,000 sucres. In March 1981 the US$1 stood at 28·10 sucres and the £ at 54·38 sucres in the official exchange.

Banking. The Central Bank of Ecuador, at Quito, with a capital of 20m. sucres, is modelled after the Federal Reserve Banks of US: through branches opened in 12 towns it now deals in mortgage bonds. On 31 July 1970 the Central Bank had gold and foreign-exchange reserves worth US$62m. Banks must hold cash equal to 21% of sight, short-term and savings deposits.

All commercial banks must be affiliated to the Central Bank; the commercial banks, 31 Oct. 1967, had capital and reserves of 463m. sucres and total assets of 4,536m. sucres. In circulation, Dec. 1972, 7,321m. sucres.

The Bank of London and Montreal, Ltd, had branches in Quito and Guayaquil.

Weights and Measures. By a law of 6 Dec. 1856 the metric system was made the legal standard but the Spanish measures are in general use. The quintal is equivalent to 101·4 lb.

The meridian of Quito has been adopted as the official time.

ENERGY AND NATURAL RESOURCES

Electricity. In 1980, total capacity of hydraulic and thermal plants was 950,000 kw. Estimated output was 2,000m. kwh.

Oil. Production of crude petroleum in 1979 was 78·2m. bbls; (1978) 73·7m. New drilling along the coast has had some success, but Ecuador has to import some crude oil. Drilling near the river Putumayo started in 1967, and oil is reported to have been found in commercial quantities.

Of 53 wells drilled in 1973 only 6 were dry. Proven oil reserves (1980, estimate) 2,000m. bbls.

Minerals. A few firms are engaged in stoping mineralized vein material for copper, gold, silver, lead and zinc. Production is small: that of silver was 2 tonnes in 1972.

The country has some copper, iron and lead. There are coal deposits in the Biblián area, but their exploitation has so far proved uneconomic. Output of sea salt in 1970 was 40,000 tonnes.

Agriculture. Ecuador is divided into two agricultural zones: the coast and lower river valleys, where tropical farming is carried on in an average temperature of from 18° to 25° C.; and the Andean highlands with a temperate climate, adapted to grazing, dairying and the production of cereals, potatoes, pyrethrum and vegetables suitable to temperate climes. Some wheat has to be imported.

124,000 acres of rich virgin land in the Santo Domingo de los Colorados area has been set aside for settlement of smallholders.

Excepting the two agricultural zones and a few arid spots on the Pacific coast, Ecuador is a vast forest. Roughly estimated, 10,000 sq. miles on the Pacific slope extending from the sea to an altitude of 5,000 ft on the Andes, and the Amazon Basin below the same level containing 80,000 sq. miles, nearly all virgin forest, are rich in valuable timber, but much of it is still not commercially accessible.

The staple export products are bananas, cacao and coffee. These make up over 82% of her exports; the value of the bananas being some 46%. The production of wheat is increasing. Sugar is becoming important; some tea is being produced, mostly for export. Main crops, in 1,000 tonnes, in 1979: Rice, 303; wheat, 19; potatoes, 545; maize, 217; coffee, 102; barley, 26; cocoa, 78; bananas, 2,391.

Livestock (1979): Cattle, 2·5m.; sheep, 2·3m.; pigs, 3·4m.

Fisheries. Fisheries and fish product exports were valued at US$9·6m. in 1970; of these, shrimps comprised about half.

INDUSTRY AND TRADE

Industry. The Industrial Development Law of 1965 has stimulated the establishment of new industries, including textiles, refrigerators, pharmaceuticals, tinned food, batteries, etc. In 1971 there were 1,053 manufacturing units employing 50,000 people who earned 1·1m. sucres. Value of gross output, 11,172m. sucres. Cement output, 1972, from the country's 3 plants was 482,000 tonnes. Production (in tonnes) of sawn wood was 792,000; fuel oils, 691; motor spirit, 407; sugar, 275.

GNP *per capita* (1975) US$635.

Commerce. Imports and exports for calendar years, in US$1m.:

	1976	1977	1978	1979	1980
Imports (c.i.f.)	860·7	1,288·7	1,630	1,997	1,552
Exports (f.o.b.)	1,127·3	1,189·4	1,494	2,192	2,471

Of the total exports (1980) bananas were US$211·1m.; cocoa, US$211m.; coffee, US$143·7m.

USA furnished 35% of imports in 1970 and took 43% of the exports.

Total trade between Ecuador and UK (British Department of Trade returns, in £1,000 sterling):

	1976	1977	1978	1979	1980
Imports to UK	2,540	4,978	4,275	6,210	8,844
Exports and re-exports from UK	23,260	59,522	33,035	33,483	30,930

Tourism. There were 240,000 visitors in 1979, mainly from South American countries.

COMMUNICATIONS

Roads. There are 17,195 km of roads of all types in this mountainous country, but most are narrow and subject to landslides. A trunk highway through the coastal plain is under construction which will link Machala in the extreme south-west with Esmeraldas in the north-west and with Quito and the northern section of the Pan-American Highway.

In 1971 there were 30,000 passenger cars and 44,300 commercial vehicles.

Railways. A 1,067 mm gauge line runs from San Lorenzo through Quito to Guayaquil and Cuenca, total 965 km.

Aviation. The following international lines operate: Air France, Avianca, Braniff, British Caledonian, Ecuatoriana de Aviación, KLM, Lufthansa, Iberia, LAN Chile, and Aerovías Peruanas. They connect Quito with Panama, Bogotá (Colombia), Guayaquil, New York and Europe. All the leading towns are connected by an almost daily service, but landing fields are small.

Shipping. Ecuador has 7 seaports, of which Guayaquil is the chief. The merchant navy comprises 39,964 tons of seagoing and 21,232 tons of river craft. In 1970 ships totalling 8·88m. GRT entered Ecuadorean ports, unloading 1·52m. tons, and loading 1·77m. tons.

There is river communication, improved by dredging, throughout the principal agricultural districts on the low ground to the west of the Cordillera by the rivers Guayas, Daule and Vinces (navigable for 200 miles by river steamers in the rainy season).

Post and Broadcasting. Quito is connected by telegraph with Colombia and Peru, and by cable with the rest of the world. The main towns in the country are connected by radio-telephone. There are over 300 radio stations.

In 1978 there were 221,578 telephones in use, 76,143 in Quito and 66,394 in Guayaquil; most were operated by the Government; 80·6% were automatic. Television was inaugurated in 1960 in Guayaquil, in 1961 in Quito and in 1967 in Cuenca. In 1971 there were 1·7m. radio receivers and 280,000 television receivers.

Cinemas (1974). Cinemas numbered about 185 with total seating capacity of 114,600.

Newspapers (1971). There were 22 daily newspapers with an aggregate daily circulation of 283,000; 7 papers in Quito and Guayaquil have the bulk of the circulation.

JUSTICE, RELIGION, EDUCATION AND WELFARE

Justice. The Supreme Court in Quito is the highest tribunal and consists of 5 justices and the Minister Fiscal. Of the 15 superior courts, 4 are composed of 6 judges and 11 of 3 judges each. There are numerous lower courts. The popular jury was abolished in 1928, and criminal cases are heard before a 'special jury' consisting of 1 judge and 3 members of the Ecuadorean bar, appointed annually by the superior courts. Capital punishment and all forms of torture are prohibited under the constitution, as are imprisonment for debt and contracts involving personal servitude or slavery. Substantial amendments expediting judicial procedure were introduced in 1936, and salaries for all judicial officials replaced remuneration by fees.

Religion. The state recognizes no religion and grants freedom of worship to all. Civil registration of births, deaths and marriages is obligatory. Divorce is permitted. Illegitimate children have the same rights as legitimate ones with respect to education and inheritance.

The Catholic Church has 1 cardinal, 3 archbishops and 18 bishops. A *modus vivendi* was concluded with the Holy See on 24 July 1937, governing the relations between the Catholic Church and the State. Protestants numbered 19,200 in 1966.

Education. Primary education is free and in principle obligatory. Private schools, both primary and secondary, are under some state supervision. There were (1976–77) primary schools with 1,318,475 pupils; secondary schools with 431,226 pupils and universities with 170,173 students.

Social Welfare. From 1 May 1964 social benefits are extended to professional men, artisans and domestic workers; and to agricultural workers from 1 May 1965. The Ministry of Social Welfare and Labour was in 1967 divided into the Ministries of Social Welfare and of Public Health. In 1970 there were 199 hospitals with 14,024 beds.

DIPLOMATIC REPRESENTATIVES

OF ECUADOR IN GREAT BRITAIN (3 Hans Crescent, London, SW1X 0LS)

Ambassador: Orlando Gabela (accredited 12 March 1980).

OF GREAT BRITAIN IN ECUADOR (Calle Gonzalez Suarez 197, Quito)

Ambassador: J. K. Hickman, CMG.

OF ECUADOR IN THE USA (2535–15th St., NW, Washington, D.C., 20009)

Ambassador: Dr Ricardo Crespo Z.

OF THE USA IN ECUADOR (120 Avenida Patria, Quito)

Ambassador: Raymond E. Gonzalez.

OF ECUADOR TO THE UNITED NATIONS

Ambassador: Dr Miguel A. Albornoz.

Books of Reference

Anurio de Legislación Ecuatoriana. Quito. Annual
Boletin del Banco Central. Quito
Boletin General de Estadistica. Tri-monthly
Boletín Mensual del Ministerio de Obras Públicas. Monthly
Informes Ministeriales. Quito. Annual
Bibliografia Nacional, 1756–1941. Quito, 1942
Invest in Ecuador. Banco Central del Ecuador, Quito, 1980
Blanksten, G. I., *Ecuador: Constitutions and Caudillos.* Univ. of California Press, 1951
Bromley, R. J., *Development Planning in Ecuador.* London, 1977
Buitrón, Aníbal, and Collier, Jr, J., *The Awakening Valley: Study of the Otavalo Indians.* New York, 1950
Holdridge, L. R., and others, *The Forests of Western and Central Ecuador.* Washington, 1947
Linke, L., *Ecuador, Country of Contrasts.* R. Inst. of Int. Affairs, 3rd ed., 1959
Luna Yepes, J., *Sintesis histórica y geográfica del Ecuador.* Madrid, 1951
Martz, J. D., *Ecuador: Conflicting Political Culture and the Quest for Progress.* Boston, 1972

ARAB REPUBLIC OF EGYPT

Capital: Cairo
Population: 40·98m. (1979)
GNP per capita: US$400 (1978)

HISTORY. On 1 Feb. 1958 President Nasser of Egypt and President Kuwatly of Syria proclaimed in Cairo the union of their countries, under one head of state, with a common legislature, a unified army and one flag.

On 8 March the Kingdom of Yemen federated with the United Arab Republic under the name of the United Arab States.

On 26–28 Sept. 1961 Syria broke away and resumed its independence. President Nasser accepted the situation on 29 Sept.

On 26 Dec. 1961 Egypt also declared the union with Yemen terminated; but in Nov. 1962 concluded a defence pact with the republican regime.

On 13 Aug. 1964 the UAR, Iraq, Kuwait, Jordan and Syria signed a document forming an Arab Common Market, which aims at the free movement of the currency and products of the member countries. The market was to come into being on 1 Jan. 1965, but this has not taken place.

Following President Sadat's visit to Israel in Nov. 1977 and considerable political activity including the Camp David (USA) summit in Sept. 1978 a Peace Treaty was signed between Israel and Egypt in Washington on 26 March 1979 and ratified in Sinai on 26 April 1979.

AREA AND POPULATION. The total area of Egypt is about 386,198 sq. miles (1m. sq. km), but the cultivated and settled area, that is, the Nile valley, delta and oases, covers only about 13,500 sq. miles (35,500 sq. km). Canals, roads, date plantations, etc., cover 1,900 sq. miles; 2,850 sq. miles constitute the surface of the Nile, marshes and lakes.

Egypt is divided into two districts—'Wagh-el-Bahari', Lower Egypt and 'El-Saïd', Upper Egypt.

The following table gives the total area, and the results of the census taken in 1966 and estimates for 1976:

Governorates	Area in sq. km	1966 census (in 1,000)	1976 estimate (in 1,000)
Sinai	60,714	131	...
Suez	17,840	264	194
Ismailia	1,442	345	352
Port Said	72	283	263
Sharqîya	4,180	2,108	2,621
Daqahlîya	3,471	2,285	2,733
Damietta	589	432	557
Kafr el Sheikh	3,437	1,118	1,403
Alexandria	2,679	1,801	2,319
Behera	4,589	1,979	2,517
Gharbîya	1,942	1,901	2,294
Menûfîya	1,612	1,458	1,711
Qalyûbîya	971	1,212	1,674
Cairo	214	4,220	5,084
Gîza	1,010	1,650	2,419
Faiyûm	1,827	935	1,140
Beni Suef	1,322	928	1,109
Minya	2,262	1,706	2,056
Asyût	1,530	1,418	1,695
Sohag	1,547	1,689	1,925
Qena	1,851	1,471	1,705
Aswân	679	521	620
Red Sea	203,685	38	...
New Valley	376,505	59	...
Matrûh	2,962	124	...
Total		30,076	36,391

The density of population was 732 per sq. km. The nomadic population of about 78,000 is not included in the table on p. 417.

The principal towns, with their estimated 1974 populations (in 1,000), are: Cairo (city only) 5,715; Alexandria, 2,259; Gîza, 854; Suez, 368; Subra-El Khema, 346; Port Said, 342; Mahalla el Kûbra, 288; Tanta, 278; Aswân, 246; Mansûra, 232; Asyût, 197; Zagazig, 195; Ismailia, 190; Damanhûr, 176; Faiyûm, 167; Minya, 131.

Estimated population in 1979 was 40·98m. (census, 1966, 30,075,858) and Greater Cairo (1978), 8·3m.

Vital statistics for 1971: Births, 1,479,000; deaths, 445,000.

CONSTITUTION AND GOVERNMENT. A provisional Constitution was proclaimed on 25 March 1964 and a new Constitution on 11 Sept. 1971.

The Constitution defines the UAR as 'a democratic socialist state' and the Egyptian people as 'part of the Arab nation'; with Islam as a state religion and Arabic as the official language. The national economy is directed by the State; the 3 sectors of state, co-operative and private ownership are supervised and controlled by the people. 'Freedom of belief is absolute; freedom of the press, printing and publication is guaranteed within the limits of the law'. Public education is free at all stages.

In May 1980 amendments to the 1971 Constitution were agreed by referendum.

The People's Assembly is elected by universal suffrage and has 360 members; the President of the Republic may appoint up to 10 additional members. The President of the Republic is nominated by the People's Assembly and confirmed by plebiscite for a 6-year term. He is the supreme commander of the armed forces and presides over the defence council.

The Constitution is supplemented by the Charter of 21 May 1962, which sketches the principles and aims of the regime since the overthrow of the monarchy on 23 July 1952; and by the Statute of the Arab Socialist Union of 7 Dec. 1962; and by the Oct. paper, presented by President Sadat in April 1974, which envisages development from now until 2000. This organization has been created as 'the socialist vanguard' for safeguarding and furthering the 'socialist revolution' on all levels of local, district and national administration.

General elections took place on 7 and 14 June 1979 for 372 of the 382 seats in the People's Assembly. There were about 11m. registered voters and voting was compulsory for men. The National Democratic Party gained 330 seats; Socialist Labour Party, 29; Liberal Socialist Party, 3; Independents, 10. In addition 10 members were nominated by the President.

President of the Republic and Prime Minister: Mohammed Anwar El Sadat (sworn in on 17 Oct. 1970 and re-elected 16 Sept. 1976).

The Cabinet in March 1981 was composed as follows:

Deputy Prime Minister: Dr Ahmed Fuad Mohieddin. *Deputy Prime Minister and Minister of Foreign Affairs:* Kamal Hassan Ali. *Deputy Prime Minister for People's Assembly Affairs:* Fikri Makram Ebeid. *Deputy Prime Minister for Public Services and Minister of the Interior:* Mohamed Nabawi Ismail. *Deputy Prime Minister for Production and Minister of Petroleum:* Ahmed Ezzeddin Hilal. *Deputy Prime Minister for Economic and Financial Affairs and Minister of Planning, Finance and Economy:* Dr Abdel Razzak Abdel Meguid. *Defence and Military Production:* Lieut.-Gen. Muhammed Abdul Halim Abu Ghazada. *Education and Scientific Research:* Dr Mustafa Kamal Helmy. *Social Insurance and Social Affairs:* Dr Amal Abdel Halim Osman. *Construction, Housing and Land Reclamation:* Hassaballah Mohamed El Kafrawi. *Foreign Affairs:* Dr Butros Butros Ghali. *Manpower and Vocational Training:* Saad Mohamed Ahmed. *Agriculture and Food Sufficiency:* Dr Mahmoud Mohamed Daoud. *Transport, Communication and Maritime Transport:* Soliman Metwalli Soliman. *Irrigation and Sudan Affairs:* Abdel Hadi Samaha. *People's Assembly Affairs:* Abdel Akhar Mohamed Amer Abdel Akhar. *Tourism and Civil Aviation:* Ali Gamal El Nazer. *Public Health:* Dr Mamdouh Kamel Gabr. *Justice:* Anwar Abdel Fattah Abou Sehti. *Culture and Information:* Mansour Mohamed Hassan. *Industry and Mineral Wealth:* Mohamed Taha Daki. *Electric*

Power: Mohamed Maher Mohamed Osman Abaza. *Supply and Home Trade:* Ahmed Ahmed Nouh. *Military Production:* Dr Mohamed Gamal Ibrahim. *Wakfs:* Dr Zakaria El Barri.

National flag: Three horizontal stripes of red, white, black, with the national emblem in the centre in gold.

DEFENCE. The total strength of the defence forces was about 367,000 in 1980. There were also paramilitary forces of 49,000.

Army. Service in the Army is compulsory for all male citizens at the age of 18. The Army comprised (1980) 2 armoured divisions, 3 mechanized infantry divisions, 5 infantry divisions, 3 independent armoured and 8 independent infantry brigades, 1 parachute brigade, 2 airborne brigades, 7 artillery brigades and 6 commando groups. Its tank strength (1980) was about 1,680, mainly USSR. Total strength is about 320,000 men; reserves totalled about 500,000.

Navy. There are 12 elderly diesel-driven submarines, 5 old destroyers, 3 old frigates, 10 fleet minesweepers, 4 inshore minesweepers, 30 torpedo boats, 24 missile boats, 12 submarine chasers, 9 coastal patrol boats, 2 training ships, 3 medium landing ships, 14 landing craft, 2 survey vessels, 10 service craft, 2 tenders, 3 hovercraft, 7 auxiliaries and 2 tugs.

The intended acquisition of surplus warships from Britain, comprising a large destroyer, 2 frigates and a diesel powered patrol submarine, in 1978, was rescinded.

The construction of 2 submarines in France, 2 frigates in Italy and 6 fast attack craft in Britain was reportedly included in the 1979 new projects programme.

Naval bases are at Alexandria, Port Said, Mersa Matru, Port Tewfik, Hurghada and Safaqa. The Naval Academy is at Abu Quir.

Naval personnel in 1981 exceeded 17,500 officers and men, including the Coastguard, but not reserves of about 12,000.

Air Force. Until 1979, the Air Force was equipped largely with aircraft of USSR design, but current re-equipment involves aircraft bought in the West, as well as some supplied by China. Current strength is about 27,000 personnel and 360 combat aircraft, of which the interceptors are operated by an independent Air Defence Command, in conjunction with many 'Guideline', 'Goa' and 'Gainful' missile batteries. There are about 23 Tu-16 twin-jet strategic bombers, some equipped to carry 'Kelt' air-to-surface missiles. The main strike force includes some Il-28 twin-jet bombers, and about 60 Su-7B and 18 Su-20 supersonic fighter-bombers. Other interceptor/ground attack fighter divisions are equipped with 45 Mirage IIIEs, 14 Mirage 5s, 35 F-4E Phantoms, 40 F-6s (Chinese-built MiG-19s), about 95 MiG-21s and 30 MiG-17s. Many other Soviet-built aircraft are in reserve. Transport units have an estimated 16 An-12 and 17 C-130H Hercules turboprop heavy freighters, 26 Il-14 twin-engined transports, a few An-24s and up to 175 Gazelle, Mi-4, Mi-6, Mi-8 and Sea King/Commando helicopters; 2 EC-130H Hercules are equipped for ECM duties. Training units are equipped with Gomhouria piston-engined trainers, Czech-built L-29 Delfin jet trainers, single-seat and two-seat versions of the MiG-15, and two-seat TF-6s, Mirage IIIs, MiG-21Us and Su-7Us.

INTERNATIONAL RELATIONS

Membership. Egypt is a member of UN, OAU, the Arab League and OAPEC.

ECONOMY

Planning. A 'permanent council of national production' was established in 1952.

The 10-year development plan 1973–83 envisages an initial investment by the public and private sectors of £E8,400m.

In 1961–62 a number of sweeping socialist measures were carried out, which contributed largely to the Syrian defection in Sept. 1961. In addition to the nationalization of banks, insurance companies, etc., about 1,000 private businessmen had their property confiscated by Jan. 1962. In 1963 complete nationalization was enforced of all cotton exporting and ginning firms, pharmaceutical factories and some 400 other companies in which the State had previously held a half-share. Share owners were compensated by government bonds redeemable over 15 years at 4% interest.

Budget. Ordinary revenue and expenditure for fiscal years ending 30 June, in £E1,000:

	1976[1]	1977[1]	1978[1]	1979[1]
Revenue	5,976	5,503	6,516	10,249
Expenditures	5,976	5,503	6,516	12,929

[1] Estimates.

Currency. By decree of 18 Oct. 1916 (20 Zi-El-Higga 1934), the monetary unit of Egypt is the gold Egyptian pound of 100 *piastres* of 1,000 *millièmes*. Coins in circulation are 20, 10, 5, 2 piastres (silver); 2, 1 piastre, 5 millièmes, 1 millième (bronze). Gold coins are no longer in circulation. Silver coin is legal tender only up to £E1, and bronze coins up to 10 piastres. The Treasury issues 5- and 10-piastre currency notes. Bank-notes are issued by the National Bank in denominations of 5, 10, 25 and 50 piastres, £E1, 5, 10, 20, and 100.

In March 1981, £1 sterling = £E1·53; US$ = £E1·449.

Banking. On 18 Aug. 1960 a Central Bank of Egypt was established by decree. It manages the note issue, the Government's banking operations and the control of commercial banks. At the same date the National Bank founded in 1898 ceased to be the central bank and became a purely commercial bank. The position of the bank at 31 Dec. 1976 was (in £E): Capital and reserves, 28,778,550; investments, securities and other investments, 78,252,590; discounts, advances and sundry debit balances, 607,652,637; deposits, 525,853,275.

Weights and Measures. In 1951 the metric system was made official with the exception of the feddân and its subdivisions.

Capacity. Kadah = 1/96th ardeb = 3·36 pints. *Rob* = 4 kadahs = 1·815 gallons. *Keila* = 8 kadahs = 3·63 gallons. *Ardeb* = 96 kadahs = 43,555 gallons, or 5·44439 bu., or 198 cu. decimetres.

Weights. Rotl = 144 dirhems = 0·9905 lb. *Oke* = 400 dirhems = 2·75137 lb. *Qantâr* or 100 rotls or 36 okes = 99·0493 lb. 1 *Qantâr* of unginned cotton = 315 lb. 1 *Qantâr* of ginned cotton = 99·05 lb. The approximate weight of the ardeb is as follows: Wheat, 150 kg; beans, 155 kg; barley, 120 kg; maize, 140 kg; cotton seed, 121 kg.

Surface. Feddân, the unit of measure for land = 4,200·8 sq. metres = 7,468·148 sq. pics = 1·03805 acres. 1 sq. pic = 6·0547 sq. ft = 0·5625 sq. metre.

ENERGY AND NATURAL RESOURCES

Electricity. Electricity generated in 1969 was 7,316m. kw.

Oil. The first commercial discovery of oil in the Middle East outside Iran was made in Egypt in 1909, but production long remained low and often insufficient to meet Egypt's domestic requirements. In 1979 production was rising again and with the newly-regained Sinai oilfields was 25·5m. tonnes. In 1976 a major exploration effort was being mounted and the Egyptian Government hoped that, as a result, production will reach 1m. bbls a day by 1981.

Policy is controlled by the Egyptian General Petroleum Corporation (EGPC) a wholly state-owned corporation answerable to the Minister of Petroleum. EGPC is whole or part-owner of the various production and refining companies and controls supplies to the domestic marketing companies.

In 1978, 24,299,000 tonnes of crude petroleum and 11,362,000 tonnes of refined products were produced.

Minerals. Production (1973 in tonnes): Phosphate rock, 553,000; iron ore, 656,000; marine salt, 454,000.

Agriculture. Rain seldom falls in Upper Egypt, and only at irregular intervals in Cairo, where the average for the year is no more than 1·2 in. At Alexandria the average is 8 in.

The cultivated area of Egypt proper was estimated in 1971 at 10·74m. feddâns (1 feddân = 1·038 acres) and of this 4,869,000 feddâns were under winter crops, 5,012,000 under summer crops and 613,000 under Nile crops.

The Agricultural Reform Decree of Sept. 1952 limits agricultural ownership to 200 feddâns, reduced to 100 feddâns in July 1961. Foreigners were debarred in 1963 from owning any land. Holdings in excess of this limit will be redistributed; compensation, equivalent to 10 times the rental value of the land, will take the form of 3% (from 1958: 1½%) bonds redeemable within 30 years (from 1958: 40 years). All national *waqfs* are to be dissolved.

Irrigation occupies a predominant place in the economic development of the country. The Aswân reservoir can now hold up to 5,500m. cu. metres of water, and the Gebel Aulia reservoir, completed in 1937, holds 2,000m. cu. metres. Barrages have been erected at Esna, Nag' Hammâdi, Asyût and Zifta, and at the bifurcation of the Nile below Cairo. Nag' Hammâdi barrage, completed in 1930, ensures full basin supplies even in low flood to Girga province, and will facilitate perennial irrigation when basin lands are converted. Asyût barrage, having been remodelled, will meet the greater demands of the area it now commands. The Esna barrage now secures basin irrigation to lands in Qena province. New barrages (Mohamed Ali barrages) have been completed at the bifurcation of the Nile below Cairo to replace the existing structures which, built in 1861, are now unable to meet the conditions following the increase in summer supplies, the reclamation of large areas of waste lands and the earlier watering of food crops.

On 8 Nov. 1959 the United Arab Republic and Sudan concluded agreements on the sharing of the Nile waters (after construction of the Aswân High Dam), and trade, payments and Customs dues. The agreement provides that from the time the High Dam started to store water (15 May 1964) Sudan will be entitled to 18,500m. cu. metres of the total annual flow and Egypt to 55,500m.

In 1979 the area (1,000 hectares) and production (1,000 tonnes) were: Wheat, 584(1,856); barley, 45(122); beans (dry), 7(13); lentils, 9(9); onions, 21(536); maize, 791(2,938); millet, 171(635); sugar-cane, 105(8,488).

The rice crop was 2·3m. tonnes in 1977.

Livestock (1979): 1·95m. cattle, 2·3m. buffaloes, 1·7m. sheep, 1·4m. goats, 105,000 camels and 15,000 pigs.

Fisheries. The catch of the Egyptian sea, Nile and lake fisheries in 1957 amounted to 102,600 tonnes. In 1952 there were 48,947 men and 16,347 boys engaged in fishing and 11,739 boats used for fishing.

INDUSTRY AND TRADE

Industry. The census of industrial production (1966) showed 875,000 persons engaged in 4,000 industrial establishments employing 10 or more persons. Total value of industrial production in 1963 was £E952·6m.

Production in 1962 of pig-iron was 99,770 tonnes; of steel ingots and castings, 149,655 tonnes.

Electricity generated in 1969 was 7,316m. kw.

Trade Unions. Trade unions were first recognized in 1942. In 1952 the acts concerning trade unions, individual contracts, and conciliation and arbitration were recast. Employment exchanges and unemployment statistics were introduced in 1953. Social insurance was enacted in 1955.

Commerce. Imports and exports for 6 years (in £E1,000):

	1973	1974	1975	1976	1977	1978
Imports	357,500	919,200	1,539,300	1,489,908	1,884,278	2,632,180
Exports	444,200	593,300	548,600	595,450	668,478	679,754

Raw cotton and cotton products represent over 60% of total exports.

Total trade between Egypt and UK (British Department of Trade returns, in £1,000 sterling):

	1976	1977	1978	1979	1980
Imports to UK	65,254	88,065	101,685	252,733	336,595
Exports and re-exports from UK	171,851	190,516	205,570	264,494	346,688

Tourism. In 1979, 1,064,000 foreigners visited Egypt.

COMMUNICATIONS

Roads. In 1980, the total length of roads was 21,637 km, of which 16,182 km were paved. Motor vehicles, in 1977, 283,000 private cars, 64,000 commercial vehicles (including buses).

Railways. In 1980 there were 4,446 km of state railways and 2,554 km of service tracks etc. The state railways have a gauge of 4 ft $8\frac{1}{2}$ in., except that to the Western Oases, which is 2 ft $5\frac{1}{2}$ in.

In 1978 the railways ran 10,760m. passenger-km.

Aviation. There is an international airport at Cairo. A new airport at Cairo began operations in 1977. The national airline Egyptair has a fleet of 20 aircraft. Egyptair operates scheduled flights connecting Cairo with Athens, Rome, Frankfurt, Zürich, London, Khartoum, Tōkyō, Bombay, Aden, Jeddah, Doha, Dharan, Kuwait, Beirut, Baghdad, Tripoli, Benghazi, Algiers, Entebbe, Nairobi, Dar-es-Salaam, Kano, Lagos, Accra, Abidjan, Damascus, Amman, Manilla, Paris, Munich, Copenhagen, Nicosia, Karachi, Aleppo, Bahrain, Abu Dhabi, Dubai, Sharjah, Sanaa and Vienna. In addition, Egyptair operates scheduled flights on a widespread domestic network connecting Cairo with Port Said, Mersa Matruh, Assiout, Luxor, Aswân.

Shipping. The Egyptian merchant navy in 1980 consisted of 75 steamers of 387,460 tons.

In 1977, 3,050 ships of 11,432,000 tons entered the port of Alexandria and 876 ships of 4,583,000 tons entered Port Said.

Suez Canal. The Suez Canal was opened for navigation on 17 Nov. 1869. By the convention of Constantinople of 29 Oct. 1888 the canal is open to vessels of all nations and is free from blockade, except in time of war, but the UAR Government did not allow Israeli ships to use the canal until May 1979, when the embargo was lifted. It is 173 km long (excluding 11 km of approach channels to the harbours), connecting the Mediterranean with the Red Sea. Its minimum width is 197 ft at a depth of 33 ft, and its depth permits the passage of vessels up to 38 ft draught.

In 1976 a 2-stage development project was started. The first stage which was completed in 1980 allowing vessels, of up to 150,000 tons, fully loaded, and up to 370,000 tons in ballast to pass through the canal and give a draught of 53 ft.

During the war with Israel in June 1967 Egypt blocked the Canal. The canal was cleared and re-opened to shipping on 5 June 1975. This is part of a programme to develop and rebuild the whole area of Suez to make it one of the largest tax-free industrial zones. Canal toll fees reached £E230m. in 1976, and in 1978 21,266 vessels (248·26m. tons) went through the canal.

On 1 Jan. 1981 charges were increased by 30%. The first tunnel below the canal, located 10 miles north of Suez City, was completed on 30 April 1980.

UNCTAD, *Economic Effects of the Closure of the Suez Canal.* Geneva, 1974
Baxter, R. R., *The Law of International Waterways.* Harvard Univ. Press, 1964
Lauterpacht, E. (ed.), *The Suez Canal Settlement, 1956–59.* London, 1960
Marlow, J., *The Making of the Suez Canal.* London, 1964

Post and Broadcasting. The telephone service was taken over by the Egyptian Government in April 1918. In 1958–59 the state telegraphs had a length of 15,381 km of wire, and telephones, 1,076,159 km. There were, in 1978, 1,590 postal agencies, 1,812 mobile offices, 1,579 government and 2,833 private post offices. Number of telephones in 1975, 503,200. Number of wireless licences in 1975, 5·12m. and 620,000 TV licences.

The internal telecommunications system is owned and operated by the Tele-communications Organization. Government landlines connect with those of the Gaza sector and the Sudan.

Cinemas (1971). There were 152 cinemas with a seating capacity of 140,900.

Newspapers. On 23 May 1960 all newspapers were nationalized.

JUSTICE, RELIGION, EDUCATION AND WELFARE

Justice. The National Courts in 1981 were as follows: Court of Cassation with a bench of 5 judges which constitutes the highest court of appeal in both criminal and civil cases; Courts of Appeal with 3 judges situated in Cairo and 4 other cities; Assize Courts with 3 judges which deal with all cases of serious crime; Central Tribunals with 3 judges which deal with ordinary civil and commercial cases; Summary Tribunals presided over by a single judge which hear civil disputes in matters up to the value of £E3,250, and criminal offences punishable by a fine or imprisonment of up to 3 years.

Religion. In 1947 the population (excluding Nomads) consisted of 17,397,946 Moslems (91·46%); 1,186,353 Orthodox Copts; 86,918 Protestant Copts; 72,764 Roman Catholic Copts; 89,062 other Orthodox; 50,200 other Roman Catholics; 16,338 other Protestants; 1,547 Jews, other and unknown.

There are in Egypt large numbers of native Christians connected with the various Oriental Churches; of these, the largest and most influential are the Copts, who adopted Christianity in the 1st century. Their head is the Coptic Patriarch. There are 25 metropolitans and bishops in Egypt; 4 metropolitans for Ethiopia, Jerusalem, Khartoum and Omdurman, and 12 bishops in Ethiopia. Priests must be married before ordination, but celibacy is imposed on monks and high dignitaries. The Copts use the Diocletian (or Martyrs') calendar, which begins in A.D. 284.

Education. Education was made compulsory for all children between the ages of 6 and 12 in 1933; primary education (6 years) was made free in 1944, secondary and technical education in 1950. Compulsory education is provided in primary schools (6 years).

In 1976–77 there were 4,151,956 primary school pupils and 125,397 teachers and 1,828,090 secondary school pupils and 52,700 teachers.

Teachers' training colleges had 32,744 students and 2,830 staff in 1976–77.

There are 12 universities in Egypt. Cairo University, founded in 1908 as a private institution and taken over by the Government in 1925; Alexandria University, founded by the Government in 1942; the Ein Shams University, founded by the Government in Cairo in 1950; Asyût University. In addition there are universities at Al-Azhar, Tanta, Mansoura, Zagazig, Helwan, Suez Canal, Menya and Menoufia. The number of students at universities was 476,537 in 1977–78.

Health. In 1966 there were about 6,000 doctors and (1970–71) 72,976 hospital beds.

DIPLOMATIC REPRESENTATIVES

OF EGYPT IN GREAT BRITAIN (26 South St.,
London, W1Y 8EL)

Ambassador: Hassan Aly Abou-Seéda (accredited 27 Feb. 1980).

OF GREAT BRITAIN IN EGYPT (Ahmed Ragheb St., Garden City, Cairo)
Ambassador: Sir Michael Weir, KCMG.

OF EGYPT IN THE USA (2310 Decatur Pl., NW,
Washington, D.C., 20008)

Ambassador: (Vacant).

OF THE USA IN EGYPT (5 Sharia Latin America, Cairo)
Ambassador: Alfred L. Atherton, Jr.

OF EGYPT TO THE UNITED NATIONS
Ambassador: Dr Ahmed Esmat Abdel Meguid.

Books of Reference

Statistical Information: The Department of Statistics and Census (15, Sharia Mansour, Cairo) was formed in 1905. *Chief:* Under-Secretary of State for Statistical Affairs, Dr Hasan M. Husein. Previously, various government departments had their own statistical sections. Estimates of population were made in 1800, 1821 and 1846; the first census took place in 1873. Among the publications of the Department are the following: *Annuaire Statistique* (Arabic and French). *Annual Return of Shipping* (Arabic and English). *Monthly Summary, and Annual Statement of Foreign Trade* (Arabic and English). *Monthly Bulletin of Agriculture and Economic Statistics* (Arabic and English). *Vital Statistics* (Arabic and English). *Statistical Pocket Year-Book* (Arabic and English).

The Egyptian Almanac. Annual

Le Mondain Egyptien (*Who's Who*). Cairo. Annual

Aatikiotos, P. J., *The Modern History of Egypt.* London, 1969

Dawisha, A. I., *Egypt in the Arab World.* London, 1976

Elias, E. A., *Modern Dictionary English–Arabic.* 5th ed. Cairo, 1946

Fedden, R., *Egypt: Land of the Valley.* London, 1977

Mabro, R., and Radwan, S., *The Industrialization of Egypt 1939–1973.* Oxford, 1976

Nelson, N., *Egypt.* London, 1976

Richmond, J. C. B., *Egypt 1798–1952.* London, 1977

Rubinstein, A. Z., *Red Star on the Nile: The Soviet–Egyptian Relationship Since the June War.* Princeton Univ. Press, 1977

Vatikiotis, P. J., *The History of Egypt: From Muhammad Ali to Sadat.* 2nd ed. London, 1980

EL SALVADOR

República de El Salvador

Capital: San Salvador
Population: 4·36m. (1979)
GNP per capita: US$600 (1978)

HISTORY. In 1839 the Central American Federation, which had comprised the states of Guatemala, El Salvador, Honduras, Nicaragua and Costa Rica, was dissolved, and El Salvador declared itself formally an independent republic in 1841.

AREA AND POPULATION. El Salvador is the smallest and most densely populated of the Central American states. Its area (including 247 sq. km of inland lakes) is estimated at 21,393 sq. km (8,236 sq. miles) with population (census 1971) of 3,712,622. Census (1979) 4,364,539. The capital is San Salvador (914,662 inhabitants in 1979).

A Treaty was signed in Peru on 30 Oct. 1980 settling the border dispute between El Salvador and Honduras which caused 4 days of fighting in July 1979.

The republic is divided into 14 departments, each under an appointed governor. Their areas (in sq. km) and populations at census 1971 were:

Department	Area	Population	Department	Area	Population
San Salvador	892	681,656	La Paz	1,155	194,196
Santa Ana	1,829	375,186	Chalatenango	2,507	186,003
San Miguel	2,532	337,325	Ahuachapán	1,281	183,682
Usulután	1,780	304,369	Marazán	1,364	170,706
La Libertad	1,650	293,076	San Vicente	1,175	160,534
Sonsonate	1,133	239,688	Cuscatlán	766	158,458
La Unión	1,738	230,103	Cabañas	1,075	139,312

Important towns (with population census 1971) are: Santa Ana, 96,306; San Miguel, 59,304; Mejicanos, 54,916; Delgado, 44,367; Nueva San Salvador, 35,106; Sonsonate, 33,562.

There has been considerable emigration into nearby states. There are no tribal Indians. The language of the country is Spanish.

CONSTITUTION AND GOVERNMENT. The latest Constitution was enacted in Jan. 1962, slightly amending that of 1950. The Executive Power is vested in a President elected for a non-renewable term of 5 years, with Ministers and Under-Secretaries appointed by him. The Legislative power is an Assembly of 52 members elected by universal suffrage and proportional representation for a term of 2 years. The judicial power is vested in a Supreme Court, of a President and 9 magistrates elected by the Legislative Assembly for renewable terms of 3 years; and subordinate courts.

A new *Partido de Conciliación Nacional* won all the seats of a new Assembly elected on 17 Dec. 1961. Its president, Dr Eusebio Cordón, was elected Provisional President of the Republic when it promulgated the new Constitution on 25 Jan. 1962. In Presidential elections on 29 April, Col. J. A. Rivera was returned without opposition and held office 1962–67. The elections of 13 March 1966 resulted in 31 *Partido de Conciliación Nacional* being elected against the opposition *Partido Demócrata Cristiano* (15) and various minor parties (6).

At the elections held 20 Feb. 1977 Col. Carlos Humberto Romero, of the ruling *Partido de Conciliación Nacional*, was elected President but on 16 Oct. 1979 Col. Romero was deposed in a *coup*. Col Jaime Abdul Gutiérrez and Col. Arnoldo Majano stated that a joint civilian–military Junta would rule the country.

430

The Junta consisted of Col. Gutiérrez and Col. Majano and 3 civilians: Dr Guillermo Manuel Ungo, Román Mayorga Quiroz and Mario Antonio Andino.

In Dec. 1980 the junta was re-organized and on 22 Dec. José Napoleón Duarte, a Christian Democrat, was sworn in as President and Col. Jaime Abdul Gutiérrez became Vice-President.

In March 1981, there was continuing fighting between government forces and guerrillas and it was estimated that 9,000 people were killed in 1980 as a result of the violence.

National flag: Blue, white, blue (horizontal): the white stripe charged with the arms of the republic.

National anthem: Saludemos la patria orgullosos (words by J. J. Cañas; tune by J. Aberle).

DEFENCE

Army. The Army is organized in 3 territorial divisions of 3 infantry brigades, 1 artillery brigade, 1 air defence battalion, 1 engineer battalion, 1 parachute battalion, and 1 cavalry squadron. Total strength (1980), 7,000 men. There are also the National Guard, the National Police and the Treasury Police. Strength, 5,000.

Navy. The Navy includes 2 patrol boats, 2 cutters and 3 other small coastguard craft. Personnel in 1981 totalled 130 officers and men.

Air Force. The Air Force underwent a major re-equipment programme in 1974–75, with most aircraft coming from Israel and US aid for transport units. Combat squadron now has 4 Super Mystère and 17 Ouragan jet fighter-bombers. Transports include 6 C-47s, 2 C-118/DC-6s and 4 Israeli-built light twin-engined Aravas, plus 3 Lama and 1 Alouette III light helicopters. Training types include 9 Israeli-built Magister jets, and about 12 piston-engined T-41Cs, T-6s and T-34s. A few Cessna liaison aircraft are also in service. Strength totalled about 150 personnel and 60 aircraft in 1980.

INTERNATIONAL RELATIONS

Membership. El Salvador is a member of UN and OAS.

ECONOMY

Budget. Revenue and expenditure for fiscal years ending 31 Dec., in 1,000 cólones (2·5 colónes = US$1):

	1975	1976	1977	1978	1979	1980
Revenue	729,700	1,069,000	1,252,000	1,252,000	1,452,000	1,676,000
Expenditure	729,700	1,069,000	1,252,000	1,252,000	1,452,000	1,676,000

External debt amounted to US$175·4m. on 30 June 1975.

Currency. The monetary unit is the *colón* (₡) of 100 *centavos*. The *colón* (₡) is issued in denominations of 1, 2, 5, 10, 25 and 100 *colónes*; 25 and 50 *centavos* (silver); 1, 2, 3, 5 and 10 *centavos* (copper–nickel and copper–zinc). In March 1981, £1 = ₡5·45; US$1 = ₡2·50.

Banking. There are 6 native commercial banks, including the Banco Salvadoreño (paid-up capital, 6m. colónes). The Bank of London and Montreal and the Citibank are the only foreign institutions. The Central Reserve Bank of El Salvador, constructed in 1934 out of the Banco Agricola Comercial, was nationalized on 20 April 1961. A stock exchange was officially inaugurated in Oct. 1962 with the declared intention of promoting investments in Central America; it began operations on 17 Aug. 1964 with a capital of 100,000 colónes subscribed by 360 shareholders. Its activities have been limited.

Weights and Measures. On 1 Jan. 1886 the metric system was made obligatory. But other units are still commonly in use, of which the principal are as follows: *Libra* = 1·014 lb. av.; *quintal* = 101·4 lb. av.; *arroba* = 25·35 lb. av.; *fanega* = 1·5745 bushels.

ENERGY AND NATURAL RESOURCES

Electricity. El Salvador's biggest national enterprise, begun in 1950, is the construction of a 200-ft high dam across the (unnavigable) Lempa River, 35 miles northeast of San Salvador, designed to double the country's electric-power resources, from 31,000 to 78,000 kw. Production in 1975, 935·3m. kwh.; consumption, 831·9m. kwh.

Oil. Production of petrol lubricants and other petroleum derivatives during 1970 totalled ₡15·8m.

Minerals. The mineral output of the republic is now negligible, but the Ministry of Public Works has recently started to investigate 2 new silver mines in the department of Morazán.

Agriculture. El Salvador is predominantly agricultural; 32·5% of its total area is used for crops and 30·2% for pasture. Area devoted to coffee is about 308,000 acres, almost entirely owned by nationals. 50% of the working population is engaged in agriculture.

Production (1977, in 1m. quintales, 46 kg each): Coffee, 2·8; cotton, 1·6; maize, 8·2. A little rubber is exported.

Livestock (1979): 1·4m. cattle, 560,000 pigs, 4,000 sheep, 14,000 goats.

Forestry. In the national forests are found dye woods and such woods as mahogany, cedar and walnut. Balsam trees also abound: El Salvador is the world's principal source of this medicinal gum.

Fisheries. In 1978, shrimp exports were valued at US$10m. (1977, US$10·5m.).

INDUSTRY AND TRADE

Industry. Total production was valued at ₡550·2m. in 1972, which included: Footwear and clothing, ₡61·3m.; textiles, ₡70·2m.; food, ₡157·7m.; chemicals, ₡42.

Labour. A decree of Aug. 1950 permits the formation of trade unions except among agricultural workers and those engaged in seasonal work such as coffee-milling and sugar-refining; trade-union posts must be filled by natives, not foreigners.

Commerce. The imports (including parcels post) and exports have been as follows in calendar years in 1,000 colónes:

	1971	1972	1973	1974	1975	1976
Imports	619,500	691,400	934,423	1,408,548	1,495,734	1,794,700
Exports	569,500	694,000	895,745	1,156,188	1,281,387	1,801,800

Of total exports, coffee furnishes about 20% by weight and 51% by value. The coffee is of the 'mild' variety; it is sold in bags of 60 kg, but trade statistics use a bag of 69 kg.

In 1976 US took 587·9m. colónes of exports and furnished 512·3m. colónes of the imports. The chief imports are normally wheat, flour, fuel-oil, fertilizers, machinery, vehicles and iron and steel manufactures. The other Central American Republics, the Federal Republic of Germany, Japan, the Netherlands and the UK are also important trading partners.

Total trade between El Salvador and UK for 5 years (British Department of Trade returns, in £1,000 sterling):

	1976	1977	1978	1979	1980
Imports to UK	1,603	3,138	2,607	3,517	2,889
Exports and re-exports from UK	12,478	11,770	11,289	9,354	4,603

Tourism. There were 285,415 visitors in 1974 (236,137 in 1973).

COMMUNICATIONS

Roads. In 1974 there were 10,972 km of national roads in the republic, including 1,373 km of paved road; 4,868 km are usable all the year round and 4,622 only in the dry season. Motor vehicles registered, 1969, 63,949.

Railways. All railways (602 km) came under the control of National Railways of El Salvador (*Fenadesal*) in 1975. Lines run from Acajutla to San Salvador, Cutuco and Santa Ana; there is also a link to the Guatemalan system.

Aviation. International air traffic is expanding and in 1972 there were 80 flights a week. The airport at Ilopango, 5 miles from San Salvador, is equipped to handle jet aeroplanes and a new international airport at Cuscatlán opened in 1979.

Shipping. The principal ports are La Unión, La Libertad and Acajutla, all on the Pacific. Passengers (and some freight) use the Guatemalan port of Puerto Barrios on the Atlantic, reaching El Salvador by rail or road.

Post and Broadcasting. The telephone and telegraph systems are government-owned; the radio-telephone systems are partly private, partly government-owned. Telephone instruments, 1978, 70,400. Two radio transmitting and receiving stations at San Salvador maintain communications with Latin America. El Salvador has, 1965, over 500,000 wireless receiving sets. In 1973, there were 3 commercial television channels and 2 educational channels sponsored by the Ministry of Education.

Cinemas (1976). Cinemas numbered 65.

Newspapers (1970). There are 4 daily newspapers in San Salvador and 1 each in Santa Ana and San Miguel.

JUSTICE, RELIGION, EDUCATION AND WELFARE

Justice. Justice is administered by the Supreme Court of Justice, courts of first and second instance, besides minor tribunals. Magistrates of the Supreme Court and courts of second instance are elected by the Legislative Assembly for a renewable 3-year term.

An anti-Communist law, effective 29 Sept. 1962, has made the propagation of totalitarian or Communist doctrines an offence punishable by imprisonment; supplementary offences, contrary to democratic principles, are punished by prison terms of from 3 to 7 years.

Religion. The dominant religion is Roman Catholicism. Under the 1962 Constitution churches are exempted from the property tax; the Catholic Church is recognized as a legal person, and other churches are entitled to secure similar recognition. There is an archbishop in San Salvador and bishops at Santa Ana, San Miguel, San Vicente, Santiago de María and Usulután.

Education. Education is free and obligatory. In 1929 the State took over control of all schools, public and private, but the provision that the teaching in government schools must be wholly secular was removed in 1945.

In Dec. 1970 there were 2,892 (2,937 in 1972) primary schools (state, municipal and private), with 531,309 (869,065 in 1974) pupils and 14,193 teachers. Secondary education was given at 860 schools (86,853 pupils). The national university and the Catholic University had 186,500 students in 1974.

Social Welfare. The Social Security Institute now administers the sickness, old age and death insurance, covering industrial workers and employees earning up to ₡700 a month. Employees in other private institutions with salaries over this amount are included but are excluded from the medical and hospital benefits.

DIPLOMATIC REPRESENTATIVES

OF EL SALVADOR IN GREAT BRITAIN (9B Portland Place, London, W1N 3AA)

Ambassador: (Vacant).

OF GREAT BRITAIN IN EL SALVADOR

Ambassador and Consul-General: J. M. Brown (resides in San José).

It was announced in Jan. 1980 that UK would close its embassy because of violence directed against diplomatic missions.

OF EL SALVADOR IN THE USA (2308 California St., NW, Washington, DC., 20008)

Ambassador: Roberto Quinonez Meza.

OF THE USA IN EL SALVADOR (25 Ave. Norte, Colnia Dueñas, San Salvador)

Ambassador: Robert E. White.

OF EL SALVADOR TO THE UNITED NATIONS

Ambassador: Dr Miguel Rafael Urquia.

Books of Reference

Statistical Information: The Dirección General de Estadistica y Censos (Villa Fermina, Calle Arce, San Salvador) dates from 1937. *Director General:* Lieut.-Col. José Castro Meléndez. Its publications include *Anuario Estadistico.* Annual from 1911.—*Boletin Estadistico.* Quarterly.—*El Salvador en Gráficas.* Annual.—*Atlas Censal de El Salvador.* 1955 only.

Angel Gallardo, M., *Cuatro Constituciones Federales de Centro América y Las Constituciones Politicas de El Salvador.* San Salvador, 1945

Browning, D., *El Salvador: Landscape and Society.* OUP, 1971

Vogt, W., *The Population of El Salvador and Its Natural Resources.* Washington, D.C., 1946

Wallich, H. C. (ed.), *Public Finance in a Developing Country: El Salvador.* Harvard Univ. Press, 1951

White, A., *El Salvador.* New York, 1973

EQUATORIAL GUINEA

Capital: Malabo
Population: 325,000 (1978)
GNP per capita: US$330 (1976)

República de Guinea Ecuatorial

HISTORY. The Republic of Equatorial Guinea became independent on 12 Oct. 1968 after having been a Spanish colony (Territorios Españoles del Golfo de Guinea) until 1959. From 1959 to 1963 the territory was made into two Spanish provinces with a status comparable to the metropolitan provinces. From 1964 to 1968 this Equatorial Region became an autonomous entity still retaining the status of two Spanish provinces, but with a certain amount of internal self-government. Serious political disturbances in Rio Muni occurred in March–April 1969. This led to the partial withdrawal of the Spanish community. Agreements for co-operation in education and economic development were signed with Spain in 1971, 1972 and 1979. While under the first President (1968–79) the republic depended heavily on the Soviet bloc including Cuba and the People's Republic of China, Spanish economic, technical and social co-operation has become essential since the overthrow of his régime in Aug. 1979.

AREA AND POPULATION. The total area is 28,051 sq. km (10,831 sq. miles). Total population, 245,989 (1960 census); 1978 estimate, 325,000.

The republic consists of 2 provinces: (1) the continental Rio Muni (26,017 sq. km including the adjacent islets of Corisco, Elobey Grande and Elobey Chico which cover 17 sq. km). The administrative and economic capital is Bata (3,548 inhabitants in 1960). Total population was 183,377, including 2,864 Europeans at the census of 1960; 1970 estimate, 290,000; (2) the island of Bioko, formerly Fernando Póo and Macías Nguema (2,034 sq. km including Pagalu, formerly Annobón, 17 sq. km). The capital is Malabo, formerly Santa Isabel, which is also the capital of the republic (19,869 inhabitants in 1960). Total population at the census of 1960 was 62,612 (including 1,415 for Pagalu), including 4,220 Europeans: 1968 estimate about 70,000–80,000 with a significant increase of Nigerian plantation workers, but there has been considerable withdrawal of Nigerian workers because of the deterioration of economic conditions since independence. In 1976 the colony of Nigerian citizens was expelled.

The majority of the Rio Munian population is Fang (Pámues in Spanish). Along the coast and in the islets are the Combes, the Bengas, the Bujebas, etc.

In Bioko the aborigines are called Bubis. These are now a minority (perhaps 15,000). Other ethnic groups are the Fernandinos (descendants of English-speaking Creoles), the Fangs, coast people from Rio Muni and formerly naturalized migrant workers from Nigeria, Cameroon and São Tomé. A fluctuating mass of plantation workers were about twice as numerous as the Equatorial Guineans. Pagalu is peopled by descendants of slaves brought by the Portuguese; they still speak a Portuguese patois. Pidgin English was the lingua franca in Bioko in spite of the official Spanish. Because of political and economic difficulties about 150,000 citizens are reported to live in neighbouring countries and Spain.

CONSTITUTION AND GOVERNMENT. Following the referendum of 11 Aug. and the elections of 22 and 29 Sept. 1968, Equatorial Guinea has become a sovereign state consisting of two provinces. The republic is administered by a President who is chief of the armed forces and head of government.

The first Assembly elected in 1968 was dissolved in 1971. The first President was appointed for life on 14 July 1972. A new Constitution was adopted in July 1973. All power rested with the Life President, Macías Nguema, and the nominal autonomy of the provinces did not exist. On 3 Aug. 1979 the President was overthrown by a 'revolutionary military council'. A 10-member cabinet has been established and the country is under military rule.

President: Lieut.-Col. Teodoro Obiang Nguema Mbasogo.
First Vice-President, Foreign Affairs: Capt. Florencio Maye.
Second Vice-President, Labour: Eulogio Eyo Riqueza.

National flag: Three horizontal stripes of green, white, red; a blue triangle based on the hoist; in the centre the national arms.

DEFENCE. Under President Macías the *Guardia Nacional* consisted mainly of Fang soldiers with Cuban and Chinese military advisers. Total strength about 1,000. Since the 1979 *coup*, Moroccan troops and Spanish military and police personnel have replaced them.

INTERNATIONAL RELATIONS

Membership. Equatorial Guinea is a member of UN, OAU and is an ACP state of EEC.

ECONOMY

Budget. Spanish subsidies normally balance the budget since 1979.

Currency. In July 1973 the Guinean *peseta* was redesignated the *Ekuele*.

Banking. The Banco Central de Guinea Ecuatorial in Malabo was established in 1969 with Spanish technical and financial assistance.

NATURAL RESOURCES

Agriculture. The chief products are cocoa (71,000 hectares in 1979), coffee (17,000 hectares) and wood; in 1979 production was about 3,000 tonnes of cocoa, most of it high-grade exported to Spain and the US. Production declined by 56%, 1965–76. Coffee, of mediocre quality, is chiefly a Fang product. Production (1975) 7,200 tonnes and is gradually decreasing. With the departure of Nigerian workers, Fang labourers from Rio Muni were recruited forcibly in 1976 and were still on the island of Bioko in late 1979.

Livestock (1979): Cattle, 4,000; sheep, 34,000; goats, 8,000; poultry, 85,000.

Forestry. Wood was almost entirely exported from Rio Muni to Spain and the Federal Republic of Germany (337,438 tonnes to Spain in 1967). Production ceased in 1969 but is slowly recovering (920,000 tonnes in 1973). Plantations in the hinterland have been abandoned by their Spanish owners and except for cocoa, commercial agriculture is under serious difficulties.

INDUSTRY AND TRADE

Industry. Bioko has very few industries. Electricity production in 1967: Bioko, 9·47m. kwh.; Rio Muni, 5·7m. kwh. Rio Muni has no industry except lumbering. In Bioko a fish-processing industry is developing. Hopes based on the 4-year development plan (1964–68) have not materialized. Post-independence political conditions have not been conducive to private investment.

Trade. In 1965 Equatorial Guinea exported 330,100 tonnes (value, 1,635·6m. pesetas; 1966, 1,817m.), of which 326,000 tonnes to Spain (value, 1,581·6m. pesetas). In 1970 total exports were 1,741m. EG pesetas, of which 91% went to Spain. Imports were 1,472m. EG pesetas, of which 80% came from Spain. In 1975 cocoa exports were US$13·4m. and coffee, US$7m.

Total trade between Equatorial Guinea and UK (British Department of Trade returns, in £1,000 sterling):

	1978	1979	1980
Imports to UK	65	—	—
Exports and re-exports from UK	742	604	54

COMMUNICATIONS

Roads. Bioko had a good tarmac road network, but Rio Muni had few surfaced roads; the main artery is Mbini–Bata–Micomeseng–Ebebiyin. Road reconstruction is envisaged.

Aviation. An international airfield exists in Malabo (28,029 passengers in 1967). Bata has more modest facilities (15,031 passengers in 1967). The line Madrid–Malabo–Bata is subsidized by Spain. Links with Douala (from Santa Isabel) and Libreville (Gabon) exist.

Shipping. Malabo is the main port. The other ports are Luba, formerly San Carlos (bananas, cocoa) in Bioko and Bata, Kogo and Mbini (wood) in Rio Muni. A new harbour in Bata has been completed. In 1966 in the 5 ports 141,600 tonnes were unloaded and 429,000 loaded.

Post and Broadcasting. Estimated number of telephones (1969), 1,451. In 1977 there were 80,000 radio and 1,000 TV receivers.

JUSTICE, RELIGION, EDUCATION AND WELFARE

Justice. The Constitution guarantees an independent judiciary. The Supreme Tribunal is the highest court of appeal and is located at Malabo.

Religion. The population of Equatorial Guinea is nominally Roman Catholic (227,517 in 1966) with influential Protestant groups in Santa Isabel and Rio Muni. By order of the President most churches were closed in 1975 and in June 1978 the Roman Catholic Church was banned. Since 1979, religious services have been restored.

Education. There were in 1974, 35,977 pupils enrolled in 559 primary schools with 630 teachers. In 1976 there were 3,984 pupils and 115 teachers in secondary schools, 370 students and 29 teachers at technical schools and 169 students and 21 teachers at teacher-training establishments.

Health. In 1967 there were 16 hospitals and dispensaries with 1,637 beds. In 1975 there were only 5 doctors, 2 midwives and 248 nursing personnel.

DIPLOMATIC REPRESENTATIVES

OF GREAT BRITAIN IN EQUATORIAL GUINEA

Ambassador: D. E. Richards (resides at Yaoundé).

OF EQUATORIAL GUINEA TO THE UNITED NATIONS

Ambassador: (Vacant).

The US Embassy was closed on 14 March 1976.

Books of Reference

Atlas Histórico y Geográfico de Africa Española. Madrid, 1955
Plan de Desarrollo Económico de la Guinea Ecuatorial. Presidencia del Gobierno. Madrid, 1963
Resumén estadístico del Africa española, 1965–66. Madrid, 1967
Berman, S., *Spanish Guinea: An Annotated Bibliography.* Microfilm Service, Catholic University. Washington, D.C. 1961
Liniger-Goumaz, M., *La Guinée équatoriale un pays méconnu.* Paris, 1980
Pélissier, R., *Les Territoires espagnols d'Afrique.* Paris, 1963.—*Los territorios españoles de Africa.* Madrid, 1964.—*Etudes Hispano–Guinéennes.* Orgeval, 1969

ETHIOPIA

Capital: Addis Ababa
Population: 30·4m. (1979)
GNP per capita: US$120 (1978)

HISTORY. The ancient empire of Ethiopia has its legendary origin in the meeting of King Solomon and the Queen of Sheba. Historically, the empire developed in the centuries before and after the birth of Christ, at Aksum in the north, as a result of Semetic immigration from South Arabia. The immigrants imposed their language and culture on a basic Hamitic stock. Ethiopia's subsequent history is one of sporadic expansion southwards and eastwards, checked from the 16th to early 19th centuries by devastating wars with Moslems and Gallas. Modern Ethiopia dates from the reign of the Emperor Theodore (1855–68).

Menelik II (1889–1913) defeated the Italians in 1896 and thereby safeguarded the empire's independence in the scramble for Africa. By successful campaigns in neighbouring kingdoms within Ethiopia (Jimma, Kaffa, Harar, etc.) he united the country under his rule and created the empire as it is today.

In 1936 Ethiopia was conquered by the Italians, who were in turn defeated by the Allied forces in 1941 when the Emperor returned.

The former Italian colony of Eritrea, from 1941 under British military administration, was in accordance with a resolution of the General Assembly of the UN, dated 2 Dec. 1950, handed over to Ethiopia on 15 Sept. 1952. Eritrea thereby became an autonomous unit within the federation of Ethiopia and Eritrea.

This federation became a unitary state on 14 Nov. 1962 when Eritrea was fully integrated with Ethiopia.

A provisional military government assumed power on 12 Sept. 1974 and deposed the Emperor. The deposed Emperor Hailé Selassié I, was born 23 July 1892; crowned King (Negus), on 7 Oct. 1928, proclaimed Emperor, after the death of the Empress Zauditu, on 2 April 1930, and crowned on 2 Nov. 1930. He married in 1911 Menen, who died on 15 Feb. 1962. The Emperor died on 27 Aug. 1975. There are a son and a daughter surviving. On 25 Jan. 1931 the eldest son, Asfa Wossen, was proclaimed Crown Prince and heir to the throne. On 14 April 1974 the Emperor named his grandson, Prince Zare Yacob as Crown Prince, but following the military takeover Asfa Wossen was invited to be crowned King, but this offer was later rescinded.

In early 1978 a reversal of the position in the armed struggle in the Ogaden area of Ethiopia with Somali forces took place. After an offensive mounted with strong USSR and Cuban support the area was recaptured and in March Somalia withdrew all troops from the area. Control was re-established by Ethiopia later in 1978 and nationalist guerrillas were pushed back.

AREA AND POPULATION. The total area of the Empire is approximately 395,000 sq. miles or 1m. sq. km (Ethiopia 350,000, Eritrea, 45,000).

The official estimate of the population in 1979 was 30·4m.

The dominant race of Ethiopia, the Amhara, inhabit the central Ethiopian highlands. To the north of them are the Tigréans, akin to the Amhara and belonging to the same Christian church, but speaking a different, though related, language. Both these races are of mixed Hamitic and Semitic origin, and further mixed by intermarriage with Galla and other races. The Gallas, some of whom are Christian, some Moslem and some pagan, comprise about 40% of the entire population, and are a pastoral and agricultural people of Hamitic origin. Somalis, another Hamitic race, inhabit the south-east of Ethiopia, in particular the Ogaden desert region. These like the closely related Afar people, are Moslem. The Afar stretch northwards from Wollo region into Eritrea.

The country is divided into 15 administrative regions, each under a Chief Administrator, and under the administrative control of the Minister of the Interior. Each region is divided into about 7 districts under a district administrator. All revenues collected in the regions are under the control of the Minister of Finance.

Region	Area (sq. km)	Population 1974	Chief town	Population 1974
Addis Ababa	...	1,083,620	—	—
Arussi	23,500	892,700	Assela	22,100
Bale	124,600	739,600	Goba	15,650
Begemdir	74,200	1,418,700	Gondar	43,040
Eritrea	117,600	2,070,100	Asmara	296,044
Gemu Goffa	39,500	730,700	Arba Minch	8,790
Gojjam	61,600	1,829,600	Debre Markos	33,730
Hararge	259,700	3,510,000	Harar	53,560
Illubabor	47,400	719,400	Mattu	7,820
Kefa	54,600	1,768,700	Jimma	52,420
Shoa	85,400	4,628,680	—	—
Sidamo	117,300	2,595,600	Awassa	19,550
Tigre	65,900	1,916,600	Mekele	34,290
Wollega	71,200	1,326,800	Lekemti	21,260
Wollo	79,400	2,570,200	Dessie	54,910

Other large towns (population, 1974): Dire Dawa, in Hararge, 72,860; Nazret, in Shoa, 50,550.

CONSTITUTION AND GOVERNMENT. On 24 Nov. 1974 the Provisional Military Government announced that on 23 Nov. it had executed 60 former military and civilian leaders including Gen. Aman Andom who was Chairman of the Provisional Military Administrative Council.

On 3 Feb. 1977 it was announced that Brig.-Gen. Teferi Bante, the Chairman of PMAC and 6 other members of the ruling military council were executed.

Chairman of the Provisional Military Administrative Council: Lieut.-Col. Mengistu Haile Mariam.

National flag: Three horizontal stripes of green, yellow and red.

National anthem: Ityopya, Ityopia Kidemi (tune by Daniel Yohannes, 1975).

DEFENCE

Army. The Army, trained by British officers from 1947 to 1951 and by Swedish officers until 1964, comprises 14 infantry divisions, including 12 tank battalions, 1 light infantry division, 4 parachute commando brigades, 30 artillery and 2 engineering battalions. It is recruited by voluntary enlistment. Five artillery battalions, 5 anti-aircraft batteries, 2 combat engineer battalions, an airborne infantry battalion and ancillary service, make up the ground forces to a total of 225,000 in 1980. This includes a People's Militia of around 150,000. This force was still being expanded in Oct. 1977.

A US military advisory and administrative group, established since 1954, working down to divisional level, was asked by the Ethiopian Government to disband in April 1977. Ethiopia's military rulers have moved away from US military assistance since they came to power and now rely on USSR for most of their military aid. Large amounts of USSR military equipment have been sent to help her in her conflict with Somalia over the Ogaden desert region. Ethiopian officers are trained at the National Military Academy, Harar, and at the National Military Training Centre, Holletta, near Addis Ababa.

Navy. The Navy, with headquarters at Addis Ababa, consists of 4 *ex*-Soviet fast missile boats, 2 *ex*-Soviet fast torpedo boats, 1 training ship (1,768 tons; *ex*-US seaplane tender), 1 *ex*-Netherlands coastal minesweeper, 4 patrol craft (*ex*-US coastguard motor gunboats), 4 new patrol boats, 1 *ex*-Yugoslav submarine chaser, 4 harbour defence craft, 2 landing craft and 4 minor landing craft. The Naval Base and College is at Massawa.

Personnel, in 1981, totalled 1,200 officers and men. It is presumed that Soviet advisers remain embarked in the 6 attack craft recently acquired until Ethiopian naval officers and ratings have sufficient expertise to operate independently the missiles and torpedoes.

Air Force. The Air Force, trained originally by Swedish and American personnel, has its headquarters at Debre Zeit, near Addis Ababa. It includes a training school and a central workshop. Before fighting with Somalia began, there were 1 bomber, 1 ground-attack, 2 day-fighter/ground-attack and 1 fighter/reconnaissance combat squadrons, equipped with Canberras, F-5s, F-86s and T-28Ds, and 1 transport squadron equipped with jet-augmented C-119Ks, C-54s, C-47s and Do 28D Sky-servants. USSR equipment since supplied is reported to include 24 MiG-23, 50 MiG-21 and 20 MiG-17 fighters. Training aircraft include two-seat F-5Bs, T-33 jet advanced trainers and piston-engined Cessna 310s, T-28s and Saab-91s. More than 30 Agusta-Bell 204, Alouette III, UH-1H, Mi-6 and Mi-8 helicopters are in service. Personnel, 3,000 officers and men.

The frontier guard patrols the Somalia border, and commando police units are being employed to assist the Army and police in border patrols and anti-terrorist operations in Eritrea. Total paramilitary force, 20,000.

INTERNATIONAL RELATIONS

Membership. Ethiopia is a member of UN, OAU and is an ACP state of EEC.

ECONOMY

Planning. The third 5-year plan (1969–73, which was extended to 1974) involved a total expenditure of EB2,865m. (of which EB565m. for industry and EB624m. for transport and communications) and hoped to achieve a growth rate of 6% per annum. Actual growth rate was below 4% and the fourth 5-year plan was replaced in 1975 by a policy statement embodying a package approach to rural development. In 1978 a new development plan was launched envisaging growth of 6% in 1979–80 and 7% in 1980–81.

Budget. Revenue and expenditure estimates for financial years (ended 7 July) were as follows (in EB1m.):

	1975–76	1976–77	1977–78	1978–79	1979–80
Revenue	1,331	1,466	1,601	2,119	2,365
Expenditure	1,331	1,466	1,601	2,119	2,365

Of the estimated revenue in 1979–80, EB1,327m. is expected to come from taxes and EB417m. from external assistance. Of the 1979–80 expenditure, EB1,655m. is on current account and EB710m. for capital expenditure.

Currency. The Ethiopian *birr*, divided into 100 cents, is the unit of currency; it is based on 5·52 grains of fine gold. It consists of notes of EB1, 5, 10, 50 and 100 denominations, and bronze 1-, 5-, 10- and 25-cent coins. The former dollar notes were replaced by the new *birr* in Oct. 1976. Currency is issued by the National Bank, and, as at 30 Sept. 1975, was notes, EB673·7m.; coins, EB169·7m. The note issue, under the Banking Proclamation of 1963, must be backed by gold and foreign securities in the international reserve fund to at least 25% of its value. Foreign currency reserves stood at US$108·5m. in June 1979. *Birr* 4·44 = £1 sterling; *Birr* 2·01 = US$1 (in March 1981).

Banking. The State Bank was renamed the National Bank of Ethiopia in Oct. 1963, when its commercial activities were transferred to the newly established Commercial Bank of Ethiopia. At the same time another new bank, the Investment Bank of Ethiopia, was set up with a capital of EB10m., of which the Government held the majority of shares. In Sept. 1965 it became the Ethiopian Investment Corporation, which is a substantial shareholder in a number of industrial and other ventures.

The Investment Corporation has now been merged with the Development Bank of Ethiopia and the two are now known as the Agricultural and Industrial Development Bank, SC.

Two Italian banks have subsidiaries in Asmara, and one has a subsidiary in Addis Ababa. The Addis Ababa Bank Share Co. is connected with National & Grindlays Bank Ltd.

On 1 Jan. 1975 the Government nationalized all banks, mortgage and insurance companies.

Weights and Measures. The metric system of weights and measures is officially in use. Traditional weights and measures vary considerably in the various provinces: the principal ones are: *Frasilla* = approximately 37½ lb.; *gasha*, the principal unit of land measure, which is normally about 100 acres but can vary between 80 and 300 acres, depending on the quality of the land.

ENERGY AND NATURAL RESOURCES

Electricity. Installed electricity generating power of the Ethiopian Electric Light and Power Authority was 185 mw in 1972 and production in 1977 totalled 427m. kwh.

Oil. A Russian built state-owned oil refinery at Assab came on stream in 1967 with a capacity of 600,000 tonnes of crude.

Minerals. Ethiopia has little proved mineral wealth. Salt (122,000 tonnes in 1974) is produced mainly in Eritrea, while a placer goldmine is worked by the Government of Adola in the south. Gold production, in 1974, was 15,754 troy oz. Small quantities of other minerals are produced including platinum. The potash deposits in the Dankali salt plains in the north-east part of the country were investigated by 2 US companies in 1966–70 but no exploitation has taken place. Japanese interests were engaged in the exploitation of significant copper deposits near Asmara, but the mine was closed down in March 1974 as a result of damage caused by ELF dissidents. A natural gas-strike was made offshore near Massawa in Dec. 1969, but it was not exploited. Traces of gas and oil have been found in south-east Ethiopia.

Agriculture. Coffee is by far the most important source of rural income. Harari coffee (long berry Mocha) is cultivated in the east; Abyssinian coffee is produced in Kaffa and the surrounding provinces, much of it growing wild.

Teff (*Eragrastis abyssinica*) is the principal food grain, followed by barley, wheat, maize and durra. Pulses and oilseeds are imported for local consumption and export. Cane sugar is an important crop.

Production (1978 in 1,000 tons): Maize, 800; sorghum, 713; barley, 600; coffee, 190; raw sugar, 146.

Livestock (1979): 25·9m. cattle, 23·2m. sheep, 17·1m. goats; smaller numbers of donkeys, horses, mules and camels. Hides and skins and butter (ghee) are important for home consumption and export. Sheep, cattle and chickens (53m.) are the main providers of meat. All agricultural land was nationalized in March 1975, and a radical land reform was carried out. Tenants were given possessory rights to the land they tilled, absentee landlords were abolished, and a ceiling on landholding was instituted.

INDUSTRY AND TRADE

Industry. The most important products of the small but growing industries are cotton yarn (9,600 tons in 1978) and fabrics, cement (100,000 tons), sugar, salt, cigarettes, canned foodstuffs, beer, building materials, footwear, pharmaceuticals, tyres and paint. Most industry is centred around Addis Ababa and Asmara. Industry around Asmara has been severely hit by actions of Eritrean guerrillas.

Commerce. Coffee is by far the most important export, followed by pulses, oilseeds, hides and skins. Imports are textiles, foodstuffs, vehicles, machinery, manufactured goods and petroleum products. Coffee exports, 1973, were 76,082 tonnes.

Imports and exports (in EB1m.) for 6 years (ending 9 Dec.):

	1974	1975	1976	1977	1978	1979
Imports	555·7	644·9	729·5	727·8	942·7	1,149·2
Exports	593·2	497·8	580·6	689·0	633·6	877·6

In 1978 the main supplying countries were: Italy (14%), Japan (11%), Federal Republic of Germany (10%), Saudi Arabia (8%), UK (7%).

The chief items of import in 1978 were: Machinery and transport equipment (EB300·3m.), petroleum products (EB129·3m.). The main items of export were: Coffee (EB502·3m.), hides and skins (EB66·3m.), pulses (EB17·3m.).

Total trade between Ethiopia and UK (British Department of Trade returns, in £1,000 sterling):

	1975	1976	1977	1978	1979	1980
Imports to UK	3,762	14,913	4,689	4,471	12,947	10,281
Exports and re-exports from UK	8,709	12,584	19,111	17,091	16,039	20,962

COMMUNICATIONS

Roads. Loans totalling EB83·75m. have been made between 1951 and 1968 by the International Bank and the International Development Agency for 3 programmes for improving and extending the road system. A fourth programme began in 1968 and is being financed by EB190m. in foreign loans and was completed in 1972. A fifth programme is near completion with a projected cost of EB60m. A sixth programme, estimated to cost EB133m., is underway which will include about 400 km of gravel-surfaced feeder roads. The Highway Authority now maintains some 7,600 km of roads and is engaged in constructing another 850 km of all-weather roads. Chief motor roads: Massawa–Asmara–Sudan; Asmara–Dessie–Addis Ababa; Asmara–Gondar–Addis Ababa; Addis Ababa–Jimma; Addis Ababa–Lekemti; Addis Ababa–Nazareth; Dire-Dawa–Hargeisa; Dessie–Assab; Addis Ababa–Adola.

Estimated number of motor vehicles (1976): Cars, 63,100; lorries and trucks, 7,000; buses, 3,500; tractors, 3,000.

Railways. The Franco-Ethiopian Railway Co., owned by the 2 governments, operates the line (782 km, metre gauge) from Jibuti to Addis Ababa. Through running from Jibuti has been suspended for some years, but trains run in Ethiopia when terrorist activity permits.

Aviation. Ethiopian Air Lines, formed in 1946, provides services to Cairo, Athens, Frankfurt, London, Khartoum, Lagos, Accra, Rome, Nairobi, Entebbe, Kinshasa, Kigali, Dar es Salaam, Jibuti, Aden, Paris, Douala, Jedda, Peking, Seychelles, Bombay, San'a and Abu Dhabi, in addition to internal services. The following airlines operate through Asmara and Addis Ababa: Alitalia, Kenya Airways, Air India, Lufthansa, China Airline, Aeroflot, Air-France, British Airways and Air Jibuti.

Shipping. A state shipping line was established in 1964. In May 1973 it owned 4 cargo vessels and 2 tankers.

Post and Broadcasting. The postal system serves 301 offices, mainly by air-mail. All the main centres are connected with Addis Ababa by telephone or radio telegraph. International telephone services are available at certain hours to most countries in Europe, North America and India. Number of telephones (1978), 78,691 and 194 telex subscribers (1972).

The Ethiopian Broadcasting Service makes sound broadcasts on the medium and short waves in English, Amharic and in the vernacular languages spoken within the country. Radio Voice of the Gospel, owned by the Lutheran World Federation, was nationalized in March 1977 and renamed Radio Voice of Revolutionary Ethiopia. It broadcasts from Addis Abba in English, French, Amharic, Arabic, Somali and Afar. Television was introduced in 1964 and programmes broadcast from Addis Ababa for a radius of about 100 miles to the south and south-east of the capital and in Asmara from June 1977.

Cinemas (1974). There were 31 cinemas, with seating capacity of about 25,600.

Newspapers. In Addis Ababa there are 1 English, 1 French and 1 Amharic dailies, and in Asmara 2 Italian dailies, 1 part-Tigrinya, part-Arabic, and 1 Amharic weekly. All the papers are government-controlled and have small circulations, varying between 2,000 and 20,000.

JUSTICE, RELIGION, EDUCATION AND WELFARE

Justice. The legal system is said to be based on the Justinian Code. A new penal code came into force in 1958 and Special Penal Law in 1974. Codes of criminal procedure, civil, commercial and maritime codes have since been promulgated.

The extra-territorial rights formerly enjoyed by foreigners have been abolished, but any person accused in an Ethiopian court has the right to have his case transferred to the High Court, provided he asks for this before any evidence has been taken in the court of first instance.

Provincial and district courts have been established, and High Court judges visit the provincial courts on circuit. The Supreme Imperial Court at Addis Ababa is presided over by the Chief Justice.

Police. In 1948 the regular police force of the capital and some provincial cities was amalgamated with the irregular territorial forces under the provincial governors-general. The total force now numbers about 32,000 officers and other ranks.

Religion. Since the conversion of the Amharas to Christianity in the 4th century they have retained their connexion with the Alexandrian Church through the Abuna, or Metropolitan who was always an Egyptian Copt, and who was appointed and consecrated by the Coptic Patriarch of Alexandria. Both the Egyptian and Ethiopian Coptic Churches are monophysite, rejecting the decrees of the Council of Chalcedon (A.D. 451). After the restoration of the Emperor relations between the Ethiopian and Egyptian churches were strained until the summer of 1948, when an agreement was reached which envisaged the appointment of an Ethiopian Archbishop, and in Jan. 1951 Abuna Basilios (who died in 1970) was elected Archbishop of Ethiopia. A further agreement in 1959 made the Ethiopian Church autocephalous, and Basilios assumed the rank of Patriarch, with seniority immediately after the Patriarch of Alexandria. Abuna Theophilos was elected to the Patriarchate by an electoral college representing clergy, laity and Government and consecrated by the Ethiopian Archbishops in May 1971. In Aug. 1976 the third Patriarch, Abuna Tekle Haimanot, was invested. Christianity is predominant in the following provinces in the north: Tigré, Gondar, Gojjam, Shoa. Wollo province in the north-east is half Christian, half Moslem. In the southern half of the country the provinces of Hararge and Arussi have Moslem majorities, while all the other southern provinces have considerable Moslem minorities. In addition, the province of Gamu Gofa on the Kenya border and parts of Sidamo and Arussi have considerable pagan elements. Eritrea is half Moslem and half Christian. Each province now forms a diocese.

Islam is widely practised in the south and east of the Empire. Moslem minorities are found in Addis Ababa and in other commercial centres. The rite is mainly shafeitic. Harar is the most important Moslem centre. There are mosques and government schools for Moslems in most towns.

Education. In the academic year 1971–72 there were more than 2,600 primary, secondary and church schools providing education for 872,000 pupils. Higher education is co-ordinated under the National University, chartered in 1961. The University College, the Engineering, Building and Theological Colleges are in Addis Ababa, the Agricultural College in Harar and the Public Health College in Gondar. It is intended to develop these provincial colleges into universities in their own right. In 1971–72 the University of Asmara had 1,500 students. Altogether they provided tuition for about 5,884 students.

Since the military takeover in 1974 education has been in a state of flux. A campaign, known as *zemetcha*, lasting from Dec. 1974 to July 1976, was launched, in which all higher academic institutions were closed and the students sent into the countryside to preach the revolution. Academic institutions are now in operation again, although it is not clear if numbers have recovered to a pre-1974 level.

The main language of instruction from the secondary level upwards is English.

A national adult literacy campaign was launched in 1979 with the aid of UNESCO. In Sept. 1980 it was claimed that 7m. adults, 70% of them women, had taken or were taking basic literacy or follow-up courses. Follow up courses provide basic education in such fields as agriculture, health, home economics, handicrafts and co-operatives, as well as ideology.

Health. In 1972 there were 350 doctors and 8,415 hospital beds.

DIPLOMATIC REPRESENTATIVES

OF ETHIOPIA IN GREAT BRITAIN (17 Prince's Gate,
London, SW7 1PZ)

Ambassador: Ato Ayalew Wolde-Giorgis.

OF GREAT BRITAIN IN ETHIOPIA (Fikre Mariam Abatechan St.,
Addis Ababa)

Ambassador: R. M. Tesh, CMG.

OF ETHIOPIA IN THE USA (2134 Kalorama Rd., NW,
Washington, D.C., 20008)

Chargé d'Affaires: Tibabu Bekele.

OF THE USA IN ETHIOPIA (Entoto St., Addis Ababa)

Ambassador: Frederic L. Chapin.

OF ETHIOPIA TO THE UNITED NATIONS

Ambassador: Mohamed Hamid Ibrahim.

Books of Reference

Area Handbook for Ethiopia. US Govt. Printing Office, Washington, 1971
Trade Directory and Guide Book of Ethiopia. Addis Ababa, 1971
Gilkes, P., *The Dying Lion: Feudalism and Modernisation in Ethiopia.* London, 1975
Hess, R. L., *Ethiopia: The Modernization of Autocracy.* Cornell Univ. Press, 1970
Holmberg, J., *Grain Marketing and Land Reform in Ethiopia.* Uppsala, 1977
Mosley, L., *Haile Selassie.* London, 1964
Scholler, H. and Brictzke, P., *Ethiopia: Revolution, Law and Politics.* New York, 1976
Thompson, B., *Ethiopia: The Country That Cut Off Its Head.* London, 1975
Trevaskis, G. K. N., *Eritrea.* London, 1960
Ullendorff, E., *The Ethiopians.* New York, 1973
Wolde-Mariam, M., *An Atlas of Ethiopia.* Rev. ed. Addis Ababa, 1970

FALKLAND ISLANDS AND DEPENDENCIES

Capital: Stanley
Population: 1,776 (1979)

HISTORY. France established a settlement in 1764 and Britain a second settlement in 1765. In 1770 Spain bought out the French and drove off the British. In 1806 Spanish rule was overthrown in Argentina, and the Argentinians claimed to succeed Spain in the French and British settlements in 1820. The British objected and reclaimed their settlement in 1832 as a Crown Colony.

AREA AND POPULATION. The Crown Colony is situated in the South Atlantic Ocean about 480 miles north-east of Cape Horn. The numerous islands cover 4,700 sq. miles. The main East Falkland Island, 2,610 sq. miles; the West Falkland, 2,090 sq. miles, including the adjacent small islands. The Dependency of South Georgia lies 800 miles south-east of the Falklands, has an area of 1,450 sq. miles; the South Sandwich group, 470 miles south-east of South Georgia, has an area of 130 sq. miles.

The population of the Falkland Islands on 31 Dec. 1979 was 1,776. The only town is Stanley, in East Falkland, with a population of just over 1,000. The population of South Georgia varies with the season, but the resident population in 1979 was 22 (males).

The South Shetlands are uninhabited.

South Georgia, once a base for whaling and sealing operations, is now occupied by members of the British Antarctic Survey at the base at King Edward Point.

The population of the Falkland Islands is nearly all of British descent, with about 80% born in the islands.

CONSTITUTION AND GOVERNMENT. The Colony is administered by a Governor, assisted by an Executive Council consisting of the Chief Secretary and Financial Secretary, both *ex-officio*; 2 members elected by the Legislature and 2 appointed members; and a Legislative Council composed of the Chief Secretary and Financial Secretary, both *ex-officio*; 3 elected members representing Stanley, 1 elected member from the East Falkland and 1 from the West Falkland and 1 representing the Camp as a whole.

Governor and Commander-in-Chief: R. M. Hunt, CMG.
Chief Secretary: F. E. Baker, OBE.
Flag: British Blue Ensign with arms of Colony on a white disc in the fly.

ECONOMY

Budget. Revenue and expenditure (in £ sterling) for fiscal years ending 30 June:

	1975–76	1976–77	1977–78	1978–79	1979–80[1]	1980–81[1]
Revenue	1,294,447	1,154,204	1,803,151	1,820,561	1,964,945	2,213,201
Expenditure	1,013,235	1,131,045	1,382,744	1,792,780	1,936,078	2,284,320

[1] Estimates.

Chief source of revenue (estimate, 1980–81): Internal revenue, £783,820; posts and telecommunications, £237,140; municipal services, £200,190; investment, £275,010; customs, £150,000.

Currency. The Falkland £ is at parity with the £ sterling.

Banking. On 30 June 1980 the government savings bank held a balance of £2,396,203. Some banking facilities are also offered by Lloyds Bank.

SHEEP FARMING. The whole acreage of the Colony is divided into large sheep runs. Wool is the principal product, but hides are exported. In 1979 there were 659,012 sheep, 8,221 cattle and 2,291 horses in the islands.

DEVELOPMENT. The economy is entirely dependent on the production of wool for export. A comprehensive economic survey, published in 1976, drew attention to the potential for exploitation of fish, kelp and possibly oil, and made recommendations for various areas of development. Work on implementing many of the long-term and short-term recommendations has begun, notably feasibility studies in horticultural expansion, tourism, investigations into commercial fishing and fish drying, tanning of hides and skins, and potential oil development as well as improvements to internal communications—roads, radio/telephone system, educational and medical facilities.

TRADE. Total imports, 1978, amounted to £1,447,502 and exports to £2,502,251.

COMMUNICATIONS

Roads. There are 13 miles of made-up roads in Stanley. Outside Stanley tracks link all the settlements which are passable in all but the worst weather. Work has continued on an all-weather road from Stanley to Darwin.

Aviation. LADE (Argentine development airline), operate a twice-weekly air service from Comodoro Rivadavia in Southern Argentina to the new Stanley Airport. The Fokker F-27 and F-28 aircraft carry passengers, mail and freight.

Shipping. A charter vessel calls 4 or 5 times a year to/from the UK. Communication with the Colony, the Dependencies and the British Antarctic Territory is kept up by the Royal research ships *John Biscoe* and *Bransfield* and by the ice-patrol vessel HMS *Endurance*.

In 1978 the total tonnage of shipping entered was 301,144 and cleared was 300,088.

Post and Broadcasting. Number of telephones (1979) 481. There is a government-operated broadcasting station at Stanley and the Government also operates a wired broadcasting service to subscribers.

EDUCATION AND WELFARE

Education. Education is compulsory between the ages of 5 and 15 years. In 1979 there were 322 children receiving education in the Colony. This includes Stanley schools, Darwin Boarding School and settlement schools, as well as pupils taught by itinerant teachers in rural areas. 17 children were being educated abroad.

Health. The Falkland Islands Medical Department, under the supervision of the senior medical officer, is responsible for the public health and sanitation of the Colony. The government medical department employs the following: 3 registered medical practitioners; 4 registered nurse/midwives; 8 partially trained nurses; 1 laboratory and X-ray technician and 1 dental surgeon. There is 1 general hospital situated in Stanley with 27 beds. There is also a routine/emergency flying doctor service operating to the outlying farm settlements.

WILD LIFE. The Falkland Islands and South Georgia are noted for their outstanding wild life, including penguin and seal. Four Nature Reserves have been declared and 18 Wild Animal and Bird Sanctuaries gazetted. The brown trout introduced between 1947 and 1952 can now be found in nearly all the rivers.

Books of Reference

Falkland Islands and Dependencies. Biennial Report: 1972–73. HMSO, 1976
Falkland Islands Journal. Stanley, from 1967
Phipps, C., *What Future for the Falklands?* London, 1977
Strange, I. J., *The Falkland Islands.* Newton Abbot, 1972

FIJI

Capital: Suva
Population: 618,979 (1979)
GNP per capita: US$1,440 (1978)

HISTORY. The Fiji Islands were discovered by Tasman in 1643 and visited by Capt. Cook in 1774, but first recorded in detail by Capt. Bligh after the mutiny of the *Bounty* (1789). In the 19th century the search for sandalwood, in which enormous profits were made, brought many ships. Deserters and shipwrecked men stayed on; fire-arms salvaged from wrecks were used in native wars, new diseases swept the islands, and rum and muskets became regular articles of trade. Tribal wars became bloody and general until Fiji was ceded to Britain on 10 Oct. 1874, after a previous offer of cession had been refused. British administrators produced order out of chaos, and since then there has been steady political, social and economic progress. Fiji gained independent status on 10 Oct. 1970.

AREA AND POPULATION. Fiji comprises about 322 islands and islets (about 106 inhabited) lying between 15° and 22° S. lat. and 174° E. and 177° W. long. The largest is Viti Levu, area 4,010 sq. miles; next is Vanua Levu, area 2,137 sq. miles. The island of Rotuma (18 sq. miles), about 12° 30′ S. lat., 178° E. long., was added to the colony in 1881. Total area, 7,055 sq. miles (18,272 sq. km).

A population census is taken every 10 years. Total population (census, Dec. 1977), 601,485; 1979 (estimate) 618,979. The 1979 total population consisted of the following: 275,737 Fijians; 300,179 Indians; 10,763 Part Europeans; 3,518 Europeans; 7,644 Rotumans; 4,579 Chinese; 5,739 other Pacific Islanders; 820 others.

Suva, the capital, is on the south coast of Viti Levu; population (1979), 64,000. Suva was proclaimed a city on 2 Oct. 1953.

Vital statistics, 1978:

	Fijians	Indians	Others [1]	Total
Births	6,953	9,329	899	17,181
Deaths	1,037	1,329	190	2,556

[1] Includes Europeans, Part-Europeans, Rotumans, Other Pacific Islanders and Chinese.

CONSTITUTION AND GOVERNMENT. Fiji became an independent nation within the Commonwealth on 10 Oct. 1970. This had been agreed at a constitutional conference held in London in April 1970. There is a Lower House, the House of Representatives, which consists of 52 elected members and an Upper House, the Senate, of 22 members (8 nominations by the Council of Chiefs, 7 by the Prime Minister, 6 by the Leader of the Opposition and 1 by the Rotuma Council).

At elections held in Sept. 1977 for the 52 seats in the House of Representatives the Alliance Party won 36 seats, two factions of the National Federation Party won 15 seats and there was 1 independent.

Local Government. The Fijian Administration, established in 1876, had jurisdiction over all Fijians.

Fiji is divided into 13 provinces, each with its own council. Elections to these councils in 90 constituencies were conducted for the first time in 1967 on a full adult franchise amongst Fijians.

The councils have wide powers to make by-laws and draw up their own budget subject to confirmation by the Fijian Affairs Board. Each council has its own treasury and levies rates to raise its revenue. These provincial rates vary from $F6 to $F9 per annum for every male adult, but those maintaining 5 or more children pay lower rates until their children become taxpayers. A start has been made, however, to change over to a system of land rating based upon the unimproved value of Fijian-owned land. This is considered to be more equitable and related to ability to pay.

These newly elected councils held their inaugural and 1968 budget meetings

447

towards the end of 1967, when the chairman for each of these 13 councils was also elected from among its members. Members were elected for 2 years and new elections were held in 1969.

At the apex of the Fijian Administration is the Great Council of Chiefs presided over by the Minister for Fijian Affairs and Rural Development. The Council of Chiefs consists of 22 Fijian members elected to the House of Representatives, 30 representatives, elected by the Provincial Councils and 15 representatives nominated by the Minister for Fijian Affairs and Rural Development.

The Council of Chiefs advises the Government generally on Fijian affairs.

Governor-General: Ratu Sir George Cakobau, GCMG, GCVO, OBE.
Prime Minister: Ratu Sir Kamisese Mara, KBE.
Flag: Light blue with the Union Flag in the canton and the shield of Fiji in the fly.

DEFENCE. The Fiji Military Forces Ordinance, 1949, provides for the maintenance of a small regular force, with territorial units and trained reserves. This force, comprising 2 infantry battalions, numbers (1980), 1,300.

Navy. A naval squadron has been raised to perform fishery protection, surveillance, hydrographic surveying and coastguard duties. Present strength is 3 coastal minesweepers (*ex*-US MSC) and 1 survey craft. Naval personnel in 1981 numbered 20 officers and 140 ratings. The naval base is HMFS *Viti* in Suva.

INTERNATIONAL RELATIONS

Membership. Fiji is a member of the UN, the Commonwealth, the Colombo Plan and is an ACP state of the EEC.

ECONOMY

Budget. The financial year corresponds with the calendar year. All figures are in $ Fijian.

	1976	1977	1978	1979	1980
Revenue	128,785,048	151,700,000	161,600,000	198,476,000	223,543,000
Expenditure	129,667,658	155,077,000	170,284,000	205,188,000	223,543,000

For budget purposes, revenue and expenditure are divided into two parts: Operating and Capital Operating. Revenue comes mainly from taxation, customs and excise duty, licences and fees. In 1978, of the total revenue collected over $F59m. was derived from customs and excise duty and over $F77m. from income tax collections. The total capital expenditure in 1978 was $F49,542,112.

GDP at factor cost in 1977 was $F649·5m. (1978, $F729·9m.), and GDP *per capita* at factor cost was $F1,090m. (1978, $F1,202m.).

Currency. Fiji changed to decimal currency on 13 Jan. 1969, with the major unit being $F1. In March 1981, £1 = $F1·80; US$ = $F0·823.

Banking. The Bank of New South Wales has 7 branches and 11 agencies; the Bank of New Zealand has 6 branches, 1 sub-branch and 17 agencies; the Australia and New Zealand Bank has 3 branches, 1 sub-branch and 1 agency and the Bank of Baroda has 7 branches and 5 agencies in Fiji. Barclays International has a branch in Suva.

The National Bank of Fiji had, at the end of 1978, deposits amounting to $F29,177,274 due to 190,621 accounts. The headquarters are at Suva, and there are 58 agencies, 4 branches and 3 sub-branches throughout Fiji.

NATURAL RESOURCES

Agriculture. Some 600,000 acres of land are in agricultural use. Sugar-cane is the principal cash crop, accounting for more than two-thirds of Fiji's export earnings; one quarter of the population depend on it directly for their livelihood. Copra, Fiji's second major cash crop, provides coconut oil and other products for export and employs nearly as many workers as the sugar industry. Ginger is the third major export crop replacing bananas which has declined through disease and hurricane. Other agricultural products include rice, cocoa, maize, tobacco and a variety of fruits and vegetables.

Fiji has a small but fast developing livestock industry.

Livestock (1979): Cattle, 170,000; horses, 39,000; goats, 55,000; pigs, 18,000; poultry, 870,000.

Forestry. Fiji supplies the bulk of its own timber requirements. A comprehensive pine scheme has been implemented with the aim of planting 186,000 acres by 1988. So far some 59,954 acres have been planted with a further 13,000 acres being developed a year. The Government provides extension and research services, agricultural subsidies, training and marketing services.

INDUSTRY AND TRADE

Industry. Major industries include 4 large sugar-mills, the goldmines (92,300 grammes in 1979) and 3 mills which process copra into coconut oil and coconut meal. There is a great variety of light industries.

Trade Unions. In 1978 there were 46 trade unions registered with the Registrar-General's office.

Commerce. Exports in 1979: Sugar, 428,000 tonnes ($F116,962,027); coconut oil, 15,000 tonnes ($F11,683,371); gold, 904,000 grammes ($F6,491,551); oil seed, cake and meal, 2,000 tonnes ($F234,000); cement, 3,000 tonnes ($F235,058).

Total trade (in $F) in calendar years:

	1975	1976	1977	1978	1979
Imports	220,967,274	238,040,052	280,960,000	300,849,000	392,821,000
Exports	142,292,948	122,523,214	162,822,000	170,726,000	215,039,000

Imports in 1979 (in $F1,000) from Australia were 138,866; New Zealand, 59,011; Japan, 56,028; UK, 34,946; Singapore, 19,112.

Exports in 1979 (in $F1,000) to UK were 79,606; New Zealand, 20,718; Australia, 17,224; Singapore, 4,556.

Total trade between Fiji and UK (British Department of Trade returns, in $1,000 sterling):

	1975	1976	1977	1978	1979	1980
Imports to UK	51,094	25,145	45,948	47,521	45,694	36,759
Exports and re-exports from UK	11,810	13,482	12,584	14,717	14,154	12,786

COMMUNICATIONS

Roads. There is a principal highway round Viti Levu, the distance from Suva to Lautoka via Ra, Tavua and Ba (King's Road) being 166 miles and via Navua and Sigatoka and Nadi (Queen's Road) being 156 miles. Branch roads run 34 miles along the Sigatoka Valley, 18 miles to Nadarivatu and Navai, 5½ miles to Vatukoula Goldfields, 35 miles to Serea and 7 miles to Vunidawa.

On Vanua Levu highways are in the neighbourhood of Labasa (Nasea) and Nasavusavu (Valeci). There are highways, 92 miles south and 36 miles west of Labasa. A highway extends to Buca Bay, 45 miles east of Nasavusavu. Coastal roads connect villages and plantations on parts of the islands of Taveuni and Ovalau. Work is now complete on the reconstruction of the new bitumen surfaced highway between Suva and Nadi except for the section between Deuba and Sigatoka. The construction of a new gravel surfaced highway on Vanua Levu to link the towns of Nasavusavu and Labasa is almost complete.

Total road mileage is 2,019, of which 218 are sealed (paved), 1,663 are gravelled and 138 are unimproved.

Railway. There is a private 2-ft-gauge railway (Fiji Sugar Corporation's Railway) of 400 miles from Tavua to Sigatoka serving most of the sugar-cane producing area.

Aviation. Fiji provides an essential staging point for long-haul trunk-route aircraft operating between North America, Australia and New Zealand. Under the South Pacific Air Transport Council, which comprises the UK, Australia, New Zealand

and Fiji, the international airport at Nadi has been developed and administered. Fourteen other airports are in use for domestic services.

Long-haul services touching Nadi airport are operated by JAL (Tōkyō, Auckland), Air New Zealand (Auckland, Pago Pago, Honolulu, Los Angeles), Qantas (Sydney, Honolulu, San Francisco; Sydney, Tahiti, Mexico), Union de Transports Aériens (Sydney, Nouméa, Tahiti, Los Angeles), Canadian Pacific Airlines (Vancouver, Honolulu, Auckland, Sydney), Continental Airlines (West Coast, USA, Hawaii, Fiji, Australia).

Domestic and regional services are operated by Air Pacific (Tonga, also including Australia (Brisbane) and New Zealand (Auckland), Vanuatu, Solomon Islands, Kiribati, Tuvalu, Western Samoa); Polynesian Airlines (Western Samoa) and Air Nauru. Fiji Air provides a domestic island service.

Shipping. In 1977, 167 vessels of 6,298 net tons were registered. Suva has 4 slipways of 100, 200, 500 and 1,500 tons, and there are 3 shipbuilding and repair firms.

Post. There are 35 post offices and 158 agencies. Overseas postal communications are excellent. There is a daily air service to the major countries of the world and frequent dispatches by sea to UK, Australia, New Zealand and North America. Overseas telephone and telegram services are available through the Commonwealth cable to most countries except those in the South Pacific, which are served by direct radio circuits. The automatic telex network operates through New Zealand into the international telex system. There are ship-to-shore radio facilities. There were 47,500 telephones in 1979.

Cinemas. In 1979 there were 48 cinemas with a seating capacity of 28,100.

JUSTICE, RELIGION AND EDUCATION

Justice. Fijian courts have been abolished and merged into the magistrates' court.

Police. The Royal Fiji Police Force had (1979) a total strength of 1,363.

Religion. The 1976 census showed: Christians, 299,960; Hindus, 234,520; Muslims, 45,247; Confucians, 731.

Education (1980). School attendance is not compulsory in Fiji. There were 828 schools scattered over 56 islands, staffed by 6,500 teachers, of whom about 88·4% were trained. There were also 140 pre-schools. The primary schools had 127,325 pupils and secondary 35,238. The technical and vocational schools had (1978) 1,930 students and the teachers' colleges 613. There were 4 teacher-training colleges, 1 medical and 1 agricultural school.

The University of the South Pacific opened in Feb. 1968 at Laucala Bay in Suva. It had 1,427 full-time students in 1980. The University has 3 schools, social and economic development, natural resources and education.

The main libraries are at Suva and Lautoka and there are also public libraries at Nadi, Ba, Sigatoka and Labasa. There is a national archives library, confined mainly to Fijiana and the Pacific.

The Fiji museum in Suva contains a fine historical and ethnological collection relating to Fiji and Western Pacific territories.

Total government expenditure on education in 1980 was over $F55·5m.

DIPLOMATIC REPRESENTATIVES

OF FIJI IN GREAT BRITAIN (34 Hyde Park Gate, London, SW7 5DN)

High Commissioner: (Vacant).

OF GREAT BRITAIN IN FIJI (Civic Centre, Stinson Parade, Suva)
High Commissioner: Viscount Dunrossil.

OF FIJI IN THE USA (United Nations Plaza, New York, NY., 1007)
Ambassador: Filipe Bole.

OF THE USA IN FIJI (31 Loftus St., Suva)
Ambassador: William Bodde, Jr.

OF FIJI TO THE UNITED NATIONS

Ambassador: Filipe Bole

.

Books of Reference

Statistical Information: A Bureau of Statistics was set up in 1950 (Government Buildings, Suva).

Trade Report. Annual (from 1887 [covering 1883–86]). Ministry of Information, Suva

Journal of the Fiji Legislative Council. Annual (from 1914 [under different title from 1885]). Suva

Fiji Today. Annually. Suva

Report of Commission of Inquiry Into Natural Resources and Population Trends in Fiji. Suva, Government Press, 1960

Ashford, J. E., *Social Security in Fiji.* Suva Government Press, 1964

Burns, Sir Alan, *Fiji.* HMSO, 1963

Capell, A., *New Fijian Dictionary.* 2nd ed. Glasgow, 1957

France, P., *The Charter of the Land.* OUP, 1969

Nayacakalou, R. R., *Leadership in Fiji.* OUP, 1976

Roth, G. K., *The Fijian Way of Life.* 2nd ed. OUP, 1973

Sahlins, M. D., *Moala: Culture and Nature on a Fijian Island.* Univ. of Michigan Press, 1962

Spate, O. H. K., *The Fijian People: Economic Problems and Prospects.* Suva, Government Press, 1959

Ward, R. G., *Land Use and Population in Fiji.* HMSO, 1965

Watters, R. F., *Koro: Economic Development and Social Change in Fiji.* OUP, 1969

FINLAND

Capital: Helsinki
Population: 4·79m. (1980)
GNP per capita: US$8,543 (1979)

Suomen Tasavalta—
Republiken Finland

HISTORY. Since the Middle Ages Finland was a part of the realm of Sweden. In the 18th century parts of south-eastern Finland were conquered by Russia, and the rest of the country was ceded to Russia by the peace treaty of Hamina in 1809. Finland became an autonomous grand-duchy which retained its previous laws and institutions under its Grand Duke, the Emperor of Russia. After the Russian revolution Finland declared itself independent on 6 Dec. 1917. The Civil War began in Jan. 1918 between the 'whites' and 'reds', the latter being supported by Russian bolshevik troops. The defeat of the red guards in May 1918 consequently meant freeing the country from Russian troops. A peace treaty with Soviet Russia was signed in 1920.

On 30 Nov. 1939 Soviet troops invaded Finland, after Finland had rejected territorial concessions demanded by the USSR. These, however, had to be made in the peace treaty of 12 March 1940, amounting to 32,806 sq. km and including the Carelian Isthmus, Viipuri and the shores of Lake Ladoga.

When the German attack on the USSR was launched in June 1941 Finland again became involved in the war against the USSR. On 19 Sept. 1944 an armistice was signed in Moscow. Finland agreed to cede to Russia the Petsamo area in addition to cessions made in 1940 (total 42,934 sq. km) and to lease to Russia for 50 years the Porkkala headland to be used as a military base. Further, Finland undertook to pay 300m. gold dollars in reparations within 6 years (later extended to 8 years). The peace treaty was signed in Paris on 10 Feb. 1947. The payment of reparations was completed on 19 Sept. 1952. The military base of Porkkala was returned to Finland on 26 Jan. 1956.

AREA AND POPULATION. The area and the population of Finland on 31 Dec. 1979 (Swedish names in brackets):

Province	Area (sq. km)[1]	Population[2]	Population per sq. km[2]
Uusimaa (Nyland)	9,859	1,119,731	113·6
Turku-Pori (Åbo-Björneborg)	21,924	701,700	32·0
Ahvenanmaa (Åland)	1,481	22,608	15·3
Häme (Tavastehus)	17,153	662,562	38·6
Kymi (Kymmene)	10,736	345,053	32·1
Mikkeli (St Michel)	16,425	209,199	12·7
Pohjois-Karjala (Norra Karelen)	17,986	176,612	9·8
Kuopio	16,719	251,715	15·1
Keski-Suomi (Mellersta Finland)	16,431	242,439	14·8
Vaasa (Vasa)	26,122	430,177	16·5
Oulu (Uleåborg)	56,706	414,436	7·3
Lappi (Lappland)	93,933	195,060	2·1
Total	305,475	4,771,292	15·6

[1] Excluding inland water area which totals 31,557 sq. km. [2] Resident population.

The growth of the population, which was 421,500 in 1750, has been:

End of year	Urban	Rural	Total	Percentage urban
1800	46,600	786,100	832,700	5·6
1900	333,300	2,322,600	2,655,900	12·5
1950	1,302,400	2,727,400	4,029,800	32·3
1960	1,707,000	2,739,200	4,446,200	38·4
1970	2,340,308	2,258,028	4,598,336	50·9
1979	2,852,164	1,919,128	4,771,292	59·8
1980	2,865,711	1,922,073	4,787,784	59·9

The population on 31 Dec. 1979 by language primarily spoken: Finnish, 4,463,032 (93·5%); Swedish, 301,554 (6·3%); other languages, 5,417; Lappish, 1,289.

The principal towns with resident census population, 31 Dec. 1979, are (Swedish names in brackets):

Helsinki (Helsingfors)—capital	483,743	Imatra	36,527
(metropolitan area)	892,960	Kajaani	34,092
Tampere (Tammerfors)	165,883	Kokkola (Gamlakarleby)	33,599
(metropolitan area)	242,587	Kouvola	30,869
Turku (Åbo)	163,903	Rauma (Raumo)	30,604
(metropolitan area)	239,932	Rovaniemi	29,720
Espoo (Esbo)	133,712	Savonlinna (Nyslott)	28,308
Vantaa (Vanda)	129,807	Mikkeli (St Michel)	28,282
Lahti	94,900	Kemi	27,093
Oulu (Uleåborg)	93,420	Varkaus	24,635
Pori (Björneborg)	79,431	Seinäjoki	24,154
Kuopio	73,899	Riihimäki	23,987
Jyväskylä	63,599	Nokia	23,584
Kotka	61,042	Kerava	23,214
Vaasa (Vasa)	53,720	Järvenpää	22,867
Lappeenranta (Villmanstrand)	53,418	Valkeakoski	22,827
Joensuu	44,318	Kuusankoski	22,531
Hämeenlinna (Tavastehus)	41,559	Iisalmi	22,321
Hyvinkää (Hyvinge)	37,215		

Vital statistics in calendar years:

	Living births	Of which illegitimate	Still-born	Marriages	Deaths (exclusive of still-born)	Emigration
1975	65,719	6,670	378	31,547	43,828	12,237
1976	66,846	7,273	376	32,004	44,786	17,346
1977	65,659	7,317	335	30,966	44,065	16,657
1978	63,983	7,263	314	29,760	43,692	15,035
1979	63,475	...	...	29,324	43,737	17,022

In 1979 the rate per 1,000 was: Births, 13·3; marriages, 6·2; deaths, 9·2, and infantile deaths (per 1,000 live births), 7·6 in 1978.

General Census of Population 1970. 16 vols. Helsinki, 1973
Population. Annual, Helsinki

CONSTITUTION AND GOVERNMENT. Finland is a republic according to the Constitution of 17 July 1919.

Parliament consists of one chamber of 200 members chosen by direct and proportional election, in which all Finnish citizens (men or women) who are 18 years have the vote (since 1969). The country is divided into 15 electoral districts with a representation proportional to their population. Every citizen over the age of 20 is eligible for Parliament, which is elected for 4 years, but can be dissolved sooner by the President.

The President is elected for 6 years by a college of 300 electors, elected by the votes of the citizens in the same way as the members of Parliament.

President of Finland: Dr Urho Kekkonen (elected 15 Feb. 1956, re-elected 15 Feb. 1962, 15 Feb. 1968, mandate extended by special law to March 1978 on 17–18 Jan. 1973 and re-elected 15 Feb. 1978 for a further 6-year term).

State of Parties for Parliament elected on 18–19 March 1979: Conservative 47; Liberals, 4; Swedish Party, 10 (including 1 for Coalition of Åland); Centre, 36; Rural, 7; Social Democratic Party, 52; Communists, 35; Christian League, 9.

The Council of State (Cabinet), appointed by the President in May 1979 was composed as follows:

Prime Minister: Mauno Koivisto.

Agriculture and Forestry: Taisto Tähkämaa. *Foreign Affairs:* Paavo Väyrynen. *Justice:* Cristoffer Taxell. *Deputy Prime Minister and Minister of Interior:* Eino Uusitalo. *Interior (Deputy):* Johannes Koikkalainen. *Defence:* Lasse Äikäs. *Finance:* Ahti Pekkala. *Economics and Finance:* Pirkko Työläjärvi. *Education:* Pär Stenbäck. *Education (Deputy):* Kalevi Kivistö. *Communications:* Veikko Saarto. *Trade and*

Industry: Ulf Sundqvist. *Social Affairs and Health:* Sinikka Luja-Penttilä. *Social Affairs and Health (Deputy):* Katri-Helena Eskelinen. *Labour:* Arvo Aalto. *Foreign Trade:* Esko Rekola.

National flag: White with a blue Scandinavian cross.

National anthem: Maamme; Swedish: Vårt land (words by J. L. Runeberg, 1843; tune by F. Pacius, 1948).

Finnish and Swedish are the official languages of Finland.

Local Government. For administrative purposes Finland is divided into 12 provinces (*lääni,* Sw.: *län*). The administration of each province is entrusted to a governor (*maaherra,* Sw.: *landshövding*) appointed by the President. He directs the activities of the provincial office (*lääninhallitus,* Sw.: *länsstyrelse*) and of local sheriffs (*nimismies,* Sw.: *länsman*). In 1979 the number of sheriff districts was 227.

The unit of local government is the commune. Main fields of communal activities are local planning, roads and harbours, sanitary services, education, health services and social aid. The communes raise taxes independent from state taxation. Two different kinds of communes are distinguished: Urban communes (*kaupunki,* Sw.: *stad*) and rural communes. In 1980 there were altogether 464 communes, of which 84 were urban and 380 rural. In all communes communal councils are elected for terms of 4 years; all inhabitants (men and women) of the commune who have reached their 18th year are entitled to vote and eligible. The executive power is in each commune vested in a board which consists of members elected by the council and one or a few chief officials of the commune. Several communes often form an association for the administration of some common institution, *e.g.,* a hospital or a vocational school.

The autonomous county (*landskap*) of Åland has a county council (*landsting*) of one chamber, elected according to rule corresponding to those for parliamentary elections. In addition to its provincial governor it has a county board with executive power in matters within the field of the autonomy of the county.

Constitution Act and Parliament Act of Finland. Helsinki, 1967
The Finnish Parliament. Porvoo, 1969
Local Self-Government in Finland and the Finnish Municipal Law. Helsinki, 1960
Democracy in Finland. Studies in Politics and Government. Political Science Association. Helsinki, 1960
Report of the Second Parliamentary Defence Committee. Helsinki, 1976

DEFENCE. The period of military training is 240 to 330 days and refresher training 40 to 100 days. Total strength of trained and equipped reserves is about 700,000.

Army. The country is divided into 7 military districts. The Army consists of 1 armoured brigade, 7 infantry brigades, 7 independent infantry battalions, 3 field-artillery regiments, 2 independent field-artillery battalions, 2 coastal artillery regiments, 3 independent coastal artillery battalions, 1 anti-aircraft regiment, 1 surface-to-air missile battalion and 4 independent anti-aircraft battalions, making a total strength in 1980, of about 34,400.

Navy. The Fleet comprises 2 frigates (*ex*-Soviet), 2 corvettes, 2 coastal minelayers, 5 missile craft, 14 fast patrol boats, 6 inshore minesweepers, 5 patrol boats capable of minelaying, 13 patrol boats, 4 coastguard patrol vessels, 3 support ships, 2 headquarters ships, 13 transport craft, 57 small transport boats, 5 coastguard cutters, 90 coastal craft, 1 training ship, 6 tugs, 10 icebreakers, 1 supply ship and a cable ship. There is a naval academy. Personnel in 1981 totalled 2,500 (200 officers and 2,300 ratings).

Air Force. The Air Force has 2 fighter squadrons, a military school of aviation and air force technical school, a depot, a transport squadron and a signal school. The fighter squadrons have MiG-21bis and Saab J35 Draken aircraft. Other equipment includes Saab-91D Safir piston-engined primary trainers (being replaced by 30 Valmet Vjinka trainers of Finnish design), Magister jet basic trainers (being replaced by 50 Hawk light attack/trainers), MiG-15UTI and MiG-21U jet advanced trainers, C-47 transport aircraft, Il-28 target tugs (being replaced by Learjets 35As) and Mi-8, Mi-4 and Hughes 500 helicopters. Personnel total 3,000 officers and men.

INTERNATIONAL RELATIONS

Membership. Finland is a member of UN, the Nordic Council, OECD and EFTA.

Treaties. A Treaty of friendship, co-operation and mutual assistance between Finland and the USSR was concluded in Moscow on 6 April 1948 for 10 years, extended on 19 Sept. 1955 to cover a period of 20 years and extended on 19 July 1970 for a further period of 20 years.

Treaty of Peace with Finland (10 Feb. 1947). Cmd. 7484

ECONOMY

Budget. Actual revenue and expenditure for the calendar years 1973–78, the ordinary budget for 1979 and the proposed budget for 1980 in 1m. marks:

	1974	1975	1976	1977	1978	1979	1980	1981
Revenue	20,931	25,108	32,132	35,168	40,393	43,319	48,710	55,937
Expenditure	21,307	27,546	31,094	35,064	38,938	48,701	48,701	55,937

Of the total revenue, 1979, 25% derived from sales tax, 19% from excise duties, 12% from other taxes and similar revenue, 11% from loans and 11% from miscellaneous sources. Of the total expenditure, 1979, 18% went to education and culture, 13% to social security, 11% to transport, 12% to agriculture and forestry, 9% to general administration, public order and safety, 8% to health, 6% to communities and housing policy, 5% to defence, 6% to promotion of industry and 13% to other expenditures.

At the end of Dec. 1979 the foreign loans totalled 8,964m. marks, of which 8,779m. were long-term loans, 185m. promissory notes to international organizations. The internal loans amounted to 6,225m. marks, of which, 6,017m. were consolidated debt and 174m. short-term loans. The cash surplus was 1,106m. marks. The total public debt was 15,189m. marks.

Currency. The unit of currency, starting 1 Jan. 1963, is the new *mark* of 100 *pennis*, equalling 100 old *marks*. The gold standard was suspended on 12 Oct. 1931. Aluminium bronze coins are 50, 20 and 10 *pennis*; copper coins, 5 and 1 *pennis*; aluminium coins, 5 and 1 *pennis*; silver, 1 *mark* pieces. Exchange rate in March 1981: 8·98 marks = £1; 4·08 marks = US$1.

Banking. The Bank of Finland (founded in 1811) is owned by the State and under the guarantee and supervision of Parliament. It is the only bank of issue, and the limit of its right to issue notes is fixed equal to the value of its assets of gold and foreign holdings plus 500m. marks. Notes of 500, 100, 50, 10, 5 and 1 marks are in circulation, and their total value at the end of 1979 was 4,020m. marks.

At the end of 1979 the deposits in banking institutions totalled 65,538m. marks and the loans granted by them 72,047m. marks. The most important groups of banking institutions were:

	Number of institutions	Number of offices	Deposits (1m. marks)	Loans (1m. marks)
Commercial banks	7	1,144	23,477	25,803
Savings banks	278	1,317	18,444	16,541
Post office savings bank	1	27 [1]	8,145	7,790
Co-operative banks	373	1,224	14,371	14,255

[1] In addition: 3,210 post offices.

Bank of Finland Monthly Bulletin. Helsinki, from 1926
Unitas. Quarterly Review, issued by Union Bank of Finland. Helsinki, from 1929
Economic Review (issued quarterly by Kansallis–Osake–Pankki). Helsinki, from 1948

Weights and Measures. The metric system of weights and measures was introduced in 1887 and is officially and universally employed.

Economic Survey of Finland. Annual

ENERGY AND NATURAL RESOURCES

Electricity. Electricity production was (in 1m. kwh.) 8,605 in 1960; 27,885 in 1976; 31,563 in 1977, 33,871 in 1978 and 37,151 in 1979, of which 29% was hydro-electric.

Minerals. The most important mines are Outokumpu (copper, discovered in 1910) and Otanmäki (iron, discovered in 1953). In 1979 the metal content (in tonnes) of the output of copper concentrates was 41,000, of zinc concentrates 54,499, of nickel concentrates 5,800, of iron concentrates and pellets 774,000 and of lead concentrates 1,390.

Agriculture. The cultivated area covers only 9% of the land and of the economically active population 15% were employed in agriculture and forestry in 1975. The arable area was divided in 1978 into 238,035 farms, and the distribution of this area by the size of the farms was: Less than 5 hectares cultivated, 78,435 farms; 5–20 hectares, 131,790 farms; 20–50 hectares, 25,066 farms; 50–100 hectares, 2,369 farms; over 100 hectares, 375 farms.

The principal crops (area in 1,000 hectares, yield in tonnes) were in 1979:

Crop	Area	Yield	Crop	Area	Yield
Rye	37	77,200	Oats	451	1,282,600
Barley	633	1,649,900	Potatoes	43	674,100
Wheat	99	208,400	Hay	471	1,864,400

The total area under cultivation in 1979 was 2,589,000 hectares. Production of dairy butter in 1979 was 74,224 tonnes, and of cheese, 70,103 tonnes.

Livestock (1980): Horses, 22,400; cattle, 1,738,100; pigs (excluding piggeries of dairies), 1,410,200; poultry, 9,375,900; reindeer, 205,000 (1979).

Forestry. The total forest land amounts to 30–31m. hectares. The productive forest land covers 19·73m. hectares. The growing stock was valued at 1,520m. cu. metres in 1971–76 and the annual growth at 57·4m. cu. metres.

In 1979 there were exported: Round timber, 1,299,989 cu. metres; sawn wood, 6,634,524 cu. metres; plywood and veneers, 867,490 cu. metres.

Census of Agriculture 1969. Helsinki, 1969
Westermarck, N., *Finnish Agriculture.* Helsinki, 1963

INDUSTRY AND TRADE

Industry. The following data cover establishments with a total personnel of 5 or more in 1979 [1]:

Industry	Establish-ments	Person-nel [2]	Value of production Gross (1m. marks)	Value added (1m. marks)
Mining and quarrying	103	7,307	1,213	824
Metal ore mining	13	4,735	766	556
Other mining	90	2,561	412	236
Manufacturing	6,746	500,245	123,946	45,955
Manufacture of food, beverages and tobacco	1,206	59,881	22,770	5,497
Textile, wearing apparel and leather industries	896	64,607	7,546	3,527
Manufacture of textiles	284	22,439	3,114	1,453
Manufacture of wearing apparel, except footwear	454	33,096	3,255	1,645
Manufacture of wood and wood products, incl. furniture	987	56,217	10,177	4,122
Manufacture of paper and paper prod., printing, publishing	851	80,566	27,143	9,969
Manufacture of paper and paper products	177	49,010	21,295	6,633
Printing, publishing, etc.	674	31,522	5,825	3,291
Manufacture of chemicals and chemical, petroleum, coal, rubber and plastic products	421	37,532	18,724	6,000
Manufacture of industrial chemicals	130	12,967	5,279	1,606
Manufacture of other chemical products	122	9,354	2,101	1,063
Petroleum refineries	3	2,908	9,029	2,111
Manufacture of non-metallic mineral products	415	19,718	3,535	1,877
Basic metal industries	96	19,634	9,363	2,677
Iron and steel basic industries	63	14,394	6,232	1,953
Non-ferrous metal basic industries	33	5,248	3,859	768
Manufacture of fabricated metal products, machinery, etc.	1,749	157,529	24,087	12,027

[1] Preliminary.

[2] Working proprietors, salaried employees and wage earners.

| | | | Value of production | |
Industry	Establish-ments	Person-nel[1]	Gross (1m. marks)	Value added (1m. marks)
Manufacture of fabricated metal products, excl. machinery	598	29,088	4,274	2,145
Manufacture of machinery, except electrical	644	57,538	8,699	4,436
Manufacture of electrical machinery, apparatus, etc.	186	29,365	4,406	2,157
Manufacture of transport equipment	256	36,896	6,185	2,927
Other manufacturing industries	125	5,155	682	357
Electricity, gas and water	491	25,231	13,509	4,900
All industry	7,340	532,783	138,668	51,679

[1] Working proprietors, salaried employees and wage earners.

GDP (at market prices) *per capita* (1979) 33,855 marks.

Industrial Statistics of Finland. Annual
Knoellinger, C. E., *Labor in Finland.* Harvard Univ. Press, 1960

Commerce. Imports and exports for calendar years, in 1m. marks:

	1976	1977	1978	1979	1980
Imports	28,555	30,708	32,338	44,222	58,239
Exports	24,505	30,931	35,206	43,430	52,793

The trade with some principal import and export countries was (in 1,000 marks):

Country	Imports		Exports	
	1978	1979	1978	1979
Australia	47,109	56,311	337,198	385,726
Austria	420,244	557,862	255,139	300,532
Belgium–Luxembourg	582,140	809,202	563,845	651,259
Brazil	224,007	290,842	165,711	182,879
Canada	142,430	301,554	177,344	207,349
China	53,622	109,942	153,995	165,574
Colombia	359,901	391,469	43,649	57,659
Czechoslovakia	162,986	217,888	153,217	120,865
Denmark	873,343	1,113,502	1,432,881	1,705,379
France	1,058,266	1,443,915	1,338,916	1,906,450
German Dem. Rep.	202,348	248,891	226,393	356,168
Germany (Fed. Rep.)	4,356,500	5,705,878	3,546,744	4,778,700
Greece	27,816	66,524	176,179	299,340
Hungary	140,237	188,635	240,635	226,017
Iran	385,723	821,859	391,221	175,114
Iraq	155,426	740,584	133,149	410,428
Ireland	57,113	90,139	239,679	332,009
Israel	107,067	136,665	170,354	211,746
Italy	732,634	1,049,245	603,684	954,692
Japan	898,585	1,210,814	517,761	466,573
Netherlands	914,183	1,191,305	1,281,709	1,813,405
Norway	896,844	1,119,952	1,771,063	2,336,752
Poland	729,995	841,629	216,693	194,771
Portugal	115,868	211,241	59,398	73,555
Saudi Arabia	631,709	1,264,519	223,167	294,788
Spain	308,124	401,925	294,285	458,241
Sweden	4,656,636	6,113,392	5,142,637	6,975,361
Switzerland	670,377	799,450	589,595	759,426
USSR	6,066,404	8,632,024	6,275,729	5,987,205
UK	2,960,985	3,818,906	4,431,678	5,678,131
USA	1,623,851	2,219,146	1,386,849	1,850,085

Principal imports 1979 (in 1m. marks): Machinery, apparatus and appliances, 11,963; mineral fuels, lubricants, etc., 11,543; chemicals, 4,242; food and live animals, 2,844; road vehicles, 2,845; crude materials, inedible, except fuels, 2,675; textile yarn, fabrics, etc., 2,111; iron and steel, 1,540.

Principal exports in 1979 (in 1m. marks): Paper and paper-board, 9,972; machinery and transport equipment, 8,614; wood shaped or simply worked, 3,908; wood pulp, 2,759; ships, 2,515; clothing, 2,170; veneers, plywood, etc., and other wood manufactures, 1,300; food and live animals, 1,078; road vehicles, 756.

Total trade between Finland and UK (British Department of Trade returns, in £1,000 sterling):

	1976	1977	1978	1979	1980
Imports to UK	562,462	593,675	636,374	794,485	793,218
Exports and re-exports from UK	288,960	345,957	349,131	410,537	525,488

Finnish Foreign Trade Directory, 1971. Helsinki, 1971

COMMUNICATIONS

Roads. In Jan. 1979 there were 74,430 km of public roads, of which 33,186 km were paved. At the end of 1979 there were 1,169,501 registered cars, 51,756 lorries, 91,339 vans and 8,826 buses.

Railways. On 31 Dec. 1979 the total length of the line operated was 6,107 km, of which all except 6 km was owned by the State. The gauge was 1,524 mm. In 1979 the number of passengers carried was 38m. and the amount of goods carried was 26·7m. tonnes. The total revenue in 1979 was 1,541m. marks and the total expenditure 2,027m. marks.

Aviation. The scheduled traffic of Finnish airlines covered 32m. km in 1979. The number of passengers was 2,352,979 and the number of passenger-km 1,984m. The air transport of freight and mail amounted to 46m. tonne-km.

Shipping. The total registered mercantile marine on 31 Dec. 1979 was 466 vessels of 2·42m. gross tons. In 1979 the total number of vessels arriving in Finland from abroad was 17,428 and the goods discharged amounted to 30·6m. tonnes. The goods loaded for export from Finland ports amounted to 17·2m. tonnes.

The lakes, rivers and canals are navigable for about 6,600 km. Timber floating is important, and there are about 41,500 km of floatable inland waterways. In 1977 bundle floating was about 8·3m. tonnes and river floating 1·3m. tonnes. In 1979, timber floated by vessels, 453,746 tonnes (rafts, 6·68m.).

On 27 Aug. 1963 the USSR leased to Finland the Russian part of the canal connecting Lake Saimaa with the Gulf of Finland. After extensive rebuilding the canal was opened for traffic in 1968. The Saimaa Canal and deepwater channels on Lake Saimaa (520 km) can be used by vessels with dimensions not larger than as follows: length 82 metres, width 11·8 metres, draught 4·4 metres and height of mast 24·5 metres.

Post and Broadcasting. In 1979 there were 3,999 post offices and 919 telegraph offices. The total length of telegraph wires was 532,904 km and that of domestic trunk and net group telephone wires 6·1m. km. The number of telephones was (1979), 2,244,055. All post and telegraph systems are administered by the State jointly with a large part of the telephone services. The total revenues from postal services were 1,163m. marks and from (wire and radio) telegraph services 1,608m. marks.

On 31 Dec. 1979 the number of television licences, 1,505,094, of which licences for colour television, 648,186. *Oy Yleisradio AB* broadcasts 2 programmes in Finnish and 1 in Swedish on long-, medium- and short-waves, and on FM. Two TV programmes (1 commercial) are broadcast.

Cinemas. In Dec. 1979 there were 336 cinemas with a seating capacity of 91,549.

Newspapers. In 1979 the number of newspapers published more often than once a week was 121, of which 108 in Finnish and 12 in Swedish.

JUSTICE, RELIGION, EDUCATION AND WELFARE

Justice. The lowest courts of justice are the municipal courts in towns and district courts in the country. Municipal courts are held by the burgomaster and at least 2 members of court, district court by judge and 5 jurors, the judge alone deciding, unless the jurors unanimously differ from him, when their decision prevails. From these courts an appeal lies to the courts of appeal (*Hovioikeus*) in Turku, Vaasa,

Kuopio, Kouvola and Helsinki. The Supreme Court (*Korkein oikeus*) sits in Helsinki. Judges can be removed only by judicial sentence.

Two functionaries, the *Oikeuskansleri* or Chancellor of Justice, and the *Oikeusasiamies*, or Solicitor-General, exercise control over the administration of justice. The former acts also as counsel and public prosecutor for the Government; while the latter, who is appointed by the Parliament, exerts a general control over all courts of law and public administration.

At the end of 1979 the prison population numbered 5,073 men and 142 women; the number of convictions in 1978 was 316,188, of which 288,954 were for minor offences with maximum penalty of fines and 27,227 with penalty of imprisonment.

Merikoski, V., *Précis du droit public de la Finlande*. Helsinki, 1954

Religion. Liberty of conscience is guaranteed to members of all religions. National churches are the Lutheran National Church and the Greek Orthodox Church of Finland. The Lutheran Church is divided into 8 bishoprics (Turku being the archiepiscopal see), 76 provostships and 593 parishes. The Greek Orthodox Church is divided into 2 bishoprics (Kuopio being the archiepiscopal see) and 25 parishes, in addition to which there are a monastery and a convent.

Percentage of the total population at the end of 1979: Lutherans, 90·4; Greek Orthodox, 1·1; others, 0·8; not members of any religion, 7·7.

Education (1978–79). *Primary and Secondary Education:*

	Number of institutions	Teachers	Students
First-level Education	4,297	25,142	406,921
(Lower sections of the comprehensive schools, grades I–VI)			
Second-level Education	1,597	32,651	446,041
General education	1,056	19,549	345,603
(Upper sections of the comprehensive schools, grades VII–IX, and senior secondary schools)			
Vocational education	541	13,102	100,438

Higher Education. Education at the third level (including universities and third level education at vocational institutes) was provided for 122,825 students. Education at universities was provided at 17 institutions with 5,581 teachers and 80,480 students.

University Education. Universities and similar types of institutions and the number of teachers and students are:

Universities	Founded	Teachers	Students Total	Students Women
Helsinki	1640	1,587	23,941	13,001
Turku (Swedish)	1919	228	3,245	1,718
Turku (Finnish)	1922	678	8,570	4,737
Jyväskylä	1958	441	5,983	3,653
Oulu	1958	677	7,255	3,376
Tampere	1966	388	8,628	5,131
Joensuu	1969	215	2,430	1,569
Kuopio	1972	174	1,130	601
Polytechnic, Lappeenranta	1969	86	747	95
Polytechnic, Helsinki	1849	517	7,343	1,207
Polytechnic, Tampere	1972	182	2,386	242
College of Veterinary Medicine, Helsinki	1946	50	254	155
Schools for Economics				
Helsinki (Finnish)	1911	140	4,086	1,820
Helsinki (Swedish)	1927	78	1,480	599
Turku (Swedish)	1927	35	612	265
Turku (Finnish)	1950	51	1,339	618
Vaasa	1968	54	1,051	690
Swedish school of social sciences and local administration	1964 [1]	20	351	252
Teachers' training colleges [2]				

[1] Previously Swedish Civic College since 1943.　　[2] Included in data for the universities above.

General adult education (at civic institutes, folk high schools and study centres) had 738,534 students.

General Education. Central Statistical Office, Helsinki (annual), *Higher Education.* Central Statistical Office, Helsinki (annual), *Vocational Education.* Helsinki (annual)

Health. In 1979 there were 8,543 physicians, 3,827 dentists and 74,150 hospital beds.

Social Security. The Social Insurance Institution administers general systems of old age pensions (to all persons over 65 years of age and disabled younger persons) and of health insurance. An additional system of compulsory old age pensions paid for by the employers is in force and works through the Central Pension Security Institute. Systems for child welfare, care of vagrants, alcoholics and drug addicts and other public aid are administered by the communes and supervised by the National Social Board and the Ministry of Social Affairs and Health.

The total cost of social security amounted to 33,487m. marks in 1978. Out of this 9,604m. (28·7%) was spent for health, 743m. (2·2%) for industrial accidents, 2,600m. (7·8%) for unemployment, 13,451m. (40·2%) for old age and disability, 5,096m. (15·2%) for family allowances and child welfare, 447m. (1·3%) for general welfare purposes, 941m. (2·8%) for war-disabled, etc., 533m. (1·8%) as tax reductions for children and 604m. (1·8%) as interest subventions for housing loans. Out of the total expenditure 28% was financed by the State, 15% by local authorities, 47% by employers, 7% by the beneficiaries and 4% by users.

Labour Protection and Legislation. Helsinki, 1977
Social Welfare and Social Allowances. Helsinki, 1976
Social Security in the Nordic Countries 1972. Statistical Reports of the Nordic Countries, vol. 29. Copenhagen, 1976
Ellala, Esa, Suominen Risto, and Kotiranta, Maija-Liisa, *The Development of Social Security in Finland from 1950 to 1974.* Official statistics of Finland, special social studies XXXII : 48. Helsinki, 1976
Suominen, R. and Arajarvi, E., *Social Expenditure in 1977 and Preliminary Data for 1978.* Official Statistics of Finland, Helsinki, 1980

DIPLOMATIC REPRESENTATIVES

OF FINLAND IN GREAT BRITAIN (38 Chesham Place,
London SW1X 8HW)

Ambassador: Dr Richard Tötterman, GCVO, OBE (accredited 20 March 1975).

OF GREAT BRITAIN IN FINLAND (16–20 Uudenmaankatu,
Helsinki 12)

Ambassador: A. C. Stuart, CMG.

OF FINLAND IN THE USA (3216 New Mexico Ave., NW,
Washington, D.C., 20016)

Ambassador: Jaakko Iloniemi (accredited 10 Sept. 1977).

OF THE USA IN FINLAND (Itäinen Puistotie 14A, Helsinki 14)
Ambassador: James E. Goodby.

OF FINLAND TO THE UNITED NATIONS
Ambassador: Ilkka Olavi Pastinen.

Books of Reference

Statistical Information: The Central Statistical Office (Tilastokeskus, Swedish: Statistikcentralen; address: PO Box 504, SF-00101 Helsinki 10) was founded in 1865 to replace earlier official statistical services dating from 1749 (in united Sweden–Finland). Statistics on foreign trade, agriculture, forestry, navigation, health and social welfare are produced by other state authorities. Its publications include: *Statistical Yearbook of Finland* (from 1879) and *Bulletin of Statistics* (monthly, from 1924). A bibliography of all official statistics of Finland is published in Finnish, Swedish and English in each *Statistical Yearbook.*

Constitution Act and Parliament Act of Finland. Helsinki, 1978
Suomen valtiokalenteri (State Calendar of Finland; a Swedish version *Finlands statskalender* is published separately). Helsinki. Annual
Facts About Finland. Helsinki. Annual (Union Bank of Finland)
Finland: Creation and Construction. London, 1968
Finland in Figures. Helsinki, Annual
Finland Press Laws. Helsinki, 1978
Statistical Yearbook of Finland. Helsinki, Annual
Yearbook of Finnish Foreign Policy. Helsinki, Annual
Finnish Foreign Policy: Studies in Foreign Politics. Political Science Association, Helsinki, 1963
Hall, W., *The Finns and Their Country.* London, 1967
Havel, J. E., *La Finlande et la Suède.* Sherbrooke, Canada, 1978
Hurme-Pesonen, *Finnish–English General Dictionary.* Helsinki, 1973
Jakobson, M., *Finnish Neutrality.* London, 1968
Jutikkala, E., and Pirinen, K., *A History of Finland.* 2nd ed. New York, 1974
Kekkonen, U., *Neutrality: The Finnish Position.* 2nd ed. London, 1973
Kirby, D. G., *Finland in the Twentieth Century.* London, 1979
Nousiainen, J., *The Finnish Political System.* Harvard Univ. Press, 1971
Puntila, L. A., *The Political History of Finland, 1809–1966.* Helsinki, 1974
Suomen Kartasto/Atlas of Finland/Atlas over Finland (ed. L. Aario). Finnish Geogr. Society, Helsinki, 1960
Suomi: Handbook of Finnish Geography. Finnish Geogr. Society, Helsinki, 1962
Törnudd, K., *The Electoral System of Finland.* London, 1968
Tuomikoski, A., and Sloor, A., *English–Finnish Dictionary.* Helsinki, 1973
Uotila, J., *The Finnish Legal System.* Helsinki, 1966
Varjo, U., *Finnish Farming: Typology and Economics.* Budapest, 1977
Wuolle, A., *Finnish–English School Dictionary.* Helsinki, 1976
Wuorinen, J. H., *A History of Finland.* Columbia Univ. Press, 1965

FRANCE

République Française

Capital: Paris
Population: 53·59m. (1980)
GNP per capita: US$8,270 (1978)

HISTORY. The republic proclaimed on the fall of the Bourbon monarchy in 1792 lasted until the First Empire, under Napoleon I, was established in 1804. The Bourbon monarchy was restored in 1814 and (with an interval during 1815) lasted until the abdication of Louis Philippe in 1848. The Second Republic was established on 12 March 1848, the Second Empire (under Louis Napoleon) on 2 Dec. 1852. The Third Republic was established on 4 Sept. 1870 following the capture and imprisonment of Louis Napoleon in the Franco-Prussian war, and lasted until the German occupation of 1940. The Fourth Republic was established on 24 Dec. 1946 and lasted until 4 Oct. 1958.

AREA AND POPULATION. France is bounded north by the English Channel (La Manche), north-east by Belgium and Luxembourg, east by Federal Republic of Germany, Switzerland and Italy, south by the Mediterranean (with Monaco as a coastal enclave), south-west by Spain and Andorra, and west by the Atlantic Ocean.

The population (present in actual boundaries) at successive censuses has been:

1801	27,349,003	1881	37,672,048	Mar. 1946	40,506,639
1821	30,461,875	1891	38,342,948	May 1954	42,777,174
1841	34,230,178	1901	38,961,945	Mar. 1962	46,519,997
1861	37,386,313	1911	39,604,992	Mar. 1968	49,778,540
1866	38,067,064	1921	39,209,518	Apr. 1975	52,655,802
1872	36,102,921	1931	41,834,923		

The 1975 total included 3,442,415 foreigners, of whom 758,925 were Portuguese, 710,690 Algerian, 497,480 Spanish and 462,940 Italian.

The latest population estimate (at 1 Jan. 1980) is 53,589,000.

Vital statistics for calendar years:

	Marriages	Divorces	Live births	Still-born	Deaths
1974	394,755	58,500	799,217	11,400	550,550
1975	387,379	61,200	745,065	8,225	560,353
1976	374,003	63,200	720,395	7,522	557,114
1977	368,000	71,000	745,830	8,600	535,900
1978	354,628	73,000	737,062	7,852	546,916
1979	339,770	...	756,960	7,570	541,050

Live birth rate in 1979 was 14·1 per 1,000 inhabitants; death rate, 10·1; marriage rate, 6·3; divorce rate, 1·3; infant mortality, 10·1 per 1,000 live births. Life expectation at birth: men, 69·7; women, 77·9.

The areas, populations and administrative centres of the 96 Metropolitan departments were as follows:

Departments	Area (sq. km)	Census April 1975	Estimate Jan. 1980	Chief town
Ain	5,762	376,477	398,000	Bourg-en-Bresse
Aisne	7,369	533,862	527,200	Laon
Allier	7,340	378,406	365,400	Moulins
Alpes-de-Haute-Provence	6,925	112,178	115,800	Digne
Alpes (Hautes-)	5,549	97,358	99,800	Gap
Alpes-Maritimes	4,299	816,681	862,600	Nice
Ardèche	5,529	257,065	252,000	Privas
Ardennes	5,229	309,306	300,700	Charleville-Mézières
Ariège	4,890	137,857	135,500	Foix
Aube	6,004	284,823	286,900	Troyes

Departments	Area (sq. km)	Census April 1975	Estimate Jan. 1980	Chief town
Aude	6,139	272,366	265,200	Carcassonne
Aveyron	8,735	278,306	268,300	Rodez
Belfort (Territoire de)	609	128,125	132,000	Belfort
Bouches-du-Rhône	5,087	1,632,974	1,715,400	Marseille
Calvados	5,548	560,967	579,100	Caen
Cantal	5,726	166,549	160,500	Aurillac
Charente	5,956	337,064	334,200	Angoulême
Charente-Maritime	6,864	497,859	499,800	La Rochelle
Cher	7,235	316,350	319,100	Bourges
Corrèze	5,857	240,363	238,600	Tulle
Corse-du-Sud	4,014	128,600	102,500[1]	Ajaccio
Corse (Haute-)	4,666	161,242	127,000[1]	Bastia
Côte-d'Or	8,763	456,070	474,100	Dijon
Côtes-du-Nord	6,878	525,556	531,700	St-Brieuc
Creuse	5,565	146,214	138,100	Guéret
Dordogne	9,060	373,179	365,800	Périgueux
Doubs	5,234	471,082	492,500	Besançon
Drôme	6,530	361,847	366,700	Valence
Essonne	1,804	923,061	1,087,600	Évry
Eure	6,040	422,952	443,800	Évreux
Eure-et-Loir	5,880	335,151	352,700	Chartres
Finistère	6,733	804,088	817,800	Quimper
Gard	5,853	494,575	500,000	Nîmes
Garonne (Haute-)	6,309	777,431	816,600	Toulouse
Gers	6,257	175,366	167,200	Auch
Gironde	10,000	1,061,474	1,089,000	Bordeaux
Hauts-de-Seine	176	1,438,930	1,350,000	Nanterre
Hérault	6,101	648,202	685,500	Montpellier
Ille-et-Vilaine	6,775	702,199	731,600	Rennes
Indre	6,791	248,523	243,000	Châteauroux
Indre-et-Loire	6,127	478,601	498,700	Tours
Isère	7,431	860,378	903,900	Grenoble
Jura	4,999	238,856	237,800	Lons-le-Saunier
Landes	9,243	288,323	292,000	Mont-de-Marsan
Loir-et-Cher	6,344	283,686	288,600	Blois
Loire	4,781	742,396	735,500	St-Étienne
Loire (Haute-)	4,977	205,491	199,300	Le Puy
Loire-Atlantique	6,815	934,499	977,700	Nantes
Loiret	6,775	490,189	521,900	Orléans
Lot	5,217	150,725	148,300	Cahors
Lot-et-Garonne	5,361	292,616	287,800	Agen
Lozère	5,167	74,825	72,300	Mende
Maine-et-Loire	7,166	629,849	652,700	Angers
Manche	5,938	451,662	444,600	Saint-Lô
Marne	8,162	530,399	553,300	Châlons-sur-Marne
Marne (Haute-)	6,211	212,304	205,700	Chaumont
Mayenne	5,175	261,789	264,700	Laval
Meurthe-et-Moselle	5,241	722,587	716,500	Nancy
Meuse	6,216	203,904	191,400	Bar-le-Duc
Morbihan	6,823	563,588	571,700	Vannes
Moselle	6,216	1,006,373	1,007,200	Metz
Nièvre	6,817	245,212	239,500	Nevers
Nord	5,742	2,510,738	2,521,300	Lille
Oise	5,860	606,320	642,100	Beauvais
Orne	6,103	293,523	290,300	Alençon
Paris (Ville de)	105	2,299,830	2,050,500	Paris
Pas-de-Calais	6,672	1,403,035	1,399,000	Arras
Puy-de-Dôme	7,970	580,033	594,300	Clermont-Ferrand
Pyrénées-Atlantiques	7,645	534,748	542,100	Pau
Pyrénées (Hautes-)	4,464	227,222	222,200	Tarbes
Pyrénées-Orientales	4,116	299,506	309,100	Perpignan
Rhin (Bas-)	4,755	882,121	904,300	Strasbourg
Rhin (Haut-)	3,525	635,209	655,700	Colmar
Rhône	3,249	1,429,647	1,478,900	Lyon
Saône (Haute-)	5,360	222,254	223,500	Vesoul

[1] Following special survey of Corsica,

Departments	Area (sq. km)	Census April 1975	Estimate Jan. 1980	Chief town
Saône-et-Loire	8,574	569,810	569,000	Mâcon
Sarthe	6,206	490,385	499,500	Le Mans
Savoie	6,028	305,118	312,400	Chambéry
Savoie (Haute-)	4,388	447,795	483,400	Annecy
Seine-et-Marne	5,915	755,762	889,400	Melun
Seine-Maritime	6,278	1,172,743	1,194,700	Rouen
Seine-Saint-Denis	236	1,322,127	1,292,400	Bobigny
Sèvres (Deux-)	5,999	335,829	338,000	Niort
Somme	6,170	538,462	545,300	Amiens
Tarn	5,758	338,024	334,900	Albi
Tarn-et-Garonne	3,718	183,314	179,100	Montauban
Val-de-Marne	245	1,215,674	1,226,000	Créteil
Val-d'Oise	1,246	840,885	921,000	Pontoise
Var	5,973	626,093	667,300	Toulon
Vaucluse	3,567	390,446	412,200	Avignon
Vendée	6,720	450,641	466,200	La Roche-sur-Yon
Vienne	6,990	357,366	365,200	Poitiers
Vienne (Haute-)	5,520	352,149	356,800	Limoges
Vosges	5,874	397,957	397,800	Épinal
Yonne	7,427	299,851	307,000	Auxerre
Yvelines	2,284	1,082,255	1,247,800	Versailles
Total	543,965	52,655,802	53,589,000	

Populations of the principal conurbations and towns at Census 1975:

	Conurbation	Town		Conurbation	Town
Paris	8,549,898	2,317,227	Limoges	167,664	147,406
Lyon	1,170,660	462,841	Avignon	162,562	93,024
Marseille	1,070,912	914,356	Mantes-la-Jolie	154,988	42,564
Lille	935,882	177,218	Amiens	152,997	135,992
Bordeaux	612,456	226,281	Béthune	145,155	28,279
Toulouse	509,939	383,176	Thionville	141,881	44,191
Nantes	453,500	263,689	Briey	133,853	—
Nice	437,566	346,620	Montbéliard	132,343	31,591
Grenoble	389,088	169,740	Nîmes	131,638	133,942
Rouen	388,711	118,332	Pau	126,859	85,860
Toulon	378,430	185,050	Troyes	126,611	75,500
Strasbourg	365,323	257,303	Besançon	126,349	126,187
Valenciennes	350,599	43,202	Bayonne	121,474	44,706
St-Étienne	334,846	221,775	Saint-Nazaire	119,418	69,769
Lens	328,741	40,281	Perpignan	117,689	107,971
Nancy	280,569	111,493	Bruay-en-Artois	116,340	25,951
Le Havre	264,422	219,583	Trappes	112,353	—
Cannes	258,479	71,080	Aix-en-Provence	110,659	114,014
Clermont-Ferrand	253,244	161,203	Lorient	105,797	71,923
Tours	245,631	145,441	Valence	104,330	70,307
Rennes	229,310	205,733	Annecy	103,543	54,954
Mulhouse	218,743	119,326	La Rochelle	100,649	77,494
Montpellier	211,430	195,603	Boulogne-sur-Mer	100,581	49,284
Douai	210,508	47,570	Angoulême	100,528	50,500
Orléans	209,234	109,956	Calais	100,327	79,369
Dijon	208,432	156,787	Poitiers	98,554	85,466
Reims	197,021	183,610	Forbach	97,970	25,385
Le Mans	192,057	155,245	Maubeuge	97,494	35,474
Brest	190,812	172,176	Béziers	88,619	85,677
Angers	188,695	142,966	Chambéry	88,081	56,788
Dunkerque	186,314	83,759	Bourges	86,041	80,379
Caen	181,390	122,794	Roanne	83,561	56,498
Metz	181,191	117,199	Colmar	83,435	67,410

Recensement de la population de 1975. Paris, Institut National de la Statistique et des Etudes Economiques, 1975

Ormsby, H., *France, a Regional and Economic Geography.* 2nd ed. London, 1950

CONSTITUTION AND GOVERNMENT. The Constitution of the Fifth Republic, superseding that of 1946, came into force on 4 Oct. 1958. It consists of a preamble, dealing with the Rights of Man, and 92 articles.

Emphasis is placed on the rôle of the President of the Republic. 'He sees that the Constitution is respected; he ensures, through his arbitration, the regular functioning of public powers as well as the continuity of the state. He is the guarantor of national independence' (Art. 5). He is elected by direct universal suffrage for a 7-year term (Art. 6). He nominates and dismisses the Prime Minister and the other members of the government (Art. 8). He can dissolve the National Assembly after consultation with the Prime Minister and the presidents of the assemblies (Art. 12). He appoints to all military and civil offices of the Republic (Art. 13). 'When the institutions of the Republic, the independence of the nation, the integrity of its territory or the fulfilment of its international commitments are threatened with immediate and grave danger, and when the regular functioning of constitutional public powers is interrupted, the President of the Republic takes the measures demanded by the circumstances, after official consultation with the Prime Minister, the presidents of the assemblies and the Constitutional Council' (Art. 16).

Previous Presidents of the Fifth Republic: Charles de Gaulle, 8 Jan. 1959–28 April 1969 (resigned); Alain Poher (interim) 28 April 1969–20 June 1969; George Pompidou, 20 June 1969–2 April 1974 (died); Alain Poher (interim) 2 April 1974–27 May 1974.

'The government determines and conducts the policy of the nation' (Art. 20); 'the government may ask parliament for authority to take, by decrees and within a limited period, such measures as are normally within the province of the law' (Art. 38). Ministers must not be members of parliament (Art. 23). Votes of censure can only be carried by a majority of the members constituting the Assembly (Art. 49). The 2 ordinary sessions in autumn and spring are curtailed to a total of 5 months (Art. 28).

The 'Constitutional Council' has to uphold the fairness of the elections and act as a guardian of the constitution. It is composed of 9 members, 3 of whom are nominated by the President of the Republic, 3 by the President of the National Assembly and 3 by the President of the Senate. In addition, past Presidents of the Republic are, by right, members of the Constitutional Council (Art. 56).

The Senate is composed of 305 members, of which one-third is elected every 3 years (for a 9-year term); it comprises 287 Senators representing Metropolitan Departments, 8 Overseas Departments, 1 Mayotte (*collectivité particulière*), 3 Overseas Territories, and 6 Frenchmen residing outside France. Following partial elections in Sept. 1980, the Senate was composed of 41 *Rassemblement Pour la République* (Gaullists); 52 *Parti Républicaine* (Giscardians); 67 *Union Centrist;* 26 *Gauche démocratique;* 13 *Mouvement des Radicaux de Gauche* (MRG); 69 *Parti Socialiste;* 23 *Parti communiste;* 13 *non-inscrits* (unaffiliated), with 1 seat vacant. In 1983 the Senate will be enlarged to 316 members.

The National Assembly comprises 491 members, composed of 474 representing Metropolitan constituencies, 11 Overseas Departments, 1 Mayotte (*collectivité particulière*), and 5 Overseas Territories. Elections took place in March 1978, resulting in a new composition of 153 RPR (Gaullists), 137 *Union de la Démocratie Française* (Giscardians and Centrist Union), 10 MRG, 104 *Parti socialiste*, 86 *Parti communiste*, and 1 far left.

President of the Republic: Valéry Giscard d'Estaing; elected 19 May 1974. Assumed office 27 May 1974.

The Cabinet, as in March 1981:

Prime Minister: Raymond Barre.
Justice: Alain Peyrefitte.
Defence and Co-operation: Robert Galley.
Foreign Affairs: Jean François-Poncet.
Economic Affairs: René Monory.
Education: Christian Beullac.
Interior: Christian Bonnet.
Labour and Participation: Jean Mattéoli.
Health and Social Security: Jacques Barrot.
Industry: André Giraud.

Environment: Michel D'Ornano.
Agriculture: Pierre Mehaignerie.
External Trade: Michel Cointat.
Budget: Maurice Papon.
Universities: Alice Saunier-Seïté.
Transport: Daniel Hoeffel.
Commerce and Artisan Industries: Maurice Charretier.
Youth and Sport: Jean-Pierre Soisson.
Culture and Communications: Jean-Philippe Lecat.
Women's Affairs: Monique Pelletier.
Administrative Reforms: Jean-François Deniau.
Technological Applications: Norbert Ségard.

There are also 18 Secretaries of State.

National flag: The Tricolour of three vertical stripes of blue, white, red.
National anthem: La Marseillaise (words and tune by C. Rouget de Lisle, 1792).

Local Government. For administrative purposes metropolitan France is divided into 22 regions for national development work, for planning and for budgetary policy. Each Region has an appointed Prefect as its executive head aided by an indirectly-elected Regional Council.

There are 96 *départements* within the 22 regions each with an appointed Prefect as the executive head, and a *Conseil Général* who is directly elected.

The *arrondissement* (324 in 1975) and the *canton* (3,509 in 1975), have (1981) little administrative significance, although the departmental prefects have a sub-prefect in each *arrondissement*.

The unit of local government is the *commune*, the size and population of which vary very much. There were, in 1975, in the 96 metropolitan departments, 36,394 communes. Most of them (31,593) had less than 1,500 inhabitants, and 16,550 had less than 300, while 229 communes had more than 30,000 inhabitants. A law of 16 July 1971 causes the smallest *communes* either to merge or to re-group themselves into combined administrative units of 'communes' or into urban communities. The local affairs of the commune are under a Municipal Council, composed of from 9 to 36 members, elected by universal suffrage, and by the *scrutin de liste* for 6 years by French citizens of 21 years or over after 6 months' residence.

Each Municipal Council elects a mayor, who is both the representative of the commune and the agent of the central government. He is the head of the local police and, with his assistants, acts under the orders of the prefect.

In Paris the *Conseil de Paris* is composed of 109 members elected from the 20 *arrondissements* which have been grouped in 9 sectors for this purpose.

d'Estaing, V. G., *French Democracy*. New York, 1977
Hayward, J., *The One and Invisible French Republic*. New York, 1973
Suleiman, E. N., *Politics, Power, and Bureaucracy in France*. Princeton Univ. Press, 1974
Wright, V., *The Government and Politics of France*. London, 1978

DEFENCE. The President of the Republic exercises command over the Armed Forces. He is assisted by the research organization of the High Council of Defence (*Conseil Supérieur de la Défense Nationale*) and two Committees (*Comité de Défense* and *Comité de Défense restreint*) which formulate directives. The Prime Minister is responsible for the national defence; he exercises his military responsibilities through the General Secretariat of National Defence (SGDN). Under the Prime Minister's authority, the *Comité d'Action Scientifique de Défense* co-ordinates research.

On 5 July 1969 the Army Ministry was replaced by the Ministry of State for National Defence which is responsible for the Army, Air Force and Navy. In addition to the powers of the Army Ministry, the Ministry of State prepares general directives for negotiations relating to defence. It has SGDN at its disposal for exercising these powers. It is assisted by the Departmental Assistant for Weapons, the Secretary-General for Administration, the Chief of Staff of the Armed Forces and the Chiefs of Staff of the 3 Armed Forces—Army, Navy and Air.

In 1962 the Armed Forces were reorganized in 3 groups: (1) nuclear strategic force; (2) operational forces; (3) home defence forces.

French forces are not formally committed to NATO.

Army. The Army consists of regular officers and n.c.o.s, long-term n.c.o.s and soldiers, and conscripts serving 12 months.

The peace-time units comprise infantry, armoured troops and cavalry, artillery, engineering, signals, transport, matériel, naval infantry and artillery. In addition, there are the Foreign Legion, mountain and airborne troops and other specialized units.

In 1980 the effective strength of the Army was 321,320 all ranks.

Higher military instruction is provided in 3 stages: the staff school (*École d'État-major*) for officers of formation staffs; the *École Supérieure de Guerre* for officers earmarked for the higher command; the *Institut des Hautes Études de Défense Nationale* where high-ranking officers and civilians study together the problems of national defence.

Light Army Aircraft. Formed in 1952, the *Aviation Légère de l'Armée de Terre* (ALAT) is a well-equipped force, with 75 light aeroplanes and more than 550 helicopters for observation, reconnaissance, combat area transport, liaison and supply duties. Effective strength, 1979, 6,450.

The *Gendarmerie* is an integral part of the Army but also co-operates with the civil administration in maintaining public order. Effective strength, 1980, 79,486.

Navy. The Navy is under the supreme direction of the Minister of Defence, being administered by the Chief and Deputy Chiefs of Naval Staff.

All naval aircraft and coastal defences are under the control of the Navy, and have been reorganized in 3 coast 'naval frontier' districts (with headquarters in Cherbourg, Brest and Toulon), in relation to the aircraft attached to the active fleet.

The French Navy is manned partly by conscription but mainly by voluntary enlistment. In 1981 the active personnel was 69,000 officers and men, including 9,000 in the Naval Air Arm.

The following is a summary of the strength of the fleet at the periods shown:

				Completed at end of					
	1972	1973	1974	1975	1976	1977	1978	1979	1980
Aircraft carriers	4[1]	4[1]	3[3]	3[3]	3[3]	3[3]	3[3]	3[3]	3[3]
Submarines	22[2]	23[2]	23[2]	24[4]	24[4]	26[4]	27[4]	29[5]	28[5]
Cruisers	2	1	1	1	1	1	1	1	1
Destroyers	16	20	22	21	20	21	22	20	19
Frigates	30	31	28	28	27	29	27	24	22

[1] Including 2 helicopter-carriers. [2] Including 3 nuclear-powered ballistic missile submarines.
[3] Including 1 helicopter-carrier. [4] Including 4 nuclear-powered ballistic missile submarines.
[5] Including 5 nuclear-powered ballistic missile submarines.

The principal surface ships of the French Navy are as follows:

Completed	Name	Standard displacement Tons	Armour Belt In.	Guns In.	Principal armament	Shaft horsepower	Speed Knots
			Aircraft Carriers				
1963	Foch ⎱	27,300	—	—	8 3·9 in.	126,000	32·0
1961	Clemenceau ⎰	(normal)			(30 aircraft)		
			Helicopter Carriers				
1964	Jeanne d'Arc[1]	10,000	—	—	4 3·9 in. (8 helicopters)	40,000	26·5

[1] Cruiser type forward, flat-topped midships to aft.

The helicopter carrier *Arromanches* (former British fixed-wing aircraft carrier *Colossus*) was listed for disposal in 1974.

					Cruisers		
1959	Colbert	8,500	—	—	1 twin 'Masurca' guided missile launcher; 2 3·9 in. AA	86,000	32·0

The command cruiser *De Grasse* was condemned in 1973.

There are also 5 nuclear-powered ballistic missile submarines of 7,500 tons, 23 diesel-powered submarines, 2 guided-missile destroyer leaders of 5,090 tons, 3 guided-missile leaders of 4,580 tons, 1 missile leader of 3,830 tons, 1 missile leader of 3,500 tons, 12 old conventional destroyers of 2,750 tons, 22 escorts (frigates), of 950 to 1,750 tons, 5 missile boats, 10 large minehunters (ex-ocean minesweepers), 5 coastal minehunters, 34 coastal minesweepers (14 used as patrol vessels), 1 inshore minesweeper (used as patrol craft), 8 surveying vessels, 1 coastal patrol craft, 2 dock landing ships, 5 tank landing ships, 14 landing craft, 30 minor landing craft, 7 maintenance, repair and depot ships, 9 oilers, 10 boom defence vessels, 5 support ships, 13 transports, 4 sail training vessels, 40 auxiliary ships and 85 tugs.

One more nuclear-powered ballistic-missile submarine, 3 nuclear-powered fleet (torpedo armed) submarines, 3 guided missile destroyers and 8 *avisos* (escorts) are under construction. A prototype nuclear-powered helicopter carrier, 4 more nuclear-powered fleet, torpedo-armed (hunter-killer) submarines, 6 fast missile craft and 14 minehunters are projected.

The naval air arm, known usually as *Aéronavale*, has 2 squadrons of nationally designed Etendard IV-M transonic fighter-bombers, 1 squadron of Etendard IV-P reconnaissance fighters, 2 squadrons of US-built Crusader all-weather fighters, 3 squadrons of Alizé turboprop anti-submarine aircraft, 5 maritime reconnaissance squadrons with Atlantic and Neptune aircraft and 3 anti-submarine and assault squadrons with Super Frelon and Sikorsky HSS-1 helicopters. Strength is 320 aircraft comprising 235 fixed-wing and 85 helicopters.

Air Force. Formed as the *Service Aéronautique* in April 1910, the *Armeé de l'Air* is organized in 7 major commands. Its bases and installations were regrouped and modernized in 1967. The *Commandement des Forces Aériennes Stratégiques* (CFAS) commands the nuclear deterrent force. The *Commandement de la Force Aérienne Tactique* (FATAC) directs the tactical air forces, commands the air force reserve and is responsible for support of the ground forces. Under FATAC the 1st *Commandement Aérien Tactique* (1^0 CATAC) controls tactical air units based in eastern France; the 2nd *Commandement Aérien Tactique* (2^0 CATAC) controls the reserve forces and the air component of the *Force d'Intervention*. The *Commandement du Transport Aérien Militaire* (COTAM) is responsible for air transport operations and for the training and transport of airborne forces. The *Commandement Air des Forces de Défense Aérienne* (CAFDA) controls air defence forces. The *Commandement des Écoles de l'Armée de l'Air* (CEAA) is responsible for training the personnel for all branches of the Air Force. The *Commandement des Transmissions* has responsibility for communications and electronic warfare. Finally, the *Commandement du Génie de l'Air*, made up mainly of Army personnel, undertakes airbase construction and maintenance under Air Force control.

The home-based French Air Force is divided territorially among 4 metropolitan air regions (Metz, Villacoublay, Bordeaux, Aix-en-Provence); overseas, small air units are integrated into the local joint-service commands. There are about 40 combat squadrons plus about 30 transport, helicopter and support squadrons, and the Air Force uses a total of 66 bases.

The strategic, tactical and air defence forces are equipped entirely with jet aircraft. The CFAS has 33 first-line Mirage IV supersonic nuclear bombers, and 14 reserves, deployed in 2 wings (each 3 squadrons) supported by 11 C-135F refuelling tanker transports. Twelve Mirage IVs are equipped for reconnaissance missions. The 1^0 CATAC deploys 7 wings (20 squadrons), consisting of about 180 Mirage III-E and 5F ground-attack and III-R reconnaissance fighters, and 120 Jaguar strike aircraft, plus 2 OCUs equipped with Mirage III-Bs and Jaguars. The air defence forces have 4 wings, with 7 squdrons of Mirage F.1 multi-mission fighters and 2 squadrons of Mirage III-Cs. The COTAM is equipped with 3 wings of turboprop Transall C.160 and Noratlas piston-engined transports, supplemented by 2 groups of DC-8, Caravelle, Nord 262, Mystère 20 and M.S. 760 Paris aircraft. Other units are equipped with Broussard observation and general-purpose monoplanes, and about 125 Alouette II/III and Puma helicopters. Training aircraft include CAP-10 piston-engined primary trainers, Magister jet basic trainers, Alpha Jet, Mystère IV (to be replaced with Alpha Jets) and Mirage III-B advanced trainers, and two-seat Jaguars.

Total personnel (1980), 103,460; 460 combat aircraft.

INTERNATIONAL RELATIONS

Membership. France is a member of UN, the Council of Europe, NATO and EEC.

ECONOMY

Planning. The post-war reconstruction and expansion of the French economy began under the guidance of the first 'Monnet plan' (1947–50), named after the then director of the planning office, Jean Monnet. This was followed by the second and third plans (1954–57, 1958–61), an intermediate plan for 1960 and 1961, the fourth plan, 1962–65, fifth plan, 1966–70, sixth plan, 1971–75, and seventh plan, 1976–80.

Caire, G., *La Planification, Techniques et Problèmes.* Paris, 1967
Carré, J.-J., Dubois, P., and Malinvaud, E., *French Economic Growth.* Stanford Univ. Press, 1975
Treize, A., *La Planification en Pratique.* Paris, 1971

Budget. Budgets (in 1m. francs) for calendar years:

Receipts	1979[1]	%	1980[2]	%
Taxation				
Income tax	100,150	19·80	116,635	20·54
Corporation tax	48,900	9·66	51,275	9·03
Other direct taxes	39,050	7·72	44,630	7·86
Registration and stamp duties	30,100	5·95	34,549	6·08
Taxes on consumption (VAT)	224,300	44·35	253,007	44·56
Customs	48,000	9·49	49,515	8·72
Other indirect taxes and excise	15,200	3·00	18,124	3·19
Gross total	505,700		567,735	
Net budget receipts (gross total				
taxes minus various deductions)	446,609		497,724	
Expenditure				
Public authorities and general				
administration	53,102	11·11	59,064	10·80
Education and culture	120,437	25·19	133,682	24·45
Social affairs, health, employment	93,137	19·48	109,123	19·96
Agriculture and countryside	15,861	3·31	17,557	3·21
Housing and town planning	23,471	4·91	26,196	4·79
Transport and communications	25,182	5·26	28,113	5·14
Industry and services	23,708	4·96	26,063	4·77
Foreign affairs	13,557	2·83	15,547	2·84
Defence	82,858	17·33	95,318	17·43
Miscellaneous expenditure	26,720	5·59	36,163	6·61
Total expenditure	477,957		546,831	

[1] Revised estimates.   [2] Initial estimates.

The accounts of revenue and expenditure are examined by a special administrative tribunal (*Cour des Comptes*), instituted in 1807.

Bloch-Laine, F., *La Zone Franc.* Paris, 1956
Mérigot, J. G., and Coulbois, P., *Le Franc, 1938–50.* Paris, 1950

Currency. The unit of currency is the *franc.* Coins are issued for 5, 10, 20 and 50 centimes, 1, 2, 5 and 10 francs; and bank-notes for 10, 50, 100 and 500 francs. In March 1981. £ sterling = 11.05 *francs*; US$1 = 4.99 *francs.*

Banking. The *Banque de France,* founded in 1800, and placed under the authority of a state-appointed Governor in 1806, has the monopoly (since 1848) of issuing bank-notes throughout France. Note circulation on 2 Jan. 1980 was 129,276m. francs.

On 2 Dec. 1945 a law was passed to nationalize the *Banque de France* and the 4 (from 1966, 3) principal deposit banks. It also established a new body, the National Credit Council, formed to regulate banking activity and consulted in all political decisions on monetary policy. This new body comprises 45 members nominated by the Government; its president is the Minister for the Economy, its vice-president is the Governor of the *Banque de France* which as a Central Bank puts monetary policy into effect and supervises its application.

The rest of the banking system comprises the deposit banks, the popular banks, the Crédit agricole, the Crédit mutuel, the Banque française du commerce exterieur and the various financial establishments. The deposit banks are (*i*) those nationalized in 1945: Crédit Lyonnais (founded 1863), Banque Nationale de Paris (founded by amalgamation 1966) and the Société Générale (founded 1864), and (*ii*) the non-nationalized banks, the principal ones being: Crédit Industriel et Commercial, Crédit Commercial de France, the Banque de Paris et des Pays-Bas and the Crédit du Nord. Total deposits and short- and medium-term bonds held by the banks on 2 Jan. 1980 was 1,057,589m. francs.

The state savings organization (*Caisse nationale d'épargne*) is administered by the post office on a giro system. On 2 Jan. 1980 the private savings banks (*Caisses d'épargne et de prévoyance*), numbering about 500 had 335,499m. francs in deposits; the state savings banks had 162,399m. francs in deposits. Deposited funds are centralized by a non-banking body, the *Caisse de Dépôts et Consignations*, which finances a large number of local authorities and state aided housing projects, and carries an important portfolio of transferable securities.

Weights and Measures. The metric system is in general use.

ENERGY AND NATURAL RESOURCES

Electricity. Production of electrical power (in 1m. kwh.): 1970, 140,708; 1971, 148,998; 1972, 163,652; 1973, 174,480; 1974, 180,022; 1975, 177,480; 1976, 191,196; 1977, 210,840; 1978, 222,552. In 1978, 37% was hydro-electric and 9% nuclear.

Oil. In 1978 about 1·1m. tonnes of crude oil were produced (1967, 2·8m. tonnes). The greater part came from the Parentis oilfield in the Landes. France has an important oil-refining industry, utilizing imported crude oil. Total yearly capacity at the end of 1977 was about 171·24m. tonnes. The principal plants are situated in Basse Seine (production in tonnes, 1972), 31·2m.; Mediterranean, 24·6m.; Atlantic, 15·4m.; Alsace, 12·6m., and Nord, 9m.

There has been considerable development of the production of natural gas and sulphur in the region of Lacq in the foothills of the Pyrenees. Production of natural gas was 7,695m. in 1977 and 7,869m. in 1978.

Minerals. Principal minerals and metals produced, in 1,000 tonnes:

	1975	1976	1977	1978		1975	1976	1977	1978
Coal	22,411	21,879	21,293	19,690	Potash salts	2,085	1,738	1,719	1,928
Lignite	3,186	3,189	3,080	2,732	Pig-iron	17,921	19,024	18,257	18,497
Iron ore	49,647	45,181	36,630	33,454	Crude steel	21,530	23,221	22,094	22,841
Bauxite	2,563	2,330	2,059	1,978	Aluminium	383	385	400	391

Agriculture. Of the total area of France (54·9m. hectares) 17·4m. were under cultivation, 13m. were pasture, 1·2m. were under vines, 14·3m. were forests and 8m. were uncultivated land in 1978.

The following table shows the area under the leading crops and the production for 4 years:

	Area (1,000 hectares)				Produce (1,000 tonnes)			
Crop	1975	1976	1977	1978	1975	1976	1977	1978
Wheat	3,876	4,274	4,126	4,167	15,013	16,126	17,546	21,057
Rye	110	118	129	138	308	310	389	432
Barley	2,770	2,780	2,909	2,814	9,344	8,530	10,319	11,414
Oats	655	652	625	611	1,898	1,431	1,938	2,194
Potatoes	279	273	279	269	6,642	4,279	8,190	7,459
Sugar-beet	598	613	585	556	23,656	22,869	24,500	24,488
Maize	1,960	1,394	1,639	1,802	8,209	5,625	8,316	9,473

Other crops in 1978 (figures for 1977 in brackets) include (in 1,000 tonnes): Rice, 37 (23); tobacco, 54 (53); flax, 297 (306).

France is the world's second largest producer of wine (after Italy); production in 1978 amounted to 5,882,000 tonnes.

The annual production of wine (in 1,000 hectolitres) appears as follows:

	Vineyards (1,000 hectares)	Wine produced		Vineyards (1,000 hectares)	Wine produced
1938	1,513	60,332	1976	1,189	73,496
1948	1,433	47,437	1977	1,180	53,137
1958	1,315	47,735	1978	1,141	58,599
1968	1,228	66,460	1979	...	80,319

The production of fruits (other than for cider making) and for 4 years was (in 1,000 tonnes) as follows:

	1975	1976	1977	1978		1975	1976	1977	1978
Apples	2,125	1,711	1,243	1,867	Cherries	89	136	53	99
Pears	410	464	273	366	Nuts	26	35	18	37
Plums	30	184	73	165	Grapes	224	246	211	234
Peaches	109	522	319	406	Strawberries	73	72	77	68
Apricots	58	132	72	81					

In 1979 the numbers of farm animals (in 1,000) were (figures for 1978 in brackets): Horses, 380 (380); cattle, 23,510 (23,762); sheep, 11,543 (11,415); goats, 1,048 (1,048); pigs, 11,745 (11,548).

Forestry. The total area of forested land (1975) was 148,640 sq. km. Timber production (1977), 8,766m. cu. metres valued at 1,099m. francs.

Fisheries. (1978). There were 28,011 fishermen, and 12,128 sailing-boats, steamers and motor-boats. Catch (in 1,000 tonnes): Fish, fresh and frozen, 424·9; crustaceans, 29·1; shell fish, 97·1; oysters, 95·3.

INDUSTRY AND TRADE

Industry. Industrial production (in 1,000 tonnes) for 3 years was as follows:

	1977	1978	1979
Sulphuric acid	4,501	4,584	5,069
Caustic acid	1,313	1,339	1,449
Sulphur	1,911	1,900	1,940
Polystyrene	233	240	269
Polyvinyl	645	665	783
Polyethylene	955	981	1,173
Ammonia	2,034	2,017	...
Wool	61	60	62
Cotton	186	179	178
Linen	3·3	3·3	2·6
Silk	48	49	52
Man-made fibres, yarns	83	76	78
Jute	14	11	9
Cheese	946	980	...
Chocolate	105	104	111
Biscuits	349	353	334
Sugar	3,927	3,740	3,968
Fish preparations	99	102	99
Jams and jellies	117	127	107
Cement	28,830	28,025	28,825

Engineering production (in 1,000 units) for 3 years:

	1977	1978	1979
Motor vehicles	3,511	3,508	3,612
Television sets	1,911	2,101	1,854
Radio sets	3,570	3,019	2,773
Tyres	46,590	46,000	49,000

See map in THE STATESMAN'S YEAR-BOOK, 1968–69, Industrial Redeployment.

Employment (1975). Out of an economically active population of 21,061,215 persons, there are 2·01m. engaged in agriculture; 1,841,083 in building and public works; 6,327,818 in other manufacturing industries; 829,289 in transport; 3,632,478 in business, banking and insurance; 3,543,881 in services; 2,522,544 in commerce. In 1979, there were 21,486,426 employed (39·4% female), of whom 1,455,681 were foreign workers; there were 1,503,994 unemployed.

Trade Unions. The main unions considered as nationally representative are the CGT (Confédération Générale du Travail), which was founded in 1895 and has about 2·35m. members; the CGT–FO (Confédération Générale du Travail–Force Ouvrière) which broke away from the CGT in 1948 as a protest against Communist influence therein and has about 900,000 members; the CFTC (Confédération Française des Travailleurs Chrétiens), which was founded in 1919 and has about 225,000 members following its break-away in 1964 from the main body of the union which continues under the new name of CFDT (Confédération Française Démocratique du Travail) and has about 890,000 members; the CGC (Confédération Générale des Cadres) formed in 1944 which only represents managerial and supervisory staff and has about 300,000 members.

Membership is estimated because unions are not required to publish figures; some publish none, others define 'membership' in different terms.

Except for the CGC unions operate within the framework of industries and not of trades. Their main fields of influence are: CGT—steel, metallurgy, building, chemicals, mining, printing, ports and dockyards, electricity and gas, railways; CGT–FO—Civil service, Paris transport, agricultural and food trades, banking, insurance, electrical engineering, building and civil engineering, clothing, leather and hides; CFDT—metallurgy, rubber, oil, textiles, electrical engineering, banking, insurance; CFTC—mining, banking, insurance, air traffic control, oil, glass, pottery.

An Outline of French Trade Unionism. French Embassy, London, 1975
Chardonnet, J., *L'Economie Française.* 2 vols. Paris, 1958–59
Jeanneney, J.-M., *Forces et faiblesses de l'économie française, 1945–59.* 2nd ed. Paris, 1959
Lorwin, V. R., *The French Labor Movement.* Harvard Univ. Press, 1955
Pilliet, G., *Inventaire économique de la France.* Annual from 1945. Paris

Commerce. Imports (c.i.f.) and exports (f.o.b.) in 1m. francs for 5 calendar years were (including gold):

	1976	1977	1978	1979	1980
Imports	308,012	346,364	368,401	457,100	569,900
Exports	266,228	312,072	344,594	414,700	470,400

The chief imports for home use and exports of home goods are to and from the following countries, in 1m. francs (including gold):

	Imports (c.i.f.)			Exports (f.o.b.)		
Countries	1977	1978	1979	1977	1978	1979
Algeria	3,894	3,204	4,858	8,786	6,913	8,216
Belgium–Luxembourg	31,131	34,064	41,127	31,063	35,558	40,891
Germany (Fed. Rep.)	64,067	70,010	82,842	53,344	59,820	71,700
Italy	33,160	37,377	46,065	32,660	37,636	47,609
Netherlands	21,133	23,010	27,534	15,940	18,799	22,305
Saudi Arabia	21,166	18,338	24,588	3,032	3,919	4,709
Spain (excluding Canary Is.)	9,683	11,167	13,399	8,145	8,294	11,153
Sweden	5,757	5,713	7,379	3,616	3,769	5,096
Switzerland (and Liechtenstein)	7,891	8,855	10,485	12,204	14,147	17,075
USSR	5,676	5,626	...	7,237	6,551	...
UK	18,061	20,297	25,599	20,240	24,960	32,029
USA	24,051	26,879	34,390	16,052	19,248	20,399

Total trade between France and UK (British Department of Trade returns, in £1,000 sterling):

	1976	1977	1978	1979	1980
Imports to UK	2,091,308	2,660,123	3,211,837	4,064,233	3,899,174
Exports and re-exports from UK	1,710,262	2,147,613	2,530,837	3,070,498	3,651,470

Tourism. In 1977 foreign visitors contributed about 21,505m. francs to the French economy.

COMMUNICATIONS

Roads. At the end of 1977 the French road system consisted of 3,873 km of motorway, 29,103 km of national roads, 345,990 km of departmental roads and 424,950 km of local roads. Total, 803,916 km.

Railways. As from 1 Jan. 1938 all the independent railway companies were merged with the existing state railway system in a Société Nationale des Chemins de Fer Français, in which the State holds 51% of the shares.

In 1979, the State railway totalled 34,444 km (9,863 km electrified) of 1,435 mm gauge, and ran 53,560m. passenger-km and 70,680m. tonne-km. A new railway for high-speed trains is under construction between Paris and Lyon, the first section due to open in 1981. In addition to the main network, there are some 2,000 km of independent or state-run minor railways.

The Paris transport network consisted in 1980 of 278 km of underground railway (métro) and regional express railways and 2,096 km of bus routes. In 1978 it carried 1,104m. passengers on the métro and 709m. by bus.

Lartilleux, H., *Géographie des chemins de fer français*. 2 vols. Paris, 1946–48
Peyret, H., *Histoire des chemins de fer en France*. Paris, 1949

Aviation. Air France, UTA and Air Inter, the national airlines, had (31 Dec. 1978) a fleet of 164 aircraft, servicing Europe, North America, Central and South America, West and East Africa, Madagascar, the Near, Middle and Far East. There are local networks in the West Indies and Central America.

In 1978 Air France, UTA and Air Inter flew 1,859m. tonne-km (excluding mail, 113m. tonne-km) and 30·5m. passenger-km (16·93m. passengers).

Shipping. French merchant ships of more than 100 tons, with gross tonnage, on 1 Jan. 1977, 504 (11·14m.); 1978, 502 (11·86m.).

Shipping (excluding fishing vessels) in foreign trade in 1978: Entered, 81,502 vessels and disembarked 232·5m. tonnes of imports; cleared, 81,102 vessels and loaded 58·2m. tonnes of exports. Total cargo traffic 290·7m. tonnes.

In 1978 there were 8,623 km of navigable rivers, waterways and canals, (of which 1,583 km accessible to vessels over 3,000 tons) with a total traffic of 91·56m. tonnes.

Post and Broadcasting. In 1977 the receipts on account of posts, telegraphs and telephones amounted to 56,275m. francs.

On 31 Dec. 1978 the telephone system (government-owned) had 19·87m. subscribers; the Paris region (including the Paris and Seine-et-Marne, Yvelines, Essonne, Hauts-de-Seine, Seine-Saint-Denis, Val-de-Marne and Val-d'Oise departments) accounted for 4,153,586 in 1978.

Radio and television broadcasting was reorganized under the Act of 7 Aug. 1974 which replaced the Office de Radiodiffusion Télévision Française with 4 broadcasting companies, a production company and an audio-visual institute. Organization, development, operation and the maintenance of networks and installations became the responsibility of the Public Broadcasting Establishment. Radio programmes are broadcast from 298 transmitters (including 260 VHF) by 3 stations: *France Inter*, *France Musique* and *France Culture*. Television programmes are broadcast from 325 transmitters and 4,661 relay stations on 3 channels. There were about 18·22m. sets in use in 1980 (of which 7·6m. in colour).

Cinemas (1979). There were 4,484 cinemas with a seating capacity (1976) of 1,676,000; attendances totalled 176·37m.

Newspapers (1977). There were 69 daily papers published in the provinces with a circulation of 7·48m. copies, and 10 published in Paris with a national circulation of 3·05m. Among Paris dailies *France-Soir* sells 671,000; *Le Monde* 546,000; *Le Parisien Libéré* 474,000; *Le Figaro* 407,000, and *L'Aurore* 347,000. Among provincial dailies *Ouest-France* (Rennes) sells 749,000; *Le Progrès* (Lyon) 436,000; *La Voix du Nord* (Lille) 389,000; *Sud-Ouest* (Bordeaux) 383,000; *La Dauphine Libérée* (Grenoble) 362,000 and *Le Provençal* (Marseilles) 345,000.

JUSTICE, RELIGION, EDUCATION AND WELFARE

Justice. Since 1976, 469 *tribunaux d'instance* (10 in overseas departments), under a single judge each and with increased material and territorial jurisdiction, have replaced the former *juges de paix* (1 in each canton); and 181 *tribunaux de grande instance* (6 in overseas departments) have taken the place of the 357 *tribunaux de première instance* (1 in each *arrondissement*).

The *tribunaux de grande instance* usually have a collegiate composition, however a law dated 10 July 1970 has allowed them to administer justice under a single judge in some civil cases.

All petty offences (*contraventions*) are disposed of in the Police Courts (*Tribunaux de Police*) presided over by a Judge on duty in the *tribunal d'instance*. The Correctional Courts pronounce upon all graver offences (*délits*), including cases involving imprisonment up to 5 years. They have no jury, and consist of 3 judges who administer both criminal and civil justice. An Act of 29 Dec. 1972 established that there is only 1 judge; in some cases, the correctional courts may consist of a single judge each. In all cases of a *délit* or a *crime* the preliminary inquiry is made in secrecy by an examining magistrate (*juge d'instruction*), who either dismisses the case or sends it for trial before a court where a public prosecutor (*Procureur*) endeavours to prove the charge.

The Conciliation Boards (*Conseils des Prud'hommes*) composed of an equal number of employers and employees deal with small trade and industrial disputes. Commercial litigation goes to the Commercial Courts (*Tribunaux de Commerce*) composed of tradesmen and manufacturers elected for 2 years. The judges hold office for 2 years and they can be re-elected; 3 years for the President.

When the decisions of any of these Tribunals are susceptible of appeal, the case goes to one of the 34 Courts of Appeal (*Cours d'Appel*), (including 3 in overseas departments and 1 in an overseas territory), composed each of a president and a variable number of members.

The Courts of Assizes (*Cours d'Assises*), composed each of a president, assisted by 2 other magistrates who are members of the Courts of Appeal, and by a jury of 9 people, sit in every *département*, when called upon to try very important criminal cases. The decisions of the Courts of Appeal and the Courts of Assizes are final; however, the Court of Cassation (*Cour de Cassation*) has discretion to verify if the law has been correctly interpreted and if the rules of procedure have been followed exactly. The Court of Cassation may annul any judgment, and the cases have to be tried again by a Court of Appeal or a Court of Assizes.

A State Security Court has been established by 2 laws dated 15 Jan. 1963. It is usually composed of 3 civilian judges, including the president, and 2 judges of general or field officer rank, and has jurisdiction to deal with subversion in peace-time.

On 24 Jan. 1973 the first Ombudsman (*médiateur*) was appointed for a 6-year period.

The French penal institutions consist of: (1) *maisons d'arrêt* and *de correction*, where persons awaiting trial as well as those condemned to short periods of imprisonment are kept; (2) central prisons (*maisons centrales*) for those sentenced to long imprisonment; (3) special establishments, namely (*a*) schools for young adults, (*b*) hostels for old and disabled offenders, (*c*) hospitals for the sick and psychopaths, (*d*) institutions for recidivists. Special attention is being paid to classified treatment and the rehabilitation and vocational re-education of prisoners including work in open-air and semi-free establishments. There are 2 penal institutions for women.

Juvenile delinquents go before special judges and courts; they are sent to public or private institutions of supervision and re-education.

The population at 1 April 1980 of all penal establishments was 37,481 men and 1,276 women.

Religion. No religion is officially recognized by the State. Under the law promulgated on 9 Dec. 1905, which separated Church and State, the adherents of all creeds are authorized to form associations for public worship (*associations culturelles*). The law of 2 Jan. 1907 provided that, failing *associations culturelles*, the buildings for public worship, together with their furniture, would continue at the disposition of the ministers of religion and the worshippers for the exercise of their religion; but in each case there was required an administrative act drawn up by the *préfet* as regards buildings belonging to the State or the departments, and by the *maire* as regards buildings belonging to the communes.

There are 18 archbishops and 92 bishops of the Roman Catholic Church, with (1974) 43,557 clergy of various grades and 45·3m. church members. The Protestants of the Augsburg confession are, in their religious affairs, governed by a General Consistory, while the Reformed Church is under a Council of Administration, the seat of which is in Paris. In 1975 communicant Protestants numbered 750,000. There were (1978) about 2m. Moslems.

Education. The primary, secondary and higher state schools constitute the 'Université de France'. The Supreme Council of 84 members has deliberative, administrative and judiciary functions, and a Consultative Committee advise respecting the working of the school system, but the inspectors-general are in direct communication with the Minister. For local education administration France is divided into 25 academic areas, each of which has an Academic Council whose members include a certain number elected by the professors or teachers. The Academic Council deals with all grades of education. Each is under a Rector, and each is provided with academy inspectors, 1 for each department.

By decree of 6 Jan. 1959 the whole system of public instruction was reorganized and the structure of the Ministry of National Education has consequently been modified. A further Education Act was passed on 11 July 1975. Compulsory education is now provided for children of 6–16. The educational stages are as follows:

  1. Non-compulsory pre-school instruction for children aged 2–5, to be given in infant schools or infant classes attached to primary schools.

  2. Compulsory elementary instruction for children aged 6–11, to be given in primary schools and certain classes of the *lycées*. It consists of 3 courses: preparatory (1 year), elementary (2 years), intermediary (2 years). Physically or mentally handicapped children are cared for in special institutions or special classes of primary schools.

  3. *Enseignement du Second Degré*, for pupils aged 11–18:

    (*a*) *Enseignement du 1er cycle du Second Degré;* 4 years of study in the *lycées*, *Collèges d'Enseignement Secondaire* or *Collèges d'Enseignement Général.*
    (*b*) *Enseignement du Second Cycle:*

    Long, général or *professionel* provided by the *lycées* and leading to the *baccalauréat* or to the *baccalauréat de technicien* after 3 years.
    Court, professional courses of 3, 2 and 1 year are taught in the *lycées* *d'enseignement professionel*, or the specialized sections of the *lycées*, CES or CEG.

The following table shows the various types of schools in 1977–78 and the numbers of enrolled pupils:

| | | Pupils | |
Description	State	Private	Total
Pre-primary	2,230,809	345,163	2,575,972
Primary	3,978,023	652,765	4,630,788
Secondary:			
First cycle	2,564,463	325,414	2,889,877
Second cycle			
'short'	582,796	113,554	696,350
'long'	882,414	570,189	1,452,603
Specialized	98,375	—	98,375
Total	4,128,048	1,009,157	5,137,205

The state schools in 1978 had 64,676 nursery, 172,969 primary, 18,908 special school, 143,572 secondary and 44,624 secondary technical school and 65,797 grammar school (*lycée*) teachers.

Higher Instruction is supplied by the State in the universities and in special schools, and by private individuals in the free faculties and schools. The law of 12 July 1875 provided for higher education free of charge. This law was modified by that of 18 March 1880, which granted the state faculties the exclusive right to confer degrees. A decree of 28 Dec. 1885 created a general council of the faculties, and the creation of universities, each consisting of several faculties, was accomplished in 1897, in virtue of the law of 10 July 1896.

The law of 12 Nov. 1968 laying down future guidelines for higher education redefined the activities and working of universities. Bringing several disciplines together, 780 units for teaching and research (UER—Unités d'Enseignement et de Récherche) were formed which decided their own teaching activities, research programmes and procedures for checking the level of knowledge gained. They and the other parts of each university must respect the rules designed to maintain the national standard of qualifications.

The UERs form the basic units of the 62 Universities, 6 Universities Centres and 3 National Polytechnic Institutes, all of which have university status. They are grouped geographically into 23 *académies* with student populations in 1977–78 as follows:

Academie	1977–78	Academie	1977–78	Academie	1977–78
Aix-Marseille	47,834	Lille	38,180	Paris	281,479
Amiens	10,611	Limoges	7,205	Poitiers	13,064
Besançon	11,274	Lyon	48,921	Reims	12,221
Bordeaux	41,231	Montpellier	34,225	Rennes	31,373
Caen	12,436	Nancy-Metz	29,168	Rouen	12,305
Clermont	14,231	Nantes	25,068	Strasbourg	26,757
Dijon	13,087	Nice	19,265	Toulouse	44,402
Grenoble	31,294	Orléans-Tours	17,869		
				Total	824,117

The following table shows the number of students by faculties, for 5 years:

Students of	1973–74	1974–75	1975–76	1976–77	1977–78
Law and economics	169,170	178,215	183,566	182,533	178,277
Medicine and dentistry	130,012	146,912	154,660	159,874	158,914
Science	118,153	117,389	121,028	122,205	125,823
Letters	236,703	233,954	251,421	252,134	254,558
Pharmacy	28,032	31,599	33,510	33,474	34,079
Technology	38,943	41,949	43,526	44,243	47,137
Multi-discipline courses	—	4,843	18,527	21,818	25,329
Total	742,074	754,861	806,238	816,281	824,117

In 1977–78 there were also 94,700 students in preparatory classes leading to the Grandes Écoles, the Sections de Techniciens Supérieurs and other bodies; there were also 27,700 students in Écoles normales d'instituteurs.

The other higher institutions under the Ministry of Public Instruction are the Collège de France (founded by Francis I in 1530), which has courses of study bearing on various subjects (literature and language, archaeology, mathematical, natural science, psychology and social science, political economy, etc.); the Museum of Natural History, giving instruction in science and natural history; the École Pratique de Hautes Études (history and philology, mathematical and physicochemical sciences, natural science, theology, economics and social science), having its seat at the Sorbonne; the École Normale Supérieure, which prepares teachers for secondary education and, since 1904, follows the curricula of the Sorbonne without special teachers of its own; the École des Chartes, which trains archivists and palaeographers; the École des Langues Orientales vivantes; the École du Louvre, devoted to art and archaeology; the Bureau des Longitudes, the central meteorological bureau; the Observatoire de Paris; and the French Schools at Athens, Rome, Cairo and South-East Asia.

Outside Paris there are 12 observatories (Meudon, Besançon, Bordeaux, etc.). The observatory at Nice belongs to the University of Paris.

There are free faculties in Paris (the Catholic Institute of Paris comprising theology and literary studies), Angers, Lille, Lyon and Toulouse.

Professional and Technical Instruction. The principal institutions of higher or technical instruction are: (*i*) The *Grandes Écoles* with 136,700 students in 1977–78, the Conservatoire des Arts et Métiers at Paris (with 20 evening courses on the applied sciences and social economy), the École Central des Arts et Manufactures (953 students in 1971–72), the École des Hautes Études Commerciales (803 students in 1972–73), 17 higher schools of commerce (4,461 pupils in 1969–70), under the Ministry of Public Instruction; (*ii*) the National Agronomic Institute at Paris, the veterinary school at Maisons-Alfort, Lyon and Toulouse, a school of forestry at

Nancy, Écoles Nationales Supérieures Agronomiques at Grignon, Rennes, Mont-
pellier, Nancy and Toulouse, 98 schools of agriculture, etc., under the Ministry of
Agriculture; (*iii*) the École Supérieure de Guerre, the École Polytechnique, the military school at Coëtquidan (formerly St Cyr), the École d'Artillerie at Fontainebleau,
the École de Cavalerie at Saumur and other schools under the Ministry of Defence;
the Naval School at Brest under the Ministry of Marine; (*iv*) the School of Mines at
Paris, the School of Civil Engineering at Paris, the School of Mines at St Etienne
and the Schools of Miners at Alès and Douai with other schools under the Ministry
of Public Works; (*v*) the École Nationale Supérieure des Beaux Arts, the École
Nationale Supérieure des Arts Décoratifs and the Conservatoire de Musique et de
Déclamation under the Department of Fine Arts, which is attached to the Ministry of
Cultural Affairs. In the provinces there are national schools of fine arts, and schools of
music, and several municipal schools, as well as free subventional schools, etc.

Health. At the end of 1978 there were 97,168 physicians, 34,887 pharmacists, 28,852
dentists and 8,999 midwives practising. There were 1,062 public hospitals (376,125
beds) including 205 public mental hospitals (120,466 beds) and 2,506 private hospitals
(175,261 beds) including 223 private mental homes (15,414 beds) at the end of 1976.

Social Welfare. An order of 4 Oct. 1945 laid down the framework of a comprehensive plan of Social Security and created a single organization which superseded the
various laws relating to social insurance, workmen's compensation, health insurance, family allowances, etc. All previous matters relating to Social Security are
dealt with in the Social Security Code, 1956; this has been revised several times, and
finally by orders laid down on 21 Aug. 1967, which were ratified on 31 July 1968.
The Social Security general scheme covers all wage-earning workers in industry and
commerce that are not covered by a special scheme of their own.

Contributions. All wage-earning workers or those of equivalent status are insured
regardless of the amount or the nature of the salary or earnings. The funds for the
general scheme are raised mainly from professional contributions, these being fixed
within the limits of a ceiling (assessed at 53,640 francs per annum on 1 Jan. 1979)
and calculated as a percentage of the salaries. The calculation of the contributions
payable for family allowances, old age and industrial injuries relates only to this
amount; on the other hand, the amount payable for sickness, maternity expenses,
disability and death is calculated partly within the limit of the 'ceiling' and partly on
the whole salary. These contributions are the responsibility of both employer and
employee, except in the case of family allowances or industrial injuries, where they
are the sole responsibility of the employer.
    Contributions and benefits paid in 1979 (in 1m. francs) were:

	Contributions	Benefits
Health service	132,809	97,193
Individual injuries	20,653	14,908
Old age pensions	68,905	64,350
Family benefits	49,659	41,818

Self-employed Workers. From 17 Jan. 1948 allowances and old-age pensions were
paid to self-employed workers by independent insurance funds set up within their
own profession, trade or business. Schemes of compulsory insurance for sickness
were instituted in 1961 for farmers and in 1966, with modifications in 1970, for
other non-wage-earning workers.

Social Insurance. The orders laid down in Aug. 1967 ensure that the whole population can benefit from the Social Security Scheme; at present all elderly persons who
have been engaged in the professions, as well as the surviving spouse, are entitled to
claim an old-age benefit; 98% of the population, both working and retired, are
covered by a compulsory scheme of insurance for sickness, the remaining 2% who
are not covered by a compulsory insurance scheme have been able to participate in
a voluntary scheme since 1967; the whole population benefit from the legislation
regarding family allowances.

Sickness Insurance refunds the costs of treatment required by the insured, of the
needs of his wife, of children under 16 and a half who are in his care and not
earning, under 18 who are apprenticed, under 20 who are still studying or who

cannot work on account of some chronic illness or infirmity, as well as relations older or younger or of similar age living under the same roof who are engaged exclusively in domestic duties and in the education of at least 2 children under 14. A decree of 12 Oct. 1976 laid down conditions on which students of 20 or over at public or private educational institutions, who do not benefit from a social security scheme in their own right, are guaranteed insurance benefits for sickness or maternity, holding their parents entitlement until the end of the academic year in which they attain their 21st birthday, provided they have proof that their studies have been interrupted by illness. The general principles relating to medical care consist of: a free choice by the patient of his doctor, his pharmaceutical chemist, his place of treatment, etc.; the medical practitioner is granted freedom of prescription. Reimbursement is not as a rule made in full; the insured person usually pays between 10% and 30% of the legal rate except in cases of exemption. The insured who is recognized as medically unfit for work receives daily allowances equal to half of the wage which has been used to calculate the contributions, or to two-thirds of this if the person has 3 or more children. These allowances may be paid for 3 years, plus 1 additional year if the insured undergoes re-adaptation treatment or takes up fresh vocational training.

Maternity Insurance covers the costs of medical treatment relating to the pregnancy, confinement and lying-in period; the beneficiaries being the insured person or the spouse. The daily allowances are equal to 90% of the salary on which contributions were calculated.

Insurance for Invalids is divided into 3 categories: (1) those who are capable of working; (2) those who cannot work; (3) those who, in addition, are in need of the help of another person. According to the category, the pension rate varies from 30 to 50% of the average salary for the last 10 years, with a minimum additional allowance for home help of 28,094·64 francs per year for the third category.

Old-age Pensions for workers were introduced in 1910 and revised in 1930, 1935, 1941 and 1945 and are now fixed by the Social Security Code of 28 Jan. 1972. Since 1975 people who have paid insurance for at least $37\frac{1}{2}$ years (150 quarters) receive at 60 a pension equal to 25% of basic annual salary, to be increased by 1·25% of the basic salary for every quarter that realization is deferred; thus at 65 the maximum pension rate is reached, equal to 50% of basic salary. People who have paid insurance for less than $37\frac{1}{2}$ years but no less than 15 years can expect a pension equal to as many 1/150ths of the full pension as their quarterly payments justify. In the event of death of the insured person, the husband or wife of the deceased person receives half the pension received by the latter. Compulsory supplementary schemes ensure for those to whom they apply benefits additional to the old-age pensions.

Family Allowances. The system comprises: (*a*) Family allowances proper, equivalent to 23% of the basic monthly salary (949 francs) for 2 dependent children, 41% for the third child, 37% for the fourth child, and 35% for the fifth and each subsequent child; a supplement equivalent to 9% of the basic monthly salary for the second and each subsequent dependent child more than 10 years old and 16% for each dependent child over 15 years. (*b*) Single wage-earner allowance (when the wife does not work), according to the number of dependent children. (*c*) Housewife allowance (when an employer's or self-employed person's wife does not work), according to the number of dependent children and the amount of net annual taxable income. (*d*) Maintenance grant for children under 3 years for families who do not receive either of the above grants, and to individual recipients whose resources are less than a maximum which varies according to the number of dependent children. (*e*) Antenatal grants. (*f*) Maternity grant equal to 260% of basic salary. (*g*) Allowance for supervision. (*h*) Allowance for specialized education of crippled minors. (*i*) Allowances for orphans. (*j*) Allowance for handicapped minors. (*k*) Allowance for opening of school term. (*l*) Allowance for accommodation, under certain circumstances (since July 1972 older persons and young workers enjoy equal benefit from the accommodation allowance). The allowance for single wage (*b*) allowance for the mother in the home (*c*) and the allowance for expenses respecting supervision have been subjected to an annual ceiling of resources. The amount is identical over the whole country.

Workmen's Compensation. The law passed by the National Assembly on 30 Oct. 1946 forms part of the Social Security Code and is administered by the Social Security Organization. Employers are invited to take preventive measures. The application of these measures is supervised by consulting engineers (assessors) of the local funds dealing with sickness insurance, who may compel employers who do not respect these measures to make additional contributions; they may, in like manner, grant rebates to employers who have in operation suitable preventive measures. The injured person receives free treatment, the insurance fund reimburses the practitioners, hospitals and suppliers chosen freely by the injured. In cases of temporary disablement the daily payments are equal to half the total daily wage received by the injured. In case of permanent disablement the injured person receives a pension, the amount of which varies according to the degree of disablement and the salary received during the past 12 months.

A law promulgated on 11 Oct. 1946 has created a medical labour service of doctors who hold a diploma of 'industrial health specialists'. These doctors are entrusted with the control of hygiene and health matters in all industrial undertakings or groups of undertakings. In addition, it is the duty of this medical service to examine wage-earners when they are engaged, to carry out periodical medical examinations and to ensure the application of the existing rules relating to safety in work.

Unemployment Benefits vary according to circumstances (full or partial unemployment) and means test. Since 1926 unemployment benefits have been paid from public funds. Full unemployment benefit amounts to 13·50 francs per day for the head of the family and 5·40 francs for the spouse or a dependent person. After 3 months the payment is reduced to 12·40 francs.

A collective agreement signed on 31 Dec. 1958 between the national council of employers and certain trade unions has established a system of special allowances for unemployed workers in industry and trade. The costs are shared by employers (1·92%) and employees (0·48%) and the benefits amount to 35% of the wages for 12 months, to be extended for workers of old age and long employment. The system is administered by commissions composed of representatives of employers and employees in equal proportion. A similar agreement of 22 Feb. 1968 extends the system to partial unemployment.

Social Security in France. I.N.S.E.E., 1970
Questions de Sécurité Sociale. Paris, 1970

DIPLOMATIC REPRESENTATIVES

OF FRANCE IN GREAT BRITAIN (58 Knightsbridge, London, SW1X 7JT)
Ambassador: Emmanuel de Margerie (accredited 27 March 1981)

OF GREAT BRITAIN IN FRANCE (35 rue du Faubourg St. Honoré, Paris)
Ambassador: Sir Reginald Hibbert, KCMG.

OF FRANCE IN THE USA (2535 Belmont Rd., NW,
Washington, D.C., 20008)
Ambassador: François de Laboulaye.

OF THE USA IN FRANCE (2 Ave. Gabriel, Paris)
Ambassador: Arthur A. Hartman.

OF FRANCE TO THE UNITED NATIONS
Ambassador: Jacques Leprette.

Books of Reference

Statistical Information: The Institut national de la Statistique et des Études économiques (18, Boulevard Adolphe Pinard, 75014 Paris) is the central office of statistics. It was established by a law of 27 April 1946, which amalgamated the Service National des Statistiques (created in 1941 by merging the Direction de la Statistique générale de la France and the Service de la Démographie) with the Institut de Conjoncture (set up in 1938) and some statistical services of the

Ministry of National Economy. The Institut comprises the following departments: Metropolitan statistics, Overseas statistics, Market research and economic studies, Documentation, Research statistics and economics, Informatics, Foreign Economic Studies.

The main publications of the Institut include:

Annuaire statistique de la France (from 1878)
Annuaire statistique des Territoires d'Outre-Mer (from 1959)
Bulletin mensuel de statistique (monthly)
Documentation économique (bi-monthly)
Données statistiques africaines et Malgaches (quarterly)
Economie et Statistique (monthly)
Tableaux de l'Economie Française (biennially, from 1956)
Tendances de la Conjoncture (monthly)

Bonnefous, E., Duroselle, J. B., and Gerbet, P., *L'année politique, économique, sociale et diplomatique en France*. Paris, 1970
Caron, F., *An Economic History of Modern France*. London, 1979
Coffey, P., *The Social Economy of France*. London, 1973
Dyer, C., *Population and Society in Twentieth Century France*. London, 1978
Hoffman, S., *Decline or Renewal? France Since the 1930's*. New York, 1973
Ouston, P. A., *France in the Twentieth Century*. London, 1972
Pinchemel, P., *La France*, 2 vols. Paris, 1969
Tint, H., *French Policy Since the Second World War*. New York, 1972

OVERSEAS DEPARTMENTS

GUADELOUPE

HISTORY. Discovered by Columbus in Nov. 1493, the two main islands were then known as *Karukera* (Isle of Beautiful Waters) to the Carib inhabitants, who resisted Spanish attempts to colonize. A French colony was established on 28 June 1635, and apart from short periods of occupancy by British forces, Guadeloupe has since remained a French possession. On 19 March 1946 the status of Guadeloupe was changed to that of an Overseas Department; in 1973 it additionally became an administrative region.

AREA AND POPULATION. Guadeloupe consists of a group of islands in the Lesser Antilles. The two main islands, Basse-Terre to the west and Grande-Terre to the east, are separated by a narrow channel, called Rivière Salée. Adjacent to these are the islands of Marie Galante (*Ceyre* to the Caribs) to the south-east, La Désirade to the east, and the Îles des Saintes to the south. The islands of St Martin and St Barthélemy lie 250 km to the north-west.

	Area in sq. km.	Census 1974	Chief town
St Martin [1]	52	6,191	Marigot
St Barthélemy	21	2,491	Gustavia
Basse-Terre	943	135,746	Basse-Terre
Îles des Saintes	14	3,084	Terre-de-Bas
Grande-Terre	570	159,424	Pointe-à-Pitre
La Désirade	21	1,682	Grande Anse
Marie-Galante	158	15,912	Grand-Bourg
	1,780	324,530	

[1] Northern part only; the southern third belongs to the Netherlands.

The total population at the 1974 Census was 324,530. The vast majority are black or mulatto, but the populations of St Barthélemy and Les Saintes are still mainly descended from 17th-century Breton and Norman settlers. French is the official language, but a Creole dialect is also widely used.

The seat of government is Basse-Terre (15,457 inhabitants) at the south-west end of that island but the largest towns are Pointe-à-Pitre (23,889 inhabitants), the economic centre with a large commercial harbour, and its suburb Abymes (53,605).

Vital statistics (1976): Births, 6,926; deaths, 2,362.

GOVERNMENT. Guadeloupe is under an appointed Prefect, an elected general council of 36 members (assisted by an Economic and Social Committee of 40 members) and an elected regional council of 41 members. It is represented in the National Assembly by 3 deputies, in the Senate by 2 senators and on the Economic and Social Council by 2 councillors. There are 3 *arrondissements*, sub-divided into 34 communes, each administered by an elected municipal council.

Prefect: Guy Maillard.

ECONOMY

Budget. The budget for 1977 balanced at 454,359,000 francs.

Banking. The Banque de Guadeloupe (founded 1851), with a capital of 2·4m. francs and reserve funds amounting to 1·44m. francs, advances loans chiefly for agricultural purposes. The Crédit Guadeloupéen has a capital of 5m. francs. The Banque Nationale de Paris has 7 branches in the department, the Crédit Agricole 6, the Banque Française Commerciale, Banque des Antilles Françaises and the Banque Populaire 2 each, and the Société Generale de Banque aux Antilles and the Chase Manhattan Bank 1 each. The Caisse Centrale de Coopération économique is the official banking institution of the department, enjoying the privilege of issuing bank-notes. Silver coin has disappeared from circulation.

ENERGY AND NATURAL RESOURCES

Electricity. Production in 1979 totalled 286·3m. kwh.

Agriculture. Chief products (1977) are bananas (128,000 tonnes), sugar (80,841 tonnes in 1978), rum (94,094 hectolitres of pure alcohol), roots (60 tonnes), aubergines (3,850 tonnes).

Livestock (1979): Cattle, 90,000; goats, 35,000; sheep, 2,500; pigs, 42,000.

Fisheries. The catch in 1979 was 7,800 tonnes.

COMMERCE. Trade for 1978 (in 1m. francs) was imports 1,909·7 and exports 498·8. In 1976, 74% of imports were from France and 5% from the USA, while 84% of exports went to France and 11% to Martinique; bananas formed 42% of the exports, sugar 35%, rum 6%. St Martin and St Bartélemy are free ports.

There are Chambers of Commerce and Industry at Basse-Terre and Pointe-à-Pitre. There is a British consular agent at Point-à-Pitre.

Tourism. In 1979 there were 140,224 tourists.

COMMUNICATIONS

Roads. In 1975 there were 323 km of national roads, 535 km of departmental roads and 1,150 km of local roads.

Aviation. Air France and 7 other airlines call at Guadeloupe. In 1979 there were 72,068 arrivals and departures of aircraft and 1,105,908 passengers at Pointe-à-Pitre airport making it the sixth most frequented French airport.

Shipping. Guadeloupe is in direct communication with France by means of 3 steam navigation companies. In 1976, 800 vessels arrived to disembark 52,349 passengers and 669,000 tonnes of freight and to embark 51,818 passengers and 266,400 tonnes of freight.

Post and Broadcasting. In 1978 there were 44 post offices and 30,730 telephones. ORTF broadcasts for 17 hours a day in French and television broadcasts for 5 hours a day. There were (1977) 13,979 radio and 19,294 TV receivers.

Newspapers. There were (1975) 2 daily newspapers with a combined circulation of 24,000.

JUSTICE, RELIGION, EDUCATION AND WELFARE

Justice. There are 4 *tribunaux d'instance* and 2 *tribunaux de grande instance* at Basse-

Terre and Pointe-à-Pitre; there is also a court of appeal and a court of assizes at Basse-Terre.

Religion. The majority of the population are Roman Catholic.

Education. In 1979–80 there were 15,360 pupils at pre-primary schools, 52,070 at primary schools and 45,532 at secondary schools. In 1977–78 there were 1,645 students in higher education. The *Centre Universitaire* had 3,408 students in 1975–76.

Health. The medical services in 1979 included 12 public hospitals (2,949 beds), 15 private clinics (1,177 beds) and 42 dispensaries. There were 378 physicians, 78 dentists, 130 pharmacists, 76 midwives and (1974) 790 nursing personnel.

Books of Reference

Information: Office du Tourisme du département, Point-à-Pitre. *Director:* R. Fortuné.
Lasserre, G., *La Guadeloupe, étude géographique.* 2 vols. Bordeaux, 1961

GUIANA
Guyane Française

HISTORY. A French settlement on the island of Cayenne was established in 1604 and the territory between the Maroni and Oyapock rivers finally became a French possession in 1817. Convicts settlements were established from 1852, that on off-shore Devil's Island being most notorious; all were closed by 1945. On 19 March 1946 the status of Guiana was changed to that of an Overseas Department.

AREA AND POPULATION. French Guiana is situated on the north-east coast of South America, and has an area of about 91,000 sq. km (35,135 sq. miles) and a population at the 1974 Census of 55,125; 1980 (estimate) 64,400, of whom 7,200 are tribal Indians. Cayenne, the chief town, has a population of (1980) 36,215. These figures are exclusive of the floating population of miners, officials and troops.

Vital statistics (1979): Live births, 1,704; deaths, 438.

GOVERNMENT. French Guiana is administered by an appointed Prefect and an elected council-general of 16 members. It is represented in the National Assembly and the Senate by 1 deputy each. There are 2 *arrondissements* (Cayenne and Saint-Laurent-du-Maroni) sub-divided into 20 communes.

Prefect: Désiré Carli.

ECONOMY

Budget. The budget for 1980 balanced at 391·35m. francs, excluding duplicated items.

Banking. The Bank of Guiana has a capital of 10m. francs and reserve fund of 2·39m. francs. Loans totalled 153·4m. francs in Sept. 1980.

AGRICULTURE. The country has immense forests (about 80,000 sq. km) rich in many kinds of timber. Only about 6,000 hectares are under cultivation. The crops consist of rice (470 tonnes in 1979), maize (1,200 tonnes), manioc (8,000 tonnes), bananas (1,000 tonnes) and sugar-cane (7,500 tonnes) as well as a large variety of fruits, vegetables and spices. The fishing of shrimps has been taken up by American companies and formed (1979) 21% of exports.

Livestock (1979): 3,000 cattle, 6,000 swine and 152,000 poultry.

COMMERCE. Trade in 1,000 tonnes and 1m. francs:

	1977		1978		1979	
	Quantity	Value	Quantity	Value	Quantity	Value
Imports	160·1	674	198·6	861	273·3	1,068
Exports	23·8	36	29·2	35	50·3	71

In 1979, 63% of imports came from France, 15% from Trinidad and Tobago and 5% from the USA, while 21% of exports went to the USA, 12% to the French Antilles and 35% to France.

Total trade between Guiana and UK (British Department of Trade returns, in £1,000 sterling):

	1976	1977	1978	1979	1980
Imports to UK	187	10	10	24	117
Exports and re-exports from UK	405	849	933	1,213	1,264

COMMUNICATIONS

Roads. Three chief and some secondary roads connect the capital with most of the coastal area by motor-car services. There are (1980) 321 km of national and 269 km of departmental roads. Connexions with the interior are made by waterways which, despite rapids, are navigable by local craft.

Aviation. Air France calls at Cayenne (Rochambeau Airport) 8 times a week, Air Martinique twice a week and Cruseiro do Sul once a week; Air Guyane services interior connexions. The airport registered 8,150 arrivals and departures of aircraft in 1979, transporting 130,000 passengers and 3,401 tonnes of freight.

Shipping. The chief ports are: Cayenne, St-Laurent-du-Maroni and Kourou. Dégrad des Cannes, the port of Cayenne is visited regularly by ships of the Compagnie General Maritime, the Compagnie Maritime des Chargeurs Reunis and Marseille Fret. There is also steamboat communication between the capital and the other towns of the department. In 1979, 584 arrivals and departures of vessels were registered in French Guiana (94,007 tonnes of petroleum products arrived and 158,489 tonnes of other freight arrived and departed).

Post and Broadcasting. An automatic telephone system connects Cayenne with 10 other communes as well as with Europe and the French West Indies. Number of telephones (1980), 15,542. There are wireless stations at Cayenne, Oyapoc, Régina, St-Laurent-du-Maroni and numerous other locations.

France-Region 3 (Guiana Radio) broadcasts for 116 hours each week on medium- and short-waves and FM in French. Television is broadcast for 43 hours each week on 7 transmitters. In 1980 there were 35,000 radio and 9,063 TV receivers.

Newspapers. There was (1980) 1 daily newspaper (*Presse de la Guyane*) with a circulation of 1,500 and a bi-weekly paper (*France-Guyane*) with a circulation of 3,500.

JUSTICE, RELIGION, EDUCATION AND WELFARE

Justice. At Cayenne there is a *tribunal d'instance* and a *tribunal de grande instance*, from which appeal is to the regional *cour d'appel* in Martinique.

Religion. The majority of the population is Roman Catholic.

Education. Primary education has been free since 1889 in lay schools for the two sexes in the communes and many villages. In 1980 public primary schools had 530 teachers and 12,010 pupils, the *lycées* and *collèges d'enseignement supérieur*, 455 teachers and 6,954 pupils. Private schools had 110 teachers and 2,235 pupils. The *Institut Henri Visioz* forms part of the *Centre Universitaire des Antilles-Guyane*.

Health. There were (1980) 59 physicians, 14 dentists, 18 pharmacists, 11 midwives and 287 nursing personnel. In 1980 there were 5 hospitals with 868 beds and 3 private clinics.

Books of Reference

Abonnec, A., Hurrault, J., Saban, R., *Bibliographie de la Guyane Française*. 2 vols. Paris, 1957
Henry, *Guyane Française, son histoire 1604–1946*. Cayenne
Hurault, J., *Guide du voyageur en Guyane*. Paris, 1949
Masse, D., *La Guyane Française: Histoire, Géographie, Possibilités*. Abbeville, 1978

MARTINIQUE

HISTORY. Discovered by Columbus in 1493, the island was known to its inhabitants as *Madinina*, from which its present name was corrupted. A French colony was established in 1635 and, apart from brief periods of British occupation, has since remained under French control. On 19 March 1946 its status was altered to that of an Overseas Department.

AREA AND POPULATION. The island, situated in the Lesser Antilles between Dominica and St Lucia, occupies an area of 1,079 sq. km (417 sq. miles). The total population, 1974 Census was 324,832 (1980, estimate, 308,169), of whom 98,807 live in Fort-de-France, the capital and chief commercial town, which has a landlocked harbour nearly 40 sq. km in extent.

French is the official language, but the majority of the population use a Creole dialect.
Vital statistics (1979): Live births 2,571; deaths 1,057.

GOVERNMENT. The department is administered by an appointed prefect and an elected general council of 36 members; there are 3 *arrondissements*, sub-divided into 34 communes, each administered by an elected municipal council. Martinique is represented in the National Assembly by 3 deputies, in the Senate by 2 senators and on the Economic and Social Council by 1 councillor.

Prefect: Marcel Julia.

ECONOMY

Budget. The budget, 1979, balanced at 925m. francs.

Banking. The Institut d'Émission des Départements d'Outre-mer is the official bank of the department. The Caisse Centrale de Coopération économique is used by the Government in assisting the economic development of the department.

The Banque des Antilles Françaises (with a capital of 10·8m. francs), the Crédit Martiniquais (11·4m. francs), branches of the Banque Nationale de Paris (22·6m. francs), Crédit Agricole, The Chase Manhattan Bank, Société Générale de Banque and Banque Française Commerciale are operating at Fort-de-France.

AGRICULTURE. Bananas, sugar and rum are the chief products, followed by pineapples, food and vegetables. In 1978 there were 7,000 hectares under sugar-cane, 10,300 hectares under bananas and 500 hectares under pineapples. There are 3 sugar works with distilleries attached, 28 agricultural distilleries producing rum and 3 factories for canning pineapples. In 1979 production of sugar was 9,375 tonnes; rum, 87,002 hectolitres.

Livestock (1979): 51,000 cattle, 49,000 sheep, 35,000 pigs, 20,000 goats and 2,000 horses.

COMMERCE. Trade in 1,000 tonnes and 1m. francs:

	1977		1978		1979	
	Quantity	Value	Quantity	Value	Quantity	Value
Imports	946	1,890	789	2,216	902	2,870
Exports	417	550	401	567	393	567

In 1978 the main items of import were foodstuffs; main items of export were sugar (2,340 tonnes), bananas (242,000 tonnes), rum (74,000 hectolitres) and pineapples (184 tonnes).

Total trade of the French West Indian Islands with UK (British Department of Trade returns, in £1,000 sterling):

	1976	1977	1978	1979	1980
Imports to UK	1,421	1,031	336	21	578
Exports and re-exports from UK	1,664	1,717	2,043	2,539	2,588

The Chamber of Commerce and Industry administers the port, airport and industrial zones.

COMMUNICATIONS

Roads. There are 252 km of national roads, 618 km of district roads and 748 km of local roads. In 1974 there were 39,200 passenger cars and 2,200 commercial vehicles.

Aviation. In 1979, 729,000 passengers arrived and departed by air.

Shipping. The island is visited regularly by French and American steamers. In 1979, 1,354 vessels called at Martinique.

Post and Broadcasting. There were, in 1978, 44 post offices and, 1980, 33,000 telephones. Radio-telephone service to Europe is available. In 1978 there were 21,230 radio and 33,171 TV receivers.

Newspapers. In 1978 there was 1 daily newspaper with a circulation of 19,000.

JUSTICE, RELIGION, EDUCATION AND WELFARE

Justice. Justice is administered by 2 *tribunaux d'instance*, a *tribunal de grande instance*, a regional court of appeal, a commercial court, a court of assizes and an administrative court.

Religion. The majority of the population is Roman Catholic.

Education. Education is compulsory between the ages of 6 and 16 years. In 1978, 129,973 children received primary and secondary education. The *Institut Henri Visioz*, which forms part of the *Centre Universitaire Antilles-Guyane*, had (1978) 2,100 students of law, politics and economics.

Health. There were (1979) 14 hospitals with 4,200 beds and in 1978 there were 316 physicians, 124 pharmacists, 120 midwives and 98 dentists.

Books of Reference

Annuaire statistique de la Martinique. Paris. (Latest issue, 1959–60)
Monographie de la Martinique. Préfecture, Martinique, 1964
Hannau, H. W., *Martinique*. Munich, 1966
Nicolas, M., *Guide Touristique de la Martinique*. 2nd ed. Martinique, 1969

MAYOTTE

HISTORY. Mayotte was a French colony from 1843 until 1914, when it was attached, with the other Comoro islands, to the government-general of Madagascar. The Comoro group was granted administrative autonomy within the French Republic and became an Overseas Territory.

When the other 3 islands voted to become independent (as the Comoro state) in 1974, Mayotte voted against this and remained a French dependency. In 1976, it became (following a further referendum) a *collectivité particulière*, being an intermediate status between Overseas Territory and Overseas Department.

AREA AND POPULATION. Mayotte, east of the Comoro Islands, has an area of 374 sq. km (144 sq. miles) and a 1978 Census population of 47,246 (1980, estimate, 50,400). The capital is Dzaoudzi (4,147 inhabitants) situated on a tiny offshore islet. The main languages are Swahili and French.

GOVERNMENT. The department is under an appointed Prefect and an elected general council of 17 members. Mayotte is represented by 1 deputy in the National Assembly and by 1 member in the Senate.

Prefect: Jean Rigotard.

ECONOMY

Budget. The budget for 1978 balanced at 34·75m. French francs.

Currency. In Feb. 1976 the currency was changed from the *franc CFA* to the (metropolitan) *French franc*.

NATURAL RESOURCES

Agriculture. The main products are vanilla, ylang-ylang, coffee and copra.

Fisheries. A lobster and shrimp industry has recently been created. Annual catch is about 2,000 tonnes.

COMMERCE. In 1976, exports totalled 5m. francs (92% to France) and imports 12m. francs (27% from Réunion and 23% from France). Total trade between Mayotte and UK (1978): Imports to UK, £10,000 and exports and re-exports from UK, £403,000.

COMMUNICATIONS

Roads. In 1979 there were 60 km of bitumenized roads and 130 km of tracks, with about 720 motor vehicles.

Aviation. In 1978, 4,300 passengers and 361 tonnes of freight arrived by air and 4,410 passengers (90 tonnes) departed.

JUSTICE, RELIGION AND EDUCATION

Justice. There is a *tribunal d'instance* and a *tribunal supérieur d'appel.*

Religion. The population is 99% Moslem, with a small Christian (mainly Roman Catholic) minority.

Education. In 1979 there were 7,253 pupils and 187 teachers in primary schools and 667 pupils and 29 teachers in secondary schools.

RÉUNION

HISTORY. The island of Réunion became a French possession in 1642 and remained so until 19 March 1946, when its status was altered to that of an Overseas Department; in 1974 it additionally became part of an administrative region.

AREA AND POPULATION. Réunion (or Bourbon), about 569 miles east of Madagascar, has an area of 2,511·6 sq. km (968·5 sq. miles) and a population of 484,924 (Dec. 1978). The capital is Saint-Denis (1974 census) 103,512.
   Vital statistics (1978): Live births, 11,946; deaths, 3,098.
   The small islands of Juan de Nova, Europa, Bassas da India, Îles Glorieuses and Tromelin, with a combined area of less than 50 sq. km, are all uninhabited and lie at various points in the Indian Ocean adjacent to Madagascar. They remained integral parts of the French Republic after Madagascar's independence in 1960, and are now administered by Réunion. In 1978 the Seychelles laid claim to Tromelin (which had been transferred by the UK from the Seychelles to France in 1954), and Madagascar to the other 4 islands.

GOVERNMENT. The région is under a prefect, an elected general council of 36 members and an elected regional council of 46 members. Réunion is represented in the National Assembly by 3 deputies, in the Senate by 2 senators, and in the Economic and Social Council by 2 councillors. There are 4 *arrondissements*, sub-divided in 24 communes each administered by an elected municipal council.
   Prefect: Bernard Landouzy.

ECONOMY

Budget. The budget for 1978 balanced at 3,573m. French francs.

Banking. The Institut d'émission des Départements d'Outre-mer has the right to issue bank-notes. Banks operating in Réunion are the Banque de la Réunion (Crédit Lyonnais), the Banque Nationale pour le Commerce et l'Industrie, the Caisse

Régionale de Crédit Agricole Mutuel de la Réunion and the Banque française Commerciale (BFC).

NATURAL RESOURCES

Agriculture (1978). The chief produce is sugar (272,634 tonnes), rum (70,000 hectolitres), maize (13,214 tonnes), potatoes (2,335 tonnes), onions (1,500 tonnes), vanilla, essences and tobacco. The forests occupy about 113,000 hectares.

Livestock (1979): 21,000 cattle, 125,000 swine, 3,000 sheep and 33,000 goats.

Fisheries. In 1978 the catch was 1,781 tonnes.

INDUSTRY AND TRADE

Industry (1978). Total number of workers (in 418 firms employing 10 or more) 20,173. The sugar industry employed (1976) 6,350.

Commerce. Trade in 1,000 tonnes and 1,000 French francs:

	1975		1976		1977		1978	
	Quantity	Value	Quantity	Value	Quantity	Value	Quantity	Value
Imports	641	1,757	809	2,152	725	2,412	793	2,659
Exports	156	257	251	450	303	561	261	519

The chief imports in 1978 were (in tonnes): Rice, 54,952; cement, 32,651. Chief exports (1978): Sugar, 210,670 tonnes; molasses, 37,250 tonnes; rum, 4,866 tonnes. In 1978 (by value) 66% of imports were from, and 78% of exports to, France.

Total trade between Réunion and UK (British Department of Trade returns, in £1,000 sterling):

	1976	1977	1978	1979	1980
Imports to UK	4,469	19,585	9,480	7,855	60
Exports and re-exports from UK	1,742	1,807	2,041	2,296	3,022

COMMUNICATIONS

Roads. There were, in 1978, 2,690 km of roads, 2,359 km of which are bitumenized. There were 78,629 passenger cars and 35,963 other vehicles in 1977.

Aviation. Air France maintains an air service 7 times a week. In 1978, 129,549 passengers and 5,070 tonnes of freight arrived and 133,282 passengers and 1,570 tonnes of freight departed at Saint-Denis-Gillot airport.

Shipping. Four shipping lines serve the island. In 1978, 374 vessels (101 of them French) visited the island to discharge 878,116 tonnes of freight and 363 passengers, and load 317,385 tonnes of freight and 277 passengers at Pointe-des-Galets.

Post and Broadcasting. There are telephone and telegraph connexions with Mauritius, Madagascar and metropolitan France. There are 50 post offices and a central telephone office; number of telephones (1978), 36,177.

France Regions 3 broadcast in French on medium- and short-waves for more than 18 hours a day. There is 1 television programme *via* 14 transmitters for 21 hours a week. In 1977 there were 53,380 radio and 59,210 TV receivers.

Newspapers. There were (1978) 3 daily newspapers with a combined circulation of 52,000 and 14 other periodicals with a circulation of 29,000.

JUSTICE, RELIGION, EDUCATION AND WELFARE

Justice. There are 3 *tribunaux d'instance,* 2 *tribunaux de grande instance*, 1 *Cour d'Appel* and 1 *tribunal administratif.*

Religion. The vast majority of the population is Roman Catholic.

Education. Réunion had (1978) 5 *lycées*, 49 *collèges*, 9 *lycées d'enseignement technique* with 58,135 pupils and 4 private secondary schools with 3,476 pupils. Primary education is given in 462 public schools with 4,046 teachers and 117,982 pupils; and in 29 private schools, 307 teachers, 9,817 pupils. University courses are given in 6 high schools to 2,688 students by 62 teachers. The *Centre Universitaire de la Réunion* (founded 1971) had 1,901 students in 1977–78.

Health. In 1972 there were 21 hospitals with 3,886 beds; in 1975 there were 296 physicians, 77 dentists, 143 pharmacists, 77 midwives and 2,029 nursing personnel.

Books of Reference

Bulletin de l'Académie de la Réunion. Biennial
Bulletin de la Chambre d'Agriculture de la Réunion
Statistiques et Indicateurs Économiques, 1976. Département de la Réunion, 1977

ST PIERRE AND MIQUELON

HISTORY. The tiny remaining fragment of the once extensive French possessions in North America, the archipelago was settled from France in the 17th century and finally became a French territory from 1816 until July 1976, when its status was altered to that of an Overseas Department.

AREA AND POPULATION. The department consists of a group of 8 small islands off the south coast of Newfoundland. Area of Saint-Pierre group, 26 sq. km (10 sq. miles); population (census 18 Feb. 1974), 5,232; area of Miquelon-Langlade group, 216 sq. km (83·5 sq. miles); population, census, 1974, 608; total area, 242 sq. km (93·5 sq. miles). Population (estimate June 1979), 6,272. The chief town is St Pierre.

Vital statistics (1979): Births, 82; marriages, 40; deaths, 30.

GOVERNMENT. The department is administered by an appointed Prefect and an elected General Council of 14 members; it is represented in the National Assembly by 1 deputy, in the Senate by 1 senator and in the Economic and Social Council by 1 councillor.

Prefect: Clement Bouhin.

BUDGET. The ordinary budget for 1979 balanced at 31·5m. francs.

INDUSTRY. The islands, being mostly barren rock, are unsuited for agriculture. The chief industry is fishing.

COMMERCE. Trade in 1,000 tonnes and 1m. francs:

	1977		1978		1979	
	Quantity	Value	Quantity	Value	Quantity	Value
Imports	63·6	126,000	58·5	134,000	56·2	140,000
Exports	2·9	17,000	2·5	17,800	2·4	19,000

The imports comprise textiles, salt, wines, coal, petrol, foodstuffs, meat; and the exports (in 1976), dried and salted fish (19 tonnes; 287,000 francs); frozen and smoked fish (1,958 tonnes; 18m. francs). In 1974, 54% of imports came from Canada and 38% from France, while 70% of exports were to Canada, 25% to the USA and 5% to France.

Total trade between St Pierre and Miquelon and UK (British Department of Trade returns, in £1,000 sterling):

	1976	1977	1978	1979	1980
Imports to UK	16	7	—	224	3
Exports and re-exports from UK	209	356	382	435	884

COMMUNICATIONS

Roads. In 1974 there were 60 km of roads, of which 20 km were paved. In 1974 there were about 1,500 passenger cars and 300 commercial vehicles.

Aviation. Air Saint-Pierre connects the department with Sydney (Nova Scotia), and there are occasional flights to and from St John's (Newfoundland), Gander and New York.

Shipping. St Pierre is in regular motor-vessel communication with North Sydney, Fortune (Newfoundland) and Halifax. In 1972, 89,000 tonnes of freight were loaded or unloaded.

Post and Broadcasting. There were 1,863 telephones in 1978. *France Regions 3* broadcasts in French on medium-waves. St Pierre is connected by radio-telecommunication with most countries of the world. Radio licences totalled 2,100 and TV 1,700 in 1975.

Cinemas. There were (1973) 2 cinemas with a seating capacity of 800.

JUSTICE, RELIGION, EDUCATION AND WELFARE

Justice. There is a *tribunal de premier instance* and a *tribunal supérieur d'appel* at St Pierre.

Religion. The population is chiefly Roman Catholic.

Education. Primary instruction is free. There were, in 1979, 7 nursery and primary schools with 1,161 pupils and 3 secondary schools (including 1 technical school) with 750 pupils.

Health. There was (1979) 1 hospital on St Pierre with 78 beds; 6 doctors, 2 dentists and 21 nurses.

Books of Reference

De Curton, E., *Saint-Pierre et Miquelon*. Paris, 1944
De La Rüe, E. A., *Saint-Pierre et Miquelon*. Paris, 1963
Ribault, J. Y., *Histoire de Saint-Pierre et Miquelon: Des Origines à 1814*. St Pierre, 1962

OVERSEAS TERRITORIES

SOUTHERN AND ANTARCTIC TERRITORIES

Terres Australes et Antarctiques Françaises

The Territory of the TAAF was created on 6 Aug. 1955. It comprises the islands of Saint Paul and Amsterdam, formerly Nouvelle Amsterdam, the Kerguelen and Crozet islands, and Terre Adélie.

The Administrator is assisted by a consultative council which meets twice yearly in Paris; its members are nominated by the Government for 5 years. Members of the Scientific Council are appointed by the Senior Administrator after approval by the Minister in charge of scientific research. The administration has its seat in Paris.

Administrateur supérieur: Francis Jacquemont.

There are 4 postal agencies; the TAAF has its own postage stamps.

The scientific stations of the TAAF which took an important part in the International Geophysical Year, 1956–58, have been made permanent; the staff of the French bases (183 in 1975) is renewed annually and forms the only population.

Kerguelen islands, situated 48–50° S. lat., 68–70° E. long., consists of 1 large and 85 smaller islands and over 200 islets and rocks with a total area of 7,215 sq. km (2,786 sq. miles), of which Grande Terre occupies 6,675 sq. km (2,577 sq. miles). It was discovered in 1772 by Yves de Kerguelen, but was effectively occupied by France only in 1949. Port-aux-Français has several scientific research stations (92 members). Reindeer, trout and sheep have been acclimatized.

Crozet islands, situated 46° S. lat., 50–52° E. long., consists of 5 larger and 15 tiny islands, with a total area of 300 sq. km (116 sq. miles); the western group includes Apostles, Pigs and Penguins islands; the eastern group, Possession and Eastern islands. The archipelago was discovered in 1772 by Marion Dufresne, whose mate, Crozet, annexed it for Louis XV. A meteorological and scientific station (28 members) on Possession Island was built in 1964.

Amsterdam Island and **Saint-Paul Island**, situated 38–39° S. lat., 77° E. long. Amsterdam, with an area of 60 sq. km (25 sq. miles) was discovered in 1522 by Magellan's companions; Saint-Paul, lying about 100 km to the south, with an area of 7 sq. km (2·7 sq. miles), was probably discovered in 1559 by Portuguese sailors. Both were first visited in 1633 by the Dutch explorer, Van Diemen, and were annexed by France in 1843. They are both extinct volcanoes, barren and uninhabited; but in 1949 an administrative office, research stations (37 members) and a hospital were established at Camp Heurtin on Amsterdam.

Terre Adélie comprises that section of the Antarctic continent between 136° and 142° E. long., south of 60° S. lat. The ice-covered plateau has an area of about 432,000 sq. km (166,800 sq. miles), and was discovered in 1840 by Dumont d'Urville. A research station (34 members) is situated at Base Dumont d'Urville, which is maintained by the French Polar Expeditions.

Books of Reference

T.A.A.F. Revue trimestrielle. Paris, 1957 ff
Expéditions Polaires Françaises. Études et Rapports. Paris, 1948–59

NEW CALEDONIA
Nouvelle Calédonie

HISTORY. New Caledonia was annexed by France in 1853 and, together with most of its former dependencies, became an Overseas Territory in 1958.

AREA AND POPULATION. The island of New Caledonia is situated between 20° 8′ and 22° 25′ S. lat., and 164° 15′ and 162° 15′ E. long. It has a total length exceeding 397 km and an average breadth of 50 km. Area, including outlying islands, 19,103 sq. km (7,374 sq. miles). In 1976 the population (census) was 133,233, including 50,757 Europeans (majority French), 55,598 Melanesians, 7,054 Vietnamese and Indonesians, 6,391 Polynesians, 9,571 Wallisians, 3,862 others; 1980 (estimate) 139,600. The capital, Nouméa had (1976) 74,335 inhabitants.

Vital statistics (1978): Live births, 3,698; deaths, 916.

GOVERNMENT. From Jan. 1976 State affairs are administrated by the High Commissioner and Territorial affairs by a Council of Government of 7 elected members (until 1976 the Council was advisory). A Territorial Assembly of 36 elected members decides the more important territorial affairs including local revenue.

New Caledonia is represented in the National Assembly by 2 deputies, in the Senate by 1 senator and in the Economic and Social Council by 1 councillor.

At territorial elections held 1 July 1979, the *Rassemblement Populaire Calédonienne pour la République* (Gaullists) gained 15 seats, *Front Indépendantiste* 14 seats, *Fédération pour une Nouvelle Société Calédonienne* 7 seats.

The Territory is divided into 4 *circonscriptions* (of which the Loyalty Islands form one), and subdivided into 32 communes which are administered by locally elected councils and mayors.

High Commissioner: Claude Charbonniaud.

ECONOMY

Budget. The budget for 1979 balanced at 17,163m. francs CFP. Revenues included special grants by France totalling 3,730m. francs CFP. 1 French franc = 18·18 francs CFP.

Banking. There are branches of the Banque de Indosuez, the Banque Nationale de Paris, the Banque de Paris et des Pays-Bas, and the Société Générale, in addition to the Banque de la Nouvelle-Calédonie (Crédit Lyonnais).

ENERGY AND NATURAL RESOURCES

Electricity. In 1977, production totalled 1,700m. kwh.

Minerals. The mineral resources are very great; nickel, chrome and iron abound; silver, gold, cobalt, lead, manganese, iron and copper have been mined at different times. The nickel deposits are of special value, being without arsenic. Production of nickel ore in 1978, 3·29m. tonnes. About 467,000 hectares of mining land are owned, and 97,000 hectares have been granted for exploitation. In 1978 the furnaces produced 17,103 tonnes of matte nickel and 19,889 tonnes of ferro-nickel.

Agriculture. Of the total area only about 6% is cultivable; about 416,000 hectares are pasture land; about 6,000 hectares are commercially cultivated and about 250,000 hectares contain forest; forest produce, 1976, 19,849 cu. metres. There are 4 forms of landownership: native reserves belonging to the local tribes, private estates, public land belonging to the New Caledonian territory and public land belonging to the metropolitan government. The chief agricultural products are beef, pork, poultry, coffee, maize, fruit and vegetables.

Livestock (1979): Cattle, 116,000; pigs, 36,000; goats, 10,000; poultry, 178,000.

INDUSTRY AND TRADE

Industry. Local industries include chlorine and oxygen plants, cement, soft drinks, barbed wire, nails, pleasure and fishing boats and clothing.

Commerce. Imports and exports in 1m. francs CFP for 5 years:

	1975	1976	1977	1978	1979
Imports	27,048	24,073	26,032	23,926	27,791
Exports	25,494	26,749	27,809	17,484	28,549

In 1979, 41% of the imports came from, and 63% of the exports went to France.

Chief imports in 1979 were (in 1m. francs CFP): Food, 5,912; fuels and minerals, 5,872; machines and electrical equipment, 3,196. Chief exports: Nickel metal, 22,391; nickel ore, 3,815.

COMMUNICATIONS

Roads. There were, in 1978, 5,481 km of roads.

Aviation. New Caledonia is connected by air routes with France (by UTA), Australia (UTA, Air Pacific and Qantas), New Zealand (UTA and Air New Zealand), Fiji (by Air Pacific), Vanuatu, Wallis archipelago and Tahiti (by UTA). In 1978, 100,520 passengers landed or departed *via* Nouméa airport.

Shipping. In 1978, 407 vessels entered Nouméa unloading 801,500 tonnes of goods and loading 1·7m. tonnes. A new harbour for deep-water alongside discharge was completed in 1974.

Post and Broadcasting. There were 52 post offices and telex, telephone, radio and television services. There were (1978) 23,130 telephones. *Radio Nouméa* belongs to *Société Mahande des Programmes* and broadcasts in French on medium- and short-waves. *Télé Nouméa* broadcasts 1 television programme 28 hours a week. Number of receivers (1978): radio, 65,000; TV, 28,000.

Cinemas. In 1978 there were 14 cinemas with a seating capacity of 3,700.

Newspapers. In 1978 there were 2 daily newspapers with a circulation of 12,000 and 16 other periodicals.

JUSTICE, RELIGION, EDUCATION AND WELFARE

Justice. There is a *tribunal de grande instance* and a *cour d'appel* in Nouméa.

Religion. Over 60% of the population are Roman Catholic and 30% Protestant.

Education. In 1978, there were 33,632 pupils in 251 primary schools, 7,948 in 28 secondary schools and 3,147 in 24 technical and vocational schools.

Health. In 1978 there were 163 physicians, 42 dentists, 33 pharmacists, 11 midwives and 423 nursing personnel. 66 hospitals had a total of 1,541 beds.

Outlying islands:

1. The Loyalty Islands, 100 km (60 miles) east of New Caledonia, consisting of 3 large islands, Maré, Lifou and Uvéa, and many small islands with a total area of about 2,353 sq. km and a population (census, 1976) of 14,518, nearly all Melanesians except on Uvéa, which is partly Polynesian. The chief culture in the islands is that of coconuts: the chief export, copra.

2. The Isle of Pines, 50 km (30 miles) to the south-east of Nouméa, with an area of 153 sq. km and a population of 1,095 (census 1976), is a tourist and fishing centre.

3. The Bélep Archipelago, about 50 km north-west of New Caledonia, with an area of 70 sq. km and a population of 551 (1969).

4. Chesterfield Islands are on the 20° S. parallel, about 550 km (342 miles) west of the northern headland of New Caledonia

5. The Huon Islands, 275 km (170 miles) north-west of New Caledonia, a barren group.

6. Walpole lies south-east of Maré (Loyalty Islands) and east of the Isle of Pines, about 150 km (93 miles) from each of these islands; Matthew and Hunter lie further east.

Books of Reference

Journal Officiel de la Nouvelle Calédonie et Dépendances
Annuaire Statistique de la Nouvelle Calédonie et Dépendances

FRENCH POLYNESIA

Polynésie Française

HISTORY. French protectorates since 1843, these islands were annexed to France 1880–82 to form 'French Settlements in Oceania', which opted in Nov. 1958 for the status of an Overseas Territory within the French Community.

AREA AND POPULATION. The total area of these 5 archipelagoes, scattered over a wide area in the Eastern Pacific is 3,941 sq. km (1,522 sq. miles). The population, Census, 1977, was 137,382; 1980, estimate, 148,000. The islands are administratively divided into 5 *circonscriptions*:

1. The **Windward Islands** (Îles du Vent) (101,392 inhabitants in 1977) comprise Tahiti with an area of 1,042 sq. km and (1977) 95,604 inhabitants; Moorea with an area of 132 sq. km and 5,788 inhabitants; and the smaller Mehetia, Tetiaroa and Tubuai Manu. The capital is Papeete (62,735 inhabitants including suburbs).

2. The **Leeward Islands** (Îles sous le Vent) (16,311 inhabitants), comprising the volcanic islands of Huahine (3,140), Raiatéa (6,376), Tahaa (3,513), Bora-Bora (2,572), Maupiti (710) together with 4 small (uninhabited) atolls, the group having a total area of 507 sq. km. The chief town is Uturoa (2,517 inhabitants) on Raiatéa.

The Windward and Leeward Islands together are called the Society Archipelago (Archipel de la Société). Tahitian, a Polynesian language, is spoken throughout the archipelago.

3. The **Tuamotu Archipelago**, consisting of two parallel ranges of 78 atolls lying between 135° and 143° W. long. and 14° and 23° S. lat., east of the Society Archi-

pelago, have a total area of 774 sq. km and a population of 8,537; its major islands are Rangiroa, Hao and Turéia. The *circonscription* (total 9,052 inhabitants) also includes the **Gambier Islands** further east (of which Mangareva is the principal), an atoll having an area of 36 sq. km and a population of 515; the chief centre is Rikitea.

4. The **Austral or Tubuai Islands**, lying south of the Society Archipelago, comprise a 1,300 km chain of volcanic islands and reefs. They include Rimatara, Rurutu, Tubuai, Raivaevae and, 500 km to the south, Rapa-Iti, with a combined area of 174 sq. km and 5,208 inhabitants; the chief centre is Mataura on Tubuai.

5. The **Marquesas Islands**, lying north of the Tuamotu Archipelago, with a total area of 1,274 sq. km and 5,419 inhabitants, comprise Nuku-Hiva, Ua Pu, Ua Huka, Hiva-Oa, Tahuata, Fatu-Hiva and 5 smaller (uninhabited) islands.

CONSTITUTION AND GOVERNMENT. Under the 1977 Constitution, the Territory is administered by a High Commissioner, a Council of Government (over which the High Commissioner presides) of 8 members, a Territorial Assembly of 30 members elected every 5 years by universal suffrage, and an advisory Economic and Social Committee. French Polynesia is represented in the National Assembly by 2 deputies, in the Senate by 1 senator, and in the Economic and Social Council by 1 councillor.

At the territorial elections held on 29 May 1977, the *Front Uni pour l'autonomie interne* and its supporters gained 16 seats in the Assembly, and the *Tahoeraa Huira-atira* (Gaullists) 10 seats, with 4 seats going to others.

High Commissioner: Paul Cousseran.

FINANCE. The ordinary budget for 1978 balanced at 13,524·7m. francs CFP.

ENERGY AND NATURAL RESOURCES

Electricity. Production in 1979 amounted to 136·97m. kwh.

Agriculture. An important product is copra (coconut trees covering the coastal plains of the mountainous islands and the greater part of the low-lying islands), production (1979) 14,513 tonnes. Tropical fruits, such as bananas, pineapples, oranges, etc., are grown only for local consumption.

Livestock (1979): Cattle, 7,000; horses, 2,000; pigs, 22,000; sheep, 3,000; goats, 3,000; poultry, 473,000.

Fisheries. The catch in 1979 amounted to 4,217 tonnes of fish.

COMMERCE. Trade in 1,000 tonnes and 1m. francs CFP:

	1977		1978		1979	
	Quantity	Value	Quantity	Value	Quantity	Value
Imports	396	29,187	407	33,070	450	36,645
Exports	11	1,464	9	2,973	12	2,252

Total trade between the French possessions in the Pacific and UK (British Department of Trade returns, in £1,000 sterling):

	1976	1977	1978	1979	1980
Imports to UK	—	11	14	6	32
Exports and re-exports from UK	1,647	1,768	2,781	2,285	2,154

Chief imports (by value) include metalwork, textiles, petrol, sugar and flour. Chief exports are coconut oil, cultured pearls, vanilla and citrus fruits. Tourism is very important, earning almost half as much as the visible exports. There were 101,194 tourists in 1979.

COMMUNICATIONS

Aviation. Five international airlines connect Tahiti with Paris, Honolulu, USA, Mexico and New Zealand. There is also a regular air service between Faaa airport (on Tahiti) and the Leeward Isles with occasional connexions to the other groups. In 1976, 657,700 passengers arrived or departed *via* Faaa airport and 210,300 *via* Moorea airport.

Shipping. Several shipping companies connect France, San Francisco, New Zealand and Australia with Papeete.

Post and Broadcasting. Number of telephones (1978), 17,302. *Radio Tahiti* belongs to *Office de Radiodiffusion-Télévision Française* and broadcasts in French, Tahitian and English on medium- and short-waves and also broadcasts 1 television programme *via* 5 transmitters. Number of receivers (1978): radio, 75,000; TV, 15,000.

Cinemas. In 1975 there were 6 cinemas with a seating capacity of 3,200.

Newspapers. In 1975 there were 4 daily newspapers with a combined circulation of 11,000 and 2 other periodicals with 2,000.

JUSTICE, RELIGION, EDUCATION AND WELFARE

Justice. There is a *tribunal de grande instance* and a *cour d'appel* at Papeete.

Religion. In 1975 it was estimated that 50% of the inhabitants were Protestants, 34% Roman Catholics and 6% Mormon.

Education. Education at primary level was re-organized in 1974 and secondary education in 1975. There were, in 1976, 160 primary schools (37,275 pupils), 14 secondary schools (7,707 pupils) and 3 technical schools (1,903 pupils).

Health. There were (1977) 117 physicians, 23 dentists, 10 pharmacists, 24 midwives and 286 nursing personnel. There was a main hospital at Mamao (on Tahiti), 6 secondary hospitals, 41 dispensaries and medical centres and 45 first aid posts.

DEPENDENCY. The uninhabited Clipperton Islands, 1,000 km off the coast of Mexico, are administered by the High Commissioner for French Polynesia but do not form part of the Territory; they comprise an atoll whose 2 islands cover 7 sq. km.

Books of Reference

Journal Officiel des Etablissements Françaises de l'Océanie, and *Supplement Containing Statistics of Commerce and Navigation*. Papeete
Andrews, E., *Comparative Dictionary of the Tahitian Language*. Chicago, 1944
Luke, Sir Harry, *The Islands of the South Pacific*. London, 1961
O'Reilly, P., and Reitman, E., *Bibliographie de Tahiti et de la Polynésie française*. Paris, 1967
O'Reilly, P., and Teissier, R., *Tahitiens. Répertoire bio-bibliographique de la Polynésie française*. Paris, 1963

WALLIS AND FUTUNA

HISTORY. French dependencies since 1842, the inhabitants of these islands voted on 22 Dec. 1959 by an overwhelming majority in favour of exchanging their status to that of an Overseas Territory, which took effect from 29 July 1961.

AREA AND POPULATION. The Territory comprises two groups of islands in the central Pacific, north-east of Fiji; the Wallis Archipelago (area 96 sq. km) and the Îles de Horn (159 sq. km). The capital of the Territory is Mata-Utu (558 inhabitants) on Uvea, the main island of the Wallis Archipelago.

The resident population (census 26 March 1976) was 9,192, comprising 6,019 on Uvea and 3,173 on Futuna in the Îles de Horn (whose other main island, Alofi, is uninhabited). About 11,000 Wallisians and Futunians live abroad, mainly in New Caledonia and Vanuatu. Uvean and Futunan are distinct Polynesian languages.

CONSTITUTION AND GOVERNMENT. The Senior Administrator carries out the duties of Head of the Territory, assisted by an elected 20-member Territorial Assembly. The territory is represented by 1 deputy in the National Assembly, by 1 senator in the Senate, and by 1 member on the Economic and Social Council.

Administrateur supérieur: Jacques de Agostini.
President of the Territorial Assembly: Manuele Lisiahi.

ECONOMY. The 1978 budget provided for expenditure of 148·45m. francs CFP.

AGRICULTURE. The chief products are copra, yams, taro roots and bananas. Livestock: Cattle, 100 (1976); pigs, 4,000 (1979); horses, 400 (1978); goats, 7,000 (1977).

COMMERCE. Imports (1976) amounted to 217m. francs CFP.

COMMUNICATIONS

Roads. In 1977 there were 100 km of roads on Uvea.

Aviation. In 1977 there were 581 aircraft arrivals and departures at Hihifo airport, on Uvea. There is a weekly flight *via* Vila (Vanuatu) to Nouméa (Vanuatu).

Post and Broadcasting. In 1979 a radio station was established on Uvea. In 1978 there were 148 telephones.

RELIGION, EDUCATION AND WELFARE

Religion. The majority of the population is Roman Catholic.

Education. In 1978, there were about 3,000 pupils in 9 primary and lower secondary schools.

Health. In 1974 there were 3 physicians and 26 nursing personnel (including 10 midwives). There were (1972) 5 small hospitals and dispensaries with 108 beds.

GABON

République Gabonaise

Capital: Libreville
Population: 1·3m. (1978)
GNP per capita: US$3,580 (1978)

HISTORY. First colonized by France in the mid-19th century, Gabon was annexed to French Congo in 1890 and became a separate colony in 1910 as one of the 4 territories of French Equatorial Africa. It achieved independence on 17 Aug. 1960. The first President, Leon M'ba, died in 1967 and was succeeded on 2 Dec. by his Vice-President, Albert-Bernard (now Omar) Bongo.

AREA AND POPULATION. Gabon is bounded west by the Atlantic ocean, north by Equatorial Guinea and Cameroon and east and south by Congo. The area covers 267,667 sq. km; its population at the 1970 census was 950,007; the latest estimate (1978) is 1,300,200, including about 12,000 Europeans. The capital is Libreville (251,400 inhabitants, 1974), other large towns being Port-Gentil (77,111) and Lambaréné (22,682).

Vital statistics (1975): Birth rate, 3·22%; death rate, 2·22%.

Provincial areas, populations (census 1970, in 1,000) and capitals are as follows:

Province	sq. km		Capital	Province	sq. km		Capital
Estuaire	20,740	195	Libreville	Nyanga	21,285	67	Tchibanga
Woleu-Ntem	38,465	148	Oyem	Ngounié	37,750	130	Mouila
Ogooué-Ivindo	46,075	60	Makokou	Ogooué-Lolo	25,380	52	Koulamoutou
Moyen-Ogooué	18,535	52	Lambaréné	Haut-Ogooué	36,547	127	Franceville
Ogooué-Maritime	22,890	120	Port-Gentil				

The largest ethnic groups are the Fang (30%) in the north, Eshira (25%) in the south-west, and the Adouma (17%) in the south-east.

CONSTITUTION AND GOVERNMENT. The 1967 Constitution (revised 1979) provides for an Executive President directly elected for a 7-year term and a unicameral National Assembly of 84 members, directly elected for a 5-year term with 9 members nominated by the President. The President appoints a Council of Ministers to assist him, and a Prefect to administer each of the country's 9 provinces (which are sub-divided into 37 *départements*).

President of the Republic: Omar Bongo (re-elected on 25 Feb. 1973 and 30 Dec. 1979).
Prime Minister: Léon Mébiame.
Foreign Minister: Martin Bongo.
Flag: Three horizontal stripes of green, yellow, blue.

French is the official language.

DEFENCE

Army. The Army consists of 1 all-arms battalion with support units, totalling (1980), 1,100 men.

Navy. The naval forces in 1981 comprised 2 fast attack craft (3 more reportedly on order), 3 patrol craft and 1 landing craft with bases at Libreville and Port-Gentil. Personnel, 170 officers and men. The Coastguard has 9 small patrol craft and 1 service tender.

Air Force. The Air Force has 3 single-seat and 2 two-seat Mirage 5 ground-attack aircraft. It has 3 Hercules turboprop transports, 2 twin-jet Gulfstream IIs and 1 twin-jet Falcon 20, 2 Cessna Skymaster communications aircraft, and 3 Puma and 4 Alouette III helicopters. Other transport aircraft are operated on a joint military/

civilian basis. On order are 2 EMBRAER EMB-110 twin-turboprop light transports and an EMB-111 maritime patrol aircraft. Personnel number 300.

INTERNATIONAL RELATIONS

Membership. Gabon is a member of UN, OAU and OPEC; it is an ACP state of the EEC.

FINANCE. The provisional budget for 1980 balanced at 313,700m. francs CFA.

ENERGY AND NATURAL RESOURCES

Electricity. The semi-public *Société d'energie et d'eau du Gabon* produced 437m. kwh. in 1978, mainly from thermal plants but increasingly from hydro-electric schemes at Kinguélé, near Libreville, and elsewhere.

Oil. The petroleum refinery at Port-Gentil, a joint venture of the governments of the 5 members of the Central African Customs and Economic Union (UDEAC) and foreign petroleum companies, began trial operations in Oct. 1967. The refinery, operated by *La Société Gabonaise de raffinerie*, produced 10·8m. tonnes of oil in 1976. A second refinery at Pointe Clairette came on stream in 1976. Production of crude petroleum totalled 10·6m. tonnes in 1978 and Gabon was (1979) Africa's fifth largest crude oil producer. Exports (1980) US$773m.

Minerals. Production 1978: Manganese ore, 1,661,000 tonnes; uranium concentrates 1,407 tonnes; natural gas, 56·17m. cu. metres; gold, 40 kg.

A large deposit of iron ore estimated at 1,000m. tonnes was discovered in 1971 at Mékambo near Bélinga.

Agriculture. Agriculture, forestry and fisheries occupy 82% of the working population. The major crops are cocoa, coffee, rice, palm products, cassava and bananas.

Livestock (1979): 3,000 cattle, 100,000 sheep, 90,000 goats, 6,000 pigs.

Forestry. Gabon's equatorial forests covering 78% of the land area produced 1,225,000 cu. metres of *okoumé* in 1978.

Fisheries. The total catch (1975) amounted to 5,700 tonnes in the Atlantic and 400 tonnes in inland waters.

TRADE. In 1978 imports totalled 139,174m. francs CFA and exports 181,144m. francs CFA. France, UK, USA, the Netherlands and the Federal Republic of Germany are Gabon's principal trading partners. Petroleum made up 79% of exports.

Total trade between Gabon and the UK (British Department of Trade returns, in £1,000 sterling):

	1975	1976	1977	1978	1979	1980
Imports to UK	3,759	9,160	3,216	4,401	12,893	10,657
Exports and re-exports from UK	2,828	4,041	5,626	7,725	8,507	9,155

COMMUNICATIONS

Roads. There were (1978) 6,929 km of roads and (1976) there were 19,000 (8,000 goods) vehicles.

Railways. A 1,435-mm gauge (Transgabonais) railway is under construction from Owendo *via* N'Djole and Booué to Franceville with a projected branch from Booué to Bélinga. The first section, to N'Djole, was opened for traffic on 27 Dec. 1978.

Aviation. There are 5 airports at Port-Gentil, Franceville, Lambaréné, Moanda and Libreville.

Shipping. Owendo (near Libreville), Mayumba and Port-Gentil are the main ports. In 1975, 5·58m. tonnes were loaded and 468,000 tonnes unloaded at the ports. In 1978 there were 15 merchant vessels of 98,645 gross tons.

Post and Broadcasting. Telephones (1973), 11,000. In 1977 there were 8,600 television and 95,000 radio licences.

Cinemas. In 1971 there were 2 cinemas with a seating capacity of 1,700.

Newspapers. There are 2 daily newspapers published in Libreville; *Gabon-Matin* has a circulation of 18,000 and *L'Union* 15,000.

JUSTICE, RELIGION, EDUCATION AND WELFARE

Justice. There are *tribuneaux de grande instance* at Libreville, Port-Gentil, Lambaréné, Mouila, Oyem, Franceville and Koulamoutou, from which cases move progressively to a central Criminal Court, Court of Appeal and Supreme Court, all 3 located in Libreville.

Civil police number about 900.

Religion. It is estimated that about 35% of the population is Christian (mainly Roman Catholic), the majority of the balance following animist beliefs. There are about 2,000 Moslems.

Education. Education is compulsory between 6–16 years. In 1977–78 there were 792 primary schools with 140,632 pupils; 59 secondary schools with 21,614 students; 9 technical schools with 3,405 students; and 13 teacher-training schools with 1,323 students. The literacy rate was about 30% in 1973.

The Université Nationale du Gabon, founded in 1970 in Libreville, had (1978) 1,284 students; about 750 Gabonese students study abroad.

Health (1971). There were 96 doctors, 4 dentists, 15 pharmacists, 99 midwives and 823 nursing personnel. In 1975 there were 41 hospitals and 4,046 beds.

DIPLOMATIC REPRESENTATIVES

OF GABON IN GREAT BRITAIN
(48 Kensington Ct., London, W8)

Ambassador: Léon N'Dong.

OF GREAT BRITAIN IN GABON
(Bâtiment Sogame, Blvd de l'Indépendance, Libreville)

Ambassador: T. Grady, MBE.

OF GABON IN THE USA
(2034 20th St., NW, Washington, D.C., 20009)

Ambassador: José-Joseph Amiar.

OF THE USA IN GABON
(Blvd de la Mer, Libreville)

Ambassador: Arthur T. Tienken.

OF GABON TO THE UNITED NATIONS

Ambassador: (Vacant).

Books of Reference

Lasserre, G., *Libreville, la ville et sa région.* Paris, 1958
Remy, M., *Gabon Today.* Paris, 1977
Thiery, Y., and Delarozière, R., *Carte ethnique du Gabon.* Paris, 1945

THE GAMBIA

Capital: Banjul
Population: 592,000 (1980)
GNP per capita: US$230 (1978)

HISTORY. The Gambia was discovered by the early Portuguese navigators, but they made no settlement. During the 17th century various companies of merchants obtained trading charters and established a settlement on the river, which, from 1807, was controlled from Sierra Leone; in 1843 it was made an independent Crown Colony; in 1866 it formed part of the West African Settlements, but in Dec. 1888 it again became a separate Crown Colony. The boundaries were delimited only after 1890. The Gambia achieved full internal self-government on 4 Oct. 1963 and became an independent member of the Commonwealth on 18 Feb. 1965.

A referendum was held in Nov. 1965 to decide whether the Gambia was to become a republic. The referendum failed, as any alteration of the Constitution requires a two-thirds majority. A further referendum was held in April 1970 and 84,968 were cast in favour of a republic and 35,683 against. The Gambia became a republic within the Commonwealth on 24 April 1970.

AREA AND POPULATION. The Gambia is bounded west by the Atlantic ocean and on all other sides by Senegal. Area of Banjul (formerly Bathurst) and environs, 87·8 sq. km; population (census 1973) 39,476. In the provinces (area, 10,601·5 sq. km) the settled population (1971) was 275,469, not including temporary immigrants. Total population (census, April 1973), 493,197. Estimate (1980) 592,000. The largest tribe is the Mandingo (186,241), followed by the Fulas (79,994), Woloffs (69,291), Jolas (41,988) and Sarahulis (38,478). The capital is Banjul, and the other chief town is Kombo St Mary (38,934). There are 1,159 non-Africans.

CONSTITUTION AND GOVERNMENT. Parliament consists of the House of Representatives which consists of a Speaker, Deputy Speaker and 32 elected members; in addition, 4 Chiefs are elected by the Chiefs in Assembly; 3 nominated members are without votes and the Attorney-General is nominated and has a vote.

At the general election of 4–5 April 1977, the People's Progressive Party obtained 27, the National Convention Party 5, and the United Party 2 seats.

The Cabinet comprises the President and 11 Ministers from the Legislature.

The Government was in Feb. 1980 composed as follows:

President: Sir Dawda Kairaba Jawara.

Vice-President: Assan Musa Camara. *Attorney-General and Minister of Justice:* Alhaji Muhammadu Lamin Saho. *External Affairs:* Alhaji Lamin Kiti Jabang. *Finance and Trade:* Alhaji Muhammadu Cadi Cham. *Information and Tourism:* Hawsoon Ousman Semega-Janneh. *Labour, Health and Social Welfare:* Momadu Cherno Jallow. *Education, Youth and Sports:* Alhai Dembo Jatta. *Agriculture and Natural Resources:* Alhaji Jerreh Lang Bumari Daffeh. *Economic Planning and Industrial Development:* Saihou Sabally. *Local Government and Lands:* Landing Jallow Sonko. *Works and Communications:* Alhaji I. B. A. Kelepha-Samba.

National flag: Three horizontal stripes of red, blue, green, with the blue edged in white.

Local Administration. The Gambia is divided into 35 districts, each traditionally under a Chief, assisted by Village Heads and advisers. These districts are grouped into 6 Area Councils containing a majority of elected members, with the Chiefs of the district as *ex-officio* members. The city of Banjul is administered by a City Council.

INTERNATIONAL RELATIONS

Membership. The Gambia is a member of UN, OAU, the Commonwealth and is an ACP state of EEC.

499

ECONOMY

Budget. Revenue and expenditure for years ending 30 June are (in 1,000 dalasi):

	1974–75	1975–76	1976–77	1977–78	1978–79[1]
Revenue	29,702	37,139	65,515	66,870	66,132
Expenditure	32,731	39,964	60,219	70,031	69,425

[1] Estimate.

Currency. In July 1971 a new currency unit (*dalasi*) was introduced. It is divided into 100 *butut*. 4 *dalasi* = £ sterling; 1·8 *dalasi* = US$1 (March 1981).

Banking. There are 4 banks in the Gambia, the Standard Bank of West Africa Ltd, Central Bank of the Gambia, Commercial and Development Bank and la Banque Internationale pour le Commerce et l'Industrie (BICI). On 30 Nov. 1978 the government savings bank had about 36,000 depositors holding approximately 992,496 dalasi.

NATURAL RESOURCES

Minerals. Heavy minerals, including ilmenite, zircon and rutile, have been discovered (1m. tons up to 31 Dec. 1980) in Sanyang, Batakunku and Kartong areas.

Agriculture. Almost all commercial activity centres upon the marketing of groundnuts, which is the only export crop of financial significance. Cotton is also exported on a limited scale. Rice is of increasing importance for local consumption.

Livestock (1979): 280,000 cattle, 92,000 goats, 95,000 sheep, 9,000 pigs and 260,000 poultry.

Fisheries. Total catch (1975) 10,800 tonnes, of which 800 tonnes were from inland waters.

LABOUR. There are 4 large and 10 small trade unions.

TRADE. Chief items of imports are textiles and clothing, vehicles and machinery, metal goods and petroleum products.

Imports and exports, in 1,000 dalasi:

	1974–75	1975–76	1976–77	1977–78	1978–79
Imports	88,349	146,013	169,082	209,094	221,014
Exports	84,833	73,186	106,713	80,219	94,913

Chief items of exports are groundnuts, palm kernels, dried and smoked fish, hides and skins and groundnut oil.

Total trade between the Gambia and UK (British Department of Trade returns, in £1,000 sterling):

	1975	1976	1977	1978	1979	1980
Imports to UK	8,240	6,761	8,503	5,721	2,357	2,417
Exports and re-exports from UK	7,554	10,865	12,362	17,332	13,953	17,792

TOURISM. In 1979–80, 24,821 tourists visited the Gambia.

COMMUNICATIONS

Roads. There are 2,990 km of motorable roads, of which 1,718 km rank as all-weather roads including 306 km of bituminous surface and 531 km of laterite gravel. Number of licensed motor vehicles (1974–75): 11,765 private cars, 5,777 commercial vehicles, 240 buses and coaches, 410 tractors and 143 trailers.

Aviation. The Gambia is served by Air Mali, British Caledonian Airways, Ghana Airways and Nigeria Airways. Air movements at Yundum Airport in 1975 numbered 2,756, including scheduled services.

Shipping. The chief port, Banjul, handled 303 ships of 686,300 DWT in 1975–76. The first phase of development of the port was completed in 1974; a new 400 ft berth will take one large vessel of up to 36 ft draught. Internal communication is maintained by steamers and launches.

The Gambia River Development Organization was founded in 1978 as a joint project with Senegal to develop the river and its basin.

Post and Broadcasting. There are several post offices and agencies; postal facilities are also afforded to all river towns by means of a travelling post office on the government river mail-steamers. Banjul is connected with St Vincent (Cape Verde islands) and with Sierra Leone by cable. Banjul is in wireless communication with London and the main centres up river. A trans-Gambia telephone system provides direct communications with Dakar and Ziguinchor. Telephones numbered 2,779 in Jan. 1978. A telex service was introduced in 1968.

Radio Gambia, a government station, broadcasts for about 12 hours a day; Radio Syd, a commercial station, broadcasts for 20 hours. Number of radio receivers (1976, estimate), 100,000.

Cinemas. In 1979 there were 10 cinemas.

Newspapers. There is an official (three times weekly) and several duplicated news-sheets.

JUSTICE, RELIGION, EDUCATION AND WELFARE

Justice. Justice is administered by a Supreme Court consisting of a chief justice and puisne judges. It has unlimited jurisdiction but there is a Court of Appeal. Two magistrates' courts and divisional courts are supplemented by a system of travelling magistrates. There are also Moslem courts, group tribunals dealing with cases concerned with customs and traditions, and one juvenile court.

Religion. About 70% of the population is Moslem. Banjul is the seat of an Anglican and a Roman Catholic bishop. There are some Methodist missions. Some sections of the population retain their original animist beliefs.

Education (1979–80). There were 133 primary schools (1,371 teachers, 37,644 pupils), 17 secondary technical schools (260 teachers, 5,274 pupils), 7 senior secondary schools (179 teachers, 3,040 pupils) and 1 post-secondary school; total number of teachers, 1,810. Brihama College, which is to replace Yundum College as a teacher-training and vocational centre, opened for agricultural students in Sept. 1979.

Health. In 1980 there were 43 government doctors, 23 private doctors and about 635 hospital beds.

DIPLOMATIC REPRESENTATIVES

OF THE GAMBIA IN GREAT BRITAIN (60 Ennismore Gdns., London, SW7)

High Commissioner: Abdullah Mamadu Kalifa Bojang (accredited 4 Nov. 1980).

OF GREAT BRITAIN IN THE GAMBIA (48 Atlantic Rd., Fajara, Banjul)

High Commissioner: E. N. Smith, CMG.

OF THE GAMBIA IN THE USA AND TO UN (2550 M St., NW, Washington, D.C., 20037)

Ambassador: Ousman A. Sallah.

OF THE USA IN THE GAMBIA (16 Buckle St., Banjul)

Ambassador: Larry G. Piper.

Books of Reference

The Gambia in Brief. Gambia Information Services, Banjul, 1979
The Gambia Independence Act, 1964
The Gambia Independence Order, 1965
The Gambia since Independence 1965–1980. Banjul, 1980
Gailey, Jr, H. A., *A History of the Gambia.* London, 1964
Rice, B., *Enter Gambia.* Sydney, 1968

GERMANY

POST-WAR HISTORY. Since the unconditional surrender of the German armed forces on 8 May 1945 there has been no central authority whose writ runs in the whole of Germany. Consequently no peace treaty has been signed with a government representing the whole of Germany, and the country is virtually partitioned between the Federal Republic of Germany and the German Democratic Republic.

By the Berlin Declaration of 5 June 1945 the governments of the USA, the UK, the USSR and France assumed supreme authority over Germany. Each of the 4 signatories was given a zone of occupation, in which the supreme power was to be exercised by the C.-in-C. in that zone (*see* map in THE STATESMAN'S YEAR-BOOK, 1947). Jointly these 4 Cs.-in-C. constituted the Allied Control Council in Berlin, which was to be competent in all 'matters affecting Germany as a whole'. The territory of Greater Berlin, divided into 4 sectors, was to be governed as an entity by the 4 occupying powers.

At the Potsdam Conference (17 July–2 Aug. 1945) the northern part of the Province of East Prussia, including its capital Königsberg (renamed Kaliningrad), was transferred to the Soviet Union, pending final ratification by a peace treaty; and it was agreed that, pending the final peace settlement, Poland should administer those parts of Germany lying east of a line running from the Baltic Sea immediately west of Swinemünde along the river Oder to its confluence with the Western Neisse and thence along the Western Neisse to the Czechoslovak frontier.

The agreements between the war-time allies concerning the occupation zones (12 Sept. 1944) and control of Germany (1 May 1945) were repudiated by the USSR on 27 Nov. 1958.

A Treaty was signed in East Berlin between the German Democratic Republic and the Federal Republic of Germany on 21 Dec. 1972 agreeing the basis of relations between the two countries.

GERMAN DEMOCRATIC REPUBLIC

Capital: Berlin (East)
Population: 16·7m. (1979)
GNP per capita: US$5,660 (1978)

Deutsche Demokratische Republik

HISTORY. For the immediate post-war history *see* p. 502.

AREA AND POPULATION. Area and population, 30 June 1979 (in 1,000):

Districts	Area in sq. km	Male	Female	Total	Per sq. km
Berlin (East)	403	520·2	613·6	1,133·9	2,814
Cottbus	8,262	420·5	461·0	881·6	107
Dresden	6,738	834·9	979·8	1,814·7	269
Erfurt	7,349	581·7	655·1	1,236·7	168
Frankfurt	7,186	335·5	364·3	699·8	97
Gera	4,004	345·7	393·2	739·0	185
Halle	8,771	867·7	978·1	1,845·9	210
Karl-Marx-Stadt	6,009	892·5	1,049·0	1,941·5	323
Leipzig	4,966	654·3	766·7	1,421·0	286
Magdeburg	11,525	597·3	675·9	1,273·1	110
Neubrandenburg	10,794	299·4	323·3	622·7	58
Potsdam	12,568	526·2	590·3	1,116·4	89
Rostock	7,074	421·6	460·4	882·0	125
Schwerin	8,672	279·3	309·7	589·0	68
Suhl	3,856	258·3	289·1	547·4	142
German Democratic Republic	*108,177*	*7,835·0*	*8,909·7*	*16,744·7*	*155*

An agreement proclaiming the Oder–Neisse line the permanent frontier between Germany and Poland was concluded between the German Democratic Republic and Poland on 6 July 1950. A protocol on the delimitation of the frontier was signed on 27 Jan. 1951.

Resident population of the principal towns as at 30 June 1979:

Berlin (East), capital	1,133,854	Halle	232,746	Gera	121,980
Leipzig	563,912	Rostock	226,667	Schwerin	117,406
Dresden	515,387	Erfurt	209,344	Cottbus	108,892
Karl-Marx-Stadt	314,951	Potsdam	126,933	Jena	102,538
Magdeburg	283,548	Zwickau	123,475	Dessau	101,290

Vital statistics:

	Live births	Marriages	Divorces	Deaths
1976	195,483	144,590	44,803	233,733
1977	223,152	147,402	43,137	226,233
1978	232,151	141,063	43,296	232,332
1979[1]	235,233	136,884	44,745	232,805

[1] Preliminary.

Crude birth rate per 1,000 population was 10·6 in 1974; 10·8 in 1975; 11·6 in 1976; 13·3 in 1977; 13·9 in 1978; 14 in 1979; marriage rate, 8·2 in 1974; 8·4 in 1975; 8·6 in 1976; 8·8 in 1977; 8·4 in 1978; 8·2 in 1979; death rate, 13·5 in 1974; 14·3 in 1975; 13·9 in 1976; 13·5 in 1977; 13·9 in 1978; 13·9 in 1979; infantile mortality per 100 live births, 1·6 in 1974 and 1975; 1·4 in 1976; 1·3 in 1977, 1978 and 1979.

CONSTITUTION AND GOVERNMENT. Upon the establishment of the Federal Republic of Germany, the People's Council of the Soviet-occupied zone, appointed in 1948, was converted into a provisional People's Chamber.

On 7 Oct. 1949 the provisional People's Chamber enacted a constitution of the 'German Democratic Republic'.

In July 1952 the 5 Länder of Mecklenburg, Saxony-Anhalt, Brandenburg, Saxony and Thuringia were replaced by 14 districts (*Bezirke*).

A new 'socialist constitution' was approved by a referendum on 6 April 1968, when 94·54% of the electorate voted for the constitution; it came into force on 8 April 1968. The People's Chamber, of 500 deputies, is 'the supreme organ of state power'; it elects the Council of State, the Council of Ministers, the National Defence Council and the judges of the Supreme Court.

Council of State. After the death of President Wilhelm Pieck (7 Sept. 1960), the People's Chamber on 12 Sept. 1960 abolished the office of president and elected instead a council of state. This consists of a chairman, 6 deputy chairmen, 18 members and a secretary. The Council is authorized to issue decisions and to interpret existing laws. The Chairman of the Council of State represents the GDR in international law. *Chairman:* Erich Honecker.

On 13 Oct. 1978 the People's Chamber passed a 'law for the defence of the GDR'; the People's Chamber is authorized to declare a 'state of defence'.

At the elections held on 16 Oct. 1976, the list of the National Front received 99·86% of the valid votes.

The cabinet was, in Dec. 1978, composed as follows:

Chairman: Willi Stoph.

First Deputy Chairmen: Alfred Neumann, Werner Krolikowski.

Deputy Chairmen: Günther Kleiber, Wolfgang Rauchfuss, Gerhard Schürer, Dr Gerhard Weiss, Dr Herbert Weiz, Manfred Flegel, Hans-Joachin Heusinger, Dr Hans Reichelt, Rudolph Schulze.

Members of the Presidium of the Council of Ministers: All members of the cabinet and Heinz Kuhrig, Walter Halbritter, Horst Sölle.

Considerable political power is exercised by the Politburo of the Socialist Unity Party (SUP).

National flag: Black, red, golden (horizontal); in the centre, on both sides, the coat of arms showing a hammer and compass with a wreath of grain entwined with a black, red and golden ribbon.

National hymn: Auferstanden aus Ruinen (words by Johannes R. Becher, tune by Hanns Eisler).

East Berlin ('Democratic Berlin') is the capital of the German Democratic Republic. *Head of the Administration (Magistrat):* Erhard Krack.

DEFENCE. On 18 Jan. 1956 the Diet passed laws for the establishment of a 'national people's army' and a defence ministry. A 12-member defence council, under the chairmanship of E. Honecker, General Secretary of the Central Committee, was set up on 10 Feb. 1960.

The 'law for the defence of the GDR', of 20 Sept. 1960, makes military service (in case of emergency) and civil defence compulsory for all citizens.

Conscription for men between 18 and 25 years was introduced on 24 Jan. 1962 (18 months' service in the army, 2 years in the navy and air force).

Twenty Soviet divisions of about 258,000 men with about 1,000 heavy tanks and 6,000 armoured vehicles are stationed in the German Democratic Republic, chiefly along the Polish border.

Army. The Army, set up on 1 March 1956, is organized in 2 army corps, including 2 armoured divisions and 4 motorized infantry divisions. Operationally these divisions are subordinate to the Soviet formations of the Warsaw Pact forces. They are armed with about 2,600 tanks (mostly Soviet T-54, T-55 and T-62), 216 self-propelled guns and ground-to-air 'Guideline' missiles. The Border Police was incorporated in the Army in Sept. 1961. Total army strength was (1980) 108,000 all ranks.

Police. The Police force (*Volkspolizei*) numbered 25,000 security and 46,500 border troops. There are also 500,000 militiamen organized in combat groups. The militia receive military instruction from the People's Police.

Navy. The 'People's Navy' includes 2 frigates, 12 missile boats, 60 torpedo boats, 13 patrol vessels, 50 coastal minesweepers, 3 intelligence ships, 18 coastguard boats, 16 tank landing ships, 4 oilers, 9 training ships (including 1 fleet minesweeper), 4 supply ships, 5 survey vessels, 19 small survey craft, 17 buoy tenders, 4 diving vessels, 1 cable layer, 2 torpedo recovery craft, 3 icebreakers, 30 auxiliary ships and service craft and 13 tugs. Personnel in 1981 totalled 17,800 officers and men, including the Coastal Frontier Guards (*Grenzbrigade Kuste*).

Air Force. The *ex*-'air-police', set up in Nov. 1950, had in 1981 a strength of about 38,000 officers and men and 300 combat aircraft. Two fighter divisions consist respectively of 2 and 4 regiments (each with at least 3 squadrons of 12 aircraft), plus a fighter training division. Operational units are equipped mainly with MiG-21 supersonic day and all-weather interceptors and reconnaissance fighters; delivery of variable-geometry MiG-23 fighters began in 1979. About 40 MiG-17 fighters remain in service, mainly for training. Mi-24 gunship helicopters have been delivered to Germany. Other units include a regiment of Mi-2, Mi-4 and Mi-8 helicopters, a regiment of Il-14, An-24/26, Tu-124 and Tu-134 transports and a Flight Training Division with Yak-18, Trener, L-29 Delfin, L-39 Albatros, MiG-15UTI and MiG-21U training aircraft. 'Guideline' and 'Goa' surface-to-air missile units are operational.

INTERNATIONAL RELATIONS

Membership. The German Democratic Republic is a member of UN and Comecon.

ECONOMY

Budget. The budget of the German Democratic Republic was as follows (in M 1m.) for calendar years:

	1974	1975	1976	1977	1978	1979
Revenue	104,645	114,662	117,588	124,543	132,612	140,633
Expenditure	103,292	114,160	117,128	124,103	132,103	140,223

Of the 1979 expenditures, 48,578m. was earmarked for health and social services, education and *Kultur*.

Currency. The circulating Reichsmark notes were in June 1948 exchanged for 'Deutsche Mark' (East), renamed 'Mark of the German Bank of Issue' (MDN) from 1 Aug. 1964 and further renamed 'the Mark of the GDR' (M) from 1967. The circulation of notes and coins at 31 Dec. 1979 was M 12,372m. Since 1 Nov. 1953 the M currency has been based on gold, the gold content of the M being fixed at 0·399902 gramme.

Banking. The most important banking institutions of the GDR are the Staatsbank der DDR Berlin, which is the bank of issue, and the Industrie- und Handelsbank der DDR. Savings, as at 31 Dec. 1979, totalled M 96,958m.

Weights and Measures. The metric system is in force.

ENERGY AND NATURAL RESOURCES

Electricity. Generation of electric power (in 1m. kwh.): 1950, 19,466; 1960, 40,305; 1970, 67,650; 1973, 76,908; 1974, 80,286; 1975, 84,505; 1976, 89,150; 1977, 91,996; 1978, 95,963; 1979, 96,843.

Minerals. In the production of lignite, the German Democratic Republic takes first place in world output. Rare metals, such as uranium, cobalt, bismuth, arsenic and antimony, are being exploited in the western Erzgebirge and eastern Thuringia.

The principal minerals raised are as follows (in 1,000 tonnes):

	1976	1977	1978	1979		1976	1977	1978	1979
Coal	457	349	85	...	Iron ore	60	63	70	...
Lignite	246,897	253,705	253,264	256,000	Potash	3,161	3,229	3,323	3,395

Agriculture. In 1979 the arable land was 4,767,300 hectares; meadows and pastures, 1,239,200 hectares; forests, 2,951,000 hectares. Since 1945, the estates of Junkers, war criminals and leading Nazis have been sequestrated; 3·1m. hectares have been distributed among farmers. In 1979 there were 3,916 collective farms of 4·7m.

hectares of land independently cultivated and 700,000 hectares of land given for co-operative cultivation and 474 state farms of 392,800 hectares.

The yield of the main crops in 1979 was as follows (in 1,000 tonnes): Potatoes, 12,243; sugar-beet, 6,695; barley, 3,323; wheat, 3,116; rye, 1,830; oats, 532.

Livestock (in 1,000) in 1979: Cattle, 5,596 (including 2,125 milch cows); pigs, 12,132; sheep, 1,979; goats (1978), 29; horses (1978), 66; laying hens, 26,500.

Fisheries. Total catch (1978) 200,633 tonnes. Inland catch (1979) was 14,936 tonnes, of which 7,715 tonnes was carp.

INDUSTRY AND TRADE

Industry. Industry produced about 61% of the national income in 1979; the nationally owned and co-operative undertakings were responsible for 97·6% of the net product. The percentage of privately owned enterprises was 32·8 in 1950 and 2·4 in 1978.

There were, at 31 Dec. 1979, 5,707 industrial establishments with 3,144,896 employees.

Production of iron and steel (in 1,000 tonnes):

	1974	1975	1976	1977	1978	1979
Crude steel	6,165	6,472	6,732	6,850	6,976	7,023
Pig-iron	2,280	2,455	2,528	2,628	2,560	...
Rolled steel	4,099	4,281	4,593	4,802	5,002	5,100

Leading chemical products in 1979 were (in 1,000 tonnes): Sulphuric acid, 952; nitrogen fertilizers, 875; calcined soda, 860; caustic soda, 548; other industrial products: cement, 12,273; passenger cars (no.), 171,000; television receivers (no.), 584,000; shoes, 78m. pairs; plastics and synthetic resins, 762.

The 340-km pipeline from Schwedt on the Oder to Leuna near Halle was completed in Jan. 1967; it carried Soviet oil direct to the industrial centre of the GDR. Total pipeline length within GDR (1979) 1,301 km.

Commerce. Total trade was as follows (in 1m. Valuta-Mark):

	Total			Total	
	Imports	Exports		Imports	Exports
1970	39,597	15,485	1977	91,726	32,456
1975	74,394	26,539	1978	96,879	34,907
1976	85,457	27,785			

Total trade between the German Democratic Republic and UK (British Department of Trade returns, in £1,000 sterling):

	1975	1976	1977	1978	1979	1980
Imports to UK	38,826	60,299	95,446	88,392	111,705	88,127
Exports and re-exports from UK	32,495	44,811	54,440	47,466	58,162	94,124

COMMUNICATIONS

Roads. There were, in 1979, 47,494 km of classified roads. Road traffic amounted to 21,567m. ton-km of goods and 22,801m. passenger-km (by buses). Motor vehicles included, 2,532,941 passenger cars, 231,228 lorries and 1·3m. motor cycles.

Railways. There were, in 1979, 14,164 km of railway line, of which 1,621 km were electrified. Traffic amounted to 54,375m. ton-km of goods and 22,284m. passenger-km.

Aviation. Interflug operates services between Berlin and Prague, Warsaw, Budapest, Bucharest, Moscow, Sofia, Belgrade, Tirana, Cairo, Baghdad, Beirut and other capitals. Passengers carried (1979), 1,242,600; freight, 28,758 tonnes.

Shipping. The port of Rostock is being reconstructed and enlarged so as to absorb the sea-going traffic of the German Democratic Republic and the Czechoslovak hinterland. In 1979 navigable inland waterways had a length of 2,302 km; they handled 1,933m. ton-km of goods. The state-owned merchant fleet had, in 1979, 194 vessels of 1,308,345 BRT.

Post and Broadcasting. In 1978 there were 11,999 post offices and agencies and 2,967,619 telephone subscribers. *Staatliches Kommittee für Rundfunk*, the governmental broadcasting station, broadcasts 4 programmes on long-, medium- and short-waves, and on FM. The foreign service is broadcast in 11 languages on medium- and short-waves, using the name Radio Berlin International. The transmitters are located at Königswusterhausen, Leipzig and Nauen. Radio Volga transmits on long-waves from Burg and broadcasts in Russian for the Soviet Armed Forces in Germany. More than 80% of the programmes are relays from Radio Moscow. Radio Moscow is using relay transmitters on medium-waves at Leipzig for programmes in German. *Deutsche Freiheitssender 904* and *Deutsche Soldatensender* are clandestine stations claiming to be operating from the Federal Republic although they are located not far from Burg. *Fernsehen der DDR* broadcasts 2 TV programmes, of which the second broadcasts in colour, using SECAM-system. Number of wireless licences, 6·29m.; TV licences, 5·63m.

Cinemas (1979). There were 837 cinemas with a seating capacity of 274,544.

Newspapers (1978). There were 39 daily newspapers with a combined circulation of 7·1m.

RELIGION, EDUCATION AND WELFARE

Religion. According to the census of 1950, 80·5% of the population were Protestants and 11% were Roman Catholics.

Education. There are 2 types of schools: (*a*) the General polytechnical secondary schools, with 10 grades (the former elementary and middle schools), numbering (1979) 5,073 with 2,314,201 pupils; (*b*) the Extended polytechnical secondary schools, with the 11th and 12th grades, numbering (1979) 282 with 46,454 pupils.

In addition there were (1979), 981 vocational schools (*Berufsschulen*) with 16,259 teachers and 462,200 pupils and 236 technical schools with 169,608 pupils. There were also 53 universities and other high schools with 129,055 students, including 62,163 women.

Health. In 1979, 559 (1978) hospitals had 176,300 beds. There were 560 polyclinics each with at least 6 special branches. There were 33,089 physicians and 9,289 dentists.

Social Welfare. Expenditure for social welfare in state budget, M 3,335m., and social insurance, M 27,375m. in 1979.

DIPLOMATIC REPRESENTATIVES

OF THE GERMAN DEMOCRATIC REPUBLIC IN GREAT BRITAIN
(34 Belgrave Sq., London, SW1X 8QB)

Ambassador: Martin Bierbach.

OF GREAT BRITAIN IN THE GERMAN DEMOCRATIC REPUBLIC
(108 Berlin, Unter den Linden 32/34)

Ambassador: P. M. Forster, CMG.

OF THE GERMAN DEMOCRATIC REPUBLIC IN THE USA
(1717 Massachusetts Ave., NW, Washington, D.C. 20036)

Ambassador: Dr Horst Grunert.

OF THE USA IN THE GERMAN DEMOCRATIC REPUBLIC
(108 Berlin, Neustädtische Kirchstrasse 4-5)

Ambassador: Herbert S. Okun.

OF THE GERMAN DEMOCRATIC REPUBLIC
TO THE UNITED NATIONS

Ambassador: Peter Florin.

Books of Reference

Statistical Information: The central statistical agency is the Staatliche Zentralverwaltung für Statistik (Hans-Beimler-Str. 70–72, 102, Berlin).

The Zentralverwaltung publishes: *Statistisches Jahrbuch der Deutschen Demokratischen Republik* (from 1956).—*Statistisches Taschenbuch der DDR* (annual, from 1959; also Arabic, English, French, Russian, Spanish editions).—*Statistische Praxis* (from 1946).
Deutsche Demokratische Republik, Handbuch. Leipzig, 1979
Jahrbuch der Deutschen Demokratischen Republik, ed. Institut für Zeitgeschichte (latest issue, 1961).

Biermann, W., *Demokratiserung in der DDR?* Cologne, 1978
Childs, D., *East Germany.* London, 1969
Jacobsen, H.-A., *Drei Jahrzehnte Aussenpolitik der DDR.* Munich, 1979
Krisch, H., *German Politics under Soviet Occupation.* New York and London, 1974
Legters, L. H., *The German Democratic Republic: A Developed Socialist Society.* Boulder, 1978

National Library: Deutsche Bücherei, Leipzig C.1. *Director:* Helmut Rötzsch.—Deutsche Staatsbibliothek, Berlin. *Director:* Professor H. Kunze.

FEDERAL REPUBLIC OF GERMANY

Capital: Bonn
Population: 61·4m. (1979)
GNP per capita: US$9,600 (1978)

Bundesrepublik Deutschland

HISTORY. The Federal Republic of Germany became a sovereign independent country on 5 May 1955 and is a member of EEC, the Council of Europe, Western European Union, NATO, the European Coal and Steel Community, Euratom, the European Monetary Agreement and the Agencies of the UN.

In June 1948 USA, UK and France agreed on a central government for the 3 western zones. An Occupation Statute, which came into force on 31 Sept. 1949, reduced the responsibilities of the occupation authorities. Formally, the Federal Republic of Germany came into existence on 21 Sept. 1949. The Petersberg Agreement of 22 Nov. 1949 freed the Federal Republic of numerous restrictions of the Occupation Statute. In 1951 USA, UK and France as well as other states terminated the state of war with Germany; the Soviet Union followed on 25 Jan. 1955. On 5 May 1955 the High Commissioners of USA, UK and France signed a proclamation revoking the Occupation Statute. On the same day, the Paris and London treaties, signed in Oct. 1954, came into force and established the sovereignty of the Federal Republic of Germany.

AREA AND POPULATION. In April 1949 some minor frontier rectifications were carried out in favour of the Netherlands (68 sq. km), Belgium (18 sq. km), Luxembourg (6 sq. km) and France (7 sq. km), subject to a final peace settlement. Belgium (1956) and the Netherlands (1963) returned most of this territory to Germany.

Area and estimated population as at 31 Dec. 1979:

| | Area in | Population | | | Per |
Länder	sq. km	Male	Female	Total	sq. km
Schleswig-Holstein	15,710	1,250,100	1,348,900	2,599,000	165
Hamburg	755	768,900	884,100	1,653,000	2,190
Lower Saxony	47,424	3,464,900	3,769,100	7,234,000	153
Bremen	404	326,500	368,700	695,100	1,722
North Rhine-Westphalia	34,069	8,122,600	8,894,400	17,017,100	499
Hessen	21,114	2,679,200	2,896,900	5,576,100	264
Rhineland-Palatinate	19,839	1,734,200	1,899,000	3,633,200	183
Baden-Württemberg	35,752	4,420,300	4,769,700	9,190,100	257
Bavaria	70,546	5,192,600	5,678,400	10,871,000	154
Saarland	2,574	505,900	562,700	1,068,600	415
Berlin (West)	480	852,000	1,050,300	1,902,300	3,961
Federal Republic	*248,667*[1]	*29,317,100*	*32,122,300*	*61,439,300*	*247*

[1] 96,005 sq. miles.

Vital statistics for calendar years:

	Marriages	Live births	Of these illegitimate	Deaths	Divorces
1976	365,728	602,851	38,251	733,140	108,258
1977	358,487	582,344	37,649	704,922	74,658[1]
1978	328,215	576,468	40,141	723,218	32,462[1]
1979	344,822	581,984	41,504	711,732	...

[1] From 1 July 1977, pursuant to the First Law on the Reform of Marriage and Family 1976.

The annual rate of the population increase or decrease (including migration) was −0·2% in 1974; −0·6% in 1975; −0·3% in 1976; −0·2% in 1977; −0·1% in 1978; +0·2% in 1979.

Crude birth rate in 1979 was 9·5 per 1,000 population; marriage rate, 5·6; death rate, 11·6; infantile mortality, 1·5 per 100 live births.

Migrants from Eastern Germany to the Federal Republic, including West Berlin, totalled about 2,022,000 between 1955 and 1961. The East German Government tried to stop the outflow by erecting a concrete wall which later became a heavily fortified barrier along the border in Berlin on 13 Aug. 1961; despite the Berlin wall, the figures registered for persons moving from Eastern Germany and East Berlin into the Federal Republic were 20,700 in 1970, 19,900 in 1971, 19,700 in 1972, 17,300 in 1973, 16,200 in 1974, 20,300 in 1975, 17,100 in 1976, 13,900 in 1977, 14,400 in 1978 and 15,400 in 1979; most of them are older people with permission to emigrate. Migrants from the Federal Republic to Eastern Germany totalled about 279,000 between 1955 and 1961, 2,500 in 1969, 2,100 in 1970, 1,900 in 1971, 1,800 in 1972, 1,700 in 1973, 1,500 in 1974, 1,400 in 1975, 1,300 in 1976, 1,200 in 1977, 1,200 in 1978 and 1,300 in 1979.

The resident population of the principal towns was estimated as follows on 31 Dec. 1979:

Town	Land	Population	Town	Land	Population
Berlin (West)	Berlin (West)	1,902,250	Herne	N. Rhine-Westph.	183,065
Hamburg	Hamburg	1,653,043	Mülheim a.d.		
München	Bavaria	1,299,693	Ruhr	N. Rhine-Westph.	182,465
Köln	N. Rhine-Westph.	976,136	Freiburg im		
Essen	N. Rhine-Westph.	652,501	Breisgau	Baden-Württ.	174,121
Frankfurt am			Hamm	N. Rhine-Westph.	171,595
Main	Hessen	628,203	Solingen	N. Rhine-Westph.	166,654
Dortmund	N. Rhine-Westph.	609,954	Leverkusen	N. Rhine-Westph.	161,453
Düsseldorf	N. Rhine-Westph.	594,770	Ludwigshafen		
Stuttgart	Baden-Württ.	581,989	am Rhein	Rhinel.-Pal.	160,479
Duisburg	N. Rhine-Westph.	559,066	Osnabrück	Lower Saxony	158,150
Bremen	Bremen	556,128	Neuss	N. Rhine-Westph.	149,333
Hannover	Lower Saxony	535,854	Bremerhaven	Bremen	138,987
Nürnberg	Bavaria	484,184	Darmstadt	Hessen	138,661
Bochum	N. Rhine-Westph.	402,988	Oldenburg	Lower Saxony	136,155
Wuppertal	N. Rhine-Westph.	394,605	Regensburg	Bavaria	132,399
Bielefeld	N. Rhine-Westph.	312,357	Remscheid	N. Rhine-Westph.	129,507
Gelsenkirchen	N. Rhine-Westph.	306,323	Heidelberg	Baden-Württ.	128,773
Mannheim	Baden-Württ.	303,247	Göttingen	Lower Saxony	128,118
Bonn	N. Rhine-Westph.	286,184	Würzburg	Bavaria	127,370
Wiesbaden	Hessen	273,267	Wolfsburg	Lower Saxony	126,942
Karlsruhe	Baden-Württ.	271,417	Recklinghausen	N. Rhine-Westph.	119,472
Münster			Bottrop	N. Rhine-Westph.	114,510
(Westf.)	N. Rhine-Westph.	267,478	Koblenz	Rhinel.-Pal.	113,795
Braunschweig	Lower Saxony	261,669	Salzgitter	Lower Saxony	113,427
Mönchenglad-			Siegen	N. Rhine-Westph.	112,740
bach	N. Rhine-Westph.	258,001	Heilbronn	Baden-Württ.	111,426
Kiel	Schleswig-Holstein	250,750	Offenbach am		
Augsburg	Bavaria	245,940	Main	Hessen	111,310
Aachen	N. Rhine-Westph.	242,971	Paderborn	N. Rhine-Westph.	109,218
Oberhausen	N. Rhine-Westph.	229,613	Pforzheim	Baden-Württ.	106,677
Krefeld	N. Rhine-Westph.	222,750	Witten	N. Rhine-Westph.	106,185
Lübeck	Schleswig-Holstein	222,120	Hildesheim	Lower Saxony	102,512
Hagen	N. Rhine-Westph.	220,676	Bergisch		
Kassel	Hessen	196,224	Gladbach	N. Rhine-Westph.	101,007
Saarbrücken	Saarland	194,452	Erlangen	Bavaria	100,760
Mainz	Rhinel.-Pal.	186,200	Moers	N. Rhine-Westph.	100,110

CONSTITUTION. The Constituent Assembly (known as the 'Parliamentary Council') met in Bonn on 1 Sept. 1948, and worked out a Basic Law which was approved by a two-thirds majority of the parliaments of the participating Länder and came into force on 23 May 1949.

The Basic Law (*Grundgesetz*) consists of a preamble and 146 articles. The first section deals with the basic rights which are legally binding for legislation, administration and jurisdiction.

The Federal Republic of Germany is a democratic and social federal state. For the time being the Basic Law applies to the Länder Baden-Württemberg, Bavaria, Bremen, Greater Berlin (temporarily suspended), Hamburg, Hessen, Lower Saxony, North Rhine-Westphalia, Rhineland-Palatinate, Saarland and Schleswig-Holstein. The Basic Law decrees that the general rules of international law form part of the federal law. The constitutions of the Länder must conform to the principles of a republican, democratic and social state based on the rule of law. Executive power is vested in the Länder, unless the Basic Law prescribes or permits otherwise. Federal law supersedes Land law.

The organs of the Federal Republic are:

The Federal Diet (*Bundestag*), elected in universal, direct, free, equal and secret elections, for a term of 4 years.

The Federal Council (*Bundesrat*), consisting of members of the governments of the Länder. Each Land has at least 3 votes. Länder with more than 2m. inhabitants have 4, Länder with more than 6m. inhabitants have 5 votes.

The Federal President (*Bundespräsident*) is elected by the Federal Assembly for a term of 5 years and represents the Federal Republic in international relations. Re-election is admissible only once. The Federal Assembly (which meets only for the election of the Federal President) consists of the members of the Federal Diet and an equal number of members elected by the popular representative bodies of the Länder according to a particular system of semi-proportional representation.

The Federal Government consists of the Federal Chancellor, elected by the Federal Diet on the proposal of the Federal President, and the Federal Ministers, who are appointed and dismissed by the Federal President upon the proposal of the Federal Chancellor.

The Federal Republic has exclusive legislation on: (1) foreign affairs; (2) federal citizenship; (3) freedom of movement, passports, immigration and emigration, and extradition; (4) currency, money and coinage, weights and measures, and regulation of time and calendar; (5) customs, commercial and navigation agreements, traffic in goods and payments with foreign countries, including customs and frontier protection; (6) federal railways and air traffic; (7) post and telecommunications; (8) the legal status of persons in the employment of the Federation and of public law corporations under direct supervision of the Federal Government; (9) trade marks, copyright and publishing rights; (10) co-operation of the Federal Republic and the Länder in the criminal police and in matters concerning the protection of the constitution, the establishment of a Federal Office of Criminal Police, as well as the combating of international crime; (11) federal statistics.

For concurrent legislation in which the Länder have legislative rights if and as far as the Federal Republic does not exercise its legislative powers, *see* THE STATESMAN'S YEAR-BOOK, 1956, p. 1038.

Federal laws are passed by the Federal Diet and after their adoption submitted to the Federal Council, which has a limited veto. The Basic Law may be amended only upon the approval of two-thirds of the members of the Federal Diet and two-thirds of the votes of the Federal Council.

The foreign service, federal finance, railways, postal services, waterways and shipping are under direct federal administration.

In the field of finance the Federal Republic has exclusive legislation on customs and financial monopolies and concurrent legislation on: (1) excise taxes and taxes on transactions, in particular, taxes on real-estate acquisition, incremented value and on fire protection; (2) taxes on income, property, inheritance and donations; (3) real estate, industrial and trade taxes, with the exception of the determining of the tax rates.

Customs, the yield of monopolies, excise taxes with the exception of the beer tax, the transportation tax, the turnover tax and property dues serving non-recurrent purposes accrue to the Federal Republic. The Federal Republic can, by federal law, claim part of the income and corporation taxes to cover its expenditures not covered by other revenues. Financial jurisdiction is uniformly regulated by federal legislation.

National flag: Three horizontal stripes of black, red, gold.

National anthem: Einigkeit und Recht und Freiheit (words by H. Hoffmann, 1841; tune by J. Haydn, 1797).

Mangoldt, H., *Das Bonner Grundgesetz* (*Kommentar*). 2nd ed. Berlin, 1960
Maunz, Th., *Deutsches Staatsrecht*. 12th ed. Munich, 1963
Schäfer, H., *Der Bundesrat*. Cologne, 1955

GOVERNMENT. The *Federal Diet*, elected on 5 Oct. 1980, is composed of 496 members. In addition, there are 22 members for Berlin (11 CDU, 10 SPD, 1 FDP), who, however, have no vote.

State of the parties: Social Democrats (SPD), 218 (1976: 214); Christian Democrats (CDU; CSU), 226 (243); Free Democrats (FDP), 53 (39); other parties failed to obtain 5% of the votes or to elect a representative in a constituency, and therefore returned no members.

Bonn on the Rhine is the capital of the Federal Republic.

Federal President: Karl Castens (elected 1 July 1979).

The Cabinet, a coalition of Social Democrats and Free Democrats, in March 1981, was as follows:

Chancellor: Helmut Schmidt (SPD).
Deputy Chancellor, Minister of Foreign Affairs: Hans-Dietrich Genscher (FDP).
Interior: Gerhard Baum (FDP).
Justice: Dr Jürgen Schmude (SPD).
Finance: Hans Matthöfer (SPD).
Economics: Dr Otto Graf Lambsdorff (FDP).
Food, Agriculture and Forests: Josef Ertl (FDP).
Labour and Social Affairs: Dr Herbert Ehrenberg (SPD).
Defence: Dr Hans Apel (SPD).
Family Affairs: Antje Huber (SPD).
Transport: Dr Volker Hauff (SPD).
Posts and Telecommunications: Kurt Gscheidle (SPD).
State and Town Planning, and Housing: Dr Dieter Haack (SPD).
Internal German Relations: Egon Franke (SPD).
Research and Technology: Dr Andreas von Bülow (SPD).
Education and Science: Björn Engholm (SPD).
Economic Co-operation: Rainer Offergeld (SPD).

DEFENCE. The Paris Treaties, which entered into force in May 1955, stipulated a contribution of the Federal Republic to western defence within the framework of NATO and the Western European Union. In 1977 the Federal Armd Forces (*Bundeswehr*) had a total strength of 489,000 all ranks (235,000 conscripts).

Army. In 1979 the Army consisted of 16 armoured brigades, 12 armoured infantry brigades, 3 Jäger brigades, 2 mountain brigades, 3 airborne brigades; total strength 335,200.

The principal combat unit is still the Brigade, however, under the 'Brigade 80' concept the number of battalions per brigade goes up, although the number of men per battalion comes down. The armoured brigade has 3,026 men and the armoured infantry 3,730. The main emphasis of the concept is to improve the anti-armour capability and the brigades will have to look to the divisional troops for reconnaissance, artillery and air-defence support in points of main effort. The Army is at present converting to the 'Brigade 80' concept. There are 3 corps and 12 divisions, each of 3 brigades. The Army has 1,342 M-48A2 Patton and 2,437 Leopard I medium tanks with a further 1,800 Leopard II tanks on order; 7,700 armoured personnel carriers; 1,400 artillery pieces; 65 *Honest John* and 26 *Lance* surface to surface missiles.

Territorial Army. The Territorial Army lies outside the Authority of Supreme Commander NATO, but is tasked with securing the freedom of manoeuvre of NATO forces under national command as well as protecting points of military relevance. There are 3 Territorial Commands and 6 Home Defence Groups. Peacetime strength, 63,000.

Navy. The Federal Navy comprises 24 diesel-powered coastal submarines, 1 old experimental oceangoing submarine, 3 US-built guided missile armed destroyers, 4 German-built destroyers, 4 ancient *ex*-US destroyers, 6 frigates, 6 corvettes, 30 fast missile boats (Exocet armed) of 265–390 tons, 10 fast torpedo boats, a light cruiser type training ship, 11 frigate-type support ships, 18 coastal minesweepers and mine-hunters, 22 fast minesweepers, 20 inshore minesweepers, 50 landing craft, 13 supply and support ships, 2 fleet replenishment ships, 7 oilers, 8 coast patrol ships, 9 coast-guard cutters, 3 repair ships, 24 tugs and 100 auxiliaries and service craft.

The construction programme includes 10 large patrol (missile) vessels. The project to build 4 guided missile frigates was cancelled, but 4 frigates (initially, to replace old *ex*-US destroyers) and eventually 8 (to replace 'Hamburg' class destroyers and 'Köln' class frigates) are projected under the new development programme.

The Naval Air Arm has 2 wings (each 2 squadrons of 18 aircraft) of F-104G Starfighters and 1 wing of Breguet Atlantic maritime patrol bombers, supplemented by an anti-submarine helicopter wing (Lynx for new frigates). Albatross amphibians and Do 27 aircraft form an air-sea rescue wing (re-equipping with Sea King helicopters).

Navy personnel in 1981 totalled 5,600 officers and 32,900 men, including 6,700 of the Naval Air Arm.

Air Force. Since Oct. 1970, the *Luftwaffe* has comprised the following commands: German Air Force Tactical Command, German Air Force Support Command (including two German Air Force Regional Support Commands—North and South) and General Air Force Office. Its strength in 1980 was approximately 106,200 officers and other ranks and about 560 first-line combat aircraft. Combat units, including 12 heavy fighter-bomber squadrons, 4 light ground attack/reconnaissance squadrons, 4 reconnaissance squadrons, 8 surface-to-surface missile squadrons, and an air defence force of 4 interceptor squadrons, 24 batteries of *Nike-Hercules* and 36 batteries of *Improved Hawk* surface-to-air missiles, are assigned to NATO. There are 4 F-4F Phantom interceptor squadrons, 8 F-104G fighter-bomber squadrons (to be re-equipped with Tornados), 4 attack squadrons of F-4Fs, 4 RF-4E Phantom reconnaissance squadrons and 4 light attack/reconnaissance squadrons of Fiat G91Rs (being replaced with 7 squadrons of Alpha Jets). Three transport squadrons (each 15 aircraft) with turboprop Transall C-160 aircraft and 1 wing of 5 helicopter squadrons with UH-1D Iroquois add to the air mobility of the *Bundeswehr*. There are also VIP, support and light transport aircraft, and Piaggio P.149D initial training aircraft. Guided weapons in service include 8 squadrons of *Pershing* surface-to-surface missiles and 6 battalions of *Nike-Hercules* and 9 battalions of *Hawk* surface-to-air missiles.

All F-104 and Phantom pilots undergo basic and advanced training in USA.

INTERNATIONAL RELATIONS

Membership. The Federal Republic of Germany is a member of UN, OECD, EEC, NATO and the Council of Europe.

External Debt. On 27 Feb. 1953 several agreements were signed in London settling Germany's external pre-war and post-war debts. These agreements entered into force on 16 Sept. 1953.

The claims arising from the post-war economic assistance given to Germany by the UK (£201·8m.), France (US$15·79m.) and the USA (US$3,014m.) were fixed at £150m., US$11·84m. and US$1,000m. respectively, of which only the claims of the USA bear interest at $2\frac{1}{2}\%$. Up to March 1961 the claims were paid off by regular and premature redemption as follows: Great Britain except for £67·5m., France except for US$5,328,000 and the USA except for US$787·37m. In April/May 1961 the Deutsche Bundesbank repaid on behalf of the Federal Republic the total claims of Great Britain and France and the amount of US$587m. to the USA. The debt still outstanding on 30 Dec. 1966 (US$195·94m.) was also repaid by the Deutsche Bundesbank on behalf of the Federal Republic.

On 31 Dec. 1968 the London Debts Agreement of 27 Feb. 1953 was in force in a total of 56 foreign countries. 90% of all debts were claims of the USA, Great Britain, France and Switzerland.

Of the approximately DM 4,000m. of public pre-war debts, the sum of DM 13m. are still to be paid at the present time. Of approximately DM 2,200m. of private pre-war debts the amount of DM 253m. had still to be paid back on 31 Dec. 1977.

ECONOMY

Budget. The budget of the Federal Government shows the following figures (in DM 1m.) for calendar years:

	1976	1977	1978	1979
Revenues				
Federal taxes and customs duties	35,647	37,130	39,343	40,656
Share of Federal Government in joint taxes and trade tax levy	95,253	106,874	114,744	125,480
Tax-like charges	0	4	2	0
Others	5,727	9,063	5,746	11,380
Total revenue	136,627	149,755	163,152	177,515
Expenditures				
Defence	33,300	34,206	36,675	38,594
Social security	59,085	62,119	67,102	69,509
Agriculture and food	1,919	1,923	2,071	2,167
Transport and communications	11,491	11,853	12,932	14,511
Electricity, gas, water supply, industries and services	3,148	3,765	5,428	5,519
Education and science	8,450	8,569	9,632	10,934
Housing and settlements	2,046	2,077	1,779	2,265
All other expenditure	43,075	47,872	53,457	59,859
Total expenditure	162,514	171,952	189,508	203,358
Balance of transitory means	+ 31	− 10	+ 43	− 210
Net financing balance	−25,856	−22,206	−26,313	−26,053
Financed from:				
Loans	−46,316	−36,755	−46,505	−54,542
Coinage	− 74	− 494	− 373	− 443
Less:				
Redemption payments	+20,533	+15,043	+20,565	+28,931
Withdrawals from reserves	—	—	—	—

The total debt of the Federal Government, the Equalization of Burdens Fund, ERP-Special Fund and the Länder was DM 322,344m., as at 31 Dec. 1979 (excluding debt of communities/local authorities).

Currency. Pursuant to the laws issued on the monetary reform by the military governors of the British, American, and French Zones, from 18 to 26 June 1948, the 'Reichmark' was replaced by the 'Deutsche Mark'. The RM notes circulated by the former Reichsbank were exchanged for DMs at the rate of 1 to 1 up to the amount of RM 60, and all amounts exceeding RM 600 as well as all bank and saving deposits at the ratio of RM 100 to DM 6·5. All RM liabilities, including securities, were depreciated at the ratio of 10 to 1.

On 31 Aug. 1980 the circulation of coins in the Federal Republic amounted to DM 7,225m.; that of notes and coins to DM 87,981m.

Banking. On 14 Feb. 1948 the Bank of German Länder (Bank deutscher Länder) was established in Frankfurt as the central bank of issue for the Federal Republic and designated the exclusive agency for issuing notes and coins.

The Land Central Banks and the Berlin Central Bank were merged with the Bank deutscher Länder as from 1 Aug. 1957. The Bank deutscher Länder became the Deutsche Bundesbank.

The most important items of the balance sheets of the Deutsche Bundesbank in Frankfurt on 31 Aug. 1980 were as follows (in DM 1m.):

Assets

Gold	13,688·0
Balances at foreign banks and money market investments abroad	42,886·3
Foreign notes, coins, bills and cheques	3,657·1
Loans to international institutions and consolidation loans	4,035·0
Domestic bills of exchange and advances against securities	37,233·1
Equalization claims [1]	8,136·4

Liabilities

Bank-notes in circulation	80,755·4
Deposits	61,964·7

[1] From the monetary reform.

Weights and Measures. The metric system is in force.

ENERGY AND NATURAL RESOURCES

Electricity. In 1979, 372,186m. kwh. were produced.

Oil. In 1979, 67,445 tonnes of petroleum and 12,097,009 tonnes of diesel oil were produced.

Minerals. The great bulk of the minerals in Germany is produced in North Rhine-Westphalia (for coal, iron and metal smelting-works), Central Germany (for brown coal), Lower Saxony (Salzgitter for iron ore; the Harz for metal ore). The chief oil-fields are in Lower Saxony (Emsland).

The quantities of the principal minerals raised in the Federal Republic were as follows (in 1,000 tonnes):

Minerals	1974	1975	1976	1977	1978	1979
Coal	94,876	92,393	89,269	84,513	83,936	86,319
Lignite	126,044	123,377	134,535	122,920	123,559	130,579
Iron ore	5,671	4,273	3,034	2,868	1,608	1,654
Metal ore	995	1,032	1,034	1,031	726	...
Potash	26,202	22,006	21,178	23,799	25,260	27,674
Crude oil	6,191	5,741	5,524	5,401	5,059	4,774

The production of iron and steel in the Federal Republic was (in 1,000 tonnes):

	1974	1975	1976	1977	1978	1979
Pig-iron	40,221	30,074	31,849	28,959	30,148	35,167
Steel ingots and castings	53,232	40,415	42,415	38,985	41,253	46,040
Rolled products finished	39,615	29,487	30,398	29,411	31,102	33,616

Agriculture. In 1979 the agricultural holdings with a farm area of 1 hectare or more in the Federal Republic of Germany cultivated an agricultural area of 12·3m. hectares, of which the arable land was 7,290,400 hectares; meadows and pastures 4,796,700 hectares; vineyards, orchards, nurseries 226,400.

The total number of agricultural holdings in the Federal Republic, and their classification by size, according to the agricultural area, were as follows (1979):

	Total	Under 1 hectare	1–5 hectares	5–20 hectares	20–100 hectares	Over 100 hectares
Schleswig-Holstein	35,509	2,249	6,072	6,610	19,535	1,043
Hamburg	2,296	850	880	324	231	11
Lower Saxony	129,962	5,427	33,085	38,735	51,202	1,513
Bremen	610	114	163	115	215	3
North Rhine-Westphalia	107,151	4,918	32,290	38,030	31,383	530
Hessen	66,943	1,999	25,667	25,859	13,223	195
Rhineland-Palatinate	74,792	10,679	26,162	25,662	12,187	102
Baden-Württemberg	152,265	10,264	59,665	59,930	22,131	275
Bavaria	274,273	5,381	72,850	142,468	53,005	569
Saarland	5,690	375	2,382	1,611	1,294	28
Berlin (West)	283	136	88	31	28	—
Federal Republic	*849,774*	*42,392*	*259,304*	*339,375*	*204,434*	*4,269*

Area (in 1,000 hectares) and yield (in 1,000 tonnes) of the main crops in the Federal Republic, were as follows:

	Area				Yield			
	1977	1978	1979	1980[1]	1977	1978	1979	1980[1]
Wheat	1,599	1,619	1,627	1,657	7,235	8,118	8,061	8,136
Rye	702	651	564	547	2,540	2,457	2,114	2,111
Barley	1,811	1,951	1,989	1,998	7,582	8,608	8,184	8,856
Oats	793	749	728	688	2,714	3,202	2,994	2,622
Potatoes	400	355	276	260	11,368	10,510	8,716	...
Sugar-beet	423	402	393	392	20,206	18,777	18,340	...

[1] Preliminary results.

Wine must production (in 1m. hectolitres): 7·4 in 1960; 9·9 in 1970; 6 in 1971; 7·5 in 1972; 10·7 in 1973; 6·8 in 1974; 9·2 in 1975; 8·7 in 1976; 10·4 in 1977; 7·3 in 1978; 8·2 in 1979.

Livestock on 3 Dec. 1979 were as follows: Cattle, 15,049,500 (including 5,442,700 milch cows); horses, 379,800; sheep, 1,145,600; pigs, 22,373,800; goats, 36,300 (1977); poultry, 87,860,400.

Forestry. Forestry is an industry of great importance, conducted under the care of the State on scientific methods. The forest area of Germany within the boundaries of 1937 was 12·9m. hectares, of which 7·2m. are now in the Federal Republic. In 1979 cuttings amounted to 27·3m. cu. metres in the Federal Republic.

Fisheries. In 1979 the yield of sea and coastal fishing in the Federal Republic was 330,200 tonnes live weight, valued at DM 343m.

At the end of 1979 the number of vessels of the fishing fleet was 47 trawlers (92,000 gross tons), 2 luggers and 684 cutters.

INDUSTRY AND TRADE

Industry. In 1979, 49,176 establishments (with 20 and more employees; production industries including handicrafts) in the Federal Republic employed 7,607,239 persons; of these 1,011,981 were employed in machine construction; 310,571 in textile industry; 969,444 in electrical engineering; 228,954 in mining; 559,729 in chemical industry (average of 12 months).

The production of important industrial products in the Federal Republic was as follows:

Products	1976	1977	1978	1979
Aluminium (1,000 tonnes)	697	742	740	742
Potassium fertilizers, K_2O (1,000 tonnes)	1,925	2,341	2,470	2,616
Sulphuric acid, SO_3 (1,000 tonnes) [1]	3,811	3,819	3,813	4,136
Soda, Na_2CO_3 (1,000 tonnes) [1]	1,364	1,351	1,230	1,401
Cement (1,000 tonnes) [1]	34,155	32,163	33,959	35,287
Rayon:				
Staple fibre (1,000 tonnes)	72	68	73	76
Continuous rayon filament (1,000 tonnes) [1]	71	66	62	62
Cotton yarn (1,000 tonnes) [1]	208	178	164	161
Woollen yarn (1,000 tonnes) [1]	60	54	53	56
Passenger cars (1,000) [2]	3,548	3,796	3,901	3,943
Commercial cars and buses (1,000)	310	294	282	297
Bicycles (1,000)	2,845	3,028	2,923	3,099

[1] Including the quantities processed in the same factories.
[2] Including dual-purpose vehicles.

Fachserie 4 Produzierendes Gewerbe. Ed. Statistisches Bundesamt, Wiesbaden
Gutmann, G., and others. *Die Wirtschaftsverfassung der Bundesrepublik.* Stuttgart, 1964

Labour. The economically active persons (excluding the armed forces) totalled 25·81m. at the 1%-sample survey of the microcensus of April 1979. Of the total, 2,339,000 were self-employed, 943,000 unpaid family workers and 22·53m. dependently employed persons. 1,441,000 were engaged in agriculture and forestry; 11,872,000 in production industries; 4,682,000 in commerce and transport; 7,817,000 in other industries; 852,000 were unemployed.

In June 1979 foreign workers numbered 1,933,651, including 540,471 Turks, 367,301 Yugoslavs, 300,442 Italians, 140,139 Greeks, 89,992 Spaniards and 495,306 others.

Commerce. The distribution of the imports and exports of the Federal Republic according to principal countries was as follows (in DM 1m.):

		Imports			Exports	
Country	1977	1978	1979	1977	1978	1979
Argentina	1,304·5	1,490·0	1,442·4	993·9	947·9	1,623·4
Australia	1,409·3	1,201·5	1,288·7	2,126·8	2,091·5	1,987·3
Austria	6,100·8	7,116·4	8,403·9	14,545·0	14,617·1	16,461·2
Belgium–Luxembourg	19,556·5	20,523·8	23,402·2	21,501·7	23,657·2	26,753·7
Brazil	2,674·2	2,299·8	2,531·4	2,240·4	2,160·4	2,379·2
Canada	2,342·4	1,963·3	3,104·0	2,195·3	2,215·1	2,326·4
Denmark	3,544·6	4,011·2	4,641·4	6,024·1	6,320·1	6,837·1
Finland	1,948·9	1,944·5	2,476·1	2,247·3	1,988·1	2,514·3
France	27,305·9	28,281·2	33,195·2	33,643·0	34,895·2	39,992·1
Greece	1,929·6	2,187·8	2,396·8	2,799·2	3,036·6	3,765·2
India	786·3	764·6	1,002·0	1,140·7	1,271·2	1,284·8
Iran	4,335·2	4,214·8	4,225·3	6,350·7	6,767·2	2,349·2
Italy	20,728·9	23,184·9	18,729·6	18,729·6	19,431·5	24,534·1
Japan	6,493·1	7,178·7	7,912·1	3,013·7	3,476·8	4,150·8
Libya	5,026·9	3,416·5	5,540·5	1,507·6	1,630·8	2,159·6
Netherlands	30,825·3	30,748·5	35,841·8	27,529·2	28,370·6	31,297·7
Norway	2,793·1	3,989·7	5,332·0	3,903·9	3,130·3	3,305·0
Rep. of South Africa	2,555·3	2,460·6	3,641·5	2,598·2	3,082·2	3,136·2
Spain	3,008·7	3,396·8	3,840·0	4,237·6	3,634·2	4,457·5
Sweden	4,833·2	5,147·1	6,152·9	8,767·0	7,674·0	9,118·9
Switzerland	7,869·0	9,484·5	10,637·1	12,574·2	14,436·0	16,398·4
USSR	4,560·8	5,438·4	7,381·2	6,450·8	6,301·4	6,623·7
UK	10,448·9	12,065·3	17,215·9	14,608·2	16,883·2	21,033·6
USA	17,020·0	17,433·6	20,274·4	18,198·7	20,179·7	20,759·3

The main items of imports in 1979 were finished manufactures (US$61,963m.) and raw materials (US$23,383m.); exports, finished manufactures (US$112,875m.) and semi-finished manufactures (US$32,059m.).

Fachserie 7 Aussenhandel. Ed. Statistisches Bundesamt, Wiesbaden

Total trade between the Federal Republic of Germany and UK (British Department of Trade returns, in £1,000 sterling):

	1976	1977	1978	1979	1980
Imports to UK	2,757,025	3,574,241	4,512,838	5,799,403	5,700,861
Exports and re-exports from UK	1,834,438	2,501,120	3,104,901	4,243,975	5,113,032

Tourism. In 1979, 10·3m. arrivals and 24·7m. 'overnights' of foreign visitors were registered. Foreign exchange receipts from international tourism amounted to DM 10,524m.

COMMUNICATIONS

Roads. On 1 Jan. 1979 the total length of classified roads in the Federal Republic was 170,661 km, including 7,029 km autobahn, 32,252 km federal highways, 65,377 km first-class and 66,003 km second-class country roads. Motor vehicles licensed in the Federal Republic on 1 July 1979 numbered 26,109,079 (including 479,100 motor cycles, 22,535,469 passenger cars, 1,236,120 trucks, 68,360 buses and 1,624,713 tractors; not including 186,814 motor cycles and motor vehicles up to 50 cm^3 cylinder capacity and 2,014,129 mopeds).

Road casualties in 1979 totalled 486,441 injured and 13,222 killed.

Railways. The total operative length of railway line in the Federal Republic was 31,711 km (28,583 Federal Railway, 3,128 private railways) on 31 Dec. 1979; of these, 11,211 km were electrified. In 1979 the railways (including ships owned by the Federal Railways) carried 1,085m. passengers and 371m. tonnes of freight.

Aviation. The Deutsche Lufthansa AG (set up on 6 Jan. 1953, as AG für Luftverkehrsbedarf and renamed on 6 Aug. 1954), with headquarters at Cologne, has capital of DM 900m. The Federal Republic owns 74·3%, Land North Rhine-Westphalia 2·2%, the Federal Railways, 0·9%, Federal Post 1·8%, Kreditanstalt für Wiederaufbau 3% and private industry 17·8%.

Lufthansa operate internal, European, African, North and South Atlantic, Near and Far East routes. In 1979 the Lufthansa carried 13·7m. passengers, 399,327 tonnes of cargo and 47,730 tonnes of mail.

Shipping. On 31 Dec. 1979 the Federal German mercantile marine comprised 1,732 ocean-going vessels of 7,877,100 BRT.

The inland-waterways fleet in the Federal Republic on 31 Dec. 1979 comprised 3·79m. tons. The length of the navigable rivers and canals in use was 4,329 km.

Sea-going ships (foreign trade only) in 1979 loaded 36m. tonnes clearing and unloaded 121m. tonnes entering in the ports of the Federal Republic. Inland waterways carried 246m. tonnes in 1979.

Post and Broadcasting. The Federal Republic had, on 31 Dec. 1979, 19,051 post and telecommunications offices. Number of telephones, 26,632,302.

The postal bus services covered, in 1979, 187m. km and carried 331m. passengers.

The post office savings banks had, on 31 Dec. 1979, 18,606,500 depositors with DM 26,906m. to their credit.

In the financial year 1978 the postal revenues amounted to DM 35,501m. and the expenditure to DM 33,406m.

Arbeitsgemeinschaft der öffentlich-rechtlichen Rundfunkanstalten der Bundesrepublik Deutschland (ARD) is an organization for co-operation between the German broadcasting stations. ARD also broadcast a common TV programme under the name *Deutsches Fernsehen* throughout the Federal Republic. In addition regional programmes are broadcast. Number of wireless licences, 21,151,540; of television licences, 19,421,539 (1979).

Cinemas (31 Dec. 1977). There were 2,698 cinemas with a seating capacity of 0·8m. and 12 drive-in cinemas for 9,978 cars.

Newspapers (1977). There were 372 daily newspapers with a combined circulation of 24m.

JUSTICE, RELIGION, EDUCATION AND WELFARE

Justice. Justice is administered by the federal courts and by the courts of the Länder. In criminal procedures, civil cases and procedures of non-contentious jurisdiction the courts on the Land level are the local courts (*Amtsgerichte*), the regional courts (*Landgerichte*) and the courts of appeal (*Oberlandesgerichte*). On the federal level decisions regarding these matters are taken by the Federal Court (*Bundesgerichtshof*) at Karlsruhe. In labour law disputes the courts of the first and second instance are the labour courts and the Land labour courts and in the third instance, the Federal Labour Court (*Bundesarbeitsgericht*) at Kassel. Disputes about public law in matters of social security, unemployment insurance, maintenance of war victims and similar cases are dealt with in the first and second instances by the social courts and the Land social courts and in the third instance by the Federal Social Court (*Bundessozialgericht*) at Kassel. In most tax matters the finance courts of the Länder are competent and in the second instance, the Federal Finance Court (*Bundesfinanzhof*) at Munich. Other controversies of public law in non-constitutional matters are decided in the first and second instance by the administrative and the higher administrative courts (*Observerwaltungsgerichte*) of the Länder, and in the third instance by the Federal Administrative Court (*Bundesverwaltungsgericht*) at Berlin.

For the inquiry into maritime accidents the admiralty courts (*Seeämter*) are competent on the Land level and in the second instance the Federal Admiralty Court (*Bundesoberseeamt*) at Hamburg.

The constitutional courts of the Länder decide on constitutional questions. The Federal Constitutional Court (*Bundesverfassungsgericht*) as the supreme German court decides such questions as loss of basic rights, unconstitutional character of political parties, validity of laws, charges against judges and complaints regarding violations of basic rights by the public force.

The death sentence is abolished.

Religion. Of the population 49% are Protestants, 44·6% Roman Catholics and 0·1% Jews (census, 1970).

The Evangelical Church in Germany consists of 18 member-churches in the Federal Republic of Germany and West Berlin (7 Lutheran Churches, 8 United-Lutheran-Reformed-Churches, 2 Reformed Churches and 1 Confederation of United member Churches: 'Church of the Union'). Its organs are the Synod, the Church Conference and the Council under the chairmanship of Bishop Dr Eduard Lohse (Hanover). The Protestants numbered about 26·5m. in 1978. There are also some 12 Evangelical Free Churches. The 8 territorial churches in German Democratic Republic established the Federation of Evangelical Churches in 1969.

There are 5 Catholic archbishops and 17 bishoprics. Chairman of the German Bishops' Conference is Cardinal Höffner, Archbishop of Cologne. A concordat between Germany and the Holy See was signed on 20 July and ratified on 10 Sept. 1933.

The 'Old Catholics', who are in full communion with the Anglican Churches, numbered about 30,000 in 1977; they have a bishop at Bonn.

Evangelische Kirche in Deutschland, Hanover, 1979
Taschenbuch der evangelischen Kirche in Deutschland. Frankfurt, 1980
Kirchliches Handbuch. Amtliches statistisches Jahrbuch der Katholischen Kirche Deutschlands. Vol. 28. Cologne, 1976
Pastoral der Kirche fremden—Eroffnungsreferat der Deutschen Bischofskonferenz 1979 in Fulda—von Kardinal Joseph Höffner. Bonn, 1979
Alt-Katholisches Jahrbuch. Bonn, 1978
Katholiken und ihre Kirche, Protestanten und ihre Kirche. Munich, 1977
Luckey, G., *Free Churches in Germany.* Bad Nauheim, 1956

Education. Schools providing general education are primary and post-primary schools (*Grund- und Hauptschulen*), special schools (*Sonderschulen*), secondary modern schools (*Realschulen*), grammar schools (*Gymnasien*) and comprehensive schools. Primary schools: Attendance is compulsory for all children having completed their 6th year of age. Compulsory education extends 9 years. After the first 4 (or 6) years at primary school children may attend post-primary schools, secondary modern schools, grammar schools and other schools of general secondary education. The secondary modern school comprises 6, the grammar school 9 years. The final Grammar School Certificate (Abitur-Higher School Certificate) entitles the holder to enter any institution of higher education. There are also special schools for retarded, physically or mentally handicapped and socially maladjusted children.

In 1979 there were in the Federal Republic 17,701 primary and post-primary schools with 5,353,998 pupils; 2,787 special schools with 370,646 pupils, 2,492 secondary modern schools with 1,365,203 pupils; 2,464 grammar schools with 2,088,771 pupils; 241 comprehensive schools (primary and secondary stage) with 213,706 pupils.

Vocational education is provided in part-time, full-time and advanced vocational schools (*Berufs-, Berufsaufbau-, Berufsfach-* and *Fachschulen,* including *Fachschulen für Technik* and *Schulen des Gesundheitswesens*). Running parallel to the occupation, part-time vocational schools offer 6 to 12 hours per week of additional compulsory schooling. All young people who are apprentices, in some other employment or even unemployed have to attend them in general up to the age of 18 years or until the completion of the practical vocational training. Full-time vocational schools comprise courses of at least one year. They prepare for commercial and domestic occupations as well as specialized occupations in the field of handicrafts. Advanced full-time vocational schools are attended by pupils having completed their 18th year of age; courses vary from 6 months to 3 or more years.

In Nov. 1979 there were 6,720 full- and part-time vocational schools with 65,013 teachers and 2,400,947 pupils (1,050,736 female); 5,096 full-time vocational schools with 574,614 pupils (316,497 female); 2,912 advanced vocational schools with 8,092 teachers and 181,694 pupils (120,896 female).

Higher Education. Universities and equivalent institutions; teacher-training colleges and equivalent institutions which train teachers for primary schools, special schools, intermediate schools and schools providing vocational education; colleges of music, fine arts and the college for physical education in Cologne.

Higher technical colleges offer highly qualified full-time vocational instruction. There were, in the winter term 1979–80, 111 higher technical colleges with 180,651 students (50,609 female).

During the winter term 1979–80 there were 228 academic institutions of higher education with 981,808 students (353,432 female; 56,601 foreigners); they comprise 64 universities with 728,334 students (258,422 female); 6 Roman Catholic theological colleges and 4 Protestant theological colleges with together 2,182 students (591 female).

In the winter term 1979–80 there were 17 teacher-training colleges and equivalent institutions with 53,665 students (36,133 female); 15 colleges of music, 10 colleges of fine arts and the college of film and television with together 16,976 students (7,677 female).

Health. There were in 1978, 3,328 hospitals with 714,879 beds in the Federal Republic. In 1978 public assistance (including aid to tuberculars) and aid to war victims amounted to DM 12,274m. or DM 200.14 per head of population.[1]

[1] All subsequent statistics relate to the end of 1978 or the calendar year 1978.

Social Welfare. *Social Health Insurance* (originally introduced in 1883). Compulsory insurants are in particular wage-earners and apprentices, salaried employees with an income below the limit of compulsory insurance and the social-insurance pensioners. Voluntary insurance is possible; insurants may voluntarily continue to insure when no longer liable to do so.

Benefits: Medical treatment, medicaments, hospital and nursing care, maternity benefits, death benefits for the insured and their families, sickness payments and out-patients' allowances.

Number of insurants, 34·4m., including compulsory insurants (19·8m.) and pensioners (10·2m.). Number of the cases of incapacity for work 23·4m. Total expenditure, DM 74,991m.

Accident Insurance (originally introduced in 1884). Insured are all persons in employment or service, apprentices and the greater part of the self-employed and the unpaid family workers.

Benefits in the case of industrial injuries and occupational diseases: Medical treatment and nursing care, sickness payments, pensions and other payments in cash and in kind, surviving dependants' pensions.

Number of insurants, 27m.; number of current pensions, 1m.; total expenditure, DM 8,916m.

Workers' and Employees' Old-age Insurance Funds (originally introduced in 1889). Compulsory insurants are all wage-earners and salaried employees, the members of certain liberal professions and—subject to certain conditions—self-employed craftsmen. Insurants may voluntarily continue to insure when no longer liable to do so or increase the insurance.

Benefits: Measures designed to maintain, improve and restore the earning capacity; pensions paid to persons incapable for work, old age and surviving dependants' pensions.

Number of pensions paid, 12m., of which pensions to insurants, 7·8m.; pensions to widows and widowers, 3·6m.; pensions to orphans, 0·5m. Total expenditure, DM 130,763m.

Miners' Pension Insurance Funds. Compulsory insurants are all persons employed in mining, excluding salaried employees functioning as employers. Insurants may voluntarily continue to insure when no longer liable to do so or increase the insurance.

Benefits: Measures designed to maintain, improve and restore the earning capacity; pensions paid to underground workers because of partial disability to work in mines, miners' pensions in the case of complete disability, miners' retirement benefits, surviving dependants' pensions.

Number of pensions paid, 0·7m., of which pensions to insurants, 0·4m.; pensions to widows and widowers, 0·3m.; pensions to orphans, 0·03m. Total expenditure, DM 12,401m.

Farmers' Old-age Pension Funds: Unemployment Insurance and *Unemployment Relief* granted to unemployed persons who are not entitled to unemployment pay. Number of insured, 0·7m.; number of current pensions, 0·3m. Total expenditure, DM 2,505m.

Assistance for War Victims (war-disabled and surviving dependants of war victims).

Benefits: Medical treatment and nursing care, aid to war victims, disablement pensions, basic and equalization pensions paid to widows and orphans, parents' pensions, allowances for nursing care, compensation for occupational detriment, funeral allowances, lump-sum indemnification and indemnification paid upon marriage.

Persons (including those with permanent residence abroad) qualifying for pensions, 2·1m., of which disabled persons, 1m.; widows and widowers, 1m.; orphans, 0·03m.; parents, 0·1m. Total expenditure, DM 12,693m.

Equalization of Burdens (public relief and compensation payments). Eligible are expellees and persons who suffered damage because of the war or in connexion with the currency reform.

Benefits: Basic compensation, war-damage pensions, compensation for household equipment, accommodation assistance, currency-conversion compensation, compensation for holders of 'old savings', training grants, loans and other promotive measures.

Number of recipients of war damage pensions, 0·3m.; payments made (1 Sept. 1952–31 Dec. 1978), DM 99,253m., including basic compensation, DM 24,235m.; war damage pension, DM 38,842m.; accommodation assistance, DM 5,611m.; compensation for household equipment, DM 9,127m.

Family Assistance. From 1 Jan. 1975, children's allowances are being paid, beginning with the first child, to all persons living in the area of application of the law, the income limit being abolished. The monthly allowance is for the first child DM 50. As from 1 Jan. 1978, the allowance has been raised for the second child from DM 70 to DM 80 and for the third and any further child from DM 120 to DM 150. Beginning with 1 Jan. 1979, the beneficiaries have been receiving for the third and any further child DM 200 each per month and as from 1 July 1979 for the second child DM 100. Before, the Federal Law on Children's Allowances (*Bundeskindergeldgesetz*) had provided that all persons living in the area of application of the law were to be paid children's allowances for the third and any further child, unless the beneficiaries were public service employees or recipients of social benefits and as such already entitled to children's allowances. For the second child allowances were paid only to persons who together with their husband/wife had a yearly income not exceeding DM 15,000 (as of 1 Jan. 1973 = DM 16,800, as of 1 Jan. 1974 = DM 18,360); this limitation did not apply in the case of persons with 3 or more children.

Accommodation Allowances for tenants, owners of a homestead, a freehold flat or a small-holder's cottage.

Public Welfare. Public assistance or welfare (the latter from 1 June 1962) for needy persons, namely livelihood aid and aid in special situations (including aid to tuberculars) provided outside and inside institutions, homes and similar establishments.

Aid provided outside institutions, DM 4,376m.; aid provided inside institutions, DM 6,973m.

Aid to War Victims. Benefits for disabled persons and members of their families as well as for surviving dependants, namely vocational assistance, education allowances, supplementary livelihood aid; recovery, accommodation and special assistance. Total expenditure, DM 925m.

Public Youth Welfare. In particular, supervision of foster children, official guardianship, assistance with adoptions and affiliations, social assistance in juvenile courts, educational assistance and correctional education under a court order. Total expenditure, DM 4,427m.

Übersicht über die soziale Sicherung. Bundesministerium für Arbeit und Sozialordnung. 9th ed. Bonn, 1977

Tietz, G., *Zahlenwerk zur Sozialversicherung in der Bundesrepublik Deutschland* (and supplements). Berlin, 1963

Arbeits- und Sozialstatistik. Bundesminister für Arbeit und Sozialordnung, Bonn (from 1950)

Fachserie 13 Sozialleistungen. Statistisches Bundesamt (from 1951)

Fachserie 12 Gesundheitswesen. Statistisches Bundesamt (from 1946)

DIPLOMATIC REPRESENTATIVES

OF THE FEDERAL REPUBLIC OF GERMANY IN GREAT BRITAIN
(21–23 Belgrave Sq., London, SW1X 8PZ)

Ambassador: Dr Jürgen Ruhfus, KBE.

OF GREAT BRITAIN IN THE FEDERAL REPUBLIC OF GERMANY
(Friedrich-Ebert-Alle 77, 5300, Bonn)

Ambassador: Sir John Taylor.

OF THE FEDERAL REPUBLIC OF GERMANY IN THE USA
(4645 Reservoir Rd, NW, Washington, D.C. 20007)

Ambassador: Berndt von Staden.

OF THE USA IN THE FEDERAL REPUBLIC OF GERMANY
(Deichmannsaue, 5300, Bonn)

Ambassador: William J. Stoessel, Jr.

FEDERAL REPUBLIC OF GERMANY TO THE UNITED NATIONS

Ambassador: Rüdiger von Wechmar.

Books of Reference

Statistical Information: The central statistical agency is the Statistisches Bundesamt, 62 Wiesbaden, Gustav Stresemann Ring 11. *President:* Franz Kroppenstedt. Its publications include:

Statistisches Jahrbuch für die Bundesrepublik Deutschland (latest issue, 1980); *Wirtschaft und Statistik* (monthly, from 1949); *Das Arbeitsgebiet der Bundesstatistik* (latest issue 1976; also in English: *Survey of German Federal Statistics*).

Documents on Germany under Occupation, 1945–54. Ed. B. Ruhm von Oppen. R. Inst. of Int. Affairs, 1955

Bluhm, G., *Die Oder-Neisse-Linie in der Deutschen Aussenpolitik.* Freiburg, 1963

Dickinson, R. E., *The Regions of Germany.* London, 1945

Grosser, A., *Germany in our Time: A Political History of the Postwar Years.* New York, 1971

Pounds, N. J. G., *The Economic Pattern of Modern Germany.* 2nd ed. London, 1966

Roberts, G. K., *West German Politics.* London, 1972

Ryder, A. J., *Twentieth-Century Germany: From Bismarck to Brandt.* London, 1973

Trene, W., *Germany Since 1884.* Bad Godesberg, 1969

Wiskemann, E., *Germany's Eastern Neighbours.* R. Inst. of Int. Affairs, 1956

National Library: Deutsche Bibliothek, Zeppelinallee 4–8; Frankfurt (Main). *Director:* Professor Dr Kurt Köster.

THE LÄNDER

BADEN-WÜRTTEMBERG

AREA AND POPULATION. Baden-Württemberg comprises 35,752 sq. km, with a population (at 31 May 1980) of 9,227,563 (4,448,137 males, 4,779,426 females).

The Land is administratively divided into 4 areas, 9 urban and 35 rural districts, and numbers 1,111 communes. The capital is Stuttgart.

Vital statistics for calendar years:

	Live births	Marriages	Divorces	Deaths
1977	90,981	50,129	10,251	90,517
1978	89,924	46,943	4,089	93,987
1979	92,425	49,491	10,305	91,513

CONSTITUTION. The Land Baden-Württemberg is a merger of the 3 Länder, Baden, Württemberg-Baden and Württemberg-Hohenzollern, which were formed in 1945. The merger was approved by a plebiscite held on 9 Dec. 1951, when 70% of the population voted in its favour.

The Diet, elected on 16 March 1980, consists of 68 Christian Democrats, 40 Social Democrats, 10 Free Democrats, 6 Ecologists.

The Government is formed by Christian Democrats, with Lothar Späth (CDU) as Prime Minister.

AGRICULTURE. Area and yield of the most important crops:

	Area (in 1,000 hectares)			Yield (in 1,000 tonnes)		
	1977	1978	1979	1977	1978	1979
Rye	21·9	21·8	21·1	76·3	78·3	77·2
Wheat	246·0	235·5	239·9	993·1	1,043·3	1,137·0
Barley	178·1	188·2	197·8	674·7	738·3	804·2
Oats	92·2	95·0	97·4	354·3	413·6	401·4
Potatoes	45·2	40·3	37·9	1,173·7	1,130·1	1,192·3
Sugar-beet	23·9	22·7	22·7	1,207·2	1,127·7	1,142·8

Livestock (1 Dec. 1979): Cattle, 1,870,139 (including 691,992 milch cows); horses, 46,050; pigs, 2,170,667; sheep, 194,862; poultry, 6,715,695.

INDUSTRY. In June 1980, 10,421 establishments (with 20 and more employees) employed 1,490,859 persons; of these, 259,315 were employed in machine construction (excluding office machines, data processing equipment and facilities); 99,916 in textile industry; 244,853 in electrical engineering; 210,611 in car building.

LABOUR. The economically active persons totalled 4,111,800 at the 1%-sample survey of the microcensus of April 1979. Of the total 347,600 were self-employed, 153,400 unpaid family workers, 3,610,800 employees; 221,300 were engaged in agriculture and forestry; 2,128,500 in power supply, mining, manufacturing and building, 578,700 in commerce and transport, 1,183,300 in other industries and services.

ROADS. On 1 Jan. 1980 there were 27,620 km of 'classified' roads, including 914 km of autobahn, 4,775 km of federal roads, 12,693 km of first-class and 9,238 km of second-class highways. Motor vehicles, at 1 July 1980, numbered 4,221,628, including 3,603,042 passenger cars, 8,492 buses, 173,683 lorries, 290,647 tractors and 75,381 motor cycles.

JUSTICE. There are a constitutional court (*Staatsgerichtshof*), 2 courts of appeal, 17 regional courts, 108 local courts, a Land labour court, 9 labour courts, a Land social court, 8 social courts, a finance court, a higher administrative court (*Verwaltungsgerichtshof*), 4 administrative courts.

RELIGION. On 1 Jan. 1980, 44·4% of the population were Protestants and 47·2% Roman Catholics.

EDUCATION. In 1980 there were 2,583 primary schools with 25,992 teachers and 762,324 pupils; 548 special schools with 6,645 teachers and 61,200 pupils; 424 intermediate schools with 9,231 teachers and 257,352 pupils; 409 high schools with 16,186 teachers and 336,977 pupils; 19 *Freie Waldorf* schools with 572 teachers and 10,255 pupils; 18 *Integrierte Gesamtschulen* (comprehensive schools) including stage of orientation, with 752 teachers and 14,821 pupils; 162 *Berufliche Gymnasien* (technical secondary schools) with 26,565 pupils; 385 part-time vocational schools with 270,311 pupils; 941 full-time vocational schools with 81,079 pupils; 195 advanced vocational schools with 9,137 pupils; 210 schools for public health occupations with

12,438 pupils; there were also 68 (full- and part-time) institutions for the training of technicians with 4,287 participants and 34 *Fachhochschulen* (colleges of engineering and others) with 26,654 students; in all vocational schools there were 13,645 teachers.

In the winter term 1979–80 there were 9 universities (Freiburg, 18,347 students; Heidelberg, 21,048; Konstanz, 3,232; Tübingen, 19,356; Karlsruhe, 11,328; Stuttgart, 12,289; Hohenheim, 3,443; Mannheim, 6,161; Ulm, 2,908); 10 teacher-training colleges with 13,924 students; 5 colleges of music and 2 colleges of fine arts, comprising together 3,172 students.

Statistical Information: Statistisches Landesamt Baden-Württemberg (P.O.B. 898, D7000 Stuttgart 1) (*President:* Prof. Klaus Szameitat), publishes: Monatsschrift 'Baden-Württemberg in Wort und Zahl'; *Jahrbücher für Statistik und Landeskunde von Baden-Württemberg; Statistik von Baden-Württemberg* (series); *Statistisches Handbuch Baden-Württemberg* (1955 and 1958); *Statistisches Taschenbuch* (latest issue 1979).

Spreng, R., and others, *Die Verfassung des Landes Baden-Württemberg*. Stuttgart, 1954

State Library: Württembergische Landesbibliothek, Konrad-Adenauer-Str. 8, 7000 Stuttgart 1. *Director:* Dr Hans-Peter Geb.

BAVARIA

Bayern

AREA AND POPULATION. Bavaria has an area of 70,546 sq. km. The capital is Munich. There are 7 areas, 96 urban and rural districts and 2,048 communes. The population (31 March 1980) numbered 10,880,274 (5,199,311 males, 5,680,963 females).

Vital statistics for calendar years:

	Live births	Marriages	Divorces	Deaths
1977	106,633	61,863	10,691	120,487
1978	106,145	59,419	4,086	124,775
1979	107,667	63,146	11,340	122,271

CONSTITUTION. The Constituent Assembly, elected on 30 June 1946, passed a constitution on the lines of the democratic constitution of 1919, but with greater emphasis on state rights; this was agreed upon by the Christian Social Union and the Social Democrats.

The elections for the Diet, held on 15 Oct. 1978, had the following results: 129 Christian Social Union, 65 Social Democrats, 10 Free Democrats. The cabinet of the Christian Social Union is headed by Minister President Dr Franz Josef Strauss (CSU).

AGRICULTURE. Area and yield of the most important products:

	Area (1,000 hectares)			*Yield (1,000 tonnes)*		
	1978	1979	1980[1]	1978	1979	1980[1]
Wheat	493·5	482·6	490·9	2,310·2	2,131·1	2,313·5
Rye	81·6	70·8	75·3	281·1	220·7	267·4
Barley	499·6	518·6	511·5	1,967·9	1,957·6	2,031·3
Oats	149·7	153·8	144·7	541·5	530·9	482·5
Potatoes	132·8	111·9	104·8	3,991·9	3,564·7	...
Sugar-beet	83·6	80·5	79·3	4,260·0	4,145·7	...

[1] Preliminary results.

Livestock (2 Dec. 1979): 4,939,700 cattle (including 1,984,700 milch cows); 55,900 horses; 288,500 sheep; 4,140,500 pigs; 15,329,100 poultry.

INDUSTRY. In July 1980, 10,035 establishments (with 20 and more employees) employed 1,384,134 persons; of these, 246,611 were employed in electrical engineering; 180,783 in mechanical engineering; 87,306 in clothing industry.

LABOUR. The economically active persons totalled 5,058,900 at the 1% sample survey of the microcensus of April 1979. Of the total, 545,600 were self-employed, 335,400 unpaid family workers, 4,177,900 employees; 2,276,200 in power supply, mining, manufacturing and building; 838,800 in commerce and transport; 1,431,500 in other industries and services.

ROADS. There were, on 1 Jan. 1980, 39,360 km of 'classified' roads, including 1,561 km of autobahn, 7,254 km of federal roads, 13,642 km of first-class and 16,903 km of second-class highways. Number of motor vehicles, at 1 July 1980, was 5,031,195, including 4,075,514 passenger cars, 219,830 lorries, 12,492 buses, 527,748 tractors, 158,541 motor cycles.

JUSTICE. There are a constitutional court (*Verfassungsgerichtshof*), a supreme Land court (*Oberstes Landesgericht*), 3 courts of appeal, 21 regional courts, 72 local courts, 2 Land labour courts, 11 labour courts, a Land social court, 7 social courts, 2 finance courts, a higher administrative court (*Verwaltungsgerichtshof*), 6 administrative courts.

RELIGION. At the census of 27 May 1970 there were 69·9% Roman Catholics and 25·7% Protestants.

EDUCATION. In 1979–80 there were 2,835 primary schools with 46,624 teachers and 1,006,865 pupils; 394 special schools with 4,463 teachers and 50,563 pupils; 327 intermediate schools with 8,067 teachers and 177,521 pupils; 393 high schools with 17,381 teachers and 327,270 pupils; 258 part-time vocational schools with 6,343 teachers and 388,901 pupils; 552 full-time vocational schools with 3,115 teachers and 64,084 pupils including 213 schools for public health occupations with 563 teachers and 13,713 pupils; 258 advanced full-time vocational schools with 1,688 teachers and 23,185 pupils; 80 vocational high schools (*Berufsoberschulen, Fachoberschulen*) with 1,242 teachers and 23,938 pupils.

In the winter term 1979–80 there were 9 universities with 106,384 students (Augsburg, 4,044; Bamberg, 2,209; Bayreuth, 1,513; Erlangen–Nürnberg, 18,150; München, 41,191; Passau, 633; Regensburg, 9,710; Würzburg, 12,840; the Technical University of München, 16,094); 3 *Gesamthochschulen* with 3,817 students and the college of philosophy, München, 278. There were also 2 colleges of music, 2 colleges of fine arts and 1 college of television and film, with together 2,023 students; 13 vocational colleges (*Fachhochschulen*) with 32,285 students.

Statistical Information: Bayerisches Statistisches Landesamt, 51 Neuhauser Str. 8000 Munich, was founded in 1833. *President:* Dr Günther Scheingraber. It publishes: *Statistisches Jahrbuch für Bayern.—Bayern* in *Zahlen.* Monthly (from Jan. 1947).—*Zeitschrift des Bayerischen Statistischen Landesamts.* July 1869–1943; 1948 ff.—*Beiträge zur Statistik Bayerns.* 1850 ff.—*Statistische Berichte.* 1951 ff.—*Schaubilderhefte.* 1951 ff.—*Kreisdaten.* 1972 ff.—*Gemeindedaten.*

Nawiasky, H., and Luesser, C., *Die Verfassung des Freistaates Bayern vom 2. Dez. 1946.* Munich, 1948; supplement, by H. Nawiasky and H. Lechner, Munich, 1953

State Library: Bayerische Staatsbibliothek, Munich 22. *Director:* Dr Franz G. Kaltwasser.

BERLIN

GOVERNMENT. Greater Berlin was under quadripartite Allied government (Kommandatura) until 1 July 1948, when the Soviet element withdrew. On 30 Nov. 1948, a separate Municipal Government was set up in the Soviet Sector (*see* p. 502).

AREA. The total area of Berlin is 883 sq. km, of which Western Berlin covers 480 sq. km and the Soviet Sector 403 sq. km. The *British Sector* includes the administrative districts of Tiergarten, Charlottenburg, Wilmersdorf and Spandau; the *American Sector* those of Kreuzberg, Neukölln, Tempelhof, Schöneberg, Zehlendorf and Steglitz; the *French Sector* covers the administrative districts of Wedding and Reinickendorf, and the *Soviet Sector,* those of Mitte, Friedrichshain, Prenzlauer

Berg, Pankow, Weissensee, Lichtenberg, Treptow and Köpenick. The British, American and French sectors form an administrative unit, called Berlin (West).

On 13 Aug. 1961 the East German Government completely severed all communications between West and East Berlin.

BERLIN (WEST)

POPULATION. Population, 31 Dec. 1979, 1,902,250 (851,979 males, 1,058,271 females). According to the census of 27 May 1970, 70·2% were Protestants and 12·5% Roman Catholics.

Vital statistics for calendar years:

	Live births	Marriages	Divorces	Deaths
1977	16,517	12,789	5,479	35,888
1978	16,678	10,804	5,600	36,060
1979	17,259	10,754	...	35,008

CONSTITUTION AND GOVERNMENT. According to the constitution of 1 Sept. 1950, Berlin is simultaneously a *Land* of the Federal Republic (though not yet formally incorporated) and a city. It is governed by a House of Representatives (at least 200 members); the executive power is vested in a Senate, consisting of the Ruling Burgomaster, the deputy Burgomaster and not more than 16 senators.

In the municipal elections, held on 18 March 1979, the Christian Democrats obtained 63 seats; the Social Democrats, 61 seats; the Free Democrats, 11 seats. The Government is a coalition of Social Democrats and Free Democrats.

Governing Mayor: Dr Hans-Jochen Vogel (Social Democrat).

ECONOMY

Currency. The legal tender of Berlin (West) is the German Mark (DM).

Banking. On 20 March 1949 when the DM (West) became the only legal tender of the Western Sectors, the Zentralbank of Berlin was established. Its functions were similar to those of the Zentralbanks of the Länder of the Federal Republic. The Berlin Central Bank was merged with the Bank deutscher Länder as from 1 Aug. 1957, when the latter became the Deutsche Bundesbank. The legal tender for the Western Sectors of Berlin is being issued by the Deutsche Bundesbank (formerly Bank deutscher Länder).

AGRICULTURE. Agricultural area (May 1979), 3,387 hectares, including 1,100 hectares arable land and 150 hectares gardens, orchards, nurseries.

Livestock (1 Dec. 1979): Cattle, 702; pigs, 3,793; horses, 2,570; sheep, 1,526.

INDUSTRY. In 1979 (monthly averages), 1,216 establishments (with 20 or more employees) employed 182,946 persons; of these, 65,163 were employed in electrical engineering, 19,853 in machine construction, 4,000 in cloth manufacture, 4,118 in steel construction.

LABOUR. The economically active persons totalled 841,900 at the 1%-sample survey of the microcensus of April 1979. Of the total, 71,900 were self-employed including unpaid family workers, 770,000 employees; 5,300 were engaged in agriculture and forestry; 274,400 in power supply, manufacturing and building; 167,600 in commerce and transport; 394,600 in other industries and services.

ROADS. There were, on 1 Jan. 1976, 117 km of 'classified' roads, including 25 km of autobahn and 92 km of federal roads. On 1 July 1980, 642,514 motor vehicles were registered, including 581,061 passenger cars, 37,080 lorries, 19,143 motor cycles, 2,224 buses and 3,006 tractors.

JUSTICE. There are a court of appeal (*Oberlandesgericht*), a regional court, 7 local courts, a Land labour court, a labour court, a Land social court, a social court, a higher administrative court, an administrative court and a finance court.

EDUCATION. In 1979 (preliminary figures) there were 449 schools providing general education (excluding special schools) with 14,443 teachers and 236,562 pupils; 64 special schools with 1,305 teachers and 10,354 pupils. There were a further 43 vocational schools with 981 teachers and 39,904 pupils; 24 full-time vocational schools with 432 teachers and 4,805 pupils; 13 *Fachoberschulen* (full-time vocational schools leading up to vocational colleges) with 115 teachers and 1,529 pupils; 34 advanced full-time vocational schools with 250 teachers and 4,754 pupils; 68 schools for public-health occupations with 340 teachers and 4,599 pupils. Moreover, there were 2 schools for technicians with 38 teachers and 543 participants.

In the winter term 1979–80 there was 1 university (137,960 students); 1 technical university (20,289); 1 theological (evangelical) college (362); 1 teacher-training college with 4,768 students; 1 college of fine arts with 2,361 students; 1 vocational college (for economics) (783); 2 colleges for social work (1,410); 1 technical college (2,732), 1 college of the Federal postal administration (349) and 1 college for public administration (1,215).

Statistical Information: The Statistisches Landesamt Berlin, formerly Statistisches Amt der Stadt Berlin, was founded in 1862 (Fehrbelliner Platz 1, 1000 Berlin 31). *Director:* Günter Appel. It publishes: *Statistisches Jahrbuch* (from 1867): *Berliner Statistik* (monthly, from 1947).—*100 Jahre Berliner Statistik* (1962).

State Library: Amerika-Gedenkbibliothek-Berliner Zentralbibliothek-, Blücherplatz 1, D1000 Berlin 61. *Director:* Dr Peter K. Liebenow.

BREMEN

Freie Hansestadt Bremen

AREA AND POPULATION. The area of the Land, consisting of the towns and ports of Bremen and Bremerhaven, is 404 sq. km. Estimated population, 31 Dec. 1979, 695,115 (326,452 males, 368,663 females).

Vital statistics for calendar years:

	Live births	Marriages	Divorces	Deaths
1977	5,947	4,187	1,581	8,924
1978	5,817	3,713	...	8,972
1979	5,640	3,671	...	8,776

CONSTITUTION. Political power is vested in the House of Burgesses (*Bürgerschaft*), which appoints the executive, called the Senate.

The elections of 7 Oct. 1979 had the following result: 52 Social Democratic Party, 33 Christian Democrats, 11 Free Democratic Party, 4 Bremer Grüne Liste. The Senate is only formed by Social Democrats; its president is Hans Koschnick (Social Democrat).

AGRICULTURE. Agricultural area comprised (1979), 14,440 hectares: yield of grain crops, 8,104 tonnes; potatoes, 516 tonnes.

Livestock (3 Dec. 1979): 16,341 cattle (including 4,535 milch cows); 5,171 pigs; 375 sheep; 1,335 horses; 29,910 poultry.

INDUSTRY. In 1979, 408 establishments (20 and more employees) employed 90,195 persons; of these, 14,913 were employed in shipbuilding (except naval engineering); 7,504 in machine construction; 11,386 in electrical engineering; 5,297 in coffee and tea processing.

LABOUR. The economically active persons totalled 292,100 at the 1%-sample survey of the microcensus of April 1979. Of the total, 18,700 were self-employed, 268,900 employees; 105,000 in power supply, mining, manufacturing and building, 78,600 in commerce and transport, 108,500 in other industries and services.

ROADS. On 1 Jan. 1976 there were 139 km of 'classified' roads, including 45 km of autobahn, 82 km of federal roads, 7 km of first-class and 5 km of second-class highways. Registered motor vehicles on 1 July 1979 numbered 260,246, including 235,244 passenger cars, 15,171 trucks, 2,216 tractors, 642 buses and 4,445 motor cycles.

SHIPPING. Vessels entered in 1979, 10,766 of 45,822,497 net tons; cleared, 10,600 of 45,485,937 net tons. Sea traffic, 1979, incoming 16,969,179 tonnes; outgoing, 11,096,263 tonnes.

JUSTICE. There are a constitutional court (*Staatsgerichtshof*), a court of appeal, a regional court, 3 local courts, a Land labour court, 2 labour courts, a Land social court, a social court, a finance court, a higher administrative court, an administrative court.

RELIGION. On 27 May 1970 (census) there were 82·4% Protestants and 10·2% Roman Catholics.

EDUCATION. In 1979 there were 331 new system schools with 5,976 teachers and 108,139 pupils; 22 special schools with 522 teachers and 4,380 pupils; 22 part-time vocational schools with 24,526 pupils; 21 full-time vocational schools with 1,357 pupils; 15 advanced vocational schools (including institutions for the training of technicians) with 1,497 pupils; 10 schools for public health occupations with 933 pupils.

In the winter term 1979–80 about 6,771 students were enrolled at the university. In addition to the university there were 7 other colleges in 1979 with about 4,344 students.

Statistical Information: Statistisches Landesamt Bremen (An der Weide 14–16 (P.B. 101309), D2800 Bremen 1), founded in 1850. *Director:* RD Volker Hannemann. Its current publications include: *Statistische Mitteilungen Freie Hansestadt Bremen* (from 1948).—*Monatliche Zwischenberichte* (1949–53); *Statistische Monatsberichte* (from 1954).—*Statistische Berichte* (from 1956).—*Statistisches Handbuch für das Land Freie Hansestadt Bremen* (*1950–60*, 1961; *1960–64*, 1967; *1965–69*, 1971; *1970–74*, 1975).—*Bremen im statistischen Zeitvergleich 1950*. 1976, 1977.—*Bremen in Zahlen*. 1980.

Beutin, L., *Bremen und Amerika*. Bremen, 1953

University Library: Klagenfurter Str., D2800 Bremen 33. *Director:* Gerhard Wenske.

HAMBURG

Freie und Hansestadt Hamburg

AREA AND POPULATION. In 1938 the territory of the town was reorganized by the amalgamation of the city and its 18 rural districts with 3 urban and 27 rural districts ceded by Prussia. Total area, 754·7 sq. km (1979), including the islands Neuwerk and Scharhörn (7 sq. km). Population (31 Dec. 1979), 1,653,043 (768,949 males, 884,094 females).

Vital statistics for calendar years:

	Live births	Marriages	Divorces	Deaths
1977	12,987	9,401	4,601	24,294
1978	12,616	7,966	1,141	24,072
1979	12,722	8,296	3,183	23,760

CONSTITUTION. The constitution of 6 June 1952 vests the supreme power in the House of Burgesses (*Bürgerschaft*) of 120 members. The executive is in the hands of the Senate, whose members are elected by the Bürgerschaft.

The elections of 4 June 1978 had the following results: Social Democrats, 69; Christian Democrats, 51. The First Burgomaster is Hans-Ulrich Klose (Social Democrat).

The territory has been divided into 7 administrative districts.

AGRICULTURE. The agricultural area comprised 25,000 hectares in 1979. Yield, in tonnes, of cereals, 22,100; potatoes, 1,100.

Livestock (3 Dec. 1979): Cattle, 13,685 (including 3,439 milch cows); pigs, 11,791; horses, 3,628; sheep, 1,334; poultry, 80,750.

FISHERIES. In 1978 the yield of sea and coastal fishing was 38,979 tonnes valued at DM 39·4m.

INDUSTRY. In June 1980, 993 establishments (with 20 and more employees) employed 167,799 persons; of these, 21,784 were employed in electrical engineering; 18,616 in machine construction; 13,945 in shipbuilding (except naval engineering); 15,514 in chemical industry.

LABOUR. The economically active persons totalled 736,200 at the 1%-sample survey of the microcensus of May 1979. Of the total, 61,800 were self-employed, 7,600 unpaid family workers, 666,800 employees; 9,300 were engaged in agriculture and forestry, 216,500 in power supply, mining, manufacturing and building, 216,000 in commerce and transport, 29,400 in other industries and services.

ROADS. On 1 Jan. 1979 there were 3,623 km of roads, including 60 km of autobahn, 157 km of federal roads. Number of motor vehicles (1 July 1980), 629,083, including 566,641 passenger cars, 36,816 lorries, 1,754 buses, 4,757 tractors, 13,235 motor cycles.

SHIPPING. Hamburg is the largest port in the Federal Republic.

Vessels		*1938*	*1958*	*1968*	*1978*	*1979*
Entered:	Number	18,149	19,033	18,802	16,636	15,903
	Tonnage	20,567,311	27,454,640	37,073,215	61,785,643	64,095,021
Cleared:	Number	19,316	20,363	19,320	17,414	16,678
	Tonnage	20,547,148	27,579,914	36,820,828	62,028,141	63,920,734

JUSTICE. There is a constitutional court (*Verfassungsgericht*), a court of appeal (*Oberlandesgericht*), a regional court (*Landgericht*), 6 local courts (*Amtsgericht*), a Land labour court, a labour court, a Land social court, a social court, a finance court, a higher administrative court, an administrative court.

RELIGION. On 25 May 1970 (census) Evangelical Church and Free Churches 73·6%, Roman Catholic Church 8·1%.

EDUCATION. In 1979 there were 405 schools of general education (not including *Internationale Schule*) with 9,243 teachers and 217,936 pupils; 63 special schools with 1,041 teachers and 9,969 pupils; 47 part-time vocational schools with 49,174 pupils; 23 schools with 1,794 pupils in their vocational preparatory year; 20 schools with 1,590 pupils in manual instruction classes; 57 full-time vocational schools with 9,010 pupils; 9 economic secondary schools with 1,890 pupils; 23 advanced vocational schools with 3,330 pupils; 41 schools for public health occupations with 2,696 pupils; 11 vocational introducing schools with 420 pupils and 23 technical superior schools with 2,076 pupils; all these vocational and technical schools have a total number of 2,481 teachers.

In the winter term 1979–80 there was 1 university with 32,097 students; 1 college of music and 1 college of fine arts with together 1,779 students; 1 high school of the

Bundeswehr with 1,986 students; 1 professional high school (*Fachhochschule*) with 7,255 students; 1 high school for economics and politics with 1,078 students; 1 high school of public administration with 371 students, as well as 1 private professional high school with 97 students.

Statistical Information: The Statistisches Landesamt der Freien und Hansestadt Hamburg (Steckelhörn 12, D2000 Hamburg 11) publishes: *Hamburg in Zahlen, Statistische Berichte, Statistisches Jahrbuch, Statistisches Taschenbuch, Statistik des Hamburgischen Staates.*
Studt, B. and Olsen, H., *Hamburg—eine kurzgefaßte Geschichte der Stadt.* Hamburg, 1964
Meyer-Marwitz, B., *Großer Hamburg.* Hamburg, 1978
State Library: Staats--und Universitätsbibliothek, Moorweidenstr. 40, D2000 Hamburg 13.
Director: Dr Horst Gronemeyer.

HESSEN

AREA AND POPULATION. The state of Hessen comprehends the areas of the former Prussian provinces Kurhessen and Nassau (excluding the exclaves belonging to Hessen and the rural counties of Westerwaldkreis and Rhine-Lahn) and of the former Volksstaat Hessen, the provinces Starkenburg (including the parts of Rheinhessen east of the river Rhine) and Oberhessen. Hessen has an area of 21,113 sq. km. Its capital is Wiesbaden. Since 1 Aug. 1979 there have been 2 areas with 5 urban and 21 rural districts and 421 communes. Population, 31 May 1980, was 5,584,874 (2,684,742 males, 2,900,132 females).

Vital statistics for calendar years:

	Live births	Marriages	Divorces	Deaths
1977	51,703	30,862	7,958	61,880
1978	51,139	28,085	2,630	64,047
1979	51,854	29,632	6,707	63,024

CONSTITUTION. The constitution was put into force by popular referendum on 1 Dec. 1946. The Diet, elected on 8 Oct. 1978, consists of 53 Christian Democrats, 50 Social Democrats, 7 Free Democrats.

The Social Democrat and Free Democrat cabinet is headed by Minister President Holger Börner (SPD).

AGRICULTURE. Area and yield of the most important crops:

	Area (in 1,000 hectares)			*Yield (in 1,000 tonnes)*		
	1977	1978	1979	1977	1978	1979
Wheat	129·8	132·2	135·9	568·7	695·2	711·2
Rye	49·7	45·6	37·7	175·1	181·1	154·2
Barley	119·5	131·2	135·9	508·5	633·1	597·4
Oats	77·7	75·3	75·8	226·0	354·7	310·1
Potatoes	21·4	18·7	15·3	605·8	533·7	473·7
Sugar-beet	22·0	23·4	21·2	1,078·6	1,063·4	1,020·7

Livestock, 1 Dec. 1979: Cattle, 886,500 (including 300,300 milch cows); horses, 32,700; pigs, 1,378,500; sheep, 122,600; poultry, 4,891,800.

INDUSTRY. In July 1980, 4,147 establishments (with 20 and more employees) employed 673,291 persons; of these, 93,050 were employed in chemical industry; 87,028 in electrical engineering; 84,533 in machine construction; 90,609 in car building; 31,799 in food industry.

LABOUR. The economically active persons totalled 2·4m. at the 1%-sample survey of the microcensus of April 1979. Of the total, 187,900 were self-employed, 65,400 unpaid family workers, 2,151,000 employees; 97,200 were engaged in agriculture and forestry, 1,101,100 in power supply, mining, manufacturing and building, 423,800 in commerce and transport, 782,200 in other industries and services.

ROADS. On 1 Jan. 1980 there were 16,425 km of 'classified' roads, including 892 km of autobahn, 3,480 km of federal highways, 7,151 km of first-class highways and 5,001 km of second-class highways. Motor vehicles licensed on 1 July 1980 totalled 2,557,522, including 2,226,252 passenger cars, 5,689 buses, 116,356 trucks, 135,005 tractors and 56,945 motor cycles.

JUSTICE. There are a constitutional court (*Staatsgerichtshof*), a court of appeal, 9 regional courts, 58 local courts, a Land labour court, 12 labour courts, a Land social court, 7 social courts, a finance court, a higher administrative court (*Verwaltungsgerichtshof*), 4 administrative courts.

RELIGION. On 27 May 1970 (census) there were 60·5% Protestants and 32·8% Roman Catholics.

EDUCATION. In 1979 there were 1,309 primary schools with 14,963 teachers and 357,960 pupils; 252 special schools with 2,752 teachers and 28,820 pupils; 163 intermediate schools with 2,985 teachers and 68,737 pupils; 150 high schools with 7,849 teachers and 150,841 pupils; 169 *Gesamtschulen* (comprehensive schools) with 10,519 teachers and 208,740 pupils; 112 part-time vocational schools with 3,027 teachers and 158,576 pupils; 223 full-time vocational schools with 2,217 teachers and 34,691 pupils; 59 advanced vocational schools with 326 teachers and 4,764 pupils; 161 schools for public health occupations with 8,352 pupils; there were a further 35 full- and part-time institutions for the training of technicians with 2,178 participants.

In the winter term 1979–80 there were 3 universities (Frankfurt/Main, 23,829 students; Giessen, 14,273; Marburg, 12,106); 1 technical university in Darmstadt (11,923); 1 *Gesamthochschule* (7,097); 10 *Fachhochschulen* (17,218); 2 Roman Catholic theological colleges and 1 Protestant theological college with together 370 students; 1 college of music and 2 colleges of fine arts with together 1,007 students.

Statistical Information: The Hessisches Statistisches Landesamt (Rheinstr. 35–37, D6200 Wiesbaden). *President:* Götz Steppuhn. Main publications: *Statistisches Handbuch für das Land Hessen* (1978–79).—*Statistisches Taschenbuch für das Land Hessen* (1980–81).—*Staat und Wirtschaft in Hessen* (monthly).—*Beiträge zur Statistik Hessens.—Statistische Berichte.—Hessische Gemeindestatistik 1960–61* (5 vols., 1963 ff.).—*Hessische Gemeindestatistik 1970* (5 vols., 1972 ff.)—*Hessische Gemeindestatistik 1980* (1 vol.).

State Library: Hessische Landesbibliothek, Rheinstr. 55–57, D6200 Wiesbaden. *Director:* Dr Helmut Schwitzgebel.

LOWER SAXONY

Niedersachsen

AREA AND POPULATION. Lower Saxony (excluding the town of Bremerhaven, and the districts on the right bank of the Elbe in the Soviet Zone) comprises 47,423 sq. km, and is divided into 4 administrative districts, 38 rural districts, 9 towns and 1,026 communes; capital, Hanover.

Estimated population, on 31 Dec. 1979, was 7,234,000 (3,464,890 males, 3,769,110 females).

Vital statistics for calendar years:

	Live births	Marriages	Divorces	Deaths
1977	69,268	40,989	8,067	84,868
1978	68,557	36,957	3,970	85,562
1979	67,637	...	...	84,169

GOVERNMENT. The Land Niedersachsen was formed on 1 Nov. 1946 by merging the former Prussian province of Hanover and the *Länder* Brunswick, Oldenburg and Schaumburg-Lippe. The Diet, elected on 4 June 1978, consists of 83 Christian Democrats and 72 Social Democrats.

The cabinet of the Christian Democratic Union is headed by Minister President Dr Ernst Albrecht (CDU).

AGRICULTURE. Area and yield of the most important crops:

	Area (in 1,000 hectares)			*Yield (in 1,000 tonnes)*		
	1977	*1978*	*1979*	*1977*	*1978*	*1979*
Wheat	250	263	281	1,291	1,357	1,467
Rye	273	255	230	1,000	946	817
Barley	438	468	494	1,921	2,152	2,007
Oats	199	189	183	715	823	802
Potatoes	92	85	76	2,617	2,618	2,502
Sugar-beet	152	145	144	6,684	2,212	5,977

Livestock, 3 Dec. 1979: Cattle, 3,077,779 (including 1,056,223 milch cows); horses, 84,647; pigs, 6,708,767; sheep, 149,314; poultry, 35,587,742.

FISHERIES. In 1978 the yield of sea and coastal fishing was 176,760 tonnes valued at DM 173m.

INDUSTRY. In Sept. 1979, 4,857 establishments (with 20 and more employees) employed 721,130 persons; of these 64,803 were employed in machine construction; 143,055 in car building; 70,091 in electrical engineering.

LABOUR. The economically active persons totalled 3,029,000 at the 1%-sample survey of the microcensus of April 1979. Of the total 279,000 were self-employed, 134,000 unpaid family workers, 2,617,000 employees; 229,000 were engaged in agriculture and forestry, 1,249,000 in power supply, mining, manufacturing and building, 555,000 in commerce and transport, 997,000 in other industries and services.

ROADS. At 1 Jan. 1979 there were 27,653 km of 'classified' roads, including 944 km of autobahn, 5,187 km of federal roads, 8,651 km of first-class and 12,871 km of second-class highways.

Number of motor vehicles, 1 Jan. 1980, was 3,145,815 including 2,661,628 passenger cars, 146,005 lorries, 8,395 buses, 241,308 tractors, 64,912 motor cycles.

JUSTICE. There are a constitutional court (*Staatsgerichtshof*), 3 courts of appeal, 11 regional courts, 79 local courts, a Land labour court, 15 labour courts, a Land social court, 8 social courts, a finance court, a higher administrative court (together with Schleswig-Holstein), 3 administrative courts.

RELIGION. On 27 May 1970 (census) there were 74·6% Protestants and 19·6% Roman Catholics.

EDUCATION. In 1979 there were 2,331 primary schools with 27,793 teachers and 547,125 pupils; 289 special schools with 4,393 teachers and 46,103 pupils; 276 stages of orientation with 170,569 pupils; 271 intermediate schools with 7,119 teachers and 169,941 pupils; 241 grammar schools with 11,890 teachers and 206,102 pupils; 9 evening high schools with 129 teachers and 1,384 pupils; 18 integrated comprehensive schools with 1,592 teachers and 23,817 pupils; 17 co-operative comprehensive schools with 1,380 teachers and 25,735 pupils; 143 part-time vocational schools with 211,148 pupils; 106 year of basic vocational training with 17,746 pupils; 640 full-time vocational schools with 38,730 pupils; 88 *Fachgymnasien* with 7,319 pupils; 120 *Fachoberschulen* with 6,499 pupils (full-time vocational schools leading up to vocational colleges); 54 vocational extension schools with 1,351 pupils; 151 advanced full-time vocational schools (including schools for technicians) with 8,968 pupils; 230 public health schools with 11,228 pupils.

In the winter term 1979–80 there were 4 universities (Göttingen, 23,956 students; Hanover, 18,284; Oldenburg, 4,961; Osnabrück, 4,162); 2 technical universities (Braunschweig, 10,940; Clausthal, 2,920); the medical college of Hanover (2,635), the veterinary college in Hanover (1,409) and the colleges of Hildesheim (983) and Lüneburg (1,001).

Statistical Information: The Niedersächsisches Landesverwaltungsamt—Statistik' (Geibelstr. 65, D3000 Hanover 1) fulfils the function of the 'Statistisches Landesamt für Niedersachsen'. *Head of Division:* Abteilungsdirektor Dr Günter Koop. Main publications are: *Statistisches Jahrbuch Niedersachsen* (from 1950).—*Statistische Monatshefte Niedersachsen* (from 1947).—*Statistik Niedersachsen.*

State Library: Niedersächsische Staats- und Universitätsbibliothek, Prinzenstr. 1, 3400, Göttingen. *Director:* Helmut Vogt; Niedersächsische Landesbibliothek, Waterloostr. 8, D3000 Hannover 1. *Director:* Dr Wilhelm Totok.

NORTH RHINE-WESTPHALIA

Nordrhein-Westfalen

AREA AND POPULATION. The Land comprises 34,069 sq. km. It is divided into 5 areas, 23 urban and 31 rural districts. Capital Düsseldorf. Population, 31 Dec. 1979, 17,017,075 (8,122,634 males, 8,894,441 females).

Vital statistics for calendar years:

	Live births	Marriages	Divorces	Deaths
1977	160,940	102,617	17,247	192,672
1978	158,478	93,067	11,434	197,249
1979	159,378	98,109	23,826	195,147

GOVERNMENT. The Land Nordrhein-Westfalen is governed by Social Democrats; Minister President, Johannes Rau (SPD). The Diet, elected on 11 May 1980, consists of 106 Social Democrats, 95 Christian Democrats.

AGRICULTURE. Area and yield of the most important crops:

	Area (in 1,000 hectares)			Yield (in 1,000 tonnes)		
	1977	1978	1979	1977	1978	1979
Wheat	214·3	213·6	216·4	871·1	1,101·6	1,139·2
Rye	118·0	107·0	86·8	434·0	425·0	382·7
Barley	336·6	362·3	373·1	1,476·8	1,727·2	1,647·3
Oats	129·5	121·1	120·1	371·5	553·5	531·4
Potatoes	37·3	32·2	22·4	1,021·2	1,028·2	681·7
Sugar-beet	89·3	84·4	84·2	4,284·2	6,441·6	3,873·7

Livestock, 1 Dec. 1979: Cattle, 1,940,775 (including 627,933 milch cows); pigs, 5,363,654; sheep, 167,382; horses, 92,611; poultry, 14,948,167.

INDUSTRY. In June 1980, 11,675 establishments (with 20 and more employees) employed 2,215,041 persons; of these, 177,403 were employed in mining; 297,082 in machine construction; 200,140 in iron and steel production; 208,420 in chemical industry; 182,819 in electrical engineering; 82,252 in textile industry.

Output and/or production in 1,000 tonnes, 1979: Hard coal, 75,911; lignite, 116,363; pig-iron, 22,748; raw steel ingots, 28,386; rolled steel, 20,144; castings (iron, steel and malleable castings), 1,842; cement, 12,811; fireproof products, 1,479; sulphuric acid (including production of cokeries), 2,308; staple fibres and rayon, 311,451; metalworking machines, 133; equipment for smelting works and rolling mills, 125; machines for mining industry, 280; cranes and hoisting machinery, 65; installation implements, 73; cables and electric lines, 256; springs of all kinds, 216; chains of all kinds, 89; locks and fittings, 280; spun yarns, 173; electric power, 174,552m. kwh. Of the total population, 13% were engaged in industry.

LABOUR. The economically active persons totalled 6,824,800 at the 1%-sample survey of the microcensus of April 1979. Of the total, 543,000 were self-employed, 120,600 unpaid family workers, 6,161,200 employees; 171,800 were engaged in agriculture and forestry, 3,289,500 in power supply, mining, manufacturing and building, 1·3m. in commerce and transport, 2,101,700 in other industries and services.

ROADS. There were (1 Jan. 1980) 29,381 km of 'classified' roads, including 1,702 km of autobahn, 5,546 km of federal roads, 12,234 km of first-class and 9,900 km of second-class highways. Number of motor vehicles, 1 July 1980, 7,091,249, including 5,888,150 passenger cars, 438,341 lorries, 321,342 motor lorries/trucks, 17,079 buses, 206,188 tractors and 176,000 motor cycles.

JUSTICE. There are a constitutional court (*Verfassungsgerichtshof*), 3 courts of appeal, 19 regional courts, 132 local courts, 2 Land labour courts, 29 labour courts, a Land social court, 8 social courts, 3 finance courts, a higher administrative court, 7 administrative courts.

RELIGION. On 27 May 1970 (census) there were 41·9% Protestants and 52·5% Roman Catholics.

EDUCATION. In 1979 there were 4,802 primary schools with 71,071 teachers and 1,478,983 pupils; 740 special schools with 12,297 teachers and 112,012 pupils; 556 intermediate schools with 15,570 teachers and 369,059 pupils; 44 *Gesamtschulen* (comprehensive schools) with 3,410 teachers and 50,706 pupils; 646 high schools with 32,590 teachers and 634,129 pupils; in 1979 there were 303 part-time vocational schools with 471,928 pupils; vocational preparatory year 270 with 37,959 pupils; 341 full-time vocational schools with 107,310 pupils; 246 full-time vocational schools leading up to vocational colleges with 29,129 pupils; 142 advanced full-time vocational schools with 11,651 pupils; 568 schools for public health occupations with 8,648 teachers and 28,013 pupils; 7 schools within the scope of a pilot system of courses with 15,222 pupils and 554 teachers.

In the winter term 1979–80 there were 7 universities (Bielefeld, 7,721 students; Bochum, 24,002; Bonn, 30,120; Dortmund, 6,571; Düsseldorf, 9,519; Cologne, 28,028; Münster, 31,057); the Technical University of Aachen (24,807); 1 Roman Catholic and 2 Protestant theological colleges with together 775 students. There were also 3 teacher-training colleges with 29,669 students; 3 colleges of music, 1 college of fine arts and the college for physical education in Cologne with together 7,833 students; 17 *Fachhochschulen* (vocational colleges) with 57,886 students, and 6 *Gesamthochschulen* with together 50,807 students.

Statistical Information: The *Landesamt für Datenverarbeitung und Statistik Nordrhein-Westfalen* (Mauerstr. 51, D4000 Düsseldorf 1) was founded in 1946, by amalgamating the provincial statistical offices of Rhineland and Westphalia. *President:* A. Benker. The Landesamt publishes: *Statistisches Jahrbuch Nordrhein-Westfalen.* From 1949.—*Statistisches Taschenbuch Nordrhein-Westfalen.* From 1955 to 1971.—More than 550 other publications yearly.

Land Library: Universitätsbibliothek, Grabbeplatz 7, Düsseldorf. *Director:* Dr G. Gattermann.

RHINELAND-PALATINATE

Rheinland-Pfalz

AREA AND POPULATION. Rhineland-Pfalz comprises 19,848 sq. km. Capital Mainz. Population (at 31 Dec. 1979), 3,633,195 (1,734,160 males, 1,899,035 females).

Vital statistics for calendar years:

	Live births	Marriages	Divorces	Deaths
1977	34,129	23,720	4,786	41,941
1978	34,346	21,613	2,137	44,029
1979	34,805	22,756	5,434	43,108

CONSTITUTION. The constitution of the Land Rheinland-Pfalz was approved by the Consultative Assembly on 25 April 1947 and by referendum on 18 May 1947, when 579,002 voted for and 514,338 against its acceptance.

The elections of 18 March 1979 returned 51 Christian Democrats, 43 Social Democrats, 6 Free Democrats.

The cabinet is headed by Bernhard Vogel (Christian Democrat).

AGRICULTURE. Area and yield of the most important products:

	Area (1,000 hectares)			Yield (1,000 tonnes)		
	1977	1978	1979	1977	1978	1979
Wheat	121·7	122·3	117·5	500·2	588·8	567·6
Rye	43·7	41·3	35·1	154·2	165·0	140·1
Barley	132·0	142·5	135·7	503·4	580·3	577·5
Oats	57·4	52·5	49·3	182·7	219·7	191·8
Potatoes	31·9	28·4	16·2	843·5	707·5	440·9
Sugar-beet	25·4	24·5	22·6	1,345·6	1,247·4	1,168·6
Wine (1,000 hectolitres)	59·2	59·7	57·5	6,829·3	5,177·7	5,395·8
Tobacco	1·3	1·3	1·2	...	...	...

Livestock (1 Dec. 1979): Cattle, 678,200 (including 235,800 milch cows); horses, 21,800; sheep, 87,600; pigs, 687,300; poultry 3,657,100.

INDUSTRY. In Sept. 1979, 2,910 establishments (with 20 and more employees) employed 398,156 persons; of these 73,008 were employed in chemical industry; 25,543 in production of leather goods and footwear; 49,826 in machine construction; 18,574 in processing stones and earthenware.

LABOUR. The economically active persons totalled 1,553,000 at the census of April 1979. Of the total, 152,000 were self-employed, 72,000 unpaid family workers, 1·33m. employees; 107,000 were engaged in agriculture and forestry, 668,000 in power supply, mining, manufacturing and building, 275,000 in commerce and transport, 503,000 in other industries and services.

ROADS. There were (1 Jan. 1980) 18,664 km of 'classified' roads, including 645 km of autobahn, 3,248 km of federal roads, 6,910 km of first-class and 7,861 km of second-class highways. Number of motor vehicles, 1 July 1980, was 1,711,704, including 1,429,892 passenger cars, 77,126 lorries, 4,793 buses, 140,886 tractors and 48,178 motor cycles.

JUSTICE. There are a constitutional court (*Verfassungsgerichtshof*), 2 courts of appeal, 8 regional courts, 47 local courts, a Land labour court, 5 labour courts, a Land social court, 4 social courts, a finance court, a higher administrative court, 4 administrative courts.

RELIGION. On 27 May 1970 (census) there were 40·7% Protestants and 55·7% Roman Catholics.

EDUCATION. In 1979 there were 1,189 primary schools with 15,781 teachers and 333,616 pupils; 158 special schools with 2,355 teachers and 18,880 pupils; 105 intermediate schools with 3,076 teachers and 69,613 pupils; 138 high schools with 6,328 teachers and 124,590 pupils; 100 vocational schools with 125,789 pupils; 123 advanced vocational schools and institutions for the training of technicians (full- and part-time) with 6,413 pupils; 109 schools for public health occupations with 270 teachers and 6,140 pupils.

In the summer term 1980 there were the University of Mainz (21,059 students), the University of Kaiserslautern (3,096 students), the University of Trier (3,293 students) and the Roman Catholic Theological College in Trier (362 students). There were also the Teacher-Training College of the Land Rheinland-Pfalz (*Erziehungswissenschaftliche Hochschule*) with 2,375 students and the *Fachhochschule des Landes Rheinland-Pfalz* (college of engineering) with 7,169 students; also 2 private colleges for social-pedagogy (739 students).

Statistical Information: The Statistisches Landesamt Rheinland-Pfalz (Mainzer Str., 15–16, D5427 Bad Ems) was established in 1948. *President:* Dr Weis. Its publications include: *Statistisches Jahrbuch für Rheinland-Pfalz* (from 1948); *Statistische Monatshefte Rheinland-Pfalz* (from 1958); *Statistik von Rheinland-Pfalz* (from 1949) 287 vols. to date; *Rheinland-Pfalz im Spiegel der Statistik* (1968); *Die kreisfreien Städte und Landkreise in Rheinland-Pfalz* (1977); *Rheinland-Pfalz heute* (from 1973); *Benutzerhandbuch des Landesinformationssystems* (1976); *Rheinland-Pfalz heute und morgen* (Mainz, 1974); *Raumordnungsbericht 1979 der Landesregierung Rheinland-Pfalz* (Mainz, 1979).

Klöpper, R., and Korber, J., *Rheinland-Pfalz in seiner Gliederung nach zentralörtlichen Bereichen.* Remagen, 1957
Süsterhenn, A., and Schäfer, H., *Verfassung von Rheinland-Pfalz: Kommentar.* Koblenz, 1950

SAARLAND

HISTORY. In 1919 the Saar territory was placed under the control of the League of Nations. Following a plebiscite, the territory reverted to Germany in 1935. In 1945 the territory became part of the French Zone of occupation, and was in 1947 accorded an international status inside an economic union with France. In pursuance of the German–French agreement signed in Luxembourg on 27 Oct. 1956 the territory returned to Germany on 1 Jan. 1957. Its re-integration with Germany was completed by 5 July 1959.

AREA AND POPULATION. Saarland has an area of 2,573 sq. km. Estimated population, 31 Dec. 1979, 1,068,555 (505,891 males, 562,664 females). The capital is Saarbrücken.

Vital statistics for calendar years:

	Live births	Marriages	Divorces	Deaths
1977	9,876	7,614	631	12,383
1978	9,574	7,069	666	13,208
1979	9,787	7,331	2,259	13,106

CONSTITUTION. Saarland now ranks as a *Land* of the Federal German Republic and is represented in the Federal Diet by 8 members. The constitution passed on 15 Dec. 1947 is being revised.

The Saar Diet, elected on 27 April 1980, is composed as follows: 24 Social Democrats, 23 Christian Democrats, 4 Free Democrats.

Saarland is governed by Christian Democrats and Free Democrats in spite of deadlock in Parliament. Minister President: Werner Zeyer (Christian Democrat).

AGRICULTURE AND FORESTRY. The cultivated area occupies 126,500 hectares or slightly more than half the total area; the forest area comprises nearly 32% of the total.

Area and yield of the most important crops:

	Area (1,000 hectares)			Yield (1,000 tonnes)		
	1977	1978	1979	1977	1978	1979
Wheat	11·1	10·5	7·7	45·1	46·1	36·9
Rye	9·2	9·8	7·7	33·9	36·2	29·8
Barley	12·4	13·8	11·8	47·3	55·2	49·3
Oats	8·6	7·9	7·2	29·7	31·8	26·8
Potatoes	6·2	5·7	1·1	178·8	158·1	31·1
Sugar-beet	...	...	...	0·9	0·6	1·0

Livestock, 3 Dec. 1979: Cattle, 72,032 (including 26,030 milch cows); pigs, 50,462; sheep, 10,000; horses, 4,300; poultry, 568,071.

INDUSTRY. In June 1979, 609 establishments (with 20 and more employees) employed 149,573 persons; of these 21,947 were engaged in coalmining, 30,145 in iron and steel production, 11,686 in machine construction, 10,067 in steel construction. In 1979 the coalmines produced 9·9m. tonnes of coal. Four iron foundries had 13 blast furnaces working and produced 4·5m. tonnes of pig-iron and 5·1m. tonnes of crude steel.

LABOUR. The economically active persons totalled 391,500 at the 1%-sample survey of the microcensus of April 1979. Of the total, 28,800 were self-employed, 9,700 unpaid family workers, 353,000 employees; 8,300 were engaged in agriculture and forestry, 202,100 in power supply, mining, manufacturing and building, 64,600 in commerce and transport, 116,500 in other industries and services.

ROADS. At 1 Jan. 1980 there were 2,127 km of 'classified' roads, including 154 km of autobahn, 441 km of federal roads, 765 km of first-class and 767 km of second-class highways. Number of motor vehicles, 1 July 1980, 465,716, including 415,112 passenger cars, 21,053 lorries, 1,525 buses, 11,855 tractors and 12,953 motor cycles.

JUSTICE. There are a constitutional court (*Verfassungsgerichtshof*), a court of appeal, a regional court, 11 local courts, a Land labour court, 3 labour courts, a Land social court, a social court, a finance court, a higher administrative court, an administrative court.

RELIGION. On 27 May 1970 (census) 73·8% of the population were Roman Catholics and 24·1% were Protestants.

EDUCATION. In 1979–80 there were 335 primary schools with 4,141 teachers and 89,577 pupils; 57 special schools with 623 teachers and 6,120 pupils; 37 intermediate schools with 1,063 teachers and 22,297 pupils; 39 high schools with 1,875 teachers and 34,136 pupils; 2 *Gesamtschule* (comprehensive schools) with 88 teachers and 1,738 pupils; 1 *Freie Waldorfschule* with 16 teachers and 304 pupils; 42 part-time vocational schools with 34,230 pupils; year of commercial basic training: 39 institutions with 123 classes and 2,528 pupils; 20 advanced full-time vocational schools and schools for technicians with 1,661 pupils; 78 full-time vocational schools with 8,214 students; 23 vocational extension schools with 2,049 pupils; 18 *Fachoberschulen* (full-time vocational schools leading up to vocational colleges) with 2,359 students; 36 schools for public health occupations with 2,038 pupils; 2 evening high schools and 1 *Saarland-Kolleg* with together 330 pupils. The number of pupils visiting the vocational schools amounts to 53,079. They are instructed by 1,520 teachers.

In the winter term 1979–80 there was the University of the Saar with 13,195 students; 1 conservatory with 276 students; 1 vocational college (economics, engineering and design) with 1,580 students; 1 *Fachhochschule* (vocational college) for social affairs with 158 students.

Statistical Information: The Statistisches Amt des Saarlandes (Hardenbergstrasse 3, D6600 Saarbrücken 1) was established on 1 April 1938. As from 1 June 1935, it was an independent agency; its predecessor, 1920–35, was the Statistical Office of the Government Commission of the Saar. *Chief:* Direktor Dr Kunkel. The most important publications are: *Statistisches Handbuch für das Saarland*, from 1950.—*Statistisches Taschenbuch für das Saarland*, from 1959.—*Saarländische Bevölkerungsund Wirtschaftszahlen*. Quarterly, from 1949.—*Saarland in Zahlen* (special issues).—*Einzelschriften zur Statistik des Saarlandes*, from 1950.

Fischer, P., *Die Saar zwischen Deutschland und Frankreich*. Frankfurt, 1959
Freymond, J., *Le Conflit sarrois, 1945–55*. Brussels, 1959. [*The Saar Conflict*. New York, 1960]
Schmidt, R. H., *Saarpolitik 1945–57*. 3 vols. Berlin, 1959–62

SCHLESWIG-HOLSTEIN

AREA AND POPULATION. The area of Schleswig-Holstein is 15,710 sq. km; it is divided into 4 urban and 11 rural districts and 1,132 communes. The capital is Kiel. The population (estimate, 31 Dec. 1979) numbered 2,599,004 (1,250,085 males, 1,348,919 females).

Vital statistics for calendar years:

	Live births	Marriages	Divorces	Deaths
1977	23,366	14,316	3,366	31,068
1978	23,185	12,579	...	31,257
1979	22,810	13,068	3,289	31,400

GOVERNMENT. The elections of 29 April 1979 gave the Christian Democrats 37, the Social Democratic Party 31, the Free Democratic Party 4 and the South Schleswig Association 1 seat. Minister President, Dr Gerhard Stoltenberg (Christian Democrat).

AGRICULTURE. Area and yield of the most important crops:

	Area (1,000 hectares)			Yield (1,000 tonnes)		
	1977	1978	1979	1977	1978	1979
Wheat	124·0	140·3	161·0	109·5	932·3	936·5
Rye	92·1	82·9	75·1	356·1	321·7	293·5
Barley	127·9	136·2	128·4	656·7	706·6	571·4
Oats	69·0	53·4	44·0	257·6	238·2	208·2
Potatoes	8·2	6·4	5·6	222·6	172·8	153·0
Sugar-beet	21·4	18·6	18·3	869·3	712·8	686·5

Livestock, 3 Dec 1979: 34,400 horses, 1,552,200 cattle (including 511,250 milch cows), 1,854,500 pigs, 123,000 sheep, 4,123,900 poultry.

FISHERIES. In 1978 the yield of small-scale deep-sea and inshore fisheries was 47,100 tonnes valued at DM 57m.

INDUSTRY. In 1979 (average), 1,647 establishments (with 20 and more employees) employed 179,920 persons; of these, 15,227 were employed in shipbuilding (except naval engineering); 29,253 in machine construction; 26,111 in food and kindred industry; 19,579 in electrical engineering.

LABOUR. The economically active persons totalled 1·25m. at the 1%-sample survey of the microcensus of April 1979. Of the total, 107,000 were self-employed, 36,400 unpaid family workers, 1,103,100 employees; 77,400 were engaged in agriculture and forestry, 362,100 in power supply, mining, manufacturing and building, 222,200 in commerce and transport, 441,400 in other industries and services.

ROADS. There were (1 Jan 1980) 9,652 km of 'classified' roads, including 313 km of autobahn, 1,982 km of federal roads, 3,511 km of first-class and 3,846 km of second-class highways. Number of motor vehicles, 1 July 1980, was 1,128,860, including 967,691 passenger cars, 55,957 lorries, 2,743 buses, 73,631 tractors, 19,981 motor cycles.

SHIPPING. The Kiel Canal, 98·7 km (51 miles) long, is on Schleswig-Holstein territory. In 1938, 53,530 vessels of 22·6m. net tons passed through it; in 1977, 57,765 vessels of 45·3m. net tons; in 1978, 57,292 vessels of 48·3m. net tons; in 1979, 55,457 vessels of 49·3m. net tons.

JUSTICE. There are a court of appeal, 4 regional courts, 43 local courts, a Land labour court, 6 labour courts, a Land social court, 4 social courts, a finance court, an administrative court.

RELIGION. On 27 May 1970 (census) there were 86·5% Protestants and 6% Roman Catholics.

EDUCATION. In 1979–80 there were 707 primary schools with 6,865 teachers and 213,352 pupils; 166 special schools with 1,602 teachers and 20,858 pupils; 170 intermediate schools with 3,420 teachers and 90,414 pupils; 94 high schools with 4,065 teachers and 87,052 pupils; 6 *Integrierte Gesamtschulen* (comprehensive schools) with 209 teachers and 3,771 pupils; 69 part-time vocational schools with 1,410 teachers and 83,397 pupils; 131 full-time vocational schools with 394 teachers and 9,680 pupils; 64 advanced vocational schools with 319 teachers and 4,870 pupils; 55 schools for public health occupations with 3,036 pupils; 41 vocational grammar schools with 313 teachers and 4,647 pupils; 5 *Fachhochschulen* (vocational colleges) with 4,538 pupils in the summer term 1980.

In the summer term 1980 the University of Kiel had 12,873 students, 2 teacher-training colleges had 2,769 students, 1 music college had 286 students and 1 *Medizinische Hochschule* in Lübeck had 425 students.

Statistical Information: Statistisches Landesamt Schleswig-Holstein (Mühlenweg 166, D2300 Kiel 1). *Director:* Dr Mohr. Publications: *Statistisches Taschenbuch Schleswig-Holstein,* since1954.— *Statistisches Jahrbuch Schleswig-Holstein,* since 1951.—*Statistische Monatshefte Schleswig-Holstein,* since 1949.—*Statistische Berichte,* since 1947.—*Beitrage zur historischen Statistik Schleswig-Holstein,* since 1967.—*Lange Reihen,* since 1977.

Baxter, R. R., *The Law of International Waterways.* Harvard Univ. Press, 1964
Brandt, O., *Grundriss der Geschichte Schleswig-Holsteins.* 5th ed. Kiel, 1957
Handbuch für Schleswig-Holstein. 16th ed. Kiel, 1972

State Library: Schleswig-Holsteinische Landesbibliothek, Kiel, Schloss. *Director:* Prof. Dr Klaus Friedland.

GHANA

Capital: Accra
Population: 11·7m. (1980)
GNP per capita: US$390 (1978)

HISTORY. The State of Ghana came into existence on 6 March 1957 when the former Colony of the Gold Coast and the Trusteeship Territory of Togoland attained Dominion status. The name of the country recalls a powerful monarchy which from the 4th to the 13th century A.D. ruled the region of the middle Niger.

The Ghana Independence Act received the royal assent on 7 Feb. 1957. The General Assembly of the United Nations in Dec. 1956 approved the termination of British administration in Togoland and the union of Togoland with the Gold Coast on the latter's attainment of independence.

The country was declared a Republic within the Commonwealth on 1 July 1960 with Dr Kwame Nkrumah as the first President. On 24 Feb. 1966 the Nkrumah regime was overthrown in a military *coup* and ruled by the National Liberation Council until 1 Oct. 1969 when the military regime handed over power to a civilian regime under a new constitution. Dr K. A. Busia was the Prime Minister of the Second Republic. In Aug. 1975 the Government announced that they would commemorate the late Dr Nkrumah as 'a great Ghanaian responsible for taking the country to independence'.

On 13 Jan. 1972 the armed forces and police took over power again from the civilian regime in a *coup*.

In Oct. 1975 the National Redemption Council was subordinated to a Supreme Military Council (SMC). In 1979 the SMC was toppled in a *coup* led by Flight-Lieut. J. Rawlings. The new government permitted elections already scheduled and these resulted in a victory for Dr Hilla Limann and his People's National Party.

AREA AND POPULATION. The area of Ghana is 92,010 sq. miles (238,305 sq. km); census population 1970, 8,559,331. Estimate (1980) 11·7m.

The capital is Accra (population, 1970, 636,067).

Ghana is divided into 9 regions:

Regions	Area (sq. km)	Population census 1970	Capital	Population census 1970
Eastern	19,833	1,262,882	Koforidua	69,804
Western	24,214	770,089	Sekondi-Takoradi	254,543
Central	9,469	890,135	Cape Coast	71,594
Ashanti	25,123	1,505,049	Kumasi	351,629
Brong-Ahafo	39,709	766,509	Sunyani	61,772
Northern	70,338	728,572	Tamale	120,000
Volta	20,651	947,012	Ho	46,348
Upper	16,877	862,723	Bolgatanga	18,896
Greater Accra	2,023	903,445	Accra	636,067

Other chief towns (population, census, 1970); Asamankese, 101,144; Nsawam, 57,350; Oda, 40,740; Obuasi, 40,001; Winneba, 36,104; Keta, 27,461; Swedru (Agona), 23,843.

Estimated birth rate, between 47 and 52 per 1,000; death rate, about 23 per 1,000.

CONSTITUTION AND GOVERNMENT. Following a bloodless *coup* on 13 Jan. 1972 the armed forces of Ghana took over the government from Dr K. A. Busia. A National Redemption Council (NRC) was established to administer the affairs of the country.

The Constitution of the Second Republic of Ghana which came into force on 22 Aug. 1969 was suspended. The office of President was abolished and the National Assembly dissolved.

On 5 July 1978 officers of the Supreme Military Council ousted Gen. I. K. Acheampong in a bloodless *coup*. They in turn were overthrown by a junior officers *coup* on 4 June 1979. An Armed Forces Revolutionary Council was formed but on 24 Sept. 1979 this made way in favour of a civilian government. The Constitution of the Third Republic provides for a unicameral legislature of 140 members.

For earlier political history of Ghana *see* THE STATESMAN'S YEAR-BOOK, 1971–72.
President: Dr Hilla Limann.
National flag: Red, gold, green (horizontal); a black star in the centre.
National anthem: Hail the name of Ghana.

DEFENCE. The Ministry of Defence is responsible for the armed services, the military academy and the border guards. The Military Academy provides a 2-year course for army officers, a 1-year course for later entrants in the flying-training school and a preliminary 6-month course for navy cadets.

Army. The Ghana Army consists of 6 infantry battalions, 1 reconnaissance battalion, 1 field engineer battalion, 1 mortar battalion, 5 with armoured cars, and ancillary units. Total strength, about 14,700. There are also 3 border battalions and a paramilitary militia of 4,000.

Navy. The Ghana Navy was formed in 1959. It comprises 2 British-built 500-ton corvettes, 4 fast attack craft, 2 patrol craft, 2 old seaward defence boats, 4 coastal patrol boats and 2 service craft. Naval personnel in 1981 numbered 2,000 officers and ratings.

Air Force. The Ghana Air Force was formed in 1959, when an Air Force Training School was established at Accra. Its first combat unit has 6 Italian-built Aermacchi M.B.326K light ground attack jets ordered in 1976. It has, for training, transport, search and rescue, and air survey operations, 5 Fokker Friendship twin-turboprop transports, and a twin-turbofan Fokker Fellowship for Presidential use, all built in the Netherlands; 6 Shorts Skyvan and 8 Britten-Norman Islander twin-engined STOL transports and 12 Bulldog primary trainers, all built in the UK; 2 Bell 212 helicopters built in the US; 4 French-built Alouette III helicopters, and 6 Aermacchi M.B.326F armed jet trainers. There are air bases at Takoradi and Tamale. Personnel strength (1981) about 1,550.

INTERNATIONAL RELATIONS

Membership. Ghana is a member of UN, the Commonwealth, OAU, ECOWAS and is an ACP state of EEC.

ECONOMY

Planning. The 1975–80 Development Plan was launched in 1977.

Budget. Revenue and expenditure for fiscal years ending 30 June (excluding Ghana Railway and Takoradi Harbour accounts), in ₵ 1,000:

	1974–75	1975–76	1976–77	1978–79
Revenue[1]	804,800	814,800	1,171,300	3,206,430
Expenditure[2]	1,161,400	1,438,572	2,015,900	3,819,420

[1] Excludes redemption of loans.
[2] Excludes contribution to sinking funds, repayment of loans, loans and refunds of revenue.

The main items of expenditure for 1976–77 were (in ₵ 1m.): Social services and health, 335·4; works and housing, 98; agriculture, 71; defence, 66; financial services administration, 227.

The development budget for 1975–76 was ₵ 422·7m.

Currency. The monetary unit is the *cedi* (₵), divided into 100 *pesewas* (P) and equivalent to £0·51 or US$0.87. Notes are issued of 1, 2, 5 and 10 ₵; copper coins of ½ and 1 P, and cupro-nickel coins of 2½, 5, 10 and 20 P. In March 1981, £1 = ₵ 6·09; US$1 = 2·75.

Banking. The Bank of Ghana was established in Feb. 1957 as the central bank of the country. The Ghana Commercial Bank, also established in Feb. 1957, is the former Bank of the Gold Coast. It is a purely commercial institution and has 120 branches in the country, 1 in London and 1 in Lomé (Togo). Barclays Bank (Ghana) Ltd has 54 branches and agencies and the Standard Bank (Ghana) Ltd has 27 branches.

The Ghana National Investment Bank, opened in June 1963, is a finance-cum-development agency. The former post office savings bank has been transformed into the Ghana Savings Bank. The Bank for Housing and Construction opened in 1973.

ENERGY AND NATURAL RESOURCES

Oil. The Government announced in Jan. 1978 that oil had been found in commercial quantities.

Minerals. In 1977 gold production was 481,000 fine oz.; diamonds, 1,851,000 carats; manganese, 268,000 tons; bauxite, 265,000 long tons. Old mines are being re-opened and exploration of mineral oil deposits, bauxite, limestone and iron ore is now extensive.

Agriculture. Cocoa is by far the most important crop and covers about 2m. acres. Production (1979–80) 300,000 tons. There has been a considerable increase in cocoa yields as a result of the Capsid control and the introduction of improved varieties. A Cocoa Affairs Ministry has been established to formulate policy and provide technical supervision for developing cocoa, coffee, shea-nuts, copra and bananas. Coffee, improved types of oil-palm and coconut are being planted on an increased scale and production from these crops is increasing. Progress has been made in the planting of Clonal rubber in south-west Ghana. In the south-east coastal belt irrigation works have been constructed and black-clay farming is being successfully undertaken in the Accra plains.

Of the main foodstuffs in south and central Ghana, maize, rice, cassava, plantain, groundnuts, yam and cocoyam predominate. Tobacco is proving an attractive and very important cash crop in food-crop producing areas.

In northern Ghana the chief food crops are groundnuts, rice, maize, guinea corn, millet and yams, with tobacco and cotton as important cash crops.

The State Farms Corporation has been reorganized and is now to concentrate on the development of large-scale tree-crop plantations such as palm-oil, rubber, coconut, kola and cashew. All its available food farms have been transferred to the newly formed Food Production Corporation. The Corporation undertakes the growing of maize, guinea corn, rice, vegetables, cassava, plantain, yams, etc.

Agricultural cash crops, *e.g.*, pepper, ginger, pineapple, avocado and citrus, etc., are being extensively cultivated for export. Active steps have also been taken to provide within the next few years industrial raw materials, *e.g.*, kenaf, cotton, tobacco, palm-oil, mango, pineapple, sugar-cane, etc., to feed the local factories. The trend is towards diversification of agriculture.

A Food Production Corporation has been established to see to the production and efficient and equitable distribution of foodstuffs throughout the country. The state farms have been transferred to the Corporation.

Production of main food crops (1977) was: Cassava, 2·3m. tons; plantain, 1,455,000 tons; coco yam, 905,000 tons; yam, 397,000 tons.

Livestock, 1979: Cattle, 930,000; sheep, 1·7m.; goats, 2m.; horses, 4,000; pigs, 400,000; poultry, 11·5m. The Central Veterinary Laboratory is located at Pong-Tamale under the Veterinary Research Officer. The efficient control of rinderpest and bovine pleuro-pneumonia, the two main killing diseases of cattle, has made it possible to quadruple the cattle in the past 20 years. The control of imported livestock is effected by 8 quarantine stations along the frontier, and newly established veterinary centres are being established.

Forestry. The total area of closed forest is 82,576 sq. km, of which 16,852·2 sq. km are reserved. Exports (1976) of logs, was 512,261 tons.

The destruction of unreserved forests by farming is threatening the timber supply for exports. Reafforestation is going ahead to counteract this and the Upper and Northern Regions included to arrest the Sahelian threat.

Fisheries. The fisheries sector of the economy is being developed, including fishing harbours and landing stages, workshops for repair and maintenance of outboard motors; development of fish culture and expansion of fish farms, establishment of fishing complexes, purchase of refrigerated vans for fish distribution and the establishment of more cold-stores.

COMMERCE. Total trade, in ₵ 1,000, for calendar years:

	1974	1975	1976	1977
Imports	943,706	909,300	968,800	1,175,900
Exports	840,933	928,260	924,300	1,105,800

Principal exports in ₵ 1,000	1973	1974	1975	1976
Cocoa	344,833	466,427	551,427	515,503
Timber (logs)	88,551	63,955	77,269	75,214
Gold	71,016	94,843	83,766	60,438
Diamonds	13,063	14,570	12,722	8,403
Manganese	7,315	10,519	16,853	19,676
Bauxite	2,574	3,465	4,333	3,396

In 1976 the most important items of imports were raw materials capital equipment, mineral fuels and food.

Total trade between Ghana and UK (British Department of Trade returns, in £1,000 sterling):

	1976	1977	1978	1979	1980
Imports to UK	82,230	126,632	110,122	89,808	104,545
Exports and re-exports from UK	79,563	100,072	118,975	88,058	88,511

West African Common Market. On 4 May 1967, 12 West African countries (Benin, Ghana, Ivory Coast, Liberia, Mali, Mauritania, Niger, Nigeria, Senegal, Sierra Leone, Togo and Upper Volta) signed articles of association in Accra, setting up a common market for goods and services among them and eliminating customs and trade barriers.

COMMUNICATIONS

Roads. The total mileage of roads maintained by the Public Works Department in 1974 was 21,762, of which 2,746 miles were bitumen surfaced and 5,016 miles gravel surfaced.

The number of vehicles in use (1976) was 110,000, of which private cars, 64,000.

Railways. Total length of railways open in 1980 was 953 km of 1,067 mm gauge. In 1976–77 railway income was ₵ 13·8m. from 6m. passenger-journeys and 1m. tonnes of freight carried.

Aviation. There are 4 major airports in Ghana, situated at Accra, Takoradi, Kumasi and Tamale; and 3 airstrips for domestic services. Accra airport is an international airport. The following airlines operate scheduled services: Ghana Airways, Air France, Nigerian Airways, Air Mali, United Arab Airlines, KLM, Swissair, PANAM, British Caledonian and several other companies. Total aircraft freight in 1975 was 3m. ton-km.

Shipping. The chief ports are Takoradi and Tema; the 'surf' ports at Accra, Winneba, Cape Coast and Keta ceased to operate when Tema harbour was opened in 1962, 18 miles east of Accra. In 1970, 4,164,329 tons of cargo were imported and 2,154,759 tons were exported by 3,116 ships.

Post and Broadcasting. There were (31 Dec. 1974) 2,190 miles of telegraph land wire, 20,948 miles of telephone trunks, 237 post offices and 710 postal agencies. There were 431 telephone exchanges and 742 call offices with (1978) 66,405 telephones in use and 29,227 miles of underground and overhead land wires in the exchange areas. There are internal wireless stations at Accra, Kumasi, Bawku, Lawra, Kete-Krachi, Tamale, Yendi, Kpandu, Tumu and Sekondi-Takoradi.

Newspapers. There are 5 daily and 7 weekly papers, 8 fortnightly and 5 monthly magazines.

JUSTICE, EDUCATION AND WELFARE

Justice. The judicial power of Ghana is vested in the Judiciary with the Chief Justice as the Head. It has jurisdiction in all civil and criminal matters.

The Courts of Ghana are constituted as follows: *Superior Courts of Ghana*, the Court of Appeal and the High Court of Justice. The Supreme Court of Ghana, created by the suspended Constitution in 1969, has been abolished and its functions taken over by the Court of Appeal.

The Court of Appeal. The Court of Appeal replaces the former Supreme Court of Ghana as the highest and final Court of Appeal in and for Ghana. It has all the power, authority and jurisdiction vested in any Court established in the country. The Court of Appeal consists of the Chief Justice, together with not less than 6 other Justices of the Appeal Court and such other Justices of Superior Courts as the Chief Justice may nominate. The Court is duly constituted by 3 justices. A full Bench of the Court of 5 Judges has jurisdiction to review and determine, among other things, a decision of the Court of Appeal or any justice or division thereof upon a question of law, including matters relating to aspects of the Chieftaincy Act 1971. Divisions of the Appeal Court may be created, subject to the discretion of the Chief Justice.

The High Court of Justice. This Court has jurisdiction in civil and criminal matters as well as those relating to industrial and labour disputes, including administrative complaints. It has supervisory jurisdiction over all interior and traditional courts, but has no power in a trial for offences involving treason, to convict any person for any offence other than treason. The High Court consists of the Chief Justice and not less than 12 other Judges as may be appointed by the Chief Justice. A High Court Judge can sit alone or with a jury.

The country has been divided into circuits, and there are Circuit Judges sitting in these courts with original jurisdiction in all criminal cases, except offences where the maximum punishment is death. The original jurisdiction in civil matters is restricted to cases where the subject-matter of the suit is not more than ₵ 8,000 or, in respect of liquidated sums, ₵ 15,000 involving ownership or occupation of land. *District Courts* (Grade I and II), sitting throughout the country in the magisterial districts. *Juvenile Courts*, dealing with persons under the age of 17, have been established in Accra, Cape Coast, Sekondi, Kumasi and Koforidua.

Police. The force was established in Oct. 1874. It is headed by an Inspector-General and consists of 7 divisions with a (1975) strength of 15,817.

Education. A complete re-organization of the system took place in 1974. There are kindergartens for the age-groups 4–6 years. Primary schools are free and attendance is compulsory. In 1973–74 there were 6,843 primary schools with 1,014,964 pupils. The 4,000 secondary schools had about 500,000 pupils. In 1975–76 there were 9,079 students at the 3 universities (University of Ghana, the University of Science and Technology and the University of the Cape Coast).

Health. Medical facilities include 50 government hospitals, 116 health centres and posts, 4 university hospitals, 3 mental hospitals, 4 leprosaria, 7 military hospitals, 1 prison hospital, 40 mission hospitals and 16 private hospitals. In addition, there are 30 nurses and midwives training schools.

There were 1,224 doctors, 7,608 nurses and 4,168 midwives at work in 1976.

DIPLOMATIC REPRESENTATIVES

OF GHANA IN GREAT BRITAIN (13 Belgrave Sq., London, SW1X 8PR)

High Commissioner: Francis Kelugu Badgie (accredited 7 Nov. 1970).

OF GREAT BRITAIN IN GHANA (Barclays Bank Bldg., High St., Accra)
High Commissioner: J. Mellon, CMG.

OF GHANA IN THE USA (2460 16th St., NW, Washington, D.C. 20009)
Ambassador: Dr Alex Quaison-Sackey.

OF THE USA IN GHANA (Liberia and Kinbu Rds., Accra)
Ambassador: Thomas W. M. Smith.

OF GHANA TO THE UNITED NATIONS
Ambassador: Henry Van Hien Sekyi.

Books of Reference

Digest of Statistics. Accra. Quarterly (from May 1953)
Ghana. Official Handbook. Annual
Trade Directory of the Republic of Ghana. 5th ed. London, 1967
The Volta River Project. 3 vols. HMSO, 1956
Acquah, L., *Accra Survey.* Univ. of London Press, 1958
Afrifa, A. A., *The Ghana Coup 24th February 1966.* London, 1966
Austin, D., *Politics in Ghana, 1946–60.* OUP, 1964
Boateng, E. A., *A Geography of Ghana.* 2nd ed. CUP, 1966
Davidson, B., *Black Star.* London, 1973
James, C. L. R., *Nkrumah and the Ghana Revolution.* London, 1977
Jones, T., *Ghana's First Republic 1960–1966.* London, 1975
Killick, T., *Development Economics in Action: A Study of Economic Policies in Ghana.* London, 1978
Lystad, R. A., *The Ashanti.* Rutgers Univ. Press, 1966
Manshard, W., *Die geographischen der Wirtschaft Ghanas.* Wiesbaden, 1961
Timothy, B., *Kwame Nkrumah: His Rise to Power.* London, 1964
Wills, J. B. (ed.), *Agriculture and Land Use in Ghana.* OUP, 1962

GIBRALTAR

Population: 29,760 (1979)
GNP per capita: US$3,660 (1978)

HISTORY. The Rock of Gibraltar was settled by Moors in 711; they named it after their chief Jebel Tariq, 'the Mountain of Tarik'. In 1462 it was taken by the Spaniards, from Granada. It was captured by Admiral Sir George Rooke on 24 July 1704, and ceded to Great Britain by the Treaty of Utrecht, 1713. The cession was confirmed by the treaties of Paris (1763) and Versailles (1783).

On 10 Sept. 1967, in pursuance of a United Nations resolution on the decolonization of Gibraltar, a referendum was held in Gibraltar in order to ascertain whether the people of Gibraltar believed that their interests lay in retaining their link with Britain or in passing under Spanish sovereignty. Out of a total electorate of 12,762, 12,138 voted to retain the British connexion, while 44 voted for Spain.

AREA AND POPULATION. Area, $2\frac{1}{2}$ sq. miles (6·5 sq. km). Total population, including port and harbour (census, 6 Oct. 1970), 26,833 (13,501 males; 13,322 females). Estimate (1979) 29,760 (15,256 males; 14,504 females). The population is mostly of Genoese, Portuguese and Maltese as well as Spanish descent.

Vital statistics (1979): Births, 472; marriages, 459; deaths, 257.

GOVERNMENT. Following a Constitutional Conference held in July 1968, a new Constitution was introduced in 1969. The Legislative and City Councils were merged to produce an enlarged legislature known as the Gibraltar House of Assembly. Executive authority is exercised by the Governor, who is also Commander-in-Chief. The Governor, while retaining certain reserved powers, is normally required to act in accordance with the advice of the Gibraltar Council, which consists of 4 *ex-officio* members (the Deputy Governor, the Deputy Fortress Commander, the Attorney-General and the Financial and Development Secretary) together with 5 elected members of the House of Assembly appointed by the Governor after consultation with the Chief Minister. Matters of primarily domestic concern are devolved to elected Ministers, with Britain responsible for other matters, including external affairs, defence and internal security. There is a Council of Ministers presided over by the Chief Minister.

The House of Assembly consists of a Speaker appointed by the Governor, 15 elected and 2 *ex-officio* members (the Attorney-General and the Financial and Development Secretary).

A Mayor of Gibraltar is elected from among the members of the Assembly by the elected members of the Assembly.

Governor and C.-in-C.: Gen. Sir William Jackson, GBE, KCB, MC.
Chief Minister: Sir Joshua Hassan, CBE, MVO, QC.
Flag: White with a red strip along the bottom, a red triple-towered castle with a gold key depending from the gateway.

DEFENCE. The Gibraltar Regiment is a part-time infantry battalion with a small regular cadre.

ECONOMY

Budget. Revenue and expenditure (in £ sterling):

	1974–75	1975–76	1976–77	1977–78	1978–79
Revenue	8,790,210	11,807,045	18,207,859	18,661,858	26,408,993
Expenditure	8,653,078	10,322,937	17,709,855	19,962,916	30,495,374

Currency. The legal currency consists of Gibraltar government notes and UK coins. The amount of local currency notes in circulation at 31 March 1979 was £5,651,410.

Banking. There are 7 banks, including 3 branches of Barclays Bank International. Government savings banks had £1,785,426 deposited at 31 March 1979.

546

INDUSTRY AND TRADE

Industry. There are a number of relatively small industrial concerns engaged in the bottling of beer and mineral waters, etc., mainly for local consumption. There is a small but important commercial ship-repair yard.

Tourism. The number of tourists in 1979 was 44,569 (1978, 39,102).

Labour. The full-time labour force in April 1979 was (estimate) 11,593. The labour supply from the local population is insufficient to meet the demand and since the withdrawal of the Spanish frontier workers in June 1969, a substantial part of the labour has had to come from other places. A quota system is in existence which takes into account the demand from the various industries and seasonal variations and the issue of employment permits is based on this. More than one-half of the local labour force is employed by the UK departments or the Gibraltar government.

A considerable proportion of the workers are organized in one or other of the 14 registered employees' trade unions, of which the Transport and General Workers Union has the largest membership; 7 of these are local branches of parent associations in the UK.

Commerce. Imports and exports (in £ sterling):

	1975	1976	1977	1978	1979
Imports	27,027,401	32,415,906	39,589,742	39,442,136	55,519,064
Exports	10,753,448	13,727,865	13,859,398	11,863,114	19,453,243

Britain and the Commonwealth provide the bulk of the imports, but fresh vegetables, fruit and fish come mainly from Morocco, Portugal and the Netherlands. Exports of local produce are negligible. Gibraltar depends largely on tourism, the entrepôt trade and the provision of supplies to visiting ships.

COMMUNICATIONS

Roads. There are 30 miles of roads including 4 miles of pedestrian way.

Aviation. There are 5 weekly flights between London and Gibraltar (3 operated by Gibraltar Airways and 2 by British Airways) during the winter; these are increased to daily flights during the summer.

The unilateral closure by Spain of their land frontier with Gibraltar makes overland travel from or to Spain impossible. However, there is a regular car ferry service and air services to Tangier and Morocco from where it is possible to cross over to the Spanish mainland.

Shipping. Gibraltar is a naval and air base of strategic importance. There is a deep Admiralty harbour of 440 acres. A total of 2,752 merchant ships, 22,931,062 NRT, entered the port during 1979. An additional 4,672 calls were made by yachts, 48,861 NRT.

Post. An automatic telephone system exists in the town; number of telephones (1979), 8,982. There is also world-wide communication *via* the cable and/or wireless circuits of Cable & Wireless Ltd. Air-mails arrive by British Airways daily. A direct air-mail service between Gibraltar and Tangier is run by Gibraltar Airways, Ltd. Surface mails arrive direct and through France, Spain and Tangier.

Cinemas. In 1978 there were 3 cinemas with a seating capacity of 2,400.

JUSTICE, RELIGION, AND EDUCATION

Justice. The judicial system is based on the English system. There is a Court of Appeal, a Supreme Court, presided over by the Chief Justice, a court of first instance and a magistrates' court.

Religion. Religion of civil population mostly Roman Catholic; 1 Anglican and 1 Roman Catholic cathedral and 2 Anglican and 6 Roman Catholic churches; 1 Presbyterian and 1 Methodist church and 4 synagogues; annual subsidy to each communion, £500.

Education. Free compulsory education is provided for children between ages 5 and 15 years. Scholarships are made available for universities, teacher-training and other higher education in Britain. The comprehensive system was introduced in Sept. 1972. There are 12 government primary schools and 2 comprehensive schools, 1 for boys and 1 for girls. There is also 1 private primary school, 1 Hebrew primary school, 2 Services primary schools and 1 school for handicapped children. Total number of pupils was 5,313, including 42 in technical and vocational schools.

Books of Reference

Annual Report on Gibraltar, 1972. London, 1974
Gibraltar Directory and Guide Book. Gibraltar, 1961
Dennis, P., *Gibraltar.* Newton Abbot, 1977
Ellicott, D., *Our Gibraltar.* Gibraltar, 1975
Garcia, J., *Gibraltar Who's Who and Year-Book, 1974–75.* Gibraltar, 1974
Garcia, S., *Gibraltar: An Analysis of How the Economy was Affected by the Spanish Restrictions 1963–72* (unpublished). Garrison Library, 1974
Hills, G., *Rock of Contention: A History of Gibraltar.* London, 1974
Howes, H. W., *The Story of Gibraltar.* London, 1946

GREECE

Elliniki Dimokratia

Capital: Athens
Population: 9·5m. (1980)
GNP per capita: US$3,270 (1978)

HISTORY. Greece gained her independence from Turkey in 1821–29, and by the Protocol of London, of 3 Feb. 1830, was declared a kingdom, under the guarantee of Great Britain, France and Russia. For details of the subsequent history to 1947 *see* THE STATESMAN'S YEAR-BOOK, 1957, pp. 1069–70 and for details of the monarchy *see* THE STATESMAN'S YEAR-BOOK, 1973–74, p. 1000.

AREA AND POPULATION. Greece is bounded north by Albania, Yugoslavia and Bulgaria, east by Turkey and the Aegean Sea, south by the Mediterranean and west by the Ionian Sea. The total area is 131,986 sq. km (50,960 sq. miles), of which the islands account for 24,761 sq. km (9,560 sq. miles).

The population was 8,768,641 according to the census of 14 March 1971. Estimate (1980), 9·5m.

Athens is the capital; population of Greater Athens, in 1971, 2,540,241.

The following table shows the prefectures (*Nomoi*) and their population:

Nomoi	Area in sq. km	Population 1971	Capital	Population 1971
Greater Athens [1]	433	2,540,241		
Central Greece and Euboea [2]	24,475	992,077		
Aetolia and Acarnania	5,447	228,989	Missolonghi	11,614
Attica [2]	2,496	201,948	Athens	867,023
Boeotia	3,211	114,675	Levadeia	15,445
Euboea	3,908	165,369	Chalcis	36,300
Evrytania	2,045	29,533	Karpenissi	4,414
Phthiotis	4,368	154,542	Lamia	37,872
Phokis	2,121	41,361	Amphissa	6,605
Piraeus [2]	879	55,660	Piraeus	187,458
Peloponnessos	21,439	986,912		
Argolis	2,214	88,698	Nauplion	9,281
Arcadia	4,419	111,263	Tripolis	20,209
Akhaïa	3,209	239,859	Patras	111,607
Elia	2,681	165,056	Pyrgos	20,599
Korinthia	2,289	113,115	Korinthos	20,773
Lakonia	3,636	95,844	Sparte	10,549
Messenia	2,991	173,077	Calamata	39,133
Ionian Islands	2,307	184,443		
Zakynthos	406	30,187	Zante	9,339
Kerkyra	641	92,933	Kerkyra	28,630
Kefallenia	935	36,742	Argostolion	7,060
Lefkas	325	24,581	Levkas	6,818
Epirus	9,203	310,344		
Arta	1,612	78,376	Arta	19,498
Thesprotia	1,515	40,684	Hegoumenitsa	4,109
Yannina	4,990	134,688	Yannina	40,130
Preveza	1,086	56,586	Preveza	11,439
Thessaly	13,904	659,913		
Karditsa	2,576	133,776	Karditsa	25,685
Larissa	5,354	232,226	Larisa	72,336
Magnessia	2,636	161,392	Volos	51,290
Trikkala	3,338	132,519	Trikkala	34,794

[1] Comprising parts of Attica and Piraeus prefectures.
[2] Excluding figures for the parts of Attica and Piraeus prefectures within Greater Athens.

Nomoi	Area in sq. km	Population 1971	Capital	Population 1971
Macedonia	*34,203*	*1,890,684*		
Grevena	2,338	35,275	Grevena	8,016
Drama	3,468	91,009	Drama	29,692
Imathia	1,699	118,103	Verria	29,528
Thessaloniki	3,560	710,352	Thessaloniki	345,799
Kavala	2,109	121,593	Kavala	46,234
Kastoria	1,685	45,711	Kastoria	15,407
Kilkis	2,597	84,375	Kilkis	10,538
Kozani	3,562	135,709	Kozani	23,240
Pella	2,506	126,085	Edessa	13,967
Pieria	1,548	91,728	Katerini	28,808
Serres	3,987	202,898	Serres	39,897
Florina	1,863	52,264	Florina	11,164
Khalkidiki	2,945	73,850	Polyghyros	3,707
Mount Athos	336	1,732	Karyai	301
Thrace	*8,578*	*329,582*		
Evros	4,242	138,988	Alexandroupolis	22,995
Xanthi	1,793	82,917	Xanthi	24,867
Rodopi	2,543	107,677	Komotini	28,896
Aegean Islands	*9,071*	*417,813*		
Cyclades	2,572	86,337	Hermoupolis	13,502
Lesvos	2,154	114,802	Mitylini	23,426
Samos	778	41,709	Limin Vatheos	5,146
Khios	904	53,948	Khios	24,084
Dodecanese	2,663	121,017	Rhodes	32,092
Crete	*8,331*	*456,642*		
Iraklion	2,641	209,670	Heraklion	77,506
Lassithi	1,818	66,226	Aghios Nikolaos	6,176
Rethymnon	1,496	60,949	Rethymnon	14,969
Canea	2,376	119,797	Canea	40,564

In 1971 cities (*i.e.*, communes of more than 10,000 inhabitants, including Greater Athens) had 4,667,489 inhabitants (53·2%), towns (*i.e.*, communes with between 2,000 and 9,999 inhabitants), 1,028,769 (11·7%), villages and rural communities (under 2,000 inhabitants), 3,072,383 (35·1%).

Mount Athos, the easternmost of the three prongs of the peninsula of Chalcidice, is a self-governing community composed of 20 monasteries. (*See* THE STATESMAN'S YEAR-BOOK, 1945, p. 983.) For centuries the peninsula has been administered by a Council of 4 members and an Assembly of 20 members, 1 deputy from each monastery. The Greek Government on 10 Sept. 1926 recognized this autonomous form of government; Articles 109–112 of the Constitution of 1927 gave legal sanction to the Charter of Mount Athos, drawn up by representatives of the 20 monasteries on 20 May 1924. Article 103 of the 1952 Constitution and Article 105 of the 1975 Constitution confirmed the special status of Mount Athos.

Vital statistics (1977): 143,739 live births; 1,566 still births; 1,918 illegitimate births; 76,228 marriages; 83,750 deaths; 16,510 emigrants (Jan.–Sept.); 12,572 immigrants (Jan.–Sept.).

GOVERNMENT AND CONSTITUTION. A *coup d'état* took place on 21 April 1967, 'to avert the danger of a communist threat against the nation'. A Military Government was formed, which suspended the 1952 Constitution. Following the unsuccessful counter-*coup* in 1967, King Constantine went abroad. Voting took place on 29 July 1973 in the referendum to change Greece from a Monarchy to a Republic and to elect a President. 77·2% of the valid votes were cast for a republican régime.

On 25 Nov. 1973, in a bloodless *coup*, President Papadopoulos was overthrown and Lieut.-Gen. Phaedon Ghizikis was sworn in. The military dictatorship collapsed on 23 July 1974 and the 1952 Constitution was reintroduced in a modified form. A new Constitution was introduced in June 1975. Parliamentary elections took place on 17 Nov. 1974.

A further referendum on the Monarchy took place on 8 Dec. 1974 and 69·2% of the valid votes were cast for an 'uncrowned democracy'.

Elections were again held on 20 Nov. 1977. The results were New Democracy,

173; Pan-Hellenic Socialist Movement, 92; Union of Democratic Centre, 15; Communists, 11; National Camp, 5; Alliance of Progressive and Left-Wing Forces, 2; Neo-Liberal Party, 2. A number of UDC deputies and both Neo-Liberal deputies subsequently joined the New Democracy Party.

President: Konstantinos Karamanlis (elected President in May 1980).

The Cabinet in Nov. 1980:

Prime Minister and Minister of Co-ordination: George Rallis.
Deputy Prime Minister: Constantine Papaconstantinou. *Minister to the Prime Minister:* Constantine Stefanopoulos. *Foreign Affairs:* Constantine Mitsotakis. *National Defence:* Evangelos Averof-Tositsas. *Interior:* Christophoros Stratos. *Justice:* George Stamatis. *Culture and Sciences:* Andreas Andrianopoulos. *Public Order:* Dimitrios Davakis. *National Education and Cults:* Athanassios Taliadouros. *Finance:* Miltiadis Evert. *Agriculture:* Athanassios Kanellopoulos. *Industry and Energy:* Stefanos Manos. *Commerce:* Aristidis Kalantzakos. *Labour:* Constantine Laskaris. *Social Services:* Spyridon Doxiadis. *Public Works:* Tzanis Tzanetakis. *Communications:* George Panayotopoulos. *Mercantile Marine:* Ioannis Fikioris. *Northern Greece:* Nikolaos Martis. *Without Portfolio (for relations with the EEC):* George Kontogeorgis. *Without Portfolio (attached to the Ministry of Co-ordination):* Stavros Dimas. *Physical Planning, Housing and Environment:* George Plytas. *Deputy Minister of Co-ordination:* Ioannis Paleokrassas.

National flag: Nine horizontal stripes of blue and white, with a canton of blue with a white cross.

National anthem: Hymn to Freedom, Imnos eis tin Eleftherian (words by Dionysios Solomos, 1824; tune by N. Mantzaros, 1828).

DEFENCE. In Aug. 1950 the Ministries of War, Marine and Military Aviation were fused into a single Ministry of National Defence. The General Staff of National Defence is directly responsible to the Minister on general defence questions, besides the special staffs for Army, Navy and Air Force. Defence expenditure in 1980 was 71,250m. drachmai.

Army. Military service is compulsory and universal. Liability begins in the 21st year and lasts up to the 50th. The normal term of service in the active Army is for 24–32 months for all arms, followed by 19 years in the first reserve of the active Army and 10 years in the second. The normal annual contingent of recruits in peace-time is about 50,000. Every 3 months a quarter of the current year's contingent is called up for service.

Since 1945, the organization and establishment of the Army units have been adapted to British models. In Feb. 1952 an American Mission took over from a British Military Mission the training of the Army.

The Army consists of 11 infantry and 1 armoured division, 1 infantry, 2 armoured and 1 para-commando brigade, and 12 artillery battalions, with a total strength of 140,000 men.

Navy. The Hellenic Navy includes 11 submarines (8 modern German (Fed. Rep.)-built small and 3 old *ex*-US large), 12 old *ex*-US destroyers, 1 *ex*-German support frigate, 4 old *ex*-US frigates (small DE type), 2 coastal minelayers, 12 fast missile boats, 14 coastal minesweepers, 12 fast torpedo boats, 7 coastal patrol boats, 1 dock landing ship, 12 landing ships, 10 landing craft, 29 minor landing craft, 2 salvage vessels, 8 oilers, 2 transports, 1 repair ship, 1 depot ship, 6 surveying craft, 2 lighthouse tenders, 6 water carriers, 1 netlayer and 17 fleet tugs.

Personnel in 1981 exceeded 2,500 officers and 17,000 ratings (called up for 2 years, or enlisted).

Air Force. The Hellenic Air Force has a strength of about 24,500 officers and men and some 230 combat aircraft, consisting of 3 squadrons of F-4E Phantom air-superiority fighters, supported by RF-4E reconnaissance fighters, 2 squadrons of F-104G Starfighters, 2 squadrons of Mirage F.1 fighters, 3 squadrons of A-7H Corsair II attack aircraft, 4 squadrons of F-5 fighters, and RF-5A reconnaissance fighters and 1 squadron of HU-16B Albatross ASW amphibians. There are also transport squadrons equipped with C-130H Hercules (12), Noratlas and C-47 aircraft, 7 Canadair CL-215 twin-engined amphibians, 39 T-2E Buckeye training/attack aircraft, other training and helicopter units, and anti-aircraft units equipped with Nike-Hercules and Hawk surface-to-air missiles.

The HAF is organized into Tactical, Training and Materiel Commands.

INTERNATIONAL RELATIONS

Membership. Greece is a member of UN, EEC, the Council of Europe and the political wing of NATO.

ECONOMY

Budget. The estimated revenue and expenditure for calendar years were as follows (in 1m. drachmai):

	1972	1973	1974	1975	1976	1977	1978
Revenue	86,230	105,240	129,380	138,320	174,362	210,234	249,202
Expenditure	86,229	105,234	129,380	170,496	210,231	252,094	300,950

Currency. On 11 Nov. 1944 the Greek currency was stabilized at 1 new *drachma* equalling 50,000m. old *drachmai*. Further readjustments took place in 1946, 1949 and 1953. A 'new issue' of notes and coins was put into circulation on 1 May 1954, 1 new drachma equalling 1,000 old drachmai (72 drachmai = £1; 30 drachmai = US$1). The 'new issue' comprises notes of 50, 100, 500 and 1,000 drachmai and metal coins of 1, 2, 5, 10 and 20 drachmai and 10, 20 and 50 *lepta*. Rate of exchange, March 1981, £1 = 112 drachmai; US$1 = 51·35.

Banking. The Bank of Greece (*Trapeza Tis Ellados*) is the bank of issue. On 31 Dec. 1978 bank-notes in circulation amounted to 228,771m. drachmai.

In 1953 the National Bank of Greece and the Bank of Athens were amalgamated; in 1957 its name was changed to National Bank of Greece (*Ethniki Trapeza tis Ellados*).

The National Investment Bank for industrial development was set up in Dec. 1963; of its capital of 180m. drachmai, the National Bank provided 60%.

Other important banks are the Ionian and Popular Bank of Greece, the Commercial Bank of Greece, the National Mortgage Bank, the Hellenic Industrial Development Bank, the Investment Bank, the Commercial Credit Bank and the General Bank of Greece.

On 31 Dec. 1978, total private bank deposits were 410,718m. drachmai (107,941m. in 1970); total money supply was 228,800m. drachmai.

Post office savings bank deposits amounted to 39,449m. drachmai in Aug. 1974.

Weights and Measures. The metric system was made obligatory in 1959; the use of other systems is prohibited. The Gregorian calendar was adopted in Feb. 1923.

ENERGY AND NATURAL RESOURCES

Electricity. Total installed capacity of the Public Power Corporation was 4,841 mw as at 31 Dec. 1978. Total net production in 1978 was 19,458m. kwh. Total production (1977) 17,401m. kwh.

Minerals. Greece produces a variety of ores and minerals, including iron-pyrites (180,000 tonnes in 1976), bauxite (2,984m. tonnes), nickel (2,205,000 tonnes), magnesite (1·5m. tonnes), dead burnt magnesite (342,000 tonnes), mixed sulphur ores (752,000 tonnes), barytes, chromite, marble (white and coloured) and various other earths, chiefly from the Laurium district, Thessaly, Euboea and the Aegean islands. There is little coal, and lignite of indifferent quality (22·2m. tonnes). Oil was struck in 1963 by British Petroleum at Kleisoura in west central Greece. Salt production (1970) 68,471 tonnes.

Agriculture. Of the total area only 33% is cultivable, but it supports about 45% of the whole population. The total area under cultivation in 1971 was 3,586,232 hectares, forest area (1965) was 2,512,418 hectares (445,715 of which were privately owned). The average holding was 3·42 hectares in 1975.

Yield (1,000 tonnes) of the chief crops (1978):

Wheat	2,660	Table grapes	224
Tobacco	128	Wine	574
Cotton	451	Citrus fruit	636
Sugar-beet	2,800	Other fruit	1,460
Currants and raisins	148	Milk	1,698
Olive oil	234	Meat and poultry	480

About 496,260 hectares of olives are under cultivation.

Rice is cultivated in Macedonia, the Peloponnese, Epirus and Central Greece. Successful experiments have been made in growing rice on alkaline land previously regarded as unfit for cultivation. The main kinds of cheese produced are sliced cheese in brine (commercially known as Fetta) and hard cheese, such as Kefalotyri.

Livestock (1979): 973,000 cattle, 3,000 buffaloes, 830,000 pigs, 8m. sheep, 4·5m. goats, 138,000 horses, 131,000 mules, 267,000 asses, 29·7m. poultry.

Fisheries. In 1977, 9,387 fishermen were active and landed 97,262 tonnes of fish. 54,146. kg of sponges were produced in 1970.

INDUSTRY AND TRADE

Industry. The main products are canned vegetables and fruit, fruit juice, beer, wine, alcoholic beverages, cigarettes, textiles, yarn, leather, shoes, synthetic timber, paper, plastics, rubber products, chemical acids, pigments, pharmaceutical products, cosmetics, soap, disinfectants, fertilizers, glassware, porcelain sanitary items, wire and power coils and household instruments.

Production, 1976 (1,000 tonnes): Textile yarns, 137; cement, 8,714; fertilizers, 1,554; ammonia, 287; iron (concrete-reinforcing bars), 589; iron–nickel, 16; alumina, 450; aluminium, 133; electrical domestic goods (1,000 pieces), 325.

Labour. Of the economically active population in 1971, 1·96m. were engaged in agriculture, 677,451 in industry and 1,000,684 in other employment.

Pepelasis, A. A., and Yotopoulos, P. A., *Surplus Labor in Greek Agriculture, 1953–60*. Athens, 1962

Trade Unions. The status of trade unions in Greece is regulated by the Associations Act 1914. Trade-union liberties are guaranteed under the Constitution, and the right to strike is subject to the Settlement of Collective Labour Disputes Act of 21 Nov. 1935, which, while not making strikes illegal, introduced the principle of compulsory arbitration.

The national body of trade unions in Greece is the Greek General Confederation of Labour.

Commerce. Foreign trade (in 1m. drachmai) for 6 calendar years was:

	1973	1974	1975	1976	1977	1978
Imports	102,979	132,181	172,041	223,159	252,150	280,000
Exports	42,812	60,891	74,441	93,811	101,330	124,000

Leading exports (1970, in 1,000 drachmai): Manufactured goods, 39,454,200; food and live animals, 19,518,588; crude materials, 7,558,652; beverages and tobacco, 5,820,228; chemicals, 2,344,680.

Textiles were the highest-valued exports in 1979. Percentage distribution of foreign trade by area (1979):

	Imports	Exports
EEC	44·3	49·1
Saudi Arabia	6·1	5·5
USA	4·8	5·5

Total trade between Greece and UK (British Department of Trade returns, in £1,000 sterling):

	1975	1976	1977	1978	1979	1980
Imports to UK	65,237	64,606	95,563	107,600	151,880	142,456
Exports and re-exports from UK	117,207	149,207	220,393	214,178	273,026	224,619

Tourism. Tourists visiting Greece in 1978 numbered 5,081,033, coming mainly from USA, UK, Federal Republic of Germany, Yugoslavia, Italy, Sweden and Switzerland. They spent the equivalent of US$1,300m. At 31 Dec. 1978 there were 247,000 hotel beds.

COMMUNICATIONS

Roads. There were, in 1977, 37,000 km of roads, of which 8,650 were national and 27,253 provincial roads.

Number of motor vehicles in Dec. 1978: 744,692 passenger cars, 406,986 goods vehicles, 15,526 buses.

Railways. In 1980 the State network, Hellenic Railways (CH), totalled 2,548 km comprising 1,565 km of 1,435 mm gauge, 961 km of 1,000 mm gauge, and 22 km of 750 mm gauge.

Aviation. Olympic Airways connects Athens with all important cities of the country, Europe, the Middle East and USA. Thirty-four foreign companies connect Athens with the principal cities of the world.

The principal airport is at Athens. In 1979, 90,700 aircraft arrived, carrying 7·7m. passengers.

Shipping. In March 1980 the merchant navy comprised 3,970 vessels of 39,327,594 GRT. Greek-owned ships under foreign flags totalled more than 11,192,683 GRT.

There is a canal (opened 9 Nov. 1893) across the Isthmus of Corinth (about 4 miles).

There is (since 1925) in the town and port of Thessaloniki a free zone, covering today a land area of 536 sq. km. In the same port there was established in 1923 and operating since 1929 a Yugoslav free zone with 94 sq. km total area of land and seaway. In 1923 there was created a free zone in the town of Piraeus, covering a land area of 181·5 sq. km.

Post and Broadcasting. In 1973 there were 3,200 telephone exchanges, 1·8m. installed capacity of telephone exchanges, handling 8,000m. calls. There were (1978) 2,319,797 telephones.

Elliniki Radiophonia Tileorasis (ERT), the Hellenic National Radio and Television Institute, is the government broadcasting station. *Ypiressia Enimerosseos Enoplon Dhynameon Helladhos* (YENED), the Greek Armed Forces Information Service, broadcasts from a central station in Athens *via* medium- and short-waves and has regional stations in 11 towns. ERT and YENED each broadcasts 1 TV programme. AFRTS broadcasts 1 TV programme in Iraklion (Crete). Number of receivers: radio, 2·8m.; television, 850,000.

Cinemas (1965). There were 1,400 cinemas.

Newspapers (1974). There were 12 daily newspapers published in Athens.

JUSTICE, RELIGION, EDUCATION AND WELFARE

Justice. There are administrative, civil and criminal courts and they are organized by special laws.

Religion. The Christian Eastern Orthodox faith is the established religion to which 98% of the population belong.

The Greek Orthodox Church is under an archbishop and 67 metropolitans, 1 archbishop and 7 metropolitans in Crete, and 4 metropolitans in the Dodecanese. The Roman Catholics have 3 archbishops (in Naxos and Corfu and, not recognized by the State, in Athens) and 1 bishop (for Syra and Santorin). The Exarchs of the Greek Catholics and the Armenians are not recognized by the State.

Complete religious freedom is recognized by the Constitution of 1968, but proselytizing from, and interference with, the Greek Orthodox Church is forbidden.

Education. Public education is provided in nursery, primary and secondary schools, starting at 6 years of age and since 1963 free at all levels.

In 1978 there were 4,417 nursery schools with 5,410 staff and 133,700 pupils; 9,654 public day primary schools with 32,638 staff and 922,740 pupils. There were 2,214 secondary schools with 26,446 staff and 586,692 pupils. There were 811 public and 720 private technical and vocational schools with 147,799 students.

In 1980 there were 6 universities at Athens, Crete, Thessaloniki, Thrace, Patras and Ioannina with 100,000 students and 6,150 lecturers.

Illiteracy in the age groups of 10 years and over was 18% in 1961 (8% among men). 1972 estimate 12%.

The Greek language consists of 2 branches, *katharevousa*, a conscious revival of classical Greek, used for official purposes and in newspapers, and *demotiki*, the spoken language.

Health (1976). There were 724 hospitals and sanatoria with a total of 58,574 beds. There were 19,340 doctors and 6,160 dentists.

DIPLOMATIC REPRESENTATIVES

OF GREECE IN GREAT BRITAIN
(1A Holland Park, London, W11 3TP)

Ambassador: Efstathios P. Lagacos.

OF GREAT BRITAIN IN GREECE
(1 Ploutarchou St., Athens 139)

Ambassador: I. J. M. Sutherland, CMG.

OF GREECE IN THE USA (2221 Massachusetts Ave., NW,
Washington, D.C. 20008)

Ambassador: Menelas D. Alexandrakis.

OF THE USA IN GREECE
(91 Vasilissis Sophia Blvd., Athens)

Ambassador: Robert J. Macloskey.

OF GREECE TO THE UNITED NATIONS

Ambassador: Nicolas Katapodis.

Books of Reference

Campbell, J., and Sherrard, P., *Modern Greece*. London, 1968

Forster, E. S., *A Short History of Modern Greece*. 3rd ed. London, 1958

Holden, D., *Greece Without Columns: The Making of the Modern Greeks*. London, 1972

Katris, J. A., *Eyewitness in Greece: The Colonels Come to Power*. St Louis, 1971

Kayser, B., *Géographie humaine de la Grèce*. Paris, Presses Universitaires, 1964

Kolodny, E. Y., *La Population des Îles de la Grèce*. Aix-en-Provence, 1973

Kousoulas, D. G., *Revolution and Defeat: The Story of the Greek Communist Party*. OUP, 1965

Kykkotis, I., *English–Modern Greek and Modern Greek–English Dictionary*. 3rd ed. London, 1957

Mouzelis, N. P., *Modern Greece*, London, 1978

Munkman, C. A., *American Aid to Greece*. New York, 1958

Phillipson, A., *Die griechischen Landschaften: eine Landeskunde*. 4 vols. Frankfurt, 1951–59

Spring, J. T., *The Oxford Dictionary of Modern Greek*. 2 vols. OUP, 1966–67

Tsoukalis, L., *Greece and the European Community*. Farnborough, 1979

Woodhouse, C. M., *The Struggle for Greece, 1941–1949*. London, 1976

Xydis, S. G., *Greece and the Great Powers, 1944–47*. Thessaloniki, 1963

Young, K., *The Greek Passion*. London, 1967

GRENADA

Capital: St. George's
Population: 110,394 (1978)
GNP per capita: US$530 (1978)

HISTORY. Grenada became an independent nation within the Commonwealth on 7 Feb. 1974. Grenada was formerly an Associated State under the West Indies Act, 1967. Independence was achieved in May 1973.

AREA AND POPULATION. Grenada is the most southerly island of the Windward Islands with an area of 133 sq. miles (344 sq. km); population, census 1970, 92,775, of which 29,860 were in the parish of St George; estimated population 1978, 110,394. The largest of the Grenadines attached to Grenada is Carriacou, area 6,500 acres; population 1970, 5,950.

Vital statistics (1978): Births, 2,521; deaths, 765; infant deaths, 73; marriages, 360.

CONSTITUTION AND GOVERNMENT. Grenada Constitution Order of 1973 was suspended on 13 March 1979 following a *coup*. The People's Revolutionary Government now comprises 23 members with a Cabinet of 7 members. Grenada has a bicameral legislature consisting of a Senate and a House of Assembly.

Governor-General: Sir Paul Scoon.
Prime Minister: Maurice Bishop.
National flag: Divided into 4 triangles of yellow, top and bottom, and green, hoist and fly; in the centre a red disc bearing a gold star; along the top and bottom edged red stripes each bearing 3 gold stars; on the green triangle near the hoist a pod of nutmeg.

INTERNATIONAL RELATIONS

Membership. Grenada is a member of the UN, OAS, Caricom, the Commonwealth and is an ACP state of EEC.

ECONOMY

Budget. The 1976 estimates balanced at EC$27,559,541. Public debt at 31 Dec. 1970 was EC$15,168,705.

Currency. The currency is the *Eastern Caribbean dollar.* In March 1981, £1 = EC$5·90; US$1 = EC$2·70.

Banking. In 1976 there were 6 commercial banks in Grenada: Barclays Bank International, Royal Bank of Canada, Bank of Nova Scotia, Canadian Imperial Bank of Commerce, Grenada National Bank and the Grenada Co-operative Bank. The Grenada Agricultural Bank was established in 1965 to encourage agricultural development.

AGRICULTURE (1979). The principal crops grown are: Cocoa (16,000 acres), nutmegs (10,000 acres), bananas (4,200 acres), coconuts (3,000 acres), corn and pigeon peas (3,000 acres), citrus (1,240 acres), sugar-cane (1,000 acres), root-crops (665 acres), and vegetables (230 acres), in addition to small scattered cultivations of cotton, cloves, cinnamon, pimento, coffee and fruit trees.

Livestock (1979): Cattle, 7,000; sheep, 13,000; goats, 12,000; pigs, 14,000; poultry, 285,000.

COMMERCE (1978). Total value of imports, EC$96,268,746; exports, EC$45,774,900. Chief exports: Cocoa (5·3m. lb.) EC$19·6m.; nutmegs (4·4m. lb.) EC$10·7m.; bananas (31·5m. lb.) EC$9·3m.; mace (600,000 lb.) EC$1·7m.

Total trade between Grenada and UK (British Department of Trade returns, in £1,000 sterling):

	1977	1978	1979	1980
Imports to UK	4,493	5,246	5,397	5,225
Exports and re-exports from UK	4,294	4,152	4,099	3,371

TOURISM. In 1978, 32,321 visitors (excluding 116,346 cruise passengers) visited the island, spending an estimated EC$25m.

COMMUNICATIONS

Roads. The scheduled road mileage is 577, of which 377 have an oiled surface and 210 are graded as third-and fourth-class roads. Vehicles registered (1979) 6,676.

Aviation. International Aeradio Ltd control by radio all plane movements within this area, and keep Pearls Airport in contact with St George's, on official airways business.

Shipping. Total shipping for 1978 was 927 motor and steamships and 166 sailing and auxiliary vessels, with a total net tonnage of 2,210,532 and 7,479 respectively.

Post and Broadcasting. The telephone system is owned and operated by the Grenada Telephone Co. Ltd. The Government of Grenada is a shareholder. The system is completely automatic, and in 1978 served 5,217 subscribers. Cable & Wireless (W.I.) Ltd operates a VHF radio system (telephone and telegraph) to Trinidad and Barbados, from where connexion is made to all principal West Indian islands and all other parts of the world.

Radio Grenada is government owned and operated. There were (1978) 63,500 radios.

JUSTICE, RELIGION AND EDUCATION.

Justice. The Grenada Supreme Court, situated in St. George's, comprises a High Court of Justice, a Court of Magisterial Appeal (which hears appeals from the lower Magistrates' Courts exercising summary jurisdiction) and an Itinerant Court of Appeal (to hear appeals from the High Court).

Religion. The majority of the population are Roman Catholic; the Anglican and Methodist churches are also well represented.

Education. There are 20 primary schools, 4 junior schools and 16 secondary schools, as well as 46 schools taking the full age range. There is a Technical Centre in each district and a Technical Institute in St. George's, where there is also a Teacher Training College and a branch of the University of the West Indies. There were 28,745 primary and 4,773 secondary school pupils in 1973.

DIPLOMATIC REPRESENTATIVES

OF GRENADA IN GREAT BRITAIN (Grand Bldgs., Trafalgar Sq., London, WC2)

High Commissioner: Fennis Augustine.

OF GREAT BRITAIN IN GRENADA

High Commissioner: J. S. Arthur, CMG (resides at Bridgetown).

OF GRENADA IN THE USA (1101 Vermont Ave., NW, Washington, DC., 20005)

Ambassador: Bernard K. Radix.

OF THE USA IN GRENADA

Ambassador: Sally Shelton (resides in Bridgetown).

OF GRENADA TO THE UNITED NATIONS

Ambassador: Bernard K. Radix.

GUATEMALA

República de Guatemala

Capital: Guatemala City
Population: 7·05m. (1979)
GNP per capita: US$910 (1978)

HISTORY. From 1524 to 1821 Guatemala was a Spanish captaincy-general, comprising the whole of Central America. It became independent in 1821 and formed part of the Confederation of Central America from 1823 to 1839, when Rafael Carrera dissolved the Confederation.

AREA AND POPULATION. Guatemala is bounded on the north and west by Mexico, south by the Pacific ocean and east by El Salvador, Honduras and Belize, and the area is 108,889 sq. km (42,042 sq. miles). In March 1936 Guatemala, El Salvador and Honduras agreed to accept the peak of Mount Montecristo as the common boundary point.

The population was 7·05m. in 1979. About 45% are pure Indians, of 21 different groups descended from the Maya; most of the remainder are mixed Indian and Spanish and these supply the ruling classes. Density of population, 1978, 63 per sq. km.

Vital statistics, 1976: Births, 266,497; deaths, 81,677; marriages, 28,555; infant deaths, 20,576.

Guatemala is administratively divided into 22 departments, each with a governor appointed by the President. Population, 1976:

Departments	Area (sq. km)	Population	Departments	Area (sq. km)	Population
Alta Verapaz	8,686	372,572	Petén	35,854	71,463
Baja Verapaz	3,124	136,747	Quezaltenango	1,951	383,470
Chimaltenango	1,979	233,287	Quiché	8,378	363,579
Chiquimula	2,376	212,869	Retalhuleu	1,858	159,085
El Progreso	1,922	92,453	Sacatepéquez	465	116,259
Escuintla	4,384	353,302	San Marcos	3,791	473,341
Guatemala	2,126	1,239,749	Santa Rosa	2,955	225,597
Huehuetenango	7,403	422,717	Sololá	1,061	156,548
Izabal	9,038	205,305	Suchitepéquez	2,510	257,439
Jalapa	2,063	145,091	Totonicapán	1,061	207,954
Jutiapa	3,219	290,511	Zacapa	2,690	138,292

The capital is Guatemala City with about 1·5m. inhabitants (1979). Other towns are Quezaltenango (65,733), Puerto Barrios (38,956), Mazatenango (38,319), Antigua (26,631), Zacapa (35,769) and Cobán (43,538). An earthquake in central Guatemala in Feb. 1976 killed 24,103 people and destroyed 200,000 dwellings.

CONSTITUTION AND GOVERNMENT. Following the revolution of June 1954 the Constitution of 1945 was replaced in Aug. 1954 by a 'Political Statute'. A new Constitution was promulgated in 1965 with effect from 6 May 1966.

President of the Republic and C.-in-C.: Gen. Romeo Lucas García, elected by Congress for a 4-year term beginning 1 July 1978.
Minister of Foreign Affairs: Rafael Castillo Valdez.

The President governs through a Cabinet of ministers; legislation is effected by a 61-member Congress and a 14-member Council of State. Congress and mayors of municipalities, with their councils, are elected.

National flag: Three vertical strips of blue, white, blue, with the national arms in the centre.

National anthem: ¡Guatemala! feliz (words by J. J. Palma; tune by R. Alvarez).

DEFENCE

Army. Military service is voluntary. The Army numbers 14,900, organized in 9 infantry, 1 parachute and 1 engineer battalions and some motorized units with some tanks. The Policía Nacional has 3,000 personnel.

Navy. A Naval force was formed in 1959. It comprises 15 small patrol craft, 1 landing craft, 2 strike troopers, 6 motor launches, 30 work boats, and 6 service craft. Since 1973 the base at Santo Tomas has had a 230-ton marine elevator (synchrolift), greatly improving naval repair facilities. Personnel in 1981 numbered 600 officers and men (including 210 marines).

Air Force. There is a small Air Force with 10 A-37B light attack aircraft, 1 DC-6, 11 C-47 and 8 Israeli-built Arava transports, 4 T-33 jet trainers and 12 PC-7 Pilatus turboprop trainers, and a number of light aircraft and helicopters, including 8 UH-1 Iroquois. Total strength is about 450 personnel and 70 aircraft.

INTERNATIONAL RELATIONS

Membership. Guatemala is a member of UN, OAS and CACM.

External Debt. In 1978 the external debt was Q.220m.

ECONOMY

Planning. In 1978 the Government announced its economic development programme and this included the continued development of agriculture, encouraging the development of agriculture-based industry and light engineering industry associated with agricultural development, promoting tourism, encouraging oil and mining development, improving roads and railway and airport facilities and continuing hydro-electric development. The 1979–82 National Economic Development Plan along these lines involves government investment of Q.1,937·5m.

Budget. The estimates of ordinary revenue and expenditure balanced as follows, in quetzales (1 quetzal = US$): 1978, 942·6m.; 1979, 1,056m.; 1980, 1,280m.; 1981, 1,467m. Income tax was introduced for the first time in 1963.

Currency. The gold *quetzal* was established 7 May 1925 equal to 60 old Guatemala paper pesos, with a gold content equal to that of the US$. Coins of 25, 10, 5 and 1 *centavos* were issued by the Banco de Guatemala on 16 Sept. 1965; they are of a lower content value than the previous ones. There are also paper notes of 100, 50, 20, 10, 5, 1 and ½ *quetzales* (50 *centavos*). In March 1981, £1, = Q.2·18; US$1 = Q.1.

Banking. By an Act effective 4 Feb. 1946 the Central Bank of Guatemala (founded in 1926 as a mixed central and commercial bank) was superseded by a new institution, the Banco de Guatemala, to operate solely as a central bank. Savings and term deposits at commercial banks were Q.882·6m. at the end of 1979. Total currency circulation (backed by a gold reserve fixed by law at a minimum of 40%) on 31 Dec. 1979 was Q.891·1m.; total net international reserves amounted to Q.632m. on 31 Dec. 1979. In July 1965 the country's quota with the IMF was increased from US$15m. to 25m.

There are 17 banks, including the Banco de Guatemala, Banco Nacional de Desarollo, set up in 1971 to promote agricultural development, its counterpart for small industries (Banco de los Trabajadores) set up in Jan. 1966 with initial capital of US$1·3m., a branch of the Bank of London and Montreal Ltd and a branch of the Bank of America.

Weights and Measures. The metric system has been officially adopted, but is little used in local commerce.

Libra of 16 oz.	= 1·014 lb.	*League*	= 3 miles
Arroba of 25 libras	= 25·35 lb.	*Vara*	= 32 in.
Quintal of 4 arrobas	= 101·40 lb.	*Manzana*	= 100 varas sq.
Tonelada of 20 quintals	= 18·10 cwt	*Caballeria* of 64 man-	
Fanega	= 1½ Imp. bushels	zanas	= 110 acres

ENERGY AND NATURAL RESOURCES

Electricity. 1,045m. kwh. of electricity were generated in 1976. A large-scale hydro-electric development is now underway and others are planned.

Oil. Guatemala began exporting crude oil in 1980. Production is from wells in Alta Verapaz department from where the oil is piped to Santo Tomas de Castilla. Further exploration is proceeding in the Petén.

Minerals. Mineral production includes zinc and lead concentrates, some antimony and tungsten, a small amount of cadmium and silver; some copper is also being mined. Exports (1979) Q.6m. In 1965 a subsidiary of International Nickel Company of Canada was granted a 40-year concession to extract and process nickel ore in northern Guatemala. Production and exports started in 1977.

Agriculture. The Cordilleras divide Guatemala into two unequal drainage areas, of which the Atlantic is much the greater. The Pacific slope, though comparatively narrow, is exceptionally well watered and fertile between the altitudes of 1,000 and 5,000 ft, and is the most densely settled part of the republic. The Atlantic slope is sparsely populated, and has little of commercial importance beyond the chicle and timber-cutting of the Petén, coffee cultivation of the Cobán region and banana-raising of the Motagua Valley and Lake Izabal district. Soil erosion is serious and a single week of heavy rains suffices to cause flooding of fields and much crop destruction.

On 17 June 1952 an 'Agrarian Reform Law' was enacted providing for the ex-propriation (with eventual compensation) of those parts of landed estates which were not under cultivation. The US Government in 1953 protested against the ex-propriation of 234,000 acres belonging to the United Fruit Company. Under the new government the expropriation was halted and the 'Agrarian Reform Law' was superseded by a 'Statute' early in 1956, which provided small holdings to several thousand peasant farmers. This distribution of land continues, now under the provisions of the 'Agrarian Transformation Law' of 1962.

The principal crop is coffee; there are about 12,000 coffee plantations with 138m. coffee trees on about 338,000 acres, but 80% of the crop comes from 1,500 large coffee farms employing 426,000 workers. Coffee exports in 1979 were valued at Q.431·9m. mainly to USA and Federal Republic of Germany.

Bananas are still an important export crop, but exports have at times been seriously reduced, partly by labour troubles and by hurricanes. Exports 1978 were worth Q.19m.

Cotton has become an important export and in 1979 was valued at Q.192·3m. Other important exports (1979) were sugar, Q.53·5m.; beef, Q.41·4m. Guatemala is, after Mexico, the largest producer of chicle gum (used for chewing-gum manufacture in USA). Rubber development schemes are under way, assisted by US funds. Guatemala is one of the largest sources of essential oils (citronella and lemon grass); exports in 1979 were valued at Q.2·2m. Cardamom, exported mainly to the Arab countries, is an increasingly important source of revenue; exports, 1979, Q.49·2m. Cattle-grounds (*potreros*) occupy about 758,000 acres. There were (1979) some 1·6m. head of cattle (mostly beef) in the country.

Forestry. The forest area has an extent of 17,784,000 acres. The department of Petén is rich in mahogany and other woods.

Fisheries. Exports were about Q.8m. in 1978.

INDUSTRY AND TRADE

Industry. The principal industries are food and beverages, tobacco, chemicals, hides and skins, textiles, garments and non-metallic minerals. New industries include electrical goods, plastic sheet and metal furniture.

Trade Unions. Trade unions are small. In 1954 the trade unions were ordered to reorganize and there are now two main federations.

Commerce. Values in Q.1,000 (1 quetzal = US$1) were:

	1974	1975	1976	1977	1978	1979
Imports (c.i.f.)	700,473	732,679	981,600	1,052,507	1,285,640	1,503,900
Exports (f.o.b.)	572,133	623,503	782,400	1,160,115	1,089,457	1,241,400

Value (in Q.1,000) of principal imports, 1977: Machinery and transport equipment, 355,191; chemicals, 191,952; petroleum products, 148,424; foodstuffs, 55,422. Chief exports are coffee, cotton, bananas, beef, essential oils, timber, chicle and shrimps. The main trading partners are USA, Japan and Federal Republic of Germany, and the partners of the Central American Common Market.

Total trade between Guatemala and UK for 6 years (British Department of Trade returns, in £1,000 sterling):

	1975	1976	1977	1978	1979	1980
Imports to UK	31,918	2,133	3,600	5,726	7,596	23,657
Exports and re-exports from UK	9,838	14,022	16,676	14,529	13,371	13,835

Tourism. There were 503,908 foreign visitors in 1979.

COMMUNICATIONS

Roads. In 1977 there were 17,139 km of roads, of which 2,765 are paved. There is a trunk highway from coast to coast *via* Guatemala City. There are 2 trunk highways from the Mexican to the Salvadorean frontier: the Pacific Highway serving the fertile coastal plain and the Pan-American Highway running through the highlands and Guatemala City. Motor vehicles number about 200,000.

Railways. The principal railway system is the government-owned (since 1968) *Ferrocarriles de Guatemala*. All railways are of 914 mm gauge. Total length of all lines is 820 km. Passengers carried, 1976, numbered 386,000, and freight carried (1976), 703,600 short tons. The bridge across the Suchiate River between Mexico and Guatemala in 1942 linked the railways of North and Central America, though differences in gauge make it necessary to change trains at Ayutla.

Aviation. The government-owned airline, Aviateca, furnishes both domestic and international services; 6 other airlines handle international traffic. In 1976 air cargo amounted to 16·1m. tons; number of passengers, 422,000.

Shipping. The chief ports on the Atlantic coast are Puerto Barrios and Santo Tomás de Castilla: on the Pacific coast, San José and Champerico. Total tonnage handled was, 1977, 2·6m. tons.

Post and Broadcasting. The Government own and operate the telegraph and telephone services; there were (1978) 70,614 telephone instruments. There are some 70 broadcasting stations. Radio receiving sets in use, 1976, numbered about 1m. There are 4 commercial TV stations, 1 government station and about 192,000 TV receivers.

Cinemas (1979). Cinemas numbered approximately 100.

Newspapers (1980). There are 8 daily newspapers.

JUSTICE, RELIGION, EDUCATION AND WELFARE

Justice. Justice is administered in a Supreme Court, 6 appeal courts and 28 courts of first instance. Supreme Court and appeal court judges are elected by Congress. Judges of first instance are appointed by the Supreme Court.

All holders of public office have to show on entering office, and again on leaving, a full account of their private property and income.

Religion. Roman Catholicism is the prevailing faith; but all other creeds have complete liberty of worship. Guatemala has an archbishopric.

Education. In 1976 there were 6,415 primary schools with 27,666 teachers and an attendance of 753,932 pupils; these figures include private schools. There are 357 secondary and other schools having 7,051 teachers and an attendance of 104,800 pupils; the autonomous University of San Carlos de Borromeo, founded in 1678, was reopened in 1910 with 7 faculties and schools and there are 4 new universities. Students at state university (1977) approximately 25,925. All education is in theory free, but owing to a grave shortage of state schools private schools flourish. The 1964 census showed that 63% of those 10 years of age and older were illiterate.

Social Welfare. A comprehensive system of social security was outlined in a law of

30 Oct. 1946. Medical personnel include about 1,250 doctors and 275 dentists for the whole republic. There are about 60 public hospitals and about 100 dispensaries.

DIPLOMATIC REPRESENTATIVES

OF GUATEMALA IN THE USA (2200 R St., NW, Washington, D.C. 20008)

Ambassador: Gen. Felipe Doroteo Monterroso.

OF THE USA IN GUATEMALA (7–01 Avenida de la Reforma, Zone 10, Guatemala City)

Ambassador: (Vacant).

OF GUATEMALA TO THE UNITED NATIONS

Ambassador: Eduardo Castíllo Arriola.

Guatemala broke off diplomatic relations with UK on 31 July 1963, but there is a British Consulate in Guatemala City.

Books of Reference

The official gazette is called *Diario de Centro America.*

Adler, J. H., and others, *Public Finance and Economic Development in Guatemala.* Stanford Univ. Press, 1952
Banco de Guatemala, *Memoria annual, Estudio económico* and *Boletin Estadistica*
Bianchi, W. J., *Belize.* New York, 1959
Bloomfield, L. M., *The British Honduras–Guatemala Dispute.* Toronto, 1953
Glassman, P., *Guatemala Guide.* Dallas, 1977
Holleran, M. P., *Church and State in Guatemala.* New York, 1949
Humphreys, R. A., *The Diplomatic History of British Honduras 1638–1901.* London, 1961
Male, P. J. E., *Economic and Commercial Conditions in Guatemala.* HMSO, 1956
Mendoza, J. L., *Britain and Her Treaties on Belize.* Guatemala, 1946
Morton, F., *Xeláhuh.* London, 1959
Plant, R., *Guatemala: Unnatural Disaster.* London, 1978
Rosenthal, M., *Guatemala.* New York, 1961
Whetton, N. L., *Guatemala: The Land and the People.* Yale Univ. Press, 1961

National Library: Biblioteca Nacional, 5a Avenida y 8a Calle, Zona 1, Guatemala City.

GUINEA

Capital: Conakry
Population: 5·13m. (1978)
GNP per capita: US$210 (1978)

République populaire et
révolutionnaire de Guinée

HISTORY. Guinea was occupied by France in 1898 and became a territory of French West Africa in 1904. The independent republic of Guinea was proclaimed on 2 Oct. 1958, after the territory of French Guinea had decided at the referendum of 28 Sept. to leave the French Community.

AREA AND POPULATION. Guinea is bounded north and east by Guinea-Bissau, Senegal and Mali, south by Liberia and Sierra Leone and the Atlantic ocean to the west.

The area is 245,857 sq. km (95,000 sq. miles), and the population, census, 1972, was 5,143,284, including an estimated 1·5m. living abroad (estimate, 1978, 5·13m.). The largest towns (populations 1972 census) are Conakry, the capital (525,671), Kankan (85,310), Kindia, (79,861), Labé (79,670), and N'Zérékoré (about 23,000).

The ethnic composition is Fulani (40·3%, predominant in Moyenne-Guinée), Malinke (or Mandingo, 25·8%, prominent in Haut-Guinée), Susu (11%, prominent in Guinée-Maritime), Kissi (6·5%) and Kpelle (4·8%) in Guinee-Forestière, and Dialonka, Loma and others (11·6%).

CONSTITUTION AND GOVERNMENT. The Constitution of 12 Nov. 1958 declared Guinea 'a democratic, secular and social republic'. The Constitution provides for the limitation or renunciation of sovereignty in favour of African unity. The President of the republic is elected for a 7-year term and can be re-elected.

President: Sékou Touré (elected Jan. 1961, re-elected Jan. 1968 and Dec. 1974).
Prime Minister: Dr. Louis Lansana Beavogni.
Foreign Affairs: Abdoulaye Touré.

The National Assembly has 210 members; they and the 33 regional governors are appointed by the National Council of the *Parti démocratique de Guinée*, the sole legal party.

The administrative division comprises 33 regions, grouped into 4 'supra-regions' which correspond to the 4 major geographical and ethnic areas: Guinée-Maritime (Lower Guinea, headquarters at Kindia); Moyenne-Guinée (Fouta Djallon, head-quarters at Labé); Haute-Guinée (Upper Guinea, headquarters at Kankan) and Guinée-Forestière (Forest-Guinea, headquarters at N'Zérékoré).

National flag: Three vertical strips of red, gold, green.

The official language is French but there are plans to replace French by either Susu or Malinké.

DEFENCE

Army. The Army of 8,500 men (1980), which comprises 1 armoured battalion, 4 infantry battalions, 1 commando and 1 engineering battalion, has been equipped with Soviet, Czech and Chinese weapons, armoured cars and artillery.

Air Force. The Air Force, formed with Soviet assistance, is reported to be equipped with 6 MiG-17 jet-fighters and 2 MiG-15UTI trainers, 2 Il-18 turboprop transports, 4 An-14 and 4 Il-14 piston-engined transports, all Russian built, plus a few helicopters, piston-engined Yak-18 and L-29 jet trainers. Personnel about 300. An operational base for Soviet maritime reconnaissance aircraft has been established at Conakry.

INTERNATIONAL RELATIONS

Membership. Guinea is a member of UN, OAU and is an ACP state of EEC.

ECONOMY

Budget. The budget for 1979 balanced at 11,250m. sylis.

Currency. The monetary unit is the *syli*, divided into 100 *cauris*, introduced in 1972. The issue consists of notes of 100, 50, 25 and 10 *sylis*, and coins of 50 *cauris*, 5, 2 and 1 *sylis*. In March 1981, £1 = 43·65 *sylis*; US$1 = 20·12 *sylis*.

Banking. The Banque Centrale de la République de Guinée, with a capital of 50m. sylis, is controlled by a governor with ministerial rank. It is the sole bank of issue. In Jan. 1962 all insurance companies and the Banque de l'Afrique Occidentale, the only private bank in Conakry, were nationalized.

ENERGY AND NATURAL RESOURCES

Electricity. Production of electrical energy was 500m. kwh. in 1976.

Minerals. Diamonds are found in the Macenta district (80,000 carats in 1976). Bauxite exists in the Los islands, the Boké district and the Kindia–Telimélé district; output, 1977, 9m. tonnes. Production of iron ore in the Kaloum peninsula was 1·04m. tonnes in 1970.

Agriculture. The chief products are rice, palm-nuts, bananas, coffee, pineapples, orange juice, groundnuts, millet. Coffee is grown in forest districts. There are experimental fruit gardens at Camayenne near Conakry, Kindia and Dalaba, 2 stations for rice selection (Kankan, Koba) and an experimental quinine station at Sérédou. Fouta Djallon contains cattle in abundance. In 1979 there were 1·7m. cattle and 825,000 sheep and goats.

Agricultural production, 1977 (in 1,000 tonnes): Bananas, 70; cassava, 484; maize, 370; rice, 320; palm oil, 37·8.

COMMERCE. In 1977 imports totalled 5,664m. sylis; exports, 6,629m. sylis. Alumina forms about 30% and bauxite 58% of the exports.

Total trade between Guinea and the UK (British Department of Trade returns, in £1,000 sterling):

	1976	1977	1978	1979	1980
Imports to UK	54	205	476	489	10,777
Exports and re-exports from UK	4,508	5,399	5,471	5,057	26,596

COMMUNICATIONS

Roads. There are 28,400 km of roads and tracks, of which 520 km are bitumenized.

Railways. A railway connects Conakry with Kankan (662 km) and may be extended to Bamako in Mali. A line 134 km long linking bauxite deposits at Sangaredi with Port Kamsar was opened in 1973 and a third line links Conakry and Fria.

Aviation. There are airports at Conakry and Kankan; in 1973, 55,000 passengers disembarked and embarked.

Shipping. Conakry port facilities were being expanded 1976–80. There are 13 vessels of 15,041 GRT in Guinea.

Post and Broadcasting. The territory is connected by cable with France and Pernambuco; also with Freetown, Monrovia and other places. There is a wireless station at Conakry affording communication with all territories of West Africa. Telephones, 1972, numbered about 7,488. There were 110,000 radio receivers in 1975; television broadcasting commenced 1977.

JUSTICE, RELIGION, EDUCATION AND WELFARE

Justice. There are *tribunaux du premier degré* at Conakry and Kankan, and a *juge de paix* at N'Zérékoré. The High Court, Court of Appeal and Superior Tribunal of

Cassation are at Conakry, while the National Assembly serves as the 'supreme revolutionary tribunal'.

Religion. About 62% of the population is Moslem, 1·5% Christian and 35% follow tribal religions.

Education. There were, in 1977, 324,165 pupils in primary schools, 124,455 in secondary schools and 6,000 in technical schools and teacher-training colleges.

Health. In 1976 there were 314 hospitals and dispensaries with 7,650 beds; there were also 277 doctors, 21 dentists, 159 pharmacists, 394 midwives and 1,533 nursing personnel.

DIPLOMATIC REPRESENTATIVES

OF GUINEA IN GREAT BRITAIN

Ambassador: Aboubacar Somparé (resides in Paris).

OF GREAT BRITAIN IN GUINEA

Ambassador: C. W. Squire, CMG, MVO (resides in Dakar).

OF GUINEA IN THE USA (2112 Leroy Pl., NW, Washington, D.C., 20008)

Ambassador: Mamady Lamine Conde.

OF THE USA IN GUINEA (2nd Blvd. and 9th Ave., Conakry)

Ambassador: Allen C. Davis.

OF GUINEA TO THE UNITED NATIONS

Ambassador: Ibrahima Fofana.

Books of Reference

Bulletin Statistique et Economique de la Guinée. Monthly. Conakry
Adamolekun, L., *Sékou Touré's Guinea.* London, 1976
Camara, S. S., *La Guinée sans la France.* Paris, 1976
Rivière, C., *Guinea: The Mobilization of a People.* Cornell Univ. Press, 1977
Taylor, F. W., *A Fulani–English Dictionary.* Oxford, 1932

GUINEA-BISSAU

Capital: Bissau
Population: 777,214 (1979)
GNP per capita: US$140 (1978)

HISTORY. Guinea-Bissau, formerly Portuguese Guinea, on the coast of Guinea, was discovered in 1446 by Nuno Tristão. It became a separate colony in 1879. It is bounded by the limits fixed by the convention of 12 May 1886 with France. In 1951 Guinea-Bissau became an overseas province of Portugal. The armed struggle against colonial rule began in 1963. Independence was declared on 24 Sept. 1973. On 10 Sept. 1974 Portugal formally recognized the independence of Guinea-Bissau.

AREA AND POPULATION. Guinea-Bissau is bounded by Senegal in the north and by Guinea in the east and south. It includes the adjacent archipelago of Bijagoz, with the island of Bolama. There are 8 administrative regions. The capital and chief port is Bissau, estimated population (census 1979), 109,486. Other ports are Bolama and Cacheu. Area is 36,125 sq. km (13,948 sq. miles); population (census, 1979), 777,214.

CONSTITUTION AND GOVERNMENT. The Constitution, as established by the National People's Assembly at independence, designated the *Partido Africano da Independencia da Guiné e Cabo Verde* (PAIGC) as the only permitted Party, and provided for eventual union between Guinea-Bissau and Cape Verde.

On 14 Nov. 1980, President Luis Cabral was overthrown in a *coup*. A Revolutionary Council was established by the former Prime Minister, João Bernardo Vieira. The aim of eventual union with Cape Verde was abandoned.

National flag: Horizontally yellow over green with red vertical strip in the hoist bearing a black star.

DEFENCE

Army. The Army consisted in 1981 of 4 infantry battalions, 1 engineer unit and 1 tank squadron. Personnel, 6,000 men.

Air Force. Formation of a small Air Force began in 1978 with the delivery of a French-built Cessna FTB-337 twin-engined counter-insurgency and general-purpose light transport. It has been followed by an Mi-8 and 2 Alouette III helicopters and 2 Dornier Do 27 utility aircraft.

Navy. The naval force comprises 2 fast attack craft, 4 coastal patrol craft, a survey ship and some auxiliaries, based at Bissau. Personnel (1980) 250.

INTERNATIONAL RELATIONS

Membership. Guinea-Bissau is a member of UN, OAU and is an ACP state of EEC.

ECONOMY

Budget. The revenue in 1976 was 463m. pesos; the expenditure, 907m. pesos.

Currency. The monetary unit is the *peso*. In March 1981, £1 = 77·82 *pesos*; US$1 = 35·88 *pesos*.

NATURAL RESOURCES

Minerals. Mining is very little developed although bauxite (200m. tonnes) has been located in the Boké area. Exploration for oil is taking place but no reports of finds have been reported.

Agriculture. Chief products are rice, palm-oil, groundnuts, coconuts, timber, hides, seeds, wax.

Livestock (1979): Cattle, 264,000; goats, 183,000; pigs, 175,000.

COMMERCE. Imports in 1978, 1,726,412 contos; exports, 422,642 contos. In 1977, 59% of exports went to Portugal (1976, 76·6%).

Total trade between Guinea-Bissau and UK (British Department of Trade returns, in £1,000 sterling):

	1977	1978	1979	1980
Imports to UK	2	562	835	1
Exports and re-exports from UK	516	3,346	600	483

COMMUNICATIONS

Roads. There were (1972) 3,570 km of roads.

Shipping. In 1972, 112 vessels of 232,912 net tons entered the ports.

Post. In 1972 there were 2,764 telephones.

Cinemas. There were 7 cinemas (1972) with a seating capacity of 3,000.

RELIGION, EDUCATION AND WELFARE

Religion. About 40% of the population are Moslem and about 4% Christian.

Education. There were, in 1978, 93,256 pupils in primary schools with 2,620 teachers; 4,612 pupils in secondary schools and 284 students in teacher-training establishments.

Health. In 1976 there were 9 hospitals with 1,056 beds and 74 doctors, 2 dentists, 2 pharmacists, 70 midwives and 292 nursing personnel.

DIPLOMATIC REPRESENTATIVES

OF GREAT BRITAIN IN GUINEA-BISSAU

Ambassador: C. W. Squire, CMG, MVO (resides in Dakar).

OF GUINEA-BISSAU IN THE USA

Ambassador: Gil Vicente Vaz Fernandes.

OF THE USA IN GUINEA-BISSAU
(Ave. Domingos Ramos, Bissau)

Ambassador: Edward Marks.

OF GUINEA-BISSAU TO THE UNITED NATIONS

Ambassador: Gil Vicente Vaz Fernandes.

Books of Reference

Anuário da Guiné Portuguesa. Bissau (latest issue, 1956–58)
Relatório e Mapas do Movimento Comercial e Maritimo da Guiné. Bolama. Annual
Guiné. Agencia-Geral do Ultramar. Lisbon, 1961
Cabral, A., *Revolution in Guinea.* London, 1969—*Return to the Source.* New York, 1973
Davidson, B., *Growing from the Grass Roots.* London, 1974
Gjerstad, O., and Sarrazin, C., *Sowing the First Harvest: National Reconstruction in Guinea-Bissau.* Oakland, 1978
Mota, T. de, *Guiné Portuguesa.* Lisbon, 1954
Rudebeck, L., *Guinea-Bissau: A Study of Political Mobilization.* Uppsala, 1974

GUYANA

Capital: Georgetown
Population: 824,000 (1978)
GNP per capita: US$550 (1978)

HISTORY. The territory, including the counties of Demerara, Essequibo and Berbice, named from the 3 rivers, was first partially settled by the Dutch West Indian Company about 1620. The Dutch retained their hold until 1796, when it was captured by the English. It was finally ceded to Great Britain in 1814 and named British Guiana. On 26 May 1966 British Guiana became an independent member of the Commonwealth under the name of Guyana and the world's first Co-operative Republic on 23 Feb. 1970.

AREA AND POPULATION. Guyana is situated on the north-east coast of South America on the Atlantic ocean, with Suriname on the east, Venezuela on the west and Brazil on the south and west. Area, 83,000 sq. miles (210,000 sq. km). Estimated population (Dec. 1978), 824,000. Births (1972), 25,065; deaths (1974), 3,418. The Greater Georgetown area had in 1978 an estimated population of 183,000.

In Nov. 1940 sites on the bank of the Demerara River, about 25 miles from the sea, and at Makouria, about 40 miles up the Essequibo River, were leased to the USA as military bases. The site on the Demerara River is being operated by the Guyana Government as a civil airport. The US Government relinquished its claims to Atkinson on Guyana's attainment of independence. On 1 May 1969 the airport and surrounding area (formerly Atkinson) were renamed Timehri.

CONSTITUTION AND GOVERNMENT. A new Constitution was promulgated in Oct. 1980. The National Assembly consists of 53 elected members. Elections are held under the single-list system of proportional representation, with the whole of the country forming one electoral area and each voter casting his vote for a party list of candidates. The legislature is elected for 5 years unless earlier dissolved.

The elections held on 15 Dec. 1980 gave the People's National Congress 41 seats, the People's Progressive Party 10 seats, the Liberator Party 2 seats. The PNC with an overall majority formed a 25-member cabinet.

The Cabinet was in Jan. 1981 composed as follows:

Executive President: L. F. S. Burnham.

First Vice-President and Prime Minister: Dr P. A. Reid. *Vice-President and Economic Planning:* H. S. Hoyte. *Vice-President and Public Welfare:* H. Green. *Vice-President and Works and Transport:* S. Narine. *Vice-President and Parliamentary Affairs:* B. Ramsaroop.

Energy and National Resources: H. O. Jack. *Trade and Consumer Protection:* F. Hope. *Agriculture:* J. Tyndall. *National Development:* R. Corbin. *Foreign Affairs:* R. Jackson. *Attorney-General and Justice:* Dr M. Shahabuddin. *Higher Education:* R. Chandisingh. *Education:* J. Thomas. *Home Affairs:* S. Moore. *Regional Development:* O. Clarke. *Information:* F. Campbell. *Health and Public Welfare:* Dr R. Van-West Charles. *Works and Transport:* C. A. Nascimento. *Co-operatives:* U. Johnson. *Public Service:* Y. Harewood-Benn. *Office of the President:* H. Raschid. *Finance:* Sallahuddin. *Fisheries:* R. Williams. *Environment and Water Supply:* J. Chowritmootoo. *Forestry:* F. Carmichael. *Crops and Livestock:* S. Prashad. *Drainage and Irrigation:* R. Van Sluytman.

There are 3 Ministers of State.

National flag: Green with a yellow triangle based on the hoist, edged in white, charged with a red triangle edged in black.

DEFENCE

Army. The Guyana Army has a strength of 7,000 (which includes all armed services), including a women's army corps. It comprises 2 infantry battalions.

Air Force. The Air Command is equipped with light aircraft and helicopters, including a turboprop Super King Air 200, 6 Islander twin-engined STOL transports and 4 Bell 206/212 light helicopters.

INTERNATIONAL RELATIONS

Membership. Guyana is a member of UN, the Commonwealth, Caricom and is an ACP state of EEC.

ECONOMY

Budget. Revenue and expenditure for calendar years (in G$1,000):

	1974	1975 [1]	1976 [1]	1977	1978	1979
Revenue	395,317	585,491	500,942	442,475	539,591	693,921
Expenditure	358,553	602,518	746,329	567,322	632,749	868,664

[1] Revised estimates.

These figures are exclusive of special receipts from the Colonial Development Fund, US grant and the related expenditure.

Chief items of revenue 1975 (in G$1,000): Customs and excise, 330,746; internal revenue, 124,071; fees, fines, etc., 4,082; posts, 3,841; rents, royalties, etc., 1,197; miscellaneous, 16,201. Expenditure: Public works, 91,522; agriculture, 60,443; education, 59,433; health, 29,248; post and telecommunications, 19,716.

Public debt, 31 Dec. 1975, was G$676·8m.

Currency. Accounts are kept in *dollars* and *cents* (£1 = G$5·56). The Bank of Guyana, established in 1965, issued Guyana dollar notes of $1, 5, 10 and 20 and coins of 1-, 5-, 10-, 25- and 50-cent pieces. The face value of Guyana notes in circulation at 31 Dec. 1977 was G$161·4m.

Banking. Barclays Bank International and the Royal Bank of Canada maintain branches in Berbice, Demerara and Essequibo while the Bank of Baroda (India) has branches in Demerara and Berbice. The Chase Manhattan Bank (USA) and the Bank of Nova Scotia each have a branch in Georgetown. The Guyana National Co-operative Bank opened in Feb. 1970 with headquarters at Georgetown and branches in Berbice, Linden and Essequibo. In 1973 the Guyana Agricultural Co-operative Bank and the Guyana Mortgage Finance Bank were established.

As at 31 Dec. 1977 the Bank of Guyana had external assets totalling G$148m.

NATURAL RESOURCES

Minerals. Placer gold mining commenced in 1884, and was followed by diamond mining in 1887. From 1884 to 1973 the output of gold was 431,413 bullion oz. (15,600 oz. in 1976). From 1901 to 1973 the production of diamonds was 4,008,211 metric carats (15,148 in 1979). There are large deposits of bauxite; 4,851,000 tons and 137,000 tons of alumina were produced in 1979. Full-scale production of manganese began in 1960 and 114,988 wet tons were produced in 1968. The North West Guyana Mining Co. Ltd, operating through the Manganese Mines Ltd, closed operation in Guyana by the end of 1968.

Agriculture. Production, 1979: Sugar-cane, 298,000 tons; rice, 142,000 tons. Other important products are coconuts, coffee, cocoa, ground provisions and citrus fruit. Other tropical fruits and vegetables are grown mostly in scattered plantings; they include mangoes, papaws, avocado pears, melons, bananas and gooseberries. Other important crops are tomatoes, cabbages, black-eye peas, peanuts, carrots, onions, turmeric, ginger, red kidney beans, soybeans, eschallot and tobacco. Large areas of unimproved land in the coastal region, which vary in width up to about 30 miles from the sea, are still available for agricultural and cattle-grazing projects.

Livestock estimate (1979): Cattle, 280,000; pigs, 132,000; sheep, 113,000; goats, 68,000; poultry, 12m.

Forestry. Guyana can be divided roughly into 3 regions: (1) A low coastal region varying in width up to about 30 miles and constituting the agricultural area; (2) an intermediate area about 100 miles wide, of slightly higher undulating land containing the chief mineral and forest resources of the country; and (3) a hinterland of several mountain ranges and extensive savannahs. Approximately 87% of the land area is forested, and about 60,000 sq. miles of this is still available for timber exploitation. Only about 20% of the forest area is at present regarded as being reasonably accessible for timber extraction on an economic basis, however. In 1972 this area accounted for the production of 8,233,743 cu. ft of wood and wood products.

COMMERCE. Imports and exports (in G$) for calendar years:

	1975	1976	1977	1978	1979
Imports	810,641,316	927,299,000	804,265,086	711,056,000	811,000,000
Exports	840,669,788	695,151,911	652,451,438	739,589,440	732,900,000

Chief imports (1978): Wheat flour, 12,891,962 lb., $4,026,671; unmilled wheat, 91,298,250 lb., $17,452,170; milk, 33,593,349 lb., $28,964,157; textile fabrics, 11·8m. sq. yd, $24,938,438; footwear, 14,921,871 doz. pairs; motor vehicles and parts, $7,453,203; split peas, 6,272,093 lb., $4,031,912.

Chief domestic exports (1978): Sugar, 280,672 tons, $234,552,873; rice, 104,761 tons, $95,982,985; rum, 1,842,569 proof gallons, $9,456,032; timber, 1,209,436 cu. ft, $9,981,892; molasses, 19,572,640 gallons, $8,917,682; diamonds, 10,999 carats, $1,471,661; shrimps, 1,682,610 lb., $12,397,056.

Imports (exclusive of transhipments), 1978, from CARICOM Territories, 28·9%; from USA, 22·5%; from UK, 21·9%; from Canada, 4·1%; exports (exclusive of transhipments) to UK, 29%; to CARICOM Territories, 15·4%; to Canada, 6·9%.

Total trade between Guyana and UK (British Department of Trade returns, in £1,000 sterling):

	1976	1977	1978	1979	1980
Imports to UK	46,414	46,447	50,623	43,009	47,143
Exports and re-exports from UK	37,977	33,441	27,292	27,607	30,191

COMMUNICATIONS

Roads. Roads and vehicular trails in the national, provincial and urban systems amount to 1,810 miles, of which 595 miles are maintained by government, 836 miles by local authorities and 269 miles by 5 municipalities. There are 422 miles of road on the coastal and lower riverain areas of which 308 miles are paved; and 651 miles of road and vehicular trail in the upper riverain and interior areas of which only 16 miles are paved. A new road, which will eventually link up with the Pan American Highway, is now under construction in the Guyana interior. The road extends from Mahdia on the Potaro River to Annai in the Rupununi. Work on the road is being undertaken on a self-help basis. Motor vehicles, as of 31 Dec. 1976, totalled 64,272, including 26,599 passenger cars, 6,979 lorries and vans, 9,072 tractors and trailers, and 19,109 motor cycles.

Railways. The 19-mile government-owned West Coast Railway ceased operation in June 1974. Passenger and cargo services between Vreed-en-Hoop on the west bank of the Demerara River and Parika at the mouth of the Essequibo River are carried out by buses owned by the Guyana Transport Services.

In addition, there is a short, government-owned railway in the North West District, while the Guyana Bauxite Co. operates a standard-gauge railway of 80 miles from Linden on the Demerara River to Ituni. In March 1967 a bridge (740 ft) across the Demerara River was opened to enable the company to resume mining operations on the west bank of the river.

Aviation. Guyana Airways Corporation operates scheduled services within the state and also a new service to Trinidad, Barbados and Miami. Other services in operation: British Airways 4 times weekly to the Caribbean, Europe and North America: PANAM 3 times weekly to North, Central and South America: Air France, to and from Guadeloupe, Paramaribo and Cayenne 4 times a week; British West Indian Airways, Ltd, to and from Trinidad 3 times a week, providing direct connexion with New York and London; Cubana Airlines once weekly. All-cargo services are provided by Guyana Airways out of Guyana through the major Caribbean countries to the USA (Miami) and also to Brazil.

Shipping. In 1975, 1,273 vessels of 2,823,912 NRT entered and 1,225 of 2,266,220 NRT cleared the port of Georgetown.

Guyana is in direct sea-communication with the UK, France, Canada, USA, the West Indies, and Netherlands and French Guiana. There are 217 nautical miles of river navigation. There are ferry services across the mouths of the Demerara, Berbice and Essequibo rivers, the last providing a link between the West Coast Railway and the islands of Leguan and Wakenaam and the mainland at Adventure, and a number of coastal and river-boat services carrying both passengers and cargo. A number of launch services are operated in the more remote areas by private concerns.

Georgetown harbour, about $\frac{1}{2}$ mile wide and $2\frac{1}{2}$ miles long, has a minimum depth of 24 ft. New Amsterdam harbour is situated at the mouth of the Berbice River; there are wharves for coastal vessels only. Bauxite is loaded on ocean-going freighters at Mackenzie, 67 miles up the Demerara River, and at Everton on the Berbice River, about 10 miles from the mouth of the waterway. The Essequibo River has several timber-loading berths ranging from 20 to 40 ft. Springlands on the Corentyne River is the point of entry and departure of passengers travelling by launch services to and from Suriname. It is also a shipping point for rice and other produce from the Corentyne to Georgetown.

Post and Broadcasting. The inland public telegraph and radio communication services are operated and maintained by the Telecommunication Corporation, established on 1 March 1967. On 31 Dec. 1976 there were 57 post offices and 94 agencies (including travelling post offices and agencies).

The telephone exchanges had at the end of 1975 a total of 17,311 direct exchange lines with (1978), 27,064 telephone instruments. The number of route miles in the coastal and inland areas was 2,982 km. 39 land-line stations were maintained at post offices in the coastal area, and 8 telegraph stations in the interior provide communication with the coastal area through a central telegraph office in Georgetown.

Overseas radio-telephone and telegraphic communication were provided by Cable & Wireless (W.I.) Ltd, but were nationalized in 1977 and the service is now provided by the Guyana International Telecommunications Corporation Ltd (Guyintel). In Georgetown a central radio station provides facilities for radio communication with 5 branch offices operated in combination with the wireless telegraph stations mentioned above. 92 stations operated by other government departments, 31 stations operated by private concerns (including mining, ranching, timber and other commercial interests) and 12 coastal ships and launches. This system is linked with the telephone system and is available to the general public.

A Tropospheric Scatter System, operated by Guyintel, was opened on 26 March 1969. It provides for a maximum of 32 channels linking Guyana with the rest of the world *via* Trinidad, the nearest point for connexion in the company's broad band system. The Guyana Broadcasting Corporation, which came into operation on 1 July 1980, has 2 channels.

Cinemas (1975). There are 51 cinemas with seating capacity of 38,375.

Newspapers (1979). There is 1 daily newspaper with a circulation of 98,000 and 4 weekly papers with a combined circulation of 157,000.

JUSTICE, EDUCATION AND WELFARE

Justice. The law, both civil and criminal, is based on the common and statute law of England, save that the principles of the Roman–Dutch law have been retained in respect of the registration, conveyance and mortgaging of land.

The Supreme Court of Judicature consists of a Court of Appeal and a High Court.

Education. In Sept. 1976 the Government assumed total responsibility for education from nursery school to university. Private education was abolished. In Sept. 1980, the total number of schools was 1,367: Nursery, 906; primary, 372; community high, 29; secondary, 60.

There are now 5 technical and vocational schools and 2 schools for the teaching of home economics and domestic crafts. Training in co-operatives is provided by the Kuru-Kuru Co-operative College and agriculture by the Guyana School of

Agriculture and the Burnham Agricultural Institute. The training of primary and secondary school teachers is undertaken by 3 institutions. Higher education is also provided by the University of Guyana which was established in 1963 with faculties of natural science, social science, art, technology and education as well as first year students in law. There were 1,889 students in July 1979.

Health. In 1977 there were 23 hospitals, 132 health centres and stations, 29 dispensaries and 13 medical outposts. There were 114 doctors and 11 dentists.

DIPLOMATIC REPRESENTATIVES

OF GUYANA IN GREAT BRITAIN (3 Palace Court, London, W2 4LP)
High Commissioner: Dr Cedric Hilburn Grant (accredited 12 Oct. 1977).

OF GREAT BRITAIN IN GUYANA (44 Main St., Georgetown)
High Commissioner: P. L. V. Mallet, CMG.

OF GUYANA IN THE USA (2490 Tracey Place, NW,
Washington, D.C., 20008)
Ambassador: Laurence E. Mann.

OF THE USA IN GUYANA (31 Main St., Georgetown)
Ambassador: George B. Roberts, Jr.

OF GUYANA TO THE UNITED NATIONS
Ambassador: Noel G. Sinclair.

Books of Reference

Daly, P. H., *From Revolution to Republic*. Georgetown, 1970
Daly, Vere T., *A Short History of the Guyanese People*. Rev. ed. London, 1975
Newman, P., *British Guiana—Problem of Cohesion in an Immigrant Society*. OUP, 1964
Report of the British Guiana Commission of Inquiry of the International Commission of Jurists on Racial Problems in the Public Service. Geneva, 1965
Smith, R. T., *British Guiana*. OUP, 1962
Swan, M., *British Guiana*. HMSO, 1957

HAITI

République d'Haiti

Capital: Port-au-Prince
Population: 5·53m. (1978)
GNP per capita: US$260 (1978)

HISTORY. Haiti occupies the western third of the large island of Hispaniola which was discovered by Christopher Columbus in 1492. The Spanish colony was ceded to France in 1697 and became her most prosperous colony. After the extirpation of the Indians by the Spaniards (by 1533) large numbers of African slaves were imported whose descendants now populate the country. The slaves obtained their liberation following the French Revolution, but subsequently Napoleon sent his brother-in-law, Gen. Leclerc, to restore French authority and re-impose slavery. Toussaint Louverture, the leader of the slaves who had been appointed a French general and governor, was kidnapped and sent to France, where he died in gaol. However, the reckless courage of the Negro troops and the ravages of yellow fever forced the French to evacuate the island and surrender to the blockading British squadron.

The country declared its independence on 1 Jan. 1804, and its successful leader, Gen. Jean-Jacques Dessalines, proclaimed himself Emperor of the newly-named Haiti. After the assassination of Dessalines (1806) a separate régime was set up in the north under Henri Christophe, a Negro general who in 1811 had himself proclaimed King Henry. In the south and west a republic was constituted, with the mulatto Alexander Pétion as its first President. Pétion died in 1818 and was succeeded by Jean-Pierre Boyer, under whom the country became re-united after Henry had committed suicide in 1820. From 1822 to 1844 Haiti and the eastern part of the island (later the Dominican Republic) were united. After one more monarchical interlude, under the Emperor Faustin (1847–59), Haiti has been a republic. From 1915 to 1934 Haiti was under United States occupation.

AREA AND POPULATION. The area is 27,750 sq. km (10,700 sq. miles), of which about three-quarters is mountainous. The population at the census in 1975 was 4,583,785 (highest density in Latin America), of which 85% are living in rural areas. The capital, Port-au-Prince (Ouest) census (1975) population 458,675. Other estimates (1975): Cap Haitien (Nord), 54,691; Gonaives (Artibonite), 36,736 (Sud); Les Cayes (Sud), 27,222; Jérémie (Sud), 25,117; Port de Paix (Nord-Ouest), 21,733; St Marc, 20,504: Jacmel, 16,449. Infant deaths per 1,000 live births in 1970 were estimated at 147.

The country is divided into 9 *Départements*: the original Nord-Ouest, Artibonite, Nord, Ouest, Sud; plus (1962) Nord Est, Centre, Sud Est and Grande Anse. The Île de la Gonave, some 40 miles long, lies in the gulf of the same name. Among other islands is La Tortue, off the north peninsula. The majority of the population are Negroes, with an important minority of mulattoes and only about 5,000 white residents, almost all foreign.

Haiti is the only French-speaking republic in the Americas. The standard French of government, parliament and the press is spoken by the small literate minority, but the great majority of the people habitually speak the dialect known as Créole.

CONSTITUTION AND GOVERNMENT. The 1950 Constitution, under which Dr François Duvalier was elected president on 22 Oct. 1957, provided that no president was immediately re-eligible. The new Constitution later in 1957 did not forbid re-election.

A single-chamber legislature of 58 deputies elected for a 6-year term was established in April 1961, and new chambers were elected in 1967, 1973 and 1979.

In 1964 the Constitution was again rewritten and Dr Duvalier named Life President (22 June); the deputies were made capable of indefinite re-election.

President of the Republic: In April 1961 elections were held for the Legislative Chamber, and afterwards it was announced that Dr Duvalier had been re-elected President for a further 6 years (on 22 June 1964 extended to 'life'), although the next presidential election was not due until 1963 and there had been neither nominations nor campaign. (For the series of *coups d'état* in 1956–57, *see* THE STATESMAN'S YEAR-BOOK, 1960, p. 1085.) Dr Duvalier died 21 April 1971. He was succeeded, as President for Life, by his son, Jean-Claude Duvalier whom he nominated as his successor under Article 102 of the 1964 Constitution as amended 14 Jan. 1971.

The Cabinet in Jan. 1981 was composed as follows:

President: Jean-Claude Duvalier.

Foreign Affairs and Worship: Edouard Francisque. *Interior and Defence:* Edouard Berrouet. *Labour and Social Affairs:* Ulysse Pierre-Louis. *Co-ordination and Information:* Jean-Marie Chanoine. *Minister to Presidency:* Henri Bayard. *Agriculture and Natural Resources:* Réné Destin. *Public Works, Transport and Communications:* Alix Cinéas. *Finance and National Economy:* Emmanuel Bros. *Public Health and Population:* Réné Charles. *Commerce and Industry:* Jacques Siméon. *Justice:* Roc Raymond. *Planning:* Raoul Berret. *Mines and Energy:* Fritz Pierre-Louis. *Education:* Joseph Bernard. *Youth and Sports:* Théodore Achille.

National flag: Vertically black and red, with a small white panel in the centre bearing the national arms.

National anthem: 'La Dessalinienne': Pour le pays, pour les ancêtres (words by J. Lhérisson; tune by N. Geffrard, 1903).

DEFENCE. The Haitian Defence Force (*Forces Armées d'Haiti*) totalling about 7,500 men, is divided into Army, Navy, and Air Force. The President is Commander-in-Chief and appoints the officers.

Army. Total strength, about 7,000, organized into 9 Military Departments and the 'Leopards'. Three of the Departments are in Port-au-Prince and consist of the Presidential Guard (4 Companies); the Dessalines Barracks (7 Companies including the Dessalines Battalion and Headquarters troops); and the Port-au-Prince Police (6 Companies in blue uniforms). The other 6 Military Departments are located outside Port-au-Prince; their troops (21 Companies) operate as District Police. The Fire Brigade and the Prison Guard Company are also part of the Armed Forces. Only the Presidential Guard, the Dessalines Battalion and the Leopards (2 companies of 'Commandos' or Special Forces) with a third company of about 200 recruits, now in training, have any potential for tactical military operations. They are armed mainly with light infantry weapons but have a few elderly pieces of light artillery, 9 light tanks and 6 V-150 commando vehicles.

Navy. The Navy/coastguard of 40 officers and 260 men has 2 *ex*-US armed tugs, 2 *ex*-USCG cutters, 5 coastal patrol boats and 11 service craft. The base is at Port-au Prince.

Air Force. Personnel strength is about 200, with about 29 aircraft of some 12 varieties. They include 8 Summit/Cessna O2-327 Sentry twin piston-engined counter-insurgency aircraft, 2 DC-3s, 5 light transports, 5 training/liaison aircraft, and 9 Hughes and Sikorsky helicopters.

Militia. There is in addition a volunteer civilian force, the *Volontaires de la Sécurité Nationale*, whose total strength is now estimated at about 14,900, about half of whom have access to antiquated rifles. This force, formerly of some importance as Dr François Duvalier's 'private army' of tough, devoted followers (sometimes called Tontons Macoute or Bogeymen) is much less prominent since his death, having been reduced in strength and reorganized under Defence Force Headquarters on lines roughly parallel to the regional Military Departments.

INTERNATIONAL RELATIONS

Membership. Haiti is a member of UN and OAS.

ECONOMY

Budget. Revenue and expenditure (fiscal year ending 30 Sept.) in US$1m. (5 gourdes = US$1), balanced as follows: 1971–72, 29·6; 1972–73, 31·3; 1973–74, 33·2; 1974–75, 38·9; 1975–76, 43·3.

Currency. The unit of currency is the *gourde* and its value fixed at 5 *gourdes* = US$1. In March 1981, £1 = 10·9 *gourdes*. There are copper–nickel coins for 50, 20, 10 and 5 *centimes* and copper–zinc–nickel coins of 10 and 5 centimes. The amount of US currency in circulation is not known, due to the fact that it is used freely with the local currency, and is legal tender.

Banking. The Banque Nationale de la République d'Haiti, owned by the State, was established 21 Oct. 1910 with a capital of US$5m., and has a monopoly of the note issue. US dollars may be included in the minimum required reserves. The Royal Bank of Canada, the Citibank, the Bank of Nova Scotia, the Bank of Boston, the Banque de l'Union Haitienne (mainly local capital with participation from American, Canadian and Dominican Republic Banks), Banque Nationale de Paris and First National Bank of Chicago all have branches in Port-au-Prince.

Weights and Measures. The metric system is officially accepted.

ENERGY AND NATURAL RESOURCES

Electricity. The hydro-electric plant at Péligre, which was inaugurated in July 1971, provides some 45m. kw. to the capital. The thermal plant in Port-au-Prince, formerly US and now state owned, is now on standby for emergencies. Generating capacity at Cap Haitien is 3·1m. kw.

Minerals. A US company is engaged in mining bauxite (792,600 tonnes in 1973–74). A Canadian firm mining copper (144,430 tonnes in 1970) had to suspend operations at the end of 1971, as uneconomical because of the world price of copper, but indications are that copper mining may start again. Haiti may possess undeveloped mineral resources of oil, gold, silver, antimony, sulphur, coal and lignite, nickel, gypsum and porphyry.

Agriculture. Only one-third of the country is arable and most people own the tiny plots they farm; the resulting pressure of population is the main cause of rural poverty. Number of farms is estimated at over 500,000.

The occupations of Haiti are nine-tenths agricultural, carried on in 7 large plains, from 200,000 to 25,000 acres, and in 15 smaller plains down to 2,000 acres. Irrigation is used in some areas. Haiti's most important product is coffee of good quality, classified as 'mild', and grown by peasants. Production in 1979 totalled about 40,000 tonnes. In 1974–75, 300,000 bags were exported. Second most important crop is sugar. Sisal is grown extensively. Much of the fibre is exported as or for cordage. New types of cotton are being tried with success. New varieties of rice should significantly boost future production, especially in the Artibonite Valley. Output of main crops in 1979 (tonnes) was: Maize, 260,000; plantains; 198,000; rice, 95,000; sugar, 70,000; sisal, 13,000; cocoa, 3,000.

Rum and other spirits are distilled. Essential oils from lime, vetiver, neroli and amyris are important. Cattle and horse breeding are encouraged.

Livestock (1979): Cattle, 1m.; sheep, 87,000; pigs, 1·9m.; goats, 1·3m.; horses, 408,000; poultry, 4·2m.

INDUSTRY AND TRADE

Industry. Light manufacturing industries assembling or finishing goods for re-export constitute the fastest growing sector. Their foreign exchange earnings are second only to those of coffee. There are 2 textile mills producing cheap denim with a total of 550 looms and 14,000 spindles. Soap factories produce laundry soap, toilet soap and detergent. A cement factory located near the capital produced 140,000 tons in 1973–74 and is extending to 300,000 tons per year. A steel plant making rods, beams and angles was opened in 1974. There are also a pharmaceutical plant, a tannery, a plastics plant, 2 paint works, 2 shoe factories, a large factory producing enamel cookingware, 2 pasta-making factories, a tomato cannery and a flour-mill, all located in or near Port-au-Prince.

Labour. Trade unions were recognized in Feb. 1946. Strong government influence is exercised over the insignificant portion of the labour force that is unionized and organized labour has virtually no strength in Haiti.

Commerce. Imports and exports for fiscal years ending 30 Sept. (in US$1m.):

	1972–73	1973–74[1]	1974–75[1]	1975–76[1]	1976–77[1]
Imports	76·7	119·9	142·5	201·0	225·4
Exports	51·3	100·8	81·1	117·5	143·3

[1] Provisional.

The leading imports are foodstuffs, textiles, machinery, mineral oils, raw materials for transformation industries and vehicles.

Total trade between Haiti and UK (British Department of Trade returns, in £1,000 sterling):

	1974	1975	1976	1977	1978	1979	1980
Imports to UK	199	139	882	1,063	635	1,118	915
Exports and re-exports from UK	2,000	2,143	2,697	3,394	4,155	3,162	2,818

Tourism. In 1976, 280,000 tourists visited Haiti.

COMMUNICATIONS

Roads. Total length of roads is some 4,000 km, little of which is practicable in ordinary motors in the rainy season. There were (1978) about 21,500 vehicles in Haiti.

Railways. The only railway is owned by the Haitian American Sugar Company.

Aviation. An airport capable of handling jets was opened at Port-au-Prince in 1965. US and French carriers provide daily direct services to New York, Miami, Jamaica, Puerto Rico and the French Antilles. There are also services to the Dominican Republic, the Bahamas and the Netherlands Antilles. A Haitian company provides a cargo service to the US and Puerto Rico. Air services connecting Port-au-Prince with other Haitian towns are operated by Haiti Air Inter, under a management contract with Turks and Caicos Airways, who provide aircraft and personnel.

Shipping. US, French, Federal Republic of Germany, Dutch, British, Canadian and Japanese lines connect Haiti with the US, Latin America (except Cuba), Canada, Jamaica, Europe and the Far East.

Post and Broadcasting. Most principal towns are connected by the government telegraph system, telephones and wireless.

The telephone company, of which the Haitian Government is now the majority stockholder, is in process of being modernized. Telephone subscribers totalled 17,800 in 1977.

In 1978 there were 100,000 radio and 15,000 television receivers.

Cinemas (1975). There were 19 cinemas and 4 drive-in cinemas in Port-au-Prince.

Newspapers (1975). There were 6 daily newspapers in Port-au-Prince, also a monthly in English and 1 weekly newspaper in Cap Haitien.

JUSTICE, RELIGION, EDUCATION AND WELFARE

Justice. Judges, both of the lower courts and the court of appeal, are appointed by the President. The legal system is basically French. The divorce law has recently been amended to permit parties to obtain 'quick and painless' divorces at a moderate cost, in the hope of attracting the US trade, now that the Mexican 'divorce mills' have closed down. This has developed a useful flow of dollar revenue.

Police. The Police number about 600 in Port-au-Prince and are part of the armed forces.

Religion. Since the Concordat of 1860, the official religion is Roman Catholicism, under an archbishop with 5 suffragan bishops. There are still quite a number of foreigners, French and French Canadians mainly, among the clergy but the first Haitian archbishop took office in 1966. The Episcopal Church now has its first

Haitian bishop who was consecrated in 1971. Other Christian churches number perhaps 10% of the population. The folk religion is Voodoo.

Education. Education is divided into primary (first 6 years), secondary (the next 7 years) and finally superior or university. The school system is modelled on that of France. The law calls for free and compulsory elementary education in the French language.

For the 1973–74 academic year, urban primary schools numbered 360 (221 lay and 139 religious) attended by 127,330 pupils with 3,532 teachers. There were, for the same period, at the secondary level, 21 public secondary *lycées* with 15,760 students (4,163 of them girls), 563 teachers (39 of them women). In the private secondary sector, 129 schools were reported with 35,414 students (16,398 girls), 1,172 teachers (107 women). Professional education is divided into 3 categories: (*a*) 41 pre-vocational schools; (*b*) 18 vocational schools which prepare trained workers, and (*c*) 5 vocational schools preparing technicians. There were also 10 licensed private commercial schools. The total number of students was 13,000, 2,000 of whom were in the private sector.

It is estimated that rural school population was about 1·3m. but only about 14% regularly attended classes in 1973–74.

Higher education is offered at the following faculties of the University of Haiti: medicine and pharmacy, odontology (dentistry), science (engineering, architecture, natural sciences, physics, chemistry, biology) with a school of surveying, law and economic sciences, agronomy and veterinary medicine, ethnology, and the Institute of Administration and Management. A new Faculty of Arts (Sciences and Humanities) was opened in Nov. 1974. The École Normal Supérieure has replaced the faculty of Letters and Pedagogy.

Health. There were, in 1972, 332 doctors and 104 dentists in practice, 44 hospitals, and 196 health centres and rural clinics. The hospitals had 3,329 beds, of which 776 were in private and charitable establishments.

DIPLOMATIC REPRESENTATIVES

OF HAITI IN GREAT BRITAIN (33 Abbots Hse., St Mary Abbots Terr., London, W14)

Chargé d'Affaires: Alec M. Toussaint.

OF GREAT BRITAIN IN HAITI
Ambassador: J. K. Drinkall, CMG (resides in Kingston).

OF HAITI IN THE USA (4400–17th St., NW, Washington, D.C., 20011)
Ambassador: Georges Salomon.

OF THE USA IN HAITI (Harry Truman Blvd., Port-au-Prince)
Ambassador: William B. Jones.

OF HAITI TO THE UNITED NATIONS
Ambassador: Alexander Verret.

Books of Reference

The official gazette is *Le Moniteur.*

Revue Agricole d'Haïti. From 1946. Quarterly
Bellegarde, D., *Histoire du Peuple Haïtien.* Port-au-Prince, 1953
De Young, M., *Man and Land in the Haitian Economy.* Univ. of Florida Press, 1958
Diedrich, B., and Burt, D., *Papa Doc.* London, 1969
Layburn, J. G., *The Haitian People.* Yale Press, 1966
Nicholls, D., *From Dessalines to Duvalier: Race, Colour and National Independence in Haiti.* CUP, 1979
Rodman, S., *Haiti, the Black Republic.* New York, 1973

National Library: Bibliothèque Nationale, Rue du Centre, Port-au-Prince.

HONDURAS

República de Honduras

Capital: Tegucigalpa
Population: 3·69m. (1980)
GNP per capita: US$520 (1980)

HISTORY. On 5 Nov. 1838 Honduras declared itself an independent sovereign state, free from the Federation of Central America, of which it had formed a part.

AREA AND POPULATION. Honduras is bounded north by the Caribbean, east and north-east by Nicaragua, west by Guatemala, south-west by El Salvador and south by the Pacific ocean. Area is 112,088 sq. km (43,227 sq. miles), with a population, census (1974) of 2,656,948. Estimate (1980) 3,691,027.

The capital of Honduras is Tegucigalpa with (1979, estimate) a population of 445,100. The next most important town is San Pedro Sula, 317,100; other towns are: El Progreso, 89,300; Choluteca, 73,400; Danli, 68,100; Olanchito, 49,700; Juticalpa, 46,500; Comayagua, 42,200; Siguatepeque, 39,900; Santa Rosa de Copan, 25,200. The main ports are Henecan on the Pacific, and, on the Atlantic coast, La Ceiba (61,700), Puerto Cortés (56,100) and Tela (56,800). The port of entry for the Bay Islands is Roatán. A new port at Puerta Costilla, on the Atlantic coast, is under construction.

The republic is divided into 18 departments with their populations (1981, estimate): Atlántida (223,023); Choluteca (272,888); Colón (118,674); Comayagua (198,044); Copán (206,653); Cortés (566,937); El Paraíso (194,840); Francisco Morazán (683,138); Gracias a Dios (32,519); Intibucá (106,963); Islas de La Bahía (17,910); La Paz (84,308); Lempira (167,690); Ocotepeque (62,943); Olancho (213,525); Santa Barbara (269,054); Valle (120,498); and Yoro (281,344).

Aboriginal tribes number over 35,000, principally Miskito, Payas and Xicaques Indians and Sambos (the latter a mixture of Miskito and Negro), each speaking a different dialect. The Spanish-speaking inhabitants are chiefly *mestizos*, Indians with an admixture of Spanish blood. Gracias a Dios is still largely unexplored and is inhabited by pure native races who speak little or no Spanish.

In 1978 there were 145,717 live births and 18,127 deaths; 14,056 marriages and 727 divorces. Infant mortality rate, 26·9 per 1,000 live births.

CONSTITUTION AND GOVERNMENT. Until a change of Government on 4 Dec. 1972, legislative power had been vested in a single chamber, the Congress of Deputies consisting of 64 members, chosen for 6 years by popular vote, in the ratio of 1 per 30,000 inhabitants. It used to meet for 180 days beginning 26 May and ending 26 Oct. A permanent commission of 5 members used to sit while Congress was not in session for the transaction of routine or emergency business. All men and women over 18 are entitled to vote.

In March 1971, Dr Ramón Ernesto Cruz (National Party) was elected President, defeating Dr Jorge Bueso Arias (Liberal Party). The former President, Gen. López, who was debarred from standing for re-election in 1971, seized power in a bloodless *coup* on 4 Dec. 1972. Since that date Congress has been suspended and Government is by decree. Gen Oswaldo López Arellano was deposed in a military *coup* in April 1975 and Gen. Juan Melgar Castro was deposed on 7 Aug. 1978. The *coup* was led by the commander of the armed forces, Gen. Policarpo Paz García, supported by Col. Domingo Alvarez Cruz (chief of Air Force) and Col. Amílcar Zelaya (chief of National Police). A Military Junta was established.

In fulfilment of their promise to restore constitutional Government, elections were held on 20 April 1980 for deputies to a National Constituent Assembly. The election results were Liberals, 35 deputies; Nationalists, 33 and Party of Innovation and Unity, 3. Roberto Suazo Córdova (Liberal), was elected President of the Assembly. The Assembly elected Gen. Paz as Provisional President until elections could be held for a Constitutional President. A new Constitution is being drafted and electoral law in preparation for elections for President, Deputies to Congress and Municipal officers in late 1981 or early 1982.

President: Gen. Policarpo Paz García.

National flag: Three horizontal stripes of blue, white, blue, with 5 blue stars in the centre.

National anthem: Tu bandera es un lampo de cielo (words by A. C. Coello; tune by C. Hartling).

DEFENCE

Army. Every male citizen is liable to serve in the Army from the age of 18 to 50. Service in the active Army is for approximately 1 year. Although there is no actual reserves programme, those men who have served on active duty for 1 year or more, are eligible for recall. The size of the regular Army is approximately 10,000 men; this does not include the National Police Force, which numbers 3,000. The Army is organized into 8 infantry battalions, 2 artillery battalions and minor units.

Air Force. Equipment, mostly of US origin, includes 12 J52-engined Super Mystère fighters acquired from Israel, 6 A-37B jet light attack aircraft, 1 or 2 F-86K jet fighters, 3 RT-33A reconnaissance aircraft, some Summit/Cessna O2-337 Sentry twin piston-engined COIN aircraft, 8 T-28S Fennec and 4 T-28E armed piston-engined trainers, 2 C-54, 6 C-47 and 3 Israeli-built Arava and 1 Westwind transports, T-33A, T-41A and T-6 trainers. Total strength is about 1,200 personnel, of whom 400 are civilian maintenance staff.

INTERNATIONAL RELATIONS

Membership. Honduras is a member of UN and OAS.

ECONOMY

Budget. The fiscal and calendar years have coincided since 1 Jan. 1957. Recent budgets (in 1m. lempiras) balance as follows: 1977, 625·7; 1978, 831·9; 1979, 1,000; 1980, 1,136·7; 1981, 1,350.

The largest sources of income (1978) were (in 1m. lempiras): Production taxes, 138; import taxes, 135·9; export taxes, 109·7; income tax, 111.

Total external debt (1978) was (in 1m. lempiras), 1,509 and net reserves of foreign currency, 233·7.

Currency. The unit of the monetary system is the *lempira* also known as a *peso*, comprising 100 *centavos*. Notes are issued by the Banco Central de Honduras which has the sole right to issue, in denominations of 100, 50, 20, 10, 5, 2 and 1 *lempiras*. Coins in circulation are 50 and 20 *centavos* in silver, 10 and 5 *centavos* in cupronickel and 2 and 1 *centavos* in copper.

Rate of exchange, March 1981: 2 *lempiras* = US$1, 4·37 *lempiras* = £1.

Banking. The central bank of issue is the Banco Central de Honduras. The Banco Atlántida has branches in Tegucigalpa, San Pedro Sula, Comayaguela, Puerto Cortés, La Ceiba, Tela, El Progreso, Choluteca and other towns. The Banco de Honduras which operates in many parts of the country is controlled by the Citibank. The Bank of America has branches in Tegucigalpa and San Pedro Sula. The Bank of London and Montreal has branches in Tegucigalpa, San Pedro Sula, Comayaguela and La Ceiba. The Central American Bank for Economic Integration has its head office in Tegucigalpa.

Weights and Measures. The metric system has been legal since 1 April 1897, but English pounds and yards and the old Spanish system are still in use: 1 *vara* = 32 in.; 1 *manzana* (10,000 sq. *varas*) = 700 sq. metres; 1 *arroba* = 25 lb.; 1 *quintal* = 100 lb.; 1 *tonelada* = 2,000 lb.

NATURAL RESOURCES

Minerals. Mineral resources include gold, silver, lead, tin, zinc and mercury, which are exported. There are probably reserves of other minerals which have not yet been exploited. The Rosario Resources Company, which owned and operated the famous Rosario mines near Tegucigalpa from 1882 to 1954, developed and now operates a mine at El Mochito (Department of Santa Barbara) while the Compañia Minera Los Angeles SA has a mine currently extracting lead, zinc and silver at Valle de Angeles (Department of Francisco Morazán).

Agriculture. Although Honduras is essentially an agricultural country, less than a quarter of the total land area is cultivated and by far the larger portion of this is on the Caribbean and Pacific coastal plains. Agriculture employs 56% of the working population and provides 80% of the exports. The main agricultural crops are: Coffee, bananas, cotton, sugar and tobacco. Exports of meat amounted to 64·5m. lempiras in 1978.

Livestock (1979): Cattle, 1·8m.; sheep, 3,000; pigs, 530,000; goats, 15,000; horses, 149,000; poultry, 4·7m.

Forestry. Forests cover nearly 45% of the total land area. Honduras has an abundance of hard- and softwoods. Large stands of mahogany and other hardwoods—granadino, guayacán, walnut and rosewood—grow in the north-eastern part of the country, in the interior valleys, and near the southern coast. Stands of pine occur almost everywhere in the interior, but are severely damaged by bark beetle and fires. In 1978, total wood exports amounted to 94m. lempiras. The Olancho Forest Development Programme involving the construction of saw- and pulp- mills was in progress in 1978.

Fisheries. Commercial fishing in territorial waters is restricted to Honduran nationals and Honduran companies in which the controlling share of the capital is owned by a Honduran national. Shrimps and lobsters are important catches.

INDUSTRY AND TRADE

Industry. Small-scale local industries include beer and mineral waters, cement, flour, vegetable lard, coconut oil, sweets, cigarettes, cigars, textiles and clothing, panama hats, plastics, nails, matches, plywood, furniture, paper bags, soap, candles, fruit juices and household chemicals. An important hydro-electric scheme has been built at Rio Lindo to serve the Central and North Coast regions. The El Cajon hydro-electric project is now under construction and will come on stream in 1985 (290 mw). A small integrated steel-mill may be erected in Agalteca (Department of Francisco Morazán). The manufacturing industry employed 13% of the working population in 1979.

Labour. The organization of trade unions was begun in 1954 with the assistance of ORIT (Inter-American Regional Organization) sponsored by the USA trade unions. In 1972 there were 166 trade unions, of which only 119 were active, with about 67,956 members. A 'Charter of Labour' was granted in Feb. 1955 and an advanced Labour Code and Social Security Bill passed into law in May 1959. A Ministry of 'Labour, Social Assistance and the Middle Class' was created in 1955; the last four words of its title were expunged in 1957.

Commerce. Imports in 1979 were valued at 2,133·7m. lempiras and exports at 1,699·3m. lempiras.

Imports (1979) in 1m. lempiras: Machinery and transport equipment, 498·5; manufactured goods, 384·3; chemicals, 277·1; mineral fuel and lubricants, 225·2; various products, 111·4; food products, 110; crude material inedible, 20; animal and vegetable oils and fats, 14·3; beverages and tobacco, 10.

Exports (1979) in 1m. lempiras: Bananas, 400·7; coffee, 393·7; refrigerated meats, 114·7; timber, 84·1; shrimps and lobster, 51·3; lead and zinc, 48·2; silver, 41·9; soap, 30·2; tobacco, 29·8; sugar, 26·9; cotton, 22·2; preserved fruit, 7·3.

Trade with main countries in 1m. lempiras (1979) was: USA, 1,529·5; Japan, 189·3; Federal Republic of Germany, 188; Guatemala, 165·5; Venezuela, 160·1; Netherlands, 140.

Total trade between Honduras and UK (British Department of Trade returns, in £1,000 sterling):

	1976	1977	1978	1979	1980
Imports to UK	483	1,107	2,219	4,000	3,687
Exports and re-exports from UK	4,580	6,965	8,443	9,013	11,835

Tourism. There were 102,353 tourists in 1979.

COMMUNICATIONS

Roads. Honduras is connected with Guatemala, El Salvador and Nicaragua by the Pan-American Highway. Out of a total of 12,316 km of road (1979), 1,681 are paved. There are good asphalted highways between Puerto Cortés in the north and Choluteca in the south passing through San Pedro Sula and Tegucigalpa with branches to Guatemala and El Salvador. In 1979 there were 5,360 motor vehicles, including 495 motor cycles.

Railways. Only 4 railways exist; they are confined to the north coastal region and are used mainly for transportation of bananas. Tegucigalpa, the capital, is not served by any railway, and there are no international railway connexions. The total railways operating in 1980 were 1,928 km of 1,067 mm and 914 mm gauge.

Aviation. Over a large part of the country the aeroplane is the normal means of transport for both passengers and freight. There are international airports at Tegucigalpa, San Pedro Sula, La Ceiba and over 30 smaller airstrips in various parts of the country.

Shipping. Sailings to the Atlantic coast port of Puerto Cortés from Europe are frequent, mainly operated by the Harrison Line, Cia Generale Transatlantique, the Royal Netherlands Steamships Co., Hapag Lloyd and vessels owned or chartered by the Tela Railroad Co., a subsidiary of United Brands, and the Standard Fruit Co.

Post and Broadcasting. The Government in April 1972 operated 18,845 km of telephone lines and 12,526 km of telegraph lines. Number of government telephones in use, 1975, 14,984; telephone exchanges, 52; number of telegraph offices, 210; combined telephone and telegraph offices, 179. In 1979 there were 514 post offices and agencies, 145 commercial broadcasting stations. Commercial television began with a station in Tegucigalpa in Sept. 1959. There were (1979) 3 commercial channels and about 27,000 receivers in use. Transmission in colour commenced mid-1973.

Cinemas (1972). Cinemas numbered about 46 with seating capacity of some 40,000.

Newspapers (1979). The 5 most important daily papers are *El Cronista, El Heraldo* and *La Tribuna* in Tegucigalpa, *La Prensa* and *El Tiempo* in San Pedro Sula. Several others exist but their circulation is low and their influence is very limited.

JUSTICE, RELIGION, EDUCATION AND WELFARE

Justice. The judicial power resides in the Supreme Court, with 7 judges elected by the National Constituent Assembly in 1980 for 6 years; it appoints the judges of the courts of appeal, labour tribunals and the district attorneys who, in turn, name the justices of the peace.

Religion. Roman Catholicism is the prevailing religion, but the constitution guarantees freedom to all creeds, and the State does not contribute to the support of any.

Education. Instruction is free, compulsory (from 7 to 15 years of age) and secular. In 1976 the 4,698 primary schools had 483,210 children (11,938 teachers); the 154 secondary, normal and technical schools had 45,000 pupils (2,983 teachers); the teachers' college had 1,025 students (59 teachers); 6 university faculties (1976) had 12,951 students (729 teachers) at Tegucigalpa offering economics, engineering, law, medicine, dentistry, chemistry and pharmacy. Other courses offered are: Public administration, journalism, business administration, auditing and accounting, nursing, psychology, mechanical engineering, social service, agronomy (La Ceiba) and economics (San Pedro Sula). The José Cecilio del Volla University in Tegucigalpa and the Private University of San Pedro Sula opened in 1978.

The illiteracy rate was 40% of those 10 years of age and older in 1978.

Health. In 1972 there were 780 doctors and 4,500 hospital beds.

DIPLOMATIC REPRESENTATIVES

OF HONDURAS IN GREAT BRITAIN (48 George St.,
London, W1H 5RF)

Ambassador: Ricardo Arturo Pineda Milla.

OF GREAT BRITAIN IN HONDURAS (Ave. República de Chile, Tegucigalpa)

Ambassador: J. B. Weymes, OBE.

OF HONDURAS IN THE USA (4301 Connecticut Ave., NW,
Washington, D.C., 20008)

Ambassador: Col. Federico Pujól.

OF THE USA IN HONDURAS (Ave. La Paz, Tegucigalpa)

Ambassador: Jack Binns.

OF HONDURAS TO THE UNITED NATIONS

Ambassador: Dr Mario Carías Zapata.

Books of Reference

The *Anuario Estadístico* (latest issue, *Comercio Exterior de Honduras*, 1967) is published by the Dirección de Estadísticas y Censos, Tegucigalpa. *Director:* Carlos Raudeles.

Banco Central de Honduras: *Monthly Bulletin*
Checchi, V. (and others), *Honduras, a Problem in Economic Development.* New York, 1959
Rubio Melhado, A., *Geografía General de la Republica de Honduras.* Tegucigalpa, 1953
Stokes, W. S., *Honduras: An Area Study in Government.* Madison, Wisc., 1950

HONG KONG

Population: 5·1m. (1980)
GDP per capita: US$3,600 (1979)

HISTORY. The Crown Colony of Hong Kong was ceded by China to Great Britain in Jan. 1841; the cession was confirmed by the treaty of Nanking in Aug. 1842, and the charter bears the date 5 April 1843. Since then Hong Kong has been under British administration, with the exception of the period from 25 Dec. 1941 to 30 Aug. 1945, when it was occupied by the Japanese.

AREA AND POPULATION. Hong Kong island is 32 km east of the mouth of the Pearl River and 130 km south-east of Canton. The area of the island is 76·2 sq. km. It is separated from the mainland by a fine natural harbour. On the opposite side is the peninsula of Kowloon (10·48 sq. km), which, with Stonecutters Island (0·75 sq. km), was added to the Colony by the Convention of Peking, 1860. By a further convention, signed at Peking on 9 June 1898, about 950 sq. km, consisting of all the immediately adjacent mainland and numerous islands in the vicinity, were leased to Great Britain by China for 99 years. This area is known as the New Territories. Total area of the territory is 1,062 sq. km (including recent reclamations), a large part of it being steep and unproductive hillside. Shortage of land suitable for development for housing and industry, is a serious problem. Since 1945, the Government has reclaimed about 1,600 hectares from the sea, principally from the seafronts of Hong Kong and Kowloon, facing the harbour. In the New Territories, the new town of Tsuen Wan, incorporating Tsuen Wan, Kwai Chung and Tsing Yi, is well advanced and already houses 644,000 of its planned ultimate population of 990,000. The construction of 5 further new towns at Sha Tin, Tuen Mun, Tai Po, Fanling/Shek Wu Hui and Yuen Long is now well underway, with population capacities of 720,000, 537,000, 219,000, 168,000 and 127,000 respectively.

The climate is sub-tropical, the winter being cool and dry and the summer hot and humid. The average rainfall is 2,246 mm. (88 in.), May to Sept. being the wettest months.

The population was 4,439,250 at 1976 census. Estimate (1980) 5·1m. During the war years the population of Hong Kong fluctuated sharply. In Sept. 1945, at the end of the Japanese occupation, it was about 600,000. In mid-1950 it was estimated at 2·24m. Since 1963 the net annual increase has been between 32,000 and 95,100. Of the present population about 37% are under 20 years of age. About 59% of the population was born in Hong Kong.

CONSTITUTION AND GOVERNMENT. The administration is in the hands of a Governor, aided by an Executive Council, composed of the Commander, British Forces, the Chief Secretary, the Attorney-General, the Secretary for Home Affairs, the Financial Secretary (who are members *ex officio*) and such other members, both official and unofficial, as may be appointed by the Queen upon the Governor's nomination. In 1980 there were, in addition to the 5 *ex-officio* members, 1 nominated official and 9 nominated unofficial members. There is also a Legislative Council, presided over by the Governor. In 1980 it consisted of 4 *ex-officio* members, namely the Chief Secretary, the Attorney-General, the Secretary for Home Affairs and the Financial Secretary, 26 nominated unofficial members and 17 official members. Chinese and English are the official languages.

Governor and C.-in-C.: Sir Murray MacLehose, GBE, KCMG, KCVO.
Commander British Forces: Maj.-Gen. John Chapple, CBE.
Chief Secretary: Sir Jack Cater, KBE.
Flag: British Blue Ensign with the arms of the Colony on a white disc in the fly.

DEFENCE. The Hong Kong Garrison, under the Commander British Forces, comprises units of all three services. Its principal role is to assist the Hong Kong Government in maintaining security and stability.

Army. The Army constitutes the bulk of the garrison. It comprises a UK battalion, based at Stanley Fort, and 3 Gurkha infantry battalions, based in the New Territories; supporting units include the Queen's Gurkha Engineers, the Queen's Gurkha Signals, the Gurkha Transport Regiment, and 660 Squadron Army Air Corps.

Navy. The Naval Base is at HMS *Tamar*. The Hong Kong Squadron comprises five patrol craft, which are converted Ton-class minesweepers. In addition, there are two SRN 6 hovercraft and a fast patrol boat. 3 Raiding Squadron Royal Marines, equipped with fast 'Sea Rider' craft, also operates from HMS *Tamar*.

Air Force. The Royal Air Force is based at Sek Kong. No. 28 (Army Co-operation) Squadron operates 8 Wessex helicopters. In addition to its operational role in support of the army and navy, the RAF carries out search and rescue and medical evacuation tasks. It is also responsible for air traffic control services at Sek Kong, and provides a territory-wide air traffic advisory service.

Auxiliary Defence Units. The local Auxiliary Defence Units, consisting of the Royal Hong Kong Regiment and the Royal Hong Kong Auxiliary Air Force, are administered by the Hong Kong Government, but, if called out, would come under the command of the Commander British Forces. The Royal Hong Kong Regiment (The Volunteers) has a strength of about 700. It is fully mobile and its role is to operate in support of regular army battalions stationed in Hong Kong. The Royal Hong Kong Auxiliary Air Force is intended mainly for internal security and air-sea rescue duties. It has a strength of about 116, operating a fleet of seven aircraft – a twin-engined Britten-Norman Islander, a twin-engined Cessna 404 Titan Courier, two Scottish Aviation Bulldog Trainers and three Aérospatiale Dauphin 365C1 helicopters. Apart from these, a Vickers Supermarine 'Spitfire' is retained for display.

ECONOMY

Budget. The public revenue and expenditure for financial years ending 31 March were as follows (in HK$):

	1976–77	1977–78	1978–79	1979–80
Revenue	7,493,500,000	10,232,600,000	12,557,000,000	16,796,000,000
Expenditure	6,590,900,000	8,996,900,000	11,090,100,000	13,872,000,000

The revenue is derived chiefly from rates, licences, duties on liquor, tobacco and hydrocarbon oils, a tax on earnings and profits, land sales and stamp duties.

Currency. The unit of currency is the Hong Kong *dollar*. Bank-notes (of denominations of $10 upwards) are issued by the Hongkong and Shanghai Banking Corporation, and the Chartered Bank. Their combined note issue was, at 31 March 1980, HK$8,350m. Subsidiary currency consisting of HK$5, HK$2, HK$1, 50-cent, 20-cent, 10-cent, 5-cent copper-nickel-alloy coins and 1-cent notes is issued by the Hong Kong Government and at 31 March 1980 totalled HK$1,007m.

Since 1975, the Hong Kong Government has issued annually a limited quantity of HK$1,000 gold coins. The first in the series was issued to commemorate the Queen's visit to Hong Kong in 1975. Gold coins have since been minted to mark the Chinese Lunar Years of the Dragon, the Snake, the Horse, the Goat, the Monkey and the Cockerel.

Banking. There are 115 licensed banks and 118 foreign banks maintaining representative offices in Hong Kong. Deposits in 1980 totalled HK$88,490m.

Weights and Measures. The *Tael* (*leung*) = $1\frac{1}{3}$ oz. avoirdupois; the *Picul* (*taam*) = $133\frac{1}{3}$ lb. (often taken as $\frac{1}{17}$ of a ton); the *Catty* (*kan*) = $1\frac{1}{3}$ lb. avoirdupois; the *Chek* (Chinese foot) = $14\frac{5}{8}$ in. (but varying from $11\frac{1}{2}$ to $14\frac{5}{8}$ in. according to the custom of various trades, the commonest equivalent being 14·14 in.); the *Tsuen* (Chinese inch) = $\frac{1}{10}$ of a *Chek*, the *Cheung* = 10 *Chek*; the *Lei* (Chinese mile) = 707–744 yd.

Besides the above weights and measures of China, Hong Kong is adopting the metric system.

AGRICULTURE. Livestock (1979): Cattle, 9,000; pigs, 510,000; poultry, 6m.

WATER. The provision of sufficient capacity to store the summer rainfall to meet water requirements, particularly during the dry winter months, has always been a serious problem. However, this has been alleviated to some extent by the raising of the Plover Cove Dams in 1973, giving the reservoir a capacity of 230m. cu. metres, and the completion in 1978 of the 273m. cu. metre High Island Reservoir which involved the conversion of another sea inlet to a fresh water lake, as was the case with Plover Cove.

Total available storage capacity now stands at 579m. cu. metres distributed in 18 impounding reservoirs. This is supplemented by water purchased from China which at present amounts to 172 m. cu. metres a year with provision for staged increases in the future. These resources can be further supplemented when necessary by up to 181,800 cu. metres of fresh water a day from a desalting plant completed in 1976 but now in a 'stand-by' state.

INDUSTRY AND TRADE

Industry. An economic policy based on free enterprise and free trade; an industrious work force; an efficient and aggressive commercial infrastructure; modern and efficient sea-port (including container shipping terminals) and airport facilities: its geographical position relative to markets in North America and its traditional trading links with Britain have all contributed to Hong Kong's success as a modern industrial complex.

In Sept. 1980, there were 45,409 factories employing 892,140 people out of a total population of approximately 5·1m. The type of factory involved ranges from the small cottage type to large highly complex modern establishments. Given the scarcity of land it is most common for light industry to operate in multi-storey buildings specially designed for this purpose. The main industry is textiles and clothing, which employs 19% of the labour force and accounts for 41% of total domestic exports. Other major light manufacturing industries include electronic products, clocks and watches, toys, plastic products, metalware, footwear, cameras and travel goods. Heavy industry includes ship-building, ship-repairing, aircraft engineering and iron and steel rolling. Agriculture, fishing and some mining are the main primary industries.

Commerce. Hong Kong's industries are mainly export oriented. The total value of domestic exports in 1980 was HK$68,171m. The major markets were USA (33%), Federal Republic of Germany (11%), UK (10%), Japan (3%), Australia (3%), and Singapore (3%). There is also a sizeable and flourishing entrepôt trade which accounted for another HK$30,072m. in 1980.

The total value of imports in 1979 was HK$85,837m., mainly from Japan (23%), China (18%), USA (12%), Taiwan (7%), Singapore (6%) and UK (5%).

The chief import items were machinery (22%), textiles (14%), foodstuffs (11%), chemicals (8%) and petroleum products (6%), crude raw materials (2%).

Imports from the Commonwealth countries (HK$13,491m. in 1979) amounted to 16% of total imports and exports to the Commonwealth countries (HK$12,733m.) accounted for 23% of Hong Kong's domestic exports.

Duties are levied only on tobacco, hydrocarbon oils, methyl alcohol and alcoholic liquors (including toilet preparations containing more than 1·2% of ethyl alcohol but excluding registered pharmaceutical products), whether imported into or manufactured in Hong Kong for local consumption.

All imports (apart from foodstuffs, which are subject to a flat charge of HK$2 per shipment) and exports are subject to a varying *ad valorem* charge.

The adverse balance on visible trade is offset by a favourable balance from exchange, shipping and insurance transactions, an inflow of capital, ship-repairing, a flourishing tourist industry, remittances from overseas Chinese, etc.

Hong Kong has a free exchange market. Foreign merchants may remit profits or repatriate capital. Import and export controls are kept to the minimum, consistent with strategic requirements.

Total trade between Hong Kong and UK (British Department of Trade returns, in £1,000 sterling) is given as follows:

	1975	1976	1977	1978	1979	1980
Imports to UK	306,967	439,605	454,056	531,368	689,252	850,340
Exports and re-exports from UK	157,376	204,430	271,194	362,444	442,452	559,420

Tourism. Tourists spent an estimated HK$6,528m. in Hong Kong in 1980. During the year tourists totalled over 2·3m.

COMMUNICATIONS

Roads. In Dec. 1980 there were 1,161 km of roads, distributed as follows: Hong Kong Island, 348; Kowloon and New Kowloon, 346, and New Territories, 467. A cross-harbour tunnel, 1·6 km in length, opened to traffic in Aug. 1972, now links Hong Kong Island with the Kowloon peninsula. The 1·4 km twin-tube Lion Rock Tunnel, which links Kowloon with Sha Tin New Town and other areas of the north-eastern New Territories, became fully operational in Oct. 1978.

Railways. There is an electric tramway of 13·2 km, and a cable tramway connecting the Peak district with the lower levels in Victoria. The government-owned Kowloon Canton Railway which has remained virtually unchanged for the past 80 years is now undergoing a massive modernization and electrification programme. The entire 34 km route which runs from the Kowloon terminus in Hung Hom to Lo Wu on the Chinese frontier is being double tracked and electrified. On 4 April 1979, a through passenger train service between Kowloon and Guangzhou was reintroduced after a lapse of 30 years; other local passenger services to Lo Wu allow for connections to be made for onward trains at Shenzhen.

An underground railway is under construction between Hong Kong Island and Kwun Tong in Kowloon with a branch to Tsuen Wan. The first section (with 15 stations and a length of 15·6 km) opened on 1 Oct. 1979. The whole Modified Initial System running from Kwun Tong across the harbour to Central became fully operational on 12 Feb. 1980. The extended system (total length 26 km with 25 stations) will be operational by the end of 1982.

Aviation. Hong Kong International Airport is situated on the north shore of Kowloon Bay. It is regularly used by 32 airlines and many charter airlines which provide frequent services throughout the Far East to Europe, North America, Africa, the Middle East, Australia and New Zealand. British Airways operates 13 services per week, to UK, Africa and Japan. Cathay Pacific Airways, the Hong Kong-based airline, operates 114 passenger services to the UK, the Far and Middle East and Australia. During 1980, British Caledonian Airways also commenced scheduled services on the Hong Kong to London route. About 960 scheduled services are operated weekly to and from Hong Kong by various airlines. In 1980, 54,569 aircraft arrived and departed on international flights, carrying 6·8m. passengers, 9,701 tonnes of mail and 257,866 tonnes of freight.

Shipping. The total vessels entering and clearing Hong Kong and engaged in foreign trade during the year ending 31 Dec. 1979 amounted to 19,710 ocean-going vessels of 102,867,200 net tons. Launches and junks engaging in local trade, totalled, 41,656 vessels of 7,103,300 net tons. 529 vessels (1,520,165 gross tons) were registered in Hong Kong as British ships.

Telecommunications, Post and Broadcasting. There were 78 post offices in 1980; postal revenue totalled HK$344m.; expenditure, HK$225m. Telephone services are provided by the Hong Kong Telephone Co. Ltd. It operates through a network of 64 fully automatic main exchanges and served (1980) 1·6m. subscribers. Cable & Wireless Ltd is responsible for all external telecommunications and also provides for marine, meteorological and aeronautical communications. Telecommunication systems employed in Hong Kong include satellite, tropospheric scatter, HF, VHF, UHF, submarine and land coaxial cables. Services provided to the community include international telephone, telegram, telex, leased circuits, data transmission, facsimile and ship-shore communications.

There is a government broadcasting station, Radio Television Hong Kong, with daily transmissions in English and Chinese. Wireless licences were abolished as from 1 March 1967. A commercial station, the Commercial Broadcasting Co. Ltd, transmits daily in English and Cantonese. Two radio stations operate 8 channels.

Television Broadcasts Ltd and Rediffusion Television Ltd transmit commercial television in English and Chinese on 4 channels, mainly in colour.

Cinemas. In 1980 there were 81 cinemas with a seating capacity of over 97,684. Attendance 65m. in 1980.

Newspapers. In 1980 there were 115 daily or weekly newspapers, registered and in circulation, including 4 daily English-language papers; the remainder are almost all in Chinese.

JUSTICE, EDUCATION AND WELFARE

Justice. There is a Supreme Court, having original, bankruptcy and companies winding-up, criminal, probate, divorce, admiralty and prize jurisdiction, and a court of appeal. There is also a District Court which, for administrative purposes, is divided into 3 geographical areas. It sits in several different buildings. There are 45 Magistrates sitting in 8 separate Magistracies. The district courts, apart from hearing civil cases where the claim does not amount to more than HK$20,000, also have jurisdiction over certain criminal matters. A tenancy tribunal hears cases covering disputes between landlord and tenant, etc. The labour tribunal provides speedy settlements to individual money claims arising from contracts of employment. The lands tribunal adjudicates on all statutory claims for compensation over land. The small claims tribunal deals with monetary claims involving amounts not exceeding HK$3,000.

Police. The Royal Hong Kong Police Force numbered, in 1980, 24,382, composed of 267 gazetted, 1,738 inspectorate officers, 18,358 junior officers and 4,019 civilians. These figures include 2,057 women police officers, who are completely integrated throughout the force. There are also 4,993 part-time officers.

The maritime force operated by the Marine Division of the Royal Hong Kong Police comprises 92 vessels ranging from sea-going patrol launches and jet boats to inflatables and logistic support craft. Personnel in 1980 numbered 1,910 (106 officers, 435 n.c.o.s and 1,369 constables).

Education. The majority of schools have to be registered with the Education Department under the Education Ordinance. They are required to comply with regulations as to staff, building, fire and health requirements. From Sept. 1971, free and compulsory primary education was introduced in government and the majority of government-aided schools. Free junior secondary education of 3 years' duration was achieved in 1978 and it was made compulsory in stages beginning in Sept. 1979.

In 1980 there were 207,856 pupils in kindergartens (all private), another 555,406 in primary schools and 510,709 in secondary schools.

There are 5 technical institutes with a total full-time and part-time enrolment of 23,288 and 4 teacher-training colleges with enrolment of 2,350.

The University of Hong Kong had 4,269 undergraduates in 1980 and the Chinese University of Hong Kong, inaugurated in Oct. 1963, had 4,397 undergraduates. The Hong Kong Polytechnic, 1980, had a total of 6,487 full-time and 15,103 part-time students.

Health. In 1980 there were 3,133 doctors and about 22,400 hospital beds.

Social Security. The Government co-ordinates and implements expanding programmes in social welfare, which include social security, family services, child care, services for the elderly, youth and community work, probation and corrections and rehabilitation. About 110 voluntary welfare agencies are subsidised by public funds.

The Government gives non-contributory cash assistance to needy families, unemployed able-bodied adults, the severely disabled and the elderly. Caseload in 1980 totalled 230,000. Victims of natural disasters, crimes of violence and traffic accidents are financially assisted.

Books of Reference

Statistical Information: The Census and Statistics Department is responsible for the preparation and collation of Government statistics. These statistics are published mainly in the Special

Supplement No. 4 to the *Hong Kong Government Gazette* at the end of each month; the Special Supplements are also available in a collected annual edition. The Department publish monthly trade statistics and economic indicators. The Commerce and Industry Department issues an annual review of overseas trade. Statistical information is also published in the annual reports of Government departments. *Hong Kong 1981*, and other government publications are available from the Hong Kong Government Publications Centre, GPO Building, Connaught Place, Hong Kong, and the Hong Kong Government Office in London, 6 Grafton Street, London, W1X 3LB.

The Hong Kong Trade Development Council, Connaught Centre, Connaught Place, Hong Kong, issues a monthly *Hong Kong Enterprise* and other publications.

Hong Kong 1981. Hong Kong Government Press, 1981

Hong Kong Bibliography. Hong Kong Government Press, 1965

Endacott, G. B., *A History of Hong Kong*. 2nd ed. OUP, 1973.—*Government and People in Hong Kong, 1841–1962. A Constitutional History*. OUP, 1965

Hopkins, K., *Hong Kong: The Industrial Colony*. OUP, 1971

Miners, N., *The Government and Politics of Hong Kong*. OUP, 1976

Rabushka, A., *The Changing Face of Hong Kong: New Departures in Public Policy*. Washington, 1973

Szcepanik, T. F., *The Economic Growth of Hong Kong*. OUP, 1958

Tregear, E. R., *Land Use in Hong Kong*. Hong Kong Univ. Press, 1958.—*Hong Kong Gazetteer*. Hong Kong Univ. Press, 1958.—*The Development of Hong Kong as Told in Maps*. Hong Kong Univ. Press, 1959

HUNGARY

Magyar Népköztársaság

Capital: Budapest
Population: 10·71m. (1980)
GNP per capita: US$3,450 (1978)

HISTORY. Hungary first became an independent kingdom in 1001. For events in Hungary since 1918 *see* THE STATESMAN'S YEAR-BOOK, 1945, pp. 1006–7, and 1957, p. 1096.

On 23 Oct. 1956 an anti-Stalinist revolution broke out, and the newly formed coalition government of Imre Nagy on 1 Nov. withdrew from the Warsaw Pact and asked the UN for protection. János Kádár, formed a counter-government on 3 Nov. and asked the USSR for support.

Russian troops suppressed the revolution and abducted Nagy and his Ministers, who were later secretly executed.

On 7 Sept. 1967 the Soviet–Hungarian treaty of friendship was renewed for 20 years.

In 1978 the crown of St Stephen, the symbol of Hungarian nationhood, which had been in US hands since 1945, was returned to Hungary.

AREA AND POPULATION. Hungary is bounded north by Czechoslovakia, north-east by the USSR, east by Romania, south by Yugoslavia and west by Austria. The peace treaty of 10 Feb. 1947 restored the frontiers as of 1 Jan. 1938. The area of Hungary is 93,032 sq. km (35,911 sq. miles).

The official language is Hungarian (Magyar), which is a member of the Finno-Ugrian group.

At the census of 1 Jan. 1970 the population was 10,322,099 (5,003,651 males). Population in 1980: 10·71m.

54% of the population is urban (20% in Budapest). Population density, 115 per sq. km. Birth rate, 1979, 15·0 per 1,000; growth rate, 0·4% per annum, 3·8% per decade; expectation of life (1978): males, 67; females, 73. In 1970 there were some 1·25m. Hungarian émigrés. There are Hungarian minorities in Romania, Yugoslavia and Czechoslovakia.

Vital statistics, 1979: Births, 161,518; marriages, 87,176; divorces, 28,000; deaths, 136,758; infant mortality, 23·7 per 1,000 live births.

Area (in sq. km) and population (in 1,000) of counties, county boroughs and county towns:

Counties (1978)	Area	Population	Chief town (1980)	Population
Baranya	4,487	434	Pécs	170
Bács-Kiskun	8,362	572	Kecskemét	93
Békés	5,632	433	Békéscsaba	66
Borsod-Abaúj-Zemplén	7,247	798	Miskolc	210
Csongrád	4,263	460	Hódmezővásárhely	54
Fejér	4,374	419	Székesfehérvár	102
Gyor-Sopron	4,012	429	Gyor	125
Hajdú-Bihar	6,212	548	Debrecen	195
Heves	3,638	346	Eger	60
Komárom	2,250	319	Tatabánya	75
Nógrád	2,544	236	Salgótarján	49
Pest	6,393	969	Budapest	2,060
Somogy	6,035	362	Kaposvár	73
Szabolcs-Szatmár	5,937	574	Nyíregyháza	107
Szolnok	5,608	445	Szolnok	77
Tolna	3,703	260	Szekszárd	34
Vas	3,337	282	Szombathely	82
Veszprém	5,186	430	Veszprém	55
Zala	3,288	265	Zalaegerszeg	55

County boroughs (1980)	Area	Population	County boroughs (1980)	Area	Population
Budapest (capital)	525	2,060	Szeged	145	175
Miskolc	224	210	Pécs	113	170
Debrecen	446	195	Gyor	175	125

Ethnic minorities in 1980 (in 1,000): Germans, 200; Slovaks, 100; Croats and Serbs, 100; Romanians, 20–25.

CONSTITUTION AND GOVERNMENT. On 1 Feb. 1946 the National Assembly proclaimed a republic.

The present People's Republic was established by a constitution adopted on 18 Aug. 1949. Supreme power is vested in Parliament. Parliament elects a Presidential Council, which exercises the functions of Parliament between sessions. It can dissolve government bodies and annul legislation. The 1949 Constitution was amended in 1972. The distinction between 'working people' and 'citizens' disappears. Citizens are stated to have both indirect (through elected representatives) and direct (through local and enterprise councils) democratic rights. State and co-operative property are recognized as co-existing with equal status. Personal property is 'recognized and protected' up to the limit set by law (this includes for private artisans, places of business and machinery).

Ethnic minorities have equal rights and education in their own tongue.

National flag: Three horizontal stripes of red, white, green.

National anthem: God bless the Hungarians—Isten áldd meg a magyart (words by Ferenc Kölcsey, tune by Ferenc Erkel).

Chairman of the Presidential Council (Head of State): Pál Losonczi, appointed on 14 April 1967. *Deputy Chairmen:* Sándor Gáspár and Rezso Trautmann.

In 1949 the Hungarian Working People's Party (Communists), the Smallholders' Party, the National Peasant Party, the Trade Union Federation, the Association of Working Peasants, the Democratic Women's Association and the Federation of Working Youth were merged in the Hungarian People's Independence Front. In 1954 a new comprehensive organization was formed, the People's Patriotic Front. The Communist Youth Association (KISZ) had 800,000 members in 1975.

The Communist Party was reorganized after the 1956 revolution and changed its name to 'Hungarian Socialist Workers' Party'. It had 754,353 members in 1975 (32% women; 46% manual workers and peasants). Supreme *de facto* power is in the hands of the Party's Politburo, composed in March 1981 of: János Kádár, *First Secretary of the Central Committee*; György Aczél; Valéria Benke; Sándor Gáspár; Ferenc Havasi; Mihály Korom; György Lázár; Pál Losonczi; László Márothy; Lajos Mehes; Károly Németh; Miklos Óvári; István Sárlos.

The Government was in March 1981 composed as follows:

Prime Minister: György Lázár.

Deputy Prime Ministers: György Aczél, János Borbándi, Lájos Faluvégi (*Chairman, State Planning Committee*), Jozsef Marjai. *Finance:* Dr István Hetényi. *Foreign Affairs:* Frigyes Puja. *Speaker, National Assembly:* Antal Apró. *Interior:* Dr István Horváth. *Culture and Education:* Dr Imre Pozsgai. *Defence:* Gen. Lájos Czinege. *Foreign Trade:* Péter Veress. *Justice:* Imre Markója.

Parliament consists of 352 deputies, elected for a 5-year term by all citizens over 18 years.

The right to select candidates is vested solely in pre-election nomination meetings open to all voters. More than one candidate is permitted to stand in each constituency. Such 'alternative' candidates must receive 30% of the votes at nomination meetings. All candidates must support the Patriotic People's Front (PPF). To be elected candidates must gain at least 50% of the votes cast.

Elections were held on 8 June 1980. Electorate, 7,661,361; votes cast, 7,577,401; votes for PPF candidates, 7,462,953; against, 54,070. Alternative candidates stood in 15 constituencies.

Local Government. Hungary is divided into the capital, Budapest, 19 counties (*megyek*) and 5 county boroughs (large towns with county status), which are subdivided into districts, towns and boroughs. All of these are administered by a hierarchy of local councils which in turn elect Executive Committees to carry on day-to-day administration. Members of county councils are elected by the lower councils. Elections are held every 5 years. The last local elections were held in June 1980.

DEFENCE. The 1947 Treaty authorized Hungary to have an army up to a strength of 65,000 personnel, and an air force of 90 aircraft, of which not more than 70 may be combat types with a personnel strength of 5,000.

By a law of 1976 the Presidential Council may establish a National Defence Council which in times of war would exercise supreme control over defence.

Men between the ages of 18 and 23 are liable for 18 months' conscription. Compulsory military service age-limits are 18 to 55 (18 to 45 women).

The security police (BKH) is controlled by the Ministry of the Interior.

The Workers' Militia is a para-military organization armed with automatic weapons. Strength (1980), 60,000.

Four Soviet divisions are stationed in Hungary.

Army. Hungary is divided into 4 army districts: Budapest, Debrecen, Kiskunféle-gyháza, Pécs. The strength of the Army was (1980) 72,000 (including 50,000 conscripts). It is organized in 1 tank and 5 motorized divisions not all up to full strength, with about 1,250 T-54 and T55 tanks.

Navy. The maritime wing of the Army in 1981 deployed 500 officers and men operating 45 vessels, including 10 patrol craft of 100 tons, 5 utility landing craft and 30 river mine-warfare vessels, troop transports, river monitors, icebreakers, tugs and watch pickets, constituting the River Guard, and Army logistic and bridging vessels are active along the Danube.

Air Force. The Air Force is an integral part of the Army, with a strength of about 21,000 officers and men and 175 combat aircraft, in 2 fighter divisions. The interceptor division has 3 regiments of MiG-21 fighters. MiG-23 and Su-7 fighter-bombers equip the other division. Transport units are equipped with An-2, An-24, An-26 and Il-14 aircraft. Other types in service include Ka-26, Mi-2, Mi-4 and Mi-8 helicopters and L-29 Delfin and MiG-15UTI trainers. 'Guideline' surface-to-air missiles are also operational.

INTERNATIONAL RELATIONS

Membership. Hungary is a member of UN, the Warsaw Pact and Comecon.

External Debt. Hungary settled its debt to the UK in 1967. By an agreement of 6 March 1973 Hungary is to meet US claims of US$18·9m. arising from war damage and nationalization in 20 yearly instalments.

ECONOMY

Planning. For details of past plans *see* THE STATESMAN'S YEAR-BOOK, 1975–76. A 'New Economic Mechanism' (NEM) came into effect on 1 Jan. 1968. It restricted central direction to overall policies, replaced direct by financial control and gave local managers more initiative. Reforms aimed ultimately at adapting the economy to world prices by reducing costs, bringing salaries into line with productivity, re-deploying labour, cutting import subsidies and encouraging exports were set in train in 1980. Since 1976, enterprises have been required to repay state investment credits in full, usually over 10 years, and to cover unscheduled increases in costs. Targets for the sixth 5-year plan (1976–80) were not met. The seventh 5-year plan (1981–85) is one of consolidation and envisages rises of only 6% in real incomes and 15% in the national income.

Budget. The budget for calendar years was as follows (in 1,000m. forints):

	1974	1975	1976	1977	1978	1979	1980
Revenue	280,807	313,264	320,384	361,272	382,900	411,600	423,500
Expenditure	284,297	316,224	322,874	364,808	386,400	415,200	428,000

1978 revenue was derived 82% from enterprises, 13% from social organizations and 5% from personnal taxation. Distribution of expenditure: Subsidies to enterprises, 22%; investment, 20%; welfare, 19%; consumer price subsidies, 11%; culture, 7%; defence, 4%.

Currency. A decree of 26 July 1946 instituted a new monetary unit, the *forint* subdivided into 100 *fillér*. The tourist rate of exchange (Dec. 1980) 57·58 forints to the £1 sterling, 22·5 forints = US$1. The commercial rate is 75·7 = £1, 31·7 = US$1, 27·9 = 1 rouble.

Banking. All banking activities are controlled by the National Bank, including the National Savings Bank, which handles local government, as well as personal, accounts. (Deposits in 1978: 124,885m. forints.) The National Bank finances investment to individual enterprises and is the main authority over foreign-exchange transactions. There is also a Foreign Trade Bank for Hungarian enterprises trading abroad. The State Development Bank (formerly Investment Bank) finances large-scale investment projects and oversees national investment trends.

The National Credit Institute of Co-operatives handles all credit transactions for farmers, artisans and co-operatives. The Hungarian International Trade Bank opened in London in 1973. In 1980 the Central European Intenational Bank was set up in Budapest with 7 Western banks holding 66% of the shares.

Weights and Measures. The metric system of weights and measures is in use. For land measure a cadastral yoke (1 acre = 0·7033 cadastral yoke) is used.

ENERGY AND NATURAL RESOURCES

Electricity. An 880-mw nuclear power station is being built with Soviet help at Paks to begin producing in 1981. A 750 kv power line linking Albertirsa in Hungary with the Soviet grid at Vinnitsa came into operation in 1978.

Oil. Oil and natural gas have been found in the Szeged basin and in Zala county. There are pipelines for crude oil ('Friendship' I and II from USSR) and natural gas totalling 4,262 km in 1978. The 2,700-km Orenburg–Hungary natural gas pipeline came on stream in 1980. Imports in 1978 (in 1,000 tonnes): Oil, 9,960; gas, 1,235. The Hungarian section of the Adria oil pipeline (from Rijeka to Czechoslovakia) came on stream 1978.

Minerals. Coal and bauxite are mined, and there is some iron ore.

Agriculture. The large private holdings which characterized pre-war agriculture were broken up by the Communist government and distributed as individual smallholdings. After 1950 this policy was superseded by collectivization. A land law of 1968 permits collectives to own land, and guarantees individuals' rights to private plots. Collectives meet in a National Council of Agricultural Co-operatives.

In 1978 the agricultural area was (in 1,000 hectares) 6,698, of which 4,869 were arable, 1,309 meadows and pastures, and 342 orchards and vineyards.

In 1980 there were 1,585 collective farms with 5·9m. hectares of land (including 596,000 hectares of household plots) and 123 state farms with 991,000 hectares of land. The irrigated area was 180,000 hectares; 57,000 tractors were in use.

Production statistics (in 1,000 tonnes):

Crops	1977	1978	1979	Crops	1977	1978	1979
Wheat	5,315	5,655	3,702	Maize	5,939	6,672	7,422
Rye	142	136	92	Potatoes	1,335	1,584	1,149
Barley	706	760	707	Sugar-beet	3,889	4,182	3,856
Oats	64	73	90	Sunflowers	212	222	416

Livestock in 1979 was (in 1,000 head) as follows: Cattle, 1,966; pigs, 8,011; poultry, 62,857; sheep, 2,863; horses, 134,000.

Livestock products (1978): Eggs, 4,755m.; milk, 2,206m. litres; wool, 10,771 tonnes; animals for slaughter, 2m. tonnes.

The north shore of Lake Balaton and the Tokai area are important wine-producing districts. Tokaj viticulture was neglected before the 1970s, but now a Reconstruction Committee has reimposed rigorous standards. Wine production in 1978 was 454m. litres.

Forestry. The area under forest in 1978 was 1·58m. hectares. 31,000 hectares were afforested and 5·7m. cu. metres of timber were cut.

Fisheries. There are fisheries in the rivers Danube and Tisza and Lake Balaton, and in 1977 there were 24,000 hectares of commercial fishponds. Catch in 1977: 23,000 tonnes.

INDUSTRY AND TRADE

Industry. For a summary of the successive stages of nationalization from 1946 to 1952, *see* THE STATESMAN'S YEAR-BOOK, 1954, p. 1115.

Production statistics (in 1,000 tonnes):

	1975	1976	1977	1978	1979
Coal[1]	24,900	25,300	25,500	25,700	25,700
Iron ore	642	602	525	534	532
Pig-iron	2,219	2,221	2,286	2,330	2,369
Crude steel	3,671	3,652	3,723	3,877	3,907
Rolled steel	2,675	2,857	3,077	3,188	3,240
Bauxite	2,800	2,918	2,949	2,899	2,976
Aluminium	70	70	71	71	72
Alumina	756	732	786	785	793
Crude oil	2,006	2,142	2,191	2,200	2,027
Natural gas (1m. cu. metres)	5,175	6,082	6,598	7,333	6,506
Electricity (1m. kwh.)	20,457	22,049	23,390	25,542	24,519
Cement	3,759	4,298	4,620	4,764	4,857
Artificial fertilizers	641	783	805	887	1,043
Synthetic materials (PVC, etc.)	124	141	148	213	294
Sulphuric acid	630	617	632	644	588
Sugar	308	363	438	496	497
Cotton cloth (1m. sq. metres)	351	353	366	365	349
Woollen (1m. sq. metres)	39	41	43	43	41
Silk and rayon (1m. sq. metres)	55	57	57	62	57
Flax and hemp (1m. sq. metres)	24	23	21	20	19
Leather footwear (1m. pairs)	43	45	46	46	45

[1] Including lignite and brown coal.

Labour. In 1979 there were 5·08m. wage-earners (2·2m. female) in the following categories (females in brackets): Manual workers, 2·9m. (1·1m.); co-operative peasants, 642,700 (259,200); industrial managers, 103,200 (13,700); farm managers, 23,400 (1,200); professional workers, 1·2m. (769,300); self-employed tradesmen, 167,300 (86,400). The labour code was modified on 1 Jan. 1980 in the interests of discipline and the more flexible deployment of manpower. Trade unions play an increased role. A 42-hour 5-day week has been introduced progressively since July 1971. Average monthly wages of employed persons in 1980: 4,500 forints. Retirement age: Men, 60; women, 55.

Trade Unions. Trade union membership was 4·3m. in 1980.

Commerce. Hungary is heavily dependent on foreign trade, which even under the 'New Economic Mechanism' remains basically under state control. Trade for calendar years (in 1m. forints):

	1974	1975	1976[1]	1977	1978	1979
Imports	51,010	61,500	230,056	267,300	300,900	308,900
Exports	46,927	52,200	204,834	238,600	240,700	282,100

[1] Official statistics for 1975 and before were expressed in exchange rate forints, but thereafter in commercial rate forints. The dramatic increase for 1976 is therefore only apparent. The index numbers are: 1975 = 100, 1976 = 96·9.

In 1979 Hungary's trade with communist countries totalled 327·7m. forints (29% with USSR). Major exports to communist countries: Machinery, industrial consumer goods, raw materials; elsewhere, raw materials and industrial consumer goods.

All exports and imports require licensing by the Ministry of Foreign Trade, and may be handled by 29 specialized foreign-trade agencies. Under a law of Oct. 1974 enterprises may handle their own foreign trade relations, set up companies abroad and participate in foreign companies. Hard currency is available through the National Bank for enterprises permitted to trade directly with foreign customers. The Marketexpo branch of the Hungarian National Market Research Institute will conduct research for foreign firms. The agency Interag acts for Western firms in Hungary. Main imports from the West are machinery, fuel and consumer goods. Hungarian indebtedness to the West was US$6,142,000 in 1978.

Joint ventures with Western firms holding up to 49% of the capital have been permitted since 1972 on Hungarian soil. Foreign companies may set up offices in Hungary. In Nov. 1978 the US and Hungary signed a most-favoured-nation trade agreement.

Total trade between Hungary and UK (British Department of Trade returns, in £1,000 sterling):

	1975	1976	1977	1978	1979	1980
Imports to UK	26,137	30,771	43,203	42,476	51,748	43,327
Exports and re-exports from UK	44,449	49,515	61,894	64,510	60,917	68,977

Tourism. In 1978, 16·96m. foreigners visited Hungary (1·68m. from the West), of whom 9·95m. were tourists (1·16m. from the West); and 5·43m. Hungarians travelled abroad (0·36m. to the West).

COMMUNICATIONS

Roads. In 1978 there were 29,912 km of roads. In 1978 passenger cars numbered 834,000 (788,000 private). 233m. tonnes of freight and 745m. passengers were transported by road in 1978 (excluding urban traffic).

Railways. Route length of public lines in 1978, 8,190 km, of which 1,307 km are electrified. 135m. tonnes of freight and 310m. passengers were carried.

Aviation. Hungarian Air Lines (Malév) operate from Ferihegy airport, 16 km from Budapest. 1978 arrivals, 796,163; departures, 825,071. Malév operates flights to Austria, Belgium, France, Federal Republic of Germany, Greece, Italy, Scandinavia, Egypt, UK and European communist capitals. 697,298 passengers were carried in 1978. British Airways, PANAM, Air France, SABENA, Swissair, OS, Lufthansa and KLM have services to Budapest.

Shipping. Permanently navigable waterways have a length of 1,302 km; 4·2m. tons of cargo were carried in 1978 and 4·6m. passengers were carried in 1975.

Post and Broadcasting. Number of post offices (1978), 2,516; number of telephones, 1,103,843 (1978). Wireless licences (1978), 2·59m.; television licences, 2,633,000. *Magyar Rádió és Televízió* broadcasts 3 programmes on medium-waves and FM and also regional programmes, including transmissions in German and Serbo-Croat. One TV programme is broadcast. Colour broadcasts are only transmitted in Budapest, using the SECAM system.

Cinemas (1978). There were 3,660 cinemas; attendance totalled 72m. 29 full-length feature films were made.

Newspapers and Books. In 1977 there were 29 dailies and 501 other periodicals. The Party daily is *Népszabadság* ('People's Freedom') (average daily circulation, 800,000). 8,556 book titles were published in 1978.

JUSTICE, RELIGION, EDUCATION AND WELFARE

Justice. The administration of justice is the responsibility of the Procurator-General, who is elected by Parliament for a term of 6 years. Civil and criminal cases fall under the jurisdiction of the district courts, county courts and the Supreme Court in Budapest. Criminal proceedings are dealt with by district courts through 3-member councils and by county courts and the Supreme Court in 5-member councils. A new Civil Code was adopted in 1978 and a new Criminal Code in 1979.

District Courts act only as courts of first instance; county courts as either courts of first instance or of appeal. The Supreme Court acts normally as an appeal court, but may act as a court of first instance in cases submitted to it by the Public Prosecutor. All courts, when acting as courts of first instance, consist of 1 professional judge and 2 lay assessors, and, as courts of appeal, of 3 professional judges. Local government Executive Committees may try petty offences.

District or county judges and assessors are elected by the district or county councils, all members of the Supreme Court by Parliament.

There are also military courts of the first instance. Military cases of the second instance go before the Supreme Court.

Judges are elected by the Presidential Council.

Religion. There are 20 authorized religious denominations which share proportionally an annual state subsidy of 70m. forints. 8·5m. of the population professed a religious faith in 1976; the number of active church members was put between 1m. and 1·5m.

Senior church appointments require the consent of the Presidential Council. Lower ones are ratified by the State Office for Church Affairs. Certain appointments become valid if the Office makes no comment within 15 days, and for the most minor church appointments neither state consent nor prior notification is required. Ecclesiastics are required to take an oath of allegiance to the state.

In 1976 there were 5·25m. Roman Catholics with 11 dioceses, 4,000 priests and 4,400 churches, and 500,000 uniates. In 1979 there were 3 seminaries and 1 uniate seminery, a theological academy, and 8 secondary schools. The Primate of Hungary is the Archbishop of Esztergom, Laszló Lekai, appointed Feb. 1976. There are also an archbishop of the diocese of Eger, a diocesan bishop of Székesfehérvár, 7 bishoprics and a uniate bishopric.

In 1976 there were 2m. Calvinists with 4 dioceses, 1,300 ministers and 1,567 churches. There were 2 theological colleges (20% of students female) with 16 teachers, and 1 secondary school. There were 500,000 Lutherans with 16 dioceses, 374 ministers and 673 churches. There is a theological college with 6 teachers. The 10 denominations in the Association of Free Churches had 37,000 members, 230 ministers and 675 churches. There are 4 Orthodox denominations with 40,000 members in 1979. The Unitarian Church has 10,000 members, 11 ministers and 6 churches. In 1979 there were 80,000–100,000 Jews (825,000 in 1939) with 130 synagogues, 26 rabbis, a rabbinical college with 6 teachers and a secondary school.

Education. Education is free and compulsory from 6 to 14. Primary schooling ends at 14; thereafter education may be continued at secondary, secondary technical or secondary vocational schools, which offer diplomas entitling students to apply for higher education, or at vocational training schools which offer tradesmen's diplomas. Students at the latter may also take the secondary school diploma examinations after 2 years of evening or correspondence study.

In 1978–79 there were 4,317 kindergartens with 25,710 teachers and 422,000 pupils; 3,856 general schools with 71,925 teachers and 1·1m. pupils; 529 secondary schools with 14,945 teachers and 198,000 pupils. There are 4 universities proper (Budapest, Pécs, Szeged, Debrecen), and 14 specialized universities (6 technical, 4 medical, 3 arts, 1 economics). At these and at 37 other institutions of higher education there were, in 1978–79, 65,000 students and 13,450 teachers.

Libraries and Museums. In 1977 there were 5,054 public and 5,440 trade union libraries. Major national libraries (1978): National Széchenyi, 5·6m. volumes; Budapest University, 3m.; Academy of Sciences, 1·5m.; National Technical Library and Documentation Centre, 1·1m. In 1978 there were 449 museums with 16·29m. visitors.

Health. In 1978 there were 29,135 doctors and dentists and 92,497 hospital beds.

Social Security. Medical treatment is free. Patients bear 15% of the cost of medicines. Sickness benefit is 75% of wages, old age pensions (at 60 for men, 55 for women) 60–70%. In 1978, 65m. forints were paid out in social insurance benefits.

Pensions were raised in Jan. 1979 and family allowances in July 1980.

DIPLOMATIC REPRESENTATIVES

OF HUNGARY IN GREAT BRITAIN (35 Eaton Place, London, SW1X 8BY)

Ambassador: János Lörincz-Nagy (accredited 10 Nov. 1976).

OF GREAT BRITAIN IN HUNGARY (Harmincad Utca 6, Budapest V)
Ambassador: B. G. Cartledge, CMG.

OF HUNGARY IN THE USA (3910 Shoemaker St., NW,
Washington, D.C., 20008)
Ambassador: Ferenc Esztergalyos.

OF THE USA IN HUNGARY (Szabadság Tér 12, Budapest V)
Ambassador: Harry E. Bergold, Jr.

OF HUNGARY TO THE UNITED NATIONS
Ambassador: Pál Rácz.

Books of Reference

Report of the Hungarian Statistical Office on the Economic Development and Plan Fulfilment.
Budapest, annual from 1973
Statisztikai Évkönyv. Budapest, annual; occasional editions in English (latest, 1972)
Statistical Pocket Book of Hungary (in English). Budapest, annual from 1962
Hungarian Digest. Budapest, 6 a year
Hungary 66 (67 etc.). Budapest, annual from 1966
Marketing in Hungary. Budapest, quarterly
Information Hungary. Budapest, 1980
Bako, E., *Guide to Hungarian Studies.* 2 vols. Stanford Univ. Press, 1973
Berend, I. T., and Ranki, G., *Hungary: A Century of Economic Development.* New York and
Newton Abbot, 1974
Enyedi, G., *Hungary: An Economic Geography.* Boulder, Colorado, 1976
Gadó, O., *The Economic Mechanism of Hungary.* Leiden and Budapest, 1976
Halász, Z., *Hungary: A Guide with a Difference.* 2nd ed. Budapest, 1979
Hegedüs, A., *The Structure of Socialist Society.* London, 1977
Ignotus, P., *Hungary.* London, 1972
Kádár, J., *For a Socialist Hungary.* Budapest, 1974
Macartney, C. A., *Hungary: A Short History.* London, 1962
Németh, G. (ed.), *Hungary: A Comprehensive Guide.* Budapest, 1980
Országh, L., *Magyar-Angol Szótár.* Budapest, 1968.—*Angol-Magyar Szótár.* Budapest, 1968
Pamlényi, E. (ed.), *A History of Hungary.* Budapest, 1975
Pécsi, M. and Sárfalvi, B., *Physical and Economic Geography of Hungary.* 2nd ed. Budapest,
1979
Shawcross, W., *Crime and Compromise: Janos Kadar and the Politics of Hungary Since the
Revolution.* London, 1974
Toma, P. A., and Volgyes, I., *Politics in Hungary.* San Francisco, 1977

ICELAND

Lýðveldið Ísland

Capital: Reykjavík
Population: 226,724 (1979)
GNP per capita: US$8,320 (1978)

HISTORY. The first settlers came to Iceland in 874. Between 930 and 1264 Iceland was an independent republic, but by the 'Old Treaty' of 1263 the country recognized the rule of the King of Norway. In 1381 Iceland, together with Norway, came under the rule of the Danish kings, but when Norway was separated from Denmark in 1814, Iceland remained under the rule of Denmark. Since 1 Dec. 1918 it has been acknowledged as a sovereign state. It was united with Denmark only through the common sovereign until it was proclaimed an independent republic on 17 June 1944.

AREA AND POPULATION. Iceland is a large island in the North Atlantic, close to the Arctic Circle, and comprises an area of about 103,000 sq. km (39,758 sq. miles), with its extreme northern point (the Rifstangi) lying in 66° 32′ N. lat., and its most southerly point (Dyrhólaey, Portland) in 63° 24′ N. lat., not including the islands north and south of the land; if these are included, the country extends from 67° 10′ N. (the Kolbeinsey) to 63° 19′ N. (Geirfuglasker, one of the Westman Islands). It stretches from 13° 30′ (the Gerpir) to 24° 32′ W. long. (Látrabjarg). The skerry *Hvalbakur* (The Whaleback) lies 13° 16′ W. long.

The 25 constituencies of the country are now grouped in 7 districts.

District	Inhabited land (sq. km)	Mountain pasture (sq. km)	Waste-land (sq. km)	Total area (sq. km)	Population (1 Dec.1979)
Reykjanes area	1,266	716	—	1,982	133,561
West	5,011	3,415	275	8,711	14,537
Western Peninsula	4,130	3,698	1,652	9,470	10,363
Northland West	4,867	5,278	2,948	13,093	10,595
Northland East	9,890	6,727	5,751	22,368	25,416
East ⎫ South ⎬	16,921	17,929	12,555	{ 21,991 { 25,214	12,763 19,489
Iceland	42,085	37,553	23,181	102,819	226,724

In 1979, 27,285 were domiciled in rural districts and 199,439 in towns and villages (of over 200 inhabitants.) The population is almost entirely Icelandic.

In 1978 foreigners numbered 3,085; of these 930 were Danish, 598 US, 301 British, 267 Norwegian and 232 German (Fed. Rep.) nationals.

The capital, Reykjavík, had on 1 Dec. 1979, a population of 83,536; other towns are Akranes, 5,017; Akureyri, 13,137; Bolungarvík, 1,249; Dalvík, 1,253; Eskifjörður, 1,056; Garðabaer, 4,731; Grindavík, 1,849; Hafnarfjörður, 12,158; Húsavík, 2,401; Ísafjörður, 3,301; Keflavík, 6,539; Kópavogur, 13,533; Neskaupstaður, 1,706; Njarðvík, 1,922; Ólafsfjörður, 1,181; Sauðarkrókur, 2,109; Selfoss, 3,329; Seltjarnarnes, 2,981; Seyðisfjörður, 1,027; Siglufjörður, 2,047; Vestmannaeyjar, 4,723.

Vital statistics for calendar years:

	Living births	Still-born	Marriages	Divorces	Deaths	Infant deaths
1975	4,384	33	1,689	397	1,412	55
1976	4,291	27	1,645	383	1,343	33
1977	3,996	25	1,568	407	1,435	38
1978	4,162	30	1,585	411	1,421	47
1979	4,475	17	1,451	394	1,482	24

597

CONSTITUTION AND GOVERNMENT. On 24 May 1944 the people of Iceland decided in a referendum to sever all ties with the Danish Crown. The voters were asked whether they were in favour of the abrogation of the Union Act, and whether they approved of the bill for a republican constitution: 70,725 voters were for severance of all political ties with Denmark and only 370 against it; 69,048 were in favour of the republican constitution, 1,042 against it and 2,505 votes were invalid. On 17 June 1944 the republic was formally proclaimed, and as the republic's first president the Alþingi elected Sveinn Björnsson for a 1-year term (re-elected 1945 and 1949; died 25 Jan. 1952). The President is now elected for a 4-year term.

President of the Republic of Iceland: Vigdís Finnbogadóttir (elected 29 June 1980, with 43,611 out of 129,049 valid votes, inaugurated 1 Aug. 1980).

National flag: Blue with a red white-bordered Scandinavian cross.

National anthem: Ó Guðvors lands (words by M. Jochumsson, 1874; tune by S. Sveinbjørnsson).

The official language is Icelandic (*islenzka*).

The *Alþingi* (Parliament) is divided into two Houses, the Upper House and the Lower House. The former is composed of one-third of the members elected by the whole Alþingi in common sitting. The remaining two-thirds of the members form the Lower House. The members of the Alþingi receive payment for their services.

The budget bills must be laid before the two Houses in joint session, but all other bills can be introduced in either of the Houses. If the Houses do not agree, they assemble in a common sitting and the final decision is given by a majority of two-thirds of the voters, with the exception of budget bills, where a simple majority is sufficient. The ministers have free access to both Houses, but can vote only in the House of which they are members.

The electoral law enacted in 1959 provides for an Alþingi of 60 members. Of these, 49 are elected in 8 constituencies by proportional representation; the remaining 11 are apportioned to the parties according to their total vote.

At the elections held on 3 Dec. 1979 the following parties were returned: Independence Party, 21; Progressives, 17; People's Alliance, 10; Social Democrats, 10; Independents, 1.

The executive power is exercised under the President by the Cabinet. The coalition Cabinet, as constituted in April 1980, was as follows:

Prime Minister: Gunnar Thoroddsen (Ind.).

Foreign Affairs: Olafur Jóhannesson (Progress). *Justice:* Fridjón Thórdarson (Ind.). *Agriculture:* Pálmi Jónsson (Ind.). *Education:* Ingvar Gíslason (Progress). *Fisheries and Communications:* Steingrímur Hermannsson (Progress). *Trade and Commerce:* Tómas Arnason (Progress). *Health and Social Security:* Svavar Gestsson (P.A.). *Finance:* Ragnar Arnalds (P.A.). *Energy and Industry:* Hjörleifur Guttormsson (P.A.).

The ministers are responsible for their acts. They can be impeached by the Alþingi, and in that case their cause will be decided by the *Landsdómur*, a special tribunal for parliamentary impeachments.

Local Administration. For administrative purposes Iceland is divided into 17 provinces (*syslur*), each under a chief executive (*syslumaður*). Each province forms one or two municipal districts with a council superintending the 203 rural municipalities. There are also 21 urban municipalities with a town council, independent of the provinces, and forming by themselves administrative districts co-ordinate with the provinces. The municipal councils are elected direct by universal suffrage (men and women over 20 years of age), in urban municipalities by proportional representation, but in rural municipalities by simple majority.

DEFENCE. Iceland possesses neither an army nor a navy. Under the North Atlantic Treaty, US forces are stationed in Iceland as the Iceland Defence Force. Four armed fishery protection vessels are maintained by the Coastguard, with 2 patrol aircraft and 2 helicopters. Coastguard Service personnel in 1980 totalled about 150 officers and men.

INTERNATIONAL RELATIONS

Membership. Iceland is a member of UN, EFTA, OECD, the Council of Europe, NATO and the Nordic Council.

ECONOMY

Budget. Current revenue and expenditure for calendar years (in 1,000 kr.):

	1975	1976	1977	1978	1979	1980
Revenue	47,625,680	60,342,390	89,956,581	139,496,000	208,950,789	346,177,300
Expenditure	47,225,533	58,857,251	89,153,247	138,473,000	202,286,419	343,240,052

Main items of the Treasury accounts for 1979 (in 1,000 kr.):

Revenue		Expenditure	
Direct taxes	54,096,279	Presidency	92,559
Indirect taxes	188,700,157	Alþingi	1,575,100
Profit from government enter-		Cabinet	227,588
prises	334,999	Justice and ecclesiastical affairs	14,883,582
		Culture and education	38,436,331
		Social affairs	8,559,593
		Commerce	24,888,126
		Foreign affairs	2,838,183
		Fisheries and agriculture	17,335,749
		Finance	9,286,023
		Communications	21,326,269

The public debt of Iceland was on 31 Dec. 1979, 118,033m. kr., of which the foreign debt amounted to 16,548m. kr. and the internal debt to 101,485m. kr.

Currency. The Icelandic monetary units are the *króna*, pl. *krónur* and the *eyrir*, pl. *aurar*. There are 100 *aurar* to the *króna*. On 1 Jan. 1981 a currency reform took place and 100 old krónur equal 1 new króna. In March 1981, US$1 = kr. 6·48; £1 = 14·192. Note and coin circulation, 31 Dec. 1979, was 15,709m. kr.

Banking. By Act of 29 March 1961 the Central Bank of Iceland was established, which took over the central bank function up to that date exercised by the *Landsbanki Íslands* (The National Bank of Iceland, owned entirely by the State). Other banks are: *Búnaðarbanki Íslands* (the Agricultural Bank of Iceland), a state bank, founded in 1930; *Útvegsbanki Íslands* (the Fisheries Bank of Iceland), founded in 1930 as a joint-stock bank, which in 1957 became a state bank; *Ísnaðarbanki Íslands* (Industrial Bank of Iceland Ltd), a joint-stock bank, established 1953, part of the shares being owned by the Government; *Verzlunarbanki Íslands* (Iceland Bank of Commerce Ltd), established in 1961; *Samvinnubanki Íslands* (The Icelandic Co-operative Bank), established in 1963; *Alþýðubankinn* (The People's Bank Ltd) established 1971. On 31 Aug. 1980 the accounts of the Central Bank balanced at 242,230m. kr.

At the end of 1979 there were 42 savings banks with deposits amounting to 36,775m. kr.

Weights and Measures. The metric system of weights and measures is obligatory.

ENERGY AND NATURAL RESOURCES

Electricity. The installed capacity of public power plants at the end of 1979 totalled 664,000 kw., of which 542,000 kw. comprised hydro-electric plants. Total energy production in public-owned plants in 1979 amounted to 2,919m. kwh.; in privately-owned plants, 5m. kwh.

Agriculture. Of the total area of Iceland, about six-sevenths is unproductive, but only about 0·5% is under cultivation, which is confined to hay, potatoes and turnips. In 1979 the total hay crop was 3,153,000 cu. metres; the crop of potatoes, 6,089 tonnes, and of turnips 271 tonnes. At the end of 1979 the livestock was as follows: Horses, 50,067; cattle, 57,172 (including 33,749 milch cows); sheep, 796,755; pigs, 11,376; poultry, 393,974.

Fisheries. Fishing vessels in Dec. 1979 numbered 868 with a gross tonnage of 104,160. Total catch in 1979, 1,644,200 tonnes; 1980, 1,483,500 tonnes.

The Icelandic Government announced that the fishery limits off Iceland were extended from 12 to 50 nautical miles from Sept. 1972. An interim agreement for 2 years signed by the UK and Iceland in Nov. 1973 expired in Nov. 1975.

On 15 July 1975 the Icelandic Government issued a decree that from 15 Oct. 1975 the fishery limits of Iceland were extended from 50 to 200 nautical miles. The Icelandic Government maintain that this extension is necessary to protect the fish stocks in Icelandic waters because the fishing industry is of vital importance to the national economy.

COMMERCE. Total value of imports and exports in 1,000 kr.:

	1975	1976	1977	1978	1979
Imports	75,062,400	85,659,600	120,969,100	184,320,600	291,307,200
Exports	47,436,600	73,499,700	101,889,300	176,285,700	278,451,500

Leading exports (in 1,000 kg and 1,000 kr.):

	1978		1979	
	Quantity	*Value*	*Quantity*	*Value*
Fish and whale products	487,159·1	134,057,600	563,989·5	207,986,900
Agricultural products	9,457·4	4,076,200	10,824·1	7,127,200

Leading imports (in 1,000 tonnes and 1,000 kr.):

	1978		1979	
	Quantity	*Value*	*Quantity*	*Value*
Ships (number)	7	5,111,000	11	9,135,400
Fuel oil	500,258·9	16,045,700	533,810·9	42,849,900
Cereals	13,489·6	1,377,300	13,846·9	1,921,600
Animal feed	73,460·4	3,535,200	84,918·2	6,052,700
Gasoline	97,953·5	3,932,800	96,949·5	10,025,600
Motor vehicles (number)	9,245	11,087,000	8,542	13,849,300
Fishing nets and other gear	2,422·3	3,137,200	2,285·4	4,217,400

Value of trade with principal countries for 3 years (in 1,000 kr.):

	1977		1978		1979	
	Imports	*Exports*	*Imports*	*Exports*	*Imports*	*Exports*
	(c.i.f.)	*(f.o.b.)*	*(c.i.f.)*	*(f.o.b.)*	*(c.i.f.)*	*(f.o.b.)*
Austria	603,355	37,832	1,295,958	76,488	1,303,480	221,598
Belgium	3,353,332	1,625,374	4,678,824	1,452,248	10,036,627	1,536,418
Brazil	1,723,633	223,532	2,168,019	1,130,305	3,702,577	709,894
Canada	346,946	259,030	683,430	780,588	1,705,670	1,520,800
Czechoslovakia	850,847	491,426	1,233,406	941,224	1,605,239	2,698,623
Denmark	12,306,487	1,999,716	18,302,248	3,385,727	25,796,017	5,124,382
Faroe Islands	320,515	743,775	30,879	967,203	30,623	1,357,686
Finland	2,262,162	2,015,647	4,131,533	3,992,453	7,015,937	5,585,416
France	3,782,184	681,789	4,046,495	1,457,274	6,691,847	8,060,837
German Dem. Rep.	320,768	171,275	630,827	38,848	758,963	214,910
Germany, Fed. Rep. of	12,346,793	7,088,287	21,054,804	13,984,022	31,213,580	23,332,748
Greece	13,792	1,475,736	16,723	1,862,489	42,143	3,429,501
Hungary	31,173	470,367	36,261	768,988	83,779	671,956
India	194,845	—	310,203	1,373,069	341,993	526,055
Irish Republic	263,250	41,656	384,604	103,637	525,712	774,806
Israel	132,887	26	196,658	20	340,610	7,008
Italy	2,736,115	2,446,853	4,092,895	4,448,630	6,015,063	10,100,709
Japan	3,851,569	1,732,758	6,249,830	2,770,297	9,076,907	8,488,381
Netherlands	9,202,103	1,950,969	14,226,150	1,826,003	22,362,312	5,102,470
Nigeria	8,832	2,058,568	6,317	6,058,562	711,889	2,507,267
Norway	12,058,449	1,854,000	15,363,127	2,679,177	24,610,753	5,412,649
Poland	2,711,563	4,026,088	1,336,901	4,669,936	1,663,427	5,827,971
Portugal	342,871	5,718,952	677,749	7,187,593	7,500,380	9,808,237
Spain	521,763	2,146,311	1,066,244	4,569,985	1,434,667	8,846,422
Sweden	8,464,344	2,404,895	17,342,626	2,991,687	21,999,702	7,139,580
Switzerland	1,118,996	2,865,402	1,974,885	5,893,496	3,795,081	9,859,609
USSR	10,885,805	7,177,959	15,571,918	6,940,549	32,621,674	10,804,664
UK	13,284,273	14,744,758	19,388,316	29,821,709	32,391,767	53,356,502
USA	7,965,159	30,813,348	13,092,829	51,627,902	19,016,526	77,910,336

Total trade between Iceland and UK (British Department of Trade returns, in £1,000 sterling):

	1976	1977	1978	1979	1980
Imports to UK	31,659	44,880	63,810	83,269	82,042
Exports and re-exports from UK	26,215	39,276	44,431	48,520	47,223

TOURISM. There were 76,912 visitors to Iceland in 1979.

COMMUNICATIONS

Roads. There are no railways in Iceland. Iceland possesses between 11,000–12,000 km of high roads and country roads. Motor vehicles registered at the end of 1979 numbered 90,015, of which 82,142 were passenger cars and 7,873 trucks; there were also 563 motor cycles. On 26 May 1968 Iceland changed from left-hand to right-hand traffic.

Aviation. One large and some small companies maintain regular services between Reykjavík and various places in Iceland (the large one 1979: 238,767 passengers; 782 tonnes of mail; 3,281 tonnes of freight). The large company maintains regular services between Iceland and the UK, the Scandinavian countries, some other European countries and USA. In 1979 the company carried in scheduled foreign flights 420,077 passengers, 970 tonnes of mail and 8,134 tonnes of freight.

Shipping. The mercantile marine of Iceland consisted in Dec. 1979 of 4 steam vessels (1,953 gross tons) and 975 motor vessels (192,511 gross tons).

Post and Broadcasting. At the end of 1978 the number of post offices was 184 and telephone and telegraph offices 152; number of telephones, 95,515. The government station, *Rikisutvarpid*, broadcasts 1 programme on long- and medium-waves and on FM. *Rikisutvarpid-Sjonvarp* uses 97 transmitters and broadcasts 1 TV programme. Number of licenced receivers: radio, 67,000; television, 60,000.

Cinemas (1976). There were 29 cinemas with a seating capacity of 9,727.

Newspapers (1978). There are 6 daily newspapers, all in Reykjavík, with a combined circulation of about 129,000.

JUSTICE, RELIGION, EDUCATION AND WELFARE

Justice. The lower courts of justice are those of the provincial magistrates (*syslumenn*) and town judges (*bæjarfógetar*). From these there is an appeal to the Supreme Court (*hæstiréttur*) in Reykjavík, which has 6 judges.

Religion. The national church, and the only one endowed by the State, is Evangelical Lutheran. But there is complete religious liberty, and no civil disabilities are attached to those not of the national religion. The affairs of the national church are under the superintendence of a bishop. In 1979, 4,099 persons (1·8%) were Dissenters and 2,710 persons (1·2%) did not belong to any religious community.

Education. There is a university in Reykjavík, inaugurated on 17 June 1911, with an enrolment of about 2,800 students. In 1975–76 there were 7 grammar schools (3,500 pupils), 124 general secondary schools (16,800 pupils), 6 vocational schools of home economics for women (178 pupils), 1 training college for primary and secondary school teachers (181 pupils) and 3 other teachers' training colleges (143 pupils); 2 agricultural and 1 horticultural school (146 pupils), 3 schools of navigation (192 pupils), 1 school of nautical engineering (398 students), 2 commercial high schools (551 pupils), 18 part-time vocational training schools for apprentices in trade (about 3,000 pupils), 1 technological college (210 pupils), 7 schools for training of nurses, midwives, etc. (435 pupils), 1 college of music (57 students), 1 arts college (139 students) and 1 drama school (42 students). There are also many part-time schools of cultural activities, such as 26 schools of music, 3 schools of arts and crafts, 3 schools of dance and drama and 1 school of athletics. There are also some courses on various subjects for adults and continuation schools for young people. Elementary instruction is compulsory for children from 7 to 15 years.

Social Welfare. The main body of the Icelandic social welfare legislation is consolidated in six main acts:

(*i*) *The social security legislation* (*a*) health insurance, including sickness benefits; (*b*) social security pensions, mainly consisting of old age pension, disablement pension and widows' pension, and also children's pension; (*c*) employment injuries insurance.

(*ii*) *The unemployment insurance legislation*, where daily allowances are paid to those who have met certain conditions.

(*iii*) *The subsistence legislation*. This is controlled by municipal government, and social assistance is granted under special circumstances, when payments from other sources are not sufficient.

(*iv*) *The tax legislation*. In 1975 family allowances were abolished and children's support included in the tax legislation, according to which a certain amount is subtracted from levied taxes for each child in a family.

(*v*) *The rehabilitation legislation.*

(*vi*) *Child and juvenile guidance.*

Health insurance covers the entire population. Citizenship is not demanded and there is no waiting period. Most hospitals are both municipally and state run, a few solely state run and all offer free medical help. Medical treatment out of hospitals is partly paid by the patient, the same applies to medicines, except medicines of life-long necessary use, which are paid in full by the health insurance. Dental care is free for the age groups 6–15, but is paid 50% for old age and disablement pensioners, pregnant women and children at the age of 3–5. Sickness benefits are paid to those who lose income because of periodical illness. The daily amount is fixed and paid from the 11th day of illness. In Oct. 1980 it was 4,259 kr. a day.

Entitlement to old age and disablement pensions at the full rates is subject to the condition that the beneficiary has been resident in Iceland for 40 years at the age period of 16–67. For shorter period of residence, the benefits are reduced proportionally. Entitled to old age pension are all those who are 67 years old, and have been residents in Iceland for 3 years of the age period of 16–67. Entitled to disablement pension are those who have lost 75% of their working capacity and have been residents in Iceland for 3 years before application or have had full working capacity at the time when they became residents. Old age and disablement pension are of equally high amount, in the year 1979 the total sum was 731,966 kr. for an individual. Married pensioners are paid 90% of two individuals' pensions. In addition to the basic amount, supplementary allowances are paid according to social circumstances and income possibilities. Widows' pensions are the same amount as old age and disablement pension, provided the applicant is over 60 when she becomes widowed. Women at the age 50–60 get reduced pension. Women under 50 are not entitled to widows' pensions.

The employment injuries insurance covers medical care, daily allowances, disablement pension and survivors' pension and is applicable to practically all employees.

All benefits within the above-mentioned laws shall go up in step with general wages within 6 months from their increase.

Social assistance is primarily municipal and granted in cases outside the social security legislation. Domestic assistance to old people and disabled is granted within this legislation, besides other services.

Child and juvenile guidance is performed by chosen committees according to special laws, such as home guidance and family assistance. In cases of parents' disablement the committees take over the guidance of the children involved.

DIPLOMATIC REPRESENTATIVES

OF ICELAND IN GREAT BRITAIN (1 Eaton Terrace, London, SW1W 8EY)

Ambassador: Sigurður Bjarnason.

OF GREAT BRITAIN IN ICELAND (Laufasvegur 49, Reykjavík)
Ambassador and Consul-General: W. R. McQuillan.

Ambassador: Hans G. Andersen.

OF THE USA IN ICELAND (Laufasvegur 21, Reykjavík)
Ambassador: Richard A. Ericson, Jr.

OF ICELAND TO THE UNITED NATIONS
Ambassador: Tómas Á. Tómasson.

Books of Reference

Statistical Information: The Icelandic Statistical Office, Hagstofa Islands (Reykjavík) was founded in 1914. *Director:* Klemens Tryggvason. Its main publications are:

Economic Statistics. Central Bank of Iceland (quarterly from 1979)

Hagskýrslur Islands. Statistics of Iceland (from 1912)

Hagtíðindi (Statistical Journal) (from 1916)

Icelandic Currency Reform January 1st 1981. Central Bank of Iceland, 1980

Statistical Bulletin. Issued quarterly by the Statistical Bureau of Iceland and the Central Bank of Iceland (from 1931 to 1962, monthly). Ceased publication May 1980

Heilbrigðisskýrslur. Public Health in Iceland (latest issue for 1977; published 1980)

Briem, Helgi P., *Iceland and the Icelanders.* Maplewood, 1945

Cleasby, R., *An Icelandic–English Dictionary.* 2nd ed. Oxford, 1957

Foss, H. (ed.), *Directory of Iceland.* Annual. Reykjavik, 1907–40, 1948 ff.

Hansson, Ólafur, *Facts about Iceland.* Reykjavík, 1951

Hermannsson, Halldór, *Islandica.* An annual relating to Iceland and the Fiske Icelandic Collection in Cornell University Library. Ithaca (from 1908)

Hood, J. C. F., *Icelandic Church Saga.* London, 1946

Leaf, H., *Iceland Yesterday and Today.* London, 1949

Magnússon, S. A., *Northern Sphinx: Iceland and the Icelanders from the Settlement to the Present.* London, 1977

Nordal, J., and Kristinsson, V. (eds), *Iceland 874–1974.* Central Board of Iceland, Reykjavík, 1975

þorðarson, Björn, *Iceland: Past and Present.* 2nd ed. Oxford, 1945

þorðarson, Matthias, *The Althing, Iceland's Thousand-Year-Old Parliament, 930–1930.* Reykjavík, 1930

þorsteinsson, þorsteinn, *Iceland, 1946: A Handbook Published on the 60th Anniversary of the National Bank of Iceland.* 4th ed. Reykjavík, 1946

Trial, G. T., *History of Education in Iceland.* Cambridge, 1945

Zoëga, G. T., *Íslensk-ensk (and Ensk-íslensk) orðabók.* 3rd ed. 2 vols. Reykjavík, 1932–51

National Library: Landsbókasafnið, Reykjavík, *Librarian:* Dr Finnbogi Guðmundsson.

INDIA

Capital: New Delhi
Population: 683m. (1981)
GNP per capita: US$159 (1979)

Bharat

HISTORY. The Indus civilization was fully developed by *c.* 2500 B.C., and collapsed *c.* 1750 B.C. An Aryan civilization spread from the west as far as the Ganges valley by 500 B.C.; separate kingdoms were established and many of these were united under the Mauryan dynasty established by Chandragupta in *c.* 320 B.C. The Mauryan Empire was succeeded by numerous small kingdoms. The Gupta dynasty (A.D. 320–600) was followed by the first Arabic invasions of the north-west. Moslem, Hindu and Buddhist states developed together with frequent conflict until the establishment of the Mogul dynasty in 1526. The first settlements by the East India Company were made after 1600 and the company established a formal system of government for Bengal in 1700. During the decline of the Moguls frequent wars between the Company, the French and the native princes led to the Company's being brought under British Government control in 1784; the first Governor-General of India was appointed in 1786. The powers of the Company were abolished by the India Act, 1858, and its functions and forces transferred to the British Crown. Representative government was introduced in 1909, and the first parliament in 1919. The separate dominions of India and Pakistan became independent within the Commonwealth in 1947 and India became a republic in 1950.

AREA AND POPULATION. India is bounded north-west by Pakistan, north by China, Tibet, Nepál and Bhután, east by Burma, south-east, south and south-west by the Indian ocean. The far eastern states and territories are almost separated from the rest by Bangladesh as it extends northwards from the Bay of Bengal. The area of the Indian Union (excluding the Pakistan and China-occupied parts of Jammu and Kashmir) is 3,166,828 sq. km. Its population according to the 1971 census was 547,949,809 (excluding Sikkim and the occupied area of Jammu and Kashmir); this represents an increase of 24·8% since 1961. Sex ratio was 929 females per 1,000 males (941 in 1961); density of population, 178 per sq. km. About 20% of the population was urban in 1971 (in Maharashtra, 30%; in Assam, Himachal Pradesh, Nagaland and Orissa, less than 10%). Estimated population (1981) 683m.

Many births and deaths go unregistered. Data from certain areas of better registration and field studies suggest that the 1975 birth rate was about 35·2 per 1,000 population, the death rate 14·7 per 1,000. In 1971 the age-group 0–14 years represented 42% of the population and only 5·2% were over 60. In 1976 expectation of life for men was 53·2 years, for women 51·9.

Marriages and divorces are not registered. The minimum age for a civil marriage is 18 for women and 21 for men; for a sacramental marriage, 14 for girls and 18 for youths.

The main details of the census of 1 March 1961 and of 1 March 1971 are:

	Land area in	Population	
Name of State	*sq. km (1971)*	*1961*	*1971*
States			
Andhra Pradesh	276,814	35,983,447	43,502,708
Assam [1]	78,523	11,872,772	14,625,152
Bihar	173,876	46,455,610	56,353,369
Gujarat	195,984	20,633,350	26,697,475
Haryana	44,222	—	10,036,808
Himachal Pradesh	55,673	1,351,144	3,460,434
Jammu and Kashmir [2]	101,283	3,560,976	4,617,000
Karnataka	191,773	23,586,772	29,299,014

[1] In 1961 population included areas now separate (Meghalaya and Mizoram).
[2] Excludes the Pakistan-occupied area.

	Land area in	Population	
Name of State	sq. km. (1971)	1961	1971
Kerala	38,864	16,903,715	21,347,375
Madhya Pradesh	442,841	32,372,408	41,654,119
Maharashtra	307,762	39,553,718	50,412,235
Manipur	22,356	780,037	1,072,753
Meghalaya	22,489	—	1,011,699
Nagaland	16,527	369,200	516,449
Orissa	155,782	17,548,846	21,944,615
Punjab [1]	50,362	20,306,812	13,551,060
Rajasthan	342,214	20,155,602	25,765,806
Tamil Nadu	130,069	33,686,953	41,199,168
Tripura	10,477	1,142,055	1,556,342
Uttar Pradesh	294,413	73,746,401	88,341,144
West Bengal	87,853	34,926,279	44,312,011
Union Territories			
Andaman and Nicobar Islands	8,293	63,548	115,133
Arunachal Pradesh	83,578	336,558	467,511
Chandigarh	114	—	257,251
Dadra and Nagar Haveli	491	57,963 [2]	74,170
Delhi	1,485	2,658,612	4,065,698
Goa, Daman and Diu	3,813	626,667 [3]	857,771
Lakshadweep	32	24,108	31,810
Mizoram	21,087	—	332,390
Pondicherry	480	369,079	471,707
Grand total	3,159,530	439,072,582	547,949,809

[1] By the creation of Haryana (1966) Punjab has lost *c.* 7m. people to the new state, 89,000 to the new Union territory of Chandigarh and a further 1·5m. to Himachal Pradesh.

[2] 1962 census.

[3] 1960 Portuguese census.

Sikkim was added to the Union as a state in 1975; area, 7,298 sq. km, population (1977 estimate), 250,000.

Greatest density occurs in Delhi (2,738 per sq. km), Chandigarh (2,257), Lakshadweep (994) and Pondicherry (983). The lowest occurs in Arunachal Pradesh (6).

There were (1971) 283,936,000 males and 264,013,200 females.

In 1971, 438·9m. were rural (*c.* 80%) and 109·1m. were urban. There were 575,721 villages: 318,611 of these had less than 500 inhabitants.

Cities and Urban Agglomerations (with states in brackets) having more than 100,000 population at the 1971 census were:

Agra (U.P.)	637,785	Bhadravati (Kar.)	101,315	Delhi	3,647,023
Ahmedabad (Guj.)	1,741,522	Bhagalpur (Bih.)	172,700	Devanagere (Kar.)	121,018
Ahmednagar		Bhavnagar (Guj.)	226,072	Dhanbad (Bih.)	433,085
(Mah.)	117,275	Bhopal (M.P.)	392,077	Dhulia (Mah.)	137,089
Ajmer (Raj.)	262,480	Bhubaneswar (Ori.)	105,514	Dindigul (T.N.)	127,406
Akola (Mah.)	168,454	Bihar (Bih.)	100,052	Durgapur (W.B.)	207,232
Aligarh (U.P.)	254,008	Bijapur (Kar.)	103,308	Durg-Bhilainagar	
Allahabad (U.P.)	513,997	Bikaner (Raj.)	188,598	(M.P.)	245,333
Alleppey (Ker.)	160,064	Bilaspur (M.P.)	130,804	Eluru (A.P.)	127,047
Alwar (Raj.)/Har.	100,791	Bokaro Steel City		Erode (T.N.)	103,704
Ambala (Har.)	102,519	(Bih.)	108,012	Faizabad (U.P.)	109,765
Amravati (Mah.)	193,636	Bombay (Mah.)	5,970,575	Farrukhabad-	
Amritsar (Pun.)	432,663	Burdwan (W.B.)	144,970	Fatehgar (U.P.)	111,373
Asansol (W.B.)	157,388	Burhanpur (M.P.)	105,349	Firozabad (U.P.)	133,945
Aurangabad		Calcutta (W.B.)	7,031,382	Gauhati (Ass.)	122,981
(Mah.)	150,514	Chandigarh (Ch.)	233,004	Gaya (Bih.)	179,826
Bangalore (Kar.)	1,653,779	Cochin (Ker.)	438,420	Ghaziabad (U.P.)	128,036
Bareilly (U.P.)	326,127	Cuddalore (T.N.)	101,345	Gorakhpur (U.P.)	230,701
Behrampur (Ori.)	117,635	Cuttack (Ori.)	194,036	Gulbarga (Kar.)	145,630
Belgaum (Kar.)	213,830	Darbhanga (Bih.)	132,129	Guntur (A.P.)	269,941
Bellary (Kar.)	125,127	Dehra Dun (U.P.)	199,443	Gwalior (M.P.)	406,755

Hubli-Dharwar		Malegaon (Mah.)	191,784	Sagar (M.P.)	154,811
(Kar.)	379,555	Mangalore (Kar.)	214,093	Saharanpur (U.P.)	225,698
Hyderabad (A.P.)	1,796,339	Mathura (U.P.)	140,468	Salem (T.N.)	308,303
Imphal (Man.)	100,605	Meerut (U.P.)	367,821	Sangli (Mah.)	115,052
Indore (M.P.)	572,622	Mirzapur (U.P.)	105,920	Shahjahanpur	
Jabalpur (M.P.)	533,751	Monghyr (Bih.)	102,462	(U.P.)	144,058
Jaipur (Raj.)	613,144	Moradabad (U.P.)	272,355	Shimoga (Kar.)	102,703
Jalgaon (Mah.)	106,739	Muzaffar Nagar		Sholapur (Mah.)	398,122
Jammu (J. & K.)	155,249	(U.P.)	114,859	Singanallur (T.N.)	113,397
Jamnagar (Guj.)	214,853	Muzaffarpur (Bih.)	127,045	Srinagar (J. & K.)	403,612
Jamshedpur (Bih.)	465,200	Mysore (Kar.)	355,636	Surat (Guj.)	471,815
Jhansi (U.P.)	198,101	Nadiad (Guj.)	108,268	Tenali (A.P.)	102,943
Jodhpur (Raj.)	318,894	Nagercoil (T.N.)	141,207	Thana (Mah.)	170,167
Jullundur (Pun.)	296,103	Nagpur (Mah.)	866,144	Thanjavur (T.N.)	140,470
Kakinada (A.P.)	164,172	Nanded (Mah.)	126,400	Tiruchirapalli	
Kanchipuram		Nasik (Mah.)	176,187	(T.N.)	306,247
(T.N.)	110,505	Nellore (A.P.)	133,607	Tirunelveli (T.N.)	108,509
Kanpur (U.P.)	1,275,242	Nizamabad (A.P.)	114,868	Tiruppur (T.N.)	113,171
Kharagpur (W.B.)	161,911	Patiala (Pun.)	151,903	Trivandrum (Ker.)	409,761
Kolhapur (Mah.)	259,068	Patna (Bih.)	490,265	Tuticorin (T.N.)	154,804
Kotah (Raj.)	213,005	Pune (Mah.)	1,135,034	Udaipur (Raj.)	162,934
Kozikhode (Ker.)	333,980	Quilon (Ker.)	124,072	Ujjain (M.P.)	209,118
Kumbakonam		Raipur (M.P.)	205,909	Ulhasnagar (Mah.)	168,128
(T.N.)	112,971	Rajahmundry		Vadodara (Guj.)	467,422
Kurnool (A.P.)	136,682	(A.P.)	188,841	Varanasi (U.P.)	582,915
Lucknow (U.P.)	826,246	Rajkot (Guj.)	300,152	Vellore (T.N.)	138,220
Ludhiana (Pun.)	401,124	Rampur (U.P.)	161,802	Vijayawada (A.P.)	343,664
Machilipatnam		Ranchi (Bih.)	256,011	Visakhapatnam	
(A.P.)	112,636	Ratlam (M.P.)	118,625	(A.P.)	362,270
Madras (T.N.)	3,169,930	Rohtak (Har.)	124,783	Warangal (A.P.)	207,130
Madurai (T.N.)	548,298	Rourkela (Ori.)	172,536		

Report of the Officials of the Government of India and the People's Republic of China on the Boundary Question. New Delhi, Ministry of External Affairs, 1961

1961 Census: Final General Totals. 1962

Census of India, 1951 and 1961: Reports and Papers, Decennial Series. (All published by Government of India.)

Annual Report on the Working of Indian Migration. Government of India, from 1956

Report of the Commissioner for Scheduled Castes and Scheduled Tribes. Government of India. Annual

Public Health. Report of the Public Health Commission with the Government of India. Annual

Agarwala, S. N., *India's Population Problems.* New York, 1973

Hutton, J. H., *Caste in India.* 4th ed. Bombay, 1963

Mamoria, C. B., *India's Population Problem.* Allahabad, 1961

Mayer, A. C., *Caste and Kinship in Central India.* London, 1960

Misra, B. B., *The Indian Middle Classes.* R. Inst. of Int. Affairs, 1961

Sovani, N. V., *Urbanization and Urban India.* London, 1966

Turner, R. (ed.), *India's Urban Future.* Univ. of California Press and CUP, 1962

CONSTITUTION AND GOVERNMENT. On 26 Jan. 1950 India became a sovereign democratic republic. India's relations with the British Commonwealth of Nations were defined at the London conference of Prime Ministers on 27 April 1949.

Unanimous agreement was reached to the effect that the Republic of India remains a full member of the Commonwealth and accepts the Queen as 'the symbol of the free association of its independent member nations and, as such, the head of the Commonwealth'. This agreement was ratified by the Constituent Assembly of India on 17 May 1949.

The constitution was passed by the Constituent Assembly on 26 Nov. 1949 and came into force on 26 Jan. 1950. It has since been amended 44 times.

India is a Union of States and comprises 22 States and 9 Union territories. Each State is administered by a Governor appointed by the President for a term of 5 years while each Union territory is administered by the President through an administrator appointed by him.

The capital is New Delhi.

Presidency. The head of the Union is the President in whom all executive power is vested, to be exercised on the advice of ministers responsible to Parliament. He is elected by an electoral college consisting of all the elected members of Parliament and of the various state legislative assemblies. He holds office for 5 years and is eligible for re-election. He must be an Indian citizen at least 35 years old and eligible for election to the Lower House. He can be removed from office by impeachment for violation of the constitution.

There is also a Vice-President who is *ex-officio* chairman of the Upper House of Parliament.

Central Legislature. The Parliament for the Union consists of the President, the Council of States (*Rajya Sabha*) and the House of the People (*Lok Sabha*). The Council of States, or the Upper House, consists of not more than 250 members; in 1980 there were 232 elected members and 12 members nominated by the President. The election to this house is indirect; the representatives of each State are elected by the elected members of the Legislative Assembly of that State. The Council of States is a permanent body not liable to dissolution, but one-third of the members retire every second year. The House of the People, or the Lower House, consists of 544 members, 525 directly elected on the basis of adult suffrage from territorial constituencies in the States, and 17 members to represent the Union territories, chosen in such manner as the Parliament may by law provide; in March 1980 there were 542 elected members and 2 members nominated by the President. The House of the People unless sooner dissolved continues for a period of 5 years from the date appointed for its first meeting; in emergency, Parliament can extend the term by 1 year.

State Legislatures. For every State there is a legislature which consists of the Governor, and (*a*) 2 Houses, a Legislative Assembly and a Legislative Council, in the States of Andhra Pradesh, Jammu and Kashmir, Karnataka, Madhya Pradesh, Maharashtra, Tamil Nadu and Uttar Pradesh, and (*b*) 1 House, a Legislative Assembly, in the other States. Every Legislative Assembly, unless sooner dissolved, continues for 5 years from the date appointed for its first meeting. In emergency the term can be extended by 1 year. Every State Legislative Council is a permanent body and is not subject to dissolution, but one-third of the members retire every year. Parliament can, however, abolish an existing Legislative Council or create a new one, if the proposal is supported by a resolution of the Legislative Assembly concerned.

Legislative Councils have one-third of the total membership of the Assemblies but not less than 40 members, of whom one-third are elected by local authorities, one-third by members of the Assembly, one-twelfth by state university graduates and one-twelfth by teachers of secondary school upwards; the rest are named by the Governor. Legislative Assemblies have between 60 and 500 directly elected members.

Legislation. The various subjects of legislation are enumerated in three lists in the seventh schedule to the constitution. List I, the Union List, consists of 97 subjects (including defence, foreign affairs, communications, currency and coinage, banking and customs) with respect to which the Union Parliament has exclusive power to make laws; the State legislature has exclusive power to make laws with respect to the 66 subjects in list II, the State List—these include police and public order, agriculture and irrigation, education, public health and local government; the powers to make laws with respect to the 47 subjects (including economic and social planning, legal questions and labour and price control) in list III, the Concurrent List, are held by both Union and State governments, though the former prevails. But Parliament may legislate with respect to any subject in the State List in circumstances when the subject assumes national importance or during emergencies.

Other provisions deal with the administrative relations between the Union and the States, interstate trade and commerce, distribution of revenues between the States and the Union, official language, etc.

Fundamental Rights. Two chapters of the constitution deal with fundamental rights and 'Directive Principles of State Policy'. 'Untouchability' is abolished, and its practice in any form is punishable. The fundamental rights can be enforced through the ordinary courts of law and through the Supreme Court of the Union. The directive principles cannot be enforced through the courts of law; they are nevertheless fundamental in the governance of the country.

Citizenship. Under the Constitution, every person who was on the 26 Jan. 1950, domiciled in India and (*a*) was born in India or (*b*) either of whose parents was born in India or (*c*) who has been ordinarily resident in the territory of India for not less than 5 years immediately preceding that date became a citizen of India. Special provision is made for migrants from Pakistan and for Indians resident abroad. Under the Citizenship Act, 1955, which supplemented the provisions of the Constitution, Indian citizenship is acquired by birth, by descent, by registration and by naturalization. The Act also provides for loss of citizenship by renunciation, termination and deprivation. The right to vote is granted to every person who is a citizen of India and who is not less than 21 years of age on a fixed date and is not otherwise disqualified.

Parliament. Parliament and the state legislatures are organized according to the following schedule (figures show distribution of seats in March 1980):

| | Parliament | | State Legislatures | |
	House of the People (*Lok Sabha*)	Council of States (*Rajya Sabha*)	Legislative Assemblies (*Vidhan Sabhas*)	Legislative Councils (*Vidhan Parishads*)
States:				
Andhra Pradesh	42	18	294	90
Assam	14	7	126	—
Bihar	54	22	324	—
Gujarat	26	11	182	—
Haryana	10	5	90	—
Himachal Pradesh	4	3	68	—
Karnataka	28	12	224	63
Kerala	20	9	140	—
Madhya Pradesh	40	16	320	90
Maharashtra	48	19	288	78
Manipur	2	1	60	—
Meghalaya	2	1	60	—
Nagaland	1	1	60	—
Orissa	21	10	147	—
Punjab	13	7	117	—
Rajasthan	25	10	200	—
Sikkim	1	1	32	—
Tamil Nadu	39	18	234	63
Tripura	2	1	60	—
Uttar Pradesh	85	34	425	108
West Bengal	42	16	294	—
Jammu and Kashmir	6	4	76[2]	36[4]
Union Territories:				
Andaman and Nicobar Islands	1	—	—	—
Arunachal Pradesh	2	1[3]	30	—
Chandigarh	1	—	—	—
Dadra and Nagar Haveli	1	—	—	—
Delhi	7	3	61	—
Goa, Daman and Diu	2	—	30	—
Lakshadweep	1	—	—	—
Mizoram	1	1	30	—
Pondicherry	1	1	30	—
Nominated by the President under Article 80 (1) (a) of the Constitution	—	12	—	—
Total	544[1]	244	4,034	528

[1] Includes 2 nominated members to represent Anglo-Indians.
[2] Excludes 25 seats for Pakistan-occupied areas of the State which are in abeyance.
[3] Nominated by the President.   [4] Excludes seats for the Pakistan-occupied areas.

The number of seats allotted to scheduled castes and scheduled tribes in the House of the People is 77 and 42 respectively. Out of the 3,864 seats allotted to the Legislative Assemblies, 521 are reserved for scheduled castes and 329 for scheduled tribes.

Following the general election of Jan. 1980 the composition of the House of the People was: Indira Congress 352, Janata 31, Lok Dal 41, Communist Party (Marxist) 36, Dravida Munnetra Kazhagam 16, Congress 13, Communist Party of India 11; others 17; vacant, 16.

The Council of States (July 1980) was composed as follows: Indira Congress 121, Congress 21, Janata 17, Bhartiya Janata 14, Lok Dal 14, CPI (Marxist) 9, CPI 7, All-India Anna DMK 6, DMK 6, Akali Dal 3, National Conference 2, Muslim League 1, Kerala Congress 1, Forward Bloc 1, NNDP 1, RSP 1, RPI (Khobragade) 1, Socialist 1, Independent 6, Nominated 8, Vacant 3.

On 2 Jan. 1978 the Congress Party split into two: Congress and Indira Congress.

National flag: Three horizontal stripes of saffron (orange), white and green, with the wheel of Asoka in the centre in blue.

National anthem: Jana-gana-mana (words by Rabindranath Tagore).

Indian Independence Act, 1947. (Ch. 30.) London, 1947

The Constitution of India (Modified up to 15 April 1967). Delhi, 1967

Appadorai, A., *Indian Political Thinking in the Twentieth Century: From Naoroji to Nehru.* OUP, 1971.—*Documents on Political Thought in Modern India.* OUP, 1974

Austin, G., *The Indian Constitution.* OUP, 1972

Basu, D. D., *Commentary on the Constitution of India.* 3rd ed. 2 vols. Calcutta, 1956

Gandhi, I., *The Speeches and Reminiscences of Indira Gandhi.* London, 1975

Mansergh, N., ed. *The Transfer of Power 1942–47.* 5 vols. HMSO, 1970–75

Menon, V. P., *Transfer of Power in India.* Bombay, 1957

More, S. S., *Practice and Procedure of Indian Parliament.* Bombay, 1960

Morris-Jones, W. H., *Parliament in India.* London, 1957.—*The Government and Politics of India.* London, 1964

Pylee, M. V., *Constitutional Government in India.* 2nd ed. Bombay, 1965

Rao, K. V., *Parliamentary Democracy of India.* 2nd ed. Calcutta, 1965

Seervali, H. M., *Constitutional Law of India.* Bombay, 1967

Sinha, S., *Indian Independence in Perspective.* London, 1965

Language. The Constitution provides that the official language of the Union shall be Hindi in the Devanagari script. It was originally provided that English should continue to be used for all official purposes until 1965. But the Official Languages Act 1963 provides that, after the expiry of this period of 15 years from the coming into force of the Constitution, English might continue to be used, in addition to Hindi, for all official purposes of the Union for which it was being used immediately before that day, and for the transaction of business in Parliament. The Official Languages Amendment Act, 1967, provides that bilingualism shall continue; central government officers will choose their medium for official business. Translations will be provided for them until they attain a working knowledge of Hindi.

The following 15 languages are included in the Eighth Schedule to the Constitution: Assamese, Bengali, Gujarati, Hindi, Kannada, Kashmiri, Malayalam, Marathi, Oriya, Punjabi, Sanskrit, Sindhi, Tamil, Telugu, Urdu.

The number of mother tongues (including 103 non-Indian languages) returned in 1961 Census was 1,652. Hindi or Urdu languages (including mother tongues grouped under each) are spoken by $30 \cdot 4\%$ and $5 \cdot 31\%$ of the population respectively.

Ferozsons English–Urdu, Urdu–English Dictionary. 2 vols. 4th ed. Lahore, 1961

Fallon, S. W., *A New English–Hindustani Dictionary.* Lahore, 1941

Grierson, Sir G. A., *Linguistic Survey of India.* 11 vols. (in 19 parts). Delhi, 1903–28

Mehta, B. N. and B. B., *Modern Gujarati–English Dictionary.* 2 vols. Baroda, 1925

Mitra, S. C., *Student's Bengali–English Dictionary.* 2nd ed. Calcutta, 1923

Scholberg, H. C., *Concise Grammar of the Hindi Language.* 3rd ed. London, 1955

University of Madras, *Tamil Lexicon.* 7 vols. Madras, 1924–39

Vyas, V. G., and Patel, S. G., *Standard English–Gujarati Dictionary.* 2 vols. Bombay, 1923

Government. *President of the Republic:* Neelam Sanjiva Reddy (sworn in Aug. 1977).

Vice-President: Mohammad Hidayatullah.

There is a Council of Ministers to aid and advise the President of the Republic in the exercise of his functions; this comprises Ministers who are members of the Cabinet, Ministers of State who are not members of the Cabinet and Deputy Ministers. A Minister who for any period of 6 consecutive months is not a member of either House of Parliament ceases to be a Minister at the expiration of that period. The Prime Minister is appointed by the President; other Ministers are appointed by the President on the Prime Minister's advice.

The salary of each Minister is Rs 27,000 per annum, and that of each Deputy Minister is Rs 21,000 per annum. Each Minister is entitled to the free use of a furnished residence throughout his term of office. At the administrative head of each Ministry is a Secretary of the Government.

Following was the composition of the Cabinet in March 1981:

Prime Minister, Defence, Atomic Energy, Science and Technology: Indira Ghandhi.

Industry and Finance: R. Venkataraman.
Home Affairs: Z. Singh.
Agriculture: R. B. Singh.
Law and Justice, Company Affairs: P. Shivshankar.
Education, Health and Family Welfare: B. Shankaranand.
External Affairs: P. V. Narasimha Rao.
Labour: T. Anjiah.
Parliamentary Affairs: B. Narain Singh.
Energy: A. B. A. Ghani Khan Chaudhury.
Shipping and Transport: A. P. Sharma.
Information, Supply and Rehabilitation: V. P. Sathe.
Commerce and Steel: P. Mukherjee.
Works and Housing: P. C. Sethi.
Communications: C. M. Stephens.
Petroleum and Chemicals: V. Patil.
Civil Supplies: V. C. Shukla.
Planning: N. D. Tewari
Railways: K. Pande.

There are also 11 Ministers of State.

Local Government. There were in 1971, 32 municipal corporations, 1,493 municipalities, 249 town area committees, 202 notified area committees and 62 cantonment boards. The municipal bodies have the care of the roads, water supply, drainage, sanitation, medical relief, vaccination and education. Their main sources of revenue are taxes on the annual rental value of land and buildings, octroi and terminal, vehicle and other taxes. The municipal councils enact their own bye-laws and frame their budgets, which in the case of municipal bodies other than corporations generally require the sanction of the State government. All municipal councils are elected on the principle of adult franchise.

For rural areas there is a 3-tier system of *panchayati raj* at village, block and district level, although the 3-tier structure may undergo some changes in State legislation to suit local conditions. All *panchayati raj* bodies are organically linked, and representation is given to special interests. Elected directly by and from among villagers, the *panchayats* are responsible for agricultural production, rural industries, medical relief, maternity and child welfare, common grazing grounds, village roads, tanks and wells, and maintenance of sanitation. In some places they also look after primary education, maintenance of village records and collection of land revenue. They have their own powers of taxation. There are some judicial *panchayats* or village courts.

Panchayati raj now cover all the States with the exception of Nagaland and Meghalaya, although Nagaland has area, range and tribal councils. They exist in all the Union Territories except Mizoram and Lakshadweep. In Pondicherry they have been created by declaring existing Municipal Communes to be Commune Panchayat Councils; this is a transition arrangement. In Arunachal Pradesh and Chandigarh the 3-tier system of *panchayati raj* has been introduced. In Jan. 1977 there were 221,727 village *panchayats* covering a population of 441·6m. In addition, there are 4,017 *panchayat samitis* (block level) and 262 *zila parishads* (district level). With most of the country covered by *panchayati raj*, the emphasis now is on consolidation and clarifying their role in rural development.

The powers and responsibilities of *panchayati raj* institutions are derived not only from State Legislatures, but also from the procedures—administrative and financial—laid down by the State governments to give effect to statutory provisions.

NAGARLOK (Municipal Affairs Quarterly). Quarterly. Institute of Public Administration. Delhi

Proceedings of the 13th Meeting of the Central Council of Local Self Government. Delhi, 1970
Report of the Committee on Budgetary Reforms in Municipal Administration. Delhi, 1974
State Machinery for Municipal Supervision. Institute of Public Administration. Delhi, 1970
Statistical Abstract of India. Annual. Delhi.
Khera, S. S., *District Administration in India*. London, 1964
Roy, N. C., *The Civil Service in India*. 2nd ed. Calcutta, 1960

DEFENCE. The Supreme Command of the Armed Forces vests in the President of the Indian Republic. Policy is decided at different levels by a number of committees, including the Political Affairs Committee presided over by the Prime Minister and the Defence Minister's Committee. Administrative and operational control rests in the respective Service Headquarters, under the control of the Ministry of Defence.

The Ministry of Defence is the central agency for formulating defence policy and for co-ordinating the work of the three services. Among the organizations directly administered by the Ministry are the Research and Development Organization, the Production Organization, the National Defence College, the National Cadet Corps and the Directorate-General of Armed Forces Medical Services.

The Research and Development Organization (headed by the Scientific Adviser to the Minister) has under it about 30 research establishments. The Production Organization controls 8 public-sector undertakings and 28 ordnance and 2 departmental factories; the total value of production in 1971–72 was estimated at Rs 352 crores.

The National Defence College, New Delhi, was established in 1960 on the pattern of the Imperial Defence College (UK): the 1-year course is for officers of the rank of brigadier or equivalent and for senior civil servants. The Defence Services Staff College, Wellington, trains officers of the three Services for higher command for staff appointments. There is an Armed Forces Medical College at Pune.

The National Defence Academy, Khadakvasla, gives a 3-year basic training course to officer cadets of the three Services prior to advanced training at the respective Service establishments.

Army. The Army Headquarters functioning directly under the Chief of the Army Staff is divided into the following main branches: General Staff Branch; Adjutant-General's Branch; Quartermaster-General's Branch; Master-General of Ordnance Branch; Engineer-in-Chief's Branch; Military Secretary's Branch.

The Army is organized into 4 commands—eastern, central, western and southern—each divided into areas, which in turn are subdivided into sub-areas.

Recruitment of permanent commissioned officers is through the Indian Military Academy, Dehra Dun. It conducts courses for ex-National Defence Academy, National Cadet Corps and direct-entry cadets, and for serving personnel and technical graduates.

The Territorial Army came into being in Sept. 1949, its role being to: (1) relieve the regular Army of static duties and, if required, support civil power; (2) provide anti-aircraft units, and (3) if and when called upon, provide units for the regular Army. The Territorial Army is composed of practically all arms of the Services.

The authorized strength of the Army is 944,000, that of the Territorial Army, 40,000. There are 2 armoured, 17 infantry and 10 mountain divisions, 5 independent armoured brigades, 1 independent infantry, 14 independent artillery brigades, 1 commando and 2 parachute brigades.

Mason, P., *A Matter of Honour*. London, 1974

Navy. Since 26 Jan. 1950 the former Royal Indian Navy, which traced its history in an unbroken line from the foundation in 1613 of the East India Company's Marine, has been known as 'Indian Navy', and the ships referred to as 'INS' instead of 'HMIS'. There are 3 commands: Eastern, Western and Southern.

Principal ships of the Indian Navy:

Completed	Name	Standard displacement Tons	Armour Belts in.	Turrets in.	Principal armament	Shaft horse-power	Speed Knots
		Aircraft Carrier					
1961	Vikrant (ex-Hercules)	16,000	—	—	15 40 mm. AA (22 aircraft)	40,000	24·5
		Cruisers [1]					
1940	Mysore (ex-Nigeria)	8,700	3–4½	2	9 6-in.; 8 4-in.	72,500	31·5

[1] The cruiser *Delhi* (ex-*Achilles*) completed in 1933, was scrapped in 1979.

The fleet also includes 8 *ex*-Soviet submarines, 6 new broad beam 'Leander' class general purpose frigates (built in India), 2 anti-submarine frigates and 3 anti-aircraft frigates (built in Great Britain), 1 old *ex*-British frigate, 12 Soviet-built escorts, 4 corvettes, 2 ocean minesweepers, 4 coastal minesweepers, 4 inshore minesweepers 16 missile boats, 4 patrol craft, 7 landing ships, 5 survey ships, a repair ship, a submarine parent ship, a submarine rescue ship, 6 oilers, 4 utility landing craft, 10 service craft and 3 tugs.

Three 'Kashin' class guided missile destroyers are being acquired from the USSR.

The major training establishments of the Navy include INS *Venduruthy* at Cochin (Basic and Divisional, Gunnery, Torpedo and Anti-Submarine, Navigation and Direction, Communication), INS *Vaisura* at Jamnagar (Electrical), INS *Shivaji* at Lonavla (Engineering), INS *Hansa* at Goa (Aviation), INS *Hamla* at Bombay (Supply and Secretariat) and INS *Circars* at Vishakhapatnam (Boys' Training).

The Fleet Requirement Unit of the Naval Aviation Station, INAS *Garuda*, is at Cochin. Some 100 aircraft include Sea Harriers, Sea Hawk fighters, Alizé anti-submarine aircraft and Sea King anti-submarine helicopters acquired for the aircraft carrier.

Naval personnel in 1981 comprised 46,000 officers and ratings, including the Naval Air Arm.

The Coast Guard was constituted as an independent para-military service by 1978 Act of Parliament. It comprises the frigates *Kirpan* and *Kuthar* and five patrol craft all transferred from the Indian Navy and 2 larger patrol vessels custom-built. It is to be augmented by new specifically built ships and aircraft, including 3 1,000-tonne offshore patrol vessels, 3 200-tonne inshore protection craft and 5 Defender aircraft. It is administered by a Director-General (retired Vice-admiral) and a Deputy Director-General (Commodore). It functions under the Defence Ministry but is funded by the Defence Department.

Air Force. The Indian Air Force Act was passed in 1932, and the first flight was formed in 1933.

The Air Headquarters, under the Chief of Air Staff, consists of 4 main branches, viz., Air Staff, Administration, Policy and Plans, and Maintenance. Units of the IAF are organized into 3 operational commands—Western at Delhi, Central at Allahabad, Eastern at Shillong—plus an operational group at Jodhpur administered directly by Air HQ. Training Command HQ is at Bangalore, Maintenance Command at Nagpur. Nominal strength in 1980 was about 113,000 personnel and 650 first-line combat aircraft in 34 squadrons, supported by 12 transport squadrons, 12 helicopter squadrons, training units and about 30 squadrons of 'Guideline' and 'Goa' surface-to-air missiles, supplemented by close-range missiles such as 'Gainful' and Tigercat.

Air defence units include 5 squadrons of Gnat fighters (being re-equipped progressively from Mk 1 Gnats to a Mk 2 version known as the Ajeet) and 14 squadrons of MiG-21s. Initial delivery of MiG-21s from the Soviet Union has been followed by large-scale licence production in India, with the new MiG-21bis version in current production. There are 4 squadrons of Sukhoi Su-7s, 4 of Canberras (3 bomber, 1 reconnaissance), 4 of Hunter F56s and 3 of Hindustan HF-24 Marut supersonic fighter-bombers. Jaguars are being acquired to re-equip Canberra bomber and Hunter squadrons. Those flying MiG-21s, HF-24s and Su-7s will receive MiG-23s; the reconnaissance squadron will re-equip with MiG-25s.

The large transport force includes An-12s, jet-boosted C-119Gs, C-47s, HS 748s, Caribou, Otters, 2 Boeing 737s, and smaller aircraft and helicopters for VIP and other duties. It will re-equip some squadrons with An-32s. Helicopter units have Mi-8s, Mi-4s, Chetaks (Aérospatiale Alouette IIIs) and licence-built Cheetahs (Aérospatiale Lamas); main training types are the Hindustan HT-2 and Kiran, Polish-built TS-11 Iskra, Hunter T.66, MiG-21UT1 and Su-7U.

Primary flying training is provided at the Elementary Flying School, Bidar, and advanced flying training at the Air Force Academy, Dundigal, Hyderabad. There is a Navigaton and Signals School at Begumpet. The IAF Technical College, Jalahalli, imparts technical training, while the IAF Administrative College, Coimbatore, trains officers of the ground duty branch. There are also land–air warfare, flying instructors' and medical schools.

INTERNATIONAL RELATIONS

Membership. India is a member of the UN, the Commonwealth and the Colombo Plan.

External Debt. At the end of financial year 1979–80 India's external public debt was Rs 12,178·42 crores.

Treaties. India pursues a general policy of non-alignment; the exception is a Treaty of Peace, Friendship and Co-operation with the USSR, 1971; the parties agreed to mutual support short of force in the event of either being attacked by a third party.

ECONOMY

Planning. The third 5-year plan ended in March 1966 and 3 annual plans, as periods of stabilization, led up to the beginning of the fourth plan in April 1969. The formal fifth plan document was placed before Parliament on 19 Dec. 1973. The fifth plan period was brought to an end with the close of the Annual Plan 1977–78. It stressed agriculture, mining and manufacturing industries and aimed at a $4\frac{1}{2}\%$ growth rate. Actual growth rates: 1975–76, 6%; 1976–77, 5·2%; 1977–78, 7·25%.

Outlay was set at Rs 66,353 crores, of which Rs 39,304 were for the public sector. Goals were an increase of 4·67% in agricultural production, 8·2% in mining and manufacturing, and 7·6% in exports.

Priority is given to increasing the income of the worst-off 30% of the population.

The sixth plan (1980/81–1984/85) involves an outlay of Rs 900,000m. in the public sector, and aims at a 5% annual growth rate.

Estimated net national product, 1977–78, Rs 732,000m.

Ministry of Agriculture. *Serving the Small Farmer: Policy Choices in Indian Agricultural Development.* 1975
Dutt, A. K. (ed.), *India: Resources, Potentialities and Planning.* Rev. ed. Dubuque, India, 1973
Singh, T., *India's Development Experience.* London, 1975

Budget. Revenue and expenditure (on revenue account) of the central government [1] for years ending 31 March, in crores of rupees:

	1976–77	1977–78	1978–79 [2]	1979–80 [2]	1980–81 [3]
Revenue	8,738·93	9,791·49	11,019·85	11,177·0	12,356·0
Expenditure	8,440·48	9,362·29	11,148·31	12,048·0	11,310·0

Under the Constitution (Part XII and 7th Schedule), the power to raise funds has been divided between the central government and the states. Generally, the sources of revenue are mutually exclusive. Certain taxes are levied by the Union for the sake of uniformity and distributed to the states. The Finance Commission (Art. 280 of the Constitution) advises the President on the distribution of the taxes which are distributable between the centre and the states, and on the principles on which grants should be made out of Union revenues to the states. The main sources of central revenue are: customs duties; those excise duties levied by the central government; corporation, income and wealth taxes; estate and succession duties on non-agricultural assets and property, and revenues from the railways and posts and telegraphs. The main heads of revenue in the states are: taxes and duties levied by the state governments (including land revenues and agricultural income tax); civil administration and civil works; state undertakings; taxes shared with the centre; and grants received from the centre.

[1] Excluding states' share of excise duties and other taxes.
[2] Revised.   [3] Budget estimates.

Important items of total (revenue and capital accounts) revenue and expenditure charged to revenue of the central government for 1980–81 (estimates), in Rs 1m.:

Revenue		Expenditure	
Net tax revenue	87,230	Development and planning	129,600
Non-tax revenue	34,060	Defence	36,000
Market loans, small savings etc.	39,000	Interest payments	25,980
External loans (IMF)	13,400		

Total capital account receipts, Rs 76,940m.; capital account disbursements, Rs 81,570m. Total (revenue and capital) receipts, Rs 200,500m.; disbursements, Rs 214, 570m.

Debt. At the end of the financial year 1977–78 the interest-bearing obligations of the Government of India were estimated to amount to Rs 25,850·22 crores, of which total obligations in India were Rs 16,733·73 crores.

Bhargava, R. N., *Indian Public Finance*. London, 1962
Cheliah, R. J., *Fiscal Policy in Underdeveloped Countries, with Special Reference to India*. London, 1960
Misra, B. R., *Indian Federal Finance*. Rev. ed. Bombay, 1960
National Council of Applied Economic Research, *Management of Public Debt in India*. New Delhi, 1965
Premchand, A., *Control of Public Expenditure in India*. New Delhi, 1963

Currency. A decimal system of coinage was introduced in 1957. The Indian *rupee* is divided into 100 *paise* (until 1964 officially described as *naye paise*), the decimal coins being 1, 2, 5, 10, 25 and 50 *paise* (or *naye paise*) and rupee.

On the devaluation of the £ in Nov. 1967, the £ became equivalent to Rs 18. Value (1979): £1 = Rs 16·1. The rupee is valued in relation to a package of main currencies.

The paper currency consists of: (1) Reserve Bank notes in denominations of Rs 2, 5, 10, 100, 1,000, 5,000 and 10,000; and (2) Government of India currency notes of denominations of Re 1 (issued in 1917), Rs 2½, 5, 10, 20, 50 and 100. Re 1 notes of a different type, issued since 1940, are deemed to be included in the expression 'rupee coin' for the purposes of the Reserve Bank of India Act, 1934. Bank and Government notes bearing the king's effigy and other earlier issues have ceased to be legal tender, 28 Oct. 1957, except at the issue department of the Reserve Bank, government treasuries and sub-treasuries, and agency branches of the State Bank of India and its subsidiaries.

According to the Reserve Bank of India, the total money supply with the public in May 1979 was Rs 223,980m.

100,000 rupees are called 1 lakh; 100 lakhs are called 1 crore. In March 1981 Rs 17·90 = £1; Rs 8·18 = US$1.

Sadeque, A., *Indian and Pakistan Currency*. Dacca, 1965

Banking. The Reserve Bank, the central bank for India, was established in 1934 and started functioning on 1 April 1935 as a shareholder's bank; it became a nationalized institution on 1 Jan. 1949. It has the sole right of issuing currency-notes. The Bank acts as adviser to the Government on financial problems and is the banker for central and state governments, commercial banks and some other financial institutions. The Bank manages the rupee public debt of central and state governments. It is the custodian of the country's exchange reserve and supervises repatriation of export proceeds and payments for imports. The Bank gives short-term loans to state governments and scheduled banks and short- and medium-term loans to state co-operative banks and industrial finance institutions. The Bank has extensive powers of regulation of the banking system, directly under the Banking Regulation Act, 1949, and indirectly by the use of variations in bank rate, variation in reserve ratios, selective credit controls and open market operations. Bank rate was raised to 9% in the financial year 1974–75. The statutory cash reserves were raised to the level of 6% from Nov. 1976 and as much as 10% of the incremental demand and time liabilities were impounded from 14 Jan. 1977. With a view to restricting to a minimum the commercial banks' use of Reserve Bank's credit facilities, the system of Net Liquidity Ratio, which regulated the cost of refinance from the Reserve Bank, was given up in Nov. 1975. Automatic recourse to borrowings from the Reserve Bank was severely cut, being limited to a basic quota equivalent to 1% of a bank's demand and time liabilities, and to a proportion of a bank's incremental lendings for public food procurement operations and for exports. All other recourse to Reserve Bank facilities, including rediscount of bills, was placed on a discretionary basis. The Bank provides short-term credit (for financing seasonal agricultural operations) to state co-operative banks at 2% below the Bank rate. The Bank also provides financial accommodation to State Co-operative Banks at the Bank rate for financing and industrial co-operative societies and industrial societies and units outside the co-operative sector. The net profit of the Reserve Bank of India for the year ended 30 June 1977 amounted to Rs 300 crores.

The commercial banking system consisted of 113 scheduled banks (*i.e.*, banks which are included in the 2nd schedule to the Reserve Bank Act) and 6 non-scheduled banks on 31 Dec. 1976; scheduled banks included 40 Regional Rural Banks. Total number of offices was 23,655. Total deposits in commercial banks, 31 Dec. 1976, stood at Rs 17,132 crores; in post office savings banks 31 March 1975 deposits were Rs 1,266 crores. The business of non-scheduled banks forms less than 1% of commercial bank business. Of the 113 scheduled banks, 14 are foreign banks which specialize in financing foreign trade but also compete for domestic business. The largest scheduled bank is the State Bank of India, constituted by nationalizing the Imperial Bank of India in 1955. The State Bank acts as the agent of the Reserve Bank and the subsidiaries of the State Bank act as the agents of the State Bank for transacting government business as well as undertaking commercial functions. Fourteen banks with aggregate deposits of not less than Rs 50 crores were nationalized on 19 July 1969. Public sector banks accounted for 85% of deposits and 86% of credit on 31 Dec. 1976. Six banks were nationalized in April 1980.

Reserve Bank of India: Report on Currency and Finance.—Report on the Trend and Progress of Banking in India.—Report of the Central Board of Directors. Annual. Bombay
Reserve Bank of India—Functions and Working. Reserve Bank of India, 1970

Weights and Measures. Uniform standards of weights and measures, based on the metric system, were established for the first time by the Standards of Weights and Measures Act, 1956, which provided for a transition period of 10 years. So far the system has been fully adopted in trade transactions but there are a few fields such as engineering, survey and land records and the building and construction industry where it has not; efforts are being made to complete the change as early as possible.

In order to align this legislation with the latest international trends an expert committee (Weights and Measures (Law Revision) Committee) was set up by the central government to suggest a revised Bill which was passed by Parliament in April 1976. The new Standards of Weights and Measures Act, 1976, has recognized the International System of Units and other units recommended by the General Conference on Weights and Measures and is in line with the recommendations of the International Organisation of Legal Metrology (OIML). The new Act also covers the system of numeration, the approval of models of weights and measures, regulation and control of inter-state trade in relation to weights and measures. The Act also protects consumers through proper indication of weight, quantity, identity, source, date and price on packaged goods. A (model) State Weights and Measures Bill has also been prepared by the committee for adoption by states on a uniform basis throughout the country and, in some states, has already been adopted.

The provisions of the Act came into force in Sept. 1977, as did the accompanying Standards of Weights and Measures (Packaged Commodities) Rules, 1977.

While the Standards of Weights and Measures are laid down in the Central Act, enforcement of weights and measures laws is the responsibility of the state governments; the central Directorate of Weights and Measures is responsible for co-ordinating activities so as to ensure national uniformity.

An Indian Institute of Legal Metrology trains officials of the Weights and Measures departments of India and different developing countries. The Institute is being modernized with technical assistance from the Federal Republic of Germany.

There are 2 Regional Reference Standards laboratories in the country which (besides calibrating secondary standards of physical measurements) also provide testing facilities in metrological and industrial measurements. These laboratories are equipped with Standards next in line to the National Standards of physical measurements which are maintained at the National Physical Laboratory in New Delhi.

For weights previously in legal use under the Standards of Weight Act, 1956, *see* THE STATESMAN'S YEAR-BOOK, 1961, p. 171.

Calendar. The dates of the Saka era (named after the north Indian dynasty of the first century A.D.) are being used alongside Gregorian dates in issues of the *Gazette of India*, news broadcasts by All-India Radio and government-issued calendars, from 22 March 1957, a date which corresponds with the first day of the year 1879 in the Saka era.

ENERGY AND NATURAL RESOURCES

Electricity. In Dec. 1979 41·8% of all villages had electricity. Total installed capacity (1980) was 31m. kw. Production of electricity was 103m. kwh. in 1979–80. There were 93 hydro-electric stations and 5 nuclear power stations. Hydro-electricity was in short supply in 1980 because of drought.

Oil and Gas. The Oil and Natural Gas Commission, Oil India Ltd and the Assam Oil Co. are the only producers of crude oil. Total production, 1979, about 12·8m. tonnes. The main fields are in Assam and offshore in the Gulf of Cambay (the Bombay High field). Natural gas production, 1979–80, 1,890m. cu. metres.

Water. The net area of 50m. hectares (1978) under irrigation exceeds that of any other country except China, and equals about 29% of the total area under cultivation. Irrigation projects have formed an important part of all three Five-Year Plans. The possibilities of diverting rivers into canals being nearly exhausted, the emphasis is now on damming the monsoon surplus flow and diverting that. Usable surface and groundwater resources were assessed (1972) at 870,000m. cu. metres. Utilization (1974) 337,000m. cu. metres. Irrigation plant in operation in 1976 could make use of 67m. hectare-metres of surface water and 26·5m. hectare-metres of ground water. Ultimate potential of irrigation is assessed at 107m. hectares, total cultivated land being 142m. hectares. In 1977 India and Bangladesh reached an agreement to share the water of the Ganges at the Farakka barrage: India needs this supply to supplement the Hooghly River in flushing silt from Calcutta port.

Minerals. Bihar, West Bengal and Madhya Pradesh produce 42%, 25% and 19% of all coal, respectively. The coal industry was nationalized in 1973; planned state investment 1976–86, Rs 4·0 crores. Production, 1979–80, 104m. tonnes; reserves (including lignite) are estimated at 83,050m. tonnes. Production of other minerals, 1979 (in 1,000 tonnes): Iron ore, 39,500; bauxite, 1,900; chromite 309; copper ore, 2,200; manganese ore, 1,800; gold, 2,636 kg. Other important minerals are lead, zinc, limestone, apatite and phosphorite, dolomite, magnesite and silver. Value of mineral production, 1979, Rs 18,366m. of which mineral fuels produced Rs 14,134m., metallic minerals Rs 2,058m. and non-metallic Rs 2,174m.

Agriculture. The chief industry of India has always been agriculture. About 70% of the people are dependent on the land for their living. In 1971 agriculture employed about 126m. people; in 1978 it provided about 40% of national income.

Agricultural commodities account for about 20% by value of Indian exports, while agricultural commodities, machinery and fertilizers account for about 25–30% of imports. Tea accounts for about 40% of agricultural exports.

An increase in food production of at least 2% per annum is necessary to keep pace with the rising population. There was no increase in foodgrain production in the first 3 years of the third Plan: 82·7m. tons in 1961–62, 78·4m. tons in 1962–63, 80·2m. tons in 1963–64; a rise to 89m. tons in 1964–65 and a severe setback because of the unprecedented drought in 1965–66, with a harvest of only 72·3m. tons.

The harvest by 1975 had risen to 99·8m. tonnes; in 1978 it was 126m. tonnes, in 1979, 130m. tonnes and 1980, 116m. tonnes.

The Indian Council of Agricultural Research, established in 1929 by the Government of India and registered as a Society under the Societies Registration Act, 1960 (21 of

1860), became a fully autonomous organization with effect from 1 April 1974. It is a National Apex Body to plan, undertake, promote and co-ordinate education and research in agriculture and animal husbandry and their application in practice.

The Council at present works through 22 Research Institutes, 2 Technological Research Laboratories and a Directorate of All India Soil and Land Use Survey, Universities (including Agricultural Universities) and other public and quasi-public research and educational bodies. It supports the establishment of at least 1 agricultural university in each of the states; it also supports research in agriculture, animal husbandry, fisheries and allied subjects through a national grid of All-India Co-ordinated Research Projects and a number of *ad-hoc* research schemes.

Land Tenure. There are three main systems of land tenure: *ryotwari* tenure, where the individual holders, usually peasant proprietors, are responsible for the payment of land revenues; *zamindari* tenure, where one or more persons own large estates and are responsible for payment (in this system there may be a number of intermediary holders); and *mahalwari* tenure, where village communities jointly hold an estate and are jointly and severally responsible for payment.

Agrarian reform, initiated in the first Five-Year Plan, being undertaken by the state governments includes: (1) The abolition of intermediaries under *zamindari* tenure. Formerly the *zamindari* system prevailed in about 43% of the country, but by 1958 it had been abolished, usually in favour of *ryotwari* tenure, in all except about 5%. The total amount payable in compensation had been estimated at Rs 570 crores, payable in cash in some states and in transferable bonds in others. (2) Tenancy legislation designed to scale down rents to $\frac{1}{4}-\frac{1}{5}$ of the value of the produce, to give permanent rights to tenants (subject to the landlord's right to resume a minimum holding for his personal cultivation), and to enable tenants to acquire ownership of their holdings (subject to the landlord's right of resumption for personal cultivation) on payment of compensation over a number of years. (3) Fixing of ceilings on existing holdings and on future acquisition following a census of land holdings. Based on the recommendations of the Central Land Reforms Committee made in July 1972, the Government of India decided to keep the holding of a family between 4·05 and 7·28 hectares if it has assured irrigation to produce two crops a year; a ceiling of 10·93 hectares for land with irrigation facilities for only one crop a year; and a ceiling of 21·85 hectares for all other categories of land. A family unit for the ceiling consists of husband, wife and 3 minor children. Additional land can be retained by large families subject to a maximum of twice the ceiling. Tea, coffee, cocoa and cardamom plantations have been exempted from the ceiling. Until Aug. 1973, 13 states had passed legislation to implement the ceiling law. (4) The consolidation of holdings in community project areas (45·3m. acres had been consolidated by 31 March 1965, mainly in the Punjab, Madhya Pradesh and Uttar Pradesh) and the prevention of fragmentation of holdings by reform of inheritance laws. (5) Promotion of farming by co-operative village management (*see* p. 620).

The average size of holding for the whole of India is 2·63 hectares. Andhra Pradesh, 2·87; Assam, 1·46; Bihar, 1·53; Gujarat, 4·49; Jammu and Kashmir, 1·43; Karnataka, 4·11; Kerala, 0·75; Madhya Pradesh, 3·99; Maharashtra, 4·65; Orissa, 1·98; Punjab, 3·85; Rajasthan, 5·5; Tamil Nadu, 1·49; Uttar Pradesh, 1·78; West Bengal, 1·56.

Of the total 71m. rural households possessing operational holdings, 34% hold on the average less than 0·20 hectare of land each.

The table on p. 618 shows, in 1,000 hectares, according to state and territories, the net area and the classification of areas of India that were in 1974 cultivated, and uncultivated, and the areas under forests and irrigation.

Agricultural production, 1977 (in 1,000 tonnes): Cardamom, an important cash crop supplying 70% of world consumption, 2·2; groundnuts, 5,262; rape seed and mustard, 1,562; sesame seed, 404; linseed, 431; cottonseed (1976), 2,100 (oil yield, 220); rice (1979–80), 48,400; wheat (1979–80), 32,000; total foodgrains (1979–80), 116,000; coffee, of which the main cash varieties are Arabica and Robusta (main growing areas Karnataka, Kerala and Tamil Nadu), 145 (1979); sugar cane (1979–80), 145,000; cotton (1978), 7·1m. bales (of 170 kg); jute is grown in West Bengal (half total yield), Bihar and Assam, yield per hectare about 1,370 kg, total yield, 1979–80, 8,000.

State or Territory	Geographical area	Reporting area	Permanent pasture and other grazing land	Area irrigated (net)	Area sown	Area cropped	Forests	Fallow land	Other uncultivated land
Andhra Pradesh	27,676	27,440	1,028	2,998	11,269	12,652	6,240	855	2,313
Assam	7,853	7,807	234	572	2,235	2,834	2,080	166	1,787
Bihar	17,388	17,330	173	2,384	8,276	10,683	2,797	903	1,080
Gujarat	19,598	18,562	1,019	1,209	9,322	9,933	1,634	392	4,200
Haryana	4,422	4,402	47	1,565	3,567	5,048	110	—	186
Himachal Pradesh	5,567	5,082	1,186	91	548	901	2,783	2	116
Jammu and Kashmir	22,224	4,523	133	264	706	861	2,776	11	244
Karnataka	19,177	18,943	1,592	1,373	10,331	10,988	2,895	644	861
Kerala	3,886	3,859	28	439	2,187	2,958	1,055	23	69
Madhya Pradesh	44,284	44,238	3,141	1,643	18,461	20,892	14,405	865	2,315
Maharashtra	30,776	30,747	1,666	1,344	16,575	17,481	5,417	1,473	1,802
Manipur	2,236	2,211	—	65	140	147	602	—	1,419
Meghalaya	2,248	2,248	—	37	162	193	187	—	1,900
Nagaland	1,653	1,351	725	12	62	63	266	—	1,023
Orissa	15,584	15,540	5	1,149	6,119	7,042	4,973	95	802
Punjab	5,036	5,031	1,805	2,955	4,076	5,724	127	—	198
Rajasthan	34,222	34,109	229	2,173	15,263	16,773	1,401	1,884	4,705
Tamil Nadu	13,007	13,004	34	2,710	6,348	7,642	2,007	540	805
Tripura	1,048	1,048	78	22	240	355	630	2	6
Uttar Pradesh	29,441	29,806		6,989	17,317	23,025	4,952	554	1,418
West Bengal	8,785	8,852		1,489	5,712	7,271	1,101	160	1,272
Andaman and Nicobar Islands	829	790	3	—	19	19	740	3	1
Arunachal Pradesh	8,358	6,353	—	23	115	130	5,154	118	37
Dadra and Nagar Haveli	49	49	4	—	23	24	21	—	—
Delhi	149	148	1	46	76	118	1	8	16
Goa, Daman and Diu	381	370	1	8	133	139	105	—	16
Lakshadweep	3	3	—	—	3	3	—	—	—
Mizoram	2,109	2,092	—	2	47	40	1,298	—	747
Pondicherry	48	47	—	26	32	55	—	—	—
	328,048	305,985	13,132	31,593	139,365	164,002	65,757	8,696	29,338

Figures are for 1973 with the following exceptions:

Assam, 1969–70. Gujarat, 1969–70. Jammu and Kashmir, 1970–71. Excludes Pakistan-occupied area. Manipur, estimates. Meghalaya (equivalent area) 1969–70. Nagaland (equivalent area) 1968–69. West Bengal, 1967–68, area cropped, estimate. Arunachal Pradesh (equivalent area) 1970–71. Mizoram (equivalent area) 1969–70. Goa, Daman and Diu, estimates.

The tea industry is important, with production concentrated in Assam, West Bengal, Tamil Nadu, Kerala and Karnataka. Total crop in 1979–80, about 560,000 tonnes from 364,000 hectares.

Production of natural rubber (1977) was 150,000 tonnes. Kerala produced about 93% of this.

Livestock (1979). Cattle, 181·8m.; sheep, 41m.; pigs, 9·9m.; horses, 760,000; asses, 1m.; goats, 71m.

There were 215,000 tractors in use in 1975.

Opium. By international agreement the poppy is cultivated under licence, and all raw opium is sold to the central government. Opium, other than for wholly medical use, is available only to registered addicts.

Fisheries. Total catch (1976) was 2·47m. tonnes, of which Kerala produced 355,000; Tamil Nadu, 510,000, and Maharashtra, 294,000. Of the total catch, 1,612,140 tonnes were marine fish. There were about 13,000 mechanized fishing boats, including trawlers, operating at the beginning of 1976.

Forestry. The lands under the control of the state forest departments are classified as 'reserved forests' (forests intended to be permanently maintained for the supply of timber, etc., or for the protection of water supply, etc.), 'protected forests' and 'unclassed' forest land.

In 1976 the total forest area was 74·6m. hectares, or 23% of the land area. Main types are teak (8·9m. hectares) and sal (11·6m.). Forests employed 13·6m. Forest revenue was Rs 1,322m. Production is low at 0·28 cu. metre per hectare per year (France, 3·9 cu. metres; Japan, 2·8 cu. metres; USA, 1·25 cu. metres). About 16% of the area is inaccessible, of which about 45% is potentially productive. Production, 1976, 22·8m. cu. metres, of which 13·7m. cu. metres are fuel wood. There are about 3,000 saw-mills. Outlay on forests for the Fifth Plan period is envisaged at about Rs 2,205m. as against Rs 930m. for the Fourth Plan. Distribution of plantations (1973–74):

Plantations of quick growing species (1,000 hectares)	510
Economic plantations of industrial and commercial uses (1,000 hectares)	850
Farm forestry (1,000 hectares)	80
Mixed plantations including fuel wood (1,000 hectares)	140
Communications (1,000 km)	45

INDUSTRY AND TRADE

Industries. The most important traditional industry, after agriculture, is the weaving of cotton cloth. Others are silk-rearing and weaving, shawl and carpet weaving, wood-carving and metal-working. Silk production, 1976, was 3m. kg of raw silk. In 1973 there were about 20m. people engaged in village industries, of whom about 5m. were in handloom industries.

Indian Government industrial policy aims to further a socialist pattern of society. Railways, air transport, armaments and atomic energy are government monopolies. In a number of industries (including the manufacture of iron and steel and mineral oils, shipbuilding and the mining of coal, iron and manganese ores, gypsum, gold and diamonds) new units are set up only by the state. In a further group of industries (road transport, manufacture of chemicals such as drugs, dyestuffs, plastics and fertilizers) the state established new undertakings, but private enterprise may develop either on its own or with state backing, which may take the form of loans or purchase of equity capital. Under the Industries (Development and Regulation) Act, 1951, as amended, industrial undertakings are required to be licensed; 162 industries are within the scope of the Act. The Government are authorized to examine the working of any undertaking, to issue directions to it and to take over its control if this be deemed necessary. A Central Advisory Council has been set up consisting of representatives of industry, labour, consumers and primary producers. There are 16 Development Councils for individual industries.

Foreign investment is encouraged by a tax holiday on income up to 6% of capital employed for 5 years. There are special depreciation allowances, and customs and excise concessions for export industries.

In the cotton industry production of yarn in 1977 was 98,100 tonnes and of cloth, 7,737m. metres (mill cloth accounts for about 58% of total production, the balance being produced by handloom and small industries). In 1976 there were about 900,000 workers in the mills and 10m. handloom weavers. There were about 700 mills with 19·5m. installed spindles and 207,750 looms. Capital investment was estimated at Rs 2,700m. and value of output at Rs 25,000m.

Oil refinery installed capacity, 1979, was 37m. tonnes; production of refined oils, 22·7m. tonnes. The Indian Oil Corporation was established in 1964 and had (1976–77) 64·6% of the market.

Industry, particularly steel, has suffered from a shortage of power and coal. There is expansion in petrochemicals, from the oil and associated gas of the Bombay High field, and gas from Bassein field. Small industries (initial outlay on capital equipment of less than Rs 2m.) are important; they employ about 7m. and produced (1980) goods worth Rs 209,000m.

Industrial production, 1977 (in 1,000 tonnes): Pig-iron and ferro-alloys, 10,010; crude steel, 8,660; finished steel, 6,880; aluminium, 208; smelted copper, 23; petroleum products, 21,900; sulphuric acid, 1,778; cement, 18,200; board and paper, 882; nitrogen fertilizer, 2,180 (1979); phosphate fertilizer, 770 (1979); jute goods, 1,040; rayon yarn, 127; diesel engines, 108,900 engines; electric motors, 3·6m. h.p.; refractories, 790; sugar, 4,810.

Labour. At the 1971 census there were 180·3m. workers, of whom 78m. were cultivators, 37·4m. agricultural labourers, 17m. in manufacturing, processing and servicing, 2·2m. in construction, 10m. in trade and commerce and 4·4m. in transport, communications and storage. There were 847 central unions registered and 19,865 state unions. In 1974, 62,833 manufacturing units (employing 10 or more persons with power, or 20 or more without power) employed 5·2m. people earning Rs 22,600m.; value added by manufacture, Rs 47,913m. Bond labour system was abolished in 1975. In the autumn of 1977 the number of unemployed was estimated at 40m. Man-days lost by industrial disputes, 1979, 37·10m., of which 6·66m. were in the public sector.

Dasgupta, A. K., *A Theory of Wage Policy*. OUP, 1976

Companies. The total number of companies limited by shares at work in India, 31 March 1979, was 51,051; aggregate paid-up capital was Rs 11,878·1 crores. There were 8,214 public limited companies with an aggregate paid-up capital of Rs 3,540·7 crores, and 42,837 private limited companies (Rs 8,337 crores). There were also 62 companies with unlimited liability.

During 1978–79, 3,488 new limited companies were registered in the Indian Union under the Companies Act 1956 with a total authorized capital of Rs 1,379·7 crores; 254 were public limited companies (Rs 105·5 crores) and 3,234 were private limited companies (Rs 229·2 crores). There were 15 private companies with unlimited liability, authorized capital Rs 0·42 crores. Of the new companies, 72 had an authorized capital of Rs 1 crore and above, and 75 of between Rs 50 lakhs and Rs 1 crore; 33 were government companies (*i.e.*, companies in which Government owns at least 51% of share capital). During 1978–79, 195 companies with an aggregate paid-up capital of Rs 9,13 lakhs went into liquidation and 188 companies (Rs 1,76 lakhs) were struck off the register.

On 31 March 1979 there were 782 government companies at work with a total paid-up capital of Rs 8,315·2 crores; 321 were public limited companies and 461 were private limited companies.

On 31 March 1979, 358 companies incorporated elsewhere were reported to have a place of business in India; of these 189 were of UK and 64 of USA origin.

Department of Company Affairs, Govt. of India. *Joint Stock Companies in India*. New Delhi

Co-operative Movement. in 1977 there were over 300,000 co-operative societies of all types with a membership of about 50m. In 1976 there were 25 state co-operative banks with share capital of Rs 63·46 lakhs and deposits of Rs 708·05 lakhs; loans advanced, Rs 2,359·36 lakhs. The central co-operative banks (including banking unions) numbered 345, total advances were Rs 1,239·6 crores, funds and deposits Rs 920·1 crores. Agricultural primary credit societies (which constitute the base of the co-operative credit structure of the country) 140,000, with a membership of 40m.; share capital of Rs 318·8 crores; loans advanced, Rs 980 crores, and deposits of Rs 112 crores. There were 19 central land development banks funding long-term improvements.

Following the recommendations (1954) of a committee appointed by the Reserve Bank of India, the co-operation movement was extended from its chief function of providing credit to include marketing, processing, warehousing, etc. In 1971–72 there were 142,597 non-credit societies including 3,654 primary marketing societies, 144 sugar factories, 1,341 agricultural processing societies, 9,605 farming societies, 12,273 primary weavers' societies, 33,736 other industrial societies; there were 13,278 primary consumers' stores.

In 1974 non-credit societies marketed agricultural produce worth Rs 809 crores, agricultural requisites worth Rs 614 crores and consumer goods worth Rs 536 crores. Co-operative sugar factories accounted for 40% of national output.

Indian Labour Guide. Monthly. Delhi
Co-operative Movement in India, Statistical Statements Relating to. Annual. Reserve Bank of India, Bombay
Das, N., *Industrial Enterprise in India.* 3rd ed. Bombay, 1961
Dube, R. N., *The Economic Geography of the Indian Republic.* Allahabad, 1954
Ghose, B. C., *Industrial Organization.* 2nd ed. OUP, 1959
Ghosh, A., *Indian Economy, its Nature and Problems.* 7th ed. Calcutta, 1963
Hough, E. M., *Co-operative Movement in India.* 4th ed. OUP, 1959
Karnik, V. B., *Indian Trade Unions.* 2nd ed. Bombay, 1966
Kust, M. J., *Foreign Enterprise in India.* Bombay, 1964
Neale, W. C., *Economic Change in Rural India.* Yale Univ. Press, 1962
Pant, S. C., *Indian Labour Problems.* Allahabad, 1965
Rangnekar, D. K., *Poverty and Capital Development in India.* OUP, 1958
Rao, R., *Surveys of Indian Industries.* 2 vols. OUP, 1957–58
Sharma, T. R., and Singh Chauhan, S. D., *Indian Industries.* 2nd ed. Agra, 1965
Sharma, V. S., *Sahayoga, or Indian Co-operation.* Hoshiarpur, 1964
Thorner, D., *Agricultural Co-operatives in India.* Bombay, 1964
Turner, R. (ed.), *India's Urban Future.* California Univ. Press, 1961
Venkatasubbiah H., *Indian Economy Since Independence.* 2nd ed. London, 1961

Commerce. The external trade of India (excluding land-borne trade with Tibet and Bhután) was as follows (in 1,000 rupees):

| | Imports | | Exports and Re-exports | |
	Merchandise [1]	Treasure	Merchandise	Treasure
1972–73	1,867,43,80	80,72	1,970,83,19	2,77
1973–74	2,955,36,92	69,12	2,523,39,98	1,39
1974–75	4,468,10,37	7,65	3,304,14,11	3,72
1975–76	5,264,77,87	7,40	4,036,25,87	4,32
1976–77	5,015,14,94	8,84 [2]	4,981,01,37	3,88 [2]
1977–78	6,026,01,24	—	5,363,18,33	—

[1] Excludes certain consignments of foodgrains and stores awaiting adjustment.
[2] Provisional.

The distribution of commerce by countries and areas was as follows in the year ended 31 March 1978 (in 1,000 rupees):

Countries	Exports to	Imports from	Countries	Exports to	Imports from
Afghánistán	29,27,69	21,39,80	German Dem.		
Argentina	2,43,00	27,92,18	Republic	34,10,95	34,28,01
Australia	82,54,69	71,95,65	Hungary	17,84,98	21,28,72
Belgium	202,21,37	157,67,70	Iran	116,58,96	548,43,92
Burma	8,52,81	2,71,50	Italy	100.52,34	86,98,32
Canada	44,77,26	81,18,14	Japan	504,73,90	427,27,64
Czechoslovakia	52,06,18	28,41,15	Kenya	28,74,26	4,25,78
Denmark	19,34,05	13,40,71	Malaysia	33,48,60	221,02,51
Federal Rep.			Nepál	58,58,76	16,61,11
of Germany	244,04,14	554,66,20	Netherlands	136,99,54	80,51,86
France	146,01,30	159,37,65	New Zealand	14,09,77	2,33,88

Countries	Exports to	Imports from	Countries	Exports to	Imports from
Poland	66,00,90	58,86,75	USSR	656,73,16	441,84,37
Saudi Arabia	123,53,20	247,76,67	UAR	71,67,63	14,03,47
Singapore	68,98,23	50,96,40	UK	522,22,21	464,77,67
Sri Lanka	54,30,80	2,27,09	USA	671,77,34	755,52,48
Sudan	35,56,53	52,56,38	Yemen	19,61,05	1,79
Sweden	21,31,32	57,73,86	Yugoslavia	63,42,03	26,42,78
Switzerland	53,26,64	67,58,31			

The value (in 1,000 rupees) of the leading articles of merchandise was as follows in the year ended 31 March 1978:

Exports	Value
Fish	170,92,33
Edible nuts and fresh fruits	163,60,76
Coffee	191,09,78
Tea and mate	555,31,69
Spices	137,02,21
Oilseed, oilnuts and oil kernels	4,40,14
Tobacco	117,24,38
Hides and skins, undressed	59,66
Wood (unworked)	13,59,59
Wool and other animal hair	1,62,03
Cotton, raw	3,81,08
Cottonwaste; shoddy	47,78
Stone, sand and gravel	10,58,84
Iron ore and concentrates	240,84,11
Iron and steel scrap	4,35,72
Ore and concentrates, non-ferrous base metals	22,90,11
Coal, coke and briquettes	12,08,75
Fixed vegetable oils	20,68,28
Leather	247,95,89
Textile yarn and thread	48,25,19
Textile fabrics (woven) except cotton and man-made fibre	152,95,17
Cotton fabrics, woven	233,64,10
Man-made fibre fabrics, woven	26,81,01
Floor coverings, tapestries, except cotton and jute	103,14,08
Manufactures of leather or artificial leather	18,90,78

Imports	
Milk and cream	24,34,56
Wheat, spelt and meslin	93,57,97
Rice	3,17,66
Edible nuts and fresh fruit	46,92,06
Pulp and waste paper	21,24,25
Wool and other animal hair	30,03,86
Cotton, raw	198,86,57
Jute	22
Vegetable fibres except cotton and jute	2,06,32
Crude fertilizers	40,58,43
Sulphur and unroasted iron pyrites	39,24,47
Petroleum, crude and partly refined	1,235,11,17
Petroleum products	320,46,86
Animal oils and fats	24,64,83
Fixed vegetable oils	711,60,69
Organic chemicals	124,63,70
Medical and pharmaceutical products	63,57,11
Manufactured fertilizers	258,19,39
Plastic materials	66,05,63
Chemical materials and products, n.e.s.	40,72,70
Paper, paperboard and manufactures	81,69,30
Pearls, precious and semi-precious stones	330,65,91
Iron and steel bars, angles, shapes, sections	34,34,89
Iron and steel universals, plates and sheets	125,62,53
Iron and steel tubes, pipes, fittings	75,14,04
Copper	51,20,59
Zinc	41,39,65
Tin	28,55,53

Imports	Value
Machinery other than electrical	682,93,81
Electrical machinery	183,14,39
Transport equipment	232,04,87

Total trade between India and UK (British Department of Trade returns, in £1,000 sterling):

	1975	1976	1977	1978	1979	1980
Imports to UK	237,136	855,074	383,462	322,056	365,843	315,858
Exports and re-exports from UK	164,535	206,918	278,098	348,639	455,606	529,007

Annual Statement of the Foreign Trade of India. 2 vols. Calcutta
Monthly Statistics of the Foreign Trade of India. Calcutta
Review of the Trade of India. Annual. Delhi
India—Handbook of Commercial Information. 3 vols. Calcutta
Guide to Official Statistics of Trade, Shipping, Customs and Excise Revenue of India. Rev. ed. Calcutta

Tourism. There were 465,275 visitors to India in 1975. They spent the equivalent of US$124m.

COMMUNICATIONS

Roads. In 1976 there were about 1,367,000 km of roads, of which 538,000 km were metalled. Roads are divided into 5 main administrative classes, namely, national highways, state highways, major district roads, district roads and village roads. The national highways (29,016 km in 1976) connect capitals of states, major ports and foreign highways. The national highway system is linked with the ESCAP (Economic and Social Commission for Asia and the Pacific) international highway system. The state highways are the main trunk roads of the states, while the major district roads connect subsidiary areas of production and markets with distribution centres, and form the main link between headquarters and neighbouring districts.

There were (31 March 1976) 2,635,000 motor vehicles in India, comprising 690,000 private cars and jeeps, 1,032,000 motor cycles and auto-rickshaws, 182,000 public service vehicles, 359,000 goods vehicles.

Railways. The Indian railway system is government-owned and (under the control of the Railway Board) is divided into 9 zones, with route-km as follows at 31 March 1977:

Zone	Headquarters	Route-km
Central	Bombay	5,900
Eastern	Calcutta	4,230
Northern	Delhi	10,686
North Eastern	Gorakhpur	5,036
North East Frontier	Gauhati	3,628
Southern	Madras	7,449
South Central	Secunderabad	6,160
South Eastern	Calcutta	6,989
Western	Bombay	10,153

Passengers carried in 1975–76 were approximately 2,946m. (1963–64, 1,892·6m.); freight, 223·3m. (192·3m.) tonnes; this includes freight carried for railway purposes. Railway staff on 31 March 1973 numbered 1·43m. Total route, 31 March 1976: 60,231 km, of which 4,649 km are electrified.

Indian Railways pay to the central government a fixed dividend of $4\frac{1}{2}\%$ on capital-at-charge.

Financial years	Gross traffic receipts (Rs crores)	Working expenses (Rs crores)	Net revenues (Rs crores)	Net surplus or deficit (Rs crores)
1979–80 [1]	2,354·44	2,100·57	253·87	− 42·10
1980–81 [2]	2,749·59	2,384·64	364·95	+ 42·71

[1] Revised estimate. [2] Budget.

Prasad, A., *Indian Railways.* Bombay and London, 1960
Saxena, K. K., *Indian Railways.* Bombay, 1962

Aviation. The air transport industry in India was nationalized in 1953 with the formation of two Air Corporations: Air India for operating long-distance international air services, and Indian Airlines for operating air services within India and to adjacent countries. A third airline, Air Messenger, was established in 1981 to serve country towns in the north-east. Air India has 7 Boeing 747s and 9 707s; it operates daily to New York *via* London with halts in the Middle East and Europe, 11 flights a week to London with halts in the Middle East and 2 flights per week to London *via* Moscow. Other scheduled flights are made to Perth and Sydney, Kuala Lumpur, Singapore, Tōkyō, Osaka, Bangkok and Hong Kong, Nairobi, Dar es Salaam, Aden and Addis Ababa, Lagos and Accra, Kuwait, Cairo, Baghdad, Mauritius, Seychelles, Dhahran, Jeddah, Bahrain, Doha, Abu Dhabi, Dubai and Muscat. A fleet of 43 aircraft consisting of Airbus A-300, Caravelle, Viscount, Boeing 737, F-27 and HS-748 aircraft are flown by Indian Airlines on 192 flights covering 43,632 route-km.

In 1978 Indian aircraft flew 79·8m. km, carrying about 6·03m. passengers and 104,636 tonnes of cargo and mail. At 31 Oct. 1979, there were 674 aircraft with certificates of registration and 260 with certificates of airworthiness.

The Civil Aviation Department maintains and operates 85 aerodromes. The management of the 4 international airports at Bombay (Santa Cruz), Calcutta (Dum Dum), Delhi (Palam) and Madras is vested in the International Airports Authority of India.

Shipping. In March 1980, 375 ships totalling 5,544,336 GRT were on the Indian Register; of these, 56 ships of 249,205 GRT were engaged in coastal trade, and 319 ships of 5,295,131 GRT in overseas trade. Traffic of major ports, 1978–79, was as follows:

Port	Ships entered	Imports (1m. tonnes)	Exports (1m. tonnes)
Calcutta	938	5·27	2·71
Bombay	2,915	12·09	4·41
Madras	1,049	5·28	4·30
Cochin	994	4·23	1·24
Marmagoa	458	0·87	9·93
Vishakhapatnam	492	3·14	6·90
Kandla	410	5·40	0·47
Paradip	130	0·18	1·98
New Mangalore	285	0·67	0·20
New Tuticorin	190	0·68	0·36
	7,861	37·81	32·50

The shipyard at Vishakhapatnam is capable of building vessels of a maximum of 21,600 DWT. Present capacity is about 57,240 DWT per year. The Cochin Shipyard can build Panamax type bulk carriers of 85,000 DWT each. On full development the capacity of the shipyard will be 2 such ships a year. Garden Reach Shipbuilders and Engineers are building bulk carriers of 26,000 DWT each while the Mazagoan Dock at Bombay has developed capacity to build ships up to 27,000 DWT each. There are about 19,811 km navigable inland waterways, of which 16,180 km are rivers and 3,631 km canals.

Post and Broadcasting. On 31 March 1978 there were 125,283 post offices and 22,876 telegraph offices (including 3,102 licensed offices, 19,440 combined offices and 334 DTOs). Of the post offices, 112,077 were rural and 13,206 urban.

The telephone system is in the hands of the Indian Posts and Telegraphs Department. On 31 March 1978 there were 6,238 departmental exchanges with 2,247,187 telephones. There were 101 telex exchanges and 14,599 subscribers.

There were (1978) 82 radio stations and 2 auxiliary centres; on 31 Dec. 1976, 17,359,710 receiver licences were in force and programmes were sent out from 155 transmitters. 'Home Service' broadcasts reach 87·75% of the population. The television service was started at Delhi, 15 Sept. 1959. There were (1974) 275,424 television receiver licences. There were 7 television centres and a relay station at Pune. Entertainment films occupy 29·3% of broadcasting time, news and current affairs, 21·3%.

Cinemas. In 1976 there were 9,017 cinemas, including about 2,660 touring cinemas: about 500 feature films were produced.

Newspapers. In Dec. 1976 the total number of newspapers and periodicals was 13,320. Maharashtra published 1,948; 4,220 papers were published in Delhi,

Bombay, Calcutta and Madras. There were 875 daily and 3,801 weekly papers. Papers in 6 principal languages included 2,765 English papers with a circulation of 7,828,000; 3,289 Hindi, 7,738,000. About 115 papers claimed a circulation of over 50,000 copies; most had under 15,000. Total circulation, 34m.

Annual Report of the Register of Newspapers for India. New Delhi
Natarajan, S., History of the Press in India. London, 1962

JUSTICE, RELIGION, EDUCATION AND WELFARE

Justice. All courts form a single hierarchy, with the Supreme Court at the head, which constitutes the highest court of appeal. Immediately below it are the high courts and subordinate courts in each state. Every court in this chain, subject to the usual pecuniary and local limits, administers the whole law of the country, whether made by Parliament or by the state legislatures.

The states of Andhra Pradesh, Assam (in common with Nagaland, Meghalaya, Manipur and Tripura and the Union territories of Arunachal Pradesh and Mizoram), Bihar, Gujarat, Himachal Pradesh, Jammu and Kashmir, Karnataka, Kerala, Madhya Pradesh, Maharashtra, Orissa, Punjab (in common with the state of Haryana and the Union Territory of Chandigarh), Rajasthan, Tamil Nadu, Uttar Pradesh, West Bengal and Sikkim have each a High Court. There is a Court of Judicial Commissioners, which is in status equivalent to a High Court, in the Union Territory of Goa. There is a separate High Court for Delhi. For the Andaman and Nicobar Islands the Calcutta High Court, for Pondicherry the High Court of Madras, and for Lakshadweep the High Court of Kerala are the highest judicial authorities; in Dadra and Nagar Haveli the High Court of Bombay is the highest judicial authority. The Allahabad High Court has a Bench at Lucknow, the Bombay High Court has a Bench at Nagpur, the Madhya Pradesh High Court has Benches at Gwalior and Indore, the Patna High Court has a Bench at Ranchi and the Rajasthan High Court has a Bench at Jaipur. Judges and Division Courts of the Gauhati High Court also sit in Meghalaya, Manipur, Nagaland and Tripura. Below the High Court each state is divided into a number of districts under the jurisdiction of district judges who preside over civil courts and courts of sessions. There are a number of judicial authorities subordinate to the district civil courts. On the criminal side magistrates of various classes act under the overall supervision of the High Court.

The Code of Criminal Procedure, 1898, has been replaced by the Code of Criminal Procedure, 1973 (2 of 1974), which came into force with effect from 1 April 1974. The new Code provides for complete separation of the Judiciary from the Executive throughout India.

Police. The states control their own police force through the state Home Ministers. The Home Minister of the central government co-ordinates the work of the states and controls the Central Detective Training School, the Central Forensic Laboratory, the Central Fingerprint Laboratory as well as the National Police Academy at Mount Abu (Rajasthan) where the Indian Police Service is trained. This service is recruited by competitive examination of university graduates and provides all senior officers for the state police forces. The Central Bureau of Investigation functions under the control of the Cabinet Secretariat.

The cities of Pune, Ahmedabad, Nagpur, Bangalore, Calcutta, Madras, Bombay and Hyderabad have separate police commissionerates.

Total sanctioned strength of police was 706,895 in 1971.

Sarkar, P. C., Civil Laws of India and Pakistan. 2 vols. Calcutta, 1953.—Criminal Laws of India and Pakistan. 2nd ed. 2 vols. Calcutta, 1956
Setalvad, M. C., The Common Law of India. London, 1960
Sharma, S. R., Supreme Court in the Indian Constitution. Delhi, 1959

Religion. The principal religions in 1971 (census) were: Hindus, 453·2m. (82·7%); Moslems, 61·4m. (11·21%); Christians, 14·2m. (2·6%); Sikhs, 10·3m. (1·89%); Buddhists, 3·8m. (0·7%); Jains, 2·6m. (0·47%).

In 1971 the Christian population consisted of 8·2m. Roman Catholics, 2·69m. Anglicans of the Church of South India, 1·37m. Anglicans of the Church of North India and about 2m. nonconformists

Sundkler, B., *Church of South India*. London, 1954

Education. *Literacy.* According to the 1971 census the literacy percentage in the country (excluding age-group, 0–4) was 34·45 (28·3 in 1961): 45·95% among males, 21·97% among females. Of the states and territories, Chandigarh (70·43%) and Kerala (69·75%) respectively have the highest rates.

Educational Organization. With some exceptions, education is the concurrent responsibility of state and Union governments. In the union territories it is the responsibility of the central government. The Union Government is directly responsible for the central universities and all institutions declared by parliament to be of national importance; the promotion of Hindi as the federal language; co-ordinating and maintaining standards in higher education, research, science and technology. Professional education rests with the Ministry or Department concerned, *e.g.*, medical education, the Ministry or Department of Health. The Union Minister of Education is in overall charge of the separate Departments of Education and Culture, assisted by a Minister of State. There are several autonomous organizations attached to the Department of Education. The Central Advisory Board of Education meets periodically (in average intervals of 1 year) to recommend directions for educational policy. The University Grants Commission is a statutory body and is responsible for the funding of the central universities and some institutions deemed to be universities, besides providing developmental assistance to the state universities as well. The Commission also influences the policies and the course curricula of the universities. The National Council of Educational Research and Training provides advisory and consultancy services in respect of school education, and also produces standard school textbooks which can be used all over the country. The Union Ministry of Education is also concerned with non-formal education, youth activities, promotion of regional languages, sports, the institution of scholarships, the award of foreign scholarships, liaison with Unesco and its organizations and promoting book production.

School Education. The school system in India can be divided into four stages: pre-primary, primary, middle and high or higher secondary.

There are as yet not many pre-primary schools in India.

Primary education is imparted either at independent primary (or junior basic) schools or primary classes attached to middle or high schools. The period of instruction in this stage varies from 4 to 5 years and the medium of instruction is the mother tongue of the child or the regional language. Free education is available for all children. Legislation for compulsory education has been passed by 16 state governments and 3 Union Territories but it is not practicable to enforce compulsion and attendance is more often ensured by incentive.

The period for the middle stage varies from 2 to 3 years and instruction is given in middle classes of high schools or middle schools, the latter having, generally, primary classes attached to them.

The high-school education extends from 2 to 4 years. Education is given in higher classes of high schools, which have middle or primary (or both) departments attached. English is generally taught as a compulsory subject. The medium of instruction is mostly the mother tongue or the regional language.

The eventual pattern is to be 10 years general school education and 2 years high secondary education with diversified courses.

There are, in addition, schools for professional subjects such as agriculture, commerce, fine arts, forestry, medicine, veterinary science, physical education, social service, teachers' training, technical, industrial and crafts subjects. There are also special schools for the physically and mentally handicapped and reformatory pupils. There are schools of oriental studies and adult education centres.

Higher Education. Higher education is given in arts, science or professional colleges, universities and all-India educational or research institutions. In 1979 there were 108 universities, 9 institutions of national importance and 10 institutions deemed as universities. Of the 108 universities, 7 are central: Aligarh Muslim University; Banaras Hindu University; University of Delhi; University of Hyderabad; Jawaharlal Nehru University; North Eastern Hill University; Visva Bharati. The rest are state universities.

Grants are paid through the University Grants Commission to the central universities and institutions deemed to be universities for their maintenance and development and to state universities for their development projects only; their maintenance is the concern of state governments. During 1978–79 the University Grants Commission sanctioned grants of Rs 68·95 crores.

Technical Education. The number of institutions awarding degrees in engineering and technology in 1979–80 was 149 (in 1947: 38), and those awarding diplomas in engineering and technology numbered 306 (in 1947: 53); the former admitted about 28,000, the latter about 47,500 students; enrolment in some has been less than capacity, following a period of unemployment in engineering. There were also 7 rural institutes and 30 Girls' Polytechnics with about 455 and 4,090 students respectively. For training high-level engineers and technologists 5 Institutes of Technology, the Indian Institute of Science, Bangalore, and 89 other institutions conduct postgraduate and research courses.

Adult Education. In spite of the improvement in the literacy rate, the number of adult illiterates over 14 was 210m. in 1971. Adult education is, therefore, being accorded a high priority. A National Adult Education Programme was launched on a massive scale throughout the country on 2 Oct. 1978. A provision of Rs 200 crores has been made for this programme in the Plan 1978–83. It is proposed to cover 100m. illiterate persons in the age-group 15–35. A National Board of Adult Education has been established for this purpose by the central government and similar boards have been established at the state level also. The Directorate of Adult Education, established in 1971, co-ordinates the programme with various states and is also responsible for producing teaching/learning materials, training and orientation, monitoring and evaluating the programme. Existing programmes include the rural functional literacy project, adult education programmes for urban workers, assistance to voluntary agencies working in the field of adult education. About 116,000 programmes were running in Jan. 1980.

Educational statistics for the year 1978–79:

Type of recognized institution	No. of institutions	No. of students on rolls	No. of teachers
Primary/junior basic schools	474,993	51,383,299	1,276,446
Middle/senior basic schools	110,902	26,671,872	821,600
High/higher secondary schools	46,859	19,552,903	759,663
Training schools and colleges	496	170,018[1]	—
Arts, Science and Commerce colleges	3,261	2,299,053[2]	—

[1] Enrolment by stages of teachers' training courses at school and college level.
[2] Enrolment by stages of all post-graduate and graduate courses.

Primary pupils represent 84·5% of the age-group 6–11; middle school pupils, 38·0% of 11s–14s; high school pupils, 18·8% of 14s–17s.

Expenditure (on recognized institutions) during the Sixth Plan (1980–85) is estimated at Rs 1,986 crores.

University Development in India: A Statistical Report, 1961–62. New Delhi, 1962
Mudaliar, A. L., *Education in India.* London, 1960
Rawat, P. L., *History of Indian Education.* 4th ed. Agra, 1965
Vakil, K. S., and Natarajan, S., *Education in India.* 3rd ed. Bombay, 1966

Health. Health programmes are primarily the responsibility of the state governments. The Union Government has sponsored and supported major schemes for disease prevention and control which are implemented nationally. These include the prevention and control of malaria, filaria, tuberculosis, leprosy, venereal diseases, smallpox, trachoma and cancer. There are also Union Government schemes in connexion with water supply and sanitation, and with nutrition. The Nutrition Advisory Committee of the Indian Council of Medical Research sponsors schemes for research and advises the Government. The National Nutrition Advisory Committee is to formulate a national nutrition policy and recommend measures for improving national standards.

Medical relief and service is primarily the responsibility of the states. In 1977 there were 5,372 primary health centres and 37,745 sub-centres. In 1975 there was 1 doctor to every 4,200 people. Medical education is also a state responsibility, but there is a co-ordinating Central Health Educational Bureau. In 1977 there were 106 medical colleges and 74 colleges for homeopathic medicine. There were 601 nursing schools. In 1977 there were 38 mental hospitals and 51 institutions for the mentally handicapped and retarded; there were 600 TB clinics.

Family planning is centrally sponsored and locally implemented. The goal is to reduce the birth-rate by means of education in family planning methods.

Health expenditure under the fifth development plan was Rs 681·66 crores, of which the greatest single item was the control of communicable diseases.

Social Security. Annual plan expenditure (estimate) 1977–78, Rs 1,286·65 lakhs: services for children in need of care, Rs 210 lakhs; assistance to voluntary organizations, Rs 375 lakhs; integrated child development services, Rs 107 lakhs; hostels for working women, Rs 161·5 lakhs; education for employment and vocational training for adult women, Rs 80 lakhs; national institute for the handicapped, Rs 65 lakhs; functional literacy, Rs 57·5 lakhs.

DIPLOMATIC REPRESENTATIVES

OF INDIA IN GREAT BRITAIN (India House, Aldwych, London, WC2 4NA)
High Commissioner: Dr V. A. Seyid Mohammed.

OF GREAT BRITAIN IN INDIA (Chanakyapuri, New Delhi 21, 1100–21)
High Commissioner: Sir John Thomson, KCMG.

OF INDIA IN THE USA (2107 Massachusetts Ave., NW, Washington, D.C., 20008)

Ambassador: K. R. Narayanan.

OF THE USA IN INDIA (Shanti Path, Chanakyapuri, New Delhi 21)

Ambassador: Robert F. Goheen.

OF INDIA TO THE UNITED NATIONS

Ambassador: Brajesh Chandra Mishra.

Books of Reference

Special works relating to States are shown under their separate headings.

The Gazetteer of India. Central Gazetteers Unit. Delhi, 1965
India: A Reference Annual. Delhi Govt. Printer. Annual
Cambridge History of India. 6 vols. CUP, 1922–47. Supp., 1953
The Times of India Directory and Yearbook. Bombay and London. Annual
Handbook for Travellers in India, Pakistan, Burma and Ceylon. 19th ed. by L. F. Rushbrook Williams. London, 1962
Bhatia, K., *Indira: A Biography of Prime Minister Gandhi.* New York, 1974
Cassen, R. H., *India: Population, Economy and Society.* London, 1978
Chatterjee, S. P., *Indian Climatology.* Calcutta, 1956.—(ed.), *National Atlas of India* (*Preliminary* [Hindi] *edition*). Calcutta, 1957
Desai, A. R., *The Social Background of Indian Nationalism.* Bombay, 1954
Frankel, F., *India's Political Economy 1947–77.* Princeton Univ. Press, 1978
Griffiths, P. J., *The British Impact on India.* London, 1952
Hanson, A. H., and Douglas, J., *India's Democracy.* London, 1972
Jones, W. M., *Politics Mainly Indian.* New Delhi, 1978
Kesavan, B. S., and Kulkarni, V. Y. (eds), *The National Bibliography of Indian Literature, 1901–53,* New Delhi, 1963 ff.
Lipton, M., and Firn, J., *The Erosion of a Relationship: India and Britain Since 1960.* OUP, 1975
Majumdar, R. C., Raychandhuri, H. C., and Datta, K., *An Advanced History of India.* 2nd ed. London, 1950
Mitra, H. N., *The Indian Annual Register.* Calcutta, from 1953
Moraes, D., *Mrs. Gandhi.* London, 1980
Nanda, B. R. (ed.), *Socialism in India.* Delhi, Bombay, Bangalore, Kanpur, London, 1972

Pachauri, R. K., *Energy and Economic Development in India*. New York, 1977
Philips, C. H. (ed.), *The Evolution of India and Pakistan: Select Documents*. OUP, 1962 ff.—
Politics and Society in India. London, 1963
Platt, R. (ed.), *India: A Compendium*. New York, 1962
Poplai, S. L. (ed.), *India, 1947–50* [select documents]. 2 vols. Bombay and London, 1959
Smith, V. E., *Oxford History of India*. 3rd ed. OUP, 1958
Spear, P., *India: A Modern History*. 2nd ed. Univ. of Michigan Press, 1972
Sukhwal, B. L., *India: A Political Geography*. Bombay and New Delhi, 1971
Sutton, S. C., *Guide to the India Office Library [founded in 1801]*. HMSO, 1952
Yasdani, C. (ed.), *Early History of the Deccan*. 2 vols. London, 1960

STATES AND TERRITORIES

The Republic of India is composed of the following 22 States and 9 centrally administered Union Territories:

States	Capital	States	Capital
Andhra Pradesh	Hyderabad	Manipur	Imphal
Assam	Dispur	Meghalaya	Shillong
Bihar	Patna	Nagaland	Kohima
Gujarat	Ahmedabad	Orissa	Bhubaneswar
Haryana	Chandigarh	Punjab	Chandigarh
Himachal Pradesh	Simla	Rajasthan	Jaipur
Jammu and Kashmir	Srinagar	Sikkim	Gangtok
Karnataka	Bangalore	Tamil Nadu	Madras
Kerala	Trivandrum	Tripura	Agartala
Madhya Pradesh	Bhopal	Uttar Pradesh	Lucknow
Maharashtra	Bombay	West Bengal	Calcutta

Union Territories

Andaman and Nicobar Islands; Arunachal Pradesh; Chandigarh; Dadra and Nagar Haveli; Delhi; Goa, Daman and Diu; Lakshadweep; Mizoram; Pondicherry.

States Reorganization. The Constitution, which came into force on 26 Jan. 1950, provided for 9 Part A States (Assam, Bihar, Bombay, Madhya Pradesh, Madras, Orissa, Punjab, Uttar Pradesh and West Bengal) which corresponded to the previous governors' provinces; 8 Part B States (Hyderabad, Jammu and Kashmir, Madhya Bharat, Mysore, Patalia–East Punjab (PEPSU), Rajasthan, Saurashtra and Travancore–Cochin) which corresponded to Indian states or unions of states; 10 Part C States (Ajmer, Bhopal, Bilaspur, Coorg, Delhi, Himachal Pradesh, Kutch, Manipur, Tripura and Vindhya Pradesh) which corresponded to the chief commissioners' provinces; and Part D Territories and other areas (*e.g.*, Andaman and Nicobar Islands). Part A States (under governors) and Part B States (under rajpramukhs) had provincial autonomy with a ministry and elected assembly. Part C States (under chief commissioners) were the direct responsibility of the Union Government, although Kutch, Manipur and Tripura had legislatures with limited powers. Andhra was formed as a Part A State on its separation from Madras in 1953. Bilaspur was merged with Himachal Pradesh in 1954.

The States Reorganization Act, 1956, abolished the distinction between Parts A, B and C States and established two categories for the units of the Indian Union to be called States and Territories. The following were the main territorial changes: the Telugu districts of Hyderabad were merged with Andhra; Mysore absorbed the whole Kannada-speaking area (including Coorg, the greater part of 4 districts of Bombay, 3 districts of Hyderabad and 1 district of Madras); Bhopal, Vindhya Pradesh and Madhya Bharat were merged with Madhya Pradesh, which ceded 8 Marathi-speaking districts to Bombay; the new state of Kerala, comprising the majority of Malayalam-speaking peoples, was formed from Travancore–Cochin with a small area from Madras; Patalia–East Punjab was included in Punjab; Kutch and Saurashtra in Bombay; and Ajmer in Rajasthan; Hyderabad ceased to exist.

On 1 May 1960 Bombay State was divided into two parts: 17 districts (including Saurashtra and Kutch) in the north and west became the new state of Gujarat; the remainder was renamed the state of Maharashtra.

In Aug. 1961 the former Portuguese territories of Dadra and Nagar Haveli became a Union territory. The Portuguese territory of Goa and the smaller territories of Daman and Diu, occupied by India in Dec. 1961, were constituted a Union territory in March 1962. In Aug. 1962 the former French territories of Pondicherry, Karikal, Mahé and Yanaon were formally transferred to India and became a Union territory. In Sept. 1962 the Naga Hills Tuensang Area was constituted a separate state under the name of Nagaland. On 1 Nov. 1966, under the Punjab Reorganization Act 1966, a new state of Haryana and a new Union Territory of Chandigarh were created from parts of Punjab (India); for details, *see* pp. 637 and 668. On 26 Jan. 1971 Himachal Pradesh became a state. In 1972 the North East Frontier Agency and Mizo hill district were made Union territories (as Arunachal Pradesh and Mizoram) and Manipur, Meghalaya and Tripura full states. Sikkim became a state in 1975.

Report of the States Reorganization Commission. Government of India. Delhi, 1956
Menon, V. P., *The Story of the Integration of the Indian [Princely] States.* London, 1956
Santhanam, K., *Union–State Relations in India.* London, 1961

ANDHRA PRADESH

HISTORY. Andhra was constituted a separate state on 1 Oct. 1953, on its partition from Madras, and consisted of the undisputed Telugu-speaking area of that state. To this region was added, on 1 Nov. 1956, the Telangana area of the former Hyderabad State, comprising the districts of Hyderabad, Medak, Nizamabad, Karimnaga, Warangal, Khammam, Nalgonda and Mahbubnaga, parts of the Adilabad district and some taluks of the Raichur, Gulbarga and Bidar districts, and some revenue circles of the Nanded district. On 1 April 1960, 221·4 sq. miles in the Chingleput and Salem districts of Madras were transferred to Andhra Pradesh in exchange for 410 sq. miles from Chittoor district. The district of Ongole was formed on 2 Feb. 1970. Hyderabad was split into 2 districts on 15 Aug. 1978. A new district, Vizianagaram, was formed in 1979.

EVENTS. A cyclone in May 1979 killed 638 people and about 400,000 head of livestock. About 680,000 houses were damaged. The cost of damage to crops was Rs 208 crores; total loss and damage, Rs 681 crores.

AREA AND POPULATION. Andhra Pradesh is in south India and is bounded south by Tamil Nadu, west by Mysore, north and north-west by Maharashtra, north-east by Madhya Pradesh and Orissa, east by the Indian ocean. The state has an area of 276,700 sq. km and a population (1971) of 43·5m. Density, 157 per sq. km. Population estimate, 1976, 47·9m. The principal language is Telugu. Cities with over 100,000 population (1971 census), *see* pp. 605–606.

CONSTITUTION AND GOVERNMENT. Andhra Pradesh has a bicameral legislature. Three regional committees composed of the elected members of Telangana, Rayalaseema and Coastal Regions are consulted by the Government on matters pertaining to those regions.

For administrative purposes there are 23 districts in the state. The capital is Hyderabad.

There are 294 seats in the Legislative Assembly and 90 in the Legislative Council. Following the elections of Feb. 1978 the state of the parties in the Legislative Assembly was: Indira Congress, 175; Janata 60; Congress 30; others 29.

Governor: K. C. Abraham.
Chief Minister: M. Channa Reddy.

BUDGET. The budget estimates for 1978–79 showed total revenue receipts of Rs 1,097 crores, and expenditure of Rs 1,160·5 crores.

ENERGY AND NATURAL RESOURCES

Electricity. There are hydro-electric plants at Machkund, Upper Sileru, Nizam Sagar, Nellore and Kothagudam. Installed capacity, 1977, 1,563 mw. In 1977 there were 14,851 electrified towns and villages; power generated, 5,148m. kwh.

Water. The Tungabhadra dam, inaugurated in 1953, has been completed, thus irrigating about 492,800 hectares in Andhra Pradesh and Karnataka. The Nagarjunsaga project, which incorporates canals and a dam (the tallest masonry dam in the world) on the Krishna River 160 km from Hyderabad, will irrigate over 1,305,000 hectares on completion of the final phase. The Pochambad dam on the Godavari River will irrigate 230,000 hectares.

Minerals (1977). Production of principal minerals (in 1,000 tonnes): Coal, 8,790; limestone, 2,888·5; barytes, 318; manganese, 151; iron ore, 84·8; clay, 36; steatite, 15; mica, 2·9. The state also has bauxite, asbestos and chromite. Value of mineral production, 1976, Rs 602·5m.

Agriculture. There were (1978) about 12·5m. hectares of cropped land, of which 31% is irrigated. Yield per hectare, in kg: Sugar-cane, 7,966; rice, 1,565; ground-nuts, 931; tobacco, 819; jowar, 621; cotton, 90. The state produces about 94% of India's Virginia tobacco and 55% of her castor.

Livestock (1977 census): Cattle, 12·04m.; buffaloes, 7·16m.; goats, 4·3m.; sheep, 7·06m.

Forests. In 1978 it was estimated that forests occupy about 22·5% of the total area of the state (64,200 sq. km); main forest products are timber and bamboo. Value of produce Rs 20,55·4 lakhs.

Fisheries. Production, 1977, 220,000 tonnes.

INDUSTRY. The main industries are textile manufacture, sugar-milling and paper-making. Other industries include cement, tanning and glass. There is an oil refinery at Vishakhapatnam, where India's only major shipbuilding yards are situated. There is an important fertilizer plant and a plant processing ferro-manganese. There were 5,798 factories in 1976.

Cottage industry includes the manufacture of carpets, wooden and lacquer toys, brocades, bidriware, filigree and lace-work. The wooden toys of Nirmal and Kondapalli are particularly well known. Sericulture is developing rapidly.

COMMUNICATIONS

Roads. In 1978 there were 31,500 km of roads, including 21,100 km of surfaced roads. Number of vehicles, 1978: 189,000.

Railways. In 1978 there were approximately 4,789 route-km of railway, of which 2,879 km were broad gauge.

Aviation. There are airports at Hyderabad, Tirupati, Vijayawada and Vishakapatnam, with regular scheduled services to Bombay, Calcutta and Madras.

Shipping. The chief port is Vishakhapatnam. There are minor ports at Kakinada, Machilipatnam, Bheemunipatnam, Narsapur, Krishnapatnam, Vadarevu and Calingapatnam.

JUSTICE, RELIGION AND EDUCATION

Justice. The High Court of Judicature at Hyderabad has a Chief Justice and 17 puisne judges.

Religion. At the 1971 census Hindus numbered 38,119,279; Moslems, 3,520,166; Christians, 1,823,436; Jains, 16,103; Sikhs, 12,591; Buddhists, 10,035.

Education. In 1971, 24·56% of the population were literate. There were, in 1977–78, 47,280 recognized educational institutions, with 6,289,000 pupils. Number of schools: 38,836 primary, 4,201 upper primary, 3,636 secondary. Education is free for children up to 14.

There were 305 junior colleges, 248 colleges for general education and 54 professional and technical colleges. There are 8 universities: Osmania University,

Hyderabad; Andhra University, Waltair; Sri Venkateswara University, Tirupati; Kakatiya University, Warangal; Nagarjuna University, Guntur; Sri Jawaharlal Nehru Technological University, Hyderabad; Central University, Hyderabad; A.P. Agricultural University, Hyderabad.

ASSAM

HISTORY. Assam first became a British Protectorate at the close of the first Burmese War in 1826. In 1832 Cachar was annexed; in 1835 the Jaintia Hills were included in the East India Company's dominions, and in 1839 Assam was annexed to Bengal. In 1874 Assam was detached from Bengal and made a separate chief commissionership. On the partition of Bengal in 1905, it was united to the Eastern Districts of Benegal under Lieut.-Governor. From 1912 the chief commissionership of Assam was revived, and in 1921 a governorship was created. On the partition of India almost the whole of the predominantly Moslem district of Sylhet was merged with East Bengal (Pakistan). Dewangiri in North Kamrup was ceded to Bhután in 1951. The Naga Hill district, administered by the Union Government since 1957, became part of Nagaland in 1962. The autonomous state of Meghalaya within Assam, comprising the districts of Garo Hills and Khasi and Jaintia Hills, came into existence on 2 April 1970, and achieved full independent statehood in Jan. 1972, when it was also decided to form a Union Territory, Mizoram, from the Mizo Hills district.

EVENTS. Agitation by the All-Assam Students Union and All-Assam Gana Sangram Parishad (for the detection and deportation of aliens) caused serious unrest in 1980; it ended by agreement in Aug. 1980.

AREA AND POPULATION. Assam is in eastern India, almost separated from central India by Bangladesh. It is bounded west by West Bengal, north by Bhután and the Territory of Arunachal Pradesh, east by Nagaland, Manipur and Burma, south by Meghalaya, Bangladesh and Tripura. The area of the state is now approximately 78,523 sq. km. Its population (1971 census) 14·6m. Estimate (1976) 17m. Principal towns with population (1971) are; Gauhati, 122,981; Dibrugarh, 80,344; Tinsukia, 55,392; Nowgong, 52,892; Silchar, 52,612. The principal language is Assamese.

CONSTITUTION AND GOVERNMENT. Assam has a unicameral legislature of 126 members; this was dissolved in Feb. 1980 and presidential rule imposed, pending elections.

Governor: L. P. Singh.
Chief Minister: J. N. Hazarika.

BUDGET. The budget estimates for 1979–80 showed total revenue receipts of Rs 271·13 crores and expenditure of Rs 277·49 crores. Outside the revenue account receipts are estimated at Rs 460·98 crores and expenditure at Rs 476·72 crores.

ENERGY AND NATURAL RESOURCES

Electricity. In 1978 there was an installed capacity of 141·5 mw and 2,260 villages (out of 21,995) with electricity. A further 583 mw capacity is to be installed by 1984. New power stations are under construction at Bongaigaon and Lakwa.

Oil. Assam contains important oilfields and produces about 50% of India's crude oil. There is also natural gas.

Water. In 1978, 88,300 hectares were irrigated and 228 projects were in hand. Intended Sixth Plan outlay, Rs 300 crores.

Minerals. Coal production (1973), 436,000 tonnes. The state also has limestone, refractory clay, dolomite, and corundum. Total value of mineral production, 1976, Rs 1,235·4m.

Agriculture. There are 756 tea plantations, and growing tea is the principal industry. Production in 1976, 276m. kg, over 50% of Indian tea. Over 72% of the cultivated area is under food crops, of which the most important is rice. Total foodgrains, 1976–77, 21·47m. tonnes. Main cash crops: jute, tea, cotton, oilseeds, sugar-cane, fruit and potatoes. Wheat has been introduced recently and yielded 71,045 tonnes in 1976–77. Cattle are important; milk production, 1976–77, 343m. litres.

Forestry. There are 1·62m. hectares of reserved forests under the administration of the Forest Department and 1,229,000 hectares of unclassed forests, altogether about 30% of the total area of the state. Revenue from forests, 1978–79, Rs 821 lakhs.

INDUSTRY. Sericulture and hand-loom weaving, both silk and cotton, are important home industries together with the manufacture of brass, cane and bamboo articles. Hand-loom weaving of silk is stimulated by state and central development schemes; outlay, Rs 18,34·5 lakhs. There is a silk-spinning mill and 2 cotton-mills. The main heavy industry is petro-chemicals; there are 3 oil refineries. Other industries include manufacturing paper, fertilizers, sugar, jute and plywood products, rice and oil milling.

COMMUNICATIONS

Roads. In 1972 there were 17,839 km of road maintained by the Public Works Department in Assam, including national highway. There were 63,616 motor vehicles in the state in 1976.

Railways. The open length of railways in 1974 was 2,193·65 km, of which 105·22 km are broad gauge.

Aviation. Daily scheduled flights connect the principal towns with the rest of India. There are airports at Gauhati, Tezpur, Jorhat, Dimapur, Silchar and Dibrugarh.

Shipping. Water transport is important in Lower Assam; the main waterway is the Brahmaputra River.

JUSTICE, RELIGION AND EDUCATION

Justice. The seat of the High Court is Gauhati. It has a Chief Justice and 6 puisne judges.

Religion. At the 1971 census Hindus numbered 10,604,618; Moslems, 3,592,124; Christians, 381,010; Buddhists, 22,565; Jains, 12,914; Sikhs, 11,920.

Education. The 1971 census showed 28·74% of the population to be literate.

In 1976 there were 26,000 primary schools; 2,504 middle schools; 1,657 high schools; 70 higher secondary schools; in 1977 there were 25,768 schools altogether, 126 general colleges and institutions for professional education, 507 vocational and technical schools, 31 teacher-training colleges and 3 universities.

Goswami, P. C., *Economic Development of Assam*. London, 1963
Reid, Sir Robert, *History of the Frontier Areas Bordering on Assam*. Shillong, 1942

BIHAR

The state contains the 2 ethnic areas of Bihar and Chota Nagpur. In 1956 certain areas of Purnea and Manbhum districts were transferred to West Bengal.

AREA AND POPULATION. Bihar is in north India and is bounded north by Nepál, east by West Bengal, south by Orissa, south-west by Madhya Pradesh and west by Uttar Pradesh. The area of Bihar is 173,876 sq. km and its population (1971 census), 56,353,369, a density of 324 per sq. km. Population estimate, 1976, 61·8m. Population of principal towns, *see* pp. 605–606.

The official language is Hindi.

CONSTITUTION AND GOVERNMENT. Bihar has a unicameral legislature. The Legislative Assembly consists of 314 elected members. Following the elections of May 1980 (310 seats contested), Congress (I) hold 166 seats; Janata (Charan Singh), 42; CPI, 23; Bhartiya Janata, 21; Congress (U), 14; others, 68.

For the purposes of administration it is divided into 5 divisions covering 23 districts. The capital is Patna; the hot-weather seat is Ranchi.

Governor: Dr A. R. Kidwai.
Chief Minister: Dr J. Mishra.

BUDGET. The budget estimates for 1980–81 show total revenue receipts of Rs 874·65 crores and expenditure of Rs 721·74 crores. Expenditure on capital account was Rs. 487·79 crores.

ENERGY AND NATURAL RESOURCES

Electricity. Installed capacity (1976) 1,551 mw. There were 16,565 villages with electricity.

Minerals. Bihar is the foremost state for mineral deposits. Value of production, 1976, Rs 3,628·2m. Coal is the principal mineral; the Jharia and Bokaro fields are (with Raniganj across the West Bengal border) the most important in India. Jharia produces coking coal. Copper, of which Bihar is the only Indian producer, iron ore, ruby mica (61% of national output), chromite, manganese, kyanite and bauxite are important. The recently discovered large deposits of pyrites in the Shahabad district are being exploited.

Agriculture. About 26% of the cultivable area is irrigated. Main crops are rice, jute, sugar-cane, oilseeds, tobacco, wheat, jowar, bajra and maize; total foodgrains (1976), 9·3m. tonnes.

Livestock (1961 census): Buffaloes, 3,698,000; other cattle, 16,104,000; sheep, 1,156,000; goats, 8,671,000; horses and ponies, 133,000.

Forests cover 17% of the state.

INDUSTRY. Main plants are the Tata Iron and Steel Co., the Tata Engineering and Locomotive Co., the steel plant at Bokaro, oil refinery at Barauni and aluminium plant at Muri. Other important industries are machine tools, fertilizers, electrical engineering, sugar-milling, paper-milling, silk-spinning, manufacturing explosives and cement. There is a copper smelter at Ghatsila and a lead-refining plant at Tundo. Industrial disputes lost 1·18m. man-days in 1979.

COMMUNICATIONS

Roads. In 1972 the state had 116,575 km of highway (including 88,040 km of un-metalled roads). Passenger transport has been nationalized in 7 districts. There were 123,461 motor vehicles in 1976.

Railways. The North Eastern and Eastern railways traverse the province.

Aviation. There are airports at Patna and Ranchi with regular scheduled services to Calcutta and Delhi.

Shipping. The length of waterways open for navigation is 900 miles.

JUSTICE, RELIGION AND EDUCATION

Justice. There is a High Court (constituted in 1916) at Patna with a Chief Justice, 17 puisne judges and 6 additional judges.

Police. The police force is under an inspector-general; there is 1 policeman to 1,211 of the population.

Religion. At the 1961 census Hindus numbered 39,347,050; Moslems, 5,785,631; Christians, 502,195; Sikhs, 44,413; Jains, 17,598; Buddhists, 2,885.

Education. At the census of 1971 the proportion of literates was 19·97%.

There were, 1971, 2,581 high and higher secondary schools with 601,000 pupils, 8,025 middle schools with 965,000 pupils, 46,582 primary schools with 5,009,000 pupils. Primary schools had 144,559 teachers, higher secondary and high schools 25,740. Education is free for children aged 6–11.

There were 7 universities in academic year 1972–73; Patna University (founded 1917) with 12,577 full-time students (1970); Bihar University, Muzaffarpur (1952) with 4 constituent colleges, 35 affiliated colleges and 41,640 students (1970); Bhagalpur University (1960) with 40,746 students (1970); Ranchi University (1960) with 36,892 students (1968–69); Darbhanga Sanskrit University (1961); Magadha University, Gaya (1962) and Mithila University (1972), Darbhanga.

GUJARAT

HISTORY. On 1 May 1960, as a result of the Bombay Reorganization Act, 1960, the state of Gujarat was formed from the north and west (predominantly Gujarati-speaking) portion of Bombay State, the remainder being renamed the state of Maharashtra. Gujarat consists of the following districts of the former state of Bombay: Banas Kantha, Mehsana, Sabar Kantha, Ahmedabad, Kaira, Panch Mahals, Vadodara, Bharuch, Surat, Dangs, Amreli, Surendranagar, Rajkot, Jamnagar, Junagadh, Bhavnagar, Kutch, Gandhinagar and Bulsar.

AREA AND POPULATION. Gujarat is in western India and is bounded north by Pakistan and Rajasthan, east by Madhya Pradesh, south-east by Maharashtra, south and west by the Indian ocean and Arabian sea. The area of the state is 195,984 sq. km and the population at the 1971 census was 26,697,475; a density of 136 per sq. km. Population estimate, 1976, 30·3m. The chief cities, see pp. 605–606. Gujarati and Hindi in the Devanagari script are the official languages.

CONSTITUTION AND GOVERNMENT. Gujarat has a unicameral legislature, the Legislative Assembly, which has 181 elected members. Following the election of May 1980, Congress (I) held 140 seats; Janata, 22; Bhartiya Janata, 9; others, 10.

The capital is Gandhinagar. There are 19 districts.

Governor: Smt. S. Mukerjee
Chief Minister: M. Solanki

BUDGET. Budget estimates, 1978–79, showed total revenue of Rs 6,35,01·45 lakhs, and expenditure of Rs 5,74,56·72 lakhs. Receipts included: Taxes on income except corporation tax, Rs 40,67·0 lakhs; state excise, Rs 2,68·0 lakhs; estate duty, Rs 48·0 lakhs; registration fees, Rs 88·0 lakhs; stamps, Rs 16,08·0 lakhs; sales tax, Rs 2,24,29·0 lakhs; vehicle taxes, Rs 16,00·0 lakhs; land revenue, Rs 7,50·0 lakhs. Expenditure included: Education, Rs 1,33,14·60 lakhs; public works and improvements, Rs 20,16·40 lakhs; irrigation, embankment, etc., Rs 43,39·48 lakhs; medical, and public health, Rs 43,44·87 lakhs; police, Rs 33,55·5 lakhs; agriculture, Rs 27,61·57 lakhs; general administration, Rs 17,67·6 lakhs; extraordinary, including community projects and local development, Rs 37,90·10 lakhs; industries, Rs 6,55·19 lakhs. Annual Plan expenditure for 1978–79 (estimate), Rs 335·0 crores, including Rs 33·5 crores for the Tribal Area Sub-plan.

ENERGY AND NATURAL RESOURCES

Electricity. In 1979 the total generating capacity was 2,334 mw of electricity, serving 9,823 towns and villages and 185,306 wells and tube-wells.

Oil and Gas. There were crude oil and gas reserves in 24 fields in 1978. Production: Crude oil, 4·2m. tonnes; gas, 7m. cu. metres.

Minerals. Chief minerals produced in 1978 (in tonnes) included chalk (76,030), limestone (2·5m), agate stone (2,897), calcite (1,428), quartz (45,689), bauxite (230,728), china clay (47,130), other clays (259,928), dolomite (195,789), crude fluorite (80,136), silica-glass sand (90,921) and lignite (134,674). Enormous reserves of coal were found under the Kalol and Mehsama oil and gas fields in May 1980. The deposit, mixed with crude petroleum, is estimated at 100,000m. tonnes, extending over 500 km.

Agriculture. Cropped area, 1973–44, was 10·5m. hectares. Area and production of principal crops, 1977–78 (in 1,000 hectares and 1,000 tonnes): Rice, 484, 669; groundnuts, 1,954, 1,723; cotton, 1,829, 1,942,000 bales of 170 kg.

Livestock (1972): Buffaloes, 3·46m.; other cattle, 6,457,284; sheep, 1,722,057; goats, 3,209,502; horses and ponies, 63,018.

Fisheries. There were (1977) about 49,227 active fishermen and (1978) 148 fishing co-operatives. There were (1978) 7,597 fishing vessels (2,545 motor vessels). The catch for 1977–78 (estimate) was 190,000 tonnes.

INDUSTRY. Gujarat is one of the 4 most industrialized states. In 1977 there were over 10,400 registered factories employing an estimated 565,110 workers. This figure includes over 2,202 textile factories. There were about 77 industrial estates. Principal industries are textiles, general and electrical engineering, vegetable oils, chemicals, soda ash and cement. Large fertilizer plants have been set up at Jawaharnagar, Kandla and Kalol. There is an oil refinery at Koyali near Vadodara, with a developing petro-chemical complex. Industrial production (1978) in tonnes: Cement, 2m.; soda ash, 223,400; caustic soda, 74,088; sugar, 297,288; sulphuric acid, 724,000; cotton yarn, 128,173; superphosphate, 93,370; paper and paper-board, 69,794; ceramics, 18,739; cotton cloth, 101·2m. metres; powered pumps, 77,000 (no.); diesel engines, 14,988 (no.); clocks, 151,909 (no.).

COMMUNICATIONS

Roads. In 1978 there were 42,359 km of roads. Gujarat State Transport Corporation operated 8,858 routes over 3·99 crore route-km.

Railways. In 1978 the state had 3,326 km metre gauge railway, 1,135 km narrow gauge and 1,155 km broad gauge.

Aviation. Ahmedabad is the main airport. There are 6 services daily between Bombay, Ahmedabad and Delhi. There are 8 other airports.

Shipping. The largest port is Kandla. There are 45 other ports, including Okha, Bedi, Bhavnagar, Verawal, Sikka and Porbandar.

Post. There were (1978) 7,423 post offices, 1,140 telegraph offices. Ahmedabad has direct dialling telephone connexion with Delhi, Bombay, Pune, Rajkot, Vadodara, Nadiad, Gandhinagar and Surat, and telex connexions with other cities.

JUSTICE, RELIGION, EDUCATION AND WELFARE

Justice. The High Court of Judicature at Ahmedabad has a Chief Justice and 10 puisne judges.

Religion. At the 1971 census Hindus numbered 23,835,471; Moslems, 2,249,055; Jains, 451,578; Christians, 109,341; Sikhs, 18,233; Buddhists, 5,469.

Education. Literacy is 35·8% of the population. Primary and secondary education are free. In 1977–78 there were 22,806 primary schools; nearly all villages with more than 500 people have one. In 1977–78 there were 2,854 secondary schools with 956,000 pupils.

There are 6 universities in the state. Gujarat University, Ahmedabad, founded in 1949, is teaching and affiliating; it has 147 affiliated colleges. The Maharaja Sayajirao University of Vadodara (1949) is residential and teaching. The Sardar Vallabhnhai Vidyapeeth, Anand (1955) has 18 constituent and affiliated colleges. The 2 newer universities (1967) are Saurashtra University at Rajkot with 60 affiliated colleges, and South Gujarat at Surat with 35. Gujarat Vidyapeeth at Ahmedabad is of university status. In 1977–78 the total number of students was 250,000. There were also 1 agricultural and 1 Ayurvedic university.

There are 7 technical institutions for degree courses (student capacity 2,290) and 19 for diploma courses (3,950).

Health. In 1978 there were 251 primary health centres and 19,881 hospital beds. The annual intake at 5 medical colleges was 675.

Rushbrook Williams, L. F., *The Black Hills: Kutch in History and Legend.* London, 1958
Desai, I. F., *Untouchability in Rural Gujarat.* Bombay, 1977

HARYANA

HISTORY. The state of Haryana, created on 1 Nov. 1966 under the Punjab Reorganization Act, 1966, was formed from the Hindi-speaking parts of the state of Punjab (India). It comprises the districts of Hissar, Mohindergarh, Gurgaon, Rohtak and Karnal; parts of Sangrur and Ambala districts; and part of Kharar tehsil.

AREA AND POPULATION. Haryana is in north India and is bounded north by Himachal Pradesh, east by Uttar Pradesh, south and west by Rajasthan and north-west by Punjab. Delhi forms an enclave on its eastern boundary. The state has an area of 44,222 sq. km and a population (1971) of 10,036,808; density, 226 per sq. km. Population estimate, 1976, 11·2m. The principal language is Hindi.

CONSTITUTION AND GOVERNMENT. The state has a unicameral legislature with 90 members. In Jan. 1980 the Chief Minister and 37 other members left the Janata party (formerly in control) and joined the India Congress party, which subsequently held 46 out of 90 seats. The state shares with Punjab (India) a High Court, a university and certain public services. The capital (shared with Punjab) is Chandigarh (*see* p 668). There are 7 districts.

Governor: G. D. Tapase.
Chief Minister: Bhajan Lal.

BUDGET. Budget estimates for 1980–81 show income of Rs 688 crores and expenditure of Rs 719 crores. Annual plan outlay, Rs 240·5 crores.

ENERGY AND NATURAL RESOURCES

Electricity. Approximately 1,000 mw are supplied to Haryana, mainly from the Bhakra Nangar system. In 1976 installed capacity was 612 mw and all the 3,302 villages had electric power.

Minerals. Minerals include iron ore, limestone, china clay and marble. Value of production, 1976, Rs 8·6m.

Agriculture. Haryana has sandy soil and erratic rainfall. Total irrigated area, 1976, was 46·8% of the cultivable area of 3,738,000 hectares; the state shares the benefit of the Sutlej–Beas scheme. Agriculture employs over 82% of the working population. During 1977 foodgrain production was 5·2m. tonnes; sugar (gur), 728,000 tonnes; oilseeds, 80,000 tonnes, and cotton, 450,000 bales (of 180 kg).
Forests cover 3·3% of the state.

INDUSTRY. Number of registered working factories (1970), 1,260, employing 83,178 workers. The main industries are cotton textiles (11 mills in 1976), agricultural machinery, woollen textiles, scientific instruments, glass, cement, paper and sugar milling.

COMMUNICATIONS

Roads. There were (1971) about 13,259 km of metalled roads and 262 km unsurfaced. Road transport was nationalized by 1971; Haryana Roadways has a fleet of 725 vehicles running on 335 routes and daily carrying 125,255 passengers over 149,630 km.

Railways. The state is crossed by lines from Delhi to Agra, Ajmer, Ferozepur and Chandigarh. The main stations are at Ambala and Kurukshetra.

Aviation. There is no airport within the state but Delhi is on its eastern boundary.

JUSTICE AND EDUCATION

Justice. Haryana shares the High Court of Punjab and Haryana at Chandigarh which had (1968) a Chief Justice and 16 puisne judges.

Education. In 1969–70 there were 5,967 schools and colleges with 1,250,590 attending. This includes 4,362 primary schools, 776 high and higher secondary schools, 777 middle schools and 47 colleges.

HIMACHAL PRADESH

HISTORY. The territory came into being on 15 April 1948 and comprised 30 former Hill States. The state of Bilaspur was merged with Himachal Pradesh in 1954. The 6 original districts were: Mahasu, Sirmur, Mandi, Chamba, Bilaspur and Kinnaur. On 1 Nov. 1966, under the Punjab Reorganization Act, 1966, certain parts of the state of Punjab (India) were transferred to Himachal Pradesh. These comprise the districts of Simla, Kulu, Kangra, and Lahaul and Spiti; and parts of Hoshiarpur and Ambala districts, with an estimated population (1967) of 1·5m.

AREA AND POPULATION. Himachal Pradesh is in north India and is bounded north by Kashmir, east by Tibet, south-east by Uttar Pradesh, south by Haryana, south-west and west by Punjab. The area of the state is 55,673 sq. km and it had a population at the 1971 census of 3,460,434. Density, 62 per sq. km. Population estimate, 1976, 3·7m. Principal language is Pahari.

CONSTITUTION AND GOVERNMENT. Full statehood was attained, as the 18th state of the Union, on 25 Jan. 1971.

On 1 Sept. 1972 districts were reorganized and 2 new districts created, Hamirpur and Una, making a total of 12. The capital is Simla.

There is a unicameral legislature.

Governor: A. A. Khan.
Chief Minister: R. Lal.

BUDGET. Budget estimates for 1980–81 showed revenue receipts of Rs 193 crores and expenditure on revenue account of Rs 161 crores. The capital account showed a deficit of Rs 73·57 crores.

ENERGY AND NATURAL RESOURCES

Electricity. In 1977 7,245 villages (out of 16,916) had electricity.

Water. An artificial confluence of the Sutlej and Beas rivers has been made, directing their united flow into Govind Sagar Lake.

Minerals. The state has rock salt, slate, gypsum, limestone, barytes, dolomite and pyrites.

Agriculture. Farming employs 76% of the people. Irrigated area is 16·7% of the area sown. Main crops are seed potatoes, wheat, maize, rice and fruits such as apples, peaches, apricots, nuts, pomegranates.

Production of foodgrains (1976) 1·13m. tonnes.

Livestock (1966 census): Buffaloes, 415,356; other cattle, 1,048,917; goats, 813,041.

Forestry. Himachal Pradesh forests cover 38·3% of the state and supply the largest quantities of coniferous timber in northern India. They are the main source of revenue of Pradesh. The forests also ensure the safety of the catchment areas of the Jumna, Sutlej, Beas, Ravi and Chenab rivers.

INDUSTRY. The main sources of employment are the forests and their related industries; there are factories making turpentine and rosin, fertilizers, cement and

TV sets. There is a foundry and a brewery. Other industries include salt production and handicrafts, including weaving.

COMMUNICATIONS

Roads. The national highway from Chandigarh runs through Simla; other main highways from Simla serve Kulu, Manali, Kangra, Chemba and Pathankot. The rest are minor roads. Pathankot is also on national highways from Punjab to Kashmir. There were 9,400 motor vehicles in 1976.

Railways. There is a line from Chandigarh to Simla, and the Jammu–Delhi line runs through Pathankot.

Aviation. The state has no airport, but Chandigarh is on its southern boundary.

JUSTICE. The state has its own High Court at Simla.

JAMMU AND KASHMIR

HISTORY. The state of Jammu and Kashmir, which had earlier been under Hindu rulers and Moslem sultans, became part of the Mogul Empire under Akbar from 1586. After a period of Afghan rule from 1756, it was annexed to the Sikh kingdom of the Punjab in 1819. In 1820 Ranjit Singh made over the territory of Jammu to Gulab Singh. After the decisive battle of Sobraon in 1846 Kashmir also was made over to Gulab Singh under the Treaty of Amritsar. British supremacy was recognized until the Indian Independence Act, 1947, when all states decided on accession to India or Pakistan. Kashmir asked for standstill agreements with both. Pakistan agreed, but India desired further discussion with the Government of Jammu and Kashmir State. In the meantime the state became subject to armed attack from the territory of Pakistan and the Maharajah acceded to India on 26 Oct. 1947, by signing the Instrument of Accession. India approached the UN in Jan. 1948; India–Pakistan conflict ended by ceasefire in Jan. 1949. Further conflict in 1965 was followed by the Tashkent Declaration on Jan. 1966. Following further hostilities between India and Pakistan a ceasefire came into effect on 17 Dec. 1971, followed by the Simla Agreement in July 1972, whereby a new line of control was delineated bilaterally through negotiations between India and Pakistan and came into force on 17 Dec. 1972.

AREA AND POPULATION. The state is in the extreme north and is bounded north by China, east by Tibet, south by Himachal Pradesh and Punjab and west by Pakistan. The area is 222,236 sq. km, of which about 78,932 sq. km is occupied by Pakistan and 42,735 sq. km by China; the population of the territory on the Indian side of the line, 1971 census, was 4,617,000. Estimate, 1976, 5·1m. For the population of Srinagar and Jammu, *see* p 606. The official language is Urdu; other commonly spoken languages are Kashmiri, Dogri, Balti, Ladakhi, Pahari and Punjabi, of which 18·59% was urban.

CONSTITUTION AND GOVERNMENT. The Maharajah's son, Yuvraj Karan Singh, took over as Regent in 1950 and, on the ending of hereditary rule (17 Oct. 1952), was sworn in as Sadar-i-Riyasat. On his father's death (26 April 1961) Yuvraj Karan Singh was recognized as Maharajah by the Indian Government; he decided not to use the title while he was elected head of state.

The permanent Constitution of the state came into force in part on 17 Nov. 1956 and fully on 26 Jan. 1957. It is unique in Indian states in that the Governor is bound by the advice of the Chief Minister. There is a bicameral legislature; the Legislative Council has 36 members and the Legislative Assembly has 76, of which 24 are reserved for the Pakistan-occupied areas. The state of the parties in the Legislative Assembly in 1978 was: Congress, 10; National Conference, 48; Janata, 13; others, 5. Since the 1967 elections the 6 representatives of Jammu and Kashmir in the central House of the People are directly elected; there are 4 representatives in the Council of States. The Council of Ministers consists of 4 Ministers, 11 Ministers of State and 1 Chief Parliamentary Secretary with the status of Minister of State.

In Nov. 1977 measures were passed allowing detention for up to 2 years without stated reason, banning entry to certain areas and censoring the press.

Kashmir Province has 4 districts and Jammu Province has 6 districts; the frontier district of Ladakh is in the former. Srinagar is the summer and Jammu the winter capital.

Governor: L. K. Jha.
Chief Minister: Shaikh Mohammed Abdullah.

BUDGET. Budget estimates for 1980–81 show revenue of Rs 576·62 crores, and expenditure of Rs 578·37 crores.

Total planning expenditure for 1980–81 was Rs 150·13 crores.

ENERGY AND NATURAL RESOURCES

Electricity. Installed capacity (1976) 103·63 mw.; 2,086 villages had electricity.

Minerals. Value of production, 1976, Rs 5·46m. Minerals include coal, bauxite and gypsum.

Agriculture. About 77% of the population are supported by agriculture. Rice, wheat, maize, barley, bajra and jawar are the major cereals. The total area under crops (1976) was estimated at 2,256,000 acres. Total foodgrains produced, 1975–76, 1m. quintals. The size of units has been limited to 12 standard acres—the standard acre being determined by soil fertility, availability of irrigation, etc. Fruit is important; exports (1975–76), 230,000 tonnes.

Livestock (1972 census): Cattle, 1,791,000; buffaloes, 493,000; sheep, 1,072,000; goats, 569,000; horses, 60,000, and poultry, 1,654,000.

Forestry. Forests cover about one-eighth of the area of the state, forming an important source of revenue, besides providing employment to a large section of the population. About 7,480 sq. km of forests yield valuable timber; output in 1974–75 was 362,320 cu. metres. Most forests yield medicinal drugs.

INDUSTRY. The chief industry is tourism, and after that sericulture, which dates back to the 16th century. It employs about 45,000 people. There are 25 main industrial units, 19 in the public sector. Of these, 18 are run by Jammu and Kashmir Minerals Ltd and Jammu and Kashmir Industries Ltd.

COMMUNICATIONS

Roads. Kashmir is linked with the rest of India by the motorable Jammu–Pathankot road. The Jawahar Tunnel, through the Banihal mountain, connects Srinagar and Jammu, and maintains road communication with the Kashmir Valley during the winter months. In 1976 there were 7,874 km of roads and 20,365 motor vehicles.

Railways. Kashmir was linked with the Indian railway system on 3 Dec. 1972 when the line between Jammu and Pathankot was opened.

Aviation. Major airports, with daily service from Delhi, are at Srinagar and Jammu. Srinagar airport accommodates jet aircraft and is linked with international routes *via* Delhi and Kábul.

Post. There were 890 post offices in 1967. In 1975 there were 51 telephone exchanges and approximately 10,000 private telephones. There is direct dialling between Srinagar, Jammu and Delhi.

JUSTICE, RELIGION, EDUCATION AND WELFARE

Justice. The High Court, at Srinagar and Jammu, has a Chief Justice and 4 puisne judges.

Religion. The majority of the population, except in Jammu, are Moslems. At the 1971 census Moslems numbered 3,040,129; Hindus, 1,404,292; Sikhs, 105,873; Buddhists, 57,956; Christians, 7,182; Jains, 1,150.

Education. The proportion of literates was 18·63% in 1972. Education is free. There are 8,246 schools and about 600,000 children attend. Jammu and Srinagar Universities (founded 1948) have 31 teaching departments and 40 affiliated colleges (1972). There are 2 medical colleges, an engineering college, 1 agricultural college, 2 polytechnics, 2 fine art colleges, 1 commercial college and an Ayurvedic college.

Health. In 1975 there were 35 hospitals, 273 primary health units and centres, about 620 clinics and dispensaries, and 307 mobile medical units. There were 1,334 doctors. Expenditure on health *per capita* was Rs 14·75 in 1973.

Bamzai, P. N. K., *A History of Kashmir.* Delhi, 1962
Birdwood, Lord, *Two Nations and Kasmir.* London, 1956
Gupta, S., *Kashmir: A Study in India–Pakistan Relations.* London, 1967
Korbel, J., *Danger in Kasmir.* Rev. ed. Princeton Univ. Press, 1966

KARNATAKA

HISTORY. The state of Karnataka, constituted as Mysore under the States Reorganization Act, 1956, brought together the Kannada-speaking people distributed in 5 states, and consisted of the territories of the old states of Mysore and Coorg, the Bijapur, Kanara and Dharwar districts and the Belgaum district (except one taluk) in former Bombay, the major portions of the Gulbarga, Raichur and Bidar districts in former Hyderabad, and South Kanara district (apart from the Kasaragod taluk) and the Kollegal taluk of the Coimbatore district in Madras. The state was renamed Karnataka in 1973.

AREA AND POPULATION. The state is in south India and is bounded north by Maharashtra, east by Andhra Pradesh, south by Tamil Nadu and Kerala, west by the Indian ocean and north-east by Goa. The area of the state is 191,773 sq. km, and its population (1971 census), 29,299,014, an increase of 24·07% since 1961. Estimate, 1976, 32·4m. Kannada is the language of administration and is spoken by about 60% of the people. Other languages include Telugu (8·7%), Urdu (8·6%), Marathi (4·5%), Tamil (3·6%), Tulu and Konkani. Principal cities, *see* pp. 605–606.

CONSTITUTION AND GOVERNMENT. Karnataka has a bicameral legislature. The Legislative Council has 63 members. The Legislative Assembly consists of 223 elected members and 1 nominated member. Seats in spring 1978: Indira Congress, 149; Congress, 3; Janata, 59; Communist Party of India, 3; independents and others, 10.

The state has 19 districts (of which Coorg is one) in 4 divisions: Bangalore, Mysore, Belgaum and Gulbarga. The capital is Bangalore.

Governor: Govind Narain.
Chief Minister: R. Gundu Rao.

BUDGET. Budget estimates for 1980–81 showed total revenue of Rs 912·44 crores; expenditure 899·81 crores.

ENERGY AND NATURAL RESOURCES

Electricity. In 1980 the state's installed capacity was to be revised (by the Kalinadi project) to 2,000 mw.

Water. About 1·26m. hectares were irrigated in 1976. A further 852,000 hectares were added in 1978.

Minerals. Karnataka has India's only sources of gold and silver. The estimated reserves of high grade iron ore are 5,000m. tonnes. These reserves are found mainly in the Chitradurga belt. The National Mineral Development Corporation of India has indicated total reserves of nearly 1,000m. tonnes of magnesite and iron ore (with an iron content ranging from 25 to 40) which have been found in Kudremukh

Ganga-Mula region in Chickmagalur District. The estimated reserves of manganese are over 100m. tonnes.

Limestone is found in many regions; deposits are about 1,500m. tonnes.

Karnataka is the largest producer of chromite. It is one of the only two states of India producing magnesite. The other minerals of industrial importance are corundum and garnet.

Agriculture. Agriculture forms the main occupation of more than three-quarters of the population. Physically, Karnataka divides itself into four regions—the coastal region, the southern and northern 'maidan' or plain country, comprising roughly the districts of Bangalore, Tumkur, Chitaldrug, Kolar, Bellary, Mandya and Mysore, and the 'malnad' or hill country, comprising the districts of Chickmagalur, Hassan and Shimoga. Rainfall is heavy in the 'malnad' tracts, and in this area there is dense forest. The greater part of the 'maidan' country is cultivated. Coorg district is essentially agricultural.

The main food crops are rice and jowar, and ragi which is also about 30% of the national crop. Sugar, groundnut, castor-seed, safflower and cotton are important cash crops. The state grows about 70% of the national coffee crop.

In 1975–76, 7·48m. hectares were under foodgrains (production, 5·53m. tonnes); other crops included oilseeds (950,000 tonnes), cotton (700,000 bales of 180 kg), arecanut (66,100 tonnes), chillies, tobacco, sugar-cane and rubber. Yield of raw rubber from 1,120 hectares, 2 tonnes per day. There were, in 1977, 730,241 hectares under cotton, 730,240 under groundnuts, 963,017 under rice, 1·8m. under jowar, 9·14m. under ragi and 362,713 under wheat.

Livestock (1977): Buffaloes, 3,215,873; other cattle, 10,018,714; sheep, 662,420; goats, 726,016.

Forestry. Total forest in the state (1979) is 18% of the land area, producing sandalwood, bamboo and other timbers, and ivory.

INDUSTRY. The Visvesvaraya Iron and Steel Works is situated at Bhadravarti, while at Bangalore are national undertakings for the manufacture of aircraft, machine tools, light engineering and electronics goods. Other industries include textiles, vehicle manufacture, cement, chemicals, sugar, paper, porcelain and soap. In addition, much of the world's sandalwood is processed, the oil being one of the most valuable productions of the state. Sericulture is a more important cottage industry giving employment, directly or indirectly, to perhaps 1m. persons; production is about 4% of the world's mulberry silk (Indian total, 5%). Industrial production, 1972 (tonnes): Iron, 180,637; steel, 290,307; paper, 71,618; cement, 1·2m. and sugar, 254,000.

COMMUNICATIONS

Roads. In 1977 the state had 89,496 km of roads. There were 195,483 motor vehicles in 1976.

Railways. In 1976 there were 2,803 km of railway (including 154 km of narrow gauge) in the state.

Aviation. There are airports at Bangalore, Mangalore and Belgaum, with regular scheduled services to Bombay, Calcutta, Delhi and Madras.

Shipping. Mangalore is a deep-water port for the export of mineral ores. Karwar is being developed as an intermediate port.

JUSTICE, RELIGION AND EDUCATION

Justice. The seat of the High Court is at Bangalore. It has a Chief Justice and 11 puisne judges.

Religion. At the 1971 census Hindus numbered 25,332,388; Moslems, 3,113,298; Christians, 613,026; Jains, 218,862; Buddhists, 114,139; Sikhs, 6,830.

Education. The proportion of literates to the total population, according to the 1971 census, was 31·52% (males, 41·62%; females, 20·97%). In 1977 the state had 33,137 primary schools, 2,326 high schools, 314 schools for professional and technical education and 30 polytechnic and engineering schools. Education is free up to pre-university level.

The University of Mysore (founded in 1916) at Mysore has 3 university colleges at Mysore and 134 affiliated colleges. Karnatak University (1950) at Dharwar has 4 constituent colleges and 95 affiliated colleges. Bangalore University (1964) has 46 constituent colleges, the University of Agricultural Sciences, Hebbal, Bangalore, (1964) has 3 constituent colleges.

The Indian Institute of Science. Bangalore, is unaffiliated; it conducts diploma courses in engineering, metallurgy and technology. There are 415 other colleges, including medical, law and commercial.

Learmouth, A. T. A., and Bhat, L. T., *Mysore State.* 2 vols. London, 1961–62

KERALA

HISTORY. The state of Kerala, created under the States Reorganization Act, 1956, consists of the previous state of Travancore–Cochin, except for 4 taluks of the Trivandrum district and a part of the Shencottah taluk of Quilon district. It took over the Malabar district (apart from the Laccadive and Minicoy Islands) and the Kasaragod taluk of South Kanara (apart from the Amindivi Islands) from Madras State.

AREA AND POPULATION. Kerala is in south India and is bounded north by Karnataka, east and south-east by Tamil Nadu, south-west and west by the Indian ocean. The state has an area of 38,855 sq. km. The 1971 census showed a population of 21,347,375; density of population was 549 per sq. km (highest of any state). Estimated population, 1976, 24m. Population of principal cities, *see* pp. 605–606.

Languages spoken in the state are Malayalam, Tamil and Kannada.

The physical features of the land fall into three well-marked divisions: (1) the hilly tracts undulating from the Western Ghats in the east and marked by long spurs, extensive ravines and dense forests; (2) the cultivated plains intersected by numerous rivers and streams; and (3) the coastal belt with dense coconut plantations and rice fields.

CONSTITUTION AND GOVERNMENT. The state has a unicameral legislature of 140 members including the Speaker. The election of Jan. 1980 was won by the Left Front coalition (CPI pro-Moscow, CPI Marxist, Revolutionary Socialist Party and 3 smaller groups).

The state has 12 districts. The capital is Trivandrum.

Governor: J. Vencatachellum.
Chief Minister: E. K. Nayanar.

BUDGET. Budget estimates for 1980–81 showed revenue account receipts of Rs 591 crores, expenditure Rs 575 crores. Total receipts, Rs 1,491·79 crores; total expenditure, Rs 1,523·54 crores. Annual Plan expenditure, Rs 206·60 crores.

ENERGY AND NATURAL RESOURCES

Electricity. Installed capacity (1979), 1,011·5 mw.; energy generated in 1978–79 was 4,730·4m. kw. Stage I of the Idukki hydro-electric plant has a capacity of 390 mw, the Sabarigiri scheme 300 mw.

Minerals. Next to Bihar, Kerala possesses the widest variety of economic mineral resources among the Indian States. The beach sands of Kerala contain monazite, ilmenite, rutile, zircon, sillimanite, etc. There are extensive white-clay deposits; other minerals of commercial importance include mica, graphite, limestone, quartz sand and lignite. Iron ore has been found at Kozhikode. Value of mineral production, 1976, Rs 11·5m.

Agriculture. The chief agricultural products of the state are rice, tapioca, coconut, arecanut, cashewnut, oilseeds, pepper, sugar-cane, rubber, tea, coffee and cardamom. About 98% of Indian black pepper and about 95% of Indian rubber is produced in Kerala. Area and production of principal crops, 1978–79 (in 1,000 hectares and 1,000 tonnes): Rice, 799·2, 1,270; black pepper, 108·3, 25·1; ginger (dry), 11, 28; arecanut, 62·8, 10,576 (million nuts); bananas and other plantains, 50·9, 615·9; cashewnuts, 135·5, 89·7; coconuts, 678·6, 3,075 (million nuts); tea, 36·1, 47·2; coffee, 51·7, 21·7; rubber, 214·4, 123·6; tapioca, 289·8, 4,226; cardamom, 51·9, 2·9.

Livestock (1972, provisional); Buffaloes, 469,515; other cattle, 2,855,856; sheep, 10,390; goats, 1,450,587.

Forestry. About a third of the area is comprised of forests, including teak, sandalwood, ebony and black-wood and varieties of softwood. Forest revenue, 1978–79, Rs 26·2 crores, from timber, bamboos, reeds and ivory.

Fisheries. Fishing is a flourishing industry; the catch in 1979 was about 398,000 tonnes.

INDUSTRIES. Most of the major industrial concerns are either owned or sponsored by the Government. The Government owns 11 industrial concerns and has substantial shares in more than 40. Among the privately owned factories are the numerous cashew and coir factories. Other important factory industries are rubber, tea, tiles, oil, textiles, ceramics, fertilizers and chemicals, zinc-smelting, sugar, cement, rayon, glass, matches, pencils, monazite, ilmenite, titanium oxide, rare earths, aluminium, electrical goods, paper, shark-liver oil, etc.

The number of factories registered under the Factories Act 1948 on 31 Dec. 1978 was 7,784, with daily average employment of 272,392. Man-days lost by industrial disputes in 1979, 3·51m.

Among the cottage industries, coir-spinning and handloom-weaving are the most important, forming the means of livelihood of a large section of the people. Other industries are the village oil industry, ivory carving, furniture-making, bell metal, brass and copper ware, leather goods, screw-pines, mat-making, rattan work, bee-keeping, pottery, etc. These have been organized on a co-operative basis.

COMMUNICATIONS

Roads. In 1979 there were 90,440 km of roads in the state; national highways, 838 km. There were 154,595 motor vehicles in 1979.

Railways. There is a coastal line from Mangalore (Karnataka) which serves Mahe, Kozhikode, Ernakulam (for Cochin) and Quilon, and connects them with main towns in Tamil Nadu. In 1980 there were 806 km broad gauge and 113 km metre gauge lines.

Aviation. There are airports at Cochin and Trivandrum with regular scheduled services to Bombay and Madras.

Shipping. Port Cochin, administered by the central government, is one of India's 6 major ports. There are 10 other ports and harbours.

JUSTICE, RELIGION AND EDUCATION

Justice. The High Court at Ernakulam has a Chief Justice and 11 puisne judges and 4 additional judges.

Religion. At the 1971 census Hindus numbered 12,683,277; Christians, 4,494,089; Moslems, 4,162,718; Jains, 3,336.

Education. Kerala is the most literate Indian State—60·42% at the 1971 census. Education is free up to the age of 14.

In 1979–80 there was a total school enrolment of 5·59m. students. There were 7,013 lower primary schools 2,739 upper primary schools and 1,680 high schools. About 62% of schools are privately run.

Kerala University (established 1937) at Trivandrum, is affiliating and teaching; in 1979 it had 79 affiliated arts and science colleges and 25 affiliated professional colleges. The University of Cochin is federal, and for post-graduate studies only.

The University of Calicut (established 1968) is teaching and affiliating and has 65 affiliated colleges. Kerala Agricultural University (established 1971) has 3 constituent colleges.

Mankekar, D. R., *The Red Riddle of Kerala*. Bombay, 1966
Pillai, V. R., and Panikar, P. G. K., *Land Reclamation in Kerala*. London, 1965
Woodcock, G., *Kerala*. London, 1968

MADHYA PRADESH

HISTORY. Under the provisions of the States Reorganization Act, 1956, the State of Madhya Pradesh was formed on 1 Nov. 1956. It consists of the 17 Hindi districts of the previous state of that name, the former state of Madhya Bharat (except the Sunel enclave of Mandsaur district), the former state of Bhopal and Vindhya Pradesh and the Sironj subdivision of Kotah district, which was an enclave of Rajasthan in Madhya Pradesh.

For information on the former states, *see* THE STATESMAN'S YEAR-BOOK, 1958, pp. 180–84.

AREA AND POPULATION. The state is in central India and is bounded north by Rajasthan and Uttar Pradesh, east by Bihar and Orissa, south by Andhra Pradesh and Maharashtra, west by Gujarat. Madhya Pradesh is the largest Indian state in size, with an area of 442,841 sq. km. In respect of population it ranks sixth. Population (1971 census), 41,654,119, an increase of 28·04% since 1961. Estimate, 1976, 47·2m.

Cities with over 100,000 population, *see* pp. 605–606.

The number of persons speaking each of the more prevalent languages (1971 census) were: Hindi, 32,873,079; Urdu, 988,275; Marathi, 1,385,952; Gujarati, 155,723.

CONSTITUTION AND GOVERNMENT. Madhya Pradesh is one of the 9 states for which the Constitution provides a bicameral legislature, but the Vidhan Parishad or Upper House (to consist of 90 members) has yet to be formed. The Vidhan Sabha or Lower House has 320 elected members. Following the election of May 1980 (318 seats contested), Congress (I) held 245; Bhartiya Janata, 59; others, 14.

For administrative purposes the state has been split into 11 divisions with a Commissioner at the head of each; the headquarters of these are located at Bhopal, Bilaspur, Gwalior (2), Hoshangabad, Indore, Jabalpur, Raipur, Rewa, Sagar and Ujjain. There are 45 districts.

The seat of government is at Bhopal.

Governor: B. D. Sharma.
Chief Minister: A. Singh.

BUDGET. Budget estimates for 1980–81 showed total revenue of Rs 11,14,87·64 lakhs, and expenditure of Rs 9,93,31·04 lakhs. Receipts included: Contributions and adjustments between central and state governments, Rs 4,23,37·33 lakhs; taxes on income, Rs 72,57 lakhs; state excise, Rs 50,00 lakhs; stamps and registration, Rs 21,35 lakhs; forests, Rs 1,40,86 lakhs; sales tax, Rs 1,70,79 lakhs; vehicles taxes, Rs 29,85 lakhs; debt services, Rs 51,85·69 lakhs; civil administration, Rs 19,41·29 lakhs; land revenue, Rs 9,33·22 lakhs. Expenditure included: Education, Rs 1,70,52·95 lakhs; public works and improvements, Rs 46,80·93 lakhs; irrigation, embankment, etc., Rs 40,64·93 lakhs; medical, and public health, Rs 1,07,68·09 lakhs; police, Rs 58,06·5 lakhs; agriculture, Rs 45,43·08 lakhs; general administration, Rs 18,52·62 lakhs; debt services, Rs 74,29·28 lakhs; community projects and local development, Rs 46,15·81 lakhs; industries, Rs 12,49·16 lakhs; forests, Rs 89,30·52 lakhs; social security and welfare, Rs 65,08·01 lakhs.

ENERGY AND NATURAL RESOURCES

Electricity. Madhya Pradesh is rich in low-grade coal suitable for power generation, and also has immense potential hydro-electric energy. The present installed capacity is 1,012·5 mw; of this 819·50 mw is from thermal and 193 mw from hydro-electric power stations. The thermal power stations are at Korba in Bilaspur district, Amarkantak in Shahdol district and Satpura in Betul district; new stations are being built. The only hydro-electric power station is at Gandhi Sagar lake in Mandsaur district; this, with a maximum water surface of 165 sq. miles, is the biggest man-made lake in Asia.

Water. Major irrigation projects include the Chambal Valley scheme (started in 1952 with Rajasthan) which irrigates some 700,000 acres, the Tawa project in Hoshangabad district (750,000 acres), the Barna and Hasdeo schemes, the Mahanadi canal system (140,000) and schemes under construction (Bargi, Narmadasagar, and Bansagar). Up to the end of the Fourth Plan period works by the state had an irrigation potential of 12·46 lakh hectares. Target for the Fifth Plan, a further 8·77 lakh.

Minerals. The state has extensive mineral deposits including coal, iron ore and manganese, bauxite, ochre, sillimanite, limestone, dolomite, rock phosphate, copper, lead, tin, fluorite, barytes, china clay and fireclay, corundum, gold, diamonds, pyrophyllite and diaspore, lepidolite, asbestos, vermiculite, mica, glass sand, quartz, felspars, bentonite and building stone.

In 1975 the output of major minerals was (in tonnes): Coal, 20,020m.; limestone, 5·3m.; dolomite, 541,000; fireclay, 74,000; diamonds, 19,927 carats; bauxite, 360,000m.; iron ore, 9·7m.; manganese ore, 177,000. Value of production, 1976, Rs 1,644m.

Agriculture. Agriculture is the mainstay of the state's economy and 83% of the people are rural. Over 42% of the land area is cultivable, of which 10·7% is irrigated. The Malwa region abounds in rich black cotton soil, the low-lying areas of Gwalior, Bundelkhand and Baghelkhand and the Chhatisgarh plains have a lighter sandy soil, while the Narmada valley is formed of deep rich alluvial deposits. Production of principal crops, 1975–76 (in tonnes): Foodgrains, 12m.; sugar-cane, 169,000; oilseeds, 604,000, and cotton, 299,000 bales (of 180 kg).

Livestock (1977 census): Buffaloes, 5,852,549; other cattle, 34,256,725; sheep, 968,595; goats, 6,573,467; horses and ponies, 121,908.

Forestry. Nearly 40% of the state's area is covered by forests. The forests are chiefly of sal, babul, salai, dhavra, tendu, mahua, bamboo, teak, anjan and harra. They are the chief source in India of best-quality teak.

INDUSTRY. The major industries are the steel plant at Bhilai, Bharat Heavy Electricals at Bhopal, the aluminium plant at Korba, the security paper mills at Hoshangabad, the Bank Note Press at Dewas, the newsprint mill at Nepanagar and alkaloid factory at Neemuch, cement factories, vehicle factory, ordnance factory, and gun carriage factory. There are also 23 textile mills, 7 of them nationalized.

The Bhilai steel plant near Durg is one of the 6 major steel mills. A power station at Korba (Bilaspur) with a capacity of 420 mw serves Bhilai, the aluminium plant and the Korba coalfield.

The heavy electricals factory was set up by the Government of India at Bhopal during the second-plan period. This is India's first heavy electrical equipment factory and also one of the largest of its type in Asia. It makes a variety of highly complicated equipment required for generation, transmission, distribution and utilization of electric power.

Other industries include cement, sugar, straw board, paper, vegetable oil, refractories, potteries, textile machinery, steel casting and rerolling, industrial gases, synthetic fibres, drugs, biscuit manufacturing, engineering, tools, rayon and art silk. The number of heavy and medium industries in the state is 193, with 181 ancillary industries; the number of small-scale industries in production is 64,630. Thirty-six out of 45 districts in the state are categorized as industrially backward districts.

The main industrial development agencies are Madhya Pradesh Financial Corporation, Madhya Pradesh Audyogik Vikas Nigam Ltd, Madhya Pradesh State Industries Corporation, Madhya Pradesh Laghu Udyog Nigam, Madhya Pradesh State Textile Corporation, Madhya Pradesh Handicrafts Board, Khadi and Village Industries Board and Madhya Pradesh State Mining Corporation.

The state is known for its traditional village and home crafts such as handloom weaving, best developed at Chanderi and Maheshwar, toys, pottery, lacework, woodwork, zari work, leather work and metal utensils. The ancillary industries of dyeing, calico printing and bleaching are centred in areas of textile production.

COMMUNICATIONS

Roads. Total length of roads in 1977 was 50,748·76 km, of which 38,101·5 km were surfaced. In 1976 there were 126,127 motor vehicles.

Railways. Bhopal, Bilaspur, Katni, Khandwar and Ratlam are important junctions for the central and northern networks.

Aviation. There are airports at Bhopal, Indore, Jabalpur, Khajuraho and Raipur with regular scheduled services to Bombay, Calcutta and Delhi.

JUSTICE, RELIGION AND EDUCATION

Justice. The High Court of Judicature at Jabalpur has a Chief Justice and 17 puisne judges.

Religion. At the 1971 census Hindus numbered 39,024,162; Moslems, 1,815,685; Christians, 286,072; Buddhists, 81,823; Sikhs, 98,973.

Education. The 1971 census showed 22·3% of the population to be literate. Education is free for children aged up to 14.

In 1975–76 there were 355 higher educational institutions. Primary schools (1974–75) had 3·5m. pupils and higher secondary schools, 620,897 pupils.

There are 10 universities in Madhya Pradesh: the University of Sagar (established 1946), at Sagar, had 53 affiliated colleges and 26,516 students in 1975; Jabalpur University (1957) had 30 affiliated colleges and 12,962 students; Vikram University (1957), at Ujjain, had 46 affiliated colleges and 38,011 students; Indira Kala Sangeet Vishwavidyalaya (1956), at Khairagarh, had 9 affiliated colleges and 1,164 students on roll (this university teaches music and fine arts); Indore University (1964) had 21 affiliated colleges and 22,915 students; Jivagi University (1963), at Gwalior, had 43 affiliated colleges and 31,462 students; Jawaharlal Nehru Krishi University (1964), at Jabalpur, had 9 affiliated colleges and 2,274 students in 1964; Ravishankar University (1964), at Raipur, had 63 affiliated colleges and 41,607 students. In 1975–76 there were 256 degree-granting colleges, 19 teacher-training colleges, and 71 professional colleges including polytechnics.

MAHARASHTRA

HISTORY. Under the States Reorganization Act, 1956, Bombay State was formed by merging the states of Kutch and Saurashtra and the Marathi-speaking areas of Hyderabad (commonly known as Marathwada) and Madhya Pradesh (also called Vidarbha) in the old state of Bombay, after the transfer from that state of the Kannada-speaking areas of the Belgaum, Bijapur, Kanara and Dharwar districts which were added to the state of Mysore, and the Abu Road taluka of Banaskantha district, which went to the state of Rajasthan.

By the Bombay Reorganization Act, 1960, which came into force 1 May 1960, 17 districts (predominantly Gujarati-speaking) in the north and west of Bombay State became the new state of Gujarat, and the remainder was renamed Maharashtra.

The state of Maharashtra consists of the following districts of the former Bombay State: Ahmednagar, Akola, Amravati, Aurangabad, Bhandara, Bhir, Buldana, Chanda, Dhulia (West Khandesh), Greater Bombay, Jalgaon (East Khandesh), Kolaba, Kolhapur, Nagpur, Nanded, Nasik, Osmanabad, Parbhani, Pune, Ratnagiri, Sangli, Satara, Sholapur, Thana, Wardha, Yeotmal; certain portions of Thana and Dhulia districts have become part of Gujarat.

AREA AND POPULATION. Maharashtra is in central India and is bounded north and east by Madhya Pradesh, south by Andhra Pradesh, Karnataka and

Goa, west by the Indian ocean and north-west by Daman and Gujarat. The state has an area of 307,762 sq. km. The population at the 1971 census was 50,412,235 (an increase of 27·45% since 1961), of whom about 30m. were Marathi-speaking. Estimate, 1976, 56·3m. The area of Greater Bombay was 603 sq. km. and its population 5,970,575. For other principal cities, *see* pp. 605–606.

CONSTITUTION AND GOVERNMENT. Maharashtra has a bicameral legislature. The Legislative Council has 78 members. The Legislative Assembly has 287 elected members and 1 member nominated by the Governor to represent the Anglo-Indian community. Following the election of May 1980 Congress (I) held 186 seats; Congress (U), 47; Janata, 17; Bhartiya Janata, 14; others, 24.

The Council of Ministers consists of the Chief Minister, 13 other Ministers, 12 Ministers of State and 5 Deputy Ministers.

The capital is Bombay.

Governor: Sadiq Ali.
Chief Minister: A. R. Antulay.

BUDGET. Budget estimates, 1980–81, show revenue receipts of Rs 1,921·97 crores. revenue account expenditure Rs 1,857·39 crores. Capital account receipts, Rs 799·03 crores; expenditure, Rs 873·33 crores.

Capital expenditure on development, 1976–77: Agriculture and allied services, Rs 2,28 lakhs; industries and minerals, Rs 5,78 lakhs; water and power development, Rs 86,51 lakhs; schemes for transport and communications, Rs 10,79 lakhs; public health, Rs 8,09 lakhs.

ENERGY AND NATURAL RESOURCES

Minerals. Value of production, 1976, Rs 26·7m. The state has coal, chromite, limestone, iron ore, manganese, bauxite.

Agriculture. About 10% of the cropped area is irrigated. Area (in 1,000 hectares) and production (in 1,000 tonnes) of principal crops in 1973–74: Rice, 1,351, 1,637; wheat, 965, 547; jowar, 6,088, 2,819; bajri, 2,215, 850; total cereals, 11,091, 6,177; total pulses, 2,762, 868; total foodgrains, 13,853, 7,045; sugar-cane, 215 (of gur, 1,544); groundnuts, 758, 566; cotton, 2,348 (1,058 bales of 180 kg). Total foodgrains, 1976, 9,119,000 tonnes. Cash crops, 1976: Sugar-cane, 2m. tonnes; cotton, 781,000 bales (of 180 kg); groundnuts, 671,000 tonnes.

Livestock (1972 census): Buffaloes, 3,300,746; other cattle, 14,705,147; sheep, 2,128,036; goats, 5,910,554; horses and ponies, 58,287; poultry, 12,216,567.

Forestry. Forests occupy 17·4% of the state.

INDUSTRY. The number of factories on 31 Dec. 1974 was 10,975 employing (daily average) 1,038,868 workers. Man-days lost by industrial disputes, 1979, 2·3m.

The textile industry is dominant in production. On 31 Dec. 1976 there were 107 cotton textile (spinning and composite) mills with 4·89m. spindles. There are 26 woollen mills employing about 6,158. There are 74 sugar mills employing about 27,364 workers daily, 775 chemical factories employing about 82,967, and in engineering there are 1,079 factories employing about 86,341 workers. The motor industry had (1976) 12 vehicle factories and 63 factories making parts. The state has important ferro-manganese processing plants.

COMMUNICATIONS

Roads. On 31 March 1975 there were 89,007 km of roads, of which 41,484 km were surfaced. There were 432,901 motor vehicles in 1976. Passenger and freight transport has been nationalized.

Railways. The total length of railway is about 5,162 km. The main junctions and termini are Bombay, Manmad, Akola, Nagpur, Pune and Sholapur.

Aviation. The main airport is Bombay, which has national and international flights. Nagpur airport is on the route from Bombay to Calcutta and there are also airports at Pune and Aurangabad.

Shipping. Maharashtra has a coastline of 720 km. Bombay is the major port, and there are 42 minor ports.

JUSTICE, RELIGION AND EDUCATION

Justice. The High Court has a Chief Justice and 27 judges. There are 8 additional judges. The seat of the High Court is Bombay, but it has a bench at Nagpur.

Religion. At the 1961 census Hindus numbered 32,530,901; Moslems, 3,034,332; Buddhists, 2,789,501; Christians, 560,594; Jains, 485,672; Sikhs, 57,617.

Education. The proportion of literates to the total population, according to the 1971 census, was 39·08% (males, 51·3%; females, 25·9%).

The total number of recognized institutions in 1975 was 56,656, with 10,528,258 students. Higher and secondary schools numbered 6,579 with 2,986,636 pupils; primary schools, 48,018, with 7,367,045 pupils; pre-primary schools, 827 with 62,781.

Bombay University, founded in 1857, is mainly an affiliating university. It has 99 constituent colleges and 21 post-graduate departments in Bombay with a total (1975–76) of 137,922 students. Colleges in Goa can affiliate to Bombay University. Nagpur University (1923) is both teaching and affiliating. In addition to the 26 post-graduate departments there were (1975–76) 140 affiliated colleges and constituent colleges with 87,153 students. Pune University, founded in 1948, is teaching and affiliating; in 1975–76 it had 103 affiliated colleges and constituent colleges, 26 post-graduate departments and a total of 88,232 students. The SNDT Women's University had, in 1975–76, 16 constituent colleges and affiliated colleges with a total of 9,911 students. Marathwada University, Aurangabad, was founded in 1958 as a teaching and affiliating body to control colleges in the Marathwada or Marathi-speaking area, previously under Osmania University; in 1975–76 there were 82 affiliated and constituent colleges and 6 post-graduate departments and 71,419 students. Shiwaji University, Kolhapur, was established in 1963 to control affiliated colleges previously under Pune University. In 1975–76 it had 84 affiliated and constituent colleges and 14 post-graduate departments and 65,526 students. There are 4 agricultural universities with 16 affiliated colleges and 6,114 students in 1975–76.

There were altogether 682 institutions for higher education in 1975–76, with 474,067 students.

Statistical Information: The Director of Publicity, Sachivalaya, Bombay.

Annual Statistical Abstract (from 1951)

State Library: Central Library, Town Hall, Bombay.

MANIPUR

HISTORY. Formerly a state under the political control of the Government of India, Manipur, on 15 Aug. 1947, entered into interim arrangements with the Indian Union and the political agency was abolished. The administration was taken over by the Government of India on 15 Oct. 1949 under a merger agreement, and it is centrally administered by the Government of India through a Chief Commissioner. In 1950–51 an Advisory form of Government was introduced. In 1957 this was replaced by a Territorial Council of 30 elected and 2 nominated members. Later in 1963 a Legislative Assembly of 30 elected and 3 nominated members was established under the Government of Union Territories Act 1963. Because of the unstable party position in the Assembly, it had to be dissolved on 16 Oct. 1969 and President's Rule introduced. The status of the administration was raised from Chief Commissioner to Lieut.-Governor with effect from 19 Dec. 1969. On the 21 Jan. 1972 Manipur became a state and the status of the administrator was changed from Lieut.-Governor to Governor.

AREA AND POPULATION. The state is in north-east India and is bounded north by Nagaland, east by Burma, south by Burma and Mizoram, and west by Assam. Manipur has an area of 22,356 sq. km and a population (1971) of 1,072,753. Density, 48 per sq. km. Estimated population, 1976, 1·2m. The valley, which is about 1,813 sq. km, is 2,600 ft above sea-level. The hills rise in places to nearly 10,000 ft, but are mostly about 5,000–6,000 ft. The average annual rainfall is 65 in. The hill areas are inhabited by various hill tribes who constitute about one-third of the total population of the state. There are about 40 tribes and sub-tribes falling into two main groups of Nagas and Kukis. A large number of dialects are spoken, while Hindi is gradually becoming prevalent.

CONSTITUTION AND GOVERNMENT. With the attainment of state-hood, Manipur has a Legislative Assembly of 60 members, of which 19 are from reserved tribal constituencies. There are 6 districts. Capital, Imphal (population, 1971, 100,366). Presidential rule was imposed in Feb. 1981.

Governor: L. P. Singh.

BUDGET. Revised estimates for 1977–78 show revenue of Rs 4,247·82 lakhs and expenditure on revenue account of Rs 4,774·24 lakhs.

ENERGY AND NATURAL RESOURCES

Electricity. Installed capacity, 1977–78, 10·4 mw. There were 212 villages with electricity.

Agriculture. Rice is the principal crop; production, 1977–78, 179,130 tonnes from 299,980 hectares. Total foodgrains, 1977–78, 193,670 tonnes.

INDUSTRY. Handloom weaving is a popular industry. Many development schemes are in progress under the 5-year plans.

COMMUNICATIONS. A national highway from Kazirangar (Assam) runs through Imphal to the Burmese frontier. There are no railways. There is an airport at Imphal with regular scheduled services to Gauhati and Calcutta.

EDUCATION AND HEALTH

Education. In 1976–77 there were 3,467 primary schools, 337 middle schools, 235 high and higher schools and 20 colleges. There were 36 trade and vocational training colleges. The number enrolled at the schools and colleges was 333,868.

Health. In 1977–78 there were 33 hospitals (including primary health centres) and 125 dispensaries (including primary health centres).

MEGHALAYA

HISTORY. The state was created under the Assam Reorganization (Meghalaya) Act 1969 and inaugurated on 2 April 1970. Its status was that of a state within the State of Assam until 21 Jan. 1972 when it became a fully independent state of the Union. It consists of the former Garo Hills district and United Khasi and Jaintia Hills district of Assam.

AREA AND POPULATION. Meghalaya is bounded north and east by Assam, south and west by Bangladesh. In 1971 (census figure) the area was 22,489 sq. km and the population 1,011,699. Density 45 per sq. km. Population estimate, 1976, 1·1m. The people are mainly of the Khasi, Jaintia and Garo tribes.

CONSTITUTION AND GOVERNMENT. Meghalaya has a unicameral legislature. The Legislative Assembly has 60 seats. State of the parties following elections in Feb. 1978: All-Party Hill Leaders' Conference, 16; Congress, 20; HSPDP, 14; independents, 10.

There are 2 districts. The capital is Shillong, shared at present with Assam.

Governor: L. P. Singh.
Chief Minister: D. D. Dohpugh.

BUDGET. Budget estimates for 1980–81 showed a surplus on revenue account of Rs 9·85 crores and a deficit on capital account of Rs 13·4 crores, giving an overall deficit of Rs 3·56 crores.

ENERGY AND NATURAL RESOURCES

Electricity. Total installed capacity (1977) was 65·2 mw. 388 villages had electricity.

Minerals. The United Khasi and Jaintia Hills district produces coal, sillimanite (95% of India's total output), limestone, white clay and corundum. The state also has deposits of coal (estimated reserves 1,200m. tonnes), limestone (2,100m.), fire-clay (100,000) and sandstone which are virtually untapped because of transport difficulties. Value of production, 1976, Rs 3·26m.

Agriculture. About 80% of the people depend on agriculture, and 27% of the cultivable area is irrigated. Principal crops are potatoes, fresh fruit and cotton. Production 1978 (in 1,000 tonnes): Foodgrains, 130; potatoes, 71; tapioca, 5; jute, 50,000 bales (of 180 kg). Annual production (in 1,000 tonnes, estimated) of pineapples, 70; oranges, 80; bananas, 35.

Forest products are the state's chief resources.

INDUSTRY. Apart from agriculture the main source of employment is the extraction and processing of minerals; there are also important timber processing mills.

COMMUNICATIONS. A national highway from Gauhati (Assam) runs through Dispur and Shillong. The state has no railways. There is no airport but Gauhati airport is on the northern boundary.

JUSTICE. There is a High Court at Shillong which is common to Assam, Meghalaya, Nagaland, Manipur, Tripura and the Union Territories of Mizoram and Arunachal Pradesh.

NAGALAND

HISTORY. The territory was constituted by the Union Government in Sept. 1962. It comprises the former Naga Hills district of Assam and the former Tuensang Frontier division of the North-East Frontier Agency; these had been made a Centrally Administered Area in 1957, administered by the President through the Governor of Assam. In Jan. 1961 the area was renamed and given the status of a state of the Indian Union, which was officially inaugurated on 1 Dec. 1963.

For some years a section of the Naga leaders sought independence. Military operations from 1960 and the prospect of self-government within the Indian Union led to a general reconciliation, but rebel activity continued. A 2-month amnesty in mid-1963 had little effect. A 'ceasefire' in Sept. 1964 was followed by talks between a Government of India delegation and rebel leaders. The peace period was extended and the 'Revolutionary Government of Nagaland' (a breakaway group from the Naga Federal Government) was dissolved in 1973. Further talks with the Naga underground movement resulted in the Shillong Peace Agreement of Nov. 1975.

AREA AND POPULATION. The state is in the extreme north-east and is bounded west and north by Assam, east by Burma and south by Manipur. Nagaland has an area of 16,527 sq. km and a population (1971 census) of 516,449.

Density 31 per sq. km. Population estimate, 1976, 600,000. Towns include Kohima, Mokokchung, Tuensang and Dimapur. The chief tribes in numerical order are: Angami, Ao, Sema, Konyak, Chakhesang, Lotha, Phom, Khiamngan, Chang, Yimchunger, Zeliang-Kuki, Rengma and Sangtam.

CONSTITUTION AND GOVERNMENT. An Interim Body (Legislative Assembly) of 42 members elected by the Naga people and an Executive Council (Council of Ministers) of 5 members were formed in 1961, and continued until the State Assembly was elected in Jan. 1964. The initial strength of this Assembly was 46, with 8 cabinet ministers. Since 1974 there have been 60 members. The Cabinet comprises the Chief Minister, 5 Cabinet Ministers and 2 Deputy Ministers. The Governor has extraordinary powers, which include special responsibility for law and order. On 5 June 1980 a Naga National Democratic Party government took office.

The state has 7 districts (Kohima, Mon, Zunheboto, Wokha, Phek, Mokokchung and Tuensang). The capital is Kohima.

Governor: L. P. Singh.
Chief Minister: J. B. Jasokie.

BUDGET. Budget estimates for 1974–75 show total revenue of Rs 47,43·32 lakhs and expenditure of Rs 47,53·19 lakhs. Receipts included: Statutory grant under the Finance Commission award, Rs 23,77 lakhs; share of central taxes and duties, Rs 1,17·18 lakhs; grants-in-aid for plan expenditure, Rs 6,40·80 lakhs; loans from the Government of India, Rs 71·20 lakhs; grant for roads, Rs 3,64·94 lakhs.

ENERGY AND NATURAL RESOURCES

Electricity. Installed capacity (1976) 2,126 kw; 176 villages (out of 814) had electricity.

Agriculture. More than 80% of the people derive their livelihood from agriculture. The Angamis, in Kohima district, practise a fixed agriculture in the shape of terraced slopes, and wet paddy cultivation in the lowlands. In the other two districts there is a traditional form of shifting cultivation (*jhumming*). About 1,223,000 hectares were under cultivation in 1977. Production of rice (1977) was 94,530 tonnes.

Forests cover 17·56% of the state.

INDUSTRY. There is a forest products factory at Tijit; a paper-mill (100 tonnes daily capacity) and a distillery unit were under construction in 1978–79. There is also a sugar-mill (1,200 tonnes daily capacity).

COMMUNICATIONS. There is a national highway from Kaziranga (Assam) to Kohima and on to Manipur. There were 3,502 motor vehicles in 1976. There are no railways, and no airports.

RELIGION AND EDUCATION

Religion. At the 1971 census Christians numbered 344,798; Hindus, 59,031; Moslems, 2,966; others, 108. The Naga Baptist Christian Convention had, 1969, 632 churches and a total church membership of 73,500.

Education. The 1971 census records 27·4% literacy. In 1976 there were 2 government and 5 private colleges, 45 government and 41 private high schools, 171 government and 88 private middle schools and 916 lower primary schools, 1 polytechnic, 3 teacher-training schools and 151 adult literary centres.

Aram, M., *Peace in Nagaland*, New Delhi, 1974
Mankekar, D. R., *Slippery Slope of Nagaland*. New Delhi, 1965
Rattan, H. R., *Nagaland is Born*. Calcutta, 1964

ORISSA

HISTORY. Orissa, ceded to the Mahrattas by Alivardi Khan in 1751, was conquered by the British in 1803. In 1804 a board of 2 commissioners was appointed to administer the province, but in the following year it was designated the district of Cuttack and was placed in charge of a collector, judge and magistrate. In 1823 it was split up into 3 regulation districts of Cuttack, Balasore and Puri, and the non-regulation tributary states which were administered by their own chiefs under the ægis of the British Government. Angul, one of these tributary states, was annexed in 1847, and with the Khondmals, ceded in 1835 by the tributary chief of the Boudh state, constituted a separate non-regulation district. Sambalpur was transferred from the Central Provinces to Orissa in 1905. These districts formed an outlying tract of the Bengal Presidency till 1912, when they were transferred to Bihar, constituting one of its divisions under a commissioner. Orissa was constituted a separate province on 1 April 1936, some portions of the Central Provinces and Madras being transferred to the old Orissa division.

The rulers of 25 Orissa states surrendered all jurisdiction and authority to the Government of India on 1 Jan. 1948, on which date the Provincial Government took over the administration. The administration of 2 states, viz., Saraikella and Kharswan, was transferred to the Government of Bihar in May 1948. By an agreement with the Dominion Government, Mayurbhanj State was finally merged with the province on 1 Jan. 1949. By the States Merger (Governors' Provinces) Order, 1949, the states were completely merged with the state of Orissa on 19 Aug. 1949.

AREA AND POPULATION. Orissa is in eastern India and is bounded north by Bihar, north-east by West Bengal, east by the Bay of Bengal, south by Andhra Pradesh and west by Madhya Pradesh. The area of the state is 155,782 sq. km, and its population (1971 census), 21,944,615, density 141 per sq. km. Population estimate, 1976, 24·4m. The second-largest city next to Cuttack (*see* pp. 605–606) is Rourkela, with 172,502 inhabitants. The principal language is Oriya.

CONSTITUTION AND GOVERNMENT. The Legislative Assembly has 147 members. State of the parties after the elections of May 1980: Congress (I), 117; Janata (Charan Singh), 13; others, 16.

The state consists of 17 districts, of which 4 are linked with other districts for administrative purposes.

The capital is Bhubaneswar (18 miles south of Cuttack).

Governor: C. M. Poonacha.
Chief Minister: J. B. Patnaik.

BUDGET. Budget estimates, 1980–81 showed total revenue of Rs 1,257·3 crores and expenditure of Rs 1,235·6 crores (capital and revenue accounts).

ENERGY AND NATURAL RESOURCES

Electricity. The Hirakud Dam Project on the river Mahanadi (started 1949) irrigates 1·8m. acres and has a scheduled capacity of 270,000 kw. The dam (the largest earth dam in the world) was completed in 1957. Hydro-electric power totalling 85,000 kw. is now serving Sambalpur, Cuttack, Puri and Dhenkanal districts. The installed capacity of the Machkund hydro-electric project (financed jointly with Andhra Pradesh) is 114,750 kw. Total installed capacity, 1979, 923 mw.; there were 15,568 electrified villages.

Minerals. The chief minerals are iron ore (7·3m. tonnes in 1979), manganese ore 661,000 tonnes, (about 20% of India's total), coal (2·5m. tonnes), chromite (236,000 tonnes), bauxite (3m. tonnes), limestone and dolomite (759,000 tonnes). About 36,000 workers are employed in the mines. Value of mineral production, 1979, Rs 608·9m.

Agriculture. The cultivation of rice is the principal occupation of nearly 80% of the population. Production amounted to 4·44m. tonnes in 1978–79; only a very small amount of other cereals is grown. Production of foodgrains (1978–79) totalled 4·9m. tonnes from 5·1m. hectares. Jute (439,000 tonnes), wheat (110,000 tonnes), oilseeds (426,950 tonnes) and sugar-cane (281,000 tonnes) are also grown. Turmeric is cultivated in the uplands of the districts of Ganjam, Phulbani and Koraput, and is exported.

Livestock (1977 census): Buffaloes, 1,571,271; other cattle, 12·6m.; sheep, 1·72m.; goats, 3·1m.; horses and ponies, 16,807.

Forests. Forests occupy about 43% of the area of the state, the most important species being sal, teak and kendu.

Fisheries. There were, in 1979, 220 fishery co-operative societies.

INDUSTRY. Fifty-five large industries have been set up (1978–79), mostly based on minerals, including the steel plant of Hindustan Steel Ltd at Rourkela, a pig-iron plant at Barbil, a ferrochrome plant, 2 ferromanganese plants at Joda and Jeypore, 1 ferrosilicon plant at Theruvelli and an aluminium smelter plant at Hirakud, 3 refractory plants at Belpahar, Rajgangpur and Laitkata and 2 cement plants at Bargarh and Rajgangpur. There are 3 large paper mills at Rayagada, Chowdwar and Brajrajnagar, a fertilizer plant at Rourkela, a caustic soda plant, a salt manufacturing unit and an industrial explosives plant.

Other industries of importance are sugar, glass, aluminium, heavy machine tools, a re-rolling mill and textile mills, and fertilizer plants.

There are cottage and small-scale industries in the state, e.g., handloom weaving and the manufacture of baskets, wooden articles, hats and nets; silver filigree work and hand-woven fabrics are specially well known.

TOURISM. Tourist traffic is concentrated mainly on the 'Golden Triangle', Konark, Puri and Bhubaneswar, and its temples. Tourists also visit the Similipal Forest and Chilka Lake.

COMMUNICATIONS

Roads. On 31 March 1978 length of roads was: State highway, 2,189 km; major district roads, 5,049 km; other district roads, 2,320 km; village roads, about 6,560 km. There were 94,156 motor vehicles in 1979. An 80-km expressway connects the Daitari mining area with Paradip Port.

Railways. The total length of railway in 1979 was 1,948 km, of which 1,310 km was single line.

Aviation. There is an airport at Bhubaneswar with regular scheduled services to New Delhi, Calcutta and Hyderabad.

Shipping. Paradip was declared a 'major' port in 1966 and has been developed to handle 2m. tons of traffic. Other minor ports at Chandbali and Gopalpur.

JUSTICE, RELIGION AND EDUCATION

Justice. The High Court of Judicature at Cuttack has a Chief Justice and 6 puisne judges.

Religion. There were in 1971: Hindus (including scheduled castes and scheduled tribes), 21,121,056; Christians, 378,888; Moslems, 326,507; Sikhs, 10,204; Buddhists, 8,462; Jains, 6,521.

Education. The percentage of literates in the population is 26·2% (males, 38·3%, females, 13·9%).

In 1977–78 there were 32,027 primary and 2,030 secondary schools.

Utkal University was established in 1943 at Cuttack and moved to Bhubaneswar in 1962; it is both teaching and affiliating. It has 2 university colleges (engineering and law) and 67 affiliated colleges. Berhampur University has 16 affiliated colleges and Orissa University of Agriculture and Technology 4 constituent colleges. Sambalpur University has 34 affiliated colleges.

PUNJAB (INDIA)

HISTORY. The Punjab was constituted an autonomous province of India in 1937. In 1947, the province was partitioned between India and Pakistan into East and West Punjab respectively, under the Indian Independence Act, 1947, the boundaries being determined under the Radcliffe Award. The name of East Punjab was changed to Punjab (India) under the Constitution of India. On 1 Nov. 1956 the erstwhile states of Punjab and Patiala and East Punjab States Union (PEPSU) were integrated to form the state of Punjab. On 1 Nov. 1966, under the Punjab Reorganization Act, 1966, the state was reconstituted as a Punjabi-speaking state comprising the districts of Gurdaspur (excluding Dalhousie), Amritsar, Kapurthala, Jullundur, Ferozepore, Bhatinda, Patiala and Ludhiana; parts of Sangrur, Hoshiarpur and Ambala districts; and part of Kharar tehsil. The remaining area comprising an area of 18,000 sq. miles and an estimated (1967) population of 8·5m. was shared between the new state of Haryana and the Union Territory of Himachal Pradesh. The existing capital of Chandigarh was made the joint capital of Punjab and Haryana.

AREA AND POPULATION. The Punjab is in north India and is bounded at its northernmost point by Kashmir, north-east by Himachal Pradesh, south-east by Haryana, south by Rajasthan, west and north-west by Pakistan. The area of the state is 50,376 sq. km, with census (1971) population of 13,551,060. Density 270 per sq. km. Population estimate, 1976, 15m. The largest cities, see pp. 605–606. The official language is Punjabi.

CONSTITUTION AND GOVERNMENT. Punjab (India) has a unicameral legislature of 117 members. The Legislative Council was abolished in Jan. 1970. The Legislative Assembly was composed as follows after the election of May 1980: Congress (I), 63; Akali Dal, 37; others, 17.

There are 12 districts. The capital is Chandigarh (see p 668). There are 104 municipalities, 116 community development blocks and 9,331 elected village *panchayats*.

Governor: J. S. Lal Hathi.
Chief Minister: D. Singh.

BUDGET. Budget estimates, 1980–81, showed a deficit of Rs 70 crores. Annual Plan outlay, 1980–81, Rs 300 crores.

ENERGY AND NATURAL RESOURCES

Electricity. Installed capacity, 1976, was 719 mw; all villages had electricity.

Agriculture. About 70% of the population depends on agriculture. Agricultural prosperity is mainly due to irrigation. The irrigated area rose from 2·21m. hectares in 1950–51 to 2·95m. hectares in 1972–73: total production of foodgrains rose from 1·99m. tonnes to 7·7m. tonnes in 1972–73. Production in 1,000 tonnes (area in 1,000 hectares) in 1972–73: Wheat, 5,361 (2,386); maize, 738 (549); rice, 1,163 (508); oilseeds, 287 (347); sugar-cane (gur), 597 (112); cotton, 961,000 bales (of 180 kg) from 499,000 hectares. Food-grain production, 1977, 9·2m. tonnes.

Livestock (1972 census): Buffaloes, 3,839,200; other cattle, 3·41m.; sheep and goats, 1,205,400; horses and ponies, 54,700; poultry, 3m.

Forestry. In 1974 there were 215,665 hectares of forest land, of which 99,849 hectares belonged to the Forest Department.

INDUSTRY. In Jan. 1974 the number of registered factories in the Punjab (India) was 5,136; 4,933 operational factories employed about 127,451 people. The chief manufactures are textiles (especially woollen hosiery), sewing machines, sports goods, sugar, starch, fertilizers, bicycles, scientific instruments, electrical goods, machine tools and pine oil. In 1977 there were 43,030 important small manufacturing units.

COMMUNICATIONS

Roads. The total length of metalled roads on 31 March 1973 was 18,207 km. State transport services cover 249,350 route km daily with a fleet of 1,405 buses carrying a daily average of 350,000 passengers. Coverage by private operators is estimated as 40%. In 1976 there were 112,653 motor vehicles.

Railways. The Punjab possesses an extensive system of railway communications, served by the Northern Railway. Total length, 3,371 km.

Aviation. There is an airport at Amritsar, and Chandigarh airport is on the north-eastern boundary; both have regular scheduled services to Delhi.

JUSTICE, RELIGION, EDUCATION AND WELFARE

Justice. The Punjab and Haryana High Court exercises jurisdiction over the states of Punjab and Haryana and the territory of Chandigarh. It is located in Chandigarh. It consists (1973) of a Chief Justice and 17 puisne judges.

Religion. At the 1971 census Hindus numbered 5,037,235; Sikhs, 8,159,172; Moslems, 114,447; Christians, 162,202; Jains, 21,383; Buddhists, 1,374.

Education. Compulsory education was introduced in April 1961; at the same time free education was introduced up to 8th class for boys and 9th class for girls as well as fee concessions. The aim is education for all children of 6–11.

In 1974–75 there were 8,969 primary schools, 1,220 middle schools and 1,478 higher secondary schools.

Punjab University was established in 1947 at Chandigarh as an examining, teaching and affiliating body. It is shared with Haryana and Himachal Pradesh. In 1962 Punjabi University was established at Patiala and an agricultural university at Ludhiana. Guru Nanak University has been established at Amritsar to mark the 500th anniversary celebrations for Guru Nanak Dev, first Guru of the Sikhs. Altogether there are 179 affiliated colleges, 151 for arts and science, 14 for teacher training, 5 medical, 1 dental, 2 engineering and 6 for other studies.

Health. Punjab claims the longest life expectancy (58·6 years for women, 63·5 for men) and lowest death rate (7·48 per 1,000). There were (1974) 888 medical institutions, including 126 hospitals, 296 Ayurvedic dispensaries, 128 primary health centres and 338 dispensaries.

Mangat Rai, E. N., *Civil Administration in the Punjab.* Cambridge, Mass., 1963
Singh, Khushwant, *A History of the Sikhs.* 2 vols. Princeton and OUP, 1964–67

RAJASTHAN

HISTORY. As a result of the implementation of the States Reorganization Act, 1956, the erstwhile state of Ajmer, Abu Taluka of Bombay State and the Sunel Tappa enclave of the former state of Madhya Bharat were transferred to the state of Rajasthan on 1 Nov. 1956, whereas the Sironj subdivision of Rajasthan was transferred to the state of Madhya Pradesh.

AREA AND POPULATION. Rajasthan is in north-west India and is bounded north by Punjab, north-east by Haryana and Uttar Pradesh, east by Madhya Pradesh, south by Gujarat and west by Pakistan. The area of the state is 342,214 sq. km and its population (1971) census, 25,765,806, density 75 per sq. km. Population estimate, 1976, 29m. The chief cities, *see* pp. 605–606.

CONSTITUTION AND GOVERNMENT. There is a unicameral legislature, the Legislative Assembly, having 200 members. The state of the parties in the Assembly after the election of May 1980, was: Congress (I), 133; Bhartiya Janata, 32; Janata, 8; Janata (Charan Singh), 7; others, 20.

The capital is Jaipur. There are 26 districts.

Governor: Raghukul Tilak.
Chief Minister: J. Pahadia.

BUDGET. Budget estimates for 1979–80 show total revenue receipts of Rs 798·48 crores, and expenditure of Rs 854·92 crores. Receipts included: share in Central taxes, Rs 154·19 crores; state excise, Rs 21·54 crores, sales tax, Rs 133 crores; vehicles taxes, Rs 9·07 crores; non-tax revenue, Rs 245·46 crores. Expenditure included: Education, Rs 125·54 crores; water and power, Rs 184·43 crores; medical and public health, Rs 41·97 crores; agriculture, Rs 126·03 crores. Budget estimates 1980–81 showed a deficit of Rs 58·04 crores; gross Plan expenditure, Rs 348·36 crores (of which Rs 193·45 crores were for irrigation and power).

ENERGY AND NATURAL RESOURCES

Electricity. Installed capacity in 1979–80, 1,150 mw. By Aug. 1979, 12,651 villages and 160,366 wells had electric power, and a number of rural electrification schemes were in progress.

Minerals. The state is rich in minerals. In 1976, 7m. tonnes of gypsum and 581,000 tonnes of rock phosphate were produced. Other minerals include silver, asbestos, felspar, copper, limestone and salt. Total value of principal mineral production in 1977 was about Rs 44 crores.

Agriculture. The sown area is (1977–78) about 16·9m. hectares, of which 3·1m. is irrigated. Production of principal crops (in 1,000 tonnes), 1977–78: Rabi, 4,777; pulses (Kharif), 2,374; sugar-cane (gur), 2,825; total oilseeds, 224; cotton, 479,000 bales (of 180 kg). Total foodgrains, 1977, 7,480. Tractors numbered 36,250 in 1978–79.

Livestock (1977): Buffaloes, 4,592,489; other cattle, 12,469,509; sheep, 8,557,295; goats, 12,162,441; horses and ponies, 48,089; poultry, 1,235,036.

INDUSTRY. In 1979 there were 5,049 (1,949 in 1965) factories subject to the Factories Act, 1948. In Jan. 1979 there were 31,292 small industrial units employing 203,819; 121 industrial estates were developed. Total capital investment in small units, Rs 1,179m. Chief manufactures are cotton textiles, cement, glass and sugar. Production, 1977 estimate: Cloth, 69m. metres; yarn, 33m. kg; cement, 208,750 tonnes; sugar, 35,190 tonnes.

COMMUNICATIONS

Roads. In 1978–79 there were 39,194 km of roads including 10,893 km of unsurfaced roads in Rajasthan; there were 2,110 km of national highway. Motor vehicles numbered 238,114 in 1978.

Railways. Jodhpur, Marwar, Udaipur, Ajmer, Jaipur and Sawai Madhopur are important junctions of the north-western network.

Aviation. There are airports at Jaipur, Jodhpur and Udaipur with regular scheduled services to Bombay and Delhi.

JUSTICE, RELIGION, EDUCATION AND WELFARE

Justice. The seat of the High Court is at Jodhpur. There is a Chief Justice and 11 puisne judges. There is also a bench of 5 judges at Jaipur.

Religion. At the 1971 census Hindus numbered 23,093,895; Moslems, 1,778,275; Jains, 513,548; Sikhs, 341,182; Christians, 30,202.

Education. The proportion of literates to the total population was 19·07% at the 1971 census.

In 1977–78 enrolment in 27,141 schools was 3,545,000; primary schools had 1·59m. students, 5,031 middle schools had 1m. students and 1,814 secondary and higher schools had 673,466. Elementary education is free but not compulsory. The percentage in 1977–78 of children attending schools in the age-group 6–11 was 57·29 (40·9 in 1961), in the 11–14 age-group 27·22 (14·4).

In 1977–78 there were 116 colleges. Enrolment at these and at the 4 universities (one deemed a university) was 125,664. Rajasthan University, established at Jaipur in 1947, is teaching and affiliating; Jodhpur University was founded in 1962; Udaipur University and Rajasthan Agricultural University are both at Udaipur. There are also 4 agricultural colleges, 1 veterinary and animal science college, 4 engineering colleges, 5 government or aided Ayurvedic colleges and 6 polytechnics.

Health. In 1979 there were 1,163 hospitals and dispensaries. Rajasthan had (1976) 1,981 doctors and 8,077 nurses and assistants. There are 5 medical colleges.

In 1979 there were 1,163 hospitals and dispensaries, 232 primary health centres, 55 Unani, 43 homoepathic and 2 naturopathy hospitals. There were 100 maternity centres, and 2,296 Ayurvedic hospitals and dispensaries.

SIKKIM

HISTORY. Sikkim became the twenty-second state of the Indian Union in May 1975. It is inhabited chiefly by the Lepchas, who are a tribe indigenous to Sikkim with their own dress and language, the Bhutias, who originally came from Tibet, and the Nepalis, who entered from Nepál in large numbers in the late 19th and early 20th century. The main languages spoken are Bhutia, Lepcha and Khaskura (Nepali). Being a small country Sikkim had frequently been involved in struggles over her territory, and as a result her boundaries have been very much reduced over the centuries. In particular the Darjeeling district was acquired from Sikkim by the British East India Company in 1839. The Namgyal dynasty had been ruling Sikkim since the 14th century; the first consecrated ruler was Phuntsog Namgya I who was consecrated in 1642 and given the title of 'Chogyal', meaning 'King ruling in accordance with religious laws', derived from Cho—religion and Gyalpo—king.

Sikkim is a land of wide variation in altitude, climate and vegetation, and is known for the great number and variety of birds, butterflies, wild flowers and orchids to be found in the different regions. It is a fertile land and to the Sikkimese is known as Denjong, The Valley of Rice.

AREA AND POPULATION. Sikkim is in the Eastern Himalayas and is bounded north by Tibet, east by Tibet and Bhután, south by West Bengal and west by Nepál. Area, 7,298 sq. km. Census population (1971), 208,609, of whom 15,000 lived in the capital, Gangtok. Population estimate, 1977, 250,000.

CONSTITUTION AND GOVERNMENT. Sikkim was joined to the British Empire by a treaty in 1886 until 1947, but that relationship ceased when Britain withdrew from India in 1947. Thereafter there was a standstill agreement between India and Sikkim until a treaty was signed on 5 Dec. 1950 between India and Sikkim by which Sikkim became a protectorate of India and India undertook to be responsible for Sikkim's defence, external relations and strategic communications.

The Chogyal had governed Sikkim with the help of the Sikkim Council, consisting of 18 elected members and 6 members nominated by the Chogyal. Sikkim parties represented were: National Party, Sikkim National Congress and, later, Sikkim Janta Congress.

Political reforms were demanded by the National Congress and the Janta Congress in March–April 1973 and Indian police took over control of law and order at the request of the Chogyal. On 13 April it was announced that the Chogyal had agreed to meet most of the political demands. Elections were held in April 1974 to a popularly-elected assembly. By the Government of Sikkim Act, June 1974, the Chogyal became a constitutional monarch with power of assent to the Assembly's legislation. By the Constitution (Thirty-Sixth Amendment) Act 1974 Sikkim became a state associated with the Indian Union. The office of Chogyal was abolished in April 1975. By the Constitution (Thirty-Eighth Amendment) Act 1975 Sikkim became the twenty-second state of the Indian Union. The Assembly has 32 members with a cabinet of 8 ministers including the Chief Minister. The Janata Parishad party holds

21 seats, the Sikkim Revolutionary Congress party holds 8, Sikkim Aajatantra Congress holds 1, Independents, 2.

Governor: **B. B. Lal.**

The official language of the Government is English. Lepcha, Bhutia and Nepali have also been declared official languages.

Sikkim is divided into 4 districts for administration purposes, Gangtok, Mangan, Namchi and Gyalshing being the headquarters for the Eastern, Northern, Southern and Western districts respectively. Each district is administered by a District Collector. Within this framework are the *Panchayats* or Village Councils, representing the villages.

ECONOMY

Planning. The sixth Five-Year Plan began in 1980.

Budget. The annual budget for 1980–81 is Rs 2,044 lakhs. This does not include centrally sponsored schemes.

ENERGY AND NATURAL RESOURCES

Electricity. There are 4 operational hydro-electric power stations; the Lagyap project is also being implemented by the Government of India as aid to meet the growing demand for electrical power for new industries. The first of its two 6 mv generators was commissioned 1 Sept. 1979.

Agriculture. The economy is mainly agricultural; main crops are rice, maize, millet, cardamom (a spice), mandarin oranges, apples, potatoes, ginger and soybean. A tea plantation has recently been started. Forests occupy about 1,000 sq. km. of the land area (excluding hill pastures) and the potential for a timber and wood-pulp industry is being explored. Some medicinal herbs are exported.

INDUSTRY AND TRADE

Industry. There is a state Industrial Development Investment Corporation and an Industrial Training Institute offering 7 trades. There is a distillery at Rangpo and a fruit preservation factory at Singtam. Copper, zinc and lead are mined by the Sikkim Mining Corporation. A recent survey by the Geological Survey of India and the Indian Bureau of Mines has confirmed further deposits of copper, zinc, silver and gold in Dikchu, North Sikkim. There is a jewel-bearing factory for the production of industrial jewels. A watch factory has been set up in collaboration with Hindustan Machine Tools (India). A number of small manufacturing units for leather, wire nails, storage cells batteries, candles, safety matches and carpets, are already producing in the private sector. Local crafts include carpet weaving, making handmade paper, wood carving and silverwork. To encourage trading in indigenous products, particularly agricultural produce, the State Trading Corporation of Sikkim has been established.

Tourism. There is great potential for the tourist industry; a 78-bed lodge at Gangtok and a 50-bed tourist lodge in West Sikkim have been opened. Tourism has been stimulated by the opening of new roads from Pemayangtse to Yuksam in West Sikkim and from Yuksam to the Dzongri Glacier.

COMMUNICATIONS

Roads. There are 1,355 miles of motorable roads, all on mountainous terrain, and 200 major bridges under the Public Works Department. Public transport and road haulage is nationalized.

Railways. The nearest railhead is at Siliguri (72 miles from Gangtok).

Aviation. The nearest airport is at Bagdogra (80 miles from Gangtok).

Post and Broadcasting. There are 790 telephones (1977) and 32 wireless stations.

RELIGION, EDUCATION AND WELFARE

Religion. The state religion is Mahayana Buddhism, but a large proportion of the population is Hindu. There are some Christians, Moslems and members of other religions.

Education. Sikkim has 100 pre-primary schools, 321 primary schools, 44 junior high schools, 29 high schools, 8 higher secondary schools. Education is free up to class XII. There is also a training institute for primary teachers, a law college and a degree college. Estimated spending on education, 1980–81, Rs 29·78m. (Rs 6·4m. in 1975).

Health. There are 4 district hospitals at Singtam, Gyalshing, Namchi and Mangan, and one central referral hospital at Gangtok, besides 15 primary health centres, 26 sub-centres and 8 dispensaries, a maternity ward, chest clinic and 2 blocks for tuberculosis patients. There are 86 doctors. Medical and hospital treatment is free; there is a health centre for every 20,000 of the population. Small-pox and Kala-azar have been completely eliminated and many schemes for the provision of safe drinking water to villages and bazaars have been implemented.

Coelho, V. H., *Sikkim and Bhutan*. New Delhi, 1970
Olschak, B. C., *Sikkim*. Zürich, 1965
Mele, F., *Sikkim*. Paris, 1974

TAMIL NADU

HISTORY. The first trading establishment made by the British in the Madras State was at Peddapali (now Nizampatnam) in 1611 and then at Masulipatnam. In 1639 the English were permitted to make a settlement at the place which is now Madras, and Fort St George was founded. By 1801 the whole of the country from the Northern Circars to Cape Comorin (with the exception of certain French and Danish settlements) had been brought under British rule.

Under the provisions of the States Reorganization Act, 1956, the Malabar district (excluding the islands of Laccadive and Minicoy) and the Kasaragod district taluk of South Kanara were transferred to the new state of Kerala; the South Kanara district (excluding Kasaragod taluk and the Amindivi Islands) and the Kollegal taluk of the Coimbatore district were transferred to the new state of Mysore; and the Laccadive, Amindivi and Minicoy Islands were constituted a separate Territory. Four taluks of the Trivandrum district and the Shencottah taluk of Quilon district were transferred from Travancore–Cochin to the new Madras State. On 1 April 1960, 405 sq. miles from the Chittoor district of Andhra Pradesh were transferred to Madras in exchange for 326 sq. miles from the Chingleput and Salem districts. In Aug. 1968 the state was renamed Tamil Nadu.

AREA AND POPULATION. Tamil Nadu is in south India and is bounded north by Karnataka and Andhra Pradesh, east and south by the Indian ocean and west by Kerala. Area, 130,357 sq. km. Population (1971 census), 41,103,125, density of 313 per sq. km. Population estimate, 1976, 45·4m. Tamil is the principal language and has been adopted as the state language with effect from 14 Jan. 1958. The principal towns, *see* pp. 605–606.

CONSTITUTION AND GOVERNMENT. The Governor is aided by a Council of 16 ministers. There is a bicameral legislature; the Legislative Council has 63 members and the Legislative Assembly has 234 members. The Legislative Assembly was composed as follows after the election of May 1980: All-India Anna DMK, 129; DMK, 38; Congress (I), 30; CPM, 11; CPI, 10; others, 16.

There are 14 districts. The capital is Madras.

Governor: S. Ali.
Chief Minister: M. G. Ramachandran.

BUDGET. Budget estimates for 1980–81, revenue receipts, Rs 982·66 crores, revenue account expenditure, Rs 967·27 crores. Capital outlay, Rs 94·21 crores; plan outlay, Rs 436·37 crores.

ENERGY AND NATURAL RESOURCES

Electricity. Installed capacity 1977 amounted to 2,634 mw; 63,289 towns, hamlets and villages were supplied with electricity.

Minerals. Value of production, 1976, Rs 306·37m. The state has coal, chromite, bauxite, limestone, manganese, mica, quartz, salt, gypsum and feldspar.

Agriculture. Agriculture engages 29% of the population. The land is a fertile plain watered by rivers flowing east from the Western Ghats, particularly the Cauvery and the Tambaraparani. Temperature ranges between 18° C. and 43° C., rainfall between 25 in. and 75 in. Of the total land area (13·01m. hectares), 7,698,000 hectares were cultivable and 3m. hectares were irrigated in 1977. The staple food crops grown are paddy, maize, jawar, bajra, pulses and millets. Important commercial crops are sugar-cane, oilseeds, cashewnuts, cotton, tobacco, coffee, tea, rubber and pepper. The production of foodgrains was 7·39m. tonnes; sugar-cane and oilseeds, 1·35m., and 1,343,000 tonnes respectively.

Livestock (1966 census): Buffaloes, 2,753,049; other cattle, 11,009,368; sheep, 6,641,843; goats, 3,796,736; swine, 874,880; horses, ponies, mules, camels, etc., 185,336; poultry, 10,898,862.

Forestry. The revenue from forests in 1973–74 was Rs 7,35·40 lakhs: sandalwood, Rs 2,82·19 lakhs; timber, Rs 1,08·24 lakhs; firewood, Rs 1,07·91 lakhs. Area of forest land, 1977, 20,910 sq. km.

Fisheries. Landings, 1976, 510,000 tonnes.

INDUSTRY AND TRADE

Industry. The contribution of the industrial sector to the state income was Rs 373 crores in 1972–73. The number of registered factories was 6,713 in 1973. The consumption of power in the industrial sector was 49·5% of total state consumption in 1974. The biggest central sector project is Salem steel plant. Man-days lost in industrial disputes, 1979, 8·38m.

Cotton textiles is one of the major industries. There are nearly 180 cotton textile mills and most of the spinning mills supplying yarn to the decentralized handloom industry. Other important industries are tanning, manufacture of textile machinery, power-driven pumps, bicycles, electrical machinery, tractors, rubber tyres and tubes, bricks and tiles and silk. Tamil Nadu is the second largest producer of cement, while its sugar industry has been expanding rapidly.

Public sector undertakings include the Neyveli lignite complex, integral coach factory, high-pressure boiler plant, photographic film factory, surgical instruments factory, teleprinter factory, oil refinery, continuous casting plant and defence vehicles manufacture. Main exports: tanned hides and skins, leather and cotton goods, tea, coffee, spices, engineering goods, motor-car ancillaries.

Tourism. In 1973, 50,074 tourists visited the state, 35,929 of whom came by air and 14,145 by sea.

COMMUNICATIONS

Roads. At the end of 1973 the state had approximately 78,463 km of roads (about 50,000 km metalled). In 1976 there were 184,475 registered motor vehicles.

Railways. In 1970 there were 6,038 km of railway. Madras and Madurai are the main centres.

Aviation. There are airports at Madras, Tiruchirapalli and Madurai, with regular scheduled services to Bombay, Calcutta and Delhi. Madras is the main centre of airline routes in South India.

Shipping. Madras is the chief port. Important minor ports are Cuddalore and Nagapattinam. There are 9 intermediate ports. A harbour is under construction at Tuticorin.

JUSTICE, RELIGION AND EDUCATION

Justice. There is a High Court at Madras with a Chief Justice and 18 judges.

Police. Strength of armed police battalions, 1973, 4,420; strength of the armed reserve (1972) in the state and in Madras, 356,461.

Religion. At the 1971 census Hindus numbered 36,674,150 (89·2%), Christians, 5·75%; Moslems, 5·11%.

Education. At the 1971 census 39·39% of the total population was literate.

Education is free up to pre-university level. In 1973–74 there were 2,823 high schools with a total enrolment of 1,627,030 students. The number of primary schools was 26,726, and their enrolment, 3,759,140; 5,773 upper primary schools had 2,113,981 pupils. Allotment of expenditure for education for 1974–75, Rs 1,08·52 crores.

There are 3 universities. Madras University (founded in 1857) is affiliating and teaching. It had (1968) 119 colleges for arts and sciences with 106,571 students. Annamalai University, Annamalainagar (founded 1928) is residential; Madurai University (founded 1966) is an affiliating and teaching university.

Statistical Information: The Department of Statistics (Fort St George, Madras) was established in 1948 and reorganized in 1953. *Director:* D. S. Rajabushanam, MA. Main publications: *Annual Statistical Abstract*; *Decennial Statistical Atlas*; *Season and Crop Report*; *Quinquennial Wages Census*; *Quarterly Abstract of Statistics*.

TRIPURA

HISTORY. A Hindu state of great antiquity having been ruled by the Maharajahs for 1,300 years before its accession to the Indian Union on 15 Oct. 1949. With the reorganization of states on 1 Sept. 1956 Tripura became a Union Territory. The Territory was made a State on 21 Jan. 1972.

EVENTS. The state's tribal population, having been under pressure from an influx of refugees from E. Pakistan and later from Bangladesh, became concerned for the forest lands which supported them in their traditional shifting cultivation. They opposed purchase of such land by immigrants; the problem led to serious rioting in June 1980.

AREA AND POPULATION. Tripura is bounded on the north, west and south by Bangladesh, and on the east by Mizoram. The major portion of the state is hilly and mainly jungle. It has an area of 10,477 sq. km and a population of 1,556,342 (1971 census); 1976 estimate, 1·7m.

GOVERNMENT. There is a Legislative Assembly of 60 members. The election of Jan. 1978 was won by the Communist Party of India (Marxist). The territory has 1 district, divided into 10 administrative sub-divisions, namely, Sadar, Khowai, Kailasahar, Dharmanagar, Sonamura, Udaipur, Belonia, Kamalpur, Sabroom and Amarpur.

The capital is Agartala (population, 1961, 54,878).

Governor: L. P. Singh.
Chief Minister: N. Chakravarty.

BUDGET. Budget estimates 1980–81 show revenue receipts of Rs 107·1 crores, and expenditure on revenue account of Rs 108·8 crores. Annual plan expenditure, Rs 35 crores.

ENERGY AND NATURAL RESOURCES

Electricity. Installed capacity (1976), 9·7 mw; there were 245 electrified villages.

Agriculture. About 8% of the cultivated area is irrigated. The tribes practise shifting cultivation, but this is being slowly replaced by modern methods. The main crops are rice, jute, mesta, potatoes, cotton, oilseeds and sugar-cane. Rice production (1976 estimate), 366,000 tonnes.

Forestry. Forests cover about 60% of the land area.

COMMUNICATIONS

Roads. Total length of motorable roads (1974) 3,692 km, of which 1,123 km were surfaced. Vehicles registered, 31 March 1975, 5,526.

Railways. There is a railway between Dharmanagar and Kalkalighat (Assam).

Aviation. There is 1 airport and 3 airstrips. The airport (Agartala) has regular scheduled services to Calcutta.

UTTAR PRADESH

HISTORY. In 1833 the then Bengal Presidency was divided into two parts, one of which became the Presidency of Agra. In 1836 the Agra area was styled the North-West Province and placed under a Lieut.-Governor. The two provinces of Agra and Oudh were placed, in 1877, under one administrator, styled Lieut.-Governor of the North-West Province and Chief Commissioner of Oudh. In 1902 the name was changed to 'United Provinces of Agra and Oudh', under a Lieut.-Governor, and the Lieut.-Governorship was altered to a Governorship in 1921. In 1935 the name was shortened to 'United Provinces'. On Independence, the states of Rampur, Banaras and Tehri-Garwhal were merged with United Provinces. In 1950 the name of the United Provinces was changed to Uttar Pradesh.

AREA AND POPULATION. Uttar Pradesh is in north India and is bounded north by Himachal Pradesh, Tibet and Nepál, east by Bihar, south by Madhya Pradesh and west by Rajasthan, Haryana and Delhi. The area of the state is 294,413 sq. km. Population (1971 census), 88,341,144, a density of 300 per sq. km. Population estimate, 1976, 96·2m. Cities with more than 100,000 population, *see* pp. 605–606. The official language is Hindi.

CONSTITUTION AND GOVERNMENT. Uttar Pradesh has had an autonomous system of government since 1937. There is a bicameral legislature. The Legislative Council has 108 members; the Legislative Assembly has 425, of which 421 were contested at the election of May 1980. Congress (I) won 306; Janata (Charan Singh), 59; Congress (U), 13; Bhartiya Janata, 11; others, 32.

There are 11 administrative divisions, each under a Commissioner, and 54 districts. The number of municipalities (1968) is 142, that of *Zila Parishads* 51 and that of *Antarim Zila Parishads* 3. On 23 March 1970 all *Zila Parishads* were dissolved for 2 years or until their reconstitution.

The capital is Lucknow.

Governor: C. P. N. Singh.
Chief Minister: V. P. Singh.

BUDGET. Budget estimates 1980–81 show revenue receipts of Rs 1,622·34 crores (Rs 504·99 crores from state taxes and Rs 597·04 crores from state's share of central taxes); revenue account expenditure, Rs 1,556·92 crores.

ENERGY AND NATURAL RESOURCES

Electricity. The State Electricity Board had, 31 March 1977, an installed capacity of 2,675 mw. There were 33,193 villages with electricity.

Minerals. Value of production, 1976, Rs 31·769m. The state has magnesite.

Agriculture. Agriculture occupies 78% of the work force. Production of foodgrains (1976), 19·46m. tonnes; sugar-cane (gur), 5·84m.; oilseeds, 1·85m. The state is one of India's main producers of sugar.

Forests cover 17·23% of the state.

INDUSTRY. Sugar production is important; other industries include textiles, distilleries, paper and chemicals. There is an aluminium smelter at Renukoot. An oil refinery at Mathura has capacity of 6m. tonnes per annum. Man-days lost by industrial disputes, 1979, 1·28m.

COMMUNICATIONS

Roads. There were, 31 March 1973, 112,243 km of roads, of which 36,437 km were metalled. (This excludes forest roads.) In 1976 there were 182,343 motor vehicles.

Railways. Lucknow is the main junction of the northern network; other important junctions are Agra, Kanpur, Allahabad and Varanasi.

Aviation. There are airports at Lucknow, Kanpur, Varanasi and Gorakhpur.

JUSTICE, RELIGION AND EDUCATION

Justice. The High Court of Judicature at Allahabad (with a bench at Lucknow) has a Chief Justice, 40 puisne judges including additional judges. There are 45 sessions divisions in the state.

Religion. At the 1971 census Hindus numbered 73,997,597; Moslems, 13,676,533; Sikhs, 369,672; Christians, 131,810; Jains, 124,728; Buddhists, 39,639.

Education. For secondary education there were, in 1973–74, an estimated 3,793 schools, with 1,193,000 scholars, and for primary education, 62,486 schools, with 11,912,000 scholars. Compulsory education for boys was in force in 95 municipalities and for girls in 10 municipalities in 1967.

Uttar Pradesh has 11 universities: Allahabad University (founded 1887) with 3 university colleges, 6 associated colleges and 8,992 students in 1973; Agra University (1927) with 68 affiliated colleges and 74,156 full-time students; the Banaras Hindu University, Varanasi (1916) with 2 constituent colleges, 4 affiliated colleges and 12,999 students; Lucknow University (1921) with 3 university colleges and 26,186 students; Aligarh Muslim University (1920) with 8,000 students in 1963; Rookee University (1948), formerly Thomason College of Civil Engineering (established in 1847) with 1,396 students; Gorakhpur University (1957), with 63 affiliated colleges and 42,524 students; Varanasaya Sanskrit Vishwavidyalaya, Varanasi (1958) with about 1,000 students, and Uttar Pradesh Agriculture University, Phoolbagh (1960) with about 1,870 students. Kanpur University and Meerut University were founded in 1966. The Indian Institute of Technology, Kanpur (1960), has university status; in 1962–63 there were 288 post-graduate students. In 1966–67 an estimated 39,775 students were studying in the universities and 65,084 in the affiliated colleges.

WEST BENGAL

HISTORY. For the history of Bengal under British rule, from 1633 to 1947, *see* THE STATESMAN'S YEAR-BOOK, 1952, p. 183.

Under the terms of the Indian Independence Act, 1947, the Province of Bengal ceased to exist. The Moslem majority districts of East Bengal, consisting of the Chittagong and Dacca Divisions and portions of the Presidency and Rajshahi Divisions, became what was then East Pakistan.

AREA AND POPULATION. West Bengal is in north-east India and is bounded north by Sikkim and Bhután, east by Assam and Bangladesh, south by the Bay of Bengal and Orissa, west by Bihar and north-west by Nepál. The total area of West Bengal is 87,853 sq. km. At the 1971 census its population was 44,312,011, an increase of 27% since 1961, the density of population 507 per sq. km. Estimated population, 1976, 49·8m. Population of chief cities, *see* pp. 605–606. The principal language is Bengali.

CONSTITUTION AND GOVERNMENT. The state of West Bengal came into existence as a result of the Indian Independence Act, 1947. The territory of

Cooch-Behar State was merged with West Bengal on 1 Jan. 1950, and the former French possession of Chandernagore became part of the state on 2 Oct. 1954. Under the States Reorganization Act, 1956, certain portions of Bihar State (an area of 3,157 sq. miles with a population of 1,446,385) were transferred to West Bengal.

The Legislative Assembly has 294 seats. Distribution March 1978: Communist Party of India (Marxist), 178; Forward Bloc, 26; Revolutionary Socialist Party, 20; others of the 'Left Front', 7; Janata, 29; Congress, 20; others of the opposition bloc, 14.

The capital is Calcutta.

For administrative purposes there are 2 divisions (Burdwan and Presidency), under which there are 15 districts, excluding Calcutta. The Calcutta Metropolitan Development Authority has been set up to co-ordinate development in the metropolitan area (1,000 sq. km). For the purposes of local self-government there are 15 district boards, 325 *anchalik parishads* (regional boards), 2,926 *anchal* (regional) *panchayats* and 19,662 *gram* (village) *panchayats*. There is no district board in Cooch-Behar district. There are 90 municipalities. The Calcutta Corporation was reconstituted in 1969 with a mayor and deputy mayor, a commissioner, aldermen and standing committees.

Governor: A. L. Dias.
Chief Minister: J. Basu.

BUDGET. The revised estimates for 1975–76 show total revenue of Rs 5,57,44·21 lakhs and expenditure of Rs 5,41,94·17 lakhs. Receipts included: Contributions and adjustments between central and state governments, Rs 1,48,97·64 lakhs; taxes on income, Rs 63,75 lakhs; state excise, Rs 26,50 lakhs; stamps, Rs 21,52 lakhs; sales tax, Rs 1,54,54 lakhs; vehicles taxes, Rs 1,00 lakhs; debt services, Rs 13,33·36 lakhs; civil administration, Rs 35,35·38 lakhs; land revenue, Rs 9,80·12 lakhs. Expenditure included: Education, Rs 1,18,59·65 lakhs; public works and improvements, Rs 17,68·67 lakhs; medical, and family planning, Rs 55,18 lakhs; police, Rs 47,04·25 lakhs; agriculture, Rs 37,31 lakhs; general administration, Rs 4,54·05 lakhs; debt services, Rs 64,13·75 lakhs; extraordinary, including community projects and local developments, Rs 11,61·49 lakhs; industries, Rs 8,21·10 lakhs.

ENERGY AND NATURAL RESOURCES

Electricity. Installed capacity, 1977, 1,367 mw; 11,241 villages had electricity.

Water. Important major irrigation and power schemes at present under construction are the Damodar Valley scheme; the Kansabati project; and the Mayurakshi River project. The Canada Dam on the Mayurakshi was opened on 1 Nov. 1955 and the reservoir irrigates 560,000 acres.

Minerals. Value of production, 1976, Rs 1,784·4m. The state has coal (the Raniganj field is one of the 3 biggest in India) including coking coal.

Agriculture. About 73% of the cultivated area is rice-paddy, one-third of it irrigated. Total foodgrain production, 1975–76, 8·6m. tonnes; oilseeds, 85,000 tonnes; jute (1977), 3·5m. bales (180 kg); wheat (1977), 1m. tonnes. The state produces about half the national output of jute.

Livestock (1971 census): 11,878,083 cattle, 824,161 buffaloes, 793,369 sheep, 5,211,445 goats, 14,548 horses and 15,491,905 poultry; tractors numbered 692.

Forests cover 13·4% of the state.

Fisheries. Landings, 1976, about 264,000 tonnes.

INDUSTRY. The jute textile industry in 1975 employed 243,799 workers. The total number of registered factories, 1975, was 5,977. The coalmining industry had 101 units employing 170,000 workers. There are about 300 tea estates which employ about 214,000 workers. Man-days lost by industrial disputes, 1979, 16·53m.

There is a large automobile factory at Uttarpara, and there are aluminium rolling-mills at Belur and Asansol. At Durgapur a major steel plant was completed in 1962. Durgapur has other industries under the state sector—a thermal power plant, coke oven plant, fertilizer factory, alloy steel plant and ophthalmic glass plant. There are a locomotive factory and cable factory at Chittaranjan and Rupnarayanpur. A refinery and fertilizer factory are operating at Haldia.

COMMUNICATIONS

Roads. In April 1972 the length of national highway was 1,481 km and of other motorable roads 75,081 km. In 1976 the state had 225,889 motor vehicles.

Railways. The length of railways within the state is 2,908 km. The main centres are Calcutta and Durgapur.

Aviation. The main airport is Calcutta which has national and international flights. The second airport is at Bagdogra in the extreme north, which has regular scheduled services to Calcutta.

Shipping. Calcutta is the chief port: a barrage is being built at Farakka to control the flow of water and to provide a rail and road link between North and South Bengal. A second port is being developed at Haldia, halfway between the present port and the sea, which is intended mainly for bulk cargoes. West Bengal possesses 779 km of navigable canals.

JUSTICE, RELIGION AND EDUCATION

Justice. The High Court of Judicature at Calcutta has a Chief Justice and 38 puisne judges. The Andaman and Nicobar Islands (*see below*) come under its jurisdiction.

Police. In 1975–76 the police force numbered 48,421, under an inspector-general. Calcutta has a separate force under a commissioner directly responsible to the Government; its strength was 19,737.

Religion. At the 1971 census Hindus numbered 34,611,864; Moslems, 9,064,338; Christians, 251,752; Buddhists, 121,504; Sikhs, 35,084; Jains, 32,203.

Education. At the 1971 census literacy was 33·05%. In 1972 recognized educational institutions numbered 42,786, with about 5m. pupils. There were 35,484 primary and junior basic schools, with about 3·5m. pupils and 4,133 secondary schools with about 1m. pupils. Primary education is free.

The University of Calcutta (founded 1857) is affiliating and teaching; in 1972–73 it had 24 constituent colleges and 283 affiliated institutions. Visva Bharati, Santiniketan, was originally established by Tagore and is residential and teaching. The University of Jadavpur, Calcutta (1955), had 5,192 students in 1970. Burdwan University was established 15 June 1960 with 31 affiliated colleges previously under the supervision of the University of Calcutta; in 1972–73 there were 196,257 students. Kalyani University was established in 1961. The University of North Bengal had 26,191 students in 1972–73. Rabindra Bharati University had 30 affiliated colleges in 1972.

UNION TERRITORIES

ANDAMAN AND NICOBAR ISLANDS. The Andaman and Nicobar Islands are administered by the President of the Republic of India acting through a Chief Commissioner. There is an Advisory Committee of 20 members associated with the Chief Commissioner and another 12 members associated with the Union Home Minister. The seat of administration is at Port Blair, which is connected with Calcutta (1,255 km away) and Madras (1,190 km) by steamer service which calls about every 10 days; there is a bi-weekly air service from Calcutta. There are 2 districts, each with a Deputy Commissioner.

The population (1971 census) was 115,133; estimate, 1976, 100,000.

Revised estimates for 1977–78 show total revenue receipts of Rs 6,12·56 lakhs, and total expenditure on revenue account of Rs 10,60·44 lakhs, and total capital expenditure of Rs 23,28·01 lakhs.

Chief Commissioner: S. M. Krishnatry.

The **Andaman Islands** lie in the Bay of Bengal, 193 km from Cape Negrais in Burma, 1,255 from Calcutta and 1,190 from Madras. Five large islands grouped together are called the Great Andamans, and to the south is the island of Little Andaman. There are some 204 islets, the two principal groups being the Ritchie Archipelago and the Labyrinth Islands. The total area is about 6,475 sq. km. The Great Andaman group is about 467 km long and, at the widest, 51 km broad.

The original inhabitants live in the forests by hunting and fishing; they are of a small Negrito type and their civilization is about that of the Stone Age. Their exact numbers are not known, as they avoid all contact with civilization. The total population of the Andaman Islands (excluding the aboriginals) was in 1951, 18,962 (12,734 males and 6,228 females). Under a central government scheme started in 1953, some 4,000 displaced families, mostly from East Pakistan, had been settled in the islands by May 1967.

Japanese forces occupied the Andaman Islands on 23 March 1942. Civil administration of the islands was resumed on 8 Oct. 1945.

From 1857 to March 1942 the islands were used by the Government of India as a penal settlement for life and long-term convicts, but the penal settlement was abolished on re-occupation in Oct. 1945.

The Great Andaman group, densely wooded, contains many valuable trees, both hardwood and softwood. The best known of the hardwoods is the *padauk* or Andaman redwood; *gurjan* is in great demand for the manufacture of plywood. Large quantities of softwood are supplied to match factories. Annually the Forest Department export about 25,000 tons of timber to the mainland. Coconut, coffee and rubber are cultivated. The islands are slowly being made self-sufficient in paddy and rice, and now grow approximately half their annual requirements. The average yield of rice in 1966–67 was 1·24 tonnes per hectare. Total livestock (1961 census) was 38,617. There is a saw-mill at Port Blair and a coconut-oil mill at Dunbar Point. There are about 338 km of black top road in the entire territory.

The islands possess a number of harbours and safe anchorages, notably Port Blair in the south, Port Cornwallis in the north and Elphinstone and Mayabandar in the middle.

The **Nicobar Islands** are situated to the south of the Andamans, 121 km from Little Andaman. The British formally took possession in 1869. There are 19 islands, 7 uninhabited; total area, 1,645 sq. km. The islands are usually divided into 3 subgroups (southern, central and northern), the chief islands in each being respectively, Great Nicobar, Camotra with Nancowrie and Car Nicobar. There is a fine landlocked harbour between the islands of Camotra and Nancowrie, known as Nancowrie Harbour.

The population numbered, in 1961, 14,563. The coconut and arecanut are the main items of trade, and coconuts are a major item in the people's diet.

The Nicobar Islands were occupied by the Japanese in July 1942; and Car Nicobar was developed as a big supply base. The Japanese built some roads in Car Nicobar and small jetties at Malacca in Car Nicobar, and in the harbour at Nancowrie. The Allies reoccupied the islands on 9 Oct. 1945.

ARUNACHAL PRADESH. On 21 Jan. 1972 the former North East Frontier Agency of Assam was created a Union Territory. The territory includes the Kameng, Tirap, Subansiri, Siang and Lohit frontier divisions and has an area of 81,426 sq. km and a population (1971 census) of 444,744; estimate, 1976, 500,000.

There is a Legislative Assembly of 30 members and a Council of Ministers. The election of 1978 was won by the Janata party.

There are 5 districts. The centre of administration is at Itanagar.

Chief Commissioner: S. M. Krishnatry.
Chief Minister: Prem Khandu Thungon.

About 60% of the land area is forest. Agriculture employs 18·5% of the people. In 1970 there were 200,000 acres under cultivation, 32,600 acres of it irrigated. Crops include rice (13,000 tonnes, 1976), rubber, coffee, coconut, arecanut, fruits and spices. There were about 100 co-operatives. The budget estimates for 1980–81 provided Rs 81·7 crores, of which Rs 1·16 crores was allotted to agriculture.

CHANDIGARH. On 1 Nov. 1966 the city of Chandigarh and the area surrounding it was constituted a Union Territory. Population (1971), 257,251; estimate, 1976, 300,000. Area, 114 sq. km. It serves as the joint capital of both Punjab (India) and the new state of Haryana, and is the seat of a High Court and of a university serving both states. The city will ultimately be the capital of just the Punjab; joint status is to last while a new capital is built for Haryana.

There is some cultivated land (foodgrain production, 1977, 8,000 tonnes) and some forest (27·5% of the territory).

Evenson, N., *Chandigarh*. Berkeley, Cal., 1966

DADRA AND NAGAR HAVELI. By the 10th amendment to the constitution the Portuguese territories of Dadra and Nagar Haveli (area, 491 sq. km; population (1971), 74,170 (males 36,964, females 37,206); density, 151 per sq. km) became a centrally administered Union Territory with effect from 11 Aug. 1961, forming an enclave at the southernmost point of the border between Gujarat and Maharashtra. Population estimate, 1976, 80,000. Formerly for administrative purposes a part of Damão (on the south Gujarat coast), they were separated from it by a 26-km strip of Indian territory. In July 1954 'nationalist volunteers' occupied Dadra and Nagar Haveli and a pro-India administration was formed; this body made a request for incorporation into the Union, 1 June 1961, and has been recognized by the Indian Government as able to exercise an advisory role on the pattern of territorial councils. The Indian Government appointed an Administrator in Oct. 1960. Headquarters are at Silvassa. Dadra has 3 villages, Nagar Haveli 69. Languages used are Bhilli, Gujarat, Bhilodi (83%), Marathi and Hindi.

Administrator: Col. P. S. Gill.

Finance. Revised estimates for 1972–73 show provision of Rs 1,68·63 lakhs.

Electricity. Electricity is supplied by Gujarat. A Silvassa sub-station is being built, and 44 villages had been electrified by 1977.

Agriculture. Farming is the chief occupation, and about 23,000 hectares were under crops in 1976–77. Much of the land is terraced and there is a 75% subsidy for soil conservation. The major food crops are rice and ragi; 9,600 hectares were under paddy cultivation and 11,285 under ragi and pulses in 1976–77. Some wheat is also grown. There is little irrigation (713 hectares). There are veterinary centres, an agricultural research centre and 2 breeding centres to improve strains of cattle and poultry. During 1977 the Administration distributed 43,000 kg of high yielding paddy seed, 16,000 kg of improved and high yielding wheat and 182 tonnes of fertilizer.

Forests. About 41·5% of the total area is forest, mainly of teak and khair. Timber production, 1977, 3,166 cu. metres including 1,151 cu. metres of teak.

Industry. An industrial estate has been set up at Piparia which had 49 operating factories in 1978 for chemical products, engineering, textiles, plastics, fertilizers and other manufactures. There were 15 units operating outside the estate. Concessions are available for small industries , and the whole Territory is included in the Rural Industrial Project. Estimated employment (total) in 1978, 1,380.

Communications. There are (1978) 167 km of motorable road. The railway line from Bombay to Ahmedabad runs through Silvassa. The nearest airport is Bombay.

Justice. The territory is under the jurisdiction of the Bombay (Maharashtra) High Court. There is a District and Sessions Court and one junior Division Civil Court at Silvassa.

Education. Literacy was 14·86% of the population at the 1971 census. In 1978 there were 11 pre-primary schools, 144 government primary schools, 12 mission schools, 1 higher secondary school and 4 high schools. Total primary enrolment was 11,357; high-school, 896.

Health. The territory has 1 hospital (27 beds), 2 primary health centres and 4 dispensaries.

DELHI. Delhi became a Union Territory on 1 Nov. 1956.

Area and Population. The territory forms an enclave inside the eastern frontier of Haryana in north India. Delhi has an area of 1,485 sq. km. At the 1971 census its population was 4,065,698 (density per sq. km, 2,738). Estimate (1979) 5,755,390. In the rural area of Delhi there are 243 inhabited and 15 deserted villages in 5 community development blocks.

Government. Delhi is administered by an elected Metropolitan Council consisting of 61 members including 5 nominated by the President of India. State of the parties after elections of June 1977: Janata, 49; Congress, 1; Congress (I), 10. The Lieut-Governor is the Administrator, assisted by 4 Executive Councillors (1 Chief Executive Councillor and 3 Executive Councillors) appointed by the President of India on the recommendation of the Union Home Ministry. The Territory is covered by 3 local bodies: Delhi Municipal Corporation, New Delhi Municipal Committee and Delhi Cantonment Board.

Lieut.-Governor: J. Mohan.
Chief Executive Councillor: Kidar Nath Sahani.

Budget. Budget estimates 1979–80 show total revenue of Rs 1,54,16·54 lakhs and expenditure of Rs 2,48,48·29 lakhs. Biggest items of expenditure were social and community services, Rs 1,80,07·76 lakhs.

Agriculture. The contribution to the economy is not significant. About 115,839 hectares are cultivated. Animal husbandry is increasing and mixed farms are common. Chief crops in 1977–78, production in 1,000 tonnes were: Wheat, 116; jowar and bajra, 6; gram, 4; sugar-cane (gur), 0·23; fruit, vegetables and flowers.

Industry. The modern city of Delhi and New Delhi is not only the largest commercial centre in northern India but is also an important industrial centre. Since 1947 a large number of industrial concerns have been established; these include factories for the manufacture of razor blades, sports goods and parts for radios, bicycles and station wagons, plastic and PVC goods including footwear. The number of industrial units functioning was about 42,000 in 1978; average number of workers employed was 348,000. Production was worth Rs 1,168 crores and investment was about Rs 625 crores.

Some traditional handicrafts, for which Delhi was formerly famous, still flourish; among them are ivory carving, miniature painting, gold and silver jewellery and papier mâché work. The handwoven textiles of Delhi were particularly fine; this craft is being successfully revived.

Roads. Three national highways pass through the city. There were (1978) 449,053 registered motor vehicles in Delhi including 5,580 taxis. The city transport service had 2,881 buses in 1978–79; this included the use of 598 private buses.

Railways. Delhi is an important rail junction with three main stations: Delhi, New Delhi, Hazart Nizamuddin.

Aviation. Palam airport operates internal and international flights.

Religion. At the 1971 census Hindus numbered 3,407,835; Sikhs, 291,123; Moslems, 263,019; Jains, 50,513; Christians, 43,720; Buddhists, 8,720.

Education. The proportion of literates to the total population was 56·61% at the 1971 census (63·71% of males and 47·75% of females).

The total number of educational institutions in 1977–78 was 2,762, with an enrolment of 1,251,135 students.

The University of Delhi was founded in 1922; it has 74 constituent colleges and institutions with, 1977, a total of 82,057 students.

GOA, DAMAN AND DIU. The coast was captured for Portugal by Afonso de Albuquerque in 1510 and the inland area was added in the 18th century. Daman (Damão) on the Gujarat coast, 70 miles north of Bombay, was seized by the

Portuguese in 1531 and ceded to them (1539) by the Shar of Gujarat. The island of Diu, captured in 1534, lies off the south-east coast of Kathiawar (Gujarat); there is a small coastal area. In Dec. 1961 the territories were occupied by India and incorporated into the Indian Union.

Area and Population. Goa, bounded on the north by Maharashtra and on the east and south by Karnataka, has a coastline of 105 km. The area of the territory is 3,813 sq. km, that of Goa itself being about 3,701 sq. km. Daman, 72 sq. km; Diu, 40 sq. km. Population (1971) 857,771: Goa, 795,120; Daman, 38,739; Diu, 23,912. Density, 225 per sq. km. Population estimate, 1976, 1m. Panaji is the largest town, population (urban agglomeration, 1971) 59,258. The languages spoken are Gujarati and Konkani.

Government. The Indian Parliament passed legislation in March 1962 by which Goa, Daman and Diu became a Union Territory with retrospective effect from 20 Dec. 1961. Goa is represented by 2 elected members in the Indian House of the People. For judicial purposes the territory comes under the High Court of Bombay. The capital is Panaji. There are 194 village *panchayats*.

There is a Legislative Assembly of 30 members.

Administrator: Col. P. S. Gill.
Chief Minister: P. R. Rane.

Budget. Annual Plan expenditure, 1980–81, Rs 312·5m.: Agriculture, Rs 45·1m.; irrigation and power, Rs 89·5m.; social services, Rs 107·4m.

Electricity. Units sold, 176·53m. kwh. in 1978–79. Thirteen towns and 351 villages were supplied with electric power by March 1979. Power is generated in neighbouring states.

Minerals. Resources include manganese ore and iron ore, both of which are exported. There are also reserves of bauxite, limestone and clay.

Agriculture. Agriculture is the main occupation; important crops are rice, wheat, ragi, pulses, groundnuts, fruit and coconuts. The net area sown is 128,429 hectares in Goa, 4,353 in Daman and 793 in Diu. Area irrigated, 11,277 hectares. Area under paddy (1979–80), 29,539 hectares of high-yielding strain (producing 142,934 tonnes). Area under wheat, 55,000 hectares; pulses, 6,500; ragi, 7,000. Government poultry and dairy farming schemes yielded 497,634 eggs and 4·36m. litres of milk in 1979–80, with 7,298 kg of butter and 1,904 kg of ghee.

Fisheries. The fishing industry is important; fish is the territory's staple food. In 1979 the catch of seafish was 39,488 tonnes (value Rs 8,18·17 lakhs). The whole territory has a coastline of about 140 km. There are about 4,950 active fishing vessels.

Industry. At 19 Jan. 1980 there were 31 large and medium industrial projects and 1,711 small units registered, the largest being a fertilizer factory (investment, Rs 500m.). There were 7 government industrial estates. Small units were mainly occupied in rice- and flour-milling, boat repairs and forest products.

Employment. In 1979 there were 71 unions with 40,200 members.

Roads. In 1980 there were 2,642 km of motorable road (national highway, 223 km). A road bridge on national highway 17 is being built at Zuari. In 1980 there were 35,552 registered vehicles.

Railways. There is a metre gauge line from the Pune–Bangalore line into Goa. There are no railways on Diu or in Daman.

Aviation. There are regular services to Bombay and Bangalore.

Shipping. The main port is Marmagoa. There is a daily steamer service between Panaji and Bombay, and weekly service between Bombay and Cochin, calling at Marmagoa. The port handled 14·5m. tonnes of cargo, mainly iron ore, in 1979–80.

Post and Telegraphs. There are (1981) 219 post offices and 27 telephone exchanges with 7,220 lines. There are 3 telex exchanges.

Justice. The territory comes under the High Court of Bombay.

Religion. About 62% of the population is Hindu, 36% Christian, 2% Muslim and other communities.

Education. The 1971 census recorded 44·53% literacy. Education is free up to grade VIII. In 1979–80 primary schools numbered 1,202 with 124,840 pupils, middle schools 375 with 67,660 pupils and secondary schools 242 with 37,312 pupils. There were 17 higher secondary schools, with 6,465 pupils, and 9 arts, commercial and science colleges with 4,387 students. There were also 7 professional colleges and 5 non-degree colleges.

Health. There are (1980) 33 government hospitals (2,261 beds) including 3 tuberculosis hospital; also mobile and specialist clinics. There were also 55 private hospitals and nursing homes. Two health centres were opened in 1972; there are about 940 doctors. There is 1 medical college.

National Council of Applied Economic Research, *Techno-economic Survey of Goa, Daman and Diu.* New Delhi, 1964

LAKSHADWEEP. The territory consists of a group of 27 islands (10 inhabited), about 300 km off the west coat of Kerala. It was constituted a Union Territory in 1956 as the Laccadive, Minicoy and Amindivi Islands, and renamed in Nov. 1973. The total area of the islands is 32 sq. km. The northern portion is called the Amindivis. The remaining islands are called the Laccadives (including Minicoy Island). Androth is the largest island, 4·8 sq. km, and is nearest to Kerala. An Advisory Committee associated with the Union Home Minister and an Advisory Council to the Administrator assist in the administration of the islands; these are constituted annually. Population (1971 census), 31,810, nearly all Moslems. Population estimate, 1976, 40,000. The language is Malayalam, but the language in Minicoy is Mahl. There were, in 1979, 7 high schools and 9 nursery schools, 17 junior basic schools, 5 senior basic schools and 1 junior college. There are 2 hospitals and 7 primary health centres. The staple products are coconut-husk fibre (coir), coconuts and fish. There is a tourist resort at Bangarem, an uninhabited island with an extensive lagoon. Headquarters of administration, Kavaratti Island.

Administrator: P. M. Nair.

MIZORAM. On 21 Jan. 1972 the former Mizo Hills District of Assam was created a Union Territory. The area is approximately 21,090 sq. km and the population approximately 400,000, of whom 53% are literate and 90% are Christian.

Serious disturbances in summer 1980 ended on 1 Aug. when the Mizo National Front agreed to negotiate a settlement of their grievances.

There is a Council of Ministers responsible to a Legislative Assembly with 30 seats. The present ministry took office in June 1978. The main town is Aizawl, which is connected by a main road (not a national highway) to Silchar, Assam; Silchar is also the nearest airport. There are no railways.

The budget for 1980–81 estimated receipts of Rs 52·28 crores on revenue account and Rs 24·50 crores on capital account. Outlay for the sixth Five-Year Plan is Rs 24·50 crores.

Agriculture employs 46% of the people and 17% of cultivated land is irrigated; there are some terraced holdings, elsewhere shifting cultivation is practised in forest clearings. Industry is based on the forests. Total installed power capacity, 1975, 3·4 mw supplying 61 villages.

Lieut.-Governor: K. A. A. Raja.
Chief Minister: Brig. Sailo.

PONDICHERRY. Formerly the chief French settlement in India, was founded by the French in 1674, taken by the Dutch in 1693 and restored to the French in 1699. The English took it in 1761, restored it in 1765, re-took it in 1778, restored it a second time in 1785, retook it a third time in 1793 and finally restored it to the French in 1814. Administration was transferred to India on 1 Nov. 1954. A Treaty of Cession (together with Karikal, Mahé and Yanaon) was signed on 28 May 1956; instruments of ratification were signed on 16 Aug. 1962 from which date (by the 14th amendment to the Indian Constitution) Pondicherry, comprising the 4 territories, became a Union Territory.

Area and Population. The territory forms an enclave on the Coromandel Coast of Tamil Nadu, with Karikal forming a separate enclave further south. The total area of Pondicherry (with Karikal, Mahé and Yanaon) is 480 sq. km, divided into 4 Municipalities and 11 Communes. Population (1971), 471,707; estimate (1976) 500,000. Pondicherry city had (1971) 90,637 inhabitants. The principal languages spoken are French, English, Tamil, Telegu and Malayalam.

Government. By the Government of Union Territories Act 1963 Pondicherry is governed by a Lieut.-Governor, appointed by the President, and a Council of Ministers (4) responsible to a Legislative Assembly of 30 members.

Lieut.-Governor: B. T. Kulkarni.
Chief Minister: D. Ramachandran.

Planning. Outlay for 1980–81 was Rs 135·1m. Of this, Rs 24·1m. was for agriculture, Rs 53·9m. for social and community services, Rs 19·7m. for irrigation, flood control and power development, Rs 13·2m. for transport and communications and Rs 7·5m. for industry.

Budget. Budget estimates for 1980–81 show revenue receipts of Rs 31,95·75.

Electricity. Power is bought from neighbouring states. All main villages have electricity. Consumption, 1979–80, 142·7m. units: 49% in industry, 28% in agriculture. Peak demand, 33·3 mw.

Agriculture. Nearly 45% of the population is engaged in agriculture and allied pursuits; 89% of the cultivated area is irrigated. The main food crop is rice. Estimated foodgrain production, 120,000 tonnes from 41,400 hectares in 1979–80, of which 99,000 tonnes was paddy; cash crops include groundnuts (10,900 tonnes), cotton (13,800 bales of 180 kg) and sugar-cane (145,000 tonnes).

Industry. There are no heavy industries or mines; manufacturing produces consumer goods such as textiles, sugar, electrical appliances, camphor, leather-goods, paper and bicycle parts. In 1980 there were about 30,000 people employed in 10 large and 13,000 small industrial units engaged in varied manufacturing.

Railways. Pondicherry is on a branch from the main Madurai–Madras line.

Aviation. The nearest airport is Madras.

Education. There were, in 1980, 42 pre-primary schools (4,140 pupils and 78 teachers), 259 primary schools (73,047 and 1,043), 83 middle schools (31,669 and 1,071), 54 high schools (12,025 and 1,336) and 9 higher secondary schools (3,769 and 335). There were 9 general education colleges, a medical college, a law college and a polytechnic; these had a total of 6,636 students; there were 9 professional and vocational colleges.

Health. In 1980 there was one doctor to each 1,500 population, and one hospital bed to each 250. There were 251 nurses.

REPUBLIC OF INDONESIA

Capital: Jakarta
Population: 148·5m. (1979)
GNP per capita: US$360 (1978)

Republik Indonesia

HISTORY. In the 16th century Portuguese traders in quest of spices settled in some of the islands, but were ejected by the British, who in turn were ousted by the Dutch (1595). From 1602 the Netherlands East India Company conquered the Netherlands East Indies, and ruled them until the dissolution of the company in 1798. Thereafter the Netherlands Government ruled the colony from 1816 to 1941, when it was occupied by the Japanese until 1945. An independent republic was proclaimed by Dr Sukarno and Dr Hatta on 17 Aug. 1945.

Complete and unconditional sovereignty was transferred to the Republic of the United States of Indonesia on 27 Dec. 1949, except for the western part of New Guinea, the status of which was to be determined through negotiations between Indonesia and the Netherlands within one year after the transfer of sovereignty. A union was created to regulate the relationship between the two countries. A settlement of the New Guinea (Irian Jaya) question was, however, delayed until 15 Aug. 1962, when, through the good offices of the United Nations, an agreement was concluded for the transfer of the territory to Indonesia on 1 May 1963. In Feb. 1956 Indonesia abrogated the union and in Aug. 1956 repudiated Indonesia's debt to the Netherlands.

During 1950 the federal system which had sprung up in 1946–48 (*see* THE STATESMAN'S YEAR-BOOK, 1950, p. 1233) was abolished, and Indonesia was again made a unitary state. The provisional constitution was passed by the Provisional House of Representatives on 14 and came into force on 17 Aug. 1950. On 5 July 1959 by Presidential decree, the Constitution of 1945 was reinstated and the Constituent Assembly dissolved.

On 12 Jan. 1960 President Sukarno issued a decree enabling him to control the political parties, with the power (on the recommendation of the Supreme Court) to dissolve them. He also set up a mass organization, the National Front, and a supreme State body called the Provisional People's Consultative Assembly.

On 6 March 1960 the President prorogued Parliament to be reorganized on the basis of the 1945 constitution. Local administrations nominated 130 members representing political parties and 153 members representing functional groups, who formed the new 'Mutual Co-operation House of Representatives'.

A communist second attempt to overthrow the government in Sept./Oct. 1965 was suppressed by the army. Some 80,000 communists are said to have been killed, and the communists killed 6 generals and several officials of the armed forces.

The 3-year 'confrontation' with Malaysia ended on 11 Aug. 1966, when an agreement was signed in Jakarta, terminating hostilities and re-establishing diplomatic relations.

AREA AND POPULATION. Indonesia, covering a total land area of 735,000 sq. miles (1,903,650 sq. km), consists of the islands of Sumatra, Java and Madura, Sulawesi (Celebes), Kalimantan (Borneo), Nusa Tenggara (Lesser Sundas), Maluku (Moluccas), Irian Jaya (the western half of New Guinea) and some 3,000 smaller islands and islets. It extends about 3,200 miles east to west through three time-zones (East, Central and West Standard time) of 1 hour's difference. Indonesia has a tropical climate with two monsoons; the dry (June–Sept.) and the wet (Oct.–April).

The total population in 1971 (census) was 119,232,499 (estimate (1979) 148·5m.), distributed as follows:

Province	Sq. km	Census 1971	Chief town
Aceh (D.I.)	59,904	2,008,918	Banda Aceh
Sumatera Utara	71,104	6,622,693	Medan
Sumatera Barat	49,333	2,793,196	Padang
Riau	124,084	1,651,591	Pakanbaru
Jambi	62,150	1,006,084	Telanaipura
Sumatera Selatan	104,363	3,443,749	Palembang
Bengkulu	20,760	519,366	Bengkulu
Lampung	33,866	2,777,085	Tanjungkarang
Sumatra	524,097	20,812,682	
Jakarta Raya (D.C.I.)	592	4,576,009	Jakarta
Jawa Barat	49,144	21,632,684	Bandung
Jawa Tengah	34,353	21,877,081	Semarang
Yogyakarta (D.I.)	3,090	2,489,998	Yogyakarta
Jawa Timur	46,865	25,526,714	Surabaya
Jawa and Madura	134,044	76,102,486	
Kalimantan Barat	157,066	2,019,936	Pontianak
Kalimantan Tengah	156,552	699,589	Palangkaraya
Kalimantan Selatan	33,966	1,699,105	Banjarmasin
Kalimantan Timur	202,619	733,536	Samarinda
Kalimantan	550,203	5,152,166	
Sulawesi Utara	24,200	1,718,155	Menado
Sulawesi Tengah	88,655	913,662	Palu
Sulawesi Selatan	83,799	5,189,227	Ujung Padang
Sulawesi Tenggara	32,454	714,120	Kendari
Sulawesi	229,108	8,535,164	
Bali	5,623	2,120,338	Denpasar
Nusu Tenggara Barat	21,740	2,202,333	Mataram
Nusu Tenggara Timur	48,889	2,294,945	Kupang
Loro Sae [1]	14,925	610,270 [2]	Dili
Maluku	83,675	1,088,945	Amboina
Irian Jaya	421,981	923,440	Jajapura
Palau–Palau Lain	596,833	9,240,271	
Totals	2,034,255	119,842,769	

[1] Formerly Portuguese East Timor.   [2] At Portuguese census 1970.

The principal ethnic groups are the Aceh, Bataks and Minangkabaus in Sumatra, the Javanese and Sundanese in Java, the Madurese in Madura, the Balinese in Bali, the Sasaks in Lombok, the Menadonese and Buginese in Sulawesi, the Dayaks in Kalimantan, Irianese in Irian Jaya and the Ambonese in the Moluccas.

Bahasa Indonesia is the official language of the Republic.

GOVERNMENT AND CONSTITUTION. Indonesia is a sovereign, independent republic.

On 11–12 March 1966 the military commanders under the leadership of Lieut.-Gen. Suharto took over the executive power while leaving President Sukarno as the head of State. The Communist Party was at once outlawed and the National Front was dissolved in Oct. 1966. On 22 Feb. 1967 Sukarno handed over all his powers to Gen. Suharto.

The People's Consultative Assembly is the supreme power. It has 920 members and it sits at least once every 5 years. The House of People's Representatives has 460 members, 360 of them elected, and sits for a 5-year term. Functional Group members have 236 seats; Muslim parties, 94; Nationalists, 20.

General elections to the 360 elected seats in the House of Representatives were held on 2 May 1977. The results were *Sekber Golkar*, 232 seats (39,750,096 votes);

Partai Persatuan Pembangunan, 99 (18,743,491); *Partai Demokrasi Indonesia*, 29 (5,504,757).

President, Prime Minister and Minister of Defence: Gen. Suharto, elected by the People's Consultative Assembly in March 1968 and re-elected in 1973 and 1978.
Vice-President: Adam Malik.

National flag: Horizontally red over white.
National anthem: Indonesia Raya (tune by Wage Rudolf Supratman, 1928).

Feith, H., *The Decline of Constitutional Democracy in Indonesia*. Cornell Univ. Press, 1962
Palmier, L. H., *Indonesia and the Dutch*. OUP, 1961
Schiller, A. A., *The Formation of Federal Indonesia, 1945–49*. The Hague, 1955

DEFENCE. The Indonesian Armed Forces were formally set up on 5 Oct. 1945. On 11 Oct. 1967 the Army, Navy, Air Force and Police were integrated under the Department of Defence and Security. Their commanders no longer hold cabinet rank. There is selective military service.

Army. There is 1 armoured cavalry brigade, 13 infantry brigades, 2 airborne infantry brigades, 4 artillery regiments, 1 engineer and 4 air defence regiments. Total strength in 1980 was 181,000.

Navy. The fleet comprises 4 diesel powered patrol submarines (2 new Fed. German built and 2 *ex*-Soviet), 11 small frigates, 9 fast missile boats, 4 fleet minesweepers, 4 fast torpedo boats, 8 coastal gunboats, 13 patrol vessels, 1 coastal minesweeper, 8 small patrol craft, 8 landing ships, 3 landing craft, 2 training ships, 4 surveying vessels, 6 oilers, 2 command and support ships, 1 destroyer depot ship, 1 repair ship, 1 cable ship, 10 auxiliaries, 60 minor landing craft, 24 service craft and 9 tugs. The (*ex*-Soviet) cruiser was discarded in 1972; and only 3 of the 10 (originally 14) old submarines and none of the 8 old destroyers acquired from the USSR remain. The construction of 2 more small submarines is being negotiated in Germany (Fed. Rep.). The naval air arm has 30 aircraft, including 15 helicopters. There are 24 customs patrol cutters.

Naval personnel in 1981 numbered 40,000 officers and men, including 1,000 naval air arm and 5,000 marine commando corps.

Air Force. Operational combat units comprise single squadrons of A-4E Skyhawk attack aircraft, F-5E Tiger II fighters, Avon-Sabre fighters provided by Australia, and OV-10F Bronco twin-turboprop counter-insurgency aircraft. There are 2 transport squadrons, equipped with turboprop C-130B Hercules, CASA Aviocar and F-27 Friendship, and piston-engined C-47 aircraft; 1 maritime patrol squadron with Albatross amphibians; and an assortment of other aircraft in transport, helicopter and training units including 8 Hawk attack/trainers and 16 T-34C-1 armed turbo-prop trainers. Personnel (1980) approximately 25,000.

INTERNATIONAL RELATIONS
Membership. Indonesia is a member of UN and ASEAN.

ECONOMY
Planning. On 15 Aug. 1960 the National Planning Council produced the draft of the First National Overall Development Plan, which the Consultative Assembly subsequently ratified. The third Five-Year Development Plan (1979–84) provides funds from central government for food production and other programmes implemented by village, region, province and municipal authority. Village projects include building and credits to farmers; regions and municipalities implement schemes to create employment, often in road-making; provinces receive sums for specific projects. Aid is also provided for school building, health centres, irrigation and fertilizer plant. The largest single programme is that for increased production of paddy, secondary and horticultural crops (7·6% of plan budget). Other important programmes are those for stimulating fisheries and stock-farming, and for generally lessening dependence on rice by encouraging other food crops.

Budget. The ordinary budget, excluding the development budget, was as follows in

1980–81 (in Rp. 1m.): Gross revenue, 10,557,000m.; gross expenditure, 10,556,000m.

Currency. The monetary unit is the *rupiah* (abbreviated Rp.), divided into 100 *sen*. There are bank-notes of 1, 2½, 5, 10, 25, 50 and 100 rupiahs and aluminium coins of 1, 5, 10, 25 and cupro-nickel coins of 50 sen.

In March 1981 there were 1,363 rupiahs = £1 sterling; 625 rupiahs = US$1.

In Sept. 1979 foreign exchange reserves stood at US$3,000m.

Banking. The Bank Indonesia, formerly the Java Bank, established in 1828, was made the central bank of Indonesia on 1 July 1953. It had an original capital of Rp. 25m.; a reserve fund of Rp. 18m. and a special reserve of Rp. 84m.

Bank Negara Indonesia is a state bank and is designed to act as a source of credit for reconstruction purposes. The Bank Pembangunan Indonesia accords long-term credits for agricultural, industrial and mining projects. The Bank Koperasi Tani & Nelayan extends credits to co-operative societies and smaller business men.

There are 7 major commercial banks and 10 foreign banks; the latter include the Chartered Bank, the Hongkong and Shanghai Banking Corporation, the Bank of America, the Citibank and the Bank of Tōkyō.

In Aug. 1973, 18,377 co-operative societies, including 17,589 primary co-operatives with 2·8m. members and savings of Rp. 4,530m. (provisional), had a combined membership of 6·8m.

Weights and Measures. The metric system of weights and measures was officially introduced in Feb. 1923, and came into full operation on 1 Jan. 1938.

The following are the old weights and measures: *Pikol* = 136·16 lb. avoirdupois; *Katti* = 1·36 lb. avoirdupois; *Bau* = 1·7536 acres; *Square Pal* = 227 hectares = 561·16 acres; *Jengkal* = 4 yd; *Pal* (Java) = 1,506 metres; *Pal* (Sumatra) = 1,852 metres.

ENERGY AND NATURAL RESOURCES

Electricity. All gas and electricity undertakings were nationalized by presidential decree of 3 Oct. 1953, retroactive from 23 Dec. 1952. Three large-scale hydro-electric plants are operating on the Jatiluhur and Brantas rivers in Java and on the Asahan River in Sumatra. Electricity generated, 1973–74, 2,932,480 mwh.

Oil. Oil plays an important part in Indonesian economy, being a major source of revenue and providing employment for some 42,000. Indonesia is the principal producer of petroleum in the Far East, production coming from Sumatra, Kalimantan (Indonesian Borneo) and Java, where Anglo-Dutch and US interests operate. Indonesia is the tenth largest OPEC producer. The 1977–78 output of crude oil was 616m. bbls. Oil refined in 1977–78: 116·2m. bbls. Production rate, 1977, 1·72m.– 1·74m. bbls per day. On 1 Nov. 1960 the Government announced a new regulation providing that all mineral oil and gas exploitation must be exclusively in the hands of Indonesian Government mining companies. Mining rights held by oil and gas companies issued before the new regulation continued.

Gas. Pertamina, the state oil company, started to pump natural gas to Jakarta in 1979.

Minerals. The high cost of extraction means that little of the large mineral resources outside Java is exploited; however, there is copper mining in Irian Jaya, nickel mining and processing on Sulawesi, aluminium smelting in northern Sumatra. The tin mines of Bangka, Billiton and Riouw are worked by the Government. In 1979 their total yield was 25,000 tonnes. Output (in tonnes) of bauxite was 1,052,000; iron sand, 380,000; coal, 279,000; copper, 129,000; silver (1978), 2,788 kg; gold (1978), 252 kg.

Agriculture. Indonesian agriculture is divided between estate and smallholders cultivation.

Rice production (1976), 15·8m. tonnes. Other main crops are maize, rubber, cassava, sweet potatoes, copra, coffee, palms. In 1976 production on estates was (in 1,000 tonnes): Copra,1,393; sugar 1,321; rubber, 786; palm oil, 481; tea, 73.

Livestock (1979): Cattle, 6·5m.; buffaloes, 2·3m.; horses, 615,000; sheep, 3·6m.; goats, 8m.; pigs, 2·9m.

Salt is a government monopoly; production in 1973, 30,000 tonnes.

Forestry. The forest area is 902,808 sq. km. Production, 1977 (provisional): All timber, 21,787 cu. metres, of which 573 was teak.

Fisheries. In 1977 (provisional) the catch of sea fisheries was 1·5m. tonnes.

INDUSTRY AND TRADE

Industry. At the beginning of Dec. 1957 the trade unions expropriated all Dutch-owned banks, trading firms, hotels, etc., which were then placed under government control. On 3 Dec. 1958 parliament passed a bill for the nationalization of all Dutch-owned businesses.

In Nov. 1963 all business enterprises owned 'wholly or partly by Malaysian nationals or Indonesian nationals domiciled in Malaysia' were sequestrated by presidential decree.

There are shipyards at Jakarta Raya, Surabaya, Semarang and Amboina. There are many textile factories (total production in 1977–78, 1,332m. metres), large paper factories (83,500 tonnes, 1977–78), match factories, automobile and bicycle assembly works, large construction works, tyre factories, glass factories, a caustic soda and other chemical factories. Production (1977–78): Cement, 2,878,500 tonnes; fertilizers, 1,083,300 tonnes; glass, 59,921,000 tonnes; 7·4m. cycle tyres; 2,339,100 motor vehicles; 6,806,000 cu. metres of oxygen; 305,000 cu. metres of acetylene.

There were (1978) 8 oil refineries with a combined capacity of 31·5m. bbls per day. Domestic consumption takes about 12% and the remainder is exported mainly to Japan and USA.

Trade Unions. The largest group of trade unions in Indonesia is the Serekat Organasasi Karyawan Seluruh Indonesia (SOKSI), the Central Council of All Indonesia Trade Unions, with a membership of 2·6m., to which 28 national unions and 832 local unions are affiliated. The second largest is the Kongres Buruh Seluruh Indonesia (KBSI), the All Indonesia Trades Union Congress, with a membership of nearly 400,000. To the KBSI 25 national unions and 54 local unions are affiliated. There are also the HISSBI (Federation of Indonesian Trade Unions) with a membership of 180,203, and the KBKI (Indonesian Democratic Labour Organization), with a membership of 94,477. In addition, there are also trade-union centres which are closely connected with the Islamic Parties, viz., Serikat Buruh Islam Indonesia, with a membership of 275,000; the Sarekat Buruh Muslimin Indonesia, with a membership of 11,950, and the Gerakan Organisasi Buruh Sjarekat Islam Indonesia, with a membership of 1,347.

Commerce. Imports and exports (including oil) in US$1m. for year April–March:

	1975	1976	1977	1978	1979
Imports	5,160	5,745	6,395	7,543	9,230
Exports	4,810	5,200	5,850	7,989	13,140

The main export items (in US$1m.) in 1977 were: Oil, 4,300; coffee, 613·6; rubber, 565; palm-oil and kernels, 186·9; tin ore, 165·4 (1976); tea, 120; tobacco, 58·9; copra, 36·2.

The main import items are non-crude oil, rice, consumer goods, fertilizer, chemicals, weaving yarn, iron and steel, industrial and business machinery.

Total trade between Indonesia and UK (British Department of Trade returns, in £1,000 sterling):

	1975	1976	1977	1978	1979	1980
Imports to UK	15,100	22,321	28,740	33,384	55,950	56,971
Exports and re-exports from UK	59,533	80,616	86,683	83,632	76,704	112,170

Tourism. In 1977 about 456,000 tourists visited Indonesia mainly from USA, Australia and Japan.

COMMUNICATIONS

Roads. The projected Trans-Sumatra trunk road will connect Aceh (north) and Lampung (south). The feeder-road between West Sumatra and Riau provinces was completed with the building of the bridge over the Kampar River at Pekanbaru in 1974. Motor vehicles, at 31 Dec. 1976, totalled 419,240 passenger cars, 220,692 vans and trucks, 39,389 buses and about 1·4m. motor cycles.

Railways. In 1980 the State Railways totalled 6,877 km, comprising 4,922 km of 1,067 mm gauge on Java, and 1,458 km of 1,067 mm gauge and 497 km of 750 mm gauge on Sumatra. In 1978, 29·2m. passengers were carried.

Aviation. The Government and KLM in 1949 set up 'Garuda Indonesian Airways' as a mixed enterprise on a 50–50 capital basis under KLM management. The agreement was to last until 1960. In 1954, however, the Government bought up the shares held by KLM for 15m. guilders and nationalized GIA; and in Jan. 1958, the Government unilaterally terminated the contracts with the technical assistants provided by KLM. GIA maintains a direct service between Jakarta and Manila, Bangkok, Hong Kong, Tōkyō and Amsterdam. In 1977–78 the company flew 59,142 km and carried 3,372,560 passengers and 32,908 tons of goods on domestic flights, and on international flights flew 17m. flying hours, carried 245m. passengers and 3,953 tons of goods.

Shipping. The national shipping company Pelajaran Nasional Indonesia (PELNI) had in 1973 a fleet of 312 vessels, and maintains interinsular communications. The Jakarta Lloyd maintains regular services between Jakarta, Amsterdam, Hamburg and London.

Post and Broadcasting. In 1974 the postal and telegraph services of Indonesia included 950 post offices. There were 660 telegraph offices which handled 3·9m. domestic and 488,000 international cables. Post offices handled 176m. letters and Rp. 250,000m. in money orders, Giro and postal cheques. Deposits with post office savings accounts, Rp. 31,210m. Number of telephones (1978), 324,546.

Radio Republik Indonesia, under the Department of Information, operates 26 stations. Television broadcasting covers 40m. people in an area of 72,100 sq. km. There were, in 1973, 6 studios broadcasting from 22 stations.

Newspapers (1973). There were 117 daily newspaper publishers with estimated circulation of 1·6m. There were 374 publishers of weekly papers with a circulation of 3·3m.

JUSTICE, RELIGION, EDUCATION AND WELFARE

Justice. There are courts of first instance, high courts of appeal in every provincial capital and a Supreme Court of Justice for the whole of Indonesia in Jakarta.

Administrative matters on judicial organization is under the direction of the Department of Justice.

In civil law the population is divided into three main groups: Indonesians, Europeans and foreign Orientals, to whom different law systems are applicable. When, however, people from different groups are involved, a system of so-called 'inter-gentile' law is applied.

The present criminal law, which has been in force since 1918, is codified and is based on European penal law. This law is equally applicable to all groups of the population. For private and commercial law, however, there are various systems applicable for the various groups of the population. For the Indonesians, a system of private and agrarian law is applicable; this is called Adat Law, and is mainly uncodified. For the other groups the prevailing private and commercial law system is codified in the Private Law Act (1847) and the Commercial Law Act (1847). These Acts have their origins in the French *Code Civile* and *Code du Commerce* through the similar Dutch codifications. These Acts are entirely applicable to Indonesian citizens and to Europeans, whereas to foreign Orientals they are applicable with some exceptions, mainly in the fields of family law and inheritance. Penal law was in the process of being codified in 1981.

Religion. Religious liberty is granted to all denominations. The majority of the

Indonesians are Moslems. There are nearly 6m. Christians; their main strength is in Central and East Java, North Sulawesi, East Nusa Tenggara, the Moluccas and Irian Jaya. There are also about 1m. Buddhists, probably for the greater part Chinese. Hinduism has 6m. members, of whom 2·5m. are on Bali.

In 1977–78 there were 419,418 Islamic houses of worship, 24,215 Christian (7,052 of them Catholic), 4,365 Hindu and 1,762 Buddhist.

Education. The following table shows the number of school and college students in 1978 (1,000):

Total population aged 7–13	23,000
Pupils in public and private elementary schools	13,612[1]
Pupils in Islamic schools	3,032[1]
Total population aged 13–18	16,196[1]
Junior high school pupils	2,056
Senior high school pupils	886
Academy and university students	401

[1]1973.

English is the first foreign language taught in schools.

There are 51 universities (23 are private).

Higher education is given at the University of Indonesia (at Jakarta and Bogor), the University of Gajah Mada (at Yogyakarta), Airlangga University (at Surabaya), Brawijaya University, 1960 (at Malang), Andalas University (1956) (at Bukittinggi, Payakumbuh, Padang and Batusangkar), Hasanuddin University (1956) (at Ujung Padang and Tondano), Pajajaran University (1958) (at Bandung), the University of North Sumatra (at Medan), and the Institute of Technology (at Bandung), the State Institute of Islam (1960) (at Yogyakarta), the Sriwijaja University (1960) (at Palembang and Tanjungkarang), the Lambung Mangkurat University (1960) (at Banjarmasin), the University of Sjah Kuala (at Banda Aceh), the University of Diponegoro (at Semarang), the University of North and Central Sulawesi (at Menado), the Institute of Technology (at Surabaya) and the new universities of Riau (at Pakanbaru), Maluku (at Amboina), East Nusa Tenggara (at Kupang), West Nusa Tenggara (at Mataram), and Cendrawasih (at Jayapura), Mulawarman (at Samarinda), Brawijaja (at Malang), Pancasila (at Jakarta) and Bung Karno (at Surakarta) universities. In 1961 a separate Department of Higher Education and Science was set up. Five training centres for technical education were opened in May 1975.

Health. In 1977 there were nearly 4,000 public health centres, 2,800 mother-and-child clinics, 4,200 polyclinics, nearly 9,000 doctors and 34,600 nurses and midwives.

DIPLOMATIC REPRESENTATIVES

OF INDONESIA IN GREAT BRITAIN
(38 Grosvenor Sq., London W1X 9AD)

Ambassador: Saleh Basarah (accredited 31 May 1978).

OF GREAT BRITAIN IN INDONESIA
(Jalan, M.H. Thamrin, 75, Jakarta)

Ambassador: Robert Brash.

OF INDONESIA IN THE USA (2020 Massachusetts Ave., NW, Washington, D.C., 20036)

Ambassador: D. Ashari.

OF THE USA IN INDONESIA (Medan Merdeka Selatan 5, Jakarta)

Ambassador: Edward E. Masters.

OF INDONESIA TO THE UNITED NATIONS

Ambassador: Abdullah Kamil.

Books of Reference

Indonesian Handbook 1978. Dept. of Information, Jakarta, 1979

Bemmelen, R. W. van, *Geology of Indonesia*. 2 vols. The Hague, 1949

Echols, J. M., and Shadily, H., *An Indonesian–English Dictionary*. 3rd ed. Cornell Univ. Press, 1975

Grant, B., *Indonesia*. Melbourne Univ. Press, 1964

Helsdingen, W. H. van, and Hoogenberk, H. (ed.), *Mission Interrupted; The Dutch in the East Indies . . . in the 20th century*. Amsterdam, 1946

Hindley, D., *The Communist Party of Indonesia, 1951–63*. California Univ. Press and CUP, 1965

Kroef, J. M. van der, *Indonesian Social Evolution*. Amsterdam, 1958.—*The Communist Party of Indonesia*. Univ. of Br. Columbia Press, 1965

Lagerberg, K., *West Iranian and Jakarta Imperialism*. London, 1979

Legge, J. D., *Sukarno: A Political Biography*. London, 1972

Neill, W. T., *Twentieth-Century Indonesia*. Columbia Univ. Press, 1973

Paauw, D. S., *Financing Economic Development: The Indonesian Case*. Glencoe, Ill., 1960

Palmier, L. H., *Social Status and Power in Java*. Athlone Press, London, 1960

Polomka, P., *Indonesia Since Sukarno*. London, 1971

Schrieke, B., *Indonesian Sociological Studies*. The Hague, 1955

Taylor, A. M., *Indonesian Independence and the United Nations*. Cornell Univ. Press, 1960

Weinstein, F. B., *Indonesian Foreign Policy and the Dilemma of Dependence*. Cornell Univ. Press, 1977

IRAN

Capital: Tehrán
Population: 34m. (1977)
GNP per capita: US$2,160 (1977)

HISTORY. Persia was ruled by the Shahs as an absolute monarchy until 1906. The name was changed to Iran in 1935, when the first Constitution was granted. Reza Khan took contol after a *coup d'etat* in 1921 and became Reza Shah Pahlavi in 1925.

Mohammad Reza Pahlavi (born 26 Oct. 1919) was sworn before the Majles on 16 Sept. 1941 on the abdication of his father Reza Shah Pahlavi (died 25 July 1944), and was elected Shah on 12 Dec. 1925. The Shah left Iran with his family on 17 Jan. 1979 and he died in Egypt on 27 July 1980. On 31 Oct. 1980 Prince Reza Pahlavi (born 31 Oct. 1960), the heir apparant, declared himself Shah.

AREA AND POPULATION. Iran is bounded north by the USSR and the Caspian Sea, east by Afghánistán and Pakistan, south by the Persian Gulf and the Gulf of Oman, west by Iraq and Turkey. Iran has an area of about 1,648,000 sq. km (634,000 sq. miles), but a vast portion is desert, and the average density is only 15 inhabitants to the sq. km.

The population of Iran was (census, 1976) 33,591,875. Estimate (1977) 34m. Population of Tehrán, the capital (1976) 4,496,159.

The principal cities and their population at census Nov. 1976 are: Esfahán, 671,825; Meshed, 670,180; Tabriz, 598,576; Shiráz, 414,408; Ahwaz, 329,006; Abadan, 296,081; Kermánsháh, 290,861; Qum, 246,831; Rasht, 187,203; Rezáyeh, 163,991; Hamadán, 155,848; Ardebil, 147,846; Khorramshahr, 146,709; Kermán, 140,309; Qazvin, 138,978; Karaj, 138,774; Yezd, 135,978.

The central province; capital Tehrán; population, 4,950,394. Khorásán; capital Meshed; population, 2,494,283. Esfáhán; capital Esfáhán; population, 1·7m. Eastern Azerbáiján; capital Tabriz; population, 2·6m. Western Azerbáiján; capital Rezáyeh; population, 1m. Khuzistán; capital Ahwáz; population, 1·6m. Mázándárán; capital Sári; population, 1·8m. Fárs; capital Shiráz; population, 1·5m. Gilán; capital Rasht; population, 1·7m. Kermán; capital Kermán; population, 773,669. Kermánsháhán; capital Kermánsháh; population, 776,409. Ports and Islands of the Sea of Oman; capital Bándár Abbás; population, 605,387. Báluchestán and Sistán; capital Záhedán; population, 454,996. Kurdestán; capital Sánándáj; population, 624,256.

CONSTITUTION AND GOVERNMENT. Following the referendum in April 1979 Iran became an Islamic Republic, the Shah having left the country, but not abdicated, in Jan. 1979. Ayatollah Ruhollah Khomeini was exiled in 1964 and by 1977 the first movements towards the overthrow of the Shah were noted which culminated in the student riots in Oct. influenced by President Carter's statements about human rights. In Jan. 1978 the Committee for the Defence of Liberty and Human Rights was established and many were killed in riots at Qom following anti-Khomeini articles in the press. In Sept. martial law was imposed and many hundreds were killed on 'Black Friday' in Jaleh Square in Tehrán. In Nov. 1978 the Shah appointed Dr Shahpour Bakhtiar to lead a civilian government. Following the Shah's departure in Jan. 1979 Ayatollah Khomeini returned in Feb. and Dr Bakhtiar resigned as Prime Minister.

Dr Mehdi Bazagan was appointed Prime Minister of the provisional Islamic Government on 5 Feb. 1979. During 1979 there was considerable difficulty in establishing where political power lay (*i.e.*, with the Islamic Revolutionary Council or with the provisional government).

A referendum on the draft Constitution was held in March 1979 and in April the Islamic Republic of Iran was proclaimed. The official result showed 20,288,021 votes for the Constitution and only 140,966 (all in Tehrán) against. Dr Bani-Sadr was elected president following elections in Jan. 1980.

In March 1980 elections took place for the Islamic parliament. There were 3,300 candidates for 270 seats.

In Sept. 1980, Iraq invaded Iran in an attempt to gain control of the Shatt al Arab waterway. The situation was not resolved in March 1981.

President: Dr Abol Hassan Bani-Sadr.
Prime Minister: Mohammad Ali Rajai.

The country is divided into 21 *ustán* (administrative provinces), 2 governor-generalships, 153 governorships and 461 districts. The provinces are divided into *shahrestán* (counties), each under a *farmándár* (governor). the *shahrestáns* are subdivided into *bakhsh* (districts) under a *bakhshdár* and *dehistán* (group of villages) under a *dehdár*. Each village has a *kadkhodá* (headman). All these officials, with the exception of the village headmen, are appointed, directly or indirectly, by the central government.

National flag: Three horizontal stripes of green, white and red; on the borders of the green and red stripes the legend *Allah Akbar* in white Kufi script repeated 22 times in all; in the centre of the white stripe the national emblem in red.

DEFENCE

Army. The Army consists of about 150,000 men organized in 3 infantry divisions, 4 independent infantry brigades, 3 armoured divisions, and auxiliary units. Two years' military service is compulsory. *Gendarmerie* strength is about 74,000. Its function is internal security in rural areas.

Navy. The Navy, which had been in a state of flux since the revolution, before the war comprised 3 destroyers, 4 frigates, 4 corvettes, 3 coastal minesweepers, 2 inshore minesweepers, 7 patrol boats, 14 hovercraft, 2 landing ships, 1 landing craft, 2 supply ships, 1 repair ship, 2 oilers, 4 survey vessels, 1 water carrier and 3 tugs. There were also 30 coastguard cutters and 2 customs craft.

The order for 6 large destroyers to be built in USA was twice reduced by 2 and finally cancelled. The order for 6 submarines to be built in the Federal Republic of Germany was also cancelled. There was tentative agreement for the transfer of 3 old diesel-powered patrol submarines from the US Navy in 1979 and 1980, but the transfers of 2 were cancelled and the takeover of the third abandoned. The construction of 12 fast missile craft in France was to have been completed by mid-1979, but later boats did not receive their missiles and the last 3 boats were embargoed in France. Two new landing ships had been projected.

The naval air arm comprised 14 patrol, transport and command aircraft and 20 helicopters.

In 1981 personnel nominally totalled 20,000 officers and ratings including cadets, apprentices and marines, but few were on active service at sea.

With the war following the revolution and the withdrawal of UK and US maintenance teams the fleet is suffering from lack of spares and materially the navy is running down, several ships being laid up. The situation is not improved by cessation of foreign help in training semi-illiterate conscripts and with poor morale following general instability and casualties the above ships do not represent the most efficient of maritime forces.

Air Force. In Aug. 1955 the Air Force became a separate and independent arm, and had a strength of about 23 first-line squadrons (each 15 aircraft, plus reserves), with 100,000 personnel before the 1979 revolution. There were 4 squadrons of F-14 Tomcat interceptors, with Phoenix missiles, 8 squadrons of F-5E Tiger II fighter-bombers, 10 squadrons of F-4D and F-4E Phantom interceptor/fighter bombers and 1 reconnaissance squadron of RF-4Es. Six P-3F Orions had been acquired for long-range anti-submarine duties. The transport wing was equipped with 54 C-130E/H Hercules and 18 F-27 Friendship turboprop transports and smaller types. Eleven Boeing 707-320C and 10 Boeing 747 transports included some adapted as tankers to support the tactical fighter and anti-submarine squadrons. The Air Force also operated some of the many hundreds of turbine-powered helicopters acquired for the Iranian services, including twin-engined CH-47C Chinooks, Super Frelons and Model 214 utility helicopters. Training aircraft included Bonanza basic trainers, T-33 advanced trainers and two-seat F-5B/Fs. Missiles in service included Rapier and Tigercat surface-to-air weapons. Strength in 1981 is uncertain.

INTERNATIONAL RELATIONS

Membership. Iran is a member of UN, OPEC and the Colombo Plan.

ECONOMY

Planning. The fifth development plan 1973–78 originally envisaged an expenditure of US$36,000m. In Aug. 1974 it was decided to increase this to $69,000m. Of this amount $23,000m. is allotted to the private sector.

Budget. Budget estimate for year commencing 21 March 1976 totalled 3,105,000 rials, of which 27% was allocated to defence.

Currency. The Iranian unit of currency is the *rial* sub-divided into 100 *dinars*.

Notes in circulation are of denominations of 50–10,000 *rials*. Coins in circulation are bronze–aluminium and copper, 50 *dinar*; silver alloy, 1, 2, 5, 10 and 20 *rials*. There are also gold *pahlavi* and $\frac{1}{2}$ *pahlavi* pieces containing 7·322382 and 3·661191 grammes of gold respectively which do not constitute part of monetary circulation, but have a market value as any other commodity.

In March 1981, US$1 = 70 *rials*; £1 = 166 *rials*.

Banking. The following banks are established in Iran: Bank Markazi (Central Bank), which was officially established in 1961 under the Monetary and Banking Law of May 1960 to implement the monetary and credit policy of the country. The Central Bank took over from the Bank Melli many of its functions, including the issue of bank-notes.

The liabilities and assets of the Bank Markazi on 20 March 1972 were as follows (in rials): Liabilities: notes in circulation, 61,500m.; assets, 324,734m.; bank deposits, 48,770m.; capital, 3,600m.

Bank Melli Iran, founded in 1927, continues to be the leading commercial bank with branches all over the country. The National Savings Bank, founded in 1939, is a branch of the Bank Melli. Bank Keshavarzi Iran (Agricultural Bank), formerly a section of the Bank Melli Iran, was made a separate establishment in 1933. It has a nominal capital of 1,500m. rials and has branches at the principal agricultural centres in Iran. The bank gives assistance for the agricultural development of the country. The Bank Sepah, founded in 1926, deals principally in inland exchange and manages army accounts; paid-up capital, 400m. rials. Bank Rahni Iran (Mortgage Bank), founded in 1939, has an authorized capital of 720m. rials and fulfils the functions of a building society. Bank Tows'eh Sanati va Madani (Industrial and Mining Development Bank) was founded in 1959 under the 7-year plan with a paid-up capital of 400m. rials with the object of assisting the modernization and development of Iran's industries. The Foreign Trade Bank of Iran, with a capital of 275m. rials, of which 51% belong to the Bank Melli, 24% to American and 12½% each to German and Italian banks. Bank Sakhtemani (Building Bank) was formed with an authorized capital of 150m. rials with the object of building and selling houses to the poorer classes. Bank Omran (Development Bank) was founded in 1953 with a nominal capital of 15m. rials to finance farmers and peasants who come into possession of land by virtue of the distribution of Crown lands. Sherkat Sahami Bimeh Iran (The Iran Insurance Co.), in 1954 inaugurated a banking department. In addition, there are 19 privately owned banks.

The Russo-Iran Bank is the oldest foreign bank operating in Iran; it finances Soviet–Iranian trade. An Irano-French bank (Bank Etabarate) opened in 1958. The Irano-British Bank, the Bank of Iran and the Middle East, the Mercantile Bank of Iran and Holland, and the Bank of Iran and Japan opened in 1959.

All insurance companies were nationalized in June 1979.

Weights and Measures. By a law passed on 8 Jan. 1933, the official weights and measures are those of the metric system.

The Iranian year is a solar year running from 21 March to 20 March; the Hejra year 1357 corresponds to the Christian year 21 March 1977–20 March 1978.

ENERGY AND NATURAL RESOURCES

Electricity. Energy produced in 1972 was 351·88m. tonnes of coal equivalent. Electric energy installed capacity, 1971, was 2,807,000 kw., and 9,100m. kwh. was generated in 1972.

Oil. The exploitation of Iran's large oil resources was undertaken by the Anglo-Persian (later Anglo-Iranian) Oil Co., which held a concession for a considerable area of southern Iran, built a large refinery and produced the following quantities of crude oil (in long tons): 1946, 19,189,551; 1948, 24,871,058; 1950, 31,750,147; 1951 (Jan.–Oct.), 16,176,000.

This concession was terminated as a result of the nationalization of the Iranian oil industry in 1951. The ensuing dispute (*see* THE STATESMAN'S YEAR-BOOK, 1954, p. 1294) led to the cessation of oil exports in June 1951, and of the company's operations in Iran in Oct. 1951. The dispute was finally settled on 5 Aug. 1954, and on 29 Oct. 1954, the date when the Shah signed it, an agreement came into force between the Iranian Government and the National Iranian Oil Co., on the one hand, and 17 international oil companies, on the other; of these, the British Petroleum Co. Ltd holds 40% of the shares. These companies came to be known collectively as the Consortium.

The agreement is for 25 years with provisions for three 5-year extensions, at the option of the Consortium under specific terms and conditions. Two operating companies—Iraanse Aardolie Exploratie en Producte Maatschappij (Iranian Oil Exploration and Producing Co.) NV and Iraanse Aardolie Raffinage Maatschappij (Iranian Oil Refining Co.) NV—were formed by Consortium member companies and they received the necessary rights and powers from Iran to be solely responsible respectively for exploration and production in a defined area in South Iran and for the operation of the Refinery of Abadan. While the National Iranian Oil Co., the shares of which are held by the Iranian Government, is the owner of the fixed assets of the oil industry in South Iran, the Operating Companies have the unrestricted use of them. The two Operating Companies do not sell the oil; their function is solely to produce and refine it. So-called Trading Companies, subsidiaries representing Consortium members, deal individually and independently of each other with the buying and selling in Iran of oil for export.

The National Iranian Oil Co. was united in Jan. 1955 with the Iran Oil Co., whose object is the exploration and production of oil throughout Iran except in regions subject to special agreements. The National Iranian Oil Co. operates the Naft-i-Shah oilfield and the Kermánsháh refinery in West Iran and is solely responsible for the distribution and marketing of oil in Iran. The net effect of the financial aspects of the sale of oil by the National Iranian Oil Co. to the Trading Companies for export is to bring about an equal sharing between Iran and each Trading Company of the profits arising in Iran from the Trading Companies operations.

The Shah signed a new 20-year agreement with a western Consortium on 31 July 1973 bringing the oil industry totally under the control of the National Iranian Oil Co.

Crude oil production figures since the Consortium began operations in Oct. 1954 have been (in tonnes): 1961, 56·3m.; 1962, 64·5m.; 1963, 66m.; 1964, 84m.; 1965, 92m.; 1966, 106m.; 1967, 121m.; 1968, 133m.; 1969, 153m.; 1970, 222m.; 1971, 227m.; 1972, 258m.; 1973, 293m.

Refining capacity in 1972 was 31m. tonnes.

Production of residual fuel oils was 11·3m. tonnes; distillate fuel oils, 4·8m.; motor spirit, 3·5m., and kerosene, 2·7m.

Minerals. Iran has substantial mineral deposits relatively underdeveloped. Production figures for 1973 (in 1,000 tonnes): Iron ore, 900; lead and zinc, 1,140; chromite, 200; salt, 500; natural gas, 17·2m. cu. metres.

Agriculture. Reliable statistics of production are not available. It is estimated, however, that out of 164·8m. hectares of land area only 16,857,000 are crop land (including 10,300 hectares fallow), 27·8m. hectares are forests and ranges and 32·7m. hectares are potentially cultivable waste.

Crop returns for 1975 (in 1,000 tonnes): Wheat, 5,507; oats, 1,438; rice, 954; sugar-beet, 4,585; tobacco, 14.

Wool comes principally from Khorásán, Kermánsháh, Mázandarán and Azerbáiján. Production, 1972, 20,000 tonnes.

Rice is grown largely on the Caspian shores.

Tobacco is grown along the shores of the Caspian. It is purchased by the Tobacco Monopoly and manufactured in the government factory at Tehrán.

Opium, until 1955, was an important export commodity in Iran. On 7 Oct. 1955 an Act was approved by Parliament to prohibit the cultivation and usage of opium. The Government has been contemplating reintroducing poppy cultivation on a limited scale and under rigid state control in an effort to fight narcotic trafficking and addiction.

Livestock (1979): 33·7m. sheep, 13·5m. goats, 7·6m. cattle, 350,000 horses, 27,000 camels, 55,000 pigs and 1·8m. donkeys.

Fisheries. The Caspian Fisheries Co. (Shilát) is a government monopoly. Exports of caviar (1975) were valued at US$72m.

INDUSTRY AND TRADE

Industry. Iran's chief natural products are oil, wool, cotton, silk, fruit, nuts, cereals, vegetables, gum, timber, oil seeds, copper and other metalliferous ores, coal, cattle, sheep and goats. Its principal manufactured or processed products are textiles, carpets, skins, casings, vegetable oil, soap, metal products, plastic products, furniture, beet sugar, tea, tobacco and cigarettes, wine, vodka, soft drinks, caviar, footwear, petroleum products, glass products, tiles, bricks, cement, leather and leather goods, dairy products and manufactured foodstuffs, and printed matter.

In 1975 there were 215,087 manufacturing units employing about 2m. people. Apart from the oil industry, the industries employing most workers are textiles, sugar refining, flour-milling, fruit processing, tea, furniture, printing, leather, matches, glass, building materials and light metal goods. The most popular carpets are manufactured in the environs of Tabriz, Kermán, Arák, Káshán, Esfahán, Shiráz and Hamadán. Esfahán is the traditional textile manufacturing centre, but in recent years important textile mills, particularly cotton, have been built in other towns, including Tehrán. A number of automobile assembly plants have been set up in recent years employing several thousand workers. A steel-mill, a machine-tool factory, a tractor plant and a huge petrochemical complex are also going into production.

In March 1975 it was decreed that 99% of shares in all state-owned factories were to be sold to their workers and the public. This did not apply to the key industries—oil, steel, copper and transport. Production, 1972, in 1,000 tonnes: Cement, 3,600 (1975, 5,145); nitrogenous fertilizers, 108; hydrochloric acid, 15·6; sugar, 598 (1975, 558); wheat flour, 3,800; cotton yarn, 42; wool yarn, 29·2; ethyl alcohol, 33,000 hectolitres; woven silks, 7m. metres; cotton fabrics, 482m. metres, and woollen fabrics, 13m. metres.

Labour. Legislation regulating conditions of employment in certain industrial undertakings was first introduced in 1949. The subsequent adoption of certain international minimum standards led to the enactment of the Labour Act of 1959, which establishes basic provisions dealing with hours of work; holidays with pay; the payment of wages, salaries and overtime; the formation, registration and activities of employers' and workers' organizations; employment contracts and collective agreements; the settlement of disputes; industrial safety, health and welfare; and labour inspection. Regulations concerning safety, health and welfare in industrial premises, conciliation procedure and the settlement of disputes, the formation, registration and activities of trade unions, the duties and powers of labour inspectors have since been promulgated. The employment of foreigners is controlled by regulations promulgated in 1960. Responsibility for the enforcement of the Labour Act, 1959, and supporting legislation is entrusted to provincial and district departments of labour.

Commerce. Imports and exports were as follows for years ending 20 March (1m. rials):

	1975	1976
Imports	400,600	694,100
Exports	1,435,800	1,370,100

Total trade between Iran and UK (British Department of Trade returns, in £1,000 sterling):

	1976	1977	1978	1979	1980
Imports to UK	1,049,263	789,819	534,388	243,589	107,176
Exports and re-exports from UK	510,901	654,661	751,265	231,798	393,335

COMMUNICATIONS

Roads. In 1970 there were 10,749 km of completely surfaced roads and 1,537 km of roads in the process of surfacing. First- and second-class (graded, all weather) roads total (1975) 16,000 km and third-class roads 30,000 km.

In 1974 passenger cars and taxis numbered 119,851; commercial vehicles, 13,193; buses, 2,611, and motor cycles, 19,785.

Railways. The State Railways total 4,567 km, comprising 4,473 km of 1,435 mm gauge and 94 km of 1,676 mm gauge. Revenue in 1978–79 was 9,119m. rials, and expenditure 13,513m. rials.

Aviation. The principal airlines which link Tehrán with Europe and the Middle East are Air France, British Airways, Ariana, Iraqi Airways, Alitalia, PANAM, Swissair, LIA, KLM, PIA, SAS, Qantas, SABENA, El Al, Lufthansa, Aeroflot and Middle East Air Lines. British Airways, Qantas, Lufthansa, PANAM and Air France also connect Tehrán with the Far East. Aryana (Afghánistán) Airline connects Tehrán with Lebanon, Syria and Afghánistán. British Airways, KLM and SAS operate services to Abadán and Iran National Airlines Corporation, registered on 29 March 1962, has monopoly rights on all internal flights and also operates in the Persian Gulf; in 1965 it inaugurated European services. The Iranian Government owns 51% of its shares.

Shipping. During the year ended 21 March 1970, 1,790 vessels of 19,369,000 tons entered at ports of the Persian Gulf, and 619 vessels totalling 195,095 tons entered ports on the Caspian Sea. In 1973, 211,005,000 tonnes of goods were loaded at Iranian ports and 3,766,000 tonnes were unloaded.

Navigation on the Lake of Rezáyeh, from Sharaf-Khaneh to Kolmankháneh, is served by some 5 tugs and 9 barges for the transport of goods and passengers. The service runs twice a week. On the river Karun likewise, from Khorramshahr to Ahwáz, an irregular service for cargo only both ways is run by the Iran Transport Co. and the Karun Navigation Co., and some local firms run daily trips by motor boat, for passengers and merchandise. By changing into lighter-draught boats at Ahwáz both can be taken up to Shallili near Shushtar.

Post and Broadcasting. Postal, telegraph and telephone services are administered by the Iranian Ministry of Posts, Telegraphs and Telephones.

The Indo-European Telegraph Co. relinquished its lines in Iran in 1931, while the telephone system was nationalized in 1952. There is wireless-telegraph communication between Tehrán and Tabriz, Meshed, Kermánsháh, Kermán, Khorramshahr, Bushehr, Yezd, Shiráz and Lingeh and a wireless-telephone link between Tehrán and Tabriz. Tehrán is also in wireless communication with Europe and is linked by wireless telephone with Baghdad, London, Berne and New York. In 1978 the number of telephones was 828,571, of which some 391,700 were in Tehrán. Wireless sets numbered 8m. in 1974, and television sets 1·5m.

Cinemas (1975). There were 430 cinemas with 299,191 seats.

Newspapers. There were in 1972, 39 daily papers in Tehrán and other cities. Their circulation is relatively small, *Ettela'át* and *Kayhán* leading with about 100,000 each. Total circulation was 750,000. Two English-language and a French-language daily ceased publication in March 1979.

JUSTICE, RELIGION, EDUCATION AND WELFARE

Justice. The judicial system was modelled on that of France, but a new legal system will be introduced in the Islamic republic. There are justices of the peace in villages and small towns, higher courts in the large towns, police magistrates in all important places, courts of appeal in Tehrán, Tabriz, Shiráz, Kermánsháh, Esfahán, Meshed, Kermán, Ahwáz, and a court of cassation, or supreme court, in Tehrán. The courts are supervised by the Ministry of Justice. New civil, criminal and commercial codes based on French and Swiss codes were introduced in the early 1930s.

Religion. The official religion is the Shia branch of Islam, known as the *Ithna-Ashariyya*, which recognizes 12 Imáms or spiritual successors of the Prophet Mohammad. Of the total population, 850,000 are of the Sunní sect, 19,816 are

Parsîs (Zartushti), 60,682 Jews, 108,421 Armenians, 20,000 Nestorians and 8,500 Protestants.

The Shia Moslems reject the *Sunna* or tradition, as distinct from the actual text of the Koran, both of which are recognized by the Sunnî Moslems. The power of the clergy had diminished, as the result of the increased power of the central government. The highest authority is the leading *ayatullah*, at present *ayatullah* Khomeini.

All mosques and shrines have some endowments (*ouqáf*, sing. *vaqf*), now devoted to charitable and educational institutions and administered by the Ministry of Education. The shrines of some favourite saints are richly endowed and own extensive property.

The Gregorian National Armenians form 3 dioceses. There are also a few thousand Roman Catholic Armenians, who have a bishop of their own rite at Esfahán, the bishop of the Latin rite residing at Rezayeh (Urmia). There is an Anglican bishop residing at Esfahán.

Education. A law providing for the gradual establishment of compulsory primary education was passed in July 1943. In 1972 schooling was available for 80% of the children of school age. The literate population is estimated at 36·9%.

The influence of the French educational system has been prominent. As in France, education is highly centralized.

The curricula for primary and secondary schools are drawn up by the Ministry of Education.

The great majority of primary and secondary schools are state schools. Grants are made to private schools. Elementary education in state schools and university education are free; small fees are charged for state-run secondary schools. Textbooks are issued free of charge to pupils in the first 4 grades of elementary schools.

In 1975–76 there were 6·63m. pupils attending 44,242 schools. Approximately 4·46m. of these were at primary schools.

Higher education is provided by universities and technical colleges. In 1975–76, 705,009 students were attending institutes of higher education. Tehrán University (with 11 constituent faculties) is the largest in Iran; it maintains a secondary teachers' training college and a midwifery school. There are also universities at Shiráz (letters, agriculture, science, medicine), Tabriz (letters, agriculture, science, medicine, pharmacy), Rezayeh (agriculture), Esfahán (letters, pharmacy, medicine), Meshed (medicine, letters, theology) and Ahwáz (agriculture, science, medicine). There are in Tehrán an Institute of Technology for the training of teachers of vocational subjects at secondary-school level; a Polytechnic with institutes of mechanical, textile and electrical engineering and building construction; and the National University, a private institution for fee-paying students. The National Iranian Oil Co. maintains an institute of technology at Abadán. The Central Treaty Organization in 1959 set up an institute of nuclear science in Tehrán (which has now been handed over to Iran), and in 1961 opened an agricultural machinery and soil conservation training centre at Karaj near Tehrán, and in 1960 a vocational training centre south of Tehrán.

Health. The Ministry of Health controls the health of the country through the Department of Public Health, which has achieved some remarkable results in the fight against malaria; large areas along the Caspian and the Persian Gulf and in Azerbáiján are now free from malaria. Opium addiction has been greatly reduced, and the cultivation of the poppy has been practically eradicated. Programmes to combat tuberculosis, smallpox, trachoma, venereal diseases, etc., have been introduced.

In 1975 about 45,604 hospital beds (half of them in Tehrán) were available in 498 hospitals. Medical personnel included 10,054 physicians and surgeons and 1,462 dentists.

Social Security. A system of social security benefits covering accident, sickness, retirement, death, marriage, maternity and childbirth and free medical attention and hospitalization for insured contributors and their families is embodied in the Workers' Social Insurance Law, 1960. This law provides for the insurance under the scheme of all workers in receipt of wages or salaries, but is at present being applied to some 683,496 workers employed mainly in industrial and mining establishments employing 10 or more workers. It also provides for the compulsory payment by employers of family allowances to workers with 2 or more children.

DIPLOMATIC REPRESENTATIVES

OF IRAN IN GREAT BRITAIN (16 Prince's Gate, London, SW7 1PX)

Ambassador: (Vacant).

OF GREAT BRITAIN IN IRAN (Ave. Ferdowsi, Tehrán)

Ambassador: (Vacant).

OF IRAN IN THE USA (3005 Massachusetts Ave., NW, Washington, D.C., 20008)

Ambassador: (Vacant).

OF THE USA IN IRAN (260 Takhte Jamshid Ave., Tehrán)

Ambassador: (Vacant).

OF IRAN TO THE UNITED NATIONS

Ambassador: (Vacant).

Books of Reference

Statistical Information: The principal statistical agencies of the Government are: (1) Department of Census, Civil Registration, and Statistics (Ministry of the Interior). *Director-General:* Sayyed Mehdi Hesabi; Publications on demographical statistics, in Persian. (2) Publicity and Information Department of the Seven-year Plan Organization. *Director:* Dr Mohammed Ali Rashti; Publications on industry, labour, agriculture, in English and Persian. (3) Statistical and Economic Research Department of the Bank Melli Iran; Publishes *Monthly Bulletin*, in English and Persian. (4) Customs Department (Ministry of Finance), publishes monthly and annual reports, in French and Persian. (5) and (6) Ministry of Labour and Ministry of Industry and Mines, publish statistical year-books.

H.M. The Shah, *Mission for My Country*. 1961.—*The White Revolution*. 1967 (both in Persian)
Adli, Abolfazi, *Aussenhandel und Aussenwirtschaftspolitik des Iran*. Berlin, 1960
Arberry, A. J. (ed.), *The Cambridge History of Iran*. 8 vols. CUP, 1968 ff.
Bharier, J., *Economic Development in Iran, 1900–1970*. OUP, 1971
Forbis, W. H., *Fall of the Peacock Throne*. New York, 1979
Graham, R., *Iran: The Illusion of Power*. London, 1978
Haim, S., *Shorter Persian–English Dictionary*. Tehran, 1958
Handley-Taylor, G., *Bibliography of Iran*. London, 1964; latest ed., 1968
Lambton, A. K. S., *Landlord and Peasant in Persia*. OUP, 1953.—*Persian Vocabulary*. CUP, 1954
Looney, R. E., *The Economic Development of Iran: A Recent Survey with Projections to 1981*. New York, 1973
Ramazani, R. K., *The Persian Gulf: Iran's Role*. Univ. Press of Virginia, 1972.—*Iran's Foreign Policy 1941–1973*. Univ. Press of Virginia, 1975
Steinglass, F. J., *A Comprehensive Persian–English Dictionary*. 2nd ed. London, 1930
Ward, P., *Touring Iran*. London, 1971
Zabih, S., *Iran's Revolutionary Upheaval: An Interpretive Essay*. San Francisco, 1979
Zakhoder, B. N. (ed.), *Sovremennyi Iran*. Moscow, 1957

IRAQ

Capital: Baghdad
Population: 12·2m. (1977)
GNP per capita: US$1,860 (1978)

al Jumhouriya al 'Iraqia

HISTORY. On 14 July 1958 the Republic of Iraq was declared by a group of Army officers, after an armed *coup d'état* in which the reigning King Faisal II and his uncle, the ex-Regent the Emir Abdul Ilah, and the Prime Minister, Nuri al Said, lost their lives. For the next 4 years the country was under the control of Gen. Qasim, who was executed on 9 Feb. 1963, following a *coup d'état* by the Army and Air Force on the previous day.

The republican régime terminated the adherence of Iraq to the Arab Federation (*see* THE STATESMAN'S YEAR-BOOK, 1958, p. 806).

The provisional constitution on 4 May 1964 declared Iraq to be an 'Arab, Islamic, independent and sovereign republic' based on democracy and socialism; complete Arab unity was the aim. The National Council for the Revolutionary Command, which took office on 8 Feb. 1963, following the overthrow of Gen. Qasim, affirmed its adherence to the spirit of the 14 July Revolution. It abolished the Sovereignty Council, which had exercised the functions of the Presidency since 1958, and appointed a new President and Cabinet. It reached agreement with Kuwait on the question of Kuwaiti sovereignty, which Gen. Qasim had disputed, but failed to find a peaceful solution to the 2-year-old Kurdish revolt. Increasing domination of the Government by Ba'ath Party members and consequent estrangement from Egypt led to a military *coup d'état* on 18 Nov. 1963. In April 1966 Field Marshal Abdul Salam Muhammad Arif, who came to power in Feb. 1963, and survived the revolution of Nov. 1963, was killed in a helicopter crash. His brother, Abdul Rahman Muhammad Arif, was elected President by the National Defence Council.

A cease-fire in Kurdistan was proclaimed on 10 Feb. 1964, but fighting was resumed in April 1965. In June 1966 the Government announced a peace plan which the Kurds accepted in principle. In March 1970 the Revolutionary Command Council announced a complete and constitutional settlement of the Kurdish issue.

AREA AND POPULATION. Iraq is bounded north by Turkey, east by Iran, south-east by the Gulf, south by Saudi Arabia, west by Jordan and Syria. The country has an area of 438,446 sq. km (171,267 sq. miles) and a population (census Oct. 1977) of 12,171,480. The capital is Baghdad (3,205,645). Other towns (estimate 1970): Basra, 333,684; Mosul, 293,079; Kirkuk, 207,852; Najaf, 179,160; al-Hillah, 128,811; Kerbela, 107,496; Arbil, 107,355; Sulaymaniyah, 98,063.

Each Governorate is administered by a Governor, and is subdivided into *qadhas* (under Qaimaqams) and *nahiyahs* (under Mudirs). The following are the area (in sq. km) and population (in 1,000, estimated, 1975) for each Governorate:

Maysan	17,945	362	Thi-Qar	13,900	549
Arbil	15,315	491	Al-Anbar	137,969	387
Baghdad	22,973	3,523	Sulaimaniya	11,993	555
Basrah	18,022	947	Al-Muthanna	74,536	152
Diyala	15,742	496	Ta'min [1]	19,543	600
Al-Qadisiya	9,359	416	Kerbela	7,170	588
Babylon	6,889	594	Neutral Zone,		
Wasit	14,814	386	water terri-		
Nineveh	38,670	909	tories	4,446	...
D'hok	9,754	168			

[1] Formerly Kirkuk governorate.

Two new governorates were announced in Feb. 1976: Salah ad-Din and Najaf.

Vital statistics, registered in 1973: Births, 166,387; deaths, 40,750, infant mortality, 4,559.

On 25 Nov. 1933 the Council of the League of Nations fixed the boundary between Iraq and Syria, including the whole of the Jebel Sinjar in Iraq.

CONSTITUTION AND GOVERNMENT. Under the 1970 Constitution supreme power is vested in the Revolutionary Command Council, which elects the President and Vice-President pending the establishment of an elected National Assembly. The only legal political movement is the National Progressive Front, a coalition between the Ba'ath Party and the Iraq Communist Party. Two amendments to the Constitution were introduced in 1973 and 1974. The second granted autonomy to the area whose population was predominantly Kurdish.

President, Chairman of the Revolutionary Command Council, Minister of Defence: Saddam Hussein al Takriti.
Vice-President: Taha Moheddin Marouf.
National flag: Three horizontal stripes of red, white, black, with 3 green stars on the white stripe.

DEFENCE. Military training is compulsory for all men when they reach the age of 18. This consists of 2 years' service with the colours and 18 years on the reserve. However, a man may volunteer for service in the army or change his conscript service into voluntary service. In such circumstances voluntary service is for 2 years, and he may extend it by periods of 2 years until he reaches the age of 45. The 2-year compulsory service can be extended in a national emergency. Many technicians and technically qualified officers serve up to 4 or 5 years.

Army. The strength of the Iraqi Army in 1980 was 200,000, organized into 4 infantry divisions, 4 mechanized divisions, 4 armoured divisions, 1 independent armoured brigade and Ministry of Defence troops.

Navy. The Navy comprises 12 *ex*-Soviet missile boats, 12 *ex*-Soviet torpedo boats, 3 *ex*-Soviet but Polish-built medium landing ships, 3 *ex*-Soviet submarine chasers, 2 fleet minesweepers, 3 inshore minesweepers, 1 training ship, 16 gunboats, 8 coastal patrol craft and 10 harbour patrol boats, 1 harbour authority craft (former presidential yacht) and a tug.

In 1981 naval personnel totalled over 3,000 officers and ratings, to be increased on the acquisition of 10 missile corvettes from the USSR.

Under 1972 treaty the Soviet fleet gained access to the Iraqui base of Umm Qasr in return for Soviet assistance to strengthen Iraq's defences. A further 1976 treaty reportedly provided for more permanent use of Umm Qasr in return for the provision of the above missile ships. In 1980 agreement with Italy provided for the building of 4 frigates and 6 corvettes with a replenishment ship.

Air Force. Except for 2 squadrons of Hunter jet fighter-bombers bought from Britain and 60 Mirage F.1E/B fighters, about 40 Alouette III, 8 Super Frelon and 40 Gazelle helicopters acquired from France, the combat and transport squadrons are equipped primarily with aircraft of Soviet design, including 12 Tu-22 supersonic medium bombers, 50 Su-7 and 35 Su-20 fighter-bombers, 80 MiG-23 and 90 MiG-21 interceptors, 41 Mi-24 gunship helicopters, Mi-4, Mi-6 and Mi-8 helicopters, and four-turbofan Il-76, turboprop An-12 and An-24/26 transports. A few Il-14s and smaller types are used in a transport/communications role, while Hunter, Jet Provost, L-29 Delfin and L-39 Albatros aircraft are employed with Swiss-built Bravo piston-engined primary trainers, Soviet MiG-15UTI trainers and other types in the Air Force College and operational conversion unit. Total strength is about 28,000 personnel and 300 combat aircraft. Soviet 'Guideline', 'Goa' and 'Gainful' surface-to-air missiles are operational.

INTERNATIONAL RELATIONS
Membership. Iraq is a member of UN and the Arab League.

ECONOMY
Planning. The 5-year plan 1976–80 envisaged expenditure of I.D. 10,000m.

Budget. Revenue and expenditure (in 1,000 Iraqi dinars) for 1980 balanced at I.D. 14,100m.

Oil revenues account for nearly 50%, customs and excise for about 26% of the total revenue.

The public debt was 260m. dinars on 31 Dec. 1972.

Currency. The monetary unit is the *Iraqi dinar* (I.D.) = 1,000 *fils* = 10 *riyals* = 20 *dirhams*. Silver alloy coins for 100 and 50 fils (*dirham*) and 25 fils are in circulation, and other coins for 10, 5 and 1 fils. Notes are for $\frac{1}{4}$, $\frac{1}{2}$ and 1 dinar, and for 5 and 10 dinars. In March 1981, £1 = 0·65 *dinar*; US$1 = 0·299 *dinar*.

Banking. All banks were nationalized on 14 July 1964. In 1941 the Rafidain Bank, financed by the Iraqi Government, was instituted to carry out normal banking transactions with head office in Baghdad and branches in the chief towns and abroad, including London. In addition, there are 4 government banks which are authorized to issue loans to companies and individuals: the Industrial Bank, the Agricultural Bank, the Estate Bank, and the Mortgage Bank.

In March 1972 post office savings amounted to 8,437,000 dinars held by 201,455 depositors.

Weights and Measures. The metric system is in general use.

ENERGY AND NATURAL RESOURCES

Oil. The greater part of Iraq's oil production comes from the Iraq Petroleum Co.'s field at Kirkuk (found in 1927). This company, an international group, has constructed pipelines to the Mediterranean, including one to Banias on the Syrian coast. The Mosul Petroleum Co. Ltd holds a concession for oil covering Iraqi territory west of the Tigris and north of the 33rd parallel of latitude. Oil was found at Ain Zalah, north-west of Mosul, and the company has laid a pipeline from there to Baiji. The Basra Petroleum Co. have been granted a concession for oil covering the southernmost part of Iraq (the old Basra vilayet). High-grade quality oil has been found here, and production started in Dec. 1951. Production at the oilfield of Rumaila started in Dec. 1954; its pipeline is linked to the Zubair–Fao system. An oilfield near Khanaqin, in the area known as the Transferred Territories near the Iranian frontier, was, until Nov. 1958, operated by the Khanaqin Oil Co., a subsidiary of the British Petroleum Co., and is now being operated by the Iraqi Government. There is a pipeline to a refinery near Khanaqin. Oil for consumption in Iraq is refined by the government oil refineries administration (GORA) and is distributed and marketed in Iraq at cheap prices by the Ministry of Oil and Minerals.

Under an agreement dated 3 Feb. 1952 between the Government and the Iraq, Basra and Mosul Petroleum Companies, the Government receives 50% of the profits before the deduction of foreign taxes, and in any case not less than I.D.25m. in 1955 and thereafter, from which date onward the minimum rate of oil-production will be 30m. tons annually. On 11 Dec. 1961, on the severance of the negotiations with the oil companies, the Iraqi Government enacted a law defining the areas in which the Iraq Petroleum Co. and its associates may carry out operations. The defined areas total less than $\frac{1}{2}$% of the concessions.

The total crude petroleum production was (1978) 2,600 bbls a day. Revenue received by the Iraqi Government from oil amounted to US$11,000m. in 1978. Production of natural gas (1976) 468,476m. cu. ft.

On 1 June 1972 President Bakr announced the nationalization of the Iraq Petroleum Co.'s concessions and the formation of a State company to manage the funds, assets and rights of IPC. IPC would be paid compensation although the company's alleged debts would be deducted from the amount. On 1 March 1973 the Mosul Petroleum Co. was amalgamated with the Iraq Petroleum Co.

On 7 Oct. 1973 the Government nationalized the 23·75% share in the Basra Petroleum Co. which was held by the American Near East Development Corporation.

Water. Iraq is a land of great potentialities. The soil of the country is rich, but there are vast areas which can be cultivated only if irrigated by canals or pumps. The Irrigation Ministry operates several canal systems, new dams have been completed and other irrigation works are under construction.

Agriculture. An Agrarian Reform Law, issued in Sept. 1958, limits land owner-ship to 1,000 *dunums* for flow-irrigated land and to 2,000 *dunums* for rain-irrigated land.

The chief winter crops (1977) are wheat, 695,700 tonnes and barley, 457,700 tonnes. The chief summer crop is rice, 199,200 tonnes. The date crop is important (1978 production, 581,000 tonnes), the country furnishing about 80% of the world's trade in dates (exports, 1975, I.D.11,493,000); the chief producing area is the totally irrigated riverain belt of the Shatt-el-Arab. Wool is also an important export (1975: I.D.1,013,000). In 1975, I.D.20,000 of cotton were exported.

Livestock (1979): Cattle, 2·7m.; buffaloes, 224,000; sheep, 11·6m.; goats, 3·6m.; horses, 65,000; camels, 235,000; chickens, 17m.

Forestry. Up to 1969, 614,953 *dunums* have been demarcated and surveyed in Arbil, Mosul and Sulaimaniya Governorates.

INDUSTRY AND TRADE

Industry. Industrial and constructional establishments in 1974 numbered 26,332. Constructional establishments employed the largest number of workers. Other large employers were the brick industry, water and electricity services, date pack-ing, the textile industry, cigarette factories, oil refining and the cement industry. Iraq is still relatively under-developed industrially but work has begun on 13 new industrial plants which are being established with Soviet equipment and tech-nical assistance.

Commerce. Imports and exports for 5 calendar years were as follows (in 1,000 Iraqi dinars):

	1973	1974	1975	1976	1977
Imports	270,317	700,087	1,044,664	1,150,898	1,151,268
Local exports	32,523	28,130	35,595	46,530	42,670
Transit	56,095	89,724	118,141	121,947	150,075

Movements of gold bullion and currency are excluded from the above table. Import values are c.i.f. plus landing charges, and include all goods cleared for home consumption whether subsequently re-exported or not. Exports do not include shipments of oil or re-exports, and are valued f.o.b.

Total trade between Iraq and UK for 5 years (British Department of Trade re-turns, in £1,000 sterling):

	1976	1977	1978	1979	1980
Imports to UK	279,530	331,714	497,341	393,738	532,483
Exports and re-exports from UK	149,853	166,940	215,509	201,176	321,883

Tourism. About 600,000 tourists visited Iraq in 1977.

COMMUNICATIONS

Roads. About 5,824 miles of roads and tracks have been developed for vehicular traffic. The main surfaced roads are: (1) the road north from Baghdad *via* Kirkuk, Arbil and Nineveh to a point near the Turkish frontier at Zakho, with branches from Kirkuk to the northern province of Sulaimaniya, from Arbil to the Iranian frontier, and from Nineveh to Sinjar; (2) about 350 miles of the main road west from Baghdad to the Jordan frontier; (3) the road east of Baghdad, which connects the road system of Iran near Khanaqin; and (4) the road south from Baghdad to Hilla and the holy city of Kerbela.

Vehicles registered in 1975 totalled 203,800, including 118,300 passenger cars, 65,500 lorries, 19,600 buses.

Railways. The Iraqi Republic Railways were originally largely metre gauge but now comprise a 1,435 mm gauge main line from Um Qasar through Basra to Baghdad, Mosul and Tel-Kotchek on the Syrian frontier, and the remaining metre gauge route from Baghdad to Khanaqin, Kirkuk and Erbil. A 1,435 mm gauge line is under construction from Baghdad to Husaiba (404 km) on the Syrian frontier, which will form part of a through route to the Mediterranean port of Latakia. A branch of 155 km will serve phosphates deposits at Akashat.

Aviation. Baghdad and Basra airports are served by British Airways, Lufthansa, Alitalia, Swissair, KLM, Middle East Air Lines, PIA, Iraqi Airways, Iranian Airways, Air Liban, United Arab Airlines and Aeroflot. In 1977 there were 728,266 passengers using Iraqi airports and 10,000 tons of cargo handled.

Shipping. In 1975, 828 vessels of 8,343,000 NRT entered the ports of Basra and Um Kaser.

Post and Broadcasting. In 1973 there were 352 post and telegraph offices. Wireless telegraph services exist with UK, USA, UAR, Lebanon and Saudi Arabia, and wireless telephone services with UK, USA, Italy, UAR and USSR. Telephones, 1978, 319,591.

Cinemas (1976). There were 24 cinemas in Baghdad.

Newspapers (1976). In Baghdad there are 5 daily newspapers (one of which is in English).

JUSTICE, RELIGION, EDUCATION AND WELFARE

Justice. The courts are established throughout the country as follows: For civil matters: the court of cassation in Baghdad; 6 courts of appeal at Baghdad (2), Basra, Babylon, Mosul and Kirkuk; 16 courts of first instance with unlimited powers and 150 courts of first instance with limited powers, all being courts of single judges. In addition, 6 peace courts have peace court jurisdiction only. Tribal law was abolished in Aug. 1958.

For *Shara'* (religious) matters: the Shara' courts at all places where there are civil courts, constituted in some places of specially appointed Qadhis (religious judges) and in other places of the judges of the civil courts. For criminal matters: the court of cassation; 6 sessions courts (2 being presided over by the judge of the local court of first instance and 4 being identical with the courts of appeal). Magistrates' courts at all places where there are civil courts, constituted of civil judges exercising magisterial powers of the first and second class. There are also a number of third-class magistrates courts, powers for this purpose being granted to municipal councils and a number of administrative officials. Some administrative officials are granted the powers of a peace judge to deal with cases of debts due from cultivators.

Special religious courts for non-Catholic Christians at Baghdad, Basra and Nineveh which dealt with matters of personal status, such as divorce, separation and maintenance between husband and wife, have now been abolished, cases being dealt with by the civil courts.

Religion. In 1965 there were 7,711,712 Moslems, 232,406 Christians (1979) 2,500 Jews, 69,653 Yazidis and 14,262 Sabians.

Education. Primary and secondary education is free and primary education became compulsory in Sept. 1976. Primary school age is 6–12. Secondary education is for 6 years, of which the first 3 are termed intermediate. The medium of instruction is Arabic; Kurdish is used in primary schools in northern districts.

There were, in 1976–77, 8,156 primary schools with 1,947,182 pupils, and 1,320 secondary schools with 555,184 pupils. Eighty-two vocational schools had 28,365 students.

There are 6 universities in Iraq and (1977) had 71,536 students.

Health. In 1974 there were 4,734 doctors (including dentists); 162 hospitals with 21,582 beds.

DIPLOMATIC REPRESENTATIVES

OF IRAQ IN GREAT BRITAIN (21–22 Queen's Gate,
London, SW7 5JG)

Ambassador: Hisham Ibrahim Al-Shawi.

OF GREAT BRITAIN IN IRAQ (Sharia Salah Ud-Din,
Karkh, Baghdad)

Ambassador: S. L. Egerton, CMG.

OF IRAQ TO THE UNITED NATIONS

Ambassador: Salah Omar Al-Ali.

Iraq broke off diplomatic relations with USA on 7 June 1967.

Books of Reference

Statistical Information: The Central Statistical Organization, Ministry of Planning, Baghdad (*President:* Dr Salah Al-Shaikhly) publishes an annual *Statistical Abstract* (latest issue 1973). Foreign Trade statistics are published annually by the Ministry of Planning.

Arfa, H., *The Kurds.* OUP, 1966
Khadduri, M., *Independent Iraq.* OUP, 1960.—*Republican Iraq.* OUP, 1970.—*Socialist Iraq: A Study of Iraqi Politics since 1968.* OUP, 1978
Langley, K. M., *The Industrialization of Iraq.* Harvard Univ. Press, 1961

IRISH REPUBLIC

Éire

Capital: Dublin
Population: 3·37m. (1979)
GNP per capita: US$4,377 (1979)

HISTORY. In April 1916 an insurrection against British rule took place and a republic was proclaimed. The armed struggle was renewed in 1919 and continued until 1921. The independence of Ireland was reaffirmed in Jan. 1919 by the National Parliament (*Dáil Éireann*), elected in Dec. 1918.

In 1920 an Act was passed by the British Parliament, under which separate Parliaments were set up for 'Southern Ireland' (26 counties) and 'Northern Ireland' (6 counties). The Unionists of the 6 counties accepted this scheme, and a Northern Parliament was duly elected on 24 May 1921. The rest of Ireland, however, ignored the Act.

On 6 Dec. 1921 a treaty was signed between Great Britain and Ireland by which Ireland accepted dominion status subject to the right of Northern Ireland to opt out. This right was exercised, and the border between *Saorstát Éireann* (26 counties) and Northern Ireland (6 counties) was fixed in Dec. 1925 as the outcome of an agreement between Great Britain, the Irish Free State and Northern Ireland. The agreement was ratified by the three parliaments.

Subsequently the constitutional links between *Saorstát Éireann* and the UK were gradually removed by the *Dáil*. The remaining formal association with the British Commonwealth by virtue of the External Relations Act, 1936, was severed when the Republic of Ireland Act, 1948, came into operation on 18 April 1949.

AREA AND POPULATION. The republic lies in the Atlantic ocean, separated from Great Britain by the Irish Sea to the east, and bounded north-east by Northern Ireland.

Counties and county boroughs	Area in sq. miles [1]	Males	Females	Total
Province of Leinster				
Carlow	346	19,743	18,925	38,668
Dublin County Borough	45	257,436	287,150	544,586
Dublin [2]	305	190,870	193,983	384,853
Dun Laoghaire Borough	7	24,798	29,446	54,244
Kildare	654	50,666	46,519	97,185
Kilkenny	796	35,688	33,468	69,156
Laoighis	664	26,192	23,744	49,936
Longford	403	16,059	14,726	30,785
Louth	317	43,061	43,074	86,135
Meath	903	46,704	44,011	90,715
Offaly	771	29,792	27,550	57,342
Westmeath	681	30,557	29,328	59,885
Wexford	908	48,974	47,447	96,421
Wicklow	782	41,969	41,981	83,950
Total of Leinster	7,580	862,509	881,352	1,743,861
Province of Munster				
Clare	1,231	43,945	40,974	84,919
Cork County Borough	14	67,091	71,176	138,267
Cork	2,866	132,055	125,796	257,851
Kerry	1,815	62,185	58,171	120,356
Limerick County Borough	7	29,593	31,072	60,665
Limerick	1,030	49,709	47,033	96,742
Tipperary, N. R.	771	30,118	28,358	58,476
Tipperary, S. R.	872	38,759	36,506	75,265

The census population, 1979 columns span Males, Females, Total.

[1] Exclusive of certain rivers, lakes and tideways.
[2] Excludes Dun Laoghaire borough.

Counties and county boroughs	Area in sq. miles[1]	Census population, 1979		
		Males	Females	Total
Province of Munster—contd.				
Waterford County Borough	4	15,942	16,675	32,617
Waterford	706	28,014	26,647	54,661
Total of Munster	9,315	497,411	482,408	979,819
Province of Connacht				
Galway	2,293	86,528	81,310	167,838
Leitrim	589	14,878	12,966	27,844
Mayo	2,084	58,489	55,530	114,019
Roscommon	951	28,475	25,714	54,189
Sligo	693	27,806	26,804	54,610
Total of Connacht	6,611	216,176	202,324	418,500
Province of Ulster (part of)				
Cavan	730	28,302	25,418	53,720
Donegal	1,865	62,629	59,312	121,941
Monaghan	498	26,245	24,131	50,376
Total of Ulster (part of)	3,093	117,176	108,861	226,037
Total	26,599[2]	1,693,272	1,674,945	3,368,217

[1] Exclusive of certain rivers, lakes and tideways.   [2] 68,893 sq. km.

The population has declined since 1841, when the 26 counties had 6,528,799 inhabitants; there were 3,221,823 in 1901; 3,139,688 in 1911; 2,971,992 in 1926; 2,968,420 in 1936; 2,955,107 in 1946; 2,898,264 in 1956; 2,884,002 in 1966; 2,978,248 in 1971, and 3,368,217 in 1979.

Vital statistics for 4 calendar years:

	Births	Marriages	Deaths		Births	Marriages	Deaths
1976	67,718	20,580	34,043	1978[1]	69,844	20,724	33,051
1977[1]	68,436	19,653	33,425	1979[1]	72,352	20,864	32,790

[1] Provisional.

Passenger movements by sea were in 1979, outward, 1,288,173; inward, 1,277,256.

CONSTITUTION AND GOVERNMENT. The Irish Republic is a sovereign independent, democratic republic. Its parliament exercises jurisdiction in 26 of the 32 counties of Ireland.

The first Constitution of the Irish Free State came into operation on 6 Dec. 1922. Certain provisions which were regarded as contrary to the national sentiments were gradually removed by successive amendments, with the result that at the end of 1936 the text differed considerably from the original document. On 14 June 1937 a new Constitution was approved by Parliament (*Dáil Éireann*) and enacted by a plebiscite on 1 July 1937. This Constitution came into operation on 29 Dec. 1937. Under it the name Ireland (Éire) was restored.

The Constitution provides that, pending the reintegration of the national territory, the laws enacted by the Parliament established by the constitution shall have the same area and extent of application as those of the Irish Free State.

The *Oireachtas* or National Parliament consists of the President and two Houses, viz., a House of Representatives, called *Dáil Éireann*, and a Senate, called *Seanad Éireann*, consisting of 60 members. The *Dáil*, consisting of 148 members, is elected by adult suffrage. Of the 60 members of the Senate, 11 are nominated by the *Taoiseach* (Prime Minister), 6 are elected by the universities and the remaining 43 are elected from 5 panels of candidates established on a vocational basis, representing the following public services and interests: (1) national language and culture, literature, art, education and such professional interests as may be defined by law for the purpose of this panel; (2) agricultural and allied interests, and fisheries; (3) labour, whether organized or unorganized; (4) industry and commerce, including banking, finance, accountancy, engineering and architecture; (5) public administration and social services, including voluntary social activities. The electing body is a college of about 900 members, comprising members of the *Dáil*, Senate, county boroughs and county councils.

A maximum period of 90 days is afforded to the Senate for the consideration or amendment of Bills sent to that House by the *Dáil*, but the Senate has no power to veto legislative proposals.

No amendment of the Constitution can be effected except with the approval of the people given at a referendum.

Agreement on the establishment of a Council of Ireland was reached at a meeting held at Sunningdale on 6–9 Dec. 1973. Members of the Irish and UK governments attended together with the Northern Ireland Executive-designate.

Irish is the first official language; English is recognized as a second official language.

For further details of the Constitution *see* THE STATESMAN'S YEAR-BOOK, 1952, pp. 1123–34.

President: Pádraig Óhlrighile (Patrick Hillery), installed on 3 Dec. 1976. The President holds office for 7 years.

Former Presidents: Dr Douglas Hyde (1938–45); Seán T. O. Ceallaigh (1945–59; 2 terms); Éamon de Valéra (1959–73; 2 terms); Erskine Childers (1973–74; died in office); Cearbhall Ó Dálaigh (1974–76; resigned).

A general election was held on 16 June 1977: Fianna Fáil, 84 (1973 election, 69); Fine Gael, 43 (54); Labour Party, 17 (19); Independents, 4 (2).

There are no formal party divisions in the Senate.

The Fianna Fáil Government consisted of the following members in Feb. 1981:

Taoiseach (*Prime Minister*): Charles J. Haughey.

Deputy Prime Minister and Energy: George Colley. *Foreign Affairs:* Brian Lenihan. *Industry, Commerce and Tourism:* Desmond O'Malley. *Justice:* Gerard Collins. *Defence:* Sylvester Barrett. *Finance and Public Service:* Gene Fitzgerald. *Education:* John Patrick Wilson. *Agriculture:* Ray MacSharry. *Irish Speaking Affairs:* Maire Geoghegan-Quinn. *Health and Social Welfare:* Michael Woods. *Fisheries and Forestry:* Patrick Power. *Posts and Telecommunications and Transport:* Albert Reynolds. *Environment:* Raphael P. Burke. *Labour:* Tom Nolan.

There were 15 Ministers of State.

National flag: Three vertical strips of green, white, orange.
National anthem: The Soldier's Song (words by P. Kearney; music by P. Heaney).

Local Government. The elected local authorities comprise 27 county councils, 4 county borough corporations, 7 borough corporations, 49 urban district councils and 23 Boards of Town Commissions. All the members of these authorities are elected under a system of proportional representation, normally every 5 years. All residents of an area who have reached the age of 18 are entitled to vote in the local election for their area. Women are eligible for election as members of local authorities in the same manner and on the same conditions as men. Elected members are not paid, but provision is made for the payment of travelling expenses and subsistence allowances.

The range of services for which local authorities are responsible is broken down into 8 main programme groups as follows: Housing and Building; Road Transportation and Safety; Water Supply and Sewerage; Development Incentives and Controls; Environmental Protection; Recreation and Amenity; Agriculture, Education, Health and Welfare and Miscellaneous Services. Because of the small size of their administrative areas the functions carried out by town commissioners and some of the smaller urban district councils have tended to become increasingly limited, and the more important tasks of local government have tended to become the responsibility of the county councils.

The local authorities have a system of government which combines an elected council and a whole-time manager. The elected members have specific functions reserved to them which include the striking of rates (local tax), the borrowing of money, the adoption of development plans, the making, amending or revoking of bye-laws and the nomination of persons to other bodies. The managers, who are paid officers of their authorities, are responsible for the performance of all functions which are not reserved to the elected members, including the employment of staff, making of contracts, management of local authority property, collection of rates and rents and the day-to-day administration of local authority affairs. The manager for a county council is manager also for every borough corporation, urban district council and board of town commissioners whose functional area is wholly within the county. A central body called the Local Appointments Commission is charged with the duty of selecting suitable persons to be appointed by local authorities to chief executive offices, professional offices and other prescribed offices. Where a prescribed office becomes vacant, the local authority must request the Commissioners to recommend to them a suitable person. The Commissioners normally select persons for appointment by the machinery of selection boards.

The revenue expenditure of local authorities is financed by a local tax, called rates, on the occupation of immovable property (other than houses), grants and subsidies from the central government and payments for certain services which they provide. Capital expenditure is financed mainly by means of borrowing from the Local Loans Fund, which is operated by the central government, and from banking and insurance institutions.

Local authorities use a scheme of combined purchasing to obtain commodities of standard quality at the lowest possible price. Official supply contractors are appointed biennially by the Minister for the Environment on the recommendation of an advisory committee.

DEFENCE. Under the direction of the President, and subject to the provisions of the Defence Act, 1954, the military command of the Defence Forces is exercisable by the Government through the Minister for Defence. To aid and counsel the Minister for Defence on all matters in relation to the business of the Department of Defence on which he may consult it, there is a Council of Defence consisting of the Minister for State at the Department of Defence, the Secretary of the Department of Defence, the Chief of Staff, the Adjutant-General and the Quartermaster-General. Establishments provide at present for a Permanent Defence Force of approximately 15,000 all ranks including the Air Corps and the Naval Service. The Defence Vote for the year ending 31 Dec. 1980 provided for approximately 22,000 all ranks of the Reserve Defence Force. Recruitment is on a voluntary basis. Minimum term of enlistment is 3 years in the Permanent Defence Force and in the Reserve.

The Defence Estimates for the year ending 31 Dec. 1979 provide for an expenditure of £116m.

Since May 1978 an Irish contingent comprising 754 men (all ranks) has formed part of the United Nations force in Lebanon. Irish officers are at present serving with the UN Truce Supervision Organization and the UN Disengagement Observer Force in the Middle East.

Army. There are at present 4 brigades in the Army. Each comprises 2 infantry battalions and an artillery regiment, and a squadron or company from each Corps (except Ordnance and Air). There are, in addition, 2 independent infantry battalions. Total strength, 13,370.

Navy. The Naval Service comprises 4 offshore patrol vessels or corvettes completed at Cork in 1972, 1978, 1979 and 1980, 3 coastal minesweepers acquired from Britain in 1971 for fishery protection, 1 supply and training ship, and 6 service craft. It is planned to have 2 patrol vessels, each carrying a helicopter, for service after 1982. The naval base is at Haulbowline Island, Cork Harbour. Naval personnel in 1981 exceeded 800 officers and ratings, rising to 1,200 (target) for 1982.

Air Force. The Air Corps has a personnel strength of approximately 870 all ranks and 36 aircraft. There are 7 Cessna FR-172H aircraft for border patrol, 6 Magister armed jet trainers and 10 SIAI-Marchetti SF.260W armed piston-engined trainers with dual combat responsibility; 8 Alouette III and 2 Gazelle helicopters; 2 twin-turboprop Super King Airs for coastal fishery patrol and a BAe 125 twin-turbofan communications aircraft.

INTERNATIONAL RELATIONS

Membership. The Irish Republic is a member of UN, OECD, the Council of Europe and EEC.

ECONOMY

Budget. Receipts and expenditures (in IR£1m.):

	1979	1980
Receipts		
Customs duties	40·6	47·3
Excise duties	602·0	850·9
Income tax	729·9	1,014·3
Corporation tax, etc.	130·3	139·8
Value-added tax	422·2	471·6
Stamp duties	43·6	48·0
Estate, etc., duties	3·4	3·0
Motor vehicle duties	19·4	25·5
Post Office	109·0	202·6
Capital taxes	12·4	14·4
Agricultural levies	4·6	4·6
Total (including other items)	2,383·9	3,155·3
Current expenditure		
Debt service	622·2	792·1
Agriculture, etc.	125·9	141·1
Education	378·9	461·4
Tourism and Transport	90·1	112·4
Post Office	122·2	181·1
Defence	111·6	142·1
Justice (including Police)	105·1	140·3
Social Welfare	375·4	485·9
Health	455·5	617·2
Superannuation	78·2	99·9
Industry and Energy	68·1	70·7
Total (including other items)	2,902·9	3,702·1

Capital expenditure amounted to £1,007·2m. in 1979, and £1,269·9m. in 1980.

On 31 Dec. 1979 the liabilities totalled £6,540·1m. The assets were: Electricity scheme, £44·8m.: local loans fund, £1,109m.; national transport organization, £29·4m.; industrial credit, £59·8m.; turf development, £30·4m.; reconstruction finance, £25·1m.; shares in companies established under state auspices, £222·1m.; exchequer balance, £614,000; other assets, £171·9m.; total, £1,693·1m.

Currency. The unit of currency is the Irish *pound* or *an punt Eirennach*. From 10 Sept. 1928 when the first Irish legal-tender notes were issued, the Irish currency was linked to Sterling on a one-for-one basis. This relationship was discontinued on 30 March 1979 when, following Ireland's adherence to the European Monetary System, market forces pushed sterling exchange rates beyond the upper intervention limit established for the Irish pound against the Belgian franc.

The Central Bank has the sole right of issuing legal tender notes; token coinage is issued by the Minister for Finance through the Bank. In March 1981, £1 = IR£1·28; US$ = IR£1·73.

The volume of legal-tender notes outstanding in Jan. 1981 was £632,404,000. Total notes and coins in circulation amounted to £718,068,000.

Banking. The Central Bank, which was established as from 1 Feb. 1943, in accordance with the Central Bank Act, 1942, replaced the Currency Commission, which was set up under the Currency Act, 1927, and had been responsible *inter alia* for the regulation of the note issue. In addition to the powers and functions of the Currency Commission the Central Bank has the power of receiving deposits from banks and public authorities, of rediscounting Exchequer bills and bills of exchange, of making advances to banks against such bills or against Government securities, of fixing and publishing rates of interest for rediscounting bills, or buying and selling certain Government securities and securities of any international bank or financial institution formed wholly or mainly by governments. The Bank also collects and publishes information relating to monetary and credit matters. The Central Bank Act, 1971, gives further powers to the Central Bank in the regulation of banking including licensing of banks, the supervision of their operations and control of liquidity and reserve ratios. The capital of the Bank is £40,000, of which £24,000 has been paid up and is held by the Minister for Finance.

The Board of Directors of the Central Bank consists of a Governor, appointed by the President of the Republic on the advice of the Government, and 8 directors, all appointed by the Minister for Finance, 6 direct and 2 from among directors of the Associated Banks (the term applied to the 4 shareholding banks associated with the former Currency Commission).

There are 4 commercial banks associated with the Central Bank: The Bank of Ireland, Allied Irish Banks Ltd, the Ulster Bank and the Northern Bank.

At 19 Nov. 1980 the Associated Banks had liabilities, within the State, of £4,398·2m. including current and deposit accounts amounting to £3,741m.; assets, within the State, amounted to £4,594·8m., of which the main components were liquid assets of £668·4m. and lending of £3,686·6m. At the same date liabilities, outside the State, stood at £3,298·1m. and assets at £3,101·5m., giving a net external liability of £196·6m. Total liabilities and assets balanced at £7,696·3m. The commercial banking system also includes 39 licensed banks not 'associated' with the Central Bank. At 19 Nov. 1980 these non-associated banks had total liabilities and assets, within the State and elsewhere, balancing at £4,432.

The post office savings bank has approximately 2·3m. (including 1m. dormant) accounts and the amount due at 31 Dec. 1980 was £258m. The trustee savings banks had deposits of £258m. at 31 Dec. 1980.

Weights and Measures. The Imperial system is in use but conversion to metric is in progress.

ENERGY AND NATURAL RESOURCES

Electricity. The generating and supplying of electricity and the construction and maintenance of the nationwide electricity distribution system is the function of the Electricity Supply Board, a State-sponsored body established in 1927. The total generating capacity is 2,895 mw. In the year ending 31 March 1979 the total sales of electricity amounted to 7,965m. units supplied to 1,015,636 consumers. Nuclear energy is not yet produced or used in the Irish energy sector but the Government has under consideration a proposal by the Electricity Supply Board for the construction of a 650 mw nuclear powered generating station. In late 1973, however, a Nuclear Energy Board was established to advise the Government on proposals for construction of nuclear power stations and on all aspects of the installation, operation and supervision of such stations.

Oil and gas. About 551,500 sq. km of the Continental Shelf has been made an exploration area; at its furthest point the limit of jurisdiction is 520 nautical miles from the coast. Since 1970, 59 exploratory oilwells have been drilled. There has been one discovery of natural gas, off the south-west coast at Kinsale Head. At a daily extraction rate of 125m. cu. ft the estimated life of the field is 20 years. Distribution is controlled by the Irish Gas Board (BGE).

Peat. The country has very little indigenous coal, but possesses large reserves of peat, the development of which is handled by *Bord na Móna* (Peat Board). A total of 200,000 acres of bogland is being developed at present. Production for 1978–79 totalled 1·43m. tonnes, of which 3,003,000 tonnes went to generate electricity and 3,857,000 tonnes for household and space heating.

Minerals. Lead and zinc concentrates are important. Metal equivalent of production, 1978: zinc, 205,000 tonnes; lead, 70,000 tonnes. Barytes is also important, and there is some copper, pyrites, gypsum, dolomite, limestone, aggregates, coal, green and black marble. About 50 companies are prospecting.

Agriculture. General distribution of surface (in hectares) in 1975: Crops and pasture, 4,689,961; other land, including grazed mountain, 2,199,269; total, 6,889,230.

Estimated area (statute acres) under certain crops, and estimated yield (in 1,000 tonnes), calculated from sample returns:

Crops	Area 1977	1978	Produce 1977	1978
Wheat	48,400	49,400	249	248
Oats	34,500	30,900	135	124
Barley	289,200	307,200	1,445	1,482
Potatoes	53,400	41,200	1,515	1,096
Sugar-beet	35,200[1]	36,500[1]	1,376	1,456

[1] Area grown under contract.

Gross agricultural output (excluding value changes in livestock) for the year 1979 was valued at £1,651,561,000.

Livestock (1979): Cattle, 7·1m.; sheep, 3·4m.; pigs, 1·1m.; horses, 75,500; poultry, 9·6m.

Forestry. The total area of state forests at 31 Dec. 1978 was 284,688 hectares.

Fisheries. The number of vessels and men engaged in fishing in 1979 were 1,539 boats propelled by outboard engines, sails and oars and 1,426 other fishing boats; men 8,711. The quantities and values of fish landed during 1979 were: Demersal fish, 21,092 tonnes, value £7,720,570; pelagic fish, 53,493 tonnes, value £9,783,479; shellfish, 11,113 tonnes, value £7,401,134. Total value, £22,905,183.

INDUSTRY AND TRADE

Industry. The census of industrial production for 1976 gives the following details of the values (in £1,000) of gross and net output for the principal manufacturing industries. The figures for net output are those of gross output minus cost of materials, including fuel, light and power, repairs to plant and machinery and amounts paid to others in connexion with products made.

	Gross output	Net output
Slaughtering, preparing and preserving meat	437,626	58,094
Dairy products	465,247	79,816
Bread, biscuit and flour confectionery	85,679	36,176
Sugar, cocoa, chocolate and sugar confectionery	153,938	50,245
Grain milling, animal and poultry foods	179,335	31,969
Brewing and malting	110,471	75,167
Tobacco products	142,273	33,943
Paper and paper products	84,351	29,930
Printing and publishing	90,072	59,504
Production and preliminary processing of metals	50,302	20,834
Manufacture of metal articles	121,642	54,034
Manufacture of non-metallic mineral products	224,284	107,207
Chemicals, including fertilizers and manmade fibres	381,221	144,942
Mechanical engineering	79,584	38,938
Manufacture of office machinery and data-processing machinery	89,540	31,536
Electrical engineering	130,226	63,233
Manufacture of motor vehicles, parts and accessories	99,687	28,638
Manufacture of other means of transport	66,549	28,638
Textiles (including knitting industry)	207,744	81,154
Footwear and clothing	127,251	61,105
Timber and wooden furniture	76,978	33,219
Processing rubber and plastics	97,601	40,266
Gas, water and electricity	222,944	113,200
All other industries [1]	400,784	227,413
Total (all industries)	4,125,332	1,528,621

[1] Including mining, fuel production, instrument engineering, various food and drink industries, etc.

Labour. The Department of Labour is responsible for legislation concerning: (i) worker protection generally with particular reference to the safety, health and welfare mainly of industrial workers, and those employed in mining and quarrying; (ii) conditions of employment and holidays with pay; (iii) National Manpower Service; (iv) industrial training; (v) redundancy payments and resettlement allowances; (vi) regulation of private employment agencies; (vii) industrial relations, promoting worker participation and industrial democracy; (viii) eliminating discrimination in employment.

An Industrial Training Authority (ANCO) was established by the Minister for Labour under the Industrial Training Act, 1967, to assist in the improvement of industrial training: ANCO's programme covers apprentice recruitment and training, the training and retraining of adult workers in industrial training centres and the designation and levying of industries for training purposes under the Act. Levy-grant schemes, the purpose of which is to stimulate training by industry itself, are in operation for 7 designated industries. CERT Ltd. trains staff for the hotel, catering and tourist industries under the aegis of the Minister for Labour.

The National Manpower Service is responsible for placement and guidance. The Service, which is organized on a regional basis, collects and maintains information on the labour market. Its main task is to help people seeking jobs to find suitable employment and to help employers find suitable employees at all levels up to professional and management level. It provides occupational guidance and advises workers, including redundant workers, about alternative jobs and training facilities. It provides financial help to workers who have to move to new areas to take up jobs offered through the Service. Careers information is also provided. The Service also administers the Employment Incentive Scheme and the Work Experience Programme.

The Labour Court was established by the Industrial Relations Act, 1946. Provisions relating to the Court's constitution and operation were amended by the Industrial Relations Acts, 1969 and 1976. The Court consists of a independent chairman and 3 deputy chairmen with employers' representatives nominated by the Federated Union of Employers and workers' representatives nominated by the Irish Congress of Trade Unions. The Court can investigate and/or conciliate in a trades dispute; assist in the formation of joint industrial councils, registered agreements between employers and trade unions and give its decision on questions of interpretation of such agreements. When a dispute is referred to the Court by either the trade unions or the employers or both the Act requires that the Court normally appoint an Industrial Relations Officer to mediate in the dispute and try to secure agreement through the medium of conciliation conferences. Should conciliation fail to find a settlement, both parties may request an investigation and recommendation by the Court. An investigation is normally held in private and neither party is under any legal obligation to accept the recommendation except in certain circumstances.

The Rights Commission Service was established under the Industrial Relations Act, 1969. The Rights Commission Service is free. A Commissioner may investigate a trade dispute referred to him by a party to a dispute. However he may not investigate a dispute without the consent of both parties, nor can he investigate disputes connected with rates of pay, hours or times of work or annual holidays of a body of workers. The Rights Commissioner's recommendation in trade disputes may be referred to the Labour Court on appeal. There are 3 Rights Commissioners. A Rights Commissioner may also hear claims under the Unfair Dismissals Act, 1977. Recommendations made in these cases may be appealed to the Employment Appeals Tribunal. The Tribunal may also deal with claims under the Unfair Dismissals Act, 1977 in areas where one of the parties concerned objects to a hearing by a Rights Commissioner.

On 5 May 1978 the Minister for Labour established a Commission of Enquiry on Industrial Relations to undertake a review of the industrial relations system and to make recommendations.

The Anti-Discrimination (Pay) Act, 1974, came into operation on 31 Dec. 1975. The 1974 Act establishes the right to equal remuneration where women and men are doing like work. The Employment Equality Act, 1977, which came into operation on 1 July 1977 prohibits discrimination in employment on grounds of sex or marital status. Equality Officers investigate disputes about equal pay and equal treatment and issue recommendations. Appeals against an Equality Officer's recommendation may be referred to the Labour Court, which then issues a binding determination.

The Employment Equality Agency, an independent body, was set up under the Employment Equality Act, 1977. The functions of the Agency are: to work towards the elimination of discrimination; to promote equality of opportunity for men and women; to keep under review the working of the Employment Equality Act, 1977 and the Anti-Discrimination (Pay) Act, 1974.

The Department of Labour co-operates with the EEC institutions in the formulation of EEC labour policy and the preparation of EEC labour legislation. It is responsible for the implementation of EEC labour legislation and for the promotion of standards contained in the Conventions and Recommendations of the International Labour Organization. It also services the Manpower and Social Affairs Committee of the OECD. It implements those articles of the European Social Charter which relate to conditions of work and which have been accepted by the Irish Republic.

Labour and Employment. The total labour force at mid-April 1979 was about 1,152,000, of which about 87,000 persons were out of work.

The number of trade unions holding negotiation licences in Oct. 1980 was 78, of which 62 were workers' trade unions and the remainder employers' trade unions. The total membership of these unions is estimated at 413,500, of whom 9,500 were in the employers' trade unions. Of the 403,900 workers in trade unions approximately 273,000 were organized in 6 general unions catering for both white collar and manual workers. Trade unions representing the majority of workers in the Public Service and their membership are not included in these figures as, generally, they are not obliged to hold negotiation licences.

European Social Fund. The Department of Labour has been designated by the Irish Government as the national agency responsible for formulating and transmitting to the EEC Commission Irish applications for assistance from the European Social Fund. Assistance is available from the Fund towards expenditure on certain schemes of training, retraining and resettlement of workers, of job creation for young persons and of vocational rehabilitation of the handicapped, provided that those schemes receive financial assistance from public funds.

Commerce. Value of imports and exports of merchandise for calendar years (in £):

	1975	1976	1977	1978	1979
Imports	1,704,113,910	2,337,932,028	3,090,886,805	3,713,098,432	4,815,708,897
Exports	1,447,366,772	1,859,077,079	2,518,170,389	2,963,180,624	3,498,514,967

The values of the chief imports and total exports are shown in the following table (in £):

	Imports		Exports	
	1978	1979	1978	1979
Live animals and food	385,950,189	495,069,108	1,140,720,112	1,229,292,323
Raw materials	128,968,752	165,928,245	1 20,283,576	170,862,609
Mineral fuels and lubricants	376,154,321	580,582,717	12,164,690	16,819,254
Chemicals	443,138,777	564,363,850	354,933,255	451,699,920
Manufactured goods	714,913,901	929,608,800	410,014,877	460,368,437
Machinery and transport equipment	1,110,469,596	1,386,153,879	410,071,219	561,199,025
Manufactured articles [1]	389,439,878	516,547,006	309,492,665	379,620,311

[1] Not elsewhere specified.

Distribution of trade, by principal countries of origin in the case of imports and destination in the case of exports (in £):

Country	Imports		Total exports	
	1978	1979	1978	1979
Argentina	4,366,680	3,410,634	3,202,366	5,130,403
Australia	2,988,716	4,680,459	21,981,892	25,313,328
Belgium and Luxembourg	69,933,254	103,310,691	150,844,912	205,062,569
Brazil	11,668,633	19,435,282	6,240,687	5,827,258
Canada	32,566,116	46,796,961	31,509,308	34,538,013
Denmark	30,854,739	37,557,530	20,502,262	24,241,723
Finland	37,670,474	51,126,795	6,056,548	10,450,433
France	189,931,410	249,812,822	263,868,890	282,627,960
Germany, Fed. Rep. of	265,531,232	359,050,039	247,645,733	306,319,455
Ghana	13,707,415	9,547,898	1,335,309	1,182,595

	Imports		Total exports	
Country	1978	1979	1978	1979
Greece	4,139,977	5,957,947	8,270,204	11,356,475
Hong Kong	10,078,589	16,191,245	2,267,041	3,748,340
India	14,867,818	16,771,386	1,959,834	5,266,057
Iran	10,839,586	17,591,384	15,614,705	7,485,478
Iraq	43,149,207	21,877,248	3,740,336	6,889,529
Israel	9,211,463	12,654,907	2,120,351	5,442,459
Italy	114,500,637	139,162,844	63,093,384	81,554,965
Japan	117,224,684	127,916,079	25,006,879	28,730,055
Kuwait	15,315,686	14,232,478	3,668,110	6,942,837
Malaysia	7,325,455	9,618,410	3,073,985	3,511,372
Morocco	2,281,926	3,143,370	6,029,756	3,143,814
Netherlands	101,642,440	151,257,041	149,547,222	186,536,561
New Zealand	9,956,773	10,297,143	1,379,423	3,480,245
Nigeria	4,642,355	8,463,388	26,745,750	22,040,803
Norway	15,808,298	19,905,140	8,192,125	10,455,293
Poland	26,280,158	32,750,016	5,885,841	3,572,347
Portugal	9,316,954	14,787,940	3,551,232	5,138,298
Saudi Arabia	41,069,355	65,609,161	17,616,351	16,110,867
South Africa, Rep. of	9,874,795	12,136,318	7,141,227	8,358,890
Spain	26,804,901	33,670,560	24,152,796	34,825,801
Sri Lanka	2,003,643	2,760,681	934,431	667,513
Sweden	64,284,332	83,034,858	32,364,580	43,605,684
Switzerland	34,810,925	40,220,146	19,493,037	23,971,339
USSR	24,922,915	42,328,739	5,533,630	22,442,118
UK	1,835,330,908	2,408,661,048	1,399,740,495	1,624,506,890
USA	312,428,566	409,355,218	182,644,533	171,080,860
Venezuela	1,240,465	3,344,035	11,106,481	8,372,899

An Anglo-Irish free-trade agreement to remove progressively all duties between July 1966 and July 1975 was signed in London on 14 Dec. 1965.

Total trade between Irish Republic and UK (British Department of Trade returns, in £1,000 sterling):

	1976	1977	1978	1979	1980
Imports to UK	1,008,434	1,282,560	1,606,308	1,689,206	1,784,329
Exports and re-exports from UK	1,246,575	1,640,311	2,044,796	2,554,839	2,660,024

Tourism. Estimated number of visits by foreigners (including cross-border movement) in 1979 was 9·8m.; they spent £257·4m.

COMMUNICATIONS

Roads. At 31 Dec. 1977 there were 57,326 miles of public roads, consisting of 3,264 miles of national roads, 6,662 miles of main (trunk and link) roads other than national roads, 45,948 miles of county roads and 1,452 miles of county borough and urban roads; of the total mileage 54,300 (95%) was paved.

Number of licensed motor vehicles at 30 Sept. 1979: Private cars, 682,958; public-service vehicles, 5,388; goods vehicles, 61,543; agricultural tractors, 64,409; motor cycles, 28,785; other vehicles, 10,128.

The total number of miles run by road motor passenger vehicles of the omnibus type during 1979 was 44,283,000. Passengers carried numbered 213,284,000 and the gross receipts from passengers were £42,041,000.

Railways. The total length of railway open for traffic at 31 Dec. 1979 was 1,978 km, all 1,600 mm gauge. Córas Iompair Éireann, the national transport undertaking, operates all rail services in the State.

Railway statistics for years ending 31 Dec.	1978	1979
Passengers (no.)	15,905,000	17,886,008
Miles run by coaching trains	5,281,000	5,534,000
Merchandise and mineral traffic conveyed (tons)	3,789,000	3,739,000
Miles run by freight trains	2,965,000	3,143,000
Receipts (£)	29,520,341	34,442,466
Expenditure (£)	57,193,972	70,278,490

Aviation. During the year ended 31 March 1980 Aer Lingus–Irish International Airlines carried 2,154,719 passengers, 46,602 short tons of cargo and 940 short tons of mail on its European services and 329,602 passengers, 18,001 short tons of cargo and 384 short tons of mail on its trans-Atlantic services.

Shipping. The total number of arrivals at ports in the country during 1978 was 16,787 of 26,246,010 NRT; of these, 2,408 of 3,693,856 NRT, were Irish registered vessels. The Irish merchant fleet, of vessels of 100 gross tons or over, consisted of 68 vessels totalling 204,535 GRT at 31 Dec. 1978.

Inland Waterways. The principal inland waterways open to navigation are the Shannon Navigation (130 miles) and the Grand Canal and Barrow Navigation (156 miles). Merchandise traffic is not now transported on them and navigation is confined to pleasure craft operated either privately or commercially.

Post and Broadcasting (31 Dec. 1980). Number of post offices, 2,096; telegraph offices, 1,340; telephones, 519,000; public telephones, 3,850; telephone exchanges, 1,023.

Radio and television broadcasting is operated by Radio Telefís Éireann, a statutory public body appointed by the Minister for Posts and Telegraphs under the Broadcasting Authority Acts. On 31 Dec. 1977 there were 595,000 holders of current monochrome television licences and 97,334 holders of current colour television licences.

Cinemas. There are 145 cinemas.

Newspapers (1980). There are 7 daily newspapers (all in English) with a combined circulation of 773,250; 5 of them are published in Dublin (circulation, 660,527).

JUSTICE, RELIGION, EDUCATION AND WELFARE

Justice. The Constitution provides that justice shall be administered in public in Courts established by law by Judges appointed by the President on the advice of the Government. The jurisdiction and organization of the Courts are dealt with in the Courts (Establishment and Constitution Act, 1961), the Courts (Supplemental Provisions) Acts, 1961–79. These Courts consist of Courts of First Instance and a Court of Final Appeal, called the Supreme Court. The Courts of First Instance are the High Court with full original jurisdiction and the Circuit and the District Courts with local and limited jurisdiction. A judge may not be removed from office except for stated misbehaviour or incapacity and then only on resolutions passed by both Houses of the *Oireachtas*. Judges of the Supreme, High and Circuit Courts are appointed from among practising barristers. Judges of the District Court (called District Justices) may be appointed from among practising barristers or practising solicitors.

The Supreme Court, which consists of the Chief Justice (who is *ex officio* an additional judge of the High Court) and 5 ordinary judges, has appellate jurisdiction from all decisions of the High Court. The President may, after consultation with the Council of State, refer a Bill, which has been passed by both Houses of the *Oireachtas* (other than a money bill and certain other bills), to the Supreme Court for a decision on the question as to whether such Bill or any provision thereof is or are repugnant to the Constitution.

The High Court, which consists of a President (who is *ex officio* an additional Judge of the Supreme Court) and (at present) 11 ordinary judges, has full original jurisdiction in and power to determine all matters and questions, whether of law or fact, civil or criminal. In all cases in which questions arise touching the validity of any law having regard to the provisions of the Constitution, the High Court alone exercises original jurisdiction. The High Court on Circuit acts as an appeal court from the Circuit Court.

The Court of Criminal Appeal consists of the Chief Justice or an ordinary Judge of the Supreme Court, together with either 2 ordinary judges of the High Court or the President and one ordinary judge of the High Court. It deals with appeals by persons convicted on indictment where the appellant obtains a certificate from the trial judge that the case is a fit one for appeal, or, in case such certificate is refused, where the court itself, on appeal from such refusal, grants leave to appeal. The decision of the Court of Criminal Appeal is final, unless that court or the Director of Public Prosecutions certifies that the decision involves a point of law of exceptional public importance, so that an appeal should be taken to the Supreme Court.

The High Court exercising criminal jurisdiction is known as the Central Criminal Court. It consists of a judge or judges of the High Court, nominated by the

President of the High Court. The Court sits in Dublin and tries criminal cases which are outside the jurisdiction of the Circuit Court or which may be sent forward to it for trial from the Circuit Court on the application of the Director of Public Prosecution or the accused person.

The country is divided into a number of circuits for the purposes of the Circuit Court. The President of the Circuit Court is *ex officio* an additional judge of the High Court. The jurisdiction of the court in civil proceedings is limited to £2,000 in contract and tort, £2,000 in actions founded on hire-purchase and credit-sale agreements, £5,000 in equity and £5,000 in probate and administration, save by consent of the parties, in which event the jurisdiction is unlimited. In criminal matters it has jurisdiction in all cases except murder, treason, piracy and allied offences. The Circuit Court acts as an appeal court from the District Court.

The District Court has a summary jurisdiction in a large number of criminal cases where the offence is not of a serious nature. In civil matters the Court has jurisdiction in contract and tort (except slander, libel, criminal conversation, seduction, slander or title, malicious prosecution and false imprisonment) where the claim does not exceed £250; in proceedings founded on hire-purchase and credit-sale agreements, the jurisdiction is £250.

All criminal cases, except those of a minor nature, are tried by a judge and a jury of 12. Juries are also used in many civil cases in the High Court. In a criminal case the jury must be unanimous in reaching a verdict, but in a civil case the agreement of 9 members is sufficient.

Religion. According to the census of population taken in 1971 the principal religious professions were as follows:

	Leinster	Munster	Connacht	Ulster (part of)	Total
Roman Catholics	1,387,644	849,382	378,613	180,027	2,795,666
Church of Ireland	60,115	17,807	6,084	13,733	97,739
Presbyterians	5,172	627	347	9,906	16,052
Methodists	3,187	1,321	248	890	5,646
Other religious denominations	6,914	1,269	272	426	8,881
Not stated or no religion	35,108	11,596	5,338	2,222	54,264

Education. *Elementary.* Elementary education is free and was given in about 3,432 national schools (including 108 special schools) in 1979. The average daily enrolment of pupils in 1979 was 550,819; the number of teachers of all classes (1979) 19,046. Average daily pupil attendance is about 90·2%. There are 6 training colleges for primary school teachers, all co-educational. The estimated state expenditure on elementary education for 1980 (1 Jan.–31 Dec.) is £190·57m., excluding the cost of administration.

Satisfactory progress is being maintained in the provision of up-to-date facilities and accommodation for primary school children; special measures are taken for disadvantaged children.

Special provision is made for handicapped and deprived children in special schools which are recognized on the same basis as primary schools, in special classes attached to ordinary schools and in certain voluntary centres where educational services appropriate to the needs of the children are provided. Categories of handicapped children catered for include visually handicapped, hearing impaired, physically handicapped, mentally handicapped, emotionally disturbed, itinerants and other socially disadvantaged children. Provision is also being made on an increasing scale for children with dual or multiple handicaps. In each case a programme suited to the needs of the particular kind of handicap is provided. The number of children in each class in such schools is very much smaller than in ordinary classes in a primary school and because of the size of the catchment areas involved an extensive system of school transport has been developed. Many handicapped children who have spent some years in a special school or class are integrated into normal schools for part of their school career, if necessary with special additional facilities such as nursing services, special equipment, etc. For others who cannot progress within the ordinary school system the special schools or classes provide both the primary and secondary level of education. In addition to the services being provided on a full-time basis many children are being catered for by the provision of part-time teaching facilities in hospitals, child guidance clinics, rehabilitation workshops, special 'Saturday-morning' centres and home teaching schemes.

Secondary. Voluntary secondary schools are under private control and are conducted in most cases by religious orders; all schools receive grants from the State and are open to inspection by the Department of Education. The number of recognized secondary schools during the school year 1979–80 was 529, and the number of pupils in attendance was 199,699. Total estimated state expenditure for 1980 (1 Jan.–31 Dec.) is £11,557,000.

Grants for the provision of a wide range of audio visual teaching aids are available to secondary schools. The schools television service, *Telefís Scoile*, provides programmes in Irish, English, history, geography, mathematics and science subjects for senior and junior pupils. The vast majority of secondary schools now have at least one television receiving set which was purchased with the aid of a state grant.

Vocational Education Committee schools provide courses of general and technical education. The number of vocational schools during the school year 1979–80 was 246, full-time students, 66,785. These centres are controlled by the local Vocational Education Committees, and are maintained partly from the rates and partly by state grants. The estimated state expenditure for 1980 (1 Jan.–31 Dec.) is £67,376,000, and the estimated expenditure from the local rates, £2,151,064.

Comprehensive Schools which are financed by the State combine academic and technical subjects in one broad curriculum so that each pupil may be offered an education structured to his needs, abilities and interests. Pupils are prepared for the State examinations and for entrance to universities and institutes of further education. To date, 15 comprehensive schools have been built with 8,239 pupils.

Community Schools continue to be established through the amalgamation of existing voluntary secondary and Vocational Education Committee schools where this is found feasible and desirable and in new areas where a single larger school is considered preferable to 2 smaller schools under separate managements. These 30 schools (16,404 pupils) cater for all aspects of second-level education and provide adult education facilities in the areas in which they are situated. They also make facilities available to voluntary organizations and to the adult community generally. The estimated State expenditure on running costs for 1979 (1 Jan.–31 Dec.) is £15·49m. for community and comprehensive schools.

Regional Technical Colleges have been set up in 10 provincial centres, Athlone, Carlow, Cork, Dundalk, Galway, Letterkenny, Limerick, Sligo, Tralee and Waterford. The colleges provide apprentice, technician, professional, general and adult education courses. The estimated State expenditure on the colleges for 1980 (1 Jan.–31 Dec.), including capital costs and student aid, is £16,545,099.

University Education is provided by the National University of Ireland, founded in Dublin in 1908, and by the University of Dublin (Trinity College), founded in 1592. The National University comprises 3 constituent colleges—University College, Dublin, University College, Cork, and University College, Galway. St Patrick's College, Maynooth, Co. Kildare, is a national seminary for Catholic priests and a pontifical university with the power to confer degrees up to doctoral level in philosophy, theology and canon law. It now admits lay students (men and women) to the courses in arts, celtic studies, science and education which it provides as a recognized college of the National University. Besides the University medical schools, the Royal College of Surgeons in Ireland, which is a long-established independent medical school, provides medical qualifications which are internationally recognized. Third-level courses with a technological bias, leading to degree, diploma and certificate qualifications are also provided by the National Institute for Higher Education, Limerick. A National Institute for Higher Education in Dublin opened in Nov. 1980 and it will also offer third-level courses with a technological bias. The Thomond College of Education, Limerick, is a specialist teacher-training institution concerned with the training of post-primary teachers in the areas of physical education, rural and general science, metalwork and engineering science and woodwork and building science.

The National Council for Educational Awards, established in 1972, is the validating and awarding authority for degree, diploma and certificate courses in the third-level non-university sector.

Agricultural. Full-time instruction in agriculture is provided for all sections of the farming community. There are 4 state agricultural colleges for young people, administered by the Department of Agriculture and Fisheries, and 7 private state-aided agricultural colleges, at each of which a 1-year course in agriculture is given. Second-year courses in farm machinery and dairying are provided at a number of the colleges. Advanced courses in pig and poultry husbandry and management are also provided. Scholarships tenable at these colleges, all of which are residential, are awarded by the County Committees of Agriculture. These Committees provide a comprehensive agricultural advisory service and also conduct winter classes in agriculture and horticulture at local centres. A more comprehensive course is provided in winter farm schools, which are intended, in general, for persons of not less than 17 years of age who are engaged in farming.

Horticultural. A 2-year course in commercial horticulture is provided at 3 residential colleges. There is also a 2-year course in amenity horticulture at the National Botanic Gardens in Dublin.

Poultry-keeping and Farm Home Management. An advanced 3-year residential course is provided at the Munster Institute, Cork, for young people who wish to qualify for teaching and advisory posts in farm home management. The farm home management course includes instruction in poultry-keeping, butter- and cheese-making, general farming and home management. A 1-year non-residential course of instruction for the training of young men and women as technicians in poultry husbandry is also provided at the Munster Institute (which is administered by the Department of Agriculture). In addition, if there are enough suitable applicants, a 6-month course in poultry husbandry and management is provided for young people at the Munster Institute.

Rural Home Economics and Rural Science. A 1-year course for young people in poultry-keeping, dairying and rural home economics is given at 5 private residential colleges of rural home economics and 1 private residential school of home economics. The County Committees of Agriculture award scholarships tenable at these institutions. Classes in poultry-keeping and farm home management are also conducted by the County Committees at local centres.

A scheme of farm apprenticeship and a trainee farmer scheme are operated by the Farm Apprenticeship Board, which represents various agricultural interests. The scheme provides for practical training on well-managed commercial farms.

Higher Education in Agriculture, Horticulture, Dairy Science and Veterinary Science. Higher education in general agriculture and horticulture is provided by University College, Dublin, and in dairy science by University College, Cork. Training in veterinary medicine and surgery is provided at the Veterinary College, Ballsbridge, Dublin.

Health Services. Persons in the lower income group (those who are unable to afford general practitioner services for themselves and their dependants) are entitled to a free comprehensive health service (family doctor, hospital and specialist services, maternity and infant-welfare services, dental, ophthalmic and aural services). Persons and dependants in the middle-income groups (less than £7,000 per annum income) are entitled to in-patient and out-patient hospital services including specialist services, free maternity care and help towards the cost of drugs and medicines. Such persons must pay a contribution of £24 a year, or £0·50 a week, towards the cost of these services. All insured persons, irrespective of income, qualify for the benefit of assistance towards the cost of prescriptions, which limits the total outlay of a family to £6·50 per month. Hospital treatment for tuberculosis and certain other infectious diseases as well as for children suffering from certain long-term diseases and disabilities is provided free of charge to all classes of the community. Persons suffering from diabetes and other specified long-term conditions are eligible for a free supply of drugs and other necessary medicines, etc.

Pupils of national (elementary) schools are provided with a free school health-examination service and are also eligible for free dental, ophthalmic and aural services for defects discovered at school health examinations.

A free child-welfare clinic service for children under 6 years of age is available in many urban areas. A disabled persons maintenance allowance is payable in cases of need to chronically disabled persons over 16 who are not living in institutions. The disabled are also entitled to free travel and in certain circumstances to a free electricity allowance and a television licence. There are also schemes which provide for the education of the blind, and for the training and placement in suitable employment of the blind and the disabled. All these services are provided by 8 regional health boards under the direction and control of the Minister for Health.

Social Security. Social-welfare services concerned primarily with income mainten-ance are under the general control of the Minister for Social Welfare. The services administered by the Department of Social Welfare are divided into Insurance and Assistance schemes.

Insurance Services. All employees irrespective of their level of earnings are com-pulsorily insured from age 16 to 66 years and are liable for pay-related social insur-ance contributions. The majority of employees pay a contribution of 4·5% of their earnings while their employers pay a further 9·8% up to a prescribed ceiling of £5,500. (The insured population is approximately 1m.) Subject to appropriate statu-tory conditions (but without regard to the recipients' means) the following flat-rate insurance benefits are available: Disability benefit, invalidity pension, unemploy-ment benefit, maternity benefit, widow's pension, deserted wife's benefit, orphan's allowance, treatment benefit, retirement pension payable at 65, old-age pension payable at 66 and a death grant. Pay-related benefit is payable with disability benefit, unemployment benefit, maternity allowance and injury benefit to persons whose employment is insurable at certain class rates of pay-related social insurance contribution. The cost of the flat-rate and pay-related benefits is met by pay-related social insurance contributions from employers and employees and by a state grant.

The insurance services also provide for payment of benefits in respect of injury, disablement or death, as well as medical care resulting from an occupational acci-dent or disease. These benefits are available to employees, irrespective of age, and are paid from an Occupational Injuries Fund which is financed by employers' con-tributions and income from investments.

Assistance Services. Children's allowances are payable without a means test in respect of each child under 16 years of age and children between 16 and 18 who are at school, in apprenticeship or incapacitated for a prolonged period. The fol-lowing Assistance services are subject to means and, sometimes, residence tests: Non-contributory widows' and orphans' pensions to the survivors of persons whose lack of insurance (or inadequate insurance record) precludes payment of contributory pen-sions; deserted wife's allowance to women under 66 years of age who have been deserted by their husbands and for whom the deserted wife's benefit is similarly precluded; allowances for unmarried mothers, prisoners' wives and single women between the ages of 58 and 66 years; old age pensions payable at age 66 to persons not entitled to insurance pensions; blind pensions (under the same general conditions as apply to old age pensions) payable at age 18; un-employment assistance payable during unemployment to persons not entitled to receive unemployment benefit; supplementary welfare allowance, payable when a person has no other resources or when such resources are insufficient to meet his needs.

DIPLOMATIC REPRESENTATIVES

OF THE IRISH REPUBLIC IN GREAT BRITAIN
(17 Grosvenor Place, London, SW1X 7HR)

Ambassador: Dr Eamon Kennedy.

OF GREAT BRITAIN IN THE IRISH REPUBLIC
(33 Merrion Rd., Dublin, 4)

Ambassador: Leonard Clifford William Figg, CMG.

OF THE IRISH REPUBLIC IN THE USA (2234 Massachusetts Ave.,
NW, Washington, D.C. 20008)
Ambassador: Seán A. Donlon.

OF THE USA IN THE IRISH REPUBLIC
(42 Elgin Rd., Ballsbridge, Dublin)
Ambassador: William V. Shannon.

OF THE IRISH REPUBLIC TO THE UNITED NATIONS
Ambassador: Noel Dorr.

Books of Reference

Statistical Information: The Central Statistics Office (Earlsfort Terrace, Dublin, 2) was established in June 1949, and is attached to the Department of the Taoiseach. *Director:* T. P. Linehan, B.E., B.Sc.

The Central Statistics Office took over the work carried out since 1922 by the Statistics Branch, Department of Industry and Commerce, which in turn had continued the statistical work carried out by the Department of Agriculture and Technical Instruction (since 1900) and by the Irish Department of the Ministry of Labour, London (since 1919). Vital statistics from 1864, annual agricultural statistics prior to 1900 and decennial census of population were compiled by the Registrar-General for Ireland. The population censuses were carried out in 1926, 1936 and 1946 by the Statistics Branch of the Department of Industry and Commerce and are now the responsibility of the Central Statistics Office, which has also, as from July 1950, taken over from the Registrar-General the compilation of Vital Statistics. The Statistics Act 1926 confers wide powers for the collection, compilation and publication of statistics. Other Acts under which statistics are collected are Workmen's Compensation Act, Merchant Shipping Act, Customs Consolidation Act and Road Transport Act.

Principal publications of the Central Statistics Office are *National Income and Expenditure* (annually), *Statistical Abstract* (annually), *Census of Population Reports, Census of Industrial Production Reports, Trade and Shipping Statistics* (annually and monthly), *Trend of Employment and Unemployment* (annually), *Reports on Vital Statistics* (annually), *Irish Statistical Bulletin* (quarterly).

Atlas of Ireland. Royal Irish Academy, Dublin, 1979
Facts About Ireland. Dublin Department of Foreign Affairs, 3rd ed. 1980
The Gill History of Ireland. 11 vols. Dublin
Bartholomew, P. C., *The Irish Judiciary.* Dublin, Institute of Public Administration, 1974
Chubb, B., *The Constitution and Constitutional Change in Ireland.* Dublin, 1978
Delaney, V. T. H., *The Administration of Justice in Ireland.* 4th ed. Dublin, Institute of Public Administration, 1975
Eager, A. R., *A Guide to Irish Bibliographical Material.* 2nd ed. London, 1980
Encyclopaedia of Ireland. Dublin, 1968
Freeman, T. W., *Ireland: A General and Regional Geography.* 4th ed. London, 1972
Harbison, P., *Guide to the National Monuments of Ireland.* Dublin, 1975
Hickey, D. J. and Doherty, J. E., *A Dictionary of Irish History since 1800.* Dublin, 1980
Johnston, T. J., and others, *A History of the Church of Ireland.* Dublin, 1953
Keatinge, P., *Formulation of Irish Foreign Policy.* Dublin, 1973.—*A Place Among the Nations: Issues of Irish Foreign Policy.* Dublin, 1978
Kee, R., *The Green Flag.* London, 1972
Kelly, J. M., *Fundamental Rights in the Irish Law and Constitution.* 2nd ed. Dublin, 1967
Lehane, B., *The Companion Guide to Ireland.* London, 1973
Lyons, F. S. L., *Ireland Since the Famine.* London, 1971
McDunphy, Michael, *The President of Ireland: His Powers, Functions and Duties.* Dublin, 1945
Meenan, J., *The Irish Economy Since 1922.* Liverpool, 1970
Nevill, W. E., *Geology and Ireland.* Dublin, 1963
O'Donnell, J. P., *How Ireland is Governed.* 5th ed. Dublin, Institute of Public Administration
O'Mahony, David, *The Irish Economy.* Rev. ed. Cork University Press, 1967
Thom's Directory of Ireland. 2 vols. (Dublin, Street Directory, Commercial). Dublin, 1979–80

ISRAEL

Medinat Israel—State of Israel

Capital: Jerusalem
Population: 3·83m. (1979)
GNP per capita: US$4,120 (1978)

HISTORY. In 1967, following some years of uneasy peace, local clashes on the Israeli-Syrian border were followed by Egyptian mass concentration of forces on the borders of Israel. The UN emergency force was expelled and a blockade of shipping to and from Israel was imposed by Egypt in the Red Sea. Israel struck out at Egypt on land and in the air on 5–9 June 1967. Jordan joined in the conflict which spread to the Syrian borders. By 11 June the Israelis had occupied the Gaza Strip and the Sinai peninsula as far as the Suez Canal in Egypt, West Jordan as far as the Jordan valley and the heights east of the Sea of Galilee, including Quneitra in Syria.

A further war broke out on 6 Oct. 1973 when an Egyptian offensive was launched across the Suez Canal and Syrian forces struck on the Golan Heights. Following UN Security Council resolutions a ceasefire finally came into being on 24 Oct. In Dec. agreement was reached by Egypt and Israel on disengagement and a disengagement agreement was signed with Syria on 31 May 1974. A further disengagement agreement was signed between Israel and Egypt in Sept. 1975.

Developments in 1977 included President Sadat of Egypt's visit to Israel and peace inititative and in March 1978 Israeli troops entered southern Lebanon but later withdrew after the arrival of a UN peace-keeping force.

In Sept. 1978 President Carter convened the Camp David conference at which Egypt and Israel agreed on frameworks for peace in the Middle East with treaties to be negotiated between Israel and her neighbours. Negotiations began in USA between Egypt and Israel in Oct. 1978 and a peace treaty was signed in Washington 26 March 1979.

Under the Israel–Egypt peace treaty signed in Washington on 26 March 1979, Israel was to withdraw from the Sinai Desert in two phases, part was achieved on 26 Jan. 1980 and the final withdrawal by 26 April 1982.

AREA AND POPULATION. The area of Israel, within the boundaries defined by the 1949 armistice agreements with Egypt, Jordan, the Lebanon and Syria, is 20,700 sq. km (7,993 sq. miles), with a population (May 1972 census) of 3·2m. (estimated, Jan. 1979, 3·83m.). The area within the ceasefire lines is 89,359 sq. km (34,493 sq. miles). Population of areas under Israeli administration as a result of the 6-day war was approximately 1m.; Judaea and Samaria (West Bank), 674,500, Gaza Strip and Northern Sinai, 418,800 and a few thousand on the Golan Heights.

Crude birth rate per 1,000 population of Jewish population (1976), 24·9; non-Jewish, 42·4; crude death rate, Jewish, 7; non-Jewish, 4·7; infant mortality rate per 1,000 live births, Jewish, 16; non-Jewish, 33·2.

Israel is administratively divided into 6 districts:

District	Area (sq. km)	Population[1]	Chief town
Northern	3,489	594,100	Nazareth
Haifa	855	557,400	Haifa
Central	1,243	766,400	Ramla
Tel Aviv	171	995,900	Tel Aviv
Jerusalem[2]	557	438,200	Jerusalem
Southern	14,387	464,600	Beersheba

[1] 1979.   [2] Includes East Jerusalem, annexed from Jordan after 1967 War.

711

On 23 Jan. 1950 the Knesset proclaimed Jerusalem the capital of the State. Population of the main towns (31 Dec. 1979): Tel-Aviv/Jaffa, 336,300; Jerusalem, 398,200; Haifa, 229,300; Ramat Gan, 120,400; Bat-Yam, 130,100; Holon, 128,400; Petach Tikva, 117,000; Beersheba, 107,000.

The official languages are Hebrew and Arabic.

Immigration. The following table shows the numbers of Jewish immigrants entering Palestine (Israel), including persons entering as travellers who subsequently registered as immigrants. For a year-by-year breakdown, *see* THE STATESMAN'S YEAR-BOOK, 1951, p. 1167.

1919–32	84,093	1940–47	92,563	1969–75	279,000
1933–39	218,099	1948–68	1,290,610	1976–79	104,799

During the period 1948–68, 45·5% of the immigrants came from Europe and America and 54·5% from Asia and Africa; during the period 1969–74, 78% came from Europe and America and 22% from Asia and Africa.

The Jewish Agency, which, in accordance with Article IV of the Palestine Mandate, played a leading role in laying the political, economic and social foundations on which the State of Israel was established, continues to be instrumental in organizing immigration.

CONSTITUTION AND GOVERNMENT. Israel is an independent sovereign republic, established by proclamation on 14 May 1948. For the history of the British Mandate, *see* THE STATESMAN'S YEAR-BOOK, 1920–49, under PALESTINE.

In 1950 the Knesset (*Parliament*), which in 1949 had passed the Transition Law dealing in general terms with the powers of the Knesset, President and Cabinet, resolved to enact from time to time fundamental laws, which eventually, taken together, would form the Constitution. The first of these fundamental laws, dealing with the Knesset, Israel Lands and the President, were passed in 1958, 1960 and 1964 respectively.

National flag: White with 2 horizontal blue stripes, the blue Shield of David in the centre.

National anthem: Hatikvah (The Hope). Words by N. N. Imber (1878); adopted as the Jewish National Anthem by the first Zionist Congress (1897).

The Knesset, a one-chamber Parliament, consists of 120 members. It is elected for a 4-year term by secret ballot and universal direct suffrage. The system of election is by proportional representation. In May 1977 the Knesset was composed as follows: Likud, 45; Labour Party-Mapam Alignment, 32; Democratic Movement for Change, 15; National Religious Party, 12; Democratic Front for Peace and Equality, 5; Agudat Israel, 4; Poalei Agudat, 1; Independent Liberal, 1; Citizens Rights Movement, 1; United Arab, 1; Flatto-Sharon, 1. Elections are to be held on 7 July 1981. The President is elected by the Knesset by secret ballot by a simple majority; his term of office is 5 years. He may be re-elected once.

Former Presidents of the State: Chaim Weizmann (1949–52); Izhak Ben-Zvi (1952–63); Zalman Shazar (1963–68); Ephraim Katzir (1963–1978).

President: Yitzhak Navon, elected 19 April 1978 by 86 votes to none with 23 abstentions.

The Cabinet in March 1981 was composed as follows:

Prime Minister and Minister of Defence: Menachem Begin (L-H).

Deputy Prime Minister: Yigael Yadin (DM). *Second Deputy Prime Minister:* Simcha Ehrlich (L-Lib). *Foreign Affairs:* Yitzhak Shamir (L-H). *Religious Affairs:* Abaron Abou Hassira (NR). *Finance and Communications:* Yoram Aridor. *Interior:* Dr Yosef Burg (NR). *Industry, Commerce and Tourism:* Gideon Patt (L-Lib). *Education and Culture:* Zevulun Hammer (NR). *Absorption and Housing:* David Levi (L-H). *Energy, Infrastructure and Communications:* Yitzhak Moday (L-Lib). *Health:* Eliezer Shostak (L-L). *Agriculture:* Ariel Sharon (L). *Justice:* Moshe Nissim (L-Lib). *Social Welfare and Labour:* Dr Israel Katz (DMC). *Transport:* Haim Landau (L).

Local Government. Local authorities are of three kinds, namely, municipal corporations, local councils and regional councils. Their status, powers and duties are prescribed by statute. Regional councils are local authorities set up in agricultural areas and include all the agricultural settlements in the area under their jurisdiction. All local authorities exercise their authority mainly by means of bye-laws approved by the Minister of the Interior. Their revenue is derived from rates and a surcharge on income tax. Local authorities are elected for a 4-year term of office concurrently with general elections.

There are 31 municipalities (2 Arab), 115 local councils (46 Arab and 6 Druze) and 49 regional councils (1 Arab) comprising 700 villages.

DEFENCE. The Defence Service Law of 8 Sept. 1949, as amended, provides a compulsory 30-month conscription (extended to 36 months in 1968) for men between the ages of 18 and 26 and a 30-month conscription for men in the age-group of 27–29 years. Unmarried women aged 18–26 serve 24 months. After their term of military service, men are on the reserves until the age of 55 years. Until they are 40, men usually report for 31 days training annually and from then until they are 55, for 14 days. Commissioned and n.c.o.s usually serve 7 extra days a year.

The Israel Defence Force is a unified force, in which army, navy and air force are subordinate to a single chief-of-staff. The Minister of Defence is *de facto* commander-in-chief but from Oct. 1973 the cabinet formed a defence committee with authority to make decisions on military operations.

Army. The regular army had a strength in 1980 of 135,000 (15,000 regulars) including 12,000 women, organized in 24 armoured, 9 mechanized, 9 infantry, 9 artillery and 5 parachute brigades. There is a reserve army of about 375,000 on mobilization.

The highest army rank is that of Lieut.-General (*Rav Alouf*), and the Chief-of-Staff, who is the C.-in-C., holds that rank. A divisional commander is a Brigadier (*Tat Alouf*), and a brigade commander a Colonel (*Alouf Mishne*).

Navy. The Navy includes 3 diesel-electric patrol submarines (built in Britain), 22 missile vessels (10 of 415 tons and 12 of 220 tons), 43 patrol craft, 2 transports, 3 medium landing ships, 6 landing craft, 1 support ship, 1 training ship, 4 coastguard cutters and 3 minor landing craft.

New construction includes 2 missile armed corvettes of 850 tons, and 6 improved guided-missile vessels of 500 tons displacement, all being built in Israel.

The former Nautical School in Haifa has been reorganized as a Naval Officers' School in Acre. Naval personnel in 1981 totalled 800 officers and 5,800 men, of whom 3,500 are conscripts, including a Naval Commando. There are also 5,000 naval reservists.

Air Force. The Air Force has a personnel strength of about 28,000, with more than 570 first-line aircraft, all jets, of Israeli, US and French manufacture. They include a few Mirage III and similar, locally-built Nesher supersonic multi-mission fighters, 200 Israeli-built Kfirs based on the Mirage airframe, 24 F-15 Eagle fighters, about 160 F-4E Phantom fighter-bombers, 12 RF-4E reconnaissance fighters and about 180 A-4E/H/N Skyhawk light attack aircraft, supported by 4 E-2C Hawkeye airborne early warning and control aircraft. An initial batch of 35 (of a total of 75) F-16A/Bs was entering service in 1980. There are transport squadrons of turboprop C-130/KC-130 Hercules, C-47, Arava, and Boeing 707 aircraft, helicopter squadrons of CH-53, Super Frelon, HueyCobra, Hughes 500M-D Defender, JetRanger, Agusta-Bell 205 and 212 aircraft, and training units with locally-built Magister jet trainers, which can be used also in a light ground attack role. Missiles in service include surface-to-air Hawks and surface-to-surface Lances.

INTERNATIONAL RELATIONS
Membership. Israel is a member of UN.

ECONOMY
Budget. The budget year runs from 1 April to 31 March (in I£1m.):

	1977–78	1978–79
Revenue	137,548·7	202,068
Revenue for development budget	27,400·0	46,700
Business enterprises	13,588·7	20,068
Expenditure	137,548·7	202,068

New economic measures were introduced in Sept. 1975; purchase tax was increased by 10% on luxury goods, and 5% on many basic consumer items. On 5 Jan. 1976, the Israeli pound was devalued from I£7.10 to the US$ to I£7.24.

In 1978–79 the main items of expenditure (in I£1m.) were: Defence, 55,300; education and culture, 11,535; health, 3,470; social welfare, 2,935.

Income tax is levied progressively up to a maximum of 71·9%. A Defence Levy of 10% on income tax paid was introduced during the 6-day war.

Currency. The unit of currency is the *shekel* equal to 10 Israeli £s. The new currency was announced in Feb. 1980. Currency in circulation on 31 Dec. 1978 was I£6,860m. (bank-notes and coins). In March 1981, £1 = 19·16 *shekel*; US$ = 8·57 *shekel*.

Banking. The Bank of Israel was established by law in 1954 as Israel's central bank. Its Governor is appointed by the President on the recommendation of the Cabinet for a 5-year term. He acts as economic adviser to the Government and has ministerial status. The assets of the Bank of Israel on 31 Dec. 1974 totalled I£20,551m., of which I£7,762m. was in foreign currencies and I£235m. in gold.

There are 21 commercial banks headed by Bank Leumi Le Israel, Bank Hapoalim and Israel Discount Bank.

Weights and Measures. The metric system is in general use. The (metrical) *dunam* = 1,000 sq. metres (about 0·25 acre).

Jewish Year. The Jewish year 5740 corresponds to 22 Sept. 1979–12 Sept. 1980; 5741 to 12 Sept. 1980–29 Sept. 1981; 5742 to 30 Sept. 1981–18 Sept. 1982.

ENERGY AND NATURAL RESOURCES

Electricity. Electric-power consumption amounted during 1974–75 to 7,915m. kwh.

Oil and Gas. Oil was first discovered in Sept. 1955 at Heletz in the Negev. Crude oil production in 1974 was 45m. litres and natural gas 66m. metres.

Minerals. The most valuable natural resources of the country are the potash, bromine and other salt deposits of the Dead Sea, which are exploited by the Dead Sea Works, Ltd. Geological research and exploration of the natural resources in the Negev are undertaken by the Israel Mining Corporation. Copper is being worked at Timna near Eilat; production in 1974 was 9,500 tons. Potash production in 1974 was 950,000 tons.

A plant for the production of 46,000 tons of magnesium and 80,000 tons of hydrochloric acid per annum is being erected in the Arad area.

Agriculture. In the coastal plain (Sharon, Emek Hefer and the Shephelah) mixed farming, poultry raising, citriculture and vineyards are the main agricultural activities. The Emek (the Valley of Jezreel) is the main agricultural centre of Israel. Mixed farming is to be found throughout the valleys; the sub-tropical Beisan and Jordan plainlands are also centres of banana plantations and fish breeding. In Galilee mixed farming, olive and tobacco plantations prevail. The Hills of Ephraim are a vineyard centre; many parts of the hill country are under afforestation. In the northern Negev farming has been aided by the Yarkon–Negev water pipeline. This has become part of the overall project of the 'National Water Carrier', which is to take water from the Sea of Galilee (Lake Kinnereth) to the south. The plan includes a number of regional projects such as the Lake Kinnereth–Negev pipeline which came into operation in 1964; it has an annual capacity of 320m. cu. metres.

A land-utilization survey has graded the country as follows: 3,392,000 dunams under dry farming and 3,938,000 dunams under irrigation suitable for all types of cultivation, 697,000 dunams under dry farming and 1,339,000 dunams under irrigation suitable for plantations, 8·49m. dunams suitable for pasture, 882,000 dunams suitable for afforestation, 470,000 dunams unfit for any type of cultivation.

The area under cultivation (in 1,000 dunams) in 1976–77 was 4,300, of which 1,920 were under irrigation. Of the total cultivated area 2,662 dunams were under field crops, 367 under vegetables, potatoes, pumpkins and melons, 885 under citrus and orchards, 49 under fish ponds and 176 under miscellaneous crops, including auxiliary farms, nurseries, flowers, etc.

Industrial crops, such as cotton and sugar-beet, have successfully been introduced. In 1976–77 the area under cotton totalled 490,400 dunams and under sugar-beet 54,000.

Livestock (1979) included 280,000 cattle, 330,000 sheep and goats, 26·2m. chickens.

Characteristic types of rural settlement are, among others, the following: (1) The *Kibbutz* and *Kvutza* (communal collective settlement), where all property and earnings are collectively owned and work is collectively organized. (2) The *Moshav Ovdim* (workers' co-operative smallholders' settlement) which is founded on the principles of mutual aid and equality of opportunity between the members, all farms being equal in size; hired labour is prohibited. (3) The *Moshav Shitufi* (co-operative settlement), which is based on collective ownership and economy as in the *Kibbutz*, but with each family having its own house and being responsible for its own domestic services. (4) The *Moshav* (smallholders' settlement), which resembles the *moshav ovdim* but lacks the latter's rigid ideological basis; hired labour, for instance, is permitted. (5) The *Moshava* (village), in which land and property are privately owned and every resident is responsible for his own well-being. In 1979, of the 808 rural settlements in Israel, 240 were kibbutzim (population, 101,600), 350 were moshavim (132,800), 27 moshavim shitufiim (6,800), 89 Arab villages (163,600, not including 53,000 Bedouin); the rest were temporary settlements and educational institutions.

INDUSTRY AND TRADE

Industry. A wide range of products is manufactured, processed or finished in the country, including chemicals, metal products, textiles, tyres, diamonds, paper, plastics, leather goods, glass and ceramics, building materials, precision instruments, tobacco, foodstuffs, electric goods, including refrigerators and radios.

Labour. The General Federation of Labour (Histadrut) founded in 1920, had, in 1973, 1,259,200 members (including 89,000 Arab and Druse members); including workers' families, this membership represents 56·1% of the population covering 85% of all wage-earners. Several trades unions of lesser importance also exist.

Histadrut participates in over 70% of Israeli agriculture and 23% of industrial production; it runs the Kuput Holim (workers' health service) and has large interests in banking, insurance, retail business, construction and building.

Commerce. External trade, in US$1,000, for calendar years:

	1972	1973	1974	1975	1976	1977	1978
Imports	1,961,362	2,968,579	4,197,856	4,151,119	4,140,400	4,815,200	5,542,000
Exports	1,146,972	1,458,990	1,824,859	1,941,202	2,414,500	3,083,500	3,680,000

In 1977, of the imports 55·4% came from Europe (EEC, EFTA and COMECON countries), 21·6% from the US and Canada, 5·8% from Asia and Africa; of the exports 46·7% went to European countries, 18·3% to Africa and Asia, 9·6% to US and Canada.

The main exportable commodities are citrus fruit and by-products, fruit-juices, wines and liquor, sweets, polished diamonds, chemicals, motor cars, tyres, textiles, electrical goods, flowers. The main exports were, in 1977 (US$1m.): Diamonds, 1,099; chemical and oil products, 270; food, beverages and tobacco, 245; citrus fruit, 191.

Total trade between Israel and UK (British Department of Trade returns, in £1,000 sterling):

	1976	1977	1978	1979	1980
Imports to UK	127,796	159,025	189,200	227,600	236,599
Exports and re-exports from UK	249,398	273,925	243,570	270,733	231,658

Tourism. In 1979 there were 1,138,000 tourists spending US$765m.

COMMUNICATIONS

Roads. There were 10,657 km of paved roads in 1976. Registered motor vehicles in 1974 totalled 408,280, including 5,615 buses, 94,758 trucks and 267,425 private cars.

Railways. Internal communications (1980) are provided by 552 km of standard gauge line. Surveys were being made (1977) of 215 km of new line linking Eilat on the Gulf of Aqaba with Sedom and the existing rail network by means of the 34 km line opened between Oron and Nahal Zin in Nov. 1977. In 1979–80, 2·8m. passengers and 5m. tonnes of freight were carried by rail.

Aviation. Air communications are centred in the airport of Lod, near Tel-Aviv. In 1974, 9,182 planes landed at Israeli airports on international flights; 870,600 passengers arrived, 876,000 departed; 28,191 tonnes of freight were loaded and 20,860 tonnes unloaded. The Israeli airline El Al maintains regular flights to London, Paris, Rome, Amsterdam, Brussels, Athens, Vienna, New York, Zürich, Munich, Nicosia, Istanbul, Tehrán, Johannesburg, Mexico, Nairobi, Frankfurt and Copenhagen. In 1977–78 El Al carried 1,089,910 passengers.

Shipping. Israel has 3 commercial ports, Haifa, Ashdod and Eilat. The deep-water port at Ashdod came into use at the end of 1965, when the ports of Tel-Aviv and Jaffa were closed for freight services. An Israel Ports Authority began to operate in 1962. In 1974, 2,991 ships anchored in Israeli ports; 9·97m. tons of freight (not including oil in bulk tankers) were handled. The Israeli merchant fleet consisted in 1974 of 106 vessels, totalling 2,304,253 GRT.

Post and Broadcasting. The Ministry of Posts controls the postal, telegraph and telephone service. In 1977 there were 599 post offices and postal agencies, 43 mobile post offices and (1978) 993,000 telephones.

The broadcasting station in Jerusalem, *Kol Israel*, is controlled by the Broadcasting Authority, established in 1965. Wireless licences in 1974 numbered approximately 460,000 and television licences 385,000.

Cinemas (1977). There were 228 cinemas with a seating capacity of approximately 157,700.

Newspapers (1974). There were 27 daily newspapers, including 13 in Hebrew, 4 in Arabic, 1 each in German, English, French, Hungarian, Yiddish, Russian, Romanian, Bulgarian, Spanish and Polish, with a total circulation of over 500,000.

JUSTICE, RELIGION, EDUCATION AND WELFARE

Justice. *Law.* Under the Law and Administration Ordinance, 5708/1948, the first law passed by the Provisional Council of State, the law of Israel is the law which was obtaining in Palestine on 14 May 1948 in so far as it is not in conflict with that Ordinance or any other law passed by the Israel legislature and with such modifications as result from the establishment of the State and its authorities.

Capital punishment was abolished in 1954, except for support given to the Nazis and for high treason.

The law of Palestine was derived from three main sources, namely, Ottoman law, English law (Common Law and Equity) and the law enacted by the Palestine legislature, which to a great extent was modelled on English law. The Ottoman law in its turn was derived from three main sources, namely, Moslem law which had survived in the Ottoman Empire, French law adapted by the Ottomans and the personal law of the non-Moslem communities.

Civil Courts. Municipal courts, established in certain municipal areas, have criminal jurisdiction over offences against municipal regulations and bye-laws and certain specified offences committed within a municipal area.

Magistrates courts, established in each district and sub-district, have limited jurisdiction in both civil and criminal matters.

District courts, sitting at Jerusalem, Tel-Aviv and Haifa, have jurisdiction, as courts of first instance, in all civil matters not within the jurisdiction of magistrates courts, and in all criminal matters, and as appellate courts from magistrates courts and municipal courts.

The Supreme Court has jurisdiction as a court of first instance (sitting as a High Court of Justice dealing mainly with administrative matters) and as an appellate court from the district courts (sitting as a Court of Civil or of Criminal Appeal).

In addition, there are various tribunals for special classes of cases, such as the Rents Tribunals and the Tribunals for the Prevention of Profiteering and Speculation. Settlement Officers deal with disputes with regard to the ownership or possession of land in settlement areas constituted under the Land (Settlement of Title) Ordinance.

Religious Courts. The rabbinical courts of the Jewish community have exclusive jurisdiction in matters of marriage and divorce, alimony and confirmation of wills of members of their community other than foreigners, concurrent jurisdiction with the civil courts in such matters of members of their community who are foreigners if they consent to the jurisdiction, and concurrent jurisdiction with the civil courts in all other matters of personal status of all members of their community, whether foreigners or not, with the consent of all parties to the action, save that such courts may not grant a decree of dissolution of marriage to a foreign subject.

The courts of the several recognized Christian communities have a similar jurisdiction over members of their respective communities.

The Moslem religious courts have exclusive jurisdiction in all matters of personal status over Moslems who are not foreigners, and over Moslems who are foreigners, if under the law of their nationality they are subject in such matters to the jurisdiction of Moslem religious courts.

Where any action of personal status involves persons of different religious communities, the President of the Supreme Court will decide which court shall have jurisdiction, and whenever a question arises as to whether or not a case is one of personal status within the exclusive jurisdiction of a religious court, the matter must be referred to a special tribunal composed of 2 judges of the Supreme Court and the president of the highest court of the religious community concerned in Israel.

Religion. Religious affairs are under the supervision of a special Ministry, with departments for the Christian and Moslem communities. The religious affairs of each community remain under the full control of the ecclesiastical authorities concerned: in the case of the Jews, the Sephardi and Ashkenazi Chief Rabbis, in the case of the Christians, the heads of the various communities, and in the case of the Moslems, the Qadis. The Druze were officially recognized in 1957 as an autonomous religious community.

In 1980 there were: Moslems, 479,000; Christians, 90,000; Druze and others, 50,000.

The Jewish Sabbath and Holy Days are observed as days of rest in the public services. Full provision is, however, made for the free exercise of other faiths, and for the observance by their adherents of their respective days of rest and Holy Days.

Education. The school system is under the direction of the Ministry of Education and Culture, and comprises kindergarten, primary, secondary and technical schools.

Laws passed by the Knesset in 1949 and 1978 provide for free and compulsory education from 5 to 16 years of age. There is free education until 18 years of age.

The State Education Law of 12 Aug. 1953 established a unified state-controlled elementary school system with a provision for special religious schools. The standard curriculum for all elementary schools is issued by the Ministry with a possibility of adding supplementary subjects comprising not more than 25% of the total syllabus. Many schools in towns are private, a number are maintained by municipalities and some are administered by teachers' co-operatives or trustees.

Statistics relating to schools under government supervision, 1974–75:

Type of School	Schools	Teachers	Pupils
Hebrew Education—Total	6,265	52,824	868,037
Kindergartens	4,279	4,637	186,625
Primary schools	1,213	24,670	374,443
Schools for handicapped children	164	1,780	11,594
Schools for working youth	80	235	2,992
Schools of intermediate division	176	6,512	50,882
Secondary schools	206 ⎤		54,878
Vocational schools	306 ⎬	15,384	64,505
Agricultural schools	27 ⎦		5,877
Teachers' training colleges	49	2,214	10,356
Arab Education—Total	355	6,371	146,377
Kindergartens	254	507	15,934
Primary schools	287	4,525	105,373
Schools for handicapped children	4	21	117
Schools for working youth	5	18	182
Schools of intermediate division	33	660	8,929
Secondary schools	77 ⎤		12,860
Vocational schools	24 ⎬	1,145	1,572
Agricultural schools	2 ⎦		687
Teachers' training colleges	2	88	723

There are also a number of private schools maintained by religious foundations—Jewish, Christian and Moslem—and also by private societies.

The Hebrew University of Jerusalem, founded in 1925, comprises faculties of the humanities, social sciences, law, science, medicine and agriculture. In 1978–79 it had a teaching staff of 2,184 and 14,000 students.

The Technion in Haifa had, in 1978–79, 21 faculties and departments with 1,500 teachers and 7,800 students. The Weizmann Institute of Science in Rehovoth is engaged in research in chemistry, mathematics, physics and biology; founded in 1949, it had a staff of 400 and 486 students in 1978–79.

In 1978–79 the Tel Aviv University had 16 faculties, some 2,388 teachers and 19,000 students. The religious Bar-Ilan University at Ramat Gan, opened in 1965 had, in 1978–79, 5 faculties (Jewish studies, humanities, natural sciences, social sciences, philology), 900 teachers and 7.600 students. The Haifa University had, in 1978–79, 29 faculties with 568 teachers and 7,522 students. The Ben Gurion University had, in 1978–79, 28 departments with 628 teachers and 4,300 students.

Social Welfare. In 1977 Israel had 126 hospitals with 24,883 beds. The 'Malben' organization cares for the aged. The Women's International Zionist Organization has a number of children's homes, crèches and kindergartens as well as vocational schools and training institutions for nurses. In addition, there are several other voluntary bodies providing specific services to the community.

The National Insurance Law, which took effect in April 1954, provides for old-age pensions, survivors' insurance, work-injury insurance, maternity insurance, family allowances and unemployment benefits.

DIPLOMATIC REPRESENTATIVES

OF ISRAEL IN GREAT BRITAIN (2 Palace Green, London, W8 4QB)
Ambassador: Shlomo Argov.

OF GREAT BRITAIN IN ISRAEL (192 Rehov Hayarkon, Tel Aviv 63405)
Ambassador: John A. Robinson, CMG.

OF ISRAEL IN THE USA (1621–22nd St., NW, Washington, D.C., 20008)
Ambassador: Ephraim Evron.

OF THE USA IN ISRAEL (71 Hayarkon St., Tel Aviv)
Ambassador: Samuel W. Lewis.

OF ISRAEL TO THE UNITED NATIONS
Ambassador: Yehuda Blum.

Books of Reference

Statistical Information: There is a Central Bureau of Statistics and Economic Research at the Prime Minister's Office, Jerusalem. It publishes monthly bulletins of economic statistics, social statistics, foreign trade statistics and an English summary.

Government Yearbook. Government Printer, Jerusalem. 1951 ff. (latest issue, 1971/72)
Facts about Israel. Government Printer, Jerusalem, 1979
Statistical Abstract of Israel. Government Printer, Jerusalem (from 1949/50)
Israel Yearbook. Tel-Aviv, 1948–49 ff.
Statistical Bulletin of Israel. 1949 ff.
Reshumoth (Official Gazette)
Middle East Record, ed. Y. Oron. London, 1960 ff.
Laws of the State of Israel. Authorized translation. Government Printer, Jerusalem, 1958 ff.
Alkalay, R., *The Complete English–Hebrew Dictionary.* 4 vols. Tel-Aviv, 1959–61
Atlas of Israel. Amsterdam, Jerusalem and London, 1970
Ben-Gurion, D., *Ben-Gurion Looks Back.* London, 1965.—*The Jews in Their Land.* London, 1966.—*Israel: A Personal History.* New York, 1971
Churchill, R. S. and W. S., *The Six-Day War.* London, 1967
Crossman, R., *Nation Reborn.* London, 1960
Eisenstadt, S. N., *Israel Society.* London, 1969
Goldman, N., *The Jewish Paradox.* New York, 1978
Horowitz, D., *The Economics of Israel.* New York and Oxford, 1967.—*The Enigma of Economic Growth: A Case Study of Israel.* New York, 1972
Hyamson, A. M., *Palestine under Mandate, 1920–48.* London, 1951
Jiryis, S., *The Arabs in Israel.* New York, 1976
Karmon, Y., *Israel: A Regional Geography.* London, 1971
Laquer, W. (ed.), *The Israel–Arab Reader.* London 1970.—*A History of Zionism.* New York, 1972
Likhovski, E. S., *Israel's Parliament: The Law of the Knesset.* Oxford, 1971
Lucas, N., *A Modern History of Israel.* London and New York, 1975
Luttwak, E., and Horowitz, D., *The Israeli Army.* London, 1975
Meir, G., *My Life.* New York, 1975
Peretz, D., *The Government and Politics of Israel.* Folkestone, 1979
Pryce-Jones, D., *The Face of Defeat: Palestinian Refugees and Guerrillas.* New York, 1973
Safran, N., *Israel: The Embattled Ally.* Harvard Univ. Press, 1978
Segal, R., *Whose Jerusalem? The Conflicts of Israel.* London, 1973
Who's Who in Israel. Tel-Aviv, 1978

National Library: The Jewish National and University Library, Jerusalem.

ITALY

Capital: Rome
Population: 57m. (1980)
GNP per capita: US$3,840 (1978)

Repubblica Italiana

HISTORY. On 10 June 1946 Italy became a republic on the announcement by the Court of Cassation that a majority of the voters at the referendum held on 2 June had voted for a republic. The final figures, announced on 18 June, showed: For a republic, 12,718,641 (54·3% of the valid votes cast, which numbered 23,437,143); for the retention of the monarchy, 10,718,502 (45·7%); invalid and contested, 1,509,735. Total 24,946,878, or 89·1% of the registered electors, who numbered 28,005,449. For the results of the polling in the 13 leading cities, *see* THE STATESMAN'S YEAR-BOOK, 1951, p. 1175. Voting was compulsory, open to both men and women 21 years of age or older, including members of the Civil Service and the Armed Forces; former active Fascists and a few other categories were excluded.

On 18 June the then Provisional Government without specifically proclaiming the republic, issued an 'Order of the Day' decreeing that all court verdicts should in future be handed down 'in the name of the Italian people', that the *Gazzetta Ufficiale del Regno d'Italia* should be re-named *Gazzetta Ufficiale della Repubblica Italiana*, that all references to the monarchy should be deleted from legal and government statements and that the shield of the House of Savoy should be removed from the Italian flag.

Thus ended the reign of the House of Savoy, whose kings had ruled over Piedmont for 9 centuries and as Kings of Italy since 18 Feb. 1861. (For fuller account of the House of Savoy, *see* THE STATESMAN'S YEAR-BOOK, 1946, p. 1021.) The Crown Prince Umberto, son of King Victor Emmanuel III, became Lieut.-Gen. (*i.e.*, Regent) of the kingdom on 5 June 1944. Following the abdication and retirement to Egypt of his father on 9 May 1946, Umberto was declared King Umberto II; his reign lasted to 13 June, when he left the country. King Victor Emmanuel III died in Alexandria on 28 Dec. 1947.

AREA AND POPULATION. The population (present in actual boundaries) at successive censuses were as follows:

31 Dec. 1871	27,577,640	21 April 1931	40,582,043
31 Dec. 1881	29,277,927	21 April 1936	42,302,680
10 Feb. 1901	33,370,138	4 Nov. 1951	47,158,738
10 June 1911	35,694,582	15 Oct. 1961	49,903,878
1 Dec. 1921	37,403,956	24 Oct. 1971	53,744,737

The following table gives area and population of the Regions (census of 24 Oct. 1971 and estimated 1980):

Regions	Area in sq. km (1971)	Resident pop. census, 1971	Resident pop. estimate, 1980	Density per sq. km (1971)
Piemonte	25,399	4,432,313	4,531,141	175
Valle d'Aosta	3,262	109,150	114,591	33
Lombardia	23,834	8,543,387	8,941,704	358
Trentino-Alto Adige	13,613	841,886	876,249	62
Bolzano-Bozen	*7,400*	*414,041*	*432,073*	*56*
Trento	*6,213*	*427,845*	*444,176*	*69*
Veneto	18,368	4,123,411	4,351,313	224
Friuli-Venezia Giulia	7,846	1,213,532	1,245,130	155
Liguria	5,413	1,853,578	1,844,779	342
Emilia Romagna	22,123	3,846,755	3,964,538	174
Toscana	22,992	3,473,097	3,600,233	151
Umbria	8,456	775,783	808,351	92
Marche	9,692	1,359,907	1,415,563	140
Lazio	17,203	4,689,482	5,059,174	273

Regions	Area in sq. km (1971)	Resident pop. census, 1971	Resident pop. estimate, 1980	Density per sq. km (1971)
Abruzzi	10,794	1,166,694	1,239,738	108
Molise	4,438	319,807	334,091	72
Campania	13,595	5,059,348	5,457,838	372
Puglia	19,347	3,582,787	3,917,029	185
Basilicata	9,992	603,064	618,703	60
Calabria	15,080	1,988,051	2,078,264	132
Sicilia	25,708	4,680,715	4,999,032	182
Sardegna	24,090	1,473,800	1,601,586	61
Total	301,245	54,136,547	56,999,047	180

Vital statistics for calendar years:

| | | | Living births | | | Deaths |
| | | | Illegiti- | | | excl. of |
	Marriages	Legitimate	mate	Total	Still-born	still-born
1973	418,334	852,427	22,119	874,456	11,668	547,487
1974	403,215	846,558	22,324	868,882	10,691	532,043
1975	373,784	806,391	21,461	827,852	9,271	554,346
1976	354,202	757,187	24,451	781,638	8,345	550,565
1977	347,928	715,414	25,689	741,103	7,219	545,694
1978	331,416	681,350	27,693	709,043	6,564	540,671
1979 [1]	325,598	644,566	25,512	670,078	5,606	534,563

[1] Provisional.

Emigrants to non-European countries, by sea and air: 1973, 24,832; 1974, 24,960; 1975, 20,641; 1976, 24,216; 1977, 22,508. Since 1960 nearly nine-tenths of these emigrants have gone to Canada, USA and Australia.

Communes of more than 100,000 inhabitants, with population resident on 31 Dec. 1979:

Roma (Rome)	2,911,671	Cagliari	241,472	Monza	123,834
Milano (Milan)	1,677,109	Brescia	212,265	Sassari	119,597
Napoli (Naples)	1,223,288	Reggio di C.	181,293	La Spezia	117,761
Torino (Turin)	1,160,686	Modena	180,428	Vicenza	117,571
Genova (Genoa)	782,476	Parma	176,945	Siracusa (Syracuse)	116,755
Palermo	693,949	Livorno (Leghorn)	176,757	Terni	113,241
Bologna	471,554	Salerno	161,997	Forli	110,523
Firenze (Florence)	462,690	Prato	158,229	Piacenza	108,888
Catania	398,426	Foggia	157,727	Ancona	108,371
Bari	387,266	Ferrara	152,752	Bolzano	106,199
Venezia (Venice)	355,865	Perugia	139,871	Pisa	103,772
Messina	271,660	Ravenna	139,392	Udine	102,973
Verona	269,763	Pescara	137,059	Cosenza	102,338
Trieste	260,291	Reggio nell'E.	130,005	Novara	101,947
Taranto	247,681	Rimini	127,714	Alessandria	101,684
Padova (Padua)	242,216	Bergamo	125,544		

CONSTITUTION AND GOVERNMENT. The new Constitution was passed by the constituent assembly by 453 votes to 62 on 22 Dec. 1947; it came into force on 1 Jan. 1948. The Constitution consists of 139 articles and 18 transitional clauses. Its main dispositions are as follows:

Italy is described as 'a democratic republic founded on work'. Parliament consists of the Chamber of Deputies and the Senate. The Chamber is elected for 5 years by universal and direct suffrage and it consists of 630 deputies. The Senate is elected for 5 years on a regional basis; each Region having at least 6 senators, consisting of 315 elected senators; the Valle d'Aosta is represented by 1 senator only. The President of the Republic can nominate 5 senators for life from eminent men in the social, scientific, artistic and literary spheres. On the expiry of his term of office, the President of the Republic becomes a senator by right and for life, unless he declines.

The President of the Republic is elected in a joint session of Chamber and Senate, to which are added 3 delegates from each Regional Council (1 from the Valle d'Aosta). A two-thirds majority is required for the election, but after a third indecisive scrutiny the absolute majority of votes is sufficient. The President must be 50 years or over; his term lasts for 7 years. The President of the Senate acts as his deputy.

The President can dissolve the chambers of parliament, except during the last 6 months of his term of office.

The Cabinet can be forced to resign only on a motivated motion of censure; the defeat of a government bill does not involve the resignation of the Government.

A Constitutional Court, consisting of 15 judges who are appointed, 5 each, by the President of the Republic, Parliament (in joint session) and the highest law and administrative courts, has rights similar to those of the Supreme Court of the USA. It can decide on the constitutionality of laws and decrees, define the powers of the State and Regions, judge conflicts between the State and Regions and between the Regions, and try the President of the Republic and the Ministers. The court was set up in Dec. 1955.

The reorganization of the Fascist Party is forbidden. Direct male descendants of King Victor Emmanuel are excluded from all public offices, have no right to vote or to be elected, and are banned from Italian territory; their estates are forfeit to the State. Titles of nobility are no longer recognized, but those existing before 28 Oct. 1922 are retained as part of the name.

National flag: Three vertical strips of green, white, red.
National anthem: Fratelli d'Italia (words by G. Mameli; tune by M. Novaro, 1847).

The peace treaty was signed in Paris on 10 Feb. 1947, and ratified on 15 Sept. 1947. Italy ceded to France 4 frontier districts on the Little St Bernard Pass, the Mont-Cenis Plateau, the Mont-Thabor and Chaberton areas, and the upper valleys of the Tinée, Vésubie and Roya (*see* map in THE STATESMAN'S YEAR-BOOK, 1948); to Yugoslavia, nearly the whole of the provinces of Venezia Giulia, the commune of Zara and the island of Pelagosa; to Greece, the Dodecanese; to Albania, the island of Saseno; to China the Italian concession at Tientsin. Italy also gave up her former colonies.

Under the peace treaty Italy was to pay reparations to the following states: Greece, US$105m.; Yugoslavia, US$125m.; USSR, US$100m.; Ethiopia, US$25m.; Albania, US$5m. By 30 Nov. 1967 the whole debt had been paid.

Head of State: On 8 July 1978 Chamber and Senate in joint session elected by an absolute majority (832 votes out of 1,008 votes cast) Alessandro Pertini (Socialist; born 1896), President of the Republic.

Former Presidents of the Republic: Luigi Einaudi (1948–55); Giovanni Gronchi (1955–62); Antonio Segni (1962–64); Giuseppe Saragat (1964–71); Giovanni Leone (1971–78).

General elections for the Senate and Chamber of Deputies took place on 3–4 June 1979.
Senate. Christian Democrats, 138; Communists, 109; Socialists, 32; Italian Social Movement, 13; Social Democrats, 9; Republicans, 6; other groups, 8. Total: 315.
Chamber. Christian Democrats, 261; Communists, 201; Socialists, 62; Italian Social Movement, 31; Republicans, 15; Social Democrats, 21; Radical Party, 18; other groups, 21. Total: 630.

The coalition government was composed as follows in March 1981.

Prime Minister: Arnaldo Forlani (CD).
Foreign Affairs: Emilio Colombo (CD).
Interior Affairs: Virginio Rognoni (CD).
Justice: Adolfo Sarti (CD).
Defence: Lelio Lagorio (Soc.).
Finance: Massimo Reviglio (Soc.).
Treasury: Beniamino Andreatta (CD).
Industry: Filippo Maria Pandolfi (CD).
Agriculture and Forestry: Giuseppe Bartolomei (CD).
Health: Aldo Aniasi (Soc.).
European Affairs: Vincenzo Scotti (CD).
Budget: Giorgio La Malfa (Rep.).

Civil Service: Clelio Darida (CD).
Regional Affairs: Roberto Mazzotta (CD).
Southern Region: Nicola Capria (Soc.).
Education: Guido Bodrato (CD).
Scientific Research: Pier Luigi Romita (Soc. D.).
Public Works: Franco Nicolazzi (Soc. D.).
Labour: Franco Foschi (CD).
Trade: Enrico Manca (Soc.).
Transport: Salvatore Formica (Soc.).
Post and Telecommunications: Michele Digiesi (Soc. D.).
Merchant Marine: Francesco Compagna (Rep.).
State Participation: Gianni De Michelis (Soc.).
Tourism: Nicola Signorello (CD).
Culture: Oddo Biasini (Rep.).
Parliamentary Relations: Antonio Gava (CD).

Adams, J. C., and Barile, P., *The Government of Republican Italy.* Boston, Mass., 1961
Allum, P. A., *Italy: Republic Without Government.* New York, 1974
Cross, E. (ed.), *La Constitution Italienne de 1948.* Paris, 1950
Ruini, M., and others, *La Nuova Costituzione Italiana.* Rome, 1947
Vedovato, G., *Il Trattato di Pace con l'Italia.* Rome, 1947

Regional Administration. Italy is administratively divided into regions (*regioni*), provinces (*province*) and municipalities (*comuni*).

Art. 116 of the 1948 constitution provided for the establishment of 5 autonomous regions with special statute (*regioni autonome con statuto speciale*) and 15 autonomous regions with ordinary statute (*regioni autonome con statuto normale*). The regions have their own parliaments (*consiglio regionale*) and governments (*giunta regionale e presidente*) with certain legislative and administrative functions adapted to the circumstances of each region.

A government commissioner co-ordinates regional and national activities. The results of the last regional elections were as follows:

Regions	Election date	Christian Democrats	Communists	Socialists	Social Movement	Social Democrats	Republicans	Liberals	Others	Total
Piemonte	8 June 1980	20	20	9	2	3	2	3	1	60
Valle d'Aosta[1]	25 June 1978	7	7	1	—	1	1	—	18[2]	35
Lombardia	8 June 1980	34	23	11	3	3	2	2	2	80
Trentino-Alto Adige[1]	19 Nov. 1978	22	7	4	2	2	1	1	31[3]	70
Veneto	8 June 1980	32	13	7	2	3	1	1	1	60
Friuli-Venezia Giulia[1]	25 June 1978	26	14	5	2	3	1	1	9[4]	61
Liguria	8 June 1980	13	15	5	2	2	1	2	—	40
Emilia-Romagna	8 June 1980	13	26	4	1	2	2	1	1	50
Toscana	8 June 1980	15	25	5	1	1	1	1	1	50
Umbria	8 June 1980	9	14	4	1	1	1	—	—	30
Marche	8 June 1980	16	15	4	1	1	1	1	1	40
Lazio	8 June 1980	22	19	6	6	3	2	1	1	60
Abruzzi	8 June 1980	20	12	4	2	1	1	—	—	40
Molise	8 June 1980	17	5	3	1	2	1	1	—	30
Campania	8 June 1980	25	15	7	7	3	1	1	1	60
Puglia	8 June 1980	22	13	6	4	2	1	1	1	50
Basilicata	8 June 1980	14	8	4	2	2	—	—	—	30
Calabria	8 June 1980	18	10	7	2	2	1	—	—	40
Sicilia[1]	20 June 1976	39	24	10	9	2	4	2	—	90
Sardegna[1]	17 June 1979	32	22	9	4	4	3	1	5[5]	80

[1] Autonomous regions with special statute.
[2] Including 4 Democrates Populaires, 9 Union Valdôtaine, 1 Union Valdôtaine Progressiste.
[3] Including 21 Südtiroler Volkspartie.
[4] Including 1 Slovenian Union, 2 Movimento Friuli.
[5] Including 3 Sardinian Action Party.

DEFENCE. Most of the restrictions imposed upon Italy in Part IV of the peace treaty signed on 10 Feb. 1947 were repudiated by the signatories on 21 Dec. 1951, only the USSR objecting.

Head of the armed forces is the Defence Chief of Staff. In 1947 the ministries of war, navy and air were merged into the ministry of defence. The technical and scientific council for defence directs all research activities.

National service lasts 12 months in the Army and Air Force, and 18 months in the Navy.

Army. The Army is divided into the expeditionary force and the national defence force. It is composed of 3 mechanized divisions, 1 armoured division (with M-47, M-60 and Leopard tanks), 5 Alpini brigades, 1 airborne brigade, 6 independent brigades, 1 rocket brigade, 2 amphibious battalions and various special and support units. Total strength (1980), 253,000.

Navy. Particulars of the principal surface ships in the Italian Navy:

Completed	Name	Standard displacement Tons	Armour Belt in.	Big guns in.	Principal armament	Torpedo tubes	Shaft horsepower	Speed Knots
			Cruisers					
1969	Vittorio Veneto	7,500	—	—	8 3-in.; twin 'Terrier'; 9 helicopters	6	73,000	32
1964 1964	Andrea Doria[1] } Caio Duilio[1] }	6,000	—	—	8 3-in.; twin 'Terrier'; } 4 helicopters }	6	60,000	31

[1] Rated as guided-missile escort cruisers.

There are also 10 diesel-powered submarines, 4 guided-missile destroyers, 1 large destroyer (*ex*-light cruiser converted), 2 anti-submarine destroyers, 14 frigates, 8 corvettes, 4 ocean minesweepers, 4 minehunters, 26 coastal minesweepers, 7 inshore minesweepers, 4 hydrofoil missile boats, 4 fast torpedo-boats, 3 fast gunboats, 2 landing ships, 4 surveying vessels, 2 salvage ships, 1 transport, 1 support ship, 4 training ships, 2 replenishment oilers, 13 water carriers, 1 net-layer, 7 repair craft, 18 auxiliaries, 9 coastal transports (landing craft), 54 motor transports (minor landing craft), and 54 tugs. The guided-missile cruiser *Giuseppe Garibaldi* was deleted from the list in 1972 but a new *Giuseppe Garibaldi* of 10,000 tons standard displacement, a flat-topped ship designed as an improved helicopter cruiser but latterly regarded as a light aircraft carrier, is in the early stages of construction.

Two diesel-powered submarines, 6 frigates, 4 minehunters and 3 missile hydrofoils are under construction.

The coastline of the peninsula is divided into zones, with headquarters at Spezia, Naples, Taranto and Ancona; all are under the jurisdiction of flag officers with the status of C.-in-C. The admirals commanding on the coasts of Sardinia and Sicily do not rank as C.-in-C.

Other localities of strategic importance under naval administration are Brindisi, where there is an admiral commanding, and Genoa, Leghorn, Augusta and Venice, each of which is under a senior naval officer.

The personnel of the Navy in 1981 numbered 41,900 officers and ratings, including the naval air arm and the marine force.

Air Force. Control is exercised through 2 regional HQ near Taranto and Milan. Units assigned to NATO comprise the 1st air brigade of Nike-Hercules surface-to-air missiles, 6 fighter-bomber, 3 light attack, 6 interceptor and 2 tactical reconnaissance squadrons, with supporting transport, search and rescue, and training units. One of the fighter-bomber squadrons has F-104G Starfighters, 3 have F-104S Starfighters, and 2 have Aeritalia G91Ys. (Starfighter squadrons will re-equip with Tornadoes). The light attack squadrons operate G91Rs. F-104S Starfighters have been standardized throughout the interceptor squadrons. The reconnaissance force operates RF-104G Starfighters.

One transport squadron has turboprop C-130H Hercules aircraft; 2 others have turboprop Aeritalia G222s. There is a VIP and personnel transport squadron, equipped with DC-9, DC-6B, PD-808 and P.166M aircraft.

ECM duties are performed by specially equipped EC-47s, C-53s, PD-808s and T-33s. Two land-based anti-submarine squadrons operate Breguet Atlantics. ASW helicopters, including Italian-built SH-3D Sea Kings, operate from ships of the Italian Navy. There are also strong support and training elements.

Air Force strength in mid-1980 was about 69,000 officers and men, about 300 combat aircraft, 500 fixed-wing second-line aircraft and over 100 helicopters.

INTERNATIONAL RELATIONS

Membership. Italy is a member of UN, NATO and EEC.

ECONOMY

Budget. Total revenue and expenditure for fiscal years, in 1m. lire:

	Revenue	Expenditure		Revenue	Expenditure
1972	15,563,400	19,102,600	1976	37,882,716	50,036,796
1973	18,640,892	23,807,890	1977	43,666,361	59,548,331
1974	22,930,800	29,557,700	1978	51,696,512	78,844,114
1975	32,312,962	40,201,458	1979	62,431,446	92,127,556

In the revenue for 1979 turnover and other business taxes accounted for 16,135,852m. lire, customs duties and indirect taxes for 9,134,933m. lire.

The public debt at 31 Dec. 1979 totalled 127,271,700m. lire, including consolidated debt of 42,200m. lire and the floating debt 69,549,100m. lire.

Currency. The standard coin is the *lira*. From 30 March 1960 the gold standard was formally established as equal to 0·00142187 gramme of gold per lira.

State metal coins are of 1, 2, 5, 10, 20, 50, 100, 200, 500 and 1,000 lire. There are also in circulation State notes of 500 and bank-notes of 1,000, 2,000, 5,000, 10,000, 20,000, 50,000 and 100,000 lire; they are neither convertible into gold as foreign moneys nor exportable abroad, nor importable from abroad into Italy (except for certain specified small amounts).

Circulation of money at 30 April 1980: State coins and notes, 653,900m. lire; bank-notes, 20,744,000m. lire.

In March 1981 the rate of exchange was 1,023·5 lire per US$1 and 2,262 lire per £1 sterling.

Banking. According to the law of 6 May 1926 there is only one bank of issue, the Banca d'Italia. Its gold reserve amounted to 20,082,900m. lire in April 1980; the foreign credit reserves of the Exchange Bureau (*Ufficio Italiano Cambi*) amounted to 12,113,900m. lire at the same date.

Since 1936, all credit institutions have been under the control of a State organ, named 'Inspectorate of Credit'; the Bank of Italy has been converted into a 'public institution', whose capital is held exclusively by corporate bodies of a public nature. Other credit institutions, totalling 1,071, are classified as: (1) 6 chartered banks (Banco di Napoli, Banco di Sicilia, Banca Nazionale del Lavoro, Monte dei Paschi di Siena, Istituto di S. Paolo di Torino, Banca di Sardegna); (2) 3 banks of national interest (Banca Commerciale Italiana in Milan, Credito Italiano in Genoa and Banco di Roma); (3) banks and credit concerns in general, including 152 joint-stock banks and 167 co-operative banks; (4) 89 savings banks and Monti di pegno (institutions granting loans against personal chattels as security); (5) 649 *Casse rurali e agrarie* (agricultural banks, established as co-operative institutions with unlimited liability of associates); (6) 5 Istituti di Categoria.

At 31 Dec. 1979 there were 310 credit institutes handling 96% of all deposits and current accounts, with capital and reserves of 9,857,385m. lire.

On 30 June 1980 the post office savings banks had deposits and current accounts of 36,362,000m. lire; credit institutions, 255,159,500m. lire.

Insurance. By a decree of 29 April 1923 life-assurance business is carried on only by the National Insurance Institute and by other institutions, national and foreign, authorized by the Government. At 31 Dec. 1976 the insurances vested in the *Istituto*

Nazionale delle Assicurazioni amounted to 4,288,000m. lire, including the decuple of life annuities.

Weights and Measures. The metric system is in general use.

ENERGY AND NATURAL RESOURCES

Electricity. Italy has greatly developed her water-power resources. In 1979 the total power generated was 181,264m. kwh., of which 48,212m. kwh. were generated by hydro-electric plants.

Oil. The Sicilian district of Ragusa, Gela and Fontanarossa is rapidly developing into one of the largest European oilfields. Production in 1979 amounted to 1,661,763 tonnes, of which 740,982 came from Sicily.

Minerals. The Italian mining industry is most developed in Sicily (Caltanissetta), in Tuscany (Arezzo, Florence and Grosseto), in Sardinia (Cagliari, Sassari and Iglesias), in Lombardy (particularly near Bergamo and Brescia) and in Piedmont.

Italy's fuel and mineral resources are wholly inadequate. Only sulphur and mercury outputs yield a substantial surplus for exports. In 1979 outputs, in tonnes, of raw steel was 24,249,836; rolled iron, 20,318,202; cast-iron ingots, 11,327,357; coal and similar fuels, 2,122,926.

Production of metals and minerals (in tonnes) was as follows:

	1974	1975	1976	1977	1978	1979
Iron pyrites	1,168,388	808,731	854,477	863,785	786,666	804,469
Iron ore	659,417	631,542	514,172	478,198	352,611	218,762
Manganese	14,008	...	4,461	9,314	9,741	9,782
Zinc	262,024	234,052	274,725	169,717	120,492	100,825
Crude sulphur	473,301	499,246	349,132	627,690	523,355	108,309
Bauxite	31,640	32,265	24,200	34,525	24,410	26,095
Mercury	896	1,094	757	14	5	—
Lead	43,460	33,197	42,601	33,152	31,110	27,237
Aluminium	212,225	190,070	205,723	255,397	270,770	266,814

Agriculture. The area of Italy in 1979 comprised 301,262 sq. km, of which 269,957 sq. km was agricultural and forest land and 31,305 sq. km was unproductive; the former was mainly distributed as follows (in 1,000 hectares): Forage and pasture, 9,228; woods, 6,355; cereals, 5,115; vines, 1,307; olive trees, 1,052; olive trees grown among other crops, 1,094; garden produce, 470; vines grown among other crops, 474; leguminous plants, 351.

At the second general census of agriculture (25 Oct. 1970) agricultural holdings numbered 3,620,799 and covered 25,091,267 hectares. 3,142,608 owners (86·8%) farmed directly 14,706,204 hectares (58·6%); 278,157 owners (7·7%) worked with hired labour on 8,523,107 hectares (34%); 130,648 share-croppers (3·6%) tilled 1,271,485 hectares (5·1%); the remaining 69,408 holdings (1·9%) of 590,471 hectares (2·3%) were operated in other ways.

According to the labour force survey in July 1978 persons engaged in agriculture numbered 3·17m. (2·02m. males and 1·15m. females).

In 1976, 909,580 farm tractors were being used.

The production of the principal crops (in 1,000 metric quintals) in 1979: Sugarbeet, 134,646; wheat, 91,395; maize, 62,600; tomatoes, 51,321; potatoes, 30,202; oranges, 17,814; rice, 10,139; barley, 8,093; lemons, 7,669; oats, 4,378; olive oil, 4,753; tangerines, 3,241; other citrus fruit, 592; rye, 372.

Production of wine, 1979, 84,337,000 hectolitres; of tobacco, 136,571 tonnes.

In 1978 consumption of chemical fertilizers in Italy was as follows (in 1,000 tons): Perphosphate, 756·5; nitrate of ammonia, 718·2; sulphate of ammonium, 495·8; potash salts, 155·2; nitrate of calcium $\frac{1}{8}$, 114·2; deposed slags, 57·3.

Livestock estimated in 1979: Cattle, 8·6m.; pigs, 9·8m.; sheep and goats, 10m.; horses, 264,240; donkeys, 151,000; mules, 109,000.

Fisheries. The Italian fishing fleet comprised in 1978, 22,388 motor boats (295,981 gross tons) and 20,371 sailing vessels (25,491 gross tons). The catch in 1979 was 379,682 tonnes.

INDUSTRY AND TRADE

Industry. The textile industry is the largest and most important. Silk culture, while flourishing most extensively in Lombardy, Piedmont and Venezia, is carried on all over Italy. The production of artificial and synthetic fibre (including staple fibre and waste) in 1979 was 500,257 tonnes in 16 factories. Output, 1979 (in tonnes): Pure cotton yarns, 174,712; jute yarns, 7,432; pure wool yarns, 62,003.

The food industry produced 1,563,910 tonnes of sugar in 1979.

The chemical industry produced, in 1979 (in tonnes): Sulphuric acid (at 50 Be), 4,728,385; mineral phosphate, 1,378,968.

Production of motor vehicles was 1,583,925 in 1977.

Labour. The census of industry and commerce, of 25 Oct. 1971, recorded 2,425,204 establishments employing 11,077,533 workers. Mining employed 71,460 workers; food and tobacco manufacture, 400,699; textile industries, 541,030; clothing, shoes, skins and leather industries, 645,310; engineering, 1,905,316; metallurgy, 245,648; chemical, rubber and paper industries, 427,586; building, 997,534; transport and communications, 894,567; commerce, 2,796,897; banking and insurance, 293,005; electricity, gas and water works, 155,156.

As at July 1978, 20·5m. persons were employed, 1·7m. unemployed (figures from a new series of statistics on the labour force, 1977, which is not comparable with previous series).

Trade Unions. Membership of the 4 main groups: Confederazione Generale Italiana del Lavoro (Communist-dominated), 4,485,930 (1977); Confederazione Italiana Sindacati Lavoratori (Catholic), 2,823,735 (1976); Unione Italiana del Lavoro, 1,151,370 (1977); Confederazione Italiana Sindacati Nazionali Lavoratori, 1,015,988 (1961).

Commerce. The territory covered by foreign trade statistics includes Italy, the Republic of San Marino, but excludes the municipalities of Livigno and Campione.

The following table shows the value of Italy's foreign trade (in 1m. lire):

	1973	1974	1975	1976	1977	1978	1979
Imports	16,343,378	26,714,957	25,199,599	36,730,621	42,429,110	47,867,899	64,650,431
Exports	12,989,282	19,826,059	22,866,426	31,166,722	39,967,593	47,505,301	59,924,812

The following table shows trade by countries in 1m. lire:

Countries	Imports into Italy from			Exports from Italy to		
	1977	1978	1979	1977	1978	1979
Argentina	476,702	452,569	592,956	189,686	303,493	395,063
Australia	370,144	349,475	460,062	238,891	263,643	361,070
Austria	806,763	899,793	1,261,122	1,015,242	1,125,533	1,506,445
Belgium–Luxembourg	1,418,562	1,598,884	2,303,718	1,420,596	1,632,760	2,046,710
France	5,894,744	6,970,012	9,094,041	5,715,144	6,774,179	8,872,662
Germany, Fed. Rep. of	7,139,535	8,312,974	11,102,471	7,413,206	9,036,773	11,333,788
Japan	563,530	575,266	736,127	318,016	438,272	650,093
Netherlands	1,767,856	2,008,287	2,707,841	1,508,032	1,945,804	2,746,607
Switzerland	1,153,149	1,441,268	1,772,828	1,601,506	1,954,348	2,561,782
USSR	1,284,586	1,412,499	1,713,963	1,086,357	959,900	1,011,900
UK	1,581,731	1,912,118	2,613,047	2,106,270	2,876,050	3,915,704
USA	2,950,075	3,238,934	4,385,390	2,666,124	3,385,204	3,874,130
Yugoslavia	447,714	519,089	659,957	655,361	753,264	1,038,581

In 1979 the main imports were maize, wood, greasy wool, metal scrap, pit-coal, petroleum, raw oils, meat, paper, rolled iron and steel, copper and alloys, mechanical and electric equipment, motor vehicles. The main exports were fruit and vegetables, fabrics, footwear and other clothing articles, rolled iron and steel, machinery, motor vehicles, plastic materials and petroleum by-products.

Italy's balance of trade (in 1,000m. lire) has been estimated as follows:

	Goods and services			Income from investments and work, balance	Net balance
	Export	Import	Balance		
1974	24,350	29,445	−5,095	− 61	−5,156
1975	28,175	28,365	− 190	−351	− 541
1976	38,160	40,320	−2,160	−437	−2,597
1977	49,412	47,277	+2,135	− 142	+1,993
1978	58,866	53,465	+5,401	+184	+5,585
1979	74,558	71,283	+3,275	+702	+3,977

Remittances from Italians abroad (in US$1m. until 1969 and then 1,000m. lire): 1950, 72; 1960, 214; 1970, 289; 1971, 336; 1972, 340; 1973, 360; 1974, 351; 1975, 338; 1976, 385; 1977, 626; 1978, 785; 1979, 956.

Total trade between Italy and UK (British Department of Trade returns, in £1,000 sterling):

	1976	1977	1978	1979	1980
Imports to UK	1,106,165	1,532,155	1,934,964	2,491,013	2,311,071
Exports and re-exports from UK	826,403	978,368	1,123,777	1,469,048	1,899,181

Tourism. In 1979, 48·7m. foreigners visited Italy; they included 10·7m. German, 8·5m. Swiss, 6·9m. French, 4·7m. Austrian, 3·8m. Yugoslav, 2m. British, 2m. Dutch and 1·8m. US citizens. They spent about 5,334,000m. lire.

COMMUNICATIONS

Roads. Italy's roads totalled (31 Dec. 1979) 294,423 km, of which 45,176 km were state roads, 101,681 km provincial roads, 141,666 km communal roads. Motor vehicles, Dec. 1979: Cars, 16·24m.; buses, 51,913; lorries, 1,297,049; motor cycles, light vans, etc., 4,414,256.

The Mont Blanc tunnel road (11·6 km) from Entreves to Les Pelerins (France) was opened on 16 July 1965.

Railways. Railway history in Italy begins in 1839, with a line between Naples and Portici (8 km). Length of railways (31 Dec. 1979), 20,083 km, including 16,152 km of state railways, of which 8,442 had not yet been electrified. The first section of a new high-speed direct railway linking Rome and Florence opened in Feb. 1977. In 1979 the state railways carried 374,940 passengers and 54,405,000 tonnes of goods. The Rome Underground opened in Feb. 1980.

Aviation. The Italian airline Alitalia (with a capital of 120,000m. lire, of which 98·7% is owned by the State) operates flights to every part of the world. Airports include 21 international, 32 national and 75 club airports. Domestic and international traffic in 1979 registered 12,973,798 passengers arrived and 12,999,743 departed, while freight and mail (excluding luggage) amounted to 170,422 tonnes unloaded and 208,870 tonnes loaded.

Shipping. The mercantile marine at 31 Dec. 1979 consisted of 3,137 vessels of 11,284,875 gross tons, not including pleasure boats (yachts, etc.), sailing and motor vessels. There were 1,466 motor vessels of 100 gross tons and over.

In 1978, 293m. tonnes of cargo were unloaded, and 103,305,000 tonnes of cargo were loaded in Italian ports.

In 1972 navigable waterways had a length of 2,237 km (849 km of which were canals).

Post and Broadcasting. On 31 Dec. 1977 there were 13,963 post offices and 13,064 telegraph offices. The maritime radio-telegraph service had 22 coast stations. On 1 Jan. 1978 the telephone service had 16,118,928 apparatus. *Radiotelevisione Italiana* broadcasts 3 programmes and additional regional programmes, including transmissions in English, French, German and Slovenian on medium- and short-waves and on FM. It also broadcasts 2 TV programmes. Radio licences numbered 532,800; television and radio licences, 13,400,609.

Cinemas. There were 7,475 cinemas in 1980.

Newspapers. There were 74 daily newspapers with a combined circulation of 6·71m. copies; of the papers 15 are published in Rome and 8 in Milan. One daily each is published in German and Slovene, and 2 in English.

JUSTICE, RELIGION, EDUCATION AND WELFARE

Justice. Italy has 1 court of cassation, in Rome, and is divided for the administration of justice into 23 appeal court districts (and 3 detached sections), subdivided into 159 tribunal districts, and these again into *mandamenti* each with its own magistracy (*Pretura*), 899 in all. There are also 89 first degree assize courts and 26 assize courts of appeal. For civil business, besides the magistracy above mentioned, *Conciliatori* have jurisdiction in petty plaints.

On 31 Dec. 1979 there were 19,486 male and 935 female prisoners in establishments for preventive custody, 5,059 males and 88 females in penal establishments and 1,871 males and 104 females in establishments for the execution of safety measures.

Religion. The treaty between the Holy See and Italy, of 11 Feb. 1929, confirmed by article 7 of the Constitution of the republic, lays down that the Catholic Apostolic Roman Religion is the only religion of the State. Other creeds are permitted, provided they do not profess principles, or follow rites, contrary to public order or moral behaviour.

The appointment of archbishops and of bishops is made by the Holy See; but the Holy See submits to the Italian Government the name of the person to be appointed in order to obtain an assurance that the latter will not raise objections of a political nature.

Catholic religious teaching is given in elementary and intermediate schools. Marriages celebrated before a Catholic priest are automatically transferred to the civil register. Marriages celebrated by clergy of other denominations must be made valid before a registrar. In 1972 there were 279 dioceses with 28,154 parishes and 43,714 priests. There were 187,153 members (154,796 women) of about 20,000 religious houses.

In 1962 there were about 100,000 Protestants and about 50,000 Jews.

Annuario Cattolico d'Italia, a cura del CNEC. 14th ed. 1969–70, Rome, 1970
Annuario di Pastorale. Rome, 1970
Burgalassi, S., *La Sociologia della Religione in Italia dalle originiul 1967.* Rome, 1967

Education. Education is compulsory from 6 to 14 years of age. An optional pre-school education is given to the children between 3 and 5 years in the preparatory schools (kindergarten schools). Illiteracy of males over 6 years was 4% in 1971, of females 6·3%.

Compulsory education can be classified as primary education (5-year course) and junior secondary education (3-year course).

Senior secondary education is subdivided in classical (*ginnasio* and classical *liceo*), scientific (scientific *liceo*), language lyceum, professional institutes and technical education: agricultural, industrial, commercial, technical, nautical institutes, institutes for surveyors, institutes for girls (5-year course) and teacher-training institutes (4-year course).

University education is given in Universities and in University Higher Institutes (4, 5, 6 years, according to degree course).

Statistics for the academic year 1979–80:

Elementary schools	No.	Pupils
Kindergarten	29,959	1,852,425
Public elementary schools	28,445	4,175,951
Private elementary schools }		
Private elementary recognized schools (*parificate*) }	2,487	342,448

Government secondary schools		Total students
Junior secondary schools	10,014	2,903,502
Classical lyceum	763	202,741
Lyceum for science	952	362,244
Language lyceum	189	34,779
Teachers' schools	196	31,592
Teachers' institutes	652	199,640
Professional institutes	1,660	433,007
Technical institutes, of which:		
Industrial institutes	638	286,696
Commercial institutes	1,053	519,390
Surveyors' institutes	489	135,509
Agricultural institutes }		
Nautical institutes }		
Technical institutes for tourism }	339	124,034
Managerial institutes }		
Girls technical schools }		
Artistic studies	239	56,110

Universities and higher institutes	Date of foundation	Students	Teachers	Universities and higher institutes	Date of foundation	Students	Teachers
Ancona	1965	6,547	282	Napoli	1224	115,191	3,377
Arezzo	1971	1,345	76	Padova	1222	47,298	2,169
Bari	1924	43,205	1,764	Palermo	1805	45,491	2,003
Bergamo	1970	1,838	119	Parma	1502	16,604	916
Bologna	1200	61,188	2,805	Pavia	1390	17,892	1,126
Brescia	1970	2,444	46	Perugia	1276	19,887	992
Cagliari	1626	19,540	1,052	Pescara	1965	7,176	161
Camerino	1727	2,594	231	Piacenza	1924	664	53
Cassino	1968	1,742	43	Pisa	1338	27,607	1,271
Catania	1434	33,754	1,333	Reggio di C.	1968	7,937	129
Chieti	1965	5,177	139	Roma	1303	150,041	5,726
Cosenza	1972	4,031	392	Salerno	1944	21,613	486
Feltre (Belluno)	1969	434	...	Sassari	1677	8,066	451
Ferrara	1391	7,231	324	Siena	1300	9,975	611
Firenze	1924	45,630	2,069	Teramo	1965	3,687	94
Genova	1243	34,118	1,795	Torino	1404	56,309	2,475
L'Aquila	1956	6,491	413	Trento	1965	2,833	165
Lecce	1959	6,837	303	Trieste	1924	11,693	853
Macerata	1290	4,124	199	Udine	1969	1,333	71
Messina	1549	24,080	1,164	Urbino	1564	11,035	375
Milano	1924	106,063	3,075	Venezia	1868	15,426	675
Modena	1678	8,655	615	Verona	1969	7,733	140

Health. In 1976 there were 130,846 doctors and 588,103 hospital beds.

Social Security. Social expenditure is made up of transfers which the central public departments, local departments and social security departments, make to families. Payment is principally for pensions, family allowances and health services. Expenditure on subsidies, public assistance to various classes of people and people injured by political events or national disasters are also included.

In 1975 government expenditure on social welfare amounted to 27,291,000m. lire.

DIPLOMATIC REPRESENTATIVES

OF ITALY IN GREAT BRITAIN (14 Three Kings Yard, London, W1Y 2EH)

Ambassador: Andrea Cagiati, GCVO. (accredited 20 Feb. 1980).

OF GREAT BRITAIN IN ITALY
(Via XX Settembre 80A, 00187, Rome)

Ambassador: Sir Ronald Arculus, KCMG.

OF ITALY IN THE USA (1601 Fuller St., NW, Washington, D.C., 20009)

Ambassador: Paulo Pansa Cedronio.

OF THE USA IN ITALY (Via Veneto 119/A, Rome)

Ambassador: Richard N. Gardner.

OF ITALY TO THE UNITED NATIONS

Ambassador: Umberto La Rocca.

Books of Reference

Statistical Information: The Istituto Centrale di Statistica (16 Via Cesare Balbo 00100 Rome) was set up by law of 9 July 1926 as the central institute in charge of census and all statistical information. *President:* Prof. Giuseppe de Meo. *Directors-General:* Dr Carlo Viterbo and Dr Luigo Pinto. Its publications include:

Annuario statistico italiano. 1979
Compendio statistico italiano. 1979
Bollettino mensile di statistica. Monthly, from 1950
Annuario di statistiche industriali. 1977
Annuario di statistiche demografiche. 1977
Popolazione e movimento anagrafico dei Comuni. Vol. XX, 1976. Vol. XXI, 1977
Annuario di statistica agraria. 1978
Statistica della navigazione marittima. 1978
Annuario statistico del commercio interno. 1976
Statistica annuale del commercio con l'estero. 1977
Statistica mensile del commercio con l'estero. Monthly
Annuario di statistiche del lavoro. 1978
Censimento generale dell'agricoltura, 1970. 7 vols.
Censimento generale della popolazione, 1971. 11 vols.
Censimento generale dell'industria e del commercio, 1971. 9 vols.
Sintesi Statistica di un Ventennio di Vita Economica Italiana, 1952–71

Italy. Documents and Notes. Servizi delle Informazioni, Rome. 1952 ff.
Italian Books and Periodicals. Bimonthly from 1958
A Quick Glimpse at Italy. Rome, 1970
Banco di Roma, *Review of the Economic Condition in Italy* (in English). Bimonthly, 1947 ff.
Credito Italiano, *The Italian Economic Situation.* Bimonthly. Milan, from June 1961 (in Italian), from June 1962 (in English)
Compendio Economico Italiano. Rome, Unione Italiana delle Camere di Commercio. Annually from 1954

Twentyfive Years of the Italian Republic, 1946–1971. Rome 1971
Allum, P. A., *Italy; Republic Without Government.* London, 1973
Almagià, R., *L'Italia.* 2 vols. Turin, 1959
Carone, G., *Il Turismo nell'economia internazionale.* Milan, 1959
Clough, S. B., *The Economic History of Modern Italy.* Columbia Univ. Press, 1964
Danielli, G., *Atlante Fisico Economico d'Italia.* Milan, 1950
Di Vittorio, G. (ed.), *I sindacati in Italia.* Bari, 1955
Grindrod, M., *The Rebuilding of Italy, 1945–55.* R. Inst. of Int. Affairs, 1955
Hildebrand, G. H., *Growth and Structure in the Economy of Modern Italy.* Harvard Univ. Press, 1965
Nichols, P., *Italia, Italia.* London, 1974
Wiskemann, E., *Italy Since 1945.* London, 1971
Woolfe, S. J. (ed.), *The Rebirth of Italy, 1943–50.* New York, 1972
Zanetti, G., and Filippi, E., *Finanze e sviluppo della grande industria in Italia.* 2 vols. Milan, 1967

National Library: Biblioteca Nazionale Centrale Vittorio Emanuele II Viale Castro Pretorio, Rome. *Director:* Dr L. M. Crisari.

IVORY COAST

République de Côte d'Ivoire

Capital: Abidjan
Population: 7·92m. (1979)
GNP per capita: US$1,253 (1979)

HISTORY. France obtained rights on the coast in 1842, but did not actively and continuously occupy the territory till 1882. On 1 Jan. 1933 a portion of Upper Volta was added to the Ivory Coast, but on 1 Jan. 1948 the districts of Bobo-Dioulasso, Gaoua, Kondougou, Ougadougou, Kaya, Tenkodogo and Dédougou were transferred to the reconstituted Upper Volta.

AREA AND POPULATION. The republic is situated between Liberia and Ghana and has common frontiers with the republics of Guinea, Mali and Upper Volta. Area, 322,463 sq. km; total population (census, 1975), 6,674,360; estimate 1979 7·92m.

The 26 departments at the census 1975 were:

Department	Sq. km	Population	Department	Sq. km	Population
Abengourou	6,713	175,891	Danané	4,650	169,589
Abidjan	14,819	1,389,978	Dimbokro	13,822	475,118
Aboisso	6,135	149,876	Divo	9,869	275,171
Adzopé	5,151	159,561	Ferkéssédougou	19,292	90,901
Agboville	3,900	139,056	Gagnoa	6,873	256,006
Biankouma	2,897	74,408	Guiglo	14,232	135,252
Bondoukou	16,465	293,838	Katiola	8,469	75,909
Bouaflé	8,362	265,875	Korhogo	12,164	276,846
Bouaké	23,405	805,356	Man	7,004	277,648
Bouna	21,470	77,705	Odienné	21,336	124,644
Boundiali	10,273	132,060	Sassandra	26,263	195,620
Dabakala	8,694	55,356	Séguéla	22,861	157,644
Daloa	13,918	367,356	Touba	8,767	77,696

The population of Abidjan (census 1975) was 685,800. Other towns (estimate 1974): Bouaké, 200,000; Daloa, 100,000; Man, 100,000.

The principal ethnical groups are the Agnis-Ashantis, Kroumen, Mandé, Baoulé, Dan-Gouro and Koua.

CONSTITUTION AND GOVERNMENT. The Republic of Ivory Coast became independent on 7 Aug. 1960, after having been a territory of French West Africa from 1904. The republic was admitted to the UN on 20 Sept. 1960.

The legislative assembly has 147 members; all of them elected on 27 Nov. 1970, belong to the *Parti Démocratique de la Côte d'Ivoire.* The republic is administratively divided into 26 departments.

The Government was in March 1981 composed as follows:

President: Félix Houphouët-Boigny. (Re-elected for a fifth 5-year term in 1980.)
Minister of State: Auguste Denise. *Minister of State responsible for Reform of State-owned Companies:* Mathieu Ekra. *Public Health and Population:* Jean-Baptiste Mockey. *Minister of State:* Nanlo Bamba. *Justice:* Camille Alliali. *Defence and Civic Service:* Kouadio M'Bahia Blé. *Interior:* Alexis Thierry-Lebbe. *Foreign Affairs:* Siméon Ake. *Economy, Finance and Planning:* Abdoulaye Koné. *Agriculture:* Denis Bra Kanon. *Scientific Research:* Jean Lorougnon Guédé. *Technical Education and Vocational Training:* Ange Barry-Battesti. *National Education:* Paul Akoto Yao. *Cultural Affairs:* Bernard Dadié. *Commerce:* Maurice Seri Gnoleba. *Construction and Town Planning:* Désiré Boni. *Animal Production:* Dicoh Garba. *Labour and 'Ivorization' of Personnel:* Albert Vanié Bi Tra. *Youth, Popular Education and Sport:* Laurent Doua Fologo. *Information:* Amadou Thiam. *Mining:* Paul Gui Dibo. *Water Resources and Forests:* Théodore Koffi Attobra. *Primary Education and*

Educational Television: Pascal N'Gouessan Dikébié. *Internal Security:* Gaston Ouassenan Koné. *Posts and Telecommunications:* Bangali Koné. *Navy:* Lamine Fadiga. *Public Service:* Emile Kei Boguinard. *Women's Affairs:* Jeanne Gervais. *Tourism:* Ibrahima Koné. *Relations with the National Assembly:* Emile Brou. *Social Affairs:* Etienne Ahin.

National flag: Three vertical strips of orange, white, green.

DEFENCE

Army. The Army consisted of 3 infantry battalions and support units in 1980; total strength, 5,700.

Air Force. The Air Force, formed in 1962, has 2 turboprop C-103H Hercules, 5 turbofan F-28 Fellowship, 1 turbofan Gulfstream II, 2 turboprop F-27 Friendship and 3 C-47 transports, 1 Falcon light jet transport, 1 Aero Commander 500 communications aircraft, 3 Reims-Cessna 150s and 3 Reims-Cessna 337s for liaison and training, and 3 SA330 Puma, 4 Dauphin 2 and 5 Alouette II/III helicopters. Being delivered are 6 Alpha Jet advanced trainers, with combat potential. Personnel total 350.

INTERNATIONAL RELATIONS

Membership. Ivory Coast is a member of UN, OAU and is an ACP state of EEC.

ECONOMY

Budget. The budget for 1978 balanced at 518,581m. francs CFA. Reserves (Dec. 1977) 546·9m. francs CFA.

Currency. The currency is the *franc CFA* divided into 100 centimes. In March 1981, £ sterling = 533 francs CFA; US$1 = 249 francs CFA.

ENERGY AND NATURAL RESOURCES

Oil. Petroleum has been produced (offshore) since Oct. 1977.

Minerals. Diamond fields are being exploited; 299,708 carats in 1973. Manganese deposits yielded 123,060 tonnes in 1970.

Agriculture. Coffee is the largest export commodity (1978–79), 277,048 tons (260,796 tons, exported). Production (1980) cocoa, 247,000 tonnes; palm oil, 848,000 tonnes. Other crops include maize, yams, sweet potatoes, cassava and plantains. The cultivation of cotton has been developed. Production (1980) 115,000 tonnes. Coconuts and a small quantity of rubber are collected. The mahogany forests inland are worked.

Several factories produce palm-oil, fruit preserves and fruit juice.

Livestock, 1979: 650,000 cattle, 1·1m. sheep, 1·2m. goats, 320,000 pigs, 1,000 horses and 1,000 donkeys.

TRADE. Trade for calendar years in 1,000m. francs CFA:

	1975	1976	1977	1978
Imports	241,396	311,608	429,566	522,515
Exports	245,572	392,501	529,212	524,380

In 1977 exports of coffee furnished 198,616m.; timber, 119,744m., and cocoa, 67,500m. Of the exports, 58% went to EEC, 26% to France and 1·2% to the USA. Of the imports, 60% came from EEC, 40% from France and 0·5% from the USA. Chief imports were metalwork, cement, wine, motor fuel and oils.

Total trade between the Ivory Coast and UK (British Department of Trade returns, in £1,000 sterling):

	1976	1977	1978	1979	1980
Imports to UK	45,105	79,541	57,983	73,622	53,563
Exports and re-exports from UK	17,848	25,173	24,572	24,001	27,916

COMMUNICATIONS

Roads. In 1978 roads totalled 3,000 km bitumenized and 44,000 km secondary. In 1978 there were 181,801 vehicles.

Railways. From Abidjan a metre-gauge railway runs to Léraba and thence through Upper Volta to Ouagadougou (1,140 km). An extension to Tambao is proposed and a new network for the export of iron ore from the port of San Pedro is under study. In 1978 the railways carried 3,364m. passenger-km and 1,069m. tonne-km of freight.

Aviation. The main airport is at Abidjan-Port-Buet. In 1978 it handled 564,830 passengers and 25,396 tonnes of freight and 1,216 tonnes of mail.

Shipping. The main ports are Abidjan, San Pedro and Tabou. In 1972 Abidjan port handled 5,925,000 tonnes.

Post. There were 78,965 telephones in 1978 and 939 telex machines.

Cinemas. There were 80 cinemas in 1972 with a seating capacity of 80,000.

JUSTICE, RELIGION, EDUCATION AND WELFARE

Justice. There are a court of first instance, 2 courts of second instance and a court of appeal.

Religion. Of the total population, 23·5% are Moslems, 12·5% Christians and 65% animists.

Education. There were, in 1977–78, 892,135 pupils in schools. The university of Abidjan had 9,651 students in 1977–78.

Health. In 1978 there were 9,962 hospital beds, 429 doctors, 36 dentists, 615 midwives, 3,052 nurses and 76 pharmacists.

DIPLOMATIC REPRESENTATIVES

OF THE IVORY COAST IN GREAT BRITAIN (2 Upper Belgrave St., London, SW1X 8BJ)

Ambassador: Dieudonné Essienne (accredited 4 Oct. 1978).

OF GREAT BRITAIN IN THE IVORY COAST (Immeuble Shell, Ave. Lamblin, Abidjan)

Ambassador: M. F. Daly.

OF THE IVORY COAST IN THE USA (2424 Massachusetts Ave., NW, Washington, D.C., 20008)

Ambassador: Timothée N'Guetta Ahoua.

OF THE USA IN THE IVORY COAST (5 Rue Jesse Owens, Abidjan)

Ambassador: Nancy V. Rawls.

OF THE IVORY COAST TO THE UNITED NATIONS

Ambassador: Amoakon E. Thiemele.

Books of Reference

Statistical Information: Service de la Statistique, Abidjan. It publishes *Bulletin Statistique Mensuel* and *Inventoire Économique de la Côte d'Ivoire.*

La Côte d'Ivoire en Chiffee. Abidjan, 1979
Panorama de la Côte d'Ivoire, 1978, ed. Direction de l'Information, Abidjan
Holas, B., *Industries et cultures en Côte d'Ivoire.* Abidjan, 1979
Zolberg, A. R., *One-Party Government in the Ivory Coast.* Rev. ed. Princeton Univ. Press, 1974

JAMAICA

Capital: Kingston
Population: 2·16m. (1979)
GNP per capita: US$1,110 (1978)

HISTORY. Jamaica was discovered by Columbus in 1494, and was occupied by the Spaniards between 1509 and 1655, when the island was captured by the English; their possession was confirmed by the Treaty of Madrid, 1670. Self-government was introduced in 1944 and gradually extended until Jamaica achieved complete independence within the Commonwealth on 6 Aug. 1962.

AREA AND POPULATION. The area of Jamaica is 4,243·6 sq. miles (10,991 sq. km). The population at the census of 7 April 1970 was 1,861,300, distributed on the basis of the 14 parishes of the island as follows: Kingston and St Andrew, 550,100 (estimate 1977, 635,100); St Thomas, 71,400 (77,400); Portland, 68,500 (74,300); St Mary, 100,000 ((108,100); St Ann, 121,300 (133,200); Trelawny, 61,300 (66,700); St James, 103,700 (119,800); Hanover, 59,000 (63,700); Westmoreland, 113,200 (120,600); St Elizabeth, 126,000 (137,300); Manchester, 123,500 (139,400); St Catherine, 186,000 (211,200); Clarendon, 176,600 (191,300).

Estimated population, in 1979, was 2·16m.

Vital statistics (1978): Births, 58,200; deaths, (1977) 14,200; infant deaths, 869; emigrants (1977) to USA, 11,501; to Canada, 6,291, and to UK, 1,029.

CONSTITUTION AND GOVERNMENT. A new Constitution was enacted with independence in Aug. 1962. The Crown is represented by a Governor-General appointed by the Crown on the advice of the Prime Minister. The Governor-General is assisted by a Privy Council.

The Legislature comprises two chambers, an elected House and a nominated Senate. The executive is chosen from both chambers.

The Executive comprises the Prime Minister, who is the leader of the majority party, and Ministers appointed by the Prime Minister. Together they form the Cabinet, which is the highest executive power. An Attorney-General is a member of the House and is legal adviser to the Cabinet.

The Senate consists of 21 senators appointed by the Governor-General, 13 on the advice of the Prime Minister, 8 on the advice of the Leader of the Opposition. The House of Representatives (60 members, Dec. 1976) is elected by universal adult suffrage for a 5-year period. Electors and elected must be Jamaican or Commonwealth citizens resident in Jamaica for at least 12 months before registration. The powers and procedure of Parliament correspond to those of the British Parliament.

The Privy Council consists of 6 members appointed by the Governor-General in consultation with the Prime Minister.

Governor-General: Florizel Augustus Glasspole.
National flag: A yellow diagonal cross dividing triangles of green, top and bottom, and black, hoist and fly.

The elections to House of Representatives, held on 30 Oct. 1980, returned 51 members of the Jamaica Labour Party and 8 members of the People's National Party. One seat unfilled.

Prime Minister: Edward Seaga.

DEFENCE

Army. The Jamaica Defence Force consists of a Regular and a Reserve Force. The Regular Force is comprised of the 1st battalion, Jamacia Regiment and Support Services which include the Air Wing and Coast Guard. The Reserve Force consists of the 3rd battalion, Jamaica Regiment. Total strength (all services, 1980), 4,000.

Air Force. The Air Wing of the Jamaica Defence Force was formed in July 1963 and has since been expanded and trained successively by the British Army Air Corps and Canadian air force personnel. Equipment for army liaison, search and rescue, police co-operation, survey and transport duties includes a Twin Otter; 2 Defender armed STOL transports; 1 Beech King Air and 1 Duke light transport; 4 JetRanger and 3 Bell 212 light helicopters; and 2 Cessna 185 Skywagons.

INTERNATIONAL RELATIONS

Membership. Jamaica is a member of UN, the Commonwealth, OAS and is an ACP state of EEC.

ECONOMY

Budget. Revenue and expenditure for fiscal years ending 31 March (in J$):

	1973–74	1974–75	1975–76	1976–77	1977–78	1978–79
Revenue	419,124,673	517,100,000	859,650,000	612,000,000	661,400,000	1,045,200,000
Expenditure	432,032,208	709,700,000	923,000,000	1,289,506,000	1,238,700,000	1,826,400,000

The chief heads of recurrent revenue are customs and excise duties, income tax, motor vehicle licences and post office receipts. Capital revenue is derived mainly from royalties.

Public debt at 31 March 1979, J$2,906·8m.

Remittances from overseas amounted to approximately J$18m. in the year ending 31 Dec. 1977.

Currency. The currency, is the *dollar*, divided into 100 cents. Currency circulation in Dec. 1978 was J$210,991,000, comprising notes of J$194,717,000 and J$16,274,000 coin. In March 1981, £1 = J$3·89; US$1 = J$1·78.

Banking. On 1 May 1961 the Bank of Jamaica opened for business as Jamaica's Central Bank. It has the sole right to issue notes and coins in Jamaica, acts as Banker to the Government and to the commercial banks, and administers the island's external reserves and exchange control.

There are 8 commercial banks with about 170 branches and agencies in operation, with main offices in Kingston. Six of these banks are subsidiaries of major British and North American banks, of which 4 are incorporated locally. The Workers' Savings and Loan Bank is owned by the Government, Trade Unions and the private sector. The National Commercial Bank (Jamaica) Ltd, formally Barclays Bank Jamaica Ltd, is 100% goverment-owned. The other 6 banks which operate are: The Bank of Nova Scotia (Jamaica) Ltd, City Bank of North America, Royal Bank (Jamaica) Ltd, Bank of Commerce, Jamaica Citizens Bank Ltd and First National Bank of Chicago (Jamaica) Ltd.

ENERGY AND NATURAL RESOURCES

Electricity. The Jamaica Public Service Co. is the public supplier of electricity. The bauxite companies, sugar estates and the Caribbean Cement Co. generate their own electricity.

Minerals. Bauxite, ceramic clays, marble, silica and gypsum are commercially valuable. Jamaica has become the world's second largest producer of bauxite and alumina. The bauxite deposits are worked by a Canadian and 4 American companies. Three companies process bauxite into alumina. In 1978, 11,736,000 tons of bauxite ore and 2,111,000 tons of alumina were mined.

Agriculture (1978). Production: Sugar, 288,000 tons; rum, 4,278,000 proof gallons; molasses, 133 tons; copra, 2,124 short tons. Exportable commodities: Bananas, 83,000 tonnes (exported); cocoa, 2·74m. lb; coffee, 179,000 boxes; citrus fruit, 398,000 boxes; pimento, 2,502 tons; ginger, 687 short tons. Agricultural exports (1978), J$158,632,000. Production of meat, fish and dairy products, 1978: Beef and veal, 255,174,000 lb.; goat flesh, 707,000 lb.; pork, 16,746,000 lb.; mutton, 64,000 lb.; poultry, 67,767,000 lb.; fish, 37m. lb.; eggs, 240m.; milk, 43m. quarts.

Livestock (1979): Cattle, 290,000; goats, 370,000; pigs, 250,000; poultry, 4·1m.

INDUSTRY AND TRADE

Industry. In 1976 there were 1,280 registered factories employing 52,633. From processing only a few agricultural products—sugar, rum, condensed milk, oils and fats, cigars and cigarettes—the island is now producing a wide range of manufactures using both local and imported raw materials. Among the manufactured goods are clothing, footwear, textiles, paints, building materials, including cement, agricultural machinery and toilet articles. An oil refinery in Kingston meets local fuel demand. In 1977 manufacturing and processing contributed J$563·9m. to the total GDP at current prices.

Commerce. Value of imports and domestic exports for calendar years (in J$1m.):

	1974[1]	1975	1976	1977	1978
Imports	850·8	1,021·4	829·8	781·6	1,260·0
Domestic exports	653·1	699·4	575·0	686·4	1,057·1

[1] Provisional.

Principal imports in 1978 (in J$1,000): Raw materials, 537·1; capital goods, 171·6; consumer goods, 184·8.

Principal exports, 1978 (in J$1m.): Alumina, 554·9; bauxite, 202·2; sugar, 92·5.

In 1978 total balance of visible trade with USA, UK and Canada amounted to J$86m.

Total trade between Jamaica and UK (British Department of Trade returns, in £1,000 sterling):

	1975	1976	1977	1978	1979	1980
Imports to UK	80,244	63,193	78,229	96,081	82,145	95,578
Exports and re-exports from UK	61,002	50,605	39,650	48,751	44,554	33,122

Tourism. In 1978, 532,864 tourists arrived in Jamaica, spending about J$148·2m.

COMMUNICATIONS

Roads (1978). The island has 2,944 miles of main roads, and over 7,264 miles of parochial and subsidiary roads. Main roads in the corporate area of Kingston and St Andrew are constructed and maintained by that corporation, those elsewhere by the Public Works Department of the Ministry of Public Utilities. Parochial or subsidiary roads are constructed and maintained by parish councils.

Railways. There are 303 km of railway open of 1,435 mm gauge, operated by the Jamaica Railway Corporation, which also operates 31 km (Alcoa Mineral Railway) on behalf of one of the bauxite companies. In 1978 total revenue was J$8·3m. and expenditure J$11·2m.

Aviation. In 1977, 13 scheduled commercial international airlines served Jamaica, operating through the Norman Manley and Sangster international airports at Palisadoes and Montego Bay. Trans-Jamaica Airlines Ltd operates internal flights. Air Jamaica, originally set up in conjunction with BOAC and BWIA in 1966, became a new company, Air Jamaica (1968) Ltd, and is affiliated to Air Canada. In 1969 it began operations as Jamaica's national airline. In 1978 Air Jamaica had a revenue of J$131,628,000 and operating expenses of J$122,033,000.

Shipping. Jamaica has 19 specified ports. In 1978 the port of Kingston unloaded 2m. tons of cargo.

Post and Broadcasting. Post and telecommunications are the responsibility of the Ministry of Works and Communications. In the financial year 1976–77 there were 316 post offices and 504 postal agencies.

The Jamaica Telephone Co. operates the telephone system. In Dec. 1977 there were 117,807 telephones in use. All telephone exchanges are automatic. Jamaica is linked to USA by a submarine telephone cable. Jamaica International Telecommunications Ltd (JAMINTEL) established in 1971, provides a wide range of international telecommunications services for Jamaica. There are 1 commercial and 1 publicly owned broadcasting stations; the latter also operates a television service.

Cinemas. In 1977 there were 25 cinemas and 1 drive-in cinema.

JUSTICE, RELIGION, EDUCATION AND WELFARE

Justice. The Judicature comprises a Supreme Court, a court of appeal, a revenue court, resident magistrates' courts, petty sessional courts, coroners' courts, a traffic court and a family court which was instituted in 1975. The Chief Justice is head of the judiciary. All prosecutions are initiated by the Director of Public Prosecutions.

Police. The Constabulary Force in 1978 stood at 5,898 officers, sub-officers and constables (men and women). There are, in addition, 1,392 district constables and 1,995 special constables.

Religion. Freedom of worship is guaranteed under the Constitution. The main Christian denominations are Anglican, Baptist, Roman Catholic, Methodist, Church of God, United Church of Jamaica, and Grand Cayman (Presbyterian–Congregational) Moravian, Seventh-day Adventists, Pentecostal, Salvation Army, Quaker, and Disciples of Christ. Pocomania is a mixture of Christianity and African survivals. Non-Christians include Hindus, Jews, Moslems and Bahai followers.

Education. In Sept. 1973 education became free for all government grant-aided schools (the majority of all schools) and for all Jamaicans entering the University of the West Indies, the College of Arts, Science and Technology and the Jamaica School of Agriculture. In 1977–78 there were 269 primary schools (167,542 pupils); 511 all-age schools (269,492 pupils).

In 1977 there were 6 vocational schools, 6 technical high schools, 7 teacher-training colleges, the College of Arts, Science and Technology and the Mona campus of the University of the West Indies.

Health. In 1978 there were about 720 doctors and 30 government hospitals with over 7,486 beds. There are several private hospitals and nursing homes.

DIPLOMATIC REPRESENTATIVES

OF JAMAICA IN GREAT BRITAIN
(50 St James's St., London, SW1A 1JS)

High Commissioner: Ernest Grafford Peart (accredited 10 Nov. 1978).

OF GREAT BRITAIN IN JAMAICA (Trafalgar Rd., Kingston 10)

High Commissioner: J. K. Drinkall, CMG.

OF JAMAICA IN THE USA (1666 Connecticut Ave., NW,
Washington, D.C., 20009)

Ambassador: Alfred A. Rattray.

OF THE USA IN JAMAICA (2 Oxford Rd., Kingston)

Ambassador: Loren E. Lawrence.

OF JAMAICA TO THE UNITED NATIONS

Ambassador: Donald O. Mills.

Books of Reference

Statistical Information: The Department of Statistics (93 Hanover St., Kingston) was set up in 1945—the nucleus being the Census Office, which undertook the operations of the 1943 Census of Jamaica and its Dependencies. *Director:* Mrs C. P. McFarlane. Publications of the Bureau include the *Bulletin of Statistics on External Trade* and the *Annual Abstract of Statistics.*

Economic and Social Survey, Jamaica 1976. National Planning Agency. Yearly
Social and Economic Studies. Institute of Social and Economic Research, Univ. of the West Indies. Quarterly
Black, C. V., *History of Jamaica.* London, 1965
Cassidy, F. G., and Le Page, R. B., *Dictionary of Jamaican English.* CUP, 1966
Clarke, C. G., *Jamaica in Maps.* London, 1974
Delattre, R., *A Guide to Jamaica Reference Material.* Kingston, 1965

Floyd, B., *Jamaica: An Island Microcosm*. London, 1979
Hurwitz, S. J. and E. F., *Jamaica: A Historical Portrait*. New York, 1971 and London, 1972
Jefferson, O., *The Post-War Economic Development of Jamaica*. Kingston, 1972
Kuper, A., *Changing Jamaica*. London and Boston, 1976
Lacey, T., *Violence and Politics in Jamaica, 1960–70*. Manchester Univ. Press, 1977
Manley, M., *A Voice at the Work Place*. London, 1975
Stone, C., *Class, Race and Political Behaviour in Urban Jamaica*. Kingston, 1973
Bibliography of Jamaica, 1900–1963. Jamaica Library Service, 1963

Libraries: Institute of Jamaica, Kingston. Jamaica Library Service, Kingston.

JAPAN

Nippon (*or* Nihon)

Capital: Tōkyō
Population: 116·1m. (1979)
GNP per capita: US$7,330 (1978)

HISTORY. The house of Yamato, from about 500 B.C. the rulers of one of several kingdoms, in about A.D. 200 united the nation; the present imperial family are their direct descendants. From 1186 until 1867 successive families of Shoguns exercised the temporal power. In 1867 the Emperor Meiji recovered the imperial power after the abdication on 14 Oct. 1867 of the fifteenth and last Tokugawa Shogun Keiki (in different pronunciation: Yoshinobu). In 1871 the feudal system (Hōken Seido) was abolished; this was the beginning of the rapid westernization.

At San Francisco on 8 Sept. 1951 a Treaty of Peace was signed by Japan and representatives of 48 countries. For details *see* THE STATESMAN'S YEAR-BOOK, 1953, p. 1169. On 26 Oct. 1951 the Japanese Diet ratified the Treaty by 307 votes to 47 votes with 112 abstentions. On the same day the Diet ratified a Security Treaty with the US by 289 votes to 71 votes with 106 abstentions. The treaty provided for the stationing of American troops in Japan until she was able to undertake her own defence. The peace treaty came into force on 28 April 1952, when Japan regained her sovereignty. In 1960 Japan signed the Japan–US Mutual Security Treaty, valid for 10 years, which was renewed in 1970. In June 1971 the Okinawa Reversion Agreement providing for the return from the US to Japan of Okinawa on 15 May 1972 was signed.

AREA AND POPULATION. Census population, 1 Oct. 1979, was 116,133,000 with density of 311·6 per sq. km (57m. males, 59m. females). Foreigners registered 30 June 1980 were 778,106, of whom 663,631 were Koreans, 51,717 Chinese, 21,272 Americans, 4,793 British, 4,921 Philippines, 2,777 Germans, 2,316 Vietnamese, 1,920 Indians, 1,676 Canadians, 2,731 stateless persons.

Japanese overseas, Oct. 1979, 435,473; of these 142,952 lived in Brazil, 115,377 in USA, 15,930 in Argentina, 12,649 in Federal Republic of Germany, 11,335 in Peru, 11,286 in Canada.

The leading cities, with census population, 31 March 1979 (in 1,000), are:

Akita	278	Kōbe	1,343	Sapporo	1,319
Amagasaki	523	Kochi	294	Sasebo	254
Aomori	281	Koriyama	276	Sendai	628
Asahikawa	343	Kumamoto	497	Shimonoseki	262
Chiba	718	Kurashiki	402	Shizuoka	455
Fujisawa	289	Kure	237	Suita	313
Fukushima	257	Kyōto	1,450	Takamatsu	309
Funabashi	456	Maebashi	261	Takatsuki	337
Gifu	407	Matsudo	383	Tokushima	245
Hachioji	363	Matsuyama	390	Tōkyō	8,220
Hakodate	315	Nagano	317	Toyama	297
Hamamatsu	485	Nagasaki	442	Toyohashi	297
Higashiosaka	498	Nagoya	2,081	Toyonaka	393
Himeji	442	Niigata	439	Urawa	349
Ichinomiya	247	Nishinomiya	394	Utsunomiya	366
Ichikawa	344	Oita	341	Wakayama	400
Iwaki	343	Okayama	537	Yao	263
Kagoshima	489	Omiya	344	Yokkaichi	252
Kanazawa	400	Osaka	2,600	Yokohama	2,724
Kawaguchi	366	Otaru	203	Yokosuka	414
Kawasaki	1,012	Sagamihara	415		
Kitakyushu	1,057	Sakai	787		

Vital statistics (in 1,000) for calendar years:

	1971	1972	1973	1974	1975	1976	1977	1978	1979
Births	2,001	2,039	2,101	2,030	1,901	1,833	1,755	1,709	1,643
Deaths	685	684	706	710	702	703	690	696	690

Crude birth rate of Japanese nationals in present area, 1979, was 14·2 per 1,000 population (1947: 3·43); crude death rate, 6; crude marriage rate, 6·8; infant mortality rate per 1,000 live births, 7·9.

EMPEROR. The Emperor bears the title of Nihon-koku Tennō ('Emperor of Japan'). **Hirohito,** born in Tōkyō, 29 April 1901; succeeded his father, Yoshihito, 25 Dec. 1926; married 26 Jan. 1924, to Princess Nagako, born 6 March 1903. Living sons: (1) Prince Akihito (Tsugunomiya), born 23 Dec. 1933; formally installed as Crown Prince on 10 Nov. 1952; married to Michiko Shoda (born 20 Oct. 1934), 10 April 1959. *Offspring:* Prince Naruhito (Hironomiya), born 23 Feb. 1960; Prince Fumihito (Ayanomiya), born 30 Nov. 1965; Princess Sayako (Norinomiya), born 18 April 1969. (2) Prince Masahito (Hitachinomiya), born 28 Nov. 1935; married to Hanako Tsugaru, 30 Sept. 1964.

By the Imperial House Law of 11 Feb. 1889, revised on 16 Jan. 1947, the succession to the throne was fixed upon the male descendants.

CONSTITUTION AND GOVERNMENT. Japan's Government is based upon the Constitution of 1947 which superseded the Meiji Constitution of 1889. In it the Japanese people pledge themselves to uphold the ideas of democracy and peace. The Emperor is the symbol of the States and of the unity of the people. Sovereign power rests with the people. The Emperor has no powers related to government. Japan renounces war as a sovereign right and the threat or the use of force as a means of settling disputes with other nations. Fundamental human rights are guaranteed.

National flag: White, with a red disc.

National anthem: Kimi ga yo wa (words 9th century, tune by Hiromori Hayashi, 1881).

Legislative power rests with the Diet, which consists of the House of Representatives (of 511 members), elected by men and women over 20 years of age for a 4-year term, and the House of Councillors of 252 members (100 elected at large and 152 from prefectural districts), one-half of its members being elected every 3 years. The Lower House controls the budget and approves treaties with foreign powers.

The former House of Peers is replaced by the House of Councillors, whose members, like those of the House of Representatives, are elected as representatives of all the people. The House of Representatives has pre-eminence over the House of Councillors.

In June 1980 the House of Representatives consisted of 286 Liberal-Democrats, 106 Socialists, 34 Komeito, 29 Communists, 33 Democratic Socialists, 12 New Liberal Club, 3 Social Democratic Federation, 8 Independents.

The Cabinet, as constituted in Sept. 1980, was as follows:

Prime Minister: Zenko Suzuki.
Justice: Seisuke Okuno.
Foreign Affairs: Masayoshi Ito.
Finance: Michio Watanabe.
Education: Tatsuo Tanaka.
Health and Welfare: Sunao Sonoda.
Agriculture, Forestry and Fishery: Takao Kameoka.
Trade and Industry: Rokusuke Tanaka.
Transport: Masajuro Shiokawa.
Postal Service: Ichiro Yamanouchi.
Labour: Masayuki Fujio.
Construction: Shigeyoshi Saito.
Home Affairs: Jiro Ishiba.

Local Government. The country is divided into 47 prefectures (*Todōfuken*), including Tōkyō-to (the capital), Ōsaka-fu and Kyōto-fu, Hokkai-dō, and 43 *Ken*. Each *Todōfuken* has its governor (*Chiji*) elected by the voters in the area. The prefectural government of Tōkyō-to is also responsible for the urban part (formerly Tōkyō-shi) of the prefecture. Each prefecture, city, town and village has a representative assembly elected by the same franchise as in parliamentary elections.

New legislation, which came into effect on 1 July 1954, has given the central government complete control of the police throughout the country.

DEFENCE

Army. The 'Ground Self-Defence Force' had in 1980 an authorized strength of 155,000 uniformed personnel, plus a reserve of 39,000 men. The Army is organized in 12 infantry divisions, 1 mechanized division, 1 airborne brigade, 1 tank brigade, 2 air defence brigades, 1 artillery, 5 engineer, 1 signal, 1 mixed and 1 helicopter brigades in addition to 8 anti-aircraft artillery groups. Equipment includes 740 tanks.

The Northern Army, stationed in Hokkaido, consists of 4 divisions (1 of which is mechanized), an artillery brigade, an anti-aircraft artillery brigade, a tank brigade and an engineering brigade. The Western Army, stationed in Kyushu, consists of 2 divisions. The North-Eastern Army (2 divisions), the Eastern Army (2 divisions) and 1 airborne brigade, the Middle Army (3 divisions). The infantry division establishment is approximately 9,000 with 4 infantry regiments or 7,000 (lower establishment) with 3 infantry regiments. Each infantry division has an artillery unit, an anti-tank unit, a tank battalion and an engineering battalion in addition to administrative units.

Navy. The 'Maritime Self-Defence Force' comprises 14 submarines, 1 large destroyer of 5,200 tons and 2 destroyers of 4,700 tons each carrying 3 helicopters, 3 guided-missile destroyers, 35 destroyers, 1 minelayer/support ship, 12 large patrol vessels, 1 modern purpose-built training ship (destroyer and frigate type, with helicopters), 33 coastal minesweepers, 2 minesweeper support ships, 4 auxiliary minesweepers, 2 submarine rescue vessels, 6 minesweeping boats, 5 fast torpedo-boats, 9 patrol boats, 6 landing ships, 1 new fleet support ship, 7 surveying vessels, 1 icebreaker (antarctic support ship), 1 cable (*ex*-minelayer), 2 oilers, 34 tugs, 12 tenders, 20 auxiliaries and 60 minor craft.

Personnel in 1980 numbered 43,000 officers and ratings including the Naval Air Arm; and 5,000 in civil maritime defence.

Coastguard. The 'Maritime Safety Agency' (Coastguard) consists of 11 regional MS headquarters, 65 MS offices, 51 MS bases, 14 air bases, 25 Detachments, 5 Control Communications Centres, 1 Traffic Advisory Service Centre, 4 hydrographic observatories and 140 navigation aids offices (with 4,816 navigation aids facilities) and controls 37 large patrol vessels, 44 medium patrol vessels, 19 small patrol vessels, 225 patrol craft, 24 hydrographic service vessels, 14 firefighting vessels, 63 guard and rescue boats and 89 navigation aids service supply vessels. Personnel in 1980 numbered 11,661 officers and men.

The Coastguard aviation service includes 19 aircraft and 29 helicopters.

Air Force. An 'Air Self-Defence Force' was inaugurated on 1 July 1954. In 1980 its equipment included 5 interceptor squadrons of F-104J Starfighters, and 5 of F-4EJ Phantoms; 3 squadrons of Mitsubishi F-1 close-support fighters; 1 squadron of RF-4E reconnaissance fighters; 3 squadrons of turbofan Kawasaki C-1 and turboprop NAMC YS-11 transports. About 30 helicopters, including S-62s and KV-107s, and MU-2S twin-turboprop aircraft perform search, rescue and general duties. Training units use piston-engined T-34 Mentor basic trainers (being replaced with Fuji T-3s), Fuji T-1 jet intermediate trainers, T-33 jet trainers and supersonic Mitsubishi T-2 jet advanced trainers. Five surface-to-air missile battalions are in service. Total strength is about 480 combat aircraft and 44,000 officers and men. Aircraft on order include 100 F-15J/DJ Eagle fighters and 4 E-2C Hawkeye AEW aircraft.

INTERNATIONAL RELATIONS

Membership. Japan is a member of UN, the Colombo Plan and OECD.

ECONOMY

Planning. The 1981–85 Plan envisages an onward growth rate of 5·5%. The real growth rate of 1980 is 4·8% and the nominal 8%. The real growth rate for 1981 is envisaged at 5·3% and the nominal 9·1%.

Budget. Ordinary revenue and expenditure for fiscal year ending 31 March 1981 balanced at 42,588,843m. yen.

Of the proposed revenue in 1980 (in 1m. yen), 26·41m. was to come from taxes and stamps, 14·27m. from public bonds. Main items of expenditure: Social security, 8,212,441; public works, 6,655,448; local government, 6,924,700; education, 4,524,955; defence, 2,230,202.

The outstanding national debt incurred by public bonds was estimated in March 1980 to be 57,300,845m. yen, including 16,351m. yen of Japan's foreign currency bonds.

Local. The estimated 1980 budgets of the prefectures and other local authorities forecast a total revenue of 41,642,600m. yen, to be made up partly by local taxes and partly by government grants and local loans.

Currency. Coins of 1, 5, 10, 50 and 100 *yen* are in circulation as well as notes of the Bank of Japan, of 100, 500, 1,000, 5,000 and 10,000 *yen*. Bank-notes for 100 *yen* are still in circulation in country districts but are gradually being replaced by coins. In March 1981, £1 = 460 *yen*; US$1 = 208 *yen*.

In Dec. 1979 the currency in circulation consisted of 19,068,622m. yen Bank of Japan notes and 932,990m. yen subsidiary coins.

Banking. The modern banking system dates from 1872. The Nippon Gingo (Bank of Japan) was founded in 1882. The Bank of Japan has undertaken to finance the Government and the banks; its function is similar to that of a Central Bank in other countries. The Bank undertakes the actual management of Treasury funds and foreign exchange control.

Gold bullion and cash holdings of the Bank of Japan at 31 Dec. 1979 stood at 211,990m. yen.

The Yokohama Specie Bank (specializing in foreign exchange) became the Bank of Tōkyō in Aug. 1954. Total assets of all banks at 31 March 1980 was 254,885,148m. yen.

The post office savings bank is modelled upon the British; deposits amounted to 51,907,486m. yen in March 1979.

Many foreign banks operate branches in Japan including: Bank of Indo-China, Hongkong & Shanghai Banking Corporation, Chartered Bank of India, Australia and China, Bank of India, Mercantile Bank of India, Bank of Korea, Bank of China, Algemene Bank Nederland NV, National Handelsbank NV, Bank of America, National City Bank of New York, Chase Manhattan Bank, Bangkok Bank and American Express Co.

Weights and Measures. The metric system was made obligatory by a law passed in March 1921, and the period of grace for its compulsory use ended on 1 April 1966.

ENERGY AND NATURAL RESOURCES

Electricity. In 1979 generating facilities were capable of an output of 131,218,000 kw.; electricity produced was 562·3m. kwh.

Oil and Gas. Output of crude petroleum, 1978, was 640,000 kl, almost entirely from oilfields on the island of Honshu, but 270·18m. kl crude oil had to be imported. Output of natural gas, 1977, 34,107,000m. kilocalories.

Minerals. Ore production in tonnes, 1978, of chromite, 8·7m.; coal, 19m.; iron, 528,000; zinc, 274·6m.; molybdenum, 145,000; manganese, 104·1m.; copper, 71,951; lead, 56,489; tungsten, 2,192; silver, 300,573 kg.; gold, 4,517 kg.

Agriculture. Agricultural workers in 1979 were 6·75m., including 0·95m. subsidiary and seasonal workers; 10% of the labour force as opposed to 24·7% in 1962. The arable land area in 1979 was 5,474,000 hectares (5,796,000 in 1970). Division of ordinary fields to non-agricultural use accounted largely for this decrease. Rice cultivation accounted for 2·5m. hectares in 1979. The area planted with industrial crops such as rapeseed, tobacco, tea, rush, etc., was 238,100 hectares in 1978.

In 1979 there were 4·3m. power cultivators and tractors in use together with 1·21m. power sprayers and 1·41m. power dusters.

Output of rice was 11·77m. in 1976, 13·1m. in 1977, 12·6m. in 1978 and 12m. in 1979.

Production in 1978 (in 1,000 tonnes) of barley was 276; wheat, 367; soybeans, 189·9. Sweet potatoes, which in the past mitigated the effects of rice famines, have, in view of rice over-production, decreased from 4,965 tons in 1965 to 1,371 tons in 1978. Domestic sugar-beet and sugar-cane production accounted for only 23% of requirement in 1978. In 1978, 2·29m. tonnes were imported, 34·8% of this being imported from Australia, 16·9% from Thailand, 21·8% from South Africa, 7·2% from Formosa, 2·4% from Philippines, 16% from Cuba.

Fruit production, 1978 (in 1,000 tonnes): Mandarins, 3,026; apples, 844; pears, 484; grapes, 327; peaches, 277; and persimmons, 286.

Livestock (1979): 4·1m. cattle (including about 1·89m. milch cows), 22,000 horses, 9·5m. pigs, 11,000 sheep, 80,000 goats, 307m. chickens. Milk output is increasing—in 1977, 574m. tonnes.

Forestry. Forests and grasslands cover about 25m. hectares (nearly 70% of the whole land area), with an estimated timber stand of 2,185·9m. cu. metres in 1976. In 1978, 42·8m. cu. metres were felled.

Fisheries. Before the War, Japanese catch represented one-half to two-thirds of the world's total fishing, in 1978 it was 15%. The catch in 1978 was 10·8m. tonnes, excluding whaling. Japan now ranks second to the USSR in whaling.

INDUSTRY AND TRADE

Industry. Japan's industrial equipment, 1977, numbered 714,177 plants of all sizes, employing 10,875,000 production workers.

Since 1920 there has been a shift from light to heavy industries. The production of electrical appliances and electronic machinery has made great strides: television sets (1979: 13·6m.), radio sets (1978: 16·3m.), cameras (1979: 12·3m.), computing machines and automation equipment are produced in increasing quantities. The chemical industry ranks third in production value after machinery and metals (1978). Production, 1978, included (in tonnes): Sulphuric acid, 6·4m.; caustic soda 2·7m.; ammonium sulphate, 1·9m.; calcium superphosphate, 551,000.

Output (1978), in 1,000 tonnes, of pig iron was 78,589; crude steel, 102,105; ordinary rolled steel, 79,749.

In 1978 paper production was 9·36m. tonnes; paperboard, 7·1m. tonnes.

Japan's textile industry before the War had 13m. cotton-yarn spindles. After the War she resumed with 2·78m. spindles; in 1964, 8·42m. spindles were operating. Output of cotton yarn, 1978, 448,000 tonnes, and of cotton cloth, 2,315m. sq. metres.

In wool, Japan aims at wool exports sufficient to pay for the imports of raw wool. Output, 1978, 109,000 tonnes of woollen yarns and 336m. sq. metres of woollen fabrics.

Output, 1978, of rayon woven fabrics, 852m. sq. metres; synthetic woven fabrics, 2,916m. sq. metres; silk fabrics, 152m. sq. metres.

Since 1956 Japan has led the world in shipbuilding, and in 1975 accounted for about 50% of the world's launchings. However, shipbuilding has been decreasing and in 1979, 4·7m. gross tons were launched (34%). In 1978, 6·3m. gross tons were launched, of which 860,000 GRT were tankers.

Labour. Total labour force, Oct. 1979, was 54·8m., of which 5·7m. were in agriculture and forestry, 450,000 in fishing, 120,000 in mining, 5·4m. in construction, 13m. in manufacturing, 14m. in commerce and finance, 3·82m. in transport and other public utilities, 9·8m. in services (including the professions) and 2·01m. in government work.

In 1979 there were 12,309,000 workers organized in 71,780 unions. The largest federation is the 'General Council of Japanese Trade Unions' (Sōhyō) with 4,553,000 members. The 'Japanese Confederation of Labour' (Dōmei Kaigi) had 2,147,000 members. The 'Federation of Independent Unions' (Chūritsu Rōren) founded in 1956 had 1,337,000 members.

In Oct. 1979, 1·11m. (2%) were unemployed. In 1979, 930,304 working days were lost in industrial stoppages.

Harari, E., *The Politics of Labor Legislation in Japan*. Univ. of California Press, 1973
Okochi, K., Karsch, B. and Levine, S. B. (eds.), *Workers and Employers in Japan*. Univ. of Tokyo Press, 1974

Commerce. Trade, excluding bullion and specie (in US$1m.; US$1 = 360 yen, 1,000 yen = US$2.77; from 1 Jan. 1972, US$1 = 308 yen, 1,000 yen = US$3.24):

	1973	1974	1975	1976	1977	1978	1979
Imports	38,314	62,110	57,863	64,799	70,808	79,343	110,672
Exports	28,930	55,536	55,753	67,225	80,494	97,543	103,031

Distribution of trade by countries (customs clearance basis) (in US$1m.):

	Exports		Imports	
	1978	1979	1978	1979
Africa	6,331	5,231	2,216	3,205
Australia	2,692	2,607	5,300	6,298
Canada	1,871	1,738	3,170	4,105
China	3,048	3,699	2,030	2,955
Fed. Rep. of Germany	3,654	4,261	1,997	2,584
Hong Kong	3,087	3,679	497	663
Latin America	3,262	3,574	2,191	3,318
Philippines	1,545	1,622	1,057	1,583
South-east Asia	16,942	19,113	14,897	22,780
Thailand	1,527	1,714	842	1,169
USSR	2,502	2,461	1,441	1,911
UK	2,341	3,097	1,378	1,681
USA	24,914	26,403	14,790	20,431

Principal items in 1979, with value in US$1m. were:

Imports, c.i.f.		Exports, f.o.b.	
Mineral fuels	45,286	Machinery and transport equipment	63,182
Foodstuffs	14,415		
Metal ores and scrap	6,850	Metals and metal products	18,379
Machinery and transport equipment	8,343	Textile products	4,908
		Chemicals	6,100
Textile fibres	2,449		

Total trade between Japan and UK (British Department of Trade returns, in £1,000 sterling):

	1976	1977	1978	1979	1980
Imports to UK	796,259	1,065,355	1,283,181	1,490,288	1,712,108
Exports and re-exports from UK	359,126	469,308	542,310	606,011	597,147

Tourism. In 1978, 1,038,900 foreigners visited Japan, 313,600 of whom came from USA, 65,800 from UK. Japanese travelling abroad totalled 3·53m. in 1978.

COMMUNICATIONS

Roads. The total length of roads (including urban and other local roads) was 1,097,248 km at 1 April 1978; the 'national' roads extended 40,196 km, of which 37,758 km were paved. Motor vehicles, at 31 Dec. 1979, numbered 35·5m., including 22·7m. passenger cars and 12·6m. commercial vehicles.

Railways. The first railway was completed in 1872, between Tōkyō and Yokohama (29 km). Total length of railways, in 1977, was 26,884 km, of which the national railways had 21,307 km (7,813 km electrified) and private railways, 5,577 km (4,929 km electrified). In 1978 the national railways carried 6,997m. passengers and 133m. tons of freight (private, 45m.).

Aviation. The principal airlines are Japan Airlines and All Nippon Airways. Japan Airlines, founded in 1953, operate international services from Tōkyō to the USA, Europe, the Middle East and Southeast Asia, including flights to London over the North Pole and to Moscow by way of Siberia. In 1977 Japanese companies carried 32·89m. passengers in domestic services and 3·74m. passengers in international services.

Shipping. On 30 June 1979 the merchant fleet consisted of 8,836 vessels (over 100 gross tons); there were 711 ships for passenger transport (1m. gross tons), 3,093 cargo ships (3·82m. gross tons) and 1,731 oil tankers (16m. gross tons).

Post and Broadcasting. The telephone services, operated by a public corporation, at 31 March 1980 had 53,634,000 instruments.

On 31 March 1980, 98·2% of all households owned colour television sets, 22·8% black and white television sets.

Cinemas (1979). Cinemas numbered 2,374 with an annual attendance of 165m. (1960: 1,014m.).

Newspapers (1980). Daily newspapers numbered 114 with aggregate circulation of 64m., including 4 major English-language newspapers.

JUSTICE, RELIGION, EDUCATION AND WELFARE

Justice. The Supreme Court is composed of the Chief Justice and 14 other judges. The Chief Justice is appointed by the Emperor, the other judges by the Cabinet. Every 10 years a justice must submit himself to the electorate. All justices and judges of the lower courts serve until they are 70 years of age.

Below the Supreme Court are 8 regional higher courts, district courts (*Chihō-saibansho*) in each prefecture (4 in Hokkaidō) and the local courts.

The Supreme Court is authorized to declare unconstitutional any act of the Legislature or the Executive which violates the Constitution.

Religion. There has normally been religious freedom, but Shintō (literally, The Way of the Gods) was given the status of *quasi*-state-religion in the 1930s; in 1945 the Allied Supreme Command ordered the Government to discontinue state support of Shintō. State subsidies have ceased for all religions, and all religious teachings are forbidden in public schools.

In Dec. 1978 Shintoism claimed 98,545,703 adherents, Buddhism 88,020,880; these figures obviously overlap. Christians numbered 950,491, of whom 578,949 are Protestants and 371,542 Catholics.

Education. Education is compulsory and free between the ages of 6 and 15. All institutions are co-educational. On 1 May 1979 there were 14,622 kindergartens with 100,300 teachers and 2,486,500 pupils; 24,888 elementary schools with 459,600 teachers and 11,629,100 pupils; 10,747 junior high schools with 246,100 teachers and 4,967,000 pupils; 5,132 senior high schools with 237,600 teachers and 4,484,900 pupils; 518 junior colleges with 16,200 teachers and 374,000 pupils.

There were also 837 special schools for handicapped children (30,900 teachers, 88,400 pupils).

Japan has 7 main state universities, formerly known as the Imperial Universities: Tōkyō University (1877); Kyōto University (1897); Tōhoku University, Sendai (1907); Kyūshū University, Fukuoka (1910); Hokkaidō University, Sapporo (1918); Osaka University (1931), and Nagoya University (1939). In addition, there are various other state and municipal as well as private universities of high standing, such as Keio (founded in 1859), Waseda, Rikkyo, Hosei, Meiji universities, and several women's universities, among which Tōkyō and Ochanomizu are most notable. There are 443 colleges and universities with (1 May 1979) 1,846,400 students and 100,700 teachers.

Social Welfare. Hospitals at the end of 1977 numbered 8,476 with 1,207,003 beds. Physicians at the end of 1977 numbered 138,316; dentists, 45,715.

There are in force various types of social security schemes, such as health insurance, unemployment insurance and old-age pensions. The total population come under one or more of these schemes.

In 1980 some 160,000 welfare commissioners were employed. In 1979 1,430,488 persons received some form of regular public assistance.

DIPLOMATIC REPRESENTATIVES

OF JAPAN IN GREAT BRITAIN (43 Grosvenor St., London, W1X OBA)

Ambassador: Naraichi Fujiyama.

OF GREAT BRITAIN IN JAPAN (1 Ichiban-cho, Chiyoda-ku, Tōkyō 102)

Ambassador: Sir James Plimsoll, CBE.

OF JAPAN IN THE USA (2520 Massachusetts Ave., NW, Washington, D.C. 20008)

Ambassador: Yoshio Ōkawara.

OF THE USA IN JAPAN (10–1, Akasaka 1-chrome, Minato-Ku, Tōkyō)

Ambassador: Michael J. Mansfield.

OF JAPAN TO THE UNITED NATIONS

Ambassador: Masahiro Nishibori.

Books of Reference

Statistics Bureau of the Prime Minister's Office: *Statistical Year-Book* (from 1949).—*Statistical Abstract* (from 1950).—*Statistical Handbook of Japan 1977.*—*Monthly Bulletin* (from April 1950)
Economic Planning Agency: *Economic Survey* (annual), *Economic Statistics* (monthly), *Economic Indicators* (monthly)
Ministry of International Trade: *Foreign Trade of Japan* (annual)
The Bank of Japan Research Department. *Money and Banking in Japan.* London, 1973
Japan Times Year Book. (*I. Year Book of Japan. II. Who's Who in Japan. III. Business Directory of Japan.*) Tokyo, first issue 1933
Treaty of Peace with Japan. (Cmd. 8392.) HMSO, 1951; (Cmd. 8601). HMSO, 1952
Ackerman, E. A., *Japan's Natural Resources.* Univ. of Chicago Press, 1953
Allen, G. C., *Short Economic History of Modern Japan.* London, 1946.—*Japan's Economic Recovery.* R. Inst. of Int. Affairs, 1957.—*Japan's Economic Expansion.* CUP, 1965
Asahi Newsprinting Co., *This is Japan.* Tokyo, annual from 1954
Baerwald, H. H., *Japan's Parliament.* CUP, 1974
Boltho, A., *Japan: An Economic Survey, 1953–1973.* OUP, 1976
Fistié, P., *La Rentrée en Scène du Japon.* Paris, 1972
Hirschmeier, J., and Tsunehiko, Y., *The Development of Japanese Business, 1600–1973.* London, 1976
Kahn, H., and Pepper, T., *The Japanese Challenge.* New York, 1979
Kenkyusha's *New Japanese–English [and English–Japanese] Dictionary.* 2 vols. New ed. Cambridge, Mass., and Berkeley, Cal., 1960
Kennedy, M. D., *A History of Japan.* London, 1963
Kitamura, H., *Choices for the Japanese Economy.* London, 1976
Langdon, F. C., *Japan's Foreign Policy.* Univ. of British Columbia Press, 1973
McNelly, T., *Politics and Government in Japan.* 2nd ed. London, 1972
Miyazaki, S., *The Japanese Dictionary Explained in English.* Tokyo, 1950
Nihon Keizai Shimbun, *Industrial Review of Japan.* Tokyo, annual, from 1956
Nippon: A Chartered Survey of Japan. Tsuneta Yano Memorial Society. Tokyo, annual
Ohkawa, K., and Rosovsky, H., *Japanese Economic Growth: Trend Acceleration in the Twentieth Century.* Stanford Univ. Press, 1973
Richardson, B. M., *The Political Culture of Japan.* Univ. of California Press, 1974
Sansom, G. B., *The Western World and Japan.* New York, 1950.—*A History of Japan.* 3 vols. London, 1958–64
Simonis, H. and U. E. (ed.), *Japan: Economic and Social Studies in Development.* Wiesbaden, 1974
Tanaka, K., *Building a New Japan: A Plan for Remodelling the Japanese Archipelago.* Tokyo, 1973
Vogel, E. F., *Japan as Number One.* Harvard Univ. Press, 1979
Yabuki, K. (ed.), *Japan Bibliographic Annual.* 2 vols. Tokyo, annual

REPUBLIC OF JIBUTI

Capital: Jibuti
Population: 300,000 (1980)

HISTORY. At a referendum held on 19 March 1967, 60% of the electorate voted for continued association with France rather than independence and the new statute for the territory came into being on 5 July 1967. In Jan. 1976, following discussions between Ali Aref and President Giscard d'Estaing, it was announced that the French Government affirmed that the Territory of the Afars and the Issas was destined for independence but no date was fixed. Legislative elections were held on 8 May and independence as the Republic of Jibuti was achieved on 27 June 1977.

AREA AND POPULATION. Jibuti is situated in the Gulf of Aden between the Somali Republic and Ethiopia. The frontier starts from Loyada, on the coast, 20 km south-east of Jibuti, passes by Djalelo, the Degoueiné Mountains, crosses the Addis Ababa railway at Kilometre 110, 6 km to the north of Daouenlé, encloses the Gobaad Plain and Lake Abbé, passes Mount Moussa Ali near Daddato, and terminates at Cape Doumeirah, opposite Perim, on the Straits of Bab el Mandeb.

Jibuti has an area of 23,000 sq. km (8,880 sq. miles). The population was estimated in 1980 at 300,000, of whom 47% were Somali, 37% Afar, 8% European and 6% Arab. Jibuti, the seat of government, had (1981) 150,000 inhabitants.

CONSTITUTION AND GOVERNMENT. On 8 May 1977 a 65-seat Chamber of Deputies was elected comprising 33 Issa (Somali), 30 Afar and 2 Arab members.

The Cabinet at 2 Oct. 1978 was composed as follows:

President: Hassan Gouled Aptidon.
Prime Minister and Ports: Barkat Gourad Hamadou.
Foreign Affairs and Co-operation: Moumin Bahdon Farah. *Interior:* Idriss Farah Abane. *Defence:* Habib Mohammed Loita. *Finance and Economy:* Ibrahim Soultan. *Justice and Religious Affairs:* Helaf Orbis. *Commerce, Transport and Tourism:* Aden Robleh Awale. *Youth and Sports:* Mohammed Djaba Elabe. *Public Health:* Mohammed Ahmed Issa (Cheiko). *Labour and Social Welfare:* Ahmed Hassan Liban (Gouhad). *Civil Service:* Mohammed Said. *Public Works:* Omar Kamil Warsama. *Industry:* Ali Mohammed Houmed. *Agriculture and Rural Development:* Mahamoud Del Wais.

National flag: Horizontally blue over green, with a white triangle based on the hoist charged with a red star.

DEFENCE

Army. The army comprises 1 infantry battalion. The armed forces, all services, number (1980), 1,000.

Air Force. As the nucleus of an air force, the French *Armée de l'Air* transferred to the Jibuti Government 2 Noratlas piston-engined tactical transport aircraft. These have since been supplemented by 2 light aircraft and an Alouette helicopter.

INTERNATIONAL RELATIONS

Membership. Jibuti is a member of UN, OAU, the Arab League and an ACP State of the EEC.

ECONOMY

Budget. The ordinary budget for 1980 envisaged an expenditure of 12,100m. Jibuti francs.

Currency. The *Jibuti franc* was introduced on 17 March 1949. The currency is covered 100% by a US dollar fund. In March 1981, £1 = 360 *Jibuti francs*; US$1 = 162·5 *Jibuti francs*.

MINERALS. Minerals supposed to exist are gypsum, mica, amethyst and sulphur.

AGRICULTURE. Mainly market gardening at the oasis of Ambouli and neat urban areas. Livestock (1979): 32,000 cattle, 310,000 sheep, 520,000 goats, 5,000 donkeys, 25,000 camels.

COMMERCE. The main economic activity is the operation of the port. The chief imports are cotton goods, sugar, cement, flour and benzene; the chief exports are hides, cattle and coffee (transit from Ethiopia). Special trade in 1m. Jibuti francs:

	1973	1974	1975
Imports	12,675	21,698	24,166
Exports	3,499	3,678	2,639

Total trade between Jibuti and UK (British Department of Trade returns, in £1,000 sterling):

	1976	1977	1978	1979	1980
Imports to UK	82	99	14	328	303
Exports and re-exports from UK	5,046	7,432	7,145	6,499	6,682

COMMUNICATIONS

Roads. There were (1978) 1,650 km of roads, of which 75 km was hard-surfaced. In 1977 there were 11,800 passenger cars and 3,300 lorries.

Railway. For the line Jibuti-Addis Ababa *see* p. 442. In 1969–70 the railway carried goods traffic of 411,460 tons and 457,000 passengers.

Aviation. Air Djibouti provides services to Addis Ababa, Nairobi, Jidda and the Gulf. Other airlines serving Jibuti airport are Ethiopian Airlines, Air France, Air Tanzania and Yemen Airways Corporation.

Shipping. In 1970 there entered at Jibuti 1,217 vessels, unloading 232,866 tons and loading 88,092 tons of merchandise.

Post and Broadcasting. Number of telephones (1978), 3,675. *Office de Radiodiffusion-Télévision Française* broadcasts on medium- and short-waves in French, Somali, Afar and Arabic. There is a television transmitter in Jibuti, broadcasting for 19 hours a week. Number of receivers (1973): radio, 10,000; TV, 2,500.

Cinemas. In 1975 there were 4 cinemas with a seating capacity of 5,800.

EDUCATION. In 1976 there were 21 public and 6 private schools with 6,210 pupils for primary education. There were 2,000 pupils receiving a secondary education in high school, technical school and private secondary schools.

HEALTH. There were (1975) 11 hospitals and dispensaries with 1,028 beds; 52 physicians.

DIPLOMATIC REPRESENTATIVES

OF JIBUTI IN GREAT BRITAIN

Ambassador: Ahmed Ibrahim Abdi (resides in Paris).

OF GREAT BRITAIN IN JIBUTI

Ambassador: J. F. Walker, MBE (resides in Sana'a).

OF THE USA IN JIBUTI (Villa Plateau du Serpent, Jibuti)

Chargé d'Affaires: Walter S. Clarke.

OF JIBUTI TO THE UNITED NATIONS

Ambassador: Saleh Haji Farah Dirir.

Books f Reference

Poinsot, J.-P., *Djibouti et la Côte française des Somalis.* Paris, 1965
Thompson, V., and Adloff, R., *Djibouti and the Horn of Africa.* Stanford Univ. Press, 1967

THE HASHEMITE KINGDOM OF JORDAN

Capital: Amman
Population: 2·15m. (1979) E. Bank
0·8m. (1976) W. Bank
GNP per capita: US$1,050 (1978)

Al Mamlaka al Urduniya al Hashemiyah

HISTORY. By a Treaty, signed in London on 22 March 1946, Britain recognized Transjordan as a sovereign independent state. A new Anglo-Transjordan treaty was signed in Amman on 15 March 1948. The treaty was to remain in force for 20 years, but by mutual consent was terminated on 13 March 1957.

The Arab Federation between the Kingdoms of Iraq and Jordan, which was concluded on 14 Feb. 1958, lapsed after the revolution in Iraq of 14 July 1958, and was officially terminated by royal decree on 1 Aug. 1958.

On 25 May 1946 the Amir Abdullah assumed the title of King, and when the treaty was ratified on 17 June 1946 the name of the territory was changed to that of 'The Hashemite Kingdom of Jordan'. The legislature consists of a lower house of 60 members elected by universal suffrage (30 from East Jordan and 30 from West Jordan), and a senate of 30 members nominated by the King.

AREA AND POPULATION. The part of Palestine remaining to the Arabs under the armistice with Israel 3 April 1949, with the exception of the Gaza strip, was in Dec. 1949 placed under Jordan rule and formally incorporated in Jordan on 24 April 1950; for the frontier lines *see* map in THE STATESMAN'S YEAR-BOOK, 1951. On 10 Aug. 1965 a treaty with Saudi Arabia provided for an exchange of about 6,000–7,000 sq. km in order to facilitate the development of the port of Aqaba.

Total East Bank area, 91,000 sq. km. West Bank enclaves 5,000 sq. km: census population (18 Nov. 1961), 1,706,226; estimate, 1976, 2,751,968 (1,951,968 in East Bank, 800,000 in West Bank). In 1961, 805,450 lived in West Jordan and 834,589 in East Jordan, including some 550,000 refugees from Palestine but excluding some 53,000 nomads. About 63,000 Jordanians live abroad. Density of population per sq. km, 51 in East Jordan, 143 in West Jordan.

The country is divided into 8 districts (*muhafaza*), viz., Amman, Irbid, Balqa, Karak, Ma'an, Jerusalem, Hebron and Nablus. The last 3 named districts are known collectively as the West Bank, which, since the hostilities of June 1967, has been occupied by Israel.

The largest towns, with estimated population, 1977: Amman, the capital, 732,587; Zarka, 269,780; Irbid, 139,780.

In 1975 registered births numbered 81,659; deaths, 6,788; marriages, 14,137; divorces, 2,345.

KING. The Kingdom is a constitutional monarchy headed by HM King **Hussein**, GCVO, eldest son of King Talal, who, being incapacitated by mental illness, was deposed by Parliament on 11 Aug. 1952 and died 8 July 1972. The King was born 14 Nov. 1935, and married Princess Dina Abdul Hamid on 19 April 1955 (divorced 1957), Toni Avril Gardiner (Muna al Hussein) on 25 May 1961 (divorced 1972), Alia Toukan on 26 Dec. 1972 (died in air crash 1977) and Elizabeth Halaby on 15 June 1978. *Offspring:* Princess Alia, born 13 Feb. 1956; Prince Abdulla, born 30 Jan. 1962; Prince Faisal, born 11 Oct. 1963; Princesses Zein and Aisha, born 23 April 1968; Princess Haya, born 3 May 1974; Prince Ali, born 23 Dec. 1975; Prince Hamzah, born 1 April 1980. *Crown Prince* (appointed 1 April 1965): Prince Hassan, younger brother of the King.

CONSTITUTION AND GOVERNMENT. The Constitution passed on 7 Nov. 1951 provides that the Cabinet is responsible to Parliament.

On 9 Nov. 1974 both Houses of Parliament approved amendments to the Constitution by which the King was empowered to dissolve Parliament and delay calling elections for 12 months.

On 5 Feb. 1976 both Houses of Parliament approved amendments to the Constitution by which the King was empowered to postpone calling elections until further notice. The lower house was dissolved. This step was taken because no elections could be held in the West Bank which has been under Israeli occupation since June 1967.

The Cabinet, in Feb. 1981, was composed as follows:

Prime Minister and Minister of Defence: Modar Badran.

Information: Adnan Abo Odeh. *Finance:* Salem Musadeh. *Culture, Youth, Tourism and Antiquities:* Maan Abu Nowwar. *Justice:* Ahmad Abdul Karim Tarawneh. *Agriculture:* Marwan Dodeen. *Communications:* Mohammad Adoub Al-Zaber. *Occupied Territories:* Hasan Ibrahim. *Awqaf and Religious Affairs:* Kamel Sharif. *Foreign Affairs:* Marwan Al-Kasim. *Interior:* Suleiman Arar. *Supplies:* Ibrahim Ayoub. *Transport, and Minister of State for Prime Minister's Affairs:* Ali Suheimat, Hikmat Alsaket. *Education:* Said El-Tall. *Health:* Zuhair Malhas. *Social Development:* Inam Mufti. *Labour:* Jawad Anani. *Industry and Commerce:* Waleed Asfour. *Public Works:* Awni Al-Masri. *Municipal and Rural Affairs:* Hasan Al-Momani.

There is also a National Consultative Council; the present 60-member council took office in April 1980 under the presidency of Ahmed Mahhud al-Tarawinah.

National flag: Three horizontal stripes of black, white, green, with a red triangle based on the hoist, bearing a white 7-pointed star.

The official language of the country is Arabic.

DEFENCE

Army. The Army is organized in 2 armoured and 2 mechanized divisions, 1 independent tank brigade, 4 artillery regiments, and 2 anti-aircraft brigades. In addition there are 3 special forces battalions. Total strength (1980) 60,000 men.

Navy. The Coastal Guard or Jordan Sea Force has 1 command boat and 9 patrol launches based at Aqaba. Personnel (1981) totalled 300 officers and ratings.

Air Force. The Air Force has 1 squadron and an OCU equipped with F-5A supersonic fighter-bombers, 2 squadrons of F-5E Tiger II interceptors and 1 squadron of F-104A Starfighter interceptors. (On order are 17 Mirage F.1 fighters.) There are 4 C-130B/H Hercules and 4 CASA Aviocar turboprop transports, S-76, Alouette III and Hughes 500D helicopters, and T-37B jet trainers. Basic training on piston-engined Bulldogs is centred at the Royal Academy of Aeronautics. Hawk surface-to-air missiles equip 14 batteries. Strength is about 7,000 officers and men.

INTERNATIONAL RELATIONS

Membership. Jordan is a member of the UN and the Arab League.

ECONOMY

Planning. A 5-year plan (1976–80) aimed at achieving a growth rate of 12% per annum; actual annual average growth, 10%.

Budget. The budget estimates for the year 1978–79 provide for revenue of JD.384·1m. and expenditure of JD.495·6m. Of revenue, JD.203·2m. was from foreign grants and aid.

Currency. The Jordan *dinar*, divided into 1,000 *fils.* The Jordan dinar equals £1·5. Jordan is a member of the sterling area. The following bank-notes and coins are in circulation: 10, 5 dinars, 1 dinar, 500 fils (notes), 250, 100, 50, 25, 20 fils (cupronickel), 10, 5, 1 fils (bronze). Circulation on 31 Dec. 1976 was JD.164·93m. In March 1981, £1 = JD.0·694; US$ = JD.0·32.

Banking. The Central Bank of Jordan started operations on 1 Oct. 1964, taking over the sterling assets and the commitments of the Jordan Currency Board. Commercial bank deposits in March 1979 were JD.508·5m.

NATURAL RESOURCES

Minerals. Phosphates production in 1979 was 2,828,100 tons. Potash is found in the Dead Sea. Reserves, over 800m. tonnes. A potash plant is being built on the south-east shore to extract compounds by solar evaporation. Cement production (1979), 623,000 tons.

Agriculture. The country east of the Hejaz Railway line is largely desert; north-western Jordan is potentially of agricultural value and an integrated Jordan Valley project began in 1973; 21,000 hectares had been irrigated by 1980. The main crops are tomatoes and other vegetables, fruit, wheat (badly affected by drought 1975–80).

Production in 1979 included (in tonnes): Tomatoes, 172,000; citrus fruit, 30,000; grapes, 23,000; wheat, 16,000.

Livestock (1979): 875,000 sheep; 382,000 goats; 33,000 cattle; 10,000 camels. 2,923 tractors and 189 cultivators were in use in 1975.

COMMERCE. Imports in 1978 were valued at JD.458·8m. and exports and re-exports at JD.90·8m. Imports: Consumer goods, JD.175·6m., raw materials, JD.117·2m. of which oil and fuel, JD.46·7m. Imported from: FRG, JD.60m.; Saudi Arabia, JD.43·5m.; UK, JD.36·5m.; USA, JD.33·6m.; Italy, JD.30·5m.; Japan, JD.31m. Exports: Raw materials (mainly phosphates), JD.23·3m.; consumer goods, JD.32·6m. Exported to: Saudi Arabia, JD.17·7m.; Syria, JD.10·4m.; Kuwait, JD.4·2m.; India, JD.3·5m.; Iraq, JD.3·4m.

Total trade between Jordan and UK (British Department of Trade returns, in £1,000 sterling):

	1976	1977	1978	1979	1980
Imports to UK	892	1,996	6,153	7,855	8,152
Exports and re-exports from UK	55,737	48,974	67,450	86,894	100,318

INDUSTRY. The most important activity is processing potash and other minerals. There is a large chemical fertilizer plant at Aqaba, an oil refinery at Zarka and a cement plant at Fuhers. Manufacturing contributed JD.61·4m. to total GNP in 1978.

TOURISM. In 1978, 1·8m. foreigners visited Jordan, generating an income of JD.104m.

COMMUNICATIONS

Roads. Asphalt roads connect Amman with all the chief towns in the country. Unmetalled roads have been constructed, making motor traffic possible from Amman to most other areas. The road from Amman to Ma'an and Aqaba (394 km) has branches to Karak, Tafileh, Shobak and Wadi Musa (Petra). The town of Jerash is joined by a good road to Amman. The normal asphalted route from Amman to Deraa (in Syria) and thence to Damascus is through Jerash. The oasis of Azraq may be reached by motor car from Mafraq, Zarka or Amman. Total length of public highways, 4,095 km. Motor vehicles in 1975 included 33,132 private passenger cars and taxis, 8,378 goods vehicles, 1,887 motor cycles, 729 buses.

Railways. The 1,050 mm gauge Hejaz Railway runs from the Syrian border at Nassib to Ma'an and Naqb Ishtar and Aqaba Port (total, 618 km). The railway linking Damascus with Ma'an passes through Amman. In 1978 the railways carried 53,000 passengers and 1m. tons of freight.

Aviation (1975). The Royal Jordanian Airlines (ALIA) maintains services from Amman to Amsterdam, Athens, Abu Dhabi, Aleppo, Aqaba, Baghdad, Bahrain, Bangkok, Beirut, Brussels, Cairo, Casablanca, Colombo, Copenhagen, Damascus, Deir ez Zor, Dubai, Dhahran, Doha, Frankfurt, Geneva, Istanbul, Jidda, Kuala Lumpur, Kuwait, London, Madrid, Oman, Paris, Rome, Singapore, Tehrán and Vienna. Alitalia, KLM, Middle East Airways, Egyptian Airlines, Saudi Arabian,

Iraqi, Kuwaiti, British Airways, Swissair, Syrian Arab Airlines, and Aeroflot also operate in Jordan.

Shipping (1978). The port of Aqaba handled 3·66m. tons of cargo.

Post. There were 53,107 telephones in 1978 (35,500 in Amman).

Cinemas (1975). Cinemas numbered 40 with a total attendance of 4,341,900.

Newspapers (1976). There were 6 daily (including 1 in English) and 5 weekly papers.

RELIGION, EDUCATION AND WELFARE

Religion. About 80% of the population are Sunni Moslems.

Education (1977, East Bank only). There were 153 pre-primary schools with 440 teachers and 14,000 pupils; 1,109 primary schools with 12,757 teachers and 414,490 pupils; secondary schools had 9,394 teachers and 200,916 pupils and all places of higher education had 17,219 students (of which 8,358 were in universities) and 1,125 teaching staff (568). The University of Jordan, inaugurated on 15 Dec. 1962 had 5,307 students (including 1,694 girls) and 302 teachers. The Yarmouk University (Irbid) was inaugurated in 1976 with (1980) 6,000 students.

In 1976 5 teacher-training colleges had 5,104 students (including 1,870 girls) and 229 teachers. Three agricultural schools had 40 teachers and 591 students; 10 industrial schools had 157 teachers and 1,911 pupils, and 3 nursing, midwifery and childcare schools had 25 teachers and 323 students. One social service institute had 6 teachers and 52 students. Six vocational centres had 32 teachers and 424 pupils.

Health (1975). There were 796 physicians, 145 dentists and 31 hospitals with 3,274 beds.

DIPLOMATIC REPRESENTATIVES

OF JORDAN IN GREAT BRITAIN (6 Chester Terr., London, NW1)

Ambassador: Ibrahim Izziddin.

OF GREAT BRITAIN IN JORDAN (Third Circle, Jebel Amman)

Ambassador: A. B. Urwick, CMG.

OF JORDAN IN THE USA (2319 Wyoming Ave., NW, Washington, D.C., 20008)

Ambassador: Abdullah Salah.

OF THE USA IN JORDAN (Jebel Amman, Amman)

Ambassador: Nicholas A. Veliotes.

OF JORDAN TO THE UNITED NATIONS

Ambassador: Dr Hazem Nuseibeh.

Books of Reference

The Department of Statistics, Ministry of National Economy, publishes a *Statistical Yearbook* (in Arabic and English), latest issue 1968, and a *Statistical Guide*, latest issue 1965.—*External Trade Statistics*, 1968.—*National Accounts and Input–Output Analysis, 1959–65*, 1967

The Constitution of the Hashemite Kingdom of Jordan. Amman, 1952

Aruri, N. H., *Jordan: A Study in Political Development (1921–1965)*. The Hague, 1972

Glubb, J. B., *The Story of the Arab Legion*. London, 1948.—*A Soldier with the Arabs*. London, 1957

Haas, J., *Husseins Königreich: Jordaniens Stellung in Nahen Osten*. Munich, 1975

Morris, J., *The Hashemite Kings*. London, 1959

Seton, C. R. W., *Legislation of Transjordan, 1918–30*. London, 1931. [Continued by the Government of Jordan as an annual publication: *Jordan Legislation*. Amman, 1932 ff.]

Toni, Y. T., and Mousa, S., *Jordan: Land and People*. Amman, 1973

DEMOCRATIC KAMPUCHEA

Capital: Phnom Penh
Population: 7·7m. (1976)
GNP per capita: No accurate
estimate available (1981)

Cambodia

Since April 1975 the situation in Democratic Kampuchea has been such that it has been impossible to obtain reliable statistical and other information.

HISTORY. The recorded history of Cambodia, starts at the beginning of the Christian era with the Kingdom of Fou-Nan, whose territories at one time included parts of Thailand, Malaya, Cochin-China and Laos. The religious, cultural and administrative inspirations of this state came from India. The Kingdom was absorbed at the end of the 6th century by the Khmers, under whose monarchs was built, between the 9th and 13th centuries, the splendid complex of shrines and temples at Angkor. Attacked on either side by the Vietnamese and the Thai from the 15th century on, Cambodia was saved from annihilation by the establishment of a French protectorate in 1863. Thailand eventually recognized the protectorate and renounced all claims to suzerainty in exchange for Cambodia's north-western provinces of Battambang and Siem Reap, which were, however, returned under a Franco-Thai convention of 1907, confirmed in the Franco-Thai treaty of 1937. In 1904 the province of Stung Treng, formerly administered as part of Laos, was attached to Cambodia. For history to 1949 *see* THE STATESMAN'S YEAR-BOOK, 1973–74, p. 1112.

In 1949 Cambodia was granted independence as an Associate State of the French Union. The transfer of the French military powers to the Cambodian Government of 9 Nov. 1953 is considered in Cambodia as the attainment of sovereign independence. In Jan. 1955 Cambodia became financially and economically independent, both of France and the other two former Associate States of French Indo-China, Vietnam and Laos.

Anti-French guerrilla bands had operated in the jungle from 1945, the most important being a nationalist group known as the Khmer Issarak led by Son Ngoc Thanh, who had, briefly, been Prime Minister during the Japanese occupation. By 1953 Communist bands drawn from the Vietnamese minority and controlled by the Vietminh were active, and in 1954 regular Vietminh forces invaded Cambodia. Fighting came to an end with the conclusion on 21 July 1954, at the Geneva Conference, of the agreement on Cambodia, which ensured the withdrawal of French and Vietminh troops, and most of the Khmer Issarak bands then surrendered.

The International Control Commission was withdrawn in Dec. 1969 at the request of Prince Sihanouk.

Following a period of increasing economic difficulties and growing indirect involvement in the Vietnamese war Prince Sihanouk was deposed in March 1970 and on 9 Oct. 1970 the Kingdom of Cambodia became the Khmer Republic. From 1970 hostilities extended throughout most of the country involving North and South Vietnamese and US forces as well as Republican and anti-Republican Khmer troops. During 1973 direct American and North Vietnamese participation in the fighting came to an end, leaving a civil war situation which continued during 1974 with large-scale fighting between forces of the Khmer Republic supported by American arms and economic aid and the forces of the United National Cambodian Front including 'Khmer Rouge' communists supported by North Vietnam and China.

After unsuccessful attempts to capture Phnom Penh in 1973 and 1974, the Khmer Rouge ended the 5-year war in April 1975, when the remnants of the republican forces surrendered the city.

From April 1975 the Khmer Rouge instituted a harsh and highly regimented régime. They cut the country off from normal contact with the world and expelled all foreigners. All cities and towns were forcibly evacuated and the population were set to work in the fields.

The régime had difficulties with the Vietnamese from 1975 and this escalated into full-scale fighting in 1977–78. On 7 Jan. 1979, in a surprise advance, Phnom Penh was captured by the Vietnamese, and the Prime Minister, Pol Pot, fled. In March 1981 the war with Vietnam was still continuing.

AREA AND POPULATION. Kampuchea is bounded north by Laos and Thailand, in the west by Thailand, east by Vietnam and south by the Gulf of Thailand. It has an area about 181,000 sq. km (71,000 sq. miles), divided into 17 provinces: Kompong Thom (population, 322,000), Kompong Cham (820,000), Battambang (551,860), Kampot (337,879), Siem Reap (313,000), Kompong Chhang (273,000), Kompong Speu (307,000), Takeo (467,000), Kratié (136,000), Stung Treng (136,000), Svay Rieng (287,000), Prey Veng (492,000), Pursat (180,000), Kandal (population, excluding Phnom Penh, 706,000), Ratanakiri (49,400), Mondolkiri (14,300), Koh Kong (38,700).

The total population of 7,735,279 (1976) included Chinese and Chams. No estimates were possible in 1978 or 1979. In the uplands and in the north-east live various groups of hillmen, known as Khmer-Loeu.

The chief towns are Phnom Penh, the capital located at the junction of the Mekong and Tonle Sap rivers, and Battambang. Populations of major towns have fluctuated greatly since 1970 by flows of refugees from rural areas and from one town to another. Phnom Penh formerly had a population of at least 2·5m. but a 1977 estimate puts it at 50,000. Khmer is the official language.

GOVERNMENT. For period 1972–75 *see* THE STATESMAN'S YEAR-BOOK, 1975–76, p. 1100.

A new Constitution was approved on 15 Dec. 1975 and on 22 March 1976 a legislature was elected consisting of 204 men and 46 women. On 5 April Prince Sihanouk resigned and Khieu Samphan became Head of State on 14 April. On 8 Jan. 1979 the Kampuchean United Front for National Salvation established an 8-man revolutionary council to administer the country. In Dec. 1979 Pol Pot was replaced by the President, Khieu Samphan, as Prime Minister, but Pol Pot still held the post of Supreme Military Commander.

National flag: Red with a silhouette of the temple of Angkor Wat in the centre in yellow.

DEFENCE. Since the end of the war in April 1975 there has been no accurate data on defence and the three sections below should be treated with severe reserve.

Army. No accurate data was available in early 1981.

Navy. The Marine Royale Khmer was established on 1 March 1954 and became Marine Nationale Khmer on 9 Oct. 1970. It includes, 23 coastal patrol craft, 25 river patrol boats and 65 small craft, converted junks, etc. Less than a third of this force is operational and the residual navy has little fighting value. Two patrol vessels and 2 support (landing) gunboats escaped from Khmer Rouge, and 2 torpedo boats were believed to have sunk. Units since stricken include 7 amphibious vessels, 8 coastal patrol craft and 40 river patrol boats.

Naval and marine personnel in 1981 did not exceed 4,000.

Air Force. In 1974 the Air Force had a strength of about 7,000 officers and men, including 120 pilots, with about 200 aircraft, none of them jets. Combat squadrons operated approximately 60 T-28 piston-engined light attack aircraft. The remaining equipment comprised C-123 and C-47 transports, UH-1H and Alouette helicopters, and U-1A, O-1A/D and AU-24A light aircraft. It is not known how many of these aircraft remain serviceable.

ECONOMY

Currency. Under the Paris agreements of 29 Dec. 1954, between the Associate States and France, the parity of the Cambodian *piastre* (henceforth to be known as a *riel*) was to be maintained for the time being at 10 francs = 1 *riel*. In 1978 money had been officially abolished and no wages or salaries were paid. In 1980 the use of money was restored.

Banking. In 1964 all bank functions were taken over by government banks. In 1972 legislation permitted the re-opening of foreign banks but by the end of Dec. 1973 only a few representational offices had opened. In 1979 there was no longer anything that could be called a normal banking system.

NATURAL RESOURCES

Minerals. A phosphate factory, jointly controlled by the State and private interests, was set up in 1966 near a deposit of an estimated 350,000 tons. Another deposit of about the same size is earmarked for exploitation. High-grade iron-ore deposits (possibly as much as 2·5m. tons) exist in Northern Khmer, but are not exploited commercially because of transportation difficulties. Some small-scale gold panning (6,687 troy oz. in 1963) and gem (mainly zircon) mining is carried out at Pailin where there is potential for considerable expansion. In Sept. 1972 a French company began drilling for oil in offshore waters.

Agriculture. The overwhelming majority of the population is normally engaged in agriculture, fishing and forestry. Of the country's total area of 44m. acres, about 20m. are cultivable and over 20m. are forest land. Some 4m. acres are cultivated, well over half being devoted to rice production. Before the spread of war the high productivity provided for a low, but well-fed standard of living for the peasant farmers, the majority of whom owned the land they worked. A relatively small proportion of the food production entered the cash economy. The war and unwise pricing policies have led to a disastrous reduction in production to a stage in which the country had become a net importer of rice in 1972 and 1973 and continued to be so in 1974. Since April 1975 a vigorous agricultural programme has been implemented to meet food shortages.

A crop of about 635,000 tonnes of paddy were produced in 1974. Rubber production in 1968 amounted to 49,000 tonnes but less than 10,000 tonnes in 1972.

Other products are maize, and, in usual order of value, livestock, timber, pepper, haricot beans, soybeans and fish.

Livestock (1979) FAO estimate: Cattle, 700,000; buffaloes, 460,000; sheep, 1,000; pigs, 500,000; horses, 8,000; poultry, 3·6m.

Forestry. Much of Kampuchea's surface is covered by potentially valuable forests, 3·8m. hectares of which are reserved by the Government to be awarded to concessionaires, and are not at present worked to an appreciable extent. The remainder is available for exploitation by the local residents, and as a result some areas are over-exploited and conservation is not practised. There are substantial reserves of pitch pine.

Fisheries. Kampuchea has the greatest fresh-water fish resources in South-East Asia but production in 1970 (30,000 tons) was about a third of that for 1966.

INDUSTRY AND TRADE

Industry. Some development of industry had taken place before the spread of open warfare in 1970. Industry established and in operation in Jan. 1970 included a motor-vehicle assembly plant, 3 cigarette manufacturing concerns, a modern factory, several metal fabricating concerns, a distillery, a saw-mill, textile, fish canning, plywood, paper, cement, sugar sack, tyre, pottery and glassware factories and a cotton-ginnery. In the private sector there are about 3,200 manufacturing enterprises, producing a wide range of goods; most of them are small family concerns. An oil refinery at Kompong Som came into production in 1969 but was put out of action by an attack in early 1971. Since April 1975 a programme for repairing factories has been started and some 70 are back in production.

Commerce. Principal imports by order of value (1972) were petroleum products, metals and machinery (including vehicles), general foodstuffs and chemicals.

The only recorded export in 1972 was 7,328 tonnes of rubber. Much of the country's trade is with Hong Kong and Singapore.

Total trade between Kampuchea and UK (British Department of Trade returns, in £1,000 sterling):

	1975	1976	1977	1978	1979	1980
Imports to UK	147	228	86	120	83	73
Exports and re-exports from UK	456	61	92	52	401	825

COMMUNICATIONS

Roads. There were, in 1970, 2,574 km of asphalt roads (including the 'Khmer–American Friendship Highway' from outside Phnom Penh to close to Kompong Som, built under the US aid programme and opened in July 1959), 359 km of macadamized roads, and about 1,213 km of improved dirt roads. Since 1970 many road bridges have been destroyed and long stretches of highway closed to traffic or open only to escorted convoys.

Railways. A line of 385 km (metre gauge) links Phnom Penh to Poipet (Thai frontier). In 1969 traffic amounted to 170m. passenger-km and 76m. ton-km. Work was completed during 1969 on a line Phnom Penh–Kompong Som *via* Takeo and Kampot. Total length, 649 km but by 1973 only a short stretch between Battambang and the Thai border remained in operation, the remainder having been closed by military action. Passenger and freight trains were running over about 80% of the network in 1980.

Aviation. The Pochentong airport is 10 km from Phnom Penh. The airport at Siem Reap has been closed to international traffic since 1971.

Shipping. The port of Phnom Penh can be reached by the Mekong (through Vietnam) by ships of between 3,000 and 4,000 tons. In 1970, 97 ocean-going vessels imported 51,300 tons of cargo at Phnom Penh and exported 86,400 tons.

A new ocean port has been built under the French aid programme at Kompong Som (formerly Sihanoukville) on the Gulf of Siam and is being increasingly used by long-distance shipping.

Post. There were 58 post offices functioning in 1968 but in 1979 it was doubtful if any offices operate. There are telephone exchanges in all the main towns; number of telephones in 1968, 6,325. Phnom Penh has a direct telephone link with Hong Kong, Paris and Tōkyō; and is linked by teletype with Hong Kong, Osaka, Paris and Saigon. Hong Kong is by far the most important link for both systems. There is an International Telex network in Phnom Penh and direct telephone and telegraphic links with Singapore.

RELIGION. The majority of the population practised Theravada Buddhism before 1975. The Constitution of 1976 ended Buddhism as the State religion. There are small Roman Catholic and Moslem minorities.

EDUCATION (1970–71). There were 1,490 primary schools (337,290 pupils) compared with 5,699 and 989,464 in 1969–70, 95 secondary schools (81,611 pupils) and 12,453 students in higher education. These figures show the disruption caused by the spread of war in 1970 which lead to the concentration of all university education in Phnom Penh and closed many schools in rural areas and provincial towns. In 1979 only a small minority receive more than basic primary education.

DIPLOMATIC REPRESENTATIVES

OF DEMOCRATIC KAMPUCHEA IN GREAT BRITAIN
(26 Townsend Rd., London, NW8 6LE)

Embassy closed.

OF GREAT BRITAIN IN DEMOCRATIC KAMPUCHEA
(96 Moha Vithei, Phnom Penh)

All staff temporarily withdrawn from post.

OF DEMOCRATIC KAMPUCHEA IN USA (4500–16th St., NW, Washington, DC., 20011)

Embassy closed.

OF THE USA IN DEMOCRATIC KAMPUCHEA

Embassy closed on 12 April 1975.

Books of Reference

Annuaire Statistique Retrospectif du Cambodge. Vol. I, 1937–57; vol. II, 1958–60. Ministry of Planning, Phnom-Penh

Indo-China: Geographical Appreciation. Department of Mines and Technical Surveys. Ottawa, 1953

Barron, J., and Paul, A., *Murder of a Gentle Land.* New York, 1977.—*Peace with Horror.* London, 1977

Debré, F., *La Révolution de la Forêt.* Paris, 1976

Herz, M. F., *A Short History of Cambodia.* New York and London, 1958

Kirk, D., *Wider War.* London, 1971

Leifer, M., *Cambodia: The Search for Security.* London, 1967

McDonald, M., *Angkor.* London, 1958

Migozzi, J., *Cambodge.* Paris, 1973

Ponchaud, F., *Cambodia, Year Zero.* London, 1978

Shawcross, W., *The Sideshow: Nixon, Kissinger and the Destruction of Cambodia.* London, 1979

KENYA

Jamhuri ya Kenya

Capital: Nairobi
Population: 15·32m. (1979)
GNP per capita: US$320 (1978)

HISTORY. Until Kenya became independent on 12 Dec. 1963, it consisted of the colony and the protectorate. The protectorate comprised the mainland dominions of the Sultan of Zanzibar, viz., a coastal strip of territory 10 miles wide, to the northern branch of the Tana River; also Mau, Kipini and the Island of Lamu, and all adjacent islands between the rivers Umba and Tana. The Sultan on 8 Oct. 1963 ceded the coastal strip to Kenya with effect from 12 Dec. 1963.

The colony and protectorate, formerly known as the East African Protectorate were, on 1 April 1905, transferred from the Foreign Office to the Colonial Office and in Nov. 1906 the protectorate was placed under the control of a governor and C.-in-C. and (except the Sultan of Zanzibar's dominions) was annexed to the Crown as from 23 July 1920 under the name of the Colony of Kenya, thus becoming a Crown Colony.

The territories on the coast became the Kenya Protectorate.

A treaty was signed (15 July 1924) with Italy under which Great Britain ceded to Italy the Juba River and a strip from 50 to 100 miles wide on the British side of the river. Cession took place on 29 June 1925. The northern boundary is defined by an agreement with Ethiopia in 1947.

AREA AND POPULATION. Kenya is bounded by Ethiopia in the north, Uganda in the west, Tanzania in the south and the Somali Republic and the Indian ocean in the east. The total area is 224,960 sq. miles (582,600 sq. km), of which 219,790 sq miles is land area. In the 1969 census, the population was 10,942,708, of which 10,735,192 were Africans, 139,037 Asians, 40,593 Europeans, 27,886 Arabs. Estimate (1979) 15·32.

On the coast the Arabs and Swahili predominate, farther inland the races speaking Bantu languages, and non-Bantu tribes, such as the Luo, the Nandi and Kipsigis, the Masai, the Somali and the Gallas. There are more than forty tribes.

Population of the provinces (1979): Rift Valley, 3·24m.; Eastern, 2,717,000; Nyanza, 2,634,000; Central, 2,348,000; Coast, 1,339,000; Western, 1,033,000; Nairobi district, 835,000; North-Eastern, 373,000.

Nairobi, the capital, was given a Royal charter on 30 March 1950; the 1969 census showed a population of 509,286, including 19,195 Europeans and 67,189 Asians. Estimate (1975) 700,000.

Population of the largest towns: Mombasa, 340,000; Kisumu, 149,000; Nakuru, 66,000; Eldoret, 30,000. A new town is being developed (in 1981) at Bura, which will be the centre of a production area using irrigated water from the Tana river.

GOVERNMENT. A Constitution conferring internal self-government was brought into force on 1 June 1963, and full independence was achieved on 12 Dec. 1963. On 12 Dec. 1964 Kenya became a republic.

President of the Republic: Daniel Arap Moi.
Vice-President and Minister of Finance: Mwai Kibaki.
Defence: J. S. Gichuru.

The House of Representatives and the Senate were in Dec. 1966 amalgamated into one National Assembly. Elections took place in 1974.

On 10 Nov. 1964 Kenya became a one-party state of the Kenya African National Union (KANU) when the voluntary dissolution of the Kenya African Democratic Union (KADU) was declared. Later a second party, the Kenya People's Union (KPU) was formed but on 30 Oct. 1969 was proscribed.

At general elections held in Oct. 1979 there were over 800 candidates for 157 seats.

National flag: Three horizontal stripes of black, red, green, with the red edged in white; bearing in the centre an African shield in black and white with 2 crossed spears behind.

Administration. The country is divided into the Nairobi Area and 7 provinces over which there are local councils with administrative functions. The provinces are: Coast, Central, Eastern, Rift Valley, Western, Nyanza and North Eastern.

Swahili became the official language in 1974 but English is in general use.

DEFENCE

Army. The Army consists of 6 infantry battalions, 2 artillery, 1 armoured car, 1 transport and 1 engineering battalion and a support group which includes a paratroop company; total strength (1980), 12,000.

Navy. The Navy in 1981 consists of 7 large patrol craft and 350 officers and ratings. The base is at Mombasa which has a dry dock.

Air Force. An air force, formed 1 June 1964, has been built up with RAF assistance. Current equipment includes 12 F-5E/F-5F supersonic combat aircraft/trainers, 5 BAC 167 Strikemaster light jet attack/trainers, 6 twin-turboprop Buffalos and 6 twin-engined Caribou for transport, air ambulance, anti-locust spraying and security duties, 6 Skyservant and 2 Navajo light twins, 14 Bulldog piston-engined primary trainers and Alouette II, Puma, Gazelle and Bell 47 helicopters. Personnel total about 2,000. In process of delivery are 12 Hawk armed trainers and 32 Hughes Defender helicopters, of which 15 are armed with TOW missiles. Personnel about 2,100 in 1981.

INTERNATIONAL RELATIONS

Membership. Kenya is a member of UN, the Commonwealth, OAU and is an ACP state of EEC.

ECONOMY

Budget. Ordinary revenue and expenditure (in K£1,000) for 1979–80: Revenue, 591,000; expenditure, 522,000.

Funded public debt at 31 March 1977 was Sh.3,569·76m.

Currency. The monetary unit is the Kenya *Shilling* divided into 100 *cents*. In March 1981, £1 = 18·08 *Shilling*; US$1 = 8·28 *Shilling*.

Banking. Banks operating in Kenya: the National & Grindlays Bank International, Ltd; the Standard Bank, Ltd; Barclays Bank International; Algemene Bank Nederland NV; Bank of India, Ltd; Bank of Baroda, Ltd; Habib Bank (Overseas), Ltd; Commercial Bank of Africa, Ltd; Citibank; The Co-operative Bank of Kenya, Ltd; National Bank of Kenya, Ltd; The Kenya Commercial Bank; The Central Bank of Kenya.

NATURAL RESOURCES

Minerals. By mid-1970 over 75% of the area of Kenya had been geologically mapped. A special and 2 ordinary oil-prospecting licences were extant at the end of 1969, together covering 22,250 sq. miles. A joint UN–Kenya Government project is investigating the mineral resources in western Kenya and the exploration and development of mineral deposits is proceeding.

Mineral production in 1975 (provisional) was: Soda ash, 91,733 tons; gold (refined), 3,062 grammes; limestone and products, 197,414 tons; diatomite, 1,799 tons; salt, 5,553 tons. Other minerals comprised barytes, magnesite, felspar, sapphires, guano, fluorspar ore, garnets, sand and raw soda.

Agriculture. As agriculture is possible from sea-level to altitudes of over 9,000 ft, tropical, sub-tropical and temperate crops can be grown and mixed farming can be advocated. Four-fifths of the country is range-land which produces mainly livestock products and wild game which constitutes the major attraction of the country's tourist industry.

The main areas of crop production are the Central, Rift Valley, Western and Nyanza Provinces and parts of Eastern and Coastal Provinces. Coffee, tea, sisal, pyrethrum, maize and wheat are crops of major importance in the Highlands, while coconuts, cashew nuts, cotton, sugar, sisal and maize are the principal crops grown at the lower altitudes. Principal crops with production for sale (in 1,000 tonnes, 1979): Wheat, 126; maize, 1,300; rice paddy, 37·5; pyrethrum extract, 113·7; sugar-cane, 3,148; clean coffee, 75; sisal, 36·5; tea, 99·3.

Livestock (1979): Cattle, 10·5m.; sheep, 4m.; goats, 4·5m.; pigs, 65,000; poultry, 17·5m.

Forestry. The total area of gazetted forest reserves in Kenya amounts to 16,800 sq. km, of which the greater part is situated between 6,000 and 11,000 ft above sea-level, mostly on Mount Kenya, the Aberdares, Mount Elgon, Tinderet, Londiani, Mau watershed, Elgeyo and Charangani ranges. These forests may be divided into coniferous, broad-leaved or hardwood and bamboo forests. The upper parts of these forests are mainly bamboo, which occurs mostly between altitudes of 8,000 and 10,000 ft and occupies some 10% of the high-altitude forests. Plantations established by 31 Dec. 1975 (provisional) total 142,500 hectares, of which 121,600 are exotic softwood. In addition 3,100 hectares of pines have been planted for pulpwood. The Forest Department employs about 11,000 men and primary forest industries about 8,000. Water catchment is no longer considered to be the primary role of forests. Revenue from timber royalties, fuel royalties and from exports of forest-based products continues to increase.

COMMERCE. Total domestic exports (1979) K£418m.; imports (1977) K£531·45m.

The chief areas of origin in 1976 were: Western Europe, K£182·6m.; Middle East, K£97·4m. Chief areas of destination: Western Europe, K£138·5m.; Africa, K£34·2m.

Total trade between Kenya and UK (British Department of Trade returns, in £1,000 sterling):

	1975	1976	1977	1978	1979	1980
Imports to UK	38,792	61,473	155,067	114,604	115,624	105,443
Exports and re-exports from UK	85,615	97,713	118,464	195,679	170,278	259,103

TOURISM. In 1979, about 350,000 overseas visitors travelled to Kenya.

COMMUNICATIONS

Roads. In 1976 there were 4,045 km of bitumen surfaced roads and 46,046 km of gravel-surfaced roads.

Railways. On 11 Feb. 1977 the independent Kenya Railways Corporation was formed following break-up of the East African Railways administration. The network totals 2,654 km of metre-gauge and extensive upgrading and re-equipment was in progress in 1980.

Aviation. Total number of passengers handled at the 4 airports (1976) was 2,188,000. Jomo Kenyatta Airport, Nairobi, handles nearly 30 international airlines as well as Kenya Airways.

Shipping. A national shipping service is planned (1981) to be based in Mombasa, the Kenyan main port at Kilindini on the Indian Ocean. The port handles cargo freight both for Kenya as well as for the neighbouring East African states. The Port Authority also runs a modern harbour college.

Post and Broadcasting. The Voice of Kenya operates 2 national services (Swahili–English) from Nairobi and regional services in Kisumu, Nairobi and Mombasa. The television service provides programmes mainly in English and Swahili. A new television station opened in Mombasa in 1970. Telephones (1978) 143,768.

Cinemas (1971). Cinemas numbered 32, with seating capacity of 18,800.

JUSTICE, RELIGION, EDUCATION AND WELFARE

Justice. The courts of justice comprise the High Court, established in 1921, with full jurisdiction both civil and criminal over all persons and all matters in Kenya, including Admiralty jurisdiction arising on the high seas and elsewhere, and Subordinate Courts. The High Court has its headquarters at Nairobi and consists of the Chief Justice and 11 puisne judges; it sits continuously at Nairobi, Mombasa, Nakuru and Kisumu; civil and criminal sessions are held regularly at Eldoret, Nyeri, Meru, Kitale, Kisii and Kericho.

The Subordinate Courts are presided over by Senior Resident, Resident or District Magistrates and are established in the main centres of all districts. They sit throughout the year. There are also Moslem Subordinate Courts established in areas where the local population is predominantly Moslem; they are presided over by Kadhis and exercise limited jurisdiction in matters governed by Moslem law.

Religion. The indigenous African background is largely influenced by belief in God in Judaic forms, but Christianity is making an important contribution to the life of the whole territory, not only through the educational and medical services of Christian missions, but by the growth of churches under African leadership, and by its impact on the thought and policy of the country. The Roman Catholic Church (about 1·5m. adherents) has been developed mainly by Irish, British, Dutch and Italian missionary bodies and is now organized in 12 dioceses under the archbishop of Nairobi.

The Protestant Churches (about 950,000 adherents) were started mainly by British and American mission societies; most of them are now linked together by the National Christian Council of Kenya. The Church of the Province of Kenya, formerly the Anglican Church Province of East Africa, was inaugurated on 3 Aug. 1970; at the same time the first Archbishop of Kenya was enthroned. The East African Yearly Meeting of Friends (Religious Society of Friends) has 90,000 adherents.

The Arabs on the coast are Moslems, and Islam has spread among some of the African coastal tribes and the cities. The Asians are Hindus and Moslems, with the exception of the Goans, who are Roman Catholics.

Education. *Primary* (1975). 8,161 primary schools (7,989 maintained, 142 assisted and 30 unaided), with together 2,881,155 children, of whom 1,319,654 were girls and 1,561,501 boys.

Secondary (1975). There were 1,160 secondary schools (379 maintained, 43 assisted and 738 unaided), with a total enrolment of 226,835, of whom 81,529 are girls and 145,306 are boys.

Technical (1976). The Kenya Polytechnic in Nairobi, with an enrolment of 1,860 students, and Mombasa Technical Institute, with an enrolment of 805 students, are the most advanced institutions.

Teacher training (1975). 8,630 students were training as primary teachers, 488 as secondary teachers (recruitment from university graduates only) and 36 teachers for the deaf.

Higher Education. The University of East Africa, which had 3 constituent Colleges, Makerere University College in Kampala, Uganda, the University College in Nairobi, Kenya, and University College in Dar es Salaam, Tanzania, was disbanded in 1970. The University of Nairobi was inaugurated on 10 Dec. 1970. The University of Nairobi is now wholly supported by Kenya Government, and provides courses in arts, science, education, agriculture, medicine, art, architecture, engineering, veterinary, law and domestic science. In 1975–76 there were some 5,950 Kenya students at college in East Africa, 4,060 of them at University of Nairobi. In 1976, 5,813 Kenya students were enrolled in diploma and degree courses in education at the universities.

Health. In 1974 beds in hospitals (including mission hospitals) totalled 16,934. 603 health centres, including sub-centres and dispensaries, were in operation. Free medical service for all children and adult out-patients was launched in 1965.

DIPLOMATIC REPRESENTATIVES

OF KENYA IN GREAT BRITAIN (45 Portland Pl., London, W1N 4AS)
High Commissioner: (Vacant).

OF GREAT BRITAIN IN KENYA (Bruce Hse., Standard St., Nairobi)
High Commissioner: J. R. Williams, CMG.

OF KENYA IN THE USA (2249 R. St., NW, Washington, D.C., 20008)
Ambassador: John P. Mbogua.

OF THE USA IN KENYA (Cotts Hse., Wabera St., Nairobi)
Ambassador: William C. Harrop.

OF KENYA TO THE UNITED NATIONS
Ambassador: Charles Gatere Maina.

Books of Reference

Statistical Abstract. Government Printer, Nairobi, 1969
Standard English–Swahili Dictionary. Ed. Inter-territorial Language Committee of East Africa. 2 vols. London, 1939
Arnold, G., *Kenyatta and the Politics of Kenya.* London, 1974
Bienen, H., *Kenya: The Politics of Participation and Control.* Princeton Univ. Press, 1974
Bolton, K., *Haramble Country: A Guide to Kenya.* London, 1970
Harbeson, J. W., *Nation-Building in Kenya: The Role of Land Reform.* Northwestern Univ. Press, 1973
Huxley, E., and Perham, M. *Race and Politics in Kenya.* Rev. ed. London, 1956
Leys, C., *Underdevelopment in Kenya.* London, 1975
Mboya, T. J., *Freedom and After.* London, 1963
Murray-Brown, J., *Kenyatta.* London, 1972
Rothchild, D., *Racial Bargaining in Independent Kenya.* OUP, 1973
Werlin, H. W., *Governing an African City: A Study in Nairobi.* New York, 1974

KIRIBATI

Capital: Tarawa
Population: 58,518 (1980)
GNP per capita: US$690 (1978)

HISTORY. The Gilbert and Ellice Islands were proclaimed a protectorate in 1892 and annexed (at the request of the native governments) as the Gilbert and Ellice Islands Colony on 10 Nov. 1915 (effective on 12 Jan. 1916). On 1 Oct. 1975 the former Ellice Islands severed its constitutional links with the Gilbert Islands and took a new name Tuvalu.

Internal self-government was obtained on 1 Nov. 1976 and independence achieved on 12 July 1979 as the Republic of Kiribati.

AREA AND POPULATION. Kiribati consists of 3 groups of coral atolls and one isolated volcanic island, spread over a large expanse of the Central Pacific with a total land area of 684 sq. km (264 sq. miles). It comprises Banaba or Ocean Island (5 sq. km), the 16 Gilbert Islands (295 sq. km), the 8 Phœnix Islands (55 sq. km), and 8 of the 11 Line Islands (329 sq.km), the other 3 Line Islands (Jarvis, Palmyra and Kingman Reef) being uninhabited dependencies of the US. Banaba, all 16 Gilbert Islands, and 3 atolls in the Line Islands (Teraina, Tabuaeran and Kiritimati—formerly Washington, Fanning and Christmas Islands respectively) are inhabited; their populations in 1980 were as follow:

Ocean Is. (Banaba)	300	Kuria	803	Arorae	1,527
Makin	1,419	Aranuki	850	Teraina	416
Butaritari	3,149	Nonouti	2,284	Tabuaeran	434
Marakei	2,335	Tabiteuea	4,157	Kiritimati	1,265
Abaiang	3,447	Beru	2,212	Aboard ships	255
Tarawa	22,148	Nikunau	1,829	In Nauru and	
Maiana	1,688	Onotoa	2,034	Overseas	2,299
Abemama	411	Tamana	1,349		
				Total	58,518

The remaining 13 atolls have no permanent population; the 8 Phœnix Islands comprise Birnie, Rawaki (formerly Phœnix), Enderbury, Kanton (or Abariringa), Manra (formerly Sydney), Orona (formerly Hull), McKean and Line Islands and Caroline, Flint and Vostok in the Southern Line Islands. The population are almost entirely micronesian, composed of Banabans on Ocean Island and Gilbertese on all the inhabited atolls.

GOVERNMENT. Under the independence Constitution the republic has a unicameral legislature, comprising 36 members elected from 20 constituencies for a 4-year term. The *Beretitenti* (President) is both Head of State and of Government.

On 20 July 1979 the following government was announced:

President: Ieremia T. Tabai, CMG.

Vice-President and Home Affairs: Teatao Teanniki. *Health and Community Affairs:* Abete Merang. *Works and Communications:* Babera Kirata, OBE. *Trade, Industry and Labour:* Taomati T. Iuta. *Finance:* Tiwau Awira. *Natural Resource Development:* Roniti Teiwaki. *Education, Training and Culture:* Ieremia Tata. *Line and Phœnix Group:* Tewe Arobati. *Attorney-General:* Michael Jennings.

Flag: Red, with blue and white wavy lines in base, and in the centre a gold rising sun and a flying frigate bird.

INTERNATIONAL RELATIONS

Membership. Kiribati is a member of UN, the Commonwealth and is an ACP state of the EEC.

ECONOMY

Budget. Revenue for the calendar year 1980 amounted to $A13,099,320; principal items: customs duties, $A2·9m.; direct taxation, $A700,000; taxation on phosphate, $A6,642,000. Expenditure in 1975 amounted to $A30,405,012.

Currency. The currency in use is the Australian *dollar*.

AGRICULTURE. The land is basically coral reefs upon which coral sand has built up, and then been enriched by humus from rotting vegetation and flotsam which has drifted ashore. The principal tree is the coconut, which grows prolifically on all the islands except some of the Phœnix Islands. Other food-bearing trees are the pandanus palm and the breadfruit. As the amount of soil is negligible, the only vegetable which grows in any quantity is a coarse calladium (alocasia) with the local name 'babai', which is cultivated most laboriously in deep pits. Pigs and fowls are kept throughout the Colony, and there is an abundance of fish.

Copra production is mainly in the hands of the individual landowner, who collects the coconut products from the trees on his own land.

Livestock (1979): Pigs, 10,000; poultry, 163,000.

TRADE. The principal imports are rice, flour, cotton piece-goods, tobacco and manufactured articles such as bicycles. The value of imports for 1977 amounted to $A11,565,685; exports, $A18,211,996. Exports are almost exclusively copra. The British Phosphate Commissioners withdrew from Banaba in Dec. 1979 and the Co-operative Federation is responsible for the export of copra.

Total trade between Kiribati and UK (British Department of Trade returns, in £1,000 sterling):

	1980
Imports to UK	47
Exports and re-exports from UK	413

COMMUNICATIONS

Shipping. The main ports are at Banaba and at Betio (Tawara). In 1977, 256 vessels were handled at Betio.

Aviation. Air Pacific operates a weekly service, Fiji–Funafuti–Tarawa and Fiji–Funafuti–Tarawa–Nauru on alternate 2 weeks, using a Boeing 737 aircraft. The BAC1-11 because of costly operations is used only at peak periods. Air Nauru operates a weekly service between Nauru and Tarawa using an F-28 aircraft. Air Pacific also runs the internal air service and there are air links between Tarawa and 6 outer islands which have airfields—Abemama, Butaritari, Tabiteuea, Marakei, Nonouti and Beru—the last 3 were recently completed under Government's plans to expand the air service internally. All 16 outer islands in the Gilberts group are served by the local airline, Air Tungaru, using Trislander and Islander aircraft. There are airfields at Maiana and Christmas Island from which local services link to Tarawa.

Post and Broadcasting. There were 866 telephones in 1978. Radio Tarawa transmits daily in English and Gilbertese.

Cinemas. In 1974 there were 5 cinemas with a seating capacity of 2,000.

Newspapers. There was (1980) 1 weekly newspaper and 1 monthly.

JUSTICE, RELIGION, EDUCATION AND WELFARE

Justice. In 1978 Kiribati had a police force of 188 under the command of a Commissioner of Police. The Commissioner of Police is also responsible for prisons, immigration, fire service (both domestic and airport) and firearms licensing.

Religion. The majority of the population belong to the Roman Catholic or Protestant (Congregational) church; there are small numbers of Seventh-day Adventist and Baha'i.

Education (1979). The Government maintains a co-educational boarding school, the King George V and Elaine Bernacchi School at Tarawa, with (1977) 211 boys and 178 girls, 87 primary schools, with a total of 13,092 pupils, 1 government secondary school with 385 pupils, and 4 community high schools with 562 pupils attending the first year of a new rurally oriented 3-year post-primary course. The Government also maintains a teachers' training college with 100 students and a marine training school with 180 full-time students. The Tarawa Technical Institute at Betio offers a variety of part-time and evening technical and commercial courses to about 500 students each year in addition to providing full-time courses for 34 students. There are in addition 4 Mission secondary schools with a total enrolment of 213 boys and 230 girls.

In 1978, 120 islanders were in overseas countries for secondary and further education or training.

Welfare. Government maintains free medical and other services. There are few towns, and the people are almost without exception landed proprietors, thus eliminating child vagrancy and housing problems to a large extent, except in the Tarawa urban area. Destitution is almost unknown.

DIPLOMATIC REPRESENTATIVE

OF GREAT BRITAIN IN KIRIBATI (Tarawa)

High Commissioner: D. H. G. Rose.

Books of Reference

Kiribati, Aspects of History. Univ. of South Pacific, 1979
Bailey, E., *The Christmas Island Story.* London, 1977.
Cowell, R., *Structure of Gilbertese.* Suva, 1950
Grimble, Sir Arthur, *A Pattern of Islands.* London, 1953.—*Return to the Islands.* London, 1957
Maude, H. E., *Of Islands and Men.* London, 1968.—*Evolution of the Gilbertese Boti.* Suva, 1977
Sabatier, E., *Astride the Equator.* Melbourne, 1978
Whincup, T., *Nareau's Nation.* London, 1979

KOREA

Han Kook

Capital: Seoul
Population: 37·02m. (1978)
GNP per capita: US$1,160 (1978)

HISTORY. Korea was united in a single kingdom under the Silla dynasty from 668. China, which claimed a vague suzerainty over Korea, recognized Korea's independence in 1895. Korea concluded trade agreements with the USA (1882), Great Britain, Germany (1883). After the Russo-Japanese war of 1904–5 Korea was virtually a Japanese protectorate until it was formally annexed by Japan on 22 Aug. 1910 thus ending the rule of the Yi dynasty which had begun in 1392.

Following the collapse of Japan in 1945, American and Russian forces entered Korea to enforce the surrender of the Japanese troops there, dividing the country for mutual military convenience into two portions separated by the 38th parallel of latitude. Negotiations between the American and Russians regarding the future of Korea broke down in May 1946.

On 25 June 1950 the North Korean forces crossed the 38th parallel and invaded South Korea. The same day, the Security Council of the United Nations asked all member states to render assistance to the Republic of Korea. When the UN forces had reached the Manchurian border Chinese troops entered the war on the side of the North Koreans on 26 Nov. 1950 and penetrated deep into the south. By the beginning of April 1951, however, the UN forces had regained the 38th parallel.

On 23 June 1951 Y. A. Malik, President of the Security Council, suggested a cease-fire, and on 10 July representatives of Gen. Ridgway met representatives of the North Koreans and of the Chinese Volunteer Army. An agreement was signed on 27 July 1953.

For the contributions of member-nations of the United Nations to the war, see THE STATESMAN'S YEAR-BOOK, 1954, p. 1195, and 1956, p. 1180.

On 16 Aug. 1953 the USA and Korea signed a mutual defence pact and on 28 Nov. 1956 a treaty of friendship, commerce and navigation.

On 4 July 1972 it was announced in Seoul and Pyongyang (North Korea) that talks had taken place aimed at 'the peaceful unification of the fatherland as early as possible'. By late 1975 no progress had been made.

On 18 Aug. 1976 North Korean soldiers killed 2 US officers of a UN command pruning a tree at Panmunjon in the demilitarized zone. This led to a North Korean–UN agreement on 6 Sept. 1976 establishing a joint security area 850 metres in diameter and divided into 2 equal parts to ensure the separation of the two sides.

AREA AND POPULATION. South Korea is bounded north by the de-militarized zone (separating it from North Korea), east by the Sea of Japan, south by the Korea Straight (separating it from Japan) and west by the Yellow Sea. After a transfer of some frontier districts by the United Nations command on 12 Aug. 1954, the area of South Korea is now 98,447 sq. km (38,002 sq. miles). The population (census, 1 Oct. 1975) was 34,678,972 (male, 17,451,946); latest estimate (1978) 37,019,000.

The areas (in sq. km) and 1975 census populations of the provinces are as follows:

Province	sq. km	1975	Province	sq. km	1975
Seoul (city)	613	6,879,464	Chollapuk	8,051	2,455,093
Kyonggi	10,958	4,034,707	Chollanam	12,060	3,982,752
Kangwon	16,712	1,860,768	Kyongsangpuk	19,798	4,855,852
Chungchongpuk	7,437	1,521,348	Kyongsangnam	11,948	3,278,718
Chungchongnam	8,699	2,947,023	Pusan (city)	373	2,450,125
Cheju	1,830	411,486			

Local government: South Korea is divided into 9 provinces (Do) and 2 cities with provincial status (Seoul and Pusan); the provinces are sub-divided into 138 districts (Gun) and 33 cities (Si).

CONSTITUTION AND GOVERNMENT. The first general election was held, under United Nations observation, on 10 May 1948. The National Assembly adopted a Constitution on 17 July, elected Dr Syngman Rhee President of the Republic on 20 July and proclaimed the Republic of Korea on 15 Aug., when US military government ended. For details of Constitutions and Governments 1948–73, *see* THE STATESMAN'S YEAR-BOOK 1980–81, pp 765–66.

The Constitution was suspended for a time in 1974, but reinstated in Aug. 1974. A new Constitution was approved by referendum on 22 Oct. 1980.

The Army assumed power in May 1980. Martial law was lifted on 16 Oct. and Presidential elections were held in March 1981.

President of the Republic: Gen. Chun Doo-Hwan (inaugurated March 1981).
Premier: Nam Duck Woo.
National flag: White charged in the centre with the *yang-yin* in red and blue and with 4 black *pa-kwa* trigrams.

DEFENCE

Army. The Army, in 1980, had 520,000 men in 20 infantry divisions, 1 mechanized division, 2 armoured brigades equipped with 840 M-47, M-48 and M-60 tanks, 7 special forces brigades, 2 air defence brigades, 7 tank battalions, 36 artillery battalions, SS and SA missile batteries. Reserves, 1·1m. and Popular Militia, 2·8m.

Navy. The Navy comprises 10 old (1943–46) *ex*-US destroyers, 7 equally old frigates (1 of destroyer-escort type and 6 former fast transports, *ex*-destroyer escorts), 9 fast missile patrol craft, 3 corvettes (*ex*-US fleet minesweepers), 6 fast attack craft, 32 patrol boats, 8 coastal minesweepers, 1 minesweeping boat, 20 landing ships, 4 landing craft, 1 repair ship, 6 surveying vessels, 4 supply ships, 4 oilers, 13 auxiliary ships, 35 service craft, 25 coastguard cutters and 2 tugs. Nearly all South Korea's naval vessels are *ex*-US ships. Personnel in 1981 exceeded 20,000 (2,400 officers and 17,600 ratings) in Navy; plus nearly 20,000 (2,300 officers and 17,700 men) in Marine Corps.

New construction includes 4 frigates reportedly to be built in South Korean yards where up to 20 light corvettes are planned.

The South Korean Coastguard operates 25 vessels including rescue craft and tugs.

Air Force. With a 1980 strength of about 32,000 men, the Air Force is undergoing rapid expansion with US assistance. Its combat aircraft include about 70 F-4D/E Phantoms, 65 F-5A/B tactical fighters, 120 F-5E Tiger II tactical fighters, 48 F-86F Sabre fighters, 10 RF-5A reconnaissance fighters, 14 O-2A forward air control aircraft, 20 Tracker anti-submarine aircraft and 134 Hughes 500-D Defender light anti-tank/observation helicopters. There are also 6 C-130H turboprop transports, C-54 and C-123 piston-engined transports, 2 VIP HS 748s, a w AH-1 Huey-Cobra, UH-19, UH-1D and Bell 212 helicopters, and T-41, T-28, a T-33 and T-37C trainers.

ECONOMY

Planning. The 5-year plan 1962–66 aimed at achieving a self-sufficient agricultural economy on which two-thirds of the population is dependent. The second 5-year plan (1967–71) envisaged an annual growth rate of 10%; emphasis is placed on industrial development. The third 5-year plan for 1972–75 has been turned into a long-range development programme, aimed at self-sufficiency by 1980.

Budget. The 1979 budget balanced at 4,533,836m. won.

Currency. Notes are issued by the Bank of Korea in denominations of 10,000, 5,000 and 500 *won* and coin in denominations of 100, 50, 10, 5 and 1 *won*. The exchange rate is determined daily by the Foreign Exchange Bank of Korea. In March 1981, 668·9 *won* = US$1; 1,476 *won* = £1 sterling.

Banking. State-run banks include the Bank of Korea, the Korean Construction Bank, the Medium Industry Bank, the Citizen's National Bank, the Foreign Exchange Bank, the National Agricultural Co-operatives Federation, Federation of Fisheries Co-operatives serving as banking and credit institutions for farmers and fishermen, Trust Bank of Korea, the Korea Housing Bank, Korea Development Finance Corporation.

There are 5 commercial banks: the Bank of Seoul Ltd, the Cho Heung Bank Ltd, the Commercial Bank of Korea, the First City Bank of Korea, the Hanil Bank, Ltd, the Taegu Bank Ltd. The Bank of Korea is the central bank and the only note-issuing bank, the authorized purchaser of domestically produced gold. All foreign exchange is held by the Foreign Exchange Bank.

In addition, there are non-bank financial institutions consisting of 19 insurance companies, the Land Bank of Korea, the Credit Guarantee Fund, 10 short-term financial companies, 211 mutual credit companies, and the Merchant Banking Corporation.

ENERGY AND NATURAL RESOURCES

Electricity. Electricity generated (1979) was 35,510m. kwh.

Minerals. In 1977, 749 mining companies employed 67,811 people. Mineral deposits are mostly small, with the exception of tungsten; the Sangdong mine is one of the world's largest deposits of tungsten. Korea's output, 1978, included (in 1,000 tonnes): Anthracite coal (1979), 20,000; iron ore, 693; tungsten concentrate, 4,803 short tons; kaolin, 550; copper ore, 4·8; lead ore, 32·2; gold refined, 852 kg; silver refined, 43,078 kg.

Agriculture. The arable land in South Korea comprises 24·4m. acres, of which over 5·5m. acres are cultivated.

The chief crops are rice (1978: 5·8m. tonnes), barley, wheat, beans, grain of all kinds and tobacco.

Output of tobacco manufactures, a government monopoly, was 144,000 tonnes in 1977.

Raising of livestock has recently become a flourishing industry. In 1979 cattle numbered 1·7m.; pigs, 1·7m.; poultry, 40·75m.

Fisheries. Deep-sea fishing fleets increased from 5 ships (600 gross tons) in 1962 to 455 ships (160,000 gross tons) in 1972 and 833 ships (316,000 gross tons) in 1975. In 1976, 849 Korean deep-sea fishing vessels were engaged based on 25 overseas fishing bases, 345 in the Atlantic, 143 in the Indian and 361 in the Pacific oceans.

The Government plans a US$404,266,000 inshore development programme up to 1981, increasing the annual incomes of fishing households by 165% in that year compared with 1975.

INDUSTRY AND TRADE

Industry. Manufacturing industry, which (Dec. 1972) employed 5m. persons, was concentrated primarily in the production of light consumer goods for domestic consumption and export. This is now shifting towards heavy and petro-chemical industries rapidly.

Output of principal products in 1977 (in tonnes): Cotton yarn, 279,000; Portland cement, 14·4m.; fertilizers, 1·1m.

Trade Unions. Membership of trade unions at 31 Dec. 1977 was 954,682.

Commerce. In 1979 the total exports were equal to US$14,702m., while imports (including 'aid goods') were US$29,267m. Japan provided 32·7% and USA 22·6% of imports; USA received 29·1% of exports, Japan 22·3%.

Total trade between Korea and UK (British Department of Trade returns, in £1,000 sterling):

	1976	1977	1978	1979	1980
Imports to UK	135,723	178,693	214,358	269,706	244,583
Exports and re-exports from UK	63,125	75,855	129,141	145,319	101,103

COMMUNICATIONS

Roads. In 1978 there were 45,955 km of roads. Motor vehicles (1978) totalled 384,536 including 161,886 trucks, 30,597 buses, 184,886 passenger cars.

Railways. In 1980, 5,723 km of railways existed, including 428 km electrified.

Shipping. In 1976, there were registered 2,226 vessels of 3,127,206 tons.

Post. Post offices total 1,981; telephones (all government-owned) were 1,978,366 in 1978; a direct distance dialling telephone system was completed in 1976.

Cinemas. In 1977 there were 560 with a seating capacity of 346,296.

Newspapers (1977). There were 30 daily papers, including 7 national dailies and 2 in English appearing in Seoul.

RELIGION, EDUCATION AND WELFARE

Religion. Basically the religions of Korea have been Animism, Buddhism (introduced A.D. 372) and Confucianism, which was the official faith from 1392 to 1910. Catholic converts from China introduced Christianity in the 18th century, but the ban on Roman Catholics was not lifted until 1882. Estimated Christian population in 1977 was 6·1m. (1,093,829 Catholics, 5,001,491 Protestants).

Education. In 1978 Korea had 5,604,365 pupils enrolled in 6,426 elementary schools, 2,298,124 pupils in 2,012 middle schools and 1,454,376 pupils in 1,253 high schools (including 499 vocational schools).

For higher education, 347,887 students who attended 215 universities, colleges and junior colleges. There are 87 graduate schools granting master's degrees in 2 years and doctor's degrees in 4 years, where 17,220 students attend.

The Korean language belongs to the Ural–Altaic group, is polysyllabic, agglutinative and highly developed syntactically. The modern Korean alphabet of 10 vowels and 14 consonants forms a script known as Hangul.

Health. In Dec. 1977 there were 21,734 physicians (including herb doctors), 2,899 dentists, 4,222 midwives, 70,504 nurses (including assistant nurses), 4,712 technicians and 21,392 pharmacists. There were 11,181 hospitals and clinics.

DIPLOMATIC REPRESENTATIVES

OF KOREA IN GREAT BRITAIN (4 Palace Gate, London, W8 5NF)
Ambassador: Dr Young Hoon Kang (accredited 25 Feb. 1981).

OF GREAT BRITAIN IN KOREA (4 Chung-Dong, Chung-Ku, Seoul)
Ambassador and Consul-General: W. S. Bates, CMG.

OF KOREA IN THE USA (2320 Massachusetts Ave., NW, Washington, D.C., 20008)
Ambassador: Yong Shik Kim.

OF THE USA IN KOREA (Sejong-Ro, Seoul)
Ambassador: William Gleysteen, Jr.

Books of Reference

Economic Planning Board. *Guide to Investment in Korea.* Seoul, 1973.—*Korean Economy: Present and Future.* Seoul, 1973
Korea Annual 1974. 11th ed. Seoul, 1973
Korea: Its Land, People and Culture of All Ages. Seoul, 1960
Korea: Past and Present. Seoul, 1972
Korea Statistical Year Book. Seoul, 1974
UNESCO Korean Survey. Seoul, 1960
Guide to Geographical Names in Korea (*Chosen*). United States Board of Geographical Names. Washington, 1945

Major Economic Indicators, 1958–69. Seoul, 1970

Monthly Statistics of Korea. Seoul, 1975

Bartz, P. M., *South Korea.* OUP, 1972

Lew, H. J., *New Life Korean–English, English–Korean Dictionary.* 2 vols. Seoul, 1947–50

Martin, S. F. (ed.), *A Korean–English Dictionary.* Yale Univ. Press, 1968

Wright, E. R., *Korean Politics in Transition.* Univ. of Washington Press, 1976

NORTH KOREA

Chosun Minchu-chui
Inmin Konghwa-guk

Capital: Pyongyang
Population: 16m. (1975)
GNP per capita: US$730 (1978)

HISTORY. In northern Korea the Russians, arriving on 8 Aug. 1945, one month ahead of the Americans, established a Communist-led 'Provisional Government'. The newly created Korean Communist Party merged in 1946 with the New National Party into the Korean Workers' Party. In July 1946 the KWP, with the remaining pro-Communist groups and non-party people, formed the United Democratic Patriotic Front. On 25 Aug. 1948 the Communists organized elections for a Supreme People's Assembly, both in Soviet-occupied North Korea (212 deputies) and in US-occupied South Korea (360 deputies, of whom a certain number went to the North and took their seats). A People's Democratic Republic was proclaimed on 9 Sept. 1948. In 1973 North Korea was admitted to WHO, and in 1973 granted observer status at the UN. Talks between North and South Korea on re-unification began in Feb. 1980, but were broken off by the North in Sept. 1980.

AREA AND POPULATION. The area of North Korea is 47,225 sq. miles (122,370 sq. km). Population in 1975, 16m. Rate of population increase, 2·8% per annum. Death rate, 1979: 4·4 per mille. Marriage is discouraged before the age of 32 for men and 29 for women. Expectation of life 1980, 70 (men), 76 (women). The capital is Pyongyang, with 1·5m. inhabitants.

The country is divided into 13 administrative units: 4 cities (Pyongyang, Chongjin, Hamheung and Kaesong) and 9 provinces (capitals in brackets): South Pyongan (Nampo), North Pyongan (Sinuiji), Jagang (Kanggye), South Hwanghai (Haeju), North Hwanghai (Sariwon), North Kangwon (Wonsan), South Hamgyong (Hamheung), North Hamgyong (Chongjin), Yanggang (Hyesan).

CONSTITUTION AND GOVERNMENT. The political structure is based upon the Constitution of 27 Dec. 1972, which supersedes that of 1948 as amended in 1954 and 1955. The Constitution provides for a Supreme People's Assembly elected every 4 years by universal suffrage. Citizens of 17 years and over can vote and be elected. Elections were held in 1948, 1957, 1962, 1972 and 11 Nov. 1977. At the latter it was claimed that 100% of the electorate voted for the candidates presented. There are 579 deputies.

In practice the country is ruled by the Korean Workers' (*i.e.,* Communist) Party which elects a Central Committee which in turn appoints a Politburo, the first 5 members of which constitute its Standing Committee. In March 1981 this was composed of: Marshal Kim Il Sung, *General Secretary of the Party, President of the Republic, Supreme Commander of the Armed Forces*; Kim Il (*Vice-President of the Republic*); O Jin U (*Defence Minister*); Kim Jong Il (Kim Il Sung's son and designated successor); Li Jong Ok (*Prime Minister*); Pak Sung Chul; Gen. Choe Hyon; Rim Chun Chu; So Chol; O Baek Ryong; Kim Jung Rin; Kim Yong Nam; Chon Mun Sop; Kim Hwan; Yon Hyong Muk; O Guk Ryol; Kye Ung Tae (*Deputy Prime Minister, Minister of Foreign Trade*); Kang Song San; Paek Hak Rim. There are also 15 'alternate members'.

Ministers not full members of the Politburo include Ho Dam (*Deputy Prime Minister, Foreign Minister*); Kim Gyong Ryon (*Finance*); Kim Il Dae (*Education*); Ro Tae Sok (*Deputy Prime Minister, Chairman, State Planning Commission*); Choe Won Ik (*Public Security*).

In 1981 the Party had some 2m. members.

There are also the puppet religious Chongu and Korean Social Democratic Parties, and various organizations combined in a Fatherland Front.

National flag: Blue, red and blue horizontal stripes separated by narrow white bands. The red stripe bears a white circle within which is a red 5-pointed star.

National anthem: The Song of General Kim Il Sung.

Local government is administered by People's Assemblies at city (or province), county (or district) and *ri* (town, workers' or rural commune) level. The latest elections were on 5 March 1981. There are 24,247 local deputies.

DEFENCE. Military service is compulsory at the age of 17 and lasts 3–4 years.

Army. In 1980 the Army was believed to number about 600,000 men, organized in 2 armoured and 38 infantry divisions, with 800 Soviet tanks and support units; it has about 300 'Guideline' surface-to-air missiles, and Soviet Sam-2 rockets and Frog-5 missiles.

Navy. The Navy comprises 16 diesel-powered patrol submarines (12 *ex*-Chinese and 4 *ex*-Soviet), 4 small frigates, 18 missile boats, 173 fast torpedo boats, 145 fast gunboats, 28 patrol vessels, 30 coastal patrol craft, 75 minor landing craft, 20 light gunboats and minesweeping boats, 30 trawlers and auxiliaries and 100 service craft and armed junks. Up to 5 small submarines are reported as built locally. Personnel in 1981 exceeded 30,000 officers and men, plus 40,000 reservists.

Air Force. With Chinese and Soviet assistance, the Air Force has been increased to a total of about 650 aircraft and 45,000 personnel. Equipment is believed to include about 150 supersonic MiG-21 interceptors, 300 MiG-17s for ground attack and reconnaissance, 30 Su-7 fighter-bombers, 60 Il-28 twin-jet light bombers, and a variety of transport and training aircraft and helicopters.

ECONOMY

Planning. Past plans: 3-year plan, 1954–56, rehabilitated the country after the Korean War (1950–53); 5-year plan, 1957–61; 7-year plan, extended in 1966 to 1970; 6-year plan, 1971–76, during which an average annual industrial growth rate of 16·3% was claimed. 1977 was a year of planning hiatus ('readjustment'), but it was finally announced in that year that all the 1971–76 plan targets had been reached, and a 7-year plan for 1978–84 was adopted which gives priority to the fuel and mining industries, foreign trade development and transport, and expects an annual industrial growth rate of 12·1%.

Budget (in 1m. won) for calendar years:

	1973	1974	1975	1976	1977	1978	1979
Revenue	8,599	10,015	11,586	12,626	13,789	15,923	17,478
Expenditure	8,313	9,672	11,367	12,326	13,349	15,923	16,972

In 1978, 15·1% of budget expenditure was on defence. Average monthly income was 70 won in 1970. Personal taxation was abolished in 1974.

Currency. The monetary unit is the *won*, divided into 100 *jun*. In March 1981, US$1 = 0·94 *won*; £1 = 2·22 *won*.

Weights and Measures. While the metric system is in force traditional measures are in frequent use. The *jungbo* = 1 hectare; the *ri* = 3,927 metres.

ENERGY AND NATURAL RESOURCES

Electricity. There are thermal power stations at Pyongyang, Unggi and Chongchongang. There are hydro-electric plants at Kanggye, Unbong and Sodusu, and another is under construction at Taedonggang. Output in 1975, was 28,000m. kwh. Hydro-electric potential exceeds 8m. kw. In 1972 thermal power generation accounted for 38% of total output. An oil pipeline from China was opened in Jan. 1976.

Minerals. North Korea is rich in minerals (coal, iron, lead, zinc, copper, tungsten, nickel, manganese and graphite) and has important metallurgical works. Oilwells went into production in 1957. Coalmines are being enlarged and modernized. There are large open-cast workings at Yonghung. 50m. tonnes of coal were mined in 1975. 7·4m. tonnes of iron ore and 12,000 tonnes of copper ore were extracted in 1969.

Agriculture. Only 2m. hectares of the land area are cultivable. Intensive water and soil conservancy is practised and land reclamation from the sea has a high priority. In 1946 all Japanese-owned and landowners' property above 5 *jungbo* was distributed among some 724,500 landless peasants and smallholders.

Collectivization took place between 1954 and 1958, when there were 13,309 'co-operatives' averaging 130 *jungbo*. In 1958 these were merged into 3,843 larger units (*ri*), averaging 500 *jungbo*, modelled on the Chinese communes. 90% of the cultivated land is farmed by co-operatives. A law of 1977 proclaims that there is no private property in land; land belongs either to the State or to co-operatives, and it is intended gradually to transform the latter into the former. Livestock farming is mainly carried on by large state farms.

Some 3m. *jungbo* are under cultivation, of which 1m. *jungbo* have regular irrigation. There were 37,600 km of irrigation canals in 1976. The 6-year plan (1971–76) extended irrigation so as to make possible 2 rice harvests a year. In 1974 the number of tractors (15 h.p. units) was between 70,000 and 80,000. The technical revolution in agriculture (nearly 95% of ploughing, etc., is mechanized) considerably increased the yield of grain (sown on 2·3m. *jungbo* of land); this was 9m. tonnes in 1979 (mainly rice). Maize is being fostered to replace millet as the major dry-field crop.

Livestock (FAO estimates for 1979): 925,000 cattle, 2m. pigs.

Forestry. Between 1961 and 1970, 800,000 hectares were afforested, 500,000 hectares of oil-bearing trees are scheduled for planting.

Fishery. The annual catch is about 1·6m. tonnes. There is a fishing fleet of about 3,400 modern motor and sailing fishing craft, equipped with factory and refrigerator ships.

INDUSTRY AND TRADE

Industry. Industries were intensively developed by the Japanese, notably cotton spinning, hydro-electric power, cotton, silk and rayon weaving, and chemical fertilizers. Production (in tonnes) in 1975: Chemical fertilizers, 3m.; cement, 8m.; steel, 4m.; textiles, 600m. sq. metres. Industrial workers make up some 40% of the total work force. There is a steel complex at Kangson with an annual productive capacity of 4m. tonnes. Average wage 1977: Workers, 70 won per month; managers, 200 won per month. Workers have 2 weeks, managers 4 weeks, annual holiday.

Commerce. Foreign trade is almost exclusively with Communist countries. In 1978 North Korea's indebtedness was estimated at US$2,000m. Trade with Japan amounted to US$272m. in 1978. An agreement regulating the repayment of North Korea's US$390m. debt to Japan over 10 years was signed in Sept. 1979. The chief exports are metal ores and products, the chief imports machinery and petroleum products.

Exports to the USSR in 1976 (and 1977) were worth 118·7m. (164m.) roubles; imports from the USSR, 181·8m. (164·7m.) roubles.

Total trade between North Korea and UK (British Department of Trade returns, in £1,000 sterling):

	1975	1976	1977	1978	1979	1980
Imports to UK	1,425	1,408	3,262	1,494	961	391
Exports and re-exports from UK	600	930	1,288	851	808	981

COMMUNICATIONS

Roads. Motor transport is very important, as about one-third of the inhabited places are without railway communications. Roads are bad and mostly unpaved; statistics about their length, etc., are lacking. In 1961 lorries and coaches transported 17·7m. tons of freight.

Railways. Extensive railway construction was carried out under the Japanese occupation. Because these lines served strategic purposes, however, and because of the separation of North and South Korea, not all of them were suitable for inclusion in the present railway network. The two trunk-lines Pyongyang–Sinuiji and Pyongyang–Myongchon are both electrified, and the Pyongyang–Sariwon trunk is in course of electrification. The 'Wonra' line runs from Wonsan to Rajin and is electrified from

Myongchon to Rajin. The Chagangsamgang-Unbong line was opened in 1980. Lines are under construction from Pukchong to Toksong, from Palwon to Kujang and Kanggye *via* Hyesan to Musan. The Hyesan–Samsok section of the latter opened to traffic in 1971. In 1979 there were some 4,400 km of track, about 35% electrified. In 1980, 87% of trains were hauled by electricity and 30·6m. tonnes were transported in 1969. Further electrification was in progress including 100 km Chongjin–Puryong–Musan line.

Aviation. There are weekly flights to Moscow and Peking. Domestic lines: Pyongyang–Hamheung–Chongjin.

Shipping. The leading ports are Chongjin and Heungnam (near Hamheung). Nampo, the port of Pyongyang, has been dredged and expanded. Pyongyang is connected to Nampo by railway and river.

The biggest navigable river is the Yalu, 698 km up to the Hyesan district.

Broadcasting. In 1961 there were 600,000 radio receivers. The Pyongyang central broadcasting station was rebuilt about 1955.

Newspapers. The party newspaper is *Nodong* (or *Rodong*) *Sinmun* (Labour Party News. Circulation about 1m.).

JUSTICE, EDUCATION AND WELFARE

Justice. The judiciary consists of the Supreme Court, whose judges are elected by the Assembly for 3 years; provincial courts; and city or county people's courts. The procurator-general, appointed by the Assembly, has supervisory powers over the judiciary and the administration; the Supreme Court controls the judicial administration.

Education. In 1975–76 the 10-year system of free compulsory universal technical education was extended to 11 years (1 pre-school year, 4 years primary education starting at the age of 6, followed by 6 years secondary).

In 1970–71, 9,260 schools of all grades were attended by 3·2m. pupils, including 214,000 students in institutes of higher education, two-thirds of whom were studying technical and engineering subjects. There were some 100,000 teachers. In 1975–76 there were 5–6m. children in the 11-year system and nearly 1m. students in higher education. In 1980 there were 170 institutes of higher education, including 3 universities—Kim Il Sung University (founded 1946), Kim Chaek Technical University, Pyongyang Medical School—and an Academy of Sciences (founded 1952).

In 1977–78 Kim Il Sung University had some 17,000 students.

Health. Medical treatment is free. In 1980 there were 23·3 doctors and 120 hospital beds per 10,000 population.

Books of Reference

Baik Bong, *Kim Il Sung: Biography*. 3 vols. New York, 1969–70

Brun, E., and Hersh, J., *Socialist Korea: A Case Study in the Strategy of Economic Development*. New York, 1976

Chung, J. S.-H., *The North Korean Economy: Structure and Development*. Stanford, 1974

Kim Han Gil, *Modern History of Korea*. Pyongyang, 1979

Kim, I. J., *Communist Policies in North Korea*. New York, 1975

Kim Il Sung, *Selected Works*. Pyongyang, 1965 in progress

Kiyosaki, W. S., *North Korea's Foreign Relations*. New York, 1976

Lee, C.-S., *The Korean Workers' Party: A Short History*. Stanford, 1978

McCormack, G., and Selden, M. (eds.), *Korea North and South: The Deepening Crisis*. New York, 1978

Rees, D., *North Korea: Undermining the Truce*. London, 1976

Scalapino, R. A., and Lee, C.-S., *Communism in Korea. Part I: The Movement. Part II: The Society*. Univ. of Calif. Press, 1972

United States Department of the Army. *Communist North Korea: A Bibliographic Survey*. Washington, 1971

KUWAIT

Dowlat al Kuwait

Capital: Kuwait
Population: 1·27m. (1979)
GNP per capita: US$14,890 (1978)

HISTORY. The independent and sovereign State of Kuwait is situated on the north-western coast of the Arabian Gulf. The ruling dynasty was founded by Shaikh Sabah al-Owel, who ruled from 1756 to 1772. In 1899 the then ruler Shaikh Mubarak concluded a treaty with Great Britain wherein, in return for the assurance of British protection, he undertook not to alienate any of his territory without the agreement of Her Majesty's Government. In 1914 the British Government recognized Kuwait as an independent government under British protection. On 19 June 1961 an agreement reaffirmed the independence and sovereignty of Kuwait and recognized the Government of Kuwait's responsibility for the conduct of internal and external affairs; the agreement of 1899 was terminated and Her Majesty's Government expressed their readiness to assist the Government of Kuwait should they request such assistance.

AREA AND POPULATION. Area, about 9,375 sq. miles (24,280 sq. km); the total population at the census of 1976 was 1,066,400, of which about 53% were non-Kuwaitis. Population estimate, 1979, 1·27m.

The country is divided into 3 governorates, Kuwait (the capital, 80,405 population 1970; metropolitan area, 217,749), Ahmadi and Hawali (106,542).

The Neutral Zone (3,560 sq. miles, 5,700 sq. km), jointly owned and administered by Kuwait and Saudi Arabia from 1922 to 1966, was partitioned between the two countries in May 1966, but the exploitation of the oil and other natural resources will continue to be shared.

RULER. HH Shaikh Jabir al-Ahmad al-Jabir al-Sabah the 13th Amir of Kuwait, succeeded on 31 Dec. 1977.

CONSTITUTION AND GOVERNMENT. Elections for a National Assembly of 50 members were held on 27 Jan. 1975 but in Aug. 1976 the Amir dissolved the Assembly and at the same time parts of the Constitution were suspended. Elections were held on 24 Feb. 1981 for the National Assembly.

The official language is Arabic; English is used as the second language.

Prime Minister: Shaikh Saad al Abdallah al-Sabah (appointed 8 Feb. 1978).

Deputy Prime Minister and Information: Jabir al Ali as Salim al-Sabah. *Deputy Prime Minister and Foreign Affairs:* Shaikh Sabah al-Ahmad al-Jabir al-Sabah. *Oil:* Ali al-Khalifah al-Sabah. *Planning:* Mohammed Youssef al-Adasani.

Flag: Three horizontal stripes of green, white, red, with a black trapezium based on the hoist.

DEFENCE

Army. Kuwait maintains a small, well-equipped and mobile army of 3 brigades (10,000 men in 1980).

Air Force. From a small initial combat force the Air Force has grown rapidly. It has 1 squadron with 17 Mirage F1-C fighters and 2 Mirage F1-B 2-seat trainers; and 2 squadrons with 36 A-4KU/TA-4KU Skyhawk attack aircraft. Other equipment includes 2 DC-9 jet transports and 1 L-100-20 Hercules turboprop transport, 9 BAC 167 Strikemaster armed jet trainers, 10 Puma and 24 missile-armed Gazelle helicopters. Hawk surface-to-air missiles are in service. Personnel strength (1980) about 1,900.

INTERNATIONAL RELATIONS

Membership. Kuwait is a member of UN, the Arab League and OPEC.

ECONOMY

Budget. The financial year runs 1 April–31 March. In 1978–79 revenue, KD 2,301m.; expenditure, KD 1,950m.

Currency. The Kuwait *dinar* of 1,000 *fils* replaced the Indian external rupee on 1 April 1961; £1 sterling = KD 0·597 (March 1981). Coins in circulation are, 1, 5, 10, 20, 50 and 100 *fils*. The amount of currency in circulation in 1974 was KD 81·7m.

Banking. Seven banks operate in Kuwait: the Bank of Kuwait and Middle East, the Kuwait National Bank, the Commercial Bank of Kuwait Ltd, the Gulf Bank of Kuwait and the Ahlly Bank, The Industrial Bank of Kuwait, Savings and Credit Bank.

Weights and Measures. The metric system was adopted in 1962.

ENERGY AND NATURAL RESOURCES

Oil. Kuwait oil comes mainly from the Burgan oilfields, the residential and administrative centre for oil operations being at Ahmadi. Oil reserves in Kuwait and its share of the neutral zone was estimated at 77,000m. bbls in 1975. The Kuwait Petroleum Gas and Energy Co. (KPGEC) formed in 1974 as a result of the Government's take-over of 60% of oil production, is controlling all oil exploration and the processing and marketing of oil and gas. Production of crude oil (in 1m. bbls): 1970, 1,091; 1971, 1,166; 1972, 1,202; 1973, 1,011; 1974, 929; 1975, 761; 1976, 785, 1977, 718.

Agriculture. Major crops are melons, tomatoes, onions, radishes, clover.
Livestock (1979): Cattle, 10,000; sheep, 149,000; goats, 103,000; poultry, 5·7m.

Fisheries. Shrimp fishing is becoming one of the important non-oil industries.

INDUSTRY AND TRADE

Industry. Industries, apart from oil, include boat building, fishing, food production, petrochemicals, gases and construction. The manufacture or import of alcoholic drinks is prohibited.

Labour. Of the working population 75% are foreigners.

Commerce. The port of Kuwait formerly served mainly as an entrepôt for goods for the interior, for the export of skins and wool, and for pearl fishing. Entrepôt trade continues but, with the development of the oil industry, is declining in importance. Pearl fishing is now on a small scale. Dhows and launches of traditional construction are still built.
In 1979 total imports were US$4,600m.; exports, US$17,564m.
Total trade between Kuwait and UK (British Department of Trade returns, in £1,000 sterling):

	1976	1977	1978	1979	1980
Imports to UK [1]	587,067	541,262	621,530	743,149	655,024
Exports and re-exports from UK	144,343	243,341	332,278	233,438	258,696

[1] Including oil.

COMMUNICATIONS

Roads. Number of private cars (1977) 379,100.

Aviation. British Airways, Kuwait Airways, Iraqi Airways, Iranian Airways, United Arab Airlines, Middle East Airlines, Saudi Arabian Airways, Lebanese International Airways, Air Liban, Air India, Lufthansa, Japanese Airlines, TWA, PIA, Aden Air Lines, Air France, Alitalia, SAS, Swiss Air, SABENA, KLM and Gulf Aviation operate scheduled air services.

Shipping. Ships of 27 lines make regular calls at Kuwait.

Post and Broadcasting. Wireless communication was taken over by the Kuwait

Government in 1956, internal postal services in Feb. 1958 and external postal services in 1959. There were (1978), 152,517 telephones in Kuwait. There are a broadcasting and a television station.

Cinemas. In 1976 there were 10 cinemas with a seating capacity of 13,000.

EDUCATION AND WELFARE

Education. In 1976 there were 201,907 pupils at 326 government schools. In 1969–70 there were 2,200 students at teacher-training institutes (354 teachers) and teacher-training colleges had 100 students (28 teachers). A technical college was opened in 1954 and in 1970 had 931 students (212 teachers). The University of Kuwait had 6,500 students in 1976.

Health. Medical services are free to all residents. There were (1976) 20 hospitals with over 4,764 beds in the State and 481 clinics and health centres. The Ministry of Health employs 1,219 physicians and 122 dentists. Expenditure on health services 1975–76, KD 45m.

DIPLOMATIC REPRESENTATIVES

OF KUWAIT IN GREAT BRITAIN (45 Queen's Gate, London, SW7)

Ambassador: Ghazi Mohammed Amin Al-Rayes (accredited 12 Feb. 1981).

OF GREAT BRITAIN IN KUWAIT (Arabian Gulf St., Kuwait)

Ambassador: S. J. G. Cambridge, CMG, CVO.

OF KUWAIT IN THE USA (2940 Tilden St., NW, Washington, D.C., 20008)

Ambassador: Khalid M. Jaffar.

OF THE USA IN KUWAIT (PO Box 77, Kuwait)

Ambassador: François M. Dickman.

OF KUWAIT TO THE UNITED NATIONS

Ambassador: Abdalla Yaccoub Bishara.

Books of Reference

Arabian Year Book. Kuwait, 1978
Annual Statistical Abstract of Kuwait. Kuwait
Education in Kuwait, 1969–70. Kuwait Government Press, 1971
Kuwait Economy 1968–69. Kuwait Government Press, 1970
The Oil of Kuwait: Facts and Figures. 3rd ed. Kuwait Government Press, 1970
Khouja, M. W., and Sadler, P. G., *The Economy of Kuwait.* London, 1979
Sabah, Y. S. F., *The Oil Economy of Kuwait.* London, 1980
Shiber, S. G., *The Kuwait Urbanization.* Kuwait Government Press, 1964
Winstone, H. V. F., and Freeth, Z., *Kuwait: Prospect and Reality.* London, 1972

LAOS

Capital: Vientiane
Population: 3·5m. (1979)
GNP per capita: US$90 (1978)

HISTORY. The Lao People's Democratic Republic was founded on 2 Dec. 1975. Until that date Laos was a Kingdom, once called Lanxang (the land of a million elephants).

In 1893 Laos became a French protectorate and in 1907 acquired its present frontiers. In 1941 French authority was suppressed by the Japanese. When the Japanese withdrew in 1945 an independence movement known as Lao Issara (Free Laos) set up a government under Prince Phetsarath, the Viceroy of Luang Prabang. This government collapsed with the return of the French in 1946 and the leaders of the movement fled to Thailand.

Under a new Constitution of 1947 Laos became a constitutional monarchy under the Luang Prabang dynasty, and in 1949 became an independent sovereign state within the French Union. Most of the Lao Issara leaders returned to Laos but a few remained in dissidence under Prince Souphanouvong, who allied himself with the Vietminh and subsequently formed the 'Pathet Lao' (Lao State) rebel movement.

The war in Laos from 1953 to 1973 between the Royal Lao Government (supported by American bombing and Thai mercenaries) and the Patriotic Front *Pathet Lao* (supported by large numbers of North Vietnamese troops) ended in 1973 when an agreement and a protocol were signed. A provisional coalition government was formed by the two sides in 1974. However, after the communist victories in neighbouring Vietnam and Cambodia in April 1975, the *Pathet Lao* took over the running of the whole country, although maintaining the façade of a coalition. On 29 Nov. 1975 HM King Savang Vatthana signed a letter of abdication and the People's Congress proclaimed a People's Democratic Republic of Laos. For the history of *Pathet Lao* and the military intervention of the Vietminh, *see* THE STATESMAN'S YEAR-BOOK, 1971–72, pp. 1126–28 and 1975–76 ed., pp. 1115–16.

AREA AND POPULATION. Laos is a land-locked country of about 91,400 sq. miles (236,800 sq. km) bordered on the north by China, the east by Vietnam, the south by the People's Republic of Democratic Kampuchea (Cambodia) and the west by Thailand and Burma. Apart from the Mekong River plains along the border of Thailand, the country is mountainous, particularly in the north, and in places densely forested. The climate is of a tropical monsoon type with a wet season from May to Oct. and a dry one from Nov. to April. Most of northern Laos receives about 40–80 in. of rainfall annually, while parts of the Bolovens Plateau in southern Laos have over 150 in.

There has been no complete census in Laos, but estimates place the population at about 3·5m. The most heavily populated areas are the Mekong River plains by the Thailand border. Otherwise, the population is sparse and scattered, particularly in the northern provinces, and the eastern part of the country has been depopulated by war. The majority of the population is officially divided into 4 groups: about 56% Lao-Lum (Valley-Lao), 34% Lao-Theung (Lao of the mountain sides); and 9% Lao-Soung (Lao of the mountain tops), who comprise the Meo and Yaoe. Other minorities include Vietnamese, Chinese, Europeans, Indians and Pakistanis.

The Lao-Lum and Lao-Tai belong to the Lao branch of the Tai peoples, who migrated into South-East Asia at the time of the Mongol invasion of South China. The valley Lao are Buddhists, following the Hinayana (Theravada) form. The majority of the Lao-Theung—a diverse group consisting of many tribes but mostly belonging to the Mon-Khmer group—are animists.

The Meo and Yaoe live in northern Laos. Far greater numbers live in both North Vietnam and China, having migrated over the last century. Their religions have strong Confucian and animistic features but some are Christians.

There are 13 provinces. Compared with other parts of Asia, Laos has few towns.

The administrative capital and largest town is Vientiane, with a population of (census, 1973) 176,637; estimate (1979) 90,000. Other important towns are Luang Prabang, the royal capital, 44,244; Pakse, 44,860, in the extreme south, and Savannakhet, 50,690.

Language: Lao is the official language of the country. The liturgical language of Theravada Buddhism is Pali.

GOVERNMENT. On 1–2 Dec. 1975 a national congress of 264 people's representatives met and declared Laos a People's Democratic Republic. A People's Supreme Council was appointed to draw up a new Constitution.

President: Prince Souphanouvong.
Prime Minister, Secretary General of the Central Committee of the Lao People's Revolutionary Party: Kaysone Phomvihane.

There are 4 deputy prime ministers.

National flag: Three horizontal stripes of red, blue, red, with blue of double width with in the centre a large white disc.
National anthem: Peng Sat Lao (Hymn of the Lao People).

Provincial Administration: All provincial administration is in the hands of the Lao People's Revolutionary Party. Orders come from the Central Committee through a series of 'People's Revolutionary Committees' at the province, town and village level.

DEFENCE

Army. Since the Communist victory in 1975 the Royal Lao Army has partly been integrated with the *Pathet Lao*, the rest being disbanded. The 'Lao People's Liberation Army', as the *Pathet Lao* is more correctly known, is about 46,000 strong. It is organized in 1 armoured, 64 infantry, 4 artillery and 4 anti-aircraft battalions. There are about 35,000 active North Vietnamese troops in Laos.

Navy. In 1981 there were nominally 4 river squadrons comprising 42 craft of 6 different types, of which 14 were in commission and 28 in reserve. Naval personnel totalled 550 officers and ratings.

Air Force. In spring 1975, the Air Force had about 139 aircraft, including T-28D piston-engined light strike aircraft, AC-47 ground-attack aircraft, C-123 and C-47 transports, UH-34 helicopters, observation and light communications aircraft. Little is known about these aircraft in 1980 but since 1975 it has received aircraft from the USSR, including 10 MiG-21 fighters, 6 An-24 and 3 An-26 turboprop transports and 10 Mi-8 helicopters. Personnel strength, about 8,000.

INTERNATIONAL RELATIONS
Membership. Laos is a member of UN.

ECONOMY

Planning. A development plan for the period 1975–78 was drawn up in Sept. 1974. The large projects include extending the Nam Ngum Dam and development of the infrastructure. Following the completion of the plan the government announced that a 5-year (1981–85) plan would be initiated.

Budget. Total revenue 1978, K.46,300m. including K.31,000m. in foreign aid (1979, K.58,000m., foreign aid, K.35,000m.); total expenditure, K.49,400m. (1979, K.59,000m.).

Currency. The National Bank issues the currency, the *kip*, whose value is normally expressed in US$. 1 *kip* (new) = 100 *kip* (old) after change in Dec. 1979. The official rate of exchange was (March 1981) K.10 = US$1; £1 = K21·8, but the black market rate in 1981 was considerably higher.

ENERGY AND NATURAL RESOURCES

Electricity. Only a few towns in Laos have an electricity service. A power plant with a capacity of 8,000 kw. is installed at Vientiane, but there are only small thermo-electric plants in other towns. The Nam Ngum Dam situated about 45 miles north of Vientiane was inaugurated in Dec. 1971 with an initial installed capacity of 30,000 kw. and a planned ultimate capacity of 130,000 kw. The generators of Phase II of the scheme were brought into operation in 1978, giving an installed capacity of 110,000 kw. Transmission lines to Vientiane and to Thailand have been constructed. Other sources of electric power are the dams on the Sedone River about 20 miles north of Pakse and on the Nam Dong about 5 miles south of Luang Prabang, with installed capacities of 2,400 and 1,200 kw. respectively. Production (1979) 840m. kwh.

Minerals. Various minerals are found, but only tin is mined to any significant extent at present, and only at 2 mines (1977 production, 480 tonnes of 50% concentrate). There are extremely rich deposits of high-quality iron in Xieng Khouang province and potash near Vientiane.

Agriculture. The chief products are rice (production in 1980, 1m.. tonnes; 1978, estimate, 420,000 tonnes), maize (production 27,200 tonnes), tobacco (4,200 tonnes), cotton (2,100 tonnes), citrus fruits, sticklack, benjohn tea and in the Boloven plateau coffee (2,070 tonnes), potatoes, cardamom and cinchara. Opium is produced but is the subject of legislation designed to control its manufacture.

Liestock (1979): Cattle, 551,000; buffaloes, 1·4m.; horses, 36,000; pigs, 1·64m.; goats, 40,000; poultry, 18·61m.

Forestry. The forests in the north produce valuable woods, teak in particular; the logs are floated southwards on the Mekong. Elephants are trained in forest work.

INDUSTRY AND TRADE

Industry. Industry is limited to beer, rubber sandals, cigarettes, matches, soft drinks, plastic bags, saw-mills, rice-mills, weaving, pottery, distilleries, ice, plywood, bricks, etc. but most factories have been working at limited capacity in recent years. Plans for increased production are limited by lack of funds and skilled machine operators.

Commerce. In 1979 imports amounted to US$88mm. and exports to US$26m. The main imports were food and beverages, petroleum products and agricultural and other machinery. The chief supplying countries were Thailand, Japan, USA and Indonesia. The main exports were timber, coffee and electricity.

Total trade between Laos and UK (British Department of Trade returns, in £1,000 sterling):

	1975	1976	1977	1978	1979	1980
Imports to UK	15	2	4	17	49	32
Exports and re-exports from UK	504	178	340	1,527	264	720

COMMUNICATIONS

Roads. In 1974 there were 3,412 km of all-weather, asphalted or permanent roads and 4,000 km of non-all-weather roads.

Railways. There is no railway in Laos, but the Thai railway system extends to Nongkhai, on the Thai bank of the Mekong, which is connected by ferry with Thadeua about 12 miles east of Vientiane and to Udon Ratchathani which is close to the southern border of Thailand/Laos.

Aviation. Lao Aviation provides scheduled domestic air services linking major towns in Laos and international services to Bangkok, Phnom Penh and Hanoi. Thai Airways, Aeroflot and Air Vietnam provide direct flights from Bangkok, Hanoi, Rangoon and Moscow.

Shipping. The river Mekong and its tributaries are an important means of transport, but rapids, waterfalls and narrow channels often impede navigation and make trans-shipments necessary.

Telecommunications. There is a radio network in Laos as well as a TV service with the main station at Vientiane.

In 1974 there were 5,506 telephones in Laos. A telephone link with Bangkok was opened in 1967, and telephonic communication was established with most parts of the world in 1968.

RELIGION, EDUCATION AND WELFARE

Religion. The majority of the population is Buddhist (Hinayana).

Education. At the end of the 1978–79 school year there were 5,900 elementary schools (451,000 pupils); 260 secondary schools (60,400 pupils); 86 senior high schools (7,800 pupils); 72 nursery schools, (3,400 pupils); 24 teacher training schools (8,300 students) and 7 technical schools (2,000 students).

There is 1 teachers' training college, 1 college of education, 1 school of medicine, 1 agricultural college and an advanced school of Pali.

Health. In 1981 there were about 30 qualified doctors and 8,729 hospital beds.

DIPLOMATIC REPRESENTATIVES

OF LAOS IN GREAT BRITAIN (5 Palace Green, London, W8 4QA)
Chargé d'Affaires: Khamthong Phonphongsavat.

OF GREAT BRITAIN IN LAOS (Rue Pandit J. Nehru, Vientiane)
Chargé d'Affaires: W. B. J. Dobbs.

OF LAOS IN USA (2222 S St., NW, Washington, D.C., 20008)
Chargé d'Affaires: Khamtan Ratanavong.

OF USA IN LAOS (Quartier That Dam, Vientiane)
Chargé d'Affaires: Leo Moser.

OF LAOS TO THE UNITED NATIONS
Ambassador: Dr Vithaya Sourinho.

Books of Reference

La Constitution du Laos. Notes et Etudes. 1957
International Conference on the Settlement of the Laotian Question. Geneva, 12th May 1961–23rd July 1962 (Cmnd. 1828). HMSO, 1962
Declaration and Protocol on the Neutrality of Laos. Geneva, 23rd July 1962 (Cmnd. 2025). HMSO, 1963
White Book on the Violations of the Geneva Accords of 1962 by the Government of North Vietnam. Ministry of Foreign Affairs, Vientiane, 1968
Berval, Rene De and others, *Kingdom of Laos.* Saigon, 1959
Halpern, Joel M., *Economy and Society of Laos: Brief Survey.* Yale University Press, 1964.— *Government, Politics and Social Structure in Laos.* Yale University Press, 1964
Zasloff, J. J., *The Pathet Lao: Leadership and Organization.* Lexington, Toronto and London, 1973

LEBANON

Capital: Beirut
Population: 2·7m. (1978)
GNP per capita: US$1,070 (1974)

al-Jumhouriya al-Lubnaniya

HISTORY. After 20 years' French mandatory regime, Lebanon was proclaimed independent at Beirut on 26 Nov. 1941. On 27 Dec. 1943 an agreement was signed between representatives of the French National Committee of Liberation and of Lebanon, by which most of the powers and capacities exercised hitherto by France were transferred as from 1 Jan. 1944 to the Lebanese Government. The evacuation of foreign troops was completed in Dec. 1946.

In early May 1958 the opposition to President Chamoun, consisting principally (though not entirely) of Moslem pro-Nasserist elements, rose in insurrection; and for 5 months the Moslem quarters of Beirut, Tripoli, Sidon and the northern Bekaa were in insurgent hands. On 15 July the US Government acceded to President Chamoun's request and landed a considerable force of army and marines who re-established the authority of the Government.

In the subsequent presidential elections, Gen. Fouad Chehab replaced President Chamoun and a return to normality enabled US forces to be withdrawn.

In 1970 Suleiman Frangié succeeded President Helou for a 6-year term.

Israeli attacks on Lebanon and some internal problems resulted from the presence and activities of armed Palestinian resistance units on Lebanese territory. But a secret Cairo agreement in 1969 regulated these activities. From Sept. 1970, after action by Jordan, thousands of Palestinians transferred to Lebanon. Agreements between the Lebanese authorities and the Palestinian leadership in 1973 and 1977 were attempts to regulate the Palestinian presence in Lebanon. From March 1975, Lebanon was beset by civil disorder causing considerable loss of life and economic life was brought to a virtual standstill.

By Nov. 1976 it was estimated that 40,000 people had been killed and up to 100,000 injured. During this period there were over 50 ceasefire agreements but, by the end of 1976, the intervention of the Syrian dominated Arab Deterrent Force had ensured sufficient security to permit Lebanon to establish quasi-normal conditions under the guidance of President Sarkis. Only the south of Lebanon remained unsettled in late 1977. However in early 1978 there was a full-scale Israeli invasion of South Lebanon in reaction to a Palestinian sea raid. Israeli troops withdrew from much of the area in March on the arrival of UN peace-keeping forces.

AREA AND POPULATION. Lebanon is a mountainous country about 135 miles long and varying between 20 and 35 miles wide, bounded on the north and east by Syria, on the west by the Mediterranean and on the south by Israel. Between the two parallel mountain ranges of Lebanon and Anti-Lebanon lies the fertile Bekaa Valley. About one-half of the country lies at an altitude of over 3,000 ft.

The area of Lebanon is estimated at 10,400 sq. km (3,400 sq. miles) and the population at 2·7m. (1978, estimate). The principal towns, with estimated population, are: Beirut (the capital), 702,000; Tripoli, 175,000; Zahlé, 46,800; Saida (Sidon), 24,740; Tyre, 14,000.

Vital statistics, 1971: Births, 76,099; deaths, 12,799; marriages, 16,516; divorces, 1,382.

The official language is Arabic. French and, increasingly, English are widely spoken in official and commercial circles.

CONSTITUTION AND GOVERNMENT. Lebanon is an independent republic and a member of the United Nations and the Arab League. The first Constitution was established under the French Mandate on 23 May 1926. It has since been amended in 1927, 1929, 1943 (twice) and 1947. It is a written constitution based on the classical separation of powers, with a President, a single chamber elected by universal adult suffrage, and an independent judiciary. The Executive consists of the President and a Prime Minister and Cabinet appointed by him. The system is, however, adapted to the peculiar communal balance on which Lebanese political life depends. This is done by the electoral law which allocates deputies according to the confessional distribution of the population, and by a series of constitutional conventions whereby, *e.g.*, the President is always a Maronite Christian, the Prime Minister a Sunni Moslem and the Speaker of the Chamber a Shia Moslem. There is no highly developed party system other than on religious confessional lines.

At a special meeting of Parliament on 11 April 1976, 89 deputies voted unanimously in favour of an amendment to the Constitution to allow a new President to be elected up to 6 months before the end of the incumbent's term. President Frangié delayed signing the amendment until 22 April.

President of the Republic: Elias Sarkis (elected on 8 May and took office on 23 Sept. 1976).

The caretaker government of Dr Selim Hoss resigned in June 1980 and a new government under the Prime Ministership of Chafik Al Wazzan was formed in Oct. In the 22-man administration only 5 Ministers of the caretaker government were retained.

Prime Minister: Chafik Al Wazzan.
Foreign Minister: Fuad Butros.

National flag: Three horizontal stripes of red, white, red, with the white of double width and bearing in the centre a green cedar of Lebanon.
National anthem: Kulluna lil watan lil 'ula lil' alam (words by Rashid Nachleh, tune by Mitri El-Murr).

DEFENCE

Army. The Army strength was officially estimated in 1980 at 22,250. The Army comprises 2 armoured reconaissance, 12 infantry and 1 artillery battalions. The *gendarmerie* was about 5,000 and the police force about 600. Army and *gendarmerie* use mainly British, American and French equipment.

Navy. The Navy consisted in 1981 of 4 patrol boats, 6 coastal patrol craft and 1 landing craft. Personnel totalled 400 officers and men.

Air Force. The Air Force has about 500 men and 50 aircraft. In addition to a single combat squadron of Hunter jet fighter-bombers, it has (in storage) 9 Mirage III supersonic fighters and 1 Mirage 2-seat trainer. Other aircraft include 1 Dove light transport, 12 Alouette II and III and 12 Agusta-Bell 212 helicopters, and Fouga Magister jet and piston-engined Bulldog trainers.

INTERNATIONAL RELATIONS

Membership. Lebanon is a member of UN and the Arab League.

ECONOMY

Planning. Since the civil war a Development and Reconstruction Council has been responsible for co-ordinating all efforts.

Budget. The budget for 1979 provides for a total expenditure of £Leb.3,103·91m. (2,583·66m. in 1978). A draft budget for 1980 envisages a total expenditure of £Leb4,109·5m.

Currency. The Lebanese *pound*, divided into 100 *piastres*, is issued by the Banque du Liban, which commenced operations on 1 April 1964. There is a fluctuating official rate of exchange, fixed monthly (March 1981: £Leb.8·60 = £1 sterling), but this in practice is used only for the calculation of *ad-valorem* customs duties on

Lebanese imports and for import statistics. For other purposes the free market is used.

On 15 Oct. 1979 the note circulation was £Leb.3,664·5m.

Banking. Beirut was an important international financial centre, and there were about 80 banks registered with the central bank in 1979, including 2 British banks, the British Bank of the Middle East and the Chartered Bank. As a result of the civil war in 1975–76, Beirut lost much of its status as an international and regional banking centre; in general only local offices for banks remain.

Weights and Measures. The use of the metric system is legal and obligatory throughout the whole of the country. In outlying districts the former weights and measures may still be in use. They are: 1 *okiya* = 0·47 lb.; 6 *okiyas* = 1 *oke* = 2·82 lb.; 2 *okes* = 1 *rottol* = 5·64 lb.; 200 *okes* = 1 *kantar*.

ENERGY AND NATURAL RESOURCES

Oil. There are 2 oil refineries in Lebanon, one at Tripoli, which refines oil brought by ship from Iraq, and the other at Sidon, which refines oil brought from Saudi Arabia by a pipeline owned by the Trans-Arabian Pipeline Co. These refineries received 2m. tonnes of crude oil in 1977 and their production is normally sufficient to meet the country's requirements of refined fuel.

Minerals. Iron ore exists but is difficult to work. Other minerals known to exist are iron pyrites, copper, bituminous shales, asphalt, phosphates, ceramic clays and glass sand; but the available information is of doubtful value.

Agriculture. Lebanon is essentially an agricultural country, although owing to its physical character only about 38% of the total area of the country is at present cultivated. The forests of the past have been denuded by exploitation and the unrestricted grazing of goats, and only about 80,000 hectares of indifferent timber remain, and soil erosion is considerable.

The estimated yield (in 1,000 tonnes) of the main crops in 1979 was as follows: Citrus fruits, 320; apples, 135; grapes, 135; potatoes, 112; sugar-beet, 108; wheat, 40; bananas, 18; olives, 15.

Livestock (estimated, 1979): Goats, 340,000; sheep, 242,000; cattle, 84,000; camels, 1,000; pigs, 26,000; horses, 4,000; donkeys, 26,000; mules, 4,000.

INDUSTRY AND TRADE

Industry. Industry suffered badly during the civil war. The manufacturing industry was small but had doubled in size in the 10 years before the war. As a result of the war some industrial concerns have closed but a few light industries had been established in 1977–79.

Commerce. Foreign as well as local wholesale and retail trade is the principal source of income in Lebanon and provides about 31% of the total. Because of the protectionist policies followed in some neighbouring countries, this sector has been declining, the sectors to gain being those of banking, real estate, government and services.

In 1978 imports were estimated at £Leb.5,220m.; exports were valued at £Leb.1,639m. Imports came mainly from USA, Federal Republic of Germany, France, Italy and UK. Exports went mainly to Saudi Arabia, Kuwait, Syria, Libya and Iraq.

Total trade between Lebanon and UK (British Department of Trade returns, in £1,000 sterling):

	1976	1977	1978	1979	1980
Imports to UK	6,065	8,365	8,058	9,892	9,076
Exports and re-exports from UK	10,052	48,591	58,893	65,793	70,692

Customs duties are usually imposed on an *ad-valorem* basis: the receipts are the Lebanese Government's main source of income; actual yield in 1978, £Leb.509m. The considerable adverse balance of trade is offset by invisible receipts, including foreign capital investment in Lebanese real estate, remittances from émigrés and receipts from tourism and international arbitrage operations.

Tourism. Receipts from tourism were £Leb.573m. in 1973; since 1975 they have been negligible, this sector having suffered badly as a result of the war.

COMMUNICATIONS

Roads. The main roads in Lebanon are good. The surface is normally of asphalt and they are well maintained in normal times. In Dec. 1971 there were 570 km of international roads, 1,420 km of main roads and 4,310 km of secondary and local roads, all asphalted. The main arterial routes are the north–south coastal road and the west–east trunk road (Beirut to Damascus).

Passenger transport outside the town of Beirut is provided by a great number of small private companies running cheap and regular bus services and long-distance taxi services but in 1978 there were no bus services. Most goods traffic is hauled by road.

At 31 Dec. 1978 there were 282,404 cars and taxis, 2,592 buses and 28,553 commercial vehicles.

Railways. There are 3 railway lines in Lebanon, all operated by the *Office des Chemins de Fer de l'Etat Libanais* (CFL): (1) Nakoura–Beirut–Tripoli (standard gauge); the Nakoura–Sidon section has been idle since the establishment of Israel: (2) a narrow-gauge line running from Beirut to Riyak in the Bekaa Valley and thence to Damascus, Syria; (3) a standard-gauge line from Tripoli to Homs and Aleppo in Syria, providing access to Ankara and Istanbul. From Homs a branch of the CFL line extends south and re-enters Lebanon, terminating at Riyak. Total length 417 km.

Aviation. Beirut International Airport is used by many international airlines which connect Lebanon with most countries in the world. Extensive local services cover the Middle East, Persian Gulf and Europe. There are 2 national airlines, Middle East Airlines/Air Liban and Trans-Mediterranean Airways. In 1978, 24,500 flights passed through Beirut international airport (1974: 44,406), carrying a total of 1,405,600 passengers (1974: 2,806,632).

Shipping. Beirut is by far the largest and busiest port. In 1978, 1,786 vessels and 1,753,000 tonnes of goods were handled. Activity in the port of Tripoli is growing due to increased movements in goods and petroleum. The small port of Sidon in the south, near to the closed Lebanese–Israeli frontier, is at present of little importance. General activity since the civil war has been reduced to about 60%, but was increasing in late 1977. However, sporadic fighting in Beirut closed the port at times in 1978 and 1979.

Post and Broadcasting. There is an automatic telephone system in Beirut, Tripoli, Sidon, Zahlé and several other towns and villages, which is being extended to all parts of the country. There are no telegraph, postal or telephone communications with Israel. Number of telephones (1978), 231,000.

The state radio transmits in Arabic, French, English and Armenian. Before 1978 there were 2 commercial television stations, transmitting in Arabic, French and English. In 1978 they were amalgamated into a new company in which the Government has a 50% shareholding. There were 325,000 sets in 1975.

Cinemas (1973). There were 161 cinemas with a seating capacity of about 77,400.

Newspapers (1977). There were about 30 daily newspapers in Arabic, 2 in French, 1 in English and 4 in Armenian, with a total circulation of 215,000.

RELIGION, EDUCATION AND WELFARE

Religion. Probably less than half the population are Christians, some of whom have been indigenous since the earliest time of Christianity. There were in 1958, 792,000 Christians, of whom 424,000 were Maronites, 150,000 Greek Orthodox, 69,000 Armenians, 91,000 Greek and Roman Catholics, 14,500 Armenian Catholics, 14,000 Protestants. Moslems numbered 536,000, of whom 286,000 were Sunnis and 250,000 Shiites. There were also 88,000 Druzes and 6,600 Jews.

Education. Government schools in 1970 comprised 1,290 primary and secondary schools. There were also 1,484 private primary and secondary schools. There are also 5 teachers' training colleges and 5 universities, namely the Lebanese (State) University, the American University of Beirut, the French University of St Joseph (founded in 1875), the Arab University, a branch of Alexandria University and Beirut University College. The French Government runs the École Supérieure de Lettres and the Centre d'Études Mathématiques. The Maronite monks run the University of the Holy Spirit at Kaslik.

The Lebanese Academy of Fine Arts includes schools of architecture, art, music, political and social science.

Health. In 1973 there were 2,300 physicians and 8,000 hospital beds.

DIPLOMATIC REPRESENTATIVES

OF LEBANON IN GREAT BRITAIN (21 Kensington
Palace Gdns., London, W8 4QM)

Ambassador: Dr Khalil Makkawi.

OF GREAT BRITAIN IN LEBANON (Ave. de Paris, Ras Beirut)
Ambassador: B. L. Strachan, CMG.

OF LEBANON IN THE USA (2560-28th St.,
Washington, D.C., 20008)

Ambassador: Khalil Itani.

OF THE USA IN LEBANON (Corniche at Rue Ain
Mreisseh, Beirut)

Ambassador: John Gunther Dean.

OF LEBANON TO THE UNITED NATIONS

Ambassador: Ghassan Tuéni.

Books of Reference

Statistical Information: Import and export figures are produced by the Conseil Supérieur des Douanes. The Service de Statistique Générale (M. A. G. Ayad, *Chef du Service*) publishes a quarterly bulletin (in French and Arabic) covering a wide range of subjects, including foreign trade, production statistics and estimates of the national income.

Binder, L. (ed.), *Politics in Lebanon*. New York, 1966
Cowan, J. M., *Dictionary of Modern Arabic*. Wiesbaden, 1961
Hitti, P. K., *A Short History of Lebanon*. London, 1965
Murray, G., *Lebanon: The New Future*. London, 1974
Naccache, G., *Les Partis libanais en 1959*. Beirut, 1959
Rizk, C., *Le Régime politique libanais*. Paris, 1966
Salem, E. A., *Modernization Without Revolution: Lebanon's Experience*. Indiana Univ. Press, 1973
Salibi, K. S., *Modern History of Lebanon*. London, 1965.—*Crossroads to Civil War: Lebanon 1958–76*. New York, 1976
Ward, P., *Touring Lebanon*. London, 1971

National Library: Dar el Kutub, Parliament Sq., Beirut.

LESOTHO

Capital: Maseru
Population: 1·28m. (1978)
GNP per capita: US$280 (1978)

HISTORY. Basutoland first received the protection of Britain in 1868 at the request of Moshesh, the first paramount chief. In 1871 the territory was annexed to the Cape Colony, but in 1884 it was restored to the direct control of the British Government through the High Commissioner for South Africa.

On 4 Oct. 1966 Basutoland became an independent and sovereign member of the Commonwealth under the name of the Kingdom of Lesotho.

AREA AND POPULATION. Lesotho is bounded on the west by the Orange Free State, on the north by the Orange Free State and Natal, on the east by Natal and East Griqualand, and on the south by the Cape Province. The altitude varies from 5,000 to 11,000 ft. The climate is dry and rigorous, with extremes of heat and cold both seasonal and diurnal. The temperature varies between 93° F. (34° C.) and 3° F. (−16° C.). The rainfall is variable, the average being about 29 in. per annum.

The area is 11,716 sq. miles (30,340 sq. km). Lesotho is a purely African territory, and the few European residents are government officials, traders, missionaries and artisans.

The census taken on 12 April 1976 showed a total population of 1,246,815 persons. Estimate (1978) 1,279,000.

The capital is Maseru (population, 1976, 45,000).

The official languages are Sesotho and English.

CONSTITUTION AND GOVERNMENT. On 4 Oct. 1966 the country became the Kingdom of Lesotho, with the Paramount Chief as King.

Parliament consists of the National Assembly (60 members elected by adult suffrage) and a Senate (22 principal chiefs and 11 members nominated by the King). The general election held on 30 April 1965 returned 31 members of the National Party, 25 members of the Congress Party and 4 members of the Marematlou Freedom Party. The elections of 27 Jan. 1970 were declared invalid on 31 Jan. Parliamentary rule, with a National Assembly of nominated members, was reintroduced in April 1973.

A Constitution is being drafted.

King of Lesotho: Moshoeshoe II.

Prime Minister: Chief Leabua Jonathan. *Deputy Prime Minister and Public Works:* Chief Sekhonyana 'Maseribane.

The College of Chiefs settles the recognition and succession of Chiefs and adjudicates cases of inefficiency, criminality and absenteeism among them.

National flag: Blue with a white Basuto hat; in the hoist 2 vertical strips of green and red.

Local Government. The country is divided into 10 districts as follows: Maseru, Qacha's Nek, Mokhotlong, Leribe, Butha-Buthe, Teyateyaneng, Mafeteng, Mohale's Hoek, Quthing, Thaba-Tseka. Each district is subdivided into wards, most of which are presided over by hereditary chiefs allied to the Moshoeshoe family.

District councils, established in 1944, were abolished on 17 Jan. 1966; their functions are now exercised by officials appointed by the Ministry of Local Government.

INTERNATIONAL RELATIONS

Membership. Lesotho is a member of UN, OAU, the Commonwealth and is an ACP state of the EEC.

ECONOMY

Budget. The financial year ends on 31 March.

	1970–71 [1]	1971–72	1972–73	1973–74	1974–75	1977–78 [1]
Revenue	11,704,510	12,409,839	16,052,000	26,516,000	33,320,000	48,906,000
Expenditure	11,041,480	12,440,471	17,187,000	20,900,800	24,203,000	34,465,000

[1] Estimates.

The major items of expenditure in 1977–78 were education (R8·8m.), agriculture (R4·6m.), internal security and justice (R4·1m.) and health (R2·8m.). The revenue situation was greatly improved by the re-negotiation of the Republic of South Africa's customs agreement in 1970. Of the 1977–78 revenue R32m. was generated from domestic sources including the customs union.

Currency. The currency is the *Loti* (plural *Maloti*) divided into 100 *Lisente* which is at par with the South African *Rand*. March 1981, £1 = 1·72 *Maloti*.

Banking. The Standard Bank of South Africa and Barclays Bank International have branches at Maseru, Mohale's Hoek and Leribe.

AGRICULTURE. The chief crops are wheat, maize and sorghum; barley, oats, beans, peas and other vegetables are also grown. The land is held in trust for the nation by the King and may not be alienated.

Soil conservation and the improvement of crops and pasture are matters of vital importance. A total area of 1,006,817 acres has been protected against soil erosion by means of terracing, training banks, tree planting and grass strips. Efforts are being made to secure the general introduction of rotational grazing in the mountain area.

Livestock (1979): Cattle, 550,000; horses, 110,000; donkeys, 85,000; sheep, 1·3m.; goats, 730,000; mules, 1,000.

INDUSTRY AND TRADE

Industry. Industrial development is progressing under the National Development Corporation. Diamond exports, 1978, were valued at R16,695,446.

Commerce. Lesotho, Botswana and Swaziland are members of the South African customs union, by agreement dated 29 June 1910.

Total values of imports and exports into and from Lesotho (in R1,000):

	1974	1975	1976	1977
Imports	79,120	117,300	179,600	199,374
Exports	9,809	9,200	14,600	12,180

Principal imports in 1977 were food, livestock, drink and tobacco (R43m.), machinery and transport equipment (R24m.), mineral fuels and lubricants (R18m.); principal exports were wool and mohair (R4·5m.) and diamonds.

The majority of international trade is with the Republic of South Africa.

Total trade between Lesotho and UK (British Department of Trade returns, in £1,000 sterling):

	1977	1978	1979	1980
Imports to UK	188	193	105	340
Exports and re-exports from UK	807	409	2,233	394

Tourism. In 1974 there were 75,000 visitors. The Lesotho National Development Corporation is helping the development of tourism and more hotels and resorts are planned.

COMMUNICATIONS

Roads. There were (1975) 125 miles of tarred roads and 529 miles of gravel-surfaced roads along the western border of Lesotho, with outlets to the border ports of exit. Regular motor services of the South African Railways operate between Zastron (OFS) and Quthing, Zastron (OFS) and Mohale's Hoek, and between Fouriesburg (OFS) and Butha Buthe. In addition to the main roads there were (1975) 1,029 miles of tracks leading to trading stations and missions. Communications into the mountainous interior are by means of bridlepaths suitable only for riding and pack animals, but a mountain road of 80 miles has been constructed, and some parts are accessible by air transport, which is being used increasingly. In 1977 there were 11,509 motor vehicles.

Railways. A railway built by the South African Railways, 1 mile long, connects Maseru with the Bloemfontein–Natal line at Marseilles.

Aviation. There is a scheduled passenger service between Maseru and Jan Smuts Airport, Johannesburg operated jointly by Lesotho National Airways and SAA. There are also 30 airstrips for light aircraft.

Post and Broadcasting. There were 3,726 telephones on 1 Jan. 1975. Radio Lesotho transmits daily in English and Sesotho. Radio receivers (1976), about 20,000.

Cinemas. In 1971 there were 2 cinemas with a seating capacity of 800.

JUSTICE, RELIGION, EDUCATION AND WELFARE

Justice. An appeal court for Lesotho was established at Maseru on 4 Oct. 1966.

The police force on 31 Dec. 1972 had an establishment of 111 officers and subordinate officers and 1,194 other ranks.

Religion. About 70% of the population are Christians, 40% being Roman Catholics.

Education. Education is largely in the hands of the 3 main missions (Paris Evangelical, Roman Catholic and English Church), under the direction of the Ministry of Education. In 1974 the total enrolment in 1,087 primary schools was 218,038; in 84 secondary schools, 14,908; in 7 teacher-training schools enrolment was 510 in 1972. University education was provided at the University of Botswana, Lesotho, Swaziland, which now has a campus in each of the 3 countries. Total enrolment in 1974–75 was 538, of which 322 were Basotho students. In 1975 a National University was established. Recurrent government expenditure on education was estimated at R3,948,700 in 1973–74. Bursaries are provided at all stages for secondary, teacher-training and university work. In 1972, 106 Basotho were studying at universities and places of higher education, outside Lesotho.

Health. The government medical staff of the territory consists of 1 Permanent Secretary for Health and chief medical officer, 1 medical superintendent, 26 medical officers, 1 medical officer of health and 6 specialist physicians and surgeons.

There are 10 government hospitals staffed by 333 matrons, sisters and nurses. There is accommodation for 2,106 patients in government hospitals. The 316-bed Queen Elizabeth II hospital in Maseru was completed in 1957. There are 9 mission hospitals subsidized by the Government with 729 beds. Health centres and mountain dispensaries provide outpatient medical facilities and maternity services to people living in remote areas. The leper settlement 5 miles out of Maseru had 189 patients at the end of 1972.

Typhus and plague occur.

DIPLOMATIC REPRESENTATIVES

OF LESOTHO IN GREAT BRITAIN (16A St James's St., London, SW1A 1EU)

High Commissioner: Mooki M. Molapo.

OF GREAT BRITAIN IN LESOTHO

High Commissioner: O. G. Griffith, OBE, MVO.

OF LESOTHO IN THE USA (1601 Connecticut Ave., NW, Washington, D.C., 20009)

Ambassador: Timothy T. Thahane.

OF THE USA IN LESOTHO

Ambassador: John R. Clingerman.

OF LESOTHO TO THE UNITED NATIONS
Ambassador: Thabo Makeka.

Books of Reference

Statistical Information: Bureau of Statistics, PO Box 455, Maseru, Lesotho.
Lesotho: Report for 1968. Maseru, 1969
Ambrose, A., *The Guide to Lesotho.* Johannesburg and Maseru, 1976
Ashton, H., *The Basuto.* 2nd ed. OUP, 1967
Hailey, Lord, *The Republic of South Africa and the High Commission Territories.* OUP, 1963
Jones, D., *Aid and Development in Southern Africa.* London, 1977
Khaketla, B. M., *Lesotho 1970.* London, 1971
Spence, J. E., *Lesotho.* OUP, 1968
Stevens, C., *Food, Aid and the Developing World.* London, 1979

LIBERIA

Capital: Monrovia
Population: 1·8m. (1979)
GNP per capita: US$460 (1978)

HISTORY. The Republic of Liberia had its origin in the efforts of several American philanthropic societies to establish freed American slaves in a colony on the West African coast. In 1822 a settlement was formed near the spot where Monrovia now stands. On 26 July 1847 the State was constituted as the Free and Independent Republic of Liberia. The new State was first recognized by Great Britain and France, and ultimately by other powers.

AREA AND POPULATION. Liberia has about 350 miles of coastline, extending from Sierra Leone, on the west, to the Ivory Coast, on the east, and it stretches inland to a distance, in some places, of about 250 miles. The boundaries were determined by the Anglo-Liberian agreement of 1885 and the Franco-Liberian agreements of 1882 and 1907–10. In 1911 the territory of Kailahun was transferred to Sierra Leone in exchange for a strip on the south side of Mano River, which now is the boundary.

The total area is about 43,000 sq. miles (112,600 sq. km). A census taken in 1978 gave the total population as 1,715,973 (872,105 males). Estimate (1979) 1·8m. The indigenous natives belong in the main to 4 principal stocks: Mendetan, West Atlantic, Mande-fu, and Kru. These are in turn subdivided into 16 major tribes, namely: Bassa, Belle, Gbandi, Mende, Gio, Dey, Mano, Gola, Kpelle, Kissi, Krahn, Kru, Loma, Mandingo, Vai and Grebo.

Monrovia, the capital, had (1978) a population of 208,629 and is administered as a city corporation by a mayor to be elected by popular vote. It is one of the 4 ports of entry along the 350 miles of coast, the others being Buchanan (Grand Bassa), River Cess, Greenville (Sinoe), Harper (Maryland). Other towns are Kolba City, Voinjama, Tubmanburg, Bentol, Zorzor, Kakata, Suakoko, Gbarnga, Ganta, Sanniquellie, Saclape, Tappita, Robertsport, Bendaja, Yekepa and Zwedru.

The country is divided into 9 counties and the federal district of Monrovia.

CONSTITUTION AND GOVERNMENT. The Constitution of the republic is modelled on that of the US. The executive power is vested in a President and the legislative power in a legislature of 2 Houses, the Senate (27 members) and the House of Representatives (71 members). The President is elected for 8 years in the first instance, the House of Representatives for 4 and the Senate for 6 years. A Legislative Act was approved on 22 July 1974, setting up a National Commission to give consideration to possible changes in the Motto, Flag, Anthem and the Constitution of Liberia.

On 12 March 1980, President Tolbert was assassinated and his government overthrown. President Tolbert's party, the True Whig Party, was formed in 1860 and had been in power since 1870. Recent economic decline and pressure for change had undermined the Government. On March 1980, the newly formed People's Progressive Party was banned and its leaders arrested. The *coup* was led by Master-Sergeant Doe who was later installed as Head of State.

Executive power is vested in the Head of State and a Cabinet of 17 which is supervised by a People's Redemption Council.

President: Samuel Doe.
Foreign Minister: Gabriel Baccus Matthews.

The official language is English.

National flag: Six red and 5 white horizontal stripes alternating. In the upper corner, nearest the staff, is a square of blue covering a depth of 5 stripes. In the centre of this blue field is a 5-pointed white star.

National anthem: All hail, Liberia, hail! (words by President Warner; tune by O. Lucas, 1860).

On 22 Dec. 1950 an agreement of assistance and co-operation was signed in Washington whereby a development programme was implemented under control of a joint American–Liberian Commission.

DEFENCE. For defence every citizen from 16 to 45 years of age capable of bearing arms is liable to serve. On 31 March 1942 an agreement was signed between the USA and Liberia by which the US were given the right to construct, control, operate and defend airports in Liberia for the duration of the war. On 8 June 1943 a further mutual aid agreement was concluded with the US, which extended lend-lease aid to Liberia for the purpose of defence and enabled it to increase its Armed Forces.

Army. The establishment organized on a militia basis numbers 5,130 (all services, 1980), divided into 5 infantry battalions with support units. There is in addition an enlisted frontier force, the Liberian National Guard, of 93 officers and 2,200 men.

Navy. The small naval service or coastguard comprises 1 motor gunboat, 3 small patrol boats, 3 new coastguard cutters and a few former landing craft for transport and general utility. Personnel in 1981 totalled 225 officers and men.

Air Force. The nucleus of an Air Force has been formed, as the Air Reconnaissance Unit, to support the Liberian Army. Equipment includes 2 C-47 transports and about 14 Cessna 172, 185, 150, 207 and 337G light aircraft.

INTERNATIONAL RELATIONS

Membership. Liberia is a member of UN, OAU and is an ACP state of EEC but the European Community had (March 1981) suspended its relations with Liberia.

ECONOMY

Budget. The budgets for calendar years were as follows (in US$1,000):

	1974	1975	1976	1977	1978
Revenue	108,600	125,343	149,800	166,500	185,500
Expenditure	108,900	122,500	136,000	194,000	227,600

Currency. The legal currency of Liberia is the *dollar* which is equivalent to US$1 which itself has been in circulation since 3 Nov. 1942, but there is a Liberian coinage in silver and copper. Official accounts are kept in dollars and cents. The Liberian coins are as follows: Silver, $1, 50-, 25-, 10- and 5-cent pieces; alloy, 2- and 1-cent pieces. The Government has not yet issued paper money. In March 1981, £1 = 2·18 Liberian $; US$1 = 1 Liberian $.

Banking. The Bank of Liberia, Inc., was founded on 28 July 1955. An Italian bank, Tradevco, started business in 1955. The International Trust Co. of Liberia opened a commercial banking department at the end of 1960. The Commercial Bank of Liberia and a branch of the Chase Manhattan Bank opened in 1961. The Union National Bank (Liberia) Inc., opened in 1962. The Liberian Bank for Development and Investment (LBDI) was founded in 1964 and began operations in 1965. The National Bank of Liberia opened on 22 July 1974, to act as a central bank. The National Housing and Savings Bank opened on 20 Jan. 1976. The Liberian Agricultural and Co-operative Development Bank started operations in 1978.

Weights and Measures. Weights and measures are the same as in UK and USA.

NATURAL RESOURCES

Minerals. Mineral resources have not been completely surveyed. The National Iron Ore Co. near the Mano River, the Liberian Swedish Mineral Co. in the Nimba Mountains and the Bong Mining Co. (DELIMCO) at Bong Mountain Range are exploiting their iron-ore concession areas. The Liberian Mining Co. at Bomi Hills, which was the first iron ore mine to be established, closed down its operations in 1977. Iron ore exports amounted to 20·05m. long tons in 1976. Gold and diamonds are found on a small scale.

A pelletizing and washing plant was inaugurated in 1968 for the American–Swedish Minerals Co. near the port of Buchanan. Another pelletizing and washing plant was inaugurated in 1971 for the Bong Mining Co.

Agriculture. The soil is productive, but due to excessive rainfall (from 160 to 180 in. per year), there are large swamp areas. Rice, cassava, coffee, citrus and sugar-cane are cultivated. Rice production is inadequate for local needs, but strenuous efforts are being made to increase production by the substitution of swamp rice for hill rice cultivation. Total rice production increased from 472,000 acres in 1975 to 495,000 acres in 1977. The Government is negotiating the financing of large-scale investment in rice production on over 50,000 acres, aimed at transforming the country from a rice-importing to a rice-exporting nation. Sugar-cane is grown for manufacture of locally consumed rum. In 1973, Liberia signed an agreement with China for the development of a sugar industry in Liberia. The project is being carried out in two phases, the first involving an investment of US$15m. on 10,000 acres of land, for the production of 10,000–12,000 tons of sugar and 3,000 tons of molasses per year, and the second entailing an investment of US$25·6m. for the production of 73,000–80,000 tons yearly. In 1977 sugar production had commenced under the management of LIBSUCO, in Maryland County. Coffee, cocoa and palm-kernels are produced mainly by the traditional agricultural sector. In 1976, the total volume of coffee and cocoa exports alone were 9·3m. lb. (US$6·6m.), and 5·5m. lb. (US$4·1m.), respectively.

The Liberia Produce Marketing Corporation (LPMC) operates an oil-mill in Monrovia, processing most of the palm-kernels. There were 2 large commercial oil-palm plantations in the country. The Liberia Industrial Co-operative (LBINC) has 6,000 acres of oil-palm (of which 5,000 acres are in production) in Grand Bassa County, and West Africa Agricultural Co. (WAAC) has 4,020 acres in production in Grand Cape Mount County.

Livestock (1979): Cattle, 38,000; pigs, 100,000; sheep, 190,000; poultry, 2·2m.

Forestry. The Firestone Plantation Co. have large rubber plantations, employing over 40,000 men. Their concession comprises about 1m. acres and expires in the year 2025. About 100,000 acres have been planted. Independent producers have a further 65,000 acres planted. In 1976 the total area under rubber cultivation was 294,400 acres, of which 195,800 acres were under actual production.

The B. F. Goodrich Co. was, on 9 July 1954, granted an 80-year concession to produce rubber; part of the 12,300 acres planted came into production in 1963. Other rubber-producing companies include Allen L. Grant, L. A. C. and Salala Rubber Co. Together, the foreign concessions produced 128m. lb. in 1975 while independent Liberian farmers produced 53·4m. lb. amounting to a total rubber production in 1975 of 181·4m. lb.

Logs and lumber are now the country's fourth most important export. A plywood industry has started in Sinoe County; production, 1977, 6,241 tons.

INDUSTRY AND TRADE

Industry. There are a number of small factories (brick and tile, soap, nails, mattresses, shoes, plastics, paint, oxygen, acetylene, tyre retreading, a brewery, soft drinks, cement, matches, candy and biscuits).

Commerce. Foreign trade for 6 calendar years was as follows (in US$1m.):

	1974	1975	1976	1977	1978	1979
Imports	289·4	331	399·2	463·5	486	537
Exports	400·3	394	457·0	447·4	481	505

The principal exports in 1977 were: Iron ore, and concentrates, US$274·7m.; rubber, US$220·7m.; logs and lumber, US$400m. The principal imports in 1976 were machinery and transport equipment (US$152·1m.) and manufactured goods (US$795·4m.). Main suppliers in 1976 were: EEC (US$142·3m.), USA (US$119·1m.), Asia (US$98·8m.), other West European countries (US$24·1m.).

Total trade between Liberia and UK (British Department of Trade returns, in £1,000 sterling):

	1976	1977	1978	1979	1980
Imports to UK	10,035	14,052	12,511	14,359	8,671
Exports and re-exports from UK	23,893	21,539	32,992	78,408	46,412

The figures for exports from the UK include the value of shipping transferred to the Liberian flag; the genuine exports are considerably lower.

Liberia was placed in the American account area in 1952.

Tourism. In 1979 a tourist industry was being developed.

COMMUNICATIONS

Roads. There are over 4,500 miles of state roads, suitable for motor traffic, as well as roads on private plantations. The principal highway connects Monrovia with the road system of Guinea, with branches leading into the Eastern and Western areas of Liberia. The latter branch reaches the Sierra Leone border and joins the Sierra Leone road system. A bridge over the St Paul River carries road and rail traffic to the iron-ore mines at Bomi Hills.

In the interior, communication is maintained by tracks, all goods being carried by native porters, but secondary roads are being constructed by local communities with state assistance, and transportation by vehicle is becoming increasingly common. A 5-year road improvement plan was in operation until 1977.

Railway. A railway (for freight only) was built in 1951, connecting Monrovia with the Bomi Hills iron-ore mines about 69 km distant; this has been extended to the National Iron Ore Co. area by 79 km. A line from Nimba to Lower Buchanan (267 km) was completed in 1963 and another line from Bong to Monrovia (78 km) was completed in 1965.

Aviation. The airport for Liberia is Roberts Airport (30 miles from Monrovia). The James Spriggs Payne Airfield, 5 miles from Monrovia, can be used by light aircraft and mini jumbo jets. Air services are maintained by PANAM, Ghana Airways, Nigeria Airways, UTA, Middle East Airlines, Air Mali, Air Afrique, SAS, KLM, Swissair, British Caledonian, Air Guinée, SABENA, Iberia Airlines, Romanian Airlines and Air Liberia.

Shipping. In 1976, 2,229 main-line ships entered Monrovia.

The Liberian merchant navy, in 1976, consisted of 2,666 ships of 76,412,842 GRT. The Liberian Government requires only a modest registration fee and an almost nominal annual charge and maintains no control over the operation of ships flying the Liberian flag.

Constructed under the auspices of the US Government under lend-lease terms, the port of Monrovia, a free port, was opened on 26 July 1948.

A modern port for the shipment of iron-ore from the mines at Nimba has been built at Lower Buchanan, capable of accommodating vessels up to 75,000 tons.

The river St Paul is navigable for a distance of 8 miles from its mouth for small craft of shallow draught. The Cavalla River is navigable for 8 miles.

Post and Broadcasting. There is cable communication (French) with Europe and America *via* Dakar, and a wireless station is maintained by the Government at Monrovia. There is a telephone service (8,420 telephones, 1978), in Monrovia, which is gradually being extended over the whole country. An earth station constructed by Itacable in 1976 is equipped for 24 telephone type channels and its traffic can be increased to 60 telephone type channels. With the aid of the satellite the average traffic each day now stands at 900.

There are wireless stations at Monrovia, Bassa, Harper, Kolahun, Cape Mount and Sinoe. The wireless stations at Harbel, Montserrado county, Maryland county, and Gedetarbo, have since 1928 been operated as a public utility by the US–Liberia Radio Corporation, a subsidiary of Firestone Plantation Co.

A commercial broadcasting station, ELBC, opened in Dec. 1959 and a television service on 1 Jan. 1964.

JUSTICE, RELIGION, EDUCATION AND WELFARE

Justice. Justice is administered by a Supreme Court of 5 judges, circuit courts and lower courts. A new Liberian code of laws has been published (5 vols. to 1956).

Religion. The main denominations represented in Liberia are Methodist, Baptist, Episcopalian, African Methodist, Pentecostal, Seventh-day Adventist, Lutheran and Roman Catholic, working through missionaries and mission schools. There is also a fairly large Moslem community.

Education. Schools are classified as: (1) Public schools, maintained and run by the Government; (2) Mission schools, supported by foreign Missions and subsidized by the Government, and operated by qualified Missionaries and Liberian teachers; (3) Private schools, maintained by endowments and sometimes subsidized by the Government.

By the end of 1978 there were estimated to be 1,441 schools with 1,360 teachers and 237,853 pupils. In 1975, 800 US Peace Corps Volunteers were teaching in schools throughout the country.

Health. There were 178 doctors in 1977 and about 3,000 hospital beds.

DIPLOMATIC REPRESENTATIVES

OF LIBERIA IN GREAT BRITAIN (21 Prince's Gate, London, SW7 1QB)
Chargé d'Affaires: James H. Stevens.

OF GREAT BRITAIN IN LIBERIA (Mamba Point, Monrovia)
Ambassador and Consul-General: D. G. Reid.

OF LIBERIA IN THE USA (5201–16th St., NW, Washington, D.C., 20011)
Ambassador: Francis A. Dennis.

OF THE USA IN LIBERIA (United Nations Drive, Monrovia)
Ambassador: Robert P. Smith.

OF LIBERIA TO THE UNITED NATIONS
Ambassador: Winston Tubman.

Books of Reference

Presidential Papers, July 1971–July 1972. Monrovia, 1973
Economic Survey of Liberia, 1977. Ministry of Planning and Economic Affairs
Clower, R. W. (ed.), *Growth Without Development: An Economic Survey of Liberia.* Evanston, North-western Univ. Press, 1966
Cole, H. B. (ed.), *The Liberian Year Book.* Monrovia, 1962
Dunn, D. E., *The Foreign Policy of Liberia during the Tubman Era, 1944–71.* London, 1979
Fraenkel, M., *Tribe and Class in Monrovia.* OUP, 1964
McLaughlin, R. U., *Foreign Investment and Development in Liberia.* New York, 1966
Welch, G., *The Jet Lighthouse.* London, 1960
Wilson, C. M., *Liberia: Black Africa in Microcosm.* New York, 1971

SOCIALIST PEOPLE'S LIBYAN ARAB JAMAHIRIYAH

Capital: Tripoli
Population: 2·94m. (1978)
GNP per capita: US$6,910 (1978)

Al-Jamahiriyah Al-Arabiya
Al-Libya Al-Shabiya
Al-Ishtirakiya

HISTORY. Tripoli fell under Turkish domination in the 16th century, and though in 1711 the Arab population secured some measure of independence, the country was in 1835 proclaimed a Turkish vilayet. In Sept. 1911 Italy occupied Tripoli and on 19 Oct. 1912, by the Treaty of Ouchy, Turkey recognized the sovereignty of Italy in Tripoli.

After the expulsion of the Germans and Italians in 1942 and 1943, Tripolitania and Cyrenaica were placed under British, and the Fezzan under French, military administration. Britain recognized the Amir Mohammed Idris Al-Senussi as Amir of Cyrenaica in June 1949.

Libya became an independent, sovereign, federal kingdom under the Amir of Cyrenaica, Mohammed Idris Al-Senussi, as King of the United Kingdom of Libya, on 24 Dec. 1951, when the British Residents in Tripolitania and Cyrenaica and the French Resident in the Fezzan transferred their remaining powers to the federal government of Libya, in pursuance of decisions passed by the United Nations in 1949 and 1950.

On 1 Sept. 1969 King Idris was deposed by a group of army officers. Twelve of the group of officers formed the Revolutionary Command Council which rules the country with the assistance of a, mainly, civilian cabinet. One member died in Aug. 1972 and has not been replaced and another member, Maj. Muhaishi, was dismissed in 1976.

The Confederation of Arab Republics, comprising Libya, Egypt and Syria was created in 1971. Libya and Egypt announced in Aug. 1972 their intention of complete union of their two countries by 1 Sept. 1973.

A decision to bring about political union between Libya and Egypt by 1 Sept. 1973 was announced on 2 Aug. 1972. A proposed merger between Tunisia and Libya was announced on 12 Jan. 1974. Neither of these proposals had been implemented by April 1979.

AREA AND POPULATION. The area is estimated at 1,759,540 sq. km (679,358 sq. miles). The population, according to the census of 1973, was 2·26m. Estimate (1978) 2·94m.

According to an arrangement with France (12 Sept. 1919) the western frontier extends in a curve from west of Ghadames to south of Tummo, including Ghat. According to the agreement with France of 7 Jan. 1935, the southern frontier runs along a line between Tummo and a cross-point indicated by 24° E. long. from Greenwich and 18° 45′ N. lat. Further frontier agreements with France were signed on 10 Aug. 1955 and 26 Dec. 1956. In 1926 Egypt ceded the oasis of Jarabub to Italy, in exchange for a rectification of the frontier near Sollum. The eastern boundary follows in general the 25° parallel E. long. (*See* map in THE STATESMAN'S YEAR-BOOK, 1952.)

The country is administratively divided into the following 10 provinces (with population, 1973, census): Tripoli (735,083), Benghazi (337,423), Sebha (113,006), Zawia (247,628), Kalig (106,647), Khoms (162,126), Misurata (177,939), Derna (122,984), Jebel Akhdar (131,940), Gharian (155,958).

The 3 most important towns are Tripoli (551,477 inhabitants), Misurata (103,302), Benghazi (282,192).

CONSTITUTION AND GOVERNMENT. Under the new 1977 Constitution, Libya is now divided into 46 municipalities and 186 'Basic People's Congresses', which form the primary level of government. The General People's Congress, created in Jan. 1976 as the national legislature, comprises 3 delegates from each of the 186 Basic People's Congresses. The General People's Committee, which replaced the Council of Ministers, is assisted by the 5-member General People's Secretariat, which replaced the Revolutionary Command Council. It was ruled by the Revolutionary Command Council (RCC) under the leadership of Col. Muammar Qadhafi.

In March 1977 a new form of direct democracy, the 'Jamahiriya' (state of the masses) was promulgated and the official name of the country was changed to Socialist Peoples Libyan Arab Jamahiriya. At local level authority is now vested in 186 Basic and 46 Municipal People's Congresses which appoint Popular Committees to execute policy. Officials of these Congresses and Committees form at national level the General People's Congress, a body of some 1,000 delegates which normally meets for about a week twice a year. This is the highest policy-making body in the country. The General People's Congress appoints its own General Secretariat and the General People's Committee, whose members head the 20 government departments which execute policy at national level. The Secretary of the General People's Committee has functions similar to those of a Prime Minister.

Following the re-organization of March 1979 Col. Qadhafi retained his position as leader of the Revolution. But neither he nor his former RCC colleagues have any formal posts in the new administration.

Arabic is the official language. Tripoli is the capital.

Secretary-General of the General Secretariat of the General People's Congress: Abdul Iati Ai-Ubaidi.

National flag: Plain green.

DEFENCE

Army. The Army, of 45,000 men (1980), is organized in 12 armoured, 1 National Guard, 24 mechanized and 5 artillery battalions.

Navy. The fleet comprises 3 diesel-driven submarines, 1 small frigate, 3 corvettes, 11 fast missile craft, 11 coastal patrol boats, 1 medium (dock type) logistic support ship, 5 landing ships, 1 maintenance repair craft, 1 diving ship and 4 tugs. Under construction or projection are 3 submarines, 2 corvettes and 14 fast missile craft.

The Libyan Government stated in Nov. 1975 that 6 submarines of the Soviet 'F' class would be provided by the USSR. The training of Libyans in the Soviet Union offered confirmation of this. First delivery was on 27 Dec. 1976, named *Badr*, the second in late-1977 and the third in 1978. The order for 4 submarines of the French 'Daphne' class is reportedly being reconsidered. An order for 2 miniature submarines is reportedly to compensate for 2 transferred to the PLO.

Personnel in 1981 was progressively upwards of 3,000 officers and ratings, including coastguard.

Libya is procuring naval equipment and weapons from both the East and the West; and the eventual considerable-sized and up-to-date fleet could constitute a force of critical importance in the Mediterranean.

Air Force. The creation of an Air Force began in 1959. In 1974, delivery was completed of a total of 110 Mirage 5 combat aircraft and trainers. They have been followed by 17 Tu-22 supersonic reconnaissance bombers, some MiG-25 reconnaissance aircraft (probably Soviet-manned), and about 100 MiG-23 variable-geometry fighters and fighter-bombers from the USSR. Other equipment includes Mi-24 gunship helicopters, 7 C-130H Hercules and 9 C-47 transports, 7 Super Frelon and 20 Agusta-built CH-47C Chinook heavy-lift helicopters, and a total of about 23 Bell 212, Bell 47, Alouette III and Mi-8 helicopters. Training is performed on piston-engined SF-260Ms from Italy, and L-39 Albatros, Galeb and Magister jet aircraft. Personnel total about 4,000. Aircraft on order include 34 Mirage F1 fighters from France and 20 G222 twin-turboprop transports from Italy.

INTERNATIONAL RELATIONS

Membership. Libya is a member of UN, OAU and the Arab League.

ECONOMY

Planning. A plan of economic and social transformation was published in 1976 covering the period 1976–78.

The 1976–80 5-year transformation Plan envisaged expenditure of (in LD1m.) 9,250; including 1,131 for housing, 978 for agricultural development, 930 for transport and communications, 1,205 for industry, 897 for electricity, 757 for municipalities, 522 for education and 276 for public health.

Budget. The administrative budget for 1979 allows for expenditure of LD770m.; development budget, LD1,573m.

Currency. The currency is the Libyan *dinar* which is divided into 1,000 *millemes*. Rate of exchange, March 1981: LD0·65 = £1.

Banking. A National Bank of Libya was established in 1955; it was renamed the Central Bank of Libya in 1972. On 31 Dec. 1976, its assets amounted to LD1,793·9m. All foreign banks were nationalized by Dec. 1970. In 1972 the Libyan Government set up the Libyan Arab Foreign Bank whose function is overseas investment and to participate in multinational banking corporations. The National Agricultural Bank, which has been set up to give loans and subsidies to farmers to develop their land and to assist them in marketing their crops, has offices in Tripoli, Benghazi, Sebha and other agricultural centres. The National Industrial and Real Estate Bank, which has been established to give loans to house buyers and to give short and medium loans to private sector industrial ventures, also has offices in Tripoli and Benghazi.

Weights and Measures. Although the metric system has been officially adopted and is obligatory for all contracts, the following weights and measures are still used: *oke* = 1·282 kg; *kantar* = 51·28 kg; *draa* = 46 cm; *handaza* = 68 cm.

ENERGY AND NATURAL RESOURCES

Electricity. Electricity output capacity in 1972 was 190 mw and was increased to 581 mw by the end of 1975.

Oil. In 1968, 41 companies were working concession areas; the most important discoveries so far made are: (i) Zelten, about 200 miles south from Benghazi and 100 miles from the nearest point on the coast; discovered by Esso (the local subsidiary of the Standard Oil Co. of New Jersey) in April 1959. Exports from this field began at the end of 1961, the oil being piped to the port of Marsa Bregha. (ii) Dahra, roughly midway between Tripoli and Benghazi and about 90 miles from the coast, discovered in 1958–59; a pipeline to Ras El Sidr was completed in 1962. (iii) Beida, about 140 miles from the coast and just east of the Tripolitanian/Cyrenaican border, discovered by Caltex in 1959. (iv) Other discoveries, either non-commercial or not yet evaluated, have been made by Mobiloil of Canada, Shell, Gulf, CPTL. British Petroleum has also discovered oil in commercial quantities in southern Cyrenaica some 400 miles from the coast, connected to the Tobruk terminal by pipeline. Occidental Oil Co. have made 2 high-yield strikes and are planning the construction of a pipeline and terminal at Zueitina.

In 1977 production averaged 2,064,000 bbls per day. On 7 Dec. 1971 the British Petroleum Exploration (Libya) Co. was nationalized and on 11 June 1973 its partner Nelson Bunker Hunt. The rights and concessions were listed in the Arabian Gulf Exploration Co. The Oasis and Occidental companies agreed in Aug. 1973 to 51% participation by the Libyan National Oil Co. in their rights and operations.

A decree of 1 Sept. 1973 nationalized 51% of the rights and assets of the following companies: Mobil, Exxon, Amoco, Amoseas and Shell. On 11 Feb. 1974 Amoco and Amoseas were totally nationalized. Compensation has been paid to Shell, BP and Nelson Bunker Hunt.

Minerals. The production of cement was 1,065,000 tonnes in 1977, though the existing 2 cement plants are being expanded to give a future combined production of 850,000 tonnes per annum. A third cement factory has been built in eastern Libya with a capacity of 1m. tonnes per year, and another one of the same capacity has also been opened. A limestone factory is also to be built shortly in Benghazi. Gypsum output (1975) 15,000 tonnes.

Agriculture. Tripolitania has 3 zones from the coast inland—the Mediterranean, the sub-desert and the desert. The first, which covers an area of about 17,231 sq. miles, is the only one properly suited for agriculture, and may be further subdivided into: (1) the oases along the coast, the richest in North Africa, in which thrive the date palm, the olive, the orange, the peanut and the potato; (2) the steppe district, suitable for cereals (barley and wheat) and pasture; it has olive, almond, vine, orange and mulberry trees and ricinus plants; (3) the dunes, which are being gradually afforested with acacia, robinia, poplar and pine; (4) the Jebel (the mountain district, Tarhuna, Garian, Nalut-Yefren), in which thrive the olive, the fig, the vine and other fruit trees, and which on the east slopes down to the sea with the fertile hills of Msellata. Of some 25m. acres of productive land in Tripolitania, nearly 20m. are used for grazing and about 1m. for static farming. The sub-desert zone produces the alfa plant. The desert zone and the Fezzan contain some fertile oases, such as those of Ghadames, Ghat, Socna, Sebha, Brak.

Cyrenaica has about 10m. acres of potentially productive land, most of which, however, is suitable only for grazing. Certain areas, chief of which is the plateau known as the Barce Plain (about 1,000 ft above sea-level), are suitable for dry farming; in addition, grapes, olives and dates are grown. With improved irrigation, production, particularly of vegetables, could be increased, but stock raising and dry farming will remain of primary importance. About 143,000 acres are used for settled farming; about 272,000 acres are covered by natural forests. The Agricultural Development Authority plans to reclaim 6,000 hectares each year for agriculture.

In the Fezzan there are about 6,700 acres of irrigated gardens and about 297,000 acres are planted with date palms.

A 10-year agricultural plan totalling over LD700m. was announced in May 1973. The plan aims to reclaim and develop land in the Gefara plain, the Jebel Akhdar, the Fezzan and the Kufra/Sarir areas.

Future agricultural activity will concentrate on building up local production of cereals, dairy farming, sheep rearing, poultry farming and the cultivation of fruits and vegetables.

Production (1975, in tonnes): Wheat, 107,000; barley, 216,000; vegetables, 620,000; milk, 85,000; meat, 46,000. Olive trees number about 3·4m. and productive date-palm trees about 3m.

Livestock (1979): 4·8m. sheep, 2·1m. goats, 201,000 cattle, 5·6m. poultry.

INDUSTRY AND TRADE

Industry. Among the traditional industries of Tripolitania and Cyrenaica are sponge fishing, tunny fishing, tobacco growing and processing, dyeing and weaving of local wool and imported cotton yarn, and olive oil. Tripolitania also produces bricks, salt, leather and esparto grass for paper-making. Home industries of both territories include the making of matting, carpets, leather articles and fabrics embroidered with gold and silver. The Government has embarked on an ambitious programme of industrial development aimed at the local manufacture of building materials (steel and aluminium pipes and fittings, electric cables, cement, bricks, glass, etc.), foodstuffs (dairy products, flour, tinned fruits and vegetables, dates, fish processing and canning, etc.), textiles and footwear (ready-made clothing, woollen and cotton cloth, blankets, leather footwear, etc.) and development of mineral deposits (iron ore, phosphates, mineral salts). Private sector industrialization is encouraged by government loans and subsidies.

Production (1975): Footwear, 680,000 pairs; hides, 70,000 sq. ft. On 21 Sept. 1969 a decree laid down that all business concerns should be 100% Libyan-owned, but oil companies and banks were excluded.

Commerce. Total imports in 1978 were valued at LD1,327m. (c.i.f.) and exports of LD2,813m. (f.o.b.), mostly crude oil.

Total trade between Libya and UK (British Department of Trade returns, in £1,000 sterling):

	1976	1977	1978	1979	1980
Imports to UK	166,608	141,472	98,230	62,167	46,528
Exports and re-exports from UK	134,647	173,333	214,697	253,153	288,358

COMMUNICATIONS

Roads. Good motor roads connect Tripoli through Zuara with Tunis, and through Homs and Misurata with Benghazi and thence with Tobruk and Alexandria. Other roads go south and south-west from Tripoli to Tiagura, Garian, Yefren, Nalut and Ghadames. A road connects Sebha in the south with the main coastal road. An ambitious road building programme is being implemented and a road will eventually link Libya with Chad and Niger through Sebha. A further main road is being built to link Kufra, a major agricultural centre in the south-eastern part of Libya with the coastal road.

Surface communication between Benghazi and Tripoli is by frequent bus service, and there are also bus services between Benghazi and Alexandria, and between Tripoli, Tunis and Algiers.

Aviation. Benghazi and Tripoli are both served by international airlines, linking them with each other and Athens, Cairo, Rome, Malta, Tunis, Frankfurt, Paris, Amsterdam, Algiers, Khartoum, Lagos and London. British Caledonian has 3 flights weekly between Tripoli and London.

A national airline, the Libyan Arab Airlines (LAA), was inaugurated on 30 Sept. 1965. Apart from internal flights LAA operate to Athens, London, Rome, Beirut, Cairo, Paris, Malta, Algiers, Khartoum, Moscow, Cotonou and Tunis.

Post and Broadcasting. Tripoli is connected by telegraph cable with Malta and by microwave link with Bengardane (Tunis). There are overseas wireless-telegraph stations at Benghazi and Tripoli, and radio-telephone services connect Libya with most countries of western Europe. In 1971 some 41,495 telephones were in use and in 1978 there were 130,000 radio sets and 155,000 television receivers.

JUSTICE, RELIGION, EDUCATION AND WELFARE

Justice. The Civil, Commercial and Criminal codes are based mainly on the Egyptian model. Matters of personal status of family or succession matters affecting Moslems are dealt with in special courts according to the Moslem law. All other matters, civil, commercial and criminal, are tried in the ordinary courts, which have jurisdiction over everyone. In 1971 the Revolutionary Command Council set up a Commission with the task of revising Libyan laws.

There are civil and penal courts in Tripoli and Benghazi, with subsidiary courts at Misurata and Derna; courts of assize in Tripoli and Benghazi, and courts of appeal in Tripoli and Benghazi.

Religion. Islam is declared the State religion, but the right of others to practise their religions is provided for.

Education. There were (1975–76) 534,209 pupils (282,451 boys and 251,758 girls) in primary schools, 116,630 in elementary schools and 16,839 in secondary schools. There were 13,517 students at the 2 universities of Al Fatah (in Tripoli) and Garyounes (in Benghazi).

There are several schools, mainly in Tripoli, providing British, French, Italian, American and Dutch curricula, mainly on elementary and intermediate levels and chiefly for the non-Libyan communities.

Social Welfare. In 1975 there were 12,241 hospital beds and 42 hospitals with surgical facilities.

DIPLOMATIC REPRESENTATIVES

OF LIBYA IN GREAT BRITAIN (5 St James's Sq.,
London, SW1)

Head of Mission: Mabruk Elgayed.

OF GREAT BRITAIN IN LIBYA (30 Sharia Gamal Abdul Nasser,
Tripoli)

Ambassador: J. M. Edes, CMG.

OF LIBYA IN THE USA (1118 22nd St., NW,
Washington, D.C., 20037)

Chargé d'Affaires: Ahmed Dia Addin Madfai.

OF THE USA IN LIBYA (Shari Mohammad Thabit, Tripoli)

Chargé d'Affaires: W. Eagleton, Jr.

OF LIBYA TO THE UNITED NATIONS

Ambassador: Mansur Rashid Kikhia.

Books of Reference

The Economic Development of Libya. International Bank, 1960
Ansell, M. O., and al-Arif, I. M., *The Libyan Revolution.* London, 1972
Bianco, M., *Gadafi: Voice from the Desert.* London, 1975
Khadduri, M., *Modern Libya.* Johns Hopkins Press, 1963
Ward, P., *Touring Libya.* 3 vols. London, 1967–69
Wright, J., *Modern Libya.* London, 1969

LIECHTENSTEIN

Capital: Vaduz
Population: 25,808 (1979)
GNP per capita: US$8,000 (1974)

HISTORY. The Principality of Liechtenstein, situated between the Austrian province of Vorarlberg and the Swiss cantons of St Gallen and Graubünden, is a sovereign state whose history dates back to 3 May 1342, when Count Hartmann III became ruler of the county of Vaduz. Additions were later made to the count's domains, and by 1434 the territory reached its present boundaries. It consists of the two former counties of Schellenberg and Vaduz (until 1806 immediate fiefs of the Roman Empire). The former in 1699 and the latter in 1712 came into the possession of the house of Liechtenstein and, by diploma of 23 Jan. 1719, granted by the Emperor Charles VI, the two counties were constituted as the Principality of Liechtenstein.

AREA AND POPULATION. Liechtenstein is bounded on the east by Austria and the west by Switzerland. Area, 160 sq. km (61·8 sq. miles); population, of Alemannic race (census 1976), 24,169, (estimate 1979), 25,808. In 1979 there were 370 births and 173 deaths. Population of Vaduz (census 1977) 4,704, (estimate 1979), 4,892.

REIGNING PRINCE. Francis Joseph II, born 16 Aug. 1906; succeeded his great uncle, 26 July 1938; married on 7 March 1943 to Countess Gina von Wilczek; there are 4 sons, Princes Hans Adam (*heir apparent,* born 14 Feb. 1945; married on 30 July 1967 to Countess Marie Kinsky), Philip Erasmus (married on 11 Sept. 1971 to Isabelle de l'Arbre de Malander), Nikolaus Ferdinand and Franz Josef Wenzel, and one daughter, Princess Nora Elisabeth. The monarchy is hereditary in the male line.

National flag: Horizontally blue over red, with a gold coronet in the first quarter.
National anthem: Oben am jungen Rhein (words by H. H. Jauch, 1850; tune, 'God save the Queen').

CONSTITUTION AND GOVERNMENT. Liechtenstein is a constitutional monarchy ruled by the hereditary princes of the House of Liechtenstein. The present constitution of 5 Oct. 1921 provides for a unicameral parliament (Diet) of 15 members elected for 4 years. Election is by universal adult male suffrage and is on the basis of proportional representation. In 2 communes (Vaduz and Gamprin) women are allowed to vote and hold office on communal basis. The prince can call and dismiss the parliament. On parliamentary recommendation, he appoints the prime minister and the 4 councillors for a 4-year term. Any group of 600 persons or any 3 communes may propose legislation (initiative). Bills passed by the parliament may be submitted to popular referendum. A law is valid when it receives a majority approval by the parliament and the prince's signed concurrence. The capital and seat of government is Vaduz and there are 10 more communes all connected by modern roads. The 11 communes are fully independent administrative bodies within the laws of the principality. They levy additional taxes to the state taxes. Since Feb. 1921 Liechtenstein has had the Swiss currency, and since 29 March 1923 has been united with Switzerland in a customs union. Switzerland has also since 1919 represented the Principality diplomatically.

At the elections for the Diet, on 3 Feb. 1978, the Fatherland Union obtained 8 seats, the opposition Progressive Citizens' Party, 7 seats.

Head of Government: Hans Brunhart.

INTERNATIONAL RELATIONS

Membership. Liechtenstein is a member of EFTA, the Council of Europe and the International Court of Justice.

ECONOMY

Budget. Budget estimates for 1980: Revenue, 203,292,000 Swiss francs; expenditure, 203,006,000 Swiss francs. There is no public debt.

Currency. The Swiss *franc*.

Banking. There were (1980) 3 banks: Liechtensteinische Landesbank, Bank in Liechtenstein Ltd, Verwaltungs- und Privatbank Ltd.

Weights and Measures. The metric system is in force.

ENERGY AND NATURAL RESOURCES

Electricity. Electricity produced in 1979 was 51,986,720 kwh.

Agriculture. The rearing of cattle, for which the fine alpine pastures are well suited, is highly developed. In April 1980 there were 6,131 cattle (including 2,945 milch cows), 112 horses, 2,000 sheep, 80 goats, 2,648 pigs. Total production of dairy produce, 1979, 8,274,570 kg.

INDUSTRY AND TRADE

Industry. The country has a great variety of light industries (textiles, ceramics, steel screws, precision instruments, canned food, pharmaceutical products, heating appliances, etc.).

Liechtenstein has during the past 30 years changed from a predominantly agricultural country to a highly industrialized country. The farming population has gone down from 70% in 1930 to only 3·9% in 1979. The rapid change-over has led to the immigration of foreign workers (Austrians, Germans, Italians, Spaniards). Industrial undertakings in 1979 employed 5,867 workers earning 201,181,000 Swiss francs.

Commerce. Exports of home produce in 1979 amounted to 760,459,922 Swiss francs. 31·7% went to EFTA countries and 42·1% to EEC countries. The biggest customer is Switzerland (181·9m., 23·9%).

Total trade with UK is included with Switzerland from 1968.

Tourism. In 1979, 73,657 foreign visitors stayed in Liechtenstein.

COMMUNICATIONS

Roads. There are 250 km of roads. Postal buses are the chief means of public transportation within the country and to Austria and Switzerland.

Railways. The 18·5 km of main railway passing through the country is operated by Austrian Federal Railways.

Post and Broadcasting. In 1979 there were 9,538 telephones, 338 telex, 6,700 wireless sets and 6,375 television sets. The post and telegraphs are administered by Switzerland.

Cinemas. There were 3 cinemas in 1980.

Newspapers. In 1980 there were 2 daily newspapers with a total circulation of 12,850.

JUSTICE, RELIGION, EDUCATION AND WELFARE

Justice. The principality has its own civil and penal codes. The lowest court is the county court, *Landgericht*, presided over by one judge, which decides minor civil cases and summary criminal offences. The criminal court, *Kriminalgericht*, with a bench of 5 judges is for major crimes. Another court of mixed jurisdiction is the court of assizes (with 3 judges) for misdemeanours. The superior court, *Obergericht*, and Supreme Court, *Oberster Gerichtshof*, are courts of appeal for civil and criminal cases (both with benches of 5 judges). An administrative court of appeal from government actions and the State Court determines the constitutionality of laws.

Police. The principality has no army. Police force, 37; auxiliary police, 29.

Religion. In 1979, 82·2% of the population was Roman Catholic and 7% was Protestant.

Education (1980). In 14 primary, 3 upper, 4 secondary and 1 grammar school there were 3,750 pupils and 188 teachers. There is also an evening technical school, a music school, 3 schools for backward children and a children's pedagogic-welfare day school.

Health. In 1980 there was 1 hospital, but Liechtenstein has an agreement with the Swiss cantons of St Gallen and Graübunden that her citizens may use certain hospitals.

DIPLOMATIC REPRESENTATIVES

British Consul-General: G. N. Smith (resident in Zürich).
USA Consul-General: Clarke N. Ellis (resident in Zürich).

Books of Reference

Statistical Information: Press and Information Service, Vaduz. *Chief:* Walter Kranz.

Rechenschaftsbericht der fürstlichen liechtensteinischen Regierung. Vaduz. Annual, from 1922
Jahrbücher der Historischen Vereins. Vaduz. Annual since 1900
The Principality of Liechtenstein. Press and Information Service, Vaduz, 1978
The Liechtenstein Economy. Press and Information Service, Vaduz, 1978
Batliner, E. H., *Das Geld- und Kreditwesen des Fürstentums Liechtenstein.* Winterthur, 1959
d'Havrincourt, H., *Liechtenstein.* Lausanne, 1964
Greene, B., *Liechtenstein, Valley of Peace.* Vaduz, 1967
Kranz, W., *Principality of Liechtenstein—Documentary Handbook.* Vaduz, 1973
Malin, G., *Kunstführer Liechtenstein.* Berne, 1977
Steger, B., *Fürst und Landtag nach Liechtensteinischen Recht.* Vaduz, 1950.—*A Survey of Liechtenstein History.* Vaduz, 1970

LUXEMBOURG

Grand-Duché de Luxembourg

Capital: Luxembourg
Population: 363,700 (1979)
GNP per capita: US$10,410 (1978)

HISTORY. The country formed part of the Holy Roman Empire until it was conquered by the French in 1795. In 1815 the Grand Duchy of Luxembourg was formed under the house of Orange-Nassau, also sovereigns of the Netherlands. In 1839 the Walloon-speaking area was joined to Belgium. In 1890 the personal union with the Netherlands ended with the accession of a member of another branch of the house of Nassau, Grand Duke Adolphe of Nassau-Weilberg.

AREA AND POPULATION. Luxembourg has an area of 2,586 sq. km (998 sq. miles) and is bounded on the west by Belgium, south by France, east by the Federal Republic of Germany. The population (1979) was 363,700. The capital, Luxembourg, had 79,600 inhabitants; Esch-Alzette, the centre of the mining district, 25,500; Differdange, 17,100; Dudelange, 14,200, and Petange, 12,300. In 1979 the foreign population was about 92,900.

Vital statistics (1979): 4,078 births, 3,985 deaths, 2,086 marriages.

REIGNING GRAND DUKE. Jean, born 5 Jan. 1921, son of Grand Duchess Charlotte and the late Prince Felix of Bourbon-Parma; succeeded 12 Nov. 1964 on the abdication of his mother; married to Princess Joséphine-Charlotte of Belgium, 9 April 1953. *Offspring:* Princess Marie Astrid, born 17 Feb. 1954; Prince Henri, *heir apparent*, born 16 April 1955, married Maria Teresa Mestre 14 Feb. 1981; Prince Jean and Princess Margaretha, born 15 May 1957; Prince Guillaume, born 1 May 1963.

The civil list is fixed at 300,000 gold francs per annum, to be reconsidered at the beginning of each reign.

On 28 Sept. 1919 a referendum was taken in Luxembourg to decide on the political and economic future of the country. The voting resulted as follows: For the reigning Grand Duchess, 66,811; for the continuance of the Nassau-Braganza dynasty under another Grand Duchess, 1,286; for another dynasty, 889; for a republic, 16,885; for an economic union with France, 60,133; for an economic union with Belgium, 22,242. But France refused in favour of Belgium, and on 22 Dec. 1921 the Chamber of the Grand Duchy passed a Bill for the economic union between Belgium and Luxembourg. The agreement, which is for 60 years, provides for the disappearance of the customs barrier between the two countries and the use of Belgian, in addition to Luxembourg, currency as legal tender in the Grand Duchy. It came into force on 1 May 1922.

The Grand Duchy was under German occupation from 10 May 1940 to 10 Sept. 1944. The Grand Duchess Charlotte and the Government carried on an independent administration in London. Civil government was restored in Oct. 1944.

National flag: Three horizontal stripes of red, white, blue.
National anthem: Ons Hemecht (words by M. Lentz, 1859; tune by J. A. Zinnen).

CONSTITUTION AND GOVERNMENT. The Grand Duchy of Luxembourg is a constitutional monarchy, the hereditary sovereignty being in the Nassau family. The constitution of 17 Oct. 1868 was revised in 1919, 1948, 1956 and 1972. The revision of 1948 has abolished the 'perpetually neutral' status of the country and introduced the concepts of right to work, social security, health services, freedom of trade and industry, and recognition of trade unions. The revision of 1956

807

provides for the devolution of executive, legislative and judicial powers to international institutions.

The national language is Luxemburgish; French, German and English are widely used.

The country forms 4 electoral districts. An elector must be a citizen (male or female) of Luxembourg and have completed 18 years of age; to be eligible for election the citizen must have completed 21 years of age.

The Chamber of Deputies consists of 24 Christian Social, 14 Socialists, 15 Democrats, 2 Social Democrats, 2 Communists, 1 Independent Socialist and 1 co-opted deputy (elections of 10 June 1979). Members are elected for 5 years; they receive a salary and a travelling allowance.

The head of the state takes part in the legislative power, exercises the executive power and has a certain part in the judicial power. The constitution leaves to the sovereign the right to organize the Government, which consists of a Minister of State, who is President of the Government, and of at least 3 Ministers.

The Cabinet was, in Nov. 1980, composed as follows:

President of the Government, Minister of State, Treasury, Culture, General Affairs, National Protection, Information and Press: Pierre Werner.

Vice-President, Foreign Affairs, External Commerce and Co-operation, Economy and Middle Classes, Justice: Colette Flesch. *Health, Public Forces, Physical Education and Sport:* Emile Krieps. *Agriculture, Viticulture, Water and Forests:* Camille Ney. *Environment, Transport, Communications and Information, Energy:* Josy Barthel. *Finance, Labour and Social Security:* Jacques Santer. *Public Works and Functions:* René Konen. *Interior, Family, Social Living and Social Solidarity:* Jean Spautz. *National Education and Tourism:* Fernand Boden. *Secretary of State for Finance:* Ernest Muhlen. *Secretary of State for Foreign Affairs, External Commerce and Co-operation, Economy and Middle Classes, Justice:* Paul Helminger.

Besides the Cabinet there is a Council of State. It deliberates on proposed laws and Bills, and on amendments; it also gives administrative decisions and expresses its opinion regarding any other question referred to it by the Grand Duke or the Government. The Council of State is composed of 21 members chosen for life by the sovereign, who also chooses a president from among them each year.

DEFENCE. A law passed by Parliament on 29 June 1967 abolished compulsory service and instituted a battalion-size army of volunteers enlisted for 3 years. Strength (1980) 660. The defence estimates for 1979 amounted to 1,475m. francs. Luxembourg is an original member of NATO and the battalion is committed to NATO ACE mobile force.

INTERNATIONAL RELATIONS

Membership. Luxembourg is a member of the UN, Benelux, the EEC, OECD, the Council of Europe, NATO and WEU.

ECONOMY

Budget. Revenue and expenditure (including extraordinary) for years ending 30 April (in 1m. francs):

	1976	1977	1978[1]	1979[1]	1980[2]	1981[3]
Revenue	33,112·4	38,401·1	42,603·6	42,579·0	45,244·5	49,745·6
Expenditure	32,796·2	37,990·6	41,586·3	43,666·8	45,872·9	51,157·0

[1] Provisional.　　　　[2] Budget.　　　　[3] Estimates.

Consolidated debt at 31 Dec. 1979 amounted to 22,547m. francs (long-term) and 2,067m. francs (short-term).

Currency. On 14 Oct. 1944 the Luxembourg *franc* was fixed at par value with the Belgian franc. Notes of the Belgian National Bank are legal tender in Luxembourg.

Banking. On 31 Dec. 1979 there were 302,524 depositors in the State Savings Bank with a total of 29,849m. francs to their credit. There are more than 110 banks established in Luxembourg which has become an international financial centre.

Weights and Measures. The metric system is in force.

ENERGY AND NATURAL RESOURCES

Electricity. Power production was 1,338m. kwh. in 1979.

Minerals. The mining and metallurgical industries are the most important. In 1979 production (in tonnes) of iron ore was 630,238; of pig-iron, 3,800,715; of steel, 4,949,698.

Agriculture. Agriculture is carried on by about 9,500 of the population; 130,415 hectares were under cultivation in 1979. The principal crops are potatoes, barley, beet, oats and wheat.

Livestock (May 1979): 1,823 horses, 224,023 cattle, 85,249 pigs, 3,759 sheep.

INDUSTRY AND TRADE

Commerce. By treaty of 5 Sept. 1944, signed in London, and the treaty of 14 March 1947, signed in The Hague, the Grand Duchy, together with Belgium and the Netherlands, became a party to the Benelux Customs Union, which came into force on 1 Jan. 1948. For further particulars *see* pp. 203 and 895.

Total trade between Luxembourg and UK included with Belgium from 1974 (*see* p. 201).

Tourism. In 1979 there were 448,782 tourists.

COMMUNICATIONS

Roads. In 1980 the network had a total of 5,093 km. Motor vehicles registered in Luxembourg on 1 Jan. 1980 included 162,802 passenger cars, 10,814 trucks, 741 buses, 16,880 tractors and special vehicles.

Railways. In 1979 there were 270 km of railway (standard gauge).

Aviation. Findel is the airport for Luxembourg.

Post and Broadcasting. In 1979 the telephone system had 4,809 km of telegraph and telephone line, 198,905 telephones, 102 post offices and 422 telegraph offices. *Compagnie Luxembourgeoise de Télédiffusion* broadcasts 1 programme in Luxembourgian on FM. Powerful transmitters on long-, medium- and short-waves are used for commercial and religious programmes in French, Dutch, German, English and Italian. Five TV programmes are broadcast. Colour transmission by SECAM system. Number of receivers (estimate): radio, 200,000; TV, 120,000.

Cinemas (1977). There were 20 cinemas.

Newspapers (1979). There were 5 daily newspapers with an aggregate circulation of 130,000.

RELIGION, EDUCATION AND WELFARE

Religion. The population is Catholic, save (31 Dec. 1970) 3,900 Protestants, 700 Jews, 2,100 belonging to other denominations and 3,700 without religion (or having given no indication on this subject). The Protestant Church is organized on an interdenominational basis.

Education (1979–80). Education is compulsory for all children between the ages of 6 and 15. The nursery schools had 7,626 pupils; primary schools had 30,112 pupils; technical secondary schools, 15,333 pupils; secondary schools, 8,749 pupils; the Superior Institute of Technology, 619 pupils; pedagogic education, 134 pupils; university studies, 284 pupils.

Health. In 1979 there were 530 doctors and 4,539 hospital beds.

DIPLOMATIC REPRESENTATIVES

OF LUXEMBOURG IN GREAT BRITAIN
(27 Wilton Crescent, London, SWIX 8SD)

Ambassador: Roger Hastert, CMG.

OF GREAT BRITAIN IN LUXEMBOURG (28 Boulevard Royal, Luxembourg)
Ambassador and Consul-General: Jeremy Cashel Thomas, CMG.

OF LUXEMBOURG IN THE USA (2200 Massachusetts Ave. NW,
Washington, D.C., 20008)
Ambassador: Adrien Meisch.

OF THE USA IN LUXEMBOURG (22 Blvd. Emmanuel
Servais, Luxembourg)
Ambassador: James G. Lowenstein.

OF LUXEMBOURG TO THE UNITED NATIONS
Ambassador: Paul Peters.

Books of Reference

Statistical Information: The Service Central de la Statistique et des Études Économiques was founded in 1900 and reorganized in 1962 (19–21 boulevard Royal, C.P. 304 Luxembourg-City). *Director:* Georges Als. Main publications: *Bulletin du Statec.—Annuaire statistique.—Cahiers économiques.*

Bulletin de Documentation. Government Information Service. From 1945 (monthly)
The Institutions of the Grand Duchy of Luxembourg. Press and Information Service, Luxembourg, 1976
Luxembourg 963–1963. Le livre du millénaire. Luxembourg, 1963
Tausend Jahre Luxemburg. Luxembourg, 1963
Calmes, C., *Au Fil de l'Histoire.* Luxembourg, 1977
Cooper-Pritchard, A. H., *History of the Grand-Duchy of Luxembourg.* Luxembourg, 1950
Heiderscheid, A., *Aspects de Sociologie Religieuse du Diocèse de Luxembourg.* 2 vols. Luxembourg, 1961
Majerus, P., *Le Luxembourg indépendant.* Luxembourg, 1948.—*L'État Luxembourgeois.* Luxembourg, 1948
Petit, J., *Luxemburg, plateforme internationale.* Luxembourg, 1960
Trausch, G., *Le Luxembourg à l'Époque Contemporaine.* Luxembourg, 1975
Weber, P., *Histoire du Grand-Duché de Luxembourg.* Brussels, 1949.—*Histoire de l'économie luxembourgeoise.* Luxembourg, 1950

Archives of the State: Luxembourg-City. *Director:* Paul Spang.
National Library: Luxembourg-City, 14a Boulevard Royal. *Director:* Gilbert Trausch.

MADAGASCAR

Capital: Antananarivo
Population: 8·8m. (1978)
GNP per capita: US$250 (1978)

The Democratic Republic of Madagascar

HISTORY. Madagascar was discovered by the Portuguese, Diego Diaz, in 1500. On the return of Diaz to Portugal the King concluded that the island must be Madagascar, about which he had read in Marco Polo's 'Voyages'. Polo, however, had not been there, but believing his Arab informants, ascribed to an island what was really the kingdom of Mogadisho, on the east coast of Africa. Mispronouncing and mis-spelling the name, he coined the word Madagascar.

The last native sovereign in Madagascar, Queen Ranavalona III (born 1845, died 1917), succeeded in 1883. The French claimed a portion of the north-west coast as having been transferred to them by local chiefs, and hostilities were carried on in 1883–85 against the Merina, who refused to recognize the cession. In 1885 peace was made, Diégo-Suarez having been surrendered to France. A French expedition was dispatched in May 1895 to enforce the claims of France and on 1 Oct. the Queen accepted the protectorate.

By a law promulgated 6 Aug. 1896 the island and its dependencies were declared a French colony.

On 14 Oct. 1958 Madagascar was proclaimed a republic. The republic was admitted to the UN on 21 Sept. 1960.

AREA AND POPULATION. Madagascar is situated off the south-east coast of Africa, from which it is separated by the Mozambique channel, the least distance between island and continent being 250 miles; its length is 980 miles; greatest breadth, 360 miles.

The area is 594,180 sq. km (229,233 sq. miles). In 1973 the population was 7,185,000 (48% under 18 years). Estimate (1978) 8,047,044.

In 1978 there were 30,000 Europeans, mainly French, resident on the island. Indians, 16,000, and Chinese, 9,000, carry on small retail trade.

Province	Area in sq. km	Population 1978	Chief town	Population 1978
Diégo-Suarez	42,725	620,228	Antseranana	48,000
Majunga	152,165	857,610	Mahajanga	57,500
Toamasina	72,212	1,254,639	Toamasina	59,100
Antananarivo	57,775	2,322,019	Antananarivo	400,000
Fianarantsoa	100,326	1,908,465	Fianarantsoa	55,500
Toliary	162,283	1,084,083	Toliary	34,000

Vital statistics, 1971: Births, 279,583; deaths, 85,129.

CONSTITUTION AND GOVERNMENT. The Constitution of the republic was promulgated on 29 April 1959 and amended in June 1960. It provided for a national assembly of 107 and a senate of 52 members. The Government consisted of a president and 38 ministers. On 18 May 1972 the Government was dissolved. A decree issued later gave Gen. Gabriel Ramanantsoa supreme power for up to 5 years. A provisional Constitutional law was issued on 8 Oct. 1972.

On 5 Feb. 1975 Col. Richard Ratsimandrava became Head of State and also held the portfolios of Defence and Planning. Col. Ratsimandrava was assassinated on 11 Feb. 1975 and the Minister of State without Portfolio, Brig.-Gen. Gilles Andriamahazo immediately declared martial law and on 12 Feb. established a National Military Directorate. Capt. Ratsiraka was sworn in as President on 21 Dec. 1975 when a new Constitution was approved.

The republic is divided into 6 provinces and each is under the supervision of a field officer. The provinces are subdivided into prefectures, subprefectures, arrondissements and cantons. Each canton comprises a number of *fokontany*.

President: Didier Ratsiraka.

The Cabinet was in Aug. 1977 composed as follows:

Prime Minister: Lieut.-Col. Désiré Rakotoarijaona.
Foreign Affairs: Richard Christian Rémi. *National Defence:* Capt. Guy Sibon. *Primary and Secondary Education:* Théophile Andrianoelisoi. *Scientific Research and Higher Education:* Ignace Rakoto. *Information and Ideological Guidance:* Georges Ruffin. *Revolutionary Art and Culture:* Giselle Rabesahala.

National flag: Horizontally red over green, in the hoist a vertical white strip.
National anthem: Ry tanindrazanay malala ô!

Malagasy, which is a language of Malayo-Polynesian origin, is the official language. French and English is understood and taught in Malagasy schools.

DEFENCE

Army. The Army in 1980 had a strength of 12,000 organized in 2 infantry battalions, and 1 engineer, 1 signals and 1 service regiment.

Air Force. Created in 1961 and maintained with French Air Force assistance, the Malagasy Air Force received its first combat equipment in 1978, with the arrival of 8 MiG-21-fighters, plus flying and ground staff instructors, from North Korea. Other equipment includes 1 An-12 and 4 An-26 turboprop transports, 1 Britten-Norman Defender armed transport, 6 C-47s, 5 Flamants, 4 Broussards, 1 Aztec, 3 Cessna Skymasters, 4 Cessna 172Ms and 6 helicopters, comprising 2 Mi-8s, 1 Bell 47, 1 Alouette II and 2 Alouette IIIs. Personnel about 350.

INTERNATIONAL RELATIONS

Membership. Madagascar is a member of UN, OAU and is an ACP state of EEC.

ECONOMY

Planning. A development plan, 1978–80, envisaged an annual growth rate of 5%. The main aim is to increase agricultural production through the rural reform plan based on the *fokonolona* communes and distributive co-operatives.

Budget. The local revenue is derived chiefly from income tax, from customs and other indirect taxes, from territorial lands, from posts and telegraphs, markets and miscellaneous sources. The chief branches of expenditure are general administration, public works, health services, education, the post office and the public debt. The general budget for 1980 provided for an expenditure of 277,600m. FMG.

Currency. The Malagasy *franc* (FMG) = 0·02 French franc.

Banking. The Banque Nationale Malagasy de Développement (BNM) created in 1963 to replace the Société Malgache d'Investissement et de Crédit is the national investment bank. The Banque de Madagascar et des Comores was formerly the bank of issue, but this privilege was, on 8 March 1962, transferred to a new national institute, the Institut d'Emission Malgache and later, in July 1973, this institute was replaced by the Central Bank. The other commercial banks are: Banque Malagasy d'Escompte et de Crédit (BAMES) (the Comptoir National d'Escompte de Paris holds 65% of its capital, the rest being owned by the Malagasy Government) with 9 offices throughout the island and 2 sub-offices in Antananarivo; the Banque Nationale pour le Commerce et l'Industrie (BNCI) with 9 offices and 2 sub-offices (in Antananarivo); the Banque Française pour le Commerce which has 1 office and 2 sub-offices in Antananarivo and 1 office in Toamasina.

Weights and Measures. The metric system is in use.

ENERGY AND NATURAL RESOURCES

Electricity. The consumption of electric power in 1971 amounted to 210m. kwh.

Minerals. Mining production (in tonnes) included: Mica (1975), 1,914; graphite

(1976), 17,402; chrome (1979), 200,000; ilmenite, 1,857; zircon, 209; beryl, 1971 (industrial), 52; gold (1971), 17 kg; garnet, 1971 (industrial), 40.

Agriculture. In 1978, 83% of the working population was employed in agriculture. The principal agricultural products in 1975 were (in 1,000 tonnes): Rice, 1,813; sugar, 1,092; coffee, 65; groundnuts, 38·6; cotton, 30·7; cape peas, 15·8; cloves, 4·5; tobacco, 3·3; pepper, 2·6; vanilla, 1·43.

Cattle breeding and agriculture are the chief occupations. There were, in 1979, 8·7m. cattle, 580,000 pigs, 658,000 sheep, 1·6m. goats and 14m. poultry.

Forestry. The forests contain many valuable woods, while gum, resins and plants for tanning, dyeing and medicinal purposes abound.

Fisheries. The fish catch in 1974 was 50,000 tonnes.

INDUSTRY AND TRADE

Industry. Industry, hitherto confined mainly to the processing of agricultural products, is now extending to cover other fields. Thus in addition to rice milling, sugar making, distilling, oil-seed crushing, meat, fruit and vegetable canning, cigarette and chewing-tobacco production, soap and rope manufactures, cotton spinning and weaving, brewing, processing of cashew nuts, fruit juices and jams and meat canning, it now includes an oil refinery, a paper-mill, 2 vehicle assembly plants, plants for the assembly of batteries, transistor radio and television sets and bicycles, a plastics factory, 2 paint factories, metal furniture and window making, tyre-retreading and foam-rubber plants, an animal-feed factory, an iron-sheeting and nail-making plant, a metal packing plant, 2 undertakings producing aluminium ware, a chemical works and 2 biscuit and confectionery factories. The oil refinery at Toamasina, which came on stream in 1966, has a capacity of 12,500 bbls a day. A second cotton-mill started production in 1970.

Commerce. Trade in 1m. FMG:

	1974	1975	1976
Imports	70,028	80,701	64,577
Exports	57,733	70,791	65,370

In 1972 the chief imports (in 1m. FMG) were: Metalware, 5,509; chemicals, 5,453; mineral products, 5,061; wines, 553; food, 17,136. The chief exports in 1972 were: Foodstuffs, 75,802; textiles, 24,962; animal products, 1,479.

Total trade between Madagascar and UK (British Department of Trade returns, in £1,000 sterling):

	1976	1977	1978	1979	1980
Imports to UK	4,032	3,826	4,162	2,963	4,148
Exports and re-exports from UK	2,698	2,786	3,592	4,152	11,817

COMMUNICATIONS

Roads. At the end of 1968 there were 40,000 km of roads suitable for motor traffic, of which 8,364 km are practicable all the year round. There is a motor-car service with a network of routes covering about 2,797 km. Motor vehicles registered at 1 Jan. 1971 included 45,992 passenger cars, 3,149 buses, 2,882 commercial vehicles, 31,147 lorries, 2,660 tractors and 4,724 motor cycles.

Railways. Four railways are operating, namely: between Antananarivo and Toamasina (376 km); between Antananarivo and Antsirabe (noted for its thermal springs), 158 km: the branch line of the Toamasina railway, from Moramanga to Lake Alaotra (168 km) and the line from Fianarantsoa to Manakara on to the east coast (165 km). All metre-gauge. In 1972, 2·2m. passengers and 623,000 tonnes of cargo were transported.

Aviation. Air France and Air Madagascar connect Antananarivo with Paris, Alitalia connects with Rome. Several weekly services operated by Air Madagascar connect the capital with the ports and the chief inland towns. The main airfields are at Ivato, Toamasina, Toliary and Mahajanga. In 1968, 67,365 passengers, 2,446 tonnes of cargo and 82 tonnes of mail departed on international flights.

Shipping. Toamasina, Mahajanga, Antseranana, Toliary, Nossi-Bé and Manakara are the principal ports. In 1968, 5,237 vessels of 1,090,846 tons entered these ports.

Post and Broadcasting. There were in 1971, 547 post offices and agencies and 55 wireless telegraph stations. The telegraph line has a length of 17,400 km. There were 66,000 km of telephone line and, in 1978, 28,686 telephone subscribers. Direct telephone communications exist between Antananarivo, Paris, Mauritius and Réunion. Wireless telegraph was established between Antananarivo and Fianarantsoa in Oct. 1962 and between Antananarivo and Paris in April 1972.

Cinemas. There were, in 1974, 31 cinemas with a seating capacity of 12,500.

RELIGION, EDUCATION AND WELFARE

Religion. Since 1818 a large portion of the Merina and other ethnic groups in the central districts have been Christianized. Many of the missionary societies which worked in Madagascar have now established churches. The 2 largest religious bodies are Roman Catholics with 1·4m. members (5,000 churches) and Fiangonan'i Jesosy Kristy eto Madagascar (FJKM) with 1·03m. members and 5,161 churches. There are also other smaller Christian churches and 75 mosques.

Education. Education is compulsory from 6 to 14 years of age in the primary schools. In 1972 there were 938,015 pupils in public primary schools and 260,726 in private schools. The total number of primary schools was 6,054. There were 508 colleges of general education and 18 *lycées* with a total of 105,320 students. There is a co-educational university at Antananarivo with faculties of Law, Science and Letters. The total student body in 1972 was 5,648.

There are also 4 agricultural schools at Nanisana, Ambatondrazaka, Marovoay and Ivoloina.

Health. In 1976 there were 886 hospitals and dispensaries with 19,781 beds; there were also 767 doctors, 93 dentists, 141 pharmacists, 1,010 midwives and 2,252 nursing personnel.

DIPLOMATIC REPRESENTATIVES

OF MADAGASCAR IN GREAT BRITAIN

Ambassador: Henri Raharijaona (resides in Paris).

OF GREAT BRITAIN IN MADAGASCAR
(Immeuble Ny Havana, Cite de 67 Ha, Antananarivo)

Ambassador: R. J. Langridge.

OF MADAGASCAR IN THE USA
(2374 Massachusetts Ave., NW, Washington, D.C., 20008)

Chargé d'Affaires: Norbert Rakotomalala.

OF THE USA IN MADAGASCAR
(14 rue Rainitovo, Antsohavola, Antananarivo)

Chargé d'Affaires: Robert S. Barett.

OF MADAGASCAR TO THE UNITED NATIONS

Ambassador: Blaise Rabetafika.

Books of Reference

Statistical Information: The Service de Statistique Générale in Antananarivo published the *Bulletin mensuel de Madagascar* (from 1971); continuation of the trimestrial *Bulletin de statistique générale* (1949–71), the *Revue de Madagascar*, the *Madagascar à travers ses provinces* (latest issue, 1953), the *Annuaire Statistique de Madagascar* (vol. 1, 1938–51, published 1953, the

Situation Economique au Janvier 1968, Population de Madagascar au 1er Jan. 1971, and the *Statistiques du Commerce Extérieur de Madagascar*).
Bulletin de l'Académie Malgache (from 1902)
Brown, M., *Madagascar Rediscovered*. London, 1978
Deschamps, H., *Histoire de Madagascar*. Paris, 1960
Heseltine, N., *Madagascar*. London and New York, 1971
Thompson, V., and Adloff, R., *The Malagasy Republic*. Stanford Univ. Press, 1965

MALAWI

Capital: Lilongwe
Population: 5·8m. (1979)
GNP per capita: US$180 (1978)

HISTORY. Malawi was formerly the Nyasaland (until 1907 British Central Africa) Protectorate, constituted on 15 May 1891.

Nyasaland became a self-governing country on 1 Feb. 1963, and on 6 July 1964 an independent member of the Commonwealth under the name of Malawi. It became a republic on 6 July 1966.

AREA AND POPULATION. Malawi lies along the southern and western shores of Lake Malawi (the third largest lake in Africa), and is otherwise bounded north by Tanzania, south by Mozambique and west by Zambia. Land area (excluding inland water of Lakes Palombe, Chilwa and Chiuta) 36,325 sq. miles, divided into 3 regions and 24 districts, each administered by a District Commissioner.

Lake Malawi waters belonging to Malawi are 9,250 sq. miles and the whole Lake Malawi (including the waters under Mozambique by an agreement made between the two countries in 1950) is 11,650 sq. miles.

The results of the census held in Aug. 1966: 4,020,724 Africans, 11,299 Asians, 7,395 Europeans, 165 undetermined; total 4,039,583 (1,913,262 males, 2,126,321 females). Estimate (1979), 5·8m. Over 90% of the population live in rural areas.

Population of main towns (census 1977) was as follows: Blantyre, 228,520; Lilongwe, 102,924; Zomba, 15,705; Mzuzu, 16,119. The capital was Zomba, and on 1 Jan. 1975 Lilongwe, in the Central Region, was officially declared the capital. All ministries were to be located there by 1977–78. A new Constitution was introduced in 1966.

Population of the regions, 1966 (and census 1977): Northern, 497,491 (643,485); Central, 1,474,952 (2,122,010); Southern, 2,067,140 (2,806,072).

CONSTITUTION AND GOVERNMENT. The President of the republic is also head of Government and of the Malawi Congress Party. Malawi is a one-party state. Parliament is composed of 87 elected members elected for up to 5 years, and up to 15 nominated members. Elections were held in June 1978.

Life President, External Affairs, Agriculture and Natural Resources, Justice, Works and Supplies: Ngwazi Dr H. Kamuzu Banda. (Took office 6 July 1966 and became Life President on 6 July 1971).

National flag: Three equal horizontal stripes of black, red, green, with a red rising sun on the centre of the black stripe.

DEFENCE

Army. The army consists of a headquarters—a large infantry battalion complete with its own supporting arms and services—and a depot back-up of an engineering workshop and an ordnance depot in Zomba, Lilongwe and at Mzuzu. The total strength is 3,600 (all services, 1980). The army is organized into 2 infantry battalions and 1 support battalion.

Navy. There are 3 small lake patrol boats and 1 gunboat. ersonnel (1981) 15.

Air Wing. To support the infantry battalion, the Air Wing has 4 C-47 transport aircraft, 1 Defender armed light transport, 6 Dornier Do27 and 12 Do28D Skyservant light transports, 6 Puma and 1 Alouette III helicopters.

INTERNATIONAL RELATIONS

Membership. Malawi is a member of UN, the Commonwealth, OAU, and is an ACP state of EEC.

ECONOMY

Planning. The Government of Malawi operates a 3-year 'rolling' public-sector investment programme, revised annually to take into account changing needs and the expected level of resources available. The greatest part of the development programme is annually financed from external aid, and priority in the use of resources has always been given to providing the counterpart contributions to funds received from external sources. The balance of these local resources is used for financing projects commanding high national priority for which no external funds can be secured.

The two tables below give a summary of the Government's Development Programme for the 3 years 1977–80 and the sources of finance (in K.1m.).

Government Development Expenditure	1977–78	1978–79	1979–80	Total 3 Years	%
Agriculture and natural resources	22·1	19·1	18·7	59·9	17·2
Transportation	50·3	58·9	51·8	161·0	46·4
Posts and telecommunications	4·2	4·4	1·4	10·0	2·9
Power	10·5	14·8	15·0	40·3	11·6
Education	5·9	6·4	5·2	17·5	5·0
Health	1·9	2·8	2·2	6·9	2·0
Water supplies and sanitation	6·4	5·5	3·1	15·0	4·3
New capital—Lilongwe	2·7	1·2	0·8	4·7	1·4
Housing	3·0	2·5	1·7	7·2	2·1
Other	8·5	11·3	4·9	24·7	7·1
Total	115·5	126·9	104·8	347·2	100·0
Finance					
British government loan	11·5	10·6	11·2	33·3	9·5
Other externally financed	2·8	1·5	—	4·3	1·2
External financed	88·1	101·2	80·4	269·7	77·7
Counterpart to external aid	8·9	9·0	8·3	26·2	7·6
Wholly locally financed projects	4·2	4·6	4·9	13·7	3·9
Total	115·5	126·9	104·8	347·2	100·0

Budget. Revenue Account receipts and expenditure (in K.1,000) for years ending 31 March:

	1974–75	1975–76	1976–77 [1]	1977–78	1978–79
Revenue	78,687	89,701	89,860	132,340	173,820
Expenditure	73,831	84,422	90,827	184,850	254,520

[1] Provisional.

Main revenue items (in K.1,000) in 1976–77 are: Direct taxes, 34,902; indirect taxes, 34,805.

Main expenditure items (in K.1,000) in 1975–76 were: Public debt charges, 12,714; education, 11,867; general administration, 9,152.

Currency. In 1971 a new decimalized currency was introduced, the *kwacha* (dawn), which is subdivided into 100 *tambala* (cockerels). From 9 June 1975 the kwacha has been pegged to Special Drawing Rights. Official exchange rate March 1981: £1 sterling = K.1·87, US$1 = K.0·8696.

Banking. In July 1964 the Reserve Bank of Malawi was set up with a capital of K.1m. to be responsible for the issue of currency and the holding of external reserves and to issue treasury bills and local registered stock on behalf of the Government. Since then, the Reserve Bank has fully assumed the responsibilities of a Central Bank.

The National Bank of Malawi has a total of 10 branches in major urban areas and 19 static and 35 mobile agencies in rural areas. The Commercial Bank of Malawi Ltd opened in 1970 and has branches at Limbe and Lilongwe and an agency in Dedza and headquarters at Blantyre.

In 1972 The Investment Development Bank of Malawi was established in Blantyre. Its resources are derived from domestic and foreign official sources and its objective is to provide medium and long-term credits to private entities considered of importance to the economy.

The post office savings bank has 223 offices conducting savings business throughout the country, and the New Building Society has agencies in Limbe, Zomba and Lilongwe with its head office in Blantyre. Two finance houses now operate in Malawi, providing longer-term industrial and consumer finance.

Weights and Measures. British measures are in use; the metric system is being introduced gradually.

ENERGY AND NATURAL RESOURCES

Electricity. The first stage of the Tedzani Project, two 8 mw sets, was commissioned in July 1973 which, together with the 24 mw Nkula hydro-electric station, will meet the power demands of the interconnected systems of the Southern Region and Lilongwe. With the completion of a barrage at Tedzani these machines will be up-rated to 10 mw each and, with the addition of thermal plant to the system, sufficient power will be available to meet forecast demands prior to the commissioning in 1977 of the second stage of the Tedzani Project, a further two 10 mw sets. The Electricity Supply Commission also operates stations at Mangochi, Mzuzu, Kasungu, Liwonde, Chikwawa and Salima. A total of 252·96m. kwh. were sold by the Electricity Supply Commission in 1976.

Minerals. The main product in 1976 was marble (149,254 tonnes) for the manufacture of cement.

Agriculture. Malawi is predominantly an agricultural country. Up to March 1977 519,300 of the rural population had been reached by self-help piped water projects, of which 427,700 were in the Southern region. In 1976 agriculture contributed 46·1% to the GDP, and agricultural produce accounted for over 79% of total exports. Of the total area of 23·3m. acres, 13·1m. could be cultivated and, in 1969, 3·36m. were being cultivated, of which 2·64m. were under maize. Maize is the main subsistence crop and is grown by over 95% of all smallholders. Almost all the surplus crops produced by smallholders are sold to the Agricultural Development and Marketing Corporation. In 1976 the corporation purchased: Tobacco, K.6·03m.; groundnuts, K.5·38m.; maize, K.3·54m.; cotton, K.3·02m.; rice, K.2·42m.; pulses, K.1·9m.

Livestock in 1979: Cattle, 790,000; sheep, 140,000; goats, 860,000; pigs, 174,000.

Forestry. In 1976 (estimate) 535,510 cu. ft of sawn timber were produced, valued at K.1·3m. The value of other forest products was K.536,986.

Fisheries. Landings in 1977 (provisional) were 66,000 short tons valued at K.6·6m.

INDUSTRY AND TRADE

Industry. Index of manufacturing output (1970 = 100): manufacturing for domestic consumption, 177·7 (186·5 in 1975); of this consumer goods were at 191·9 (194·8) and intermediate goods mainly for building and construction were at 128·6 (157·6). Manufacturing for export, 172·3 (154).

Labour:

		1976	
	Private	Government	Total
Agriculture, forestry, fishing	70,934	6,947	79,227
Mining and quarrying	707	3	710
Manufacturing	32,319	1,116	33,435
Electricity and water	2,196	878	3,074
Building and construction	15,735	5,389	21,124
Trade, hotels, restaurants	21,558	—	21,558
Transport, storage, communications	9,476	2,926	12,402
Financial services	3,231	68	3,299
Community, social, personal services	10,354	51,819	62,173
Total	166,510	70,492	237,002

Commerce. The main items of export in 1976 were (in K.): Tobacco, 65·2m.; tea, 26·2m.; sugar, 17·4m.; groundnuts, 11·3m. Malawi's imports in the same year included capital equipment, 58·8m.; means of transport, 26·4m.; consumer goods, 25·2m.; building materials, 19·5m.

Trade statistics for calendar years are (in US$1m.):

	1976	1977	1978	1979
Imports	181·4	204·2	297·0	354·4
Exports	166·0	199·7	186·2	232·5

Total trade between Malawi and UK (British Department of Trade returns, in £1,000 sterling):

	1977	1978	1979	1980
Imports to UK	51,040	47,727	46,464	45,651
Exports and re-exports from UK	18,359	22,348	27,088	25,749

Tourism. There were 43,000 visitors to Malawi in 1977. They spent about K.70·36 per person.

COMMUNICATIONS

Roads. In 1976 there were 1,877 miles of main road, of which 772 were bitumen-surfaced and 206 gravel; 1,520 miles of secondary roads, of which 215 were surfaced; 3,426 miles of district and other roads, of which 148 were surfaced. Motor vehicles licensed, 29,085, of which 10,222 were cars and 10,642 goods vehicles.

Railways. Malawi Railways (67 km—1,067 mm gauge) operates a main line from Salima to the Mozambique border near Nsanje, from which running powers over the Trans-Zambesia Railway allow access to the port of Beira; a branch opened in 1970 runs eastwards from a point 16 km south of Balaka to the Mozambique border to give a direct route to the deep-water port of Nacala. The 26-km section from Nsanje to the border is operated by the Central Africa Railway Co. Ltd. An extension of 111 km from Salima to the new state capital of Lilongwe was opened in Feb. 1979, and a further extension to Mchinji on the Zambian border (120 km) was under construction in 1980. In 1978, 1·2m. tons hauled, 67m. passenger-km.

Aviation. In 1976 Chileka airport handled 173,468 passengers and 11,451·8 tonnes of freight. Lilongwe airport handled 28,752 and 324·6 tonnes.

Shipping. In 1976 lake ships carried 131,000 passengers and 33,000 short tons of freight.

Post. Number of telephones (1978) 22,582.

Newspapers (1977). *The Daily Times* (English, Monday to Friday); 5,700–6,300 copies daily. *Malawi News* (English and Chichewa, Saturdays); 6,700 copies weekly. *The African* (English and Chichewa, fortnightly).

JUSTICE, RELIGION, EDUCATION AND WELFARE

Justice. Justice is administered in the High Court, the magistrates' courts and traditional courts. There are 23 magistrates' courts, 176 traditional courts and 23 local appeal courts.

Appeals from traditional courts are dealt with in the traditional appeal courts and in the national traditional appeal court. Appeals from magistrates' courts lie to the High Court, and appeals from the High Court to Malawi's Supreme Court of Appeal.

Religion. In 1972 the Roman Catholic Church claimed 1,073,000 members; the Presbyterian Church of Central Africa, 846,000; the Diocese of Malawi (part of the Province of Central Africa of the Anglican Communion), 79,000; Seventh-day Adventist Church, 93,000; Zambezi Evangelical Church (formerly Nayas Mission), 36,000; Assemblies of God, 7,000; Seventh-day Baptists (Central Africa conference), 11,000; Churches of Christ, 21,000; African Evangelical Church, 7,000; Evangelical Church of Malawi, 18,000. Moslems are estimated to number between 500,000 and 1m.

Education (1975–76). The Ministry of Education controls all aspects of education.

The number of pupils in the 2,091 primary schools was 641,709; in the 61 secondary schools, 14,489. There were 10,588 teachers in primary schools and 748 in secondary schools. The primary school course is of 8 years duration, followed by a 4-year secondary course. English is taught from the 1st year and becomes the general medium of instruction from the 4th year.

Teacher-training is undertaken in 8 residential colleges, 2 of which are directly controlled by the Ministry; the others receive grants in aid as assisted institutions. Courses last 3 years. Enrolment 1,100. Technical and trade courses are offered in commerce, building, woodwork and mechanical engineering, as well as home craft for girls; 1,904 trainees undertook courses at government and voluntary schools in 1966.

The University of Malawi was inaugurated on 6 Oct. 1965. In 1975–76 there were 1,148 students taking degree and diploma courses.

Health. In 1975 there were 482 medical institutions and 8,991 hospital beds.

DIPLOMATIC REPRESENTATIVES

OF MALAWI IN GREAT BRITAIN
(33 Grosvenor St., London, W1)

High Commissioner: N. T. Mizere.

OF GREAT BRITAIN IN MALAWI (Lingadzi Hse., Lilongwe, 3)

High Commissioner: William Peters, CMG, MVO, MBE.

OF MALAWI IN THE USA (1400 20th St., NW,
Washington, D.C., 20036)

Ambassador: Jacob T. X. Muwamba.

OF THE USA IN MALAWI (PO Box 30016, Lilongwe)

Chargé d'Affaires: Robert M. Maxim.

OF MALAWI TO THE UNITED NATIONS

Ambassador: T. J. X. Muwamba.

Books of Reference

General Information: The Chief Information Officer, PO Box 494, Blantyre.

Clutton-Brock, G., *Dawn in Nyasaland.* London, 1964
Debenham, F., *Nyasaland.* HMSO, 1964
Gelfand, M., *Lakeside Pioneers. Socio-medical Study of Nyasaland, 1875–1920.* Oxford, 1964
Jones, G., *Britain and Nyasaland.* London, 1964
McMaster, C., *Malawi: Foreign Policy and Development.* London, 1974
Pike, J. G., *Malawi, A Political History.* London, 1967
Pike and Rimmington, *Malawi, A Geographical Study.* Oxford, 1965
Read, F. E., *Malawi, Land of Promise.* Govt. Dept. of Information, 1967.—*Malawi, Land of Progress.* Govt. Dept. of Information, 1969
Williams, T. D., *Malawi: The Politics of Despair.* Cornell Univ. Press, 1979

MALAYSIA

Capital: Kuala Lumpur
Population: 13·3m. (1978)
GNP per capita: US$1,090 (1978)

HISTORY. On 16 Sept. 1963 Malaysia came into being, consisting of the Federation of Malaya, the State of Singapore and the colonies of North Borneo (renamed Sabah) and Sarawak. The agreement between the UK and the 4 territories was signed on 9 July (Cmnd. 2094); by it, the UK relinquished sovereignty over Singapore, North Borneo and Sarawak from independence day and extended the 1957 defence agreement with Malaya to apply to Malaysia. Malaysia became automatically a member of the Commonwealth of Nations. *See* map in THE STATESMAN'S YEAR-BOOK, 1964–65.

On 9 Aug. 1965, by a mutual agreement dated 7 Aug. 1965 between Malaysia and Singapore, Singapore seceded from Malaysia to become an independent Sovereign nation.

POPULATION. The 1970 census gave a total of 8,809,557. Estimates, 1977, 12,945,820; 10,882,222 for Peninsular Malaysia; 903,776 in Sabah, and 1,159,822 in Sarawak. Total estimated population (1978) 13·3m.

CONSTITUTION AND GOVERNMENT. The Constitution of Malaysia is based on the Constitution of the former Federation of Malaya, but includes safeguards for the special interests of Sabah and Sarawak.

The federal capital is Kuala Lumpur, established on 1 Feb. 1974 with an area of approximately 94 sq. miles. The official language is Malay.

The Constitution provides for one of the 9 Rulers of the Malay States to be elected from among themselves to be the *Yang di-Pertuan Agong* (Supreme Head of the Federation). He holds office for a period of 5 years. The Rulers also elect from among themselves a Deputy Supreme Head of State, also for a period of 5 years.

Supreme Head of State (Yang di-Pertuan Agong): HM Sultan Haji Ahmad Shah Al-Musta'in Billah Ibni Al-Marhum Sultan Abu Bakar Ri'Ayatuddin Al-Mu'Adzam Shah, DKM, DKP, DK, SSAP, SIMP, DMN, SPCM, SPMJ, elected as 7th *Yang di-Pertuan Agong* from 26 April 1979.

Raja of Perlis: HRH Tuanku Syed Putra ibni Al-Marhum Syed Hassan Jamalullail, DK, DKM, DMN, SMN, SPMP, SPDK, acceded 12 March 1949.

Sultan of Kedah: HRH Tuanku Haji Abdul Halim Mu'adzam Shah ibni Al-Marhum Sultan Badlishah, DK, DKH, DKM, DMN, DUK, SPMK, SSDK, acceded 20 Feb. 1959.

Sultan of Johore: HRH Sultan Ismail ibni Al-Marhum Sultan Ibrahim, DK, DMN, SMN, SPMJ, SSIJ, SPMK, acceded 10 Feb. 1960.

Sultan of Selangor: HRH Sultan Salahuddin Abdul Aziz Shah ibni Al-Marhum Sultan Hisamuddin 'Alam Shah Al-Haj, DK, DMN, SPMS, SPDK, acceded 28 June 1961.

Sultan of Perak: HRH Sultan Idris Al-Mutawakkil Alallahi Shah ibni Al-Marhum Sultan Iskandar Shah Kadasallah, DK, DMN, SPMP, SPCM, SPTS, CMG, PJK, acceded 26 Oct. 1963.

Yang di-Pertuan Besar of Negeri Sembilan: HRH Tuanku Ja'afar ibni Al-Marhum Tuanku Abdul Rahman, DMN, DK, acceded 8 April, 1968.

Regent of Kelantan: HRH Sultan Ismail Petra ibni Al-Marhum Sultan Yahya Petra, DK, SPMK, SJMK, SPSM, appointed 29 March 1979.

Sultan of Trengganu: HRH Sultan Mahmud ibni Al-Marhum Tuanku Al-Sultan Ismail Nasiruddin Shah, DK, SPMT, SPCM, appointed 20 Sept. 1979.

Acting Sultan of Pahang: HRH Tengku Abdullah Ibni Sultan Haji Ahmad Shah Al-Musta'in Billah, DK, SSAP, SIMP, appointed 14 April 1979.

Yang di-Pertua Negeri Pulau Pinang: HE Tun Datuk Haji Sardon bin Haji Jubir, SMN, PMN, DUPN, SPMJ, SPMK, appointed 5 Feb. 1975; re-appointed 5 Feb. 1979.

Governor of Malacca: HE Tun Haji Syed Zahiruddin bin Syed Hassan, DUNM, PSM, SMN, SPMP, JMN, PJK, appointed 23 May 1975; re-appointed 23 May 1979.

Yang di-Pertua Negeri Sarawak: HE Datuk Pattinggi Abang Haji Muhammed Salahuddin, SMN, SPMP, appointed 2 April 1977.

Yang di-Pertua Negeri Sabah: HE Datuk Mohamad Adnan Robert, SMN, SPDK, appointed 26 June 1978.

Parliament consists of the *Yang di-Pertuan Agong* and two *Majlis* (Houses of Parliament) known as the *Dewan Negara* (Senate) of 68 members and *Dewan Rakyat* (House of Representatives) of 154 members. There are 149 members from the states in Malaysia and 5 from the Federal Territory. Appointment to the Senate is for 3 years. The maximum life of the House of Representatives is 5 years, subject to its dissolution at any time by the *Yang di-Pertuan Agong* on the advice of his Ministers.

National flag: Fourteen horizontal stripes of red and white, with a blue quarter bearing a crescent and a star of 14 points, all in gold.

The elections to the House of Representatives held on 8 July 1978, returned the following members: National Front, 130; Democratic Action Party, 16; PAS, 5; Sarawak People's Organisation, 1; Independent, 2.

The Cabinet was in Sept. 1980 composed as follows:

Prime Minister and Minister of Defence: Dato Hussein bin Onn, DK.

Deputy Prime Minister, Commerce and Industry: Dato Seri Dr Mahathir bin Mohammad, SSDK, SPMJ, SPMS, SSAP, DP. *Agriculture:* Dato Abdul Manan bin Othman, DPMT, PPT. *Works and Public Utilities:* Dato S. Samy Vellu, PMN, PCM, AMN. *Transport:* Dato Lee San Choon, SPMJ, SSIJ, KMN. *Housing and Local Government:* Dato Dr Neo Yee Pan, SPMJ, DPMJ. *Home Affairs:* Tan Sri Haji Muhammad Ghazali bin Shafie, PMN, SSAP, SIMP, SDPK. *Health:* Tan Sri Chong Hon Nyan, PSM, JMN. *Land and Regional Development:* Dato Shariff Ahmad, DSAP, DIMP, JMN. *Welfare Services:* Datin Paduka Hajjah Aishah binti Haji Abdul Ghani, DPMS, JMN. *Culture, Youth and Sports:* Dato Mokhtar bin Haji Hashim, DSNS. *Foreign Affairs:* Y. M. Tengku Dato Ahmad Rithauddeen Al-Haj bin Tengku Ismail, SPMP, PMK. *Science, Technology and Environment:* Tan Sri Ong Kee Hui, PMN, PNBS, PGDK. *Primary Industry:* Dato Paul Leong Khee Seong, DPCM. *Education:* Dato Musa bin Hitam, SPMJ, SSIJ. *Finance:* Y. M. Tengku Razaleigh Hamzah, DK, SPMK, PSM. *Information:* Dato Mohamed bin Rahmat, SPMJ, SSIJ, DPMJ, KMN. *Labour and Manpower:* Dato Richard Ho Ung Hun, DPMP. *Public Enterprises:* Datin Paduka Rafidah Aziz, DPMS, AMN. *Energy, Telecommunications and Post:* Datuk Leo Moggie anak Irok, PNBS. *Without Portfolio:* Dato Haji Mohammad bin Nasir, SPMK, JMN, JP; Datuk Pengiran Othman bin Haji Pengiran Rauf, PGDK, ADK. *Federal Territory;* Dato Amar Haji Abdul Taib bin Mahmud, DA, SPMJ, PGDK.

DEFENCE. The Malaysian Armed Forces is made up of the Malaysian Army, the Royal Malaysian Navy and the Royal Malaysian Air Force. Each Service has its own component of reserves.

The Malaysian Constitution provides for the *Yang di-Pertuan Agong* (Supreme Head of State) to be the Supreme Commander of the Armed Forces who exercises his powers and authority in accordance with the advice of the Cabinet. Under the general authority of the Yang di-Pertuan Agong and the Cabinet, there is the Armed Forces Council which is responsible for the command, discipline and administration of all other matters relating to the Armed Forces, other than those relating to its operational use.

The Armed Forces Council is chaired by the Minister of Defence and its membership consists of the chief of the Armed Forces Staff, the 3 Service Chiefs and 2 other senior military officers, the Secretary-General of the Ministry of Defence, a representative of State Rulers and an appointed member.

The chief of the Armed Forces Staff is the professional head of the Armed Forces and the senior military member in the Armed Forces Council. He is the principal adviser to the Minister of Defence on the military aspects of all defence matters. The chief of the Armed Forces Staff's committee, established under the authority of the Armed Forces Council, is the highest level at which joint planning and co-ordination with the Armed Forces are carried out. The Committee is chaired by the chief of the Armed Forces Staff and its membership consists of the chief of the Army, Navy and Air Force, the chief of Personnel Staff, the chief of logistic Staff and the chief of Staff of the Ministry of Defence.

Army. The Malaysian Army is made up of both regular and volunteer Force. The regular force comprises 11 Infantry brigade groups in 3 Divisions and 1 semi-independent regional security command. Each brigade consists of Infantry, reconnaissance, artillery, signals, engineers and is supported by adequate logistics units. The Malaysian army is still in the process of implementing its expansion programme. The regular force has a total strength of approximately 60,000.

The Volunteer Force has one division made up of combatant reserve units and manpower reserve pool with an approximately total strength of 25,000. Reserve Officer Training Units (ROTU) are also being set up in all Institutions of higher learning to act as officers reserve pool in time of emergency.

The Royal Military College (RMC) at Sungei Besi near Kuala Lumpur and Officer Cadet School (OCS) at Port Dickson train regular and short service commissioned officers respectively. The RMC has a Boys' Wing (Academic Wing) which shapes-up young Malaysians to be officers in the Armed Forces, Officers in the higher divisions of the public service and as leaders in the professional, commercial and industrial life of the country.

Navy. The Royal Malaysian Navy is commanded by the Chief of the Naval Staff from the integrated Ministry of Defence in Kuala Lumpur. The main naval bases are KD Malaya situated on Singapore Island and KD Sri Labuan on Labuan Island. These establishments are responsible for the operation and administration of the ships, and KD Malaya for the training of personnel.

The ships include 2 British (Jarrow)-built frigates (including the former HMS *Mermaid*), 5 coastal minesweepers, 8 fast missile craft, 6 fast gunboats, 22 patrol craft, 3 landing ships, 1 diving tender and 1 survey vessel. The peace-time tasks include fishery protection and anti-piracy patrols. There are also 30 armed patrol launches, 28 operated by the Royal Malaysian Police and 2 by the Government of Sabah (North Borneo) which also operates 4 patrol boats and a yacht. Naval personnel in 1981 exceeded 6,000 officers and ratings, plus 1,000 reservists and 800 volunteer reserve.

Future plans include the provision of 4 corvettes, 4 mine countermeasures vessels, 6 coastguard patrol craft and 6 marine patrol boats.

Air Force. Formed on 1 June 1958, the Royal Malaysian Air Force is equipped primarily to provide air defence and air support for the Army, Navy and Police. Its secondary rôle is to render assistance to Government departments and civilian organizations, especially during periods of national disasters. There are 12 squadrons, of which 8 operate transport aircraft and helicopters. Equipment includes 88 A-4 Skyhawk attack aircraft, 12 F-5E Tiger II jet fighter-bombers, 2 F-5B and 6 F-5F trainers, 16 Canadair CL-41G Tebuan dual-purpose light jet strike and training aircraft, 9 C-130H-MP Hercules four-turboprop heavy transports and maritime reconnaissance aircraft, 2 F.28 Fellowship VIP transports, 15 Caribou twin-engined STOL transports, 35 Sikorsky S-61A-4 Nuri heavy troop and cargo transport helicopters, 22 Alouette III, 3 Agusta-Bell 212, 9 Bell 47 and 5 Bell 206B JetRanger helicopters, 12 Cessna 402Bs for twin-engine training and liaison, 13 piston-engined Bulldog basic trainers and 2 H.S. 125 Merpati twin-jet executive transports. Personnel (1980) totalled about 6,000.

Volunteer Forces. The Army Volunteer Force (Territorial Army) consists of first-line infantry, signals, engineer and logistics units able to take the field with the active army, and a second-line organization to provide local defence. There is also a small Naval Volunteer Reserve with Headquarters in Penang and Kuala Lumpur. The Royal Malaysian Air Force Volunteer Reserve has both air and ground elements.

INTERNATIONAL RELATIONS

Membership. Malaysia is a member of UN, the Commonwealth and the Colombo Plan.

ECONOMY

Planning. The first 5-year plan, 1966–70, envisaged an outlay of M$14,742m. The second 5-year plan, 1971–75, envisaged an expenditure of M$16,150m. and aimed at the eradication of poverty and the restructuring of society. The third 5-year plan, 1976–80, envisaged an expenditure of M$18,555m.

Budget. Revenue and expenditure for calendar years, in M$1m.:

	1976	1977	1978	1979 [1]	1980 [2]
Revenue	6,157	7,760	8,827	10,220	11,383
Operating expenditure [3]	5,828	7,398	8,028	9,910	10,868
Development expenditure	2,378	3,217	3,763	4,720	6,340

[1] Latest estimate. [2] Budget estimate.
[3] Including contribution to sinking fund from 1975.

Currency. Bank Negara Malaysia (Central Bank of Malaysia) assumed sole currency issuing authority in Malaysia on 12 June 1967. The unit of currency issued by Bank Negara Malaysia is the Malaysian *ringgit* ($) which is divided into 100 *sen*. Currency notes are of denominations of $1, 5, 10, 50, 100 and $1,000. Coins are of denominations of 1 *sen*, 5, 10, 20, 50 *sen* and $1, $5, $10, $15, $25, $100, $200, $250 and $500. The circulation of currency on 31 Dec. 1979 was M$4,361·84m.

Banking. Thirty-eight banks were operating in Dec. 1979; of these 21 were domestic banks with a total of 381 banking offices. Five were banks incorporated in Singapore with 63 banking offices and the remaining 12 banks were foreign incorporated with 85 banking offices. Total deposits amounted to M$19,141·6m. on 31 Dec. 1979 and loans and advances amounted to M$15,259·8m.

The National Savings Bank (formerly known as the post office savings bank) held M$973·8m. due to 3,600,948 depositors at 31 Dec. 1978.

TRADE. Total trade of Malaysia with UK (British Department of Trade returns, in £1,000 sterling):

	1977	1978	1979	1980
Imports to UK	223,558	199,926	221,488	187,050
Exports and re-exports from UK	147,450	186,599	187,425	223,516

COMMUNICATIONS

Post. The Postal Services in Malaysia are under the Ministry of Power, Telecommunications and Post and are headed by the Director-General of Post, Malaysia.

Cinemas. In 1974 there were 500 cinemas with a seating capacity of 345,400.

JUSTICE. By virtue of Art. 121(1) of the Federal Constitution judicial power in the Federation is vested on 2 High Courts of co-ordinate jurisdiction and status namely the High Court of Malaya and the High Court of Borneo, and the inferior courts. The Federal Court with its principal registry in Kuala Lumpur is the Supreme Court of authority in the country.

The Lord President as the supreme head of the Judiciary, the 2 Chief Justices of the High Courts and 6 other Judges form the constitution of the Federal Court. Apart from having exclusive jurisdiction to determine appeals from decisions of a High Court Judge or a Judge thereof, the Federal Court is also conferred with such original and consultative jurisdiction as is laid out in Articles 128 and 130 of the Constitution.

A panel of 3 Judges or such greater uneven number as may be determined by the Lord President preside in every proceeding in the Federal Court.

The right of appeal to the Yang di-Pertuan Agong (who in turn refers the appeal to the Judicial Committee of the British Privy Council) from a decision of the Federal Court in respect of criminal matters was abolished on 1 July 1978.

DIPLOMATIC REPRESENTATIVES

OF MALAYSIA IN GREAT BRITAIN
(45 Belgrave Sq., London, SW1X 8QT)

High Commissioner: Raja Tan Sri Aznam bin Haji Ahmad.

OF GREAT BRITAIN IN MALAYSIA (Wisma Damansara,
Jalan Semantan, Kuala Lumpur)

High Commissioner: William Bentley, CMG.

OF MALAYSIA IN THE USA (2401 Massachusetts Ave., NW,
Washington, D.C., 20008)

Ambassador: Datuk Zain Azraai bin Zainal Abidin.

OF THE USA IN MALAYSIA
(A.I.A. Bldg., Jalan Ampang, Kuala Lumpur)

Ambassador: Barbara M. Watson.

OF MALAYSIA TO THE UNITED NATIONS

Ambassador: Dato Zainal Abidin bin Sulong.

Books of Reference

Statistical Information: The Department of Statistics, Malaysia, Kuala Lumpur, was set up in 1963, taking over from the Department of Statistics, States of Malaya. *Chief Statistician:* Khoo Teik Huat. Main publications: *Peninsular Malaysia Monthly* and *Annual Statistics of External Trade*; *Malaysia External Trade* (quarterly); *Peninsular Malaysia Statistical Bulletin* (monthly); *Rubber Statistics* (monthly); *Rubber Statistics Handbook* (annual); *Oil Palm Statistics* (monthly); *Oil Palm, Coconut and Tea Statistics* (annual); *Survey of Manufacturing Industries, 1974*; *National Accounts Statistics, 1973–1977*; *Malaysia Industrial Classification, 1972*; *Monthly Industrial Statistics, Malaysia*; *Census of Selected Service Trades, 1973*.

Books About Malaysia. Singapore, National Library, 1965
The Economic Aspects of Malaysia. Report by the International Bank. Singapore, 1963
Means, G. P., *Malaysian Politics.* 2nd ed. London, 1976

PENINSULAR MALAYSIA

AREA AND POPULATION. The total area of Peninsular Malaysia is about 50,806 sq. miles (131,587 sq. km). The federal capital is Kuala Lumpur (94 sq. miles).

State	Area (sq. miles)	Population (1970 Census)	Capital	Population (1970 Census)
Johore	7,330	1,277,180	Johore Bharu	136,229
Kedah	3,639	954,947	Alor Star	66,260
Kelantan	5,765	684,738	Kota Bharu	55,124
Malacca	637	404,125	Malacca	87,160
Negeri Sembilan	2,565	481,563	Seremban	80,921
Pahang	13,886	504,945	Kuantan	43,358
Penang	399	776,124	Georgetown	269,247
Perak	8,110	1,569,139	Ipoh	247,969
Perlis	307	121,062	Kangar	8,758
Selangor	3,074	1,178,556	Shah Alam	—
Trengganu	5,002	405,368	Kuala Trengganu	53,320
Federal Territory	94	451,801	Kuala Lumpur	451,801
Peninsular Malaysia	50,806	8,809,557		

Population by races (1970 Census): 4,671,874 Malays; 3,131,320 Chinese; 936,341 Indians and Pakistani; 70,022 others. In 1974 Kuala Lumpur became a Federal District. Shah Alam became capital of Selangor. Vital statistics (1978): Births, 323,541; deaths, 63,176.

CONSTITUTION AND GOVERNMENT. The States of the Federation of Malaya, now known as Peninsular Malaysia, comprises the 11 States of Johore, Pahang, Negeri Sembilan, Selangor, Perak, Kedah, Perlis, Kelantan, Trengganu, Penang and Malacca. On 31 Aug. 1957 the Federation became the 11th sovereign member-state of the Commonwealth of Nations.

For earlier history of the States and Settlements *see* THE STATESMAN'S YEAR-BOOK, 1957, p. 241.

The Constitution is based on the agreements reached at the London conference of Jan.–Feb. 1956, between HM Government in the UK, the Rulers of the Malay states and the Alliance Party (which at the first federal elections on 27 July 1955 obtained 51 of the 52 elected members), and subsequently worked out by the Constitutional Commission appointed after that conference.

ECONOMY

Budget. Revenue and expenditure for calendar years, in M$1m.:

	1973	1974 [2]	1975 [2]
Revenue	525·6	663·6	664·1
Current expenditure [1]	572·1	730·6	761·2
Development expenditure	165·7	254·9	490·6
Less Federal reimbursement	22·6	28·8	47·1

[1] Excluding contribution to development and water supply funds but including recurrent expenditure from water supply fund, loan repayments and interest.
[2] Estimates.

Weights and Measures. The standard measures are the imperial yard, pound and gallon. The Weights and Measures Act of 1972 provides for a 10-year transition to the metric system, to be completed by 31 Dec. 1981.

ENERGY AND NATURAL RESOURCES

Electricity. In 1979, 8,150·7m. kwh. were generated; commerce and industry are the main consumers.

Minerals. Production (in 1,000 tonnes): Tin-in-concentrates: 1978, 62·6; 1979, 63. Iron ore: 1978, 320; 1979, 350. Bauxite: 1978, 615·1; 1979, 386·5. Ilmenite (exports): 1978, 166·6; 1979, 199·8. Gold: 1978, 5,805 troy oz.; 1979, 5,273.

Agriculture. Total area under agricultural crops, 1974, 8m. acres. This included 536,300 acres of second season rice crops.

Rice: Production in 1976, 1,117,900 tons from 1,433,400 acres, which includes second crop acreage.

Rubber: Production in 1979, 1,528,044 tonnes. Oil-palms: Production in 1979, 2,032,335 tonnes of palm oil; 441,040 tonnes of kernels; 61,755 tonnes of coconut oil.

Tea: Production in 1979, 4,041,000 kg.

Livestock: (1979) Cattle, 430,000; buffaloes, 293,000; sheep, 46,000; swine, 1,171,000; goats, 380,000.

Forestry (1979). Reserved forests, 12·8m. acres; productive, 8·1m. acres. Production of logs, 10,606,000 cu. metres; sawn timber, 4,811,000 cu. metres; plywood, 83,344,000 sq. metres (5mm thickness). Exports of veneer, 29,657,000 sq. metres (5mm thickness).

Fisheries. Landings in 1978, 564,908 tons; 1977, 497,952 tons. Number of vessels in 1979, 21,439 powered, 5,955 non-powered.

INDUSTRY AND TRADE

Trade Unions. There were, on 31 Dec. 1979, 385 registered trade unions with 568,419 members in Malaysia.

Commerce. Imports and exports for calendar years in M$1m.:

	1974	1975	1976	1977	1978	1979
Imports	8,550·0	7,516·1	8,513·5	9,880·7	12,156·7	15,365·8
Exports	8,437·5	7,695·8	10,042·7	11,230·9	13,680·3	19,049·6

Chief imports (1979): Machinery and transport equipment, M$5,413·8m.; manufactured goods, M$2,617·9m.; food, M$1,716m.

Chief exports (1979): Rubber, 1,577,840 tonnes (M$4,314·1m.); tin metal and tin-in-concentrates, 72,122 tonnes (M$2,315·7m.); sawn timber, 2,826,925 cu. metres (M$1,092·5m.); palm-oil, crude, 703,842 tonnes (M$955m.); palm olein, 496,918 tonnes (M$699·2m.); saw logs, 201,719 cu. metres (M$22·3m.); bauxite, 470,151 tonnes (M$13,408,657).

In 1978 imports came chiefly from Japan (M$3,150·5m.), USA (M$2,300·3m.), Singapore (M$1,180·9m.), UK (M$994·3m.), Australia (M$989m.), Thailand (M$546·2m.), Saudi Arabia (M$540·7m.), China (M$342·5m.), Indonesia (M$137·5m.), Federal Republic of Germany (M$7·9m.). Exports went mainly to Singapore (M$3,493·7m.), USA (M$3,221·5m.), Japan (M$2,310m.), Netherlands (M$1,279·9m.), UK (M$817m.), Sabah (M$768m.), Sarawak (M$613·8m.), USSR (M$567m.), France (M$392·1m.), Italy (M$368·9m.), Federal Republic of Germany (M$44·8m.).

Tourism. In 1978, 3,017,864 foreigners visited Peninsular Malaysia.

COMMUNICATIONS

Roads. In 1979 the Public Works Department maintained 13,609 miles (21,774 km) of public roads, of which 10,008 miles (16,012 km) was of bituminous metalled surface, 71 (114) waterbound metalled surface, 1,230 (1,968) hard surface bitumen sealed, 57 (90) hard surface waterbound and 743 (1,189) earth surface.

In 1979, 201,392 motor vehicles were registered, including 63,928 private cars, 713 buses, 12,737 lorries and vans, 117,018 motor cycles.

Railways. The Malayan Railway main line runs from Singapore to Butterworth opposite Penang Island. From Bukit Mertajam 8 miles south of Butterworth a branch line connects Peninsular Malaysia with the State Railways of Thailand at the frontier station of Padang Besar. Other branch lines connect the main line with Port of Klang, Teluk Anson, Port Dickson and Ampang. The east-coast line, branching off the main line at Gemas, runs for over 300 miles to Tumpat, Kelantan's northernmost coastal town; a short branch line linking Pasir Mas with Sungei Golok makes a second connexion with Thailand.

The route mileage in 1980 was 1,337 (metre gauge) and the annual budget is about M$$147m.

Aviation (1979). There are 9 airports used by scheduled air services in Peninsular Malaysia. International air services are operated into Kuala Lumpur and Penang airports. The national carrier, Malaysian Airlines System (MAS), began operation on 1 Oct. 1972 to provide both domestic and international services. The Malaysian Airlines System (MAS) operate international services to Bandar Seri Begawan, Bangkok, Frankfurt, Haadyai, Hong Kong, Jakarta, Jeddah, Kuwait, London, Madras, Manila, Medan, Melbourne, Perth, Seoul, Singapore, Sydney, Taipei and Tōkyō. The number of domestic points served by the airline is 36. Charter services are provided within Peninsular Malaysia by Malaysia Air Charter Co., Pan Malaysia Air Charter, Wira Kris, Genting Helicopter Service and Kris Udara Malaysia. The following airlines operate scheduled services through Kuala Lumpur besides MAS: Air Lanka, Cargoluse Airways, Bangladesh Beiman, Iraqui Airways, Philippine Airlines, PIA, Aeroflot Soviet Airlines, Air India, British Airways, Cathay Pacific Airways, China Airlines, Czechoslovakia Airlines, Garuda Indonesian Airways, Japan Airlines, KLM, PANAM, Qantas Airways, SAS, Sabena, Singapore Airlines, Thai International Airways and Trans Mediterranean Airways. The airlines operating scheduled services through Penang besides MAS are Merpati Nusantara Airlines, Cathay Pacific Airways, Thai Airways Co. and Thai Airways International.

Civil aviation statistics for airports in Peninsular Malaysia (1979): Aircraft movements, 76,638; terminal passengers, 3,153,017; freight, 30,288 tonnes; mail, 3,293 tonnes.

Shipping. The major ports of Peninsular Malaysia are Penang, Malacca, Port Klang, Pasir Gudang, Port Dickson and Kuantan. The volume of shipping (vessels of over 75 NRT only) handled at these ports, exclusive of coasting trade, was as follows (in 1,000 NRT):

		Arrivals		Departures	
Ports		Number	Tonnage	Number	Tonnage
Penang	1978	1,923	7,989	1,926	8,001
	1979	1,711	7,236	1,720	7,244
Port Klang	1978	2,978	17,222	2,963	17,181
	197919	2,794	16,463	2,799	16,434
Total (all ports)	78	5,721	32,727	5,691	32,567
	1979	5,399	34,103	5,408	34,090

The total cargo handled in all ports during 1978 was 22·82m. tonnes; 1979, 25·37m. tonnes.

Post and Broadcasting. As at 31 Dec. 1979, 445 post offices, 1,381 postal agencies, 177 mobile post offices and 1 riverine postal office were operating in Malaysia, and the cash turnover for the year amounted to M$4,688,113,241.

There were 374,676 telephones on 1 Jan. 1978 serviced by 299 exchanges with 15 satellite exchanges. In 1979, 208,731 wireless licences were issued and 818,842 television licences were issued.

JUSTICE, RELIGION, EDUCATION AND WELFARE

Justice. Unlike the Federal Court and the High Court which were established under the Constitution, the subordinate courts in Peninsular Malaysia comprising the sessions court, the Magistrate's court and the Penghulu's court were established under a Federal Law (the subordinate Courts Act, 1948 (Revised 1972)).

All offences punished with death are tried before a Sessions Court President who is empowered to pass any sentence allowed by law other than the sentence of death. In civil matters, the sessions court has jurisdiction to hear all actions and suits where the amount in dispute does not exceed M$25,000.

A First Class Magistrate's criminal jurisdiction is limited to offences for which the maximum term provided by law does not exceed 10 years imprisonment and to certain specified offences where the term of imprisonment provided for may be extended to 14 years imprisonment or which are punishable with fine only.

Juvenile courts established under the Juvenile Courts Act, 1947 for juvenile offenders below the age of 18 are presided over by a First Class Magistrate assisted by 2 advisers.

There are 30 penal institutions, including Borstal establishments and an open prison camp. The average prison population (1979) was 9,254.

Religion. More than half the population are Muslims, and Islam is the official religion. In 1970 there were 4,673,670 Muslims, 765,250 Hindus, 220,897 Christians and 2,495,739 Buddhists.

Education (1977). The number of schools (fully assisted, partially assisted and private) of all types, of teachers and pupils of both sexes were (as at 31 Jan.) as follows:

Primary schools	Medium of instruction				
	Malay	English	Chinese	Tamil	Total
Schools	2,354	386	988	600	4,328
Teachers	24,057	8,384	14,551	3,539	50,531
Pupils	734,236	302,449	493,809	78,841	1,609,335

Secondary schools	Medium of instruction			
			Malay and	
	Malay	English	English	Total
Schools	249	303	172	724
Teachers	8,390	14,133	7,787	30,310
Pupils	233,701	373,659	218,730	826,090

Upper secondary vocational training is given in 23 assisted secondary vocational schools (8,891 pupils), and upper secondary technical education in 9 assisted secondary technical schools (5,147 pupils).

Post-secondary professional education (1977–78) is given at the University of Technology (formerly the National Institute of Technology), Kuala Lumpur (350 lecturers and tutors, 2,907 students), the University of Agriculture (426 lecturers and tutors, 3,210 students), Ungku Omar Polytechnic, Ipoh (95 lecturers and instructors, 1,297 students), Mara Institute of Technology, Shah Alam (605 lecturers and instructors, 6,513 students), Tunku Abdul Rahman College (148 lecturers and instructors, 5,990 students), University of Science (formerly University of Penang), Penang (361 lecturers, tutors, researchers and language teachers, 2,431 full-time students), University Kebangsaan, Kuala Lumpur (608 lecturers, readers and tutors, 3,847 students) and the University of Malaya, Kuala Lumpur (955 lecturers, readers, tutors and language teachers, 8,586 students).

Teachers are trained at the Sultan Idris Teachers' College in Perak (928 students), the Malay Women's Teachers' College in Malacca (811 students), the Kota Bharu Teachers' College, Kelantan (859 students), Seri Kota Teachers' College, Kuala Lumpur (491 students), Sri Pinang Teachers' College, Penang (391 students), Mohd. Khalid Teachers' College, Johore (538 students), Raja Melewar Teachers' College, Negri Sembilan (676 students), Kinta Teachers' College, Perak (580 students), Health Education and Nutrition Teachers' Training College, Trengganu (240 students).

The Malayan Teachers' College in Penang (969 students), Temenggong Ibrahim Teachers' College, Johore (946 students), the Language Institute, Kuala Lumpur (648 students), the Specialist Teachers' Training College, Kuala Lumpur (671 students), the Technical Teachers' Training College, Kuala Lumpur (680 students), Raja Muda Teachers' College, Kuala Lumpur (650 students) and 4 other colleges which together have 1,470 students.

In 1974 further education classes were provided by the Government throughout the country (119 centres, 710 classes, 2,012 teachers and 20,368 students).

Health. In 1977 Government maintained 59 general, district hospitals with 19,456 beds, 2 institutions with 2,688 beds for the treatment of Hensens' disease, 2 mental institutions with 6,577 beds and 1 institution (293 beds) for tuberculosis treatment. For the care of the rural population there were 3,131 medical and health facilities comprising 65 main health centres, 254 health sub-centres, 1,375 midwives' clinics, 414 static, 284 travelling dispensaries, 739 dental clinics, 41 maternal and child health clinics. The Government also maintains an Institute for Medical Research with 2 branch laboratories at Ipoh and Penang.

Books of Reference

Gullick, J. M., *Malaya*. 2nd ed. London, 1965
Jin-Bee, Ooi, *Land, People and Economy in Malaya*. London, 1963
Kennedy, J., *A History of Malaya*. London, 1962
O'Ballance, E., *Malaya: The Communist Insurgent War, 1948–60*. London, 1966
Ratnam, K. J., *Communalism and the Political Process in Malaya*. OUP, 1965
Wilkinson, R. J., *Malay–English Dictionary*. 2 vols. New ed. London, 1956
Winstedt, Sir R., *Malaya and Its History*. 3rd ed. London, 1953.—*An English–Malay Dictionary*. 3rd ed. Singapore, 1949.—*The Malays: A Cultural History*. London, 1959

SABAH

HISTORY. The territory now named Sabah, but until Sept. 1963 known as North Borneo, was in 1877–78 ceded by the Sultans of Brunei and Sulu and various other rulers to a British syndicate, which in 1881 was chartered as the British North Borneo (Chartered) Company. The Company's sovereign rights and assets were transferred to the Crown with effect from 15 July 1946. On that date, the island of Labuan (ceded to Britain in 1846 by the Sultan of Brunei) became part of the new Colony of North Borneo. On 16 Sept. 1963 North Borneo joined the new Federation of Malaysia and became the State of Sabah.

AREA AND POPULATION. Area, about 29,388 sq. miles (80,520 sq. km), with a coastline of about 900 miles. The interior is mountainous, Mount Kinabalu being 13,455 ft (4,175 metres) high. Population (1970 census), 655,295, of whom 421,962 were natives, 140,969 Chinese, 2,489 Europeans and 97,717 others. The native population comprises Kadazans (largest and mainly agricultural), Bajaus and Bruneis (agriculture and fishing), Muruts (hill tribes), Suluks (mainly seafaring) and several smaller tribes.

The island of Labuan, 35 sq. miles (75 sq. km) in area, lying 6 miles off the north-west coast of Borneo is a free port. It has a fine port, Victoria Harbour.

The principal towns are situated on or near the coast. They include Kota Kinabalu, the capital (formerly Jesselton), 1970 census population, 40,939, Sandakan (41,413), Tawau (24,247), Kudat (5,089); and Keningau in the hinterland (2,037).

CONSTITUTION AND GOVERNMENT. The Constitution of the State of Sabah provides for a Head of State, called the *Yang Dipertua Negeri Sabah*. Executive authority is vested in the State Cabinet headed by the Chief Minister.

Head of State: Tun Mohamed Adam Robert, SMN, SPDK.

Flag: Four horizontal stripes of red, white, yellow and blue, with a green quarter bearing an outline of Mount Kinabalu in brown.

The Cabinet was composed as follows in Nov. 1979:

Chief Minister and Minister of Natural Resources: Datuk Harris bin Mohd. Salleh, SPDK.
Deputy Chief Minister/Industrial and Rural Development: Datuk James Peter Ongkili, DIMP. *Finance:* Datuk Hj. Mohd. Noor Mansoor, PGDK. *Agriculture and Fisheries:* Datuk Lim Guan Sing, DPMK. *Work and Utilities:* Datuk Suffian Koroh, PGDK. *Social Welfare and National Unity:* Toh Puan Hajjah Rahimah Stephens, PGDK. *Local Government and Housing:* Datuk Joseph Pairin Kitingan, PGDK. *Manpower and Environmental Development:* Datuk Yap Pak Leong, PGDK. *Culture, Youth and Sports:* Datu Abdul Hamid bin Tun Datu Haji Mustapha.

The Legislative Assembly consists of the Speaker, 48 elected members and not more than 6 nominated members.

The official language was English for a period of 10 years from Sept. 1963 but in Aug. 1973 Bahasa Malaysia was introduced and in 1974 was declared the official language.

ECONOMY

Budget. Budgets for calendar years, in M$:

Ordinary Budget	1972	1973	1974	1975	1976
Revenue	168,522,766	299,239,434	380,349,513	265,757,626	427,683,597
Expenditure [1]	234,833,994	213,361,906	345,645,805	414,619,046	299,707,169

Development Budget					
Revenue [2]	119,695,040	94,319,970	135,836,231	133,855,491	137,946,010
Expenditure [2]	93,384,695	93,084,147	124,263,362	160,517,426	140,033,443

[1] Includes contributions to Development Budget: 1972, M$80m.; 1973, M$65m.; 1974, Nil; 1975, M$85m.; 1976, M$95m.
[2] Excluding federal accounts on federal subjects in the State.

Banking. There are branches of The Chartered Bank at Kota Kinabalu, Sandakan, Tawau, Labuan, Kudat, Tenom and Lahad Datu. The Hongkong and Shanghai Bank has branches at Kota Kinabalu, Sandakan, Labuan, Beaufort, Papar and Tawau. The Hock Hua Bank (S) has branches at Kota Kinabalu, Sandakan and Tawau. The Chung Khiaw Bank has branches at Kota Kinabalu, Tuaran and Sandakan. Malayan Banking Ltd has branches at Kota Kinabalu, Tawau, Semporna and Sandakan. United Overseas Bank and the Overseas Chinese Banking Corporation have each a branch at Kota Kinabalu. Bank Bumiputra Malaysia has branches at Kota Kinabalu, Lahad Datu, Sandakan and Keningau. Overseas Union Bank and the Development and Commercial Bank have each a branch at Sandakan. The Sabah Bank Berhad and Sabah Development Bank were established in Kota Kinabalu in 1979.

The National Savings Bank has taken over the functions of the post office savings bank as from 1 Dec. 1974 and had (1976) M$12·9m. due to 47,348 depositors. It also provides additional services to depositors including the granting of loans for housing.

COMMERCE. The main imports are machinery, tobacco, provisions, petroleum products, metals, rice, textiles and apparel, vehicles, sugar, building material. Statistics for calendar years, in M$:

	1974	1975	1976	1977	1978
Imports	1,192,314,365	1,011,576,867	1,191,720,000	1,233,017,652	1,527,640,000
Exports	1,193,509,274	1,011,229,092	2,233,550,000	2,704,317,201	2,709,779,873

The main imports and exports were (in M$1m.):

Imports	1955	1960	1970	1974	1975
Rice	6·4	8·4	15·4	48·0	42·0
Provisins	13·0	22·3	45·7	89·9	93·6
Textiles and apparel	5·9	9·2	20·5	39·4	50·2
Tobacco, cigars and cigarettes	4·2	12·8	32·9	43·2	47·4
Sugar	2·5	3·5	6·7	28·2	31·6
Vehicles	2·2	8·1	47·6	117·3	70·0
Machinery	6·9	30·0	109·0	244·4	129·8
Petroleum products	5·0	16·1	28·6	85·5	95·2
Metals	7·5	12·1	36·8	169·8	134·6
Building materials	2·1	2·8	11·6	30·8	14·2
Exports					
Rubber	45·9	49·5	36·5	50·5	40·0
Timber	21·6	90·7	396·8	871·4	568·6
Hemp	2·2	5·2	0·3	—	—
Fish, fresh, dried and salted	0·4	0·9	8·0	13·3	13·6
Copra (including re-exports)	14·2	40·2	6·8	10·7	14·4
Cocoa beans	—	15·8	4·4	16·0	17·0
Veneer sheets	—	0·5	2·5	8·5	3·0
Palm oil	—	—	18·1	105·5	131·0
Copper concentrates	—	—	—	—	11·3

TOURIM. In 1976 some 71,262 tourists visited Sabah.

COMMUNICATIONS

Roads (1975). There were 2,381 miles of roads, of which 664 miles were bitumen surfaced, 1,428 miles gravel surfaced and 289 miles of earth road. Work is in progress on a network of roads, notably the Kota Kinabalu–Sandakan and Sandakan–Lahad Datu road links.

Railways. A metre-gauge railway, 140 km, runs from Kota Kinabalu on Gaya Bay to Tenom in the interior.

Aviation. External communications are provided from the international airport at Kota Kinabalu by Cathay Pacific Airways Ltd to Hong Kong; Malaysian Airways to Hong Kong, Manila, Brunei, Kuching, Singapore and Kuala Lumpur; Brunei Airways to Brunei and Kuching and Philippine Airlines to Manila.

The total air traffic handled at Sabah airports during 1976 was 1,249,499 passengers, 11,673,568 kg freight and 2,351,013 kg mail.

Shipping (1976). Merchant shipping totalling 14,952,441 gross tons used the ports, handling 8,021,950 tons of cargo.

Post. As at 31 Dec. 1976 there were 32 post offices, 13 mobile post offices and 84 postal agencies. There were 23,068 telephones in Jan. 1977.

JUSTICE, EDUCATION AND WELFARE

Justice. Pursuant to the Subordinate Courts Ordinance (Cap. 20) (1951) Courts of a Magistrate of the First Class, Second Class and Third Class were established to adjudicate upon the administration of civil and criminal law. The civil jurisdiction of a First Class Magistrate is limited to cases where the amount in dispute does not exceed M$1,000. but provision is made for the Chief Justice to enlarge that jurisdiction to M$3,000. This has been established so as to confer this jurisdiction on all stipendiary magistrates. A Second Class Magistrate can only try suits where the amount involved does not exceed M$500 and a Third Class Magistrate where it does not exceed M$100.

The criminal jurisdiction of these Magistrates' Courts is limited to offences of a less serious nature although stipendiary magistrates have enhanced jurisdiction. There are no Juvenile Courts.

There are also Native Courts with jurisdiction to try cases arising from breach of native law and custom (including Moslem Law and custom) where all parties are natives or one of the party is a native (if the matter is a religious, matrimonial or sexual one). Appeals from Native Courts lie to a District Judge or a Native Court of Appeal presided over by a Judge.

In 1975, 1,341 convictions were obtained in 2,258 cases taken to court.

Education. In 1976, there were 127,271 primary and 52,152 secondary pupils. There are 803 primary schools (613 government, 181 grant-aided and 9 private), and 94 general secondary schools (44 government, 37 grant-aided and 13 private) throughout the State. There are 3 teacher-training colleges, Gaya College (298 students), Kent College (327 students) and Sandakan Teacher Training College (152 students).

The Government also runs 2 vocational schools in Kota Kinabalu and Sandakan offering carpentry, motor mechanics, electrical installation, fitting/turning, radio and television and heavy plant fitting.

The Department of Education also runs further education classes in most towns and districts. The main medium of instruction in primary schools is Bahasa Malaysia although there are some Chinese medium primary schools. Secondary education is principally English but this is progressively being replaced by Bahasa Malaysia.

Health. The principal diseases are malaria, pulmonary tuberculosis and intestinal infestations. Specific control programmes for malaria and tuberculosis have drastically reduced the incidence of these two diseases.

There are 3 general hospitals (893 beds) with specialist facilities and 11 district hospitals (739 beds). Forty-three dispensaries in outlying districts providing in-patient and out-patient care are staffed by hospital assistants under the supervision of district medical officers. There is a mental hospital at Sandakan (330 beds). A new mental hospital at Kota Kinabalu with 300 beds was opened in 1972. There are 15 district health centres and 163 village group sub-centres throughout the State roviding maternal and child health care.

Book of Reference

Statistical Information: Director, Federal Department of Information, Kota Kinabalu.

Tregonning, K. G., *North Borneo*. HMSO, 1960

SARAWAK

HISTORY. The Government of part of the present territory was obtained on 24 Sept. 1841 by Sir James Brooke from the Sultan of Brunei. Various accessions were made between 1861 and 1905. In 1888 Sarawak was placed under British protection. On 16 Dec. 1941 Sarawak was occupied by the Japanese. After the liberation the Rajah took over his administration from the British military authorities on 15 April 1946. The Council Negri, on 17 May 1946, authorized the Act of Cession to the British Crown by 19 to 16 votes, and the Rajah ceded Sarawak to the British Crown on 1 July 1946.

On 16 Sept. 1963 Sarawak joined the Federation of Malaysia.

AREA AND POPULATION. The area is about 48,250 sq. miles (121,400 sq. km), with a coastline of 450 miles and many navigable rivers.

The population at 1970 census was 975,918 (1978 estimate, 1,173,906), including 386,260 Dayaks; 182,700 Malays; 103,194 other natives; 294,020 Chinese; 9,735 others. The annual rate of increase is 2·8% (estimate). Working population (1970), 361,171.

The chief towns are the capital, Kuching, about 21 miles inland, on the Sarawak River (1970 population: 63,535), Sibu, 80 miles up the Rejang River, which is navigable by large steamers (1970 population: 50,635), and Miri, the headquarters of the Sarawak Shell Ltd (1970 population: 35,702).

CONSTITUTION AND GOVERNMENT. On 24 Sept. 1941 the Rajah began to rule through a constitution. Since 1855 two bodies, known as Majlis Mesyuarat Kerajaan Negeri (Supreme Council) and the Dewan Undangan Negeri (State Legislature), had been in existence. By the constitution of 1941 they were given, by the Rajah, powers roughly corresponding to those of a colonial executive council and legislative council respectively. Sarawak has retained a considerable measure of local autonomy in state affairs. The State or Legislature consists of 48 elected members and sits for 5 years unless sooner dissolved.

A ministerial system of government was introduced in 1963. The Chief Minister presides over the Supreme Council, which contains no more than 8 other Council Negri members, all of whom are Ministers.

Elections to the State Legislature on 22 Sept. 1979 returned 3 Independents and 45 members of the Sarawak Barisan Nasional comprising the Party Pesaka Bumiputra Bersatu, the Sarawak United Peoples' Party, and Sarawak National Party.

Sarawak has 24 seats in the Malaysia House of Representatives (154 members) and 5 seats in the Senate (58 members).

Sarawak has 7 divisions each under a Resident.

Head of State: Tun Datuk Patinggi Abang Haji Muhammad Salahuddin, SMN, SPMP.

Chief Minister: Datuk Patinggi Tan Sri Haji Abdul Rahman Ya'kub, DP, PMN, SPMJ, SPMK, SIMP, SPMS, SSDK, SPMP, SPDK, PNBS.

Deputy Chief Ministers: Datuk Amar Sim Kheng Hong, DA, PNBS (*Finance and Development*), Daniel Tajem Anak Miri (*Communications and Works*), Datuk Alfred Jabu Anak Numpang, PNBS (*Lands and Mineral Resources*). *Agriculture and Community Development:* Datuk Dr Wong Soon Kai, PNBS. *Culture, Youth and Sports:* Celestine Ujang Anak Jilan. *Local Government:* Joseph Balan Seling. *Forestry:* Datuk Haji Noor Tahin.

State Secretary: Datuk Amar Abang Haji Yusuf Puteh, DA, PNBS, JSM. *State Attorney-General:* Datuk Jemuri Serjan, PNBS, JBS. *State Financial Secretary:* Datuk Haji Bujang mohd Nor, PNBS, JBS, JSM.

The official languages are Malay and English. The continuing use of English as official language in Sarawak will be reviewed in 1985.

Flag: Horizontally red over white with a blue triangle based on the hoist.

ECONOMY

Budget. In 1979 State revenue was M\$242·5m.; expenditure, M\$281·5m. The revenue is mainly derived from royalties on oil and timber.

The third Malaysian 5-year development plan (1976–80) provides for Sarawak an expenditure of M\$2,500m.; of this sum M\$1,034·5m. is to be spent on roads and bridges, land development, port development, education, electricity and water supply and agriculture.

Currency. The Malaysian *dollar* is on a par of £0·22 or US\$0.43.

Banking. The post office savings bank had 57,514 depositors at the beginning of 1979; the amount to their credit was M\$30·4m. There is a branch of Bank Negara Malaysia in Kuching, and branches of the Chartered Bank, the Hongkong & Shanghai Bank, the Overseas Chinese Banking Corporation, the Malayan Bank and 9 other banks.

PRODUCTION. The State produces rubber (exports, 1978, 39,609 net tons, M\$74m.; 1979, 42,000 net tons, M\$94·9m.), timber logs (exports, 1978, 4·2m. tons, M\$321m.; 1979, 5·9m. tons, M\$798·5m.), sawn timber (exports, 1978, 191m. tons, M\$78·3m.; 1979, 184m. tons, M\$113m.), palm oil (exports, 1978, 17,485 tons, M\$26·4m.; 1979, 18,376 tons, M\$27·9m.), pepper (exports, 1978, 30,780 tons, M\$131·8m.; 1979, 35,400 tons, M\$132·2m.), and other jungle produce. There are also gold (1978, 971 troy oz.; 1977, 742 troy oz.) and antimony ore (1978, 432 tons; 1977, 436 tons).

COMMERCE. Export of crude oil in 1979 was 4·01m. tons (M\$1,392m.), about

56% of total exports. The bulk of crude production was exported to Japan, USA, Philippines and Thailand.

Total import value, 1978, M$1,152m.; 1979, M$1,629m. Export, 1978, M$1,908m.; 1979, M$3,029m.

COMMUNICATIONS

Roads. There are no railways. In 1978 there were 2,823 miles of roads, consisting of 886 miles of bitumen surfaced, 1,250 miles of gravel or stone surfaced and 687 miles of earth roads.

Aviation. There are daily Malaysian Airline System (MAS) B737 flights between Kuching and Kuala Lumpur via Singapore, and also scheduled flights between Kuching, Brunei and Hong Kong. Major towns in Sarawak are linked up by internal air routes.

Shipping. In 1978 Sarawak ports loaded 9·92m. tons (1977: 7·25m. tons) and discharged 710,000 tons (1977: 1·13m. tons). New Kuching wharf, operational since Dec. 1974, can accommodate vessels up to 15,000 tons.

Post and Broadcasting. There are 46 post offices (including 3 mobile offices) and wireless-telegraph stations and 53 agencies. A telephone system with 57 exchanges (41,356 telephones) covers the country. There is communication by wireless with Singapore and other Commonwealth countries. The government radio and television service had, at the end of 1978, 32,596 registered receivers.

Newspapers (1979). There are 1 Malay, 3 English and 7 Chinese daily; 1 Malay weekly; 1 Malay and 1 Iban (Sea Dayak) monthly newspapers as well as a weekly news review in Malay and Iban published by Government.

JUSTICE, RELIGION, EDUCATION AND WELFARE

Justice (1979). In Sarawak subordinate courts were established pursuant to the Subordinate Courts Ordinance (Cap. 42) (1952). The limits of civil and criminal jurisdiction of a First Class, Second Class and Third Class Magistrate are the same as in Sabah. As in Sabah, here too there is provision for the Chief Justice to enhance the jurisdiction of a First Class Magistrate in civil and criminal matters, the reason being that there are no Sessions Courts in both Sabah and Sarawak.

Native Courts were set up under the Native Courts Ordinance (Cap. 43) (1955) with the same limited jurisdiction as Native Courts in Sabah. In addition these courts have jurisdiction to try civil cases where the amount in dispute does not exceed M$50. Appeals from Native Courts lie to a Resident's Native Court and, subject to some limitations, to the Native Court of Appeal which is presided over by a High Court Judge. There are no Juvenile Courts. There are 6 prisons. There were 2,498 admissions, of whom 1,376 were sentenced to penal imprisonment and 883 committed on remand or awaiting trial, and 47 paid fines. Daily average prison population was 322.

Police. There is a Royal Malaysia Police, Sarawak Component, with a total establishment of about 7,800 regular officers and men.

Religion. There are Church of England, Roman Catholic, American Methodist, Seventh-day Adventist and Borneo Evangelical missions. There is a large Moslem population and many Buddhists. Islam is the national religion.

Education (1978). All schools (government, missions, private) numbered 1,383 with 262,167 pupils, of whom 77,658 were in secondary classes. There are 3 teacher-training centres and an agricultural university campus conducting pre-university courses.

Health. At the end of 1978 there were 15 government and private hospitals (2,576 beds), 119 static and 53 travelling dispensaries, 1 urban health centre, 88 public dental and school dental clinics and 180 maternal and child health centres. There were 151 registered doctors.

Books of Reference

Population and Housing Census of Malaysia, 1970. Dept. of Statistics, Kuala Lumpur
Sarawak Annual of Statistics. Dept. of Statistics, Kuching, 1979
Sarawak Annual External Trade Statistics. Dept. of Statistics, Kuching, 1979
1980 Sarawak Budget. Information Dept., Sarawak
Dickson, M. G., *Sarawak and its People.* New ed. Kuching, 1962
MacDonald, M., *Borneo People.* London, 1956
Milne, R. S., and Ratnam, K. J., *Malaysia, New States in a New Nation: Political Development of Sarawak and Sabah in Malaysia.* London, 1974
Runciman, S., *The White Rajahs.* CUP, 1960
Scott, N. C., *Sea Dyak Dictionary.* Govt. Printing Office, Kuching, 1956

National Library: The Sarawak Central Library, Kuching.

REPUBLIC OF MALDIVES

Capital: Malé
Population: 143,046 (1978)
GNP per capita: US$147 (1978)

HISTORY. The islands were under British protection from 1887 to mid-1965. They now enjoy complete independence under the agreement signed in Colombo on 26 July 1965. Maldives became a republic on 11 Nov. 1968.

AREA AND POPULATION. The Republic of Maldives, 400 miles to the south-west of Sri Lanka, consists of some 2,000 low-lying coral islands (only 220 inhabited), grouped into 12 clearly defined clusters of atolls but divided into 19 for administrative purposes. Area 115 sq. miles (298 sq. km). Population (census 1978), 143,046. Capital Malé (29,600 inhabitants).

CONSTITUTION AND GOVERNMENT. The President is elected every 5 years by universal adult suffrage. He is assisted by the Ministers' *Majlis*, a cabinet of ministers of his own choice whom he may dismiss at will. There is also a Citizens' *Majlis* (House of Representatives) which consists of 48 members, 8 nominated by the President, 2 elected from Malé and 2 elected from each of the 19 atolls. The life of the Citizens' *Majlis* is 5 years.

President and Prime Minister: Maumoon Abdul Gayoom.

The people are Moslems, and Islam is reflected in the constitution and judicial system. The official language is Divehi, which is akin to Elu or old Sinhalese.

National flag: Red with a green panel bearing a white crescent.

ECONOMY. The islands are covered with coconut palms and yield millet and fruit as well as coconut produce.

The Maldivian economy is based on the fishing industry. Bonito ('Maldive fish') is the main export commodity and Japan the main buyer. Tourism, introduced in 1972, is expanding and there were 35,000 visitors in 1978–79. There is no direct taxation. The Maldives joined the Asian Development Bank, the World Bank and the IMF in 1978. Exports (1978) US$4·1m.; imports, US$13·1m. Exports to UK (1980), £294,000; imports, £1,121,000.

COMMUNICATIONS

Aviation. The Maldives' national airline, Maldives International Airlines, was established in 1977, and is a joint venture between the Maldives' government and Indian Airlines. It replaced an earlier airline, Air Maldives which was wound up in 1977. The airline operates one Boeing 737, leased from Indian Airlines, from Hulule airport on Malé atoll. Hulule airport is being extended. The Maldives' government hopes to reactivate the former RAF staging post on Gan in order to attract additional tourist traffic.

Shipping. The merchant fleet consists of about 50 vessels of 200,000 GRT.

Post and Broadcasting. In Jan. 1980 there were 822 telephones, 4,147 radio receivers and 365 television receivers. Telex was established in 1977 and in Aug. 1979 there were 35 subscribers.

EDUCATION. In 1977 there were 4,411 pupils in primary and 641 in secondary schools.

DIPLOMATIC REPRESENTATIVES

OF GREAT BRITAIN IN THE REPUBLIC OF MALDIVES

Ambassador: J. W. Nicholas, CMG (resides in Colombo).

OF THE REPUBLIC OF MALDIVES TO THE UNITED NATIONS

Ambassador: Ahmed Zaki.

Book of Reference

Bell, H. C. P., *History, Archaeology and Epigraphy of the Maldive Islands.* Ceylon Govt. Press, Colombo, 1940

MALI

République du Mali

Capital: Bamako
Population: 6·47m. (1979)
GNP per capita: US$120 (1978)

HISTORY. Annexed by France, it formed from 1895 the territory of French Sudan as a part of French West Africa. It became an autonomous state within the French Community on 24 Nov. 1958, and on 4 April 1959 joined with Senegal to form the Federation of Mali. The Federation of Mali achieved independence on 20 June 1960, but Senegal seceded from the Federation on 22 Aug. and Mali proclaimed itself an independent republic on 22 Sept. The National Assembly was dissolved on 17 Jan. 1968 by President Modibo Keita, whose government was then overthrown by an Army *coup* on 19 Nov. 1968. The Republic of Mali became independent on 22 Sept. 1960, after having been the territory of French Sudan and, from Jan. 1959 to 22 Sept. 1960, a partner (together with Senegal) of the Federation of Mali. The republic was admitted to the UN on 29 Sept. 1960.

AREA AND POPULATION. The frontiers of the former territory were readjusted in 1904, 1933, 1948 and 1954 (*see* THE STATESMAN'S YEAR-BOOK, 1959, p. 1011). The republic is bounded north-west by Mauritania, north-east by Algeria and east by Niger and covers an area of 1,204,021 sq. km with a census population of 6,035,272 in 1976. Estimate (1979) 6·47m. Capital District of Bamako (census 1976, 404,022) other towns Mopti, 35,000; Ségou, 31,000; Kayes, 29,000.

CONSTITUTION AND GOVERNMENT. A new constitution was announced on 26 April 1974 and approved by a national referendum on 21 June; it provides for a single legal political party, and an elected President and National Assembly. The Military Committee for National Liberation remained in power for a transitional period of 5 years.

The new ruling party, the *Union démocratique du peuple malien* (UDPM), was formally constituted on 30 March 1979, with a 137-member National Council as its central body. On 18 May this nominated Moussa Traoré as the sole presidential candidate and 82 candidates for the National Assembly, and all were elected for 4-year terms on 19 June.

French is the official language and Bambara is the language of 60% of the inhabitants.

Chief of State, President of the Government: Gen. Moussa Traoré.
Foreign Affairs: Alioune Blondin Beye.
National flag: Three vertical stripes of green, yellow, red.

Local Government: Mali is divided into the Capital District of Bamako and 7 regions: Kayes, Koulikoro, Sikasso, Segou, Mopti, Tombouctou and Gao; the regions are sub-divided into 46 *cercles* and then into 279 *arrondissements*.

DEFENCE

Army. The Army consists of 5 infantry battalions and 1 artillery battalion with support units; strength, 4,600 (1980).

Air Force. The Air Force has received 5 MiG-17 jet fighters, 2 MiG-15UTI jet trainers, some Yak-18 piston-engined trainers, 6 An-24, 2 Il-14 and 3 An-2 transports, and 3 Mi-8 and Mi-4 helicopters from USSR, Yak-12M liaison aircraft from Poland and 2 C-47 transports from USA. Personnel total about 300.

INTERNATIONAL RELATIONS

Membership. Mali is a member of UN, OAU and is an ACP state of EEC.

ECONOMY

Planning. The 1974–79 development plan envisaged expenditure of MF 386,000m. and a 7·1% annual increase in GDP (estimated to be MF 166,000m. in 1971).

Budget. The ordinary budget for 1979 envisaged expenditure of MF 70,100m. and revenue, MF 69,400m.

Currency. On 5 May 1967 the Mali *franc* was devalued from MF 246·853 to MF 493·706 per US$. In March 1968 the Mali franc became convertible at the rate of MF 100 to 1 French franc. In March 1981, £1 = MF 1,105; US$1 = MF 498·9.

AGRICULTURE. roduction of cotton increased from 22,000 tons (1969) to 48,000 tons (1979).

Production in 1976–77 included (in 1,000 tonnes) millet and sorghum (950), rice (264), groundnuts (160), maize (130). In 1979 there were 4·5m. head of cattle, 180,000 horses, 489,000 asses, 6·1m. sheep, 5·8m. goats and 208,000 camels.

Important irrigation schemes have been carried out in the Ségou and Mopti districts on the Niger River, of which the Sansanding Barrage is the centre; 50,000 hectares of cotton and rice lands are being irrigated.

TRADE. Imports in 1978 totalled MF 91,300m., exports, 42,500m. Chief imports are foodstuffs, automobiles, petrol, building material, sugar, salt, beer; in 1976, 40% were from France, 14% from Ivory Coast, 10% from Senegal, 7% from China. Chief exports (1976) were cotton (50% of total), livestock, peanuts, dried fish and skins; 31% went to France, 13% to Ivory Coast, 11% to Federal Republic of Germany, 10% to China.

Total trade between Mali and UK (British Department of Trade returns, in £1,000 sterling):

	1976	1977	1978	1979	1980
Imports to UK	1,797	2,124	3,257	12,108	11,318
Exports and re-exports from UK	1,453	1,554	3,245	6,120	7,878

COMMUNICATIONS

Roads. There are 14,000 km of roads, of which 7,500 km are usable in all seasons; they include 2,606 km of metalled road Dakar–Niger (1,250 km). There were 2,002 road vehicles in 1971.

Railways. Mali has a railway from Kayes to Koulikoro by way of Bamako, a continuation of the Dakar–Kayes line in Senegal. An agreement was signed in May 1968 between Mali, Guinea and China to extend the railway from Kourousa–Kankan in Guinea to Bamako, though no work had been done by early 1981. Total length 645 km.

Aviation. Air services connect the republic with Paris, Dakar and Abidjan. The chief airport is at Bamako. In 1973 aircraft disembarked and embarked 63,000 passengers and 3,945 tonnes of freight and mail.

Shipping. For about 7 months in the year small steamboats perform the service from Koulikoro to Tombouctou and Gao, and from Bamako to Kouroussa.

Post and Broadcasting. There were, in 1976, 8,000 telephones and 82,000 radio receivers.

RELIGION, EDUCATION AND WELFARE

Religion. In 1979, 65% of the population were Sunni Moslems, 30% animists and 2% Christians.

Education. There were in 1977, 29,966 pupils in primary schools, 8,915 in secondary schools, 2,609 in technical schools, 1,839 in teacher-training colleges and (1975) 2,920 students in higher educational establishments.

Health. In 1976 there were 200 hospitals and medical centres with 4,177 beds; there were also 144 doctors, 12 dentists, 18 pharmacists, 157 midwives and 1,923 nursing personnel.

DIPLOMATIC REPRESENTATIVES

OF MALI IN GREAT BRITAIN

Ambassador: Yaya Diarra (resides in Brussels).

OF GREAT BRITAIN IN MALI

Ambassador: C. W. Squire, CMG, MVO (resides in Dakar).

OF MALI IN THE USA (2130 R. St., NW, Washington, D.C., 20008)

Ambassador: Maki Koreissi Aguibou Tall.

OF THE USA IN MALI (Rue Testard and Rue Mohamed V, Bamako)

Ambassador: Anne F. Holloway.

OF MALI TO THE UNITED NATIONS

Ambassador: Seydou Traoré.

Book of Reference

Hopkins, N. S., *Popular Government in an African Town*. Univ. of Chicago Press, 1972

MALTA

Capital: Valletta
Population: 316,850 (1980)

Repubblika Ta Malta

HISTORY. Malta was held in turn by Phoenicians, Carthaginians and Romans, and was conquered by Arabs in 870. From 1090 it was joined to Sicily until 1530, when it was handed over to the Knights of St John, who ruled until dispersed by Napoleon in 1798. The Maltese rose in rebellion against the French and the island was subsequently blockaded by the British aided by the Maltese from 1798 to 1800. The Maltese people freely requested the protection of the British Crown in 1802 on condition that their rights and privileges be preserved. The islands were finally annexed to the British Crown by the Treaty of Paris in 1814.

On 15 April 1942, in recognition of the steadfastness and fortitude of the people of Malta during the Second World War, King George VI awarded the George Cross to the island.

AREA AND POPULATION. The area of Malta is 246 sq. km (94·9 sq. miles); Gozo, 67 sq. km (25·9 sq. miles); Comino, 3 sq. km (1·1 sq. miles); total area, 316 sq. km (121·9 sq. miles). Population, census 27 Nov. 1967, 314,216; estimate (30 June 1980) 316,850. Malta, 292,197; Gozo and Comino, 24,653. Chief town and port, Valletta, population 14,042 (1979).

Vital statistics, 1980, estimate: Births, 5,453; deaths, 3,195; marriages, 2,890; net emigration, 986 (1979); gross emigration (including emigrants who later returned), 1,303.

CONSTITUTION AND GOVERNMENT. Malta became independent on 21 Sept. 1964 and, became a republic within the Commonwealth on 13 Dec. 1974. For earlier constitutional and government history *see* THE STATESMAN'S YEAR-BOOK, 1980–81, p. 837.

In 1971 Malta began to follow a policy of strict non-alignment and closed the NATO base. In March 1972 agreement was reached on the phasing out of the British Military base which was closed down completely on 31 March 1979.

Malta is a democratic republic and the Constitution, which was amended in 1965, 1966, 1970, 1972 and 1974, provides for a parliament consisting of a House of Representatives of elected members and a Cabinet consisting of the Prime Minister and such number of Ministers as may be appointed. The 1974 Constitution which is founded on work, makes provision for the protection of fundamental rights and freedom of the individual, and ensures that all persons in Malta shall have full freedom of conscience and religious worship.

Maltese and English, and such other language as may be prescribed by Parliament, are the official languages.

Elections were held on 17 and 18 Sept. 1976. State of parties in Sept. 1976: Malta Labour Party, 34; Nationalist Party, 31.

President: Dr Anton Buttigieg.

The Cabinet (Malta Labour Party) was as at March 1981:

Prime Minister, Minister of Foreign Affairs and Minister of the Interior: Dom Mintoff.

Finance, Customs and People's Financial Investments: Dr Joseph Cassar. *Labour, Culture and Welfare:* Agatha Barbara. *Works and Sport:* Lorry Sant. *Development, Energy, Ports and Telecommunications:* Wistin Abela. *Fisheries and Agriculture:* Freddie Micallef. *Trade, Industry and Parastatal and People's Industries:* Dr Patrick Holland. *Health and Environment:* Dr Vincent Moran. *Tourism:* Danny Cremona.

Education: Dr Philip Muscat. *Justice, Lands, Housing and Parliamentary Affairs:* Dr Joseph Brincat.

National flag: Vertically white and red, with a representation of the George Cross medal in the canton.

DEFENCE. The Maltese armed forces are reported to have 3 Bell 47G–2 and 1 JetRanger light helicopters received in 1971–73. Libya has given 1 Super Frelon and 3 armed Alouette III helicopters. Personnel (1980) numbered 1,000 organized into 2 regiments. There was also a para-military force of 1,400.

A coastal patrol force of small craft has been formed. It is manned by the Maltese Regiment and primarily employed as a coastguard. In 1981 it comprised 15 patrol craft and customs launches manned by 130 officers and men.

All UK forces were withdrawn in March 1979.

INTERNATIONAL RELATIONS

Membership. Malta is a member of UN, the Commonwealth and the Council of Europe.

ECONOMY

Planning. Most of the economic objectives of the 1973–80 development plan have been reached. The manufacturing industry has been expanded and is largely oriented towards the export markets. Progress in tourism has surpassed plan projections while agriculture has continued to grow. The development of Malta as a leading ship-repairing and shipbuilding centre has been further enhanced by the completion of the new giant dock which is capable of taking vessels up to 300,000 DWT while works on the new Marsa shipbuilding yard for the construction of vessels of up to 120,000 tons are at an advanced stage. Intensive efforts are also under way to turn the island into a major transhipment centre by the development of a new harbour at Marsaxlokk Bay.

Budget. Revenue and expenditure (in £M) for financial years ending 31 March:

	1976–77	1977–78	1978–79	1979 [1]	1980 [2, 3]
Revenue	100,820,470	97,349,476	110,268,917	98,709,000	194,058,000
Expenditure	96,097,392	92,966,747	107,780,619	105,603,000	189,044,000

[1] Nine months. April–Dec.   [2] Calender year.   [3] Estimate.

The most important sources of revenue are customs duties, income tax, receipts from the Central Bank of Malta and until 1979, rent from defence facilities.

Currency. Central Bank of Malta notes of £M1, £M5 and £M10 denominations are in circulation. On 16 May 1972 a new decimal system was introduced and UK coinage previously in circulation ceased to be legal tender in Malta after 4 Oct. 1972. Malta coins are issued in the following denominations: 50, 25, 10, 5, 2 and 1 cents; 5, 3 and 2 *mils.* Total notes in circulation on 31 Dec. 1980 was £M206·3m.; coins, £M4·6m. In March 1981, £1 sterling = £M0·831.

Banking. The Central Bank of Malta was founded in 1968. Commercial banking facilities are provided by Bank of Valletta Ltd, Lombard Bank Malta Ltd and Mid Med Bank Ltd. The other domestic banking institutions are the Government Savings bank, the Investment Finance Bank, the Apostleship of Prayer Savings Bank Ltd, Lohombus Corporation Ltd and Singer and Friedlander (Malta) Ltd.

ENERGY AND NATURAL RESOURCES

Electricity. All towns and villages in Malta and Gozo are provided with electric current. Up to Sept. 1978 the islands obtained their electricity power supplies from 2 interconnected power stations located at Marsa (Malta) having a total installed capacity of 115 mw. The bigger power station with a generating capacity of 85 mw is also equipped with distillation plant capable of also producing fresh water for public consumption at the rate of 4·5m. gallons per day. An expansion programme is currently under way for the erection of two 30 mw turbo-generating sets and boiler plant which will increase the installed capacity to 175 mw.

In Oct. 1978 another power station, which was formerly used to supply foreign military installations on the Island, was handed over to the Government of Malta and has been integrated in the national electricity supply system. The station has a generating capacity of 12 mw.

The gross electricity generated in 1979 was 500·8m. kwh.

Agriculture. In 1979 agriculture contributed £M11·1m. to the Gross Domestic Product as against £M10·6m. in 1978. (The 1979 figure represents a share of 3·8% in the GDP.) In 1979 there was a slight decrease in the cultivable area, which totalled 12,353 hectares as against 12,585 hectares in 1978. In 1979 agriculture employed 5,643 full-time farmers, 411 full-time wage earners and 10,432 part-time farmers against 6,070, 435 and 10,498 respectively in 1978. (The 1979 figure for full-time farmers and full-time wage earners represents 5·1% of the gainfully occupied population.)

In 1979 the value of Malta's main agricultural exports reached £M2·6m. as against £M1·9m. in 1978. The 1979 exports consisted of: Potatoes, £M1,385,075; seeds, cutflowers and plants, £M533,703; wine, £M306,118; meat and meat products, £M107,424; onions, £M203,745; hides and skins, £M101,365; live animals, £M8,095.

Livestock (1979): Cattle, 14,000; pigs, 5,000; goats, 6,000; poultry, 1·4m.

Fisheries. In 1980 the fishing industry occupied 964 power propelled and 105 other fishing boats, engaging 336 full-time and 763 part-time fishermen. The catch in 1980 was 1,054 tonnes valued at £M961,328 at first sale, of which 73 tonnes valued at £M48,757 were landed by the trawlers of the Maltese-Libyan Arab Fishing Co. Ltd and of the government.

INDUSTRY AND TRADE

Industry. Investors in industry in Malta are offered the following advantages: political stability, excellent industrial relations, a strategic geographic location, a special association agreement with the EEC, a fully developed and highly functional infrastructure, free repatriation of profits and capital, easily trainable and highly adaptable labour force, financing facilities at favourable rates of interest, readybuilt factories at attractive rents. About 258 aided projects are in operation in various industrial sectors, of which the majority are foreign-owned or have foreign interests. The Malta Development Corporation is the Government agency responsible for promoting and implementing new industrial projects, including joint ventures. The Corporation may also participate by way of equity capital, in certain projects jointly with Maltese or foreign industrialists.

Labour. The total work force in Aug. 1980 was 123,623; males, 91,655; females, 31,968, distributed as follows: Agriculture and fisheries, 7,232; manufacturing, 34,467; building, construction and quarrying, 6,079; services, 38,816; electricity, gas and drydocks, 6,050; government, 24,432; armed forces, 810; Izra u Rabbi and auxiliary workers, 1,442. The number of registered unemployed under Part I of the Employment Register was 3,289, and under Part II, 1,006.

There were 42 trade unions registered as at 30 June 1980, with a total membership of 39,238 and 18 employers' associations with a total membership of 3,528.

Commerce. Imports and exports including bullion and specie (in £M1,000):

	1973	1974	1975	1976	1977	1978	1979
Imports	88,100	138,969	144,448	179,923	217,681	221,505	271,960
Exports	35,961	51,582	63,899	97,409	121,791	131,049	136,830

In 1979 the principal items of imports were: Semi-manufactures, £M96·1m.; machinery and transport, £M47·6m.; food, £M41m.; manufactures, £M25·1m.; fuels, £M17·9m.; chemicals, £M20·3m.; others, £M23·9m. Of domestic exports: Manufactures, £M95·5m.; semi-manufactures, £M17·6m.; machinery and transport, £M10·9m.; food, £M5m.; beverages and tobacco, £M5m.; others, £M2·8m.

In 1979, £M59·9m. of the imports came from Italy, £M57·9m. from UK, £M38·6m. from Federal Republic of Germany, £M18·7m. from Asia, £M17m. from USA, £M11·4m. from the EFTA, £M4·6m. from Oceania, £M3·4m. from Africa, £M54·4m. from other European countries; of domestic exports, £M50·9m. to Federal Republic of Germany, £M29·1m. to UK, £M12·7m. to Africa, £M5·6m. to

Italy, £M5m. to EFTA, £M3m. to Asia, £M2·9m. to USA and £M26·7m. to other European countries.

Total trade between Malta and UK (British Department of Trade returns, in £1,000 sterling):

	1977	1978	1979	1980
Imports to UK	34,041	39,167	53,569	46,609
Exports and re-exports from UK	64,339	69,164	79,083	87,527

Tourism. In 1979, 618,310 tourists visited Malta, 434,694 from UK, 27,290 from Italy, 24,569 from Libya, 22,710 from Federal Republic of Germany, 20,616 from Scandinavia, 12,100 from France and 8,398 from USA. In 1979, gross tourist expenditure was £M76·2m. (estimate).

COMMUNICATIONS

Roads. Every town and village is served by motor omnibuses. There are ferry services running between Malta and Gozo; cars can be transported on the ferries. Motor vehicles registered at 31 Dec. 1979 totalled 86,179, of which 62,298 were private cars, 3,950 hire cars, 13,793 commercial vehicles, 559 buses, 5,070 motor cycles and 509 other motor vehicles.

Aviation. In 1980 the principal airlines, Air Malta, Alitalia, British Airways, Libyan Arab Airlines, Union de Transports Aeriens, Yugoslav Air Transport and Tunisavia, operated scheduled services between Malta and UK, Italy, France, Libya, Yugoslavia and Tunis. In 1979 there were 13,992 civil aircraft movements at Luqa Airport. 1,068,667 passengers and 6,474 tonnes of freight (excluding mail) were handled.

Shipping. The number of ships registered in Malta on 31 Dec. 1979 was 276, 138,555·9 GRT. Ships entering harbour during 1979, 3,108.

Post and Telecommunications. Telegraph and telephone services are administered by Telemalta Corporation with exchanges at Malta and Gozo. On 31 Dec. 1979 there were 77,330 telephones. A world-wide cable and telex service is also operated.

Cinemas (1979). There were 36 cinemas with a seating capacity of 26,038.

Newspapers. There are 2 English, 3 Maltese daily newspapers and 3 Sunday papers.

JUSTICE, RELIGION, EDUCATION AND WELFARE

Justice. The number of persons convicted of crimes in 1980 was 1,301; those convicted for contraventions against various laws and regulations numbered 5,337. Sixty-six were committed to prison and 2,749 were awarded fines.

Police. On 31 Dec. 1980 police numbered 41 officers and 1,243 other ranks, including 21 women police.

Religion. The majority of the population belong to the Roman Catholic Church.

Education. Education in Malta is compulsory between the ages of 6 and 16 and free in government schools. In 1980 there were 197 kindergarten groups, with nearly 3,933 children in 62 centres throughout Malta and Gozo. The primary level enrols children between 5 and 11 years in a 6-year course. There were 24,766 children (12,853 boys and 11,913 girls) in 80 government schools. There were 31 government secondary schools with a total of 14,509 (6,601 boys, 7,908 girls). Secondary schools run 5-year courses leading to GCE 'O' level. Two-year courses leading to GCE 'A' level on a worker/pupil system which alternates work with study periods are provided for in the New Lyceum, *i.e.*, upper secondary schools (722 students). Enrolment in craft and technician courses in 3 technical institutes amounted to 1,207, while 3,198 (2,240 boys and 958 girls) were enrolled in the 12 trade schools for boys and 6 trade schools for girls. Another 146 students are enrolled in specialized vocational schools. Trade schools offer 2- to 4-year courses in specialized trades and are open to students who finish their third year of secondary education. The number of children in special education amounted to 723.

There were 80 private schools with a population of 3,972 at the nursery level,

8,681 at the primary level and 7,553 at the secondary level. Government subsidises recognized private secondary schools on a *per capita* basis.

4,800 students attended evening courses in academic, commercial, technical and practical subjects established in 82 centres. The School of Art had an enrolment of 284 students while another 2,061 students enrolled in courses organized by the School of Music.

The University of Malta consists of 6 faculties: Law, Medicine and Surgery, Engineering and Architecture, Dental Surgery, Education and Management Studies (1,089 students in 1981). Degrees in Law, Mechanical Engineering, Electrical Engineering, Engineering and Architecture, Accountancy, Business Management, Administration, Education, Medicine and Surgery, Pharmacy and Dental Surgery are conferred by the University. 197 students are pursuing Arts and Science courses previously held in the Faculties of Arts and of Science. These courses are in the process of being phased out.

Welfare. The National Insurance Act, 1956, provides cash benefits for marriage (women only), sickness, unemployment, widowhood, orphanhood, invalidity, old age, children's allowances and industrial injury. An agreement, signed on 26 Oct. 1956, established reciprocity in matters of social insurance between Malta and the UK.

The total number of persons in receipt of benefits on 31 Dec. 1979 was 75,338, viz., 838 in receipt of sickness benefit, 377 unemployment benefit, 197 injury benefit, 193 disablement benefit, 108 death benefit, 18,796 retirement pensions, 6,504 widows' pensions, 20 guardian's allowance, 2,990 invalidity pensions and 45,315 children's allowances.

The National Assistance Act, 1956, provides for the payment of social assistance and medical assistance, while the Old Age Pensions Act of 1948 provides for the payment of non-contributory old-age pensions to persons over 60 years of age and to blind persons over the age of 14 years.

The number of households in receipt of social assistance and of medical assistance on 31 Dec. 1979 was 3,759 and 4,240 respectively, and the number of old-age pensioners under the Old Age Pensions Act, 1948, was 8,464.

DIPLOMATIC REPRESENTATIVES

OF MALTA IN GREAT BRITAIN (24 Haymarket, London, SW1Y 4DJ)
Acting High Commissioner: Michael F. Gauci.

OF GREAT BRITAIN IN MALTA (7 St Anne St., Floriana)
High Commissioner: David P. Aiers, CMG.

OF MALTA IN THE USA (2017 Connecticut Ave., NW, Washington, D.C., 20008)
Chargé d'Affaires: Emanuel C. Farrugia.

OF THE USA IN MALTA (Development Hse., St Anne St., Floriana)
Ambassador: Joan M. Clark.

OF MALTA TO THE UNITED NATIONS
Permanent Representative: Victor J. Gauci.

Books of Reference

Statistical Information: The Central Office of Statistics (Auberge de Castille, Valletta) was set up in 1947. It publishes *Statistical Abstracts of the Maltese Islands*, a quarterly digest of statistics, quarterly and annual trade returns, annual vital statistics and annual publications on shipping and aviation, education, agriculture and industry and National Accounts and Balance of Payments.

Government publications: The Department of Information (Auberge de Castille, Valletta), set up in 1955, publishes *The Malta Government Gazette* (twice weekly), *Il Gzejjer* (monthly), *Malta*

Today (bi-monthly), *Malta Handbook, Economic Survey, Development Plan for Malta 1973–80* and *Supplement Paper Currency in Malta, Heritage of an Island, Reports on the Working of Government Departments*. Malta, 1980.

Malta Independence Constitution (Cmnd 2406). HMSO, 1964
Constitution of the Republic of Malta. Department of Information, 1975
Malta Manufacturers and Exporters. Department of Industry, 1980
Malta Who's Who. Malta, 1969–70
Economic Report 1980. Malta, 1980
The Year Book. Malta from 1952
Malta Handbook 1978–79. Department of Information, 1979
Blouet, Brian, *The Story of Malta*. London, 1967
Busuttil, E. D., *Kalepin Dizzjunarju Malti-Ingliz*. Valletta, 1971.—*Kalepin Dizzjunarji Ingliz-Malti*. 1976
Cassar, P., *Medical History of Malta*. London, 1966
Cremona, J. J., *The Malta Constitution of 1835 and its Historical Background*. Malta, 1959.—*The Constitutional Developments of Malta under British Rule*. Malta University Press, 1963.—*Human Rights Documentation in Malta*. Malta University Press, 1966
Dobie, E., *Malta's Road to Independence*. University of Oklahoma, Norman, USA, 1967
Gerada, E. and Zuber, C., *Malta: An Island Republic*. Paris, 1979
Luke, Sir Harry, *Malta*. 2nd ed. London, 1962
Price, G. A., *Malta and the Maltese: A Study in 19th-century Migration*. Melbourne, 1954
Smith, Harrison, *Britain in Malta*. 2 vols. Malta, 1954

MAURITANIA

République Islamique de Mauritanie

Capital: Nouakchott
Population: 1·54m. (1979)
GNP per capita: US$270 (1978)

HISTORY. Mauritania became a French protectorate in 1903 and a colony in 1920. It became an autonomous republic within the French Community on 28 Nov. 1958 and achieved full independence on 28 Nov. 1960. Under its first President, Moktar Ould Daddah, Mauritania became a one-party state in 1964, but following his deposition by a military *coup* on 10 July 1978, the ruling *Parti du peuple mauritanien* was dissolved.

Following the Spanish withdrawal from Western Sahara on 28 Feb. 1976, Mauritania occupied the southern part (88,667 sq. km) of this territory and incorporated it under the name of Tiris el Gharbia; on 8 Aug. seven additional members of the National Assembly were nominated to represent this territory. However in Aug. 1979 Mauritania renounced sovereignty and withdrew from Tiris el Gharbia.

AREA AND POPULATION. Mauritania is bounded west by the Atlantic ocean, north by Western Sahara, north-east by Algeria, east and south-east by Mali, and south by Senegal. The total area is 1,030,700 sq. km (398,000 sq. miles), and the population at the Census of 1976 was 1,419,939; latest estimate (1978) 1·54m. The main towns (with 1976 populations) are the capital Nouakchott (134,986), Nouâdhibou (21,961), Kaédi (20,848), Zouérate (17,474), Rosso (16,466) and Atâr (16,326).

The official languages are French and Arabic. The population is 80% Arabic and 20% Bantu.

CONSTITUTION AND GOVERNMENT. Following the *coup* of 10 July 1978, power has been in the hands of a Military Committee for National Recovery (CMRN); the constitution was suspended and the 70-member National Assembly dissolved. Col. Mustafa Ould Salek, Head of the CMRN, assumed the Presidency on 20 March 1979, and on 6 April the CMRN was replaced by a Military Committee for National Salvation (CMSN), which adopted a new Constitutional Charter on 11 April, separating the functions of President and Prime Minister. On 3 June Col. Salek was replaced as President by Lieut.-Col. Mohamed Mahmoud Ould Ahmed Louly, who was in turn replaced on 4 Jan. 1980 by his Prime Minister, Lieut.-Col. Mohamed Khouna Ould Kaydalla, thus recombining the two offices.

President: Lieut.-Col. Mohamed Khouna Ould Kaydalla.

The Cabinet formed on 15 Dec. 1980 is composed as follows:
Prime Minister: Sid Ahmed Ould Bneijara.
Secretary of State for Defence: Lieut.-Col. Soumare Silmane. *Foreign Affairs and Co-operation:* Mohamed El Mokhtar Ould Zamel. *Justice and Islamic Affairs:* Abdel Aziz Ould Ahmed. *Interior:* Baham Ould Mohamed Laghaf. *Information and Telecommunications:* Ahmedou Ould Sidi Henena. *Fisheries:* Soumare Oumar. *Mines and Energy:* Sidahmed Ould Taya. *Economy and Finance:* Ahmed Ould Zein. *Industry and Commerce:* Mamadou Cissoko. *Transport and Equipment:* Daffa Bakary. *Water and Housing:* Dr Louleid Ould Weddad. *Rural Development:* Mohamed Ould Amar. *Education:* Hassiny Ould Didi. *Employment and Training of Cadres:* Yahya Ould Menkouss. *Health and Social Affairs:* Dr Youssef Dia Jana. *Culture, Youth and Sports:* Ba Mahmadoud. *Secretary-General of Presidency and Government:* Mohammed Yedih Ould Bredelleil.

National flag: Green, with a crescent beneath a star in yellow in the centre.

Local government: Mauritania is divided into the District of Nouakchott and 12 regions—Hodh ech Chargui, Hodh el Gharbi, Assaba, Gorgol, Brakna, Trarza, Adrar, Dakhlet Nouâdhibou, Tagent, Guidimaka, Tiris Zemmour and Inchiri.

DEFENCE

Army. The Army consists of 1 infantry and 1 artillery battalion, 2 armoured car squadrons and support units; total strength, 7,500 in 1980.

Navy. The Navy consists of 2 corvettes, 6 large and 2 small patrol craft. Personnel (1980) 300.

Air Force. The Air Force has 7 Britten-Norman Defender armed light transports, 2 Islander, 1 C-54, 3 C-47, 1 Caravelle, 1 Buffalo and 2 Skyvan transports and 2 Broussard, 4 Reims-Cessna 337 Milirole and 1 Aermacchi AL.60 light aircraft. Personnel 150.

INTERNATIONAL RELATIONS

Membership. Mauritania is a member of UN, OAU, the Arab League and is an ACP state of EEC.

ECONOMY

Budget. The ordinary budget for 1974 balanced at 7,750m. ougiyas.

Currency. The monetary unit is *ouguiya* which is divided into 5 *khoums*. Bank-notes of 1,000, 200 and 100 *ouguiya* and coins of 20, 10, 5 and 1 *ouguiya* and 1 *khoum* are in circulation. In March 1981, £1 = 107 *ouguiya*; US$1 = 49·89 *ouguiya*.

NATURAL RESOURCES

Minerals. Huge deposits of iron ore (Fort Gouraud) and copper (Akjoujt) are being exploited. Iron ore exports in 1972, 8·6m. tonnes; copper 5·3m. tonnes.

Agriculture. Chief products are cattle, millet, gum, salt, niébé (a kind of haricot), béref (*citrullus vulgaris*), and dried and salted fish.
    Production (tonnes) (1979) of millet, 35,000; dates, 14,000; potatoes, 4,000; maize, 5,000; sweet potatoes, 2,000; rice, 4,000. Rubber production (1970–71) 5,464 tonnes.
    In 1979 there were 720,000 camels, 1·6m. cattle, 220,000 asses, 23,000 horses, 8·4m. sheep and goats.

Fisheries. Export of salted and dried fish in 1971, 4,958 tonnes.

TRADE. In 1978 imports totalled 7,400m. ouguiya, and exports, 5,499 ouguiya.
    Total trade between Mauritania and UK (British Department of Trade returns, in £1,000 sterling):

	1976	1977	1978	1979	1980
Imports to UK	14,948	11,825	7,595	7,450	9,438
Exports and re-exports from UK	6,176	4,364	3,258	2,845	5,647

COMMUNICATIONS

Roads. There were 6,904 km of roads in 1975.

Railways. A mineral railway was opened between the port of Nouadhibou and Tazadit (650 km, 1,435 mm gauge) in 1963. Passenger trains also run.

Aviation. In 1973 aircraft disembarked and embarked 55,000 passengers and 1,495 tonnes of freight and mail.

Post and Broadcasting. There were, in 1977, over 2,000 telephones and 82,000 radio receivers.

Cinemas. In 1971 there were 10 cinemas with a seating capacity of 1,000.

RELIGION, EDUCATION AND WELFARE

Religion. All Mauritanians are Moslem, mainly of the Qadiriyah sect.

Education. In 1979 there were 82,408 pupils in primary schools, 11,957 in secondary schools, and (in 1975) 1,591 in technical schools.

Health. In 1976 there were 9 hospitals with 567 beds; there were 71 doctors, 4 dentists, 5 pharmacists, 20 midwives and 560 nursing personnel.

DIPLOMATIC REPRESENTATIVES

OF MAURITANIA IN GREAT BRITAIN

Ambassador: (Vacant).

OF GREAT BRITAIN IN MAURITANIA

Ambassador: C. W. Squire, CMG, MVO (resides in Dakar).

OF MAURITANIA IN THE USA (2129 Leroy Pl., NW, Washington, D.C., 20008)

Ambassador: Sidi Bouna Ould Sidi.

OF THE USA IN MAURITANIA (PO Box 222, Nouakchott)

Chargé d'Affaires: Charles F. Dunbar, Jr.

OF MAURITANIA TO THE UNITED NATIONS

Ambassador: Sid'Ahmed Ould Taya.

MAURITIUS

Capital: Port Louis
Population: 924,243 (1979)
GNP per capita: US$830 (1978)

HISTORY. Mauritius was known to Arab navigators probably not later than the 10th century. It was probably visited by Malays in the 15th century, and was discovered by the Portuguese between 1507 and 1512, but the Dutch were the first settlers (1598). In 1710 they abandoned the island, which was occupied by the French under the name of Ile de France (1715). The British occupied the island in 1810, and it was formally ceded to Great Britain by the Treaty of Paris, 1814. Mauritius attained independence on 12 March 1968.

AREA AND POPULATION. The island, situated 20° S. lat., $57\frac{1}{2}$° E. long., is of volcanic origin. The climate is free from extremes of weather, except for tropical cyclones at times. Yearly rainfall varies from 30 in. on the north-west coast to 200 in. in the uplands.

Mauritius has an area of about 720 sq. miles (1,865 sq. km). According to the census of 30 June 1972, the population of the island was 826,199 (413,580 males, 412,619 females); that of the dependencies was 25,135 (30 June 1972). The estimated population of the island at the end of 1979 was 924,243, and the population of Port Louis, the capital with its suburbs, numbered 146,101. Port Louis was granted city status on 25 Aug. 1966. Other towns: Beau Bassin-Rose Hill, 83,983; Curepipe, 54,549; Quatre Bornes, 53,891; Vascoas-Phoenix, 51,595.

Rodrigues (formerly a dependency but now a part of Mauritius) is about 350 miles east of Mauritius, $9\frac{1}{2}$ miles long, $4\frac{1}{2}$ miles broad. Area, 40 sq. miles (103·6 sq. km). Population (31 Dec. 1979, estimate), 29,623. Imports, 1977, Rs 48,733,477; 1978, Rs 54,605,564. Exports, 1977, Rs 2,773,689; 1978, Rs 2,872,012. There are 3 government, 5 aided primary, 1 private and 1 state secondary school.

Vital statistics, June 1979: Births, 25,100 (27·5 per 1,000); marriages, 9,100; deaths, 6,600 (7·3 per 1,000).

The official language is English.

Dependencies. Agalega and St Brandon Group. St Brandon is 250 miles from Mauritius. Area, 71 sq. km. Total population of the dependencies, census 1972, 366; estimated population on 31 Dec. 1978, 350. The main exports (to Mauritius) in 1974 were 227 tonnes of salted fish.

In 1965 the Chagos Archipelago was transferred to the newly created colony of British Indian Ocean Territory (*see* SEYCHELLES, p. 1052).

CONSTITUTION AND GOVERNMENT. Mauritius became an independent state and a monarchial member of the British Commonwealth on 12 March 1968 after 7 months of internal self-government. The Governor-General is the local representative of HM the Queen, who remains the Head of the State.

In accordance with the Mauritius Independence Order 1968 the Cabinet is presided over by the Prime Minister. Each of the other 20 members of the Cabinet is responsible for the administration of specified departments or subjects and is bound by the rule of collective responsibility. There are also 9 Parliamentary Secretaries appointed by the Governor-General on the advice of the Prime Minister.

The Legislative Assembly consists of a Speaker and 62 elected members (3 each for the 20 constituencies of Mauritius and 2 for Rodrigues) and 8 additional seats in order to ensure a fair and adequate representation of each community within the Assembly. General Elections are held every 5 years on the basis of universal adult suffrage.

The Constitution also provides for the Public Service Commission and the Judicial and Legal Service Commission, which have both assumed executive powers for appointments to the Public Service. An Ombudsman assumed office on 2 March 1970. Adequate provision is also made for the protection of fundamental rights and freedoms of the individual.

Governor-General: Sir Dayendranath Burrenchobay, KBE, CMG, CVO.
Prime Minister: Dr The Rt. Hon. Sir Seewoosagur Ramgoolam, GCMG.
National flag: Horizontally 4 stripes of red, blue, yellow and green.

DEFENCE. The Mauritius Police, which is responsible for defence, is equipped with arms; its strength at 31 Dec. 1979 was 3,974 officers and men.

INTERNATIONAL RELATIONS

Membership. Mauritius is a member of UN, the Commonwealth, OAU and is an ACP state of EEC.

ECONOMY

Budget. Revenue and expenditure (in Rs) for years ending 30 June:

	1976–77	1977–78	1978–79	1979–80	1980–81[1]
Revenue	1,210,676,709	1,260,764,057	1,486,394,583	1,882,000,000	2,200,058,000
Expenditure	1,260,978,369	1,441,291,537	1,769,964,582	2,035,000,000	2,293,622,000

[1] Estimate.

Principal sources of revenue, June 1979: Direct taxes, Rs 391,199,998; indirect taxes, Rs 880,875,072; receipts from public utilities, Rs 60,469,523; receipts from public services Rs 50,943,133; interest and royalties, Rs 66,943,270; reimbursement, Rs 27,145,388. Capital expenditure, June 1979, was Rs 669,309,999. Capital revenue, Rs 718,863,086.

On 30 June 1979 the public debt of Mauritius was Rs 2,228,247,550 after deducting the value of accumulated sinking funds.

Currency. The unit of currency is the Mauritius *Rupee*, divided into 100 *cents*.

The currency consists of: (i) Bank of Mauritius notes of Rs 50, 25, 10 and 5; (ii) Cupro-nickel coins of 1 rupee, ½ rupee, ¼ rupee and 10 cents; (iii) Bronze coins of 5 cents, 2 cents and 1 cent.

Notes and coins in circulation as at 31 Dec. 1979 amounted to Rs 803·5m. and Rs 28·3m. respectively.

Banking. The Bank of Mauritius was established in 1966, with an authorized capital of Rs 10m., to exercise the function of a central bank. There are 10 commercial banks, the Mauritius Commercial Bank Ltd (established 1838), Barclays Bank International, the Bank of Baroda Ltd, The Mercantile Bank Ltd, the Mauritius Co-operative Central Bank Ltd, Banque Nationale de Commerce et d'Industrie (Ocean Indien), the Habib Bank (Overseas) Ltd, Citibank, the State Commercial Bank and the Bank of Credit and Commerce International SA. Other financial institutions include the Mauritius Housing Corporation, the Development Bank of Mauritius and the post office savings bank.

On 30 June 1980 the post office savings bank held deposits amounting to Rs 107·1m., belonging to 168,673 depositors.

NATURAL RESOURCES

Agriculture (1979). The area planted with sugar-cane was 20,300 arpents. There were 21 factories in operation and the amount of sugar produced was: Raw sugar, 645,488 tonnes; white sugar, 42,895 tonnes; molasses, 209,483 tonnes.

The main secondary crops are tea (9,800·9 arpents, yielding 5,071,974 kg of black tea), tobacco (1,905 acres, yielding 705 tonnes of tobacco), potatoes (8,329 tonnes) and onions (1,900 tonnes).

Livestock (1979): Cattle, 56,000; goats, 70,000; poultry, 1·4m.

Forestry. The total forest area is estimated at 21,027 hectares including some 10,845 hectares of plantations; if scrub and grazing lands are included the total area is approximately 56,110 hectares.

In 1979 sales of forest produce from Crown land totalled 21,180 cu. metres, round wood.

INDUSTRY AND TRADE

Labour. There were on 31 Dec. 1979, 283 registered trade unions with a total membership of 61,031 (on roll).

Commerce. Total trade (in Rs) for calendar years:

	1975	1976	1977	1978	1979
Imports[1]	1,995,300,000	2,398,700,000	2,950,800,000	3,076,400,000	3,634,400,000
Exports[2]	1,838,900,000	1,769,800,000	2,041,200,000	1,987,100,000	2,432,700,000

[1] Excluding bullion and specie.
[2] Including value of sugar quota certificates.

In 1979, Rs 495·9m. of the imports came from South Africa, Rs 489·6m. from UK, and Rs 181·4m. from Australia; Rs 1,545·9m. of the exports went to UK, Rs 316·2m. to USA and Rs 20·7m. to Canada.

Sugar exports in 1979, 650,511 tonnes (Rs 2,005·2m.); 1978, 617,800 tonnes (Rs 1,504m.).

Total trade between Mauritius and UK (British Department of Trade returns, in £1,000 sterling):

	1975	1976	1977	1978	1979	1980
Imports to UK	103,080	99,995	102,906	122,892	116,004	145,227
Exports and re-exports from UK	23,934	27,766	34,403	31,705	30,370	24,688

Tourism. In 1979, 128,360 tourists visited Mauritius, spending about Rs 300m.

COMMUNICATIONS

Roads. There are 9·5 miles of motorway, 523 miles of main roads, 361 miles of urban roads and 216 miles of rural roads. All the main urban and rural roads have a bitumen surface. At 30 June 1980 there were 25,229 cars, including 3,434 for public hire, 1,436 buses, 8,132 motor cycles and 17,283 auto cycles. Commercial vehicles comprised 12,039 lorries and vans.

Aviation. Mauritius is linked by air with Europe, Africa, Asia and Australia by the following airlines: Air France, Air India, Air Malawi, Air Mauritius, Alitalia, British Airways, Kenya Airways, Lufthansa, South African Airways, Zambia Airways, Air Tanzania and Royal Swazi National Airways. In addition to passenger services a weekly cargo flight is operated by Air France on the Mauritius–Paris route. The Government is presently planning for the construction of a new airport at Plaine des Roches.

Air Mauritius operates a Boeing 707 service to London *via* Nairobi and Rome and to Bombay *via* the Seychelles, and Twin Otter services to Réunion and Rodrigues. The company has commercial arrangements with Air France, Lufthansa, Alitalia, Zambia Airways and Air Malawi for the operation of services to Paris, Frankfurt, Rome, Lusaka and Blantyre.

Shipping. The registered shipping, as at 31 Dec. 1979, consisted of 15 motor vessels (21,805 NRT). In 1979, 1,147 vessels of 2,585,748 NRT entered and 1,021 vessels of 2,163,803 NRT cleared Mauritius.

Post and Broadcasting. In Dec. 1979 there were 30 telephone exchanges and 35,500 individual telephone installations in Mauritius and Rodrigues. Communication with other parts of the world is established *via* radio links. A radio-telephone service operates with countries all over the world.

Television was introduced in Feb. 1965. At 31 Dec. 1979 there were 73,612 television sets and 100,615 radio sets; 2,765 licences were issued.

Cinemas (1974). There were 50 cinemas, with a seating capacity of 48,000.

Newspapers. There are 6 French daily papers (with occasional articles in English) and 2 Chinese daily papers with a combined circulation of about 75,000.

RELIGION, EDUCATION AND WELFARE

Religion. At the 1972 census there were 245,570 Roman Catholics, 7,050 Protestants (Church of England and Church of Scotland). The Hindus numbered 421,707 and the Moslems, 136,997. State aid is granted to the churches and Rs 4m. is budgeted for 1980–81.

Education. Primary education is free but not compulsory, though under the Education Ordinance of 1957 compulsion may be introduced as circumstances permit. In 1979 there were 205 government and 50 state-aided primary schools. Enrolment at government schools was 93,940 and at state-aided primary schools 27,779. There were 3 junior technical schools for boys and girls providing a free 4-year post-primary pre-vocational course with emphasis on handicraft and homecraft, 75 unaided primary schools and 6 grant-aided secondary schools with primary sections with an enrolment of 3,300.

For secondary education there were in 1979, 4 government boys' schools (one of which has technical and commercial streams), 16 junior secondary schools and 3 government girls' schools with 7,673 pupils, and 125 aided (including Mahatma Gandhi Institute) with 74,204 pupils and 1 unaided secondary school with a roll of 69.

There is also a teachers' training college, known as the Mauritius College of Education, 433 on roll and 9 vocational and technical training centres, 1,040 on roll including students following part-time courses.

Government recurrent expenditure on education in 1980–81 is estimated at Rs 360m.

Health. In 1979 there were 410 doctors, including 100 specialists, and 2,836 hospital beds.

DIPLOMATIC REPRESENTATIVES

OF MAURITIUS IN GREAT BRITAIN (32–33 Elvaston Pl., London, SW7)
High Commissioner: Sir Leckraz Teelock, CBE.

OF GREAT BRITAIN IN MAURITIUS (Cerné Hse.,
Chausée, Port Louis)
High Commissioner: James Nicholas Allan, CBE.

OF MAURITIUS IN THE USA (4301 Connecticut Ave., NW,
Washington, D.C., 20008)
Ambassador: (Vacant).

OF THE USA IN MAURITIUS (Rogers Hse., John Kennedy St.,
Port Louis)
Ambassador: Roger C. F. Gordon.

OF MAURITIUS TO THE UNITED NATIONS
Ambassador: Radha Krishna Ramphul.

Books of Reference

Statistical Information: The Central Statistical Information Office (Rose Hill, Mauritius) was founded in July 1945. Its main publication is the *Bi-annual Digest of Statistics.*

Barnwell, P. J., and Toussaint, A., *A Short History of Mauritius.* London, 1949
Brouard, N. R., *A History of Woods and Forests in Mauritius.* Government Printer, 1964
Buckory, S., *Our Constitution.* Port Louis, 1971.—*An Outline of Local Government.* Port Louis, 1970
Central Statistical Office, *Population Census of Mauritius and its Dependencies.* 2 vols. 1962
Chelin, A., *Une île et son passé (1507–1947).* Mauritius Printing, 1973
Fougere, H., *A Survey of the Fisheries of Mauritius.* Government Printer, 1964
Jessop, A., *A History of the Mauritius Government Railways 1864–1964.* Government Printer, 1964
Leys, Colin, *The Development of a University College of Mauritius.* Government Printer, 1964
Lockwood, J. F., *An Examination of the Possibility of Setting up a University College in Mauritius.* London, 1962

Meade, J. E., *The Economic and Social Structure of Mauritius*. Government Printer, 1960

Ministry of Industry. *Handbook of Commerce and Industry*. Port Louis, 1970

Ministry of Information and Broadcasting, *Mauritius at a Glance*. Mauritius Printing, 1972

Napal, D., *Les constitutions de l'ile Maurice*. Port Louis, 1962

Société de l'Histoire de l'Ile Maurice. *Dictionnaire de biographie mauricienne*. Port Louis, 1967

Titmuss, R., and Abel-Smith, B., *Social Politics and Population Growth in Mauritius*. London, 1961

Toussaint, A., *History of Mauritius*. London, 1978

Toussaint, A., and Adolphe, H., *Bibliography of Mauritius (1502–1954)*. Port Louis, 1956

The Census of Industrial Production, 1964. Government Printer, 1965

10 années de réalisations. Ministry of Information and Broadcasting, 1967

Bi-annual Survey of Employment and Earnings in Large Establishments, 30 March 1972. Government Printer, 1972

Development Strategy (1971–1980), Ministry of Economic Planning and Development, Port Louis, 1970

4-Year Plan for Social and Economic Development 1971–75. Government Printer, 1971

5-Year Plan for Social and Economic Development 1975–80. Government Printer, 1975

2-Year Plan for Social and Economic Development 1980–82. Government Printer, 1980

Library: The Mauritius Institute Public Library, Port Louis.

MEXICO

Estados Unidos Mexicanos

Capital: Mexico City
Population: 69·4m. (1979)
GNP per capita: US$1,290 (1978)

HISTORY. Mexico's history falls into four epochs: the era of the Indian empires (before 1521), the Spanish colonial phase (1521–1810), the period of national formation (1810–1910), which includes the war of independence (1810–21) and the long presidency of Porfirio Díaz (1876–80, 1884–1911), and the present period which began with the social revolution of 1910–21 and is regarded by Mexicans as the period of social and national consolidation.

AREA AND POPULATION. Mexico is at the southern extremity of North America and is bounded in the north by USA, west and south-west by the Pacific, south by Guatemala and Belize and east by the Gulf of Mexico and comprises 1,967,183 sq. km (761,530 sq. miles), excluding inland waters and uninhabited islands (5,363 sq. km) offshore. The language is Spanish.

Census results for 1970 and estimates for 1977 are shown in the following table (capital of states in brackets):

States	Area (sq. km)	Census 1970	Estimate 1977	Approx. density per sq. km in 1970
Aguascalientes (Aguascalientes)	5,589	338,142	447,639	60·50
Baja California (Mexicali)	70,113	870,421	1,320,310	12·41
Baja California, T.S. (La Paz)	73,677	128,019	187,970	1·74
Campeche (Campeche)	56,114	251,556	349,456	4·85
Coahuila (Saltillo)	151,571	1,114,956	1,363,588	7·36
Colima (Colima)	5,455	241,153	332,015	44·21
Chiapas (Tuxtla Guitiérrez)	73,887	1,569,053	1,984,340	21·24
Chihuahua (Chihuahua)	247,087	1,612,525	2,062,499	6·53
Distrito Federal (México City)	1,499	6,874,165	9,233,770	4,585·83
Durango (Durango)	119,648	939,208	1,149,134	7·85
Guanajuato (Guanajuato)	30,589	2,270,370	2,895,767	74·22
Guerrero (Chilpancingo)	63,794	1,597,360	2,074,772	25·04
Hidalgo (Pachuca)	20,987	1,193,845	1,435,288	56·88
Jalisco (Guadalajara)	80,137	3,296,586	4,294,236	41·14
México (Toluca)	21,461	3,833,185	6,684,229	178·61
Michoacán (Morelia)	59,864	2,324,226	2,872,513	38·83
Morelos (Cuernavaca)	4,941	616,119	905,614	124·70
Nayarit (Tepic)	27,621	544,031	725,395	19·70
Nuevo León (Monterrey)	64,555	1,694,689	2,456,525	26·25
Oaxaca (Oaxaca)	95,364	2,015,424	2,377,720	21·13
Puebla (Puebla)	33,919	2,508,226	3,133,474	73·95
Querétaro (Querétaro)	11,769	485,523	638,839	41·25
Quintana Roo (Chetumal)	42,030	88,150	138,878	1·75
San Luis Potosi (San Luis Potosi)	62,848	1,281,996	1,560,601	20·40
Sinaloa (Culiacán)	58,092	1,266,528	1,786,681	21·80
Sonora (Hermosillo)	184,934	1,098,720	1,468,231	5·94
Tabasco (Villa Hermosa)	24,661	768,387	1,101,335	31·16
Tamaulipas (Ciudad Victoria)	79,829	1,456,858	1,968,837	18·25
Tlaxcala (Tlaxcala)	3,914	420,638	512,234	107·47
Veracruz (Jalapa)	72,815	3,815,422	5,091,331	52·40
Yucatán (Mérida)	43,379	758,355	926,283	19·28
Zacatecas (Zacatecas)	75,040	951,462	1,114,898	12·68
Total	1,967,183[1]	48,225,238	64,594,402	24·51

[1] Excludes islands (5,363 sq. km).

At the census of 28 Jan. 1970, 24,065,614 were males and 24,159,624 females (1976, estimate, 31,466,000 males and 30,863,000 females). Urban population, 1974, was 26m. and rural population was 33m. There are five basic language groups (Náhuatl, Maya, Zapotec, Otomi and Mixtec) from which are derived a total of 59 dialects spoken by 3,111,415 inhabitants (1970 census).

Estimates (1977) of the largest cities (proper) were:

México [1]	9,618,346	San Luis Potosí	303,571	Nuevo Laredo	214,028
Guadalajara [2]	1,725,107	Veracruz Llave	288,813	Durango	209,014
Monterrey [3]	1,132,050	Culiacán	281,667	Jalapa	195,235
Ciudad Juárez	570,401	Hermosillo	281,317	Matamoros	187,031
Léon de los Aldamas	557,030	Torreón	262,744	Poza Rica de Hidalgo	178,911
Puebla de Zaragoza	516,197	Mérida	250,206	Ciudad Obregón	170,275
Acapulco de Juárez	456,655	Tampico	240,540	Mazatlán	169,459
Tijuana	438,023	Aguascalientes	238,694	Querétaro	167,078
Chihuahua	386,645	Saltillo	233,613	Villahermosa	162,742
Mexicali	360,556	Morelia	230,350	Toluca de Lerdo	153,703
Cuernavaca	357,636	Reynosa	220,100	Irapuato	150,339

[1] Greater México City, 13·9m.　　[2] Greater Guadalajara, 2,194,715.
[3] Greater Monterrey, 1,823,684.

Movement of population for 3 years:

	Marriages	Births	Deaths	Immigration	Emigration
1971	378,222	2,231,999	458,323	3,035,115	2,400,617
1972	612,057 [1]	2,346,002	476,206	3,530,918	2,797,048
1973	452,640	2,572,287	458,915	3,986,574	3,118,598

[1] This figure is composed of 423,776 registered marriages plus 198,281 marriages registered in 1972 during the government 'Mexican Family' campaign among indigenous classes.

Crude birth rate has been maintained at approximately 42 per 1,000 population for several years; crude death rate (1978), 6 (26·1 in 1932); infant mortality rate, 77 per 1,000 live births (375 in 1933); crude marriage rate (1978), 6·6 per 1,000 population; divorces (1973), 13,517, or 3·2% of marriages.

For the regulations governing immigration, see THE STATESMAN'S YEAR-BOOK, 1951, p. 1234. An Immigration Tax law came into effect 1 Jan. 1951. The net immigration in 1975 included: 693 US subjects; 611 Spaniards; 182 Germans (GDR); 86 Argentinians; 85 Cubans; 82 Italians; 69 French; 63 Canadians; 38 Colombians; 37 British; 33 Japanese; 28 Swedish; 26 Swiss; 22 Germans (FRG).

CONSTITUTION AND GOVERNMENT. A new Constitution, amending the Constitution of 1857, was promulgated on 5 Feb. 1917, and has been amended from time to time. Mexico is a federal republic, divided into 31 states and 1 federal district, each of which has the right to manage its own local affairs. Citizenship, including the right of suffrage, is vested in all nationals who are 18 years old and have 'an honourable means of livelihood'; women were given equal citizenship and suffrage with men in 1952–53. Thumbprints are taken of registered voters.

Congress consists of a Chamber of Deputies elected for 3 years by universal suffrage, and a Senate of 64 members, 2 for each state and the federal district, elected for 6 years. Since 1964 additional 'party deputies' have also been elected to the Chamber according to a system of partial proportional representation. There were (1979) 400 seats, of which 100 are allocated by proportional representation. Senators and deputies are ineligible for re-election until another term has elapsed. Congress sits from 1 Sept. to 31 Dec. During the recess there is a permanent committee consisting of 14 senators and 15 representatives appointed by the respective Houses.

The President is elected by direct popular vote in a general election, and holds office for 6 years. He can never be re-elected. If the office falls vacant during the first 2 years a general election must be held; if after the first 2 years, then Congress elects a successor who completes the term. The administration is carried on under the direction of the President and a cabinet formed by the secretaries of 15 ministries, the Attorney-General and the heads of 3 departments.

The names of the presidents from 1920 are as follows:

Gen. Alvaro Obregón, 1 Dec. 1920–30 Nov. 1924

Gen. Plutarco Elias Calles, 1 Dec. 1924–30 Nov. 1928.

Emilio Portes Gil (Provisional).[1] 1 Dec. 1928–4 Feb. 1930.

Pascual Oritz Rubio, 5 Feb 1930–3 Sept. 1932.[2]

Gen. Abelardo L. Rodriguez, 4 Sept. 1932–30 Nov. 1934.

Gen. Lázaro Cárdenas, 1 Dec. 1934–30 Nov. 1940.

Gen. Manuel Avila Camacho, 1 Dec. 1940–30 Nov. 1946.

Miguel Alemán Valdés, 1 Dec. 1946–30 Nov. 1952.

Adolfo Ruiz Cortines, 1 Dec 1952–30 Nov. 1958.

Adolfo Lopez Mateos, 1 Dec. 1958–30 Nov. 1964.

Gustavo Diaz Ordaz, 1 Dec. 1964–30 Nov. 1970.

Luis Echeverría Alvarez, 1 Dec 1970–30 Nov. 1976.

[1] Took office after the assassination on 17 July 1928, of Gen. Obregón, the President-elect.
[2] Resigned.

President: José Lopez Portillo (born in 1916), formerly Minister of Finance, elected 4 July 1976 to serve for 6 years. He polled 17,695,043 votes out of the total of 25,913,215 (assumed office on 1 Dec. 1976).

Minister of the Interior: Enrique Olivares Santana. *Foreign Affairs:* Jorge Castañeda. *National Defence:* Félix Galvan López. *Navy:* Adm. Ricardo Cházaro Lara. *Finance:* David Ibarra Munõz. *National Property:* José Andrés Oteyza. *Industry and Commerce:* Jorge de la Vega Domínguez. *Agriculture and Livestock:* Francisco Merino Rábago. *Communications and Transport:* Emilio Mujica Montoya. *Public Works:* Pedro Ramírez Vázquez. *Public Education:* Fernando Solanda Morales. *Labour and Social Affairs:* Pedro Ojeda Paullada. *Secretariat of Programming and Budget:* Miguel de la Madrid. *Agrarian Reform:* Antonio Toledo Corro. *Health and Public Welfare:* Emilio Martinez Manautou. *Tourism:* Guillermo Rossel de la Lama. *Attorney-General of the Republic:* Oscar Flores Sánchez. *Regent of the Federal District:* Carlos Hank González. *Attorney-General of the Federal District:* Augustín Alanís Fuentes.

National flag: Three vertical strips of green, white, red, with the national arms in the centre.

National anthem: Mexicanos, al grito de guerra (words by F. González Bocanegra; tune by Jaime Nunó, 1854).

Local Government. Mexico is divided into 31 states, 1 federal district (comprising México City and 10 surrounding towns). Each state has its own constitution, government taxes and laws, and its governor, legislature and judicial officers popularly elected. Inter-state customs duties are not permitted. The President appoints the chief of the federal district.

DEFENCE. Supreme command is vested in the President, exercised through the Ministries of Defence (for Army and Air Force) and Marine.

Army. The country is divided into 35 zones in which both the regular army and volunteer corps are trained. The Army, in 1980, had 1 mechanized, 2 infantry and 1 parachute brigade, 64 independent garrison battalions and 23 independent cavalry regiments. Peace-time strength is 83,000. Military education is provided for officers, at the National Military School, the Application Centre for Army Officers and the Staff College, as well as in other specialized schools. To combat illiteracy in the Army, schools have been established in every regular and volunteer group.

Navy. The Navy consists of 2 (former US) destroyers, 5 frigates (including 4 former US destroyer escort transports), 1 armed transport and 4 armed tugs used as patrol ships, 18 fleet minesweepers, 16 escort minesweepers, 21 new fishery protection cutters of 130 tons built in Britain in 1974–76 and 10 built in Mexico in 1978–81, 14 patrol boats, 2 survey ships, 1 transport, 3 landing ships (2 used for rescue and 1 for light forces repair), 2 oilers, 14 auxiliary vessels and 6 tugs. There are 5 naval zones on the Gulf and 7 on the Pacific coast. Naval personnel in 1981 totalled 16,000 officers and men including naval air force and coastguard. There were 4,000 marines on active duty, with 1 regiment in reserve, formed by military service conscripts.

Air Force. The Air Force has a strength of about 4,000 officers and men, and 260 aircraft. These include 14 T-33A dual purpose jet-trainer/fighter-bombers, Boeing 727 (VIP), Buffalo, C-118A, C-54, C-47 and Israeli-built Arava transports, 45 T-28A and 20 T-6 armed piston-engined trainers and 3 Puma, 3 Bell 212, 10 Bell 205 Iroquois, 5 JetRanger II and other light helicopters. One HS 125, a JetStar, 3 Skyvans and 12 Islanders are employed on general and VIP transport duties. Primary trainers comprise 20 Beech Musketeers and 20 Bonanzas. Thirty-eight Swiss-built Pilatus Turbo-trainers are used for advanced training, with 22 more on order.

INTERNATIONAL RELATIONS

Membership. Mexico is a member of UN, OAS and LAIA (formerly LAFTA).

External Debt. The public sector external debt (June 1980) was US$27,939m.

ECONOMY

Budget. The 1980 budget envisaged an expenditure of 1,683,000m. pesos (1979, 1,124,000m.), of which 844,000m. was for the public sector, 549,000m. for federal government expenditure and 197,000m. to service the public debt.

Currency. The monetary unit is the *peso* divided into 100 *centavos.*
There are coins for 1, 5 and 10 pesos and 50, 20, 10 and 5 centavos; notes for 10,000, 5,000, 500, 100, 50, 20, 10 and 5 pesos.
Rate of exchange, March 1981: 23·59 pesos = US$1; 51·30 pesos = £1.

Banking. The Bank of Mexico, established 1 Sept. 1925, is the central bank of issue; it is modelled on the Federal Reserve system, with large powers to 'manage' the currency. The Government holds 51% of the capital stock.
In 1978 there were 7 state banks, 10 commora banks, 8 private development banks, 7 investment banks, 5 mortgage, capitalization and trustee banks and 6 foreign banks operating in Mexico.
In 1979 the total outstanding public external debt was US$29,757m.

Weights and Measures. The metric system was introduced in 1896, and its sole use is enjoined by law of 14 Dec. 1928.

ENERGY AND NATURAL RESOURCES

Electricity. In 1976 the 3,008 electric generating plants had installed capacity of 12·2m. kw.; consumption, including imports, was 46·5m. kwh.

Oil. The chief Mexican oilfields had proven reserves of oil and gas, in 1979, of 200,000m. bbls. In 1973 the oil industry generated 4·2% of the GNP; employed 75,000 persons; and supplied about 92% of the energy consumed in the country. Since the nationalization of the industry in 1938, Petróleos, Mexicanos, a government-owned enterprise, has exclusive rights to the exploitation, refining and sale of oil and its by-products. PEMEX is exploiting mainly the rich Poza Rica and Faja de Oro fields in the state of Veracruz (discovered in 1938), which extend into the Gulf of Mexico shelf and the nearby fields in Escolín and Mecatepec. New discoveries in Reforma, state of Chiapas, and Samaria, state of Tabasco, however, increased oil production in 1974 over the previous year by 25%. 43% of the current national yield is obtained from these two states. Exploration has been intensified in various states throughout Mexico leading to important discoveries in Cotaxtla, state of Veracruz, and Chac, state of Campeche. Crude petroleum output was 2·1m. bbls per day in 1980. Natural gas production came to 2,300m. cu. ft. Mexico exports crude oil but still imports petrol, gasoil (diesel), fuel oil and some petroleum gas.

Minerals. Mining is an important industry and, of the 48 principal non-metallic minerals in the world, Mexico produces at least 23. However, in view of the international price of mineral-metallurgical products, mining production, lacking incentives, has been both sluggish and fluctuating. Mining policy is aimed at the rational exploitation and increased industrialization of its mineral resources, procuring, at the same time, to completely Mexicanize the firms dedicated to this activity. This policy is implemented by the law regulating Article 27 of the Constitution regarding the exploitation and use of mineral resources. Based on this legislation, 769 mining companies had been Mexicanized by the end of Aug. 1972. The contribution, in monetary terms, of the Mexican mining companies to total national mining output soared from 26% in 1964 to 98% in Aug. 1972. In addition to the uranium deposits discovered in the states of Chihuahua, Durango, Sonora and Querétaro announced in 1959, rich deposits have been located at General Bravo, state of Nuevo León, with up to 450 tonnes of uranium oxide. Total reserves (estimate 1976) 2,860 tonnes of uranium 308.

Silver output (in tonnes) was 1,500 in 1979; 1,600 in 1978. About half the production is minted, including a 'token' coin (1949) weighing 1 troy oz. Gold output: 1976, 5,064 kg; 1975, 4,501 kg.

Mexico has large coal resources, calculated at 675m. tonnes, including high-grade coking coal at Sabinas in Coahuila; output of coke alone reached 2,066,025 tonnes in 1975. 744,673m. cu. metres of natural gas were produced in 1975. There are large underdeveloped reserves of iron ore with known reserves of 300m. tonnes; the new Peña Colorado field in Colima State seems to be promising. Output, 1976 (in tonnes): Iron ore, 3,437,000; billet steel, 5,224,000; and in 1979: lead, 169,900; copper, 88,900; zinc, 239,500; fluorite, 978,000.

Agriculture. About 80% of Mexico's territory is made up of arid and semi-arid lands. Irrigation is needed, 43% of the land having less than 500 mm of rain a year. The 1970 census indicated Mexico had 24m. hectares of arable land, of which 13·9m. hectares were cultivated and 10·6m. harvested. In 1975, land under cultivation came to 17·77m. hectares and the total area covered by irrigation was almost 900,000 hectares. Grains occupy 68% of the cultivated land, with about 53% given to maize and about 9% to wheat. In the 1970 census there were 91,354 tractors. It is estimated that Mexico should be self-supporting with at least 17m. hectares of land under irrigation and 20·3m. hectares under cultivation. Government agricultural programmes are being carried out by the National Basic Commodities Company (CONASUPO) and the National Deposit Warehouses (ANDSA) which regulate the market, intervening in the marketing process and protecting the low-income producers as well as the low-income consumer by assuring him access to basic commodities. ANDSA has undertaken the construction of silos, warehouses, storage, machinery and equipment.

The volume of credit channelled towards agriculture is dealt with by the National Ejidal Credit Bank. In addition, the Fund for Technical Assistance and Agricultural Credit Guarantees was set up in recent years to assist government and private banks in projects to finance and provide technical assistance, organizational counselling, primary industrialization and marketing to small farm producers.

Livestock (1979): Cattle, 29·9m.; sheep, 7·85m.; pigs, 12·6m.; horses, 6·4m.; goats, 8·1; mules, 3·2m.; donkeys, 3·2m.

Production of hides reached 9·5m. in 1976; production of meat, 909,733 tonnes.

Mexico's basic food crop is maize, and a rapid expansion of this crop is one of the chief aims of Mexican agricultural policy, balanced by the demand for 'cash crops' for export, such as cotton, sugar, garbanzos (chick peas), bananas, winter vegetables and coffee. Local production of nitrogen fertilizers in 1973 was 1,161,000 tonnes, and of phosphatic, 485,100 tonnes.

Principal products in tonnes for 1979 were: Maize, 8,752,000; rice, 481,000; sugarcane, 35,415,000; wheat, 2,272,000; and in 1975 coffee, 3·75m.; beans, 1,202,000; tomatoes, 1,127,000; oranges, 2,477,000; mangoes, 360,000; bananas, 1,241,000; cotton, 231,000; sorghum, 3,419,000; safflower, 531,000; soybeans, 545,000.

Sugar-cane is linked closely with the export markets, although not to the same degree as coffee, in view of the fact that despite the large crop, the national consumption of sugar, at approximately 35 kg a year per person, is one of the highest in the world. Exports have however remained more or less stable; 1972 exports represented 25% of total output.

The Yucatán peninsula produces about 50% of the world's supply of sisal (known locally as henequén).

Forestry. Timber lands represent 22% of the Mexican territory and are estimated to extend over 43m. hectares (about 43% of commercial importance), containing pine, spruce, cedar, mahogany, logwood and rosewood. Despite the existence of forests that would support a higher production, output for 20 years up to 1973, averaged an annual growth of only 1·1%. In 1973 only 15·7% of the productive capacity of the country's forests was being exploited. Reckless lumbering had destroyed the timber stands on many watersheds, resulting in spring floods and lowered water supplies in summer. In 1951 federal edicts had halted all timbercutting in 22 states, regardless of concessions; but they have been resumed under strict supervision. There are 14 forest reserves (nearly 800,000 hectares) and 47 national park forests of 750,000 hectares. In 1973 wood products amounted to 4,026,000 cu. metres; others in tonnes: chicle, 1,312; pitch, 10,640; resins, 54,338; turpentine, 2,250; ixtle, 4,120; other fibres, 3,261; vegetable waxes, 1,428; tree barks, 896.

Fisheries. Fishing is important because of Mexico's 9,903 km of coastline. Catch (1976, tonnes): Sardine, 64,182; shrimp, 47,244; oysters, 29,226; tuna, 15,016; sea bass, 10,974; sea perch, 11,178; mackerel, 7,463; bonito, 8,273; shark, 7,128. Total catch in 1979 was 900,000 tonnes.

INDUSTRY AND TRADE

Industry. In 1979 the economically active population was 19,650,000, 40% of which were engaged in agriculture. GDP contribution by agriculture, 9·7%; industry and construction, 29·9%; mining, 4·2%; electricity, gas, water, transport, communications and other services, 56·2%.

Commerce. Trade for calendar years in 1m. pesos:

	1973	1974	1975	1976	1977	1978
Imports	47,668	75,709	82,131	90,900	124,000	183,329
Exports	25,880	35,625	35,762	51,905	92,000	135,845

Export figures for metals and for certain foreign-owned agricultural products are heavily undervalued to reduce export taxes.

Of total imports (1m. pesos) in 1976, 56,848 came from USA, 6,327 from Federal Republic of Germany, 4,822 from Japan, 2,758 from France, 2,732 from UK, and 2,058 from Canada. Leading imports were cereals, machine tools, iron and steel products, electrical machinery and parts, car parts and components.

Of total exports (1m. pesos) in 1976, 32,257 went to USA, 2,726 to Japan, 1,374 to Federal Republic of Germany, 531 to France, 440 to UK and 153 to Switzerland. The main visible exports were manufactured products, petroleum, coffee, sugar and cotton.

Total trade between Mexico and UK (British Department of Trade returns, in £1,000 sterling):

	1976	1977	1978	1979	1980
Imports to UK	25,432	40,312	41,593	36,336	111,636
Exports and re-exports from UK	119,889	79,006	108,585	134,816	188,133

Tourism. Tourism is the largest single source of dollar income and, in 1978, 3·7m. tourists visited Mexico. Tourist net revenue in 1978, including border visitors, amounted to US$1,117m.

COMMUNICATIONS

Roads. Total length, 31 Dec. 1978, 208,180 km, of which 62,930 km were paved and 53,320 km gravelled.

Motor vehicles registered at 31 Dec. 1975 included 2,669,213 passenger cars, 49,264 buses, 874,758 trucks and 238,472 motor cycles.

Railways. In 1937 the main railway lines were nationalized. The two principal groups were then the National Railways and the Pacific Railroad. In 1977 a merger was announced between the National, Pacific and 3 other large railways, but unification will not be complete until 1982. In 1979, the National Railways carried 55m. tonnes of freight and 18·6m. passengers.

Aviation. Mexico has an excellent air service. Each of the larger states has a local airline which links them with main airports, which, in turn, furnish services to US, Central and South America and Europe. Thirty companies in 1976 maintained international services, of these 2 were Mexican. Domestic flights are handled by 77 companies. In 1975 commercial aircraft carried 9·63m. national and international passengers with 127,025 tonnes of baggage and some 97,923 tonnes of mail and freight.

Shipping. Mexico has 49 ocean ports, of which, on the Gulf coast, the most important include Tampico, Veracruz, Coatzacoalcos, Progreso and Yucalpletón. On the Pacific are Ensenada, La Paz, Santa Rosalía, Guaymas, Mazatlán, Manzanillo, Acapulco and Salina Cruz.

Merchant shipping loaded 39·8m. tonnes and unloaded 30·7m. tonnes in 1976. Passengers (1976), embarked, 375,042; landed, 373,320.

Post and Broadcasting. On 31 Dec. 1975 the federal, state and private telegraph and telephone system had 5,938 offices and 220,442 km of telegraph lines and 16·2m. km of telephone line. *Teléfonos de México*, a state-controlled company, controls about 98% of all the telephone service. Telephones in use, Jan. 1978, 3,712,407; 98·3% were automatic.

In 1979 there were 736 commercial broadcasting stations and 34 cultural government radio stations which reached about 8·5m. homes. Commercial television stations numbered 105 and cultural stations 3; there were about 4·5m. homes with receiving sets.

Cinemas (1975). Cinemas numbered 1,783 with annual attendance of 257m.

Newspapers (1974). There were 178 dailies and 21 weeklies, with an aggregate circulation in excess of 5m.; 23 in México City have about half of the total circulation.

JUSTICE, RELIGION, EDUCATION AND WELFARE

Justice. Magistrates of the Supreme Court are appointed for 6 years by the President and confirmed by the Senate; but the judges of the Supreme Court can be removed only on impeachment. The courts include the Supreme Court with 21 magistrates, 6 circuit courts with 3 judges each, 6 unitary and 47 district courts with 1 judge each.

The penal code of 1 Jan. 1930 abolished the death penalty, except for the Army, and set up a commission of alienists and other specialists, in place of courts, to deal with criminal cases (for federal offences); each state also appoints its own local magistrates.

The Mexican Constitution provides a guarantee of individual rights by means of a judicial procedure known as *amparo*, which gives any injured person whose constitutional rights have, in his opinion, been infringed, right to immediate access to the courts and full remedy, combining the swiftness of the Anglo-Saxon writ of *habeas corpus* and the breadth of remedy available through the injunction.

Religion. The prevailing religion is the Roman Catholic (46·38m. members at the census of 1970); with (1976) 2 cardinals, 9 archbishops and 84 bishops, but by the constitution of 1857, the Church was separated from the State, and the constitution of 1917 provided strict regulation of this and all other religions. No ecclesiastical body may acquire landed property, and since 1917 the property of the Church has been held to belong to the State. In the 1920s the Government suppressed the political influence of the priesthood and temporarily (1929–31) closed the churches. An understanding between State and Church was, however, reached, and all churches eschewing public affairs flourish freely. At the 1970 census 876,879 Protestants, 49,181 Jews and 150,329 members of other religions were also numbered.

Education. Primary and secondary education is free and compulsory, and secular. Clergy are forbidden to establish primary schools. All private schools must conform to government standards. Military drill is compulsory for boys of 18 years. In the Federal District education is controlled by the national government; elsewhere by the state authorities.

In 1975–76 there were:

	Schools	Pupils
Kindergarten	4,156	537,090
Primary	55,618	11,461,415
Secondary	8,778	2,141,127
Preparatory/Vocational	1,145	607,961
Professional and special	645	189,884
University level	531	543,112

There are 507 institutes of higher education, of which 48 are for post-graduate studies only.

The most important university is the Universidad Nacional Autónoma de México (UNAM) in México City which, with its associated universities and schools, had, in 1974–75, 238,375 pupils and 10,800 teachers. UNAM was founded in 1551, re-organized in 1910, and granted full autonomy in 1920. Other universities of particular importance in México City are El Colegio de México, a small, independent university concentrating on research in the humanities and social sciences, the Instituto Politecnico Nacional, specializing in applied science, Universidad Autónoma Metropolitana, recently opened by the federal government in order to meet the demand for higher education institutions in the federal district, and the Universidad Iberoamericana, a private university. Outside México City the more notable universities are, in Monterrey, the Universidad de Nuevo León and the Instituto Tecnólogico de Estudios Superiores de Monterrey; in Guadalajara, the Universidad de Guadalajara and the Universidad Autónoma de Guadalajara; and in Xalapa, the Universidad Veracruzana.

Health. In 1974 Mexico had 45,322 physicians; there were 5,469 state and private hospitals and clinics with 76,413 beds.

DIPLOMATIC REPRESENTATIVES

OF MEXICO IN GREAT BRITAIN (8 Halkin St., London, SW1X 7DW)

Ambassador: Dr José Juan de Olloqui (accredited 21 Feb. 1980).

OF GREAT BRITAIN IN MEXICO (Lerma 71, Col. Cuauhtémoc, México City 5, D.F.)

Ambassador: N. E. Cox, CMG.

OF MEXICO IN THE USA (2829–16th St., NW, Washington, D.C., 20009)

Ambassador: Hugo B. Margáin, GCVO.

OF THE USA IN MEXICO (Paseo de la Reforma 305, México City 5, D.F.)

Ambassador: Julian Nava.

OF MEXICO TO THE UNITED NATIONS

Ambassador: Porfirio Muñoz Ledo.

Books of Reference

Anuario Estadístico de los Estados Unidos Mexicanos. Annual (latest issue 1965)
México A Vuelo de Pajaro. Secretaria de la Presidencia, 1976
Mexico Statistical Data. Banco National de México, 1975
Petroleos Mexicanos: Anuario Estadistico, 1975. México City
Revista de Estadística (Monthly); *Revista de Economia* (Monthly)
Alba, V., *A Concise History of México.* London, 1973
Banco de México S.A., Annual report (latest, 42nd, 1964)
Banco Nacional de Comercio Exterior. *Comercio Exterior,* monthly.—*Mexico 1973.* Annual (in Spanish or English)
Bazant, J., *A Concise History of Mexico.* CUP, 1977

Bulletin of the International Commission of Jurists, No. 24, Dec. 1965: *Mexico, Constitutional Changes in the Electoral System*

Calvert, P., *Mexico*. London, 1973

Cheetham, N., *New Spain, the Birth of Modern Mexico*. London, 1974

Davies, N., *The Aztecs*. London, 1973

Johnson, K. F., *Mexican Democracy: A Critical View*. Rev. ed. New York, 1978

Ker, A. M., *Mexican Government Publications: A Guide, 1821–1936*. Washington, 1940

López-Portillo, J., *Mexico in Facts and Figures*. México City, 1976

Parkes, H. B., *A History of Mexico*. Rev. ed. Boston, 1950

Peña, M. T. de la, *El Pueblo y su Tierra*. México City, 1964

Ross, J. B., *The Economic System of Mexico*. Stanford, 1971

Smith, B., *Mexico: A History in Art*. London, 1975

MONACO

Capital: Monaco
Population: 25,029 (1975)

HISTORY. Monaco is a small Principality on the Mediterranean, surrounded by the French Department of Alpes Maritimes except on the side towards the sea. From 1297 it belonged to the house of Grimaldi. In 1731 it passed into the female line, Louise Hippolyte, daughter of Antoine I, heiress of Monaco, marrying Jacques de Goyon Matignon, Count of Torigni, who took the name and arms of Grimaldi. The Principality was placed under the protection of the Kingdom of Sardinia by the Treaty of Vienna, 1815, and under that of France in 1861. Prince Albert I (reigned 1889–1922) acquired fame as an oceanographer; and his son Louis II (1922–49) was instrumental in establishing the International Hydrographic Bureau.

AREA AND POPULATION. The area is 190 hectares or 467 acres. The Principality is divided into 4 districts: Monaco-Ville, la Condamine, Monte-Carlo and Fontvieille. Population (1975), 25,029. The official language is French.

REIGNING PRINCE. Rainier III, born 31 May 1923, son of Princess Charlotte, Duchess of Valentinois, daughter of Prince Louis II, 1898–1977 (married 19 March 1920 to Prince Pierre, Comte de Polignac, who had taken the name Grimaldi, from whom she was divorced 18 Feb. 1933). Prince Rainier succeeded his grandfather Louis II, who died on 9 May 1949. He married on 19 April 1956 Miss Grace Kelly, a citizen of the USA. *Issue:* Princess Caroline Louise Marguerite, born 23 Jan. 1957; married Philippe Junot on 28 June 1978, divorced, 9 Oct. 1980. Prince Albert Alexandre Louis Pierre, born 14 March 1958 (*heir apparent*); Princess Stephanie Marie Elisabeth, born 1 Feb. 1965.

CONSTITUTION AND GOVERNMENT. Prince Rainier III on 28 Jan. 1959 suspended the Constitution of 5 Jan. 1911, thereby dissolving the National Council and the Communal Council. On 28 March 1962 the National Council (18 members elected every 5 years, last elections 1978) and the Communal Council (16 members elected every 4 years, last elections 1979) were re-established as elected bodies.

On 17 Dec. 1962 a new constitution was promulgated. It maintains the hereditary monarchy, though Prince Rainier renounces the principle of divine right. The supreme tribunal becomes the custodian of fundamental liberties, and guarantees are given for the right of association, trade union freedom and the right to strike. It provides for votes for women and the abolition of the death penalty.

The constitution can be modified only with the approval of the elected National Council. Women were given the vote in 1945.

Monegasque relations with France were based on a convention of neighbourhood and administrative assistance of 1951. This was terminated by France on 11 Oct. 1962, but has been replaced by several new conventions signed on 18 May 1963.

National flag: Horizontally red over white.

ECONOMY

Planning. A 55-acre site has been reclaimed from the sea at Fontvieille. This land has been earmarked for office and residential development. The present industrial zone is to be reorganized and developed with a view to attracting new light industry to the Principality.

Budget. The budget (in 1,000 francs) was as follows:

	1975	1976	1977	1978	1979
Revenue	426,604	528,246	595,874	671,035	784,319
Expenditure	385,894	464,421	515,207	518,129	551,632

Currency. The monetary unit is the French *franc* divided into 100 *centimes*.

Weights and Measures. The metric system is in use.

INDUSTRY AND TRADE

Tourism. There were 224,000 tourists in 1978; 218,000 in 1979.

Trade Unions. Membership of trade unions is estimated at 4,500 out of a work force of 21,306 (1978).

Commerce. International trade is included with France.

COMMUNICATIONS

Roads. There were 46 km of roads in 1976.

Railways. The 1·6m. km of main line passing through the country is operated by the French National Railways (SNCF).

Aviation. The nearest airport is at Nice, France.

Shipping. The harbour has an area of 47 acres, depth at the entrance 90 ft, and alongside the quay 24 ft at least. In 1975 there were 2 registered ships with a total of 14,588 GRT.

Post and Broadcasting. Telephones numbered 32,000 in 1978. Monaco issues its own postage-stamps.

Radio Monte Carlo broadcasts 2 commercial programmes in French (long and medium waves) and Italian (medium waves). Radio Monte Carlo owns 55% of Radio Monte Carlo Relay Station on Cyprus and 83·34% of Radio Monte Carlo is owned by France. The foreign service is dedicated exclusively to religious broadcasts and is maintained by free-will contributions. It operates in 36 languages under the name 'Trans World Radio' and has relay facilities on Bonaire, West Indies, and is planning to build relay facilities in the southern parts of Africa. *Télé Monte-Carlo* broadcasts 1 TV programme. Number of receivers: radio, 6,700; TV, 16,000.

Cinemas. In 1974 there were 2 cinemas with seating capacity of 800.

JUSTICE, RELIGION, EDUCATION AND WELFARE

Justice. The Code Louis, adopted in 1919, is based upon the French codes. There is a Court of First Instance as well as a Juge de Paix's Court. A semi-military police force has taken the place of the 'guard of honour' and troops formerly maintained.

Religion. There has been since 1887 a Roman Catholic bishop, directly dependent on the Holy See.

Education. In 1978 there were 4,899 pupils with over 383 teachers.

Health. In 1978 there were 390 hospital beds and 58 physicians.

DIPLOMATIC REPRESENTATIVES

British Consul-General (resident in Marseille): E. A. W. Bullock.
Consul-General for Monaco in London: I. S. Ivanovic.

Books of Reference

Journal de Monaco. Bulletin Officiel. 1858 ff.
Handley-Taylor, G., *Bibliography of Monaco.* London, 1968
La Gorce, P. M. de, *Monaco.* Lausanne, 1969

MONGOLIAN PEOPLE'S REPUBLIC

Capital: Ulan Bator.
Population: 1·64m. (1980)
GNP per capita: US$940 (1978)

Bügd Nayramdakh
Mongol Ard Uls

HISTORY. Outer Mongolia was a Chinese province from 1691 to 1911, an autonomous state under Russian protection from 1912 to 1919 and again a Chinese province from 1919 to 1921. On 13 March 1921 a Provisional People's Government was established which declared the independence of Mongolia and on 5 Nov. 1921 signed a treaty with Soviet Russia annulling all previous unequal treaties and establishing friendly relations. On 26 Nov. 1924 the Government proclaimed the country the Mongolian People's Republic.

On 5 Jan. 1946 China recognized the independence of Outer Mongolia after a plebiscite in Mongolia (20 Oct. 1945) had resulted in an overwhelming vote for independence. A Sino-Soviet treaty of 14 Feb. 1950 guaranteed this independence.

AREA AND POPULATION. Mongolia is bounded north by the USSR, east and south and west by China. Area, 1,565,000 sq. km (604,250 sq. miles); population (1980) 1,641,100 (in 1977 719,000 urban; 51% male). Density, 0·97 per sq. km. Birth rate (1976), 37 per 1,000; death rate, 10 per 1,000. Rate of increase, 1971–75, 3%. The population is predominantly made up of Mongolian peoples (75% Khalkha). There is a Turkic Kazakh minority (5·2% of the population) and 8 Mongol minorities. The official language is Mongol.

The republic is administratively divided into 3 cities (Ulan Bator, the capital, population, 400,000 in 1978, and Darkhan, 57,000 and Erdenet 35,000), and 18 provinces (*aimag*). Local government is administered by People's Deputies' Khurals. The provinces are subdivided into districts (*somon*).

CONSTITUTION AND GOVERNMENT. According to the fourth Constitution (1960) power is vested in the *Great People's Khural* of deputies elected for 4 years by universal suffrage of voters over 18 years of age on a basis of 1 deputy per 2,500 inhabitants. It elects from its number 9 members of the Presidium, which carries on current state affairs. *De facto* power is in the hands of the only political party, the Mongolian People's Revolutionary (*i.e.*, Communist) Party, which had 67,000 members and candidates in 1976. The youth organization had over 140,000 members in 1975.

The last general election took place on 19 June 1977; 99% of an electorate of 694,855 were said to have voted for the 354 deputies (152 professional, 104 agricultural and 98 industrial workers; 82 women).

The *Chairman of the Presidium of the Khural* and head of state is Yumjagiin Tsedenbal, who is also *First Secretary of the People's Revolutionary Party*. The *Prime Minister* is Dr Jambyn Batmunkh. The other members of the Politburo of the Party are: D. Maydar, *First Deputy Prime Minister and Chairman, State Committee for Science and Technology*; T. Ragchaa, *First Deputy Prime Minister*; N. Luvsanravdan, D. Molomjamts, S. Jalanaajav, N. Jagvaral, D. Gombojav, B.-O. Altangerel. Ministers not in the Politburo include: *Chairman, State Planning Commission:* D. Sodnom; *Minister of Defence:* Col.-Gen. J. Avkhia; *Minister of*

866

Public Security: Col. Gen. Bugyn Dezhid; *Foreign Minister:* Mangalyn Dügesüren; *Minister of Foreign Trade:* Yĕ Ochir. *Minister of Agriculture:* L. Rinchin.

National flag: Red–sky-blue–red (vertical), with a golden 5-pointed star and under it the golden *soyonbo* emblem on the red stripe nearest to the flag-pole.

DEFENCE. Military service is 2 years. The Army was estimated to number some 25,000 in 1980. It is equipped with Soviet weapons and includes mechanized units, 1 construction and 2 infantry brigades. The Air Force has about 3,100 personnel and 50 aircraft, including 10 MiG-17 fighters, 15 An-2, 4 An-24 and 5 Il-14 transports used mainly on civil air services; 3 Wilga utility aircraft; 10 Mi-4 and 3 Mi-8 helicopters; and Yakovlev trainers. There is a para-military security force of about 10,000 men. A civil defence force was set up in 1970. There are some 25,000 Soviet service personnel in the country.

INTERNATIONAL RELATIONS

Membership. Mongolia is a member of UN and Comecon.

Aid. Mongolia receives economic aid from the USSR and other communist countries. There is also a UN development aid programme running at US$2m. per annum.

Treaties. Relations with the USSR were based on treaties of friendship and mutual aid (27 Feb. 1946), trade (17 Dec. 1957), economic and technical assistance (9 Sept. 1960), now replaced by a 20-year treaty of friendship, co-operation and mutual assistance (15 Jan. 1966).

Relations with China were based on treaties of economic and cultural co-operation (4 Oct. 1952), economic and technical aid (29 Aug. 1956), friendship and mutual aid (31 May 1960), commerce (26 April 1961 and 18 March 1963) and a border agreement (26 Dec. 1962). Sino-Mongolian relations have deteriorated since the estrangement between China and USSR.

On 28 Oct. 1961 Mongolia was admitted to the United Nations.

ECONOMY

Planning. Mongolia has had for centuries a traditional nomadic pastoral economy, which the Government aims to transform into an 'agricultural–industrial economy'. For earlier plans *see* THE STATESMAN'S YEAR-BOOK, 1976–77, p. 1156. The 5-year plan (1976–80) aimed to increase national income by 42%, industrial production by 63%, agricultural production by 30% and livestock by 7–9%. The seventh 5-year plan is running from 1981 to 1985. Emphasis is placed on the development of state farms, the extension of the arable area, mining and house building. Electricity output of 1,440m. kwh. is scheduled for 1980.

Budget (in 1m. tugriks):

	1973	1974	1975	1976	1977	1978	1980
Revenue	2,678	2,716	2,696	2,988	3,312	3,660	4,070
Expenditure	2,530	2,670	2,686	2,973	3,300	3,650	4,058

In the 1971–75 planning period 7,010m. tugriks were invested in the national economy. During the 1976–80 plan period overall investment was expected to double.

Currency. 100 *möngö* = 1 *tugrik*. Official exchange rates: £1 = 6·33 *tugriks*; 1 rouble = 4·44 *tugriks*; US$1 = 3·36 *tugriks*.

Weights and Measures. The metric system is in use.

ENERGY AND NATURAL RESOURCES

Electricity. There are maor power statins at Ulan Bator, hoybalsan, Sükh Bator and Darkhan. Production of electricity, 1976, 937m. kwh.

Minerals. Large deposits of copper, molybdenum, phosphorites, tin, fluorite and other minerals are claimed. Joint Sovet–Monol enterpriss re constructing a copper–molybdenum complex at Erdenet and a phosphorite mine at Hobsgol. Wolfram and fluorspar are exported. There are major coalmines near Ulan Bator and

Darkhan. Coal production in 1977 was 3·43m. tonnes. Oil was produced in the eastern Gobi desert at Dzüünbayan (production was 45,000 tonnes in 1969), but is no longer being extracted. There are reports of uranium and gold deposits.

Agriculture. The economy remains predominantly agricultural (mainly stock-raising). In 1979 there were 2m. horses, 620,000 camels, 2·5m. cattle, 14m. sheep and 4·7m. goats. Pastures occupy 84% of the total area, forests 10·5%. In 1978 there were 257 collective farms and 57 state farms. All cultivated land and 80% of livestock belong to collective or state farms. Farms cover vast areas. In 1978 collective farms averaged 64,000 head of cattle and state farms about 36,000.

Collectivization was carried through at the end of the 1950s. In the 1960s a virgin lands campaign to grow grain was instituted.

The sown area in 1978 was some 680,000 hectares, 500,000 hectares of which were sown to grain. The 1979 crop was 320,000 tonnes of grain. Production of hay fodder was 1·04m tonnes in 1977. In 1976 each state farm had an average of 240 tractors (15 h.p. units), 45 grain harvesters and 33 lorries.

Forestry. Forests, chiefly larch, cedar, fir and birch, occupy 150,000 sq. km. Production, 1976: 1,067,000 cu. metres of timber.

INDUSTRY AND TRADE

Industry. Industry though still small in scale and local in character, is being vigorously developed and now accounts for a greater share of GNP than agriculture. The main industrial centre is Ulan Bator; others are being built at Darkhan, Erdenet and Choybalsan. Production figures (1976): Fluorspar, 322,000 tonnes; washed wool, 11,400 tonnes; leather footwear, 2m. pairs; processed leather, 2·2m. sq. metres; woollen textiles, 898,500 sq. metres; processed meat, 58,600 tonnes.

Employment. The labour force was 259,200 in 1976.

There is a serious labour shortage necessitating the employment of military personnel, and workers from the USSR and Eastern Europe.

Commerce. Foreign trade is a state monopoly. Trade figures for 1976 (in 1m. tugriks): exports, 775; imports, 1,007, Mongolia has been a member of Comecon since 1962. The main exports are live cattle and horses, wool and hair, meat, grain, hides, furs, ores, and butter. 98·5% of foreign trade is with communist countries (80% with USSR). There is a chronic trade deficit. Just over 25% of imports are consumer goods and the remainder are machinery and industrial raw materials. In 1976 trade with China was 28m. tugriks. Trade with Japan, previously valued at US$1m. per annum, increased slightly after the establishment of diplomatic relations in 1972.

Mongolia exported goods to the UK valued at £2,091,000 in 1979 (1970: £2,000) and imported from the UK goods valued at £62,000 (1970: nil) (British Department of Trade and Industry returns). In 1972 contracts were placed for UK agricultural and textile machinery and exports of furs to UK increased. Exports to USSR in 1976 (and 1975): 139·8m. (125·3m.) roubles; imports: 474·7m. (355·1m.) roubles.

COMMUNICATIONS

Roads. There are surfaced roads in and around Ulan Bator, from Ulan Bator to Darkhan and at points on the frontier with USSR. Truck services run throughout the country where there are no surfaced roads. 98·2m. passengers and 15·2m. tonnes of freight were carried in 1976.

Railways. The Trans-Mongolian Railway (1,425 km in 1973) connects Ulan Bator with the Soviet Union and China. The Moscow–Ulan Bator–Peking express runs each way once a week. There are spur lines to Erdenet and to the coalmines at Nalaykha and Sharin Gol. A separate line connects Choybalsan in the east with Borzya on the Trans-Siberian railway. 1·1m. passengers and 8·1m. tonnes of freight were carried in 1976.

Aviation. Mongolair operates internal services and a flight to Irkutsk which links with the Moscow service. 7,000 tons of freight were carried in 1976 and 370,000 passengers. Soviet airlines (Aeroflot) and Mongolair jointly operate an approximately twice-weekly service to Moscow.

Shipping. There is a steamer service on the Selenge River and a tug and barge service on Hobsgol Lake. 3,000 tonnes of freight were carried in 1976.

Post and Broadcasting. There were, in 1976, 382 post offices and 218 telephone exchanges. Number of telephones (1977), 37,792.

There are wireless stations at Ulan Bator, Gobi Altai and Olgiy. In 1978 there were 128,000 radio and 3,800 television receivers. Television services began in 1967. A Mongolian television station opened in 1970.

Cinemas. In 1976 there were 23 cinemas, 439 mobile cinemas and 14 theatres.

Newspapers. In 1980, 70 newspapers and journals were published. The Party daily paper *Ünen* ('Truth') had a circulation of 112,000 in 1978.

JUSTICE, RELIGION, EDUCATION AND WELFARE

Justice. The Procurator-General is appointed, and the Supreme Court elected, by the *Khural* for 4 years. There are also courts at province, town and district level. Lay assessors sit with professional judges.

Religion. Tibetan Buddhist Lamaism was the prevalent form of religion. The Church was suppressed in the 1930s, and only one functioning monastery exists today, at Ulan Bator.

Education. Schooling begins at the age of 8. There are 8- and 10-year schools. In 1976 there were 30,000 children in kindergartens, 302,000 pupils in 559 'general' schools and 17,000 teachers and scientists engaged in public education. There is a state university (founded 1942) at Ulan Bator (40 professors, 240 lecturers and 2,500 students in 1967), and other institutes of higher learning (teacher training, medicine, agriculture, economics, etc.) under the supervision of an Academy of Sciences (founded 1953; reorganized, 1961). In 1977 there were 23,550 students in institutes of higher learning, and some 6,000 students a year are sent to study abroad, principally in the USSR.

In 1946 the Mongolian alphabet was replaced by one based on Russian, but now enjoys a limited revival.

Health. In 1980 there was 1 doctor per 464 inhabitants and 105 hospital beds per 10,000 inhabitants.

DIPLOMATIC REPRESENTATIVES

OF MONGOLIA IN GREAT BRITAIN
(7 Kensington Ct., London, W8 5DL)

Ambassador: Oyuny Hosbayar.

OF GREAT BRITAIN IN MONGOLIA
(30 Enkh Taivny Gudamzh, Ulan Bator)

Ambassador and Consul General: T. N. Haining.

OF MONGOLIA TO THE UNITED NATIONS

Ambassador: Buyantiyn Dashtseren.

Books of Reference

The Central Statistical Office: *Economic Statistics of the MPR for 40 Years.* 1961.—*40 Years of the MPR Revolution.* 1961.—*National Economy MPR 1973.* 1974
Bawden, C. R., *The Modern History of Mongolia.* London, 1968
Boberg, F., *Mongolian–English, English–Mongolian Dictionary.* 3 vols. Stockholm, 1954–55
Haltod, M. (ed.), *Mongolian–English Dictionary.* Berkeley, Cal., 1961
Jagchid, S., and Hyer, P. *Mongolia's Culture and Society.* Folkstone, 1979
Lattimore, O., *Nationalism and Revolution in Mongolia.* Leiden, 1955.—*Nomads and Commissars.* OUP, 1963
News from Mongolia. Ulan Bator, fortnightly, Jan. 1980

Petrov. V. P., *Mongolia: A Profile.* London, 1971

Rupen, R. A., *How Mongolia is Really Ruled: A Political History of the Mongolian People's Republic, 1900–1978.* Stanford, 1979

Sanders, A. J. K., *The People's Republic of Mongolia: A General Reference Guide.* OUP, 1968

Shirendev, B., and Sanjdorj, M. (eds.), *History of the Mongolian People's Republic.* Vol. 3 (vols. 1 and 2 not translated). Harvard Univ. Press, 1976

MONTSERRAT

Capital: Plymouth
Population: 12,073 (1980)
GNP per capita: US$920 (1978)

HISTORY. Montserrat was discovered by Colombus in 1493 and colonized by Irish settlers in 1632.

AREA AND POPULATION. Montserrat is situated in the Caribbean Sea 25 miles south-west of Antigua. The area is 39·5 sq. miles (106 sq. km). Population, 1980, 12,073. Chief town, Plymouth, 3,200 inhabitants.

CONSTITUTION AND GOVERNMENT. Montserrat is a crown colony. The Executive Council is composed of 4 unofficial members (the Chief Minister and 3 other Ministers) and 2 official members (Attorney-General and Financial Secretary). The Legislative Council consists of 7 elected and 2 official members (the Attorney-General and Financial Secretary) and 2 nominated members. The Executive Council is presided over by the Governor and the Legislative Council by the Speaker.

Governor: D. K. H. Dale, CBE.
Chief Minister: Dr J. A. Osborne.
Flag: The British Blue Ensign with the shield of Montserrat in the fly.

FINANCE. In 1979 the budget estimates balanced at EC$19,764,216 (including grant-in-aid).

AGRICULTURE. Agriculture has been in decline for several years, but is likely to recover with the progress of the Integrated Sea Island Cotton Project and revised land tenure and settlement arrangements associated with the government's acquisition of a number of estates.

Livestock (1979); Cattle, 8,000; pigs, 3,000; sheep, 3,000; goats, 3,000; poultry, 30,000.

TRADE. Imports in 1978 totalled EC$26,927,266; domestic exports, EC$1,921,052. Chief imports were manufactured goods, food and beverages. Chief exports in 1979 were hot peppers, tomatoes and manufactured articles.

Total trade between Montserrat and UK (British Department of Trade returns, in £1,000 sterling):

	1980
Imports to UK	125
Exports and re-exports from UK	1,351

TOURISM. In 1979, 14,405 tourists arrived in Montserrat.

COMMUNICATIONS

Aviation. At the modernized Blackburne airport 2,513 aircraft landed in 1978, disembarking 25,017 passengers and 467 tons of cargo.

Shipping. In 1979, 344 vessels arrived, landing 31,326 and loading 3,114 tons of cargo.

Post. Number of telephones (1979), 2,167.

JUSTICE, EDUCATION AND WELFARE

Justice. There are 2 magistrates' courts, at Plymouth and Cudjoe Head. Strength of the police force (1979), 2 gazetted officers, 4 inspectors and 88 other ranks.

871

Education. There are 12 government elementary, 1 government secondary, 2 grant-aided denominational elementary schools, 2 junior secondary schools, 2 preparatory private schools for children between the ages of 5 and 12 and 11 nursery schools. In 1979, 1,740 children were enrolled in the primary schools, with 87 teachers; 920 in the secondary schools, with 68 teachers. There was 1 technical college with 56 students and 8 teachers.

Health. In 1978 there were 9 doctors and 65 hospital beds.

Books of Reference

Overseas Trade 1976. Montserrat Government
Statistical Digest 1977. Montserrat Government

Library: Public Library, Plymouth. *Librarian:* Miss J. Grell.

MOROCCO

al-Mamlaka al-Maghrebia

Capital: Rabat
Population: 19·5m. (1979)
GNP per capita: US$670 (1978)

HISTORY. From 1912 to 1956 Morocco was divided into a French protectorate (established by the treaty of Fez concluded between France and the Sultan on 30 March 1912), a Spanish protectorate (established by the Franco-Spanish convention of 27 Nov. 1912) and the international zone of Tangier (set up by France, Spain and Great Britain on 18 Dec. 1923).

On 2 March 1956 France and the Sultan terminated the treaty of Fez; on 7 April 1956 Spain relinquished her protectorate, and on 29 Oct. 1956 France, Spain, Great Britain, Italy, USA, Belgium, the Netherlands, Sweden and Portugal abolished the international status of the Tangier Zone.

A tripartite agreement was announced on 14 Nov. 1975 providing for the transfer of power from Spanish Sahara (Western Sahara) to the Moroccan and Mauritanean governments on 28 Feb. 1976. Spanish troops left El Aaiún on 20 Dec. 1975. On 14 April 1976 a Convention was signed by Mauritania and Morocco in which the 2 countries agreed on their borders in Western Sahara. On 14 Aug. 1979 the Wad Ed-Dahab province was added to the Kingdom when Mauritania renounced its claim to Tiris El-Gharbia.

AREA AND POPULATION. As the south-eastern boundaries of Morocco have not been delimited, no exact figure can be given, but the total area is officially given as 659,970 sq. km. On 30 June 1969 the former Spanish province of Ifni was returned to Morocco, *see* THE STATESMAN'S YEAR-BOOK, 1969–70, p. 1322.

The population (census) June 1971 totalled 16,309,000, of whom 5·4m. were urban and 9·97m. rural; foreigners numbered 145,675. Estimate (1979) 19·47m.

The population of the largest municipalities (census) June 1971: Casablanca, 1,506,373; Rabat (capital), 367,620; Marrakesh, 332,741; Fez, 325,327; Meknès, 248,369; Tangier, 187,894; Oujda, 175,532; Salè, 155,557; Kénitra, 139,206; Tétuan, 139,105; Safi, 129,113; Khouribga, 73,667; Mohammedia, 70,392; Agadir, 61,192; El Jadida, 55,501.

The prefectures and provinces (and their Moslem population 1979, Rabat-Sale and Casablanca being urban prefectures) are Casablanca (2,357,200), Marrakesh (1,224,100), Kenitra (1,192,200), Agadir (933,300), Rabat-Sale (865,100), Meknès (774,100), Oujda (769,100), Fez (744,900), El Jadida (703,200), Settat (694,100), Tetuan (682,100), Safi (652,200), Taza (618,000), Nador (609,400), Ouarzazate (587,900), Beni-Mellal (572,600), Taounate (560,800), El Kelâa-Sraghna (559,100), Essaouira (456,300), Khémisset (427,700), Khouribga (424,800), Errachidia (405,000), Azilal (395,500), Tangier (377,600), Tiznit (336,400), Al Hoceima (306,400), Chaouen (300,200), Khénifra (299,100), Ben Slimane (180,200), Boulemane (127,800), Figuig (107,800), Tata (106,100), Guelmin (93,200), Tan-Tan (26,500).

With the incorporation of the southern portion of the former Spanish Sahara, administrative changes have resulted in the creation of 3 new provinces. Wad Ed-Dahab was added as a province in 1979.

The official language is Arabic; French and Spanish are considered subsidiary languages.

REIGNING KING. Hassan II, born on 9 July 1929, succeeded on 3 March 1961, on the death of his father Mohammed V, who reigned 1927–61. The royal style was changed from 'His Sherifian Majesty the Sultan' to 'His Majesty the King' on 18 Aug. 1957. *Heir apparent:* Crown Prince Sidi Mohammed, born 21 Aug. 1963.

The King holds supreme civil and religious authority; the latter in his capacity of Emir-el-Muminin or Commander of the Faithful. He resides usually at Rabat, but occasionally in one of the other traditional capitals, Fez (founded in 808), Marrakesh (founded in 1062), or at Skhirat.

CONSTITUTION AND GOVERNMENT. The Constitution was approved by referendum on 7 Dec. 1962 (3,919,737 for, 113,199 against, 72,722 void) and was promulgated on 14 Dec. 1962. In July 1970 a modification of the 1962 constitution was approved by referendum. A new constitution was approved by referendum in March 1972 and were approved by referendum in May 1980 amendments. The Kingdom of Morocco is a constitutional monarchy with a legislature of a single chamber composed of 266 deputies. Deputies for 88 seats are elected by indirect vote through an electoral college representing the town councils, the regional assemblies, the chambers of commerce, industry and agriculture, and the trade unions. Deputies for the remaining 176 seats are by general election. The King, as sovereign head of State, appoints the Prime Minister and other Ministers, has the right to dissolve Parliament and approves legislation.

National flag: Red, with a green pentacle star in the centre.

Cabinet in Feb. 1980:

Prime Minister and Minister of Justice: Maati Bouabid.

Foreign Affairs and Co-operation: Mohamed Boucetta. *Post and Telecommunications:* Mahjoubi Ahardane. *Culture:* Mohamed Bahnini. *Parliamentary Relations:* Haddou Chiguer. *Interior:* Driss Basri. *Finance:* Abdel Kamel Reghaye. *Agriculture and Agrarian Reform:* Abdellatif Ghissassi. *Commerce and Industry:* Azzeddine Guessous. *Mines and Energy:* Moussa Saadi. *Supply and National Promotion:* Mohamed Douiri. *Transport:* Mohand Naceur. *Education and Executive Training:* Azzeddine Laaraki. *Information:* Abdelwahed Belakziz. *Public Health:* Dr Ahmed Ramzi. *Labour and Professional Training:* Arsalane Al Jadidi. *Urban Affairs and Housing:* Abbès Fassi. *Tourism:* Moulay Ahmed Alaoui. *Administrative Affairs:* Mansouri Ben Ali. *Youth and Sports:* Abdelhafid Kadiri. *Handicrafts and Social Affairs:* Abdallah Gharnit. *Without Portfolio:* Abdellatif Jouahri. *Secretaries of State:* Abderrahman Baddou (*Foreign Affairs*); Said Belbachir (*Higher Education*); Abdelhaq Tazi (*Co-operation*); Khalli Henna Ould Errachid (*Saharan Affairs*); Tayeb Bencheikh (*Planning*); Abbas El Kaissi (*Government*).

The country is administratively divided into 35 provinces and 2 urban prefectures. The provinces are: Agadir, Alhouceima, Azilal, Beni Mellal, Benslimane, Bonjdour, Boulmane, Chaouen, El Jadida, El Kalâa Sraghna, Errachidia, Essaouira, Es Semara, Fez, Figuig, Guelmi, Kenitra, Khemisset, Khenifra, Khouribga, Laâyoune, Marrakesh, Meknes, Nador, Ouar Zazate, Oued Ed-Dahab, Oujda, Safi, Settat, Ta-Ta, Tangier, Tantan, Taza, Tetouan, Tiznit. The prefectures are: Casablanca and Rabat-Salé.

DEFENCE

Army. The Army numbers 90,000 officers and men, organized in 9 motorized infantry battalions, 5 armoured battalions, 1 light security brigade, 2 engineer battalions, 1 paratroop brigade, 18 infantry battalions and desert troops.

Navy. The Navy includes 2 new large patrol vessels or small corvettes, 1 coastal minesweeper, 1 patrol vessel, 1 gunboat, 1 seaward patrol craft, 9 coastal patrol boats, 4 landing craft acquired from France and 1 yacht training vessel. Personnel in 1981 totalled 1,800 officers and ratings including 500 marines. There are also 12 small customs cutters and a coastguard picket. A frigate, 4 fast gunboats (2 more planned) and 6 coastal patrol boats are under construction.

Air Force. The Air Force was formed in Nov. 1956. Equipment in current use is mainly of US and West European origin. It includes 50 Mirage F1 and 12 F-5A supersonic fighter-bombers, 2 RF-5A reconnaissance-fighters and 2 two-seat F-5Bs, 6 OV-10 Bronco counter-insurgency aircraft and 24 Hughes 500MD Defender armed helicopters, 22 Magister armed jet basic trainers, 12 T-34C-1 turboprop armed basic trainers, 10 Swiss-built Bravo primary trainers, 90 Agusta-Bell 205 and 212,

Puma and JetRanger helicopters, 12 C-130H turboprop transport aircraft and 6 turboprop King Air light transports. Personnel strength is about 7,000. Delivery has begun of 24 Alpha Jet advanced trainers. On order are 20 F-5E Tiger II fighter-bombers, 10 Do 28D Skyservants for coastal patrol and 6 CH-47C heavy-lift helicopters.

INTERNATIONAL RELATIONS

Membership. Morocco is a member of UN, OAU and the Arab League.

ECONOMY

Planning. A 5-year plan (1973–77) envisaged a total investment of 11,751,874m. DH. A new 3-year plan (1978–80) was approved in Dec. 1978.

GDP *per capita* (1977) 2,600 DH.

Budget. The ordinary budget for 1980 envisaged revenue of 15,300m. DH and expenditure of 23,500m. DH.

Currency. In Oct. 1959, a national currency was introduced. Its unit is the *dirham* (abbreviated DH), equalling 100 *centimes* (1 French franc = 1·025 DH; US$1 = 5·01 DH; £1 = 10·135 DH. Notes: 5, 10, 50, 100 DH; coins: 0·02, 0·05, 0·10; 0·20, 0·50, 1 DH. The exchange rate in March 1981 was £1 sterling = 10·25 DH.

Banking. The bank of issue is the Banque du Maroc in Rabat. Other important institutions are the Banque Marocaine du Commerce Extérieur (Casablanca), the Banque Nationale pour le Développement Economique (Rabat), Crédit Populaire and the Crédit Immobilier et Hotelier (Casablanca). There are 23 other banks in Casablanca, 3 in Tangier and 1 each in Tetouan, Fez, Kenitra, Meknès, Oujda and Rabat.

Weights and Measures. The metric system of weights and measures is the sole legal system.

ENERGY AND NATURAL RESOURCES

Electricity. Electric power-plants produced 4,105·6m. kwh. in 1979.

Oil. Crude oil production, 18,600 tonnes in 1979.

Minerals. The principal mineral exploited is phosphate, the output of which (under a state monopoly) was 20·03m. tonnes in 1979. Other important minerals (in 1,000 tonnes) are: Iron ore (61·7), lead (165·3), cobalt (8), zinc (12·9), manganese (135·7), silver (30·7). Production of minerals (1978) 2,829,284m. dirhams.

Agriculture. Agriculture is by far the most important industry, on which 70% of the population exists. The principal crops are cereals, especially wheat and barley; beans, chickpeas, fenugreek and other legumens; canary seed; cumin and coriander; linseed; olives; almonds and other fruits, especially citrus. The almost universal wild palmetto is put to various uses, including the manufacture of *crin végétal*. The trees include cork, cedar, arar, argon, oak and various conifers. Wine production, 1975, 830,000 hectolitres. Tizra wood is exported for tanning purposes. Stock-raising is an important industry.

Production (in 1,000 tonnes) in 1978–79: Barley, 18,862; wheat, 17,964; maize, 4,116; sugar-cane, 2,887; vegetables, 2,626; citrus fruit, 917.

Livestock (in 1,000 heads), 1979: Camels, 220; horses, 320; cattle, 3,650; pigs, 12; sheep, 13,500; goats, 5,650; poultry, 22m.

Fishing. The chief fishing centres are Agadir, Safi, Essaouira and Casablanca. There are over 5,000 fishing vessels and about 100 freezing and processing plants. The industry employs 50,000 workers. Total catch in 1979 was 279,583 tonnes.

COMMERCE. Imports and exports were (in 1m. DH):

	1975	1976	1977	1978	1979
Imports	10,394	11,555	14,401	12,361	14,327
Exports	6,238	5,580	5,860	6,262	7,622

Main imports, 1979, consumer goods and industrial products. Main exports, 1979, unrefined minerals (3,095,511 dirhams), and food products and tobacco (2,282,560 dirhams).

Main trading partners (1979): Exports, France (27·4%), Federal Republic of Germany (10·6%), Spain (6·2%). Imports, France (27·7%), Spain (9·4%), Iraq (9·3%).

A royal proclamation of 30 Aug. 1959 abrogated the former economic status of Tangier and integrated the zone in the kingdom. However, Tangier was declared a free port from 1 Jan. 1962; and commercial transactions within the free zone were further liberalized by decree of 8 Nov. 1965.

Total trade between Morocco and UK (British Department of Trade returns, in £1,000 sterling):

	1975	1976	1977	1978	1979	1980
Imports to UK	51,910	56,784	46,268	44,079	50,392	62,582
Exports and re-exports from UK	35,474	60,498	67,971	76,535	67,604	69,223

TOURISM. In 1979, 1,435,996 foreign visitors came to Morocco.

COMMUNICATIONS

Roads. In 1979 there were 56,203 km of classified roads, of which (1978) 27,671 km were surfaced. At the end of 1978 there were in use 179,272 lorries, 394,497 private cars and 17,820 motor cycles.

Railways. In 1978 there were 1,756 km of railways, of which 708 km were electrified. The principal standard-gauge lines are from Casablanca eastward to the Algerian border, forming part of the continuous rail line to Tunis; Casablanca to Marrakesh with 2 important branches, one eastward to Oued Zem tapping the Khouribga phosphate mines, the other westward to the port of Safi. Another branch serves the manganese mines at Bou Arfa. Two new double-track electrified lines are to serve a new deep-water port at Jorf Lasfar, and a 650 km south-east extension from Marakesh to Laayoun in the south Sahara is planned.

In 1979 Moroccan railways carried 803·5m. passenger-km and 3,853·5m. tonne-km of goods.

Aviation. There are 19 airfields, of which Casablanca–Arfa and Casablanca–Nouaceur are the most important. Total international air services in 1979 comprised 3,303,115 passengers arrived and departed and 28,761 tonnes of freight including mail.

Shipping. In 1979, 18,711 vessels of 46m. net tons entered and cleared the ports of Morocco. In 1979 Casablanca handled 25,589,000 tonnes of maritime traffic.

Post and Broadcasting. Communication with Europe is maintained by cables between Casablanca and Brest, Tangier–Casablanca–Le Havre, Tangier–Gilbraltar, Tangier–Cádiz, Larache–Cádiz via Algeciras.

Telephone subscribers totalled 210,000 in 1978; of these, 54,500 were in Casablanca and 34,700 in Rabat.

Broadcasting is done in Arabic, Berber, French, Spanish and English from Rabat and Tangier; television in Arabic and French began in 1962.

Cinemas. There were about 235 cinemas in 1971.

JUSTICE, RELIGION, EDUCATION AND WELFARE

Justice. A uniform legal system is being organized, based mainly on French and Islamic law codes and French legal procedure. The judiciary consists of a Supreme Court, courts of appeal, regional tribunals and magistrates' courts.

Religion. Islam is the established state religion. The majority of the Moroccans are Sunni Moslems of the Malekite school. The French and Spanish settlers are Roman Catholics under the Archbishop of Rabat. The once large Jewish population is diminishing.

Education. In 1959 a standardization of the various school systems (French,

Spanish, Israeli, Moslem, etc.) was begun. Education has been made compulsory from the age of 7 to 13.

In 1979–80, 1,984,665 children were enrolled in state primary schools, 678,095 in state secondary schools.

The language of instruction in primary schools is Arabic during the first 2 years, and half-Arabic and half-French during the following 3 years; in secondary schools lessons are in French and Arabic. A third language of the choice of the student is learnt during the last 3 years of secondary education.

There are six universities, Mohamed V at Rabat, Hassan II at Casablanca, Mohamed Ben Abdallah at Fez, Quaraouyine at Fez, Oujda and Marrakesh with a total enrolment of 73,833 in 1979–80.

Health. In 1979 there were 1,091 doctors and 24,453 hospital beds.

DIPLOMATIC REPRESENTATIVES

OF MOROCCO IN GREAT BRITAIN (49 Queen's Gate Gdns., London, SW7 5NE)

Ambassador: (Vacant).

OF GREAT BRITAIN IN MOROCCO (17 Blvd de la Tour Hassan, Rabat)

Ambassador: S. Y. Dawbarn, CMG.

OF MOROCCO IN THE USA (1601 21st St., NW, Washington, D.C., 20009)

Ambassador: Ali Benjelloun.

OF THE USA IN MOROCCO (2 Ave. de Marrakech, Rabat)

Ambassador: Angier B. Duke.

OF MOROCCO TO THE UNITED NATIONS

Ambassador: Dr Abdellatif Filali.

Books of Reference

Statistical Information: The Service Central des Statistiques (BP 178, Rabat) was set up in 1942. Its publications include: *Annuaire de Statistique Générale.—La Conjoncture Économique Marocaine* (monthly; with annual synthesis).—*Résultats du Recensement général de la population de 1971.—Bulletin économique et social du Maroc* (trimestral).—*La situation Economique du Maroc, 1975*

Bulletin Official (in Arabic and French). Rabat. Weekly
La situation Economique du Maroc en 1970. Rabat, 1971
Ashford, D. E., *Political Change in Morocco.* Princeton University Press, 1961
Barber, N., *Survey of North Africa,* 2nd ed. OUP, 1962.—*Morocco.* London, 1965
Decroux, P., *Les sociétés au Maroc.* Paris, 1950
D'Étienne, J., and others, *L'évolution sociale du Maroc.* Paris, 1950
Drague, G., *Esquisse d'histoire religieuse du Maroc.* Paris, 1951
Joly, F., and others, *Géographie du Maroc.* Paris, 1949
Kinross, Lord, and Hales-Gary, D., *Morocco.* London, 1971
Mercier, H., *Dictionnaire arabic–français.* Rabat, 1951
Miège, J.-L., *Morocco.* New York, 1953
Rivière, P. L., *Précis de Législation marocaine.* New ed. in collaboration with G. Catteriz. 2 vols. Caen, 1942–46
Sonnier, E., *Code des eaux du Maroc.* Rabat, 1954

National Library: Bibliothèque Générale et Archives, Rabat.

MOZAMBIQUE

The People's Republic of Mozambique

Capital: Maputo
Population: 11·75m. (1979)
GNP per capita: US$140 (1978)

HISTORY. Mozambique was discovered by Vasco da Gama's fleet on 1 March 1498, and was first colonized in 1505. The frontier with British Central and South Africa was fixed between Great Britain and Portugal in June 1891. The border with Tanzania, according to agreements of 1886 and 1890, runs from Cape Delgado at 10° 40′ S. lat. till it meets the courses of the Rovuma, which it follows to the point of its confluence with the 'Msinje, the boundary thence to Lake Nyasa being the parallel of latitude of this point. The Treaty of Versailles, 1919, allotted to Portugal the original Portuguese territory south of the Rovuma, known as the 'Kionga Triangle' (formerly part of German East Africa).

After 10 years of conflict preceding the *coup* in Portugal talks took place June–Sept. 1974 between *Frente de Libertação de Moçambique*, FRELIMO and Portugal and a transitional government was sworn in on 20 Sept. 1974 comprising FRELIMO and Portuguese elements. Complete independence was achieved on 25 June 1975.

AREA AND POPULATION. Mozambique is bounded east by the Indian ocean, south by South Africa, south-west by Swaziland, west by South Africa and Rhodesia and north by Zambia, Malawi and Tanzania. It has an area of 784,961 sq. km (303,070 sq. miles) and a population, according to the census of 1970, of 8,233,834. Estimate (1979) 11·75m. The country is divided into 10 provinces. The capital is Maputo with population (1970 census) 354,684; Beira, 113,770. The official language is Portuguese. The climate is mainly tropical.

CONSTITUTION AND GOVERNMENT. A Constitution was published on 25 June 1975. The legislative organ is the People's Assembly of 210 members. The Council of Ministers in April 1980 consisted of:

President: Samora Moïses Machel (assumed office 25 June 1975).

Planning: Mario Muchungo. *Foreign Affairs:* Joaquim Alberto Chissano. *Defence:* Alberto Joaquim Chipande. *Information:* José Luis Cabaco. *Interior:* Mariano de Araujo Matsinhe. *President's Office:* José Oscar Monteiro. *Agriculture:* Mario da Graca Manchungo. *Finance:* Rui Baltazar dos Santos Alves. *Foreign Trade:* Solomao Munguambe. *Internal Trade:* Manuel dos Santos. *Labour:* Alberto Cassimo. *Justice:* Teodato Hunguana. *Industry and Energy:* Julio Zamith Carrilho. *Public Works and Housing:* João Baptista Cosme. *Transport and Communications:* (Vacant). *Education:* Graca Machel. *Health:* Helder Fernandes Brigido Martins. *Fisheries:* Smart Catawala. *Director of the National Commission for Communal Villages:* Job Chambal. *Governor of the Bank of Mozambique:* Sergio Vieira. *Vice-Governor of the Bank of Mozambique:* Prakash Ratilal.

Flag: Four rays coloured green, red, black and yellow, with white fimbriations, radiating from the upper hoist corner, in which is placed over all the national emblem in colour.

DEFENCE. Substantial Soviet arms deliveries were made in 1977. The FPLM (Mozambique People's Liberation Forces) consist of an Army of about 22,800 men, armed with Chinese and Soviet light weapons, medium armour and some SAM missiles, and a fledgling Air Force and Navy. The former is reported to have 30–50 MiG-17 and MiG-21 fighters, probably flown by Cuban pilots, a few An-26 turbo-prop transports and Mi-8 helicopters, Zlin 326 primary trainers and *ex*-Portuguese

Air Force aircraft. The Navy comprises 6 former Portuguese coastal patrol boats, 2 *ex*-Soviet gunboats, 1 *ex*-Portuguese (*ex*-Canadian) survey ship (former fleet mine-sweeper) and 1 *ex*-Portuguese landing craft (used as a transport). Naval personnel in 1981 totalled 700 officers and men.

INTERNATIONAL RELATIONS

Membership. Mozambique is a member of UN and OAU.

Aid. After UN appeals in 1976 assistance was received from countries including Sweden, UK and USA. There are also technical co-operation agreements with China, Cuba, the German Democratic Republic, the USSR and Portugal.

ECONOMY

Budget. In 1978 the revenue was 10,042,500 contos; expenditure, 12,642,500 contos (deficit 2·6m. contos).

Currency. In June 1980 the currency became the *metical* (pl. *meticais*) divided into 100 *centavos*. The *metical* was established at par with the former *escudo*. In March 1981, £1 = 64·60 *meticais*; US$1 = 29·61 *meticais*.

Banking. Most banks had been nationalized by 1979.

Weights and Measures. The metric system is in force.

ENERGY AND NATURAL RESOURCES

Minerals. Coal mining is the main mineral being exploited. Output reached 565,000 tonnes in 1975 but has since fallen. Coal reserves (estimate) 400m. tonnes. Small quantities of bauxite, gold, titanium, fluorite and colombo-tantalite are produced. Iron ore deposits are known to exist.

Agriculture. Production in tonnes (1979): cereals, 573,000; tea, 16,000; tobacco, 3,000; cotton fibre, 15,000; rice, 35,000; maize, 350,000; bananas, 36,000; sisal, 18,000.

Livestock 1979: 1·38m. cattle, 330,000 goats, 105,000 sheep, 110,000 pigs, 20,000 asses.

Fisheries. In 1975, 4,801 tonnes of sea products were exported.

INDUSTRY AND TRADE

Industry. Although the country is overwhelmingly rural, there is some substantial industry in and around Maputo (steel, engineering, textiles, processing, docks and railways).

Commerce. Imports in 1979 totalled 23,000m. meticals and exports 12,700m. meticals. 15·3% of imports came from the Republic of South Africa and 12·7% from the Federal Republic of Germany. Exports (1976 in tonnes): Coal, 204,843; petroleum, 93,986; molasses, 76,059; sugar, 71,945; copra 41,104. Portugal took 25% of exports and USA 23·7%.

Total trade between Mozambique and UK (British Department of Trade returns, in £1,000 sterling):

	1977	1978	1979	1980
Imports to UK	41,650	10,769	11,039	11,416
Exports and re-exports from UK	18,163	17,757	15,730	11,345

COMMUNICATIONS

Roads. There were, in 1973, 38,560 km of roads, of which 11,423 km are main roads. Motor vehicles, in 1971, included 83,841 passenger cars, 20,215 lorries and buses and 4,081 motor cycles. These numbers have been reduced by the exodus of Portuguese settlers. The Government is devoting effort to constructing a new North/South road link, and to improving provincial rural feeder road systems.

Railways. The Mozambique State Railways consist of 5 independent networks known as the Maputo, Mozambique, Sofala (Beira), Inhambane and Gaza, and

Quelimane systems. The Maputo system has links with the Republic of South Africa, Swaziland and Zimbabwe railways; the Sofala system links with Zimbabwe at Machipanda and by way of the Trans-Zambesia Railway with Malawi at Dona Ana; and the Mozambique system links with Malawi at Entre Lagos. The Inhambane and Quelimane systems have no international connections. Total route-km (1980), 3,696 km (1,067 mm gauge), and 147 km (762 mm gauge). Trans-Zambesia Railway, 318 km (1,067 mm gauge). In 1977, 9,032,000 passengers and 7,886,000 tonnes of goods were carried. Rail links with Zimbabwe reopened in 1979.

Aviation. Regular air services exist between Maputo and Berlin, Brazzaville, Johannesburg, Luanda, Mbabane, Lusaka, Paris, Rome, Tananarive, Manzini, Dar es Salaam and Lisbon; and between Beira and Blantyre.

Shipping. The total tonnage handled by Mozambique ports (1977) was 10,554,660. The principal ports are: Maputo (1,880 vessels of 9,522,105 net tons handled in 1972), Beira (1,043 vessels of 4,254,728 net tons), Mozambique (71 vessels of 263,841 net tons) and Nacala (345 vessels of 1,261,379 net tons).

Post and Broadcasting. Maputo is connected by telegraph with the Transvaal system. Quelimane has telegraphic communication with Chiromo. In 1971 there were 103,533 km of telegraph line, 37 wireless stations, 125 telephone stations and 217 telegraph stations; length of telephone lines, 103,533 km, including 86,018 km of conductor wires in cable; number of telephones (1977), 52,270.

Radio Moçambique broadcasts 5 programmes in Portuguese, English, Afrikaans, Ronga and Shangane as well as 4 regional programmes in 8 languages. Number of receivers (1974): radio, 110,000; TV, 1,000.

Cinemas. There were, in 1971, 31 cinemas with a seating capacity of 20,195.

Newspapers. There are 2 daily newspapers in Mozambique: *Noticias*, published in Maputo, and *Noticias de Beira*. There is also a weekly magazine, *Tempo*. The Mozambique Information Agency (*AIM*) was established in 1976.

EDUCATION AND WELFARE

Education. Efforts are being made to expand primary and secondary schooling, and institute an adult literacy programme, despite a lack of trained teachers. There are also a number of professional and technical schools, and 1 university, *Universidade Eduardo Mondlane*, in Maputo.

Health. There were (1972) about 500 doctors and 12,500 hospital beds. Most Portuguese doctors left at independence and by 1975 there were only 80 doctors.

DIPLOMATIC REPRESENTATIVES

OF GREAT BRITAIN IN MOZAMBIQUE (Ave. Vladimir 1 Lenine, 310, Maputo)

Ambassador: J. A. B. Stewart, CMG, OBE.

OF USA IN MOZAMBIQUE (35 Rua Da Mesquita, Maputo)

Ambassador: Willard A. De Pree.

OF MOZAMBIQUE TO THE UNITED NATIONS

Ambassador: José Carlos Lobo.

Books of Reference

Boletim da Republica (Government Gazette). Maputo, 1975
Boletim Mensal de Estatistica. Maputo, 1976
Central Committee Report to the Third Congress of FRELIMO. London, 1978
Henriksen, T. H., *Mozambique: A History.* London and Cape Town, 1978
Houser, G., and Shore, H., *Mozambique: Dream the Size of Freedom.* New York, 1975
Isaacman, A., *A Luta Continua: Building a New Society in Mozambique.* New York, 1978

NAURU

HISTORY. The island was discovered by Capt. Fearn in 1798, annexed by Germany in Oct. 1888, and surrendered to the Australian forces in 1914. It was administered under a mandate, effective from 17 Dec. 1920, conferred on the British Empire and approved by the League of Nations until 1 Nov. 1947, when the United Nations General Assembly approved a trusteeship agreement with the governments of Australia, New Zealand and UK as joint administering authority. Independence was gained in 1968.

AREA AND POPULATION. The island is situated 0° 32′ S. lat. and 166° 56′ E. long. Area, 5,263 acres (2,130 hectares). It is an oval-shaped upheaval coral island of approximately 12 miles in circumference, surrounded by a reef which is exposed at low tide. There is no deep water harbour but offshore moorings, reputedly the deepest in the world, are capable of holding medium-sized vessels, including 30,000 tonne capacity bulk carriers. On the seaward side the reef dips abruptly into the deep waters of the Pacific at an angle of 45°. On the landward side of the reef there is a sandy beach interspersed with coral pinnacles. From the sandy beach the ground rises gradually, forming a fertile section ranging in width from 150 to 300 yd and completely encircling the island. On the inner side of the fertile section there is a coral cliff which rises to a height of 200 ft. Above the cliff there is an extensive plateau bearing phosphate of a high grade, the mining rights of which were vested in the British Phosphate Commissioners until 1 July 1970, subject to the rights of the Nauruan landowners. In July 1970 the Nauru Phosphate Corporation assumed control and management of the enterprise. It is chiefly on the fertile section of land between the sandy beach and the plateau that the Nauruans have established themselves. With the exception of a small fringe round a shallow lagoon, about 1 mile inland, the plateau, which contains the phosphate deposits, has few food-bearing trees and is not settled by the Nauruans.

At the census held on 22 Jan. 1977 the population totalled 7,254, of whom 4,174 were Nauruans.

Vital statistics, 1977: Births, 226 (137 Nauruan); deaths, 47 (33 Nauruan).

CONSTITUTION AND GOVERNMENT. A Legislative Council was established by the Nauru Act, passed by the Australian Parliament in Dec. 1965 and was inaugurated on 31 Jan. 1966. The trusteeship agreement terminated on 31 Jan. 1968, on which day Nauru became an independent republic but having special relationship with the Commonwealth. An 18-member Parliament is elected on a 3-yearly basis.

President and Minister for Foreign Affairs: Hammer DeRoburt, OBE.

National flag: Blue with a narrow horizontal gold stripe across the centre, beneath this near the hoist a white star of 12 points.

FINANCE. Revenue and expenditure (in $A) for financial year ending 30 June 1977: revenue, 22,643,375; expenditure, 28,052,000 (health, 715,110; education, 1,179,581).

The interests in the phosphate deposits were purchased in 1919 from the Pacific Phosphate Company by the governments of the UK, the Commonwealth of Australia and New Zealand, at a cost of £Stg3·5m., and a Board of Commissioners representing the 3 governments was appointed to manage and control the working of the deposits. In May 1967, in Canberra, the British Phosphate Corporation agreed to hand over the phosphate industry to Nauru and on 15 June 1967 agreement was reached that the Nauruans could buy the assets of the B.P.C. for approximately $A20m. over 3 years. Final payment was made on 23 April 1969 and control was handed over on 1 July 1970.

It is estimated that the deposits will be exhausted by the end of the century.

COMMERCE. The export trade consists almost entirely of phosphate shipped to Australia, New Zealand and Japan. Phosphate exported, 1976–77, 1m. tonnes. The imports consist almost entirely of food supplies, building construction materials and machinery for the phosphate industry. Value of imports, 1973–74, $A10m.

Total trade between Nauru and UK (British Department of Trade returns, in £1,000 sterling):

	1976	1977	1978	1979	1980
Imports to UK	2	4	135	160	70
Exports from UK	367	484	351	619	821

COMMUNICATIONS

Aviation. There is an airfield on the island capable of accepting medium size jet aircraft. Air Nauru, a wholly owned government subsidiary, operates services with Boeing 727 and 737 aircraft to Melbourne, Hong Kong, Apia, Honiara, Guam, Tarawa, Majuro, Kagoshima, Noumea, Port Vila, Fiji, Ponape, Manila and Taipei.

Shipping. The Nauru Local Government Council, through its agency the Nauru Pacific Shipping Line, owns 5 ships and has 3 on charter. These ships ply between Australia, Pacific Islands, west coast of USA, and Japan. Other shipping coming to the island consists of those under charter to the phosphate industry.

Telecommunications. An earth satellite station became operational in 1976, offering 24 hour telephone, telegram and telex services world-wide. Number of telephones (1978) 1,500. Direct daily high frequency service is maintained with Tarawa and both long- and short-wave transmissions with merchant shipping. A separate tele-radio service exists between Nauru and Ocean Island.

Cinemas. In 1978 there were 7 cinemas with an approximate seating capacity of 1,500.

EDUCATION. Attendance at school is compulsory for all children between the ages of 6 and 15 (if European) and 6 and 16 (if Nauruan). In June 1978 there were 8 infant and primary schools and 2 secondary schools. There were 129 teachers and 2,139 pupils in infant, primary and secondary schools. In addition, there is a trade school with 4 instructors and an enrolment of 61 trainees. Scholarships are available for Nauruan children to receive secondary and higher education and vocational training in Australia and New Zealand. In June 1978, 75 Nauruans were receiving secondary education abroad in Australia and New Zealand and 12 were enrolled in university and vocational training courses in Australia, New Zealand and Fiji.

DIPLOMATIC REPRESENTATIVE

OF GREAT BRITAIN IN NAURU

High Commisioner: Viscount Dunrossil (resides in Suva).

Books of Reference

Report to the General Assembly of the United Nations on the Administration of the Territory of Nauru. 1949–1968

Text of Trusteeship Agreement. (Cmd. 7290; Treaty Series No. 89, 1947)

Territory of Nauru—Annual Report. Dept. of Territories. Canberra, 1920–40 and from 1947–48

Packett, C. N., *Guide to the Republic of Nauru.* Bradford, 1970

Pittman, G. A., *Nauru, the Phosphate Island.* London, 1959

Viviani, N., *Phosphate and Political Progress.* Canberra, 1970

NEPÁL

Capital: Káthmándu
Population: 13·42m. (1978)
GNP per capita: US$120 (1978)

HISTORY. From 1846 to 1951 Nepál was virtually ruled by the Ráná family, a member of which always held the office of prime minister, the succession being determined by special rules. The last Ráná prime minister (and, until 18 Feb. 1951, Supreme C.-in-C.) was HH Máhárája Mohan Shumsher Jung Bahádur Ráná, who resigned in Nov. 1951.

AREA AND POPULATION. Nepál, situated between 26° 20′ and 30° 10′ N. lat. and between 80° 15′ and 88° 15′ E. long., is bounded on the north by Tibet, on the east by Sikkim and West Bengal, on the south and west by Bihar and Uttar Pradesh. On 5 Oct. 1961 a treaty was signed in Peking, according to which the Chinese–Nepalese boundary line 'runs generally south-eastwards along the mountain ridge, passing through Cho Oyu mountain, Pumoli mountain, Mount Chomo Lungma (the Chinese name for Everest) and Lhotse Too Makalu mountain'. Nepál gained about 300 sq. miles of territory. Area about 54,600 sq. miles (141,400 sq. km); population (estimate, 1978), 13·42m.

Capital, Káthmándu, 75 miles from the Indian frontier; population about 195,260. Other towns (1971) include Pátan (also called Lalitpur), 48,577; Moráng (Biratnagar), 44,938; Bhádgáon (Bhaktapur), 40,112.

The aboriginal stock is Mongolian with a considerable admixture of Hindu blood from India. They were originally divided into numerous hill clans and petty principalities, one of which, Gorkha or Gurkha, became predominant in 1559 and has since given its name to men from all parts of Nepál. The 15 feudal chieftainships were integrated into the kingdom on 10 April 1961.

The country is administratively divided into 14 zones and 75 development districts.

RULING KING. The sovereign is HM Mahárájádhirája **Birendra Bir Bikram Sháh Dev**, who succeeded his father Mahendra Bir Bikram Sháh Dev on 31 Jan. 1972.

CONSTITUTION AND GOVERNMENT. On 18 Feb. 1951 the King proclaimed a constitutional monarchy, and on 16 Dec. 1962 a new Constitution of the 'Constitutional Monarchical Hindu State'. The village and town *panchayat*, recognized as the basic units of democracy, elect the district *panchayat*, these elect the zonal *panchayat*, and these finally the 112 members of the national *panchayat*. The Constitution was amended in 1975. In addition, 23 representatives of professional organizations and royal nominees not exceeding 15% of the elected members, will be included in the national *panchayat*. The executive power is vested in the King, who appoints a council of ministers from the national *panchayat*. A state council will advise the King and proclaim the successor or, if the heir is a minor, a regency council. Art. 81 empowers the King to declare a state of emergency and to suspend the Constitution.

On 25 Aug. 1963 the King formed a National Guidance Council and in Jan. 1973 appointed a new cabinet which was reshuffled Nov. 1974.

Relations with the UK are regulated by the treaty of peace and friendship signed on 29 Oct. 1950, which supersedes the treaties of 1792, 1815 and 1923. Diplomatic relations with the USA were established in 1947.

The Cabinet appointed in June 1980 was as follows:

Prime Minister, Royal Palace Affairs and Defence: Surya Bahadur Thapa.
Law and Justice: Nayan Bahadur Swanr. *Home and Panchayat Affairs:* Nava Raj Subedi. *Works and Transport:* Jog Meher Shrestha. *Water Resources:* Harish Chandra Mahat. *General Administration:* Netra Bikram Thapa. *Local Development:* Balaram Gharti Magar. *Education:* Marich Man Singh. *Foreign Affairs:* K. B. Shahi.

Land Reforms: Hem Bahadur Malla. *Food and Agriculture:* Vijaya Prakash Thebe. *Forests:* Makeswar Prashad Singh. *Health:* Ramananda Prashad Yadav.

There are also 8 Ministers of State.

National flag: Two triangular parts of red, with a blue border all round, bearing symbols of the moon and the sun in white.

National anthem: 'May glory crown our illustrious sovereign' (1952).

DEFENCE

Army. The Army consists of about 22,000 men, mainly infantry, all of whom are regulars. There are 5 infantry brigades, 1 paratroop battalion and support units. It is being modernized with the aid of Britain and USA. The army flight is being expanded into an Air Force and has taken over 2 Skyvan and 1 Turbo-Porter transport aircraft, 1 Puma helicopter and 3 Alouette III helicopters. An H.S. 748 turboprop transport and a Puma helicopter are operated by the Royal Flight.

INTERNATIONAL RELATIONS

Membership. Nepál is a member of UN and the Colombo Plan.

ECONOMY

Planning. The fifth plan runs from 1975 to 1980. Its cost is estimated at NRs 10,110m. Priority is being given to transport, communications, power, agriculture, irrigation, training of technicians and schools.

Budget. The general budget for the fiscal year 1974–75 envisages total expenditure of NRs 1,740·8m., of which development expenditure amounts to NRs 1,153·3m. Current revenues are estimated at NRs 959·7m. The deficit is to be financed by foreign aid and loans. The main sources of foreign aid are India, USA, People's Republic of China, UK and Federal Republic of Germany.

Currency. The Nepalese *rupee* is 171 grains in weight, as compared with the Indian rupee, which weighs 180 grains. The rate of exchange is 135 Nepalese rupees for 100 Indian rupees. 100 Nepalese *pice* = 1 Nepalese rupee. Coins of all denominations are minted. The Rástra Bank also issues notes of 1, 5, 10, 100 and 1,000 rupees.

AGRICULTURE. Nepál has valuable forests in the southern part of the country. In the northern part, on the slopes of the Himálayas, there grow large quantities of medicinal herbs which find a world-wide market. Of the total area, nearly one-third (11·2m. acres) is under forest; 5·4m. acres is covered by perpetual snow; 9·6m. acres is under paddy, 2·9m. maize and millet, 800,000 wheat. Production (1978–79 in tonnes): Rice, 2·33m.; maize, 743,000; wheat, 454,000.

Livestock (1979): Cattle, 6·85m., including about 3·2m. cows; 4·2m. buffaloes; sheep and goats, 4·8m.; pigs, 350,000; poultry, 21·5m.

INDUSTRY AND TRADE

Industry. New industries, such as jute- and sugar-mills, match, leather, cigarette, and shoe factories, and chemical works have been established, including two industrial estates at Pátan and Balaju. The third economic plan envisages a 60,000-kw. capacity from hydro-electric plants.

Commerce. The principal articles of export are food grains, jute, timber, oilseeds, ghee (clarified butter), potatoes, medicinal herbs, hides and skins, cattle. The chief imports are textiles, cigarettes, salt, petrol and kerosene, sugar, machinery, medicines, boots and shoes, paper, cement, iron and steel, tea. The trade is mostly financed by the Nepál Bank, Ltd (established in 1937) and the Rástra Bank of Nepál (established in 1956). A large proportion of international trade is with India.

Imports and exports in NRs 1,000:

	1977	1978
Imports	2,003,900	2,549,200
Exports	1,007,200	2,003,900

Total trade between Nepál and UK (British Department of Trade returns, in £1,000 sterling):

	1975	1976	1977	1978	1979	1980
Imports to UK	473	539	680	642	1,591	2,253
Exports and re-exports from UK	2,253	1,532	2,747	1,572	5,096	2,956

Tourism. There were 90,000 (estimate) tourists in 1974.

COMMUNICATIONS

Roads. With the co-operation of India and the USA 900 miles of motorable roads are being constructed, including the East–West Highway through southern Nepál. A road from the Tibetan border to Káthmándu was recently completed with Chinese aid.

There are about 1,300 miles of motorable roads. A ropeway for the carriage of goods covers the 14 miles from Dhursing above Bhimphedi into the Káthmándu valley.

A road connects Káthmándu with Birgung.

Railways. Railways (762 mm gauge) connect Jayanagar on the North Eastern Indian Railway with Janakpur and thence with Bijulpura (48 km).

Aviation. The Royal Nepál Airline Corporation has linked Káthmándu, the capital, with 11 districts of Nepál; and 23 more airfields are under construction. The Royal Nepalese Airline Corporation has services between Káthmándu and Calcutta, Patna, New Delhi, Bangkok, Rangoon and Dacca, employing Boeing 727 jet aircraft.

Post and Broadcasting. Káthmándu is connected by telephone with Birganj and Raxaul (North Eastern Indian Railway) on the southern frontier with Bihar; and with the eastern part of the Terai foothills; an extension to the western districts is being completed. Number of telephones (1978) 9,425, of which 5,431 were in Káthmándu. Under an agreement with India and the USA, a network of 91 wireless stations exists in Nepál, with further stations in Calcutta and New Delhi. Radio Nepál at Káthmándu broadcasts in Nepáli and English. Wireless telecommunication was inaugurated on 1 Oct. 1964.

All post, telephone and telegraph services have been taken over from India. The Indian, originally English, post office, established in 1816, closed on 13 April 1965.

JUSTICE, RELIGION, EDUCATION AND WELFARE

Justice. The Supreme Court Act, 1956, established a uniform judicial system, culminating in a supreme court of a Chief Justice and no more than 6 judges. Special courts to deal with minor offences may be established at the discretion of the Government.

Religion. Sánáton of Pauranic, *i.e.*, traditional or ancient Hinduism, and Buddhism are the religions of the bulk of the people. Christian missions are admitted, but conversion is forbidden.

The royal family is Hindu.

Education. In 1970 there were 7,256 primary schools, 1,036 secondary schools, 49 colleges and the Tribhuvan University (founded 1960).

About 16% of the population are literate. The national language is Nepáli.

Health. There were 130 doctors and 2,000 hospital beds in 1972.

DIPLOMATIC REPRESENTATIVES

OF NEPÁL IN GREAT BRITAIN (12a Kensington Palace Gdns., London, W8 4QU)

Ambassador: Jharendra Narayan Singha, GCVO (accredited 9 Feb. 1978).

OF GREAT BRITAIN IN NEPÁL (Láincháur, Káthmándu)

Ambassador: J. B. Denson, CMG, OBE.

OF NEPÁL IN THE USA (2131 Leroy Pl. NW,
Washington, D.C., 20008)

Ambassador: Padma Badahur Khatri.

OF THE USA IN NEPÁL (Pani Pokhari, Káthmándu)

Ambassador: Phillip R. Trimble.

OF NEPÁL TO THE UNITED NATIONS

Ambassador: (Vacant).

Books of Reference

Statistical Information: A Department of Statistics was set up in Káthmándu in 1950.

Baral, L. S., *Political Development in Nepal.* London, 1980
Karan, P. P., and Jenkins, W. M., *Nepal: A Cultural and Physical Geography.* Univ. of Kentucky Press, 1960
Muni, S. D., *Foreign Policy of Nepal.* New Delhi, 1973
Regmi, D. R., *Modern Nepal.* Calcutta, 1961
Shaha, R., *Nepali Politics: Retrospect and Prospect.* OUP, 1975
Turner, R. L., *Nepali Dictionary. 1980*

THE NETHERLANDS

Capital: Amsterdam
Seat of Government: The Hague
Population: 14·09m. (1980)
GNP per capita: US$8,390 (1978)

Koninkrijk der Nederlanden

HISTORY. William of Orange (1533–84), as the German count of Nassau, inherited vast possessions in the Netherlands and the Princedom of Orange in France. He was the initiator of the struggle for independence from Spain (1568–1648); in the Republic of the United Netherlands he and his successors became the 'first servants of the Republic' with the title of 'Stadhouder' (governor). In 1689 William III acceded to the throne of England, becoming joint sovereign with Mary II, his wife. William III died in 1702 without issue, and after a stadhouderless period a member of the Frisian branch of Orange-Nassau was nominated hereditary stadhouder in 1747; but his successor, Willem V, had to take refuge in England, in 1795, at the invasion of the French Army. In Nov. 1813 the United Provinces were freed from French domination.

The Congress of Vienna joined the Belgian provinces, the 'Austrian Netherlands' before the French Revolution, to the Northern Netherlands. The son of the former stadhouder Willem V was proclaimed King of the Netherlands at The Hague on 16 March 1815 as Willem I. The union was dissolved by the Belgian revolution of 1830, and the treaty of London, 19 April 1839, constituted Belgium an independent kingdom.

Netherlands Sovereigns

Willem I	1815–40 (died 1843)	Wilhelmina	1890–1948 (died 1962)
Willem II	1840–1849	Juliana	1948–80
Willem III	1849–1890	Beatrix	1980–

AREA AND POPULATION. The Netherlands is bounded north and west by the North Sea, south by Belgium and east by the Federal Republic of Germany. Growth of census population:

1829	2,613,298	1909	5,858,175	1960	11,461,964
1849	3,056,879	1920	6,865,314	1971	13,060,115
1869	3,579,529	1930	7,935,565		
1889	4,511,415	1947	9,625,499		

Area, density and estimated population on 1 Jan. 1979 and 1980:

Province	Land area (in sq. km) 1980	Population 1979	Population 1980	Density per sq. km 1980
Groningen	2,337·89	551,315	553,709	237
Friesland	3,352·59	578,203	583,989	174
Drenthe	2,654·07	415,978	418,479	158
Overijssel	3,812·52	1,009,651	1,018,208	267
Gelderland	5,009·95	1,680,629	1,694,416	338
Utrecht	1,331·87	885,756	895,464	672
Noord-Holland	2,669·78	2,299,175	2,307,646	864
Zuid-Holland	2,900·64	3,063,625	3,083,555	1,063
Zeeland	1,785·14	344,388	348,268	195
Noord-Brabant	4,958·02	2,030,920	2,051,195	414
Limburg	2,171·46	1,065,483	1,069,038	492
Dronten [1]	329·64	18,973	19,658	60
Lelystad [1]	220·38	—	38,971	177

[1] Dronten and Lelystad are municipalities and have not been incorporated into any province.

Province	Land area (in sq. km) 1980	Population 1979	1980	Density per sq. km 1980
Zuideijke Ijsselmeerpolders [1]	404·47	39,745	6,872	17
Central Register of population [2]	—	1,685	1,546	—
Total	33,938·42	13,985,526	14,091,014	415

[1] The Zuidelijke Ijsselmeerpolders (drained in 1957) are part of the former Zuiderzee, now called Ijsselmeer; they have not been incorporated into any province.
[2] The Central population register includes persons who are residents of the Netherlands but who have no fixed residence in any particular municipality (living in caravans and houseboats, population on inland vessels, etc.).

Of the total population on 1 Jan. 1980, 6,994,280 were males, 7,096,734 females.

The total area of the Netherlands up to the low water line (i.e., sea-level at low tide) is 41,160 sq. km (15,892 sq. miles), of which 33,938·42 sq. km (13,103·65 sq. miles) is land area.

On 14 June 1918 a law was passed concerning the reclamation of the Zuiderzee. The work was begun in 1920; the following sections have been completed: 1. The Noordholland–Wieringen Barrage (2·5 km), 1924; 2. The Wieringermeer Polder (210 sq. km), 1930 (inundated by the Germans in 1945, but drained again in the same year); 3. The Wieringen–Friesland Barrage (30 km), 1932; 4. The Noordoost Polder (501 sq. km), 1942; 5. Oost Flevoland (651 sq. km), 1957; 6. Zuidelijk Flevoland (428 sq. km), 1967.

The polder Markerwaard (400 sq. km) is being reclaimed. A portion of what used to be the Zuiderzee behind the barrage will remain a fresh-water lake: Ijsselmeer (1,250 sq. km). The 'Delta-project', scheduled to be completed in about 1980, comprises the building of enclosure dams in the estuaries between the islands in the south-western part of the country, excluding the sea-entrances to the ports of Rotterdam and Antwerp; it will also create fresh-water reservoirs. See map in THE STATESMAN'S YEAR-BOOK, 1959.

Vital statistics for calendar years:

	Live births Total	Illegitimate	Still births	Marriages	Divorces	Deaths	Net migration
1977	173,296	4,747	1,317	93,280	21,483	110,093	+22,848
1978	175,550	5,359	1,259	89,090	22,257	114,415	+28,067
1979	174,979	5,962	1,240	85,648	23,748	112,565	+44,774

Population of principal municipalities on 1 Jan. 1980:

Achtharspelen	26,169	Doetinchem	36,995	Heerhugowaard	31,459
Alkmaar	71,245	Dordrecht	107,453	Heerlen	71,102
Almelo	63,381	Ede (Gld.)	82,829	Den Helder	61,761
Alphen a/d Rijn	51,780	Eindhoven	194,451	Hellendoorn	32,940
Amersfoort	88,097	Emmen	89,763	Helmond	58,490
Amstelveen	69,488	Enschede	143,042	Hengelo (O.)	75,216
Amsterdam	716,919	Epe	33,071	's-Hertogenbosch	87,897
Apeldoorn	138,164	Etten-Leur	28,523	Hilversum	92,964
Arnhem	127,846	Geldrop	26,474	Hoogeveen	43,645
Assen	45,036	Geleen	35,371	Hoogezand-	
Barneveld	36,451	Goes	30,193	Sappemeer	35,884
Bergen op Zoom	43,715	Gorinchem	28,957	Hoorn	39,300
Beverwijk	35,980	Gouda	58,784	Huizen	29,335
De Bilt	32,397	's-Gravenhage	456,886	Kampen	30,353
Breda	117,259	Groningen	161,322	Katwijk	38,163
Brunssum	26,281	Haarlem	158,291	Kerkrade	47,001
Bussum	35,316	Haarlemmermeer	77,657	Krimpen a/d Ijssel	27,875
Capelle a/d Ijssel	41,834	Hardenberg	30,869	Leeuwarden	84,518
Delft	83,939	Harderwijk	30,174	Leiden	103,046
Delfzijl	25,433	Heemskerk	31,783	Leidschendam	30,016
Deurne	27,718	Heemstede	26,729	Lelystad	38,971
Deventer	64,561	Heerenveen	36,729	Maarssen	28,185

Maassluis	32,937	Rÿswÿk (Z.-H.)	52,605	Velsen	61,202
Maastricht	109,285	Schiedam	74,895	Venlo	62,595
Middelburg	38,077	Sittard	33,702	Venray	32,825
Naaldwijk	25,156	Smallingerland	48,472	Vlaardingen	79,531
Nieuwegein	37,134	Sneek	28,457	Vlissingen	45,726
Noordoostpolder	37,403	Soest	40,581	Voorburg	44,227
Nijmegen	147,614	Spÿkenisse	36,863	Waalwÿk	28,514
Oldenzaal	28,134	Stadskanaal	33,995	Wageningen	30,447
Oosterhout	43,462	Terneuzen	35,393	Wassenaar	26,989
Opsterland	25,442	Tiel	28,919	Weert	38,311
Oss	46,866	Tietjerksteradeel	29,670	Winterswÿk	27,670
Purmerend	32,565	Tilburg	151,799	Zaanstad	128,809
Renkum	34,166	Uden	32,734	Zeist	61,532
Rheden	48,637	Utrecht	237,037	Zevenaar	27,422
Ridderkerk	45,908	Valkenswaard	27,441	Zoetermeer	63,832
Roermond	37,539	Veendam	28,169	Zutphen	31,767
Roosendaal	54,838	Veenendaal	39,210	Zwolle	82,190
Rotterdam	579,194	Veldhoven	33,382	Zwijndrecht	39,641

Urban agglomerations as at 1 Jan. 1980: Rotterdam, 1,017,531; Amsterdam, 1,015,107; The Hague, 674,555; Utrecht, 481,875; Eindhoven, 369,352; Arnhem, 287,305; Heerlen-Kerkrade, 267,003; Enschede-Hengelo, 244,065; Haarlem, 225,127; Nijmegen, 217,951; Tilburg, 216,873; Groningen, 200,467; Dordrecht-Zwijndrecht, 195,792; 's-Hertogenbosch, 183,583; Geleen-Sittard, 181,250; Leiden, 173,386; Breda, 151,236; Maastricht, 145,346; Zaanstad, 141,119; Velsen-Beverwijk, 128,965; Hilversum, 110,236.

REIGNING QUEEN. Beatrix Wilhelmina Armgard, born 31 Jan. 1938 daughter of Queen Juliana and Prince Bernhard; married to Claus von Amsberg on 10 March 1966; succeeded to the crown on 1 May 1980, on the abdication of her mother. *Offspring:* Prince Willem-Alexander, born 27 April 1967; Prince Johan Friso, born 25 Sept. 1968; Prince Constantijn, born 11 Oct. 1969.

Mother of the Queen: Queen Juliana Louise Emma Marie Wilhelmina, born 30 April 1909, daughter of Queen Wilhelmina (born 31 Aug. 1880, died 28 Nov. 1962) and Prince Henry of Mecklenburg-Schwerin (born April 1876, died 3 July 1934); married to Prince Bernhard Leopold Frederick Everhard Julius Coert Karel Godfried Pieter of Lippe-Biesterfeld (born 29 June 1911) on 7 Jan. 1937. Abdicated in favour of her daughter, the Reigning Queen, on 30 April 1980.

Sisters of the Queen: Princess Irene Emma Elisabeth, born 5 Aug. 1939, married to Prince Charles Hugues de Bourbon-Parma on 29 April 1964 (*sons:* Prince Carlos Javier Bernardo, born 27 Jan. 1970; Prince Jaime Bernardo, born 13 Oct. 1972; *daughters:* Princess Margarita Maria Beatriz, born 13 Oct. 1972; Princess Maria Carolina Christina, born 23 June 1974); Princess Margriet Francisca, born in Ottawa, 19 Jan. 1943, married to Pieter van Vollenhoven on 10 Jan. 1967 (*sons:* Prince Maurits, born 17 April 1968; Prince Bernhard, born 25 Dec. 1969; Prince Pieter-Christiaan, born 22 March 1972; Prince Floris, born 10 April 1975); Princess Maria Christina, born 18 Feb. 1947, married to Jorge Guillermo on 28 June 1975 (*son:* Bernardo, born 17 June 1977).

CONSTITUTION AND GOVERNMENT. According to the Constitution of the Kingdom of the Netherlands, the Kingdom consists of the Netherlands and the Netherlands Antilles. Their relations are regulated by the 'Statute' for the Kingdom, which came into force on 29 Dec. 1954. Each part enjoys full autonomy; they are united, on a footing of equality, for mutual assistance and the protection of their common interests.

The first Constitution of the Netherlands after its restoration as a Sovereign State was promulgated in 1814. It was revised in 1815 (after the addition of the Belgian provinces, and the assumption by the Sovereign of the title of King), 1840 (after the secession of the Belgian provinces), 1848, 1884, 1887, 1917, 1922, 1938, 1946, 1948, 1953, 1956, 1963 and 1972.

The Netherlands is a constitutional and hereditary monarchy. The royal succession is in the direct male line in the order of primogeniture; in default of male heirs, the female line ascends the throne. The Sovereign comes of age on reaching his 18th year. During his minority the royal power is vested in a Regent—designated by law—and in some cases in the Council of State.

The central executive power of the State rests with the Crown, while the central legislative power is vested in the Crown and Parliament (the *Staten-Generaal*), consisting of 2 Chambers. After the 1956 revision of the Constitution the Upper or First Chamber is composed of 75 members, elected by the members of the Provincial States, and the Second Chamber consists of 150 deputies, who are elected directly. Members of the States-General must be Netherlanders or recognized as Netherlands subjects and 25 years of age or over; they may be men or women. They receive an allowance.

First Chamber (as constituted in 1977): Labour Party, 25; Christian Democrats, 24; Party for Freedom and Democracy, 15; Radicals, 5; Communists, 2; Political Calvinist Party, 1; Farmers' Party, 1; Calvinist Political Association, 1; Pacifist Socialists, 1.

Second Chamber (elected on 25 May 1977): Labour Party, 53; Christian Democrats, 49; Party for Freedom and Democracy, 28; Democrats 1966, 8; Radicals, 3; Farmers' Party, 1; Democratic Socialists, 1970, 1; Pacifist Socialist Party, 1; Political Calvinist Party, 3; Communists, 2; Calvinist Political Association, 1.

The revised Constitution of 1917 has introduced an electoral system based on universal suffrage and proportional representation. Under its provisions, members of the Second Chamber are directly elected by citizens of both sexes who are Netherlands subjects not under 18 years (since 1972). Criminals, lunatics and certain others are disqualified; for certain crimes and misdemeanours there may be temporary disqualification.

The members of the Second Chamber are elected for 4 years, and retire in a body, whereas the First Chamber is elected for 6 years, and every 3 years one-half retires by rotation. The Sovereign has the power to dissolve both Chambers of Parliament, or one of them, subject to the condition that new elections take place within 40 days, and the new House or Houses be convoked within 3 months.

The Sovereign and the Second Chamber may propose Bills; the First Chamber can only approve or reject them without inserting amendments. The meetings of both Chambers are public, though each of them may by a majority vote decide on a secret session. It is a fixed custom, that Ministers and Secretaries of State, on their own initiative or upon invitation of the Parliament, attend the sessions to defend their policy, their budget, their proposals of Bills, etc., when these are in discussion. A Minister or Secretary of State, however, cannot be a member of Parliament at the same time.

The Constitution can be revised only by a Bill declaring that there is reason for introducing such revision and containing the proposed alterations. The passing of this Bill is followed by a dissolution of both Chambers and a second confirmation by the new States-General by two-thirds of the votes. Unless it is expressly stated, all laws concern only the realm in Europe, and not the overseas parts of the kingdom.

Every act of the Sovereign has to be covered by a responsible Minister.

The Ministry was composed as follows in March 1980:

Prime Minister, Minister of General Affairs: Andreas van Agt (CDA).
Deputy Prime Minister, Minister of the Interior: Hans Wiegel (VVD). *Foreign Affairs:* Christoph van der Klaauw (VVD). *Justice:* Job de Ruiter (CDA). *Education and Science:* Arie Pais (VVD). *Finance:* Fons van der Stee (CDA). *Economic Affairs:* Gijsbert van Aardenne (VVD). *Social Affairs:* Willem Albeda (CDA). *Housing and Planning:* Pieter Beelaerts van Blokland (CDA). *Defence:* Willem Scholten. *Agriculture and Fisheries, Antilles Affairs:* Alfons van der Stee (CDA). *Culture, Recreation and Social Work:* Mathilda Gardeniers-Berendsen (CDA). *Public Health and Environment:* Leendert Ginjaar (VVD). *Transport and Public Works:* Daniel Tuynman (VVD). *Minister without Portfolio for Development Aid:* Jan de Koning (CDA). *Minister without Portfolio for Science Policy:* Anton van Trier.

There are also 16 state secretaries (10 from CDA and 6 from VVD).

The Council of State (*Raad van State*), appointed and presided over by the Sovereign, is composed of a vice-president and not more than 16 members. It can be consulted on all legislative matters. Decisions of the Crown in administrative disputes are prepared by a special committee of the Council.

The Hague is the seat of the Court, Government and Parliament.

National flag: Three horizontal stripes of red, white, blue.

National anthem: Wilhelmus van Nassouen (words by Philip Marnix van St Aldegonde, c. 1570).

Local Government. The kingdom is divided in 11 provinces and about 840 municipalities. Each province has its own representative body, the Provincial States. The members are elected for 4 years, directly from the Netherlands inhabitants of the province who are 21 years of age. The electoral register is the same as for the Second Chamber. The members retire in a body and are subject to re-election. The number of members varies according to the population of the province, from 83 for South Holland to 43 for Zeeland. The Provincial States are entitled to issue ordinances concerning the welfare of the province, and to raise taxes pursuant to legal provisions. The provincial budgets and the provincial ordinances and resolutions relating to provincial property, loans, taxes, etc., must be approved by the Crown. The members of the Provincial States elect the First Chamber of the States-General. They meet twice a year, as a rule in public. A permanent commission composed of 6 of their members, called the 'Deputy States', is charged with the executive power and, if required, with the enforcement of the law in the province. Deputy as well as Provincial States are presided over by a Commissioner of the Sovereign, who in the former assembly has a deciding vote, but attends the latter in only a deliberative capacity. He is the chief magistrate in the province. The Commissioner and the members of the Deputy States receive an allowance.

Each municipality forms a Corporation with its own interests and rights, subject to the general law, and is governed by a Municipal Council, directly elected for 4 years, by the electorate registered for the Provincial States, provided they are residents of the municipality. All Netherlands inhabitants 21 years of age are eligible, the number of members varying from 7 to 45, according to the population. The Municipal Council has the right to issue bye-laws concerning the communal welfare. The Council may levy taxes pursuant to legal provisions; these ordinances must be approved by the Crown. All bye-laws may be vetoed by the Crown. The Municipal Budget and resolutions to alienate municipal property require the approbation of the Deputy States of the province. The Council meets in public as often as may be necessary, and is presided over by a Burgomaster, appointed by the Sovereign. The day-to-day administration is carried out by the Burgomaster and 2–7 Aldermen (*wethouders*), elected by and from the Council; this body is also charged with the enforcement of the law. The Burgomaster may suspend the execution of a resolution of the council for 30 days, but is bound to notify the Deputy States of the province. In maintaining public order, the Burgomaster acts as the chief of police. The Burgomaster and Aldermen receive allowances.

DEFENCE. The Netherlands are bordered on the south by Belgium, on the east by the Federal Republic of Germany. On both sides the country is quite level and has no natural defences, except the barriers of some large rivers, running east to west and south to north. The country has an excellent roadnet and a vast railway system, enabling rapid movement. The west part of the country is densely populated.

Army. Service is partly voluntary and partly compulsory; the voluntary enlistments bear a small proportion to the compulsory. The total peacetime strength amounts to 72,000, including Military Police. The number of regulars is 24,000 (officers, n.c.o.s and technical specialists). The technical specialists serve for a period of 4–6 years and receive military and vocational training. On completing the latter training they will be given an official civilian certificate. The Army also employs 13,500 civilians. The legal period of active service for national servicemen is 22–24 months; the actual service period is 14 months for enlisted personnel and 16 months for reserve-officers and n.c.o.s. The balance may be spent at will as 'short-term leave'. After their period of actual service the conscript personnel are granted long-term leave.

However, they will be liable to being called up for refresher training or in case of mobilization until they have reached the age of 35 (n.c.o.s 40, reserve officers 45).

The Netherlands have the 1st Netherlands Army Corps assigned to NATO. It consists of active and mobilizable units.

The active part of the Corps comprises 2 armoured brigades, 4 armoured infantry brigades and 40% of the Corps troops (headquarters, combat-support and service-support units); the brigades and the division-type headquarters may be grouped into 2 mechanized divisions. Part of this force is stationed in the Federal Republic of Germany. The peacetime strength of the active brigades is 80% of the war-authorized strength.

The mobilizable part of the Corps comprises 1 mechanized infantry division, 1 independent infantry brigade and the remaining Corps troops.

The mechanized units comprise tank battalions (Leopard and Centurion), armoured infantry battalions, heavy (175 mm) and medium (155 mm and 105 mm) artillery battalions (mainly self-propelled), armoured engineer units, armoured reconnaissance units and armoured tank-destroyer units. Helicopter squadrons are also available.

The National Territorial Command forces consist of territorial units, security forces, some logistical units and staffs. The major part of the national logistic units is placed under the National Logistic Command. In event of mobilization, territorial brigades with support and logistical units are called up. Some units in the Netherlands are earmarked for assignment to the United Nations as peace-keeping forces. A group of officers is permanently attached to the UN Truce Supervision Organization force in the Middle East. For civil defence purposes there are a number of military (mobilizable) fire-fighting, rescue and medical battalions. In time of war these units turn to the command of the National Commander of the Civil Defence.

Navy. The Royal Netherlands Navy has its main base in the Netherlands at Den Helder and minor bases at Flushing and Curaçao (Netherlands Antilles).

Principal surface ships of the Royal Netherlands Navy:

Completed	Name	Standard displacement (tons)	Shaft horse-power	Max. speed (knots)
1975	Tromp ⎫	4,300	50,000	30
1976	De Ruyter ⎭			

There are also 6 diesel-electric patrol submarines, 4 general-purpose missile-armed frigates, 4 destroyers, 6 anti-submarine missile-armed frigates, 2 fast combat support ships, 6 corvettes, 3 mine countermeasures support ships (ex-ocean mine-sweepers), 11 coastal minesweepers, 4 coastal minehunters, 3 diving vessels, 16 in-shore minesweepers, 1 torpedo maintenance vessel (ex-ocean minesweeper), 5 patrol vessels, 3 hydrographic survey ships, 10 landing craft, 2 training ships 11 tugs and 59 small auxiliary ships.

Nine missile armed general purpose frigates and 2 diesel-electric patrol submarines are under construction. The future construction programme includes 15 mine countermeasure vessels, in close co-operation with Belgium and France.

On 1 Jan. 1980 naval personnel provided for totalled 16,900 officers and other ranks, including the Naval Air Service and the Royal Netherlands Marine Corps.

The naval air service maintains 12 Lockheed Neptunes (SP-2H), 7 Breguet Atlantics (SP-13A), 6 Westland Lynx and 10 Westland Wasp helicopters. 16 Lynx helicopters for delivery in 1980 were ordered to replace the Wasp helicopters and to augment the anti-submarine warfare capacity. 13 P3C Orion maritime patrol aircraft, for delivery from 1981 onwards, are ordered to replace the Neptune aircraft.

Naval estimates (in 1m. guilders): 1973, 1,254; 1974, 1,362; 1975, 1,618; 1976, 1,683; 1977, 1,885; 1978, 2,069; 1979, 2,075; 1980, 2,006; 1981, 2,218.

Air Force. The Royal Netherlands Air Force was established 1 July 1913. Its current strength is approximately 19,000 personnel and it has a first-line combat force of 9 squadrons of aircraft and 12 squadrons of surface-to-air missiles. All squadrons are operated by Tactical Air Command. Aircraft operated are F-104G Starfighter (2 squadrons air defence, 2 squadrons ground attack), RF-104 (1 squadron for tactical reconnaissance) and NF-5A/B fighter-bombers (4 squadrons). The F-104s are being replaced with F-16s. Also under control of Tactical Air Command is 1 squadron of the USAF, flying F-15C Eagles in the air defence role. Other aircraft operated by the RNethAF are 3 squadrons of Alouette III and Bölkow BO 105C helicopters; these are under control of the Royal Netherlands Army, but flown and maintained by the RNethAF for use in the communications and observation roles. Also operated is 1 squadron of F.27 Friendship/Troopship transport aircraft.

Training of RNethAF pilots is undertaken in Canada and the USA. The 12 squadrons of surface-to-air missiles consist of 4 squadrons of Nike Hercules (high altitude) and 8 squadrons of Hawk (low and medium altitude).

INTERNATIONAL RELATIONS

Membership. The Netherlands is a member of UN, EEC, OECD, the Council of Europe and NATO.

ECONOMY

Budget. The revenue and expenditure of the central government (ordinary and extraordinary) were, in 1m. guilders, for calendar years:

	1975[2]	1976[2]	1977[3]	1978[3]	1979[4]	1980[4]	1981[6]
Revenue[1]	61,752	74,206	84,513	93,015	101,106	112,271	117,148
Expenditure[5]	69,420	83,046	91,014	101,980	109,750	127,201	130,153

[1] Without the revenue of loans. [2] Accounts. [3] Preliminary accounts.
[4] Revised budget figures. [5] Without redemption of loans. [6] Budget figures.

The revenue and expenditure of the Agriculture Equalization Fund, the Fund for Central Government roads, the Property Acquisition Fund (established in 1971), the Fund for the Development of a Fast Breeder Reactor (established in 1972) and of the Investment Account Fund (established in 1978) have been incorporated in the general budget.

The national debt, in 1m. guilders, was on 31 Dec.:

	1974	1975	1976	1977	1978	1979
Internal funded debt	29,880	34,765	40,983	47,029	55,180	64,086
„ floating „	11,411	12,000	14,023	14,683	17,356	20,314
External funded „	23	12	...	...	...	...
Total	41,314	46,777	55,006	61,712	72,537	84,400

Currency. The monetary unit is the *gulden* (guilder, florin) of 100 *cents*. In March 1981 the rate of exchange was US$1 = 2·34 guilders; £1 = 5·18 guilders.

Legal tender are bank-notes, silver 10-guilder pieces, nickel 2½- and 1-guilder pieces, 25-cent, 10-cent pieces, bronze 5-cent and 1-cent pieces. Note circulation, 31 Dec. 1978, 18,701m. guilders and 31 Dec. 1979, 20,016m.

Banking. The Netherlands Bank, founded as a private institution, was nationalized on 1 Aug. 1948, the shareholders receiving, for a share of 1,000 guilders, a security of 2,000 guilders on the 2½% National Debt. Since 1863 the bank has the sole right of issuing bank-notes. The bank does the same business as other banks, but with more guarantees. The capital amounts to 20m. guilders.

In the year 1976 the state post office savings bank had deposits of 4,055m. guilders and withdrawals of 3,532m. guilders. Private savings banks: Deposits, 8,551m. guilders; withdrawals, 8,136m. guilders.

Weights and Measures. The metric system of weights and measures was adopted in the Netherlands in 1820.

ENERGY AND NATURAL RESOURCES

Electricity. The total production of electrical energy (in 1m. kwh.) amounted in 1938 to 3,688; 1958, 13,854; 1970, 40,859; 1976, 58,138; 1977, 58,285; 1978, 61,596; 1979, 64,464.

Gas. Production of manufactured gas (milliard k joule): 1976, 181,259; 1977, 160,953; 1978, 181,033; 1979, 233,553. Production of natural gas in 1950, 8m. cu. metres; 1955, 139; 1960, 384; 1970, 31,688; 1976, 97,302; 1977, 96,889; 1978, 88,730; 1979, 96,488.

Minerals. On 1 Jan. 1975 all coalmines were closed.

The production of crude petroleum (in 1,000 tonnes) amounted in 1943 (first year) to 0·2; 1953, 820; 1970, 1,919; 1974, 1,461; 1975, 1,419; 1976, 1,371; 1977, 1,382; 1978, 1,402; 1979, 1,316.

There are saltmines at Hengelo and Delfzijl; production (in 1,000 tonnes), 1950, 412·6; 1960, 1,096; 1970, 2,871; 1974, 3,387; 1975, 2,690; 1976, 3,026; 1977, 3,111; 1978, 2,939; 1979, 3,951.

Agriculture. The net area of all holdings was divided as follows (in hectares):

	1976[1]	1977[1]	1978[1]	1979[1]	1980[1]
Field crops	683,315	698,474	698,518	700,126	704,710
Grass	1,270,103	1,238,984	1,221,458	1,212,634	1,197,592
Market gardening	91,894	95,269	96,218	89,706	87,121
Land for flower bulbs	12,743	12,927	13,498	13,949	14,307
Flower cultivation	4,248	4,315	4,548	4,829	5,180
Nurseries	5,360	5,513	5,924	6,049	6,228
Fallow land	5,442	4,798	5,255	6,190	5,099
Total	2,073,105	2,060,280	2,045,419	2,033,483	2,020,237

[1] Excluding holdings of less than 10 SFU (SFU = standard farm unit). 10 SFU is equal to a computed net value added at factor cost of about 2,000 guilders, in 1968.

The net areas [1] under special crops were as follows (in hectares):

Products	1979	1980	Products	1979	1980
Autumn wheat	125,542	128,144	Colza	6,885	7,939
Spring wheat	15,195	14,117	Flax	3,605	4,058
Rye	12,323	9,744	Agricultural seeds	17,436	19,710
Autumn barley	11,215	12,306	Potatoes, edible[2]	97,393	102,191
Spring barley	51,809	41,119	Potatoes, industrial[3]	68,896	70,623
Oats	20,875	18,119	Sugar-beet	123,576	120,647
Peas	4,065	4,025	Fodder-beet	1,720	1,667

[1] Excluding non-agrarian holdings of less than 10 SFU.
[2] Including early and seed potatoes.
[3] Including seed potatoes.

The yield of the more important products, in tonnes, was as follows:

Crop	Average 1940–49	Average 1950–58	1977[1]	1978[1]	1979
Wheat	322,003	348,464	661,173	792,238	835,593
Rye	439,055	454,992	73,541	67,713	49,288
Barley	145,892	258,049	286,554	355,048	287,729
Oats	315,642	464,041	94,152	140,073	109,030
Field beans	15,799	5,693	...	...	...
Peas	65,460	93,664	13,232	18,360	14,407
Colza	24,763	18,358	30,401	23,431	18,093
Flax, unrippled	82,906	138,165	43,699	42,960	28,575
Potatoes, edible[2]	2,861,793	2,745,505	3,233,352	3,396,680	3,504,128
Potatoes, industrial	1,242,326	1,003,994	2,518,693	2,834,044	2,772,710
Sugar-beet	1,667,711	2,935,881	6,016,635	6,323,872	5,491,283
Fodder-beet	...	...	210,265	168,532	135,811

[1] Excluding holdings of less than 10 SFU.   [2] Including early potatoes.

Livestock, May 1980: 5,225,857 cattle, 10,137,516 pigs; 46,802 horses, 3 years old and over, 858,084 sheep, 81·2m. poultry.

In 1979 the production of butter, under state control, amounted to 202,686 tonnes; that of cheese, under state control, to 424,606 tonnes. Export value of arable crops amounted to 11,684m. guilders; animal produce, 12,250m. guilders and horticultural produce, 5,669m. guilders.

Fisheries. The total produce of fish landed from the sea and inshore fisheries in 1979 was valued at 471m. guilders; the total weight amounted to 292,774 tonnes. In 1979 the herring fishery had a value of 8m. guilders and a weight of 3,160 tonnes. The quantity of oysters produced in 1979 amounted to 1,075 tonnes (15m. guilders).

INDUSTRY AND TRADE

Industry. Numbers employed (in 1,000) and turnover (in 1m. guilders) in manufacturing enterprises with 10 employees and more, excluding building:

Class in industry	Numbers employed		Turnover	
	1977	1978	1977	1978
Mining and quarrying	6·9	6·8	14,080	13,890
Manufacturing industry	934·0	907·7	162,410	166,180
Foodstuffs and tobacco products	151·3	148·3	47,110	48,700
Textile industry	43·0	37·8	4,310	4,360
Clothing	22·6	20·9	1,850	1,880
Leather and footwear	9·0	8·4	740	740
Wood and furniture industry	37·1	36·5	3,790	3,820
Paper industry	28·2	26·8	3,940	3,960
Graphic industry, publishers	60·8	62·5	7,460	8,220
Petroleum industry	10·2	9·7	14,770	14,260
Chemical industry, artificial yarns and fibre industry	88·8	86·4	20,480	21,240
Rubber and synthetic materials processing industry	25·4	24·7	3,230	3,200
Building materials, earthenware and glass	38·1	37·2	4,660	4,970
Basic metal industry	37·5	36·4	6,540	6,630
Metals products (excl. machinery and means of transport)	86·7	84·0	9,070	9,020
Machinery	87·5	84·6	9,480	9,600
Electrical industry	114·8	114·4	13,740	14,830
Means of transport	77·6	73·8	9,410	8,810
Instrument making and optical industry	10·2	10·0	1,360	1,430
Other industries	5·3	5·4	480	510
Public utilities	44·7	44·9	11,000	12,050

Commerce. On 5 Sept. 1944 and 14 March 1947 the Netherlands signed agreements with Belgium and Luxembourg for the establishment of a customs union. On 1 Jan. 1948 this union came into force and the existing customs tariffs of the Belgium–Luxembourg Economic Union and of the Netherlands were superseded by the joint Benelux Customs Union Tariff. It applies to imports into the 3 countries from outside sources, and exempts from customs duties all imports into each of the 3 countries from the other two. The Benelux tariff has 991 items and 2,400 separate specifications.

Returns of special imports and special exports (including parcel post and diamond trade, excluding unrefined and partly-worked gold, gold coins and coins in current circulation made of other metal) for calendar years (in 1,000 guilders):

	Imports	Exports		Imports	Exports
1949	5,331,569	3,851,126	1976 [1]	104,249,868	106,016,987
1959	14,968,454	13,702,927	1977 [1]	111,973,874	107,195,386
1969	39,955,406	36,205,110	1978 [1]	114,371,926	108,205,427
1975 [1]	88,010,009	88,655,462	1979 [1]	134,828,391	127,630,182

[1] Including unrefined and partly worked gold and gold coins.

Value of the trade (including parcel post and diamond trade, excluding unrefined and partly-worked gold, gold coins and coins in current circulation made of other metal) with leading countries (in 1,000 guilders):

Country	Imports			Exports		
	1977	1978	1979	1977	1978	1979
Belgium–Luxembourg	13,362,547	14,392,353	16,445,112	15,719,097	16,088,356	19,773,617
France	7,856,630	8,643,207	9,836,507	11,252,722	11,589,705	13,598,728
Germany (Fed. Rep.)	27,423,198	29,041,970	32,664,727	33,089,255	33,344,416	38,922,380
Indonesia	510,162	403,715	527,885	624,142	476,297	408,810
Italy	3,903,487	4,326,903	4,910,921	5,120,554	5,389,766	6,721,876
Kuwait	1,776,912	1,561,430	2,852,928	196,335	149,041	169,820
Sweden	2,028,181	2,148,631	2,600,676	2,210,127	1,825,091	2,346,703

Country	Imports 1977	1978	1979	Exports 1977	1978	1979
UK	7,503,661	7,659,985	10,343,796	8,007,356	8,099,438	10,735,460
USA	9,546,466	9,845,452	11,351,673	3,674,724	3,581,505	3,578,672
Venezuela	75,421	92,079	170,088	283,428	294,403	267,075

Total trade between the Netherlands and UK (British Department of Trade returns, in £1,000 sterling):

	1976	1977	1978	1979	1980
Imports to UK	2,427,921	2,491,986	2,524,634	3,446,271	3,406,928
Exports and re-exports from UK	1,500,350	2,138,789	2,255,980	3,062,642	3,845,412

Tourism. There were 2·87m. foreign visitors in 1978 (hotels and boarding houses only). Total income from tourism (1979) US$1,311m.

COMMUNICATIONS

Roads. In 1978 the length of the Netherlands network of surfaced inter-urban roads was 52,677 km, of which 1,700 km were motor highways. Buses and trams transported in 1979, 953m. passengers, 642m. of them in local traffic. Number of private cars (1979), 4·18m.

Railways. All railways are run by the mixed company 'N.V. Nederlandsche Spoorwegen'. Length of line in 1979 was 2,880 km, of which 1,759 km were electrified. Passengers carried (1979), 187m.; goods transported, 21·8m. tonnes.

Aviation. The Royal Dutch Airlines (KLM) was founded on 7 Oct. 1919. The company has a paid-up capital of 799m. guilders (1979–80). Revenue traffic, 1979–80: Passengers, 4·4m.; freight, 218m. kg; mail, 10m. kg.

Sea-going Shipping. Survey of the Netherlands mercantile marine as at 1 Jan. (capacity in 1,000 GRT):

Ships under Netherlands flag (including Netherlands Antilles)	1979 Number	Capacity	1980 Number	Capacity
Passenger ships[1]	8	109	8	109
Freighters (500 GRT and over)	439	2,384	464	2,603
Freighters (under 500 GRT)	105	47	86	38
Tankers	82	2,221	82	2,345
	634	4,761	640	5,095

[1] With accommodation for 13 or more cabin passengers.

In 1979, 43,063 sea-going ships of 355·1m. gross tons entered Netherlands ports (1978, 43,531 ships of 328·5m. gross tons).

Total goods traffic by sea-going ships in 1979 (with 1978 figures in brackets), in 1m. tonnes, amounted to 274·3 (246·5) unloaded, of which 153 (138·1) tankshipping, and 84·5 (73) loaded, of which 44·3 (31·4) tankshipping. The total seaborne freight traffic at Rotterdam was 292m. (264m.) and at Amsterdam 19·8m. (17m.) tonnes.

The number of containers at Rotterdam in 1979 was: unloaded from ships, 587,400, of which 195,600 from North America, and 599,300 loaded into ships, of which 137,300 to North America.

Inland Shipping. The total length of navigable rivers and canals is 4,387 km, of which about 1,974 km is for ships with a capacity of 1,000 and more tonnes. On 1 Jan. 1979 the Netherlands inland fleet actually used for transport (with carrying capacity in 1,000 tonnes) was composed as follows:

	Number	Capacity
Self-propelled barges	5,738	3,615
Dumb barges	514	577
Pushed barges	379	648
	6,631	4,840

In 1979, 268m. (1978: 278m.) tonnes of goods were transported on rivers and canals, of which 181m. (185m.) was international traffic. Goods transport on the

Rhine across the Dutch–German frontier near Lobith amounted to 133m. (140m.) tonnes.

Post and Broadcasting. On 1 Jan. 1980 there were 6·8m. telephone connexions (48·3 per 100 inhabitants). Number of telex lines, 31,429; teleprinters, 33,424. *Nederlandse Omroep Stichting* (NOS) provides 4 programmes on medium-waves and FM in co-operation with broadcasting organizations. Regional programmes are also broadcast.

Advertisements are transmitted. NOS broadcasts 2 TV programmes. Advertisements (31 Dec. 1979) are restricted to 217 minutes weekly. Television sets (1 Aug. 1980) totalled 4·2m.; holders of television licences may, in addition, have wireless receiving sets.

Cinemas (end 1979). There were 507 cinemas with a seating capacity of 158,000.

Newspapers (31 Dec. 1979). There were 91 daily newspapers with a total circulation of over 4·6m.

JUSTICE, RELIGION, EDUCATION AND WELFARE

Justice. Justice is administered by the High Court of the Netherlands (Court of Cassation), by 5 courts of justice (Courts of Appeal), by 19 district courts and by 62 cantonal courts; trial by jury is unknown. The Cantonal Court, which deals with minor offences, is formed by a single judge; the more serious cases are tried by the district courts, formed as a rule by 3 judges (in some cases one judge is sufficient); the courts of appeal are constituted of 3 and the High Court of 5 judges. All judges are appointed for life by the Sovereign (the judges of the High Court from a list prepared by the Second Chamber of the States-General). They can be removed only by a decision of the High Court.

At the district court the juvenile judge is specially appointed to try children's civil cases and at the same time charged with administration of justice for criminal actions committed by young persons between 12 and 18 years old, unless imprisonment of 6 months or more ought to be inflicted; such cases are tried by 3 judges.

Number of persons convicted including those who paid a fine to the public prosecutor to evade prosecution (tax offenders excluded):

Major offences	1975	1976	1977	Minor offences	1977	1978	1979
Males	46,183	49,904	53,386	Males	1,558,106	1,519,822	1,298,410
Females	3,573	3,785	4,082	Females	254,589	235,786	201,720

In addition, prosecution was evaded by paying a fine to the police in 926,415 cases in 1976, 1,003,717 in 1977, 1,206,142 in 1978 and 1,159,025 in 1979.

Police. There are both State and Municipal Police. The State Police, about 7,400 men strong, serves 680, and the Municipal Police, about 18,800 men strong, serves 140 municipalities. The State Police includes ordinary as well as water, mounted and motor police. The State Police Corps is under the jurisdiction of the Police Department of the Ministry of Justice, which also includes the Central Criminal Investigation Office, which deals with serious crimes throughout the country, and the International Criminal Investigation Office, which informs foreign countries of international crimes.

Religion. Entire liberty of conscience is granted to the members of all denominations. The royal family belong to the Dutch Reformed Church.

The number of adherents of the Churches according to the census of 1971 was: Dutch Reformed Church, 3,075,565; Reformed Churches (excluding other reformed denominations), 937,840; Roman Catholics, 5,273,665; other creeds (including other reformed denominations), 694,405; no religion, 3,078,640; total, 13,060,115.

The government of the Reformed Church is Presbyterian. On 1 July 1972 the Dutch Reformed Church had 1 synod, 11 provincial districts, 54 classes, 147 districts and 1,905 parishes.

Their clergy numbered 2,000. The Roman Catholic Church had, Jan. 1973, 1 archbishop (of Utrecht), 6 bishops and 1,815 parishes and rectorships. The Old Catholics had (1 July 1972) 1 archbishop (Utrecht), 2 bishops and 29 parishes. The Jews had, in 1970, 46 communities.

Education. Statistics for the scholastic year 1978–79:

	Full-time			Part-time[1]		
		Pupils			Pupils	
	Schools	Total	Female	Schools	Total	Female
Nursery schools	7,897	438,175	213,451	—	—	—
Primary Schools	8,690	1,413,277	696,244	—	—	—
Special schools	939	87,253	27,567	—	—	—
Secondary general schools	1,530	820,634	417,237	77	65,983	45,859
Secondary vocational schools:						
Junior—						
Technical, nautical	387	198,520	8,555	...[1]	126,301[1]	34,987[1]
Agricultural	130	27,181	5,053	237	4,249	874
Domestic science	583	134,590	131,701	41	2,172	2,165
Other	191	49,035	25,606	15	578	2
Senior—						
Technical, nautical	122	53,005	2,985	68	6,161	184
Agricultural	48	11,687	1,513	24	1,209	105
Domestic science	203	37,918	36,536	18	3,524	3,473
Teachers' training (nursery						
schools)	50	8,877	8,816	49	4,158	4,142
Other	124	35,437	14,456	84	15,828	11,929
Third level non-university						
training:						
Technical, nautical	61	31,208	3,377	41	4,523	405
Agricultural	14	4,194	593	—	—	—
Arts	37	10,628	4,888	23	3,722	1,312
Teachers' training:						
Primary schools	91	22,167	12,927	—	—	—
Secondary general schools	30	20,658	9,083	96	29,920	14,955
Secondary vocational schools	16	363	290	34	5,361	721
Other	99	37,672	20,697	54	15,392	7,368

[1] Including apprenticeship schemes, young workers' educational institutes.

Full-time: 1979–80 [1]

		Pupils	
	Schools	Total	Female
University education:			
Humanities		27,394	12,934
Social sciences		63,455	20,741
Natural sciences	14	15,827	2,956
Technical sciences		17,778	870
Medical sciences		17,825	5,046
Agricultural sciences		5,311	1,381

[1] Provisional figures.

Health. On 1 Jan. 1980 there were 25,947 doctors and 73,008 hospital beds.

DIPLOMATIC REPRESENTATIVES

OF THE NETHERLANDS IN GREAT BRITAIN
(38 Hyde Park Gate, London, SW7 5DP)

Ambassador: Robbert Fack.

OF GREAT BRITAIN IN THE NETHERLANDS
(Lange Voorhout, 10, The Hague)

Ambassador: Sir Jock Taylor, KCMG.

OF THE NETHERLANDS IN THE USA (4200 Linnean Ave., NW,
Washington, D.C., 20008)

Ambassador: A. R. Tammenoms Bakker.

OF THE USA IN THE NETHERLANDS (Lange Voorhout, 102, The Hague)

Ambassador: G. M. Joseph.

OF THE NETHERLANDS TO THE UNITED NATIONS

Ambassador: Hugo Scheltema.

Books of Reference

Statistical Information: The 'Centraal Bureau voor de Statistiek' at Voorburg, near The Hague, is the official Netherlands statistical service. *Director-General of Statistics:* Prof. Dr W. Begeer.

The Bureau was founded in 1899. Prior to that year, statistical publications were compiled by the 'Centrale commissie voor de statistiek', the 'Vereniging voor staathuishoudkunde en statistiek' and various government departments. These activities have gradually been taken over and co-ordinated by the Central Bureau, which now compiles practically all government statistics.

Its current publications include:

Statistical Yearbook of the Netherlands. From 1923/24 (preceded by *Jaarciifers voor het Koninkrijk der Nederlanden, 1898–1922*); latest issue, 1979

Statistisch zakboek (Pocket Year Book). From 1899/1924 (1 vol.); latest issue, 1979

Maandstatistiek van de buitenlandse handel (monthly statistical bulletin of foreign trade). From 1917

Nationale Rekeningen (National Accounts). From 1948–50; latest issue, 1979

Uitkomsten van de 14^e Algemene volkstelling, annex woningtelling, 28 Feb. 1971 (Results of the Fourteenth Census, Population and Housing, 28 Feb. 1971)

Statistische onderzoekingen (Statistical Studies). From 1977

Other Official Publications

Central Economic Plan. Centraal Plan-bureau, The Hague (Dutch text), annually, from 1946

Netherlands. Organization for Economic Co-operation and Development. Paris, annual from 1964

Staatsalmanak voor het Koninkrijk der Nederlanden. Annual. The Hague, from 1814

Staatsblad van het Koninkrijk der Nederlanden. The Hague, from 1814

Staatscourant (State Gazette). The Hague, from 1813

Atlas van Nederland. Government Printing Office, The Hague, 1970 and supplements up to and including 1973

De Nederlandse Economie in 1980. Centraal Planbureau, The Hague, 1976

Memoranda on the Condition of the Netherlands State Finances. Ministry of Finance, The Hague, from 1906

Basic Guide to the Establishing of Industrial Operations in the Netherlands 1976. Ministry of Economic Affairs, The Hague, 1976

The Kingdom of the Netherlands. Ministry of Foreign Affairs, The Hague, 1974–75

Huggett, F. E., *The Dutch Today.* Ministry of Foreign Affairs, The Hague, 1973

Aspects of Dutch Agriculture. Ministry of Agriculture and Fisheries, The Hague, 1976

Non-Official Publications

Huggett, F. E., *The Modern Netherlands.* London, 1971

Jansonius, H., *Groot Nederlands–Engels Woordenboek Voor Studie en Praktijk.* 3 vols. Leiden, 1972 (Vols. 1 and 2)

Newton, G., *The Netherlands: An Historical and Cultural Survey, 1795–1977.* Boulder, 1978

Pinder, D., *The Netherlands.* Folkestone, 1976

Veldman, J., *Agriculture in the Netherlands.* Utrecht, 1974

Pyttersen's Nederlandse Almanak. Zaltbommel, annual, from 1899

Commerce and Industry in the Netherlands. Amsterdam–Rotterdam Bank. Amsterdam, 1977

Foreign Investment in the Netherlands. The Hague, 1975

The Information You Need When Planning a Business in the Netherlands. Algemene Bank Nederland. Amsterdam, 1975

A Compact Geography of the Netherlands. Utrecht, 1974

De Economische Geschiedenis van Nederland. Groningen, 1977

Netherlands and Netherlands Antilles 1977. Rotterdam, 1977

National Library: De Koninklijke Bibliotheek, Lange Voorhout 34, The Hague. *Director:* Dr C. Reedijk.

THE NETHERLANDS ANTILLES

De Nederlandse Antillen

AREA AND POPULATION. The Netherlands Antilles are an integral part of the Netherlands and comprises two groups of islands, viz., the Leeward Islands, Curaçao, Aruba and Bonaire, and the Windward Islands, St Maarten, St Eustatius and Saba. The Leeward Islands are situated 40–70 miles north of the Venezuelan coast between 12° and 13° N. lat. and 68° and 71° W. long. The Windward group lies east of Puerto Rico. For the constitutional position of the Netherlands Antilles *see* p. 889. The total area is 993 sq. km (383 sq. miles) and the population was 256,000 in 1979.

Leeward group	Sq. km	Popula-tion	Windward group	Sq. km	Popula-tion
Curaçao	444	160,625	St Maarten (St Martin) [1]	34	11,379
Aruba	193	62,288	St Eustatius	21	1,355
Bonaire	288	8,845	Saba	13	979

[1] The southern part belongs to the Netherlands Antilles, the northern to France.

The capital is Willemstad on Curaçao, population (1970) 50,000.

In 1972, 4,941 births, 1,138 deaths, 1,471 marriages and 350 divorces were registered.

GOVERNMENT. Since Dec. 1954, the Netherlands Antilles have been fully autonomous in internal affairs, and constitutionally equal with the Netherlands and Surinam. The Sovereign of the Kingdom of the Netherlands is Head of the Government of the Netherlands Antilles and is represented by a Governor.

The executive power in internal affairs rests with the Governor and the Council of Ministers, who together form the Government. The Ministers are responsible to the unicameral legislature (*Staten*). This consists of 22 members (12 from Curaçao, 8 from Aruba, 1 from Bonaire, 1 from the Windward Islands) and is elected by general suffrage. It was agreed in 1977 that the 2 smallest islands, Saba and St Eustatius would each have a representative (non-voting) in the *Staten*.

The executive power in external affairs is vested in the Council of Ministers of the Kingdom, in which the Antilles is represented by a Minister Plenipotentiary with full voting powers.

In 1951 the Netherlands Antilles Islands Regulation provided for self-government of each of the 4 insular communities Aruba, Bonaire, Curaçao and the Windward Islands. The autonomous powers of the insular communities are divided between the Island Council (elected by general suffrage), the Executive Council and the Lieut.-Governor (*Gezaghebber*), who is responsible for maintaining public peace and order.

At the general election held in July 1979, the *Movimiento Antijas Nobo* won 7 seats, the *Movimiento Electoral di Puebla* 5, the Democratic Party 3, other parties 5 seats; the 2 non-voting seats for Sint Eustatius and Saba were not filled, no candidate being nominated by these 2 islands.

Governor: Dr B. M. Leito.

Prime Minister: S. G. M. Rozendal.
Deputy Prime Minister: L. A. I. Chance.

Flag: White, with a red vertical strip crossed by a blue horizontal strip bearing 6 white stars.

Dutch is the official language. Spanish and English are also spoken. In addition a 'lingua franca', *Papiamento*, has evolved out of Spanish, Dutch and some other languages.

FINANCE. The central budget for 1972 envisaged 121,796,700 guilders revenue and 121,231,500 guilders expenditure.

The public debt was 252m. guilders as at 31 Dec. 1971.

The official rate of exchange was £1 = 3·90 *Antillian guilder*; US$1 = 1·80 *Antillian guilder* in March 1981.

ENERGY AND NATURAL RESOURCES

Oil. The economy of the Netherlands Antilles is almost entirely based on the refining of oil imported from Venezuela to Curaçao and Aruba. About 25% (Curaçao) and 30% (Aruba) of the gainfully occupied are working at the refineries or their shipping establishments. On account of the activities of the oil companies (affiliated to the Royal Dutch/Shell and the Standard Oil of New Jersey), the prosperity on Curaçao and Aruba is good in comparison with the other islands.

Minerals. About 100,000 tons of calcium phosphate are annually mined in Curaçao.

Agriculture. Livestock (1979): Cattle, 8,000; goats, 20,000; poultry, 110,000.

INDUSTRY AND TRADE

Industry. In Aruba there are some petrochemical factories; Curaçao has a paint factory, 2 cigarette factories, a textile factory, a brewery and some smaller industries. The Texas Instruments Co. and Electronic Fabriek have established electronic factories. Almost all products needed for consumption and production are imported, as the rocky soil permits little agriculture and local fishing is insufficient for home consumption. Bonaire has a textile factory and a modern-equipped salt plant. St Maarten has a rum factory and fishing is important. St Eustatius and Saba are of less economic importance.

Trade (1978). Total imports amounted to US$3,537m., total exports to US$3,035m.

Total trade between the Netherlands Antilles and UK (British Department of Trade returns, in £1,000 sterling):

	1976	1977	1978	1979	1980
Imports to UK	49,675	26,075	25,646	44,841	36,243
Exports and re-exports from UK	14,945	71,096	107,784	59,070	33,375

The Free-Zones Ordinance of 1956 has established free zones in the ports of Curaçao and Aruba.

Tourism. In 1977, 302,000 foreign tourists visited the Netherlands Antilles and in addition there were 381,000 cruise tourists.

COMMUNICATIONS

Roads. In 1972 the Netherlands Antilles had 1,150 km of surfaced highway distributed as follows: Curaçao, 929; Aruba, 389; Bonaire, 125; St Maarten, 60. Number of motor vehicles (31 Dec. 1975): 41,955 in Curaçao, 15,393 in Aruba.

Shipping (1971). There entered the port of Curaçao, 5,333 vessels of 42m. gross tons; Aruba, 2,394 vessels of 34·8m. gross tons. Curaçao has a dry dock of 120,000 tons.

Post and Broadcasting. Number of telephones, 1 Jan. 1978, 49,633. Eight radio stations are operating on medium-waves from Curaçao, Aruba, Bonaire, and St Maarten. These stations broadcast in *Papiamento*, Dutch, English and Spanish and are mainly financed by income from advertisements. In addition, Radio Nederland and Trans World Radio have powerful relay stations operating on medium- and short-waves from Bonaire. There were (1975) 132,000 radio and 35,000 TV receivers.

Cinemas (1973). Curaçao and Aruba had 13 cinemas with a seating capacity of 11,000. There is a drive-in for 500 cars in Curaçao, for 200 cars in St Maarten and for 350 cars in Aruba.

RELIGION, EDUCATION AND WELFARE

Religion. In 1960, 82% of the population were Roman Catholics, 8% were Protestants.

Education (1972). Schools numbered 280, with 66,409 pupils and 2,516 teachers.

Health. In June 1973 there were 155 physicians, 55 specialists, 33 dentists and 18 pharmacists. In 1973, 11 hospitals had 2,037 beds.

DIPLOMATIC REPRESENTATIVE

USA Consul-General: Alta F. Fowler.

The British consulate closed on 1 Sept. 1976.

Books of Reference

Statistical Information: Statistical publications (on population, trade, cost of living, etc., are obtainable on request from the Statistical Office, Willemstad, Curaçao. *Statistical Jaarboek 1970* (text in Dutch, English and Spanish).

De West Indische Gids. The Hague. Monthly from 1919
Braam, H. L., *Hoe ons land geregeerd wordt.* Willemstad, 4th ed. 1972
Hartog, J., *Aruba.* Oranjestad, 1953.—*Bonaire.* Oranjestad, 1958.—*Curaçao.* Oranjestad, 1961
Nordlohne, E., *De Economisch-geographische Structuur der Benedenwindse Eilanden.* Rotterdam, 1951
Poll, W. van de, *De Nederlandse Antillen.* The Hague, 1950
Walle, J. van de, *De Nederlandse Antillen.* Willemstad, 1954
Westerman, J. H., *Overzicht van de geologische en mijnbouwkundige kennis der Nederlandse Antillen.* Amsterdam, 1949

NEW ZEALAND

Capital: Wellington
Population: 3·1m. (1980)
GNP per capita: US$4,790 (1978)

HISTORY. The first European to discover New Zealand was Tasman in 1642. The coast was explored by Capt. Cook in 1769. From about 1800 onwards, New Zealand became a resort for whalers and traders, chiefly from Australia. By the Treaty of Waitangi, in 1840, between Governor William Hobson and the representatives of the Maori race, the Maori chiefs ceded the sovereignty to the British Crown and the islands became a British colony. Then followed a steady stream of British settlers.

The Maoris are a branch of the Polynesian race, having emigrated from the eastern Pacific before and during the 14th century. Between 1845 and 1848, and between 1860 and 1870, misunderstandings over land led to war, but peace was permanently established in 1871, and the development of New Zealand has been marked by racial harmony and integration.

AREA AND POPULATION. New Zealand lies south-east of Australia in the south Pacific, Wellington being 1,233 miles from Sydney by sea. There are two principal islands, the North and South Islands, besides Stewart Island, Chatham Islands and small outlying islands, as well as the territories overseas (*see* pp. 918–20).

New Zealand (*i.e.*, North, South and Stewart Islands) extends over 1,750 km from north to south. Area, excluding territories overseas, 268,704 sq. km.; North Island, 11,469,000 hectares; South Island, 15,046,000 hectares; Stewart Island, 174,000 hectares; Chatham Islands, 96,000 hectares; minor islands, 82,900 hectares. Census population, exclusive of territories overseas:

	Total population	Average annual increase %		Total population	Average annual increase %
1858	115,462	—	1921	1,271,644	2·27
1874	344,984	—	1926	1,408,139	2·06
1878	458,007	7·33	1936	1,573,810	1·13
1881	534,030	5·10	1945 [1]	1,702,298	0·83
1886	620,451	3·05	1951 [1]	1,939,472	2·37
1891	668,632	1·50	1956 [1]	2,174,062	2·31
1896	743,207	2·13	1961 [1]	2,414,984	2·12
1901 [1]	815,853	1·89	1966 [1]	2,676,919	2·10
1906	936,304	2·75	1971 [1]	2,862,631	1·34
1911	1,058,308	2·52	1976 [1]	3,129,383	1·71
1916 [1]	1,149,225	1·50			

The census of New Zealand is quinquennial, but the census falling in 1931 was abandoned as an act of national economy, and owing to war conditions the census due in 1941 was not taken until 25 Sept. 1945.

[1] Excluding members of the Armed Forces overseas.

The areas and populations of statistical areas (with principal centres) estimated at 31 March 1979 were as follows [1]:

Statistical area [2]	Sq. km	Total population
Northland (Whangarei)	12,629	107,500
Central Auckland (Auckland)	5,594	805,900
South Auckland—Bay of Plenty (Hamilton)	36,760	477,100
East Coast (Gisborne)	10,880	47,500
Hawke's Bay (Napier, Hastings)	11,303	146,200
Taranaki (New Plymouth)	9,721	106,600
Wellington (Wellington)	27,705	592,900
Total, North Island	*114,592*	*2,283,700*

[1] For statistical purposes, the 9 provincial districts have now been replaced by 13 statistical areas.

[2] Listed from north to south.

Statistical area [1]	Sq. km	Total population
Marlborough (Blenheim)	10,859	35,400
Nelson (Nelson)	18,046	75,700
Westland (Greymouth)	15,415	23,900
Canterbury (Christchurch)	43,371	429,800
Otago (Dunedin)	37,100	188,300
Southland (Invercargill)	29,136	107,800
Total, South Island	*153,927*	*860,900*
Total, New Zealand	268,519	3,144,600

[1] Listed from north to south.

New Zealand-born residents made up 83·25% of the population at the 1976 census. Foreign-born: UK, 291,490; Australia, 61,810; Netherlands, 21,990; Western Samoa, 19,430; Cook Islands, 11,000; USA, 8,440; Republic of Ireland, 5,930; others, 105,220.

Maori population: 1896, 42,113; 1936, 82,326; 1945, 98,744; 1951, 115,676; 1961, 171,553; 1966, 201,159; 1971, 227,414; 1976, 270,035.

Populations of statistical divisions and urban areas at 31 March 1979 (estimated) were as follows:

Auckland	805,900	Invercargill	53,800
Christchurch	327,300	Masterton	21,100
Dunedin	119,600	Nelson	42,800
Hamilton	157,900	New Plymouth	44,600
Napier–Hastings	110,600	Rotorua	47,400
Palmerston North	89,800	Tauranga	49,000
Wellington	350,100	Timaru	30,100
Urban areas:		Wanganui	39,800
Gisborne	32,000	Whangarei	39,600

Vital statistics for calendar years:

	Total live births	Ex-nuptial births	Deaths	Marriages	Divorces (decrees absolute)
1977	54,179	10,265	25,961	22,589	5,381
1978	51,029	10,254	24,669	22,426	5,772
1979	52,279	10,942	25,410	22,332	6,101

Birth rate, 1979, 16·73 per 1,000; death rate, 8·13 per 1,000; marriage rate, 7·14 per 1,000; infant mortality, 12·57 per 1,000 live births.

External migration (exclusive of crews and through passengers) for years ended 31 March:

	Arrivals	Departures		Arrivals	Departures
1975	678,655	649,514	1978	715,780	737,936
1976	678,664	673,472	1979	805,876	832,420
1977	667,224	683,494	1980	925,939	947,253

Population and Migration: Part B—External Migration. Dept. of Statistics, Wellington, Annually

CONSTITUTION AND GOVERNMENT. Definition was given the status of New Zealand by the (Imperial) Statute of Westminster of Dec. 1931, which had received the antecedent approval of the New Zealand Parliament in July 1931. The Governor-General's assent was given to the Statute of Westminster Adoption Bill on 25 Nov. 1947.

The powers, duties and responsibilities of the Governor-General and the Executive Council under the present system of responsible government are set out in Royal Letters Patent and Instructions thereunder of 11 May 1917, published in the *New Zealand Gazette* of 24 April 1919. In the execution of the powers vested in him the Governor-General must be guided by the advice of the Executive Council.

The following is a list of Governors-General, the title prior to June 1917 being Governor:

Earl of Liverpool	1917–20	Lord Norrie	1952–57
Viscount Jellicoe	1920–24	Viscount Cobham	1957–62
Sir Charles Fergusson, Bt	1924–30	Sir Bernard Fergusson	1962–67
Lord Bledisloe	1930–35	Sir Arthur Porrit, Bt	1967–72
Viscount Galway	1935–41	Sir Denis Blundell	1972–77
Sir Cyril Newall	1941–46	Sir Keith Holyoake	1977–
Lord Freyberg, VC	1946–52		

National flag: The British Blue Ensign with 4 stars of the Southern Cross in red, edged in white, in the fly.

National anthems: God Save the Queen; God Defend New Zealand (words by Thomas Bracken, music by John J. Woods).

Since Nov. 1977 both 'God Save the Queen' and 'God Defend New Zealand' have equal status as national anthems.

Parliament consists of the House of Representatives, the former Legislative Council having been abolished since 1 Jan. 1951.

The statute law on elections and the life of Parliament is contained in the Electoral Act, 1956. In 1974 the voting age was reduced from 20 to 18 years.

The House of Representatives from Nov. 1978 consists of 92 members, including 4 members representing Maori electorates, elected by the people for 3 years. The 4 Maori electoral districts cover the whole country and adult Maoris of half or more Maori descent are the electors. From 1976 a descendant of a Maori is entitled to register either for a general or a Maori electoral district. Women's suffrage was instituted in 1893: women became eligible as members of the House of Representatives in 1919. The House in 1979 included 4 women members.

During Parliamentary sittings the proceedings of the House are broadcast regularly on sound radio.

House of Representatives as composed following the General Election in Nov. 1978: National Party, 51; Labour, 40; Social Credit, 1.

The Executive Council was composed as follows in March 1980:

Governor-General and C.-in-C.: The Hon. Sir David Beattie, KCMG (from Oct. 1980).

Prime Minister, Minister of Finance, Minister in charge of the Legislative Department, Minister in charge of Audit Department, Minister in charge of the New Zealand Security Intelligence Service: R. D. Muldoon.

Deputy Prime Minister, Minister of Foreign Affairs, Minister of Overseas Trade: B. E. Talboys.

Minister of Agriculture and Fisheries: D. MacIntyre.

Minister of Trade and Industry: L. R. Adams-Schneider.

Minister of State, Minister of Defence, Leader of the House of Representatives and Minister of State Services: D. S. Thomson.

Minister of Health and Social Welfare: G. F. Gair.

Minister of Customs, Broadcasting and Statistics, Deputy Minister of Finance: H. C. Templeton.

Minister of Labour and Immigration: J. B. Bolger.

Minister of Transport, Minister of Civil Aviation and Meteorological Services, Minister of Railways: C. C. A. McLachlan.

Minister of Works and Development: W. L. Young.

Minister of Lands, Minister of Forests, Minister for the Environment, Minister in charge of the Valuation Department: V. S. Young.

Minister of Internal Affairs, Minister of Local Government, Minister of Recreation and Sport, Minister of Civil Defence, Minister for the Arts: D. A. Highet.

Minister of Energy, Minister of National Development, Minister of Science and Technology: W. F. Birch.

Minister of Education: M. L. Wellington.

Attorney-General, Minister of Justice: J. K. McLay.

Minister of Housing, Associate Minister of Finance: D. F. Quigley.

Minister of Police, Minister of Maori Affairs: M. B. R. Couch.

Minister of Tourism, Minister of Regional Development and Postmaster-General: W. E. Cooper.

The Prime Minister (provided with residence) had at Aug. 1980 a salary of NZ$60,091 plus a tax-free expense allowance of $10,725 per annum; Ministers with portfolio, $41,546 plus a tax-free expense allowance of $4,400 (Minister of Foreign Affairs $8,250) per annum; Ministers without portfolio, $33,598 plus a tax-free expense allowance of $3,465 per annum; Parliamentary Under-Secretaries, $32,273 plus an expense allowance of $3,465 per annum. In addition, Ministers and Parliamentary Under-Secretaries not provided with residence at the seat of Government receive $600 per annum house allowance. An allowance of $44 per day while travelling within New Zealand on public service is payable to Ministers.

The Speaker of the House of Representatives receives $38,565 plus an expense allowance of $7,370 per annum in addition to his electorate allowance, and residential quarters in Parliament House, and the Leader of the Opposition $41,546 plus expense allowance of $4,400 per annum, and allowances for travelling and housing.

Members were paid $24,326 per annum, plus an expense allowance varying from $5,590 to $8,500 according to the area of electorate represented.

There is a compulsory contributory superannuation scheme for members; retiring allowances are payable to a member after 9 years' service and the attainment of 50 years of age.

Dollimore, H. N., *The Parliament of New Zealand and Parliament House*. 3rd ed. Wellington, 1973
Milne, R. S., *Political Parties in New Zealand*. OUP, 1966
Scott, K. J., *The New Zealand Constitution*. OUP, 1962

Local Government. For purposes of local government New Zealand is divided into counties, district councils, boroughs and town districts. Some counties are subdivided into ridings. There are also numerous other local authorities created for specific functions, such as electric-power districts, river (*i.e.*, river protection) districts, pest destruction districts, etc.

DEFENCE. The control and co-ordination of defence activities is obtained through the Ministry of Defence. This is a unitary department combining not only all joint-Service functions but also the former Departments of Army, Navy and Air.

Army. The Army is organized into a Home Command and a Field Force Command, each of which is responsible to Defence Headquarters. A regular force battalion is stationed in Malaysia.

Regular personnel, in 1980, totalled 5,666 all ranks; territorial personnel totalled 8,047; the cadet corps totalled (1979) 4,299 cadets.

Navy. The Royal New Zealand Navy is administered by the Chief of Naval Staff and the Deputy Chief of Naval Staff at Defence Headquarters.

The RNZN ships include 4 frigates, 1 surveying vessel, 4 patrol craft, 6 old harbour defence motor launches, 2 survey boats, 1 oceanographic research ship, 1 tug and 1 tender.

Personnel, in 1981, totalled 2,730 officers and ratings and 385 in the naval reserve.

Air Force. The Chief of Air Staff and Air Officer Commanding the RNZAF exercises command and administration of the RNZAF. Operational units of the RNZAF comprise a utility helicopter support unit (UH-1H Iroquois) based in Singapore as part of the NZ force, South-east Asia; maritime (P-3B Orion), long and medium-range transport (C-130H Hercules, Andover, F.27 Friendship) and helicopter (Sioux, Iroquois, Wasp) squadrons based at RNZAF Base Auckland; and offensive support (A-4K Skyhawk) and medium-range transport/communications squadrons (Andover, F.27 Friendship) at RNZAF Base Ohakea. Flying training units (Airtrainer, Strikemaster, TA-4K Skyhawks, Sioux) are located at RNZAF Bases Wigram and Ohakea; ground training is carried out at RNZAF Bases Auckland, Woodbourne and Wigram.

The strength in 1981 was 4,300 regular personnel, 1,470 non-regular personnel.

INTERNATIONAL RELATIONS

Membership. New Zealand is a member of UN, the Commonwealth, OECD and the Colombo Plan.

ECONOMY

Budget. The following tables of revenue and expenditure relate to the Consolidated Account, which covers the ordinary revenue and expenditure of the general government—*i.e.*, apart from capital items, commercial and special undertakings, advances, etc. Revenue in the Account (in NZ$1m.) was as follows:

Year ended 31 March	Customs and excise	Sales tax	Income tax	Other taxes	Trading profits and departmental receipts	Interest	Total
1977	299·3	353·3	2,828·5	256·7	149·4	227·9	4,164·9
1978	331·5	371·5	3,482·8	314·3	174·5	364·6	5,039·2
1979	345·0	449·7	3,655·2	380·2	371·6 [1]	450·3	5,652·2
1980	389·8	624·1	4,465·6	401·0	418·8	539·0	6,838·3

[1] Includes amounts previously recorded in the Works Trading Account.

Expenditure from Consolidated Account, year ended 31 March, was as follows (in NZ$1m.):

	Debt services	Social services [1]	Industrial development	Defence	Total (including other)
1977	431·3	2,411·1	304·0	214·8	4,225·1
1978	536·3	3,059·2	340·1	252·2	5,073·8
1979	670·2	3,809·4 [2]	779·8 [2]	299·5	6,512·8
1980	825·6	4,353·8	814·2	346·1	7,545·4

[1] Includes education, health and social welfare.
[2] Includes amounts previously recorded in the Works Trading Account.

Taxation receipts in 1979–80 for all purposes amounted to $6,020m., giving an average of $1,927 per head of mean population. Included in the total taxation is $139·5m. National Roads Fund taxation. The estimate for 1980–81 is $7,154m., the total being inclusive of an estimated $182m. of National Roads Fund taxation.

The gross public debt at 31 March 1980 was $10,346m., of which $6,779m. was held in New Zealand, $2,995·6m. in London, Europe and Asia, $537m. in USA and $35m. with the World Bank. The gross annual interest charge on the public debt at 31 March 1980 was $757,793,000.

New Zealand System of National Accounts. This replaces the National Income and Expenditure Accounts which have been produced since 1948. National Accounts aggregates for 4 years are given in the following table (in NZ$1m.):

Year ended 31 March	Gross domestic product	Gross national product	National income
1976	11,487	11,322	10,375
1977	13,809	13,546	12,465
1978	15,236	14,899	13,704
1979	17,648	17,227	15,919

Currency. The monetary unit is the New Zealand *dollar*, divided into 100 *cents*. In March 1981, £1 = 2·38NZ$; US$1 = 1·086NZ$1.

Banking. The Reserve Bank is the sole note-issuing authority. Six denominations of Reserve Bank notes are issued: NZ$1, 2, 5, 10, 20, 100.

The New Zealand banking system comprises a central bank—the Reserve Bank of New Zealand—5 commercial or trading banks and 18 savings banks (including the post office savings bank). The trading banks have operated savings-bank facilities from 1 Oct. 1964.

The primary functions of the Reserve Bank are to act as the central bank, to advise the Government on matters relating to monetary policy, banking and overseas exchange, and to give effect to the monetary policy of the Government.

Of the 5 trading banks 3 are primarily Australian concerns, 1 until recently had its head office in London and the Bank of New Zealand has been state owned since 1 Nov. 1945.

At the end of March 1979 the amount on deposit at trading banks was NZ$4,573·2m., while advances amounted to NZ$3,211·8m. The weekly average of bank debits for 1979 was $2,658m. excluding government.

The number of accounts with the post office savings bank at 31 March 1979 was 3·11m.; amount deposited during year ended March 1979, $1,977m.; withdrawn, $1,858m., total amount to credit of depositors at end of year, $1,618m. At 31 March 1979, $1,403m. was on deposit in 12 Trustee Savings Banks to the credit of 2·3m. depositors. The amount to the credit of depositors with savings accounts in the trading banks was $853·2m. at 31 March 1979.

Weights and Measures. Conversion to the metric system of weights and measures has been completed.

ENERGY AND NATURAL RESOURCES

Electricity. The general policy of the Government in regard to electric power is to supply power in bulk, leaving the reticulation and retail supply in the hands of local authorities; some of these are cities and boroughs but most are electric power boards. Hydro energy provides over 70% of the national electricity supply, the balance coming from coal, oil, natural gas and geothermal energy. The last is obtained from Wairakei in the thermal region; natural steam is used to drive the turbines.

The transmission systems of the North and South Islands are linked by a high-voltage direct-current transmission and 40 km of submarine cable in Cook Strait.

Principal statistics for 4 years ended 31 March are:

	1975	1976	1977	1978
Number of establishments	77	79	79	80
Generators (capacity) AC (1,000 kw.)	4,784	5,038	5,366	5,633
Units generated (1m. kwh.)	18,352	20,071	20,914	21,268
Revenue ($1,000)	328,935	377,520	542,164	743,509
Expenditure:				
Operating ($1,000)	188,649	202,520	320,215	432,189
Management, etc. ($1,000)	35,260	57,643	63,642	70,027
Capital charges ($1,000)	111,434	127,666	168,623	183,155
Capital outlay:				
During year ($1,000)	188,727	265,047	285,083	355,600
To date ($1,000)	1,913,187	2,178,634	2,463,995	2,733,900

Natural Gas. Resources discovered in the Taranaki area of the North Island in 1961 are now supplying gas for household use to North Island cities including Auckland and Wellington. The much larger Maui offshore gasfield was discovered in 1969 and is at present being developed.

Minerals. New Zealand's production of minerals in 1977 included 223 kg of gold, 1,113 tonnes of diatomite earth, 2,633 tonnes of bentonite, 173,008 tonnes of clay for bricks, tiles, etc., 94,742 tonnes of potters' clays, 2,954,394 tonnes of iron sand, 1,731,742 tonnes of limestone for agriculture and 170,356 tonnes of limestone for industry, 1,590,173 tonnes of limestone, marl, etc., for cement, 28,550 tonnes of pumice, 89,006 tonnes of serpentine, 146,486 tonnes of silica sand. Mineral fuel production amounted to 2,368,909 tonnes of coal, 860,973 cu. metres of petroleum condensate and 2,256·6m. cu. metres of natural gas. Salt produced by the solar evaporation of sea water amounted to 53,000 tonnes. Mineral production for the year was valued at $140·43m.

Agriculture. Two-thirds of the surface of New Zealand is suitable for agriculture and grazing. The total area under cultivation at 30 June 1977 was 10,132,300 hectares (including residential area and domestic orchards). There were 9,397,900 hectares of sown pasture, including areas sown with crops, and 734,400 hectares of timber plantations. The area of Crown lands (other than reserves) leased under various tenures at 31 March 1979 was 5,776,255 hectares.

The largest freehold estates are held in the South Island. The extent of occupied holdings as at 30 June 1976 (exclusive of holdings within borough boundaries) was as follows:

Size of holdings (hectares)	Number	Aggregate area (hectares)	Size of holdings (hectares)	Number	Aggregate area (hectares)
Under 5	5,535	16,900	400–799	4,375	2,394,400
5–19	9,036	91,900	800–999	809	717,500
20–39	6,423	189,000	1,000–1,199	468	514,500
40–79	13,137	753,300	1,200–1,999	964	1,473,100
80–99	4,502	398,100	2,000–3,999	581	1,590,700
100–149	7,067	865,300	4,000 and over	610	8,780,800
150–199	4,888	847,500			
200–299	6,251	1,515,600	Total	67,774	21,223,700
300–399	3,128	1,076,900			

The area and yield for each of the principal crops are given as follows (area and yield for threshing only, not including that grown for chaff, hay, silage, etc.):

Crop years	Wheat Area (1,000 hectares)	Wheat Yield (1,000 tonnes)	Maize Area (1,000 hectares)	Maize Yield (1,000 tonnes)	Barley Area (1,000 hectares)	Barley Yield (1,000 tonnes)
1978	91·0	328·8	24·8	174·5	70·8	258·7
1979	87·2	295·0	22·3	179·0	77·5	263·6

Private air companies are carrying out such aerial work as top-dressing, spraying and crop-dusting, seed-sowing, rabbit poisoning, aerial photography and surveying, and dropping supplies to deer cullers and dropping fencing materials in remote areas. The main aerial activity was top-dressing, statistics for the year ended March 1978 being: Hours flown, 153,530; lime and solid fertilizer distributed, 1·23m. tonnes.

Livestock at 31 Jan. 1979: 8,499,000 cattle (including 2·04m. milch cows), 78m. sheep and 503,000 pigs. Total meat produced in the year ended 30 Sept. 1979 was estimated at 1·12m. tonnes (including 490,500 tonnes of beef and 351,000 tonnes of lamb). Total liquid milk produced in the year ended 31 May 1979 was 6,176m. litres; of this, 5,658m. were used for butter and cheese products.

Production of wool for the 12 months ended 30 June 1979, 321,000 tonnes (greasy basis).

Agricultural Statistics. Dept. of Statistics, Wellington. Annual
New Zealand Agriculture. Ministry of Agriculture and Fisheries, Wellington, 1974
Allsop, F., *The First Fifty Years of New Zealand's Forest Service.* Wellington, 1973
Evans, B. L., *A History of Agricultural Production and Marketing.* Palmerston North, 1969
Levy, E. B., *Grasslands of New Zealand.* Wellington, 1970

Forestry. Of the 6·2m. hectares of indigenous forest only about 1m. hectares are merchantable; they are being depleted at the rate of 5,000 hectares a year (although the rate of cutting is diminishing) and mainly for sawn timber. There are about 740,000 hectares of productive exotic forest, and this produces far more timber than the indigenous forests. Introduced conifer pines form the bulk of the large exotic forest estate and among these radiata pine is the best multi-purpose tree, reaching saw-log size in 25–30 years. Other major species are Douglas fir, Corsican pine and ponderosa pine. The table below shows the quantities of timber produced in 1,000 cu. metres for years ending 31 March:

	Softwoods Indigenous	Softwoods Exotic	Hardwoods Indigenous	Hardwoods Exotic	Total
1976	326	1,618	48	11	2,003
1977	296	1,867	47	2	2,212
1978	223	1,704	32	2	1,961
1979	173	1,654	35	3	1,865

Forest industries consist of 377 saw-mills, 9 plywood and veneer plants, 3 particle board mills, 7 pulp and paper mills and 2 fibreboard mills.

The basic products of the pulp and paper mills are mechanical and chemical pulp which are converted into newsprint, kraft and other papers, paperboard and fibreboard. Production of woodpulp, calendar year 1979, amounted to 1·2m. tonnes and of paper (including newsprint paper and paperboard) to 724,000 tonnes.

Fisheries. At the peak of the 1976 season about 400 foreign vessels were within New Zealand's 200 miles fisheries management zone. The annual catch (in tonnes) of all species was about 300,000, mainly tuna and squid; New Zealand catch, about 60,000.

Exports of fisheries products for the year ended 30 June 1979 had a value of $73·8m., of which the value of rock lobster exports of 2,010 tonnes was $22·7m. Live eel exports of 379 tonnes were worth $732,224 and paua (abalone) exports of 461 tonnes, $2·7m.

INDUSTRY AND TRADE

Industry. Major industrial developments in recent years have included the establishment of an oil refinery, an iron and steel industry using New Zealand iron sands and an aluminium smelter using hydro-electric power.

Statistics of manufacturing industries for 3 years:

Production year	Persons engaged	Salaries and wages paid (NZ$1,000)	Cost of materials (NZ$1,000)	Value of production (NZ$1,000)	Net output (net value added) (NZ$1,000)
1974–75	300,945	1,391,000	4,665,000	6,499,000	2,210,000
1975–76	298,692	1,576,250	4,992,516	7,264,434	2,350,654
1976–77	306,177	1,801,717	6,381,347	8,987,242	2,865,278

The following is a statement of the provisional value of the products (including repairs) of the principal industries for the year 1976–77 (in NZ$1,000):

Industry group	Value of production	Industry group	Value of production
Food manufacturing	2,366,961	Pottery, china and earthenware	15,433
Beverages	185,706	Glass and glass products	69,345
Tobacco manufactures	66,305	Other non-metallic mineral products	270,370
Textiles	439,285	Iron and steel	201,258
Wearing apparel	259,994	Non-ferrous metal	157,076
Fur and leather	82,818	Metal products (except machinery and equipment)	704,584
Footwear (except rubber, plastic or wooden)	74,245	Machinery (except electrical)	386,108
Wood and cork products	457,358	Electrical machinery, apparatus, appliances and supplies	458,009
Furniture	144,236	Transport equipment	569,415
Paper and paper products	594,180	Measuring and controlling equipment, etc	21,488
Printing and publishing	318,112	Other manufacturing industries	81,762
Industrial chemicals	316,758		
Other chemical products	256,321		
Petroleum refineries	53,105	Total	8,856,465
Petroleum and coal products	14,917		
Rubber products	140,846		
Plastic products not elsewhere specified	150,470		

Industrial Production. Dept. of Statistics, Wellington. Annual

Labour. In Dec. 1979 there were 279 industrial unions of workers with a total of 506,963 members.

The industrial distribution of the labour force as estimated in April 1977 was: Primary industries, 145,500; manufacturing, 308,400; construction, 91,200; commerce, 192,900; transport and communication, 110,500; services, 271,300; armed forces, 11,000; unemployed, 4,100; total labour force, 1,230,100.

By the Accident Compensation Act 1972 immediate compensation without proof of fault is provided for every injured person and wherever the accident occurred. Compensation is paid both for permanent physical disability and also—in the case of earners—for income losses on an income related basis. Regular adjustment in the level of payment is provided for in accordance with variations in the value of money. Non-earners such as tourists, housewives, children, students, retired people do not normally qualify for earnings related compensation but are eligible for all other benefits. These are not taxable. Housewives—including visiting women from overseas—who are non-earners are eligible for the benefits available to non-earners and home help can be paid for or the husband compensated for loss of earnings while he is looking after the home until the injured wife can resume her duties.

After the first week's incapacity and for the ensuing 4 weeks the earner can be paid 80% of his average earnings for the 28 days preceding the accident; after that the 80% is related to average earnings over the 12 preceding months. In addition—for earners—lump sums are payable for impairment, pain and disfigurement and for funeral expenses and weekly sums and lump payments to their widows and dependent children. All employees are covered by the Accident Compensation Act 1972.

Commerce. Trade (excluding specie and bullion) in NZ$1,000 for 12 months ended 30 June:

	Total merchandise imported (v.f.d.)[2]	Exports of domestic produce	Re-exports	Total merchandise exported (f.o.b.)
1976–77	3,244,356	3,096,719	131,974	3,228,692
1977–78	3,018,158	3,141,043	172,453	3,313,496
1978–79	3,574,139	3,945,961	121,417	4,067,378
1979–80[1]	4,770,596	5,012,614	139,375	5,151,989

[1] Provisional figures.　　[2] Value for duty.

The principal imports for the 12 months ended 30 June 1980 (provisional):

Commodity	Value (NZ$1,000) (v.f.d.)
Cereals and cereal preparations	12,996
Fruit and vegetables	52,252
Sugar and sugar preparations	45,074
Coffee, tea, cocoa, spices, etc.	57,275
Beverages	30,349
Tobacco and manufactures	15,011
Crude rubber	30,875
Textile fibres	18,040
Crude fertilizers and minerals other than coal	70,295
Petroleum and petroleum products	943,196
Chemical elements and compounds	174,128
Dyeing, tanning, etc. materials	29,221
Medicinal and pharmaceutical products	113,229
Fertilizers, manufactured	31,337
Plastic materials, etc.	172,966
Miscellaneous chemical materials and products	56,193
Rubber manufactures[1]	37,487
Paper and paperboard manufactures	59,467
Textile yarn and fabrics, etc.	326,545
Non-metallic mineral manufactures[1]	57,935
Iron and steel	262,360
Nonferrous metals	93,624
Manufactures of metals	116,615
Machinery, other than electric	659,869
Electric machinery	201,346
Transport equipment	539,141
Scientific instruments, watches, etc.	141,306
Miscellaneous manufactured articles[1]	168,082
Commodities not classified (mainly arms of war)	34,613

[1] Not elsewhere specified.

The principal exports of New Zealand produce for the 12 months ended 30 June 1980 (provisional) were:

Commodity	Quantity (in tonnes)	Value (NZ$1,000)	Commodity	Quantity (in tonnes)	Value (NZ$1,000)
Meat			Dairy products		
Beef and veal	215,584	528,067	Milk and cream	...	219,092
Lamb	318,417	486,191	Butter	231,392	360,754
Mutton	87,374	98,280	Cheese	69,212	105,642
Edible offals	37,796	62,015	Fish	...	130,085
			Cereals	...	21,102

Commodity	Quantity (in tonnes)	Value (NZ$1,000)	Commodity	Quantity (in tonnes)	Value (NZ$1,000)
Apples	92,292	35,651	Casein	67,875	133,860
Animal feeding stuff	101,971	30,895	Newsprint	...	80,989
Hides and skins	...	180,359	Textile yarn	7,118	40,186
Wood and cork	...	126,013	Carpets	...	41,562
Pulp and waste paper	483,341	120,747	Aluminium	124,958	162,815
Wool	285,890	931,525	Metal manufactures	...	59,171
Sausage casings (hanks)	6,900,000	33,549	Machinery, other than electric	...	71,720
Tallow	85,594	43,454	Electric machinery, etc.	...	54,873

The following table shows the trade with different countries (in NZ$1,000):

Countries	Imports v.f.d. from 1979	1980[1]	Exports and re-exports f.o.b. to 1979	1980[1]
Australia	798,513	912,509	501,190	634,741
Bahrain	46,735	68,433	4,507	6,470
Belgium	20,279	23,216	44,533	51,990
Canada	85,417	94,902	101,350	97,822
China	21,130	41,531	78,849	118,446
Fiji	11,547	26,949	55,019	71,214
France	44,866	54,065	94,513	126,641
Germany (Fed. Rep. of)	231,044	208,545	102,480	116,113
Greece	3,819	725	48,586	55,335
Hong Kong	52,313	65,073	50,792	79,365
India	20,043	33,818	13,329	11,237
Iran	41,214	50,656	24,441	129,405
Italy	47,115	70,611	107,973	128,120
Japan	495,154	600,035	600,583	635,181
Korea, South	23,412	23,217	68,676	63,969
Kuwait	54,548	99,193	3,564	7,565
Malaysia	38,853	66,467	43,904	57,944
Netherlands	48,272	61,352	65,741	84,154
Philippines	2,871	4,812	42,275	69,498
Saudi Arabia	86,239	218,529	12,734	35,634
Singapore	67,753	273,233	42,978	74,212
Sweden	29,793	64,044	3,723	7,372
UK	542,819	691,339	676,733	715,091
USSR	5,346	5,995	129,134	251,400
USA	489,562	649,639	632,176	721,367

[1] Provisional.

Total trade between New Zealand and UK was as follows (British Department of Trade returns, in £1,000 sterling):

	1977	1978	1979	1980
Imports to UK	383,163	434,471	415,432	414,630
Exports and re-exports from UK	286,891	268,180	314,354	250,413

Tourism. The country has a growing tourist industry. In the year ended 31 March 1980, 445,195 travellers visited New Zealand (including 339,465 tourists), compared with 418,744 (including 286,408 tourists) in 1978–79.

COMMUNICATIONS

Roads. Total length of formed roads and streets in New Zealand at 31 March 1976 was 96,034 km. There were 13,397 bridges of over 3 metres in length with a total length of 300,889 metres at 31 March 1976. The network of state highways comprised, at 31 March 1976, 11,287 km, including the principal arterial traffic routes.

Total expenditure on roads, streets and bridges by the central government and local authorities combined for the financial year 1977–78 amounted to $211·86m.

In the main, roads are financed from the National Roads Fund which is administered by the National Roads Board. This fund which is derived largely from petrol tax is used for the maintenance and improvement of existing roads. The board's income is currently of the order of $140m. per annum, and is apportioned according to fixed percentages, with 50% allocated to state highways, 23% to counties and 16% to municipalities. These sector percentages have been varied twice in the last 10 years in the light of changing needs.

At 31 March 1980 motor vehicles licensed numbered 2,157,516, of which 1,297,253 were cars, 4,793 omnibuses and contract vehicles, 253,564 goods service vehicles. Included in the remaining number were 123,365 motor cycles, 2,001 power cycles and 90,345 farm tractors, road graders, etc. Licensed road goods services for the year ended 31 March 1977 recorded total vehicle journeys of 624m. km. Total revenue amounted to $449m. The road passenger services journeys amounted to 140·9m. km.

Railways. On 31 March 1980 there were 4,478 km of 1,067 mm gauge railway open for traffic. Operating earnings from government railways, 1979–80, $274,368,822; operating expenses, $331,359,816. In 1979–80 the tonnage of goods (including livestock) carried was 11,754,879 tonnes, and passengers numbered 16,011,376. In addition, the railways road motor services carried 20m. passengers. Four rail/road ferries maintain a regular service between the North and South Islands.

The total revenue (including road motor and other subsidiary services) amounted to $349,126,142, and total expenditure $404,930,697 in 1979–80.

Aviation. International services are operated to and from New Zealand by a state-owned company, Air New Zealand Ltd, and by a number of overseas companies. Air New Zealand Ltd also operates most domestic scheduled passenger services. Non-scheduled services are run by the main companies and also by a number of small operators and aero clubs.

Domestic scheduled services during the 12 months ended Dec. 1979: Passengers carried, 2,627,000. International services: Passengers carried, 1,682,000; mail, 2,665 tonnes; freight, 56,977 tonnes.

Shipping. Container ships operate from Auckland, Wellington, Lyttelton and Port Chalmers to the UK, Europe, North America and Japan. The government-owned New Zealand Shipping Corporation has begun to increase its activity into New Zealand–UK and Pacific trades.

Entrances and clearances of vessels from overseas:

	Entrances		Clearances	
	No.	Tons	No.	Tons
1977	3,400	22,317,000	3,409	22,296,000
1978	3,251	23,134,000	3,261	23,186,000
1979	3,438	25,199,000	3,433	25,313,000

Post and Broadcasting. Receipts of the Post Office for year ended 31 March 1980 were $604·3m.; total expenditure was $533·4m. Personnel numbered 39,465.

The telegraph and telephone systems are operated by the Post Office. At 31 March 1980 there were 1,114,910 telephone subscribers and 1,729,999 telephones. The telecommunications receipts for the year 1979–80 were $470·2m.

An earth satellite station has been built north of Auckland to link with the Pacific satellite Intelsat III to augment the Compac and Seacon telecommunications systems which link New Zealand with overseas countries.

There are 2 TV channels both operated by the state-owned New Zealand Broadcasting Corporation, which also operates most of the broadcasting stations. Over 85% of New Zealand households have TV sets. There are 65 medium-wave broadcasting stations and 2 short-wave transmitters. Some commercial material is broadcast by both sound and TV services. Number of TV receiving licences at 31 March 1980 was 883,021.

Cinemas. There were in 1975, 203 cinemas with a seating capacity of 119,000.

Newspapers. There were (1979), 32 daily newspapers (8 morning and 24 evening) with a combined circulation of 1,043,000. Seven of these newspapers (2 each in Auckland, Wellington and Christchurch and 1 in Dunedin) had a circulation of 718,000.

JUSTICE, RELIGION, EDUCATION AND WELFARE

Justice. The judiciary consists of the Chief Justice, 3 judges of the Court of Appeal and 22 Supreme Court judges. At the end of March 1979 the gaols and Borstal institutions contained 2,687 prisoners, 2,547 males and 140 females. In 1978, 4,597 persons were received into all penal institutions. The death penalty for murder was replaced by life imprisonment in 1961.

The Criminal Injuries Act, 1963, which came into force on 1 Jan. 1964, provided for compensation of persons injured by certain criminal acts and the dependants of persons killed by such acts. However, this has now been phased out in favour of the Accident Compensation Act, 1972, except in the residual area of property damage caused by escapers. Since 1970 legal aid in civil proceedings (except divorce) has been available for persons of small or moderate means. For the year ended 31 March 1979 expenditure amounted to $2,215,143 and 13,570 applications for aid were granted.

Police. The police in New Zealand are a national body maintained wholly by the central government. The total strength at 31 March 1980 was 4,961, the proportion of police to population being 1 to 630. The total cost of police services for the year 1979–80 was NZ$111m., equivalent to $36 per head of population. In New Zealand the police do not control traffic.

Ombudsmen. The office of Ombudsman was created in 1962. From 1975 additional Ombudsmen have been authorized. There are currently three. Ombudsmen's functions are to investigate complaints from members of the public relating to administrative decisions of government departments, local authorities and statutory organizations.

From 1 Oct. 1962 to 31 March 1980, 19,920 complaints were received, 2,196 of which were held to be justified and were acted upon by the department or organization concerned. No complaint of actual malpractice has been found justified.

Religion. No direct state aid is given to any form of religion. For the Church of England the country is divided into 7 dioceses, with a separate bishopric (Aotearoa) for the Maoris. The Presbyterian Church is divided into 23 presbyteries and the Maori Synod. The Moderator is elected annually. The Methodist Church is divided into 10 districts; the President is elected annually. The Roman Catholic Church is divided into 4 dioceses, with the Archbishop of Wellington as Metropolitan Archbishop.

Religious denomination	Number of clergy (April 1977)	Number of adherents 1971 census	1976 census
Church of England	780	895,839	915,202
Presbyterian	686	583,701	566,569
Roman Catholic (including 'Catholic' undefined)	931	449,974	478,530
Methodist	349	182,727	173,526
Baptist	254	47,350	49,442
Brethren	187	25,768	24,414
Ratana	142	30,156	35,082
Protestant (undefined)	—	37,475	33,309
Salvation Army	241	19,371	22,019
Church of Christ	54	8,930	8,087
Latter-day Saints (Mormon)	162	29,785	36,130
Congregationalist	10	7,704	6,600
Seventh-day Adventist	55	10,477	11,958
Ringatu	88	5,635	6,230
Christian (undefined)	—	33,187	52,478
Christian Scientist		816	583
Jehovah's Witnesses	125	10,318	13,392
Hebrew	7	3,803	3,921
Lutheran	15	5,930	6,297
Other bodies [1]	626	65,648	106,512
Unspecified	—	103,533	39,380
Object to state	—	247,019	438,511
No religion (so returned)	—	57,485	101,211
Total	4,712	2,862,631	3,129,383

[1] Including the Society of Friends with 996 members in 1971 and 1,074 in 1976.

Education. New Zealand has 6 universities, the University of Auckland, University of Waikato (at Hamilton), Victoria University of Wellington, Massey University (at Palmerston North), the University of Canterbury (at Christchurch) and the University of Otago (at Dunedin). There is, in addition, Lincoln College near Christchurch, a university college of agriculture, which is a constituent college of the University of Canterbury. The number of students in 1979 was 49,188. There were 8 teachers' training colleges with 5,820 students in 1979.

At 1 July 1979 there were 259 state secondary schools with 12,253 full-time teachers and 193,860 pupils. There were also 36 district high schools with 2,747 scholars in the secondary division. At 1 July 1979, 101,068 part-time pupils attended technical classes, and 29,415 received part-time instruction from the technical correspondence institute. At 1 July 1979, 912 pupils received tuition from the secondary department of the correspondence school. There were 100 registered private secondary schools with 1,137 teachers and 32,004 pupils.

At 1 July 1979, there were 2,489 state primary schools (including intermediate schools and departments), with 467,060 pupils; the number of teachers was 18,928. A correspondence school for children in remote areas and those otherwise unable to attend school had 1,654 primary pupils. There were 327 registered private primary schools with 1,894 teachers and 48,476 pupils.

Education is compulsory between the ages of 6 and 15. Children aged 3 and 4 years may enrol at the 511 free kindergartens maintained by Free Kindergarten Associations, which receive government assistance. There are also 694 play centres which also receive government subsidy. In July 1979 there were 38,595 and 17,765 children on the rolls respectively.

Total expenditure out of government funds in 1979–80 upon education was NZ$1,009·3m.

The universities and the affiliated agricultural colleges are autonomous bodies. Most secondary schools are controlled by their own boards. Virtually all state primary schools are controlled by the district education boards: there are 10 education districts. The Department of Education exercises certain defined functions in connexion with the general supervision of the education provided in state primary and secondary schools and disburses the government grants payable to controlling authorities for the running of those schools. Education in state schools is free for children under 19 years of age. Private schools are regularly visited by state school inspectors.

Report of the Minister of Education ('E.1. Report'). Annually. Wellington, Government Printer

NZ Committee on Secondary Education. *Towards Partnership*. Dept. of Education, 1976

Bates, R. J. (ed.), *Prospects in New Zealand Education*. Auckland, 1970

Ewing, J. L. *Compulsory Education in New Zealand*. Paris, UNESCO, 1969

Watson, J. E., *Intermediate Schooling in New Zealand*. Wellington, 1964

Social Welfare. New Zealand's record for progressive legislation reaches back to 1898, when it was second only to Denmark in introducing non-contributory old-age pensions.

The present system came into operation from 1 April 1972. It provides for retirement, unemployment, widowhood, invalidity and sickness, as well as hospital and other medical care. Since 1 April 1969 the scheme has been financed from general taxation. Previously there was a special social security tax on virtually all income of individuals and companies in excess of $4 a week which met approximately three-quarters of the cost of the scheme, the balance being met from general taxation.

At 31 March 1980 the current weekly rates of widows', invalids', sickness, domestic purposes, unemployment and miners' benefits were $94·70 for a married couple and $56·82 for an unmarried person.

There are additional payments for dependent children.

All benefits except superannuation and family allowances are subject to an income test.

Family Benefit. A family benefit of $6 a week is payable for each dependent child.

Unemployment Benefit. The payment is subject to the condition that the applicant is capable and willing to undertake suitable employment.

Sickness Benefit. Payment is subject to medical evidence of incapacity of a person who has suffered a loss of weekly earnings as a result.

Other benefits include emergency benefits and additional benefits for those in need but who either do not qualify for one of the standard benefits or who have special needs or commitments for which a benefit at the standard rate is insufficient.

Medical, Hospital and Related Benefits. Medical, hospital and other related benefits are also provided under the Social Welfare scheme. These consist mainly of the payment of certain fees for medical attention by private practitioners, free treatment in public and mental hospitals, certain fees for treatment in private hospitals, maternity benefits (including ante-natal and post-natal treatment and services of doctors and nurses at confinements), pharmaceutical benefits (medicines, drugs, etc., prescribed by medical practitioners), etc. There are also benefits in connexion with dental services up to the age of 16, X-ray diagnosis, massage, home-nursing, artificial aids, etc.

Pensions. Provision is made for the payment of pensions and allowances to members or dependants of disabled, deceased or missing members, of the New Zealand Forces who served in the South African War, the two World Wars, the Korean War and the Vietnam War, to members of the New Zealand Mercantile Marine during the Second World War, or in connexion with any emergency whether arising out of the obligations undertaken by New Zealand in the Charter of the United Nations or otherwise. Principal rates are: War pensions are payable to widows at a rate of $27.55 a week, together with a mother's allowance of $31.88 a week, increased by $4 a week for each additional child, in addition to the normal child allowances of $6 per week for each child. The rate for total disablement is $37.35. These rates may be increased by an amount not exceeding $22.45 per week if the pensioner is suffering from total blindness, two or more serious disabilities or one extremely severe disability.

An 'economic pension' is defined as a supplementary pension granted on economic grounds and is additional to any pension payable as of right in respect of death or disablement. The maximum weekly rates are $47.35 to a married person (if unmarried, $56.82); to the widow or dependent widowed mother of a member, $56.82.

War veterans' allowances are $56.82 weekly for a single person and $47.35 for a married person, plus an equal amount to a wife, increased by $1.50 a week each at age 65, subject to income qualifications.

Domestic Purposes Benefit. A domestic purposes benefit is payable to unsupported male and female solo parents including divorced, separated and unmarried persons, prisoners' spouses and also to those who are required to give full-time care to a person (other than their spouse) who would otherwise have to be admitted to hospital.

Death Benefit. A death benefit of $1,000 is payable to a widow or widower if totally dependent on the deceased plus $500 for each dependent child but not exceeding $1,500.

Social Welfare Benefits and War Pensions:

Benefits	Number in force at 31 March 1980	Total payments 1979–80 (NZ$1,000)
SOCIAL WELFARE:		
Monetary—		
Superannuation	405,834	1,334,115
Widows	16,120	53,342
Orphans	413	778
Family	460,897	220,854
Invalids	15,647	40,924
Miners	21	76
Unemployment	20,850	66,077
Sickness	7,504	33,236
Domestic purposes	37,040	169,449
Total	964,326	1,919,851

Benefits	Number in force at 31 March 1980	Total payments 1979–80 (NZ$1,000)
SOCIAL WELFARE (*contd*.):		
Health, etc.—		
Medical		47,094
Hospital		26,726
Maternity		7,077
Pharmaceutical		132,797
Supplementary		28,307
Total		242,002
WAR PENSION, ETC.:		
First World War	3,560	9,202
Second World War	22,069	47,078
Korean War	274	298
Vietnam War	246	125
War veterans' allowances	3,874	16,957
Mercantile Marine	20	40
Other	6,749	…
Total	36,792	73,700

Reciprocity with Other Countries. There are reciprocal arrangements between New Zealand and Australia in respect of age, invalids', widows', family, unemployment and sickness benefits, and between New Zealand and the UK in respect of family, age, superannuation, widows', orphans', invalids', sickness and unemployment benefits.

Superannuation. Following the change of Government in Dec. 1975 the earnings-related superannuation scheme described in THE STATESMAN'S YEAR-BOOK, 1977–78, was abolished. Under the new system (operative from Feb. 1977) superannuation is payable to all New Zealanders on reaching the age of 60. It is taxable but not subject to an income test. The rates are based on the national average wage, of which married couples now receive 80% and single persons 60% of the married rate.

Health. In 1978 there were 7,395 doctors on the medical register. At 31 March 1978 there were 32,900 hospital beds, of which 2,718 were for maternity cases.

MINOR ISLANDS

The minor islands (total area, 320 sq. miles, 775 sq. km) included within the geographical boundaries of New Zealand are the following: Kermadec Islands, Three Kings Islands, Auckland Islands, Campbell Island, Antipodes Islands, Bounty Islands, Snares Islands, Solander Island. With the exception of Raoul Island in the Kermadec Group (population, 12) and Campbell Island (population, 10) none of these islands is inhabited.

The **Kermadec Islands**, which were annexed to New Zealand in 1887, have no separate administration and all New Zealand laws apply to them. Situation, 29° 10′ to 131° 30′ S. lat., 177° 45′ to 179° W. long., 600 miles NNE of New Zealand. Area, 13 sq. miles (33·5 sq. km). The largest of the group is Raoul or Sunday Island, 20 miles in circuit, while Macaulay Island is 3 miles in circuit.

A meteorological station and an aeradio station have been established on Raoul Island, the official staff of 12 being the only inhabitants.

TERRITORIES OVERSEAS

Territories Overseas coming within the jurisdiction of New Zealand consist of Tokelau and the Ross Dependency.

Tokelau. Situated some 480 km to the north of Western Samoa between 8° and 10° S. lat., and between 171° and 173° W. long., are the 3 atoll islands of Atafu, Nukunonu and Fakaofo of the Tokelau (Union) group. Formerly part of the Gilbert and Ellice Islands Colony, the group was transferred to the jurisdiction of New Zealand on 11 Feb. 1926. By legislation enacted in 1948, the Tokelau Islands were declared part of New Zealand as from 1 Jan. 1949. The area of the group is 1,011 hectares; the population at 25 Oct. 1976 was 1,575.

By the Tokelau Islands Act 1948 the Tokelau Group was included within the territorial boundaries of New Zealand; legislative powers are now invested in the Governor-General in Council. The inhabitants are British subjects and New Zealand citizens. In Dec. 1976 the territory was officially renamed 'Tokelau', the name by which it has customarily been known to its inhabitants.

From 8 Nov. 1974 the office of Administrator was invested in the Secretary of Foreign Affairs. Certain powers are delegated to the district officer in Apia, Western Samoa.

Because of the very restricted economic and social future in the atolls, the islanders agreed to a proposal put to them by the Minister of Island Territories in 1965 that over a period of years most of the population be resettled in New Zealand. Up to March 1975, 528 migrants entered New Zealand as permanent residents under Government sponsorship. At the request of the people the scheme has now been suspended.

New Zealand Government aid to Tokelau totalled $900,000 for 1977–78.

Ross Dependency. By Imperial Order in Council, dated 30 July 1923, the territories between 160° E. long. and 150° W. long. and south of 60° S. lat. were brought within the jurisdiction of the New Zealand Government. The region was named the Ross Dependency. From time to time laws for the Dependency have been made by regulations promulgated by the Governor-General of New Zealand.

The mainland area is estimated at 400,000–450,000 sq. km and is mostly ice-covered. In Jan. 1957 a New Zealand expedition under Sir Edmund Hillary established a base in the Dependency. In Jan. 1958 Sir Edmund Hillary and 4 other New Zealanders reached the South Pole.

The main base—Scott Base—at Pram Point, Ross Island—is manned throughout the year, about 12 people being present during winter. Vanda Station in the dry ice-free Wright Valley is manned every summer.

Quartermain, L. B., *New Zealand and the Antarctic.* Wellington, 1971

SELF-GOVERNING TERRITORY OVERSEAS

THE COOK ISLANDS

HISTORY. The Cook Islands, which lie between 8° and 23° S. lat., and 156° and 167° W. long., were proclaimed a British protectorate in 1888, and on 11 June 1901 were annexed and proclaimed part of New Zealand. The islands within the territory fall roughly into two groups—the scattered islands towards the north (Northern group) and the islands towards the south known as the Lower group.

AREA AND POPULATION. The names of the islands with their populations as at the census of 1 Dec. 1976 were as follows:

Lower Group—	Area sq. km	Population	Northern Group—	Area sq. km	Population
Rarotonga	67·2	9,811	Nassau	1·2	113
Mangaia	51·8	1,530	Palmerston (Avarau)	2·0	53
Atiu	26·9	1,312	Penrhyn (Tongareva)	9·8	531

Lower Group (contd.)—	*Area* *sq. km*	*Population*	*Northern Group* (contd.)—	*Area* *sq. km*	*Population*
Aitutaki	18·0	2,414	Manihiki (Humphrey)	5·4	263
Mauke (Parry Is.)	18·4	710	Rakahanga (Reirson)	4·1	283
Mitiaro	22·3	305	Pukapuka (Danger)	5·1	786
Manuae and Te au-o-tu	...	—	Suwarrow (Anchorage)	0·4	1
			Total		18,112

In 1978, 520 live births and 162 deaths were registered.

CONSTITUTION AND GOVERNMENT. The Cook Islands Constitution Act 1964, which provides for the establishment of internal self-government in the Cook Islands, came into force on 4 Aug. 1965.

The Act establishes the Cook Islands as fully self-governing but linked to New Zealand by a common Head of State, the Queen, and a common citizenship, that of New Zealand. It provides for a ministerial system of government with a Cabinet consisting of a Premier and 6 other Ministers. The Resident Commissioner became the High Commissioner of the Cook Islands, who exercises the dual functions of representative of the Queen and of the New Zealand Government. New Zealand continues to be responsible for the external affairs and defence of the Cook Islands, subject to consultation between the New Zealand Prime Minister and the Premier. The changed status of the Islands does not affect the consideration of subsidies or the right of free entry into New Zealand for exports from the group.

Prime Minister: Dr Thomas Davis.

ECONOMY AND TRADE

Budget. Revenue is derived chiefly from customs duties which follow the New Zealand customs tariff, income tax and stamp sales.

Grants from New Zealand, mainly for medical, educational and general administrative purposes totalled $6,168,000 in 1977–78.

Agriculture. Livestock (1979): Pigs, 17,000; goats, 3,000; poultry, 65,000.

Commerce. Exports, mainly to New Zealand, were valued at $2·41m. in 1978. Main items of export were fruit juice, canned pineapple, copra and clothing. Imports from New Zealand in the year ending June 1979 (including re-exports from New Zealand) totalled $13,651,000. The main items were foodstuffs, drapery and piece-goods, motor vehicles, petrol and oil.

COMMUNICATIONS

Aviation. New Zealand has financed the construction of an international airport at Rarotonga which became operational for jet services in Sept. 1973.

Shipping. A monthly passenger-cargo shipping service is provided between New Zealand and Rarotonga.

Telecommunications. Wireless stations are maintained at all the permanently inhabited islands. In 1978 there were 1,186 telephones.

EDUCATION AND HEALTH

Education. Twenty-nine primary schools are established in the various islands. There are also 6 Roman Catholic missionary schools and a Seventh-day Adventist mission school. Post-primary education is provided for by 4 government and 2 mission schools on Rarotonga. The instruction given in government schools is similar to that of the New Zealand state schools, but with a special syllabus suited to the requirements of the people. Regular instruction is given in the Maori language in all classes, while during the first 2 years all instruction is in the vernacular, English being taught only as a subject. Numbers of pupils on the rolls (31 March 1977): 6,487. At the same date 88 students were receiving education or vocational training in New Zealand.

Health. All Cook Islanders receive free medical and surgical treatment in their villages, the hospital and the tuberculosis sanatorium. Cook Island Maori patients in the hospital and the sanatorium and all schoolchildren receive free dental treatment.

NIUE ISLAND

History. Niue Island achieved internal self-government in Oct. 1974.

Area and Population. Distance from Auckland, New Zealand, 1,343 miles; from Rarotonga, 580 miles. Area, 100 sq. miles; circumference, 40 miles; height above sea-level, 220 ft. Population at 31 Dec. 1976 was 3,954. During 1973 live births registered numbered 105, deaths 26. Migration to New Zealand is the main factor in population change.

Government. There is an Island Assembly, and legislative measures apply as in the case of the Cook Islands.

Budget. Financial aid from New Zealand, 1977–78, totalled $2·8m.

Agriculture. The most important products of the island are copra, passion fruit, honey and limes.

Trade. Exports, 1976, $152,690; imports, $1,599,419.

Communications. There is a wireless station at Alofi, the port of the island. A weekly commercial air service links Niue with Tonga and Western Samoa.

Education. There were 10 government schools with 1,369 pupils in 1976.

Quarterly Statistical Bulletin. Statistics Office, Rarotonga
Buck, P. H., *Vikings of the Sunrise.* New York, 1938.—*The Coming of the Maori.* Wellington, 1950
Ross, A. (ed.), *New Zealand's Record in the Pacific Islands in the Twentieth Century.* Auckland, 1969

DIPLOMATIC REPRESENTATIVES

OF NEW ZEALAND IN GREAT BRITAIN (New Zealand Hse, Haymarket, London, SW1Y 4TQ)

High Commissioner: L. W. Gandar.

OF GREAT BRITAIN IN NEW ZEALAND
(Reserve Bank of New Zealand Bldg., 2 The Terrace, Wellington, 1)

High Commissioner: R. J. Stratton, CMG.

OF NEW ZEALAND IN THE USA (37 Observatory Cir., NW, Washington, D.C., 20008)

Ambassador: T. F. Gill.

OF THE USA IN NEW ZEALAND
(29 Fitzherbert Terrace, Wellington)

Ambassador: Anne C. Martindell.

OF NEW ZEALAND TO THE UNITED NATIONS
Ambassador: Harold H. Francis.

Books of Reference

Statistical Information: The central statistical office for New Zealand is the Department of Statistics (Wellington, 1).

The beginning of a statistical service may be seen in the early 'Blue books' prepared annually from 1840 onwards under the direction of the Colonial Secretary, and designed primarily for the information of the Colonial Office in England. A permanent statistical authority was created in 1858. The Department of Statistics functions under the Statistics Act 1975 and reports to

Parliament through the Minister of Statistics. A comprehensive statistical service has been developed to meet national requirements, and close contact is maintained with the United Nations Statistical Office and other international statistical organizations; through the Conference of Asian Statisticians assistance is being given with the development of statistics in the region.

The oldest publications consist of (*a*) census results from 1858 onwards and (*b*) annual volumes of statistics (first published 1858 but covering years back to 1853). Main current publications:

New Zealand Official Yearbook. Annual, from 1893
Catalogue of New Zealand Statistics. 1972
Statistical Reports of New Zealand. Annual
Monthly Abstract of Statistics. From 1914
Pocket Digest of Statistics. Annual, 1927–31, 1938 ff.

Parliamentary Reports of Government Departments. Annual
Pacific Islands Yearbook. Sydney, 1977
Dictionary of New Zealand Biography. 2 vols. Wellington, 1940
Encyclopaedia of New Zealand. 3 vols. Wellington, 1966
National Bibliography. Wellington, 1968
New Zealand Financial System. Wellington, 1966
Oxford New Zealand Encyclopaedia. London, 1965
Best, Elsdon, *The Maori As He Was.* Wellington, 1974
Bright, T. N., *Banking Law and Practice in New Zealand.* 2nd ed. Wellington, 1969
Firth, R., *Economics of the New Zealand Maori.* Wellington, Government Printer, 1959
Hall, D. O. W., *Portrait of New Zealand.* 3rd ed. Wellington, 1961
Holcroft, M. H., *New Zealand.* Wellington, 1968
Holmes, F. W., *Money, Finance and the Economy.* Auckland, 1972
Institute of Public Administration. *Administration in New Zealand's Multi-racial Society.* Wellington, 1968
Kennaway, R., *New Zealand Foreign Policy, 1951–71.* Wellington and London, 1973
Levine, S. (ed.), *Politics in New Zealand.* London, 1978
Metge, J., *The Maoris of New Zealand.* London, 1976
Morrell, W. P., and Hall, D. O. W., *A History of New Zealand Life.* Christchurch and London, 1957
Oliver, W. H., *The Story of New Zealand.* London, 1963
Polaschek, R. J. (ed.), *Local Government in New Zealand.* Wellington, 1956.—*Government Administration in New Zealand.* Wellington, 1958
Robson, J. L. (ed.), *New Zealand: The Development of its Laws and Constitution.* 2nd ed. London, 1967
Rowe, J. W. and M. A., *New Zealand.* London, 1967
Shadbolt, M. F. R., *The Shell Guide to New Zealand.* Christchurch, 1976
Sinclair, K., *A History of New Zealand.* Penguin, 1969
Traue, J. E., *Who's Who in New Zealand.* 11th ed. Wellington, 1977
Wards, I., *A Descriptive Atlas of New Zealand.* Wellington, Government Printer, 1976
Watters, R. F. (ed.), *Land and Society in New Zealand.* Wellington, 1965
Wise's New Zealand Guide. 7th ed. Auckland, 1979

NICARAGUA

República de Nicaragua

Capital: Managua
Population: 2·5m. (1980)
GNP per capita: US$840 (1978)

HISTORY. Active colonization of the Pacific coast was undertaken by Spaniards from Panama, beginning in 1523. After links with other Central American territories, and Mexico, Nicaragua became completely independent in 1838, but subject to a prolonged feud between the 'Liberals' of León and the 'Conservatives' of Granada. Mosquitia remained an autonomous kingdom on the Atlantic coast, under British protection until 1860.

On 5 Aug. 1914 the Bryan–Chamarro treaty between Nicaragua and the US was signed, under which the US in return for US$3m. acquired a permanent option for a canal route through Nicaragua and a 99-year option for a naval base in the Bay of Fonseca on the Pacific coast and Corn Island on the Atlantic coast. It was ratified by Nicaragua on 7 April 1916 and by the US on 22 June 1916. US Marines finally left in 1933.

The Bryan–Chamarro treaty was abrogated on 14 July 1970.

AREA AND POPULATION. Area estimated at 148,000 sq. km (57,143 sq. miles) or 139,000 sq. km (54,296 sq. miles) if the lakes are excluded. The coastline runs 336 miles on the Atlantic and 219 miles on the Pacific. Population at the census of April 1971 was 1,911,543 (922,433 males, 989,110 females). Estimate (1980) 2,568,000.

Nicaragua is the largest in area and most thinly populated of the Central American republics. Crude birth rate, 1977, 42·31 per 1,000 population; crude death rate, 5·54; infantile mortality rate, 36·98 per 1,000 live births; crude marriage rate, 5·48 per 1,000 population.

In 1977 about 52% of the inhabitants lived in urban areas and 48% in rural areas.

The people of the western half of the republic are principally of mixed Spanish and Indian extraction, some of pure Spanish descent and many Indians. The population of the eastern half is composed mainly of Mosquito and other Indians and Zambos, and Negroes from Jamaica and other islands of the Caribbean. The main ethnic groups in 1974 were: Mestizo, 69%; white, 19%; Negro, 9%; Indio, 5%.

Nicaragua is administratively divided into the following 16 departments with population as on 31 Dec. 1978:

Boaco	79,641	Jinotega	112,591	Matagalpa	199,433
Carazo	97,388	Leon	220,878	Nueva Segovia	85,025
Chinandega	199,156	Madriz	64,491	Río San Juan	25,481
Chontales	81,416	Managua	677,963	Rivas	96,546
Esteli	96,119	Masaya	131,518	Zelaya	176,921
Granada	99,537				

Of the 134 *municipios*, 98 have from 2,000 to 50,000 inhabitants. The capital is Managua, situated on the lake of the same name, 180 ft above sea level, with (1978) 552,900 inhabitants. Other cities: León, 81,647; Granada, 56,232; Masaya, 47,276; Chinandega, 44,435; Matagalpa, 26,986; Estelí, 26,892; Bluefields, 18,252; Jinotega, 14,088; Juigalpa, 13,468; Boaco, 8,684.

CONSTITUTION AND GOVERNMENT. On 31 Aug. 1971 the Congress voted in favour of dissolution and the abrogation of the Constitution.

On 14 March 1974 a new Constitution came into force and provided for a national congress consisting of a Chamber of Deputies of 70 members and a

Senate of 30 members but on 20 July 1979, following the fall of Gen. Somoza, a Government Junta abrogated the Constitution; members of the Junta are Violeta B. de Chamorro, Sergio Ramirez Mercado, Moisés Hassan M, Alfonso Robelo Callejas and Daniel Ortega Saavedra.

In Aug. 1980 it was announced that elections had been postponed until 1985.

The republic is divided into 16 departments, each of which is under a political head (appointed by the President), who has supervision of finance, education and other matters. The departments have 134 *municipios*, headed by a mayor (*alcalde*). The Mosquito Reserve now forms part of the departments of Zelaya and Río San Juan.

National flag: Three horizontal stripes of blue, white, blue, with the national arms in the centre.

National anthem: Salve a ti Nicaragua (words by S. Ibarra Mayorga, 1937).

DEFENCE

Army. The National Guard (which functions as police force and army) numbered (1979) 8,000 officers and other ranks, besides 4,000 in the trained reserve. Period of enlistment, 3 years, but military service may be made compulsory at any time. A new force was being reconstituted in 1980.

Navy. Four coastguard cutters and 11 coastal patrol craft operated by the marine section of the National Guard picket the east and west coasts. An ancient patrol boat was used for training. Personnel in 1981 totalled 200 officers and men.

Air Force. Formed in June 1938 as the Nicaraguan Army Air Force, the Air Force has been semi-independent since 1947. Its combat units have 10 Summit 02–337 Sentry counter-insurgency aircraft, 4 T-33 armed jet trainers, and 3 T-28 armed piston-engined trainers. Other equipment includes some C-47s, 5 Spanish-built Aviocar and 2 Israeli-built Arava STOL transports and smaller communications aircraft and helicopters. Approximate strength is 200 personnel and 50 aircraft.

INTERNATIONAL RELATIONS

Membership. Nicaragua is a member of the UN, OAS and the Central American Common Market.

ECONOMY

Planning. The objects of the National Reconstruction Plan 1975–79 included the reconstruction of Managua which took one-third of the US$6,000m. envisaged for the plan.

Budget. Revenue and expenditure for fiscal years, ending 31 Dec., in 1m. córdobas:

	1974	1975	1976	1977	1978	1979
Revenue	2,093·2	1,820·3	2,052·3	2,774·3	3,255·3	3,760·1
Expenditure	1,710·3	1,881·9	2,223·1	2,427·6	3,433·8	3,409·0

The 1979 budget included 371·1m. for defence, 358·2m. for education, 120·8m. for the Ministry of Finance and Public Credit, 111·2m. for health and 60·6m. córdobas for commerce and public works,

The external debt at the end of 1978 was 556·8m. córdobas; the internal debt was 17·6m. córdobas.

Currency. The monetary unit is the *córdoba* (C$), divided into 100 *centavos*. Its exchange parity with gold is managed by the Central Bank of Nicaragua and the Government. On 31 Dec. 1978 total money supply was 1,887·8m. córdobas. Bills form the greater part of the currency, in denominations from 1,000 córdobas to 1 córdoba. Silver coins struck, but now out of circulation, are 50, 25 and 10 centavos; copper–nickel and copper–zinc coins, 1 córdoba, 50, 25, 10 and 5 centavos.

Banking. The National Bank of Nicaragua at Managua, founded in 1912, owned by the Government since 1924 was reorganized in July 1979, becoming the National Development Bank and including the National Development Institute (INFONAC) and Special Fund for Development (FED). This new law gave it increased responsibilities as a development bank. The Central Bank of Nicaragua came into operation on 1 Jan. 1961 as an autonomous bank of issue, absorbing the issue department of the National Bank.

In July 1979 private financial banking was nationalized and branches of foreign banks were prohibited from receiving deposits.

Weights and Measures. Since 1893 the metric system of weights and measures has been recommended.

ENERGY AND NATURAL RESOURCES

Electricity. Installed capacity for electric energy was 357,700 kw. in 1977 and 1,180·3 kwh. was produced.

Minerals. Production of gold in 1978 was 67,355 troy oz.; of silver, 603,627 troy oz.; of copper, 3,000 tonnes. There is no iron or coalmining. Large deposits of tungsten in Nueva Segovia were announced in 1961. Exploration for petroleum began off the Pacific and Atlantic coasts in 1965. A petroleum refinery of 650,000 tonnes capacity is functioning at Managua.

Agriculture. Agriculture is the principal source of national wealth, finding work for 65% of the labour force, and furnishing, 1975, 22% of the GNP.

Of the total land area (about 36·5m. acres), about 17·5m. acres are under timber, 0·9m. acres are used for grazing and 2·1m. acres are arable. The unit of area used locally is the *manzana* (= 1·73 acres). Of the arable only 1·2m. acres are actively cultivated, 780,000 in annual crops such as cotton and rice and the remainder in perennial crops such as coffee and sugar-cane, or in two harvests a year in the cases of maize, sorghum and beans.

The products of the western half are varied, the most important being cotton, coffee, now under the aegis of the new *Instituto del Café*, sugar-cane, cocoa, maize, sesame and beans. Production (1979–80.): Coffee (in bags of 60 kg) 860,000; sugar (tonnes) 200,000; cotton (bales of 478lb.) 100,000.

There were about 2·8m. head of cattle in 1979. There are now 4 modern meat-packing plants; slaughterings were 481,700 heads in 1978. There were 725,000 pigs (1979). Beef exports in 1978 were valued at US$67·7m.

Forestry. Timber production has been declining, though the forests, which cover 10m. acres and 4 distinct zones, contain mahogany and cedar, which were formerly largely exported, three varieties of rosewoods, guayacán (*lignum vitae*) and dye-woods. In 1968–69 exploitation of these vast areas of timber with a potential production of 300,000 tonnes per annum was begun. Production of sawn wood in 1978, 270,000 tonnes.

Fishery. On the Atlantic coast fisheries are an important subsistence activity. Over 6·4m. lb. of shrimps were exported in 1978 and were processed in 3 plants at Schooner Cay, El Bluff and Corn Island. The fishing limit off the coast has been defined as 200 nautical miles. Within that limit, fishing is subject to the provisions of the National Resources Exploration Law.

INDUSTRY AND TRADE

Industry. Chief local industries are cane sugar, cooking oil, cigarettes, beer, leather products, plastics, textiles, chemical products, metal products, cement (210,600 tonnes in 1977), strong and soft drinks, soluble coffee, dairy products, meat, ply-wood. Production of oil products, in 1978, was valued at 526m. córdobas; food products, 3,338·4m.; beverages, 565·8m.; textiles, 328·7m.; chemical substances and products, 1,054m.

Labour. In 1975 there were some 654,683 persons gainfully employed; of these: agriculture, 47·9%; manufacturing, construction, mining and power, 15·4%; services, transport and commerce, 35%.

Commerce. The foreign trade of Nicaragua, in US$1m., was as follows in calendar years:

	1976	1977	1978	1979	1980
Imports	532·1	761·9	553·0	388·0	700·0
Exports	541·9	636·8	645·9	598·0	524·0

The main imports in 1977 (in US$1m.) were: Machinery and vehicles, 239·9; chemicals, 161·4; crude oil, 77·9; foodstuffs, 33·2. These were supplied mainly by USA, Venezuela, Federal Republic of Germany, Japan, Costa Rica and Guatemala.

In 1978 the main exports (in US$1m.) were: Coffee, 199·6; cotton, 140·9; meat, 67·7; chemical products, 52·2; sugar, 19·6.

Total trade between Nicaragua and UK (British Department of Trade returns, in £1,000 sterling):

	1975	1976	1977	1978	1979	1980
Imports to UK	9,890	1,174	1,393	1,414	895	1,510
Exports and re-exports from UK	5,247	8,335	8,841	7,560	3,229	2,478

COMMUNICATIONS

Roads. In 1978, 1,570 km were paved, out of a total of 18,197 km. The whole 368·5 km of the Nicaraguan section of the Pan-American Highway is now paved. The all-weather Roosevelt Highway linking Managua with the river port Rama was completed in 1968, to provide the first overland link with the Atlantic coast. There are paved roads to San Juan del Sur, Puerto Somoza and Corinto. In 1977 there were 46,381 passenger cars and vans in use.

Railways. The Pacific Railroad of Nicaragua, owned and operated by the Government, has a total length of 373 km, all single-track, and connects Corinto, Chinandega, León, Managua, Masaya and Granada. Passengers carried (1978) 448,932; freight, 66,452 tonnes.

Aviation. LANICA, the Nicaraguan airline, has daily flights to Miami and 6 flights a week to Guatemala and to the inner cities of Bluefields, Puerto Cabezas and the mining towns of Siuna and Bonanza. PANAM and TACA (Transportes Aéreos Centroamericanos), COPA (Compañía Panameña de Aviacíon), have daily services to Panama, Mexico, the other Central American countries and USA. SAM (Servicio Aéreo de Medellín) has 3 flights a week to Nicaragua and Colombia. In 1977, 223,420 passengers and 24·2m. tonnes of cargo were carried.

Shipping. The Pacific ports are Corinto (the largest), San Juan del Sur and Puerto Saudino through which pass most of the external trade. The chief eastern ports are El Bluff (for Bluefields) and Puerto Cabezas. The merchant marine consists solely of the Mamenic Line with 8 vessels. In 1977, 724,966 short tons of goods were loaded and 1·42m. tonnes unloaded at Nicaraguan ports.

Post and Broadcasting. There are (1977) 16,000 km of (government-owned) telegraph line and 328 offices and (1978) there were 55,803 telephones.

The Tropical Radio Telegraph Company maintains a powerful station at Managua, and branch stations at Bluefields and Puerto Cabezas. The Government operates the National Radio with 47 broadcasting stations: there are 31 commercial stations and some 70 others. Number of wireless sets in 1972 was 115,000 and television sets 60,000. There are 2 television stations at Managua.

Cinemas. Cinemas numbered over 100 in 1977 and seated over 60,000.

Newspapers. There are 3 daily newspapers (2 in Managua and 1 in León), with a total circulation of about 105,000.

JUSTICE, RELIGION, EDUCATION AND WELFARE

Justice. The judicial power is vested in a Supreme Court of Justice at Managua, 5 chambers of second instance (León, Masaya, Granada, Matagalpa and Bluefields) and 153 judges of inferior tribunals.

Religion. The prevailing form of religion is Roman Catholic, but religious liberty is guaranteed by the Constitution. The republic constitutes 1 archbishopric (seat at Managua) and 7 bishoprics (Léon, Granada, Estelí, Matagalpa, Juigalpa, Masaya and Puerto Cabezas). Protestants, established principally on the Atlantic coast, numbered 54,100 in 1966.

Education. There were, in 1977, 2,334 elementary schools, with a total of 368,895 pupils and 9,729 teachers; and 275 secondary schools, with 105,429 pupils and 2,954 teachers. Illiterate persons, of all ages, number 63·7% of the population. In 1977 there were 6 universities and technical colleges with 1,204 professors and 23,171 students.

Social Welfare. In 1977 the minimum daily wage ranged from 6·58 to 21·60 córdobas daily according to different zones and workers' classifications. In 1977 there were 41 hospitals with 4,670 beds.

DIPLOMATIC REPRESENTATIVES

OF NICARAGUA IN GREAT BRITAIN (8 Gloucester Rd., London, SW7 4PP)

Ambassador: Gonzalo Murillo-Romero (accredited 14 Dec. 1979).

OF GREAT BRITAIN IN NICARAGUA

Ambassador and Consul-General: J. Michael Brown (resides in San José).

OF NICARAGUA IN THE USA (1627 New Hampshire Ave., NW, Washington, D.C., 20009)

Chargé d'Affaires: Dionisio Saul Arana.

OF THE USA IN NICARAGUA (Km. 4½ Carretera Sur., Managua)

Ambassador: Lawrence A. Pezzullo.

OF NICARAGUA TO THE UNITED NATIONS

Ambassador: Victor Hugo Tinoco Fonseca.

Books of Reference

Dirección General Estadística y Censos, *Boletín de Estadística* (irregular intervals); and *Indicadores Economicos.*
Boletín de la Superintendencia de Bancos. Banco Central, Managua
Nicaragua Comercio Exterior, 1978. Managua, 1979

National Library: Biblioteca Nacional, Managua, D.N.

NIGER

République du Niger

Capital: Niamey
Population: 5·3m. (1979)
GNP per capita: US$220 (1978)

HISTORY. The Republic of the Niger became independent on 3 Aug. 1960, after having been a territory of French West Africa from 1904.

AREA AND POPULATION. Niger is bounded north by Algeria and Libya, east by Chad, south by Nigeria, south-west by Dahomey and Upper Volta and west by Mali. The area, 1,186,408 sq. km (458,075 sq. miles), divided into 7 *départements* with 38 *arrondissements*. Population (1979), 5·3m. The major towns (populations 1975) are: Niamey, the capital (130,299 inhabitants), Maradi (42,000), Zinder (41,000), Tahoua (31,000). The population is composed chiefly of Hausa (54%), Songhai and Djerma (23%), Fulani (10%), Beriberi-Manga (9%) and Tuareg (3%). Precipitation determines the geographical division into a southern zone of agriculture, a central zone of pasturage and a desert-like northern zone. The country lacks water, with the exception of the western districts, which are watered by the Niger and its tributaries, and the southern zone, where there are a number of wells.

The official language is French.

CONSTITUTION AND GOVERNMENT. On 15 April 1974 President Hamani was overthrown in a military *coup*. Lieut.-Col. Seyni Kountché suspended the Constitution, dissolved the National Assembly and banned political groups.

President: Col. Seyni Kountché.
Foreign Affairs: Daouda Diallo.

National flag: Three horizontal strips of orange, white and green, with an orange disc in the middle of the white strip.

DEFENCE

Army. The Army consists of 1 paratroop, 1 engineer and 4 infantry companies and 2 armoured-car squadrons; total strength (1980), 2,150.

Air Force. The Air Force has 70 officers and men, 4 ex-*Luftwaffe* Noratlas transports, 2 C-130H, 2 DC-6B, 1 C-54, and 2 C-47 transports, 1 Boeing 737 VIP transport, 1 Flamant light transport, 2 Cessna Skymasters, 5 Do 28D Skyservants, 4 Broussards and 1 Aero Commander 500 for communications duties.

INTERNATIONAL RELATIONS

Membership. Niger is a member of UN, OAU and is an ACP state of the EEC.

ECONOMY

Planning. An economic development plan, covering the period 1965–68 was followed by a 3-year preparatory plan and was part of a 10-year economic programme (1965–74). This was followed by a further 10-year plan (1973–82).

Investments under the 1965–68 plan totalled 43,000m. francs CFA. Some 4,000m. francs CFA was used for the development of water resources and 5,000m. francs CFA for the general improvement of agricultural production. No investment figures have been published for the 1973–82 plan.

Budget. The ordinary budget for 1980 balanced at 80,600m. francs CFA.

NATURAL RESOURCES

Minerals. Large uranium deposits have been discovered at Arlit, about 200 miles north of Agadez. A mining company has been formed with the Government of

927

Niger and the French Atomic Energy Commission. The construction of a uranium-ore concentrate plant was begun in 1968, with production starting in 1970. Production (1977) 1,609 tonnes. Salt and natron are produced at Manga and Agadez, tin ore in Aïr.

Agriculture. The chief agricultural products in 1978 were millet (1,000 tonnes), pulses (1,091 tonnes), sorghum (361 tonnes) and cassava (200 tonnes); in the river districts, cotton and rice. Gum arabic at Gouré, nearly all of which is exported to Nigeria. In 1979 there were 230,000 horses, 3m. cattle, 8·9m. sheep and goats, 440,000 asses, 330,000 camels.

TRADE. Imports in 1976 were valued at 30,383m. francs CFA and exports at 31,976m. francs CFA.

Total trade between Niger and UK (British Department of Trade returns, in £1,000 sterling):

	1976	1977	1978	1979	1980
Imports to UK	820	450	235	297	184
Exports and re-exports from UK	1,101	3,549	11,930	16,576	7,885

COMMUNICATIONS

Roads. In 1977 there were 7,587 km of roads. Niamey and Zinder are the termini of two trans-Sahara motor routes; the Hoggar–Aïr–Zinder road extends to Kano and N'djamena. There were (1977), 18,825 private cars and 3,321 goods vehicles.

Aviation. At Niamey airport 56,900 passengers and 6,770 tonnes of freight and mail were dealt with in 1973. Other international airports are at Zinder and Maradi.

Post and Broadcasting. There were (1977) 8,147 telephones. In 1975 there were 100,000 radio receivers.

Cinemas. In 1970 there were 4 cinemas with a seating capacity of 3,800.

RELIGION, EDUCATION AND WELFARE

Religion. In 1979, 85% of the population was Moslem and the remainder followed animist beliefs. There were about 20,000 Christians.

Education. There were, in 1978, 177,620 pupils in 1,401 primary schools, 21,944 in 53 secondary schools, 333 in the technical school in Maradi and 782 at the University of Niamey.

Health. In 1974 there were 56 hospitals with 3,734 beds. In 1976 there were 110 doctors.

DIPLOMATIC REPRESENTATIVES

OF NIGER IN GREAT BRITAIN

Ambassador: Amadou Seydou (accredited 5 Nov. 1975, resides in Paris).

OF GREAT BRITAIN IN NIGER

Ambassador and Consul-General: M. F. Daly (resides in Abidjan).

OF NIGER IN THE USA (2204 R. St., NW, Washington, D.C. 20008)

Ambassador: André Wright.

OF THE USA IN NIGER (PO Box 11201, Niamey)

Ambassador: James K. Bishop.

OF NIGER TO THE UNITED NATIONS

Ambassador: Idé Oumarou.

Books of Reference

Bonardi, P., *La République du Niger*. Paris, 1960
Séré de Rivières, E., *Histoire du Niger*. Paris, 1965

NIGERIA

Federal Republic of Nigeria

Capital: Lagos
Population: 81m. (1978)
GNP per capita: US$560 (1978)

HISTORY. The Federal Republic comprises a number of areas formerly under separate administrations. Lagos, ceded in Aug. 1861 by King Dosunmu, was placed under the Governor of Sierra Leone in 1866. In 1874 it was detached, together with Gold Coast Colony, and formed part of the latter until Jan. 1886, when a separate 'colony and protectorate of Lagos' was constituted. Meanwhile the United African Company had established British interests in the Niger valley, and in July 1886 the company obtained a charter under the name of the Royal Niger Company. This company surrendered its charter to the Crown on 31 Dec. 1899, and on 1 Jan. 1900 the greater part of its territories was formed into the protectorate of Northern Nigeria. Along the coast the Oil Rivers protectorate had been declared in June 1885. This was enlarged and renamed the Niger Coast protectorate in 1893; and on 1 Jan. 1900, on its absorbing the remainder of the territories of the Royal Niger Company, it became the protectorate of Southern Nigeria. In Feb. 1906 Lagos and Southern Nigeria were united into the 'colony and protectorate of Southern Nigeria', and on 1 Jan. 1914 the latter was amalgamated with the protectorate of Northern Nigeria to form the 'colony and protectorate of Nigeria', under a Governor. On 1 Oct. 1954 Nigeria became a federation under a Governor-General.

On 1 Oct. 1960 Nigeria became sovereign and independent and a member of the Commonwealth and on 1 Oct. 1963 Nigeria became a republic.

For the history of Nigeria from 1961 to 1978, *see* THE STATESMAN'S YEAR-BOOK, 1979–80, pp. 923–924.

AREA AND POPULATION. Area approximately 356,669 sq. miles (923,773 sq. km). Census population, Nov. 1963, 55,670,052.
There are 19 states:

States	Area (in sq. km)	Population	States	Area (in sq. km)	Population
Anambra	17,675	3,596,618	Kwara	66,869	1,714,485
Bauchi	64,605	2,431,296	Lagos	3,345	1,443,568
Bendel	35,500	2,460,962	Niger	65,037	1,194,508
Benue	45,174	2,427,017	Ogun	16,762	1,550,966
Borno	116,400	2,997,498	Ondo	20,959	2,729,690
Cross River	27,237	3,478,131	Oyo	37,705	5,208,884
Gongola	91,390	2,605,263	Plateau	58,030	2,026,657
Imo	11,850	3,672,654	Rivers	21,850	1,719,925
Kaduna	70,245	4,098,306	Sokoto	102,535	4,538,787
Kano	43,285	5,774,840			

See map in THE STATESMAN'S YEAR-BOOK, 1977–78.
The results of the 1973 census were abandoned in Aug. 1975 because they 'will not command general acceptance throughout the country'. There is considerable uncertainty over the total population, but one estimate based on electoral registration in 1978 is 95m. and the World Bank give an estimate of 81,039,000.

The populations of the largest towns were (1975 estimate) as follows: Lagos, 1,060,848; and (in 1,000) Ibadan, 847; Ogbomosho, 432; Kano, 399; Oshogbo, 282; Ilorin, 282; Abeokuta, 253; Port Harcourt, 242; Zaria, 224; Ilesha, 224; Onitsha, 220; Iwo, 214; Ado-Ekiti, 213; Kaduna, 202; Mushin, 197; Maiduguri, 189; Enugu, 187; Ede, 182; Aba, 177; Ife, 176; Ila, 155; Oyo, 152; Ikere-Ekiti, 145; Benin, 136; Iseyin, 129.

It was announced in Feb. 1976 that the federal capital would be moved inland from Lagos to Abuja area (federal district, 8,094 sq. km) north of river Niger.

Topography and Climate. A belt of mangrove swamp forest lies along the entire coastline. North of this there is a zone of tropical rain forest and oil-palm bush some 50–100 miles wide. Farther inland the country rises and the vegetation changes to open woodland and savannah. In the extreme north the country is almost desert. There are few mountains except along the eastern boundary and on the northern plateau, where peaks of over 5,000 ft occur. The Niger, Benue and Cross are the main rivers.

The climate varies with the types of country, but Nigeria lies wholly within the tropics, and temperatures are high. Temperatures of over 100°C are common in the north; coast temperatures are seldom over 90°C, but the humidity at the coast is much higher than in the north. Most of the rain falls between April and Sept. in the north and between March and Nov. in the south; rainfall varies from under 25 in. a year to 150 in. During the dry-season the 'harmattan' wind, laden with fine particles of dust, blows from the north-east.

CONSTITUTION AND GOVERNMENT. Under the Constitution drafted and ratified in 1977–78 by the Constitution Drafting Committee (CDC) and the Constituent Assembly respectively, Nigeria is a sovereign, federal republic comprising 19 states and a federal capital district. The Head of State is the President, in whom all executive power is vested; the President and Vice-President are directly elected.

President: Alhaji Shehu Shagari (elected 11 Aug. 1979, taking office 1 Oct.).
Vice-President: Dr Alex Ifeanyichukwu Ekwueme.

The two central legislative bodies are collectively referred to as the National Assembly which consists of a Senate of 96 members (5 from each of the 19 states) and the House of Representatives of 449 members. In the general elections of 1979, the election for the Senate took place on 7 July, for the States House of Assemblies and the House of Representatives on 14 July, for the Gubernatorial on 28 July, and the Presidential election on 10 Aug. resulting in the following composition (by Party):

Senate: National Party of Nigeria (NPN), 36; Unity Party of Nigeria (UPN), 28; NPP, 16; GNPP, 8; PRP, 7.
House of Representatives: NPN, 168; UPN, 111; NPP, 78; GNPP, 43; PRP, 49.

The official language is English but Hausa, Igbo and Yoruba languages are also used in the National Assembly, *i.e.* the Senate and the House of Representatives as well as in each of the State Houses of Assembly.

National flag: Three vertical strips of green, white, green.

Local Government: Elections were held on 21 July 1979 for the House of Assembly in each State. Beneath the State is a third tier of government. In Dec. 1976, the local government elections were held in all the states of the republic.

DEFENCE

Army. The Army consists of 4 infantry divisions, 4 reconnaissance regiments, 4 artillery and 4 engineer brigades. Total strength (1980) 130,000.

Navy. The Nigerian Navy was established in 1958. Administered by a vice-admiral as Chief of Naval Staff and a captain as Chief of Operations, the Navy includes the frigate *Nigeria* (built in the Netherlands in 1964–65), 4 corvettes built in Britain in 1970–72 (*Dorina* and *Otobo*), and 1975–80 (*Erinmi* and *Enyimiri*), 12 patrol craft, 18 coastal patrol boats, 2 medium landing ships, 1 supply ship, 1 survey ship, 1 training ship, 50 launches and 2 tugs. There are also 8 small patrol launches operated by the Nigerian Police. New construction includes 1 large missile-armed frigate being built in Germany (Fed. Rep.), 6 fast missile-armed attack craft (3 in Germany (Fed. Rep.) and 3 in France) and 2 landing craft from France. Naval personnel in

1981 totalled 510 officers and 3,140 ratings, and there were 2,000 reservists.

Air Force. The Nigerian Air Force was established in Jan. 1964. Pilots were trained initially in Canada, India and Ethiopia. The Air Force was built up subsequently with the aid of a Federal Republic of Germany mission; much first-line equipment has since been received from the Soviet Union. It includes 18 MiG-21 supersonic jet-fighters, about 3 MiG-17 fighter-bombers, a few MiG-15UTI and MiG-21U fighter-trainers, 12 Alpha Jet and some L-29 Delfin armed jet trainers from Czechoslovakia. About 20 BO 105 twin-turbine helicopters have been acquired from the Federal Republic of Germany for search and rescue. Transport units operate 6 C-130H Hercules 4-turboprop heavy transports, a Fokker F.28 Fellowship twin-turbofan airliner for Presidential use, 2 turboprop Friendships, 2 Navajos and a Navajo Chieftain. Training types include 32 Bulldog primary trainers, plus Do 27s and Dornier Skyservants for instrument training, transport and ambulance duties. Thirteen medium-lift Aérospatiale Pumas and a few light helicopters are also in service. Personnel (1980) total about 8,000.

INTERNATIONAL RELATIONS

Membership. Nigeria is a member of UN, the Commonwealth, ECOWAS, OAU, OPEC and is an ACP state of EEC.

ECONOMY

Planning. The first national development plan ran from 1962 to 1968; the second plan (1970–74) provided for a total expenditure of £1,596m. The third national development plan ran from 1975 to 1980 and provided for an expenditure of ₦40,000m. The fourth plan (1981–85) was launched in 1981.

Budget. Expenditure 1979–80 totalled ₦9,510m. Education (10%) and defence (14%). Budgets are to run for calendar years from 1981.

In July 1980 external reserves were ₦5,200m.

Currency. Since 1 Jan. 1973 a decimal currency has been issued by the Central Bank of Nigeria, consisting of *Naira* (₦) and divided into 100 *kobo* (k). Notes in circulation ₦20, ₦10, ₦5, ₦1, 50k. Coins, 25k, 10k, 5k, 1k, ½k.

In March 1980, £1 = ₦1·24; US$1 = 0·58.

Banking. In Aug. 1967 the statutory foreign-exchange cover of the Central Bank was reduced from 40 to 25%, and the percentage of government securities the Bank is permitted to hold was raised from 33½ to 50% of its total liabilities.

There are 20 commercial banks including the First Bank of Nigeria (formerly Standard), Union Bank of Nigeria (formerly Barclays) and the United Bank of Africa. Eleven of the banks are indigenous. There are 3 merchant banks and 3 government-owned development banks in addition to the Post Office Savings Bank. All banks are required to be registered as Nigerian companies from 1969. In 1976 the Government took a 60% shareholding in all foreign banks.

Weights and Measures. The metric system is in force and the transitional period from the imperial system ended in 1977.

ENERGY AND NATURAL RESOURCES

Electricity. The National Electric Power Authority generated 4,712m. kwh. in 1977–78. The Niger dams at Kainji were completed in early 1969 (investment of £87m.) and provide cheap hydro-electricity for rapid industrialization.

Oil. There are refineries at Port Harcourt, Warri and at Kaduna. Oil represents 93% of exports. Production, 1978, 697,737,000 bbls.

Gas. Natural gas is being used at electric power stations at Afam and Ughelli. Production, 1972, 601,237,000 cu. ft. Reserves: 1,422,000m. cu.metres.

Minerals. Production (1977): Tin, 4,400 tonnes; columbite (the world's largest producer), 800 tonnes; coal, 267,000 tonnes. There are large deposits of iron ore, coal (reserves estimate 245m. tonnes), lead and zinc. There are small quantities of gold and uranium.

Agriculture. Groundnuts, cotton and soybean come mainly or wholly from the north, palm produce, cocoa, timber and rubber from the south. Tobacco is grown in commercial quantities. Production (estimates) 1979 were (in tonnes): Groundnuts (unshelled), 621,000; cocoa, 170,000; cereals, 9·4m.

Livestock (1979). There were 12m. cattle, 8·5m. sheep, 24·5m. goats, 1·1m. pigs and 110m. poultry.

Forestries. There are plywood factories at Epe, Sapele and Calabar, and numerous saw-mills. The most important timber species include mahogany, iroko, obeche, abwa, ebony and camwood. Exports (1977) logs and sawn timber, 170,000 cu. metres.

INDUSTRY AND TRADE

Industry. Timber and hides and skins are other major export commodities. Industrial products include soap, cigarettes, beer, margarine, groundnut oil, meat and cake, concentrated fruit juices, soft drinks, canned food, metal containers, plywood, textiles, ceramic products and cement. Of growing importance is the local assembly of motor vehicles, bicycles, radio equipment, electrical goods and sewing machines.

Under a decree on indigenization Nigerians must have a minimum of 40% shareholding in all foreign enterprises.

Trade Unions. All trade unions were dissolved in 1976 and 42 new unions, each organized around a particular occupation, have since been created.

Commerce. There is a great deal of internal commerce in local foodstuffs and imported goods moving by rail, lorry and pack animals overland, and by launches, rafts and canoes along an extensive and complex network of inland waterways. Kano is still, as it has been for centuries, the focus of caravan routes linking a territory which stretches from the Sudan in the east to Senegal in the west, with branches northwards across the Sahara.

Total trade in US$1m. for 4 years:

	1976	1977	1978	1979
Imports (c.i.f.)	8,213	11,021	12,378	9,728
Exports and re-exports (f.o.b.)	10,771	11,823	10,881	17,832

Total trade between Nigeria and UK (according to British Department of Trade returns, in £1,000 sterling):

	1976	1977	1978	1979	1980
Imports to UK	316,697	219,286	286,212	186,046	151,563
Exports and re-exports from UK	774,179	1,068,707	1,133,373	638,239	1,204,358

COMMUNICATIONS

Roads (1977). There were 105,000 km of maintained roads, of which 43,360 km are paved.

In 1976, 410,315 vehicles were registered. Bus services, by private owners, operate in the larger towns and between the main towns in southern Nigeria, but the bulk of passenger and goods traffic by road is carried in lorries (mammy wagons). Taxis are available in the large towns.

Railways. There are 3,505 route-km of line 1,067 mm gauge. A 690 km (1,435 mm gauge) line is under survey from Port Harcourt to Oturkpo and Ajaokuta.

Aviation. There is an extensive system of internal and international air routes, serving Europe, USA, Middle East and South and West Africa. Regular services are operated by Nigerian Airways (WAAC), British Caledonian, UTA, KLM, SABENA, Swissair, PANAM and other lines. Aircraft arrivals from outside Nigeria in 1961 totalled 3,804, carrying 726 tons of freight. In 1962, 60,036 passengers and 924 tons of mail and freight were carried on internal services. In 1972, 112,000 passengers arrived at Nigerian airports and 119,000 passengers departed.

Shipping. The principal ports are Lagos, Port Harcourt, Warri and Calabar.

Post and Broadcasting. Postal facilities are provided at 1,667 offices and agencies; telegraph, money order and savings bank services are provided at 280 of these. Most internal letter mail is carried by air at normal postage rates. External telegraph services are owned and operated by Nigerian External Telecommunications, Ltd, at Lagos, from which telegraphic communication is maintained with all parts of the world. There were 128,352 telephones in use in 1978, of which 45,433 were in Lagos and 9,949 in Ibadan. There is also a telex service.

Federal and some state governments have established commercial corporations for sound and television broadcasting, which are widely used in schools.

Cinemas (1974). There were 120 cinemas, with a seating capacity of 60,000. Mobile cinemas are used by the Federal and States Information Services.

Newspapers. There are over 119 newspapers, magazines and periodicals; the highest circulation of a daily is about 125,000. Most of the papers are published in English but some in the vernaculars.

JUSTICE, RELIGION, EDUCATION AND WELFARE

Justice. The highest court is the Federal Supreme Court, which consists of the Chief Justice of the Republic, not less than 2 Federal Judges and the Chief Justice of each State. It has original jurisdiction in any dispute between the Federal Republic and any State or between States; and to hear and determine appeals from any of the High Courts and from any court or tribunal established by Parliament. It may be given powers of advisory jurisdiction by Parliament in respect of the exercise of the prerogative of mercy by the Heads of State of the Republic or the States.

High Courts, presided over by a Chief Justice, are established in most of the states. Magistrates' courts are established throughout the Republic, and customary law courts in southern Nigeria. In northern States of Nigeria there are the Sharia Court of Appeal and the Court of Resolution. Moslem Law has been codified in a Penal Code and is applied through Alkali courts.

The Advisory Judicial committee has powers of appointment and discipline.

Religion. The 1963 census figures were: Moslems, 26·2m.; Christians, 19·2m.; others, 10·1m. Northern Nigeria is mainly Moslem; Southern Nigeria is predominantly Christian. The Protestant and Roman Catholic Churches have 2·5m. each.

Education. Free education for all primary school children within the 6–12-year age group was implemented in the Western State in Jan. 1955 and in Lagos and the Eastern State in Jan. 1957 and in Sept. 1976 primary education became free throughout the country. Literacy rate (1973) 25%.

In 1973 there were 14,525 primary schools with 4·7m. pupils and (1971) 116,640 teachers. The demand for secondary education continues to exceed the number of places available, particularly in southern States and in Lagos. In 1973 there were 1,499 secondary schools, including some secondary modern schools, with 448,904 pupils and (1971) 18,351 teachers. All external examinations of the Universities of London and Cambridge have been taken over by the West African Examination Council.

Teacher-training institutions totalled 157 in 1973. There were also 67 trade centres and vocational training institutes for sub-professional technicians and tradesmen.

There are 13 universities in Nigeria, providing 3–5-year courses leading to the award of a first degree in various disciplines. Three technical universities at Benue, Imo and Bauchi opened in 1980–81. There are also opportunities for taking higher degrees. Free tuition was provided from 1977. The total number of students (1978) was 43,551.

University	Students	University	Students
Ahmadu Bello, Zaria (1962)	7,366	Jos (1975)	2,555
Bayero, Kano (1975)	2,128	Lagos (1962)	5,586
Benin (1970)	3,942	Maiduguri (1975)	1,013
Calabar (1975)	1,559	Nigeria, Nsukka and Enugu (1960)	6,790
Ibadan (1948)	7,348	Port Harcourt (1975)	707
Ife (1961)	7,726	Sokoto (1975)	389
Ilorin (1975)	442		

Health. Most tropical diseases are endemic to Nigeria. Blindness, yaws, leprosy, sleeping sickness, worm infections, malaria are major health problems which, however, are yielding to remedial and preventative measures. In co-operation with the World Health Organization river blindness and malaria are being tackled on a large scale, while annual campaigns are undertaken against the danger of smallpox epidemics. Over 33m. people were vaccinated against smallpox in 1968. Dispensaries and travelling dispensaries are found in most parts of the country.

The teaching hospital at Lagos University has 350 beds; there is also a nursing school and a teaching hospital at Ibadan University. There are medical courses at Ahmadu Bello University, University of Ife, Benin University and at Nsukka.

DIPLOMATIC REPRESENTATIVES

OF NIGERIA IN GREAT BRITAIN
(9 Northumberland Ave., London, WC2N 5BX)

High Commissioner: Shuaib Uthman Yolah (accredited 19 Oct. 1979).

OF GREAT BRITAIN IN NIGERIA
(11 Eleke Cres., Victoria Island, Lagos)

High Commissioner: M. Brown, CMG, OBE.

OF NIGERIA IN THE USA (2201 M. St., NW,
Washington, D.C., 20037)

Ambassador: O. Jolaoso.

OF THE USA IN NIGERIA (2 Eleke Cres., Lagos)

Ambassador: Stephen Low.

OF NIGERIA TO THE UNITED NATIONS

Ambassador: B. Akporode Clark.

Books of Reference

National Development Plan, 1962–68. Ministry of Economic Development, 1962
Nigeria Digest of Statistics. Lagos, 1951 ff. (quarterly)
Annual Abstract of Statistics. Federal Office of Statistics. Lagos, 1960 ff.
Nigeria Trade Journal. Federal Ministry of Commerce and Industries (quarterly)
Nigeria Handbook 1975–76. Ministry of Information, Lagos, 1975

Afolabi Ojo, G. J., *Yoruba Culture.* Univ. of London Press, 1967
Arnold, G., *Modern Nigeria.* London, 1977
Blitz, F. (ed.), *The Politics and Administration of Nigerian Government.* Lagos and London, 1965
Burns, Sir Alan, *History of Nigeria.* 8th ed. London, 1972
Crowder, M., *The Story of Nigeria.* 3rd ed. London, 1973
Damachi, U. G., *Nigerian Modernization: The Colonial Legacy.* New York, 1972
Isichei, E., *History of the Igbo People.* London, 1976
Luckham, R., *The Nigerian Military: A Sociological Analysis of Authority and Revolt, 1960–67.* CUP, 1971
Nwabueze, B. O., *The Machinery of Justice in Nigeria.* London, 1964
Olaloku, F. A., (ed.) *Structure of the Nigerian Economy.* London, 1980
Oyediran, O., *Nigerian Government and Politics under Military Rule, 1966–1979.* New York, 1980
Panter-Brick, S. K., *Nigerian Politics and Military Rule: Prelude to Civil War.* London, 1970
Peil, M., *Nigerian Politics: The People's View.* London, 1976
Williams, G., *Nigeria: Economy and Society.* London, 1977

NORWAY

Kongeriket Norge

Capital: Oslo
Population: 4·07m. (1980)
GNP per capita: US$10,886 (1979)

HISTORY. By the Treaty of 14 Jan. 1814 Norway was ceded to the King of Sweden by the King of Denmark, but the Norwegian people declared themselves independent and elected Prince Christian Frederik of Denmark as their king. The foreign Powers refused to recognize this election, and on 14 Aug. a convention proclaimed the independence of Norway in a personal union with Sweden. This was followed on 4 Nov. by the election of Karl XIII (II) as King of Norway. Norway declared this union dissolved, 7 June 1905, and Sweden agreed to the repeal of the union on 26 Oct. 1905. The throne was offered to a prince of the reigning house of Sweden, who declined. After a plebiscite, Prince Carl of Denmark was formally elected King on 18 Nov. 1905, and took the name of Haakon VII.

Norwegian Sovereigns

Inge Baardssøn	1204	Erik of Pomerania	1389
Haakon Haakonssøn	1217	Kristofer af Bavaria	1442
Magnus Lagabøter	1263	Karl Knutssøn	1449
Eirik Magnussøn	1280	Same Sovereigns as in Denmark	1450–1814
Haakon V Magnussøn	1299	Christian Frederik	1814
Magnus Erikssøn	1319	Same Sovereigns as in Sweden	1814–1905
Haakon VI Magnussøn	1355	Haakon VII	1905
Olav Haakonssøn	1381	Olav V	1957
Margreta	1388		

AREA AND POPULATION. Norway is bounded north by the Arctic ocean, east by the USSR, Finland and Sweden, south by the Skagerrak Straits and west by the North Sea.

Fylker (counties)	Area (sq. km)	Census population 1 Nov. 1970	Population 1 Jan. 1980	Pop. per sq. km (total area) 1979
Oslo (City)	453·70	477,898	454,872	1,002·6
Akershus	4,916·70	322,321	366,673	74·6
Østfold	4,183·43	220,892	232,400	55·6
Hedmark	27,388·30	178,923	186,698	6·8
Oppland	25,259·60	172,163	180,285	7·1
Buskerud	14,933·22	198,225	213,608	14·3
Vestfold	2,215·77	174,640	185,922	83·9
Telemark	15,315·32	156,405	161,673	10·6
Aust-Agder	9,211·80	80,575	89,733	9·7
Vest-Agder	7,280·33	124,013	135,696	18·6
Rogaland	9,140·57	268,171	302,386	33·1
Hordaland	15,633·73	372,172	390,526	25·0
Sogn og Fjordane	18,633·50	100,761	105,271	5·6
Møre og Romsdal	15,104·20	223,360	235,719	15·6
Sør-Trøndelag	18,831·40	233,420	243,709	12·9
Nord-Trøndelag	22,463·25	117,718	125,233	5·6
Nordland	38,327·01	240,461	243,808	6·4
Troms	25,953·88	136,224	145,996	5·6
Finnmark	48,649·00	75,791	78,692	1·6
Total	323,894·71 [1]	3,874,133	4,078,900	12·6

[1] 125,056 sq. miles.

On 1 Jan. 1980, 2,301,618 persons lived in rural municipalities and 1,777,282 in towns.
Conjugal condition of the domiciled population over 15 years of age, 1979: Unmarried: 486,602 males, 384,711 females; married: 952,462 males, 950,619 females; separated, widowed or divorced: 115,255 males, 276,764 females.

Population of the principal towns at 1 Jan. 1980:

Oslo	454,872	Sandnes	36,255	Halden	26,696
Bergen	208,910	Sandefjord	34,758	Gjøvik	26,127
Trondheim	134,726	Ålesund	34,674	Moss	25,455
Stavanger	89,913	Bodø	32,567	Lillehammer	21,982
Kristiansand	60,738	Porsgrunn	31,378	Harstad	21,605
Drammen	49,660	Fredrikstad	27,968	Molde	20,904
Skien	47,435	Haugesund	27,114	Kongsberg	20,504
Tromsø	45,833	Ringerike	26,856	Steinkjer	20,509

Vital statistics for calendar years:

	Marriages	Divorces	Births	Still-born	Illegitimate[2]	Deaths
1977	24,022	6,099	50,877	394	5,903	39,824
1978	23,690	6,246	51,749	346	6,150	40,682
1979	23,055	6,608	51,580	382	6,729	41,567[1]

[1] Provisional figures.   [2] Excluding still-born.

REIGNING KING. Olav V, born 2 July 1903, married on 21 March 1929 to Princess Märtha of Sweden (born 28 March 1901, died 5 April 1954), daughter of the late Prince Carl (son of King Oscar II). He succeeded on the death of his father, King Haakon VII, on 21 Sept. 1957. *Offspring:* Princess Ragnhild Alexandra, born 9 June 1930 (married, 1953, Hr. Erling Lorentzen); Princess Astrid Maud Ingeborg, born 12 Feb. 1932 (married, 12 Jan. 1961, Hr. Johan Martin Ferner); Crown Prince Harald, born 21 Feb. 1937, married, 29 Aug. 1968, Sonja Haraldsen. *Offspring:* Princess Märtha Louise, born 22 Sept. 1971; Prince Haakon Magnus, born 20 July 1973.

CONSTITUTION AND GOVERNMENT. Norway is a constitutional and hereditary monarchy. The royal succession is in direct male line in the order of primogeniture. In default of male heirs the King may propose a successor to the Storting, but this assembly has the right to nominate another, if it does not agree with the proposal.

The Constitution, voted by the constituent assembly at Eidsvoll on 17 May 1814 and modified at various times, vests the legislative power of the realm in the Storting (Parliament). The royal veto may be exercised twice; but if the same Bill passes three Stortings formed by separate and subsequent elections it becomes the law of the land without the assent of the sovereign. The King has the command of the land, sea and air forces, and makes all appointments.

Since June 1938 all branches of the Government service, including the state church, are open to women.

National flag: Red with a blue white-bordered Scandinavian cross.

National anthem: Ja, vi elsker dette landet (words by B. Bjørnson, 1865; tune by R. Nordraak, 1865).

The Storting assembles every year. The meetings take place *suo jure*, and not by any writ from the King or the executive. They begin on the first weekday in Oct. each year, until June the following year. Every Norwegian subject of 18 years of age is entitled to vote, unless he is disqualified for a special cause. Women are, since 1913, entitled to vote under the same conditions as men. The mode of election is direct and the method of election is proportional. The country is divided into 19 districts, each electing from 4 to 15 representatives.

At the elections for the Storting held on 11–12 Sept. 1977 the following parties were elected: Labour, 76; Conservative, 41; Centre Party, 12; Christian Democratic Party, 22; Socialist Left Party, 2, and Liberal, 2.

The Storting, when assembled, divides itself by election into the *Lagting* and the *Odelsting*. The former is composed of one-fourth of the members of the Storting, and the other of the remaining three-fourths. Each Ting (the Storting, the Odelsting and the Lagting) nominates its own president. Most questions are decided by the Storting, but questions relating to legislation must be considered and decided by the Odelsting and the Lagting separately. Only when the Odelsting and the Lagting disagree, the Bill has to be considered by the Storting in plenary sitting, and a new law can then only be decided by a majority of two-thirds of the voters. The same majority is required for alterations of the Constitution, which can only be decided by the Storting in plenary sitting. The Storting elects 5 delegates, whose duty it is to revise the public accounts. The Lagting and the ordinary members of the Supreme Court of Justice (the *Høyesterett*) form a High Court of the Realm (the *Riksrett*) for the trial of ministers, members of the *Høyesterett* and members of the Storting. The impeachment before the *Riksrett* can only be decided by the Odelsting.

The executive is represented by the King, who exercises his authority through the Cabinet or Council of State (*Statsråd*), composed of a Prime Minister (*Statsminister*) and (at present) 16 ministers (*Statsråder*). The ministers are entitled to be present in the Storting and to take part in the discussions, but without a vote.

A Labour Government was formed and took office on 15 Jan. 1976; in March 1981 the members of the Government were:

Prime Minister: Dr Gro Harlem Brundtland.
Foreign Affairs: Knut Frydenlund. *Agriculture:* Oskar Øksnes. *Commerce and Shipping:* Reiulf Steen. *Justice:* Oddvar Berrefjord. *Ecclesiastical Affairs and Education:* Einar Førde. *Local Government and Labour:* Harriet Andreassen. *Industry:* Lars Skytøen. *Communications:* Ronald Bye. *Environment:* Rolf Hansen. *Social Affairs:* Arne Nilsen. *Consumer Affairs and Government Administration:* Sissel Rønbeck. *Fisheries:* Eivind Bolle. *Finance:* Ulf Sand. *Defence:* Thorvald Stoltenberg. *Oil and Energy:* Arvid Johanson. *Planning:* Per Kleppe.

The official languages are Bokmål (or Riksmål) and Nynorsk (or Landsmål).

Local Government. For the purposes of administration the country is divided into 19 counties (*fylker*), in each of which the central government is represented by a county governor (*fylkesmannen*). In addition, there are 47 urban districts (*bykommuner*) and 407 rural districts (*herredskommuner*), each of which usually corresponds in size to a parish (*prestegjeld*). The districts are administered by district councils (*kommunestyrer*), whose membership may vary between 13 and 85 councillors, and by a committee (*formannskap*) which is elected by and from the members of the council. The council is four times the size of the committee. The council elects a chairman and a vice-chairman from among its members. Councillors are elected in accordance with rules which are in most cases identical with the rules governing election to Parliament.

Each of the 18 counties forms a county district (*fylkeskommune*), while the remaining one, Oslo, comprises an urban district. The supreme authority in a county district is the county council (*fylkesting*). Every district council has until now elected its district representatives in the proportion of one to every 6,000 inhabitants, though no one district may elect more than one-third of the total number of representatives in the county council. From 1 Jan. 1976, members of the county council are elected directly by the electors of the county and the number of representatives varies between 25 and 85. In a county district the county committee (*fylkesutvalg*) occupies a position corresponding to that of the committee (*formannskap*) in the primary districts. The county committee is elected by and from among the members of the county council. The number of county committee members is one-fourth of the membership of the county council, but must be not more than 15. The county council elects from among the members of the county committee a county sheriff (*fylkesordfører*) and a deputy sheriff.

DEFENCE. Service is universal and compulsory, liability in peace-time commencing at the age of 19 and continuing till the age of 44. The training period in the Army is 12 months, in the Navy and Air Force, 15 months. The Norwegian Defence forces are ganized into 2 integrated regional commands.

Army. Major units are organized mainly in Regimental Combat Teams. Peace establishment includes 1 RCT, a number of independent unis and supporting eements a well as training units. Tanks include Leopard, M-48 med and NM-116 tanks (M-24/90). Total strength (1980), 18,000 officers and men.

Navy. The Navy consists of the coastal batteries and other static defence systems and the following naval units: 15 coastal submarines, 5 frigates, 2 minelayers, 2 corvettes, 9 coastal minesweepers, 45 fast attack boats, 1 coastal mine hunter, 7 landing craft, 1 depot ship and auxiliary vessels.

Personnel in 1980 totalled 9,000 officers and ratings including 1,600 in the Coast Artillery.

Coastguard. The Coastguard was established in 1977 within the framework of the Naval and Defence Command. Main tasks are fisheries surveillance, fishing protection and monitoring activities on the continental shelf. The Coastguard assists other government agencies in rescue service, environment protection and police duties. Present resources are 6 regular Coastguard ships, 7 chartered ships partly manned by the Navy and about 20 fishing-gear protection vessels (chartered). Procurement plan 1978–81 comprises P-3B Orion MP A/C, 3 new construction ships (2,800 tons full load) and Naval Lynx H/C. The ships are being fitted to accommodate the Naval Lynx H/C, and great emphasis is placed on seaworthiness, communications, navigation and command and control functions.

Air Force. The Royal Norwegian Air Force consists of 3 squadrons of F-5 supersonic fighter-bombers, 1 squadron equipped with RF-5A reconnaissance fighters, 2 squadrons of F-104G and CF-104 Starfighters, 1 maritime patrol squadron of P-3B Orions, 1 squadron of C-130H Hercules transports, and a number of UH-1B Iroquois helicopter, communications and training units, as well as 4 Nike surface-to-air missile batteries and several light anti-aircraft artillery units. Ten Westland Sea King helicopters are used for search and rescue duties; 6 Lynx helicopters are shipborne for fishing protection, search and rescue and oilrig surveillance duties. Aircraft on order include 72 F-16A/Bs.

Total strength is approximately 10,000 officers and men.

Home Guard. The Home Guard is organized in small units equipped and trained for special tasks in their home area. Compulsory service after basic training is 50 hours a year. The total strength is approximately 85,000.

INTERNATIONAL RELATIONS

Membership. Norway is a member of UN, NATO, EFTA, OECD, the Council of Europe and the Nordic Council.

ECONOMY

Budget. Current revenue and expenditure for years ending 31 Dec. (in 1,000 kroner):

	1975	1976	1977	1978[1]	1979[2]	1980
Revenue	34,667,531	41,663,412	48,600,912	55,895,000	61,512,000	74,621,000
Expenditure	44,024,575	52,655,159	64,299,932	73,100,314	78,137,000	92,898,000

[1] Voted budget.   [2] Estimate.

National debt[1] for years ending 31 Dec. (in 1,000 kroner):

1971	21,636,900	1974	33,943,000	1977	66,786,000
1972	25,671,200	1975	41,082,800	1978	86,556,000
1973	29,521,000	1976	50,290,300	1979	103,605,000

[1] At the rate of par on foreign loans: including treasury bills (in 1m. kroner) which amounted to 2,733 in 1973; 2,229 in 1974; 499 in 1975; 3,592 in 1976; 8,690 in 1977 and 6,000 in 1978.

Currency. The Norwegian *krone*, of 100 øre, is of the value of about 11 *kroner* to £1 sterling. National bank-notes of 10, 50, 100, 500 and 1,000 *kroner* are legal means of payment.

On 31 Oct. 1980 the nominal value of the coin in circulation was 806m. kroner; notes in circulation, 18,214m. kroner.

Banking. The Norges Bank is a joint-stock bank; in 1949 the state acquired all the shares hitherto privately owned. The bank is governed by laws enacted by the State, and its directors are elected by the Storting, except the president and vice-president of the head office, who are nominated by the King. It is the only bank of issue.

At the end of 1979 there were 26 private joint-stock banks. Their total amount of capital and funds was 3,851m. kroner (capital 2,139m., funds 1,712m.). Deposits amounted to 66,593m. kroner, of which 17,325m. kroner were at call and notice, and 49,268m. kroner on time.

The number of savings banks at the end of 1979 was 345. The total amount of funds of the savings banks amounted to 2,490m. kroner, and total deposits 55,485m. kroner, of which 8,614m. kroner were at call and notice and 46,871m. kroner on time.

Weights and Measures. The metric system of weights and measures has been obligatory since 1875.

ENERGY AND NATURAL RESOURCES

Electricity. Norway is a large producer of hydro-electric energy. The potential total hydro-electric power, for a whole year at regulated minimum water flow and by 82% efficiency, is estimated at 15m. kw. or about 131,000m. kwh. annually. About 60% of the water power suitable for development consists of waterfalls with a height of at least 900 ft.

By the end of 1978 the capacity of the installations for production of thermo-electric energy amounted to only 155,307 kw. On 31 Dec. 1978, the total capacity of generators (of hydro-electric plants) was 21·06m. kva.

In 1978 the total production of electricity amounted to 80,864m. kwh., of which 99·8% was produced by hydro-electric plants.

Most of the electricity is used for industrial purposes, especially by the chemical and basic metal industries for production of nitrate of calcium and other nitrogen products, carbide, ferrosilicon and other ferro-alloys, aluminium and zinc. The paper and pulp industries are also big consumers of electricity.

Bjerve, P. J., *Planning in Norway 1947–1956*. Amsterdam, 1959
Bourneuf, A., *Norway, the Planned Revival*. Cambridge, Mass., 1958
Galenson, W., *Labor in Norway*. Cambridge, Mass., and London, 1949
Leiserson, M. W., *Wages and Economic Control in Norway, 1945–57*. Harvard Univ. Press, 1959

Minerals. Production and value of the chief concentrates, metals and alloys were:

	1977		1978	
Concentrates and minerals	*Tonnes*	*1,000 kroner*	*Tonnes*	*1,000 kroner*
Copper concentrates	113,268	112,079	113,230	115,452
Pyrites	308,338	16,120	293,289	19,493
Iron ore and titaniferous concentrates	4,463,382	...	4,539,627	...
Zinc and lead concentrates	65,243	58,173	61,821	43,439
Metals and alloys				
Copper	26,575	...	20,061	...
Nickel	38,222	...	23,739	...
Aluminium	622,730	3,380,806	638,559	3,595,250
Ferro-alloys	647,980[1]	1,332,822	719,146	1,429,106
Pig-iron	512,353	...	554,395	...
Zinc	69,790	...	71,628	...
Lead and tin	965	...	961	...

[1] Exclusive own use for ferromanganese, ferrochromium, ferrosilisium and ferrosilico-mangan.

Agriculture. Norway, including Svalbard and Jan Mayen, is a barren and mountainous country. The arable soil is found in comparatively narrow strips, gathered in deep and narrow valleys and around fiords and lakes. Large, continuous tracts fit for cultivation do not exist. Of the total area, 80% is unproductive, 18% productive forest and 2% under cultivation.

		Area (hectares)		Produce (tonnes, holdings with at least 5 decares land in use)		
Principal crops	1977	1978	1979	1977	1978	1979
Wheat	20,987	20,508	16,700	77,998	79,806	65,779
Rye	2,472	2,230	1,300	8,431	7,544	3,996
Barley	179,376	185,416	196,500	630,167	668,251	637,236
Oats	99,260	97,409	95,300	360,093	367,352	360,764
Mixed corn	314	702	700	1,196	2,597	2,116
Potatoes	28,018	25,047	22,000	604,987	575,599	406,366
Hay	369,379	378,320	392,700	2,499,458	2,666,600	2,604,320

Livestock, 1979: 19,000 horses, 971,000 cattle (about 378,000 milch cows), 1,919,000 sheep, 74,000 goats, 711,000 pigs, 3,744,000 hens.

Fur production in 1979–80 was as follows (1978–79 in brackets): Silver fox, 5,000 (4,000); blue fox, 350,000 (315,000); mink, 900,000 (950,000).

Forestry. The forests are one of the chief natural sources of wealth. The total area covered with forests is estimated at 83,300 sq. km, of which 64,800 sq. km is productive forest. 81% of the productive forest area consisted of conifers and 19% of broadleaves. Forests in public ownership cover 8,970 sq. km of productive forests and 5,820 sq. km of unproductive forests. Besides the home consumption of timber and fuel wood, the essential part of the cut is consumed as raw material in sawmills and the pulp and paper industry. The annual natural increase is about 13·2m. cu. metres. In 1978–79, 7·8m. cu. metres were cut for production of pulp, sawn timber and other industrial wood products.

Fisheries. The total number of persons engaged in fisheries in 1979 was 33,955, of whom 9,081 had another chief occupation. The number of fishing vessels with motor was 25,874 in 1979, and of these, 17,869 were open boats.

The value of sea fisheries in 1m. kroner in 1979 was: Cod, 968; capelin, 523; mackerel, 138; coal-fish (saithe), 283; deep-water prawn, 305; haddock, 195; herring, 36; dogfish, 19. The catch totalled in 1979, 2·5m. tonnes, valued at 3,125m. kroner.

From 1 Jan. 1977 Norway established an economic zone of 200 nautical miles, and from 3 June 1977 a fishery protection zone of 200 nautical miles around Svalbard.

INDUSTRY AND TRADE

Industry. Industry is chiefly based on raw materials produced within the country (wood, fish, etc.) and on water power, of which the country possesses a large amount. Crude petroleum and natural gas production, the manufacture of paper and paper products, industrial chemicals and basic metals are the most important export manufactures. In the following table are given figures for industrial establishments in 1978, excluding one-man units. Electrical plants, construction and building industry are not included. The values are given in 1m. kroner.

Industries	Establishments	Number of Salaried staff	Wage earners	Gross value of production	Value added
Coalmining	1	192	585	106	55
Crude petroleum and natural gas	3	1,770	1,735	14,568	13,233
Metal-mining	15	845	3,259	900	325
Other-mining	560	531	2,709	1,045	545
Food manufacturing	2,551	9,650	40,465	23,931	1,442
Beverages	69	1,266	3,827	2,004	1,308
Tobacco	6	546	657	1,001	790
Textiles	489	2,144	9,878	2,357	890
Clothing, etc.	396	1,304	6,985	1,224	528
Footwear	50	167	1,301	220	98
Leather	80	171	902	213	84
Wood	1,624	4,828	19,006	7,622	2,393
Furniture and fixtures	614	1,790	8,445	2,334	936
Pulp and paper	193	4,201	13,917	6,828	1,883
Printing and publishing	1,522	12,207	22,737	6,760	2,992
Chemical, industrial	62	4,030	5,520	4,585	1,216
Chemical, other	187	3,502	4,463	2,729	984

Industries	Establish-ments	Number of Salaried staff	Number of Wage earners	Gross value of produc-tion	Value added
Petroleum, refined	7	311	425	6,076	683
Petroleum and coal	52	439	1,233	909	230
Rubber	83	510	1,739	440	183
Plastics	309	2,482	5,653	1,897	725
Ceramics	34	302	1,150	209	127
Glass	59	552	1,722	549	237
Other mineral products	502	2,119	6,732	3,186	1,287
Iron, steel and ferro-alloys	55	3,092	9,838	4,062	1,237
Non-ferrous metals	80	3,371	9,213	6,671	2,086
Metal products, except machinery	1,493	5,407	20,418	5,803	2,663
Machinery and equipment	1,017	9,814	21,333	11,172	3,769
Electrical apparatus and supplies	381	7,936	14,160	5,776	2,713
Transport equipment	1,029	9,444	40,216	12,585	4,996
Professional and scientific instruments, photographic and optical goods	57	510	1,071	361	197
Other manufacturing industries	293	744	2,872	734	330
Total (all included)	13,873	96,177	284,166	138,857	51,162

The following table sets forth the estimated value of net production, at factor cost by industries, in 1m. kroner:

	1974	1975	1976	1977	1978 [1]	1979 [1]
Agriculture	3,343	4,044	5,159	6,703	7,461	7,628
Forestry	1,119	1,435	1,397	1,349	1,413	1,465
Fishing	1,167	767	1,338	1,381	1,096	1,045
Mining and quarrying	678	739	728	779	746	784
Manufacturing	26,478	30,188	32,376	34,008	35,250	37,925
Crude petroleum and gas production	−546	2,485	3,692	4,116	8,184	15,084
Electricity, gas and water	2,353	2,522	2,895	2,912	4,001	4,371
Construction [2]	8,486	9,472	10,213	11,927	13,086	13,556
Wholesale and retail trade	11,011	12,530	15,012	16,489	17,838	19,307
Restaurants and hotels	1,287	1,567	1,824	2,190	2,406	2,498
Water transport	6,870	4,564	3,080	2,230	2,719	3,960
Other transport [3]	5,010	5,682	6,665	7,303	8,351	9,068
Financial institutions	3,930	4,430	5,322	5,977	6,991	7,960
Real estate	4,027	4,596	5,281	6,113	6,875	7,390
Business services	2,198	2,704	3,128	3,843	4,417	4,850
Government services, social and personal services	22,027	26,751	31,890	36,567	40,899	43,391
Imputed bank service charge	−3,635	−4,061	−4,959	−5,629	−6,165	−7,322
Net production at factor cost	95,803	110,415	125,041	138,258	155,568	172,960
+ Indirect taxes	22,741	26,455	31,012	36,327	37,708	40,097
− Subsidies	7,514	9,258	11,624	14,111	16,620	16,908
Net domestic product (market price)	111,030	127,612	144,429	160,474	176,656	196,149

[1] Provisional figures.
[2] Including drilling of crude oil and natural gas wells.
[3] Including pipeline transport of oil and gas.

Labour. The distribution of the population according to professions in 1970, showed 296,667 (7·7%) dependent on agriculture, forestry and gardening; 1,300,490 (33·6%) on mining, manufacturing, building, etc.; 447,248 (11·5%) on commerce; 353,207 (9·1%) on transport; 68,627 (1·8%) on fishery, sealing and whaling; 653,450 (16·9%) on public administration, liberal professions and services.

Commerce. Total imports and exports in calendar years (in 1,000 kroner):

	1974	197	1976	1977	1978	1979
Imports	46,555,707	50,544,836	60,532,915	68,579,245	60,168,613	69,338,924
Exports	34,731,723	37,922,338	43,330,277	46,438,663	57,083,799	68,527,167

Trading according to countries was as follows (in 1,000 kroner):

Countries	1978		1979	
	Imports	Exports	Imports	Exports
Argentina	84,091	107,513	130,600	79,710
Australia and New Zealand	338,869	202,222	450,965	257,271
Belgium and Luxembourg	1,621,076	676,301	2,251,537	710,593
Brazil	788,739	547,830	776,793	455,900
Canada	800,997	237,554	1,409,810	1,364,620
Czechoslovakia	179,579	108,494	184,066	97,198
Denmark	4,000,997	3,060,285	4,277,071	3,671,094
Fed. Republic of Germany	8,548,810	7,538,056	9,644,644	9,736,919
Finland	2,414,972	1,011,522	3,230,785	1,241,764
France	1,952,631	1,664,905	2,581,868	1,629,804
India	77,677	122,125	100,498	139,121
Italy	1,334,326	899,146	1,537,968	1,090,327
Netherlands	2,318,962	1,637,919	2,432,329	1,991,944
Poland	432,784	392,471	725,924	450,174
Portugal	328,633	248,324	400,860	214,993
Spain	417,295	261,429	533,905	307,517
Sweden	11,013,956	5,721,516	12,285,568	7,712,398
Switzerland	1,167,767	464,340	1,175,453	513,660
UK	7,184,678	19,982,197	9,571,492	24,968,915
USA	4,064,056	2,856,455	4,993,500	2,755,890
USSR	570,251	465,555	742,487	441,354

Principal items of import in 1978 (in 1,000 kroner): Machinery, transport equipment, etc., 20,219,352; fuel oil, etc., 7,354,691; base metals and manufactures thereof, 6,307,300; chemicals and related products, 3,967,190; textiles, 2,015,685.

Principal items of export in 1978 (in 1,000 kroner): Machinery and transport equipment, 15,694,961; base metals and manufactures thereof, 9,549,560; crude oil, 8,796,328; edible animal products, 3,334,080; pulp and paper, 3,155,573.

Total trade between Norway and UK (British Department of Trade returns, in £1,000 sterling):

	1976	1977	1978	1979	1980
Imports to UK	622,816	846,669	1,444,752	1,327,212	1,441,418
Exports and re-exports from UK	473,539	761,851	650,106	768,815	791,530

COMMUNICATIONS

Roads. On 31 Dec. 1979 the length of the public roads (including roads in towns) was 80,911 km. Of these, 56,646 km were main roads; 44,473 km had some kind of paving, mostly bituminous and oil-gravel treatment, the rest being gravel-surfaced.

Number of registered motor vehicles (31 Dec. 1979) was 1,630,123, including 1,189,754 passenger cars (including taxis), 151,697 lorries and vans, 11,443 buses, 142,781 motor cycles and mopeds. The scheduled bus and lorry services in 1978 drove 3,930m. passenger-km and 404m. net ton-km.

Railways. The length of state railways on 31 Dec. 1979 was 4,239 km; of private companies, 16 km. On 2,440 km of state and 16 km of private railways electric power is installed. Total receipts of the state railways and road traffic in 1979 were 1,749m. kroner; total expenses (excluding interest on capital), 2,250m. kroner. The state railways carried 33·5m. tonnes of freight (of which 22·3m. was iron ore on the Ofoten railway) and 35·4m. passengers.

Aviation. Det Norske Luftfartselskap (DNL) started its post-war activities on 1 April 1946. On 1 Aug. 1946 DNL, together with DDL (Danish Airlines) and ABA/SILA (Swedish Airlines), formed the 'Scandinavian Airlines System'—SAS. The 3 companies remained independent units, but all services were co-ordinated. In 1951 a new agreement was signed (retroactive from 1 Oct. 1950) according to which the 3 national companies became holding partners in a new organization which took over the entire operational system. Denmark and Norway hold each two-sevenths and Sweden three-sevenths of the capital, but they have joint responsibility towards third parties.

In the autumn of 1980 SAS had a fleet of 77 jet planes. Length of route network, about 252,000 km. Scheduled air services are run by SAS, Braathens South-American and Far East Air transport service (SAFE) and Wideroes Flyveselskap service. The Norwegian share of the scheduled air service run by SAS is two-sevenths of the SAS service on international routes and the total SAS service in Norway.

	1,000 km flown	Passengers carried	1,000 passenger-km	Post, luggage, freight and passengers (1,000 ton-km) Total	Of which post
1976	52,266	3,853,483	3,180,000	397,000	13,000
1977	53,823	4,192,516	3,441,000	433,000	15,000
1978	56,525	4,487,440	3,789,000	476,000	16,000
1979	58,950	4,866,926	4,070,000	497,000	16,000

Shipping. The total registered mercantile marine on 1 Jan. 1980 was 1,730 vessels, 21·5m. gross tons (steam and motor vessels above 100 gross tons). These figures do not include fishing and catching boats, tugs, salvage vessels, ice-breakers and similar special types of vessels, totalling 846 vessels of 367,000 gross tons.

Vessels in foreign trade 1977	No.	Total Net tons
Norwegian	8,883	13,733,000
Foreign	8,280	20,066,000
Total entered	17,163	33,839,000

Goods (in 1,000 tonnes) in 1979 discharged, 22,554; loaded, 39,490, of which 21,250 was Swedish iron ore shipped from Narvik.

Post and Broadcasting. Number of telephones on 31 Dec. 1979 was 1,725,066 (42 per 100 of population). Receipts, 3,709·3m. kroner; expenses, 3,623·9m. kroner (interest on capital included). *Norsk Rikskringkasting* is a non-commercial enterprise operated by an independent state organization and broadcasts 1 programme on long-, medium-, and short-waves and on FM. Local programmes are also broadcast. It broadcasts 1 TV programme from 1,211 transmitters. Colour programmes are broadcast by PAL system. Number of television licences, 1,173,060.

Cinemas. There were 455 cinemas with a seating capacity of 141,673 in 1978.

Newspapers. There were 72 daily newspapers with a combined circulation of 1,747,000 in 1979.

JUSTICE, RELIGION, EDUCATION AND WELFARE

Justice. The judicature in Norway is common to both civil and criminal cases. The same judges, who are state officials, preside over both kinds of cases. The participation of lay assessors and jurors, summoned for each case, varies according to the civil or criminal nature of the case.

The ordinary Court of First Instance (*Herreds- og byrett*) is presided over by a judge who in criminal cases is, and in civil cases may be, assisted by 2 lay assessors, chosen by ballot from a panel elected by the district council. In criminal matters the Court of First Instance is generally competent in cases where the maximum penalty incurred is 5 years imprisonment. Altogether there are 100 Courts of First Instance. There is a Conciliation Council (*Forliksråd*) for each community, consisting of 3 men or women, elected by the district council, before which, as a general rule, civil cases must first be brought for mediation.

The Court of Second Instance (*Lagmannsrett*) is presided over by a judge, together with 2 other judges. In civil matters they may be assisted by lay assessors, ordinarily 4 but in some cases 2, chosen and elected in the same way as mentioned above. In criminal cases the lay element is a jury composed of 10 jurors deciding the question of guilt. This court is an ordinary court of appeal in civil cases. In criminal cases competence of the court is limited to appeals directed against alleged mistakes by the lower court in its adjudication of the question of guilt and in such cases a renewed trial will take place. (If the complaint is only based on other alleged mistakes by the lower court the appeal goes to the Supreme Court, see below.) In addition, as a court of first instance, this court takes cognizance of all criminal cases (other than those coming under the *Riksrett*—the court for impeachments) which do not come under the competence of the Court of First Instance. The kingdom is divided into 5 districts (*Lagdømmer*) for the purpose of the Courts of Second Instance.

The Supreme Court (*Høyesterett*) is the ultimate court of appeal. In criminal cases competence of the court, however, is limited to complaints against the application of laws, measuring out of the penalty and trial of the case of the subordinate courts. The Supreme Court consists of a president and 17 judges. In each single case the court consists of 5 judges. Criminal procedure is at present under revision.

All serious offences are prosecuted by the State. The public prosecution is led by a general prosecutor (*riksadvokat*) and there are 19 district prosecutors (*statsadvokater*). Counsel for the defence is, generally, paid by the State.

There are 3 central penal and correctional institutions for delinquents in which were detained (12 Oct. 1980), 317 persons. There are also 35 local prisons in which were detained (12 Oct. 1980) 1,499 persons.

Religion. There is complete freedom of religion, the Evangelical Lutheran Church, however, being the national church, endowed by the State. Its clergy are nominated by the King. Ecclesiastically Norway is divided into 10 *Bispedømmer* (bishoprics), 89 *Prostier* (provostships or archdeaconries) and 606 *Prestegjeld* (clerical districts). There were 124,552 members of registered religious communities outside the Evangelical Lutheran Church, subsidized by central government and local authorities in 1978. The Roman Catholics are under a Bishop at Oslo, a Vicar Apostolic at Trondheim and a Vicar Apostolic at Tromsø.

Education. In Norway the children normally start their school attendance the year they complete 7 and finish compulsory school the year they complete 16.

On 1 Oct. 1979 the number of primary schools and pupils were as follows: 3,500 primary schools, 593,579 pupils; 97 special schools for the handicapped, 3,658 pupils.

On 1 Oct. 1979 the number of pupils in upper secondary schools, *i.e.*, folk high schools, secondary general schools and vocational schools, was 178,514.

There are in Norway 4 universities and 8 institutions equivalent to universities. In autumn 1979 the total number of students was 40,643. The University of Oslo, founded in 1811, had 19,147 students. The University of Bergen, founded in 1948, had 7,432 students. The University of Trondheim consists of the Norwegian Institute of Technology, founded in 1910, and the College of Arts and Science, founded in 1925. At each of them the number of students was in autumn 1979, 4,708 and 3,403 respectively. The University of Tromsø was established in 1968; 1,569 students were registered in autumn 1979. The other university institutions had 4,384 students.

In addition there were at other schools of higher education, 31,409 students. These included 12,734 at colleges for teachers, 6,261 at colleges for engineers and 4,597 at district colleges.

In 1979 there were 4,323 Norwegian students and pupils attending foreign universities and schools.

Health. In 1978 there were 8,345 doctors and 63,082 hospital beds.

Social Security. In 1979, 36,087m. kroner were paid under different social insurance schemes, amounting to 18% of the net national income.

The National Insurance Act of 17 June 1966, which came into force on 1 Jan. 1967, replaced the schemes relating to old age pensions, disability benefits, widows' and mothers' pensions, benefits to unmarried women, 'survivors' benefit for children and rehabilitation aid. Schemes relating to health insurance, unemployment insurance and occupational injury insurance were revised and incorporated in National Insurance Scheme on 1 Jan. 1971.

The following conspectus gives a survey of schemes established by law. Many municipalities grant additional benefits to old-age, disablement and survivor's pensions.

Type of scheme	Intro-duced[1]	Scope	Principal benefits as from 1 May 1980
National insurance	1967 (1980)		
Sickness benefits[2]	1911	All residents	Medical benefits: hospital expenses; about ¾ of doctors' fees, important medicines, etc., daily sickness allowances: kr. 13 to 505 per day cash. The new sickness allowance scheme (1 July 1978) entitles employees to a daily allowance equal to 100% of their gross earned income (within certain limits) from and including the first day of absence; the allowances are taxable
Unemployment benefits[2]	1939	Nearly all wage-earners	Daily allowance during unemployment kr. 28 to 316 per day, taxable as from 1 Jan. 1980. Contributions to training and retraining, removal expenses, wage subsidies in the case of relief work
Rehabilitation benefits[3]	1961	Persons unfit for work because of disablement and persons who have a substantially limited general functional capacity	Training; treatment; rehabilitation allowance grants and loans Full rehabilitation allowance equals old age pension
Disability benefits[3]	1961	All residents disabled before the age of 67	A basic grant (15, 23 or 30% of the basic amount) and an assistance grant (25% of the basic amount) to persons with special needs. In certain cases the benefits may be increased. Disability pension to persons between 16 and 67 years of age, occupationally disabled by at least 50%, unfit for rehabilitation Full disability pension equals old age pension
Occupational injury benefits[2] (industrial workers 1895; fishermen 1909; seamen 1913; military personnel 1953, combined in the act of occupational injury insurance 1960)	1960	All employed persons, school children and students; self-employed on a voluntary basis	The ordinary benefits of the National Insurance, e.g., sickness and rehabilitation benefits, basic grants, assistance grants, disability pensions, and benefits to survivors granted according to special rules which in almost all cases are more favourable for the insured person—or his survivors than the ordinary rules An occupational injury compensation, alone or in addition to a disability pension
Old age pensions[3]	1937	All persons above 67 years of age	Basic pensions: Single, kr. 16,900; couples, kr. 25,350 per annum; supplementary pensions based on previous pensionable income; basic grant; assistance grant; various allowances
Death grants	1967	All residents	25% of basic amount, i.e. kr. 4,225

For notes see bottom of table overleaf.

Type of scheme	Intro-duced[1]	Scope	Principal benefits as from 1 May 1980
Survivors' benefits[3]	1965	All residents	Full pension = kr. 16,900 per annum + 55% of the supplementary pension due to the deceased, *transitional benefits*, assistance grant and educational allowances
Children's pension[3]	1958	Under 18 years of age, after loss of one or both parents	40% of basic amount (kr. 6,760) for first child, 25% (kr. 4,225) for each additional child. If both parents are dead, full survivors' pension for first, 40% of basic amount for second, 25% third, etc., child
Benefits for unmarried mothers[3]	1965	Unmarried mothers	Maternity grant kr. 6,253, transitional benefit, full amount kr. 16,900 per annum, assistance grant and educational allowances
Benefits to unmarried persons forced to live at home[3]	1965	Unmarried persons under 67 years of age having stayed at home for at least 5 years to give necessary care and attention to parents or other near relatives	Transitional benefit or a pension that equals the basic amount, educational allowances
Special supplement to National Insurance pensions or transitional benefits	1969 (1980)	Pensioners and persons with transitional allowance on basic rates	Full special supplement to married pensioner 41% of basic amount, others 44% of basic amount
Compensation supplement to National Insurance pensions or transitional benefits	1970	Pensioners, persons with transitional benefits (except unmarried mothers) or rehabilitation allowances	Full compensation supplement kr. 500 for single persons and kr. 750 for married couples
Family allowances	1946 (1980)	All families with children under 16 years of age	Kr. 2,100, for the first child, kr. 3,324 for the second, kr. 4,344 for the third, kr. 4,620 for the fourth and kr. 4,908 for the fifth and each additional child. Single supporters receive benefit for one more child than the actual number of children
War pensions	1946 (1980)	War victims, 1939–45	Pensions up to kr. 79,344 per annum; widows' and children's pensions
Special pension schemes:		Persons with at least:[4]	Maximum old-age pension for couples:
Seamen	1948 (1980)	150 months service (360 ,, ,,)	Kr. 55,390[5] per annum (officers) Kr. 39,564[5] ,, ,, (others)
Forestry workers	1952 (1980)	750 premium weeks (1,500 ,, ,,)	Kr. 18,000 per annum
Fishermen	1958 (1979)	750 premium weeks (1,500 ,, ,,)	Kr. 22,500 ,, ,,

[1] Date of latest revision in brackets.
[2] Transferred to national insurance scheme and revised in 1971.
[3] Transferred to national insurance scheme and revised in 1967.
[4] Requirements for maximum pensions in brackets.
[5] Supplements for service during war not included.

Provisions have been laid down for the integration of more than one benefit, pension, etc., so as to limit the total amount.

SVALBARD

An archipelago situated between 10° and 35° E. long. and between 74° and 81° N. lat. Total area, 62,000 sq. km (24,000 sq. miles).

The main islands of the archipelago are Spitsbergen (formerly called Vestspitsbergen), Nordaustlandet, Edgeøya, Barentsøya, Prins Karls Forland, Bjørnøya, Hopen, Kong Karls Land, Kvitøya, and many small islands. The arctic climate is tempered by mild winds from the Atlantic.

The archipelago was probably discovered by Norsemen in 1194 and rediscovered by the Dutch navigator Barents in 1596. In the 17th century the very lucrative whale-hunting caused rival Dutch, British and Danish–Norwegian claims to sovereignty and quarrels about the hunting-places. But when in the 18th century the whale-hunting ended, the question of the sovereignty of Svalbard lost its significance; it was again raised in the 20th century, owing to the discovery and exploitation of coalfields. By a treaty, signed on 9 Feb. 1920 in Paris, Norway's sovereignty over the archipelago was recognized. On 14 Aug. 1925 the archipelago was officially incorporated in Norway.

Coal is the principal product. Of the 3 Norwegian and 3 Soviet mining camps, only 1 Norwegian and 2 Soviet camps are operating. A second Norwegian mining camp, Sveagruva, is being prepared for re-opening. Total population on 31 Dec. 1979 was 3,650, of which 1,190 in Norwegian communities, and 2,460 in Soviet communities. In 1979, 315,210 tonnes of coal were exported from the Norwegian and 477,311 tonnes from the Soviet mines.

Norwegian and foreign companies have been prospecting for oil. So far 5 deep drillings have been made, but oil and gas finds have not been reported.

There are Norwegian meteorological and radio stations at the following places: Bjørnøya (since 1920), Hopen (1945), Isfjord (1934), Longyearbyen (1930), Svalbard Lufthavn (1975) and Ny-Ålesund (1961). A research station, administered by Norsk Polarinstitutt, was erected at Ny-Ålesund in 1968 for various observations and investigations. An airport near Longyearbyen (Svalbard Lufthavn) opened in 1975.

Norsk Polarinstitutt, Skrifter. Oslo, from 1948 (under different titles from 1922)
Greve, T., *Svalbard: Norway in the Arctic.* Oslo, 1975
Hisdal, V., *Geography of Svalbard.* Norsk Polarinstitutt, Oslo, 1976
Orvin, A. K., 'Twenty-five Years of Norwegian Sovereignty in Svalbard 1925–1950' (in *The Polar Record, 1951*)

JAN MAYEN

This bleak, desolate and mountainous island of volcanic origin and partly covered by a glacier, is situated 71° N. lat. and 8° 30′ W. long., 300 miles NNE of Iceland. The total area is 380 sq. km (147 sq. miles). Beerenberg, its highest peak, reaches a height of 2,277 metres. Volcanic activity, which had been dormant, was reactivated in Sept. 1970.

The island was possibly discovered by Henry Hudson in 1608, and it was first named Hudson's Tutches (Touches). It was again and again rediscovered and renamed. Its present name derives from the Dutch whaling captain Jan Jacobsz May, who indisputably discovered the island in 1614. It was uninhabited, but occasionally visited by seal hunters and trappers, until 1921 when Norway established a radio and meteorological station. On 8 May 1929 Jan Mayen was officially proclaimed as incorporated in the Kingdom of Norway. Its relation to Norway was finally settled by law of 27 Feb. 1930. A LORAN station (1959) and a CONSOL station (1968) have been established.

BOUVET ISLAND
Bouvetøya

This uninhabited volcanic island, mostly covered by glaciers and situated 54° 25′ S. lat. and 3° 21′ E. long., was discovered in 1739 by a French naval officer, Jean

Baptiste Lozier Bouvet, but no flag was hoisted till, in 1825, Capt. Norris raised the Union Jack. In 1928 Great Britain waived its claim to the island in favour of Norway, which in Dec. 1927 had occupied it. A law of 27 Feb. 1930 declared Bouvetøya a Norwegian dependency. The area is 48 sq. km (19 sq. miles). From 1977 Norway has had automatic meteorological stations on the island, and 5 men operated a meteorological station there during the 1978–79 season.

PETER I ISLAND
Peter I Øy

This uninhabited island, situated 68° 48′ S. lat. and 90° 35′ W. long., was sighted in 1821 by the Russian explorer, Admiral von Bellingshausen. The first landing was made in 1929 by a Norwegian expedition which hoisted the Norwegian flag. On 1 May 1931 Peter I Island was placed under Norwegian sovereignty, and on 24 March 1933 it was incorporated in Norway as a dependency. The area is 180 sq. km (69 sq. miles).

QUEEN MAUD LAND
Dronning Maud Land

On 14 Jan. 1939 the Norwegian Cabinet placed that part of the Antarctic Continent from the border of Falkland Islands dependencies in the west to the border of the Australian Antarctic Dependency in the east (between 20° W. and 45° E.) under Norwegian sovereignty. The territory had been explored only by Norwegians and hitherto been ownerless. Since 1949 expeditions from various countries have explored the area. In 1957 Dronning Maud Land was given the status of a Norwegian dependency.

DIPLOMATIC REPRESENTATIVES

OF NORWAY IN GREAT BRITAIN (25 Belgrave Sq.,
London, SW1X 8QD)

Ambassador: Frithjof Jacobsen.

OF GREAT BRITAIN IN NORWAY (Thomas Heftyesgate 8, Oslo, 2)
Ambassador: Gillian Garda Brown.

OF NORWAY IN THE USA (2720 34th Street, NW,
Washington, D.C., 20008)

Ambassador: Knut Hedemann.

OF THE USA IN NORWAY (Drammensveien 18, Oslo, 2)
Ambassador: Sidney A. Rand.

OF NORWAY TO THE UNITED NATIONS
Ambassador: Ole Ålgård.

Books of Reference

Statistical Information: The Central Bureau of Statistics, Statistisk Sentralbyrå (Dronningensgate 16, Oslo 1), was founded in 1876 as an independent state institution. *Director:* Arne Øien. The earliest census of population was taken in 1769. The Sentralbyrå publishes the series *Norges Offisielle Statistikk*, Norway's official statistics (from 1828), and *Social Economic Studies* (from 1954). The main publications are:

Statistisk Årbok for Norge (annual, from 1880; from 1952 bilingual Norwegian–English)

Økonomisk Utsyn (annual, from 1935; with English summary from 1952)
Historisk Statistikk 1978 (historical statistics; bilingual Norwegian–English)
Statistisk Månedshefte (monthly, from 1880; with English index)

Norges Statskalender. From 1816; annual from 1877
Facts about Norway. Ed. by Aftenposten. 16th ed. Oslo, 1977–78, revised 1979
Derry, T. K., *A History of Modern Norway, 1814–1972.* OUP, 1973.—*A History of Scandinavia.* London, 1979
Ekeland, S., *Norway in the Modern World.* Oslo, 1976
Glässer, E., *Norwegen* [bibliography] Darmstadt, 1978
Gleditsch, Th., *Engelsk–norsk ordbok,* 2nd ed. Oslo, 1948
Grønland, E., *Norway in English. Books on Norway . . . 1742–1959.* Oslo, 1961
Haugen, E., *Norwegian–English Dictionary,* Oslo, 1965
Helvig, M., *Norway: Land, People, Industries, a Brief Geography.* 3rd ed. Oslo, 1970
Holtedahl, O. (ed.), *Geology of Norway.* Oslo, 1960
Hove, O., *The System of Education.* Oslo, 1968
Knudsen, O., *Norway at Work.* Oslo, 1972
Larsen, K., *A History of Norway,* New York, 1948
Midgaard, J., *A Brief History of Norway.* Oslo, 1969
Nielsen, K., and Nesheim, A., *Lapp Dictionary: Lapp–English–Norwegian.* 5 vols., Oslo 1963
Orvik, N. (ed.), *Fears and Expectations: Norwegian Attitudes Toward European Integration.* Oslo, 1972
Paine, R., *Coast Lapp Society.* 2 vols. Tromsø, 1957–65
Popperwell, R. G., *Norway.* London, 1972
Udgaard, N. M., *Great Power Politics and Norwegian Foreign Policy.* Oslo, 1973
Vorren, Ø. (ed.), *Norway North of 65.* Oslo, 1960

National Library: The University Library, Drammensvein 42b, Oslo. *Director:* John Brandrud.

OMAN

Sultanate of Oman

Capital: Muscat
Population: 820,000 (1980)
GNP per capita: US$2,570 (1978)

AREA AND POPULATION. The Sultanate of Oman, known as the Sultanate of Muscat and Oman until 1970, is an independent sovereign state, situated in south-east Arabia. Its coastline is over 1,000 miles long and extends from the Ras al Khaimah Shaikdom near Bukha on the west side of the Musandum Peninsula to Ras Dharbat Ali, which marks the boundary between Oman and the territory of the People's Democratic Republic of Yemen. The Sultanate extends inland to the borders of the Rub' al Khali ('Empty Quarter') across three geographical divisions—a coastal plain, a range of hills and a plateau. The coastal plain varies in width from 10 miles near Suwaiq to practically nothing in the vicinity of Mutrah and Muscat towns, where the hills descend abruptly into the sea. These hills are for the most part barren except at the highest part of the mountainous region of the Jebel Akhdar (summit 9,998 ft) where there is some cultivation. The plateau has an average height of 1,000 ft. With the exception of oases there is little or no cultivation. North-west of Muscat the coastal plain, known as the Batinah, is fertile and prosperous. The date gardens extend for over 150 miles. Whereas the coastline between the capital, Muscat, and the southern province of Dhofar is barren, Dhofar itself is highly fertile. Its principal town is Salalah on the coast which is served by the port of Rasut.

In the valleys of the interior, as well as on the Batinah, date cultivation has reached a high level, and there are possibilities of agricultural development subject to present water resources and soil surveys. The average annual crop of dates is estimated at 50,000 tons, most of which is exported to India. Camels are bred in large numbers by the inland tribes. There are no industries of any importance, although a copper industry was being established in 1980, and fishing, water resources, soil and agricultural surveys are being undertaken.

The area has been estimated at about 105,000 sq. miles and the population at 820,000, chiefly Arabs; of these, some 40,000 live in Dhofar. The town of Muscat is the capital which, while formerly of some commercial importance, has now lost most of its trade to the adjacent port of Mutrah (combined populations, 25,000), the starting point for the trade routes into the interior. The population of both towns consists of pure Arabs, Indians, Pakistanis and Negroes; numerous merchants are Khojas (from Sind and Kutch) and Hindus (mostly from Gujarat and Bombay). Other ports are Sohar, Khaburah and Sur, Rasut in the south; none, however, affords shelter from bad weather.

The port of Gwadur and a small tract of country on the Balúchistán coast of the Gulf of Oman were handed over to Pakistan on 8 Sept. 1958.

The **Kuria Muria** islands were ceded to the UK in 1854 by the Sultan of Muscat and Oman for the purpose of a cable station. On 30 Nov. 1967 the islands were retroceded to the Sultan of Muscat and Oman, in accordance with the wishes of the population.

RULER. The present Sultan is Qaboos bin Said (born Nov. 1940). He took over from his father Said bin Taimur, on 23 July 1970 in a Palace *coup.*

National flag: Red, with a white panel in the upper fly and a green one in the lower fly, and in the canton the national emblem in white.

The Treaty of Friendship, Commerce and Navigation between Britain and the Sultan, signed on 20 Dec. 1951, reaffirmed the close ties which have existed between the British Government and the Sultanate of Oman for over a century and a half.

950

DEFENCE

Army. The Army is of 8 infantry battalions with personnel of 16,200 with an artillery regiment, a signals regiment, a sapper company, a paratrooper squadron and an armoured-car squadron.

Navy. The Navy comprises 2 fast missile armed patrol boats, 4 fast gunboats, 1 corvette (converted royal yacht), a logistic support ship, 1 supply ship, 6 landing craft, 2 training ships and 13 coastal patrol craft. Naval personnel in 1981 totalled 1,500 officers and ratings.

Air Force. The Air Force, formed in 1959, had in 1980 a strike/interceptor squadron of Jaguars, a ground attack/interceptor squadron of Hunters, a squadron of Strikemaster light jet training/attack aircraft, 3 BAC One-Eleven twin-turbofan transports, 1 Falcon VIP transport, 1 C-130H Hercules, 1 twin-turboprop Buffalo, 7 Defender and 34 Skyvan light transports, 34 Agusta-Bell 205, 212, 214B and JetRanger helicopters for security duties and 2 Bravo piston-engined trainers. Further Jaguars are on order. Air defence force has batteries of Rapier low-level surface-to-air missiles. Personnel (1980) 2,100.

INTERNATIONAL RELATIONS

Membership. Oman is a member of UN and the Arab League.

ECONOMY

Planning. The 5-year development plan (1976–80) envisaged expenditure of R.O. 2,556m. and a plan for 1980–85 has been announced.

Budget. Revenue (1980) R.O. 993m. (800m. from oil); expenditure, 971m. (defence, 250m.).

Currency. The *Rial Omani* was introduced in Nov. 1972 replacing the *Rial Saidi*. It is divided into 1,000 *baiza*. There are notes of 100, 250 and 500 *baiza* and 1, 5 and 10 *Rial Omani* and coins of 2, 5, 10, 20, 50 and 100 *baiza*. The exchange rate in March 1981 was £1 = 751 *baiza*; US$1 = 345 *baiza*.

Weights and Measures. The metric system of measurement is being gradually introduced. The weights in use are 1 *kiyas* = the weight of 6 dollars of 5·9375 oz.; 24 kiyas = 1 Muscat *maund*; 10 maunds = 1 *farásala*; 200 maunds = 1 *bahár*. Rice is sold by the bag; other cereals by the following measures: 40 *palis* = 1 *ferrah*; 20 ferrah = 1 *khandi*.

OIL. The economy of Oman is dominated by the oil industry, which provides nearly all Government revenue. Known reserves (1974) 6,000m. bbls. In 1937 Petroleum Concessions (Oman) Ltd, a subsidiary of the Iraq Petroleum Co., was granted a 75-year oil concession extending over the whole area except the district of Dhofar. A concession covering Dhofar was granted in 1953 to Dhofar Cities Service Petroleum Corporation; it expires in 25 years from the date of commercial production, with option to renew for another 25 years.

In 1964 Petroleum Development (Oman) Ltd, re-formed in 1967 as a subsidiary of Royal Dutch Shell (with an 85% interest), Compagnie Française des Pétroles (with 10%) and Gulbenkian interests with their traditional 5% announced that drilling had proved sufficient reserves for the company to go into commercial production. The production of oil began in 1967 at a rate of 200,000 bbls per day and expanded to 360,000 bbls per day by the end of 1969. However, during late 1970 and early 1971 technical difficulties affected production and the 1971 production of 105·56m. bbls was 15m. down on 1970. Production (1977) was 124·1m. bbls valued at US$1,593m.

In 1973 the 4 connected oilfields at Fahud, Natih, Yibal and Al-Huwaisah together produced at an average rate of 292,947 bbls per day. The average rose to about 375,000 bbls per day from Jan. 1975, when the 3 Ghaba fields started producing. It is expected that Oman will maintain oil production at about 350,000 bbls per day throughout the 1980s.

Petroleum Development (Oman) Ltd is also drilling at Marmul in the north of Dhofar, where quantities of relatively heavy oil are known to exist. Production was expected to start in 1980.

The German company Wintershall A.G. heads a consortium exploring an off-shore concession in the Gulf of Oman. Other offshore concessions are held by Sun Oil (south-west of Masirah Island) and ELF–ERAP (off the Musandam coast). None of these companies has yet announced finds.

Early in 1974 the Oman Government purchased a 25% share in Petroleum Development (Oman) Ltd, increasing this in July to 60%. Shell interest is now only 34%. Oman is not a member of the Organization of Petroleum Exporting Companies (OPEC) nor of the Organization of Arab Petroleum Exporting Countries (OAPEC), but under the terms of the concessions granted to the companies the Government of the Sultanate is assured of treatment equal to that received by members of OPEC.

COMMERCE. Trade is mainly with UK, India, Australia, Japan and the neighbouring Gulf States. Total imports for 1977 were valued at US$1,135m., mainly rice, wheat, flour, milk and milk products, machinery, cement, vehicles and accessories, electrical goods, petroleum products and building materials. The main countries exporting to Oman in 1973 were UK, UAE, Japan, India, Australia, Netherlands and the Federal Republic of Germany.

Exports, which, excluding oil, consisted of dates, limes, dried fish, tobacco leaf, fruits and vegetables, were valued at R.O. 347m. in 1975 (non-oil, R.O. 1·1m.).

Total trade between Oman and UK (British Department of Trade returns, in £1,000 sterling):

	1975	1976	1977	1978	1979	1980
Imports to UK	113,997	73,234	15,147	41,942	31,844	28,728
Exports and re-exports from UK	97,994	102,288	172,856	125,721	129,729	131,094

COMMUNICATIONS

Roads. A network of adequate graded roads links all the main sectors of population, and only a few mountain villages are not accessible by Land-Rover. A rapid road construction programme began in 1976, and by the end of the year there were 1,272 km of paved roads and 8,500 km of graded roads. The road from Sohar to Buraimi is complete. In Dhofar tarmac roads have been completed from Raysut through Salalah to Taqa and also Bid Bid to Sur. Proposed future contracts for tarmac roads include: Al Qabil to Ibri, 140 miles; Ibri to Nizwa, 80 miles.

Aviation. Gulf Air run regional services in and out of Seeb international airport (20 miles from Muscat) to Bahrain, Doha, Abu Dhabi, Dubai, Karachi and Bombay. They and British Airways each operate daily flights to and from London. Other airlines serving Muscat are MEA, Kuwait Airlines, PIA, Air India, Iran Air, TMA (cargo) and Trade Winds (cargo).

Shipping. In Mutrah the new deep-water port (named Mina Qaboos) was completed in 1974 at a cost of R.O. 18·2m. It provides 12 berths, 9 of which are deep-water berths, warehousing facilities and a harbour for dhows and coastal vessels. The annual handling capacity has been raised to 1·5m. tons.

Post and Broadcasting. There are Sultanate post offices in Muscat and Mutrah, relying solely upon a Post Office Box system for delivery. Omantel maintain a telegraph office at Muscat and an automatic telephone exchange (13,068 lines, 1978) which includes Mutrah, Bait-al-Falaj and Mina al-Fahal, the oil company terminal. A high-frequency radio link with Bahrain was opened in Aug. 1972 providing communications with other parts of the world. Internally, there are radio telephone, telex and telegraph services direct between Salalah and Muscat, and a VHF radio link between Seeb international airport and Muscat. The airport is also served by a SITA telex system.

A colour television service covering Muscat and the surrounding area started transmission in Nov. 1974. A television service for Dhofar opened in 1975.

EDUCATION AND WELFARE

Education. Until 1970 there were only 3 schools in Oman, and it has been estimated that as many as 80% of Omanis are still illiterate. In 1978 there were 257 primary schools with about 78,000 pupils. Secondary education is still extremely limited with only 9 secondary schools, total number of students, 685. All Omanis desiring further education must obtain it abroad, but plans are being implemented for the development of technical and agricultural training and craft training at intermediate and secondary level. There are also programmes to combat adult illiteracy.

Health. Health services in 1980 were widely spread with 13 hospitals in use and 2 more planned, 12 health centres and 47 dispensaries. There are also Save the Children Fund Welfare Clinics at Sohar and Sur.

DIPLOMATIC REPRESENTATIVES

OF OMAN IN GREAT BRITAIN (64 Ennismore Gdns, London, SW7 5DN)

Ambassador: Malallah Habib (accredited 6 Nov. 1980).

OF GREAT BRITAIN IN OMAN (PO Box 300, Muscat)

Ambassador: Hon. Ivor Lewis, CMG.

OF OMAN IN THE USA (2342 Massachusetts Ave., NW, Washington, DC., 20008)

Ambassador: Farid Mubarak Al-Hinai.

OF THE USA IN OMAN (PO Box 966, Muscat)

Ambassador: Marshall W. Willey.

OF OMAN TO THE UNITED NATIONS

Ambassador: Mahoud Aboul-Nasr.

Books of Reference

Achievements. Ministry of Health. Oman, 1975
Hawley, D., *Oman and its Rennaissance.* London, 1977
Morris, J., *Sultan in Oman.* London, 1966
Peterson, J. E., *Oman in the Twentieth Century.* London and New York, 1978
Phillips, W., *Unknown Oman.* London, 1967.—*Oman: A History.* London, 1968
Shannon, M. O., *Oman and Southeastern Arabia: A Bibliographic Survey.* Boston, 1978
Skeet, I., *Muscat and Oman: The End of an Era.* London and New York, 1974
Thesiger, W., *Arabian Sands.* London, 1959
Townsend, J., *Oman: The Making of the Modern State.* New York and London, 1977

PAKISTAN

Islamic Republic of Pakistan

Capital: Islamabad
Population: 80·2m. (1980)
GNP per capita: US$230 (1978)

HISTORY. Pakistan was constituted as a Dominion on 14 Aug. 1947, under the provisions of the Indian Independence Act, 1947, which received the royal assent on 18 July 1947. The Dominion consisted of the following former territories of British India: Balúchistán, East Bengal (including almost the whole of Sylhet, a former district of Assam), North-West Frontier, West Punjab and Sind; and those States which had acceded to Pakistan.

On 23 March 1956 an Islamic republic was proclaimed after the Constituent Assembly had adopted the draft constitution on 29 Feb.

On 7 Oct. 1958 President Mirza declared martial law in Pakistan, dismissed the central and provincial Governments, abolished all political parties and abrogated the constitution of 23 March 1956. Field Marshal Mohammad Ayub Khan, the Army Commander-in-Chief, was appointed as chief martial law administrator and assumed office on 28 Oct. 1958, after Maj.-Gen. Iskander Mirza had handed all powers to him. His authority was confirmed by a ballot in Feb. 1960. He proclaimed a new constitution on 1 March 1962.

On 25 March 1969 President Ayub Khan resigned and handed over power to the army under the leadership of Maj.-Gen. Agha Muhammad Yahya Khan who immediately proclaimed martial law throughout the country, appointing himself chief martial law administrator on the same day. On 29 March 1970 the Legal Framework Order was published, defining a new constitution: Pakistan to be a federal republic with a Moslem Head of State; the National Assembly and Provincial Assemblies to be elected in free and periodical elections, the first of which was held on 7 Dec. 1970.

At the general election the Awami League based in East Pakistan and led by Sheikh Mujibur Rahman gained 167 seats and the Peoples' Party 90. Martial law continued pending the settlement of differences between East and West, which developed into civil war in March 1971. The war ended in Dec. 1971 and the Eastern province declared itself an independent state, Bangladesh. On 20 Dec. 1971 President Yahya Khan resigned and Mr Z. A. Bhutto became President and chief martial law administrator. On 30 Jan. 1972, Pakistan withdrew from the Commonwealth.

A new Constitution was adopted by the National Assembly on 10 April 1973 and enforced on 14 Aug. 1973. It provided for a federal parliamentary system with the President as constitutional head and the Prime Minister as chief executive. President Bhutto stepped down to become Prime Minister and Fazal Elahi Chaudhry was elected President.

The Chief of the Army Staff, Gen. M. Zia-ul-Haq, proclaimed martial law on 5 July 1977 and the armed forces took control of the administration; scheduled elections were postponed. Mr Bhutto was hanged (for conspiracy to murder) on 4 April 1979. Gen. M. Zia-ul-Haq succeeded Fazai Elahi Chaudhry as President in Sept. 1978.

Governors-General of Pakistan: Quaid-I-Azam Mohammed Ali Jinnah (14 Aug. 1947–11 Sept. 1948); Khawaja Nazimuddin (11 Sept. 1948–18 Oct. 1951; took over the premiership after the assassination of Liaquat Ali Khan); Ghulam Mohammad (19 Oct. 1951–6 Oct. 1955); Maj.-Gen. Iskander Mirza (assumed office of President on 6 Oct. 1955, elected President on 5 March 1956).

EVENTS. On 16 Oct. 1979 President Zia-ul-Haq announced the stringent enforcement of martial law, the dissolution of all political parties and the indefinite postponement of elections to Parliament.

954

AREA AND POPULATION. Pakistan is bounded north-west by Afghánistán, north by the USSR and China, east by India and south by the Arabian Sea. The total area of Pakistan is 310,400 sq. miles (803,943 sq. km); population (1972 census), 64·89m.; males, 34,417,000; females, 30,475,000. Density, 212 per sq. mile. Estimate (1980) 80·2m. This excludes Jammu and Kashmir, Gilgit and Baltistan, Junagadh, Manavadar and Pakistan enclaves in India. Annual average growth rate, 1978–80, 3%.

The population of the principal cities (census of 1972) is:

Bahawalpur	133,956	Jhang	135,722	Multan	542,195	Sargoda	201,407
Gujranwala	360,419	Karachi	3,498,634	Peshawar	268,368	Faisalabad	822,263
Gujrat	100,581	Kasur	102,531	Quetta	156,000	Sialkot	203,779
Hyderabad	628,310	Lahore	2,165,372	Rawalpindi	615,392	Sukkur	158,876
Islamabad	77,318	Mardan	115,218	Sahiwal	106,213		

Population of the provinces (census of 1972) was:

	Area (sq. miles)	Total population (1,000)	Male (1,000)	Female (1,000)	Density per sq. mile
North-West Frontier Province	28,773	8,402	4,376	4,026	296
Federally Administered Tribal Areas	10,510	2,507	1,291	1,216	237
Federal Capital Territory Islamabad	350	235	130	105	671
Punjab	79,284	37,374	19,871	17,503	475
Sind	54,407	13,965	7,474	6,491	260
Balúchistán	134,050	2,409	1,275	1,134	18

Language. The commonest languages are Urdu and Punjabi. Urdu is the national language while English is used in business and in central government. Provincial languages are Punjabi, Sindhi, Pushtu (North-West Frontier Province), Baluchi and Brahvi.

CONSTITUTION AND GOVERNMENT. Under the Constitution of 1973 Parliament is bi-cameral, comprising the National Assembly and the Senate. The strength of the National Assembly is 210 including 10 women. The Senate consists of 63 members, 14 from each province, 5 from Federally Administered Tribal Areas and 2 from the federal capital area, elected by the members of the Provincial Assemblies. A constitutional amendment of 29 March 1976 provided 6 National Assembly seats reserved for non-Moslem minority representatives.

With the proclamation of martial law the Constitution has been kept in abeyance, but not abrogated: it is subject to the laws (Continuance in Force) Order, 1977, and any Order made by the President and any Regulation issued by the Chief Martial Law Administrator. All existing laws, other than the Constitution (subject to any Order of the President or Regulation made by the Chief Martial Law Administrator and until altered, amended or repealed by the competent authority) will continue in force.

Article 31 of the Constitution obliges the Government to use such ways and means as may enable the people to order their lives collectively and individually in accordance with the principles of Islam. The Council of Islamic Ideology was set up to this end under article 228 of the Constitution.

President and Chief Martial Law Administrator, Chairman of the Planning Commission, Science and Technology, States and Frontier Regions, Establishment: Gen. M. Zia-ul-Haq.

Federal Cabinet at 31 March 1981:

Finance and Economic Affairs: G. Ishaq Khan. *Foreign Affairs:* A. Shahi. *Attorney-General:* S. Pirzada. *Interior:* M. A. Haroon. *Defence:* A. A. Talpur. *Housing and Works:* Air Marshal I. Haq Khan. *Water and Power:* R. Sikandar Zaman. *Industry:* E. Bux Soomro. *Culture, Sports and Tourism:* A. Niaz Mohammad. *Local Government and Rural Development:* F. Imam. *Labour, Manpower and Overseas*

Pakistanis: G. Dastegir Khan. *Kashmir and Northern Affairs:* Maj.-Gen. J. Dar. *Education:* M. Ali Khan. *Food, Agriculture and Co-operatives:* Vice-Adm. M. F. Janjua. *Communications:* M. Baluch. *Health and Social Welfare:* N. ud-Din Jogezai. *Petroleum and Natural Resources:* Maj.-Gen. R. F. Ali Khan. *Production and National Logistics:* Lieut.-Gen. S. Oadir. *Information and Broadcasting:* Zafarul Haq. *Without portfolio:* A. M. A. Khan Abbas.

National flag: Green, charged at the centre, with a white crescent and white 5-pointed star, a white vertical stripe at the mast to one-quarter of the flag.

Local Government. Pakistan comprises the provinces of the Punjab, the North-West Frontier, Sind and Balúchistán, the states of Bahawalpur and Khairpur, the Balúchistán States Union, the frontier states and the tribal areas of Balúchistán and the north-west. These were merged into a single unit on 14 Oct. 1955. In July 1970 the single unit was dissolved into the original 4 provinces. The provincial capitals are Peshawar (NW Frontier Province), Lahore (Punjab), Karachi (Sind) and Quetta (Balúchistán). Provincial governors are appointed by the President and are assisted by elected provincial councils.

Within the provinces there are divisions (14 in 1978) administered by Commissioners appointed by the President; the divisions are divided into districts and agencies (55 in 1978) administered by Deputy Commissioners or Political Agents who are responsible to the Provincial Governments.

Kashmir. Between one-third and one-half of Kashmir is controlled by Pakistan. This area is known as Azad (Free) Kashmir, and is the northern and western portion of the country. It has an area of 83,806 sq. km. and a population of about 1·3m. Under a United Nations resolution of 1949 its future was to be decided by plebiscite; it is still a disputed territory. The people of Azad Kashmir have their own Assembly (42 members including 2 women), their own Council (of 14 members), High Court and Supreme Court. There is a Parliamentary form of Government with a Prime Minister as the executive head and the President as the Constitutional head.

The Pakistan Government is directly responsible for Gilgit and Baltistan.

Chief Executive: Brig. Mohammad Hayat Khan.

Elections to the Legislative's 40 general seats are to be held within 10 days of the general elections in Pakistan, according to a presidential proclamation of 8 Oct. 1977. The seat of government is Muzaffarabad.

DEFENCE

Army. The Pakistan Army consists of 16 infantry divisions and 2 armoured divisions, 4 independent armoured brigades, 4 independent infantry brigades, 6 artillery and 2 air defence brigades. Total strength (1981), 408,000. General headquarters is at Rawalpindi. The entire officers cadre receives its precommission training in the Military Academy at Kakul.

Navy. The fleet comprises 6 diesel-powered patrol submarines (completed in France in 1969–79), 6 midget submarines, 1 light cruiser (cadet training ship), 6 destroyers, 1 fast anti-submarine frigate, 12 fast gunboats, 4 fast (hydrofoil) torpedo boats, 1 survey ship (*ex*-frigate), 6 coastal minesweepers, 4 patrol craft, 1 oiler, 1 rescue ship, 1 water carrier and 3 tugs.

Two 'Whitby' class frigates to have been acquired from Britain were not taken up; instead 2 destroyers were purchased from USA in 1977.

The principal naval base and dockyard are at Karachi. Naval personnel in 1981 totalled 1,000 officers and 10,000 ratings.

The submarine *Ghazi* (*ex*-USS *Diablo*), transferred from the US Navy in 1964, was sunk during the India–Pakistan war on Dec. 1971, as were the destroyer *Khaibar* (*ex*-HMS *Cadiz*), purchased from Britain in 1956, 3 patrol craft built in Britain in 1965 and a coastal minesweeper acquired from USA in 1955.

Air Force. The Pakistan Air Force came into being on 14 Aug. 1947. It has its headquarters at Peshawar and is organized within 3 air defence sectors, in the northern, central and southern areas of the country. Tactical units include 1 squadron of B-57B (Canberra) bombers, 4 squadrons of Mirage III-EP/5 supersonic fighters, 5 squadrons of MiG-19 (F-6) supersonic fighter-bombers acquired from China, 3 squadrons equipped with Canadair Sabre 6 fighters, Mirage III-RP and RT-33 jet reconnaissance aircraft and C-130 Hercules turboprop transports. On order are 32 more Mirages to equip 2 squadrons in 1981–83. Flying training schools are equipped with Saab Supporter armed piston-engined primary trainers, T-37B/C jet trainers supplied by the USA, Mirage III-DPs, MiG-15UTIs, Sabres and T-33s. Three Breguet Atlantics, 2 Albatross amphibians and 4 Super Frelon helicopters, plus a small number of Alouette III helicopters, are available to perform maritime reconnaissance, search and rescue duties in co-operation with Sea King helicopters of the Pakistan Navy Air Arm. There is a flying college at Risalpur and an apprentices' college at Korangi Creek. Total strength in 1980 was about 275 combat aircraft and 17,600 all ranks.

INTERNATIONAL RELATIONS

External Debt (Sept. 1979), about US$7,000m., of which US$2,000m. to the World Bank and the rest to USA, OPEC and Islamic consortia. The IMF authorised a further US$1,700m. in Nov. 1980.

Membership. Pakistan is a member of the UN, the Colombo Plan, and Regional Co-operation for Development.

Treaties. A mutual defence assistance agreement between Pakistan and the USA was signed in Karachi on 19 May 1954.

ECONOMY

Planning. The fifth 5-year plan (1978–83) envisages a total fixed investment of Rs 204,000m. including Rs 61,670m. in the private sector. Real growth in GDP is planned at 7·2% annually (agriculture 6%; industry 10%). Expenditure will be met mainly (75%) from internal resources. Allocations for new industrial capacity (Rs 31,841m.), industrial improvement (Rs 7,467m.), and public sector development in health (Rs 6,600m.), education, (Rs 10,280m.), transport and communications (Rs 27,400m.) and water and power (Rs 45,050m.) have been made.

Budget. The following table shows the budget for the years 1979–80 and 1980–81 in Rs 1m.:

	1979–80 Revised	1980–81 Budget
Gross revenue receipts	38,712	44,353
Less provincial share in federal taxes	6,050	7,172
Net federal revenue	32,662	37,181
Non-development revenue expenditure	26,937	31,349
Capital:		
Total resources	18,108	19,528
Development outlay	21,916	26,464

Currency. The monetary unit is the Pakistan *rupee*. The official rate (March 1981) is Rs 21·32 = £1. Decimal coinage was introduced on 1 Jan. 1961. The rupee, which previously consisted of 64 *pice*, now consists of 100 *paisas*. The notes are of Rs 100, 50, 10 and 5 denominations issued by the State Bank in the name of the Government, and Rs 1 issued by the State Bank incurring no liability; the coinage in the decimal series is 0·5, 0·25, 0·1, 0·05 and 0·01 rupee.

Total monetary assets (including currency in circulation and deposits) in March 1980 amounted to Rs 93,087m. Currency in circulation, Oct. 1980, Rs 30,812·4m.

Banking. The State Bank of Pakistan is the central bank; it came into operation as the Central Bank on 1 July 1948 with an authorized capital of Rs 30m. and was nationalized in Jan. 1974. As on 28 June 1979 total assets or liabilities of the issue department amounted to Rs 25,250m. and those of the banking department Rs 24,297m.; reserve fund, Rs 2,120m. and total deposits, Rs 12,989m. It is the sole bank of issue for Pakistan, custodian of foreign exchange reserves and banker for the federal and provincial governments and for scheduled banks. It also manages the rupee public debt of federal and provincial governments. It provides short-term loans to the Government and commercial banks and short- and medium-term loans to Provincial Co-operative banks and specialized banks. The State Bank raised the bank rate from 9 to 10% with effect from 7 June 1977, but it provides finance for export sales of locally manufactured machinery at 2% per annum and for other export sales at 3% per annum.

There were 24 scheduled banks (banks with capital and reserves of an aggregate value of not less than Rs 500,000) in Pakistan on 30 June 1979. Of these 9 were Pakistani including 5 commercial banks (National Bank of Pakistan, Habib Bank Ltd, United Bank Ltd, Muslim Commercial Bank Ltd and Allied Bank Ltd), 2 specialized banks (Agricultural Development Bank of Pakistan and Industrial Development Bank of Pakistan) and 2 co-operative banks (Punjab Provincial Co-operative Bank and Federal Bank for Co-operatives). Pakistani scheduled banks were nationalized in Jan. 1974. In addition, there were 15 foreign banks operating in Pakistan on 30 June 1979. In 1980 foreign banks were given the option of meeting part or all of their reserve requirements with the State Bank in specified foreign currencies. The total number of offices of scheduled banks was 6,956. Total deposits of all the scheduled banks stood at Rs 56,173m. and total assets at Rs 98,179·5m. on 30 Aug. 1979. The National Bank of Pakistan acts as an agent of the State Bank for transacting Government business and managing currency chests at places where the State Bank has no offices of its own.

Weights and Measures. The metric system is in general use.

ENERGY AND NATURAL RESOURCES

Electricity. Installed capacity (1979) by type of generation: Thermal 1,648,830 kw.; hydro-electric, 1,567,200 kw.; nuclear, 137,000 kw. Total generated electrical energy at the end of 1979, 14,174m. kwh.

Oil. Oil comes mainly from the Potowar Plain, from fields at Meyal, Tut, Balkassar, Joya Mair and Dhullian. Production in 1978–79, 3·75m. bbls. Oil reserves were also found at Dhodak in Dec. 1976. Exploitation is mainly through government incentives and concessions to foreign private sector companies. Investment 1978–79 was Rs 244m., of which the Government provided Rs 51m.

Gas. Gas pipelines from Sui to Karachi (345 miles) and Multan (200) supply natural gas to industry and domestic consumers. A pipeline between Quetta and Shikarpur was approved in 1980, to be constructed in 1982. There are 4 other productive fields. Reserves (1978), 22,621,341m. cu. ft; production (1978–79), 214,421m. cu. ft; consumption (1978–79), 192,804m. cu. ft.

Water. The Indus water treaty of 1960, concluded between India and Pakistan, has created the basis for a large-scale development programme. The Indus Basin Development Fund Agreement has been subscribed by Australia, Canada, Federal Republic of Germany, New Zealand, UK and USA and is administered by the International Bank; the works to be constructed call for expenditure of US$1,000m. The main purpose of the treaty is the division of the water power of the Indus and its 5 tributaries between India and Pakistan. After the construction of some 460 miles of canals, the Indus and the 2 western tributaries will serve Pakistan and the entire flow of the 3 eastern tributaries will be released for use in India.

The largest project is the construction of the Tarbela Dam, an earth-and-rock-filled dam on the river Indus, 485 ft high, which has a gross storage capacity of 11·1m. acre feet of water for irrigation. It also provides (1979–80) about 40% of national power generated.

The Lloyd Barrage and Canal Construction Scheme, which consists of a barrage across the river Indus at Sukkur and 7 canals—4 on the left and 3 on the right bank—is designed to provide an assured supply of water to an area of about 1·83m. acres in territory which used to be dependent upon inundation canals. It also brings under irrigation a further area of 3·62m. acres in Sind, the Khairpur state and the Nasirabad tehsil in Balúchistán.

Another barrage across the Indus, 4½ miles north of Kotri, called the Ghulam Muhammad Barrage, was completed in 1955; the fourth and last of the main canals taking off it was opened in 1958. The irrigable area to be served by this scheme is about 2·75m. acres in the Lower Sind area.

The Taunsa barrage on the Indus, 80 miles downstream of Kalabagh, was completed in 1958. It will eventually irrigate 1·4m. acres in the Muzaffargah and Dera Ghazi Khan districts.

The Gudu barrage, 10 miles from Kashmore, serves 2·6m. acres of the rice-growing tracts north of Sukkur; it was completed in 1962.

The province of the Punjab set up in 1949 the Thal Development Authority to colonize the Thal desert between the Indus and Jhelum rivers. The project envisages the irrigation of some 2m. acres and the establishment of a balanced economy of agriculture, trade and industry.

The Chashma canal, to be completed by 1982, will carry water 172 miles across Dera Ismail Khan from the Chashma barrage on the Indus, irrigating 350,000 acres of virgin land. The canal will extend into Punjab and there irrigate 220,000 acres.

The Mangla Dam on the Jhelum was inaugurated in Nov. 1967; it generates 400,000 kw. of hydro-electric power.

Minerals. The main agencies are the Pakistan Mineral Development Corporation, the Resource Development Corporation and the Gemstone Corporation of Pakistan. Coal is mined at Sharigh and Harnai on the Sind–Pishin railway and in the Bolan pass, also in Sor Range and Degari in the Quetta–Pishin district and in the Punjab; total recoverable reserves, about 480m. tonnes, mainly low-grade. A further 55m. tonnes was found at Lakhra in 1980. Chromite is extracted in and near Muslimbagh. Limestone is quarried generally. Gypsum is mined in the Sibi district and elsewhere; reserves, about 350m. tonnes. Iron ore is being worked in Kalabagh and elsewhere; reserves, about 400m. tonnes, low-grade. Uranium has been found in Dera Ghazi Khan. At Saindak a foreign consortium proposes to mine and process copper (1·69m. tonnes recoverable metal), gold (2·24m. oz.), silver (2·49m. oz.), and magnetite (128m. tonnes). The quantity (in 1,000 tonnes) of the chief minerals produced in 1978 was as follows: Coal, 1,282,000; limestone, 3,580; rock salt, 490; chromite, 11. Other minerals of which useful deposits have been found are magnesite, sulphur, barites, china clay, marble, bauxite, antimony ore, bentonite, celestite, dolomite, fireclay, fluorite, fuller's earth, phosphate rock, silica sand and soapstone.

Agriculture. The entire area in the north and west is covered by great mountain ranges. The rest of the country consists of a fertile plain watered by 5 big rivers and their tributaries. Agriculture is dependent almost entirely on the irrigation system based on these rivers. It employs 53% of labour and provides about 30% of GNP and 36% of foreign exchange earnings. Growth rate, 1979–80, 6%. The main crops are wheat, cotton, maize, sugar-cane and rice, while the Quetta and Kalat divisions (Balúchistán) are known for their fruits and dates.

By 31 March 1977, 3·34m. acres of land had been taken away from landlords, and 1·48m. acres had been distributed to 137,005 tenants. An ordinance of Jan. 1977 reduced the upper limit of land holding to 100 irrigated or 200 non-irrigated acres; it also replaced the former land revenue system with a new agricultural income tax, from which holders of up to 25 irrigated or 50 unirrigated acres are exempt. Land resumed by the Government, unless required for public purposes, is granted free to tenants who were in possession and cultivating during certain seasons of 1975 and 1976. About 9·5m. of the 10m. landowners held less than 25 acres; about 35,000 landowners would have had to surrender land. Of the surveyed area of 156m. acres, cultivated land accounts for 63m. acres, of which 11m. acres consist of fallow land, so that the net area sown is 52m. acres. The Mangla Dam scheme has begun the reclamation of 3m. acres of salt-affected land; this and other schemes had reclaimed between 7m. and 8m. acres by 1976. The main problem in agriculture is pest control; pesticide imports for 1976–77 are estimated at 6,045 tonnes valued at Rs 293·8m., increasing the acreage sprayed from 8·56m. to 11·92m.

Production, 1979–80 (in 1,000 tons): Rice (cleaned), 3,204; wheat, 10,870; sugar-cane (gur), 27,440; cotton (lint, 1,000 bales), 4,200.

Livestock (FAO estimate, 1979): Cattle, 15m.; buffaloes, 11·31m.; sheep, 24·2m.; goats, 27·8m.; poultry, 48·9m.

Forestry. There were (1976) 7·3m. acres of reserved and protected forests and 10·6m. acres managed as pasture ranges by the Forest Department. Of the forests 1·5m. acres are in Punjab, 1·66m. in Balúchistán, 1·46m. in Sind and 2·65m. in the North-West Frontier Province. Forests produce an annual average of over 20m. cu. ft of timber and 16m. cu. ft of fuel. Annual value of this and other produce, about Rs. 60m. Forest lands are also used as national parks, wildlife and game reserves.

Fisheries. Landings (1975) in inland waters, 37,600 tonnes; of sea fish, 161,500 tonnes.

INDUSTRY AND TRADE

Industry. Industry employs about 10% of the population. Public sector new investment, 1979–80, Rs 22,480m.; private sector, Rs 11,720m. Woollen and other cottage industries, especially cotton weaving (with 220,000 workers) and carpet weaving, have made great strides. The population engaged in the fishing industry is about 39,000. In 1972 public sector companies were re-organized under a Board of Industrial Management. In 1976 all cotton-ginning, rice-husking and flour-milling plants were nationalized (except small flour-mills of less than 6 rollers outside Balúchistán). Pakistan is self-sufficient in cotton cloth and sugar. Capacity of chemical fertilizer plants in 1976–77 was 335,000 tons; cement plants, 3·4m. tons; both are being expanded. A public sector steel-mill has been built at Port Qasim near Karachi, capacity 1·1m. tons; trial production began in autumn 1979. Also recently completed are a heavy mechanical complex and a heavy forge and foundry plant at Taxila. There are plants processing barites and china clay. A private sector ferrous alloys plant has been approved near Peshawar, capacity 40 tonnes of ferrous silicon and manganese per day.

Production 1979–80: Cotton cloth, 340m. sq. metres; cotton yarn, 366m. kg.; cement, 3·2m. tonnes; fertilizers (urea), 630,000 tonnes.

Labour. The Labour Force Survey of 1974–75 gave the total work force as 20·42m., of whom 54·8% (11·22m.) were engaged in agriculture, forestry and fishing, 13·6% (2·8m.) in manufacturing; the textile industry was the largest single manufacturing employer. Estimates (1979–80) gave a labour force of 22·97m., 5·6m. of them urban.

Commerce. Total value of exports during 1979–80 amounted to Rs 23,176m., and the total value of imports to Rs 48,114m. The value of the chief articles imported into and exported from Pakistan in 1978–79 was (in Rs 1m.):

Imports		*Exports*	
Petroleum and products	5,427	Cotton, raw	655
Non-electrical machinery	4,251	Cotton manufactures	4,091
Grains, pulses and flour	3,507	Rice	3,380
Oil vegetables	2,953	Leather	1,247
Chemical fertilizers	2,808	Petroleum and products	608
		Carpets and rugs	1,765

Total trade between Pakistan and UK (British Department of Trade returns, in £1,000 sterling):

	1975	1976	1977	1978	1979	1980
Imports to UK	38,012	40,421	48,790	54,387	68,021	58,289
Exports and re-exports from UK	77,203	92,723	121,051	112,395	139,759	139,692

Mutual trade relations with India were re-established in Jan. 1975.

Tourism. Earnings in 1979, US$100m. There were 135,694 overland tourists and 182,486 travelled by air. Expenditure per tourist, US$314.

COMMUNICATIONS

Roads. At the end of financial year 1975–76 Pakistan had 31,029 miles of roads, of which 16,875 miles were all-weather roads. The fourth plan allocated Rs 100m. to building and improving 3,500 miles. The Karakoram highway to the Chinese border, through Kohiston and the Hunza valley, was opened in 1978. An all-weather road linking Skardu and the remote NE Indus valley to the highway was built in 1980.

Railways. Pakistan Railways had (1980) a route of 8,815 km mainly on 1,676 mm. gauge, with some metre gauge and narrow gauge line. Railway budget, 1980–81: revenue account receipts, Rs 3,300m.; expenditure, Rs 3,254m.

Aviation. Karachi is served by British Airways, KLM, PANAM, Lufthansa, Swissair, SAS, Iran National Airlines, Air France, Garuda, Gulf Air and by Philippine, Japanese, Chinese, East African, Syrian, Iraqui, Kuwait, Jordanian, Saudi Arabian, Romanian, Egyptian and Russian airlines.

Pakistan International Airlines (founded 1955; the majority of shares is held by the Government) had 4 DC-10s, 7 Boeing 707Cs, 5 720Bs, 2 747Bs and 8 Fokker F-27s in 1977; 2 other Boeing 720Bs were on lease to Air Malta. Services operate to 20 home airports, New York, Paris, Amsterdam, Copenhagen, İstanbul, Athens, Rome, Cairo, Tripoli, Nairobi, Dhahran, Damascus, Amman, Baghdad, Persian Gulf points, Tōkyō, Peking, Zahedan, Singapore, Manila, Kuala Lumpur, Bangkok, Colombo, London, Frankfurt, Bombay, Delhi, Dacca, Kábul, Tehrán and Jeddah.

Shipping. There is a seaport at Karachi. A second port is being built at Phitti Creek on the Makram coast, 26 miles east of Karachi, to be called Port Muhammad Bin Qasim; this port will have iron and coal berths for Pakistan Steel Mills, multi-purpose berths, bulk-cargo handling, oil and container-traffic terminals; the first phase (handling bulk and bagged cargo) will be operational it is hoped in 1983. The merchant fleet consists of 41 dry cargo vessels with a capacity of 509,665 tons, 3 passenger-cargo ships (17,866 tons), 4 cargo-passenger vessels (36,579 tons); total carrying capacity 4,709 passengers. National flag carriers now operate between Pakistan and UK (10 ships normally employed); USA and Canada (8); the Far East (12); the (Persian) Gulf, Arabian Gulf, Red Sea, Black Sea and Mekran Coast (4); Continental Europe and the Middle East (4). Ten ships are normally operating under charter. The Karachi Shipyard and Engineering Works Ltd construct all types of vessels up to 27,000 DWT and repairs all types; dry-dock and under-water repairs can be done on vessels up to 29,000 DWT, above-water repairs on vessels and drilling rigs of all sizes.

Post and Broadcasting. The telegraph and telephone system is government-owned. Telephones, on 30 June 1979, numbered 312,247; a nationwide dialling system is in operation between 46 cities. In 1979 there were 10,488 post offices (8,193 rural) and 93 main telegraph offices; emphasis was laid on improving rural communications and 28 public call offices and 47 small exchanges were opened. Pakistan has international telephone connections by 102 satellite, 7 HF, 4 microwave and 10 carrier circuits. An international direct-dialling exchange with 25,000 connections was opened in July 1980. Television stations operate in Lahore, Karachi, Peshawar, Quetta and Rawalpindi–Islamabad.

Cinemas (1972). There are 578 cinemas seating 300,000.

Newspapers. Dailies and periodicals numbered 1,200 in 1973: 19 were English language dailies, 83 were vernacular dailies and the rest were periodicals in English and regional languages.

JUSTICE, RELIGION, EDUCATION AND WELFARE

Justice. The Central Judiciary consists of the Supreme Court of Pakistan, which is a court of record and has three-fold jurisdiction, namely, original, appellate and advisory. There are 4 High Courts in Lahore, Peshawar, Quetta and Karachi. Under the Constitution, each has power to issue directions of writs of *Habeas Corpus*, *Mandamus*, *Certiorari* and others. Under them are district and sessions courts of first instance in each division; they have also some appellate jurisdiction. Criminal cases not being sessions cases are tried by district magistrates and subordinate magistrates. There are subordinate civil courts also.

Jurisdiction of the Judicial Committee of the Privy Council ceased on 30 April 1950.

The Constitution provides for an independent judiciary, as the greatest safeguard of citizens' rights. The Laws (Continuance in Force) (Eleventh Amendment) Order, 1980, prescribed the date of 14 Aug. 1981 by which the judiciary shall be separated from the executive. There is an Attorney-General, appointed by the President, who has right of audience in all courts.

A Federal Shariat Court at the Supreme Court level has been established to decide whether any law is wholly or partially un-Islamic. Islamic law is to be enforced as the law of the state; penalties for offences involving intoxicating liquor, offences against property and sexual offences have been specified. Imprisonment remains as a penalty in general use, but some offences in all the above categories are liable to whipping and some property offences, to amputation.

Religion. Religious groups (1972 census): Moslems, 63·28m.; Christians, 907,861; Scheduled Castes, 603,369; Caste Hindus, 296,837; Parsees, 9,589; Buddhists, 4,318; others, 205,250. There is a Ministry to safeguard the constitutional rights of religious minorities.

Education. At the census of 1972, there were about 9·3m. people in Pakistan who were able to read and write, representing 21·7% of the population over 10 years old.

The principle of free and compulsory primary education has been accepted as the responsibility of the state. The duration of primary education has been fixed provisionally at 5 years. It is hoped that all boys aged 5 will be enrolled in schools by 1982 and girls by 1987. Adult literacy programmes have been established. Present policy stresses vocational and technical education, disseminating a common culture based on Islamic ideology.

Number of schools, enrolments and teachers, 1978–79 (estimate): Primary schools, 55,173 (6·17m. enrolments; 150,000 teachers); secondary schools, 8,376 (1·86m.; 109,400); vocational secondary schools, 167 (30,000; 2,100).

There were also 445 general colleges (241,000 enrolments; 12,684 teachers); 91 professional colleges (57,500; 3,200); 89 teacher-training colleges (10,100; 1,080); 15 universities, including the open university at Islamabad (26,000; 2,600).

Health. In 1980 there were 536 hospitals (42,469 beds) and about 23,000 doctors.

DIPLOMATIC REPRESENTATIVES

OF PAKISTAN IN GREAT BRITAIN (35–36 Lowndes Sq., London, SW1X 9JN)

Ambassador: Ali Arshad (accredited 13 Feb. 1981).

OF GREAT BRITAIN IN PAKISTAN (Diplomatic Enclave, Ramna 5, Islamabad)

Ambassador: O. G. Forster, CMG, MVO.

OF PAKISTAN ON THE USA (2315 Massachusetts Ave., NW, Washington, D.C., 20008)

Ambassador: Sultan Mohammad Khan.

OF THE USA IN PAKISTAN (Diplomatic Enclave, Ramna 4, Islamabad)

Ambassador: Arthur W. Hummel, Jr.

OF PAKISTAN TO THE UNITED NATIONS

Ambassador: Niaz A. Naik.

Books of Reference

Pakistan Year-Book 1973
Ahmad, K. S., *A Geography of Pakistan.* OUP, 1964
Anwar, M. R., *Presidential Government in Pakistan.* 2nd ed. Lahore, 1964
Burke, S. M., *Pakistan's Foreign Policy.* OUP, 1973
Burki, S. J., *Pakistan Under Bhutto.* London, 1980
Feldman, H., *Pakistan: An Introduction.* OUP, 1968.—*Revolution in Pakistan: A Study of the Martial-law Administration.* OUP, 1957
Griffin, K., and Khan, A. R. (ed.), *Growth and Inequality in Pakistan.* London and New York, 1972

Hasan, M., (ed.) *Pakistan in a Changing World*. Karachi, 1978

Jennings, Sir Ivor, *Constitutional Problems in Pakistan*. CUP, 1957

Khalid bin Sayeed, *Pakistan, the Formative Phase*. Karachi, 1961

Office of the Economic Adviser, *Pakistan—Basic Facts*. Rawalpindi, 1973–74

Papnek, G. F., *Pakistan's Development—Social Goods and Private Incentives*. OUP, 1968

Siddiqui, K., *Conflict, Crisis and War in Pakistan*. London, 1972

Stephens, I., *Pakistan*. New York, 1963

Suleri, Zia-ud-din Ahmad, *Politicians and Ayub: A Survey of Pakistani Politics from 1948 to 1964*. Lahore, 1965

Tayyeb, A., *Pakistan: A Political Geography*. OUP, 1966

Williams, L. F. R., *The State of Pakistan*. 2nd ed. CUP, 1966

PANAMA

República de Panamá

Capital: Panama City
Population: 1·89m. (1980)
GNP per capita: US$1,290 (1978)

HISTORY. A revolution, inspired by the USA, led to the separation of Panama from the United States of Colombia and the declaration of its independence on 3 Nov. 1903. The *de facto* Government was on 13 Nov. recognized by the USA, and soon afterwards by the other Powers. In 1914 Colombia agreed to recognize the independence of Panama. This treaty was ratified by the USA and Colombia in 1921, and on 8 May 1924 diplomatic relations between Colombia and Panama were established. On 10 Oct. 1979 Panama assumed sovereignty over what was previously known as the Panama Canal Zone and now called the Canal Area.

For the treaties regulating the relations between Panama and the USA *see* pp. 967–8.

AREA AND POPULATION. Panama is bounded north by the Caribbean, east by Colombia, south by the Pacific and west by Costa Rica. Extreme length is about 480 miles (772 km); breadth between 37 (60) and 110 miles (177 km); coastline, 426 miles (685 km) on the Atlantic and 767 (1,234 km) on the Pacific; total area (excluding the Canal Zone) is 29,761 sq. miles (77,082 sq. km); population according to the census of 10 May 1970 was 1,428,082 (estimated population in Jan. 1980 was 1·89m.). Over 75% are of mixed blood and the remainder Indians, negroid, white and Asiatic.

There are approximately 8,000 British Commonwealth citizens from the Caribbean area.

The capital is Panama City, on the Pacific coast; estimated population, 1980, 467,000. There are 9 provinces (with populations, 1970, and estimated population 1980 in brackets) as follows (the capitals in brackets): Bocas del Toro (Bocas del Toro), 50,300 (58,000); Chiriquí (David), 265,000 (294,000); Coclé (Penonomé), 133,000 (149,000); Colón (Colón), 152,000 (170,000); Los Santos (Las Tablas), 75,000 (75,000); Herrera (Chitré), 79,000 (85,000); Darién (La Palma), 24,000 (26,000); Panama (Panama City), 737,000 (850,000); Veraguas (Santiago), 162,900 (177,000). The port of Colón on the Atlantic coast had 95,300 (78,000). Smaller ports on the Pacific are Aguadulce, Pedregal, Montijo, Puerto Mutis and Puerto Armuelles; in the Atlantic, Bocas del Toro, Almirante, Portobello, Mandinga and Permé. A new fishing port came into operation at Vacamonte in Aug. 1979.

Birth rate, 1977, was 28 per 1,000 population.

CONSTITUTION AND GOVERNMENT. The constitution of 1946 contained provisions for a National Assembly of 42 members with a mandate for 4 years. The term of the President of the Republic, elected by direct vote, was 4 years, he was not eligible for the two succeeding terms. Women had equal rights with men.

There were normally 2 vice-presidents, elected every 4 years by direct popular vote, and a cabinet of 7 ministers nominated by the President, who might attend and address the legislature but could not vote. The Comptroller-General was elected by the National Assembly for 4 years.

On 11 Oct. 1968, however, the newly elected President, Dr Arnulfo Arias, was deposed after only 11 days in office, in a *coup* conducted by the National Guard. The National Assembly was suspended and a provisional government set up consisting of a two-man military Junta and a civilian cabinet. In Dec. 1969 the military members of the Junta resigned and were replaced by civilians after an abortive attempt to depose the Commander of the National Guard, Brig.-Gen. Omar Torrijos.

A new Constitution which came into force in 1972, as amended in 1978, provides for an Assembly of 505 representatives of municipal districts elected on a community rather than a party basis, a Legislative Council of 54 members, 36 of whom are elected by the Assembly (the other 18 are to be elected on party tickets in partial elections due to be held in 1980) and a directly-elected President and Vice-President; the present incumbents were indirectly elected in Oct. 1978 and the first direct elections under these arrangements are due to take place in 1984. The formation of political parties is now permitted, subject to statutory regulations, and 3 such parties had achieved full legal recognition by Nov. 1979.

Elections, the first to be held in Panama for 12 years, for the National Legislative Council were held in Sept. 1980. The Democratic Republic Revolutionary Party (PRD) gained 11 of the 19 seats; Liberals, 5; Christian Democrats, 2; Independent, 1.

President of the Republic: Aristides Royo.
Vice-President of the Republic: Ricardo de la Espriella.
Minister for Foreign Affairs: Jorge Illueca.
Commander-in-Chief of the National Guard: Brig.-Gen. Omar Torrijos.

The official language is Spanish.

National flag: Quarterly: first a white panel with a blue star, second red, third blue, fourth white with a red star.

National anthem: Alcanzamos por fin la victoria (words by J. de la Ossa; tune by Santos Jorge, 1903).

Local government: The 9 provinces are sub-divided into 64 municipal districts and 2 *comarcas* (special districts).

DEFENCE

Army. The *Guardia Nacional* is the only military type force with police as well as military and para-military functions. It has a strength of about 11,000 and includes a coastguard section.

Air Force. The air force has 1 Lockheed Electra, 1 DC-6, 4 C-47s, 2 Islanders, 1 Twin Otter transport, 11 Cessna and 5 DHC-3 Otter liaison aircraft, a Shorts Skyvan, a Westwind VIP jet transport, a Falcon VIP jet transport, and 23 UH-1B/D/H Iroquois, twin-engined UH-1N and FH-1100 helicopters.

INTERNATIONAL RELATIONS

Membership. Panama is a member of UN and OAS.

ECONOMY

Budget. The 1979 budget balanced at 649m. balboas.

Net receipts from transactions with the Panama Canal Zone were estimated at 246m. balboas in 1977.

Consolidated public sector debt was 956m. balboas in Dec. 1977.

Currency. The monetary unit is the *balboa*, which is of the same size and fineness as the US silver dollar but is maintained equivalent to the gold dollar. Other coins whose metallic content is required by law to correspond exactly to that of similar US coins are the half-balboa (equal to 50 cents US); the quarter and tenth of a balboa piece; a cupro-nickel coin of 5 cents, and a copper coin of 1 cent. US coinage is also legal tender. Volume of the currency has not been disclosed since 31 Dec. 1950, when it stood at 1·5m. balboas. The only paper currency used is that of the USA.

Banking. There is no statutory central bank. The Government accounts are handled through the *Banco Nacional de Panama*. The number of commercial banks rose from 9 in 1964 to 93 by Sept. 1980; 52 have a general licence, 29 an international licence and 12 a representational licence. Leading banks are the Citibank, The Bank of London and South America, and the Chase Manhattan Bank of New York. Other foreign-owned banks include the Bank of America, as well as Canadian,

Columbian, Swiss, Federal German, French, Spanish, Dutch, Taiwan, Japanese and Brazilian banks.

Weights and Measures. English weights and measures are in general use; those of the metric system are also used.

ENERGY AND NATURAL RESOURCES

Electricity. Production of electric energy, 1977, amounted to 1,501·1m. kwh. (Panama City and Colón).

Minerals. There are known to be copper deposits in the provinces of Chiriquí, Colón and Darien. The most important, containing possibly the largest undeveloped reserves in the world, is Cerro Colorado (Chiriquí) on which a feasibility study by Texasgulf was completed in 1978. It is expected that an annual production of 180,000 tons, value US$125m., will be achieved within a few years. The Petaquilla (Colón) exploration concession contract was awarded to a Japanese group.

Agriculture. Of the whole area (1975) 18·5% is cultivated, 57·1% is natural or artificial pasture land and 9·5% is fallow. Of the remainder only a small part is cultivated, though the land is rich in resources. About 60% of the country's food requirements are imported. The Ministry of Agricultural Development (MIDA) buys leading crops at field prices. Of the land under cultivation, 26·4% is owned and 44·7% is usufructuary. The most important export products are bananas, grown by an affiliate of the United Brands Company and sugar from 4 state-owned and 2 private mills. Value of exports of these commodities in 1977 was 66·5m. balboas and 21·9m. balboas respectively. Most important food crop, for home consumption, is rice, grown on 80% of the farms; Panama's *per capita* consumption is very high. Output of rough rice from 109,980 hectares, was 4·1m. quintals in 1977–78. Other products are maize (82,780 hectares, yielding 1·8m. quintals in 1977–78), cocoa, coffee and coconuts. Beer, whisky, rum, 'seco', anise and gin are produced. Coffee is mainly grown in the province of Chiriquí, near the Costa Rican frontier; total production in 1977–78 was 121,200 quintals, and small amounts were exported. The country has great timber resources, notably mahogany. According to the livestock estimate of 1979 there were 1·4m. cattle, 205,000 pigs and 4·9m. poultry. Hides are among minor articles of export.

INDUSTRY AND TRADE

Industry. Local industries include cigarettes, clothing, food processing, shoes, soap, cement factories; foreign firms are being encouraged to establish industries, and a petrol refinery is operating in Colón.

GDP *per capita* (1978) 1,030 balboas.

Commerce. The imports and exports (including re-exports) for the Republic of Panama, for 6 calendar years are as follows (in 1,000 balboas; 1 balboa = US$1):

	Imports	Exports		Imports	Exports
1974	730,900	200,500	1977	777,761	243,051
1975	789,700	262,000	1978	862,000	381,700
1976	783,500	378,200	1979	1,185,000	288,000

The huge adverse visible trade balance is mainly with the USA and is due to the heavy import of consumer goods, most of it covered by a large invisible surplus. In 1977 the USA furnished 29·7% of Panama's imports and took 43·2% of her exports. The UK was the eighth largest supplier.

A Free Zone exists at Colón for the storage, processing, repacking and re-exporting or sale of goods in transit. The imports and exports (including re-exports) for the Colón Free Zone, for 6 calendar years are as follows (in 1,000 balboas):

	Imports	Exports		Imports	Exports
1973	311,101	378,881	1976	558,033	651,020
1974	475,900	510,800	1977	786,804	905,451
1975	415,700	543,100	1978	1,095,000	1,230,000

Chief exports (virtually all to the USA) in 1977 (in 1m. balboas) were: Petroleum products, 168·3; bananas, 66·5; sugar, 21·9; shrimps, 29·9.

Chief imports, 1977, were valued (in 1m. balboas f.o.b.): Machinery and transport material, 148; manufactured goods, 203·6; fuel, minerals and similar, 268·9; chemicals, 79·4; food, 58·4.

Total trade between Panama (including Colón Free Zone) and UK (British Department of Trade returns, in £1,000 sterling):

	1976	1977	1978	1979	1980
Imports to UK	1,068	732	982	4,131	3,941
Exports and re-exports from UK [1]	18,995	16,928	19,758	26,384	24,032

[1] Including new ships built for foreign owners and registered in Panama.

Tourism. In 1978, 373,600 people visited Panama earning 118·6m. balboas.

COMMUNICATIONS

Roads. Panama had on 31 Dec. 1977, 7,840 km of roads. The road from Panama City westward to the cities of David and Concepción and to the Costa Rican frontier, with several branches, is part of the Pan-American Highway. In 1972 work was started on the Pan-American Highway link with Colombia and has reached a point about 70 miles east of Panama City. The Darien gap prevents through transit. A concrete highway connects Panama City and Colón.

On 31 Dec. 1977 registered motor vehicles, private and commercial, numbered 98,970, this excludes vehicles owned by government departments. Vehicles registered in the Canal Zone numbered 20,100 (1976–77).

Railways. The *Ferrocarril de Panama* (Panama Railroad) (1,524 mm gauge) (through the Canal area), which connects Ancón on the Pacific with Cristóbal on the Atlantic, is the principal railway. It is 76 km long and runs along the banks of the Canal. As most vessels unload their cargo at Cristóbal (Colón), on the Atlantic side, the greater portion of the merchandise destined for Panama City is brought overland by the *Ferrocarril de Panama.* The United Brands owned railway runs from Almirante to Guabito on the Costa Rica border and on to Fields in Costa Rica (82 km).

The Chiriquí National Railroad (914 mm gauge) operates 169 km between David and Puerto Armuelles (United Brands).

Aviation. Commercial aviation has developed rapidly. PANAM, Braniff Airways, British Airways, KLM and other international companies operate at Tocumen Airport, 17 miles from Panama City. Air Panama provides services between Panama City and New York, Los Angeles, Miami, Central America and some countries in South America. The *Compañía Panameña de Aviación* (COPA) and *Aerolineas Las Perlas* provide a local service between Panama City and the provincial towns. COPA also provides an international service to Central America. In 1977 a total of 381,616 passengers arrived by air, excluding direct transits.

Shipping. Ships under Panamanian registry on 31 Dec. 1976 numbered 10,947 of 25,465,740 gross tons; most of these ships elect Panamanian registry because fees are low and labour laws lenient. All the international maritime traffic for Colón and Panama runs through the Canal ports of Cristóbal, Balboa and Bahia Las Minas (Colón); Almirante is used for both the provincial and international trade. There is an oil transfer terminal at Puerto Armuelles on the Pacific coast.

Panama Canal. On 18 Nov. 1903 a treaty between the USA and the Republic of Panama was signed making it possible for the US to build and operate a canal connecting the Atlantic and Pacific oceans through the Isthmus of Panama. The treaty granted the US in perpetuity the use, occupation and control of a Canal Zone, approximately 10 miles wide, in which the US would possess full sovereign rights 'to the entire exclusion of the exercise by the Republic of Panama of any such sovereign rights, power or authority'. In return the US guaranteed the independence of the republic and agreed to pay the republic $10m. and an annuity of $250,000. The US purchased the French rights and properties—the French had been labouring from 1879 to 1899 in an effort to build the Canal—for $40m. and in addition, paid private landholders within what would be the Canal Zone a mutually agreeable price for their properties.

Two new treaties between Panama and USA were agreed on 10 Aug. and signed on 7 Sept. 1977. One deals with the operation and defence of the canal until the end of 1999 and the other guarantees permanent neutrality.

The USA maintains control over all lands, waters and installations, including military bases, necessary to manage, operate and defend the canal until 31 Dec. 1999. A new agency of the US Government operates the canal, replacing the Panama Canal Co., and assuring US control of the canal to the end of the century; a policy-making board of 5 US and 4 Panamanian serves on the board of directors. Until 1990 the canal administrator would be a US citizen and the deputy would be Panamanian. After that date the position would be reversed.

Six months after the exchange of instruments of ratification Panama would assume general territorial jurisdiction over the former Canal Zone and would be able to use portions of the area not needed for the operation and defence of the canal. Panamanian penal and civil codes would be applicable. Within 30 months of the treaty entering into force responsibility for the police, transport, education, postal services, ship repairs and supplies, lock duties and the unloading of goods and passengers would be among other areas formerly administered by the Canal Co. and the Canal Zone Government for which Panama would assume responsibility.

66% of the electorate of Panama agreed to the ratification of the treaties when a referendum was held on 23 Oct. 1977 and on 18 April 1978 the treaty was ratified by the US Congress. The treaty went into effect on 1 Oct. 1979.

The treaty of 1936 increased the annuity to US$430,000 and, as desired by Panama, withdrew the guarantee of independence. In 1955 the annuity was increased to US$1·93m., and the Panama Canal Co. turned over to the Republic the Panama City railroad yards and other properties valued at US$22m. At the end of 1962 the US completed the construction of a high-level bridge over the Pacific entrance to the Canal, and the flags of Panama and the US were flown jointly over areas of the Canal Zone under civilian authority. Following the devaluation of the dollar in 1972 and 1973, the annuity was adjusted proportionally to US$2·1m. and US$2·33m., respectively.

The Panama Canal Commission, a US Government Agency, is concerned primarily with the actual operation of the Canal. On 8 July 1974 and 18 Nov. 1976 tolls were increased. These were the first increases of toll rates in the history of the Canal. Tolls were raised again on 1 Oct. 1979. The new rates are US$1.67 a Panama Canal ton for vessels carrying passengers or cargo. A Panama Canal ton is equivalent to 100 cu. ft of actual earning capacity. The new toll rate for warships, colliers, hospital ships and supply ships, which pay on a displacement basis, is 93 US cents a ton.

The changes were designed to continue the approximately break-even financial operating results after paying its own expenses for reimbursing the US Treasury for the net cost of the Canal Zone Government and paying interest on the net direct investment of the US in the Canal.

Administrator of the Panama Canal Commission: Lieut.-Gen. Dennis P. McAuliffe (US Army).

Deputy Administrator: Fernando Manfredo (Panama).

The total civilian and military population of the Canal Zone is 34,700 (estimate), of whom about 30,750 are US citizens. The total force employed by the Panama Canal Commission is 7,976, comprising 2,105 US citizens, 5,521 Panamanians and 350 others.

There are 144·4 miles of improved streets and highways in the zone, exclusive of those within Armed Forces reservations. Motor vehicles number over 25,000.

The Canal was opened to commerce on 15 Aug. 1914. It is 85 ft above sea-level. It is 51·2 statute miles in length from deep water in the Caribbean Sea to deep water in the Pacific ocean, and 36 statute miles from shore to shore. The channel ranges in bottom-width from 500 to 1,000 ft; the widening of Gaillard Cut to a minimum width of 500 ft was completed in 1969. Normally, the average time of a vessel in Canal waters is 18·5 hours, 8 of which are in transit through the Canal proper. The Canal is expected to reach the limits of its capacity in 2010 and proposals have been advanced by USA and Japan for a new sea-level canal. A map showing the Panama, Suez and Kiel canals on the same scale will be found in THE STATESMAN'S YEAR-BOOK, 1959 and a new map in the 1978–79 edition.

Particulars of the ocean-going commercial traffic through the canal are given as follows (vessels of 300 tons Panama Canal net and 500 displacement tons and over; cargo in long tons):

Fiscal year ending 30 June	North-bound (Pacific to Atlantic)		South-bound (Atlantic to Pacific)		Total		Tolls levied (in US$)
	Vessels	Cargo	Vessels	Cargo	Vessels	Cargo	
1975	6,859	56,009,293	6,750	84,092,166	13,609	140,101,459	141,898,218
1976	5,988	51,216,598	6,169	65,995,668	12,157	117,212,266	134,204,402
[1]	1,439	13,316,894	1,598	17,571,406	3,037	30,888,300	35,272,300
1977[2]	5,811	53,446,552	6,015	69,532,233	11,896	122,978,785	163,826,571
1978[2]	6,283	74,413,939	6,394	68,104,349	12,677	142,518,288	194,773,111

[1] Transition quarter.   [2] Year-ending 30 Sept.

In the fiscal year ending 30 Sept. 1978, of the 12,677 ships which passed through the Canal, 1,847 were Liberian; 1,633 US; 1,316 Greek; 1,093 British; 975 Panamanian; 912 Japanese; 525 Federal German; 523 Norwegian; 281 Danish; 262 Russian.

Statistical Information: The Panama Canal Information Office; *Information Officer:* Victor G. Canel.

Annual Reports on the Panama Canal, by the Administrator of the Panama Canal Commission.
Rules and Regulations Governing Navigation of the Panama Canal. The Panama Canal Commission, Miama, Florida *or* Washington, DC
Baxter, R. R., *The Law of International Waterways.* Harvard Univ. Press, 1964
Cameron, I., *The Impossible Dream.* London, 1972
Du Val, M. P., *Cadiz to Cathay: The Diplomatic Struggle for the Panama Canal.* 2nd ed. Stanford Univ. Press, 1947.—*And the Mountains will Move: The Building of the Panama Canal.* Stanford Univ. Press, 1947
Le Feber, W., *The Panama Canal: The Crisis in Historical Perspective.* OUP, 1978
McCullough, D., *The Patch Between the Seas.* New York and London, 1978

Post and Broadcasting. There are telegraph cables from Panama to North America and Central and South American ports, and from Colón to the USA and Europe. There is also inter-continental communication by satellite. There are 93 licensed commercial broadcasting stations, nearly all operated by private companies, one of which functions in the canal. There are 3 television stations, one of them run by the US Army at Fort Clayton. On 1 Jan. 1978 there were 156,668 telephones installed not including those in the canal.

Cinemas. In 1977 there were 52 cinemas in the district of Panama. All films must have Spanish subtitles.

Newspapers. There are 1 English language and 3 Spanish language daily morning newspapers and 1 English/Spanish evening newspaper.

JUSTICE, RELIGION, EDUCATION AND WELFARE

Justice. The Supreme Court consists of 9 justices appointed by the executive. There is no death penalty.

Religion. 95% of the population is Roman Catholic and 5% Protestant. There is freedom of religious worship and separation of Church and State. Clergymen may teach in the schools but may not hold public office.

Education. Elementary education is compulsory for all children from 7 to 15 years of age, with an estimated 545,800 students in schools throughout the Republic in 1977. The University of Panama at Panama City, inaugurated on 7 Oct. 1935, had a total enrolment (1978) of 32,868 students. The Catholic university Sta. Maria La Antigua, inaugurated on 27 May 1965, had 1,916 students in Sept. 1978.

In 1978, 16% of the population over 10 years old were illiterate, excluding the tribal Indians.

DIPLOMATIC REPRESENTATIVES

OF PANAMA IN GREAT BRITAIN (109 Jermyn St.,
London, SW1)

Ambassador: Dr Santiago A. Harris.

OF GREAT BRITAIN IN PANAMA (Apartado 889, Panama City 1)

Ambassador: Stanley Stephenson.

OF PANAMA IN THE USA (2862 McGill Terr., NW,
Washington, D.C., 20008)

Ambassador: Dr Carlos Lopez Guevara.

OF THE USA IN PANAMA
(Ave. Balboa y Calle 38, Panama City)

Ambassador: Ambler H. Moss, Jr.

OF PANAMA TO THE UNITED NATIONS

Ambassador: Carlos Ozores.

Books of Reference

Statistical Information: The Comptroller-General of the Republic (Contraloria General de la
República, Calle 35 y Avenida 6, Panama City) publishes an annual report and other statistical
publications.

Fiscal Survey of Panamá. Johns Hopkins Press, 1964
Biesanz, J. M., *The People of Panama.* Columbia Univ. Press, 1955
Castillero, Ernesto J., *Historia de Panamá.* 5th ed. Panama City, 1965
Howarth, D., *The Golden Isthmus.* London, 1966
Larsen, H. and M., *The Forests of Panama.* London, 1964
Susto, J. A., *An Introduction to Panamanian Bibliography* (Publications of the National Library,
No. 4). Panama, 1946

National Library: Biblioteca Nacional, Departamento de Información. Calle 22, Panama.

PAPUA NEW GUINEA

Capital: Port Moresby
Population: 3·08m. (1979)
GNP per capita: US$560 (1978)

HISTORY. To prevent that portion of the island of New Guinea not claimed by the Netherlands from passing into the hands of a foreign power, the Government of Queensland annexed Papua in 1883. This step was not sanctioned by the Imperial Government, but on 6 Nov. 1884 a British Protectorate was proclaimed over the southern portion of the eastern half of New Guinea, and in 1887 Queensland, New South Wales and Victoria undertook to defray the cost of administration, and the territory was annexed to the Crown the following year. The federal government took over the control in 1901; the political transfer was completed by the Papua Act of the federal parliament in Nov. 1905, and on 1 Sept. 1906 a proclamation was issued by the Governor-General of Australia declaring that British New Guinea was to be known henceforth as the Territory of Papua. The northern portion of New Guinea was a German colony until the First World War. It became a League of Nations mandated territory in 1921, administered by Australia, and later a UN Trust Territory (of New Guinea).

The Papua New Guinea Act 1949–1972 provides for the administration of the UN Australian Trust Territory of New Guinea in an administrative union with the Territory of Papua, in accordance with Art. 5 of the New Guinea Trusteeship Agreement, under the title of Papua New Guinea.

Australia granted Papua New Guinea self-government on 1 Dec. 1973 and, on 16 Sept. 1975, Papua New Guinea became a fully independent state.

AREA AND POPULATION. Papua New Guinea extends from the equator to Cape Baganowa in the Louisiade Archipelago to 11° 40′ S. lat. and from the border of West Irian to 160° E. long. with a total area of 462,840 sq. km. According to the census the 1971 population was 2,489,935 (1979, estimated, 3·08m.), 1,797,803 resided in New Guinea and 692,132 in Papua. Port Moresby, estimate (1979) 122,000; Lae, 51,000; Rabaul, 32,000; Madang, 22,000; Mount Hagen, 16,000. Area and population of the provinces:

Provinces	Sq. km	Census 1971	Estimate 1980	Capital
Milne Bay	14,000	109,460	139,500	Alotau
Northern	22,800	66,514	88,600	Popondetta
Central	29,500	117,330	144,200	Port Moresby
National Capital District	240	76,507	122,300	—
Gulf	34,500	58,564	73,100	Kerema
Western	99,300	70,898	94,100	Daru
Southern Highlands	23,800	192,854	227,200	Mendi
Enga	12,800 ⎱	346,032	⎧ 167,200	Wabag
Western Highlands	8,500 ⎰		⎩ 272,800	Mount Hagen
Chimbu	6,100	160,245	170,900	Kundiawa
Eastern Highlands	11,200	239,640	300,800	Goroka
Morobe	34,500	249,032	327,600	Lae
Madang	29,000	170,953	212,600	Madang
East Sepik	42,800	181,893	213,500	Wewak
West Sepik	36,300	93,978	109,800	Vanimo
Manus	2,100	24,866	36,600	Lorengau
West New Britain	21,000	61,515	100,000	Kimbe
East New Britain	15,500	113,750	127,700	Rabaul
New Ireland	9,600	59,543	76,900	Kavieng
North Solomons	9,300	96,363	134,300	Arawa

Vital statistics (1977): Crude birth rate, 44·8 per 1,000; crude death rate, 15·6.

CONSTITUTION AND GOVERNMENT. Papua New Guinea has a Westminster type of government. A single legislative house, known as the National

971

Parliament, is made up of 109 members from all parts of the country. The members are elected under universal suffrage and general elections are held every 5 years. All persons over the age of 18 who are Papua New Guinea citizens are eligible to vote and stand for election. Voting is by secret ballot and follows the preferential system.

The First Legislative Council was established in 1951. It was abolished in 1964 and replaced with the House of Assembly. In 1950 the first village council was formed which established the basis of the now extensive local government system. A system of provincial government was introduced in 1976.

The elections in 1972 saw the formation of the first indigenous controlled central government in the history of the country. It also saw the emergence of four major political parties—the Pangu Pati, United Party, People's Progress Party and the New Guinea National Party. A number of other parties had also been formed before these elections. A coalition group was formed and the group was able to place its members in the ministerial positions, and with its combined majority in the House of Assembly, also formed a working government.

Also in 1972, the coalition government appointed a constitutional planning committee to make recommendations for a Constitution specifically suited to conditions in the country. The committee's final report was presented to the House of Assembly in 1974 and provided the basis for the Constitution of the Independent State of Papua New Guinea introduced in 1975. In 1977, following the first general election since independence, the Pangu Pati, the People's Progress Party and independent members formed a coalition with support from 69 members of Parliament.

The administrative centre and capital is located at Port Moresby. National administration is carried out by a public service of 20 departments. In accordance with the decentralization provisions of the Constitution, the country has been divided into the National Capital District and 19 provinces: Western, Gulf, Central, Milne Bay, Northern, Southern Highlands, Enga, Western Highlands, Chimbu, Eastern Highlands, Morobe, Madang, East Sepik, West Sepik, Manus, New Ireland, East New Britain, West New Britain, and North Solomons. Each of the provincial governments has a secretariat headed by an Administrative Secretary. In many provinces the system of local governments still operates, although the provinces may make changes to this if they wish.

Governor-General: Sir Tore Lokoloko, GCMG, OBE.

The Cabinet at 13 March 1980 was as follows:

Prime Minister: Sir Julius Chan, PC.
Deputy Prime Minister, Minister for Transport and Civil Aviation: Iambakey Okuk. *Finance:* John Kaputin. *National Planning and Development:* Galeva Kwarara. *Primary Industry:* Roy Evara. *Foreign Affairs and Trade:* Noel Levi. *Lands:* Thomas Kavali. *Urban Development:* Goasa Damena. *Decentralization:* John Momis. *Forests:* Josephn Aoae. *Police:* Warren Dutton. *Works and Supply:* Mark Ipuia. *Minerals and Energy:* Gabriel Bakani. *Education:* Sam Tulo. *Commerce and Industry:* Opai Kunangel. *Public Utilities:* Wiwa Korowi. *Corrective Institutions and Liquor Licensing:* Akepa Miakwe. *Justice:* Paul Torato. *Health:* John Jaminan. *Labour and Employment:* Jacob Lemeki. *Media:* Clement Poye. *Defence:* Gerega Pepena. *Environment and Conservation:* Ibne Kor. *Home Affairs:* Zibang Zurecnuoc. *Science, Culture and Tourism:* Stephen Tago.

The seat of the Government is at Port Moresby.

National flag: Diagonally ochre-red over black, on the red a bird of paradise in gold, and on the black 5 stars of the Southern Cross in white.

DEFENCE. The Papua New Guinea Defence Force has a total strength of 3,500 (1979) consisting of land, maritime and air elements. The Army is organized in 2 infantry battalions, 1 engineer and 1 signals battalion with logistic units. The nucleus of an Air Force was formed by 3 C-47 piston-engined transports delivered from Australia in 1975. They have been followed by 3 Australian-built Mission Master twin-turboprop support transports, 2 Search Master maritime patrol aircraft and 3 more C-47s. Personnel total 82.

INTERNATIONAL RELATIONS

Membership. Papua New Guinea is a member of UN, the Commonwealth, the Colombo Plan and is an ACP state of EEC.

ECONOMY

Budget. Revenue (in K1,000) for calendar years was:

Source	1978	1979
Customs and excise	84,220	97,512
Other taxes	121,567	108,698
Foreign government grants [1]	171,939	174,835
Loans	29,081	108,101
Other revenue	71,961	78,519
Total	478,768	567,665

[1] Mainly from Australia.

Expenditure (in K1,000) for the same periods:

Source	1978	1979
Departmental	273,941	298,652
Capital works and services	73,409	64,898
Other expenditure	145,894	198,854
Total	493,244	560,404

Currency. The unit of currency is the *kina* divided into 100 *toea* and is the sole legal tender. In March 1981, £1 = K1·44; US$1 = K0·66.

Banking. The Bank of Papua New Guinea assumed the central banking functions formerly undertaken by the Reserve Bank of Australia on 1 Nov. 1973.

A national banking institution, which has been named the Papua New Guinea Banking Corporation, has been established. This bank has assumed the Papua New Guinea business of the Commonwealth Trading Bank of Australia except where certain accounts give rise to special financial or contractual problems.

The subsidiaries of 3 Australian commercial banks also operate in Papua New Guinea. These are the Australia and New Zealand Banking Group (PNG) Ltd, the Bank of New South Wales (PNG) Ltd, and the Bank of South Pacific Ltd, all of which offer trading and savings facilities. As from 1 Nov. 1973 these banks operated under Papua New Guinea banking legislation.

In addition to the subsidiaries of Australian banks operating in Papua New Guinea, the Papua New Guinea Development Bank has provided long-term development finance with particular attention to the needs of small-scale enterprises since 1967 and during its first 10 years has lent K71·7m.

Weights and Measures. The metric system is in force.

ENERGY AND NATURAL RESOURCES

Electricity. In 1977 installed capacity was 296,500 kw, production 1,185m. kwh.

Minerals. Copper is the main mineral product. Oil companies have been searching for oil, but no commercial deposits have yet been found. Several wells of natural gas have been discovered in commercial quantities. In Papua New Guinea gold, copper and silver are the only minerals produced in quantity. Major copper deposits in the Kieta district of Bougainville have proven reserves of about 800m. tonnes. Copper deposits have been found in the Star mountains of the Western Province and mining is expected to begin in the early 1980s. Production of copper concentrates for export began in 1972. In 1978, 434,000 tonnes of concentrate was exported containing approximately 193,000 tonnes of copper, 22·7 tonnes of gold and 51·1 tonnes of silver.

Sales revenue for 1978 was K96m.

Agriculture. Agricultural activity in Papua New Guinea is carried out by non-indigenous and indigenous occupiers on plantations and by indigenous smallholders. At 30 June 1980, the total area of larger holdings was 380,000 hectares, of which 171,000 hectares were for agricultural purposes, the principal crops being coffee, copra and cocoa. Rubber production is declining but production of palm oil is of growing importance. Minor commercial crops include pyrethrum, tea, peanuts and spices. Locally consumed food crops include sweet potatoes, taro, bananas, rice and sago. Tropical fruits grow abundantly. There is extensive grassland and a sugar industry and a beef-cattle industry is being developed.

Livestock (1979): Cattle, 136,000; pigs, 1·39m.; goats, 15,000; poultry, 1·1m.

Forestry. Timber production is of growing importance for both local consumption and export. In 1978, about 1,186,000 cu. metres of logs were harvested; logs exported, 440,157 cu. metres.

Production of sawn timber, 1980, 136,000 cu. metres; exports of woodchips, 123,908 tonnes.

Fisheries. Tuna, both skipjack and yellowfin species, is the major fisheries resource; in 1978 the catch was 49,000 tonnes. Exports of various crustacea, 1978, 871 tonnes, value K4·6m.

INDUSTRY AND TRADE

Industry. Secondary and service industries are expanding for the local market. Industries include the manufacture of paint, gases, concrete, twist tobacco and cigarettes, matches, soap, brewing, boat-building, furniture and the assembly of electrical appliances. In 1977 there were 735 factories employing 18,969 persons. Value of output K361m.

Labour. In 1976 about 352,000 indigenous wage-earners were in regular employment.

Trade. Imports (in K1,000) for years ended 30 June:

	1973	1974	1975	1976
Food and live animals	47,734	57,404	71,364	73,098
Beverages and tobacco	5,025	4,289	5,597	5,810
Crude materials, inedible, except fuels	749	769	1,246	1,109
Mineral fuels, lubricants and related materials	11,102	19,642	38,292	47,220
Oils and fats (animal and vegetable)	357	471	805	846
Chemicals	12,435	13,624	22,939	18,945
Manufactured goods, chiefly by material	39,214	38,964	61,631	48,051
Machinery and transport equipment	73,533	61,666	112,151	109,192
Miscellaneous manufactured articles	21,791	22,202	30,117	27,992
Commodities and transactions of merchandise trade, not elsewhere specified	13,556	6,950	9,278	10,748
Total, excluding outside packages	225,495	225,982	353,421	343,000
Outside packages	3,604	2,893	3,974	3,397
Total imports	228,815	228,875	357,395	346,397

Exports (in K1,000) for calendar years:

	1977	1978	1979
Coconut and copra products—			
Copra	22,960	23,023	38,162
Copra (coconut) oil	12,578	12,449	20,599
Copra oil pellets	1,207	1,060	1,951
Total	36,745	36,531	60,712
Coffee beans	143,441	107,225	124,996
Cocoa beans	86,349	62,955	60,872
Crude rubber	2,896	2,630	3,497
Tea	9,765	7,833	7,982
Pyrethrum extract	145	118	202

	1977	1978	1979
Forest and timber products—			
Logs	10,970	11,846	20,883
Sawn timber	5,417	4,171	7,683
Veneers	224	293	259
Plywood	2,083	2,858	3,819
Other	4,689	6,534	4,951
Total	24,111	25,702	37,595
Crocodile skins	814	1,231	1,610
Crayfish and prawns	4,632	4,130	6,210
Gold	2,184	2,623	4,141
Other domestic produce	228,298[1]	253,516[2]	322,153[3]
Total domestic produce	539,380	504,496	629,970
Re-exports	31,562	45,860	56,914
Total exports	570,942	550,356	686,884

[1] Includes K201,050 for copper ore concentrate.   [2] Includes K217,238 for copper ore concentrate.
[3] Includes K288,065 for copper ore and concentrate.

Total trade between Papua New Guinea and UK (British Department of Trade returns, in £1,000 sterling):

	1975	1976	1977	1978	1979	1980
Imports to UK	13,693	16,453	30,577	24,469	30,148	22,861
Exports and re-exports from UK	5,834	7,079	10,038	10,185	10,409	10,978

Tourism. In 1977, there were 15,084 visitors.

COMMUNICATIONS

Roads. In Sept. 1976 there were approximately 19,538 km of roads including approximately 1,016 km of urban roads. Motor vehicles numbered (1977) 43,763 including 12,936 cars.

Aviation. Frequent air services operate to and from Australia (Sydney, Brisbane and Cairns), and there are regular flights to Djayapura (Indonesia), Manila, Hong Kong, Kagoshima (Japan), Djakarta and Honolulu. A service is also maintained to Honiara in the Solomon Islands. In addition to Air Niugini, the national flag carrier, Qantas, Philippine Airlines and Cathay Pacific operate in and out of Papua New Guinea.

Shipping. There are regular shipping services between Australia and Papua New Guinea ports, and also services to New Zealand, Japan, Hong Kong, US west coast, Singapore, Solomon Islands, Taiwan, Philippines and Europe. Small coastal vessels run between the various ports. In 1978 cargo discharged from overseas was 1·5m. tonnes; cargo loaded for overseas was 1·8m. tonnes.

Post and Broadcasting. Telephones numbered 45,152 on 1 Jan. 1980. The National Broadcasting Commission broadcasts on short-wave and medium-wave from Port Moresby, Rabaul, Wewak, Goroka, Lae, Daru, Alotau, Vanimo and Madang. There are 11 other stations broadcasting on short-wave only, at a number of centres, broadcasting programmes in several local languages.

Cinemas (1972): 28 with a total seating capacity of 18,800

JUSTICE, EDUCATION AND WELFARE

Justice. In 1977, 937 cases were heard in the National Court and 45,289 cases in the district courts.

Police. Total strength (1977) 4,395.

Education. At 30 June 1978 about 262,700 children attended 1,961 primary schools and 41,500 enrolled in 192 secondary, technical and vocational schools. The University of Papua New Guinea and the Papua New Guinea University of Technology had 2,948 students in 1977.

Health. In 1977, there were 20 hospitals, 365 health centres and 200 doctors.

DIPLOMATIC REPRESENTATIVES

OF PAPUA NEW GUINEA IN GREAT BRITAIN
(14 Waterloo Pl., London, SW1R 4AR)

High Commissioner: Dr Alexis Sarei.

OF GREAT BRITAIN IN PAPUA NEW GUINEA (Douglas St., Port Moresby)
High Commissioner: D. K. Middleton.

OF PAPUA NEW GUINEA IN THE USA (1776 Massachusetts Ave., NW,
Washington D.C., 20036)

Ambassador: Kuplan Los.

OF THE USA IN PAPUA NEW GUINEA
(Armit St., Port Moresby)

Ambassador: Harvey J. Feldman.

OF PAPUA NEW GUINEA TO THE UNITED NATIONS

Ambassador: Ilinome Tarua.

Books of Reference

The Territory of Papua. Annual Report. Commonwealth of Australia. 1906–1940–41 and from
  1945–46
The Territory of New Guinea. Annual Report. Commonwealth of Australia. 1914–1940–41 and
  from 1946–47
Papua New Guinea, Annual Report. From 1970–71
Report on New Guinea. UN visiting missions to . . . Nauru and New Guinea. New York, 1962
Bettison, D. G., and others, *Independence of Papua–New Guinea,* Sydney, 1962.—*The Papua–
  New Guinea Elections 1964.* Canberra, 1966
Essal, B., *Papua and New Guinea.* Melbourne, 1961
Hasluck, P., *A Time for Building.* Melbourne Univ. Press, 1976
Hastings, P. (ed.), *Papua New Guinea: Prospero's Other Island.* London, 1971
Ross, A. C., and Langmore, J., *Alternative Strategies for Papua New Guinea.* OUP, 1974
Ryan, J., *The Hot Land.* London, 1970
Ryan, P. (ed.), *Encyclopaedia of Papua and New Guinea.* Melbourne Univ. Press, 1972
Simpson, C., *Plumes and Arrows Inside New Guinea.* Sydney, 1962
Wilkes, J. (ed.), *New Guinea and Australia.* Austral. Inst. of Political Science, 1959

PARAGUAY

República del Paraguay

Capital: Asunción
Population: 3m. (1980)
GNP per capita: US$850 (1978)

HISTORY. The Republic of Paraguay gained its independence from Spain on 14 May 1811. In 1814 Dr José Gaspar Rodríguez de Francia was elected dictator, and in 1816 perpetual dictator by the National Assembly. He died 20 Sept. 1840. In 1844 a new constitution was adopted, under which Carlos Antonio López (first elected in 1842, died 10 Sept. 1862) and his son, Francisco Solano López, ruled until 1870. During the devastating war against Brazil, Argentina and Uruguay (1865–70) Paraguay's population was reduced from about 600,000 to 232,000. Argentina, in Aug. 1942, and Brazil, in May 1943, voided the reparations which Paraguay had never paid. Further severe losses were incurred during the war with Bolivia (1932–35) over territorial claims in the Chaco. A peace treaty by which Paraguay obtained most of the area her troops had conquered was signed in July 1938.

AREA AND POPULATION. The area of the Oriental province is officially estimated at 159,827 sq. km (61,705 sq. miles) and the Occidental province at 246,925 sq. km (95,337 sq. miles), making the total area of the republic 406,752 sq. km (157,042 sq. miles).

The population according to official estimates in 1980 was 3m. The capital, Asunción, had 462,776 inhabitants in 1977. Other towns: Caaguazú (70,174), Coronel Oviedo (64,368), Pedro Juan Caballero (58,742), Concepción (57,917) and Encarnación (48,395).

The 16 provinces had the following populations in 1972:

Central	310,101	Caazapá	103,002
Caaguazú	213,356	Alto Paraná	78,037
Paraguari	211,704	Neembucu	72,978
Itapua	201,776	Misiones	69,315
Cordillera	194,365	Amambay	65,527
San Pedro	138,091	Presidente Hayes	38,515
Guairá	124,843	Boquerón	26,142
Concepción	108,198	Olimpo	5,368

Number of births, 1976, was 88,371; deaths, 13,754.

The population is overwhelmingly *mestizo* (mixed Spanish and Guaraní Indian) forming a homogeneous stock. There are some 46,700 unassimilated Indians of other tribal origin, in the Chaco and the forests of eastern Paraguay. There are some small traces of Negro descent. About half the population speak only Guaraní; some 4% speak only Spanish; the rest are bilingual.

Mennonites who arrived in 3 groups (1927, 1930 and 1947) are settled in the Chaco and Oriental Paraguay and were estimated in 1969 to number 13,000, of whom 2,000 came from Canada and 11,000 from Germany. The Japanese colonists in the Oriental section, who first came in 1935, were reckoned to number 7,000 in 1969. Under an agreement signed with Japan in 1959 up to 85,000 Japanese were to be admitted over 30 years. An agreement with Korea was signed in 1966 and there are now (1978) about 3,000 Korean families living in Paraguay.

CONSTITUTION AND GOVERNMENT. A new constitution replacing that of 1940 was drawn up by a Constituent Convention in which all legally re-cognized political parties were represented and was signed into law on 25 Aug. 1967. It provides for a two-chamber parliament consisting of a 30-seat Senate and a 60-seat Chamber of Deputies. Two-thirds of the seats in each Chamber are allo-cated to the majority party and the remaining one-third shared among the minority

977

parties in proportion to the votes cast. Voting is compulsory for all citizens over 18. The President appoints the Cabinet and during parliamentary recess can govern by decree through the Council of State, the members of which are representatives of the Government, the armed forces and other bodies.

On 6 Feb. 1977 elections were held for a 60-member Constitutional Assembly to revise the 1967 Constitution.

President: Gen. Alfredo Stroessner, Commander-in-Chief, elected 11 July 1954 to complete the presidential period of his predecessor. He was re-elected as 'Colorado' candidate in 1958, 1963, 1968, 1973 and 1978.

The following is a list of past presidents since 1940, with the date on which each took office:

Gen. Higinio Morínigo, 7 Sept. 1940 (resigned).
Dr Juan Manuel Frutos, 3 June 1948.[1]
Dr J. Natalicio González, 15 Aug. 1948 (deposed).
Gen. Raimundo Rolón, 30 Jan. 1949.

Dr Felipe Molas López, 26 Feb. 1949[1] (resigned).
Dr Federico Chávez, 16 July 1950 (resigned).
Tomás Romero Pereira, 4 May 1954.

[1] Provisional, *i.e.,* following a *coup d'état.*

The President has a cabinet of 11 ministers.

Interior: Dr Sabino A. Montanaro. *Foreign Affairs:* Dr Alberto Nogués. *Finance:* César Barrientos. *Education and Worship:* Dr Raúl Peña. *Public Works and Communications:* Gral. Juan A. Cáceres. *Agriculture and Livestock:* Ing. Hernando Bertoni. *National Defence:* Gral. Marcial Samaniego. *Public Health and Social Welfare:* Dr Adan Godoy Giménez. *Justice and Labour:* Dr Saúl González. *Industry and Commerce:* Dr Delfín Ugarte Centurión. *Without Portfolio:* Tomás Romero Pereira.

National flag: Red, white, blue (horizontal); the white stripe charged with the arms of the republic on the obverse, and, on the reverse, with a lion and the inscription *Paz y Justicia*—the only flag in the world with different obverse and reverse.

National anthem: ¡Paraguayos, república o muerte! (words by F. Acuña de Figueroa; tune by F. Dupey).

The country is divided into 2 provinces: the 'Oriental', east of Paraguay River, and the 'Occidental', west of the same river. The Oriental section is divided into 13 departments and the capital. The more important departments are supervised by a *Delegado* appointed by and directly responsible to the central government. The Occidental province, or Chaco, is divided into 3 departments.

DEFENCE. The army, navy and air forces are separate services under a single command. The President of the Republic is the active Commander-in-Chief. The armed forces total about 15,500 officers and men. Of these, the Army account for about 12,500 (75% conscripts), the Navy about 2,000 (25% conscripts) and the Air Force about 1,000 (25% conscripts). There are also about 4,000 armed police (75% conscripts). Military service is compulsory between the ages of 18 and 20 but there are many exemptions.

Army. The main units of the Army are: a Presidential escort battalion, 6 infantry battalions, a cavalry brigade with 2 regiments and a battalion, 1 artillery regiment and an engineer command with 5 battalions. Strength (1979), 12,500.

Navy. The Navy consists of 5 armoured river defence gunboats (2 monitors of 636 tons built in Italy and 3 *ex*-Argentinian minesweepers of 620 tons), 1 helicopter lighter, 1 river patrol boat, 2 patrol launches, 6 coastal patrol craft, 2 landing craft, 1 survey craft, 1 training ship, 12 service craft and 2 tugs. Personnel (1981) totalled 2,000 officers and men including coastguard and 500 marines.

Air Force. The Air Force came into being in the early thirties. After operating only transport and training aircraft for a number of years, it received 6 A-37B light jet attack aircraft from USA in 1978 and ordered 9 Xavante light jet strike/training aircraft from Brazil in 1979. Other types in service include a total of about 17 DC-6B and C-54 four-engined and C-47 twin-engined transports, 3 Convair 240s, a Twin Otter, an Otter, 8 Brazilian-built Uirapuru primary trainers, 22 T-6 Texan armed basic trainers and a number of light aircraft and helicopters. HQ and flying school are at Campo Grande, Asunción. Personnel total about 1,000.

INTERNATIONAL RELATIONS

Membership. Paraguay is a member of UN, OAS and LAIA (formerly LAFTA).

ECONOMY

Budget. In 1980 revenue was Gs.54,496m. and expenditure Gs.53,494m.
The 1980 budget provided Gs.7,137m. for national defence, Gs.6,267·2m. for education and worship and Gs.1,848m. for public health and social welfare. Total external debt outstanding at the end of Dec. 1979 was US$574m.

Currency. The *guaraní* was established on 5 Oct. 1943 equal to 100 old paper pesos. Total monetary circulation was Gs.50,400m. in Dec. 1978.
Rate of exchange, March 1981: 137 *guaraníes* = US$1; 274 *guaraníes* = £1.

Banking. The Banco Central del Paraguay opened 1 July 1952 to take over the central banking functions previously assigned to the National Bank of Paraguay, which had opened in March 1943 and been reorganized as the Banco del Paraguay in Sept. 1944 with a monetary, a banking and a mortgage department. The Banco del Paraguay closed in Nov. 1961 and has been replaced, with the aid of a US loan of US$3m., by the Banco Nacional de Fomento; the latter's assets in Jan. 1979 were Gs.27,546m.
The Banco Central in Jan. 1980 had gold and exchange reserves amounting to Gs.74·2m.; contribution to the IMF was Gs.1,318m. and other investments amounted to Gs.9,257m.
The Banco Nacional de Fomento, Bank of London and South America, Ltd, Banco Exterior do Brasil, Citibank, Banco de Asunción, Banco Exterior SA, Banco Unión SA, Banco Paraguayo de Comercio, Banco Real del Paraguay SA, Banco Aleman Transatlantico, Banco Holandés Unido, Banco Nacional del Estado de São Paulo, Yegros y Azara, Bank of America, Chase Manhattan Bank, Bank of Boston and Interbanco all have agencies in Asunción and branches in some main towns.

Weights and Measures. The metric system was officially adopted on 1 Jan. 1901.

ENERGY AND NATURAL RESOURCES

Electricity. Electricity from a 90,000 kw. hydro-electric plant at Acaray, with an output of 180,000 kw. (1979), supplies Asunción and 70 small towns and villages. Electricity is exported to Argentina and Brazil. Paraguay has signed agreements with Brazil to build jointly a 10m. kw. scheme on the river Paraná which will be in operation in 1982, and with Argentina another which will yield approximately 3m. kw.

Oil. The oil refinery at Villa Elisa, which has been in operation since 1966, has a production of about 3,500 bbls a day. Exploration for petroleum in the Chaco yielded negative results but prospecting was continuing in 1979.

Minerals. Iron, manganese and other minerals have been reported but have not been shown to be commercially exploitable. There are large deposits of limestone, and also salt, kaolin and apatite. *Pennzoil Paraguay* and other national and international firms have acquired licences to prospect for oil and natural gas in the Chaco. A uranium survey was being carried out in 1978 in the Oriental region.

Agriculture. In 1976 it was estimated that agriculture absorbs some 1·5m. hectares.
Area (in hectares) and yield (in tonnes per hectare) of the main agricultural products in 1978:

	Area	Yield		Area	Yield
Cotton	318,000	285,000	Soybeans	228,000	330,000
Maize	290,800	360,000	Mandioca	171,200	...
Tobacco	21,000	20,000	Rice (Paddy)	19,600	36,000
Wheat	31,000	30,000			

Wheat, soybean (600,000 tons, 1979), cotton, sugar, tobacco, coffee are increasing in importance, as are also essential oils and oilseeds. *Yerba maté*, or strongly flavoured Paraguayan tea, continues to be produced but is declining in importance; 142 tons were exported in 1979.

The principal sources of finance for agricultural development are USAID and Interamerican Development Bank loans and, for the wheat programme, suppliers' or other credits administered by the National Development Bank.

Livestock (1979). Paraguay had about 5·2m. cattle, 334,000 horses, 1·27m. pigs, 423,000 sheep. Exports of meat products in 1979 amounted to US$5·5m. In 1979 meat packing plants slaughtered 25,000 head of cattle for processing.

Forestry. In the Oriental section there are huge reserves of hardwoods and cedars that have scarcely been exploited. Palms, tung and other trees are exploited for their oils. The Japanese are experimenting with mulberries for silk growing. Pines and firs have been introduced under a United Nations project. In the Chaco the accessible Quebracho forests have nearly been worked out but plans are being made to open up new areas. In 1979, 5,206 tons of timber were exported and 393 tons of quebracho.

INDUSTRY AND TRADE

Industry. Production, 1978 (tons): Hides, 14; preserved meat, 11; animal fat, 1; bone meal, 4; frozen meat, 2; cotton fibre, 91; tannin, 17; petit grain, 330; tung oil, 12; cement, 166; sugar, 69; cigarettes (1m. packets), 41; matches (1,000 boxes), 23. There are 3 main meat-packing plants and other factories producing vegetable oils. A textile industry in Pilar and Asunción meets a large part of local needs. As a result of government restrictions on the export of logs the sawmilling and woodworking industry has recently been expanding. A cement works at Valle-mi, with a capacity of 7,000 bags a day, was inaugurated in Jan. 1970. In 1978 the GDP was estimated at about Gs.157,563m., an increase of 10·3% over 1977. Foreign investment is encouraged by industries being exempted from 30–50% of their tax bill for 5 years. In development areas this may be increased up to 100% for 10 years. Various degrees of duty exemption are permitted on capital equipment and raw materials.

Labour. Trade unionists number about 30,000 (*Confederación Paraguaya de Trabajadores* and *Confederación Cristiana de Trabajadores*).

Commerce. Imports and exports (in US$1m.):

	1973	1974	1975	1976	1977	1978	1979
Imports	83·2	198·3	212·7	180·2	250·4	375	402
Exports	65·0	169·8	176·2	181·8	278·9	285	276

Chief exports in 1979 included (in US$1m.): Cotton, 98·5; soybeans, 81·3; timber, 42·2; tung oil, 11·2; tobacco, 8·5; vegetable oils, 7·8; meat products, 5·5; sugar, 4·2; fruit, 3·5; tannin, 3·2; yerba maté, 1·1; palm shoots, 80.

Chief imports 1978 in (US$1m.): Vehicles and accessories, 60·1; fuels and lubricants, 59·6; machinery and apparatus, 53·8; drink and tobacco, 28·9; iron and manufactures, 14·6; foodstuffs, 14·5.

Imports and exports (in US$), by country, 1979:

Country	Imports	Exports
Algeria	50,069	...
Argentina	74,040	51,009
Belgium	1,820	1,811
Brazil	96,370	29,103
Federal Republic of Germany	31,665	46,407
France	8,776	5,907
Italy	5,371	21,688
Japan	36,085	16,407
Netherlands	2,172	45,344
Spain	1,820	5,569
Sweden	4,137	...
Switzerland	2,296	21,789
UK	24,191	625
Uruguay	14,275	13,611
USA	49,809	17,628

Total trade between Paraguay and UK (British Department of Trade returns, in £1,000 sterling):

	1975	1976	1977	1978	1979	1980
Imports to UK	6,837	7,897	8,183	7,418	2,107	1,279
Exports and re-exports from UK	6,484	5,478	8,318	11,772	12,746	13,384

Tourism. Visitors numbered 93,023 in 1972; 95,086 in 1973.

COMMUNICATIONS

Roads. In 1978 there were 12,000 km of roads, of which 1,200 were paved, 582 of gravel and 6,990 of earth. The principal paved roads are Route No. 2/7 running from Asunción to the bridge over the Paraná at Puerto Presidente Stroessner, and thence down to the ocean at Paranaguá; and Route No. 1 to Encarnación in the south. The other main arteries are Coronel Oviedo-Pedro Juan Caballero road (unpaved from Coronel Oviedo) in the north and the Trans-Chaco road which starts from the bridge across the river Paraguay north of Asunción and ends at Nueva Asunción on the Bolivian border, 200 km of this are paved and work is continuing. Unpaved roads are closed when it rains. In the Argentine, a paved road starts from Pilcomayo, opposite Asunción, and provides good communication with Buenos Aires. Motor cars, 1976, numbered 17,600; commercial vehicles, 15,200, and passenger vehicles, 7,580.

Railways. The President Carlos Antonio López (formerly Paraguay Central) Railway runs from Asunción to Encarnación, on the Río Alto Paraná, with a length of 441 km (1,435 mm gauge). Traffic fell sharply in 1976 to 16m. passenger-km and 16·1m. tonne-km.

Aviation. International services are operated by 9 airlines (domestic and foreign) and internal routes by military airlines and some small private lines.

Shipping. In flood the Paraguay River, which divides the country into two distinct parts, is navigable for 12-ft-draught vessels as far as Concepción, 180 miles north of Asunción, and for smaller vessels for a further distance of 600 miles northward. Drought conditions often restrict navigation to lighter traffic. The Paraná River is navigable by large boats from Corrientes up to Puerto Aguirre, at the mouth of the Yguazú River. Boats of a few hundred tons capacity navigate the tributary rivers.

Asunción, the chief port, is 950 miles from the sea. In June 1945 the Government formed—after a break of 80 years—a national merchant marine which operates in the river Plate basin, connecting with Argentine, Uruguayan and Brazilian ports. The cargo fleet includes 25 vessels of 300–1,000 tons, 3 tankers of 1,100–1,700 tons, 2 passenger river boats and 1 ocean-going freighter of 713 tons.

Post and Broadcasting. The national telegraph (137 offices) connects Asunción with Corrientes and Posadas in the Argentine Republic, and thus with the outside world; new direct links have been opened with the Federal Republic of Germany, USA, Bolivia and Chile. In addition, 34 stations are operated by the President Carlos Antonio López Railway; total, 2,070 miles. Three companies (12 stations) offer radio-telegraph and telex services to several countries. The telephone system has been under government control since 5 Oct. 1945; a new government agency, the National Telephone Administration, took over the telecommunication services in July 1947. Telephone lines, 1949, 5,225 miles; instruments, 1977, 41,644, of which 33,501 were in Asunción and were automatic. There are 1 state and 9 commercial radio stations in Asunción, 22 in provincial towns, and a commercial television station in Asunción and Encarnación in the south.

Cinemas (1974). Cinemas numbered 65 in Asunción. The larger country towns usually have an outdoor cinema.

Newspapers (1980). There are 5 daily newspapers in Asunción with an aggregate circulation of about 200,000.

JUSTICE, RELIGION AND EDUCATION

Justice. The highest court is the Supreme Court with 5 members. There are special Chambers of Appeal for civil and commercial cases, and criminal cases. Judges of first instance deal with civil, commercial and criminal cases in 6 departments. Minor cases are dealt with by Justices of the Peace.

The Attorney-General represents the State in all jurisdictions, with representatives in each judicial department and in every jurisdiction. In matters of revenue, taxes, etc., the State is represented by the *Abogado del Tesoro*.

Religion. Religious liberty is guaranteed by the 1967 constitution. Article 6 thereof recognizes Roman Catholicism as the official religion of the country. The same article disposes that relations between Paraguay and the Holy See shall be regulated by concordats or other bilateral agreements, but no such agreements have yet been negotiated.

The Roman Catholic Church is organized into the Archdiocese of Asunción, 3 other dioceses (San Juan Bautista de las Misiones, Concepción and Villarrica); 4 Prelatures (Coronel Oviedo, Encarnación, Alto Paraná and Caacupé); and 2 Vicariates Apostolic (Chaco and Pilcomayo). The bishops meet in a Conference of Paraguayan Bishops. Only civil marriages are legally valid. There are numerous non-catholic communities, the largest of whom are the Mennonites. There is a small Anglican church in Asunción, with missions in the Chaco, which comes under the jurisdiction of an Anglican Bishop resident in Asunción.

Education. Education is free and nominally compulsory, but schools are not everywhere available, and the system has been extensively revised to provide, *inter alia*, primary education for adults. Illiteracy is estimated at 22% (urban) and 30% (rural). In 1973 there were 2,288 government primary schools and 421 private schools, with 459,393 pupils and 15,871 teachers; 652 secondary schools had 66,746 students and 6,729 teachers. In 1978 there was an intensive school building programme in progress. The National University in Asunción had, in 1973, 7,919 students and 1,209 professors. In 1973 the Catholic University and associated colleges had 4,546 students and 355 professors.

DIPLOMATIC REPRESENTATIVES

OF PARAGUAY IN GREAT BRITAIN
(51 Cornwall Gdns, London, SW7 4AQ)
Ambassador: (Vacant).

OF GREAT BRITAIN IN PARAGUAY (Calle Presidente Franco, 706, Asunción)
Ambassador and Consul-General: Derrick Mellor.

OF PARAGUAY IN THE USA (2400 Massachusetts Ave., NW, Washington, D.C., 20008)
Ambassador: Dr Mario López Escobar.

OF THE USA IN PARAGUAY (1776 Mariscal López Ave., Asunción)
Ambassador: Lyle F. Lane.

OF PARAGUAY TO THE UNITED NATIONS
Ambassador: Dr Luis Gonzalez Arias.

Books of Reference

Gaceta Oficial, published by Imprenta Nacional, Estrella y Estero Bellaco, Asunción
Anuario Daumas. Asunción
Anuario Estadistico de la República del Paraguay. Asunción. Annual
Report of the Council of the Corporation of Foreign Bondholders. Annual. London
Lewis, P. H., *Paraguay under Stroessner*. Univ. of North Carolina Press, 1980
Pendle, G., *Paraguay, A Riverside Nation*. R. Inst. of Int. Affairs, 3rd ed., 1967
Raine, P., *Paraguay*. New Brunswick, N.J., 1956
National Library: Biblioteca Nacional, De la Rosidenta, Asunción.

PERU

Capital: Lima
Population: 17·3m. (1979)
GNP per capita: US$740 (1978)

República del Perú

HISTORY. The Republic of Peru, formerly the most important of the Spanish vice-royalties in South America, declared its independence on 28 July 1821; but it was not till after a war, protracted till 1824, that the country gained its actual freedom.

AREA AND POPULATION. The total area of Peru is estimated to be 1,285,215 sq. km (496,093 sq. miles).

The long-standing dispute with Chile over the provinces of Tacna and Arica (*see* THE STATESMAN'S YEAR-BOOK, 1928, p. 1198) reached an amicable settlement on 3 June 1929 at Lima, Tacna going to Peru and Arica to Chile. In response to demands by Bolivia for permanent access to the Pacific Coast, proposals for a Bolivian corridor to the sea and a new Bolivian port to be built in the disputed area have been put forward by Chile and Peru. To date, little progress has been made. One result has been increased tension along the Chilean–Peruvian border, with reports of an arms build-up by both countries. For an account of the settlement of other boundary disputes, *see* THE STATESMAN'S YEAR-BOOK, 1948, p. 1173.

A map of the boundary with Ecuador is to be found in THE STATESMAN'S YEAR-BOOK, 1942.

The census taken in 1979 gave the population as 17,293,100. Children under 15 years, 7·2m. (45% of total population). Birth rate, 4·2%; death rate, 1·3%. Lima, the capital, had 3,158,417 population. Other major cities (with census population 1972), are Callao (296,220), Arequipa (304,653), Trujillo (241,882), Chiclayo (189,685), Chimbote (159,045), Piura (126,702), Cuzco (120,881), Huancayo (115,693), Iquitos (111,327). The language is Spanish, but the Indian population speak either Quechua (the second official language) or Aymará.

The area of the 23 departments and the constitutional province of Callao are given below with the population, according to the official census of 1961 and 1972. The area of the department of Puno includes the Peruvian zone of Lake Titicaca, 4,996·28 sq. km. The chief towns are shown in brackets:

Departments	Area (sq. km) 1959	2 July 1961 (census)	2 June 1972 census (provisional)	Pop. per sq. km 1961
Amazonas (Chachapoyas)	41,297·1	129,003	196,469	2·85
Ancash (Huaraz)	36,308·3	605,548	726,665	16·20
Apurímac (Abancay)	20,654·6	303,648	307,805	16·36
Arequipa (Arequipa)	63,527·6	407,163	530,528	6·47
Ayacucho (Ayacucho)	45,503·1	430,289	459,747	9·85
Cajamarca (Cajamarca)	35,417·8	786,599	916,331	21·15
Callao (Callao) [1]	73·8	219,420	315,605	2,901·46
Cuzco (Cuzco)	84,140·9	648,168	708,719	7·30
Huancavelica (Huancavelica)	22,870·9	315,730	331,155	13·07
Huánuco (Huánuco)	35,314·6	355,003	420,764	10·24
Ica (Ica)	21,251·4	261,126	357,973	11·48
Junín (Huancayo)	32,354·4	548,662	691,216	15·64
La Libertad (Trujillo)	23,241·3	609,105	806,368	25·29
Lambayeque (Chiclayo)	16,585·9	353,657	515,363	20·93
Lima (Lima)	33,894·9	2,093,435	3,485,411	68·42
Loreto (Iquitos)	478,336·2	411,340	494,895	0·69

[1] With province.

	Area	Population 2 July 1961	2 June 1972 census	Pop. per sq. km.
Departments	(sq. km.) 1959	(census)	(provisional)	1961
Madre de Dios (Maldonado)	78,402·7	25,269	21,968	0·19
Moquegua (Moquegua)	16,174·7	53,260	74,573	3·60
Pasco (Cerro de Pasco)	21,854·1	150,575	176,750	5·79
Piura (Piura)	33,067·1	692,414	854,668	21·68
Puno (Puno)	72,382·4	727,309	779,594	10·20
San Martín (Moyobamba)	53,063·6	170,456	224,310	3·06
Tacna (Tacna)	14,766·6	67,800	95,623	4·68
Tumbes (Tumbes)	4,731·5	57,378	75,399	21·10
Total	1,285,215·6	10,420,357	13,567,939	8·06

A new department of Ucayali is to be created in the central Amazon area, to include the provinces of Coronel Portillo and Ucayali, which were previously part of the department of Loreto. Pucallpa will be the capital of the new department.

CONSTITUTION AND GOVERNMENT. On 3 Oct. 1968 a military junta overthrew the government of President Fernando Belaúnde Terry and installed Gen. Juan Velasco Alvarado as President of a 'Revolutionary Government' with a cabinet composed entirely of officers of the armed services. Gen. Velasco was ousted in a bloodless *coup* in Aug. 1975 and was replaced by Gen. Francisco Morales Bermudez. The new democratic government, under President Fernando Belaúnde Terry, took office on 28 July 1980.

The new Constitution, which became effective when a civilian government was installed in July 1980, provides for a Legislature consisting of a Senate (60 members) and a Chamber of Deputies (180 members) and an Executive formed of the President of the Republic and a Council of Ministers appointed by him. Elections were held in May 1980. They will be held every 5 years with the President and Congress elected, at the same time, by separate ballots. All Peruvians over the age of 18 are eligible to vote; in Dec. 1970 the number of registered voters was 2,829,728, including 1m. in Lima province. Voting is compulsory; women were fully enfranchised in 1955.

Augusto Bernardino Leguia, 4 July 1919–24 Aug. 1930.[1]

Gen. Manuel Ponce (Acting), 24 Aug. 1930–28 Aug. 1930.[2]

Col. Louis M. Sánchez Cerro (Acting), 28 Aug. 1930–1 March 1931.[2]

Richardo Leoncio Elias (Acting), 1 March 1931–5 March 1931.[2]

Col. Gustavo A. Jiménez (Acting), 5 March 1931–10 March 1931.[2]

David Samanez Ocampo (Acting), 10 March 1931–8 Dec. 1931.

Gen. Luis M. Sánchez Cerro (Constitutional), 8 Dec. 1931–30 April 1933.[3]

Gen. Oscar Raimundo Benavides, 30 April 1933–8 Dec. 1939.

Dr Manuel Pradoy Ugarteche, 8 Dec. 1939–28 July 1945.

Dr José Luis Bustamante y Rivero, 28 July 1945–27 Oct. 1948.[1]

Gen. Manuel A. Odría (Acting), 27 Oct. 1948–1 June 1950.[2]

Gen. Zenón Noriega, 1 June 1950–28 July 1950.

Gen. Manuel A. Odría, 28 July 1950–28 July 1956.

Dr Manuel Prado y Ugarteche, 28 July 1956–July 1962.

Gen. Ricardo Pérez Godoy, 18 July 1962–3 March 1963.[1]

Gen. Nicolás Lindley López, 3 March–28 July 1963.

Fernando Belaúnde Terry, 28 July 1963–3 Oct. 1968.[1]

Gen. Juan Velasco Alvarado, 3 Oct. 1968–29 Aug. 1975.[1]

Gen. Francisco Moralis Bermudez, 29 Aug. 1975–28 July 1980.

[1] Deposed.   [2] Resigned.   [3] Assassinated.

President: Fernando Belaúnde Terry.

The Cabinet was in 29 Jan. 1981 composed as follows:

Prime Minister, and Minister of Economy, Finance and Commerce: Dr Manuel Ulloa (AP).

Foreign Affairs: Dr Javier Arias Stella (AP). *Interior:* Dr José María de la Jara y Ureta (AP). *Education:* Dr Luis Felipe Alarco (AP). *Transport and Communications:* Fernando Chávez Belaúnde (AP). *Agriculture:* Dr Niels Ericson (AP). *Health:*

Dr Uriel García Cáceres (AP). *Labour:* Dr Alfonso Grados Bertorini (Ind.). *Justice:* Dr Felipe Osterling Parodi (PPC). *Industry, Integration and Tourism:* Dr Roberto Rotondo Mendoza (PPC). *Housing and Construction:* Arq Javier Velarde Aspillaga (AP). *Fisheries:* Ing René Deústua (AP). *Energy and Mines:* Econ Pedro Pablo Kuczynski (Ind.). *War:* Gen. Jorge Muñiz. *Navy:* Adm. Mario Castro Mendoza. *Air Force:* Gen. José Gagliardi. *Institute of National Planning and Popular Co-operation:* Arq Carlos Pestana (AP).

As of 30 June 1965 the 23 departments are divided into 148 provinces (plus the constitutional province of Callao) and 1,662 districts; the province of Callao has some of the functions of a department.

National flag: Three vertical strips of red, white, red, with the national arms in the centre.

National anthem: Somos Libres, seámoslo siempre (words by J. de la Torre Ugarte; tune by J. B. Alcedo, 1821).

DEFENCE. The national budget for 1980 included a defence estimate of S/.96,000m.

Army. While military service is compulsory youths are only conscripted to fill the annual quota. The term of service is 2 years and all males of 20–25 years of age are liable. The country is divided into 5 military regions.

The Army comprises (1980) approximately 75,000 all ranks, of which some 6,000 are regular officers. There are 8 infantry and mechanized brigades, 1 paracommando and 2 armoured brigades, 1 jungle brigade, 3 armoured reconaissance squadrons and 10 artillery and 4 engineer battalions. There is an air element of 4 Helio Courier 395 communications aircraft. Equipment consists of approximately 420 tanks (T-54/-55, M-4 and AMX-13), over 100 light armoured fighting vehicles and 105-mm./155-mm. field artillery.

The section of the national police force with a para-military role is known as the *Guardia Civil* and comprises approximately 25,000 personnel.

Navy. The Peruvian Navy consists of 9 submarines comprising 3 German (FRG)-built completed in 1975–80, 4 completed in USA in 1954–57 and 2 older *ex*-USN; 4 cruisers, *Aguirre* (ex-*De Zeven Provincien*) and *Almirante Grau* (ex-*De Ruyter*) acquired from the Netherlands in 1976 and 1973, *Capitan Quinones*[1] (ex-*Almirante Grau*, ex-*Newfoundland*), now used as harbour training ship, and *Coronel Bolognesi* (ex-*Ceylon*), acquired from Great Britain in 1959–60; 2 reconstructed 'Daring' class destroyers delivered from Britain during 1973; 2 old destroyers acquired from USA during 1960–61; 1 old destroyer purchased from the Netherlands in 1978, 2 new Italian-built frigates, 6 new French-built fast missile-armed corvettes, 1 training ship and 1 submarine accommodation ship (both old *ex*-US destroyer escorts); 3 landing ships; 2 medium landing ships; 3 river patrol launches; 5 river gunboats; 6 small patrol craft; 2 transports; 3 hospital craft; 1 research craft; 7 oilers; 3 survey vessels; 3 floating docks; 3 water carriers, and 5 tugs.

[1] When the Dutch cruiser *De Ruyter* was purchased in 1973 she was re-named *Almirante Grau* after Peru's principal naval hero. In consequence the cruiser whose name had been changed from *Newfoundland* to *Almirante Grau* when she was purchased from Britain in 1959 was again re-named *Capitan Quinones*, after an air force hero.

All naval training takes place in the Callao area at various schools. The main naval base and dockyard are also in Callao. Smaller bases are at Iquitos on the Amazon, and at San Lorenzo. Naval personnel in 1981 totalled 2,050 officers and 18,500 men including the Naval Air Arm. There is also a brigade of 1,400 marines.

The new construction programme includes 2 frigates being built in Peru (sister ships of 2 completed in Italy in 1978–80), 3 patrol submarines to be built in the Federal Republic of Germany, and 6 coastal patrol boats.

The Coast Guard includes 2 corvettes (*ex*-fleet minesweepers acquired from the US Navy in 1960–61), 2 new patrol vessels built in Peru, 6 fast patrol craft built in Britain in 1964–65, 2 former US gunboats and 4 coastal patrol boats.

Air Force. The Air Force is under the direction of the Air Minister, who is also C.-in-C.

The operational force consists of 3 combat groups. No. 13 Group has 2 squadrons of Mirage 5 jet fighters and 1 squadron of A-37B light attack aircraft; No. 21 Group has 2 squadrons of Canberra light jet bombers and 1 squadron of A-37Bs; No. 12 Group has 12 MiG-21s for conversion training and 52 Soviet-built Su-22 variable-geometry fighter bombers in 2 operational squadrons. Other aircraft in service include medium transports (DC-9, 4 F.28 Fellowship, 16 An-26, 4 C-54, 6 C-130 and 5 C-118), light transports (6 Twin Otter, 15 Buffalo and 12 Turbo-Porter), helicopters (6 Mi-6 and a total of 60 Mi-8, Bell 212, Alouette III and Bell 47G), 75 training aircraft (including T-6, T-33, T-34, T-37 and T-41D) and a small number of miscellaneous types for photographic and communications duties. Aircraft on order include 14 Aermacchi MB 339 jet trainers. The 2 DC-9s and some of the C-54 and C-130 aircraft are used by the Air Force to run a commercial airline network (SATCO). There are military airfields at Talara, Chiclayo, Piura, Pisco, Lima (2), Iquitos and La Joya, and a seaplane base at Iquitos. All officers and pilots are trained at the Air Academy at Lima (Las Palmas). The approximate strength of the Peruvian Air Force is 10,000 personnel and 132 combat aircraft.

INTERNATIONAL RELATIONS

Membership. Peru is a member of UN, OAS, Andean Group and LAIA (formerly LAFTA).

ECONOMY

Planning. Peru has had a National Planning Institute since 1963. The plans it has published are of an indicative nature. The Institute announced in May 1975 a comprehensive plan for economic and social development in the years 1975–78. The plan provides for an annual growth rate of 6·5%.

Budget. The authorized budget for 1981 envisaged expenditure of S/.1,859,000m. and income of S/.1,634,000m.

The external debt was US$8,864m. in Dec. 1978.

Currency. The monetary unit is the *sol*. On 28 June 1976 the *sol* was devalued to the rate of 65 = US$1, and on 20 Sept. 1976 there was introduced a policy of frequent mini-devaluations which brought the exchange rate to 372.50 = US$1 in March 1981. In May 1970 exchange control was imposed on the small free exchange market. Foreign residents were exempted from a number of the regulations but Peruvian citizens were required to repatriate overseas bank deposits and declare all foreign assets. The official exchange rate was S/.811 = £1 for normal transactions in March 1981.

Coins include 50,000 soles (gold) and 10,000 soles (silver) coins as well as 10- and 5-sole pieces (copper 75%; nickel 25%), the sol and half sol (copper 30%; zinc 70%); the 20, 10 and 5 centavos (copper–zinc) and the 2- and 1-centavo pieces (zinc) have been discontinued. Peru has a paper currency issued by the Banco Central de la Reserva in denominations of 5,000, 1,000, 500, 200, 100 and 50. The 10 and 5 soles notes have been discontinued. Money in circulation at 30 June 1972 was S/.22,318·2m.

Banking. The government bank of issue is the Banco Central de la Reserva del Perú, which was established in 1922. A new charter for the bank was promulgated in Aug. 1968; this, *inter alia*, extended the bank's authority with regard to the organization of the commercial banking system. This bank also regulates the certificate exchange market through which import, export and foreign currency loan operations are channelled. As at March 1971 its paid-up capital and reserves stood at S/.311m. Net foreign currency reserves at June 1980 were US$1,794·6m.

The Government's fiscal agent is the Banco de la Nación which, since May 1970, has control of the 'giro' market through which most non-trade foreign currency transactions are channelled.

Banks, domestic and foreign, are supervised by the Superintendent of Banks and Insurance. There were in March 1971, 7 state banks, 11 commercial banks (of which 3 were controlled by the Banco de la Nación), 6 regional banks (with head office outside Lima or Callao) and 4 foreign banks (1 British, 2 American and 1

Japanese). In Dec. 1978 Peruvian currency deposits of the banking system (excluding state banks) amounted to S/.131,915,000 and advances to S/.116,046,000.

Weights and Measures. The metric system of weights and measures was established by law in 1869, and since 1916 has come into general use.

ENERGY AND NATURAL RESOURCES

Electricity. In 1972 control of electricity production and distribution passed to ELECTROPERU, a state company. In 1979 the production of electric energy was 8,261 gwh. An electrification programme to construct a series of large hydro-electric power stations, is now under way.

Oil. Proven oil reserves in the jungle region amount to about 500m. bbls. A further 75m. tonnes have been found in the north-west, some of it offshore. The new 850 km pipeline, linking the new jungle oilfields to coastal terminals, was opened in 1977. Output amounted to 192,000 bbls per day by 1979 and Peru became an oil exporter in that same year. The total value of exports in 1979 of petroleum and derivatives was US$700m.

Minerals. Mineral exports are expected to account for about 50% of value of exports in 1979. Lead, copper, iron, silver, zinc and petroleum are the chief minerals exploited. Mineral exports in 1978: Copper, US$423m.; lead, US$162m.; zinc, US$131m.; silver, US$118m.; iron ore, US$74m. Crude petroleum output in 1978 was 69·35m. bbls. Mineral production (in tonnes, 1978) of iron, 3,275,325; zinc, 386,453; copper, 336,254; lead, 160,708; antimony, 745; silver, 634·3 (refined); bismuth, 610·7; molybdenum, 586·9; cadmium, 514·1; tungsten, 396·9; tin, 458; tellurium, 15·4; selenium, 12·9; gold, 3·5; indium, 106,000 oz.

In Sept. 1969 a law was introduced to force the major mining companies to work their hitherto unexploited concessions or lose them. In June 1971 a Mining Law was published which introduced a new tax structure for the industry and stated that as a matter of policy the State would undertake the marketing and refining of minerals.

Agriculture. There are 4 natural zones: the coast strip, with an average width of 80 km; the Sierra or Uplands, formed by the coast range of mountains and the Andes proper; the Montaña or high wooded region which lies on the eastern slopes of the Andes, and the jungle in the Amazon Basin, known as the Selva. Land under cultivation, 1967, was about 2·75m. hectares. There are 4 fertilizer factories, near Callao and in Cuzco.

Peru is a substantial importer of foodstuffs, chiefly cereals (1977, US$130·3m.), but also fats and oil, meat and dairy products.

Nearly half of the population is dependent on agriculture, which accounted for 13% of the GDP in 1978. Peru's third land reform law, that of June 1969, is one of the most comprehensive. It provides for the large sugar estates in the north of Peru to be turned into co-operatives. Maximum permitted sizes for other types of land holding are stipulated for the various regions of the country. These range from 150 hectares for irrigated land on the coast to an area capable of supporting 5,000 sheep for pasture land in the Sierra. These sizes may be increased if certain efficiency criteria are met. Holdings too small to be economically viable are to be consolidated into co-operative units. The chief agricultural productions of Peru are, in the order named: Sugar, cotton, coffee and wool. The cotton industry was nationalized on 1 Oct. 1974.

Production in 1978 (in 1,000 tonnes): Sugar-cane, 8,452; sugar, 614; cotton, 107; coffee, 66; wool, 9 (1976).

Output of cattle hides (in tonnes), 1970, 1,200; sheepskins, 1,110; goatskins, 953. Output of sheep wool in 1976 was 9,000 tonnes. Exports, 1970, were sheep wool, unwashed, 606 tonnes; llama, alpaca and vicuña wool, 1,537 tonnes.

Livestock (1979): 648,000 horses, 4·19m. cattle, 2m. goats, 14·5m. sheep, 2·2m. swine, 36m. poultry.

Fisheries. Until the early 1970s Peru was the world's foremost fishing nation in terms of value of catch, due mainly to anchoveta which was converted into fishmeal for export as animal feed. Peru produced almost 45% of the world's fishmeal supplies, or nearly 2m. tonnes a year. However, abnormal marine conditions and over-fishing combined had, by 1977, reduced the anchoveta catch to 792,000 tonnes compared to 12·28m. tonnes in 1970.

Since then the industry has been partly denationalized and the number of fishing vessels reduced by approximately 50%, to some 700. Increased attention has been paid to fishing for human consumption.

Fish production 1978 (1,000 tonnes): Anchoveta, 1,156; other species, 1,589. Fresh, 151·3; frozen, 186·7; dried salted, 15·4; conserves, 226·2. Fish caught include (1978, tonnes): Anchoveta, 1,156,628; sardine, 1,074,519; jurel, 462,250; hake, 420,903; horse mackerel, 97,165; dogfish, 10,155.

INDUSTRY AND TRADE

Industry. The Industrial Promotion Law, 1959, succeeded in encouraging local enterprises. The manufacturing industry has been the fastest growing sector of the economy in recent years. The average compounded annual growth rate for the period 1968–72 was 9·2% per annum. In 1970 it was estimated that the manufacturing industries accounted for 20% of the GNP. In July 1970 a new Law of Industry was promulgated. This classifies industries according to national priorities and defines certain basic industries which it will be in the interests of the economy for the State to control. It also provides for worker participation in industrial companies to the extent that they share both in the profits and ultimately, through the industrial community, hold up to one-third of non-voting shares. In future foreign owned companies must either become Peruvianized or operate under a special contract with the Government, which will enable them to recover their investment and reasonable profits, but eventually for the enterprise to pass to the hands of the Peruvian Government. The Government in an attempt to rationalize the industry, has stipulated that as from 1 Jan. 1971 there will only be 5 plants assembling automobiles. Manufacturers are currently negotiating new contracts with the Government to take account of the Andean Pact automotive industry programming. The aim of the Government is progressively to increase the proportion of nationally produced vehicle parts and components. About 70% of Peru's manufacturing industries are located in or around the Lima/Callao metropolitan area.

Peru's first iron and steel mill came into production at Chimbote in April 1958. Products include pig-iron, blooms, billets, largets, round and round-deformed bars, wire rod, black and galvanized sheets and galvanized roofing sheets. Refractories are manufactured at Lima.

The Government has a monopoly of the import and/or local manufacture and sale of guano, salt, alcohol and explosives. The monopoly of matches was abandoned in 1954 and that of tobacco in June 1955.

Peru's manufacturing industry has stagnated since 1972 but by 1980 had recovered substantially, mainly due to exports of non-traditional goods. Output fell in 1977 by 6%. In 1977 production in the following industries was (in tonnes):

Cement	1,964,000	Refined lead	169,000
Tyres (units)	700,000	TV receivers (units)	100,000
Refined zinc	389,000	Sulphuric acid	60,000
Refined copper	350,000	Vehicle assembly	11,300
Crude steel	347,000		

In 1972 the Andean Group allocated 24 different metal manufacturing industries to Peru for meeting the Group's needs in those industries by 1980. Allocations were revised in 1979.

Labour. In 1976 the total labour force was considered to number 5m. persons, of which 40% was either under-employed or unemployed. This was 52% of the urban population of the country or about 30% of the country's population. The population was distributed roughly as follows in 1972: Agriculture, stock-raising and fishing, 2m.; manufacturing industry, 611,000; construction, 183,000; mining, 98,000; government, 317,000; commerce, 475,000; services, 477,000.

Trade Unions. Trade unions have about 2m. members (approximately 1·5m. in peasant organizations and 500,000 in industrial). The major trade union organization is the *Confederación de Trabajadores del Perú*, which was reconstituted in 1959 after being in abeyance for some years. The other labour organizations recognized by the

Government are the *Confederación General de Trabajadores del Perú*, the *Confederación Nacional de Trabajadores* and the *Central de Trabajadores de la Revolución Peruana*.

Commerce. The value of trade has been as follows (in US$1m.):

	1974	1975	1976	1977	1978	1979
Imports	1,276	1,380	1,360	1,726	1,601	2,090
Exports	1,511	2,480	2,100	2,095	1,941	3,474

On 26 May 1969 Peru signed the Cartagena Agreement between Bolivia, Colombia, Chile and Ecuador establishing the Andean Group the aim of which is to accelerate the process of economic integration and development on a sub-regional basis within the ambit of LAFTA. Venezuela joined in 1973 but Chile withdrew in Oct. 1976.

In 1979 the principal imports were: Machinery and appliances (46·3%); fuel, lubricants and other non-metallic minerals (2·5%); foodstuffs (9·5%).

The principal exports were: Minerals and metals (41·9%); marine products (6·8%); petroleum (18·6%); coffee (7·1%); sugar (1%); cotton (1·4%); wool (1%); miscellaneous (22·2%).

The major suppliers were (in S/.1m.):

| | Imports from | | Exports to | |
	1976	1977	1976	1977
USA	32,391	45,426	18,959	45,538
Ecuador	11,377	13,878	1,037	1,879
Germany (Fed. Rep.)	10,424	11,691	5,379	5,876
Japan	8,118	11,551	10,125	16,336
UK	3,906	7,001	4,885	5,076

Principal exports in 1976 and 1977 (in S/.1m.):

	1976	1977		1976	1977
Copper	13,028	30,448	Petroleum	1,621	3,477
Iron (ore)	3,236	7,104	Fish and fish products	10,926	16,821
Silver (metal content)	8,603	14,398	Sugar	5,085	7,374
Zinc (metal content)	9,081	10,597	Coffee	6,371	16,401
Lead (metal content)	3,047	6,531			

Total trade between Peru and UK (British Department of Trade returns, in £1,000 sterling):

	1976	1977	1978	1979	1980
Imports to UK	41,873	34,634	29,022	61,518	77,487
Exports and re-exports from UK	35,761	34,585	25,183	23,949	46,541

COMMUNICATIONS

Roads. There were at 30 June 1966, 45,549 km, of which 17,114 km were made up and 4,547 km asphalted. Work on the Carretera Marginal de la Selva (South American Marginal Forest Highway) started in 1965; the 5,600 km road between the Colombian–Venezuelan border and Sta. Cruz, Bolivia, of which the Peruvian portion consists of 394 km already existing, 503 km now under construction and 1,565 km outstanding, to make a sectional total of some 2,460 km.

In 1974 there were 266,910 private cars and 139,950 commercial vehicles.

Railways. Since 1972 all public railways are nationalized and run by Peruvian National Railways (ENAFER). Total length (1980), 1,628 km on 1,435- and 914-mm gauges.

Aviation. Air services connect Lima and the capitals of every South American republic.

Shipping. In 1966, 6,900 vessels of 26,602,270 tons entered, and 6,871 of 26,610,772 tons cleared the ports. Since 1928 the coasting trade has been largely reserved for Peruvian-owned vessels with Peruvian crews; in 1960 it handled 2,246,000 tonnes, valued at S/.1,665m.

Post and Broadcasting. An earth satellite ground communication station at Lurin connects Peru through Intelsat. III to the US and Europe. In 1978 there were 402,459 telephones, 301,333 in Lima. Length of telegraph lines was 26,121 km. In 1970 the Lima Telephone Co. was nationalized and the Government have announced their intention to nationalize progressively the entire telephone and communications network. Radio-telephone circuits connect Lima with distant towns. Three submarine telegraph cables connect Peru and Chile, and one connects Peru and the republics to the north. There are 153 broadcasting stations, of which 29 are in Lima. Wireless receiving sets, about 2m. There are 7 television stations in Lima, 16 in the provinces and 45 relay stations. All radio and television stations are controlled by the Government.

Cinemas. In 1972 there were 276 cinemas.

Newspapers. The main Lima newspapers are *La Prensa, El Comercio, Expreso, Correo* and *La Crónica.*

JUSTICE, RELIGION, EDUCATION AND WELFARE

Justice. The Peruvian judicial system is a pyramid at the base of which are the justices of the peace who decide minor criminal cases and civil cases involving small sums of money. The apex is the Supreme Court with 17 members; in between are the judges of first instance, who usually sit in the provincial capitals, and the superior courts of which there are 18.

The Revolutionary Government decreed in Dec. 1969 that all judges, except justices of the peace, will in future be elected by the National Council of Justice, composed of representatives of the Executive, the Legislature, the Judiciary, the National Federation of the College of Lawyers and 2 of the university law faculties. Justices of the peace will be appointed, as before, by the superior courts.

Religion. Religious liberty exists, but the Roman Catholic religion is protected by the State, and since 1929 only Roman Catholic religious instruction is permitted in schools, state or private. In 1972 there were 1 Roman Catholic cardinal, 7 archbishops, 14 bishops, 3 vicars-general, 8 vicars apostolic, 2,672 priests, 506 cloistered monks and 4,558 members of religious orders.

Protestants numbered 128,000 in 1966.

All marriages must be civil, regardless of religion and preceded by medical examination; there are liberal divorce regulations, including divorce for 'absence without just cause for more than 2 years', and by mutual consent. Divorcees may remarry immediately. A law of 1936 emphasizes that the religious obligations of marriage are fully recognized.

Education. A new law for education was promulgated in March 1972. Elementary education is compulsory and free for both sexes between the ages of 7 and 16; secondary education is also free. But schools, despite substantial increases, are still too few. The system is highly centralized; all teaching appointments are made by the Minister of Education for the public schools; for the private schools he supervises plant and equipment and limits fees but does not appoint teachers.

In 1970 there were 20,034 public, private and primary schools, with 64,004 teachers and 2·75m. pupils; 1,452 secondary schools, with 21,863 teachers and 674,000 students. Training in 414 public technical schools is also free; in 1970 they had 6,333 teachers and 223,300 pupils. The 90 teacher-training schools had 1,075 teachers and 18,000 pupils. Total literacy (1975) was 68% of total population. Because of the increase in the number of pupils state schools have divided their teaching timetable into three divisions, morning, afternoon and evening. Those pupils in the last shift have to spend an extra year at school to make up for the difference in the length of the daily timetable.

In 1970 the total number of university students was 105,600.

Social Welfare. Contributory social security schemes exist for employees and workers. These are administered by the Ministry of Labour. There were in 1975, 182 hospitals (33,350 beds). In addition in 1969 there were 63 health centres, 307 medical posts and 842 sanitary posts, all administered by the authorities. In 1975 there were 9,445 doctors, 2,119 obstetricians, 115 chemists and 8,920 trained nurses.

DIPLOMATIC REPRESENTATIVES

OF PERU IN GREAT BRITAIN (52 Sloane St., London, SW1X 9SP)
Ambassador: Carlos Vásquez-Ayllón.

OF GREAT BRITAIN IN PERU
(Edificio El Pacifico Washington, Ave. Arequipa, Lima)
Ambassador: C. W. Wallace, CVO.

OF PERU IN THE USA (1700 Massachusetts Ave., NW,
Washington, D.C., 20036)
Ambassador: (Vacant).

OF THE USA IN PERU (PO Box 1995, Lima)
Ambassador: Harry W. Shlaudeman.

OF PERU TO THE UNITED NATIONS
Ambassador: (Vacant).

Books of Reference

The official gazette is *El Peruano*, Lima.

Anario Estadistico del Perú. Annual.—*Boletin de Estadistica Peruana.* Quarterly.—*Demarcarción Política del Perú.* (Dirección Nacional de Estadística), Lima
Censo Nacional Población, 4 June 1972. Lima, 1972
Estadistica del Comercio Exterior (Superintendencia de Aduanas). Lima
Banco Central de Reserva. Monthly Bulletin.—*Renta Nacional del Perú.* Annual, Lima

Ministerio de Fomento Lima publishes separate annual statistics on the mining and petroleum industries and on general industry; the wool textile and cotton textile industries, Peruvian Chamber of Commerce furnish annual studies.

Alba, V., *Peru.* Boulder, 1977
Bourricaud, F., *Pouvoir et Société dans le Pérou contemporain.* Paris, 1965
Fitzgerald, E. V. K., *The State and Economic Development: Peru Since 1968.* CUP, 1976.—*The Political Economy of Peru 1958–78.* CUP, 1979
Hemming, J., *The Conquest of the Incas.* London, 1970
Lowenthal, A. F., *The Peruvian Experiment.* Princeton Univ. Press, 1975
Marrett, Sir R., *Peru.* London, 1969
Mejía Baca, J., and Tauro, A., *Diccionário Enciclopédico del Perú.* 3 vols. 1966
Philip, G. D. E., *The Rise and Fall of the Peruvian Military Radicals, 1968–1976.* London, 1978
Pike, *A Modern History of Peru.* London, 1967
Sharp, D. A. (ed.), *US Foreign Policy and Peru.* Univ. of Texas Press, 1972
Thorp, R., and Bertram, G., *Peru 1890–1977.* London, 1978
Vargas, Padre, *Historia General del Perú.* Lima, 1967
Webb, R. C., *Government Policy and the Distribution of Income in Peru, 1963–1973.* Harvard Univ. Press, 1977

National Library: Avenida Abancay, Lima.

REPUBLIC OF THE PHILIPPINES

Capital: Manila
Population: 47·91m. (1980)
GNP per capita: US$620 (1979)

República de Filipinas—
Republika ñg Pilipinas

HISTORY. Before the Spanish discovery of the Philippines, the native Filipinos came in contact with India, China and Arabia. According to the early records of China, 'some Filipinos from the country of Ma-i arrived in Canton and sold their merchandise' as early as 982. The Philippine islands were discovered by Magellan in 1521 and conquered by Spain in 1565. Following the Spanish–American war, the islands were ceded to the USA on 10 Dec. 1898, after the Filipinos had tried in vain to establish an independent republic in 1896.

The Republic of the Philippines came into existence on 4 July 1946, by agreement with the US Government embodied in an Act of Congress signed by President Roosevelt on 24 March 1934, accepted by the Philippine Legislature on 1 May 1934 and ratified at a plebiscite on 14 May 1935. This Act established a 10-year transitional period, designated as that of the Philippine Commonwealth, at the end of which complete independence was automatically effective.

AREA AND POPULATION. The Philippines is situated between 21° 25′ and 4° 23′ N. lat. and between 116° and 127° E. long. It is composed of 7,100 islands and islets, 2,773 of which are named. Approximate land area, 115,830 sq. miles (300,000 sq. km). The 16 most important islands with their areas (in sq. miles) are: Luzon, 40,420; Mindanao, 36,537; Samar, 5,050; Negros, 4,906; Palawan, 4,550; Panay, 4,446; Mindoro, 3,759; Leyte, 2,786; Cebu, 1,707; Bohol, 1,492; Masbate, 1,262; Sulu group, 379; Tawi-tawi, 229; Romblon, 32; Marinduque, 347, and Siquijor, 129.

Census population 1980 was 47,914,017.

The population of Manila, the present capital, in 1980 was 1,626,249 (metropolitan Manila, 5·9m.). The old capital, Quezon City, just north-east of Manila, had a population of 1,165,990. Other cities, with their population in May 1980 are: Iloilo on Panay, 244,211; Cebu on Cebu, 489,208; Zamboanga on Mindanao, 344,275; Davao on Mindanao, 611,311; Bacolod on Negros, 266,604; San Carlos on Negros Occidental, 93,268; San Carlos on Pangasinan, 101,254; Pasay on Rizal, 286,497.

On 7 June 1946 the President of the Philippines approved a law, effective 4 July 1946, making a new language (Pilipino) based on Tagalog (a Malayan dialect) the official national language of the republic. In 1970 about 16,409,133 people spoke English and about 1,335,945 Spanish; for government and commercial purposes these two languages are commonly used. Some 77 native languages are spoken in the Philippines, of which 9 are of major importance; they belong to the Malayo-Polynesian family.

CONSTITUTION AND GOVERNMENT. The republic was governed by a constitution adopted on 14 May 1935 and amended in 1940 and 1946. On 17 Jan. 1973 a new constitution was ratified naming President Marcos President and Prime Minister without a fixed term of office. The President is assisted by 25 ministers in charge of Foreign Affairs, Finance, Justice, Agriculture, Public Works, Transportation and Communications, Education and Culture, Labour, National Defence, Energy, Trade, Health, Social Services and Development, Agrarian Reform, Public Information, Local Government and Community Development, Tourism, Industry, Public Highways, Natural Resources, Youth and Sports Development, Human

Settlements, National Economic and Development Authority, Budget, National Science Development Board and by other officials with cabinet rank, namely, the Presidential Executive Assistant, Senior Presidential Assistant, Presidential Assistant on National Minorities and the Solicitor-General.

President and Prime Minister: Ferdinand E. Marcos.

Martial law was introduced on 21 Sept. 1972. A referendum held in Dec. 1977 decreed that President Marcos should remain in power. On 12 June 1978 a limited experiment in parliamentary democracy began and the President also became Prime Minister. Limited power to legislate was given to the new Assembly but the right to legislate by decree was retained by the President and no date was given for lifting the martial law. Presidential elections are to be held in May 1981.

The 1973 Constitution provides that all male and female citizens 15 years of age or older who can read or write Spanish, English or a native dialect and who meet certain residential qualifications are entitled to vote.

The constitution vests in the republic all ownership of the country's natural resources, which, apart from public agricultural land, may not be alienated. An agreement with the USA signed on 4 July 1946, ratified by plebiscite on 11 March 1948 and expired in 1974, granted American interests or companies the exploitation of any resources and public-utility business open to Filipinos. Concessions and leases are limited to 25 years; maximum area of agricultural public land which any corporation may acquire or lease is 1,024 hectares (2,529 acres) and not more than 2,000 hectares (4,940 acres) are used for grazing purposes.

National flag: Horizontally blue over red, with a white triangle based on the hoist bearing a gold sun of 8 rays and 3 gold stars.

National hymn: 'Tierra Adorado', 'Land of the morning', lyric in English by M. A. Sane and C. Osias, in Spanish by José Palma (1899), tune by Julian Felipe (1898); 'Pambansang Awit ñg Pilipinas', Tagalog lyric by the Institute of National Language, music by Julian Felipe.

Local Government. The country is administratively divided into 13 regions, 73 provinces, 60 cities, 1,484 municipalities, 21 municipal districts, 39,926 *barangays* with 252,000 councilmen. On 14 Nov. 1975 the name of provincial boards and city or municipal boards or councils was changed into *Sangguniang Bayan.* The latter assumes all the powers and responsibilities on matters of legislation of the defunct provincial, city or municipal boards.

The *Sangguniang Pambayan* is the direct successor of the old municipal council; *Sangguniang Panglunsod* for the old city council; *Sangguniang Panlalawigan* for the old provincial council and *Batasang Pambansa* for the defunct Congress.

DEFENCE. On 14 March 1947 the Philippine and US Governments signed a 99-year military-base arrangement since reduced to 25 years and will end in 1991. The USA was granted the use of a series of army, navy and air bases, with the right to use a number of others on mutual agreement. On 21 March a second agreement provided for a US Military Advisory Group as well as military assistance. A treaty of mutual assistance was signed in Washington on 30 Aug. 1951; the instruments of ratification were exchanged in Manila on 27 Aug. 1952. The Philippines is also a signatory of the S.E. Asia Collective Defence Treaty.

The Chief of Staff of the Armed Forces has overall command over the Army, Air Force, Navy and Constabulary.

Army. The Army consists of 70,000 officers and men in the active force. It is organized in 4 light infantry divisions and 1 independent, 1 Special Services and 2 engineer brigades, equipped with M-41 tanks.

Navy. The Navy includes 10 old frigates (4 former US destroyer escorts and 4 *ex*-USCG cutters, *ex*-USN seaplane tenders); 11 corvettes (3 *ex*-US fleet minesweepers and 8 *ex*-US escorts), 2 *ex*-US PC-type patrol vessels, 6 gunboats, 57 coastal patrol craft, 21 landing ships, 4 medium landing ships, 6 landing craft (3 LSSL and 3 LCU), 3 repair ships, 3 oilers, 3 water carriers, 1 supply ship, 4 survey ships, 5 tenders, 68 minor landing craft, 3 yachts (command ships), 8 tugs, 13 auxiliaries and 33 coastguard utility cutters, all *ex*-USA.

Naval personnel in 1981 totalled 1,600 officers and 13,000 men. There are also 330 officers and 6,500 enlisted men in the marine corps, and 300 officers and 1,700 men in the Coastguard.

The Philippine Navy was considerably increased in 1976 by taking over many vessels (nearly all former US warships) from the Vietnamese Navy which escaped from Indo-China when the Saigon government collapsed in 1975. They included 3 destroyer escorts, 6 frigate-size coastguard cutters, 2 fleet minesweepers, 3 escorts, 1 patrol vessel, 1 gunboat, 13 landing ships, 3 medium landing ships, 6 landing craft, 2 repair ships, 5 oilers, 3 water carriers and several auxiliary ships.

Air Force. The Air Force has a strength of 16,800 officers and men, with 375 aircraft, and was built up with US assistance. Its fighter-bomber wing is equipped with 2 squadrons of supersonic F-5A/Bs and 1 squadron of F-8H Crusaders. There are transport, observation, air/sea rescue, helicopter and training units, for which recently acquired equipment has included 3 Fokker F27 Maritime patrol aircraft, 12 Australian-built Mission Master twin-turboprop STOL light transports, 8 HU-16 Albatross amphibians and a total of 48 Italian-built SF.260WP (armed) and SF.260MP piston-engined trainers. Many of the Air Force's other trainers are armed for counter-insurgency duties. No. 16 and 18 squadrons of the 15th Strike Wing each operate 16 T-28Ds. No. 17 has 16 SF.260WPs.

Police. Public order is maintained partly through the Philippine constabulary and partly through the local police forces. The constabulary now forms part of the Armed Forces and has 27,000 personnel.

INTERNATIONAL RELATIONS

Membership. The Republic of the Philippines is a member of UN and the Colombo Plan.

External Debt. At 31 March 1979 the external debt amounted to US$5,592·6m.

ECONOMY

Budget. The revenues and expenditures of the central government for calendar years were, in 1m. Philippine pesos, as follows:

	1976	1977	1978[1]	1979[1]
Revenue	18,300	21,138	28,730	31,844
Expenditure	21,300	22,597[1]	30,464	34,289

[1] Estimate.

Expenditure (1979) included (in 1m. pesos): National defence and police, 4,977; education, health and welfare, 8,183; economic development, 12,794; public debt, 7,853.

At 31 Dec. 1979 the total internal public debt outstanding of the national and local governments, including those of the government corporations, stood at P.36,458m.

Currency. Total money supply, Oct. 1980, was P.19,389·3m., of which P.8,571·1m. was currency in circulation and P.10,818·2m. were demand deposits. The coins used are: 5 *peso*, 1 *peso*, one-half *peso*, quarter *peso*, media *peseta* (10 *centavos*), all contain 70 grammes copper, 18 grammes zinc and 12 grammes nickel; 5 *centavo* in copper and zinc, and 1 *centavo* in aluminium and magnesium zinc. Central Bank notes are issued in 2, 5, 10, 20, 50, 100 *pesos* denominations.

In March 1981, £1 = 16·28 *pesos*; US$1 = 7·65 *pesos*.

Banking. On 31 March 1980 there were 1,411 branches of commercial banks operating under 32 head offices, with 4 overseas, 1 each in New York, Hong Kong, Taipei and London. Agencies exist in Honolulu, San Francisco and Los Angeles. Total deposits of the commercial banks in 1979 were P.55,997·2m.

Under the law passed 15 June 1948 the Central Bank of the Philippines was created to have sole control of the credit and monetary supply, independent of the Treasury. It has a capital of P.10m. furnished solely by the Government. Its total assets, at 30 June 1979 were P.52,640m.

Weights and Measures. The metric system of weights and measures was established by law in 1869, and since 1916 has come into general use.

ENERGY AND NATURAL RESOURCES

Electricity. Government and private electric systems furnish the Philippines with electric power, with total generating capacity of 2,794,279 mw (1979). The Manila Electric Co., was bought by the Government in July 1978. MECO plants generated a total of 2,207,964 mwh. in 1979 while the Government's National Power Corporation produced 10,282,411 mwh.; others, 303,073 mwh.

Minerals. Mineral production in 1979 (in tonnes): Lead concentrate, 3,322; nickel metal, 21,478; nickel concentrate, 9,204 (1978); nickel direct shipping ore, 513,466; zinc concentrate, 17,545; copper concentrate, 1,061,549; copper direct shipping ore, 1,732; cobalt metal, 1,370; coal, 263,132; salt, 322,131; gold, 16,646 kg; silver, 56,167 kg. Other minerals include cement, rock asphalt, sand and gravel.

Agriculture. Of the total area of 30m. hectares, 7·17m. hectares are commercial forests; 5,491,000 hectares non-commercial forests; 876,000 hectares open grassland; 118,000 hectares mangrove and marshes; 14,523,000 hectares cultivated.

About 98·4% of the total cultivated area is owned by Filipinos; the average size of the farm is 3·21 hectares. The principal products are unhusked rice (palay), Manila hemp (abaca), copra, sugar-cane, maize and tobacco. On 30 Sept. 1979, 7,875,000 persons were employed in agriculture (47·6% of the working population).

The products (in tonnes) are (1979, provisional): Rough rice, 7·2m.; copra, 2·94m. (1978); coconut, 4·28m.; sugar (muscovado and centrifugal), 3·2m.; shelled corn, 3·17m.; tobacco, 51,100; abaca fibre, 114,000.

Minor crops are fruits, nuts, root crops, vegetables, onions, beans, coffee, cacao, peanuts, ramie, rubber, maguey and kapok.

Livestock, estimated in 1979: 3m. carabaos (water buffaloes), 1·9m. cattle, 7·3m. pigs, 1·4m. goats and 60m. poultry.

Forestry. The forests covered some 12,661,000 hectares in 1979. Log production, 6,557,864 cu. metres, of which 1,247,973 cu. metres were exported in 1979.

Fisheries. Fish production from all sources was 1,581,303 tonnes and was valued at P.10,536,747 in 1979.

INDUSTRY AND TRADE

Industry. Manufacturing is a major source of economic development contributing 24·5% to GNP in 1979. Leading growth sectors were textile, footwear and wearing apparel, chemical and chemical products, beverage industries and food manufacture. In 1978 (census), there were 9,976 large manufacturing establishments (employing 20 or more workers), of which 2,282 were engaged in food; 1,018 wearing apparel; 237 footwear; 440 industrial chemicals and other chemical products; 96 beverages; 5 petroleum refineries; 388 transport equipment, and 1,368 wood and wood and cork products including furniture. The non-agricultural labour force during the last quarter of 1979 was 8,826,050 out of a total of 17,794,450 employed.

Commerce. The values of imports and exports (f.o.b.) for calendar years are stated as follows in US$1m.:

	1976	1977	1978	1979
Imports	3,633	3,914	4,732	6,142
Exports	2,574	3,151	3,425	4,601

The principal exports in 1979 were (in US$1m.): Coconut oil (crude), 742·5; copper concentrates, 440·4; sugar, 211·6; lumber, 198·3; logs, 144·4; iron ore agglomerates, 120; plywood, 107·2; desiccated coconut, 103·3; gold from copper ore and concentrates, 96·7; copra, 89·1.

Main imports in 1979 (in US$1m.): Mineral fuels, lubricants and related materials, 1,385; machinery other than electric, 935; base metals, 547; transport equipment, 544; materials for the manufacture of electrical and electronic machinery, 351; chemical elements and compounds, 249; electrical machinery, apparatus and appliances, 229; explosives and miscellaneous chemical materials and products, 195; cereals and cereal preparations, 144; metal manufactures, 128.

For over a half-century the foreign trade has been chiefly with the USA. The trade relationship of the two countries is governed by the Philippine Trade Act of 1946 as amended.

Philippine products entering the USA paid 10% of the US tariff in 1959–61, 20% in 1962–64, 40% in 1965–67, 60% in 1968–70, 80% in 1971–73 and 100% from 1 Jan. 1974.

Total trade between the Philippines and UK (British Department of Trade returns, in £1,000 sterling):

	1975	1976	1977	1978	1979	1980
Imports to UK	40,574	33,485	44,696	63,447	81,122	99,018
Exports and re-exports from UK	54,606	86,180	92,721	115,038	105,709	88,998

Tourism. In 1979, 966,873 tourists visited the Philippines spending US$238·01m.

COMMUNICATIONS

Roads. In 1979 highways totalled 135,291·32 km; of this, 9,620·49 km were concrete; 16,528·33, asphalt; 45,863·57, earth; 63,278·93, macadam. In 1979 there were registered 1,186,796 motor vehicles of all types.

Railways. The National Railways totals 1,027 km of 1,067 mm gauge on Luzon, and Phividec Railways operates 116 km on Panay Island. In 1979, 8,531,627 passengers and 179,139 tonnes of freight were carried by rail.

Aviation. The Philippine Air Lines, Inc., with a working capital of P.250m., in 1978 carried 3,443,207 passengers, 31,575,196 kg of cargo and 649,346 kg of mail.

Shipping. In 1979, 88,266 vessels of 64,374,670 net tons entered and 88,921 vessels of 65,427,906 net tons cleared all ports.

Post and Broadcasting. In 1979 there were in operation 1,954 post offices and 1,413 telecommunication stations. The Philippine Long Distance Telephone Co. had 519,642 telephones in service in 1979 while the Government Telephone System which operates 13 automatic exchanges within the Greater Manila Area had 33,042 subscribers.

Licensed radio stations at 31 May 1979 numbered 17,872, including 1,372 ship stations and 687 aircraft stations.

Newspapers (1979). There were 300 registered publications (210 published in Manila), 15 of which were dailies.

JUSTICE, RELIGION, EDUCATION AND WELFARE

Justice. There is a Supreme Court which is composed of a chief justice and 14 associate justices; it can declare a law or treaty unconstitutional by the concurrent votes of the majority sitting. There is a court of appeal, headed by a presiding justice, with 35 associate justices. There are 16 judicial districts sub-divided into 357 branches, each with a presiding judge of first instance. Every city has a city court and every municipality has 1 municipal judge. In addition, the juvenile and domestic relations court in Manila has exclusive jurisdiction to try all cases involving minors and matrimonial disputes.

Religion. In 1970 there were 31,169,488 Roman Catholics, 1,434,688 Aglipayans, 1,584,963 Moslems, 1,122,999 Protestants, 475,407 members of the Iglesia ni Kristo, 33,639 Buddhists and 863,302 others.

The Roman Catholics are organized in 12 archbishoprics, 30 bishoprics, 12 prelatures nullius, 4 apostolic vicariates, 4 apostolic prefectures and some 1,633 parishes. The Philippine Independent Church, founded in 1902, and comprising about 3·9% of the population, denies the spiritual authority of the Roman Pontiff. It is divided into two groups, one of which has accepted ordinations by the Episcopalian Church.

Education. Formal education consists of 3 levels: elementary, secondary and further education. Public elementary education is free and public elementary schools are established in almost every *barangay* or *barrio*. The majority of the secondary and post-secondary schools are private, sectarian or non-sectarian. The number of years required to complete the elementary and secondary levels are 6 and 4 years respectively, while the tertiary level requires at least 4 years for an academic degree. Pre-school education is also offered mostly in private schools to children from ages 3–6.

Non-formal education consists of adult literacy classes, agricultural and farming training programmes, occupation skills training, youth clubs, and community programmes of instructions in health, nutrition, family planning and co-operatives.

Public and private schools in 1978–79 enrolled 8·2m. pupils in primary schools, 2·8m. in secondary schools and 1·1m. students in further education. The University of the Philippines (founded in 1908) had 27,558 students in 1978–79.

Health. In 1979 there were 41,425 registered physicians and 86,550 hospital beds.

Social Welfare. The Government programme includes the construction of urban and rural housing units for lease or sale to middle and low-income families to ease the housing problem, the settlement of landless families, the opening of rural farm-to-market roads, the setting up of rural schools and rural health units, the granting of loans to farmers, fishermen and small cottage industries, self-employment assistance to the most disadvantaged persons and practical skills development and job placement services to out-of-school youths, jobless family heads and disabled persons, and the extension of emergency services like rescue and relief operations in times of typhoons, earthquakes, fires and other calamities.

DIPLOMATIC REPRESENTATIVES

OF THE PHILIPPINES IN GREAT BRITAIN (9A Palace Green, London, W8 4QE)

Ambassador: José Manuel Stilianopoulos.

OF GREAT BRITAIN IN THE PHILIPPINES (115 Esteban St., Manila)

Ambassador: M. H. Morgan.

OF THE PHILIPPINES IN THE USA (1617 Massachusetts Ave., NW, Washington, D.C., 20036)

Ambassador: Eduardo Z. Romualdez.

OF THE USA IN THE PHILIPPINES (1201 Roxas Blvd., Manila)

Ambassador: Richard W. Murphy.

OF THE PHILIPPINES TO THE UNITED NATIONS

Ambassador: Alejandro D. Yango.

Books of Reference

Philippine Yearbook 1981. National Census and Statistics Office, Manila, 1981
Gazetteer of the Philippine Islands. United States Department of Commerce. Washington, 1945
Foreign Trade Statistics of the Philippines, 1979. National Census and Statistics Office, Manila, 1979
Burley, T. M., *The Philippines. An Economic and Social Geography.* London, 1973
Chapman, A., *Philippine Nationalism.* New York, 1950
Golay, F. H., *The Philippines: Public Policy and National Economic Development.* Cornell Univ. Press, 1961
Hainsworth, R. G., and Moyser, R. T., *Agricultural Geography of the Philippine Islands.* Washington, 1945
Lightfort, K., *The Philippines.* London, 1973
Meyer, M. W., *A Diplomatic History of the Philippine Republic.* Univ. of Hawaii Press, 1965

PITCAIRN
ISLAND

HISTORY. It was discovered by Carteret in 1767, but remained uninhabited until 1790, when it was occupied by 9 mutineers of HMS *Bounty*, with 12 women and 6 men from Tahiti. Nothing was known of their existence until the island was visited in 1808. In 1856 the population having become too large for the island's resources, the inhabitants (194 in number) were, at their own request, removed to Norfolk Island; but 43 of them returned in 1859–64.

AREA AND POPULATION. Pitcairn Island (1·75 sq. miles; 4·6 sq. km) is situated in the Pacific Ocean, nearly equidistant from New Zealand and Panama (25° 04′ S. lat., 130° 06′ W. long). The population has been declining and on 30 June 1980 it was 63.

The uninhabited islands of Henderson (12 sq. miles), Ducie (1½ sq. miles) and Oeno (2 sq. miles) were annexed in 1902 and are included in the Pitcairn group.

CONSTITUTION. Pitcairn was brought within the jurisdiction of the High Commissioner for the Western Pacific in 1898 and transferred to the Governor of Fiji in 1952. When Fiji became independent in Oct. 1970, the British High Commissioner in New Zealand was appointed Governor.

The Local Government Ordinance of 1964 constitutes a Council of 10 members, of whom 4 are elected, 5 are nominated (3 by the 4 elected members and 2 by the Governor) and the Island Secretary is an *ex-officio* member. The Island Magistrate, who is elected triennially, presides over the Council; other members hold office for only 1 year. Liaison between Governor and Council is through a Commissioner in the Auckland, New Zealand, office of the British Consulate-General.

TRADE. Fruit, vegetables and curios are sold to passing ships; fuel oil, machinery, building materials, flour, sugar and other foodstuffs are imported.

Governor: R. J. Stratton, CMG (resides in Wellington).
Island Magistrate: Ivan Christian (re-elected Dec. 1978).

Books of Reference

A Guide to Pitcairn. Pitcairn Island Administration, Auckland, revised ed. 1976
Ball, I., *Pitcairn: Children of the Bounty*. London, 1973
Ross, A. S. C., and Moverly, A. W., *The Pitcairnese Language*. London, 1964

POLAND

Polska Rzeczpospolita Ludowa

Capital: Warsaw
Population: 35·38m. (1980)
GNP per capita: US$3,660 (1978)

HISTORY. In 1966 Poland celebrated its millennium, but modern Polish history begins with the partitions of the once-powerful kingdom between Russia, Austria and Prussia in 1772, 1793 and 1795. For 19th cent. events *see* THE STATESMAN'S YEAR-BOOK 1980–81.

On 10 Nov. 1918 independence was proclaimed by Józef Piłsudski, the founder of the Polish Legions during the war. On 28 June 1919 the Treaty of Versailles recognized the independence of Poland.

On 1 Sept. 1939 Germany invaded Poland, on 17 Sept. 1939 Russian troops entered eastern Poland, and on 29 Sept. 1939 the fourth partition of Poland took place. After the German attack on Russia, the Germans occupied the whole of Poland. By March 1945 the country had been liberated by the Russians.

In July 1944 the USSR recognized the Polish Committee of National Liberation (*Polski Komitet Wyzwolenia Narodowego*) established in Lublin as an executive organ of the National Council of the Homeland (*Krajowa Rada Narodowa*). The Committee was transformed into the Provisional Government in Dec. 1944, and on 28 June 1945, supplemented by members of the Polish Government in London (which had been recognized by the UK and USA), it was re-established—in Moscow—as the Polish Provisional Government of National Unity and on 6 July recognized as such by the UK and USA.

Elections were held on 19 Jan. 1947. Of the 12·7m. votes cast, 11·24m. were recognized as valid and 9m. were given for the Communist-dominated 'Democratic Bloc'.

After riots in Poznań in June 1956 nationalist anti-Stalinist elements gained control of the Communist Party, under the leadership of Władysław Gomułka.

In 1970 the Federal Republic of Germany recognized Poland's western boundary as laid down by the Potsdam Conference of 1945 (the 'Oder–Neisse line').

In Dec. 1970 strikes and riots in Gdańsk, Szczecin and Gdynia led to the resignation of a number of leaders including Gomułka. He was replaced by Edward Gierek.

The introduction of price rises in June 1976 was again followed by strikes and riots. The rises were withdrawn and demonstrators were given severe sentences. In the campaign of protest which followed a Committee for the Defence of the Workers (KOR) was formed. All prisoners were released by July 1977. Subsequently the KOR was broadened into the Committee for Social Self-Defence (KSS) and a Movement for the Rights of Man and the Citizen appeared (ROPCIO).

The raising of meat prices on 1 July 1980 resulted in a wave of strikes which progressively broadened into generalized wage demands and eventually by mid-Aug. acquired a political character. Workers in Gdańsk, Gdynia and Sopot elected a joint strike committee, led by Lech Wałęsa, demanding the right to strike and form independent Trade Unions, the abolition of censorship, access to the media and the release of political prisoners.

Gierek offered pay rises, but no political concessions, a Government commission refused at first to negotiate with the joint strike committee, and some KOR protesters were arrested.

However, on 22 Aug. the Government negotiator was replaced by First Deputy Prime Minister Jagielski. On 24 Aug. Gierek reshuffled the Party and Government leadership, and Józef Pińkowski replaced Edward Babinch as Prime Minister. On 31 Aug. Jagielski and Wałęsa signed the 'Gdańsk Agreements' permitting the formation of independent Trade Unions, the strikers returned to work and members of KOR were freed from arrest.

On 5 Sept. Gierek suffered a heart attack and was replaced as First Secretary by Stanisław Kania. On 17 Sept. various Trade Unions decided to form a national confederation ('Solidarity') and applied for legal status. On 3 Oct. Solidarity called a one-hour strike because the Government was failing to honour its promises, and on 7 Oct. Kania dismissed some Party leaders and promised reforms.

On 24 Oct. a Warsaw court granted Solidarity legal status, but only after unilaterally inserting into its charter a reference to the supremacy of the Party. Solidarity appealed to the Supreme Court, which removed the offending clause on 10 Nov.

Jan. 1981 saw a further conflict between Solidarity and the authorities over the issue of Saturday working, which was resolved by an agreement on a 42-hour week to include one Saturday a month. On 9 Feb. Pińkowski was replaced as Prime Minister by the Defence Minister, Gen. Wojciech Jaruzelski, who called upon Solidarity to give the Government a three-month truce in order to deal with the economic and political crisis.

AREA AND POPULATION. Poland is bounded north by the Baltic and the RSFSR, east by Lithuania, White Russia and the Ukraine, south by Czechoslovakia and west by the German Democratic Republic. Poland comprises an area of 312,683 sq. km (120,628 sq. miles). In 1975 the administrative structure was reorganized. (For previous administrative divisions see THE STATESMAN'S YEAR-BOOK, 1975–76.) The country is divided into 49 voivodships (*wojewodztwo*) (including 3 urban: Warsaw, Kraków and Łódź) and these in turn are divided into 803 towns and 2,070 wards (*gmina*). The capital is Warsaw (Warszawa).

Area (in sq. km) and population (in 1,000, with percentage urban in brackets) in 1979:

Voivodship	Area	Population	Voivodship	Area	Population
Biała Podlaska	5,348	285 (29)	Opole	8,535	968 (49)
Białystok	10,055	636 (53)	Ostrołęka	6,498	368 (28)
Bielsko–Biała	3,703	819 (48)	Piła	8,205	432 (52)
Bydgoszcz	10,349	1,027 (62)	Piotrków	6,262	600 (41)
Chełm	3,865	230 (36)	Płock	5,117	492 (42)
Ciechanów	6,362	403 (30)	Poznań	8,151	1,222 (69)
Częstochowa	6,182	746 (49)	Przemyśl	4,436	378 (34)
Elbląg	6,099	436 (57)	Radom	7,297	698 (41)
Gdańsk	7,394	1,313 (76)	Rzeszów	4,398	641 (34)
Gorzów	8,484	450 (58)	Siedlce	8,499	613 (25)
Jelenia Góra	4,378	490 (64)	Sieradz	4,869	392 (30)
Kalisz	6,512	662 (43)	Skierniewice	3,960	395 (39)
Katowice	6,650	3,677 (87)	Słupsk	7,453	365 (52)
Kielce	9,211	1,062 (42)	Suwałki	10,489	419 (46)
Konin	5,139	5,139 (36)	Szczecin	9,981	887 (74)
Koszalin	8,470	456 (60)	Tarnobrzeg	6,283	551 (30)
Kraków (Cracow)	3,255	1,154 (68)	Tarnów	4,151	602 (32)
Krosno	5,701	443 (31)	Toruń	5,348	604 (59)
Legnica	4,037	449 (62)	Wałbrzych	4,169	715 (72)
Leszno	4,154	355 (44)	Warsaw	3,788	2,288 (88)
Łódź	1,526	1,122 (91)	Włocławek	4,402	414 (43)
Łomża	6,684	324 (31)	Wrocław	6,287	1,065 (72)
Lublin	6,792	925 (53)	Zamość	6,980	472 (22)
Nowy Sącz	5,577	622 (35)	Zielona Góra	8,868	603 (57)
Olsztyn	12,331	675 (54)			

Population (in 1,000) of the largest towns (1979):

Warsaw	1,572	Bydgoszcz	344	Zabrze	196
Łódź	832	Lublin	298	Radom	188
Kraków (Cracow)	705	Sosnowiec	241	Kielce	184
Wrocław (Breslau)	608	Częstochowa	233	Toruń	170
Poznań	544	Bytom	232	Tychy	160
Gdańsk (Danzig)	448	Gdynia	231	Bielsko-Biała	160
Szczecin (Stettin)	388	Białystok	218	Ruda Staska	158
Katowice	353	Gliwice	196	Chorzów	150

At the census of 7 Dec. 1978 the population was 35,032,000 (17m. males; 58% urban). Population on 1 Jan. 1980, 35,382,000 (18·1m. females; 20·6m urban) density,

113 per sq. km. Vital statistics, 1979 (per 1,000): Marriages, 9·1; divorces, 1·1 live births, 19·5; deaths, 9·2, infant mortality (per 1,000 live births), 21·3.

The rate of natural growth, 1979, 10·3 per 1,000. Expectation of life in 1977 was 67·3 years for males, 75 years for females. In 1979, 50% of the population was under 30.

Ethnic minorities in 1963: 180,000 Ukrainians, 165,000 Byelorussians, 21,000 Slovaks, 10,000 Lithuanians. There were 10,000 Jews in 1977. By a treaty of March 1976, Poland agreed to repatriate 125,000 ethnic Germans by 1980 and thereafter to issue exit permits to the remaining 155,000.

In 1969, 10·33m. Poles lived abroad (6·5m. in USA, 1·4m. in USSR, 150,000 (1976) in UK). In 1977 there were 1,600 immigrants and 28,900 emigrants.

CONSTITUTION AND GOVERNMENT. The present Constitution was adopted on 22 July 1952. Constitutional amendments were adopted in Feb. 1976. Two amendments referring to the leading role of the Communist Party and the special relationship with the USSR provoked a wave of protest when circulated in draft form and were adopted in a modified form.

The titular head of state is the Chairman of the Council of State, Henryk Jabłoński.

The Constitution defines the position of political parties as follows: 'The leading political force in Polish society is the Polish United Workers' Party. Co-operation between the Polish United Workers' Party, the United Peasants' Party and the Democratic Party constitutes the basis for the National Unity Front.'

Supreme *de facto* power is in the hands of the Politburo of the Polish United Workers' (*i.e.*, Communist) Party, in April 1981 composed as follows: Stanisław Kania, *First Secretary*; Henryk Jabloński; Mieczysław Jagielski (*First Deputy Prime Minister*); Gen. Wojciech Jaruzelski (*Prime Minister and Minister of Defence*); Stefan Olszowski; Józef Pińkowski; Kazimierz Barcikowski; Andrzej Zabiński; Gen. Mieczysław Moczar (*Chairman, Supreme Chamber of Control*); Tadeusz Grabski. Candidate members: Emil Wojtaszek; Jerzy Waszczuk; Władysław Kruk; Roman Ney; Tadeusz Fizbach. Ministers not in the Politburo include: Jerzy Bafia (*Minister of Justice*); Józef Czyrek (*Foreign Minister*); Henryk Kisiel (*Chairman, Planning Commission*); Mieczysław Rakowski (*Deputy Prime Minister*); Stanisław Jedynak (*Deputy Prime Minister*); Marian Krzak (*Finance Minister*); Stanisław Mach (*Deputy Prime Minister*); Mirosław Milewski (*Minister of the Interior*); Jerzy Ozdowski (*a Catholic representative, Deputy Prime Minister*); Tadeusz Pyka (*Deputy Prime Minister*); Tadeusz Wraszczyk (*Deputy Prime Minister*).

In 1979 the Polish United Workers' Party had 3,044,000 members, the United Peasants' Party 458,600, and the Democratic Party, 109,400.

The authority of the republic is vested in the Sejm, elected for 4 years by all citizens over 18. The Sejm elects a Council of State, composed of a Chairman, the Secretary and 14 members, including 4 vice-chairmen; and a Council of Ministers. Local government is carried out by People's Councils elected every 4 years at voivodship and community level. Alongside these are the offices of state administration. The chairman of the People's Council is the Secretary of the regional Party organization for the area.

The last local elections were held on 23 March 1980.

The last elections for the Sejm were held on 23 March 1980. 646 candidates stood on the single list of the National Unity Front and obtained 99·52% of the vote. 98·87% of the electorate voted. The 460 seats are distributed as follows: 261 United Workers' Party, 113 United Peasants' Party, 37 Democratic Party, 49 independents, including 5 Catholic representatives nominated by the Government but repudiated by the Church. There are 95 women deputies.

National flag: Horizontally white over red.

National anthem: Jeszcze Polska nie zginęła (words by J. Wybicki, 1797; tune by M. Ogiński, 1796).

DEFENCE. Poland is divided into 3 military districts: Warsaw (the eastern part of Poland); Pomerania (Baltic coast, part of central Poland; headquarters at Bydgoszcz); Silesia (Silesia and southern Poland; headquarters at Wrocław).

The armed forces are on Soviet lines and divided into army and air force (2 years' service), navy (3 years), anti-aircraft, rocket and radio-technological units (3 years) and internal security forces (2 years). In 1965 the security forces were taken away from the Ministry of Internal Affairs and placed under the Defence Ministry. The military age extends from the 19th to the 50th year. The strength of the armed forces is estimated at 317,500, plus 95,000 security and frontier forces. Security forces include armoured brigades.

Army. The Army consists of 5 armoured, 8 motorized, 1 airborne and 1 amphibious assault divisions (not all at full strength) with support units. Total strength, 210,000. Tanks (mostly T-54) number 3,600.

Navy. The Navy comprises 4 submarines, 1 destroyer, 24 fleet minesweepers, 13 missile craft, 25 patrol boats, 16 torpedo boats, 21 coast patrol boats, 23 medium landing ships, 7 training ships, 3 intelligence ships, 2 salvage ships, 2 torpedo recovery vessels, 16 minor landing craft, 20 minesweeping boats, 2 surveying vessels, 8 oilers, 20 tugs and 40 auxiliaries and tenders. The Fleet Air Arm has 50 fixed-wing aircraft (mostly MiG-17 and IL-28) and helicopters. Personnel in 1981 totalled 2,800 officers and 22,200 men.

Air Force. The Air Force has a strength of some 85,000 officers and men and 640 first-line jet aircraft of Soviet design. There are 3 divisions (more than 30 16-aircraft squadrons) of MiG-21 supersonic interceptors, and 6 regiments (at least 15 squadrons) operating variable-geometry MiG-23BM and Su-20, Su-7B and some MiG-17 close-support fighters. Another fighter division supports the Navy. There are also reconnaissance, ECM, transport, helicopter (including Mi-24 gunship) and training units. Soviet 'Guideline' 'Goa', 'Gainful' and 'Gaskin' surface-to-air missiles are operational.

Two Soviet armoured divisions are stationed on Polish territory.

INTERNATIONAL RELATIONS

Membership. Poland is a member of UN, Comecon and the Warsaw Pact.

ECONOMY

Planning. Before 1940 Poland was a predominantly agricultural country, but by 1975 only 27% of the population made a living by agriculture. In the mid-1960s some steps were taken towards decentralizing the economy. In 1973 the former three-tier hierarchy of industry (ministries–industrial associations–enterprises) began to be modified to include specializing combines and large enterprises ('big economic organizations') containing 'inner units'. By 1975 these proposals had been extended to firms producing two-thirds of the country's output, but the system was then suspended on the grounds that it was causing economic disequilibrium by its excessive demands on labour and investment resources and a tendency to generate imports. To restore the balance between supply and demand the system was modified on 18 March 1977 to increase the authority of the various economic ministries as intermediaries between the 'big economic organizations' and the central planning body. The modified system was put into effect first in the machine, chemical and light industries. In 1978 an agency scheme was introduced in retailing whereby the bulk of small shops are to be handed over to private persons.

Growth targets under the 1981–85 plan: National income, 14–18%; industry, 20–24%; agriculture, 12–13%. Actual increases for 1978: National income, 3%; industry, 5·8%; agriculture, 4·2%.

Budget. Budget in 1m. złotys, for calendar years:

	1974	1975	1976	1977	1978	1979
Revenue	604,100	720,140	881,401	993,948	1,103,457	1,154,800
Expenditure	602,300	701,663	799,494	887,599	994,158	1,107,700

Main items of 1979 revenue (in 1m. złotys): Sales tax and profits tax from state enterprises, 882,700; finance and insurance, 222,900; income tax, 12,600.

Main items of 1979 expenditure (in 1m. złotys): State enterprises, 640,100; welfare, 79,500; defence, 63,300; administration, 46,500; education, 71,600.

In 1975 a 'wealth tax' of 10–50% on assets over 700,000 złotys was instituted.

Polish debts to UK have been fully repaid. Poland does not accept liability for the £495,000 debts of Danzig (Gdańsk). Gold seized by the Nazis from Danzig was returned to Poland by the USA in 1976.

Currency. The currency unit is the *złoty*, divided into 100 *groszy*. The currency consists of notes of 50, 100, 500, 1,000 and 2,000 złotys; and of coins of 10, 20 and 50 groszy and 1, 2, 5, 10 and 20 złotys. In March 1981, £1 sterling = 76·18 złotys, US$1 = 31 złotys.

Banking. The National Bank of Poland (established 1945) is the central bank, has exclusive authority to issue currency, is charged with control of money and credit, and has responsibility for financial implementation of the national economic plan. Since its merger with the former Investment Bank on 1 Jan. 1970 it exercises centralized control over investment financing. The Agricultural Bank (Bank Rolny) has exclusive responsibility for direct financing of rural areas through both short-term and investment loans. It operates banks. The General Savings Bank (Powszechna Kasa Oszczedności) exercises central control over savings activities, transfers and checking transactions, including activities of workers' co-operative banks.

In addition to the National Bank of Poland, other authorized foreign-exchange banks are: Bank for the National Economy, the Polish Welfare Bank (Bank Polska Kasa Opieki SA) and the Commercial Bank of Warsaw (Bank Handlowy w Warszawie SA).

Deposits in savings institutions amounted to 456,632m. złotys on 31 Dec. 1979.

Weights and Measures. The metric system is in general use.

ENERGY AND NATURAL RESOURCES

Energy. Power sources in 1979: Coal, 76%; lignite, 22%; hydroelectric, 2%. A nuclear power station is being built at Zarnowiec.

Minerals. Poland is a major producer of coal (reserves of some 71,000m. tonnes) and sulphur. Copper reserves are estimated at 10m. tonnes. There is also iron ore, lead and zinc. Production in 1979 (in 1,000 tonnes): Coal, 201,000; brown coal, 38,100; copper ore, 25,572; zinc-lead ores, 5,497; iron ore, 249.

Agriculture. In 1979 there were 18·9m. hectares of agricultural land, of which 14·3m. hectares were in private hands, 3·6m. in state farms, 0.65m. in co-operatives and 0·36m. in agricultural circles. There were 3·1m. private farms in 1980. Private holdings average 5·3 hectares, and may not exceed 100 hectares. 15·9m. hectares were arable, 262,100 orchards, 2·4m. meadows, 1·8m. pasture lands.

Collectivization has been largely abandoned but remains a long-term aim and the number of co-operatives has been increasing: 1975, 1,092; 1978, 1,697; 1979, 2,000. A new agricultural policy of 1981 gives more autonomy to co-operatives, links wages to productivity and equalizes resources between the state and private sectors. The new peasant's organization 'Rural Solidarity' has not been accorded the status of trade union. A compulsory contributory pension scheme was introduced in 1978 for farmers who turn over their farms to their successors or the State. 250,000 such pensions ha been paid by June 1980. 'Agricultural circles' numbered 35,100 with 2·66m. members in 1979. In 1979 there were 4,490 state agricultural holdings.

Crops	Area (1,000 hectares)			Yield (1,000 tonnes)		
	1977	1978	1979	1977	1978	1979
Wheat	1,834	1,853	1,549	5,308	6,029	4,187
Rye	3,116	3,030	2,868	6,250	7,434	5,201
Barley	1,235	1,203	1,470	3,396	3,636	3,731
Oats	1,097	1,030	1,094	2,552	2,492	2,186
Potatoes	2,437	2,360	2,441	41,148	46,648	49,572
Sugar-beet	532	523	455	15,640	15,707	14,154

Livestock (1979): 13m. cattle (6m. cows), 21m. pigs, 4·2m. sheep, 1·9m. horses, 85m. poultry. Milk production in 1979 was 16,500m. litres.

Tractors in use in 1979: 789,600 (in 15-h.p. units).

Forestry. In 1979, 8·6m. hectares were forests (predominantly coniferous). 101,700 hectares were afforested in 1979, and 21·8m. cu. metres of timber gained.

Fisheries. In 1978 the fishing fleet had 120 deep-sea vessels totalling 235,100 GRT. In 1979 the catch was 605,000 tonnes.

In 1966 Poland joined the Fisheries Convention of 1964, extending the fishing limits from 3 to 12 miles.

INDUSTRY AND TRADE

Industry. Production in 1979 (and 1978) (in 1,000 tonnes): Coke, 20,000 (20,200); pig-iron, 11,527 (11,668); crude steel, 19,218 (19,251); rolled steel, 13,577 (13,565); cement, 19,200 (21,700); sulphuric acid (100%), 2,982 (3,172); fertilizers, 2,431 (2,621); aluminium, 97 (100); electrolytic copper, 336 (332); lead, 84·2 (86·7); zinc, 209 (222); crude oil, 331 (363); salt, 4,429 (4,393); sugar, 1,586 (1,605); electricity, 111,000m. kwh. (116,000m.); natural gas, 7,335m. cu. metres (7,991m.). In 1979, 67 ships over 100 DWT were built (602,000 DWT), 350,000 cars, 50,600 lorries and 13,200 buses were built in 1979.

Output of light industry in 1979 (and 1978): Cotton fabrics, 885m. metres (919); woollen fabrics, 123m. metres (124); silk and synthetic fibres, 163m. metres (168); shoes, 159m. pairs (159); household glass, 74,600 tonnes (83,900); paper, 1,010,000 tonnes (1,084,000); 761,000 washing machines, 767,000 refrigerators and 915,000 TV sets were produced in 1979.

Labour. In 1979 the total number in employment was 16·5m., of whom 12·7m. worked in the state-controlled sector and 3·8m. in the private sector, and including in agriculture 4·3m., industry 5·2m., building 1·4m., trade 1·3m. and transport and communications 1·1m. 5m. women were employed in the state-controlled sector. Since its foundation in Aug. 1980 the 'independent self-governing union' organization Solidarity had an estimated 8–10m. members in March 1981. The former trade unions have been reformed and had some 2m. members. Average wage in 1979, 5,098 złotys per month. The Government and Solidarity agreed on a 42-hour working week in 1981.

Commerce. Trade statistics for calendar years (in 1m. złotys):

	1974	1975	1976	1977	1978	1979
Imports	34,823	41,645	46,100	48,600	50,938	54,015
Exports	27,625	34,161	36,600	40,800	44,685	50,141

Main imports in 1979 (in tonnes): Petroleum and products, 20·5m.; iron ore, 18·7m.; fertilizers, 5·1m.; wheat, 2·9m.; coal, 1m.; passenger cars, 23,500 units.

Main exports in 1978 (in tonnes): Coal, 40·2m.; lignite, 3·4m.; coke, 2·1m.; sawn softwood, 780,000 cu. m.; ships, 642,265 DWT.

57·7% of Poland's trade is with Communist countries. UK is Poland's fifth largest trade partner after USSR, the German Democratic Republic, the Federal Republic of Germany and Czechoslovakia.

Foreign trade deals should be made directly with the appropriate foreign trade enterprise. Information may be obtained from the Polish Chamber of Foreign Trade, Trebacka 4, 00–950 Warsaw. Joint ventures with Western firms are encouraged both at home and abroad. The Western partner may own up to 49% of the shares of ventures on Polish soil, and is guaranteed a share of profits and interest.

An over-ambitious programme of importing goods for capital investment coinciding with a world recession and the rise in oil prices left Poland with a balance of payments deficit of some £11,000m. in 1980. Inspired partly by a desire to maintain political stability, massive programmes of credit and aid were offered in 1980 by the USSR, USA and EEC. The USSR has also agreed to defer until 1985 repayment of Polish credits granted 1976–80, and a meeting of Western creditor nations in Feb. 1981 agreed to the rescheduling of Polands debts.

Soviet exports include plant and equipment and raw materials; Polish exports, machinery, ships, coal, chemicals and consumer goods.

Total trade between Poland and UK for 5 years (British Department of Trade returns, in £1,000 sterling):

	1976	1977	1978	1979	1980
Imports to UK	154,150	174,265	212,239	229,318	194,523
Exports and re-exports from UK	189,473	200,409	265,911	260,606	296,254

An Anglo-Polish 10-year agreement on the development of economic, industrial, scientific and technical co-operation was signed on 20 March 1973, and a 10-year programme implementing this was signed on 4 Sept. 1975. A UK–Polish 5-year economic agreement was signed in Dec. 1976. Some Polish imports are subject to quota restrictions.

Six co-operative agreements were signed with the USA in 1974. Under these, a Polish–American Economic Council was set up. In 1976 the Federal Republic of Germany made available to Poland credits of DM 1,000m. at 2·5% interest, and is paying DM 1,300m. in settlement of Polish pension claims.

Tourism. In 1979, 9,131,000 tourists visited Poland (1,016,000 from the West) and 10,296,000 Polish citizens made visits abroad (601,000 to the West).

COMMUNICATIONS

Roads. In 1979 Poland had 146,911 km. of hard-surfaced roads. A road-improvement programme is bringing 75% of all roads up to suitability for heavy traffic. Number of motor vehicles: Passenger cars, 2,002,400 (of which, 1,955,300 private); lorries, 579,800 (122,600 private); motor cycles, 1,845,300.

In 1979 road transport carried 2,304m. passengers and 2,193m. tonnes of freight.

Railways. The length of the standard gauge railway system was (1980) 27,232 km (7,100 km electrified), comprising 23,975 km of 1,435 mm gauge, 2,860 km of narrow gauge, and 397 km of 1,524 mm (Soviet) gauge. In 1980 the railways carried 489m. tons of freight and (1979) 1,099m. passengers.

Aviation. In 1976 the state airline 'Lot' had 35 aircraft including Il-62s, operated 11 internal routes and in 1979 flew services to 36 countries. 1,993,000 passengers were flown and 17,000 tonnes of freight. There are British Airways, SABENA, KLM, PANAM, Alitalia, Swissair, Air France, Austrian Airlines and Lufthansa services to Okęcie (Warsaw) airport.

Shipping. The principal ports are Gdynia, Gdańsk (Danzig) and Szczecin (Stettin). A new port (Port Północny) to take ships of 100,000 DWT is under construction near Gdańsk. The merchant marine is grouped into Polish Ocean Lines (179 vessels totalling 1·04m. DWT in 1975), based on Gdynia and operating regular liner services, and the Polish Shipping Company based on Szczecin and operating cargo services. Poland also has a share in the Gdynia America Line. There are 4,572 km of inland navigable waterways. 23·2m. tonnes of freight were carried in 1979.

In 1979 the merchant marine had 322 vessels totalling 2,875,200 GRT (including 32 vessels over 20,000 tons). There are regular lines to London, Hull, China, Indonesia, Australia, Vietnam and some African and Latin-American countries.

Total shipping entering Polish ports in 1979 was 12,287 vessels of 32·9m. NRT. Freight traffic in 1979 was 39·2m. tonnes.

Pipeline. In 1979 there were 1,975km of oil pipeline.

Post and Broadcasting. In 1979 there were 8,125 post offices and 1,851,500 telephone subscribers, including over 1,180,000 private persons.

Polskie Radio i Telewizja broadcasts 3 programmes in Polish on long-, medium- and short-waves and on FM. There are 2 TV programmes. Colour programmes are transmitted by SECAM system. Wireless licences in 1979 numbered 8·56m.; television licences, 7·71m.

Cinemas and Theatres. In 1979 there were 2,255 cinemas, 98 theatre and 46 concert halls. Cinema attendance was 108m.; theatre and concert halls, 36m.

Newspapers (1979). There were 81 papers with an overall circulation of 2,650m.

2,350 periodicals were published. The Party newspaper is *Trybuna Ludu* (People's Tribune), weekend circulation 1·1m.

JUSTICE, RELIGION, EDUCATION AND WELFARE

Justice. A new penal code was adopted in 1969. Espionage and treason carry the severest penalties and severer punishment is provided for 'serious crimes'. For minor crimes there is more provision for probation sentences and fines.

There exist the following courts: The Supreme Court; voivodship, district and special courts. Judges and lay assessors are elected. The State Council elects the judges of the Supreme Court for a term of 5 years, and appoints the Prosecutor-General. The office of the Prosecutor-General is separate from the judiciary.

Family courts were established (1977) for cases involving divorce and domestic relations.

Religion. In 1978, 93% of the population was baptized into the Roman Catholic Church, and 78% of the population attended church regularly. Church–State relations are regulated by agreements of 1950, 1956 and 1972. A joint government-episcopal commission was reactivated in Sept. 1980, and religious broadcasting began. The Church has a university (Lublin), an Academy of Catholic Theology and a seminary in every diocese. Religious education of children is conducted in 'catechism centres', of which there were 18,254 in 1973–74.

The archbishop of Warsaw and Gniezno is the primate of Poland (since 1948, Stefan, Cardinal Wyszyński). The Vatican considers the archbishops of Lwów and Vilnius (incorporated in the USSR in 1940) as still being under Polish jurisdiction. In 1977 there were 5 archbishoprics, 27 dioceses and 6,716 parishes, 75 bishops, 19,642 priests, 30,162 monks and nuns and 14,162 churches and chapels. In 1975 some 4,000 students were studying for the priesthood. In 1973, 557 priests were ordained. In Oct. 1978 Cardinal Karol Wojtyla, archbishop of Cracow, was elected Pope as John Paul II.

On 28 June 1972 the Vatican adjusted the Church boundaries, to coincide with the State's western frontier ('Oder–Neisse line') and the 4 apostolic administrators in the former German territories became bishops.

Figures for other churches in 1977: Polish Autocephalous Orthodox, 4 dioceses, 233 parishes, 301 churches, 221 priests, 2 monasteries (460,000 adherents in 1975). Lutheran, 6 dioceses, 122 parishes, 310 churches, 100 parsons (100,000 adherents in 1975). Uniate, 3 dioceses, 84 parishes, 89 churches, 90 priests (200,000 adherents in 1975). Old-Catholic Mariavite, 3 dioceses, 42 parishes, 56 churches, 33 priests (30,000 adherents in 1975). Methodist, 5 districts, 66 parishes, 65 chapels, 39 parsons (4,133 adherents in 1975). United Evangelical, 222 congregations, 68 chapels, 215 parsons. Seventh-day Adventist, 124 communities, 122 churches, 66 parsons. Baptist, 127 congregations, 53 chapels, 60 parsons (2,300 adherents in 1975). Moslems, 6 communities, 2 mosques, 6 imams. Jews, 16 congregations, 24 synagogues (12,000 adherents in 1978). Epiphany World Mission, 80 communities, 157 churches, 427 priests.

Education. Basic education from 7 to 15 is free and compulsory. Free secondary education is then optional in general or vocational schools. Primary schools are organized in complexes based on wards under one director ('gmina collective schools'). In 1979–80 there were: Kindergartens, 25,872 with 1,180,000 pupils and 65,000 teachers; primary schools, 3,717 (of which 1,757 gmina collective schools) with 4,217,200 pupils and 196,400 teachers; secondary schools, 1,260 with 450,100 pupils and 23,100 teachers; vocational schools, 10,937 with 1,941,800 pupils and 76,800 teachers, and 91 institutions of higher education (including 10 universities, 18 polytechnics, 9 agricultural schools, 6 schools of economics, 11 teachers' training colleges and 10 medical schools) with 466,400 students (241,418 women in 1978–79) and 53,538 teaching staff.

Beginning in 1978–79 the 8-year primary school is being progressively replaced by a 10-year general secondary school.

Health. In 1979 there were 677 hospitals (including 39 mental hospitals) with

236,321 beds, 5,966 dispensaries and 3,205 health centres. There were 66,700 doctors and 18,000 dentists.

Social Security. In 1979, 130,845m. złotys were paid out in 4·17m. retirement pensions and 54·7m. złotys in family allowances and sick pay. Family allowances and pensions were raised on 1 Jan. 1981.

DIPLOMATIC REPRESENTATIVES

OF POLAND IN GREAT BRITAIN (47 Portland Place,
London, W1N 3AG)

Ambassador: Jan Bisztyga.

OF GREAT BRITAIN IN POLAND (Aleje Roz No. 1,
Warsaw)

Ambassador: K. R. C. Pridham, CMG.

OF POLAND IN THE USA (2640–16th St., NW,
Washington, D.C., 20009)

Ambassador: Romuald Spasowski.

OF THE USA IN POLAND (Aleje Ujazdowskie 29/31,
Warsaw)

Ambassador: William E. Schaufele, Jr.

OF POLAND TO THE UNITED NATIONS

Ambassador: Henryk Jaroszek.

Books of Reference

Statistical Information: The Central Statistical Office, Warsaw (Wawelska 1–3), publishes *Statistical News* (Aug. 1945–49; restarted Sept. 1956, bimonthly); *Statistical Studies and Works* (from 1950); *Statistics of Poland* (20 vols. 1946–51; restarted 1957 as *Biuletyn statystyczny*, monthly); *Rocznik statystyczny* (annual); *Concise Statistical Year Book of Poland.*

Constitution of the Polish People's Republic. Warsaw, 1964
Beneš, V. L., and Pounds, N. G. J., *Poland.* London, 1970
Blazynski, G., *Flashpoint Poland.* Oxford and New York, 1980
Bromke, A., and Strong, J. W. (eds.) *Gierek's Poland.* New York, 1973
Budrewicz, O., *Poland for Beginners.* 3rd ed. Warsaw, 1969
Bulas, K., and others, *English–Polish and Polish–English Dictionary.* 2 vols. The Hague, 1959–61
Burda, A., *Parliament of the Polish People's Republic.* Wrocław, 1978
Davies, N., *Poland, Past and Present: A Select Bibliography of Works in English.* Newtonville, 1977
Dziewanowski, M. K., *Poland in the Twentieth Century.* Columbia Univ. Press, 1977
Gieysztor, A., and others, *History of Poland.* Warsaw, 1969
Halecki, O., *A History of Poland.* 3rd ed. London, 1978.—(ed.), *Poland.* New York, 1957
Kieniewicz, S. (ed.) *History of Poland.* 2nd ed. Warsaw, 1979
Lane, D., and Kolankiewicz, G. (ed.) *Social Groups in Polish Society.* London, 1973
Leslie, R. F., (ed.) *The History of Poland since 1863.* CUP, 1980
Portes, R., *The Polish Crisis: Western Economic Party Options.* London, 1981
Raina, P., *Political Opposition in Poland, 1954–1977.* London, 1978
Roos, H., *A History of Modern Poland.* London, 1966
Wielka Encyklopedia Powszechna. 13 vols. Warsaw, 1962–70
Woiciechowski, B., *Foreign Trade of Poland: Its Growth, Structure and Economic System.* Warsaw, 1974
Zielinski, J. G., *Economic Reforms in Polish Industry.* OUP, 1973

National Library: Biblioteka Narodowa, Rakowiecka 6, Warsaw.

PORTUGAL

República Portuguesa

Capital: Lisbon
Population: 9·86m. (1979)
GNP per capita: US$2,020 (1978)

HISTORY. Portugal has been an independent state since the 12th century. The Portuguese Republic was proclaimed on 5 Oct. 1910 after the deposition of King Manuel II. A military dictatorship set up in 1926 was replaced in 1932 by a civil dictatorship under Antonio Salazar.

AREA AND POPULATION.

		Population	
	Area	*1970*	*1979*
	(sq. km)	*(census)*	*(estimate)*
Continent	88,500	8,108,214	9,337,800
Islands	3,131	540,155	524,900
Portugal (total)	91,631 [1]	8,648,369	9,862,700
Districts:			
Aveiro	2,708	548,039	638,600
Beja	10,240	204,816	184,700
Braga	2,730	612,710	719,900
Bragança	6,545	179,763	196,300
Castelo Branco	6,704	255,575	244,000
Coimbra	3,956	401,160	434,300
Évora	7,393	178,538	175,800
Faro	5,072	268,440	308,800
Guarda	5,496	213,538	216,300
Leiria	3,516	379,429	415,800
Lisboa	2,762	1,577,390	2,019,700
Portalegre	5,882	145,929	137,600
Porto	2,282	1,312,392	1,575,000
Santarém	6,689	430,885	460,300
Setúbal	5,152	467,946	626,200
Viana do Castelo	2,108	251,219	261,900
Vila Real	4,239	267,079	287,300
Viseu	5,019	413,366	435,300
Islands:			
Angra do Heroismo	703	86,458	77,400
Funchal	796	251,059	265,100
Horta	780	41,422	35,800
Ponta Delgada	852	161,216	146,600

[1] 34,861 sq. miles.

In 1970 (based on 20% of 1970 census figures) the population consisted of 4,109,360 males and 4,553,892 females, or 109 females to every 100 males.

The Azores islands are divided into 3 widely separated groups, with clear channels between, São Miguel together with Santa Maria being the most easterly. About 100 miles north-west of them lies the central cluster of Terceira, Graciosa, São Jorge, Pico and Faial. Still another 150 miles to the north-west are Flores and Corvo, the latter being the most isolated and primitive of the islands. São Miguel, Terceira and Pico are the largest, the first measuring 41 miles in length and 9 in breadth, and containing over half the total population of the archipelago. For political and administrative purposes they are divided into 3 districts, each sending its representatives to the Chamber at Lisbon. The capitals of the 3 districts are the chief seaports, Ponta Delgada on São Miguel Island, Horta on Faial Island and Angra do Heroísmo on Terceira Island.

Vital statistics for calendar years:

	Births	Still-births	Marriages	Divorces	Deaths	Emigrants
1977	181,064	2,682	91,403	...	96,201[1]	19,543
1978	167,467	2,319	81,111	...	96,380[1]	...
1979	160,318	2,154	...	...	92,987	...

[1] Provisional.

In 1978 the births included 87,124 (1977: 94,040) boys and 80,343 (1977: 87,024) girls; deaths, 49,725 (1977: 50,555) males and 46,655 (1977: 45,646) females.

At the census of 15 Dec. 1970 the population of Lisbon (capital) was 769,044 (metropolitan area, 1,034,141); Porto, 306,176 (metropolitan area, 693,170). According to 1970 census: Amadora, 66,189; Coimbra, 56,568; Barreiro, 53,200; Setúbal, 50,730; Vila Nova de Gaia, 50,219; Braga, 49,693; Almada, 38,714; Covilhã, 27,018; Guimarães, 25,113; Evora, 24,003; Matosinhos, 22,475; Moscavide, 21,647; Faro, 20,687.

In 1976, 837 emigrants went to Brazil and 7,496 to USA.

CONSTITUTION AND GOVERNMENT. Portugal has been an independent state since the 12th century; until 1910 it was a monarchy. The last King was Manuel II of the house of Braganza-Coburg, born 15 Nov. 1889, died 2 July 1932. On 5 Oct. 1910 the republic was proclaimed with Dr Teófilo Braga as the provisional president (5 Oct. 1910 to 24 Aug. 1911). Thereafter there were duly elected presidents, as follows:

Dr Manuel de Arriaga, 24 Aug. 1911–29 May 1915.[1]

Dr Joaquim Teófilo Braga, 29 May 1915–5 Oct. 1915.

Dr Bernardino Luis Machado Guimarães, 5 Oct. 1915–11 Dec. 1917.[2]

Dr Sidonio Bernardino Cardoso da Silva Pais, 11 Dec. 1917–14 Dec. 1918.[3]

Adm. João de Canto e Castro Silva Antunes, 16 Dec. 1918–5 Oct. 1919.

Dr António José de Almeida, 5 Oct. 1919–5 Oct. 1923.

Manuel Teixeira Gomes, 5 Oct. 1923–11 Dec. 1925.[1]

Dr Bernardino Luís Machado Guimarães, 11 Dec. 1925–1 June 1926.[1]

Provisional government, 1 June–29 Nov. 1926.

Marshal António Oscar Fragoso Carmona, 29 Nov. 1926–18 April 1951.

Marshal Francisco Higino Craveiro Lopes, 22 July 1951–9 Aug. 1958.

Rear-Adm. Américo de Deus Rodrigues Tomás, 9 Aug. 1958–25 April 1974.[2]

Gen. Antonio de Spinola, 25 April 1974–30 Sept. 1974.[4]

Gen. Francisco da Costa Gomes, 30 Sept. 1974–27 June 1976.[4]

Gen. Antonio Ramalho Eanes, 14 July 1976–

[1] Resigned. [2] Deposed. [3] Assassinated. [4] Not elected.

National flag: Vertical green and red, with the red of double width, and over all on the dividing line the national arms.

National anthem: A Portuguesa (words by Lopes de Mendonça, 1890; tune by Alfredo Keil).

In 1933 a constitution declared that the Portuguese state was a unitary and corporative republic, and the Constitution was adopted by plebiscite. The president was to be elected for 7 years by an electoral college, constituted of members of the National Assembly and the Corporative Chamber, with representatives of municipalities and oversea legislative councils.

On 25 April 1974 a military *coup* led by Gen Antonio de Spinola overthrew the government of Dr Caetano. Gen. Spinola announced on 26 April that there would be elections within 12 months, that political prisoners would be released and that there would be freedom of expression and the Press. The deposed President, Rear-Adm. Tomás and deposed Prime Minister, Dr Caetano, were taken to Madeira.

General Spinola resigned as President on 30 Sept. 1974.

Several military officers attempted to overthrow the Portuguese Government on 11 March 1975. Gen. Spinola went into exile but denied taking part in the *coup*.

At the legislative elections held on 2 Dec. April 1979 the Democratic Alliance gained 45% of the votes and 125 seats in the Assembly; Socialists, 27%; 73 seats; Communist Party, 19%, 47 seats; Democratic Popular Union, 2%, 1 seat.

At the presidential elections held on 7 Dec. 1980 Gen. Ramalho Eanes gained

56·43% of the votes cast; Gen. Soares Carneiro, 40·25%; Maj. Carvalho, 1·48%; Gen. Galvão de Melo, 0·84%; Col. Pires Veloso, 0·78%; Aires Rodrigues, 0·22%.

President: Gen. Antonio Ramalho Eanes.
Prime Minister: Francisco Pinto Balsemão.
Foreign Affairs: André Gonçalves Pereira. *European Intergration:* Álvaro Barreto. *Internal Administration:* Fernando do Amaral. *Defence:* Luis Azevedo Coutinho. *Justice:* José Meneres Pimentel. *Finance and Planning:* João Morais Leitão. *Education and Science:* Victor Crespo. *Labour:* Henrique Nascimento Rodrigues. *Social Affairs:* Carlos Macedo. *Agriculture and Fisheries:* António Cardoso e Cunha. *Trade and Tourism:* Alexandre Vaz Pinto. *Industry and Energy:* Ricardo Baião Horta. *Housing and Public Works:* Luis Barbosa. *Transport and Communication:* José Viana Baptista. *Quality of Life:* Augusto Ferreira do Amaral.

DEFENCE. Continental Portugal is divided into 4 military regions with headquarters at Coimbra, Oporto, Évora, Lisbon and insular Portugal territorial military command of Madeira and the Azores.

Every Portuguese citizen in good physical condition is subject to compulsory military service from the age of 20 to 45 years for a period of 15 months.

Pre-military training is entrusted to the *Colégio Militar* and the *Instituto Técnico e Profissional dos Pupilos do Exército*, with particular emphasis on physical and moral training of youths aged from 9 to 19 years.

Army. The Army consists of 1 infantry brigade, 1 tank, 3 cavalry and 15 infantry regiments, 4 artillery, 1 commando, 2 engineer and 1 signals regiments. Effective strength (1980), 37,000 all ranks. In 1979 the Republican Guard (*Guarda Nacional Republicana*) consisted of 13,000 all ranks, the Police (*Policia de Legurança Pública*) of 16,400 all ranks and the Fiscal Guard (*Guarda Fiscal*) of 6,900 all ranks.

Navy. The Navy comprises 3 small French-built diesel-powered patrol submarines, 17 frigates, 10 patrol vessels, 4 coastal minesweepers, 17 patrol launches, 1 sail training ship, 4 surveying vessels, 1 fleet oiler, 2 landing craft, 12 minor landing craft, 3 tugs and 1 harbour tanker. The navy personnel in 1981 totalled 14,000 officers and men including 2,000 marines.

Following the withdrawal from Africa there was a considerable disposal list of some 80 warships and the Navy became comparatively small.

Air Force. Formed in 1912, the Air Force has been independent since 1952, when it was combined with the naval air service and given equal status with the Army and Navy. In 1980, it had a strength of about 9,500 officers and men, with 34 first-line aircraft.

Equipment comprises a light strike unit of G-91Rs (to be replaced with A-7P Corsair IIs in 1981); 1 squadron of 5 C-130H Hercules for transport and secondary maritime surveillance duties; 2 transport squadrons, a survey squadron and an OCU equipped with 23 Spanish-built CASA 212 Aviocars, of which 4 are equipped for photographic duties; 32 Cessna 337 Skymasters for counter-insurgency and liaison duties; and a force of Puma and Alouette III helicopters. Other aircraft in service include Chipmunk piston-engined trainers, T-37C jet basic trainers, T-33, T-38A Talon and G-91T jet advanced trainers. Aircraft on order include 12 Agusta A109A light observation and anti-tank helicopters.

There is a parachute regiment of 2,000, which comes under Air Force command.

INTERNATIONAL RELATIONS
Membership. Portugal is a member of UN, EFTA, OECD and NATO.

ECONOMY
Planning. For 1977 investment included (in 1m. escudos): Education, 2·8m.; housing and urbanization, 15·2m.; agriculture, forestry and livestock, 5·1m.; transport and communications, 7·7m.

Budget. Revenue and expenditure for calendar years (in 1,000 contos):

	1971	1972	1973	1974	1975	1976	1977[1]
Revenue	36,930	42,103	50,034	61,274	79,683	125,373	159,173
Expenditure	36,648	40,868	48,894	63,415	86,620	124,688	159,173

[1] Estimates.

Main items of estimated revenue and expenditure (in 1,000 escudos):

Revenue	1977	Expenditure	1977
Current revenue	98,420,977	General charges	8,170,251
Direct taxes	30,087,501	Defence	18,179,855
Indirect taxes	61,209,070	Planning and economic	
Taxes, fines and other penalties	809,367	co-ordination	2,949,109
Property incomes	3,847,406	Domestic administration	16,431,665
Transferences	1,017,488	Justice	1,038,333
Permanent properties sale	11,826	Finance [1]	27,264,878
Services and other non-permanent		Foreign affairs	1,687,825
properties sale	1,428,319	Education and scientific	
Other current revenues	10,000	research	25,026,294
Capital revenues	54,347,681	Labour	365,017
Investment properties sale	7,426	Social affairs	14,241,713
Transferences	4,898,293	Commerce and tourism	1,951,285
Financial assets	604,711	Agriculture and fisheries	5,656,324
Financial viabilities		Industry and technology	2,449,978
Repositions non-deducted in	48,837,251	Public works	12,388,636
payment	1,152,141	Housing, urbanization and	
Memorandum item	4,820,636	construction	7,629,714
		Transport and communications	13,310,558
Total	158,741,435	Total	158,741,435

[1] Includes 13,355m. escudos for servicing the public debt.

On 31 Dec. 1978 the public debt was as follows: Consolidated debt: 4% (1940) (centenarios), 1,034,221 contos; 3½% (1941), 377,620 contos; 3% (1942), 2,536,189 contos; 2¾% (1943), 905,234 contos; public debt certificates (4%), 6·48m. contos; public debt certificates (5%), 6,143,500 contos. The internal redeemable debt was as follows: Titles, 203,614,010 contos; Caixa Geralde Depósitos, 232,517 contos. Public debt certificate: 8,553,337 contos. External redeemable debt: 48,665,401 contos.

Currency. The unit of currency is the *escudo* of 100 *centavos*, which contains 0·66567 gramme of fine gold. It was stabilized on 9 June 1931, and the paper currency re-linked to gold when the notes of the Bank of Portugal became payable in gold or its equivalent in foreign currency. 1,000 escudos is called a *conto*.

At present there are silver coins of 50, 25, 20, 10 and 5 escudos; 10, 5 and 2½ escudos (nickel and copper); alpaca coins of 1 and ½ escudo (50 centavos), bronze coins of 1 and ½ escudo and 20 and 10 centavos and aluminium coins of 10 centavos.

In March 1981, £1 = 125 *escudos*; US$1 = 56·90 *escudos*.

Banking. The one bank of issue for the mainland of the country and adjacent islands is the Bank of Portugal, founded 19 Nov. 1846. It was nationalized on 13 Sept. 1974 and its organic law came into force on 15 Nov. 1975. The capital of the bank was fixed at 200m. escudos and it is the central bank of the republic. The bank issues notes of 1,000, 500, 100, 50 and 20 escudos. All other Portuguese banks and insurance companies were nationalized on 14 March 1975.

The National Development Bank began operations on 4 Jan. 1960. Its total capital is 1,500m. escudos.

There are 11 commercial banks registered on the mainland and 1 in the islands, with cash in hand on 31 Dec. 1979, 9,913m. escudos; bills, loans and other credits, 551,644m. escudos; deposits, 656,965m. escudos. The deposits in the savings banks including the general deposit bank (state) amounted to 253,236m. escudos.

There are also 3 foreign banks, the Bank of Brazil, Bank of London and South America and Crédit Franco-Portugais.

Weights and Measures. The metric system of weights and measures is the legal standard.

ENERGY AND NATURAL RESOURCES

Electricity. Total production of electrical power in 1977 was 13,818m. kwh. (1978:

14,653,006); the installed capacity totalled 4,475,150 kva. (1978: 4,660,034), of which 2,683,604 kva. (1976: 2,523,604) were hydro-electric. New power plants were inaugurated in 1951 (Castelo do Bode, Venda Nova, Belver), 1953 (Salamonde), 1954 (Cabrill), 1955 (Caniçada and Bouçã), 1958 (Picote), 1960 (Miranda), 1964 (Bemposta), 1965 (Tàvora), 1970 (Drives and Bugalheira), 1971 (Carrapatelo) and 1975 (France, Fratel, Valeira).

Minerals. Portugal possesses considerable mineral wealth. Production in tonnes:

	1977	1978	1979		1977	1978	1979
Coal	195,265	180,101	179,118	Gold (refined)	0·275	0·284	0·320
Cupriferous pyrites	359,687	313,845	349,172	Wolframite	1,703	1,873	2,348
Tin ores	379	403	346	Hematite	21,669	19,761	22,198
Kaolin	72,860	73,555	80,039				

Uranium mining commenced in Aug. 1979. Annual production, 115 tonnes; reserves, 7,000 tonnes.

Agriculture. The following figures show the area (in hectares) and yield (in tonnes) of the chief crops:

	1976		1977		1978	
Crop	Area	Yield	Area	Yield	Area	Yield
Wheat	531,805	685,744	258,693	224,346	354,873	249,922
Maize	348,671	378,529	360,696	441,884	369,226	449,437
Oats	215,241	126,714	145,176	59,541	176,981	63,994
Barley	143,137	116,771	67,164	39,385	85,556	43,877
Rye	218,619	164,842	189,781	102,727	213,289	122,617
Rice	22,284	97,235	34,303	101,669	32,933	134,906
Dried beans	269,956	31,742	266,902	37,743	281,526	41,856
Potatoes	116,124	918,103	124,900	1,200,626	119,358	1,127,823

Wine production (in hectolitres), 1978, 6,361,959; 1977, 6,586,891; olive oil (hectolitres), 1978, 438,970; 1977, 327,347. In 1955, 228,996 hectolitres of port wine were exported; 1970, 352,090; 1972, 445,741; 1973 (tonnes), 48,244; 1974, 43,063; 1975, 37,713; 1976, 41,209; 1977, 48,622; 1978, 51,937.

Livestock (1979). Portugal (continental only) possessed 30,000 horses, 87,000 mules, 175,000 asses, 1m. cattle, 745,000 goats, 5·2m. sheep and 2·5m. pigs.

Forestry. Forest area covers 3m. hectares, of which 1·33m. are pine, 652,580 cork oak, 576,070 other oak, 213,960 eucalyptus, 29,730 chestnut and 366,660 other species.

Portugal surpasses the rest of the world in the production of cork (in tonnes): 1975, 133,707; 1976, 107,900; 1977, 177,759; 1978, 145,206. Most of it is exported crude; exports of cork and cork products totalled (in tonnes) 162,227 in 1972; 153,702 in 1973; 138,421 in 1974; 103,967 in 1975. Production of resin (in tonnes) was 137,662 in 1973; 146,968 in 1974; 137,774 in 1975; 100,319 in 1976; 123,968 in 1977; more than two-thirds are exported. Exports of turpentine (in tonnes) were 14,229 in 1972; 12,953 in 1973; 14,012 in 1974; 6,816 in 1975.

Fisheries. The fishing industry for the continent and adjacent isles is of importance. At 31 July 1979 there were 37,422 men and boys employed, with 10,936 boats. The sardine catch, 1979, was 90,523 tonnes valued at 1,480,113 contos; 1978, 83,548 tonnes valued at 1,184,299 contos. Exports of tinned sardines (in tonnes) amounted to 22,001 in 1974, 23,293 in 1975 and 28,577 in 1976. The most important centres of the sardine industry are at Matosinhos, Peniche, Setubal, Portimão and Olhão.

TRADE

Commerce. Imports for consumption and exports (exclusive of coin and bullion and re-exports) for calendar years, in 1,000 escudos:

	1974	1975	1976	1977	1978	1979
Imports	118,094,938	99,474,040	130,858,582	190,684,496	230,128,372	331,926,551
Exports	58,014,289	49,328,112	55,088,512	77,685,327	106,450,574	176,050,692

The principal articles of imports and exports (in 1,000 escudos):

Imports	1977	1978	1979	Exports	1977	1978	1979
Dried cod	821,592	718,719	663,187	Sardines	1,621,475	2,394,185	2,664,829
Wheat	2,012,385	4,181,804	6,411,769	Cork	5,711,320	7,249,380	10,230,318
Tobacco, un-				Wine	5,033,404	2,202,834	10,203,750
manuf'd	543,911	722,058	1,009,686	Olive oil	187,658	230,273	343,508
Oil seeds	5,034,665	6,366,582	8,966,033	Resin	1,006,660	1,794,162	2,210,914
Coffee	2,046,331	1,329,430	2,067,958	Turpentine	109,163	159,416	289,046
Sugar	2,326,586	2,326,831	2,729,241	Pyrites	239	49	61
Hides	1,706,014	1,567,487	3,687,319	Wolfram	680,720	777,757	860,717
Ammonium				Pit-props	42,612	51,878	56,649
sulphate	1,257	1,568	1,437	Pulpwood	3,648,988	3,219,750	5,804,639
Ingots (iron)	9,987,838	11,834,166	1,833,883	Fuel and			
Manuf'd (iron)	2,150,768	3,365,569	3,043,621	gas oils	277,470	835,410	3,097,363
Coal etc.	1,289,939	1,811,337	9,303,744	Rubber tyres			
Cotton, raw	7,245,961	6,915,167	10,046,152	and tubes	140,615	183,137	433,934
Dyes	554,487	731,411	973,123				
Motor vehicles	11,089,055	12,394,733	17,481,404				
Petroleum	23,302,379	12,917,867	51,505,979				
Fuel and gas oil	1,052,775	1,590,691	3,626,413				

The distribution of the imports and exports (in 1,000 escudos):

	Imports from			Exports to		
From or to	1977	1978	1979	1977	1978	1979
Angola	923,205	321,823	777,993	2,430,511	2,899,357	5,872,874
Belgium	5,921,075	7,325,535	9,164,821	2,840,793	3,442,644	5,631,832
France	15,400,463	20,724,091	28,389,285	6,176,074	9,598,629	17,079,442
Germany, Fed.						
Rep. of	23,689,269	31,905,410	41,822,440	9,177,774	14,044,798	21,575,018
Italy	10,228,884	12,626,116	17,054,902	2,904,048	6,124,198	10,361,450
Mozambique	844,476	893,300	2,029,206	1,377,490	1,527,000	1,128,784
Netherlands	8,494,849	8,147,004	11,113,963	2,658,880	4,391,544	8,242,548
Spain	9,217,698	12,513,460	19,258,798	1,608,881	2,255,396	5,068,528
UK	19,845,909	23,197,417	30,747,430	14,173,782	19,430,507	31,421,884
USA	19,438,003	27,151,118	38,958,800	5,211,029	7,512,813	10,783,354

Total trade between Portugal (excluding the Azores and Madeira) and UK (British Department of Trade returns, in £1,000 sterling):

	1975	1976	1977	1978	1979	1980
Imports to UK	201,081	199,124	229,889	256,222	338,337	335,112
Exports and re-exports from UK	157,606	223,317	299,321	286,488	307,670	389,849

Trade Unions. 331 unions had in 1976 a membership of 1,436,142.

Tourism. Tourism is of increasing importance for the invisible balance of payments. In 1977, 3m. visitors (1978: 3m.) spent about 15,514m. escudos (1978: 26,353m.); they included, in 1978, 327,872 British and 161,545 US citizens.

COMMUNICATIONS

Roads (1978). There were 33,634 km of road. There were registered in continental Portugal in 1979, 1,522,653 motor vehicles, including 92,030 motor cycles and 97,508 tractors; not counting vehicles used by the armed forces.

Railways. In 1979 total railway length was 3,588 km (1,668 mm and metre gauges), of which 430 km of broad-gauge was electrified. In 1979, 210,657,000 passengers were carried and 3·38m. tons of merchandise transported.

Aviation. Regular services connect Lisbon with Caracas, Rio de Janeiro, São Paulo, San Salvador, Recife, Montreal, Boston, New York, Sal Island, Bissau, Luanda, Maputo, Johannesburg, Kinshasa, Brazzaville, Madrid, Paris, London, Barcelona, Brussels, Luxembourg, Amsterdam, Copenhagen, Frankfurt, Dusseldorf, Milan, Rome, Lyon and Zürich. These lines in 1979 carried 2·1m. passengers and 40,307 tonnes of freight. The national airline changed its name to Air Portugal in 1979.

Shipping. In 1979, 13,659 vessels of 69,474,165 tons entered the ports (continental and islands). Of those entering 5,522 (14,598,113 tons) were Portuguese, 627 (5,796,988 tons) British and 612 (2,083,121 tons) Spanish. On 31 Dec. 1978 the merchant marine consisted of 99 transport vessels of 1,075,224 tons.

Post and Broadcasting (1978). The number of telegraph offices was 1,735. The State owned (1979) 5,526,742 km of telephone line and the *Telefones de Lisboa e Porto* (nationalized in 1977) owned 2,521,718 km of lines. Number of telephones was 1,305,580 (1979).

Radio Difusão Portuguesa broadcasts 3 programmes on medium waves and on FM as well as 3 regional services. *Radiotelevisão Portuguesa SARL* broadcasts 2 commercial TV programmes. *Radio Clube Português* is a commercial, nationwide network. In addition there are 6 local, commercial stations, operating on medium-waves. Radio Trans Europe is a high-powered short-wave station, retransmitting programmes of different broadcasting organizations, e.g., IBRA, Radio Canada and Deutsche Welle. Radio Free Europe also has relay facilities on short-waves in Portugal. Number of receivers (1975): Radio, 1,510,703; TV, 722,315.

Cinemas (1978). There were 448 cinemas with a seating capacity of 249,348.

Newspapers (1978). There were 34 daily newspapers with a combined circulation of 196,002; 15 of these, with a combined circulation of 120,641, appeared in Lisbon.

JUSTICE, RELIGION AND EDUCATION

Justice. Portuguese law distinguishes civil (including commercial) and penal, labour, administrative and fiscal law, each branch having its lower courts, courts of appeal and the Supreme Court.

The republic is divided for civil and penal cases into 214 *comarcas*; in every comarca there is a lower court. In the comarca of Lisbon there are 38 lower courts (22 for criminal procedure and 16 for civil or commercial cases); in the comarca of Oporto there are 21 lower courts (12 for criminal and 9 for civil or commercial cases); at Coimbra, Setúbal, Sintra and Vila Nova de Gaia there are 4 courts; at Almada, Braga, Cascais, Funchal, Guimarães, Leiria, Loures, Matosinhos, Oeiras, Santarém and Viseu there are 3 courts; 19 comarcas have 2 courts each. There are 4 courts of appeal (*Tribunal de Relação*) at Lisbon, Coimbra, Evora and Oporto, and a Supreme Court in Lisbon (*Supremo Tribunal de Justiça*).

Capital punishment was abolished completely after the new constitution of 1976. The prison population as at 31 Dec. 1979 was 5,385.

Religion. The predominant faith is the Roman Catholic, but there is freedom of worship, both in public and private, with the exception of creeds incompatible with morals and the life and physical integrity of the people.

Education. According to the latest statistics, 70% of the population over 7 years could read and write. Compulsory education has been in force since 1911. In 1978–79 there were 9,290 public primary schools with 870,712 pupils and 36,568 teachers. In 1977–78 private elementary schools numbered 627 with 57,635 pupils and 2,366 teachers. Basic preparatory schools numbered 1,765 with 294,266 pupils. Secondary instruction is supplied in two types of schools: in the *liceus* and other grammar schools, and in schools of technical instruction. In 1977–78 there were 422 *liceus* and 185 institutions of *liceu* standard, with 146,634 pupils, and 164 professional and technical secondary schools, with 77,335 pupils. There were also (1978–79) 19 schools which taught art activities (cinema, music and theatre) with 5,049 students. For higher education there are 6 universities; at Aveiro (founded in 1973), Lisbon (founded in 1911), Coimbra (founded 1290), Porto (founded 1911), Minho (founded 1974) and a new university at Lisbon (founded 1974). In 1978–79 the number of students at the universities was 50,579; and the Technical University at Lisbon (founded in 1930) had 11,837 students. There are also a military and a naval school, art schools in Lisbon and Porto (3,013 students) and 1 college of music (257 students). At upper level there are other colleges, public and private, which were attended by 15,309 and 2,477 students respectively.

DIPLOMATIC REPRESENTATIVES

OF PORTUGAL IN GREAT BRITAIN
(11 Belgrave Sq., London, SW1X 8PP)

Ambassador: João C. L. C. de Freitas-Cruz (accredited 6 March 1980).

OF GREAT BRITAIN IN PORTUGAL (35–39 Rua S.
Domingos à Lapa, Lisbon)
Ambassador: H. C. Byatt.

OF PORTUGAL IN THE USA (2125 Kalorama Rd., NW,
Washington, D.C., 20008)
Ambassador: João Manuel Hall Themido.

OF THE USA IN PORTUGAL (Ave. Duque de Loule 39, Lisbon)
Ambassador: Richard J. Bloomfield.

OF PORTUGAL TO THE UNITED NATIONS
Ambassador: Vasco Futscher Pereira.

Books of Reference

Statistical Information: The Instituto Nacional de Estatistica (Avenida Dr António José de Almeida, Lisbon) was set up in 1935 in succession to the Direcção-Geral de Estatistica. The Centro de Estudos Económicos and the Centro de Estudos Demográficos were affiliated to the Instituto in 1944. The main publications are the following:

Anuário Estatístico. Annuaire statistique. Annual, from 1875
Estatísticas do Comércio Externo. 2 vols. Annual from 1967 (replacing *Comércio Externo,* 1936–66, and *Estatística Comercial,* 1865–1935)
Censo da População de Portugal. 1864 ff. Decennial (latest ed. 1972)
Estatística da Organização Corporativa. 1938–49. Estatísticas da Organização Corporativa e Previdência Social. 1950 ff.
Estatísticas das Finanças, Publicas and *Estatísticas Nometárias.* 1969 ff. (replacing *Estatísticas Financeiras.* 1947–68 and *Situação Bancária,* 1919–46)
Estatísticas Agrícolas. Statistique Agricole. 1943–64; replaced by *Estatísticas Agrícolas e Alimentares.* From 1965. Annual
Estatísticas Industrials. 1967 ff. (replacing *Estatística Industrial. Statistique Industrielle.* 1943–66)
Estatísticas Demográficas. From 1967 (replacing *Anuário Demográfico,* 1929–66)
Boletim Mensal do Instituto Nacional de Estatística. Monthly since 1929
Centro de Estudos Económicos. Revista. 1945 ff.
Centro de Estudos Demográficos. Revista. 1945 ff.
Estatísticas das Contribuições e Impostos. Annual from 1967 (replacing *Anuário Estatístico das Contribuições e Impostos,* 1936–66)
Estatísticas da Educação. 1940 ff.
Estatísticas da Justica. 1968 ff. (replacing *Estatísticas Judiciária.* 1936–66)
Estatísticas das Sociedades. 1939 ff.
Estatísticas do Turismo. 1969 ff.
Estatísticas do Energia. 1969 ff.

Azevedo, Gonzaga de, *Historia de Portugal.* 6 vols. Lisbon, 1935–44
Bradford, S., *Portugal.* London, 1973
Brazão, E., *The Anglo-Portuguese Alliance.* London, 1957
Bruce, N., *Portugal: The Last Empire.* Newton Abbot, 1975
Ferreira, J. A., *Dictionário inglês-portugês.* 2 vols. Porto, 1948
Figueiredo, A. de, *Fifty Years of Dictatorship.* Harmondsworth, 1975
Guerreiro, A. D. (ed.), *Bibliografia sobre a economia portuguesa, 1948–69.* 21 vols. Lisbon, 1958–72
Harvey R., *Portugal: Birth of a Democracy.* London, 1978
Livermore, H. V., *Portugal: A Short History.* Edinburgh, 1973
Marques, A. H. de O., *History of Portugal.* 2 vols. Columbia Univ. Press, 1973
Mota, J. G., *A Resistência.* Lisbon, 1976
Pereira, A. M., *Organização politica e administrativa de Portugal.* Oporto, 1949
Robinson, R., *Contemporary Portugal.* London, 1979

Rodrigues, A., Borga, C. and Cardosa, M., *Portugal depois de Abril*. Lisbon, 1976
Rogers, F. M., *Atlantic Islanders of the Azores and Madeiras*. North Quincy, 1979
Salazar, A. de O., *Doctrine and Action: Integral and Foreign Policy of the New Portugal, 1928–39*. London, 1939.—*Discursos, 1928–58*. 5 vols. 5th ed. Coimbra, 1958.—*Política Portuguesa*. Santiago de Chile, 1952
Soares, M., *Le Portugal Bâillonné: Une Témoignage*. Paris, 1972
Sobel, L. A. (ed.), *Portuguese Revolution 1974–76*. New York, 1976
Spinola, A. de, *Portugal e o Futoro*. Lisbon, 1974
Stanislawski, D., *The Individuality of Portugal: A Study in Historical-Political Geography*. Univ. of Texas Press, 1959
Taylor, J. L., *Portuguese–English Dictionary*. London, 1959

National Library: Biblioteca Nacional, Campo Grande, Lisbon. *Director:* A. H. C. Marques.

OVERSEAS TERRITORIES

On 11 June 1951 the status of the Portuguese overseas possessions was changed from 'colonies' to 'overseas territories'. In 1972 greater autonomy was granted to the overseas territories. Angola and Mozambique became States instead of overseas provinces and had their own legislative assemblies. A Governor-General from each State would continue to be appointed by Lisbon but he would have the rank of Minister of State. On 6 Sept. 1961 all Africans were given full Portuguese citizenship, thereby achieving the same status as the inhabitants of Portuguese India and the other provinces. On 27 July 1974 Gen. Spinola announced that Portugal was prepared to offer independence to her African overseas territories of Angola, Mozambique and Portuguese Guinea (Guinea-Bissau) and to 'recognize the right of the populations of our overseas territories to take their destinies into their own hands'. A new constitutional law on decolonization, published on 24 July, formally repealed the section of 1933 Constitution which forbade the surrender of Portugal's overseas territories.

During 1974–76 independence was achieved by Angola (11 Nov. 1975); Cape Verde (5 July 1975); Guinea-Bissau (10 Sept. 1974); Mozambique (25 July 1975); São Tomé e Principe (12 July 1975).

East Timor was invaded by Indonesian forces on 7 Dec. 1975 after civil war had raged since August. On 17 July 1976 East Timor became a province of Indonesia and was renamed Loro Sae.

Approval has also been given for greater autonomy in Madeira and the Azores.

Books of Reference

Atlas de Portugal Ultramarino. Lisbon: Ministério das Colónais. 1948
Anuàrio Estatístico, II: Ultramar. Annuaire statistique, II: Outre-mer. Lisbon, 1961 ff (1950–60 under the title *Anuário Estatístico do Ultramar*)
Boletin da Agência Geral do Ultramar. Lisbon. Monthly
Documentacão ultramarina portuguesa. Centro de Estudos Históricos Ultramarinos. Lisbon, 1960
Andrade, A. A., *O Tradicional Anti-Racismo da Acção Civilizadora Portuguesa* (in Portuguese and English). Lisbon, 1953
Bahia dos Santos, F., *Unidade e cooperação entre a metrópole e o ultramar*. Lisbon, 1953
Boxer, C. R., *Race Relations in the Portuguese Empire*. OUP, 1963
Caetano, M., *Tradições, Princípios e Métodos da Colonização Portuguesa* (in Portuguese, French and English). Lisbon, 1951
Cunha, S., *O Sistema Português de Política Indigena*. Lisbon, 1953
Duffy, J., *Portuguese Africa*. Harvard Univ. Press, 1959.—*Portugal in Africa*. Harmondsworth, 1962
Freyer, G., *The Portuguese and the Tropics*. Lisbon, 1961
Galvão, H., and Selvagem, C., *Império Ultramarino Português*. 4 vols. Lisbon, 1950–53
Nogueira, F., *The United Nations and Portugal*. London, 1963
Oliveira, J. da Costa, *Aplicação de capitais nas provincias ultramarinas*. Lisbon, 1961
Pattee, R., *Portugal na Africa contemporânea*. Coimbra, 1959

MACAO

AREA AND POPULATION. Macao, in China, situated on a peninsula of the same name at the mouth of the Canton River, which came into possession of the Portuguese in 1557, forms with the 2 small adjacent islands of Taipa and Colôane a province, divided into 2 wards, each having its own administrator. The boundaries have not yet been definitely agreed upon; at present Portugal holds the territory in virtue of the treaty with China of 1 Dec. 1887. Talks took place in Macao in Oct. 1974, but no firm plans emerged for granting independence or decolonization. An 'organic statute' was published on 17 Feb. 1976. It defined the territory as a collective entity, *pessoa colectiva*, with internal legislative authority which, while remaining subject to Portuguese constitutional laws, would otherwise enjoy administrative, economic and financial autonomy. The area of the province is 16 sq. km (6 sq. miles). The population, according to the census of 1970, is 248,636. Estimate (1975) 260,227.

BUDGET. Revenue in 1972 was 464,510 contos; expenditure, 432,002 contos, and public debt, 258,244 contos. The currency is the *pataca.*

COMMERCE. The trade, mostly transit, is handled by Chinese merchants. Imports, in 1973, 3,713,976 contos; exports, 2,460,471 contos.

COMMUNICATIONS. The province is served by a Portuguese and various British and Dutch steamship lines. In 1977, 24,815 vessels of 7,151,287 gross tons entered the port.

The province has 1,577 km of telephone line (12,993 instruments in 1978). One government and 1 private commercial radio station are in operation on mediumwaves broadcasting in Portuguese and Chinese. Number of receivers (1974), 65,000.

EDUCATION. Education (1976–77) is provided at 23 secondary schools (9,701 pupils), 62 elementary schools, 4 secondary preparatory schools (1,191 pupils), 29 technical schools (4,360 pupils) and 2 art schools (22 pupils). A university has been established in Macao.

Governor: (Vacant).

Books of Reference

Anuário Estatístico de Macau. Macao
Brazáo, E., *Macau.* Lisbon, 1957

STATE OF QATAR

Capital: Doha
Population: over 200,000 (1978)
GNP per capita: US$12,740 (1978)

HISTORY. The State of Qatar declared its independence from Britain on 1 Sept. 1971, ending the Treaty of 3 Nov. 1916 which was replaced by a Treaty of friendship between the 2 countries.

AREA AND POPULATION. The State of Qatar, which includes the whole of the Qatar peninsula, extends on the landward side from Khor al Odeid to the boundaries of the Saudi Arabian province of Hasa. Area, about 4,247 sq. miles (11,000 sq. km); population estimate in 1978 over 200,000, including a number of migrant labourers from neighbouring states.

The capital is Doha (population, 130,000), which is the main port. Other towns are Dukhan, the centre of oil production, Umm Said, oil-terminal of Qatar and Ruwais, Wakra, Al-Khour and Umm-Bab.

RULER. *The Amir:* HH Shaikh Khalifa bin Hamad Al-Thani, assumed power on 22 Feb. 1972. On 31 May 1977, HH Shaikh Hamed bin Khalifa Al-Thani, was appointed Heir Apparent of the State of Qatar, the portfolio of Minister of Defence was added to his existing responsibility of Commander-in-Chief of the Armed Forces.

Foreign Minister: Shaikh Suhaim bin Hamad Al-Thani.
Flag: Maroon, with white serrated border on hoist.

DEFENCE

Army. The Army consists of 2 armoured car regiments, 1 Guards' infantry battalion, 1 tank, 2 infantry and 2 artillery battalions. Personnel (1980) 4,000.

Air Force. The Air Force has 2 Hunter jet fighter-bombers, 1 Hunter 2-seat trainer, 4 Commando, 2 Whirlwind, 2 Gazelle and 3 Lynx helicopters, 1 Islander twin-engined light transport and Tigercat surface-to-air missile systems. Under delivery are 6 Alpha Jet armed trainers and some Puma helicopters. Personnel (1981) 300.

INTERNATIONAL RELATIONS

Membership. Qatar is a member of UN and the Arab League.

ECONOMY

Budget. Revenue (1980) 13,745m. riyals of which oil 12,621m.; expenditure (1980) 12,174 riyals.

Currency. On 13 May 1973 the Qatar *Riyal* was introduced. In March 1981, £1 = 7·91 *riyals*, US$1 = 3·64 *riyals*.

Banking. Banks operating in Qatar include: Qatar National Bank, the Commercial Bank of Qatar (also Qatari-owned), the Arab Bank, Bank Al Mashrek, Bank Saderat Iran, Banque de Paris et des Pays Bas, British Bank of the Middle East, the Chartered Bank, the First National City Bank, Grindlays Bank, the Bank of Oman and United Bank.

ENERGY AND NATURAL RESOURCES

Oil. On 9 Feb. 1977 Qatar gained national control over its 2 natural resources, oil and gas, with the signing of an agreement with Shell Qatar over the procedure for the transfer to the State of the company's remaining 40% share. A similar agreement had been reached with the Qatar Petroleum Co. on 16 Sept. 1976.

The Qatar General Petroleum Corporation (QGPC) had been established by decree in July 1974 to assume overall responsibility for the State's domestic and foreign oil interests and operations. On 16 Oct. 1976 the Qatar Petroleum Producing

Authority (QPPA) was established to serve as the executive arm of the QGPC. A subsidiary of the QGPC, the QPPA, oversees onshore and offshore oil operations.

Production, 1980, 84,233,605m. bbls. Reserves (1974) 6,000m. bbls.

The North West Dome oilfield is being developed which contains 12% of the known world gas reserves.

Agriculture. 10% of the working population is engaged in agriculture and between Jan.–May Qatar is self-sufficient in fruit and vegetables.

Livestock (1979): Cattle, 6,000; camels, 10,000; sheep, 43,000; goats, 50,000; poultry, 58,000.

INDUSTRY AND TRADE

Industry. Several major projects have been established or were under construction in 1979 including the production of ammonia, urea and cement. The Qatar Iron and Steel Co. factory was opened in April 1978.

Commerce. In 1979 exports totalled 13,537·9m. riyals, and imports, 5,377·7m. riyals.

Total trade between Qatar and UK (British Department of Trade returns, in £1,000 sterling):

	1976	1977	1978	1979	1980
Imports to UK	248,813	100,761	30,437	40,503	44,654
Exports and re-exports from UK	86,696	116,611	90,781	101,486	101,898

Tourism. Tourism was being developed in 1978.

COMMUNICATIONS

Roads. There are 550 miles of road.

Aviation. The Gulf Aviation Co., Ltd (owned equally by Qatar, Bahrain, Oman and the UAE), operates daily services from Bahrain; British Airways, Middle East and about 15 other airlines operate regular international flights from Doha airport.

Shipping. Ships of several lines used to call at Umm Said; with the completion in 1969 of the new Doha port, it has become the main port of Qatar.

Post. Telephone and radio-telephone services connect Qatar with Europe and America; there were 29,217 telephones in Jan. 1978. An earth satellite station was inaugurated in March 1976.

Cinemas. In 1978 there were 8 cinemas with a seating capacity of 7,000.

EDUCATION AND WELFARE

Education. There were, in 1975–76, 17,479 boys at 63 elementary schools with 1,056 teachers; 59 girls' schools had 13,680 pupils and 896 teachers. Total number of pupils in schools (1976–77) 32,400. In addition, 1,915 boys and 895 girls were attending 4 secondary schools. Students in higher institutions and universities numbered 1,800, of whom 767 attended the 2 colleges of education in Doha, the nucleus of the University of the Lower Gulf. 231 university students graduated, including 117 from the colleges of education. Post-graduate students abroad numbered 53.

Health. There are 5 hospitals (including 1 for women and 1 for gynaecology and obstetrics) with a total of 682 beds. The 660-bed hospital at Doha is nearing completion and clinics are being built throughout the State.

DIPLOMATIC REPRESENTATIVES

OF QATAR IN GREAT BRITAIN (27 Chesham Pl., London, SWIX 8HG)

Ambassador: Sharida Sa'ad Jubran Al Ka'abi (accredited 26 March 1981).

OF GREAT BRITAIN IN QATAR (Doha, Qatar)

Ambassador: C. T. Brant, CVO.

OF QATAR IN THE USA (600 New Hampshire Ave., NW, Washington, D.C., 20037)

Ambassador: Abdullah Saleh Al-Mana.

OF THE USA IN QATAR (Farig Bin Omran, Doha, Qatar)

Ambassador: Charles E. Marthinsen.

OF QATAR TO THE UNITED NATIONS

Ambassador: Jasim Yousif Jamal.

Books of Reference

Qatar into the Seventies. Information Ministry, Doha, 1973
El Mallakh, R., *Qatar: The Development of an Oil Economy.* New York, 1979

ROMANIA

Republica Socialistă România

Capital: Bucharest
Population: 22·05m. (1979)
GNP per capita: US$1,750 (1978)

HISTORY. 1918 is celebrated as the year of foundation of the 'unitary national Romanian state'. For the history and constitution of Romania from 1859 to 1947, *see* THE STATESMAN'S YEAR-BOOK, 1947, pp. 1187–89. On 30 Dec. 1947 King Michael abdicated under Communist pressure and parliament proclaimed the 'People's Republic'.

AREA AND POPULATION. The area of Romania is 237,500 sq. km (91,699 sq. miles). Pre-war Romania had an area of 113,918 sq. miles. Population at censuses: 1930, 18,057,208 (14,280,729 within present-day Romania); 1948, 15,872,624 (48·3% male); 1966, 19,103,163 (49% male, 38·2% urban); 1975, 21,559,416 (49·3% male, 47·5% urban).

On 1 July 1979 the population was 22·05m., density per sq. km, 92. Vital statistics, 1978 (per 1,000 population): Live births, 19·1; deaths, 9·7; marriages, 9·2; divorces, 1·52; stillborn (per 1,000 live births), 9·3; infant mortality (per 1,000 live births), 30·3; population growth rate, 10 per 1,000.

Administratively, Romania is divided into 40 counties (*judeţ*), 236 towns (*oraş*) (of which 56 are municipalities) and 2,705 local authorities (*comune*). The capital is Bucharest (Bucureşti) a municipality with county status.

District	Area in sq. km	Population 1979	Capital	Population 1979
Alba	6,231	413,715	Alba Iulia	46,020
Arad	7,654	510,686	Arad	172,669
Argeş	6,801	647,209	Piteşti	133,179
Bacău	6,603	684,696	Bacău	141,981
Bihor	7,535	641,908	Oradea	178,407
Bistriţa-Năsăud	5,305	297,672	Bistriţa	51,467
Botoşani	4,965	461,495	Botoşani	75,542
Braşov	5,351	631,161	Braşov	299,172
Brăila	4,724	386,713	Brăila	203,983
Buzău	6,072	517,543	Buzău	106,738
Caraş-Severin	8,514	392,117	Reşiţa	90,698
Cluj	6,650	727,772	Cluj-Napoca	274,095
Constanţa	7,055	643,167	Constanţa	279,308
Covasna	3,705	211,011	Sf. Gheorghe	51,210
Dîmboviţa	3,738	512,269	Tîrgovişte	71,533
Dolj	7,413	758,594	Craiova	220,893
Galaţi	4,425	600,460	Galaţi	252,884
Gorj	5,641	355,128	Tîrgu Jiu	70,629
Harghita	6,610	341,230	Miercurea Ciuc	38,097
Hunedoara	7,016	530,005	Deva	68,290
Ialomiţa	6,211	385,128	Slobozia	35,207
Iaşi	5,469	745,778	Iaşi	262,493
Ilfov	8,225	790,269	Bucharest (*see below*)	
Maramureş	6,215	510,484	Baia Mare	112,893
Mehedinţi	4,900	326,688	Drobeta-Turnu Severin	80,114
Mureş	6,696	607,116	Tîrgu Mureş	129,284
Neamţ	5,890	547,580	Piatra Neamţ	84,192
Olt	5,507	529,799	Slatina	54,954
Prahova	4,694	835,822	Ploieşti	207,009
Satu Mare	4,405	400,074	Satu Mare	108,152
Sălaj	3,850	265,440	Zalău	36,158
Sibiu	5,422	492,181	Sibiu	156,854
Suceava	8,555	648,319	Suceava	66,857

District	Area in sq. km	Population 1979	Capital	Population 1979
Teleorman	5,872	525,826	Alexandria	38,296
Timiş	8,678	708,861	Timişoara	281,320
Tulcea	8,430	259,307	Tulcea	67,091
Vaslui	5,300	447,623	Vaslui	44,134
Vîlcea	5,705	419,609	Rîmnicu Vîlcea	75,070
Vrancea	4,863	377,753	Focşani	62,275
Bucharest [1]	605	1,960,097	Bucharest [2]	1,832,015

[1] Total conurbation.   [2] Central area.

Ethnic groups: In 1978 there were 1·7m. Hungarians, mainly in Transylvania, and and some 400,000 Germans. The official language is Romanian.

CONSTITUTION AND GOVERNMENT. The present Constitution was adopted on 21 Aug. 1965 and supersedes those of 13 April 1948 and 24 Sept. 1952. Under it Romania becomes a 'Socialist' (as opposed to 'People's') Republic. The leading role of the Communist Party is reaffirmed. The Grand National Assembly of 369 is elected for 5 years (before 1972 for 4 years). It holds short sessions twice a year, and between sessions delegates its legislative rights to the State Council (the President, head of state; 4 Vice-presidents, 1 secretary and 20 members).

All citizens of 18 and over have the right to vote and electoral law provides for the nomination of 'one or more' candidates in each constituency.

Local government is carried out by people's councils at all administrative levels (*see* p. 1018) elected at the same time as the Grand National Assembly. In 1980, 123,243 candidates stood for 61,772 seats.

The National Council of the Socialist Democracy and Unity Front functions as a consultative body on home and foreign affairs. It has central and local councils in which workers, peasants, professional bodies, ethnic minorities and the Communist Party are represented. It replaces the Popular Democratic Front (*see* STATESMAN'S YEAR-BOOK, 1979–80).

Elections were held on 30 Nov. 1952, 3 Feb 1957, 5 March 1961, 7 March 1965, 2 March 1969, 9 March 1975 and 9 March 1980.

At the 1980 elections 99·9% of the 15·6m. electorate voted, 98·52% of these for the Socialist Democracy and Unity Front. 2 candidates stood in 151, and 3 in 39, constituencies.

In 1965 the Romanian Workers' Party was renamed the Romanian Communist Party. The Party Congress elects the General Secretary, and its Central Committee elects the Executive Political Committee (27 full and 18 candidate members), the Permanent Bureau (*see below*) and the Secretariat (General Secretary and 8 secretaries). The Party had 2,960,917 members in 1980 (of whom 53% workers, 28% women).

President of the Republic and Chairman of the State Council: Nicolae Ceauşescu, succeeded Chivu Stoica in Dec. 1967. *Vice-Chairmen:* Stefan Voitec, Gheorghe Radulescu, Maria Ciocan, Petru Enache, Iosif Kovacs.

In April 1981 the Permanent Bureau of the Party consisted of: Nicolae Ceauşescu (*General Secretary*); Ştefan Andrei; Iosif Banc; Emil Bobu; Cornel Burtică; Virgil Cazacu; Elena Ceauşescu; Nicolae Constantin; Constantin Dăscălescu; Paul Niculescu; Gheorghe Oprea; Ion Păţan; Dumitru Popescu; Gheorghe Rădulescu; Ilie Verdeţ.

Council of Ministers (April 1981). *Chairman* (*Prime Minister*): Ilie Verdeţ. *First Deputy Prime Ministers:* Elena Ceauşescu, Gheorghe Oprea, Ion Dinca; *Deputy Prime Ministers:* Janos Fazekaş, Cornelia Filipaş, Col.-Gen. Ion Ioniţa, Cornel Burtică (*Minister of Foreign Trade*); Nicolas Constantin (*Chairman, State Planning Committee*); Angelo Miculescu (*Minister of Agriculture*); Paul Niculescu (*Minister of Finance*); Ion Păţan (*Minister of Technical Supplies*); Virgil Trofin (*Minister of Mines, Oil and Geology*). Ştefan Andrei (*Foreign Minister*); Maj.-Gen. Constantin Olteanu (*Defence Minister*); Gheorghe Homoştean (*Minister of the Interior*).

In July 1970 Romania signed a treaty of friendship, co-operation and mutual assistance with the USSR. A previous such treaty had expired in 1968. Since the mid-1960s Romania has been taking an increasingly independent stand in foreign affairs, and in Nov. 1978 publicized its refusal of a Soviet request to intregrate its armed forces into a more unified Warsaw Pact command structure and step up its financial contributions.

National flag: Three vertical strips of blue, yellow, red, with the national arms in the centre.

National anthem: Trei culori (Three colours). Introduced, 1977. Music by Ciprian Porumbescu.

DEFENCE. Defence is the responsibility of the Defence Council, which is controlled by the Council of State and headed by President Ceauşescu. Defence spending was reduced by 2,000m. lei in 1981.

Army. Service is 16 months. Strength in 1980 was 140,000 men plus 37,000 in paramilitary forces (frontier troops, internal-security troops, militia, military firemen).

Units of the Ministry of the National Defence are under one of the 3 military regions of Iaşi, Bucharest and Cluj. There are 2 tank and 8 motorized divisions (not all at full strength), 3 mountain brigades, 2 artillery brigades, 2 SSM brigades and 1 airborne regiment. The AA artillery consists of 2 regiments. There are 1,700 T-34, T-54, T55 and T-72 tanks. A Territorial Defence Force was set up in 1970.

Navy. The fleet comprises 3 coastal escorts, 5 missile boats, 32 torpedo boats, 28 fast gunboats, 3 old patrol vessels, 4 old minesweepers, 16 inshore minesweepers, 2 training ships, 8 minesweeping boats, 40 river patrol craft, 12 landing craft, 2 survey vessels, 10 transports, 3 oilers and 4 tugs. Headquarters of the Navy is at Mangalia, and of the Danube flotilla at the main river port of Brăila. The naval school is in Constanţa. Personnel in 1981 totalled 10,000 officers and ratings including 2,000 Coastal Defence. National service is 2 years.

Air Force. Service is 2 years. The Air Force numbers some 34,000 men, with 290 combat aircraft. These are organized into 5 fighter regiments with MiG-21 fighters and 2 ground-attack regiments and other close-support squadrons with MiG-17 fighters. There are also 310 reconnaissance and training aircraft, transports and helicopters. Under delivery are 1AR-93 close-support/interceptors and 90 Puma helicopters. 'Guideline' and 'Gaskin' surface-to-air missiles are operational, and short-range surface-to-surface missiles have been displayed.

INTERNATIONAL RELATIONS

Membership. Romania is a member of UN, Comecon and the Warsaw Pact.

ECONOMY

Planning. Annual growth targets of the sixth 5-year plan (1981–85): GNP, 9%; national income, 10%; industrial production, 10%; agricultural production, 24·5–27·5%. Romania is committed to intensive industrialization and President Ceauşescu admitted in Feb. 1981 that agriculture had been neglected. Industries scheduled for particular development: machine-building, iron and steel, non-ferrous metals, chemicals and electric power. A 10-year programme introduced in 1980 is designed to make Romania self-sufficient in energy. (For previous plans *see* THE STATESMAN'S YEAR-BOOK, 1976–77.)

There is no move towards any fundamental decentralization of planning authority but limited devolutions of reponsibility in an attempt to improve efficiency were introduced in 1967 and 1979. There are 102 economic units intermediate between ministeries and enterprises.

Budget. Revenue and expenditure (in 1m. lei) for calendar years:

	1973	1974	1975	1976	1977	1978	1979
Revenue	175,972	210,111	238,553	254,528	281,980	300,836	339,309
Expenditure	168,091	207,322	236,169	250,148	280,423	299,314	337,629

In 1979 sources of revenue (in 1m. lei) included: Profit payments of state enterprises, 149,397; turnover tax, 34,674; personal taxes, 35,397; insurance contributions, 29,987. Expenditure: National economy, 241,155; social and cultural, 65,557; defence, 11,835.

Revenues of local councils yielded 53,127m. lei in 1979; expenditure, 51,545m.

In 1974 a Court of Preventive Financial control was set up to oversee most official transactions and combat waste and corruption.

By an agreement signed 12 Jan. 1976 Romania is to pay £3·5m. as 'full and final settlement' of defaulted Romanian bonds held by UK citizens in 4 annual instalments of £875,000 starting at the end of 1976. Payments of £1·25m. in settlement of UK claims arising out of the peace treaty were completed by 31 Jan. 1967.

Currency. The monetary unit is the *leu*, pl. *lei* (of 100 *bani*). On 1 Feb. 1954 the gold content of the leu was changed to 0·148112 gramme of fine gold. Exchange rates: £1 = 14·4 lei; US$1 = 6 lei; 1 rouble = 6·67 lei. Tourist rates: £1 = 28 lei; US$1 = 18 lei; 1 rouble = 8·30 lei.

Bank-notes of 1, 5, 10, 25, 50 and 100 *lei* are issued by the National Bank, and there are coins of 5, 10, 15 and 25 *bani* and 1, 3 and 5 *lei*.

Banking. The National Bank of Romania (founded 1880, nationalized 1946) is the State Bank under the Minister of Finance. Half its profits are allotted to the State budget. There are also a Bank of Investments, a Foreign Trade Bank, an Agriculture and Food Industry Bank and a Savings Bank. In 1972 Romania joined IMF. The US Export-Import Bank has granted Romania borrowing rights. In 1974 the American bank Manufactures Hanover Trust Co. opened a branch in Bucharest, the first Western bank to do so in a Communist country.

Weights and Measures. The Gregorian calendar was adopted in 1919. The metric system is in use. Tubes and pipes are measured in *tol* (= 1 inch).

ENERGY AND NATURAL RESOURCES

Electricity. Installed electric power in 1978: 14,145,000 kw.; output (1979), 64,933m. kwh. A joint Romanian–Yugoslav hydro-electric power plant on the Danube at the 'Iron Gates' was opened in 1972; yearly output is 11,000m. kwh. A nuclear power programme has been subject to cut-backs and delays. A nuclear power station (capacity 660,000 kw.) is due to open in 1985.

Oil. The oilfields are in the Prahova, Bǎcau, Gorj, Crişana and Argeş districts. Petrol prices were raised by 60% and restrictions placed on official and private car use in 1979. Oil imports are approximately equivalent to domestic production. Oil reserves are expected to be exhausted by the mid-1990s.

Minerals. The principal minerals are oil and natural gas, salt, brown coal, lignite, iron and copper ores, bauxite, chromium, manganese and uranium. Salt is mined in the lower Carpathians and in Transylvania; production in 1979 was 4·7m. tonnes.

Output, 1978 (and 1979) (in 1,000 tonnes): Iron ore, 2,511 (2,523); crude oil, 13,724 (12,323); coal, 31,454 (34,888); methane gas (cu. metres), 28,973m. (27,189m.). The share of coal in the overall production of energy rose from 28% in 1975 to 40% in 1980, and is expected to reach 60% by 1990.

Agriculture. There were 14·97m. hectares of agricultural land in 1979, including (in 1,000 hectares): Arable, 9,817; meadows and pasture, 4,486; vineyards and fruit trees, 664.

Production in 1979 (in 1,000 tonnes): Wheat and rye, 4,716; barley, 2,043; maize, 12,425; potatoes, 4,562; oilseed crops, 956; sugar-beet, 6,109.

Livestock (1980): 6·5m. cattle, 10·9m. pigs, 15·8m. sheep and 95·4m. poultry.

In 1979 there were 4,923 collective farms, with 9m. hectares of land (7·2m. arable; 935,000 in private plots). State farms numbered 396, with 2m. hectares of land, of which 1·65m. hectares were arable. A further 2·5m. hectares of land were in the hands of other state agricultural organizations. There were 709 agriculture mechanization stations with 137,521 tractors. Individual holdings totalled 1·41m. hectares. The National Union of Agricultural Co-operatives promotes self-management in collective farms, and gives guidance on planning and marketing. A minimum income is guaranteed to peasants. In 1979 there were 2,253,000 hectares of irrigated land.

Forestry. Total forest area was 6·33m. hectares in 1979. In 1978, 70,733 hectares were afforested.

INDUSTRY AND TRADE

Industry. Output of main products in 1978 (and 1979) (in 1,000 tonnes): Pig-iron,

8,155 (8,879); steel, 11,779 (12,909); steel tubes, 1,419 (1,500); blast furnace coke, 3,458 (3,066); rolled steel, 8,958 (9,482); chemical fertilizers, 2,469 (2,522); washing soda, 899 (893); caustic soda, 725 (704); paper, 794 (819); cement, 13,892 (14,656); sugar, 555 (525); edible oils, 341 (375); butter, 44 (40). Fabrics (in 1m. sq. metres): Cotton, 717 (707); woollens, 123 (125); man-made fibres, 197,467 (196,200). In 1,000 units: Radio sets, 664 (757); TV sets, 516 (574); bicycles, 214 (205); washing machines, 272 (294); refrigerators, 451 (446); motor cars, 81,375 (75,020); footwear, 99m. pairs (104m.).

Labour. The employed population in 1979 was 10·32m., of whom 3·17m. worked in agriculture and 4·52m. industry and building. Wage differentials are in accordance with the 'social evaluation' of the work and a range of incentives for productivity. The average monthly wage was 2,256 lei in 1980. Minimum monthly wage 1,425 lei in 1980. The working week is of 44 hours with alternate Saturdays free. Men retire at 62, women at 57. The chairman of the trade union organization exercises the functions of Minister of Labour. An independent trade union movement which emerged in Feb. 1979 has been subject to police prosecution.

Commerce. Some 60% of external trade is with Communist countries (15% with the USSR).

In 1979 exports totalled 43,466m. lei and imports 48,792m. lei.

Principal exports in 1979 were (in 1,000 tonnes): Petroleum products, 7,396; cement, 2,738; cereals, 628; tractors, 41,882 units; oilfield equipment, 1,669m. lei; equipment for cement mills, 36m. lei; equipment for chemical factories, 223m lei; shipbuilding, 204m. lei. Principal imports (in 1,000 tonnes): Iron ore, 15,065; industrial coke, 2,896; rolled ferrous metals, 1,511; electrical equipment, 1,262m. lei; motor cars, 13,658 units, and industrial and agricultural equipment.

In 1979 Romania's main trading partners (trade in 1m. lei) were: USSR (14,529), Federal Republic of Germany (8,342), German Democratic Republic (5,657), USA (5,049), China (4,720), Iraq (4,441), Czechoslovakia (4,072).

Total trade between Romania and UK for calendar years (British Department of Trade returns, in £1,000 sterling):

	1976	1977	1978	1979	1980
Imports to UK	49,514	52,448	51,724	65,914	64,795
Exports and re-exports from UK	49,173	80,477	74,965	70,372	98,914

On 18 Sept. 1975 Romania and the UK signed a 10-year economic co-operation agreement. In Nov. 1976 Romania and the USA signed a 10-year commercial agreement. Both the UK and the USA have joint economic commissions with Romania. Romania's indebtedness to the West was estimated at US$2·22m. in 1978.

Joint companies with Western firms have been set up; at least 51% of the capital must be in Romanian hands. The 'Romconsult' and 'Publicom' agencies will carry out respectively market research and publicity campaigns on behalf of foreign firms.

Romania has a trade link with EEC under the generalized preference system.

Agreements with the EEC on industrial products and establishing a joint economic commission were reached in March 1980.

On 1 Jan. 1975 a 2-tier tariff system was introduced, graded according to the grant of most favoured nation status to Romania.

COMMUNICATIONS

Roads. There were in 1979, 14,676 km of national roads, of which 11,369 km were modernized. Freight carried, 414m. tons; passengers, 1,026m.

Railways. Length of route (1,435 mm gauge) in 1979 was 11,113 km and (narrow-gauge), 559 km. A total of 2,202 km is electrified. Freight carried, 273m. tons; passengers, 351m.

Aviation. TAROM (*Transporturi Aeriene Române*), the state airline, operates all internal services, and also services to Amsterdam, Athens, Beirut, Belgrade, Berlin, Brussels, Budapest, Cairo, Cologne, Copenhagen, Düsseldorf, Frankfurt, Istanbul, London, Moscow, Paris, Prague, Rome, Sofia, Tel-Aviv, Vienna, Warsaw and Zürich. Bucharest is also served by British Airways, PANAM, SABENA, Aeroflot,

Air France, Interflug, ČSA, MALEV, Austrian Air Lines, SAS, Lot, TABSO, El Al, Alitalia, Lufthansa and Swissair. An air agreement with China was signed in 1973.

Bucharest's airports are at Băneasa (internal flights) and Otopeni (international flights; 12 miles from Bucharest). Air transport in 1979 carried 1,908,000 passengers and 56,000 tons of freight.

Shipping. The main ports are Constanţa on the Black Sea and Galaţi and Brăila on the Danube. A new port is under construction at Mangalia on the Black Sea. The largest shipyard is at Galaţi.

In 1975 the mercantile marine (NAVROM) had 94 ships totalling 1,365,000 DWT. In 1979 sea-going transport carried 13·22m. tons of freight; river transport, 9·7m. tons.

Post and Broadcasting. *Radio-televiziunea Româna* broadcasts 3 programmes on medium-waves and FM. There are also 6 regional programmes, including transmission in Hungarian, German and Serbo-Croat. Two TV programmes are broadcast. Number of telephone subscribers, in 1979, 1,479,627. Radio receiving sets, in 1979, 3·2m.; TV sets, 3·6m.

Cinemas and Theatres. There were, in 1979, 5,785 cinemas and 147 theatres and concert halls. 28 full-length feature films were made in 1979.

Newspapers. There were, in 1979, 59 newspapers and 431 periodicals. These figures include 38 in minority languages. The party newspaper is *Scînteia* ('The Spark').

JUSTICE, RELIGION, EDUCATION AND WELFARE

Justice. Justice is administered by the Supreme Court, the 40 district courts, and lower courts. Lay assessors (elected for 4 years) participate in most court trials, collaborating with the judges. The Procurator-General exercises 'supreme supervisory power to ensure the observance of the law' by all authorities, central and local, and all citizens. The Procurator's Office and its organs are independent of any organs of justice or administration, and only responsible to the Grand National Assembly (which appoints the Procurator-General for 4 years) and between its sessions, to the State Council. The Ministry of the Interior is responsible for ordinary police work. State security is the responsibility of the State Security Council. A new penal code came into force on 1 Jan. 1969. It is based on 'the rule of law' and is aimed at preventing illegal trials. The death penalty is retained for 'specially serious offences' (treason, some classes of murder, theft of state property having serious consequences).

Religion. Churches are organized and function in accordance with art. 30 of the Constitution. Churches administer their own affairs and run seminaries for the training of priests. Expenses and salaries are paid by the State. There are 14 Churches, all under the control of the 'Department of Cults'. The largest is the Romanian Orthodox Church, which claimed 13·67m. members in 1950. It is autocephalous, but retains dogmatic unity with the Eastern Orthodox Church. It is administered by the consultative Holy Synod and National Ecclesiastical Assembly and the executive National Ecclesiastical Council and Patriarchal Administration. It is organized into 12 dioceses grouped into 5 metropolitan bishoprics (Hungaro-Wallachia; Moldavia-Suceava; Transylvania; Olt; Banat), and headed by Patriarch Justin Moisescu (since May 1948). There are some 11,800 churches, 2 theological colleges and 6 'schools of cantors', as well as seminaries.

The Uniate (Greek Catholic) Church (which severed its connexion with the Vatican in 1698) was suppressed in 1948. It had 1·6m. adherents and 1,818 priests. Estimates for 1973: 700,000 adherents and 600 priests.

Other churches: Serbs have a Serbian Orthodox Vicariate at Timişoara. In 1979 there were 1·4m. Roman Catholics, mainly among the Hungarian and German minorities. There is a bishop of Alba Iulia. There were 820 priests and 254 monks in 1958. The Church has not secured approval for a Statute and has no hierarchical ties with the Vatican.

Calvinists (780,000; mainly Hungarian) have bishoprics at Cluj and Oradea; Lutherans (250,000, mainly Germans) a bishopric at Sibiu and Unitarians bishoprics at Cluj and Timişoara. These sects share a seminary at Cluj.

In 1973 there were 70 Jewish communities comprising some 90,000 persons under a Chief Rabbi (Moses Rosen). There were 130 synagogues.
Moslems have a Muftiate at Constanţa.

Education. Education is free and compulsory for 10 years (6 to 16), consisting of 8 years of primary school and 2 years of secondary (gymnasium). Further secondary education is available at *lycées*, professional schools or advanced technical schools.

In 1979–80 [1] there were 13,536 kindergartens with 37,770 teachers and 911,746 children; 14,487 primary and secondary schools with 153,568 teachers and 3,289,108 pupils; 977 *lycées* with 50,201 teachers and 1,030,120 pupils; 595 professional schools with 2,553 teachers and 143,636 pupils; and 265 advanced technical schools with 237 teachers and 24,085 pupils. There are general and secondary schools for minorities, with over 250,000 pupils.

There are universities at Iaşi (founded 1860), Bucharest (1864), Cluj (1919), Timişoara (1962), Craiova (1965) and Braşov (1971). In 1979–80 there were in all 134 faculties of higher education, with a student population of 192,546.

The Academy, with seat at Bucharest, has 2 branches at Iaşi and Cluj. The National Council for Scientific Research co-ordinates research.

[1] Figures include evening classes.

Health. In 1979 there were 206,316 hospital beds and 38,075 doctors.

DIPLOMATIC REPRESENTATIVES

OF ROMANIA IN GREAT BRITAIN (4 Palace Green, London, W8 4QD)

Ambassador: Vasile Gliga.

OF GREAT BRITAIN IN ROMANIA (24 Strada Jules Michelet, Bucharest)

Ambassador: P. C. H. Holmer, CMG.

OF ROMANIA IN THE USA (1607–23rd St., NW, Washington, D.C., 20008)

Ambassador: Nicolae Ionescu.

OF THE USA IN ROMANIA (7–9 Strada Tudor Arghezi, Bucharest)
Ambassador: O. Rudolph Aggrey.

OF ROMANIA TO THE UNITED NATIONS
Ambassador: Teodor Marinescu.

Books of Reference

Anuarul Statistic al R.S.R. Bucharest, annual
Atlas Geografic Republica Socialistă România. Bucharest, 1965
Dicţionar Enciclopedic Român. Bucharest, 1962–66
Economic and Commercial Guide to Romania. Bucharest, annual since 1969
Mic Dicţionar Enciclopedic. Bucharest, 1973
Revista de Statistică. Bucharest, monthly
Romania: An Encyclopaedic Survey. Bucharest, 1980
Romania Facts and Figures. Bucharest, 1980
Academia Republicii Socialiste România. *Dicţionar Englez-Român.* Bucharest, 1974
Braun, A., *Romanian Foreign Policy Since 1965.* New York, 1978
Catchlove, D., *Romania's Ceausescu.* Tunbridge Wells, 1972
Ceauşescu, N.,. *Romania on the Way of Completing Socialist Construction.* 3 vols. Bucharest, 1968–69.—*Romania on the Way of Completing the Many-sided Developed Socialist Society.* Bucharest, 1970–
Confederation of British Industry, *Romania: An Opportunity for Joint Investment.* London, 1974
Fischer-Galati, S. A., *Rumania: A Bibliographical Guide.* Library of Congress, 1963.—*The New*

Rumania. Mass. Inst. of Technology, 1968.—*The Socialist Republic of Rumania*. Baltimore, 1969.—*Twentieth Century Rumania*. New York, 1970

Gilberg, T., *Modernization in Romania Since World War II*. New York, 1975

Giurescu, C. C. (ed.), *Chronological History of Romania*. 2nd ed. Bucharest, 1974

Hemy, G. W., *Romania: Business Opportunities*. London, 1977

Ionescu, A. (ed.), *The Grand National Assembly of the Socialist Republic of Romania: A Brief Outline*. Bucharest, 1974

Morariu, T., and others, *The Geography of Rumania*. 2nd ed. Bucharest, 1969

Levițchi, L., *Dicționar Român-Englez*. 2nd ed. Bucharest, 1965

Spigler, I., *Economic Reform in Rumanian Industry*. OUP, 1973

Turnock, D., *An Economic Geography of Romania*. London, 1974

RWANDA

Capital: Kigali
Population: 4·65m. (1979)
GNP per capita: US$180 (1978)

HISTORY. From the 16th century to 1959 the Tutsi kingdom of Rwanda shared the history of Burundi (*see* p. 258). In 1959 an uprising of the Hutu destroyed the Tutsi feudal hierarchy and led to the departure of the Mwami Kigeri V. Elections and a referendum under the auspices of the United Nations in Sept. 1961 resulted in an overwhelming majority for the republican party, the Parmehutu (Parti du Mouvement de l'Emancipation du Bahutu), and the rejection of the institution of the Mwami. The republic proclaimed by the Parmehutu on 28 Jan. 1961 was recognized by the Belgian administration (but not by the United Nations) in Oct. 1961. Internal self-government was granted on 1 Jan. 1962, and by decision of the General Assembly of the UN the Republic of Rwanda became independent on 1 July 1962. An agreement, signed with Burundi under United Nations auspices at Addis Ababa in April 192, provided for a monetary and customs union. These and other common organizations came to an end by 1 Oct. 1964.

AREA AND POPULATION. Rwanda lies between lat. 1° and 3° S. and long. 29° and 31° E., with an area of 26,330 sq. km (10,166 sq. miles). The Nile–Congo mountain divide (about 9,000 ft) and the Kirunga volcanoes (Mt. Karisimbi, 14,825 ft), rising steeply from Lake Kivu in the west, slope down first to a hilly central plateau (7,000–5,000 ft) and farther eastwards to a complex of marshy lakes in the upper reaches of the Kagera River. Rwanda is bounded in the south by Burundi, in the west by Lake Kivu and the Congo, in the north by Uganda and in the east by Tanzania.

The population, the densest in Africa outside the Nile delta (182 inhabitants per sq. km) was estimated (1979) at 4·65m. There are 3 ethnic groups, the Tutsi (Nilotic), the Hutu (Bantu) and a few Twa (pygmoid). The Tutsi, traditionally the ruling caste and about 15% of the population have greatly diminished in number since the troubles of 1959–61, as a result of which over 140,000 took refuge in neighbouring territories. In Jan. 1964 several thousand Tutsi were massacred by the Hutu, and an exodus of 12,000 more Tutsi followed. The Tutsi now form only 9% of the population. There are some 1,200 Europeans and 750 Asians.

Kigali, the capital, had an estimated population of 118,000 in 1978. Nyanza (between Kigali and Butare) is the seat of the High Court. Other centres are Gisenyi and Cyangugu on Lake Kivu, Butare, and Gitarama.

GOVERNMENT. Rwanda is a republic with an executive President as Head of State, assisted by a Council of 12 Ministers. The National Assembly consists of 47 members elected by universal suffrage for 4 years. The administrative divisions are 10 prefectures (Kigali, Kibungo, Byumba, Ruhengeri, Gisenyi, Kibuye, Gitarama, Gikongoro, Butare, Cyangugu) and 144 communes.

On 5 July 1973 President Gégoire Kayibanda who had been in office since 1961 was deposed in a bloodless *coup*. A new Constitution was introduced in Dec. 1978.

President: Maj.-Gen Juvénal Habyarimana (confirmed in office for 5-year term in Dec. 1978).

Foreign Affairs: François Ngarukiyintwari.

Flag: Three equal vertical panels of red, yellow and green (left to right), the letter 'R' in black superimposed on the centre panel.

DEFENCE

Army. The national army has a strength of 3,500 all ranks, including a Belgian cadre.

Air Force. Initial equipment ordered for the Air Force in 1972 comprised 3 Italian-built Aeritalia/Aermacchi AM.3C liaison aircraft, now supplemented by 1 armed

Magister jet trainer, 3 C-47 transports, 2 Islander light transports and 2 Alouette III helicopters. Personnel, about 150.

INTERNATIONAL RELATIONS

Membership. Rwanda is a member of UN, OAU and is an ACP state of EEC. With Burundi and Zaïre it forms part of the Economic Community of Countries of the Great Lakes.

ECONOMY

Planning. The 1977–81 Development Plan gave priority to rural development.

Budget. The budget for 1978 envisaged expenditure of 6,367m. Rwanda francs.

Currency. The currency is the *Rwanda franc*. The official rate of Rwanda francs 205 = £1; 92·84 = US$1 (March 1981).

Banking. On 5 April 1967 the Development Bank of Rwanda (*Banque Rwandaise de Développement—BRD*) was created with a capital of 50m. Rwanda francs. On 1 Sept. 1978 the share capital was expanded to 416m. Rwanda francs with ownership distributed as follows: Public sector 62·5%, domestic private sector 15·8%, foreign shareholders 21·7%. Other banks are the Central Bank (*Banque Nationale du Rwanda*); 2 commercial banks which are majority foreign owned—the *Banque Commerciale du Rwanda* and the *Banque de Kigali*; the People's Bank, the Savings Association and the *Caisse Hypothécaire*.

AGRICULTURE. Subsistence agriculture accounts for most of the gross national product. Staple food crops are beans, cassava, maize, sweet potatoes, peas, groundnuts and sorghum. The annual rainfall varies from under 40 in. in the north-east to 60 in. in the west and over 70 in. in the extreme north-west.

The main cash crop is *aravica* coffee as in Burundi; the 1980 crop was about 430,000 sacks (60 kg). Tea and pyrethrum are also produced. There is a pilot rice-growing project.

On 30 July 1964 the Rwanda Industrial Produce Bureau was established, which is responsible for organizing and controlling the quality of Rwandese agricultural exports, notably coffee. Coffee exports (1978) 23,700 tons earning 4,200m. Rwanda francs.

Tea plantations are being developed and projects are being financed by the World Bank and the African Development Bank. Fresh vegetables are produced for export (600 tonnes, 1975).

Long-horned Ankole cattle, 640,000 head in 1979, play an important traditional role. Efforts are being made to improve their present negligible economic value. There were (1979) 686,000 goats and some 257,000 sheep.

INDUSTRY. There are about 100 small-sized modern manufacturing enterprises in the country. Food manufacturing is the dominant industrial activity (64%) followed by construction (15·3%) and mining (9%). There are 4 hydro-electric installations and a large modern brewery. The industrial sector's contribution to GDP in 1976 was 23%.

COMMERCE. Imports (1978) 9,334m. Rwanda francs and exports 9,264m. Rwanda francs.

Total trade between Rwanda and UK (British Department of Trade returns, in £1,000 sterling):

	1976	1977	1978	1979	1980
Imports to UK	3,924	6,115	3,576	4,145	4,666
Exports and re-exports from UK	844	1,085	1,220	1,508	1,245

COMMUNICATIONS

Roads. There are about (1975) 8,000 miles of main and 3,500 miles of secondary roads. There are road links with Burundi, Uganda, Tanzania and Zaïre. There were in 1976 3,352 cars and 4,456 trucks. Most imports and exports travel to and from Mombasa *via* Uganda.

Shipping. Shipping on Lake Kivu in 1967 amounted to 70,000 tonnes. Kigali has an international airport, with services to Bujumbura, Bukavu *via* Kamembe, Entebbe, Goma, Lubumbashi, Athens and Brussels.

Post. Telephones (1978) 4,543.

Cinemas. In 1975 there were 3 cinemas with a seating capacity of 1,000.

RELIGION AND EDUCATION

Religion. The population is predominantly Roman Catholic; there is an archbishop (Kabgayi) and 3 bishops. The Ruanda Mission of the Church Missionary Society have 4 stations.

Education. In 1977 there were 450,000 children attending primary schools. There were secondary schools of various types with a total of 12,500 pupils. The National University opened at Butare in 1963.

The local language is Kinyarwanda, a Bantu language. French is also an official language, and Kiswahili is spoken in the commercial centres.

DIPLOMATIC REPRESENTATIVES

OF RWANDA IN GREAT BRITAIN
Ambassador: Callixte Hatungimana (resides in Brussels).

OF GREAT BRITAIN IN RWANDA
Ambassador: J. M. O. Snodgrass (resides in Kinshasa).

OF RWANDA IN THE USA
(1714 New Hampshire Ave, NW, Washington, D.C., 20009)
Ambassador: Bonaventure Ubalijoro.

OF THE USA IN RWANDA (Blvd. de la Revolution, Kigali)
Ambassador: Harry R. Melone.

OF RWANDA TO THE UNITED NATIONS
Ambassador: Ignace Karuhije.

Books of Reference

Hance, W. A., *African Economic Development*. London, 1967
Lacroix, B., *Le Rwanda*. Montreal, 1966
Northumb, D., *Un Humanisme Africain*. Brussels, 1965

ST HELENA

Capital: Jamestown
Population: 5,223 (1979)

HISTORY. The island was administered by the East India Company from 1673 and became a British colony in 1833.

AREA AND POPULATION. St Helena, of volcanic origin, is 1,200 miles from the west coast of Africa. Area, 47 sq. miles (121·7 sq. km), with a cultivable area of about 600 acres (243 hectares). The port of the island is Jamestown, population (1976) 1,516.

Population (1979), 5,223. Births, 95; deaths, 49; marriages, 45.

GOVERNMENT. The Government of St Helena is administered by a Governor, with the aid of a Legislative Council consisting of the Governor, 2 *ex-officio* members (the Government Secretary and the Treasurer) and 12 elected members. Committees of the Legislative Council are responsible for the general oversight of the activities of government departments and have, in addition, statutory and administrative functions.

The Governor is also assisted by an Executive Council consisting of the 2 *ex-officio* members and the chairmen of the Council committees.

Governor and C.-in-C.: J. D. Massingham.
Government Secretary: P. Dale, OBE.

Flag: The British Blue Ensign with the shield of the colony in the fly.

FINANCE AND TRADE, for years from 1 April–31 March, in £ sterling:

	1974–75	1975–76	1976–77	1977–78	1978–79	1979–80
Revenue [1]	1,356,049	1,481,539	2,014,981	2,244,550	2,683,681	4,226,899
Expenditure [1]	1,520,101	1,544,027	1,952,642	2,200,299	2,764,150	4,325,910
Imports [2]	1,115,341	1,192,418	1,430,168	1,758,337	1,164,437	1,835,000

[1] Including imperial grants (1974–75, £937,888; 1975–76, £1,060,342; 1976–77, £1,461,739; 1977–78, £1,657,231; 1978–79, £1,771,618; 1979–80, £3,347,631).

[2] Including government stores.

The revenue from customs was, in 1974–75, £91,998; 1975–76, £93,039; 1976–77, £122,029; 1977–78, £150,438; 1978–79, £193,576; 1979–80, £215,995.

The colony's liabilities at 31 March 1980 exceeded the assets by £88,243.

Total trade between Ascension and St Helena and UK (British Department of Trade returns, in £1,000 sterling):

	1975	1976	1977	1978	1979	1980
Imports to UK	120	109	156	192	207	476
Exports and re-exports from UK	1,675	1,632	2,387	2,031	2,570	3,016

BANKING. Savings-bank deposits on 31 March 1980, £1,102,283, belonging to 3,209 depositors.

COMMUNICATIONS

Roads. There were 83 km of all-weather motor roads.

Shipping. The number of merchant vessels that called in 1979–80 was 19; total tonnage entered and cleared was 47,000.

Post and Broadcasting. The Cable & Wireless Ltd cable connects St Helena with Cape Town and Ascension Island. There is a telephone service with 85 miles of wire and (1978), 344 telephones.

St Helena Government Broadcasting Station broadcasts in English on medium-waves. Number of radio receivers (1978), 900.

JUSTICE, RELIGION, EDUCATION AND WELFARE

Justice. Police force, 32; cases dealt with by police magistrate, 231 in 1979.

Religion. There are 10 Anglican churches and 4 Baptist chapels.

Education. Three pre-school playgroups, 8 primary, 3 senior and 1 secondary schools controlled by the Government had 1,400 pupils in March 1980.

Health. There were 3 doctors and 55 hospital beds in 1978.

Ascension is a small island of volcanic origin, of 34 sq. miles (88 sq. km), 700 miles north-west of St Helena. In Nov. 1922 the administration was transferred from the Admiralty to the Colonial Office and annexed to the colony of St Helena. There are 10 acres under cultivation providing vegetables and fruit. Population, 31 Dec. 1946, was 292; St. Helenians 719 (1976), others 460.

The island is the resort of sea turtles, which come to lay their eggs in the sand annually between Jan. and May. Rabbits, wild goats and partridges are more or less numerous on the island, which is, besides, the breeding ground of the sooty tern or 'wideawake', these birds coming in vast numbers to lay their eggs every eighth month.

Cable & Wireless Ltd own and operate a cable station, connecting the island with St Helena, Sierra Leone, St Vincent, Rio de Janeiro and Buenos Aires. There is an airstrip (Miracle Mile) near the settlement of Georgetown.

Administrator: B. E. Pauncefort.

Tristan da Cunha, a small group of islands in the Atlantic, half-way between the Cape and South America, in 37° 6′ S. lat., 12° 1′ W. long. Besides Tristan da Cunha and Gough Island, there are Inaccessible and Nightingale Islands, the former 2 and the latter 1 mile long, and a number of rocks. As from 12 Jan. 1938 the 4 islands have become dependencies of St Helena.

Tristan consists of a volcano rising to a height of 6,760 ft, with a circumference at its base of 21 miles. The volcano, believed to be extinct, erupted unexpectedly early in Oct. 1961. The whole population was evacuated without loss and settled temporarily in the UK. In 1963 they returned to Tristan.

Before the disaster occurred the habitable area was a small plateau on the north-west side of about 12 sq. miles, 100 ft above sea-level. Only about 30 acres was under cultivation, three-quarters of it for potatoes. There were apple and peach trees; bullocks, sheep and geese were reared, and fish are plentiful.

The island is extremely lonely, but the community is growing. In 1880 it numbered 109, in 1976, 304. The original inhabitants were shipwrecked sailors and soldiers who remained behind when the garrison from St Helena was withdrawn in 1817.

At the end of April 1942 Tristan da Cunha was commissioned as HMS *Atlantic Isle*, and became an important meteorological and radio station. In Jan. 1949 a South African company commenced crawfishing operations. An Administrator was appointed at the end of 1948 and a body of basic law brought into operation. The Island Council, which was set up in 1932, consists of 3 nominated and 8 elected members under the chairmanship of the Administrator, with the Society for the Propagation of the Gospel in Foreign Parts' missionary and the company manager as *ex-officio* members. Women's affairs are discussed by the Island Women's Council, which presents them for consideration to the general council.

Administrator: E. C. Brooks.

Books of Reference

Booy, D. M., *Rock of Exile: A Narrative of Tristan da Cunha*. London, 1957
Goss, A., *Saint Helena*. Newton Abbot, 1981
Holdgate, M., *Mountains in the Sea*. London, 1958
Munch, P. A., *Sociology of Tristan da Cunha*. Oslo, 1945
Stonehouse, B., *Wideawake Island* [Ascension]. London, 1960

ST LUCIA

Capital: Castries
Population: 113,000 (1979)
GNP per capita: US$630 (1978)

HISTORY. St Lucia was discovered about 1500 A.D. Attempts to colonize the island by the English took place in 1605 and 1638. The French settled in 1650 and St Lucia was ceded to Britain in 1814. Self-government was achieved in 1967 and independence on 22 Feb. 1979.

AREA AND POPULATION. St Lucia is a small island of the Lesser Antilles situated in the Eastern Caribbean, 238 sq. miles (616 sq. km); population (1979) 113,000. The capital is Castries (population, 45,000). Vital statistics (1974): Births, 3,909; deaths, 829.

CONSTITUTION AND GOVERNMENT. Independence was achieved on 22 Feb. 1979. There is a 17-seat House of Assembly and in 1979 the United Workers' Party held 10 seats and there is also an 11-seat Senate appointed by the Governor-General, 6 on the advice of the Prime Minister, 3 on the advice of the Leader of the Opposition, and 2 'after consultation with appropriate religious, economic or social bodies or associations'.

Governor-General: Sir Allen Montgomery Lewis, GCMG.
Prime Minister: Allan F. L. Louisy.
Flag: Blue with a design of a black triangle edged in white, bearing a smaller yellow triangle, in the centre.

INTERNATIONAL RELATIONS

Membership. St Lucia is a member of UN, the Commonwealth and is an ACP state of the EEC.

ECONOMY

Budget. The budget in 1978–79 amounted to EC$93·9m. expenditure, of which EC$49·8m. was recurrent expenditure and EC$44·1m. capital expenditure.
Public debt, 31 Dec. 1974, EC$2·5m.

Banking. There are Barclays Bank International with 2 branches and 4 agencies, the Royal Bank of Canada, the Bank of Nova Scotia and the Canadian Imperial Bank of Commerce (all of which have 1 branch each), the Chase Manhattan Bank, the St Lucia Co-operative Bank and the Government Savings Bank. The Government Savings Bank (end of 1974), 8,400 depositors, $359,086 deposits.

INDUSTRY AND TRADE

Agriculture. Bananas, cocoa, copra and coconut oil are the chief products.
Livestock (1979): Cattle, 16,000; pigs, 10,000; sheep, 11,000; goats, 9,000; poultry, 85,000.

Trade. Value of imports (1974), $91,114,926; of exports, $32,908,783, including coconut oil, cocoa beans, copra and bananas. Main items of imports were artificial silk and cotton piece-goods, cement, plastic goods, iron and steel products, hardware, motor vehicles, agricultural machinery, fertilizers, wheat flour, codfish and rice, meat and meat preparation.

Tourism. The total number of visitors during 1978 was 107,000.

COMMUNICATIONS

Roads. The island has 500 miles of main and secondary roads.

Aviation. The island is served on a scheduled basis by Leeward Islands Air

Transport, British West Indian Airways and Eastern Airline. There are 2 airfields—Hewanorra International Airport, with 9,000 ft runway, and Vigie.

Shipping. Registered fleet (31 Dec. 1974): 3 motor vessels (94 gross tons). In 1974, 2,798 vessels of 3·5m. gross tons entered Castries and Vieux Fort.

Post and Broadcasting. There are 104 miles of telephone trunk lines, plus 300 miles of local lines. There were (1978) 7,157 telephone instruments coupled to some 3,423 exchange lines. They operate through 12 automatic exchanges. There were 1,700 TV and 82,000 radio receivers in 1975.

Cinemas. There were 9 cinemas in 1970 with a seating capacity of 9,500.

JUSTICE AND EDUCATION

Justice. The island is divided into 2 judicial districts, and there are 9 magistrates' courts. Appeals lie with the Court of Appeal of the Windward and Leeward Islands, subject to exceptions and conditions as may be enacted by the St Lucia legislature.
  Police establishment in 1974 was 11 officers, 11 inspectors and 267 others.

Education (31 Dec. 1974). 74 primary schools (51 Roman Catholic, 3 Anglican, 3 Methodist, 17 government), with 30,000 pupils on roll; government expenditure, 1974, $5,526,945. Primary education is free and compulsory by law, but the legislation is not enforced. There are 12 secondary schools (2 Roman Catholic, 1 Seventh-day Adventist, 9 government) with 4,600 pupils. There is 1 technical college with 250 students.

Library: The Central Library, Castries. *Librarian:* Mrs Mary Prescod.

DIPLOMATIC REPRESENTATIVES

OF ST LUCIA IN GREAT BRITAIN
(10 Kensington Ct., London, W8)
High Commissioner: Dr Claudius C. Thomas, CMG.

OF GREAT BRITAIN IN ST LUCIA
(George Gordon Bldg., Castries)
High Commissioner: J. S. Arthur, CMG.

OF ST LUCIA TO THE UNITED NATIONS
Ambassador: Dr Barry B. L. Auguste.

ST VINCENT AND THE GRENADINES

Population: 117,646 (1978)
Capital: Kingstown
GNP per capita: US$380 (1978)

HISTORY. The date of the discovery of St Vincent is not known. In 1969 St Vincent became a self-governing Associated State of UK and acquired full independence on 27 Oct. 1979.

AREA AND POPULATION. The total area of 389 sq. km (150·3 sq. miles) comprises the island of St Vincent itself (345 sq. km) and the Northern Grenadines (44 sq. km) of which the largest are Bequia, Mustique, Canouan, Mayreau and Union. Population, estimate, 1978, 117,646. Capital, Kingstown, population, 22,782. Vital statistics (1979): Live births, 3,409; still births, 49; deaths 693; marriages, 384.

CONSTITUTION AND GOVERNMENT. Independence from the UK was achieved on 27 Oct. 1979. The House of Assembly consists of 13 elected members, directly elected for a 5-year term from single-member constituencies, the Attorney-General (*ex-officio*) and 6 Senators appointed by the Governor-General (4 on the advice of the Prime Minister and 2 on the advice of the Leader of the Opposition).

Governor-General: Sir Sydney Gun-Munro.
Prime Minister: Robert Milton Cato, PC.

National Flag: Three vertical stripes of blue, yellow, green, with white fimbriations, charged in the centre with a green leaf of bread-fruit bearing the arms of St Vincent.

INTERNATIONAL RELATIONS

Membership. St Vincent is a member of UN, the Commonwealth, and is an ACP state of EEC.

ECONOMY

Budget. Revenue (estimate), 1980–81, $48,228,689, excluding budgetary assistance, $500,000; development aid, $11,552,900, and other sources, $43,741,457; expenditure, $47,894,112; recurrent, $11,552,900 on colonial development and welfare schemes and $43,741,457 on other schemes. Public debt at the end of the financial year 1979–80 was $10,249,900.

Currency. The currency is the Eastern Caribbean *dollar*. In March 1981, £1 = EC$5·90; US$1 = EC$2·70.

Banking. There are branches of Barclays Bank International, the Royal Bank of Canada, the Canadian Imperial Bank of Commerce, the National Commercial Bank, the Bank of Nova Scotia, St Vincent Co-operative Bank and the St Vincent Agricultural Credit and Loan Bank at Kingstown.

ENERGY AND NATURAL RESOURCES

Electricity. The electricity system is owned jointly by the Government (49%) and the Commonwealth Development Corporation (51%) and operated by the St Vincent Electricity Services (CDC). The system consists of 4 power stations: South Rivers Hydro (800 kw.); Cane Hall Diesel (3,650 kw.); Kingstown Diesel (115 kw.) and Richmond Hydro (1,040 kw.), which are linked by 11,000-volt transmission lines covering the island from Richmond through Kingstown to Georgetown. In Bequia there is one diesel station (800 kw.) with transmission at 11,000, 3,300 and 400 volts to Hamilton and Port Elizabeth. Current is supplied at 400 volts 3-phase, 50 cycles for industrial purposes and 230 volts single phase for domestic purposes.

At 31 Dec. 1979 there were 10,800 consumers in St Vincent, 900 in Bequia and 300 in Union Island.

Agriculture. The estimated alienated area is about 47,000 of the total acreage of 85,120. 34,000 acres are under forest and woodland; of these about 5,000 acres are used for grazing; 3,000 are considered potentially productive for agriculture and 5,000 for forestry. About 14,000 acres are considered unsuitable for either agriculture or forestry. Of the total alienated area, 34,000 acres are considered arable land, of which 20,000 acres are under temporary crops, 4,000 acres under temporary meadows, 300 acres devoted to market-garden crops with temporary fallow and all other arable land making up a further 9,700 acres. About 2,000 acres are under permanent meadow, of which 750 are cultivated.

Bananas, arrowroot flour, copra, carrots, sweet potatoes, yams, tannias and other starchy roots, nutmegs and mace and small amounts of peanuts are produced. The Territory is largely self-supporting in vegetables. St Vincent is renowned for its arrowroot starch.

Land ownership: Crown, 38,000 acres; planters, 17,000 acres; small farmers, 25,500 acres; settlements, 6,000 acres.

Livestock (1979): Cattle, 7,000; pigs, 6,000; sheep, 10,000; goats, 4,000; poultry, 148,000.

INDUSTRY AND TRADE

Trade (1979). Imports, EC$125,201,660; exports, EC$39,825,778. Value of imports from the UK (1978), EC$24,746,980; of exports to the UK (1978), EC$24,239,790. Principal exports, 1979:

		EC$			EC$
Arrowroot starch	1,418,500 lb.	1,784,707	Coconuts	4,033,500 nuts	1,410,371
Eddoes	2,652,700 lb.	698,220	Copra	716,800 lb.	343,196
Bananas	49,236,978 lb.	15,883,460	Coconut oil	47,325 gals.	592,351
Sweet potatoes	2,560,640 lb.	920,328	Tannias	1,098,697 lb.	703,484

Labour (1979). The Department of Labour serves both workers and employers' organizations as a conciliatory body in case of dispute. Conciliatory meetings are held on dispute matters such as delay in the recognition of a union as collective bargaining agent for the workers, dismissals, overtime pay, delay in finalizing collective agreement and other conditions of work. There are 8 registered trade unions: the St Vincent Union of Teachers, the Civil Service Association, the Commercial, Technical and Allied Workers' Union, the St Vincent Workers' Union, the National Workers' Movement, the Farmers' and National General Workers' Union, the Workers' and Peasants' Union and the National Progressive Workers' Union. The St Vincent Employers Federation continued to render services on behalf of the employers.

Tourism. There were 63,440 visitors in 1979.

COMMUNICATIONS

Roads. There are 200 miles of all-weather roads, 260 miles of rough motorable roads and 250 miles of tracks.

Aviation. Scheduled services are operated daily by LIAT and Air Martinique. Passengers are able to travel daily through the chain of islands stretching as far north as San Juan, Puerto Rico and south to Trinidad. Connexions to the USA, Canada, South America and Europe are possible *via* Barbados, Antigua and Trinidad.

Shipping (1979): (*a*) 67 auxiliary sailing vessels of 2,474 NRT entered, while 62 of 2,069 NRT cleared. (*b*) 571 steamships of 729,787 NRT entered the territory. (*c*) 595 steamships and motor vessels of 628,800 NRT cleared. (*d*) 7 cargo motor tankers bringing 11,193 tons of fuel entered. A deep-water harbour at Kingstown was completed in 1964.

Post and Broadcasting. There is a General Post Office at Kingstown and 46 district post offices. There is a telephone system with 2,000 miles of line and (1980), 3,548 subscribers; 5,523 stations and a radio telephone service to Bequia, Mustique, Union

Island and Canouan. In 1974 there were 600 TV and 30,000 radio receivers.

Cinemas. There were 3 cinemas in 1979 with a seating capacity of 2,400.

JUSTICE AND EDUCATION

Justice (1979). There were 3,350 criminal matters disposed of in the 3 magistrates' courts. Strength of police force (1980), 489 (including 11 officers).

Education (1979). Sixty-one primary schools; pupils on roll, 24,222, average attendance, 19,377. Expenditure on primary education, $3,178,775. There is also a secondary school for girls (677 pupils, 1979), a co-educational school (574 pupils, 1979), as well as 11 assisted secondary schools (2,703 pupils) and 4 junior secondary schools with 1,413 pupils. Expenditure on secondary education, $1,781,175.

Library: St Vincent Public Library, Kingstown. *Librarian:* Mrs Lorna Small.

DIPLOMATIC REPRESENTATIVES

OF ST VINCENT AND THE GRENADINES IN GREAT BRITAIN
(10 Kensington Ct, London, W8)

High Commissioner: Dr Claudius C. Thomas, CMG.

OF GREAT BRITAIN IN ST VINCENT AND THE GRENADINES

High Commissioner: J. S. Arthur, CMG (resides in Bridgetown).

OF ST VINCENT AND THE GRENADINES IN
THE USA AND TO THE UNITED NATIONS

Ambassador: H. K. Tannis.

SAN MARINO

Capital: San Marino
Population: 19,168 (1974)

Repubblica di San Marino

HISTORY. On 22 March 1862 San Marino concluded a treaty of friendship and co-operation, including a *de facto* customs union with the kingdom of Italy, preserving the independence of the ancient republic, although completely surrounded by Italian territory. The treaty was renewed on 27 March 1872, 28 June 1897 and 31 March 1939, with 7 amendments in 1942–71.

The republic has extradition treaties with Belgium, France, the Netherlands, UK and USA.

AREA AND POPULATION. San Marino is a land-locked state in central Italy, 20 km from the Adriatic. The frontier line is 38·6 km in length, area is 61·19 sq. km (24·1 sq. miles) and the population (30 June 1974), 19,168; some 20,000 citizens live abroad.

CONSTITUTION AND GOVERNMENT. The legislative power is vested in the Great and General Council of 60 members elected every 5 years by popular vote, 2 of whom are appointed every 6 months to act as regents (*Capitani reggenti*).

The elections held on 28 May 1978 gave 26 seats to the Christian Democrats, 8 to the Left-wing Socialists, 16 to the Communists, 15 to Socialist parties, 3 to others. A political crisis arose following the election and a 'Government of Democratic Collaboration' was established finally on 17 July 1978.

The regents exercise executive power together with the Congress of State (*Congresso di Stato*), which comprises 10 departments, and through Commissions on social welfare, public works, etc.

National flag: Horizontally white over light blue, with the national arms over all in the centre.

DEFENCE. The militia consists, in case of necessity, of all able-bodied citizens between the ages of 16 and 55, with certain exceptions (teachers and students, etc.).

ECONOMY. The budget (ordinary and extraordinary) for the financial year ending 31 Dec. 1973 balanced at 14,912,266,209 lire.

The chief exports are wine, textiles, tiles, varnishes, ceramics and the building stone quarried on Mount Titano.

Italian and Vatican City currency is in general use, but the republic issues its own postage stamps.

In 1973, 2·58m. tourists visited San Marino.

COMMUNICATIONS

Roads. A bus service connects San Marino with Rimini.

Aviation. There is a helicopter service to Rimini in summer.

Post. In 1978 there were 6,276 telephones.

Cinemas. In 1974 there were 8 cinemas with a seating capacity of 2,300.

JUSTICE. Law is administered by a Commissioner for civil and commercial cases and a Commissioner for criminal cases (acting with a penal judge), from whom appeals can be made to a civil appeals judge and a criminal appeals judge respectively. The highest legal authority is, in certain cases, the *Consiglio dei XII*.

EDUCATION. There are 16 infant schools, 16 elementary schools, a secondary school and a grammar school, the diplomas of which are recognized by Italian universities. Civil marriage was instituted in Sept. 1953.

DIPLOMATIC REPRESENTATIVES

British Consul-General (resides at Florence): R. A. Vining, MBE.
USA Consul-General (resides at Florence): Robert C. F. Gordon.
Consul-General in London: Charles Forte.

Books of Reference

Information: Segreteria di Stato per gli Affari Esteri; Ente Governativo per il Turismo.

Garbeletto, A., *Evoluzione storica della costituzione di S. Marino*. Milan, 1956
Packett, C. N., *Guide to the Republic of San Marino*. Bradford, 1970
Rossi, G., *San Marino*. San Marino, 1954

SÃO TOMÉ E PRINCIPE

Capital: São Tomé
Population: 82,750 (1977)
GNP per capita: US$490 (1978)

HISTORY. The islands of São Tomé and Principe, were discovered in 1471 by Pedro Escobar and João Gomes, and from 1522 until independence had constituted a province of Portugal.

On 26 Nov. 1974 the Government of Portugal and the liberation movement of São Tomé e Principe signed an agreement granting independence to the archipelago on 12 Juy 1975 to become the Democratic Republic of São Tomé e Principe.

AREA AND POPULATION. The republic, which lies about 200 km off the west coast of Gabon, in the Gulf of Guinea, comprises the main islands of São Tomé (845 sq. km) and Principe and several smaller islets including Pedras Tinhosas and Rolas. It has a total area of 964 sq. km (372 sq. miles). Total population (census, 1970) 73,631 (São Tomé, 60,032; Principe, 4,599). Estimate (1977) 82,750.

Vital statistics (1972): Births, 3,392; deaths, 840; marriages, 141.

CONSTITUTION AND GOVERNMENT. A new constitution was approved by the Constitutional Assembly (elected 6 July 1975) on 12 Dec. 1975. Under it, the sole legal party is the *Movimento de Libertação de São Tomé e Principe*, who nominate candidates for the Presidency and People's Assembly. The President is elected by the People's Assembly for a 4-year term; he is also head of government and appoints a Cabinet of Ministers to assist him. The 33-member People's Assembly is also elected for 4 years.

The Cabinet was composed as follows in Jan. 1981:

President, Minister of Administration: Dr Manuel Pinto da Costa.

Foreign Affairs and Education: Maria do Nascimento da Graça Amorim. *Information and Culture:* Maria de Rosário Lima Barros. *Health:* Carlos Alberto Tini. *Defence and Security:* Maj. Daniel Lima dos Santos Diao. *Industry and Fishing:* Aurélio Santo. *Commerce:* Carlos Gomes. *Planning:* Enrique Pinto da Costa. *Justice:* Celestino Rocha da Costa. *Construction, Transport and Communications:* Lieut. Oscar de Sousa Aguiar. *Island of Principe:* Manuel Quaresma dos Santos Costa.

Flag: Three horizontal stripes of green, yellow, green, with the yellow of double width and bearing 2 black stars; in the hoist a red triangle over all.

INTERNATIONAL RELATIONS

Membership. São Tomé e Principe is a member of UN, OAU and is an ACP state of EEC.

DEFENCE. Armed forces strength (estimate, 1976) 160.

ECONOMY

Budget. In 1977 the budget envisaged revenue of 167·5m. dobra and expenditure of 405·5m. dobra.

Currency. The currency is the *dobra*, introduced in 1977, divided into 100 *centavos*. In March 1981, £1 = 83·03.

AGRICULTURE. The chief commercial products are cacao, copra, coconut, coffee, palm-oil and cinchona. In 1979 there were 2,000 goats, 1,000 sheep, 3,000 pigs and 3,000 cattle.

COMMERCE. Imports in 1975 amounted to 288,469,000 dobras and exports to 180,432,000 dobras, the main exports being cocoa (87%), copra (8%), coffee, bananas and palm-oil. In 1975 Portugal provided 61% of imports and Angola 13%, while the Netherlands took 52% ofexports and Portugal 33%.

Total trade between São Tomé e Principe and UK (British Department of Trade returns, in £1,000 sterling):

	1977	1978	1979	1980
Imports to UK	9	104	525	99
Exports and r-exports fro UK	701	506	1,036	2,103

COMMUNICATIONS

Roads. There were 288 km of roads in 1973.

Shipping. In 1973, 220 vessels of 435,971 net tons entered the ports.

Post. There were, in 1973, 3 wireless stations with (1976) 12,000 radio receivers, 352 km of telephone lines and a telephone exchange (with 727 instruments in 1976).

Cinemas. In 1972 there was 1 cinema with a seating capacity of 1,000.

RELIGION, EDUCATION AND WELFARE.

Religion. The vast majority of the population are Roman Catholic.

Education. In 1977 there were 14,162 pupils and 527 teachers in primary schools, 3,012 pupils and 81 teachers in secondary schools, and 155 students and 30 teachers in technical schools.

Health. In 1976 there were 11 hospitals and dispensaries with 530 beds. In 1973 there were 12 doctors, 6 midwives and 63 nursing personnel.

DIPLOMATIC REPRESENTATIVES

OF GREAT BRITAIN IN SÃO TOMÉ AND PRINCIPE

Ambassador: Francis Kennedy (resides in Luanda).

OF SÃO TOMÉ AND PRINCIPE TO THE UNITED NATIONS

Chargé d'Affaires: Helder Barros.

Book of Reference

S. Tomé e Príncipe. Agência-Geral do Ultramar, 1964

SAUDI ARABIA

al-Mamlaka al-'Arabiya
as-Sa'udiya

Capital: Riyadh
Population: 9·52m. (1977)
GNP per capita: US$8,040 (1978)

HISTORY. Saudi Arabia was founded by Abdul-Aziz ibn Abdur-Rahman al-Faisal Al Sa'ud, GCB, GCIE (born about 1880; died 9 Nov. 1953), who had been proclaimed King of the Hejaz on 8 Jan. 1926 and had in 1927 changed his title of Sultan of Nejd and its dependencies to that of king, thus becoming 'King of the Hejaz and of Nejd and its Dependencies'. On 20 May 1927 a treaty was signed at Jidda between Great Britain and Ibn Sa'ud, by which the former recognized the complete independence of the dominions of the latter. The name of the State was changed to 'The Saudi Arabian Kingdom' by decree of 23 Sept. 1932.

In Nov. 1937 a general agreement between Saudi Arabia and the Yemen concerning the settlement of disputes was ratified, and an agreement regarding the delimitation of the frontiers was negotiated.

In March 1953 the treaty of Taif, first signed with the Yemen in May 1934, was extended for 20 lunar years.

In 1942 Saudi Arabia and the British Government, acting on behalf of the Shaikh of Kuwait, signed agreements for friendship and neighbourly relations, for the extradition of offenders and for the regulation of trade between Saudi Arabia and Kuwait.

In Aug. 1962 Saudi Arabia and Jordan agreed on measures of co-operation in the military, political and economic fields.

King Faisal ibn Abdul-Aziz was assassinated on 25 March 1975 by his nephew. There appeared to be no political motive.

AREA AND POPULATION. The total area of Saudi Arabia is estimated to be 927,000 sq. miles (2·4m. sq. km).

The principal cities of the Hejaz are: Mecca, 366,801; Jidda, 561,104; Medina, 198,186, and Taif, 204,857; of the Nejd are: Riyadh, the capital, 666,840; Buraida, 69,940; Anaiza, Hail, Jauf and Sakaka; of the Hasa are: Dammam, 127,844; Hofuf, 101,271, and Al-Khobar, 44,817. The largest city of the Asir, the fourth of the traditional divisions, is Abha, 30,150. New cities were being built (1980) including Jubail (future pop. 300,000) and Yanbu (150,000).

Taif, about 3,800 ft above sea-level and some 50 miles from Mecca, is a summer resort.

The total population was (1974 census) 7,012,642, of which 5,128,655 were categorized as settled and 1,883,987 as nomadic. Estimate (1976) 9·16m.

Slavery was declared illegal in Nov. 1962.

KING. Khalid ibn Abdul-Aziz; succeeded on 25 March 1975, after King Faisal's assassination. *Crown Prince:* Prince Fahd ibn Abdul Aziz, Deputy Prime Minster, younger brother of the King.

National flag: Green, with the text 'There is no God but Allah and Mohammed is his prophet' in white Arabic script, and beneath this a white sabre.

GOVERNMENT AND CONSTITUTION. The Kingdom has been welded together from Hejaz, Nejd, Asir and Al-Hassa. Riyadh is the political capital and Mecca the religious capital. There is no formal Constitution.

In May 1958 a 'Cabinet system' was instituted under which, from 1962, effective power devolved upon the President of the Council of Ministers.

The King has the post of Prime Minister.

Deputy Prime Minister: Crown Prince Fahd ibn Abdul Aziz.
Second Deputy Prime Minister and Commander of the National Guards: Prince Abdullah ibn Abdul Aziz.

Defence and Aviation: Prince Sultan ibn Abdul Aziz.
Foreign Minister: Prince Saud al Faisal.
Interior: Prince Nayef ibn Abdul Aziz.
Petroleum and Natural Resources: Sheikh Ahmed Zaki Yamani.
Finance and Economy: Sheikh Muhammad Ali Aba al Khail.

The religious law of Islam is the common law of the land, and is administered by religious courts, at the head of which is a chief judge, who is responsible for the Department of Sharia (legal) Affairs. There are provisions for the setting up of certain advisory councils, comprising a consultative Legislative Assembly in Mecca, municipal councils in each of the towns of Mecca, Medina and Jidda, and village and tribal councils throughout the provinces. The country is divided for administrative purposes into 6 major and 12 minor provinces.

DEFENCE. In 1937 a Ministry of Defence and a training school for officers were established. British Military and Civil Air Missions helped in training the Army and civil aviation from 1947 to 1951. The US now maintains a Military Mission (with an Air Force element) as do France and Pakistan. UK provides small army and air force teams. Personnel are trained in Saudi Arabia, UK and the USA.

Army. The Army comprises 3 infantry, 1 mechanized and 1 armoured brigade, and 2 parachute, 1 Royal Guard and 3 artillery battalions, 18 AA batteries and 10 Hawk missile batteries. Service is voluntary and the strength (1980) 31,000; para-military, 26,500.

Navy. The Navy, given recent impetus under the aegis of USA, comprises 4 missile-armed corvettes, 7 fast missile craft (all completed in 1980–81 in USA), 3 *ex*-German torpedo boats, 4 new US MSC-type coastal minesweepers, 1 *ex*-US coastguard cutter, 8 new French-built patrol craft, 44 coastal patrol boats, 73 small patrol launches, 8 hovercraft, 2 air-sea rescue launches, 1 training ship, 4 landing craft, 1 salvage vessel, 2 tugs and the royal yacht. New construction includes 2 more fast missile craft in USA. An intensive training programme is under-way.

Naval personnel in 1981 exceeded 2,600 officers and men plus instructors and trainees.

Air Force. Formed as a small army support unit in 1932, the Air Force has been built up considerably with British and US assistance since 1946. Complete re-equipment began in 1966 and delivery of 60 F-15 Eagles to equip 3 air superiority squadrons was to begin in 1981. Current combat units include 1 squadron of Lightning F.53 supersonic interceptors, supported by 2-seat fighter-trainers. There are 3 squadrons of F-5E Tiger II supersonic fighter-bombers, supported by a conversion unit with F-5B/F combat trainers. Two squadrons of Strikemaster light jet attack/trainers are based at the King Faisal Air Academy, Riyadh, together with 12 Reims/Cessna FR172 piston-engined primary trainers. Other types in current service include 31 C-130E/H and 6 KC-130H Hercules transports and tankers, 1 Boeing 747 SP, 1 Boeing 707, 2 JetStar VIP jet transports, more than 50 Agusta-Bell 205, 212 and JetRanger helicopters, 2 Agusta AS-61A-4 VIP transport helicopters, 6 Kawasaki-Boeing Vertol KV-107 helicopters, and communications aircraft. On order are 40 Aviocar twin-turboprop transports and 24 Dauphin 2 anti-submarine helicopters. Personnel, about 8,000.

INTERNATIONAL RELATIONS

Membership. Saudi Arabia is a member of UN, the Arab League and OPEC.

ECONOMY

Planning. The second development plan covered 1975–80. Growth rate of GDP was 16·3% per annum during the first plan, and was expected to be 10·2% during the second (actual figures 1976–77, 14·8%, 1977–78, 5·9%, 1978–79, 7·5%). Expenditure anticipated under the second plan amounted to 498,000m. rials, of which 92,000m. for the development of economic resources, 80,000m. for education and training, 33,000m. for social welfare facilities and 113,000m. for physical infrastructure. The third development plan will run 1980–85 and is expected to emphasize industrial development. Expenditure anticipated under the third plan is 783,000m. rials, of which 292,000m. for the development of economic resources, 149,000m. for education and training, 64,000m. for social welfare facilities and 278,000m. for physical infrastructure.

Budget. The fiscal year runs from 1 Rajab to 30 Jumad II in the lunar calendar, and consequently starts approximately 10 days earlier each year. Main expenditure allocations in 1980–81 budget were 68,900m. rials for defence, 32,100m. for physical communications and telecommunications, 31,500m. for public works, 22,600m. for education and training, 12,300m. for social welfare and 38,900m. for development of economic resources (agriculture, industry, petroleum and minerals) equally divided between direct finance and loans funds available to private investors.

Currency. The paper *rial* is divided into 100 *halalas*. Money supply at March 1968 was 2,500m. *rials* and 53,100m. at Dec. 1978 (end of Hijri years 1387 and 1398).

Banking. There are 2 commercial banks of Saudi Arabian origin: the National Commercial Bank and the Riyadh Bank. It is government policy to encourage foreign banks operating in the kingdom to become Saudized. By 1980 there were 6 banks in which foreign capital represents only 40%: al Jazira Bank (National Bank of Pakistan), Saudi Dutch Bank (Algemene Bank Nederland), Saudi French Bank (Banque de l'Indochine et de Suez), Saudi British Bank (British Bank of the Middle East), Saudi Cairo Bank (Banque du Caire) and the Saudi-American Bank (Citibank). All these banks are entitled to open branches nationwide.

In addition the following commercial banks have branches in the kingdom: the Arab Bank (of Jordan) in Jeddah, Riyadh, Dammam and Al Khobar; the Banque du Liban et d'Outremer and the Bank Melli in Jeddah; the United Bank (of Pakistan) in Dammam.

ENERGY AND NATURAL RESOURCES

Electricity. 5,712m. kwh. was generated by the main electricity companies in 1976, 7,010m. kwh. in 1977 and 9,435m. kwh. in 1978.

Oil. The first general geologic–geographical survey of Saudi Arabia was completed in 1961 under the joint sponsorship of the Saudi Arabian and US governments but surveying continues.

The original oil concession agreement was signed in 1933 with Standard Oil Co. of California. The name Aramco appeared in 1944, and by 1948 Exxon, Texaco and Mobil held shares in the company. In 1973 the Saudi Arabian Government acquired a 25% interest in Aramco: this became 60% in 1974, and in 1979 it was announced that the Government had taken full control of Aramco equity retroactively from Jan. 1976. By 1973 Aramco retained only 85,000 sq. miles or 17% of the original concession areas.

Two other companies have concessions of Saudi Arabia's oil rights in the Kuwait/Saudi Arabian Neutral Zone. Getty Oil's concession dates from 1953 and that of the Arabian Oil Co. (Japanese) from 1958.

Crude oil production in 1978 was 3,038m. bbls, of which Aramco accounted for 97·2%, Arabian Oil for 1·85% and Getty Oil 0·97%. Crude oil exports in 1978 were 2,807m. bbls, of which Aramco provided 97·4%, Arabian Oil 1·65% and Getty Oil 0·54%. 1978 oil exports earned US$37,390m. (94·5m. for crude) and Aramco earned 97·1% of this total.

In Dec. 1978 Aramco's proven oil reserves amounted to 113,300m. bbls, and probable reserves to 177,800m. bbls.

The agency responsible for co-ordination of national oil policy is Petromin (General Petroleum and Minerals Organization). Petromin manages exploration and concession agreements, oil refineries (except that of Aramco at Ras Tanura) and the distribution and marketing of oil and oil products.

In 1978, when Aramco produced 2,944m. bbls of crude oil, 149m. (5·1%) were processed by the Ras Tanura refinery, 120m. (3·43%) were sent by pipeline to Bahrain and by Tapline to the Mediterranean port of Saida, and 2,653m. (90·1%) were shipped out *via* Gulf terminals. This pattern will change as the national refining capacity increases. In 1977 capacity at Ras Tanura (Aramco) was 565,000 bbls per day, 15,000 bbls per day at Riyadh and 13,000 bbls per day at Jeddah (both Petromin). During 1980 contracts were signed for the establishment of 3 new refineries of an initial capacity of 250,000 bbls per day each at Jubail and Yanbu (the latter to be connected with the eastern oilfields by a 48-in. pipeline, construction of which was scheduled for completion in 1980) and 325,000 bbls per day at Rabigh. In 1978, 275m. bbls of refined products were produced by Saudi Arabian refineries, of which fuel oil accounted for 95m., gasoline, 65m., LPG, 55m. and diesel oil, 35m.

The gas collection programme under Petromin management was initiated in 1975. The first phase was scheduled to come on stream in 1980, and the entire system is planned to be completed by 1985. It will provide fuel gas for local industry, feedstock for petrochemical plants, and a surplus for export. The programme includes a pipeline to carry gas to the industrial zone at Yanbu, which is to be constructed by 1981. In 1978 Aramco produced 91m. bbls of natural gas liquids, obtained in association with crude production.

Minerals. Surveys were launched during the second development plan to investigate potential mineral wealth other than oil. Viable deposits of several minerals including gold have been found. There are also reports of uranium deposits.

Agriculture. The Saudi Arabian Agricultural Bank in Riyadh had (1974) capital of SR103m. Most of the loans granted were for agricultural equipment or for drilling or deepening wells. SR300m. has been allocated to major projects of desert reclamation, including irrigation schemes, land preparation and sowing, drainage and control of surface water, control of moving sands and distribution of undeveloped land to farmers. A full survey of water resources is in progress; in 1980 there were 11 seawater desalination plants working in 7 towns, another 6 units under construction and a further 14 at various stages of planning. The use of greenhouses and hydroponics is increasing.

In 1977 the most productive provinces were Jizan, the West, Asir, Riyadh and Qasim. The principal crops (in tons) were: Dates, 322,000; water melons, 283; tomatoes, 197; sorghum, 139; wheat, 125; dry onions, 106; grapes, 42; squash, 33 and melons, 23.

Livestock estimates for 1979 include 440,000 cattle, 110,000 asses, 2·8m. sheep and 1·9m. goats.

INDUSTRY AND TRADE

Industry. The Government actively encourages the establishment of manufacturing industries in the country. The policy includes the provision of industrial estates and loans covering 50% of capital investment. The Government has also established two industrial poles at Jubail and Yanbu, to be the focus of heavy industrial development. Linked by gas and oil pipelines both are to have petrochemical complexes producing, initially, ethylene and methanol, for which agreements have been signed with American companies. In addition an integrated steel complex and a urea fertilizer factory are under construction in Jubail with Federal German and Taiwanese partners.

Commerce. Exports amounted to 153,000m. rials in 1978 and imports 52,000m. rials. In 1978 the USA was the main supplier, accounting for 20·9% of the total. Other major supplying countries were Japan (15·4%), Federal Republic of Germany (10·8%) and the UK (7·4%). The main imports were machinery and electrical equipment (29%), metal articles (14%), transport equipment (13%) and foodstuffs (11%).

Total trade between Saudi Arabia and UK (British Department of Trade returns, in £1,000 sterling):

	1976	1977	1978	1979	1980
Imports to UK	978,472	1,095,116	870,537	1,108,644	1,927,583
Exports and re-exports from UK	400,399	576,904	786,265	893,600	1,050,145

COMMUNICATIONS

Roads. All the main regions and population centres of the Kingdom are linked by asphalted roads, of which there were 20,134 km in 1979. There are road links with Yemen, Jordan, Kuwait and Qatar, and plans for a causeway link to Bahrain. There were a further 20,119 km of graded, unpaved agricultural roads in 1979. In 1977 there were 153,000 cars, 182,000 commercial vehicles and 3,000 buses.

Railways. A railway from Riyadh to Dammam on the Gulf (571 km, 1,435 mm gauge) *via* Dhahran and the oilfields Abqaiq, Ithmaniya (near Hofuf) and Haradh was completed in Oct. 1951. That section of the Hejaz Railway which is in Saudi Arabian territory is not now in working order, but studies have been initiated to restore the whole line from Damascus to Medina.

Aviation. Saudi Arabian Air Lines, a government-owned company managed in conjunction with Trans-World Airlines, operates regular internal air services, and international routes to Africa, the Middle East, Europe and India, as well as special flights for pilgrims. The pilots are mainly Saudi-Arabians. There are 3 international airports at Jidda, Dhahran and Riyadh and 19 domestic airports. In 1978, 6·5m. passengers and 48,000 tonnes of cargo were carried.

Shipping. The ports of Dammam and Jubail on the Gulf and Jidda and Yanbu on the Red Sea have deep-water piers. In 1979, 24·3m. tonnes were discharged.

Post and Broadcasting. Jidda, Mecca, Taif, Riyadh and Dammam are linked by telephone, Jidda and Cairo by radio-telephone. An international radio-telephone station at Riyadh was opened in 1956. Number of telephones (1978), 185,000. Number of post offices (1970) about 400. In 1971 there were 87,000 radio receivers and 18,000 television receivers.

Newspapers. There are 6 daily newspapers in Arabic and 2 in English.

EDUCATION AND WELFARE

Education. Administration is in educational districts. Schooling is in three stages, primary, intermediate and secondary which is to prepare older pupils for university; pre-primary schools are being introduced. Education is free in all these stages; monthly scholarships are paid to students in higher education. Girls' education is separate. In 1977 there were 103 pre-primary schools with 16,007 pupils, 3,874 primary schools with 726,062 pupils and 38,185 teachers, 1,147 intermediate/secondary schools with 253,228 students and 15,004 teachers and 22 technical education schools with 4,548 students and 705 teachers. There are also adult literacy classes (99,352 students in 1977, 30% women), special schools, commercial, agricultural and industrial schools including the Royal Vocational Institute in Riyadh which can take 8,000 students on two daily shifts.

There were 62 teacher-training schools in 1976.

University courses concentrating on science, engineering, agriculture and medicine, but also covering education, commerce and arts, are available at the Riyadh University, King Abdulaziz University, Jidda, and King Faisal University, Dammam and Hofuf. New general universities are to be created in Abha and Mecca. Specialized engineering studies are available at the University of Petroleum and Minerals, Dhahran, and Arabic and Sharia law studies at the Islamic University, Medina and the Imam Muhammad bin Saud University, Riyadh.

Welfare. The Ministry of Health is responsible for 10 administrative districts, serving both Saudi citizens and pilgrims. In 1977 there were 64 hospitals with 10,182 beds (1,200 private), 799 clinics and health centres, 2,820 doctors, 5,740 nurses and midwives, 1,000 pharmacists and assistants and 913 X-ray and laboratory technicians. Five new hospitals with 2,275 beds opened in 1980 and construction for a further 800 beds was in progress. The Jidda Quarantine Centre, designed by WHO and primarily for pilgrims, can take 2,400 patients. In 1975 there were 4 nursing schools and 3 sanitation training institutes. There is a strict system of health controls for visiting pilgrims and strict supervision of sanitation and water supply.

DIPLOMATIC REPRESENTATIVES

OF SAUDI ARABIA IN GREAT BRITAIN
(30 Belgrave Sq., London, SW1X 8QB)

Ambassador: Sheikh Nasser H. Almanqour.

OF GREAT BRITAIN IN SAUDI ARABIA (PO Box 393, Jedda)

Ambassador: A. J. M. Craig, CMG.

OF SAUDI ARABIA IN THE USA (1520–18th Street, NW, Washington, D.C., 20036)

Ambassador: Faisal al Hegelan.

OF THE USA IN SAUDI ARABIA (Palestine Rd., Ruwais, Jedda)

Ambassador: John C. West.

OF SAUDI ARABIA TO THE UNITED NATIONS

Ambassador: (Vacant).

Books of Reference

The Business Directory of Saudi Arabia. London, 1974
The Gulf Handbook. Bath (annual)
Doughty, C. M., *Travels in Arabia Deserta*. 2 vols. London, 1936
Hobday, P., *Saudi Arabia Today: An Introduction to the Richest Oil Power*. London, 1978
Katakura, M., *Bedouin Village*. Univ. of Toyko Press, 1977
Lewis, B., *Handbook of Diplomatic and Political Arabic*. London, 1947
McMaster, B., *The Definitive Guide to Living in Saudi Arabia*. London, 1980
Meulen, D. van der, *The Wells of Ibn Sa'ud*. London, 1957
Pesce, A., *Jiddah: Portrait of an Arabian City*. 3rd ed. Cambridge, 1978
Philby, H. St. J. B., *Arabian Jubilee*. London, 1952.—*Sa'udi Arabia*. London, 1955
Purdy, A. (ed.), *The Businessman's Guide to Saudi Arabia*. 1976
Stacey International (ed.) *The Kingdom of Saudi Arabia*. (4th ed.) London, 1979
Troeller, G., *The Birth of Saudi Arabia: Britain and the Rise of the House of Sa'ud*. London, 1976

SENEGAL

République du Sénégal

Capital: Dakar
Population: 5·66m. (1980)
GNP per capita: US$360 (1979)

HISTORY. The Republic of Senegal became independent on 20 Aug. 1960, after having been a French territory (1659 foundation of Saint-Louis, 1854–65 occupation of the hinterland), a member state of the French Community (from 25 Nov. 1958) and, from Jan. 1959 to 20 Aug. 1960, a partner (together with Sudan) of the Federation of Mali.

AREA AND POPULATION. The republic has a total area of 196,722 sq. km; the population (estimate, 1980) 5·66m. The capital is Dakar (population (1979), 978,553), Thiès (126,886), Kaolack (115,679), Saint-Louis (96,594), Ziguinchor (79,464) and Diourbel (55,307) are other important towns. The country is divided in 8 regions sub-divided into 28 departments.

The principal autochthonous tribes are the Ouolofs (about 700,000, mostly Moslems), Bambaras, Mandingos, Peuls (Fulbés) and Toucouleurs.

CONSTITUTION AND GOVERNMENT. The republic is administered by a government council of 7 ministers and 2 secretaries of state and 8 other ministers. The national assembly consists of 100 members, elected by universal suffrage, under a proportional representation system, for a 5-year term. In the general election of Feb. 1978 the *Parti socialiste* gained 82 seats and the *Parti démocratique sénégalais* 18 seats.

President of the Republic: Abdou Diouf (took office on 1 Jan. 1981).
Prime Minister: Habib Thiam.
Foreign Minister: Mustapha Niasse.
National flag: Three vertical strips of green, yellow, red, with a green star in the centre.

DEFENCE

Army. The Army has a strength of 8,500, organized in 5 infantry battalions, 1 engineer battalion and minor units.

Navy. The Navy has 4 patrol boats, 3 fast gunboats, 12 small patrol craft, 1 fishery protection trawler, 4 coastal patrol launches, 1 landing craft, 2 minor amphibious craft and 1 training tender. Personnel (1981) 350.

Air Force. The Senegal Air Force, formed with French assistance, has 1 Summit O2-337 Sentry counter-insurgency aircraft, 2 Magister jet trainers, 1 Boeing 727 VIP transport, 5 DC-3/C-47 transports, 6 F.27 twin-turboprop transports, 1 Aztec light transport, 2 Broussard liaison aircraft, 2 Puma, 1 Gazelle and 2 Alouette II helicopters. Personnel total about 160.

INTERNATIONAL RELATIONS

Membership. Senegal is a member of UN, OAU and is an ACP state of EEC.

ECONOMY

Planning. The 1977–81, 4-year plan includes investment in mineral exploration, tourism, cotton, fishing, livestock, seed selection, rice growing and fertilizers.

Budget. The budget for 1978–79 envisaged expenditure of 100,526m. francs CFA.

Currency. The currency is the *franc CFA*.

Banking. Under an agreement with the Crédit Lyonnais a new commercial bank, the Union Sénégalaise de la Banque pour le Commerce et l'Industrie, was established in Sept. 1961; the Senegal Government holds the larger part of its capital. At 31 Dec. 1979 the savings banks had deposits of 122,378m. francs CFA.

AGRICULTURE. The soil is generally sandy. Production (1979) in 1,000 tonnes: Millet, 805; maize, 53; rice, 146; groundnuts, 1m.

Livestock (1979): 2·9m. sheep and goats, 2·8m. cattle, 182,000 pigs, 202,000 asses, 4,000 camels and 271,000 horses.

INDUSTRY. Dakar has numerous industrial works. In 1979 the production of phosphate rock was 1·85m. tonnes; cement, 311,507 tonnes. The discovery of iron-ore deposits at La Faleme has created the possibility that Senegal could become one of Africa's major producers. Reserves are estimated at 980m. tonnes.

TRADE. The chief imports (1978) (in tonnes): Rice (238,996), sugar (55,647), petroleum products (921,771), textiles and machinery.

Imports in 1977 totalled 187,500m. francs CFA; exports, 152,900m.

Total trade between Senegal and UK (British Department of Trade returns, in £1,000 sterling):

	1976	1977	1978	1979	1980
Imports to UK	22,738	31,369	15,334	18,088	15,440
Exports and re-exports from UK	9,385	9,521	10,109	11,000	16,030

Tourism. In 1979, 198,433 tourists visited Senegal.

COMMUNICATIONS

Roads. The length of roads (1979) was 13,869 km.

Railways. There are 5 railway lines: Dakar–Kidira (continuing in Mali), Thiès–Saint-Louis (193 km), Guinguinéo–Kaolack (22 km), Louga–Linguère (129 km), and Diourbel–Touba (46 km). Total length, 1,034 km (metre gauge).

Aviation. In 1979 aircraft disembarked 297,170 and embarked 322,921 passengers and disembarked 7,676 tonnes and embarked 5,605 tonnes of freight at Yoff (Dakar).

Shipping. In 1978, 4,870 vessels entered the port of Dakar. There is a river service on the Senegal from Saint-Louis to Podor (363 km) open throughout the year, and to Kayes (924 km) open from July to Oct. The Senegal River is closed to foreign flags. The Saloum River is navigable as far as Kaolack, the Casamance River as far as Ziguinchor.

Post and Broadcasting. There were, in 1972, 74 post offices. Telephones in 1978 numbered 42,105, of which 33,863 were in Dakar. In 1975 there were 287,000 radio receivers and 1,800 television sets.

Cinemas. In 1975 there were 77 with a seating capacity of 33,500.

JUSTICE, RELIGION, EDUCATION AND WELFARE

Justice. There are *juges de paix* in each *département* and a court of first instance in each region. Assize courts are suituated in Dakar, Kaolack, Saint-Louis and Ziguinchor, while the Court of Appeal resides in Dakar.

Religion. The population is 80% Moslem, 10% Christian (mainly Roman Catholic) and 10% animist.

Education. Secondary education is provided at 11 *lycées*, 66 *collèges d'enseignement secondaire*, 2 *lycées techniques*, 2 *écoles normales* and 3 *cours normaux*. Total pupils in the elementary schools in 1979 was 370,412, including 44,262 attending private schools; in the secondary schools, 82,631 (of whom 15,969 attend private colleges). The University in Dakar was established on 24 Feb. 1957, with faculties of law, science, the arts and a school of medicine and pharmacy; it had 10,309 students in 1979.

Health. In 1979 there were 43 hospitals woth 6,025 beds; also 311 doctors, 37 dentists, 90 pharmacists, 380 midwives and 3,080 nursing personnel.

DIPLOMATIC REPRESENTATIVES

OF SENEGAL IN GREAT BRITAIN (11 Phillimore Gdns., London, W8 7QG)

Ambassador: Saliou Diodj Faye.

OF GREAT BRITAIN IN SENEGAL (20 Rue du Docteur Guillet, Dakar)

Ambassador: C. W. Squire, CMG, MVO.

OF SENEGAL IN THE USA (2112 Wyoming Ave., NW, Washington, D.C., 20008)

Ambassador: André Coulbary.

OF THE USA IN SENEGAL (Ave. Jean XXIII, Dakar)

Ambassador: Walter C. Carrington.

OF SENEGAL TO THE UNITED NATIONS

Ambassador: Falilou Kane.

Books of Reference

Crowder, M., *Senegal: A Study in French Assimilation.* OUP, 1962
Samb, M. (ed.), *Spotlight on Senegal.* Dakar, 1972

SEYCHELLES

Capital: Victoria
Population: 61,900 (1977)
GNP per capita: US$1,060 (1978)

HISTORY. The islands were first colonized by the French in the middle of the 18th century, in order to establish plantations of spices to compete with the Dutch monopoly. They were captured by the English in 1794 and incorporated as a dependency of Mauritius in 1814. In 1888 the office of administrator was created, with an Executive Council and a Legislative Council. In 1897 the Administrator was given full powers as Governor, and in Nov. 1903 he was raised to the rank of Governor with the Seychelles archipelago becoming a separate colony. In June 1976, Seychelles attained independence and is now a republic within the Commonwealth.

British Indian Ocean Territory, a British colony created in 1965, consisted of the Chagos Archipelago (formerly a dependency of Mauritius). Aldabra, Farquhar and Desroches. These latter 3 islands returned to Seychelles in June 1976.

AREA AND POPULATION. The Seychelles consists of 92 islands and islets in the Indian ocean, north of Madagascar, with a combined area of 156 sq. miles (404 sq. km) within two distinct groups. The Mahé or Granitic group of 32 islands cover 87 sq. miles (234 sq. km); the principal island is Mahé, with 56 sq. miles (144 sq. km) and 45,204 inhabitants at the 1971 census, the other inhabited islands of the group being Praslin, La Digue, Silhouette, Frigate and North, which together have 6,660 inhabitants.

The Outer or Coralline group comprises 60 islands spread over a wide area of ocean between the Mahé group and Madagascar, with a total land area of 69 sq. miles and a population of less than 1,000. The main islands are the Amirante Isles (including Desroches, Poivre, Daros and Alphonse), Coetivy Island and Platte Island, all lying south of the Mahé group; the Farquhar, St Pierre and Providence Islands, north of Madagascar; and Aldabra, Astove, Assumption and the Cosmoledo Islands, about 1,000 km south-west of the Mahé group. Aldabra (whose lagoon covers 55 sq. miles), Farquhar and Desroches were transferred to the new British Indian Ocean Territory in 1965, but were returned by Britain to the Seychelles on the latter's independence in 1976. Population (1977, estimate) 61,900.

Vital statistics (1976): Births, 1,642; deaths, 466.

CONSTITUTION AND GOVERNMENT. A new Constitution was introduced in Nov. 1970. The Legislative Assembly consists of 15 elected members, 3 *ex-officio* members and a Speaker. In the election, the Seychelles Democratic Party obtained 10 seats and the Seychelles People's United Party 5 seats. In the 1974 elections the Seychelles Democratic Party obtained 13 seats and the Seychelles People's United Party 2 seats. A Constitutional Conference opened in London in March 1975. A coalition government was formed on 1 June 1975 with 11 ministers, including the Prime Minister, 7 from the Seychelles Democratic Party and 4 Ministers from the Seychelles People's United Party. On 5 June 1977 President Mancham was deposed in a *coup* and F. Albert René became president forming a government entirely from the Seychelles People's United Party. On 1 Oct. 1975 Seychelles became internally self-governing. Independence was granted in June 1976.

The official languages are English and French.

President: Hon. F. Albert René.

National flag: Divided horizontally red over green by a wavy white stripe, with red of double width.

INTERNATIONAL RELATIONS

Membership. Seychelles is a member of UN, the Commonwealth, OAU and is an ACP state of EEC.

ECONOMY

Budget, in rupees, for calendar years, excluding Overseas Aid Scheme:

	1972	1973	1974	1975	1976
Total revenue	79,921,000	83,895,000	97,804,000	111,205,000	164,739,000
of which overseas loans and grants	37,734,000	28,990,000	32,832,000	32,676,000	52,563,000
Total expenditure	81,233,000	87,839,000	98,829,000	123,497,000	165,131,000
of which capital expenditure	38,142,000	29,119,000	32,683,000	33,735,000	44,965,000

Chief items of revenue, 1976: Customs, Rs 35m.; direct taxes, Rs 24m.; fees and fines, Rs 7m.

Chief items of expenditure, 1974: Education, Rs 8,924,000; agriculture, Rs 6,884,000; electricity, Rs 6,683,000; medical, Rs 6,463,000; police, Rs 4,983,000.

Currency. The currency is the Seychelles *rupee.* In March 1981, £1 = 14·85 *rupees*; US$1 = 6·02 *rupees.*

Banking. Barclays Bank International, Standard Bank, Bank of Credit and Commerce, Banque Française Commerciale, Habib Bank, Bank of Baroda and Seychelles Development Bank, have branches in Victoria, Mahé.

AGRICULTURE. Chief products are copra and cinnamon bark. Food crop production is being increased for home consumption and fishing is actively pursued mainly for home consumption but also for export as frozen fish.

Livestock (1979): Cattle, 2,000; pigs, 11,000; poultry, 127,000.

INDUSTRY AND TRADE

Industry. Local industry is expanding, the largest development in recent years being the brewery, but steel fabricated goods, furniture, plastics, soap manufacturing form a growing element.

Commerce. Total trade, in rupees, for calendar years:

	1975	1976	1977	1978
Imports (less re-exports)	191,350,000	290,620,000	349,743,000	402,100,000
Domestic exports	12,903,000	17,408,000	24,385,000	96,300,000

Principal imports (1977): Food, Rs 67·22m., of which rice, Rs 9·6m.; fruit and vegetables, Rs 3·76m.; other major imports, mineral fuels, Rs 67·78m.; manufactured goods, Rs 58·8m.

Principal exports (1977): Copra, Rs 14·5m.; cinnamon bark, Rs 3·76m.; frozen fish, Rs 3·16m.; guano, Rs 1·32m.; coconuts, Rs 1·14m.

Imports (1977) from: UK, Rs 94·59m.; Kenya, Rs 40·79m.; Republic of South Africa, Rs 31·85m.; Singapore, Rs 21·22m.; Australia, Rs 18·44m.

Exports (1977) to: Pakistan, Rs 14·04m.; Mauritius, Rs 2·6m.; USA, Rs 671,292.

Tourism. Tourism has now established itself as an important sector of the economy. The number of visitors has grown very rapidly since the opening of the international airport in 1978 and in 1977 there were 65,000. The number of hotel beds available has expanded under a strictly controlled hotel construction programme and there are now 5 hotels with over 200 beds each and the total number of hotel beds available in Seychelles was about 2,010 in 1977.

COMMUNICATIONS

Roads. There is a good system of tarmac (84 miles) and earth roads (21 miles) in Mahé; Praslin and La Digue have 28 miles (9 miles tarmac); extensive roadmaking is being undertaken.

Aviation. British Airways operates 3 services a week between London and Seychelles, twice weekly from Colombo, Hong Kong and Tōkyō, and once a week from Mauritius and Johannesburg. Air France operates 2 services a week, Air India, Air Tanzania, Air Madagascar, Ethiopian Airlines, Somalia Airlines and Condor Airlines operate a weekly service. Kenya Airways operates a service 3 times a week. 1978 aircraft movements were 13,448; passenger movements, 228,000 (including domestic flights).

Shipping. Shipping (1977), goods unloaded, 132,500 tonnes, of which petroleum, 49,700, and cement, 13,300; goods loaded, 13,000 tonnes, of which guano, 5,300. There are regular cargo vessels from Australia and the Far East, South Africa and Europe. The vessel *Nordvaer* travels to and from Mombasa and visits the outlying islands.

Post and Broadcasting. Services operated by Cable & Wireless Ltd provide telegraphic communications with all parts of the world by satellite, the company's radio-telephone service also extends to all principal countries in the world. In 1978, an automatic dialling telex system was introduced. Telephones in Jan. 1978 numbered 4,560.

Cinemas. In 1978 there was 1 cinema with seating capacity of 500.

JUSTICE, EDUCATION AND WELFARE

Justice. In 1977, 6,337 criminal and other cases were recorded by the police. The police force numbered 492 all ranks and 69 special constabulary.

Education. Equality of educational opportunity exists for all children for a minimum of 9 years. In Jan. 1977 there were 35 primary schools, 14 junior secondary schools, 3 secondary grammar schools, 4 vocational and technical schools and 1 teacher-training college.

In Jan. 1977 there were 4,947 boys and 5,054 girls in primary schools, 1,886 boys and 2,331 girls in junior secondary and secondary grammar schools, 147 boys and 160 girls in vocational and technical schools and 141 in the teacher-training college. A total of 122 students were undergoing training overseas, mainly in the UK; 68 were in university, 35 were undergoing professional/technical training, 12 teacher-training and 7 nursing.

Health. In 1978 there was 1 hospital with 230 beds and 21 doctors in government service.

DIPLOMATIC REPRESENTATIVES

OF SEYCHELLES IN GREAT BRITAIN
(2 Mill St., London, W1R 9TE)

Acting High Commissioner: M. J. Delcy.

OF GREAT BRITAIN IN SEYCHELLES (Victoria Hse., Victoria)

High Commissioner: Eric Young, OBE.

OF SEYCHELLES IN USA

Ambassador: (Vacant).

OF THE USA IN SEYCHELLES

Ambassador: William C. Harrop (resides in Nairobi).

Books of Reference

Statistical Information: Information Office, 52 Kingsgate House, Victoria, Mahé.
Report of Seychelles Constitutional Conference. HMSO, 1970
Population Census 1960.—Agricultural Census 1960. Government Printer, 1961
Seychelles Handbook. Government Printer, 1976
Benedict, B., *People of the Seychelles.* HMSO, 1966
Lionnet, G., *The Seychelles.* Newton Abbot, 1972
Webb, A. W. T., *Story of Seychelles.* Government Printer, 1965

SIERRA LEONE

Capital: Freetown
Population: 3·47m. (1978)
GNP per capita: US$210 (1978)

HISTORY. The Colony of Sierra Leone originated in the sale and cession, in 1787, by native chiefs to English settlers, of a piece of land intended as a home for natives of Africa who were waifs in London, and later it was used as a settlement for Africans rescued from slave-ships. The hinterland was declared a British protectorate on 21 Aug. 1896. Sierra Leone became independent as a member state of the Commonwealth on 27 April 1961, and a republic on 19 April 1971.

AREA AND POPULATION. Sierra Leone is bounded on the north-west, north and north-east by the Republic of Guinea, on the south-east by Liberia and on the south-west by the Atlantic ocean. The coastline extends from the boundary of the Republic of Guinea to the north of the mouth of the Great Scarcies River to the boundary of Liberia at the mouth of the Mano River, a distance of about 212 miles (341 km).

The area of Sierra Leone is 27,925 sq. miles (73,326 sq. km). Population (census Dec. 1974, provisional), 3,002,426, of whom about 2,000 are Europeans, 3,500 Asiatics and 30,000 non-native Africans. Estimate (1978) 3·47m. The capital is Freetown, with 274,000 inhabitants.

Sierra Leone is divided into 3 provinces and the Western Area:

	Sq. km	Estimate 1976	Capital	Census 1974
Western Area	663	400,000	Freetown	274,000
Southern Province	20,378	744,000	Bo	42,000
Eastern Province	15,219	970,000	Kenema	34,000
Northern Province	36,066	1,126,000	Makeni	28,500

The principal peoples are the Temnes, Limbas, Lokos and Korankos in the north, the Temnes in the centre, the Mendis in the south, and the Kissis and Konos in the east.

CONSTITUTION AND GOVERNMENT. For earlier Constitutional history see THE STATESMAN'S YEAR-BOOK 1978–79, p. 1046. Following a referendum in June 1978, a new Constitution was instituted under which the ruling All People's Congress (APC) became the sole legal Party. The 100-member Parliament elected in July 1977 comprised 74 members of the APC and 11 of the opposition Sierra Leone People's Party, who joined the APC rather than lose their seats; there are also 15 nominated members including 12 Paramount Chiefs.

President: Dr Siaka Probyn Stevens.
Vice-Presidents: Sorie Ibrahim Koroma, Dr Sama Siama Banya.
Foreign Affairs: Dr Abdulai Conteh.

The Cabinet, led by the President, consists of 32 members with 7 Ministers of State (including the commanders of the army and of the police, and 3 Paramount Chiefs) and 3 Resident Ministers (one for each Province).

National flag: Three horizontal stripes of green, white, blue.

Local Government. The provinces are administered through the Ministry of the Interior and divided into 167 Chiefdoms, each under the control of a Paramount Chief and Council of Elders known as the Tribal Authorities, who are responsible for the maintenance of law and order and for the administration of justice (except for serious crimes). 143 of these Chiefdoms have been organized into local government units, empowered to raise and disburse funds for the development of the Chiefdom concerned.

DEFENCE

Army. The Army consists of 2 infantry battalions with supporting services including an engineer squadron. Strength (1980), 2,500 officers and men.

Navy. There are 3 fast attack craft and a naval base at Freetown. Personnel (1980), 150.

Air Force. The nucleus of an air arm for the defence forces came into existence in 1973. It operates currently a single **MBB BO** 105 helicopter.

INTERNATIONAL RELATIONS

Membership. Sierra Leone is a member of UN, OAU, the Commonwealth and is an ACP state of EEC.

ECONOMY

Planning. A 5-year plan (1974–79) was launched to develop industry and plantation agriculture but failed its main objectives.

Budget. Revenue and expenditure (in leone) for years ending 30 June:

	1970–71	*1971–72*	*1972–73*	*1973–74*	*1974–75*
Revenue	51,000,000	54,000,000	59,100,000	82,500,000	86,700,000
Expenditure	41,300,000	55,000,000	58,200,000	82,500,000	86,700,000

Currency. The Bank of Sierra Leone, which was established on 4 Aug. 1964, is responsible for providing the currency in the country. It introduced on 4 Aug. 1964 a decimal currency, the *leone* and the *cent*. The paper currency consists of 1, 2, 5 *leone* and 50-*cent* notes; the coinage of 1, 5, 10, 20 and 50 *cents*.

At 30 June 1976 total Sierra Leone notes and coins in circulation was Le. 39·19m. In March 1981, £1 = 2·48 *leone*; US$1 = 1·29 *leone*.

Banking. The Standard Bank Sierra Leone, the National Commercial Bank and Barclays Bank Sierra Leone have their headquarters at Freetown; the Standard Bank has 13 and Barclays Bank 12 branches and agencies.

NATURAL RESOURCES

Minerals. The chief minerals mined are diamonds (850,000 carats, 1978) and bauxite (750,000 tonnes, 1978). Molybdenite and gold are being prospected. Rutile production started in 1979 with expected production of 54,000 tonnes per annum and a potential of 100,000 tonnes per annum.

Agriculture. In the western area farming is largely confined to the production of cassava and garden crops, such as maize and vegetables, for local consumption. In the provincial areas the principal products include rice, which is the staple food of the country, and export crops such as palm-kernels, cocoa beans, coffee and ginger. Cattle production is important in the northern part of the country, and most of the poultry, eggs and pork are produced in the Western Area.

The second agricultural statistical survey showed that in 1970–71 there were 286,137 smallholdings cultivating 1,286,348 acres; large farmers cultivated 18,806 acres. Rice plantations covered 807,557 acres; groundnuts, 34,128 acres; coffee, 176,078 acres.

Livestock (1979): Cattle, 270,000; goats, 175,000m.; sheep, 60,000; chickens, 3·6m.

Fisheries. There has been a gradual expansion of the fishing industry due to the introduction of new fishing techniques and gear. The estimated tonnage of catch of all species of fish during 1973–74 was over 50,000 tonnes. The FAO has carried out a 5-year survey of pelagic fish resources along the coastline and continental shelf.

Total catch of fish is still below the demand of the country. In 1975, 94,601 cwt of fish were imported. Total catch for 1975 was 206,000 tons.

INDUSTRY AND TRADE

Industry. Four pioneer oil-mills for the expressing of palm-oil are operated by the Sierra Leone Produce Marketing Board. Government also operates 4 rice-mills, and there are a number of privately owned mills. At Kenema the Government Department of Forest Industries produces sawn timber, joinery products (including prefabricated buildings) and high-class furniture. In addition, there is a smaller privately owned saw-mill at Panguma and several small furniture workshops throughout the country. All these products are used internally. Village industries include fishing, fish curing and smoking, weaving and hand methods of expressing palm-oil and cracking palm kernels.

Labour. A large proportion of the population was engaged in agriculture and about 125,000 workers were in wage-earning employment. The number of workers in establishments employing 6 or more persons was 72,314 in 1975, distributed as follows: Services, 33·2%; mining and quarrying, 15%; transport, storage and communications, 14·9%; construction, 12·4%; commerce, 8·7%; manufacturing, 8·1%; agriculture, forestry and fishing, 5·1%; electricity and water services, 2·6%.

There are 27 registered trade unions (22 workers and 5 employers). The number of persons registered for employment at the end of 1971 was 7,210, excluding maritime, articled and the dock workers who are registered in the Port Labour (Maritime, Articled and Harbour) Pools; registrations in these Pools numbered 8,471.

Commerce. Total trade (in leone) for calendar years:

	1975	1976	1977	1978
Imports	152,760,000	171,258,000	206,228,000	290,844,000
Exports	116,470,000	109,312,000	156,734,000	194,000,000

Of the imports (1971) 28·8% came from UK, 10·2% from Japan, 7·1% from Federal Republic of Germany. Of the exports (1971) 62·8% went to UK, 9·4% to Netherlands, 6·8% to Japan and 6·5% to the USA.

Total trade between Sierra Leone and UK (British Department of Trade returns, in £1,000 sterling):

	1975	1976	1977	1978	1979	1980
Imports to UK	32,608	35,531	40,053	39,093	75,744	65,697
Exports and re-exports from UK	21,104	17,935	19,669	31,702	32,753	36,785

Tourism. Tourism is being developed and was a major growth industry in 1981.

COMMUNICATIONS

Roads. There were (1977) about 4,406 miles of main roads, of which 665 miles are surfaced with bitumen.

Motor vehicles licensed in 1975 totalled 21, 135: passenger cars, 14,267; buses and trucks, 3,384, and motor cycles, 3,484.

Railways (1977). The government railway closed in 1974, and an 84-km mineral line of 1,067-mm gauge connecting Marampa with the port of Pepel is now used only occasionally.

Aviation. Freetown Airport (Lungi), situated north of Freetown in the Port Loko District, is the only international airport in Sierra Leone and all aircraft entering and leaving the country must land at Lungi.

The airport is served by Sierra Leone Airways, Ghana/Nigeria Airways, British Caledonian, Union de Transport Aériens, KLM, Air Afrique, United Arab Airlines and Czechoslovakia Airlines. A once weekly non-stop flight from London (Gatwick) to Freetown and vice versa is also provided.

Sierra Leone Airways provide domestic flights daily (except Sundays) from Hastings (14 miles from Freetown) to Gbangbatoke, Bo, Kenema, Yengema, twice weekly to Bonthe and occasional flights to Marampa and Port Loko on charter basis.

Shipping. During 1975 the total imports handled by the port of Freetown amounted to 361,454 freight-tons and exports 110,316 freight-tons; a total of 704 vessels called at Freetown; 699 were cargo vessels and 5 were tourist ships with a total of 793 passengers.

Bonthe-Sherbro, 80 miles south of Freetown, is used for the shipment of piassava, palm kernels, rutile and bauxite. Pepel lies some 12 miles from Freetown but is no longer in use.

Post and Broadcasting. The Posts and Telecommunications Department maintains a trunk network of radio and overhead telephone and telegraph routes of approximately 3,000 miles linking the Western Area with the other provinces. Automatic telephone exchanges have been introduced at the provincial centres of Bo, Kenema and Makeni; microwave radio relay link now replaces overhead open wire on main trunk routes. An extension programme to link important mining areas at Koidu and Mokanji to the national network by microwave links is well on the way.

The wired broadcasting relay service was replaced in Jan. 1964 by a transistor radio service. Approximately 20,000 transistor radios purchased under this scheme are now in service.

Number of telephones (1977) 11,600. Telegraphic facilities are provided at 58 offices.

There are 137 post offices and postal agencies.

The number of private wireless-licence holders at 30 June 1972 was 23,958 and 732 television sets were in operation.

JUSTICE, RELIGION, EDUCATION AND WELFARE

Justice. The High Court has jurisdiction in civil and criminal matters. Subordinate courts are held by magistrates in the various districts. Native Courts, headed by court Chairmen, apply native law and custom under a criminal and civil jurisdiction. Appeals from the decisions of magistrates' courts are heard by the High Court. Appeals from the decisions of the High Court are heard by the Sierra Leone Court of Appeal. Appeal lies from the Sierra Leone Court of Appeal to the Supreme Court which is the highest court.

Police. The police force at 31 Dec. 1975 had an authorized strength of 82 superior police officers, 211 junior police officers and 3,833 other ranks including 382 women. In the provinces each Chiefdom keeps an additional force known as Chiefdom Police.

A non-pensionable force, known as the Auxiliary Force and consisting of 2 junior police officers and 272 other ranks, are helping the regular force in maintaining law and order in the diamond protected area in the Eastern Province.

Religion. The majority of the population follow traditional tribal religions. Islam was brought to the region by the nomadic cattle-rearing Fula people from the north around 1600. The Temne people in the north-west form the main part of the Moslem community who were estimated in 1977 to comprise about 20% of the population.

Christianity came to West Africa in the 16th century from Portugal and Spain. The Roman Catholics have 2 dioceses in Sierra Leone and number about 25,000 (1977).

The Evangelical group who led the anti-slavery movement in England founded the Sierra Leone Company in 1791 to settle freed slaves in and around Freetown. In 1966 there were 16 Protestant denominations with a total community of 77,000. Members of the Sierra Leone Church (Anglican) were 25,000 in 1977.

Education (1975–76). There were over 1,974 registered primary schools with a total enrolment of over 205,910. Primary education is as yet neither free nor compulsory but parents and guardians are urged to send their children and wards to school. School attendance varies considerably in different parts of the country. There were 132 secondary schools with a total enrolment of 48,609 pupils; 71 of these schools are fully assisted by the Government. Technical education was provided in 2 technical institutes, 2 trade centres and in the technical training establishments of the mining companies. There is also a rural institute.

Non-graduate teacher-training is offered at two levels: the teachers certificate trains teachers for primary schools and the higher teachers certificate trains teachers for the lower forms of secondary schools.

Fourah Bay College (1,016 students) and Njala University College (586 students) are the 2 constituent colleges of the University of Sierra Leone. The Institute of Education, which is part of the University, is now responsible for teacher education, educational research and curriculum development in the country.

Health (1977). In the Western Area there are 12 government hospitals (1,108 beds and 217 cots), including a maternity hospital, a children's hospital and an infectious diseases hospital near Freetown. There are 6 government health centres in the Western Area. Three private hospitals are located in Freetown with 108 beds. A mental hospital at Kissy has accommodation for 224 patients. In the provinces there are 14 government hospitals, 4 hospitals associated with mining companies and 7 mission hospitals. There is a school of nursing in Freetown. There are 156 government dispensaries and health treatment centres and two military hospitals with 124 beds.

DIPLOMATIC REPRESENTATIVES

OF SIERRA LEONE IN GREAT BRITAIN
(33 Portland Pl., London, W1N 3AG)

High Commissioner: Victor E. Sumner.

OF GREAT BRITAIN IN SIERRA LEONE (Standard Bank of
Sierra Leone Ltd Bldg., Lightfoot Boston St., Freetown)

High Commissioner: T. D. O'Leary.

OF SIERRA LEONE IN THE USA (1701 19th St., NW,
Washington, D.C., 20009)

Ambassador: Mohamed Morlai Turay.

OF THE USA IN SIERRA LEONE
(Corner Walpole and Siaka Stevens St., Freetown)

Ambassador: Theresa A. Healy.

OF SIERRA LEONE TO THE UNITED NATIONS

Ambassador: George Gelaga-King.

Books of Reference

Atlas of Sierra Leone. Ed. Survey and Lands Dept. Freetown, 1953
Sierra Leone Studies. Ed. J. D. Hargreaves. Freetown, 1953 ff.
Fyfe, C., *A History of Sierra Leone.* OUP, 1962.—Fyfe, C., and Jones, E. (ed.), *Freetown.* Sierra Leone Univ. Press and OUP, 1968
Fyfe, C. N. and Jones, E. D., *A Krio–English Dictionary.* OUP and Sierra Leone Univ. Press, 1980
Kup, A. P., *Sierra Leone.* Newton Abbot, 1975
Porter, A. T., *Creoledom: A Study in the Development of Freetown Society.* OUP, 1963
Saylor, R. G., *The Economic System of Sierra Leone.* Duke Univ. Press, 1968

REPUBLIC OF SINGAPORE

Population: 2·39m. (1980)
GNP per capita: US$6,515 (1980)

HISTORY. For the early history of the settlement (1819) and colony (1867) *see* THE STATESMAN'S YEAR-BOOK, 1959, pp. 246 f.

By an agreement entered into between the Governments of Malaysia and of the State of Singapore on 7 Aug. 1965, effective on 9 Aug. 1965, Singapore ceased to be one of the 14 states of the Federation of Malaysia and became an independent sovereign state. The separation was ratified by the Constitution and Malaysia (Singapore Amendment) Act of the Malaysian Parliament on 9 Aug. The 2 governments agreed to enter into a treaty on external defence and mutual assistance. The Singapore Government retains its executive authority and legislative powers under its State Constitution and took over the powers of the Malaysian Government under the Malaysian Constitution in Singapore. The sovereignty and jurisdiction of the head of the Malaysian State was transferred to the Singapore Government. Civil servants working in Singapore for the Federal Departments became Singapore civil servants. Singapore citizens ceased to be Malaysian citizens.

Singapore accepted responsibility for international agreements entered into by the Malaysian Government on its behalf.

AREA AND POPULATION. The Republic of Singapore consists of Singapore Island itself, and some 54 islets.

Singapore Island is situated off the southern extremity of the Malay peninsula, to which it is joined by a causeway carrying a road, railway and water pipeline. The Straits of Johore between the island and the mainland are about three-quarters of a mile wide. The island is some 26 miles (41·8 km) in length and 14 miles (22·5 km) in breadth, and about 237·8 sq. miles (616 sq. km) in area, including the adjacent islets.

Census of population (1970): 1,579,866 Chinese, 311,379 Malays, 145,196 Indians and 38,093 others; total 2,074,507. Estimate (mid-1980), 2,390,800.

Report on the Census of Population 1970. Dept. of Statistics, Singapore, 1973

CONSTITUTION AND GOVERNMENT. By a constitutional amendment the name of the state was changed to 'Republic of Singapore', the head of state was named 'President of Singapore' and the legislative assembly was renamed 'Parliament'.

Malay, Chinese, Tamil and English are the official languages; English is the language of administration.

Parliament consists of 75 members, elected by secret ballot from single-member constituencies, and is presided over by a Speaker, chosen by Parliament from its own members or from outside the Assembly. In the latter case, the Speaker has no vote. With the customary exception of those serving criminal sentences, all citizens over 21 are eligible to vote irrespective of sex, race, education or property qualification. There is a common roll without communal electorates. Citizenship is automatic by birth; it can also be acquired by registration or by naturalization.

A Presidential Council was established under Part IVA of the Constitution enacted on 9 Jan. 1970. The general function of the Council is to consider and report on matters affecting persons of any racial or religious community in Singapore as referred to it by Parliament or the Government. The Council will draw attention to any bill or subsidiary legislation which in the opinion of the Council is a differentiating measure.

Parliament, elected on 23 Dec. 1980, is composed of 75 People's Action Party members.

President of Singapore: Dr Benjamin Henry Sheares (sworn in 2 Jan. 1971).

The People's Action Party Cabinet at Jan. 1981 was composed as follows:

Prime Minister: Lee Kuan Yew.
First Deputy Prime Minister: Dr Goh Keng Swee. *Second Deputy Prime Minister:* S. Rajaratnam. *Education:* Dr Tony Tan Keng Yam. *Culture and Communications:* Ong Teng Cheong. *Foreign Affairs:* S. Dhanabalan. *Labour:* Ong Pang Boon. *National Development:* Teh Cheang Wan. *Law and Science and Technology:* E. W. Barker. *Health:* Dr Toh Chin Chye. *Home Affairs:* Chua Sian Chin. *Social Affairs:* Dr Ahmad Mattar. *Finance:* Hon Sui Sen. *Defence:* Howe Yoon Chong. *Environment:* Lim Kim San. *Trade and Industry:* Goh Chok Tong. There are also 5 Senior Ministers of State and 3 Ministers of State.

National flag: Horizontally red over white, charged in the canton with a crescent and a circle of 5 stars, all in white.

DEFENCE. The Ministry of Defence exercises command and control over all armed forces in the republic. It comprises 5 major divisions, *i.e.*, the general staff, manpower, logistic, security and intelligence and finance divisions. Compulsory military service in peace-time was introduced in 1967.

The governments of Australia, Britain, Malaysia, New Zealand and Singapore continue to co-operate closely in defence arrangements and have agreed on a new 5-nation defence set-up in SE Asia designed to protect Malaysia and Singapore against outside attack. The new defence arrangement came into force on 1 Nov. 1971.

Army. Nine active infantry battalions have been raised and they are organized into 3 infantry brigades. The support arms of the artillery, the engineers and the signals have been expanded. There is an armoured unit of light tanks and armoured assault vehicles. In addition to the battalions which are performing full-time duties, reserve battalions have also been raised as full-time national servicemen are released into reserve service. The People's Defence Force consists of 6 infantry battalions, 2 volunteer battalions and a PDF women's company. Regular strength, 35,000, and reserves, 50,000.

Navy. Naval vessels comprise 6 missile boats of German design, 6 fast patrol craft built by Vosper Thornycroft (2 at Portsmouth, Britain, and 4 in Singapore), 2 *ex*-US coastal minesweepers, 1 seaward defence boat, 1 training vessel, 6 landing ships (*ex*-USN LST) and 6 small landing craft (*ex*-Australian). Personnel in 1981 numbered 3,000 officers and men. There are 10 coastal patrol craft operated by the marine police and 3 survey craft operated by the Singapore Port Authority.

Air Defence Command. The formation of an Air Defence Command began in 1968. The Republic of Singapore Air Force now has 1 squadron of F-5E supersonic fighters; 2 fighter-bomber squadrons equipped with A-4S Skyhawks, supported by TA-4S two-seat trainers; 2 squadrons of Hunter jet fighters and reconnaissance-fighters, supported by Hunter 2-seat trainers, a radar unit and a Bloodhound surface-to-air missile squadron; a transport squadron of C-130s; Skyvans; a squadron of Bell UH-1H Iroquois and Bell 212 helicopters. Personnel strength about 4,000.

INTERNATIONAL RELATIONS

Membership. Singapore is a member of UN, the Commonwealth and the Colombo Plan.

ECONOMY

Planning. The GDP in 1979, at current factor cost was $18,140·9m., an increase of 11·3% over 1978.

Budget. Public revenue and expenditure for financial years (in S$1m.):

	1975	1976	1977	1978	1979
Revenue	3,055	3,131	3,416	3,671	5,037
Expenditure	4,190	4,832	5,545	5,878	4,767

Currency. The *Singapore dollar* (S$) is divided in 100 *cents*. Gross circulation on 30 June 1980 was S$3,237·5m.

Banking. The functions of the Commissioner of Banking have been assumed by the Monetary Authority of Singapore from 1 Jan. 1971.

The Development Bank of Singapore was established in 1968, primarily to provide long-term financing of manufacturing and other industries. In Dec. 1979 it had a paid up capital of S$130·7m. and shareholders' funds amounted to S$326·7m.

There were 89 commercial banks with 288 banking offices operating in Singapore on 31 Dec. 1979. The total assets/liabilities amounted to S$26,700m. on 31 Dec. 1979. Total deposits of non-bank customers amounted to S$12,200m. while loans and advances including bills financing, totalled S$16,000m.

In June 1980, the total balances of the Singapore Post Office Savings Bank was S$2,532·2m.

Weights and Measures. The metric system or the International System of Units (SI) was introduced in 1971 in Singapore.

ENERGY AND NATURAL RESOURCES

Electricity. The Public Utilities Board is responsible for the provision of electricity, gas and water. Electrical power is generated by 6 power stations, with a total generating capacity of 2,060 mw at the end of 1979.

Fisheries. As the prospect of increasing fish production from inshore waters is poor, in 1967 various projects were introduced, with the aim of making Singapore self-sufficient in fish as well as a major fishing base in the region.

The Jurong fishing port and fish market began operating 26 Feb. 1969. A Fishery Training Institute was established at Changi with the assistance of the United Nations Development Programme (Special Fund) to train youths and fishermen in modern fishing techniques. At Changi, too, a Marine Fisheries Research Department was set up under the sponsorship of the South-East Asian Fisheries Development Centre. Research on fish culture and ornamental fish was carried out at the Freshwater Fisheries Laboratory at Sembawang. Ornamental fish industry is fast becoming a valuable foreign exchange earner. Export of ornamental fish in 1979, S$35m. The local catch of fresh fish in 1979 was 16,443 tonnes.

INDUSTRY AND TRADE

Industry. The largest industrial area is the Jurong Industrial Estate with 1,004 factories employing 94,000 workers.

Industries in Jurong include shipbuilding and those manufacturing steel rods, steel pipes, tyres, chemicals, pharmaceuticals, plywood and veneer, plastics, cement, bricks, cables, textiles and wiremesh. Smaller industrial estates have light industry factories producing food, paper and miscellaneous consumer goods.

Labour. In June 1979, 1,018,300 persons were employed, of whom 850,700 were employees, 41,100 were employers, 94,200 were self-employed and 32,300 were unpaid family workers. The majority were working in manufacturing, 293,300; commerce, 236,500; community, social and personal services, 216,200; transport, storage and communications, 118,800.

There were 136 registered trade unions comprising 85 employee unions, 50 employer unions and 1 federation of trade unions as at 31 Dec. 1979. The total membership of employee unions numbered 249,710, of whom 236,699 (95%) of the unionized workers belonged to 51 employee unions affiliated to the National Trades Union Congress. Members of employer unions numbered 6,798.

The Employment Act and the Industrial Relations Act provide principal terms and conditions of employment such as hours of work, sick leave and other fringe benefits. A new labour legislation was introduced allowing youths of 14–16 years to work in industrial establishments, and also children from 12–14 years to be employed in approved apprenticeship schemes. A trade dispute may be referred to the Industrial Arbitration Court which was established in 1960.

The Ministry of Labour operates 3 employment exchanges to assist job seekers to obtain suitable employment and employers to recruit suitable workers. The Central Provident Fund was established in 1955 to make provision for employees in their old age. At Dec. 1979 there were 1,435,564 members with S$7,515·5m. standing to their credit in the fund. The total number of employers registered with the board was 67,169.

Commerce. The principal trading countries for 1979 were Japan (13·7% of total trade), USA (14·1%) and Malaysia (14·2%). In 1979, imports (S$38,334·4m.) rose by 29·5%, mainly due to more imports of raw materials and semi-manufactured goods. Exports rose from S$22,985·5m. in 1978 to S$30,940·1m. in 1979, mainly due to increases in petroleum products, electronic products, crude rubber, machinery and transport equipment and furniture.

In the following table (British Department of Trade returns, in £1,000 sterling) the imports include produce from Borneo, Sarawak and other eastern places, transhipped at Singapore, which is thus entered as the place of export:

	1976	1977	1978	1979	1980
Imports to UK	94,358	102,611	116,747	185,290	535,915
Exports and re-exports from UK	168,235	201,162	255,908	270,718	328,112

COMMUNICATIONS

Roads. Singapore has 2,285 km of public roads, of which 1,957 km are asphalt-paved. In 1979 motor vehicles registered in Singapore numbered 338,729, of which 145,137 were private cars, 6,217 buses including 298 private hire buses, 8,518 taxis and 108,051 motor cycles and scooters.

Railways. A 16-mile (25·8-km) main line runs through Singapore, connecting with the States of Malaysia and as far as Bangkok. Branch lines serve the port of Singapore and the industrial estate at Jurong.

Aviation. The new international airport at Changi was under construction in 1978 and is to be completed in 1981. Thirty-three international airlines operated 444 scheduled services a week, totalling 65,775 aircraft movements at Singapore International Airport in 1979. Freight handled (1979) 154,852 tonnes and there were 6·4m. passengers.

Shipping. A total of 47,425 vessels of 299·5m. NRT entered into and cleared from Singapore during 1979.

Post. In 1979, 66 post offices and 56 postal agencies were in operation. Telephones numbered 625,130 in Feb. 1979.

Cinemas (1979). There were 74 cinemas and 1 drive-in cinema, with a seating capacity of 69,655.

Newspapers (1979). There were 11 daily newspapers, in 5 languages, with a total daily circulation of 587,600.

JUSTICE, EDUCATION AND WELFARE

Justice. There is a Supreme Court in Singapore which consists of the High Court, the Court of Appeal and the Court of Criminal Appeal. The Supreme Court is composed of a Chief Justice and 6 Judges. An appeal from the High Court lies to the Court of Appeal in civil matters and to the Court of Criminal Appeal in criminal matters. Further appeal can in certain cases be made to the Judicial Committee of the Privy Council. The High Court has original civil and criminal jurisdiction as well as appellate civil and criminal jurisdiction in respect of appeals from the Subordinate Courts. There are 8 district courts, 10 magistrates' courts, 1 juvenile court and 1 coroner's court.

Education. Statistics of registered institutions at 30 June 1979:

Classification	Schools	Enrolment	Teachers
Government schools	273	443,180	13,909
Government-aided schools	207	129,262	5,479
Private schools	6	1,952	82
Total	486	574,394	19,470

The University of Singapore has 7 faculties: Arts and social sciences, law, science, medicine, dentistry, engineering, architecture and building; 4 schools: accountancy and business administration, post-graduate medical and dental studies, and school of management; and 1 department: Department of Extramural Studies. It numbered 6,751 students (excluding 124 non-graduating) in 1979. The Nanyang University, established in 1953 and began functioning in 1956, has 4 Colleges of Arts, Science, Commerce and Graduate Studies in addition to a Computer Centre. There were 1,636 students in 1979, and non-degree course students, 67. The Singapore Polytechnic had 7,450 students and the Ngee Ann Technical College had 2,103 students in 1979–80. The Institute of Education, established on 1 April 1973, is now the only institution responsible for teacher education in Singapore and for promoting research in education. There were 2,153 students in 1978–79. There were also 11 vocational institutes and a technical institute with an enrolment of 9,830 students in 1978. The Adult Education Board conducts secondary education classes as well as language, technical, commercial and recreational courses. Enrolment in 1977 totalled 31,000.

The Adult Education Board and the Industrial Training Board were merged to form the Vocational and Industrial Training Board, on 1 April 1979. The VITB has taken over all the functions and responsibilities in vocational training and continuing education. The VITB runs 18 training institutes and centres offering full-time and part-time courses.

The University of Singapore and the Nanyang University were merged in July 1980 and became the National University of Singapore. The first batch of joint campus students who will graduate in April 1981 will receive NUS degrees. The Nanyang Technological Institute, which will be part of the NUS, will be sited in the Nanyang University Campus in Jurong. It will be developed into a University of Technology by 1992.

Health. There were 13 government hospitals with a total of 8,485 beds in 1979. Another 1,261 beds were available in 8 private hospitals. There were 1,852 doctors.

DIPLOMATIC REPRESENTATIVES

OF SINGAPORE IN GREAT BRITAIN
(2 Wilton Cres., London, SW1X 8RW)

High Commissioner: Jek Yeun Thong (accredited 1 Dec. 1977).

OF GREAT BRITAIN IN SINGAPORE
(Tanglin Rd, Singapore, 1024)

High Commissioner: J. D. Hennings, CMG.

OF SINGAPORE IN THE USA (1824 R St., NW,
Washington, D.C., 20009)

Ambassador: P. Coomaraswamy.

OF THE USA IN SINGAPORE
(30 Hill St., Singapore, 0617)

Ambassador: Richard F. Kneip.

OF SINGAPORE TO THE UNITED NATIONS

Ambassador: T. T. B. Koh.

Books of Reference

Statistical Information: The Department of Statistics (PO Box 3010, Singapore) was established 1 Jan. 1922. Its publications include: *Singapore External Trade Statistics* (quarterly), *Monthly Digest of Statistics, Yearbook of Statistics, Population Estimates of Singapore* (bi-annual). *Census of Population 1970. Singapore Yearbook of Labour Statistics. Acting Chief Statistician:* Khoo Chian Kim.

National Library. *Books About Singapore.* Singapore. Biennial
National Trades Union Congress, *Singapore. Towards Tomorrow.* Singapore, 1973
Singapore. Constitution. The Constitution of Singapore. Singapore, 1966

Singapore. Singapore, Publicity Division, Ministry of Culture (formerly *Annual Report*)
Singapore. Government Gazette (published weekly with supplement)
Economic Survey of Singapore, 1979. Ministry of Finance, Singapore, 1980
Facts and Pictures. Singapore, Publicity Division, Ministry of Culture (annual)
Singapore Government Directory. Singapore, Publicity Division, Ministry of Culture
The Statutes of the Republic of Singapore. 8 vols., 1970 (with annual supplements)
Buchanan, I., *Singapore in South East Asia: An Economic and Political Appraisal*. London,
    1972
George, T. J. S., *Lee Kuan Yew's Singapore*. London, 1973
Goh, K. S., *The Economics of Modernisation*. Singapore, 1972
Gramer, R. E., *The Politics of Urban Development in Singapore*. OUP, 1972
Josey, A., *Lee Kuan Yew, The Struggle for Singapore*. Sydney, 1974.—*Singapore: Its Past, Present
    and Future*. Singapore, 1979
Lee, S. Y., *Public Finance and Public Investment in Singapore*. Singapore, 1978
Ooi, J. B. (ed.), *Modern Singapore*. Singapore, 1969
Tan, C. H., *Financial Institutions in Singapore*. Singapore, 1978
Turnbull, C. M., *A History of Singapore, 1819–1975*. OUP, 1977
Wee, T.-B. (ed.), *The Future of Singapore; The Global City*. Singapore, 1977
Wilson, R., *The Future Role of Singapore*. OUP, 1972

National Library: National Library, Stamford Rd, Singapore. *Director:* Mrs Hedwig Anuar.

SOLOMON ISLANDS

Capital: Honiara
Population: 215,000 (1978)
GNP per capita: US$430 (1978)

HISTORY. The Solomon Islands were discovered in 1568 by Alvaro de Mendana, on a voyage of discovery from Peru; 200 years passed before European contact was again made with the Solomons. The Solomon Islands lie within the area 5° to 12° 30′ S. lat. and 155° 30′ to 169° 45′ E. long. The group includes the main islands of Guadalcanal, Malaita, San Cristobal, New Georgia, Santa Isabel and Choiseul; the smaller Florida and Russell groups; the Shortland, Mono (or Treasury), Vella La Vella, Kolombangara, Ranongga, Gizo and Rendova Islands; to the east, Santa Cruz, Tikopia, the Reef and Duff groups; Rennell and Bellona in the south; Ontong Java or Lord Howe to the north; and innumerable smaller islands.

The 4 first-named were placed under British protection in 1893; the other islands were added in 1898 and 1899.

AREA AND POPULATION. The land area of the Solomons is estimated at 11,500 sq. miles (29,785 sq. km). The larger islands are mountainous and forest-clad, with flood-prone rivers of considerable energy potential. Guadalcanal has the largest land area and the greatest amount of flat coastal plain.

The population of Guadalcanal (including Honiara the main town) was 46,619 at census date (Feb. 1976); Malaita (58,721).

Population of the Solomon Islands was (1978) 215,000. Census (1976) 196,823, over 50% being under 20 years (183,665 Melanesians, 7,821 Polynesians, 452 Chinese, 1,359 Europeans, 2,753 Gilbertese and 773 others).

The islands are administratively divided into 4 districts with Central 70,615, Malaita 60,043, Western 40,329 and Eastern 25,836. However, while the administrative breakdown still exists more important now is the Council system. Eight Councils cover the local administration and are virtually in charge of the development of their areas. The population at census 1976 of each of these was as follows: Malaita 60,043, Western 40,329, Guadalcanal 31,677, Honiara 14,942, Makira and Ulawa 14,891, Central Islands 13,576, Eastern Islands 10,945 and Isabel 10,420.

The capital, Honiara, on Guadalcanal, is the largest urban area, with census population in 1976 of 14,942. Rainfall at Honiara (which lies in a rain shadow) is 90 in. per annum; elsewhere as high as 300 in.; the average is 120–140 in.

CONSTITUTION AND GOVERNMENT. In 1960, a Legislative Council was established, with an Executive Council.

1969 saw a further change in the Constitution, making provision for an elected majority in a single Governing Council with an Executive Council. Elections were held in 1970 with the newly constituted council consisting of 3 *ex officio*, 6 public service and 17 elected members. By the end of 1971, the 6 public service members were withdrawn and a Solomon Islander appointed as chairman presiding over public meetings.

The transition to a ministerial form of government took place during 1974. The Governing Council became the Legislative Assembly, and in Aug. the elected members chose a Chief Minister.

A Council of Ministers was also appointed, and the High Commissioner re-designated Governor. He, in consultation with the elected members, appointed the first Solomon Islander Speaker of the Assembly.

Constitutional changes and developments are aimed at protecting the fundamental rights and freedoms of individual Solomon Islanders, to provide an independent Public Service Commission to oversee the Public Service in replacement of the Public Service Advisory Board established in 1968, and to see that its islands move smoothly and flexibly towards self-government.

The Solomon Islands achieved internal self-government on 2 Jan. 1976. In the same year a general election was held and 38 members were returned to the Legislative Assembly. These members elected a chief minister who appointed from them the 8 ministers who with the chief minister form the Council of Ministers (*i.e.*, Cabinet). The Constitution provides for 2 additional ministers if required.

The Governor retains control over security, defence and external affairs, but on all other matters his powers are exercised in accordance with the advice of the Council of Ministers.

A Constitutional Conference was held in London during Sept. 1977, where it was agreed that there should be full independence for the Solomon Islands and this was granted on 7 July 1978.

Considerable control over local affairs has been devolved on the 5 district councils whose members are elected under popular franchise.

Governor General: Baddeley Devisi.
Prime Minister: Peter Kenilorea.
National flag: Divided blue over green by a diagonal yellow band, and in the canton 5 white stars.

INTERNATIONAL RELATIONS

Membership. The Solomon Islands is a member of UN and is an ACP state of EEC.

ECONOMY

Planning. The overall objective of the $A60m. first National Development Plan covering the years 1975–79 was to provide guidelines for the development of the country. A review of the first 2 years of operation of the plan has shown that many of the targets have been met, while the prospects for the rest of the Plan period appear cautiously optimistic, with increased production and export earnings, a likely favourable balance of trade and improved revenue.

Budget. The budget for 1977 envisaged revenue of SI$14m. (including SI$2m. as grant-in-aid from UK) and expenditure SI$10·3m.

Currency. The medium of exchange is Australian decimal currency introduced in Feb. 1966, but the Solomon Island dollar (SI$) was introduced in 1977. The estimated amount of currency in circulation at the end of Dec. 1970 was $A4·3m.

NATURAL RESOURCES

Agriculture. Coconuts, cocoa, rice and other minor crops are grown. Oil-palm is being developed successfully with a total of about 6,800 acres having been planted. Production of copra (1976), 22,500 tonnes.

An oil-mill became operational in 1976 and 3,205 hectares of oil-palms have been planted. 3,500 tons of palm-oil out of 300 tons of palm-kernels were exported in 1976.

Rice-cropping in 1976 from 834 hectares yielded 1,850 tonnes of milled rice.

Timber extraction is an important development in the Solomons. Timber (logs, sawn timber and veneer sheets) exports for 1976 were 242,700 cu. metres ($A6,244,000), an increase of 12,300 cu. metres over 1975 exports.

Livestock (1979): Cattle, 26,000; pigs, 37,000; poultry, 140,000.

Fisheries. A total catch of 20,700 tonnes of skipjack was made in 1978. Exports of fish totalled $A9·11m. in 1976.

COMMERCE (1976). The main imports were food, fuels and capital goods and totalled $A21m. Exports comprised copra (23,015 tonnes), frozen fish (12,160 tonnes), rough timber (241,000 cu. metres), canned fish (672 tonnes), palm-oil (3,799 tonnes), marine shell, cocoa and manufactured tobacco. Australia supplied 38% of the imports; Japan, 13%; Singapore, 10%, and of the exports, 36% went to Japan, 13% to UK, 11% to Puerto Rico and 11% to American Samoa.

COMMUNICATIONS

Aviation. Regular flights from Fiji and Australia (*via* Papua New Guinea) provide the main communication link. Solair, the internal airline, and innumerable small ships, provide inter-island transport.

Shipping. Shipping services are maintained with Australia, New Zealand, UK and the Far East.

Post. Number of telephones (Jan. 1978), 1,984. A VHF radio telephone service operates internally as well as overseas.

Newspapers. There are 4 weekly newspapers, 1 with a circulation of 4,000 and the other 3 with 3,000.

EDUCATION AND WELFARE

Education. In 1974, a Ministry of Education and Cultural Affairs was created. Library, museum services, sociological researches, the national archives and church schools come under this ministry.

Primary education is still largely in the hands of the churches. Of the 323 registered schools in 1974, 5 were run by the Government, 35 by local councils, 6 by others and 277 by the churches. The enrolment at primary schools was 24,088. There are 6 secondary schools of which 5 are run by the churches. The enrolment was 1,566.

In 1974, the Government's recurrent expenditure on education totalled $A1·5m. $A700,000 of this went in grants to various kinds of schools controlled by churches, the local councils and other authorities. About $A543,500 was spent on various school capital projects under the Sixth Development Plan (1971–74), and a further $A357,000 provided scholarships to students overseas.

Health. In 1971 there were 1,413 hospital beds.

DIPLOMATIC REPRESENTATIVES

OF THE SOLOMON ISLANDS IN GREAT BRITAIN

High Commissioner: Francis Bugotu, CBE.

OF GREAT BRITAIN IN THE SOLOMON ISLANDS
(Sotel House, Mendana Ave., Honiara)

High Commissioner: G. J. A. Slater.

Books of Reference

B.S.I.P. Annual Report, 1969. Honiara, 1970
Pacific Islands Year Book and Who's Who. Sydney, 1968
Building the Nation. Honiara, 1975
Amhurst, Lord, and Thompson, B., *The Discovery of the Solomon Islands in 1568.* London, 1967
Fox, C. E., *The Threshold of the Pacific.* London, 1924
Kent, J., *The Solomon Islands.* Newton Abbot, 1972
Miller, J., *Guadalcanal: The First Offensive.* Washington, 1949

SOMALI DEMOCRATIC REPUBLIC

Capital: Mogadiscio
Population: 3·64m. (1980)
GNP per capita: US$130 (1978)

Al-Jumhouriya
As-Somaliya
Al-Domocradia

HISTORY. The Somali Republic came into being on 1 July 1960 as a result of the merger of the British Somaliland Protectorate, which became independent on 26 June 1960, and the Italian Trusteeship Territory of Somalia.

For the previous history of these territories *see* THE STATESMAN'S YEAR-BOOK, 1960, pp. 337 and 1367.

AREA AND POPULATION. The Somali Republic has a total area of about 630,000 sq. km (246,000 sq. miles) with an estimated population (1980) of 3·64m. Mogadiscio is the capital (population, 400,000). Other towns: Hargeisa (70,000), Kisimayu (70,000), Merca (60,000), Berbera (65,000). There has never been a census.

There are long-standing territorial disputes with Kenya and Ethiopia.

CONSTITUTION AND GOVERNMENT. A new Constitution was approved by referendum on 23 Aug. 1979 and came into force on 23 Sept. The sole legal Party (since 1 July 1976) is the Somali Revolutionary Socialist Party, administered by a 73-member Central Committee. There is an Executive President nominated by the Central Committee and elected for a 6-year term by the People's Assembly; the latter consists of 121 members elected by universal suffrage for a 5-year term and a further 6 members appointed by the President. *President:* Maj.-Gen. Mohammed Siyad Barre.

The Council of Ministers, appointed and led by the President, also includes:
Presidential Advisors: Maj. Gen. Hussein Kulmia Afrah (*Government Affairs*), Brig.-Gen. Ahmed Suleyman Abdulle (*National Security*). *Minister of Defence:* Brig.-Gen. Mohamed Ali Samater. (These 3, together with the President and the Chairman of the People's Assembly, Gen. Ismael Ali Aboker, constitute the Political Bureau of the SRSP.) *Foreign Affairs:* Dr. Abderrahman Jama Barreh.

National flag: Light blue with a white star in the centre.

The national language is Somali. Arabic is also an official language and English and Italian are extensively spoken.

DEFENCE

Army. The Army of 60,000, plus 20,000 militia, includes 3 tank brigades, 16 infantry brigades, 13 field artillery, 10 AA artillery battalions and 3 commando brigade. Border guards number 1,500.

Navy. The Navy has 4 submarine chasers (fast-attack/torpedo/patrol craft), 2 fast missile craft, 4 fast torpedo boats, 5 patrol craft, 1 medium landing ship and 4 minor landing craft. All are former Soviet naval units. Personnel (1981) 350.

Air Force. Formed with a nucleus of aircraft taken over from the former Italian Air Corps of Somalia, in 1960, the Air Corps was built up with Soviet aid. Current equipment includes 7 MiG-21 supersonic fighters, about 15 MiG-17 and MiG-15 jet-fighters and two-seat advanced trainers, a few Il-28 light jet bombers, and small transport, helicopter and training units. Personnel total about 1,000.

INTERNATIONAL RELATIONS

Membership. Somalia is a member of UN, OAU, the Arab League and is an ACP state of EEC.

ECONOMY

Planning. The 1979–81 development plan envisages expenditure of Som.Sh.7,000m., of which 37% is allocated to livestock, agriculture and mineral development, 7% to health and education.

Budget. The budget for 1980 envisaged Som.Sh.2,479m. expenditure.

Currency. The currency is the *Somali shilling*, divided into 100 cents. The money is issued in notes of 1, 5, 10, 20 and 100 shillings and coins of 1, 5, 10, 50 cents and 1 shilling. Currency in circulation (1979) Som.Sh.1152·6m. In March 1981 £1 = 13·15 Som.Sh.; US$1 = 6·02 Som.Sh.

Banking. The Banco di Roma, Napoli, National & Grindlays Bank and Banco di Portsaid have all more than one branch each in the country. The Somali National Bank and the Somali Development Bank are both state-owned.

Weights and Measures. The metric system is in use.

ENERGY AND NATURAL RESOURCES

Electricity. Electricity production (1977) was 45m. kwh.

Minerals. Deposits of iron ore in the south and gypsum in the north are known to exist. Beryl and columbite are also found in the north. None are commercially exploited. Several firms hold exploration and drilling licences for oil. Uranium is found in Juiba region.

Agriculture. Somalia is essentially a pastoral country, and about 80% of the inhabitants depend on livestock-rearing (cattle, sheep, goats and camels). In Southern Somalia, especially along the Shebeli and Giuba rivers, there are Somali and Italian plantations with a cultivated area of some 90,000 hectares. Estimated production, 1978 (in 1,000 tons): Sugar, 200; bananas, 150; maize, 100; sorghum, 130; grapefruit, 6; cotton, 1 Fresh fruit and oil seeds are grown in increasing quantities.

Livestock (1979): 16m. goats; 10m. sheep; 5·4m. camels; 3·8m. cattle; 1,000 horses, 23,000 asses and 23,000 mules.

INDUSTRY AND TRADE

Industry. In 1975, 275 industrial establishments employed 10,383 workers and produced a gross output of Som.Sh.405m., of which Som.Sh.157m. was in food manufacturing. In 1971 a sugar refinery at Jowhar had 5,300 workers; a textile factory at Balad employed 750; and a meat canning plant at Kisimayu employed 500; there is also a fish processing plant at Las Korey, and a milk bottling plant at Mogadiscio.

Trade. In 1978 imports were Som.Sh.1,519m. and exports Som.Sh.670·8m. The chief exports are fresh fruit, livestock, hides and skins.

Total trade between the Somali Republic and UK (British Department of Trade returns, in £1,000 sterling):

	1975	1976	1977	1978	1979	1980
Imports to UK	239	766	257	274	96	303
Exports and re-exports from UK	3,829	5,628	14,198	19,980	20,959	6,682

COMMUNICATIONS

Roads. Somalia has no developed transport system. Internal freight and passenger transport is almost entirely by means of road haulage. There are 8,115 miles of roads (1,243 miles are paved). In 1973 there were 8,200 passenger cars and 5,200 commercial vehicles, including buses.

The Chinese have constructed a 649-mile road from Beletwein to Burao.

Aviation. There is a commercial national airline, Somali Airlines. Mogadiscio airport is used by Alitalia, Alyemda, Aeroflot and Kenya Airways. Through Nairobi to the south and Khartoum and Jedda to the north there are reasonable connexions for travelling to any part of the world.

Shipping. There are 3 deep-water harbours at Kisimayu, Berbera and Mogadiscio. Because of the shape of the country, coastal shipping is an important form of internal transport. The merchant fleet (1973) is 1,613,000 gross tons. In 1973, 900,000 tonnes of international seaborne goods were handled in the main ports.

Post and Broadcasting. There is a manual telephone system in several towns, but Mogadiscio has an automatic system; number of telephones (1971), about 4,740. The state radio stations transmit in Somali, Arabic, English and Italian from Mogadiscio, Hargeisa, Anhazic, Koti.

Cinemas. In 1970 there were 26 cinemas with a seating capacity of 23,000.

RELIGION, EDUCATION AND WELFARE

Religion. The population is almost entirely Sunni Moslems. There are very few Roman Catholics, mainly in the capital.

Education. The nomadic life of a large percentage of the population inhibits education progress. In 1976–77 there were 268,414 primary pupils, 41,735 intermediate pupils, 16,794 secondary pupils and 2,668 vocational students. In 1972 the Somali script was introduced and in 1975 a mass literacy campaign was launched. Teachers in training (1974) 900.

The National University of Somalia in Mogadiscio (founded 1959) had 2,809 students in 1975.

Health. In 1976 there were 179 doctors, 21 pharmacists (1972), 586 medical assistants, 480 nurses (1972), 193 midwives (1972), 75 hospitals and 187 dispensaries (1972). There was a total of 5,691 beds.

DIPLOMATIC REPRESENTATIVES

OF SOMALIA IN GREAT BRITAIN (60 Portland Place, London, WIN 3DG)

Ambassador: Mohamed Jama Elmi.

OF GREAT BRITAIN IN SOMALIA (Waddada Xasan Geeddi Abtoow 7/8, Mogadiscio)

Ambassador: R. M. Purcell.

OF SOMALIA IN USA (600 New Hampshire Ave., NW, Washington, D.C., 20037)

Ambassador: Dr Adbullahi Ahmed Addou.

OF USA IN SOMALIA (Corso Primo Luglio, Mogadiscio)

Ambassador: Donald K. Petterson.

OF SOMALIA TO THE UNITED NATIONS

Ambassador: Mohamed Sharif.

Books of Reference

Background to the Liberation Struggle of the Western Somalis. Ministry of Foreign Affairs, Mogadiscio, 1978
The Agricultural Economy of Somalia. US Dept. of Agriculture, Washington, 1971
Drysdale, J., *The Somali Dispute.* London, 1964

Karp, M., *The Economics of Trusteeship in Somalia.* Boston Univ. Press, 1960
Legum, C. and Lee, B., *Conflict in the Horn of Africa.* London, 1977
Lewis, I. M., *A Pastoral Democracy.* London, 1962.—*The Modern History of Somaliland.* London, 1965
Lytton, The Earl of, *The Stolen Desert.* London, 1966
Touval, S., *Somali Nationalism.* Harvard Univ. Press and OUP, 1963

REPUBLIC OF SOUTH AFRICA

Capital: Pretoria
Population: 24m. (1979)
GNP per capita: US$1,480 (1978)

Republiek van Suid-Afrika

HISTORY. The Union of South Africa was formed in 1910 and comprised the former self-governing British colonies of the Cape of Good Hope, Natal, the Transvaal and the Orange Free State.

The Union remained a member of the British Commonwealth until it became a republic on 31 May 1961.

AREA AND POPULATION. South Africa is bounded north by South West Africa, Botswana and Rhodesia, north-east by Mozambique and Swaziland, east by the Indian ocean, south and west by the South Atlantic. Lesotho forms an enclave between the Orange Free State and Natal. The total area of the republic is 440,355[1] sq. miles (1,140,519 sq. km), divided between the provinces as follows: Cape Province, 253,529 (656,641); Natal, 33,578 (86,967); Transvaal, 103,829 (268,918); Orange Free State, 49,418 (127,993).

On 25 Dec. 1947 the Union formally took possession of Prince Edward Island and, on 30 Dec., of Marion Island, about 1,200 miles south-east of Cape Town.

[1] Excludes Walvis Bay (434 sq. miles), which is an integral part of the Cape Province but is administered under Act No. 24 of 1922 by South West Africa, and Transkei (16,675 miles, 43,188 km).

The census taken in 1904 in each of the 4 colonies was the first simultaneous census taken in South Africa. In 1911 the first Union census was taken.

		All races		Whites		Non-whites	
	Total	*Whites*	*Non-Whites*	*Males*	*Females*	*Males*	*Females*
1904	5,174,827	1,117,234	4,057,593	635,317	481,917	2,046,370	2,011,223
1911	5,972,757	1,276,319	4,696,438	685,206	591,113	2,383,879	2,312,559
1921	6,927,403	1,521,343	5,406,060	783,006	738,337	2,753,188	2,652,872
1936	9,587,863	2,003,334	7,584,529	1,017,557	985,777	3,818,211	3,766,318
1946	11,415,925	2,372,044	9,043,881	1,194,201	1,177,843	4,610,862	4,433,019
1951	12,671,452	2,641,689	10,029,763	1,322,754	1,318,935	5,109,331	4,920,432
1960	15,994,181	3,080,159	12,914,022	1,534,923	1,545,236	6,504,317	6,409,705
1970[1]	21,402,470	3,726,540	17,675,930	1,856,180	1,870,360	8,689,920	8,986,010

[1] Census, May 1970.

Of the non-White population in 1979, 16·32m. were Bantu, 2,533,000 Coloured and 792,000 Asiatic. The numerically leading Bantu nations are the Zulu (5·39m.), Xhosa (3·1m.), Sepedi (North Sotho) (2m.), Seshoeshoe (South Sotho) (1·7m.), Tswana (1·4m.). White population, 1979, 4,446,000.

In 1970 Afrikaans was the home language of 2,146,902 Whites, English of 1,404,479 Whites. Of the 15,036,360 Bantu about 50% could read and write, and 3·2m. (80%) of Bantu children of school-going age were attending school in 1972.

Vital statistics for calendar years:

	Whites					Asians and Coloureds		
	Births	*Deaths*	*Marriages*	*Immi-grants*	*Emigrants*	*Births*	*Deaths*	*Marriages*
1975	80,026	35,035	41,333	50,464	10,255	87,835	32,449	24,632
1976	78,568	36,508	40,483	46,239	15,641	85,899	33,533	25,705
1977	74,037	35,280	38,537	24,822	26,000	83,995	30,217	26,442
1978	73,216	35,877	41,048	18,669	20,686	85,843	27,097	26,796

The registration of Bantu essential data was introduced on a compulsory basis many years ago. However, despite serious efforts on the part of the registering authorities, the Bantu are still largely reluctant to have their essential data registered. Consequently no complete vital statistics are available for this population group.

Principal cities (excluding suburbs) according to the latest statistics (1970) are:

Town	Whites	Africans	Coloureds	Asians	Total
Alberton	26,802	2,567	793	160	30,322
Benoni	43,928	98,183	389	7,063	149,563
Bloemfontein	74,516	95,510	10,152	1	180,179
Boksburg	37,038	56,041	10,876	329	104,284
Brakpan	30,374	82,560	178	3	113,115
Cape Town	378,505	107,877	598,952	11,263	1,096,597
Carletonville	22,025	70,077	932	31	93,065
Durban	257,780	224,819	43,699	317,029	843,327
East London	56,809	51,244	13,249	1,994	123,294
Germiston	95,768	29,886	4,461	2,158	132,273
Johannesburg	501,061	809,595	82,639	39,348	1,432,643
Kempton Park	32,349	3,239	138	41	35,767
Kimberley	29,397	48,797	24,657	938	103,789
Krugersdorp	34,844	52,600	3,047	711	91,202
Pietermaritzburg	45,503	68,262	8,756	36,400	158,921
Port Elizabeth	149,569	201,574	112,154	5,280	468,577
Pretoria	304,618	234,695	11,343	11,047	561,703
Roodepoort Maraisburg	56,734	54,217	2,174	1,066	114,191
Springs	44,627	55,892	2,234	1,337	104,090
Vereeniging	34,568	122,052	1,951	1,982	169,553
Welkom	31,381	98,988	1,398	—	131,767

Bruwer, J. P., *Die Bantoe van Suid-Afrika*. Johannesburg, 1958
Millin, Sarah G., *The People of South Africa*. London, 1951
Patterson, Sheila, *Colour and Culture in South Africa*. London, 1953
Ritter, E. A., *Shaka Zulu*. London, 1955
Saron, G., and Hotz, L., *The Jews in South Africa*. London, 1955
Schapera, I., *The Bantu-speaking Tribes of South Africa*. Cape Town, 1953

CONSTITUTION AND GOVERNMENT. The Republic of South Africa Constitution Act 1961 established with effect from 31 May 1961, the republic, consisting of the 4 provinces—the Cape of Good Hope, Natal, the Transvaal and the Orange Free State—which until then comprised the Union of South Africa.

On 5 Oct. 1960 a referendum was held among the white voters (1,800,426 on roll) to decide whether the Union should become a republic. Of the 1,634,240 votes polled, 850,458 were in favour of a republican constitution, 775,878 against it; 7,904 votes were invalid. The voting was as follows: Transvaal, 406,632 for, 325,041 against; Cape Province, 271,418 for, 269,784 against; Orange Free State, 110,171 for, 33,438 against; Natal, 42,299 for, 135,598 against; South West Africa, 19,938 for, 12,017 against.

The head of the republic is the State President; he is elected for a 7-year term (at a meeting specially convened for the purpose) by an electoral college consisting of the members of the House of Assembly and presided over by the Chief Justice or a judge of appeal designated by him.

On 29 May 1980 the Republic of South Africa Constitution Fifth Amendment Bill was passed and became operative on 1 Jan. 1981. The Senate was abolished from 1 Jan. 1981 and a 60-member President's Council was formed. It consists of White, Coloured, Indian and Chinese representatives nominated by the President for a 5-year term. It was envisaged that a separate advisory council would represent Black views.

A session of Parliament must be held once at least in every year.

The House of Assembly consists of 165 members chosen in electoral divisions as follows: Transvaal, 76; Cape of Good Hope, 55; Natal, 20; Orange Free State, 14.

A member of the House of Assembly must be a white South African citizen, qualified as a voter and resident for 5 years within the republic. Every House of Assembly continues for 5 years unless sooner dissolved.

Only the House of Assembly can originate money bills, but may not pass a bill for taxation or appropriation unless it has been recommended by the State President during the session. Restrictions are placed on the amendment of money bills by the Senate. Provision is made respecting disagreements between the Houses and the State President's assent to bills.

To hold an office of profit under the State (with certain exceptions) is a disqualification for membership of either House, as are also insolvency, crime and insanity. Pretoria is the seat of government, and Cape Town is the seat of legislature.

The state of the parties in the House of Assembly after the general election of Nov. 1977 was as follows: National Party, 134; Progressive Federal Party, 17; New Republic Party, 10; South African Party, 3.

Elections were held in April 1981.

State President: Marais Viljoen.

The Executive Council (National Party) was, Oct. 1980, composed as follows:

Prime Minister, Minister of National Security: P. W. Botha.

Manpower Utilisation: S. P. Botha. *Co-operation and Development:* Dr P. G. J. Koornhof. *Transport:* H. Schoeman. *Industrial Affairs and Trade and Tourism:* D. J. de Villiers. *Finance:* O. P. F. Horwood. *Internal Affairs:* J. C. Heunis. *Coloured Relations and Indian Affairs:* S. J. M. Steyn. *Justice:* H. J. Coetzee. *Water Affairs and Forestry:* Dr C. V. van der Merwe. *Posts and Telecommunications:* H. H. Smit. *Foreign Affairs and Information:* R. F. Botha. *Mines and Energy:* F. W. de Klerk. *Police and Prisons:* L. le Grange. *National Education:* Dr G. V. N. Viljoen. *State Administration and Statistics:* Dr A. P. Treurnicht. *Health and Social Welfare and Pensions:* Dr L. A. P. A. Munnik. *Education and Training:* Dr. F. Hartzenberg.

The following are deputy ministers without Cabinet rank:

Defence and National Security: H. J. Coetsee. *Agriculture:* A. A. S. Hayward. *Interior and Community Development:* S. F. Kotze. *Finance:* P. T. C. du Plessis. *Co-operation and Development:* G. De V. Morrison, J. J. G. Wentzel.

The Prime Minister receives an annual salary of R43,000 and a reimbursive allowance of R20,000; a member of the Cabinet an annual salary of R23,500 and a reimbursive allowance of R6,500; and a Deputy Minister an annual salary of R19,000 and a reimbursive allowance of R6,500.

The English and Afrikaans languages are both official, subject to amendments carried by a two-thirds majority in joint session of both Houses of Parliament.

National flag: Three horizontal stripes of orange, white, blue, with the flags of the Orange Free State and the Transvaal, and the Union Jack side by side in the centre.

National anthem: The Call of South Africa/Die Stem van Suid-Afrika (words by C. J. Langenhoven, 1918; tune by M. L. de Villiers, 1921).

Provincial Administration. In each province there is an Administrator appointed by the State President-in-Council for 5 years, and a provincial council elected for 5 years, each council electing an executive committee of 4 (either members or not of the council), the Administrator acting as chairman. Members of the provincial council are elected on the same system as members of Parliament. The provincial committees and councils have authority to deal with local matters, of which provincial finance, education (primary and secondary, other than higher education and technical education), hospitals, roads and bridges, townships, horse and other racing, and game and fish preservation are the most important. In 1953 the administration and control of Black education was transferred from the provincial councils to the central government. All ordinances passed by a provincial council are subject to the veto of the State President-in-Council.

Bantu Administration. In 1951 the Bantu Authorities Act was enacted to provide a system of Bantu tribal, regional and territorial authorities. These were given limited administrative, executive and judicial functions and limited legislative powers. In 1959 the main ethnic groups received legislative recognition by the passing of the Promotion of Bantu Self-Government Act, which provided *inter alia* for the various ethnic groups to develop into self-governing national units, each with a Commissioner-General representing the Government of the Republic.

As the territorial authorities became experienced an executive body in the form of a government service was set up for each authority to increase their administrative power.

As the Act envisages eventual political autonomy for each of the various national units and as representation in the highest White governing bodies is regarded as a retarding factor, the representation of Bantu by Whites in Parliament and the Cape Provincial Administration was abolished with effect from 30 June 1960.

In 1968 the Ciskei (whose people are also Xhosa-speaking) and the Tswana Territorial Authorities were established, followed by the Lebowa (North Sotho), Machangana (Tsonga-Shangaan), Venda and South Sotho Territorial Authorities in 1969 and the Zulu Territorial Authority in 1970.

During 1971 these authorities, with the exception of the Zulu, were granted increased powers in terms of the Bantu Homelands Constitution Act 1971. In terms of the provisions of part I of this Act, 6 of the existing 7 territorial authorities in the Republic of South Africa (the Transkei became a self-governing territory in 1963 by virtue of the provisions of the Transkei Constitution Act of 1963) have been converted to Legislative Assemblies with extended legislative and administrative powers.

Part II of the Bantu Homelands Constitution Act makes provision for the areas of these legislative assemblies to be proclaimed self-governing territories with *inter alia* the power to repeal or amend, with minor exceptions, acts of the Republican Parliament. Executive power is vested in an Executive Council. These Councils, each headed by a Chief Councillor, consist of 6 members, except in the case of the South Sotho, where there are only 4. Each of these Councillors is responsible for the administration of a Department. A civil service has been established in each instance, staffed by citizens of the respective homelands. White officials will serve the homeland governments on secondment, until trained Bantu citizens are able to take over all duties.

In 1961 the ex-chief of the Umvoti Mission reserve, Albert Luthuli, was awarded the Nobel Peace Prize for his advocacy of peaceful means in the achievement of Black aspirations.

The Coloured Peoples Representative Council consists of 40 elected and 20 nominated members. Elections took place in Sept. 1969 and Tom Swartz, leader of the Federal Party, was appointed Chairman of the Council by the State President. On his death in 1975 he was succeeded by Dr W. Bergins. The Council has legislative powers and its Executive, consisting of 5 members, is responsible on behalf of the Coloured community for the management of finance, education, community welfare and pensions, local government and rural areas and settlements. The Administration of Coloured Affairs has approximately 20,000 administrative and professional posts for Coloureds.

The South African Indian Council is a statutory body consisting of 25 nominated representatives of Indian communities in the Transvaal, Natal and the Cape Province. It advises the Government on the economic, social, cultural and political interests of the Indian population. The S.A. Indian Council Amendment Bill of 1972 enlarges the Council to 30 representatives, the additional 5 to be elected. Voters rolls are being compiled. The number of elected representatives can be amended in the future.

In 1971 the Zulus established a Legislative Assembly. Their seat of government is Ulundi.

The Transkei, territory of the Xhosa nation, became independent on 25 Oct. 1976 (*see* p. 1100), Bophuthatswana on 6 Dec. 1977 (*see* p. 1098) and Venda on 13 Sept. 1979 (*see* p. 1100).

Rhoodie, N. J., and Venter, H. J., *Apartheid: A Socio-Historical Exposition of the Origin and Development of the Apartheid Idea.* Cape Town, 1959

DEFENCE. The South African Defence Force comprises a Permanent Force, a Citizen Force and a Commando organization. The Permanent Force consists of professional soldiers, airmen and seamen who are responsible for the administration and training of the whole Defence Force in peace-time, but who are gradually absorbed into the Citizen Force in time of war. The Permanent Force and the Citizen Force consist of Army, Air Force and Naval components; the Commando organization is an army and air organization.

Every white male citizen between 18 and 65 is liable to undergo training and to render personal service in time of war. Those between the ages of 16 and 25 are liable to undergo a compulsory course of peace training. Peace-time training in Commando organizations extends over a period of 16 years' intermittent training. Training in the Citizen Force takes the form of 2 years of continuous training, followed by 9 years during which training takes place at regular intervals.

Aliens have become liable for military service after 5 years' residence by Act of Parliament, 1967.

The S.A. Defence Force is administered by the Chief of the Defence Force, his advisers being the Chief of the Army, Chief of the Air Force and Chief of the Navy, Chief of Staff Operations, Chief of Staff Personnel, the Chief of Staff Management Services and the Surgeon-General.

Army. South Africa is divided into 9 territorial Commands: Western Province, Eastern Province, Natal, Orange Free State, North Western, Northern Transvaal, Witwatersrand, South West Africa and Southern Cape Commands. Within the various Commands are training units, of which members of the Permanent Force form the permanent staff. Courses of various types are held also at the S.A. Military College. The Army includes 1 armoured, 2 mechanized, 4 motorized and 1 parachute brigade. Equipment includes 250 Centurion and 20 Comet tanks. Total strength (1980), 71,000 and 120,000 Citizen Force.

Navy. The South African Navy has its headquarters at Pretoria. The Navy includes 3 French-built diesel-powered patrol submarines, 3 British-built anti-submarine frigates, 6 fast missile armed patrol vessels (3 built in Durban and 3 in Israel), 10 coastal minesweepers, 5 seaward defence boats (1 used for surveying), 1 modern British-built survey ship, 1 fleet replenishment ship, 1 boom defence vessel, 1 small training vessel, 1 torpedo recovery vessel, 4 rescue launches and 2 tugs.

Naval personnel in 1981 totalled 560 officers and 3,400 ratings, including 1,400 national service men.

New construction included 2 small frigates of the French 'A 69' class armed with Exocet missiles built in Lorient and 2 ocean-going diesel-electric patrol submarines of the French 'Agosta' class built in Nantes, but delivery was stayed by UN resolution. Six missile-armed fast attack craft are being built in South Africa.

A custom-built submarine complex incorporating an operations centre alongside a Syncholift marine elevator capable of docking all South African warships except the large tanker, was opened at Simonstown in July 1972, known as SAS *Drommedaris.* A new maritime headquarters was opened at Silvermine in March 1973.

Air Force. Units of the South African Air Force are organized in Strike, Transport, Maritime, Light Aircraft, Training and Air Logistics Commands. There is 1 light bomber squadron with 6 Canberra B.12 and 3 Canberra T.4; 1 light bomber squadron with 6 Buccaneer Mk.50; 1 maritime reconnaissance squadron equipped with 7 Shackletons; 1 coastal patrol squadron with 18 Piaggio P.166S; 1 fighter-bomber squadron with 32 Mirage F1-AZ ground attack aircraft; 1 general-purpose fighter squadron with Mirage IIICZ interceptors and Mirage IIIRZ reconnaissance fighters; and 1 squadron with Mirage F1-CZ interceptors. Transport squadrons have 9 Transall C-160s, 7 C-130B/E Hercules, 26 C-47s, 4 C-54s, 1

Viscount, 4 twin-jet HS.125s and 5 twin-turboprop Merlin IVA light transports. Four helicopter squadrons and No. 22 Flight have 40 Alouette IIIs, 11 Wasps, 60 Pumas and 14 Super Frelons. T-6Gs are used for primary training, followed by advanced training on Impalas and Mirage IIIEZ/DZ, weapons training on Impalas, and multi-engine/crew training on C-47s. Built under licence in the Republic of South Africa, about 150 two-seat Impala Mk. 1s are being followed by 75 single-seat Impala Mk. 2s, based on the Aermacchi MB.326M and 326K respectively. Two squadrons operate Cessna 185, C4M Kudu and AM.3C Bosbok liaison aircraft.

The Citizen Force has 5 squadrons of Impalas and 1 of Harvards for counter-insurgency duties and 1 squadron of C4M Kudu and AM.3C Bosbok liaison aircraft. CF personnel have additional functions in regular SAAF squadrons, notably those equipped with C-47 transports and P.166 light transport/coastal patrol aircraft. Total strength (1980) was about 6,300 regular officers and men and 4,000 Citizen Force.

INTERNATIONAL RELATIONS

Membership. The Republic of South Africa is a member of UN.

ECONOMY

Budget. A new basis of subsidy has, with effect from the 1971–72 financial year, been brought into operation by the Government following the investigation of the commission of enquiry into the financial relations between the central government and the provinces. The formula on which this subsidy is based is mainly derived from the calculation of: (1) The needs of the various provinces in respect of the services which they have to provide in the fields of education, health, roads and miscellaneous services; (2) the capacity to pay of the various provinces in respect of the different sources from which their 'own' revenue has to be derived; (3) the deficit which arises when the available revenue of each province, as reflected in its capacity to pay, is subtracted from its expenditure, as adjusted in accordance with its needs.

Ordinary revenue and expenditure of the central government (excluding Railways and Harbours Administration) in R1m.:

	1973–74	1974–75	1975–76	1976–77	1977–78
Revenue	3,800·2	4,474·7	5,046·0	6,051·8	8,083·3
Expenditure [1]	3,466·7	5,622·8	6,787·8	7,932·9	8,990·3

[1] Excluding subsidies.

Details of ordinary revenue and expenditure (1978–79) of the central government for years ended 31 March (in R1,000):

Revenue		Expenditure	
Customs	330,000	Plural relations and	
Excise	891,700	development	578,023
Income tax	4,205,200	Foreign affairs	183,766
General sales tax	395,000	Defence	1,554,375
Interest	640,014	Education	326,354
		Social welfare and pensions	449,710
		Public health	148,858
		Police	220,450
		Indian affairs	98,994
		Coloured relations—Rehoboth	
		affairs	283,646

Public debt on 31 March 1979, R16,154m., of which R485m. was foreign debt; internal debt, R15,669m.

Currency. Decimal coinage was introduced in 1959, the units being the *rand* (abbreviated as R) and the *cent* (abbreviated as c). The rand/cent coinage system came into operation on 14 Feb. 1961. The decimal coins are: *Gold coins.* 2 rand; 1 rand. *Silver coins.* 50 cents; 20 cents; 10 cents; 5 cents. *Bronze coins.* 2 cents; 1 cent. In March 1981, £1 = R1·72; US$1 = R0·78.

Banking. Statistics of the South African Reserve Bank,[1] Dec. 1979, are as follows (in R1m.):

Liabilities		Assets	
Notes in circulation	1,631	Gold coin and bullion	3,680
Deposits:		Foreign assets	...
Bankers	366	Domestic discounts and advances	1,028
Government and others	457	Government Securities	64

[1] In Dec. 1920, under the South African Currency and Banking Act, 1920, a Central Reserve Bank was established at Pretoria. It commenced operations in June 1921, and began to issue notes in April 1922. The bank has branches in Pretoria (Head Office), Johannesburg, Cape Town, Durban, Port Elizabeth, East London, Bloemfontein, Pietermaritzburg and Windhoek.

Ratio of legal reserve to liabilities to the public was 22% on 30 April 1977.

The number of depositors in the post office savings bank at the end of March 1979 was 2,176,000, and the amount standing to their credit R200·51m.

Weights and Measures. Prior to 1969 the imperial system of weights and measures was generally used in the country. However, during 1969 the Weights and Measures Act was amended to provide for the gradual change-over to the metric system of weights and measures.

ENERGY AND NATURAL RESOURCES

Electricity. The total capacity of the power plants controlled by the Electricity Supply Commission was 16,837 mw at the end of 1978; production, 82,703 Gwh.; average price per kw. sold, 1·78 cents. Total generation by all power stations (1977), 709,751 Gwh. Power sold in 1978 was 72,797m. kwh.

Water. The government activities in respect of the control and utilization of water are governed by the Water Act, 1956 (as amended), which is administered by the Department of Water Affairs. The Department's expenditure for 1976–77 is: Capital works, R115·5m.; operating costs, R34·5m.; loans and subsidies, R6·54m.; improvements and drainage, R3·42m.

The Orange River Project, launched in 1966, is near completion of its first phase. It is to embrace 3 major dams on the Orange River, 9 smaller dams or weirs, a 51½-mile tunnel, 20 hydro-electric power stations and a system of canals. The first of the major dams—the Hendrik Verwoerd Dam—was built 5 miles upstream from Norvalspont. A Water Research Commission was established in 1971 to co-ordinate and promote research; it is responsible for hydrological research, major water resource development, water pollution control.

Minerals. Value of the mineral production sales (in R1,000):

	1976	1977	1978	1979
Antimony	22,329	17,700	10,881	21,636
Asbestos	117,647	137,778	121,682	106,421
Chrome ore	60,841	72,134	88,444	88,752
Coal	517,776	755,500	875,748	1,145,878
Copper	171,794	209,229	210,296	270,989
Diamonds	215,073	257,592	452,670	524,678
Fluorspar	26,565	17,719	23,312	30,131
Gold	2,380,170	2,814,991	3,666,425	5,844,041
Granite	11,184	19,189	15,623	16,720
Iron ore	60,092	197,261	219,735	293,829
Iron pyrites	9,136	8,259	8,441	...
Lime and limestone	50,279	62,569	79,297	92,508
Manganese	131,309	119,588	117,136	175,522
Nickel	80,620	87,830	32,056	...
Phosphate	26,565	44,567	51,067	62,714
Silver	10,618	12,607	14,693	29,608
Tin	14,579	24,117	29,973	29,362
Vanadium	49,742	52,648	...	...
Vermiculite	6,246	5,860	7,487	6,458
Zinc	22,344	19,649	14,920	...

Mineral production 1979: Coal, 103,458,000 tonnes; iron ore, 31,565,000 tonnes; phosphates, 19,295,700 tonnes; manganese ore, 5,209,000 tonnes; chromite, 3,297,000 tonnes; asbestos, 247,000 tonnes; copper, 189,900 tonnes; vermiculite, 191,600 tonnes; zinc concentrates (1978), 130,318 tonnes; nickel (1977), 21,955 tonnes; vanadium (pentoxide content) (1977), 20,061 tonnes; gold, 703,273 kg; silver, 98,812 kg; diamonds, 8,392,000 carats.

In 1979 the number of persons engaged in mining was 692,209. Of these, 457,792 were engaged in goldmining. Total salaries R1,830,632,000.

The Mineral Resources of the Union of South Africa, With a Summary of the Mineral Resources of South West Africa. Geological Survey, Department of Mines. 5th ed. Pretoria, 1976
Minerals. A Quarterly Report of Production and Sales. Department of Mines. Pretoria, from 1936

Agriculture. The number of farms in white areas in 1976 was 75,562 with an area of 85,719,000 hectares.

South African farmers produced mainly the following crops for the years indicated:

Product (1,000 tonnes)	1974–75	1975–76	1976–77	1977–78
Maize	9,131	7,314	9,612	9,780
Sorghum	401	280	374	444
Wheat	1,596	1,792	2,239	1,815
Barley	50	51	...	...
Oats	103	99	85	72
Lucerne hay	...	1,284	1,294	1,294
Groundnuts	179	102	164	205
Sunflower seed	209	270	464	534
Sugar-cane	16,895	16,814	19,220	19,009
Deciduous fruit	1,729[1]	1,478	1,264	1,458
Citrus fruit	656	712	652	851
Subtropical fruit	339	280	246	257
Vegetables	1,889	1,307	1,392	1,262

[1] Preliminary.

Livestock, in 1,000 (1979): 13,200 cattle, 31,500 sheep, 5,300 goats, 1,500 pigs. In 1977–78, 2m. cattle and 6·4m. sheep and goats were slaughtered.

The 1979 production of butter was 15,135 tonnes; condensed milk, 40,700 tonnes; milk powder, 9,140 tonnes; cheese, 30,150 tonnes.

Wool sold in 1979 was 98,800 tonnes.

Cotton-growing is now undertaken by many farmers, the plant being found a better drought resistant than either tobacco or maize.

During 1974–75, 589·6m. litres of wine were produced, of which 292·7m. litres were distilled.

In 1977–78 the gross value of agricultural production was R3,794m. (field crops, R1,832m.; livestock products, R1,385m.; horticultural products, R577m.).

Forestry. The commercial forests occupy about 1·62m. hectares, of which 148,000 hectares are indigenous trees and the rest exotic trees (pine, gum, wattle). The annual output of forest products is about 85m. cu. metres. Production now meets about 90% of domestic need. Capital invested is about R1,100m., and the number of employees about 100,000.

Fisheries. South Africa is no longer engaged in whaling.

In 1979, 715,674,000 tonnes of fish were landed, including 83,181,000 tonnes of pilchards and 580,852,000 of anchovies.

INDUSTRY AND TRADE

Industry. Net value of sales of the principal groups of industries (in R1,000) in 1979: Food, beverages and tobacco, 10,508,954; motor vehicles, 1,686,117; basic metals, 4,885,571; chemicals and products, 6,842,261; non-electrical machinery, 2,126,420; non-metallic mineral products, 2,276,153; electrical machinery, 1,558,267; clothing, 1,079,566; paper and products, 1,456,414; textiles, 1,615,003; total net value including other groups, 46,495,383. Manufacturing industry contributed 24·8% to gross domestic product in 1976.

Industrial employment (except mining) in 1979: Manufacturing employed 1,352,200 workers (earning R5,467,116,000); construction, 411,200 (R1,247,042,000); transport, communications, 341,249 (R1,548,391,000); trade and accommodation services, 737,764 (R2,419,553,000); government and services, 916,126 (R3,523,886,000).

Of the above figures the following proportion of jobs and salaries were held by white South Africans: Total jobs in manufacturing, 306,900 (earning R2,966,087,000); construction, 55,200 (R539,589,000); transport, communications, 158,807 (R1,194,067,000); trade and accommodation services, 273,938 (R1,602,716,000); government and services, 337,806 (R2,323,827,000).

In 1979 in private manufacturing 165,900 workers were employed in the food industry (earning R480,502,000); textiles employed 111,800 (R287,063,000); clothing, 109,900 (R222,293,000); transport equipment, 99,900 (R484,975,000); non-metallic mineral products, 85,900 (R275,183,000).

Communications comprises the Department of Posts and Telegraphs. Transport comprises South African Railways and Harbours.

Trade Unions. At the end of 1977 there were 174 trade unions with an estimated total membership of 440,000 Whites and 231,000 Coloureds and Asians.

The total revenue of trade unions in 1964–65 was R3,857,545; their total assets were valued at R10,624,661.

Although there is no legal provision for Black trade unions, there is no legal prohibition of trade unions by Black workers. However, the vast majority of Black workers have not shown much interest in trade unionism.

The Wage Board inquires into the wage levels of numerous categories of workers, particularly Black, and it fixes minimum levels of pay and other conditions of employment. Special machinery exists under the Bantu Labour (Settlement of Disputes) Act to safeguard the interests of Black workers. This Act provides for the establishment by Black workers of local labour committees which are linked with regional committees.

The latter committees are in contact with the Central Bantu Labour Board, which, together with Bantu Labour Officers, attends the meetings of the Wage Board and the other industrial bodies. Bantu Labour Officers also maintain close contact with employers of Black workers.

Horrell, M., *South African Trade Unionism.* Johannesburg, 1961
Walker, I. D., and Weinbren, B., *2000 Casualties: A History of the Trade Unions and the Labour Movement in the Union of South Africa.* Johannesburg, 1961

Commerce. South Africa, Botswana, Lesotho, Swaziland and Transkei are members of a customs union and the foreign trade statistics shown below represent the combined imports and exports of these countries. The total value of the imports and exports, exclusive of specie and gold bullion, was as follows (in R1m.):

	Imports		Exports
1974	4,908·9	1974	3,350·1
1975	5,561·8	1975	3,989·6
1976	5,875·7	1976	4,471·7
1977	5,134·6	1977	5,477·6
1978	6,272·2	1978	6,354·6

Agricultural products valued at R1,183·8m. were exported in 1975. Processed products accounted for half of this figure. Maize, sugar, wool and fruit provide the bulk of agricultural exports, while rice, tea, raw rubber, coffee and cocoa are the major agricultural imports. Total agricultural imports for 1975 were R103·6m.

The principal commodity groups of imports and exports (in R1m.) in 1978 were:

Imports		Exports	
Food, beverages and tobacco	255·0	Manufactured goods	2,341·9
Chemicals	745·9	Machinery and transport equipment	282·5
Manufactured goods	876·6	Inedible raw materials (excl. fuels)	1,223·7
Metals and metal manufactures	373·6	Food, beverages and tobacco	1,169·6
Machinery and transport equipment	3,517·0		

The geographical origin of South Africa's imports and the direction of its export trade were mainly as follows (in R1m.) in 1978:

Imports				Exports			
Africa	245·3	America	1,074·7	Africa	537·8	America	942·5
Europe	3,726·0	USA	986·5	Europe	3,216·3	USA	812·6
UK	1,043·4	Asia	1,069·5	UK	1,250·9	Asia	1,393·4
Fed. Rep. of		Japan	823·6	Fed. Rep. of		Japan	765·7
Germany	1,274·8			Germany	471·3		

Total trade between South Africa and UK (British Department of Trade returns, i7 £1,000 sterling):

	1976	1977	1978	1979	1980
Imports to UK	612,992	879,724	767,770	533,659	756,397
Exports and re-exports from UK	645,363	581,063	667,052	713,466	1,002,073

Tourism. In 1978, 641,588 tourists visited the Republic of South Africa, spending approximately R330m.

COMMUNICATIONS

Roads. The railway administration operated road motor services over 51,231 route-km in 1979; during that year 12·9m. passengers were conveyed and 2·9m. tons of goods were carried.

There were at 31 March 1979, 185,262 km of roads, of which some 1,577 km of national roads and 43,335 km of provincial roads were tarred.

Motor vehicles in operation in 1978 (provisional) included 2,237,416 passenger cars, 846,152 commercial vehicles, 85,756 buses and 142,814 motor cycles. Motor vehicles licensed in 1978, 3,526,891.

Railways. Railway history in South Africa begins in 1860 with the line Durban–Point. With the formation of the Union in 1910, the state-owned lines in the 4 provinces (12,194 km) were amalgamated into one state undertaking, which also took over the control of the harbours—the South African Railways and Harbours Administration.

Government-owned lines operated by the administration (1980) totalled 23,328 km, of which 6,778 km were electrified. Two important lines were completed during 1976: a privately owned railway linking Sishen with the port of Saldanha Bay (860 km) for the export of iron ore; and a 509 km link comprising new construction and upgraded lines between Broodsnyersplaas and the new deep-water port of Richards Bay, for the export of coal. Passenger journeys, 1979, 622m.; goods traffic, 1979, 154·9m. tonnes.

Aviation. Civil aviation in South Africa is controlled by the Department of Transport, which administers the following state-owned airports: Jan Smuts Airport, Johannesburg; D. F. Malan Airport, Cape Town; Louis Botha Airport, Durban; J. B. M. Hertzog Airport, Bloemfontein; J. G. Strydom Airport, Windhoek; Ben Schoeman Airport, East London; H. F. Verwoerd Airport, Port Elizabeth; B. J. Vorster Airport, Kimberley; J. G. H. van der Wath Airport, Keetmanshoop; Upington Airport. At 13 other airports the Department provides air navigation services.

South African Airways, as the national air carrier, operate scheduled international air services within Africa and to Europe, South America, the USA, the Far East and Australia. Twenty-three other lines also operate scheduled international air services; they include British Airways, PANAM, KLM, SAS, TAP, Swissair, Olympic Air, El-Al, Alitalia, Sabena, Lufthansa, Deta, Air Rhodesia, Iberia, DJA, UTA, Luxair, Lesotho Airways, Swazi Air, Air Malawi, Air Madagascar. Luxavia operate international non-scheduled flights.

South African Airways, Pacair, Avne, Margate Air Services, Protea Airways, National Airways, The John Andrew Co., Avex Air, Commercial Air Services Ltd, Suidwes Lugdiens and Namakwaland-lugdiens operate scheduled air services within South Africa.

During 1976–77 South African Airways carried 2,975,862 passengers and 55,649 tons of freight and mail.

Shipping. The 4 main ports are Durban, Cape Town, Port Elizabeth and East London. Smaller ports are Mossel Bay, Port Nolloth, Saldanha, Richards Bay, Walvis Bay and Lüderitz. During 1977–78 these ports handled 80·8m. tons of cargo, of which Durban handled 35,429,906 tons.

Post and Broadcasting. On 31 March 1979 there were in South Africa 2,335 post and telegraph offices. In 1977 post office assets amounted to R1,136m.

In 1977 the international telex switchboard enabled 13,558 telex subscribers in South Africa to communicate with telex subscribers in 177 countries. There were 424 automatic telephone exchanges, 70,000 trunk (long-distance) circuits in operation in 1977. There were 25,527 public call offices and 2,503,804 telephones in 1979.

The South African Broadcasting Corporation had, in Sept. 1979, 2·18m. listeners' licences.

On 5 Jan. 1976 the South African Television Service began official transmissions. There were 610,000 sets in 1976.

Cinemas (1971). There were 686 with 498,000 seats.

Newspapers (1978). There are 9 Afrikaans and 16 English daily newspapers with a combined circulation of about 1,288,000, of which 939,000 are English.

JUSTICE, RELIGION, EDUCATION AND WELFARE

Justice. The common law of the republic is the Roman–Dutch law—that is, the uncodified law of Holland as it was at the date of the cession of the Cape in 1806. The law of England as such is not recognized as authoritative, though by statute the principles of English law relating to evidence and to mercantile matters, *e.g.*, companies, patents, trademarks, insolvency and the like, have been introduced. In shipping and insurance, English law is followed in the Cape Province, and it has also largely influenced civil and criminal procedure throughout the republic. In all other matters, family relations, property, succession, contract, etc., Roman–Dutch law rules, English decisions being valued only so far as they agree therewith.

The Supreme Court of South Africa is constituted as follows: (i) The Appellate Division, consisting of the Chief Justice and as many Judges of Appeal as the State President may stipulate, is the highest court and its decisions are binding on all courts. It has no original jurisdiction, but is purely a Court of Appeal. (ii) The Provincial Divisions: In each province there is a provincial division of the Supreme Court, while in the Cape there are three such divisions possessing both original and appellate jurisdiction. (iii) The Local Divisions: There is a local division each in the Transvaal and Natal exercising the same original jurisdiction within limited areas as the provincial divisions. The judges hold office till they attain the age of 70 years. No judge can be removed from office except by the State President upon an address from both Houses of Parliament on the ground of misbehaviour or incapacity. The circuit system is fully developed.

The Bantu appeal courts and 3 Bantu divorce courts have jurisdiction to some extent concurrent with and in certain respects exclusive of that of the Supreme Court in cases in which the parties are Bantu.

Each province is further divided into districts with a magistrate's court having a prescribed civil and criminal jurisdiction. From this court there is an appeal to the provincial divisions of the Supreme Court, and thence to the appellate division. Magistrates' convictions carrying sentences above a prescribed limit are subject to automatic review by a judge. In addition, several regional divisions consisting of a number of districts have been constituted. Convictions of such courts are not subject to automatic review by a judge.

Courts of Bantu affairs commissioners have been constituted in defined areas to hear all civil cases and matters between Bantu and Bantu only. An appeal lies to the

Bantu appeal court, whose decision is final, unless the court consents to an appeal to the appellate division of the Supreme Court on a point stated by the court itself. Bantu affairs commissioners have concurrent criminal jurisdiction with magistrates' courts in respect of certain offences committed by Bantu, while a limited civil and criminal jurisdiction is conferred upon the Bantu chief or headman over his own tribe.

Police. In 1971 the police force consisted of 1,703 White officers and 6,674 n.c.o.s, 7 Coloured officers and 250 n.c.o.s, 11 Bantu officers and 2,036 n.c.o.s, 3 Indian officers and 139 n.c.o.s. There were 8,397 White, 1,150 Coloured, 11,148 Bantu and 590 Indian constables.

Religion. A sample tabulation of the 1970 census results as regards religious denominations shows the following: *Whites:* Nederduits Gereformeerde Kerk, 1,512,066; Anglicans, 404,024; Methodists, 361,727; Roman Catholics, 309,572; Nederduits Hervormde Kerk, 225,283; Presbyterians, 118,782; Jews, 118,200; Gereformeerde Kerk, 110,277; Apostolics, 72,904; Congregationalists, 21,373; other Christians, 404,264; others, 114,810. *Non-Whites:* Bantu Churches, 2,758,001; Methodists, 1,944,563; Roman Catholics, 1,587,839; Afrikaans Churches, 1,571,114; Anglicans, 1,312,165; Lutherans, 907,433; Presbyterians, 459,545; Hindus, 432,528; Congregationalists, 373,656; Mohammedans, 268,970; Apostolics, 146,703; other Christians, 1,825,104; others and unspecified, 4,433,425.

Education. *Higher Education.* There are 16 universities in the republic: (1) The University of Cape Town. (2) The University of Natal, Durban and Pietermaritzburg. (3) The University of the Orange Free State at Bloemfontein. (4) Potchefstroom University for Christian Higher Education, Potchefstroom. (5) The University of Pretoria. (6) Rhodes University, Grahamstown, C.P. (7) The University of Stellenbosch. (8) The University of the Witwatersrand, Johannesburg. (9) The University of South Africa, with its seat in Pretoria, which conducts a Division of External Studies by means of correspondence and vacation courses; it is also an examining body. (10) The University of Port Elizabeth. (11) Rand Afrikaans University, Johannesburg.

The University of Fort Hare (12), the University of the North (13) near Pietersburg and the University of Zululand (14) near Empangeni, Natal, are operated by the Department of Education and Training and provide education at university level for Blacks, the University of the Western Cape (15), Bellville (Cape), offers university facilities to the Coloured population and is administered by the Department of Coloured Affairs; while the University for Indians (16), the University of Durban-Westville, at Durban falls under the Department of Indian Affairs. The Medical University of South Africa is for Black students.

The following statistics refer to 1977:

University	Students	University	Students
Cape Town	9,274	Rand Afrikaans	3,251
Fort Hare	1,628	Rhodes	2,654
Natal	8,353	South Africa	46,714
North	1,816	Stellenbosch	10,623
Orange Free State	7,830	West Cape	2,744
Port Elizabeth	2,700	Witwatersrand	11,341
Potchefstroom	6,560	Zululand	1,084
Pretoria	16,192		

In 1978 there were 10 White universities with 78,442 students and 6 non-White with 14,813 students; there were also 47,578 part-time students, of whom 34,045 were White, and 7,463 Black.

Technical and Vocational Education. Technical, vocational and special education for persons other than those for whom specific provisions is made (*e.g.,* Black): The Department of National Education is responsible for the maintenance, management and control of or the payment of subsidies to colleges for advanced technical education, technical colleges, technical institutes, special schools, schools of industries and reform schools. Colleges for advanced technical education provide education on an advanced level for a variety of technical, commercial and general courses of study as well as secondary education on a part-time basis. Technical colleges and technical institutes are mainly responsible for the training of apprentices and the education, on a part-time basis, of persons not subject to compulsory school attendance. Special schools for handicapped children cater for the educational needs of those who are blind, partially sighted, deaf, hard of hearing, epileptic, cerebral palsied and physically handicapped. Children found to be in need of care by a children's court, are admitted to schools of industries and reform schools.

The Department of Coloured Affairs has taken over all schools of this nature for Coloureds.

In 1978, 70 technical colleges for Whites had 73,909 students; 8 for Coloureds had 2,359 students; 1 for Asians had 3,094 students. In addition there are 15 teacher-training colleges for Coloureds and Asians. Provision is made for technical education for Black students at 4 institutions for advanced technical education and 29 industrial or trade schools; total enrolment at these institutions was 8,582 in 1978. Forty-six schools for the physically handicapped had 6,729 pupils in 1975.

State and State-aided Education other than Higher Education. Primary and secondary public education, other than that specifically provided elsewhere, falls under the Provincial Administration. In terms of the National Education Policy Act, 1967, the Minister of Education, Arts and Science may, after consultation with the Provincial Administrators and the National Advisory Education Council, determine general educational policy within the framework of the Act. Black education is the responsibility of the Department of Black Education and Training, while education for Coloureds and Indians is controlled by the Departments of Coloured Affairs and Indian Affairs respectively.

Public schools in 1978: 2,277 for Whites with 44,602 teachers and 903,442 pupils; (1977) 2,281 for Coloureds and Asians with 30,402 teachers and 879,033 pupils; 10,857 for Blacks (in the republic) with 66,146 teachers and 3,228,326 pupils.

Private Schools. To a certain extent the activities of private schools are controlled by government regulations. Their pupils generally sit for the state schools' examinations. These schools make provision for kindergarten, elementary and preparatory, general primary, secondary and commercial education.

In 1978, 143 private or aided schools for Whites had 2,822 teachers and 40,363 students. In 1977, 14 schools for Coloureds had 130 teachers and 2,946 students; 4 for Asians had 33 teachers and 899 students; in 1975 416 for Bantu had 1,878 teachers and 80,904 students.

Teacher-training colleges in 1978: 19 for Whites had 1,252 teachers and 14,585 students; (1977) 16 for Coloureds and Asians had 437 teachers and 5,263 students; 33 for Bantu had 14,170 students.

Health. In 1978 there were 14,526 medical practitioners, 3,567 specialists, 1,766 hospital interns, 2,369 dental specialists and dentists; in 1975 there were 117,411 hospital beds, excluding private and mission hospitals. More tuberculosis patients were treated as outpatients than in hospital.

Social Welfare. *Social Security.* Pensions paid in 1979:

	Beneficiaries	Amount (R1,000)
Old age	429,361	241,599
War veterans	21,998	20,668
Blind	7,413	2,949
Disability grants	174,987	80,627
Maintenance	77,617	71,371

Welfare Services. South Africa is not a welfare state, yet provides many services for the community. Welfare work on behalf of the Government is done by the

Departments of Social Welfare and Pensions, Coloured Affairs, Indian Affairs, and Plural Relations and Development.

There are also a great number of voluntary welfare societies which undertake a variety of welfare services. Social assistance is not based on compulsory insurance but is financed from taxation.

The Department of Social Welfare and Pensions formulates the broad policy and takes care of the co-ordination of the various welfare services. The National Council for Welfare, a statutory body set up under the National Welfare Act of 1965, among others, is used by the Government for the execution of this policy. Four specialized commissions serve under the National Council. These are: the Social Work Commission, the Commission for Family Life, the Commission for Welfare Planning and the Commission for Welfare Organizations. The Department also provides such personal services as pensions and allowances, and practical assistance to individuals or families who may have social problems, neglected and un-cared-for children, juvenile delinquents, adults needing special guidance and alcoholics. There is assistance for mental or physical disability, death or absence of the breadwinner. There are professional field services and institutions available as well as financial help.

Voluntary Welfare Societies. These organizations supply supplementary services to those provided by the Government. Voluntary welfare organizations must register at the Department of Social Welfare and Pensions under the National Welfare Act of 1965. There are more than 2,000 registered welfare organizations; they have organized themselves into national and provincial councils so as to co-ordinate their activities.

Funds for these voluntary services are raised from Government subsidies and by public subscription.

In the past the State, with the assistance of local authorities, voluntary welfare agencies and church organizations, provided welfare services for the Blacks, the voluntary agencies being controlled by White committees. However, this situation is gradually changing as more Blacks are taking an interest in welfare work. The various Black nations are being encouraged and assisted to form their own voluntary agencies and so to provide, as far as possible, welfare services for their own people. As far as is practicable, the institutions required for the care of the aged and the disabled and for needy children are sited in the homelands, and are staffed by Blacks.

Child and Family Welfare. Welfare or professional officers employed by the State are responsible for the implementation and administration of the Children's Act (amended and consolidated in 1960). This Act makes provision for the prevention and treatment of neglected and maladjusted children, with the full integration of the services of voluntary child and family welfare organizations. Children's institutions, mainly established and controlled by private organizations, are subsidized by the State, as are crèches, community centres and other projects in aid of child and family welfare.

DIPLOMATIC REPRESENTATIVES

OF SOUTH AFRICA IN GREAT BRITAIN (South Africa Hse., Trafalgar Sq., London, WC2N 5DP)

Ambassador: Marais Steyn (accredited 27 Nov. 1980).

OF GREAT BRITAIN IN SOUTH AFRICA
(6 Hill St., Arcadia, Pretoria, 0002)

Ambassador: J. H. G. Leahy, CMG.

OF SOUTH AFRICA IN THE USA (3051 Massachusetts Ave., NW, Washington, D.C., 20008)

Ambassador: D. B. Sole.

OF THE USA IN SOUTH AFRICA (225 Pretorius St., Pretoria)
Ambassador: William B. Edmundson.

OF SOUTH AFRICA TO THE UNITED NATIONS
Ambassador: Jacobus Adriaan.

Books of Reference

Statistical Information: The Bureau (formerly Office) of Census and Statistics (Schoeman St., Pretoria), established on 1 April 1917 as a division of the Department of the Interior and now directly under the Minister of Economic Affairs, is based mainly on the Consolidated Census Act, No. 76, of 1957, and the Consolidated Statistics Act, No. 73, of 1957. Main publications:

> *Official Year Book of the Union of South Africa and of Basutoland, Bechuanaland Protectorate and Swaziland.* From 1918 (preceded by the *Statistical Year Book, 1913–17*)
> *Union Statistics for 50 Years: Jubilee Issue, 1910–1960* (1960)
> *Statistical Year Book.* From 1964
> *Statistics of Production: Industrial.* Annual, from 1915/16 (but suspended from 1929/30 to 1931/32 and from 1938 to 1942)
> *Statistics of Production: Agricultural.* Annual, from 1917/18 (but suspended from 1920/30 to 1931/32 and from 1939 to 1946)
> *Monthly Bulletin of Statistics* (from 1922)
> *Population Census, 1970.* (Various special reports in course of publication)
> South African Reserve Bank, *Quarterly Bulletin of Statistics*
> *South Africa 1979.* Official Yearbook of the Republic of South Africa
> *Official South African Municipal Year Book 1977*
> *Homelands: The Role of the Corporations in the Republic of South Africa,* Johannesburg, 1976

The Customs and Excise Office, Pretoria, publishes *Monthly Abstract of Trade Statistics* (from 1946) and *Trade and Shipping of the Union of South Africa* (annually, 1910–55); *Foreign Trade Statistics* (annually, from 1956)

Barber, J., *South Africa's Foreign Policy.* OUP, 1973
Bate, H. M., *South Africa Without Prejudice.* London, 1956
Bissell, R. E., and Crocker, C. A., *South Africa in the 1980s.* Boulder, 1979
Bosman, D. B., *Tweetalige Woordeboek.* 2 vols. Cape Town, 1946–49
Branford, J., *A Dictionary of South African English.* Rev. ed. OUP, 1980
Brotz, H., *The Politics of South Africa: Democracy and Racial Diversity.* OUP, 1977
Davenport, T. R. H., *South Africa: A Modern History.* London, 1977
de Villiers, L., *South Africa: A Skunk Among Nations.* London, 1975
Friedman, B., *Smuts: A Reappraisal.* London, 1975
Heard, K. A., *General Elections in South Africa, 1943–70.* OUP, 1974
Hepple, A., *Verwoerd.* Harmondsworth, 1967
Kruger, D. W., *The Making of a Nation.* Johannesburg, 1969
Lacour-Gayet, R., A History of South Africa. London, 1977
Metrowich, F. R., *Africa in the Sixties.* Pretoria, 1970
Muller, C. F. J., *500 Years of South African History.* Pretoria, 1969
Talbot, A. M. and W. J., *Atlas of South African History.* Pretoria, 1969
Troup, F., *South Africa: An Historical Introduction.* London, 1972
Walker, E. A., *History of Southern Africa.* London, 1957
The Oxford History of South Africa. OUP, Vol. 1, 1969; Vol. 2, 1971

PROVINCE OF THE CAPE OF GOOD HOPE

Kaapprovinsie

HISTORY. The colony of the Cape of Good Hope was founded by the Dutch in the year 1652. Britain took possession of it from 1795 to 1803 and again in 1806, and it was formally ceded to Great Britain by the Convention of London, 13 Aug. 1814. Letters patent issued in 1850 declared that in the colony there should be a Parliament which should consist of the Governor, a Legislative Council and a House of Assembly. On 31 May 1910 the colony was merged in the Union of South Africa, thereafter forming an original province of the Union.

AREA AND POPULATION. The following table gives the population of the Cape of Good Hope[1] (area (1980) 250,311 sq. miles) at the last census:

		All races		Whites		Non-Whites	
	Total	Males	Females	Males	Females	Males	Females
1936	3,527,865	1,663,169	1,864,796	396,058	394,993	1,267,011	1,469,803
1946	4,051,424	1,924,334	2,127,090	433,849	436,300	1,490,485	1,690,790
1951	4,426,726	2,110,674	2,316,052	463,917	471,168	1,646,757	1,844,884
1960	5,360,234	2,553,245	2,806,989	493,370	507,398	2,059,875	2,299,591
1970[2]	4,293,726	2,151,629	2,142,097	546,761	567,448	1,604,868	1,579,649
1980[2]	4,007,875	2,427,137	2,480,738	592,413	619,315	1,834,724	1,861,423

[1] Including Walvis Bay (434 sq. miles).
[2] Excluding Republic of Transkei.

Present area (excluding Griqualand East, which was transferred to Natal in April 1978), 250,311 sq. miles.

Of the non-White population in 1980, 27,695 were Asians, 1,477,127 were Blacks and 2,191,325 Coloureds.

Vital statistics for calendar years:

	Whites			Asians and Coloureds		
	Births	Deaths	Marriages	Births	Deaths	Marriages
1962	22,231	9,737	8,315	68,852	21,586	8,592
1966	21,818	10,290	10,055	72,771	24,110	9,758
1978	17,993	11,859	11,129	58,421	19,274	16,711

ADMINISTRATION. The division of parties in the Provisional Council (Feb. 1981) was: National Party, 46; Progressive Federal Party, 6; New Republic Party, 2; 1 vacancy.

Cape Town is the seat of the provincial administration.

Administrator: Eugene Louw.

The province is divided into 126 magisterial districts and 38 divisional council divisions. Each division has a council of at least 6 members (15 in the Cape Division) elected quinquennially by the owners or occupiers of immovable property. The duties devolving upon divisional councils include the construction and maintenance of roads and bridges, local rating, vehicle taxation (except motor vehicle taxation) and preservation of public health. There are 226 municipalities, each governed by a mayor and councillors. Municipal elections are held biennially. There are also 73 village management boards and 9 local boards.

FINANCE. In 1980–81 revenue amounted to R886,468,000 and expenditure to R908,753,000.

MINING. For mineral production, *see* pp. 1079–80.

AGRICULTURE. Viticulture in the republic is almost exclusively confined to the Cape Province, but practically all other forms of agricultural and pastoral activity are pursued.

INDUSTRY. The province has brick, tile and pottery works, saw-mills, engineering works, foundries, grain-mills, distilleries and wineries, clothing factories, furniture, boot and shoe factories, etc.

RELIGION. Sample tabulation, 1970 census. *Whites:* Nederduits Gereformeerde Kerk, 553,548; Gereformeerde Kerk, 11,771; Nederduits Hervormde Kerk, 7,102; Anglicans, 141,858; Presbyterians, 34,243; Congregationalists, 11,590; Methodists, 98,717; Lutherans, 12,433; Roman Catholics, 77,608; Apostolics, 33,044; other Christians, 67,149; Jews, 32,076; others, 28,070. *Non-Whites:* Afrikaans Churches, 585,570; Anglicans, 397,668; Presbyterians, 50,863; Congregationalists, 189,823; Methodists, 393,843; Lutherans, 101,881; Roman Catholics, 198,692; Apostolics, 149,801; Black Christian Churches, 253,055; other Christians, 185,096; Islam, 127,523; Hindus, 5,722; others, 551,422.

EDUCATION. *Training.* Higher education is under the control of the Department of National Education, Pretoria. Primary and secondary education (including vocational education and the training of primary teachers) are controlled by the Provincial Administration in respect of White pupils, by the Department of Education and Training in respect of Black pupils and by the Department of Internal Affairs in respect of Coloured pupils. Education is compulsory for all White children. Primary and secondary education is free to the end of the calendar year in which the age of 19 years is attained.

Whites (1980). There were 863 government and aided schools with 13,945 teachers and 238,667 pupils; 8 teacher-training colleges with 333 lecturers and 2,505 students; 56 private schools with 12,202 pupils.

Coloureds (1977). There were 1,982 government and aided schools with 26,435 teachers and 734,130 pupils; 14 teacher-training schools with 4,746 students (Coloured and Asian); 14 private schools with 2,777 pupils.

Black (1980). There were 1,029 public and private schools with 4,274 teachers and 230,174 pupils.

Asians (1979–80). There were 6 government schools with 158 teachers and 3,487 pupils.

Books of Reference

Official Guide. Cape Town, 1953
Du Toit, P.S., *Onderwys in Kaapland, 1652–1939*. Pretoria, 1940
Kilpin, R., *The Parliament of the Cape*. London, 1939
Marais, J. S., *The Cape Coloured People, 1652–1937*. London, 1939

PROVINCE OF NATAL

HISTORY. Natal was annexed to Cape Colony in 1844, placed under separate government in 1845, and on 15 July 1856 established as a separate colony. By this charter partially representative institutions were established, and in 1893 the colony obtained responsible government. The province of Zululand was annexed to Natal on 30 Dec. 1897. The districts of Vryheid, Utrecht and part of Wakkerstroom, formerly belonging to the Transvaal, were annexed in Jan. 1903. On 31 May 1910 the colony was merged in the Union of South Africa as an original province of the Union.

AREA AND POPULATION. The province (including Zululand, 10,375 sq. miles) has an area of 33,578 sq. miles, with a seaboard of about 360 miles. The climate is sub-tropical on the coast and somewhat colder inland. The province is divided into 45 magisterial districts.

The returns of the total population at the census were:

	All races			Whites		Non-Whites	
	Total	Males	Females	Males	Females	Males	Females
1921	1,429,398	707,600	721,798	70,506	66,381	637,094	655,417
1936	1,946,468	944,220	1,002,248	95,157	95,392	849,063	906,856
1946	2,202,392	1,073,510	1,128,882	117,425	119,272	956,085	1,009,600
1951	2,415,318	1,182,931	1,232,387	136,300	137,940	1,046,631	1,094,447
1960	2,977,034	1,443,561	1,535,473	166,404	222,750	1,277,157	1,362,468
1970	4,236,770	2,009,410	2,227,360	171,005	214,960	1,794,430	2,004,610

Of the non-White population in 1967, 514,803 were Asians, 66,821 Coloureds and 1,114,184 Bantu.

Vital statistics for calendar years:

	Whites			Asians and Coloureds		
	Births	Deaths	Marriages	Births	Deaths	Marriages
1961	7,301 [1]	3,412	2,803	19,234 [1]	3,509	3,617
1962	7,622 [1]	3,561 [1]	...	18,575 [1]	3,728	...
1966 [1]	...	3,901	3,612	...	4,008	4,446

[1] Preliminary.

ADMINISTRATION. At the provincial council elections in 1977 there were returned: United Party, 12; National Party, 8.

The seat of provincial government in Natal is Pietermaritzburg. In April 1978 the area of East Griqualand was transferred to Natal from Cape Province.

Administrator: The Hon. Jan Christoffel Greyling Botha.

FINANCE. In 1979–80 revenue amounted to R342·35m. and expenditure to R338·22m.

MINING. The province is rich in mineral wealth, particularly coal. For figures of mineral production, *see* pp. 1079–80.

AGRICULTURE. Sugar and citrus growing are of major importance. On the coast and in Zululand there are vast plantations of sugar-cane (about 800,000 acres), producing, in 1967, 15,547,000 tons. Cereals of all kinds (especially maize), fruits, vegetables, the *Acacia molissima* (the bark of which is much used for tanning purposes) and other crops are produced. Large areas are being afforested.

INDUSTRY. Natal is highly industrialized. There are metallurgical, chemical, paper, rayon and food-processing plants, iron and steel foundries, petrol refineries, pulp-mills, explosives and fertilizer plants, milk- and meat-canning factories.

RELIGION. Sample tabulation, 1960 census. *Whites:* Nederduits Gereformeerde Kerk, 64,052; Gereformeerde Kerk, 2,895; Nederduitse Hervormde Kerk, 5,319; Anglicans, 94,349; Presbyterians, 25,852; Congregationalists, 4,652; Methodists, 53,283; Lutherans, 7,226; Roman Catholics, 35,747; Apostolics, 9,827; other Christians, 18,973; Jews, 6,266; others, 11,794. *Non-Whites:* Afrikaans Churches, 25,411; Anglicans, 128,400; Presbyterians, 35,013; Congregationalists, 16,267; Methodists, 173,088; Lutherans, 122,052; Roman Catholics, 270,744; Apostolics, 25,229; Bantu Churches, 495,747; other Christians, 95,828; Mohammedans, 59,957; Hindus, 282,797; others, 909,152.

EDUCATION. The Natal Provincial Administration controls primary and secondary technical and vocational education for Whites. Higher technical and vocational education for all races is provided by the central government. *See also* pp. 1084–85.

Whites (1980). There were 307 government and aided schools with 110,890 pupils; 3 teacher-training colleges with 1,282 students; 21 private schools with 1,625 pupils.

Coloureds (1980). There were 65 government and aided schools with 1,075 teachers and 29,498 pupils; 1 teacher-training college with 266 students.

Blacks (1977). There were 993 school sections with 3,863 teachers and 182,470 pupils.

Asians (1977). There were 300 government and aided schools with 3,863 teachers and 182,470 pupils.

Books of Reference

Town and Regional Planning Commission, Natal: *The Tugela Basin* (1952), *Towards a Plan for the Tugela Basin* (1960), *The Population and Labour Resources of Natal* (1960)

Cullingvorsh's *Natal Almanac*. Annual. Durban

Doke, C. M., and Vilakazi, B. W., *Zulu–English Dictionary*. Johannesburg, 1948

Fair, T. J. D., *Natal Regional Survey*. 3 vols. OUP, 1955

Kuper, H., *Indian People in Natal*. Natal Univ. Press, 1960

Tatlow, A. H., *Natal Province: Descriptive Guide and Official Handbook*. Durban and London. Annual

PROVINCE OF THE TRANSVAAL

HISTORY. The Transvaal was one of the territories colonized by the Boers who left the Cape Colony during the Great Trek in 1831 and following years. In 1852, by the Sand River Treaty, Great Britain recognized the independence of the Transvaal, which, in 1853, took the name of the South African Republic. In 1877 the republic was annexed by Great Britain, but the Boers took up arms towards the end of 1880. In 1881 peace was made and self-government, subject to British suzerainty and certain stipulated restrictions, was restored to the Boers. The London Convention of 1884 removed the suzerainty and a number of these restrictions but reserved to Great Britain the right of approval of the Transvaal's foreign relations, excepting with regard to the Orange Free State. In 1886 gold was discovered on the Witwatersrand, and this discovery, together with the great influx of foreigners which it occasioned, gave rise to many grave problems. Eventually, in 1899, war broke out between Great Britain and the Transvaal. Peace was concluded on 31 May 1902, the Transvaal and the Orange Free State both losing their independence. The Transvaal was governed as a crown colony until 12 Jan. 1907, when responsible government came into force. On 31 May 1910 the Transvaal became one of the four provinces of the Union.

AREA AND POPULATION. The area of the province is 103,829 sq. miles, divided into 53 districts. The following table shows the population at each of the last censuses:

		All races		Whites		Non-Whites	
	Total	Males	Females	Males	Females	Males	Females
1921	2,087,636	1,159,430	928,206	285,185	259,788	874,245	668,418
1936	3,341,470	1,846,576	1,494,894	424,470	396,286	1,422,108	1,098,608
1946	4,283,038	2,374,323	1,908,715	541,053	522,068	1,833,270	1,386,647
1951	4,812,838	2,619,314	2,193,524	737,194	731,111	2,575,119	2,230,053
1960	6,270,711	3,310,948	2,959,763	735,845	729,730	2,575,103	2,230,034
1970	8,717,530	4,460,130	4,257,400	946,430	938,210	3,513,700	3,319,190

Of the non-White population in 1970, 4,264,775 were Bantu, 80,556 Asians and 150,831 Coloureds.

Important towns of the province are listed on p. 1074.

Vital statistics for calendar years:

	Whites			Asians and Coloureds		
	Births	Deaths	Marriages	Births	Deaths	Marriages
1951	39,725 [1]	11,658	14,555	6,194 [1]	1,900	941
1962	40,199 [1]	12,600 [1]	...	6,330 [1]	2,242 [1]	...
1966	...	13,440	...	...	2,322	1,290

[1] Preliminary.

ADMINISTRATION. At the provincial council election in 1977 there were returned: National Party, 65; Progressive Federal Party, 10; New Republic Party, 1.

The seat of provincial government is at Pretoria, which is also the administrative capital of the Republic of South Africa.

Administrator: Willem Cruywagen.

FINANCE. In 1976–77 revenue amounted to R560,953,000 and expenditure to R667,523,000.

MINING. For mineral production, *see* pp. 1078–79. Gold output in 1967 was 19,591,000 oz. worth R492,978,000.

AGRICULTURE. The province is in the main a stock-raising country, though there are considerable areas well adapted for agriculture, including the growing of tropical crops.

INDUSTRY. The province has iron and brass foundries and engineering works, grain-mills, breweries, brick, tile and pottery works, tobacco, soap, and candle factories, coach and wagon works, clothing factories, etc.

RELIGION. Sample tabulation, 1960 census. *Whites:* Nederduits Gereformeerde Kerk, 539,491; Gereformeerde Kerk, 72,404; Nederduits Hervormde Kerk, 167,693; Anglicans, 137,207; Presbyterians, 50,196; Congregationalists, 3,071; Methodists, 123,218; Lutherans, 13,880; Roman Catholics, 91,235; Apostolics, 67,550; other Christians, 90,504; Jews, 74,221; others, 37,635. *Non-Whites:* Afrikaans Churches, 278,006; Anglicans, 309,047; Presbyterians, 50,924; Congregationalists, 29,839; Methodists, 318,424; Lutherans, 365,836; Roman Catholics, 270,493; Apostolics, 179,739; Bantu Churches, 1,030,853; other Christians, 310,162; Mohammedans, 42,707; Hindus, 23,190; others, 1,595,952.

EDUCATION. All education for Whites except that of universities is under the provincial authority. The province has been divided for the purposes of local control and management into 21 school districts. Instruction in government schools, both primary and secondary, is free. The medium of instruction is the home language of the pupil. The teaching of the other language begins at the earliest stage at which it is appropriate on educational grounds. Both languages are taught as examination subjects to every pupil.

Whites (1977). There were 990 public schools with 22,897 teachers and 509,533 pupils; 4 teacher-training colleges with 6,929 students; 92 private schools with 1,835 teachers and 27,224 pupils.

Coloureds (1977). There were 81 state and state-aided schools with 1,594 teachers and 49,631 pupils; 1 teacher-training college with 220 students.

Asians (1977). There were 62 public schools with 945 teachers and 23,940 pupils; 1 teacher-training college with 25 teachers and 184 students.

Blacks (1977). There were 2,170 public and private school sections with 15,450 teachers and 735,325 pupils (Homelands excluded).

Books of Reference

Transvaal Official Guide. Cape Town, 1955
Eliovson, E., *Johannesburg, the Fabulous City*. Cape Town, 1956
Symonds, F. A., *The Johannesburg Story*. London, 1953

PROVINCE OF THE ORANGE FREE STATE

Oranje-Vrystaat

HISTORY. The Orange River was first crossed by Europeans in the middle of the 18th century. Between 1810 and 1820, settlements were made in the southern parts of the Orange Free State, and the Great Trek greatly increased the number of settlers during and after 1836. In 1848, Sir Harry Smith proclaimed the whole territory between the Orange and Vaal rivers as a British possession called the 'Orange River sovereignty'. However, in 1854, by the Convention of Bloemfontein, British sovereignty was withdrawn and the independence of the country was recognized.

During the first 5 years of its existence the Orange Free State was much harassed by incessant raids by the Basutos. These were at length conquered, but, owing to the intervention of the British Government, the treaty of Aliwal North incorporated only part of the territory of the Basutos in the Orange Free State.

On account of the treaty with the South African Republic, the Orange Free State took a prominent part in the South African War (1899–1902) and was annexed on 28 May 1900 as the Orange River Colony. Crown colony government continued until 1907, when responsible government was introduced. On 31 March 1910 the Orange River Colony was merged in the Union of South Africa as the province of the Orange Free State.

AREA AND POPULATION. The area of the province is 49,418 sq. miles; it is divided into 34 administrative and 57 magisterial districts. The census population has varied as follows:

	Total	All races Males	Females	Whites Males	Females	Non-Whites Males	Females
1921	628,827	321,373	307,454	97,948	90,900	223,425	216,554
1936	772,060	381,903	390,157	101,872	99,106	280,031	291,051
1946	879,071	432,896	446,175	101,874	100,203	331,022	345,972
1951	1,016,570	519,166	497,404	115,637	112,015	403,529	385,389
1960	1,386,202	731,486	654,716	139,304	137,103	601,182	553,613
1970	1,716,350	899,140	817,210	148,110	148,030	751,030	669,180

Of the non-White population in 1970, 1,319,510 were Bantu, 36,192 Coloureds and 5 Asians.

Vital statistics for calendar years:

	Whites Births	Deaths	Marriages	Asians and Coloured Births	Deaths	Marriages
1961	7,136[1]	2,297	2,314	781[1]	467	126
1962	7,088[1]	2,441[1]	…	858[1]	527[1]	…
1966	…	2,450[1]	2,855[1]	…	…	…

[1] Preliminary.

ADMINISTRATION. At the provincial council election in 1977 there were returned 28 National Party.

The seat of provincial government is at Bloemfontein. There are 68 municipalities and 8 village management boards.

Administrator: A. C. van Wyk.

FINANCE. In 1976–77 revenues amounted to R134,288,000 and expenditure to R159,883,000.

MINING. For mineral statistics, *see* pp. 1078–79. The production of the goldfields in the province has increased tremendously since 1951, when the output was 18,545 oz. valued at R230,186. The output in 1961 was 7,235,647 oz. valued at R181,320,401.

AGRICULTURE. The province consists of undulating plains, affording excellent grazing and wide tracts for agricultural purposes. The rainfall is moderate. The country was mainly devoted to stock-farming, but now a rapidly increasing quantity of grain is being raised, especially in the eastern districts.

INDUSTRY. The more important manufacturing industries in the province are the oil-from-coal factory (as well as industries based on its by-products) at Sasolburg; fertilizer, agricultural implements, blanket and woollen products, clothing, hosiery, cement and pharmaceutical factories, grain-mills and brick, tile and pottery works.

RELIGION. Sample tabulation, 1960 census. *Whites:* Nederduits Gereformeerde Kerk, 190,458; Gereformeerde Kerk, 14,018; Nederduits Hervormde Kerk, 9,297; Anglicans, 11,433; Presbyterians, 3,926; Congregationalists, 109; Methodists, 14,226; Lutherans, 1,281; Roman Catholics, 7,303; Apostolics, 8,344; other Christians, 10,480; Jews, 3,190; others, 2,680. *Non-Whites:* Afrikaans Churches, 210,379; Anglicans, 80,554; Presbyterians, 21,414; Congregationalists, 8,309; Methodists, 193,439; Lutherans, 16,504; Roman Catholics, 119,629; Apostolics, 78,001; Bantu Churches, 183,109; other Christians, 52,083; others, 146,374.

EDUCATION. *Whites.* Primary, secondary and vocational education and the training of primary teachers are controlled and financed by the Provincial Administration. The province is divided into 11 school board areas.

Education is free in all public schools up to the university matriculation standard. Attendance is compulsory between the ages of 7 and 16, but exemption may be granted in special cases. The home language of the pupil is the medium of instruction.

Whites (1977). There were 217 government and aided schools with 4,223 teachers and 72,469 pupils.

Coloureds (1977). There were 41 government and aided schools with 359 teachers and 10,945 pupils.

Blacks (1977). There were 2,026 school sections with 5,880 teachers and 302,286 pupils (Homelands excluded).

Books of Reference

Orange Free State Official Guide. Cape Town, 1956
Orange Free State Bulletin. 1961 ff.

SOUTH WEST AFRICA
Suidwes-Afrika—Namibia

HISTORY. The territory (excluding Walvis Bay and certain islands) was proclaimed a German protectorate in 1884, but was surrendered to the Forces of the Union of South Africa on 9 July 1915 at Khorab. The administration was vested in the Government of the Union of South Africa by mandate of the League of Nations dated 17 Dec. 1920. In 1921 the Governor-General delegated certain of his functions to the Administrator of the Territory, who was assisted by an Advisory Council and, from 1925, by an Executive Committee and the Legislative Assembly. On 18 July 1966 the International Court of Justice decided, by the President's casting vote, that Ethiopia and Liberia had no legal right in applying for a decision on the international status of South West Africa. In 1971 the International Court of Justice ruled in an advisory opinion that the Republic of South Africa's presence in South West Africa was illegal. In Dec. 1973 the UN appointed Sean McBride as UN Commissioner for Namibia. The Republic of South Africa was given until May 1975 to declare its intentions on the future of Namibia, by the UN.

Independence was envisaged for 31 Dec. 1978. However in Dec. 1978 an election for a Constituent Assembly was held without UN supervision. The Democratic Turnhalle Alliance Party gained 41 of the 50 seats. The South West Africa People's Organisation (SWAPO) boycotted the election. The Constituent Assembly was not recognized by the UN, the Western Powers or SWAPO. UN plans for a ceasefire and UN-supervised elections were rejected by the Constituent Assembly on 20 April 1979. Discussions continued during 1980 aiming at solutions to the Namibia problem and in Jan. 1981 a UN conference was held in Geneva but this also ended in failure.

AREA AND POPULATION. The total area of the Territory, including the Caprivi-Zipfel, is 318,827 sq. miles (823,145 sq. km); this figure includes that of Walvis Bay, administered by South West Africa, 434 sq. miles (1,124 sq. km).

The country is bounded on the north by Angola and Zambia, on the west by the Atlantic ocean, on the south and southern portion of the eastern boundary by the Cape Province, and on the remainder of the eastern boundary by Botswana and Zambia. There are 3 main regions: the Namib, an extremely arid and desolate region stretching along the entire coastline to a width of between 80 to 130 km. The major portion of the Namib receives an annual rainfall of less than 50 mm. per annum; the Central Plateau is the region lying to the east of the Namib. It varies in altitude between 1,000 and 2,000 metres and offers a diversified landscape of rugged mountains, rocky outcrops, sand-filled valleys and plains. It covers approximately 50% of the total area; the Kalahari covers the eastern, north-eastern and northern areas of South West Africa.

The rainfall increases steadily from less than 50 mm. in the west and south-west up to 600 mm. in the Caprivi Strip.

The Kunene River and the Okavango, which form portions of the northern border of the country, the Zambesi, which forms the eastern boundary of the Caprivi-Zipfel, the Kwando or Mashi, which flows through the Caprivi-Zipfel from the north between the Okavango and the Zambesi, and the Orange River in the south, are the only permanently running streams. But there is a system of great, sandy, dry river-beds throughout the country, in which water can generally be obtained by sinking shallow wells. In the Grootfontein area there are large supplies of underground water, but except for a few springs, mostly hot, there is no surface water in the country.

On 13 Oct. 1964 and 29 Jan. 1969 the Republic of South Africa and Portugal signed agreements on the common use of the Kunene River.

Owing to the difficulty of satisfactorily controlling that part of the Caprivi-Zipfel, east of the line running due south from Beacon 22, situated west of the Kwando (or Mashi) River, the control of this area was in Aug. 1939 transferred to the Union Department of Native Affairs.

The population at the census 1960 and 1970 and estimate 1977 was:

	1960	1970	1977
Ovambos	239,363	342,455	418,300
Whites	73,464	90,658	105,600
Damaras	44,353	64,973	80,500
Hereros	35,354	49,203	58,900
Namas	34,806	32,853	40,400
Kavangos	27,871	49,577	61,400
East Caprivians	15,840	25,009	31,200
Coloureds	12,708	28,275	34,000
Rehobothers	11,257	16,474	20,800
Bushmen	11,762	21,909	27,500
Tswana and others	9,992	18,400	22,500
Kaokovelders	9,234	6,467	7,200
	526,004	746,328	908,800

The population grew at a rate of 3·7% per annum between 1960 and 1970.

The Ovambos are a Bantu race and are both agriculturists and owners of stock. They still possess tribal organization to its full extent.

The Hereros are a pastoral people who formerly owned enormous herds of cattle. Wars with Namas and Germans destroyed their tribal organization. Under the

Union and Republic administration, reserves have been set apart and they have considerably increased in numbers and in animal wealth.

The ethnic origin of the Bergdamaras or Damara is still not certain. They were alternatively the slaves of the Hereros and the Namas, whose language they now speak, in pre-European days.

The Namas consist of 2 distinct sections: one, the Hamitic, whose remnants are found in the central portions of the country, being of pure native extraction, is thought to have migrated from the region of the Central African lakes in prehistoric times; the other, the Khoisan, is composed of tribes whose members are descended from persons born in the Cape a couple of centuries ago with an admixture of European and Nama blood.

The Bushmen are among the oldest inhabitants of southern Africa.

In the centre of the country just south of the Windhoek district is the Rehoboth Gebiet, occupied by a race known as the Basters, who are of mixed Nama–European descent and whose ordinary language is Afrikaans.

ADMINISTRATION. The South West Africa Affairs Amendment Act, 1949, abolished the Advisory Council and the nominated members of the Legislative Assembly. All 18 members of the Assembly are now elected by the registered voters of the Territory.

The election held on 24 April 1974 returned 18 Nationalists.

Until 1977 the Territory was represented in the South African House of Assembly by 6 members elected by the registered voters of the Territory, and in the Senate by 4 Senators, of which number 2 were elected by the members of the Legislative Assembly and the representatives of the Territory in the House of Assembly, and 2 nominated by the President of the Republic. Under the South West Africa Constitution Amendment Act 1977 this representation was abolished.

A commission of inquiry, appointed by the South African Government, in 1964 recommended the establishment of 'homeland areas' for the non-White groups. All these areas should be governed by legislative councils, headed by executive committees; franchise should be granted to males and females over 18 years who qualify for citizenship in their respective homelands.

On 17 Oct. 1968, 22 Oct. 1970 and 15 March 1973 respectively the first sessions of the Legislative Councils of Ovambo (77 members), Kavango (30 members) and Eastern Caprivi (28 members) were opened.

On 1 May 1973 and 9 May 1973 respectively Ovambo and Kavango obtained self-government.

On 13 Oct. 1966 the security and apartheid laws of the Republic of South Africa were extended to South West Africa, retrospective to 1950. The Legislative Assembly adopted a resolution on 22 Nov. 1974 inviting the representatives of the various population groups to deliberate with the representatives of the Whites on the manner in which they should exercise their right of self-determination in view of the South African government's desire that the inhabitants of South West Africa should themselves decide upon their future.

The seat of the White administration is Windhoek. The country is divided into 19 districts controlled by magistrates and commissioners.

Administrator-General: Danie Hough.

ECONOMY

Budget. The revenue and expenditure (in R1,000) were:

	1972–73	1973–74	1974–75	1975–76	1976–77
Revenue	112,863	161,048	181,252	227,787	256,514
Expenditure	132,166	159,138	174,626	233,946	265,145

Banking. Barclays Bank International, Volkskas Bank, Standard Bank, French Bank, Netherlands Bank, Trust Bank, South African Reserve Bank and Boland Bank have branches in the Territory. The only indigenous bank, The Bank of South West Africa, was established in 1973.

NATURAL RESOURCES

Minerals. Mineral export/sales amounted to R458,511,020 in 1977. Diamonds, which constitute the principal production, are mainly recovered from alluvial terraces on a 60-mile stretch along the coastline from the Orange River mouth northward.

Agriculture. South West Africa is essentially a stock-raising country, the scarcity of water and poor rainfall rendering agriculture, except in the northern and north-eastern portions, almost impossible. Generally speaking, the southern half is suited for the raising of small stock, while the central and northern portions are better fitted for cattle.

Livestock (1979): 3m. cattle, 5·15m. sheep, 2·15m. goats. In 1977, 199,757 head of cattle and 74,855 beef carcasses and 275,937 head of small stock were exported.

In 1977–78, 188,402 kg of butter and 115,197 kg of factory cheese were manufactured. Other products produced are maize, 45,000 bags (1976); wheat, 25,000 bags (1977); sunflower, 2,000 tons (1977); peanuts, 500 tons (1977).

The production of karakul pelts is of increasing importance. In 1977–78, 2·5m. pelts, worth R31,893,000 were exported.

Fisheries. The total catch in 1977 was 425,000 tonnes. The sales value of fish products was R67m.

COMMERCE. The statistics concerning the external trade of South West Africa are included in those of the Republic of South Africa (*see* p. 1081–82).

The bulk of the direct imports into the country is landed at Walvis Bay.

Total trade between South West Africa and UK (British Department of Trade returns, in £1,000 sterling):

	1976	1977	1978	1979	1980
Imports to UK	33,323	26,122	14,844	20,446	18,898
Exports and re-exports from UK	2,914	1,348	2,215	1,593	2,726

COMMUNICATIONS

Roads. In 1978 there were 3,892 km of trunk roads, 19,579 km of district roads, of which 3,252 km are bitumen surfaced. In 1974 there were 71,272 registered motor vehicles.

Railways. The South West Africa system connects with the main system of the South African Railways at De Aar. The total length of the line inside South West Africa is 2,340 km of 1,065 mm gauge.

Aviation. In 1977 the Territory's 4 major airports handled 177,901 passengers.

Shipping. In 1976–77 Walvis Bay harbour handled 838,157 tons of cargo and Luderitz, 23,875.

Post and Broadcasting. At 31 March 1978 there were 84 post offices and postal agencies, and 1,150 private bag services distributed by rail or road transport.

There were 30,030 circuit km of trunk lines, 356,756 km of carrier circuits, 277,835 km of telegraph circuits and 47,245 km of farm telephone lines; 85 telegraph offices, 149 telephone exchanges, and 45,130 telephones. There are 1,256 licensed radio stations in operation.

In 1977, 56,698 wireless licences were issued. There were 11,049 km of broadcast circuits.

A post office savings bank was established in 1916. The number of accounts open at 31 March 1974 was 38,364 with a credit of R4,249,889. Savings certificates of a value of R200 are also issued. The balance due to holders as at 31 March 1974 amounted to R429,000.

EDUCATION AND WELFARE

Education (1978). There were 845 schools for all races, 173,316 pupils and 5,388 teachers. This included 17 academic high schools, a centre for handicapped children and 2 agricultural colleges.

Health (1977–78). There were 132 hospitals and clinics. The ratio of beds per population was 8·2 per 1,000 and the ratio of doctors to population was 1 per 4,000 inhabitants (excluding the Eastern Caprivi). Nursing staff numbered 2,261.

Books of Reference

The Territory of South West Africa. (In *Official Year Book of the Republic of South Africa*)
Department of Mines: *Quarterly Information Circulars: Industrial Minerals*
Cockram, G.-M., *South West African Mandate.* Cape Town, 1976
Serfontein, J. H. P., *Namibia?* London, 1977
Thomas, W. H., *Economic Development in Namibia.* Munich, 1978
Tötemeyer, G. *Namibia Old and New.* New York, 1979
Wipplinger, O., *The Storage of Water in Sand.* Windhoek, 1959
Vigne, R., *A Dwelling Place of Our Own: The Story of the Namibian Nation.* London, 1973

BOPHUTHATSWANA

HISTORY. Bophuthatswana was first to obtain self-government under the Bantu Homelands Constitution Act of 1971 and is the second black homeland to ask the Republic of South Africa for full independence, which was granted on 6 Dec. 1977.

AREA AND POPULATION. The total area is 40,000 sq. km.

In 1976 Bophuthatswana had a *de jure* population of 2,103,000, of which 65% lived in the White areas. The remaining 35% (736,000) lived in the homeland. In addition, the homeland has a further population of about 300,000 non-Tswanas, giving the homeland a *de facto* population of about 1,036,000.

CONSTITUTION AND GOVERNMENT. The Bophuthatswana Government is a compromise between the traditional chief-in-council system and a democratic electoral system. There are 48 nominated and 48 elected members in the Legislative Assembly. Self-government was granted in 1972. Each regional authority (coinciding with the 12 districts of the homeland) nominates 4 members, and each district elects the same number to the Legislative Assembly.

Executive power vests in the President, who is elected by the Assembly, and he elects his Cabinet.

The first general election was held in Oct. 1972, 2 political parties taking part. Chief Lucas Mangope's Bophuthatswana National Party (BNP) won 20 of the 24 contested seats, but in 1974 he formed the Bophuthatswana Democratic Party which in 1979 held two-thirds of the seats in the Assembly.

Members of regional authorities are elected from among the tribal and community authorities in their area.

The Cabinet in Oct. 1980 consisted of:

President and Minister of Economic Affairs: Chief L. L. M. Mangope.

Education: M. Setlogelo. *Foreign Affairs:* T. M. Molatlhwa. *Works:* Chief B. L. M. I. Motsatsi. *Agriculture and Community Development:* Chief E. M. Mokgoko. *Urban Affairs, Land Tenure and Housing:* D. C. M. Mokale. *Law and Order:* A. T. Gaelejwe. *Communications:* M. A. Kgomongwe. *Internal Affairs:* G. J. Makodi. *Finance:* Sir C. Hatty. *Defence:* Brig. H. F. Riekert. *Health and Social Welfare:* Dr K. P. Mokhobo.

Flag: Blue, crossed by a diagonal orange stripe, and in the canton a white disc charged with a leopard's face in black and white.

INTERNATIONAL RELATIONS

Aid. The Republic of South Africa granted aid of R22m. in 1978–79.

ECONOMY

Budget. The 1980–81 budget balanced at R300m.

Currency. South African Rand.

NATURAL RESOURCES

Water. The Department of Agriculture inherited the following improvements from

South Africa: 2,833 reservoirs; 6,845 boreholes, of which more than 4,000 have been equipped; 648 earth dams.

Minerals. The territory is particularly rich in minerals. In 1976 there were 34 mines employing 53,000 people. Minerals include platinum, asbestos, iron ore, manganese, chrome, vanadium, limestone, diamonds and fluorspar.

Exploration for more platinum, chrome and coal is currently being carried out both by the private sector and by the Bantu Mining Corporation. The platinum mines around Rustenburg produce about 66% of the free world's total production. The major chrome mines are near Rustenburg and Marico, while vanadium is mined in the Odi district near Brits.

The Rustenburg, Western and Impala Platinum mines which Bophuthatswana shares with the Republic of South Africa produce about 1·9m. oz. a year.

AGRICULTURE. Bophuthatswana is a semi-arid area of bushveld and grass veld suitable for stock farming. The annual rainfall is 300 mm in the west and 700 mm in the east and there are 3 river catchment areas—those of the Molopo, Limpopo and Vaal rivers.

Although the land tenure system militates against establishing large farms, some land which is unsuitable for building on is leased by the Government to successful farmers.

Livestock (1977): Cattle, 380,000.

Only 6·6% of the territory is suited to dryland cropping, but crop yields have shown a steady improvement in recent years. Plant production in 1972 yielded R2·4m. In the Ditsobotla district, 3,500 hectares of fertile land has been developed by 3 primary co-operatives comprising 190 Tswana farmers.

INDUSTRY. The first industries were started on an agency basis at Babelegi; the fastest growing industrial area in the homeland, in 1977 it covered 183 hectares and by March 1976 more than R56m. had been invested in the project. Other industries include 2 breweries at Thlabane and Garankuwa. There is also a furniture factory near Heystekrand, and a tannery at Montshiwa. Border industries are also promoted by the central government, notably Rosslyn where 128 industries had been established by Dec. 1975.

COMMUNICATIONS

Roads. Total length (1977) 6,300 km, of which 63 km are tarred. 1976–77, 32 km were covered by bus, and 116m. passengers transported.

EDUCATION AND WELFARE

Education. In 1978 the territory's total school attendance was 413,548 at 1,056 educational institutions which include special schools and technical schools. Primary school attendance grew from 252,000 (1970) to 327,000 (1976) and secondary school enrolment increased from 15,000 (1970) to 56,000 (1976). The number of pupils to one teacher was 55 in 1976, but the situation should improve since 3,000 pupil teachers entered the 6 training colleges, and 6,967 qualified in that year.

Education is free apart from a nominal contribution to school funds, and hostel fees at post-primary schools.

Instruction from Grade I to Standard 2 is in Setswana, while Standard 4 to senior standards are taught in English. The education is controlled by the Department of Education.

Health. In 1979 Bophuthatswana had 11 hospitals, 140 clinics, 6,000 hospital beds, 127 doctors and 2,805 nurses. The health budget in 1979–80 was R30m.

Book of Reference

The Independence of Bophuthatswana. Dept. of Information, South African Embassy, London

TRANSKEI

HISTORY. Transkei is the homeland of the Xhosa nation and was granted self-government by the Republic of South Africa in 1963. Over 1·5m. Transkeians live permanently in the Republic of South Africa but were deprived of their South African citizenship on independence.

AREA AND POPULATION. The total area is 16,910 sq. miles (43,798 sq. km). Population (1976 estimate) 1·9m., of which Coloured 7,650 and Whites 10,000. The capital is Umtata (population (1976) 24,805; 20,196 Blacks, 1,067 Coloured and 3,542 Whites). Other towns include Gcuwa, Kwabhaca and Umzimvubu.

CONSTITUTION AND GOVERNMENT. The Status of Transkei Bill passed its third reading in the South African House of Assembly on 11 June 1976 and received its second reading in the Senate on 17 June. The Bill gave Transkei a unicameral National Assembly instead of the then existing Legislative Assembly.

General elections were held on 29 Sept. 1976 and the Transkei National Independence Party gained 69 of the 75 elective seats in the National Assembly. Members were elected for a 5-year period. In addition there are 75 traditional (co-opted) members (70 chiefs and 5 paramount chiefs).

President: Chief Botha Sigcau.

Prime Minister: Paramount Chief Kaiser Matanzima.
Foreign Affairs and Information: Digby S. Koyana. *Deputy Prime Minister, Justice, Police and Prisons:* Chief George Matanzima. *Finance and Auditor-General:* Tsepo Letlaka. *Planning and Commerce:* Ramsay Madikizela. *Interior:* Hamilton Pamla. *Local Government and Land Tenure:* Chief George S. Naabankulu. *Posts and Telecommunications, and Transport:* Armstrong N. Jonas. *Education:* W. Silas Mbanga. *Health and Welfare:* T. Vike. *Agriculture and Forestry:* Saul Ndzumo. *Works and Energy:* Hubert L. Mlonyeni.

Flag: Three horizontal stripes of ochre, white, green.

FINANCE. The budget (1976–77) balanced at R136m.

AGRICULTURE. Livestock (1976): Cattle, 1·3m.; sheep, 2·5m.; goats, 1·25m.

COMMUNICATIONS

Roads. There are above 8,800 km of roads.

Railways. There is a 209 km railway line linking Umtata with the port of East London in the Republic of South Africa.

Aviation. An international airport exists at Umtata.

Shipping. A start was made in 1978 on a 'free port' at Mnganzana. It will be completed in 5–6 years at a cost of R125m. by a French consortium.

Post. There were 11,498 telephones in 1978.

DIPLOMATIC REPRESENTATIVES

No country, other than the Republic of South Africa, recognized Transkei as an independent state and in April 1978 Transkei severed diplomatic relations with the republic.

VENDA

HISTORY. Traditionally the territory of the Vhavenda, the country was granted self-government in 1973, and became the third black homeland to be granted independence by the Republic of South Africa on 13 Sept. 1979.

AREA AND POPULATION. The total area is 6,500 sq. km. Of the 381,000 Vhavenda living in the Republic of South Africa in 1970, nearly 70% lived in Venda. In 1978 the *de jure* population of Venda was estimated at 510,000, the *de facto* population at 360,000.

CONSTITUTION AND GOVERNMENT. Executive power is vested in the President, who is elected for the duration of each Parliament, which consists of the President and the National Assembly; legislative power is vested in Parliament. In addition to the National Assembly there is an Executive Council, or Cabinet, and a judiciary independent of the Executive. The National Assembly comprises the 25 chiefs and 2 headmen, 15 members designated by 4 regional councils, and 42 members elected by popular vote. A new Assembly must be elected after every 5 years, but it may be dissolved at any time by the President. All existing tribal, community and regional councils were retained with their status and powers unchanged, like those of the tribal leaders.

The first general election was held in Aug. 1973; the sole political party, the Venda Independence People's Party (VIPP) won 10 of the 18 contested seats. Shortly after, the Chief Minister, Chief Mphephu, formed the Venda National Party (VNP); in the second general election of July 1978 the VIPP won 31 of the 42 contested seats, VNP the remaining 11. Chief Mphephu was re-elected Chief Minister.

President: Chief P. Mphephu.

Minister of the Interior: Chief A. M. Madzivhandila. *Justice:* Chief J. R. Rambuda. *Education and Culture:* Headman E. R. B. Nesengani. *Agriculture and Forestry:* Chief C. A. Nelwamondo. *Health and Social Welfare:* Vacant. *Works:* Headman F. N. Ravele.

Flag: Three horizontal stripes of green, yellow, and brown, with a brown V on the yellow stripe, and a blue vertical strip in the hoist.

INTERNATIONAL RELATIONS

Aid. The Republic of South Africa granted aid of R20·4m. in 1978–79.

ECONOMY

Budget. The 1979–80 budget balanced at about R37m.

Currency. South African Rand.

NATURAL RESOURCES

Water. In Sept. 1979 there were 78 km of canals, 210 dams and 507 boreholes.

Minerals. Venda is relatively poor in mineral resources, although there are large supplies of stone for construction. Coal is the most important mineral; there are large deposits in the west near Makhado and in the north-east, bordering on the Kruger National Park, which it is hoped will soon be exploited. In addition there are deposits of graphite, copper sulphides, phosphates and magnesite; in 1978 the 2 graphite and 2 magnesite mines provided employment for 233 people, and the value of their output was R963,900.

Agriculture. About 85% of Venda is suitable only for the raising of livestock because of insufficient rainfall and poor soils, while some 10% is suited to dry-land crop production. Over 4,000 hectares have been given over to forest, mainly pine and eucalyptus. Eighteen irrigation schemes are being developed and there is extensive reclamation and conservation of eroded or overgrazed land; nearly R500,000 were spent on these projects in 1977–78. Only maize is grown on a comparatively large scale, but tea, sisal, groundnuts, coffee and sub-tropical fruits are increasing in importance. A fish-breeding project produced 1 tonne in 1976–77.

Over 80% of the working population are engaged in agriculture.

INDUSTRY. Industrial development is still in its early stages, and since Venda's location is unfavourable, the Government is concentrating on the promotion of agro-industries utilizing local produce, and small-scale industries. A chutney factory has recently been established, in addition to a tea processing plant, a furniture factory and several saw-mills. A copper-chrome arsenate preservation plant has been established at Phiphidi. At Shayandima a 20-hectare industrial area has been prepared. The construction industry is particularly important owing to the substantial increase in the demand for buildings caused by the recent expansion of government, educational and health services.

In March 1978 total investment in industry was estimated at R4·2m. The Venda Development Corporation was established in 1975 to promote and finance economic developments.

COMMUNICATIONS

Roads. There were (1979) 1,200 km of roads, of which 46 km had a permanent surface.

Post and Broadcasting. In 1980 there were 29 post offices and postal agencies. Telephones (1980) numbered, 857.

EDUCATION AND WELFARE

Education. The Department of Education and Culture assumed responsibility for education on independence. Education is free, and pupils are taught in the native tongue, Luvenda, for the first 4 years (up to Standard 3), after which English is gradually introduced. Secondary education comprises Standards 6 to 10.

The number of primary schools increased from 233 (1970) to 325 (1978), the number of pupils from 65,500 (1970) to 107,711 (1978) and the number of teachers from 956 (1970) to 2,300 (1978).

In 1970 there were 12 secondary schools, which had increased to 55 by 1979. Pupils numbered 2,465 in 1970, 23,460 in 1979, while the number of teachers increased from 100 (1970) to 555 (1979).

In addition there is a technical school at Sibasa with about 300 pupils, an agricultural school at Dimani with 278 pupils, and a school for the handicapped at Shayandima. There are 2 teacher-training colleges; enrolment was 270 in 1970, and 674 in 1978.

Health. In 1979 there were 3 hospitals with 1,310 beds and 40 clinics. White doctors numbered 10, while there were, in 1978, 327 nurses.

Welfare. In 1978–79 the Government spent R4,097,385 on grants and pensions to 19,252 recipients.

SPAIN

Estado Español

Capital: Madrid
Population: 37·7m. (1977)
GNP per capita: US$3,520 (1978)

HISTORY. The Spanish State was established by Gen. Franco on 1 Oct. 1936. For a short account of the Civil War in Spain, 17 July 1936 to 1 April 1939, *see* THE STATESMAN'S YEAR-BOOK, 1939, pp. 1325–26.

On 19 April 1937 the various political groups in the Nationalist Movement were united by Gen. Franco into one single political party, under the title *Falange Española Tradicionalista y de las Juntas de Ofensiva Nacional Sindicalistas* comprising the *falange española* created on 29 Oct. 1933 by José Antonio Primo de Rivera, eldest son of the general who was dictator of Spain from 1923 to 1930, and the traditionalists. On 30 Jan. 1938 the first civil government was proclaimed, with Gen. Franco, possessing dictatorial powers, at its head.

On 31 March 1947 Gen. Franco announced that Spain would eventually become a monarchy, with a regency council and himself as the head of state.

On 6 July 1947 the 'Law of Succession' was approved by a referendum; out of a total of 17,178,812 electors, 14,145,163 voted for, and 722,656 against it; 351,744 votes were invalid.

In July 1969, Prince Don Juan Carlos de Borbón y Borbón was sworn in as successor to the Head of State and he had the title of HRH Prince of Spain until he became King.

Prince Juan Carlos was appointed acting Head of State on 30 Oct. 1975 because of Gen. Franco's illness.

Gen. Francisco Franco y Bahamonde died on 20 Nov. 1975 and on 22 Nov. Prince Juan Carlos de Borbón y Borbón took the oath as Juan Carlos I, King of Spain.

AREA AND POPULATION. Spain is bounded north by the Bay of Biscay and the Pyrenees (which form the frontier with France), east and south by the Mediterranean and the Straits of Gibraltar, south-west by the Atlantic and west by Portugal and the Atlantic. Continental Spain has an area of 492,592 sq. km, and including the Balearic and Canary Islands 504,879 sq. km (194,883 sq. miles).

The growth of the population has been as follows:

Census year	Population	Rate of annual increase	Census year	Population	Rate of annual increase
1860	15,655,467	0·34	1940	25,877,971	0·98
1910	19,927,150	0·72	1950	27,976,755	0·81
1920	21,303,162	0·69	1960	30,903,137	0·88
1930	23,563,867	1·06	1970	33,823,918	...

Area and registered population of the provinces, as at (census) 1970:

Province	Area (sq. km)	Population	Per sq. km	Province	Area (sq. km)	Population	Per sq. km
Alava	3,047	204,323	67	Cádiz	7,385	885,433	120
Albacete	14,858	335,026	23	Castellón	6,679	385,823	58
Alicante	5,863	920,105	157	Ciudad-Real	19,749	507,650	26
Almeria	8,774	375,004	43	Córdoba	13,718	724,116	53
Avila	8,048	203,798	25	Coruña (La)	7,876	1,004,188	127
Badajoz	21,657	687,599	32	Cuenca	17,061	247,158	14
Baleares	5,014	558,287	111	Gerona	5,886	414,397	70
Barcelona	7,733	3,929,194	508	Granada	12,531	733,375	59
Burgos	14,369	358,075	25	Guadalajara	12,190	147,732	12
Cáceres	19,945	457,777	23	Guipúzcoa	1,997	631,003	316

SPAIN

Province	Area (sq. km)	Population	Per sq. km	Province	Area (sq. km)	Population	Per sq. km
Huelva	10,085	397,683	39	Santa Cruz de			
Huesca	15,671	222,238	14	Tenerife	3,208	590,514	184
Jaén	13,498	661,146	49	Santander	5,289	467,138	88
León	15,468	548,721	35	Segovia	6,949	162,770	23
Lérida	12,028	347,015	29	Sevilla	14,001	1,327,190	95
Logroño	5,034	235,713	47	Soria	10,287	114,956	11
Lugo	9,803	415,052	42	Tarragona	6,283	431,961	69
Madrid	7,995	3,792,561	474	Teruel	14,804	170,284	12
Málaga	7,276	867,330	119	Toledo	15,368	468,925	31
Murcia	11,317	832,313	74	Valencia	10,763	1,767,327	164
Navarra	10,421	464,867	45	Valladolid	8,202	412,572	50
Orense	7,278	413,733	57	Vizcaya	2,217	1,043,310	471
Oviedo	10,565	1,045,635	99	Zamora	10,559	251,934	24
Palencia	8,029	198,763	25	Zaragoza	17,194	760,186	44
Palmas (Las)	4,065	579,710	143				
Pontevedra	4,477	750,701	168				
Salamanca	12,336	371,607	30	Total	504,750	33,823,918	70

In 1970 there were 16,619,144 males and 17,413,657 females.

By decree of 21 Sept. 1927 the islands which form the Canary Archipelago were divided into 2 provinces, under the name of their respective capitals: Santa Cruz de Tenerife and Las Palmas de Gran Canaria. The province of Santa Cruz de Tenerife is constituted by the islands of Tenerife, Palma, Gomera and Hierro, and that of Las Palmas by Gran Canaria, Lanzarote and Fuerteventura, with the small barren islands of Alegranza, Roque del Este, Roque del Oeste, Graciosa, Montaña Clara and Lobos. The area of the islands is 7,273 sq. km; population (census 1970), 1,138,801. Places under Spanish sovereignty in Morocco are: Alhucemas, Ceuta, Chafarinas, Melilla and Peñón de Vélez.

The following were the registered populations of principal towns at census 1970:

Town	Population	Town	Population	Town	Population
Albacete	93,233	Hospitalet	241,978	Palma de Mallorca	234,098
Alcoy	61,371	Huelva	96,689	Pamplona	147,168
Algeciras	81,662	Jaén	78,156	Pontevedra	52,452
Alicante	184,716	Jérez de la Frontera	149,867	Puertollano	53,001
Almería	114,510	La Coruña	189,654	Rens	59,095
Avilés	81,710	La Laguna	79,963	Sabadell	159,408
Badajoz	101,710	Langreo	58,864	Salamanca	125,220
Badalona	162,888	Las Palmas	287,038	San Fernando	60,187
Baracaldo	108,757	Leganés	57,537	San Sebastián	165,829
Barcelona	1,745,142	León	105,235	Sta Coloma de	
Bilbao	410,490	Lérida	90,884	Grammanet	106,711
Burgos	119,915	Linares	50,516	Sta Cruz de	
Cáceres	56,064	Logroño	84,456	Tenerife	151,361
Cádiz	135,743	Lorca	60,609	Santander	149,704
Cartagena	146,904	Lugo	63,830	Santiago de Com-	
Castellón	93,968	Madrid	3,146,071	postela	70,893
Córdoba	253,632	Málaga	374,452	Sevilla	548,072
Cornellá	77,314	Manresa	57,846	Tarragona	78,238
Elche	122,663	Mataró	73,129	Tarrasa	138,697
El Ferrol	87,736	Mieres	64,552	Valencia	653,690
Gerona	50,338	Murcia	243,759	Valladolid	236,341
Getafe	69,424	Orense	73,379	Vigo	197,144
Gijón	187,612	Oviedo	154,117	Vitoria	136,873
Granada	190,429	Palencia	58,370	Zaragoza	479,845

Vital statistics for calendar years:

	Marriages	Births	Deaths
1974	267,171	682,010	295,275
1975	271,347	669,378	298,192
1976	260,974	677,456	299,007
1977	262,015	656,357	294,324
1978[1]	257,395	632,975	290,042
1979[1]	245,856	597,252	289,316

[1] Provisional figures.

KING. Juan Carlos I, born 5 June 1938. The eldest son of Don Juan, Conde de Barcelona. Juan Carlos was given precedence over his father as pretender to the Spanish throne in an agreement in 1954 between Don Juan and Gen. Franco. King Juan Carlos married, in 1962, Princess Sophia of Greece, daughter of the late King Paul of the Hellenes and Queen Frederika. *Offspring:* Elena, born 20 Dec. 1963; Cristana, 13 June 1965; Felipe, 30 Jan. 1968.

GOVERNMENT AND CONSTITUTION. The constitutional regulations contained in the Law of the Cortes, the Succession Act, the Fuero of the Spaniards, the Fuero of Labour, etc. (*see* THE STATESMAN'S YEAR-BOOK, 1966–67, pp. 1425 f.) were consolidated and partly modified by the 'Organic Law of the Spanish State' (*La Ley Orgánica del Estado Español*), unanimously approved by the Cortes on 22 Nov. 1966 and ratified by a national referendum on 14 Dec. 1966.

On 27 Dec. 1978 a new Constitution was ratified by the King and it came into force on 29 Dec. On 11 Jan. 1980 the Basque and Catalan Communities were established. Voting took place in Dec. 1980 for the third autonomous zone of Galicia to be established.

A general election took place on 1 March 1979.

Congress of Deputies (350 members): Centre Democrats, 167; Socialist Workers, 120; Communists, 23; Popular Alliance, 9; Catalan Democrats, 9; PNV, 8; Union National, 8; Herri Batasuna, 3; others, 10.

Senate (248 members): Centre Democrats, 105; Socialist Workers, 35; Communists, 12; Democratic Senate, 12; others, 12. In addition there are 41 senators appointed by the King.

The Cabinet in March 1981 was composed as follows:

Prime Minister (Presidente del Gobierno): Leopoldo Calvo Sotelo.
First Deputy Prime Minister and Minister of Defence: Manuel Gutiérrez Mellado. *Second Deputy Prime Minister and Minister of Economics:* Leopoldo Calvo Sotelo. *Foreign Affairs:* José Pedro Pérez-Llorca. *Finance:* Jaime Garcia Añoveros. *Justice:* Francisco Fernández Ordóñez. *Interior:* Juan José Rosón. *Public Works and Urbanization:* Jesús Sáncho Rof. *Education:* Juan Antonio Ortega y Diaz Ambrona. *Labour:* Félix Manuel Pérez Miyares. *Industry and Energy:* Ignacio Bayón. *Agriculture:* Jaime Lamo de Espinosa. *Transport and Communications:* José Luis Alvarez. *Culture:* Iñigo Cavero. *Health and Social Security:* Alberto Oliart. *Territorial Administration:* Rodolfo Martin Villa. *Minister for Relations with the EEC:* Eduardo Punset Casals. *Economy and Commerce:* Juan Antonio Garcia Diez. *Universities and Investigations:* Luis Gonzáles Seara. *Presidency of Government:* Rafael Arias Salgado. *Defence:* Agustin Rodriguez Sahagún. *Office of the President:* Pio Cabanillas. *Public Administration:* Sebastián Martin Retortillo.

National flag: Three horizontal stripes of red, yellow, red, with the yellow of double width, and charged over all in the hoist with the national arms.
National anthem: Marcha real.

Local Government. The provinces are constituted by the association of municipalities (8,655 in 1970). All municipalities are autonomous in their respective spheres, and at their heads stands the *Ayuntamiento*. The municipal councils are elected by the heads of family. The *Alcalde* or Mayor is appointed by the Minister of the Interior in municipalities of over 10,000 inhabitants, and elsewhere by the Civil Governors. The *Diputaciones Provinciales* have entire jurisdiction over their own province and are their sole administrators. Each island of the Canaries has a corporation known as *Cabildo Insular*, to rule their special interests; the Balearic Islands have the same provincial administration as the mainland. Each province of Spain has its own Assembly, the *Diputación Provincial*.

The reconstruction of devastated regions is under the care of the *Instituto de la Vivienda* and by the *Banco de Crédito a la Reconstrucción*, whose duty is to grant and administer loans approved for reconstructing buildings, and the *Banco de Crédito Agricola* and *Banco de Crédito Industrial* with regard to industries, agriculture, commerce and mining, and merchant vessels.

DEFENCE. On 26 Sept. 1953 the US and Spain signed three agreements covering the construction and use of military facilities in Spain by the US, economic assistance, and military end-item assistance. These agreements were renewed for another 5 years on 26 Sept. 1963. The American naval and air base at Rota (near Cádiz) is connected by pipelines with the American bomber bases at Morón de la Frontera (near Seville), Torrejón (near Madrid) and Zaragoza.

A further agreement was signed on 6 Aug. 1970 replacing the one signed in 1953 which was due to expire on 26 Sept. 1970 having been extended for 18 months in 1969.

Length of service is 16 months in the army, 24 months in the navy and 18 months in the air force.

Army. The Army consists of 1 armoured division with AMX-30, M-47 and M-48 tanks, 2 mechanized infantry divisions, 2 mountain divisions, 10 independent infantry brigades, 1 armoured cavalry brigade, 1 high mountain brigade, 1 parachute brigade, 1 airportable brigade and 1 battalion with surface-to-air missiles.

Army personnel consisted (1979) of 240,000 officers and other ranks. Total strength in Africa, about 35,000 men, including 3 regiments of the Foreign Legion.

Navy. Particulars of the principal ship:

Completed	Name	Standard displacement Tons	Principal armament	Aircraft	Shaft horsepower	Speed Knots
			Helicopter Carrier			
1943	Dedalo [1]	13,000	26 40-mm. A.A.	7 Vstol aircraft and 20 helicopters	100,000	32

[1] The former US fixed-wing aircraft carrier *Cabot*, converted in 1966 and transferred to Spain on loan in 1967 and purchased in 1973.

There are also 8 diesel-powered patrol submarines (4 new French-built and 4 old *ex*-US), 14 destroyers, 12 frigates, 4 old corvettes, 12 new fast patrol craft, 7 patrol vessels, 4 ocean minesweepers, 11 coastal minesweepers, 20 coastal patrol craft, 50 inshore patrol launches, 1 dock landing ship, 6 survey ships, 3 landing ships, 9 landing craft, 84 minor landing craft, 15 oilers, 2 attack vehicle and troop transports, 2 tenders, 1 training ship, 1 boom defence vessel, 31 tugs, 1 royal yacht and 50 service craft.

The Spanish Navy is being renewed and modernized. Ships under construction include 1 small aircraft carrier, 4 more patrol submarines of French design, 2 more small frigates and 7 fishery protection cutters. Ships projected include 3 missile armed frigates and 8 corvettes, although a modified new construction programme is being considered.

The heavy cruiser *Canarias* was placed on the ineffective list at the end of 1976.

The anti-aircraft cruiser *Méndez Núñez* was stricken from the list in 1963 and the cruisers *Almirante Cervera*, *Galicia* and *Miguel de Cervantes* in 1964–66.

Shipbuilding is mainly carried on at the dockyards at El Ferrol and Cartagena, Cádiz having a smaller share in it.

There are naval radio telegraphic stations at Cádiz, Barcelona, Mahón, Pontevedra, Cartagena and El Ferrol.

Barcelona, Bilbao, Seville and Cádiz are the chief naval yards.

In 1981 naval personnel totalled 55,400, comprising 4,100 naval officers, 32,700 ratings, 8,000 civil branch, 600 marine officers and 10,000 marine other ranks.

Air Force. The Air Force is organized as an independent service, dating from 1939. It is administered through 4 operational commands. These comprise Air Combat Command which controls interceptor squadrons (including USAF elements) and the control and warning radar network, Tactical and Transport Commands, and Air Command of the Canaries. Strength is about 38,000 and 150 combat aircraft.

The Tactical Air Command has 1 fighter-bomber squadron of Spanish-built Northrop SF-5s, 1 squadron of HA-220 Super Saeta light attack jet aircraft of Spanish design and manufacture, 1 aero-naval co-operation squadron with 6 P-3A Orion anti-submarine aircraft, and a liaison squadron at Tablada with CASA 127s and Bird Dogs. Air Defence Command has 2 squadrons of Mirage III-Es, 2 squadrons of F-4C/RF-4C Phantom IIs and 2 squadrons of Mirage F1-Cs, plus a squadron of CASA 127 liaison aircraft. Four KC-130H tankers support the F-4C squadrons. Three wings of Air Transport Command operate C-130 Hercules, Caribou and Spanish-built CASA Aviocars. Air Command of the Canaries has 11 squadrons, equipped with Aviocar transports; SF-5 fighter-bombers; F27 Maritime aircraft and a variety of helicopters for search and rescue; 2 DC-8s, 4 Falcons, a Navajo and helicopters for VIP transport; and aircraft for photographic, firefighting, target training and research duties.

American-built Bonanza, T-34A and T-6 piston-engined aircraft are used for basic training, together with HA-200 Saeta twin-jet training aircraft which are being replaced by CASA C-101s in 1980–81. T-33A jet aircraft and 2-seat versions of operational types are used as advanced trainers.

INTERNATIONAL RELATIONS

Membership. Spain is a member of UN and OECD.

ECONOMY

Budget. Revenue and expenditure in 1m. pesetas:

	1974	1975	1976	1977	1978	1979
Revenue	551,698	656,000	785,000	967,250	1,433,000	1,680,000
Expenditure	551,698	656,000	785,000	967,250	1,433,000	1,680,000

The budget is made up as follows (in 1m. pesetas):

Revenue (1979)		Expenditure (1979)	
Direct taxes	730,135	Chief of State	...
Indirect taxes	693,050	Regency council	...
Levies and taxes	99,586	Cortes	2,592
Current transactions	47,215	National Council	...
Investment income	84,943	Court of Accounts	180
		Public Debt	39,740
		National fund	68,155
		Presidency of the Government	48,703
		Ministry of Foreign Affairs	9,824
		„ Justice	34,668
		„ Defence	236,812
		„ Interior	115,750
		„ Public Works	128,857
		„ Education	301,683
		„ Labour	5,928
		„ Industry	41,265
		„ Agriculture	73,698
		„ Commerce and Tourism	17,576
		„ Finance	26,003
		„ Economy	2,668
		„ Transport and Communications	134,635
		„ Health and Social Security	185,501
		„ Culture	27,030
		Other charges	151,761

Currency. The *peseta* of 100 *céntimos* had the nominal value of a pre-war franc, 25·22 *pesetas* to the £ sterling.

Bank-notes of 1,000, 500, 100, 50, 25, 5 and 1 *peseta* and coins of 5 and 10 *céntimos* (aluminium, tin and copper), 1 *peseta* (copper and aluminium), 5, 25, 50 *pesetas* (nickel and copper) and 100 *pesetas* (silver) are in circulation. In 1979 the circulation of bank-notes was 1,160,745m. *pesetas* and of coins, 36,568m. *pesetas*.

Banking. On 1 Jan. 1922 the Bank of Spain came under the Bank Ordinance Law, according to which the Government participate in its net profits.

In 1963 the Banco Central set up the Banco de Fomento (capital, 225m. pesetas) for long-term financing; the new bank is to absorb the Banco Central's investment company (Hispana de Inversiones), after which its capital is to be increased by 75m.

In 1979 the gold and foreign currency holdings of the Bank of Spain amounted to US$13,107·7m. (paper). A decree of 11 July 1941 established the voluntary nation- alization of foreign banks in Spain, and the transference and amalgama- tion of the business of national banks.

Savings bank deposits (Popular Savings Banks) in Spain, 31 Dec. 1970, amounted to 325,661m. pesetas. Post office savings banks opened on 12 March 1916. Deposits, 31 Dec. 1967, amounted to 37,965m. pesetas; private banks saving deposits, 564,468m. pesetas.

By a decree of 20 Nov. 1941 the post office savings bank opens an account with an initial entry of 1 peseta for every Spanish child born.

Weights and Measures. On 1 Jan. 1859 the metric system of weights and measures was introduced.

ENERGY AND NATURAL RESOURCES

Electricity. Electric power-stations in 1971 had a total installed capacity of 19m. kw., of which 8m. was hydro-electric. The total output 1978, amounted to 99,534m. kwh of which 41,497m. hydro-electric and 7,649m. nuclear. Gas production in 1977 was 783m. cu. metres.

Minerals. Spain is rich in minerals. The production of the more important minerals in 1978 were as follows (in 1,000 tonnes):

Anthracite	3,831	Iron ore	8,580	Tin ore	1·1
Coal	7,668	Lead ore	104	Zinc ore	261·9
Lignite	8,272	Copper	148	Wolfram ore	0·6

Agriculture. Spain is mainly an agricultural country. In 1977 the total value of agricultural produce was 690m. pesetas; of livestock, 482m.; of forestry, 61·8m. Land under cultivation in 1978 (in 1,000 hectares) included: Cereals, 7,514; vegetables, 572; potatoes, 843. In 1976, 400,928 tractors and 41,168 harvesters were in use.

Principal crops	Area (in 1,000 hectares)				Yield (in 1,000 tonnes)			
	1975[1]	1976[1]	1977[1]	1978[1]	1975[1]	1976[1]	1977[1]	1978[1]
Wheat	2,661	2,772	2,715	2,752	4,302	4,436	4,064	4,806
Barley	3,262	3,240	3,348	3,519	6,728	5,473	6,766	8,068
Oats	457	455	406	442	609	528	418	553
Rye	228	224	236	228	240	214	228	251
Rice	62	64	68	68	378	406	379	401
Maize	485	432	442	443	1,793	1,544	1,892	1,969
Potatoes	385	391	403	371	5,337	5,658	5,881	5,364
Sugar-beet	200	293	253	235	6,336	10,166	8,307	8,292
Tomatoes	81	68	73	72	2,488	2,078	2,358	2,223

[1] Provisional.

In 1978, 1,639,000 hectares were under vines; in 1977 production of wine was 21m. hectolitres. The area of onions in 1978 was 35,000 hectares, yielding 996,000 tons. Production of oranges and mandarines in 1978 was 2,544,000 tons. Other products are esparto, flax, hemp and pulse. Spain has important industries connected with the preparation of wine and fruits. Silk culture is carried on in Murcia, Alicante and other provinces; 3,000 tons were produced in 1977. Spain produced in 1968, 8,951 tons of honey and 500 tons of beeswax. Alcoholic beverages produced totalled 137·2m. litres in 1976.

Tobacco crop in 1978 was 29,000 tons; sugar-cane, 316,000 tons.

Livestock (1979): Horses, 260,000; mules, 257,000; asses, 238,000; cattle, 4·65m.; sheep, 14·5m.; goats, 2·3m.; pigs, 9·9m.; poultry, 53·3m.

Forestry. Total forests (1977) 26m. hectares; production value, 36,010m. pesetas.

Fisheries. The most important catches are those of sardines, tunny fish and cod. The total catch amounted in 1978 to 1·25m. tons, representing a value of 106,425·1m. pesetas. In the tinned fish industry there were, in 1972, 495 factories, producing 106,944 tons. The Spanish fishing fleet in 1978 consisted of 17,174 vessels of 785,642 tons.

INDUSTRY AND TRADE

Industry. The manufacture of cotton and woollen goods is important, principally in Catalonia. In 1970 there were 3,626 textile factories in operation. Production, in

1,000 tonnes (1976): Wool yarn, 27; cotton (yarn, 65; fabrics, 57); rayon fabrics, 6. 275 paper-mills produced in 1975, 1·9m. tonnes of writing, printing, packing and other paper. The production of cork and cork products was 51,300 tonnes. The production of cement reached 23,968,090 tonnes in 1975.

Spanish shipyards launched 1,002,119 BRT in 1978. In 1978, 1,431,052 vehicles were built, including 984,954 passenger cars.

Labour. The daily minimum wage for workers is 759 pesetas (June 1980).

The economically active population numbered 13,413,900 at the end of 1975. Of these, 2·9m. were occupied in agriculture and fishing, 3·6m. in manufactures, 1·4m. in trade, 5·2m. in public and personal services.

Commerce. Foreign trade of Spain (Peninsula, Baleares, Canaries, Ceuta, Melilla) (in 1m. pesetas):

	1973	1974	1975	1976	1977	1978
Imports	561,543	888,688	931,986	1,169,412	1,350,352	1,431,538
Exports	302,670	407,972	441,091	583,222	775,150	1,001,599

In 1977 the most important items of import were (in 1m. pesetas): Manufactures, 608,935; mineral fuels and lubricants, 382,141; animal and vegetable oils and fats, 179,333; food, drink and tobacco, 159,878. The main items of exports were: Manufactured goods, 558,300; food, drink, tobacco, 157,156.

In 1977 the main supplying countries were (in 1m. pesetas): USA, 163,018; Federal Republic of Germany, 136,034; France, 113,094; UK, 71,337; Italy, 68,170. The main receiving countries were (in 1m. pesetas): France, 123,639; Federal Republic of Germany, 82,015; USA, 76,222; UK, 49,037; Italy, 39,367.

Of the 115·9m. litres of sherry exported in 1972, 57·9m. went to the UK. In 1972, 113·6m. litres of wine were exported.

Total trade between Spain and UK (British Department of Trade returns, in £1,000 sterling):

	1975	1976	1977	1978	1979	1980
Imports to UK	277,830	360,354	435,176	505,894	710,901	804,232
Exports and re-exports from UK	294,796	368,483	464,829	472,035	573,015	708,998

Total trade of the Spanish territories and UK (British Department of Trade returns, in £1,000 sterling):

	Imports to UK			Exports from UK		
	1978	1979	1980	1978	1979	1980
Canary Islands	55,904	55,548	61,565	40,888	48,419	46,108
North Africa	4	—	7	5,122	5,060	6,860

Tourism. In 1979, 38·9m. foreigners visited Spain.

COMMUNICATIONS

Roads. In 1977 the total length of highways and roads in Spain was 145,997 km, of which 56,106 km were macadamized. Number of motor cars was 8,952,628 in 1978.

Railways. The total length of the state railways in 1980 was 13,533 km, mostly 1,676-mm gauge. There are 4,956 km of lines electrified. On 1 Feb. 1941 the Spanish railways, of broad gauge only, passed into state ownership; they are under a board known as the *Red Nacional de Ferrocarriles Españoles* (RENFE). The gauge of the principal Spanish railways has, for strategic reasons, been kept different from that of France; passengers therefore must change trains at the frontier stations except by certain trains having variable gauge axles. Number of passengers carried in 1979 by government-owned lines was 205m.; freight carried was 35·7m. tonnes. A further 2,757 km of route was electrified during 1974–77 development plan period and a high-speed 1,435-mm gauge line from the French frontier at Port Bou to Barcelona and Madrid is planned.

Aviation. The most important Spanish airline is 'Iberia': it maintains a regular service with Tangier, Morocco, the Balearic and Canary Islands, Lisbon, Switzerland, London, Buenos Aires, Venezuela, Cuba, Canada and USA. There are 37 civilian and 7 military airports.

Aircraft movements in 1979 (provisional), 370,638 internal and 243,193 international, carrying 49·2m. passengers and 378,062 tonnes of merchandise.

Shipping. The merchant navy in 1978 contained 1,111 vessels of a gross tonnage of 7,712,000.

1978, 106,567 ships entered Spanish ports, carrying 8,110,615 passengers and discharging 403,265,000 tons of cargo.

Post and Broadcasting. The receipts of the post office in 1978 were 16,497m. pesetas; expenses, 28,657m. pesetas. There were in 1978, 12,803 post offices and 9,527,781 telephones, all privately operated.

The length of telegraph lines in 1977 was 34,236 km; number of telegraph offices, 6,580. Total receipts (1978), 4,895m. pesetas; expenses, 11,210m. pesetas.

The 'Compañia Nacional de Telegrafia sin Hilos' holds the government concession for the public service with ships, and between the Peninsula and the Canary Islands, and the international service with UK, Italy, France, Switzerland and USA, as well as various special press services. The National Radio Service 'Redera' operates a broadcasting station at Arganda, 15 miles from Madrid.

The overseas radio-telegraph circuits are operated in Spain mainly by Trans-radio Española, SA. Under an agreement with Cable and Wireless, Ltd, London, Transradio Española lease and operate the Bilbao end of the Bilbao–Great Britain cable and the Barcelona end of the Barcelona–Marseilles cable.

Radio Nacional de España broadcasts 4 programmes on medium-waves and FM, as well as 4 regional programmes. *Television Española* broadcasts 2 programmes. Colour transmissions are carried by PAL system. Number of receivers: radio, 5·1m.; television, 4·4m. (including 3,000 colour sets).

Cinemas (1977). There were 5,684 cinemas with an estimated seating capacity of 4m.

Newspapers (1977). There appeared 167 daily newspapers with a total daily circulation of about 5·7m. copies. Thirteen of them were published in Madrid and 10 in Barcelona; all must be printed in Castilian.

JUSTICE, RELIGION, EDUCATION AND WELFARE

Justice. Justice is administered by *Tribunales* and *Juzgados* (Tribunals and Courts), which conjointly form the *Poder Judicial* (Judicial Power). Judges and magistrates cannot be removed, suspended or transferred except as set forth by law.

The Judicature is composed of the *Tribunal Supremo* (Supreme High Court); 15 *Audiencias Territoriales* (Division High Courts); 50 *Audiencias Provinciales* (Provincial High Courts); 579 *Juzgados de Primera Instancia* (Courts of First Instance); and 9,203 *Juzgados Municipales, Comarcales y de paz* (District Court, or Court of Lowest Jurisdiction held by Justices of the Peace).

The *Tribunal Supremo* consists of a President (appointed by the Government) and various judges distributed among 6 chambers: 1 for trying civil matters, 3 for administrative purposes, 1 for criminal trials and 1 for social matters. The *Tribunal Supremo* has disciplinary faculties; is court of cassation in civil criminal trials; for administrative purposes decides in first and second instance disputes arising between private individuals and the State, and in social matters resolves in the last instance all cases involving over 100,000 pesetas.

The *Audiencias Territoriales* have power to try in second instance sentences passed by judges in civil matters.

The *Audiencias Provinciales* try and pass sentence in first instance on all cases filed for delinquency. The jury system is in operation except for military trials.

The *Juzgados Municipales* try small civil cases and petty offences. The *Juzgados Comarcales* deal with the same charges, but their jurisdiction embraces larger districts.

Military cases are tried by the *Tribunal Supremo de Justicia Militar*.

The prison population was, on 31 Dec. 1979, 13,627.

Police. The Minister of the Interior (*Gobernación*) controls the armed police, the secret police and the para-military *Guardia Civil*.

Religion. Catholicism is again established as the religion of the State. Religious bodies have recovered their legal status; confiscated property has been returned;

allowances to clergy are again paid by the State; divorce is suppressed; cemeteries are brought back to ecclesiastical jurisdiction. There are 10 metropolitan sees and 64 suffragan sees, the chief being Toledo, where the Primate resides.

A concordat was signed in Rome on 27 Aug. 1953 to replace the concordat of 1851, which the republic had denounced in 1931.

There are about 26,000 Protestants, with 200 churches and chapels, outside which no public ceremonies are permitted. The British and Foreign Bible Society was, on 10 March 1963, allowed to resume its activities.

The first synagogue since the expulsion of the Jews in 1492 was opened in Madrid on 2 Oct. 1959. The number of Jews is estimated at about 1,000.

Education. Spain is divided into 12 educational districts, with the universities as centres. Primary education is compulsory and free. The *Frente de Juventudes* (Youth Front) was created by law of 6 Dec. 1940; it comprises 3 sections (educational, labour, rural). There is also the University Militia for army training under conscription.

In 1973–74 there were 138,114 primary schools attended by 4,945,774 pupils, with 169,977 teachers. Secondary education is conducted by 4,312 middle schools, with 56,379 teachers and 1,012,945 pupils. For higher education, there are 410 centres with 399,500 pupils and 26,800 teachers. There are 13 universities, attended (1965–66) by 125,771 students, with 3,078 teachers. The universities are at Barcelona, Granada, Madrid, Murcia, Oviedo, Salamanca, Santiago, Sevilla, Valencia, Valladolid, Zaragoza, Pamplona and La Laguna (Canaries). There is, besides, a medical and science faculty at Cádiz in connexion with the University of Seville.

In 1972 the Government announced the creation of 4 new universities at Málaga, Córdoba, Santander and the first 'university of the air'. A further 2 universities are envisaged.

Social Security. Schemes of wide social range include the Labour Charter (*Fuero del Trabajo*) of 9 March 1938, for a better distribution and remuneration of the working classes, with uninterrupted Sunday and feast-day wages. The law of Family Subsidy (*Subsidio Familiar*), which came into force on 1 March 1939, makes all working people contribute 1% of their earnings, plus an additional 6% from the employers, in a system of social insurance which entitles all families with from 2 to 12 children under 14 years of age to a proportional monthly allowance ranging from 60 to 4,500 pesetas, with an additional 3,000 pesetas for each child in excess of 12 (2 Sept. 1955). Married workers receive an additional bonus. Since 1949, old age pensions and health and maternity insurances have been added; workers contribute 1% and employers 5%.

A decree of 22 Feb. 1941 established state loans on marriage to help large families, and the institution known as *Auxilio Social*, the funds of which are derived among other channels from a fortnightly public collection throughout the country, for supplying food and clothing to needy persons and the maintenance of nurseries and infirmaries. A national health insurance for all workers is now also in operation.

By a law dated 27 Feb. 1908 the *Instituto Nacional de Previsión* was founded for the purpose of granting old age pensions and administering a system of social insurance. The family-allowance and health-insurance schemes, described above, have been incorporated in the *Instituto*.

DIPLOMATIC REPRESENTATIVES

OF SPAIN IN GREAT BRITAIN (24 Belgrave Sq., London SW1X 8QA)

Ambassador: Fernando Arias-Salgado (accredited 11 March 1981).

OF GREAT BRITAIN IN SPAIN (Calle de Fernando el Santo, 16, Madrid, 4)

Ambassador: R. E. Parsons, CMG.

OF SPAIN IN THE USA (2700–15th St., NW, Washington, D.C., 20009)

Ambassador: José Llado.

OF THE USA IN SPAIN (Serrano 75, Madrid)

Ambassador: Terence A. Todman.

OF SPAIN TO THE UNITED NATIONS

Ambassador: Jaime de Pinies.

Books of Reference

Statistical Information: The Instituto Nacional de Estadistica (Generalisimo 91, Madrid) combines the administrative work of a government department attached to the Presidency of the Government with a centre of statistical studies. *Director-General:* Benito Martinez-Echevarria. Its publications include: *Anuario Estadístico de España.* Annual (latest vol., 1966). *Edición manual* (latest vol., 1973).—*Reseñas estadisticos provinciales.*—*Nomenclator de las ciudades, villas lugares, aldeas, y demás entidades de población de España.* 6 vols. Madrid, 1963.—*Censo de Población de España.* Madrid, 1960.—*Diccionario Corográfico de España.* 4 vols. Madrid, 1948.—*Boletín de Estadística.* Madrid. (No. 1, Jan.–March 1939: monthly from 1948).— *Estadística española. Revista trimestral* (from 1959).

Spain at a Glance, 1972. Servicio Informativo Español, Madrid, 1972

Aguilar (ed.), *Nuevo Atlas de España.* Madrid, 1961
Altamira y Crevea, R., *A History of Spain.* New York and London, 1950
Anuario del Mercado Español. Madrid, 1965
Enciclopedia Universal Ilustrada. 70 vols., 10 appendices, 10 supplements. Madrid
Garcia Venero, M., *Historia del Nacionalismo Vasco, 1793–1936.* Madrid, 1945
Hermet, G., *L'Espagne de Franco.* Paris, 1974
Lafuente, M., and Valera, J., *Historia General de España.* New ed. 25 vols. Barcelona, 1925
López Oliván, J., *Repertorio Diplomático Español.* [*Collection of treaties, 1125–1935.*] Madrid, 1944
Morris, J., *Spain.* London, 1979
Roman, M., *The Limits of Economic Growth in Spain.* New York, 1971 and London, 1972
Russell, P. E. (ed.), *Spain: A Companion to Spanish Studies.* 6th ed. London, 1973
Vicens Vives, J., *Historia Económica de España.* 5 vols. Barcelona, 1959
Wright, A., *The Spanish Economy 1959–1976.* London, 1977

National Library: Biblioteca Nacional, Madrid. *Director:* Guillermo Cuastavino Callent.

FORMER PROVINCE IN AFRICA (WESTERN SAHARA)

It was announced in Madrid on 14 Nov. 1975 that Spain, Morocco and Mauritania had reached agreement on the transfer of power over Western Sahara to Morocco and Mauritania on 28 Feb. 1976. Morocco occupied El Aiaún in late Nov. and on 12 Jan. 1976 the Spanish army withdrew from Western Sahara which had ceased to be a Spanish province on 31 Dec. 1975. The country was partitioned by Morocco and Mauritania. In Aug. 1979 Mauritania withdrew from the territory it took over in 1976. The area was taken over by Morocco and reorganized into Moroccan provinces.

Algeria stated that the former province should be handed over to the people of the territory, objected to the partition and is (1981) backing the claims of *Frente Polisario* for an independent state. In spite of occupation of all centres by Moroccan troops, Saharan guerrillas based in Algeria continue to attempt to liberate their country. They have renamed it the Democratic Saharan Arab Republic.

The area was 266,000 sq. km (102,680 sq. miles). The population at the census (1970) was 76,425; Saharans, 59,777 and 16,648 Europeans. The capital was El Aaiún (Laayoune) (population, 24,048).

Rich phosphate deposits were discovered in 1963 at Bu Craa. Morocco holds 65% of the shares of the former Spanish state-controlled company. While production reached 5·6m. tonnes in 1975, exploitation has been severely reduced by guerrilla activity in 1976 and 1977. After a nearly complete collapse, production and transportation of phosphate resumed in 1978.

Books of Reference

Atlas Histórico y Geográfico de Africa Española. Madrid, 1955
Resumén estadistico del Africa española. 1965–66. Madrid, 1967
Caro Baroja, J., *Estudios saharianos*. Madrid, 1955
Hernández-Pacheco, E., and others, *El Sahara español*. Madrid, 1949
Mercer, J., *Spanish Sahara*. London, 1976
Pélissier, R., *Les Territoires Espagnols d'Afrique*. Paris, 1963.—*Los Territorios Españoles de Africa*. Madrid, 1964
Rumeu de Armas, A., *España en el Africa Atlántica*. 2 vols. Madrid, 1956–57
Thompson, V. and Adloff, R., *The Western Saharans*. London, 1980

SRI LANKA

Ceylon

Capital: Colombo
Population: 14·47m. (1979)
GNP per capita: US$200 (1979)

HISTORY. According to the Mahawansa chronicle, an Indian prince from the valley of the Ganges, named Vijaya, arrived in the 6th century B.C. and became the first king of the Sinhalese. The monarchical form of government continued until the beginning of the 19th century when the British subjugated the Kandyan Kingdom in the central highlands.

In 1505 the Portuguese formed settlements on the west and south, which were taken from them about the middle of the next century by the Dutch. In 1796 the British Government annexed the foreign settlements to the presidency of Madras. In 1802 Ceylon was constituted a separate colony.

Ceylon reached fully responsible status within the British Commonwealth when the Ceylon Independence Act, 1947, came into force on 4 Feb. 1948. Sri Lanka became a republic in 1972.

AREA AND POPULATION. Sri Lanka lies off the south-east coast of the Indian State of Tamil Nadu, separated from it by the Indian ocean but almost joined to it by the chain of islands called Adam's Bridge. On 28 June 1974 the frontier between India and Sri Lanka in the Palk Strait was re-defined, giving to Sri Lanka the island of Kachchativu. Area (in sq. miles) and census population on 9 Oct. 1971:

Provinces	Area	Population	Provinces	Area	Population
Western	1,432	3,401,779	North-Central	4,140	552,423
Central	2,158	1,953,044	Uva	3,874	808,425
Southern	2,146	1,661,870	Sabaragamuwa	1,892	1,316,096
Northern	3,429	874,626			
Eastern	3,242	717,571	Total	25,332[1]	12,689,897
North-Western	3,016	1,404,063			

[1] 65,610 sq. km.

Population (1971 census), 12,689,897, an increase of 19·9% since 1963. Estimate (1979) 14·47m. Population (in 1,000) according to race and nationality at the 1971 census: 9,131 Sinhalese, 1,424 Ceylon Tamils, 828 Ceylon Moors, 45 Burghers and Eurasians, 43 Malays, 1,175 Indian Tamils, 27 Indian Moors. Non-nationals of Sri Lanka totalled 1,202,000. By agreement with the Government of India in 1964 and 1974, Indian nationals who have not been granted Sri Lanka citizenship were to be repatriated. The 1964 agreement covered 525,000 people; the 1974 agreement, 150,000.

Vital statistics, 1979: birth-rate (per 1,000 population), 26; death-rate, 7·4; infant death-rate (per 1,000 live births), 43·7.

The urban population is 22·4% of the total population. The principal towns and their population according to the census of 1971 are: Colombo, 562,160 (1978 estimate, 624,000); Dehiwela–Mt. Lavinia, 154,785 (171,000); Jaffna, 107,663 (120,000); Kotte, 92,042 (104,000); Kandy, 93,602 (104,000); Galle, 72,720 (79,000); Moratuwa, 96,489 (107,000); Negombo, 57,115 (64,000); Kurunegala, 25,189 (27,000); Nuwara Eliya, 16,347 (19,000).

The national languages are Sinhala and Tamil; Sinhala is the official language and Tamil is used in the northern and eastern provinces.

CONSTITUTION AND GOVERNMENT. Prior to independence the Ceylon and UK governments concluded agreements on defence, external affairs and public officers. The defence agreement provided that the UK and Ceylon would give

1114

to each other such military assistance as it may be in their mutual interest to provide. The UK may base such naval and air forces and maintain such land forces in Ceylon as may be required for these purposes, and as may be mutually agreed. The UK naval base at Trincomalee and the air base at Katunayake were taken over by Ceylon on 15 Oct. and 1 Nov. 1957 respectively.

The agreement on external affairs declared the readiness of Ceylon to adopt and follow the resolutions of past imperial conferences; provides that in external affairs generally the two governments will conform to the principles and practice observed by other members of the Commonwealth; provides that Ceylon will enjoy reciprocal rights and benefits enjoyed by the UK, and bear the obligations carried by the UK, which arise out of any valid international instrument which applies to Ceylon.

The public officers agreement protected the positions of specified classes of person holding office in the public service of Ceylon.

Parliament consists of one chamber, composed of 168 members elected by universal suffrage, and 6 are nominated. An amendment to the constitution (Jan. 1981) providing for 169 members, remains inchoate. The Senate was abolished by constitutional amendment in Sept. 1971.

The House of Representatives as a Constituent Assembly framed a new republican constitution providing for a President and a Council of Ministers headed by the Prime Minister and responsible to a National Assembly.

This constitution came into force on 22 May 1972. Sovereignty is vested entirely in the National Assembly, which sits for 6 years and combines legislative and executive functions.

In Oct. 1977 the constitution was amended to provide a presidential form of government. The office of President would be held by the then Prime Minister: Mr Jayawardene took office on 4 Feb. 1978 for a 6-year term with wide executive powers, including the right to preside over the cabinet and to assign any ministry to himself.

A new constitution for the Democratic Socialist Republic of Sri Lanka was promulgated in Sept. 1978.

The electorate consists of all who are 18 years of age and over.

National flag: A yellow field bearing 2 panels: in the hoist 2 vertical strips of green and orange; in the fly, dark red with a gold lion holding a sword and in each corner a gold 'bo' leaf.

The Cabinet formed in Feb. 1980 was as follows:

President, Defence, Higher Education, Janata Estates, State Plantations, and Planning: J. R. Jayawardene.

Prime Minister, Local Government, Highways, Housing and Construction: Ranasingle Premadasa.

Land, Land Development and Mahaweli Development: Gamini Dissanayake. *Foreign Affairs:* A. C. S. Hameed. *Home Affairs:* K. W. Devanayagam. *Trade and Shipping:* Lalith Athulathmudali. *Rural Development:* Wimala Kannangara. *Justice:* N. P. Wijeyeratna. *Finance and Planning:* Ronnie de Mel. *Labour:* Capt. C. P. J. Seneviratne. *Industries and Scientific Affairs:* Cyril Mathew. *Cultural Affairs:* E. L. B. Hurulle. *Fisheries:* F. Perera. *Health:* Gamini Jayasooriya. *Power and Energy, Post and Telecommunications:* D. B. Wijetunge. *Parliamentary Affairs and Sports:* M. Vincent Perera. *Transport:* H. M. Mohamed. *Agricultural Development and Research:* E. L. Senanayake. *Public Administration and Plantation Industries:* M. Jayawickrene. *Textile Industry:* Wijepala Mendis. *Social Services:* Asoka Karunaratne. *Food and Co-operatives:* S. B. Herath. *Rural Industrial Development:* R. S. Thondaman. *Youth Affairs, Education and Employment:* R. Wickremasinghe. *State:* A. de Alwis. *Regional Development:* C. Rajadurai.

For purposes of general administration, the island is divided into 24 districts, each presided over by a government agent with assistants. There are 12 municipalities, with 39 urban councils, 85 town councils and 542 village committees. People's Committees inaugurated on 1 Sept. 1971, consisting of 11 members drawn from cooperatives, trade unions, rural development societies and local government bodies have been abandoned.

The capital is Colombo.

DEFENCE

Army. The Army was constituted on 10 Oct. 1949 and consists of the Regular Force, the Regular Reserve, the Volunteer Force and the Volunteer Reserve. Strength (1980), 10,000, organized into 1 infantry brigade of 4 battalions, 1 reconnaissance, 1 engineer, 1 signals and 1 artillery regiment. Reserves, 10,000.

Navy. The Navy was constituted on 9 Dec. 1950. It comprises 6 (1 *ex*-Soviet and 5 *ex*-Chinese) fast gunboats, 21 small patrol boats and 4 survey craft. The *ex*-Canadian frigate sold by Israel to Ceylon in 1959 was written off in 1979. *Gemunu* and *Rangalla* are commissioned as shore establishments. Personnel in 1981 numbered 200 officers and 2,680 ratings. Naval personnel are sent to the UK for training. There is also a Naval Reserve of 45 officers and 540 ratings, and a Voluntary Naval Reserve.

Air Force. The Air Force was formed on 10 Oct. 1950. Its flying bases are at Katunayake and China Bay, Trincomalee. Equipment include 4 MiG-17F jet fighter-bombers, 1 MiG-15UTI jet trainer, 3 Jet Provosts (armed), 7 Chipmunk and 4 Cessna 150 trainers, 3 Heron and 3 Dove light transports, 1 HS748, 1 Convair 440, 2 DC-3s, 4 Cessna Skymasters for coastal reconnaissance and transport, and 2 Dauphin, 7 JetRanger and 5 Bell 47G helicopters for internal security operations. Total strength about 2,200 officers and airmen. There is also an Air Force Reserve.

INTERNATIONAL RELATIONS

Membership. Sri Lanka is a member of UN, the Commonwealth and the Colombo Plan.

External debt. External debt in 1980 was over Rs 16,250m.

Agreement. In 1978 Sri Lanka and China signed a trade agreement replacing the 'Rice–Rubber Agreement' of 1952 with a general trade including petroleum.

ECONOMY

Planning. The 1979–83 plan aims at 5·5% annual growth rate. Investment allocated is mainly for manufacturing (private sector), the Greater Colombo Development Plan (public sector) and the Mahaweli energy and irrigation scheme. Total investment, about Rs 81,000m.

Budget. Revenue and expenditure of central government in Rs 1m. for financial years ending 30 Sept.:

		Expenditure		
Year	Revenue	Recurrent	Capital	Total
1975–76	4,493·6	4,593·2	1,968·4	6,651·6
1976–77	6,497·0	6,195·0	3,054·0	9,249·0
1977–78 [1]	10,830·0	10,070·0	5,180·0	15,250·0
1978–79 [1]	11,431·0	10,991·7	7,294·8	18,286·5

[1] Estimate.

The principal sources of revenue in 1978–79 were (in Rs 1m.): Income tax, 1,152; import duties, 1,475; export duties, 4,500; other indirect taxes, 2,025.

The principal items of expenditure in 1978–79 (in Rs 1m.): Administration including defence, 1,783·2; food subsidies, 2,332·9; education, social services and health, 1,818·2. Capital expenditure on agriculture, 526·8; communications, 1,271·1.

Currency. The Monetary Law (Amendment) Act No. 16 of 1967 provides that the standard monetary unit is the Ceylon *rupee* having a par value equal to 0·149297 of a grain of fine gold. Following the devaluation of sterling in Nov. 1967, the Ceylon rupee was devalued by 20%.

The Central Bank is the sole authority for the issue of currency and all currency notes and coins issued by the Central Bank are legal tender for the payment of any amount. Currency notes are issued in the denominations of Re 1, Rs 2, 5, 10, 50 and 100. The following coins are legal tender: (1) nickel brass, 10 and 5 cents; (2) cupro-nickel, Re 1, 50 and 25 cents; (3) aluminium, 2 and 1 cent, and copper, ½ cent. The total circulation Rs 3,800m. on 31 Dec. 1979. In March 1981, £1 = Rs 38·66; US$1 = Rs 17·56.

Banking. The money supply at 31 Dec. 1979 stood at Rs 7,669m.

The leading banks in Sri Lanka are: The Bank of Ceylon and the People's Bank (state-managed), the Mercantile Bank Ltd, the State Bank of India, National & Grindlays Bank, the Hongkong and Shanghai Banking Corporation, the Chartered Bank, the Commercial Bank of Ceylon, the Hatton Bank, the Habib Bank (Overseas) Ltd and the Indian Overseas Bank Ltd. Total assets of commercial banks at 31 Dec. 1979, Rs 18,653·2m.

The state-owned Ceylon Insurance Corporation has a monopoly of all insurance business.

The Sri Lanka Savings Bank had deposits amounting to Rs 180m. in March 1972. It has been amalgamated with the post office savings bank and Ceylon Savings Movement to form the Sri Lanka National Savings Bank. In Dec. 1979 the bank had a balance to depositors' credit of Rs 1,890·6m. The loans granted by the Sri Lanka State Mortgage and Investment Bank were outstanding at Rs 112·8m. in Dec. 1979.

Weights and Measures. The metric system has been established by the Weights and Measures (Amendment) Law No. 24 of 1974.

ENERGY AND NATURAL RESOURCES

Electricity. Installed capacity of electric energy (1979), 401,000 kw. Energy produced, 1,525·5m. kwh.

Water. The Mahaweli Ganga power and irrigation scheme entered phase 2. It is to be completed within 5 years and will benefit 896,000 acres. Two major diversions, at Polgolla near Kandy and at Bowatenna on the Amban Ganga River, will benefit 120,000 acres of land already cultivated and irrigate an extra 104,000 acres of new land. There is a Water Resources Board (set up in 1966) and a National Water Supply and Drainage Board (1974). Water supply to the city and area of Colombo comes from the Labugama and Kalatuwawa reservoirs. Consumption within Colombo city limits is estimated at 10,000m. gallons a year.

All domestic consumers receive a free water allowance; commercial consumers do not.

Water supply to Kandy was complete in 1966, and to 20 other cities in 1976.

Minerals. Gems are among the chief minerals mined and exported. Precious and semi-precious stones are found among the layers of older alluvium and river gravels of quarternary age in the valleys of the Ratnapura district in the southwest. The most important are sapphire, ruby, crysoberyl, beryl, topaz, spinel, garnet, ziran and tourmaline. Estimated value of gemstones exported in 1979, Rs 490m.

Graphite is also important. The State Graphite Corporation was set up in 1971. There were 3 large mines (Bogala, Kahatagaha and Kalangaha), and several smaller mines working at the end of 1976. Graphite produced (1979), 9,526 tonnes. 1980 (provisional), 7,300.

The Ceylon Mineral Sands Corporation was established in 1957, mainly to extract ilmenite. Production of ilmenite, 1979, 55,370 tonnes. Some rutile is also produced (14,825 tonnes in 1979). Provisional figures, 1980: ilmenite 30,844, rutile 12,789.

Salt extraction is the oldest industry in Sri Lanka and is now controlled by the National Salt Corporation. The method is solar evaporation of sea-water. Production, 1979, 123,356 tonnes.

Agriculture. The area of the island is approximately 6,560,962·6 hectares, of which 2,353,221·2 hectares are under cultivation. The main crops in 1979 were as follows: Paddy, 1·92m. tonnes from 789,562 hectares; rubber, tea, coffee and maize.

In March 1976 the Sri Lanka State Plantation Corporation took over management of all private tea and rubber estates. Compensation is paid on condition that it be re-invested in Sri Lanka. The Sri Lanka Tea Corporation was formed in March 1972. Tea production (1979) 208,000 tonnes; rubber, 153,000 tonnes.

Livestock in 1979: 1·6m. cattle, 844,000 buffaloes, 49,000 swine, 461,000 goats, 24,000, sheep, 4·9m. poultry.

Fisheries. The Government is implementing a programme for the development of fisheries. Production for 1980 was 160,316 tons of marine fish, 20,000 tons of fresh water fish. In 1979 there were approximately 23,350 fishing craft, of which 10 were trawlers and 14,190 were not motorized.

INDUSTRY AND TRADE

Industry. The Business Undertakings (Acquisition) Act was passed in May 1971 empowering the Government to acquire any business for the state. The British Ceylon Corporation Ltd and its subsidiaries were nationalized in Feb. 1972. The nationalization of the oil industry was completed in Dec. 1971. The first objective was the development of heavy industry through state investment in small companies and the setting up of public corporations. Three such corporations have been established for the mining and processing of graphite; the importing, manufacture and distribution of pharmaceuticals; the importing and distribution of materials for textile manufacture. Other important manufactures are ceramics, vegetable oils, fertilizers, cement, wood and paper products, leather, rubber products and sugar. The government has set up Investment Promotion Zones; by Aug. 1980 these had 119 projects employing over 7,600; the main industry was clothing manufacture. Foreign investment is encouraged by a tax holiday of up to 10 years for approved industries. Export profits may have a 3-year tax holiday.

Trade unions. The registration and control of trade unions are regulated by the Trade Unions Ordinance (Ch. 138 of the Legislative Enactments). In 1979 there were 105 registered trade unions with a membership of 1,440,720.

Commerce. State Trading Corporations handle all imports and the private sector handles most exports. The values of total imports and exports (both including bullion, specie and postal articles; exports, including re-exports and ship's stores) for calendar years (in Rs 1,000):

	1976	1977	1978	1979
Imports	4,392,000	5,436,000	13,542,000	20,271,000
Exports	4,840,000	6,570,000	13,193,000	15,282,000

Principal exports (domestic) in 1978 (in Rs 1m.): Tea, 6,401; rubber, 2,021; copra, coconut oil and desiccated coconut, coir fibre products, 972; other crops, 658; industrial products, 1,891; precious and semi-precious stones, 531.

Principal imports in 1978 were food and drink, consumer goods, investment goods and intermediate goods.

In 1978 the principal sources of imports were (in Rs 1m.): Saudi Arabia, 1,385; Japan, 1,590; UK, 1,396; Australia, 738; USA, 1,205; India, 1,242; Iraq, 858; China, 453.

Principal export destinations (1978) were (in Rs 1m.): UK, 1,048; China, 956; USA, 926; Japan, 772; Pakistan, 689; FRG, 565; Egypt, 560.

Total trade between Sri Lanka and UK (British Department of Trade returns, in £1,000 sterling):

	1976	1977	1978	1979	1980
Imports to UK	35,518	50,793	39,659	40,826	53,681
Exports and re-exports from UK	17,913	27,872	49,110	55,260	76,831

Tourism. About 300,000 tourists visited the country in 1980.

COMMUNICATIONS

Roads. There are about 16,649 miles of motorable roads, of which 12,039 are black-topped.

Number of motor vehicles, 31 Dec. 1979, 274,080, including 114,453 private cars and cabs, 51,665 lorries and vans, 45,558 tractors, 45,087 motor cycles, 17,317 buses.

Railways. In 1980 there were about 1,435 km of railway open, of which 1,394 km were broad gauge and 59 narrow gauge.

Aviation. Air Lanka operates internal and international services.

Foreign airlines which operate scheduled services to Sri Lanka are British

Airways, UTA, Qantas, India Airlines Corporation, Swissair, Aeroflot, Garuda, KLM, Singapore Airlines, Thai Airways International, Pakistan International Airlines; various others operate charter services. In 1978 aircraft flew 2·5m. km and carried a total of 100,000 passengers.

Shipping. In 1977, merchant vessels totalling 9,179,000 NRT entered and vessels of 8,658,000 NRT cleared the ports of Sri Lanka. The Sri Lanka Shipping Corporation began functioning as ship-owners, charterers, brokers and shipping agents in 1979; shipping fleet, 85,966 DWT. Net profit for 1978, Rs 73m.; 1979, Rs 69·8m.

Post and Broadcasting. In 1979 there were 1,711 post and telegraph offices. There were (1979) 53,461 telephones. Throughout the Greater Colombo Area inter-dialling facilities are now available between 19 stations.

The Overseas Telecommunication Service operates telegraph and telephone services through submarine cables and/or VHF radio circuits to most parts of the world. There is a telex service to 66 countries. Broadcasting is provided by the Sri Lanka Broadcasting Corporation, which assumed the functions of Radio Ceylon on 5 Jan. 1967.

Cinemas. In 1979 there were 349 cinemas with a seating capacity of about 184,950. The State Film Corporation established in 1971 has exclusive rights to import films and equipment and arranges distribution of foreign and local films. Films released, 1979, 128.

Newspapers. There are 4 main newspaper groups: Associated Newspapers of Ceylon Ltd (5 daily and 10 weekly papers and other periodicals); Times of Ceylon Ltd (2 daily, 2 weekly and other periodicals); Express Newspapers (Ceylon) Ltd (2 daily and 2 weekly papers); Independent Newspapers Ltd.

There are 3 daily and 8 weekly papers in Sinhala; 3 daily and 3 weekly in Tamil; 3 daily and 3 weekly in English. In 1976, 150 papers were registered.

JUSTICE, RELIGION, EDUCATION AND WELFARE

Justice. The systems of law which obtain in Sri Lanka are the Roman-Dutch law, the English law, the Tesawalamai, the Moslem law and the Kandyan law.

The Kandyan law applies to the Kandyan Sinhalese in the Central, North-Central, Uva and Sabaragamuwa provinces in respect of all matters relating to inheritance, matrimonial rights and donations. The law of England is observed in most commercial matters. The law of Tesawalamai is applied to all Tamil inhabitants of Jaffna, in all matters relating to inheritance, marriages, gifts, donations, purchases and sales of land. The Moslem law is applied to all Moslems in respect of succession, donations not involving Fidei Commissa, marriage, divorce and maintenance. These customary and religious laws have been modified in many respects by local enactments.

The court of original jurisdiction are the High Courts, district courts and magistrates' courts. The High Courts try major crimes and also exercise election and admiralty jurisdiction in addition to their power to grant injunctions. The district court has unlimited civil jurisdiction and criminal jurisdiction carrying punitive power to impose sentences of imprisonment up to 5 years and fines up to Rs 5,000. The magistrates' courts exercise civil jurisdiction where the value of the subject-matter does not exceed Rs 1,500, and has criminal jurisdiction carrying the power to impose terms of imprisonment not exceeding 18 months and fines not exceeding Rs 1,500. The Supreme Court is the sole appellate tribunal to which a single appeal lies from decisions of any court. A system of mandatory conciliation also obtains since the establishment of conciliation boards in 1958. The Minister of Justice appoints panels of conciliators from which the conciliation boards are constituted. Wherever such a panel has been appointed all civil disputes and specified criminal offences must be submitted to these boards for conciliation before recourse can be had to the regular courts of law.

Police. The strength of the police service on 31 Dec. 1976 was 16,556.

Religion. Buddhism was introduced from India in the 3rd century B.C.. and is the religion of 67·3% of the inhabitants. There were (1971) 8,537,000 Buddhists, 2,239,000 Hindus, 1,004,000 Christians, 902,000 Moslems and 8,000 others.

Education. Education is free from the kindergarten to the university and is imparted in the medium of the mother tongue.

In 1979 there were 9,626 schools including 9,052 government schools; the rest were private and estate schools. The government schools had 138,488 teachers and 3·1m. students from grades I to XII. Department of Education expenditure, Rs 1,206·3m. Education is now administered under 17 regional directors.

The overall control of the education regions is vested in the Ministry of Education.

In 1972 the 4 universities and the College of Technology at Katubedde were amalgamated as the University of Ceylon, with a Vice-Chancellor, and a President for each of 5 campuses (the 4 universities and 1 college). A sixth campus was established at Jaffna in 1975 and a seventh at Matara in 1978. Since 1979 the seven function as autonomous universities.

In 1979 there were 16,254 students on the 6 existing campuses, and 2,498 teachers. There were 14 institutions for technical education, 7 of which were polytechnics. There is also a law college controlled by the Incorporated Council of Legal Education; there were 249 admissions in 1976.

Health. In 1979 there were 347 hospitals, 95 cottage and maternity homes and 719 dispensaries. Hospitals had 41,585 beds and there were 3,703 Department of Health doctors (one to every 3,830 population). Total state budget expenditure on health, 1979, Rs 19,376·8m.

Social Security. The activities of the Department of Social Services fall into five main divisions:

Public assistance (monthly allowances); casual relief; relief to leprosy and tuberculosis patients and their dependants.

Relief of widespread distress due to failure of crops, floods, storms, etc., including relief to individual cases of distress among fishermen due to acts of God such as fire, storms and accidents; rehabilitation and resettlement of flood victims.

State homes for the aged; grants-in-aid to voluntary agencies and local authorities for the running of charitable and welfare institutions, homes for children, homes for the aged and crèches.

Services for orthopaedically handicapped persons; services for the deaf and blind; vagrancy and administration of the house of detention.

The payment of compensation to workmen meeting with accidents in the course of their work is provided for under the Workmen's Compensation Ordinance No. 19 of 1934, as amended in 1957, 1959 and 1966. It was brought into operation in 1935, and has been administered by the Director of Social Services, who is Commissioner for Workmen's Compensation, since 1948.

DIPLOMATIC REPRESENTATIVES

OF SRI LANKA IN GREAT BRITAIN (13 Hyde Park Gdns., London, W2 2LX)

High Commissioner: Arambamoorthy T. Moorthy (accredited 18 Feb. 1981).

OF GREAT BRITAIN IN SRI LANKA (Galle Rd., Kollupitiya, Colombo 3)

High Commissioner: J. W. Nicholas, CMG.

OF SRI LANKA IN THE USA (2148 Wyoming Ave., NW, Washington, D.C., 20008)

Ambassador: Dr W. S. Karunarakne.

OF THE USA IN SRI LANKA (44 Galle Rd., Kollupitiya, Colombo 3)

Ambassador: Donald R. Toussaint.

OF SRI LANKA TO THE UNITED NATIONS

Ambassador: B. J. Fernando.

Books of Reference

The Sri Lanka Year Book
Census Publications from 1871
Performance 1980. Ministry of Plan Implementation, Colombo. 1981
Review of the Economy. Central Bank of Ceylon. Annual
Statistical Pocket-Book. Department of Census and Statistics. Colombo, 1980

de Silva, K. M. (ed.), *Sri Lanka: A Survey*. London, 1977.—*A History of Sri Lanka*. 1980
Ferguson's *Ceylon Directory*. Annual (from 1858)
Jennings, Sir I., *The Constitution of Ceylon*. 3rd ed. London, 1953
Kearney, R. N., *The Politics of Ceylon (Sri Lanka)*. Cornell Univ. Press, 1973
Ludowyk, E. F. G., *The Story of Ceylon*. London, 1962
Pickens, V. L., *Serendipity*. New York, 1964
Pyatt, G. and Roe, A., *Social Accounting for Development Planning with Special Reference to Sri Lanka*. CUP, 1977
Ratnasuriya, M. D., and Wijeratne, P. B. F., *Shorter Sinhalese–English Dictionary*. Colombo, 1949
Robinson, M. S., *Political Structure in a Changing Sinhalese Village*. CUP, 1975
Snodgrass, D. R., *Ceylon: An Export Economy in Transition*. Homewood, Ill., 1966
Williams, H., *Ceylon*. London, 1963
Wilson, A. J., *Politics in Sri Lanka 1947–73*. London, 1974
Wriggins, W. H., *Ceylon: Dilemma of a New Nation*. Princeton Univ. Press, 1960

THE
DEMOCRATIC
REPUBLIC OF
THE SUDAN

Capital: Khartoum
Population: 18·4m. (1980)
GNP per capita: US$320 (1978)

Jamhuryat es-Sudan
Al Democratia

HISTORY. Sudan was proclaimed a sovereign independent republic on 1 Jan. 1956. On 19 Dec. 1955 the Sudanese parliament passed unanimously a declaration that a fully independent state should be set up forthwith, and that a Council of State of 5 should temporarily assume the duties of Head of State. The Co-domini, the UK and Egypt, gave their assent on 31 Dec. 1955.

For the history of the Condominium and the steps leading to independence, *see* THE STATESMAN'S YEAR-BOOK, 1955, pp. 340–341.

On 8 July 1965 the Constituent Assembly elected Ismail El-Azhari as President of the Supreme Council. Following a crisis in the coalition Cabinet the Prime Minister, Mohammed Ahmed Mahgoub resigned on 23 April 1969. For political history *see* THE STATESMAN'S YEAR-BOOK, 1973–74, p. 1333. The Government was taken over by a 10-man Revolutionary Council on 25 May 1969 under the Chairmanship of Col. Jaafar M. al Nemery. This Council was dissolved in 1972.

AREA AND POPULATION. Sudan is bounded north by Egypt, north-east by the Red Sea, east by Eritrea and Ethiopia, south by Kenya, Uganda and Zaïre, west by the Central African Republic and Chad, north-west by Libya. Sudan covers an area of 967,500 sq. miles (2·5m. sq. km). The Eritrea–Sudan frontier and the frontier with the Chad and Central African Republic have been delimited and demarcated, as also has the greater part of the frontier with Ethiopia.

The population according to the 1973 census was 14,171,732 (estimate (1980) 18,400,000), and consists mainly (two-thirds to four-fifths) of Moslem Arabs, and Nubians in the north and Nilotic and Negro tribes in the south.

The capital is Khartoum (census, 1973, 333,921; estimate, 1980, 1m.). Other important cities are: Omdurman (299,401), Khartoum North (150,991), Port Sudan (132,631), Wadi Medani (106,776), Kassala (98,751), El Obeid (90,060), Al-Qadarif (66,465), Atbara (66,116), Kosti (65,257).

In 1980 there were 15 provinces.

CONSTITUTION AND GOVERNMENT. A new Constitution was introduced in 1973 (amended in 1975). Legislative power lies with a People's Assembly of 304 members. The President nominates 30 and 274 are elected for 4-year terms by universal adult suffrage. Executive power lies with the President.

A measure of autonomy has been given to southern Sudan and a People's Assembly of 60 was elected in May 1980. The Assembly is situated at Juba.

President and Prime Minister: Jaafar M. al Nemery (re-elected for a second term in April 1977).

Vice-President, Minister of Defence: Lt.-Gen. Abdul Magid Hamid Khalil. *Vice-President, President of the High Executive Council of the Southern Region:* Abel Alier. *Energy and Mining:* Dr Sharif el Tuhami. *Industry:* Izzeldin Hamid. *Public Services:* Hayder Khabsoun. *Irrigation and Hydroelectric Power:* El Rayah el Amin. *Co-operation, Trade and Supply:* Faroug Ibrahim al Magboul. *Finance:*

Badreldin Sulayman. *National Planning:* Maj.-Gen. Nasr el Din Mustafa. *Communication:* Dr Ahmed el Sayed Hamad. *Transport:* Mustafa Osman Harrar. *Education and Orientation:* Dafalla el Haj Yusuf. *Health:* Maj.-Gen. Khalid Hassan Abbas. *Food, Agriculture and Natural Resources:* Omer el Amin. *Culture and Information:* Dr Ismael el Haj Musa. *Construction and Public Works:* Mohammed Sid Ahmed Abdalla. *Presidential Affairs:* Dr Baha el Din Mohammed Idris. *Cabinet Affairs:* Abu Bakr Osman Mohammed Salih. *National Security:* Maj.-Gen. Umar Mohammed el Tayib. *Attorney General:* Dr Hassan Abdalla al Turabi. *Chairman of the High Council of Religious Affairs:* Dr Awn Sharif Gasim. *Chairman of the High Council for Popular Sports:* Ali Shummu. *Internal Affairs:* Ahmed Abdel Rahman. *State Minister of Foreign Affairs:* Mohammed Mirghani.

On 9 Dec. 1965 the Constituent Assembly proscribed the Communist Party.

National flag: Three horizontal stripes of red, white, black, with a green triangle based on the hoist.

DEFENCE

Army. The Army is organized in 2 armoured, 1 parachute and 7 infantry brigades, with 6 artillery and 1 engineer regiment. There are about 130 Russian tanks. Total strength (1980), 65,000.

Navy. The Navy was established in 1962 with 4 patrol boats built in Yugoslavia and a 10-year training mission from the Yugoslav Navy. Since then 2 more patrol boats, 6 fast gun (*ex*-torpedo) boats, 5 landing craft (3 in service), an oiler, a water carrier and a survey ship have been acquired from Yugoslavia and 3 coastguard cutters from Iran. Personnel in 1981 totalled 600 officers and men.

Air Force. The Air Force was built up with Soviet and Chinese assistance. Two combat squadrons are equipped with about 12 MiG-21 supersonic fighters and 12 F-4 (Chinese-built MiG-17) fighter-bombers. There is 1 transport squadron, with 6 C-130H Hercules, 4 DHC-5D Buffalo, 5 An-24 and 2 F.27 Friendship turboprop transports; 8 Turbo-Porter light transports; 1 helicopter squadron with 10 Mi-8s and 6 BO 105s; and 5 armed Jet Provost trainers. Ten Puma helicopters have been ordered. Personnel total about 1,500.

INTERNATIONAL RELATIONS

Membership. Sudan is a member of UN, OAU, the Arab League and is an ACP state of EEC.

ECONOMY

Planning. The 1978–83 6-year development plan was published in 1977 and envisaged a total investment of £S2,670m.

Budget. Revenue and expenditure in Sudanese pounds for financial years ending 30 June:

	1978–79	1979–80
Revenue	686,100,000	908,400,000
Expenditure	842,000,000	1,105,500,000

The external debt was US$1,300m. in 1979 (US$312m. in 1973).

Currency. The monetary unit is the Sudanese *pound* (£S) divided into 100 *piastres* and 1,000 *milliemes*. Sudanese bank-notes of £S10, £S5, £S1, 50 and 25 *piastres* and Sudanese coins of P. 10, 5, 2; m/ms 10, 5, 2, 1 are in circulation. In March 1981, £1 = £S1·74.

Banking. The Bank of Sudan opened in Feb. 1960 with an authorized capital of £S1·5m. as the central bank of the country; it has the sole right to issue currency. Its foreign reserves stood at £S12,631,000m. as at 31 Dec. 1978. All foreign banks were nationalized in 1970. The post office savings bank had 212,090 depositors each with an average balance of £S61 as at 31 May 1974.

Weights and Measures. The metric system is in use.

ENERGY AND NATURAL RESOURCES

Oil. Two oil wells in the south-west produce 15,000 bbls per day of high quality oil. An oil refinery is being constructed and 2 oil companies are prospecting for oil and natural gas in the Red Sea area.

Minerals. The following minerals are known to exist in Sudan: gold, graphite, sulphur, chromium-ore (estimate, 13,000m. tonnes in 1977), iron-ore, manganese-ore, copper-ore, zinc-ore, fluorspar, natron, gypsum and anhydrite, magnesite, asbestos, talc, halite, kaolin, white mica, coal, diatomite (kieselguhr), limestone and dolomite, pumice, lead-ore, wollastonite, black sands, vermiculite pyrites.

Gold is being exploited on a small scale at Gabeit and at Abirkateib (in Kassala Province); alluvial gold is occasionally exploited in Southern Fung and Equatoria. Total production of good ores was 9 kg in 1977. Iron-ore was discovered in Red Sea area in 1976 with estimated reserves of 250m. tonnes.

About 10m. tons of copper ore were proved at Hofrat-en-Nahas, an ancient copper working. Manganese mining activities started in the 1950s but this industry did not develop well and in 1977 only 400 tonnes was produced. Processed and scrap white mica have been mined since the late fifties; it went out of production for almost a decade, but started again in 1970 when 170 tonnes were produced; 1977, 400 tonnes. A big deposit of vermiculite and a medium-sized deposit of pyrophyllite are known to occur in the Sinkat District. Reserves of metallurgical grade chromite occur in the Ingessana Hills, Blue Nile Province, but only 47,060 tonnes of this mineral were exported in 1970. Huge reserves of chrysotile asbestos are proved in this vicinity and also in Qala El Nahal area, Kassala Province. Deposits of magnesite, with or without talc, are known to occur in the Ingessana Hills and Qala El Nahal areas in addition to other occurrences in the Halaib area, Red Sea Province, but only 400 tonnes of magnesite were shipped in 1970.

Reserves of high grade gypsum and anhydrite are known to occur in the Red Sea Province 40 miles north of Port Sudan. Salt pans at Port Sudan supply the whole needs of the country and a surplus of about 70,000 tonnes was shipped in 1970; production, 1977 (estimate), 92,000 tonnes. High grade quartz for the glass industry occurs in the Sinkat area and reserves of limestone occur in the Atbara and Rabak areas supplying the needs of cement factories in these areas. Wolfram and tin occur in the Halaib area and nickel, with or without platinum, occurs in the Halaib and Ingessana Hills areas.

Agriculture. The Sudan is a predominantly agricultural country; in 1974–75 agriculture contributed 40·6% of GDP (manufacturing, 9·6%). Cotton is by far the most important cash crop on which the Sudan depends for earning foreign currency. The two types of cotton grown in the Sudan are: (*a*) long staple sakellaridis and sakel types (derivatives of sakellaridis), grown in Gezira, White Nile, Abdel Magid and private pump schemes; (*b*) short staple, mainly American types, in Equatoria and Nuba Mountains, generally by rain cultivation.

Production (1979) in 1,000 tonnes: Sorghum, 1,970; sugar-cane, 1,700 (estimate); groundnuts, (1978–79) 1,050; cotton, 131 (estimate); millet, 370; wheat, 266; sesame, 210 (estimate); cotton seed, 320.

One of the largest sugar complexes in the world was opened at Kenana in March 1981. It is capable of processing 330,000 tonnes a year.

Livestock (1979): Cattle, 17·3m.; sheep, 17·2m.; goats, 12·2m.; poultry, 26m.

Forestry. The forests of Sudan, their extent and dominant species are approximately as follows: (1) desert, 728,800 sq. km; (2) semi-desert, 491,000 sq. km (*Acacia Tortilis, Maerua crassifolia*); (3) woodland savannah: (*a*) low rain, 691,000 sq. km (*Acacia melifera, Acacia seyal, Acacia senegal, cambretum*), (*b*) high rain, 347,000 sq. km (*Anogeissus, Khaya, Isoberlinia*); (4) flood region, 246,000 sq. km (*Papyrus*); (5) montane vegetation, 6,000 sq. km (*Podocarpus, Olea*).

Gum arabic, mainly hashab gum from *Acacia senegal*, is the sole forest produce exported from the Sudan on a major scale. 26,508 tons (80% of the total world supply) was exported in 1978–79. Production is declining as trees are cut down for higher priority agriculture. It ranks as the fourth cash crop after cotton, groundnuts and sesame. The bulk of gum production originates from the central provinces.

A forest research and education institute has been established by the Sudan Government in co-operation with the United Nations Special Fund.

COMMERCE. Total trade for calendar years, in £S:

	1975	1976	1977
Imports[1]	321,320,000	304,810,000	368,980,000
Exports	152,470,000	193,010,000	330,180,000

[1] Including government imports.

Principal items of imports and exports in 1975 (quantities in tonnes, value in £S1,000):

	Quantity	Value
Imports:		
Cotton fabrics	187,085	72,669
Sugar	...	111,210
Motor vehicles (number)	125	3,294
Tea	11,075	12,324
Wheat flour	3,686	531
Coffee	7,759	7,178
Cigarettes and tobacco	720	8,879
Machinery	...	...
Fertilizers	167,150	21,052
Exports:		
Cotton, ginned	143,939	191,806
Gum arabic	...	24,131
Oil seeds and nuts	291,848	140,463
Animal feeding stuff	165,951	11,695
Vegetable oils (not processed)	156,495	11,240
Sheep (number)	77,221	3,146
Hides and skins	4,752	8,574

Principal sources of import into the Sudan in 1976: UK (20·3%), USA (9·9%), Federal Republic of Germany (8·4%). Principal countries of export from the Sudan: Italy (19·7%), Japan (7·5%), France (6·6%), Federal Republic of Germany (6·6%).

Total trade between Sudan and UK (British Department of Trade returns, in £1,000 sterling):

	1976	1977	1978	1979	1980
Imports to UK	14,209	13,164	19,470	19,747	13,362
Exports and re-exports from UK	91,975	86,234	114,079	106,403	124,697

COMMUNICATIONS

Roads. In the Northern Sudan there are about 550 km of asphalted roads, other than town roads. The remaining roads are only cleared tracks mostly impassable directly after rain. The El Gedaref to Kassala road (1,190 km) opened in 1980, and the section from Khartoum to Port Sudan was almost complete in 1980. In Upper Nile Province motor traffic is limited mostly to the months Jan.–May. In the other 5 southern provinces there are a number of good gravelled roads with permanent bridges which can be used all the year round, though minor roads become impassable after rain. Private cars (1972) 29,000; commercial vehicles, 21,500.

Railways. The main railway lines run from Khartoum to El Obeid *via* Wad Medani, Sennar Junction, Kosti and El Rahad (701 km); El Rahad to Nyala *via* Abu Zabad, Babanousa and Ed-Daein (698 km); Sennar Junction to Kassala *via* Gedaref (455 km) and to Roseires *via* Singa (220 km); Kassala to Port Sudan *via* Haiya Junction and Sinkat (550 km); Khartoum to Wadi Halfa *via* Shendi, El Dammer, Atbara, Berber and Abu Hamad Junction (924 km); Abu Hamad to Karima (248 km); Atbara to Haiya Junction (271 km); Babanousa to Wau (444 km). The main flow of exports and imports is to and from Port Sudan *via* Atbara and Kassala. The total length of line open for traffic (1980) was 1,786 km. The gauge is 1,067 mm. Several new lines are planned, including a link from Wadi Halfa across the Egyptian border. In 1978–79, the railways carried 1,060m. passenger-km and 1,821m. tonne-km.

Aviation. Sudan Airways is a government-owned airline, with its headquarters in Khartoum, operating domestic and international services. The latter include services to Asmara, Addis Ababa, Aden, Jiddah, Cairo, Athens, Rome, London, Beirut, Nairobi, N'djamena, Tripoli and Entebbe. In 1977 Sudan Airways carried 379,000 passengers and 10·3m. kg of mail and freight.

Shipping. Supplementing the railways are regular river steamer services of the Sudan Railways, between Karima and Dongola, 319 km; from Khartoum to Kosti, 319 km; from Kosti to Juba, 1,436 km, and from Kosti to Gambeila, 1,069 km. Port Sudan is the country's only seaport; it is equipped with 13 berths. A modernization programme began in Feb. 1980.

Post and Broadcasting (1975). There are 213 permanent post and telegraph offices, 24 travelling post and telegraph offices and 372 agencies. There are 27 wireless telegraph and 99 radio-telephone stations, 36 automatic telephone exchanges and 340 telephone call boxes; number of telephones in 1978 was 62,297 (40,131 in Greater Khartoum). Radio receivers (1977) 1·4m. The television service broadcasts for 35 hours per week. There were (1978) 95,000 TV receivers and 4 colour transmitters.

Cinemas. In 1975 there were 58, seating capacity 112,000 and also 43 mobile units.

JUSTICE, RELIGION, EDUCATION AND WELFARE

Justice. The judiciary is a separate and independent department of state directly and solely responsible to the President of the Republic. The general administrative supervision and control of the judiciary is vested in the High Judicial Council.

Civil Justice is administered by the courts constituted under the Civil Justice Ordinance, namely the High Court of Justice—consisting of the Court of Appeal and Judges of the High Court, sitting as courts of original jurisdiction—and Province Courts—consisting of the Courts of Province and District Judges. The law administered is 'justice, equity and good conscience' in all cases where there is no special enactment. Procedure is governed by the Civil Justice Ordinance.

Justice in personal matters for the Moslem population is administered by the Mohammedan law courts, which form the Sharia Divisions of the Court of Appeal, High Courts and Kadis Courts; President of the Sharia Division is the Grand Kadi. The religious law of Islam is administered by these courts in the matters of inheritance, marriage, divorce, family relationship and charitable trusts.

Criminal Justice is administered by the courts constituted under the Code of Criminal Procedure, namely major courts, minor courts and magistrates' courts. Serious crimes are tried by major courts, which are composed of a President and 2 members and have the power to pass the death sentence. Major Courts are, as a rule, presided over by a Judge of the High Court appointed to a Provincial Circuit or a Province Judge. There is a right of appeal to the Chief Justice against any decision or order of a Major Court, and all its findings and sentences are subject to confirmation by him.

The President of the Supreme Council of the Armed Forces has power to commute a capital sentence. The Chief Justice has power to remit any case subject to confirmation by him to the Court of Criminal Appeal composed of the Chief Justice and 2 Magistrates of the first class, one of whom has to be a Judge of the High Court.

Lesser crimes are tried by Minor Courts consisting of 3 Magistrates and presided over by a Second Class Magistrate, and by Magistrates' Courts consisting of a single Magistrate or a bench of lay magistrates. In provinces in which circuits of the High Court exist the High Court Judge, in other cases the Province Judge, exercises an appellate jurisdiction and a general supervision over these courts. The greater part of the criminal law is codified in the Sudan Penal Code.

Religion. The population of the 12 northern provinces is almost entirely Moslem (Sunni), the majority of the 6 southern provinces is pagan. There are small Christian communities, with 2 Coptic Bishops, a Greek Orthodox metropolitan, 4 Anglican bishops, 4 Roman Catholic bishops and Greek Evangelical, Evangelical and Maronite congregations.

Education (1977). 4,945 elementary schools had 1,302,040 pupils (41% female); there were 326,250 pupils in secondary schools and 24,109 in tertiary education. In 1979 Khartoum University with 10 faculties had 8,777 students. The Khartoum branch of Cairo University with 4 faculties had about 5,000 students and the Islamic University of Omdurman with 3 faculties had 1,472 students. Juba University, founded in 1975 with 5 faculties had 425 students.

Health. In 1976 the Ministry of Health maintained 151 hospitals, 1,500 dispensaries and dressing stations, 139 health centres and 620 clinics (with together 17,324 beds) and 1,652 doctors.

DIPLOMATIC REPRESENTATIVES

OF SUDAN IN GREAT BRITAIN (3 Cleveland Row, London, SW1A 1DD)

Ambassador: Sayed Amir El-Sawi.

OF GREAT BRITAIN IN SUDAN (New Aboulela Bldg, Barlaman Ave., Khartoum)

Ambassador: R. A. Fyjis-Walker, CMG, CVO.

OF SUDAN IN THE USA (600 New Hampshire Ave., NW, Washington, D.C., 20037)

Ambassador: Omer Salih Eissa.

OF THE USA IN SUDAN (Gamhouria Ave., Khartoum)

Ambassador: C. William Kontos.

OF SUDAN TO THE UNITED NATIONS

Ambassador: (Vacant).

Books of Reference

Sudan Almanac. Khartoum (annual)
al Rahim, M. Abd, *Changing Patterns of Civilian-Military Relations in the Sudan.* Uppsala, 1978
Barnett, T., *The Gezira Scheme: An Illusion of Development.* London, 1977
Duncan, J. S. B., *The Sudan's Path to Independence.* London, 1957
El Bushra, El.-S., *An Atlas of Khartoum Conurbation.* Khartoum Univ Press, 1976
Fabunni, L. A., *The Sudan in Anglo-Egyptian Relations.* London and New York, 1960
Fawzi, Saad Ed-Din, *The Labour Movement in the Sudan, 1946–55.* R. Inst. of Int. Affairs, 1957
Gaitskell, A., *Gezira: A Story of Development in the Sudan.* London and New York, 1959
Henderson, K. D. D., *The Sudan Republic.* London, 1965
Hill, R., *Sudan Tansport: A History of Railway, Marine and River Services.* OUP, 1965
Holt, P. M., *A Modern History of the Sudan.* New York, 3rd ed. 1979
Lebon, J. H. G., *Land Use in Sudan.* Bude, 1965
Lees, F. A., *The Economic and Political Development of the Sudan.* London, 1977
Macmichael, Sir H. A., *The Anglo-Egyptian Sudan.* London, 1954
Nimeiri, S., *Evaluation of the Six Year Development Plan 1977–78—1982–83.* Khartoum, 1978
Trimingham, J. S., *Islam in the Sudan.* London, 1949
Wai, D. M. (ed.), *The Southern Sudan: The Problem of National Integration.* London, 1973
Wickens, G. E., *The Flora of Jebel Marra.* London, 1977
Woodward, P., *Condominium and Sudanese Nationalism.* London, 1979

SURINAME

Capital: Paramaribo
Population: 375,000 (1979)
GNP per capita: US$2,340 (1978)

HISTORY. At the peace of Breda (1667) between Great Britain and the United Netherlands, Suriname was assigned to the Netherlands in exchange for the colony of New Netherland in North America, and this was confirmed by the treaty of Westminster of Feb. 1674. Since then Suriname has been twice in British possession, 1799–1802 (when it was restored to the Batavian Republic at the peace of Amiens) and 1804–16, when it was returned to the Kingdom of the Netherlands according to the convention of London of 13 Aug. 1814, confirmed at the peace of Paris of 20 Nov. 1815. On 25 Nov. 1975, Suriname gained full independence and was admitted to the UN on 4 Dec. 1975.

AREA AND POPULATION. Suriname is situated on the north coast of South America and bounded on the north by the Atlantic ocean, on the east by the Marowijne River, which separates it from French Guiana, on the west by the Corantijn River, which separates it from Guyana, and on the south by forests and savannas, which separate it from Brazil.

Area, 163,265 sq. km. Census population (1971), 384,900 (estimate (1979) 375,000), including 39,500 Bush Negroes and 10,200 aboriginal Indians. The capital, Paramaribo, had (1971 census) 151,500 inhabitants. Annual rate of growth decreased from 4·34% during 1950–64 to 2·3% during 1964–71, mainly through severe migration primarily to the Netherlands. It is estimated that Suriname lost a total of 150,000 persons by migration (1975–80).

Suriname is divided into 9 districts: Paramaribo (urban district), Commewijne, Coronie, Marowijne, Nickerie, Saramacca, Suriname, Brokopondo and Para.

Birth rate 32·8 per 1,000, death rate 6·4 per 1,000.

The official languages are Dutch and English. English is widely spoken next to Hindi, Javanese and Chinese as inter-group communication. A vernacular, called 'Sranan Tongo' or 'Surinamese', is used as a lingua franca. In 1976 the Government announced that Spanish would become the nation's principal working language.

CONSTITUTION AND GOVERNMENT. A new Constitution was being drafted in March 1981. The Government consists of the President of the Republic of Suriname and the Council of Ministers. The Governor is the constitutional head of the Government. He is assisted by an Advisory Council of 6 members.

On 25 Feb. 1980 the Prime Minister, Henck Arron, was ousted in a *coup*. A National Military Council was established under the leadership of Lieut. Michel Van Rey. In Sept. 1980 the Cabinet was composed as follows:

Prime Minister and General Affairs: Dr Henk Chin-a-Sen.

Deputy Prime Minister, Foreign Affairs, Justice, Army and Police: André Haakmat. *Internal Afffairs:* Franklin Leeflang. *Finance and Economic Affairs:* M. J. B. Chehin. *Education and People's Development:* Harold Rusland. *Agriculture, Husbandry, Fisheries and Forestry:* Albert van Dijk. *Social Affairs and Housing:* Siegmien Power-Staphorst. *Public Works and Communications:* Mohamed Ataoellah. *Labour and Health:* Henry Illes. *Construction:* Herman Adhin. *Youth, Sport and Culture:* André Kamperveen.

There is a council of 13 ministers who are responsible to the Legislative Council (*Staten van Suriname*). The Legislative Council (39 members) is elected for a 4-year period by universal adult suffrage. Seven political parties are represented in the Legislative Council.

Flag: Horizontally green, red, green with the red of double width with yellow 5-pointed star in centre of red bar.

DEFENCE. Armed forces of the Republic of Suriname consist of regular local officers and conscripted personnel with a strength of about 600 at the time of independence.

INTERNATIONAL RELATIONS

Membership. Suriname is a member of UN, OAS and is an ACP state of the EEC.

ECONOMY

Planning. For 15 years from independence approximately 3,500m. guilders is available from the Netherlands to carry out an extensive social and economic development programme devised by a joint Dutch and Surinamese team of experts. This programme envisaged, the creation of greater employment and the improvement of the living conditions of the people, but by 1980 only a third of the aid had been spent.

Budget. The expenditures and local revenues (derived from import, export and excise duties, taxes on houses and estates, personal imports and some indirect taxes) are as follows (in 1,000 Suriname guilders):

	1973	1974 [1]	1975	1976	1977	1978
Revenues	185,000	204,579	234,600	354,600	541,100	623,100
Expenditures	219,000	249,700	363,900	404,900	581,500	650,500

[1] Provisional figures.

Outstanding loans in 1974: Local, 31·7m.; foreign, 184·9m. Suriname guilders. Public debt as at 30 March 1974, 216·6m. Suriname guilders.

Currency. Notes ranging from 5 to 1,000 *Suriname guilders* are legal tender. Currency notes of 1·00 and 2·50 guilders are issued by the Government. In March 1981, US$1 = 1·80 Suriname guilders; £1 sterling = 3 Suriname guilders.

Banking. The Central Bank of Suriname is a bankers' bank and also a bank of issue; the Surinaamsche Bank, the Algemene Bank Nederland and the O.R.G. Vervuurt's Banking Corporation Ltd, are commercial banks; the Suriname People's Credit Bank operates under the auspices of the Government; Surinaamse Postspaarbank (postal savings bank); Surinaamse Hypotheekbank NV (mortgage bank); Surinaamse Investerings Mij. NV (investment bank); Agentschap van de Maatschappij tot financiering van het Nationaal Herstel NV (long-term investments); National Development Bank; The Agrarian Bank.

Weights and Measures. The metric system is in force.

NATURAL RESOURCES

Minerals. Bauxite is the most important mineral; it is being mined in the Suriname and Marowijne districts. Fresh deposits have been found in the western areas. The ore is exported mainly to USA, but partly processed locally into alumina and aluminium. Production in 1975: Bauxite, 4·75m. tonnes; alumina, 1,148,602 tonnes; aluminium, 39,964 tonnes; gold (1973), 14 kg.

Agriculture. Agriculture is restricted to the alluvial coastal zone; cultivated area in 1973, 54,656 hectares. The staple food crop is rice; 46,471 hectares of paddy were planted in 1973, chiefly in the Nickerie, Commewijne, Saramacca and Coronie districts.

Principal products (in 1,000 units) in 1975:

Sugar-cane (kg)	159,543	Maize on cob (kg)	365	Oranges (pieces)	15,036
Cocoa (kg)	55	Bananas (kg)	43,095	Grapefruit (pieces)	5,530
Coffee (kg)	88	Rum 50% (litres)	2,422	Coconuts (pieces)	5,525
Paddy (kg)	174,845	Molasses (kg)	5,727		

Livestock (1979): 27,000 head of cattle, 10,000 sheep and goats, 19,000 pigs, 1m. poultry.

Forestry. Suriname has great timber resources. Production 1975 included 29 tonnes of balata, 12,775 cu. metres of sleepers, 1,397 cu. metres of fuel wood, 14,225 cu.

metres of plywood and 9,054 cu. metres of particle board, chiefly from the Suriname and Marowijne districts.

Fishery. The catch in 1975 amounted to 2,634 tonnes.

INDUSTRY AND TRADE

Industry. There are 3 large bauxite plants, 1 alumina and 1 aluminium smelting plants, sugar- and rice-mills, 2 paint factories, a fruit-juice plant, 2 shrimp freezing plants, a plywood factory, timber-mills, a milk pasteurization plant, a butter and margarine factory and a number of various medium and small industries. Shortage of skilled personnel inhibits expansion.

Commerce. Imports and exports in calendar years (in US$1m.):

	1976	1977	1978	1979
Imports	259	324	344	370
Exports	304	346	411	444

Principal exports in 1973 (value in 1,000 Suriname guilders): Alumina, 143,600; bauxite, 85,000; aluminium, 44,800; rice, 20,600; citrus fruits, 12,500; plywood, 6,384; bananas, 3,800; particle board, 2,157; shrimp and other fisheries products, 1,300.

Principal imports in 1973 (value in 1,000 Suriname guilders): Raw and auxiliary materials, 108,600; investment goods, 48,500; fuels and lubricants, 36,100; textile yarn and fabrics, 7,300; foodstuffs, cars and motor cycles, 6,300.

Total trade between Suriname and UK (British Department of Trade returns, in £1,000 sterling):

	1976	1977	1978	1979	1980
Imports to UK	24,030	16,525	14,992	16,825	20,181
Exports and re-exports from UK	6,109	9,458	9,719	7,707	8,112

COMMUNICATIONS

Roads. There are 1,335 km of main roads. Two of them lead from Paramaribo to the bauxite centres of Smalkalden (29 km) and Paranam (30 km) and to the airport of Zanderij (49 km). Another main road runs across the districts of Saramacca (71 km) and Coronie (68 km), a fourth across the Commewijne district (41 km) and a fifth in the Marowijne district, from the bauxite centre Moengo to Albina (45 km).

The 'East–West connexion' is almost completed, linking the Corantijn and the Marowijne rivers (375 km).

In 1974 there were 23,227 passenger cars, 5,369 trucks, 1,898 buses, 34,799 powered bicycles and 4,354 motor cycles and scooters.

Railway. There is one single-track railway, running from Onverwacht to Bronsweg (86 km); part of the track, from Paramaribo to Onverwacht (34 km) has been removed.

Aviation. Regular air services are maintained by KLM, SLM, Air France and Cruzeiro do Sul. The international airfield at Zanderij is capable of handling all types of planes.

Suriname Airways Ltd provides daily services between all major districts and maintains also a charter service.

In 1975, 1,205 aircraft landed at Zanderij airport with 40,416 passengers and 1,225 tons of incoming mail and freight.

Shipping. The Royal Netherlands Steamship Co. plies between Amsterdam, Rotterdam, Antwerp, Hamburg and Paramaribo, and New York, Baltimore, New Orleans and Paramaribo. Regular sailings are made to Georgetown, Ciudad Bolivar and most Caribbean ports. The Suriname Navigation Co. maintains services from Paramaribo to Georgetown and Cayenne, and once a month to the Caribbean area. A French and an Italian company maintain passenger services to Europe. The Alcoa Steamship Co. has a fortnightly service to New York, Baltimore, Mobile and New Orleans; a Japanese line sails once a month from Hong Kong and Yokohama to Paramaribo; the Boomerang Line maintains a monthly freight and passenger service between Suriname and Australia. In 1974, 615 vessels totalling 3·58m. GRT entered and in 1975 1,172 of 6·5m. GRT cleared Paramaribo.

Post and Broadcasting. Automatic telephone service links most of the districts in the interior. In 1978 there were 20,787 telephones. Wireless telephone connects Suriname with the Netherlands, USA, Curaçao, Guyana, French Guiana and Trinidad. There are 6 broadcasting and 1 television stations. In 1974 there were 170,000 radios and 36,000 TV sets. Automatic telex was established in 1972.

Cinemas (1973). There are 31 cinemas with a seating capacity of 19,000, and 1 drive-in cinema.

Newspapers (1974). There are 5 daily newspapers and 5 weeklies with a combined circulation of over 24,000.

JUSTICE, RELIGION, EDUCATION AND WELFARE

Justice. There is a court of justice, whose members are nominated by the President. There are 3 cantonal courts.

Religion. There is entire religious liberty. At the end of 1971 the various religious bodies were: Hindus, 112,047; Moslems, 74,078; Roman Catholics, 70,175; Moravian Brethren, 51,868; Reformed and Lutheran, 3,911; Confucians, 80; others, 27,228.

Education. During school-year 1975–76 there were 413 schools with a total of 134,656 pupils and 4,813 teachers. There are also a University with faculties of medicine and law, social and economic studies, 3 technical schools and 5 teachers' training colleges.

Schooling is compulsory from 6 to 12 years of age. Primary education is free and is undertaken by the Government in public schools and by the Roman Catholic and Protestant Missions in denominational schools.

Social Security. The Government subsidizes orphanages and other religious or philanthropical institutions, and maintains an almshouse and institutions for delinquent boys and girls. There are 13 modern hospitals in the country, 4 of which are operated by missions, 2 by a private company, 1 by the military forces and 6 by the Government.

DIPLOMATIC REPRESENTATIVES

OF GREAT BRITAIN IN SURINAME

Ambassador: P. L. V. Mallet, CMG (resides in Georgetown).

OF SURINAME IN THE USA (2600 Virginia Ave., NW, Washington, D.C. 20037)

Ambassador: Roel F. Karamat.

OF THE USA IN SURINAME (Dr Sophie Redmondstraat 13, Paramaribo)

Ambassador: John J. Crowley, Jr.

OF SURINAME TO THE UNITED NATIONS

Ambassador: Henricus A. F. Heidweiller.

Books of Reference

Statistical Information: The General Bureau of Statistics in Paramaribo was established on 1 Jan. 1947. Its publications comprise trade statistics, *Suriname in Figures* (including, from 1953, the former *Handelsstatistiek*) and *Statistische Berichten.*

Economische Voorlichting Suriname. Ministry of Economic Affairs, Paramaribo
Annual Report of the Central Bank of Suriname

SWAZILAND

Capital: Mbabane
Population: 563,733 (1979)
GNP per capita: US$590 (1978)

HISTORY. The Swazi migrated into the country to which they have given their name, in the last half of the 18th century. They settled first in what is now southern Swaziland, but moved northwards under their chief, Sobhuza—known also to the Swazi as Somhlolo. Sobhuza died in 1838 and was succeeded by Mswati. The further order of succession has been Mbandzeni and Bhunu, whose son, Sobhuza II, was installed as King of the Swazi nation in 1921 after a long minority.

The independence of the Swazis was guaranteed in the conventions of 1881 and 1884 between the British Government and the Government of the South African Republic. In 1890, soon after the death of Mbandzeni, a provisional government was established representative of the Swazis, the British and the South African Republic Governments. In 1894 the South African Republic was given powers of protection and administration. In 1902, after the conclusion of the Boer War, a special commissioner took charge, and under an order-in-council in 1903 the Governor of the Transvaal administered the territory, through the Special Commissioner.

AREA AND POPULATION. Swaziland is bounded on the north, west and south by the Transvaal Province, and on the east by Mozambique and Zululand. The area is 6,705 sq. miles (17,400 sq. km).

The country is divided geographically into 4 longitudinal regions running from north to south; 3 of roughly equal width—Highveld (westernmost), Middleveld, Lowveld—and the Lubombo plateau in the east. The mountainous region on the west rises to an altitude of over 6,000 ft (1,800 metres). The Middleveld is mostly between 1,700 and 3,000 ft, while the Lowveld has an average height of not more than 1,000 ft (300 metres). The whole country is now virtually free from malaria. The Highveld and the Middleveld are well watered. Innumerable small streams unite with the large rivers, notably the Usutu and Komati, which traverse the country from west to east. Except for these the Lowveld is not very well watered. The climate is good except for a few months in summer, when the heat is somewhat excessive in low-lying parts.

Population (census 1976), 527,791. Estimate (1979) 563,733. Mbabane, the administrative capital (22,262). The main urban areas with 1971 populations are: Manzini (16,000); Havelock Mine (4,500); Siteki (3,600); Big Bend (2,900); Mhlume (2,200); Nhlangano (1,700) and Pigg's Peak (1,400).

CONSTITUTION AND GOVERNMENT. Swaziland became independent on 6 Sept. 1968.

On 25 April 1967 the British Government gave the country internal self-government. It changed the country's status to that of a protected state with the Ngwenyama, Sobhuza II, recognized as King of Swaziland and head of state. Britain's protection ended at independence, when a Constitution similar to the 1967 Constitution was brought into force. The general elections (by universal adult franchise) in April 1967 gave the royalist and traditional Imbokodvo National Movement all 24 seats. The Parliament consists of a House of Assembly, with 24 elected and 6 nominated members and the Attorney-General, who has no vote, and a Senate comprising 12 members, 6 of whom are elected by the House of Assembly and 6 appointed by the King. The executive authority is vested in the King and exercised through a Cabinet presided over by the Prime Minister, and consisting of the Prime Minister, the Deputy Prime Minister and up to 8 other ministers. In April 1973 the King assumed supreme power and the Constitution was suspended and in 1976 it was abolished. On 27 Oct. 1978 a general election took place to elect an electoral college of 80 members. This college elected 40 members for the National Assembly. The King nominated 10 additional members.

His Majesty the King: Sobhuza II, KBE.
In April 1980, the Cabinet was composed as follows:
Prime Minister: Prince Mabandla N. F. Dlamini.
Deputy Prime Minister: B. Sibandze. *Home Affairs:* Prince Gabheni Dlamini.
Agriculture and Co-operatives: A. K. Hlophe. *Health:* S. C. Dlamini. *Education:* S.
Hynd. *Finance:* J. L. F. Simelane. *Justice:* P. L. Dlamini. *Power and Telecommunications:* Dr V. S. Leibrandt. *Commerce, Industry, Mines and Tourism:* Prince
Nquaba Dlamini. *Foreign Affairs:* L. M. Mncina. *Establishments and Training:*
E. B. Simelane.

National flag. Horizontally 5 unequal stripes of blue, yellow, red, yellow, blue; in
the centre of the red strip an African shield of black and white, behind which are 2
assegais and a staff, all laid horizontally.

Local Government. In Dec. 1963 the former 6 districts were replaced by the 4 districts of Shiselweni, Lubombo, Manzini and Hhohho. They are administered by
District Commissioners.

DEFENCE

Air Force. First military aircraft acquired by Swaziland, in mid-1979, was an
Israeli-built Arava light twin-turboprop transport.

INTERNATIONAL RELATIONS

Membership. Swaziland is a member of UN, OAU, the Commonwealth and is an
ACP state of EEC.

ECONOMY

Budget. Revenue and expenditure (in 1,000 emalangeni) for financial years ending
31 March:

	1977–78	1978–79	1979–80
Revenue	79,000	87,000	115,000
Expenditure	124,000	169,000	169,000

Chief items of estimated revenue, 1975–76: Customs and excise, E18m.; income
tax, E20·2m.
The external public debt expenditure was estimated at E71m. in 1977.

Currency. The currency in circulation in Swaziland, from 1974, is the *emalangeni*,
but remains in the rand monetary area. In March 1981, £1 = 1·71 *emalangeni*;
US$1 = 0·783 *emalangeni*.

Banking. Barclays Bank International and the Standard Bank Ltd maintain
branches at Mbabane and Manzini; sub-branches and agencies are operated in 17
other places. Bank rates are those in force throughout South Africa and are prescribed by the main South African offices of the 2 banks. The Swaziland Credit and
Savings Bank, now known as The Swazi Bank, a statutory body, was opened in
1965. It specializes in credit for agriculture and low-cost housing. Its head office is
in Mbabane and it has branches or agencies at 3 other places. A fourth bank, The
Bank of Credit and Commerce International opened in Sept. 1978; its head office is
in Manzini and it has a branch in Mbabane.

ENERGY AND NATURAL RESOURCES

Minerals. Swaziland produced a large tonnage of iron ore from the Ngwenya mine
near Mbabane (but mining has now ceased) and asbestos from the Havelock Mine
(38,046 tons in 1977). Coal is mined at Mpaka (150,000 tons in 1980). Small quantities
of quarry stone, kaolin, barytes and pyrophyllite are also mined. Total mineral
production was valued in 1968, R18,277,300.
A railway has been built from the Ngwenya hæmatite deposits to Goba, in
Mozambique, chiefly for the transportation of iron ore. The extensive deposits of
low-volatile bituminous coal in the Lowveld are being worked to provide coal for
the railway, sugar-mills and export.

Agriculture. Some 60% of the country, which covers 4,290,944 acres, is reserved for occupation by the Swazi. The main crops are sugar (employing 13,000 people), citrus and rice, all of which are grown under irrigation, and cotton, maize (the staple product), sorghum, tobacco and pineapples. It is usually necessary to import maize from South Africa. Sugar, first produced in 1958, and wood-pulp and other forest products are the two main agricultural exports (worth E80m. and E12·5m respectively in 1975).

Livestock (1979): Cattle, 650,000; goats, 265,000; sheep, 33,000; poultry, 600,000.

COMMERCE. By agreement with the Republic of South Africa, Swaziland is united in a customs union with the republic and receives a *pro rata* share of the customs dues collected.

Total exports in 1976 amounted to E163m. The chief items were: Sugar, E54·5m.; wood-pulp and other forest products, E47·6m.; asbestos, E13·8m.; iron ore, E12·1m.; citrus fruit, E4·5m.; meat and meat products, E500,000. Imports in 1976 were E174·1m.

Total trade between Swaziland and UK (British Department of Trade returns, in £1,000 sterling):

	1975	1976	1977	1978	1979	1980
Imports to UK	30,538	30,188	13,340	34,021	37,361	30,438
Exports and re-exports from UK	521	710	559	1,580	1,333	691

Tourism. There were 115,000 visitors in 1975.

COMMUNICATIONS

Roads. There is daily (except Sundays) communication by railway motor-buses between Manzini, Mbabane and Breyten; Manzini, Mankayana and Piet Retief. There are 241 km of tarred trunk roads. Total length of roads 2,750 km.

Railways. Swaziland's railway, constructed in 1962–64, is 316 km long, starting at Kadake, operated by Mozambique State Railways, and connecting at the Mozambique frontier with an extension to the Mozambique State Railways between Maputo and Goba. A rail link from Phuzumoya to Lavumisa was opened in 1980, connecting Swaziland to Richards Bay, South Africa.

Aviation. The country's chief airport is at Matsapa. It is served by Royal Swazi National Airways connecting with Johannesburg, Durban, Lusaka, Nairobi, Mauritius and Salisbury and South African Airways, connecting with Johannesburg and Durban. Lesotho National Airways flies from Matsapa to Maseru.

Post. There were (1975) 28 post offices, 2 telephone–telegraph agencies and 10 telephone agencies. There were, in Jan. 1978, 9,190 telephones in the country.

Cinemas. There were 4 cinemas in 1975 with a total seating capacity of 1,300.

Newspapers. There are no daily newspapers but South African dailies are available.

JUSTICE, RELIGION, EDUCATION AND WELFARE

Justice. The judiciary is headed by the Chief Justice. A High Court having full jurisdiction and subordinate courts presided over by Magistrates and District Officers are in existence. During 1969 there were 6,624 convictions in subordinate courts and 36 convictions in the High Court.

There is a Court of Appeal with a President and 3 Judges. It deals with appeals from the High Court. There are 16 Swazi courts of first instance, 2 Swazi courts of appeal and a Higher Swazi Court of Appeal. The channel of appeal lies from Swazi Court of first instance to Swazi Court of Appeal, to Higher Swazi Court of Appeal, to the Judicial Commissioner and thence to the High Court of Swaziland.

Police. The police force in 1969 had a strength of 30 senior and 188 subordinate officers and 448 other ranks.

Religion. In 1975 there were about 95,000 Christians and about 50,000 adults holding traditional beliefs. A large number of churches and missionary societies are established throughout the country and, in addition to evangelism, are doing important work in the fields of education and medicine. In the larger centres there are churches of several denominations—Protestant, Roman Catholics and others.

Education. In 1976 there were 487 schools with 92,721 pupils in primary classes and 17,396 in secondary classes. The Swaziland Agricultural College and University Centre at Luyengo was opened in Oct. 1966. Technical and vocational training classes are run at the Government's Industrial Training Institute and its Staff Training Institute. The Government also operates a police college. There are 2 teacher-training colleges. In 1975 Botswana and Swaziland formed a joint university with campuses in each territory.

Health. In 1976 there were 51 doctors and about 1,462 hospital beds.

DIPLOMATIC REPRESENTATIVES

OF SWAZILAND IN GREAT BRITAIN (58 Pont St., London SW1X 0AE)

High Commissioner: George Mbikwakhe Mamba (accredited 16 Feb. 1978).

OF GREAT BRITAIN IN SWAZILAND (Allister Miller St., Mbabane)

High Commissioner: Desmond M. Kerr, OBE.

OF SWAZILAND IN THE USA (4301 Connecticut Ave., NW, Washington, D.C., 20008)

Chargé d'Affaires: Norman Vilakati.

OF THE USA IN SWAZILAND (PO Box 199, Mbabane)

Ambassador: Richard C. Matheron.

OF SWAZILAND TO THE UNITED NATIONS

Ambassador: N. M. Malinga.

Books of Reference

The Kingdom of Swaziland. Swaziland Government Information Services, 1968
Post Independence Development Plan. Mbabane, 1969
Barker, D., *Swaziland.* HMSO, 1965
Grotpeter, J. J., *Historical Dictionary of Swaziland.* Metuchen, 1975
Holleman, J. F. (ed.), *Experiment in Swaziland: Sample Survey 1960.* OUP, 1964
Jones, D., *Aid and Development in Southern Africa.* London, 1977
Kuper, H., *An African Aristocracy.* New ed. London, 1961.—*The Uniform of Colour.* Johannesburg, 1947.—*The Swazi: An Ethnographical Survey.* London, 1952
Matsebula, J. S. M., *A History of Swaziland.* London, 1972
Potholm, C. P., *Swaziland: The Dynamics of Political Modernization.* Univ. of California Press, 1972

SWEDEN

Konungariket Sverige

Capital: Stockholm
Population: 8·3m. (1979)
GNP per capita: US$10,210 (1978)

HISTORY. Organized as an independent unified state in the 10th century, Sweden became a constitutional monarchy in 1809. In 1809 she also ceded Finland to Russia. In 1815 German possessions were ceded to Prussia and Sweden was united with Norway, which union lasted until 1905.

AREA AND POPULATION. The first census took place in 1749, and it was repeated at first every third year, and, after 1775, every fifth year. Since 1860 a general census has been taken every 10 years and, in addition, in 1935, 1945, 1965 and 1975.

Latest census figures: 1940, 6,371,432 (annual increase since 1935: 0·38%); 1945, 6,673,749 (0·94% since 1940); 1950, 7,041,829 (1·1% since 1945); 1960, 7,495,316 (0·64% since 1950); 1965, 7,766,424 (1·04% since 1960); 1970, 8,076,903 (1·04% since 1965); 1975, 8,208,544 (1·02% since 1970).

Counties (*Län*)	*Land area:* sq. km	*Census population* 1 Nov. 1975	*Estimated population* 31 Dec. 1979	*Pop. per* sq. km 1 Jan. 1978
Stockholm (city)[1] Stockholm (county)[1] }	6,488	1,493,546	1,524,266	235
Uppsala	6,989	230,028	241,722	35
Södermanland	6,060	251,913	252,026	42
Östergötland	10,569	387,088	392,390	37
Jönköping	9,944	301,986	302,475	30
Kronoberg	8,453	169,438	172,401	20
Kalmar	11,168	240,724	241,448	22
Gotland	3,140	54,400	55,261	18
Blekinge	2,919	155,336	154,135	53
Kristianstad	6,054	272,014	278,917	46
Malmöhus	4,929	740,069	743,133	151
Halland	5,454	219,780	229,211	42
Göteborg and Bohus	5,112	715,012	713,242	140
Älvsborg	11,394	418,026	424,240	37
Skaraborg	7,938	263,218	268,720	34
Värmland	17,609	284,249	284,615	16
Örebro	8,515	273,923	274,223	32
Västmanland	6,302	259,921	259,670	41
Kopparberg	28,344	281,109	285,545	10
Gävleborg	18,191	294,412	293,959	16
Västernorrland	21,786	268,034	267,895	12
Jämtland	49,917	133,433	134,653	3
Västerbotten	55,432	236,397	241,898	4
Norrbotten	98,906	264,386	266,983	3
Total	411,615	8,208,442	8,303,010	20

[1] From Jan. 1968 Stockholm city and Stockholm county have been united in Stockholm county.

On 31 Dec. 1979 there were 4,115,522 males and 4,187,488 females.

On 1 July 1976 aliens employed in Sweden numbered 266,677. Of these, 117,972 were Finns, 30,963 Yugoslavs, 21,997 Danes, 14,347 Greeks, 13,791 Norwegians, 12,718 Germans, 4,576 Italians and 3,092 Austrians.

Vital statistics for calendar years:

	Total living births	Of which illegitimate [1]	Still-born	Marriages	Divorces	Deaths exclusive of still-born
1977	96,057	33,300	492	40,370	20,391	88,202
1978	93,248	33,512	455	37,844	20,317	89,681
1979	96,255	36,123	445	37,273	20,314	91,074

[1] From 1977 children born to women who were single, divorced or widowed.

Immigration: 1977, 44,005; 1978, 36,187; 1979, 37,025. Emigration: 1977, 21,078; 1978, 22,168; 1979, 23,467.

In 1860 the urban population numbered 435,000 (11% of the total population) and on 31 Dec. 1965, 4,177,212 (54%); including other densely populated areas, the urbanized population in 1965 was 77·4%.

On 1 Nov. 1975, population in densely populated areas was 6,789,432 (82·7%).

Population of largest communities, 31 Dec. 1978:

Stockholm	653,929	Karlstad	73,619	Hässleholm	48,812
Göteborg	436,985	Skellefteå	73,441	Mölndal	47,536
Malmö	236,716	Kristianstad	68,152	Uddevalla	46,294
Uppsala	143,386	Luleå	67,180	Borlänge	45,850
Norrköping	120,251	Huddinge	65,299	Skövde	45,734
Västerås	117,599	Nyköping	63,499	Sollentuna	45,686
Örebo	116,817	Växjö	63,340	Täby	45,157
Linköping	111,424	Örnsköldsvik	60,752	Varberg	43,671
Jönköping	108,179	Karlskrona	60,238	Sandviken	43,078
Borås	103,387	Haninge	56,128	Kungsbacka	42,041
Helsingborg	101,046	Nacka	55,927	Västervik	41,238
Sundsvall	94,375	Östersund	55,403	Norrtälje	39,987
Eskilstuna	91,097	Gotland	54,435	Piteå	37,556
Gävle	87,491	Kalmar	52,751	Landskrona	37,438
Umeå	78,568	Järfälla	52,307	Lidingö	37,333
Södertälje	78,827	Solna	51,518	Karlskoga	37,252
Lund	77,550	Trollhättan	49,947	Hudiksvall	37,084
Halmstad	75,290	Motala	49,742	Lidköping	34,812
Botkyrka	75,267	Falun	49,585	Vänersborg	34,697

Befolkningsförändringar (Population Changes). Annual. 3 vols. National Central Bureau of Statistics, Stockholm

Folkmängd 31 Dec. (Population). Annual. 3 vols. National Central Bureau of Statistics, Stockholm

Historisk statistik för Sverige. I: Befolkning (Population), 1720–1967. 2nd ed. National Central Bureau of Statistics, Stockholm, 1969

REIGNING KING. Carl XVI Gustaf, born 30 April 1946, succeeded on the death of his grandfather Gustaf VI Adolf, 15 Sept. 1973, married 19 June 1976 to *Silvia* Renate Sommerlath, born 23 Dec. 1943 (Queen of Sweden). *Daughter:* Crown Princess Victoria Ingrid Alice Désirée, Duchess of Västergötland, born 14 July 1977; *son:* Prince Carl Philip Edmund Bertil, Duke of Värmland, heir-presumptive, born 13 May 1979.

Sisters of the King. Princess Margaretha, born 31 Oct. 1934, married 30 June 1964 to Mr John Ambler; Princess Birgitta (Princess of Sweden), born 19 Jan. 1937, married 25 May 1961 (civil marriage) and 30 May 1961 (religious ceremony) to Johann Georg, Prince of Hohenzollern; Princess Désirée, born 2 June 1938, married 5 June 1964 to Baron Niclas Silfverschiöld; Princess Christina, born 3 Aug. 1943, married 15 June 1974 to Tord Magnuson.

Uncles of the King. Sigvard, Count of Wisborg, born on 7 June 1907; Prince Bertil, Duke of Halland, born on 28 Feb. 1912, married 7 Dec. 1976 to Lilian May Davies, born 30 Aug. 1915 (Princess of Sweden, Duchess of Halland); Carl Johan, Count of Wisborg, born on 31 Oct. 1916.

Aunt of the King. Princess Ingrid (Princess of Sweden), born 28 March 1910, married 24 May 1935 to Frederik, Crown Prince of Denmark (King Frederik IX), died 14 Jan. 1972.

The following is a list of the kings and queens of Sweden, with the dates of their accession from the accession of the House of Vasa:

House of Vasa		House of Pfalz-Zwei-brücken (contd.)		House of Bernadotte	
Gustaf I	1523	Carl XII	1697	Carl XIV Johan	1818
Eric XIV	1560	Ulrica Eleonora	1718	Oscar I	1844
Johan III	1568			Carl XV	1859
Sigismund	1592			Oscar II	1872
Carl IX	1600	*House of Hesse*		Gustaf V	1907
Gustaf II Adolf	1611	Fredrik I	1720	Gustaf VI Adolf	1950
Christina	1632			Carl XVI Gustaf	1973
		House of Holstein-Gottorp			
House of Pfalz-Zwei-brücken		Adolf Fredrik	1751		
		Gustaf III	1771		
Carl X Gustaf	1654	Gustaf IV Adolf	1792		
Carl XI	1660	Carl XIII	1809		

The royal family of Sweden have a civil list of 8·2m. kronor; this does not include the maintenance of the royal palaces.

CONSTITUTION AND GOVERNMENT. Sweden's present Constitution came into force in 1975 and replaced the 1809 Constitution. Under the present Constitution Sweden is a representative and parliamentary democracy. Parliament (*Riksdag*) is declared to be the central organ of government. The executive power of the country is vested in the Government, which is responsible to Parliament. The King is Head of State, but he does not participate in the government of the country. Since 1971 Parliament has consisted of one chamber. It has 349 members, who are elected for a period of 3 years in direct, general elections.

Every man and woman who has reached the age of 18 years on election-day itself, and who is not under wardship has the right to vote and to stand for election.

The manner of election to the *Riksdag* is proportional. The country is divided into 28 constituencies. In these constituencies 310 members are elected. The remaining 39 seats constitute a nation-wide pool intended to give absolute proportionality to parties that receive at least 4% of the votes. A party receiving less than 4% of the votes in the country is, however, entitled to participate in the distribution of seats in a constituency, if it has obtained at least 12% of the votes cast there.

A state subsidy is given to all political parties which have obtained at least one seat in the *Riksdag* at the last election. The subvention (53·1m. kr. in 1977–78) is distributed in the ratio of 115,000 kr. per seat. Furthermore a municipal subsidy may be decided by the regional councils and the local councils. The subsidy is distributed in a fixed ratio per seat in the council. The counties subsidy is estimated at 30,136,700 kr. for 1977 and the municipalities at 38·5m. kr. for 1974.

The *Riksdag*, elected 16 Sept. 1979, has 154 Social Democrats, 73 Conservatives, 64 Centre Party, 38 Liberals and 20 Communists.

A new Coalition Cabinet was appointed on 12 Oct. 1979, composed as follows:

Prime Minister: Thorbjörn Fälldin.
Foreign Affairs: Ola Ullsten. *Justice:* Håkan Winberg. *Defence:* Eric Krönmark. *Health and Social Affairs:* Karin Söder. *Communications:* Ulf Adelsohn. *Economy:* Gösta Bohman. *Finance:* Rolf Wirtén. *Education:* Jan Erik Wikström. *Agriculture:* Anders Dahlgren. *Commerce:* Staffan Burenstam Linder. *Labour:* Ingemar Eliasson. *Housing:* Birgit Friggebo. *Industry:* Nils G. Åsling. *Local Government:* Karl Boo. *Without Portfolio:* Elisabet Holm, Olof Johansson, Britt Mogård, Karin Andersson, Georg Danell, Carl Akel Petri.

All the members of the Cabinet are responsible for the acts of the Government.

Public administration in Sweden is characterized by a unique degree of functional decentralization. The Ministries are not really administrative agencies. They prepare bills for the *Riksdag*, issue general directives and make higher appointments, but, as a rule, do not take individual administrative decisions. The routine administrative work is attended to by the central boards (*centrala ämbetsverk*). Each board's sphere of activity depends partly on its organization which is decided by the appropriations granted by the Riksdag. The Government often asks the boards' opinion on proposed measures.

National flag: Blue with a yellow Scandinavian cross.

National anthem: Du gamla, du fria, du fjällhöga nord (words by R. Dybeck, 1844; folk-tune).

The official language is Swedish. The capital is Stockholm.

Local Government. For administrative purposes Sweden is divided into 24 counties (*län*), in each of which the central government is represented by a county administrative board (*länsstyrelse*). The governor (*landshövding*), appointed by the government, is chairman of the board, which in addition to the governor has 14 members elected by the county council.

Local government and the levying of local taxes are based on the fundamental law and are regulated by the municipal law and special acts. According to the municipal law Sweden is divided into municipalities in which all men and women who have reached the age of 18 on election-day itself, and not under wardship, are entitled to elect the municipal council. These councils are named *kommunfullmäktige*. The number of municipalities has, since 1951, been reduced from about 2,500 to 279. The municipalities deal with a great variety of different tasks such as social welfare, education and culture, public health, town planning, housing etc. Each county, except Gotland, which consists of only one municipality, has a county council (*landsting*) elected by men and women who enjoy municipal suffrage. The county councils chiefly administer the health service. The municipalities of Gothenburg and Malmö do not belong to county councils. Ecclesiastical affairs in all parishes with more than 1,000 inhabitants are dealt with by church councils (*kyrkofullmäktige*); smaller parishes may make the same arrangement. All elections are conducted on a proportional basis.

Andrén, N., *Modern Swedish Government*. 2nd ed. Stockholm, 1968
Elder, N. C. M., *Government in Sweden: The Executive at Work*. Oxford, 1970
Lewin, L., Jansson, B., and Sörbom, D., *The Swedish Electorate 1887–1968*. Stockholm, 1972
Ministry of Local Government, *Local Government in Sweden*. Stockholm, 1978
Vinde, P., *Swedish Government Administration: An Introduction*. Stockholm, 1971

DEFENCE. A Supreme Commander is, under the Government, in command of the three services. He is assisted by the Defence Staff under a chief of staff.

The military forces are recruited on the principle of national service, supplemented by voluntarily enlisted personnel who form the permanent cadres for training purposes, staff duties, etc.

Liability to service commences at the age of 18, and lasts till the end of the 47th year. The period of training for the Army and Navy is 7½–15 months and for the Airforce 8–15 months.

The territorial organization consists of 6 military commands each one under a general officer commanding.

Army. The C.-in-C. of the Royal Swedish Army has at his disposal the Army Staff under a chief of staff. The peace-time Army consists for training purposes of 16 infantry, 8 armour, 7 artillery, 6 AA, 3 engineer, 3 signal and 4 Army Service Corps units, most of which are called 'regiments' (*regementen*).

The Army is organized and equipped with regard to the varying geographical and climatic conditions of the country. The voluntary Home Guard (*Hemvärnet*) with a total strength of more than 100,000 men ready for action within 2 hours, raised during the War continues to be in force.

Sweden's ground forces, total 700,000 men, can be said to consist of an Army which for the most part is on indefinite leave, but which on short notice can be ready for action. One of the basic principles of the Swedish system of mobilization is the local recruitment of as many units as possible. The storage of equipment and supplies is decentralized on more than 1,500 places.

The active personnel of the Army comprises about 44,500, including 36,000 conscripts doing basic training.

Navy. The C.-in-C. of the Royal Swedish Navy is assisted by the Chief of Naval Staff, the Chief of Naval Materiel Department and the C.-in-C. of Coastal Fleet. The Navy is divided into two branches, the Royal Swedish Navy and the Royal Coast Artillery. There are 3 Naval Base Areas: those of the southern, eastern and western coasts.

There are 14 submarines, 6 destroyers, 2 frigates, 10 fast missile boats, 22 fast torpedo craft, 3 minelayers, 9 coastal minelayers, 12 coastal minesweepers, 6 patrol vessels (ex-minesweepers), 18 inshore minesweepers, 27 patrol craft, 2 mine transports, 36 minelaying boats, 3 torpedo recovery vessels, 12 tenders, 6 surveying vessels, 8 icebreakers, 1 oiler, 1 salvage vessel, 9 artillery landing craft, 81 utility landing craft, 54 minor landing craft, 2 sail training ships, 1 supply ship, 2 water carriers and 19 tugs.

The Naval Air Arm comprises 10 Boeing Vertol 107 helicopters, 10 JetRanger helicopters and 5 Alouette II training helicopters.

The coast artillery defence areas are those of the Stockholm archipelago, Blekinge, Gothenburg, Gotland and Norrland. There are 5 coastal artillery regiments. The personnel of the navy and coast artillery in 1981 totalled 14,900 officers and men, comprising 4,800 regulars, 3,100 reservists and 7,000 national servicemen (additionally 8,000 conscripts train annually).

The Swedish Fleet has been progressively reduced over the last few years, the cruiser, 8 destroyers and frigates, and 12 submarines having been disposed of, and with the imminent disposal of the remaining destroyers and frigates, the largest remaining surface ships being minelayers, will constitute a coastal defence navy.

Air Force. The C-in-C. of the Royal Swedish Air Force has at his disposal the Air Staff under a chief of staff. Directly subordinate to the C.-in-C. of the Air Force are also the Inspectors of Air Base Control and Reporting Services, and of Flying Safety.

The combat force consists of 6 fighter-interceptor, 3 ground-attack and one mixed interceptor/attack wings (flottiljer), each with 2–3 squadrons of 12–15 aircraft, including 3 reconnaissance squadrons (divisioner). Total peace-time strength of the combat units is 21 squadrons with nearly 400 first-line aircraft.

Standard night and all-weather fighter is the Swedish-built Saab J35 Draken, equipping 11 squadrons; the remaining squadron has JA37 Viggens. The ground-attack wings have 5 squadrons of Saab AJ37 Viggens, and there is provision for 5 light ground-attack squadrons of twin-jet Saab-105s (Sk60s), most of which could be withdrawn in wartime from training units. One Sk60 squadron is designated as part of the primary ground-attack force. The 3 reconnaissance squadrons have SF37 (overland) and SH37 (maritime) Viggen reconnaissance aircraft; the fighter-interceptor force will have eventually 8 squadrons of JA37 Viggens; plus transport, helicopter and other support units, as at present. The Sk60A is the Air Force's standard advanced trainer, to which pupils progress after initial training on piston-engined Bulldogs. Other trainers in service include the Sk35C Draken and Sk37 Viggen.

Active strength consists of about 9,800 personnel, including 4,600 conscripts.

INTERNATIONAL RELATIONS

Membership. Sweden is a member of UN and EFTA.

ECONOMY

Budget. Revenue and expenditure of the ordinary budget for fiscal years ending 30 June (in 1,000 kr.):

	Revenue	Expenditure		Revenue	Expenditure
1975–76	91,367,610	89,228,047	1978–79	116,263,786	148,375,628
1976–77	101,974,916	106,705,827	1979–80[1]	128,562,962	170,695,356
1977–78	109,286,130	125,936,282	1980–81[2]	155,459,136	209,276,513

[1] Estimate.

[2] By the introduction of a reformed budget system, the current budget and the capital budget have been consolidated.

The estimated actual revenue and expenditure (current accounts) for the financial year 1 July 1979 to 30 June 1980 was as follows (in 1,000 kr.):

Current revenue:		Current expenditure:	
Income and property taxes	57,623,374	Royal household	19,917
Death duty and other stamp-		Justice	6,182,642
duties	2,199,007	Foreign affairs	4,692,851
Motor-car duty	7,628,369	Defence	15,159,825

Current revenue (contd.):		*Current expenditure* (contd.):	
Special employer's fee	67,375	Social welfare	47,964,251
Customs duties	1,145,044	Communications	7,051,361
Purchase tax	32,252,201	Economy	380,097
Excise on spirits, tobacco, etc.	14,007,264	Budget	9,863,930
Civil service fees, etc.	3,377,622	Education	22,360,016
Miscellaneous	2,158,413	Agriculture	6,145,219
		Commerce	1,127,424
Net receipts from state capital		Labour	12,037,394
funds:		Housing and physical planning	7,195,880
State enterprises:		Industry	6,281,420
Posts, Telecommunications	235,426	Local government	2,470,520
Hydro-electric power	1,116,298	Expenses for the Diet, etc.	287,171
Forests	41,646	Unforeseen expenses	5,464
Railways	...		
Defence factories	61,003	*Expenditure on state funds:*	
Civil aviation	48,170	National debt (interest, etc.)	14,508,895
Real estate funds	996,854	Depreciation of new capital	
Interest on state-owned		investment	3,118,190
shares	94,278	Appropriation for covering	
Interest on outstanding		capital losses	3,842,890
loans	4,331,383		
Other funds	429,233		
Shares in the profits of			
Bank of Sweden	750,000		

[1] By the introduction of a reformed budget system for fiscal year 1980–81, the current budget and the capital budget have been consolidated.

Net capital investments (in 1,000 kr.): 1975–76, 5,437,236; 1976–77, 5,647,438; 1977–78, 7,567,757; 1978–79, 6,829,951; 1979–80[1], 6,823,944.

Revenue and expenditure of state business enterprises (in 1m. kr.):

	Revenue	Expenditure		Revenue	Expenditure
Forest Service, 1978	1,264·8	973·4	Post Office, 1977–78 [1]	4,798·4	4,768·2
Power Administration,			Telecommunications,		
1977–78	4,035·4	2,970·1	1977–78	5,813·3	4,330·6
Railways, 1977–78	4,926·7	5,219·6			

[1] Not comparable with previous years.

On 31 Dec. 1979 the national debt amounted to 175,146m. kr.

Riksgäldskontoret [National Debt Office], *årsbok*. Annual. Stockholm, from 1920
Riksskatteverket [National Tax Board], *årsbok*. Annual. Stockholm, from 1971
The Swedish Budget. Ministry of Economic Affairs and Ministry of the Budget, from 1962/63

Currency. The monetary unit is the Swedish *krona*, of 100 *öre*. In March 1981, £1 = 10·18 *krona*; US$1 = 4·62 *krona*.

Gold coins do not exist as a currency. Central bank-notes for 5, 10, 50, 100, 1,000 and 10,000 kr. are legal means of payment.

Banking. The Riksbank, or Central Bank of Sweden, belongs entirely to the State and is managed by directors elected for 3 years by the Parliament, except the chairman, who is designated by the Government. The bank is under the guarantee of the Parliament, its capital and reserve capital are fixed by its constitution. Since 1904, only the Riksbank has the right to issue notes. On 31 Dec. 1979 its note circulation amounted to 31,580m. kr.; its combined gold and net foreign-exchange holdings (including surplus value of gold) totalled 15,209m. kr.

There are 14 commercial banks. On 31 Dec. 1979 their total deposits amounted to 151,640m. kr.; advances to the public amounted to 133,920m. kr.

The savings-banks statistics (exclusive of post office) are as follows, at the end of the year:

	1973	1974	1975	1976	1977	1978	1979
Depositors' accounts, 1,000	9,380	9,574	9,711	9,943	10,357	10,850	...
Deposits, 1m. kr.[1]	42,682	46,907	52,224	56,554	61,857	69,751	78,580
Capital and reserve funds,							
1m. kr.	1,173	1,219	1,252	1,294	1,340	1,395	...

[1] Including interest.

On 30 June 1974 the post office bank had 5·6m. depositors and 11,553m. kr. of deposits, including interest.

On 1 July 1974 the Swedish Credit Bank and parts of the Post Office Bank were merged into the Swedish Post Office and Credit Bank.

Sveriges Riksbank, årsbok. Annual. Stockholm, from 1908
Skandinaviska Enskilda Banken, Kvartalskrift. Quarterly Review (in English). Stockholm, from 1920

Weights and Measures. The metric system is obligatory.

ENERGY AND NATURAL RESOURCES

Electricity. Sweden is rich in water power resources. The total electric energy production in 1979 was 95,204m. kwh. About 64% of this energy was produced in hydro-electric plants. The development of water power will in the future be insignificant and the new plants must be based on thermal power, mainly nuclear.

Minerals. Sweden is one of the leading exporters of iron ore. The largest deposits are found north of the polar circle in the area of Kiruna and Gällivare–Malmberget. The ore is exported *via* the Norwegian port of Narvik and the Swedish port of Luleå. There are also important resources of iron ore in southern Sweden (Bergslagen). The most important fields are Grängesberg and Stråssa and the ores are shipped *via* the port of Oxelösund. Some of the southern deposits have, in contrast to the fields in North Sweden, a low phosphorus content.

There are also some deposits of copper, lead and zinc ores especially in the Boliden area in the north of Sweden. These ores are often found together with pyrites. Nonferrous ores, except zinc ores, are used in the Swedish metal industry and barely satisfy domestic needs.

The total production of iron ores amounted to 21·1m. tons in 1978 and exports to 17·9m. tons. The production of copper ore was 196,577 tons, of lead ore 117,516 tons, of zinc ore 299,962 tons.

There are also deposits of raw materials for aluminium not worked at present. In southern Sweden there are big resources of alum shale, containing oil and uranium.

Agriculture. According to the farm register which is revised annually the following data was provided for 1979. The number of farms in cultivation of more than 2 hectares of arable land, was 120,631; of these there were 75,588 of 2–20 hectares; 41,874 of 20–100 hectares; 3,169 of above 100 hectares. Of the total land area of Sweden (41,161,500 hectares), 2,996,515 hectares (except kitchen gardens and fruit gardens) were arable land, 250,623 hectares cultivated pastures and 22,598,565 hectares forests.

	Area (1,000 hectares)[1]			Production (1,000 tonnes)		
Chief crops	1977	1978	1979	1977	1978	1979
Wheat	376·3	297·2	251·0	1,522	1,290	1,030
Rye	112·3	83·2	60·4	338	297	195
Barley	641·3	721·9	754·1	1,966	2,434	2,346
Oats	491·2	486·2	489·5	1,416	1,550	1,524
Mixed grain	62·6	62·3	59·1	153	170	148
Peas and vetches	11·0	11·6	12·7	23	25	26
Potatoes	46·8	44·2	41·2	1,279	1,339	1,284
Sugar-beet	53·5	52·5	51·9	2,199	2,247	2,206
Tame hay	682·8	695·5	701·6	2,656[2]	2,807[2]	2,826[2]
Oil seed	125·3	157·0	160·3	269	329	302

[1] Figures refer to holdings of more than 2 hectares of arable land.
[2] Figures refer only to the first harvest.

Area of rotation meadows for pasture was (in 1,000 hectares): 1977, 204; 1978, 197; 1979, 192.

Total production of milk (in 1,000 tonnes):1977, 3,257; 1978, 3,311; 1979, 3,408. Butter production in the same years was (in 1,000 tonnes): 62, 63, 65; and cheese, 87, 94, 96.

Livestock (1979): Cattle, 1·9m.; sheep, 384,000; pigs, 2·7m.; poultry, 11·65m.

Number of farm tractors in 1976, 209,186; combines in 1976, 50,040.

The number of pelts produced in 1977 was as follows: Fox, 46,848; mink, 1·1m.; others, 800,000.

Forestry. Nearly 23·5m. hectares or 57% of the total land area are covered with forests. The total amount of standing timber is estimated at 2,472m. cu. metres with bark; 83% of this volume consists of coniferous wood (pine and spruce). Half of the forest area is privately owned, the other half is equally divided between public authorities (Crown, Church, communities, etc.) and joint-stock companies. The total cut in 1977 was 45m. cu. metres solid volume (without bark); of these, 22m. were coniferous timber, 21m. pulpwood, 1m. fuel wood and 1m. other wood. In 1976 the total cut was 53m. cu. metres.

In 1973 there were about 900 saw-mills with 5 or more workers, the total production of which—representing some 90% of the country's total production—amounted to 11·3m. cu. metres sawn and planed wood. The production of the 89 pulp-mills in Sweden in 1977 amounted to 7·7m. tonnes pulp (dry weight). There was an export of approximately 900,000 cu. metres of roundwood; exports of sawn coniferous wood amounted to 6·1m. cu. metres, of plywood (including blockboards) to 17,300 tonnes, of pulp 3m. tonnes and of particle board 306,700 tonnes.

Fisheries. In 1979 the total value of the catches of the sea fisheries was 430m. kr.; of this sum, 205m. kr. came from west coast fisheries.

INDUSTRY AND TRADE

Manufacturing. The most important sector of Swedish manufacturing is the production of metals, metal products, machinery and transport equipment, covering almost half of the total value added by manufacturing. Production of high-quality steel is an old Swedish speciality. A large part of this production is exported. The production of ordinary steel is slightly decreasing and is still short of domestic demand. The total production of steel amounted to 3·9m. tons in 1977, 29% of which was high-quality steel. There is also a large production of other metals (aluminium, lead, copper) and rolled semi-manufactured goods of these metals.

These basic metal industries are an important basis for the production of more developed metal products, machinery and equipment, which are to a large extent sold on the world market, *i.e.*, hand tools, mining drills, ball-bearings, turbines, pneumatic machinery, refrigerating equipment, machinery for pulp and paper industries, etc., sewing machines, machine tools, office machinery, high-voltage electric machinery, telephone equipment, cars and trucks, ships and aeroplanes.

Another important manufacturing sector is based on Sweden's forest resources. This sector includes saw-mills, plywood factories, joinery industries, pulp- and paper-mills, wallboard and particle board factories, accounting for about 15% of the total value of manufacturing. A fast increasing sector is the chemical industry, especially the petro-chemical branch. Minerals industries include production of building materials, decorative arts products of glass and china.

Industry groups	No. of establishments		Average no. of wage-earners		Sales value of production (gross) in 1m. kr.	
	1977	1978	1977	1978	1977	1978
Mining and quarrying	159	151	11,280	10,266	2,799	2,445
Metal-ore mining	53	47	9,957	8,941	2,420	2,033
Other mining	106	104	1,323	1,325	379	421
Manufacturing	11,383	10,794	634,241	608,468	215,747	233,050
Manufacture of food, beverages and tobacco	1,084	1,039	54,006	54,259	31,750	34,483
Textile, wearing apparel and leather industries	1,038	931	39,476	34,794	7,361	7,028
Manufacture of wood products including furniture	1,967	1,874	60,044	58,939	17,937	19,249
Manufacture of paper and paper products, printing and publishing	1,159	1,132	73,186	71,409	27,426	30,393
Manufacture of chemicals and chemical, petroleum, coal, rubber and plastic products	762	735	42,631	41,677	25,474	28,136
Manufacture of non-metallic mineral products, except products of petroleum and coal	604	558	22,775	21,523	5,963	6,303
Basic metal industries	181	177	49,443	46,193	15,425	17,899

Industry groups	No. of establishments		Average no. of wage-earners		Sales value of production (gross) in 1m. kr.	
	1977	1978	1977	1978	1977	1978
Manufacture of fabricated metal products, machinery and equipment	4,439	4,218	288,225	275,216	83,446	88,542
Other manufacturing industries	149	...	4,455	...	965	...
Electricity, gas and water	*967*	*948*	*11,468*	*11,395*	*22,971*	*27,195*
Electricity, gas and steam	809	806	10,437	10,451	22,046	26,146
Water works and supply	158	142	1,031	944	925	1,049

Arbetsmarknadsstatistik (*Labour Market Statistics*). Monthly. National Labour Market Board, Stockholm, from 1963

Arbetsmarknadsstatistisk Årsbok (*Year Book of Labour Statistics*). National Central Bureau of Statistics, Stockholm, from 1973

Carlson, B., *Trade Unions in Sweden*. Stockholm, 1969

Historisk statistik för Sverige, II (Climate, land surveying, agriculture, forestry, fisheries). National Central Bureau of Statistics, Stockholm, 1959

Johansson, Ö., *The Gross Domestic Product of Sweden and its Composition 1861–1955*. Stockholm, 1967

Jörberg, L., *A History of Prices in Sweden 1732–1914*. 2 vols. Stockholm, 1972

Jordbruksekonomiska meddelanden (Journal of Agricultural Economics, published monthly by the National Agricultural Market Board). Stockholm, from 1939

Jordbruksstatistisk årsbok (Yearbook of Agricultural Statistics). National Central Bureau of Statistics, Stockholm, from 1965

The Swedish Economy. Ministry of Economic Affairs and National Institute of Economic Research. Stockholm, from 1960

The 1,000 Largest Companies in Sweden. Stockholm, from 1972

Commerce. The imports and exports of Sweden, unwrought gold and coin not included, have been as follows (in 1m. kr.):

	1973	1974	1975	1976	1977	1978	1979
Imports	46,336	72,800	74,000	84,000	90,246	92,717	122,952
Exports	53,153	70,514	72,012	80,195	85,678	98,205	118,147

On 1 Jan. 1974 a new Customs procedure for the imports was introduced. This means that a great part of the imports are now recorded in the statistics with an extra delay of up to 2 weeks as compared to the registration before 1974. The import values for the first months of 1974 and especially Jan. are, therefore, underestimated.

A series of monthly totals, for 1974, 1975 and 1976, preliminary adjusted for the effects of the time-lags, have been calculated in order to facilitate comparisons with earlier years and to show the development of the trade balance. For 1974 the adjusted import value is about 72,800m. kr. The registered import value is 69,949·52m. kr. For 1975 the adjusted import value is about 74,000m. kr. The registered import value is 74,865,378,000 kr. For 1976 the adjusted import value is about 84,000m. kr. The registered import value is 83,225,897,000 kr.

Adjustments have not been made by commodity and country. For this reason the adjusted import value is used in the summary table only, while the data in the other tables are unadjusted.

Imports and exports by products (in 1m. kr.):

	Imports		Exports	
	1978	1979	1978	1979
Food and live animals chiefly for food	7,238	7,934	1,943	2,266
Cereals and cereal preparations	355	397	672	746
Vegetables and fruit	2,127	2,313	202	213
Coffee, tea, cocoa, spices and manufactures thereof	2,157	2,177	174	191
Feeding stuff for animals (not including unmilled cereals)	751	834	27	40
Beverages and tobacco	795	873	84	90
Crude materials, inedible, except fuels	3,876	5,285	12,535	14,762
Hides, skins and furskins, raw	252	324	313	412
Crude rubber (including synthetic and reclaimed)	282	374	53	57
Cork and wood	562	938	4,615	5,336
Pulp and waste paper	62	151	5,220	5,772
Textile fibres (other than wool tops) and their wastes (not manufactured into yarn or fabric)	189	208	206	232

	Imports		Exports	
	1978	1979	1978	1979
Crude fertilizers and crude minerals (excluding coal, petroleum and precious stones)	604	719	186	214
Metalliferous ores and metal scrap	1,060	1,657	1,773	2,430
Mineral fuels, lubricants and related materials	15,119	27,038	1,941	3,739
Coal, coke and briquettes	600	870	47	38
Petroleum, petroleum products and related materials	14,329	25,689	1,579	3,212
Chemicals and related products, n.e.s.	8,383	10,887	5,041	6,289
Artificial resins and plastic materials, and cellulose esters and ethers	2,317	3,200	1,566	2,143
Manufactured goods classified chiefly by material	16,824	21,318	27,257	33,131
Paper, paperboard, and articles of paper pulp, of paper or of paperboard	935	1,106	9,255	11,475
Textile yarn, fabrics, made-up articles, n.e.s., and related products	3,292	3,908	1,368	1,591
Non-metallic mineral manufactures, n.e.s.	1,479	1,791	1,000	1,214
Iron and steel	4,245	5,665	7,621	9,252
Non-ferrous metals	2,242	3,096	2,029	2,694
Manufactures of metal, n.e.s.	2,721	3,309	3,871	4,411
Machinery and transport equipment	27,819	34,046	41,785	48,532
Power generating machinery and equipment	2,213	2,762	2,662	3,060
Machinery specialized for particular industries	2,907	3,438	5,104	5,937
Metalworking machinery	836	996	1,190	1,411
General industrial machinery and equipment, n.e.s. and machine parts, n.e.s.	4,825	5,594	7,139	8,376
Office machines and automatic data processing equipment	2,285	3,148	2,011	2,494
Telecommunications and sound recording and reproducing apparatus and equipment	1,963	2,097	4,036	4,497
Electrical machinery apparatus and appliances, n.e.s., and electrical parts thereof (including non-electrical counterparts, n.e.s., of electrical household type equipment)	4,841	5,748	3,867	4,510
Road vehicles (including air cushion vehicles)	6,310	8,082	11,728	14,774
Other transport equipment	1,639	2,180	4,046	3,474
Miscellaneous manufactured articles	11,938	14,585	6,631	7,801

Principal import and export countries (in 1m. kr.):

	Imports from		Exports to	
	1978	1979	1978	1979
Belgium–Luxembourg	2,844	4,128	2,762	3,793
Denmark	6,537	8,098	8,935	10,663
Federal Republic of Germany	17,112	21,248	10,776	13,330
Finland	5,718	7,906	5,621	7,361
France	3,997	5,254	4,831	6,332
Italy	2,641	3,499	3,233	3,804
Netherlands	3,695	5,559	4,637	5,609
Norway	5,047	6,656	10,081	11,218
Switzerland	2,200	2,354	1,988	2,578
USSR	2,472	4,564	957	1,453
UK	10,326	14,902	10,636	13,629
USA	6,777	9,005	6,201	7,022

Total trade between Sweden and UK (British Department of Trade returns, in £1,000 sterling):

	1976	1977	1978	1979	1980
Imports to UK	1,187,887	1,259,859	1,343,864	1,605,942	1,475,506
Exports and re-exports from UK	1,045,046	1,196,773	1,170,893	1,542,197	1,623,511

Historisk Statistik för Sverige, III: Utrikeshandel (Foreign Trade), *1732–1970*. National Central
  Bureau of Statistics, Stockholm, 1972
Utrikeshandel (Foreign Trade). National Central Bureau of Statistics, Stockholm. Annually, 2
  vols, from 1911
Utrikeshandel, kvartalsstatistik (Foreign Trade, Quarterly Bulletin). National Central Bureau of
  Statistics, Stockholm, from 1961. From 1976 published in *Statistical Reports*, Series H
Utrikeshandel, månadsstatistik (Foreign Trade, Monthly Bulletin). National Central Bureau of
  Statistics, Stockholm, from 1913. From 1976 published in *Statistical Reports*, Series H

COMMUNICATIONS

Roads. On 1 Jan. 1980 there were 183,408 km of public roads comprising State-
administered roads, 97,475 km, municipal, 17,603 km, private roads with subsidies,
68,330 km, of which 81,955 km were surfaced. Motor vehicles on 31 Dec. 1979
included 2,868,302 passenger cars, 190,523 buses and lorries and 15,569 heavy motor
cycles (all in use).

Railways. At the end of 1979 the total length of railways was 11,898 km, of which
11,377 km belonged to the State; 7,583 km were electrified. In 1979 the number of
passengers on the railways was 81m.; weight of goods, including Lapland ore, 61m.
tonnes.

Aviation. Commercial air traffic is maintained in (1) Sweden and other parts of the
world by Scandinavian Airlines System (SAS), of which AB Aerotransport
(ABA = Swedish Air Lines) is the Swedish partner (DDL = Danish Air Lines and
DNL = Norwegian Air Lines being the other two); (2) only within Sweden by
Linjeflyg AB. Scandinavian Airlines System have a joint paid-up capital of about
Sw. kronor 990m. Capitalization of ABA, Sw. kronor 364m., of which 50% is
owned by the Government and 50% by private enterprises. Capitalization of
Linjeflyg, Sw. kronor 87m., of which 50% is owned by SAS and 50% by ABA.
  In scheduled air traffic during 1979 the total number of km flown was 68·1m.;
passenger-km, 5,298·2m.; goods, 182·3m. ton-km; mail, 19·2m. ton-km. These
figures represent the Swedish share of the SAS traffic (Swedish domestic and three-
sevenths of international traffic) and the Linjeflyg traffic.

Shipping. The Swedish mercantile marine consisted on 1 Jan. 1980 of 513 vessels of
4·31m. gross tons (only vessels of at least 100 gross tons, and excluding fishing
vessels and tugs). Stockholm and Göteborg, with together 242 vessels of 3·41m.
gross tons in Jan. 1980 are the two largest ports.
  Vessels entered from and cleared for foreign countries, exclusive of passenger
liners and ferries, with cargoes and in ballast, in 1979, are as follows (only vessels of
at least 40 net tons included): With cargoes, 28,934 of 53·7m. net tons; in ballast,
14,824 of 33·3m. net tons.

Post and Broadcasting. The length of telegraph circuits in Dec. 1978 was 1,591,000
km. The circuits of the telephone had a length of 27·4m. km. On 1 Jan. 1979 there
were 6·16m. instruments employed in the telephone service.
  Number of combined radio and television reception fees paid at the end of 1978
was 3,077,000, of which 2·21m. included extra fees for colour television; radio reception fees paid, 214,000. As from 1 April 1978, special sound broadcasting licences
were discontinued.
  Sveriges Radio AB is a non-commercial semi-governmental corporation, transmitting 3 programmes on long-, medium-, and short-waves and on FM. There
are also regional programmes. It also broadcasts 2 TV programmes. Colour programmes are broadcast by PAL system.
  The overseas radio-telegraph and radio-telephone services are conducted by the
Swedish Telecommunications Administration.
  The number of post offices at the end of 1978 was 1,988. For receipts of the post
and telecommunication services *see* the section on *Economy*.

Cinemas (1980). There were 1,189 cinemas.

Newspapers (1979). There were 161 daily newspapers with a total circulation of
4·9m.

JUSTICE, RELIGION, EDUCATION AND WELFARE

Justice. The administration of justice is entirely independent of the Government. The *Justitiekansler*, or Chancellor of Justice (a royal appointment) and the *Justitieombudsmän* (Judicial Commissioners appointed by the Diet), exercise a control over the administration. In 1968 a reform was carried through which meant that the offices of the former *Justitieombudsman* (Ombudsman for civil affairs) and the *Militieombudsman* (Ombudsman for military affairs) were turned into one sole institution with 3 Ombudsmen, each styled *Justitieombudsman*. They exert a general supervision over all courts of law, the civil service, military laws and the military services. In 1979–80 they received altogether 3,361 cases; of these, 140 were instituted on their own initiative and 3,211 on complaints. They dismissed 1,205 cases, investigated 1,424 without taking direct action, offered criticisms in 417 cases and instituted 6 prosecutions.

Bruzelius, A., and Ginsburg, R. B., *The Swedish Code of Judicial Procedure.* South Hackensack, 1968

Justitieombudsmännens ämbetsberättelse avgiven till Riksdagen. Annual. Stockholm

The Penal Code of Sweden: As Amended 1 Jan. 1972. South Hackensack, 1972

Rowat, D. C., *The Ombudsman: Citizen's Defender.* London, 1965

Rättsstatistisk årsbok (Year Book of Legal Statistics). National Central Bureau of Statistics, Stockholm, from 1975

The *Riksåklagaren* (a royal appointment) is the chief public prosecutor.

The kingdom has a Supreme Court of Judicature and is divided into 6 Courts of Appeal districts and 100 district-court divisions (*tingsrätter*). Regarding rent and tribunal cases the kingdom has an Apartment Appeal Court and 12 rent and tenancy tribunals.

Of the district courts 27 also serve as real estate courts and 6 as water rights courts. These district courts (or courts of first instance) deal with both civil and criminal cases. More serious criminal cases are generally tried by a judge and a jury (*nämnd*) of 4–5 members (lay judges); petty cases are tried by the judge alone. Civil cases are tried as a rule by 3 to 4 judges or in minor cases by 1 judge. Disputes of greater consequence relating to the Marriage Code and the Code relating to Parenthood and Guardianship are tried by a judge and a *nämnd*. When cases concerning real estate are being tried the court consists of 2 qualified lawyers, 1 specialist on technical matters and 2 lay assessors.

In trials by *nämnd* the judge decides the case except when the majority of the *nämnd* (at least 4 members of 5 or 3 members of 4) differs from him, in which case the decision of the *nämnd* prevails. The cases in Courts of Appeal are generally tried by 4 or 5 judges, but the same cases, which are tried with a judge and a *nämnd* in the first instance, are tried by 3 or 4 judges and a *nämnd* of 2–3 members (lay judges). The court consists in cases concerning real estate of a specialist on technical matters instead of one of the judges and in water-right cases of 3 or 4 judges and 1 or 2 specialists on technical water matters.

Those with low incomes can receive free legal aid out of public funds. In criminal cases a suspected person has the right to a defence counsel, paid out of public funds.

The Attorney-General (*Justitiekanslern*) and the Parliamentary Commissioner (*Justitieombudsmannen*) for the Judiciary and Civil Administration supervises the application in the public sector of acts of parliament and regulations. The Attorney-General is the Government's legal adviser and also the Public Prosecutor.

The holders of the office of Parliamentary Commissioner, now 4 in number, are appointed by Parliament.

There were 72 penal and correctional institutions for delinquents, with 3,203 male and 108 female inmates on 1 Jan. 1980. Besides, there were 18 institutions with 469 places for children and juveniles in need of care owing to viciousness, maladjustment or delinquency on 31 Dec. 1979.

Religion. The overwhelming majority of the population belong to the Evangelical Lutheran Church, which is the established national church. There were 13 bishoprics (Uppsala being the metropolitan see) and 2,575 parishes at the beginning of 1979. The clergy are chiefly supported from the parishes and the proceeds of the church lands. The nonconformists mostly still adhere to the national church. The largest denominations, on 1 Jan. 1979, were: Pentecost Movement, 97,203; Swedish Missionary Society, 80,768; Salvation Army, 35,622; Evangelical National Missionary Society, 25,106; Swedish Baptist Church, 21,678; Orebro Missionary Society, 19,545; Swedish Alliance Missionary Society, 13,210; Holiness Mission, 6,006; Methodists, 5,924.

There were also 91,856 Roman Catholics (under a Bishop resident at Stockholm), about 35,000 Orthodox Catholics (1978) and about 15,000 Jews (1978).

Parliament and Convocation (*Kyrkomötet*) decided in 1958 to admit women to ordination as priests.

Murray, R., *L'église Suédoise. Son Histoire et Son Organisation*. Stockholm, 1970

Education. By the Swedish Higher Educational Act of 1977 a unified educational system was created by integrating institutions which had previously been administered separately. This new *högskola* includes not only traditional university studies but also those of various professional colleges (state, local government and private) as well as a number of study programmes previously offered by the secondary school system. One of the goals of the 1977 university reform was to introduce an increased element of professional training into Swedish higher education. A Certificate of Education is awarded on completion of a general study programme. This certificate states the number of courses taken as well as the points and grades obtained on each course in the study programme.

In Dec. 1979 there were, in these new integrated institutions for higher education, *högskola*, 95,700 registered for undergraduate studies at general study programmes, that is programmes offering vocational education, usually of at least 3 years duration, and 64,000 registered at (*a*) seperate courses, that is short courses aiming to meet the need for further education and training, (*b*) specialized continuation courses, (*c*) local or individual study programmes. The number of registered students at each of the five sectors into which the general study programmes are organized is as follows: Education for technical professions, 22,800; education for social work and economic and administrative professions, 23,500; education for medical and paramedical professions, 22,200; education for the teaching professions, 22,800; and education for information, communication and cultural professions, 4,400. The number of students enrolled for post-graduate studies was 12,700.

In autumn term in the school year 1979–80 there were 677,000 pupils in primary education (grades 1–6 in compulsory comprehensive schools). Secondary education at the lower stage (grades 7–9 in compulsory comprehensive schools) comprised 366,000 pupils. In secondary education at the higher stage (the integrated upper secondary school), there were 225,000 pupils (excluding about 28,500 pupils in the 4-year technical group regarded as third-level education). The folk high schools, 'people's colleges', had 14,100 pupils in courses of more than 15 weeks.

In municipal adult education there were 152,000 pupils (corresponding to a gross number of 322,000 participants) and in state adult education there were about 23,000 pupils (of which 19,000 taking correspondence courses).

There are also special schools for pupils with visual and hearing handicaps and those who are mentally retarded (about 14,000 pupils in all).

Goals for Educational Policy in Sweden. OECD, Paris, 1980
Higher Education for Visiting Students.—Series Studying in Sweden.—National Board of Universities and Colleges. Stockholm, 1978
Gotberg, B., and Svard, S., *The Swedish 'Folk High School': Its Background and its Present Situation*.
Marklund, S. and Bergendal, G., *Trends in Swedish Educational Policy*. Stockholm, 1979
Paulston, R. G., *Educational Change in Sweden: Planning and Accepting the Comprehensive School Reforms*. New York, 1968
Stenholm, B., *Education in Sweden*. Stockholm, 1970

Social Welfare. The social security schemes are greatly expanding. Supported by a referendum, the Diet in 1958 and 1959 decided that the national pensions should be increased successively until 1968 and supplementary pensions paid from 1963. These pensions are of invariable value. In 1969 the Diet decided that as from 1 July 1969 an increment to the basic pension was to be paid to persons without supplementary pensions, and this amount is to be successively increased in a 10-year period. The basic and supplementary pensions consist of old-age and family pensions, as well as pensions paid to the disabled. The financing of the supplementary system is based on the current-cost method.

The most important social welfare schemes are described in the conspectus below.

Type of scheme	Intro- duced	Scope	Principal benefits
Sickness insurance (compulsory—current law, 1962)	1955	All residents	Hospital fees, most private doctors charge the insured person normally 30 kr., district physicians and doctors in hospitals charge the insured person only 20 kr. for full medical treatment, some reimbursement of cost of transportation as well as costs of physiotherapy, convalescent care, etc., medicines at reduced prices or free of charge. During sickness daily allowance 90% of the yearly income in between 6,000 and 104,250 kr. There is generally no maximum benefit period. Dental care is available to all residents from 17 years of age, the maximum payable by the patient being 50%.
Employment injury insurance (compulsory—current law, 1976)	1901	All employed persons	Medical treatment, medicine and medical appliances, hospital care, sickness benefit 100% of the yearly income in between 6,000 and 104,250 kr. (first 90 days covered by sickness insurance), disability annuities, funeral benefit and survivor's pensions.
Unemployment insurance (current law, 1973)	1935	Members of recognized unemployment insurance societies (about 70% of all employees)	80–195 kr. per day subject to tax.
Basic pensions (current law, 1962)			
Old-age	1914	All citizens	Payable from the age of 65 or, at a reduced rate, from the age of 60. 36,458 kr. per annum for married couples, 20,944 kr. for others (including the special increment of 12,628 kr. and 6,314 kr. respectively for those without supplementary pension); about half of them receive municipal housing supplement.
Disability	1914	All citizens	Payable before the age of 65. Full pension 27,258 kr. per annum (including the special increment of 12,628 kr.).
Survivors	1948	All citizens	Widow's pension is payable before the age of 65. The pension is 20,944 kr. (including the special increment of 6,314 kr.) but less for those who have become widows before the age of 50 and have no child below 16. Many of them receive municipal housing supplements.

Type of scheme	Intro-duced	Scope	Principal benefits
Survivors (cont.)			Child pension is payable before the age of 18. The pension amounts to 6,160 kr. (fatherless or motherless) and 9,240 kr. (orphans).
Supplementary pensions (current law, 1962) *Old-age*	1960	All gainfully occupied persons	Payable from the same age as the basic pension (*see above*). The pension is in principle 60% of the insured person's average annual earnings during the best 15 years except an amount corresponding to the basic pension and subject to a ceiling.
Disability	1960	All gainfully occupied persons	Payable before the age of 65. Full pension corresponds in principle to supplementary old-age pension.
Survivors	1960	All gainfully occupied persons	Payable to widow and children, before the age of 19, of a deceased person as a certain percentage of the deceased's supplementary pension.
Partial pensions (current law, 1975)	1976	All employees between 60–65 years of age	The pension is payable between 60–65 years of age. The insured must have reduced his working time by 5 hours on an average a week and the part-time work must thereafter comprise at least 17 hours per week. Furthermore the insured must have worked during at least 5 of the last 12 months and achieved a right to supplementary pension for 10 years after the age of 45. The partial pension is paid out by 65% of the loss of income in connection with the change-over to part-time work.
Parents benefit	1974	All resident parents in connection with confinement	Parents cash benefit of 37 kr. a day during 180 days. Employed parents entitled to daily parents cash benefit of 90% of the daily income (in between 6,000–104,250 kr. yearly) for 180 days. Maximum daily parents cash benefit 257 kr.
Special parents benefit	1978	All resident parents	Special parents cash benefit with the same amount as for parents cash benefit for care of each child during 90 days for the parents together until the child reaches 8 years of age or until the end of the child's first school year if that is later.
Children's allowances	1948	All children below 16	3,000 kr. per annum.
		Children at school 16–18	233 kr. per month during school-courses. Children at school (16–19 years) living more than 6 km from school may receive supplementary allowance of 140–345 kr. per month; other allowance income-tested up to 155 kr. per month and means-tested up to 215 kr. per month.

Total social expenditure, including also hygiene, care of the sick and social assistance, amounted to 122,664m. kr. in 1978, representing 32·2% of the GDP.

The Cost and Financing of the Social Services in Sweden, 1974. Stockholm, 1976
Modern Trends in Swedish Pension Systems. Stockholm, 1968
Socialnytt (Official Journal of the National Board of Health and Welfare). Stockholm, from 1968
Social Benefits in Sweden. Stockholm, 1974
Faramond, G. de, *La Suède et la qualité de la Vie.* Paris, 1975
Fors, Å., *Social Policy and How it Works.* Stockholm, 1972
Heclo, H., *Modern Social Politics in Britain and Sweden: From Relief to Income Maintenance.* New Haven, 1974
Michanek, E., *For and Against the Welfare State: Swedish Experiences.* Stockholm, 1964
Mollstedt, B., *Public Health in Sweden. Health Services, Environmental Hygiene and Health Education.* Stockholm, 1972
Rosenthal, A.-H., *The Social Programs of Sweden, A Search for Security in a Free Society.* Minneapolis, 1967

DIPLOMATIC REPRESENTATIVES

OF SWEDEN IN GREAT BRITAIN (23 North Row, London, W1R 2DN)
Ambassador: Per E. Lind.

OF GREAT BRITAIN IN SWEDEN (Skarpögatan 6–8, 115 27 Stockholm)
Ambassador: Donald Frederick Murray, CMG.

OF SWEDEN IN THE USA (600 New Hampshire Ave., NW, Suite 1200, Washington, D.C., 20037)
Ambassador: Count Wilhelm H. F. Wachtmeister.

OF THE USA IN SWEDEN (Strandvägen 101, 115 27 Stockholm)
Ambassador: (Vacant).

OF SWEDEN TO THE UNITED NATIONS
Ambassador: Anders I. Thunborg.

Books of Reference

Statistical Information: The National Central Bureau of Statistics (Statistiska, Centralbyrån, Fack, S-10250 Stockholm 27) was founded in 1858, in succession to the Kungl. Tabellkommissionen, which had been set up in 1756. *Director-General:* Lennart Nilsson. Its publications include:
   Levnadsförhållanden, årsbok (Living Conditions). Annual. From 1975.—*Rapport.* from 1976
   Statistik årsbok för Sverige (Statistical Abstract of Sweden). From 1914
   Siffror om Sverige (Sweden). From 1971. Also in English as *Sweden*
   Historisk statistik för Sverige (Historical Statistics of Sweden). 1955 ff. (4 vols. to date)
   Sveriges officiella statistik (Official Statistics of Sweden). From 1911. (With summary in French; from 1952 in English)
   Allmän månadsstatistik (Monthly Digest of Swedish Statistics). From 1963
   Statistiska meddelanden (Statistical Reports). From 1963
Ahlmann, H. W. (ed.), *Sverige, Land och Folk.* 3 vols. Stockholm, 1967
Andersson, I., *A History of Sweden.* Stockholm, 1962
Atlas över Sverige. Stockholm, 1953–71. [Publ. in separate parts dealing with population, economics, etc.]
Bastide, F.-R., *Suède.* Paris, 1969
Britten Austin, P., *The Swedes: How They Live and Work.* Newton Abbot, 1970
Courtier, E., *En Suède.* Montreal, 1970
Documentation on Sweden. Stockholm, 1976
Documents on Swedish Foreign Policy, 1973. Stockholm, 1976
Faramond, G. de, *Un Politique du Bien-Être.* Paris, 1972
Fleisher, F., *The New Sweden.* New York, 1967
Fullerton, B., and Williams, A. F., *Scandinavia.* London, 1972
Furer, H. B. (ed.), *The Scandinavians in America 986–1970. A Chronology and Fact Book.* Dobbs Ferry, 1972

Gullberg, I. E., *Swedish–English Dictionary of Technical Terms.—Svensk-Engelsk Fackordbok.* Stockholm, 2nd ed. 1977

Hancock, M. D., *Sweden. The Politics of Post-Industrial Change.* Hinsdale, Ill., 1972

Heilborn, A., *Travel, Study and Research in Sweden.* 6th ed. Stockholm, 1965

Mead, W. R., and Hall, W., *Scandinavia.* London, 1972

Nobel, The Man and His Prizes. Published by the Nobel Foundation. Stockholm, 1950

Nordic Council, *Yearbook of Nordic Statistics.* From 1962 (in English and one Nordic Language)

Nording, R., *Suède Socialiste et Libre Entreprise.* Paris, 1970

Parent, J., *Le Modèle Suédois.* Paris, 1970

Paul, W. W., *The Story of Scandanavia.* Cincinnati, 1971

Scobbie, I., *Sweden.* London, 1972

Stomberg, A. A., *A History of Sweden.* New York, 1970

Scott, F. D., *Sweden: The Nation's History.* Univ of Minnesota Press, 1977

Tomason, R. F., *Sweden: Prototype of Modern Society.* New York, 1970

Toyne, S. M., *The Scandanavians in History.* Freeport, 1970

Turner, B., *Sweden.* London, 1976

Sveriges statskalender. Published by Vetenskapsakademien. Annual, from 1813

National Library: Kungliga Biblioteket, Stockholm. *Director:* Lars Tynell.

SWITZERLAND

Schweiz—Suisse—Svizzera

Capital: Bern
Population: 6·3m. (1979)
GNP per capita: US$12,100 (1978)

HISTORY. On 1 Aug. 1291 the men of Uri, Schwyz and Unterwalden entered into a defensive league. In 1353 the league included 8 members and in 1513, 13. Various territories were acquired either by single cantons or by several in common, and in 1648 the league became formally independent of the Holy Roman Empire, but no addition was made to the number of cantons till 1798. In that year, under the influence of France, the unified Helvetic Republic was formed. This failed to satisfy the Swiss, and in 1803 Napoleon Bonaparte, in the Act of Mediation, gave a new Constitution, and out of the lands formerly allied or subject increased the number of cantons to 19. In 1815 the perpetual neutrality of Switzerland and the inviolability of her territory were guaranteed by Austria, France, Great Britain, Portugal, Prussia, Russia, Spain and Sweden, and the Federal Pact, which included 3 new cantons, was accepted by the Congress of Vienna. In 1848 a new Constitution was passed. The 22 cantons set up a Federal Government (consisting of a Federal Parliament and a Federal Council) and a Federal Tribunal. This Constitution, in turn, was on 29 May 1874 superseded by the present Constitution. In a national referendum held in Sept. 1978, 69·9% voted in favour of the establishment of a new canton, Jura, which was established on 1 Jan. 1979.

AREA AND POPULATION. Area and population, according to the census held on 1 Dec. 1960 and the census held on 1 Dec. 1970.

Canton	Area (sq. km)	Census population 1 Dec. 1960	Census population 1 Dec. 1970	Pop. per sq. km, 1970
Zürich (Zurich) (1351)	1,729	952,304	1,107,788	641
Bern (Berne) (1553)	6,887	889,523	983,296	143
Luzern (Lucerne) (1332)	1,494	253,446	289,641	194
Uri (1291)	1,075	32,021	34,091	32
Schwyz (1291)	908	78,048	92,072	101
Obwalden (Obwald) (1291)	492	23,135	24,509	50
Nidwalden (Nidwald) (1291)	274	22,188	25,634	94
Glarus (Glaris) (1352)	684	40,148	38,155	56
Zug (Zoug) (1352)	239	52,489	67,996	285
Fribourg (Freiburg) (1481)	1,670	159,194	180,309	108
Solothurn (Soleure) (1481)	791	200,816	224,133	283
Basel-Stadt (Bâle-V.) (1501)	37	225,588	234,945	6,338
Basel-Land (Bâle-C.) (1501)	428	148,282	204,889	479
Schaffhausen (Schaffhouse) (1501)	298	65,981	72,854	244
Appenzell A.-Rh. (Rh.-Ext.) (1513)	243	48,920	49,023	202
Appenzell I.-Rh. (Rh.-Int.) (1513)	172	12,943	13,124	76
St Gallen (St Gall) (1803)	2,016	339,489	384,475	191
Graubünden (Grisons) (1803)	7,109	147,458	162,086	23
Aargau (Argovie) (1803)	1,404	360,940	433,284	309
Thurgau (Thurgovie) (1803)	1,006	166,420	182,835	182
Ticino (Tessin) (1803)	2,811	195,566	245,458	87
Vaud (Waadt) (1803)	3,211	429,512	511,851	159
Valais (Wallis) (1815)	5,231	177,783	206,563	39
Neuchâtel (Neuenburg) (1815)	797	147,633	169,173	212
Genève (Genf) (1815)	282	259,234	331,599	1,175
Total	41,288 [1]	5,429,061	6,269,783	152

[1] 15,941 sq. miles.

Population (1979 estimate) 6,356,300.

The German language is spoken by the majority of inhabitants in 19 of the 25 cantons above (French names given in brackets), the French in 6 (Fribourg, Vaud, Valais, Neuchâtel, Jura and Genève, for which the German names are given in brackets), the Italian in 1 (Ticino). In 1970, 64·9% spoke German, 18·1% French, 11·9% Italian, 0·8% Romansch and 1·4% other languages; counting only Swiss nationals, the percentages were 74·5, 20·1, 4, 1 and 0·4. On 8 July 1937 Romansch was made the fourth national language; it is spoken mostly in Graubünden.

At the end of 1979 the population figures of the principal towns (and their 'agglomérations' or conurbations, estimate 1980) were as follows: Zürich, 377,300 (707,300); Basel, 183,200 (363,700); Geneva, 152,700 (327,100); Bern, 142,900 (282,400); Lausanne, 131,000 (225,200); Winterthur, 86,700 (106,800); St Gallen, 74,700 (85,900); Luzern, 63,200 (156,400); Biel, 57,200 (87,000); La Chaux-de-Fonds, 38,500.

The number of foreigners resident in Switzerland at 31 Dec. 1979 was 883,837. Of these, 180,836 were in Zürich canton, 98,669 in Vaud and 96,722 in Geneva.

Vital statistics for calendar years:

| | Live births | | | | | |
	Total	Illegitimate	Marriages	Divorces	Still births	Deaths
1977	72,829	...	33,032	...	...	55,658
1978	71,375	2,921	32,120	10,497	435	57,718
1979	71,986	3,190	33,987	10,394	412	57,454

The excess of emigrants over remigrants was: 1972, 882; 1973, 1,928; 1974, 2,087; 1975, 2,967; 1976, 3,873; 1977, 3,510; 1978, 3,209.

Historisch-Biographisches Lexikon der Schweiz. 7 vols. Neuenburg, 1919–34. (Also in French)

Früh, J., *Geographie der Schweiz.* 3 vols. St Gallen, 1930–38

Jacot, A., *Neues Schweizerisches Orts-Lexikon mit Verkehrs-Karte.* Lucerne, 1949

Leeman, Walter, *Landeskunde der Schweiz.* Zürich, 1939

CONSTITUTION AND GOVERNMENT. Switzerland is a republic. The highest authority is vested in the electorate, *i.e.*, all Swiss citizens of over 20. This electorate—besides electing its representatives to the Parliament—has the voting power on amendments to, or on the revision of, the Constitution. It also takes decisions on laws and international treaties if requested by 30,000 voters or 8 cantons (facultative referendum), and it has the right of initiating constitutional amendments, the support required for such demands being 50,000 voters (popular initiative).

The Federal Government is supreme in matters of peace, war and treaties; it regulates the army, the railway, telecommunication systems, the coining of money, the issue and repayment of bank-notes and the weights and measures of the republic. It also legislates on matters of copyright, bankruptcy, patents, sanitary policy in dangerous epidemics, and it may create and subsidize, besides the Polytechnic School at Zürich and at Lausanne, 2 federal universities and other educational institutions. There has also been entrusted to it the authority to decide concerning public works for the whole or great part of Switzerland, such as those relating to rivers, forests and the construction of national highways and railways. By referendum of 13 Nov. 1898 it is also the authority in the entire spheres of common law. In 1957 the Federation was empowered to legislate on atomic energy matters and in 1961 on the construction of pipelines of petroleum and gas.

National flag: Red with a white couped cross.

National anthem: Trittst im Morgenrot daher (words by Leonard Widmer, 1808–68; tune by Alberik Zwyssig, 1808–54); adopted by the Federal Council in 1962.

The legislative authority is vested in a parliament of 2 chambers, a *Ständerat*, or Council of States, and a *Nationalrat*, or National Council.

The *Ständerat* is composed of 44 members, chosen and paid by the 22 cantons of the Confederation, 2 for each canton. The mode of their election and the term of membership depend entirely on the canton. Three of the cantons are politically divided—Basel into Stadt and Land, Appenzell into Ausser-Rhoden and Inner-

Rhoden, and Unterwalden into Obwalden and Nidwalden. Each of these 'half-cantons' sends 1 member to the State Council.

The *Nationalrat*—after the referendum taken on 4 Nov. 1962—consists of 200 National Councillors, directly elected for 4 years, in proportion to the population of the cantons, with the proviso that each canton or half-canton is represented by at least 1 member. The members are paid from federal funds at the rate of 150 francs for each day during the session and a nominal sum of 10,000 francs per annum.

In 1980 the 200 members were distributed among the cantons[1] as follows:

Zürich (Zurich)	35	Appenzell—Outer- and Inner-Rhoden	3
Bern (Berne)	29	St Gallen (St Gall)	12
Luzern (Lucerne)	9	Graubünden (Grisons)	5
Uri	1	Aargau (Argovie)	14
Schwyz	3	Thurgau (Thurgovie)	6
Unterwalden—Upper and Lower	2	Ticino (Tessin)	8
Glarus (Glaris)	1	Vaud (Waadt)	16
Zug (Zoug)	2	Valais (Wallis)	7
Fribourg (Freiburg)	6	Neuchâtel (Neuenburg)	5
Solothurn (Soleure)	7	Genève (Genf)	11
Basel (Bâle)—town and country	14	Jura	2
Schaffhausen (Schaffhouse)	2		

[1] The name of the canton is given in German, French or Italian, according to the language most spoken in it, and alternative names are given in brackets.

At the elections held on 21 Oct. 1979 the following parties were returned to the National Council: Social Democrats, 51; Radicals, 51; Christian-Democratic People's Party, 44; Central Democrats, 23; Independents, 8; Protestant Party, 3; Liberal Democrats, 8; Communists, 3; Action Party, 3; Independent Socialists, 6.

Council of States (1975): Catholic Democrats, 17; Radicals, 15; Socialists, 5; Central Democrats, 5; Liberals, 1; Independents, 1.

A general election takes place by ballot every 4 years. Every citizen of the republic who has entered on his 20th year is entitled to a vote, and any voter, not a clergyman, may be elected a deputy. Laws passed by both chambers may be submitted to direct popular vote, when 50,000 citizens or 8 cantons demand it; the vote can be only 'Yes' or 'No'. This principle, called the *referendum*, is frequently acted on.

Women's suffrage, although advocated by the Federal Council and the Federal Assembly, was on 1 Feb. 1959 rejected, but in a subsequent referendum, held on 7 Feb. 1971, women's suffrage was carried.

The chief executive authority is deputed to the *Bundesrat*, or Federal Council, consisting of 7 members, elected from 7 different cantons for 4 years by the *Vereinigte Bundesversammlung, i.e.,* joint sessions of both chambers. The members of this council must not hold any other office in the Confederation or cantons, nor engage in any calling or business. In the Federal Parliament legislation may be introduced either by a member, or by either House, or by the Federal Council (but not by the people). Every citizen who has a vote for the National Council is eligible for becoming a member of the executive.

The President of the Federal Council (called President of the Confederation) and the Vice-President are the first magistrates of the Confederation. Both are elected by the Federal Assembly for 1 calendar year and are not immediately re-eligible to the same offices. The Vice-President, however, may be, and usually is, elected to succeed the outgoing President.

President of the Confederation for 1981: Kurt Furgler.

The 7 members of the Federal Council—each of whom has a salary of 203,000 francs per annum, while the President has 215,000 francs—act as ministers, or chiefs of the 7 administrative departments of the republic. The city of Berne is the seat of the Federal Council and the central administrative authorities.

The Federal Council is composed as follows (1 Jan. 1979):

Foreign Affairs: Pierre Aubert.
Interior: Hans Hürlimann.
Justice and Police: Kurt Furgler.

Military: Georges-André Chevallaz.
Finance: Willi Ritschard.
Public Economy: Fritz Honegger.
Transport, Communications and Energy: Léon Schlumpf.

Local Government. Each of the cantons and demi-cantons is sovereign, so far as its independence and legislative powers are not restricted by the federal constitution; all cantonal governments, though different in organization (membership varies from 5 to 11, and terms of office from 1 to 5 years), are based on the principle of sovereignty of the people.

In all cantons a body chosen by universal suffrage, usually called *der Grosse Rat,* or *Kantonsrat,* exercises the functions of a parliament. In all the cantonal constitutions, however, except those of the cantons which have a *Landsgemeinde,* the referendum has a place. By this principle, where it is most fully developed, as in Zürich, all laws and concordats, or agreements with other cantons, and the chief matters of finance, as well as all revisions of the Constitution, must be submitted to the popular vote. In Appenzell, Glarus and Unterwalden the people exercise their powers direct in the *Landsgemeinde, i.e.,* the assembly in the open air of all male citizens of full age. In all the cantons the *popular initiative* for constitutional affairs, as well as for legislation, has been introduced, except in Lucerne, where the *initiative* exists only for constitutional affairs. In most cantons there are districts (*Amtsbezirke*) consisting of a number of communes grouped together, each district having a Prefect (*Regierungsstatthalter*) representing the cantonal government. In the larger communes, for local affairs, there is an Assembly (legislative) and a Council (executive) with a president, maire or syndic, and not less than 4 other members. In the smaller communes there is a council only, with its proper officials.

Basler Handelskammer, *La neutralité suisse,* 1962
Bonjour, E., *Swiss Neutrality.* London, 1946
Huber, H., *How Switzerland is Governed.* Zürich, 1947
Hughes, C., *The Federal Constitution of Switzerland. Translation and Commentary.* Oxford, 1954
Hughes, C. J., *The Parliament of Switzerland.* Hansard Society, 1962
Marx, Dr Paul, *Systematisches Register zu den geltenden Staatsverträgen der schweizerischen Eidgenossenschaft und der Kantone mit dem Auslande.* Zürich, 1918. *Appendix,* 1934
Rappard, W. E., *La Constitution fédérale de la Suisse.* Zürich, 1948.—*Collective Security in Swiss Experience.* London, 1948
Ruck, Erwin, *Schweizerisches Staatsrecht.* Zürich, 1933
Silbernagel-Caloyanni, Alfred, *Suisse: Organisation Politique, Administrative et Judiciaire de la Confédération Helvétique et de Chaque Canton.* Paris, 1936

DEFENCE. There are fortifications in all entrances to the Alps and on the important passes crossing the Alps and the Jura. Large-scale destructions of bridges, tunnels and defiles are prepared for an emergency.

Army. Switzerland depends for defence upon a *national militia.* Service in this force is compulsory and universal, with few exemptions except for physical disability. Those excused or rejected pay certain taxes in lieu. Liability extends from the 20th to the end of the 50th year for soldiers and of the 55th year for officers. The first 12 years are spent in the first line, called the *Auszug,* or *Élite,* the next 10 in the *Landwehr* and 8 in the *Landsturm.* The unarmed *Hilfsdienst* comprises all male males between 20 and 50 whose services can be made available for non-combatant duties of any description.

The initial training of the Swiss militia soldier is carried out in recruits' schools, and the periods are 118 days for infantry, engineers, artillery, etc. The subsequent trainings, called 'repetition courses', are 20 days annually; but after going through 8 courses further attendance is excused for all under the rank of sergeant. The *Landwehr* men are called up for training courses of 13 days every 2 years, and the *Landsturm* men have to undergo a refresher course of 13 days.

The Army is divided into 3 field corps each of 1 armoured and 2 infantry divisions, 11 independent frontier brigades, 3 mountain divisions, and independent redoubt-, fortress- and territorial-brigades, organized in 4 army corps. Strength on mobilization: 580,000, and 621,500 reserves.

The administration of the Swiss Army is partly in the hands of the Cantonal authorities, who can promote officers up to the rank of captain. But the Federal Government is concerned with all general questions and makes all the higher appointments.

In peace-time the Swiss Army has no general; only in time of war the Federal Assembly in joint session of both Houses appoints a general.

The Swiss infantry are armed with the Swiss automatic rifle and with machine-guns, bazookas and mortars. The field artillery is armed with a Q.F. shielded 10·5 Bofors and field howitzers of 10·5 cm calibre. The heavy artillery is armed with guns of 10·5 cm and howitzers of 15 cm calibre. The armoured troops are equipped with the light French AMX, the British Centurion and a modern Swiss tank.

Air Force. The Air Force has 3 flying regiments, made up of 20 first-line squadrons with about 340 combat aircraft. The fighter squadrons are equipped with Swiss-built F-5E Tiger IIs (4 squadrons), Mirage IIIS supersonic interceptor/ground-attack (2 squadrons), Mirage IIIRS fighter/reconnaissance (1 squadron), Venom ground-attack (3 squadrons) and Hunter interceptor/ground-attack (9 squadrons) aircraft. Bloodhound surface-to-air missile batteries are operational.

Training aircraft are Pilatus P-2 and P-3 and Vampire; there are also communications and transport aircraft and helicopters. Personnel numbers, 3,000 regulars, 6,000 conscripts and 40,000 reservists.

INTERNATIONAL RELATIONS

Membership. Switzerland is a member of OECD, EFTA and the Council of Europe.

ECONOMY

Budget. Revenue and expenditure of the Confederation, in 1m. francs, for calendar years:

	1974	1975	1976	1977	1978	1979
Revenue	13,052	13,541	14,287	14,026	15,106	15,050
Expenditure	12,012	12,232	15,863	15,493	15,824	16,764

The public debt, comprising consolidated debt and flowing debt, of the Confederation on 31 Dec. 1977 amounted to 13,658m. francs. The floating debt in 1979 was 3,623·2m. francs.

Schweizerisches Finanz-Jahrbuch. Bern. Annual. From 1899
Staatsicchnung der Schweizerischen Eidgenossenschaft. Bern, 1976

Currency. The *franc* of 100 *Rappen* or *centimes* is the monetary unit. By law of 17 Dec. 1952, which came into force on 20 April 1953, the value of the franc was fixed at 0·20322 gramme of fine gold. On 10 May 1971 there was a revaluation to 0·21759 gramme of fine gold.

The legal gold coins are 20- and 10-franc pieces; cupro-nickel coins are 5, 2, 1 and ½ franc, 20, 10 and 5 centimes; bronze, 2 and 1 centime. Notes are of 1,000, 500, 100, 50, 20, 10 and 5 francs.

On 10 July 1979 the notes in circulation (of francs of nominal value) was as follows: In 1,000 franc notes, 10,024·2m. francs; in 500, 4,777·3m. francs; in 100, 6,737m. francs; in 50, 1,021·2m. francs, and in lower denominations, 1,201·2m.

Banking. The National Bank, with headquarters divided between Bern and Zürich, opened on 20 June 1907. It has the exclusive right to issue bank-notes. In 1979 the condition of the bank was as follows (in 1m. francs): Gold, 11,903·9, foreign exchange (currency), 26,391; currency in circulation, 23,761.

In 1976 there were 1,740 banking institutions with total assets of 347,710·5m. Swiss francs. They included 28 cantonal banks (79,376m. francs), 5 big banks (161,382m.), 225 regional banks (38,138m.), 185 other banks (43,267m.).

On 31 Dec. 1976 the total amount of savings deposits in Swiss banks was 73,903m. francs, with 11·2m. depositors.

National Bank: Bulletin mensuel.—Das schweizerische Bankwesen. Yearly. From 1920

Weights and Measures. The metric system of weights and measures was made compulsory by the federal law on 3 July 1875 and since 1 Jan. 1887 only metric units have been legal. By the federal law of 24 June 1909 the international electric units were also adopted.

ENERGY AND NATURAL RESOURCES

Electricity. In 1978 Switzerland had electrical power-plants with a capacity of 31,825m. kwh. The total production of energy amounted to 42,194m. kwh. in 1978–79 (Oct.–Sept.); 30,790m. kwh. were generated by hydro-electric plants.

Gas. The production of gas in 1979 was 52·55m. cu. metres (total consumption, 646m. cu. metres).

Minerals. There are 2 salt-mining districts; that in Bex (Vaud) belongs to the canton, but is worked by a private company, and those at Schweizerhalle, Rheinfelden and Ryburg are worked by a joint-stock company formed by the cantons interested. The output of salt of all kinds in 1979 was 384,691 tonnes.

Agriculture. Of the total area of the country of 4,129,315 hectares, about 1,057,794 hectares (25·6%) are unproductive. Of the productive area of 3,071,521 hectares, 1,051,991 hectares are wooded. The agricultural area, in 1975, consisted of 274,093 hectares arable land (including vineyards), 102,634 hectares artificial meadows and 660,776 hectares permanent meadow. In 1975 there were 136,708 farms with a total area of 1,055,627 hectares. The gross value of agricultural products was estimated at 6,402·7m. in 1975 and 6,685·9m. in 1977.

In 1975, 177,804 hectares were planted with cereals, of which 86,225 hectares were wheat; barley, 44,697; rye, 6,196; potatoes, 23,811; sugar-beet, 10,641; vegetables, 6,214; tobacco, 713. Production, 1978 (in 1,000 tonnes): Potatoes, 893; sugar-beet, 633; wheat, 384; barley, 215; rye, 44; tobacco, 1. Milk production (in 1,000 tonnes): 1960, 3,112; 1970, 3,204; 1976, 3,473; 1977, 3,511; 1978, 3,542; 1979, 3,666.

The fruit production (in 1,000 tonnes) in 1977 was: Apples, 260; pears, 112; plums, 46; cherries, 28·5; nuts, 6.

Wine is produced in 18 of the cantons. In 1979 Swiss vineyards (13,525 hectares) yielded 1,108,343 hectolitres of wine, valued at 410,706 francs.

Livestock (1979): 45,000 horses, 361,000 sheep, 2,038,000 cattle (including about 896,900 milch cows), 2,062,000 pigs, 6,337,000 poultry.

Forestry. Of the forest area of 986,668 hectares, 55,381 were owned by the Federation or the cantons, 631,077 by communes and 300,210 by private persons or companies in 1979. The utilization of timber, in 1978, was 4,026,088 cu. metres, of which 313,331 in state-owned, 2,640,745 in communal and 1,072,012 in private forests.

INDUSTRY AND TRADE

Industry. The chief food producing industries, based on Swiss agriculture, are the manufacture of cheese, butter, sugar and meat. The production in 1978 was (in tonnes): Cheese, 119,800; butter, 32,500; sugar, 98,582. There are 46 breweries, producing in 1978, 4·05m. hectolitres of beer. Tobacco products in 1978: Cigars, 388·91m.; cigarettes, 29,282m.

Among the other industries, the manufacture of textiles, wearing apparel and footwear, chemicals and pharmaceutical products, bricks, glass and cement, the manufacture of basic iron and steel and of other metal products, the production of machinery (including electrical machinery and scientific and optical instruments) and watch and clock making are the most important. In 1979 there were 8,944 factories with 678,179 workers. Of these, 36,682 were working in textile industries, 36,502 in the manufacture of textile goods and clothing, 62,263 in chemical works, 19,034 in the manufacture of stone and clay products, 91,738 in manufacture of metal products, 227,216 in the manufacture of machinery and 45,148 in watch and clock making and in the manufacture of jewellery.

Production in 1979 was: Woollen and blended yarn, 14,349 tonnes; woollen and blended cloth, 9,256 metres; footwear, 5·83m. pairs; cement, 3,933,664 tonnes; raw aluminium, 82,974 tonnes; chocolate, 62,939 tonnes. 30·35m. watches and clocks were exported.

Labour. According to the census of industries, 1975, the total working population was reduced to about 2·7m., of which 6·3% were active in agriculture and forestry, 44·7% in manufacture and construction and 48·9% in services. In all non-agricultural sectors there were 288,470 establishments (including 594 being shut down) with 2,537,738 occupied persons, divided in 159,289 occupants and 2,378,449 employees.

The main groups show the following numbers of gainfully occupied persons: Engineering, 254,185; retail trade, 228,751; construction 225,533; metalwork, 175,983; agriculture and forestry, 172,649; transport and postal services, 171,081; catering, 158,500; wholesale trade, 113,197; banking and insurance, 105,106; food processing, 103,306; textiles, 89,660; chemical industry, 68,975; watchmaking, 61,058.

The foreign labour force with permit of temporary residence was 320,112 in Aug. 1979. Of the number recorded 101,256 were Italians, 47,130 Spaniards, 44,548 Frenchmen, 26,581 Germans and 9,657 Austrians. 83,261 were construction workers, 43,189 metalworkers and mechanics and 44,313 housekeepers, hotel and restaurant workers.

The Swiss Federal Union of Administrative and Public Service Workers had, in 1979, a membership of 124,777. The Federation of Trade Unions had about 458,978 members.

Commerce. The special commerce, excluding gold (bullion and coins) and silver (coins), was (in 1m. Swiss francs) as follows:

	1973	1974	1975	1976	1977	1978	1979
Imports	36,589	42,929	34,268	36,871	43,026	42,299	48,730
Exports	29,948	35,353	33,430	37,045	42,159	41,779	44,024

The following table, in 1m. francs, shows the distribution of the special trade of Switzerland among the principal countries:

Countries	Imports from				Exports to			
	1976	1977	1978	1979	1976	1977	1978	1979
Federal Rep. of								
Germany	10,470·0	12,144·5	12,233·5	13,946·5	5,761·2	6,968·9	7,537·2	8,642·6
France	4,891·1	5,263·6	5,285·6	6,273·3	3,365·9	3,686·9	3,612·5	3,845·2
Italy	3,564·0	4,201·1	4,147·7	5,054·9	2,758·0	3,399·7	2,633·7	3,127·2
Netherlands	1,362·9	1,682·2	1,544·9	2,089·3	992·0	1,227·9	1,210·2	1,240·9
Belgium–Luxembourg	1,311·8	1,726·0	1,629·9	2,003·2	1,007·8	1,119·1	1,185·8	1,255·5
UK	2,482·7	3,148·0	3,377·6	3,754·9	2,181·8	2,400·4	2,869·3	3,090·9
Denmark	372·2	396·3	383·7	417·6	545·6	548·0	583·5	532·1
Irish Republic	70·1	83·2	100·0	114·7	66·5	68·0	104·7	113·5
EEC Total	24,524·8	28,644·9	28,702·9	33,654·4	16,678·8	19,418·9	19,736·9	21,847·9
Austria	1,511·4	1,629·3	1,649·4	1,830·0	1,972·8	2,245·2	1,938·8	2,010·9
Norway	167·2	196·0	151·9	178·9	473·1	502·3	395·8	373·1
Sweden	876·6	913·8	875·4	1,041·1	1,054·5	1,002·5	889·4	933·1
Portugal	130·5	134·8	104·7	127·6	356·2	371·4	324·8	339·7
Finland	201·9	238·4	230·5	274·0	389·7	348·5	288·4	326·3
Iceland	29·1	39·3	40·1	44·3	10·4	11·9	12·3	13·9
EFTA	2,916·7	3,151·6	3,052·0	3,495·9	4,256·7	4,481·8	3,849·5	3,997·0
Spain	397·6	432·8	440·0	490·9	894·1	847·8	763·3	840·8
Gibraltar, Malta	2·3	2·4	3·9	3·2	14·0	19·0	14·0	23·1
German Dem. Republic	51·7	59·0	55·9	56·4	212·6	213·5	196·0	242·7
Poland	88·1	104·9	142·5	137·7	444·9	438·2	334·3	320·5
Czechoslovakia	152·0	167·2	122·5	165·9	259·3	251·0	217·2	207·5

		Imports from				Exports to		
Countries	1976	1977	1978	1979	1976	1977	1978	1979
Hungary	170·4	148·6	159·9	150·7	268·3	310·2	325·4	285·3
Yugoslavia	124·4	132·5	124·8	154·1	505·8	602·2	540·1	587·9
Greece	52·4	64·7	56·5	77·0	248·9	287·4	252·5	294·2
Bulgaria	26·0	29·6	25·3	24·9	129·1	108·3	98·9	100·5
Romania	111·6	64·0	75·5	53·9	163·8	229·6	248·5	178·0
USSR	644·5	863·1	917·5	1,296·7	504·2	559·7	475·6	441·2
Turkey	134·6	106·9	92·3	94·4	281·6	274·5	239·4	175·7
Other European countries	2·6	3·3	4·0	4·2	15·4	20·2	17·7	24·3
Europe Total	29,399·7	33,975·5	33,975·5	39,860·3	24,877·5	28,062·3	27,309·3	29,566·6
Egypt	35·2	34·6	42·7	33·5	190·2	219·0	221·2	280·0
Sudan	23·4	13·3	11·2	4·1	24·4	39·7	40·2	49·8
Libya	91·7	94·1	190·5	258·6	193·7	190·6	188·6	89·7
Tunisia	6·6	8·4	7·6	56·0	32·5	42·4	33·3	35·8
Algeria	124·7	125·3	34·8	151·4	191·5	336·1	197·1	231·4
Morocco	28·7	28·7	27·7	28·3	97·8	100·7	85·0	73·7
Ivory Coast	29·0	39·3	54·6	37·9	30·0	70·1	52·1	44·4
Guinea	7·0	1·2	0·2	1·5	10·7	12·7	12·8	9·3
Ghana	31·1	24·1	55·8	42·8	44·4	119·9	137·8	23·5
Nigeria	215·3	193·1	118·1	137·0	274·1	391·7	421·4	263·2
Zaire	15·9	47·7	23·0	21·7	42·6	39·4	32·2	23·6
SW Africa	14·7	24·6	18·9	7·9	19·8	29·9	35·6	19·0
S Africa, Rep. of	69·0	127·0	109·1	142·8	371·1	350·4	362·4	382·7
Zambia	10·2	11·7	23·2	32·4	14·5	16·1	10·8	16·9
Rhodesia	19·1	20·4	19·5	11·4	5·0	4·6	3·3	3·6
Tanzania	3·9	6·8	6·0	7·6	15·5	24·7	19·9	20·3
Kenya	24·4	59·2	23·2	19·6	20·4	41·5	31·7	38·3
Other African countries	106·1	120·9	83·5	84·5	162·1	215·5	254·0	171·0
Africa Total	856·0	980·4	849·6	1,079·0	1,740·3	2,245·0	2,139·4	1,776·2
Syria	9·6	10·1	8·8	11·4	158·6	97·9	76·8	98·5
Lebanon	7·5	9·0	5·1	34·9	45·0	92·4	76·6	124·3
Israel	156·7	160·7	175·2	196·7	650·5	899·6	963·4	973·0
Iraq	0·2	0·1	0·2	0·3	146·7	187·2	220·3	229·6
Kuwait	25·0	7·4	14·3	24·8	103·6	147·8	164·4	132·5
Iran	192·3	237·5	145·9	79·3	761·3	870·3	686·2	368·0
Saudi Arabia	44·0	47·9	72·0	186·5	600·4	795·7	928·9	951·6
UAE	389·4	496·1	276·0	374·4	178·9	225·5	172·9	154·3
Pakistan	20·3	22·8	23·9	23·2	60·5	61·5	55·1	67·9
India	278·6	196·8	157·1	139·0	137·0	165·5	195·7	214·9
Thailand	47·3	60·2	52·4	107·3	59·5	77·5	71·1	87·2
Malaysia	21·0	33·4	25·7	41·1	28·5	43·3	40·3	52·4
Singapore	42·9	46·4	49·1	47·9	141·8	199·3	194·1	219·1
China	90·8	94·1	88·8	90·7	130·1	134·6	167·3	197·3
Hong Kong	323·6	366·4	323·6	378·9	567·8	651·1	766·1	800·7
Korea, Rep. of	74·8	103·2	103·6	107·5	73·2	142·4	111·2	172·1
Taiwan	100·0	124·3	86·0	86·0	97·5	69·1	173·2	267·4
Japan	971·4	1,289·8	1,220·2	1,338·6	1,010·2	1,018·6	1,185·0	1,300·4
Philippines	22·3	29·4	24·2	22·0	62·7	73·9	78·0	75·9
Indonesia	73·5	97·0	62·1	62·6	79·8	79·2	84·3	89·4
Other Asian countries	36·9	50·5	55·0	87·7	213·1	255·6	223·1	236·0
Asia Total	2,928·1	3,483·1	2,969·2	3,440·8	5,306·7	6,288·0	6,634·0	6,812·5
Canada	240·6	247·4	202·9	220·0	369·6	465·4	381·3	384·3
USA	2,520·2	2,887·8	3,170·8	3,048·8	2,521·2	2,768·4	2,974·2	2,992·8
Mexico	101·7	99·5	68·4	65·2	267·5	222·5	229·7	281·2
Guatemala	29·8	71·3	64·0	53·4	29·2	37·9	48·4	57·1
Honduras	21·2	39·3	28·6	29·9	5·8	9·9	13·0	9·7
Costa Rica	37·0	66·5	56·4	44·1	22·1	18·2	12·6	17·0

	Imports from				Exports to			
Countries	1976	1977	1978	1979	1976	1977	1978	1979
Panama	70·2	289·5	267·5	215·9	88·3	138·9	222·8	224·3
Cuba	12·4	19·1	10·6	12·7	24·4	62·3	57·5	43·5
Colombia	62·8	73·7	50·3	56·7	78·8	98·2	112·1	112·1
Venezuela	8·7	18·7	18·7	12·1	246·2	298·5	242·4	200·4
Brazil	166·1	230·7	143·9	210·4	538·7	426·9	446·7	483·8
Uruguay	21·4	16·0	17·2	14·4	19·8	21·9	16·9	30·6
Argentina	115·4	158·7	148·3	115·4	176·4	259·4	229·8	309·0
Chile	10·8	35·4	17·8	13·5	37·7	58·9	73·2	57·6
Bolivia	1·7	1·9	1·2	2·5	27·4	28·1	23·9	28·8
Peru	59·5	56·6	44·6	31·9	96·8	76·0	62·1	74·3
Ecuador	16·9	34·9	21·6	21·8	41·6	73·0	59·7	70·9
Other American countries	88·5	114·8	79·7	93·0	127·2	135·5	133·2	130·5
Australia and Oceania	102·5	125·3	93·1	88·4	401·6	363·3	357·3	361·3

Custom receipts (in 1,000 francs): 1975, 2,939,161; 1976, 2,833,305; 1977, 2,920,800; 1978, 2,989,707; 1979, 3,002,117.

Total trade between Switzerland (including Liechtenstein) and UK for calendar years (British Department of Trade, in £1,000 sterling):

	1976	1977	1978	1979	1980
Imports to UK	962,877	1,319,281	2,156,014	2,564,773	2,614,690
Exports and re-exports from UK	1,000,360	1,421,382	1,913,744	2,407,328	3,076,337

Federal Customs Office, *Statistique mensuelle du commerce extérieur de la Suisse*. From 1925.—*Statistique annuelle du commerce extérieur de la Suisse*. 2 vols. From 1840.—*Rapport annuel de la statistique du commerce Suisse*. From 1889
Handbuch der schweizerischen Volkswirtschaft. 2 vols. Bern, 1955

Tourism. Tourism is an important industry. In 1979, overnight stays in hotels and sanatoria were 31,861,000 (17·26m. by foreign visitors) and in other accommodation 35·46m. (12·8m.).

COMMUNICATIONS

Roads. There are (1978) 63,893 km of main roads, including 1,035 km of 'national roads' for motor cars only. There is a postal autobus service, which, in 1976, carried 53·7m. passengers. Motor vehicles, as at 30 Sept. 1979, numbered 2,577,194, including 2,154,274 private cars, 45,331 trucks, 120,427 motor cycles, 10,945 buses and 94,849 agricultural tractors and special cars.

Railways. Railway history in Switzerland begins in 1847. In 1978 the length of the general traffic railways was 4,991 km, and of special lines (funiculars etc.), 814·2 km. The operating receipts of general traffic lines amounted to (1977) 2,969,581,000 francs; operating expenses, 3,349,945,000 francs. Traffic was 52·15m. tonnes and 297·39m. passengers.

There are many privately-owned lines, the most important of which are the Bern-Lotschberg–Simplon (115 km) and Rhaetian (363 km) networks.

Aviation. In 1979 civil aviation on domestic and international routes carried 11,545,072 passengers, 323,607 tonnes of mail, freight and luggage.

The air transport organization Swissair (founded in 1931) in 1980 carried 178,000 tonnes of freight and 6,954,000 passengers. Swissair had a capital of 422m. francs on 15 May 1977. Its fleet consisted of 50 aircraft on 27 Jan. 1981.

Shipping. A merchant marine was created by a decree of the Swiss Government dated 9 April 1941, the place of registry of its vessels being Basel. In 1979 it consisted of 32 vessels with a total of 279,287 GRT. In 1979, 8,280,286 tonnes of goods were handled in the port of Basel.

Post and Broadcasting. In 1979 there were 3,930 post offices. On 1 Jan. 1979 there were 4,446,205 telephones, all integrated in one dial system.

Wireless communication is furnished by 3 main medium-wave stations and 1 short-wave station. There are 3 television studios and more than 100 transmitters.

TV programmes are financed by licence fees and advertisements. Advertisements are limited to 15 minutes each day. All stations are operated by the Federal Post, Telephone and Telegraph (PTT) services. Radio-telegraph circuits are operated by Radio Suisse SA, radio-telephone circuits by the PTT. Radio licences, 1979, 2,209,828; television licences, 1,937,450.

The total expenditure of the PTT in 1979 was 5,499·8m. francs, the total gross receipts 5,875·6m. francs.

Cinemas (1979). There were 486 cinemas with a seating capacity of 167,236.

Newspapers (1970). The number of daily newspapers was estimated to be 118 with a combined circulation of 2·5m.

JUSTICE, RELIGION, EDUCATION AND WELFARE

Justice. The Federal Tribunal (*Bundes-Gericht*), which sits at Lausanne, consists of 26–28 members, with 11–13 supplementary judges, appointed by the Federal Assembly for 6 years and eligible for re-election; the President and Vice-President serve for 2 years and cannot be re-elected. The President has a salary of 170,000 francs a year, and the other members 158,000 francs. The Tribunal has original and final jurisdiction in suits between the Confederation and cantons; between cantons and cantons; between the Confederation or cantons and corporations or individuals, the value in dispute being not less than 8,000 francs; between parties who refer their case to it, the value in dispute being at least 20,000 francs; in such suits as the constitution or legislation of cantons places within its authority; and in many classes of railway suits. It is a court of appeal against decisions of other federal authorities, and of cantonal authorities applying federal laws. The Tribunal also tries persons accused of treason or other offences against the Confederation. For this purpose it is divided into 4 chambers: Chamber of Accusation, Criminal Chamber (*Cour d'Assises*), Federal Penal Court and Court of Cassation. The jurors who serve in the Assize Courts are elected by the people, and are paid 100 francs a day when serving.

On 3 July 1938 the Swiss electorate accepted a new federal penal code, to take the place of the separate cantonal penal codes. The new code, which abolished capital punishment, came into force on 1 Jan. 1942.

By federal law of 5 Oct. 1950 several articles of the penal code concerning crime against the independence of the state have been amended with a view to reinforcing the security of the State.

Thormann, P., and Overbeck, A. (ed.), *Das Schweizerische Strafgesetzbuch*. Zürich, 1939
Williams, Ivy, *The Swiss Civil Code*. English version. Oxford, 1925

Religion. There is complete and absolute liberty of conscience and of creed. No one is bound to pay taxes specially appropriated to defraying the expenses of a creed to which he does not belong. No bishoprics can be created on Swiss territory without the approbation of the Confederation. The Society of Jesus and its affiliated societies cannot be received in any part of Switzerland.

According to the census of 1 Dec. 1970 Roman Catholics numbered 3,097,000 (49·4%) of the population; Protestants, 2,992,000 (47·7%) and others, 181,000 (2·9%). In 1960 Protestants were in a majority in 10 of the cantons and Catholics in 12. Of the more populous cantons, Zürich, Bern, Vaud, Neuchâtel and Basel (town and land) were mainly Protestant, while Luzern, Fribourg, Ticino, Valais and the Forest Cantons are mainly Catholic. The Roman Catholics are under 6 Bishops, viz., of Basel (resident at Solothurn), Chur, St Gallen, Lugano, Lausanne–Geneva–Fribourg (resident at Fribourg) and Sitten (Sion), all of them immediately subject to the Holy See. The Old Catholics have a theological faculty at the university of Bern.

Lampert, U., *Kirche und Staat in der Schweiz*. 2 vols. Freiburg, 1937

Education. Education is administered by the cantons. Before the year 1848 most of the cantons had organized a system of primary schools, and since that year elementary education has steadily advanced. In 1874 it was made obligatory for the whole country (the school age varying in the different cantons) and placed under the civil authority. In some cantons the cost falls almost entirely on the communes, in others it is divided between the canton and communes. In all the cantons primary instruction is free.

In most cantons there are also secondary schools for youths of from 12 to 15, gymnasia, higher schools for girls, teachers' seminaries, commercial and administrative schools, trade schools, art schools, technical schools, schools for the instruction of girls in domestic economy and other subjects, agricultural schools, schools for horticulture, for viticulture, for arboriculture and for dairy management. There are also institutions for the blind, the deaf and dumb and feeble-minded.

There are 7 universities in Switzerland. These universities are organized on the model of those of Germany, governed by a rector and a senate, and divided into 4 faculties of theology, jurisprudence, philosophy and medicine. In 1979–80 the Federal Institute of Technology at Zürich (founded in 1855) had 770 teachers and 7,176 matriculated students; the Federal Institute of Technology at Lausanne, independent of the university since 1946, had 211 teachers and 2,001 students; the St Gall School of Economics and Social Sciences, founded in 1899, had 136 teachers and 1,889 matriculated students.

University statistics in the winter of 1979–80:

	The-ology	Law	Eco-nomics	Medi-cine	Science	Others	Total	Teach-ing staff
Basel (1460)	163	831	479	1,660	1,074	1,416	5,623	588
Zürich (1523 & 1833)	198	2,461	989	2,920	2,046	5,702	14,316	1,575
Bern (1528 & 1834)	164	1,435	529	1,794	1,340	2,048	7,310	695
Genève (1559[1] & 1873[1])	93	896	653	1,469	1,270	4,953	9,334	791
Lausanne (1537[1] & 1890[2])	94	779	680	1,403	695	1,582	5,233	409
Fribourg (1889)	344	625	568	335	521	1,616	4,009	443
Neuchâtel (1866 & 1909)	40	242	195	75	409	926	1,887	211

[1] Founded as an academy.   [2] Reorganized as a university.

These numbers are exclusive of 'visitors', but inclusive of women students.

Social Security. The Federal Insurance Law against illness and accident, of 13 June 1911, entitles all Swiss citizens to insurance against illness; foreigners may be admitted to the benefits. Compulsory insurance against illness does not exist as yet, but cantons and communities are entitled to declare insurance obligatory for certain classes or to establish public benefit (sick fund) associations, and to make employers responsible for the payment of the premiums of their employees. In 1978 the 512 societies insuring against illness had 6,659,723 members.

Unemployment insurance is based since 13 June 1976 upon a Constitution amendment which stipulates unemployment insurance as compulsory for all wage-earners. A federal law was in preparation in 1976. At 30 Sept. 1975 there existed 123 public and private unemployment insurance organizations with a total membership (31 March 1977) of 1,435,577 (53·5% of working population).

Insurance against accident is compulsory for all officials, employees and workmen of all the factories, trades, etc., which are under the federal liability law. The Swiss Accident Insurance Institution commenced operations on 1 April 1918.

On 6 July 1947 a federal law was accepted by a referendum, providing compulsory old age and widows and widowers insurance for the whole population, as from 1 Jan. 1948. In March 1979 the number of normal pensioners was 941,688, the number of interim pensioners, 39,749. On 1 Jan. 1960 the old-age insurance scheme was extended to cover invalidity. In March 1979, 100,555 invalids received a regular annuity and 17,649 invalids an interim annuity.

DIPLOMATIC REPRESENTATIVES

OF SWITZERLAND IN GREAT BRITAIN
(16–18 Montagu Place, London, W1H 2BQ)

Ambassador: Claude Caillat.

OF GREAT BRITAIN IN SWITZERLAND (Thunstrasse 50, 3005 Berne)
Ambassador: C. S. R. Giffard, CMG.

OF SWITZERLAND IN THE USA (2900 Cathedral Ave., NW, Washington, D.C., 20008)

Ambassador: (Vacant).

OF THE USA IN SWITZERLAND (Jubilaeumstrasse 93, 3005, Bern)

Ambassador: Richard David Vine.

Books of Reference

Statistical Information: The Bureau fédéral de statistique (15 Hallwyl St, Bern) was established in 1860. *Director:* J.-J. Senglet. Its principal publications are:

Annuaire statistique de la Suisse. Bâle. From 1891
Statistique de la Suisse. From 1930
Contributions à la Statistique Suisse. From 1930
Bibliographie Suisse de statistique et d'économie politique. Annual, from 1937

Swiss Confederation
Annuaire; Budget; Message du Budget; Compte d'Etat (annual) *Feuille Fédérale; Recueil des Lois fédérales* (weekly)
Recueil systématique des lois et ordonnances, 1848–1947 (in German, French and Italian). Bern, 1951
Sammlung der Bundes- und Kantonsverfassungen (in German, French and Italian). Bern, 1937

Federal Department of Economics
La vie économique (and supplements). Monthly. From 1928
Législation sociale de la Suisse. Annual, from 1928

Behrendt, R. F. (ed.), *Strukturwandlugen der schweizerischen Wirtschaft und Gesellschaft.* Bern, 1962
Bonjour, E., Offler, H. S., and Potter, G. R., *A Short History of Switzerland.* Oxford, 1952
Dürrenmatt, P., *Schweizer Geschichte.* Zürich, 1963.—*Schweiz.* Zürich, 1962.—*Wir Schweizer und der totale Krieg.* Zürich, 1960
Imhof, E. (ed.), *Atlas der Schweiz.* Bern, 1965 ff.
Riklin, A., *et al, Handbuch der schweizerischen Aussenpolitik.* Bern, 1975
Sorell, W., *The Swiss: A Cultural Panorama of Switzerland.* Indianapolis, 1972. London, 1973
Tschäni, H., *Profil der Schweiz.* Zürich, 1967
Unser Schweizer Standpunkt 1914, 1939, 1964. Bern, 1964
Who's Who in Switzerland. Ed. H. and E. Girsberger. Zürich, 1952

National Library: Bibliothèque Nationale Suisse, 15 Hallwyl St, Bern. *Director:* F. G. Maier.

SYRIA

al-Jamhouriya al Arabia as-Souriya

Capital: Damascus
Population: 8·33m. (1979)
GNP per capita: US$930 (1978)

HISTORY. For the history of Syria from 1920 to 1946 *see* THE STATESMAN'S YEAR-BOOK, 1957, pp. 1408 f. For the union with Egypt concluded on 1 Feb. 1958, *see* THE STATESMAN'S YEAR-BOOK, 1961, pp. 1527 ff. On 28 Sept. 1961 a national revolution broke out, and on 5 Oct. President Nasser acknowledged the dissolution of the union. Syria was re-admitted to the United Nations (13 Oct.) and the Arab League.

AREA AND POPULATION. Syria is bounded by the Mediterranean and the Lebanese Republic on the west, by Israel and Jordan on the south, by Iraq on the east and by Turkey on the north. The frontier between Syria and Turkey (Nisibim-Jeziret ibn Omar) was settled by the Franco-Turkish agreement of 22 June 1929.

The administrative districts of Syria consist of the *mohafazets* of Damascus, the city of Damascus, Hama, Homs, Derá, Aleppo, Lattakia, Deir-el-Zor, Sweida, Hassakeh, Raqqa, Idlib, Kunaitra and Tartous.

The area of Syria is 185,680 sq. km (71,772 sq. miles), of which 35,000 sq. km have been surveyed. The census of 17 Sept. 1970 gave a total population of 6,304,685, showing about 10% less than the estimates. Estimate (1979) 8·33m. The 14 *mohafaza* (administrative districts) with population, 1975, are: City of Damascus, 1,042,000; Damascus, excluding city, 732,000; Aleppo, 1,523,000; Homs, 629,000; Hama, 514,748; Lattakia, 389,552; Deir-el-Zor, 332,000; Idlib, 428,000; Hassakeh, 532,000; Raqqa, 281,000; Sweida, 162,000; Derá, 282,000; Tartous, 348,000; Kunaitra, 19,000.

Principal towns (census 1970), Damascus, 836,668; Aleppo, 639,428; Homs, 215,423; Hama, 137,421; Lattakia, 125,716; Deir-el-Zor, 66,143.

Arabic is the official language.

CONSTITUTION AND GOVERNMENT. On 8 March 1963 a National Council of Revolution seized power, probably in collusion with the revolutionary junta in Iraq and President Nasser of Egypt.

Lieut.-Gen. Hafez al Assad seized power on 16 Nov. 1970 and formed a cabinet on 21 Nov. A provisional Constitution was published and on 16 Feb. 1971 a People's Council of 173 members was nominated by presidential decree. Lieut.-Gen. Assad was sworn in as President on 14 March 1971. On 12 March 1973 a plebiscite was held to approve a new Constitution.

President: Lieut.-Gen. Hafez al Assad (re-elected for further 7-year term in 1978).

Prime Minister: Dr Abdul Rauf al-Kasn.

National flag: Three horizontal stripes of red, white, black, with 2 green stars on the white stripe.

DEFENCE

Army. The Army in 1980 was composed of about 200,000 trained men, the *gendarmerie* of 8,000, the Bedouin Control Force of about 1,500 and the Palestine Liberation Army Brigade of 6,000. The USSR supplies technical advisers and equipment, which include over 2,000 tanks (600 T-62). The Army was organized (1980) into 3 armoured and 2 mechanized infantry divisions, 2 armoured, 4 mechanized, 2 artillery brigades, 5 commando and 1 parachute regiment and 32 surface-to-air missile batteries.

Navy. The Navy includes 2 small frigates, 14 missile boats, 8 torpedo boats, 1 minesweeper, 2 coastal minesweepers and 1 diving ship (all *ex*-Soviet) and the 3 patrol vessels (*ex*-French) transferred in 1962 to form the nucleus of the Syrian Navy. Personnel in 1981 totalled 2,500 officers and men.

Air Force. The Air Force, including Air Defence Command, is believed to have about 45,000 personnel and about 450 first-line jet combat aircraft, made up of about 250 MiG-21 supersonic interceptors, 45 MiG-23 and 60 Su-7 supersonic fighter-bombers and 50 MiG-17 fighter-bombers, supplemented by 20 Mach 3 MiG-25s and 30 variable-geometry Su-22s delivered in 1979. Training units have Soviet Yak-18 and Spanish-built Flamingo piston-engined primary trainers and Czechoslovakian L-29 Delfin jet basic trainers. There are also transport units with An-12, An-24/26, Il-14 and other types, and helicopter units with Soviet-built Ka-25s, Mi-4s, Mi-6s and Mi-8s, and French-built Gazelles. 'Guideline', 'Goa', 'Gainful' and 'Gaskin' surface-to-air missiles are widely deployed in Syria by Air Defence Command.

INTERNATIONAL RELATIONS

Membership. Syria is a member of UN and the Arab League.

ECONOMY

Planning. A 5-year development plan for 1960/61–1964/65 incorporated many of the features in the 7-year expenditure development project of 1955 and the 10-year plan of 1958 (*see* THE STATESMAN'S YEAR-BOOK, 1958, p. 1426, and 1961, p. 1541). The total expenditure in the second 5-year plan was estimated at £Syr.4,955m. The expenditure in the third 5-year development plan for 1971–75 is estimated at £Syr.8,120m. 19% of the total spent on Euphrates project, 4·3% on irrigation and reclamation, 6·3% on communication and transportation, 6·3% on agriculture, 22·7% on industry and mining, 17·6% on power and fuel, 7·4% on public services and 12% on internal trade.

Budget. The ordinary budget for the calendar year 1980 gave revenue at £Syr.29,000m. and ordinary and development expenditure at £Syr.29,000m.

Currency. The monetary unit is the Syrian *pound*, divided into 100 *piastres*. In March 1981, £1 = £Syr.8·56; US$1 = £Syr.3·93.

Banking. The Central Bank has the sole right of issuing currency. Other banks were nationalized in March 1963, namely, the Omaya Bank and its subsidiary, the Popular Mortgage Bank; the Orient Arab Bank; the Bank of Syria and Overseas; the Agricultural Bank; the Arab World Bank. Number of branches, 1973: Central Bank of Syria, 9; Commercial Bank of Syria, 22; Industrial Bank, 3; Agricultural Co-operative Bank, 50; Real Estate Bank, 3; Bank of Popular Discount, 27.

Weights and Measures. A decree dated 22 Aug. 1935 makes the use of the metric system legal and obligatory throughout the whole of the country. In outlying districts the former weights and measures may still be in use. They are: 1 *okiya* = 0·47 lb.; 6 *okiyas* = 1 *oke* = 2·82 lb.; 2 *okes* = 1 *rottol* = 5·64 lb.; 200 *okes* = 1 *kantar*.

ENERGY AND NATURAL RESOURCES

Oil. A branch of the Iraq Petroleum Co.'s oil pipeline from Kirkuk crosses Syria between Makaleb in the east and Nahr el Kebir valley in the west. The Iraq Petroleum Co. has constructed a new pipeline from Kirkuk to the small fishing port of Banias (south of Lattakia), which came into use in April 1952; the Trans-Arabian Pipeline Co.'s line to Sidon crosses southern Syria. Another pipeline is being constructed from the Karachouk oilfield *via* Homs to the port of Tartous.

On 8 Dec. 1955 the Syrian Parliament ratified a Supplemental Convention concluded with the Iraq Petroleum Co. By the terms of the Convention, Syria will receive an annual payment of approximately £6·5m. sterling as transit dues and a sum of £8·5m. in settlement of claims for back payment.

Search for petroleum in the Lattakia and Deir El Zor regions continues. Oil has been discovered in the Jezirah region. Crude oil production (1976), 11m. tonnes.

Minerals. Syria is poorer in minerals than in other resources, but this may be due to insufficient exploration.

Phosphate deposits have been discovered at two places near al-Shargiya and at Khneifis. Production, 1975, 857,000 tonnes; other minerals were salt, 34,000; natural asphalt, 31,000. There are indications of lead, copper, antimony, nickel, chrome and other minerals widely distributed. Manganese ore was mined before 1914. Sodium chloride and bitumen deposits are being worked. There is abundance of good calcareous building stone and basalt. Deposits of natural gas have been discovered in the Jezirah.

Agriculture. Syria is an agricultural country but is moving towards greater industrialization, the bulk of the population being engaged in the cultivation of the soil and in cattle breeding. In 1977 the irrigated area was 531,000 hectares; in 1975, 2m. hectares under cotton and 1,692,000 hectares were under wheat, 1,011,000 hectares under barley. The total cultivable area was 5·95m. hectares, including 455,000 hectares of forest and 8,631,000 hectares of steppe and pasture.

The Agrarian Reform Law of 1958, as modified by 1963, allows proprietors a maximum of 15–50 hectares of irrigated land and 80 hectares of uncultivated land, taking into account irrigation possibilities, rainfall, size of families, etc.

Yield of principal crops, 1975 (in 1,000 tonnes): Wheat, 1,550; barley, 597; cotton, 414 (ginned, 141·5); olives, 157; lentils, 66·6; millet, 14·5; sugar-beet, 14·5; tobacco, 12.

Livestock (1979): Cattle, 705,000; asses, 270,000; sheep, 7·6m.; goats, 1m.; poultry, 12·7m.

INDUSTRY AND TRADE

Industry. The most important industries are flour, oils, soap, cement, tanning, tobacco, textiles, knitwear, glassware, spinning, sugar, margarine, hosiery, footwear and brassware. Limited nationalization of certain basic industries was decreed in March 1963. On 3 Jan. 1965, 22 companies were completely nationalized, the owners of 61 companies were allowed to keep a quarter share and those of 24 companies to retain a tenth of their property.

Industrial production in 1975 included (in 1,000 tonnes): Woollen fabrics, 1,254; cement, 994; sugar, 117; cottoncake, 103; salt, 34; cotton yarn, 31·6; vegetable oil, 22·1; manufactured tobacco, 6·7. In addition, 3·7m. pairs of shoes were manufactured and 50,040 refrigerators assembled.

Commerce. In April 1965 a state trading company (SIMEX) was set up to handle the nationalized imports and exports.

Trade in calendar years in £Syr.1m. was as follows:

	1973	1974	1975	1976	1977	1978
Imports	2,342	4,571	6,173	...	9,719	8,935
Exports	1,341	2,914	3,441	...	4,199	4,160

Cotton is one of the chief exports (£Syr.502·4m., 1975). Others include oil, cereals, live animals and, since 1972, phosphates. Imports include industrial raw materials, machinery, chemicals and electrical equipment.

Total trade between Syria and UK (British Department of Trade returns, in £1,000 sterling):

	1976	1977	1978	1979	1980
Imports to UK	7,673	5,351	4,285	7,001	12,241
Exports and re-exports from UK	64,398	57,203	57,977	66,667	81,584

Tourism. In 1976, 1,389,079 tourists visited Syria.

COMMUNICATIONS

Roads. In 1975 there were 10,740 km of asphalted roads, 1,500 km of paved non-asphalted road and 2,364 km of levelled roads. The first-class roads are capable of carrying all types of modern motor transport and are usable all the year round, while the second-class roads are usable during the dry season only, *i.e.*, for about 9 months. The Nairn Transport Company operate a trans-desert pullman motor coach service between Damascus and Baghdad. There are also two pullman transport companies (Elkarnak, Syrian, and Jett, Jordanian) operating a joint service between Damascus and Amman. The motor vehicles registered at the end of 1975 totalled 100,972, including 11,125 motor cycles, 4,192 buses, 49,674 cars and 19,184 goods vehicles.

Railways. In Syria the following railways are open (in addition to those listed under LEBANON (p. 787): Standard gauge from Aleppo to Meidan-Ekbes (Turkish frontier), 116 km; Aleppo to Tel-Kotchek (Iraq frontier), 523 km; narrow gauge from Damascus to El Hammé, 195 km; Damascus to Dera'a (Jordan frontier), 130 km. Two lines have recently been constructed: a standard gauge from Akari to Tartous, 42 km, and the 755-km Aleppo–Kamechli, opened to traffic in 1976. Work is in progress on the Mhein–Palmyra line and the Akari–Homs–Damascus line; lines between Deir El Zor and Al-Boukamal, Palmyra and Deir El Zor, Lattakia and Tartous are planned.

Aviation. In 1975, 7,582 aircraft arrived at Damascus and Aleppo airports, disembarking 346,552 passengers and embarking 359,711. Syrian Air carried 480,000 passengers in 1976.

Shipping. The amount of cargo discharged in 1975 was 38,982,000 NRT and the amount loaded 38,532,000 NRT. A deep water harbour at Lattakia was built by a Yugoslav firm and in 1976 it was announced that further extensions would take place.

Tartous remains a fishing port and Banias is used as an oil terminal and loading port by the Iraq Petroleum Co. Ltd. Movement of vessels through Syrian ports in 1975:

	Cleared		Entered	
	Sailing	Steam	Sailing	Steam
Harbours	vessels	vessels	vessels	vessels
Lattakia	44	2,043	47	2,062
Jableh	1	1	1	1
Banias	37	594	40	601
Tartous	25	1,278	26	1,338
Erwad	128	233	134	240

Post and Broadcasting. An automatic telephone system has been installed in Damascus, and most other towns. Number of telephones (1978), 193,044; of these, 76,035 were in Damascus and 37,797 in Aleppo. There are 1·6m. radio sets.

Newspapers. There were (1977) 3 national daily newspapers in Damascus; other dailies and periodicals appear in Hama, Homs, Aleppo and Lattakia.

RELIGION, EDUCATION AND WELFARE

Religion. The population is composed mainly of Sunni Moslems and there are also Shiites and Ismailis. There are also Druzes and Alawites. Christians include Greek Orthodox, Greek Catholics, Armenian Orthodox, Syrian Orthodox, Armenian Catholics, Protestants, Maronites, Syrian Catholics, Latins, Nestorians and Assyrians. There are also Jews and Yezides.

Education. The Syrian University was founded in 1924, although the faculties of law and of medicine had existed previously. In 1975 there were 3 universities comprised of 25 faculties with 61,156 students. In 1974–75 there were 42,204 students at the University of Damascus; 15,805 at the University of Aleppo; 3,147 at the University of Teshreen.

In 1975, 6,760 primary schools had 34,995 teachers and 1,211,570 pupils; 1,050 secondary and intermediate schools, 20,479 teachers and 314,272 pupils; 58 vocational schools, 2,304 teachers and 21,211 pupils; 23 teacher-training colleges, 506 teachers and 5,913 students; 95 various schools and mining institutes, 4,449 teachers and 15,719 students.

Health. In 1977 there were 7,479 hospital beds (1 per 983 persons) in 31 state hospitals, 69 private hospitals and 4 sanatoria.

DIPLOMATIC REPRESENTATIVES

OF SYRIA IN GREAT BRITAIN
(8 Belgrave Sq., London, SW1X 8PH)

Ambassador: (Vacant).

OF GREAT BRITAIN IN SYRIA (Quarter Malki,
11 Mohammed Kurd Ali St., Damascus)

Ambassador: P. H. R. Wright, CMG.

OF SYRIA IN THE USA (2215 Wyoming Ave., NW,
Washington, D.C., 20008)

Ambassador: Dr Sabah Kabbani.

OF THE USA IN SYRIA (Abu Rumaneh, Al Monsur St., Damascus)

Ambassador: Talcott W. Seelye.

OF SYRIA TO THE UNITED NATIONS

Chargé d'Affaires: Mohammad Samir Mansouri.

Books of Reference

Statistical Information: There is a Central Statistics Bureau affiliated to the Council of Ministers, Damascus. It publishes a monthly summary and an annual Statistical Abstract (in Arabic and English).

Census of Population 1960. 15 vols. Ministry of Planning, Damascus, 1961–65
The Economic Development of Syria. International Bank Report. Baltimore, 1955
Asfour, E. Y., *Syria: Development and Monetary Policy.* Harvard Univ. Press, 1959
Barthélemy, A., *Dictionnaire arabe-français. Dialectes de Syrie.* 4 vols. Paris, 1935–50
Hourani, A. H., *Syria and Lebanon.* 2nd ed. R. Inst. of Int. Affairs, 1954
Petran, T., *Syria.* London, 1972

UNITED REPUBLIC OF TANZANIA

Capital: Dodoma
Population: 17·6m. (1979)
GNP per capita: US$230 (1978)

HISTORY. German East Africa was occupied by German colonialists from 1884 and placed under the protection of the German Empire in 1891. It was conquered in the First World War and subsequently divided between the British and Belgians. The latter received the territories of Ruanda and Urundi and the British the remainder, except for the Kionga triangle, which went to Portugal. The country was administered as a League of Nations mandate until 1946 and then as a UN trusteeship territory until 9 Dec. 1961.

Tanganyika achieved responsible government in Sept. 1960 and full self-government on 1 May 1961. On 9 Dec. 1961 Tanganyika became a sovereign independent member state of the Commonwealth of Nations. It adopted a republican form of government on 9 Dec. 1962.

At the end of the 17th century the inhabitants of Zanzibar drove out the Portuguese with the assistance of the Arabs of Oman. Thereafter an Arab governor from Oman was sent to Zanzibar, but the government of the interior remained in the hands of a local ruler. In 1832 Seyyid Said bin Sultan, ruler of Oman, established his capital at Zanzibar, and thereafter the whole of that island and the island of Pemba together with a large strip of the East African mainland coast came under his effective rule. Seyyid Said died in 1856. Five years later his former African possessions were, under an arbitration award made by Lord Canning (then Governor-General of India), declared to be independent of Oman. In 1887 the Sultan of Zanzibar handed over the administration of his possessions to the north of Vanga on the African continent to the British East Africa Association. These territories eventually passed to the British Government and are now part of Kenya. In 1888 a similar concession was granted to the German East Africa Association of the Sultan's mainland territories between the river Umba and Cape Delgado. In 1890 the German Government bought these territories outright for 4m. marks. In 1892 the administration of the Benadir Ports (which had in 1889 been conceded to the British East Africa Association) was, with the consent of the Sultan, transferred to the Italian Government in consideration of a quarterly payment of Rs 40,000. The Sultan renounced in 1886 in favour of Portugal all claims to the coast to the south of Cape Delgado.

In 1890 the islands of Zanzibar and Pemba were placed under British protection by the Sultan, Seyyid Ali bin Said.

On 24 June 1963 Zanzibar became an internal self-governing state and on 9 Dec. 1963 she became independent. On 24 June 1963 the Legislative Council was replaced by a National Assembly.

On 12 Jan. 1964 the sultanate was overthrown and the sultan sent into exile by a revolt of the Afro-Shirazi Party leaders who established the People's Republic of Zanzibar.

On 26 April 1964 Tanganyika, Zanzibar and Pemba combined to form the United Republic of Tanganyika and Zanzibar (named Tanzania on 29 Oct.).

AREA AND POPULATION. Tanzania is bounded north-east by Kenya, north by Lake Victoria and Uganda, north-west by Rwanda and Burundi, west by Lake Tanganyika, south-west by Zambia and Malawi and south by Mozambique. The census of Aug. 1978 gave 17,551,925 for the United Republic, of which 17,076,270 were counted in mainland Tanzania and 475,655 in Zanzibar. Estimate (1979) 17·6m.

Dar es Salaam is the chief port (population, 1978, 870,020). Dodoma in central Tanzania is now being developed as the country's new capital to be completed in 1983.

1170

A Ministry of Capital Development was established in 1975 to supervise gradual transfer of the government secretariat. Other towns include Mwanza (170,883), Tanga (143,878), Zanzibar Town (90,000), Arusha (88,155), Kigoma, Iringa, Morogoro and Lindi.

Swahili is generally spoken and understood throughout Tanzania.

CONSTITUTION AND GOVERNMENT. An 'interim constitution' was approved by parliament on 5 July 1965 and assented to by the President on 8 July 1965. A new Constitution was approved in April 1977.

The country is a one-party state. The Tanganyika African National Union and the Afro-Shirazi Party in Zanzibar merged into one revolutionary party, *Chama cha Mapinduzi*, in Jan. 1977.

The President of the United Republic is head of state, chairman of the party and commander-in-chief of the armed forces. The vice-president is head of the executive in Zanzibar and vice-chairman of the party; the Prime Minister is also the leader of the National Assembly.

The National Assembly is composed of 111 elected members, 32 Parliament Members from the Zanzibar Revolutionary Council, 20 Nominated Members from Zanzibar, 25 National Members representing regions, 15 National Members representing mass organizations affiliated to the party, 10 Nominated Members from the mainland and 25 regional secretaries who are *ex-officio* members.

In Dec. 1979 a separate Constitution for Zanzibar was approved. Although at present (1981) under the same Constitution as Tanzania Zanzibar has, in fact, been ruled by decree since 1964.

The Government was in Jan. 1981 composed as follows:

President of the United Republic: Dr Julius K. Nyerere (re-elected for a further 5-year term in Oct. 1980).

Vice-President: Aboud Jumbe. *Prime Minister:* Cleopa Msuya.

Foreign Affairs: Salim Ahmed Salim. *Defence and National Service:* Abdallah Twalipo. *Home Affairs:* Brig. Muhiddin Kimaryo. *Finance:* Amir Jamal. *Agriculture:* Joseph Mungai. *Justice:* Julie Manning. *Industry:* Basil Mramba. *Land, Housing and Urban Development:* Mustafa Nyang'anyi. *Labour and Social Welfare:* Alfred Tandau. *National Education:* Tabitha Siwale. *Commerce:* Ibrahim Kaduma. *Water and Energy:* Al Noor Kassimu. *Mines:* John W. Malecela. *Communication and Transport:* Augustine Mwingira. *Information and Culture:* Ben Mkapa. *Animal Husbandry:* Herman Kirigini. *Works:* Samuel Sitta. *Health:* Aaron D. Chiduo. *Natural Resources and Tourism:* Isaac Sepetu. *Ministers of State:* Timothy Shindika, George Kahama (*President's Office*); Aboud Aboud, Kighoma Malima (*Vice-President's Office*); Jackson Makweta, Abel Mwanga (*Prime Minister's Office*). *Without Portfolio:* Rashid Kawawa, Abdallah Natepe, Daniel Machemba.

National flag: Divided diagonally green, black, blue, with the black strip edged in yellow.

DEFENCE

Army. The Army consists of 1 tank and 1 engineer regiment, 9 infantry battalions and 9 artillery battalions. Strength, 50,000.

Air Force. The Tanzanian People's Defence Force Air Wing was built up initially with the help of Canada, but combat equipment is now being acquired from China. Personnel totalled about 1,000 in 1980, with about 8 F-7 (MiG-21), 9 F-6 (MiG-19) and 3 F-4 (MiG-17) jet fighters; 1 F28 Fellowship VIP transport; 6 Buffalo twin-engined STOL transports; 3 HS 748 turboprop transports; 1 An-2 light transport; 4 Agusta-Bell JetRanger and 2 Bell 47G light helicopters; and Piper Cherokee, Cessna 310 and F-2 (MiG-15UTI) trainers.

INTERNATIONAL RELATIONS

Membership. Tanzania is a member of UN, OAU, the Commonwealth and is an ACP state of EEC.

ECONOMY

Planning. The first 5-year plan ran from 1964 to 1969. The second plan for economic and social development ran from 1969 to 1974. The third 5-year plan starting 1977 envisaged small but actively growing industrial factories to manufacture small parts with the object of improving foreign exchange earnings.

Budget. Revenue and expenditure (in Tanzanian Sh. 1m.) for financial years ending 30 June:

	1975–76	1976–77	1977–78	1978–79	1979–80	1980–81 [1]
Revenue	4,390·2	7,883·0	9,556·2	9,523·0	7,270·0	9,200·9
Expenditure	5,888·9	7,228·0	9,556·0	12,267·2	9,100·0	9,342·0

[1] Estimate.

Import duties in 1978–79 amounted to Sh. 950m. and income tax to Sh. 1,574m. The main items of expenditure for the year 1969–70 were communications, transport and labour (Sh. 278·5m.), education (Sh. 56·2m.) and agriculture, food and co-operatives (Sh. 109·9m.).

Development expenditure, 1978–79, was Sh. 5,549m.

Total national debt on 30 June 1978 amounted to Sh. 962·8m.

Currency. The monetary unit is the *Tanzanian shilling* divided into 100 *cents.* The Tanzanian coinage has denominations of 5, 20, 50 cents., 1 Sh. and 5 Sh. Notes and coins in circulation at the end of Dec. 1978 were Sh. 3,143m. In 1966 the country left the East African Currency Board, establishing its own national currency, the Tanzanian shilling (£1 = Sh. 18·10 in March 1981).

Banking. On 14 June 1966 the central bank called the Bank of Tanzania, with a government-owned capital of Sh. 20m., began operations.

On 6 Feb. 1967 all commercial banks with the exception of National Co-operative Banks were nationalized and their interests vested in the National Bank of Commerce on the mainland and the Peoples' Bank in Zanzibar.

Weights. Tanzania has adopted the International System of Weights and Measures (SI), which has been introduced progressively since 1969. An important local unit of weight is the frasla (or frasila) = 35 lb. av.

ENERGY AND NATURAL RESOURCES

Electricity. A hydro-electric station on the Pangani River near Tanga has been built; £3m. of its estimated cost of £5·25m. is being provided by the Commonwealth Development Corporation. The second phase of the Kidatu power-station in Morogoro region is nearing completion; total power generated, 200 mw. Kiwira River power project, estimated to cost Sh.55m., has been completed, total capacity 24 mw. The Musoma power-station has also been completed with a capacity of 6 mw. The Mbeya-Iyunga power-station, capacity 12·5 mw, started in Nov. 1979, was nearing completion in late 1980.

Minerals. The value of mineral exports in 1976 was Sh. 550m. Principal exports, 1977, were (in Sh. 1m.): Diamonds, 181·3; gold, 50·9; salt, 12; gemstones, 1·8. New discoveries of coal and iron ore were made in the south while copper, cobalt, nickel and tin deposits have been found in Western Tanganyika. Gas, at shallow depths, has been found off the coast.

Agriculture. Production of main agricultural crops in 1978 (in 1,000 tons) was: Maize, 200; sisal, 188; cotton, 151; sugar, 100; coffee, 44·9; wheat, 34·5; tobacco, 23. Production of sisal has been declining since 1967. The Tanganyika Sisal Corporation has embarked on a diversification programme by introducing various new crops. Crops already planned are cardamon, beans, cashew nuts, citrus, cocoa, coconuts, cotton, maize and timber. Cattle ranching, dairying and twine spinning have also been introduced.

Zanzibar provides the greater part of the world's supply of cloves. There are about 40,000 hectares under cloves with about 1·5m. trees; five-sixths of the clove output is produced on Pemba. Cloves and clove oil (distilled from the stems) form more than half Zanzibar's exports. In recent years cloves production has decreased from an average annual figure of 12,000 tons to 4,000 in 1974 but reached 10,000 tons in 1976.

The coconut industry ranks next in importance. There are about 5·5m. bearing trees in both islands. Chillies, cocoa, limes, other tropical fruits and coil tobacco are also cultivated. The chief food crops are rice, bananas, cassava, pulses, maize and sorghum.

Livestock (1979, including Zanzibar): 15·3m. cattle, 3m. sheep, 4·7m. goats, 20·7m. poultry.

Forestry. In 1973 work continued on planting new areas with hard-woods and soft-woods. Hard-woods could be planted in old sisal estates that are now reverting to bush.

Fisheries. A Fisheries Development Co. is catching sardines and tuna for export. In 1976, 400 tons were exported valued at Sh. 3·5m.

INDUSTRY AND TRADE

Industry. Industry is limited and is mainly textiles, food processing, tobacco and brewing.

Commerce. Total trade (in Sh. 1m.):

	1974	1975	1976	1977	1978	1979
Imports	5,258	5,710	5,350	6,200	8,582	8,941
Exports	2,681	2,764	4,108	4,537	3,514	4,296

In 1977 imports (in Sh. 1m.) were: UK, 933; Federal Republic of Germany, 700; Japan, 700; USA, 287. Exports: Federal Republic of Germany, 795; UK, 675; USA, 600.

Major export items 1979 (in Sh. 1m.): Coffee, 1,228; cotton, 484; sisal, 253; cloves, 219; tea, 165; tobacco, 149.

Total trade between Tanzania and UK (British Department of Trade returns, in £1,000 sterling):

	1977	1978	1979	1980
Imports to UK	45,460	41,692	43,655	36,501
Exports and re-exports from UK	72,060	112,218	121,504	110,910

Tourism. In 1978 about 148,400 tourists visited Tanzania and spent Sh. 83·8m.

COMMUNICATIONS

Roads. Motor traffic is possible over 25,000 miles of road during dry season and at almost all times over 21,500 miles. In Zanzibar there are 279 miles of tarmac roads and 70 miles of all-weather unsealed roads; in Pemba there are 86 miles of tarmac roads and 184 miles of dry-weather earth roads.

Railways. On 23 Sept. 1977 the independent Tanzanian Railway Corporation was formed following the break-up of the East African Railways administration. The network totals 2,480 km (metre-gauge), excluding the Tan-Zam Railway 969 km in Tanzania (1,067 mm gauge) operated by a separate administration.

Aviation. There are 53 aerodromes and landing strips maintained or licensed by Government; of these, 2 are of international standards category and 18 are suitable for Dakotas. Air Tanzania Corporation provide regular and frequent services to all the more important towns within the territory and to Mozambique, Zambia, Seychelles, Comoro, Rwanda, Burundi and Madagascar. In 1976, 322,000 passengers and 4·3m. kg of freight were handled at Dar es Salaam airport. This airport and the one at Kilimanjaro can handle Jumbo-jets and 6 further airports are being modified to handle Fokker Friendship aircraft. In 1975 passengers for Dar es Salaam were 345,688 and for Kilimanjaro 92,335.

There is an all-weather landing-ground in Zanzibar and a smaller all-weather landing-ground in Pemba.

Shipping. In 1976 there were 1,586 ships of 5m. NRT.

Post and Broadcasting. In 1978 there were 74,264 telephones. There are 2 broadcasting stations and colour television operates in Zanzibar.

Newspapers (1976). There were 2 dailies, 1 Sunday newspaper, 2 fortnightlies and several monthly magazines.

EDUCATION AND WELFARE

Education. The educational system has been integrated on non-racial lines. Schools are maintained by the Government, private and agencies, including missions.

In 1980–81, 560,330 children enrolled to start primary school education.

Technical and vocational education is provided at several secondary and technical schools and at the Dar es Salaam Technical College.

There were, in 1980, 34 colleges of national education, including the college at Chang'ombe for secondary-school teachers and 170 secondary schools.

In 1980, the Dar es Salaam University had a total of 3,054 students. In the 4 years (1972–76) illiteracy was reduced to about 31%. The University of Dar es Salaam, independent since 1970, has faculties of science, law, arts, social sciences, medicine, agriculture, engineering, veterinary science and forestry.

Health. In 1976 there were 765 doctors and 25,000 hospital beds.

DIPLOMATIC REPRESENTATIVES

OF TANZANIA IN GREAT BRITAIN
(43 Hertford St., London, W1)

High Commissioner: Amon James Nsekela.

OF GREAT BRITAIN IN TANZANIA (Permanent Hse, Independence Ave., Dar es Salaam)

High Commissioner: Sir Peter Moon, KCVO, CMG.

OF TANZANIA IN THE USA (2139 R St., NW, Washington, D.C., 20008)

Ambassador: Paul Bomani.

OF THE USA IN TANZANIA
(National Bank of Commerce Bldg, Dar es Salaam)

Ambassador: Richard N. Viets.

OF TANZANIA TO THE UNITED NATIONS

Ambassador: Salim Ahmed Salim.

Books of Reference

Atlas of Tanganyika. 3rd ed. Dar es Salaam, 1956
Tanganyika Notes and Records. Tanganyika Society, Dar es Salaam. (Twice yearly, from 1936)
The Economic Development of Tanganyika. Report . . . by the International Bank. Johns Hopkins Univ. Press and OUP, 1961
Ayany, S. G., *A History of Zanzibar.* Nairobi, 1970
Ingle, C. R., *From Village to State in Tanzania.* London, 1973
Lofchie, M. F., *Zanzibar: Background to Revolution.* Princeton Univ. Press, 1965
Mwansasu, B., *Towards Socialism in Tanzania.* Univ. of Toronto Press, 1979
Nellis, J. R., *A Theory of Ideology: The Tanzanian Example.* New York, OUP, 1972
Nyerere, J., *Freedom and Development.* New York, 1976
Ommanney, F. D., *Isle of Cloves.* London, 1955
Samoff, J., *Tanzania: Local Politics and the Structure of Power.* Univ. of Wisconsin Press, 1975
Yu, G. T., *China's African Policy: A Study of Tanzania.* New York, 1975

THAILAND

Prathes Thai, or Muang-Thai

Capital: Bangkok
Population: 45m. (1979)
GNP per capita: US$490 (1978)

HISTORY. Until 24 June 1932 Siam was an absolute monarchy. On that date a *coup d'état* was effected and a Provisional Constitution Act was promulgated on 27 June. This was replaced by the constitution of 10 Dec. 1932, which in turn was superseded by new constitutions.

AREA AND POPULATION. The area of Thailand is 514,000 sq. km (198,250 sq. miles) and is bounded west by Burma and the Indian Ocean, east by the Gulf of Thailand, Democratic Kampuchea and east and north by Laos.

At the census taken in 1979 the registration gave a population of 45,221,625 (22,775,852 males, 22,445,773 females), of whom 30·4% lived in the Central region, 35·2% in the North-East region, 12·5% in the South region, 21·9% in the North region. Of the 1960 population, 1·6% were Chinese. Estimate (1979) 45m.

Vital statistics, 1979: Birth rate, 25 per 1,000 population; infant mortality, 56; death rate, 5 per thousand live births.

Bangkok Metropolis is the capital (population 1979, 4,870,509). Other towns (1979 estimate) are Chiang Mai (105,230), Nakhon Ratchasima (87,371), Khon Kaen, (80,286), Udon Thani (76,173), Pitsanulok (73,175), Hat Yai (67,117), Songkhla (65,523), Nakhon Si Thammarat (61,049), Nakhon Sawan (55,741).

REIGNING KING. Bhumibol Adulyadej, born 5 Dec. 1927, younger brother of King Ananda Mahidol, who died on 9 June 1946. King Bhumibol married on 28 April 1950 Princess Sirikit, and was crowned 5 May 1950. Children: Princess Ubol Ratana (born 5 April 1951), Crown-Prince Vajiralongkorn (born 28 July 1952, married 3 Jan. 1977 Soamsawali Kitiyakra), Princess Maha Chakri Sirindhorn (born 2 April 1955), Princess Chulabhorn (born 4 July 1957).

CONSTITUTION AND GOVERNMENT. The military government resigned on 14 Oct. 1973 and a new government was formed. New Constitutions were enacted on 7 Oct. 1974 and on 9 Nov 1977. However on 20 Oct. 1977 a further military *coup* took place in order to return more swiftly to democracy. A new Constitution designed to restore democracy was promulgated in Dec. 1978 and elections took place on 22 April 1979.

Prime Minister: Gen. Prem Tinsulanond.

Deputy Prime Ministers: Maj.-Gen. Pramarn Adireksarn; Gen. Serm Na Nakorn; Dr Thanat Khoman; Boonchu Rojanasathien.

National flag: Five horizontal stripes of red, white, blue, white, red, with the blue of double width.

Local Government. For purposes of administration Thailand is divided into 72 provinces (*changwads*), each under the control of a *changwad* governor. The *changwads* are subdivided into 576 districts (*amphurs*) and 80 sub-districts (*king amphurs*), 5,317 communes (*tambons*) and 49,841 villages (*moobans*). Local legislative and executive bodies with limited powers are being established with functions, procedure and method of election modelled on those of central Assembly.

DEFENCE. Under the Ministry of Defence Organization Act of 1960 the Ministry of Defence has assumed the Supreme Command and the control of the Army, Navy and Air Force with the advice of the Defence Council headed by the

Ministry of Defence. The National Defence College, the Armed Forces Staff College and the Military Preparatory School serve the education of officers. Each service has its own C.-in-C., service council, schools of arms and Command and General Staff College.

Under the Military Service Act of 1954 every able-bodied man between the ages of 21 and 30 is liable to serve 2 years with the colours; 7 years in the first reserve; 10 years in the second reserve; 6 years in the third reserve.

Army. The Army is organized in 6 infantry divisions (including 4 tank battalions), 1 cavalry division and 3 independent regimental combat teams with support units. Equipment includes light American armoured vehicles. Peace-time strength is 145,000.

Navy. The Fleet includes 4 frigates (1 modern built in Britain, 2 old *ex*-US, and 1 old *ex*-US destroyer escort), 2 corvettes (small frigates), 2 coastal minelayers, 4 coastal minesweepers, 6 new fast missile craft, 11 patrol vessels, 1 minesweeper support ship, 18 coastal gunboats, 18 coastal patrol boats, 8 landing ships, 9 landing craft, 32 minor landing craft, 10 minesweeping boats, 1 surveying ship, 3 surveying boats, 2 transports, 4 oilers, 3 training ships (old frigate, old corvette, old escort minesweeper), 18 coastguard vessels, 2 water carriers and 4 tugs.

This is an aged fleet, only 1 frigate, 2 corvettes, 6 missile craft and a few coastal patrol craft being under 10 years of age. Replacement of most of the other vessels is overdue.

Naval personnel in 1981 totalled 20,000, including the Marine Corps of 7,000. There is a Royal Naval Academy at Paknam.

At the mouth of the Chao Praya River are the Paknam forts. The naval dockyard was reconstructed; a large new graving dock was under consideration.

Air Force. The Royal Thai Air Force was reorganized with the assistance of a US Military Air Advisory Group. It has a strength of about 42,000 personnel, and is made up of a headquarters and Combat, Logistics Support, Training and Special Services Groups. The 3 squadrons of 1st Wing form the primary combat element, equipped with 37 F-5A/E supersonic fighter-bombers, some of the 38 OV-10C Bronco light reconnaissance/attack aircraft, and 24 T-33A/RT-33A and 4 RF-5A armed reconnaissance aircraft acquired from the USA. Six light attack squadrons in 2nd Wing operate the remaining OV-10Cs, about 45 T-28 armed piston-engined trainers, 16 A-37B light jet attack aircraft and 25 AU-23A Peacemakers, for security duties. There are transport units equipped with about 70 C-130H Hercules, HS 748, C-123 Provider, C-47 and smaller aircraft; training units with Airtrainer CT/4 primary trainers built in New Zealand, Italian-built SF.260MTs, T-37 intermediate and T-33A advanced trainers; and large numbers of helicopters for assault and rescue duties.

INTERNATIONAL RELATIONS

Planning. The Fourth National Development Plan, 1977–81 envisages a revival of the economy after the 1974–76 slump and a more equal distribution of income between the urban and rural population. Total investment envisaged 252,500m. baht.

Membership. Thailand is a member of UN, ASEAN and the Colombo Plan.

ECONOMY

Budget. Ordinary expenditures in 1977–78 (in 1m. baht): Defence, 15,809·4; agriculture, 7,528·7; communications, 7,053·7; education, 16,293; public health, 8,835·1.

Revenue in 1976–77 derived from taxes and duties, sales and charges and government enterprises, 81,000m. baht.

In March 1976 the national internal debt was 44,852·9m. baht. External debt in March 1976 totalled 4,859·4m. baht, including US$5,646·4m. and DM 616·9m.

Currency. The unit of currency is the *baht*, formerly called in English the *tical*, which is divided into 100 *satang*. Silver coins have gone out of circulation. Only nickel, copper, tin and bronze coins are now minted, in denominations of 1, 5 *baht*, 50, 25, 10 and 5 *satang*. Currency notes, first issued in 1902, now comprise, 5, 10, 20, 100, 500 *baht* notes.

On 31 March 1976 the total amount of notes and coins in circulation was 30,280m. baht.

In March 1981, £1 = 44·47 *baht*; US$1 = 20·50 *baht*.

Banking. In 1942 the Bank of Thailand was established under the Bank of Thailand Act, B.E. 2485 (1942) and began operations on 10 Dec. 1942, with the functions of a central bank. The Bank was organized on similar lines to the Bank of England, having its banking activities entirely separate from the management of the note issue. The Bank also took over the note issue previously performed by the Treasury Department of the Ministry of Finance. Although the entire capital is owned by the Government, the Bank is an independent body. Its gold and foreign-exchange reserves, at the end of Dec. 1973, amounted to US$1,082m.

In Jan. 1966 the Agricultural Bank and the Provincial Bank merged in the Krung Thai Bank (capital 105m. baht, of which 80% is owned by the Government).

Banks incorporated under Thai law include the Bangkok Bank Ltd, the Bangkok Bank of Commerce Ltd, the Bank of Asia for Industry & Commerce Ltd, the Bank of Ayudhya Ltd, Bangkok Metropolitan Bank Ltd, the Laem Thong Bank Ltd, the Siam City Bank Ltd, the Siam Commercial Bank Ltd, First Bangkok City Bank Ltd, Union Bank of Bangkok Ltd and the Wang Lee Chan Bank Ltd. Foreign banks include the Chartered Bank, the Hongkong and Shanghai Banking Corporation, the Mercantile Bank Ltd, Banque de l'Indochine, Bank of Canton Ltd, Bank of China Ltd, Bank of America, N.T. & S.A., the Mitsui Bank Ltd, The Asia Trust Bank Ltd, Bharat Overseas Bank Ltd, The Chase Manhattan Bank, United Malayan Banking Corporation and the Bank of Tokyo Ltd.

The commercial Thai banks had, in 1974, 846 branches in Thailand and 12 abroad; only Mae Hongson province has no commercial bank services. The deposits held by commercial banks in Jan. 1974 amounted to 73,480m. baht.

The Government Savings Bank, which was established as an independent organization in 1947, originated in 1913 when the Government Savings Office was established.

Weights and Measures. The metric system was made compulsory by a law promulgated on 17 Dec. 1923. The actual weights and measures prescribed by law are: Units of weight: 1 *standard picul* = 60 kg; 1 *standard catty* ($\frac{1}{100}$ picul) = 600 grammes; 1 *standard carat* = 20 centigrammes. Units of length: 1 *sen* = 40 metres; 1 *wah* ($\frac{1}{20}$ sen) = 2 metres; 1 *sauk* ($\frac{1}{4}$ wah) = 0·50 metre; 1 *keup* ($\frac{1}{2}$ sawk) = 0·25 metre. Units of square measure: 1 *rai* (1 sq. sen) = 1,600 sq. metres; 1 *ngan* ($\frac{1}{4}$ rai) = 400 sq. metres; 1 *sq. wah* ($\frac{1}{100}$ ngan) = 4 sq. metres. Units of capacity: 1 *standard kwien* = 2,000 litres; 1 *standard ban* ($\frac{1}{2}$ kwien) = 1,000 litres; 1 *standard sat* ($\frac{1}{50}$ ban) = 20 litres; 1 *standard tanan* ($\frac{1}{20}$ sat) = 1 litre.

Legislation passed in 1940 provided that the calendar year shall coincide with the Christian Year, and that the year of the Buddhist era 2484 shall begin on 1 Jan. 1941. (The New Year's Day was previously 1 April.) The years B.E. 2514–2518 therefore correspond to A.D. 1974 and 1975.

ENERGY AND NATURAL RESOURCES

Electricity. In 1977, steam power accounted for 55% of production (81% of the fuel being imported) and 29% hydro-electric. Only 20% of the population had access to electricity on 31 Dec. 1976

Oil. Extensive oil and gas exploration in the Gulf of Thailand is expected to produce commercial quantities in the early 1980s.

Minerals. The mineral resources are extensive and varied, including cassiterite (tin ore), wolfram, scheelite, antimony, coal, copper, gold, iron, lead, manganese, molybdenum, rubies, sapphires, silver, zinc and zircons. By far the most important are tin and wolfram. Ore output in 1978 (in tonnes): Iron, 88,121; manganese, 72,211; tin, 41,210; lead, 39,121; antimony, 6,759; wolfram, 5,815; lignite (1978), 638,942; gypsum (1978), 280,905.

Agriculture. The chief produce of the country is rice, which forms the national food and the staple article of export. The area under paddy is about 18m. acres. With the completion of the Chao Phya dam located near Chai-nat in 1957 the irrigable area in the Central Plain had by 1962 been extended to about 8,409,000 rai (3,363,600 acres). Additional projects now under construction will bring the irrigable lands to the total of about 11,605,900 rai (4,642,360 acres). Tank irrigation projects which were designed to ensure water supply for upland crop cultivation, especially in the north-eastern part, irrigate 325,418 rai (130,167 acres).

Output of the major crops in 1975–76 was (in tonnes): Paddy, 15·1m.; maize, 5·3m.; sugar-cane, 13·4m.; kenaf, 250,000; tobacco, 36m. kg; tapioca-root, 7·2m.; soybeans, 180,000.

Livestock, 1979 (in 1,000): Elephants (1967), 11,500; horses, 167; buffaloes, 5,500; cattle, 4,850; swine, 5,386; poultry, 65,324.

Forestry. About 60% of the land area of Thailand is under forest. In the north, mixed deciduous forests with teak (*Tectona grandis, Linn.*), growing in mixture with several other species, predominate. In the north-eastern section hardwood of the *Dipterocarpus* species, especially *Shorea obtusa* and *Pentacme Siamensis, Kurz* exist in most parts. In all other regions of the country tropical evergreen forests are found, with the well-known timber of commerce, Yang (*Dipterocarpus alatus, Roxb* and *Dipterocarpus* spp.) as the outstanding crops. Most of the teak timber exploited in northern Thailand is floated down to Bangkok. Some of them, however, are exported through the Salween into Burma.

About one-third of the teak-forest area is being exploited by the Forest Industry Organization, and the remaining two-thirds is to be worked by timber company lessees and other private enterprises.

Output of main forestry products in 1977 was (in 1,000 cu. metres): Teak, 138; yang, 900; other woods, 2,212; firewood, 1,057; charcoal, 287.

Rubber production (in 1,000 tonnes), 1955, 133·3; 1960, 170·8; 1968, 259; 1969, 281·8; 1973, 384; 1976, 393; 1977, 440; 1978, 470.

Fisheries. In 1976 the catch of sea fish was 1·5m. tonnes; of freshwater fish, 147,294 tonnes, and of marine prawns, shrimps and crabs, 160,000 tonnes.

INDUSTRY AND TRADE

Industry. Production of manufactured goods in 1978 included 5,004,490 tonnes of cement, 46,818 tonnes of white cement, 1,584,453 tonnes of sugar, 149·8m. gunny bags, 39,721 tonnes of paper, 23,905 tonnes of cigarettes, 95,363 tonnes of sweetened condensed milk, 15,830 tonnes of evaporated milk, 108·3m. litres of beer, 875m. sq. yd of cotton textiles, 887·2m. sq. yd of man-made textiles, 4,673,432 sheets of plywood and 1,166,614 sq. metres of vinyl tiles.

Trade Unions. The Thai National Trade Union Congress is a member of the International Confederation of Free Trade Unions.

Commerce. The foreign trade (in 1m. baht) was as follows:

	1973	1974	1975	1976	1977	1978
Imports (c.i.f.)	42,184	64,044	66,835	72,877	94,091	108,899
Exports (f.o.b.)	32,226	49,799	45,007	60,797	71,258	83,065

In 1978 the main items of imports were (in 1m. baht): Machinery, 33,636; mineral fuels and lubricants, 22,851; manufactured goods, 18,479; chemicals, 14,979; crude materials, 7,316; food, 2,846; beverages and tobacco, 1,013; animal and vegetable oil and fats, 272; miscellaneous commodities, 1,830.

In 1978 exports of rice were 1,606,732 tonnes (10,425m. baht); rubber, 442,191 tonnes (8,030m. baht); maize, 1,972,446 tonnes (4,275m. baht); tin, 28,943 tonnes (7,229m. baht); teak, 15,393 tonnes (253m. baht); jute and kenaf, 91,059 tonnes (448m. baht); tapioca products, 6,287,965 tons (10,892m. baht); shrimps, 15,378 tons (1,500m. baht); tobacco leaves, 34,811 tons (1,160m. baht); sugar, 1,090,050 tons (3,969m. baht); mung beans, 160,606 tons (1,160m. baht); fluorite, 205,697 tons (206m. baht); sorghum, 158,066 tons (370m. baht); cement, 22,607 tons (34m. baht).

Total trade between Thailand and UK (British Department of Trade returns, in £1,000 sterling):

	1976	1977	1978	1979	1980
Imports to UK	25,461	34,904	37,289	52,188	52,004
Exports and re-exports from UK	59,142	82,448	86,428	94,115	96,926

Tourism. In 1978 about 1,453,839 foreigners visited Thailand, including 331,321 neighbouring visitors and 1,122,518 overseas visitors.

COMMUNICATIONS

Roads. In 1978 the length of highways and provincial roads open to traffic was 25,065 km, of which about 13,226 km were concrete or asphalt-surfaced. Motor vehicles registered in 1975 included 248,561 passenger cars, 22,079 buses, 178,425 lorries and 456,651 motor cycles.

Railways. In 1980 there were 3,765 km of state railways (metre gauge) open to traffic.

The northern line runs from Bangkok to Chiang Mai (741 km), the extreme northern terminus. The southern line (990 km) runs from Bangkok down the Peninsula to the frontier station of Padang Besar, where it connects with the Malayan railway from Penang, and to Singapore. Another line (214 km) branching off from Haad Yai on the southern line runs along the east coast of the peninsula to Su-gnai Kolok, where it connects with the Malayan railway line. There are branch lines (totalling 190 km) to Song Khla, Nakhon-Si Thammarat, Kan Tang and Tha-Kanon. The extensions of the north-eastern line (264 km) from Nakhon Ratsima (Korat) to Nong Khai (360 km) and from Kaeng Koi to Buayai (250 km) have been completed. The Nakhon Ratsima–Ubol line (311 km) has been completed as far as Ubol Rat Thani. The eastern line (255 km) runs from Makkasan to Aran Pradet on the Kampuchea frontier. The northern and southern railway systems are linked by a railway bridge over the Menam Chao Phya, and both systems terminate in Bangkok. All state railways are under one management.

Aviation. Thai Airways Co. Ltd (TAC), established in 1947, is the sole Thai air transport enterprise, with authorized capital of 300m. baht. The Company operates 11 domestic routes and 3 international routes. On 24 Aug. 1959 Thai Airways and the Scandinavian Airlines System set up a new company, Thai International Airways, to operate the international air services from Thailand.

Shipping. In 1977, 2,449 vessels of 10,606,677 NRT entered and 2,712 of 9,677,801 NRT cleared the port of Bangkok.

The port of Bangkok, about 30 km from the mouth of the Chao Phya River, is capable of berthing ocean-going vessels of 10,000 gross tons and 28 ft draught. Bangkok is now a port of entry for Laos, and goods arriving in transit are sent up by rail to Nong Khai and ferried across the river Mekhong to Vientiane.

In 1973 there were 3 Thai steamship companies: Thai Navigation Co. Ltd (7 vessels); Thai Maritime Navigation Co. Ltd (3 vessels); Thai Lines Ltd (10 vessels). There are also 40 foreign steamship lines serving the port.

Post and Broadcasting. In 1974 there were 555 post offices proper, 341 licensed and Amphur post offices and 545 railway-station post offices. In 1967, the length of telegraph lines was 21,203 km. In 1979 there were 427,588 telephones, of which 318,613 were in Bangkok.

A ground satellite station at Sriracha, Chon Buri was completed in 1968. It provides a 24-hour service for telecommunications to all parts of the world and also receives and transmits live television programmes to and from other countries. The second station, at the same site, was opened in April 1970 and covers the Indian ocean. In 1979, there were 235 radio stations and 4 television stations.

Cinemas (1978). There were 366 cinemas with a seating capacity of 263,738.

Newspapers (1979). There are 20 daily newspapers in Bangkok, including 4 in English and 5 in Chinese, with a combined circulation of more than 800,000.

JUSTICE, RELIGION, EDUCATION AND WELFARE

Justice. The judicial power is exercised in the name of the King, by (a) courts of first instance, (b) the court of appeal (*Uthorn*) and (c) the Supreme Court (*Dika*). The

King appoints, transfers and dismisses judges, who are independent in conducting trials and giving judgment in accordance with the law.

Courts of first instance are subdivided into 20 magistrates' courts (*Kwaeng*) with limited civil and minor criminal jurisdiction; 85 provincial courts (*Changwad*) with unlimited civil and criminal jurisdiction; the criminal and civil courts with exclusive jurisdiction in Bangkok; the central juvenile courts for persons under 18 years of age in Bangkok.

The court of appeal exercises appellate jurisdiction in civil and criminal cases from all courts of first instance. From it appeals lie to Dika Court on any point of law and, in certain cases, on questions of fact.

The Supreme Court is the supreme tribunal of the land. Besides its normal appellate jurisdiction in civil and criminal matters, it has semi-original jurisdiction over general election petitions. The decisions of Dika Court are final. Every person has the right to present a petition to the Government who will deal with all matters of grievance.

Religion. About 94% of the population are Buddhists, 4% Moslems, 2% Christians, Hindus and others.

Education. Primary education is compulsory for children between the ages of 7–14 and free in local municipal schools. In 1977 there were 7,196,223 students enrolled in 31,516 government schools and 1,134,138 in 2,422 private schools. There were 43 teachers' training schools with 4,588 teachers and 146,966 students and 179 government vocational schools with 7,680 teachers and 130,079 students. In 1978 there were 12 universities: Chulalongkorn University (1917), Thammasat University (1934), Universities of Medical Science, Agriculture and Fine Arts; Ramkamhaeng University (1971)—all in Bangkok; Chiengmai University (1964), the Khon Kaen University (1966) in the north-east and Prince of Songkhla University (1968) in the south.

The literacy of the population 10 years of age and over was 70·8% in 1960 (53·7% in 1947).

Health. In 1976 there were 3,833 hospitals and health centres throughout the country. In 1976 there were 5,210 physicians, 925 dentists and 1,978 pharmacists.

DIPLOMATIC REPRESENTATIVES

OF THAILAND IN GREAT BRITAIN (30 Queen's Gate, London, SW7 5JB)

Ambassador: Phan Wannamethee (accredited 19 Dec. 1977).

OF GREAT BRITAIN IN THAILAND (Wireless Rd., Bangkok)

Ambassador: John Peter Tripp, CMG.

OF THAILAND IN THE USA (2300 Kalorama Rd., NW, Washington, D.C., 20008)

Ambassador: Prok Amaranond.

OF THE USA IN THAILAND (95 Wireless Rd., Bangkok)

Ambassador: Morton I. Abramowitz.

OF THAILAND TO THE UNITED NATIONS

Ambassador: M. L. Birabhongse Kasemsri.

Books of Reference

Thailand into the 80's. Office of the Prime Minister, Bangkok, 1979
Thailand Statistical Yearbook 1978. National Statistical Office, Bangkok
Thailand: Facts and Figures. Government's Public Relations Department, Bangkok, 1974
Thailand in Brief. Government's Public Relations Department, Bangkok, 1977
Thailand Official Yearbook 1968. Government Printer, Bangkok

Bibliography of Materials About Thailand in Western Languages. Chulalongkorn University, Bangkok, 1960

Douner, W., *The Five Faces of Thailand.* Hamburg and London, 1978

Exell, F. K., *The Land and People of Thailand.* London, 1960

Haas, M. R., *Thai–English Student's Dictionary.* OUP, 1966

Kirkup, J., *Bangkok.* London, 1968

Muscat, R. J., *Development Strategy in Thailand: A Case Study of Economic Modernization.* London, 1966

Phloyphrom, P., *Modern Standard Thai–English Dictionary.* Bangkok, 1958

Silcock, T. H. (ed.), *Thailand: Social and Economic Studies.* Canberra, 1967

TOGO

República Togolaise

Capital: Lomé
Population: 2·47m. (1979)
GNP per capita: US$320 (1978)

HISTORY. The Republic of Togo became independent on 27 April 1960, after having been a German protectorate (1894–1914, subsequently divided between the French and the British), a mandate of the League of Nations (20 July 1922) and a trusteeship territory of the United Nations (14 Dec. 1946).

On 28 Oct. 1956 a plebiscite was held to determine the status of the territory. Out of 438,175 registered voters, 313,458 voted for an autonomous republic within the French Union and the end of the trusteeship system. The trusteeship was abolished on the achievement of independence on 27 April 1960.

On 13 Jan. 1963 the President Sylvanus Olympio was murdered by n.c.o.s. of the army. Nicolas Grunitzky, a former prime minister and Olympio's brother-in-law, was appointed President of the Republic and head of government. On 13 Jan. 1967 in a bloodless *coup* the army under Col. Etienne Eyadéma made President Grunitzky 'voluntarily withdraw'. On 14 April 1967 Col. Eyadéma assumed the offices of President and Defence.

AREA AND POPULATION. Togo is bounded north by Upper Volta, east by Dahomey, south by the Bight of Benin and west by Ghana. Area, about 56,000 sq. km. The population of Togo in 1977 was 2,348,000. The capital is Lomé (population, 1979, 247,000), other towns being Sokodé (33,500), Palimé (25,500), Atakpamé (21,800), Bassari (17,500), Tsévié (15,900) and Anécho (13,300).

The southern part of Togo is peopled by tribes using several different languages, of which the principal are Ewe and Mina; these may be regarded as an offshoot of the Bantu peoples. The northern half contains, ethnologically, a totally different population descended largely from Hamitic tribes and speaking a fairly large number of different languages, of which Dagomba, Tim and Cabrais are the most important.

CONSTITUTION AND GOVERNMENT. Following approval in a referendum on 30 Dec. 1979, a new Constitution came into force on 13 Jan. 1980, when the Third Togolese Republic was proclaimed. It provides for an Executive President, directly elected for a 7-year term, and for a National Assembly of 67 deputies, elected on a regional list system, elections were held on 30 Dec. 1979.

All candidates are nominated by the *Rassemblement du peuple togolais*, the sole legal Party since 1969; it is administered by a 33-member Central Committee and a 9-member Political Bureau appointed by the President.

The government in June 1980 was composed as follows:

President, Minister of Defence: Gen. Gnassingbe Eyadéma.

Foreign Affairs: Dr Anani Kuma Akakpo-Ahianyo. *Planning and Administrative Reform:* Koudjolou Dogo. *Interior and Information:* Kpotivi Tevi-Djidjogbe Lacle. *Youth, Culture and Sports:* Koffi Voule-Frititi. *Economy and Finance:* Tete Tevi Benissan. *Public Works, Mines, Energy and Hydraulic Resources:* Barry Moussa Barque. *Rural Planning:* Samon Kortho. *Health:* Hodabalo Bodjona. *National Education:* Vigniko Amede-gnato. *Higher Education:* Boumbera Alassounouma. *Rural Development:* Anani Gassou. *Industries and State Enterprises:* Kwasivi Kpetigo. *Commerce and Transport:* Koffi Douala. *Social Affairs:* Abra Amedome. *Labour and Civil Service:* Komla Tsatsu. *Justice:* Akanyo Awouner Kodjovi.

National flag: Five horizontal stripes of green and yellow, a red quarter with a white star.

Local government: There are 4 regions (Maritime, Des Plateaux, Centrale and Des Savanes), each under an inspector appointed by the President; they are divided into

19 *circonscriptions*, each administered by a district chief assisted by an elected district council.

DEFENCE

Army. The Army consists of 3 infantry, 2 parachute and 1 commando battalion of 3,400 men. There is also a para-military force of about 1,500.

Navy. In 1981 there were 2 patrol craft and a naval base at Lomé. Personnel, 200.

Air Force. An Air Force, established with French assistance, has 6 Brazilian-built EMB-326 Xavante (Aermacchi MB.326) armed jet trainers; 1 four-turboprop Hercules, 1 twin-turbofan F28 Fellowship, 2 turboprop Buffalo and 2 C-47 transports; 2 Cessna Skymaster and 1 Do27 communications aircraft; 5 Magister jet trainers; 1 Puma and 1 Lama helicopter. On order are 5 Alpha Jet advanced trainers, with strike capacity.

INTERNATIONAL RELATIONS

Membership. Togo is a member of UN, OAU and is an ACP state of EEC.

ECONOMY

Planning. A first 5-year development plan (1966–70) was adopted by the National Assembly in 1965. A second 5-year development plan (1971–75) aimed at economic independence and the third (1976–80) provides for investment of 250,600m. francs CFA primarily in industry and rural development.

Budget. The ordinary budget for 1980 balanced at 67,000m. francs CFA.

Currency. The unit of currency is the *franc CFA* divided into 100 centimes. The rate of exchange (March 1981) was 552·6 francs CFA to £1.

Banking. In Dec. 1966 the Crédit du Togo was reorganized as a national development bank, named Banque Togolaise de Développement, with a capital of 300m. francs CFA (1,000m. in 1979), of which the Government's share is 60%.

NATURAL RESOURCES

Minerals. A Mines Department was set up in 1953 after the discovery of very rich deposits of phosphate and bauxite; mining began in 1961. Output of phosphate rock (1977) 2,857,000 tonnes. Other mineral deposits are limestone, estimated at 28m. tons; iron ore, estimated at 550m. tons with iron content varying between 40% and 55%, and 3 magnesian limestone deposits, estimated at about 170m. tons.

Agriculture. Inland the country is hilly, rising to 3,600 ft, with streams and waterfalls. There are long stretches of forest and brushwood, while dry plains alternate with arable land. Maize, yams, cassava, plantains, groundnuts, etc., are cultivated; oil palms and dye-woods grow in the forests; but the main commerce is based on coffee, cocoa, palm-oil, palm-kernels, copra, groundnuts, cotton, manioc. There are considerable plantations of oil and cocoa palms, coffee, cacao, kola, cassava and cotton. Production, 1977 (in 1,000 tonnes): Cassava, 468; maize, 140; millet and sorghum, 120

Livestock (1979): Cattle, 250,000; sheep, 835,000; swine, 275,000; horses, 3,000; asses, 1,000; goats, 748,000.

INDUSTRY AND TRADE

Industry. There is a cement works (production, 1978; 300,000 tonnes); a second is being built in co-operation with Ghana and Ivory Coast with a capacity of 1·2m. tonnes per annum. An oil refinery of 1m. tonne capacity opened in Lomé in 1978 and a steel mill (20,000 tonne capacity) in 1979. Industry, though small, is developing and there are about 40 medium sized enterprises in the public and private sectors, including textile and food processing plants.

Trade (in 1m. francs CFA):

	1973	1974	1975	1976	1977
Imports	22,388	28,612	37,300	44,420	...
Exports	12,755	45,174	27,000	24,914	39,000

In 1976, of the exports, phosphates amounted to 53%, cocoa beans 17% and coffee 16% by value; of the imports, transport equipment constituted 16% and cotton fabrics 11%. France and the Netherlands were Togo's main trading partners.

Total trade between Togo and UK (British Department of Trade returns, in £1,000 sterling):

	1976	1977	1978	1979	1980
Imports to UK	577	48	5,175	3,991	7,395
Exports and re-exports from UK	82,721	16,133	18,156	18,773	28,967

COMMUNICATIONS

Roads. There were, in 1977, 7,170 km of roads, of which 1,137 km were paved.

Railways. There are 3 metre-gauge railways connecting Lomé with Anécho, Palimé and Blitta; total, 443 km.

Aviation: Air services connect Lomé with Paris, Dakar, Abidjan, Douala, Accra, Lagos, Cotonou and Niamey. In 1972 aircraft disembarked 19,350 passengers and 477 tonnes of freight.

Shipping. In 1977, 777 vessels landed 663,392 tonnes and cleared 61,894 tonnes at Lomé. The merchant marine comprises 4 vessels of 15,498 gross tons.

Post and Broadcasting. There were (1972) 39 post offices and 16 postal agencies and (1978), 4,749 telephones. Togo is connected by telegraph and telephone with Ghana, Benin, Abidjan and Dakar, and by wireless telegraphy with Europe and America. There are 5,000 television and 30,000 radio receivers.

RELIGION, EDUCATION AND WELFARE

Religion. In 1975 there were 521,185 Christians, of which 402,476 were Catholics and 118,709 Protestants. There were 226,186 Mohammedans.

Education. In 1977 there were 395,381 pupils and 6,528 teachers in primary schools, 74,567 pupils and 1,832 teachers in secondary schools, 6,478 students and 305 teachers in technical schools and 329 students and 24 teachers at the teacher-training college. The University of Benin at Lomé had 2,186 students (117 teaching staff).

Health. In 1977 there were 61 hospitals with 3,438 beds; there were also 128 doctors, 5 dentists, 26 pharmacists, 517 midwives and 880 nursing staff.

DIPLOMATIC REPRESENTATIVES

OF TOGO IN GREAT BRITAIN (116 Knightsbridge, London SW1)
Ambassador: Ayivi Mawuko Ajavon.

OF GREAT BRITAIN IN TOGO
Ambassador: J. Mellon, CMG (resides in Accra).

OF TOGO IN THE USA (2208 Massachusetts Ave., NW, Washington, D.C., 20008)
Ambassador: Yao Grunitzky.

OF THE USA IN TOGO (Rue Pelletier Caventou, Lomé)
Ambassador: Marilyn P. Johnson.

OF TOGO TO THE UNITED NATIONS
Ambassador: Akanyi-Awunyo Kodjovi.

Book of Reference

Cornevin, R., *Histoire du Togo*. Paris, 1959

TONGA

Friendly Islands

Capital: Nuku'alofa
Population: 90,128 (1976)
GNP per capita: US$430 (1978)

HISTORY. The Kingdom of Tonga attained unity under Taufa'ahau Tupou (George I) who became ruler of his native Ha'apai in 1820, of Vava'u in 1833 and of Tongatapu in 1845. By 1860 the kingdom had become converted to Christianity (George himself having been baptized in 1831). In 1862 the king granted freedom to the people from arbitrary rule of minor chiefs and gave them the right to the allocation of land for their own needs. These institutional changes, together with the establishment of a parliament of chiefs, paved the way towards the democratic constitution under which the kingdom is now governed, and provided a background of stability against which Tonga was able to develop her agricultural economy.

The kingdom continued up to 1899 to be a neutral region in accordance with the Declaration of Berlin, 6 April 1886. By the Anglo-German Agreement of 14 Nov. 1899 subsequently accepted by the USA, the Tonga Islands were left under the Protectorate of Great Britain.

A protectorate was proclaimed on 18 May 1900, and a British Agent and Consul appointed.

AREA AND POPULATION. The kingdom consists of some 169 islands and islets with a total area of 270 sq. miles (700 sq. km; including inland waters), and lies between 15° and 23° 30′ S. lat and 173° and 177° W. long., its western boundary being the eastern boundary of Fiji. The islands are split up into the following groups reading from north to south: The Niuas, Vava'u, Ha'apai, Kotu, Nomuka, Otu Tolu and Tongatapu. The 3 main groups, both from historical and administrative significance, are Tongatapu in the south, Ha'apai in the centre and Vava'u in the north. The Tongatapu group was discovered by Tasman in 1643.

The capital is Nuku'alofa on Tongatapu (18,312).

The islands to the east, being mostly of limestone formation, are low lying and with but a few exceptions seldom exceed 100 ft above sea-level. The islands to the west are of a volcanic nature, approximately 11, average between 350 and 3,433 ft in height. After a violent volcanic eruption in Sept. 1946 on the island of Niuafo'ou (Tin Can Island to philatelists, so named because of the method that was used of collecting and delivering mail) the 1,300 inhabitants were evacuated, most of them to Tongatapu and 'Eua, but more than 600 have returned since 1958. It was thought that a new island had been born when an eruption took place on the Metis Shoal on 12 Dec. 1967; during the volcanic activity a small rocky mass reached a maximum elevation of about 50 ft, but by Feb. 1968 the area was once more awash.

The climate is mild and healthy, malaria being unknown. The temperature from May to Nov. rarely exceeds 84° F. in the shade, with a minimum temperature of 52° F. Census population (1976) 90,128 (males, 46,029).

CONSTITUTION AND GOVERNMENT. Relations between the UK and Tonga have been governed by the 1900 Treaty of Friendship and Protection and several subsequent revisions. For earlier history of this relationship *see* THE STATESMAN'S YEAR-BOOK, 1970–71. By exchange of letters on 19 May 1970 it was agreed that the UK Government should, as from 4 June 1970, cease to have any responsibility for the external relations of the Kingdom of Tonga.

King: HM King Taufa'ahau Tupou IV, GCVO, GCMG, KBE, born 4 July 1918, succeeded on 16 Dec. 1965 on the death of his mother, Queen Salote Tupou III; his coronation took place on 4 July 1967.

Prime Minister: HRH Prince Tu'ipelehake, KCMG, KBE, younger brother of the King.

National flag: Red with a white quarter bearing a red couped cross.

The present Constitution is almost identical with that granted in 1875 by King George Tupou I. There is a Privy Council, Cabinet, Legislative Assembly and Judiciary. The legislative assembly, which meets annually, is composed of 7 nobles elected by their peers, 7 elected representatives of the people and the Privy Councillors (numbering 8); the King appoints one of the 7 nobles to be the Speaker. The elections are held triennially. In 1960, women voted for the first time.

INTERNATIONAL RELATIONS

Membership. Tonga is a member of UN, the Commonwealth and is an ACP state of EEC.

ECONOMY

Planning. Since 1965 Tonga has organized its development effort around a 5-year development Plan. The Second Plan 1970–75 laid greater stress than its predecessor on developing the economic potential of the kingdom with expenditure of T$4·4m. Urgent social needs were largely met in the First Plan 1965–70.

The Third Plan 1975–80 is the kingdom's first attempt at formal, comprehensive indicative planning covering both the public and private sectors. The plan places considerable emphasis on investment in the productive sectors of the economy particularly agriculture, fisheries, manufacturing and tourism and on the development of supporting infrastructure and policies. Estimated expenditure for the public sector during the plan period amounts to T$31m. A Central Planning Office has been established to co-ordinate the implementation of the Third Plan and to formulate future development plans. A Fourth Plan, 1980–85, is in preparation.

Budget. Revenue and expenditure in T$1,000:

	1974–75	1975–76	1976–77	1977–78	1978–79
Revenue	5,530	5,054	6,462	8,628	8,046
Expenditure	4,773	5,873	6,961	8,515	8,602

Currency. There is a government note issue of *pa'anga* (T$)10, 5, 2, 1 and ½ and coin issue of T$2, T$1 and *seniti* 50, 20, 10, 5, 2 and 1. The change-over to decimal currency took place on 3 April 1967. In Sept. 1974, following devaluation by Australia, the Australian dollar equalled 88 *seniti*. In April 1963 gold coins were issued in denominations of 1, ½ and ¼ *koula* (1 *koula* = T$20) and in July 1967, Coronation Palladium coins of 1, ½ and ¼ *hau* (1 *hau* = T$100). In Nov. 1975, gold coins (T$100, 75, 50 and 25) and silver coins (T$20, 10 and 5) were issued to commemorate the centenary of the Constitution. In July 1978, 2 silver coins (T$2 and T$1) were issued to commemorate the sixtieth birthday of the King.

AGRICULTURE. Tongan produce (exports 1977) consists of copra (T$3,931,390); packaged desiccated coconut (T$866,942); bananas (T$401,519); swamp taros (T$246,485).

Livestock (1979): Cattle, 6,000; horses, 9,000; pigs, 83,000; goats, 11,000; poultry, 120,000.

COMMERCE. Imports in 1971 were valued at T$6,305,000; exports, T$2·2m.

Total trade between Tonga and UK (British Department of Trade returns, in £1,000 sterling):

	1977	1978	1979	1980
Imports to UK	1,003	794	145	9
Exports and re-exports from UK	434	714	710	821

COMMUNICATIONS

Aviation. International air service connexions to Tongatapu are now provided by Air Pacific and Polynesian Airlines with 5 flights per week to Auckland, 3 to Fiji, 5 to Western Samoa and 2 to Niue. South Pacific Island Airways provide a service 3 times per week from Pago Pago, American Samoa, TonVava'u in the Northern

Group and through to Tongatapu. Internal air service flights are operated daily, except Sundays to 'Eua, Ha'apai and Vava'u island groups.

Shipping. The Union Steamship Co. of New Zealand maintains a fortnightly service New Zealand–Fiji–Samoa–Tonga, and cargo steamers visit the group from time to time for shipments of copra. Shipping cleared at all ports in 1977, 102 cargo vessels, 30 cruise vessels, 3 gas vessels and 12 tankers.

Cruise ships from the following lines call at Vava'u and Nuku'alofa: P & O, Chandris, Sitmar, Royal Viking, Shaw Savill, Pacific Far East Line. The Pacific Navigation Co. Ltd maintains a regular inter-island shipping service between 'Eua, Ha'apai and Vava'u.

Post. The kingdom has its own issue of postage stamps. Telephones numbered 1,285 in 1978.

JUSTICE, RELIGION AND EDUCATION

Justice. Now that British extra-territorial jurisdiction has lapsed British and foreign nationals charged with an offence against the laws of Tonga (the enforcement of which is a responsibility of the Minister of Police) are fully subject to the jurisdiction of the Tongan courts to which they are already subject in all civil matters.

Religion. The Tongans are Christian, the vast majority being adherents of the Wesleyan Church.

Education. The Tongans enjoy free education, free medical attendance and dental treatment. In 1977 there were 95 government and 19 denominational primary schools, with a total of 19,416 pupils. There are 2 government and 39 mission schools and 1 private school at which post-primary education is provided for both boys and girls, with a total roll of 12,157. The Atenisi Institute University Division opened in 1975 and in 1977 there were 15 students with 11 staff.

DIPLOMATIC REPRESENTATIVES

OF TONGA IN GREAT BRITAIN (New Zealand Hse., Haymarket, London, SW1Y 4TE)

High Commissioner: 'I. F. Faletau (also Ambassador to Washington, USA).

OF GREAT BRITAIN IN TONGA (Nuku'alofa)

High Commissioner: H. A. Arthington-Davy, MVO, OBE.

OF THE USA IN TONGA

Ambassador: A. I. Selden, Jr (resides in Wellington).

Books of Reference

Tonga Government Departmental Reports, 1972
Biennial Report, 1962–63. HMSO, 1965
Bain, K. R., *Royal Visit to Tonga: Tonga Government Official Record.* London, 1954.—*The Friendly Islanders.* London, 1967
Churchward, C. M., *Tongan Dictionary.* London, 1959
Luke, Sir Harry, *Queen Salote and Her Kingdom.* London, 1954
Morrell, W. P., *Britain in the Pacific Islands.* OUP, 1960
Wood, A. H., *A History and Geography of Tonga.* Rev. ed. Nuku'alofa, 1963

TRINIDAD AND TOBAGO

Capital: Port-of-Spain
Population: 1·16m. (1979)
GNP per capita: US$2,910 (1978)

HISTORY. Trinidad was discovered by Columbus in 1498 and colonized by the Spaniards in the 16th century. During the French Revolution a large number of French families settled in the island. In 1797, Great Britain being at war with Spain, Trinidad was occupied by the British and ceded to Great Britain by the Treaty of Amiens in 1802. Trinidad and Tobago were joined in 1889.

Under the Bases Agreement concluded between the governments of the UK and the USA on 27 March 1941, and the concomitant Trinidad–US Bases Lease of 22 April 1941, defence bases were leased to the US Government for 99 years. On 8 Dec. 1960 the US agreed to abandon 21,000 acres of leased land and the US has since given up the remaining territory, except for a small tracking station.

AREA AND POPULATION. Area: Trinidad, 1,864 sq. miles (4,828 sq. km); Tobago, 116 sq. miles (300 sq. km). Population (census 7 April 1970): 931,071 (459,512 males and 471,559 females) (Trinidad, 892,317; Tobago, 38,754). Capital, Port-of-Spain, 62,680; other important towns, San Fernando (36,879) and Arima (11,636). The majority are of African descent (42·83%), the balance being made up of Indians (40·11%), mixed races (14·17%), Chinese (0·86%) and Syrian Lebanese (0·11%). English is spoken generally.

Estimated population in mid-1979, 1,157,000.

Vital statistics (rate per 1,000), 1978: Births, 25·3; deaths, 6·6; infant deaths, 28·6. Proportion of population under 15 years (1978) 36%.

Tobago is situated about 21 miles north-east of Trinidad. Main town is Scarborough.

Principal goods shipped from Tobago to Trinidad are copra, cocoa, livestock and poultry, fresh vegetables, coconut oil and coconut fibre.

CONSTITUTION AND GOVERNMENT. On 31 Aug. 1962 Trinidad and Tobago became an independent member state of the British Commonwealth. A Republican Constitution was adopted on 26 Oct. 1976.

The Constitution provides for a bicameral legislature of a Senate and a House of Representatives. The Senate consists of 31 members, 16 being appointed by the President on the advice of the Prime Minister, 6 on the advice of the Leader of the Opposition and 9 at the discretion of the President.

The voting age in the 1976 election was reduced from 21 to 18 years and ballot boxes were re-introduced in place of the voting machines used in previous elections.

The House of Representatives consists of 36 elected members and a Speaker elected from outside the House.

The Cabinet consists of the Prime Minister, appointed by the President, and other Ministers, including the Attorney-General (15 in 1974).

In July 1979 the People's National Movement held the 24 seats.

President: Sir Ellis Clarke.
Acting Prime Minister and Minister of Finance: George Chambers.
National flag: Red with a diagonal black strip edged in white.

DEFENCE. The Defence Force has a small air element, equipped with 2 Cessna Skymaster light transports and a JetRanger helicopter. Two S-76 helicopters were on order in 1981.

INTERNATIONAL RELATIONS

Membership. Trinidad and Tobago is a member of UN, the Commonwealth, Caricom and is an ACP state of EEC.

ECONOMY

Budget. Statistics of 5 calendar years (in TT$1,000):

	1974	1975	1976	1977	1978	1979
Revenue	1,397,700	1,769,000	...	3,212,000	3,226,000	3,592,000
Expenditure	1,301,400	1,768,800	...	2,066,500	3,140,100	3,592,000
Public debt	628,700	634,800	613,600	1,057,220	1,355,600	1,448,600

The principal item of revenue during 1978 was direct taxes, $1,982·9m.
Public debt at 31 Dec. 1978, TT$1,341·8m.

Currency. The currency is the *Trinidad and Tobago dollar* of 100 *cents*. £1 = TT$5·23; US$1 = TT$2·40 (March 1981).

Banking. Banks operating: Barclays Bank of Trinidad and Tobago Ltd; Royal Bank of Trinidad and Tobago Ltd; Bank of Commerce, Trinidad and Tobago Ltd; Bank of Nova Scotia; Chase Manhattan Bank; Citibank; National Commercial Bank of Trinidad and Tobago; Workers' Bank of Trinidad and Tobago. A Central Bank began operations in Dec. 1964.

Government savings banks are established in 62 offices, with a head office in Port-of-Spain, the amount of deposits at the end of 1973 being $8,316,739, and the total number of depositors, 137,349.

ENERGY AND NATURAL RESOURCES

Oil. Oil production is one of Trinidad's leading industries and an important source of revenue. Commercial production began in 1909; production of crude oil in 1978 was 83·7m. bbls. Trinidad also possesses 3 refineries, with throughput capacity of 144·2m. bbls annually; crude oil is imported from Venezuela, Indonesia, Ecuador, Nigeria, Brazil, and Saudi Arabia and refined in Trinidad. The 'Pitch Lake' is an important source of asphalt.

Agriculture. Of the total area of 1,267,236 acres (Trinidad, 1,192,844 acres, and Tobago, 74,392 acres), about half has been alienated. Acres under cultivation and care include (1973): Forest, 685,604; cocoa, 119,703; sugar, 118,703; coconuts, 35,797; citrus, 13,667; tonca beans, 1,735. Sugar production in 1980 was 110,000 (1976: 200,000) tons. The territory is still largely dependent on imported food supplies, especially rice, dairy products, meat and rice. Areas have been irrigated for rice, and soil and forest conservation is practised.

Livestock (1979): Cattle, 77,000; sheep, 11,000; goats, 45,000; pigs, 58,000; poultry, 7·2m.

INDUSTRY AND TRADE

Labour. The working population in 1978 was 439,000 (132,400 women) and unemployment was 53,500 (12%), 23,600 women.

Commerce. Chief imports, 1978:

	TT$1,000		TT$1,000
Mineral fuels, lubricants, etc.	1,915,100	Manufactured goods	723,900
Machinery and transport		Food	438,200
equipment	1,021,900		

The principal domestic exports during 1978 were (in TT$1,000): Petroleum products, 4,383,400; chemicals, 204,500; food, 138,000.

The chief country of origin of imports was USA ($968·7m.). Exports were shipped chiefly to USA ($3,228·3m.).

Total trade of Trinidad and Tobago with UK (British Department of Trade returns, in £1,000 sterling):

	1976	1977	1978	1979	1980
Imports to UK	48,255	29,500	31,630	41,243	35,088
Exports and re-exports from UK	73,834	97,308	110,788	104,562	120,270

Tourism. In 1978, 176,100 foreigners visited Trinidad and Tobago spending TT$266·3m.

COMMUNICATIONS

Roads. There are 2,630 miles of main and local roads. Motor vehicles registered in 1978 totalled 176,895, including 112,572 private cars, 18,895 hired and rented cars, and 27,399 goods vehicles.

Aviation. The following airlines operate scheduled passenger, mail and freight services. British West Indian Airways, Ltd, Air Canada, PANAM, KLM, Linea Aeropostal Venezolana, Aerolinas Argentinas, Leeward Islands Air Transport, Air France, ASPA, Air India, Caribair and British Airways.

Shipping. In 1969, 6,539 vessels arrived at Port-of-Spain.

Post and Broadcasting. International communications to all parts of the world are provided by Trinidad and Tobago External Telecommunications Co. Ltd (TEXTEL) by means of a satellite earth station and various high quality radio circuits. The marine radio service is also maintained by TEXTEL. Number of post offices (1979), 63; postal agencies offering limited services, 175; number of telephones (1978), 74,908.

Four wireless stations are maintained by the Trinidad Government and 3 by airline companies. A meteorological station is maintained at Piarco airport.

Cinemas (1973). There are 72 cinemas and 4 drive-in cinemas.

Newspapers (1973). There are 2 daily newspapers with an average daily circulation of 90,000, 3 Sunday newspapers with an average circulation of 146,000, 1 evening paper and 5 weekly newspapers.

JUSTICE, RELIGION, EDUCATION AND WELFARE

Justice. The High Court consists of the Chief Justice and not fewer than 10 puisne judges. In criminal cases a judge of the High Court sits with a jury of 12 in cases of treason and murder, and with 9 jurors in other cases. The Court of Appeal consists of the Chief Justice and 3 Justices of Appeal; there is a limited right of appeal from it to the Privy Council. There are 10 High Courts and 28 magistrates' courts.

Police. At the end of 1970 the police force consisted of 63 officers, 72 inspectors and 2,446 other ranks.

Religion. In 1970, 18·1% of the population were Anglicans (under the Bishop of Trinidad and Tobago), 35·6% Roman Catholics (under the Archbishop of Port-of-Spain), 4·2% Presbyterians, 24·7% Hindus and 6·3% Moslems.

Education. In 1972–73 there were 476 primary and intermediate schools (government assisted) and (1971–72) 116 secondary schools (47 government and assisted and 69 private).

There were 222,928 pupils on roll in the primary and intermediate schools and 35,302 in the secondary schools (government and assisted). Education in government and assisted secondary schools was made free in 1960. There are also 5 training colleges. Technical and commercial education is provided by 4 government sponsored technical schools.

Health. State medical services are free and in 1972 a National Insurance Scheme was established.

DIPLOMATIC REPRESENTATIVES

OF TRINIDAD AND TOBAGO IN GREAT BRITAIN
(42 Belgrave Sq., London, SW1X 8NT)

High Commissioner: Eustace Seignoret.

OF GREAT BRITAIN IN TRINIDAD AND TOBAGO
(Furness Hse., 90 Independence Sq., Port-of-Spain)

High Commissioner: D. N. Lane.

OF TRINIDAD AND TOBAGO IN THE USA
(1708 Massachusetts Ave., NW, Washington, D.C., 20036)

Ambassador: Victor C. McIntyre.

OF THE USA IN TRINIDAD AND TOBAGO
(15 Queen's Park West, Port-of-Spain)

Ambassador: Irving G. Cheslaw.

OF TRINIDAD AND TOBAGO TO THE UNITED NATIONS

Ambassador: Frank Owen Abdulah.

Books of Reference

Statistical Information: The Central Statistical Office, Government of Trinidad and Tobago, 2 Edward St., Port-of-Spain. *Director:* J. Harewood. Publications include *Annual Statistical Digest, Quarterly Economic Report, Annual Overseas Trade Report, Population and Vital Statistics Annual Report.*

Report of the Trinidad and Tobago Independence Conference, 1962. (Cmnd. 1757.) HMSO, 1962

Development Plan for Tobago. HMSO, 1957

Economic Survey of Trinidad and Tobago, 1953–58. Government Printer, Port-of-Spain, 1959
Facts on Trinidad and Tobago. Public Relations Division, Prime Minister's Office, Port-of-Spain, 1978

Five Year Development Programme, 1958–1962. Government Printer, Port-of-Spain, 1958
Third Five Year Plan, 1969–73. Government Printer, Port-of-Spain, 1970
Trinidad and Tobago Year Book. Port-of-Spain. Annual (from 1865)
Trade Dictionary of Trinidad and Tobago. 2nd ed. London, 1966
Anthony, M., *Profile Trinidad: A Historical Survey from the Discovery to 1900.* London, 1975

Central Library: The Central Library of Trinidad and Tobago, Queen's Park East, Port-of-Spain. *Acting Librarian:* Mrs L. Hutchinson.

TUNISIA

Capital: Tunis
Population: 6·03m (1978)
GNP per capita: US$950 (1978)

Al-Djoumhouria
Attunusia

HISTORY. Tunisia was a French protectorate from 1881 and achieved independence on 20 March 1956. The Constituent Assembly, elected on 25 March 1956, abolished the monarchy (of the Bey of Tunis) on 25 July 1957 and proclaimed a republic.

AREA AND POPULATION. The boundaries are on the north and east the Mediterranean Sea, on the west Algeria and on the south Libya. The area is about 164,150 sq. km (63,362 sq. miles), including that portion of the Sahara which is to the east of the Djerid, extending towards Ghadamès.

At the census of 8 May 1975 there were 5,588,209 inhabitants (2,840,913 males and 2,747,209 females). Estimate (1978) 6·03m.

The census populations of the *gouvernorats* were as follows as at 8 May 1975 (in 1,000): Tunis North (945), Sfax (479), Nabeul (374), Kairouan (337), Bizerta (336), Jendouba (300), Médénine (292), Gabès (259), Sousse (253), Béja (246), Kassérine (237), Gafsa (236), Le Kef (236), Sidi Bouzid (215), Mahdia (214), Monastir (221); Tunis South (204), Siliana (193).

Tunis, the capital, had (census, 1975) 505,404 inhabitants: Sfax, 171,297; Sousse, 69,530; Bizerta, 62,856; Djerba, 70,217; Kairouan, a holy city of the Moslems, 54,546; Gabès, 40,585; Béja, 39,226.

Vital statistics (1976). Births, 208,728; deaths, 36,912; marriages, 47,940.

CONSTITUTION AND GOVERNMENT. The Constitution of the republic was promulgated on 1 June 1959. The President and the National Assembly are elected simultaneously by direct universal suffrage for a period of 5 years. The President cannot be re-elected more than 3 times consecutively. An amendment to the Constitution in 1969 gives the Prime Minister power to act as President in case of a sudden vacancy of the Presidency.

It was announced on 12 Jan. 1974 by the President that Tunisia and Libya would be merged into a single state eventually but this proposal collapsed in the same year.

President of the Republic and Head of Government: Habib Bourguiba (elected 25 July 1957, re-elected 8 Nov. 1959, 8 Nov. 1964, 2 Nov. 1969 and elected President for life in Nov. 1974).

The Cabinet in April 1980 was composed as follows:

Prime Minister: Mohammed M'Zali.
Special Adviser to the President: Habib Bourguiba, Jr. *Justice:* M'hamed Chaker. *Foreign Affairs:* Hassan Belkhodja. *Interior:* Idris Guiga. *Defence:* Salaheddine Bali. *Planning and Finance:* Mansour Moalla. *National Economy:* Abdelaziz Lasram. *Equipment and Housing:* Mohamed Sayah. *Information and Culture:* Fouad M'Baza. *National Education:* Mohamed Frej Chedli. *Higher Education and Scientific Research:* Abdelaziz Ben Dhia. *Agriculture:* Lassaad Ben Osman. *Public Health:* Rashid Sfar. *Transport and Communications:* Sadok Ben Jamaa. *Social Affairs:* Mohamed Ennaceur. *Youth and Sports:* Hedi Zeghala. *Minister-Delegate responsible for Prime Minister's Office:* Mongi Kooli. *Minister-Delegate attached to Prime Minister responsible for Civil Service and Administrative Reform:* Moncef Belhadj Amor. *Secretary of State for Posts and Telecommunications:* Brahim Khouaja.

By decree of 21 July 1956 the country was divided into *gouvernorats*, each subdivided into *délégations, communes* and *imadas.* The official language is Arabic.

Flag: Red with a white circle in the middle, on which is a 5-pointed red star encircled by a red crescent.

DEFENCE. A Tunisian National Army was created in 1956. It consisted in 1980 of about 24,000 officers and men. Selective military service is 1 year. Officer-cadets are being trained in France. Defence expenditure in 1979 was 59m. dinars.

Army. The Army consists of 2 combined arms and 3 armoured regiments, 2 para-commando, 1 desert, 2 artillery and 1 engineer battalion.

Navy. The Navy consists of 1 frigate (*ex*-US old destroyer-escort), 2 fast gunboats (*ex*-Chinese), 2 fast attack craft (British-built in 1977), 2 coastal minesweepers, 4 patrol vessels (French built), 10 patrol boats and 3 tugs. In 1981 naval personnel totalled 2,600 officers and ratings.

Air Force. Equipment of the Air Force, acquired from various Western sources, includes single squadrons of Aermacchi M.B.326K jet light attack aircraft and SF.260W piston-engined light trainer/attack aircraft, 1 C-130H Hercules transport, 4 S.208 liaison aircraft, 6 SF.260M trainers, 12 T-6 Texan advanced trainers, 12 M.B.326B/LT jet trainers, 1 Puma, 18 Agusta-Bell AB205, 6 Bell UH-1N and about 12 Alouette II and III helicopters. Personnel, about 2,000.

INTERNATIONAL RELATIONS

Membership. Tunisia is a member of UN, OAU and the Arab League.

ECONOMY

Planning. A fifth development plan (1977–81) envisaged investment of 4,200m. dinars.

Budget (in 1,000 dinars). Ordinary receipts and expenditure for calendar years balanced as follows: 1975, 92,000; 1976, 105,000; 1977, 110,000; 1978, 120,000. Budget estimates, 1979, revenue, 625,100; expenditure, 481,600.

Currency. On 1 Nov. 1958 a new currency, the *dinar,* divided into 1,000 *millimes,* was established. The Central Bank of Tunisia is the note-issuing agency. Note circulation, July 1974, was 374·56m. *dinars.*

Currency consists of coins of 1, 2, 5, 10, 20, 50, 100 and 500 *millimes,* and notes of 500 *millimes,* 1 *dinar,* 5 and 10 *dinars.* £1 = 0·94 *dinar;* US$1 = 0·40 *dinar* (March 1981).

Banking. In 1977 there were 14 banks operating in Tunisia, including 3 French and 1 British banks. Bank deposits amounted to 475·4m. dinars at 31 Dec. 1975.

Weights and Measures. The metric system of weights and measures has almost entirely taken the place of those of Tunisia, but corn is still sold in *kaffis* and *wibas.* The *kfiz* (of 16 *wiba,* each of 12 *sa')* = 16 bushels. The *ounce* = 31·487 grammes.

The principal measure of length is the metre.

ENERGY AND NATURAL RESOURCES

Electricity. The electricity, gas and water services, formerly run by a French company, were nationalized on 26 Nov. 1959 and are now run respectively by the Société Tunisienne d'Electricité et du Gaz (STEG) and the Société Nationale d'Exploitation et de Distribution du Eaux (SONEDE).

Electrical energy generated was 1,346m. kwh. in 1977, of which 1,145m. was produced by STEG.

Minerals. Mineral production (in 1,000 tonnes) in 1977 (and 1975): Phosphate, 3,614 (3,511); iron ore, 343 (616); lead ore, 16·5 (17); zinc ore, 10·5 (8).

Processed minerals (in 1,000 tonnes) in 1976: Phosphates, 3,301; lead, 17; iron ore, 494. Crude oil production, 1977, 4,264,000 tonnes.

Agriculture. Tunisia may be divided into 5 districts—the north, characterized by its mountainous formation, having large and fertile valleys (*e.g.,* the valley of the Medjerdah and the plains of Mornag, Mateur and Béja); the north-east, with the peninsula of Cap Bon, the soil being specially suited for the cultivation of oranges, lemons and tangerines; the Sahel, where olive trees abound; the centre, the region of high table lands and pastures, and the desert of the south, famous for its oases and gardens, where dates grow in profusion.

Agriculture is the chief industry, and large estates predominate. Of the total area of 15,583,000 hectares, about 9m. hectares are productive, including 2m. under cereals, 3·6m. used as pasturage, 900,000 forests and 1·3m. uncultivated.

Products		1976	1977	1978
Hard wheat		700	486	573
Soft wheat		180	126	132
Barley		270	133	199
Olive oil	(in 1,000	180	90	130
Oranges and	tonnes)			
lemons		163	160	220
Dates		45	42	33
Wine (in 1,000 hectolitres)		650	850	1,150

Other products are apricots, pears, apples, peaches, plums, figs, pomegranates, almonds, shaddocks, pistachios, esparto grass, henna and cork. Agricultural tractors numbered 35,000 in 1977.

Livestock (1979): Horses, 112,000; asses, 204,000; mules, 69,000; cattle, 910,000; sheep, 3·7m.; goats, 950,000; camels, 221,000; pigs, 4,000.

Fisheries. In 1977, 5,961 boats with 22,555 men were engaged in fishing. In 1976 the catch amounted to 50,000 tonnes; 1977, 56,000.

INDUSTRY AND TRADE

Industry. Major modern plants include a sugar refinery in Béja (57,700 tonnes in 1975), a cellulose plant in Kassérine (22,000 tonnes in 1976), a petroleum refinery in Bizerta and a steel plant at Menzel Bourguiba. There is a marble work plant and a tyre factory at Mégrine.

In 1972 a phosphoric acid plant opened at Ghannouche with an annual capacity of 120,000 tonnes.

The index of industrial production stood at 137 in 1976 (1970 = 100).

Production, 1977 (in 1,000 tonnes): Refined oil, 1,130; cement, 680; metal castings, 200; steel, 200; rounded bars, 145; paper pulp, 22.

Trade Unions. The Union Générale des Travailleurs Tunisiens was placed under government control in Aug. 1965. There are also the Union Tunisienne de l'Industrie, du Commerce et de l'Artisanat (UTICA, the employers' union) and the Union National des Agriculteurs (UNA, farmers' union).

Commerce. The imports and exports for calendar years (in 1,000 dinars) were as follows:

	1972	1973	1974	1975	1976	1977	1978
Imports	222,219	265,947	488,658	572,800	656,700	735,000	834,000
Exports	150,327	168,653	397,695	345,600	338,300	390,000	440,000

Exports to France in 1976 totalled 57·7m. dinars, and imports from France, 210·9m. dinars and exports to USA were valued at 46·5m. dinars and imports from USA were valued at 40·8m. dinars.

In 1977 exports of iron ore totalled 55,000 tonnes; lime phosphates, and hyperphosphates, 2,087,400; crude petroleum, 4,144,900.

Total trade between Tunisia and UK (British Department of Trade returns, in £1,000 sterling):

	1976	1977	1978	1979	1980
Imports to UK	3,116	12,641	11,964	9,084	17,566
Exports and re-exports from UK	22,969	28,371	21,365	24,660	29,872

Tourism. In 1977, 1,016,000 tourists visited Tunisia, not counting ships' passengers in transit.

COMMUNICATIONS

Roads. In 1975 there were 16,695 km of roads, of which 10,645 km were main roads.

Number of motor vehicles, 1977, included 110,002 private cars, 81,370 commercial cars, 10,764 motor cycles and 35,598 tractors.

Railways. In 1980 there were 2,013 km of railways, owned by the state Société Nationale des Chemins de Fer Tunisiens. Traffic in 1979 was 25m. passengers and 7·6m. tonnes of freight.

Aviation. The national airline is 'Tunis-Air'. The main airport is at Tunis-Carthage. In 1977, 1,126,766 passengers were carried.

Shipping. The main port is Tunis, and its outer port is Tunis-Goulette. These two ports and Sfax, Sousse and Bizerta are directly accessible to ocean going vessels. The port of La Skhirra, in the south, is used for the shipping of Algerian and Tunisian oil.

In 1976, 5,304 ships of 16·4m. tons entered Tunisian ports.

Post and Broadcasting. There were, in 1978, 144,116 telephones, of which 36,378 were in Tunis. There were, in 1978, 403 post offices, and 6 wireless transmitting stations. Wireless sets in use in 1976 were 1,124,000. Television began in 1966 and in 1976 there were 209,000 sets.

Cinemas (1976). There were 175 cinemas with a seating capacity of 44,000.

Newspapers. There are 2 Arabic and 3 French daily newspapers.

JUSTICE, RELIGION, EDUCATION AND WELFARE

Justice. The Government has abolished the multiple jurisdictions of religious (shara'ic and rabbinic) tribunals. These have been integrated into the civil courts so as to form a single three-level jurisdiction (courts of primary jurisdiction, courts of appeal and the High Court).

A Personal Status Code was promulgated on 13 Aug. 1956 and applied to Tunisians from 1 Jan. 1957. This raised the status of women, made divorce subject to a court decision, abolished polygamy and decreed a minimum marriage age.

Religion. The constitution recognizes Islam as the state religion. There are about 14,000 Roman Catholics, under the Prelate of Tunis. The Greek Church, the French Protestants and the English Church are also represented.

Education. All education was in 1956 made dependent on the Ministry of National Education. The 208 independent koranic schools have been nationalized and the distinction between religious and public schools has been abolished. All education is free from primary schools to university. A teachers' training college (*école normale supérieure*) was established in 1955. There are also a high school of law, 2 centres of economic studies, 2 schools of engineering, 2 medical schools, a faculty of agriculture and 2 institutes of business administration.

In 1977–78 primary schools had 1,012,800 pupils; secondary, technical and vocational schools had 229,100 pupils; higher education mainly at the University of Tunis had 26,781 students.

Health. In 1976 there were 268 hospitals (13,145 beds). The registered medical personnel in Tunisia comprised 1,210 doctors (843 Tunisians and 367 foreigners), 313 pharmacists, 176 dentists and 60 veterinaries.

Social Security. A system of social security was set up in 1950 (amended 1963, 1964 and 1970).

DIPLOMATIC REPRESENTATIVES

OF TUNISIA IN GREAT BRITAIN (29 Prince's Gate, London, SW7 1QG)
Ambassador: Faika Farouk, GCVO.

OF GREAT BRITAIN IN TUNISIA (5 Place de la Victoire, Tunis)
Ambassador and Consul-General: A. J. D. Stirling.

OF TUNISIA IN THE USA (2408 Massachusetts Ave., NW, Washington, D.C., 20008)

Ambassador: Ali Hedda.

OF THE USA IN TUNISIA (144 Ave. de la Liberté, Tunis)

Ambassador: Stephen W. Bosworth.

OF TUNISIA TO THE UNITED NATIONS

Ambassador: M'Hamed Essaafi.

Books of Reference

Statistical Information: Institut National de la Statistique (27 Rue de Liban, Tunis) was set up on 13 March 1947. Its main publications are: *Annuaire statistique de la Tunisie* (latest issue, 1975).

Journal Officiel de la République Tunisienne (in Arabic and French)
Tunisie, 1953. (*L'Encyclopédie d'outre-mer.*) Paris, 1953
Bannour, A. (ed.), *Economic Yearbook of Tunisia.* 2nd ed. Tunis, 1966
Garas, F., *Bourguiba et la Naissance d'une Nation.* Paris, 1956
Knapp, W., *Tunisia.* London, 1970
Ling, D. L., *Tunisia: From Protectorate to Republic.* Indiana Univ. Press, 1967
Rossi, P., *Bourguiba's Tunisia.* Tunis, 1967
Rudebeck, L., *The Tunisian Experience: Party and People.* London, 1970
Sylvester, A., *Tunisia.* London, 1969
Tlatli, S. E., *Tunisie Nouvelle: Problèmes et Perspectives.* Tunis, 1957
Vibert, J., *Tableau de l'Économie Tunisienne.* Tunis, 1955

TURKEY

Türkiye Cumhuriyeti

Capital: Ankara
Population: 45·4m. (1980)
GNP per capita: US$1,210 (1978)

HISTORY. The Turkish War of Independence (1919–22), following the disintegration of the Ottoman Empire, was led and won by Mustafa Kemal (Atatürk) on behalf of the Grand National Assembly which first met in Ankara on 23 April 1920. On 20 Jan. 1921 the Grand National Assembly voted a constitution which declared that all sovereignty belonged to the people and vested all power, both executive and legislative, in the Grand National Assembly. The name 'Ottoman Empire' was later replaced by 'Turkey'. On 1 Nov. 1922 the Grand National Assembly abolished the office of Sultan and Turkey became a republic on 29 Oct. 1923.

On 27 May 1960 the Turkish Army, directed by a National Unity Committee under the leadership of Gen. Cemal Gürsel, overthrew the government of the Democratic Party. The Grand National Assembly was dissolved and party activities were suspended. Party activities were legally resumed on 12 Jan. 1961. A new constitution was approved in a referendum held on 9 July 1961 and general elections were held the same year.

AREA AND POPULATION. The Treaty of Peace between the Allied Powers and Turkey, which was signed at Lausanne on 24 July 1923, defined the European frontier of the new Turkey and to some extent her Asiatic frontiers. This treaty was ratified by the Grand National Assembly in Ankara on 23 Aug. 1923 and entered into force 6 Aug. 1924.

The Treaty of Lausanne and the conventions attached to it provided for the demilitarization of zones adjoining the European frontier, the Dardanelles and the Bosphorus, subject to the right to maintain a garrison at Istanbul, for the demilitarization of İmroz, Bozcaada (Tenedos) and Tavşan Islands, as well as the islands in the Sea of Marmora with one exception and for a special administrative regime in İmroz and Bozcaada.

On 10 July 1936 a new Straits Convention was signed at Montreux (ratified on 9 Nov. 1936) to take the place of the 1923 Convention, whereby Turkey obtained the right of re-militarizing the zone of the Straits, and this area was re-occupied by Turkish troops on 21 July 1936. The International Commission of the Straits ceased to function on 30 Sept. 1936.

By an agreement between the Turkish and French Governments concluded at Ankara on 23 June 1939, the Sanjak of Alexandretta (the Hatay) was incorporated in the Turkish Republic.

The area of Turkey (including lakes) is 779,452 sq. km (300,947 sq. miles). Area in Europe (Trakya), 23,764 sq. km. Area in Asia (Anadolu), 755,855 sq. km; population, 1975, 40,197,670; in 1980 estimated at 45,442,000.

The census population of Turkey is given as follows:

	Males	Females	Total	Increase %
1935	7,936,770	8,221,248	16,158,018	21·2
1940	8,898,912	8,922,038	17,820,950	17·3
1945	9,446,580	9,343,594	18,790,174	10·5
1950	10,527,085	10,420,103	20,947,188	22·9
1955	12,233,421	11,831,342	24,064,763	29·7
1960	14,163,888	13,590,932	27,754,820	28·9
1965	15,996,964	15,394,457	31,391,421	24·9
1970	18,006,986	17,598,190	35,605,176	25·1
1975	20,412,200	19,780,470	40,197,670	25·4

The population of the provinces, at the census of Oct. 1980, was as follows:

Adana	1,467,346	Erzincan	298,186	Maraş	743,465
Adıyaman	368,780	Erzurum	802,288	Mardin	568,039
Afyonkarahisar	598,462	Eskişehir	543,753	Muğla	436,959
Ağrı	369,272	Gaziantep	807,093	Muş	298,757
Amasya	337,955	Gireşun	478,389	Nevşehir	254,849
Ankara	3,196,460	Gümüşane	278,063	Niğde	506,614
Antalya	753,596	Hakkari	177,936	Ordu	717,977
Artvin	227,906	Hatay	863,645	Rize	359,199
Aydin	651,526	İsparta	356,826	Sakarya	551,116
Balıkesir	851,381	İçel	842,817	Samsun	998,417
Bilecik	147,702	İstanbul	4,870,747	Siirt	445,486
Bingöl	228,452	İzmir	1,968,614	Sinop	276,445
Bitlis	258,247	Kars	701,196	Sivas	749,055
Bolu	473,168	Kastamonu	448,363	Tekirdağ	363,017
Burdur	236,526	Kayseri	768,413	Tokat	623,300
Bursa	1,161,553	Kırklareli	281,412	Trabzon	725,942
Çanakkale	401,363	Kırşehir	240,108	Tunceli	157,236
Çankırı	258,467	Kocaeli	591,848	Urfa	607,425
Çorum	570,518	Konya	1,560,968	Uşak	245,778
Denizli	601,492	Kütahya	498,660	Van	471,019
Diyarbakir	770,763	Malatya	609,452	Yozgat	499,410
Edirne	361,888	Manisa	940,408	Zonguldak	972,856
Elâziğ	428,687				

The population of towns of over 70,000 inhabitants was as follows in 1970:

İstanbul	2,132,407	Samsun	134,081	Antalya	95,616
Ankara	1,236,152	Sivas	133,979	Kırıkkale	91,658
İzmir	520,838	Erzurum	133,494	Balıkesir	85,004
Adana	347,454	Malatya	128,891	Denizli	82,372
Bursa	275,953	Kocaeli	120,694	Trabzon	80,795
Gaziantep	227,652	İçel	112,982	İskenderun	79,291
Eskişehir	216,373	Maraş	110,761	Zonguldak	77,135
Konya	200,444	Elaziğ	107,368	Tarsus	74,510
Kayseri	160,958	Adapazarı	101,483	Manisa	72,276
Diyarbakir	149,566	Urfa	100,654		

The population of Turkey according to 'mother tongue' (1965 census) comprises 28,289,680 Turks, 2,219,502 Kurds, 365,340 Arabs, 57,337 Circassians, 48,143 Greeks, 48,096 Armenians, 33,094 Georgians, 23,715 Lazes and 9,124 Spanish-speaking Jews.

CONSTITUTION AND GOVERNMENT. The Constitution of 9 July 1961 has consolidated the modernizing reforms: the abolition of the Caliphate and of old-style religious education (1924), the prohibition of oriental headgear (1925), the suppression of the dervish orders (1925), the introduction of the Western civil code, ending polygamy (1926), the substitution of the Latin for the Arabic alphabet (1928), the abolition of old-style titles (1934) and the prohibition of clerical garb (1934).

Religious courts were abolished in 1924, Islam ceased to be the official state religion in 1928, women were given the franchise and western-style surnames were adopted in 1934.

Thirty-five Articles of the 1961 Constitution were amended in Sept. 1971 and 9 temporary articles added. Five more articles were amended in 1973 and a further one in 1974.

Following the military takeover on 12 Sept. 1980, the National Security Council is the supreme body with legislative power. The Constitution and Grand National Assembly were abolished.

Executive power is vested in the Head of State, and in the Council of Ministers. The Head of State is the Chairman of the NSC and Chief of the General Staff of the Turkish Armed Forces.

Turkish men and women are entitled to vote at the age of 21 and to become deputies at the age of 30 and second members of Senate at the age of 40. Secret ballot was introduced by law on 10 July 1948.

Elections held on 5 June 1977 resulted in the following composition of the National Assembly: Republican People's Party, 213; Justice Party, 189; Republican

Reliance Party, 3; National Salvation Party, 24; National Action Party, 16; Democratic Party, 1; Independents, 4; Total, 450.

The Senate (150 members elected by direct vote, 15 nominated by the President of the Republic, and 19 life senators, formerly members of the National Unity Committee) is composed of (after 5 June 1977 elections): Republican People's Party, 78; Justice Party, 64; National Salvation Party, 6; National Action Party, 1; Republican Reliance Party, 4; Independents, 1; Nominees of the President of the Republic, 11; former President of the Republic, 1.

National flag: A white crescent and star on red.

National anthem: Korkma! Sönmez bu şafaklarda yüzen al sancak (words by Mehmed Akif Ersoy; tune by Zeki Güngör; adopted 12 March 1921).

Past Presidents of the Republic: Mustafa Kemal Atatürk (29 Oct, 1923–10 Nov. 1938), İsmet İnönü (11 Nov. 1938–21 May 1950), Celâl Bayar (22 May 1950–27 May 1960), Cemal Gürsel (26 Oct. 1961–27 March 1966), Cevdet Sunay (29 March 1966–28 March 1973), Fahri S. Korutürk (6 April 1973–6 April 1980).

Head of State, Head of National Security Council and Chief of General Staff: Gen. Kenan Evren.

Members of the Council: Gen. Nurettin Ersin; Gen. Tahsin Sahinkaya; Adm. Nejat Tümer. *Secretary-General:* Gen. Haydar Saltik.

The Council of Ministers was in Sept. 1980 constituted as follows:

Prime Minister: Bulend Ulusu.

Ministers of State: Zeyyad Baykara (*Deputy Prime Minister*), Turgut Özal (*Deputy Prime Minister*), Mehmet Özgünes, Nimet Ozdas, Ilhan Oztrak. *Justice:* Cevdet Mentes. *Defence:* Haluk Bayulken. *Foreign Affairs:* Ilter Turkmen. *Finance:* Kaya Erdem. *Education:* Hasan Sağlam. *Interior:* Selahattin Çetiner. *Public Works:* Tarhin Önalp. *Trade:* Kemal Cantürk. *Public Health:* Necmi Ayanoglu. *Customs and Monopolies:* Recai Baturalp. *Agriculture and Forestry:* Sabahattin Ozbek. *Transport and Communications:* Necmi Özcül. *Labour:* Turhan Esener. *Industry and Technology:* Sahap Kocatopcu. *Energy and Natural Resources:* Serbülent Bingül. *Tourism and Information:* Ilhan Evliyaoglu. *Housing and Reconstruction:* Serif Tuten. *Rural Affairs:* Munir Güney. *Youth and Sports:* Vecdi Özgül. *Social Security:* Sadik Şide. *Culture:* Cihad Baban.

Local Government. The Constitution of 1921 provided for the administrative division of the country into *Il,* province (now 67 in number), divided into *Ilçe* (district), subdivided in their turn into *Bucak* (township or commune). At the head of each Il is a Vali representing the Government. Each Il has its own elective council.

The Ilçe is regarded as a mere grouping of Bucaks for certain purposes of general administration. The Bucak or commune is an autonomous entity and possesses an elective council charged with the administration of such matters as are not reserved to the State.

According to the municipal law passed in 1930, Turkish women have the right to be electors and to be elected at municipal elections.

DEFENCE. Several bills for the reorganization of the armed forces were passed in June 1961 by the Grand National Assembly. One of these placed all organizations connected with national defence under the authority of the Minister of National Defence. Another created a Supreme Council of National Security, under the chairmanship of the Prime Minister, with the object of co-ordinating the resources of the country in case of war. Besides the Minister of National Defence and the Chief of the General Staff, the heads of economic Ministries are members of this council

Military service in Army, Air Force and Navy is 18 months for officers and 20 months for other ranks. Men are called up when they reach the age of 20. The average number of men liable to be called up is 175,000 every year. The strength of the forces is about 567,000 officers and men. The total number that could be mobilized is estimated at over 2m.

Army. The land forces contain 16 infantry divisions (2 mechanized), 1 armoured division and 6 armoured brigades (M-48 tanks), 1 commando and 7 infantry brigades, 4 mechanized infantry brigades, 1 parachute brigade. The units are largely equipped with 10·5 cm, 15·5 cm and 20·3 cm howitzer guns. Ground forces have been assigned to the South-Eastern Command of Nato, of which Izmir is the headquarters. Total strength (1980), 470,000; conscripts, 310,000.

Navy. The Navy includes 14 diesel-powered submarines (4 new designed in Federal Republic of Germany and 10 old *ex*-US patrol submarines), 12 old *ex*-US destroyers, 2 new Turkish-built frigates, 1 minelayer, 6 coastal minelayers, 8 fast missile craft, 13 fast torpedo boats, 6 fast attack craft, 21 coastal minesweepers, 8 patrol vessels, 4 inshore minesweepers, 9 minehunting boats, 38 patrol craft, 3 repair ships, 2 submarine support ships, 1 training ship (*ex*-German support frigate), 5 landing ships, 52 landing craft, 20 minor landing craft, 3 submarine rescue ships, 6 oilers, 3 transports, 2 survey ships, 2 survey boats, 4 boom defence vessels, 3 gate vessels, 14 auxiliary vessels, 9 tugs and 2 tenders.

Ships under construction include a fifth diesel-electric patrol submarine designed in the Federal Republic of Germany, but being built in Turkey (and 7 more are planned); 4 more fast missile craft and 8 fast attack craft.

The naval bases are at Gölcük in the Gulf of İzmit, at İskenderun, at Taskizak (İstanbul) and at İzmir.

Personnel strength in 1981 totalled 45,000 officers and ratings.

Air Force. The Air Force is under the control of the General Staff and, operationally, under 6 ATAF. It is organized as 2 tactical air forces, with F-5s equipping 5 fighter-bomber/interceptor and 2 reconnaissance squadrons: F-100 Super Sabres in 3 fighter-bomber squadrons; F-104G and F-104S Starfighters in 4 squadrons; F-4E Phantoms in 3 squadrons; and RF-4E Phantoms in 1 squadron; plus Nike-Hercules surface-to-air missile batteries. The 7 transport squadrons are equipped with Transall C-160, C-130 Hercules, Viscount and C-47 aircraft, and UH-1H helicopters. Training types include T-33A and T-37 and T-38 advanced trainers and T-41 primary trainers. Personnel strength is about 52,000, with 290 combat aircraft.

INTERNATIONAL RELATIONS

Membership. Turkey is a member of UN, OECD, Nato and Council of Europe and an Associate of EEC.

ECONOMY

Planning. The first 5-year development plan, 1963–67, provided for investments of TL68,000m. (at 1965 prices); TL64,000m. were invested, the gross national product increasing at the rate of 6·7% per annum. The second 5-year plan (1968–72) aimed at achieving an annual growth of 7%; external financing amounting to US$1,716m. The third 5-year plan (1973–78) sets out to achieve an annual growth of 7·4%. The fourth 5-year plan (1979–83) sets out to achieve an annual growth of 8%.

Budget. Estimates of revenue and expenditure (in TL1,000) for financial years 1 March–28/29 Feb.:

	1976–77	1977–78	1978–79	1979–80
Revenue	139,719,980	203,449,003	308,350,000	395,871,000
Expenditure	153,637,351	222,949,003	341,173,000	406,876,000

Currency. The Turkish *Lira* (TL) is divided into 100 *kuruş* (*piastres*). Coins in general circulation are of the following values: 5, 10, 25 and 50 *kuruş*; 1, 2½ and 5 *Lira*. Bank-notes in circulation are as follows: 5, 10, 20, 50, 100, 500 and 1,000 *Lira*.

Banking. The Turkish banking system is composed of the Central Bank of the Republic of Turkey (Merkez Bankası) and 45 other banks. Thirteen (including the Central Bank) are established by special laws.

The 13 banks established by special laws carry out specialized banking activities beside their general banking transactions. Five of them are state economic enterprises whose capital is owned wholly by the State. They include: Ziraat Bankası (rural credits, capital: TL1,500m.), Sümerbank (textiles, etc., capital: TL2,250m.),

Etibank (mining, energy, capital: TL3,250m.), İller Bankası (urban works, capital: TL2,000m.), İstanbul Emniyet Sandığı (savings bank). Six of them are joint-stock companies; the majority of their share capital is owned by the public sector. They include: the Emlâk Kredi Bankası (housing, capital: TL1,000m.), Denizcilik Bankası (shipping, capital: TL2,000m.), Türkiye Vakıflar Bankası (investments of pious foundations, funds, capital: TL200m.), Türkiye Halk Bankası (small business, capital: TL1,000m.); Türkiye Öğretmenler Bankası (teachers' housing, capital: TL30m.), T. C. Turizm Bankası (tourism, capital: TL1,000m.).

The development banks are: Devlet Yatırım Bankası (investment credits to state economic enterprises, capital: TL1,000m.), Türkiye Sınaî Kalkınma Bankası (investment credit to the private sector, capital: TL328·66m.), Sınaî Yatırım ve Kredi Bankası (industrial medium-term credit, capital: TL40m.).

Of the 31 commercial banks, 5 are foreign banks established in Turkey, and one is a bank whose capital is shared by a foreign bank.

The total credit volume of banks at 31 Dec. 1978 amounted to TL463,310m.

Weights and Measures. The metric system came into force on 1 Jan. 1934. On 24 May 1928 the Grand National Assembly made European numerals obligatory as from 1 June 1929.

On 1 March 1917 the Gregorian calendar was introduced into Turkey, to be used side by side with the Hegira calendar, while as from 26 Dec. 1925 it was decided finally to adopt the Gregorian calendar alone.

ENERGY AND NATURAL RESOURCES

Electricity. The potential hydro-electric power in Turkey is estimated at 56,000m. kwh. In 1978 the electrical power plants (hydro-electric or thermal) produced 21,596m. kwh.

Oil. Oil is being produced in Garzan and Raman by the Turkish Petroleum Co. Under the oil law of 14 Oct. 1954 private companies can explore and produce oil. Turkish companies produced 991,000 tons in 1978 and foreign companies 1,662,000 tonnes. The 3 refineries refined 12m. tons of crude oil in 1975. With a fourth refinery, introduced in 1973, total refining capacity now reaches 24m. tons a year. The oil pipeline Batman–Iskenderun (494 km) was opened on 4 Jan. 1967. Imports (refined locally) in 1978 were 10,762,000 tons.

Minerals. The Turkish provinces, especially those in Asia, are reported rich in minerals. Turkey is one of the four principal producers of chrome in the world.

Production of principal minerals (in 1,000 tonnes) was:

	1974	1975	1976	1977	1978
Coal (S and P)	8,554	8,365	4,632	8,042	7,751
Lignite (S and P)	11,161	11,851	7,440	9,391	11,454
Chrome (S and P)	726	946	830	268	293
Sulphur (S)	19	19	21	...	...
Manganese (P)	4	35	21	...	...
Iron ore (S and P)	2,285	2,297	2,739	1,939	2,396
Copper (Blister) (S)	19	16	28	31	27
Petroleum (S and P) (tons)	3,430	3,095	2,592	13,111 [1]	11,966 [1]

(S) State; (P) Private enterprise. [1] Petroleum products.

Of the Government organizations producing these ores, Zonguldak coal mines operate under the Turkish State Coal Exploitation; while the copper mines at Murgul and Ergani, the Eastern chromite mines, Keçiborlu sulphur, Emet colemanite, Küre pyrite and cupriferous pyrite, Keban argentiferous lead mines operate under the Etibank.

Agriculture. The number of people aged 15 and over engaged in agriculture in 1975 was 9,463,310.

In 1976, 240,570 sq. km were cultivated land, 163,100 sq. km of its own and 77,470 sq. km fallow; vineyards, fruit orchards and olive groves occupied 34,600 sq. km; forest occupied 201,700 sq. km.

The soil for the most part is very fertile; the principal products are cotton, tobacco, cereals (especially wheat), figs, silk, olives and olive oil, dried fruits, liquorice root, nuts, almonds, mohair, skins and hides, furs, wool, gums, canary seed, linseed and sesame. The principal tobacco districts are Samsun, Bafra, Çarsamba, İzmit and İzmir. Two-thirds of the exports of leaf tobacco goes to the USA. The principal centre for silk production is Bursa. The production of olive oil, mainly confined to the Ils of Aydın and Balıkesir, is very important (74,000 tonnes in 1979). Sugar production (refined) in 1978 was 1,126,000 tonnes. Agricultural production (in tonnes) in 1979 included 3,485,000 grapes, 980,000 oranges and lemons, 270,000 hazelnuts, 1·2m. apples, 411,000 olives, 1m. onions, 2·9m. potatoes. Tea production (fresh leaves) was 117,000 tonnes.

Turkey produced 2,000 tonnes of flax fibre and 8,000 tonnes of hemp fibre in 1979. Cotton production was 475,000 tonnes in 1978. Agricultural tractors numbered 370,259 in 1978.

Yield (in 1,000 tonnes) of principal crops:

	1975	1976	1977	1978	1979
Wheat	14,750	16,500	16,720	16,769	17,631
Barley	4,500	4,916	4,750	4,750	5,217
Maize	1,200	1,310	1,265	1,300	1,358
Rye	750	740	690	620	620
Tobacco	193	315	248	288	287
Oats	390	400	370	370	371
Rice	150	158	270	305	224

On 7 June 1945 the Grand National Assembly passed the Land Reform Bill under which large tracts of agricultural land are being distributed to peasants without land or with insufficient for their subsistence.

Livestock (1979): 43,942,000 sheep, 18,447,000 goats, 14·9m. cattle, 1,371,000 asses, 812,000 horses, 1,023,000 buffaloes.

In 1977 Turkey produced 88,800 tonnes of wool, 794,300 tonnes of cattle and sheep meat and 185,400 tonnes of poultry.

Forestry. On 8 Feb. 1937 a new forest law was voted, providing for state control of all forests, including those under private ownership. It contains measures for planting, protection against fire, marauders and insects, and lays down penalties for infringements of its clauses. The most wooded Ils are Kastamonu, Aydın, Bursa, Bolu, Trabzon, Konya and Balıkesir. Of the forest land, 10,417,560 hectares belonged to the State in 1951. In 1975 total forest land was 20·17m. hectares.

Fisheries. On 25 Aug. 1964 Turkey extended her waters in which she has exclusive fishing rights to 12 nautical miles. In 1978, 300,000 tonnes of sea and fresh water food was produced.

INDUSTRY AND TRADE

Industry. Production in 1978 included 15,129,000 tonnes of cement and 304,000 tonnes of paper. Industrial plants number about 30,000.

In 1978 Turkey produced (in tonnes) 2,595,000 of iron and steel, 11,466,000 of petroleum products, 2,735,000 of crude oil, 2,346,000 of iron ore, 11,454,000 of lignite (clean), 7,751,000 of coal (clean), 243,000 of chrome, 27,000 of copper, 828,000 of boron. There are steel works at Karabük, Ereğli and Iskenderun.

Labour. On 27 June 1945 a Ministry of Labour was set up, superseding the Department of Labour under the control of the Ministry of Economic Affairs. According to the strikes and lock-outs law, which came into effect on 24 Aug. 1963, strikes and lock-outs may be declared only after due effort has been made to negotiate and after the local authorities as well as the Ministry of Labour have been informed.

Conditions of work are regulated by the Labour Act of 12 Aug. 1967, which covers all places of work, employing more than 3 persons, outside agriculture. Children under 16 must not be employed for more than 8 hours a day, and employment should not impede school attendance. The Act provides for annual paid holidays of 12–24 working days and regulates overtime payment.

The trade-union movement began in 1947. There are 4 national confederations (including Türk-İş and Disk) and 6 federations. There are 35 unions affiliated to Türk-İş and 17 employers' federations affiliated to Disk, whose activities were banned on 12 Sept. 1980. In 1972, labour unions totalled 660 and employers' unions, 109.

Employment, 1975: Manufacturing, 1,243,567; construction, 447,342; transport, communications and warehousing, 512,327; mining, 108,506; services, 176,207. There were 157,466 manufacturing firms, 236,995 trading establishments and 580,635 service establishments.

Commerce. Imports and exports (in US$1m.) for calendar years:

	1975	1976	1977	1978
Imports	4,739	5,128	5,218	4,599
Exports	1,401	1,960	1,487	2,288

Exports (1978) in US$1m.: Cotton, 398·4; hazelnuts, 330·9; tobacco, 225·3; cotton yarn, 179·7; raisins, 99·7; chromium ores, 30; leather, 29; olive oil, 0·4.

Imports (1978) in US$1m.: Crude oil, 1,093·5; machinery, 792·2; chemicals, 762·1; motor vehicles, 450·8; iron and steel, 409·8; petroleum products, 289·1; electrical appliances, 223·6; rubber and plastics, 159·7.

Total trade between Turkey and UK (British Department of Trade returns, in £1,000 sterling):

	1976	1977	1978	1979	1980
Imports to UK	60,395	56,733	64,574	67,060	49,243
Exports and re-exports from UK	210,897	210,181	110,571	135,734	147,118

Tourism. A tourist industry is developing. The number of foreign tourists was over 1·75m. in 1978.

COMMUNICATIONS

Roads. Turkey had, in 1978, 59,718 km of national highways, of which 52,675 were hard surfaced. In 1978 there were registered 1,005,900 motor vehicles, including 629,000 passenger cars and 29,200 buses.

Railways. The total length of railway lines in 1980 was 8,141 km, all state-owned; 202 km are electrified.

In 1978 Turkish railways carried 13·2m. tonnes.

Aviation. The State Airways Administration, formed in 1938, has been converted into the mixed company Turkish Airlines (Türk Havayollari Anonim Ortaklığı); British Airways became a partner in July 1957. It conducts foreign services to Athens, Beirut, Brussels, Amsterdam, Munich, Rome, Frankfurt, Vienna, London, Paris, Belgrade, Nicosia, Tel-Aviv and Baghdad.

In 1977 Turkish Airlines carried 6,545,000 passengers, 1·39m. kg of mail (1972) and 144·5m. kg of freight (1972). İstanbul or Ankara are connected with all the principal countries by 27 national airlines.

Shipping. In 1977 Turkish Maritime Lines and private companies had a gross tonnage of 1,699,910, with a total of 347 ships. The main ports in order of tonnage capacity are: İstanbul, İzmir, Samsun, Mersin, İskenderun and Trabzon.

Ports built or extended since 1950 are İskenderun, Ereğli, Trabzon, Samsun, Mersin, Zonguldak, Giresun, Hopa, Antalya and Bandirma. New facilities have been provided at Haydarpaşa, Salıpazari, Hopa, Yarımca and İzmir.

Post and Broadcasting. Number of telephones in 1978 was 1,378,620; İstanbul, 395,791; Ankara, 288,600.

In 1977 there were 4,260,563 licensed wireless sets. There were 2,271,781 television receivers.

Newspapers. In 1975 there were 2,362 daily newspapers and periodicals in the Turkish language, 2 in Greek, 1 in French and 1 in English. In 1976, 27 dailies were published in Ankara, 40 dailies in İstanbul, 6 dailies in İzmir, 5 dailies in Bursa and 4 dailies in Konya.

JUSTICE, RELIGION, EDUCATION AND WELFARE

Justice. The unified legal system consists of: (1) justices of the peace (single judges with limited but summary penal and civil jurisdiction); (2) courts of first instance (single judges, dealing with cases outside the jurisdiction of (3) and (4)); (3) central criminal courts (a president and 2 judges, dealing with cases where the crime is punishable by imprisonment over 5 years); (4) commercial courts (3 judges); (5) state security courts, to prosecute offences against the integrity of the state (a president and 4 judges, 2 of the latter being military).

The civil and military Courts of Cassation sit at Ankara.

The Council of State is the highest administration tribunal; it consists of 5 chambers. Its 31 judges are nominated from among high-ranking personalities in politics, economy, law, the army, etc.

The Military Court of Cassation in Ankara is the highest military tribunal. The Military Administrative Court deals with the judicial control of administrative acts and deeds concerning military personnel.

The Constitutional Court, set up under the Constitution, can review and annul legislation and try the President of the Republic, Ministers and senior judges. It consists of 15 regular and 5 alternate members.

The Civil Code and the Code of Obligations have been adapted from the corresponding Swiss codes. The Penal Code is largely based upon the Italian Penal Code, and the Code of Civil Procedure closely resembles that of the Canton of Neuchâtel. The Commercial Code is based on the German.

Religion. Freedom of religion is guaranteed by the Constitution. Although Islam is not the official state religion of Turkey, Moslems form 98·2% of the population. The administration of the Moslem religious organizations is in charge of the Presidency of Religious Affairs, attached to the Prime Minister's office. The Turkish Republic is a secular state.

İstanbul is the seat of the Œcumenical Patriarch, who is the head of the Orthodox Church in Turkey. The Armenian Church (Gregorian) is ruled by a Patriarch in İstanbul who is subordinate to the Katholikos of Etchmiadzin, the spiritual head of all Armenians. The Armenian Apostolic Church is ruled by the Patriarch of Cilicia. The Chaldeans (Nestorian Uniats) have a Bishop at Mardin. The Syrian Uniats have a See of Mardin and Amida, but it is united with their Patriarchate of Antioch (residence, Damascus). Greek Uniats (Byzantine Rite) have as their Ordinary in Istanbul, the Titular Bishop of Gratianopolis. The Latins have an Apostolic Delegate in İstanbul and an Archbishop in İzmir, but their Patriarch of İstanbul is titular and non-resident. There is a Grand Rabbi (Hahambaşı) in Istanbul for the Jews, who are nearly all Sephardim.

At the 1965 census there were in Turkey 31,391,421 Moslems, 73,725 Orthodox, 69,526 Gregorians, 25,833 Roman Catholics, 22,883 Protestants, 14,758 other Christians (unspecified), 38,267 Jews, 14,661 adherents of other religions, 1,212 without religion, 602 undeclared or unknown.

A law passed in Dec. 1934 forbids the wearing of clerical garb for those other than religious leaders except in places of worship and during divine service. The constitution forbids the political exploitation of religion or any impairment of the secular character of the republic.

In lieu of religious formulae, all citizens take oaths on their honour.

Education. Elementary education is compulsory and co-educational and, in state schools, free. All children from 7 to 12 are to receive primary instruction, which may be given in state schools, schools maintained by communities, or private schools, or, subject to certain tests, at home. The state schools are under the direct control of the Ministry of Education. They include primary schools, secondary or middle schools, and *lycées* or secondary schools of a superior kind. There are also training schools for male and female teachers, and technical schools. In 1979 there were 18 universities and 102 other institutes of higher education. The important non-Moslem communities in Istanbul maintain their own schools, which, like all 'private' schools, are subject to the supervision of the Ministry of Education.

Literacy of the population of 6 years and over was 10·6% in 1927, 19·2% in 1935, 29% in 1945, 40·9% in 1955, 48·7% in 1965, 49% in 1970, 61·7% in 1975.

Religious instruction in schools, hitherto prohibited, was made optional in elementary and middle schools in May 1948. There are many training schools for Moslem clergy as well as a Faculty of Theology in Ankara.

Statistics for 1979–80	Number	Teachers	Students
Primary schools (state and private)	42,886	182,679	5,502,000
Middle schools (state and private)	3,055	22,301	1,054,000
Lycées (state and private)	929	29,025	429,000
Professional and technical schools	1,389	22,728	436,000
Faculties (university and higher education)	314	16,981	340,000

On 1 Nov. 1928 the Grand National Assembly voted a law for the adoption of Latin characters as from 1 Dec. 1928. The publication of books in Arabic characters was forbidden after 1 Jan. 1929.

Health. Public health is the responsibility of the Ministry of Health and Social Welfare, established in 1920; social insurance for workers comes under the Workers' Insurance Institution attached to the Ministry of Labour. A law promulgated in 1961 and being implemented from 1963 provides for the nationalization of the health services within 15 years. In 1972, 1·52m. workers and employees were covered by social insurance, including free medical care.

In 1977 there were 23,920 doctors and 87,232 beds in some 807 hospitals.

The counterpart of the Red Cross in Turkey is the Red Crescent Society founded in 1877.

DIPLOMATIC REPRESENTATIVES

OF TURKEY IN GREAT BRITAIN (43 Belgrave Sq., London, SW1X 8PA)

Ambassador: Vahap Aşıroğlu (accredited 16 Nov. 1978).

OF GREAT BRITAIN IN TURKEY (Sehit Ersan Caddesi 46/A, Cankaya, Ankara)

Ambassador: P. H. Laurence, CMG, MC.

OF TURKEY IN THE USA (1606–23rd St., NW, Washington, D.C., 20008)

Ambassador: Şükrü Elekdağ.

OF THE USA IN TURKEY (110 Ataturk Blvd., Ankara)

Ambassador: James W. Spain.

OF TURKEY TO THE UNITED NATIONS

Ambassador: Orhan Eralp.

Books of Reference

Statistical Information: The State Institute of Statistics in Ankara consists of a research bureau and 10 sections dealing with agriculture, education, foreign trade, etc. It published an *Annuaire Statistique/Istatistik Yılığı* (1928–53) and *Aylık Istatistik Bülteni*, Monthly Bulletin of Statistics.

Almanac: Turkey Annex
The Turkish Constitution, 1971. Ankara, 1972
Resmî Gazete, Official Gazette. Ankara
Konjonktür. Ministry of Commerce (three times a year, from 1940)
Banque Centrale de la République de Turquie. *Bulletin Mensuel* (from Jan. 1953)
Bulletins of the Chambers of Commerce of Istanbul and Izmir
Turkish Trade Directory, 1971–72. Istanbul, 1971
Ahmad, F., *The Turkish Experiment in Democracy.* London, 1977
Akurgal, E., *Ancient Civilizations and Ruins of Turkey.* Ankara, 1973
Aslanapa, O., *Turkish Art and Architecture.* London, 1971
Cenani, Rasim, *Foreign Capital Investments in Turkey.* 2nd ed. Istanbul, 1958
Dewdney, J. C., *Turkey.* London, 1971
Economic News Digest. Ankara, 1971
Frey, F. W., *The Turkish Political Elite.* M.I.T. Press, 1965
Goodwin, G., *A History of Ottoman Architecture.* London, 1971

Hotham, D., *The Turks*. London, 1973
Kinross, Lord, *Atatürk*. London, 1964
Koray, Enver, *Türkiye Tarih Yayınları Bibliografyası 1729–1950* (*Bibliography of Historical Works on Turkey*). Ankara, 1952
Kortepeter, C. M., *Ottoman Imperialism During Reformation: Europe and the Caucasus*. London, 1972
Landau, J. M., *Radical Politics in Modern Turkey*. Leiden, 1974
Lewis, B., *The Emergence of Modern Turkey*. OUP, 1961
Lewis, G., *Turkey*. 3rd ed. London, 1965
Lewis, R., *Everyday Life in Ottoman Turkey*. London, 1971
Mair, C., *A Time in Turkey*. London, 1973
Mango, A., *Discovering Turkey*. London, 1971
Newman, B., *Turkey and the Turks*. London, 1968
Price, M. P., *A History of Turkey*. London, 1968
Robinson, D. R., *The First Turkish Republic*. Harvard Univ. Press and OUP, 1964
Sezer, D. B., *Turkey's Security Policies*. London, 1981
Tamkoç, M., *The Warrior Diplomats*. Univ. of Utah Press, 1976
Weiker W., *Political Tutelage and Democracy in Turkey*. Leiden, 1972
Williams, G., *Turkey: A Traveller's Guide and History*. London, 1967

State Library: MilliKütüphane Müdürlüğü, Ankara. *Director-General:* Müjgân Cunbur.

THE TURKS AND CAICOS ISLANDS

Capital: Grand Turk
Population: 7,200 (1977)

HISTORY. The islands were ceded to Britain by Spain in 1670 and became dependencies of Jamaica in 1848.

AREA AND POPULATION. The Turks and Caicos Islands are geographically a portion of the Bahamas, of which they form the two south-eastern groups. There are upwards of 30 small cays; area 192 sq. miles (430 sq. km). Only 6 are inhabited; the largest, Grand Caicos, is 30 miles long by 2 to 3 miles broad. The seat of government is at Grand Turk, 7 miles long by 1·25 broad; 2,900 inhabitants (estimate). Population, 1970 census, 5,558 (1977, estimate, 7,200). South Caicos, 1,018 (1,300); Middle Caicos, 362 (400); North Caicos, 989 (1,200); Providenciales, 558 (900).

Vital statistics (1977): Births, 194; marriages, 39 (1976); deaths, 41.

CONSTITUTION AND GOVERNMENT. A new Constitution was introduced in Sept. 1976, providing for an Executive Council and a Legislative Council. The Governor retains responsibility for external affairs, internal security, defence and certain other matters. The Executive Council comprises 3 official members: the Chief Secretary, the Financial Secretary and the Attorney-General; a Chief Minister and 3 other ministers from among the elected members of the Legislative Council; and is presided over by the Governor. The Legislative Council consists of a Speaker, the 3 official members of the Executive Council, 11 elected members and 2 nominated members.

Governor: J. C. Strong.
Flag: British Blue Ensign with the shield of the Colony in the fly.

ECONOMY

Budget. 1978–79 revenue (revised) US$6,343,000 including $2,378,797 budgetary aid; expenditure (revised) $5,753,767.

1979–80 revenue (revised) US$6,495,610 including $2,265,000 budgetary aid; expenditure (estimated) $5,420,469.

Currency. The currency in circulation is US$.

Banking. The Government Savings Bank has 3 branches. Barclays Bank International and the Oxford International Bank and Trust Co. Ltd have offices in Grand Turk with branches in South Caicos, North Caicos and Providenciales.

COMMERCE (1978). Exports, US$1,703,954, and imports, US$7,082,883. Principal imports, food, drink, tobacco and clothing. Exports, 1977–78 season, crawfish, US$803,590; conch, US$834,817; miscellaneous, US$65,547.

Total trade between Turks and Caicos Islands and UK (British Department of Trade returns, in £1,000 sterling):

	1977	1978	1979	1980
Imports to UK	6	1,044	257	8
Exports and re-exports from UK	321	238	276	295

TOURISM. Number of hotels and guest houses, 16 (beds 194). Number of visitors, 1978, 12,331.

COMMUNICATIONS

Aviation. There is a 5,500 ft paved airfield on Grand Turk under the control of the US Air Force but open to civil aviation. On South Caicos there is a 7,000 ft paved airstrip and on Providenciales a 5,000 ft paved airstrip. There are small unpaved airstrips on the other 3 inhabited islands. Air Florida Airlines operate a twice or thrice weekly passenger service to Miami. Bahamas Air operate a twice weekly scheduled passenger service to the Bahamas. Air Turks and Caicos operate a twice daily service to the islands and 2 flights a week to Cap Haitien (Haiti). Turks Air Ltd operates a regular weekly cargo service to Miami.

Shipping. Registered shipping (1978), 157 sailing vessels of 2,060 tons and 32 motor vessels of 2,367 tons.

Post and Broadcasting. Air-mail is received and dispatched by Miami twice or thrice weekly. Surface mail from all parts of the world is routed *via* the US arriving at 3 weekly intervals from Miami, Florida. There is no regular outgoing surface mail. Cable & Wireless (West Indies) provide internal and international cable, telephone, telex and telegraph services and also operate telephone and telegraph services to ships at sea. There were (1978) 721 telephones. North Caicos and Salt Cay are linked with the Providenciales and Grand Turk exchanges respectively. The Government operates a radio broadcasting service from the Islands to Grand Turk, call sign VSI radio Turks and Caicos, for a total of 72 hours a week on 1,500 KHZ medium wave. Number of receivers, approximately 6,000.

EDUCATION AND WELFARE

Education. Education is free and compulsory up to 15 years of age in the 14 government primary and 3 government secondary schools. There is also 1 private primary school. Number on rolls, 1 Jan. 1979, primary, 1,897 (including 144 private); secondary, 689. Expenditure on education 1977 (revised) US$702,303 recurrent, US$64,098 capital.

Health. In 1978 there were 2 doctors and 30 hospital beds.

TUVALU

HISTORY. Formerly the Ellice Islands, a British Protectorate since 1892. On the recommendation of a Commissioner, appointed by the British Government, to consider requests that the island group be separated from the Gilbert Islands, a referendum was held in 1974. There was a large majority in favour of separation and this took place in Oct. 1975.

AREA AND POPULATION. Tuvalu (formerly the Ellice Islands) lie between 5° 30′ and 11° S. lat. and 176° and 180° E. long. and comprise Nanumea, Nanumanga, Niutao, Nui, Vaitupu, Nukufetau, Funafuti (administrative centre), Nukulaelae and Niulakita. Population (census 1979) 7,349. Area approximately 9½ sq. miles (24 sq. km). The population is of a Polynesian race.

CONSTITUTION AND GOVERNMENT. The Constitution provides for a Prime Minister and 4 other Ministers to be elected from among the 12 elected members of the House of Assembly, for which general elections took place on 29 Aug. 1977. The Cabinet, chaired by the Prime Minister, consists of the 4 ministers and 2 *ex officio* members, the Attorney-General and the Financial Secretary, who are also *ex officio* members of the House of Assembly. Independence was achieved on 1 Oct. 1978. Local Government services are provided by an elected Island Council on each of the 8 atolls.

Governor-General: Fiatau Penitala Teo, GCMG, MBE.
Prime Minister, Minister for Finance and Foreign Affairs: Toaripi Lauti.
Social Services: Taui Finikaso. *Commerce and Natural Resources:* Toomu Sione. *Communications and Transport:* Ilaoa Imo. *Works and Local Government:* Maheu Naniseni.

National flag: Light blue with the Union Jack in the canton, and 9 gold stars in the fly arranged in the same pattern as the 9 islands.

Local Government. There is a town council on Funafuti and island councils on the 7 other main islands, each consisting of 6 elected members including a president.

ECONOMY

Budget. In 1979 the budget envisaged expenditure of $A2m.; $A750,000 provided by UK by a grant-in-aid.

Currency. The unit of currency is the Australian *dollar* although Tuvaluan coins up to $A1 are in local circulation.

Banking. The Bank of Tuvalu was established at Funafuti in 1980.

NATURAL RESOURCES

Agriculture. Coconut palms are the main crop. Fruit and vegetables are grown for local consumption.

Fisheries. Sea fishing is excellent but is largely unexploited.

INDUSTRY AND TRADE

Industry. The main sources of income are from overseas remittances from Tuvaluans working abroad, philatelic and copra sales, and handicrafts.

Employment. The majority of the population are employed in the phosphate industry on Nauru. The remainder are engaged in harvesting coconuts and fishing.

Commerce. Commerce is dominated by co-operative societies, the Tuvalu Co-operative Wholesale Society being the main importer.

Total trade between Tuvalu and UK (British Department of Trade returns, in £1,000 sterling):

	1979	1980
Imports to UK	174	34
Exports and re-exports from UK	67	362

COMMUNICATIONS

Aviation. Tuvalu is linked to the outside world by Air Pacific HS748 which operates weekly, arriving on Wednesday and leaving on Thursday.

Shpping. Funafuti is the ony port n a deep-water wharf was opened in 1980. Inter-island communication is by ship; a limited service using an amphibious plane came into operation in 1980.

Post and Broadcastin. TheTuvalu Broadcastin Service transmits daily in Tuvaluan and English and all islands have daily radio communication with Funafuti.

JUSTICE, RELIGION, EDUCATION AND WELFARE

Justice. There is a High Court presided over by the Chief Justice of the Solomon Islands. Appeals lie to the Fiji Court of Appeal.

Religion. The majority of the population are Christians mainly Protestant but with small groups of Roman Catholics, Seventh Day Adventists and Jehovah's Witnesses.

Education. In 1980 there was 1 secondary school jointly administered by the Government and the Church. In addition there were 8 primary schools with (1977) 1,558 pupils run by Island Councils and subsidized by the central government. In 1979, a maritime school was opened on Amatuku islet. Tuvaluans requiring further education must seek it abroad.

Health. In 1978 there was 1 central hospital with 36 beds situated at Funafuti. There were 3 doctors.

DIPLOMATIC REPRESENTATIVE

OF GREAT BRITAIN IN TUVALU

High Commissioner: Viscount Dunrossil (resides in Suva).

UGANDA

Capital: Kampala
Population: 13·22m. (1979)
GNP per capita: US$270 (1977)

HISTORY. Uganda became a British Protectorate in 1894, the province of Buganda being recognized as a native kingdom under its Kabaka. In 1961 Uganda was granted internal self-government with federal status for Buganda. The country became independent in 1962.

AREA AND POPULATION. Uganda is bounded on the north by Sudan, on east by Kenya, on south by Tanzania and west by Zaïre. Total area 91,343 sq. miles (236,860 sq. km), including 15,217 sq. miles (39,459 sq. km) of swamp and water.

The population of Uganda was 13·22m. (1979 estimate). On 4 Aug. 1972 President Amin announced that he would ask the UK to take responsibility for Asians in Uganda holding British passports. Later that year 27,200 Asians had left Uganda for Britain. The majority of the Africans (1,044,000) are Baganda, the tribe from which the country takes its name.

About 3m. Africans speak Bantu languages; there are a few Congo pygmies living near the Semliki River; the rest of the Africans belong to the Hamitic, Nilotic and Sudanese groups. Ki-Swahili is generally understood in trading centres. The capital is Kampala; the population of greater Kampala (1975), 332,000.

The official language is English.

CONSTITUTION AND GOVERNMENT. Uganda became a fully independent member of the Commonwealth on 9 Oct. 1962 after nearly 70 years of British rule. Full sovereign status was granted by the Uganda Independence Act, 1962, and the Constitution is embodied in the Uganda (Independence) Order in Council, 1962. The post of Governor-General was on 9 Oct. 1963 replaced by that of President as head of state, elected by the National Assembly for a 5-year term.

Uganda became a republic on 8 Sept. 1967. Under the 1967 Constitution, the executive authority is vested in the President.

In 1971, Dr A. Milton Obote was overthrown by troops led by Gen. Idi Amin.

In April 1979 a force of the Tanzanian Army and Ugandan exiles advanced into Uganda taking Kampala on 11 April. On 14 April Dr Yusuf Lule was sworn in as President and the country is to be administered, initially, by the Uganda National Liberation Front.

The former Attorney-General, Godfrey Lukongwa Binaisa, QC, was appointed President by the National Consultative Council on 20 June 1979. Dr Lule subsequently left the country. Dr Binaisa was subsequently overthrown in May 1980 by the army. At the elections held on 10–11 Dec. 1980, the Uganda People's Congress was declared to have held 72 of the 124 elective seats in the new Parliament, the Democratic Party 51 seats, and the Uganda Patriotic Movement 1 seat.

President, Minister of Foreign Affairs and Finance: Dr Milton Obote.
Vice-President, Minister of Defence: Paulo Muwanga.
Prime Minister: Otema Alimadi.

National flag: Six horizontal stripes of black, yellow, red, black, yellow, red, in the centre a small white disc bearing a representation of a Balearic Crested Crane.

For administrative purposes Uganda is divided into 10 provinces, subdivided into 38 districts. The provinces are: Busoga, Central, Eastern, Karamoja, Nile, North Buganda, Northern, South Buganda, Southern, Western.

DEFENCE

Army. The Army had a strength of 20,000 in 1979 and was organized into 2 brigades (each of 4 infantry battalions), 2 reconnaissance, 1 mechanized, 1 commando and 1 training battalion. Accurate statistics unavailable in early 1981.

Navy. A small lake patrol was initiated in 1977.

Air Force. The Air Force was formed in 1964 and later underwent rapid expansion with the assistance of Israeli and Czechoslovakian training missions. Prior to the events of 1979 equipment included about 10 MiG-21 and 12 MiG-17 jet fighter-bombers, 2 MiG-15 UTI two-seat trainers, about 5 L-29 Delfin and 8 Israeli-built Magister armed jet trainers, 11 Super Cub liaison aircraft, 5 Piaggio P 149 piston-engined trainers, 6 Swiss-built Bravo primary trainers, 6 Agusta-Bell 205, 2 Agusta-Bell 206 JetRanger and some Mi-8 helicopters. Personnel numbered about 1,000. In addition the Police Air Wing had 1 Twin Otter and 1 Caribou twin-engined STOL transports, 1 Turbo-Beaver and 1 Piper Aztec light transports, and about 7 Bell 205, JetRanger, Bell 212 and Scout helicopters. The status of these aircraft was unknown in early 1981.

INTERNATIONAL RELATIONS

Membership. Uganda is a member of UN, OAU, the Commonwealth and is an ACP state of EEC.

ECONOMY

Budget. The revenue and expenditure (exclusive of loan disbursements) for fiscal years (1 July–30 June) were (in Uganda Sh. 1m.):

	1976–77	1977–78	1978–79	1979–80
Revenue	4,305	5,856	3,197	4,871
Expenditure	5,201	6,287	5,441	6,805

Currency. East African Currency Board notes ceased to be legal tender from 14 Sept. 1967. The monetary unit is the *Uganda shilling* divided into 100 *cents*. In March 1981, £1 = 18·08 Uganda shillings; US$1 = 7·88 Uganda shillings.

Banking. The Bank of Uganda was set up on 16 May 1966; its external assets as at 31 Aug. 1967 were £9m. The Uganda Credit and Savings Bank, set up in 1950, was on 9 Oct. 1965 reconstituted as the Uganda Commercial Bank, with its capital fully owned by the Government.

Barclays Bank International has 11 branches and 7 agencies; National & Grindlays Bank Ltd has 12 branches and 12 agencies; the Standard Bank Ltd has 6 branches and 2 agencies; the Bank of Baroda Ltd has 3 branches; the Bank of India Ltd has 2 branches. Other banks operating in Uganda are the Algemene Bank Nederland NV and the Commercial Bank of Africa.

ENERGY AND NATURAL RESOURCES

Electricity. Industrial expansion is based on hydro-electric power provided by the Owen Falls scheme, which has a capacity of 150,000 kwh. Production (1976) 696m. kwh.

Minerals. With the opening of the Kilembe mine in 1956, copper has become Uganda's most valuable mineral export. Production (1978) in tonnes: Blister copper, 600; tin, 120; phosphate rock (1977) 5,000.

Agriculture. In 1980, agriculture was still recovering from the administration of 1971–79. Cotton and coffee are the principal exports, the former being grown entirely and the latter very largely by African farmers. Production (1978) in 1,000 tonnes: Groundnuts, 250; coffee, 121; cotton lint, 15; tea,10; sugar, 8; millet, 480.

Livestock (1979): Cattle, 5·4m.; asses, 16,000; sheep, 1·1m.; goats, 2·1m.; pigs, 225,000; poultry, 13·m.

Forestry. Exploitable forests consist almost entirely of hardwoods. Internal consumption is rising. During 1964–65 approximately 28,000 tons of sawn timber were produced. About half of the timber exported goes to the UK and another quarter to Kenya and Tanganyika, from which the bulk of the softwood imports are obtained.

Fishery. With its 13,600 sq. miles of lakes and many rivers, Uganda possesses one of the largest fresh-water fisheries in the world. In 1966 fish production was 80,000 tons with a retail value of £6·5m. Fish farming (especially carp and tilapia) is a growing industry.

COMMERCE. In 1977 the main exports (in Uganda Sh.) were: Coffee, 4,536m.; raw cotton, 126m.; tea, 103m.

Trade (in Uganda Sh.1m.):

	1975	1976	1977	1978
Imports	1,469	1,424	2,712	1,963
Exports	1,912	3,009	4,634	2,682

Total trade between Uganda and UK (British Department of Trade returns, in £1,000 sterling):

	1976	1977	1978	1979	1980
Imports to UK	32,448	33,402	47,651	19,189	30,735
Exports and re-exports from UK	11,171	21,227	39,358	18,881	33,526

COMMUNICATIONS

Roads. There are 3,876 miles of all-weather roads maintained by the Ministry of Works, of which 796 miles are two-lane bitumenized highways, and some 11,230 miles of other roads, maintained by district governments.

Railways. On 26 Aug. 1977 Uganda Railways was formed following break-up of the East African Railways administration. The network totals 1,120 km (metre gauge).

Aviation. Entebbe had a first-class international airport which had direct flights to Europe, Rhodesia, Sudan, Kenya, Burundi, Ghana, Ethiopia, Zaïre, Nigeria, USSR, and Rwanda by Sudan Airways, Air Congo, SABENA, Air France, Ethiopian Airlines, Air Zaïre and Aeroflot. The airport was damaged during the 1979 invasion. Eleven other government airfields are used for internal communications.

Posts. There were 48,884 telephones in use at 1 Jan. 1978.

Cinemas. In 1971 there were 16 cinemas with a seating capacity of 8,000.

JUSTICE, EDUCATION AND WELFARE

Justice. The High Court of Uganda, presided over by the Chief Justice and 12 puisne judges, exercises original and appellate jurisdiction throughout Uganda. Subordinate courts, presided over by Chief Magistrates and Magistrates of the first, second and third grade, are established in all areas: jurisdiction varies with the grade of Magistrate. Chief and first-grade Magistrates are professionally qualified; second- and third-grade Magistrates are trained to diploma level at the Law School, Entebbe.

Chief Magistrates exercise supervision over and hear appeals from second- and third-grade courts.

The Court of Appeal for Eastern Africa was re-established on 9 Dec. 1962 as the Court of Appeal for Uganda; it hears appeals from the High Court.

A law school has been established at Entebbe to train magistrates in civil and criminal law.

The African courts have been integrated with the Central Government Courts so that a unified courts system has been established.

Education. Education is a joint undertaking by the Government, local authorities and, to some extent, voluntary agencies. The education system is divided into 3 sectors, primary, secondary and post-secondary. The primary course covers 7 years. There were 786,899 pupils in grant-aided primary schools in 1972. Education at secondary level falls into 4 categories, namely, secondary schools, which are the grammar type of schools with a course extending over 6 years to Higher School Certificate; technical schools; farm schools; and primary teacher-training colleges. Further education is provided at the Uganda Technical College, the National Teachers' College, the Uganda College of Commerce and Agricultural Colleges.

There are also several Departmental Training Schools for training staff for different departments.

The medical department has 8 such schools for training nurses, midwives, medical assistants, health inspectors, and other medical staff.

University level education is available at Makerere University College and the 2 other constituent Colleges of the University of East Africa; the University College, Nairobi, in Kenya, and the University College, Dar es Salaam, in Tanzania. Uganda students also go to universities and colleges outside East Africa for higher education.

Health. In 1973 there were 300 doctors and over 15,000 hospital beds.

DIPLOMATIC REPRESENTATIVES

OF UGANDA IN GREAT BRITAIN
(Uganda Hse., Trafalgar Sq., London, WC2N 5DX)

High Commissioner: Shafiq Arain (also Minister of Portfolio in Ugandan cabinet).

OF GREAT BRITAIN IN UGANDA (10/12 Parliament Ave., Kampala)

High Commissioner: B. A. Flack, CMG.

OF UGANDA IN THE USA (5909, 16th St., NW, Washington, D.C., 20011)

Chargé d'Affaires: A. C. Nabeta.

OF UGANDA TO THE UNITED NATIONS

Ambassador: E. Kanyanya Wapenyi.

Books of Reference

Atlas of Uganda. Dept. of Lands and Surveys. Kampala, 1962
Faller, L. A. (ed.), *The King's Men.* OUP, 1964
Gukiina, P. M., *Uganda: A Case Study in African Political Development.* Univ. of Notre Dame Press, 1972
Hills, D., *The White Pumpkin.* New York, 1976
Ingham, K., *The Making of Modern Uganda.* London, 1957
Kendall, H., *Town Planning in Uganda.* London, 1955
Kitching, A. L., and Blackledge, G. R., *A Luganda–English and English–Luganda Dictionary.* Kampala, 1925
Larimore, A. E., *The Alien Town: Patterns of Settlement in Uganda.* Chicago, 1959
Listowel, J., *Amin.* Irish Univ. Press, 1973

UNION OF SOVIET SOCIALIST REPUBLICS

Capital: Moscow
Population: 264·5m. (1980)

Soyuz Sovyetskikh Sotsialisticheskikh Respublik

POST-REVOLUTION HISTORY. Up to 12 March 1917 the territory now forming the USSR, together with that of Finland, Poland and certain tracts ceded in 1918 to Turkey, but less the territories then forming part of the German, Austro-Hungarian and Japanese empires—East Prussia, Eastern Galicia, Transcarpathia, Bukovina, South Sakhalin and Kurile Islands—which were acquired during and after the Second World War, was constituted as the Russian Empire. It was governed as an autocracy under the Tsar, with the aid of Ministers responsible to himself and a State Duma with limited legislative powers, elected by provincial assemblies chosen by indirect elections on a restricted franchise.

On 12 March 1917 a revolution broke out. The Duma parties, the same day, set up a Provisional Committee of the State Duma, while the factory workmen and the insurgent garrison of Petrograd elected a Council (Soviet) of Workers' and Soldiers' Deputies. Soviets were also elected by the workmen in other towns, in the Army and Navy and, as time went on, by the peasantry. On 15 March 1917 the Tsar abdicated, and the Provisional Committee, by agreement with the Petrograd Soviet, appointed a Provisional Government and, on 14 Sept., proclaimed a republic. However, a political struggle went on between the supporters of the Provisional Government—the Mensheviks and the Socialist-Revolutionaries—and the Bolsheviks, who advocated the assumption of power by the Soviets. When they had won majorities in the Soviets of the principal cities and of the armed forces on several fronts, the Bolsheviks organized an insurrection through a Military-Revolutionary Committee of the Petrograd Soviet. On 7 Nov. 1917 the Committee arrested the Provisional Government and transferred power to the second All-Russian Congress of Soviets. This elected a new government, the Council of People's Commissars, headed by Lenin.

On 31 Jan. 1918 the third All Russian Congress of Soviets issued a Declaration of Rights of the Toiling and Exploited Masses, which proclaimed Russia a Republic of Soviets of Workers', Soldiers' and Peasants' Deputies; and on 10 July 1918 the fifth Congress adopted a Constitution for the Russian Socialist Federal Soviet Republic. In the course of the civil war other Soviet Republics were set up in the Ukraine, Belorussia and Transcaucasia. These first entered into treaty relations with the RSFSR and then, in 1922, joined with it in a closely integrated Union.

AREA AND POPULATION. The total area of the Soviet Union in April, 1965 was 22·4m. sq. km (8·65m. sq. miles). The census population on 15 Jan. 1970 was 241·7m. (111·3m. males, 130·4m. females; 136m. urban, 105·7m. rural). The census population on 17 Jan. 1979 was 262·4m. (122·3m. males, 140·1m. females, 163·6m. urban, 98·8m. rural). The increase of 27·6m. in urban population between 1970 and 1979 was due to natural increase and 15·6m. rural dwellers becoming part of the urban population resulting from migration because of the development of industry and transport, and increased farm mechanization, and from the urbanization of large rural centres. Consequently, despite a natural increase of 8·7m. in rural areas, there was a net decrease of 6·9m. over this period. Population at 1 Jan. 1980, 264·5m. (123·3m. males, 141·2m. females; 166·1m. urban; 98·4m. rural).

Regions, towns, streets, factories, schools, etc., named after Stalin were renamed in Nov. 1961 when Stalin's body was removed from the Lenin–Stalin tomb in Red

Square in Moscow. Similarly, in Jan. 1962 towns bearing the names of Molotov, Kaganovich and Malenkov were renamed.

The areas (in 1,000 sq. km) and population (in 1m., in Jan. 1980) of the constituent republics are as follows (capitals in brackets):

Constituent Republics	Area	Popu-lation	Constituent Republics	Area	Popu-lation
RSFSR (Moscow)	17,075	138·4	Tadzhikistan (Dushanbe)	143	3·9
Ukraine (Kiev)	604	50·0	Kirgizia (Frunze)	198	3·6
Uzbekistan (Tashkent)	447	15·8	Lithuania (Vilnius)	65	3·4
Kazakhstan (Alma-Ata)	2,717	14·9	Armenia (Yerevan)	30	3·0
Belorussia (Minsk)	208	9·6	Turkmenistan (Ashkhabad)	488	2·8
Azerbaijan (Baku)	87	6·1	Latvia (Riga)	64	2·5
Georgia (Tbilisi)	70	5·0	Estonia (Tallinn)	45	1·5
Moldavia (Kishinev)	34	4·0			

Nationalities. The most numerous nationalities at the 1979 census were: 137m. Russians, 42m. Ukrainians, 12·5m. Uzbeks, 9·4m. Belorussians, 6·5m. Kazakhs, 6·3m. Tatars, 5·4m. Azerbaijanians, 4·1m. Armenians, 3·6m. Georgians, 3m. Moldavians, 2·9m. Tadzhiks, 2·8m. Lithuanians, 2m. Turkmenians, 1·9m. Germans, 1·9m. Kirgiz, 1·8m. Jews, 1·8m. Chuvashes, 1·4m. Latvians, 1·4m. Bashkirs, 1·2m. Mordovians, 1·2m. Poles, 1m. Estonians. The great majority (in each case 84–99%) indicated the language of their nationality as their native tongue; exceptions were the Bashkirs (66%), Poles (33%) and Jews (17·7%).

Estimated losses of population in the Second World War, 20m., of which 7m. were military losses.

The following tables show the growth of the population in Russia:

1897 (Russian Empire)	126,900,000	1959 (census)	208,826,000
1913 (Russian Empire)	170,900,000	1970 (census)	241,748,000
1913 (present frontiers)	159,200,000	1979 (census)	262,436,000
1939 (census)	170,600,000		

The following was the population on 1 Jan. 1980 of the larger towns (in 1,000):

Aktyubinsk	197	Engels	161	Kramatorsk	180
Alma-Ata	928	Ferghana	177	Krasnodar	572
Andizhan	233	Frunze	543	Krasnoyarsk	807
Angarsk	241	Gomel	393	Kremenchug	212
Arkhangelsk	387	Gorlovka	337	Krivoi Rog	657
Armavir	163	Gorky	1,358	Kuibyshev	1,226
Ashkhabad	318	Grodno	202	Kurgan	316
Astrakhan	465	Grozny	377	Kursk	383
Baku	1,030	Irkutsk	561	Kustanai	169
Barnaul	542	Ivanovo	466	Kutaisi	197
Belgorod	248	Izhevsk	562	Kzyl-Orda	159
Berezniki	186	Kalinin	416	Leninakan	210
Biisk	213	Kaliningrad	361	Leningrad	4,638
Blagoveshchensk	175	Kaluga	270	Lipetsk	405
Bobruisk	197	Kamensk-Uralski	189	Lvov	676
Bratsk	219	Karaganda	577	Lyubertsy	162
Brest	186	Kaunas	377	Magnitogorsk	410
Bryansk	401	Kazan	1,002	Makeyevka	439
Bukhara	188	Kemerovo	478	Makhachkala	261
Cheboksary	323	Kerch	158	Melitopol	163
Chelyabinsk	1,042	Khabarovsk	538	Miass	152
Cherepovetz	274	Kharkov	1,464	Minsk	1,295
Cherkassy	234	Kherson	324	Mogilev	300
Chernigov	245	Kiev	2,192	Moscow	8,099
Chernovtzy	221	Kirov	392	Murmansk	388
Chimkent	327	Kirovabad		Naberezhnye Chelny	319
Chita	308	(Azerbaijan)	237	Nalchik	211
Djambul	270	Kirovograd	242	Namangan	234
Dneprodzerzhinsk	253	Kishinev	519	Nikolayev	449
Dnepropetrovsk	1,083	Klaipeda	178	Nizhni Tagil	400
Donetsk	1,032	Kokand	154	Norilsk	182
Dushanbe	501	Komsomolsk-on-		Novgorod	192
Dzerzhinsk (Gorky		Amur	269	Novocherkassk	185
region)	260	Kostroma	255	Novokuznetsk	545

Novorossiisk	162	Ryazan	462	Tomsk	431
Novosibirsk	1,328	Rybinsk	241	Tselinograd	234
Odessa	1,057	Samarkand	481	Tula	518
Omsk	1,028	Saransk	271	Tyumen	369
Ordzhonikidze		Saratov	864	Ufa	986
(Vladikavkaz)	283	Semipalatinsk	286	Ulan-Ude	305
Orel	309	Sevastopol	308	Ulyanovsk	473
Orenburg	471	Severodvinsk	203	Uralsk	170
Orsk	252	Shakhty	212	Ust-Kamenogorsk	280
Osh	173	Simferopol	307	Vilnius	492
Pavlodar	281	Smolensk	305	Vinnitsa	323
Penza	490	Sochi	291	Vitebsk	303
Perm	1,008	Stavropol	265	Vladimir	301
Petropavlovsk-		Sterlitamak	224	Vladivostok	558
Kamchatski	219	Sumgait	196	Volgograd	939
Petropavlovsk (North		Sumy	233	Vologda	214
Kazakhstan)	209	Sverdlovsk	1,225	Volzhsk	241
Petrozavodsk	238	Syktyvkar	175	Voronezh	796
Podolsk	203	Syzran	168	Voroshilovgrad	469
Poltava	282	Taganrog	278	Yaroslavl	597
Prokopyevsk	266	Tallinn	436	Yerevan	1,036
Pskov	177	Tambov	273	Yoshkar-Ola	201
Riga	843	Tashkent	1,816	Zaporozhye	799
Rostov-on-Don	946	Tbilisi	1,080	Zhdanov	507
Rovno	185	Temirtau	215	Zhitomir	250
Rubtsovsk	158	Togliatti	517	Zlatoust	199

Balzac, Vasyutin and Felgin, *Economic Geography of the USSR*. London, 1951
Baransky, N. N., *Economic Geography of the USSR*. Moscow, 1956 (in English)
Cole, J. P., and German, F. C., *A Geography of the USSR*. London, 1961
Leimbach, W., *Die Sowjet-Union*, Stuttgart, 1950
Narodnoye Hoziaistvo SSSR 1979. Moscow, 1980
The Oxford Regional Atlas of the USSR. Clarendon Press, Oxford, 1956
Yezhegodnik BSE, 1979

CONSTITUTION

Constituent Republics. The Union of Soviet Socialist Republics was formed by the union of the RSFSR, the Ukrainian Soviet Socialist Republic, the Belorussian Soviet Socialist Republic and the Transcaucasian Soviet Socialist Republic; the Treaty of Union was adopted by the first Soviet Congress of the USSR on 30 Dec. 1922. In May 1925 the Uzbek and Turkmen Autonomous Soviet Socialist Republics and in Dec. 1929 the Tadzhik Autonomous Soviet Socialist Republic were declared constituent members of the USSR, becoming Union Republics.

At the 8th Congress of the Soviets, on 5 Dec. 1936, a new constitution of the USSR was adopted. The Transcaucasian Republic was split up into the Armenian Soviet Socialist Republic, the Azerbaijan Soviet Socialist Republic and the Georgian Soviet Socialist Republic, each of which became constituent republics of the Union. At the same time the Kazakh Soviet Socialist Republic and the Kirghiz Soviet Socialist Republic, previously autonomous republics within the RSFSR, were proclaimed constituent republics of the USSR.

In Sept. 1939 Soviet troops occupied eastern Poland as far as the 'Curzon line', which in 1919 had been drawn on ethnographical grounds as the eastern frontier of Poland, and incorporated it into the Ukrainian and Belorussian Soviet Socialist Republics. In Feb. 1951 some districts of the Drogobych Region of the Ukraine and the Lublin Voivodship of Poland were exchanged.

On 31 March 1940 territory ceded by Finland was joined to that of the Autonomous Soviet Socialist Republic of Karelia to form the Karelo-Finnish Soviet Socialist Republic, which was admitted into the Union as the 12th Union Republic. On the 16 July 1956 the Supreme Soviet of the USSR adopted a law altering the status of the Karelo-Finnish Republic from that of a Union (constituent) Republic of the USSR to that of an Autonomous (Karelian) Republic within the RSFSR.

On 2 Aug. 1940 the Moldavian Soviet Socialist Republic was constituted as the 13th Union Republic. It comprised the former Moldavian Autonomous Soviet Socialist Republic and Bessarabia (44,290 sq. km, ceded by Romania on 28 June

1940), except for the districts of Khotin, Akerman and Ismail, which, together with Northern Bukovina (10,440 sq. km), were incorporated in the Ukrainian Soviet Republic. The Soviet–Romanian frontier thus constituted was confirmed by the peace treaty with Romania, signed on 10 Feb. 1947. On 29 June 1945 Ruthenia (Sub-Carpathian Russia, 12,742 sq. km) was by treaty with Czechoslovakia embodied in the Ukrainian Soviet Socialist Republic.

On 3 Aug. 1940 Estonia, Latvia and Lithuania were incorporated in the Soviet Union as the 14th, 15th and 16th Union Republics. The change in the status of the Karelo-Finnish Republic has reduced the number of Union Republics to 15.

After the defeat of Germany it was agreed by the governments of the UK, the USA and the USSR (by the Potsdam declaration) that part of East Prussia should be embodied in the USSR. The area (11,655 sq. km), which includes the towns of Königsberg (renamed Kaliningrad), Tilsit (renamed Sovietsk) and Insterburg (renamed Chernyakhovsk) was joined to the RSFSR by decree of 7 April 1946.

By the peace treaty with Finland, signed on 10 Feb. 1947, the province of Petsamo (Pechenga), ceded to Finland on 14 Oct. 1920 and 12 March 1946, was returned to the Soviet Union. On 19 Sept. 1955 the Soviet Union renounced its treaty rights to the naval base of Porkkala-Udd and on 26 Jan. 1956 completed the withdrawal of the forces from Finnish territory.

In 1945, after the defeat of Japan, the southern half of Sakhalin (36,000 sq. km) and the Kurile Islands (10,200 sq. km) were, by agreement with the Allies, incorporated in the USSR.[1]

[1] However, Japan asks for the return of the Etorofu and Kunashiri Islands as not belonging to the Kurile Islands proper. The Soviet Government informed Japan on 27 Jan. 1960 that the Habomai Islands and Shikotan would be handed back to Japan on the withdrawal of the American troops from Japan.

GOVERNMENT. The Soviet Union is a socialist state of the whole people (1977 constitution), the political units of which are the Soviets of Working People's Deputies. All central and local authority is vested in these Soviets.

The economic foundation of the USSR is the socialist system of economy and the socialist ownership of the means of production. There are two forms of socialist property: (1) state property (property of the whole people); (2) co-operative and collective farm (*Kolhoz*) property (property of individual collective farms and property of co-operative associations). The land, mineral deposits, waters, forests, mills, factories, mines, railways, water and air transport, banks, means of communication, large state-organized agricultural enterprises, such as state farms (*Sovhozy*), machine-repair stations and the like, as well as municipal enterprises and the principal dwelling-house properties in the cities and industrial localities, are state property, but the land occupied by collective farmers is secured to them in perpetuity so long as they use it in accordance with the laws of the country. The members of the *Kolhozy* may have small plots of land attached to their dwellings for their own use. Peasants unwilling to enter a Kolhoz may retain their individual farms, but they are not allowed to employ hired labour. The right of personal property of citizens in their income from work and in their savings, in their dwelling-houses and auxiliary household economy, their domestic furniture and utensils and objects of personal use and comfort, as well as the right of inheritance of personal property of citizens, are protected by law. The constitution recognizes the right of all citizens to work, rest, leisure, education, health protection, housing, maintenance in old age, sickness or incapacity, without distinction of sex, race or nationality, and lays down that any direct or indirect restriction of the rights of, or conversely, the establishment of direct or indirect privileges for, citizens on account of their race, religion or nationality, as well as the advocacy of racial or national exclusiveness or hatred and contempt, is punishable by law. The franchise is enjoyed by all citizens of the USSR, including members of the Armed Forces, who have reached the age of 18, irrespective of sex, with the exception of the insane and of persons convicted by court of law to sentences including deprivation of rights. Candidates for election to the Supreme Soviet of the USSR must be 21 years of age; for all other authorities the minimum age for candidates is 18. A member of any

Soviet may be recalled by a decision of a majority of his or her electors if he or she fails to give satisfaction (law on procedure for this, 30 Oct. 1959).

The USSR consists of 15 Union Republics, each inhabited by a major nationality which gives its name to the republic. These are divided into 127 territories and regions, and these again into 3,150 districts and 2,052 towns and 3,811 urban settlements (1 Jan. 1977). Within the districts there are 41,175 rural districts (usually each including a number of villages). The territories and regions also include a number of smaller nationalities, forming their own self-governing units—20 Autonomous Republics, 8 Autonomous Regions and 10 Autonomous Areas.

The highest legislative organ is the Supreme Soviet of the USSR. It consists of 2 chambers with equal legislative rights, elected for a term of 5 years: the Soviet of the Union and the Soviet of Nationalities.

The Soviet of the Union is elected by the citizens of the USSR on the basis of 1 deputy for every 300,000 of the population. The Chamber elected on 4 March 1979 consists of 750 members (*Chairman*, A. P. Shitikov).

The Soviet of Nationalities is elected by the citizens of the USSR, voting by Union and Autonomous Republics, Autonomous Regions and Autonomous Areas on the basis of 32 (from June 1966) deputies from each Union Republic, 11 deputies from each Autonomous Republic, 5 deputies from each Autonomous Region and 1 deputy from each Autonomous Area. The Chamber elected on 4 March 1979 consists of 750 members (*Chairman*, V. P. Rubenis).

Each chamber has 14 standing committees: planning and budget; industry; transport and communications; building; agriculture; health and social welfare; education, science and culture; trade and services; draft legislation; foreign affairs; youth affairs; natural environment; credentials; consumer goods.

The highest executive and administrative organ is the Council of Ministers (called People's Commissars before 16 March 1946); they are appointed by the Supreme Soviet.

The Presidium of the Supreme Soviet of the USSR is elected at a joint session of both chambers of the Supreme Soviet and consists of the chairman, first vice-chairman, 15 vice-chairmen (1 from each of the Union Republics), 21 members and the secretary. It acts as the supreme state authority between sessions of the Supreme Soviet and is accountable to the latter for all its activities.

Deputies are elected by the voters on the basis of universal, equal and direct suffrage by secret ballot. The only legal political party is the Communist Party; non-members are classed as non-party citizens. Candidates up to the present have been selected at a preliminary 'constituency electoral consultation' (selection conference), to which organizations which have put forward nominations send delegates, who discuss the various nominees. As a consequence, so far, a single candidate has been arrived at in each constituency, whose name has appeared on the ballot paper, to be struck out or approved by a cross as the voter desires. This procedure, however, is not laid down by the Constitution, and may be altered. At the election held on 4 March 1979, 174,920,221 electors voted. The Supreme Soviet elected on that day consists of 1,075 Communist and 425 non-party deputies; 487 were women, 522 manual workers in industry and state farms, and 244 collective farmers.

On 1 Feb. 1944 each of the constituent republics of the Union was given the right to have separate Commissariats (now Ministries) for Defence and Foreign Affairs. After the death of Stalin, 5 March 1953, a number of Ministries comprising different branches of trade, engineering, transport and electricity were merged into single Ministries. In 1957 the number of Ministries in the central government was reduced from 52 to 19, and in Dec. 1959 to 15; but in Oct. 1964 it was again increased to 47, in Aug. 1966 to 48 and in 1968 to 56.

Elections to Supreme Soviets and local authorities in Union and Autonomous Republics took place on 24 Feb. 1980.

The Council of Ministers, in July 1976 included 13 vice-chairmen, the Premiers of the 15 Union Republics, the head of the Central Statistical Department, the chairmen of 8 commissions of the Presidium of the Council of Ministers (4 of them vice-chairmen of the Council), of the Committee for People's Control, State Planning Committee, the Agricultural Technique Organization and of 7 other State Committees; 62 Ministers; and the chairman of the State Bank.

Soon after the adoption of the 1936 Constitution all the constituent republics of the Union held their Soviet congresses, at which they adopted their own constitutions based in all essentials on the Constitution of the Union, but adapted where necessary to national and local requirements. Article 73 of the 1977 Constitution reserves to the central government the spheres of war and peace, diplomatic relations, defence, foreign trade, state security, economic planning, education, criminal and civil codes, etc. The right of the constituent republics to withdraw from the Union is expressly recognized. In April 1978 the Supreme Soviets of the constituent republics adopted new constitutions based on the new Constitution of the USSR.

The 20 Autonomous Republics include 16 in the RSFSR, 1 in Azerbaijan, 2 in Georgia, 1 in Uzbekistan. Five Autonomous Regions are in the RSFSR, 1 each in Georgia, Azerbaijan, Tadzhikistan; all 10 Autonomous Areas are in the RSFSR.

The Autonomous Republics are governed by their own Supreme Soviet and Council of Ministers: the regions and territories, districts, towns and rural areas have their own Soviets, elected for a term of $2\frac{1}{2}$ years. In June 1975, 9,259 deputies were elected to the Supreme Soviets of Union and of Autonomous Republics: 3,393 (36·6%) were women, 3,126 (33·8%) non-Party, 3,055 (33%) industrial workers and 1,604 (17·3%) collective farmers. To the regional, district and other local Soviets in June 1977, 2,229,641 deputies were elected, 1,093,235 of them women (42·3%), 1,266,949 non-Party (56·8%), 943,240 (42·3%) industrial workers and 582,373 (26·1%) collective farmers (June 1977).

In June 1977 there were 47,412 rural and urban Soviets with 1·96m. deputies, 1·7m. voluntary co-opted members participating in their standing committees and 43,000 women were chairmen or secretaries of Soviets.

State flag: Red, with sickle and hammer in gold in the upper corner near the staff, and above them a 5-pointed star bordered in gold.

National anthem: Soyuz nerushimy respublik svobodnykh (words by S. Mikhalkov and El-Registan; music by A. V. Alexandrov; 1944).

The Presidium of the Supreme Soviet may, within the framework of the constitution, issue edicts (*ukazy*) interpreting existing legislation or amending it, subject to ratification subsequently by the Supreme Soviet.

Legislation by decree and executive authority is vested in the Council of Ministers. The Council of Ministers is responsible to the Supreme Soviet of the USSR and in the intervals between sessions to the Presidium of the Supreme Soviet.

President of the Presidium of the Supreme Soviet of the USSR: Leonid Ilyich Brezhnev (June 1977).

First Vice-President: Victor Vasilievich Kuznetsov (Oct. 1977).

Secretary of the Presidium: M. P. Georgadze.

Chairman of the Council of Ministers: Nikolai Alexandrovich Tikhonov (Oct. 1980).

First Vice-Chairman: I. V. Arkhipov (Dec. 1980).

Minister of Defence: Marshal D. F. Ustinov. *Minister of Foreign Trade:* N. S. Patolichev. *Minister for Foreign Affairs:* A. A. Gromyko.

Yezhegodnik BSE. Moscow (annual)
Denisov, A., and Kirichenko, M., *Soviet State Law.* Moscow, 1960
Hazard, J. N., *The Soviet System of Government.* Univ. of Chicago Press, 1957
Meyer, A. G., *The Soviet Political System: An Interpretation.* New York, 1965

Communist Party. According to the rules adopted by the 22nd Congress of the Party on 31 Oct. 1961, the Communist Party of the Soviet Union 'unites, on a voluntary basis, the more advanced, politically more conscious section of the working class, collective-farm peasantry and intelligentsia of the USSR', whose principal objects are to build a Communist society by means of gradual transition from Socialism to Communism, to raise the material and cultural level of the people, to organize the defence of the country and to strengthen ties with the workers of other countries.

The Party is built on the territorial-industrial principle. The supreme organ is the Party Congress. Ordinary congresses are convened not less than once in 4 years. The Congress elects a Central Committee which meets at least every 6 months, carries on the work of the Party between congresses, and guides the work of central Soviet and public organizations through Party groups within them.

The Central Committee forms a Political Bureau to direct the work of the Central Committee between plenary meetings, a Secretariat to direct current work and a Commission of Party Control to consider appeals against decisions about expulsion. Similar rules hold for the Regional, Territorial and Republican Party organizations.

Over 414,000 primary Party organizations exist in mills, factories, state tractor repair stations and other economic establishments, in collective farms, units of the Soviet Army and Navy, in villages, offices, educational establishments, etc., where there are at least 3 Party members. In March 1980 over 43% of the members were industrial workers, 13% were collective farmers and 44% office and professional workers. 25·1% were women.

The Central Committee elected by the 26th Congress in March 1980 consisted of 319 members and 151 candidate members.

In March 1981 the Political Bureau of the Central Committee consisted of the following members: Y. V. Andropov, L. I. Brezhnev, K. U. Chernenko, M. S. Gorbachov, V. V. Grishin, A. A. Gromyko, A. P. Kirilenko, D. A. Kunayev, A. Y. Pelshe, G. V. Romanov, M. A. Suslov, D. F. Ustinov, V. V. Shcherbitsky, N. A. Tikhonov, and the following alternate members: G. A. Aliev, P. N. Demichev, T. Y. Kiselev, V. V. Kuznetsov, B. N. Ponomaryov, S. R. Rashidov, E. A. Shevardnadze, M. S. Solomentsev.

Secretariat: L. I. Brezhnev (*General-Secretary*); K. U. Chernenko; V. I. Dolgikh; I. V. Kapitonov; A. P. Kirilenko; B. N. Ponomaryov; M. S. Gorbachov; K. V. Rusakov; M. A. Suslov; M. V. Zymianin.

Chairman of the Commission of Party Control: A. Y. Pelshe.
Vice-Chairman: Z. T. Serdyuk.

In March 1980 the Communist Party had 17·5m. members. Membership of the Young Communist League was 37·8m. in April 1978.

The Communist International (the Comintern), founded on the initiative of the Russian Communist Party in 1919, was dissolved on 15 May 1943. In Oct. 1947 a Communist Information Bureau (Cominform) was set up in Belgrade to serve the Communist parties of Bulgaria, Czechoslovakia, France, Hungary, Italy, Poland, Romania, USSR and Yugoslavia. On 28 June 1948 Yugoslavia was expelled from the Cominform and the bureau was transferred to Bucharest. The Cominform was on 17 April 1956 declared dissolved.

Hammond, T. T. (ed.), *Soviet Foreign Relations and World Communism*. Princeton and OUP, 1965

Hunt, R. N. C., *Books on Communism* [in English]. London, 1960

Kassof, A., *The Soviet Youth Program*. Harvard and OUP, 1965

Schapiro, L., *The Communist Party of the Soviet Union*. New York, 1960.—*The Government and Politics of the Soviet Union*. New York, 1965

History of the Communist Party of the Soviet Union (English ed.). Moscow, 1960; rev. Russian ed., Moscow, 1965

DEFENCE. On 26 Feb. 1946 the control of the Soviet Armed Forces was unified under a single Ministry of the Armed Forces. On 25 Feb. 1950 the Defence Ministry was divided into a War Ministry and a Navy Ministry; on 15 March 1953 a single Ministry of Defence was reconstituted.

In 1955 the Air Defence Command and in 1960 the Strategic Rocket Forces were established as the 4th and 5th 'branches' of the armed forces beside the army, navy and air force.

The direction of Party and political work in the Armed Forces is exercised by the Central Committee of the Communist Party of the Soviet Union through the chief political directorate of the Ministry of Defence. The chiefs of the political departments of military commands, fleets and armies must be Party members of 5 years' standing and the chiefs of political departments of divisions and regiments Party members of 3 years' standing. Nearly 90% of the officers are members of the Communist Party or Young Communist League, and 45% have had an engineering and technical education.

Military service begins at the age of 19 (or 18 for graduates of secondary schools). Active service lasts 2 years for privates in the Army and M.V.D. troops, 3 years for n.c.o.s in the Army and M.V.D. troops and for privates and n.c.o.s in the Air Force, 4 years for privates and n.c.o.s in the Coastal Defence, 5 years for ratings in the Navy. Reserve service lasts up to the ages of 35, 45 or 50 years according to fitness, family status and other considerations. Conscientious objection is treated as a criminal offence. Students in places of higher education are freed from military service, but receive military instruction. About half the service personnel have had higher, or 10-year, education and over 80% are members of the Communist Party.

In Jan. 1960 Prime Minister Khrushchov quoted the following figures of the armed forces of the Soviet Union: 1927, 586,000; 1937, 1,433,000; 1941, 4,207,000; May 1945, 11,365,000; 1948, 2,874,000; 1955, 5,763,000; 1959, 3,623,000; 1960, 2,423,000. The reduction, according to Khrushchov, was mainly due to the switch-over to rocket and nuclear weapons.

The estimated expenditure on defence (in 1m. new roubles) for 1961 was 9,255; 1970, 17,900; 1971, 17,900; 1972, 17,900; 1973, 17,900; 1974, 17,700; 1975, 17,400; 1976, 17,400; 1977, 17,200; 1978, 17,200; 1979, 17,200.

Eastern Security Treaty. On 14 May 1955 the USSR, Albania, Bulgaria, Czechoslovakia, the German Democratic Republic, Hungary, Poland and Romania signed in Warsaw a 20-year treaty of friendship and collaboration, after the USSR had (on 7 May) annulled the 20-year treaties of alliance with the UK (1942) and France (1944). The main provisions of the treaty are as follows:

ARTICLE 4. In case of armed aggression in Europe against one or several States party to the pact by a State or group of States, each State member of the pact ... will afford to the State or States which are the object of such aggression immediate assistance ... with all means which appear necessary, including the use of armed force.... These measures will cease as soon as the Security Council takes measures necessary for establishing and preserving international peace and security.

ARTICLE 5. The contracting Powers agree to set up a joint command of their armed forces to be allotted by agreement between the Powers, at the disposal of this command and used on the basis of jointly established principles. They will also take over agreed measures necessary to strengthen their defences.

ARTICLE 9. The present treaty is open to other States, irrespective of their social or Government regime, who declare their readiness to abide by the terms of the treaty in order to safeguard peace and security of the peoples.

ARTICLE 11. In the event of a system of collective security being set up in Europe and a pact to this effect being signed—to which each party to this treaty will direct its efforts—the present treaty will lapse from the day such a collective security treaty comes into force.

It is estimated (1978) that the armed forces of the Warsaw pact countries total 3·83m., including 3·45m. Russians, compared with 4·82m. NATO forces.

Marshal Grechko was from July 1960 to April 1967 C.-in-C. of the united Armed Forces, with headquarters in Moscow. He was succeeded by Marshal I. I. Yakubovsky in 1967 and by Marshal V. G. Kulikov in Jan. 1977.

In 1962 Albania was no longer invited to the Warsaw Pact meetings, without being formally expelled.

Two Soviet divisions are stationed in Poland, 20 divisions in German Democratic Republic, 4 divisions in Hungary and 5 in Czechoslovakia.

Army. The Army was, in 1980, thought to consist of about 173 divisions, of which some 100 are of combat readiness, numbering about 1,825,000 men.

The mechanized and tank divisions are equipped with the T54 medium tank, mounting an 85-mm gun, and with the Stalin III heavy tank, mounting a 122-mm gun. The T54 is being replaced by the T62 medium tank mounting a 115-mm gun. Rocket units are stated to be 'the main force' of the Army.

In addition to the Soviet Army, there are some 460,000 security and border troops.

Navy. The Soviet Fleet is steadily expanding and progressively modernizing under a continuity of policy and technology given by the quarter century in office of Admiral of the Fleet of the Soviet Union Sergei Georgiyevich Gorshkov, C.-in-C. of the Soviet Navy and Deputy Minister of Defence. The overall picture is of an unprecedentedly powerful and well-balanced navy, the capacity of which is increasing annually by scientific application if not by numerical strength.

The principal surface ships of the Soviet Navy are as follows:

Completed	Name	Standard displacement Tons	Armour Belt In.	Armour Guns In.	Principal armament	Shaft horse-power	Speed Knots

Aircraft Carriers[1]

Completed	Name	Standard displacement Tons	Belt In.	Guns In.	Principal armament	Shaft horse-power	Speed Knots
1980 1978 1976	Novorossiisk Minsk Kiev	40,000	—	—	4 twin SS missile launchers; 4 twin SA missile launchers; 1 twin AS missile launcher; 13 fixed-wing aircraft; 22 helicopters; 4 76-mm AA guns	180,000	32

[1] See Aircraft carriers under construction, successors of *Kiev* and *Minsk*, next page. Projected fourth name was *Kharkov*.

Battle Cruisers[1]

Completed	Name	Standard displacement Tons	Belt In.	Guns In.	Principal armament	Shaft horse-power	Speed Knots
1980	Kirov	27,000			4 SS missile launchers; 10 SA missile launchers; 4 AS missile launchers; 2 100-mm guns	120,000	32

[1] A sister ship is under construction. The first battle cruisers, and the largest combatant warships, apart from aircraft carriers, to be built for any navy since the Second World War.

Helicopter Carriers

Completed	Name	Standard displacement Tons	Belt In.	Guns In.	Principal armament	Shaft horse-power	Speed Knots
1968 1967	Leningrad Moskva	15,000	5	4	2 twin SA missile launchers; 1 twin AS missile launcher; 2 twin 57-mm AA guns 18 helicopters	100,000	30

Cruisers

Completed	Name	Standard displacement Tons	Belt In.	Guns In.	Principal armament	Shaft horse-power	Speed Knots
1980	Sovietsky Soyuz	14,000	—	—	SS, SA and AS missile launchers	100,000	32
1979 1978 1977 1976 1975 1974 1973	Tashkent Tallin Petropavlovsk Azov[3] Kerch Ochakov Nikolaiev	8,000	—	—	2 quadruple SS missile launchers; 8 twin SA missile launchers; 4 76-mm AA guns	120,000	34
1958 1957 1956 1956 1956 1955 1954 1954 1953 1953 1953 1953	Admiral Senyavin[1] Mikhail Kutuzov Dimitri Pojarski Oktyabrskaya Revolutsiya (ex-Molotovsk) Admiral Lazarev Alexandr Suvorov Admiral Ushakov Dzerzhinski[2] Alexandr Nevski Murmansk Zhdanov[1] Sverdlov	15,450	5	4	12 6-in.; 12 3·9-in.	110,000	30
1950	Komsomolets[4]	11,500			12 6-in.; 8 3·9-in.	113,000	35

¹ *Admiral Senyavin* now has a helicopter pad and hangar ('X' and 'Y' turrets removed) while *Zhdanov* has high deckhouse ('X' turret removed). Each carries twin surface-air missile launchers. Both latterly employed as command and communications ships.

² *Dzerzhinski* has only nine 6-in. guns in 3 triple turrets, 'X' turret having been replaced by a twin surface-air missile launcher.

³ *Azov* of this class is reported to be of a modified design.

⁴ Used as training ship. Of sister ships, *Kirov* and *Slava* (ex-*Molotov*) were deleted from the effective list in 1976–77 and *Zheleznyakov* in 1978.

Submarines

75	SSBN	Nuclear powered	Ballistic missile armed¹
19	SSB	Diesel-electric powered	Ballistic missile armed
47	SSGN	Nuclear powered	Cruise (guided) missile armed
23	SSG	Diesel-electric powered	Cruise missile armed
51	SSN	Nuclear powered	Torpedo (only) armed
275²	SS	Conventionally (diesel) powered	Conventionally (torpedo) armed

¹ All missile-carrying submarines are also armed with torpedoes.
² Including some 125 patrol submarines in reserve or used for training only.

There are also 1 very large new aircraft carrier support ship, 14 missile-armed light cruisers, 43 missile-armed destroyers, 50 gun-armed destroyers, 30 missile-armed frigates, 50 gun-armed frigates, 60 missile-armed corvettes, 150 gun-armed corvettes, 150 fleet minesweepers, 90 coastal minesweepers, 33 minehunters, 110 inshore minesweepers, 130 fast missile craft, 40 torpedo boats, 70 anti-submarine boats, 55 patrol craft, 50 hydrofoil gunboats, 25 coastal patrol launches, 80 river patrol boats, 2 dock landing ships, 30 tank landing ships, 70 medium landing ships, 60 utility landing craft, 100 minor landing craft, 65 intelligence collecting ships, 65 major support ships, 20 space associated ships, 130 survey ships, 60 research ships, 4 nuclear powered icebreakers, 50 icebreakers, 20 training ships, 200 fishery protection ships, 10 fleet replenishment ships, 50 oilers, 13 special tankers, 25 salvage vessels, 80 transports, 25 rescue ships, 135 tenders, 10 lifting ships, 10 cable ships, 80 fleet tugs, 50 hovercraft and thousands of auxiliaries, para-military ships and service craft.

The new construction programme includes 2 medium aircraft carriers (successors of *Kiev* and *Minsk*), 1 considerably larger aircraft carrier, 1 large battle cruiser, 6 nuclear powered ballistic missile submarines, 2 nuclear powered cruise missile submarines, 6 nuclear powered torpedo-armed submarines and 9 guided missile cruisers.

In the revised forward procurement programme more aircraft carriers of improved 'Kiev' class are envisaged, together with nuclear powered surface ships and specialized support ships, to fit into the Soviet global and strategic maritime pattern.

There are 5 shipyards in and near Leningrad; Black Sea yards are at Nikolaiev and Sevastopol, new shipyards are at Molotovsk in the White Sea region and at Komsomolsk on the Amur.

The completion of a through canal system between the Baltic and White Seas, allowing regular traffic *via* the North-East Passage (during the ice-free season), facilitates the navigation of suitable ships between the Baltic and Far East.

Estimated number of personnel in 1981 totalled 450,000, including naval aviation, naval infantry, coastal defence, cadets and apprentices (but excluding 75,000 civilians in administration and new construction); only 18% are volunteers, *i.e.*, officers and petty officers, the remainder comprising national service men serving 3 years at sea and 2 if ashore.

Air Force. The Soviet Air Force (excluding PVO air defence force) is believed to consist, in 1980, of over 470,000 officers and men and some 8,500 first-line aircraft, excluding second-line and training types. To supplement long-range rocket missiles (limited by SALT I interim agreement to 1,618 ICBM, 600 MRBM/IRBM), the DA strategic bomber force has still 113 Tupolev Tu-95 ('Bear')¹ 4-turboprop bombers, 74 Myasishchev M-4 4-jet bombers and flight-refuelling tankers ('Bison'), 420 twin-jet Tupolev Tu-16 ('Badger'), and 140 supersonic Tupolev Tu-22 ('Blinder') bombers, ECM and reconnaissance aircraft, and at least 100 Tupolev ('Backfire')

¹ For convenience Soviet aircraft and missiles are usually referred to by invented English names in non-Soviet military writings.

swing-wing bombers. All types are used also by the Naval Air Force for long-range maritime reconnaissance; the Tu-16, Tu-95, Tu-22 and 'Backfire' can carry air-to-surface guided self-propelled missiles and all 5 types have provision for flight refuelling.

The FA tactical air forces, under local army command in the field, have an estimated total of 5,000 ground attack and reconnaissance aircraft, including 1,400 MiG-23/27 ('Flogger') and 500 two-seat Sukhoi Su-24 ('Fencer') supersonic swing-wing aircraft, 220 twin-jet Yakovlev Yak-28 ('Brewer') multi-purpose combat aircraft, 200 single-jet Sukhoi Su-7B ('Fitter-A'), 650 swing-wing Su-17 ('Fitter-C/D/G/H'), and 1,000 MiG-21 ('Fishbed') fighter-bombers, 300 MiG-21 and 170 MiG-25 ('Foxbat') reconnaissance aircraft, with strong interceptor, transport and helicopter support. In service in large numbers is the Mi-24 ('Hind') assault helicopter, in transport and gunship versions. The PVO defence forces, organized as a separate service, have an estimated total of 2,600 jet interceptors. A high proportion of the squadrons are equipped with the latest MiG-23 ('Flogger'), Su-15 ('Flagon') and MiG-25 ('Foxbat') all-weather interceptors, armed with air-to-air missiles. The single-seat single-engined Su-9 and Su-11 ('Fishpot') and twin-jet Yak-28P ('Firebar') and Tu-28P ('Fiddler') make up the balance of the force. Early warning and fighter-control duties are performed by radar-carrying adaptations of the Tu-114 turboprop transport, redesignated Tu-126 ('Moss'). Very large numbers of surface-to-air guided missiles are operational, on some 10,000 launchers, including the 'Guild', 'Guideline', 'Goa', 'Gainful' and 'Ganef', the long-range 'Gammon' and the 'Galosh' which is deployed around Moscow on 64 launchers and has anti-missile capability.

Soviet Air Force transport squadrons have an estimated total of 1,550 aircraft, consisting primarily of 600 An-12 ('Cub') 4 turboprop transports and 40 An-24s ('Coke') and An-26s ('Curl'), with 40 very large An-22s ('Cock'), 75 new Il-76 ('Candid') heavy four-jet freighters, a variety of older and smaller types and over 3,200 helicopters, including the turbine-powered Mi-6, Mi-8 and Mi-10 flying crane. Training aircraft include the piston-engined Yak-18 primary trainer, the Czech-built L-29 Delfin and L-39 jet basic trainers and versions of operational types such as MiG-21, MiG-23, MiG-25, MiG-15, Su-7, Su-9, Su-17, Yak-28 and Tu-22.

Naval Air Force. Operating 1,425 fixed-wing aircraft and helicopters, the Soviet Navy has the world's second largest naval air arm. Under the control of the various naval commands, *i.e.*, Baltic, Black Sea and Pacific, the Naval Air Arm has an estimated 620 land-based maritime patrol bombers and 80 flying-boats. Primary offensive aircraft are 280 Tu-16 ('Badger') twin-jet bombers, and 50 'Backfire' swing-wing bombers, able to carry air-to-surface missiles, 40 supersonic twin-jet Tu-22 ('Blinder') reconnaissance bombers and 80 Beriev M-12 ('Mail') maritime patrol amphibians. Some 75 Tu-142 ('Bear') 4-engined bombers, as well as Tu-16s, Il-18s ('Coot-A') and 55 Il-38s ('May'), are used for long-range over-water reconnaissance and electronic intelligence missions. The Tu-142 also has an important targeting role for ships fitted with anti-shipping missile launchers. Over 250 anti-submarine helicopters, notably the Ka-25 ('Hormone'), are carried in naval vessels, including 2 aircraft carriers (which also operate Yak-36 ('Forger') VTOL attack/reconnaissance aircraft) and 2 helicopter carriers. Several hundred transport, utility and training fixed-wing aircraft and shore-based ASW helicopters are also under Navy control.

Berman, H. J., and Kerner, M. (ed.), *Soviet Military Law and Administration*. 2 vols. Harvard Univ. Press, 1955
Gouré, L., Kohler, F. D., and Harvey, M. L., *The Role of Nuclear Forces in Current Soviet Strategy*. Washington, 1974
Kilmarx, R. A., *A History of Soviet Air Power*. London, 1962
O'Ballance, E., *The Red Army*. London, 1964
Scott, H. F., and Scott, W. F., *The Armed Forces of the USSR*. Boulder, 1979

INTERNATIONAL RELATIONS

Membership. USSR is a member of UN, Comecon and the Warsaw Pact.

External Debt. The debts contracted by the tsarist régime, *i.e.*, before 1917, have been repudiated by the Soviet Government.

After the Second World War the USSR has become one of the biggest creditor countries in the world. Between 1945 and Jan. 1978 economic aid in the form of 2% or 2½% loans to be repaid, as a rule, over 12 years has been advanced for 2,628 industrial and agricultural enterprises in Socialist countries and 1,035 enterprises in developing countries; the latter including loans (in 1m. old roubles): India, 2,500m.; Egypt, 2,300m.; Iraq, 550m.; Afghánistán, 480m.; Indonesia, 443m.; Argentina, 400m.; Ethiopia, 400m.; Guinea, 140m.; Cuba, US$100m. 76% of aid is for industrial development and 14% for agriculture and transport. 1,403 industrial plants have been completed in these countries, and nearly as many are being completed; 340,000 native skilled workers have been trained by Soviet specialists in Africa and Asia alone, and many thousands more in the USSR. Agreements for economic co-operation operate with 45 developing countries in all.

ECONOMY

Planning. Planning is based on public ownership in industry and trade, and on mixed public and collective (co-operative) ownership in agriculture. The first plan drawn up by Gosplan (the State Planning Commission) was the 'Goelro' drawn up in 1920. This was to be the basis for the economic development of the country and for the construction of a system of electrical power plants with an aggregate capacity of 1·75m. kw., in the course of 15 years. By 1927–28 the capacity of the electrical stations in operation was already 1,792,000 kw. with an output of 5,160m. kwh.

In 1925 Gosplan started to draw up annual plans for the national economy, and in 1927–29 undertook to draw up the first 5-year plan, which was to have run from 1 Oct. 1928 to 30 Sept. 1933. It was considered completed in Dec. 1932, when 93·7% of the planned industrial output for the 5 years had been carried out. Stress was laid on the development of the heavy industries, particularly in the outlying areas rich in natural resources and inhabited by the national minorities.

The second 5-year plan ran from 1933 to 1937. It aimed at strengthening the defensive capacity of the Soviet Union, and more stress was laid than in the first 5-year plan on increasing the output and improving the quality of consumer goods. About one-half of the total investments in new heavy industrial constructions was allocated to the eastern areas. By the end of 1937 the plan for large-scale industry was overfulfilled by 4%, but the target for the light industries and consumer goods was not reached.

The third 5-year plan, 1938–42, envisaged an average annual increase in output of 13·5%, but that of the means of production was to be 15·25% and the means of consumption 11%; stress was to be laid on war industry. During the first 3½ years, industrial output was increasing annually by an average of 13%. In the Urals, the Volga area, Siberia and Central Asia industrial output increased during 1938–40 by about 50%. One of the richest grain-growing areas of the Soviet Union was created in the eastern part of the country. Capital construction amounted in value to a total of 130,000m. roubles; more than one-third fell to the eastern areas. The plan was interrupted in June 1941, when Hitler attacked the USSR. The whole of the national economy was switched to help the war effort, and whole industries were shifted from the western areas to the east.

For details of the fourth 5-year plan, 1946–50, see THE STATESMAN'S YEAR-BOOK, 1952, pp. 1424 f. The 1950 target of the gross output of industry was exceeded by 2%.

On 10 Oct, 1952 the 19th Congress of the Communist Party issued directives for the fifth 5-year plan, 1951–55; for details, see THE STATESMAN'S YEAR-BOOK, 1953, pp. 1435–36. During Sept. and Oct. 1953 the Government issued a number of decrees to stimulate the development of agriculture, the output of consumer goods and the expansion of the home trade. For details of these decrees, see THE STATESMAN'S YEAR-BOOK, 1955, pp. 1448–50.

The directive for the sixth 5-year plan, 1956–60, was adopted by the 20th Congress of the Communist Party on 25 Feb. 1956; for details see THE STATESMAN'S YEAR-BOOK, 1958, p. 1472.

In May 1955 Gosplan was reorganized to consist of 2 state commissions for long-term planning (Gosplan) and for current planning (Goseconomcommissya); at the same time a committee was set up to improve the application to industry of advanced science and technology (Gostekhnika).

Between 1954 and 1956 considerable changes were made in planning methods. In March 1954 collective farms were given greater authority over planning their own output, only the quantities required by the State in fixed deliveries being determined beforehand, and voluntary sales by contract. In 1955 they were authorized to make changes in their statutes, which had followed a fixed model since 1935. In 1955–57 over 15,000 industrial establishments in various basic industries, previously controlled by the Union Government, and later a number of entire light industries were turned over to the Constituent (Union) Republics. By 1962 they controlled from 95 to 100% of all industrial output.

In 1957 a comprehensive plan for decentralization of management of industry was initiated. Industrial establishments responsible for about 71% of all Soviet industrial output were turned over to Economic Councils set up in 104 (in 1963: 47) economic administrative areas. These in 1962 controlled 73% of all industrial production. The Ministries previously responsible for the industries concerned were either abolished or transformed into purely planning and supervisory bodies. The State Committee for current planning was abolished, and Gosplan was given wider powers.

In consequence of this change a 7-year plan for 1959–65 was adopted by the 21st Congress of the Communist Party in Feb. 1959. Industrial output was to increase by 80%; it was in fact, in 1965, 84% above that of 1959. Capital investments would roughly equal the total for 1917–58: special attention was to be given to mechanization of agriculture and arduous industrial labour, automation and new technological processes, and housing. Diesel or electric traction of railway freight was to rise to 85%. Real incomes were to rise 40%, the 7-hour day (6 hours for miners) became general in 1960 and the 40-hour week in 1961, and introduction of the 35-hour week (30 hours for miners) began in 1964.

In Oct. 1965 the regional and Republic Economic Councils were abolished and also 28 Ministries for various branches of industry (17 Union-Republican, *i.e.*, corresponding to similar Ministries in the Union Republics, and 11 all-Union).

A 20-year plan was adopted by the 22nd Congress of the Communist Party on 31 Oct. 1961, which envisaged a ninefold growth in electricity output and big increases in production of steel, oil, coal, machinery and cement, and also in grain, milk and meat. Two new iron and steel centres were to be developed in Kazakhstan and in Kursk region. A single deepwater system was to link the main inland waterways in the European USSR. Some rivers in northern Asia were to be diverted south for irrigation purposes. A 6-hour day for a 6-day week or 35 hours for a 5-day week were to be achieved by 1970. Housing, water, gas, heating, public urban transport and school meals were to be free by 1980. These and cognate measures were to provide 'the material and technical basis of communism'.

The 23rd Congress of the Communist Party in April 1966 adopted 'directives' for a 5-year plan for 1966–70. Under these, power output was to reach 830,000–850,000m. kwh.; oil, 345–355m. tons; coal, 665–675m. tons; steel, 124–129m. tons; mineral fertilizers, 62–65m. tons; machine-tools, 220,000–230,000; cars, 700,000–800,000; tractors, 600,000–625,000; paper, 5–5·3m. tons; cement, 100–105m. tons; fabrics, 9·5–9·8m. sq. metres; leather footwear, 610–630m. pairs; meat, 5·9–6·2m. tons; butter, 1·2m. tons; sugar, 9·8–10m. tons. The average annual output of grain was to increase 30% over 1964–65. 7,000 km of new railway line, 63,000 km of new motor roads and 35–40 new airports were to be built; marine tonnage was to be increased by 50%.

The 9th Five-Year Plan adopted in 1971 provided for an increase in electric power output to 1,065,000m. kwh.; oil to 496m. tons; gas, 320,000m. cu. metres; steel, 146m. tons; coal, 695m. tons; mineral fertilizers, 90m. tons; tractors, 575,000; passenger cars, 1·26m., and lorries, 750,000. Grain output was to rise to 195m. tons in 1975; meat, approximately 16m. tons; milk, 100m. tons; textiles, 11,000m. sq. metres; leather footwear, 830m. pairs. Average wages were to increase by 22%, incomes of collective farmers 30–35%, and the average of real incomes by 31%. 3,400 miles of new railway tracks were to be built and 3,700 miles electrified, with 17,000 miles of new oil pipelines, and 40% more cargo carried by sea. Over 16m. flats and houses were to be built.

By July 1972, 43,000 industrial plants had been transferred to the new system of decentralized cost-accounting; they produced 94% of total output of Soviet industry and 95% of its total profit. All public establishments in trade and catering and all the state farms have gone over to the new system.

On 29 Oct. 1976, the Supreme Soviet adopted the 10th Five-Year Plan (1976–80). This provided for an increase of industrial output from 104·3% of the 1975 level to 136%, an average annual increase of agricultural output by 16%, freight traffic (all forms) from 105·7% to 132%, state capital investments from 105·1% of the 1975 level in 1976 to 114·6% in 1980, real income per head from 103·7% to 121%, retail commodity turnover from 103·6% to 128·7%. 550m. sq. metres of new housing were to be built. Children in pre-school establishments would increase by 104·4% in 1976 and 125·5% in 1980, pupils in day schools from 108·9% to 148·8%, and students in higher education from 100·4% to 105·4%. Hospital beds were to increase from 102·2% in the first year to 109·7% in the final year.

A far-reaching plan for land improvement, increasing of agricultural, housing and road facilities and expansion of village amenities, from 1976 to 1980, in the 'Non-Black-Earth Zone' (northern and central European Russia), was begun in 1975–76, at a total cost of 35,000m. roubles.

In 1979 it was decided that from 1981 detailed plans would be drawn up at the outset for each year of a 5-year plan, so that enterprises could spread their potential more rationally over the whole period.

The National Economy of the USSR in 1978. (Statistical annual in Russian). Moscow, 1980
Directives of the 5-Year Economic Plan, 1971–1975. Moscow, 1971 (in English)
Guidelines for the Development of the National Economy of the USSR for 1976–1980. Moscow, 1976 (in English)
Bandera, U. N., and Melnyk, Z. L. (ed.), *The Soviet Economy in Regional Perspective.* New York, 1973
Conyngham, W. J., *Industrial Management in the Soviet Union.* Stanford, California, 1973
Dobb, M., *Soviet Economic Development Since 1917.* London, 1966
Krylov, C. A., *The Soviet Economy.* Toronto, 1979

Budget. Revenue and expenditure in 1,000m. new roubles for calendar years:

	1974	1975	1976	1977	1978	1979
Revenue	201,300	218,800	232,200	247,800	265,800	275,600
Expenditure	197,400	214,500	226,700	242,800	260,200	275,100

The 1979 budget allotted 150,500m. roubles to the national economy, 17,200m. to defence and 92,300m. to social and cultural services.

The social insurance budget, which is controlled by the Central Council for Trade Unions and its affiliated bodies, was 22,169m. in 1974, 26,100m. in 1975, 27,992m. in 1976, 29,476m. in 1977 and 31,179m. in 1978.

The national income was assessed (in 1,000m. roubles) at 152·9 in 1961, 225 in 1967, 261·9 in 1969, 289·9 in 1970, 305 in 1971, 313·6 in 1972, 337·8 in 1973, 353·7 in 1974, 363·3 in 1975, 385·7 in 1976, 403 in 1977, 422·5 in 1978 and 430 in 1979.

Income tax was abolished on 1 Oct. 1961 for earnings up to 60 roubles per month and reduced for earnings between 61 and 70 roubles; in Dec. 1967 further cuts of 25% were made for earnings from 61 to 80 roubles; in 1972 earnings up to 70 roubles were freed of income tax, and taxes on incomes up to 90 roubles were cut by about 33⅓%.

Capital investment (1979) was 130,600m. roubles, including 117,100m. by State and co-operative enterprises, 11,800m. by collective farms and 1,700m. by individuals (on housing).

Currency. As from 1 Jan. 1961 the gold content of the *rouble* was raised from 0·222 168 to 0·987 412 gramme. The official exchange rates (Feb. 1981) 1·666 *roubles* = £1; 0·654 *roubles* = US$1.

The gold holdings of the USSR were, in Dec. 1955, estimated at about 200m. fine oz. (US$7,000m.), or about 20% of the world total of monetary gold.

The currency in circulation is: (1) State Bank notes in denominations of 10, 25, 50 and 100 *roubles*; (2) Treasury notes in denominations of 1, 3 and 5 *roubles*; (3) cupronickel coins in denominations of 10, 15, 20 and 50 *kopeks* and 1 *rouble*; (4) cupro-zinc coins in denominations of 1, 2, 3 and 5 *kopeks*.

Banking. The State Bank began operations on 16 Nov. 1921. By an edict of 7 April 1959 a number of specialized banks for planned long-term investments, which had existed since 1932, were abolished. The State Bank, in addition to short-term credits, effects long-term investments in agriculture and in individual rural house-building. The Bank for Financing Capital Investments (*Stroibank*) covers industry, transport, urban housing schemes and public utilities and individual house-building in towns.

Deposits in 80,500 savings banks were over 135,500m. new roubles to the credit of 135·5m. depositors at 1 Jan. 1980.

Weights and Measures. The metric system has been in use since 1 Jan. 1927. The Gregorian Calendar was adopted as from 14 Feb. 1918.

ENERGY AND NATURAL RESOURCES

Electricity. Many hydro-electrical power stations are being constructed. The Irkutsk station (4,500m. kwh. output per annum) is in operation; Bratsk (4·5m. kw. capacity) was completed in 1967. Ust-Ilimskaya, of 3·6m. kw. capacity (Central Siberia) was completed in Nov. 1977. Krasnoyarsk (6m. kw. capacity) was completed and began full production in July 1972. A 1·26m. kw. power station was completed on the Pechora (far north) by Dec. 1978. The first unit of Sayano-Shushenskaya was in operation by Nov. 1978 (6·4m. kw.). Three units at the Inguri hydro-electrical station and a 500,000 kw. unit at the Reftinskaya state district thermal power station, Sverdlovsk region, were also commissioned in 1978.

The Kremenchug power station (625,000 kw. capacity) was completed in Nov. 1960, rendering the Dnieper navigable for large vessels from Kaney to the Black Sea (over 800 km). Two power stations in Central Asia are under construction: at Nurek on the Amu-Darya (2·7m. kw.) and at Toktogul in the Syr-Darya basin (1·2m. kw.). Their reservoirs will irrigate 1·5m. hectares. A large hydroelectric station was under construction (1981) on the river Kureika in Siberia which will provide energy for the mining and metallurgical centre at Norilska in the Arctic.

Total installed capacity of power stations in 1938 was 8·7m. kw. and 245·4m. kw. in 1978. Industry consumes about 70% of the total electricity. Over 35,000 small rural power stations have been closed in recent years owing to supply from State stations becoming available, but there are still many operating in the countryside. 800 towns and urban settlements were heated by central thermal plants.

A nuclear power station, with capacity of 5,000 kw., was put into operation at Obninsk (Kaluga region), 27 June 1954; the Novo-Voronezh station (now 1·5m. kw.) began operating Dec. 1964, and Beloyarsk (1m. kw.) 1965. A fast neutron reactor, with a capacity of 600,000 kw., was started up at the Beloyarsk nuclear power station in 1980. The fourth 1m. kw. reactor at the Leningrad nuclear power station became operational in 1981. By 31 Dec. 1980, 12 nuclear power stations were operational. An experimental tidal energy station is working at Kislaya Guba (Murman coast).

The country's integrated power grid is now in operation, covering over 700 power stations with a total capacity of 220m. kw., which are handled by a central control panel.

A unified power grid ('Mir') with all the Socialist countries of eastern Europe was built up between 1962 and 1967. Total capacity (1972) was 58m. kw.

Oil. In the 1930s practically all Soviet oil came from the Caucasian fields, of which the Baku fields yielded 75–80% and the Grozny and Maikop fields between them 15%. Since then, the distribution has considerably changed. The Ural–Volga area, the 'Second Baku', has 4 large centres in operation, at Samarska Luka (Kuibyshev), Tuimazy (Bashkiria), Ishimbaev (Bashkiria) and Perm.

A large new oilfield has been developed in the Trans-Volga area of the Saratov region. The Tyumen (West Siberian) complex, now accounts for over 50% of the USSR's oil output. In 1980 the USSR extracted over 600m. tonnes of oil.

The total length of pipeline on 1 Jan. 1939 was 4,212 km, divided as follows: Baku–Batumi, 1,717 km; Grozny–Mahachkala, 150 km; Grozny–Armavir–Tuapse, 618 km; Armavir–Trudovaya, 488 km; Guriev–Orsk, 845 km, and other, 394 km. One pipeline (1,700 km) was completed in 1955, connecting Tuimazy in Bashkiria with the refineries of Omsk. In 1957 the Almetyevsk–Gorky pipeline (580 km) and

479 km of the Stavropol–Moscow pipeline were completed. At the end of 1979 there were 67,400 km of pipeline, through which (in 1979) were conveyed over 600m. tonnes of oil.

The construction of the 'Druzhba' pipeline of about 5,327 km from the oilfields near Kuibyshev to Poland and the German Democratic Republic (northern branch) and to Czechoslovakia and Hungary (southern branch)—separating in Belorussia—begun in 1960, was completed in 1965.

In 1976 the USSR exported 111m. tonnes of crude oil and oil products.

Gas. A natural-gas pipeline from Gazli, near Khiva, to Voskresensk, near Moscow (2,750 km), with a planned capacity of 100m. cu. metres per day, began operating in Oct. 1967. Since then it has been extended to Czechoslovakia, where a 1,000-km extension, for transmission of Soviet gas to Austria, Italy and German Democratic Republic and Federal Republic of Germany, is under construction and another to Bulgaria. Another natural-gas pipeline, over 3,000 km from Medvezhye (Tyumen Region) to Moscow, began operating in Oct. 1974. A second pipeline from this region, linking the Urengoi deposit with Petrovsky in the Central European area of the USSR, became operational in 1980, and is to be continued to the southern Ukraine, to a total length of 3,000 km. A gas pipeline starting from Orenburg (Urals), passing across the Volga at Kamyshin, and continuing across the Ukraine *via* Kremenchug and Vinnitsa to Czechoslovakia (2,750 km), reached the Soviet frontier in Jan. 1979. When completed, it is to supply Czechoslovakia, Poland, Bulgaria and Hungary with 14,000m. cu. metres annually and Romania with 1,500m. A unified gas-grid exceeding 124,000 km now exists.

Minerals. Mining experts are trained in 6 mining, 3 oil and 1 peat institutes, the mining faculties of 17 higher educational establishments, oil faculties of 2 industrial institutes and a peat faculty at the Belorussian Polytechnical Institute.

The Soviet Union is rich in minerals. Soviet scientists claim that it contains 58% of the world's coal deposits, 58·7% of its oil, 41% of its iron ore, 76·7% of its apatite, 25% of all timber land, 88% of its manganese, 54% of its potassium salts and nearly one-third of its phosphates.

Estimated output (in tonnes) in 1962: Copper, 634,900; zinc, 399,000; lead, 363,000; tungsten, 10,500; antimony, 5,980; silver, 27m. fine oz. Output in 1963: Baryte, 199,500; magnesium, 31,745; aluminium, 961,400; manganese ore (1977), 8·6m.; graphite, 54,000; bauxite, 4·3m.; asbestos, 1·3m.; phosphate rock, 3·7m. (plus 7·4m. apatite); chromite, 1·23m.; gold, 12·5m. fine oz.; molybdenum, 12·5m. lb.; cadmium (1956), 160.

Output of iron and steel in the USSR (in 1m. tonnes):

	Pig-iron	Ingot steel	Rolled steel		Pig-iron	Ingot steel	Rolled steel
1913	4·2	4·2	3·5	1960	46·8	65·3	50·9
1928–29	4·0	4·8	3·9	1965	66·2	91·0	61·7
1932	6·2	5·9	4·4	1970	85·9	115·9	80·6
1940	14·9	18·3	13·1	1977	107·4	146·7	102·1
1946	10·0	13·4	9·6	1978	111·0	151·0	122·0
1950	19·2	27·3	20·9	1979	109·0	149·0	119·0

Coal production (in 1m. tonnes) was 29·1 in 1913, 64·4 in 1932, 165·9 in 1940, 261·1 in 1950, 513 in 1960, 624 in 1970, 668 in 1973, 685 in 1974, 701 in 1975, 711 in 1976, 722 in 1977, 724 in 1978, 719 in 1979, 716 in 1980.

The main centre of the atomic industry is at Ust-Kamenogorsk in the Altai Mountains. Uranium deposits are being worked near Taboshar (south-east of Tashkent), Andizhan (in the Tynya-Muyan Mountains), Slyudianka (near Lake Baikal), on the Kolyma River and in Southern Armenia.

Output of natural gas reached 407,000m. cu. metres in 1979; oil (including gas condensate), 586m. tonnes.

Agriculture. The Soviet Union, up to about 1928 predominantly agricultural in character, has become an industrial–agricultural country. Of the gross social product, industry and transport accounted for 42·1% in 1913 and 78·8% in 1977; agriculture for 57·9% in 1913 and 14·6% in 1977. Of the total state land fund of 2,227·5m. hectares, agricultural land in use in 1979 amounted to 1,050·3m., state forests and state reserves to 1,114·4m. hectares. 21% of all gainfully employed in 1979 were engaged in agriculture (1913, 75%).

The total area under cultivation (including single-owner peasant farms, state farms and collective farms) was (in the same territory) 118·8m. hectares in 1913, 129·7m. in 1933, 146·3m. in 1950, 203m. in 1960, 206·7m. in 1970, 217·9 in 1976, 217·6m. in 1977, 226·9m. in 1978, 226·3m. in 1979.

Collective farms on 1 Nov. 1979 possessed 245·9m. hectares, of which 103·1m. were under crops of various kinds; state farms and other state agricultural undertakings possessed 793·4m. hectares, of which 119·9m. were under crops; manual and clerical workers held 4m. hectares as allotments.

In Nov. 1969 the Third Congress of collective farmers adopted a new model constitution, considerably enlarging the planning powers of collective farms and making payments to their members a priority.

Since 1969 conferences of collective farms have elected 2,417 district collective farm councils with 85,000 members, to study and co-ordinate local experience in methods and finance. Processing and other joint agricultural productive establishments in 1978 numbered 8,906.

Produce marketed (after consumption by collective farmers) was, in 1m. tonnes, for the present area of the USSR:

	1950	1960	1970	1979		1950	1960	1970	1979
Grain	38·2	54·1	80·8	74·7	Meat [2] and fats	2·5	6·0	9·4	12·4
Raw cotton [1]	3·5	4·3	6·9	9·2	Milk and milk				
Sugar-beet	19·7	52·2	71·4	69·3	products	11·4	29·1	48·0	61·5
Potatoes	14·0	13·7	18·1	22·3	Wool	138·0	319·0	395·0	468·0
Other vegetables	4·3	8·0	13·8	20·6	Eggs (1,000m.)	3·5	10·5	22·1	44·7

[1] Seed-cotton unginned.   [2] Slaughter weight.

Since 1954 grain crops have been measured in 'barn crop' (*i.e.*, net quantities delivered to barns) and not in 'gross harvest' or 'biological yield' (*i.e.*, calculated as growing crops) as previously. Average annual crops (in 1m. tonnes): 1909–13, 72·5; 1946–50, 64·8; 1951–55, 88·5; 1956–60, 121·5; 1961–65, 130·3; 1966–70, 167·5; 1971–75, 181·6; 1978–79, 179; 1979–80, 189·2.

Other produce (in 1m. tonnes) in 1979: Milk, 93·3; sugar-beet, 90·3; potatoes, 76; vegetables, 25·8; meat (slaughter weight), 15·5; raw cotton, 9·2; sunflower, 5·4; 61,180m. eggs.

In Dec. 1963 collective farms comprised 99·7% of all peasant holdings. In 1978 they produced 90% of all sugar-beet, cotton 70%, milk 52%, marketed grain 45%, meat 41%, potatoes 30%, other vegetables 31%, eggs 11%.

Between 1953 and 1 Jan. 1980 the number of collective farms was reduced, mainly by amalgamation and partly by transformation into state farms, from 93,300 to 26,000, their cultivated area falling from 132m. hectares to 95·5m. The number of state farms rose in the same period from 4,857 to 20,800, their cultivated area from 15·2m. hectares to 119·9m.

State purchases in 1979 (in 1m. tonnes; 1978 figures in brackets): Grain, 62·8 (95·9); sugar-beet, 69·3 (80·1); milk, 59 (60·4); meat (slaughter weight), 10·4 (10·6); cotton, 9·2 (8·5); eggs (1,000m.), 41 (39·3).

By 1978 the main field work on state and collective farms and joint inter-farm enterprises (ploughing, sowing of grain, cotton and sugar-beet, and the harvesting of grain and silage crops) was fully mechanized; 83% of sugar-beet pulling and 65% of cotton-picking were mechanized, as was 87% of the milking.

Rural power stations in 1940 had a capacity of 265,000 kw.; in 1976, 2·9m. kw. 99·9% of collective farms and 99·9% of state farms were using electric power in 1973. In 1979 agriculture consumed 102,300m. kwh. of electric power.

Investments in agriculture in 1979 were 21,600m. roubles by the state and 10,200m. by collective farms. Total agricultural output in 1979 was valued at 123,500m. roubles.

In 1913 the total of irrigated land was 4m. hectares; in 1953, 11m.; in 1979, 17m. The total of land drained was 8·4m. hectares in 1956 and 16·3m. in 1979. In 1975 nearly 85m. hectares were treated from the air against weed, pest and disease.

In 1913, 188,000 tonnes of mineral fertilizers were used; in 1950, 5·3m. tonnes, and in 1980, 82m. On 1 Jan. 1980 there were 2·5m. tractors, 706,300 grain combine harvesters and 1·6m. lorries in the countryside.

An All-Union Academy of Agricultural Sciences, founded in 1929, has regional branches in Siberia and Central Asia and 196 research institutes.

Livestock (1 Jan. 1980), in 1m. head: Cattle, 115 (including 43 milch cows); pigs, 73·7; sheep, 143. Since 1957 the enumeration of livestock has been made on 1 Jan. instead of 1 Oct., *i.e.*, after the winter sales and slaughter for the market. Percentage of farm production in 1978:

	All grain	Cotton	Sugar-beet	Pota-toes	Other vegetables	Meat	Milk	Eggs	Wool
State	60	33	10	29	56	46	43	83	48
Collective	40	67	90	30	30	40	51	10	33
Private [1]	0	0	0	41	14	14	6	7	19

[1] *I.e.*, household plots of collective farmers.

Forestry. On the 747m. hectares of forest land of the USSR, a large portion is administered and worked by the State, and the other, about 38m. hectares in extent, is granted for use to the peasantry free of charge.

The largest forest areas are 515m. hectares in the Asiatic part of USSR, 51·4m. along the northern seaboard, 25·4m. in the Urals and 17·95m. in the north-west.

On 24 Oct. 1948 a plan was published for planting crop-protecting forest belts, introducing crop rotation with grasses and building of ponds and water reservoirs in the steppe and forest-steppe areas of the European part of the USSR. By the middle of 1952 some 2·6m. hectares had been planted with shelter-belt trees and 13,500 ponds and reservoirs had been built. The planting of the shelter belts in the Kamyshin–Volgograd and Byelgorod–Don areas has in the main been completed. A Volga forest belt has been planted along 1,200 km of railway. Re-afforestation was carried out on 2·2m. hectares of land in 1980.

Fisheries. The fishing catch including whaling (in 1,000 tonnes): 1913, 1,051; 1940, 1,422; 1960, 3,541; 1979, 9,359.

Belov, F., *The History of a Soviet Collective Farm*. New York, 1956
Simush, P., *The Soviet Collective Farm* (in English). Moscow, 1971
Symons, L., *Russian Agriculture: A Geographic Survey*. London, 1972
Vasiliev, P., and Kozlovsky, V., *Forest Wealth of the USSR* (in Russian). Moscow, 1959

INDUSTRY AND TRADE

Industry. The organization of industry in the USSR is based on state ownership and control, administered by a separate Ministry for each large industry.

Under the successive 5-year plans, large-scale modern industrial works have been constructed, namely: 1st, over 1,500; 2nd, 4,500; 3rd (up to June 1941), 3,000; wartime, 3,500 (apart from reconstruction of destroyed plants); 4th, 6,200; 5th, 3,200; 6th, 2,700; 7th (1959–65), 5,470; 8th (1966–70), 1,870; 9th (1971–75), 2,000.

Output of some heavy industries was as follows:

Industry	1913	1940	1950	1960	1978	1979
Iron ore (1m. tonnes)	9·2	29·9	39·7	106·2	244·0	242·0
Oil (1m. tonnes)	9·2	31·1	37·9	148·0	572·0	586·0
Electric power (1,000m. kwh.)	1·9	48·3	91·2	292·0	1,202·0	1,239·0
Mineral fertilizers (1m. tonnes)	0·07	3·0	5·5	13·8	98·0	94·5
Machine tools (1,000)	1·5	58·4	70·6	154·0	236·0	231·0
Steam and gas turbines (1,000 kw.)	5·9	972·0	2,381·0	9,200·0	19,500·0	20,000·0
Oil industry equipment (1,000 tonnes)	—	15·5	47·9	92·8	180·0	188·0
Diesel locomotives (1,000 h.p.)	—	5·0	125·0	1,303·0	3,705·0	3,704·0
Electric locomotives (1,000 h.p.)	—	29·0	2,428·0	2,972·0	3,475·0	3,254·0
Lorries and buses (1,000)	—	136·0	294·4	385·0	839·4	859·2
Tractors (1,000)	—	31·6	108·8	238·5	576·0	557·0
Looms (1,000)	4·6	1·8	8·7	16·4	21·2	22·2
Excavators (no.)	—	274·0	3,540·0	12,290·0	41,100·1	41,100·1
Timber (hauled, 1m. cu. metres) [1]	27·2	117·9	161·0	261·5	361·0	270·0
Cement (1m. tonnes)	1·8	5·7	10·2	45·5	127·0	123·0

[1] Excluding collective farm production.

The process of industrial mechanization and the installation of automatic remote control is being pushed ahead. About 90% of Soviet pig-iron and 87% of the steel is produced in fully automatic furnaces. All hydro-electric plants (in terms of capacity) are fully automatic. Coal production in open-cast mines has been completely mechanized; hydraulic mining is coming into general use. Coal-cutting and underground haulage was over 99% mechanized by the end of 1962 (loading on inclined seams 56%); peat-cutting, 100%, and loading, nearly 80%; timber-cutting, 98%; haulage to loading centres, 93%, and despatch, 97%.

Output in some consumer industries was as follows:

Industry	1913	1940	1950	1960	1978	1979
Cotton fabrics (1m. linear metres)	2,672·0	3,954·0	3,899·2	6,387	8,049·0	6,974·0
Woollen fabrics (1m. linear metres)	107·7	119·7	155·5	342	579·0	774·0
Silk fabrics (1m. linear metres)	42·6	77·3	129·7	810	1,619·0	1,725·0
Leather footwear (1m. pairs)	60·0	211·0	203·4	419	740·0	739·0
Clocks and watches (1m.)	0·7	2·8	7·6	26	63·3	64·5
Radio and television sets (1,000)	—	161·0	1,083·0	5,900	15,893·0	15,723·0
Bicycles and mopeds (1,000)	4·9	255·0	649·3	2,800	5,414·0	5,420·0
Paper (1,000 tonnes)	269·0	812·0	1,193·0	2,334	5,548·0	5,249·0
Meat (abattoirs) (1,000 tonnes)[1]	1,042·0	1,501·0	1,556·0	4,400	9,581·0	9,544·0
Butter (1,000 tonnes)[1]	104·0	226·0	336·0	737	1,381·0	1,325·0
Granulated sugar (1,000 tonnes)	1,363·0	2,165·0	2,523·0	6,360	12,207·0	10,600·0
Canned foods (1m. tins)	116·0	1,113·0	1,113·0	4,864	14,998·0	16,100·0

[1] Excluding collective farm and other home production, home-killed meat, etc.

Since 1945 the cotton industry has expanded, especially in the Urals, Central Asia and Siberia. Large mills have been built at Kamyshin, Kherson, Barnaul, Engels, Alma-Ata, Chernigov and Frunze.

Trade Unions and Labour. Trade unions are organized on an industrial basis, all workers, whether manual or brain, in every branch of a given industry being eligible for membership of the same union. Collective farmers may join trade unions.

Since 1933 the trade unions have carried out the functions of the former Labour Commissariat; they control and supervise the application of labour laws, introduce new labour laws for approval by the Government and administer social insurance and factory inspection. Social insurance is non-contributory. The All-Union Congress has met at irregular intervals; the 14th Congress met in 1968, the 15th in 1972 and the 16th in 1977. Membership (1978) 121m.

In 1944 there were 176 unions. This number was reduced by amalgamation of unions to 22 in 1958, but increased to 30 in 1977. Contributions range from 0·5 to 6% of wages. There are 167 regional and Republican Trades Councils.

Chairman, Central Council of Trade Unions: A. I. Shibayev.

The average number of industrial and clerical workers engaged (1979) in the whole national economy of the Soviet Union was 110·6m., 51% of them women. The 7-hour day (6 hours for miners underground and other heavy trades) was generally in operation by the end of 1960. The average working week since 1970 has been 39·4 hours and the working day in industry 6·93 hours. The 5-day week (without reduction of total working hours) was introduced in 1967.

New 'Fundamentals of Labour Legislation', intended to codify and extend labour laws adopted in the last 40 years, were adopted by the Supreme Soviet in July 1970. They lay down, *inter alia*, the right to receive wages irrespective of the income of the enterprise concerned, the right to free vocational and advanced technical training; the right to form trade unions without state registration; the right of trade unions to participate in and supervise management and planning, labour legislation, safety regulation and housing, fixing of working conditions and wages, etc. Pensioners in Jan. 1980 numbered 48·7m., including 33·1m. old age. Average monthly wages were 180 roubles in 1980.

The Trade Union Situation in the USSR. International Labour Office, 1960
From the 14th Congress to the 15th Congress of the Soviet Trade Unions (in Russian). Moscow, 1972
Costello, M., *Workers' Participation in the Soviet Union.* Moscow, 1977
Swiainiewicz, S., *Forced Labour and Economic Development.* OUP, 1965

Commerce. Retail home trade takes three forms—state, co-operative and the free market, *i.e.*, sales by individual collective-farm members and by the collective farms of their surplus products, after having fulfilled their statutory deliveries and made their regular allocations to their members.

In 1979 the consumer co-operative societies had 63m. members and did over 23% of the retail trade of the USSR. They were organized in 5,100 societies, employing about 3m. workers, with 369,000 retail shops, 90,000 catering establishments, 12,700 bakeries and 324 canneries. Their central union is affiliated to the International Co-operative Alliance. Retail trade by the State and co-operatives totalled 252,200m. roubles in 1979; by collective farm markets (agricultural produce), 6,200m. roubles. Total state and co-operative retail trade turnover represented (in comparable prices) an increase of 1% on 1976.

Foreign trade is organized as a state monopoly. Importation and exportation of goods are effected under licences issued by the Ministry for Foreign Trade and its respective departments in pursuance of a plan annually sanctioned by the Government. The right of purchasing goods for importation, and that of selling Soviet exports abroad, is vested in Trade Delegations and representatives of the appropriate state corporations in foreign countries.

There are 29 state import and export organizations, including chartering and tourist corporations (one, Vostokintorg, dealing with Mongolia, Sinkiang and Afghánistán). The Central Union of Consumers' Societies (Centrosoyuz) is also authorized to conduct foreign trade operations.

For foreign trade up to 1938 see THE STATESMAN'S YEAR-BOOK, 1951, p. 1465. The Central Statistical Department of the USSR estimates that, in comparable prices, the volume of foreign trade in 1938 was less than one-third that of 1913, but was in 1978, 31 times as large as in 1913. Exports in 1979 were valued at 42,400m. roubles (23,600m. to the Socialist countries), and imports at 37,900m. roubles (21,500m. from the Socialist countries).

Russia's imports of fuel and raw materials, between 1913 and 1977, declined from 43·5 to 21·7%, of machinery and equipment increased from 16·6 to 38·1%; imports of foodstuffs and manufactured consumer goods increased from 31·5% in 1913 to 33·7% in 1977.

Main items of exports in 1974:

Oil (1m. tonnes)	116·2	Cotton (1,000 tonnes)	739·0
Coal (1m. tonnes)	26·2	Vegetable oil (1,000 tonnes)	513·0
Iron ore (1m. tonnes)	43·3	Tractors (1,000)	40·1
Iron and rolled metal (1m. tonnes)	11·3	Motor cars and lorries (1,000)	327·4
Manganese ore (1,000 tonnes)	1,500·0	Clocks and watches (1,000)	15,700·0
Paper (1,000 tonnes)	650·0	Grain (1m. tonnes)	4·9

Total trade between the USSR and UK for calendar years (British Department of Trade returns, in £1,000 sterling):

	1977	1978	1979	1980
Imports to UK	780,572	688,170	827,629	786,176
Exports and re-exports from UK	347,432	423,085	419,042	455,310

Tourism. Pre-revolutionary Russia was never a country for any but the most hardy and better-off tourists, as the introductory pages of Baedeker's guide made clear. For her subjects, too, touring was no more inviting. Acute shortage of hotels and boarding-houses, poor roads, lack of ordinary services for visitors were among the least of their difficulties.

These have not by any means been fully overcome: but very great efforts to meet them have been made.

	1972	1973	1974	1975
Foreign visitors to the USSR	2,316,974	2,909,158	3,446,933	3,690,751
Of whom, from non-Socialist countries	875,395	1,309,979	1,558,522	1,582,741
Soviet visitors abroad	1,973,333	2,082,385	2,224,601	2,450,087
Of whom, to non-Socialist countries	854,792	868,725	893,059	932,119

Within the USSR, tourism by Soviet citizens has been much encouraged by the trade unions, which are developing an extensive network of facilities, particularly for hikers, campers and climbers. These facilities number more than 10,000 tourist camps, 650 tourist 'bases' (supply depots for hiring equipment), and over 4,000 cabins for anglers, hunters and mountaineers. The Central Council of Trade Unions also owns or controls 137 river or seagoing ships, 120 trains and 8,000 motor coaches exclusively for tourist use.

Soviet tourists recorded by this network numbered 40,000 in 1950; 1,997,000 in 1965; 5,041,000 in 1970 and about 19m. in 1978.

COMMUNICATIONS

Roads. By 1941 there were over 1·5m. km of constructed roads, of which 143,000 km were suitable for motor traffic. The total length of motor roads in 1979 was 770,000 km. Road freights by lorry amounted to 859m. tonnes in 1940 and 23,175m. tonnes in 1979. Passengers carried were 590m. in 1940 and 41,300m. in 1979. In 1979, 21,800 inter-urban bus routes had a total length of 3,205,000 km.

Railways. The length of railways in Jan. 1980 was 141,125 km (1913: 58,500). By the end of 1979, 140,500 km of main-line railways had changed to electric and diesel traction, 42,461 km wholly electrified, and 99·9% of railway freight went by these means. In 1979, 60% of all goods traffic and 40% of passenger transport went by rail (in 1913, 57% and 91% respectively). The Moscow–Donetz, Leningrad–Leninakan (3,400 km) and western frontier–Baikal (7,500 km) lines have been electrified.

There are 43 main railway systems which may be grouped as follows:

In the west: Estonian (1,388 km), Latvian (3,100 km) and Lithuanian (2,100 km), Kalinin (2,064 km, Moscow–Orsha and Moscow–Zilupe, centre at Smolensk), Belorussian (5,800 km), October (Moscow–Leningrad, centre Leningrad, 3,857 km), Lvov (south-western Ukraine, 4,257 km), South-Western (centre Kiev–western Ukraine and southern Belorussia, 3,888 km), Moscow–Kiev (centre Kaluga–western Russia, eastern Belorussia, north-Ukraine, western 3,821 km).

In the north: Northern (Moscow and north European Russia, centre Yaroslavl, 3,750 km), Pechora (centre Kotlas: north-eastern European Russia, 1,953 km), Kirov (Murmansk–Petrozavodsk–Volhovstroi, centre Petrozavodsk, 3,587 km).

In the European south: Moscow–Kursk–Donbass (centre Moscow, 3,027 km), Southern (centre Kharkov: eastern Ukraine, south-eastern Russia, 3,304 km), South-Eastern (centre Voronezh: Ukraine–Urals, Rostov–Penza regions, 2,579 km), Odessa (south-eastern Ukraine–south-western Moldavia, centre Odessa, 3,839 km), Moldavian (Kishinev, 1,200 km), Stalin (centre Dnepropetrovsk, links this heavy-industry area with the Black Sea coast, 3,298 km), North Caucasus (centre Rostov-on-Don, 3,391 km), Ordzhonikidze (links northern Caucasus Autonomous Republics with Caspian coast, centre Ordzhonikidze, 1,708 km). Donetz (centre Donetsk, served the Donetz coalfield, 2,862 km). The entire route from Leningrad to Simferopol (Crimea) was electrified during 1970.

In eastern European Russia: Moscow–Ryazan (centre Moscow, 2,089 km), Kazan (centre Kazan, links Volga with Urals, 2,783 km), Gorky (Moscow–Ryazan–north-eastern Russia, centre Gorky, 1,543 km), Ufa (links Bashkir and Tartar Republics and northern Volga regions, centre Ufa, 1,866 km), Kuibyshev (centre Kuibyshev, links Volga regions with Urals, 2,012 km), Volga (centre Saratov, links it with Volgograd and Astrakhan, 3,149 km).

In the Urals and western Asia: Sverdlovsk (centre Sverdlovsk, links northern Urals with western Siberia, 4,000 km), South Urals (centre Chelyabinsk, links eastern regions of Russia in Europe with northern Kazakhstan, 2,875 km), Orenburg (centre Orenburg, links southern Urals with Siberia, 3,150 km), Omsk (centre Omsk, links western Siberia with northern Kazakhstan and Altai, 2,050 km), Tomsk (centre Novosibirsk, links western Siberia, Kemerovo coalfield and Altai, 3,039 km).

In south-western Asia: Transcaucasian (centre Tbilisi, links Black Sea coast with Yerevan, 1,887 km), Azerbaijan (centre Baku, 1,650 km).

In Central Asia: Tashkent (centre Tashkent, links Tadjik, Uzbek, Kirgiz and Kazakh republics with Orenburg, 2,420 km), Ashkhabad (centre Ashkhabad, links Caspian coast and Turkmen Republic with Uzbekistan, 2,647 km), Kazakh (centre Alma-Ata, 9,000 km). The 334-km Guriev–Astrakhan railway, across the Caspian desert, began operating on 1 Jan. 1971, shortening the route from Central Asia to the Caucasus by nearly 700 km. New lines, Kokchetav–Volodarskoye and Kustanai–Uritskoye, are under construction in Kazakhstan, and a Termez–Yavan line in Tadjikistan.

In central and eastern Siberia: Krasnoyarsk (centre Krasnoyarsk, a part of Trans-Siberian line but with new branches serving the Khakass and Tuva republics, 1,279 km), East Siberia (centre Irkutsk, serves Irkutsk region and Buryat Republic with link to Mongolian People's Republic, 1,696 km), Transbaikal (centre Chita, part of Trans-Siberian line but serving Buryatia and linked with China and Mongolia, 3,320 km). The Abakan–Taishet line, connecting the South-Siberian and main Trans-Siberian lines and linking the Bratsk and Kuznetzk industrial areas (640 km), began operating in 1964 with electric traction. A Tyumen–Surgut–Nizhnevartovsk (on the upper Ob) line, of nearly 1,000 km is under construction.

A line from Khrebtovaya, on the Taishet–Zena railway in East Siberia, to Ust-Ilimskaya on the Angara (215 km) has been opened, as the first section of a new North Siberian main line, skirting the northern shore of Lake Baikal, and stretching from Lena, on the Lena River, 3,145 km to Komsomolsk-on-Amur. This line is scheduled for full electrification and operation in 1982. Electrification of the first 640 km began in June 1975.

The Baikal–Amur Magistral (BAM) will provide a more direct route to the Pacific ports of Nakhodka and Vladivostok than that offered by the Trans-Siberian railway and much of its route will lie several hundred km north of the Trans-Siberian railway, avoiding the latter's lengthy detour round Lake Baikal. It will give access to valuable raw materials such as coal, iron ore, copper, nickel and timber. The Baikal–Amur Magistral will ease the very heavy pressure on the Trans-Siberian route, which is only partially electrified and is not double-track throughout. Development of new port facilities on the east coast will create even greater strain on the existing facilities and the Baikal–Amur Magistral will become the principal route for export traffic to these ports. Oil from the Tyumen fields will be among the major commodities.

Construction of the Baikal–Amur Magistral is the most arduous railway-building project ever tackled by Soviet engineers and the greatest drawback to development of the region has been its severe climatic and geological conditions. There is permafrost throughout the area, and winter temperatures fall to $-60°$ C. Severe danger exists in the mountains in winter from avalanches and in summer freak streams of mud fill river beds and valleys, hindering construction.

Work is being carried out from 7 major construction sites, each equipped with its own reinforced concrete plant, steel fabrication works and extensive engineering plant. When the line is completed in 1982 these sites will remain to form the nucleus of new heavy industry towns.

Over 3,200 bridges, tunnels and culverts are being built for the Baikal–Amur Magistral, including 140 major river crossings and a 1,200-metre bridge 40 metres high over the river Zeya reservoir. One of the first projects tackled was the 1,450-metre-long crossing of the river Amur near Komsomolsk. Extraordinary conditions here necessitated development of entirely new construction techniques. Large bridge spans are being used wherever possible to minimize the number of piles to be driven in permafrost conditions. Two tunnels are of particular note—a 15-km bore through the Severo-Muisky range, and one of 7 km through the Baikal ridge.

A 180-km link from the Trans-Siberian railway at Skovorodino to Tyndin, about midway between Ust-Kut and Komsomolsk, was opened in 1975, and a northwards extension of this route, to Berkakit, was opened in 1978. This line will reach the rich Chulman coalfields, allowing exploitation to begin well ahead of completion of the Baikal–Amur Magistral. The 700-km eastern section of the line from Urgal to Komsomolsk-on-Amur, was opened to service traffic in June 1979. About 2,000 km of line have been laid since work started in 1975.

Many thousands of workers are involved in this major project, but despite the huge commitment of labour and equipment construction of at least a further 1,500 km of lines is due to begin during the next 5 years. Two major extensions of the Tyumen–Surgut line will exploit oil, natural gas and timber in Northern Siberia. One will serve Nizhne-Vartovskoye on the river Ob, while the other will reach Urengoi on the river Pur. Survey work has also been completed for a 400-km line in the Yamal Peninsula from Khal'mer-Yu to Cape Kharasavei. This will extend to more than $73°$ North on the coast of the Kara Sea, making it the world's most northerly railway. Included is a 600-km crossing of the Baydaratskaya Gulf, which will be achieved by ice-breaking train ferries.

See map in THE STATEMAN'S YEAR-BOOK, 1977–78.

In the Far East: Far Eastern (centre Khabarovsk, serves Maritime regions, 1,712 km), Amur (centre Blagoveshchensk, part of Trans-Siberian line, serves the Amur valley, 2,468 km), South Sahalin (centre Yuzhno-Sahalinsk, 752 km).

Underground railways have been built in Moscow, Leningrad, Kiev, Tbilisi, Kharkov, Tashkent, Baku and Yerevan. Others are under construction at Minsk, Novosibirsk and Gorky. Surveys are in progress for lines in Kuibyshev, Riga, Sverdlovsk and Dnepropetrovsk.

Aviation. In 1979 total length of internal airlines in the USSR was approximately 957,000 km; 102m. passengers were carried internally and externally. The Central Asian Airways in some instances provide the only means of communication across the desert and mountainous regions of the local republics. An 8,500-km air service was opened in Feb. 1941 between Moscow and Anadyr (Eastern Siberia), through Archangel, Igarka, Khatanga, Tiksi Bay and Cape Schmidt, *i.e.*, along the entire course of the Northern Sea Route. There are also other Arctic airlines, *e.g.*, Igarka–Gulf of Kozhevnikov; Igarka–Dickson Island; Yakutsk–Tiksi Bay; Yakutsk–Viluisk; Yakutsk–Verkhoiansk.

Direct air services are maintained throughout the year between Moscow and the capitals of all Soviet republics as well as London, New York, Montreal, Tōkyō, Delhi, Rangoon, Belgrade, Peking, Pyongyang, Ulan Bator, Kábul, Tirana, Paris, Warsaw, Prague, Budapest, Bucharest, Sofia, Vienna, Berlin, Helsinki, Stockholm, Copenhagen, Jakarta, Dakar and Gander. During 1979 direct services have been opened from Kiev to Paris and Dusseldorf; Leningrad to Vienna and Gdansk; Moscow to Saigon, Kinshasa, Kuwait and Kingston (Jamaica); Yerevan to Aleppo.

Soviet air services reach 62 countries, and 20 foreign lines have regular services to the USSR, including British Airways, KLM, SAS, Air France, SABENA, Air India, PANAM.

MacDonald, H., *Aeroflot: Soviet Air Transport Since 1923.* London, 1975

Shipping. In 1977 the Soviet mercantile marine comprised 7,000 self-propelled vessels, of which 80% were built between 1957 and 1966. By May 1977 the gross cargo capacity was (including fishing vessels) 20·8m. registered tonnes (16m. tonnes deadweight).

Freights carried were: In 1913 (present frontiers), 15·1m. tonnes; in 1940, 32·9m. tonnes; in 1950, 33·7m. tonnes, and in 1977, 220m. tonnes; 51·9m. passengers were carried. The Soviet share in world marine tonnage was 2% in 1960 and 6% in 1977. Deep-sea ports are under construction at Vostochny (Far East) and Grigorevsky (Black Sea) with new deep-sea wharves at Ventspils (Latvia), Murmansk and Archangel (for Arctic traffic). Archangel is kept open by icebreakers all the year round from 1979. Foreign freights in 1977 totalled 14% of all Soviet seaborne trade.

The North Sea route affords convenient communication between the European USSR and the Far East along the Soviet coast, for the produce of the basins of the Ob, Yenissei, Lena and Kolyma rivers.

The length of navigable rivers and canals in exploitation was (1977) 143,100 km, of which the length of floatable rivers is 89,500 km. There are several thousand miles of canals and other artificial waterways; among them the Baltic and White Sea Canal (235 km), the Moscow–Volga Canal (130 km). Goods turnover on inland waterways was 28,900m. tonne-km in 1913, 35,900m. in 1940, 45,900m. in 1950 and 230,700m. in 1977; freight carried rose from 35·1m. tonnes in 1913 to 521m. tonnes in 1977.

The Volga–Don Shipping Canal was opened for traffic in 1952. The Volga–Don waterway from Volgograd to Rostov is 540 km long, of which the Volga–Don canal comprises 101 km. The canal has transformed the section of the river from Kalach, where the Don is joined by the Volga–Don canal, to Rostov into a deep-water highway suitable for big Volga shipping. The canal links the White, Baltic, Caspian, Azov and Black Seas into a single water transport system. In Oct. 1964 the 2,430-km Baltic–Volga waterway, linking Klaipeda on the Baltic to Kakhovka at the mouth of the Dnieper and suitable for 5,000-tonne vessels, was begun. Reconstruction of the 18th-century Mariinsky canal system in north-west Russia was completed, providing a through waterway from Leningrad to Rybinsk (on the Upper Volga) and cutting the passage of freight from 18 to 2½ days.

At the end of 1977 the longest train ferry route in the world was opened between the Soviet Union and Bulgaria (Ilyichovsk–Varna).

The first section of Vostochny port, in Wrangel Bay on the Pacific coast, is completed. It will be the country's largest deep-sea port.

In 1962 a canal was completed across the Kara-Kum desert in southern Turkmenistan (replacing an earlier project for a more costly scheme across the north of the republic. The canal, from Bussag on the river Amu-Darya to Archnan, north-west of Ashkhabad, through the Murgab oasis, 900 km long, supplies water to an area exceeding 200,000 hectares, suitable for cotton, fruit, vineyards and livestock. An extension to the Caspian (500 km) is under construction: the complete system will irrigate 1m. hectares.

An irrigation canal system (250 miles), bringing water from Kakhovka on the Dnieper to the North Crimea, is nearing completion. Work to divert water from the Pechora and Vychegda rivers (flowing into the White Sea) south to the Volga is in progress. Work has begun on a 300-mile canal which will supply water from the Irtysh to Karaganda in Central Kazakhstan, irrigating over 150,000 acres; the first 37 miles were opened in 1965 and another 45 miles in Dec. 1967. Most of the 11 reservoirs required had been completed by 1 Jan. 1972. Other irrigation canals under construction are Kuibyshev (279 km long, to supply over 100,000 hectares) and Stavropol (481 km, irrigating 200,000 hectares); the second section of the latter went into commission in Nov. 1974, 14 months ahead of schedule. In Sept. 1972 the Saratov Canal (irrigating 1m. hectares) went into commission.

By 1 Jan. 1979, over 29m. hectares of land reclaimed by irrigation or drainage were under crops (nearly 25% of total output). In 1980 the reclaimed area was brought up to 33m. hectares.

Post and Broadcasting. In Dec. 1979 the number of post, telegraph and telephone offices was 90,000 and of public telephones 22·3m.

The international radio-telecommunications services are operated by the Ministry of Communications of the USSR. The Great Northern Telegraph Co., Ltd, of Denmark, operates cables connecting Denmark with Leningrad, whence connexion is made by means of a trans-Siberian landline with Vladivostok. From the latter place the Great Northern Telegraph Co. owns cables connecting with Japan, China and Hong Kong. Direct radio and telephone communication with India is provided for in an agreement concluded in 1955.

The State Committee for Broadcasting and Television produces 3 programmes in Moscow, broadcasting throughout the Union. In addition the regional radio stations produce 1, 2 or 3 programmes for the republics as well as local programmes for a town or region. The foreign service from Moscow is beamed to all parts of the world, in 64 languages. Chinese is broadcast for 28½ hours a day. In addition, several republics have their own foreign services. English is broadcast from Moscow, Kiev, Tashkent, Vilnius and Yerevan. There are 122 TV centres in the USSR, several of them producing more than 1 programme. In Moscow there are 4 programmes. Colour programmes are broadcast by SECAM system. A nationwide system of space telecommunications, consisting of satellites and ground stations, takes TV broadcasts to distant parts of the country.

Number of receivers, Jan. 1980: radio, 66m.; television, 64·3m.

Cinemas and theatres (Jan. 1980). There were 144,000 permanent and 8,800 mobile cinemas. In Jan. 1980 there were 596 theatres, to which 119·3m. visits were made in 1979.

Newspapers. In 1979, 8,019 newspapers with a total circulation of 173m. copies were published in 57 languages of the USSR.

JUSTICE, RELIGION, EDUCATION AND WELFARE

Justice. The basis of the judiciary system is the same throughout the Soviet Union, but the constituent republics have the right to introduce modifications and to make their own rules for the application of the code of laws. The Supreme Court of the USSR is the chief court and supervising organ for all constituent republics and is elected by the Supreme Soviet of the USSR for 5 years. Supreme Courts of the Union and Autonomous Republics are elected by the Supreme Soviets of these republics, and Territorial, Regional and Area Courts by the respective Soviets, each for a term of 5 years.

Court proceedings are conducted in the local language with full interpreting facilities as required. All cases are heard in public, unless otherwise provided for by law, and the accused is guaranteed the right of defence.

Laws establishing common principles of criminal legislation, criminal responsibility for state and military crimes, judicial and criminal procedure and military tribunals were adopted by the Supreme Soviet on 25 Dec. 1958 for the courts both of the USSR and the constituent Republics.

The Law Courts are divided into People's Courts and higher courts. The People's Courts consist of the People's Judge and 2 Assessors, and their function is to examine, as the first instance, most of the civil and criminal cases, except the more important ones, some of which are tried at the Regional Court, and those of the highest importance at the Supreme Court. The Regional Courts supervise the activities of the People's Courts and also act as Courts of Appeal from the decisions of the People's Court. Special chambers of the higher courts deal with offences committed in the Army and the public transport services.

People's Judges and Assessors, who serve on a rota basis, are elected directly by the citizens of each constituency: judges for 5 years, assessors for 2½. Should a judge be found not to perform his duties conscientiously and in accordance with the mandate of the people, he may be recalled by his electors.

The People's Assessors are called upon for duty for 2 weeks in a year. The People's Assessors for the Regional Court must have had at least 2 years' experience in public or trade-union work. The list of Assessors for the Supreme Court is drawn up by the Supreme Soviet of the republic.

The Labour Session of the People's Court supervises the regulations relating to the working conditions and the protection of labour and gives decisions on conflicts arising between managements and employees, or the violation of regulations.

Disputes between State institutions must be referred to an arbitration commission. Disputes between Soviet State institutions and foreign business firms may be referred by agreement to a Foreign Trade Arbitration Commission of the All-Union Chamber of Commerce.

The Procurator-General of the USSR is appointed for 5 years by the Supreme Soviet. All procurators of the republics, autonomous republics and autonomous regions are appointed by the Procurator-General of the USSR for a term of 5 years. The procurators supervise the correct application of the law by all state organs, and have special responsibility for the observance of the law in places of detention. The procurators of the Union republics are subordinate to the Procurator-General of the USSR, whose duty it is to see that acts of all institutions of the USSR are legal, that the law is correctly interpreted and uniformly applied; he has to participate in important cases in the capacity of State Prosecutor.

Capital punishment was abolished on 26 May 1947, but was restored on 12 Jan. 1950 for treason, espionage and sabotage, on 7 May 1954 for certain categories of murder, in Dec. 1958 for terrorism and banditry, on 7 May 1961 for embezzlement of public property, counterfeiting and attack on prison warders and, in particular circumstances, for attacks on the police and public order volunteers and for rape (15 Feb. 1962) and for accepting bribes (20 Feb. 1962).

In view of criminal abuses, extending over many years, discovered in the security system, the powers of administrative trial and exile previously vested in the security authorities (MVD) were abolished in 1953; accelerated procedures for trial on charges of high treason, espionage, wrecking, etc., by the Supreme Court were abolished in 1955; and extensive powers of protection of persons under arrest or serving prison terms were vested in the Procurator-General's Office (1955). Supervisory commissions, composed of representatives of trade unions, youth organizations and local authorities, were set up in 1956 to inspect places of detention.

Further reforms of the civil and criminal codes were decreed on 25 Dec. 1958.

Thereby the age of criminal responsibility has been raised from 14 to 16 years; deportation and banishment have been abolished; a presumption of innocence is not accepted, but the burden of proof of guilt has been placed upon the prosecutor; secret trials and the charge of 'enemy of the people' have been abolished.

Religion. With the Revolution the Orthodox Church lost its position as the dominant religion and all religions were placed on an equal footing. Article 52 of the 1977 Soviet Constitution reads as follows: 'Citizens of the USSR are guaranteed freedom of conscience; that is, the right to profess or not to profess any religion, and to conduct religious worship or atheistic propaganda. Incitement of hostility or hatred on religious grounds is prohibited. In the USSR the church is separated from the state and school from the church.'

By decree of 23 Jan. 1918 the Orthodox Church was disestablished; its property, together with that of all other denominations, was nationalized. The congregations themselves have to maintain their churches and clergy, regardless of confession or denomination, and may organize a minimum of 20 persons, which may request and receive the use of a church building, free of charge, except for maintenance, insurance, land taxes, etc. About two-thirds of all the churches have been closed. Religious instruction may be given in private, but otherwise only in church classes. The income of religious communities is not subject to taxation. The state supplies paper and printing facilities to all denominations for producing the Bible, the Koran, prayer books, missals, etc.

Relations between the religious communities of all creeds and the Government are maintained through a Council for Religious Affairs (*Chairman*, V. A. Kuroyedov).

The Russian Orthodox Church, represented by the Patriarchate of Moscow, had, in 1967, 30m. regular worshippers. There are still many Old Believers, whose schism from the Orthodox Church dates from the 17th century. The Russian Church is headed by the Patriarch of Moscow and All Russia, assisted by the Holy Synod, which has 6 members—the Patriarch himself and the Metropolitans of Krutitsy and Kolomna (Moscow), Leningrad and Kiev *ex officio*, and 3 bishops alternating for 6 months in order of seniority from the 3 regions forming the Moscow Patriarchate. In 1967 there were 20,000 places of worship (54,000 before the Revolution). Religious instruction in classes for persons under 18 is forbidden. The Patriarchate of Moscow maintains jurisdiction over a few parishes of Russian Orthodox abroad, at Tehrán, Jerusalem, German Democratic Republic, France (1 archbishop), England, North and South America (2 bishops). There are 20 monasteries and nunneries, and 6 Orthodox academies and seminaries with 6 journals.

After the Russian Orthodox Church the next Christian community in importance are the Armenians; their Catholicos (Patriarch), whose seat is at Etchmiadzin, is head of all the Armenian (Gregorian) communities throughout the world.

There is an Armenian Orthodox academy and a seminary.

The Georgian Church has its own organization under a Catholicos (Patriarch) and a seminary.

Protestantism is represented chiefly by the Evangelical Christian Baptists, with over 512,000 baptized adult members and some 5,000 churches: the Lutherans are concentrated mainly in the Baltic States (350,000 in Estonia, 600,000 in Latvia), the Reformed in the Transcarpathian Region of the Ukraine (70,000). Both Baptists and Lutherans conduct theological courses.

The Roman Catholics are most numerous in Lithuania and the western Ukraine. There are 2 Roman Catholic archepiscopates and 4 episcopates in Lithuania with 630 churches and a seminary at Kaunas providing a 5-year course. In 1946 some 3·5m. Uniates in the USSR withdrew their allegiance to Rome and came under the jurisdiction of the Orthodox Patriarchate in Moscow. In Latvia there are an archepiscopate and 1 episcopate (Riga and Liepaja) of the Roman Catholic Church.

The Moslems, mainly Sunnis, are divided into 4 administrative regions; 3 of them (Central Asia, European Russia and Siberia, Northern Caucasus) headed by a Mufti; the largest (Transcaucasia, with its centre at Baku) by a Shaikh-ul-Islam.

There is a Moslem academy and a madrasah in Central Asia. Several editions of the Koran have appeared in recent years.

There are various Jewish communities, the chief being in Moscow and Kiev.

Large synagogues maintain bakeries for producing unleavened bread. There is a Jewish Yeshiva. The Central Buddhist Council of the USSR is headed by a Lama with communities in Buryatia, Tuva, Kalmykia and in the national (minority) areas of the Chita and Irkutsk regions.

Bordeaux, M., *Opium of the People. The Christian Religion in the USSR.* London, 1965.— *Religious Ferment in Russia.* London, 1968
Braham, R. L., *Jews in the Communist World; a bibliography, 1945–1960.* New York, 1961
Conquest, R. (ed.), *Religion in the USSR.* London, 1968
Curtiss, J. S., *The Russian Church and the Soviet State, 1917–50.* New York, 1953
Fejtö, F., *Les Juifs et l'antisémitisme dans les pays communistes.* Paris, 1960
Fletcher, W. C., *A Study in Survival: The Church in Russia 1927–43.* New York, 1965
Goldberg, B. Z., *The Jewish Problem in the Soviet Union.* New York, 1961
Kolarz, W., *Religion in the Soviet Union.* London, 1961
Leneman, L., *La Tragédie des Juifs en URSS.* Bruges, 1959
Novosti Press Agency (ed.), *Soviet Jews: Fact and Fiction.* Moscow, 1970
Struve, N., *Les Chrétiens en URSS.* Paris, 1963

Education. Education is free and compulsory from 7 to 16/17. Co-education was reintroduced in all schools on 1 Sept. 1954. There are 2 types of general schools— with an 8-year or a 10-year curriculum; the minimum school-leaving age is now 17. Pupils who leave an 8-year school continue their education at either a 10-year school or a vocational training school. A 10-year school pupil may also transfer to vocational school after the 8th year. Vocational school pupils must reach the same standard of general education as those at 10-year general schools, and so stay on at school longer. Instruction is given in more than 100 languages.

In 1979–80 there were 147,000 primary and secondary schools. Pupils in general educational schools numbered 44·4m. (10·2m. of them in the 16–18 age-groups) and the teachers 2·6m. Those at vocational and specialized technical secondary schools numbered 6·7m.

At the end of 1940 labour reserve schools (both vocational and industrial) were organized, admitting applicants from 14 to 17 years of age. From 1959 onwards these and other technical schools were reorganized as town and rural vocational and technical schools, at which pupils stay for a year longer than at general schools, combining completion of general secondary education with vocational training. From 1940 to 1977 inclusive they trained 35m. skilled workers. In 1978, 2·3m. graduated from such schools, including 628,000 for agriculture; 600,000 agricultural mechanics were trained in state and collective farms. Over 6,900 vocational training schools existed in 1979, training 3·5m. boys and girls, about one-third providing full secondary education. In 1979, 13·9m. children of from 3 to 7 years of age attended kindergartens. Children in boarding schools numbered over 800,000 in 1972–73.

In 1979–80 there were 4,357 technical colleges with 4·6m. students, and 870 universities, institutes and other places of higher education, with 5·2m. students (including 1·74m. taking correspondence or evening courses). 68,000 part-time students from factories, collective farms, or the armed forces were attending preparatory courses at 524 places of higher education (similar to the 'workers' faculties' of early Soviet years).

Among the 65 university towns are: Moscow, Leningrad, Kharkov, Odessa, Tartu, Kazan, Saratov, Tomsk, Kiev, Sverdlovsk, Tbilisi, Alma-Ata, Tashkent, Minsk, Gorky and Vladivostok. On 1 Jan. 1980 there were 1·34m. scientific workers in places of higher education, research institutes and Academies of Sciences. There are 33,000 foreign students from 130 countries.

The Academy of Sciences of the USSR had 753 members and corresponding members. Total learned institutions under the USSR Academy of Sciences number 244, with 46,000 scientific staff. Fourteen of the Union Republics have their own Academies of Sciences, with scientific staff numbering 47,340. There are also Siberian, Far Eastern and other branches of the USSR Academy. On 1 Jan. 1980 there were 96,075 post-graduate students.

The Academy of Pedagogical Sciences had 14 research institutes with 1,700 staff.

In Jan. 1980 there were employed in the national economy 11·1m. specialists with a completed higher education and 15·3m. with a completed secondary technical education.

In 1979–80 about 98·3m. people were studying at schools, colleges and training or correspondence courses. 100 per 1,000 of the employed population had a higher education (1939, 13; 1959, 33).

Health and Social Security. All health services are free of charge; but private practice exists. Health is administered by the Ministry of Health of the USSR, which supervises the work of the Health Ministries of the Union Republics and the Autonomous Republics.

In 1944 an Academy of Medical Sciences was formed; it has under its direct control 42 research institutes. In all, there were, in 1976, 393 medical research institutions with 70,000 research staff. Smallpox, trachoma and malaria have been virtually eliminated.

In 1979–80, 98 institutes and medical faculties had a total of 374,400 students taking a 6-year course.

In Dec. 1979 there were 23,200 civil hospitals with 3·3m. beds. There were 1m. infants in day nurseries and another 2·7m. in the crèche-sections of kindergartens. 960,000 doctors (including dentists) were in the health service. All confinements in towns and 75% in the country were in hospital.

There were 35,961 outpatients' clinics, apart from the 24,000 women's consultation centres and children's clinics.

The death-rate in the USSR in 1979 was 10·1 per 1,000, and the birth rate 18·2 per 1,000. Infant death rate was 27·9 (per 1,000 live births) in 1974, compared with 273 in 1913, 184 in 1940 and 81 in 1950. Average expectation of life, 70 (1913, 32).

Social insurance is administered by the trade unions, through social insurance councils elected in places of work and social insurance sub-committees of factory committees: about 5m. volunteers are engaged in this work. 37·7m. people were sent to holiday sanatoria or rest homes in 1979. 48·7m. people, including 11·4m. collective farmers, were receiving state pensions in Jan. 1980; of these, 10m. were old-age pensioners.

Total number of holiday sanatoria providing toning-up treatment at resorts in 1979 was 2,355, with accommodation for 542,000; in addition, there were 2,481 overnight sanatoria at large plants for treatment of mild disorders without absence from work, accommodating 201,000. There were also 1,208 trade union-managed holiday hotels with a capacity of 380,000, holidays being partly or wholly at trade unions' expense.

State expenditure (in 1m. new roubles) on health services proper, 1960, 4,800; 1970, 9,300; 1976, 11,800; 1977, 12,500; 1978, 13,500; 1979, 14,100.

Between 1950 and 1977 56,748,000 apartments (in towns) and houses (in rural areas) were built. In 1979, 2·5m. apartments and houses were built. By the end of 1977, 71% of all housing in urban settlements and 65% in villages, had gas supply installed.

DIPLOMATIC REPRESENTATIVES

OF THE USSR IN GREAT BRITAIN (13 Kensington
Palace Gdns., London, W8 4QX)

Ambassador: Victor Popov.

OF GREAT BRITAIN IN THE USSR (Naberezhnaya Morisa
Toreza 14, Moscow 72)

Ambassador: Sir Curtis Keeble, KCMG.

OF THE USSR IN THE USA (1125–16th St., NW,
Washington, D.C., 20036)

Ambassador: Anatoly F. Dobrynin.

OF THE USA IN THE USSR (Ulitsa Chaikovskogo 19, Moscow)

Ambassador: Thomas J. Watson, Jr.

OF THE USSR TO THE UNITED NATIONS

Ambassador: Oleg Alexsandrovich Troyanovsky.

Books of Reference

Narodnoye Hozyaistvo SSSR 1922–1974 (National Economy of the USSR). Statistical Summary. 1975

SSSR v Tsifrakh. Central Statistical Department, 1975

Pravda [Truth]. Daily organ of the Central Committee of the Communist Party

Izvestia [News]. Daily organ of the Presidium of the Supreme Soviet of the USSR

Viedomosti Verkhovnovo Sovieta. Bulletin of the Supreme Soviet of the USSR, in the languages of the 16 republics

Sovietskaia Torgovlia. Thrice-weekly publication of the Ministry of Trade of the USSR

Planovoye Khoziaistvo. Monthly. Moscow

Voprosy Torgovli. A monthly journal published by the Ministry of Trade of the USSR

Vneshnaya Torgovlya. Published by the Ministry for Foreign Trade. Monthly. Moscow

Trud. The daily organ of the All-Union Central Council of Trade Unions

Professionalnye Soyuzy. A trade union fortnightly. Moscow

Kommunist. A fortnightly organ of the Communist Party of the Soviet Union

Finansy i Khoziaistov. A weekly publication of the Ministry for Finance

Sotsialititcheskoye Zemledelie. A daily publication of the Ministry of Agriculture

Soviet Foreign Policy During the Patriotic War; Documents and Materials. 2 vols. (translated by A. Rothstein). London, 1946–47

History of the USSR. Published by the Soviet Academy of Sciences. 3 vols. Moscow, 1948–57. (In Russian.) German edition, *Geschichte der Völker der Sowjetunion.* Basle, 1945

Bolshaya Sovietskaya Entsiklopedia. 65 vols. Moscow, 1926–47; 2nd ed., 51 vols. Moscow, 1949–58; annual supplement (*Yezhegodnik*)

Soviet Union. A monthly pictorial. Moscow. (In English)

Soviet Import–Export Dictionary (in Russian, with English, etc., terms). Moscow, 1952

Velikaia Otechestvennaya Voina Sovetskogo Soyuza. Moscow, 1965

Soviet Studies; a Quarterly Review. Ed. J. Miller and R. J. A. Schlesinger. Oxford, 1949 ff.

The Current Digest of the Soviet Press. Published by Joint Committee on Slavic Studies. Weekly. Washington, D.C.

Beloff, M., *The Foreign Policy of Soviet Russia, 1929–41.* 2 vols. 1947–49.—*Soviet Policy in the Far East.* Oxford, 1953.—*Soviet Policy in Asia, 1944–52.* Oxford, 1953

Brown, A., and Kaser, M., *The Soviet Union Since the Fall of Krushchev.* London, 1975

Carr, E. H., *The Bolshevik Revolution.* 8 vols. London, 1950–64

Coates, W. P., and Coates, Zelda K., *A History of Anglo-Soviet Relations.* 2 vols. London, 1944–58

Degras, J. (compiler), *Soviet Documents on Foreign Policy, 1917–41.* 3 vols. London, 1948–52

Deutscher, K., *Trotsky.* 3 vols. OUP, 1954 ff.

Ellman, M., *Soviet Planning Today.* CUP, 1971

Fitzsimmons, T., and others, *USSR; Its People, Its Society, Its Culture.* New Haven, 1960

Galperin, I. R., *New English–Russian Dictionary.* 2 vols. Moscow, 1972

Hough, J. F. and Fainsod, M., *How the Soviet Union is Governed.* Rev. ed. Harvard Univ. Press, 1979

Hutchings, R., *Soviet Economic Development.* New York, 1971

Jones, D. L., *Books in English in the Soviet Union 1917–73: A Bibliography.* London and New York, 1975

Kaiser, R. G., *Russia: The People and the Power.* London, 1976

Kelly, D. R., (ed.) *Soviet Politics in the Brezhnev Era.* London, 1980

Kirby, E. S., *The Soviet Far East.* London, 1971

Lenin, V. L., *Collected Works.* 45 vols. London, 1960–70

Lydolph, P. E., *Geography of the USSR.* New York, 1970

Maynard, J., *Russia in Flux.* London, 1941.—*The Russian Peasant: and Other Studies.* London, 1942.—*Russia in Flux* (abridged ed. of the two foregoing books). New York, 1948

Miller, W., *Who are the Russians? A History of the Russian People.* London, 1973

Moore, Harriet L., *Soviet Far Eastern Policy, 1931–45.* Princeton and Oxford, 1946

Müller, V. K., *Anglo-russkii slovar.* 13th ed. Moscow, 1967

Nove, A., *The Soviet Economic System.* London, 1977

Pares, Sir B., *A History of Russia.* London, 1962

Preobrazhensky, A. G., *Etymological Dictionary of the Russian Language.* Columbia Univ. Press, 1951

Riasanovsky, N. V., *A History of Russia.* 3rd ed. OUP, 1977

Rothstein, A., *A History of the USSR.* 2nd ed. London, 1951

Shabad, T., and Mote, V.L., *Gateway to Siberian Resources* (*The BAM*). New York and London, 1977

Shinkarev, L., *The Land Beyond the Mountains: Siberia and its People Today.* London, 1973

Slusser, R. M., and Triska, J. F., *A Calendar of Soviet Treaties, 1917–57.* Stanford Univ. Press, 1959

Smirnitzky, A. I. (ed.) *Rusko–angliiskii slovar.* 4th ed. Moscow 1959

Stalin, J. V., *Collected Works.* 13 vols. London, 1952–55

Thompson, A., *Russia/USSR: A Selective Annotated Bibliography of Books in English.* Oxford and Santa Barbara, 1979

Utechin, S. V. (ed.), *Everyman's Concise Encyclopaedia of Russia*. London, 1961
Vernadsky, G., *A History of Russia*. 4th ed. Yale Univ. Press, 1954
Wheeler, M., *The Oxford Russian–English Dictionary*. OUP, 1972

RUSSIAN SOVIET FEDERAL SOCIALIST REPUBLIC (RSFSR)
Rossiskaya Sovietskaya Federativnay Sotsialisticheskaya Respublika

AREA AND POPULATION. The RSFSR occupies over 76% of the total area of the USSR stretching from the Far North to the Black Sea in the south and from the Far East to Kaliningrad in the west. 82·6% of its population in Jan. 1979 were Russians, the rest being 38 national minorities such as the Tartars, Jews, Mordovians, Chuvashis, Bashkirs, Poles, Germans, Udmurts, Buryats, Mari, Yakuts and Ossetians. The 2 principal cities are Moscow, the capital, with a population (Jan. 1980) of 8·1m. (without suburbs, 7,914,000) and Leningrad, the second capital, 4,636,000 (without suburbs, 4,073,000). Among other important large towns are Gorki, Rostov-on-Don, Volgograd, Sverdlovsk, Novosibirsk, Chelyabinsk, Kazan, Omsk and Kuibyshev.

The RSFSR has a variety of climates (ranging from arctic to sub-tropical) and of geographical conditions (tundra, forest lands, steppes and rich agricultural soil). It also contains great mineral resources: iron ore in the Urals, the Kerch Peninsula and Siberia; coal in the Kuznetz Basin, Eastern Siberia, Urals and the sub-Moscow Basin; oil in the Urals, Azov–Black Sea area, Bashkiria, and West Siberia. It also has abundant deposits of gold, platinum, copper, zinc, lead, tin and rare metals.

The RSFSR produces about 70% of the total industrial and agricultural output of the Soviet Union. Industrial and office workers averaged 64·7m. in 1979.

CONSTITUTION AND GOVERNMENT. The RSFSR adopted its present constitution at a meeting of the Supreme Soviet in April 1978, following 330,000 town and country meetings in which 25m. citizens took part.

President, Presidium of the Supreme Soviet: M. A. Yasnov.
Chairman, Council of Ministers: M. S. Solomentsev.
Foreign Minister: F. E. Titov.

A special bureau of the Central Committee of the Communist Party of the USSR has been set up for the RSFSR.

The RSFSR consists of:

(1) *Territories:* Altai, Khabarovsk, Krasnodar, Krasnoyarsk, Primorye, Stavropol.

(2) *Regions:* Amur, Archangel, Astrakhan, Belgorod, Briansk, Chelyabinsk, Chita, Gorki, Irkutsk, Ivanovo, Kaluga, Kalinin, Kaliningrad, Kamchatka, Kemerovo, Kirov, Kostroma, Kuibyshev, Kurgan, Kursk, Leningrad, Lipetsk, Magadan, Moscow, Murmansk, Novgorod, Novosibirsk, Omsk, Orel, Orenburg, Penza, Perm, Pskov, Rostov, Ryazan, Sakhalin, Saratov, Smolensk, Sverdlovsk, Tambov, Tomsk, Tula, Tyumen, Ulyanovsk, Vladimir, Volgograd, Vologda, Voronezh, Yaroslavl.

(3) *Autonomous Soviet Socialist Republics:* Bashkir, Buryat, Checheno-Ingush, Chuvash, Daghestan, Kabardino-Balkar, Kalmyk, Karelian, Komi, Mari, Mordovian, North Ossetia, Tartar, Tuva, Udmurt, Yakut.

(4) *Autonomous Regions:* Adygei, Karachayevo-Cherkess, Gorno-Altai, Jewish, Khakass.

(5) *National Areas:* Aginsky-Buryat, Chukot, Evenki, Khanty-Mansi, Komi-Permyak, Koryak, Nenetz, Taimyr (Dolgano-Nenetz), Ust-Ordynsky-Buryat, Yamalo-Nenetz.

The Supreme Soviet, elected in Feb. 1980, consisted of 975 deputies (1 per 150,000 population); 650 were Communists, 341 women, 591 workers and collective farmers.

On 19 June 1977, 1,116,025 deputies were elected to local authorities; 559,843 (50·2%) were women, 645,589 (57·8%) non-Party and 745,250 (66·8%) industrial workers and collective farmers.

FINANCE. Revenue and expenditure balanced as follows (in 1m. new roubles): 1971, 44,113 (surplus 639m.); 1977, 66,243 (1,442); 1978, 68,166; 1980, 67,205; 1981 (estimate), 71,072. These figures, and those for the other 14 Union Republics, include grants from the Union Budget.

COMMUNICATIONS. Length of railways on 1 Jan. 1980 was 82,030 km, inland waterways, 126,000 km, hard-surface motor roads, 333,600 km.

Newspapers. In 1979 there were 4,370 newspapers, 4,066 of them in Russian. Circulation of Russian-language newspapers, 113·6m., other languages, 3m.

EDUCATION. In 1979–80 there were 20·4m. pupils in primary and secondary schools; 3,025,400 students in 488 higher educational establishments (including correspondence students) and 2,688,400 students in 2,499 technical colleges of all kinds (including correspondence students). There were 7·6m. children attending pre-school institutions. There were, on 1 Jan. 1979, 918,000 scientific staff in 3,009 learned and scientific institutions.

In 1957 a Siberian branch of the Academy of Sciences was organized, in charge of all scientific research institutions from the Urals to the Pacific.

There is an Academy of Municipal Economy (with 5 research institutions and a staff of 437).

HEALTH. Doctors at the end of 1980 numbered 541,000, and hospital beds 1·77m. (133,400 in 1913 and 482,000 in 1940); 2·96m. infants in crèches.

BASHKIR AUTONOMOUS SOVIET SOCIALIST REPUBLIC

Area 143,600 sq. km (55,430 sq. miles), population (Jan. 1980) 3·86m. Capital, Ufa. Bashkiria was annexed to Russia in 1557. It was constituted as an Autonomous Soviet Republic on 23 March 1919. Population, on 5 Jan. 1970, included 23·5% Bashkirians, 40·5% Russians, 29% Tartars and Chuvashes.

280 deputies were elected on 24 Feb. 1980, 109 of them women.

In 1979–80 there were over 5,000 schools with 746,000 pupils. There is a state university and a branch of the USSR Academy of Sciences with 8 learned institutions (511 research workers). There were 126,000 students in technical colleges and higher schools.

In Jan. 1979 there were 11,400 doctors and 46,205 hospital beds.

There are expanding chemical, coal, steel, electrical engineering, timber and paper industries. There were 631 collective farms and 160 state farms in 1977. Crop area was 4,573,000 hectares. Bashkiria is a major oil producer in USSR.

BURIAT AUTONOMOUS SOVIET SOCIALIST REPUBLIC

The area is 351,300 sq. km (135,650 sq. miles). The Buriat Republic, situated to the south of the Yakut Republic, adopted the Soviet system on 1 March 1920. This area was penetrated by the Russians in the 17th century and finally annexed from China by the treaties of Nerchinsk (1689) and Kyakhta (1727). The population (Jan. 1980) was 917,500. Capital, Ulan-Udé. The name of the republic was changed from 'Buriat-Mongol' on 7 July 1958. The population includes 22% Buriats and 73·5% Russians.

170 deputies were elected on 24 Feb. 1980, 59 of them women.

The main industries are coal, timber, building materials, fisheries, sheep and cattle farming. In 1977 there were 100 state and 59 collective farms. Crop area was 888,700 hectares. Gold, molybdenum and wolfram are mined.

In 1979–80 there were over 700 schools with 157,000 pupils, 16 technical colleges with 219,000 students and 2 higher educational institutions with 22,400 students. A branch of the Siberian Department of the Academy of Sciences had 4 learned institutions with 281 research workers.

At the end of 1979 there were 2,700 doctors and (1978) 11,102 hospital beds.

CHECHENO-INGUSH AUTONOMOUS SOVIET SOCIALIST REPUBLIC

Area, 19,300 sq. km (7,350 sq. miles); population (Jan. 1980), 1,158,000. Capital, Grozny. After 70 years of almost continuous fighting, the Chechens and Ingushes were conquered by Russia in the late 1850s. In 1918 each nationality separately established its 'National Soviet' within the Terek Autonomous Republic, and in 1920 (after the Civil War) were constituted areas within the Mountain Republic. The Chechens separated out as an Autonomous Region on 30 Nov. 1922 and the Ingushes on 7 July 1924. In Jan. 1934 the two regions were united, and on 5 Dec. 1936 constituted as an Autonomous Republic. This was dissolved in 1944, but reconstituted on 9 Jan. 1957: 232,000 Chechens and Ingushes returned to their homes in the next 2 years. The population includes 47·8% Chechens, 10·7% Ingushes, 34·5% Russians.

175 deputies were elected on 24 Feb. 1980, 95 of them women.

The republic has one of the major Soviet oilfields: also a number of large engineering works, chemical factories, building materials works and food canneries. There is an expanding timber, woodworking and furniture industry. In 1977–78 there were 100 state and 45 collective farms. Crop area was 460,400 hectares.

There were, in 1979–80, 534 schools with 259,000 pupils, 12 technical colleges with 14,400 students and 2 places of higher education with 12,100 students.

In 1977 there were 75 hospitals, 2,900 (1980) doctors and 11,210 hospital beds.

CHUVASH AUTONOMOUS SOVIET SOCIALIST REPUBLIC

Area, 18,300 sq. km (7,064 sq. miles); population (Jan. 1980), 1,301,000. Capital, Cheboksary. The territory was annexed by Russia in the middle of the 16th century. On 24 June 1920 it was constituted as an Autonomous Region, and on 21 April 1925 as an Autonomous Republic. The population includes Chuvashes (70%), Russians (24·5%), Tartars and Mordovians (4·7%).

200 deputies were elected on 24 Feb. 1980, 79 of them women.

Like most of the Autonomous Republics, Chuvashia before 1914 was a region of primitive agriculture, with a certain development of the timber industry. Today it has several big railway repair works, an expanding electrical and other engineering industry, building materials, chemicals, textiles and food industries; timber felling and haulage are largely mechanized. In 1977 there were 210 collective farms and 96 state farms. Grain crops account for nearly two-thirds of all sowings and fodder crops for nearly a quarter. Fruit and wine-growing are a developing branch of agriculture. Crop area was 829,300 hectares.

In 1979–80 there were 254,200 pupils at school, 24,500 students at technical colleges and 14,300 students undertaking higher education.

There were 2,901 doctors and 13,950 hospital beds.

DAGESTAN AUTONOMOUS SOVIET SOCIALIST REPUBLIC

Area, 50,300 sq. km (19,416 sq. miles); population (Jan. 1980), 1·6m. Capital, Makhachkala. Over 30 nationalities inhabit this republic apart from Russians

(14·7%); the most numerous are the Avartsy (24·5%), Dargintsy (14·5%), Lezginy (11·4%), Kumyki (11·8%), Laki (5·1%), Tabasarany (3·7%) and Azerbaidjanis (3·8%). Annexed from Persia in 1723, Dagestan was constituted an Autonomous Republic on 20 Jan. 1921.

210 deputies were elected on 24 Feb. 1980, 82 of them women.

There are large engineering, oil, chemical, woodworking, textile, food and other light industries. Agriculture is very varied, ranging from wheat to grapes, with sheep farming and cattle breeding; in 1977 there were 311 collective farms and 233 state farms. Crop area was 413,900 hectares. A chain of power stations is under construction in the Sulak River (total capacity 2·5m. kw.).

In 1977–78 there were 1,576 schools with 475,900 pupils, 33,800 technical students (1979–80) and 4 higher educational establishments with 23,400 students; and a branch of the USSR Academy of Sciences with 4 learned institutions (373 research workers). Doctors numbered 5,300 and hospital beds 17,300.

KABARDINO-BALKAR AUTONOMOUS SOVIET SOCIALIST REPUBLIC

Area, 12,500 sq. km (4,825 sq. miles); population (Jan. 1980), 683,000. Capital, Nalchik. Kabarda was annexed to Russia in 1557. The republic was constituted on 5 Dec. 1936. Population includes Kabardinians (45%), Balkars (8·7%), Russians (37·2%).

160 deputies were elected on 24 Feb. 1980, 70 of them women.

Main industries are ore-mining, timber, engineering, coal, food processing, timber and light industries, building materials. Grain, livestock breeding, dairy farming and wine-growing are the principal branches of agriculture. There were, in 1977, 54 state and 74 collective farms.

In 1979–80 there were 250 schools with 144,000 pupils, 11,600 students in 11 technical colleges and 8,600 students receiving higher education; 2,500 doctors and 7,530 hospital beds.

KALMYK AUTONOMOUS SOVIET SOCIALIST REPUBLIC

The Kalmyks migrated from western China to Russia (Nogai Steppe) in the early 17th century. The territory was constituted an Autonomous Region on 4 Nov. 1920, and an Autonomous Republic on 22 Oct. 1935; this was dissolved in 1943. On 9 Jan. 1957 it was reconstituted as an Autonomous Region and on 29 July 1958 as an Autonomous Republic once more.

Area, 75,900 sq. km (29,300 sq. miles); population (Jan. 1980), 297,000. Capital, Elista (64,000). The population includes 41% Kalmyks, 45·8% Russians, 6·9% Kazakhs, Chechens and Dagestanis.

130 deputies were elected on 24 Feb. 1980, 54 of them women.

Main industries are fishing, canning and building materials. Cattle breeding and irrigated farming (mainly fodder crops) are the principal branches of agriculture. In 1977 there were 90 state and 23 collective farms. Crop area was 831,400 hectares.

In 1979–80 there were 60,500 pupils in 242 schools, 7,902 students in technical colleges and 4,800 in higher education; 858 doctors and 4,355 hospital beds.

KARELIAN AUTONOMOUS SOVIET SOCIALIST REPUBLIC

HISTORY. Before 1917, Karelia (then known as the Olonetz Province) was noted chiefly as a place of exile for political and other prisoners.

After the November Revolution of 1917, Karelia formed part of the RSFSR. In June 1920 a Karelian Labour Commune was formed and in July 1923 this was transformed into the Karelian Autonomous Soviet Socialist Republic (one of the autonomous republics of the RSFSR). On 31 March 1940, after the Soviet–Finnish war, practically all the territory (with the exception of a small section in the neighbourhood of the Leningrad area) which had been ceded by Finland to the USSR was added to Karelia and the Karelian Autonomous Republic was transformed into the Karelo-Finnish Soviet Socialist Republic as the 12th republic of the USSR. In 1946, however, the southern part of the republic, including its whole seaboard and the town of Viipuri (Vyborg) and Keksholm, was attached to the RSFSR. In 1956 the status of the republic was changed (*see* p. 1217).

AREA AND POPULATION. The Karelian Autonomous Republic, capital Petrozavodsk, covers an area of 172,400 sq. km, with a population of 740,000 (Jan. 1980). Karelians represent 11·8% of the population, Russians 68·1%, Belorussians 9·3%, Finns 3·1%.
150 deputies were elected on 24 Feb. 1980, 53 of them women.

NATURAL RESOURCES. Karelia is chiefly noted for its wealth of timber, some 70% of its territory being forest land. It is also rich in other natural resources, having large deposits of diabase, spar, quartz, marble, mica, granite, zinc, lead, silver, copper, molybdenum, tin, baryta, iron ore, etc. Karelia takes first place in the USSR for the production of mica. It has 43,643 lakes, which, as well as its rivers, are rich in fish.

Agriculture. There were 10 collective fisheries and 60 state farms in 1976. Livestock on 1 Jan. 1980 included 93,400 cattle, 40,000 pigs, 100,000 sheep and goats.

INDUSTRY. The republic has some 25 large-scale enterprises, such as timbermills, paper-cellulose works, mica, chemical plants, power stations and furniture factories. Output, 1977: Timber, 12·3m. cu. metres; paper and cellulose, 1,733,700 tonnes; power, 2,796m. kwh.; canned fish, 12·3m. tins.
The construction of the White Sea–Baltic Canal had a powerful influence on the economic development of Karelia. New refrigerating plants, cellulose factories and timber industry equipment began working in 1970.

COMMUNICATIONS. A railway between Petrozavodsk and Suoyarvi connects the capital and the Murmansk Railway with the main railway line Sortavala–Vyborg. A railway line was also laid between Kandalaksha and Kuolayarvi. Length of track, 1,600 km.

EDUCATION. In 1979–80 there were 115,600 pupils in 747 schools. There were 10,200 students in 3 places of higher education and 10,200 in 10 technical colleges.
There are in Petrozavodsk a university (4,028 full-time students, 2,036 taking correspondence courses and 622 evening students in 1971), 2 other higher institutes and a teachers' training college. A branch of the Academy of Sciences was set up in 1949 with 8 learned institutions (349 research workers).

HEALTH. There were over 3,000 doctors in 1980, and 11,600 hospital beds.

KOMI AUTONOMOUS SOVIET SOCIALIST REPUBLIC

Area, 415,900 sq. km (160,540 sq. miles); population (Jan. 1980), 1,138,000. Capital, Syktyvkar (176,500). Annexed by the princes of Moscow in the 14th century and occupied by British and American forces in 1918–19, the territory was constituted as an Autonomous Region on 22 Aug. 1921 and as an Autonomous Republic on 5 Dec. 1936. The population includes Komi (28·6%), Russians (53·1%), Ukrainians and Belorussians (11·2%).
180 deputies were elected on 24 Feb. 1980, 59 of them women.
There are large coal, oil, timber, gas, asphalt and building materials industries; light industry is expanding. Livestock breeding (including dairy farming) is the main branch of agriculture. There were 51 state farms in 1977. Crop area, 92,000 hectares.

In 1979–80 there were 189,000 pupils in 789 schools, 12,000 students receiving higher education, 18,400 students in 13 technical colleges; and a branch of the Academy of Sciences with 4 learned institutions (297 research workers).

There were 3,900 doctors and 16,200 hospital beds.

MARI AUTONOMOUS SOVIET SOCIALIST REPUBLIC

Area, 23,200 sq. km (8,955 sq. miles); population (Jan. 1980), 708,000. Capital, Yoshkar-Ola. The Mari people were annexed to Russia, with other peoples of the Kazan Tartar Khanate, when the latter was overthrown in 1552. On 25 Nov. 1920 the territory was constituted as an Autonomous Region, and on 5 Dec. 1936 as an Autonomous Republic. The population includes Mari (43·7%), Tartars (5·9%), Chuvashes (1·3%), Russians (46·9%).

150 deputies were elected on 24 Feb. 1980, 57 of them women.

There are over 300 modern factories. The main industries are metalworking, timber, paper, woodworking and food processing. In 1977 there were 105 collective farms and 72 state farms. Over 69% of cultivated land is under grain, but flax, potatoes, fruit and vegetables are also expanding branches of agriculture, as is also livestock farming. 625,300 hectares were under crops.

Estimated reserves of the Pechora coalfield are 262,000m. tons.

In 1979–80 there were 714 schools with 130,100 pupils. Technical colleges and higher educational establishments had a total of 33,300 students. There were 3,000 doctors and 8,500 hospital beds.

MORDOVIAN AUTONOMOUS SOVIET SOCIALIST REPUBLIC

Area, 26,200 sq. km (10,110 sq. miles); population (Jan. 1980), 986,000. Capital, Saransk. By the 13th century the Mordovian tribes had been subjugated by the Russian princes of Ryazan and Nizhni-Novgorod. In 1928 the territory was constituted as a Mordovian Area within the Middle-Volga Territory, on 10 Jan. 1930 as an Autonomous Region and on 20 Dec. 1934 as an Autonomous Republic. The population includes Mordovians (35·4%), Russians (58·9%), Tartars (4·4%).

175 deputies were elected on 24 Feb. 1980, 74 of them women.

The Republic has a wide range of industries: Electrical, timber, cable, building materials, furniture, textile, leather and other light industries. Agriculture is devoted chiefly to grain, sugar-beet, sheep and dairy farming. In 1977 there were 76 state and 275 collective farms.

There were 173,800 children at school, 38,100 students in technical colleges and at the state university and institutes, in 1979–80. There were 2,835 doctors and 12,400 hospital beds.

NORTH OSSETIAN AUTONOMOUS SOVIET SOCIALIST REPUBLIC

Area, 8,000 sq. km (3,088 sq. miles); population (Jan. 1980), 602,000. Capital, Ordzhonikidze (formerly Vladikavkaz). The Ossetians, known to antiquity as Alani (who were also called by their immediate neighbours 'Ossi' or 'Yassi'), were annexed to Russia after the latter's treaty of Kuchuk-Kainardji with Turkey, and in 1784 the key fortress of Vladikavkaz was founded on their territory (given the name of Terek region in 1861). On 4 March 1918 the latter was proclaimed an Autonomous Soviet Republic, and after the Civil War this territory with others was set up as the Mountain Autonomous Republic (20 Jan. 1921), with North Ossetia as the Ossetian (Vladikavkaz) Area within it. On 7 July 1924 the latter was constituted as an Autonomous Region and on 5 Dec. 1936 as an Autonomous Republic. The population comprises chiefly Ossetians (48·7%), Russians (36·6%), Ingushi and other Caucasian nationalities (10%).

150 deputies were elected on 24 Feb. 1980, 68 of them women.

The main industries are non-ferrous metals (mining and metallurgy), maize-processing (at the Beslan Works, the largest in Europe), timber and woodworking, textiles, building materials, distilleries and food processing. There is also a prosperous and varied agriculture. In 1977 there were 36 state and 44 collective farms.

There were in 1979–80, 106,700 children in 205 schools, 15,100 students in technical colleges and 18,800 students in 4 higher educational establishments (pedagogical, agriculture, medical and mining-metallurgical institutes). There were over 3,000 doctors and over 7,000 hospital beds.

TARTAR AUTONOMOUS SOVIET SOCIALIST REPUBLIC

Area, 68,000 sq. km (26,250 sq. miles); population (Jan. 1980), 3,454,000. Capital, Kazan. From the 10th to the 13th centuries this was the territory of the flourishing Volga-Kama Bulgar State; conquered by the Mongols, it became the seat of the Kazan (Tartar) Khans when the Mongol Empire broke up in the 15th century, and in 1552 was conquered again by Russia. On 27 May 1920 it was constituted as an Autonomous Republic. The population includes Tartars (49·1%), Chuvashes, Mordovians and Udmurts (6·7%), Russians (42·4%).

250 deputies were elected on 24 Feb. 1980, 97 of them women.

The Republic has highly developed engineering, oil and chemical industries, while timber, building materials, textiles, clothing and food industries are also expanding. The Kama works at Naberejnye Chelny plan to produce 400,000 vehicles annually. In 1977, 552 collective and 238 state farms served a total area under crops of 3·8m. hectares.

In 1979–80 there were 3,492 schools with 638,000 pupils, 39 technical colleges with 62,000 students and 12 higher educational establishments with 71,000 students (including a state university). There is a branch of the USSR Academy of Sciences with 5 learned institutions (512 research workers).

Doctors at the end of 1979 numbered 11,000 and hospital beds 40,000.

TUVA AUTONOMOUS SOVIET SOCIALIST REPUBLIC

Area, 170,500 sq. km (65,810 sq. miles); population (Jan. 1980), 269,000. Capital, Kizyl (59,000). Tuva was incorporated in the USSR as an autonomous region on 13 Oct. 1944 and elevated to an Autonomous Republic on 10 Oct. 1961. It is situated to the north-west of Mongolia, between 50° and 53° N. lat. and between 90° and 100° E. long. It is bounded to the east, west and north by Siberia, and to the south by the Republic of Mongolia. The Tuvans are a Turkic people, formerly ruled by hereditary or elective tribal chiefs. (For the earlier history of the former Tannu-Tuva Republic, see THE STATESMAN'S YEAR-BOOK, 1946, p. 798.) The population includes Tuvans (58·6%) and Russians (38·3%).

130 deputies were elected to its Supreme Soviet on 24 Feb. 1980, 53 of them women.

Tuva is well-watered and has much good pastoral land; 47 hydro-electric stations have been set into operation. The Tuvans are mainly herdsmen and cattle farmers, but, in 1977, 376,000 hectares were under crops. There are deposits of gold, cobalt and asbestos. The main exports are hair, hides and wool, and the imports manufactured goods and iron. There are 60 state farms. Mining, woodworking, garment, leather, food and other industries are rapidly developing.

In 1979–80 there were 194 schools with 71,500 pupils; 5 technical colleges with 4,200 students, and an Institute of Linguistics, Literature and History with 2,700 students; 11 newspapers (2 in Russian). There were 860 doctors and 4,530 hospital beds.

A Soviet steamer-service along the river Yenisei maintains communication with Minussinsk, in Central Siberia. Internal transport is chiefly by lorry and motor coach. There is an air service from Kizyl to Krasnoyarsk.

UDMURT AUTONOMOUS SOVIET SOCIALIST REPUBLIC

Area, 42,100 sq. km (16,250 sq. miles); population (Jan. 1980), 1,506,000. Capital, Izhevsk. The Udmurts (formerly known as 'Votyaks') were annexed by the Russians in the 15th and 16th centuries. On 4 Nov. 1920 the Votyak Autonomous Region was constituted (the name was changed to Udmurt—used by the people themselves—in 1932), and on 28 Dec. 1934 it was raised to the status of an Autonomous Republic. The population includes Udmurts (34·2%), Tartars (6·1%), Russians (57·1%).

200 deputies were elected on 24 Feb. 1980, 78 of them women.

Heavy industry includes the manufacture of locomotives, machine tools and other engineering products, timber and building materials. There are also light industries—clothing, leather, furniture, food, etc.

There were 95 state and 261 collective farms in 1977; crop area 1·4m. hectares.

In 1979–80 there were 513 schools with 252,000 pupils; 5,800 finished technical colleges and 3,800 schools of higher education.

There were over 5,000 doctors and over 16,000 hospital beds.

YAKUT AUTONOMOUS SOVIET SOCIALIST REPUBLIC

The area is 3,103,000 sq. km (1,197,760 sq. miles); population (Jan. 1980), 859,000. Capital, Yakutsk (149,000). The Yakuts were subjugated by the Russians in the 17th century. The territory was constituted an Autonomous Republic on 27 April 1922. The population includes Yakuts (43%), other northern peoples (3%), Russians (47·3%).

205 deputies were elected on 24 Feb. 1980, 92 of them women.

The principal industries are mining (gold, tin, mica, coal) and livestock-breeding. The Soviet Soyuz-Zoloto Trust and a number of individual prospectors are working the fields. Silver- and lead-bearing ores and coal are worked; large diamond fields have been opened up. Timber and food industries are developing. There was 1 collective farm in 1975 with 82 state farms, with an area under crops of 95,000 hectares. Trapping and breeding of fur-bearing animals (sable, squirrel, silver fox, etc.) are an important source of income. A severe climate and lack of railways are serious obstacles to the economic development of the republic. There are, however, 10,000 km of roads and internal airlines totalling 10,000 km. There is an air service between Irkutsk and Yakutsk.

In 1979–80 there were 179,800 secondary school pupils, 10,200 technical college students and 6,600 at university and teacher training colleges.

There were 3,094 doctors and 12,700 hospital beds.

ADYGEI AUTONOMOUS REGION

Part of Krasnodar Territory. Area, 7,600 sq. km (2,934 sq. miles); population (Jan. 1980), 405,300. Centre, Maikop (128,000). Established 27 July 1922.

Chief industries are timber, woodworking, food processing; but engineering is rapidly expanding. Cattle breeding predominates in agriculture. There were 39 collective and 26 state farms in 1976.

In 1977–78 there were 267 schools with (1980) 68,900 pupils, 6 technical colleges with (1980) 13,100 students and a pedagogical institute with 4,000 students. Regional newspapers are in Adygei and Russian. There were 1,089 doctors and 5,240 hospital beds.

GORNO-ALTAI AUTONOMOUS REGION

Part of Altai Territory. Area, 92,600 sq. km (35,740 sq. miles); population (Jan. 1980), 173,000. Capital, Gorno-Altaisk (39,000). Established 1 June 1922 as Oirot Autonomous Region; renamed 7 Jan. 1948.

Chief industries are gold, mercury and brown-coal mining, timber, chemicals and dairying. Cattle breeding predominates; pasturages and hay meadows cover over 1m. hectares, but 142,000 hectares are under crops. There were 20 collective and 33 state farms in 1977.

In 1979–80 there were 29,500 school pupils; technical colleges had 4,540 students and 3,539 students were receiving higher education. There were 410 doctors and 2,470 hospital beds.

JEWISH AUTONOMOUS REGION

Part of Khabarovsk Territory. Area, 36,000 sq. km (13,895 sq. miles); population (Jan. 1980), 193,400 (Russians, 128,000; Ukrainians, 14,000; Jews, 15,000). Capital, Birobidjan (67,000). Established as Jewish National District in 1928, became an autonomous region 7 May 1934.

Chief industries are non-ferrous metallurgy, building materials, timber, engineering, textiles, paper and food processing. There were in 1977, 50 factories, 156,000 hectares under crops, 88,500 cattle and 39,000 pigs. There were 35 state farms and 2 collective farms in 1976.

In 1979–80 there were 31,900 schoolchildren; students in technical colleges numbered 5,500. There are a Yiddish national theatre, a Yiddish newspaper and a Yiddish broadcasting service. Doctors numbered 488 and hospital beds 2,860.

KARACHAYEVO-CHERKESS AUTONOMOUS REGION

Part of Stavropol Territory. Area, 14,300 sq. km (5,442 sq. miles); population (Jan. 1980), 370,000. Capital, Cherkessk (89,000). A Karachai Autonomous Region was established on 26 April 1926 (out of a previously united Karachayevo–Cherkess Autonomous Region created in 1922), and dissolved in 1943. A Cherkess Autonomous Region was established on 30 April 1928. The present Autonomous Region was re-established on 9 Jan. 1957.

Ore-mining, engineering, chemical and woodworking industries have been built up since 1917. There are 70 large factories, and a copper works and sugar factory are under construction. A large irrigation scheme, Kuban–Kalaussi, is being developed, to irrigate 200,000 hectares. Livestock breeding and grain growing predominate in agriculture; crop area in 1977 was 197,900 hectares. There were 14 collective farms and 40 state farms in 1976.

In 1979–80 there were 73,000 pupils in (1977–78) 220 schools, 6 technical colleges (1977–78) with 6,500 students and 2 institutes with 3,300 students; 935 doctors and (1977–78) 3,720 hospital beds.

KHAKASS AUTONOMOUS REGION

Part of Krasnoyarsk Territory. Area, 61,900 sq. km (23,855 sq. miles); population (Jan. 1980), 503,000. Capital, Abakan (123,000). Established 20 Oct. 1930.

Coal- and ore-mining, timber and woodworking industries have been highly developed since 1917. The region is linked by rail with the Trans-Siberian line. Large textile and sugar factories are being built.

In 1979, 619,200 hectares were under crops. Livestock breeding, dairy and vegetable farming are developed. There are 58 state farms.

In 1979–80 there were 70,900 pupils in (1977–78) 363 schools, 7 (1977–78) technical colleges with 9,300 students and 5,800 students in higher educational establishments;

1,170 doctors and 6,800 hospital beds. A Khakass alphabet was created after the Revolution.

Books of Reference

Armstrong, T., *Russian Settlement in the North*. CUP, 1965
Dallin, D. J., *The Rise of Russia in Asia*. New York, 1949.—*Soviet Russia and the Far East*, London, 1949
Kolarz, W., *The Peoples of the Soviet Far East*. London, 1954
Leprince-Ringuet, F., *L'Avenir de l'Asie russe*. Paris, 1951
Mikhailov, N. L., *Sibir*. Moscow, 1955
Thiel, E., *The Soviet Far East*. London, 1957

UKRAINE
Ukrainska Radyanska Sotsialistichna Respublika

HISTORY. The Ukrainian Soviet Socialist Republic was proclaimed on 27 Dec. 1917 and was finally established in Dec. 1919. In Dec. 1920 it concluded a military and economic alliance with the RSFSR and on 6 July 1923 formed, together with the other Soviet Socialist Republics, the Union of Soviet Socialist Republics. On 1 Nov. 1939 Western Ukraine (about 88,000 sq. km) was incorporated in the Ukrainian SSR. On 2 Aug. 1940 Northern Bukovina (about 6,000 sq. km) ceded to the USSR by Romania 28 June 1940, and the Khotin, Akkerman and Izmail provinces of Bessarabia were included in the Ukrainian SSR, and on 29 June 1945 Ruthenia (Sub-Carpathian Russia), about 7,000 sq. km, was also incorporated. From the new territories 2 new regions (provinces) were formed, Chernovitz and Izmail.

AREA AND POPULATION. The Ukraine is in south-west USSR; it has a Black Sea coast and western frontiers with Romania, Hungary, Poland and Czechoslovakia. It is bounded north by Belorussia and otherwise by the RSFSR. In 1938 the Ukrainian SSR covered an area of 445,000 sq. km (171,770 sq. miles); it now covers 603,700 sq. km (231,990 sq. miles).

The population in Jan. 1959 was 41,869,000. Population, Jan. 1980, 49,936,000 (in 1970, 75% Ukrainians, 19·4% Russians, 1·6% Jews, 0·8% Belorussians).

The principal towns are the capital Kiev, Kharkov, Donetsk, Odessa, Dniepropetrovsk, Lvov, Zaporozhye and Krivoi Rog.

The Ukrainian Soviet Socialist Republic consists of the following regions: Cherkassy, Chernigov, Chernovtzy, Crimea (transferred from the RSFSR on 19 Feb. 1954), Dniepropetrovsk, Donetsk, Ivan Franko, Khmelnitsky (formerly Kamenetz-Podolsk), Kharkov, Kherson, Kiev, Kirovograd, Lvov, Nikolayev, Odessa, Poltava, Rovno, Sumy, Ternopol, Vinnitza, Volhynia, Voroshilovgrad, Zakarpatskaya (Transcarpathia), Zaporozhye, Zhitomir.

CONSTITUTION AND GOVERNMENT. The Supreme Soviet, elected on 24 Feb. 1980, consists of 650 deputies (1 per 90,000 population); 447 are Communists and 234 women. A new Constitution, based on that of the USSR, was adopted in April 1978.

At elections to regional, district, urban and rural Soviets (19 June 1977), out of 521,984 deputies returned, 248,260 (47·6%) were women, 286,142 (54·8%) non-Party and 378,018 (72·4%) industrial workers and collective farmers.

President, Presidium of the Supreme Soviet: K. M. Sytnik.
Chairman, Council of Ministers: A. P. Lyashko.
Foreign Minister: G. G. Shevel.
First Secretary, Communist Party: V. V. Shcherbitsky.

FINANCE. Budget estimates (in 1m. new roubles), 1965, 10,223; 1970, 13,550; 1980, 20,832; 1981, 23,223.

AGRICULTURE. The Ukraine contains some of the richest land in the USSR.

It raises wheat, buckwheat, beet, sunflower, cotton, flax, tobacco, soya, hops, the rubber plant kok-sagyz, fruit and vegetables, and in 1976 provided nearly 20% of the grain production in the USSR and over 62% of the sugar-beet. Nine-tenths of the grain exported from USSR came from the Ukraine. The area under cultivation was 27·9m. hectares in 1913, 27m. in 1939 before the new territories were added, and 34·2m. in 1978.

Output (in 1m. tonnes) in 1979 (1913 figures in tons in brackets): Sugar-beet, 47·1 (9·3); sunflower seed, 2·4 (0·07); flax, 0·014 (0·004); potatoes, 23·9 (8·5); meat and fats, 3·6 (1·1); milk, 22·5 (4·7); wool, 0·028 (0·015); 13,747m. eggs (3,005m.); grain, 50·6m.

On 1 Jan. 1979 there were 25·4m. cattle, 20·7m. pigs, 9·2m. sheep and goats. In 1949 silver-fox breeding farms were started.

On 1 Jan. 1980 there were 2,104 state farms and 6,963 collective farms.

Irrigation networks supplied 1·82m. hectares of land; 2·2m. hectares were drained.

Tractors numbered 403,700 at 31 Jan. 1979 and combine harvesters, 86,900.

INDUSTRY. Coal in the Donetz field (25,900 sq. km stretching from Donetsk to Rostov), estimated to contain 60% of the bituminous and anthracite-coal reserves of the USSR, yielded, in 1961, 186·1m. tonnes—about 36% of the USSR production. Large new seams have been found near Novo-Moskovsk (Dniepropetrovsk region), Kharkov, Lugansk (beyond the Don) and on the left bank of the Dnieper. Within the present frontiers of the Ukraine, coal output was 22·8m. tons in 1913, 83·8m. tons in 1940, 78m. tons in 1950 and 217m. tons in 1977.

Combining coal from the Donetz field with the iron-ore from the mines in Krivoi Rog has made possible the development of a large ferrous metallurgical industry in the Ukraine. Output of iron ore was 6·9m. tons in 1913, 18·9m. tons in 1940 and 126m. tons in 1977.

Manganese is also available at Nikopol; output in 1976, 6·7m. tons.

Pig-iron output was 2·9m. tons in 1913, 9·6m. tons in 1940, 9·2m. tons in 1950 and 46·4m. tons in 1975. Steel output (in the present frontiers) was 2·4m. tons in 1913, 8·9m. in 1940, 8·4m. in 1950 and 53·7m. in 1977.

The Ukraine also contains oil, rich deposits of salt and various important chemicals. Oil output was 1m. tons in 1913 (in present frontiers), 353,000 tons in 1940 and 10·5m. tons in 1977; with 68·7m. cu. metres of natural gas.

The Ukraine has highly developed chemical and machine-construction industries producing one-fifth of the total output of machinery and chemicals in the USSR. 142,000 tractors and 3,500 main-line diesel locomotives were produced in 1979.

In Northern Bukovina there are deposits of gypsum, oil, alabaster, brown coal and timber. Output of mineral fertilizers was 36,000 tons in 1913 and 19·5m. tons in 1979; cement output increased in the same years from 269,000 to 22·5m. tons (in present frontiers in both cases). Paper output in 1977 was 250,000 tons (1913: 26,900).

Consumer goods and food industries are important. Output of cotton fabrics was (in present frontiers) 4·7m. linear metres in 1913, 13·8m. in 1940, 20·6m. in 1950 and 429·4m. in 1975. Granulated sugar output was 1913, 1·1m. tons; 1940, 1·6m. tons; 1950, 1·8m. tons, and 1977, 6·8m. tons. Leather footwear manufactured in 1940 totalled 40·8m. pairs; 1979, 176m.

The number of industrial and office workers at the end of 1950 was 6·9m., and the average in 1979, 19·8m. There were 1,816,000 specialists with a higher education.

During the first 5-year plan (1929–32) the Dnieper power-station was built; destroyed during the War, it was restored during the fourth plan (1946–50). Another large hydro-electric station at Kahovka began operations during the fifth plan (1951–55). Power output (in 1,000m. kwh.) increased as follows: 1913, 0·5; 1940, 12·4; 1950, 14·7; 1978, 222.

COMMUNICATIONS. The total length of railways of the Ukrainian SSR in 1978 was 22,440 km, and the navigable rivers, 3,900 km. Length of hard-surface motor roads was 127,900 km.

Airlines connect Kiev, Lvov, Chernovtsy and Odessa with Crimean and Caucasian spas, Kiev with Tbilisi, Odessa with Riga and Donetsk.

Newspapers (1979). Out of 1,755 newspapers, 1,304 were in Ukrainian. Circulation of Ukrainian-language newspapers, 16m., other languages, 8m.

RELIGION. Several Christian Churches have their adherents in the Ukraine, the chief being the Orthodox Greek Church and the Catholic Church. The Western Ukraine Uniate Church, which in 1596 had been forced by the Poles to establish unity with the Roman Church, severed this connexion in March 1946 and joined the Orthodox Church. There are also some Protestants as well as Jews and others.

EDUCATION. In 1979–80 the number of pupils in 23,400 primary, secondary and special schools was 7·6m.; 145 higher educational establishments had 876,400 students, and 725 technical colleges 802,900 students; 2·3m. children were attending 17,400 pre-school institutions.

The Ukrainian Academy of Sciences was established in 1919; in 1977 it had 70 institutions with 12,444 scientific staff. There is an academy of building and architecture. Total scientific staff in 814 learned institutions numbered 185,100.

HEALTH. Doctors numbered 176,800 in 1979, and hospital beds, 616,600.

Books of Reference

Allen, W. E. D., *The Ukraine: A History*. London, 1940
Andrusyshen, C. H. (ed.), *Ukrainian–English Dictionary*. Toronto, 1955
Brégy, Pierre, and Obolensky, Prince S., *The Ukraine: A Russian Land*. London, 1940
Chamberlin, W. H., *The Ukraine*. New York, 1945
Chirovsky, N. L., *The Ukrainian Economy*. New York, Paris, Toronto, 1965
Doroshenko, D., *History of the Ukraine*. 2nd ed. Edmonton (Alberta), 1941
Holubnychy, V., *The Industrial Output of the Ukraine, 1913–56*. Munich, 1957
Hrushevsky, M., *A History of the Ukraine*. New Haven, 1941
Manning, C. A., *Twentieth-century Ukraine*. New York, 1951
Mirchuk, L. (ed.), *Ukraine and its People*. London, 1949
Soviet Ukraine. (English ed.) Ukrainian Soviet Encyclopaedia, 1970

BELORUSSIA
Belaruskaya Sovietskaya Sotsialistychnaya Respublika

HISTORY. The Belorussian Soviet Socialist Republic was set up on 1 Jan. 1919. It forms one of the constituent republics of the USSR.

AREA AND POPULATION. Belorussia is situated along the Western Dvina and Dnieper. It is bounded west by Poland, north by Latvia and Lithuania, east by the RSFSR and south by the Ukraine. The area is 207,600 sq. km (80,134 sq. miles). The capital is Minsk. Other important towns are Gomel, Vitebsk, Mogilev, Bobruisk, Grodno and Brest. On 2 Nov. 1939 western Belorussia was incorporated with an area of over 108,000 sq. km and a population of 4·8m. The population (Jan. 1980) was 9·6m. About 81% of this population in 1970 were Belorussians, 10·4% Poles, 2·1% Russians, 4·3% Ukrainians and 1·6% Jews.

Belorussia now comprises the following regions: Brest, Gomel, Grodno, Mogilev, Minsk, Vitebsk.

CONSTITUTION AND GOVERNMENT. The Supreme Soviet, elected in 1980, consists of 485 deputies (1 per 20,000 population); 328 are Communists and 180 women. A new Constitution was adopted in April 1978.

At elections to regional, district, urban and rural Soviets (19 June 1977), of 79,815 deputies returned, 38,233 (47·9%) were women, 45,096 (56·5%) non-Party and 54,001 (67·7%) industrial workers and collective farmers.

President, Presidium of the Supreme Soviet: I. E. Poliakov.
Chairman, Council of Ministers: A. N. Aksyonov.
Foreign Minister: A. E. Gurinovich.
First Secretary, Communist Party: T. Y. Kiselyov.

FINANCE. Budget estimates (in 1m. new roubles), 1965, 1,960; 1970, 3,506; 1978, 4,730; 1980, 5,227; 1981, 5,613.

NATURAL RESOURCES. Belorussia is hilly, with a general slope towards the south. It contains large tracts of marsh land, particularly to the south-west, and valuable forest land wooded with oak, elm, maple and white beech: there are over 6,500 peat deposits.

AGRICULTURE. Agriculturally, Belorussia may be divided into three main sections—Northern: growing flax, fodder, grasses and breeding cattle for meat and dairy produce; Central: potato growing and pig breeding; Southern: good natural pasture land, hemp cultivation and cattle breeding for meat and dairy produce. The area under cultivation (in hectares) was 4·5m. in 1913, 5·2m. in 1940 and 6·3m. in 1979. There were 6·8m. cattle, 4·6m. pigs and 540,000 sheep and goats on 1 Jan. 1980.

Output of main agricultural products (in 1,000 tonnes) in 1979 (1913 figures in brackets): Flax, 78 (33); sugar-beet, 1,383 (0); potatoes, 15,253 (4,024); meat, 915 (219); milk, 6·3 (1·4); wool, 1·1 (2·3); grain 4·6 (2·6); 2,894m. eggs (413m.).

At the end of 1977 there were 1,887 collective farms and 894 state farms. About 2·5m. hectares of marsh land had been drained for agricultural use, 828,200 of these for crops. This land has been found to be as rich as the soil of the Black Earth Zone, and yields good harvests of grain, fodder, potatoes, koksagyz and other crops. In Jan. 1980, 2·6m. hectares were drained and 36,300 hectares of land irrigated.

In Jan. 1980 there were 27,700 tractors and grain combine harvesters.

INDUSTRY. Industry in this republic was almost completely destroyed during the years 1941–45. By 1956, aggregate industrial output was three times what it had been in 1940. Plants producing tip-lorries, machine-tools and agricultural machinery are prominent.

The republic also contains timber works; a match factory in Borisov; building materials, machine, pre-fabricated house construction, glass-blowing and other factories; canneries, creameries and other food industries; chemical, textiles, artificial-silk, flax-spinning and leather works.

The automobile and tractor industry produced 89,100 tractors and 32,500 lorries in 1979. Cement output, 33,000 tons in 1913, was 2·17m. tons in 1975. Leather footwear output, 9·8m. pairs in 1940, was 41·6m. pairs in 1979. Linen fabrics, 13,000 linear metres in 1913, 68·4m. in 1975; woollens, 37,000 linear metres in 1913, 29m. in 1975.

Particular attention has been paid to the development of the peat industry with a view to making Belorussia as far as possible self-supporting in fuel, and in 1939 local peat provided 67·5% of her total requirements of fuel. The average annual output is about 18m. tonnes.

There are also rich deposits of rock salt. In 1951 the first sugar refinery in Belorussia was opened in Grodno; sugar output in 1979 was 313,900 tonnes.

Output of electricity in 1978, 32,700m. kwh. (508m. in 1940). New power-plants have been built in Baranovichi, Grodno, Molodechno and Lida.

The number of industrial and office workers at the end of 1979 was 3·9m.

COMMUNICATIONS. In 1978 there were 5,520 km of railways, 71,700 km of motor roads (39,000 km hard-surface) and 3,900 km of navigable waterways.

Newspapers (1979). Of 193 newspapers published 128 were in Belorussian. Circulation of Belorussian-language newspapers, 1·7m., other languages, 1·3m.

EDUCATION. In 1979–80 there were 173,800 students in 31 places of higher education and 163,500 students in 133 technical colleges. There were 36,500 scientific personnel in 178 institutions, and 340,000 specialists with a higher education employed in the national economy. The Belorussian Academy of Sciences controlled 32 learned institutions with 5,297 scientific staff. The number of children in primary, secondary and special schools was 489,000 in 1914–15, and 1·5m. in 1979–80. 462,000 children were attending pre-school institutions in 1979–80.

HEALTH. In 1979–80 there were 33,000 doctors (900 in 1913, within present frontiers), and 123,400 hospital beds (6,400 in 1913).

Books of Reference

Vakar, N. P., *Belorussia.* Harvard Univ. Press, 1956.—*A Bibliographical Guide to Belorussia.* Harvard Univ. Press, 1956

AZERBAIJAN
Azarbaijchan Soviet Sotsialistik Respublikasy

HISTORY. The 'Mussavat' (Nationalist) party, which dominated the National Council or Constituent Assembly of the Tartars, declared the independence of Azerbaijan on 28 May 1918, with a capital, first at Ganja (Elizavetpol) and later at Baku. On 28 April 1920 Azerbaijan was proclaimed a Soviet Socialist Republic. With Georgia and Armenia it formed the Transcaucasian Soviet Federal Socialist Republic. In 1936 it assumed the status of one of the Union (constituent) republics of the USSR.

AREA AND POPULATION. Azerbaijan covers an area of 86,600 sq. km (33,430 sq. miles) and has a population (Jan. 1980) of 6,117,000. Its capital is Baku. Other important towns are Kirovabad and Sumgait. Nahichevan is the capital of the Autonomous Republic of the same name.

Azerbaijan includes the Nahichevan Autonomous Republic and the Nagorno-Karabagh Autonomous Region. Situated in the eastern area of Transcaucasia, it is protected by mountains in the west and north, washed by the Caspian Sea in the east and bounded by Iran in the south. Its climate is inclined to drought.

In 1970 about 74% of the population were Azerbaijanis. Other nationalities were Russians (10%), Armenians (9%) and Georgians (2·7%).

CONSTITUTION AND GOVERNMENT. The Supreme Soviet, elected in 1980, consists of 450 deputies (1 per 10,000 population); 312 are Communists and 179 women. A new Constitution was adopted in April 1978.

At elections to the Nagorno-Karabagh regional Soviet and the district, urban and rural Soviets (19 June 1977), of 48,911 deputies returned, 22,731 (46·5%) were women, 26,841 (54·9%) non-Party and 32,061 (65·6%) industrial workers and collective farmers.

President, Presidium of the Supreme Soviet: K. A. Halilov.
Chairman, Council of Ministers: A. I. Ibrahimov.
First Secretary, Communist Party: G. A. Aliev.

FINANCE (in 1m. new roubles). Estimate, 1965, 1,033; 1970, 1,520; 1978, 1,782; 1980, 1,953; 1981, 2,129.

AGRICULTURE. The chief agricultural products are grain, cotton, rice, grapes, fruit, vegetables, tobacco and silk. The Mexican rubber plant *grayule* has been acclimatized. A new kind of high-yielding winter wheat has been produced for use in mountainous parts of the republic.

Livestock on 1 Jan. 1979: Cattle, 1·7m.; pigs, 167,000; sheep and goats, 5·3m.

Output of main agricultural products (in 1,000 tonnes) in 1978 (1913 figures in brackets): Cotton, 742 (4); potatoes, 131 (38); tea, 20 (0); meat, 136 (40); milk, 768 (203); wool, 10·2 (4·1); grapes, 1,045; fruit, 217; 691m. eggs (97m.).

Azerbaijan has become an important cotton-growing and sub-tropical base. About 70% of cultivated land is irrigated. On the irrigated land crops of Egyptian and Sea-Island cotton are obtained. Here, too, rice and lucerne are cultivated, and in the mountain valleys there are also orchards, vineyards and silk cultures.

In the south along the coast of the Caspian, where the climate is more moist, there are tea plantations, and citrus fruits and other sub-tropical plants are grown.

In 1941 a scientific research institute for sub-tropical research was opened to develop the culture of sub-tropical plants in Azerbaijan and other parts of Transcaucasia. A forestry research institute was opened in 1949.

There were on 1 Jan. 1980, 625 collective farms, 676 state farms, 34,500 tractors and 4,400 grain combine harvesters.

INDUSTRY. The republic is rich in natural resources: oil, iron, aluminium, copper, lead, zinc, precious metals, sulphur pyrites, limestone and salt. Iron and steel and aluminium works have been built at Sumgait.

The most important industry is the oil industry, especially in the Baku region. The output of oil was 7·7m. tonnes in 1913, 22·2m. tonnes in 1940 and 16·5m. tonnes in 1976. The largest producing area lies along the western shore of the Caspian Sea, north and south of Baku, where the largest refineries are located. Other wells lie west of Baku, and some have been drilled in the Caspian itself, off the Apsheron Peninsula. Baku is connected by a double pipeline with Batum on the Black Sea. All the oilfields have been electrified and are connected with Baku.

Azerbaijan has also copper, chemical, cement and building material, food, timber, salt, textiles and fishing industries. 788,000 tonnes of steel were produced in 1976, 1·4m. tons of cement, 130·4m. linear metres of cotton fabrics, 15·8m. pairs leather footwear, 32·3m. linear metres of silk fabrics, 1·3m. tons of iron ore.

In addition to Baku, among the important industrial centres are Kirovabad, Nukha, Stepanakert, Nahichevan, Lenkoran.

In 1979 electric power output was 15,200m. kwh. Output of gas, which began in 1928 with 176m. cu. metres, was 10,989m. in 1976. Pipelines from Karadag to Baku and Sumgait supply gas fuel for all oil-cracking factories and most engineering works.

Synthetic rubber works (Sumgait), tyre works and a worsted combine (Baku) and a large textile combine (Mingechaur) have been built.

The number of industrial and office workers in 1979 (average for year) was 1·75m.

COMMUNICATIONS. Railway lines, apart from narrow gauge, 1,880 km. The first electrical railway (42 km) in the USSR was constructed in Azerbaijan in 1924; in 1949, 27 km was added, and the line now runs Baku–Surakhany–Sabunchi–Buzovny–Baku. The capital is also linked by rail with Tbilisi, Yerevan, Derbent, Julfa and Astara. There were, in 1978, 23,800 km of motor roads (17,100 km hard-surface) and 500 km of inland waterways.

Newspapers (1979). There were 123 newspapers, 98 of them in the Azerbaijani language (circulation 2·2m.), other languages, 2·5m.

EDUCATION. In 1979–80 there were 1·6m. pupils in 4,300 elementary and secondary schools and 144,000 children attending pre-school institutions. There were 75 technical colleges with 79,800 students, 17 higher educational institutions, including a state university at Baku, with 105,200 students (including correspondence students).

The Azerbaijan Academy of Sciences has 28 research institutions with 4,249 research workers. There are 142 learned and scientific institutions, with 21,500 research workers in all.

HEALTH. In 1979 there were 19,700 doctors and 58,900 hospital beds. There were also 619 maternity and infant welfare centres.

NAHICHEVAN AUTONOMOUS SOVIET SOCIALIST REPUBLIC

Area, 5,500 sq. km (2,120 sq. miles), population (Jan. 1980), 243,000. Capital, Nahichevan (37,000). This territory, on the borders of Turkey and Iran, forms part of the Azerbaijan SSR although separated from it by the territory of Soviet Armenia. Its population, mainly Azerbaijanis, had a chequered history for 1,500 years under the ancient Persians, Arabs, Seljuk Turks, Mongols, Ottoman Turks and modern Persians before being annexed by Russia in 1828. On 9 Feb. 1924 it was constituted as an Autonomous Republic within Azerbaijan. Its Supreme Soviet, elected 24 Feb. 1980, has 110 members including 52 women.

The republic has silk, clothing, cotton, canning, meat-packing and other factories. Nearly 70% of the people are engaged in agriculture, of which the main branches are cotton and tobacco growing. Fruit and grapes are also produced in increasing quantity. There are 47 collective and 26 state farms. Crop area 37,400 hectares.

In 1977–78 there were 225 (218, 1979–80) primary, 8-year and 11-year schools with 70,800 pupils. There were 1,700 pupils in 4 technical colleges and a pedagogical institute with 2,400 students.

Doctors numbered 503, and hospital beds, 2,378.

NAGORNO-KARABAGH AUTONOMOUS REGION

Area, 4,400 sq. km (1,700 sq. miles); population (Jan. 1980), 162,600. Capital, Stepanakert (33,000). Populated by Armenians and Azerbaijanis, a separate khanate in the 18th century, it was established on 7 July 1923 as an Autonomous Region within Azerbaijan.

Main industries are silk, wine, dairying and building materials. Crop area is 67,200 hectares; cotton, grapes and winter wheat are grown. There are 53 collective and 21 state farms.

In 1979–80 there were 188 schools, 5 technical colleges, a teacher training college and a higher educational institution with 42,000 students; 402 doctors and 1,720 hospital beds.

Books of Reference

Baddeley, J. F., *The Rugged Flanks of Caucasus*. 2 vols. Oxford, 1941
Tutaeff, D., *The Soviet Caucasus*. London, 1942

GEORGIA
Sakartvelos Sabchota Sotsialisturi Respublica

HISTORY. The independence of the Georgian Social Democratic Republic was declared at Tiflis on 26 May 1918 by the National Council, elected by the National Assembly of Georgia on 22 Nov. 1917. The independence of Georgia was recognized by the USSR on 7 May 1920. On 12 Feb. 1921 a rising broke out in Mingrelia, Abhazia and Adjaria, and Soviet troops invaded the country, which, on 25 Feb. 1921, was proclaimed the Georgian Soviet Socialist Republic. At the first Transcaucasian Soviet Congress, 15 Dec. 1922, Georgia, together with Armenia and Azerbaijan, united to form the Transcaucasian Soviet Federal Socialist Republic, and a federal constitution was adopted and published 10 Jan. 1923. In 1936 the Georgian Soviet Socialist Republic became one of the constituent republics of the USSR and, like other republics of USSR, adopted a new Constitution.

AREA AND POPULATION. Georgia is bounded west by the Black Sea and south by Turkey, Armenia and Azerbaijan. It occupies the whole of the western part of Transcaucasia and covers an area of 69,700 sq. km (26,900 sq. miles). Its population on 1 Jan. 1980 was 5m. The capital is Tbilisi (Tiflis). Other important towns are Kutaisi (194,000), Rustavi (129,000), Batumi (124,000), Sukhumi (114,000), Poti (54,000), Gori (54,000).

Protected from the north by the Caucasian mountains, and receiving in the west the warm, moist winds from the Black Sea, into which most of its rivers flow, Georgia is outstanding for its fine, warm climate and its natural wealth, variety and beauty. It has the highest snow-capped peaks of the Caucasian mountains. Georgia contains valuable sulphur and other medicinal springs. Georgians, an ancient people, were (1970) 66·8% of the population; Armenians, 9·7%; Russians, 8·5%; Azerbaijanis, 4·6%; Ossetians, 3·2%; Abhazians, 1·7%.

CONSTITUTION AND GOVERNMENT. The Georgian Soviet Socialist Republic includes the Abhazian ASSR, the Adjarian ASSR and the South Ossetian Autonomous Region.

The Supreme Soviet, elected in 1980, consists of 440 deputies (1 per 10,000 population); 158 are women, 290 Communists. A new Constitution was adopted in April 1978.

At elections to the district, rural and urban Soviets, and that of the South Ossetian region (19 June 1977), of 49,371 deputies returned 23,903 (48·5%) were women, 28,064 (56·8%) non-Party and 33,303 (67·3%) industrial workers and collective farmers.

President, Presidium of the Supreme Soviet: P. G. Gilashvili.
Chairman, Council of Ministers: Z. A. Pataridze.
First Secretary, Communist Party: E. A. Shevardnadze.

FINANCE (in 1m. new roubles). Budget estimates, 1965, 1,049; 1970, 1,491; 1978, 1,873; 1980, 1,953; 1981, 2,232.

AGRICULTURE. There are 3 main agricultural areas: (1) The moist sub-tropical area along the Black Sea coast, where are cultivated tea, citrus fruits (lemons, oranges, mandarins, etc.), the tung tree (which yields special industrial oils), eucalyptus, bamboo, high-quality tobacco; (2) Imeretia (the Kutais region), where the chief cultures are grapes and silk, and (3) Kakhetia, along the Alazani (a tributary of the Kura River), famed for its orchards and wines. Land (in hectares) under cultivation was 748,000 in 1913, 896,000 in 1940, 778,000 in 1961, 800,000 in 1979.

Output of main agricultural products (in 1,000 tonnes) in 1978 (1913 figures in brackets): Sugar-beet, 115 (0); fruit, 811; grapes, 784; tea in leaf, 454; meat, 133 (49); wool, 5·5 (3·4); milk, 631 (222); wine, 19·9m. decalitres; 629m. eggs (119m.).

On 1 Jan. 1980 there were 686 collective farms working over 66% of all agricultural land, 471 state farms working nearly 34% of such land. In the Colchis area 115,000 hectares of extremely rich land have been reclaimed. There are 389,000 hectares of irrigated land. 151,400 hectares of marsh land have been drained. Tractors numbered 25,200; grain combines, 1,700.

Livestock on 1 Jan. 1980: Cattle, 1·5m.; pigs, 940,400; sheep and goats, 2m.

Georgia is rich in forest lands where fine varieties of timber are grown. Area covered by forests, 2·4m. hectares.

INDUSTRY. The most important mining industry of Georgia is the exploitation of the manganese deposits, the richest of which lie in the Chiatura region, where 1·6m. tonnes of ore were produced in 1971. Manganese deposits in Georgia are calculated at 250m. tonnes, distributed over an area of 140 sq. km. The most important coal seams are at Tkvarcheli (deposits estimated at 250m. tonnes) and Tkibuli (deposits of 80m. tonnes). Other important minerals are baryta, the best in the USSR, fire-resisting and other clays, diatomite shale, oil, agate, marble, cement, alabaster, iron and other ores, building stone, arsenic, molybdenum, tungsten and mercury. In 1941 a goldfield was discovered. Output of coal in 1976 was 1·9m. tonnes (625,000 in 1940).

Since the Second World War the Transcaucasian Metallurgical Plant has been built at Rustavi (near Tbilisi) and a motor works at Kutaisi. There are modern factories for processing green tea-leaves, creameries and breweries; Georgia has also textile and silk industries.

In 1977, 784,000 tonnes of pig-iron, 1·5m. tonnes of steel, 1,334,000 tonnes of rolled metal were produced; also 1·7m. tonnes of cement, 748,000 tonnes of mineral fertilizer, 56·7m. linear metres of cotton fabrics, 43·8m. linear metres of silk fabrics, 14·8m. pairs of leather footwear and 46,200 tons of granulated sugar.

Georgia's fast flowing rivers form an abundant source of energy. One of the most

powerful stations completed in recent years is Tbilisi (1m. kw.). Power output in 1979 was 13,800m. kwh. (742m. in 1940).
There were 1·9m. industrial and office workers in 1979.

COMMUNICATIONS. Length of railways in 1978 was 1,420 km. The trunk line leading from Batumi through Tbilisi to Baku on the Caspian Sea has several narrow-gauge branches on Georgian territory to the coalmines of Tkibuli, to the port of Poti, to the manganese mines of Chiatura, to the mineral springs of Borjom and the health resort Bakuriani, to the towns Signakh and Telavi, in Kakhetia, and to the Armenian frontier, across the coalmine district of Alaverdi. The last branch divides in Armenia, going on the one side to Tabriz in Iran, and on the other to Erzerum in Anatolia. A railway line from Akhal-Senaki along the Black Sea coast, through Sukhumi to Tuapse, was completed in 1946. All lines are electrified or work on diesel traction. In 1978 there were 22,000 km of motor roads, 18,500 km of them hard-surfaced.

Newspapers (1979). Out of 141 newspapers, 123 were in Georgian. Circulation in Georgian language newspapers, 2·4m., other languages, 483,000.

EDUCATION. In 1979–80 there were 1m. pupils in 4,000 primary and secondary schools, 53,900 in 93 technical colleges and 85,500 students in 19 higher educational institutions. Tbilisi University has 16,300 students. In towns, 11 years' education is usual. In Abastuman there is an astro-physical observatory. In 1936 a branch of the Academy of Sciences of the USSR was formed in Tbilisi, and in Feb. 1941 a Georgian Academy of Sciences was opened, which in 1979 had 43 institutions with scientific staff totalling 5,488. There were in all 194 research institutions with 25,500 scientific staff.
In 1979, 165,000 children were attending pre-school institutions.

HEALTH. There were 22,500 doctors and 53,300 hospital beds in 1979.

ABHAZIAN AUTONOMOUS SOVIET SOCIALIST REPUBLIC

Area, 8,600 km (3,320 sq. miles); population (Jan. 1980), 507,000. Capital Sukhumi. This area, the ancient Colchis, included Greek colonies from the 6th century B.C. onwards. From the 2nd century B.C. onwards, it was a prey to many invaders—Romans, Byzantines, Arabs, Ottoman Turks—before accepting a Russian protectorate in 1810. However, from the 4th century A.D. a West Georgian kingdom was established by the Lazi princes in the territory (known to the Romans as 'Lazica') and by the 8th century the prevailing language was Georgian and the name Abhazia.

On 4 March 1921 a congress of local Soviets proclaimed it a Soviet Republic, and its status as an Autonomous Republic, within Georgia, was confirmed on 17 April 1930.

140 deputies were elected on 24 Feb. 1980, 57 of them women.

The Abhazian coast (along the Black Sea) possesses a famous chain of health resorts—Gagra, Sukhumi, Akhali-Antoni, Gulripsha and Gudauta—sheltered by thickly forested mountains.

The republic has coal, electric power, building materials and light industries. In 1976 there were 93 collective farms and 48 state farms; main crops are tobacco, tea, grapes, oranges, tangerines and lemons. Crop area 41,400 hectares.

Livestock, 1 Jan. 1980: 32,500 cattle, 16,200 pigs, 9,200 sheep and goats.

101,500 pupils were attending 460 schools in 1976–77. There were 7 technical colleges with 3,100 students; 6,100 students were receiving higher education (including correspondence courses). A university has been opened in Sukhumi.

There were 152,700 industrial and office workers, and 13,200 specialists with a higher education in the national economy in 1978. Doctors, 1,883; hospital beds, 5,800.

ADJARIAN AUTONOMOUS SOVIET SOCIALIST REPUBLIC

Area, 3,000 sq. km (1,160 sq. miles); population (Jan. 1980), 359,000. Capital, Batumi. After a history similar to that of Abhazia, it fell under Turkish rule in the 17th century, and was annexed to Russia (rejoining Georgia) after the Berlin Treaty of 1878. On 16 June 1921 the territory was constituted as an Autonomous Republic within the Georgian SSR.

110 deputies were elected on 24 Feb. 1980, 43 of them women.

The republic specializes in sub-tropical agricultural products. These include tea, mandarines and lemons, grapes, bamboo, eucalyptus, etc. Livestock: 116,000 cattle, 10,000 sheep and goats. In 1976 there were 77 collective farms and 21 state farms.

There are shipyards at Batumi, modern oil-refining plant (the pipeline from the Baku oilfields ends at Batumi), food-processing and canning factories, clothing, building materials, drug factories, etc.

Health resorts are Kobuleti, Tsihis-Dari, Batumi on the coast and Beshumi in the hills. The sub-tropical climate and flora, and the combination of mountains and sea, make this republic (like Abhazia) a favourite holiday country.

In 1979 there were 76,400 pupils at school, several technical colleges with 3,500 students, a pedagogical institute and several research institutions. 2,000 students were receiving a higher education.

There were (1978) 92,700 industrial and office workers, and 10,500 specialists with a higher education in the national economy. Doctors, 1,097; hospital beds, 3,695.

SOUTH OSSETIAN AUTONOMOUS REGION

This area was populated by Ossetians from across the Caucasus (North Ossetia), driven out by the Mongols in the 13th century. The region was set up within the Georgian SSR on 20 April 1922. Area, 3,900 sq. km (1,505 sq. miles); population (Jan. 1980), 98,000. Capital, Tskhinvali (34,000).

Main industries are mining, timber, electrical engineering and building materials. Crop area, chiefly grains, was 21,700 hectares in 1979; other pursuits are sheep-farming (103,500 sheep and goats) and vine-growing. There were 14 collective farms and 13 state farms.

There are a pedagogical institute (2,345 students) and several technical colleges (700 students). In 1976 there were 24,000 pupils in elementary and secondary schools.

There were (1978) 34,900 industrial and office workers, and 3,800 specialists with a higher education in the national economy. Doctors, 401; hospital beds, 1,350.

Books of Reference

Avalishvill, Zourab, *The Independence of Georgia in International Politics, 1918–21*. London, 1940
Gvesiani, G. G., and Klopotovsky, B. A., *Gruzinskaya SSR*. Moscow, 1955
Lang, D. M., *A Modern History of Georgia*. London, 1962
Tutaeff, D., *The Soviet Caucasus*. London, 1942

ARMENIA
Haikakan Sovetakan Sotsialistakan Respublika

HISTORY. On 29 Nov. 1920 Armenia was proclaimed a Soviet Socialist Republic. The Armenian Soviet Government, with the Russian Soviet Government, was a party to the Treaty of Kars (March 1921), which confirmed the Turkish possession of the former Government of Kars and of the Surmali District of the Government of Yerevan. From 1922 to 1936 it formed part of the Transcaucasian

Soviet Federal Socialist Republic. In 1936 Armenia was proclaimed a constituent republic of the USSR.

AREA AND POPULATION. Armenia covers an area of 29,800 sq. km (11,490 sq. miles). It is bounded in the north by Georgia, in the east by Azerbaijan and in the south and west by Turkey and Iran. It is a very mountainous country with but little forest land, has many turbulent rivers and a highly fertile soil, but subject to drought. In Jan. 1980 the population was 3·08m. About 89% of the population are Armenians, the rest are Russians (2·7%), Kurds (1·5%), Azerbaijanians (5·9%) (1970 census). The capital is Yerevan. Other large towns are Leninakan (210,000) and Kirovakan (149,000).

CONSTITUTION AND GOVERNMENT. The Supreme Soviet, elected in 1980, consists of 340 deputies (1 per 5,000 population); 121 are women, 218 Communists. A new Constitution was adopted in April 1978.

At elections to the district, urban and rural Soviets (19 June 1977), of 26,592 deputies returned 12,952 (48·7%) were women, 15,317 (57·6%) non-Party and 18,436 (69·3%) industrial workers and collective farmers.

President, Presidium of the Supreme Soviet: B. E. Sarkisov.
Chairman, Council of Ministers: F. T. Sarkisian.
First Secretary, Communist Party: K. S. Demirchian.

FINANCE. Budget estimates (in 1m. new roubles), 1965, 699; 1970, 1,130; 1977, 1,198; 1978, 1,244; 1980, 1,337; 1981, 1,492.

AGRICULTURE. The chief agricultural area is the valley of the Arax and the area around Yerevan. Here there are considerable cotton plantations as well as orchards and vineyards. Sub-tropical plants, such as almonds and figs, are also grown. Olive groves and pomegranate plantations occupy large areas; experiments are being made to naturalize cork oak. In the mountainous areas the chief pursuit is livestock raising. In 1913 the total cultivated area of Armenia amounted to 346,000 hectares; in 1940, 434,000; in 1965, 400,000; in 1970, 409,000; in 1978, 500,000.

Output of main agricultural products (in 1,000 tonnes) in 1978 (1913 figures in brackets): Wheat, 318 (110); sugar-beet, 162 (0); potatoes, 223 (47); fruit, 157; grapes, 244; meat, 83·5 (19); milk, 495 (129); wool, 5 (2·3); and 440m. eggs (54m.).

Area of irrigated land in Armenia in 1979 was 270,000 hectares.

There were, in Dec. 1979, 314 collective farms, and these together with the 434 state farms tilled 99·9% of the total cultivated area. Livestock included 233,000 pigs, 772,100 cattle and 2·3m. sheep and goats. All the state farms and collective farms had been electrified by the end of 1960. There were 12,800 tractors and 1,500 grain and cotton combines in Jan. 1979.

INDUSTRY. Armenia contains large deposits of copper, zinc, aluminium, molybdenum and other metals. It is also rich in marble, granite, cement and other building materials. The mining of these minerals is becoming more and more important. Among other industries are the chemical, producing chiefly synthetic rubber and fertilizers, and the extraction and processing of building materials such as cement, pumice-stone, tuffs, marble, volcanic basalt and fire-proof clay, ginning- and textile-mills, carpet weaving, food, including wine-making, fruit, meat-canning and creameries. Machine-tool and electrical engineering works have also been established. Among the industrial centres are Yerevan, Leninakan, Alaverdi, Kafan, Kirovakan, Daval, Megri and Oktemberyan. Output of electricity in 1979 was 12,100m. kwh. A chain ('cascade') of 8 hydro-electric stations on the river Razdan, as it falls about 3,300 ft from the mountain lake Sevan to its junction with the Arax, has been completed.

In 1977 there were produced 1,828,000 tons of cement, 416,000 tons of mineral fertilizers, 95·6m. linear metres of cotton fabrics, 18·5m. linear metres of silk fabrics, 11·8m. pairs of leather footwear, 13,900 tons of granulated sugar and 8·9m. decalitres of wine (excluding collective farm output).

There were 1,151,000 industrial and office workers employed in the national economy in 1979.

COMMUNICATIONS. Length of railways in 1978, 710 km; motor roads, 8,700 km (hard surface, 6,300); airlines, 570 km.

Newspapers (1978). Out of 83 newspapers 73 appeared in Armenian. Circulation of Armenian-language newspapers, 1·4m., other languages, 115,000.

EDUCATION. In 1979–80 there were 600,000 pupils in 1,535 primary, secondary and special schools; 65 technical colleges with 54,100 students; 13 higher educational institutions with 57,600 students (including correspondence students). Erevan houses the Armenian Academy of Sciences, 43 scientific institutes, a medical institute and other technical colleges, and a state university. 31 learned institutions with 2,960 scientific staff are under the Academy of Sciences. Scientific workers totalled 17,700 in 101 institutions in 1978.

In 1979 there were 131,000 children in pre-school institutions.

HEALTH. In 1979 there were 10,700 doctors and 26,000 hospital beds.

Books of Reference

Aslanyan, A., Bagdasarian, A., *et al., L'Arménie Sovietique.* Moscow, 1972
Baghdasarian, A. B. (ed.) *Atlas Armyanskoi SSR.* Moscow, 1961
Kurkjian, V., *A History of Armenia.* New York, 1958
Missakian, J., *A Searchlight on the Armenian Question, 1878–1950.* Boston. Mass., 1950
Shaginyan, M., *A Journey Through Soviet Armenia.* Moscow (English ed., 1954)

MOLDAVIAN SOVIET SOCIALIST REPUBLIC
Respublika Sovietike Sochialiste Moldovenyaske

HISTORY. The Moldavian Soviet Socialist Republic, capital Kishinev, was formed by the union of part of the former Moldavian Autonomous Soviet Socialist Republic (organized 12 Oct. 1924), formerly included in the Ukrainian Soviet Socialist Republic, and the areas of Bessarabia (ceded by Romania to the USSR, 28 June 1940) with a mainly Moldavian population. As from 2 Aug. 1940 the MSSR includes the following regions of the former Moldavian Autonomous Soviet Socialist Republic: Grigoriopol, Dubossarsk, Kamensk, Rybnitz, Slobedzeisk and Tiraspol, and the following districts of Bessarabia: Beltsk, Bendery, Kagulsk, Kishinev, Orgeev and Sorok. The republic, however, is divided not into regions but into 36 rural districts, 21 towns and 40 urban settlements.

AREA AND POPULATION. Moldavia is bounded in the east and south by the Ukraine and on the west by Romania. The area is 33,700 sq. km (13,000 sq. miles). In Jan. 1980 the population was 4m., of whom 65% are Moldavians. Others include Ukrainians (14%), Russians (11·6%), Gagauzi (3·5%), Jews (2·7%). Apart from Kishinev, larger towns are Tiraspol (142,000), Beltsy (128,000) and Bendery (104,000).

CONSTITUTION AND GOVERNMENT. The Supreme Soviet, elected in 1980, consists of 380 deputies (1 per 10,000 population); 138 are women, 253 Communists. A new Constitution was adopted in April 1978.

At elections to the district, urban and rural Soviets (19 June 1977), of 34,361 deputies returned, 16,994 (49·5%) were women, 18,759 (54·6%) non-Party and 23,840 (69·4%) industrial workers and collective farmers.

President, Presidium of the Supreme Soviet: K. F. Ilyashenko.
Chairman, Council of Ministers and Foreign Minister: I. I. Bodyul.
First Secretary, Communist Party: S. K. Grossu.

FINANCE. Budget estimates (in 1m. new roubles), 1965, 598; 1970, 967; 1977, 1,342; 1978, 1,442; 1980, 1,639; 1981, 1,750.

AGRICULTURE. On 1 Jan. 1979 there were 422 collective farms and 291 state farms. All ploughing and sowing is mechanized. Livestock included (1 Jan. 1979) 1·1m. cattle, 2m. pigs and 1·2m. sheep and goats. There were 49,300 tractors and 3,600 combine harvesters.

Output of main agricultural products (in 1,000 tonnes) in 1978 (1913 figures in tons in brackets): Wheat, 1,288 (526); maize, 1,165 (639); sugar-beet, 2,807 (15), sunflower seeds, 350 (9); potatoes, 335 (119); other vegetables, 1,227; fruit, 929; grapes, 1,377; meat, 253 (53); milk, 1,200 (210); wool, 2·5 (3); 880m. eggs (275m.).

Bessarabia has an equable climate and very fertile soil. It contains nearly one-quarter of the vineyards of the USSR. Bessarabia is also rich in fish in the south: sturgeon, mackerel, brill.

INDUSTRY. There are canning plants, wine-making plants, woodworking and metallurgical factories, a factory of ferro-concrete building materials, and footwear and textile plants. Moldavia takes third place in the USSR in the production of wine, tobacco and food-canning. Power output in 1978 was 13,600m. kwh. Production in 1977 included 28·9m. linear metres of silk fabrics, 16·3m. pairs of leather footwear, 424,100 tons of granulated sugar, 1,525m. tins of preserves and 24·7m. decalitres of wine. Meat and dairy produce are rapidly expanding food industries.

There are lignite, phosphorites, gypsum and valuable building materials.

In 1979 there were 1·4m. industrial and office workers working in the national economy.

COMMUNICATIONS. Length of railways, 1,110 km. There is direct air communication with Leningrad, Moscow, Kiev, Lvov and across the Black Sea. There are 10,500 km of motor roads (8,700 hard surface), and 1,100 km of inland waterways.

Newspapers (1979). There were 163 newspapers, of which 69 were in Moldavian. Circulation of Moldavian-language newspapers, 1·2m., other languages, 784,000.

EDUCATION. In 1979–80 there were 700,000 pupils in 1,800 primary, secondary and special schools, 59,400 students in 50 technical colleges and 50,500 students in 8 higher educational institutions including the state university. A Moldavian Academy of Sciences was established in 1961: it had 17 research institutions and a scientific staff of 962 in 1979. In all, there are 68 learned institutions with 8,100 scientific staff. In 1979 there were 253,000 children attending pre-school institutions.

HEALTH. Moldavia has 800 medical centres, many district hospitals, a state medical institute and 9 medical schools with over 2,500 students. Doctors in 1979 numbered 12,000; hospital beds, 46,900.

Book of Reference

Zlatova, Y., and Kotelnikov, V., *Across Moldavia* [English ed.]. Moscow, 1959

ESTONIA
Eesti Nõukogude Sotsialistlik Vabariik

HISTORY. The workers' and soldiers' Soviets in Estonia took over power on 8 Nov. 1917, were overthrown by the German occupying forces in March 1918, and were restored to power as the Germans withdrew in Nov. 1918, establishing the 'Estland Labour Commune'. It was overthrown with the assistance of British naval forces in May 1919, and a democratic republic proclaimed.

The secret protocol of the Soviet–German agreement of 23 Aug. 1939 assigned Estonia to the Soviet sphere of interest. An ultimatum (16 June 1940) led to the formation of a government acceptable to the USSR; on 21 July the State Duma proclaimed Soviet power and applied to join the USSR: on 6 Aug. the Supreme Soviet accepted the application. The incorporation has been accorded *de facto* recognition by the British Government, but not by the US Government, which continues to recognize an Estonian consul-general in New York.

AREA AND POPULATION. Estonia is bounded west and north by the Baltic, east by the RSFSR and south by Latvia. Area, 45,100 sq. km (17,410 sq. miles); population, 1·47m. (Jan. 1980). 68·2% are Estonians, 24·7% Russians, 1·4% Finns. The capital is Tallinn. Other large towns are Tartu (106,000), Pärnu, Narva (74,000). There are 15 districts, 33 towns and 26 urban settlements.

CONSTITUTION AND GOVERNMENT. The Supreme Soviet, elected in 1980, consists of 285 deputies (1 per 10,000 population); 101 are women, 193 Communists. A new Constitution was adopted in April 1978.

At elections to district, urban and rural Soviets (19 June 1977), out of 10,880 deputies returned 5,330 (49%) were women, 6,035 (55·5%) non-Party and 7,294 (67%) industrial workers and collective farmers.

President, Presidium of the Supreme Soviet: I. G. Kebin.
Chairman, Council of Ministers: V. I. Klauson.
First Secretary, Communist Party: K. G. Vaino.

FINANCE. Budget estimates (in 1m. new roubles), 1965, 480; 1970, 708; 1977, 883; 1978, 931; 1980, 1,028; 1981, 1,087.

AGRICULTURE. Agriculture and dairy farming are the chief occupations. Area under cultivation was 697,000 hectares in 1913, 918,000 hectares in 1940 and 954,000 hectares in 1978. There were 143 agricultural and 8 fishery collectives and 158 state farms in 1979 using 19,300 tractors and 3,400 grain combines. 97% of state farms and 70% of collective farms were receiving electric power.

On 1 Jan. 1980 there were 822,000 head of cattle, 150,000 sheep and goats, 1,052,000 pigs and 5·8m. poultry.

Output of main agricultural products (in 1,000 tonnes) in 1979 (1913 figures in brackets): Potatoes, 1,243 (689); grains, 1,052 (428); other vegetables, 109; meat (slaughter weight), 188 (60); milk, 1,138 (415); wool, 0·3 (0·7); 493m. eggs (67m.).

INDUSTRY. Some 22% of the territory is covered by forests which provide good material for its sawmills, furniture, match and pulp industries, as well as wood fuel. Since the end of the War, 80,000 hectares have been afforested. 966,700 hectares of marsh land had been reclaimed by 1977.

Estonia has rich high-quality shale deposits (particularly in the north-east) which are estimated at 3,700m. tons. Shale output was 1·9m. tons in 1940 and 30m. in 1977. A factory for the production of gas from shale and a pipeline (208 km long) from Kohtla-Järve supplies shale gas to Leningrad and Tallinn. Estonian factories are now turning out agricultural and peat-digging machines, complex control and measuring instruments. The 'Volta' factory in Tallinn produces electric motors.

In the neighbourhood of Tallinn, phosphorites have been found, and in 1947 a plant for refining and for the production of superphosphates was started. Estonia also contains valuable peat deposits, and some of her electrical stations work on peat. A hydro-electric station was erected in 1955 on the Narva. There are 350 rural electric stations. Output of mineral fertilizers in 1977 was 1·4m. tons; cement, 1·26m. tons; paper, 106,000 tons; cotton fabrics, 196m. linear metres; linen fabrics, 6·1m. linear metres; sawn timber, 733,000 cu. metres; leather footwear, 6·1m. pairs; electric production (1979), 19,400m. kwh.

In 1979 there were 690,000 industrial and office workers and 62,000 specialists with a higher education engaged in the national economy.

COMMUNICATIONS. Length of main railways 970 km, of secondary lines 730 km. Estonia has 20 ports, but Tallinn handles four-fifths of the total sea-going transport. Inland waterways total 500 km; motor roads, 29,700 km (hard surface, 23,500 km). Airlines link Tallinn with Moscow, Leningrad, Riga and the Estonian islands.

Newspapers (1978). There were 42 newspapers, 31 of them in Estonian. Circulation of Estonian-language newspapers, 988,000, other languages, 179,000.

EDUCATION. Estonia has retained an 11-year school curriculum, when it was reduced to 10 years elsewhere in the USSR. In 1979–80 pupils in 600 primary, secondary and special schools numbered 216,000. There were 25,400 students in 6 higher educational establishments, including Tartu (Dorpat) University, founded in 1632, and 24,500 students in 37 technical colleges.

The Estonian Academy of Sciences, founded in 1946, has 24 institutions with 985 scientific staff; in all, 6,000 scientists are working in 72 institutions.

In 1979 there were 83,000 children attending pre-school institutions.

HEALTH. In 1979 there were 6,000 doctors and 17,600 hospital beds.

Books of Reference

Druzhinin, V., *Soviet Estonia.* Moscow, 1953 (in English)
Estonia. Basic Facts on Geography, History and Economy. Stockholm, 1948
Jackson, J. H., *Estonia.* London, 1948
Kareda, E., *Estonia in the Soviet Grip.* London, 1949
Küng, A., *A Dream of Freedom.* Cardiff, 1980
Pranspill, A., *Estonian Anthology.* Milford, Conn., 1957
Silvet, J., *Inglise–eesti sõnaraamat.* Vadstena, 1949
Varetz, E. F., and Tarmisto, V. Y., *Estonia.* Moscow, 1967 (in Russian)
Woods, E. G., *The Baltic Region: A Study in Physical and Human Geography.* London, 1945

LATVIA
Latvijas Padomju Socialistiska Republika

HISTORY. In the part of Latvia unoccupied by the Germans, the Bolsheviks won 72% of the votes in the Constituent Assembly elections (Nov. 1917). Soviet power was proclaimed in Dec. 1917, but was overthrown when the Germans occupied all Latvia (Feb. 1918). Restored when they withdrew (Dec. 1918), it was overthrown once more by combined British naval and German military forces (May–Dec. 1919), and a democratic government set up.

The secret protocol of the Soviet–German agreement of 23 Aug. 1939 assigned Latvia to the Soviet sphere of interest. An ultimatum (16 June 1940) led to the formation of a government acceptable to the USSR; on 21 July a People's Diet established Soviet power and applied to join the USSR: the Supreme Soviet accepted the application on 5 Aug. The incorporation has been accorded *de facto* recognition by the British Government, but not by the US Government, which continues to recognize the *Chargé d'Affaires* in Washington, D.C.

AREA AND POPULATION. Latvia is bounded north by Estonia and the Baltic Sea, west by the Baltic, south by Lithuania and Belorussia and east by the RSFSR. Latvia has a total area of 63,700 sq. km (25,590 sq. miles). Population, Jan. 1980, 2·5m., of whom 57% are Letts and 30% Russians. There are 26 districts, 56 towns and 36 urban settlements.

The chief town is Riga (the capital); other principal towns are Daugavpils (Dvinsk) (117,000), Liepāja (108,000), Jelgava (Mitau) (69,000) and Ventspils (Windau).

CONSTITUTION AND GOVERNMENT. The Supreme Soviet, elected in 1980, consists of 325 deputies (1 per 10,000 population); 113 are women, 218 Communists. A new Constitution was adopted in April 1978.

At elections to district, urban and rural Soviets (19 June 1977), of 23,081 deputies returned, 11,339 (49·1%) were women, 12,324 (53·4%) non-Party and 15,287 (63%) industrial workers and collective farmers.

President, Presidium of the Supreme Soviet: P. Y. Strautmanis.
Chairman, Council of Ministers: Y. Y. Ruben.
First Secretary, Communist Party: A. E. Voss.

FINANCE. Budget estimates (in 1m. new roubles), 1965, 678; 1970, 1,047; 1977, 1,371; 1978, 1,396; 1980, 1,568; 1981, 1,606.

AGRICULTURE. Latvia is now no longer mainly an agricultural country. The urban population, 35% of the total in 1939, was 67% in Jan. 1978.

Latvian forest lands, state and private (2·4m. hectares), produced in 1937–38, 3·4m. cu. metres of timber; 1977 output, 3·9m. cu. metres.

Area under cultivation was 1·4m. hectares in 1913, 2m. in 1940, 1·7m. in 1978. 1·8m. hectares of marsh land have been drained (1979).

Cattle breeding and dairy farming are the chief agricultural occupations. Oats, barley, rye, potatoes and flax are the main crops.

After the establishment of the Soviet regime about 960,000 hectares were distributed among the landless peasants or those with very small holdings. On 1 Jan. 1979 there were 243 state farms and 347 collective farms. There were 32,200 tractors and 6,500 grain combine harvesters. By 1 Jan. 1964, all state farms and collective farms were using electric power.

Livestock (1 Jan. 1980): Cattle, 1·4m. (1939: 1·3m.); sheep, 211,000 (1939: 1·5m.); pigs, 1·4m. (1939: 891,500).

Output of main agricultural products (in 1,000 tonnes) in 1979 (1913 figures in brackets): Sugar-beet, 195 (0); potatoes, 1,626 (645); all grains, 1,171 (880); other vegetables, 147; fruit, 35; meat and fats, 25 (122); milk, 1,664 (673); wool, 0·5 (1·4); flax, 4·1 (21); 720m. eggs (136m.).

INDUSTRY. Latvia is the main producer of electric railway passenger cars and long-distance telephone exchanges in the USSR, fourth in output of paper and woollen goods, fifth of sawn timber, sixth of mineral fertilizers.

Industrial output in 1977 (in 1,000 tons) included: Steel, 502; rolled metal, 630; cement, 903; granulated sugar, 271; paper, 169; fish catch, 550; cotton fabrics, 62·8m. linear metres; linen fabrics, 21·3m. linear metres; woollens, 14m. linear metres; silks, 19·9m. linear metres; leather footwear, 10·2m. pairs; radio sets, 2·4m. (no.). Electric power output was 3,300m. kwh.

The peat deposits extend over 645,000 hectares or about 10% of the total area, and it is estimated that the total deposits of peat are 3,000–4,000m. tons; output, 1971, 2·3m. tons. There are also gypsum deposits; amber is frequently found in the coastal districts.

In 1978 industrial and office workers numbered 1·2m.

COMMUNICATIONS. In 1978 the length of railways was 2,450 km, and motor roads, 24,300 km (hard surface, 14,900 km). Riga is the largest port in the Baltic after Leningrad.

Newspapers (1979). There were 99 newspapers (60 in Lettish). Circulation of Lettish-language newspapers, 1·1m., other languages 430,000.

RELIGION. The Latvian Lutheran Church numbered 600,000 members in 1956.

EDUCATION. In 1979–80 there were 900 primary, continuation and secondary schools, with a total of 300,000 pupils: 108,000 children attended pre-school institutions. Ten places of higher education had 47,700 students, 54 technical colleges had 42,700 students; there were also 21 music and art schools, 3 teachers' training colleges and an agricultural academy. In 1946 an Academy of Sciences was opened which in 1979 had 16 research institutes with a staff of 1,700 scientific workers; there were over 12,000 scientific workers in 101 research institutions.

HEALTH. There were 11,000 doctors and 33,900 hospital beds in 1979.

Books of Reference

Latvian Academy of Sciences, *Istoria Latviiskoi SSR*. Riga, 1952–58
Central Statistical Department, Latvian Branch, *Latviiskaya SSR v Tsifrakh*. Riga
Bilmanis, A., *A History of Latvia*. Princeton Univ. Press, 1951
Roze, B. and K., *Latviska–Angliska Vārdnicā*. Göppingen, 1948
Skujenicks, M., *Atlas Statistique de la Lettone*. Riga, 1938
Spekke, A., *History of Latvia*. Stockholm, 1951
Turkina, E., *Angliski–Latviska Vārdnīca*. Riga, 1948.—*Latviešu-Anglu Vārdnīca*. Riga, 1962

LITHUANIA
Lietuvos Tarybu Socialistine Respublika

HISTORY. In 1914–15 the German army occupied the whole of Lithuania. On its withdrawal (Dec. 1918) Soviets were elected in all towns and a Soviet republic was proclaimed. In the summer of 1919 it was overthrown by Polish, German and nationalist Lithuanian forces, and a democratic republic established.

The secret protocol of the Soviet–German frontier treaty of 28 Sept. 1939 assigned the greater part of Lithuania to the Soviet sphere of influence. In Oct. 1939 the province and city of Vilnius (in Polish occupation 1920–39) were ceded by the USSR. An ultimatum (16 June 1940) led to the formation of a government acceptable to the USSR. A people's Diet, elected on 14–15 July, applied for Lithuania's admission to the Soviet Union on 22 July, which was effected by decree of the Supreme Soviet on 3 Aug. and included also those parts of Lithuania which had been reserved for inclusion in Germany. This incorporation has been accorded *de facto* recognition by the British Government, but not by the US Government, which continues to recognize a Lithuanian *Chargé d'Affaires* in Washington, D.C.

AREA AND POPULATION. Lithuania is bounded north by Latvia, east and south by Belorussia, west by Poland, the Kaliningrad area of the RSFSR and the Baltic Sea. The total area of Lithuania is 65,200 sq. km (25,170 sq. miles) and the population (Jan. 1980) 3·4m., of whom 80% were Lithuanians, 8·6% Russians and 7·7% Poles.

The capital is Vilnius (Vilna). Other large towns are Kaunas (Kovno), Klaipėda (Memel), Šiauliai (121,000) and Panevėžys (104,000). There are 44 rural districts, 92 towns and 21 urban settlements.

CONSTITUTION AND GOVERNMENT. The Supreme Soviet, elected in 1980, consists of 350 deputies (1 per 15,000 population); 125 are women, 235 Communists. A new Constitution was adopted in April 1978.

At elections to district, urban and rural Soviets (19 June 1977), of 28,276 deputies returned, 13,832 (48·9%) were women, 15,870 (56·1%) non-Party and 18,951 (67%) industrial workers and collective farmers.

President, Presidium of the Supreme Soviet: A. S. Barkauskas.
Chairman, Council of Ministers: J. A. Maniušis.
First Secretary, Communist Party: P. P. Griškevičius.

FINANCE. Budget estimates (in 1m. new roubles), 1965, 944; 1970, 1,665; 1977, 2,073; 1978, 2,194; 1980, 2,330; 1981, 2,443.

AGRICULTURE. Lithuania before 1940 was a mainly agricultural country, but has since been considerably industrialized. The urban population was 23% of the total in 1937 and 59% in Jan. 1978. The resources of the country consist of timber and agricultural produce. Of the total area, 49·1% is arable land, 22·2% meadow and pasture land, 16·3% forests and 12·4% unproductive lands.

Area under cultivation in 1913 was 1·9m.; in 1938, 2·7m.; in 1977, 2·4m. hectares. By 1978 over 2·5m. hectares of swamps had been drained.

Output of main agricultural products (in 1,000 tonnes) in 1978 (1913 figures in brackets): All grains, 2,225 (1,449); sugar-beet, 803 (0); flax, 12 (17); potatoes, 2,313 (1,375); other vegetables, 365; fruit, 153; meat and fats, 463 (159); milk, 2,681 (832); wool, 0·2 (1·5); 943m. eggs (264m.).

On 1 Jan. 1980 there were 2·2m. cattle, 2·6m. pigs, 60,000 sheep and goats.

Forests cover 1,554,000 hectares; 70% of the forests consist of conifers, mostly pines. Peat reserves total 4,000m. cu. metres.

Between 1940 and 1947 about 575,500 hectares (about 1·4m. acres) were distributed among the landless and poor peasant farmers. In 1979 there were 45,800 tractors and 10,300 grain combines serving 787 collective farms and 327 state farms.

INDUSTRY. Heavy engineering, shipbuilding and building material industries are developing. Industrial output included, in 1977: Cement, 2·99m. tons; granulated sugar, 207,100 tons; paper, 124,000 tons; cotton fabrics, 86·3m. linear metres; linens, 19m. linear metres; woollens, 12·4m. linear metres; sawn timber, 1m. cu. metres; leather footwear, 9·4m. pairs; electric power, 10·7m. kwh.

In 1979 there were 1·4m. industrial and office workers employed in the national economy.

COMMUNICATIONS. Length of railways, 2,030 km. Vilnius has one of the largest airports of the USSR. There are 32,100 km of motor roads (19,900 km hard surface) and 600 km of inland waterways. Klaipėda, as a non-freezing harbour and fishery base, is of national importance.

Newspapers (1979). Of 123 newspapers, 96 were in Lithuanian. Circulation of Lithuanian-language newspapers, 2·1m., other languages, 1·9m.

RELIGION. In 1956, the Lithuanian Lutheran Church had 215,000 members; Roman Catholics, including those in Estonia and Latvia, numbered 2·5m.

EDUCATION. In 1979–80 there were 600,000 pupils in 2,400 primary, secondary and special schools. The University of Vytautas the Great, at Kaunas, was opened on 16 Feb. 1922. On 15 Jan. 1940 certain faculties were transferred to Vilnius to join the ancient University of Vilnius. In 1979–80 there were 12 higher educational institutions with 70,000 students: in 72 technical colleges of all kinds there were 69,100 students. The Lithuanian Academy of Sciences, founded in 1941, had 11 institutions with a total scientific staff of 1,679; there were 88 scientific institutions with 13,500 research personnel. 142,000 children in 1979 were attending pre-school institutions.

HEALTH. In 1979 there were 13,000 doctors and 40,000 hospital beds.

Books of Reference

Griškevičius, P. P., *Land on the Nemunas.* Moscow, 1977
Jurgėla, C. R., *History of the Lithuanian Nation.* New York, 1948
Kantantas, F. *A Lithuanian Bibliography.* Univ. of Alberta Press, 1975
Peteraitis, V., *Lithuanian–English Dictionary.* 2 vols. Chicago, 1960

SOVIET CENTRAL ASIA

Soviet Central Asia embraces the Kazakh Soviet Socialist Republic, the Uzbek Soviet Socialist Republic, the Turkmen Soviet Socialist Republic, the Tadzhik Soviet Socialist Republic and the Kirghiz Soviet Socialist Republic.

Turkestan (by which name part of this territory was then known) was conquered by the Russians in the 1860s. In 1866 Tashkent was occupied and in 1868 Samarkand, and subsequently further territory was conquered and united with Russian Turkestan. In the 1870s Bokhara was subjugated, the emir, by the agreement of 1873, recognizing the suzerainty of Russia. In the same year Khiva became a vassal state to Russia. Until 1917 Russian Central Asia was divided politically into the Khanate of Khiva, the Emirate of Bokhara and the Governor-Generalship of Turkestan.

In the summer of 1919 the authority of the Soviet Government became definitely established in these regions. The Khan of Khiva was deposed in Feb. 1920, and a People's Soviet Republic was set up, the medieval name of Khorezm being revived. In Aug. 1920 the Emir of Bokhara suffered the same fate, and a similar regime was set up in Bokhara. The former Governor-Generalship of Turkestan was constituted an Autonomous Soviet Socialist Republic within the RSFSR on 11 April 1921.

In the autumn of 1924 the Soviets of the Turkestan, Bokhara and Khiva Republics decided to redistribute the territories of these republics on a nationality basis; at the same time Bokhara and Khiva became Socialist Republics. The redistribution was completed in May 1925, when the new states of Uzbekistan, Turkmenistan and Tadzhikistan and several autonomous regions were established. The remaining districts of Turkestan populated by Kazakhs were united with Kazakhstan. Kirghizia, until then part of the RSFSR, was established as a Union Republic in 1936.

Books of Reference

Nove, A. and Newth, J. A., *The Soviet Middle East*. London, 1967
Vaidyanathy, R., *The Formation of the Soviet Central Asian Republics*. New Delhi, 1967
Wheeler, G., *The Modern History of Soviet Central Asia*. London, 1964
Yuldashev, M. (ed.), *Oktiabrskaya Sotsialisticheskaya Revolutsia i Grajdanskaya Voina v Turkestane*. Tashkent, 1957
Zevelyov, A. (ed.), *Za Sovetski Turkestan*. Tashkent, 1963

KAZAKHSTAN
Kazak Soviettik Sotzialistik Respublikasy

HISTORY. On 26 Aug. 1920 Uralsk, Turgai, Akmolinsk and Semipalatinsk provinces formed the Kazakh Soviet Socialist Republic within the RSFSR. It was made a constituent republic of the USSR on 5 Dec. 1936. To this republic were added the parts of the former Governorship of Turkestan inhabited by a majority of Kazakhs. It consists of the following regions: Aktyubinsk, Alma-Ata, Chimkent, Dzhambul, Dzhezkazgan, East Kazakhstan, Guryev, Karaganda, Kokchetav, Kustanai, Kzyl-Orda, Mangyshlak, North Kazakhstan, Pavlodar, Semipalatinsk, Taldy-Kurgan, Tselinograd, Turgai, Uralsk.

AREA AND POPULATION. Kazakhstan is bounded on the west by the Caspian Sea and the RSFSR, on the east by China, on the north by the RSFSR and on the south by Uzbekistan and Kirghizia. The area of the republic is 2,717,300 sq. km (1,049,155 sq. miles). It is the next in size to the RSFSR, is far larger than all the other Central Asian Soviet Republics combined and stretches nearly 3,000 km from west to east and over 1,500 km from north to south. Population (Jan. 1980) 14·8m., of whom 55% live in urban areas. The Kazakhs form 32·6%, Russians 42% and Ukrainians 7·2% (owing to the industrialization of the country since 1941 and the opening of virgin lands since 1945). The population includes over 100 nationalities.

The capital is Alma-Ata, formerly Verny; other large towns are Karaganda, Semipalatinsk, Chimkent and Petropavlovsk. In all there are 82 towns, 189 urban settlements and 218 rural districts.

CONSTITUTION AND GOVERNMENT. The Supreme Soviet, elected in 1980, consists of 510 deputies (1 per 20,000 population); 182 are women, 336 Communists. A new Constitution was adopted in April 1978.

At elections to the regional, district, urban and rural Soviets (19 June 1977), out of 123,266 deputies returned, 59,341 (48·1%) were women, 73,554 (59·7%) non-Party and 83,725 (67·9%) industrial workers and collective farmers.

President, Presidium of the Supreme Soviet: S. B. Niyazbekov.
Chairman, Council of Ministers: B. A. Ashimov.
First Secretary, Communist Party: D. A. Kunayev.

FINANCE. The budget (in 1m. new roubles) balanced as follows: 1965, 4,689; 1970, 6,072; 1977, 7,056; 1978, 7,234; 1980, 8,400; 1981, 8,784.

AGRICULTURE. Kazakh agriculture has changed from primarily nomad cattle breeding to production of grain, cotton and other industrial crops. In 1978 the crop area was 35·3m. hectares—over 16% of the total cultivated area of the USSR (1913, 4·2m.; 1940, 6·8m.).

1,827,000 hectares of land have an irrigation network.

The 'Ukrainka' winter wheat has been transformed into a spring wheat suitable for cultivation in Kazakhstan. Tobacco, rubber plants and mustard are also cultivated. Kazakhstan has rich orchards and vineyards; 25,000 hectares were under vines and 101,000 under orchards in 1978. Between 1954 and 1959, over 23m. hectares of virgin and long fallow land were opened up, 544 new state grain farms being organized for the purpose. Grain deliveries to the state were 10·5m. tons in 1960; 2·4m. in 1965; 13·4m. in 1970; 5·1m. in 1975; 8·2m. in 1977; 16,784 in 1978.

Kazakhstan is noted for its livestock, particularly its sheep, from which excellent quality wool is obtained. The Akharomerino is a newly developed crossbreed of merino sheep and the wild Akhar mountain ram. Livestock on 1 Jan. 1979 included 8·01m. cattle, 34·2m. sheep and goats and 2·6m. pigs.

There were, on 1 Jan. 1979, 418 collective farms and 2,035 state farms with 239,700 tractors and 112,400 grain combine harvesters. There were 5,293 rural power stations of 307,800 kwh. capacity.

Output of main agricultural products (in 1m. tonnes) in 1978 (1913 figures in brackets): All grains, 34·5 (2·2); cotton, 0·3 (0·015); sugar-beet, 2·5 (0); potatoes, 1·83 (0·18); other vegetables, 2·29; meat, 1 (0·44); milk, 4·4 (0·85); 3,352m. eggs (233m.); wool, 0·1 (0·04).

INDUSTRY. Kazakhstan is extremely rich in mineral resources. Coal and tungsten in Karaganda (in the centre), oil along the river Emba (in the west), copper, lead and zinc—Kazakhstan contains about one-half of the total deposits of these three metals contained in the USSR—Iceland spar (in the south), nickel and chromium in the Kustanai and Semipalatinsk regions, molybdenum and other minerals.

In 1943 big deposits of manganese were found in Eastern Kazakhstan; new coal seams were also discovered there. In South Kazakhstan new copper and bauxite deposits have been found.

Coal, oil, non-ferrous metallurgy, heavy engineering and chemical industries have brought Kazakhstan to the third place among the industrial republics of the USSR.

Coal output in 1977 was 93·7m. tons; oil, 23·3m. tons; steel, 5·6m. tons; rolled metal, 4·4m. tons; cement, 6·8m. tons; mineral fertilizers, 6·5m. tons; cotton fabrics, 101·2m. linear metres; leather footwear, 31·2m. pairs; woollen fabrics, 16·7m. linear metres; granulated sugar, 120,100 tons. The Leninogorsk and Chimkent lead plants, the Balkhash, Irtysh and Karaskpai copper-smelting works and others supply the country with nonferrous metals. A meat-packing plant has been built in Semipalatinsk, a fish cannery in Guryev, a chemical plant in Aktyubinsk, a tractor works at Pavlodar, and a superphosphate plant in Dzhambul. The oil industry in Emba and Aktyubinsk yields high-quality aviation oil. Iron ore output in 1977 was 23·4m. tons.

Aviation plays an important part in agriculture. About 14m. hectares were in 1970 treated from the air (destruction of pests, surface feeding of sugar-beet plantations, pollination of orchards, etc.).

Among recent enterprises are a large textile combine at Kustanai, hosiery factories at Djezkazgan, Leninogorsk and Aktyiubinsk, a sugar factory at Aksu, meat canneries at Djetygar and Kzyl-Orda.

Electric power output in 1979 was 59,700m. kwh.

There were, in 1979, 5·9m. (average for year) industrial and office workers in the national economy.

COMMUNICATIONS

Roads. In 1978 there were 97,400 km of motor roads (66,900 km hard surface).

Railways. A 430-km railway line between the settlements of Mointi and Chu in Kazakhstan to complete the Transkazakh trunk line, connecting Petropavlovsk, Akmolinsk, Karaganda and Balkhash, was opened in 1953. The new line links the Transkazakh trunk line with the Turkestan–Siberian railway carrying Karaganda coal to South Kazakhstan. The Akmolinsk–Pavlodar railway (438 km), a section of the South Siberian line, was opened in Dec. 1953. Other lines in operation are Dzhambul–Chalaktan, Akmolinsk–Kartaly, Uralsk–Iletsk, Guriev–Kandagach. In 1977 the total length of railways in operation was 14,160 km. Over 600 km of narrow-gauge line and 700 km of broad-gauge line were built in the virgin lands area in 1951–57.

Inland waterways. Total length 5,500 km.

Newspapers (1979). Of 429 newspapers, 157 were in the Kazakh language. Circulation of Kazakh-language newspapers, 1·8m., other languages, 3·5m.

EDUCATION. Nearly the whole population is literate. In 1979–80 there were 3·3m. pupils at 8,800 elementary and secondary schools; 231 technical colleges with 260,200 students, 53 higher educational institutions with 251,000 students, and 207 research institutes with 34,700 scientific personnel. The Kazakh Academy of Sciences, founded in 1945, had, in 1978, 31 institutions, the scientific staff of which numbered 3,728. 846,000 children were attending pre-school institutions.

HEALTH. In 1979 there were 45,700 doctors and 192,600 hospital beds.

Books of Reference

Central Statistical Dept. of Kazakh SSR., *Narodnoye Hoziaistvo Kazakhstana*. Alma-Ata, 1968
Alampiev, P., *Soviet Kazakhstan*. Moscow, 1958.—*Where Economic Inequality is No More*. Moscow, 1959
Grauman, J., and others, *The Kazakhs under Changing Russian Regimes*. Washington, 1951
Lias, G., *Kazak Exodus*. London, 1956

TURKMENISTAN
Tiurkmenostan Soviet Sotsialistik Respublikasy

HISTORY. The Turkmen Soviet Socialist Republic was formed on 27 Oct. 1924 and covers the territory of the former Trans-Caspian Region of Turkestan, the Charjiui vilayet of Bokhara and a part of Khiva situated on the right bank of the Oxus. In May 1925 the Turkmen Republic entered the Soviet Union as one of its constituent republics.

AREA AND POPULATION. Turkmenistan is bounded on the north by the Autonomous Kara-Kalpak Republic, a constituent of Uzbekistan, by Iran and Afghánistán on the south, by the Uzbek Republic on the east and the Caspian Sea on the west. The principal Turkmen tribes are the Tekkés of Merv and the Tekkés of the Attok, the Ersaris, Yomuds and Goklans. All speak closely related varieties of a Turkic language (of the south-western group); many are Sunni Mohammedans.

The country passed under Russian control in 1881, after the fall of the Turkoman stronghold of Gök-Tépé. 66% of the population are Turkmenians, most of whom were nomads before the First World War. 14·5% are Russians living mostly in urban areas, and 8·3% Uzbeks. There are also Kazakhs (3·2%), Tartars, Ukrainians, Armenians and others (1970 census).

The area of Turkmenistan is 488,100 sq. km (186,400 sq. miles), and its population in Jan. 1980 was 2·84m.

There are 5 regions: Chardzhou, Maruy, Ashkhabad, Tashauz and Krasnovodsk, comprising 42 rural districts, 15 towns and 74 urban settlements.

The capital is Ashkhabad (Poltoratsk); other large towns are Chardzhou (140,000), Maruy (Merv) (72,000), Nebit-Dag (67,000) and Krasnovodsk (55,000).

CONSTITUTION AND GOVERNMENT. The Supreme Soviet, elected in 1980, consists of 330 deputies (1 per 5,000 population); 107 are women, 224 Communists. A new Constitution was adopted in April 1978.

At elections to regional, district, urban and rural Soviets (19 June 1977), of 22,367 deputies returned, 10,506 (47%) were women, 12,708 (56·8%) non-Party and 15,425 (69%) industrial workers and collective farmers.

President, Presidium of the Supreme Soviet: A. M. Klychev.
Chairman, Council of Ministers and Foreign Minister: B. Yazkuliev.
First Secretary, Communist Party: M. G. Gapurov.

FINANCE. Budget estimates (in 1m. new roubles), 1965, 557; 1970, 724; 1977, 845; 1978, 861; 1980, 982; 1981, 1,078.

AGRICULTURE. The main occupation of the people is agriculture, based on irrigation. Turkmenistan produces cotton, wool, Astrakhan fur, etc. It is also famous for its carpets, and produces a special breed of Turkoman horses and the famous Karakul sheep.

There were 318 collective farms and 78 state farms in 1979, with 35,100 tractors and 1,000 grain combines. There were 608 rural power stations.

A considerable area is under Egyptian cotton, and from it has been evolved an original Soviet long-fibred cotton.

The main grain grown is maize. Sericulture, fruit and vegetable growing are also important; dates, olives, figs, sesame and other southern plants are grown. There is fishing in the Caspian. 900,000 hectares were under cultivation in 1978 (1913, 318,000; 1940, 411,000).

Between 1958 and 1970 the Kara-Kum Canal was extended to 860 km. In 1971 the fourth section, to reach the Caspian, was begun to reach 1,000 km. By 1978 over 892,000 hectares had been irrigated.

Livestock on 1 Jan. 1980: Cattle, 602,000; pigs, 158,000; sheep and goats, 4·5m.

Output of main agricultural products (in 1,000 tonnes) in 1978 (1913 figures in brackets): Wheat, 281 (113); cotton, 1,215 (69); vegetables, 284; grapes, 63; fruit, 39; meat, 67 (58); milk, 307 (63); wool, 15·3 (9·7); 243m. eggs (18m.).

INDUSTRY. Turkmenistan is rich in minerals, such as ozocerite, oil, coal, sulphur and salt. Industry is being developed, and there are now chemical, tailoring, textile, light, food, agricultural implements, cement and other factories, oil refineries, as well as ore-mining.

In the Kara-Kum Desert deposits of magnesium, minerals and coal were discovered, as well as some 50 new saltmines. Here a new oil town, Nebit-Dag, has sprung up. On the Kara-Bogaz bay a sulphate industry has been developed. Industrial output in 1977 included 14·8m. tons of oil, 564,000 tons of cement, 23·1m. linear metres of cotton fabrics, 3·5m. pairs of leather footwear. Electric power output was 5,700m. kwh. (in 1940): 62,581m. cu. metres of natural gas were produced.

In 1979 there were 678,000 industrial and office workers in the national economy.

COMMUNICATIONS. Length of motor roads 9,900 km (7,800 km hard surface). Motor communication exists between Ashkhabad and Meshed (Iran).

Length of railways, 2,120 km. The line Chardzhou–Kungrad crosses the Chardzhou and Tashauz regions of Turkmenia and runs across Uzbekistan. Another line connects Chardzhou and Urgench. Inland waterways, 1,300 km.

Airlines connect Leninsk and Tashauz, and Ashkhabad and remote areas in the west, north and east.

Newspapers (1979). Of 58 newspapers, 45 were in the Turkmen language. Circulation of Turkmenian-language newspapers, 787,000, other languages, 219,000.

EDUCATION. In 1979–80 there were 1,800 primary and secondary schools with 700,000 pupils, 6 higher educational institutions with 34,400 students, 34 technical colleges with 33,000 students, and 11 music and art schools. The Turkmen Academy of Sciences directs the work of 14 learned institutions with a staff of 923 scientists; there were 58 research institutions in all, with 5,000 research workers, in

1978. A Turkmenian State University was opened in 1951: in 1973 it had 10,124 students.
In 1979, 131,000 children were attending pre-school institutions.

HEALTH. In 1979 there were 7,700 doctors and 29,400 hospital beds.

UZBEKISTAN
Ozbekiston Soviet Sotsialistik Respublikasy

HISTORY. In Oct. 1917 the Tashkent Soviet assumed authority, and in the following years established its power throughout Turkestan. The semi-independent Khanates of Khiva and Bokhara were first (1920) transformed into 'People's Republics', then (1923–24) into Soviet Socialist Republics and finally merged in the Uzbek SSR and other republics.

The Uzbek Soviet Socialist Republic was formed on 27 Oct. 1924 from lands formerly included in Turkestan. It includes a large part of the Samarkand region, the southern part of the Syr Darya, Western Ferghana, the western plains of Bukhara, the Kara-Kalpak ASSR and the Uzbek regions of Khorezm. In May 1925 Uzbekistan, by the decision of the Congress of Soviets of the USSR, was accepted as one of the constituent republics in the Soviet Union.

AREA AND POPULATION. Uzbekistan is bordered on the north by the Kazakh Soviet Socialist Republic, on the east by the Kirghiz Soviet Socialist Republic and the Tadzhik Soviet Socialist Republic, on the south by Afghánistán and on the west by the Turkmen Soviet Socialist Republic. The Uzbeks, who form 65% of the population, were the ruling race in Central Asia, until the arrival of the Russians during the third quarter of the 19th century. The several native states over which Uzbek dynasties formerly ruled were founded in the 15th century upon the ruins of Tamerlane's empire. The Uzbek speak Jagatai Turkish, which is related to Osmanli and Azerbaijan Turkish; many are Sunni Moslems. Russians number 12·5%, other Central Asians 10·7%, Tartars 4·9%.

The area of Uzbekistan is 447,400 sq. km (172,741 sq. miles). The population in Jan. 1980 was 15,774,000 (40% urban). The country comprises the following regions: Andizhan, Bukhara, Dzhizak (formed 29 Dec. 1973), Ferghana, Kashkadar, Khorezm, Namangan, Samarkand, Surkhan-Darya, Syr-Darya (formed 16 Feb. 1963), Tashkent and the Autonomous Soviet Republic of Kara Kalpakia. The capital of the Republic is Tashkent; other large towns are Samarkand, Andizhan, Namangan. There are 87 towns, 84 urban settlements and 138 rural districts.

On 19 Sept. 1963 the Supreme Soviet of the USSR confirmed decisions of the Supreme Soviets of Kazakhstan and Uzbekistan, transferring over 40,000 sq. km from the former to the latter to ensure more efficient use of the 'Hungry Steppe'.

CONSTITUTION AND GOVERNMENT. The Supreme Soviet, elected in 1980, consists of 510 deputies (1 per 15,000 population); 178 are women, 346 Communists. A new Constitution was adopted in April 1978.

At elections to the regional, district, urban and rural Soviets (19 June 1977), of 93,430 deputies returned, 44,953 (48·1%) were women, 51,691 (55·3%) non-Party and 64,600 (69·1%) industrial workers and collective farmers.

President, Presidium of the Supreme Soviet: I. B. Usmanhodjayev (Dec. 1978).
Chairman, Council of Ministers: N. D. Hudaiberdyev.
First Secretary, Communist Party: S. R. Rashidov.

FINANCE. Budget estimates (in 1m. new roubles), 1965, 2,133; 1970, 3,228; 1977, 4,465; 1978, 4,636; 1980, 5,225; 1981, 5,659.

AGRICULTURE. Uzbekistan is a land of intensive farming, based on artificial irrigation. It is the chief cotton-growing area in the USSR and the third in the world. About 3·3m. hectares of collective and state farmland have irrigation networks, totalling 150,000 km in length, and all are in full use.

In 1939 the Ferghana Canal (270 km) was built. During 1940, among the irrigation canals completed were: the North Ferghana Canal (165 km), and Andreyev South Ferghana Canal (108 km) and the first section of the Tashkent Canal (63 km). A canal from the Amu-Darya to Bokhara across the Kzyl-Kum and Ust-Urt deserts (180 km) was completed in 1965. A 200-km canal joining the river Zeravshan with the Kashka Darya at the village of Paruz was completed in Aug. 1955; it is part of the Iski–Angara Canal. The first section (93 km) of a canal irrigating the southern 'Hungry Steppe' was opened in 1960; 500,000 hectares of this desert were under cultivation in 1967.

Agriculture flourishes, particularly in the well-watered, warm, rich oases areas, such as the Ferghana valley, Zeravshan, Tashkent and Khorezm, where cotton, fruit, silk and rice are cultivated. In the higher-lying plains grain is grown; the wide desert and semi-desert area of Western Uzbekistan is mainly given to pasture land and the breeding of the Karakul sheep; there is a Karakul institute at Samarkand.

Orchards occupied 195,000 hectares and the vineyards 70,000 hectares in 1977. The Central Asian Branch of the Scientific Research Institute of Viticulture in Tashkent has produced new frost resistant grapes by crossing the wild Amur grape with Central Asian and European types. In 1979 there were 927 collective farms and 744 state farms, with 151,800 tractors and 27,400 cotton picking and grain combines. Ploughing, cotton-sowing and cultivation are completely mechanized; cotton-picking over 46%.

Uzbekistan provides 67% of the total cotton, 50% of the total rice and 60% of the total lucerne grown in the USSR. The area under crops was 2,189,000 hectares in 1913, 3,036,000 hectares in 1940 and 3·9m. hectares in 1978.

Livestock on 1 Jan. 1979: 3·23m. cattle, 8·1m. sheep and goats and 368,000 pigs.

Output of main agricultural products (in 1,000 tonnes) in 1978 (1913 figures in tons in brackets): Wheat, 757 (513); maize, 1,052 (39); cotton, 5,763 (517); potatoes, 227 (46); fruit, 124; grapes, 103; meat, 302 (89); milk, 2,073 (231); wool, 28·4 (5·3); 1,397m. eggs (87m.).

Afforestation over an area of 50,000 hectares has been carried out to protect the Bokhara and Karakul oases from the advancing Kzyl-Kum sands and to stop the sand-drifts in a number of districts of Central Ferghana.

INDUSTRY. Of its mineral resources, in addition to oil and coal, copper and building materials and ozocerite deposits are now also exploited. New very rich coal deposits were discovered in 1944 and 1947 near Tashkent.

There are nearly 1,600 factories and mills. They include a factory of agricultural machinery (in Tashkent), a cement factory, a sulphur-mine, an oxygen factory, a paper-mill, a leather factory, textile-mills, clothing factories, iron and steel works, the Chirchik electro-chemical plant, a superphosphate plant in Kokand and oil refineries, coalmines, etc. Output in 1977 included 5·4m. tons of coal, 411,000 tons of steel, 1·4m. tons of oil, 3·54m. tons of cement, 5·9m. tons of mineral fertilizers, 223·1m. linear metres of cotton fabrics, 107m. linear metres of silk fabrics, 27·1m. pairs of leather footwear, 784,000 hectolitres of wine (apart from collective farm output). Gold is being worked at Muruntau, Chadak and Kochbulak.

The Tashkent power station (2m. kw.) was completed in 1971. Power output in 1977 was 34,900m. kwh. (481m. kwh. in 1940). Two natural-gas pipelines (Djaikak–Tashkent, Ferghana–Kokand) and a third from Bokhara to the Urals are operating. Natural gas output (1976) was 36,100m. cu. metres.

In 1979 there were 4m. industrial and office workers in the national economy.

COMMUNICATIONS. The total length of railway in 1978 was 3,390 km. Branches lead to Karshe-Kitab, Kerki-Termez, Jalal-Abad, Namangan, Andijan and other centres. In 1947–55 a new line was built from Chardzhou to Kungrad.

The Great Uzbek Highway was completed in April 1941. Total length of motor roads in 1978 was 51,900 km (hard surface, 31,800 km). Inland waterways, 1,100 km.

An airline, serving all of Central Asia, is most developed in Uzbekistan.

Newspapers (1979). There were 185 newspapers in the Uzbek and Kara-Kalpak languages out of a total of 267. Circulation of Uzbek-language newspapers, 3·7m., other languages, 1·1m.

EDUCATION. In 1979–80 there were 9,400 elementary and secondary schools with 4m. pupils, 43 higher educational establishments with 272,900 students and 213 technical colleges with 226,600 students. Uzbekistan has an Academy of Sciences and 188 research institutes with 33,600 scientific staff, 3,783 of them in 30 institutions of the Uzbek Academy of Sciences. There are universities and medical schools in Tashkent and Samarkand. In 1979, 849,000 children were attending pre-school institutions.

The Uzbek Arabic script was in 1929 replaced by the Latin alphabet which in 1940 was superseded by one based on the Cyrillic alphabet.

HEALTH. In 1979 there were 43,700 doctors and 176,500 hospital beds.

Books of Reference

Istoria Uzbekskoi SSSR. 2 vols. Tashkent, 1955–57
Pobeda Oktiabrskoi Revolutsii v Uzbekistane. Vol. I. Tashkent, 1963

KARA-KALPAK AUTONOMOUS SOVIET SOCIALIST REPUBLIC

Area, 165,600 sq. km (63,920 sq. miles); population (Jan. 1980), 930,000. Capital, Nukus (113,400). The Karakalpaks are first mentioned in written records in the 16th century as tributary to Bokhara, and later to the Kazakh Khanate. In the second half of the 19th century, as a result of the Russian conquest of Central Asia, they came under Russian rule. On 11 May 1925 the territory was constituted within the then Kazakh Autonomous Republic (of the Russian Federation) as an Autonomous Region. On 20 March 1932 it became an Autonomous Republic within the Russian Federation, and on 5 Dec. 1936 it became part of the Uzbek SSR.

185 deputies were elected to its Supreme Soviet on 20 Feb. 1980, of whom 68 are women and 118 Communists.

Its manufactures are in the field of light industry—bricks, leather goods, furniture, canning, wine. Output of cotton in 1977 was 371,000 tons (in 1913, 8,000 tons). There were 4,217 tractors. Cattle numbered 308,000 and sheep and goats 621,000. There were 43 collective and 84 state farms. 218,300 industrial and office workers, and 14,800 specialists with a higher education, were employed in the national economy.

In 1979–80 there were 256,400 pupils at schools, 24,718 at technical colleges, and 5,543 at university. There is a branch of the Uzbek Academy of Sciences with 190 scientific staff.

There were 1,878 doctors and 8,920 hospital beds.

TADZHIKISTAN
Respublikai Sovieth Sotsialistii Tojikiston

HISTORY. The Tadzhik Soviet Socialist Republic was formed from those regions of Bokhara and Turkestan where the population consisted mainly of Tadzhiks. It was admitted as a constituent republic of the Soviet Union on 5 Dec. 1929.

AREA AND POPULATION. Tadzhikistan is situated between 39° 40′ and 36° 40′ N. lat. and 67° 20′ and 75° E. long., north of the Oxus (Amu-Darya). On the west and north it is bordered by Uzbekistan and by the Kirghiz Soviet Socialist Republic; on the east by Chinese Turkestan and on the south by Afghánistán. It includes three regions (Leninabad, Kurgan-Tyube and Kulyab) and 41 rural districts, 18 towns and 49 urban settlements, together with the Gorno-Badakhshan Autonomous Region. Its highest mountains are Communism Peak (7,495 metres) and Lenin Peak (7,127 metres). Even the lowest valleys in the Pamirs are not below 3,500 metres above sea-level. The huge mountain glaciers are the source of many rapid rivers—the tributaries of the Amu-Darya, which flows from east to west along the southern border of Tadzhikistan. About 56% of the population are Tadzhiks. They speak an Iranian dialect, little different from Persian, and they are considered to be the descendants of the original Aryan population of Turkestan. Unlike the Persians, the Tadzhiks are mostly Sunnis. Of the rest, 23% are Uzbeks living in the north-west of the republic. Russians and Ukrainians number 13% (1970 census).

The area of the territory is 143,100 sq. km (55,240 sq. miles). Population (Jan. 1980), 3·9m. The capital is Dushanbe. Other large towns are Leninabad (130,000), Kurgan-Tyube, Kulyab.

CONSTITUTION AND GOVERNMENT. The Supreme Soviet, elected in 1980, consists of 349 deputies (1 per 5,000 population); 123 are women and 238 Communists. A new Constitution was adopted in April 1978.

At elections to the district, urban and rural Soviets and the regional Soviet of Gorno-Badakhshan (19 June 1977), out of 24,890 deputies returned, 11,813 (47·5%) were women, 13,817 (55·5%) non-Party and 17,239 (69·2%) industrial workers and collective farmers.

President, Presidium of the Supreme Soviet: Makhmadullo Kholov.
Chairman, Council of Ministers and Foreign Minister: R. Nabiev.
First Secretary, Communist Party: D. Rasulov.

FINANCE. Budget estimates (in 1m. new roubles), 1965, 553; 1970, 827; 1977, 1,077; 1978, 1,117; 1980, 1,256; 1981, 1,229.

AGRICULTURE. The occupations of the population are mainly farming, horticulture and cattle breeding. Area under crops in 1978 was 800,000 hectares (1913, 494,000; 1940, 807,000). Wine production, 1976, was 450,000 hectolitres.

There are 43,000 km of irrigation canals: the irrigation networks cover about 602,000 hectares of land.

Tadzhikistan grows many varieties of fruit, including apricots, figs, olives, pomegranates, a local variety of lemons and oranges, and in the south sugar-cane has been grown. Even on the highest mountain plateaux of the Pamirs, 'the roof of the world', the biological station of Tadzhikistan (3,860 metres above sea-level) has succeeded in raising crops of 60 varieties of barley, 10 varieties of oats, 4 of wheat, as well as vegetables. Eucalyptus and geranium are grown for the perfumery industry. Jute, rice and millet are also grown.

Tadzhikistan contains rich pasture lands, and cattle breeding is a very important branch of its agriculture. Livestock on 1 Jan. 1979: 1·1m. cattle, 2·9m. sheep and goats and 123,000 pigs.

The Gissar sheep is famous in the south for its meat and fat; the Karakul sheep is widely bred for its wool.

There were 179 collective farms (all with electric power) and 198 state farms in 1979, with 29,800 tractors and 2,900 cotton and grain combine harvesters.

Output of main agricultural products (in 1,000 tonnes) in 1978 (1913 figures in tons in brackets): Wheat, 183 (133); maize, 48 (2); cotton, 903 (32); potatoes, 142 (10); other vegetables, 340; fruit, 287; grapes, 175; meat, 92·4 (48); milk, 461 (102); wool, 5·6 (2·1); 337m. eggs (20m.).

INDUSTRY. The original small-scale handicraft industries have been replaced by big industrial enterprises, including mining, engineering, food, textile, clothing and silk factories.

There are rich deposits of brown coal, lead, zinc and oil (in the north of the republic), rare elements, such as uranium, radium, arsenic and bismuth. Asbestos, mica, corundum and emery, lapis lazuli, potassium salts, sulphur and other minerals have been found in other parts of the republic.

Industrial output in 1977 included: 800,000 tons of coal, 274,000 tons of oil, 1·01m. tons of cement, 116m. linear metres of cotton fabrics, 58m. linear metres of silk fabrics; leather footwear, 7·3m. pairs; refrigerators, 134,400.

There are 80 big electrical stations. The hydro-electric Varzob station began to operate in 1954, that at Kairak-Kum on the Syr Darya River was completed in 1957 and 2 more at Murgab in 1964. Output in 1979 was 10,533m. kwh. (in 1940, 62m. kwh.).

Construction of an electro-chemical combine, the largest in the USSR, has begun in the Yavan steppe in south Tadzhikistan, and the 3·2m. kw. power station in the upper reaches of the Vakhsh River was near completion in 1979.

In 1979 there were 905,000 industrial and office workers in the national economy.

COMMUNICATIONS

Roads. There are 13,200 km of motor roads. Of these, 10,500 km are hard surface, including the Osh–Khorog (700 km), Yasui–Bazar–Charm (107 km) and Dushanbe–Khorog in the Pamirs (557 km) roads.

Railways. A railway line between Termez and Dushanbe (258 km) connects the republic with the railway system of the USSR. The mountainous nature of the republic makes ordinary railway construction difficult; accordingly 345 km of narrow gauge railways have been constructed (Kurgan–Tyube–Piandzh and Dushanbe–Kurgan–Tyube, connecting Dushanbe with the cotton-growing Vakhsh valley are particularly important).

Aviation. Dushanbe is connected by air with Moscow, Tashkent, Baku and the regional and district centres of the republic.

Shipping. A steamship line on the Amu-Darya runs between Termez, Sarava and Jilikulam on the river Vakhsh (200 km).

Newspapers. (1979). 55 newspapers had a total circulation of 1,285,000. Of these, 51 with 938,000 circulation, were in Tadzhik.

EDUCATION. In 1979–80 there were 3,000 primary and secondary schools with 1m. pupils, 9 higher educational institutions with 55,000 students and 38 technical colleges with 40,100 students; the Tadzhik state university had 12,467 students. In 1979, 105,000 children were attending pre-school institutions. In 1951 an Academy of Sciences was established; it has 17 institutions, the scientific staff of which numbers 1,267; there are 61 research institutions in all, with 6,900 scientific personnel. The Pamir research station is the highest altitude meteorological observatory in the world.

In 1940 a new alphabet based on Cyrillic was introduced.

HEALTH. There are 277 hospitals as well as maternity homes, clinics and special institutes to combat tropical diseases. There were 8,200 doctors in 1977 and 37,400 hospital beds.

GORNO-BADAKHSHAN AUTONOMOUS REGION

Comprising the Pamir massif along the borders of Afghánistán and China, the region was set up on 2 Jan. 1925. Area, 63,700 sq. km (24,590 sq. miles); population (Jan. 1979), 127,000 (83% Tadjiks, 11% Kirghiz). Capital, Khorog (14,800).

There were 36,800 pupils in 268 schools in 1977–78 and 170 students in technical colleges, 151 doctors and 1,005 hospital beds.

Mining industries are developed (gold, rock-crystal, mica, coal, salt). Wheat, fruit and fodder crops are grown and cattle and sheep are bred in the western parts. In 1978 there were 65,500 cattle, 347,000 sheep and goats.

In 1976 there were 17 collective farms and 15 state (livestock) farms.

Books of Reference

Academy of Science of Tadzhikistan, *Istoria Tadzhikskogo Naroda.* 3 vols. Moscow, 1963–65
Chumichev, D. A., *Tadzhikskaya SSR.* Moscow, 1954
Luknitsky, P., *Soviet Taikistan* [In English]. Moscow, 1954

KIRGHIZIA
Kyrgyz Sovietik Sotsialistik Respublikasy

HISTORY. After the establishment of the Soviet regime in Russia, Kirghizia was part of Soviet Turkestan, which itself became an Autonomous Soviet Socialist Republic within the RSFSR in April 1921. In 1924, when Central Asia was reorganized territorially on a national basis, Kirghizia was separated from Turkestan and formed into an autonomous region within the RSFSR. On 1 Feb. 1926 the Government of the RSFSR transformed Kirghizia into an Autonomous Soviet Socialist Republic within the RSFSR, and finally in Dec. 1936 Kirghizia was proclaimed one of the constituent Soviet Socialist Republics of the USSR.

AREA AND POPULATION. The territory of Kirghizia covers 198,500 sq. km (76,460 sq. miles), and its population in Jan. 1980 was 3·6m. The republic comprises 3 regions: Issyk-Kul, Naryn and Osh. There are 18 towns, 31 urban settlements and 37 rural districts. Its capital is Frunze (formerly Pishpek). Other large towns are Osh (173,000), Przhevalsk (52,000), Kyzyl-Kia, Tokmak.

Kirghizia is situated on the Tian-Shan mountains and bordered on the east by China, on the west by Kazakhstan and Uzbekistan, on the north by Kazakhstan and in the south by Tadzhikistan. The Kirghizians are of Turkic origin and form 44% of the population; the rest are Russians (29%), Ukrainians (4%), Uzbeks (11·3%) and others (1970 census).

CONSTITUTION AND GOVERNMENT. The Supreme Soviet, elected in 1980, consists of 350 deputies (1 per 5,000 population); 126 are women, 235 Communists. A new Constitution was adopted in April 1978.

At elections to the regional, district, urban and rural Soviets (19 June 1977), of the 24,890 deputies returned, 11,813 (47·5%) were women, 13,817 (55·5%) non-Party and 17,239 (69·2%) industrial workers and collective farmers.

President, Presidium of the Supreme Soviet: S. I. Ibraimov.
Chairman, Council of Ministers: A. S. Suyumbayev.
First Secretary, Communist Party: T. U. Usubaliev.

FINANCE. Budget estimates (in 1m. new roubles), 1965, 603; 1970, 886; 1977, 1,201; 1978, 1,254; 1980, 1,440; 1981, 1,478.

AGRICULTURE. Kirghizia is famed for its livestock breeding. On 1 Jan. 1979 there were 957,000 cattle, 298,000 pigs, 10m. sheep and goats. Yaks are bred as meat and dairy cattle, and graze on high altitudes unsuitable for other cattle. Crossed with domestic cattle, hybrids are produced much heavier than ordinary Kirghiz cattle and giving twice the yield of milk. The Kirghizian horse is famed for its endurance, but it is of small stature; it has in recent years been crossed with Don, Arab and other breeds.

On 1 Jan. 1979 there were 182 collective and 214 state farms. Area under crops (1978), 1·3m. hectares (1913, 640,000; 1940, 1,056,000). There were 25,900 tractors and 4,200 grain combine harvesters and 1,600 cotton combines in 1978; nearly all collective and state farms received electric power.

Kirghizia raises wheat sufficient for its own use and other grains and fodder, particularly lucerne; also sugar-beet, hemp, kenaf, kendyr, tobacco, medicinal plants and rice. Sericulture, fruit, grapes and vegetables and bee-keeping are major branches of Kirghiz agriculture. Agriculture is highly mechanized; nearly all the area under crops is worked by tractors. In 1977 irrigation networks in collective and state farms covered 933,000 hectares; practically all were in use. A canal in the western Tien-Shan ranges and a reservoir in the Urto-Tokoi mountains are being constructed.

The health resorts of Jety-Oguz (7,200 ft) and Jalal-Abad are famous for their mild alpine climate and mineral springs.

Output of main agricultural products (in 1,000 tonnes) in 1979 (1913 figures in tons in brackets): Wheat, 767 (250); maize, 193 (37); cotton, 28 (28); sugar-beet,

SOVIET CENTRAL ASIA 1281

1,418 (0); potatoes, 227 (19); other vegetables, 361; fruit, 177; grapes, 70; meat, 154 (39); milk, 662 (91); wool, 33 (4·7); 416m. eggs (19m.).

INDUSTRY. Kirghizia contains 500 large modern industrial enterprises, including sugar refineries, tanneries, cotton and wool-cleansing works, flour-mills, a tobacco factory, food, timber, textile, engineering, metallurgical, oil and mining enterprises.

The output of coal in 1976 was 4·3m. tons; oil, 230,000 tons; silk fabrics, 9·7m. linear metres; cotton fabrics, 64m. linear metres.

Granulated sugar, (1977) 270,000 tons; leather footwear, 10·1m. pairs.

Hydro-electric power stations are being built in the Central Tien-Shans and the cotton-growing districts in the Osh Region, the Chui valley and on the shore of Lake Issyk-Kul. Power output (1979) was 7,760m. kwh.

There were, in 1979, 1,076,000 industrial and office workers in the national economy.

COMMUNICATIONS. In the north a railway runs from Lugovaya through Frunze to Rybachi on Lake Issyk-Kul. Towns in the southern valleys are linked by short lines with the Ursatyevskaya–Andizhan railway in Uzbekistan. Total length of railway is 370 km. Most of the traffic is by road; there were 22,300 km of motor roads (15,200 hard surface) in 1978. A road tunnel through the Tien Shan mountains at an altitude of 9,600 ft, connecting Frunze and Osh, is being constructed. Inland waterways, 600 km. Airlines link Frunze with Moscow and Tashkent.

Newspapers (1979). Of 108 newspapers with 1,237,000 circulation, 60 with 772,000 circulation are in the Kirghiz language.

EDUCATION. Kirghizia had 1,700 primary, continuation (8-year) and secondary schools with 1m. pupils in 1979–80; 140,000 children attended 853 pre-school institutions. There were also 9 higher educational institutions with 55,100 students, 39 technical and teachers' training colleges with 48,300 students, as well as music and art schools. The Kirghizian Academy of Sciences was established in 1954. In 1978 there were 65 research institutes, 18 of them, with 1,423 scientific staff, under the Kirghiz Academy of Sciences; the others have scientist staffs of 6,225. A university was opened in 1951. It has 13,370 students, 6,268 full-time, 1,054 evening and 6,048 correspondence students taking a full degree course. In Sept. 1940 a new alphabet, based on Cyrillic, was introduced.

HEALTH. In 1979 there were 10,000 doctors and 42,200 hospital beds.

Books of Reference

Istoria Kirgizii. Frunze, 1956
Ryazantsev, S. N., *Kirghizia.* Moscow, 1951

UNITED ARAB EMIRATES

Population: 1·04m. (1980)
GNP per capita: US$14,230 (1978)

HISTORY. From Sha'am, 35 miles south-west of Ras Musam dam, for nearly 400 miles to Khor al Odeid at the south-eastern end of the peninsula of Qatar, the coast, formerly known as the Trucial Coast, of the Gulf (together with 50 miles of the coast of the Gulf of Oman) belongs to the rulers of the 7 Trucial States. In 1820 these rulers signed a treaty prescribing peace with the British Government. This treaty was followed by further agreements providing for the suppression of the slave trade and by a series of other engagements, of which the most important are the Perpetual Maritime Truce (May 1853) and the Exclusive Agreement (March 1892). Under the latter, the sheikhs, on behalf of themselves, their heirs and successors, undertook that they would on no account enter into any agreement or correspondence with any power other than the British Government, receive foreign agents, cede, sell or give for occupation any part of their territory save to the British Government.

British forces withdrew from the Gulf at the end of 1971 and the treaties whereby Britain had been responsible for the defence and foreign relations of the Trucial States were terminated, being replaced on 2 Dec. 1971 by a treaty of friendship between Britain and the United Arab Emirates. The United Arab Emirates (formed 2 Dec. 1971) consists of the former Trucial States: Abu Dhabi, Dubai, Sharjah, Ajman, Umm al Qawain, Ras al Khaimah (joined in Feb. 1972) and Fujairah. The small state of Kalba was merged with Sharjah in 1952. *See* map in THE STATESMAN'S YEAR-BOOK, 1972–73, The Gulf States of the Middle East.

AREA AND POPULATION. The Emirates are bounded north by the Persian Gulf, east by Oman, south and west by Saudi Arabia, north-west by Qatar. The area of these states is approximately 32,300 sq. miles (92,100 sq. km). The total population at census (1980), 1,040,275. About one-tenth are nomads.

Population (1978 estimate): Abu Dhabi, 235,662; Ajman, 21,566; Dubai, 206,861; Fujairah, 26,498; Ras al Khaimah, 57,282; Sharjah, 88,188; Umm al Quawain, 16,789.

GOVERNMENT. The Emirates are a federation, headed by a Supreme Council which is composed of the 7 rulers and which in turn appoints a Council of Ministers. The Council of Ministers drafts legislation and a federal budget; its proposals are submitted to a federal National Council of 40 elected members which may propose amendments but has no executive power.

President: HH Sheikh Zayed bin Sultan al Nahyan, Ruler of Abu Dhabi.

Members of the Supreme Council of Rulers:

HH Sheikh Rashid bin Saeed al-Maktoum, Vice-President and Ruler of Dubai.
HH Sheikh Sultan bin Mohammed al-Qasimi, Ruler of Sharjah.
HH Sheikh Saqr bin Mohammed al-Qasimi, Ruler of Ras al Khaimah.
HH Sheikh Rashid bin Ahmed al-Mualla, Ruler of Umm al Qaiwain.
HH Sheikh Hamad bin Mohammed al Sharqi, Ruler of Fujairah.
HH Sheikh Rashid bin Humaid al-Nuaimi, Ruler of Ajman.

The Council of Ministers formed in July 1979 was:

Prime Minister: Sheikh Zayed bin Sultan al Nahyan.
Deputy Prime Ministers: Sheikh Maktoum bin Rashid al-Maktoum; Sheikh Hamdan bin Mohammed al-Nahyan.
Interior: Sheikh Mubarak bin Mohammed al-Nayhan. *Finance and Industry:* Sheikh Hamdan bin Rashid al-Maktoum. *Defence:* Sheikh Mohammed bin Rashid

al-Maktoum. *Foreign Affairs:* Ahmed Khalifa al-Suweidi. *Petroleum and Mineral Resources:* Dr Mana Said al-Otaiba. *Economy and Commerce:* Sheikh Sultan bin Ahmed al-Mualla. *Information and Culture:* Sheikh Ahmed bin Hamed. *Communications:* Mohammed Said al-Mualla. *Internal Affairs:* Hamouda bin Ali Dhariri. *Public Works and Housing:* Mohammed Khalifa al-Kindi. *Education and Youth:* Sayyed Said Salman. *Minister of State:* Sheikh Ahmad Sultan al-Qasimi (*Without Portfolio*). *Planning:* Said al-Ghobash. *Cabinet Affairs:* Said al-Ghaith. *Minister of State for Supreme Council Affairs:* Sheikh Abdul Aziz al-Qasimi. *Justice, Islamic Affairs and AWQAF:* Mohammed Abdul Rahman al-Bakr. *Agriculture and Fisheries:* Said al-Raqbani. *Minister of State for Foreign Affairs:* Rashid Abdullah. *Water and Electricity:* Humaid Nasser al-Owais. *Labour and Social Affairs:* Saif al-Jarwan. *Health:* Hamad Abdul Rahman al-Madfa.

National flag: Three horizontal stripes of green, white, black, with a vertical red strip in the hoist.

DEFENCE

Army. The Army consists of 1 Royal Guard brigade, 4 armoured, 7 infantry, 3 artillery and 3 air defence battalions. The strength was (1979) 23,500.

Navy. The Navy has 6 large and 9 small patrol craft and 15 light launches and tenders. Four fast attack craft are on order from the Federal Republic of Germany. Personnel (1980) numbered 1,000 officers and ratings.

Air Force. Formation of an air wing in Abu Dhabi, to support land forces, began in 1968 with the purchase of 2 Britten-Norman Islander light STOL transports and some light helicopters. Expansion has been rapid. Current equipment includes 26 Mirage 5 supersonic fighter-bombers, 3 Mirage 5R tactical reconnaissance aircraft and 3 Mirage 5D 2-seat trainers; 7 Hunter fighters and reconnaissance fighters and 2 Hunter 2-seat trainers; 2 C-130 Hercules and 4 Buffalo turboprop transports; 3 Caribou and 4 Islander transports; and about 20 Alouette III, Puma and Agusta-Bell 205 light helicopters. Initial personnel were mostly British but considerable assistance is now being received from Arab countries and from Pakistan. The air wing became the Air Force of Abu Dhabi in 1972, in which year 3 JetRanger helicopters were transferred to the air wing of the Union Defence Force, since combined with the Dubai Police Air Wing to form a single component of the United Emirates Air Force. Current equipment of the Dubai Air Wing of the UEAF, bought mainly in Italy, comprises 9 Aermacchi MB 326K jet light attack aircraft, 1 Aeritalia G222 twin-turboprop transport, 1 piston-engined SF-260W armed basic trainer and 2MB 326L jet trainers, 4 Bell 205A-1, 3 Bell 212 and 6 JetRanger helicopters and 1 Cessna 182 liaison aircraft, plus a Boeing 720B transport for VIP use.

INTERNATIONAL RELATIONS

Membership. The UAE became a member of the Arab League on 6 Dec. and of the UN on 9 Dec. 1971.

External Debt. The UAE (mainly the government of Dubai) borrowed about $205m. on Eurocurrency markets in 1976 and about $850m. in 1977.

Aid. Abu Dhabi committed 25% of government oil revenues to external aid 1971–76; this included aid to other Arab countries and loans at concessionary rates through the Abu Dhabi Fund for Arab Economic Development. The Government of Abu Dhabi has also committed funds to the IMF and the World Bank.

ECONOMY

Planning. Public projects completed include the 15-berth Port Rashid harbour opened 1972. A municipal sewerage scheme is under way and a police headquarters is planned. Further developments include reclamation of part of the seafront, improvement of the creek unloading facilities, a traffic tunnel, and additional bridge over the creek. In Sharjah, Mina Khalid is now operational and ships are using the new jetty, while improvement of the creek entrance and additional wharfage are now being undertaken. There are plans for a cement works and a flour-mill in Dubai in the near future and a large deep-water harbour is being constructed in Abu Dhabi.

Budget. Revenue is principally derived from oil-concession payments. The federal budget (1980) UD 15,972m.

Currency. The UAE issued its own currency in 1972 based on the *dirham.* 1 UAE *dirham* = 10 *dinar* = 1,000 *fils.* There are notes of 1, 5, 10, 50, 100 and 1,000 *dirham* and coins of 1, 5, 10, 25, 50 and 100 *fils.* Rate of exchange, March 1981: £1 = 7·48 *dirham;* US$1 = 3·672 *dirham.*

Banking. The British Bank of the Middle East has branches in Dubai, Abu Dhabi, Sharjah, Fujairah, Ajman and Ras al Khaimah; the Chartered Bank has branches in Dubai, Sharjah, Abu Dhabi and Al Ain; the National & Grindlays Bank (Ottoman Branch) has branches in Abu Dhabi and Sharjah. The Arab Bank has branches in Ajman, Ras al Khaimah, Sharjah, Abu Dhabi and Dubai; the Citibank has branches in Dubai, Sharjah and Abu Dhabi; the Habib Bank of Pakistan has branches in Abu Dhabi, Dubai and Sharjah and the United Bank Ltd of Pakistan branches in Dubai, Sharjah, Abu Dhabi and Al Ain. Barclays Bank International has branches in Abu Dhabi, Dubai, Ras Al Khaimah and Sharjah. There is also the National Bank of Dubai, formed in 1963, which has a branch in Abu Dhabi and Umm al Qaiwain, and the Bank of Oman Ltd, formed in 1967, which has branches in Ajman, Abu Dhabi and Dubai. The Commercial Bank opened in Dubai in 1969. The Bank Sadarat of Iran has branches in Abu Dhabi, Dubai and Sharjah. The National Bank of Abu Dhabi, formed in 1967, has its head office in Abu Dhabi and a branch office in Dubai.

The UAE is to become the headquarters of the new Arab Monetary Fund, which will have an initial capital of 250m. Arab Dinar units of account, worth about US$900m., and is providing 15m. units of account as its contribution.

ENERGY AND NATURAL RESOURCES

Oil. *Abu Dhabi.* Until the end of 1972 production was in the hands of 2 major companies, the Abu Dhabi Petroleum Co. and the Abu Dhabi Marine Area. The Government has acquired a 60% interest in both companies. Ownership in 1976 was as follows: *ADPC*, 60% Government; 9·5% BP; 9·5% Shell; 9·5% CFP; 4·75% Mobil; 2% Partex. *ADMA*, 60% Government; 26·7% BP/Japan Oil Development Co.; 13·3% CFP. A Japanese company, Abu Dhabi Oil Co. (ADOCO) began production from its Mubarraz field in 1973. There are other companies which have concessions in the State: Japan's Middle East Oil; a US consortium led by Pan Ocean Oil and Sunningdale Oils of Canada. A State Petroleum Co., the Abu Dhabi National Oil Co. (ADNOC), was formed in 1971 and began to set up its own tanker fleet known as the Abu Dhabi National Tankers Co. (ADNATCO). At the end of 1972 Abu Dhabi signed a participation agreement which would have given it an immediate 25% interest in the companies, rising to 51% by 1982. Oil production, 1979, 534·1m. bbls.

Dubai. In July 1975 Dubai decided to take full control of all foreign oil and gas operations in the State. The companies were to remain however. A Dubai producing group was set up to comprise the foreign interests—US and continental companies. Dubai Petroleum Co. (DPC—a subsidiary of Continental Oil) has a 30% interest in this group; the other members are Dubai Marine Areas (*Compagnie Française des Pétroles*) with 50%; Deutsche Texaco with 10%; Dubai Sun Oil 5%; and Delfzee Dubai Petroleum (Wintershall) 5%. Oil production, 1979, 129·3m. bbls.

Sharjah In Sharjah the concession is given to Crescent Oil, its shareholders are: Ashland Oil, Skelly Oil, Kerr-McGee, Cities Services and Juniper. Other oil concessions have recently been given to the Crystal Oil Co. of USA and the Reserves Oil and Gas Co. Oil production, 1979, 3·1m. bbls.

Ajman. An oil concession was awarded to United Refining in 1974.

Umm al Quawain. The concession here was given to US Occidental Petroleum; another was awarded to a consortium led by the US company United Refinery.

Ras al Khaimah. The Dutch oil firm Vitol took over Union's concession in 1973. Shell began prospecting in 1969 but pulled out in 1971. A concession in the same area was awarded to Peninsula Petroleum, a subsidiary of the US California Time Group, in 1973.

Gas. Abu Dhabi has reserves of natural gas, nationalized in 1976. The Abu Dhabi Gas Liquefaction Plant at Das Island (51% ADNOC) has a capacity of 2m. tons LNG, 1m. tons LPG, 220,000 tons of light distillate and 230,000 tons of pelletized sulphur.

Agriculture. The fertile Buraimi Oasis, known as Al Ain, is largely in Abu Dhabi territory, but owing to lack of water and good soil there is little agriculture in the rest of UAE. There are 15,000 hectares of cultivated land. However, since the establishment of an agricultural trials station and an agricultural school in Ras al Khaimah the number of gardens under cultivation has more than doubled and there have been remarkable increases in the variety of crops and the length of the agricultural season. An experimental agricultural farm exists in Al Ain which produces vegetables for Abu Dhabi.

Livestock (1979): Cattle, 25,000; camels, 50,000; sheep, 125,000; goats, 290,000.

Fisheries. The industry is still a major employer. Sharjah exports shrimps and prawns; a fishmeal plant is operating in Ras al Khaimah and plants are planned for Ajman and Sharjah.

INDUSTRY. Main industries in Abu Dhabi relate to the construction industry and to oil and gas extraction; there is also a steel rolling mill. Dubai has a cement factory of 500,000 tons annual capacity, and a dry dock. Work has also begun on a complex at Jebal Ali consisting of a liquefied petroleum gas plant. An aluminium smelter with power station and desalination plant was opened in Feb. 1979. Sharjah has a cement factory and various manufacturing estates. Ras al Khaimah also produces cement and crushed rock.

COMMERCE. Imports in 1979 for UAE were US$6,483m. Exports and re-exports totalled 13,475·1m. Oil exports accounted for 95% of the total.

Total trade between the UAE (excluding Abu Dhabi) and UK (British Department of Trade returns, in £1,000 sterling):

	1976	1977	1978	1979	1980
Imports to UK	121,923	137,779	146,435	143,071	239,519
Exports and re-exports from UK	188,697	190,514	273,160	328,773	287,615

Total trade between Abu Dhabi and UK (British Department of Trade returns, in £1,000 sterling):

	1976	1977	1978	1979	1980
Imports to UK	77,752	121,276	123,376	93,990	246,422
Exports and re-exports from UK	125,692	264,463	125,150	159,426	214,309

COMMUNICATIONS

Aviation. International airports at Dubai and Abu Dhabi are served by a large number of major airlines, as well as by Gulf Air partially owned by the Government of the UAE. Plans are underway for the construction of a new Abu Dhabi airport. A new international airport was inaugurated at Sharjah in 1979. A Ras al Khaimah international airport was opened early in 1976 although it initially had only one scheduled service by Kuwait Airways. An airstrip exists at Al Ain, in the Buraimi Oasis, and in the oilfields, both onshore and offshore, on Das Island, while construction of a strip at Khor Fakkan is planned.

Abu Dhabi and Dubai are served by Alia, Air France, Air India, British Airways, Egyptair, Iran Air, Kuwait Airways, Middle East Airlines, PIA, KLM, Gulf Air, Iraqi Airways, Olympic, Sabena, Saudia, Syrian Arab Airlines and TMA. Lufthansa and Singapore Airlines initiated scheduled flights to Dubai in mid-1976, while Sharjah is served by Gulf Air and TMA. A number of cargo airlines also fly regularly to the country's major airports. An air-taxi service, Emirates Air Services, flying between Abu Dhabi and Dubai, began in June 1976.

Shipping. British and European shipping lines call at Dubai (30–40 vessels a month) and Abu Dhabi. In 1972 Port Rashid, equipped with 15 deep-water berths, was opened, making Dubai harbour the largest in the Middle East, and a new contract was granted to a British company in 1976 to build a further 22 berths. A major dry dock, capable of handling super-tankers has also been built. Abu Dhabi has also become an important port since the opening of the first stage of its artificial harbour, Port Zayed, which, when completed, will have 17 deep-water berths.

In 1976, the Government of the UAE joined with Qatar, Bahrain, Saudi Arabia, Kuwait and Iraq in forming the United Arab Shipping Co.

Post and Broadcasting. In 1978 there were 96,847 telephones, of which 32,071 were in Abu Dhabi. In Sharjah a new telephone company has been formed and the other Northern States are now linked by telephone. The new Cable and Wireless Station at Jebel Ali in the State of Dubai links the system with the international communication network.

Television stations are at Abu Dhabi and Dubai, with extension of the service well advanced to the rest of the Emirates. Stations for The Voice of the United Arab Emirates began broadcasting in 1972 at Abu Dhabi, Dubai, Ras al Khaimah and Sharjah. Estimated radios (1976) 50,000 and television sets over 16,000.

The UAE is a founder member of the New Arab Space Communications Organization, having one satellite ground station at Jebel Ali in Dubai connected to the Indian ocean satellite; another is building and a link with the Atlantic ocean satellite is well underway.

Newspapers (1978). There are a number of daily and weekly publications mostly in Arabic, but some in English, notably *The Emirates News* of Abu Dhabi, and *The Gulf Mirror*, a weekly, published in Bahrain.

JUSTICE, RELIGION, EDUCATION AND WELFARE

Justice. UAE subjects and citizens of all Arab and Moslem states are subject to the jurisdiction of the local courts. In the local courts the rules of Islamic law prevail. A new code of law is being produced for Abu Dhabi. In Dubai there is a court run by a *qadi*, while in some of the other States all legal cases are referred immediately to the Ruler or a member of his family, who will refer to a *qadi* only if he cannot settle the matter himself. In Abu Dhabi a professional Jordanian judge presides over the Ruler's Court. The 95th article of the provisional Constitution of 1971 provided for the setting up of a Union Supreme Court and Union Primary Tribunals.

Religion. Nearly all the inhabitants are Moslems of the Sunni and Shi'ite sects.

Education (1977–78). Primary and secondary education for boys and girls is available in the UAE, and there are now 206 schools with over 86,000 pupils, with 10 under construction. There are 4 junior colleges and 112 adult education centres, established in order to eliminate illiteracy. The education system is the same as that followed in Kuwait, and many of the teachers are supplied by the Kuwait, Qatar, Egypt, Jordan and Bahrain education departments. The oil companies in Abu Dhabi operate apprentice training schools and there is also a vocational training institute. A vocational training centre is under construction.

There are trade schools in Sharjah, Dubai and Ras al Khaimah. The UAE university had 519 students (205 females) in 1977–78.

Health. A tuberculosis sanatorium is to be constructed by the State of Kuwait in Sharjah. In 1978 there were 20 hospitals (1,503 beds) and 47 clinics. There were 774 doctors.

DIPLOMATIC REPRESENTATIVES

OF THE UAE IN GREAT BRITAIN
(30 Prince's Gate, London, SW7 1PT)

Ambassador: Sayed Mohamed Mahdi Al-Tajir.

OF GREAT BRITAIN IN THE UAE

Ambassador: David A. Roberts, CMG, CVO (at the British Embassy, Abu Dhabi).

OF THE UAE IN THE USA (600 New Hampshire Ave., NW, Washington, D.C., 20037)

Ambassador: Mohammed Abdul Rahman Al Madfa.

OF THE USA IN THE UAE (Sheikh Khalid Bldg., Corniche Rd., Abu Dhabi)

Ambassador: William D. Wolle.

OF THE UAE TO THE UNITED NATIONS

Ambassador: Dr Ali Humaidan.

Books of Reference

Middle East Annual Review. London
Al-Baharna, H. M., *The Legal Status of the Arabian Gulf States.* Manchester, 1969
Busch, B. C., *Britain and the Persian Gulf 1894–1914.* California, 1967
Daniel, John, *Abu Dhabi: A Portrait.* London, 1974
Fenelon, K. G., *The United Arab Emirates: An Economic and Social Survey.* London, 1973
Hawley, D. F., *Courtesies in the Trucial States.* 1965.—*The Trucial States.* London, 1971
Hopwood, D., *The Arabian Peninsula.* London, 1972
Izzard, M., *The Gulf,* 1980
Khalifa, A. M., *The U.A.E.: Energy Development.* London, 1980
Mann, C., *Abu Dhabi: Birth of an Oil Sheikhdom.* Beirut, 1964
Marlowe, J., *The Persian Gulf in the 20th Century.* London, 1962
Miles, S. B., *The Countries and Tribes of the Persian Gulf.* 3rd ed. London, 1966
Sadiq, M. T. *with* W. P. Snavely, *Bahrain, Qatar and the UAE: Colonial Past, Present Problems and Future Prospects.* Lexington, Mass., 1972
Soffan, L. U., *Women of the United Arab Emirates.* London, 1980
Wilson, Sir A. T., *The Persian Gulf.* 1928
Zahlan, R. S., *The Origins of the United Arab Emirates.* London, 1978

UNITED KINGDOM OF GREAT BRITAIN AND NORTHERN IRELAND

Capital: London
Population: 55·93m. (1976)
GNP per capita: US$5,030 (1978)

'Great Britain' is a geographical term describing the main island of the British Isles which comprises England, Scotland and Wales (so called to distinguish it from 'Little Britain' or Brittany). By the Act of Union, 1801, Great Britain and Ireland formed a legislative union as the United Kingdom of Great Britain and Ireland. Since the separation of Great Britain and Ireland in 1921 Northern Ireland remained within the Union which is now the United Kingdom of Great Britain and Northern Ireland. The United Kingdom does not include the Channel Islands or the Isle of Man which are direct dependencies of the Crown with their own legislative and taxation systems.

GREAT BRITAIN

AREA AND POPULATION. Area (in sq. miles) and population at the census taken 25 April 1971:

Divisions	Area	Males	Females	Total
England	50,331	22,299,460	23,580,210	46,019,000
Wales (incl. Monmouthshire)	8,016	1,324,205	1,400,070	2,731,000
Scotland	30,405	2,514,622	2,514,341	5,228,963
Isle of Man	211	24,461	29,828	56,289
Channel Islands	75	59,648	63,415	123,063
	89,038 [1]	26,224,396	27,787,864	54,158,315 [1]

[1] 230,609 sq. km.

Population at the 4 previous decennial censuses:

Divisions	1921	1931	1951	1961
England	35,230,225	37,359,045	41,159,213	43,460,525
Wales	2,656,474	2,158,374	2,598,675	2,644,023
Scotland	4,882,497	4,842,980	5,096,415	5,178,490
Isle of Man	60,284	49,308	55,253	48,151
Channel Islands	90,230	93,205	102,806	104,378
Army, Navy and Merchant Seamen abroad	256,811	434,532	—	—
Total	43,176,521	44,937,444	50,383,283	52,867,716

In 1971 in Wales and Monmouthshire 32,725 persons 3 years of age and upwards were able to speak Welsh only, and 509,700 able to speak Welsh and English: these totals represent 20% of the total population. In Scotland in 1971, 338 persons could speak Gaelic only, and 88,415 could speak Gaelic and English, totalling 1·8% of the population.

At the census of 1971, in England and Wales, there were 16,509,905 private households; in Great Britain, 18,195,965.

The age distribution in 1971 of the population of England and Wales and Scotland was as follows (in 1,000):

Age-group		England and Wales	Scotland	Great Britain
Under	5	3,904	444	4,349
5 and under 10		4,044	468	4,512
10	,, 15	3,627	442	4,069
15	,, 20	3,313	392	3,705
20	,, 25	3,731	390	4,121
25	,, 35	6,062	616	6,676
35	,, 45	5,721	611	6,333
45	,, 55	6,022	617	6,651
55	,, 65	5,815	598	6,414
65	,, 70	2,399	247	2,647
70	,, 75	1,778	179	1,957
75	,, 85	1,892	180	2,072
85 and upwards		424	36	461
Total		48,749	5,228	53,978

At 30 June 1979 the estimated sex distribution of the population of England and Wales was: between 0 and 15, 5,379,300 males, 5,093,900 females; 15 and under 65, 15,752,400 males; 15 and under 60, 14,292,300 females; aged 65 and over, 2·87m. males; 60 and over, 5,735,600 females.

Estimated total home population of Great Britain at 30 June:

	England and Wales [1]	Scotland [2]	Total of Great Britain
1976	49,184,400	5,205,100	54,389,500
1977	49,119,500	5,196,000	54,315,500
1978	49,117,300	5,179,000	54,296,300
1979	49,170,800	5,167,000	54,337,800

[1] The home population of England and Wales is the population of all types, actually in the country. [2] Excluding merchant seamen overseas.

England and Wales: The census population of England and Wales 1801 to 1961:

Date of enumeration	Population	Pop. per sq. mile	Date of enumeration	Population	Pop. per sq. mile
1801	8,892,536	152	1881	25,974,439	445
1811	10,164,256	174	1891	29,002,525	497
1821	12,000,236	206	1901	32,527,843	558
1831	13,896,797	238	1911	36,070,492	618
1841	15,914,148	273	1921	37,886,699	649
1851	17,927,609	307	1931	39,952,377	685
1861	20,066,224	344	1951	43,757,888	750
1871	22,712,266	389	1961	46,104,548	791

There is only one other major country in Europe, Netherlands (population density 893 persons per sq. mile), more crowded than England and Wales.

Population of the administrative counties and county boroughs in 1971 (for areas of administrative counties, etc., 1931, *see* THE STATESMAN'S YEAR-BOOK, 1950, p. 51):

ENGLAND			
Bedfordshire	463,493	Herefordshire	138,425
Berkshire	633,457	Hertfordshire	922,188
Buckinghamshire	586,211	Huntingdonshire	202,337 [1]
Cambridgeshire	302,507	Kent	1,396,030
Isle of Ely	—	Lancashire	5,106,123
Cheshire	1,542,624	Leicestershire	771,213
Cornwall	379,892	Lincolnshire	
Cumberland	292,009	The parts of Holland	105,643
Derbyshire	884,339	The parts of Kesteven	232,215
Devonshire	896,245	The parts of Lindsey	470,526
Dorsetshire	361,213	London	7,379,014 [2]
Durham	1,408,103	Middlesex	—
Essex	1,353,564	Norfolk	616,427
Gloucestershire	1,069,454	Northamptonshire	467,843
Hampshire	1,561,605	Soke of Peterborough	—
Isle of Wight	109,284	Northumberland	794,975
		Nottinghamshire	974,640

[1] Includes Peterborough.   [2] Greater London.

ENGLAND—contd.		WALES	
Oxfordshire	380,814	Anglesey	59,705
Rutlandshire	27,463	Breconshire	53,234
Shropshire	336,934	Caernarvonshire	122,852
Somerset	681,974	Cardiganshire	54,844
Staffordshire	1,856,890	Carmarthenshire	162,313
Suffolk, East	380,524	Denbighshire	184,824
Suffolk, West	164,201	Flintshire	175,396
Surrey	999,588	Glamorganshire	1,255,374
Sussex, East	750,312	Merionethshire	35,277
Sussex, West	491,020	Monmouthshire	461,459
Warwickshire	2,079,799	Montgomeryshire	42,761
Westmorland	72,724	Pembrokeshire	97,295
Wiltshire	486,048	Radnorshire	18,262
Worcestershire	692,605		
Yorkshire, East Riding	542,565	Total Wales (13 counties)	2,723,596
Yorkshire, North Riding	724,463		
Yorkshire, West Riding	3,780,539	Total—England and Wales	48,593,658
Total	45,870,062		

Local authority areas in being from April 1974. Area in sq. km. and population estimate 1979:

ENGLAND	Area		Non-Metropolitan	Area	
Metropolitan counties	sq. km	Population	counties—contd.	sq. km	Population
Greater London	1,580	6,877,100	Leicestershire	2,553	836,300
Greater Manchester	1,286	2,648,300	Lincolnshire	5,885	533,800
Merseyside	652	1,531,600	Norfolk	5,355	686,300
South Yorkshire	1,560	1,301,300	Northamptonshire	2,367	523,300
Tyne and Wear	540	1,155,900	Northumberland	5,033	289,800
West Midlands	899	2,696,000	North Yorkshire	8,317	663,200
West Yorkshire	2,039	2,064,100	Nottinghamshire	2,164	974,100
			Oxfordshire	2,611	542,100
Non-metropolitan			Shropshire	3,490	369,500
counties			Somerset	3,458	415,500
Avon	1,338	924,200	Staffordshire	2,716	999,900
Bedfordshire	1,235	498,800	Suffolk	3,800	597,600
Berkshire	1,256	682,000	Surrey	1,655	993,700
Buckinghamshire	1,883	535,800	Warwickshire	1,981	468,900
Cambridgeshire	3,409	579,300	West Sussex	2,016	643,800
Cheshire	2,322	926,500	Wiltshire	3,481	516,400
Cleveland	583	568,600			
Cornwall and Isles of			Total		46,396,100
Scilly	3,546	419,300			
Cumbria	6,809	469,900			
Derbyshire	2,631	898,300	WALES		
Devon	6,715	952,100	Clwyd	2,425	385,100
Dorset	2,654	591,100	Dyfed	5,765	325,600
Durham	2,436	603,200	Gwent	1,376	435,900
East Sussex	1,795	654,600	Gwynedd	3,868	226,300
Essex	3,674	1,446,700	Mid-Glamorgan	1,019	537,500
Gloucestershire	2,638	497,100	Powys	5,077	107,100
Hampshire	3,772	1,459,500	South Glamorgan	416	390,600
Hereford and Worcester	3,927	617,900	West Glamorgan	815	366,600
Hertfordshire	1,634	952,000			
Humberside	3,512	849,600	Total Wales		2,774,700
Isle of Wight	381	115,300			
Kent	3,732	1,456,100	Total—England		
Lancashire	3,043	1,369,700	and Wales		49,170,800

County districts with populations of over 90,000 (1979 estimates):

ENGLAND		Barnsley	221,800
Allerdale	93,700	Basildon	148,200
Amber Valley	106,700	Basingstoke and Deane	127,200
Arun	115,200	Bassetlaw	98,600
Ashfield	105,000	Beverley	106,600
Aylesbury Vale	126,600	Birmingham	1,033,900

ENGLAND—*contd.*

Blackburn	142,500
Blackpool	145,400
Bolton	260,100
Bournemouth	144,200
Bradford	461,600
Braintree	111,100
Breckland	97,800
Brighton	152,700
Bristol	408,000
Broadland	96,000
Broxtowe	102,500
Burnley	92,300
Bury	178,600
Calderdale	189,400
Cambridge	101,600
Canterbury	118,600
Carlisle	98,300
Charnwood	130,900
Chelmsford	134,600
Cherwell	109,900
Chester	116,300
Chesterfield	96,300
Chichester	96,500
Colchester	137,500
Coventry	339,300
Crewe and Nantwich	97,500
Dacorum	128,900
Darlington	95,000
Derby	215,900
Doncaster	286,500
Dover	98,700
Dudley	296,000
East Devon	105,400
East Hertfordshire	107,000
East Lindsey	102,100
East Staffordshire	93,700
Elmbridge	110,000
Epping Forest	113,800
Erewash	101,900
Exeter	95,600
Gateshead	212,200
Gedling	102,800
Gillingham	92,800
Gloucester	91,300
Gravesham	95,900
Grimsby	91,900
Guildford	117,400
Halton	120,700
Harrogate	134,500
Hartlepool	95,100
Havant	116,100
Horsham	97,600
Huntingdon	125,500
Ipswich	118,900
Kingston upon Hull	274,500
Kirklees	379,100
Knowsley	179,700
Lancaster	123,400
Langbaurgh	148,700
Leeds	724,300
Leicester	276,600
Liverpool	520,200
Luton	160,300
Macclesfield	149,800
Maidstone	128,700
Manchester	479,100
Mansfield	97,900

ENGLAND—*contd.*

Mid-Bedfordshire	103,300
Middlesbrough	153,000
Mid-Sussex	114,400
Newark	100,800
Newbury	123,400
Newcastle under Lyme	116,700
Newcastle upon Tyne	287,300
New Forest	142,000
Northampton	154,900
Northavon	118,100
North Bedfordshire	129,300
North-East Derbyshire	94,700
North Hertfordshire	105,000
North Tyneside	193,000
North Wiltshire	105,500
Norwich	119,300
Nottingham	278,600
Nuneaton	110,300
Oldham	223,500
Oxford	122,400
Peterborough	129,300
Plymouth	255,500
Poole	115,500
Portsmouth	191,000
Preston	126,200
Reading	138,400
Reigate and Banstead	114,000
Rochdale	209,000
Rochester upon Medway	147,400
Rotherham	248,800
St Albans	124,300
St Helens	188,700
Salford	252,600
Salisbury	103,100
Sandwell	306,900
Scarborough	99,900
Sedgefield	93,300
Sefton	300,700
Sevenoaks	108,600
Sheffield	544,200
Slough	98,400
Solihull	198,300
Southampton	207,800
South Bedfordshire	105,900
South Cambridgeshire	103,800
Southend on Sea	154,700
South Kesteven	93,400
South Lakeland	94,500
South Norfolk	92,800
South Oxfordshire	134,700
South Ribble	96,100
South Staffordshire	93,600
South Tyneside	162,600
Spelthorne	93,500
Stafford	113,700
Staffordshire Moorlands	94,400
Stockport	291,700
Stockton on Tees	171,800
Stoke on Trent	257,200
Stratford on Avon	99,200
Stroud	99,900
Suffolk Coastal	98,600
Sunderland	300,800
Swale	107,300
Tameside	218,500
Teignbridge	95,200
Tendring	110,400

Test Valley	92,400	Wirral	342,300
Thamesdown	143,800	Wokingham	111,000
Thanet	119,500	Wolverhampton	258,200
Thurrock	127,100	Woodspring	156,600
Tonbridge and Malling	94,100	Worthing	90,600
Torbay	108,700	Wrekin	122,400
Trafford	224,000	Wychavon	91,800
Tunbridge Wells	95,700	Wycombe	151,300
Vale of White Horse	96,800	Wyre	98,200
Vale Royal	110,000	Wyre Forest	91,800
Wakefield	309,700	Yeovil	129,300
Walsall	263,400	York	100,900
Warrington	168,200		
Warwick	116,000	WALES	
Waveney	97,700	Cardiff	282,000
Waverley	108,200	Newport	132,800
Wealden	116,700	Ogwr	128,000
Welwyn Hatfield	92,800	Rhymney Valley	107,100
West Lancashire	108,300	Swansea	186,900
West Norfolk	119,100	Taff Ely	92,700
West Wiltshire	98,800	Torfaen	90,400
Wigan	311,200	Vale of Glamorgan	108,600
Windsor and Maidenhead	131,500	Wrexham Maelor	109,300

The following table shows the distribution of the urban and rural population of England and Wales in 1951, 1961 and 1971.

		Population		Percentage	
	England and Wales	Urban districts [1]	Rural districts [1]	Urban [1]	Rural
1951	43,757,888	35,335,721	8,422,167	80·8	19·2
1961	46,071,604	36,838,442	9,233,162	80·0	20·0
1971	48,755,000	38,151,000	10,598,000	78·2	21·5

[1] As existing at each census.

Conurbations. These are aggregates of local-authority areas with high population densities. In April 1971 there were 7 in England and Wales, with a population of 16m. (33·2% of total population). Excluding the London conurbation, their populations were: Tyneside, 0·8m.; W. Yorks., 1·73m.; S.E. Lancs., 2·39m.; Merseyside, 1·26m.; W. Midlands, 2·37m.; S.E. Wales, 1·83m. The municipal and parliamentary City of London, coinciding with the registration City of London, has an area of 677 acres. The registration County of London (the London for purposes of the census, the registration of births, deaths and marriages, and for poor law purposes), coinciding with the former administrative county, has an area of 74,898 acres, and nearly coincides with the collective area of the London parliamentary boroughs. The population of registration London, of the 'Outer Ring', and of 'Greater London' (the area covered by the City and Metropolitan police) at the dates of the census, was:

	1931	1941	1961	1971
Registration London	4,397,003	3,347,982	3,200,484	2,145,185
'Outer Ring'	3,818,670	5,000,041	4,982,066	5,307,160
'Greater London' [1]	8,215,673	8,348,023	8,182,550	7,452,345

[1] Area 461,885 acres (1961).

Greater London Boroughs. Estimated population in June 1979:

Barking	149,300	Haringey	223,900	Merton	162,100
Barnet	290,400	Harrow	196,600	Newham	224,300
Bexley	213,000	Havering	239,900	Redbridge	225,800
Brent	251,900	Hillingdon	228,700	Richmond-on-	
Bromley	290,700	Hounslow	201,300	Thames	161,700
Camden	190,900	Islington	167,400	Southwark	219,200
Croydon	320,500	Kensington and		Sutton	166,600
Ealing	289,400	Chelsea	149,900	Tower Hamlets	149,200
Enfield	258,800	Kingston upon		Waltham Forest	218,400
Greenwich	204,400	Thames	135,700	Wandsworth	272,800
Hackney	190,700	Lambeth	266,400	Westminster	211,900
Hammersmith	161,800	Lewisham	238,000		

Census of England and Wales, 1961. HMSO. 1961–65
Royal Commission on Local Government in Greater London, Report. HMSO 1960 (Cmnd. 1164)
Census 1971, England and Wales, Preliminary Report. HMSO, 1971
Census 1971, Great Britain; Advance Analysis. HMSO, 1972

Scotland: Area 29,796 sq. miles, including its islands, 186 in number, but excluding inland water 609 sq. miles.

Population (including military in the barracks and seamen on board vessels in the harbours) at the dates of each census:

Date of enumeration	Population	Pop. per sq. mile	Date of enumeration	Population	Pop. per sq. mile
1811	1,805,864	60	1891	4,025,647	135
1821	2,091,521	70	1901	4,472,103	150
1831	2,364,386	79	1911	4,760,904	160
1841	2,620,184	88	1921	4,882,497	164
1851	2,888,742	97	1931	4,842,980	163
1861	3,062,294	100	1951	5,096,415	171
1871	3,360,018	113	1961	5,179,344	174
1881	3,735,573	125	1971	5,229,963	175

The 1971 population included 2,514,622 males, 2,714,341 females.
The 33 civil counties were as follows:

	Area in statute acres (1931)	Census population 1931	1951	1961	Estimated population[1] June 1974
1. Aberdeen	1,261,521	300,436	308,008	321,783	324,574
2. Angus	559,037	270,190	274,876	278,399	281,131
3. Argyll	1,999,472	63,050	63,361	59,390	59,926
4. Ayr	724,523	285,217	321,237	342,822	369,636
5. Banff	403,053	54,907	50,148	46,454	43,767
6. Berwick	292,535	26,612	25,086	22,437	21,224
7. Bute	139,658	18,823	19,283	15,170	12,743
8. Caithness	438,833	25,656	22,710	27,370	27,901
9. Clackmannan	34,927	31,948	37,532	41,394	46,611
10. Dumfries	686,302	81,220	85,660	88,440	88,540
11. Dunbarton	157,433	146,723	164,269	184,559	244,354
12. East Lothian	170,971	47,338	52,258	52,677	56,966
13. Fife	322,844	276,368	306,778	320,692	337,690
14. Inverness	2,695,094	82,108	84,930	83,480	91,698
15. Kincardine	244,482	39,865	47,403	48,810	27,188
16. Kinross	52,410	7,454	7,418	6,702	7,090
17. Kirkcudbright	575,832	30,168	30,725	28,870	27,761
18. Lanark	562,821	1,587,665	1,614,363	1,626,424	1,456,151
19. Midlothian	234,325	526,296	565,735	580,329	603,615
20. Moray	304,931	40,805	48,218	49,170	54,833
21. Nairn	104,252	8,294	8,719	8,423	8,906
22. Orkney	240,847	22,077	21,255	18,747	17,462
23. Peebles	222,240	15,051	15,232	14,156	13,584
24. Perth	1,595,802	120,793	128,029	127,056	128,692
25. Renfrew	153,332	287,991	324,660	338,872	366,485
26. Ross and Cromarty	1,977,248	62,799	60,508	57,642	61,464
27. Roxburgh	426,028	45,685	45,557	43,183	42,255
28. Selkirk	170,793	22,711	21,729	21,052	20,743
29. Shetland (Zetland)	352,319	21,421	19,352	17,812	18,445
30. Stirling	288,842	166,447	187,527	194,878	211,994
31. Sutherland	1,297,914	16,101	13,670	13,507	12,728
32. West Lothian (Linlithgow)	76,861	81,431	88,577	92,768	112,833
33. Wigtown	311,984	29,331	31,620	29,124	27,410
Total Scotland	19,070,466	4,842,980	5,096,415	5,179,344	5,226,400

[1] Home population.

Population estimates, 1979 (and area in sq. km) for Scottish regions: Borders, 99,902 (4,670); Central, 271,023 (2,621); Dumfries and Galloway, 142,427 (6,369); Fife, 332,933 (1,305); Grampian, 463,130 (8,702); Highland, 189,858 (25,141); Lothian, 747,737 (1,753); Strathclyde, 2,424,189 (13,849); Tayside, 400,451 (7,501).

Island Authorities: Orkney, 18,055 (905); Shetland, 21,835 (1,429); Western Isles, 29,255 (2,898).

Population of cities and large burghs (1971) was 2,669,000 (50·1% of the total).

Burghs	Census population			Burghs	Census population		
	1951	1961	1971		1951	1961	1971
Glasgow	1,079,000	1,055,017	893,790	Kirkcaldy	51,800	52,390	50,091
Edinburgh	470,800	468,361	453,025	Clydebank	44,638	49,651	48,170
Dundee	181,800	182,978	182,930	Dunfermline	44,719	47,151	51,738
Aberdeen	186,900	185,390	181,785	Kilmarnock	42,123	47,509	48,992
Paisley	97,200	95,750	95,067	Ayr	42,377	45,276	48,021
Motherwell	73,100	72,794	74,038	Hamilton	40,174	41,928	46,376
Greenock	78,400	74,560	69,171	Perth	40,487	41,196	42,438
Coatbridge	54,300	53,825	51,985	Falkirk	37,535	38,044	37,489

Population (estimate, 1979): Glasgow, 792,616; Edinburgh, 453,348; Aberdeen, 208,539; Dundee, 190,596.

The birthplaces of the 1971 population were: Scotland, 4,759,475; England, 279,340; Wales, 11,905; Northern Ireland, 32,790; Irish Republic 31,260; Commonwealth, 43,600; foreign countries, 51,345 (including 7,470 aliens).

The population of the Central Clydeside conurbation in 1971 was 1,731,048.

At 30 June 1979 the estimated sex distribution of the population in Scotland was: between 0 and 14, 593,547 males, 561,774 females; 15 and 65, 1,624,314 males, 15 and 60, 1,536,308 females; 65 and over, 271,600 males, 60 and over, 579,457 females.

Isle of Man and Channel Islands:

Islands	Area in statute acres, 1951	Census population		
		1951	1961	1971
Isle of Man	141,263	55,253	48,151	56,289
Jersey	28,717	57,310	57,200	69,329
Guernsey, Herm and Jethou	16,068 ⎫			
Alderney	1,962 ⎬	45,496	47,178	53,734
Sark, Brechou and Lihou	1,386 ⎭			
Total	189,396	158,059	152,529	179,352

Vital statistics for England and Wales:

	Estimated home population at 30 June [1]	Total live births	Illegitimate live births	Deaths	Marriages	Divorces, annulments and dissolutions
1973	49,153,800	675,953	58,097	587,478	400,435	106,003
1974	49,158,900	639,885	56,486	585,292	384,389	113,500
1975	49,157,100	603,445	54,891	582,851	380,620	120,522
1976	49,142,400	584,270	53,766	598,494	358,567	126,694
1977	49,119,500	569,259	55,379	575,928	356,954	129,053
1978	49,117,300	596,418	60,637	585,901	368,258	143,667
1979	49,170,800	638,028	69,467	592,853	368,853	138,706

[1] The population actually in England and Wales.

In 1979 the proportion of male to female births was 1,060 male to 1,000 female; the live birth rate was 13·0 and the death rate 12·1 per 1,000 of the population; infant mortality rate, 12·8 per 1,000 of live births. The average age at marriage (1979) was 29·4 years for males and 26·6 years for females.

Vital statistics for Scotland:

	Estimated home population at 30 June [1]	Total births	Illegitimate births	Deaths	Marriages	Divorces, annulments and dissolutions
1973	5,211,700	74,392	6,520	64,545	42,018	7,135
1974	5,226,400	70,093	6,349	64,740	41,174	7,221
1975	5,206,200	67,943	6,314	63,125	39,191	8,319
1976	5,205,100	64,895	6,025	65,253	37,543	8,692
1977	5,195,000	62,342	5,968	62,294	37,288	8,823
1978	5,179,400	64,295	6,304	65,123	37,814	8,458
1979	5,167,000	68,366	6,960	65,747	37,860	8,833

[1] Includes merchant navy at home and forces stationed in Scotland.

In 1979 the proportion of male to female births was 1,071 male to 1,000 female; the live birth rate was 13·2 and the death rate 12·7 per 1,000 of the population; infant mortality rate, 13 per 1,000 live births. The average age of marriage was 27 years for males and 25 years for females.

Emigration and Immigration. The UK has traditionally been a net exporter of population. In the two 30-year periods 1871–1901 and 1901–31 there was a net loss of population due to emigration of 1·6m. and 2·4m. persons respectively. Since then there have been two periods when this trend was reversed. During the 1930s there was an inflow of refugees from Europe and during the decade centred on 1960 there was an inflow from the new Commonwealth countries. More recently there has been a return to the traditional pattern with a new outflow during the period 1965–75 of 700,000 persons.

The following table shows a summary of migration statistics for 1979 based on the International Passenger Survey which is conducted by the Office of Population Censuses and Surveys for the Department of Trade and Industry and covers all the principal air and sea routes to the UK except those to and from the Irish Republic.

UK migration 1979 (in 1,000):

By country of last or future intended residence	Into UK	Out from UK	Balance
All Countries	194·8	188·6	+ 6·2
Australia, New Zealand, Canada	30·7	50·2	− 19·5
India, Bangladesh, Sri Lanka	18·9	4·0	+ 14·9
Other Commonwealth	42·3	22·0	+ 20·3
EEC	22·6	28·8	− 6·3
USA	13·4	26·3	− 12·8
South Africa	11·1	6·1	+ 5·0
Rest of World	55·7	51·2	+ 4·6
By sex/age			
Males 0–14	19·9	15·7	+ 4·2
15–24	31·0	26·3	+ 4·7
25–44	43·4	54·6	− 11·1
45 and over	9·1	9·8	− 0·7
All ages	103·4	106·4	− 3·0
Females 0–14	15·6	13·7	+ 1·9
15–24	32·2	24·9	+ 8·4
25–44	34·5	35·8	− 1·2
45 and over	8·0	7·9	+ 0·1
All ages	91·4	82·3	+ 9·1

QUEEN, HEAD OF THE COMMONWEALTH. Elizabeth II Alexandra Mary, born 21 April 1926 daughter of King George VI and Queen Elizabeth; married on 20 Nov. 1947 Lieut. Philip Mountbatten (formerly Prince Philip of Greece), created Duke of Edinburgh, Earl of Merioneth and Baron Greenwich on the same day and created Prince Philip, Duke of Edinburgh, 22 Feb. 1957; succeeded to the crown on the death of her father, on 6 Feb. 1952. Offspring: *Charles* Philip Arthur George, Prince of Wales, born 14 Nov. 1948, married Lady Diana Spencer on 29 July 1981 (Heir Apparent); Princess *Anne* Elizabeth Alice Louise, born 15 Aug. 1950, married Mark Anthony Peter Phillips on 14 Nov. 1973. Offspring: *Peter* Mark Andrew, born 15 Nov. 1977. Prince *Andrew* Albert Christian Edward, born 19 Feb. 1960; Prince *Edward* Antony Richard Louis, born 10 March 1964.

The Queen Mother: Queen Elizabeth, born 4 Aug. 1900, daughter of the 14th Earl of Strathmore and Kinghorne; married the Duke of York, afterwards King George VI, on 26 April 1923.

Sister of the Queen: Princess Margaret Rose, born 12 Aug. 1930; married Antony Armstrong-Jones (created Earl of Snowdon, 3 Oct. 1961) on 6 May 1960; divorced, 1978. Offspring: *David* Albert Charles (Viscount Linley), born 3 Nov. 1961; Lady *Sarah* Frances Elizabeth Armstrong-Jones, born 1 May 1964.

Children of the late Duke of Gloucester (died 10 June 1974): William Henry Andrew Frederick, born 18 Dec. 1941, died 28 Aug. 1972; Richard Alexander Walter George, Duke of Gloucester, born 26 Aug. 1944, married Birgitte van Deurs on 8 July 1972 (offspring: Alexander Patrick Gregers Richard Windsor, Earl of Ulster, born 24 Oct. 1974; Davina Elizabeth Alice Benedikte Windsor, born 19 Nov. 1977; Rose Victoria Birgitte Louise Windsor, born 1 March 1980).

Children of the late Duke of Kent (died 25 Aug. 1942): Edward George Nicholas Patrick, Duke of Kent, born 9 Oct. 1935; married Katharine Worsley on 8 June 1961 (offspring: George Philip Nicholas, Earl of St Andrews, born 26 June 1962; Lady Helen Windsor, born 28 April 1964; Lord Nicholas Charles Edward Jonathan Windsor, born 25 July 1970). Alexandra Helen Elizabeth Olga Christabel, born 25 Dec. 1936; married 24 April 1963, Angus Ogilvy (offspring: James Robert Bruce, born 29 Feb. 1964; Marina Victoria Alexandra, born 31 July 1966). Michael George Charles Franklin, born 4 July 1942; married Marie-Christine von Reibnitz on 30 June 1978 (offspring: Lord Frederick Michael George David Louis Windsor, born 6 April 1979).

The Queen's legal title rests on the statute of 12 and 13 Will. III, c. 3, by which the succession to the Crown of Great Britain and Ireland was settled on the Princess Sophia of Hanover and the 'heirs of her body being Protestants'. By proclamation of 17 July 1917 the royal family became known as the House and Family of Windsor. On 8 Feb. 1960 the Queen issued a declaration varying her confirmatory declaration of 9 April 1952 to the effect that while the Queen and her children should continue to be known as the House of Windsor, her descendants, other than descendants entitled to the style of Royal Highness and the title of Prince or Princess, and female descendants who marry and their descendants should bear the name of Mountbatten-Windsor. The Royal Style and Titles of Queen Elizabeth are: In *Australia*: 'Elizabeth the Second, by the Grace of God Queen of Australia and Her other Realms and Territories, Head of the Commonwealth'. In the *Bahamas*: 'Elizabeth the Second, by the Grace of God, Queen of the Commonwealth of the Bahamas and of Her other Realms and Territories, Head of the Commonwealth'. In *Barbados*: 'Elizabeth the Second, by the Grace of God, Queen of Barbados and of Her other Realms and Territories, Head of the Commonwealth'. In *Canada*: 'Elizabeth the Second, by the Grace of God of the United Kingdom, Canada and Her other Realms and Territories Queen, Head of the Commonwealth, Defender of the Faith'. In *Fiji*: 'Elizabeth the Second, by the Grace of God, Queen of Fiji and of Her other Realms and Territories, Head of the Commonwealth'. In *Grenada*: 'Elizabeth the Second, by the Grace of God, Queen of the United Kingdom of Great Britain and Northern Ireland and of Grenada and Her other Realms and Territories, Head of the Commonwealth'. In *Jamaica*: 'Elizabeth the Second, by the Grace of God of Jamaica and of Her other Realms and Territories Queen, Head of the Commonwealth'. In *Mauritius*: 'Elizabeth the Second, Queen of Mauritius and of Her other Realms and Territories, Head of the Commonwealth'. In *New Zealand*: 'Elizabeth the Second, by the Grace of God Queen of New Zealand and Her Other Realms and Territories, Head of the Commonwealth, Defender of the Faith'. In *Papua New Guinea*: 'Elizabeth the Second, Queen of Papua New Guinea and Her other Realms and Territories, Head of the Commonwealth'. *Saint Lucia:* 'Elizabeth the Second, by the Grace of God, Queen of Saint Lucia and of Her other Realms and Territories, Head of Commonwealth'. *Saint Vincent and the Grenadines:* 'Elizabeth the Second, by the Grace of God, Queen of Saint Vincent and the Grenadines and of Her other Realms and Territories, Head of the Commonwealth'. *Solomon Islands:* 'Elizabeth the Second by the Grace of God Queen of Solomon Islands and of Her other Realms and Territories, Head of the Commonwealth'. *Tuvalu:* 'Elizabeth the Second by the Grace of God Queen of Tuvalu and Her other Realms and Territories, Head of the Commonwealth'. In the *United Kingdom*: 'Elizabeth the Second, by the Grace of God of the United Kingdom of Great Britain and Northern Ireland and of Her other Realms and Territories Queen, Head of the Commonwealth, Defender of the Faith'.

By letters patent of 30 Nov. 1917 the titles of Royal Highness and Prince or Princess are restricted to the Sovereign's children, the children of the Sovereign's sons and the eldest living son of the eldest son of the Prince of Wales.

Provision is made for the support of the royal household by the settlement of the Civil List soon after the beginning of each reign. (For historical details, *see* THE

STATESMAN'S YEAR-BOOK, 1908, p. 5, and 1935, p. 4.) According to the Civil List Act of 1 Jan. 1972 and the Civil List (Increase of Financial Provision) Order 1975, the Civil List of the Queen, after the usual surrender of hereditary revenues, was (1981) £3,964,000.

The Civil List Acts of 1981 provide for an annuity of £100,000 to the Princess Anne; £286,000 to Queen Elizabeth (the Queen Mother); £98,000 to the Princess Margaret.

Sovereigns of Great Britain, from the Restoration (with dates of accession):

House of Stewart		George III	25 Oct. 1760
Charles II	29 May 1660	George IV	29 Jan. 1820
James II	6 Feb. 1685	William IV	26 June 1830
		Victoria	20 June 1837
House of Stewart-Orange			
William and Mary	13 Feb. 1689	*House of Saxe-Coburg and Gotha*	
William III	28 Dec. 1694	Edward VII	22 Jan. 1901
House of Stewart			
Anne	19 March 1702	*House of Windsor*	
		George V	6 May 1910
House of Hanover		Edward VIII	20 Jan. 1936
George I	1 Aug. 1714	George VI	11 Dec. 1936
George II	11 June 1727	Elizabeth II	6 Feb. 1952

CONSTITUTION AND GOVERNMENT. The supreme legislative power is vested in Parliament, which in its present form, as divided into two Houses of Legislature, the Lords and the Commons, dates from the middle of the 14th century.

Parliament is summoned by the writ of the sovereign issued out of Chancery, by advice of the Privy Council, at least 20 days previous to its assembling. Every session must end with a prorogation, and all Bills which have not been passed during the session then lapse.

A dissolution may occur by the will of the sovereign, or, as is most usual, during the recess, by proclamation, or finally by lapse of time, the statutory limit of the duration of any Parliament being 5 years.

Under the Parliament Acts 1911 (1 and 2 Geo. V, ch. 13) and 1949 (12, 13 and 14 Geo. VI, ch. 103), all Money Bills (so certified by the Speaker of the House of Commons), if not passed by the House of Lords without amendment, may become law without their concurrence on the royal assent being signified within 1 month. Public Bills, other than Money Bills or a Bill extending the maximum duration of Parliament, if passed by the House of Commons in 2 successive sessions, whether of the same Parliament or not, and rejected each time, or not passed, by the House of Lords, may become law without their concurrence on the royal assent being signified, provided that 1 year has elapsed between the second reading in the first session of the House of Commons and the third reading in the second session. All Bills coming under this Act must reach the House of Lords at least 1 month before the end of the session.

The House of Lords consists of: (1) 808 hereditary peers and peeresses sitting by virtue of creation or descent, other than those who have disclaimed their titles for life under the provisions of the Peerage Act, 1963; (2) life peers being (*a*) 18 Lords of Appeal (active and retired), under the Appellate Jurisdiction Act, 1876, as amended; (*b*) (Jan. 1981) 316 life peers and peeresses under the Life Peerages Act, 1958: (3) 2 archbishops and 24 bishops of the Church of England (as long as they hold their sees).

The full House thus consists of 1,168, and the average attendance is about 300; in Jan. 1981 169 peers were on leave of absence and 87 peers (including 6 minors) were without writs of summons.

The House of Commons consists of members representing county and borough constituencies. Persons under 21 years of age, Clergymen of the Church of England, Ministers of the Church of Scotland, Roman Catholic clergymen, civil servants, members of the regular armed forces, policemen and most judicial officers are disqualified from sitting in the House of Commons. No English or Scottish peer can be elected to the House of Commons unless he has disclaimed his title for life under the Peerage Act, 1963, but Irish peers and holders of courtesy titles, who are not members of the House of Lords, are eligible. Under the Parliament (Qualification of Women) Act, 1918, women are also eligible.

In Aug. 1911 provision was first made for the payment of a salary of £400 per annum to members, other than those already in receipt of salaries as officers of the House, as Ministers or as officers of Her Majesty's household. As from June 1980 the salaries of members are £10,725 per annum, with income-tax relief on expenses incurred in the course of parliamentary duties. There is a secretarial allowance of up to £4,600 per annum and a living allowance, for an additional home, of up to £3,886 per annum. Members of the House of Lords are entitled to recover expenses incurred for the purpose of attendance at sittings of the House within a maximum of £11 for each day's attendance. For those Lords who incur the additional expense of overnight accommodation away from their main residence the limit is £23 for each day of such attendance and for general office expenses or on secretarial and research assistance, £10 for each day's attendance. Members of the House may also recover travelling expenses incurred between permanent places of residence and London.

The Representation of the People Act, 1948, abolished the business premises and University franchises, and the only persons entitled to vote at Parliamentary elections are those registered as residents or as service voters. No person may vote in more than one constituency at a general election. Persons may apply on certain grounds to vote by post or by proxy.

All persons over 17 years old and not subject to any legal incapacity to vote and who are either British subjects or citizens of the Irish Republic are entitled to be included in the register of electors for the constituency containing the address at which they were residing on the qualifying date for the register and are entitled to vote at elections held during the period for which the register remains in force. The current register was published in Feb. 1980.

Members of the armed forces, Crown servants employed abroad, and the wives accompanying their husbands, are entitled, if otherwise qualified, to be registered as 'service voters' provided they make a 'service declaration'. To be effective for a particular register, the declaration must be made on or before the qualifying date for that register.

The Representation of the People Act, 1969, abolished the occupier's qualification for voting in Local Government elections.

The House of Commons (Redistribution of Seats) Acts, 1944, 1949 and 1958, provided for the setting up of Boundary Commissions for England, Wales, Scotland and Northern Ireland. The Commissions are required to make general reports at intervals of not less than 3 and not more than 7 years and to submit reports from time to time with respect to the area comprised in any particular constituency or constituencies where some change appears necessary. Any changes giving effect to reports of the Commissions are to be made by Orders in Council laid before Parliament for approval by resolution of each House. The electorate of the United Kingdom and Northern Ireland in the register used at the election of 3 May 1979 numbered 41,569,787, of whom 34,608,491 were in England, 2,083,771 in Wales, 3,837,019 in Scotland and 1,040,506 in Northern Ireland.

At the general election held in May 1979, 635 members were returned, 516 from England, 71 from Scotland, 36 from Wales and 12 from Northern Ireland. Every constituency returns a single member.

Devolution in Wales and Scotland was decided by referendum on 1 March 1979. In Wales the result was 956,330 against a regional Assembly and 243,048 for. In Scotland 1,230,937 (32·85% of those entitled to vote) voted for an Assembly and 1,153,502 against. However, the Scotland and Wales Acts stated that the relevant Secretary of State must lay order for the repeal of legislation if less than 40% of those entitled to vote, voted 'Yes' and the Act was repealed in June 1979.

The following is a table of the duration of Parliaments called since the accession of King Edward VII.

Reign	When met	When dissolved	Duration (years and days)	
Edward VII	13 Feb. 1906	10 Jan. 1910	3	328
Edward VII and George V	15 Feb. 1910	28 Nov. 1910	0	287
George V	31 Jan. 1911	25 Nov. 1918	7	301
,,	4 Feb. 1919	26 Oct. 1922	3	269
,,	20 Nov. 1922	16 Nov. 1923	0	362
,,	8 Jan. 1924	9 Oct. 1924	0	276
,,	2 Dec. 1924	10 May 1929	4	161
,,	25 June 1929	7 Oct. 1931	2	75
,,	3 Nov. 1931	25 Oct. 1935	3	358
George V, Edward VIII and George VI	26 Nov. 1935	15 June 1945	9	205
George VI	1 Aug. 1945	3 Feb. 1950	4	188
,,	1 Mar. 1950	5 Oct. 1951	1	219
George VI and Elizabeth II	31 Oct. 1951	6 May 1955	3	188
Elizabeth II	7 June 1955	18 Sept. 1959	4	105
,,	20 Oct. 1959	25 Sept. 1964	4	341
,,	27 Oct. 1964	10 Mar. 1966	1	134
,,	18 Apr. 1966	29 May 1970	4	81
,,	29 June 1970	8 Feb. 1974	3	225
,,	12 Mar. 1974	20 Sept. 1974	0	224
,,	22 Oct. 1974	7 April 1979	4	167
,,	15 May 1979	—	—	

The executive government is vested nominally in the Crown, but practically in a committee of Ministers, called the Cabinet, which is dependent on the support of a majority in the House of Commons.

The head of the Ministry is the Prime Minister, a position first constitutionally recognized, and special precedence accorded to the holder, in 1905. His colleagues in the Ministry are appointed on his recommendation, and he dispenses the greater portion of the patronage of the Crown.

Heads of the Administrations since 1908 (C. = Conservative, L. = Liberal, Lab. = Labour, Nat. = National, Coal. = Coalition, Care. = Caretaker):

H. H. Asquith (L.)	8 Apr. 1908	W. S. Churchill (Care.)	23 May 1945
H. H. Asquith (Coal.)	25 May 1915	C. R. Attlee (Lab.)	26 July 1945
D. Lloyd George (Coal.)	7 Dec. 1916	W. S. Churchill (C.)	26 Oct. 1951
A. Bonar Law (C.)	23 Oct. 1922	Sir Anthony Eden (C.)	6 Apr. 1955
S. Baldwin (C.)	22 May 1923	H. Macmillan (C.)	10 Jan. 1957
J. R. MacDonald (Lab.)	22 Jan. 1924	Sir Alec Douglas-Home (C.)	18 Oct. 1963
S. Baldwin (C.)	4 Nov. 1924	H. Wilson (Lab.)	16 Oct. 1964
J. R. MacDonald (Lab.)	5 June 1929	E. Heath (C.)	19 June 1970
J. R. MacDonald (Nat.)	25 Aug. 1931	H. Wilson (Lab.)	12 Mar. 1974
S. Baldwin (Nat.)	7 June 1935	J. Callaghan (Lab.)	5 Apr. 1976
N. Chamberlain (Nat.)	28 May 1937	M. Thatcher (C.)	4 May 1979
W. S. Churchill (Coal.)	10 May 1940		

In April 1981 the Government consisted of the following members:

(a) MEMBERS OF THE CABINET

1. *Prime Minister and First Lord of the Treasury and Minister for Civil Service:* Rt Hon. Margaret Thatcher, MP, born 1925. (Salary £26,250 per annum.)

2. *Secretary of State for the Home Department:* Rt Hon. William Whitelaw, CH, MC, MP, born 1918. (£26,250.)

3. *Lord High Chancellor of Great Britain:* Rt Hon. The Lord Hailsham, CH, born 1907. (£26,250.)

4. *Secretary of State for Foreign and Commonwealth Affairs, Minister of Overseas Development:* Rt Hon. The Lord Carrington KCMG, MC, born 1919. (£26,250.)

5. *Chancellor of the Exchequer:* Rt Hon. Sir Geoffrey Howe, QC, MP, born 1926. (£26,250.)

6. *Secretary of State for Industry:* Rt Hon. Sir Keith Joseph, Bt, MP, born 1918. (£26,250.)

7. *Chancellor of the Duchy of Lancaster and Paymaster-General:* Rt Hon. Francis Pym, MC, MP, born 1922. (£26,250.)

8. *Lord President of the Council:* Rt Hon. The Lord Soames, GCMG, GCVO, CH, CBE, born 1920. (£26,250.)

9. *Secretary of State for Employment:* Rt Hon. James Prior, MP, born 1927. (£26,250.)

10. *Secretary of State for Defence:* Rt Hon. John Nott, MP, born 1932. (£26,250.)

11. *Lord Privy Seal:* Rt Hon. Sir Ian Gilmour, Bt, MP, born 1926. (£26,250.)

12. *Minister of Agriculture, Fisheries and Food:* Rt Hon. Peter Walker, MBE, MP, born 1932. (£26,250.)

13. *Secretary of State for the Environment:* Rt Hon. Michael Heseltine, MP, born 1933. (£26,250.)

14. *Secretary of State for Scotland:* Rt Hon. George Younger, MP, born 1931. (£26,250.)

15. *Secretary of State for Wales:* Rt Hon. Nicholas Edwards, MP born 1934. (£26,250.)

16. *Secretary of State for Northern Ireland:* Rt Hon. Humphrey Atkins, MP, born 1922. (£26,250.)

17. *Secretary of State for the Social Services:* Rt Hon. Patrick Jenkin, MP, born 1926. (£26,250.)

18. *Secretary of State for Trade:* Rt Hon. John Biffen, MP, born 1930. (£26,250.)

19. *Secretary of State for Energy:* Rt Hon. David Howell, MP, born 1936. (£26,250.)

20. *Secretary of State for Education and Science:* Rt Hon. Mark Carlisle, QC, MP, born 1929. (£26,250.)

21. *Secretary of State for Transport:* Rt Hon. Norman Fowler, MP, born 1938. (£26,250.)

22. *Chief Secretary to the Treasury:* Rt Hon. Leon Brittan, QC, MP, born 1939. (£26,250.)

(b) LAW OFFICERS

23. *Attorney-General:* Rt Hon. Sir Michael Havers, QC, MP, born 1923. (£27,850.)

24. *Lord Advocate:* Baron MacKay of Glashfern of Eddarachis, born 1927. (£23,000.)

25. *Solicitor-General:* Sir Ian Percival, QC, MP, born 1921. (£23,000.)

26. *Solicitor-General for Scotland:* Nicholas Fairbairn, QC, MP, born 1933. (£19,750.)

(c) MINISTERS NOT IN THE CABINET

27. *Parliamentary Secretary, Treasury:* Rt Hon. Michael Jopling, MP, born 1930. (£21,900.)

28. *Minister of State, Home Office:* Timothy Raison, MP, born 1929. (£18,650.)

29. *Minister of State, Home Office:* Patrick Mayhew, QC, MP, born 1929. (£18,650.)

30. *Minister of State, Foreign and Commonwealth Office:* Hon. Douglas Hurd, CBE, MP, born 1930. (£18,650.)

31. *Minister of State, Foreign and Commonwealth Office:* Hon. Nicholas Ridley, MP, born 1929. (£18,650.)

32. *Minister of State, Foreign and Commonwealth Office:* Peter Blaker, MP, born 1922. (£18,650.)

33. *Minister of State, Foreign and Commonwealth Office and Minister for Overseas Development:* Neil Marten, MP, born 1916. (£18,650.)

34. *Financial Secretary, Treasury:* Nigel Lawson, MP, born 1932. (£18,650.)

35. *Minister of State, Treasury:* Peter Rees, QC, MP, born 1926. (£18,650.)

36. *Minister of State, Treasury:* The Lord Cockfield, born 1916. (£18,650.)

37. *Minister of State, Department of Industry:* Norman Tebbit, MP, born 1931. (£18,650.)

38. *Minister of State, Department of Industry:* Kenneth Baker, MP, born 1934. (£18,650.)

39. *Minister of State, Ministry of Defence:* The Viscount Trenchard, MC, born 1923. (£18,650.)

40. *Minister of State, Civil Service Department:* Barney Hayhoe, MP, born 1925. (£18,650.)

41. *Minister of State, Department of Employment:* The Earl of Gowrie, born 1939. (18,650.)

42. *Minister of State, Ministry of Agriculture, Fisheries and Food:* The Earl Ferrers, born 1929. (£18,650.)

43. *Minister of State, Ministry of Agriculture, Fisheries and Food:* Alick Buchanan-Smith, MP, born 1932. (£18,650.)

44. *Minister of State, Department of the Environment, Minister of Local Government and Environmental Services:* Rt Hon. Tom King, MP, born 1933. (£18,650.)

45. *Minister of State, Department of the Environment, Minister for Housing and Construction:* John Stanley, MP, born 1942. (£18,650.)

46. *Minister of State, Scottish Office:* The Earl of Mansfield, born 1930. (£18,650.)

47. *Minister of State, Northern Ireland Office:* Michael Alison, MP, born 1926. (£18,650.)

48. *Minister of State, Northern Ireland Office:* Hon. Adam Butler, MP, born 1931. (£18,650.)

49. *Minister of State, Department of Health and Social Security, Minister for Health:* Dr Gerard Vaughan, MP, born 1923. (£18,650.)

50. *Minister of State, Department of Health and Social Security, Minister for Social Security:* Hugh Rossi, MP, born 1927. (£18,650.)

51. *Minister of State, Department of Trade, Minister for Consumer Affairs:* Rt Hon. Sally Oppenheim, MP, born 1930. (£18,650.)

52. *Minister of State, Department of Trade, Minister for Trade:* Cecil Parkinson, MP, born 1931. (£18,650.)

53. *Minister of State, Department of Energy:* Hamish Gray, MP, born 1927. (£18,650.)

54. *Minister of State, Department of Education and Science, Minister for the Arts:* Rt Hon. Paul Channon, MP, born 1935. (£18,650.)

55. *Minister of State, Department of Education and Science:* Baroness Young, born 1926. (£18,650.)

Leader of the Opposition in the House of Commons: The Rt Hon. Michael Foot, MP, born 1914. (£24,100.)

Leader of the Opposition in the House of Lords: The Rt Hon. The Lord Peart, born 1915. (£14,250.)

The constitution of the House of Commons after the general election held on 3 May 1979 was as follows: Conservative, 339; Labour, 268; Liberal, 11; Others, 17; total, 635. The numbers of votes cast were: Conservative, 13,697,753 (43·9% of poll); Labour, 11,509,524 (36·9%); Liberals, 4,313,931 (13·8%); Others, 1,699,582 (5·4%).

Beloff, M. and Peele, G., *The Government of the United Kingdom.* London, 1980
Blake, R. N. W., *The Office of Prime Minister.* OUP, 1975
Butler, D. E. and Sloman A., *British Political Facts 1900–1979.* London 1980
Butler, D. E. and Kavanagh, D., *The British General Election of 1979.* London, 1980
Butler D. E. and Stokes, D., *Political Change in Britain: The Evolution of Electoral Choice.* London, 1975
Butt, R., *The Power of Parliament.* 2nd ed. London, 1969
Cook, C., *A Short History of the Liberal Party.* London, 1976
Cook, C., and Ramsden, J., *By-Elections in British Politics.* London, 1973

Craig, F. W. S., *British Electoral Facts 1885–1975*. London, 1976.—*The Most Gracious Speeches to Parliament 1900–1974*. London, 1975
Ford, P. and G., *A Guide to Parliamentary Papers*. New ed. OUP, 1956
Herman, V., and Att, J. E., *Cabinet Studies*. London, 1976
Jennings, Sir I., *Cabinet Government*. 3rd. ed. CUP, 1959.—*The British Constitution*. 5th ed. CUP, 1966.—*Parliament*. 2nd ed. CUP, 1957.—*Party Politics*. 3 vols. CUP, 1960–62
Jones, J. M., *British Nationality Law*. Rev. ed. London, 1955
King, A. (ed.), *The British Prime Minister*. London, 1969.—*British Members of Parliament*. London, 1974
Laundy, P., *The Office of Speaker*. London, 1964
Lindsay, T. F., *The Conservative Party 1918–1970*. London, 1976
Mackintosh, J. P., *The British Cabinet*. 3rd ed. London, 1977.—*The Government and Politics of Britain*. 4th ed. London, 1977
May, Sir T. E., *Treatise on the Law, Privileges, Proceedings and Usage of Parliament*. 19th ed., London, 1976
Mitchell, B. R., and Boehm, K. H., *British Parliamentary Elections, 1950–64*. CUP, 1966
Pelling, H., *A Short History of the Labour Party*. London, 1976
Rush, M., and Shaw, M., *House of Commons*. London, 1974
Stacey, F., *British Government 1966–1975*. London, 1975
Taylor, E., *The House of Commons at Work*. 7th ed. London, 1967
Wilding, N., and Laundy, P., *An Encyclopaedia of Parliament*. 4th ed. London, 1972
Young, R., *The British Parliament*. London, 1962

European Parliament: On 7 June 1979 Great Britain elected 81 representatives to the European Parliament, of which 66 came from England, 8 from Scotland and 4 from Wales, each constituency returning a single member by a first past the post system. Northern Ireland returned 3 members by single transferable vote. 13,446,076 votes were cast, on a 33% poll. The seats were won as follows: Conservative 60, Labour 17, Scottish Nationalists 1, Ulster Unionists 1, Democratic Unionists 1, Social, Democratic and Labour Party 1.

Local Government. Local Administration is carried out by four different types of bodies, namely: (i) local branches of some central ministries, such as the Department of Health and Social Security; (ii) local sub-managements of nationalized industries (coal, electricity, gas, public transport and the post office); (iii) specialist authorities such as water authorities; and (iv) the system of *local government* described below. The phrase 'local government' has come to mean that part of the local administration conducted by elected councils.

There are two separate systems: one for England and Wales and one for Scotland, but both systems are financed by a species of tax on property, levied locally, combined with government grants which, in the aggregate, amount to more than the yield of the local tax. This local tax is called 'the rate'. The system of financing local government was the subject of a major review in 1975.

Local Government: England and Wales—*Outside London.* England and Wales have slightly differing systems. Each country has three types of councils namely, county, district and English parish or Welsh Community Councils. In addition, England has some metropolitan county and district councils.

Councillors are elected by their local electors for 4 years. The chairman of the council is one of the councillors elected by the rest. In a district with the status of city or borough his title is mayor, or in a few famous places Lord Mayor. Any parish or community council can by simple resolution adopt the style 'town council' and the status of town for the parish or community with the town mayor as chairman.

Counties and Districts: There are 47 non-metropolitan counties (of which 8 are in Wales) and 6 metropolitan counties (Greater Manchester, Merseyside, South Yorkshire, Tyne and Wear, West Yorkshire and West Midlands). Within the counties there are 369 districts (36 metropolitan and 333 non-metropolitan, of which 37 are in Wales).

Parishes and Communities: There are some 10,000 parishes within the English districts, of which 7,000 or so have councils. About 300 are former small boroughs or urban districts which became successor parishes. Parishes generally, however, remain comparatively unaffected by reorganization.

In Wales, parishes have been replaced by communities. Unlike England, where many areas are not in any parish, communities have been established for the whole of Wales. There is one for each former parish, county borough, borough or urban district (or part thereof where the former area is divided by a new boundary). There are 1,004 communities altogether, of which 800 or so have councils.

The Local Government Act 1972 laid down the boundaries for all the counties and districts in England and Wales except the English non-metropolitan districts.

Permanent Local Government Commissions for England and for Wales advise the Secretary of State on boundaries and electoral arrangements.

A council has only those powers which have been conferred upon it expressly by Act of Parliament, and no more. The relationship between the different types of council is one of specialization, not of hierarchy. The larger do not supervise the smaller; each being, within its own sphere, entitled to make its own decisions. Government sanction, however, is required to borrow money and to sell land below its market value, and certain types of land use are subject to planning control.

Councils are kept within the law by a system of publicly regulated audit, and in the last resort they can be restrained from exceeding their powers by the courts.

Local government functions may be classified into county, district and parish or community functions, but whereas county and district functions are distinct, the parish and community functions are mostly concurrent with those of the districts. Arrangements may, however, be made so that any council may discharge functions of any other as its agent.

The following is the classification of powers given above: *Parish and Community Functions.* Allotments, burial and cremation, halls, meeting places and entertainments, facilities for exercise and recreation, public lavatories, street lighting, off-street vehicle parking, footpaths, the support of local arts and crafts, the encouragement of tourism and the right to be consulted by the district council on planning application and certain byelaws. *District Functions.* In addition to the Parish and Community functions, aerodromes, civic restaurants, housing, markets, refuse collection, the administration of planning control, the formulation of local plans, sewerage, on behalf of the water authority, museums, the licensing of places of entertainment and refreshment, and the constitutional oversight of parishes and communities. *County Functions.* The formulation of structure plans, traffic, transportation and roads, education, public libraries and museums, youth employment and social services.

There are, in addition, a number of special arrangements. Four district councils in Wales have been designated as library authorities and Welsh district councils have powers in relation to allotments currently with community councils. The county councils in England and Wales separately or jointly appoint the fire and police authorities, and the bodies responsible for national parks. In Metropolitan counties the district not the county councils are responsible for education, social services and libraries.

The total number of local government electors in England and Wales was 36,927,947 in 1980.

Greater London. Since 1965 London has been governed by the Greater London Council covering the whole metropolitan area, and by 32 London Boroughs and the City of London, each with responsibilities in its own area. In the City and the 12 boroughs covering the inner part of Greater London education is the responsibility of the Inner London Education Authority, a special Committee of the GLC but independent of it, while in the 20 outer boroughs the London Borough Council is the education authority. Other functions are divided between the GLC and the boroughs. The main responsibilities of the GLC are strategic planning, major roads, public transport (through the London Transport Executive, which is responsible to it), housing, major parks and open spaces, the fire service, refuse disposal and Thames flood prevention. The boroughs are the primary housing authorities in their own areas, while the GLC is concerned with matters affecting the whole of London. The City has preserved a large measure of independence and has its own powers regarding police, justice, bridges, sanitation, etc. Except in the City the police authority covering the whole of Greater London is the Metropolitan Police, which is responsible direct to the Central Government.

Estimated population of Greater London in June 1980 was 6,916,495, and rateable value at 1 April 1980 (estimate) was £1,935,826,000. Estimated gross revenue expenditure of the GLC in 1980–81 was £2,198·2m. (including £709·7m. for the ILEA and £547m. for London Transport). Estimated gross capital expenditure, 1980–82 was £490m., including ILEA £18m., London Transport £110m. and £92m. for housing loans. The GLC outstanding debt at 1 April 1980 was £1,805,455,000; ILEA, £188,542,000.

Scotland. Under the system, which came into effect in 1975, the Scots mainland is divided into 9 regions, and in addition there are the 3 islands areas of Orkney, Shetland and the Western Isles. There is no equivalent to the English metropolitan county. The regions are divided into districts which total 53. All these units have a council consisting of councillors elected for 4 years and a chairman elected by the councillors for 4 years. Community councils have been established under schemes submitted by district and island councils. These community councils cannot claim public funds as of right, nor do they have powers directly conferred by Statute: consequently they are not local authorities in the sense that Welsh Community Councils are.

As in England and Wales a permanent Local Government Boundary Commission advises the Secretary of State on Local Authority Boundaries and electoral arrangements.

On the mainland, functions are allocated between regional and district authorities, in the same way (with minor exceptions) as they are allocated between English counties on the one hand and English districts and parishes on the other, but the councils of the islands areas, which have no districts, perform both sets of functions.

Despite differences of nomenclature the effect of the reforms of 1972 (England) and 1973 (Scotland) is to assimilate the systems of mainland Scotland and of England and Wales more closely than has been the case in the past.

The total number of local government electors in Scotland was 3,860,551 in 1980.

Complaints. Under both systems, complaints, by members of the public, of maladministration may be investigated by a Commissioner for Local Administration. Initially a complaint must be referred to him through a councillor, but a direct approach to him is possible if this fails. He can deal only with matters for which there is no other remedy; he reports to the council concerned and may publish his report.

For map of regions *see* THE STATESMAN'S YEAR-BOOK, 1974–75.

Our Changing Democracy: Devolution to Scotland and Wales. HMSO, 1975
Arnold-Baker, C., *The Local Government Act 1972.* London, 1973

DEFENCE. The Defence Council was established on 1 April 1964 under the chairmanship of the Secretary of State for Defence, who is responsible to the Sovereign and Parliament for the defence of the realm. Vested in the Defence Council are the functions of commanding and administering the Armed Forces. The Secretary of State heads the Ministry of Defence as a Department of State. There are 4 subordinate Ministers: The Minister of State for Defence and 3 Parliamentary Under-Secretaries of State, 1 for each of the Services.

Defence Council membership comprises the Secretary of State, the Minister of State, the 3 Parliamentary Under-Secretaries, the Chief of the Defence Staff, the 3 single Service Chiefs of Staff, the Vice Chief of Defence Staff (Personnel and Logistics), the Chief of Defence Procurement, the Chief Scientific Adviser and the Permanent Under-Secretary of State.

There are 3 Service Boards, each of which enjoys delegated powers for the administration of matters relating to the naval, military and air forces respectively.

Defence policy decision making is a collective Governmental responsibility. Important matters of policy are considered by the full Cabinet or, more frequently, by the Defence and Oversea Policy Committee under the chairmanship of the Prime Minister. Other members of this Committee include the Secretary of State for Defence, the Foreign and Commonwealth Secretary and the Home Secretary.

Logistics Services. Since the inception of a unified Ministry of Defence in 1964, progress has been made in the rationalization of the logistics services of the Royal Navy, the Army and the Royal Air Force. Airfield construction for all Services is now the responsibility of the Army's Royal Engineers; the Air Force Department is responsible for accommodation stores for maintenance and for the initial furnishing of new buildings; the Army Department is the single management authority for the design, development, procurement and inspection of clothing other than certain specialized clothing; the Navy Department has for some time been responsible for ration policy provisioning, procurement, storing and distribution of food to main depots and to Army forward supply depots in BAOR and is responsible for water transport to its tri-service responsibilities. The supply of Naval air stores has been integrated with those of the RAF. Considerable savings in money and in Service and civilian manpower have already been realized and are expected to continue.

The Procurement Executive. An important development in 1971 was the creation of a Procurement Executive to combine the Defence Procurement responsibilities of the Ministry of Defence and the former Ministry of Aviation Supply.

Service Strengths at 1 Jan. 1981, all ranks, males and females, UK personnel only: Royal Navy and Royal Marines, 73,627; Army, 167,311; Royal Air Force, 92,977; Total, 333,915.

Defence Budget Estimates: 1980–81, £11,300m.; 1980–81, £12,138m.

Army. Control of the British Army is vested in the Defence Council and is exercised through the Army Board, which consists of 6 civilian and 5 military members. The Secretary of State for Defence is Chairman of the Army Board. The other civilian members are the Minister of State for Defence and the Parliamentary Under-Secretary of State for Defence for the Army, the Chief Scientist (Army) and the Deputy Under-Secretary of State (Army) and the Second Permanent Under-Secretary of State who attend meetings as appropriate.

The Military members of the Army Board are the Chief of the General Staff, the Adjutant-General, the Quartermaster-General, the Master-General of the Ordnance and the Vice-Chief of the General Staff. The Chief of the General Staff is the professional head of his Service and the professional adviser to Ministers on the Army aspects of military problems. He is responsible for the fighting efficiency of his Service; for the consideration of all Army aspects of policy planning; for Army advice on the conduct of operations; and for the issuing of such single Service operational orders as may be appropriate resulting from defence policy decisions. He is also responsible for the Territorial Army. The Chief of the General Staff is a member of the Chiefs of Staff Committee which is collectively responsible to HM Government for professional advice on strategy and military operations and on the military implication of defence policy. This advice is tendered to the Secretary of State for Defence by the Chairman of the Chiefs of Staff Committee, the Chief of the Defence Staff. In exercise of his General Staff responsibilities the Chief of the General Staff is assisted by the Vice-Chief of the General Staff. The Adjutant-General is responsible for Army manpower within the policy set up by the General Staff; for recruiting and selection; for the administration and individual training of military personnel; for the discipline of the Army; for pay and allowances and pensions; for Army medical services; for dental and nursing services; for legal services; for the veterinary and remount services; for the Army Cadet Forces; for questions of Army welfare and education including school children overseas; and for resettlement and sports. The Quartermaster-General is responsible for logistic planning for the Army; for the storage, distribution, maintenance, repair and inspection of equipment, stores and ammunition; for development of stores; for supply, transport and accommodation; for the development, production and inspection of clothing; for military movements and transportation; for the Army postal, catering, salvage and fire services; and for questions connected with canteens, institutes and military labour. The Master General of the Ordnance is a member of both of the Army Board and of the Procurement Executive Management Board. He is responsible to the Chief of Defence Procurement for the financial and technical management of the approved programme for the procurement of land service equipment for the Armed Services, and to the Army Board for the co-ordination of the Army's total equipment programme. The Chief Scientist (Army) is responsible for providing scientific advice to the Army Board and its members and for ensuring that the Defence Research Programme properly reflects their needs. He is also a member of the Procurement Executive as Deputy Controller, Research and Development Establishments, and Research (B). The Deputy Under-Secretary of State (Army) is responsible for the general co-ordination of Army Board business and, under the Permanent Under-Secretary of State and the Second Permanent Under-Secretary of State, for providing the Board with financial and administrative guidance.

Headquarters United Kingdom Land Forces at Wilton commands all Army units in UK except Ministry of Defence controlled units. The Ministry of Defence retains direct operational control of units in Northern Ireland. Command by HQ United Kingdom Land Forces is exercised through 9 district headquarters. There are 3 major overseas Commands: Land Forces Cyprus, Hong Kong and the British Army of the Rhine. There are also garrisons in Berlin, Gibraltar and Belize.

The strength of the Regular Army (less the Brigade of Gurkhas and locally enlisted personnel) on 1 Jan. 1981 was 160,697 men and 6,632 women. The citizen force is the Territorial Army.

The Territorial Army has an establishment of about 73,000. Its role is to provide a national reserve for employment on specific tasks at home and overseas and to meet the unexpected when required; and, in particular, to complete the Army Order of Battle of NATO committed forces and to provide certain units for the support of NATO Headquarters, to assist in maintaining a secure UK base in support of forces deployed on the Continent of Europe and to provide a framework for any future expansion of the Reserves. In addition, men who have completed service in the Regular Army normally have some liability to serve in the Regular Reserve. All members of the TA and Regular Reserve may be called out by a Queen's Order in time of emergency or imminent national danger and most of the TA and a large proportion of the Regular Reserve may be called out by a Queen's Order when warlike operations are in preparation or in progress. There is a special reserve force in Northern Ireland, the Ulster Defence Regiment, 7,500 strong, which gives support to the regular army.

Men, women and juniors enlist in the Army for 22 years' active and reserve service. However, under a scheme introduced in May 1981 they are entitled to give 12 months' notice to leave active service provided they serve for a minimum of 3 years. Alternatively, they can agree to serve for 6 or 9 years to receive the benefit of higher rates of pay. Those enlisting in certain technical trades must agree to serve for a minimum of 6 years. Recruits under the age of $17\frac{1}{2}$ on reaching the age of 18 are entitled either to confirm their original engagement or to reduce their period of service to 3 years.

Women serve in both the Regular Army and the TA in the Queen Alexandra's Royal Army Nursing Corps, the Ulster Defence Regiment and the Women's Royal Army Corps, the latter's employments including communications, motor transport, clerical and catering duties. Some officers of the Women's Royal Army Corps are employed on the staffs of military headquarters.

Barnett, C., *Britain and her Army 1509–1970*. London, 1970
Blaxford, G., *The Regiments Depart: A History of the British Army 1945–70*. London, 1971
Fortescue, J. W., *History of the British Army*. 14 vols. London, 1899–1930
Haswell, J., *The British Army*. London, 1975
Johnson, F. A., *Defence by Ministry: The British Ministry of Defence 1944–1974*. London, 1980
Sheppard, E. W., *Short History of the British Army*. 4th ed. London, 1950
Stanhope, H., *The Soldiers: An Anatomy of the British Army*. London, 1979

Navy. The Royal Navy is a permanent establishment, governed by the Admiralty Board of the Defence Council. The Secretary of State for Defence is Chairman of the Admiralty Board; the Minister of State for Defence is Vice-Chairman. The members of the Admiralty Board and their responsibilities are as follows: The Parliamentary Under-Secretary of State for Defence for the Royal Navy; The Chief of the Naval Staff and First Sea Lord (professional head of the Royal Navy), assisted by the Vice-Chief of the Naval Staff, responsible for fighting efficiency, policy planning and operations advice; The Chief of Naval Personnel and Second Sea Lord, responsible for the manning of the Fleet, service conditions, training, discipline and welfare; The Controller of the Navy (formerly also Third Sea Lord), responsible for research and development, design, production, inspection, repair and maintenance of ships, their weapons and equipment; The Chief of Fleet Support, known until 1968 as Chief of Naval Supplies and Transport and Vice-Controller (formerly also Fourth Sea Lord), responsible for the provision of naval armament, victualling and medical stores and fuels, and for the movement of transport of persons and material, and superintending Dockyard organization and maintenance of the Fleet; and The Chief Scientist (Royal Navy), responsible for super-intending the conduct of all research and development and the deployment of scientific effort. The post of Second Permanent Under-Secretary of State (Royal Navy) (form-erly Permanent Secretary) lapsed in 1968 (he was Civil Service head, responsible for general co-ordination of the Admiralty Board business, the interior economy of the Navy department, Navy contracts and the administration of civil staff, and account-ing officer for Navy Votes responsible for the control of expenditure and adviser to the Admiralty Board on financial questions). Thus the office of Samuel Pepys, of which the last holder was the 33rd, passed into history. The Deputy Under-Secretary of State (Navy) is the Board Member now responsible for some of these functions. Financial and staff control is vested in the Second Permanent Under-Secretary for Administration and the Second Permanent Under-Secretary for Equipment.

The following is a summary of the more important units:

Category	1972	1973	1974	1975	1976	1977	1978	1979	1980
				Completed by the end of					
Aircraft carriers	4[2]	3[1]	3[1]	3[1]	3[3]	3[3]	3[3]	3[4]	3
Submarines	35	34	32	30	31	31	30	31	31
Cruisers	2	2	2	2	2	2	2	2[5]	1
Destroyers	12	9	10	10	10	10	11	14	14
Frigates	65	62	60	58	56	56	54	56	55

[1] Included 2 commando carriers.

[2] Included 3 commando carriers.

[3] Included 1 helicopter/V/STOL carrier and 1 commando carrier in reserve.

[4] Includes the new anti-submarine cruiser/carrier of Sea Harrier V/STOL aircraft and Sea King helicopters.

[5] Old ships with reduced complements while laid up in reserve.

There are also 2 assault ships, 3 maintenance ships, 1 ice patrol ship, 1 fast patrol craft, 3 fast training boats, 2 seaward defence boats, 13 surveying vessels, 5 coastal patrol vessels (*ex*-coastal minesweepers), 17 minehunters, 17 coastal minesweepers, 2 trawler minesweepers, 5 inshore minesweepers, 1 mine countermeasures support ship, 6 trials ships, 1 helicopter support ship, 1 submarine tender (ocean-going tug type), 7 offshore patrol vessels (fishery protection), 4 inshore patrol boats, 11 moor-ing, salvage and boom vessels, 10 fleet support and supply ships, 14 fleet oilers, 52 other auxiliaries, 6 logistic landing ships, 60 minor landing craft, 12 fleet tugs, 58 other tugs, and 53 tenders. In the following table the principal surface warships are grouped in classes, in descending order of modernity.

Com-pleted	Name	Standard displace-ment Tons	Aircraft	Armament	Shaft horse-power	Speed knots
		Helicopter and V/STOL Aircraft Carriers				
1959	Hermes[2]	23,900	5 V/STOL plus 9 helicopters	2 'Seacat'	78,000	28·0
1954	Bulwark[1]	23,300	20 helicopters	Light AA	78,000	28·0

[1] Converted from fixed wing aircraft carrier to commando carrier 1959–60 and reduced to care and maintenance reserve in April 1976: brought forward in Jan. 1978 for unwrapping, refit, re-storing and docking before re-commissioning for operational service in Feb. 1979 as an anti-submarine helicopter carrier with V/STOL aircraft capability. Her sister ship *Albion*, converted in 1961–62, was de-commissioned in May 1973 and towed away for disposal in Dec. 1973.

[2] Converted from fixed wing aircraft carrier to commando carrier 1971–73. Converted to anti-submarine helicopter and V/STOL aircraft role in 1976–77. Fitted with 'Ski-jump' launching ramp during 1980–81 refit.

The large fixed-wing aircraft carrier *Ark Royal*, 43,060 tons, returned to Devonport from her last active service mission on 4 Dec. 1978 and was decommissioned in 1979 for disposal. She was towed to Scotland in Sept. 1980 for breaking up.

Her sister ship *Eagle*, reconstructed Dec. 1959 to May 1964, was de-stored in 1972 and laid up at Devonport (providing spares for *Ark Royal*) until Oct. 1978 when she was towed to Scotland for breaking up.

The aircraft carrier *Victorious*, scheduled for disposal in Nov. 1967, decommisioned on 13 March 1968 and left Portsmouth for breaking up at Faslane on 11 July 1969. The aircraft carrier *Centaur* used 1965–1970 as accommodation ship for aircraft carriers and commando carriers refitting, was officially declared for disposal in Feb. 1971 and broken up in 1973.

Com- pleted	Name	Standard displace- ment Tons	Aircraft	Armament	Shaft horse- power	Speed knots
			Anti-Submarine Cruisers/Carriers			
1980	Invincible*	16,000	8 V/Stol plus 10 helicopters	Twin Sea Dart	112,000	28

* Originally designed as 'Command Cruiser', subsequently re-rated as 'Through-deck Cruiser' (meaning flat-top or near full-length flight deck) and later designated 'Anti-Submarine Cruiser' officially listed as ASW carrier in 1980.

			Cruisers			
1961	Blake[1]	9,550	4 helicopters	2 6-in; 2 3-in.	80,000	31·5

[1] Partially converted (aft) into a helicopter carrier 1965–69. Standby Reserve 1980.

[2] Sister ship *Tiger*, partially converted (aft) into a helicopter carrier 1968–72. Reduced to Reserve in 1979. Approved for disposal in 1980. Sister ship *Lion*, not converted into a helicopter carrier (reconstruction rescinded in Oct. 1970), was scheduled for disposal in 1972, and broken up in 1975.

The cruiser *Belfast*, reclassified as harbour accommodation ship in June 1966, ceased in this capacity in Feb. 1971, and on 21 Oct. 1971 became museum ship on the Thames.

The cruisers *Ceylon* and *Newfoundland* were sold to Peru in 1959. *Birmingham* scrapped in 1960; *Jamaica* and *Superb* in 1961; *Kenya* and *Swiftsure* in 1962; *Bermuda* and *Mauritius* in 1965. *Sheffield* towed to the shipbreakers in 1967; *Gambia* in 1968.

Submarines are of the following classes: 'Resolution' (nuclear powered and Polaris missile armed), 4; 'Swiftsure' (nuclear powered), 5; 'Churchill' (nuclear powered), 3; 'Valiant' (nuclear powered), 2; 'Dreadnought' (nuclear powered), 1; 'Oberon', 13; 'Porpoise', 3. Surface displacements range from 2,030 to 7,500 tons.

The first nuclear-powered fleet submarine, *Dreadnought*, was commissioned on 17 April 1963; and the first nuclear powered ballistic missile submarine, *Resolution*, was accepted in Oct. 1967.

The destroyers of the Royal Navy are of the following classes: 'Sheffield', 7; 'Bristol', 1; 'County', 6. Standard displacements range from 3,150 to 6,100 tons.

Frigates are of the following classes: 'Broadsword', 2; 'Amazon', 8; 'Leander', 26; 'Tribal', 7; 'Rothesay', 9; 'Salisbury', 1; 'Leopard', 1; 'Whitby', 1. Displacements range from 2,150 to 3,500 tons.

Ships under construction or on order include 4 nuclear powered submarines, 7 guided missile armed destroyers, 4 frigates, 4 mine counter measures vessels and 2 offshore patrol vessels. The 'through-deck' (flat-top) 'anti-submarine cruiser' (small vertical aircraft/helicopter carrier) *Invincible*, ordered in April 1973, laid down in July 1973 and launched in May 1977 was commissioned on 11 July 1980; and a sister ship, *Illustrious*, ordered in 1976, was launched on 1 Dec. 1978, when the third ship of the class, to be named *Ark Royal*, was ordered, perpetuating the name of the large aircraft carrier broken up in 1980–81.

The Navy Estimates are now included in a total Defence Budget which in the 1979–80 White Paper Statement amounted to £8,557·7m. and in 1980–81 to £10,785m.

The total number of officers and ratings provided for was (in 1,000) 1974–75, 78·3; 1975–76, 77·4; 1976–77, 76·5; 1977–78, 76·1; 1978–79, 75·5; 1979–80, 74·5; 1980–81, 72·6 (including 3,900 service-women).

Blackman, R. V. B., *The World's Warships*. London, 1969
Blackman, R. V. B., *Ships of the Royal Navy*. London, 1975
Moore, J. E. (ed.), *Jane's Fighting Ships*. London, annual

Air Force. In May 1912 the Royal Flying Corps first came into existence with military and naval wings, of which the latter became the independent Royal Naval Air Service in July 1914. On 2 Jan. 1918 an Air Ministry was formed, and on 1 April 1918 the Royal Flying Corps and the Royal Naval Air Service were amalgamated, under the Air Ministry, as the Royal Air Force.

In 1937 the units based on aircraft carriers and naval shore stations again passed to the operational and administrative control of the Admiralty, as the Fleet Air Arm. In 1964 control of the Royal Air Force became a responsibility of the unified Ministry of Defence.

The Royal Air Force is administered by the Air Force Board, of which the Secretary of State for Defence is Chairman. The Minister of State for Defence is Vice-Chairman, as is the Under-Secretary of State for Defence for the Royal Air Force, who normally acts as Chairman on behalf of the Secretary of State. Other members of the Board are, Chief of the Air Staff, who is assisted by, Vice-Chief of the Air Staff, Air Member for Personnel, Air Member for Supply and Organization, Controller of Aircraft, Chief Scientist (Royal Air Force), Deputy Under-Secretary of State (Air) and Second Permanent Under-Secretary of State for Administration. The Royal Air Force is organized into commands:

Home Commands. Strike and Support Commands. The Air Training Corps and the Air Sections of the Combined Cadet Force are under the administrative control of Support Command and functionally controlled by the Ministry of Defence.

Overseas Commands. Royal Air Force Germany. Small units in Gibraltar, Cyprus and Hong Kong.

The RAF College, which trains general-duties, engineering, and supply and secretarial graduates for permanent commissions, is at Cranwell. The RAF Staff College is at Bracknell. The Department of Air Warfare is at Cranwell. The RAF Central Flying School is at Leeming. Estimated strength in April 1980, including WRAF and boys, was 87,500.

There is a single multi-role operational command in the UK, known as Strike Command, made up of 5 Groups. No. 1 Group is responsible for control and training of the strike/attack, air-to-air refuelling and reconnaissance forces. There are home-based squadrons of Vulcan Mk. 2 medium bombers; Buccaneer low-level strike and maritime attack aircraft; Victor flight refuelling tankers; and reconnaissance squadrons of Vulcan SR. Mk. 2 and Canberra aircraft. No. 11 Group controls air defence squadrons of Lightning and Phantom supersonic all-weather fighters armed with air-to-air missiles, and their associated communications and ground environment radars, including the Ballistic Missile Early Warning System station at Fylingdales. No. 11 Group also has Shackleton AEW. Mk. 2 airborne early warning aircraft, and Bloodhound surface-to-air missiles. No. 18 Group has Nimrod MR. Mk. 1 and 2 maritime reconnaissance aircraft and Whirlwind, Wessex and Sea King helicopters for search and rescue. No. 38 Group is responsible for the UK ground attack force of Jaguars and V/STOL Harriers; reconnaissance Jaguars; VC10 jets, turboprop Hercules transports, and smaller communications aircraft; and the Queen's Flight, with 3 Andover and 2 Wessex helicopters; Wessex and Puma helicopters for tactical and logistic support in the battlefield area; RAF Regiment UK squadrons, equipped with Bofors L40/70 guns, Tigercat and Rapier missiles, and other weapons for airfield defence; and the Tactical Communications Wing. Strike Command has NATO commitments, but is available for overseas reinforcement. Its fifth Group is Military Air Traffic Operations. The training element of RAF Support Command utilizes Bulldog and Chipmunk primary trainers, Jet Provost basic trainers, Hawk and Hunter advanced trainers, Jetstreams for multi-engine pilot training, twin-jet Dominies for training navigators and other non-pilot aircrew, and Gazelle, Wessex and Whirlwind helicopters.

Squadrons of RAF Germany, which forms part of NATO's 2nd Allied Tactical Air Force under SACEUR, have Harrier V/STOL and Jaguar attack and reconnaissance aircraft, Phantom fighters, Buccaneer strike aircraft, Wessex helicopters, Pembroke communications aircraft and Rapier surface-to-air missiles. A squadron of Wessex helicopters is based in Hong Kong. New types of aircraft under development include the Tornado multi-role combat aircraft, an AEW conversion of the Nimrod, a version of the Chinook helicopter, and flight refuelling tanker conversions of the VC10.

The Royal Air Force, 1939–45. Vols. I, II, III. HMSO, 1953–54
Taylor, J. W. R. (ed.), *Jane's All the World's Aircraft.* London. Annual from 1909
Taylor, J. W. R., *Military Aircraft of the World.* London 1979

INTERNATIONAL RELATIONS

Membership. The UK is a member of UN, the Commonwealth, EEC, OECD, the Council of Europe, NATO and the Colombo Plan.

ECONOMY

Budget. Revenue and expenditure for years ending 31 March, in £ sterling:

Revenue	Estimated in the Budgets	Actual receipts into the Exchequer	More than estimates
1977	33,197,000,000	33,797,000,000	600,000,000
1978	37,742,000,000	38,773,000,000	1,031,000,000
1979	42,746,000,000	43,088,000,000	342,000,000
1980	51,013,000,000	53,369,000,000	2,256,000,000
1981	65,415,000,000	66,814,000,000	1,399,000,000

The Budget estimate of ordinary revenue for 1981–82 is £75,524m.

Expenditure	Budget and supplementary estimates	Actual payments out of the Exchequer	More (+) or less (−) than estimates
1977	39,915,000,000	39,402,000,000	− 513,000,000
1978	43,489,000,000	43,989,000,000	+ 500,000,000
1979	51,378,000,000	51,469,000,000	+ 91,000,000
1980	59,371,000,000	60,753,000,000	+ 1,382,000,000
1981	73,175,000,000	76,728,000,000	+ 3,553,000,000

The Budget estimate of ordinary expenditure for 1981–82 is £83,697m.

The imperial revenue in detail for 1980–81 and the expenditure, are given below, as is the budget estimate for 1981–82 (in £1m.):

Sources of revenue	Net receipts 1980–81	Budget estimate 1981–82
Inland Revenue:		
Income	24,704	28,202
Surtax	5	3
Corporation tax	4,650	4,600
Petroleum revenue tax	2,420	2,210
Supplementary petroleum duty	—	1,850
Capital Gains tax	520	575
Development land tax	24	25
Estate duties	27	15
Capital transfer tax	415	445
Stamp duties	635	775
Special tax on banking deposits	—	400
Total Inland Revenue	33,400	39,100
Customs and Excise:		
Value Added Tax	11,300	12,650
Spirits, beer and wine	2,600	3,200
Oil	3,550	4,800
Tobacco	2,750	3,220
Betting and gaming	465	510
Car tax	455	550
Other revenue duties	10	25
Customs duties	800	835
Agricultural levies	205	210
Total Customs and Excise	22,135	26,000
Vehicle Excise duties	1,403	1,628
National insurance surcharge	3,585	3,809
Total taxation	60,523	70,537
Miscellaneous receipts:		
Broadcasting receiving licences	529	552
Interest and dividends	246	222
Other	5,516	4,218
Total	66,814	75,524

The following are the branches of expenditure and the issues out of the Exchequer for year ended 31 March 1981 and the estimates for the year 1981–82 (in £1m.):

Supply Services

	Estimates 1980–81	Estimates 1981–82
Defence		
Defence	11,300	12,138
Civil supply:		
Overseas Services	1,397	1,581
Agriculture, Fisheries, and Forestry	709	652
Trade, Industry, Energy and Employment	5,741	4,906
Government Investment in Nationalized Industries	1,390	926
Roads and Transport	1,516	1,733
Housing	3,030	2,360
Other Environmental Services	423	520
Law, Order and Protective Services	1,945	2,229
Education and Libraries, Science and Arts	2,463	2,632
Health and Personal Social Services	8,823	9,572
Social Security	7,311	9,438
Other Public Services	1,070	1,216
House of Commons Administration	13	14
Common Services	1,592	1,922
Scotland	2,606	2,737
Wales	1,014	1,101
Northern Ireland	959	1,118
Rate Support Grant, Financial Transactions, etc.	15,056	15,315
Total Civil Supply	68,358	72,110
Supplementary provision	—	1,631
Total Supply Services	68,358	73,741

Consolidated Fund Standing Services

Payment to the National Loans Funds in respect of service of the National Debt	5,180	6,200
Northern Ireland—share of taxes, etc.	1,236	1,279
Payments to European Communities	1,930	2,450
Other Services	24	27
Total	76,728	83,697

A single graduated income tax came into operation on 6 April 1973, replacing the existing income tax and surtax.

Rates of Personal Tax from 6 April 1981 Income between	%
£0–11,250	30
£11,251–£13,250	40
£13,251–£16,750	45
£16,751–£22,250	50
£22,251–£27,750	55
Over £27,750	60

Surcharge on investment income from 1980–81 is at the single rate of 15% on income in excess of £5,500. There is no separate exemption level for taxpayers who are 65 or over.

Under the tax system, the amounts of the personal allowances are adjusted so that they retain their equivalent in relation to earned income.

	1981–82 £
Personal Allowances	
Single person ⎫ Wife's earned income ⎭	1,375
Married man	2,145
Additional allowance	770

	1981–82
Personal Allowances (contd.)	£
Dependent relative:	
Single woman claimant	145
Others	100
Housekeeper	100
Relative taking charge of younger brother	
or sister	100
Daughter's services	55
Blind person	360

Deductions of tax under PAYE extend over the full range of unified tax rates and not merely the basic rate. Similarly, assessment on business profits and on other income which was directly assessed to tax, such as rents and interest on bank deposits, are made by reference to the full scale of rates, including where appropriate the investment income surcharge.

The standard rate of 30% is the rate at which tax is deducted from payments of interest, etc., and corresponds under the new corporation tax system, to the tax credit on dividends. Where an individual's total income is such that he is liable on this taxed investment income at rates exceeding 30%, or if his investment income is high enough to make him liable to the surcharge, the higher rate or surcharge liability on this taxed investment income will in general be assessed separately after the end of the tax year.

Corporation Tax. Corporation Tax applies, with certain exceptions, to trades or businesses carried on by bodies corporate or by unincorporated societies or other bodies and this tax came into force from April 1966 replacing Profits Tax. The rate of this tax for 1969–71, 45%; but in Oct. 1970 this was reduced to 42·5% for financial year 1969–70 and reduced again to 40% in 1970–71. There are reduced rates of Corporation Tax for small companies and for 1981–82 the rate is 42% and the limit for that rate £80,000, limit for marginal relief £200,000.

Capital Gains Tax. Gains resulting from the disposal of capital assets (other than British Government and Government guaranteed securities and certain exempted forms of property such as a private car and personal residences) are taxed under the Finance Act 1965. In 1980–81 exemption was granted for all gains made in a financial year which in total did not exceed £3,000 and a lower rate of 15% and most trusts on the first £1,500.

Value Added Tax. Value Added Tax was introduced from 1 April 1973 at the rate of 10% on the supply of goods (with certain exceptions) and services. From 18 June 1979 the rate of tax was fixed at 15%.

Kay, J. A. and King, M. A., *The British Tax System.* OUP, 1980

Local Taxation. The rateable value on which rates were leviable in England and Wales on 1 April 1980 was £7,318m. In England and Wales, the average amount of the rates collected per £ of rateable value was £0·34 in 1913–14; and estimated to be 109·16p for 1980–81. In Scotland the rateable value on which rates are leviable on 1 April 1980 was £1,281m. and the average amount per £ of rateable value of the rates was 81p. The average water rate was 6·6p in the £.

Under the Local Government Planning and Land Act 1980, the Government gives general financial assistance to local authorities by means of rate support grants. The Rate Support Grant Report (England) 1980 deals with the distribution of these grants to local authorities in England only. The grants for 1981–82 contain (i) Block Grant £8,364m., the object of which is to give authorities sufficient grant to put them in a position where they can provide similar standards of service for a similar rate in the £, and (ii) Domestic Grant £663m., which will provide a relief of 18½p for domestic ratepayers. There is also provisions in the 1980 Act for payment of National Parks Supplementary Grant (£4·5m.) to county councils with all r part of a national park in their area, and Transport Supplementary Grant (£416·5m.) payable to county councils and the Greater London Council. Grants are also payable on revenue expenditure for specific services, including police and housing, and capital expenditure on certain services also attracts grant.

In Scotland, rate support grants are paid under the Local Government (Scotland) Act 1966, as amended by the Local Government (Scotland) Act 1975. The total rate support grant and the amounts of the component parts for the local authority financial year 1981–82, as prescribed in the Rate Support Grant (Scotland) Order 1980 are as follows: £1,503·1m.; needs element £1,340·2m.; resources element £148·9m.; domestic element £14m. The domestic element is paid to rating authorities to offset the cost of reducing by 3p in the £ the rates payable on domestic properties. A small part of the needs element, £10·8m. in 1981–82, is apportioned among those local authorities incurring extraordinary expenses in connection with developments relating to exploration for or exploitation of offshore petroleum. Payments under Part V of the Local Government Act 1948 have been repealed in so far as they relate to years commencing on or after 1 April 1978. The lands and heritages concerned are now valued by formula as prescribed by Order. As in England and Wales capital and revenue grants are also payable on expenditure for certain specific services.

Local authority loan debt at 31 March 1974 amounted to £19,391m.

The rateable value of Greater London was £1,909,619,000 on 1 April 1979. The outstanding debt of the Greater London Council on 1 April 1979 was £1,667,718,000 and the Inner London Education Authority, £187,063,000.

Rates and Rateable Values, 1974–75. HMSO
Rates and Rateable Values in Scotland, 1977–78. HMSO
Estimates, 1978–79. GLC
Analysis of Rateable Values List. GLC, 1977
Report on Rate Support Grant Order 1979. HMSO

Gross National Product:

	1946	1950	1960	1970	1978
Expenditure (£1m.)					
Consumers' expenditure	7,273	9,400	16,939	31,773	96,086
Central government final consumption	2,282	2,123	4,206	8,961	32,693
Gross domestic fixed capital formation	925	1,700	4,190	9,462	29,218
Value of physical increase in stocks and work in progress	−126	−210	562	425	1,528
Total domestic expenditure at market prices	10,354	13,013	25,897	50,581	159,525
Exports of goods and services	1,775	3,807	5,153	11,533	47,636
Less Imports of goods and services	−2,083	−3,492	−5,549	−11,122	−45,522
Less Taxes on expenditure	−1,573	−2,065	−3,378	−8,416	−23,238
Subsidies	384	474	493	884	3,598
Gross domestic product at factor cost	8,855	11,737	22,616	43,460	141,999
Factor incomes (£1m.)					
Income from employment	5,758	7,627	15,174	30,404	98,156
Income from self-employment [1]	1,126	1,389	2,008	3,735	13,245
Gross trading profits of companies [1]	1,476	2,126	3,730	5,935	17,055
Gross trading surplus of public corporations [1]	20	196	534	1,447	5,412
Gross trading surplus of other public enterprises [1]	86	139	189	151	184
Rent [2]	429	539	1,086	2,833	9,842

[1] Before providing for depreciation and stock appreciation.
[2] Before providing for depreciation.

	1946	1950	1960	1970	1978
Total domestic income before providing for depreciation and stock appreciation	8,895	12,016	22,863	44,837	145,177
Less Stock appreciation	−125	−650	−122	−1,090	−4,249
Residual error	...	− 25	−125	−287	1,071
Gross domestic product at factor cost	8,770	11,341	22,616	43,460	141,999
Net property income from abroad	85	396	233	559	836
Gross national product	8,855	11,737	22,849	44,019	142,835
Less Capital consumption	...	−953	−2,047	−4,420	−18,310
National income	...	10,784	20,802	39,599	124,525

National Economic Development Council. The NEDC (Neddy), which first met in 1962, is the national forum for economic consultation between government, management and unions. It includes leading representatives of the Government, CBI and TUC and also chairmen of nationalized industries and independent members. It meets usually under the chairmanship of the Chancellor of the Exchequer although the Prime Minister takes the chair from time to time. Discussions at the monthly council meetings are normally based on papers, presented by the participating parties, which deal primarily with questions of medium-term national economic performance and prospects, besides seeking to agree on ways of improving industrial efficiency. Council meetings are held in private to encourage the frank exchange of views between members, and discussions are summarized at a press conference taken by the Director-General of the National Economic Development Office (NEDO) following each meeting. The Economic Development Committees (Little Neddies), and the Sector Working Parties, like the NEDC, bring together representatives of management and unions and officials from Government, who use this neutral meeting place to study the efficiency and prospects of individual industries and sectors and to suggest ways in which these could be improved. The National Economic Development Office (NEDO) provides the professional staff for the NEDC, the EDCs and the Sector Working Parties.

Currency. The monetary unit of Great Britain is the *pound sterling.* A gold standard was adopted in 1816, the sovereign or twenty-shilling piece weighing 7·98805 grammes 0·916⅔ fine. Currency notes for £1 and 10s. were first issued by the Treasury in 1914, replacing the circulation of sovereigns. The issue of £1 and 10s. notes was taken over by the Bank of England in 1928. The issue of 10s. notes ceased on the issue of the 50p coin in 1969.

Following the post-war fluctuations in the value of the pound, Great Britain returned to the Gold Standard in 1925 with the pound fixed at the pre-war parity of US$4.8665. But the world financial crisis of 1931 forced the country off the Gold Standard again, and in the following year the Exchange Equalization Account was set up for the purpose of checking undue fluctuations in the exchange value of the pound. With the relative stability of the pound which followed, a 'Sterling Bloc' emerged consisting of most Empire countries and those others who voluntarily pegged their currencies to the pound.

The Bloc was superseded at the outbreak of the Second World War by the 'Sterling Area'. The pound was then fixed at $4.03 and remained at that rate until Sept. 1949, when it was devalued to $2.80. On 18 Nov. 1967 it was further devalued to $2.40. Following the general international currency re-alignment of Dec. 1971, the rate for the pound, in terms of the US$, was fixed at £1 = $2.6057 but in June 1972 the pound was allowed to float.

When the pound was floated in June 1972 measures were also introduced to control payments between the 'Scheduled Territories' (*i.e.,* the UK including the Channel Islands, the Isle of Man and the Irish Republic), and the rest of the Sterling Area as well as the rest of the world. Exchange control restrictions were lifted in Oct. 1979 except for Rhodesia (Zimbabwe) and these were lifted in Dec. 1979.

Coinage. The sovereign (£1) weighs 123·27447 grains, or 7·98805 grammes, 0·916¾ (or eleven-twelfths) fine, and consequently it contains 113·00159 grains or 7·32238 grammes of fine gold. On 15 Feb. 1971 (Decimalization Day) a decimal currency system was introduced retaining the *pound sterling* as the major unit but now divided into 100 *new pence* instead of 240 old pence. The decimal coins are the 50p (equilateral curve heptagon, 30 mm diameter, 13·5 grammes weight); 10p (28·5 mm, 11·31 grammes); 5p (23·6 mm, 5·65 grammes); 2p (25·9 mm, 7·12 grammes); 1p (20·3 mm, 3·56 grammes) and ½p (17·1 mm, 1·78 grammes). The Decimal Currency Act, 1967 and the Proclamation of 27 Dec. 1968 required that the 50p, 10p and 5p be made of three-quarters copper and one-quarter nickel (75/25 cupro-nickel) and the 2p, 1p and ½p of mixed metal; copper, tin and zinc (bronze). The Decimal Currency Act, 1969, provided that the coins of the Queen's Maundy Money should continue to be made in silver to a millesimal fineness of 925; and, if issued before Decimalization Day, should be treated as denominated in the same number of new pence in which they were de-nominated.

By Proclamation dated 28 July 1971, which came into force on 30 Aug. 1971, the crown, double-florin, the florin, the shilling and the sixpence are to be treated as coins of the new currency and as being of the denominations respectively of 25, 20, 10, 5 and 2½ new pence.

The Coinage Act, 1971, specified that the legal tender limits for coins were: Gold coins, for payment of any amount; coins of cupro-nickel and silver of denominations of more than 10p, for payment of any amount not exceeding £10; coins of cupro-nickel and silver of not more than 10p, for payment of any amount not exceeding £5; coins of bronze, for payment of any amount not exceeding 20p.

The value of money issued in the 12 months up to March 1978 was, cupro-nickel £38·4m., and bronze £6·8m.

By the end of 1975 the transfer to Llantrisant of all of the functions of the London Mint had been completed.

UK coins produced in 1977–78 totalled 806·7m., as follows, in millions: 50p 35·7, 25p 25·5, 10p 41·8, 5p 39, 2p 127·1, 1p 326·2, ½p 211·4.

It is estimated that the following coins were in circulation in the UK at 31 March 1978, in millions: 50p 349·8, 25p 66·6, 10p 1,901·6, 5p 1,588, 2½p 173·6, 2p 1,572, 1p 2,453, ½p 2,218 making a total of 10,322·6m. coins with a face value of £532·5m

Bank-notes. The Bank of England issues notes in denominations of £1, £5, £10, £20 and £50 for the amount of the fiduciary note issue. Under the provisions of the Currency and Bank Notes Act, 1954, which came into force on 22 Feb. 1954, the amount of the fiduciary note issue was fixed at £1,575m., but this figure might be altered by direction of HM Treasury and after representations made by the Bank of England.

All Bank of England notes are legal tender in England and Wales, and notes of denominations less than £5 are legal tender in Scotland and Northern Ireland. The banks in Scotland and Northern Ireland have certain note-issuing powers. The average circulations of such notes were £483m. (Scotland—15 Oct. 1980) and £51m. (Northern Ireland—15 Oct. 1980).

The total amount of notes issued at 31 Dec. 1980 was £10,825m., of which £10,819m. were in the hands of other banks and the public and £6m. in the Banking Department of the Bank of England.

Banking. The Bank of England, Threadneedle Street, London, is the Government's banker and the 'banker's bank'. It has the sole right of note issue in England and Wales and manages the National Debt. The Bank operates under royal charters of 1694 and 1946 and the Bank of England Act, 1946. The capital stock has, since 1 March 1946, been held by the Treasury.

The statutory return is published weekly. End-December figures for the past 6 years are as follows (in £1m.):

	Notes in circulation	Notes and coin in Banking Department	Public deposits (government)	Other deposits [1]
1975	6,341	10	22	1,818
1976	7,291	9	16	2,799
1977	8,302	23	30	2,219
1978	9,551	24	28	2,135
1979	10,750	25	26	1,948
1980	10,819	6	36	1,292

[1] Including Special Deposits.

The fiduciary note issue was £10,825m. at 31 Dec. 1980. All the profits of the note issue are passed on to the National Loans Fund.

Official reserves of gold and convertible currencies, SDR and reserve position in the IMF at 31 Dec. 1980 were US$27,476m.

The value of paper debit bank clearings for 1980, £4,457m. Paper credit clearings for 1980, £26m. Automatic direct debits, 1980, £26m.; automatic credit transfers, 1980, £65m.

The following statistics relate to the 6 London clearing banks at mid-Dec. 1980. Total deposits (sterling and currency), £53,596m.; reserve assets, £4,552m.; sterling market loans (other than reserve assets), £7,312m.; advances (sterling and currency), £31,293m.; sterling investments (other than reserve assets), £3,475m.

Total net profits from the operations of clearing bank groups in 1980 amounted to £1,027m., of which £167m. in gross dividends, £861m. transferred to reserves.

Most commercial banking business in Britain is conducted by clearing banks. Industrial and overseas trading business is handled primarily by the merchant banks, who also deal with such matters as the issue of shares to the public for new companies and act as registrars for public companies.

Trustee Savings Banks. Trustee Savings Banks started in Scotland in 1810. They are managed by Boards of Trustees, under the terms of the Trustee Savings Bank Acts 1969, 1976 and 1978. There are 16 banks with a network of 1,650 branches throughout the UK and the Channel Islands. The banks are supervised by the TSB Central Board, a statutory body established by the TSB Act 1976.

On 20 Nov. 1980 the funds of all Trustee Savings Banks totalled £5,700m., the total number of accounts exceeded 14m.

National Savings Bank. Statistics for 1978 and 1979:

	Ordinary accounts		Investment accounts	
	1978	1979	1978	1979
Accounts open at 31 Dec.	20,436,644 [1]	20,796,788 [1]	1,108,171	1,344,160
Amounts—	*£1,000*	*£1,000*	*£1,000*	*£1,000*
Received	704,329	656,435	387,289	469,083
Interest credited	81,339	87,061	116,127	153,270
Paid	619,690	709,086	718,388	296,038
Due to depositors at 31 Dec.	1,798,934	1,833,344	1,203,663	1,529,978
Average amount due to each depositor in active accounts	£87·73	£87·87	£1,086·17	£1,138·24

[1] Excluding accounts with balances of less than £1 which have been inactive for 3 years or more.

The amount due to depositors in Ordinary Accounts on 1 Jan. 1981 was approximately £1,752,656,954 and in Investment Accounts £1,843,685,910.

Bank of England Quarterly Bulletin. Bank of England
Bank of England Annual Report. Bank of England
British Banking and other Financial Institutions. HMSO, 1977
Central Statistical Office, Financial Statistics. HMSO (monthly)
Report of the Committee on the Working of the Monetary System. HMSO, 1959

Report of the Select Committee on Nationalised Industries—The Bank of England. HMSO, 1970
The Royal Mint. 6th ed. HMSO, 1977
Clapham, Sir J. H., *The Bank of England: A History.* 2 vols. CUP, 1944
Craig, J., *The Mint.* Cambridge, 1953
Horne, H. O., *History of Savings Banks.* London, 1947
Sayers, R. H., *The Bank of England 1891–1944.* CUP, 1976

Weights and Measures. Conversions to the metric system was in progress (1978) which will replace the imperial system at present in force.

ENERGY AND NATURAL RESOURCES

Electricity. The electricity industry was vested in the British Electricity Authority on 1 April 1948. Following the re-organization of the electricity supply industry after the passing of the Electricity Act, 1957, the statutory bodies comprising the electricity service in England and Wales are the Electricity Council, the Central Electricity Generating Board and the 12 Area Electricity Boards.

The Electricity Council has functioned from Jan. 1958 as the central council for the supply industry in England and Wales for consultation on, and formulation of, general policy; its main functions are to advise the Secretary of State for Energy on all matters affecting the supply industry, and to promote and assist the maintenance and development by the Central Electricity Generating Board and the Area Boards (known collectively as Electricity Boards) of an efficient, co-ordinated and economical system of electricity supply. The Council can also perform services for the Boards, and, in addition, has certain specific functions, particularly in matters of finance, research and industrial relations.

The Central Electricity Generating Board is responsible for the generation and bulk supply of electricity to the 12 Area Boards in England and Wales. It therefore plans the provision of new generating and transmission capacity, including the siting and construction of new generating stations, both conventional and nuclear, and is responsible for the operation and maintenance of generating stations and the main transmission system.

Area Electricity Boards. Each of the 12 Area Electricity Boards acquires bulk supplies of electricity from the Generating Board and is responsible for distribution networks and sales of electricity to its Area consumers. Thus distribution and utilization of electricity, and also the contracting and sale of appliances side of the industry, are their responsibilities.

The number of power stations owned by the Generating Board in England and Wales on 31 March 1980 was 132 with a total output capacity of 57,029 mw. Total number of consumers in England and Wales on 31 March 1979 was 20,118,057 (on 31 March 1980, 20,334,146).

Electricity sold in England and Wales in 1979–80 amounted to 204,762m. units. Revenue from sales of electricity in 1979–80 was £5,742m. Coal used for electricity generation in 1979–80 amounted to 80·4m. tonnes (75·2m. tonnes in 1978–9). Total fuel (coal equivalent) used in 1979–80 amounted to 104·7m. tonnes and in 1978–79 to 104·2m. tonnes. Nine nuclear stations of total output capacity 4,427 mw provided 11·4% of total units supplied in 1979–80. Eight of these are gas-cooled graphite-moderated stations using natural uranium fuel canned in magnesium alloy (Magnox) and 1 is an advanced gas-cooled station (AGR). With 3 AGR stations under construction, installed capacity will reach 7,400 mw by Dec. 1985.

The number of persons employed by the Generating Board, the Electricity Council and Area Boards at the end of March 1980 was 158,780.

The North of Scotland Hydro-Electric Board, established under the Hydro-Electric Development (Scotland) Act 1943, is the nationalized authority responsible not only for generating and transmitting electricity but also for distributing and selling it to over 500,000 consumers.

The Board's district covers a quarter of the land mass of Great Britain and lies generally north and west of a line joining the firths of Clyde and Tay as well as all the island groups extending to the Outer Hebrides, Orkney and Shetland. About 99% of potential consumers have now been provided with supply. On the mainland the Board operates generating stations with a total installed generating capacity of 2,116 mw consisting of 1,752 mw of hydro power and pumped storage, together with 240 mw of steam. Diesel stations with a total installed capacity of 121 mw supply the principal island groups while a further 1,320 mw of oil/gas fired thermal plant is nearing completion at Peterhead.

The main transmission system consists of 5,097 circuit km of 275 kv and 132 kv lines linking the power stations and the bulk supply points serving the distribution networks. The system control centre at Pitlochry co-ordinates the operation of the transmission system and power stations together with the continuous interchange of power with the South of Scotland Electricity Board. The number of staff at the end of the year was 4,146.

The South of Scotland Electricity Board was established in April 1955 by the Electricity Reorganisation (Scotland) Act 1954, replacing in South Scotland 2 Electricity Boards and 2 Divisions of the British Electricity Authority. The area of Scotland served by the Board lies south of a line from the Firth of Clyde to the Firth of Tay and extends to about 8,000 sq. miles, including the industrial belt of Scotland, with a population of 4m. By special arrangement a small part of North-East England is also supplied. The remainder of Scotland is served by the North of Scotland Hydro-Electric Board.

The Board differs from those established in England and Wales in that its responsibilities cover not only the distribution of electricity and retail sale of electrical appliances but also the generation and transmission of bulk power within South Scotland.

At 31 March 1980 the Board operated 17 generating stations (including 2 nuclear and 7 hydro-electric stations) with a total output capacity of 7,826 mw. In 1979–80 the Board sold 18,374m. units to more than 1·5m. consumers and had a total revenue of £519m. The number of staff employed at the end of the year was 13,658.

Oil. Production 1979, in 1,000 tons (1978 in brackets): Throughput of crude and process oils, 97,854 (96,390); refinery use, 6,538 (6,423); gases, 1,772 (1,760); naphtha, 5,242 (4,626); motor spirits, 16,111 (15,958); kerosene, 7,945 (7,397); diesel oil, 25,450 (24,024); fuel oil, 28,600 (30,518); lubricating oils, 1,330 (1,203); bitumen, 2,065 (1,886). Total output, 90,583 (89,156). 1979 investment in North Sea oil and gas production: £2,062m. (£2,168m.).

Gas. The British gas industry, nationalized in 1949, was reorganized as the British Gas Corporation on 1 Jan. 1973. Under the terms of the Gas Act 1972, the Corporation has the general duty 'to develop and maintain an efficient, co-ordinated and economical system of gas supply'. The chairman and members of the Corporation are appointed by the Secretary of State for Energy. British Gas explores for and produces natural gas, manufactures substitute natural gas, transmits, distributes and sells gas, and sells, installs and maintains gas appliances.

Gas Council (Exploration) Ltd and Hydrocarbons Great Britain Ltd, wholly owned subsidiaries of British Gas, have been involved in exploration for oil and gas in the Irish Sea, the English Channel and Celtic Sea and, in partnership with oil companies, in the North Sea and onshore. British Gas is a partner in gasfields in the southern North Sea, and the Beryl, Hutton and Montrose oilfields in the northern North Sea and discovered the Morecambe gasfield in the Irish Sea and the Wytch Farm oilfield in Dorset.

In 1979–80, British Gas sold 16,736m. therms of gas. Conversion to natural gas was completed in 1977. There were 14·69m. domestic customers, who used 8,163m. therms; 78,000 industrial customers, who used 6,513m. therms; and 492,000 commercial customers, who used 2,060m. therms.

The turnover of British Gas in 1979–80 was £3,513m. and the average capital employed was £2,379m. The surplus for the year was £426m. before tax. In March 1980, there were 104,400 employees.

Minerals. The number of National Coal Board mines producing coal on 31 March 1980 was 219. Statistics of the coalmining industry (including licensed mines) for recent years are as follows:

	1976–77[1]	1977–78[1]	1978–79	1979–80
Saleable output of coal:				
Total deep-mined (1m. tonnes)	109·4	107·3	106·4	110·3
Opencast (1m. tonnes)	11·4	13·6	13·5	13·0
Average weekly number of wage-earners on colliery books:				
All workers (NCB only)	242,000	240,500	234,900	232,500
Underground workers (NCB only)	192,206	190,744	186,390	184,367
Coal exports:				
Total (1m. tonnes)	1·46	1·84	2·07	2·52

[1] 12-month period ending March.

Total stocks of coal on 31 March 1980 amounted to 28m. tonnes (15·9m. tonnes distributed, 12·1m. tonnes undistributed). Trading profit made by the NCB for the year ended 31 March 1980 amounted to £27·6m. Interest payable was £184·7m., of which to the Secretary of State for Energy, £101·1m. There was a Deficit grant of £159·3m. from the Government for the year ended 31 March 1980 (which was not applicable in the year 1978–79).

Production of coke (including coke breeze) amounted in 1979–80 to 4·4m. tonnes.

In 1979–80 inland consumption (in 1,000 tonnes) of coal is estimated to have been 128,327, some of the principal users being: Power stations, 89,187; coke ovens, 14,258; domestic, 10,270; other conversion industries, 2,919; collieries, 756; industry, 8,956.

Ezra, D., *Coal and Energy*. London, 1980

The UK is the eighth largest steel producing country in the world. Output in recent years was as follows (in 1,000 tonnes):

	Iron ore	Pig-iron	Crude steel	Home consumption[1]
1974	3,602	13,903	22,323	23,240
1975	4,490	12,131	20,098	21,539
1976	4,582	13,835	22,274	21,130
1977	3,745	12,232	20,411	20,520
1978	4,239	11,434	20,311	20,540
1979	4,269	12,898	21,464	20,140

[1] Finished steel (ingot equivalent).

In 1979 imports of iron ore amounted to 17·69m. tonnes. Exports of finished steel products were 4·4m. tonnes in 1979.

Iron Castings. Production of iron castings was 2·7m. tonnes in 1979 (2·7m. tonnes in 1978).

The industry is divided between the 'public sector' and the 'private sector'.

The British Steel Corporation, which was established by the Iron and Steel Act 1967, took over the 14 largest UK iron and steel making concerns (and their subsidiaries) in July 1967 and merged them into a single publicly owned business. With a turnover of more than £3,105m. and a liquid steel output of 14·1m. tonnes in 1979–80, the British Steel Corporation ranks as one of Britain's major manufacturing industries and is one of the world's largest steel makers. The number of employees as at 29 March 1980 was 166,400. A substantial part of the British steel industry remains in private ownership and although responsible for only 20% of UK crude steel production, produces about half the UK requirements of engineering steels and much higher proportions of steel in finished form. For some products such as bright bars, wire, open-die forgings and high speed and tool steels, nearly all

UK production is in the private sector. Because of the private sector involvement in higher value steels it accounts for over a third of the total turnover of the British steel industry but employs a smaller proportion of the total labour force at about 70,000 people. Private sector companies have been engaged in recent years in a heavy programme of investment, particularly in crude steel production, and a number of new companies, some with overseas ownership, have become established in the UK for this purpose.

Production of non-ferrous metals in 1979 (in 1,000 tonnes): Refined copper, 121·7 (125·6 in 1978); refined lead, 244·2 (222·9 in 1978); tin metal, 11·2 (1978); virgin aluminium, 359·5 (346·2 in 1978); slab zinc, 76·7 (73·6 in 1978).

Agriculture. General distribution of the surface, in acres (1970):

Divisions	Total land surface	Rough grazing land	Permanent pasture	Arable land
England	32,030,000	3,116,000	8,059,000	13,167,000
Wales and Monmouth	5,100,000	1,554,000	1,826,000	738,000
Scotland	19,071,000	11,328,000	1,018,000	3,140,000
Isle of Man	141,000	45,000	24,000	54,000

Distribution of the cultivated area in the UK (in 1,000 hectares):

	1978	1979
Corn crops [1]	3,785	3,850
Green crops [2]	969	923
Hops	6	6
Fruit	64	65
Bare fallow	67	72
Rotation grasses including lucerne	2,069	1,920
Permanent pasture	5,002	5,127

[1] Includes wheat, barley and oats.
[2] Green crops include beans, potatoes, turnips and swedes, mangolds, sugar-beet, cabbage, etc., for fodder, vegetables, and all other crops.

The number of workers employed in agriculture, forestry and fishing in the UK was, in June 1979, 366,000; 344,000 were solely engaged in agriculture; there were also (June 1979 provisional) 293,400 farmers, partners and directors (213,500 full-time).

In Dec. 1978 there were about 406,000 tractors and 48,800 combine harvesters in use.

Principal crops in the UK as at June in each year:

	Wheat	Barley	Oats	Beans	Potatoes	Fodder crops [1]	Man-gold	Sugar-beet
	Acreage (1,000 acres and 1,000 hectares from 1976)							
1975	2,557	5,794	575	138	504	264	17	488
1976	1,231	2,182	235	62	222	103	6	206
1977	1,076	2,400	195	55	233	97	7	202
1978	1,257	2,348	180	55	214	223	—	209
1979	1,371	2,343	136	60	204	204	—	214
	Total product (1,000 tons and 1,000 tonnes from 1976)							
1975	4,368	8,309	789	226	4,445	5,940	404	4,787
1976	4,470	7,648	764	195	4,789	4,816	360	6,325
1977	5,244	10,738	778	269	6,632	5,869	457	6,382
1978	6,610	9,850	705	285	7,330	9,835	—	7,080
1979	7,140	9,550	535	286	6,485	9,049	—	7,660

[1] Includes mangolds from 1978.

Livestock in the UK as at June in each year (in 1,000):

	1975	1976	1977	1978	1979
Cattle	14,717	14,069	13,854	13,625	13,543
Sheep	28,270	28,265	28,104	29,686	29,860
Pigs	7,532	7,947	7,736	7,708	7,844
Poultry	136,572	142,222	134,286	137,329	134,700

Forestry. On 31 March 1980 the productive woodland in Britain was 1,749,000 hectares. The Forestry Commission was responsible for 884,000 hectares, mainly softwood plantations. The Forestry Commission employed 2,179 non-industrial and 5,950 industrial workers on 31 March 1980.

Fisheries. Quantity (in 1,000 tons and 1,000 tonnes from 1976) and value (in £1,000) of fish of British taking landed in Great Britain (excluding salmon and sea-trout):

Quantity	1975	1976	1977	1978	1979
Wet fish	792·0	839·4	830·4	880·6	764·1
Shell fish	63·4	77·8	73·9	64·4	62·5
	855·4	917·2	904·3	945·0	826·6
Value					
Wet fish	136,642	184,950	222,130	219,412	211,892
Shell fish	12,707	21,539	25,189	30,492	35,545
	149,349	206,489	247,319	249,904	247,437

The fishing fleet of England and Wales comprised (1979) 4,405 vessels including 1,741 trawlers and 723 line fishing vessels; the Scottish fleet (1979) 2,517 vessels including 772 trawlers and 1,011 creel fishing vessels.

INDUSTRY AND TRADE

Industry. Statistics of a cross-section of industrial production are as follows (in 1,000 tonnes):

	1977	1978	1979
Sulphuric acid	3,405	3,453	3,498
Synthetic resins	2,711	2,760	2,647
Tractors (no.)	147,200	113,000	120,900
Commercial motor vehicles (no. 1,000)	398	384	408
Cotton single yarn	84	79	79
Wool tops (1m. kg)	98	92	79
Woollen yarn (1m. kg)	106	106	105
Man-made fibres (rayon, nylon, etc.)	552	607	596
Newsprint	301	319	364
Other paper and board	3,845	3,877	3,889
Fertilizers, phosphate, super phosphate, basic slag and compounds (1,000 tons)	2,847	3,145	2,858
Cement	15,457	15,916	16,140
Fabricated aluminium (to consumers)	539	526	574

Engineering. In 1979 the number (in 1,000) of passenger cars produced amounted to 1,070 (1978: 1,223); computers, value £1,053m. (1978: £825m.).

Electrical Goods. Production (in £1m.) for 1979 (1978 in brackets): Radio and electronic components, 1,203·9 (1,039·4); broadcasting receiving and sound reproducing equipment, 534·7 (520); gramophone records and tape recordings, 132 (127·3); television sets, 2·48m. units (2·42); domestic electrical appliances, 876·4 (778).

Textile Manufacturers. Production for 1979 (1978 in brackets): Woven cloth, cotton (1m. metres), 365 (380); man-made fibres (1m. metres), 385·6 (377·8); woven woollen and worsted fabrics (1m. sq. metres), deliveries, 137·8 (144).

Construction. Total value (in £1m.) of constructional work by all agencies in 1979 was 18,866 (16,147 in 1978), including new housing, 4,505. Value of industrial buildings for private developers completed in 1979 was £2,362m. New work (other than housing) for public authorities was valued at £3,272m.

Annual Abstract of Statistics. HMSO
Chester, Sir N., *The Nationalisation of British Industry, 1945–51.* HMSO, 1976
Kelf-Cohen, R., *British Nationalization: 1945–1973.* New York, 1973
Stamp, L. D., *The Land of Britain: Its Use and Misuse.* 3rd ed. London, 1962
Statistical Summary of the Mineral Industry. HMSO, annual
Worswick, G. D. N., and Ady, P. H. (ed.), *The British Economy, 1945–50.* OUP, 1952.—*The British Economy in the Nineteen-Fifties.* OUP, 1962

Labour. The distribution of total manpower in Great Britain was in June 1979 (in 1,000): Total working populaion, 25,731 (15,678 males, 10,054 females). Total employed in armed forces and women's services, 314. Total engaged in civil employment, 22,311, including agriculture, 336; mining and quarrying, 335; metal manufacture, 449; national and local government service, 1,580; transport and communications, 1,461; construction, 1,255; distributive trades, 2,749; insurance, banking, business, professional and scientific services, 1,181.

The average monthly numbers (in 1,000) of registered unemployed in Great Britain were: 1974, 600 (males 501; females, 99); 1975, 936 (males, 747; females, 188); 1976, 1,304 (11 months total; males, 988; females, 315); 1977, 1,423 (males, 1,027; females, 395); 1978, 1,410 (males, 995; females, 414); 1979, 1,326 (males, 920; females, 406).

Trade Unions. In Dec. 1980 there were 109 unions affiliated to the Trades Union Congress with a total membership of 12,172,508 (including (1976) 3,033,591 women). The unions affiliated to the TUC in 1980 ranged in size from the Transport and General Workers' Union, with 2,086,281 members, to the Cloth Pressers' Society with 30 members. Non-manual workers accounted for nearly a third of the total TUC membership.

The TUC's executive body, the General Council, is elected at the annual Congress. It is composed of 41 members elected from 18 industrial groupings of unions (railways, mining and quarrying, etc.), to ensure that the Council is broadly representative of the whole trade union movement. Two members are elected to represent women workers.

The General Secretary is elected by the Congress but is not subject to annual re-election.

The TUC General Council appoints committees, which draw upon the services of specialist departments in preparing policies on economic, education, international, employment, industrial organization, and social questions.

The TUC is affiliated to the International Confederation of Free Trade Unions, the Trade Union Advisory Committee of OECD, the Commonwealth Trade Union Council and the European Trade Union Confederation. The TUC provides a service of trade union education. It provides members to serve, with representatives of employers, on joint committees advising the Government on issues of national importance (*e.g.*, National Economic Development Council and various Royal Commissions) and on the managing boards of such bodies as the Health and Safety Commission; Advisory, Conciliation and Arbitration Service; and Manpower Services Commission.

The following table is a statistical summary relating to trade disputes for recent years:

	No. of stoppages	No. of workers involved	Working days lost through stoppages
1977	2,703	1,165,800	10,142,000
1978	2,471	1,041,500	9,405,000
1979	2,045	4,454,100	29,116,000

Lovell, J., and Robert, B. C., *A Short History of the T.U.C.* London, 1968
Pelling, H., *A History of British Trade Unionism*. 2nd ed. London, 1972

Commerce. Value of the imports and exports of merchandise (excluding bullion and specie and foreign merchandise transhipped under bond) of the UK for 6 recent years (in £1,000):

	Total imports	Total exports		Total imports	Total exports
1975	24,028,143	19,762,403	1978	40,969,066	37,362,739
1976	31,212,619	25,777,537	1979	48,467,400	42,803,609
1977	36,493,152	32,951,476	1980	51,650,267	49,510,791

The value of goods imported is generally taken to be that at the port and time of entry, including all incidental expenses (cost, insurance and freight) up to the landing on the quay. For goods consigned for sale, the market value in this country is

required and recorded in the returns. For exports, the value at the port of shipment (including the charges of delivering the goods on board) is taken. Imports
are entered as from the country whence the goods were consigned to the UK,
which may, or may not, be the country whence the goods were last shipped.
Exports are credited to the country of ultimate destination as declared by the
exporters.

For details of imports and exports for 1979 and 1980, *see* pp. 1325–26.

Trade according to countries for 1979 and 1980 (in £1,000):

Countries	Imports of merchandise from		Exports of merchandise to	
	1979[1]	1980[1]	1979[1]	1980[1]
Foreign countries				
Europe and Overseas Possessions—				
Albania	62	107	701	1,478
Austria	345,446	307,267	259,251	279,681
Belgium and Luxembourg	2,324,561	2,596,962	2,467,631	2,624,108
Bulgaria	12,082	14,425	27,324	35,242
Czechoslovakia	96,577	87,812	73,801	81,026
Denmark and Faroe Islands	1,091,916	1,114,149	1,020,592	1,034,959
Finland	794,485	793,218	410,537	525,488
France	4,064,233	3,899,174	3,070,498	3,651,470
German Dem. Rep.	111,705	88,127	58,162	94,124
Germany (Fed. Rep. of)	5,799,403	5,700,861	4,243,975	5,113,032
Greece	151,880	142,456	273,026	224,619
Hungary	51,748	43,327	60,917	68,977
Iceland	83,269	82,042	48,520	47,223
Italy	2,491,013	2,311,071	1,469,048	1,899,181
Netherlands	3,446,271	3,406,928	3,062,642	3,845,412
Netherlands Antilles	44,841	36,243	59,070	33,375
Norway	1,327,212	1,441,418	768,815	791,530
Poland	229,318	194,523	260,606	296,254
Portugal, Azores and Madeira	338,337	335,112	307,670	389,849
Romania	65,914	64,795	70,372	98,914
Spain	710,901	804,232	573,015	708,998
Canary Islands	55,548	61,565	48,419	46,108
Sweden	1,605,942	1,475,506	1,542,197	1,623,511
Switzerland and Liechtenstein	2,564,773	2,614,690	2,407,328	3,076,337
Turkey	67,060	49,243	135,734	147,118
USSR	827,629	786,176	419,042	455,310
EEC	20,895,933	20,802,915	17,885,036	20,825,802
EFTA	7,059,464	7,049,252	5,744,318	6,733,619
Yugoslavia	51,331	56,802	173,954	190,503
Africa—				
Algeria	87,526	114,054	115,016	142,552
Angola	49,469	83,125	30,561	27,811
Burundi	710	1,881	1,158	583
Cameroon	16,278	9,798	18,811	17,470
Egypt	252,733	336,595	264,494	346,688
Ethiopia	12,947	10,281	16,039	20,962
Ivory Coast	73,622	53,563	24,001	27,916
Liberia	14,359	8,671	78,408	46,412
Libya	62,167	46,528	253,153	288,385
Mali	12,108	11,318	6,120	7,878
Mauritania	7,450	9,438	2,845	5,647
Morocco	50,392	62,582	67,604	69,223
Mozambique	11,039	11,416	15,730	11,345
Rwanda	4,145	4,666	1,508	1,245
Senegal	18,088	15,440	11,000	16,030
South Africa, Republic of	533,659	756,397	713,466	1,002,073
S.W. Africa/Namibia	20,446	18,898	1,593	2,726
Sudan	19,747	13,362	106,403	124,697
Tunisia	9,084	17,566	24,660	29,872
Zaïre	67,006	52,585	22,246	27,629

[1] Provisional figures.

Countries	Imports of merchandise from		Exports of merchandise to	
	1979[1]	1980[1]	1979[1]	1980[1]
Asia—				
Afghánistán	20,276	20,174	9,567	6,818
Bahrain	22,780	25,063	123,467	115,569
Burma	6,000	5,379	18,641	20,494
China	137,891	153,433	213,039	169,500
Indonesia	55,950	56,971	76,704	112,170
Iran	243,589	107,176	231,798	393,335
Iraq	393,738	532,483	201,176	321,883
Israel	227,600	236,599	270,733	231,658
Japan	1,490,288	1,712,108	606,011	597,147
Jordan	7,855	8,152	86,894	100,318
Korea (South)	269,706	244,583	145,319	101,103
Kuwait	743,149	655,024	233,438	258,696
Lebanon	9,892	9,076	65,793	70,692
Pakistan	68,021	58,289	139,759	139,692
Philippines	81,122	99,018	105,709	88,998
Qatar	40,503	44,654	101,486	101,898
Saudi Arabia	1,108,644	1,927,583	893,600	1,050,145
Syria	7,001	12,241	66,667	81,584
Thailand	52,188	52,004	94,115	96,920
America				
Argentina	145,064	114,286	128,278	172,830
Bolivia	37,619	33,179	9,594	8,684
Brazil	400,378	296,430	286,481	218,159
Chile	131,218	126,273	45,640	55,741
Colombia	23,874	34,289	52,258	41,920
Costa Rica	3,123	5,424	9,752	8,302
Cuba	14,970	26,208	36,112	35,272
Dominican Republic	5,174	4,788	9,627	11,514
Ecuador	6,210	8,844	33,483	30,930
El Salvador	3,517	2,889	9,354	4,603
Guatemala	7,596	23,657	13,371	13,835
Haiti	1,118	915	3,162	2,818
Honduras (not British)	4,000	3,687	9,013	11,835
Mexico	36,336	111,636	134,816	188,133
Nicaragua	895	1,510	3,229	2,478
Panama	4,131	3,941	26,384	24,032
Paraguay	2,107	1,279	12,746	13,384
Peru	61,518	77,487	23,949	46,541
Puerto Rico	40,807	33,002	18,332	16,970
Uruguay	13,416	16,884	24,735	26,619
USA	4,919,882	6,043,774	4,047,158	4,668,342
Venezuela	100,823	117,614	137,722	131,684
Total (including those not specified above)	41,688,388	44,145,486	34,948,450	40,547,007
Commonwealth countries:				
In Europe—				
Cyprus	115,636	128,386	120,101	153,754
Gibraltar	2,463	3,285	26,015	26,672
Malta	53,569	46,609	79,083	87,527
In Africa—				
West Africa:				
Gambia	2,357	2,417	13,953	17,792
Ghana	89,808	104,545	88,058	88,511
Nigeria, Federation of	186,046	151,563	638,239	1,204,358
Sierra Leone	75,744	65,697	32,753	36,785
South Africa:				
Botswana	26,264	4,044	3,845	2,644
Lesotho	105	340	2,233	394
Malawi	46,464	45,651	27,088	25,749
Zimbabwe	325	28,632	1,497	16,209

[1] Provisional figures.

Countries Commonwealth Countries (contd.) In Africa—(contd.)	Imports of merchandise from 1979[1]	1980[1]	Exports of merchandise to 1979[1]	1980[1]
South Africa (contd.)				
Swaziland	37,361	30,438	1,333	691
Zambia	103,570	94,610	85,458	103,941
East Africa:				
Kenya	115,624	105,443	170,278	259,103
Mauritius	116,004	145,227	30,370	24,688
Uganda	19,189	30,735	13,881	33,526
Tanzania	43,655	36,501	121,504	110,910
Seychelles	371	601	8,084	9,772
St Helena	207	476	2,570	3,016
In Asia—				
Bangladesh	60,421	73,084	90,071	110,408
Hong Kong	690,699	850,340	442,232	559,420
India	365,843	315,858	455,606	529,007
Malaysia	221,488	187,050	187,425	223,516
Singapore	185,290	535,915	270,718	328,112
Sri Lanka	40,826	53,681	55,260	76,831
In Oceania—				
Australia	474,902	484,112	839,871	815,652
Fiji Islands	45,694	36,759	14,154	12,786
Nauru	160	70	619	821
New Zealand	415,432	414,630	314,354	250,413
Papua New Guinea	30,148	22,861	10,409	10,978
Western Samoa	837	572	619	710
In America—				
Bahamas	21,758	59,123	79,851	77,366
Barbados	8,414	7,630	27,253	29,860
Belize	13,515	13,168	10,347	11,824
Bermuda	3,794	2,900	17,209	24,499
Canada	1,260,057	1,412,156	766,430	758,367
Falkland Islands	3,331	2,846	2,344	2,083
Guyana	43,009	47,143	27,607	30,191
Jamaica	82,145	95,578	44,554	33,122
Leeward Islands	5,333	4,533	15,065	14,915
Trinidad and Tobago	41,243	35,088	104,562	120,270
Windward Islands	25,126	25,704	17,112	21,344
Total, Commonwealth countries (including those not specified above)	5,089,806	5,720,452	5,300,320	6,303,710
Irish Republic	1,689,206	1,784,329	2,554,839	2,660,074
Grand Total	48,467,400	51,650,267	42,803,609	49,510,791

[1] Provisional figures.

Imports and exports for 1979 and 1980 (Great Britain and Northern Ireland) (in £1,000):

Import values c.i.f. Export values f.o.b. 0. Food and Live Animals	Total imports 1979[1]	1980[1]	Domestic exports 1979[1]	1980[1]
Live animals (excluding zoo animals, dogs and cats)	88,298	105,324	170,863	139,971
Meat and meat preparations	1,258,411	1,225,862	275,464	327,180
Dairy products and eggs	533,937	500,211	226,454	298,477
Fish and fish preparations	324,628	349,253	152,571	154,519
Cereals and cereal preparations	664,353	604,031	264,450	456,213
Fruit and vegetables	1,175,233	1,240,114	148,498	153,195
Sugar, sugar preparations, honey	405,916	403,012	103,569	112,220
Coffee, tea, cocoa, spices	791,346	677,035	268,297	262,576

[1] Provisional figures.

Import values c.i.f.	Total imports		Domestic exports	
Export values f.o.b.	1979[1]	1980[1]	1979[1]	1980[1]
0. *Food and Live Animals*—(contd.)				
Feeding stuff for animals	276,817	249,231	56,887	63,655
Miscellaneous food preparations	172,658	148,775	84,968	94,608
Total of Section 0	5,691,597	5,502,849	1,752,020	2,062,613
1. *Beverages and Tobacco*				
Beverages	478,507	439,929	854,320	898,035
Tobacco and tobacco manufactures	350,423	235,198	340,997	307,966
Total of Section 1	828,930	675,127	1,195,317	1,206,001
2. *Crude Materials, Inedible, except Fuels*				
Hides, skins and furskins, undressed	224,652	226,970	221,513	189,920
Oil seeds, oil nuts and oil kernels	260,831	265,149	3,122	2,888
Crude rubber (including synthetic and reclaimed)	185,324	182,699	79,166	75,645
Wood and cork	742,978	684,077	13,539	16,236
Pulp and waste paper	390,187	398,944	13,797	22,796
Textile fibres and their waste	477,611	376,199	315,848	313,077
Crude fertilizers and crude minerals (excluding fuels)	312,870	302,892	218,719	235,288
Metalliferous ores and metal scrap	856,934	968,082	273,433	471,702
Crude animal and vegetable materials, not elsewhere specified	198,684	184,789	43,811	48,613
Total of Section 2	3,650,070	3,589,801	1,182,948	1,376,165
3. *Mineral Fuels, Lubricants and Related Materials*				
Coal, coke and briquettes	156,822	238,944	100,713	180,024
Petroleum and petroleum products	5,225,207	6,101,877	4,153,100	6,121,316
Gas, natural and manufactured; electric energy	396,711	566,943	64,709	115,920
Total of Section 3	5,778,740	6,907,764	4,318,522	6,417,260
4. *Animal and Vegetable Oils and Fats*	315,013	260,418	65,682	71,073
5. *Chemicals*				
Chemical elements and compounds	1,469,615	1,330,953	1,920,481	1,918,565
Dyeing, tanning and colouring materials	167,841	145,883	392,016	433,062
Medicinal and pharmaceutical products	232,765	222,488	638,663	745,415
Essential oils and perfume; toilet and cleansing preparations	177,134	174,580	408,239	464,703
Fertilizers, manufactured	96,534	90,048	58,237	52,267
Plastic materials	830,814	763,883	778,959	874,939
Total[2] of Section 5	3,404,099	3,148,323	4,914,231	5,290,010
6. *Manufactured Goods Classified Chiefly by Material*				
Leather and dressed furs	197,007	137,257	223,586	212,275
Rubber	259,136	264,490	363,348	447,293
Wood and cork (excluding furniture)	465,019	369,125	75,992	84,221

[1] Provisional figures.   [2] Includes items not specified here.

Import values c.i.f.	*Total imports*		*Domestic exports*	
Export values f.o.b.	1979[1]	1980[1]	1979[1]	1980[1]
6. *Manufactured Goods Classified Chiefly by Materials*—(contd.)				
Paper, paperboard	1,241,755	1,287,926	435,602	475,033
Textile yarn, fabrics	1,691,738	1,544,866	1,339,830	1,363,425
Non-metallic mineral manufactures	3,067,715	3,422,410	3,397,778	3,550,426
Iron and steel	1,216,412	1,448,892	1,277,685	984,234
Non-ferrous metals	1,564,888	2,487,368	1,140,453	1,759,757
Manufactures of metal, not elsewhere specified	774,003	866,360	1,192,499	1,309,570
Total of Section 6	10,477,674	11,828,693	9,446,772	10,186,233
7. *Machinery and Transport Equipment*				
Boilers, engines, motors and power-units	852,773	962,701	1,788,721	2,233,023
Agricultural and industrial machinery	3,041,078	3,029,493	4,662,067	5,379,910
Office machinery	1,331,099	1,396,221	1,164,400	1,347,247
Electrical machinery, apparatus, not elsewhere specified	2,209,545	2,344,353	2,191,707	2,512,833
Transport equipment	5,329,042	5,317,892	4,951,481	5,535,909
Total of Section 7	12,763,538	12,763,538	14,758,377	17,008,922
8. *Miscellaneous Manufactured Articles*				
Sanitary, plumbing, heating and lighting fixtures	81,117	78,432	89,930	109,071
Furniture	255,070	283,436	231,107	239,197
Travel goods, handbags and similar articles	92,288	95,049	16,676	19,488
Clothing	1,194,446	1,231,122	751,088	807,558
Footwear	353,060	354,653	113,368	130,389
Scientific instruments; watches and clocks	1,244,727	1,400,834	1,222,380	1,468,193
Miscellaneous manufactured articles, not elsewhere specified	1,575,347	1,733,441	1,550,725	1,730,549
Total of Section 8	4,796,055	5,176,967	3,975,275	4,504,446
9. *Commodities and Transactions not Classified According to Kind*				
Post parcels	165,168	171,117	495,154	550,460
Special transactions	255,063	275,569	239,940	251,946
Total[2] of Section 9	761,655	1,509,664	1,194,464	1,388,069
Total[2] of all classes	48,467,400	51,650,267	42,803,609	49,510,791

[1] Provisional figures.   [2] Includes items not specified here.

Tourism. There were an estimated 12·5m. overseas visitors in 1979. Foreign exchange from tourism was £3,500m. including £650m. from fares to British air and shipping lines.

COMMUNICATIONS

Roads. Central government responsibility for highways in England rests with the Secretary of State for Transport. His responsibilities are administered by the Department of Transport through a number of Directorates at Headquarters together with 8 Regional Offices and 6 Road Construction Units. For Welsh and Scottish roads central government responsibility rests with the Secretaries of State for Wales and Scotland respectively.

The Secretary of State is responsible for all trunk roads. Under the local government system introduced in 1974, the responsible authorities for principal roads are the County Councils. District Councils may claim maintenance powers for urban roads which are neither trunk roads nor classified roads. In London responsibility is shared between the Greater London Council and the London Boroughs.

The Secretary of State has powers to provide roads designed for limited classes of motor traffic, and to confirm schemes for the provision of such special roads by local authorities. The former have the status of trunk roads; the latter principal roads. They are generally referred to as motorways. About 1,350 miles of motorways in England were open to traffic by Sept. 1979 and some 500 miles are under construction.

The Road Construction Units' responsibilities for the design and supervision of the construction of major trunk roads (including motorways) are being transferred to firms of consulting engineers, and to county councils who will act as the Secretary of State's agents. The six Road Construction Unit Headquarters will continue to perform work which proceeds directly from the Secretary of State's statutory and financial responsibilities. Units are responsible for designing and supervising the construction of major trunk roads (including motorways). Regional Controllers (Roads and Transportation) are responsible for smaller trunk road schemes (generally those costing under £2·5m.) and for the maintenance of all trunk roads (including motorways). Local authorities act as the Secretary of State's agents for construction and maintenance, the work being carried out by them or by contractors acting on their behalf. Central government bears the full cost.

On 1 April 1975 specific grants to local authorities for the construction or improvement of principal roads were abolished. All aid to local authorities for transport expenditure is now given through the rate support grant and through a transport supplementary grant which is paid to County Councils whose expenditure for the year, as accepted by the Secretary of State, exceeds the level determined by a formula prescribed in the Rate Support Grant Order.

Public highways in Great Britain at 1 April 1979, excluding mileages of unsurfaced roads (green lanes), had a total length of 210,046 miles (England, 160,112 miles; Wales, 19,400; Scotland, 30,533). There were 7,744 miles of all-purpose trunk roads, 1,544 of motorways (both trunk and principal), 21,442 were principal roads and 179,389 were other roads.

At 1 April 1974 there were about 6,000 miles of unsurfaced roads (green lanes) in England and 2,000 in Wales.

Motor vehicles for which licences were current under the Vehicles (Excise) Act, 1971, numbered, at 31 Dec. 1979, 18·6m., including 14·5m. cars, 1·3m. mopeds, scooters and motor cycles, 111,000 public transport vehicles (including taxis) and 1·8m. goods vehicles.

New vehicle registrations in 1980 numbered 2·16m.

Road casualties in Great Britain numbered in 1979, 335,000 (47,400 under 15) including 6,352 killed; in 1978, 350,000 (50,800 under 15) including 6,831 killed.

Railways. The nationalized railway system, known as 'British Rail', together with British Transport Hotels Ltd, British Rail Engineering Ltd, British Rail Hovercraft Ltd, Freightliners Ltd, Transportation Systems and Market Research Ltd (Transmark), Sealink UK Ltd and the British Rail Property Board are owned and managed by a public authority, the British Railways Board. The Board is required to direct its affairs in such a way as to ensure that standards of public service and safety are maintained while at the same time keeping within specified financial constraints.

The role of the British Railways Board is to determine policies and objectives, establish the organization to carry them out, monitor performance and take major decisions.

The management of the railways, which forms the bulk of the Board's activity, is the responsibility of the Chief Executive (Railways). In this role he establishes plans and budgets for the achievement of objectives set by the Board, monitors and achieves results against those plans and budgets and directs the organization and deployment of manpower resources. He is assisted by Executive Board Members with functional responsibility for Engineering and Research, Finance and Planning, Marketing, Operating and Productivity, and Personnel.

He also directs the General Managers of the 5 operating Regions of the railways. The responsibilities of these managers are for the day-to-day operation of the passenger and freight railway systems throughout the country.

The management of each subsidiary activity is the responsibility of each Managing Director, directed by a Subsidiary Board.

The Transport Act, 1968, reduced the railways commencing debt from £1,562m. to £300m. The Act also enabled the Secretary of State for the Environment to make grants for the maintenance of unremunerative passenger services and, additionally, to make grants, until 1973, towards the cost of surplus track and signalling equipment. The Railways Act, 1974, introduced a new system of financial support in accordance with EEC Regulations 1191/69 and 1192/69. On 1 Jan. 1975, the Board's capital debt was reduced to £250m. and their borrowing limit, including commencing debt, was increased to £600m. extendable to £900m. The power to make grants for unremunerative passenger services was withdrawn. The Secretary of State is authorized to impose general obligations on the Board in respect of passenger services and is empowered to compensate the Board for providing adequate transport services. Aggregate compensation is limited to £900m., extendable to £1,500m. subject to Parliamentary approval.

In 1979 the total freight traffic amounted to 169·3m. tonnes, comprising coal and coke 93·5m. tonnes, iron and steel 25m. tonnes and other freight, excluding carryings for Freightliners Ltd and National Carriers Ltd, for which tonnage figures are not available, 50·8m. tonnes. Passenger journeys amounted to 736·2m. Rolling stock (standard gauge) at the end of 1979 included 3,712 locomotives (including 136 high speed power units), 17,175 passenger-carrying vehicles (including Pullman carriages), 4,336 luggage and parcel vans and 137,589 freight vehicles. At the end of the year 11,123 (standard gauge) route-miles were open to traffic.

The London Transport Executive, in Jan. 1980, had 241 route-miles of railway open for traffic and also operated over 19 miles of track owned by British Rail. Rolling stock owned: Underground, 4,228 (2,843 motor cars, 1,385 trailer cars); buses, 6,481. Total number of miles run in passenger service (1979) was 367m. miles. The number of passengers carried in 1979 was: Underground, 594m.; buses, 1,234m. Average takings per passenger journey (1979) were: Underground, 34·5p; buses, 13·2p.

Under the provisions of the Transport Act, 1947, the 4 main-line railways, together with their associated lines, docks, steamships and hotels, the London Passenger Transport Board and the major canal undertakings, passed on 1 Jan. 1948 into the ownership of the British Transport Commission, as the instrument of the State.

The Transport Act, 1962, dissolved the Commission and created in its stead separate Boards for British Railways, London Transport, British Transport Docks and British Waterways. The new Boards assumed their responsibilities as from 1 Jan. 1963. Other main provisions of the Act reconstructed the finances of the Boards and gave them a greater measure of commercial freedom.

The Transport Act, 1968, set up 3 new state-owned transport organizations. The National Freight Corporation inherited the road haulage subsidiaries of the THC, British Rail sundries division, now National Carriers Ltd, and 51% of BR's freight-liner company. The National Bus Company acquired the assets of 65 companies, mainly concerned with road passenger transport in England and Wales, including those companies operated by the THC.

From 1 Jan. 1969 the Scottish Transport Group acquired the assets of the THC's road passenger transport companies in Scotland, and also certain ships, ferry services and British Railways domestic Scottish shipping services.

On 1 Jan. 1970, the responsibility for the London Transport Board was transferred to the Greater London Council and renamed London Transport Executive. The LTB Country Bus services and Green Line services were transferred at the same time to the National Bus Company and renamed London Country Buses.

Gross receipts in 1979 for these Boards were: British Railways Board, from 1975 the Railways Act 1974 introduced, *inter alia*, new arrangements for the financial support of the railway passenger system and provided for the reconstruction of the finances of the Board, £1,775·1m.[1]; London Transport Executive, £368·1m.[1]; British Transport Docks Board, £131·2m.; National Bus Company, £4,603m.[1]; National Freight Corporation, £417m., and British Waterways Board, £13·1m.[1]

On 4 Aug. 1978, Freightliners Ltd became a wholly owned subsidiary of the British Railways Board.

[1] Excludes support grants.

Aviation. The British Airways Board was set up by the Civil Aviation Act 1971 to incorporate the 2 state-owned airlines (BOAC and BEA) as the British Airways divisions of a larger group to be known as the British Airways Group.

The British Overseas Airways Corporation (BOAC) was set up under the British Overseas Airways Act 1939 and British European Airways (BEA) was established under the Civil Aviation Act 1946. In addition to the nationalized corporation, there are about 20 independent air transport operators.

British Airways is engaged on long-haul operations. Its scheduled services link Britain with Europe, the Middle East, the Far East, Australasia, Africa and North America. It co-operates closely with airlines of several other Commonwealth countries and has financial interests in companies operating local and regional services adjacent to its main routes as well. British Airways also operates a network of short-haul services to over 150 places in Britain, Europe, North Africa and the Middle East. It also has a financial interest in several associated companies both in Britain and abroad, most of which collaborate in providing local services.

The 2 State Corporations had a statutory monopoly up to 1961, although there was an arrangement by which independent operators could provide services as private companies associated with the Corporations. There has been a significant expansion by independent operators who have carried increasing numbers of passengers and volumes of freight on a network of scheduled and non-scheduled domestic and international services, in particular British Caledonian Airways has emerged as the principal independent scheduled airline.

British Airways carried 17·3m. passengers in 1979–80. In March 1980 there were 215 aircraft and 56,866 personnel were employed.

Following the Civil Aviation Act 1971, the Civil Aviation Authority was established as an independent public body responsible for the economic and safety regulation of British civil aviation. It took over the responsibilities of the former Air Transport Licensing Board and Air Registration Board, and also runs the National Air Traffic Services in conjunction with the Ministry of Defence.

In addition to the public transport operators there are a number of companies engaged in miscellaneous aviation activities such as crop-spraying, aerial survey and photography, and flying instruction.

The operating and traffic statistics of the UK airlines on scheduled services during the calendar year 1978 (and 1979) are as follows: Aircraft km flown, 347m. (373m.); revenue passengers carried, 20·3m. (22m.); cargo (freight and mail) carried 278,016 (294,000) tonnes.

Traffic between the UK airports and places abroad in 1977 (and 1978) included 479,000 (499,000) air transport aircraft movements.

There were 6,534 civil aircraft registered in the UK at 1 Jan. 1981.

Shipping. The UK flag merchant fleet in July 1980 totalled 43m. DWT (dry cargo, 16·9m. DWT; tankers, 26·1m. DWT) representing 6·4% of the world fleet. The total number of UK flag ships was 1,698. The number of UK nationality seafarers was about 66,000 as at 30 Sept. 1980.

Capital investment in new tonnage and facilities by British shipping companies 1970–79 (inclusive) was over £4,600m. In 1979 capital expenditure was an estimated £228m. The average age of UK owned and registered tonnage in mid-1980 was 8 years.

Total gross earnings by UK owned and registered ships in 1979 amounted to £2,193m. The net contribution to UK balance of payments was £1,139m. and, in addition, there were gross import savings of £525m.

On 30 Nov. 1980, 22 UK flag ships (1·4m. DWT) were laid up out of a world total of 401 ships (10·6m. DWT).

GCBS Facts and Figures 1980. 1980
Committee of Inquiry into Shipping. Cmnd 4337. HMSO, 1970
Bird, J., *The Major Seaports of the United Kingdom.* London, 1963
Rees, H., *British Ports and Shipping.* London, 1958
Sturmey, S. G., *British Shipping and World Competition.* London, 1962
Thornton, R. H., *British Shipping.* 2nd ed. CUP, 1958

Inland Waterways. There are approximately 2,500 miles of navigable canals and locked river navigations in Great Britain. Of these, the British Waterways Board is responsible for some 300 miles of commercial waterways (maintained for freight traffic) and some 1,100 miles of cruising waterways (maintained for pleasure cruising, fishing and amenity). The Board is also responsible for a further 600 miles of canals, some of which are no longer navigable and whose future is being considered in conjunction with local authorities; a number of these lengths have been restored for cruising or as local amenities. The Board's gross receipts for the year 1979 were £13·1m. The total traffic on their waterways was 5·2m. tonnes.

The most important of the river navigations and canals under other authorities include the rivers Thames, Great Ouse, Nene and Yorkshire Ouse, the Norfolk Broads and the Manchester Ship Canal.

Manchester, one of the leading ports in the UK, was opened to maritime traffic in 1894 by the construction of the Manchester Ship Canal, which is 35¼ miles in length and owned and operated by the Manchester Ship Canal Company. The entrance lock is 80 ft (24·38 metres) wide and the maximum width of other locks within the canal is 65 ft (19·81 metres). Ships up to 28 ft 10 in. (8·78 metres) fresh-water draught can navigate to Ince Oil Berth; between Ince Oil Berth and Manchester the maximum draught is 26 ft 6 in. (8·07 metres) in fresh water.

The Port of Manchester includes the Queen Elizabeth II Oil Dock at Eastham (separate entrance lock 100 ft wide), the oil docks at Stanlow and a considerable number of public and private wharves and installations along the canal, as well as the terminal docks at Manchester. Total sea-borne and barge traffic in 1980 amounted to 12·5m. tonnes; operating revenue, £25·54m.; operating deficit, £2,092,000. The total issued capital at 31 Dec. 1980 was £19,457,000.

Edwards, L. A., *Inland Waterways of Great Britain and Northern Ireland*. 5th ed. St. Ives, 1972
Farnie, D. A., *The Manchester Ship Canal and the Rise of the Port of Manchester*. Manchester Univ. Press, 1980
Hadfield, C., *British Canals*. 6th ed. Newton Abbot, 1979
McKnight, H., *The Shell Book of Inland Waterways*. Newton Abbot, 1975
Paget-Tomlinson, E. W., *Complete Book of Canal and River Navigations*. Albrighton, 1978
The Last Ten Years. British Waterways Board, 1973

Posts and Telecommunications. Number of post offices at 31 March 1980 was 22,639; number of posting boxes including those at post offices, over 100,000; staff employed, 443,958 (including 21,056 sub-postmasters employed on an agency basis).

	1976–77 (1m.)	1977–78 (1m.)	1978–79 (1m.)	1979–80 (1m.)
Correspondence (incl. registered items) posted	9,458	9,485	9,965	10,208
Parcels handled	152	160	172	180
Telegrams handled	19	17	16	16
Telex: Inland (units)	407	421	462	483
Overseas (minutes)	267	293	336	368

Weight (kg) of air-mail traffic (all services) dispatched abroad:

	1977	1978	1979	1980
Letters, printed paper, datapost, etc.	15,149,000	15,747,000	16,585,000	17,184,000
Parcels	7,312,000	7,425,000	7,843,000	7,545,000

In 1979–80 the total value of postal orders was £536m.

On 31 March 1980 the total number of telegraph acceptance offices was 8,824 and the London Telecommunications Region had 508 local exchanges, 37 auto-manual and dedicated main network switching centres, 10,865 call offices and 5,706,049 telephone stations. In the provinces there were 5,792 local exchanges, 245 auto-manual and dedicated main network switching centres, 66,202 call offices and 20,763,648 telephone stations. The accrued revenue derived in 1979–80 from private telephone circuits amounted to £105·2m.

1977, 1978, 1979 and 1980 resulted in a surplus of income over expenditure of £298·5m., £366·5m., £373·8m. and £295·3m. respectively.

Broadcasting. Radio and television services are provided by the BBC and by the Independent Broadcasting Authority and its programme contractors. The BBC, constituted by Royal Charter until 31 July 1981, has responsibility for providing domestic and external broadcast services, the former financed from the television licence revenue, the latter by Government grant. The domestic services include 2 national television services, 4 national radio network services and an expanding local radio service.

The IBA constituted by statute provides an independent television service serving the franchise areas, covering the country, of its programme contractors. The Broadcasting Act 1980 provides for the establishment of a fourth television channel. It also provides independent local radio services. These services are financed by the sale of broadcast advertising time.

The BBC's domestic radio services are available on LF, MF and VHF; those of the IBA on MF and VHF. The television services of the 2 authorities BBC1, BBC2 and ITV are broadcast at UHF in 625-line definition and in colour.

The broadcasting authorities, whose governing bodies are appointed (by HM the Queen in the case of the BBC and by the Home Secretary in the case of the IBA) as trustees for the public interest in broadcasting, are independent of government in matters of programme content and are publicly accountable to Parliament for the discharge of their responsibilities.

The number of broadcast receiving licences in force on 31 Dec. 1980 was 18·52m., including 13·49m. for colour.

25 Years of ITV. London, 1980

Cinemas. In 1979 there were 1,607 cinemas and 112m. admissions with box office takings of £127m.

Newspapers. In 1978 there were 9 national dailies with a circulation of over 13m.

Benn's Press Directory. Tunbridge Wells, Annual

JUSTICE, RELIGION, EDUCATION AND WELFARE

Justice. *England and Wales.* The legal system of England and Wales, divided into civil and criminal courts has at the head of the superior courts, as the ultimate court of appeal, the House of Lords, which hears each year a number of appeals in civil matters, including a certain number from Scotland and Northern Ireland, as well as some appeals in criminal cases. In order that civil cases may go from the Court of Appeal to the House of Lords, it is necessary to obtain the leave of either the Court of Appeal or the House itself, although in certain cases an appeal may lie direct to the House of Lords from the decision of the High Court. An appeal can be brought from a decision of the Court of Appeal or the Divisional Court of the Queen's Bench Division of the High Court in a criminal case provided that the Court is satisfied that a point of law 'of general public importance' is involved, and either the Court or the House of Lords is of the opinion that it is desirable in the public interest that a further appeal should be brought. As a judicial body, the House of Lords consists of the Lord Chancellor, the Lords of Appeal in Ordinary, commonly called Law Lords, and such other members of the House as hold or have held high judicial office. The final court of appeal for certain of the Commonwealth countries is the Judicial Committee of the Privy Council which, in addition to Privy Counsellors who are or have held high judicial office in the UK, includes others who are or have been Chief Justices or Judges of the Superior Courts of Commonwealth countries.

Civil Law. The main courts of original civil jurisdiction are the county courts for less important cases, and the High Court for the more important ones.

There are about 300 county courts located throughout the country, grouped in districts, and each presided over by a circuit judge. They have a general jurisdiction (subject to certain rights of transfer to the High Court given to defendants) to determine all actions founded on contract or tort involving sums of not more than £2,000. Certain matters, such as actions of libel and slander, are entirely reserved for the High Court. In addition, certain designated county courts have jurisdiction in matrimonial proceedings. Divorce proceedings must now commence in these courts and, subject to being transferred to the High Court upon becoming defended, are determined in the County Court.

The High Court has both appellate and original jurisdiction, covering virtually all civil causes not determined in the county court. The judges of the High Court are attached to one of its 3 divisions: Chancery; Queen's Bench; and Family; each with its separate field of jurisdiction. There are 75 such judges, called puisne judges. For the hearing of cases at first instance, the High Court judges sit singly. Appellate jurisdiction is usually exercised by Divisional Courts consisting of 3 (sometimes 2) judges, though in certain circumstances a judge sitting alone may hear the appeal.

The Restrictive Practices Court was set up in 1956 under the Restrictive Trade Practices Act, and is responsible for deciding whether a restrictive trade agreement is in the public interest. It is presided over by a judge, but laymen sit on the bench also.

The Court of Appeal (Civil Division) hears appeals in civil actions from both the High Court and County Courts. It includes the Lord Chancellor, who is President of the Chancery Division, and the heads of the other 2 divisions (the Lord Chief Justice and the President) of the High Court, but effectively the head of the Civil Division is the Master of the Rolls, aided by 17 Lords Justices of Appeal sitting in 5 divisions.

Civil proceedings are instituted by the aggrieved person, but, as they are a private matter, they are frequently settled by the parties to a dispute through their lawyers before the matter actually comes to court. In some cases, at the instance of either party, a jury may sit to decide questions of fact and award of damages.

Criminal Law. At the base of the system of criminal courts are the lay justices who try the great proportion of minor offenders (over 98% of all criminal cases) as well as undertaking a small proportion of civil work. Magistrates' courts are comprised of 3 lay justices who are unpaid and need not possess legal qualifications (though they undergo a course of training, though they do have the assistance on points of law of a professional clerk to justices. In central London and large cities there exist stipendiary magistrates, paid for their duties. These are professional lawyers and usually sit alone. Exercising summary jurisdiction in petty sessions, justices have power to pass sentences of imprisonment up to, in general, 6 months, and to impose fines up to, in general, £1,000. One of their functions is to examine persons charged with indictable offences and to determine whether they should be committed for trial at the Crown Court. Justices deal each year with almost 2m. cases, including thefts, assaults, road traffic infringements, drug abuse, breaches of licensing laws, etc. There are some 21,964 justices who are appointed to the Commission of the Peace by the Lord Chancellor, and some 3,471 justices appointed by the Chancellor of the Duchy of Lancaster; each assisted by advisory committees. Women are eligible to be appointed justices, and the number on the Commission of the Peace is 9,484.

Specially qualified justices sit in juvenile courts to deal with cases involving persons under 17 years of age charged with criminal offences (other than homicide and other grave offences) or brought before the court as being in need of care or control. These courts normally sit with 3 justices, including 1 woman, and are accommodated separately from other courts.

Specially qualified justices also sit in the domestic courts to deal with matrimonial proceedings, custody, guardianship and maintenance of children, affiliation and adoption. These courts normally sit with 3 justices including 1 woman.

Above the magistrates' courts is the Crown Court. This was set up by the Courts Act 1971 to replace quarter sessions and assizes. Unlike quarter sessions and assizes, which were individual courts, the Crown Court is a single court which is capable of sitting anywhere in England and Wales. It has power to deal with all trials on indictment and has inherited the jurisdiction of quarter sessions to hear appeals, proceedings on committal of persons for sentence, and certain original proceedings on civil matters under individual statutes.

The jurisdiction of the Crown Court is exercisable by a High Court judge, a

Circuit judge or a Recorder (who is a part-time judge) sitting alone, or, in specified circumstances, with justices of the peace. The Lord Chief Justice has given directions as to the types of case to be allocated to High Court judges (the more serious cases) and to Circuit judges or Recorders respectively.

Appeals from magistrates' courts go either to a Divisional Court of the High Court (when a point of law alone is involved) or to the Crown Court which is empowered to deal with appeals against conviction and/or sentence. Appeals from the Crown Court lie to the Court of Appeal (Criminal Division). Appeals on questions of law go by right, and appeals on other matters by leave. The Lord Chief Justice and the other judges of the High Court may sit with the Master of the Rolls and the Lords Justices to constitute this court.

There remains as a last resort the invocation of the royal prerogative exercised on the advice of the Home Secretary. In 1965 the death penalty was abolished for murder.

All contested criminal trials, except those which come before the magistrates' courts, are tried by a judge and a jury consisting of 12 members. The defence may object, without showing cause, to up to 3 jurors. The prosecution may ask that any number may 'stand by' until the jury panel is exhausted, and only then need to show cause. When these peremptory challenges have been exhausted further challenges may only be made for cause and this rarely happens. The jury decides whether the accused is guilty or not. The judge is responsible for summing up on the facts and explaining the law; he sentences convicted offenders. If, after at least 2 hours of deliberation, a jury is unable to reach a unanimous verdict it may, provided that in a full jury of 12 at least 10 of its members are agreed, bring in a majority verdict. The failure of a jury to agree on a unanimous verdict or to bring in a majority verdict involves the retrial of the case before a new jury.

The Employment Appeal Tribunal. The Employment Appeal Tribunal which is a superior Court of Record with the like powers, rights, privileges and authority of the High Court, was set up in 1976 to hear appeals on questions of law against decisions of industrial tribunals and on questions of fact and law against decisions of the Certification Officer. The appeals are heard by a High Court Judge sitting with 2 members (in exceptional cases 4) appointed for their special knowledge or experience of industrial relations either on the employer or the trade union side, with always an equal number on each side. Industrial tribunals are responsible for deciding questions under Employment Protection (Consolidation) Act, 1978, Equal Pay Act, 1970, Sex Discrimination Act 1975, Employment Protection Act 1975, Employment Act 1980 and Race Relations Act, 1976. The great bulk of their work is concerned with the problems which can arise between employees and their employers. The Certification Officer is responsible for deciding questions under the Trade Union Act 1913, the Trade Union (Amalgamations, etc.) Act 1964, the Trade Union and Labour Relations Act 1974 and the Employment Protection Act 1975.

Military Courts. Offences by persons subject to service law against the system of military law created under the powers of the Army Act, Air Force Act or Naval Discipline Act are dealt with either summarily or by courts-martial. Petitions may be made to the Defence Council. Subsequent appeals lie to a Courts-Martial Appeals Court, and from that court an appeal may lie to the House of Lords.

The Personnel of the Law. All judicial officers except the Lord Chancellor (who is a member of the Cabinet) are independent of Parliament and the Executive. They are all appointed by the Crown on the advice of the Prime Minister or the Lord Chancellor and hold office until retiring age. The legal profession is divided; barristers, who advise on legal problems and conduct cases in court, usually act for the public only through solicitors, who deal directly with the legal business brought to them by the public. Most judicial appointments are made from barristers of long standing, though solicitors are eligible for appointment as Recorders, who may, after 3 years, be appointed Circuit Judges.

There are 2 kinds of civil legal aid. Firstly there is legal advice and assistance, otherwise known as the 'Green Form' scheme. This includes advice and help on anything that is normally regarded as being within a solicitor's practice but except in rare circumstances it does not cover representation. Secondly, there is legal aid for civil court proceedings which covers all the work up to and including the court proceedings and representation. Under the provisions of the Legal Aid Act 1974, aid is available to those of low or moderate means either free or subject to a contribution, depending on means. In 1979–80 there were over 430,000 applications for advice and assistance under the Legal Advice and Assistance Scheme and over 189,000 applications for legal aid. The cost of legal aid in civil cases is met from (a) contributions from assisted persons; (b) the operation of the statutory charge which gives the Law Society a first charge on money or property recovered or preserved for an assisted person to the extent of that person's liability for his own costs; (c) costs recovered from opposing parties and (d) a grant from the Exchequer. The cost of civil legal aid to the state in the year 1979–80 amounted to £35·8m. and the cost of the legal advice and assistance scheme was £11·8m.

Under Part II of the Legal Aid Act 1974 a court dealing with criminal proceedings may order legal aid to be given if it considers it is desirable in the interests of justice and if it also considers that the defendant (or appellant) requires financial assistance in meeting the costs he may incur. The interests of justice are not statutorily defined but may include, for example, situations where the defendant is in real danger of going to prison or losing his job, where substantial questions of law are to be argued or where the defendant is unable to follow the proceedings and explain his case due to inadequate knowledge of English, mental illness or other mental or physical disability. Legal aid must be granted where a person is committed for trial on a charge of murder or where the prosecutor appeals or applies for leave to appeal from the criminal division of the Court of Appeal or the Courts-Martial Appeal Court to the House of Lords.

The costs of legal aid in criminal proceedings are paid by the central government, but courts have power to require legally aided persons to contribute towards the cost of legal aid given to them. The cost of legal aid in criminal proceedings in the year 1979–80 was £61m., £31·5m. of this was for legal aid in the higher courts which is paid for out of the Home Office vote and £29·5m. for legal aid in the magistrates' courts which is paid from the legal aid fund.

Under the Parliamentary Commissioner Act, passed 22 March 1967, M.P.s may refer to the Parliamentary Commissioner complaints received from the public regarding improper or inequitable administration in most spheres of central government affairs. Generally, other available remedies (such as legal action) must be exhausted before a complaint can be investigated. If a complaint is found to require a remedy the Parliamentary Commissioner makes a report to Parliament.

Commissions for Local Administration in England and Wales were set up under the Local Government Act 1974. The Commissioners carry out similar functions in relation to local government bodies to those the Parliamentary Commissioner discharges with regard to maladministration in central government.

Police. The authorized strength of the police force in England and Wales in Dec. 1980 was 120,261: the actual strength was 106,993 men and 10,430 women. In addition there were 15,067 special constables (including 2,629 women). Total police net expenditure (estimated) in England and Wales for 1978–79 was £1,060·8m.

Blom-Cooper, L., and Drewry, G., *Final Appeal: A Study of the House of Lords in its Judicial Capacity.* OUP, 1972
Critchley, T. A., *A History of Police in England and Wales.* Rev. ed. London, 1978

SCOTLAND. The High Court of Justiciary is the supreme criminal court in Scotland and has jurisdiction in all cases of crime committed in any part of Scotland, unless expressly excluded by statute. It consists of the Lord Justice-General, the Lord Justice-Clerk and 19 other judges, who are the same judges as of the Court of Session, the Scottish supreme civil court. The Court, which is presided over by the Lord Justice-General, whom failing, the Lord Justice-Clerk, exercises an appellate jurisdiction as well as one of first instance, sits as business requires in Edinburgh as a Court of Appeal (the *quorum* being 3 judges) and on circuit as a court of first instance. The decisions of the Court in either case are not subject to review by the House of Lords. One judge sitting with a jury of 15 persons can, and usually does, try cases, but 2 or more (with a jury) may do so in important or complex cases. It has a privative jurisdiction over cases of treason, murder, rape, deforcement of messengers and breach of duty by magistrates. It also, in practice, is the only court which tries cases of incest, sodomy and other serious or aggravated crimes against person or property and generally those cases in which a sentence greater than imprisonment for 2 years may be imposed either under statute or common law. Moreover, the Court has inherent power to try and to punish all acts which are plainly criminal though previously unknown and not dealt with by any statute.

The appellate jurisdiction of the High Court of Justiciary extends to all cases tried on indictment, whether in the High Court or the Sheriff Court, and persons so convicted may appeal to the Court on any ground involving a question of law alone, or apply for leave to appeal, on any question of fact or of mixed law and fact, or on any other sufficient ground, and also against sentence unless it is one fixed by law. It is also a court of review from courts of summary criminal jurisdiction, and on the final determination of any summary prosecution either party may appeal to the Court by way of stated case on questions of law, procedure, etc., but not on questions of fact. A further or complementary form of process of review which can be resorted to by convicted persons in these courts is by Bill of Suspension (and Liberation), but it is of strictly limited application. A prosecutor in these courts may also bring under review a decision in law, prior to final judgment of the case, by way of Bill of Advocation, but this process is infrequently resorted to. The Court also hears appeals under the Courts-Martial (Appeals) Act 1951.

The Sheriff Court has an inherent universal criminal jurisdiction (as well as an extensive civil one) limited in general to crimes and offences committed within a sheriffdom (a specifically defined region), which has, however, been curtailed by statute or practice under which the High Court of Justiciary has exclusive jurisdiction in relation to the crimes above-mentioned. This Court is presided over by a Sheriff-Principal or a Sheriff, and when trying cases on indictment sits with a jury of 15 persons. His power of awarding punishment involving imprisonment is restricted to 2 years in the maximum, but he may under certain statutory powers remit the prisoner to the High Court for sentence. The Sheriff also exercises a wide summary criminal jurisdiction and when doing so sits without a jury; and he has concurrent jurisdiction with every other court within his sheriffdom in regard to all offences competent for trial in summary courts. The great majority of offences which come before the courts are of a minor nature and, as such, are disposed of in the Sheriff Courts. In cases indicated for trial in the High Court of Justiciary the Pleading, or First Diet, is always held in the Sheriff Court and, in these cases, the Sheriff may dispose of any objection of a preliminary nature, whether to the competency or relevancy or otherwise, or may refrain from doing so. In either case the Sheriff's decision can be reviewed by the High Court at the second, or trial, Diet.

New procedures will be introduced during 1981 by the introduction of the Criminal Justice (Scotland) Act 1980.

District Courts in each local authority district have jurisdiction in minor offences occurring within the district. These courts are presided over by lay magistrates, known as justices, and have limited powers of fine and imprisonment.

The Court of Session, presided over by the Lord President (the Lord Justice-General in criminal cases), is divided into an Inner House comprising 2 divisions of 4 judges each with mainly appellate function, and an Outer House comprising 13 single judges, sitting individually at first instance; it exercises the highest civil jurisdiction in Scotland, with the House of Lords as a court of appeal.

Police. The police forces in Scotland at the end of 1979 had an authorized establishment of 13,274; the strength was 12,424 men and 790 women. Whole-time 'additional' policemen numbered 148, and there were 3,128 part-time special constables. The total police net expenditure in Scotland was £118·2m. for 1978–79.

CIVIL JUDICIAL STATISTICS

ENGLAND AND WALES	1977	1978	1979
Appellate Courts	*Appeals*	*Appeals*	*Appeals*
Judicial Committee of the Privy Council	48	52	46
House of Lords	64	83	76
Court of Appeal	1,359	1,401	1,419
High Court of Justice (appeals and special cases from inferior courts)	1,029	1,081	916
Courts of First Instance			
High Court of Justice:			
Chancery Division [1]	14,615	13,745	13,848
Queen's Bench Division	176,128	143,577	149,244
Family Division	2,836	1,561	1,041
County courts: Divorce	170,149	166,178	167,511
Other	1,682,771	1,526,033	1,482,553
Other courts [2]	6,694	6,540	6,321
SCOTLAND			
House of Lords (Appeals from Court of Sessions)	5	8	5
Court of Session—General Department	24,112	26,643	27,497
Sheriff's Ordinary Court	29,989	27,126	26,563
Summary Cause	160,034	150,020	137,734

[1] Including contentious probate, 3rd Patents Court.

[2] From Jan. 1972 certain 'other' courts, namely, the Palatine Chancery Court o Lancaster and Durham were merged with the High Court; the Mayor's and City of London Court became a County Court; Borough Courts of Record were abolished. The figure 6,321 for 1979 represents: Court of Protection, 4,157; Restrictive Practices Court, 7; Transport Tribunal, 19; Lands Tribunal, 1,543; Employment Appeal Tribunal, 595.

CRIMINAL STATISTICS

ENGLAND AND WALES	Total number of offenders		Indictable/triable either-way offences [1]	
	1978	1979	1978	1979
Aged 10 and over				
Proceeded against	2,018,596	2,048,878	460,769	460,337
Found guilty at magistrates' courts	1,821,978	1,847,480	359,516	361,674
Found guilty at the Crown Court	56,979	50,672	56,979	50,672
Cautioned [2]	141,474	136,599	102,974	96,789
Aged 10 and under 17				
Proceeded against	134,315	125,764	96,402	88,468
Found guilty at magistrates' courts	123,534	115,519	88,331	80,998
Found guilty at the Crown Court	1,353	957	1,353	957
Cautioned [2]	103,404	98,226	87,492	82,223

SCOTLAND	1977	1978	1979
Crimes—			
Number of persons proceeded against in all courts	42,302	44,218	40,522
Number of persons proceeded against summarily	39,028	41,086	37,673
Miscellaneous offences—			
Proceedings taken	170,534	183,923	182,728
Children [3]—			
Proceeded against in court	1,727	1,639	1,055
Police warnings and referred to reporter	25,935	23,403	22,614

[1] Includes offences which can be tried either at the Crown Court or at magistrates' courts.

[2] Offenders who, on admission of guilt, are given an oral caution by or on the instruction of a senior police officer as an alternative to court proceedings. Such cautions are not given for motoring offences.

[3] Young persons under 16 years of age.

Average population in prisons, borstals and detention centres (1979) in England and Wales was 42,220 (convicted 37,704; untried 4,019, and 497 non-criminal prisoners); in Scotland (1979), 4,585 (sentenced, 3,894; remanded, 691).

Royal Commission on Criminal Procedure. HMSO, 1981

Religion. The Anglican Communion has originated from the Church of England and parallels in its fellowship of autonomous churches the evolution of British influence beyond the seas from colonies to dominions and independent nations. There is no terrestrial head of the Anglican Communion; the Archbishop of Canterbury presides as *primus inter pares* at the decennial meetings of the bishops of the Anglican Communion at the Lambeth Conference.

The Anglican churches, in addition to the Church of England, comprise the churches, councils, and provinces in communion with the see of Canterbury; which are situated in Wales; Ireland; Scotland; United States of America; Canada; Australia; New Zealand; West Indies; Brazil; South Africa; Central Africa; West and East Africa; Jerusalem and the Middle East; South East Asia; Burma; Sri Lanka; Japan; South America; China.

In addition to the dioceses included within the Provinces of Canterbury and York, there are several dioceses overseas over which the Archbishop of Canterbury exercises metropolitical jurisdiction, while Church of England chaplaincies in North and Central Europe formerly under the jurisdiction of the Bishop of London now form the new diocese of Europe.

England and Wales. The established Church of England, which baptizes about 40% of the children born in England (*i.e.*, excluding Wales but including the Isle of Man and the Channel Islands), is Protestant Episcopal. Civil disabilities on account of religion do not attach to any class of British subject. Under the Welsh Church Acts, 1914 and 1919, the Church in Wales and Monmouthshire was disestablished as from 1 April 1920, and Wales was formed into a seperate Province.

The Queen is, under God, the supreme governor of the Church of England, with the right, regulated by statute, to nominate to the vacant archbishoprics and bishoprics. The Queen, on the advice of the First Lord of the Treasury, also appoints to such deaneries, prebendaries and canonries as are in the gift of the Crown, while a large number of livings and also some canonries are in the gift of the Lord Chancellor.

There are 2 archbishops (at the head of the 2 Provinces of Canterbury and York), and 42 diocesan bishops and including the bishop of the diocese of Europe, which is part of the Province of Canterbury. Each archbishop has also his own particular diocese, wherein he exercises episcopal, as in his Province he exercises metropolitan, jurisdiction. In Dec. 1980 there were 67 suffrogan and assistant bishops, 37 deans and provosts of cathedrals and 104 archdeacons. The General Synod, in England, consists of a House of Bishops, a House of Clergy and a House of Laity, and has power to frame legislation regarding Church matters. The first two Houses consist of the members of the Convocations of Canterbury and York, each of which consists of the diocesan bishops and elected representatives of the suffragan bishops, 6 for Canterbury province and 3 for York (forming an Upper House), deans, provosts, and archdeacons, and a certain number of proctors elected as the representatives of the inferior clergy, together with, in the case of Canterbury Convocation, representatives of the Universities of Oxford, Cambridge and London and in the case of York a representative for the Universities of Durham and Newcastle; the chaplains in the Forces (forming the Lower House). They are elected by their fellow suffragans. The House of Laity is elected by the lay members of the Deanery Synods. Parochial affairs are managed by annual parochial church meetings and parochial church councils. Every Measure passed by the General Synod must be submitted to the Ecclesiastical Committee, consisting of 15 members of the House of Lords nominated by the Lord Chancellor and 15 members of the House of Commons nominated by the Speaker. This committee reports on each Measure to Parliament, and the Measure receives the Royal Assent and becomes law if each House of Parliament resolves that the Measure be presented to the Queen.

At 31 Dec. 1978 there were 13,750 ecclesiastical parishes, inclusive of the Isle of Man and the Channel Islands. These parishes do not, in many cases, coincide with civil parishes. Owing to the pastoral re-organization, although most parishes have their own churches, not every parish nowadays can have its own incumbent or minister; so that in some areas one or more parishes may be served by a clergyman, who must be in priest's orders, and in these cases he holds the parishes in plurality. In 1979 there were 10,815 parochial incumbencies in which 1,899 benefices were under suspension of presentation. In 1980 there were 7,380 beneficed clergymen excluding dignitaries, 1,368 other clergymen of incumbent status and 1,815 assistant curates working in the parishes.

Private persons possess the right of presentation to over 2,000 benefices; the patronage of the others belongs mainly to the Queen, the bishops and cathedrals, the Lord Chancellor, and the universities of Oxford and Cambridge. In addition to the 10,563 parochial incumbents and assistant curates, there were (1980) 371 dignitaries, 308 non-parochial clergymen working within the diocesan framework and approximately 2,000 non-parochial clergymen outside the framework.

The membership of the Church at 30 June 1979 was estimated to be 26·8m. baptized members, of whom 8·7m. were confirmed.

Of the 40,508 churches and chapels registered for the solemnization of marriages at 30 June 1980, 16,721 belonged to the Established Church and the Church in Wales and 23,787 to other religious denominations. Of the 368,853 marriages celebrated in 1979 (368,258 in 1978), 32% were in the Established Church and the Church in Wales, 17% in churches or chapels of other denominations and 51% were civil marriages in a Register Office.

Roman Catholics in England and Wales were 4,298,050 in 1980. There were 5 archdioceses and 16 dioceses, 7,016 clergy and 2,602 parish churches and 1,173 other churches open to the public. Convents, 1,296.

The Unitarians have about 330 places of worship, the Catholic Apostolic Church over 80, the New Jerusalem Church about 75. The Salvation Army, a religious body with a quasi-military organization, carries on both spiritual and social work at home and abroad, and had, in British Territory, 1973, 2,100 officers, 1,035 corps, 31 Red Shield Centres and 51 Red Shield Mobile Units. There were also 38 eventide homes, 13 maternity homes, 2 maternity hospitals, 46 hostels for men, 14 hostels for women and girls, and 9 approved and training schools.

The following is a summary of statistics of certain churches in England and Wales, Channel Islands and Isle of Man:

Denomination	Full members	Ministers in charge	Local and lay preachers
Methodist	557,249	3,865	16,962
Independent Methodist	5,367	189	—
Wesleyan Reform Union	4,523	22	237
United Reform	187,408	1,837	—
Baptist	187,144	1,572	—
Calvinistic Methodist Church of Wales	99,288	290	—
Moravian	3,500	40	—
Society of Friends	20,242	—	—

There are about 410,000 Jews in the UK with about 240 synagogues.

Scotland. The Church of Scotland (established in 1560 at the Reformation and re-established in 1688 as part of the Revolution Settlement) is Presbyterian, the ministers all being of equal rank. There is in each parish a kirk session, consisting of the minister and a number of laymen called elders. There are presbyteries (formed by groups of parishes), meeting frequently throughout the year, and these are again grouped in synods, which meet half-yearly and can be appealed to against the decisions of the presbyteries.

The supreme court is the General Assembly, which now consists of some 1,250 members, half clerical and half lay, chosen by the different presbyteries. It meets annually in May (under the presidency of a Moderator appointed by the Assembly, the Sovereign being present or represented by a Lord High Commissioner, appointed by the Queen on the nomination of the Government of the day), and sits for 7 days. Any matters not decided during this period may be left to a Commission which sits at stated intervals until the meeting of the next General Assembly.

On 2 Oct. 1929 the Church of Scotland and the United Free Church of Scotland were reunited under the name of The Church of Scotland, and the two bodies met in General Assembly in Edinburgh as one. The united Church had, in Scotland, on 31 Dec. 1979, 1,873 congregations, 970,741 members; 20,740 teachers and 127,256 scholars in attendance in Sunday schools. The Church courts are the General Assembly, 12 synods, 47 presbyteries in Scotland, 1 in England and 2 on the Continent. Income in 1977 was £26,231,984. There are divinity faculties in 4 Scottish universities of Edinburgh, Glasgow, Aberdeen and St Andrews, with 60 professors and lecturers who are mostly ministers of the Church of Scotland.

The Episcopal Church of Scotland is a province of the Anglican Church and is one of the historic Scottish churches. It consists of 7 dioceses. As at 31 Dec. 1980 it had 296 churches and missions, 201 clergy and 71,422 members, of whom 41,044 were communicants.

There are in Scotland some small outstanding Presbyterian bodies and also Baptists, Congregationalists, Methodists and Unitarians.

The Roman Catholic Church which celebrated the centenary of the restoration of the hierarchy in 1978, had in Scotland (1979) 1 cardinal, 1 archbishop and 9 bishops, 1,173 clergy, 474 parishes, and 823,600 adherents.

The proportion of marriages in Scotland according to the rites of the various Churches in 1979 was: Church of Scotland, 40·3%; Roman Catholic, 15%; Episcopal, 1·3%; United Free, 0·5%; others, 4·2%; civil, 38·7%.

Bossy, J., *The English Catholic Community, 1570–1850*. London, 1975
Davies, H., *The English Free Churches*. 2nd ed. London, 1963
Mayfield, G., *The Church of England: Its Members and its Business*. 2nd ed. OUP, 1963
Moorman, J. R. H., *A History of the Church in England*. London, 1973

Education. *The Publicly Maintained System of Education in England and Wales:* Compulsory schooling begins at the age of 5 and the minimum leaving age for all pupils is 16.[1] No tuition fees are payable in any publicly maintained school (but it is open to parents, if they choose, to pay for their children to attend other schools). The post-school stage, which is voluntary, includes universities, polytechnics and other further education establishments (including those which provide courses for the training of teachers), as well as adult education and the youth service. Financial assistance is generally available to students on higher education courses in the university and non-university sectors and to many students on other courses in further education.

Nursery Education. Children under 5 may be provided for in nursery schools and nursery classes in primary schools. In the public sector no fees are payable and there were (1980) 596 such nursery schools accommodating about 48,456 children while some 4,027 nursery classes accommodate about 166,995 children. Over 78% of all these children attend on a part-time basis. There are also nearly 213,469 children under the compulsory school age attending maintained primary schools.

Primary Schools. Children normally begin primary school when they are 5. Nearly half of the 20,482 primary schools take the complete age-range from 5 upwards. About 3,900 take infants only, up to about 7 years; the rest take juniors only, from 7 or 8 on. The great majority of primary schools take both boys and girls. Nearly 13,000 of these schools had between 100 and 300 pupils each; of the remainder, over half had 100 pupils or less.

There are 1,930 primary schools in Wales. In those primary schools (and some secondary schools) which are in the predominantly Welsh-speaking areas, the main language of instruction is Welsh. There are also 'Welsh', or, more accurately, bilingual schools in mainly English-speaking parts of Wales. Generally children transfer from primary to secondary schools at 11.

Middle Schools. In some areas middle schools are being developed. These cover the age-ranges 8 to 12, 9 to 12, 9 to 13, 10 to 13 or 10 to 14. In Jan. 1980 there were 1,396 middle schools (there were only 15 in 1969) and more are planned as local education authorities introduce a 3-tier system of comprehensive education to replace the traditional 2-tier system.

Secondary Education. In some areas, pupils are still selected at 11 for grammar schools on the basis of ability. The grammar schools, of which there were 254 at

[1] As a result of the Education (School Leaving Dates) Act 1976, one of the two former leaving dates was amended. This means that pupils whose dates of birth fall between 1 Feb. and 31 Aug. (inclusive) cease to be of compulsory school age on the Friday before the last Monday in May. Some of these pupils will leave school before their 16th birthdays. Pupils whose dates of birth fall between 1 Sept. and 31 Jan. (inclusive) remain of compulsory school age until the end of the Easter term following their 16th birthdays.

Jan. 1980, provide a mainly academic course from age 11 to 18. There were also a small number of technical schools which are the academic equals of grammar schools but can specialize to a greater or lesser extent in technical studies. Modern schools provide a general education up to the minimum school leaving age, though some pupils can, and increasingly do, stay on beyond that age. At Jan. 1980 there were 433 of these schools. There are also a small number of other schools which are various combinations of grammar, technical and modern schools.

Many authorities now operate comprehensive schools to which pupils are admitted without reference to ability or aptitude. In Jan. 1980 there were 3,318 fully comprehensive schools with over 3·14m. pupils, in comparison with 221 such schools with about 210,000 pupils in 1965. With the development of comprehensive education various patterns of secondary school organization have come into operation, of which the main ones are: all through schools with an age-range of 11–18 or 11–16 (with possible transfer to an 11–18 school or to a sixth form college (i.e., 16–19) for further studies); 3-tier systems, which incorporate middle schools with a transfer age of 12, 13 or 14, and corresponding 12–18, 13–18 or 14–18 schools; or a system of junior and senior comprehensive schools, catering for the 11–18 age group with a transfer age of 13 or 14.

Direct Grant Grammar Schools. These schools receive grants direct from the Department of Education and Science for their secondary departments (or 'upper schools') and are independent of local education authorities. In 1975 the Government decided to phase out direct grant and invited the schools to join the maintained sector as comprehensive schools. 51 out of the total of 170 schools in England and Wales decided to accept the invitation, but a small number of these schools are now expected either to close or to become independent along with 118 other schools (1 closed in July 1976) which originally opted for independent status. By Sept. 1979, 35 schools had entered the maintained sector.

Pupils who were admitted before Sept. 1976, to those schools which are becoming independent will continue to attract grant aid (thereby paying lower fees), and will also be eligible for fee remission related to their parents' income until they leave. An assisted places scheme is to operate from Sept. 1981.

Special Schools. Special education is provided for children who are deaf, partially hearing, blind, partially sighted, physically handicapped, educationally sub-normal, epileptic, delicate, maladjusted, autistic or suffering from speech defects not due to deafness. The educationally sub-normal are the largest category in this group. Some handicapped children attend ordinary schools. Others attend special schools: there are at present nearly 1,500 of these, catering (in Jan. 1980) for about 125,000 pupils, including about 4,700 pupils in schools in hospitals for children receiving medical treatment as in-patients. In addition nearly 7,500 pupils attend independent schools catering wholly or mainly for handicapped pupils (the majority placed by local education authorities) and a further 16,000 attend classes in ordinary county or voluntary schools. Special education is intended to enable handicapped children to overcome their difficulties in order that they may, as far as possible, take their place in society. To this end special schools have a more generous staffing ratio and provide physiotherapy, speech therapy and other medical treatment as well as special teaching facilities. Over three-quarters of the maintained special schools are day schools. For children with severe handicaps, for whom day special schools cannot cater, and for children who live out of reach of a suitable day school, free boarding education is provided. Attendance is compulsory from 5 to 16. In addition, local authorities can provide special educational treatment below the age of 5 for those ascertained as being in need of it and until the age of 18 for those who want it (education from 16–18 may be provided either in a school or a college of further education). In addition to the provision in special schools, authorities make special arrangements for educating children at home, in small groups or in hospitals when there is no special school. In Jan. 1980 about 4,800 pupils were being educated otherwise than at school. There are also some establishments which provide further education, pre-vocational training and for assessment for employment purely for handicapped school leavers (these students are usually those who cannot attend ordinary establishments for further education).

Ancillary Services. Local education authorities may provide registered pupils at any school maintained by them with milk, meals and refreshment and they may make such charges as they think fit for anything they provide. For pupils whose parents are in receipt of supplementary benefit or family income supplement, however, authorities are required to ensure that such provision is made for the pupil at mid-day as appears to be requisite and anything which is provided must be free of charge. Authorities are also required to remit the charge for anything they provide for other pupils if having regard to the circumstances, they consider it appropriate to do so. Facilities must also be provided, free of charge, for consuming any meals or other refreshments which pupils bring to school themselves.

Local education authorities also have power to provide milk, meals and refreshment for pupils in non-maintained schools, if they wish to do so, under such terms as may be agreed with the proprietors as long as the cost does not exceed what it would have been if the pupils had been at a school maintained by an authority.

Further Education. In Nov. 1979 there were about 590 institutions in England and Wales providing courses of further education, ranging from shorthand instruction to degree-level, postgraduate work and courses of teacher-training. Course enrolments numbered nearly 496,000 full-time (including 58,000 sandwich students) and 1·48m. part-time and evening; students released by their employers numbered 581,000. There were in addition nearly 4,900 adult education centres (formerly known as evening institutes), which provided mainly part-time courses of non-advanced general education and were attended by 1·85m. students. At the top end of this range are the 23 polytechnics, these are engaged almost entirely in higher education, offering degrees of a standard comparable to those of universities, professional qualifications and courses in a wide range of disciplines leading to Higher National Diplomas and Certificates and to awards of the Technician Education Council and Business Education Council. Many other colleges of further education are however involved to a greater or lesser extent in the higher education sector of further education; and all polytechnics and most further education colleges cater for full-time, part-time and sandwich students, whose periods of study at college alternate with periods of practical training in industry.

Courses were also provided by the Workers' Educational Association (6,581), the University extramural departments (7,832) and the Welsh National Council of YMCAs (80). The total number of students registered at these courses was 272,973.

Education at institutions of further education is not free, but fees are generally low, and are remitted for most students under the age of 18 by the local authority.

The Youth Service. A wide range of facilities for the leisure-time recreation and informal special education of young people primarily of post-school age is provided by local education authorities and voluntary youth organizations. A duty is laid upon local education authorities by the provisions of the 1944 Education Act to secure the adequacy of such facilities for young people in their areas; to this end they either provide, maintain and staff youth clubs, centres and other facilities from their own resources or assist voluntary agencies to do so.

Grants to voluntary agencies to help meet the cost of capital projects and to national voluntary bodies towards their headquarters and training expenses are made by the Government.

Awards to Students. Local education authorities are responsible for making mandatory awards to suitably qualified students taking first-degree and comparable courses, courses of initial teacher-training and certain other advanced level courses. These awards cover fees and maintenance but the maintenance grants are subject to the income of the student and his parents or spouse. In addition scholarships may be available both from universities and other sources. The authorities may also give discretionary awards to students who do not qualify for mandatory awards including those taking non-degree level courses.

In 1978–79 there were 369,246 full value awards current in all, 50% at university and 51,300 were for teacher-training courses. These include awards to students at university departments of education for which responsibility was transferred to local authorities in 1975–76. Lesser value awards, for which the maximum rate of grant payable is below the full cost of the student's fees and maintenance, were also made by the authorities. There were 62,748 awards taken up in the calendar year 1978–79.

The Research Councils (generally in science and social science subjects) and the Department of Education and Science (generally in the arts and the humanities) make awards to students at postgraduate level. The Research Councils gave 6,170 new awards in 1980–81 and there were 12,350 current awards in that academic year. The Department gave 2,126 new awards (state studentships and state bursaries) in 1978–79 and current awards totalled about 3,414.

Teachers. In order to qualify for work in maintained schools, most teachers take a course of professional training. Graduates and holders of some specialist qualifications obtained before 1 Jan. 1970 are regarded as qualified to teach without training, but anyone obtaining these qualifications after that date is obliged to take a training course before being appointed for the first time to a primary school, and since 1 Jan. 1974 before first appointment to a secondary school. For the time being, however, this requirement has been waived for graduates in science and mathematics because of the acute shortage of teachers in these subjects.

In 1980 there were some 60 non-university institutions (including 23 polytechnics) and 30 university departments of education providing courses of initial teaching in England and Wales.

In Oct. 1980 there were about 34,000 students on initial teacher-training courses.

On 30 Sept. 1980, 430,928 full-time teachers (176,794 men and 254,134 women) were employed by local education authorities in maintained nursery, primary and secondary schools in England and Wales.

Finance. Total current and capital expenditure on education in England from public funds (excluding university education) is estimated at £7,009m. for 1979–80 as compared with £6,955m. for 1978–79.

Scotland. The statistics on schools relate to education authority and grant-aided schools. From 1974–75 all teachers employed in theseschools require to be qualified.

Nursery Education. In Sept. 1978 there were 493 nursery schools and departments, with a total enrolment of 31,461 pupils.

Primary Education. In Sept. 1978 there were 2,554 primary schools and departments and the number on the registers was 575,696.

In Sept. 1978, 26,945 teachers were employed in primary schools and departments.

Secondary Education. In Sept. 1978 there were 466 secondary schools with 422,263 pupils. Of these schools, 355 were all-through comprehensive establishments providing the full range of Scottish Certificate of Education courses and also non-certificate courses. A further 81 schools were comprehensive in intake and provided both non-certificate and certificate courses, the latter however only up to Ordinary grade. Of the remaining 31 schools, these were selective in intake, 20 provided certificate courses only (Ordinary grade and Higher grade) and 10 non-certificate and certificate courses, the latter again not extending beyond Ordinary grade. Pupils who start their secondary education in schools which do not cater for courses beyond Ordinary grade may in the light of their performance, or for other reasons, be transferred at the end of their second or fourth year to schools providing Higher grade courses.

There were 29,068 teachers in secondary schools at Sept. 1978.

Special Schools. In Sept. 1978 there were 319 special schools and departments. The total number of handicapped children under instruction was 12,999, of which 9,928 were mentally handicapped, 982 were physically handicapped, 356 were blind or partially blind and 718 were deaf or partially deaf, and 1,015 were otherwise handicapped.

At Sept. 1978 there were 26 'List D' schools (these establishments correspond to Community Homes in England and Wales) with a total enrolment of 1,304.

Further Education. Centres and colleges for formal further education numbered 177 in 1978–79.

The student population was 176,538, of whom 38,151 attended full-time (advanced courses, 19,100; non-advanced, 19,051) and 138,387 part-time (advanced courses, 14,670; non-advanced, 123,717).

Teacher-Training. In Nov. 1978 there were 5,438 students in 10 colleges of education on pre-service courses of teacher-training.

Finance. Total expenditure on education met from revenue in 1978–79 was £792·1m. (excluding university education and loan charges).

Independent Schools. Outside the state system of education there were in England and Wales nearly 2,300 independent schools in Jan. 1980, ranging from large 'public' schools to small local ones; there were (1980) 435,058 full-time and 10,605 part-time pupils in these schools. Fees are charged by all these schools, which receive no grant from central government sources. Recognized as efficient status has been discontinued but the requirement for the registration of all independent schools by the Department and their inspection by HM Inspectors, remains unchanged. The term 'public schools' refers to independent schools in membership of the Headmasters' Conference, Governing Bodies Association or the Governing Bodies of Girls' Schools Association. Qualifications under which a school may be represented at the Headmasters' Conference include the measure of independence enjoyed by the governing body and the amount of advanced courses undertaken. Some of these schools are for boarders only, but the majority include non-resident 'day-pupils'. In Scotland there were 95 independent schools, with a total of 16,652 pupils in Sept. 1978. A small number of the Scottish independent schools are of the 'public school' type but they are not known as 'public schools' since in Scotland this term is used to denote education authority (*i.e.*, state) schools.

The earliest of the schools were founded by, and attached to, the medieval churches. Many were founded as 'grammar' (classical) schools in the 16th century, receiving charters from the reigning sovereign. Reformed mainly in the middle of the 19th century, these schools now provide the highest form of English pre-university education. Among the most well-known independent schools are Eton College, founded in 1440 by Henry VI, with 1,250 boys; Winchester College, 1394, founded by William of Wykeham, Bishop of Winchester, 600 boys; Harrow School, founded in 1560 as a grammar school by John Lyon, a yeoman, 740 boys; Charterhouse, 1611, 670 boys. Among the earliest foundations are King's School, Canterbury, founded 600; King's School, Rochester, 604; St Peter's, York, 627.

Universities. In *England* there are 33 traditional degree-giving universities. In addition there are the University of Manchester Institute of Science and Technology; the London and Manchester Business Schools and the Open University. Eight new universities have been established since 1961.

In *Wales* there is 1 university, the University of Wales, with colleges at Aberystwyth, Bangor, Cardiff, Lampeter and Swansea. The Welsh National School of Medicine is a school of the University, and the University of Wales Institute of Science and Technology became a constituent college in Nov. 1967.

In *Scotland* there are 8 universities, Aberdeen, Dundee, Edinburgh, Stirling, Strathclyde, Heriot-Watt, Glasgow and St Andrews. The Carnegie Trust for Scottish Universities (founded, 1901) has a capital (1980) of £7m. and an annual income of £490,000; 50% of the income is devoted to the improvement and expansion of Scottish Universities and 50% to assist students with their fees.

All these universities and colleges are independent, self-governing institutions, although they receive substantial aid from the State (in the case of the Open University by direct grant from the Department of Education and Science, and the traditional universities through the University Grants Committee). The UGC is a committee appointed by the Secretary of State for Education and Science designed to advise the Government on the needs of the universities, and to prepare plans for future development. The members are drawn from education and industry. The Government receives advice on the universities' requirements for central computing facilities from the Computer Board for the Universities and Research Councils whose members are also drawn from the universities and industry.

The Royal College of Art and the Cranfield Institute of Technology are postgraduate institutions which award higher degrees under charters granted in 1967 and 1969 respectively. They receive grants direct from the Department of Education and Science.

The local education authorities have no responsibility for universities.

The Open University received its charter on 1 June 1969 and is an independent, self-governing institution, awarding its own degrees. It is financed by the Government through the Department of Education and Science and by the receipt of students' fees.

Tuition is by means of correspondence textbooks, radio and television broadcasts and summer schools. Students can also attend one of 260 local study centres. No formal qualifications are required for entry to undergraduate or associate student courses.

Anyone resident in the UK aged 21 or over may apply. In the 1980 Feb.–Oct. teaching year there were 60,000 undergraduates and 8,000 associate students; 5,600 part-time tutors and counsellors; 413 full-time academic staff at the University's headquarters in Milton Keynes and 282 full-time academic staff (*i.e.*, in tutorial and counselling posts) based in 13 regional offices.

The University College at Buckingham, an independent institution of higher education, took its first students in Feb. 1976. It offers a first degree (licence) in 2 academic years of 40 weeks each (the academic year Jan.–Dec. and has 4 terms). There are schools of study: Law; economics; politics, economics and law; history, politics and English literature; accounting and financial management; biology and society; European studies. The licence in European studies takes 3 years including 1 year abroad. In 1980 there were 350 full-time students.

All universities charge fees, but financial help is available to students from several sources.

The universities themselves provide scholarships of various kinds and all local education authorities have a system of awards to help suitable students to attend university.

The amount of aid given generally depends upon the parents' means. The majority of the students at the English and Welsh universities are in receipt of some form of financial assistance.

Awards known as state studentships are offered on a competitive basis by the Department from among candidates considered by the universities to be qualified for post-graduate studies in the humanities; similar awards, tenable at universities or technical colleges, are offered by the Research Councils to students studying science, mathematics and technology at the post-graduate level.

The following table gives the approximate number of professors, lecturers, etc., and students (full-time and sandwich courses) for 1978–79:

University or college	Students	Staff	University or college	Students	Staff
Aston	5,557	606	Brunel	2,722	332
Bath	3,561	417	Cambridge	11,299	1,177
Birmingham	8,919	1,400	City	2,834	352
Bradford	4,934	543	Durham	4,301	513
Bristol	6,755	1,073	East Anglia	3,872	364

University or college	Students	Staff	University or college	Students	Staff
Essex	2,795	330	Warwick	5,032	584
Exeter	4,949	563	York	3,163	402
Hull	5,192	541			
Keele	2,690	337			
Kent	3,809	467	*Wales—*		
Lancaster	4,531	525	Aberystwyth U.C.	3,173	425
Leeds	10,297	1,334	Bangor U.C.	2,978	409
Leicester	4,208	576	Cardiff U.C.	5,347	699
Liverpool	7,435	1,071	St David's, Lampeter	665	69
London Business School	224	67	Swansea U.C.	3,846	499
London	39,337	7,444	Welsh Nat. School of		
Loughborough	5,151	571	Medicine	778	221
Manchester Business School	138	40	Univ. of Wales Institute of		
Manchester	10,982	1,598	Science and Technology	2,808	323
Univ. of Manchester Inst. of					
Science and Technology	3,862	539			
Newcastle	7,619	1,092	*Scotland—*		
Nottingham	6,500	884	Aberdeen	5,457	856
Oxford	12,203	1,937	Dundee	2,867	513
Reading	5,849	742	Edinburgh	9,869	1,500
Salford	4,376	510	Glasgow	9,404	1,466
Sheffield	7,576	995	Heriot-Watt	3,066	335
Southampton	6,106	925	St Andrews	3,277	364
Surrey	3,309	449	Stirling	2,645	287
Sussex	4,321	672	Strathclyde	6,455	876

Women students are admitted on equal terms with men. Number of women students: England, 78,530; Wales, 7,436; Scotland, 16,724. There are, however, colleges exclusively for female students at Oxford and Cambridge. Numbers of students at institutions receiving aid from the University Grants Committee: England, 226,408; Wales, 19,595; Scotland, 43,040; total, 289,043.

McIntosh, N. E., Calder, J. A. and Swift, B., *A Degree of Difference*. London, 1976
Perry, W., *Open University: A Personal Account*. Open Univ. Press, 1976
Tunstall, J., *The Open University*. London, 1974

The British Council. The British Council was established in Nov. 1934 and incorporated by Royal Charter in 1940. Its aims are the promotion of a wider knowledge of Britain and the English language abroad and the development of closer cultural relations between Britain and other countries.

The Council's expenditure in 1979–80 amounted to £109·3m. Funds were provided by a grant-in-aid of £28·9m. from the Overseas Information (Foreign and Commonwealth Office) vote and a contribution of £16m. from the Overseas Aid Vote. A further £43·6m. was provided by the Overseas Development Administration to cover the cost of administration of, and the reimbursement of sums expended on technical co-operation schemes. The balance of £20·8m. was derived from Council earnings and from international agencies, overseas governments, etc. for educational services.

The Council is governed by a board consisting of up to 30 members, 6 of whom are nominated by Ministers. There are advisory committees for Scotland and Wales and also advisory committees or panels for the main branches of the Council's work. In Jan. 1981 the Council had staff in 79 countries.

The Council is designated by the British Government to carry out over 30 bilateral cultural agreements, including that with the Soviet Union. The Council's work broadly divides into English language teaching and other educational work, the promotion of wider use and availability of British books and periodicals, the development of personal contacts and the exchange of information, especially in the fields of education, medicine, science, technology and the arts.

The general policy in the field of English language teaching is to advise and assist education authorities overseas, particularly in curriculum and materials development and the training of local teachers of English; courses are provided in Britain and abroad for the further training of English language teaching experts from overseas. In many countries the Council runs its own English teaching centres. The Council acts as a centre for the dissemination of information about British educational thought and practice at all levels and, through its complement of education specialists working overseas, it has become closely involved with the administration of aid on behalf of the Overseas Development Administration. It assists in producing English teaching and other educational television and radio programmes overseas and arranges training courses in TV, radio and audio-visual aids both in Britain and overseas. A prominent aspect of its education work is the assistance given in developing countries to the adoption of modern and locally relevant methods of science and mathematics teaching in schools, and for this work the Council maintains a growing group of science educationists and administers the ODA funded Aid for Commonwealth Teaching of Science scheme. Over 800 lecturers etc., mainly in the field of English language, are working overseas, having been recruited by the British Council on behalf of universities, schools etc. in over 100 different countries. The Council is concerned to promote closer international academic collaboration through a variety of interchange and linking schemes, and through the provision of information and advice on educational institutions; it also administers the British Government's Technical Co-operation Training Programme and scholarship programmes on behalf of a large number of international organizations, notably UN and EEC. It administers examinations on behalf of a number of British examining boards; and it also circulates films for general educational purposes.

During recent years the Council has collaborated with British educational institutions and firms in designing and implementing a wide range of education projects, for which overseas authorities or multilateral agencies pay the full cost.

The sciences, including medicine, technology and agriculture, form an increasingly important part of Council work. Contacts are built up and information collected and distributed through the specialist departments in London and the qualified scientists serving overseas, who also advise on training in Britain and the provision of experts abroad.

The importance of the arts as a medium for fostering cultural relations is reflected in the Council's encouragement of the appreciation of British achievements in the performing and the visual arts, both by supporting local activity and by sending theatre and ballet companies, orchestras and chamber groups, and exhibitions both of fine arts and photographs, from Britain on tours overseas. The Council also produces booklets, records and tapes on a wide range of literary and artistic subjects.

The Council runs, or is associated with, over 100 libraries in the countries in which it is represented. It arranges touring exhibitions of new British books and periodicals (some 95,000 books were exhibited in 290 exhibitions in 1979–80). Additional publicity for British books is provided by the publication *British Book News*, the distribution of specialized book lists and the operation of a review scheme. The Council also administers for ODA funds (approximately £3m. in 1979–80) for library development, the presentation of books and periodicals to educational institutions in developing countries and the subsidized publication of low-priced books for students under the imprint of the English Language Book Society.

The Council arranges short advisory tours overseas by British experts. In a number of countries it is also the overseas administrative arm of the British Volunteer Programme. It awards scholarships and bursaries and arranges study programmes for some 30,000 visitors a year in Britain. It administers central government funds for youth exchanges with other countries.

In Britain the Council administers the programmes of award schemes for overseas students, meets many students on arrival from overseas, and provides an accommodation service, mainly for students from overseas for whom it has a special responsibility. The Council runs offices in Britain, mainly in university cities, for these purposes.

The Council is increasingly called on to administer training schemes and educational services financed by overseas authorities, or by multilateral agencies, on a contractual basis. The Council's specialist courses and summer schools provide advanced study in a number of fields, notably medicine, science, literature and the arts, English language and education. Payment is made by the student, or his parent organization, or by some other sponsor.

The Council publishes the following periodicals: *British Medical Bulletin, Educational Broadcasting International* and *British Book News.* Other publications produced include the series *Writers and their Work, Notes on Literature, British Education, British Books and Libraries;* a number of booklets including *Higher Education in the United Kingdom, Introducing Wales, How to Live in Britain* and *Statistics of Overseas Students in Britain.* The Council has sponsored two major series of literature recordings, *The Complete Works of Shakespeare* and *The English Poets from Chaucer to Yeats.*

Chairman: Sir Charles Troughton, CBE, MC, TD.
Director-General: J. C. Burgh, CB.
Headquarters: 10 Spring Gdns., London, SW1A 2BN.

Arts Council of Great Britain. The Arts Council is an independent organization established by Royal Charter in 1946, and is one of the principal channels for British Government aid to the arts. The Council's objects are to develop and improve the knowledge, understanding and practice of the arts, to increase their accessibility to the public, and to advise and co-operate with government departments, local authorities and other organizations.

The Council consists of a Chairman and not more than 19 other members who are appointed by the Secretary of State for Education and Science, after consultation with the Secretaries of State for Scotland and Wales. The Council is advised by panels and committees concerned with different aspects of the arts. With the approval of the appropriate Minister, the Council appoints committees for Scotland and Wales known respectively as the Scottish Arts Council and the Welsh Arts Council.

The Council receives a grant-in-aid from the Government voted annually by Parliament. The grant-in-aid for 1981–82 is £80m., including £1m. for special capital purposes and £1½m. for the Housing the Arts Fund.

As well as giving financial help and advice to 1,200 artistic organizations from the major opera, dance, drama companies, orchestras and festivals, to the smallest touring theatre and experimental group, the Council encourages such diverse interests as contemporary dance, photography, art films, and helps professional creative writers, dramatists, poets, musicians, composers, artists and photographers by means of bursary and award schemes. The Council provides funds for specialist training courses in the arts, and assists projects for the construction of new buildings, or improvements to existing ones under its 'Housing the Arts' scheme.

A growing proportion of the Council's funds is channelled to the network of regional arts associations which practically covers the whole of England and Wales. The regional arts associations are not branches of the Arts Council, but are autonomous bodies, financed by a combination of Arts Council, local authority and private funds.

The Council mounts art exhibitions at the Hayward and Serpentine and other galleries in London and also in the regions. Other direct promotions include tours of opera and drama companies, of the Council's own films on the arts and of music groups under the Contemporary Music Network scheme. The Council has a library of contemporary British poetry at 9 Long Acre, London, WC2E 9LG.

Chairman: Rt Hon. Kenneth Robinson, PC.
Secretary-General: Sir Roy Shaw.
Headquarters: 105 Piccadilly, London, W1V 0AU. *The Scottish Arts Council:* 19–20 Charlotte Sq., Edinburgh, EH2 4DF. *The Welsh Arts Council:* 9 Museum Place, Cardiff, CF1 3NX.

National Insurance. The National Insurance Act, 1946, came into operation on 5 July 1948, repealing the existing schemes of health, pensions and unemployment insurance. This Act, along with later legislation, was consolidated as the National Insurance Act, 1965.

The Social Security Act 1975 introduced, from 6 April 1975, a new system of national insurance contributions to replace the previous system of flat-rate and graduated contributions. Since 6 April 1975, Class 1 contributions have been related to the employee's earnings and are collected with PAYE income tax, instead of by affixing stamps to a card. Class 2 and Class 3 contributions remain flat-rate, but, in addition to Class 2 contributions, those who are self-employed may be liable to pay Class 4 contributions, which for the year 1981–82 will be at the rate of 5·75% on profits or gains between £3,150 and £10,000, which are assessable for income tax under Schedule D. The non-employed and others whose contribution record is not sufficient to give entitlement to benefits are able to pay a Class 3 contribution voluntarily to qualify for a limited range of benefits. Class 2 contributions for 1981–82 are £3·40 a week for men and women. Class 3 contributions are £3·30 a week.

From 6 April 1978 the Social Security Pensions Act 1975 introduced earnings-related retirement, invalidity and widows' pensions. Employee's national insurance contribution liability depends on whether he is in contracted out or not contracted out employment. The not-contracted out employee pays 7·75% on all earnings up to £200 a week. The employer's rate is 10·2% and a 3½% surcharge of the same earnings. An employee's contracted-out contribution is 7·75% of the first £27 a week of earnings and 5·25% of earnings between £27 and £200 a week. The employer's contribution is 10·2% (and the 3½% surcharge) of the first £27 of weekly earnings and 5·7 (and the 3½% surcharge) of earnings up to £200 a week.

The State supplements the contributions paid by contributors and employers, from general taxation. Contributions (other than the surcharge) and supplement together with interest on investments form the income of the National Insurance Fund from which benefits are paid.

Benefits. The range of benefits are unaffected by the new arrangements from 5 April 1975. The benefits are: (1) Unemployment benefit; (2) Sickness benefit; (3) Invalidity benefit; (4) Maternity benefit; (5) Widow's benefit; (6) Guardian's allowance; (7) Child's special allowance; (8) Retirement pension; (9) Death grant.

Employed persons may qualify for all the benefits; self-employed may qualify for all except unemployment; non-employed may qualify for all except unemployment, sickness, invalidity and maternity allowance. Qualification for any benefit depends upon the fulfilment of the appropriate contribution and other conditions.

Sickness and Unemployment Benefit. From 23 Nov. 1981 the normal rate is £22·50 a week plus £13·90 a week for an adult dependant, plus £0·80 for each child for whom child benefit is in payment. An earnings-related supplement may be payable from the 13th to 168th day of a period of interruption of employment to persons under minimum pension age (65 for men, 60 for women) who are entitled to standard-rate sickness benefit, unemployment benefit or maternity allowance and who have paid Class 1 (employee's) National Insurance contributions on earnings of more than 50 times the lower weekly earnings limit for contributions in the relevant income-tax year.

Unemployment benefit is paid through the local unemployment benefit offices of the Department of Employment.

Invalidity Benefit replaces sickness benefit after 168 days of entitlement. It comprises a basic invalidity pension of £28·35 weekly and an invalidity allowance of £6·20 if incapacity began before age 40: £4 if incapacity began between 40 and 50 or £2 if it began between 50 and 60 (55 for women). Increases are: £17 for an adult dependant plus £7·70 for each child for whom child benefit is payable.

Maternity Benefit. For a confinement a woman may receive a maternity grant of £25 and, where 2 or more children are born at the confinement, a further grant of £25 for each additional child who is alive 12 hours after its birth. If the woman has been gainfully employed or self-employed, and has paid sufficient full-rate national insurance contributions in the relevant income tax year, she may receive a maternity allowance of £22·50 a week normally payable for 18 weeks commencing 11 weeks before the expected week of confinement, provided she does not work during this period. Maternity allowance may be increased in certain circumstances in respect of dependants in the same way as sickness and unemployment benefits and an earnings-related supplement may be payable.

Widow's Benefit. On her husband's death a widow normally qualifies for 26 weeks for an allowance of £41·40 a week for herself plus an increase for each child for whom child benefit is payable at £7·70 a week. An earnings related addition based on the amount on which her late husband had paid Class 1 (employee's) contributions in the relevant tax year may also be paid, but ceased after 2 Jan. 1982. At the end of the 26 weeks she may qualify for a widowed mother's allowance of £29·60 for herself, and the increases for the children for whom child benefit is payable continue at the same rate as for the first 26 weeks of widowhood. She may also receive her allowance at the personal rate of £29·60 a week if she has living with her a son or daughter who is under 19. The child increase for widow's allowance and widowed mother's allowance is, generally speaking, payable only in respect of a child for whom child benefit is payable.

A widow's pension may be paid to: (i) A widow after the termination of her widow's allowance, if she does not qualify for widowed mother's allowance and was over the age of 40 when her husband died. (ii) A widow after she ceases to be entitled to a widowed mother's allowance if she is then over the age of 40. The standard rate of this pension is £29·60 a week if the widow was over 50 when her husband died or when her entitlement to widowed mother's allowance ended. If she was between 40 and 50, however, the standard rates of total pension range in 7% steps from 93% of the full age-50 rate (*i.e.*, £27·53 a week) for the widow who was 49 at that time to 30% (*i.e.*, £8·88 a week) for the widow who was then 40.

Child's Special Allowance. An allowance may be payable for the children of divorced parents where the father has died. It is payable to the mother if she has not remarried and her former husband was contributing, or legally liable to contribute, at least 25p a week towards the children's support in cash or kind or if she took reasonable steps to enforce maintenance and she was entitled to child benefit for the child(ren) when her former husband died or it is her child by her former husband and he was entitled to child benefit for the child(ren) when he died. It is similar to the increases for widow's children and is payable at the same rates.

Guardian's Allowance. A person who is responsible for an orphan child may be entitled to a guardian's allowance of £7·70 a week in addition to the amount of child benefit payable in respect of that child. Normally both the child's parents must be dead but when the child is illegitimate, or the parents were divorced, or one parent is missing, or serving a long sentence of imprisonment, the allowance may, in certain circumstances, be paid on the death of one parent only.

Retirement Pension. In order to receive a retirement pension, men between 65 and 70, and women between 60 and 65 must have retired from regular employment. From 6 April 1979 a woman divorced over the age of 60 must satisfy the retired conditions before a pension is payable. The standard rates of basic pensions are £29·60 a week for a man or a woman on his or her own contributions and £17·75 for a married woman through her husband's contributions. Proportionately reduced pensions are payable where contribution records are deficient. For a person who reaches pension age on or after 6 April 1979, additional pension may also be payable. This is based on the earnings on which he or she has paid Class 1 contributions in each complete tax year between April 1978 and pension age. If the person has been a member of a contracted-out occupational pension scheme, that scheme will be responsible for paying the whole or part of the additional pension. An increase of £17·75 a week may be payable for a dependent wife. If she resides with the beneficiary the increase is gradually reduced for earnings over £52 a week. If she does not reside with the beneficiary an increase is not payable if she earns more than £17·75 a week. In addition £7·70 a week may be payable for each child for whom child benefit is payable. In certain circumstances an increase of £17·75 a week may be payable for a woman having care of the pensioner's children. In addition, a man who had paid graduated contributions receives 3·54p per week for every £7·50 of graduated contributions paid, and a woman 3·54p per week for every £9 paid. Although no further graduated contributions have been paid after April 1975, pension already earned will be paid along with the basic pension in the normal way. If, after being awarded a retirement pension, a man under 70 or a woman under 65 earns more than £52 in a calendar week the pension for the next pension week, including any increase for dependants, will be reduced by 5p for every 10p earned between £52 and £56 and by 5p for every 5p earned over £56. If retirement is postponed after minimum pension age increments of basic pension can be earned for periods of deferred retirement: Between 6 April 1975 and 5 April 1979 increments were earned at the rate of one-eighth penny per £1 of the pension rate for every 6 days (excluding Sundays) for which the pension had been forgone. From 6 April 1979 increments are earned at the rate of one-seventh penny per £1 of basic pension for every 6 days (excluding Sundays) for which pension has been forgone. Any days for which another benefit has been paid will not count. These increments must be at least 1% of the pension rate unless the minimum was earned under the arrangements which applied before 6 April 1979. For periods between 6 April 1975 and that date, the rate was one-eighth penny per £1 of the basic pension rate for every 6 days and for periods of deferred retirement before 6 April 1975 increments were based on the number of contributions paid as an employed or self-employed person. At age 70 for a man (65 for a woman) the pension for which a person has qualified may be paid in full whether a person continues in work or not irrespective of the amount of earnings. At the age of 80 an age addition of £0·25 a week is payable. In addition non-contributory pensions are now payable, subject to residence conditions, to persons aged 80 and over who do not qualify for a retirement pension or qualify for one at a low rate. The rates of these pensions, which are financed by Exchequer funds, are £17·75 a week for a single person and £10·65 for a married woman. These amounts do not include the £0·25 age addition.

Death Grant. This is a lump sum paid on the death of an insured person or his close relative. The normal amount of the payment is: For an adult, £30; for a child aged 6 but under 18, £22·50; for a child aged 3 but under 6, £15; for a child under 3, £9. For the death of a person who was within 10 years of pensionable age on 5 July 1948 (*i.e.*, a man over 55 and a woman over 50 on that date) only half the standard amount is payable. No grant is payable for the death of a person who was over the pensionable age on 5 July 1948.

The Industrial Injuries Provisions of the Social Security Act, 1975. The Industrial Injuries Act, which also came into operation on 5 July 1948, with its later amending Acts, was consolidated as the National Insurance (Industrial Injuries) Act, 1965. This legislation was incorporated in the Social Security Act, 1975. The scheme provides a system of insurance against 'personal injury by accident arising out of and in the course of employment' and against certain prescribed diseases and injuries due to the nature of the employment. It takes the place of the Workmen's Compensation Acts and covers persons who are employed earners under the Social Security Act. There are no contribution conditions for the payment of benefit. Three types of benefit are provided:

(*1*) *Injury benefit*, payable for incapacity for work due to an industrial accident or certain of the prescribed diseases for a maximum of 26 weeks from the date of the accident or the development of the disease. The rate of this benefit is £25·25 a week, with increases of £13·90 for 1 adult dependant and £0·80 for each child for whom child benefit is payable. An earnings-related supplement may be payable where there would otherwise be entitlement to earnings-related supplement of sickness benefit or maternity allowance. If the employed earner is under 18 years of age and is not entitled to a dependant's increase, benefit will be payable at a reduced rate—£22·50. For children under 16 years of age in part-time employment, the rate is £6·80.

(*2*) *Disablement benefit.* This is payable where, as the result of an industrial accident or prescribed disease, there is a loss of faculty usually after injury benefit ceases to be payable. The loss of faculty will be assessed at a percentage by comparison with a person of the same age and sex whose condition is normal. If the assessment is 20%, or more, benefit will be a pension varying according to the assessment, from £8·90 a week to £48·30 a week. If the assessment is under 20% benefit will normally be a gratuity of an amount not exceeding £2,950. Unemployability supplement plus age additions similar to invalidity allowance, may be payable to a disablement pensioner who, as a result of the relevant loss of faculty is incapable of work and likely to remain permanently so incapable. Increases for dependants at the same rates as for invalidity pension are also payable to a disablement pensioner who is entitled to unemployability supplement. The supplement cannot be paid at the same time as certain other benefits payable under the Social Security Act or out of public funds. Other increases of disablement benefit may be payable where the loss of faculty causes special hardship, *i.e.*, it prevents the beneficiary from undertaking his regular job or one of an equivalent standard of earnings; where there is a need for constant attendance; where there is exceptionally severe disablement and the need for constant attendance is likely to be permanent or where disablement is assessed at less than 100% and the beneficiary is in hospital for treatment for his injury or prescribed disease. Pensions for persons under 18 are reduced similarly to injury benefit.

(3) *Death Benefit.* On the death of a person as the result of an industrial accident or a prescribed disease, certain dependants may qualify for benefit. Benefit for a widow is a pension normally of £41·40 weekly for the first 26 weeks and thereafter £30·15, depending on such factors as age, entitlement to a child's allowance and permanent incapacity for self-support. If the conditions for pension at the higher rate are not satisfied the widow may receive a pension of £8·88 a week. Child allowances may be payable to the widow, or other person, entitled to child benefit for children of the deceased. For widows, these allowances are usually at the rate of £7·70 a week for each child; for other persons, the rate is £0·80 for each child. An allowance of £1 is payable to a woman having care of a child of the deceased. Benefit for widowers, parents and certain other relatives takes the form of pensions, allowances or gratuities according to the relationship to, and degree of maintenance by, the deceased.

War Pensions. The number of beneficiaries in receipt of war (1914–18) pensions or allowances as at 26 Sept. 1980 was 38,000. The number of beneficiaries in receipt of war (1939–45 and later) pensions or allowances in payment as at 26 Sept. 1980 was 317,300. The estimated expenditure for both wars for 1980–81 was £429m. The expenditure is exclusive of administrative expenses.

National Insurance Fund. At 1 April 1979 the balance of the National Insurance Fund amounted to £4,090,473,000. Income during the period 1 April 1979 to 31 March 1980, consisting of contributions from insured persons and employers, payments from the Exchequer and interest on investments, etc., was £13,297·45m. Payments of benefit in respect of unemployment were £652,881,000; sickness, £594,659,000; invalidity, £994,829,000; maternity, £141m.; widows, £563m.; guardian's allowance and child's special allowance, £1·9m.; retirement pension, £8,814·42m.; death grants, £16·08m.; injury benefit, £46,548,000; disablement benefits, £244,185,000; death benefit, £36m.; pensioners' lump sum payments, £95·65m. Included in these figures are the following estimated amounts of earnings-related supplement: unemployment benefit, £88m.; sickness benefit, £138m.; maternity allowance, £28m.; widow's benefit, £13m.; graduated retirement benefit, £124m.; additional component, £4m. Administrative and other payments cost approximately £560,996,000. The balance at 31 March 1980 was £4,625,775,000.

From 1 April 1975 the National Insurance Reserve Fund and the Industrial Injuries Fund were merged with the National Insurance Fund. All basic scheme contributions payable under the 1975 Social Security Act are paid into the single fund out of which the existing range of benefits will continue to be financed. The new national insurance fund will continue to receive a Treasury Supplement set at a level of 18% of total contribution income.

Child Benefit. Child benefit is a tax-free cash allowance for all children. The weekly rate for each child is £5·25 from Nov. 1981. Child benefit is payable for all children under age 16 and for those under age 19 receiving full-time non-advanced education at a college or school. Child Benefit Increase (One Parent Benefit). This is a tax-free cash allowance for certain people bringing up children alone. It is payable for the first or only child in the family in addition to child benefit. The weekly rate from Nov. 1980 is £3.

Family Income Supplement. Family income supplement is payable to families with at least 1 dependent child where the head of the household is in remunerative work for at least 30 hours a week (24 hours for lone parents), and where the family's normal gross weekly income (but excluding child benefits) is below a prescribed amount. The prescribed amount for a 1-child family is £74, this amount being increased by £8 for each additional child in the family. The weekly rate of benefit payable is one-half of the difference between the prescribed amount and the family's normal income, subject to a maximum weekly payment of £18·50 for families with 1 child, increasing by £1·50 for each additional child. Benefit is usually payable for 52 weeks and is not affected by changes in circumstances. The prescribed amounts are the same for both 1- and 2-parent families.

Attendance allowance. This is a tax-free allowance for severely disabled people, including children aged 2 or over, who require a lot of help from another person. There are 2 rates, the higher rate of £23·65 a week for those who require attention or supervision by day and night, and the lower rate of £15·75 a week for those who need the attendance either by day or night. In addition to the medical re-quirements a simple test of residence and presence in Great Britain must also be satisfied.

Invalid Care Allowance. Payable to those under pensionable age for caring for a severely disabled relative. Current rate £16·30 a week.

Supplementary Benefit. Under the Supplementary Benefits Act, 1976, as amended by the Social Security Act 1980, benefit is payable to any persons in Great Britain aged 16 years or over (excluding persons at school or college or anyone directly involved in a trade dispute) who are not in full-time remunerative work and who are without resources, or whose resources (including national insurance benefits) need to be supplemented in order to meet their requirements. A person who is excluded from benefit under the normal rules may, nevertheless, receive payments to meet urgent need. The general standards by reference to which supplementary benefit is granted are determined by statutory regulations approved by Parliament. Persons who are dissatisfied with the amount of benefit granted to them may appeal to an independent Appeal Tribunal established under the Act.

During the financial year 1979–80 net payments on supplementary benefit amounted to £2,155m.

Newman, T. S., *Digest of British Social Insurance.* London, 1947 (and supplements, to date)

National Health. The National Health Service in England and Wales started on 5 July 1948 under the National Health Service Act, 1946. There is a separate Act for Scotland and also one for Northern Ireland, where the Health Services are run on similar lines to those in England and Wales.

The National Health Service, which is available to every man, woman and child, is a charge on the national incme in the same way as the armed forces and other facilities.

Every person normally resident in this country is entitled to use any complete part of the services, and no insurance qualification is necessary.

Most of the cost of running the service is met from the national exchequer, *i.e.,* from taxes.

Since Sept. 1957 a small weekly National Health Service contribution has been payable by contributors and where applicable by their employers. For convenience this contribution is collected with the National Insurance contribution and for 1980–81 is estimated to be £990m. for Great Britain.

Organization. Under the provisions of the National Health Service Act 1977, the administration of the National Health Service in England and Wales is organized under a system of regional and area health authorities accountable to the Secretary of State for the Social Services and the Secretary of State for Wales. In Scotland the National Health Service is administered under the National Health Service (Scotland) Act 1978, by 15 Health Boards and a Common Services Agency all accountable to the Secretary of State for Scotland.

There are 90 area health authorities in England responsible for the administration and development of allthe health services in thir areas. Fourteen regional health authorities, each consisting of a number of complete health areas, are responsible for allocating resources between the area health authorities in their regions and for monitoring their performance. The regional health authorities are responsible for developing strategic plans and priorities and for carrying out certain executive functions.

Services. The National Health Service broadly consists of hospital and specialist services, general medical, dental and ophthalmic services, pharmaceutical services, community health services and school health services. All these services are free of charge except for such things as prescriptions, spectacles, dentures and dental treatment, amenity beds in hospitals and for some of the community services, for which charges are made with certain exemptions.

The total cost of the Health and Personal Social Services (England and Wales) is estimated at £12,081m. for 1980–81 and the estimated net expenditure of the Exchequer (except for the Local Authority Personal Social Services, where the rates and the Exchequer grants are estimated at about £1,334m.) in 1980–81 is £9,373m.

The number of abortion notifications received in 1979 under the provisions of the Abortion Act, 1967, was 147,451, of which 120,611 related to England and Wales residents. Of these 119,028 notifications, 62,000 (51·9%) were to single women, 43,278 (35·9%) were to married women, and 14,540 (12·2%) were to widowed, divorced or separated women and to women who did not state their marital status.

The number of abortion notifications received in Scotland in 1979 under the provisions of the Abortion Act 1967, was 7,754, of which 7,668 related to Scottish residents. Of these 7,754 notifications, 3,831 (49·4%) were to single women, 2,954 (38·1%) were to married women, and 969 (12·5%) were to widowed, divorced or separated women and to women who did not state their marital status.

In 1977 there were 26,810 general medical practitioners, 13,564 general dental practitioners and 219,900 qualified nurses and midwives. There were (1977) 469,849 allocated hospital beds.

Personal Social Services. Under the Local Authority Social Services Act 1970 and in Scotland the Social Work (Scotland) Act 1968 the welfare and social work services provided by local authorities were made the responsibility of a new local authority department—the Social Services Department in England and Wales, and Social Work Departments in Scotland headed by a Director of Social Work. The social services thus administered include: the fostering, care and adoption of children, welfare services and social workers for the mentally disordered, the disabled and the aged, and accommodation for those needing residential care services. In Scotland the social work departments' functions also include the supervision of persons on probation, of adult offenders and of persons released from penal institutions or subject to fine supervision orders.

The number of persons in residential and temporary accommodation provided by or on behalf of local authoriies was as follows:

England and Wales (31 March)	Residential accommodation Adults
1975	127,937
1976	134,000
1977	135,000
1978	136,000
1979	135,000

Scotland	Residential accommodation Adults and Children	Temporary accommodation Adults	Children	Total Adults and Children
1977[1]	17,543	76	153	17,772
1978[1]	17,302	65	94	17,461
1979[1]	16,717	—	—	16,717

[1] Year ending 31 March.

England and Wales. Expenditure and income relating to the personal social services administered by local authorities (in £ sterling):

Year ended 31 March	Expenditure (including loan charges)	Income (including payments by recipients of services)	Net Expenditure
1976	963,380,000	144,571,000	818,809,000
1977	1,131,223,000	176,001,000	955,222,000
1978	1,267,079,000	206,654,000	1,060,425,000
1979	1,440,931,000	240,577,000	1,200,354,000
1980 [1]	1,752,094,000	283,746,000	1,468,348,000

[1] Provisional.

Scotland. The total local authority expenditure for 1978–79 in respect of residential accommodation and welfare services under the Social Work (Scotland) Act, 1968, was £143·6m. Central Government expenditure on social work totalled £6m.

Social Security Statistics 1980 (incorporating 1979). HMSO, 1980
Watkin, B., *The National Health Service.* London, 1978

DIPLOMATIC REPRESENTATIVES

OF THE USA IN GREAT BRITAIN (Grosvenor Sq., London, W1A 1AE)
Ambassador: John J. Louis, Jr.

OF GREAT BRITAIN IN THE USA (3100 Massachusetts Ave., Washington, D.C., 20008)
Ambassador: Sir Nicholas Henderson, GCMG.

OF GREAT BRITAIN TO THE UNITED NATIONS
Ambassador: Sir Anthony Parsons, KCMG, MVO, MC.

Books of Reference

The annual and other publications of the various Public Departments, and the Reports, etc. of Royal Commissions and Parliamentary Committees. (These may be obtained from HM Stationery Office.)

Allen, G. C., *British Industries and their Organization.* 4th ed. London, 1959
Bickmore, D. P., and Shaw, M. A. (ed.), *The Atlas of Great Britain and Northern Ireland.* OUP, 1963
Burn, D., *The Structure of British Industry.* 2 vols. CUP, 1958
Central Statistical Office. *Annual Abstract of Statistics.* HMSO.—*Monthly Digest of Statistics.* HMSO
Central Office of Information. *Britain: An Official Handbook.* HMSO, 1978.—*Britain in Brief* 18th ed. HMSO, 1977
Demangeon, A., *The British Isles.* 3rd ed. London, 1952
Directory of British Associations. Beckenham, annual
Government Statistical Service. *Social Trends.* HMSO, 1979—*Regional Statistics.* HMSO, 1979
Halsey, A. H., *Trends in British Society Since 1900.* London, 1972
History of the Second World War. HMSO, 1949 ff.
Kendall, M. G. (ed.), *The Source and Nature of the Statistics of the United Kingdom.* 2 vols. London, 1952–1957
Mitchell, B. R., *Abstract of British Historical Statistics.* OUP, 1962
Oxford History of England. 15 vols. OUP, 1936 ff.
Stamp, L. D., and Beaver, S. H., *The British Isles: A Geographic and Economic Survey.* 4th ed., London, 1954
Woodward, Sir E. L., and Butler, R., *Documents on British Foreign Policy, 1919–39.* HMSO, 1957 ff.

Scotland

Scottish Council (Development and Industry). *Inquiry into the Scottish Economy, 1900–61.* Edinburgh, 1961

Scottish Office. *Scottish Economic Bulletin*. HMSO (quarterly).—*Scottish Abstract of Statistics.* HMSO (annual)
The New Scottish Local Authorities: Organisation and Management Structures. HMSO, 1973
Brand, J., *The National Movement in Scotland*. London, 1978
Campbell, R. H., *The Rise and Fall of Scottish Industry, 1707–1939*. Edinburgh, 1981
Donaldson, G. (ed.) *The Edinburgh History of Scotland*. 4 vols. Edinburgh, 1965–75
Drucker, N. and H. M., *The Scottish Government Year Book*. London, 1980
Hogg, A., and Hutcheson, A. MacG., *Scotland and Oil*. 2nd ed. Edinburgh, 1975
Johnston, T. L., *Structure and Growth in the Scottish Economy*. London, 1971
Kellas, J. G., *The Scottish Political System*. 2nd ed. CUP, 1975
Meikle, H. W. (ed.), *Scotland: A Description of Scotland and Scottish Life*. London, 1947
Turnock, D., *Patterns of Highland Development*. London, 1970

Wales

Wales: The Way Ahead (Cmnd 3334.) HMSO, 1971
Wales: Employment and the Economy. Cardiff, 1972
Digest of Welsh Statistics. HMSO (annual)
Thomas, B. (ed.), *The Welsh Economy*. Cardiff, 1962
Williams, D., *A History of Modern Wales*. New ed. London, 1977
Williams, G., (ed.) *Social and Cultural Change in Contemporary Wales*. London, 1978

NORTHERN IRELAND

AREA AND POPULATION. Area (revised by the Ordnance Survey Department) and population at the census of 25 April 1971 were as follows:

Counties and county boroughs	Area in hectares	Males	Females	Total
Antrim	304,526	175,177	180,539	355,716
Armagh	132,697	66,917	67,052	133,969
Belfast C.B.	7,305	172,397	189,685	362,082
Down	246,624	152,622	159,254	311,876
Fermanagh	185,097	25,830	24,425	50,255
Londonderry	210,782	65,827	65,062	130,889
Londonderry C.B.	1,044	25,331	26,874	52,205
Tyrone	326,550	70,575	68,498	139,073
Northern Ireland	1,414,625	754,676	781,389	1,536,065

Vital statistics for calendar years:

	Marriages	Divorces	Births	Deaths
1974	10,783	382	27,160	17,327
1975	10,867	437	26,130	16,511
1976	9,914	574	26,361	17,030
1977	9,696	569	25,437	16,921
1978	10,304	599	26,239	16,153

CONSTITUTION AND GOVERNMENT. The Northern Ireland Constitution Act 1973 as amended by the Northern Ireland Constitution (Amendment) Act 1973 and the Northern Ireland Assembly Act 1973 provide for a Northern Ireland Assembly of 78 members and a Northern Ireland Executive of not more than 11 members (including the Chief Executive Member). The Secretary of State appointed this full number to take office from 1 Jan. 1974. He may also, under the Amendment Act, appoint others to carry out particular functions in the Administration up to a total (including members of the Executive) of 15. This additional number were appointed.

Devolution of legislative and executive responsibility to the Northern Ireland Assembly and the new Administration under Section 2 of the Constitution Act was given effect by the Northern Ireland Constitution (Devolution) Order 1973 from 1

Jan. 1974 ('the appointed day'). On that day, Section 1 of the Northern Ireland (Temporary Provisions) Act 1972 expired and, with it, the power to legislate for Northern Ireland by Order in Council under that Act.

Power to make laws (to be known as Measures) in respect of 'transferred' matters, that is on matters other than those listed in Schedules 2 and 3 to the Constitution Act was vested in the Assembly subject to the overriding power of the UK Parliament to legislate on such matters and subject to Section 17 of the Constitution Act which declares void any provision which discriminates against any person or class of persons on the ground of religious belief or political opinion. The procedure for Measures is set out in the Standing Orders of the Assembly. All Measures require the approval of the Queen in Council before they become law. The first election of Members to the 78 seats in the Northern Ireland Assembly was held in 1973. The state of the parties following the election was: Social Democratic and Labour Party 19; Democratic Unionist Loyalist Coalition 8; Official Unionist 24; Northern Ireland Labour 1; Other Unionist 8; Alliance 8; Vanguard Unionist Coalition 7; Other Loyalist Coalition 2; Other Loyalist 1. Northern Ireland also returns 12 members of the UK House of Commons.

On 28 May 1974 the Unionist members of the Administration resigned, as a result of which the Secretary of State terminated the appointments of members, and HM the Queen prorogued the Assembly for a period of 4 months (thus preventing it from legislating). Parliament subsequently enacted the Northern Ireland Act 1974 extending the prorogation of the Assembly and providing for its dissolution. The Act also reintroduced the power to legislate for Northern Ireland by Order in Council.

The Assembly was dissolved on 28 March 1975, and an election, provided for under the 1974 Act, of a Constitutional Convention took place on 1 May 1975. The Convention had the purpose of considering what provision for the government of Northern Ireland was likely to command the most widespread acceptance throughout the community there. The Convention was dissolved on 5 March 1976 as there was no prospect of agreement. Direct rule continues in being under the terms of the Northern Ireland Act 1974.

In Jan. 1980, the main political parties were invited by the Secretary of State to take part in a Conference with the object of seeking the highest level of agreement on the future government of the Province. The conference, which was attended by 3 of the 4 main parties was adjourned in March 1980.

What began ostensibly as a Civil Rights campaign in 1968, escalated into a full-scale offensive designed to overthrow the State. This offensive was originally mounted by an illegal organization, the Irish Republican Army (not to be confused with the legitimate Army of the Republic of Ireland). At times countermeasures have required the services of over 20,000 regular troops, in addition to the Royal Ulster Constabulary, the RUC Reserve and the part-time Ulster Defence Regiment.

Secretary of State for Northern Ireland: Right Hon. Humphrey Atkins, MP.

Local Government. Northern Ireland has a single-tier system of 26 district councils based on main centres of population.

The district councils are responsible for the provision of a wide range of local services including refuse collection and disposal, street cleansing, litter prevention, consumer protection, environmental health, miscellaneous licensing, the provision and management of recreational and cultural facilities, the promotion of tourist development schemes, the enforcement of building regulations and gas supply. They have in addition both a representative role in which they send forward representatives to sit as members of statutory bodies including the Northern Ireland Housing Council, the Fire Authority and the Area Boards for health and personal social services and education and libraries; and a consultative role under which the Department of Environment (NI) and the Northern Ireland Housing Executive, among others, have an obligation to consult them regarding the provision of the regional services for which these bodies are responsible.

Regional development strategy in Northern Ireland throughout the late sixties and early seventies was based on the *Matthew Report* of 1963, which marked the beginning of a new era in regional planning in the Province. This in turn was endorsed by the economic plan prepared by Professor Wilson in 1965, which modified and up-dated a number of the original Matthew proposals. The Northern Ireland Development Programme 1970–75 extended the scope of the regional strategy and basically identified two categories of interest: (*i*) centres of accelerated growth consisting of the greater Belfast area (including the Belfast Urban Area, Craigavon, Antrim, Bangor, Carrickfergus and Newtownards), Londonderry and Ballymena.

These were centres where a proportionately large expansion was deliberately planned and where population growth was to be actively encouraged. (*ii*) Eight key centres which were to be made as attractive as possible to potential new industry and where significant expansion was anticipated. The 8 centres were the provincial towns of Newry, Dungannon, Coleraine, Enniskillen, Omagh, Larne, Downpatrick and Strabane. This growth and key centre policy had a twofold purpose: to maintain a Development Stopline around Belfast and to encourage movement of population from the city and elsewhere to the major towns outside the Belfast Urban Area.

In 1975 the Development Programme of 1970 having run its full course, the Government published a discussion paper which outlined and evaluated 6 very broad options for the future development of the Province for the period 1975–95. Following comments from a wide variety of sources the Government announced its decision to adopt in principle the District Towns Strategy. Basically the strategy advocates that the growth and key centre strategy should be extended to embrace the major town in each local government district. A detailed exposition *Northern Ireland Regional Physical Development Strategy 1975–95* was published in May 1977.

While the physical strategy sets out the Government's aims and objectives on a regional basis, the details required to pursue these aims and objectives at local level are promulgated in Area Plans. These have been published for the Belfast Urban Area, the North Down, Londonderry, West Tyrone, Newry, Limavady, Armagh, East Antrim, East Tyrone, Magherafelt, Fermanagh and the north-east of the Province which incorporates the Coleraine–Portrush–Portstewart area. Work is continuing on the preparation of a plan for the Lisburn, Banbridge, Mourne, and Downpatrick areas. Statements of the Department's conclusions and decisions have been published on the Belfast Urban, North Down, Londonderry, Armagh, Newry, West Tyrone, Limavady, East Antrim and East Tyrone Plans following consideration of the Reports of Public Inquiries held into objections to the Plans, and the latter 8 Plans have been adopted as statutory development plans under Article 7(2) of the Planning (NI) Order 1972. Public Inquiries have been held into the North-East and Magherafelt Area Plans. A major review of the Belfast Urban Area Transportation Strategy has been carried out and a public inquiry held. A statement has been issued by the Department of the Environment (NI) indicating the future system of transport in Belfast.

Provisions in Part VII of the Planning (NI) Order 1972 enable the Department of the Environment (NI) to deal with areas requiring to be developed or redeveloped in overall schemes involving the participation of several agencies. Land when acquired is not normally developed by the Department itself but is disposed of to other agencies for the carrying out of their development. The Department is currently using these powers for two main purposes, the promotion of commercial redevelopment of certain town centre sites and the acquisition overall of large areas, principally in Belfast, which are in need of redevelopment and are proposed to be redeveloped for mainly other than housing purposes. Where land is to be developed by the private sector then disposal by the Department is on the basis of a lease rather than by transfer of the freehold.

The legislative framework for planning in Northern Ireland is contained in the Planning (NI) Order 1972 and the Planning (Amendment) (NI) Order 1978. Under the 1972 Order the Department of the Environment (NI) is the sole planning authority for Northern Ireland. The Order includes procedures for the preparation of plans and development control, establishes a Planning Appeals Commission, contains provisions for the protection of buildings of special architectural or historic merit and trees and gives powers for the carrying out of town-centre redevelopment.

FINANCE. There exists a separate Northern Ireland Consolidated Fund from which is met the expenditure of Northern Ireland Departments. Its main sources of revenue are: (*i*) The Northern Ireland attributed share of UK taxes; (*ii*) A non-specific grant in aid of Northern Ireland's revenue, payable by the Secretary of State for Northern Ireland; (*iii*) Rates and other receipts of Northern Ireland Departments.

The general principle underlying the financial arrangements is that Northern Ireland should have parity of taxation and services with Great Britain.

Since the financial year 1978–79 the income of the Northern Ireland Consolidated Fund has been as follows (in £ sterling):

	1978–79	1979–80[1]	1980–81[2]
Attributed share of UK taxes	765,171,204[1]	986,837,073	1,142,300,000
Payments by UK Government:			
Grant in Aid	560,000,000	589,500,000	682,257,000
Refund of value added tax	8,090,919	11,687,571	15,000,000
Regional and district rates	96,650,000	109,350,000	135,800,000
Other receipts	136,287,494	160,294,610	179,224,600
Total	1,566,199,617	1,857,669,259	2,154,581,600

[1] Including final adjustment for 1977–78.
[2] Provisional.

The public debt at 31 March 1980 was as follows: Northern Ireland 7% Exchequer Stock 1982–84, £20m.; Ulster Savings Certificates, £98,143,000; Ulster Development Bonds, £8,199,000; borrowing from UK Government, £598,843,147; borrowing from Northern Ireland Government Funds, £165,672,000; borrowing from bank, £1m.; borrowing from building societies, £17m.; European Investment Bank Loan, £14,714,458; total, £923,571,605.

The above amount of public debt is offset by equal assets in the form of loans from Government to public and local bodies and of cash balances.

ENERGY AND NATURAL RESOURCES

Electricity. The planning, generation and distribution of electricity supplies are the responsibility of the Northern Ireland Electricity Service.

The installed capacity of the system is 1,845 mw largely provided from 3 thermal power-stations. Work is in progress on the construction of a power-station designed to accommodate four 300 mw turbines and one 60 mw gas turbine in Kilroot, Co. Antrim. This station is due for commissioning progressively from early 1981.

The total sales of electricity in Northern Ireland in the year ended 31 March 1980 amounted to 5,051m. units supplied to a total of 522,192 consumers.

Water Supplies and Sewerage. The Water Service Division of the Department of the Environment (NI) is responsible for water supply and sewerage. Over 140m. gallons of water a day are supplied throughout the Province. More than 90% of the population have a mains supply of water and about 85% live in property connected to public sewers.

The Department is also responsible for the conservation and planned development of water resources in Northern Ireland.

Minerals. The output of minerals (in 1,000 tonnes) during 1979 was approximately: Basalt and igneous rock (other than granite), 7,080; chalk, 320; clay and shale, 257; grit and conglomerate, 3,025; limestone, 2,602; sand and gravel, 4,300; and other minerals (rocksalt, flint, sandstone, diatomite and granite), 388.

Agriculture. Estimated gross output in 1979:

	Quantity (1,000)	Value (£m.)			Quantity (1,000)	Value (£m.)
Fat cattle ⎫	545	194·5	Grass seed ⎫		—	—
Calves	24	3·5	Hay and straw		13	0·8
Store cattle	10	3·0	Fruit	⎬ tonnes	28	3·6
Exports of breeding ⎬ head			Vegetables		36	4·1
livestock	8	2·0	Mushrooms ⎭		5	5·5
Fat sheep and lambs	364	12·7	Flowers		—	1·7
Fat pigs ⎭	1,243	69·0	Sundry		—	1·9
Poultry (tonnes)	48	26·8				
Eggs: for human						
consumption (dozen)	110,400	33·8				
Wool (kg)	1,388	1·3	Total receipts			515·9
Milk (litres)	1,138,400	120·6	Value of changes in			
Potatoes ⎫	258	20·5	stocks due to volume			−19·6
Oats ⎬ tonnes	5	0·5				
Barley	65	6·4	Gross output			496·3
Wheat ⎭	1	0·1				

Area (in 1,000 hectares) of crops at June census (1978 and 1979):

	1978	1979		1978	1979
Oats	5·1	4·2	Other crops	2·1	2·7
Barley	55·8	52·3	Fruit	2·6	2·6
Other cereals and pulses	1·9	1·9	Grass for mowing	262·1	263·0
Potatoes	14·1	14·3	Grass for grazing	504·3	504·4
Turnips, swedes, kale			Rough grazing (excluding		
and cabbage[1]	0·9	0·8	common land)	200·8	208·2
Vegetables	1·2	1·1			

[1] Stock feeding only.

Livestock (1,000) at June census (1978 and 1979):

	1978	1979		1978	1979
Dairy cows	257	264	Total sheep	974	1,000
Beef cows	261	245	Breeding sows	78	77
Total cattle	1,548	1,541	Total pigs	683	722
Breeding ewes	498	513	Total poultry	11,936	11,884

INDUSTRY AND TRADE

Industry. Industry makes a considerable contribution to the Northern Ireland economy. In 1979 employment in manufacturing and construction amounted to 177,700, some 35% of the total workforce. Of this number, 41,600 (23%) were engaged in the engineering and allied industries, which include shipbuilding and aircraft manufacture. The former predominance of shipbuilding has diminished, and the engineering sector now produces an impressive variety of goods: from textile machinery, air-conditioning plant and oilfield equipment to automobile and aero-engine components, data-processing and sound-reproduction equipment, and electronic components. The textile industry, with a workforce of 30,000, has traditionally been associated with linen, but man-made fibre production has brought diversification to the sector and now accounts for a quarter of the total output of synthetic and artificial fibres in the UK. The related clothing and footwear trades employ 18,900 people. Taken together, food, drink and tobacco account for 22,700 jobs, the remainder of the manufacturing sector comprising a multiplicity of trades, such as chemicals and oil-refining, rubber and plastic goods, and furniture accounting for 26,900. The construction industry employs over 37,600 people. The Government offers special encouragement towards the establishment of new and the expansion of existing industry, including substantial grants towards capital investment and the provision of government-built factories at a low rent or on repayment terms. At 31 Dec. 1979 there were 190 new firms and 441 schemes of expansion by existing firms, giving employment to over 61,000 workers.

Labour. The main source of statistics of employees in Northern Ireland is the census of employment which was conducted annually from 1971 to 1978. This provides industrial analyses of employees distinguishing between full-time and part-time employees. The census is supplemented by a less detailed sample quaterly enquiry which since 1979 has been used to provide the main mid-year employment estimate. This showed that at June 1980 there were 503,350 jobs for employees in Northern Ireland; of which 279,950 were taken up by males.

Statistics of persons registered as unemployed in Northern Ireland are compiled monthly. The average rate of unemployment in Northern Irelandn 1980 was 13·8% compared with 11·3% in 1979. The average numbers registered as unemployed was 78,824. The Department of Manpower Services provides an all-age guidance and placement service through a network of Employment Service Offices and Jobmarkets situated in the principal towns of Northern Ireland. They maintain registers of persons seeking employment (either full- or part-time) and those already in employment who wish to change their job. In 1979 the number of vacancies filled in Northern Ireland by te Employment Service was 29,842 (adults and young persons).

Assistance is available to employers who transfer key workers temporarily or permanently to Northern Ireland from other countries or within Norhern Ireland in connection with the establishment or expansion of an industrial undertaking.

The Department of ManpowerServices maintains a register of disabled persons who are in the employment field and under the provisions of the Disabled Persons (Employment) Acts (NI) 1945 and 1960, makes efforts to find suitable work for those who are unemployed. Employment rehabilitation courses are provided at the Employment Rehabilitation Unit at Mill Road, Newtownabbey to assist unemployed disabled persons to readjust themselves to working conditions and to enhance their prospects of obtaining suitable employment. Allowances are paid to persons attending these courses.

Enterprise Ulster is a direct labor organization whose objective is to recruit workers from the unemployed register. Work is carried out mainly for public bodies and projects are of a ommunity and amenity nature such as play areas, parks, playing fields, etc. In Sept. 1980, more than 80 schemes were in operation providing employment for 1,426 people.

There are 13 Government Training Centres in Northern Ireland which now provide some 3,300 training places and are capable of an annual output of over 5,000 trainees. Two of the centres provide 100 training places in traditionally female occupations. Apprentice training accounts for approximately two-thirds of training places. Most of the remaining places are reserved for adults but there are also special courses for young people under 18 years who have been unable to obtain an apprenticeship.

In the sphere of indstrial relations a new independent and statutory body entitled The Labour Relations Agency was established under the Industrial Relations (NI) Order 1976 with the general duty to promote the improvement of industrial relations and to encourage the extension, development and, where necessary, the reform of collective bargaining machinery. The Agency is empowered to undertake research and provide an advisory service on industrial relations matters and to act as a forum for discussion of matters of mutual concern to management and unions. It also has a range of specific functions in the industrial relations field, including the settlement of disputes concerning trade-union recognition. In addition, the Agency has a major role in relation to the provision of conciliation and arbitration services. This means that, upplementing the procedures within industry for the prevention and settlement of disputes, the Agency plays an important part as an impartial third party in helping the sides to clarify issues in dispute and to settle their differences by agreement. Where conciliation fails, the Agency may arrange, if the parties agree, for independent arbitration by one or more persons appointed by the Agency or by the Industrial Court. Occasionally a settlement is promoted by the appointment of a Court of Inquiry. However, the great majority of industrial disputes are settled without stoppage of work, and Northern Ireland's record of days lost due to industrial disputes bears favourable comparison with that of the rest of the UK.

The Fair Employment Agency for Northern Ireland was established under the Fair Employment (NI) Act 1976, with the duties of promoting equality of opportunity in employments and occupations as between persons of different religious beliefs (including people without any religious belief), of working for the elimination of religious and political discrimination (made unlawful by the Act) in employments and occupations, and of keeping under review patterns and trends of employment and occupations.

The Equal Opportunities Commission for Northern Ireland was established under the Sex Discrimination (NI) Order 1976 with the duties of working towards the elimination of sex discrimination in the fields covered by the Order, of promoting equality of opportunity between men and women generally and of keeping under review the working of the Order and equal pay legislation.

The Department of Manpower Services is responsible for the administration of the Health and Safety at Work (NI) Order 1978 which came into force 1 May 1979. Existing statutory provisions including the Factories Act (NI) 1965 and the Office and Shop Premises Act (NI) 1966 together with many new provisions for the health, safety and welfare of persons at work are enforced by the Department's Health and Safety Inspectorate. The 1978 Order extends to all persons at work with the exception of private domestic employment and applies to persons at work in over 40,000 employment situations. The 1978 Order lays duties on employers, employees, self-employed, manufacturers and suppliers of materials and persons having control of buildings. Employers and self-employed have duties in regard to persons not employed by them but who may be affected by their operations at work. Provisions relating to quarries are enforced by the Department of Commerce and agricultural provisions by the Department of Agriculture. Some existing statutory provisions under factories and shops legislation continue to be enforced by district councils with some additional duties.

COMMERCE. Northern Ireland has a substantial export trade with countries overseas, but as a large part of it is routed through Great Britain, separate details are not available. The main markets outside the UK are the Irish Republic, USA, Saudi Arabia, Algeria, Japan, Romania, the EEC and EFTA. From 1975 no detailed trade figures of Northern Ireland were compiled.

Imports and exports, including trade with Great Britain (in £1m. sterling), for calendar years:

	1967	1968	1969	1970	1971	1972	1973	1974
Imports	552	660	728	829	892	937	1,304	1,734
Exports	507	596	669	745	843	917	1,175	1,368

In 1974, 74% of the total imports (by value) came from Great Britain or from foreign countries *via* Great Britain; 12% from the Irish Republic. Of the exports, 82% (by value) went to Great Britain or to foreign countries *via* Great Britain; 13% to the Irish Republic.

Principal imports in 1974 (including imports from Great Britain) were valued at: Textiles, fibres, yarns and fabrics, £341m.; machinery, £214m.; transport equipment, £158m.; petroleum and petroleum products, £115m.; chemicals, £90m.; manufactures of metal, fruit and vegetables, fresh and processed, £43m.

Principal exports in 1974 (including exports to Great Britain) were valued at: Textiles, fibres, yarns and fabrics, £485m.; machinery, £134m.; meat and meat preparations, £77m.; transport equipment, £65m.; clothing, £62m.

Tourism. Tourism earns a substantial amount of revenue for Northern Ireland and total spending by some 728,000 visitors in 1979 was estimated at £57m. Altogether tourism provides over 8,000 permanent jobs and some 3,000 temporary or seasonal jobs. The Northern Ireland Tourist Board plays a major role in promoting the development of tourist traffic in Northern Ireland.

The protection of scenic beauty, scientific and nature interest, and wildlife is fostered under the Amenity Lands Act (NI) 1965 and the Wild Birds Protection Acts (NI) 1931 to 1968 by the Department of the Environment for Northern Ireland, which is advised by the Ulster Countryside Committee, the Nature Reserves Committee and the Wild Birds Advisory Committee. Eight Areas of Outstanding Natural Beauty and 46 Areas of Scientific Interest have been designated, and in these areas special attention is given respectively to the amenity and scientific aspects of planning applications. Country Parks have been established at Crawfordsburn and Scrabo, Co. Down, and the Roe Valley and Ness Wood, Co. Londonderry, Castle Archdale, Co. Fermanagh. Land for further parks has been acquired at Redburn, Co. Down and The Birches in N. Armagh. The Lagan Valley between Belfast and Lisburn is being administered as Northern Ireland's first Regional Park. Thirty-six National Nature Reserves have been declared, and steady progress is being made with the acquisition of further reserves. Nine areas have been designated as Bird Sanctuaries.

The Department is advised by the Historic Monuments Council on the exercise of its powers under the Historic Monuments Act (NI) 1971 in respect of the conservation of historic monuments and the preservation of objects of archaeological or historic interest. At present there are 148 monuments in State care, either in the Department's ownership or guardianship. The Department, advised by the Historic Buildings Council, is also responsible for listing buildings of special architectural or historic interest and for designating areas of similar interest the character or appearance of which it is desirable to preserve or enhance. To date some 4,600 buildings have been listed and 13 areas have been designated. Grants are payable by the Department to assist in the repair or maintenance of listed buildings.

COMMUNICATIONS

Road and Rail. All train services are operated by the Northern Ireland Railways Co. Ltd which is a subsidiary of the Northern Ireland Transport Holding Co. In Oct. 1979 there were 337 km (1,600 mm gauge) of railway open. Most bus services are operated by two other subsidiaries, Ulsterbus Ltd and Citybus Ltd. Ulsterbus runs services outside the Belfast area (except for a few services provided by privately owned bus undertakings) while all the services within the Belfast area are run by Citybus.

A public sector/private enterprise system under licence is in operation for the carriage of goods by road for reward. Approximately 1,853 operators and 4,032 vehicles have been licensed; the biggest single operator is Northern Ireland Carriers Ltd.

The number of motor vehicles licensed at 30 Sept. 1977 was 428,956, comprising private cars, 347,091; motor cycles, 17,006; hackney vehicles, 1,858; goods vehicles, 39,658; agricultural tractors, 14,030. In addition, there were 9,283 vehicles which were not subject to licence duty.

The Department of the Environment (NI) is responsible for the provision and maintenance of all public roads, bridges and street lighting in the Province, the provision and operation of car parks, and for the operation of the Strangford Lough Ferry. In addition to a Headquarters Unit the Roads Service of the Department operates through Divisional Offices in Ballymena, Belfast, Coleraine, Craigavon, Downpatrick and Omagh and smaller offices in other centres.

At 1 April 1979 the total mileage of roads was 14,549, graded for administrative purposes as follows: Motorway, 67 miles; all purpose trunk, 332 miles; Class I, 1,037 miles; Class II, 1,757 miles; Class III, 2,946 miles; unclassified, 8,410 miles.

Aviation. Northern Ireland Airports Ltd is responsible for the operation of Belfast Airport. A major development programme, which will double the size of the terminal building and improve other operational facilities, is now under construction. In 1979, 1·4m. passengers and 16,000 tonnes of freight and mail were handled.

Passenger services operate between Belfast and London, Birmingham, Blackpool, Bristol, Cardiff, East Midlands, Edinburgh, Exeter, Glasgow, Leeds/Bradford, Liverpool, Manchester, Newcastle upon Tyne, Southampton, Isle of Man, Prestwick, Luton, Kirkwall, Sumburgh, Stornaway and Scotsta.

Shipping. Passenger services operate between Belfast and Liverpool and between Larne and (i) Cairnryan and (ii) Stranraer. Conventional cargo services have given way in many cases to container, unit load and drive on/drive off services. The latter type of service now operates between Belfast, Larne and Warrenpoint to various ports in UK.

JUSTICE, RELIGION, EDUCATION AND WELFARE

Justice. The Lord Chancellor has responsibility for the administration of all courts in Northern Ireland through the Northern Ireland Court Service, and is responsible for the appointment of judges and resident magistrates.

The Court structure in Northern Ireland has 3 tiers—the Supreme Court of Judicature of Northern Ireland (comprising the Court of Appeal, the High Court and the Crown Court), the County Courts and the Magistrates' Courts. There are 25 Petty Sessions which when grouped together for administration purposes form 8 County Court Divisions and 4 Circuits.

The County Court has general civil jurisdiction subject to an upper monetary limit of £2,000. Appeals from the Magistrates' Courts lie to the County Court, while appeals from the County Court lie to the High Court. Circuit Registrars have jurisdiction to deal with most defended actions up to £500 and undefended actions up to £1,000. They also deal, by an informal arbitration procedure, with small claims whose value does not exceed £200. An appeal from the decision of a Registrar lies to the High Court.

Police. The police force consists of the Royal Ulster Constabulary, supported by the Royal Ulster Constabulary Reserve, a mainly part-time force.

Religion. The religious professions at the census of 1971 were: Roman Catholics, 477,919; Presbyterians, 405,719; Church of Ireland, 334,318 (including Church of England and Episcopal Church of Scotland); Methodists, 71,235; others and not stated, 230,449.

Education. Education in Northern Ireland is administered centrally by the Department of Education and locally by 5 education and library boards. The Department is concerned with the whole range of education from nursery education through to higher education and continuing education; for sport and recreation; for youth services; for the arts and culture (including libraries) and for community relations and community development. District councils are the main providers of sport, recreation and community facilities and the education and library boards have a responsibility where the facilities are intended primarily for education and youth service activities. The Department assists with grants as far as the district councils are concerned and meets the full cost in relation to education and library boards.

The 5 education and library boards which took over responsibility for the local administration of the education and library services on 1 Oct. 1973 are required to ensure that there are sufficient schools of all kinds to meet the needs of their area. They provide primary and secondary schools, special schools for handicapped pupils and institutions of further education. The boards also make contributions towards the cost of maintaining voluntary schools; award university and other scholarships; meet the tuition fees of the great majority of pupils attending grammar schools; provide milk and meals; free books and transport for pupils; enforce school attendance; regulate the employment of children and young people and secure the provision of recreational and youth service facilities. They are also required to develop a comprehensive and efficient library service for their areas. The following are the statistics for the 1978–79 academic year:

Universities. The Queen's University of Belfast (founded in 1849 as a college of the Queen's University of Ireland and reconstituted as a separate university in 1908) had 100 professors, 237 readers and senior lecturers, 468 lecturers and tutors and 5,816 full-time students.

The New University of Ulster at Coleraine, of which Magee University College, Londonderry, is now an integral part, had 28 professors, 38 readers and senior lecturers, 178 lecturers and demonstrators and 1,693 full-time students.

The Ulster Polytechnic is a central institution providing higher non-university education for the whole of Northern Ireland with a full-time academic staff of 537, 3,558 full-time and 2,936 part-time students on vocational and professional courses and 381 students on specialist teacher-training courses.

Secondary Education. 78 grammar schools with 57,582 pupils and 3,378 full-time teachers; 183 secondary (intermediate) schools with 106,155 pupils and 6,968 full-time teachers: the last technical intermediate school closed in June 1974.

Primary Education. 1,069 primary schools with 200,866 pupils and 8,446 teachers; 61 nursery schools with 3,260 pupils and 110 teachers.

Further Education. 27 institutions of further education with 1,685 full-time and 2,105 part-time teachers and an enrolment of 11,442 full-time, 12,273 part-time day and 17,322 evening students on vocational courses; and over 37,800 students on non-vocational (mostly evening) courses.

Special Educational Treatment. 31 special schools, including hospital schools, with 2,709 pupils and 321 teachers.

Teachers. There were 20,908 full-time teachers (8,471 men and 12,437 women) in grant-aided schools and institutions of further education. The minimum general teacher-training course is of 3 years' duration and there were 2,831 students (878 men and 1,953 women) in training; these included students following teacher-training courses at university establishments and at Ulster Polytechnic.

Expenditure. Expenditure by the Department of Education in 1978–79 was £335·2m.

Health and Personal Social Services. Under the provisions of the Health and Personal Social Services (NI) Order 1972, the Department of Health and Social Services is responsible for the provision of integrated health and personal social services in Northern Ireland, designed to promote the physical and mental health of the people of Northern Ireland through the prevention, diagnosis and treatment of illness, and also to promote their social welfare. Four Health and Social Services Boards, Eastern, Northern, Southern and Western, established under the above Order, administer health and personal social services, as the Department directs, within their designated areas.

Social Security. The social security schemes in Northern Ireland are similar to those in force in Great Britain.

The system of social security established by the Social Security Acts 1975 to 1980, and the corresponding system established by the Social Security (NI) Acts 1975 to 1980, operate, by virtue of a reciprocal arrangement between Great Britain and Northern Ireland, as a single system throughout the UK. The National Insurance Joint Authority, consisting of the Secretary of State for Social Services and the Head of the Department of Health and Social Services for Northern Ireland is responsible under this reciprocal arrangement for making any necessary financial adjustments between the National Insurance funds of the two countries and also has responsibility for determining the administrative procedures necessary for the purpose of giving effect to the provisions of the reciprocal arrangement. There are comprehensive reciprocal agreements with the Isle of Man, and agreements covering reciprocity in respect of most benefits have been made by the Government of the UK, applying to the schemes in both Great Britain and Northern Ireland, with Australia, Austria, Belgium, Canada, Cyprus, Denmark, Finland, France, Germany (Fed. Rep.), Gibraltar, Guernsey, Irish Republic, Israel, Italy, Jamaica, Jersey, Luxembourg, Malta, the Netherlands, New Zealand, Norway, Portugal, Spain, Sweden, Switzerland, Turkey and Yugoslavia. There are also limited agreements with Bermuda and the USA.

Since 1 April 1973 the reciprocal agreements between the UK and the other members of the EEC have been largely superseded by the Social Security Regulations of the Community.

National Insurance. During the year ended 31 March 1980, £27·5m. sickness benefit was paid to an average of 17,000 persons and £29·2m. unemployment benefit was paid to an average of 25,000 persons. Widows' benefits amounting to £20m. were paid to 16,000 persons and retirement pensions totalling £189·1m. were paid to an average of 182,000 persons. Invalidity pensions and allowances totalling £51·3m. were paid to approximately 30,000 persons. Accidents in respect of which claims to benefit are made occur at the rate of 280 per week and £1·3m. industrial injury benefit was paid in 1979–80 to an average of 870 persons. Industrial disablement benefit amounting to £6m. was paid to an average of 5,000 persons. Maternity benefit totalling £5·3m. was paid to approximately 25,000 persons. Receipts, including an item related to the financial adjustments mentioned above of the Northern Ireland Insurance Fund in the year ended 31 March 1979 were £309·7m. and payments were £305·4m.

Child Benefit. During the year ended 31 March 1980, £104·7m. was paid to an average of 208,800 families.

Supplementary Benefits. In 1979–80, £96·4m. was paid to an average of 121,000 persons.

Family Income Supplement. In 1979–80, £3·6m. was paid to an average of 8,000 persons.

Books of Reference

The annual and other publications of the various Departments and the Reports, etc., of Parliamentary Committees may be obtained from HM Stationery Office, Belfast.

Ulster Year Book, 1979. Belfast, HMSO, 1980
Census of Population Reports, Northern Ireland. Belfast, HMSO, 1971
Digest of Statistics. Belfast, HMSO (bi-annual)
Northern Ireland Development 1970–75. Belfast, HMSO, 1970
Social and Economic Trends. Belfast, HMSO (annual)
Who Makes What in Northern Ireland: A Trade Directory. Belfast, HMSO, 10th ed. 1979
Reports on the Census of Production of Northern Ireland. Belfast, HMSO, 1976
The Education, Initial Training and Probation of Teachers in Northern Ireland Schools and Institutions of Further Education (Lelievre Report). Belfast, HMSO, 1973
Re-organization of Secondary Education in Northern Ireland. Belfast, HMSO, 1976
Bell, G., *The Protestants of Ulster.* London, 1976
Bew, P., Gibbon, P. and Patterson, H., *The State in Northern Ireland, 1921–1972.* New York, 1980
Biggs-Davison, J., *The Hand is Red.* London, 1974
Budge, I., and O'Leary, C., *Belfast: Approach to Crisis.* London, 1973
Farrell, M., *Northern Ireland: The Orange State.* London, 1976
Flackes, W. D., *Northern Ireland: Political Directory 1968–79.* London, 1980
Heskin, K., *Northern Ireland: A Psychological Analysis.* Dublin, 1980
Hull, R. H., *The Irish Triangle.* Princeton Univ. Press, 1976
Lawrence, R. J., *The Government of Northern Ireland: Public Finance and Public Services.* OUP, 1965
Quekett, Sir A. S., *The Constitution of Northern Ireland.* 3 pts. Belfast, 1928–47
Rose, R., *Northern Ireland: A Time of Choice.* London, 1976
Winchester, S., *Northern Ireland in Crisis: Reporting the Ulster Troubles.* New York, 1975

ISLE OF MAN

AREA AND POPULATION. Area, 227 sq. miles (572 sq. km); resident population census April 1976, 60,496. The principal towns are Douglas (population, 19,897), Ramsey (5,372), Peel, (3,295), Castletown (2,788). Vital statistics, 1979: Births, 758; deaths, 972; marriages, 417. The number of Manx-speaking people was 284 in 1971 (165 in 1961 and 4,657 in 1901), all of whom were bilingual.

CONSTITUTION AND GOVERNMENT. The Isle of Man is administered in accordance with its own laws by the Court of Tynwald, consisting of the Governor, appointed by the Crown; the Legislative Council, composed of the Lord Bishop of Sodor and Man, the Attorney-General (who does not vote) and 8 members selected by the House of Keys, total 11 members, including the Governor; and the House of Keys, a representative assembly of 24 members chosen on adult suffrage with 12 months' residence for 5 years by the 6 'sheadings' or local subdivisions, and the 4 municipalities. The Island is not bound by Acts of the Imperial Parliament unless specially mentioned in them.

A special relationship exists between the Isle of Man and the European Economic Community providing for free trade and adoption by the Isle of Man of the EEC's external trade policies with third countries. The Island remains free to levy its own system of rates and taxes.

The elections to the House of Keys, Nov. 1976, resulted in the return of 20 Independents, 3 Labour and 1 Manx Nationalist. Number of voters, 44,324. By-elections held in Dec. 1978 and March 1980 did not change this distribution of seats.

An Executive Council to act with the Governor on all matters of government was set up under the Isle of Man Constitution Act, 1961. It consists at present of 5 members of the House of Keys and 2 of the Legislative Council.

Lieut.-Governor: Rear-Adm. Sir Nigel Cecil, KBE, CB (term of office began Sept. 1980).

Government Secretary: P. J. Hulme.

Government Treasurer: W. Dawson.

Flag: Red, with 3 steel-coloured legs armoured and spurred (knees and spurs, yellow) in the centre.

ECONOMY

Budget. Revenue is derived from customs duties, value added tax and from income tax. In 1980–81 the budget allowed for gross revenue and capital expenditure of £96,237,750. Income tax was 20p in the £. No death duties or surtaxes are levied. Company registration tax is levied at a flat rate of £200 on every company incorporated in the Isle of Man which trades and is controlled outside the island. A Land Speculation Tax has recently been introduced at the same rate as income tax.

The Island currently makes an annual contribution to the UK Government of $2 \cdot 5\%$ of net 'common purse' receipts (share of customs and excise duties and VAT received by Treasury) towards cost of defence and other common services provided by the UK Government. That contribution currently amounts to about £730,000.

Currency. Notes to the value of £20, £10, £5, £1 and 50p are issued by the Isle of Man Government. Annual minting of decimal coinage takes place, and in 1973, 1974, 1977 and 1979 legal tender gold coins in half sovereign, sovereign, £2 and £5 pieces were issued. Commemorative crowns have also been issued since 1970, and silver and platinum decimal sets have been minted more recently. In 1978 and 1979 £1 coins were minted for general circulation.

AGRICULTURE. The principal agricultural produce of the Island consists of oats, wheat, barley, potatoes, grasses, fatstock dairy products. The total area under crops in 1979 was 78,923 acres and of rough grazings, 40,446 acres. The total area under cereals was 12,030 acres, including 1,911 under oats, 1,259 under wheat and 8,434 under barley or bere. There were also 1,143 acres under turnips and swedes, 861 under potatoes, 7,279 under hay and 31,253 of permanent grass for both grazing and silage.

Livestock in 1979: 908 horses, 34,839 cattle, 99,495 sheep and 5,002 pigs.

TOURISM. In 1978–79 tourism contributed 11% of national income and about 6,000 were employed in the industry.

COMMUNICATIONS

Roads. There are 500 miles of good roads. The International TT Motor Cycle Races and cycle races take place annually. Omnibus services operate to all parts of the island.

Number of vehicles (31 March 1980): 26,332 cars, 3,861 goods vehicles and engineering plant, 1,052 agricultural vehicles, 2,758 motor cycles and scooters and 916 taxis and public service vehicles.

Railways. Several novel transport systems operate on the Island during the summer season, including 100-year-old horse-drawn trams, and the Manx Electric Railway, linking Douglas, Ramsey and Snaefell Mountain (2,036 ft). The Isle of Man Steam Railway also operates between Douglas and Port Erin.

Aviation. Ronaldsway Airport handles scheduled services operated by Air UK, Dan-Air and British Midland Airways to and from London, Manchester, Belfast, Dublin, Glasgow, Liverpool, Birmingham, Blackpool, Newcastle upon Tyne, etc. Air taxi services also operate.

Shipping. Car ferries of the Isle of Man Steam Packet Co. link the Island with Liverpool throughout the year and similar services operate to Fleetwood, Ardrossan, Dublin and Belfast during the summer season, while a passenger-only summer service operates to Llandudno.

Manx Line provides a roll-on roll-off service between Douglas and Heysham.

Broadcasting. The first constitutionally licensed commercial radio station in the British Isles, Manx Radio, is operated by Government on medium and VHF wavelengths from Douglas.

Newspapers. In 1980 there were 5 weekly newspapers.

JUSTICE AND EDUCATION

Police. The police force numbered 142 all ranks and 14 cadets in 1980.

Education. Education is compulsory between the ages of 5 and 15. In Jan. 1980 there were 37 primary schools. The enrolled pupils numbered 5,874. The net expenditure on education for 1978–79 amounted to £6·5m.; in addition, capital expenditure of £1·7m. was made for school buildings. There are 7 secondary schools, 5 provided by the Education Board (4,261 registered pupils), 1 direct grant school for girls (380 registered pupils), 1 independent public school for boys (460 registered pupils), 1 college of further education (285 full- and 3,184 part-time and evening pupils).

Books of Reference

Isle of Man Digest of Economic and Social Statistics, 1980. Isle of Man Government, 1980
A Report Comprising the Isle of Man Index, the Family Expenditure Survey and a Cost of Living Comparison with the United Kingdom. 2nd. ed. Isle of Man Government, 1980
Manx Tourism 77, Isle of Man Government, 1977
Kinvig, R. H., *History of the Isle of Man*. Oxford, 1945.—*The Isle of Man: A Social, Cultural and Political History*. Liverpool Univ. Press, 1975
Mais, S. P. B., *Isle of Man*. London, 1954
Solly, M., *Anatomy of a Tax Haven. The Isle of Man and Manx Income Tax*, 2 vols. Douglas, 1980
Stenning, E. H., *Portrait of the Isle of Man*. London, 1958

CHANNEL ISLANDS

AREA. The Channel Islands are situated off the north-west coast of France and are the only portions of the 'Duchy of Normandy' now belonging to the Crown of England, to which they have been attached since the Conquest. They consist of Jersey (28,717 acres), Guernsey (15,654 acres) and the following dependencies of Guernsey—Alderney (1,962), Brechou (74), Great Sark (1,035), Little Sark (239), Herm (320), Jethou (44) and Lihou (38), a total of 48,083 acres, or 75 sq. miles (194 sq. km).

The climate is mild. Total rainfall (1979), Jersey, 998·2 mm; Guernsey, 885·4 mm. Temperature registered (1979): highest, Jersey, 24·5° C.; Guernsey, 23° C.; lowest, Jersey, −4·3° C.; Guernsey, −3·4° C.

CONSTITUTION. The Lieut.-Governors and Cs.-in-C. of Jersey and Guernsey are the personal representatives of the Sovereign, the Commanders of the Armed Forces of the Crown and the channel-communication between H.M. Government in the UK and the insular governments. They are appointed by the Crown and have a voice but no vote in the Assemblies of the States (the insular legislatures). The Secretaries to the Lieut.-Governors are their staff officers.

The Bailiffs are appointed by the Crown and are Presidents both of the Assembly of the States and of the Royal Courts of Jersey and Guernsey. They have in the States a casting vote.

LANGUAGE. The official languages are French and English, but English is gradually supplanting French. The language commonly used is English, but in the country districts of Jersey and Guernsey and throughout Sark some people also speak a Norman-French dialect; that of Alderney has died out.

TRADE. From 1958 the trade of the Channel Islands with the UK has been regarded as internal trade.

COMMUNICATIONS

Road. Omnibus services operate in all parts of Jersey and Guernsey.

Aviation. Scheduled air services are maintained by Air UK, Jersey European, British Midland, Aurigny Air Services, Caledonian and other companies between the islands and airports in the UK, Irish Republic, the Netherlands and France. During the summer months these services are greatly increased, both in the number of airports served and in the frequency of flights.

Shipping. Passenger and cargo steam services between Jersey, Guernsey and England are maintained by British Rail; between Guernsey, Jersey and England and St Malo by the Commodore Shipping Co.; between Guernsey, Jersey, Alderney and France by Condor Ltd (hydrofoil), and between Guernsey and Alderney and England and Guernsey and Sark by local companies.

Post and Broadcasting. Postal and overseas telephone and telegraph services are maintained by the respective Postal Administrations of each bailiwick. The local telephone services are maintained by the insular authorities. There were, in 1979, 30,183 subscribers in Jersey and 21,827 in Guernsey.

There is an independent television station in Jersey.

JUSTICE AND RELIGION

Justice. Justice is administered by the Royal Courts of Jersey and Guernsey, each of which consists of the Bailiff and 12 Jurats, the latter being elected by an electoral college. There is an appeal from the Royal Courts to the Courts of Appeal of Jersey and of Guernsey. A final appeal lies to the Privy Council in certain cases. A stipendiary magistrate in each, Jersey and Guernsey, deals with minor civil and criminal cases.

Church. Jersey and Guernsey each constitutes a deanery within the diocese of Winchester. The rectories (12 in Jersey; 10 in Guernsey) are in the gift of the Crown. The Roman Catholic and various Nonconformist Churches are represented.

Books of Reference

Ambrière, F., *Les Iles Anglo-Normandes*. Paris, 1971
Coysh, V., *The Channel Islands: A New Study*. Newton Abbot, 1977
Cruickshank, C., *The German Occupation of the Channel Islands*. London, 1975
Lempière, R., *Portrait of the Channel Islands*. London, 1970.—*History of the Channel Islands*. London, 1974
Lockley, R. M., *The Channel Islands*. London, 1968
Myhill, H., *Introducing the Channel Islands*. London, 1964
Uttley, J., *The Story of the Channel Islands*. London, 1966

JERSEY

POPULATION (census, 1977), 74,382. In the year ended 31 Dec. 1979 there were 914 births and 984 deaths. The town is St Helier on the south coast.

CONSTITUTION. The States consist of 12 senators (elected for 6 years, 6 retiring every third year), 12 Constables (triennial) and 28 Deputies (triennial), all elected on universal suffrage by the people.

The island legislature is 'The States of Jersey'. The States comprises the Bailiff, the Lieut.-Governor, 12 Senators, the Constables of the 12 parishes of the island, 28 Deputies, the Dean of Jersey, the Attorney-General and the Solicitor-General. They all have the right to speak in the Assembly, but only the 52 elected members (the

Senators, Constables and Deputies) have the right to vote; the Bailiff has a casting vote. General elections for Senators and Deputies are held every third year. Except in specific instances, enactments passed by the States require the sanction of The Queen-in-Council. The Lieut.-Governor has the power of veto on certain forms of legislation.

Flag: White with a red saltire.

Lieut.-Governor and C.-in-C. of Jersey: Gen. Sir Peter Whiteley, GCB, OBE.
Secretary and ADC to the Lieut.-Governor: Lieut.-Cdr O. M. B. de Las Casas, MVO, OBE, RN (Retd).

Bailiff of Jersey and President of the States: Sir Frank Ereaut.
Deputy Bailiff: P. L. Crill, CBE.

ECONOMY

Budget (year ending 31 Dec. 1979). Revenue, £84,698,669; expenditure, £67,919,841; public debt, £1,343,689. The standard rate of income tax is 20p in the pound. No super-tax or death duties are levied. Parochial rates of moderate amount are payable by owners and occupiers.

Currency. The States issue bank-notes in denominations of £10, £5 and £1.

INDUSTRY AND TRADE

Industry. Principal activities: Tourism; total number of hotel and guesthouse beds (1979), 25,108; expenditure of tourists (1979), £115m. Agriculture, total output (1979), £22m. Light industry, mainly electrical goods, textiles and clothing. Total exports (1979), £27m. Banking and finance, total bank deposits (1979), £7,700m., including parent companies.

Commerce (1979). Principal imports: Machinery and transport equipment, £61·8m.; manufactured goods, £37·8m.; food, £38·9m.; mineral fuels, £20·8m.; chemicals, £14·4m. Principal exports (1979): Food, £21·3m.; machinery and transport equipment, £30·3m.; manufactured goods, £12·2m., and miscellaneous, £20·2m.

COMMUNICATIONS

Aviation. The Jersey airport is situated at St Peter. It covers approximately 375 acres. Number of aircraft movements (1979) 25,813; number of passenger arrivals, 740,927.

Shipping (1979). All vessels arriving in Jersey from outside Jersey waters report at St Helier or Gorey on first arrival. There is a harbour of minor importance at St Aubin. Number of commercial vessels entering St Helier, 4,896; number of registered craft (of 15 ft and over), 1,437. Passengers arrived in 1979, 687,070.

EDUCATION (1979). There are 7 secondary schools and 27 primary schools (including fee-paying preparatory departments); 4,675 pupils attend the primary schools, 4,460 the secondary schools. Highlands College offers full- and part-time courses to Ordinary and National Certificate and Diploma levels or similar standards and, together with Les Quennevais Adult Community Centre, evening classes in technical and recreational subjects.

Books of Reference

Balleine, G. R., *Biographical Dictionary of Jersey.* London, 1948.—*A History of the Island of Jersey.* London, 1950.—*The Bailiwick of Jersey.* 3rd ed. London, 1970
Bois, F. de L., *The Constitutional History of Jersey.* Jersey, 1970
Carre, A. L., *English–Jersey Language Vocabulary.* Jersey, 1972
Le Maistre, F., *Dictionnaire Jersiais-Français.* Jersey, 1966
Powell, G. C., *Economic Survey of Jersey.* Jersey, 1971

States of Jersey Library: Royal Square, St Helier. *Librarian:* J. K. Antill, FLA.

GUERNSEY

POPULATION. Census population, 1976, was 54,256. Births during 1979 were 646; deaths, 638. The town is St Peter Port.

CONSTITUTION. The government of the island is conducted by committees appointed by the States.

The States of Deliberation, the Parliament of Guernsey, is composed of the following members: The Bailiff, who is President *ex officio*; 12 Conseillers; H.M. Procureur and H.M. Comptroller (Law Officers of the Crown), who have a voice but no vote; 33 People's Deputies elected by popular franchise; 10 Douzaine Representatives elected by their Parochial Douzaines; 2 representatives of the States of Alderney.

The States of Election, an electoral college, elects the Jurats and Conseillers. It is composed of the following members: The Bailiff (President *ex officio*); the 12 Jurats or 'Jurés-Justiciers'; the 12 Conseillers; H.M. Procureur and H.M. Comptroller; the 33 People's Deputies; 34 Douzaine Representatives; and (for the election of Conseillers) 4 representatives of the States of Alderney.

Since Jan. 1949 all legislative powers and functions (with minor exceptions) formerly exercised by the Royal Court have been vested in the States of Deliberation. Projets de Loi (Bills) require the sanction of The Queen-in-Council.

Flag: White with a red cross.

Lieut.-Governor and C.-in-C. of Guernsey and its Dependencies: Air Chief Marshal Sir Peter Le Cheminant, GBE, KCB, DFC.

ADC to the Lieut.-Governor: Capt. D. P. L. Hodgetts. *Secretary to the Lieut.-Governor:* R. J. Williams.

Bailiff of Guernsey and President of the States: Sir John Loveridge, CBE.
Deputy Bailiff of Guernsey: C. K. Frossard.

FINANCE (year ending 31 Dec. 1979). Revenue, £37,097,370 (including £1,293,522 for Alderney); expenditure, £30,966,511. (including £1,015,302 for Alderney), States' funded debt less sinking fund provisions, £1,415,673; note and coin issue, £20,140,854. The standard rate of income tax is 20p in the pound. States and parochial rates are very moderate. No super-tax or death duties are levied.

COMMERCE (1979). Principal imports: Coal, 18,969 tonnes; petrol and oils, 220,317,627 litres. Principal exports: Tomatoes (1979), £22·73m.; flowers and fern, £11,419,909; sweet peppers, £102,019.

COMMUNICATIONS

Aviation. The airport in Guernsey, situated at La Villiaze, has a landing area of approximately 124 acres and a tarmac runway of 4,800 ft. In 1979, 216,712 passengers arrived from places outside the Channel Islands.

Shipping. The principal harbour is that of St Peter Port, and there is a harbour at St Sampson's (used mainly for commercial shipping). In 1979 the number of ship tonnes gross entering and leaving Guernsey was 10,026,766. 132,193 passengers arrived from places outside the Channel Islands. Ships registered in Guernsey at 31 Dec. 1979 numbered 538 and 534 fishing vessels. Small craft registered, 3,920. In 1979, 9,916 yachts visited Guernsey.

EDUCATION. There are 2 public schools in the island: Elizabeth College, founded by Queen Elizabeth in 1563, for boys, and the Ladies' College, for girls. The States grammar schools provide for education up to University entrance requirements, and there are numerous modern secondary and primary schools and a College of Further Education. The total number of school children is 9,400. Facilities are available for the study of art, domestic science and many other subjects of a technical nature. There is also a convent school with boarding facilities for girls.

ALDERNEY. Population (census, 1971), 1,686 (1978 estimate, 2,000). The island has an airport. The constitution of the island (reformed 1949) provides for its own popularly elected President and States (12 members), and its own Court. The town is St Anne's.

Flag: White with a red cross with the island badge in the centre.

President of the States: J. Kay-Mouat.
Clerk of the States: W. R. Jones, MA.
Clerk of the Court: K. K. Lacey, DSC.

SARK. Population (census, 1971), 584 (1978 estimate, 600). The Constitution is a mixture of feudal and popular government with its Chief Pleas (parliament), consisting of 40 tenants and 12 popularly elected deputies, presided over by the Seneschal. The head of the island is the Seigneur. Sark has no income tax. Motor vehicles, except tractors, are not allowed.

Flag: White with a red cross and a red first quarter bearing two gold lions.

The Seigneur: J. M. Beaumont.
Greffier: H. Carre, MBE.

Books of Reference

Carteret, A. R. de, *The Story of Sark*. London, 1956
Clark, L., *Sark Discovered*. London, 1956
Coysh, V., *Alderney*. Newton Abbot, 1974
Durand, R., *Guernsey, Present and Past*. Guernsey, 1933.—*Guernsey under German Rule*. London, 1946
A Short History of and Guide to Alderney. New ed. Guernsey, 1968
Hathaway, Sybil, *Dame of Sark: An Autobiography*. London, 1961
Le Huray, C. P., *The Bailiwick of Guernsey*. London, 1952
Robinson, G. W. S., *Guernsey*. Newton Abbot, 1977
Wood, A. and M. S., *Islands in Danger*. 2nd ed. London, 1957
Wood, J., *Herm, Our Island Home*. London, 1973

UNITED STATES OF AMERICA

Capital: Washington, D.C.
Population: 226·5m. (1980)
GNP per capita: US$9,700 (1978)

HISTORY. The Declaration of Independence of the 13 states of which the American Union then consisted was adopted by Congress on 4 July 1776. On 30 Nov. 1782 Great Britain acknowledged the independence of the USA, and on 3 Sept. 1783 the treaty of peace was concluded and was ratified by the USA on 14 Jan. 1784.

AREA AND POPULATION. Population of conterminous USA at each census from 1790 to 1950, and for USA including Alaska and Hawaii, 1960 and 1970. Residents of Puerto Rico, the Philippine Islands, Guam, American Samoa, Virgin Islands of the USA and Panama Canal Zone, and persons in the military and naval service stationed abroad are not included in the figures of this table. Residents of Hawaii and Alaska are excluded prior to 1960. Residents of Indian reservations are excluded prior to 1890.

	White	Negroes[1]	Other races[2]	Total	Decennial increase %
1790	3,172,464[3]	757,208	—	3,929,672	—
1800	4,306,446	1,002,037	—	5,308,483	35·1
1810	5,862,073	1,377,808	—	7,239,881	36·4
1820	7,866,797	1,771,562	—	9,638,359	33·1
1830	10,537,378	2,328,642	—	12,866,020	33·5
1840	14,195,805	2,873,648	—	17,069,453	32·7
1850	19,553,068	3,638,808	—	23,191,876	35·9
1860	26,922,537	4,441,830	78,954[4]	31,443,321	35·6
1870[5]	33,589,377	4,880,009	88,985	38,558,371	22·6
1870[5]	*34,337,292*	*5,392,172*	*88,985*	*39,818,449*	*26·6*
1880	43,402,970	6,580,793	172,020	50,155,783	30·1
1890	55,101,258	7,488,676	357,780	62,947,714	25·5
1900	66,809,196	8,833,994	351,385	75,994,575	21·0
1910	81,731,957	9,827,763	412,546	91,972,266	21·0
1920	94,820,915	10,463,131	426,574	105,710,620	14·9[6]
1930	110,286,740[7]	11,891,143	597,163	122,775,046	16·1[6]
1940	118,214,870	12,865,518	588,887	131,669,275	7·3
1950	134,942,028	15,042,286	713,047	150,697,361	14·5
1960[8]	158,831,732	18,871,831	1,619,612	179,323,175	18·5
1970	177,748,975	22,580,289	2,882,662	203,211,926	13·3
1980	—	—	—	226,504,825	11·4

[1] Seventeen southern states (including D.C.) in 1900 had 7,922,969 Negroes (89·7% of the total Negro population); in 1920, 8,912,231 (85·2%); in 1940, 9,904,619 (77%); in 1950, 10,225,407 (68%); in 1960, 11,311,607 (59·9%); in 1970, 11,969,961 (53%).

[2] 1870: 63,199 Chinese, 55 Japanese and 25,731 Indians; 1880, 105,465 Chinese, 148 Japanese and 66,407 Indians; 1890, 107,488 Chinese, 2,039 Japanese and 248,253 Indians; 1900, 89,863 Chinese, 24,326 Japanese and 237,196 Indians; 1910, 71,531 Chinese, 72,157 Japanese, 265,683 Indians and 3,175 other races; 1920, 61,639 Chinese, 111,010 Japanese, 244,437 Indians and 9,488 other races; 1930, 332,397 Indians, 74,954 Chinese, 138,834 Japanese and 50,978 other races; 1940, 333,969 Indians, 77,504 Chinese, 126,947 Japanese and 50,467 other races; 1950, 343,410 Indians, 141,768 Japanese, 117,629 Chinese, 110,240 other races; 1960, 523,591 Indians, 464,332 Japanese, 237,292 Chinese, 176,310 Filipino, 218,087 other races; 1970, 792,730 Indians, 591,290 Japanese, 435,062 Chinese, 343,060 Filipino, 720,520 other races.

[3] Made up of Anglo-Scottish, 89·1%; German, 5·6%; Dutch, 2·5%; Irish, 1·9%; French, 0·6%.

[4] 34,933 Chinese and 44,021 Indians.

[5] Enumeration in 1870 incomplete. Figures in italics represent estimated corrected population.

[*Footnotes continued on p. 1374.*]

Total population in 1970 at 203,211,926 comprised 98,912,192 males and 104,299,734 females; 149,324,930 were urban and 53,886,996 were rural. Negroes, 10,748,316 males and 11,831,973 females.

Estimated population, including Alaska and Hawaii, and armed forces overseas, on 1 July 1950, 152,271,000; 1955, 165,931,000; 1960, 180,671,000; 1965, 194,303,000; 1968, 200,706,000; 1969, 202,677,000; 1970, 204,878,000; 1971, 207,053,000; 1972, 208,846,000; 1973, 210,410,000; 1974, 211,901,000; 1975, 213,559,000; 1976, 215,142,000; 1977, 216,817,000; 1978, 218,059,000.

The age distribution by sex of the total population of the US (excluding armed forces overseas, US population abroad and outlying areas) at the 1970 census was as follows:

Age-group	Male	Female	Total
Under 5	8,745,499	8,408,838	17,154,337
5–9	10,168,496	9,787,751	19,956,247
10–14	10,590,737	10,198,731	20,789,468
15–19	9,633,847	9,436,501	19,070,348
20–24	7,917,269	8,453,752	16,371,021
25–34	12,217,357	12,690,072	24,907,429
35–44	11,221,236	11,856,569	23,087,805
45–54	11,199,250	12,020,701	23,219,951
55–59	4,765,821	5,207,207	9,973,028
60–64	4,026,972	4,589,812	8,616,784
65–74	5,437,084	6,998,372	12,425,456
75 and over	2,978,624	4,651,422	7,630,046
Total	98,912,192	104,299,734	203,211,926

The following table includes population statistics, the year in which each of the original 13 states ratified the constitution, and the year when each of the other states was admitted into the Union. Postal abbreviations for the names of the states are shown in brackets. Land area includes land temporarily or partially covered by water, and lakes, etc., of less than 40 acres. (For census population by states and regions in 1940 and 1950 see THE STATESMAN'S YEAR-BOOK, 1952, pp. 552 and 553.)

Geographic divisions and states		Land area: sq. miles, 1970	Census population 1 April 1970	Census population 1 April 1980	Pop. per sq. mile, 1970
United States		3,536,855	203,235,298	226,504,825	57·5
New England		62,951	11,847,186	...	188·1
Maine (1820)	(*Me.*)	30,920	993,663	1,124,660	32·1
New Hampshire (1788)	(*N.H.*)	9,027	737,681	920,610	81·7
Vermont (1791)	(*Vt.*)	9,267	444,732	511,456	47·9
Massachusetts (1788)	(*Mass.*)	7,826	5,689,170	5,737,037	727·0
Rhode Island (1790)	(*R.I.*)	1,049	949,723	947,154	902·5
Connecticut (1788)	(*Conn.*)	4,862	3,032,217	3,107,576	623·6
Middle Atlantic		100,318	37,283,339	...	370·8
New York (1788)	(*N.Y.*)	47,831	18,241,266	17,557,288	380·3
New Jersey (1787)	(*N.J.*)	7,521	7,168,164	7,364,158	953·1
Pennsylvania (1787)	(*Pa.*)	44,966	11,793,909	11,866,728	262·3

[6] Between the 1910 census (15 April 1910) and the 1920 census (1 Jan. 1920), the period covered was 116 months (less than a full decade). Adjusting for this, the exact rate of increase for the decade was 15·4%. Similarly correcting for the 123 months between the 1920 and 1930 censuses, the true rate of increase was 15·7%.

[7] Figures for 1930 have been revised to include Mexicans (1,422,533), who were classified with 'Other Races' in the 1930 census reports.

[8] Figures for 1960 strictly comparable with those given for other years (*i.e.*, excluding Alaska and Hawaii) are: White, 158,454,956; Negroes, 18,860,117; other races, 1,149,163; total, 178,464,236; decennial increase, 18·4%.

Geographic divisions and states		Land area: sq. miles 1970	Census population 1 April 1970	Census population 1 April 1980	Pop. per sq. mile 1970
East North Central		244,101	40,252,678	...	164·9
Ohio (1803)	(*Oh.*)	40,975	10,652,017	10,797,419	260·0
Indiana (1816)	(*Ind.*)	36,097	5,193,669	5,490,179	143·9
Illinois (1818)	(*Ill.*)	55,748	11,113,976	11,418,461	199·4
Michigan (1837)	(*Mich.*)	56,817	8,875,083	9,258,344	156·2
Wisconsin (1848)	(*Wis.*)	54,464	4,417,933	4,705,335	81·1
West North Central		507,723	16,344,389	...	32·1
Minnesota (1858)	(*Minn.*)	79,289	3,805,069	4,077,148	48·0
Iowa (1846)	(*Ia.*)	55,941	2,825,041	2,913,387	50·5
Missouri (1821)	(*Mo.*)	68,995	4,677,399	4,917,444	67·8
North Dakota (1889)	(*N.D.*)	69,273	617,761	652,695	8·9
South Dakota (1889)	(*S.D.*)	75,955	666,257	690,178	8·8
Nebraska (1867)	(*Nebr.*)	76,483	1,483,791	1,570,006	19·4
Kansas (1861)	(*Kans.*)	81,787	2,249,071	2,363,208	27·5
South Atlantic		266,970	30,671,337	...	114·9
Delaware (1787)	(*Del.*)	1,982	548,104	595,225	276·5
Maryland (1788)	(*Md.*)	9,891	3,922,399	4,216,446	396·6
Dist. of Columbia (1791)	(*D.C.*)	61	756,510	637,651	12,401·8
Virginia (1788)	(*Va.*)	39,780	4,648,494	5,346,279	116·9
West Virginia (1863)	(*W. Va.*)	24,070	1,744,237	1,949,644	72·5
North Carolina (1789)	(*N.C.*)	48,798	5,082,059	5,874,429	104·1
South Carolina (1788)	(*S.C.*)	30,225	2,590,516	3,119,208	85·7
Georgia (1788)	(*Ga.*)	58,073	4,589,575	5,464,265	79·0
Florida (1845)	(*Fla.*)	54,090	6,789,443	9,739,992	125·5
East South Central		178,982	12,804,552	...	71·5
Kentucky (1792)	(*Ky.*)	39,650	3,219,311	3,661,433	81·2
Tennessee (1796)	(*Tenn.*)	41,328	3,924,164	4,590,750	94·9
Alabama (1819)	(*Al.*)	50,708	3,444,165	3,890,061	67·9
Mississippi (1817)	(*Miss.*)	47,296	2,216,912	2,520,638	46·9
West South Central		427,791	19,322,458	...	45·2
Arkansas (1836)	(*Ark.*)	51,945	1,923,295	2,285,513	37·0
Louisiana (1812)	(*La.*)	44,930	3,643,180	4,203,972	81·0
Oklahoma (1907)	(*Okla.*)	68,782	2,559,253	3,025,266	37·2
Texas (1845)	(*Tex.*)	262,134	11,196,730	14,228,383	42·7
Mountain		856,047	8,283,585	...	9·7
Montana (1889)	(*Mont.*)	145,587	694,409	786,690	4·8
Idaho (1890)	(*Id.*)	82,677	713,008	943,935	8·6
Wyoming (1890)	(*Wyo.*)	97,203	332,416	470,816	3·4
Colorado (1876)	(*Colo.*)	103,766	2,207,259	2,888,834	21·3
New Mexico (1912)	(*N. Mex.*)	121,412	1,016,000	1,299,968	8·4
Arizona (1912)	(*Ariz.*)	113,417	1,772,482	2,717,866	15·6
Utah (1896)	(*Ut.*)	82,096	1,059,273	1,461,037	12·9
Nevada (1864)	(*Nev.*)	109,889	488,738	799,184	4·4
Pacific		891,972	26,525,774	...	29·7
Washington (1889)	(*Wash.*)	66,570	3,409,169	4,130,163	51·2
Oregon (1859)	(*Oreg.*)	96,184	2,091,385	2,632,663	21·7
California (1850)	(*Calif.*)	156,361	19,953,134	23,668,562	127·6
Alaska (1959)	(*Ak.*)	566,432	302,173	400,481	0·5
Hawaii (1960)	(*Hi.*)	6,425	769,913	965,000	119·8

Geographic divisions and states	Land area sq. miles, 1970	Census population 1 April 1960	Census population 1 April 1970	Pop.per sq. mile, 1970
Outlying Territories, total	4,610	3,917,812	4,720,306	...
Puerto Rico (1898)	3,435	8,349,544	8,712,033	789
Virgin Islands (1917)	132	32,099	62,438	473
American Samoa (1900)	76	20,051	27,159	357
Guam (1898)	209	67,044	84,996	407
Northern Marianas (1947)	184		9,640	52
Palau Islands (1947)	192	70,724	11,210	57
Micronesia, Fed. States of (1947)	271		47,202	174
Marshall Islands (1947)	70	—	22,888	327
Midway Islands (1867)	2	2,356	2,220	1,110
Wake Island (1898)	3	1,097	1,647	549
Johnston and Sand Islands (1858)	—	156	1,007	2,000
Other Islands	9	—	—	—
Canton and Enderbury Islands	27	320	—	—
US population abroad	—	1,374,421	1,737,836	—

The 1970 census showed 8,733,770 foreign-born Whites. The 8 countries contributing the largest numbers who were foreign-born were Italy, 1,005,687; Germany, 830,498; Canada, 798,782; Mexico, 746,327; UK, 681,140; Poland, 547,010; USSR, 461,444; Irish Republic, 250,492.

Increase or decrease of native White, and foreign-born White, population from 1860 to 1970, by decades:

	Native White			Foreign-born White		
	Total	Increase	Per cent. increase	Total	Increase or decrease (−)	Per cent. change
1860	22,825,784	5,513,251	31·8	4,096,753	1,856,218	82·8
1870	28,095,665	5,269,881	23·1	5,493,712	1,396,959	34·1
1880	36,843,291	8,747,626	31·1	6,559,679	1,065,967	19·4
1890	45,979,391	9,018,732[1]	24·5	9,121,867	2,562,188	39·1
1900	56,595,379	10,615,988	23·1	10,213,817	1,091,950	12·0
1910	68,386,412	11,791,033	20·8	13,345,545	3,131,728	30·7
1920	81,108,161	12,721,749	18·6	13,712,754	367,209	2·8
1930	96,303,335	15,195,174	18·7	13,983,405	270,651	2·0
1940	106,795,732	10,492,397	10·9	11,419,138	−2,564,267	−18·3
1950	124,780,860	17,985,128	16·8	10,161,168	−1,257,970	−11·0
1960	149,543,638	24,762,778	19·8	9,293,992	− 867,176	− 8·5
1970	169,385,451	19,841,813	13·3	8,773,770	− 560,222	6·0

[1] Exclusive of population specially enumerated in 1890 in Indian Territory and on Indian reservations.

Principal cities in 1910, 1960 and 1970:

	No. of cities[1]			Combined population[1]		
Cities with	1910	1960	1970	1910	1960	1970
250,000 or more	19	51	56	15,461,680	39,360,931	42,177,800
100,000–250,000	31	81	100	4,840,458	11,652,426	14,286,033
50,000–100,000	60	201	240	4,213,098	13,835,902	16,723,878
25,000–50,000	119	432	520	4,023,397	14,950,612	17,848,297
25,000 or more	229	765	916	28,504,450	79,799,871	91,036,008

[1] Exclusive of Honolulu (Hawaii) in 1910 and 1950 and San Juan (Puerto Rico) in 1910, 1950 and 1970.

The population of leading cities (with over 100,000 inhabitants) at the censuses of 1970 and 1980 were as follows:

Cities	1 April 1970	1 April 1980	Cities	1 April 1970	1 April 1980
New York, N.Y.	7,895,563	7,015,608	Detroit, Mich.	1,514,063	1,192,222
Chicago, Ill.	3,369,357	2,969,570	Dallas,Tex.	844,401	901,450
Los Angeles, Calif.	2,811,801	2,950,010	San Diego, Calif.	697,471	870,006
Philadelphia, Pa.	1,949,996	1,680,235	Baltimore, Md.	905,787	783,320
Houston, Tex.	1,233,473	1,544,992	San Antonio, Tex.	645,153	783,296

Cities	1 April 1970	1 April 1980	Cities	1 April 1970	1 April 1980
Phoenix, Ariz.	584,303	781,443	Des Moines, Iowa	201,404	190,910
Indianapolis, Ind.	746,992	695,040	Knoxville, Tenn.	174,587	182,161
Honolulu, Hawaii	630,528	681,004	Grand Rapids, Mich.	197,649	181,602
San Francisco, Calif.	715,674	674,063	Montgomery, Ala.	133,386	176,781
Memphis, Tenn.	623,988	644,838	Lubbock, Tex.	149,101	174,157
Washington, D.C.	756,668	635,185	Anchorage, Alaska.	126,385	173,992
Milwaukee, Wisc.	717,372	632,989	Lincoln, Nebr.	149,518	171,787
San José, Calif.	459,913	625,763	Fort Wayne, Ind.	178,269	171,036
Cleveland, Ohio	750,879	572,532	Spokane, Wash.	170,516	170,993
Boston, Mass.	641,071	562,118	Madison, Wisc.	171,809	170,669
Columbus, Ohio	540,025	561,943	Huntington Beach,		
New Orleans, La.	593,471	556,913	Calif.	115,960	170,597
Jacksonville, Fla.	504,265	541,269	Syracuse, N.Y.	197,297	170,292
Seattle, Wash.	530,831	491,897	Riverside, Calif.	140,089	169,677
Denver, Colo.	514,678	488,765	Columbus, Ga.	155,028	168,598
St Louis, Mo.	622,236	448,640	Chattanooga, Tenn.	119,923	165,328
Kansas City, Mo.	507,330	446,562	Las Vegas, Nev.	125,787	164,275
Nashville-Davidson,			Salt Lake City, Utah	175,885	162,960
Tenn.	426,029	439,599	Worcester, Mass.	176,572	161,384
El Paso, Tex.	322,261	424,522	Warren, Mich.	179,260	161,173
Pittsburgh, Pa.	520,089	423,962	Kansas City, Kans.	168,213	159,972
Atlanta, Ga.	495,039	422,293	Flint, Mich.	193,317	159,576
Oklahoma City, Okla.	368,164	401,002	Arlington, Tex.	90,229	159,117
Cincinnati, Ohio	453,514	383,058	Aurora, Colo.	74,974	158,143
Fort Worth, Tex.	393,455	382,349	Tacoma, Wash.	154,407	158,101
Minneapolis, Minn.	434,400	370,091	Providence, R. I.	179,116	156,421
Portland, Oregon	379,967	364,246	Greensboro, N.C.	144,076	154,763
Buffalo, N.Y.	462,768	357,002	Fort Lauderdale, Fla.	139,590	154,028
Long Beach, Calif.	358,879	356,906	Little Rock, Ark.	132,483	153,467
Tulsa, Okla.	330,350	355,500	Springfield, Mass.	163,905	152,212
Toledo, Ohio	383,062	354,265	Gary, Ind.	175,415	151,557
Austin, Tex.	251,808	343,390	Mesa, Ariz.	62,852	149,328
Oakland, Calif.	361,561	338,721	Amarillo, Tex.	127,010	149,167
Miami, Fla.	334,859	335,360	Raleigh, N.C.	122,830	148,299
Tucson, Ariz.	262,933	331,506	Stockton, Calif.	109,963	145,841
Newark, N.J.	381,930	329,498	Newport News, Va.	138,177	144,795
Albuquerque, N. Mex.	244,501	328,829	Hialeah, Fla.	102,452	143,596
Omaha, Nebr.	346,929	312,929	Bridgeport, Conn.	156,542	142,459
Charlotte, N.C.	241,420	310,799	Huntsville, Ala.	139,282	142,238
Louisville, Ky.	361,706	298,161	Rockford, Ill.	147,370	139,206
Birmingham, Ala.	300,910	282,068	Garland, Tex.	81,437	138,749
Wichita, Kans.	276,554	279,352	Paterson, N.J.	144,824	138,025
Sacramento, Calif.	257,105	274,488	Glendale, Calif.	132,664	137,229
Tampa, Fla.	277,714	268,709	Hartford, Conn.	158,017	136,319
St Paul, Minn.	309,866	268,248	Savannah, Ga.	118,349	133,672
Norfolk, Va.	307,951	262,803	Springfield, Mo.	120,096	132,014
Virginia Beach, Va.	172,106	260,680	Fremont, Calif.	100,869	131,486
Rochester, N.Y.	295,011	241,509	Winston-Salem, N.C.	133,683	131,211
Akron, Ohio	275,425	236,820	Lansing, Mich.	131,403	130,208
St Petersburg, Fla.	216,159	233,532	Evansville, Ind.	138,764	129,665
Corpus Christi, Tex.	204,525	230,715	Torrance, Calif.	134,968	129,511
Jersey City, N.J.	260,350	222,764	Orlando, Fla.	99,006	127,811
Richmond, Va.	249,332	219,429	New Haven, Conn.	137,707	125,787
Baton Rouge, La.	165,921	219,164	Garden Grove, Calif.	121,155	125,085
Fresno, Calif.	165,655	216,365	Peoria, Ill.	126,963	123,571
Anaheim, Calif.	166,408	214,688	Hampton, Va.	120,779	122,383
Colorado Springs,			Erie, Pa.	129,265	118,964
Colo.	135,517	206,939	San Bernardino, Calif.	106,869	118,092
Santa Ana, Calif.	155,710	204,089	Beaumont, Tex.	117,548	118,031
Lexington-Fayette,			Pasadena, Calif.	112,951	117,861
Ky.	108,137	203,082	Hollywood, Fla.	106,873	116,832
Jackson, Miss.	153,968	200,338	Macon, Ga.	122,423	116,044
Mobile, Ala.	190,026	199,392	Topeka, Kans.	125,011	115,996
Yonkers, N.Y.	204,297	194,557	Oxnard, Calif.	71,225	115,692
Shreveport, La.	182,064	194,506	Youngstown, Ohio	140,909	115,429
Dayton, Ohio	243,023	193,319	Lakewood, Colo.	92,743	113,787

Cities	1 April 1970	1 April 1980	Cities	1 April 1970	1 April 1980
Chesapeake, Va.	89,580	113,746	Allentown, Pa.	109,871	103,634
Pasadena, Tex.	89,957	111,884	Ann Arbor, Mich.	100,035	103,583
Independence, Mo.	111,630	111,760	Fullerton, Calif.	85,987	103,334
Bakersfield, Calif.	69,515	111,485	Berkeley, Calif.	114,019	103,134
Cedar Rapids, Iowa	110,642	110,124	Davenport, Iowa	98,469	103,036
Irving, Tex.	97,260	109,575	Sunnyvale, Calif.	95,976	103,023
Sterling Hgts, Mich.	61,365	108,998	Alexandria, Va.	110,927	102,494
South Bend, Ind.	125,580	108,185	Waterbury, Conn.	108,033	102,230
Temep, Ariz.	63,550	106,306	Boise City, Idaho	74,990	102,125
Modesto, Calif.	61,712	105,409	Concord, Calif.	85,164	101,862
Elizabeth, N.J.	112,654	105,384	Albany, N.Y.	115,781	101,767
Eugene, Oregon	79,028	104,672	Stamford, Conn.	108,798	101,636
Livonia, Mich.	110,109	104,660	Pueblo, Colo.	97,774	101,504
Portsmouth, Va.	110,963	104,068	Waco, Tex.	95,326	101,267

Vital Statistics: Vital statistics are based on records of births, deaths, fœtal deaths, marriages and divorces filed with registration officials of states and cities. Figures for the US include Alaska beginning with 1959 and Hawaii beginning with 1960.

Annual collection of mortality records from a national death-registration area was inaugurated in 1900. A national birth-registration area was established in 1915. These areas, which at their inception comprised 10 states and the District of Columbia, expanded gradually until 1933, when both the birth- and death-registration areas covered the entire continental US. Marriage and divorce statistics are compiled from reports furnished by state and local officials. Data on annulments are included in the divorce statistics. The marriage-registration area was established in 1957 with 29 states and 4 other areas. The divorce-registration area was established in 1958 with 14 states and 3 other areas. In Jan. 1972 the marriage-registration area included 41 states and 5 other areas, and the divorce-registration area included 29 states and one other area.

	Live births[1]	Deaths[2]	Marriages[3]	Divorces[4]	Maternal deaths[5]	Deaths under 1 year[6]
1900	—	343,217	709,000	56,000	—	—
1910	2,777,000	696,856	948,000	83,000	—	—
1920	2,950,000	1,118,070	1,274,476	170,505	16,320	170,911
1930	2,618,000	1,327,240	1,126,856	195,961	14,915	143,201
1940	2,559,000	1,417,269	1,595,874	264,000	8,876	110,984
1950	3,632,000	1,452,454	1,667,231	385,144	2,960	103,825
1960	4,257,850[7]	1,711,982	1,523,000	393,000	1,579	110,873
1970	3,731,386	1,921,031	2,158,802	708,000	803	74,667
1974	3,159,958	1,934,388	2,229,667	977,000	462	52,776
1975	3,144,198	1,892,879	2,152,662	1,036,000	403	50,525
1976	3,167,788	1,909,440	2,154,807	1,083,000	390	48,265
1977	3,326,632	1,899,597	2,178,367	1,091,000	373	46,975
1978[8]	3,329,000	1,924,000	2,243,000	1,128,000	320	45,300

[1] Figures through 1959 include adjustment for under-registration (the 1959 registered count was 4,244,796); beginning 1960 figures represent number registered.
[2] Excluding fœtal deaths and deaths among the armed forces overseas.
[3] Estimates for all years except 1970.
[4] Includes reported annulments. Estimated for all years except 1930.
[5] Deaths for 1968–74 (Eighth Revision, International Classification of Diseases, adapted, 1965). Deaths from deliveries and complications of pregnancy, childbirth and the puerperium. Deaths for 1958–67 were classified according to the Seventh Revision of the International Lists of Diseases and Causes of Death, those for 1949–57 according to the Sixth Revision and those for 1939–48, according to the Fifth Revision.
[6] Excluding fœtal deaths.   [7] Based on a 50% sample.   [8] Provisional.

The crude birth rate, based on total live-birth estimates per 1,000 total population, fell from 29·5 in 1915 to 18·4 in 1933; it rose to a peak of 26·6 in 1947—its highest for 25 years. This peak reflects demobilization (1945–46), the record number of marriages that followed, and the high levels of employment and income. The decrease in the following 3 years was moderate. In 1951 the rate moved upward and levelled off in 1957 at about 25 per 1,000 population. Since 1957 the crude birth rate has declined every year to 18·4 live births per 1,000 population in 1966. The crude birth rate for 1977 was 15·4. Estimated number of illegitimate births in 1977 was 515,700, a ratio of 155 illegitimate births per 1,000 registered live births.

Deaths, excluding fœtal deaths (per 1,000 population), declined from 17·2 in 1900 to 10 in 1946. The death rate has been below 10 per 1,000 since 1947, fluctuating slightly from year to year, mainly under the impact of occurrences of outbreaks of severe respiratory diseases. Since the record low of 9·2 in 1954 the rate has changed only between 9·3 and 9·7. The rate for 1970, 9·5; for 1971, 9·3; for 1972, 9·4; for 1973, 9·4; for 1974, 9·2; for 1975, 8·9; for 1976, 8·9; for 1977, 8·8.

Leading causes of death, 1977, per 100,000 population: Diseases of heart, 332·3; malignant neoplasms, 178·7; cerebrovascular diseases, 84·1; accidents, 47·7. Suicides in 1977 were 13·3 per 100,000 population; homicides, 9·2.

The marriage rate per 1,000 population for selected years are: 1920, 12; 1932, 7·9; 1946, 16·4; 1951, 10·4; 1961, 8·5; 1964, 9; 1965, 9·3; 1969, 10·6; 1970, 10·6; 1971, 10·6; 1975, 10·1; 1976, 10; 1977, 10·1. The divorce rates per 1,000 population for selected years are: 1920, 1·6; 1946, 4·3; 1951, 2·5; 1961, 2·3; 1965, 2·5; 1971, 3·7; 1975, 4·9; 1976, 5; 1977, 5.

Maternal mortality rates (deaths of mothers from conditions associated with deliveries and complications of pregnancy, childbirth and the puerperium) per 100,000 live births, were 1915–19, 727·9 and thereafter declined: 493·9 for 1935–39; 376 for 1940; 207·2 for 1945; 83·3 for 1950; 52·4 for 1954; 47 for 1955; 37·1 for 1960; 31·6 for 1965; 21·5 for 1970; 12·8 for 1975; 12·3 for 1976; 11·2 for 1977. The 1977 rate for white women was 7·7 and for all other women 26. By state, the average maternal mortality rate for 1971–73 was highest for Mississippi (38·1) and lowest for Rhode Island (4·9).

The infant mortality rates, per 1,000 live births were: 1915–19, 95·7; 1920–24, 76·7; 1925–29, 69; 1930–34, 60·4; 38·3 in 1945; 29·2 in 1950; 26·4 in 1955; 26 in 1960; 20·9 in 1969; 20 in 1970; 16·7 in 1974; 16·1 in 1975; 15·2 in 1976; 14·1 in 1977. In 1977 the rate for whites was 12·3; for all other, 21·7.

Immigration: The Immigration and Nationality Act, as amended by Public Law 89–236, establishes a numerical ceiling of 170,000 visas for the Eastern Hemisphere and 120,000 for the Western Hemisphere, with a maximum of 20,000 visas available for any one country. The visas are allocated under a system of 7 preference categories, 4 of which are designed to reunite close relatives of US citizens and resident aliens of the US, 2 for skilled and professional workers and 1 for refugees. Visa numbers not used in any of the preference categories are made available to qualified nonpreference immigrants. Spouses, children and parents of US citizens from both hemispheres are exempt from the numerical limitations.

During the year ended 30 Sept. 1977, 462,315 aliens became permanent residents of the US. Of the total immigrants admitted, 407,792 had obtained visas abroad and entered the US while aliens who were already in the US had their status adjusted to that of permanent residents.

Immigrant aliens admitted to US for permanent residence, by country or region of birth.

| Country or region of birth | Immigrants admitted | | | |
	1975	1976	1977[1]	1978
All countries	386,194	398,613	462,315	601,442
Europe	73,996	72,404	70,010	73,198
Germany (GDR and FRG)	5,154	5,836	6,372	6,739
Greece	9,984	8,417	7,838	7,035
Italy	11,552	8,380	7,510	7,415
Poland	3,941	3,805	4,010	5,050
Portugal	11,845	10,511	9,657	10,445
Spain	2,549	2,254	2,487	2,297
UK	10,807	11,392	10,416	14,245
Yugoslavia	3,524	2,820	2,791	2,621
Other Europe	14,640	18,989	18,929	17,351

[1] Year ending 30 Sept.

			Immigrants admitted	
Country or region of birth	*1975*	*1976*	*1977*[1]	*1978*
Asia	132,469	149,881	157,759	249,776[1]
China and Taiwan	18,536	18,823	19,764	21,315
Hong Kong	4,891	5,766	5,632	5,158
India	15,773	17,487	18,613	20,753
Japan	4,274	4,258	4,178	4,010
Korea (North and South)	28,362	30,803	30,917	29,288
Philippines	31,751	37,281	39,111	37,216
Thailand	4,217	6,923	3,945	3,574
Other Asia	24,665	28,540	35,599	31,873
North America	146,668	142,307	187,345	220,778
Canada	7,308	7,638	12,688	16,863
Mexico	62,205	57,863	44,079	92,367
Cuba	25,955	29,233	69,708	29,754
Dominican Republic	14,066	12,526	11,655	19,458
Haiti	5,145	5,410	5,441	6,470
Jamaica	11,076	9,026	11,501	19,265
Trinidad and Tobago	5,982	4,839	6,106	5,973
Other West Indies	5,206	5,805	9,600	10,441
Central America	9,696	9,912	16,485	20,153
Other North America	29	55	82	34
South America	22,984	22,706	32,954	41,764
Colombia	6,434	5,742	8,272	11,032
Ecuador	4,727	4,504	5,302	5,732
Other South America	11,823	12,460	19,380	25,000
Africa	6,729	7,723	10,155	11,524
Australia and New Zealand	1,500	1,796	1,986	2,184
Other countries	1,848	1,796	2,106	2,218

[1] Year ending 30 Sept.

The total number of immigrants admitted from 1820 up to 30 Sept. 1977 was 48,063,523; this included 6,970,176 from Germany (GDR and FRG), and from Italy 5,287,386.

Aliens coming to the US for temporary periods of time are classified as non-immigrants. In the year ending 30 Sept. 1977, a total of 8,036,916 non-immigrants were admitted as tourists, students, exchange visitors, aliens in transit, representatives of foreign governments, foreign information media, temporary workers and their children, and intracompany transferees and their spouses and children. This is exclusive of multiple entries at land borders and of alien crewmen. Tourists, primarily from Mexico, Japan, the UK, the West Indies, Germany (GDR and FRG) and Canada numbered 3,744,233. There were 897,243 aliens expelled during fiscal year 1977. Of this number, 30,228 were deported and 867,015 were required to depart without formal orders of deportation.

In accordance with the Immigration and Nationality Act, 4,980,480 aliens reported their address in Jan. 1978. Of this total, 4,280,364 were permanent residents and 700,116 were aliens here temporarily. The permanent resident aliens who reported were nationals of the following countries: Mexico, 942,092; Cuba, 295,053; Canada, 293,328; UK, 276,497; Philippines, 204,417; Italy, 181,937; Germany (GDR and FRG), 153,306. Over 75% of the permanent resident aliens reported their states of residence as: California, 1,283,598; New York, 796,454; Texas, 392,094; Florida, 370,238; Illinois, 287,777; New Jersey, 275,852; Massachusetts, 168,787, and Michigan, 135,522.

In the year ended 30 Sept. 1978, 173,535 persons became US citizens through naturalization; this includes, 143,133 naturalized under the general provisions of 5-year residence in the US, 25,242 spouses and children of US citizens, 5,126 military and 34 who were naturalized under other provisions. Of the total, there were 16,053 former nationals of Cuba, 20,218 of the Philippines, 11,303 of China and Taiwan, 12,575 of Korea, 9,118 of UK, 8,180 of Italy and 8,662 of Mexico.

US Depart. of Commerce. *Population of the United States: Trends and Prospects, 1500–1990.* Washington, 1974
Coale, A. J., and Zelnik, M., *New Estimates of Fertility and Population in the United States.* Princeton Univ. Press, 1963
Divine, R. A., *American Immigration Policy, 1924–52.* Yale Univ. Press, 1957
Hutchinson, E. P., *Immigrants and Their Children, 1850–1950.* New York, 1956
Jones, M. A., *American Immigration.* Univ. of Chicago Press, 1960
Okun, B., *Trends in Birth Rates in the US Since 1870.* Johns Hopkins Univ. Press, 1958

CONSTITUTION AND GOVERNMENT. The form of government of the USA is based on the constitution of 17 Sept. 1787.

By the constitution the government of the nation is composed of three co-ordinate branches, the executive, the legislative and the judicial.

The National Government has authority in matters of general taxation, treaties and other dealings with foreign Powers, foreign and inter-state commerce, bankruptcy, postal service, coinage, weights and measures, patents and copyright, the armed forces (including, to a certain extent, the militia), and crimes against the USA; it has sole legislative authority over the District of Columbia and the possessions of the US.

The 5th article of the constitution provides that Congress may, on a two-thirds vote of both houses, propose amendments to the constitution, or, on the application of the legislatures of two-thirds of all the states, call a convention for proposing amendments, which in either case shall be valid as part of the constitution when ratified by the legislatures of three-fourths of the several states, or by conventions in three-fourths thereof, whichever mode of ratification may be proposed by Congress. Ten amendments (called collectively 'the Bill of Rights') to the constitution were added 15 Dec. 1791; two in 1795 and 1804; a 13th amendment, 6 Dec. 1865, abolishing slavery; a 14th in 1868, including the important 'due process' clause; a 15th, 3 Feb. 1870, establishing equal voting rights for white and coloured; a 16th, 3 Feb. 1913, authorizing the income tax; a 17th, 8 April 1913, providing for popular election of senators; an 18th, 16 Jan. 1919, prohibiting alcoholic liquors; a 19th, 18 Aug. 1920, establishing woman suffrage; a 20th, 23 Jan. 1933, advancing the date of the President's and Vice-President's inauguration and abolishing the 'lame-duck' sessions of Congress; a 21st, 5 Dec. 1933, repealing the 18th amendment; a 22nd, 26 Feb. 1951, limiting a President's tenure of office to 2 terms, or to 2 terms plus 2 years in the case of a Vice-President who has succeeded to the office of a President; a 23rd, 30 March 1961, granting citizens of the District of Columbia the right to vote in national elections; a 24th, 4 Feb. 1964, banning the use of the poll-tax in federal elections; a 25th, 10 Feb. 1967, dealing with Presidential disability and succession; a 26th, 22 June 1970, establishing the right of citizens who are 18 years of age and older to vote.

National flag: Seven red and 6 white alternating stripes, horizontal; with a blue canton, extending down to the lower edge of the 4th red stripe from the top, and displaying 50 white 5-pointed stars, one for each state. The stars have one point directed vertically upward, and they are arranged in 6 rows of 5 each, alternating with 5 rows of 4 each. On the admission of additional states, stars are added, effective on 4 July following the date of admission. Congress, by law of 22 Dec. 1942, has codified 'existing rules and customs' pertaining to the display of the flag, for civilians.

National anthem: The Star-spangled Banner, 'Oh say, can you see by the dawn's early light' (words by F. S. Key, 1814; tune by J. S. Smith; formally adopted by Congress 3 March 1931).

National motto: 'In God we trust'; formally adopted by Congress 30 July 1956.

Presidency. The executive power is vested in a president, who holds office for 4 years, and is elected, together with a vice-president chosen for the same term, by electors from each state, equal to the whole number of senators and representatives to which the state may be entitled in the Congress. The President must be a natural-born citizen, resident in the country for 14 years, and at least 35 years old.

The presidential election is held every fourth (leap) year on the Tuesday after the first Monday in November. Technically, this is an election of presidential electors, not of a president directly; the electors thus chosen meet and give their votes (for the candidate to whom they are pledged, in some states by law, but in most states by custom and prudent politics) at their respective state capitals on the first Monday after the second Wednesday in December next following their election; and the votes of the electors of all the states are opened and counted in the presence of both Houses of Congress on the sixth day of January. The total electorate vote is one for each senator and representative.

If the successful candidate for President dies before taking office the Vice-President-elect becomes President; if no candidate has a majority or if the successful candidate fails to qualify, then, by the 20th amendment, the Vice-President acts as President until a president qualifies. The duties of the Presidency, in absence of the President and Vice-President by reason of death, resignation, removal, inability or failure to qualify, devolve upon the Speaker of the House under legislation enacted 18 July 1947. And in case of absence of a Speaker for like reason, the presidential duties devolve upon the President *pro tem.* of the Senate and successively upon those members of the Cabinet in order of precedence, who have the constitutional qualifications for President.

The presidential term, by the 20th amendment to the constitution, begins at noon on 20 Jan. of the inaugural year. This amendment also installs the newly elected Congress in office on 3 Jan. instead of—as formerly—in the following December. The President's salary is $200,000 per year, plus $50,000 to assist in defraying expenses resulting from official duties. Also $40,000 non-taxable for travel and official entertainment. The office of Vice-President carries a salary of $62,500, plus $10,000 allowance for travel.

The President is C.-in-C. of the Army, Navy and Air Force, and of the militia when in the service of the Union. The Vice-President is *ex-officio* President of the Senate, and in the case of 'the removal of the President, or of his death, resignation, or inability to discharge the powers and duties of his office', he becomes the President for the remainder of the term.

President of the United States: Ronald Reagan, of California, born at Tampico, Illinois, in 1911; Governor of California, 1967–75.

At the Presidential election on 4 Nov. 1980 total vote cast, including men and women in the armed services, was 86,513,296, of which Ronald Reagan (R.) received 43,901,812 (50·7%), James Earl Carter (D.) 35,483,820 (41%) and John Anderson 5,719,722 (6·6%). Electoral college votes: Reagan 489; Carter 49; Anderson 0.

PRESIDENTS OF THE USA

Name	From state	Term of service	Born	Died
George Washington	Virginia	1789–97	1732	1799
John Adams	Massachusetts	1797–1801	1735	1826
Thomas Jefferson	Virginia	1801–09	1743	1826
James Madison	Virginia	1809–17	1751	1836
James Monroe	Virginia	1817–25	1759	1831
John Quincy Adams	Massachusetts	1825–29	1767	1848
Andrew Jackson	Tennessee	1829–37	1767	1845
Martin Van Buren	New York	1837–41	1782	1862
William H. Harrison	Ohio	Mar.–Apr. 1841	1773	1841
John Tyler	Virginia	1841–45	1790	1862
James K. Polk	Tennessee	1845–49	1795	1849
Zachary Taylor	Louisiana	1849–July 1850	1784	1850
Millard Fillmore	New York	1850–53	1800	1874
Franklin Pierce	New Hampshire	1853–57	1804	1869
James Buchanan	Pennsylvania	1857–61	1791	1868
Abraham Lincoln	Illinois	1861–Apr. 1865	1809	1865
Andrew Johnson	Tennessee	1865–69	1808	1875
Ulysses S. Grant	Illinois	1869–77	1822	1885
Rutherford B. Hayes	Ohio	1877–81	1822	1893
James A. Garfield	Ohio	Mar.–Sept. 1881	1831	1881

Name	From state	Term of service	Born	Died
Chester A. Arthur	New York	1881–85	1830	1886
Grover Cleveland	New York	1885–89	1837	1908
Benjamin Harrison	Indiana	1889–93	1833	1901
Grover Cleveland	New York	1893–97	1837	1908
William McKinley	Ohio	1897–Sept. 1901	1843	1901
Theodore Roosevelt	New York	1901–09	1858	1919
William H. Taft	Ohio	1909–13	1857	1930
Woodrow Wilson	New Jersey	1913–21	1856	1924
Warren Gamaliel Harding	Ohio	1921–Aug. 1923	1865	1923
Calvin Coolidge	Massachusetts	1923–29	1872	1933
Herbert C. Hoover	California	1929–33	1874	1964
Franklin D. Roosevelt	New York	1933–Apr. 1945	1882	1945
Harry S. Truman	Missouri	1945–53	1884	1972
Dwight D. Eisenhower	New York	1953–61	1890	1969
John F. Kennedy	Massachusetts	1961–Nov. 1963	1917	1963
Lyndon B. Johnson	Texas	1963–69	1908	1973
Richard M. Nixon	California	1969–74	1913	—
Gerald R. Ford	Michigan	1974–77	1913	—
James Earl Carter	Georgia	1977–81	1924	—
Ronald Reagan	California	1981–	1911	—

VICE-PRESIDENTS OF THE USA

Name	From state	Term of service	Born	Died
John Adams	Massachusetts	1789–97	1735	1826
Thomas Jefferson	Virginia	1797–1801	1743	1826
Aaron Burr	New York	1801–05	1756	1836
George Clinton	New York	1805–12 [1]	1739	1812
Elbridge Gerry	Massachusetts	1813–14 [1]	1744	1814
Daniel D. Tompkins	New York	1817–25	1774	1825
John C. Calhoun	South Carolina	1825–32 [1]	1782	1850
Martin Van Buren	New York	1833–37	1782	1862
Richard M. Johnson	Kentucky	1837–41	1780	1850
John Tyler	Virginia	Mar.–Apr. 1841 [1]	1790	1862
George M. Dallas	Pennsylvania	1845–49	1792	1864
Millard Fillmore	New York	1849–50 [1]	1800	1874
William R. King	Alabama	Mar.–Apr. 1853 [1]	1786	1853
John C. Breckinridge	Kentucky	1857–61	1821	1875
Hannibal Hamlin	Maine	1861–65	1809	1891
Andrew Johnson	Tennessee	Mar.–Apr. 1865 [1]	1808	1875
Schuyler Colfax	Indiana	1869–73	1823	1885
Henry Wilson	Massachusetts	1873–75 [1]	1812	1875
William A. Wheeler	New York	1877–81	1819	1887
Chester A. Arthur	New York	Mar.–Sept. 1881 [1]	1830	1886
Thomas A. Hendricks	Indiana	Mar.–Nov. 1885 [1]	1819	1885
Levi P. Morton	New York	1889–93	1824	1920
Adlai Stevenson	Illinois	1893–97	1835	1914
Garret A. Hobart	New Jersey	1897–99 [1]	1844	1899
Theodore Roosevelt	New York	Mar.–Sept. 1901 [1]	1858	1919
Charles W. Fairbanks	Indiana	1905–09	1855	1920
James S. Sherman	New York	1909–12 [1]	1855	1912
Thomas R. Marshall	Indiana	1913–21	1854	1925
Calvin Coolidge	Massachusetts	1921–Aug. 1923 [1]	1872	1933
Charles G. Dawes	Illinois	1925–29	1865	1951
Charles Curtis	Kansas	1929–33	1860	1935
John N. Garner	Texas	1933–41	1868	1967
Henry A. Wallace	Iowa	1941–45	1888	1965
Harry S. Truman	Missouri	1945–Apr. 1945 [1]	1884	1972
Alben W. Barkley	Kentucky	1949–53	1877	1956
Richard M. Nixon	California	1953–61	1913	—

[1] Position vacant thereafter until commencement of the next presidential term.

Name	From state	Term of service	Born	Died
Lyndon B. Johnson	Texas	1961–Nov. 1963 [1]	1908	1973
Hubert H. Humphrey	Minnesota	1965–69	1911	1978
Spiro T. Agnew	Maryland	1969–73	1918	—
Gerald R. Ford	Michigan	1973–74	1913	—
Nelson Rockefeller	New York	1974–77	1908	1979
Walter Mondale	Minnesota	1977–81	1928	—
George Bush	Texas	1981–	1924	—

[1] Position vacant thereafter until commencement of the next presidential term.

Cabinet. The administrative business of the nation has been traditionally vested in several executive departments, the heads of which, unofficially and *ex officio*, formed the President's Cabinet. Beginning with the Interstate Commerce Commission in 1887, however, an increasing amount of executive business has been entrusted to some 60 so-called independent agencies, such as the Veterans Administration, Housing and Home Finance Agency, Tariff Commission, etc.

All heads of departments and of the 60 or more administrative agencies are appointed by the President, but must be confirmed by the Senate.

The Cabinet consisted of the following (Jan. 1981):

1. *Secretary of State* (created 1789). Alexander M. Haig; President of the United Technologies Corporation; former Chief of Staff (1973–74) and Supreme Allied Commander NATO (1974–79); born 1924.

2. *Secretary of the Treasury* (1789). Donald Regan, of New York; Chairman of Merrill Lynch and Company, securities; born 1918.

3. *Secretary of Defense* (1947). Caspar Weinberger, Vice-President of the Bechtel Power Corporation; lawyer, former Secretary of Health, Education and Welfare; born 1917.

4. *Attorney-General* (Department of Justice, 1870). William French Smith, of California; lawyer; born 1917.

5. *Secretary of the Interior* (1849). James G. Watt, of Wyoming; lawyer; born 1938.

6. *Secretary of Agriculture* (1889). John R. Block, of Illinois; farmer; director of the Illinois Farm Bureau; born 1935.

7. *Secretary of Commerce* (1903). Malcolm Baldrige, of Connecticut; manufacturer; born 1922.

8. *Secretary of Labor* (1913). Raymond J. Donovan, of New Jersey; construction company executive; born 1930.

9. *Secretary of Health and Human Services* (1953). Richard Schweiker, of Pennsylvania; State Senator; born 1926.

10. *Secretary of Housing and Urban Development* (1966). Samuel J. Pierce, of New York; lawyer; born 1922.

11. *Secretary of Transportation* (1967). Andrew L. Lewis, of Pennsylvania; management consultant, railway company trustee; born 1931.

12. *Secretary of Energy* (1977). James B. Edwards, of South Carolina; former Governor of South Carolina; born 1927.

Each of the above Cabinet officers receives an annual salary of $69,630 and holds office during the pleasure of the President.

Congress: The legislative power is vested by the Constitution in a Congress, consisting of a Senate and House of Representatives.

Electorate: By amendments of the constitution, disqualification of voters on the ground of race, colour or sex is forbidden. Accordingly, the electorate consists theoretically of all citizens of both sexes over 18 years of age, but the franchise is not universal. There are requirements of residence varying in the several states as to length from 6 months to 2 years and differing requirements as to registration. In 20 states the ability to read (usually an extract from the constitution) is required—in

Alaska the ability to read English; in Hawaii, English or Hawaiian; in Louisiana, English or one's native tongue. In Alabama the voter must take an 'anti-Communist oath' and fill out a questionnaire to the satisfaction of the registrars. In some southern states voters are required to give a reasonable explanation of what they read. Estimate of Negroes registered in the 11 southern states of Ala., Ark., Fla., La., Miss., N.C., Okla., S.C., Tex., Tenn. and Va.: 1947, 595,000; 1956, 1,238,000; 1960, 1,414,000; 1970, 3,324,000; 1972, 5,678,939. In 1972 there were about 14·2m. registered Negro voters in the USA. In most states convicts are excluded from the franchise, in some states duellists and fraudulent voters.

Legislation designed to discourage the rise of third parties has been adopted in a few states. In Illinois a new party must present a petition signed by at least 25,000 voters, including at least 200 in each of 50 of the 102 counties.

The method of balloting varies greatly. Seventeen states use different ballots for federal, state and local elections. In Delaware and South Carolina the various political parties furnish their own ballot-papers to the voters as he or she enters the polling-booth.

Senate: The Senate consists of 2 members from each state, chosen by popular vote for 6 years, one-third retiring or seeking re-election every 2 years. Senators must be no less than 30 years of age; must have been citizens of the USA for 9 years, and be residents in the states for which they are chosen. The Senate has complete freedom to initiate legislation, except revenue bills (which must originate in the House of Representatives); it may, however, amend or reject any legislation originating in the lower house. The Senate is also entrusted with the power of giving or withholding its 'advice and consent' to the ratification of all treaties initiated by the President with foreign Powers, a two-thirds majority of senators present being required for approval. (However, it has no control over 'international executive agreements' made by the President with foreign governments; such 'agreements', representing an important but very recent development, cover a wide range and are actually more numerous than formal treaties.) It also has the power of confirming or rejecting major appointments to office made by the President, but it has no direct control over the appointment by the President of 'personal representatives' or 'personal envoys' on missions abroad. Members of the Senate constitute a High Court of Impeachment, with power, by a two-thirds vote, to remove from office and disqualify any civil officer of the USA impeached by the House of Representatives, which has the sole power of impeachment.

The Senate has 16 Standing Committees to which all bills are referred for study revision or rejection. The House of Representatives has 21 such committees. In both Houses each Standing Committee has a chairman and a majority representing the majority party of the whole House; each has numerous sub-committees. The jurisdictions of these Committees correspond largely to those of the appropriate executive departments and agencies. Both Houses also have a few special Committees with limited duration; there are some Joint Committees.

House of Representatives: The House of Representatives consists of 435 members elected every second year. The number of each state's representatives is determined by the decennial census, in the absence of specific Congressional legislation affecting the basis. The states, in 1979, had the following representatives:

Alabama	7	Indiana	11	Nebraska	3	South Carolina	6
Alaska	1	Iowa	6	Nevada	1	South Dakota	2
Arizona	4	Kansas	5	New Hampshire	2	Tennessee	8
Arkansas	4	Kentucky	7	New Jersey	15	Texas	24
California	43	Louisiana	8	New Mexico	2	Utah	2
Colorado	5	Maine	2	New York	39	Vermont	1
Connecticut	6	Maryland	8	North Carolina	11	Virginia	10
Delaware	1	Massachusetts	12	North Dakota	1	Washington	7
Florida	15	Michigan	19	Ohio	23	West Virginia	4
Georgia	10	Minnesota	8	Oklahoma	6	Wisconsin	9
Hawaii	2	Mississippi	5	Oregon	4	Wyoming	1
Idaho	2	Missouri	10	Pennsylvania	25		
Illinois	24	Montana	2	Rhode Island	2		

The Supreme Court decided on 17 Feb. 1964, that the federal constitution requires congressional districts within each state to be substantially equal in population. By almost invariable custom the representative lives in the district from which he is elected.

Representatives must be not less than 25 years of age, citizens of the USA for 7 years and residents in the states from which they are chosen. The District of Columbia, Guam and the Virgin Islands have one non-voting delegate each. The House also admits a 'resident commissioner' from Puerto Rico, who has the right to speak on any subject and to make motions, but not to vote; he is elected in the same manner as the representatives but for a 4-year term. Each of the two Houses of Congress is sole 'judge of the elections, returns and qualifications of its own members'; and each of the Houses may, with the concurrence of two-thirds, expel a member. The period usually termed 'a Congress' in legislative language continues for 2 years, terminating at noon on 3 Jan.

The salary of a senator or representative, also that of a resident commissioner in Congress, is $60,662 per annum, with tax-free expense allowance and allowances for travelling expenses and for clerical hire. The salary of the Speaker of the House of Representatives is $79,125 per annum, with a taxable allowance.

No senator or representative can, during the time for which he is elected, be appointed to any *civil* office under authority of the USA which shall have been created or the emoluments of which shall have been increased during such time; and no person holding *any* office under the USA can be a member of either House during his continuance in office. No religious test may be required as a qualification to any office or public trust under the USA or in any state.

The 97th Congress (1981–83) was constituted (Jan. 1981) as follows: Senate, 53 Republicans, 46 Democrats, 1 Independent; House of Representatives, 243 Democrats, 192 Republicans.

Indians: By an Act passed on 2 June 1924 full citizenship was granted to all Indians born in the USA, though those remaining in tribal units were still under special federal jurisdiction. Those remaining in tribal units constitute from one-half to three-fourths of the Indian population. The Indian Reorganization Act of 1934 gave the tribal Indians, at their own option, substantial opportunities to self-government and of self-controlled corporate enterprises empowered to borrow money, buy land, machinery and equipment; these corporations are controlled by democratically elected tribal councils; by 1945 roughly a third of the Indians had taken advantage of this Act. Recently a trend towards releasing Indians from federal supervision has resulted in legislation terminating supervision over specific tribes. Indian lands (1965) amounted to 55,319,000 acres, of which about 71% was tribally owned and 20% in trust allotments, with the remainder owned by the Government. Indian lands are held free of taxes. Indian population under jurisdiction of the Indian Bureau was about 343,000 in 1950; nearly one-half were in the three states of Oklahoma, Arizona and New Mexico. Total Indian population at the 1970 census was 791,839, of which Oklahoma, Arizona, California, North Carolina and New Mexico accounted for 53%.

State and Local Government: The Union comprises 13 original states, 7 states which were admitted without having been previously organized as territories, and 30 states which had been territories—50 states in all. Each state has its own constitution (which the USA guarantees shall be republican in form), deriving its authority, not from Congress, but from the people of the state. Admission of states into the Union has been granted by special Acts of Congress, either (1) in the form of 'enabling Acts' providing for the drafting and ratification of a state constitution by the people, in which case the territory becomes a state as soon as the conditions are fulfilled, or (2) accepting a constitution already framed, and at once granting admission.

Each state is provided with a legislature of two Houses (except Nebraska, which since 1937 has had a single-chamber legislature), a governor and other executive officials, and a judicial system. Both Houses of the legislature are elective, but the senators (having larger electoral districts usually covering 2 or 3 counties compared with the single county or, in some states, the town, which sends 1 representative to the Lower House) are less numerous than the representatives, while in 38 states their terms are 4 years; in 12 states the term is 2 years. Of the 4-year senates, Illinois,

Montana and New Jersey provide for two 4-year terms and one 2-year term in each decade. Terms of the lower houses are usually shorter; in 45 states, 2 years.

Members of both Houses are paid at the same rate, which varies from $200 per biennium (New Hampshire) to $64,140 per biennium (California). The trend is towards annual sessions of state legislatures; in 1976, 36 were constitutionally required to meet annually (in 1939, only 4), the other 14 holding biennial sessions, 12 in the odd-numbered and 2 in the even-numbered years. Of these 14, 6 met annually in practice by invoking flexible constitutional powers to reconvene at intervals during the biennium.

The Governor has power to summon an extraordinary session, but not to dissolve or adjourn. The duties of the two Houses are similar, but in many states money bills must be introduced first in the Lower House. The Senate sits as a court for the trial of officials impeached by the other House, and often has power to confirm or reject appointments made by the Governor.

State legislatures are competent to deal with all matters not reserved for the federal government by the federal constitution nor specifically prohibited by the federal or state constitutions. Among their powers are the determination of the qualifications for the right of suffrage, and the control of all elections to public office, including elections of members of Congress and electors of President and Vice-President; the criminal law, both in its enactment and in its execution, with unimportant exceptions, and the administration of prisons; the civil law, including all matters pertaining to the possession and transfer of, and succession to, property; marriage and divorce, and all other civil relations; the chartering and control of all manufacturing, trading, transportation and other corporations, subject only to the right of Congress to regulate commerce passing from one state to another; labour; education; charities; licensing; fisheries within state waters, and game laws (apart from the hunting of migratory birds, which is a federal concern under treaties with Canada and Mexico). Taxes on income were left to the states until 1913, when the 16th amendment authorized the imposition of federal taxes on income without regard to apportionment.

The Governor is chosen by direct vote of the people over the whole state. His term of office varies in the several states from 2 to 4 years, and his salary from $10,000 (Arkansas) to $85,000 (New York). His duty is to see to the faithful administration of the law, and he has command of the military forces of the state. He may recommend measures but does not present bills to the legislature. In some states he presents estimates. In all but one of the states (North Carolina) the Governor has a veto upon legislation, which may, however, be overridden by the two Houses, in some states by a simple majority, in others by a three-fifths or two-thirds majority. In some states the Governor, on his death or resignation, is succeeded by a Lieut.-Governor who was elected at the same time and has been presiding over the state Senate. In several states the Speaker of the Lower House succeeds the Governor.

The chief officials by whom the administration of state affairs is carried on (secretaries, treasurers, members of boards of commissioners, etc.) are usually chosen by the people at the general state elections for terms similar to those for which governors hold office. State employees, Oct. 1970, numbered 2,755,033, earning $1,612·1m. monthly; education accounted for 1·18m. employees (43%). Local government employees numbered 7,392,437, earning $4,294·2m. monthly.

Local Government: The chief unit of local government is the county, of which there were (1976) 3,088 with definite functions; in addition, Rhode Island has 5 'counties' which have no functions; Alaska does not have 'counties' as such and, since Oct. 1960, there has been no active county government in Connecticut. Louisiana has 64 'parishes'. The counties maintain public order through the sheriff and his deputies, who may, in a crisis, be drawn temporarily from willing citizens; in many states the counties maintain the smaller local highways; other functions are the granting of licences and the apportionment and collection of taxes. In a few states they also manage the schools.

The unit of local government in New England is the rural township, governed directly by the voters, who assemble annually or oftener if necessary, and legislate in local affairs, levy taxes, make appropriations and appoint and instruct the local officials (selectmen, clerk, school-committee, etc.). Townships are grouped to form counties. Where cities exist, the township government is superseded by the city government.

The **District of Columbia,** ceded by the State of Maryland for the purposes of government in 1791, is the seat of the US Government. It includes the city of Washington, and embraces a land area of 61 sq. miles. The Reorganization Plan No. 3 of 1967 instituted a Mayor Council form of government with appointed officers. In 1973 an elected Mayor and elected councillors were introduced; in 1974 they received power to legislate in local matters. Congress retains power to enact legislation and to veto or supersede the Council's acts. Since 1961 citizens have had the right to vote in national elections. On 23 Aug. 1978 the Senate approved a constitutional amendment giving the District full voting representation in Congress. This has still to be ratified.

The **Commonwealth of Puerto Rico, Guam and the Virgin Islands** each have a local legislature, whose acts may be modified or annulled by Congress, though in practice this has seldom been done. The President appoints the Governor and Federal District Judge in Guam. Puerto Rico since its attainment of commonwealth status on 25 July 1952, enjoys practically complete self-government, including the election of its governor and other officials. The conduct of foreign relations, however, is still a federal function and federal bureaus and agencies still operate in the island.

General supervision of territorial administration is exercised by the Office of Territories in the Department of Interior.

The Book of the States 1978–79. Council of State Governments, Lexington, 1978

Constitution of the US, National and State. 2 vols. [with subsequent amendments]. Dobbs Ferry, 1962

Adrian, C. R., *State and Local Government.* 4th ed. New York, 1977

Barber, J. D. (ed.), *The 44th American Assembly, New York 1973.—Choosing the President.* Englewood Cliffs, 1974

Barone, M. (ed.). *The Almanac of American Politics.* Rev. ed. New York and London, 1976

Beloff, M., and Vale, V. (eds.), *American Political Institutions in the 1970s.* London, 1975

Berger, M., *Equality by Statute; The Revolution in Civil Rights.* Rev. ed. Gordon City, N.Y., 1968

Binkley, W. E., *American Political Parties.* 4th ed. New York, 1963

Bone, H. A., *American Politics and the Party System.* 4th ed. New York, 1971

Cater, D., *Power in Washington.* London, 1964

Corwin, E. S., *Presidential Power and the Constitution.* Cornell Univ. Press, 1976

Coyle, D. C., *The United States Political System and How it Works.* Rev. ed. New York, 1963

Dumbauld, E., *The Constitution of the United States.* Univ. of Oklahoma Press, 1965

Egger, R. A., *The President of the United States.* 2nd ed. New York, 1972

Ferguson, J. H., and McHenry, D. E., *Elements of American Government.* 6th ed. New York, 1963.—*The American Federal Government.* 12th ed. New York, 1973.—*The American System of Government.* 12th ed. New York, 1973

Fisher, L., *Presidential Spending Power.* Princeton Univ. Press, 1975

Hardin, C. M., *Presidential Power and Accountability: Towards a New Constitution.* Univ. of Chicago Press, 1974

Kelly, A. H., and Harbison, W. A., *The American Constitution, Its Origin and Development.* 4th ed. New York, 1970

Koenig, L. W., *The Chief Executive.* 3rd ed. New York, 1975

Levine, E. L., *An Introduction to American Government.* 2nd ed. New York, 1974

Maddox, R. W., and Fuquay, R. F., *State and Local Government.* 3rd ed. New York, 1975

Mayer, G. H., *The Republican Party, 1854–1966.* 2nd ed. OUP, 1967

Moe, R. C., *Congress and the President, Allies and Adversaries.* Pacific Palisades, 1971

Ogg, F. A., and Ray, P. O., *Introduction to American Government.* 12th ed. New York, 1962.—*Essentials of American National Government.* 10th ed. New York, 1969.—*Essentials of American State and Local Government.* 10th ed. New York, 1969

Pritchett, C. H., *The American Constitution.* 2nd ed. New York, 1968.—*The American Constitutional System.* New York, 1977

Redford, E. S., *Democracy in the Administrative State.* OUP, 1969

Ripley, R. B., *American National Government and Public Policy.* New York, 1974

Robinson, J. A., *State Legislative Innovation.* New York, 1973

Rossiter, C., *Parties and Politics in America.* Cornell Univ. Press, 1964

Scammon, R. M. (ed.). *America Votes. Handbook of Contemporary Election Statistics.* Pittsburg, 1975

Scheer, R. *America after Nixon: The Politics of the New World Order.* New York, 1975
Schlesinger, A. M., *Congress and the Presidency: Their Role in Modern Times.* Washington, 1967
Tugwell, R. G., *The Enlargement of the Presidency.* Garden City, N.Y., 1960.—*The Emerging Constitution.*
Tugwell, R. G., and Cronin, T. E., *Presidency Reappraised.* New York, 1974
White, T. H., *The Making of the President.* New York, 1960.—*The Making of the President, 1964.* New York, 1965.—*The Making of the President, 1968.* New York, 1969

DEFENCE. The President is C.-in-C. of the Army, Navy and Air Force.

The National Security Act of 1947 provides for the unification of the Army, Navy and Air Forces under a single Secretary of Defense with cabinet rank. The President is also advised by a National Security Council and the Office of Civil and Defense Mobilization.

The major components of the Department of Defense are the Office of the Secretary of Defense and the Joint Chiefs of Staff, who provide immediate staff assistance and advice to the Secretary; the departments of the Army, Navy and Air Force, each separately organized under a civilian head (not of cabinet rank); and the unified and specified commands.

Army. *Secretary of the Army:* John Marsh.

Central Administration. The Secretary of the Army is the head of the Department of the Army. Subject to the authority of the President as C.-in-C. and of the Secretary of Defense, he is responsible for all affairs of the Department.

The Secretary of the Army is assisted by the Under Secretary of the Army, 4 Assistant Secretaries of the Army (Installations, Logistics and Financial Management; Research and Development; Manpower and Reserve Affairs, and Civil Works), the General Counsel, an Administrative Assistant, Chief of Legislative Liaison, Chief of Public Affairs and the Army Staff headed by the Chief of Staff, US Army. The office of the Under Secretary of the Army includes a Deputy Under Secretary (Operations Research).

The Chief of Staff is the principal military adviser of the Secretary of the Army, and performs his duties under the direction of the Secretary of the Army, except as otherwise prescribed by law, by the President or by the Secretary of Defense. He has supervision of all members and organizations of the Army. The Vice Chief of Staff assists and advises the Chief of Staff.

The Army General Staff is the principal element of the Army Staff and includes the offices of the Chief of Staff, Vice Chief of Staff, Director of Staff, the 4 Deputy Chiefs of Staff (Military Operations, Personnel, Logistics, and Research, Development and Acquisition), the Comptroller of the Army, the Assistant Chief of Staff for Intelligence, the Ballistic Missile Defense Program Manager and the Army Reserve Forces Policy Committee. Other elements of the Army Staff are the offices of the Judge Advocate General, Surgeon General, Adjutant General, Inspector General and Auditor General, Chief of Chaplains, Chief, Army Reserve, Chief, National Guard Bureau, and Chief of Engineers.

The Army consists of the Regular Army, the Army National Guard of the US, the Army Reserve and civilian workforce; and all persons appointed to or enlisted into the Army without component; and all persons serving under call or conscription, including members of the National Guard of the States, etc., when in the service of the US.

Department of the Army active authorized strength, including cadets, was (1979) 774,000, including 55,000 women, comprised, in major combat units, or 16 divisions and several separate brigades and regiments.

The US Army Forces Command, with headquarters at Fort McPherson, Georgia, commands the continental US Armies and all assigned Active Army and US Army Reserve troop units in the continental US, Alaska, Hawaii, Panama, Guam, Johnston Island, the Commonwealth of Puerto Rico, and the Virgin Islands of the USA. The headquarters of the continental US Armies are: First US Army, Fort George G. Meade, Maryland; Fifth US Army, Fort Sam Houston, Texas; Sixth US Army, Presidio of San Francisco, California. The US Army Training and Doctrine Command, with headquarters at Fort Monroe, Virginia, co-ordinates and integrates the total combat development effort of the Army as well as developing, managing and supervising the training of individuals of the US Army and authorized foreign nationals. The US Army Health Services Command, with headquarters at Fort Sam Houston, Texas, provides health services in the continental US for the US Army and provides professional education and training for medical personnel of the US Army and authorized foreign national personnel. The US Army Materiel Development and Readiness Command, with headquarters in Alexandria, Virginia, is responsible for all US Army operations dealing with equipment development, procurement, delivery, supply and maintenance. The US Army Communications Command, with headquarters at Fort Huachuca, Arizona, provides worldwide communications to the Department of the Army and supports the Defense Communications Systems. The US Army Military District of Washington, with headquarters at Fort McNair, Washington, D.C. provides support to the Department of the Army and the Department of Defense at the seat of Government.

Some 35% of the Army is deployed overseas. Two divisions two-thirds of which are located in the USA keeps equipment in the Federal Republic of Germany and can be flown there in 48–72 hours. Headquarters of US Seventh and Eighth Armies are in Europe and Korea respectively.

Operational Commands and Weapons. The larger commands are the theater army and the corps. The typical theater army may consist of a variable number of corps; combat forces of armour and infantry; air defense artillery (*Nike-Hercules* and *Hawk* and short-range missile battalions); field artillery and Pershing missile battalions; combat support forces of aviation, engineer and signal elements; and combat service support forces. A typical corps consists of a variable number and mixture of infantry, mechanized infantry, armoured, airmobile, and airborne divisions; one or more separate infantry brigades; one or more armoured cavalry regiments; corps artillery (155-mm howitzer, 8-in. howitzer, 175-mm gun, *Lance* missile battalions); an air defense element of a size commensurate with the hostile air threat (*Nike-Hercules, Hawk* and *Chaparral/Vulcan* battalions), and a target acquisition unit; combat support and combat service support forces.

US Army Divisions have a common base (containing command, aviation divisional artillery, combat, combat support units and combat service support units) and a varying mixture of 'combat manoeuvre battalions' (usually 10 or 11 in number in 3 brigades) to make up airborne, infantry, armoured, mechanized infantry and airmobile divisions. Divisions can in this way be 'tailored' to fit a variety of strategic or tactical situations. An infantry division, with about 16,900 men, may have 8 infantry battalions, an armoured battalion and a mechanized infantry battalion; a mechanized infantry division, with about 16,600 men, may have 6 mechanized infantry battalions and 4 armoured battalions; an armoured division, with about 16,900 men, may have 5 mechanized infantry battalions and 6 armoured battalions; an airborne division, with 13,000 men, may have 9 infantry (airborne) battalions.

Small arms include the M-16, which fires a 5·56-mm cartridge. The standard general-purpose machine-gun is the M-60 (23 lb.; 550 rounds of 7·63-mm per minute). Infantry weapons also include M-203 grenade launcher attachment for the M16A1 rifle, which fire a 40-mm grenade up to 400 metres, the *Tow* and *Dragon* anti-tank missile system, and the M-72 rocket, a light anti-tank weapon.

Combat vehicles of the US Army are the tank, armoured personnel carrier, armoured reconnaissance airborne assault vehicle and the armoured command and reconnaissance vehicle. The first-line tanks are the XM-1 Abrams tank, M-60A3 with 105-mm main armament. The M-60A2, a version of the M-60 series tank, fires both the *Shillelagh* missile and conventional ammunition. The standard armoured personnel carrier is the M-113A1; it carries a mechanized infantry squad. The M-113A1 is also being utilized as the ground scout vehicle in armoured cavalry regiments, squadrons and in scout platoons of armoured and mechanized infantry battalions. The M-551 'Sheridan' is an armoured reconnaissance airborne assault vehicle in armoured cavalry units and light armour battalions; it fires both *Shillelagh* missiles and conventional ammunition. Combat vehicles under development are mechanized infantry combat vehicle and armoured reconnaissance scout vehicle.

The approved calibres of artillery are: light, 105-mm howitzer, medium 155-mm howitzer; the heavy, 175-mm gun and 8-in. howitzer. The 4·2-in. mortars and the 81-mm mortar are used by combat manoeuvre elements. The 90-mm, 106-mm recoilless rifles are being replaced by the *Dragon* and *Tow* anti-tank missile systems which are the primary anti-tank weapons. *Chaparral* and *Vulcan*, forward-area air-defence weapons, provide the capability of low-altitude defence against high-performance aircraft.

The Army has two categories of missiles—surface-to-surface (field artillery) and surface-to-air (air defence artillery). Surface-to-surface missiles are: *Pershing*, ballistic, nuclear warhead, range about 400 miles operational; *Lance*, guided, nuclear warhead, storable, liquid propellant, operational. Surface-to-air missiles, for air defence, are: *Nike-Hercules*, guided, field or fixed installation, nuclear warhead, operational; *Hawk*, homing type, low-to-mid-altitude, field, operational (an improved system has replaced the basic *Hawk*); *Chaparral*, infra-red homing, low-altitude, forward area, operational (improvements to the basic system are under development); *Redeye*, hand-held, infra-red homing, low-altitude, forward area, operational; *Patriot*, mid-to-high-altitude, replacement for *Hawk* and *Nike-Hercules*, under limited production; *Stinger*, hand-held infra-red homing, low-altitude, forward area, replacement for *Redeye* is under development. Anti-tank missiles are: *Tow*, tube launched, optically tracked, wire guided, anti-armour, forward area, operational; *Hellfire*, terminal homing under development.

The Army employs rotary- and fixed-wing aircraft as organic elements of its ground formations where their use is required on a full-time basis and their immediate and constant availability is essential. The front line commander exploits the benefits of aviation technology to perform traditional land battle tasks in the third dimension. This concept of airmobility for ground formation utilizes aerial vehicles as a highly integrated team to perform all five functions of land combat: reconnaissance, command and control, logistics and that inseparable combination, firepower and manoeuvre.

Enlistment, Terms of Service. Since 1974 the Army has operated a 'zero draft' system making it, in effect, an all-regular force. Terms of service may be 3, 4, 5 or 6 years.

Men who enlist incur a 6-year obligation and must serve in the reserve any part of the period not served on active duty.

The Army National Guard is a reserve military component with a dual status and role. Enlistment is voluntary. The members are recruited by each state, but are equipped and paid by the federal government. Training is supervised by the active Army (FORSCOM), and unit organization parallels that for the active army; training facilities are made available by the USA and each state. As the organized militia of the several states, the District of Columbia, Puerto Rico and the Territory of the Virgin Islands, the Guard may be called into service for local emergencies by the sovereigns in those jurisdictions; and may be called into federal service by the President to thwart invasion or rebellion or to enforce federal law. In its role as a reserve component of the Army, the Guard is subject to the order of the President in the event of national emergency. The Air Guard provide 100% of the air defence of Hawaii.

The Army Reserve is designed to supply qualified and experienced units and individuals in an emergency. US Army Forces Command is charged with the command, support and training supervision of US Army Reserve units. Members are assigned to one of 3 categories: the Ready, Standby or Retired Reserve. A limited number of Ready Reservists is subject to call by the President in case of national emergency without declaration of war by Congress. The Standby Reserve and the Retired Reserve may be called only after declaration of war or national emergency by Congress.

Army 1968 Green Book. Association of the U.S. Army, Washington, D.C.
The Army Almanac. Dept. of the Army, Washington, D.C.
Dupuy, R. E. and T. N., *Military Heritage of America.* New York, 1956
Forman, S., *West Point.* New York, 1950
ROTCM 145–20, Department of the Army ROTC Manual, *American Military History, 1607–1953.* Washington, 1956

Navy. *Secretary of the Navy:* John F. Lehman, Jr.

The Department of the Navy is administered under the Secretary of Defense by the Secretary of the Navy, assisted by an Under Secretary, 3 Assistant Secretaries, the Chief of Naval Operations, and the Commandant of the Marine Corps. The 3 divisions of the Department of the Navy are:

Central Executive Authority: comprising staff offices of the Secretary, dealing with financial management, administration, general counsel, programme appraisal, information, Judge Advocate General, and legislative affairs, Assistant Secretary of the Navy (Manpower, Reserve Affairs and Logistics), Assistant Secretary of the Navy (Research, Engineering and Systems); Office of the Chief of Naval Operations (comprising the Vice Chief, Assistant Vice Chief/Director of Naval Administration, 6 Deputy Chiefs, 8 Directors, the Naval Inspector General and the Surgeon General); Headquarters, US Marine Corps; Headquarters, Naval Material Command; Bureau of Naval Personnel; and Bureau of Medicine and Surgery.

Operating Forces: comprising the US Naval Forces, Europe; Atlantic and Pacific Fleets, including Fleet Marine Forces; Military Sealift Command; other Navy and Marine Corps forces and commands not otherwise assigned.

Shore Establishment: comprising commands dealing with systems (air, electronic, facilities engineering, sea and supply) and naval telecommunications; intelligence; security group, oceanographer, education and training, reserve, data automation, civilian personnel, naval district headquarters; and supporting establishment of the Marine Corps and Marine Corps Reserve.

Major shore activities include 5 shipyards, 32 air stations and facilities, 1 amphibious base, 2 submarine bases and 13 naval stations and bases. By agreement dated 2 Sept. 1940, Britain granted leases for naval and air bases in Newfoundland, Bermuda, Bahamas, Jamaica, St Lucia, Trinidad, Antigua and Guyana; but these are not all now active.

Naval appropriations in recent fiscal years: 1974, \$26,860m.; 1975, \$27,426m.; 1976, \$28,752m.; 1977, \$32,800m.; 1978, \$39,639m.; 1979, \$41,530m.; 1980, \$47,038m.; 1981, \$51,036m.

The active personnel on duty on 1 Jan. 1981 was 528,200 Navy officers and enlisted men, plus 185,200 Marine Corp officers and men.

The following is a tabulated statement of US vessels listed on 31 Dec.:

Category	1973	1974	1975	1976	1977	1978	1979	1980
Multi-purpose aircraft carriers	15	15	15	15	15	15	15	15
Anti-submarine carriers	7	5[1]	5[1]	5[1]	5[1]	5[1]	5[1]	5[1]
Helicopter carriers	7	7	7	9	9	10	11	12[2]
Command ships	2	3[3]	3[3]	3[3]	3[3]	3[3]	3[3]	3[3]
Nuclear powered submarines	106	107	107	108	109	113	115	118
Submarines (conventional)	33	18	15	15	15	13	10	10
Battleships	4	4	4	4	4	4	4	4
Cruisers	23	14	35[4]	35[4]	35[4]	36[4]	32[4]	29[4]
Frigates (Destroyer leaders)	33	32	—	—	—	—	—	—
Destroyers	173	156	112[5]	101[5]	97[5]	93[5]	96[5]	98[5]
Frigates (former Escort ships)	105	82	71[6]	65[6]	65[6]	65[6]	69[6]	67[6]

[1] Comprises 1 training carrier and 4 anti-submarine warfare support carriers in reserve.

[2] Comprises 5 flat-top hangar/dock heavy amphibious assault ships and 7 lighter flat-top hangar ships.

[3] Includes 1 Middle East Flagship (converted amphibious transport dock).

[4] Includes 22 frigates reclassified as cruisers in 1975.

[5] Includes 10 frigates reclassified as destroyers in 1975.

[6] Includes 65 escort ships reclassified as frigates on 1 July 1975.

The table below shows principal surface ships, guns under 3-in. calibre not given:

Com-pleted	Name	Standard displace-ment Tons	Armour Belt In.	Armour Guns In.	Principal armament	Shaft horse-power	Speed Knots
Multi-Purpose (Former Attack) Aircraft Carriers							
1977	Eisenhower	81,600	—	—	Guided missiles (90 aircraft)	260,000	33
1975	Nimitz	81,600	—	—	Guided missiles (90 aircraft)	260,000	33
1968	John F. Kennedy	61,000	—	—	Guided missiles (85 aircraft)	280,000	34
1965	America	60,300	—	—	Guided missiles (85 aircraft)	280,000	34

Completed	Name	Standard displacement Tons	Armour Belt In.	Armour Guns In.	Principal armament	Shaft horsepower	Speed Knots
1962	Enterprise	75,700	—	—	85 aircraft	300,000 (nuclear power) } 35	
1962	Constellation	61,000	—	—⎫			
1961	Kitty Hawk	61,000	—	—⎪			
1959	Independence	60,000	—	—⎬ Guided missiles (75 to 80 aircraft) } 280,000			34
1957	Ranger	60,000	—	—⎪			
1956	Saratoga	59,100	—	—⎭			
1955	Forrestal	59,100	—	—{ Guided missiles (70 aircraft) } 260,000			33
1950	Oriskany [1]	33,250	3	—	2 5-in. (70 aircraft)	150,000	33
1947	Coral Sea [2]	52,500	—	—	3 5-in. (75 aircraft)	212,000	33
1945	Midway [2]	51,000	—	—	3 5-in. (75 aircraft)	212,000	33
1944	{ Bon Homme Richard [1]	33,100	3	—	4 5-in. (70 aircraft)	150,000	33

[1] In reserve.   [2] Sister ship *Franklin D. Roosevelt* has been stricken.

Anti-Submarine Support Aircraft Carriers [1]

1944	{ Bennington { Shangri-La	} 33,000	3	—	{ 4 5-in. (45 aircraft— more or fewer, according to size and type }	} 150,000	33
1943	{ Hornet { Intrepid						

Training Carrier

1943	Lexington	32,800	3	—	Removed	150,000	33

The 'Essex' class originally comprised 24 ships, the *Essex, Yorktown, Intrepid, Hornet, Franklin, Lexington, Bunker Hill, Wasp, Ticonderoga, Hancock, Randolph, Bennington, Bon Homme Richard, Shangri-La, Tarawa, Antietam, Boxer, Kearsarge, Lake Champlain, Leyte, Philippine Sea, Princeton, Valley Forge, Oriskany.* (Five were rated as attack aircraft carriers, 11 as anti-submarine warfare aircraft carriers, 5 as auxiliary aircraft transports and 3 as amphibious assault ships.)

Of the auxiliary aircraft transports, *ex*-support aircraft carriers of the 'Essex' class, *Franklin* was stricken in Oct. 1964, *Bunker Hill* in Nov. 1966, *Tarawa* in June 1967, *Leyte* in June 1969 and *Philippine Sea* in Dec. 1969.

[1] All in reserve. *Lake Champlain* was stricken from the Navy List in Dec. 1969, *Wasp* in July 1972, *Antietam* and *Kearsarge* in May 1973, *Essex, Randolph* and *Yorktown* in June 1973, *Ticonderoga* in Nov. 1973 and *Hancock* on 31 Jan. 1975.

Aircraft Ferry Ships (ex-Escort Carriers) [1]

[1] The 'Commencement Bay' class comprising the *Kula Gulf, Rabaul* and *Point Cruz,* and the 'Bogue' class comprising the *Breton, Card, Core* and *Croatan* were deleted in 1972–73.

Helicopter Carriers (Amphibious Assault Ships)

1981	Pelileu						
1980	Nassau				{ 26 to 42 helicopters (or		
1978	Belleau Wood	39,300 (full load)	—	—	V/STOL aircraft); 3 5-in. guns;	} 140,000	24
1977	Saipan				2 missile launchers		
1976	Tarawa						
1970	Inchon						
1968	New Orleans						
1966	Tripoli						
1965	Guam [1]	17,000	—	—	20 to 26 helicopters (or V/STOL aircraft)	23,000	23
1963	Guadalcanal						
1962	Okinawa						
1961	Iwojima						

[1] *Guam* was modified in 1971–72 as 'interim' sea control ship but reverted to the amphibious role in 1974. (The Amphibious Assault ship *Thetis Bay*, former Escort Aircraft Carrier, was stricken in 1964 and *Valley Forge, Boxer* and *Princeton*, all of the 'Essex' class in 1969.)

Completed	Name	Standard displacement Tons	Armour Belt In.	Guns In.	Principal armament	Shaft horsepower	Speed Knots

Command Ships [1]

| 1971 | Mount Whitney | 19,100 | — | — | 2 missile launchers; | 22,000 | 23 |
| 1970 | Blue Ridge | (full load) | — | — | 4 3-in guns (twin); 1 helicopter | | |

[1] *Northampton*, originally designed as a heavy cruiser; redesigned as a tactical command ship; reclassified as a command ship in 1961 and: *Wright*, originally built as light fleet aircraft carrier, reclassified as aircraft transport in 1959; reclassified and converted into Command Ship in 1962–63, were stricken from the Navy List in 1977–78.

Major Communications Relay Ships (ex-*Carriers*) [1]

[1] The former Auxiliary Aircraft Transport *Saipan* (ex-Aircraft Carrier completed in 1946), converted to Major Communications Relay Ship (instead of Command Ship) and renamed *Arlington* in 1963–64 was stricken on 15 Aug. 1975.
The former Aircraft Ferry Ship *Gilbert Islands* (ex-Escort Carrier) converted to Major Communications Relay Ship 1962–64 and renamed *Annapolis* was stricken on 15 Oct. 1976.

Battleships

| 1944 | Missouri [1] Wisconsin [1] | 45,000 | 19 | 18 | 9 16-in.; 20 5-in. | 212,000 | 33 |
| 1943 | Iowa [1] New Jersey [2] | | | | | | |

[1] All laid up in reserve since 1955–58.   [2] Reactivated in 1968–69, reserve since.

Cruisers

1961	Long Beach	14,200	—	—	1 twin 'Talos' and 2 twin 'Terrier'; guided missile launchers: 2 5-in.	80,000 (nuclear power)	30
1949	Salem*	17,000	8	3–5	9 8-in.; 12 5-in.; 20 3-in.	130,000	33
1948	Des Moines						

*Sister ship *Newport News* was stricken from the Navy List on 31 July 1978, possibly to become a memorial.
[1] Of two other unconverted heavy cruisers, *Oregon City* was stricken from the Navy List in Nov. 1970 and *Rochester* in 1974.
[2] *St Paul*, sole survivor of the 'Baltimore' class, was stricken on 31 July 1978. Of 9 sister ships *Macon* was stricken in 1969, *Baltimore* and *Fall River* in 1971, *Bremerton*, *Pittsburg* and *Quincy* in 1973, and *Helena*, *Los Angeles* and *Toledo* in 1974.

The *Boston* and *Canberra* were reclassified as guided-missile cruisers in 1955 (*Boston* was stricken in Nov. 1973 and *Canberra* on 31 July 1978). The *Albany* (originally of the 'Oregon City' class), reclassed guided-missile cruiser in 1958 for conversion, completed by Nov. 1962 was stricken at the end of 1980. The *Chicago* and *Columbus* reclassed guided-missile cruisers in 1958–59 for conversion, completed in 1964 and 1963, respectively, were stricken in 1980 and 1976.
Of the 6 'Cleveland' class converted into guided-missile cruisers in 1958–60 *Topeka* and *Galveston* were stricken in Dec. 1973 and *Little Rock* on 22 Dec. 1976 to become memorial at Buffalo, N.Y. on 21 June 1977, *Providence* and *Springfield* were stricken on 31 July 1978, and *Oklahoma City* in 1980.
Of the original 'Cleveland' class *Amsterdam*, *Pasadena*, *Portsmouth* and *Wilkes-Barr* were stricken from the Navy List in 1970–71, *Astoria* in 1969 and *Vincennes* in 1966. *Atlanta* of this class, was converted for support of Pacific experiments before being discarded as a target. *Fargo* was stricken from the Navy List in 1970.
Of the 'Juneau' class anti-aircraft light cruisers *San Diego*, *San Juan*, *Oakland*, *Reno* and *Juneau* were stricken in 1959, *Fresno* and *Flint* in 1965, and *Tucson* in 1966. The remaining ship, *Spokane*, was converted into a sonar test ship in 1967.

Cruisers, Former Frigates (Destroyer Leaders)

1980	Arkansas	9,000	—	—	2 twin 'Tartar/ASROC'; 2 5-in.	80,000 (nuclear power)	30
1978	Mississippi						
1977	Texas						
1976	Virginia						
1974	South Carolina	9,560	—	—	2 single 'Tartar'; 2 5-in.;	70,000 (nuclear power)	30
1973	California						

Completed	Name	Standard displacement Tons	Armour Belt In.	Guns In.	Principal armament	Shaft horse-power	Speed Knots
1967	Truxtun	8,200	—	—	1 twin 'Terrier'; 1 5-in.; 2 3-in.	60,000 (nuclear power)	30
1962	Bainbridge	7,600	—	—	2 twin 'Terrier'; 4 3-in.		
1964–67	9 Belknap Class [1]	6,570	—	—	1 twin 'Terrier'; 1 5-in.; 2 3-in.	85,000	34
1962–64	9 Leahy Class [2]	5,670	—	—	2 twin 'Terrier'; 4 3-in.	85,000	34

[1] The 'Belknap' class comprises *Belknap, Biddle, Fox, Horne, Josephus, Daniels, Jouett, Sterett, Wainwright* and *William H. Standley*. The *Belknap* was severely damaged by collision with the aircraft carrier *John F. Kennedy* on 22 Nov. 1975 in the Mediterranean and towed to the United States for 2-year re-building from 1978 to 1980 (including repairs and modernization).

[2] The 'Leahy' class comprises *Dale, England, Gridley, Halsey, Harry E. Yarnell, Leahy, Reeves, Richmond K. Turner* and *Worden*.

Destroyers, Former Frigates (Destroyer Leaders)*

| 1959–62 | 10 Coontz Class [1] | 4,700 | — | — | 1 twin 'Terrier'; 1 5-in.; 4 3-in. | 85,000 | 34 |

*Of the original 4 'frigates' (DL—destroyer leaders) of the 'Mitscher' class, *John S. McCain* and *Mitscher*, converted into guided-missile destroyers in 1968–69, and *Wilkinson* and *Willis A. Lee*, both unconverted, were discarded in 1973–74.

[1] The 'Coontz' class comprises *Coontz, Dahlgren, Dewey, Farragut, King, Luce, Macdonough, Mahan, Preble* and *William V. Pratt*. They were reclassified from frigates (DLG) to destroyers (DDG) on 1 July 1975.

The *Norfolk*, designed as a special anti-submarine cruiser (*Cruiser, Hunter, Killer Ship*), reclassified as a destroyer leader in 1951 and as a frigate in 1955, was stricken in Nov. 1973.

In addition to the above named ships there are 118 nuclear-powered submarines, 10 conventional submarines, 88 other destroyers, 67 frigates, 25 ocean minesweepers, 4 patrol vessels, 2 hydrofoil patrol craft, 4 fast patrol boats, 60 amphibious warfare ships, 30 replenishment ships, 70 sealift ships, 95 fleet support ships and auxiliaries and 1,100 service craft.

Ships under construction include 7 submarines of 18,700 tons submerged with nuclear power and ballistic missiles, 22 nuclear powered attack submarines of 6,900 tons submerged; the giant nuclear powered aircraft carrier *Carl Vinson* of 93,400 tons war load; 1 cruiser, 8 destroyers and 32 guided missile frigates.

Projected new construction includes 8 more 'Ohio' class nuclear powered deterrent or 'strategic' submarines; 8 more nuclear powered fleet or 'attack' submarines; 1 large aircraft carrier; 15 guided missile destroyers and 33 guided missile frigates.

The US Coast Guard operates under the Department of Transportation in time of peace and as a part of the Navy in time of war or when directed by the President. The act of establishment stated the Coast Guard 'shall be a military service and branch of the armed forces of the United States at all times'. The Coast Guard did operate as part of the Navy during the First and Second World Wars. It also had some units serving in Vietnam. It comprises 260 ships including cutters of destroyer, frigate, corvette and patrol vessel types, powerful icebreakers, and para-military auxiliaries and tenders. It also maintains 50 fixed-wing aircraft and 120 helicopters. The Coast Guard missions include maintenance of aids to navigation, enforcement of maritime laws, enforcement of international treaties, environmental protection (especially waterway pollution), commercial vessel safety programmes, recreational boating safety, and search and rescue efforts. In the new construction programme are 9 cutters of frigate size and utility each capable of carrying a helicopter. The strength of personnel on 1 Jan. 1981 was 4,900 officers, 1,430 warrant officers and 31,300 enlisted men.

Air Force. *Secretary of the Air Force:* Verne Orr.

The Department of the Air Force was activated within the Department of Defense on 18 Sept. 1947, under the terms of the National Security Act of 1947. It is administered by a Secretary of the Air Force, assisted by an Under Secretary and 3 Assistant Secretaries (Research, Development and Logistics; Financial Management; and Manpower, Reserve Affairs and Installations). The USAF, under the administration of the Department of the Air Force, is supervised by a Chief of Staff, who is a member of the Joint Chiefs of Staff. He is assisted by a Vice Chief of Staff, Assistant Vice Chief of Staff, and 5 Deputy Chiefs of Staff (Manpower and Personnel; Programs and Evaluation; Research, Development and Acquisition; Operations, Plans and Readiness; and Logistics and Engineering).

The USAF consists of active duty Air Force officers and airmen, civilian employees, the Air National Guard and the Air Force Reserve. For operational purposes the service is organized into 11 major commands and 13 separate operating agencies. The Strategic Air Command, equipped with long-range bombers based both in the USA and overseas, and with intercontinental ballistic missiles, is maintained primarily for strategic air operations anywhere on the globe. Tactical Air Command is the Air Force's mobile strike force, able to deploy US general-purpose air forces anywhere in the world for tactical air combat operations. The Military Airlift Command provides air transportation of personnel and cargo for all military services on a worldwide basis; and is also responsible for Air Force audio-visual products, weather service, and aerospace rescue and recovery operations.

The other functional commands are the Air Force Systems Command, Air Force Logistics Command, Air Force Communications Command, Electronic Security Command, and Air Training Command.

The overseas commands are the Pacific Air Forces, the US Air Forces in Europe and the Alaskan Air Command. These commands conduct, control and co-ordinate offensive and defensive air operations according to tasks assigned by their respective theatre commanders. There are also a number of separate operating agencies which include the Air Force Accounting and Finance Center, Air Force Audit Agency, Air Force Commissary Service, Air Force Engineering and Services Center, Air Force Inspection and Safety Center, Air Force Intelligence Service, Air Force Office of Security Police, Air Force Manpower and Personnel Center, Air Force Medical Service Center, Air Force Service Information and News Center, Air Force Legal Services Center, Air Force Office of Special Investigations, and Air Force Test and Evaluation Center. The Air Force has several other direct reporting units, including the Air Force Academy, Air Force Reserve, and Aerospace Defense Center.

Of the fighter and interceptor aircraft in service, the F-15 Eagle, F-5 Tiger II, F-16 Fighting Falcon, F-105 Thunderchief, F-106 Delta Dart, F-111 and F-4 Phantom II fly faster than the speed of sound in level flight and can carry a variety of armament. The E-3A AWACS is a large long range airborne warning and control aircraft. The subsonic A-7 Corsair II and the A-10 Thunderbolt II are close-support aircraft. Strategic bombers are the B-52 Stratofortress heavy bomber and the 'swing-wing' FB-111A. The Strategic Air Command also operates the KC-135 Stratotanker for aerial refuelling and the SR-71 Blackbird and U-2 for strategic reconnaissance. Current transport types include the C-141 StarLifter, the C-5 Galaxy and the turboprop-powered C-130 Hercules. Intercontinental ballistic missiles in USAF service are Titan II and Minuteman II and III.

In 1981, the Air Force had 564,000 personnel. Total 1981 aircraft strength is 9,263.

American Defense Policy. 3rd ed. Johns Hopkins Univ. Press, 1975
The Army Air Forces in World War II. 7 vols. Univ. of Chicago Press, 1948 ff.
Goldberg, A., *A History of the US Air Force, 1907–57.* New York, 1957

INTERNATIONAL RELATIONS

Membership. USA is a member of UN, OAS, NATO, OECD and the Colombo Plan.

ECONOMY

Budget. The budget covers virtually all the programmes of federal government, including those financed through trust funds, such as for social security, Medicare and highway construction. Receipts of the Government include all income from its sovereign or compulsory powers; income from business-type or market-orientated activities of the Government is offset against outlays. Budget receipts and outlays (in $1m.):

Year ending 30 June	Receipts	Outlays	Surplus (+) or deficit (−)
1945	45,216	92,690	−47,474
1950	39,485	42,597	− 3,112
1955	65,469	68,509	− 3,041
1960	92,492	92,223	+ 269
1970	193,743	196,588	− 2,845
1979 [1]	465,940	493,673	−27,733
1980 [2]	517,892	578,774	−60,882
1981 [2]	604,026	633,791	−29,765

[1] From 1977 the fiscal year changed from a 1 July–30 June basis to a 1 Oct.–30 Sept. basis.
[2] Estimate.

Budget receipts, by source, for fiscal years (in $1m.):

Source	1979[1]	1980[1,2]	1981[1,2]
Individual income taxes	217,841	240,713	278,152
Corporation income taxes	65,677	65,481	66,383
Social insurance taxes and contributions	141,591	160,512	184,519
Excise taxes	18,745	25,379	48,656
Estate and gift taxes	5,411	6,100	6,284
Customs	7,439	7,050	7,510
Miscellaneous	9,237	12,657	12,522
Total	465,940	517,892	604,026

[1] From 1977, the fiscal year changed from a 1 July–30 June basis to a 1 Oct.–30 Sept. basis.
[2] Estimate.

Budget outlays, by function, for fiscal years (in $1m.):

Source	1979[1]	1980[1,4]	1981[1,4]
National defence [2]	117,681	135,611	157,513
International affairs	6,091	10,897	10,290
General science, space, and technology	5,041	5,726	6,183
Energy	6,856	6,513	7,227
Natural resources and environment	12,091	13,739	13,100
Agriculture	6,238	5,843	2,223
Commerce and housing credit	2,565	8,274	654
Transportation	17,459	20,795	19,244
Community and regional development	9,482	9,479	9,330
Education, training, employment and social services	29,685	29,893	30,921
Health	49,614	56,913	63,411
Income security	160,198	193,548	230,366
Veterans benefits and services	19,928	20,893	21,770
Administration of justice	4,153	4,617	4,563
General government	4,153	5,014	4,698
General purpose fiscal assistance	8,372	8,632	7,264
Interest	52,556	64,284	67,640
Allowances [3]	...	−22	1,400
Undistributed offsetting receipts	−18,488	−21,876	−24,005
Total budget outlays	493,673	578,774	633,791

[1] From 1977, the fiscal year changed from a 1 July–30 June basis to a 1 Oct.–30 Sept. basis.
[2] Includes allowances for civilian and military pay raises for the Department of Defense.
[3] Includes allowances for civilian agency pay raises and contingencies.
[4] Estimate.

Budget outlays, by agency, for fiscal years (in $1m.):

Agency	1979[1]	1980[1,2]	1981[1,2]
Legislative branch	1,077	1,311	1,314
The judiciary	480	597	649
Executive Office of the President	80	100	116
Funds appropriated to the President	2,623	7,577	5,964
Agriculture	20,636	25,727	20,786
Commerce	4,072	3,768	2,884
Defence—Military	115,013	132,600	153,879
Defence—Civil	2,908	3,453	3,080
Education	10,879	12,454	13,337
Energy	7,893	6,549	8,400
Health and Human Services	170,303	194,119	224,069
Housing and Urban Development	9,213	12,551	11,919
Interior	4,087	4,005	3,996
Justice	2,522	2,688	2,551
Labour	22,649	29,593	39,356
State	1,548	1,920	2,163
Transportation	15,486	18,573	17,687
Treasury	65,044	76,479	78,296
Environmental Protection Agency	4,800	5,662	5,519
General Services Administration	4,187	4,851	5,208
National Aeronautics and Space Administration	19,887	20,838	21,737
Veterans Administration	12,654	14,939	17,023
Other independent agencies:			
Office of Personnel Management	1,787	1,677	1,343
Postal Service	4,365	4,799	5,318
Railroad Retirement Board	7,970	13,841	9,804
All other	...	−22	1,400
Undistributed offsetting receipts	−18,488	−21,876	−24,005
Total budget outlays	493,673	578,774	633,791

[1] From 1977, the fiscal year changed from a 1 July–30 June basis to a 1 Oct.–30 Sept. basis.
[2] Estimate.

National Debt: Gross federal debt outstanding (in $1m.), and *per capita* debt (in $1) on 30 June to 1970 and then on 30 Sept:

	Public debt	Per capita[2]		Public debt	Per capita[2]
1919[1]	25,485	243	1950	256,853	1,687
1920	24,299	228	1960	290,862	1,610
1930[1]	16,185	132	1970	382,603	1,867
1940	50,696	382	1979	833,751	3,773

[1] On 31 Aug. 1919 gross debt reached its First World War (1914–18) peak of $26,596,702,000, which was the highest ever reached up to 1934; on 31 Dec. 1930 it had declined to $16,026m., the lowest it has been since the First World War. On the 30 Nov. 1941, just preceding Pearl Harbor, debt stood at $61,363,867,932. The highest Second World War debt was $279,764,369,348 on 28 Feb. 1946.
[2] *Per capita* figures, beginning with 1960, have been revised; they are based on the Census Bureau's estimates of the total population of the US, including Alaska and Hawaii.

State and Local Finance: Revenue of the 50 states and all local governments (79,913 in 1977) from their own sources amounted to $329,770m. in fiscal year 1978–79; in addition they received $75,164m. in revenue from fiscal aid, shared revenues and reimbursements from the federal government, bringing total revenue from all sources to $404,934m. Of the revenue from state and local sources, taxes provided $205,514m., of which property taxes (mainly imposed by local governments) yielded $64,944m. or 32% of all tax revenue; and sales taxes, both general sales taxes and selective excises, provided $74,248m. (36%).

State tax revenue totalled $124,908m. in fiscal year 1979. Largest sources of state tax revenue are general sales taxes (imposed during 1979 by 45 states), motor fuel sales taxes (all states), individual income (44 states), motor vehicle and operators' licences (49 states), corporation income (46 states), tobacco products (all states) and alcoholic beverage sales taxes (all states).

General revenue of local units from own sources in fiscal year 1978–79 totalled $139,853m. In addition they received $94,778m. from state and federal aids. Property taxes provided 29% of total general revenue.

Total expenditures of state and local governments were $381,867m. in 1978–79, of which approximately 72% was for current operation. Education took $119,448m. in current and capital expenditure; highways, $28,440m.; welfare (chiefly public assistance), $41,898m., and health and hospitals, $28,218m. Capital outlays (construction, equipment and land purchases) totalled $53,196m.

Gross debt of state and local governments totalled $304,103m. or $1,381 *per capita* at the close of their 1978–79 fiscal year. Total cash and investment assets of state and local governments were $362,359m., about 24% being in cash and deposits, and the remainder in investments, mainly non-governmental securities.

US Bureau of the Census, *Governmental Finances in 1978–79*. Washington, 1979
American Economic Association, *Readings in Fiscal Policy*. Homewood, Ill., 1955
Brookings Institute and National Bureau of Economic Research, *Role of Direct and Indirect Taxes in the Federal Revenue System*. Washington, D.C., 1964
National Bureau of Economic Research, *National Economic Accounts of the US; Review, Appraisal and Recommendations*. 1958
Burkhead, J., *Government Budgeting*. New York, 1956
Kimmell, L. H., *Federal Budget and Fiscal Policy, 1789–1958*. Washington and London, 1959
Lewis, W., *Federal Fiscal Policy in the Post-war Recessions*. New York, 1963

National Income. The Bureau of Economic Analysis of the Department of Commerce prepares detailed estimates on the national income and product of the United States. The principal tables are published monthly in *Survey of Current Business*; the complete set of national income and product tables are published in the *Survey* regularly each July, showing data for recent years. *The National Income and Product Accounts of the United States, 1929–1974: Statistical Tables* (1976) contains a complete set of tables from 1929 through 1974. The conceptual framework and statistical methods underlying the US accounts were described in *National Income, 1954*. Subsequent limited changes were described in *US Income and Output* (1958), and in *Survey of Current Business* (Aug. 1965 and Jan. 1976).

These latest figures [1] in $1,000m. for various years are as follows:

	1929 [2]	1933 [3]	1950	1960	1970	1978	1979
I. Gross National Product	103·4	55·8	286·2	506·0	982·4	2,127·6	2,368·8
(a) Personal consumption expenditures	77·3	45·8	192·0	324·9	618·8	1,350·8	1,509·8
(b) Gross private domestic investment	16·2	1·4	53·8	76·4	140·8	351·5	387·2
(c) Net exports of goods and services	1·1	0·4	1·9	4·4	3·9	−10·3	−4·6
(d) Government purchases of goods and services	8·8	8·2	38·5	100·3	218·9	435·6	476·4
1. GNP *less* capital consumption allowances with capital consumption adjustment, indirect business tax and non-tax liability, business transfer payments, statistical discrepancy, *plus* subsidies *less* current surplus of government enterprises, equals:							
2. National Income	84·8	39·9	236·2	412·0	798·4	1,724·3	1,924·8
which, *less* corporate profits with inventory valuation and capital consumption adjustments, contributions for social insurance, wage accruals *less* disbursements, *plus* government transfer payments to persons, interest paid by government to persons and business *less* interest received by government, interest paid by consumers, dividends, business transfer payments, equals:							

[1] The inclusion of statistics for Alaska and Hawaii in 1960 does not significantly affect the comparability of the data.

[2] Peak year between First and Second World Wars.   [3] Low point of the depression.

	1929[1]	1933[2]	1950	1960	1970	1978	1979
3. Personal income	84·9	46·9	226·1	399·7	801·3	1,717·4	1,924·2
whereof							
4. Personal tax and non-tax payments take	2·6	1·4	20·6	50·4	115·3	259·0	299·9
leaving							
5. Disposal personal income divided into	82·3	45·5	205·5	349·4	685·9	1,458·4	1,624·3
(e) Personal outlays[3]	79·1	46·5	194·7	332·3	635·4	1,386·4	1,550·5
(f) Personal saving	3·1	−1·0	10·8	17·1	50·6	72·0	73·8
IA. GNP in constant (1972) $s	314·6	222·1	533·5	736·8	1,075·3	1,399·2	1,431·6
(a) Personal consumption expenditures	215·6	170·7	338·1	453·0	668·9	900·8	924·5
(b) Gross private domestic investment	55·9	8·4	93·7	105·4	154·7	214·3	215·2
(c) Net exports of goods and services	2·2	0·2	4·0	5·5	1·4	11·0	17·6
(d) Government purchases of goods and services	40·9	42·8	97·7	172·9	250·2	273·2	274·3
II. National Income	84·8	39·9	236·2	412·0	798·4	1,724·3	1,924·8
composed of							
Compensation of employees	*51·1*	*29·5*	*154·8*	*294·9*	*609·2*	*1,304·5*	*1,459·2*
(g) Salaries and wages	50·5	29·0	147·0	271·9	546·5	1,103·5	1,227·4
(h) Supplements to wages and salaries	0·6	0·5	7·8	23·0	62·7	201·0	231·8
Proprietors' income	*14·9*	*5·8*	*38·4*	*47·0*	*65·1*	*116·8*	*130·8*
(i) Farm	6·2	2·6	13·5	11·4	13·9	27·7	32·8
(j) Business and professional	8·8	3·2	24·9	35·6	51·2	89·1	98·0
Personal income from rents	*4·9*	*2·2*	*7·1*	*13·8*	*18·6*	*25·9*	*26·9*
Net interest	*4·7*	*4·1*	*2·3*	*9·8*	*37·5*	*109·5*	*129·7*
Corporate profits with inventory valuation and capital consumption adjustments	*9·2*	*−1·7*	*33·7*	*46·6*	*67·9*	*167·7*	*178·2*
(k) Tax liabilities	1·4	0·5	17·9	22·7	34·5	84·5	92·5
(l) Inventory valuation adjustment	0·5	−2·1	−5·0	0·3	−5·1	−25·2	−41·8
(m) Capital consumption adjustment	−1·3	0·5	−4·0	−2·3	1·5	−13·1	−16·7
(n) Dividends	5·8	2·0	8·8	12·9	22·9	47·2	52·7
(o) Undistributed profits	2·8	−1·6	15·9	13·0	14·1	74·3	91·4

[1] Peak year between First and Second World Wars.

[2] Low point of the depression.

[3] Includes personal consumption expenditures, interest paid by consumers and personal transfer payments to foreigners (net).

Currency. Prior to the banking crisis that occurred early in 1933, the monetary system had been on the gold standard for more than 50 years. An Act of 14 March 1900 required the Secretary of the Treasury to maintain at a parity with gold all forms of money issued by the USA. For a description of these, *see* THE STATESMAN'S YEAR-BOOK, 1934, p. 491.

The old gold dollar had a par value of 49·32d., or $4·8666 to the £ sterling; it contained 25·8 grains (or 1·6718 grammes) of gold 0·900 fine. By the act of 12 May 1933 the President of the USA was given authority to reduce the gold content of the dollar by not more than 50% and by the Gold Reserve Act of 30 Jan. 1934 the minimum reduction which he could make was fixed at 40%; on 31 Jan. 1934 he fixed its value at 59·06%, or 15$\frac{5}{21}$ grains of gold 0·900 fine. This was equal to a price for gold of $35 a fine oz. (old price, $20·67183). The President's power to alter the gold content of the dollar to 50% of its value, which was extended by Congress in 1937, 1939 and 1941, was not again extended in 1943.

The Par Value Modification Act (Public Law 92–268), enacted on 31 March 1972, authorized and directed the Secretary of the Treasury to take the steps necessary to establish a new par value of the dollar of $1 = 0·818513 gramme of fine gold or $38 per fine troy oz. of gold. The Secretary of the Treasury, pursuant to the statutory directive, proposed the new par value for the US dollar to the International Monetary Fund, which par value became effective on 8 May 1972.

In Public Law 93–110, enacted on 21 Sept. 1973, Congress amended the Par Value Modification Act of 1972, and authorized and directed the Secretary of the Treasury to take the steps necessary to establish a new par value of $1 equals 0·828948 Special Drawing Right or 1/42$\frac{2}{9}$ of a fine troy ounce of gold. Pursuant to the statutory directive, the Secretary of the Treasury notified the International Monetary Fund that, effective 18 Oct. 1973, the par value of the dollar would be changed from 1/38 to 1/42$\frac{9}{10}$ a fine troy ounce of gold. Expressed in terms of gold, the new par value of the dollar is 0·736662 gramme of gold per dollar, or $42.222 per fine troy ounce of gold. Expressed in percentage, the change in the par value of the dollar amounted to a reduction of 10% in the former gold content of the dollar. This is the equivalent to an 11·1% increase in the former dollar price of gold.

The USA, on 1 April 1978, accepted the second amendment to the Articles of Agreement of the International Monetary Fund. The par value of the dollar is no longer defined in terms of the Special Drawing Right and gold, and the USA is not obliged to establish and maintain a par value for the dollar.

At the time of the banking crisis in March 1933 gold payments by banks and the Treasury were suspended by the Government, and an embargo was placed on gold exports. Steps were taken to withdraw from circulation all gold coin and gold certificates and to prohibit the private ownership of all gold coin except for numismatic purposes. Public Law 93–373, 14 Aug. 1974, amended the Par Value Modification Act so as to provide for the termination of all governmental restrictions on private ownership of gold, including gold coins, no later than 31 Dec. 1974.

Currency in the USA for many years has comprised several varieties. Prior to May 1933 the legal tender qualities of the classes varied, but in that month all types of currency were made equally legal tender. Under the Coinage Act of 1965, all coins and currencies of the USA, regardless of when coined or issued, are legal tender for all debts, public and private.

Only two of the eight kinds of notes outstanding are now significant: Federal Reserve notes in denominations of $1, $2, $5, $10, $20, $50 and $100; and US notes in denominations of $100. The issue of (a) $500, $1,000, $5,000 and $10,000 Federal Reserve notes; of (b) silver certificates, and of (c) $5 and $2 US notes have been discontinued, although they are still in general circulation. The following issues were stopped many years ago and are in process of retirement: (1) Federal Reserve Bank notes; (2) National Bank notes; (3) Treasury notes of 1890; (4) fractional currency.

Federal Reserve notes are obligations of the USA and a first lien on the assets of the Federal Reserve Banks, through which they are issued. Each of the 12 banks issues them against the security of an equal volume of collateral.

Gold coins (of the old weight and fineness) were $20, $10, $5 and $2½ pieces called *double eagles, eagles, half-eagles* and *quarter-eagles*. The old eagle weighed 258 grains or 16·7181 grammes 0·900 fine, and therefore contained 232·2 grains or 15·0463 grammes of fine gold. Except for collector's holdings, these are no longer in circulation. The stock of gold bullion held by the Treasury on 31 Oct. 1978 was 276·1m. fine oz., valued at $11,700m.; stock of silver bullion was 39·2m. fine oz. (excluding 139·5m. fine oz. held for defence stockpile). Estimated stock of domestic coin on 30 Sept. 1978 was $10,355m., of which $482m. were standard silver dollars and the remainder silver and other subsidiary coin.

The silver dollar weighs 412·5 grains or 26·7296 grammes 0·900 fine, and contains 371·25 grains or 24·0566 grammes of fine silver. Subsidiary, 0·900 fine, silver coins contain 347·22 grains of fine silver per dollar. These are the half-dollar, quarter-dollar and dime (one-tenth). Minor coins currently issued are the cupro-nickel 5-cent piece and the bronze 1-cent piece. Pursuant to the Coinage Act of 1965, Congress authorized the minting and issuance of new silver clad half-dollars containing 40% silver and cupro-nickel quarter-dollars and dimes containing no silver. In an amendment to the Coinage Act enacted on 31 Dec. 1970, Congress provided that all coins minted thereafter, including dollar and half-dollar coins, be made of cupro-nickel composition. However, a provision in the 1970 law permitted the coining of 1·500 inch dollar coins containing 40% silver. These dollar coins, which bear the likeness of the late President Eisenhower, are sold at premium price to coin collectors. In Oct. 1978 there was authorization of a new dollar bearing the likeness of suffragette Susan B. Anthony. The new dollars, which are 1·043 inches in diameter and weigh 8·1 grammes, replace the cupro-nickel Eisenhower dollars.

Banking. On 31 Dec. 1979 there were 15,171 domestic banks doing a general deposit business with the public and having aggregate deposits of $1,241,596m. Of these,

4,448 with deposits of $594,970m. were national banks operating under charters granted by the federal government; the remaining banks, including trust companies and savings banks, were organized under the laws of the various states. Of the total number, 5,425 were members of the Federal Reserve System, namely, all the 4,448 national banks and 977 state banks admitted to membership.

The Federal Reserve System, established under an Act of 1913, comprises the Board of 7 Governors, the 12 regional Federal Reserve Banks with their 25 branches, the Federal Open Market Committee and the Federal Advisory Council. The 7 members of the Board of Governors are appointed by the President by and with the consent of the Senate. Each Governor is appointed to a full term of 14 years or an unexpired portion of a term, one term expiring every 2 years. No two may come from the same Federal Reserve District. The Board supervises the Reserve Banks and the issue and retirement of Federal Reserve notes; it designates 3 of the 9 directors of each Reserve Bank one of whom is designated Chairman; it passes on the admission of state banks to the System and has power to correct unsound conditions in State member banks or violations of banking law by them, including, if necessary, disciplinary action to remove officers and directors for unsafe or unsound banking practices or for continuous violations of banking laws; it also authorizes State member bank branches and approves mergers and consolidations if the acquiring, assuming or resulting bank is to be a State member; and it has power to control the expansion of bank holding companies and to require divestment of certain non-banking interests. The 12 members of the Federal Open Market Committee include the 7 members of the Board of Governors and 5 of the 12 Federal Reserve Bank presidents. The latter serve 1-year terms on the Committee in rotation except for the President of the Federal Reserve Bank of New York, who is a permanent member. The Federal Open Market Committee influences credit market conditions, money and bank credit, by buying or selling US Government securities; and it also supervises System operations in foreign currencies for the purpose of helping to safeguard the value of the dollar in international exchange markets and facilitating co-operation and efficiency in the international monetary system. The Board also influences credit conditions through powers to set member-bank reserve requirements, to approve discount rates at Federal Reserve Banks, and to fix margin requirements on stock-market credit.

The 12 Reserve Banks (one for each district) implement Federal Reserve policies, chiefly through their dealings with member banks, which, although outnumbered by non-member banks, hold about 73% of the country's total commercial banking deposits. The Reserve Banks hold bank reserves, advance funds to member banks, issue Federal Reserve notes, which are the principal form of currency in the US, act as fiscal agent for the Government and afford nation-wide cheque-clearing and fund transfer arrangements. They may issue notes, fully secured; discount paper for member banks; increase or reduce the country's supply of reserve funds by buying or selling Government securities and other obligations at the direction of the Federal Open Market Committee. Their capital stock is held by the member banks, but it carries no voting rights except in the election of directors.

Every member bank is required to subscribe to stock in the Reserve Bank of its district in an amount equal to 6% of its paid-up capital and surplus. Only one-half of the par value of the stock is paid in, the other half remaining subject to call by the Board of Governors. However, no call has been made for the second half of the subscription. The reserve balances which member banks must carry with Reserve Banks are based on the volume of their net demand and time deposits. The Board of Governors has the power to alter these requirements within limits. The Board of Governors also has authority to limit the rate of interest payable by member banks on time and savings deposits. Under provisions of the Defense Production Act of 1950 the Board of Governors prescribes regulations under which the Federal Reserve Banks act as fiscal agents of certain Government departments and agencies in guaranteeing loans made by banks and other private financing institutions to finance contracts for the procurement of materials or services which the guaranteeing agencies consider necessary for the national defence.

Under the Credit Control Act of 1969 the President is empowered to authorize the Board of Governors to institute selective credit controls when necessary to curb inflation.

Beginning in 1968, the Congress passed a number of consumer credit protection acts, the first of which was the Truth in Lending Act (and including the Equal Credit Opportunity Act), Home Mortgage Disclosure Act, Consumer Leasing Act and the Fair Credit Billing Act, for which it has directed the Board to write implementing regulations and assume partial enforcement responsibility. To manage these responsibilities the Board has established a Consumers Affairs Division. To assist it, the Board consults with a Consumer Advisory Council, established by the Congress as a statutory part of the Federal Reserve System.

Another statutory body, the Federal Advisory Council, consists of 12 members (one from each district); it meets in Washington four times a year (or oftener) to advise the Board of Governors on general business and financial conditions.

Banks which participate in the federal deposit insurance fund have their deposits insured against loss up to $40,000 for each depositor. The fund is administered by the Federal Deposit Insurance Corporation established in 1933; it obtains resources through annual assessments on participating banks.

All members of the Federal Reserve System are required to insure their deposits through the Corporation, and non-member banks may apply and qualify for insurance. On 31 Dec. 1979, 14,351 commercial banks with deposits of $1,085,739m. were members of the insurance fund. This insurance also covered 324 mutual savings banks with deposits of $132,338m. There were 496 uninsured banks comprising 357 commercial banks and trust companies and 139 mutual savings banks with deposits of $23,519m. (in 1975 this figure included mutual savings banks only).

There are also banks which operate solely in the field of agricultural credits under the Farm Credit Administration; Federal Home Loan Banks makes advances to financial associations and institutions upon the security of home mortgages.

US Board of Governors of the Federal Reserve System. *The Federal Reserve System Purposes and Functions.* 6th ed., 1974.—*Federal Reserve Bulletin.* Monthly.—*Annual Report.—Annual Statistical Digest.—The Federal Reserve Act, As Amended Through 1978*

Beckhart, B. H., *Federal Reserve System.* New York, 1972

Chandler, L. V., *Economics of Money and Banking.* 7th ed. New York, 1977

Clifford, A. J., *The Independence of the Federal Reserve System.* Philadelphia, 1965

Friedman and Swartz, *A Monetary History of the United States,* 1867–1960, National Bureau of Economic Research, New York, 1963

Horovitz, P. M., *Monetary Policy and the Financial System.* 4th ed. Englewood Cliffs, 1979

Maisel, S. J., *Managing the Dollar.* New York, 1973

Myers, M. G., *A Financial History of the United States.* Columbia Univ. Press, 1970

Timberlake, R. H., *The Origins of Central Banking in the United States.* Cambridge, Massachusetts, 1978

Young, R. A., *Instruments of Monetary Policy in the United States; the Role of the Federal Reserve System.* Washington, 1973

Weights and Measures. British weights and measures are usually employed, but the old Winchester bushel and wine gallon are used instead of the new or Imperial standards: *Wine gallon* = 0·83268 Imperial gallon; *Bushel* = 0·9690 Imperial bushel. Instead of the British cwt of 112 lb., one of 100 lb. is used; the *short* or *net ton* contains 2,000 lb.; the *long* or *gross ton*, 2,240 lb.

ENERGY AND NATURAL RESOURCES

Minerals. Total value of non-fuel minerals produced in US (including Alaska and Hawaii) in 1979 was estimated at $23,966m. ($19,821m. in 1978). Details are given in the following tables.

Production of metallic minerals (long tons, 2,240 lb.; short tons, 2,000 lb.):

	1978		1979	
Metallic minerals	*Quantity*	*Value ($1,000)*	*Quantity*	*Value ($1,000)*
Bauxite (dried equiv.) tonnes	1,669,000	23,186	1,821,000	24,875
Copper (recoverable content), tonnes	1,357,579	1,990,323	1,441,148	2,955,737
Gold (recoverable content), troy oz.	998,832	193,325	919,783	282,833
Iron ore (usable),[1] 1,000 long tons, gross	82,826	2,387,965	86,130	2,811,574
Lead (recoverable content), tonnes	529,661	393,516	525,569	609,929

[1] Excluding by-product iron sinter.

	1978		1979	
		Value		*Value*
Metallic minerals (contd.)	*Quantity*	*($1,000)*	*Quantity*	*($1,000)*
Molybdenum (content of concentrate), 1,000 lb.	130,694	607,950	143,504	871,067
Silver (recoverable content), 1,000 troy oz.	39,385	212,681	38,055	422,032
Zinc (recoverable content), tonnes	302,669	206,854	267,341	219,841
Other metals	—	979,724	—	318,805
Total metals	—	6,296,000	—	8,517,000

The two world wars and record levels of industrial production have hastened the depletion of once abundant supplies of metal and US is increasingly an importer. US is wholly or almost wholly dependent upon imports for industrial diamonds, bauxite, tin, chromite, nickel, strategic-grade mica and long-fibre asbestos; it imports the bulk of its tantalum, platinum, manganese, mercury, tungsten, cobalt and flake graphite, and substantial quantities of antimony, cadmium, arsenic, fluorspar, zinc, gypsum and bismuth.

In 1977 precious metals were mined mainly in Idaho, Arizona, Colorado, Utah, Montana and Missouri (in order of combined output of gold and silver). US output of gold (troy oz.), 1930–39, 31,453,370; 1940–49, 24,171,646; 1950–59, 18,817,241; total 1792–1970, 316,620,436. Output of silver (troy oz.), 1930–39, 466,412,499; 1940–49, 434,656,631; 1950–59, 374,055,521; total 1792–1970, 4,701,429,507.

Statistics of important non-metallic minerals and mineral fuels are:

	1978		1979	
		Value		*Value*
Non-metallic minerals	*Quantity*	*($1,000)*	*Quantity*	*($1,000)*
Boron minerals, short tons	1,554,000	279,927	1,590,000	310,211
Cement:				
Portland, 1,000 short tons	80,010	3,239,580	78,978	3,650,436
Masonry, 1,000 short tons	4,123	208,566	3,748	204,797
Clays, 1,000 short tons	56,822	717,274	54,689	846,089
Gypsum, 1,000 short tons	14,891	92,726	14,630	99,868
Lime, 1,000 short tons	20,443	749,667	20,945	862,459
Phosphate rock, 1,000 tonnes	50,037	928,820	51,611	1,045,655
Potassium salts, 1,000 tonnes (K_2O equivalent)	2,307	226,468	2,388	279,199
Salt (common), 1,000 short tons	42,869	499,345	45,793	538,352
Sand and gravel, 1,000 short tons	996,200	2,302,000	979,000	2,427,000
Stone, 1,000 short tons	1,050,960	2,885,689	1,098,617	3,398,968
Sulphur (Frasch-process), 1,000 tonnes	5,736	279,918	7,507	449,433
Other non-metallic minerals	—	1,115,472	—	1,336,371
Total non-metallic minerals	—	13,525,000	—	15,449,000

Mineral fuels	1977		1978	
Coal: Bitum. and lignite, 1,000 short tons	678,685	13,189,481	...	...
Pennsylv. anthracite,[1] 1,000 short tons	6,228	209,234	...	...
Gas: Natural gas,[2] 1m. cu. ft	19,952,438	11,571,776	20,025,463	15,825,954
Natural gasoline and cycle products, 1,000 bbls of 42 gallons } L.P. gases, 1,000 bbls of 42 gallons	587,045	3,284,089	590,455	4,047,473
Petroleum (crude), 1,000 bbls of 42 gallons	2,976,180	24,229,540	3,009,265	25,790,732

[1] Includes a small quantity of anthracite mined in states other than Pennsylvania.
[2] Value at wells.

Minerals Yearbook. Bureau of Mines. Washington, D.C. Annual from 1932–33; containing the *Mineral Resources of the United States* series (1866–1931); from 1963 in 3 vols. (*Metals, Minerals, Fuels; Area Reports, Domestic; and Area Reports, International*)

Agriculture. Agriculture in the USA is characterized by its ability to adapt to widely varying conditions, and still produce an abundance and variety of agricultural products. From colonial times to about 1920 the major increases in farm production were brought about by adding to the number of farms and the amount of land under cultivation. During this period nearly 320m. acres of virgin forest were converted to crop land or pasture, and extensive areas of grass lands were ploughed. Improvident use of soil and water resources was evident in many areas.

During the next 20 years the number of farms reached a plateau of about 6·5m., and the acreage planted to crops held relatively stable around 330m. acres. The major source of increase in farm output arose from the substitution of power-driven machines for horses and mules. Greater emphasis was placed on development and improvement of land, and the need for conservation of basic agricultural resources was recognized. A successful conservation programme, highly co-ordinated and on a national scale—to prevent further erosion, to restore the native fertility of damaged land and to adjust land uses to production capabilities and needs—has been in operation since early in the 1930s.

Following the Second World War the uptrend in farm output has been greatly accelerated by increased production per acre and per farm animal. These increases are associated with a higher degree of mechanization; greater use of lime and fertilizer; improved varieties, including hybrid maize and grain sorghums; more effective control of insects and disease; improved strains of livestock and poultry; and wider use of good husbandry practices, such as nutritionally balanced feeds, use of superior sites and better housing. During this period land included in farms decreased slowly, crop land harvested declined somewhat more rapidly, but the number of farms declined sharply.

Some significant changes during these transitions are:

All land in farms totalled less than 500m. acres in 1870, rose to a peak of over 1,200m. acres in the 1950s and declined to 1,088m. acres in 1974, even with the addition of the new States of Alaska and Hawaii in 1960. The number of farms declined from 6·35m. in 1940 to 2·68m. in 1978, as the acreage size of farms doubled. The average size of farms in 1978 was 400 acres, but ranged from 3 to many thousand acres. In 1969, 162,111 farms (170,706 in 1974) were 10 acres or less; 473,465 (453,187), 10–49 acres; 1,001,706 (852,800), 50–179 acres; 726,363 (612,176), 180–499 acres; 215,659 (205,970), 500–999 acres; 91,039 (92,653), 1,000–1,999 acres; 59,907 (62,634) over 2,000 acres.

Farms operated by owners or part-owners, 1974, were 2,052,000 (89% of all farms), by all tenants, 262,000 (11%). The proportion of farms operated by tenants is declining, and currently is three-tenths of the peak recorded in 1930. The average size of farms in 1974 was 252 acres for full-owners, 852 acres for part-owners and 467 acres for tenants. Farms with white operators numbered 1,631,926, and non-white operators 30,616. A higher proportion of non-white operators were tenants and operated a significantly smaller acreage than white operators.

Farms also vary widely in degree of specialization and output. About 60% of all farms received over half their farm income from a single enterprise, such as dairying, or from a single crop, such as cotton, wheat, tobacco or fruit. In 1978 (with 1960 figures in parentheses) large-scale, highly mechanized farms with sales of agricultural products totalling over $20,000 per farm made up 33·7% (9%) of all farms and accounted for 91·2% (51%) of the value of farm products sold. Farms selling between $2,500 and $20,000 worth of products per farm were 32% (45%) of all farms and sold 8% (43%) of all sales. The remaining 34·3% (46%) of farms sold less than $1,100 worth of products per farm in 1978, 0·9% (6%) of total sales. Many farms in this lowest sales class are called part-time or part-retirement farms. Operators in every sales category received off-farm income, but operators selling less than $2,500 per year received 90·9% of their average income of $18,943 from non-farm sources.

A century ago three-quarters of the total US population was rural, and practically all rural people lived on farms. In April 1978 less than 30% of the population was rural, and the 8m. farm residents comprised less than 4% of the total population.

Hired farm workers in 1978 averaged about 1·3m., and farm family workers, including operators, about 2·7m. In 1950 there were nearly 10m. farm workers. At that time each farm worker supplied farm products for 15 people; in 1974, 56 people, and in 1977, 59 people.

Cash receipts from farm marketings and government payments (in $1m.):

	Crops	Livestock and livestock products	Government payments	Total
1932	1,996	2,752	—	4,748
1945	9,655	12,008	742	22,405
1950	12,356	16,105	283	28,744
1960	15,259	18,989	702	34,950
1970	20,976	29,563	3,717	54,256
1975	45,150	43,059	807	89,016
1976	48,349	46,152	734	95,235
1977	48,519	47,565	1,819	97,903
1978	53,482	59,038	3,000	115,520
1979	62,820	68,639	1,400	132,859

Realized gross farm income (including government payments), in $1m., was 108,535 in 1977, compared with 125,976 in 1978; net income of farm operators, 19,759 (27,880). Farm-mortgage debt, on 1 Jan. 1979, was estimated at $72,232m.

US agricultural exports, fiscal year, totalled: 1970–71, $7,758m.; 1971–72, $8,049m.; 1972–73, $12,901m.; 1973–74, $21,321m.; 1974–75, $21,999m.; 1975–76, $21,884m.; 1976–77, $22,996m.; 1977–78, $23,671.

Total area of farm land under irrigation in 1969 was 39,121,693 acres (257,147 farms); in 1974: 40,218,000 acres and 239,000 farms.

Federal income taxes paid by farm people was $15m. in 1941, $1,365m. in 1948, $1,182m. in 1967, $3,434m. in 1971, $5,309m. in 1972, $8,364m. in 1973 and $8,277m. in 1974. Total taxes levied on farm real estate were $2,463m. in 1972, $2,514m. in 1973, $2,652m. in 1974, $2,855 in 1975, $3,098 in 1976 and $3,243 in 1977.

According to census returns and estimates of the Economic Research Service, the acreage and specified values of farms has been as follows (area in 1,000 acres; value in $1,000):

	Farm area[1]	Crop land available for crops	Value, land, bldgs, machinery, livestock	Value of products sold in preceding year
1910	878,798	432,000	41,089,000	...
1930	986,771	480,000	57,815,000	9,609,924
1940	1,060,852	467,000	41,829,000	6,681,581
1950	1,158,566	478,000	99,366,000	22,051,129
1959	1,125,508	448,100	164,200,000	30,492,721
1969	1,063,346	459,048	206,751,000	44,519,658
1974	1,017,030	465,084	414,345,000	89,675,000

[1] Acreages are for the preceding year except for 1959.

The areas and production of the principal crops for 3 years were:

	1977 Harvested 1,000 acres	1977 Production 1,000 bu.	1977 Yield per acre bu.	1978 Harvested 1,000 acres	1978 Production 1,000 bu.	1978 Yield per acre bu.	1979 Harvested 1,000 acres	1979 Production 1,000 bu.	1979 Yield per acre bu.
Corn for grain	70,872	6,425,457	90·7	69,970	7,081,849	101·2	70,984	7,763,771	109·4
Oats	13,452	750,901	55·8	11,531	601,477	52·2	9,831	534,386	54·4
Barley	9,564	420,159	43·9	9,233	447,008	48·4	7,468	378,067	50·6
All wheat	66,461	2,036,318	30·6	56,839	1,798,712	31·6	62,600	2,141,732	34·2
Rice (cwt)	2,249	99,223	4,412	3,059	137,805	4,505	2,869	131,574	4,586
Soybeans for beans	57,612	1,761,755	30·6	63,003	1,842,647	29·2	70,524	2,267,589	32·2
Flaxseed	1,314	15,105	11·5	860	10,921	12·7	1,018	13,539	13·3
Cotton lint (bale)	13,275	14,389	520	12,370	10,856	421	12,816	14,629	548
Potatoes (cwt)	1,359	354,576	261	1,368	360,467	263	1,276	342,958	269
Tobacco (lb.)	957·5	1,912,114	1,997	949·1	2,026,124	2,135	826·3	1,526,682	1,848

Wheat. The chief wheat-growing states (1978) were (estimated yield in 1,000 bu.): Kansas, 306,000; N. Dakota, 286,065; Montana, 146,050; Oklahoma, 145,800; Washington, 133,980; Minnesota, 93,225; Nebraska, 81,600; Idaho, 74,730; S. Dakota, 66,000; Colorado, 57,268; Texas, 54,000; Oregon, 51,925.

Cotton. Leading production, 1978, by state (in 1,000 bales, 480 lb. net weight) was: Texas, 3,792; California, 1,940; Mississippi, 1,378; Arizona, 1,068; Arkansas, 660; Louisiana, 478; Oklahoma, 355; Alabama, 291; Tennessee, 235; Missouri, 188.

Tobacco. Output (1,000 lb.) of the chief tobacco-growing states (92% of the crop) was, in 1978: N. Carolina, 849,431; Kentucky, 469,658; S. Carolina, 150,520; Tennessee, 142,099; Virginia, 135,157; Georgia, 125,660.

Fruit. A wide variety of fruits are grown; the chief products are as follows:

| | 1976 | | 1977 | | 1978[1] | |
	Production 1,000 tons	Value $1,000	Production 1,000 tons	Value $1,000	Production 1,000 tons	Value $1,000
Apples	3,237	586,577	3,336	698,890	3,817	779,369
Citrus Fruit	14,788	...	15,242	...	14,212	...
Grapes	4,398	635,570	4,298	834,794	4,567	997,213

[1] At 1 Dec.

Dairy produce. In 1977, production of milk was 122,698m. lbs.; milkfat, 4,483m. lbs.; cheese, 3,358,535,000 lbs.; butter, 1,085,595,000 lbs.; eggs, 64,600m.

Livestock. Number of farm animals (in 1,000) on farms on 1 Jan.:

	1977	1978	1979
Cattle of all kinds	122,810	116,375	110,864
Sheep and lambs	12,786	12,348	12,224
Swine (hogs and pigs)[1]	54,934	52,539	59,860

[1] At 1 Dec.

The value (in $1,000) was:

	1977	1978	1979
Cattle of all kinds	25,252,000	27,055,000	44,661,000
Sheep and lambs	541,000	636,000	876,000
Swine (hogs and pigs)	2,583,000	3,575,000	4,986,000

Total value of livestock, excluding poultry and, from 1961, horses and mules (in $1m.) on farms in the USA on 1 Jan. was: 1930, 6,061; 1933 (low point of the agricultural depression), 2,733; 1970, 22,886; 1974, 45,836; 1975, 24,581; 1976, 29,483; 1977, 29,053; 1978, 31,952; 1979, 51,256.

In 1977 the production of shorn wool was 107·2m. lb. from 13·2m. sheep (average 1970–74, 320m. lb. from 18·2m. sheep); of pulled wool, 1·7m. lb. (1970–74, 10·1m. lb.).

Fact Book of US Agriculture. US Dept. of Agriculture, 1976
Cochrane, W. W., *The City Man's Guide to the Farm Problem.* Minneapolis, 1965
Higbee, E. C., *American Agriculture: Geography, Resources, Conservation.* New York, 1958
Paarlberg, D., *American Farm Policy.* New York, 1964
Tweeton, L., *Foundations of Farm Policy.* Lincoln, 1970
Wilcox, W. W., *Economics of American Agriculture.* 2nd ed. New York, 1960

Forestry. In 1977 the US forest lands, including Alaska and Hawaii, capable of producing timber for commercial use, covered 482,485,900 acres (more than one-fifth of the land area), classified as follows: Saw-timber stands, 215,435,700 acres; pole timber stands, 135,609,900 acres; seedling and sapling stands, 115,032,100 acres; non-stocked and other areas, 16,408,200 acres. Ownership of commercial forest land is distributed as follows: Federal government, 99,410,400 acres; state, county, municipal and Indian, 36,311,200 acres; privately owned, 346,764,300 acres, including 115,777,100 acres on farms. Of the saw-timber stand (2,578,940m. bd ft) Douglas fir constitutes 514,317; Southern yellow pine, 321,563; Western yellow (ponderosa and jeffrey) pine, 192,638; other softwoods, 956,890; hardwoods, 593,532. In 1976 growing stock timber removals amounted to 14,229,023,000 cu. ft compared to net annual growth of about 21,664,316,000 cu. ft. Saw-timber removals amounted to 65,176,618,000 bd ft against an annual growth of 74,620,832,000 bd ft. The net area of the 154 national forests and other areas in USA and Puerto Rico administered by the US Forest Service, including commercial and non-commercial forest land, was on 30 Sept. 1979, 187,450,840 acres.

Fire takes a heavy annual toll in the forest; total area burned over in 1979 was 2,986,826 acres, of which 21% was commercial forest; 1,463,745,000 acres of land are now under organized fire-protection service. The area planted or seeded in forest and wind barrier nursery stock in the year ending 30 Sept. 1978 was 2,088,568 acres, an increase of 110,398 acres over the previous year.

Forest Statistics of the United States. Forest Service, US Dept. of Agriculture, 1977
Land Areas of National Forest System. Forest Service, US Dept. of agriculture, 1981
Report of the Forest Service, 1977

Fisheries. The main fishing industries are in California (anchovy, tuna and sole); Alaska (notably salmon); Washington (salmon and halibut); Florida (the main source of turtles and sponges); Massachusetts, Maine, North Carolina and Oregon. Total catch, 1975, 5,350m. lb. tons valued at $1,353m.

Tennessee Valley Authority. Established by Act of Congress, 1933, the TVA is a multiple-purpose federal agency which carries out its duties in an area embracing some 41,000 sq. miles, in 125 counties (aggregate population, about 7·2m.) in the 7 Tennessee River Valley states: Tennessee, Kentucky, Mississippi, Alabama, North Carolina, Georgia and Virginia. In addition, 76 counties outside the Valley are served by TVA power distributors. Its 3 directors are appointed by the President, with the consent of the Senate; headquarters are in Knoxville, Tenn. There were 48,800 employees in Aug. 1979.

Under the Act its chief duties are flood control; the maintenance of navigation; generation, transmission and sale of electric power; the development and production of fertilizers and munitions; assistance in forestry development; and related activities in a single unified approach to resource development. There are 59 dams and reservoirs (29 built by TVA) operating in TVA's integrated water control system. A navigable channel 650 miles long, connecting with the American system of inland waterways, in 1977 carried 26·6m. tons of traffic in iron and steel products, grains, coal, petroleum, chemicals and other products. Flood damages averted by river control exceed $1,900m.

TVA supplies electric power to 160 local distribution systems serving 2·7m. customers in an area of 80,000 sq. miles. The TVA power system originated with the water-power development of the Tennessee River, but has become predominantly a coal-fired system as power requirements have outgrown the region's hydro-electric potential. In fiscal year 1978 the TVA system generated 117,370m. kwh.; the same region used 1,500m. kwh. in 1933 before TVA operations began. Installed capacity, 1978, was about 28·3m. kw., with another 19·6m. kw. under construction in nuclear and pumped-storage installations. Residential consumers served by TVA power distributors used an average of 16,190 kwh. in fiscal year 1978 at an average rate of about 2·7 cents per kwh.; US averages were 8,849 kwh. and about 4 cents.

Another activity is experimentation in the development and manufacture of mineral fertilizers accompanied by programmes designed to encourage proper fertilizer use in all parts of the country. The TVA works closely with other federal agencies, and with state and local authorities in combating soil erosion, improving forest resources, improving agriculture and to the development of local industries based on natural resources.

In the depression year, 1933, the average *per capita* income in the Valley region was $168 compared with the national average of $375; in 1977 the region's *per capita* income had multiplied over 33 times to $5,630 while the national average had increased 18 times.

Other TVA activities include demonstration of effective ways of reclaiming strip-mined areas, development of new and improved methods of controlling air and water pollution, and a leading role in the US programme of energy development and conservation.

Power operations are financially self-supporting from revenues. In fiscal year 1978 power revenues were $2,350·1m. and net income $216·6m. Power facilities are financed from revenues and the sale of revenue bonds and notes, and TVA is repaying appropriations previously invested in power facilities. In fiscal year 1978 TVA paid the US Treasury $20m. as a capital repayment and $61·7m. in dividends on the remaining appropriation investment, making a total of $1,505m. to date paid to the Treasury from power revenues. Other TVA resource development programmes continue to be financed primarily from appropriations, which amounted to $138m. in fiscal year 1978.

Annual Report of the TVA. Knoxville, 1934 to date
Clapp, G. R., *The TVA; An Approach to the Development of a Region.* Univ. of Chicago Press, 1955
Lilienthal, D. E., *TVA; Democracy on the March.* 20th Anniversary ed. New York and London, 1953
Munger, M. E., *Valley of Vision: The TVA Years.* New York, 1969
Owen, M., *The Tennessee Valley Authority.* New York, 1973
Tennessee Valley Authority. *Director of TVA Environment Programs, 1976.—Short History of the TVA.* Knoxville, Tennessee, 1973.—*TVA: The First Twenty Years* (ed. R. C. Martin), Univ. of Tennessee Press, 1956

INDUSTRY AND TRADE

Industry. The following table presents industry statistics of manufactures as reported at various censuses from 1909 to 1977 and from the Annual Survey of Manufactures for years in which no census was taken. The figures for 1958 to 1977 include data for some establishments previously classified as non-manufacturing. The figures for 1939, but not for earlier years, have been revised to exclude data for establishments classified as non-manufacturing in 1954. The figures for 1909–33 were previously revised by the deduction of data for industries excluded from manufacturing during that period.

The statistics for 1958, 1963, 1967, 1972 and 1977 relate to all establishments employing 1 or more persons anytime during the year; for 1950, 1956–57, 1959–62, 1964–66 and 1968–74 on a representative sample of manufacturing establishments of 1 or more employees; for 1929 through 1939, those reporting products valued at $5,000 or more; and for 1909 and 1919, those reporting products valued at $500 or more. These differences in the minimum size of establishments included in the census affect only very slightly the year-to-year comparability of the figures.

The annual Surveys of Manufactures carry forward the key measures of manufacturing activity which are covered in detail by the Census of Manufactures. The estimate for 1950 is based on reports for approximately 45,000 plants out of a total of more than 260,000 operating manufacturing establishments; those for 1956–57 on about 50,000, and those for 1959–62, 1964–66 and 1968–74 on about 60,000 out of about 300,000. Included are all large plants and representative samples of the much more numerous small plants. The large plants in the surveys account for approximately two-thirds of the total employment in operating manufacturing establishments in the US.

	Number of establishments	Production workers (average for year)	Production workers' wages total ($1,000)	Value added by manufacture[1] ($1,000)
1909	264,810	6,261,736	3,205,213	8,160,075
1919	270,231	8,464,916	9,664,009	23,841,624
1929	206,663	8,369,705	10,884,919	30,591,435
1933	139,325	5,787,611	4,940,146	14,007,540
1939	173,802	7,808,205	8,997,515	24,487,304
1950	260,000	11,778,803	34,600,025	89,749,765
1960	...	12,209,514	55,555,452	163,998,531
1961	...	11,778,518	54,764,619	164,291,080
1962	...	12,126,500	59,134,100	179,071,100
1963	306,617	12,232,041	62,093,601	192,103,102
1964	...	12,403,300	65,838,900	206,193,600
1965	...	13,076,000	71,361,500	226,939,900
1966	...	13,826,500	78,256,400	250,880,100
1967	305,680	13,955,300	81,393,600	261,983,800
1968	...	14,042,500	87,485,400	285,016,200
1969	...	14,359,600	93,459,600	304,308,200
1970	...	13,258,000	91,609,000	300,227,600
1971	...	12,874,900	93,063,200	314,151,700
1972	320,710	13,527,900	105,501,800	353,994,000
1973	...	14,233,100	118,332,300	405,623,500
1974	...	13,970,900	124,983,200	452,468,400
1975	...	12,567,900	121,427,200	442,485,800
1976	...	13,051,200	137,564,600	511,470,900
1977	359,928	13,690,800	157,163,600	585,096,100

[1] For the period 1954–67 value added represents adjusted value added and for earlier years unadjusted value added. Unadjusted value is obtained by subtracting cost of materials, supplies and containers, fuel, electricity and contract work from the value of shipments for products manufactured plus receipts for services rendered. Adjusted value added also takes into account value added by merchandizing operations plus net change in finished goods and work-in-process inventories between the beginning and end of the year.

For comparison of broad types of manufacturing, the industries covered by the Census of Manufactures have been divided into 20 general groups according to the

Standard Industrial Classification. This was revised in 1972; 1967 figures are not therefore strictly comparable.

Code No.	Industry group	Census year	Production workers (average for year)	Production workers' wages, total ($1,000)	Value added by manufacture[1] ($1,000)
20.	Food and kindred products	1967	1,121,700	6,062,600	26,620,900
		1972	1,085,400	8,007,400	35,616,600
		1977	1,065,600	11,740,000	56,232,800
21.	Tobacco manufactures	1967	66,200	303,600	2,032,000
		1972	57,400	400,900	2,637,200
		1977	50,400	570,600	4,343,500
22.	Textile mill products	1967	828,200	3,556,600	8,153,000
		1972	836,200	4,807,200	11,718,000
		1977	759,400	6,140,400	15,965,200
23.	Apparel and related products	1967	1,200,000	4,340,600	10,064,400
		1972	1,198,300	5,461,100	13,487,500
		1977	1,151,800	7,223,500	19,448,100
24.	Lumber and wood products	1967	495,700	2,290,600	4,973,400
		1972	601,100	3,932,900	10,309,400
		1977	588,300	5,778,800	16,168,000
25.	Furniture and fixtures	1967	357,500	1,653,700	4,169,500
		1972	383,800	2,321,300	6,089,500
		1977	379,500	3,158,100	8,797,500
26.	Paper and allied products	1967	507,500	3,205,500	9,756,300
		1972	498,800	4,320,200	13,064,100
		1977	484,100	6,306,200	21,718,800
27.	Printing and publishing	1967	631,600	4,011,300	14,355,100
		1972	637,400	5,459,300	20,197,100
		1977	614,400	7,277,600	31,543,600
28.	Chemical and allied products	1967	541,400	3,555,200	23,550,100
		1972	525,000	4,753,900	32,413,900
		1977	540,500	7,412,000	56,522,500
29.	Petroleum and coal products	1967	99,400	786,400	5,425,800
		1972	97,900	1,064,000	5,793,100
		1977	101,800	1,776,700	16,223,700
30.	Rubber and plastics products, not elsewhere classified[2]	1967	410,100	2,312,500	6,799,500
		1972	486,800	3,605,000	11,653,300
		1977	560,700	5,823,100	19,834,300
31.	Leather and leather products	1967	293,300	1,147,000	2,626,500
		1972	240,400	1,230,800	2,917,200
		1977	208,600	1,391,900	3,650,500
32.	Stone, clay and glass products	1967	469,300	2,784,100	8,333,400
		1972	492,600	4,037,300	12,586,500
		1977	477,200	5,692,900	18,800,100
33.	Primary and metal industries	1967	1,041,500	7,457,300	19,978,200
		1972	922,700	9,202,400	23,258,100
		1977	887,700	14,096,300	37,298,200
34.	Fabricated metal products[2]	1967	1,056,900	6,541,600	18,042,600
		1972	1,148,000	9,544,400	26,945,800
		1977	1,177,300	14,305,400	44,943,000
35.	Machinery (except electrical)	1967	1,349,000	9,236,100	27,836,400
		1972	1,266,900	11,358,600	37,562,900
		1977	1,407,300	18,266,400	67,406,000
36.	Electrical machinery[2]	1967	1,323,800	7,607,000	24,587,000
		1972	1,160,800	8,822,600	30,583,600
		1977	1,180,500	12,835,900	49,708,300
37.	Transportation equipment[2]	1967	1,336,500	9,918,200	28,173,900
		1972	1,246,200	12,848,600	39,799,400
		1977	1,280,800	20,232,700	64,166,400
38.	Instruments and related products[2]	1967	265,900	1,569,000	6,418,400
		1972	292,000	2,237,100	10,583,700
		1977	344,100	3,719,600	18,692,100
39.	Miscellaneous manufacturing	1967	344,400	1,552,500	4,599,400
		1972	350,200	2,086,700	6,777,000
		1977	333,000	2,724,100	10,197,700

For footnotes see opposite.

Iron and Steel: Output of the iron and steel industries (in net tons of 2,000 lb.), according to figures supplied by the American Iron and Steel Institute, was:

	Fur-naces in blast 31 Dec.	Pig-iron (including ferro-alloys)	Raw steel	Steel by method of production[1]			
				Open hearth	Bessemer	Electric[2]	Basic Oxygen
1932[3]	44	9,835,227	15,322,901	13,336,210	1,715,925	270,044	...
1939	195	35,677,097	52,798,714	48,409,800	3,358,916	1,029,067	...
1944[4]	218	62,866,198	89,641,600	80,363,953	5,039,923	4,237,699	...
1950	234	66,400,311	96,336,075	86,262,509	4,534,558	6,039,008	...
1960	114	68,566,384	99,281,601	86,367,506	1,189,196	8,378,743	3,346,156
1970	152	87,933,000	131,514,000	48,022,000	—	20,162,000	63,330,000
1977	179	83,082,000	125,333,000	20,043,000	—	27,882,000	77,408,000
1978	168	89,351,000	137,031,000	21,310,000	—	32,237,000	83,484,000
1979	...	89,011,000	136,341,000	19,158,000	—	33,927,000	83,256,000

[1] The sum of these 4 items should equal the total in the preceding column; any difference appearing is due to the very small production of crucible steel, omitted prior to 1950.
[2] Includes crucible production beginning 1950.
[3] Low point of the depression.
[4] Peak year of war production.

Wholesale price index of iron and steel (1967 = 100) was: 1950, 59·4; 1960, 96·4; 1970, 114·3; 1975, 197·2; 1976, 209·8; 1977, 229·9; 1978, 254·4; 1979, 280·4.

Leading producers of pig-iron in 1978 were: Indiana, 18·81m. net tons; Pennsylvania, 18·15m.; Ohio, 14·3m.; Illinois, 6·9m.

Consumption of ore, 1979, was 128·57m. net tons, of which blast-furnaces took 104·7m. tons; agglomerating plants, 22·79m. tons; and steel producing furnaces, 1,039,000 tons.

The iron and steel industry in 1979 employed 341,931 wage-earners (compared with 449,888 in 1960), who worked an average of 37·5 hours per week and earned an average of $12.55 per hour: total wages were $8,397m. and total salaries for 111,250 employees were $3,085m.

Annual Statistics Report. American Iron and Steel Institute
Adams, W. (ed.), *The Structure of American Industry.* 3rd ed. New York, 1961
Alderfer, E. B., and Michl, H. E., *Economics of American Industry.* 3rd ed. New York, 1957
Fuchs, V. R., *Changes in the Location of Manufacturing Since 1929.* Yale Univ. Press, 1962
Glover, J. G. (ed.), *The Development of American Industries.* 4th ed. New York, 1959
Resources for the Future. *Regions, Resources and Economic Growth.* Baltimore, 1960

Labour. The American trade unions comprise about 174 national and international unions plus a large number of small independent local or single-firm unions. In 1979 total membership was approximately 21·7m., including 1·5m. Canadian workers affiliated with American unions and under 120,000 others outside the USA. The American Federation of Labor (founded 1881 and taking its name in 1886) and the Congress of Industrial Organizations merged into one organization, named the AFL–CIO, in Dec. 1955, representing 17m. workers in 1978.

Unaffiliated or independent unions, inter-state in scope, including those organizing coalminers, teamsters and government employees and railroad workers, had an estimated total membership excluding all foreign members (1978) of about 4·5m. In addition, 34 professional and state employee associations represent approximately 2·6m. members for collective bargaining purposes. Together, unions affiliated with the AFL–CIO, unaffiliated unions and professional and state employee associations represented 22·7m. workers or 22·3% of the labour force in 1978.

The Labor–Management Relations (Taft–Hartley) Act, 1947, applicable to industries affecting inter-state commerce, prohibits the closed shop, but permits union shop arrangements except where forbidden by state laws. Statutes regulating, restricting or prohibiting closed shop or other types of union security agreements are

[1] Figures represent adjusted value added. For definitions see footnote to previous table, p.1409.
[2] Figures for 1967 are not comparable to 1972 due to revisions in the Standard Industrial Classification System.

in effect in 20 states which ban all types of union security agreements (Alabama, Arizona, Arkansas, Florida, Georgia, Iowa, Kansas, Louisiana, Mississippi, Nebraska, Nevada, North Carolina, North Dakota, South Carolina, South Dakota, Tennessee, Texas, Utah, Virginia and Wyoming). Colorado and Wisconsin ban all-union agreements unless a certain percentage of employees have voted for them; in Hawaii an all-union agreement may be entered into unless a majority of employees votes against it. Thirteen states have acts to prevent industrial disputes between public utilities and their employees by means of compulsory arbitration or seizure; however, a number of these laws have been declared unconstitutional in so far as industries in inter-state commerce are concerned. Laws to restrict or regulate picketing or other strike activities have been enacted in over half the states. About one-half of the states also prohibit certain types of strikes, as 'sit down', jurisdictional or sympathy strikes.

The Employee Retirement Income Security Act of 1974 protects the interests of workers and their beneficiaries who are entitled to benefits from employee pension and welfare plans. The law requires disclosure of plan provisions and financial information and establishes standards of conduct for trustees and administrators of welfare and pension plans. It provides funding, participation and vesting requirements for pension plans and makes termination insurance available for most pension plans. The Department of Labor and the Internal Revenue Service share administration of the law. The pension plan termination insurance programme is administered by the Pension Benefit Guaranty Corporation.

The law does not require a company to establish a welfare or pension plan. But it does provide that any employee not covered by a pension plan, other than Social Security, may put aside a certain amount of his income, tax-free, to take care of his retirement needs.

Minimum wage laws governing private employers are in operation in 45 jurisdictions: 41 states, the District of Columbia, Guam, Puerto Rico and the Virgin Islands have minimum wage laws and minimum wage rates. As of 1 Aug. 1978, all but one of the laws cover men, women and, usually, minors. The exception covers only women and minors. The minimum wage rate under federal law is $3.35 per hour for employees who are engaged in commerce, in the production of goods for commerce or in certain enterprises which are engaged in commerce as well as federal employees.

A total of 4,825 strikes and lockouts occurred in 1979, involving 1·7m. workers and 34·8m. idle days; the number of idle days was 0·15% of the year's total working time of all workers.

There are 3 federal agencies which provide formal machinery for the adjustment of labour disputes: (1) The Federal Mediation and Conciliation Service, now an independent agency, whose mediation services are available 'in any labor dispute in any industry affecting commerce'; under Executive Order 11491, as amended, to federal agencies and organizations of federal employees involved in negotiation disputes; and in state and local government collective bargaining disputes when adequate dispute resolution machinery is not available to the parties. Its aim is to prevent and minimize work stoppages. (2) The National Mediation Board (1934) provides much the same facilities for the railroad and air-transport industries pursuant to the Railway Labor Act. (3) The National Railroad Adjustment Board (1934) acts as a board of final appeal for grievances arising over the interpretation of existing collective agreements under the Railway Labor Act; its decisions are binding upon both sides and enforceable by the courts.

The National Labor Relations Act, as amended by the Labor–Management Relations (Taft–Hartley) Act, 1947 (see THE STATESMAN'S YEAR-BOOK, 1955, p. 617), was amended by the Labor–Management Reporting and Disclosure Act, 1959, and again amended in 1974. The 1959 Act requires extensive reporting and disclosure of certain financial and administrative practices of labour organizations, employers and labour relations consultants. In addition, certain powers are vested in the Secretary of Labor to prevent abuses in the administration of trusteeships by labour organizations, to provide minimum standards and procedures for the election of union officers and to establish rules prescribing minimum standards for determining the adequacy of union procedures for the removal of officers. Other provisions impose a fiduciary responsibility upon union officers and provide for the exclusion of those convicted of certain named felonies from office for specified periods; more stringently regulate secondary boycotts and banning of 'hot' cargo agreements; put limitations upon organizational and recognition picketing and permit States to assert jurisdiction over labour disputes where the National Labor Relations Board declines to act. The Act also contains a 'Bill of Rights' for union members (enforceable directly by them) dealing with such things as equal rights in the nomination and election of union officers, freedom of speech and assembly subject to reasonable union rules, and safeguards against improper disciplinary action.

The Census of Population (1 April 1970) showed that the total labour force was 82,048,781 (58·2% of those 16 years and over); the armed forces accounted for 1,997,735 and the civilian labour force for 80,051,046, of whom 76,553,599 were employed and 3,497,447—or 4·4%—were unemployed. The following table shows employment by industry group and sex and percentage distribution of the total:

Industry Group	Male	Female	Total	Percentage distribution
Employed (1,000 persons):	47,624	28,930	76,554	100·0
Agriculture, forestry and fisheries	2,521	320	2,841	3·7
Mining }	4,885	318	{ 631	0·8
Construction }			{ 4,572	6·0
Manufacturing:				
Durable goods	9,248	2,493	11,741	15·3
Non-durable (including not specified)	4,925	3,171	8,096	10·6
Transportation, communication and other public utilities	4,072	1,114	5,186	6·8
Wholesale and retail trade	9,039	6,334	15,373	20·1
Finance, insurance and real estate	1,925	1,913	3,838	5·0
Business and repair services	1,719	676	2,395	3·1
Personal services	1,007	2,530	3,537	4·6
Entertainment and recreation services	407	224	631	0·8
Professional and related services	4,954	8,557	13,511	17·6
Public administration	2,921	1,281	4,202	5·5

The Bureau of Labor Statistics estimated the average total labour force (including armed forces) during 1979 at 105m., of the civilian labour force (102·91m.), 6m. persons (6%) were unemployed; 3·3m. were working in agriculture and 94m. in non-agricultural industries. The Bureau estimated that an average of 21·06m. persons were employed in manufacturing, 20,269,000 in trade and 15·92m. in civilian government services.

Bureau of Labor Statistics, US Dept. of Labor. *Directory of National Unions and Employee Associations in the US.* 1979.—*Brief History of the American Labor Movement.* 1976.— *Analysis of Work Stoppages.* 1979.—*Employment and Earnings.* Monthly
A Guide to Basic Law and Procedures under the National Labor Relations Act, National Labor Relations Board, Washington, D.C., 1976
Commons, J. R. (ed.), *History of Labor in the United States.* 4 vols. New York, 1918–36
Hardman, J. B. S., and Neufeld, M. S. (ed.), *The House of Labor; Internal Operation of American Unions.* New York, 1951
Lebergott, S., *Manpower in Economic Growth: The American Record Since 1800.* New York and London, 1963
Millis, H. A., and Brown, E. C., *From the Wagner Act to Taft–Hartley.* Chicago, 1950
Peterson, F., *American Labor Unions.* Rev. ed. New York and London, 1963
Taft, P., *The Structure and Government of Labor Unions.* Harvard Univ. Press, 1954.— *Organized Labor in American History.* New York, 1964

Commerce. The subjoined table gives the total value of the imports and exports of merchandise by yearly average or by year (in $1m.):

	Exports Total	Exports US mdse.[1]	General imports		Exports Total	Exports US mdse.[1]	General imports
1946–50	11,829	11,673	6,659	1975	108,050	106,561	97,356
1951–55	15,333	15,196	10,832	1976	115,340	113,666	122,126
1956–60	19,204	19,029	13,650	1977	121,212	119,006	148,718
1961–65	24,006	24,707	17,659	1978	143,663	141,126	173,250
1970	43,224	42,590	39,952	1979	181,802	178,578	207,131

[1] Excludes re-exports.

For a description of how imports and exports are valued, see *Explanation of Statistics of Report FT990, Highlights of US Export and Import Trade*, Bureau of the Census, US Department of Commerce, Washington, D.C., 1946.

The 'most favoured nation' treatment in commerce between Great Britain and US was agreed to for 4 years by the treaty of 1815, was extended for 10 years by the treaty of 1818, and indefinitely (subject to 12 months' notice) by that of 1827.

Imports and exports of gold and silver bullion and specie in calendar years (in $1,000):

	Gold		Silver	
	Exports	Imports	Exports	Imports
1932	809,528	363,315	13,850	19,650
1940	4,995	4,749,467	3,674	58,434
1944	959,228	113,836	126,915	23,373
1955	7,257	104,592	8,331	72,932
1960	1,647	335,032	25,789	57,438
1965	1,285,097	101,669	54,061	64,769
1970	36,887	227,472	53,003	58,838
1974	179,070	350,706	27,694	432,864
1975	429,278	406,583	104,086	274,106
1976	333,425	311,011	32,586	289,032
1977	1,055,234	638,707	39,165	315,393
1978	1,024,912	857,488	54,594	324,714
1979	4,620,503	1,400,669	237,542	840,731

The domestic exports of US produce, including military, and the imports for consumption by economic classes for 3 calendar years were (in $m.):

	Exports (US merchandise)			Imports for consumption		
	1977	1978	1979	1977	1978	1979
Food and live animals	14,136	18,311	22,245	12,410	13,521	15,171
Crude materials	13,080	15,555	20,755	7,581	9,294	10,651
Machinery and transport equipment	50,257	59,268	70,491	36,392	47,590	53,678
Chemicals	10,823	12,623	17,306	5,430	6,430	7,485
Total	88,296	105,757	130,797	61,813	76,835	86,985

Leading exports of US merchandise are listed below for the calendar year 1979: Special category merchandise is included. Data for major subdivisions of certain classes are also given:

Commodity	$1m.	Commodity	$1m.
Machinery, total	70,491	Chemicals	17,306
Power generating machinery	6,840	Chemical elements and compounds	7,704
Metalworking machinery	1,391	Plastic materials and resins	3,241
Agricultural machines and tractors	2,636	Soybeans	5,708
Office machines	6,475	Cotton	2,198
Electrical apparatus	8,635	Textiles and apparel	3,189
Telecommunications apparatus	2,957	Tobacco and manufactures	1,184
Electrical power machinery and switchgear	1,802	Iron and steel-mill products	2,227
		Non-ferrous base metals and alloys	1,609
Automobiles (and parts)	15,077	Pulp, paper and products	1,644
Aircraft (and parts)	9,719	Coal	3,496
Grains and preparations	14,451	Fruits, nuts and vegetables	2,130
Wheat (and flour)	5,491	Petroleum and products	1,914
Maize	7,804	Firearms of war and ammunition	1,854

Chief imports for 28 commodity classes for consumption for the calendar year 1979:

Commodity	$1m.	Commodity	$1m.
Petroleum and products	56,046	Fertilizers	976
Petroleum	46,100	Sugar	974
Petroleum products	9,946	Iron and steel-mill products	6,764
Nonferrous base metals	1,672	Cattle, meat and preparations	2,776
Copper	984	Automobiles and parts	16,870
Aluminium	1,029	Fish (and shellfish)	2,639
Nickel	635	Fruit, nuts and vegetables	2,062
Bauxite, crude	398	Alcholic beverages	2,013
Tin	720	Wool and other hair	134
Pulp, paper and products	4,863	Metal manufactures	3,671
Newsprint	2,322	Diamonds (excl. industrial)	1,862
Wood pulp	1,506	Rubber	897

Commodity	$1m.	Commodity	$1m.
Textiles and apparel	2,216	Plywood	855
Clothing	5,876	Oils and oilseeds	59
Cotton fabrics, woven	380	Cocoa (and cacao beans)	555
Machinery, total	28,045	Glass and pottery	1,097
Electrical apparatus	6,588	Footwear	2,859
Agricultural machines and tractors	1,419	Toys and sports goods	1,664
Office machines	2,500	Furs, undressed	183
Coffee	3,820	Scientific/telecommunications	
Chemicals	7,485	apparatus	7,333
Chemical elements and compounds	4,218	Artworks and antiques	1,487
Uranium oxide	459	Grains and animal feeds	298

Total trade beween the USA and the UK for 5 years (British Department of Trade returns, in £1,000 sterling):

	1976	1977	1978	1979	1980
Imports to UK	3,044,259	3,662,505	4,222,555	4,919,882	6,043,774
Exports and re-exports from UK	2,448,751	3,087,279	3,477,231	4,047,158	6,668,342

Imports and exports by continents, areas and selected countries for calendar years (in $1m.):

	General imports		Exports incl. re-exports[1]	
Area and country	1978	1979	1978	1979
Canada	33,736	37,984	28,374[2]	33,096[2]
20 American Republics	18,578	24,816	20,185[2]	26,257[2]
Western Europe	36,959	42,357	39,929[2]	54,331[2]
Western Hemisphere	56,711	68,500	50,394	61,553
Canada	33,736	37,984	28,374	33,096
20 American Republics	18,578	24,816	20,185	26,257
Central American Common Market	1,481	1,901	1,571	1,655
Costa Rica	297	391	335	413
El Salvador	293	444	366	352
Guatemala	342	413	398	467
Honduras	338	418	288	324
Nicaragua	211	235	184	100
Panama	154	192	438	528
Latin American FTA	16,213	21,833	17,499	23,221
Argentina	564	586	842	1,890
Brazil	2,828	3,120	2,981	3,442
Chile	385	440	725	886
Colombia	1,052	1,218	1,046	1,409
Ecuador	741	816	609	696
Mexico	6,102	8,829	6,680	9,847
Paraguay	51	164	90	128
Peru	653	1,181	501	720
Uruguay	123	90	90	127
Dominican Republic	536	668	473	610
Haiti	194	222	204	243
Bolivia	169	222	208	146
Venezuela	3,546	5,167	3,728	3,931
Bahamas	977	1,589	284	334
Netherlands Antilles	1,262	1,830	377	412
Jamaica	387	375	289	292
Trinidad and Tobago	1,425	1,560	330	462
Europe				
Western Europe	36,959	42,357	39,929	54,331
OECD Countries	36,547	41,945	39,405	53,502
European Economic Community	29,429	33,890	32,048	42,582
Belgium and Luxembourg	1,776	1,756	3,653	5,186
Denmark	699	713	585	732

[1] Data include exports of commodities classed for security reasons as 'special category' except as indicated.
[2] 'Special category' exports are included in these totals.

Area and country	General imports 1978	1979	Exports incl. re-exports[1] 1978	1979
Europe (*contd.*)				
France	4,135	4,884	4,166	5,587
Germany (Fed. Rep.)	10,140	11,186	6,957	8,482
Irish Republic	327	329	527	695
Italy	4,173	5,047	3,361	4,359
Netherlands	1,619	1,867	5,683	6,907
UK	6,561	8,107	7,116	10,635
Greece	168	183	699	812
Turkey	175	201	358	354
EFTA countries	...	...	...	...
Austria	412	383	260	312
Norway	1,189	1,266	558	688
Portugal	181	245	525	691
Sweden	1,343	1,673	1,091	1,513
Switzerland	1,836	2,099	1,728	3,660
Finland	372	455	215	337
Iceland	174	225	39	48
Spain	1,268	1,326	1,884	2,507
Yugoslavia	396	392	475	757
Soviet bloc.	1,838	2,469	4,503	7,408
Poland	439	427	680	793
USSR	539	873	2,252	3,607
Asia [2,3]	58,773	66,925	39,630	48,771
Near East	11,804	14,985	12,412	11,030
Egypt	103	382	1,134	1,433
Iran	2,876	2,783	3,685	1,019
Iraq	243	618	317	442
Israel	721	751	1,925	1,857
Kuwait	50	87	745	765
Lebanon	15	15	142	227
Saudi Arabia	5,306	7,982	4,370	4,875
Japan	24,933	26,398	12,885	17,579
Other Asia	33,546	39,945	25,921	29,467
Bangladesh	79	88	170	204
Hong Kong	3,450	3,974	1,625	2,083
India	983	1,043	948	1,167
Indonesia	3,604	3,623	751	982
Korea, Republic of	3,818	4,102	3,160	4,191
Malaysia	1,525	2,153	728	932
Singapore	1,075	1,480	1,462	2,331
Pakistan	84	120	496	529
Philippines	1,211	1,491	1,041	1,570
Sri Lanka	60	100	63	57
Thailand	439	600	629	961
Taiwan (Formosa)	5,182	5,897	2,342	3,271
Vietnam	1	1	2	1
China	324	592	822	1,724
Oceania	2,351	3,074	3,464	4,319
Australia	1,660	2,166	2,912	3,617
New Zealand and W. Samoa	527	709	409	534
Africa [4]	16,905	24,381	4,753	4,866
Algeria	3,482	4,940	374	404
Ethiopia	96	109	24	104
Libya	3,776	5,256	425	468
Morocco	43	40	406	271
Ghana	215	225	126	91
Liberia	133	136	108	108

[1] See note on previous page.
[2] Includes Egypt.
[3] Excludes Yemen (Aden) (formerly Southern Yemen), and Bahrain.
[4] Excludes Egypt.

| Area and country | General imports | | Exports incl. re-exports[1] | |
	1978	1979	1978	1979
Africa (*contd.*)				
Nigeria	4,712	8,161	985	632
Kenya	51	50	138	61
Zaire	225	286	83	113
South Africa, Republic of[2]	2,271	2,627	1,090	1,423

[1] See note on p. 1415. [2] Includes also South-West Africa (Namibia).

US Department of Commerce, Bureau of Census. Report FT 990, Highlights of US Export and Import Trade
US Department of Commerce. Bureau of International Commerce Overseas Business Reports

Tourism. In 1975, 15,698,000 tourists visited the USA and spent $4,875m. They came mainly from Canada (9·9m.), Mexico (2·15m.), Japan (746,000), the UK (438,000) and the Federal Republic of Germany (298,000).

COMMUNICATIONS

Roads. On 31 Dec. 1978 the total US highway mileage, including rural and urban roads, amounted to 3,885,452 miles, of which 3,202,799 miles were surfaced roads. The total mileage cited includes 704,421 miles of rural roads under control of the states, 2,255,526 miles of local roads, 230,850 miles of federal park and forest roads, and 694,655 miles of municipal roads and streets. Expenditures for construction and maintenance amounted to $23,874m. in 1978.

By the end of 1978, toll roads, financed by private capital through bond issues and administered by state toll authorities, totalled 4,812 miles (including some under construction) compared with 344 miles in 1940. Additional toll-road programmes contemplated at present will add approximately 1,578 miles to the toll-road network.

Motor vehicles registered in the calendar year 1978 were (Federal Highways Administration) 148,777,965, including 116,574,999 automobiles, 500,362 buses and 31,702,604 trucks.

Road haulage of goods by motor lorries and trucks in 1978 used 31,702,604 vehicles (250,048 in 1916). The motor vehicle-related industry (1977) employed 13·9m. workers, or 1 out of every 5 employed in the USA.

Inter-city trucks (private and for hire) averaged 602,000m. revenue net ton-miles in 1978. Of the 500,362 buses in service in 1978, 396,387 were school buses. Inter-city service operated a total of 1,082m. bus-miles and carried a total of 4,406m. revenue passengers in 1978.

There were 49,500 deaths in road accidents in 1977.

Railways. Railway history in the USA commences in 1828, but the first railway to convey both freight and passengers in regular service (between Baltimore and Ellicott's Mills, Md., 13 miles) dates from 24 May 1830. Mileage rose to 52,922 miles in 1870; to 167,191 miles in 1890, and to a peak of 266,381 miles in 1916, falling thereafter to 261,871 in 1925; 246,739 in 1940 and 222,164 in 1969 (these include some duplication under trackage rights and some mileage operated in Canada by US companies). The ordinary gauge is 4 ft 8½ in. (about 99·6% of total mileage). The USA has about 29% of the world's railway mileage.

In addition to the independent railroad companies, railway service is provided by two federally-assisted organizations, the National Railroad Passenger Corporation (Amtrak), and the Consolidated Rail Corporation (Conrail).

Amtrak was set up on 1 May 1971 to maintain a basic network of inter-city passenger trains with government assistance, and is responsible for almost all non-commuter services with 27,000 miles of route.

Conrail is the organization established on 1 April 1976 to run freight services in the industrial north-east formerly operated by the bankrupt Penn Central, Reading, Lehigh Valley, Central of New Jersey, Erie Lackawanna, Lehigh & Hudson railroads, and Pennyslvania-Reading Seashore Lines.

The following table, based on the figures of the Interstate Commerce Commission, shows some railway statistics for 4 calendar years:

	1960	1970	1978[2]	1979[1,2]
Classes I and II Railroads				
Mileage owned (first main tracks)	223,779	204,621	170,862	157,905
Revenue freight originated (1m. short tons)	1,421	1,572	1,431	1,502
Freight ton-mileage (1m. ton-miles)	591,550	771,012	867,832	900,853
Passengers carried (1,000)	488,019	289,469	262,094	273,466
Passenger-miles (1m.)	31,790	10,786	6,263	6,333
Operating revenues ($1m.)	9,587	12,209	22,138	25,219
Operating expenses ($1m.)	7,135	9,806	21,424	23,994
Net railway operating income ($1m.)	1,055	506	451	837
Net income after fixed charges ($1m.)	855	126	695	1,377
Class I Railroads:				
Locomotives in service	40,949	27,086	27,238	27,304
Steam locomotives	25,640	—	—	—
Freight-train cars (excluding caboose cars)	1,721,269	1,423,921	1,167,259	1,118,381
Passenger-train cars	57,146	11,177	2,242	2,215
Average number of employees	1,220,784	566,282	471,519	482,962
Average wage per week ($1)	72.59	188.71	390.13	434.17

[1] Class I railroads only.   [2] Data for National Railroad Passenger Corporation excluded.

Aviation. In civil aviation there were, on 31 Dec. 1979, 814,667 certified pilots (including 210,180 student pilots) and 251,516 registered civil aircraft.

Airports on 31 Dec. 1979: Air carrier, 730; general aviation, 14,016. Of these airports, 12,064 were conventional land-based, while 524 were seaplane bases, 2,107 were heliports and 50 stolports (STOL—Short Take-Off and Landing).

Statistics from the Civil Aeronautics Board indicate that for 12 months ended June 1979 on US flag carriers in scheduled international service there were 24·4m. enplanements with 319m. aircraft miles (excluding all-cargo) for a total of 53,953m. revenue passenger-miles. The non-scheduled airlines had a total of 6,526m. revenue passenger-miles internationally. Domestically US scheduled airlines in 1979 had 286·7m. enplanements with a total of 2,443m. aircraft miles for 207,430m. revenue passenger-miles. Non-scheduled airlines in the US recorded 454m. revenue passenger-miles in 1979. (A revenue passenger-mile is one paying passenger carried per mile.)

Shipping. On 1 Sept. 1979 the US merchant marine included 870 sea-going vessels of 1,000 gross tons or over, with aggregate dead-weight tonnage of 23m. This included 305 tankers of 15·2m. DWT.

On 1 Sept. 1979 US merchant ocean-going vessels were employed as follows: Active, 558 of 19m. DWT, of which 266 of 9·2m. tons were foreign trade, 226 of 8·6m. tons in domestic trade and 66 of 1·2m. tons in other US agency operations. Inactive vessels totalled 4m. DWT; 42 of 1·2m. DWT privately owned were laid up and 270 of 2·7m. tons were in the National Defense reserve fleet. Of the total vessels in the US fleet, 576 of 20m. DWT were privately owned.

US exports and imports carried on dry cargo and tanker vessels in the year 1977 totalled 775·3m. long tons, of which 34·8m. long tons or 4·5% were carried in US flag vessels.

Post and Broadcasting. The telephone business is largely in the hands of the American Telephone and Telegraph Company and its telephone operating subsidiaries, which together are known as the Bell Telephone System. There are, however, many hundreds of smaller telephone companies having no common ownership affiliation with the Bell companies, but which connect with them for universal service, countrywide and worldwide. The message telegraph and telex services are in the hands of The Western Union Telegraph Company, but it competes with the telephone industry in providing private leased lines.

The number of telephones in service in the USA has increased in the period since the close of the Second World War much more proportionately than has the population. Among principal reasons there may be cited the facts that an increasingly high percentage of families have telephones installed in their homes, and extension phones associated with the main home telephones have become increasingly common.

In marked contrast, the number of public telegrams has decreased by more than 80%. Telegrams have lost favour due to shifts in user preference to the air-mail and to the telephone. The telex services of the telegraph company have also found broad acceptance in place of telegrams for business purposes. The following table contains key data items on a comparative basis for the domestic telephone and message telegram services:

	1950	1960	1970	1978
All telephone systems:				
Total telephones	43,131,000	74,342,000	120,218,000	169,027,000
Bell Telephone System:				
Total telephones	35,343,400	60,735,100	96,561,000	133,436,000
Average daily telephone calls	140,782,000	219,093,000	368,363,000	546,673,000
Local	134,870,000	209,373,000	346,505,000	502,269,000
Long distance	5,912,000	9,720,000	21,858,000	44,404,000
Total plant in service ($1,000)	10,101,522	24,072,499	54,813,202	110,500,685
Total operating revenues ($1,000)	3,271,029	7,958,125	17,094,846	41,343,539
Employees, number	523,251	580,405	772,980	804,285
Western Union Telegraph System:				
Public telegrams for year	153,054,000	102,931,000	46,083,860	35,549,828
Total plant ($1,000)	294,451	398,023	1,029,149	1,898,664
Revenue from public telegrams				
($1,000)	132,281	160,746	126,739	91,218
Total operating revenues ($1,000)	177,994	262,365	402,456	576,455
Employees, number	40,482	32,655	24,293	12,137

International communication services, providing overseas connexions with all parts of the world, are furnished principally by the American Telephone and Telegraph Company and three telegraph companies. The old-type telegraph-only-transmission-capability ocean cables have all been abandoned in favour of using telegraph circuits derived from voice channels in the newer telephone ocean cables which have also made inroads on the use of high-frequency radio. More recently, satellite communications facilities have been utilized not only for telephone and telegraph services but for television transmission as well.

International overseas telegrams, inbound to and outbound from the continental US, numbered 12·5m. in 1978 (13·2m. in 1976). This service has tended to decline in volume in recent years. It has lost ground to the air-mail and, in addition, in more recent years to the telex and telephone services. For the US and its possessions the volume of international overseas telephone calls has grown enormously with the availability of the excellent voice-transmission qualities provided in the telephone ocean cables and in the satellite radio relays. Whereas, international telephone calls were 990,000 in 1955, the last year in which there was no cable service available, there were 94·6m. such calls in 1978.

Postal business for the years ended 30 Sept. included the following items:

	1976	1977	1978	1979
Number of post offices, on 30 June [1]	30,528	30,521	30,518	30,449
Postal revenue ($1,000) [2]	11,199,211	12,997,873	14,133,056	16,106,085
Postal expenses ($1,000) [3]	13,922,736	15,310,169	16,219,619	17,529,303

[1] The US Postal Service was established 1 July 1971. Financial statements prior to that date are those of the Post Office Department. Such statements for 1968–71 have been restated to be in a format and on an accounting principle basis generally consistent with 1972.

[2] Operating revenue excludes government appropriations, operating reimbursements and other income.

[3] Operating expenses are stated net of operating reimbursements and exclude certain costs financed by revenue.

On 1 Jan. 1975 there were in the USA and Territories, 7,068 authorized commercial radio stations, 711 commercial television stations: of non-commercial stations 717 were for radio, 241 for television.

Cinemas. Cinemas increased from 17,003 in 1940 to 20,239 in 1950 and decreased to 12,187 in 1967.

Newspapers. Of the daily newspapers being published in the USA in 1971, 339 were morning papers with a circulation of 26,116,000, and 1,425 were evening papers with a circulation of 36,115,000. The 590 Sunday papers had a total circulation of 49·7m.

JUSTICE, RELIGION, EDUCATION AND WELFARE

Justice. Legal controversies may be decided in two systems of courts: the federal courts, with jurisdiction confined to certain matters enumerated in Article III of the Constitution, and the state courts, with jurisdiction in all other proceedings. The federal courts have jurisdiction exclusive of the state courts in criminal prosecutions for the violation of federal statutes, in civil cases involving the government, in bankruptcy cases and in admiralty proceedings, and have jurisdiction concurrent with the state courts over suits between parties from different states, and certain suits involving questions of federal law.

The highest court is the Supreme Court of the US, which reviews cases from the lower federal courts and certain cases originating in state courts involving questions of federal law. It is the final arbiter of all questions involving federal statutes and the Constitution; and it has the power to invalidate any federal or state law or executive action which it finds repugnant to the Constitution. This court, consisting of 9 justices who receive salaries of $60,000 a year (the Chief Justice, $62,500), meets from Oct. until June every year and disposes of about 3,380 cases, deciding about 380 on their merits. In the remainder of cases it either summarily affirms lower court decisions or declines to review. A few suits, usually brought by state governments, originate in the Supreme Court, but issues of fact are mostly referred to a master.

The US courts of appeals number 11 (in 10 circuits composed of 3 or more states and 1 circuit for the District of Columbia); the 97 circuit judges receive salaries of $42,500 a year. Any party to a suit in a lower federal court usually has a right of appeal to one of these courts. In addition, there are direct appeals to these courts from many federal administrative agencies. In the year ending 30 June 1976 more than 18,400 appeals were filed in the courts of appeals.

The trial courts in the federal system are the US district courts, of which there are 89 in the 50 states, 1 in the District of Columbia and 1 each in the territories of Puerto Rico, Virgin Islands, Canal Zone and Guam. Each state has at least 1 US district court, and 3 states have 4 apiece. Each district court has from 1 to 27 judgeships. There are 400 US district judges ($40,000 a year), who handle about 130,600 civil cases and 55,000 criminal defendants every year.

In addition to these courts of general jurisdiction, there are special federal courts of limited jurisdiction. The Court of Claims (7 judges at $42,500 a year) decides claims for money damages against the federal government in a wide variety of matters; the Customs Court (9 judges at $40,000 a year) determines controversies concerning the classification and valuation of imported merchandise; and the Court of Customs and Patent Appeals (5 judges at $42,500 a year) hears appeals from the Customs Court, the Tariff Commission and the Patent Office.

The judges of all these courts are appointed by the President with the approval of the Senate; to assure their independence, they hold office during good behaviour and cannot have their salaries reduced. This does not apply to the territorial judges, who hold their offices for a term of years. The judges may retire with full pay at the age of 70 years if they have served a period of 10 years, or at 65 if they have 15 years of service, but they are subject to call for such judicial duties as they are willing to undertake. Only 9 US judges up to 1974 have been involved in impeachment proceedings, of whom 3 district judges and 1 commerce judge were convicted and removed from office.

Of the 130,597 civil cases filed in the district courts in the year ending 30 June 1976, about 70,372 arose under various federal statutes (such as labour, social security, tax, patent, securities, antitrust and civil rights laws); 25,736 involved personal injury or property damage claims; 23,998 dealt with contracts; and 8,475 were actions concerning real property.

Of the 37,667 criminal cases filed in the district courts in the year ending 30 June 1974, about 1,900 were charged with alleged infractions of the immigration laws; 3,000, the transport of stolen motor vehicles; about 3,225 larceny and theft; 4,700, embezzlement and fraud; about 650, liquor laws, and 7,400 narcotics laws.

Persons convicted of federal crimes are either fined, released on probation under the supervision of the probation officers of the federal courts, confined in prison for a period of up to 6 months and then put on probation (known as split sentencing) or confined in one of the following institutions: 3 for juvenile and youths; 7 for young adults; 7 for intermediate term adults; 7 for short-term adults; 2 for females; 1 hospital and 15 community service centres. In addition, prisoners are confined in centres operated by the National Institutes of Mental Health. In addition, prisoner drug addicts may be committed to US Public Health Service hospitals for treatment. In 1972–73 about 1,500 of the federal prison population were placed on work release, that is, they were confined in community treatment centres at night and permitted to work at gainful employment during the weekdays. Prisoners confined in institutions operated by the US Bureau of Prisons for the year ending 30 June 1973, numbered 23,336.

The state courts have jurisdiction over all civil and criminal cases arising under state laws, but decisions of the state courts of last resort as to the validity of treaties or of laws of the US, or on other questions arising under the Constitution, are subject to review by the Supreme Court of the US. The state court systems are generally similar to the federal system, to the extent that they generally have a number of trial courts and intermediate appellate courts, and a single court of last resort. The highest court in each state is usually called the Supreme Court or Court of Appeals with a Chief Justice and Associate Justices, usually elected but sometimes appointed by the Governor with the advice and consent of the State Senate or other advisory body; they usually hold office for a term of years, but in some instances for life or during good behaviour. Their salaries range from $14,000 to $40,000 a year. The lowest tribunals are usually those of Justices of the Peace; many towns and cities have municipal and police courts, with power to commit for trial in criminal matters and to determine misdemeanours for violation of the municipal ordinances; they frequently try civil cases involving limited amounts.

The Federal Bureau of Investigation estimates the number of major crimes in the US and its possessions as follows:

Crime index classification	1959–61 average	1975	Crime index classification	1959–61 average	1975
Murder	8,670	20,510	Burglary	789,300	3,252,100
Forcible rape	15,860	56,090	Larceny over $50	464,300	5,977,700
Robbery	87,570	464,970	Motor car theft	312,000	1,000,500
Aggravated assault	129,400	484,710			
			Total	1,807,100	11,256,600

The death penalty is illegal in Alaska, Hawaii, Iowa, Maine, Minnesota, Oregon, West Virgina, Wisconsin and Michigan; in North Dakota it is legal only for treason and first-degree murder committed by a prisoner serving a life sentence for first-degree murder, in Rhode Island only for murder committed by a prisoner serving a life sentence and in Vermont and New York for the murder of a peace officer in the line of duty and for first-degree murder by those who kill while serving a life sentence for murder. The death penalty, although still legal in most states, has fallen into disuse and has been abolished *de facto* in many states. The US Supreme Court has held the death penalty, as applied in general criminal statutes, to contravene the eighth and fourteenth amendments of the US constitution, as a cruel and unusual punishment when used so irregularly and rarely as to destroy its deterrent value.

In 1967 only 2 persons were executed under civil authority; both for murder. There were no executions 1968–76. In 1977 a convicted murderer requested that he should be executed and after a lengthy legal dispute the sentence was carried out at Utah state prison. In Jan. 1977, 350 prisoners were reported under sentence of death.

The total number of civilian executions carried out in the US from 1930 to 1967 was 3,859, including 1,751 white persons (20 women), 2,066 Negroes (12 women) and 42 persons of other races.

Federal 'Political' Crimes. Prosecutions for what may be loosely described as 'political' offences, or crimes directed towards the overthrow by violence of the federal government, which were somewhat numerous in the early 1950s, have declined sharply over the last 15 years and are now exceedingly rare. During the fiscal year 1975–76 the following number of defendants appeared in federal courts: Espionage, none; Subversive Activities Control Act, 1950, none; contempt of Congress, none.

A Guide to Court Systems. Institute of Judicial Administration. New York, 1960

The United States Courts (88th Congress, 1st Session, House Document No. 180). US Government Printing Office, 1975

The Challenge of Crime in a Free Society. Report of the President's Commission on Law Enforcement and Administration of Justice. US Government Printing Office, 1967

Hart and Wechsler, *The Federal Courts and the Federal System.* Brooklyn, N.Y., 1953

Hurst, J. Willard, *The Growth of American Law.* New York, 1950

Huston, L. A., *The Department of Justice.* New York, 1967

Huston, L. A., and others. *Roles of the Attorney General of the United States.* New York, 1968

McCloskey, R. G., *The Modern Supreme Court.* Harvard Univ. Press, 1972

Mayers, L., *The American Legal System.* Rev. ed. New York, 1964

Murphy, W. F., *Congress and the Court.* Univ. of Chicago Press, 1962

Smith, B., *Police Systems in the US.* Rev. ed. New York, 1960

Vanderbilt, A. T., *Minimum Standards of Judicial Administration.* New York, 1949

Warren, Charles, *The Supreme Court in United States History.* 2 vols. Rev. ed. Boston, Mass, 1960

Religion. *The Yearbook of American and Canadian Churches for 1980,* published by the National Council of the Churches of Christ in the USA, New York, presents the latest figures available from official statisticians of church bodies. The large majority of reports are for the calendar year 1978, or a fiscal year ending 1978. The 1978 reports indicated that there were 133,388,776 members with 332,970 local churches. There were 282,501 clergymen having local congregations. The principal religious bodies (numerically or historically) or groups of religious bodies are shown below:

Denominations	Local churches	Total membership
Summary:		
Protestant bodies	300,676	72,944,162
Roman Catholic Church	25,542	49,602,035
Jewish Congregations [1]	3,500	5,781,000
Eastern Churches	1,583	3,632,555
Old Catholic, Polish National Catholic and Armenian	421	808,684
Buddhists	60	60,000
Miscellaneous [2]	1,188	160,340
1979 totals	332,970	133,388,776 [3]

Protestant Church Membership	Total membership
Baptist bodies	
Southern Baptist Convention	13,191,394
National Baptist Convention, USA	5,500,000
National Baptist Convention of America, Inc.	2,668,799
National Primitive Baptist Convention	250,000
American Baptist Churches in the USA	1,316,760
American Baptist Association	1,500,000
Progressive National Baptist Convention	521,692
Conservative Baptist Association of America	300,000
Regular Baptist Churches	240,000
Free Will Baptists	216,831
Baptist Missionary Association of America	219,697
Christian Church (Disciples of Christ)	1,231,817
Christian Churches and Churches of Christ	1,054,266
Church of the Nazarene	462,724
Churches of Christ	3,000,000
The Episcopal Church	2,815,359
Latter-Day Saints:	
Church of Jesus Christ of Latter-Day Saints	2,592,200
Reorganized Church of Jesus Christ of Latter-Day Saints	185,636
Lutheran Bodies:	
Lutheran Church in America	2,942,002
The Lutheran Church-Missouri Synod	2,631,374

[1] Includes Orthodox, Conservative and Reformed bodies.

[2] Includes non-Christian bodies such as Spiritualists, Ethical Culture, Unitarian-Universalists.

[3] Care should be taken in interpreting membership statistics for the US Churches. Some statistics are accurately compiled and others are estimates. Also statistics are not always comparable.

Protestant Church Membership	Total membership
Lutheran Bodies (*contd.*):	
The American Lutheran Church	2,377,235
Wisconsin Evangelical Lutheran Synod	402,972
Methodist Bodies:	
United Methodist Church	9,731,779
African Methodist Episcopal Church	1,970,000
African Methodist Episcopal Zion Church	1,093,001
Christian Methodist Episcopal Church	466,718
Pentecostal Bodies:	
Assemblies of God	1,293,394
Church of God in Christ, International	501,000
Church of God in Christ	425,000
Church of God (Cleveland, Tenn.)	392,551
United Pentecostal Church, International, Inc.	450,000
Presbyterian Bodies:	
United Presbyterian Church in the USA	2,520,367
Presbyterian Church in the US	862,416
Reformed Churches:	
Reformed Church in America	348,080
Christian Reformed Church	211,302
The Salvation Army	414,035
Seventh-day Adventists	535,705
United Church of Christ	1,769,104

Yearbook of American and Canadian Churches. Annual, from 1951. New York
Clarke, E. T., *The Small Sects in America*. Rev. ed. New York, 1949
Johnson, A. W., and Yost, F. H., *Separation of Church and State in the United States*. Minneapolis and London, 1949
Mead, F. S., *Handbook of Denominations in the US*. 6th ed. Nashville, 1975
Moehiman, C. H., *The Wall of Separation between Church and State*. Boston, 1951
Roemer, T., *The Catholic Church in the United States*. Rev. ed. New York, 1961
Sperry, W. L., *Religion in America*. London, 1945
Stokes, A. P., and Pfeffer, L., *Church and State in the US*. New York, 1964
Sweet, W. W., *The Story of Religion in America*. 2nd ed. New York, 1950

Education. Under the system of government in the USA, elementary and secondary education is committed in the main to the several states. Each of the 50 states and the District of Columbia has a system of free public schools, established by law, with courses covering 12 years plus kindergarten. There are 3 structural patterns in common use: the K8–4 plan, meaning kindergarten plus 8 elementary grades followed by 4 high school grades; the K6–3–3 plan, or kindergarten plus 6 elementary grades followed by a 3-year junior high school and a 3-year senior high school; and the K6–6 plan, kindergarten plus 6 elementary grades followed by a 6-year high school. All plans lead to high-school graduation, usually at age 17 or 18. Vocational education is an integral part of secondary education. In addition, some states have, as part of the free public school system, 2-year colleges in which education is provided at a nominal cost. Each state has delegated a large degree of control of the educational programme to local school districts (numbering 15,929 in autumn 1979), each with a board of education (usually 3 to 9 members) elected locally and serving mostly without pay. The school policies of the local school districts must be in accord with the laws and the regulations of their state Departments of Education. While regulations differ from one jurisdiction to another, in general it may be said that school attendance is compulsory between the ages of 7 to 16.

The Census Bureau estimates that in Nov. 1969 only 1,433,000 or 1% of the 143m. persons who were 14 years of age or older were unable to read and write; in 1930 the percentage was 4·8. In 1940 a new category was established—the 'functionally illiterate', meaning those who had completed fewer than 5 years of elementary schooling; for persons 25 years of age or over this percentage was 3·5 in March 1979 (for the non-white population alone it was 9·2%); it was 1 for white and 0·9% for non-whites in the 25–29-year-old group. The Bureau reported that in March 1979 the median years of school completed by all persons 25 years old and over was 12·5, and that 16·4% had completed 4 or more years of college. For the 25–29-year-old group, the median school years completed was 12·9 and 23·1% had completed 4 or more years of college.

In the autumn of 1979, 11,569,899 students (5,682,877 men and 5,887,022 women) were enrolled in 3,150 colleges and universities; 2,502,896 were first-time students. Total enrolment in colleges and universities represents a number equal to 39·5 per 100 persons between the ages of 18 and 24.

Public elementary and secondary school revenue is supplied from the county and other local sources (44·5% in 1978–79), state sources (45·7%) and federal sources (9·8%). In 1978–79 expenditure for public elementary and secondary education totalled about $89,000m., including $79,300m. for regular day school programmes, $1,200m. for other programmes, $5,900m. for capital outlay and $2,600m. for interest on school debt. The current expenditure per pupil in average daily attendance was about $2,062. The total cost per pupil, also including capital outlay and interest, amounted to about $2,284. Estimated total expenditures, for private elementary and secondary schools in 1978–79 were $10,600m. In 1978–79 the 3,134 universities and colleges expended $50,721m. from current funds, of which $33,733m. was spent by institutions under public control. The federal government contributed 15·1% of total current-fund revenue; state governments, 31·6%; student tuition and fees, 20·6%; and all other sources, 32·7%.

Vocational education below college grade, including the training of teachers to conduct such education, has been federally aided since 1918. During the school year 1978–79 enrolments in the vocational classes were: Agriculture, 971,726; distributive occupations, 942,057; health occupations, 798,520; home economics, 4,300,124; trade and industry, 3,436,089; technical education, 484,076; office occupations, 3,469,134; other programmes, 2,866,316. Federal support funds were $550,896,000.

Summary of statistics of regular schools (public and non-public), teachers and pupils in autumn 1979 (compiled by the US National Center for Education Statistics):

Schools by level	Number of schools 1978–79	Teachers autumn 1979	Enrolment autumn 1979
Elementary schools:			
Public	62,644[1]	1,171,000	24,840,000
Non-public	16,097	180,000	3,550,000
Secondary schools:			
Public	25,378[1]	1,010,000	16,740,000
Non-public	5,766	90,000	1,510,000
Higher education:			
Public	1,474	602,000	9,037,000
Non-public	1,660	220,000	2,533,000
Total	113,019	3,273,000	58,210,000

[1] 1976–77.

Most of the non-public elementary and secondary schools are affiliated with religious denominations. Of the children attending non-public elementary and secondary schools in 1978–79, 3·27m. or 64·3% were enrolled in Roman Catholic schools.

During the school year 1978–79 high-school graduates numbered 3,134,000 (1,532,000 boys and 1,602,000 girls). Institutions of higher education conferred 921,390 bachelor's degrees for the academic year 1978–79, 477,344 to men and 444,046 to women; 301,079 master's degrees, 153,370 to men and 147,709 to women; 32,730 doctorates, 23,541 to men and 9,189 to women; and 68,848 first professional degrees, 52,652 to men and 16,196 to women.

During the academic year, 1978–79, 263,940 foreign students were enrolled in American colleges and universities. The percentages of students coming from various areas were: Asia, 55·7; Latin America, 15·6; Africa, 12·9; Europe, 8·2; North America, 5·9; Oceania, 1·6.

School enrolment, Oct. 1979, embraced 96% of the children who were 5 and 6 years old; 99% of the children aged 7–13 years; 94% of those aged 14–17, 45% of those aged 18 and 19, 30% of those aged 20 and 21, and 16% of those aged 22–24 years.

The US National Center for Education Statistics estimates the total enrolment in the autumn of 1980 at all of the country's regular educational institutions (public and non-public) at 58m. (58,491,000 in the autumn of 1979); this was 26·5% of the total population of the USA as of 1 Sept. 1979.

Enrolment at the elementary and secondary school level is expected to be down by 1·9% in autumn 1980 and total enrolment in the colleges and universities to rise by 3·2%.

The number of teachers in the public and non-public elementary and secondary schools in the autumn of 1980 is expected to decrease slightly to 2·45m. The average annual salary of the public school teachers was about $16,100 in 1979–80.

Digest of Educational Statistics. Annual. Dept. of Education, Washington 20202, D.C. (from 1962)

American Junior Colleges. 6th ed. American Council of Education. Washington, 1963

American Universities and Colleges. 9th ed. American Council of Education. Washington, 1964

Ayer's Directory of Newspapers and Periodicals. Annual, from 1880. Philadelphia

Berelson, B., *Graduate Education in the United States.* New York, 1960

De Young, C. A., and Wynn, D. R., *American Education.* 5th ed. New York, 1964

Douglass, H. R., *Secondary Education in the US.* 2nd ed. New York, 1964

French, W. M., *America's Educational Tradition.* Boston, 1964

Good, H. G., *History of American Education.* 2nd ed. New York and London, 1962

Hofstadter, R., and Smith, W., *American Higher Education: A Documentary History.* 2 vols. Univ. of Chicago Press, 1962

Health and Welfare. Admission to the practice of medicine (for both doctors of medicine and doctors of osteopathic medicine) is controlled in each state by examining boards directly representing the profession and acting with authority conferred by state law. Although there are an increasing number of variations, the usual time now required to complete basic training is 8 years beyond the secondary school with an additional year of graduate training. Certification as a specialist may require as much as 5 more years of graduate training plus experience in practice. In academic year 1979–80 the 140 US schools (including 14 osteopathic and 126 medical) graduated 15,970 physicians. About 27% of first-year students were women. In Dec. 1979 the total estimated number of active physicians (MD and DO—in all forms of practice) in the US, Puerto Rico and outlying US areas was 598,340. The distribution of physicians throughout the country is uneven, both by state and by urban–rural areas.

In 1979–80 the 60 dental schools graduated 5,424 dentists. Active dentists in Dec. 1979 numbered 118,330. New York state had 1 active civilian dentist to 1,479 population and Mississippi, 1 to 3,458.

In Oct. 1979, there were 1,374 registered nursing programmes in the US and (1978), 77,132 graduates of registered nursing programmes. In Dec. 1979 an estimated 1,119,100 registered nurses were employed full- or part-time (1 to 198 inhabitants).

Number of hospitals listed by the American Hospital Association in 1978 was 7,015, with 1,381,000 beds and 37,243,000 admissions during the year; average daily census was 1,020,000. Of the total, 370 hospitals with 122,000 beds were operated by the federal government; 1,843 with 215,000 beds by state and local government; 3,360 with 684,000 beds by non-profit organizations (including church groups); 732 with 81,000 beds are proprietary. The categories of non-federal hospitals are 5,935 short-term general and special hospitals with 980,000 beds; 169 non-federal long-term general and special hospitals with 41,000 beds; 526 psychiatric hospitals with 235,000 beds; 15 tuberculosis hospitals with 3,000 beds. Hospital beds in short-term general facilities range from 2 (Alaska) to 6·2 (North Dakota) hospital beds per 1,000 population[1]; the national average is 4·4. It was estimated that, in 1979, more than 130,000 additional beds in general hospitals and 127,429 additional long-term care beds (nursing homes and chronic disease hospitals) were needed.

[1] Excluding District of Columbia.

Social welfare legislation was chiefly the province of the various states until the adoption of the Social Security Act of 14 Aug. 1935. This as amended provides for a federal system of old-age, survivors and disability insurance; health insurance for the aged and disabled; supplemental security income for the aged, blind and disabled; federal state unemployment insurance; and federal grants to states for public assistance (medical assistance for the aged and aid to families with dependent children generally) and for maternal and child-health and child-welfare services. The Social Security Administration of the Department of Health, Education and Welfare has responsibility for the programmes—old-age, survivors and disability insurance, supplemental security income and aid to families with dependent children. The Health Care Financing Administration, an agency of the same Department, has federal responsibility for health insurance for the aged and disabled (Medicare) and medical assistance (Medicaid). The Department's Office of Human Development administers all human development and social services programmes, and its Public Health Service is responsible for maternal and child-health services. Unemployment insurance is the responsibility of the Department of Labor.

The Social Security Act provides for protection against the cost of medical care through the two-part programme of health insurance for people 65 and over and for certain disabled people under 65, who receive disability insurance payments or who have permanent kidney failure (Medicare). During fiscal year 1978, payments totalling $17,400m. were made under the hospital insurance part of Medicare on behalf of 6m. people. During the same period, $6,900m. was paid under the voluntary medical insurance part of Medicare on behalf of 15·6m. people.

In 1978 about 110m. persons worked in employment covered by old-age, survivors and disability insurance.

In June 1978, over 34m. beneficiaries were on the rolls, and the average benefit paid to a retired worker (not counting any paid to his dependants) was about $260 per month.

Benefits paid during fiscal year 1978 totalled $88,600m., including $11,900m. paid to disabled workers and their dependants.

In calendar year 1977, over 11m. persons (adults and children) were receiving payments under aid to families with dependent children (average monthly payment, $237.97 per family). Total payments under aid to families with dependent children were $10,200m. for the calendar year.

In Sept. 1978, more than 4·2m. persons were receiving supplemental security income payments, including over 1·9m. persons aged 65 or over; 77,258 blind persons, and over 2·1m. disabled persons. Payments, including supplemental amounts from various states, totalled $550m.

During the fiscal year 1970–71 federal appropriations for grants to states were made for maternal and child health services amounting to $59·2m.; for crippled children's services, $58·6m., and for child welfare services, $46m. Additional appropriations for grants for research projects relating to maternal and child health and crippled children's services were $5·7m.; research, training and demonstration projects in the field of child welfare, $10·2m.; maternity and infant care projects, $38·6m.; projects to provide comprehensive health care for school and pre-school children, $43·8m.; and training personnel for health care of mothers and children, $11·2m.

Burns, E. M., *Social Security and Public Policy*. New York, 1956 (Repr. 1976).—*Health Services for Tomorrow*. New York, 1973
Friedlander, W. A., *Introduction to Social Welfare*. 4th ed. New York, 1974
Grob, G. N., ed., *Social Problems and Social Policy Series*. 51 vols. New York, 1975
Grob, G. N., et al., eds., *Mental Illness and Social Policy: The American Experience*. 41 books. New York, 1973
Grod, F. P., *Public Health Law Manual*. New York, 1965
Schottland, C. A., *The Social Security Program in the US*. 2nd ed. New York, 1970
Smillie, W. G., *Public Health, Its Promise For the Future*. New York, 1976

DIPLOMATIC REPRESENTATIVES

OF THE UNITED STATES IN GREAT BRITAIN (Grosvenor Sq., London, W1A 1AE)

Ambassador: John J. Louis, Jr.

OF GREAT BRITAIN IN THE USA (3100 Massachusetts Ave., Washington, D.C., 20008)

Ambassador: Sir Nicholas Henderson, GCMG.

Ambassador: Jeane Kirkpatrick.

Books of Reference

I. STATISTICAL INFORMATION

Within the federal government of the USA, responsibilities for the collection, compilation, analysis and publication of statistics are decentralized among a number of agencies, with specified responsibilities for general-purpose statistics in particular areas. In addition, most agencies of the Government collect statistical data as a by-product of their administrative or operating responsibilities in specific fields. Responsibility for co-ordinating the decentralized statistical activities rests in the Office of Statistical Standards, Bureau of the Budget, Washington 25, D.C., as a part of the Executive Office of the President. This Office reviews all proposed collections of statistical data to avoid duplication or overlapping; promotes the use of improved statistical techniques; develops standard definitions and classifications so that the data collected by different agencies are comparable; serves as liaison between federal agencies and international organizations and as an information centre on government statistical programmes. The Division does not itself collect or publish statistics.

The major general-purpose statistical agencies and their principal areas of responsibility are:

(1) Bureau of the Census in the Department of Commerce (A. Ross Eckler, Director). Decennial censuses of population and housing and quinquennial censuses of agriculture, manufactures and business; current statistics on population and the labour force, manufacturing activity and commodity production, retail and wholesale trade and services, foreign trade, and state and local government finances and operations.

(2) Bureau of Labor Statistics in the Department of Labor (Geoffrey H. Moore, Commissioner). Current statistics on employment, earnings, man-hours, labour turnover, industrial accidents, work stoppages, wage rates; collective bargaining agreements; construction; industrial productivity; wholesale prices, retail prices and urban consumers' price indexes; income and expenditures of urban families.

(3) Statistical Reporting Service and Economic Research Service in the Department of Agriculture. Statistics on crop and livestock production and inventories; crop forecasts; food processing and food consumption; farm population, labour and wages; farm management; farm ownership values, transfers; taxation and finance; prices farmers pay and receive; farm income; accidents; studies of land and water uses.

(4) National Center for Health Statistics in the Public Health Service, Department of Health, Education and Welfare (Theodore D. Woolsey, Chief). Current statistics on births, deaths, marriages and divorce.

(5) Bureau of Mines in the Department of the Interior (John F. O'Leary, Director). Statistics on production, consumption and stocks of metals and minerals, and on injuries in mineral industries.

Other agencies in which statistics are an important by-product of regulatory or other administrative functions include: Social Security Administration in the Department of Health, Education and Welfare; Internal Revenue Service in the Treasury Department; Federal Power Commission; Federal Trade Commission; Interstate Commerce Commission, and the Securities and Exchange Commission.

Among the more important statistical publications of a fairly general nature are:

Statistical Abstract of the United States, published by the Bureau of the Census, Department of Commerce. Annual. Important summary statistics on the industrial, social, political and economic organization of the USA, with a representative selection from most of the important statistical publications. *Survey of Current Business*, published by the Office of Business Economics, Department of Commerce. Monthly. Interpretative text and charts reviewing business trends, etc.; official estimates of national income. *Economic Indicators*, prepared by the Council of Economic Advisers and published by the Congressional Joint Committee on the Economic Report. Monthly. Tables and charts presenting current data on the total output of the economy; prices; employment and wages; production and business activity; purchasing power; money, banking and federal finance. *Monthly Labor Review*, published by the Bureau of Labor Statistics, Department of Labor. *Federal Reserve Bulletin*, published by the Board of Governors of the Federal Reserve System. Monthly. Current data on money and banking and selected other economic series. Federal Reserve indexes of industrial production, etc.; international financial statistics. *Treasury Bulletin*, published by the Office of the Secretary, Department of the Treasury. Monthly. Current coverage of federal fiscal statistics; international capital movements. *Minerals Yearbook*, published by the Bureau of Mines, Department of the Interior. Annual. *Agricultural Statistics*, published by the Department of Agriculture. Annual. *Crops and Markets*, published by the Bureau of Agricultural Economics in the Department of Agriculture. Monthly. Crop report and market statistics. *Foreign Agriculture*, published by the

Office of Foreign Agriculture Service, Department of Agriculture. Monthly. Foreign agricultural production, foreign government policies relating to agriculture and international trade in agricultural products. *Vital Statistics of the United States*, published by the Public Health Service, US Department of Health, Education and Welfare. Monthly and Annual. Natality and mortality data tabulated by place of occurrence, with supplemental tables for Puerto Rico and the Virgin Islands; and tabulated by place of residence.

An annotated bibliography of about 100 periodical statistical publications is included in *Statistical Services of the United States Government*, a pamphlet issued by the Division of Statistical Standards, Bureau of the Budget, describing the general organization of the statistical system of the USA and the principal types of economic statistics.

II. OTHER OFFICIAL PUBLICATIONS

Guide to the Study of the United States of America. General Reference and Bibliography Division, Library of Congress. 1960.

Historical Statistics of the United States, Colonial Times to 1957: A Statistical Abstract Supplement. Washington, 1960.—*Continuation to 1962 and Revisions*. 1965.

United States Government Manual. Washington. Annual.

The official publications of the USA are issued by the US Government Printing Office and are distributed by the Superintendent of Documents, who issued in 1940 a cumulative *Catalog of the Public Documents of the . . . Congress and of All the Departments of the Government of the United States*. This *Catalog* is kept up to date by *United States Government Publications, Monthly Catalog* with annual index and supplemented by *Price Lists*. Each *Price List* is devoted to a special subject or type of material, *e.g.*, *American History* or *Census*. Useful guides are Schmeckebier, L. F., and Eastin, R. B. (eds.), *Government Publications and Their Use*. 2nd ed., Washington, D.C., 1961; Boyd, A. M., *United States Government Publications*. 3rd ed. New York, 1949, and Leidy, W. P., *Popular Guide to Government Publications*. 2nd ed. New York and London, 1963.

Treaties and other International Acts of the United States of America (Edited by Hunter Miller), 8 vols. Washington, 1929–48. This edition stops in 1863. It may be supplemented by *Treaties, Conventions . . . Between the US and Other Powers, 1776–1937* (Edited by William M. Malloy and others). 4 vols. 1909–38. A new Treaty Series, *US Treaties and Other International Agreements* was started in 1950.

Writings on American History. Washington, annual from 1902 (except 1904–5 and 1941–47).

III. NON-OFFICIAL PUBLICATIONS

A. Handbooks

National Historical Publications Commission. *Guide to Archives and Manuscripts in the United States*, ed. P. M. Hamer. Yale Univ. Press, 1961

Adams, J. T. (ed.), *Dictionary of American History*. 2nd ed. 7 vols. New York, 1942

Dictionary of American Biography, ed. A. Johnson and D. Malone. 23 vols. New York, 1929–64.—*Concise Dictionary of American Biography*. New York, 1964

Current Biography. New York, annual from 1940; monthly supplements

Handlin, O., and others. *Harvard Guide to American History*. Cambridge, Mass., 1954

Kreutz, B., and Fleming, E., *Introducing America*. London, 1963

Lord, C. L. and E. H., *Historical Atlas of the US*. Rev. ed. New York, 1969

Who's Who in America. Chicago, 1899–1900 to date; monthly Supplement. 1940 to date

B. General History

Barck, Jr, O. T., and Blake, N. M., *Since 1900: A History of the United States*. 5th ed. New York, 1974

Bellot, H. H., *American History and American Historians*. London, 1952, repr. 1974

Billington, R. A., *Westward Expansion*. 4th ed. New York, 1974

Carman, H. J., and others, *A History of the American People*. 3rd ed. 2 vols. New York, 1967

Commager, H. S. (ed.), *Documents of American History*. 8th ed. New York, 1966

Divine, R. A., *Since 1945: Politics and Diplomacy in Recent American History*. New York, 1975

Hicks, J. D., *The American Nation, A History of the United States from 1865*. 5th ed. Boston, 1971

Link, A. S., and Catton, W. B., *American Epoch: A History of the United States Since the 1890s*. 4th ed. New York, 1967

Morison, S. E., *The Oxford History of the American People*. OUP, 1968

Morison, S. E., with Commager, H. S., *The Growth of the American Republic*. 2 vols. 5th ed. OUP, 1962–63

Nicholas, H. G., *The Nature of American Politics*. OUP, 1980

Parkes, H. B., *The United States of America, A History*. 3rd ed. New York, 1968

Scammon, R. N. (ed.), *American Votes: A Handbook of Contemporary American Election Statistics*. Washington, D.C., 1956 to date (biennial)

Schlesinger, A. M., *The Rise of Modern America, 1865–1951*. 4th ed. New York, 1951.—*The Age of Roosevelt*. 4 vols. New York and London, 1957–62.—*A Thousand Days: John F. Kennedy in the White House*. New York and London, 1965

Snowman, D., *America Since 1920*. London, 1978

Watson, R. A., *The Promise and Performance of American Democracy*. 2nd ed. New York, 1975

Wish, H., *Society and Thought in America*. 2 vols. OUP, 1962

C. Minorities

Bennett, M. T., *American Immigration Policies: A History*. Washington, D.C., 1963

Burma, J. J., *Spanish-speaking Groups in the US*. Duke University Press, 1954, repr. 1974

Burns, W. H., *The Voices of Negro Protest in America*. OUP, 1963

Frazier, E. F., *The Negro Family in the United States*. Chicago Univ. Press, 1966

McNickle, D., *The Indian Tribes of the United States*. OUP, 1962.—*Native American Tribalism*. OUP, 1973

Sklare, M., *The Jew in American Society*. New York, 1974

Wissler, Clark, *Indians of the United States*. Rev. ed. New York, 1966

D. Economic History

The Economic History of the United States. 9 vols. New York, 1946 ff.

Bining, A. C., and Cochran, T. C., *The Rise of American Economic Life*. 4th ed. New York, 1963

Dorfman, J., *The Economic Mind in American Civilization*. 5 vols. New York, 1946–59

Faulkner, H. U., *American Economic History*. 8th ed. New York, 1960

Friedman, M., and Schwartz, A. J., *A Monetary History of the United States, 1867–1960*. New York, 1963

Jones, P. d'A., *America's Wealth*. London, 1963.—*An Economic History of the United States Since 1783*. London, 1969

Landsberg, H. H., and others, *Resources in America's Future: Patterns of Requirements and Availabilities, 1960–2000*. Washington, D.C., 1963

Mund, V. A., *Government and Business*. 4th ed. New York, 1965

E. Foreign Relations

Documents on American Foreign Relations. Princeton, from 1948. Annual

The United States in World Affairs. 1931 ff. Council on Foreign Relations. New York, from 1932. Annual

Allison, G., and Szanton, P., *Remaking Foreign Policy: The Organizations Connection*. New York, 1976

Bartlett, R. (ed.), *The Record of American Diplomacy; Documents and Readings in the History of American Foreign Relations*. 4th ed. New York, 1964

Beloff, M., *The United States and the Unity of Europe*. London, 1963, repr. 1976

Bemis, S. F., *Diplomatic History of the US*. 4th ed. New York, 1955.—*Short History of American Foreign Policy and Diplomacy*. Rev. ed. New York, 1959.—*The United States as a World Power: A Diplomatic History*. Rev. ed. New York, 1955

Connell-Smith, G., *The United States and Latin America*. London, 1975

DeConde, A., *The American Secretary of State*. London, 1963, repr. 1976

Graebner, N. A. (ed.), *An Uncertain Tradition: American Secretaries of State in the 20th Century*. New York, 1961.—*Cold War Diplomacy: American Foreign Policy, 1945–60*. Princeton, 1962

Hyde, L. K., *The United States and the United Nations*. New York, 1960

Lary, H. B., *Problems of the United States as World Trader and Banker*. New York, 1963

Leopold, R. W., *The Growth of American Foreign Policy: A History*. New York, 1962

Morgan, R., *The United States and West Germany, 1945–73*. OUP, 1975

Pratt, J. W., *A History of United States Foreign Policy*. 3rd ed. New York, 1972

Rostow, W. W., *The United States in the World Arena: An Essay in Recent History*. New York, 1960

Smith, R. F., *The United States and Cuba: Business and Diplomacy, 1917–1960*. New York, 1962

Spanier, J. W., *American Foreign Policy Since World War II*. 6th ed. London, 1973

Stebbins, R. P., and Adam, E. A., *Documents of American Foreign Relations, 1968–69*. New York, 1972

Stuart, Graham H., *Latin America and the United States*. 6th ed. New York, 1975

Wilcox, F. O., and Frank, R. A., *The Constitution and the Conduct of Foreign Policy*. New York, 1976

F. National Character

Coan, O. W., *America in Fiction, An Annotated List of Novels*. 5th ed. Stanford Univ. Press, 1967

Curti, M. B., *The Growth of American Thought*. 3rd ed. New York, 1964

Degler, C. N., *Out of Our Past: The Forces That Shaped Modern America*. Rev. ed. New York, 1970

Duigan, P. and Rabushka A., (eds.) *The United States in the 1980s*. Stanford, 1980

Hertzler, J. O., *American Social Institutions: A Sociological Analysis*. Boston, 1961

Lerner, M., *America as a Civilization: Life and Thought in the United States Today*. 2 vols. New York, 1961

Riesman, D., with R. Denny and N. Glazer, *The Lonely Crowd: A Study of the Changing American Character*. Rev. ed. Yale Univ. Press, 1969

Rossiter, C. L., *Conservatism in America*. 2nd ed. New York, 1962

Wish, H., *Society and Thought in America*. 2nd ed. 2 vols. New York [1962].—*Contemporary America*. 3rd ed. New York, 1961

National Library: The Library of Congress. Washington 25, D.C. *Librarian:* Lawrence Quincy Mumford, AB, MA, BS.

STATES AND TERRITORIES

For information as to State and Local Government, *see under* UNITED STATES, *pp.* 1386–88.

Against the names of the Governors and the Secretaries of State, (D.) stands for Democrat and (R.) for Republican.

Figures for the revenues and expenditures of the various states are those of the Federal Bureau of the Census unless otherwise stated, which takes the original state figures and arranges them on a common pattern so that those of one state can be compared with those of any other.

Official publications of the various states and insular possessions are listed in the *Monthly Check-List of State Publications*, issued by the Library of Congress since 1910. Their character and contents are discussed in J. K. Wilcox's *Manual on the Use of State Publications* (1940). Of great importance bibliographically are the publications of the Historical Records Survey and the American Imprints Inventory, which record local archives, official publications and state imprints. These publications supplement those of state historical societies which usually publish journals and monographs on state and local history. An outstanding source of statistical data is the material issued by the various state planning boards and commissions, to which should be added the annual *Governmental Finances* issued by the US Bureau of the Census.

The Book of the States. Biennial. Council of State Governments, Lexington, 1953 ff.

County and City Data Book. Dept. of Commerce, 1967

State Government Finances. Annual. Dept. of Commerce, 1966 ff.

Regionalism

Bogue, D. J., and Beale, C. L., *Economic Areas of the United States*. New York, 1961

Jensen, M. (ed.), *Regionalism in America*. Univ. of Wisconsin Press, 1965

Odum, H. W., *American Regionalism, A Cultural–Historical Approach to National Integration*. New York, 1938

Visher, S. X., *Climatic Atlas of the USA*. Harvard Univ. Press., 1954

A. North-East

Gottman, J., *Megalopolis, the Urbanized North-eastern Seaboard of the US*. New York, 1964

B. The South

Cash, W. J., *The Mind of the South*. New York, 1960

Clark, T. D., *The Emerging South*. New York, 1961

Clement, E., *A History of the Old South*. New York, 1949

Ezell, J. S., *The South Since 1865*. New York and London, 1963

Heseltine, W. B., and Smiley, D. L., *The South in American History*. 2nd ed. Englewood Cliffs, 1960

Sindler, A. P. (ed.), *Change in the Contemporary South*. Duke Univ. Press, 1963

Stephenson, W. H., and Coulter, E. M. (ed.), *A History of the South*. 10 vols. Louisiana State Univ. Press, 1947–67

C. The Middle West

Lynd, R. S. and H. M., *Middletown: A Study in Contemporary American Culture*. New York and London, 1929.—*Middletown in Transition: A Study in Cultural Conflicts*. New York and London, 1937

Nye, R. B., *Midwestern Progressive Politics, 1870–1938*. Michigan State Univ. Press, 1959

D. The West
Fogelson, R. U., *The Fragmented Metropolis: Los Angeles, 1850–1930*. Harvard Univ. Press, 1967
Fuller, G. W., *History of the Pacific Northwest*. 2nd ed. New York, 1938
Johansen, D. O., and Gates, C. M., *Empire of the Columbia: A History of the Pacific North-
    West*. New York, 1957
Parrish, P. H., *Before the Covered Wagon*. Portland, Oreg., 1931
Quiett, G. C., *They Built the West, An Epic of Rails and Cities*. New York and London, 1934
Scott, H. W., *History of the Oregon Country*. 6 vols. Cambridge, Mass, 1924
Winther, O. O., *The Great Northwest: A History*. 2nd ed., rev. New York, 1950

ALABAMA

HISTORY. Alabama, settled in 1702 as part of the French Province of Louisiana, and ceded to the British in 1763, was organized as a Territory, 1817, and admitted into the Union on 14 Dec. 1819.

AREA AND POPULATION. Alabama is bounded north by Tennessee, east by Georgia, south by Florida and the Gulf of Mexico and west by Mississippi. Area, 51,609 sq. miles, including 901 sq. miles of inland water. Census population, 1 April 1980, 3,861,466, an increase of 12·1% over that of 1970. Births, 1978, 60,108 (16·1 per 1,000 population); deaths, 34,489 (9·2); infant deaths (under 28 days), 655 (10·9 per 1,000 live births); marriages, 47,720 (12·8); divorces, 25,059 (6·7).

Population in 5 census years (with distribution by sex, 1970) was:

	White	Negro	Indian	Asiatic	Total	Per sq. mile
1910	1,228,832	908,282	909	70	2,138,093	41·4
1930	1,700,844	944,834	465	105	2,646,248	51·3
1950	2,079,591	979,617	928	669	3,061,743	59·9
1960	2,283,609	980,271	1,726	915	3,266,740	64·0
			All others			
1970	2,533,831	903,469	6,867		3,444,165	66·7
Male	1,235,489	423,083	3,369		1,661,941	—
Female	1,298,342	480,384	3,498		1,782,224	—

Of the total population in 1970, 2,011,941 (58·4%) were urban (54·8% in 1960). Those 21 years or older numbered 2,020,959; 65 years or older, 325,961. Foreign-born whites numbered 15,988 in 1970. In 10 of the 67 counties Negroes constitute 50% or more of the population.

The large cities (1980 census, preliminary) were: Birmingham, 282,068 (metropolitan area, (1977 estimate) 807,955); Mobile, 199,392 (424,491); Huntsville, 142,238 (290,442); Montgomery (capital), 176,781 (254,154); Tuscaloosa, 73,228 (123,895).

CONSTITUTION AND GOVERNMENT. The present constitution dates from 1901; it has had 393 amendments. The legislature consists of a Senate of 35 members and a House of Representatives of 105 members, all elected for 4 years. The Governor and Lieut.-Governor are elected for 4 years.

The state is represented in Congress by 2 senators and 7 representatives. Applicants for registration must take an 'anti-communist oath' and fill out a questionnaire to the satisfaction of the registrars. In the 1980 presidential election Reagan polled 654,192 votes, Carter, 636,730 and Anderson, 15,844.

Montgomery is the capital.

Governor: Forrest H. James Jr. (D.), 1979–83 ($50,000).
Lieut.-Governor: George McMillan ($11,835).
Secretary of State: Don Siegelman (D.) ($25,800).

BUDGET. The total receipts for the fiscal year ending 30 Sept. 1979 were $4,858·2m.; total expenditure was $4,820·3m.

The net long-term debt on 30 Sept. 1979 amounted to $1,184·6m.
Per capita income (1979) was $6,962.

ENERGY AND NATURAL RESOURCES

Minerals. Production of principal minerals (1979): Coal, about 23·72m. short tons; Portland cement, 3·3m. short tons. Total (non-fuel) mineral output (1978) was valued at $319m.

Agriculture. The number of farms in 1979 was 54,000, covering 13·2m. acres; average farm had 244 acres and was valued at $117,000.

Cash receipts from farm marketings, 1979: Crops, $810·6m.; livestock and products, $1,292·1m.; and total, $2,102·7m. Principal crops: soybeans, cotton, corn and peanuts; potatoes, tomatoes, hay and wheat are also important. In 1978, poultry accounted for the largest percentage of cash receipts from farm marketings; cattle and calves were second, hogs third, dairy products fourth. Soybeans are the most valuable crop.

Forestry. Area of national forest lands Dec. 1978, 642,820 acres.

INDUSTRY. Alabama is predominantly industrial. In 1980, 5,850 manufacturing establishments employed 370,650 production workers, earning over $5,200m. Pig-iron, 1978, amounted to 3·4m. net tons.

TOURISM is rapidly expanding and is considered the largest single industry. Total receipts of tourism amounted to $2·2m. in 1979.

COMMUNICATIONS

Roads. Paved roads of all classes in 1978 totalled 57,329 miles; total highways, 87,013 miles.

Railways. In 1978 the railways had a length of 4,437 miles.

Aviation. In 1978 the state had 202 airfields.

Shipping. The only port is Mobile, with a large ocean-going trade; imports (1979–80), 25,138,556 tons; exports, 16,478,024 tons. The 9-ft channel of the Tennessee River traverses North Alabama for 200 miles; the Warrior–Tombigbee Waterway (476 miles) connects the Birmingham industrial area with Mobile and also with the Gulf Intracoastal Waterway; the Chattahoochee River 9-ft channel extends from the Gulf to Phenix City (Alabama). In 1971 a 9-ft channel was completed which connects Montgomery and Mobile through the Alabama River System. The Alabama State Docks also operates a system of 14 inland docks; there is 1 privately-run inland dock.

JUSTICE, RELIGION, EDUCATION AND WELFARE

Justice. The prison population on 30 Sept. 1980 was 6,133.

From 1927 to 1965 there were 153 executions (electrocution): 121 for murder, 25 for rape, 5 for armed robbery, 1 for burglary and 1 for carnal knowledge.

The transport system is now integrated.

In 39 counties the state controls the sale of alcoholic beverage, while 28 counties remain 'bone dry'.

Religion. Chief religious bodies (in 1971) are: Southern Baptists (948,769), National (Black) Baptists (550,000), Church of Christ (350,000), United Methodist (274,531), Roman Catholic (85,991), Presbyterian (39,513), Episcopalian (32,303).

Education. In 1977–78 the 1,323 public elementary and high schools required 39,513 teachers to teach 773,051 pupils enrolled in grades K–12. In 1978–79 the 14 senior or 4-year universities had 98,506 students and 4,027 full-time faculty members. The 21 junior colleges had 37,837 students and 1,064 teachers, 28 vocational technical schools 16,500 students and 850 teachers.

Health. In 1980 there were 137 hospitals (120,260 beds) licensed by the State Board of Health. In 1979 hospitals for mental diseases had approximately 1,000 beds.

Pensions and Security. In Aug. 1980 Alabama paid supplements (to federal welfare payments) to 12,405 recipients of old-age assistance, receiving an average of $59.83 a month; 3,840 permanently and totally disabled, $63.67; 137 blind, $59.83. Combined state–federal aid to dependent children was paid to 62,819 families, average $108.77 per family per month.

Books of Reference

Alabama Official and Statistical Register. Montgomery. Quadrennial
Alabama Encyclopædia. Vol. I. Northport, 1965
Economic Abstract of Alabama. Center for Business and Economic Research, Univ. of Alabama, 1975
The Deep South in Transformation: A Symposium. Univ. of Alabama Press, 1964
Farmer, H., *The Legislative Process in Alabama.* Univ. of Alabama, 1949

ALASKA

HISTORY. Discovered in 1741 by Vitus Bering, its first settlement, on Kodiak Island, was in 1784. The area known as Russian America with its capital (1806) at Sitka was ruled by a Russo-American fur company and vaguely claimed as a Russian colony. Alaska was purchased by the United States from Russia under the treaty of 30 March 1867 for $7·2m. It was not organized until 1884, when it became a 'district' governed by the code of the state of Oregon. By Act of Congress approved 24 Aug. 1912 Alaska became an incorporated Territory; its first legislature in 1913 granted votes to women, 7 years in advance of the Constitutional Amendment.

Alaska officially became the 49th state of the Union on 3 Jan. 1959.

AREA AND POPULATION. Alaska is bounded north by the Beaufort Sea, west and south by the Pacific and east by Canada. It has the largest area of any state, being more than twice the size of Texas. The gross area (land and water) is 586,400 sq. miles; the land area is 571,065 sq. miles, of which 96·4% was in federal ownership in 1975. Census population, 1 April 1980 (preliminary), was 400,481, including military personnel, an increase of 32·5% over 1970. Births, 1978 (provisional), were 8,761 (21·7 per 1,000 population); deaths, 1,762 (4·4); infant deaths, 143 (16·3 per 1,000 live births); marriages, 5,102 (12·7); divorces, 3,353 (8·3).

Census population: 1880, 33,426; 1900, 63,592; 1910, 64,356; 1940, 72,526; 1950, 128,643; 1960, 226,167; 1970, 302,173; 1980 (preliminary), 400,481.

The white population in 1970 numbered 236,767 (163,258 males and 137,124 females); Indians, Aleuts, Eskimos and others, 54,704; Negroes, 8,911.

The largest town is Anchorage, which had a 1980 census population of 173,992. Metropolitan area populations (1976), Anchorage, 185,200; Fairbanks, 51,500; Juneau, 18,800; Ketchikan, 11,400. There are 11 major incorporated boroughs. The total assessed valuation of cities and boroughs was $8,607·2m. in 1977. There were 11 home-rule cities, 20 first-class cities and about 110 second-class cities in Jan. 1976.

CONSTITUTION AND GOVERNMENT. An important provision of the Enabling Act is that the state has the right to select 103·55m. acres of vacant and unappropriated public lands in order to establish 'a tax basis'; it can open these lands to prospectors for minerals, and the state is to derive the principal advantage in all gains resulting from the discovery of minerals. In addition, certain federally administered lands reserved for conservation of fisheries and wild life have been transferred to the state. Special provision is made for federal control of land for defence in areas of high strategic importance.

The constitution of Alaska was adopted by public vote, 24 April 1956. The state legislature consists of a Senate of 20 members (elected for 4 years) and a House of

Representatives of 40 members (elected for 2 years). The state sends 2 senators and 1 representative to Congress. The franchise may be exercised by all citizens over 18 years of age.

The capital is Juneau. A new capital site near Anchorage was chosen in 1976.

In the 1980 presidential election Reagan polled 86,112 votes, Carter 41,842.

Governor: Jay S. Hammond (R.), 1979– ($50,000).
Lieut.-Governor: Lowell Thomas, Jr (R.) ($44,000).

ECONOMY

Budget. Total state government revenue for the year ended 30 June 1978 (Annual Financial Report figures) was $1,095m. ($544·4m. from taxation, $310·6.m from federal sources). Total expenditure was $1,152m. (including $317·2m. for personal services and $446m. for grants, claims and shared revenue).

In 1976 a Permanent Fund was set up for the deposit of at least 25% of all mineral-related revenue. Cash and investment holdings at 30 Sept. 1978, $73·7m.

Net bonded debt on 30 June 1973 was $274m.

Per capita income (1977) was $10,438.

Banking. Total assets at 30 Sept. 1978 were $2,198m., total deposits $1,858m.

ENERGY AND NATURAL RESOURCES

Oil and Gas. Commercial production of crude petroleum began in 1959 and by 1961 had become the most important mineral by value. Production: 1961, 6,327,000 bbls (of 42 gallons); 1965, 11m. bbls; 1976, 67m. bbls; 1977, 169m. bbls, value $989m. Estimate for 1978, the first full year of production for the Prudhoe Bay oilfield, 450m. bbls. Oil comes mainly from Prudhoe Bay, the McArthur River field and several Cook Inlet fields. Natural gas production, 1977, 187,889m. cu. ft, value $75·5m. Alaska receives 90% of all royalties (12·5%) from oil, gas and coal production on federal lands and the full 12·5% royalty for oil and gas production in state lands (coal royalties are being negotiated). Revenue to the state from oil and gas production tax in 1977 was $23·9m. and from reserves tax $720·6m. In 1969, the state conducted a major competitive lease sale for the arctic coastal region where reserves are estimated to be as large as 50,000m. bbls.

Oil from the Prudhoe Bay arctic field is now carried by the Trans-Alaska pipeline to Prince William Sound on the south coast, where a tanker terminal has been built at Valdez.

Minerals. Value of production, 1977, $160m.: sand and gravel (66m. short tons), $134·25m.; gold (18,962 troy oz.), $2·81m.; others, including silver, gemstones, lead, copper, tin, barite and platinum group minerals, $22·79m.

Agriculture. In some parts of the state the climate during the brief spring and summer (about 100 days in major areas and 152 days in the south-eastern coastal area) is suitable for agricultural operations, thanks to the long hours of sunlight, but Alaska is a food-importing area. In 1964, 1,959,440 acres were classified as agricultural land, 90% of this was unimproved pasture primarily government leases for grazing of sheep and beef cattle in south-west Alaska. In 1977 about 20,000 acres was cultivated. In 1979 (preliminary) there were 8,500 cattle, 3,900 milch cows, 1,100 hogs and 5,500 sheep stock.

Farm production in 1978: Milk, $2·6m.; eggs, $458,000; silage, $457,000; potatoes, $932,000.; hay, $2·65m.; beef and veal, $435,000; barley, $570,000; vegetables, $560,000.

There were about 31,000 reindeer in western Alaska in 1969, owned by individual Eskimo herders except for 750 at Nome owned by the Government. Reindeer meat production, 1977, $275,000.

Forestry. In south-eastern Alaska timber fringes the shore of the mainland and all the islands extending inland to a depth of 5 miles. The state's enormous forests could produce an estimated annual sustained yield of 1,500m. bd ft of lumber, nearly twice Alaska's record 1973 cut. Alaska has 2 national forests: the Tongass of 16·8m. acres and the Chugach of 4·8m. acres. An estimated total of 602·4m. bd ft was cut in 1977, of which 491·5m. came from national forests and 60·2m. from state forests. Alaska has 2 large pulp-mills at Ketchikan and Sitka.

Fisheries. The catch for 1977 (estimate) was 674·5m. lb. of fish and shellfish having a value to fishermen of $350·8m. This compares with 471m. lb. in 1971 with a value of $85·5m. Salmon remains the highest per unit value species, with a catch in 1977 of 306·7m. lb. valued to the fishermen at $173·2m.

INDUSTRY. Main industries with employment, 1977: Government, 50,700; trade, 28,500; services, 27,400; contract construction, 19,500; manufacturing, 10,900; oil and gas 4,600.

The major manufacturing industry was food processing, followed by timber industries. Total employment outside agriculture, 166,000. Total wages and salaries, $3,538,881,000.

A gas liquefaction plant is under construction on the Kenai Peninsula; there is already a fertilizer plant in Kenai. An oil refinery and petrochemical complex is being built at Valdez.

TOURISM. About 430,000 tourists visited the state in 1978.

COMMUNICATIONS

Roads. Alaska's highway and road system, 1974, totalled 9,848 miles, including marine highway systems, local service roads, borough and city streets, national park, forest and reservation roads and military roads, of which 4,692 miles were surfaced primary roads; unsurfaced secondary roads totalled 3,654 miles. Registered motor vehicles, 1977, 329,672.

The Alaska Highway extends 1,523 miles from Dawson Creek, British Columbia, to Fairbanks, Alaska. It was built by the US Army in 1942, at a cost of $138m. The greater portion of it, because it lies in Canada, is maintained by the Canadian Government.

Railways. There is a railway of 111 miles from Skagway to the town of Whitehorse, in the Canadian Yukon region. The government-owned Alaska Railroad runs from Seward to Fairbanks, a distance of 471 miles.

Aviation. In 1974 the state had about 766 airports, of which about 545 were publicly owned. Passengers by air to and from Alaska's international airports Anchorage and Fairbanks (1977) numbered 2·8m. at Anchorage and 548,600 at Fairbanks; freight handled, 132,500 short tons at Anchorage and 76,300 at Fairbanks. General aviation aircraft in the state per 1,000 population was about ten times the US average.

Shipping. Regular shipping services to and from the US are furnished by 2 steamship lines and several barge lines operating out of Seattle and other Pacific coast ports. Two Canadian companies also furnish a regular service from Vancouver, B.C. Freight handled at the Port of Anchorage, 1977 (short tons): Bulk petroleum, 1·13m.; vans, flats and containers, 978,584; cement and drilling mud, 37,943; vehicles, 40,360; total 2·2m.

A 490-mile ferry system for motor cars and passengers (the 'Marine Highway') operates from Seattle, Washington and Prince Rupert (British Columbia) to Juneau, Haines (for access to the Alaska Highway) and Skagway. A second system extends throughout the south-central region of Alaska linking the Cook Inlet area with Kodiak Island and Prince William Sound.

JUSTICE, RELIGION, EDUCATION AND WELFARE

Justice. There is no death penalty in Alaska.

Religion. In Alaska are many religious missions representing the Russian Orthodox, Roman Catholic, Episcopalian, Presbyterian, Methodist and other denominations.

Education. During 1977–78 there were 87,094 pupils at public schools, 3,178 at private schools. The Bureau of Indian Affairs schools had 2,983 pupils attending schools in the state. The University of Alaska (founded in 1922) had (1978) 4,382 students on the main campus, 3,341 at its branches in Anchorage and Juneau and 13,958 in community colleges. Other colleges had 674 students in 1978.

Welfare. Old-age assistance was established under the Federal Social Security Act; in 1976 aid to dependent children funds covered a monthly average of 13,299 persons; dependent children received an average of $76 per month; adult public assistance (including old age assistance, aid to the blind and to the disabled) was given to a monthly average of 3,469 persons receiving on average $109 per month.

Health. In 1974 there were 26 civilian hospitals with 1,600 beds, of which 11 were federal public health hospitals; there were 2 mental hospitals and 3 regional mental health clinics.

Books of Reference

Statistical Information: Department of Commerce and Economic Development, Division of Economic Enterprise, Pouch EE, Juneau.

Alaska Economic Information. Reporting Service, Division of Economic Enterprise, Juneau 99811. Quarterly
Alaska Economy, The. Division of Economic Enterprise, Juneau. Annual
Alaskan Earthquake, preliminary report. Civil Defense Office (Army), Washington, 1964
Establishing a Business in Alaska. Division of Economic Enterprise, Juneau, 1976
Look North. Department of Economic Development, Juneau, 1970
Adams, B., *The Last Frontier.* New York, 1961
Gardey, J., *Alaska: The Sophisticated Wilderness.* London, 1976
Hulley, Clarence C., *Alaska Past and Present.* Portland, Oregon, 1970
Rogers, G. W., *Alaska in Transition: the south-east region.* Johns Hopkins Univ. Press, 1960.— *The Future of Alaska.* Johns Hopkins Univ. Press, 1962

State Library: Pouch G, Juneau. *Librarian:* Richard Engen.—Alaska Historical Library, Pouch G, Juneau. *Librarian:* Phyllis Nottingham.

ARIZONA

HISTORY. Arizona was settled in 1752, organized as a Territory in 1863 and became a state on 14 Feb. 1912.

AREA AND POPULATION. Arizona is bounded north by Utah, east by New Mexico, south by Mexico, west by California and Nevada. Area, 113,909 sq. miles, including 346·6 sq. miles of inland water. Of the total area (72,680,320 acres) 32,336,577 were owned by the federal government in 1970, including 19,623,000 acres held by the Office of Indian Affairs. Census population on 1 April 1980 (preliminary) was 2,717,866, an increase of 53·4% over 1970. Births, 1979, 46,549; deaths, 19,648; infant deaths, 559; marriages, 29,603; divorces, 19,982.

Population in 5 census years (with distribution by sex, 1970):

	White	Negro	Indian	Chinese	Japanese	Total	Per sq. mile
1910	171,468	2,009	29,201	1,305	371	204,354	1·8
1930	378,551	10,749	43,726	1,110	879	435,573	3·8
1950	654,511	25,974	65,761	1,951	780	749,587	6·6
1960	1,169,517	43,403	83,387	2,937	1,501	1,302,161	11·3
				All others			
1970	1,604,498	53,344	95,812	16,640		1,772,482	15·6

			All others		
Male	587,872	22,252	44,804	654,928	—
Female	581,645	21,151	44,437	647,233	—

Of the total population in 1970, 1,408,864 (79·6%) were urban (74·5% in 1960). The 1980 (preliminary) census population of Phoenix was 781,443; Tucson, 331,506; Scottsdale, 87,700; Tempe, 106,306; Mesa, 149,328; Glendale, 92,797.

CONSTITUTION AND GOVERNMENT. The state constitution (1910, with now 70 amendments) placed the government under direct control of the people through the Initiative, Referendum and the Recall. The state Senate consists of 30 members, and the House of Representatives of 60, all elected for 2 years. Arizona sends to Congress 2 senators and 5 representatives. In the 1980 presidential election Reagan polled 529,688 votes, Carter 246,843, Anderson 76,952, Clark 18,784 and DeBerry 1,094.

The state capital is Phoenix. The state is divided into 14 counties.

Governor: Bruce Babbitt (D.), 1978– ($35,000).
Secretary of State: Rose Mofford (D.).

BUDGET. General revenues, year ending 30 June 1979 (US Census Bureau figures), were $1,703·8m. (taxation, $1,172m. and federal aid, $317·3m.); general expenditures, $1,612·9m. (education, $813·4m.; highways, $456·6m., and public welfare, $263·9m.).

Per capita income (1979) was $8,305.

NATURAL RESOURCES

Minerals. The mining industries of the state are important, but less so than agriculture and manufacturing. By value the most important mineral produced is copper. Production (1979): Copper (1,042,788 short tons); gold (101,015 troy oz.) and silver (7,300,000 troy oz.) are both largely recovered from copper ore. Other minerals include sand and gravel (28m. short tons), zinc (4,460 short tons in 1977) and lead (445 short tons in 1978). Total value of minerals mined in 1979 was $2,487,995,000.

Agriculture. Arizona, despite its dry climate, is well suited for agriculture along the water-courses and where irrigation is practised on a large scale from great reservoirs constructed by the US as well as by the state government and private interests. Irrigated area, 1977, 4·3m. acre-feet. The wide pasture lands are favourable for the rearing of cattle and sheep, but numbers are either stationary or declining compared with 1920.

In 1976 Arizona contained 5,900 farms and ranches with 1·3m. acres (1979 estimate) of crop land, out of a total farm and pastoral area of 37·2m. acres. The average farm (1977) was estimated at 6,640 acres. Farming is highly commercialized and mechanized and concentrated largely on cotton (1,500 cotton farms 1976) picked by machines and by Indian, Mexican and migratory workers.

Areas under cotton (1979), 618,300 acres; 1·3m. bales (of 500 lb.) of upland and 67,000 bales of American Pima cotton were harvested in 1979.

Cash income, 1979, from crops, $905m.; from livestock, $827m. Most important cereals are grain sorghums and barley; other crops include oranges, grapefruit and lettuce. On 1 Jan. 1979 there were 1·2m. all cattle, 14,850 milch cows, 60,000 sheep and 125,000 swine. The wool clip in 1979 amounted to 2·57m. lb.

Forestry. The national forests in the state had an area (1976) of 11·36m. acres.

INDUSTRY. Manufacturing establishments (numbering 2,562 in 1979) had 142,100 production workers, earning $2,237·4m.; value of output (1979) $4,800m.

TOURISM. In 1979 total estimated tourist business in the state was $4,040m.

COMMUNICATIONS

Roads. In 1978 there were 36,700 miles of public roads and streets maintained by counties and cities, and 18,000 miles maintained by federal agencies.

Aviation. Airports, 1979, numbered 206, of which 105 were for public use.

JUSTICE, RELIGION, EDUCATION AND WELFARE

Justice. A 'right-to-work' amendment to the constitution, adopted 5 Nov. 1946, makes illegal any concessions to trade-union demands for a 'closed shop'.

The Arizona state prison 30 June 1980 held 1,945. There have been no executions since 1963; from 1930 to 1963 there were 38 executions (lethal gas) all for murder, and all men (28 whites, 10 Negro).

Religion. The leading religious bodies are Roman Catholics and Mormons (Latter Day Saints); others include Methodists, Presbyterians, Baptists and Episcopalians. No recent statistics of membership are available.

Education. School attendance is compulsory between the ages of 8 and 16 years, and instruction is free for pupils from 6 to 21 years of age. The enrolled pupils in 1978–79 in the elementary schools were 339,045 and public high schools had 163,134 pupils. Teachers for both elementary and high schools totalled (1978) 26,116. The total expenditure for public schools was $1,046·5m. Teachers' salaries averaged (1978) $10,925. The state maintains 3 universities at Tucson, Tempe and Flagstaff and 16 junior colleges.

Health. In 1978 there were 72 hospitals reported by the State Department of Health; capacity 10,263 beds. Resident patients in mental hospitals on 30 June 1979 numbered 176.

Social Security. Old-age assistance (maximum depending on the programme) is given, with federal aid, to needy citizens 65 years of age or older. In June 1980, 2,300 people were receiving general assistance at an average of $105.29 a month; 18,875 families (52,642 recipients), $61.55 per recipient in aid to dependent children; in the supplemental payment programme 1,200 old persons received $86.38 per month; 6 blind, $61.17; 663 totally disabled, $36.44.

Books of Reference

Arizona Statistical Review. 36th ed. Valley National Bank, Phoenix, 1980
Federal Writers' Project. *Arizona: The Grand Canyon State.* 4th ed. New York, 1966
Cross, J. L., ed., *Arizona, its People and Resources.* Tucson, 1960
Goff, J. S., *Arizona Civilization.* 2nd ed. Cave Creek, 1970
Mason, B. B., and Hink, H., *Constitutional Government of Arizona.* 6th ed. Tempe, 1979
Morey, R. D., *Politics and Legislation: The Office of Governor in Arizona.* Tucson, 1965
Wyllys, R. K., *Arizona: The History of a Frontier State.* Phoenix, 1951

State Library: Department of Library, Archives and Public Records, Capitol, Phoenix 85007.
Acting Director: Sharon G. Womack.

ARKANSAS

HISTORY. Arkansas was settled in 1686, made a Territory in 1819 and admitted into the Union on 15 June 1836. The name originated with the Quapaw Indian tribe. The constitution, which dates from 1874, has been amended 57 times.

AREA AND POPULATION. Arkansas is bounded north by Missouri, east by Tennessee and Mississippi, south by Louisiana, south-west by Texas and west by Oklahoma. Area, 53,104 sq. miles (1,159 sq. miles being inland water). Census population on 1 April 1980 (preliminary) was 2,285,513, an increase of 18·8% from that of 1970. Births, 1978, were 34,747 (15·9 per 1,000 population); deaths, 21,826 (10); infant deaths, 562 (16·2 per 1,000 live births); marriages, 25,096 (11·5); divorces 19,964 (9·1).

Population in 5 census years (with distribution by sex, 1970) was:

	White	Negro	Indian	Asiatic	Total	Per sq. mile
1910	1,131,026	442,891	460	72	1,574,449	30·0
1930	1,375,315	478,463	408	296	1,854,482	35·2
1950	1,481,507	426,639	533	832	1,909,511	36·3
1960	1,395,703	388,787	580	1,202	1,786,272	34·0
			All others			
1970	1,565,915	352,445	4,935		1,923,295	37·0
Male	762,982	167,019	2,309		932,310	—
Female	802,933	185,426	2,626		990,985	—

Of the total population in 1970, 960,865 persons (50%) were urban (43% in 1960); 1,169,498 were 21 years of age or older. Foreign-born numbered 8,287.

Little Rock (capital) had a population of 153,467 in 1980 (preliminary); Fort Smith, 71,515; North Little Rock, 34,319; Pine Bluff, 56,811; Hot Springs, 35,513; Fayetteville, 36,165; Jonesboro, 31,228; West Memphis, 28,198. The population of the largest standard metropolitan statistical areas: Little Rock–North Little Rock, 391,910; Fort Smith (Arkansas portion), 131,656; Fayetteville–Springdale, 177,474; Pine Bluff, 90,761.

GOVERNMENT. The General Assembly consists of a Senate of 35 members elected for 4 years, partially renewed every 2 years, and a House of Representatives of 100 members elected for 2 years. The sessions are biennial and usually limited to 60 days. The Governor and Lieut.-Governor are elected for 2 years. The state is represented in Congress by 2 senators and 4 representatives.

In the 1980 presidential election Reagan polled 402,945 votes, Carter 379,919.

The state is divided into 75 counties; the capital is Little Rock.

Governor: Frank White (R.), 1981–82 ($35,000).
Lieut.-Governor: Winston Bryant (D.) ($14,000).
Secretary of State: Paul Riviere (D.) ($22,500).

FINANCE

Budget. The state's general revenue for the fiscal year 1979 was $1,798·3m., of which taxation furnished $994·6m. and federal aid, $637·7m. General expenditure was $1,773·5m., of which education took $681·2m.; highways, $299·8m., and public welfare, $307·7m.

Net long-term debt on 30 June 1979 was $216·2m.

Per capita income (1979) was $6,933.

Banking. At 30 June 1979 total bank deposits were $8,239·9m.

ENERGY AND NATURAL RESOURCES

Minerals. In 1979 crude petroleum amounted to 18·9m. bbls; natural gas, 132·4m. cu. ft; bromine brine, 234·7m. bbls; crushed stone, 14m. tons; sand and gravel, 13·1m. tons. Arkansas produces about 90% of the country's supply of bauxite for aluminium; production 1978, 1·9m. tons dried bauxite equivalent. The state has a large coal area; 224,655 short tons were mined in 1979. Total mineral output in 1979 was valued at $667·9m.

Agriculture. Arkansas is an agricultural state. In 1978 (Federal Census Preliminary Report), 58,788 farms had a total area of 15·6m. acres; average farm was of 265 acres; 7·7m. acres were harvested cropland; 1,689,052 acres were irrigated.

The largest source of income in 1979 was soybeans ($825·6m.), chickens including broilers ($694·9m), cattle and calves ($455·8m.); rice ($399·8m.); eggs ($211·6m.) and cotton ($192·1m.). Cash farm income (1979) was $3,171·7m.; from crops, $1,538·9m., and from livestock, $1,623·8m.

Livestock on 1 Jan. 1980 included 2m. all cattle, 88,000 milch cows, 4,900 sheep (1978) and 600,000 swine.

INDUSTRY. In June 1980 total employment averaged 884,000 (61,350 agricultural, 212,150 manufacturing, 161,550 wholesale and retail trade, 144,650 government). The Arkansas Department of Labor estimated that 168,100 factory production workers earned an average $221.52 per week (39 hours). The most important manufacturing group was food and kindred products employing 32,450, followed by electric and electronic equipment (24,300) and lumber and wood products (20,000). Construction employed 36,550.

COMMUNICATIONS

Roads. Total road mileage, 79,424 miles. State-maintained highways (1 Jan. 1979) total 15,997 miles; local county highways, 47,722 miles; city streets, 8,717 miles. In 1978 there were 1,478,617 registered motor vehicles.

Railways. In 1979 there were in the state 5,308·4 miles of commercial railway.

Aviation. Five air carrier and 5 commuter airlines serve the state; there were, in 1978, 244 airports (78 publicly-owned and 166 private).

Waterways. There are 1,237 miles of navigable streams including the Kerr-McClellan Channel which bisects the state and gives access to the sea *via* the Mississippi River.

EDUCATION, RELIGION AND WELFARE

Education. In the school year 1978–79 elementary and secondary schools had 475,891 enrolled pupils and 22,837 classroom teachers. Average salaries of teachers in elementary and secondary schools was $11,006. Expenditure on elementary and secondary education was $636m.

An educational TV network began operating in 1966 with a full 12-hour-day telecasting.

Higher education is provided at 31 institutions: 9 state universities, 1 medical college, 12 private or church colleges, 9 community and junior colleges. Total enrolment in institutions of higher education, 1980–81, was 74,018.

There were (1979–80) 23 vocational-technical schools with 58,540 students, including extension class students. Total expenditure, 1979–80, $14·9m.

Religion. The most numerous religious bodies in the state are Baptist (601,200 members estimated in 1979), Methodist (219,398), Roman Catholic (53,555) and Assembly of God (26,910). Total known membership, all denominations, 976,867.

Social Welfare. In 1980, 44,846 persons were drawing old-age assistance at an average amount of $87.07 per month; 29,203 families (62,149 children), $150.91 per family; 1,529 blind persons, $141.32; 33,351 totally and permanently disabled, $133.58.

There were 100 licensed hospitals (with 11,578 beds) in 1980, and 221 licensed nursing homes (21,255 beds); resident patients in mental hospitals, numbered 875.

State prisons in Oct. 1980 had 2,752 inmates (12·6 per 100,000 population).

Books of Reference

State and County Economic Data for Arkansas. Industrial Research and Extension Center, Little Rock

Ferguson and Atkinson, *Historic Arkansas.* Little Rock, 1966

Fletcher, J. G., *Arkansas.* Univ. of N. Carolina, Chapel Hill, 1947

CALIFORNIA

HISTORY. California, first settled in July 1769, was from its discovery down to 1846 politically associated with Mexico. On 7 July 1846 the American flag was hoisted at Monterey, and a proclamation was issued declaring California to be a portion of the US, and on 2 Feb. 1848, by the treaty of Guadalupe–Hidalgo, the territory was formally ceded by Mexico to the US, and was admitted to the Union 9 Sept. 1850 as the thirty-first state, with boundaries as at present.

AREA AND POPULATION. Area, 158,693 sq. miles (2,120 sq. miles being inland water). In 1974 the federal government owned 45m. acres (45·03% of the land area); in 1975, 546,000 acres were under jurisdiction of the Bureau of Indian Affairs, of which 472,000 acres were tribal. Public lands, vacant in 1975, totalled 15,607,125 acres, practically all either mountains or deserts.

Census population, 1 April 1980 (preliminary), 23,668,562, an increase of 18·6% over 1970, making California the most populous state of the USA (New York: 17,557,288). Births in 1977, 347,434 (16 per 1,000 population); deaths, 170,755 (8·1); infant deaths, 4,196 (12·1 per 1,000 live births); marriages, 149,416 (6·8); divorces, dissolutions and nullities, 132,193 (6·0).

Population in 5 census years (with distribution by sex, 1970) was:

	White	Negro	Japanese	Chinese	Total (incl. all others)	Per sq. mile
1910	2,259,672	21,645	41,356	36,248	2,377,549	15·3
1930	5,408,260	81,048	97,456	37,361	5,677,251	36·2
1950	9,915,173	462,172	84,956	58,324	10,586,223	67·5
1960	14,455,230	883,861	157,317	95,600	15,717,204	100·4
1970	17,761,032	1,400,143	213,280	170,131	19,953,134	125·7
Male	8,731,367	683,026	99,567	87,835	9,816,685	—
Female	9,029,665	717,117	113,713	82,296	10,136,449	—

Of the 1970 population 90·9% were urban (86·4% in 1960). The largest county, Los Angeles, had (1 July 1976) 6,970,100. Those 21 years old or older numbered 12·25m.; foreign-born whites were 1,512,435.

The largest cities with 1980 (preliminary) census population are:

Los Angeles	2,950,010	Fresno	216,365	Fremont	131,486
San Diego	870,006	Anaheim	214,688	Torrance	129,511
San Francisco	674,063	Santa Ana	204,089	Garden Grove	125,085
San José	625,763	Huntington Beach	170,597	San Bernardino	118,092
Long Beach	356,906	Riverside	169,677	Pasadena	117,861
Oakland	338,721	Stockton	145,841	Berkeley	103,134
Sacramento	274,488	Glendale	137,279		

Urbanized areas (1970 census): Los Angeles–Long Beach, 8,351,266; San Francisco–Oakland, 2,987,850; San Diego, 1,198,323; San José, 1,025,273; Sacramento, 633,732; San Bernardino–Riverside, 583,597; Fresno, 262,908.

CONSTITUTION AND GOVERNMENT. The present constitution became effective from 4 July 1879; it has had numerous amendments since 1962. The Senate is composed of 40 members elected for 4 years—half being elected each 2 years—and the Assembly, of 80 members, elected for 2 years. Two-year regular sessions convene in Dec. of each even-numbered year. The Governor and Lieut.-Governor are elected for 4 years.

California is represented in Congress by 2 senators and 45 representatives.

In the 1980 presidential election Reagan polled 4,524,835 votes, Carter 3,083,652 and Anderson 739,832.

The capital is Sacramento. The state is divided into 58 counties.

Governor: Edmund G. Brown, Jr (D.), 1978 ($49,100).
Lieut.-Governor: Mike Curb (R.), 1978 ($42,500).
Secretary of State: March Fong Eu (D.) ($42,500).

BUDGET. For the year ending 30 June 1980 (estimates) total revenues were $20,293m.; total expenditures were $21,752m. ($7,816m. for education, $5,685m. for health and welfare).

The long-term state debt (general obligation bonds outstanding) was $6,017m. on 30 June 1979.

Per capita personal income (1979) was $10,018.

ENERGY AND NATURAL RESOURCES

Minerals. California is one of the three most important petroleum-producing states of the US (Texas and Louisiana being the other two); crude oil output was estimated at 341,000,000 bbls in 1979. Output of natural gas was 343,000m. cu. ft; of natural gas liquids, (1977) 8,117,000 bbls. Gold output was 7·6m. troy oz.; asbestos (1978), 70,730 short tons; boron minerals, diatomite, tungsten, sand and gravel, salt, magnesium compounds, lead, zinc, copper and iron ore are also produced. The estimated value of all the minerals produced (other than petroleum) was $1,740m.

Agriculture. Extending 700 miles from north to south, and intersected by several ranges of mountains, California has almost every variety of climate, from the very wet to the very dry, and from the temperate to the semi-tropical. Of the total surface area (100,313,600 acres), estimates (1971) show 5·9m. acres to be seriously eroded, 35·4m. acres moderately affected and 58·8m. with little or no erosion.

In 1974 there were 63,000 farms, comprising 36·2m. acres; average farm, 574 acres. Cotton, fruit, poultry and vegetables are important. Cash receipts, 1979, from crops, $7,230m.; from livestock and poultry, $4,170m. Cattle, dairy produce, cotton, grapes, hay, tomatoes (in that order) are the main sources of farm income.

Production of cotton lint, 1978, was 465,600 short tons; other field crops included sugar-beet (4·8m. short tons). Cereal crops include barley, 45·6m. bu.; wheat, 37·2m. bu., and rice, 26·2m. cwt in 1978. Principle crops (1978) include wine, table and raisin grapes (3,879,000 short tons); peaches (815,500 short tons); pears (288,200 short tons); apricots (123,000 short tons); prunes (131,000 short tons); plums, nectarines, avocados, olives and cherries. Citrus fruit crops were: Oranges, 47·1m. boxes; lemons, 47m. boxes; grapefruit, 8m. boxes.

On 1 Jan. 1979 the farm animals were: 860,000 milch cows, 4·7m. all cattle, 965,000 sheep and 190,000 swine.

Forestry. Total forest area in 1975 was 36,549,000 acres, of which 16,299,000 acres was commercial forest. California ranks third to Oregon and Washington in volume of standing timber (278,000m. bd ft); total annual cut is about 4,731·3m. bd ft (1976). National forest service land in 1975 was 20,250,000 acres.

Fishery. California ranks first as a fishing state (by value of fish caught). The catch in 1977 was 1,047m. lb.; leading species were anchovy, tuna and mackerel.

INDUSTRY. In 1979, manufacturing employed about 2m. The fastest-growing industries were instruments and related products, non-electrical machinery, electric and electronic equipment, transport equipment and fabricated metal products. The aerospace industry is important, as is also food-processing.

COMMUNICATIONS

Roads. In 1978 California had 51,108 miles of roads inside cities and 125,201 miles outside. In 1980 there were about 12m. registered cars and over 3m. commercial vehicles, leading all states in all items by a wide margin.

Railways. Total mileage of railways, 1 Jan. 1977, was 7,600 miles. There are 2 systems: Amtrack and Southern Pacific Railroad commuter trains. Amtrack carries about 900,000 passengers per year, Southern Pacific about 5m.

Aviation. In 1980 there were 311 public airports and 950 private airstrips.

Shipping. The chief ports are San Francisco and Los Angeles.

JUSTICE, RELIGION, EDUCATION AND WELFARE

Justice. State prisons, 31 Dec. 1978, had 19,116 inmates. From 1893 to 1942, 307 inmates were executed by hanging. From 1938 to 1976, 194 inmates were executed by lethal gas. No further death sentences were passed until 1980.

Religion. The Roman Catholic Church, with 2,483,411 adherents in 1954, is much stronger than any other single church; next are the Jewish congregations with an estimated 431,471 members, Methodists, Presbyterians and Baptists. There were 210,000 Episcopalians in 1973.

Education. Full-time attendance at school is compulsory for children from 6 to 16 years of age for a minimum of 175 days per annum, and part-time attendance is required from 16 to 18 years. In autumn 1977 there were 2,815,552 pupils enrolled in elementary schools and 1,341,448 pupils in secondary schools. Estimated expenditure on public schools, 1978–79, was $3,626·4m.

Community Colleges had 1,170,773 students in autumn 1978.

California has two publicly supported higher education systems: the University of California (1868) and the California State University and Colleges. In Jan. 1980, the University of California with campuses for resident instruction and research at Berkeley, Los Angeles, San Francisco and 6 other centres, had 121,489 full-time students. California State University and Colleges with campuses at Sacramento,

Long Beach, Los Angeles, San Francisco and 15 other cities had 229,350 full-time students in Jan. 1980. In addition to the 28 publicly supported institutions for higher education there are 266 private colleges and universities which had a total estimated enrolment of 129,567 in the autumn of 1978.

Health. In 1978 there were 562 general hospitals; capacity, 107,889 beds. On 30 June 1980 state hospitals for the mentally disabled had 4,836 patients and state hospitals for the developmentally disabled had 8,522 patients.

Social Security. On 1 Jan. 1974 the federal government (Social Security Administration) assumed responsibility for the Supplemental Security Income/State Supplemental Program which replaced the State Old-Age Security. The SSI/SSP provides financial assistance for needy aged (65 years or older), blind or disabled persons. An individual recipient may own assets up to $1,500; a couple up to $2,250, subject to specific exclusions. There are federal, state and county programmes assisting the aged, the blind, the disabled and needy children. In 1977–78, 470,657 families with one or more children were receiving an average of $314.15 per month per family.

Books of Reference

California Statistical Abstract. 19th ed. Dept. of Finance, Sacramento, 1978
Economic Report of the Governor. Annual. Governor's Office, Sacramento
Arnold, R. K. (ed.), *The California Economy 1947–1980.* Menlo Park, 1961
Crouch, W. E., and others, *California Government and Politics.* 2nd ed. New York, 1960
Turner, H. A., and Veig, J. A., *The Government and Politics of California.* 2nd ed. New York, 1964

State Library: The California State Library, Library-Courts Bldg, Sacramento 95814.

COLORADO

HISTORY. Colorado was first settled in 1858, made a Territory in 1861 and admitted into the Union on 1 Aug. 1876.

AREA AND POPULATION. Colorado is bounded north by Wyoming, north-east by Nebraska, east by Kansas, south-east by Oklahoma, south by New Mexico and west by Utah. Area, 104,247 sq. miles (450 sq. miles being inland water). Federal lands, 1974, 23,974,000 acres (36% of the land area).

Census population, 1 April 1980 (preliminary), was 2,888,834, an increase of 681,575 or 30·9% since 1970. Births, 1978, were 44,387 (16·6 per 1,000 population); deaths, 18,944 (7·1); infant deaths, 529 (11·9 per 1,000 live births); marriages, 30,362 (11·4); dissolutions, 17,524 (6·6).

Population in 5 census years (with distribution by sex, 1970) was:

	White	Negro	Indian	Asiatic	Total	Per sq. mile
1910	783,415	11,453	1,482	2,674	799,024	7·7
1930	1,018,793	11,828	1,395	3,775	1,035,791	10·0
1950	1,296,653	20,177	1,567	5,870	1,325,089	12·7
1960	1,700,700	39,992	4,288	8,967	1,753,947	16·7
1970	2,112,352	66,411	8,836	10,388	2,207,259	21·3
Male	1,041,364	34,047	4,513	4,861	1,089,377	—
Female	1,070,988	32,364	4,323	5,527	1,117,882	—

Of the total population in 1970, 1,581,739 (71·7%) were urban (73·7% in 1960); those 21 years or older were 1,301,577. Denver, the capital, had a 1980 census population of 488,765. Other cities with 1980 population: Colorado Springs, 206,939; Lakewood, 113,787; Aurora, 158,143; Pueblo, 101,504; Boulder, 76,228; Arvada, 77,749; Fort Collins, 66,235; Greeley, 52,480.

GOVERNMENT AND CONSTITUTION. The constitution adopted in 1876 is still in effect with (1970) 78 amendments. The General Assembly consists of a Senate of 35 members elected for 4 years, one-half retiring every 2 years, and of a House of Representatives of 65 members elected for 2 years. Sessions are annual, beginning 1951. The Governor, Lieut.-Governor, Attorney-General and Secretary of State are elected for 4 years. Qualified as electors are all citizens, male and female (except criminals and insane), 18 years of age, who have resided in the state for 32 days immediately preceding the election. The state is divided into 63 counties. The state sends to Congress 2 senators and 6 representatives.

In the 1980 presidential election Reagan polled 652,264 votes, Carter 368,009 and Anderson 130,633.

The capital is Denver.

Governor: Richard D. Lamm (D.), 1979 ($40,000).
Lieut.-Governor: Nancy Dick (D.) ($20,000).
Secretary of State: Mary E. Buchanan (R.) ($20,000).

BUDGET. The state's total budget, 1976–77, is $1,985m., of which taxation and other revenue furnish $979·7m. and federal grants $551·6m. Education takes $956·7m.; health, welfare and rehabilitation, $481·4m., and highways, $198·1m. Total state and local taxes *per capita* (1975–76) were $728.

The state has no general debt. The net long-term debt (in revenue bond) on 30 June 1974 was $126·7m.

Per capita personal income (1977) was $7,160.

ENERGY AND NATURAL RESOURCES

Minerals. Colorado has a variety of mineral resources. Among the most important are crude oil, coal and molybdenum. The world's largest molybdenum mine is at Climax; output since 1914 has been about 72% of the country's cumulative total. Mineral production, 1977, was: Gold, 72,668 oz. ($10·8m.); silver, 4·663m. oz. ($21·5m.); coal, 12·3m. tons ($197·3m.); lead, 23,000 tons ($14·1m.); zinc, 40,267 tons ($27·7m.); petroleum, 39·928m. bbls ($397·3m.); natural gas, 190,600m. cu. ft ($139m.); molybdenum, 75m. lb. ($276·5m.); uranium ore, 1·82m. lb ($33·4m.); vanadium, 12·275m. lb. ($25m.). Total mineral output in 1977 was valued at $1,346m.

Agriculture. Farms number about 29,000, with a total area of 39·0m. acres in 1978 (58·4% of the land area); 5,915,000 acres (1977) were harvested crop land; average farm, 1,345 acres (1978). Cash income, 1978, from crops, $560m.; from livestock, $2,074m. In 1974 there were 2,874,000 acres under irrigation.

Production of principal crops in 1978: Maize, 79m. bu. (from 695,000 acres); wheat, 57·3m. bu. (2·575m.); hay, 3m. tons (1·3m.); dry beans, 1·5m. cwt (150,000); potatoes, 11m. cwt (43,400); sugar-beet, 1·5m. tons (72,000); oats, rye, sorghums and broomcorn are grown, as well as fruit.

On 1 Jan. 1978 the number of farm animals was: 71,000 milch cows, 3·18m. all cattle, 810,000 sheep, 320,000 swine. The wool clip in 1977 yielded 8·8m. lb. of wool.

INDUSTRY. The 2,842 manufacturers (1972 census) had 132,600 employees, who earned $1,298·2m., value added by manufacture was $2,509·6m. Wholesale trade (1972) had 4,757 establishments with 49,435 employees, who earned $435·7m.; total value of wholesale sales was $8,030m. Retail trade (1972) had 24,335 establishments with 146,202 employees, who earned $709·9m.; total value of retail sales was $5,869m. Service industries had 24,011 establishments with 74,083 employees, who earned $398·6m.; total value of receipts of service industries was $1,234m. Distribution of employment in 1976 was: Government, 214,200; services, 194,200; retail trade, 193,600; manufacturing, 142,600; transport and utilities, 60,300.

TOURISM. During 1977 visitors to Colorado totalled 9·5m., including 6·65m. for ski-ing; there are 54 mountain peaks over 14,000 ft high, 27 of which rank among the 50 highest in the US. Tourist expenditures, $862m.

COMMUNICATIONS

Roads. The state highway system (1974) included 9,318 miles of highway. County roads totalled 67,572, and city streets, 7,634 miles. Total road mileage, 84,524, of which 9,892 miles are unmaintained county and city roads.

Railways. In 1973 there were in the state 3,492 miles of main-track and branch railway.

Aviation. There were (1973) 62 public airports and 42 private airports for general use.

JUSTICE, RELIGION, EDUCATION AND WELFARE

Justice. State prisons during 1974 had 1,350 inmates in the State Penitentiary and 685 in the State Reformatory. In 1967 there was 1 execution; since 1930 executions (by lethal gas) numbered 47, including 41 whites, 5 Negroes and 1 other; all were for murder.

Colorado has a Civil Rights Act (1935) forbidding places of public accommodation to discriminate against any persons on the grounds of race, religion, sex, colour or nationality. No religious test may be applied to teachers or students in the public schools, 'nor shall any distinction or classification of pupils be made on account of race or colour'. In 1957 the General Assembly prohibited discrimination in employment of persons in private industry and in 1959 adopted the Fair Housing Act to discourage discrimination in housing. A 1957 Act permits marriages between white persons and Negroes or mulattoes.

Religion. In 1970 the Roman Catholic Church had 412,000 members; the 100 Protestant and independent Churches totalled 404,000 members; the Jewish community had 26,000 members. Buddhism is among other religions represented.

Education. In autumn 1977 the public elementary and secondary schools had 561,807 pupils and 34,838 teachers and administrators; total instructional salaries averaged $14,838. Enrolments in universities and larger colleges, 1977, were: US Air Force Academy (Colorado Springs), 4,572 students; University of Colorado (Boulder), 21,767; University of Colorado (Denver), 8,832; University of Colorado (Colorado Springs), 4,127; University of Colorado (Medical Center), 1,477; Colorado State University (Fort Collins), 17,812; University of Denver (Denver), 7,753; Colorado School of Mines (Golden), 2,584; University of Northern Colorado (Greeley), 11,048; University of Southern Colorado (Pueblo), 5,166; Western State College (Gunnison), 3,152; Adams State College (Alamosa), 2,345; Metropolitan State College (Denver), 12,587; Colorado College (Colorado Springs), 1,928; Fort Lewis College (Durango), 2,787; Mesa College, 3,068.

Health. Approved hospitals, 1976, numbered 93 with 12,691 beds. In 1976, there were 26 public mental health centres, clinics and hospitals with 28,436 patients (1,102 per 100,000 population).

Social Security. A constitutional amendment, adopted 1956, provides for minimum old age pensions of $100 per month, which may be raised on a cost-of-living basis ($201 for 1976); for a $5m. stabilization fund and for a $10m. medical and health fund for pensioners. Old-age assistance is available to citizens 60 years of age and resident for stated periods, with assets not exceeding $1,000 (excluding home ownership). In 1975–76 an average of 21,754 persons were drawing an average of $36.46 per month. There were 150,032 recipients of medical assistance and 160,673 recipients of food stamp assistance.

Books of Reference

Directory of Colorado Manufacturers, 1979. Business Research Division, School of Business, University of Colorado, Boulder, 1979

Economic Outlook Forum, 1979. Colorado Division of Commerce and Development, and the College of Business, University of Colorado, Denver, 1978

State Library: Colorado State Library, State Capitol, Denver, 80203. *State Librarian:* Anne Marie Falsone.

CONNECTICUT

HISTORY. Connecticut was first settled in 1635 and has been an organized commonwealth since 1637. In 1629 a written constitution was adopted which, it is claimed, was the first in the history of the world formed under the concept of a social compact. This constitution was confirmed by a charter from Charles II in 1662, and replaced in 1818 by a state constitution, framed that year by a constitutional convention.

AREA AND POPULATION. Connecticut is bounded north and east by Massachusetts, south by the Atlantic and west by New York. Area, 4,862 sq. miles (110 sq. miles being inland water).

Census population, 1 April 1980 (preliminary), 3,107,576, an increase of 3% since 1970. Births (1978) were 35,695 (11·5 per 1,000 population); deaths, 26,104 (8·4); infant deaths, 342 (9·6 per 1,000 live births); marriages, 23,731 (7·7); divorces, 12,678 (4·1).

Population in 5 census years (with distribution by sex, 1970) was:

	White	Negro	Indian	Asiatic	Total	Per sq. mile
1910	1,098,897	15,174	152	533	1,114,756	231·3
1930	1,576,700	29,354	162	687	1,606,903	328·0
1950	1,952,329	53,472	333	1,146	2,007,280	409·7
1960	2,423,816	107,449	923	3,046	2,535,234	517·5
			All others			
1970	2,838,690	181,474	10,545		3,031,709	629·0
Male	1,378,771	85,975	5,772		1,470,518	—
Female	1,459,919	95,499	4,773		1,561,191	—

In 1970 foreign-born whites numbered 251,844. Of the total population, 2,343,578 persons (74%) were urban (78·3% in 1960). Those 21 years old or older numbered 1,866,908.

The chief cities and towns, with census population 1 April 1980, are:

Bridgeport	142,459	Bristol	57,177
Hartford	136,319	Meriden	56,506
New Haven	125,787	West Haven	53,128
Waterbury	102,230	Milford	50,886
Stamford	101,636		
Norwalk	76,730		
New Britain	73,684		
Danbury	59,303		

Larger urbanized areas, 1970 census: Hartford, 657,104; Bridgeport, 385,746; New Haven, 348,424; Waterbury, 206,625; Stamford, 204,888.

CONSTITUTION AND GOVERNMENT. The 1818 Constitution was revised in June 1953 effective 1 Jan. 1955. On 30 Dec. 1965 a new constitution went into effect, having been framed by a constitutional convention in the summer of 1965 and approved by the voters in Dec. 1965.

The 1965 Constitution provides for 30 to 50 members of the Senate (instead of 24 to 36) and for 125 to 225 members of the House of Representatives, to be elected from assembly districts, rather than 2 or 1 from each town, as in the former constitution. The convention has added a new provision for a 3-day session following each regular or special session, solely to reconsider bills vetoed by the Governor.

The General Assembly consists of a Senate of 36 members and a House of Representatives of 177 members. Members of each House are elected for the term of 2 years (annual salary $6,500 first year, $4,500 second year; expenses $1,000 and travel expenses). Legislative sessions are annual. The Governor and Lieut.-Governor are elected for 4 years. All citizens (with necessary exceptions and the usual residential requirements) have the right of suffrage.

Connecticut is one of the original 13 states of the Union. The state is represented in Congress by 2 senators and 6 representatives.

In the 1980 presidential election Reagan polled 677,210 votes, Carter 541,732. The state capital is Hartford.

Governor: Mrs Ella Grasso (D.), 1979–83 ($42,000).
Lieut.-Governor: William A. O'Neill (D.) ($18,000).
Secretary of State: Barbara M. Kennelly (D.) ($20,000).

BUDGET. For the year ending 30 June 1974 (state government figures) general revenues were $1,421,876,633 (taxation, $916·1m., and federal aid, $151·5m.); general expenditures were $1,252,929,660 (education, $4,759,983, highways, $260,449,380, and public welfare, $296,643,097).

The total net long-term debt on 30 June 1976 was $1,850,315,000.

Per capita income, 1973, was $5,889.

NATURAL RESOURCES

Minerals. The state has some mineral resources: sheet mica, sand, gravel, clays and stone; total production in 1972 was valued at $33,123,000.

Agriculture. In 1975 the state had 4,400 farms with a total area of 540,000 acres; average farm was of 123 acres, valued at $1,737 per acre. Of the farms, 2,795 were commercial in 1974 (4,500 in 1971) and 1,505 were residential or part-time. Total cash income, 1978, was $229·9m., including $89·5m. from crops and $140·5m. from livestock and products (mainly from dairy products and poultry). Principal crops are tobacco, hay, oats, maize, potatoes, apples, peaches, pears, vegetables and small fruit.

Livestock (1 Jan. 1973): 113,000 all cattle (value $38·9m.), 4,800 sheep ($134,000), 6,800 swine ($270,000) and 5m. poultry ($10m.).

Forestry. The state had (1975) 170,000 acres of state forest land, which is about 4·3% of the total land area.

INDUSTRY. Manufacturing establishments employed 420,800 production workers in Dec. 1974 who earned average weekly wages of $185.76; value added by manufacture (1973), $3·6m. Total non-agricultural employment in Dec. 1974 was 1,221,100.

COMMUNICATIONS

Roads. The state (1974) maintains 3,994 miles of highways, all surfaced. Motor vehicles registered 1 July 1973 numbered 2,103,813 (licences issued 1973, 1,213,141).

Railways. On 30 June 1974 there were 664 miles of railway track.

Aviation. In 1974 there were 68 airports (28 commercial including 5 state-owned, and 22 heliports).

JUSTICE, RELIGION, EDUCATION AND WELFARE

Justice. In 1970 there were no executions; since 1930 there have been 22 executions (19 by electrocution, 3 by hanging), including 19 whites and 3 Negroes, all for murder. The 6 community correctional centres, 1974, had 1,508 inmates; 5 correctional institutions had 1,136 inmates.

The Civil Rights Act makes it a punishable offence to discriminate against any person or persons 'on account of alienage, colour or race' and to hold up to ridicule any persons 'on account of creed, religion, colour, denomination, nationality or race'. Places of public resort are forbidden to discriminate. Insurance companies are forbidden to charge higher premiums to persons 'wholly or partially of African descent'. Schools must be open to all 'without discrimination on account of race or colour'.

Religion. The leading religious denominations (1974) in the state are the Roman Catholic (1,372,712 members), United Churches of Christ (124,042), Protestant Episcopal (111,489), Jewish (110,000), Greek Orthodox (60,000), Methodist (53,892), Baptist (42,270), Presbyterian (10,200).

Education. Elementary instruction is free for all children between the ages of 4 and 16 years, and compulsory for all children between the ages of 7 and 16 years. In 1974–75 the 847 public elementary schools had 449,407 enrolled pupils; the 146 high schools had 189,973 pupils; the 15 vocational technical state schools, 8,907 pupils. Expenditure of the state Board of Education for grants-in-aid, 1973–74, was $143,169,480; local expenditure, 1973–74, $549,047,011. Average salary of teachers in public schools, 1973–74, $12,061.

Connecticut has 47 colleges, 4 state teachers' colleges and 8 regional community colleges. The University of Connecticut at Storrs, founded 1881, had 1,078 faculty and 20,048 students in 1974. Yale University, New Haven, founded in 1701, had 1,395 faculty and 8,665 students. Wesleyan University, Middletown, founded 1831, had 278 faculty and 1,530 students. Trinity College, Hartford, founded 1823, had 152 faculty and 1,525 students. Connecticut College for Women, New London, founded 1915, had 186 faculty and 1,500 students. The University of Hartford had 186 faculty and 2,323 students. The regional community colleges (2-year course) had 857 staff and 21,500 students.

Health. Hospitals listed by the American Hospital Association, 1974, numbered 67 (including 5 federal), with 20,874 beds, and an average daily census of 343 persons per hospital. Average daily census of the 11 state psychiatric hospitals was 902 per hospital. In July 1970 the state controlled 4 hospitals for the mentally retarded, 1 institution for the deaf and 3 chronic disease hospitals.

Social Security. Disbursements during the year ending 30 June 1974 amounted to $5,096,756 for old-age assistance, and medical aid to the aged, $66,068,000. In June 1974, 3,671 old people were receiving $68.60 monthly; 35,975 families were receiving $257.18 per family on aid to dependent children; 6,466 totally disabled, $69.26.

Books of Reference

Connecticut in Focus. League of Women Voters of Connecticut. 2nd ed. Hamden, 1974
The Register and Manual of Connecticut. Secretary of State. Hartford. Annual
The Structure of Connecticut's State Government. Connecticut Public Expenditure Council. Hartford, 1973
Adams, V. Q., *Connecticut: The Story of Your State Government.* Chester, 1973
Hoyt, J. R., *The Connecticut Story.* New Haven, 1961
Smith, Allen R., *Connecticut, a Thematic Atlas.* Newington, 1974

State Library: Connecticut State Library, Capitol Avenue, Hartford, 06015. *State Librarian:* Charles E. Funk.

DELAWARE

HISTORY. Delaware, permanently settled in 1638, is one of the original 13 states of the Union, and the first one to ratify the Federal Constitution.

AREA AND POPULATION. Delaware is bounded north by Pennsylvania, north-east by New Jersey, east by Delaware Bay, south and west by Maryland. Area 2,399 sq. miles (437 sq. miles being inland water). Census population, 1 April 1980 (preliminary), was 595,225, an increase of 47,121 or 8·6% since 1970. Births in 1977, 8,771; deaths, 4,884; infant deaths, 103; marriages, 3,999; divorces, 3,044.

Population in 5 census years (with distribution by sex, 1970) was:

	White	Negro	Indian	Asiatic	Total	Per sq. mile
1910	171,102	31,181	5	34	202,322	103·0
1930	205,718	32,602	5	55	238,380	120·5
1950	273,878	43,598	—	87	266,505	134·7
1960	384,327	60,688	597	410	446,292	224·0
			All others			
1970	466,459	78,276	3,369		548,104	276·5
Male	227,978	37,646	1,708		267,332	—
Female	238,481	40,630	1,661		280,772	—

Of the total population in 1960, 292,994 (65·7%) were urban (62·6% in 1950); households, 158,582. Those 18 years old or older numbered 283,253; foreign-born whites, 14,307.

The 1980 census figures show Wilmington with population of 70,363. The 1970 figures: Newark, 21,078; Dover, 17,488; Wilmington Manor, 10,134; Elsmere, 8,415; Dover Air Force Base, 8,106.

CONSTITUTION AND GOVERNMENT. The present constitution (the fourth) dates from 1897, and has had 51 amendments; it was not ratified by the electorate but promulgated by the Constitutional Convention. The General Assembly consists of a Senate of 19 members elected for 4 years and a House of Representatives of 39 members elected for 2 years. The Governor and Lieut.-Governor are elected for 4 years.

With necessary exceptions, all adult citizens, registered as voters, who have resided in the state 1 year, and complied with local residential requirements, have the right to vote; those who have attained the age of 18 since 1900 must be able to read English and to write their names. Citizens resident for 3 months or over may vote for President and Vice-President only.

Delaware is represented in Congress by 2 senators and 1 representative, elected by the voters of the whole state.

In the 1980 presidential election Reagan polled 111,252 votes, Carter 105,754.

The state capital is Dover. Delaware is divided into 3 counties.

Governor: Pierre S. du Pont (R.), 1981–85 ($35,000).
Lieut.-Governor: James D. McGinnis (D.) ($9,000).
Secretary of State: Glenn C. Kenton (R.) ($18,000) (appointed by the Governor).

FINANCE. For the year ending 30 June 1974 general receipts were $680·98m., of which taxes furnished $359·56m. and federal grants $138·2m. General expenditure was $668m. (education, $249·9m.; highways, $70·8m.; health and public welfare, $100·7m.).

On 30 June 1973 the operating cash deficit was $6,023,690.

Per capita income (1975) was $6,748.

ENERGY AND NATURAL RESOURCES

Minerals. The mineral resources of Delaware are not extensive, consisting chiefly of clay products, stone, sand and gravel. Value of mineral production in 1974 (preliminary) was $3·3m.

Agriculture. Delaware is mainly an industrial state, but about 50% of the land area is in farms (698,000 acres), which in 1974 numbered 3,600; average farm (1969) was of 181·6 acres and valued (land and buildings) at $90,632.

Cash income, 1978, from crops and livestock, $319·8m., of which $218m. was from livestock and products. The chief crops are corn and soybeans.

INDUSTRY. In 1973–74 manufacturing establishments (numbering 573) employed 74,500 people, earning $948m.

COMMUNICATIONS

Roads. The state in 1978 maintained 4,591 miles of roads and streets and 1,365 miles of federally-aided highways. There were also 585 miles of municipal maintained streets. Vehicles registered in 1978, 412,358.

Railways. In 1978 the state had 291 miles of railway.

Aviation. Delaware had 48 airports, of which 13 were for general use in 1978.

JUSTICE, RELIGION, EDUCATION AND WELFARE

Justice. State prisons, 1 July 1977–30 June 1978, had daily average of 1,038 inmates. The death penalty was illegal from 2 April 1958 to 18 Dec. 1961. Executions since 1930 (by hanging) have totalled 12 (none since 1946).

Religion. Membership, 1973–74: Methodists, 101,239; Roman Catholics, 98,637; Episcopalians, 19,935; Presbyterians, 17,191; Lutherans, 10,000.

Education. The state has free public schools and compulsory school attendance. In Sept. 1977 the elementary and secondary public schools had an estimated number of 118,000 enrolled pupils and 6,023 classroom teachers. Appropriation for public schools (financial year 1977–78) was about $172m. Average salary of classroom teachers (financial year 1977–78), $13,736. The state supports the University of Delaware at Newark (1834) which had approximately 820 faculty members and 19,000 students in Sept. 1977, and Delaware State College, Dover (1892), with 131 faculty members and 2,079 students.

Health. In 1973 there were 15 hospitals (5,002 beds) listed by the American Hospital Association. In Oct. 1973 patients in mental hospitals numbered 1,734.

Social Security. In 1974 the federal Supplemental Security Income (SSI) programme lessened state responsibility for the aged, blind and disabled. Provisions are also made for the care of dependent children in (June 1978) 10,611 cases totalling 30,434 recipients ($73.36 per person); general assistance, 1,422 cases totalling 1,868 persons ($41.59 per person). The total state programme for the year ending 30 June 1978 was $13·5m. for the care of dependent children, $919,815 in general assistance and $603,698 for Supplemental Security Income. Total federal aid, $21m.

Books of Reference

Information: Division of Historical and Cultural Affairs, Hall of Records, Dover.

State Manual, Containing Official List of Officers, Commissions and County Officers. Secretary of State, Dover. Annual

The Delaware Economy, 1939–58. Bureau of Economic & Business Research, Univ. of Delaware, 1961

Topical History of Delaware. Division of Historical and Cultural Affairs. Dover, 1977

Dolan, P., *The Government and Administration of Delaware.* New York, 1956

Federal Writers' Project. *Delaware: A Guide to the First State.* Rev. ed. New York, 1955

DISTRICT OF COLUMBIA

HISTORY. The District of Columbia, organized in 1790, is the seat of the Government of the US, for which the land was ceded by the state of Maryland to the US as a site for the national capital. It was established under Acts of Congress in 1790 and 1791. Congress first met in it in 1800 and federal authority over it became vested in 1801.

AREA AND POPULATION. The District forms an enclave on the Potomac River, where the river forms the south-west boundary of Maryland. The area of the District of Columbia is 69·245 sq. miles, 8 sq. miles being inland water. The federal government on 30 June 1968 owned 13,314 acres (43·3% of the land area).

Census population, 1 April 1980 (preliminary), was 637,651, a decrease of 15·6% from that of 1970. Metropolitan statistical area of Washington, D.C.–Md–Va. (1978 estimate), 3·5m. Estimated average annual growth rate, 50,000. Density of population in the District, 1978, 10,627 per sq. mile. Births, 1978, in the District were 19,054 (28·3 per 1,000 population); resident deaths, 8,737 (13·0); infant deaths, 440 (23·1 per 1,000 live births); marriages, 4,618 (7); divorces, 3,492 (5·2).

Population in 5 census years (with distribution by sex, 1960) was:

	White	Negro	Indian	Chinese and Japanese	Total	Per sq. mile
1910	236,128	94,446	68	427	331,069	5,517·8
1930	353,981	132,068	40	780	486,869	7,981·5
1950	517,865	280,803	330	2,178	802,178	13,150·5
1960	345,263	411,737	587	3,532	763,956	12,523·9
			All others			
1970	209,272	537,712	9,526		756,510	12,321·0
Male	158,124	196,257	3,790		358,171	—
Female	187,139	215,480	3,166		405,785	—

GOVERNMENT. Local government, from 1 July 1878 until Aug. 1967, was that of a municipal corporation administered by a board of 3 commissioners, of whom 2 were appointed from civil life by the President, and confirmed by the Senate, for a term of 3 years each. The other commissioner was detailed by the President from the Engineer Corps of the Army. Reorganization Plan No. 3 of 1967 submitted by the President to Congress on 1 June 1967 abolished the Commission form of government and instituted a new Mayor Council form of government with officers appointed by the President with the advice and consent of the Senate. On 24 Dec. 1973 the appointed officers were replaced by an elected Mayor and councillors, with full legislative powers in local matters as from 1974. Congress retains the right to legislate, to veto or supersede the Council's acts. The 23rd amendment to the federal constitution (1961) conferred the right to vote in national elections; in the 1980 presidential election Carter polled 130,231 votes, Reagan, 23,313. On 23 Aug. 1978 the Senate approved a constitutional amendment giving the District full voting representation in Congress. In order to become part of the constitution the amendment must be ratified by 38 state legislatures within 7 years. It would give the District 2 senators and a number of representatives according to population.

BUDGET. The District's revenues are derived from a tax on real and personal property, sales taxes, taxes on corporations and companies, licences for conducting various businesses and from federal payments.

The District of Columbia has no bonded debt not covered by its accumulated sinking fund.

INDUSTRY. The District's main industries are government service, food processing, printing and tourism. In 1978 there were about 303,000 non-government employees; total employment was 618,100 at the census of 1972.

COMMUNICATIONS

Roads. Within the District are 340 miles of bus routes.

Railways. There is a rapid rail transit system including a town subway system.

Aviation. The District is served by 2 general airports; across the Potomac River in Arlington, Va., is National Airport, and in Chantilly, Va., is Dulles International Airport.

JUSTICE, RELIGION AND EDUCATION

Justice. Since 1958 there have been no executions; from 1930 to 1957 there were 40 executions (electrocution) including 3 whites for murder and 35 Negroes for murder and 2 for rape.

Religion. The largest churches are the Protestant and Roman Catholic Christian churches; there are also Jewish, Eastern Orthodox and Islamic congregations.

Education. In 1977 there were 128 elementary schools, 29 junior high schools and 12 high schools. Expenditure per pupil, 1977–78, $2,033. Segregation was abolished in 1954. Higher education is given in Georgetown University, founded in 1795 by the Jesuit Order; George Washington University, non-sectarian, founded in 1821; Howard University, founded in 1867; Catholic University of America, founded in 1884; American University (Methodist).

Books of Reference

Statistical Information: The Metropolitan Washington Board of Trade publications, *New Dynamism in the Nation's Capital* and *The Case for Washington.*
Reports of the Commissioners of the District of Columbia. Annual. Washington
Federal Writers' Project. *Washington, D.C.: A Guide to the Nation's Capital.* N
National Capital Park and Planning Commission. *Monographs on Washington, Present and Future.* Washington, D.C., 1950
Rutherford, G. W., *Administration Problems in a Metropolitan Area: The National Capital Region.* Chicago, 1952

FLORIDA

HISTORY. White men, probably Spaniards but possibly English, saw Florida for the first time in the period 1497–1512. Juan Ponce de Leon sighted Florida on 27 March 1513. Going ashore between 2 and 8 April in the vicinity of what is now St Augustine, he named the land 'Pasqua de Flores' because his landing was 'in the time of the Feast of Flowers'. The first permanent settlement in the entire US was made at St Augustine, 8 Sept. 1565. It was claimed by Spain until 1763, then ceded to England; back to Spain in 1783, and to the US in 1821. Florida became a Territory in 1821 and was admitted into the Union on 3 March 1845.

AREA AND POPULATION. Florida is a peninsula bounded west by the Gulf of Mexico, south by the Straits of Florida, east by the Atlantic, north by Georgia and north-west by Alabama. Area, 58,560 sq. miles, including 4,424 sq. miles of inland water. Census population, 1 April 1980 (preliminary), was 9,739,992, an increase of 43·4% since 1970. Births in 1978 were 112,987 (13·1 per 1,000 population); deaths, 97,791 (11·4); infant deaths, 1,610 (14·2 per 1,000 live births); marriages, 94,423 (11); divorces, 66,011 (7·7).

Population in 5 federal census years (with distribution by sex, 1970) was:

	White	Negro	Indian	Asiatic	Total	Per sq. mile
1910	443,634	308,669	74	242	752,619	13·7
1930	1,035,390	431,828	587	406	1,468,211	27·1
1950	2,166,051	603,101	1,011	1,142	2,771,305	51·1
1960	4,063,881	880,186	2,504	4,990	4,951,560	84·6
			All others			
1970	5,711,411	1,049,578	28,454		6,789,443	115·9
Male	2,762,779	498,695	14,097		3,275,571	—
Female	2,956,564	542,956	14,352		3,513,872	—

Of the population in 1970, 80% were urban (73·9% in 1960); 3,962,178 were 21 years of age or over; in 1960, 255,071 were foreign-born whites.

The largest cities in the state (1980 census) are: Jacksonville, 541,269; Miami, 335,360 (urbanized area, 1972, 1,340,700); Tampa, 268,709; St Petersburg, 233,532; Fort Lauderdale, 154,028; Hialeah, 143,596; Orlando, 127,811; Hollywood, 116,832; Miami Beach, 90,836; Clearwater, 87,246; Tallahassee, 80,820; West Palm Beach, 58,424; Pensacola, 57,130; Daytona Beach, 53,608.

CONSTITUTION AND GOVERNMENT. The 1968 Legislature revised the constitution of 1885. The state legislature consists of a Senate of 40 members, elected for 4 years, and House of Representatives with 120 members elected for 2 years. Sessions are held annually, and are limited to 60 days. The Governor is elected for 4 years, and can hold two terms in office. Two senators and 19 representatives are elected to Congress.

In the 1980 presidential election Reagan polled 2,046,951 votes and Carter 1,419,475.

The state capital is Tallahassee. The state is divided into 67 counties.

Governor: Robert Graham (D), 1979–83 ($50,000).
Lieut.-Governor: Wayne Mixson (D.), 1979–83 ($40,000).
Secretary of State: George Firestone (D.), 1979–83 ($40,000).

FINANCE. There is no state income tax on individuals. For the year ending 30 June 1977 the state had a general revenue of $5,707·07m. General expenditure was $5,391,507,000, of which education took $2,205,579,000; public welfare, $442,093,000; and highways, $584,523,000.

Net long-term debt, 30 June 1974, amounted to $1,234m.

Per capita personal income (1977) was $6,684.

NATURAL RESOURCES

Minerals. Chief mineral is phosphate rock, of which marketable production in 1977 was 42m. short tons, leading all states (Florida produces 84% of national and 30% of world demand). Total value of mineral production, 1977, $1,604·6m.

Agriculture. In 1974, 34,000 farms had a total acreage of 14·5m.; net income per farm was $25,249. Total cash receipts from crops and livestock (1978), $3,238m., of which crops provided $2,383m. Oranges, grapefruit, melons and vegetables are important. Other crops are maize ($40m.); soybeans ($65m.); sugar-cane, tobacco and peanuts. On 1 Jan. 1978 the state had 2·35m. cattle, including 269,000 milch cows and 320,000 swine.

The national forests area in June 1967 was 1,076,000 acres.

Fisheries. Florida has extensive fisheries for oysters, shrimp, red snapper, crabs, mackerel and mullet. Catch (1976), 156m. lb. valued at $88m.

INDUSTRY. In 1976 there were 9,760 manufacturers. They employed 348,108 persons with value added by manufacture, about $5,000m. The metal-working, lumber, chemical, woodpulp, food-processing and instruments industries are important.

TOURISM. During 1977 over 29m. tourists visited Florida. They spent over $11,200m. making tourism one of the biggest industries in the state. There are 74 state parks, 4 state forests, 1 national park and 9 national forests. The state parks were visited by 10·8m. people in 1976, 1·3m. of them campers.

COMMUNICATIONS

Roads. The state (1975) had over 98,000 miles of road and streets and 20,190 miles of federally-aided highways.

In 1976, 8·2m. vehicle licence plates were issued.

Railways. In 1975 there were 4,075 miles of railway.

Aviation. In 1975 Florida had 330 airports, including 6 seaplane bases.

JUSTICE, RELIGION, EDUCATION AND WELFARE

Justice. Since 1968 there has been 1 execution, by electrocution, for murder; from 1930 to 1968 there were 168 executions (electrocution), including 130 for murder, 37 for rape and 1 for kidnapping. State prisons, 7 Nov. 1978, had 20,074 inmates.

Religion. In 1960, 30·3% of the population were members of 6 churches: Baptists (455,175), Roman Catholics (466,028), Methodists (223,151), Presbyterians (105,834) and Episcopalians (83,656). Jews numbered 159,337.

Education. Attendance at school is compulsory between 7 and 16.

In 1977 the public elementary and secondary schools had 1,534,041 enrolled pupils. State expenditure on public schools (1976–77) was $2,206·5m.; on higher education, $489·6m. The state maintains 28 community colleges with 543,162 students (1977).

There are 9 universities in the state system, namely the University of Florida at Gainesville (founded 1853) with 27,554 students in 1977; the Florida State University (founded at Tallahassee in 1857) with 21,372 students; the University of South Florida at Tampa (founded 1960) with 22,307 students; Florida A. & M. University at Tallahassee (founded 1887) with 5,632 students; Florida Atlantic University (founded 1964) at Boca Raton with 6,994 students; the University of West Florida at Pensacola with 4,972 students; the Florida Technological University at Orlando with 9,504 students; the University of North Florida at Jacksonville with 4,214 students; Florida International University at Miami with 10,178 students.

Health. Hospitals, 1973, numbered 234 with 50,629 beds; there were 214 general, 18 special and 2 tuberculosis hospitals.

Social Security. From 1974 aid to the aged, blind and disabled became a federal responsibility. The state continued to give aid to families with dependent children and general assistance. Monthly payments 1975: aid to 2,374 blind averaged $122; aid to 192,837 dependent children averaged $38; aid to 54,610 disabled averaged $115; aid to 92,217 aged averaged $88.

Books of Reference

1973 Legislative Economic Bulletin. Comptroller's Office, Tallahassee, 1973
Florida Statistical Abstract. Univ. of Florida Press, 1977
Florida Tourist Study. Florida Department of Commerce, Tallahassee. Annual
Report. Florida Secretary of State. Tallahassee. Biennial
Report of the Comptroller. Tallahassee, 1977–78. Biennial
Dimensions. Bureau of Business and Economic Research, Univ. of Florida, Gainesville. Monthly
Morris, Allen, *The Florida Handbook.* Tallahassee, 1977–78. Biennial
Raisz, E. J., and others, *Atlas of Florida.* Univ. of Florida Press, 1974

State Library: Gray Building, Tallahassee. *Librarian:* Barratt Wilkins.

GEORGIA

HISTORY. Georgia (so named from George II) was founded in 1733 as the 13th original colony; she became the 4th original state.

AREA AND POPULATION. Georgia is bounded north by Tennessee and North Carolina, north-east by South Carolina, east by the Atlantic, south by Florida and west by Alabama. Area, 58,876 sq. mile, of which 602 sq. miles are inland water. Census population, 1 April 1980 (preliminary), was 5,464,000. Births, 1978, were 83,784 (16·5 per 1,000 population); deaths, 43,416 (8·5); infant deaths, 1,229 (14·7 per 1,000 live births); marriages, 67,593 (13·3); divorces and annulments, 31,421 (6·2).

Population in 5 census years (with distribution by sex, 1960) was:

	White	Negro	Indian	Asiatic	Total	Per sq. mile
1910	1,431,802	1,176,987	95	237	2,609,121	44·4
1930	1,837,021	1,071,125	43	317	2,908,506	49·7
1950	2,380,577	1,062,762	333	—	3,444,578	58·9
1960	2,817,223	1,122,596	749	2,004	3,943,116	67·7
			All others			
1970	3,391,242	1,187,149	11,184		4,589,575	79·0
Male	1,391,735	532,509	1,669		1,925,913	—
Female	1,425,488	590,087	1,628		2,017,203	—

Of the 1970 population, 2,759,255 (60%) were urban (55·3% in 1960); those 21 years of age and over numbered 2,685,290; foreign-born whites, 32,988.

The largest cities are: Atlanta (capital), with population, 1980 census, of 422,293 (urbanized area, 1970, 1,370,164); Columbus, 168,598 (193,190); Savannah, 133,672 (187,767); Macon, 116,044 (206,423); Albany, 74,471 (89,369).

CONSTITUTION AND GOVERNMENT. A new constitution was ratified in the general election of 2 Nov. 1976, proclaimed on 22 Dec. 1976 and became effective 1 Jan. 1977. The General Assembly consists of a Senate of 56 members and a House of Representatives of 180 members, both elected for 2 years. The Governor and Lieut.-Governor are elected for 4 years. Legislative sessions are annual, beginning the 2nd Monday in January and lasting for 40 days.

Georgia was the first state to extend the franchise to all citizens 18 years old and above. The state is represented in Congress by 2 senators and 10 representatives.

Registered voters, 1976, numbered 2,178,623. At the 1980 presidential election Carter polled 890,955 votes, Reagan 654,168 and Anderson 36,055.

The state capital is Atlanta. Georgia is divided into 159 counties.

Governor: George Busbee (D.), 1979–82 ($50,000).
Lieut.-Governor: Zell Miller (D.) ($25,000).
Secretary of State: David B. Poythress (D.) ($35,000).

BUDGET. For the fiscal year ending 30 June 1978 general revenue was $2,262,816,271 ($2,218,055,593 from taxes and $44,760,678 in federal aid); general expenditure was $2,197,726,699 out of total available funds of $2,398,629,323.

On 30 June 1978 total liability, reserves, bonded indebtedness and surplus was $1,187,287,907.

Estimated *per capita* personal income (1976), was $5,571.

NATURAL RESOURCES

Minerals. Georgia is the leading producer of kaolin; production 1975 had a value of $177·6m. The state ranks first in production of crushed and dimensional granite, second in production of fuller's earth and marble (crushed and dimensional).

Mineral products, 1976, had a record value of $389·2m.

Agriculture. In 1977, 70,000 farms had an area of 17m. acres; average farm was of 243 acres. For 1976 cotton output was 199,000 bales (of 480 lb.) (valued at $59·3m.). Other crops, 1976, included tobacco, 123·8m. lb ($138·3m.); corn, 133·9m. bu. ($176·2m.); peanuts, 1,554m. lb. ($311·5m.); pecans, 52m. lb. ($40m.). Cash income, 1976, $2,279m: from crops, $1,103·3m.; from livestock, $1,165·7m.

On 1 Jan. 1977 farm animals included 2·3m. all cattle, including 129,000 milch cows, 3,600 sheep, 34m. chickens and 1·6m. swine.

Forestry. The national forest area in 1974 was 855,000 acres.

INDUSTRY. In 1977 the state had approximately 8,630 manufacturing establishments employing 484,400 workers; the value added by manufacture was $12,500m.

TOURISM. In 1979 the tourist industry employed 182,370 earning $1,100m. Tourists spent $2,200m. and tax revenue was $95·9m. Number of tourists, 67m.

COMMUNICATIONS

Roads. Total road mileage (1976) was 101,656 (city, county and state); paved mileage totalled 55,976. Motor vehicles registered, 1976, numbered 3,706,288.

Railways. In 1976 there were 5,417 miles of railways.

Aviation. Airports numbered 140 (107 publicly owned, 33 privately owned but open to the public) in 1977.

Shipping. The principal port is Savannah.

JUSTICE, RELIGION, EDUCATION AND WELFARE

Justice. State prisons, 1 Sept. 1977, had 11,800 inmates. Since 1964 there have been no executions. From 1924 to 1964 there were 415 executions (electrocution), including 75 whites and 268 Negroes for murder, 3 whites and 63 Negroes for rape and 6 Negroes for armed robbery.

Under a Local Option Act, the sale of alcoholic beverages (not including malt beverages and light wines) is prohibited in more than half the counties.

Religion. An estimated 78% of the population are church members. Of the total population, 74·3% are Protestant, 3·2% are Roman Catholic and 1·5% Jewish.

Education. Since 1945 education has been compulsory; tuition is free for pupils between the ages of 6 and 18 years. At the end of the 1975–76 school year the 346 high schools, 33 junior high schools, 1,287 elementary schools and 104 combination junior high and elementary schools had 1,192,129 pupils and 54,673 teachers and principals. Teachers' salaries averaged $10,729. Integration in public schools is now an accepted practice.

The University of Georgia (Athens) was founded in 1785 and was the first chartered State University in the US. Other institutions of higher learning include Georgia Institute of Technology (Atlanta), Emory University (Atlanta), Agnes Scott College (Decatur), Georgia College (Milledgeville), Georgia State University (Atlanta) and Mercer University (Macon). The Atlanta University Center, devoted primarily to Negro education, includes Clark College and Morris Brown College, co-educational, Morehouse, a liberal arts college for men, Interdenominational Theological Center, a co-educational theological school, and Spelman College, the first liberal arts college for Negro women in the US. Atlanta University serves as the graduate school centre for the complex. Wesleyan College near Macon is the oldest chartered women's college in the US. Total enrolment, 1976–77, was 166,756 in 61 institutions of higher education.

Health. Hospitals licensed by the Department of Human Resources, 1 July 1977, numbered 222 with 38,941 beds.

Social Security. In Aug. 1977, 85,235 persons were receiving old-age assistance of an average $84.77 per month; 83,413 families were receiving as aid to dependent children an average of $105.61 per family; aid to the blind went to 2,733 persons (averaging $131.33 monthly); aid to 73,678 disabled persons was $121.70 monthly.

Books of Reference

Georgia History in Outline. Univ. of Georgia Press, Athens, 1978
Bonner, J. C., and Roberts, L. E., eds., *Studies in Georgia History and Government.* Reprint Company, Spartanburg, 1940 Repr.
Pound, M. B., and Saye, A. B., *Handbook on the Constitution of the U.S. and Georgia.* Univ. of Georgia Press, Athens, 1978
Rowland, A. R., *A Bibliography of the Writings on Georgia History.* Hamden, Conn., 1978
Saye, A. B., *A Constitutional History of Georgia, 1732–1968.* Univ. of Georgia, Athens, Rev. ed., 1970

State Library: Judicial Building, Capital Sq., Atlanta. *State Librarian:* John D. M. Folger.

HAWAII

HISTORY. The Hawaiian Islands, formerly known as the Sandwich Islands, were discovered by Capt. James Cook in Aug. 1778. During the greater part of the 19th century the islands formed an independent kingdom, but in 1893 the reigning Queen, Liliuokalani (died 11 Nov. 1917), was deposed and a provisional government formed; in 1894 a Republic was proclaimed, and in accordance with the request of the people of Hawaii expressed through the Legislature of the Republic, and a resolution of the US Congress of 6 July 1898 (signed 7 July by President McKinley), the islands were on 12 Aug. 1898 formally annexed to the US. On 14 June 1900 the islands were constituted as a Territory of Hawaii.

Statehood was granted to Hawaii on 18 March 1959.

AREA AND POPULATION. The Hawaiian Islands lie in the North Pacific Ocean, between 18° 50′ and 28° 15′ N. lat. and 154° 40′ and 178° 15′ W. long., about 2,090 nautical miles south-west of San Francisco. There are more than 20 islands in the group, of which 7 are inhabited. The land and inland water area of the state is 6,424 sq. miles, with census population, 1 April 1980, of 963,617, an increase of 193,704 or 25·2% since 1970; density was 150 per sq. mile.

The principal islands are Hawaii, 4,038 sq. miles (population, 1980, 92,206); Maui, 729 (71,337); Oahu, 608 (761,964); Kauai, 553 (39,117); Molokai, 261 (6,076); Lanai, 140 (2,125); Niihau, 73 (226); Kahoolawe, 45 (0). The capital Honolulu, on the island of Oahu, had a population in 1980 of 365,114 and Hilo on the island of Hawaii, 44,011.

Figures for racial groups, 1976, are: 286,894 Caucasians, 242,465 Japanese,

112,913 Filipinos, 48,449 Chinese, 9,594 Negroes, 151,510 all others. Of the total, approximately 92% were citizens of the US.

Inter-marriage between the races is popular. Of the 10,376 persons married in the calendar year 1978, 37·9% married a wife or husband of a different race. Births, 1978, were 16,762; deaths, 4,859; infant deaths, 220; marriages, 10,731; divorces and annulments, 4,837.

CONSTITUTION AND GOVERNMENT. The constitution took effect on 21 Aug. 1959.

The Legislature consists of a Senate of 25 members elected for 4 years, and a House of Representatives of 51 members elected for 2 years. The constitution provides for annual meetings of the legislature with 60-day regular sessions. The Governor and Lieut.-Governor are elected for 4 years. The registered voters, 1980, numbered 402,795.

The state sends to Congress 2 senators and 2 representatives.

In the 1980 presidential election Carter polled 135,879 votes, Reagan, 130,112.

Governor: George R. Ariyoshi (D.), 1978–81 ($50,000).

BUDGET. Revenue is derived mainly from taxation of sales and gross receipts, real property, corporate and personal income, and inheritance taxes, licences, public land sales and leases. For the year ending 30 June 1979 state general fund receipts amounted to $892·7m.; special fund receipts, $678·5m., and federal grants, $6·7m. State expenditures were $1,482,995,300 (education, $471,496,500; highways, $46,682,200; public welfare, $243,717,200; figures include both special and general funds).

Net long-term debt, 31 Dec. 1979, amounted to $1,971·9m.

Estimated *per capita* personal income (1978) was $8,437.

NATURAL RESOURCES

Minerals. Total value of mineral production, 1978, amounted to $52·7m. Cement shipped from plants amounted to 452,000 short tons (valued at $26·5m.); stone, 6·03m. short tons (value $23·8m.).

Agriculture. Farming is highly commercialized, aiming at export to the American market, and highly mechanized. In 1978 there were 4,312 farms with an acreage of 2m.

Sugar and pineapples are the staple crops. Income from crop sales, 1979, was $287m., and from livestock, $78m. The sugar crop was valued at $217·6m.; pineapple, $69·5m.; other crops, $73·8m.

Forestry. Commercial forests totalled 1·2m. acres (1976); state lands, 1·4m. acres. Land held by the federal government totalled 402,900 acres in 1978.

INDUSTRY AND TRADE

Industry. In 1977 manufacturing establishments employed 25,100 production workers who earned an estimated $276·4m.; value added by manufacture was estimated at $790·9m.

Commerce. In 1978 imports of newsprint, fertilizer, lumber, feed, crude oil and other products from foreign countries such as Saudi Arabia, Indonesia and Japan exceeded $1,126·4m. In 1978 exports, primarily food and manufactures, amounted to $137·8m. About 68% of Hawaii's overseas trade is with the mainland USA.

Tourism. Tourism is an outstanding factor in Hawaii's economy. Tourist arrivals numbered 109,798 in 1955, and reached 3·96m. in 1979. Tourist expenditures, totalling $55m. in 1955, contributed $2,620m. to the state's economy in 1979.

COMMUNICATIONS

Roads. In 1979 there were 610,570 motor vehicles, and a total of 3,874 miles of highways (including 1,085 miles of federally assisted highways and federal highways in national parks).

Aviation. There were 11 commercial airports in 1979; passengers arriving overseas numbered 4·25m., and there were 7·6m. passengers between the islands.

Shipping. Several lines of steamers connect the islands with the mainland USA, Canada, Australia, the Philippines, China and Japan. In 1978, 10,344 inbound vessels entered Hawaiian ports; cargo arriving, 1977, 9·5m. tons; passengers arriving, 14,073.

Post. There were 684,812 telephones at 1 Jan. 1980.

JUSTICE, RELIGION, EDUCATION AND WELFARE

Justice. There is no capital punishment in Hawaii.

Religion. The residents of Hawaii are mainly Christians, though there are many Buddhists. A sample survey in 1979 showed that 31% were Roman Catholic, 34% Protestant, 12% Buddhist, 2·5% Latter Day Saints.

Education. Education is free, and compulsory for children between the ages of 6 and 18. The language in the schools is English. In 1978–79 there were 229 public schools (170,515 pupils with 7,930 teachers) and 136 private schools (36,297 pupils) ranging from kindergarten through the 12th grade. The University of Hawaii, founded in 1907, had 20,833 day students in 1979; total university and college attendance 1979–80, 43,875.

Social Security. During 1979 the state spent $244·9m., the federal government met 41% of this fund. In 1979 there were 30 non-military hospitals (3,270 beds in 1977) listed by the Department of Health. During 1979 the average number of persons served by major welfare programmes was 72,928. In early 1980, 6·6% of all welfare recipients were recent migrants to Hawaii.

Books of Reference

Government in Hawaii. Tax Foundation of Hawaii. Honolulu, 1980
Guide to Government in Hawaii. 7th ed. Legislative Reference Bureau. State of Hawaii, Honolulu, 1980
All About Hawaii: Thrum's Hawaiian Annual and Standard Guide. Honolulu, 1875 to date
Current Hawaiiana (quarterly bibliography). Hawaii Library Association, Honolulu
The State of Hawaii Data Book 1978 and 1979: A Statistical Abstract. Dept. of Planning and Economic Development, Honolulu, 1978, 1979
Allen, G. E., *Hawaii's War Years.* 2 vols. Hawaii Univ. Press, 1950–52
Catton, M. M. L., *Social Service in Hawaii.* Palo Alto, 1959
Day, A. Grove, *Hawaii and Its People.* New York, 1955.—and Stroven, C., *A Hawaiian Reader.* New York, 1961
Fodor, E., ed., *Hawaii, 1965.* New York, 1965
Fuchs, L. E., *Hawaii Pono: A Social History.* New York, 1961
Kamins, Robert M., *Hawaii's Revised Tax System.* Honolulu, 1957
Kuykendall, R. S., and Day, A. G., *Hawaii, A History.* Rev. ed. New Jersey, 1961
Lind, A. W., *Hawaii's People.* Honolulu, 1955
Mann, A. F., *Hawaii: The Fiftieth State: Government and Economy.* Honolulu, 1960
Pukui, M. K., and Elbert, S. H., *Hawaiian–English Dictionary.* Honolulu, 1957
Smith, Branford, *Yankees in Paradise: The New England Impact on Hawaii.* Philadelphia, 1956

IDAHO

HISTORY. Idaho was first permanently settled in 1860, although there was a mission for Indians in 1836 and a Mormon settlement in 1855. It was organized as a Territory in 1863 and admitted into the Union as a state on 3 July 1890.

AREA AND POPULATION. Idaho is bounded north by Canada, east by the Rocky Mountains of Montana and Wyoming, south by Nevada and Utah, west by Oregon and Washington. Area, 83,557 sq. miles, of which 788 sq. miles are inland water. In 1970 the federal government owned 33,979,389 acres (64% of the state

IDAHO 1459

area). Census population, 1 April 1980 (preliminary), 943,935, an increase of 32·3% since 1970.

Births, 1979, 19,919 (22 per 1,000 population); deaths, 6,386 (7·1); infant deaths, 202 (10·1 per 1,000 live births); marriages, 13,429 (14·8); divorces, 6,449 (7·1).

Population in 5 census years (with distribution by sex, 1970) was:

	White	Negro	Indian	Asiatic	Total	Per sq. mile
1910	319,221	651	3,488	2,234	325,594	3·9
1930	438,840	668	3,638	1,886	445,032	5·4
1950	581,395	1,050	3,800	2,392	588,637	7·1
1960	657,383	1,502	5,231	2,958	667,191	8·1
1970	693,375	3,655	5,413	2,526	713,008	8·5

		All others	
Male	350,613	5,123	355,736	—
Female	352,146	4,685	356,831	—

Of the total 1970 population, 588,387 (80%) were urban (57·5% in 1960). Those 20 years of age or older were 431,343, foreign-born whites numbered 12,572.

The largest cities are Boise (capital) with 1980 census population of 102,125; Pocatello, 46,736 others, 1977 estimate: Idaho Falls, 38,457; Lewiston, 25,788; Twin Falls, 24,157; Nampa, 26,841.

CONSTITUTION AND GOVERNMENT. The constitution adopted in 1890 is still in force; it has had 79 amendments. A new constitutional study is under revision. The Legislature consists of a Senate of 35 members and a House of Representatives of 70 members, all the legislators being elected for 2 years. Annual sessions last for 60 days and 30 days for extraordinary sessions. The Governor, Lieut.-Governor and Secretary of State are elected for 4 years. Voters are citizens, over the age of 18 years. The state is represented in Congress by 2 senators and 2 representatives.

In the 1980 presidential election Reagan polled 290,699 votes, Carter 110,192. The state is divided into 44 counties. The capital is Boise.

Governor: John V. Evans (D.), 1979–82 ($33,000).
Lieut.-Governor: Phil Batt (R.), 1979–82 ($8,000).
Secretary of State: Pete Cenarrusa (R.), 1979–82 ($21,500).

BUDGET. For the year ending 30 June 1979 (State Auditor's Office) general revenues were $356·8m. and general expenditures included education, $332·7m., highways, $148·2m., and public welfare, $180·9m.

Per capita personal income (1979) was $7,571.

NATURAL RESOURCES

Minerals. Production of the most important minerals (1979): Lead, 42,636 short tons; silver, 17,144 troy oz.; zinc, 29,660 tonnes; copper, 3,618 tonnes; gold, 24,140 troy oz. There is some tungsten, antimony and vadium. Non-metallic minerals include phosphate rock, barite, clay, garnet, gypsum, perlite, lime, cement, pumice, sand and gravel and dimension stone. Value of total mineral output was $437m.

Agriculture. Agriculture is the leading industry, although a great part of the state is naturally arid. Extensive irrigation works have been carried out, bringing an estimated 2·9m. acres under irrigation; 83 reservoirs have a total capacity of 10·4m. acre-ft, 7·3m. acre-ft of which is primarily used for irrigation.

In 1980 there were 23,300 farms with a total area of 15·4m. acres (32% of the land area); average farm had 661 acres with land and buildings valued at approximately $7,500m.

On 30 June 1978 there were 51 soil conservation districts, managed by local farmers and ranchers, embracing 52·69m. acres.

Cash income, 1979, was $1,883m. ($958m. from major crops and livestock $925m.). The most important crops are potatoes and wheat—potatoes leading all states; in 1979 the production amounted to 85m. cwt., cash receipts $246m. Other crops are sugar-beet, alfalfa, oats, barley, field peas, dry beans, apples, prunes and hops. On 1

Jan. 1980 the number of sheep was 468,000; milch cows, 142,000; all cattle, 1·86m.; swine, 110,000.

Forestry. In 1979 a total of 20,635,700 acres (37·6% of the state's area) was in forests; 13,540,600 acres of this was commercial (non-reserved) forest. The volume of sawtimber in commercial forests was 139,600m. bd ft. The stumpage value of forest products was about $172m., and an additional $315m. was added by process. Ownership of commercial forests is 70% federal, 6·5% state and local government, 0·5% Indian, 22·3% private. Some 15,000 workers are involved in forestry.

INDUSTRY. In 1979 there were about 1,515 manufacturing establishments and they employed 55,000 production workers; value added by manufacture (1978) was $1,525m.

TOURISM. Money spent by travellers in 1979 was about $810m. Estimated local tax receipts from tourism, $3·2m., state receipts, $30m. Jobs generated, 24,000 (payroll over $218m.).

COMMUNICATIONS

Roads. The state maintained in 1979, 4,932 miles of the total of 63,006 miles of public roads; 666,204 passenger vehicles were registered.

Railways. The state had (1979) 2,504 miles of railways (including 2 AMTRAK routes) operated by 7 companies.

Aviation. There were 85 municipally owned airports in 1979.

Shipping. Water transport is provided from the Pacific to Lewiston, by way of the Columbia and Snake rivers, a distance of 464 miles.

JUSTICE, RELIGION, EDUCATION AND WELFARE

Justice. The death penalty is mandatory for first degree murder, but has been used sparingly. Since 1926 only 3 men (white) have been executed, by hanging (2 in 1951 and 1 in 1957). The state prison, 1 Nov. 1980, had 867 inmates.

Religion. The leading religious denomination is the Church of Jesus Christ of Latter Day Saints (Mormon Church), with 191,286 adherents; Roman Catholics have 53,104; Methodists, 19,017; Presbyterians, 14,130; Episcopalians, 5,000, and Lutherans, 4,602.

Education. In 1979–80 public elementary schools (grades 1 to 6) had 110,782 pupils and 5,186 classroom teachers; secondary schools had 91,976 pupils and 4,679 classroom teachers.

Average salary, 1979–80, of elementary and secondary classroom teachers, $13,609. The University of Idaho, founded at Moscow in 1889, had 383 professors in 1979–80 and 8,698 students. There are 9 other institutions of higher education; 5 of them are public institutions with a total enrolment (1979–80) of 21,109 (excluding vocational-technical colleges).

Social Welfare. Old-age assistance is granted to needy persons 65 years of age. In Aug. 1980, 1,555 persons were drawing an average of $70.16 per month; 7,773 families with 14,377 children were drawing an average of $258.32 per case (or $94.78 per eligible person); 32 blind persons, $63.56; 632 children were receiving $331.27 per child for foster care.

Health. In Aug. 1980 skilled nursing covered 889 beds; intermediate care, 1,619; mental intermediate care, 325.

Books of Reference

Biennial Report. Secretary of State. Boise
Idaho. Idaho First National Bank
Idaho Almanac. Division of Economic and Community Affairs, 1977
Idaho's Yesterdays. State Historical Society. Quarterly
Martin and Barber, *Idaho in the Pacific Northwest.* Boise, 1956

ILLINOIS

HISTORY. Illinois was first discovered by Joliet and Marquette, two French explorers, in 1673, and settled in 1720. In 1763 the country was ceded by the French to the British. In 1783 Great Britain recognized the title of the US to Illinois, which was organized as a Territory in 1809 and admitted into the Union on 3 Dec. 1818.

AREA AND POPULATION. Illinois is bounded north by Wisconsin, north-east by Lake Michigan, east by Indiana, south-east by the Ohio River (forming the boundary with Kentucky), west by the Mississippi River (forming the boundary with Missouri and Iowa). Area, 56,400 sq. miles, of which 470 sq. miles are inland water. Census population, 1970, 11,418,461, an increase of 2·71% since 1970. Births in 1978 were 174,212; deaths, 100,363; infant deaths, 2,568; marriages 105,605; divorces, 47,676.

Population in 5 census years (with distribution by sex, 1970) was:

	White	Negro	Indian	All others	Total	Per sq. mile
1910	5,526,962	109,049	188	2,392	5,638,591	100·6
1930	7,295,267	328,972	469	5,946	7,630,654	136·4
1950	8,064,058	645,980	1,443	18,695	8,712,176	155·8
1960	9,010,252	1,037,470	4,704	28,732	10,081,158	180·3
			All others			
1970	9,600,381	1,425,674	87,921		11,113,976	199·4
Male	4,674,899	673,097	5,463	38,377	5,391,836	—
Female	4,925,482	752,577	5,950	38,131	5,722,140	—

Of the total population in 1970, 9,229,321 persons (83%) were urban (80·7% in 1960); 6,756,755 were 21 years of age or older; foreign-born whites numbered 2,139,784 in 1970.

The most populous cities with population (1970 census), are:

Chicago	2,969,570	Cicero	
Rockford	139,206	Oaklawn	
Peoria	123,571	Skokie (1964)	
Springfield (cap.)	99,098	Champaign	
Decatur	92,643	East St Louis	
Joliet	78,165	Oak Park	
Aurora	77,014		
Evanston	73,278		
Waukegan	67,095		
Elgin	63,249		

Standard Metropolitan Statistical Area population (1970 census): Chicago, 6,979,000; St Louis, Mo.–Ill., 2,363,000; Davenport–Rock Island–Moline, Iowa–Ill., 363,000; Peoria, 342,000; Rockford, 272,000.

CONSTITUTION AND GOVERNMENT. The present constitution became effective 1 July 1971. The General Assembly consists of a House of Representatives of 177 members, elected for 2 years and a Senate of 59 members who serve 2 terms of 4 years and 1 of 2 years during a decade. Sessions are annual. The Governor and Lieut.-Governor are elected as a team for 4 years; the Comptroller and Secretary of State are elected for 4 years. Electors are citizens 18 years of age, having the usual residential qualifications.

The state is divided into legislative districts, in each of which 1 senator and 3 representatives are chosen; for the election of the latter each elector has 3 votes, of which he may cast 3 for 1 candidate or distribute them equally among no more than 3 candidates.

Illinois is represented in Congress by 2 senators and 22 representatives.

In the 1980 presidential election Reagan polled 2,358,094 votes, Carter 1,981,413. The capital is Springfield. The state has 102 counties.

Governor: James R. Thompson (R.), 1979–81 ($50,000).
Lieut.-Governor: Dave O'Neal (R.), 1979–81 ($37,500).
Secretary of State: Alan J. Dixon (D.), 1979–81 ($42,000).

BUDGET. For the year ending 30 June 1978 general revenues were $11,869m. and general expenditures were $11,689m.

Total net long-term debt, 1 July 1978, was $2,735m.

Per capita personal income (1977) was $6,487.

ENERGY AND NATURAL RESOURCES

Minerals. Chief mineral product is coal; 55 operative mines had an output (1977) of 58·2m. tons. Mineral production also included: Crude petroleum, 26·2m. bbls; fluorspar, 142,666 short tons. Total value of mineral products, 1977, was $1,581m.

Agriculture. In 1978, 117,000 farms had an area of 28·9m. acres; the average farm was 247 acres.

Cash receipts, 1978, from crops, $3,984·5m.; from livestock and livestock products, $2,138·7m. Illinois is a large producer of soybeans, the state's leading cash commodity. Output, 1978, was 303m. bu. Other crops were, in 1978, maize, 1,191m. bu.; wheat, 35·3m. bu; potatoes, hay, barley, rye and buckwheat are also grown. In Jan. 1977 there were 234,000 milch cows, 3·4m. all cattle, 180,000 sheep and 5·6m. swine. The wool clip in 1977 was 1·38m. lb.

Forestry. National forest area under the US Forest Service administration, 1977, was 257,000 acres.

INDUSTRY AND TRADE

Industry. In 1976, 17,668 manufacturing establishments employed 1,255,800 workers, earning $16,831·3m.; value added by manufacture was $36,084m. Largest industry was machinery (excluding electrical). Pig-iron production in 1974 was 7·17m. short tons; steel, 12,939,000 net tons.

Labour. In 1976, 57,860 retail establishments had total sales of $5,603m. and 1m. employees; 20,250 wholesale establishments had total sales of $52,100m. and 285,798 employees; 57,204 selected service establishments with total receipts of $10,703m. employed 760,204 persons. In May 1975 there were 4,311,400 employees on non-agricultural payrolls. In 1973 there were 945,400 production workers in manufacturing earning $8,657,400.

COMMUNICATIONS

Roads. In 1978 there were 5·5m. passenger cars, 1·2m. trucks and buses, 924,372 trailers and 227,301 motor cycles registered in the state. In 1977 there were 13,338 miles of state administered main roads, 73,714 miles of state administered rural roads and 115,908 miles of locally administered roads. There were 4,652 miles of interstate or freeway roads.

Railways. There were 1978, 10,672 miles of main line railway.

Shipping. In 1974 the seaport of Chicago handled exports of 594,291 short tons and imports of 1·23m. short tons. Overseas grain exports were 481,424 short tons.

Aviation. There were (1976) 510 certified airports, 125 heliports and 569 restricted landing areas.

Post. In 1976 there were 9,110,273 telephones in the state.

JUSTICE, RELIGION, EDUCATION AND WELFARE

Justice. In 1978 there were no executions; since 1930 there have been 90 executions (electrocution), including 58 white men, 1 white woman and 31 Negro men, all for murder. In 1976 the total average daily prison population was 9,500.

A Civil Rights Act (1941), as amended, bans all forms of discrimination by places of public accommodation, including inns, restaurants, retail stores, railroads, aeroplanes, buses, etc., against persons on account of 'race, religion, colour, national ancestry or physical or mental handicap'; another section similarly mentions 'race or colour.'

The Fair Employment Practices Act of 1961, as amended, prohibits discrimination in employment based on race, colour, sex, religion, national origin or ancestry, by employers, employment agencies, labour organizations and others. These principles are embodied in the 1971 constitution.

Religion. Among the larger religious denominations (1976) are: Roman Catholic, 9,051,153; Jewish, 6,115,000; United Presbyterian Church, USA, 1,040,444; Lutheran Church in America, 782,558; Lutheran Church Missouri Synod, 723,787; American Baptist, 500,000; Disciples of Christ, 124,120; Methodist, 114,007.

Education. Education is free and compulsory for children between 7 and 16 years of age. In 1978 there were 1,021 school districts. Public school elementary enrolments (1976–77) were 1,338,716 pupils and 65,368 teachers; secondary enrolments, 881,819 pupils and 34,326 teachers. Enrolment (1976–77) in non-public schools was 274,038 elementary and 98,717 secondary. Teachers' salaries, 1976–77, averaged $14,419. Total expenditure on public schools, 1976–77, $3,670m. Total enrolment in institutions of higher education (autumn 1976) was 609,342.

Colleges and universities with over 3,000 students:

Founded	Name	Place	Control	Autumn 1977 Enrolment
1851	Northwestern University	Evanston	Methodist	9,992
1857	Illinois State University	Normal	Public	19,049
1867	University of Illinois	Urbana	Public	58,299
1869	Chicago State University [1]	Chicago	Public	6,870
1869	Southern Illinois University	Carbondale	Public	24,317
1870	Loyola University	Chicago	Roman Catholic	13,007
1890	University of Chicago	Chicago	Non-Sect.	8,355
1895	Eastern Illinois University	Charleston	Public	9,252
1895	Northern Illinois University	DeKalb	Public	21,650
1897	Bradley University	Peoria	Non-Sect.	4,893
1898	DePaul University	Chicago	Roman Catholic	10,000
1899	Western Illinois University	Macomb	Public	14,237
1940	Illinois Institute of Technology [2]	Chicago	Non-Sect.	6,720
1945	Roosevelt University	Chicago	Non-Sect.	4,965
1961	Northeastern Illinois University [3]	Chicago	Public	10,179
1970	Sangamon State University	Springfield	Public	3,377

[1] Formerly Illinois Teachers College (South).
[2] Illinois Institute of Technology formed in 1940 by merger of two older technical schools.
[3] Formerly Illinois Teachers' College (North).

Health. In 1978 hospitals listed by the American Hospital Association numbered 286, with 76,135 beds. In 1978 state institutions for the mentally retarded had 6,653 residents and state hospitals for the mentally ill, 5,474.

Social Security. In 1978, 41,967 persons were drawing old age assistance totalling $3·9m., 767,399 were drawing aid to dependent children totalling $60·4m., 1,623 persons blind assistance totalling $0·2m. and 85,429 persons assistance to the disabled totalling $13·3m.

Books of Reference

Blue Book of the State of Illinois. Edited by Secretary of State. Springfield. Biennial
Federal Writers' Project. *Illinois: A Descriptive an Historical Guide.* Rev. ed. Chicago, 1947
Angle, P. M., and Beyer, R. L., *A Handbook of Illinois History.* Illinois State Historical Society, Springfield, 1943
Pease, T. C., *The Story of Illinois.* 3rd ed. Chicago, 1965

The Illinois State Library: Centennial Building, Springfield. *State Librarian:* Alan J. Dixon.

INDIANA

HISTORY. Indiana, first settled in 1732–33, was made a Territory in 1800 and admitted into the Union on 11 Dec. 1816.

AREA AND POPULATION. Indiana is bounded west by Illinois, north by Michigan and Lake Michigan, east by Ohio and south by Kentucky across the Ohio

River. Area, 36,291 sq. miles, of which 194 sq. miles are inland water. Census population, 1 April 1978 (preliminary), was 5,490,179, an increase of 296,510 or 5·7% since 1970. In 1978 (provisional figures) births were 83,348 (15·5 per 1,000 population); deaths 47,437 (8·8); infant deaths, 1,065 (12·8 per 1,000 live births); marriages 58,050 (10·6).

Population in 5 census years (with distribution by sex, 1970) was:

	White	Negro	Indian	Asiatic	Total	Per sq. mile
1910	2,639,961	60,320	279	316	2,700,876	74·9
1930	3,125,778	111,982	285	458	3,238,503	89·4
1950	3,758,512	174,168	438	1,106	3,934,224	108·7
1960	4,388,554	269,275	948	2,447	4,662,498	128·9
			All others			
1970	4,820,324	357,464	15,881		5,193,669	143·9
Male	2,351,540	171,942	7,688		2,531,170	—
Female	2,468,784	185,522	8,193		2,662,499	—

Of the total in 1970, 3,372,060 (65%) were urban (62·4% in 1960); in 1970, 3,072,025 were 21 years of age or older; foreign-born whites numbered 78,232.

The largest cities with population (census 1980) are: Indianapolis (capital), 695,040; Fort Wayne, 171,036; Gary, 151,557; Evansville, 129,665; South Bend, 108,185; Hammond, 93,440; Muncie, 74,051; Anderson, 64,421; Terre Haute, 61,006.

CONSTITUTION AND GOVERNMENT. The present constitution (the second) dates from 1851; it has had (as of Nov. 1978) 34 amendments. The General Assembly consists of a Senate of 50 members elected for 4 years, and a House of Representatives of 100 members elected for 2 years.

A constitutional amendment of 1970 allows the legislators to set the length and frequency of sessions, which are currently held annually. The Governor and Lieut.-Governor are elected for 4 years. The state is represented in Congress by 2 senators and 10 representatives.

In the 1980 presidential election Reagan polled 1,255,656 votes, Carter 844,197.

The state capital is Indianapolis. The state is divided into 92 counties and 1,008 townships.

Governor: Robert D. Orr (R.), 1981–85 ($36,000 plus $12,000 expenses).
Secretary of State: Edwin Simcox (R.), 1978–82 ($34,000).

BUDGET. In the fiscal year 1976–77 (US Census Bureau figures) general revenues were $3,437m. ($770m. from federal government, $2,162·9m. from taxes), general expenditures were $3,186·5m. ($1·4m. for education, $390·7m. for public welfare and $442·6m. for highways).

Total long-term debt, on 30 June 1976, was $585·5m.

Per capita personal income (1977) was $6,922.

ENERGY AND NATURAL RESOURCES

Minerals. The state produced 28·6m. tons of crushed limestone and 240,000 tons of dimension limestone in 1978; the output of coal was 23,942,000 short tons; petroleum, 5·42m. bbls (of 42 gallons). The total mineral output in 1978 was valued at $741·4m.

Agriculture. Indiana is largely agricultural, about 75% of its total area being in farms. In 1978, 95,000 farms had 17m. acres (average, 180 acres). Cash income, 1978, from crops, $1,921·5m.; from livestock and products, $1,556·7m.

The chief crops (1978) were maize (637·2m. bu.), winter wheat (31·78m. bu.), oats (8·91m. bu.), soybeans (140·42m. bu.), popcorn, rye, barley, hay (alfalfa, clover, timothy), lespedeza seed, mint, clover seed, apples, strawberries, tomatoes, watermelons and tobacco.

The livestock on 1 Jan. 1979 included 1·75m. all cattle, 202,000 milch cows, 171,000 sheep and lambs, 4·4m. swine, 21m. chickens. In 1978 the wool clip yielded 1·29m. lb. of wool from 172,000 sheep.

Forestry. The national forests area, 30 Sept. 1978, was 181,806 acres; 13 state forests totalled 140,956 acres.

INDUSTRY. Manufacturing establishments employed, in 1976, 498,300 workers, earning $6,107·7m.; value added by manufacture was $19,982·8m. The steel industry is the third largest in the country. Production of pig-iron, 1975, was 15·66m. short tons.
    Refinery production, 1975, included 79m. bbls of petrol.

COMMUNICATIONS

Roads. In 1979 there were 91,074 miles of highways, roads and streets, of which 66,313 miles were county highways and 11,183 miles state highways. Motor vehicles registered, 1978, 4,238,839.

Railways. In 1979 there were 5,269 miles of mainline railway and 2,796 miles of branch lines.

Aviation. Of airports, 1979, 130 were for public use, 350 were private and 1 was military.

JUSTICE, RELIGION, EDUCATION AND WELFARE

Justice. In 1963–80 there were no executions; since 1930 there have been 2 executions (electrocution), both for murder. State correctional institutions, 1978–79, had daily average of 5,685 inmates.
    The Civil Rights Act of 1885 forbids places of public accommodation to bar any persons on grounds not applicable to all citizens alike; no citizen may be disqualified for jury service 'on account of race or colour'. An Act of 1947 makes it an offence to spread religious or racial hatred.
    A 1961 Act provided 'all ... citizens equal opportunity for education, employment and access to public conveniences and accommodations' and created a Civil Rights Commission.

Religion. Religious denominations include Methodists, Roman Catholic, Disciples of Christ, Baptists, Evangelical United Brethren, Presbyterian churches, Society of Friends.

Education. School attendance is compulsory from 7 to 16 years of age. In 1978–79 public elementary schools, nursery school to grade 6, had 555,884 pupils and 24,115 teachers; public secondary schools, grades 7 to 12, had 527,052 pupils and 25,881 teachers. Teachers' salaries, grades 1–12, averaged $14,332. Total expenditure for public schools, 1978–79, $1,885·9m.
    The principal institutions for higher education are (1977):

Founded	Institution	Control	Teachers	Students (full-time)
1824	Indiana University, Bloomington	State	3,223	77,948
1837	De Pauw University, Greencastle	Methodist	145	2,384
1942	University of Notre Dame	R.C.	780	8,556
1850	Butler University, Indianapolis	—	360	4,117
1859	Valparaiso University, Valparaiso	Evangelical Lutheran Church	343	3,537
1870	Indiana State University, Terre Haute	State	700	15,593
1874	Purdue University, Lafayette	State	2,376	40,997
1898	Ball State University, Muncie	State	881	17,547

Health. Hospitals listed by the Indiana State Board of Health (1979) numbered 120 (23,467 beds). On 30 June 1979, 11 state mental hospitals had 8,052 patients enrolled (5,233 present).

Social Security. Old-age assistance, assistance to the blind and to the disabled were transferred from state to federal programmes in June 1974. In Jan.–June 1979, state supplemental assistance and/or Federal Supplemental Security assistance was paid to an average of 17,019 elderly persons per month (total $7·3m.), 1,053 blind ($744,868) and 22,548 disabled ($15m.). Assistance was given to 50,872 families with 106,097 dependent children, at an average of $183.38 per family per month.

Books of Reference

Indiana State Chamber of Commerce. *Here is Your Indiana Government.* 18th ed. Indianapolis, 1977

Martin, J. B., *Indiana: An Interpretation.* New York, 1947

State Library: Indiana State Library, 140 North Senate, Indianapolis 46204. *Director:* C. Ray Ewick.

IOWA

HISTORY. Iowa, first settled in 1788, was made a Territory in 1838 and admitted into the Union on 28 Dec. 1846.

AREA AND POPULATION. Iowa is bounded east by the Mississippi River (forming the boundary with Wisconsin and Illinois), south by Missouri, west by the Missouri River (forming the boundary with Nebraska), north-west by the Big Sioux River (forming the boundary with South Dakota) and north by Minnesota. Area, 56,290 sq. miles, including 247 sq. miles of inland water. Census population, 1 April 1980, 2,908,797, an increase of 2·9% since 1970. Births, 1979, were 46,763; deaths, 26,816; infant deaths, 496; marriages, 27,925; dissolutions of marriages, 11,426.

Population in 5 census years (with distribution by sex, 1970) was:

	White	Negro	Indian	Asiatic	Total	Per sq. mile
1870	1,188,207	5,762	48	3	1,194,020	21·5
1930	2,452,677	17,380	660	222	2,470,939	44·1
1950	2,599,546	19,692	1,084	620	2,621,073	46·8
1960	2,729,286	25,354	1,708	1,022	2,757,537	49·2
			All others			
1970	2,782,762[1]	32,596[1]	9,018[1]		2,825,041	50·5
Male	1,344,933	12,373	1,741		1,359,047	—
Female	1,383,776	12,981	1,733		1,398,490	—

[1] Preliminary figure.

At the census of 1970, 1,616,405 persons (57·2%) were urban (53% in 1960).

The largest cities in the state, with their census population in 1980 are: Des Moines (capital), 190,910; Cedar Rapids, 110,124; Davenport, 103,036; Sioux City, 81,434; Waterloo, 75,535; Dubuque, 61,779; Council Bluffs, 56,269; Iowa City, 50,489; Ames, 45,820; Clinton, 32,779; Mason City, 30,100; Burlington, 29,440; Fort Dodge, 29,280; Ottumwa, 27,354.

CONSTITUTION AND GOVERNMENT. The constitution of 1857 still exists; it has had 37 amendments. The General Assembly comprises a Senate of 50 and a House of Representatives of 100 members, meeting annually for an unlimited session. Senators are elected for 4 years, half retiring every second year: representatives for 2 years. The Governor and Lieut.-Governor are elected for 4 years. The state is represented in Congress by 2 senators and 6 representatives. Iowa is divided into 99 counties; the capital is Des Moines.

In the 1980 presidential election Reagan polled 676,026 votes, Carter 508,672.

Governor: Robert Ray (R.), 1979–82 ($55,000).
Lieut.-Governor: Terry Branstad (R.) ($18,000).
Secretary of State: Melvin D. Synhorst (R.) ($33,000).

BUDGET. For fiscal year 1979 state tax revenue was $1,569·3m. General expenditures were $2,736·9m. (education, $1,175·7m.; highways, $477·2m.; public welfare, $407·6m.; health, $240m. and hospitals, $171·1m.).

On 30 June 1979 the net long-term debt was $299·3m.

Per capita personal income (1979) was $8,772.

ENERGY AND NATURAL RESOURCES

Minerals. The leading products by value are cement (2·74m. tons in 1978) and limestone (29·9m. tons in 1978). Coalfields produced 350,000 tons in 1978. The value of mineral products, 1978, was $262·9m.

Agriculture. Iowa is the wealthiest of the agricultural states, partly because nearly the whole area (95·5%) is arable and included in farms. It has escaped large-scale commercial farming. The average farm (in 1979) was 281 acres.

In 1979, 121,000 farms had 34m. acres of farm land.

Cash farm income (1979 estimate) was $9,569m. (ranks second); from livestock, $5,819·5m., and from crops, $3,749·5m. Production of corn grain in 1979 was 1,625·6m. bu. Red meat production in 1979 totalled 6,230m. lb. On 1 Dec. 1979 livestock included swine, 16·2m. (leading all states); milch cows, 372,000; all cattle, 7·2m., and sheep and lambs, 408,000. The wool clip (1979) yielded 3m. lb. of wool.

INDUSTRY. In 1977 manufacturing establishments employed 239,900 people with annual payroll at $3,375·4m., value added by manufacture was $8,715·8m. in 1977.

COMMUNICATIONS

Roads. On 1 Jan. 1979 the number of miles of streets and highways was 113,000; there were 1·9m. licensed drivers and 2·2m. registered vehicles.

Railways. The state, 1979, had 10,333 miles of track, 8 Class I railways and 10 Class II railways.

Aviation. Airports (1979), numbered 355, including 133 lighted airports and 88 all-weather runways. There were 3,000 private aircraft.

JUSTICE, RELIGION, EDUCATION AND WELFARE

Justice. There is now no capital punishment in Iowa. State prisons, 10 Oct. 1980, had 2,489 inmates.

Religion. Chief religious bodies in 1979 were: Roman Catholic (541,950 members); United Methodists, 261,751; American Lutheran, 201,558 baptised members; United Presbyterians, 84,983; United Church of Christ, 50,575.

Education. School attendance is compulsory for 24 consecutive weeks annually during school age (7–16). In 1979–80 547,199 were attending primary and secondary schools; 53,067 pupils attending non-public schools. Classroom teachers (1978–79) numbered 33,610 with average salary of $15,150. Total expenditure on public schools in 1978–79 was $1,218,603,000. Leading institutions for higher education (1979–80) were:

Founded	Institution	Control	Professors and full-time instructors	Undergraduate Students (full-time)
1847	University of Iowa, Iowa City	State	1,046	13,132
1847	Grinnell College, Grinnell	Independent	105	1,232
1852	Wartburg College, Waverly	American Lutheran	76	1,061
1853	Cornell College, Mount Vernon	Independent	68	893
1858	Iowa State University, Ames	State	1,234	18,080
1876	Univ. of Northern Iowa, Cedar Falls	State	549	7,768
1881	Drake University, Des Moines	Independent	262	3,869
1881	Coe College, Cedar Rapids	Independent	75	1,080
1894	Morningside College, Sioux City	Methodist	74	1,081

Health. In 1980, the state had 138 hospitals (about 19,042 beds). On 30 July 1979 hospitals for mental diseases had 1,038 resident patients.

Social Security. Iowa has a Civil Rights Act (1939) which makes it a misdemeanour for any place of public accommodation to deprive any person of 'full and equal enjoyment' of the facilities it offers the public.

Old-age assistance was established in 1934 for citizens 65 years of age or older; in July 1980, 11,141 persons were drawing an average of $83.98 per month. Aid to dependent children, established 1974, was received by 38,630 families ($309.59 per family) representing 106,523 persons; aid to disabled was paid to 13,605 persons (average, $148.18); 1,013 recipients of aid to the blind averaged $152.99.

Books of Reference

Statistical Information: State Departments of Health, Public Instruction and Social Services; State Aeronautics, Commerce and Development Commissions; Crop and Livestock Reporting Services, Des Moines; State Highway Commission, Ames; Geological Survey, Iowa City; Iowa College Aid Commission.

Annual Survey of Manufactures. US Department of Commerce
Government Finance. US Department of Commerce
Official Register. Secretary of State. Des Moines. Biennial
Petersen, W. J., *Iowa History Reference Guide.* Iowa City, 1952
Transplan '79. Iowa Department of Transportation

Iowa State Library: Des Moines 50319. *Librarian:* Frances Desmond.

KANSAS

HISTORY. Kansas, first settled in 1727, was made a Territory (along with part of Colorado) in 1854, and was admitted into the Union with its present area on 29 Jan. 1861.

AREA AND POPULATION. Kansas is bounded north by Nebraska, east by Missouri, with the Missouri River as boundary in the north-east, south by Oklahoma and west by Colorado. Area, 82,264 sq. miles, including 216 sq. miles of inland water. Census population, 1 April 1980 (preliminary), 2,363,208, an increase of 5·1% since 1970. Vital statistics, 1978: Births, 34,747 (14·8 per 1,000 population); deaths, 21,001 (8·9); infant deaths, 398 (11·5 per 1,000 live births); marriages, 23,901 (10·2); divorces 12,737 (5·4).

Population in 5 federal census years (with distribution by sex, 1960) was:

	White	Negro	Indian	Asiatic	Total	Per sq. mile
1870	346,377	17,108	914	—	364,399	4·5
1930	1,811,997	66,344	2,454	204	1,880,999	22·9
1950	1,828,961	73,158	2,381	431	1,905,299	23·2
1960	2,078,666	91,445	5,069	2,271	2,178,611	26·3
			All others			
1970	2,122,068	106,977	17,533		2,249,071	27·5
Male	1,031,409	45,743	4,225		1,081,377	—
Female	1,047,257	45,702	4,275		1,097,234	—

Of the total population in 1960, 1,328,741 were urban (61% compared with 52·1% in 1950). Households were 672,907. Those 21 years of age or older numbered 1,321,835; foreign-born whites numbered 31,098.

Cities, with 1980 census population, are Wichita, 279,352; Kansas City, 159,972; Topeka (capital), 115,996; Overland Park, 81,385; Lawrence, 52,003.

CONSTITUTION AND GOVERNMENT. The year 1861 saw the adoption of the present constitution; it has had 54 amendments. The Legislature includes a Senate of 40 members, elected for 4 years, and a House of Representatives of 125 members, elected for 2 years. Sessions are annual. The Governor and Lieut.-Governor are elected for 2 years. The right to vote (with the usual exceptions) is possessed by all citizens. The state is represented in Congress by 2 senators and 5 representatives.

The state was the first (of 42 states) to establish in 1933 a Legislative Council of 10 senators and 15 representatives to sit continuously between sessions for the study of legislative problems.

In the 1980 presidential election Reagan polled 566,812 votes, Carter 326,150. The capital is Topeka. The state is divided into 105 counties.

Governor: John Carlin (D.), 1979–82 ($35,000).
Lieut.-Governor: Paul V. Dugan (R.) ($12,275).
Secretary of State: Jack H. Brier (R.) ($18,500).

BUDGET. For the year ending 30 June 1974 (US Census Bureau figures) general revenue was $1,234,503,000, of which taxation furnished $702,709,000. General expenditures were $1,112,219,000 ($439m. for education, $182,529,000 for highways and $160,696,000 for public welfare).

Total net long-term debt, 30 June 1974, amounted to $174·57m.

Per capita personal income (1969) was $3,488.

ENERGY AND NATURAL RESOURCES

Minerals. Important minerals are coal, petroleum, natural gas, lead and zinc.

Agriculture. Kansas is pre-eminently agricultural, but sometimes suffers from lack of rainfall in the west. In 1974, 83,000 farms had an area of 49·9m. acres; average farm (1969) was 568 acres, value of lands and buildings (1959) $48,084; in 1959, 10,070 farms had 1,000 acres or more and 10,562 farms had 49 acres or less. The national grassland area, 30 June 1968, was 107,708 acres.

Cash income, 1978, from crops was $1,490m.; from livestock and products, $2,955m.

Kansas is a great wheat-producing state. Its output in 1978 was 306m. bu. Other crops in 1978 (in bushels) were maize, 153m.; grain sorghums, 209m.; soybeans, 26m.; oats, 4·6m.; barley, 2·6m.; rye, 315,000. The state has an extensive livestock industry, comprising, on 1 Jan. 1979, 136,000 milch cows, 6,200,000 all cattle, 208,000 sheep and lambs and 1,960,000 swine. Wool clip (1978), 1,612,000 lb. from 219,000 sheep.

INDUSTRY. In 1967 there were 2,564 manufacturing establishments, 107,000 production workers earned $655m.; value added by manufacture was $2,108m. The slaughtering industry, manufacture of transport equipment and petroleum refining are important.

COMMUNICATIONS

Roads. The state in 1974 had 10,891 miles of roads and streets and 32,329 miles of federally-aided highways.

Railways. There were 7,621 miles of railway in 1974.

Aviation. There were 272 airports in 1969, of which 119 were public and 163 were private.

JUSTICE, RELIGION, EDUCATION AND WELFARE

Justice. There were 2,042 sentenced prisoners in state institutions, Dec. 1969. The death penalty (by hanging) for murder was abolished in 1907 and restored in 1935; there were no executions in 1968; total executions 1934 to 1968 have been 15 (all for murder).

For the various Civil Rights Acts forbidding racial or political discrimination, *see* THE STATESMAN'S YEAR-BOOK, 1955, p. 666. The 1965 Kansas Act against Discrimination declared that it is the policy of the state to eliminate and prevent discrimination in all employment relations, and to eliminate and prevent discrimination, segregation or separation in all places of public accommodations covered by the Act.

Religion. The most numerous religious bodies are Roman Catholic, with 157,292 adherents in 1936, Methodists (140,792), and Disciples of Christ (65,740). Total membership, all denominations, was 691,438.

Education. In 1974–75 organized school districts had 449,564 enrolled pupils in elementary and secondary schools. There were 113,352 students in higher education.

Kansas has 6 state supported institutions of higher education: the University of Kansas, Lawrence, founded in 1865; Kansas State University of Agriculture and Applied Science, Manhattan (1863); Kansas State Teachers' College, Emporia (1865); Kansas State College of Pittsburg, Pittsburg (1903); Fort Hays State College, Hays (1901) and Wichita State University (1964), an associate of the University of Kansas. There is one municipal university, Washburn University, Topeka (1944).

Health. In 1969 the state had 165 hospitals (19,900 beds) listed by the American Hospital Association; psychiatric hospitals had an average daily census of 4,317.

Social Security. In June 1975, 103,142 persons received state and federal aid under programmes of aid to the aged, blind or disabled, aid to dependent children, general assistance, and medical assistance. Total payments amounted to $7,386,396.

Books of Reference

Annual Economic Report of the Governor. Topeka
Directory of State Officers, Boards and Commissioners and Interesting Facts Concerning Kansas. Topeka. Biennial
Drury, J. W., *The Government of Kansas*. Lawrence, Univ. of Kansas, 1970
Hornbaker, Allison L., *The Kansas Mineral Industry, 1967*. Lawrence, Univ. of Kansas, State Geological Survey, 1968
Howes, C. C., *This Place Called Kansas*. Univ. of Oklahoma, Norman, Okla., 1952
Zornow, W. F., *Kansas: A History of the Jayhawk State*. Norman, Okla., 1957

State Library: Kansas State Library, Topeka. *State Librarian:* Denny Stephens.

KENTUCKY

HISTORY. Kentucky, first settled in 1765, was originally part of Virginia; it was admitted into the Union on 1 June 1792 and its first legislature met on 4 June.

AREA AND POPULATION. Kentucky is bounded north by the Ohio River (forming the boundary with Illinois, Indiana and Ohio), north-east by the Sandy River (forming the boundary with West Virginia), east by Virginia, south by Tennessee and west by the Mississippi River (forming the boundary with Missouri). Area, 40,395 sq. miles, of which 745 sq. miles are water. Census population, 1980 (preliminary), 3,661,433, an increase of 13·7% since 1970. Births in 1978, 58,359 (16·7 per 1,000 population); deaths, 33,108 (9·6); infant deaths, 700 (12 per 1,000 live births); marriages, 34,104 (9·7); divorces, 14,043 (4).

Population in 4 census years (with distribution by sex, 1970) was:

	White	Negro	All others	Total	Per sq. mile
1930	2,388,452	226,040	97	2,614,589	65·2
1950	2,742,090	201,921	195	2,944,806	73·9
1960	2,820,083	215,949	1,689	3,038,156	75·6
1970	2,971,425	241,448	6,438	3,219,311	79·7
Male	1,464,399	111,642	2,995	1,579,036	—
Female	1,517,367	119,151	3,152	1,639,670	—

Of the total population in 1970, 1,684,053 (52·3%) were urban (44·5% in 1960). Those 21 years old or older numbered 1,918,642; foreign-born whites numbered 16,096.

The principal cities with census population in 1980 are: Louisville, 298,161 (urbanized area, 1970, 695,055); Lexington-Fayette, 203,082. 1970 figures: Covington,

52,535; Owensboro, 50,329; Bowling Green, 36,705; Paducah, 31,627; Ashland, 30,386; Frankfort (capital), 21,902.

CONSTITUTION AND GOVERNMENT. The constitution dates from 1891; there had been 3 preceding it. The 1891 constitution was promulgated by convention and provides that amendments be submitted to the electorate for ratification. The General Assembly consists of a Senate of 38 members elected for 4 years, one-half retiring every 2 years, and a House of Representatives of 100 members elected for 2 years. Sessions are biennial. The Governor and Lieut.-Governor are elected for 4 years. All citizens are (with necessary exceptions) qualified as electors; the voting age was in 1955 reduced from 21 to 18 years. Registered votes, Sept. 1980: 1,740,585. In the 1980 presidential election Reagan polled 635,274 votes, Carter 617,417.

The state is represented in Congress by 2 senators and 7 representatives.

The capital is Frankfort. The state is divided into 120 counties.

Governor: John Y. Brown, Jr. (D.), 1979–83 ($45,000).
Lieut.-Governor: Martha Layne Collins (D.) ($38,640).
Secretary of State: Frances Jones Mills (D.) ($38,640).

BUDGET. For the fiscal year ending 30 June 1979 general revenues were $1,698m. (federal grants, $6,872m.). General expenditures for the year ending 30 June 1979, included education, $840·4m.; public welfare, $664·9m.; transport, $551m.

The total net long-term debt on 30 June 1979 was $298·8m.

Per capita personal income (1979) was $7,390.

ENERGY AND NATURAL RESOURCES

Minerals. The principal mineral product of Kentucky is coal, 147·8m. tons mined in 1977. Output of petroleum, 7m. bbls (of 42 gallons); natural gas, 72·7m. cu. ft; stone, 33·8m. short tons; clay 831,000 short tons. Total value of mineral products in 1977 was $3,533·9m. Other minerals include fluorspar, ball clay, lead, zinc, cement, natural gas liquids and quartzite.

Agriculture. In 1976, 124,000 farms had an area of 16m. acres. The average farm was 129 acres.

Cash income, 1977, from crops, $1,064·6m., and from livestock $714,185,000. The chief crop is tobacco: production, in 1976, 425·1m. lb., ranking second to N. Carolina in US. Other principal crops include corn, hay, soybeans, wheat, sorghum grain, rye, barley, popcorn and oats.

Stock-raising is important in Kentucky, which has long been famous for its horses. The livestock in 1977 included 278,000 milch cows, 3·3m. all cattle, 28,000 sheep, 1m. swine.

Forestry. Total forests area, 1978, 12,160,800 acres. Total commercial forest land, 1978, 11,901,900 acres; 92% is privately owned.

INDUSTRY. In 1979 the state's 3,291 manufacturing plants had 216,118 production workers.; value added by manufacture in 1977 was $9,440m. The leading manufacturing industries are electrical equipment, apparel and other fabric products, non-electrical machinery and foods. Direct foreign investment in manufacturing by foreign investors was $640m. in 1979.

COMMERCE. Exports in 1976 included manufactured and agricultural products valued at $500m.

COMMUNICATIONS

Roads. In 1979 the state had over 69,047 miles of federal, state and local roads. There were 2,671,969 motor vehicle registrations in 1979.

Railways. In 1979 there were 3,259 miles of railway.

Aviation. There are (1980) 95 licensed airports and heliports and 1,950 aircraft in Kentucky. Five air-carrier airports served 6m. passengers in 1979.

Shipping. There is an increasing amount of barge traffic on 1,453·8 miles of navigable rivers. There are 5 river ports and 4 are being developed.

JUSTICE, RELIGION, EDUCATION AND WELFARE

Justice. There are 11 correctional institutions and 2 camps for adults. Juvenile offenders are placed in custody of the Bureau for Social Services, Department for Human Resources, which maintains 34 institutions.

In 1979–80 the prisons had an average of 3,436 inmates. There has been no execution since 1962. A session of Congress in 1976 limited the death penalty to cases of kidnap and murder.

Total executions, 1911–62, were 162, including 76 whites and 86 Negroes; 144 were for murder, 7 for rape, 6 for criminal offences, 5 for armed robbery.

Religion. The chief religious denominations in 1975 were: Baptists (Southern and General), with 715,469 members, Roman Catholic (347,365), Methodists (201,748), Christian Church (82,848) and Disciples of Christ (52,369).

Education. Attendance at school between the ages of 6 and 15 years (inclusive) is compulsory, the normal term being 175 days. In 1979–80, 21,132 teachers were employed in public elementary and 12,216 in secondary schools, in which 435,874 and 241,249 pupils enrolled respectively. Expenditure on elementary and secondary day schools in 1979–80 was about $1,085,000; public school classroom teachers' salaries (1979–80) averaged $14,520.

There were also 4,054 teachers working in private elementary and secondary schools with 75,164 students.

The state has 23 universities and senior colleges, 6 junior colleges and 13 community colleges, with a total (autumn 1979) of 129,167 students. Of these universities and colleges, 22 are state-supported, and the remainder are supported privately. The largest of the institutions of higher learning are (autumn 1979): University of Kentucky, with 23,058 students; University of Louisville, 19,238 students; Western Kentucky University, 13,532 students; Eastern Kentucky University, 13,668 students; Murray State University, 7,836 students; Morehead State University, 7,029 students; Northern Kentucky University, 7,527 students. Four of the several privately endowed colleges of standing are Berea College, Berea; Centre College, Danville, Transylvania University, Lexington, and Bellarmine College, Louisville.

Health. In 1979 the state had 106 general hospitals (12,720 beds), 8 hospitals for mental diseases (1,707 beds) and 3 children's hospitals (320 beds).

Welfare. In Oct. 1979 there were 262,661 persons receiving financial assistance; 8,912 of these persons received the Federal Supplemental Security Income (SSI); 5,447 of them were aged, 110 blind, 3,355 disabled. The average monthly SSI payment in each group is as follows: $114.70 to aged, $79.35 to blind and $120.81 to disabled. Also, in the all state funded Supplementation programme payments were made in June 1978 to 8,663 persons, of which 5,352 were aged, 106 blind and 3,205 disabled. The average State Supplementation payment was $109.11 to aged, $81.14 to blind and $115.67 to disabled.

In the Aid to Families with Dependent Children Programme as of June 1979, aid was given to 163,972 persons in 60,617 families. The average payment per person was $60.97, per family $164.94. The Unemployed Father segment of the AFDC Programme was discontinued in July 1977 when employment rates improved.

In addition to money payments, medical assistance, food stamps and social services are available.

Books of Reference

Kentucky Deskbook of Economic Statistics. 15th ed. Department of Commerce, Frankfort, 1978
Directory for the Use of Courts, State and County Officials and General Assembly of the State of Kentucky. Frankfort. Biennial

Vital Statistics. Kentucky Department for Human Resources, 66th Annual Report, 1973
Federal Writers' Project. *Kentucky: A Guide to the Bluegrass State.* Rev. ed. New York, 1954
Coleman, J. W., *A Bibliography of Kentucky History.* Univ. of Kentucky, Lexington, 1949
Schwendeman, J. R., *Geography of Kentucky.* Oklahoma City, 1958

LOUISIANA

HISTORY. Louisiana was first settled in 1699. That part lying east of the Mississippi River was organized in 1804 as the Territory of New Orleans, and admitted into the Union on 30 April 1812. The section west of the river was added very shortly thereafter.

AREA AND POPULATION. Louisiana is bounded north by Arkansas, east by Mississippi, with the Mississippi River forming the boundary in the north-east, south by the Gulf of Mexico and west by Texas, with the Sabine River forming most of the boundary. Area, 48,523 sq. miles, including 3,417 sq. miles of inland water. Census population, 1 April 1980 (preliminary), 4,203,972, an increase of 15·4% since 1970. Births, 1978, 74,221 (18·7 per 1,000 population); deaths, 34,953 (8·8); infant deaths, 1,283 (17·3 per 1,000 live births); marriages (1977), 38,645; divorces (1977), 12,965.

Population in 5 census years (with distribution by sex, 1970) was:

	White	Negro	Indian	Asiatic	Total	Per sq. mile
1910	941,086	713,874	780	648	1,656,388	36·5
1930	1,322,712	776,326	1,536	1,019	2,101,593	46·5
1950	1,796,683	882,428	409	3,996	2,683,516	59·4
1960	2,211,715	1,039,207	3,587	2,004	3,257,022	72·2
			All others			
1970	2,541,498	1,086,832	12,976		3,641,306	81·1
Male	1,249,632	515,231	6,621		1,771,484	—
Female	1,291,866	571,601	6,355		1,869,822	—

Of the 1970 total, 2,406,150 (66·1%) were urban (63·3% in 1960); those 21 years of age or older were 2,040,776; foreign-born whites numbered 36,146.

The largest cities with their 1980 census population are: New Orleans, 557,761 (urban area, 1,183,606); Shreveport, 194,773 (376,704); Baton Rouge (capital), 219,164 (497,087); Lake Charles, 75,621; Lafayette, 79,511; Monroe, 56,338; Bossier, 50,866; Alexandria, 51,579, Kenner, 66,241.

CONSTITUTION AND GOVERNMENT. The present constitution dates from 1974.

The Legislature consists of a Senate of 39 members and a House of Representatives of 105 members, both chosen for 4 years. Sessions are annual; a fiscal session is held in odd years. The Governor and Lieut.-Governor are elected for 4 years.

A Governor may serve a second consecutive term. Qualified electors are (with the usual exceptions) all registered citizens with the usual residential qualifications.

In the 1980 presidential election Reagan polled 792,853 votes, Carter 708,453.

The state sends to Congress 2 senators and 8 representatives. Louisiana is divided into 64 parishes (corresponding with the counties of other states).

Governor: David C. Treen (D.), 1980–84 ($68,000).
Lieut.-Governor: Robert Freeman (D.), 1980–84 ($58,673).
Secretary of State: James Brown (D.), 1980–84 ($55,712).

BUDGET. For the fiscal year ending 30 June 1980 (Louisiana State Budget Office figures) general revenues were $5,191,587,082, of which $1,283,763,509 were federal funds; total expenditures were $4,676,383,509 (education, $1,582,423,353; transport and development, $248,278,704; health, hospitals and public welfare, $1,269,624,470).

Per capita personal income (1979) was $7,477.

ENERGY AND NATURAL RESOURCES

Minerals. The yield in 1977 of crude petroleum was 562·9m. bbls; natural gas, 7m. cu. ft. Rich sulphur mines are found in the state, and wells for the extraction of sulphur by means of hot water and compressed air are in operation; output, 1977, 2·6m. long tons.

Output of salt (1977) was 13·54m. short tons. Total output of raw, non-fuel minerals in 1978 was valued at $329m.

Agriculture. The state is divided into two parts, the uplands and the alluvial and swamp regions of the coast. A delta occupies about one-third of the total area. Manufacturing is the leading industry, but agriculture is important. In 1977 there were 35,466 farms; average farm, 257 acres.

Cash income, 1977, from crops $851,024,000; from livestock, $405,994,000. Production of sugar-cane was valued at $101,599,000; rice, $170,888,000; sweet potatoes, $16·56m.; soybeans, $319,047,000; pecans, $14·27m.; cotton, $179·5m.; strawberries, $2,236,000.

In 1978 the state contained 132,000 milch cows, 1·7m. all cattle, 13,000 sheep and 140,000 swine.

Forestry. Forests, 14·5m. acres, represent 47% of the state's area. Income from manufactured products exceeds $2,400m. annually. In 1978 pulpwood cut, 3,586,625 cords; sawtimber cut, 1,358m. bd ft.

INDUSTRY. The manufacturing industries are chiefly those associated with petroleum, chemicals, lumber, food, paper. Investment in manufacturing, 1977–80, about $8,000m.

TOURISM. Travellers spent an estimated $2,500m. in 1979 and generated 74,000 jobs with earnings of $524m. State and local tax revenue, $134m.

COMMUNICATIONS

Roads. The state has more than 52,000 miles of public roads. In 1978, 1·8m. automobiles were registered in the state.

Railways. In 1978 the railways in the state had a length of about 3,700 miles.

Aviation. There were, 1978, 240 commercial and private airports.

Shipping. New Orleans is the second largest seaport of the US handling (1979) 163m. tons of cargo. The Mississippi and other waterways provide 7,500 miles of navigable water.

JUSTICE, RELIGION, EDUCATION AND WELFARE

Justice. Prisons, Oct. 1980, had 7,414 inmates.

Since 1961 there have been no executions; total executions by electrocution since 1930 were 135.

Religion. The Roman Catholic Church is the largest denomination in Louisiana, with 1,316,441 members in 1979. The leading Protestant Churches are Southern Baptist, with (1979) 524,566 members; Methodist, (1979) 136,972.

Education. School attendance is compulsory between the ages of 7 and 15, both inclusive. In 1978–79 there were 1,485 public elementary and high schools which had 845,813 pupils with a current expenditure of $1,535 per pupil. Private schools (449) had 153,220. In 1978–79, instructional staff had an average salary of $12,864. Total expenditure on elementary and secondary schools (1978–79), $1,361,124,301.

There are 16 four year public colleges and universities and 12 non-public four-year institutions of higher learning. There are 53 state trade and vocational-technical schools. Superior instruction is given in the Louisiana State University system with 49,661 students (1979). Tulane University in New Orleans had 9,717 students (1979). The Roman Catholic Loyola University in New Orleans had 4,400 students (1979). Dillard University in New Orleans (1,248 students in 1979) and the Southern University system (11,385 students in 1979) were formerly for Negroes.

Health. In 1978 the state had 155 licensed hospitals (25,289 beds); 3 mental hospitals cared for 12,381 patients.

Social Security. In Dec. 1978, 86,641 persons were receiving old-age assistance to the average of $93 per month; 61,931 families with dependent children were receiving an average of $127 per month; 1,665 blind persons, $144 per month; 53,408 totally disabled persons, $137. Aid was from state and federal sources.

Books of Reference

Louisiana Almanac. New Orleans, 1979–80

The History and Government of Louisiana. Legislative Council, Baton Rouge, 1975

Louisiana State Agencies Handbook. Public Affairs Research Council of Louisiana. Baton Rouge, 1979

The State of the State: an Economic and Social Report to the Governor. Louisiana State Planning Office, New Orleans, 1978

Statistical Abstract of Louisiana. Division of Business and Economic Research. University of New Orleans, 1977

Davis, E. A., *Louisiana, the Pelican State.* Louisiana State Univ. Press, Baton Rouge, 1975

Hansen, H., ed., *Louisiana, a Guide to the State.* Rev. ed. New York, 1971

Kniffen, F. B., *Louisiana, its Land and People.* Louisiana State Univ. Press, Baton Rouge, 1968

State Library: The Louisiana State Library, Baton Rouge, Louisiana. *State Librarian:* Thomas F. Jaques.

MAINE

HISTORY. After a first attempt in 1607, Maine was settled in 1623. From 1652 to 1820 it was part of Massachusetts and was admitted into the Union on 15 March 1820.

AREA AND POPULATION. Maine is bounded west, north and east by Canada, south-east by the Atlantic, south and south-west by New Hampshire. Area, 33,215 sq. miles, of which 2,282 are inland water. Of the state's total area, about 17·2m. acres (87%) are in timber and wood lots. Census population, 1 April 1980 (preliminary), 1,124,660, an increase of 13·1% since 1970. In 1978 live births numbered 15,919; deaths, 10,168; infant deaths, 162; marriages, 11,658; divorces 5,751.

Population for 5 census years (with distribution by sex, 1970):

	White	Negro	Indian	Asiatic	Total	Per sq. mile
1910	739,995	1,363	892	121	742,371	24·8
1930	795,185	1,096	1,012	130	797,423	25·7
1950	910,846	1,221	1,522	185	913,774	29·4
1960	963,291	3,318	1,879	597	969,265	31·3
			All others			
1970	985,276[1]	2,800[1]	3,972		993,663	32·1
Male	479,241	1,618	2,006		482,865	—
Female	506,035	1,182	1,966		509,183	—

[1] Preliminary.

The urban population was 504,157 or 53·9% of the total (51·3% in 1960); those 21 years or older numbered 595,938.

The largest city in the state is Portland with a census population of 65,120 in 1970. Other cities (with population in 1970) are: Lewiston, 41,780; Bangor, 33,170; Auburn, 24,150; South Portland, 23,270; Augusta (capital), 21,950; Biddeford, 19,980; Waterville, 18,190.

CONSTITUTION AND GOVERNMENT. The constitution of 1820 is still in force, but it has been amended 140 times. In 1951, 1965 and 1973 the Legislature approved recodifications of the constitution as arranged by the Chief Justice under special authority.

The Legislature consists of the Senate with 33 members and the House of Representatives with 151 members, both Houses being elected simultaneously for 2 years. Apart from these legislators and the Governor (elected for 4 years), no other state officers are elected. The Justices of the Supreme Judicial Court give their opinion upon important questions of law and upon solemn occasions when required by the Governor, Senate or House of Representatives. The suffrage is possessed by all citizens, 18 years of age; persons under guardianship for reasons of mental illness have no vote. Indians residing on tribal reservations and otherwise qualified have the vote in all county, state and national elections, but retain the right to elect their own tribal representative to the legislature.

In the 1980 presidential election Reagan polled 238,522 votes, Carter 220,974 and Anderson 53,327.

The state sends to Congress 2 senators and 2 representatives.

The capital is Augusta. The state is divided into 16 counties.

Governor: Joseph E. Brennan (D.), 1979–83 ($35,000).
Secretary of State: Rodney S. Quinn (D.), 1979–83 ($25,000).

BUDGET. For the financial year ending 30 June 1978 total general revenue was $938,956,000 and expenditure was $922,254,000.

Total net long-term debt on 30 June 1978 was $273·7m.
Per capita personal income (1976) was $5,367.

NATURAL RESOURCES

Minerals. Minerals include sand and gravel, stone, lead, clay, copper, peat, silver and zinc. Mineral output, 1980, was valued at over $40m.

Agriculture. In 1979, 7,800 farms occupied 1·6m. acres; the average farm was 210 acres.

Cash receipts, 1979, $440m., of which $93·8m. came from potatoes; Maine is the third largest producer of potatoes (about 7% of the country's total); production in 1979 was 27·7m. cwt. Other important items include broilers ($92·7m.), eggs ($110·8m.) and dairy products ($81·7m.); these with potatoes provide 86% of receipts. Sweet corn, peas and beans, oats, hay, apples and blueberries are also grown. On 1 Jan. 1979 the farm animals included 57,000 milch cows, 124,000 all other cattle, 13,000 sheep, 13,000 swine.

Forestry. Lumber, wood turnings and pulp are important. In 1979 the cut of softwood was 921,722m. bd ft; hardwood, 187,461m. bd ft, and pulpwood (1977), 2,810,192 cords. Spruce and fir, white pine, hemlock, white and yellow birch, sugar maple, northern white cedar, beech and red oak are the most important species cut. There were (1974) 16,894,300 acres of commercial forest (98% in private ownership). National forests comprise 37,500 acres; other federal, 35,800 acres; state forests, 163,000 acres; municipal, 75,200 acres. Wood products industries are of great economic importance; in 1978 the paper, lumber and wood industries' production was valued at $2,379·5m. (54·5% of total industrial production). There were (1980) 388 primary manufacturers and over 470 secondary.

Fisheries. In 1977, 182,188,922 lb. of fish and shellfish (valued at $62,001,398 were landed; the catch included 18,487,138 lb. of lobsters (valued at $32,101,423). 25·54m. lb. of sardines were packed in 1977 valued at $27·49m.

INDUSTRY. In 1978, 2,663 manufacturing establishments reported 102,320 workers, earning $1,237·7m., gross value of production, $5,665·1m. (increase of 14·7%

from 1977). Leading industry is paper with 51 plants, 17,641 workers and output valued at $1,809·7m. (31·9% of the state's total manufactures).

COMMUNICATIONS

Roads. In 1980 there were 21,744 miles of roads, of which 3,964 miles were state highways and 7,651 miles were state-aided; town streets and miscellaneous, 10,129 miles. In 1978, 1,136,476 motor vehicles were registered, including 552,826 passenger vehicles.

Railways. In 1980 there were nearly 2,000 miles of railway tracks.

Aviation. Commercially licensed airports, 1980, numbered 200, including 3 international, 2 county and 1 state; there were 2 military airports, 11 private landing strips (1 being state-owned), 14 licensed commercial seaplane bases and 3 registered non-commercial seaplane bases.

JUSTICE, RELIGION, EDUCATION AND WELFARE

Justice. The state's penal system in July 1980 held 424 adults in the state prison, 286 in the Correctional Institute and 307 juveniles in the Youth Centre. There is no capital punishment. Inmates serving life sentences are eligible for parole consideration after 15 years, less remission for good conduct, provided they were imprisoned before the passage of a new Criminal Code by the 107th Maine Legislature, which abolished the parole system.

Religion. The largest religious bodies are: Roman Catholic (270,283 members), Baptists (36,808 members) and Congregationalists (40,750 members), and other Christian Churches (34,066 members).

Education. Education is free for pupils from 5 to 21 years of age, and compulsory from 7 to 17. In 1978–79 the 806 public schools (661 elementary, 91 secondary and 54 combined elementary and secondary) had 12,563 staff and 234,073 enrolled pupils. In 1978–79 there were 111 private schools with 1,106 teachers and 17,932 pupils. Public school teachers' salaries, 1978–79, averaged $13,071. Total public expenditure on public elementary and secondary education in 1978–79, $342,479,102.

The state University of Maine, founded in 1865, had (1978–79) 966 professors and 28,319 students at 7 locations; Portland campus is now called the University of Southern Maine; Bowdoin College, founded in 1794 at Brunswick, had 96 professors and 1,375 students; Bates College at Lewiston, 97 professors and 1,471 students; Colby College at Waterville, 116 professors and 1,692 students; Nasson College at Springvale, 39 professors and 601 students; Husson College, 35 professors and 1,296 students; Thomas College, 20 professors and 905 students; Westbrook College at Westbrook, 37 professors and 935 students; Unity College at Unity, 25 professors and 652 students, and the University of New England (formerly St Francis College) at Biddeford, 23 professors and 490 students.

Health. In Oct. 1978 the state had 53 general hospitals including 10 non-accredited, (5,402 beds); 3 hospitals for mental diseases, acute and psychiatric care (559 beds); 18 nursing homes and units (596 beds).

Social Security. Supplemental Security Income (SSI) (maximum payment for single person, $189.40 per month) is administered by the Social Security Administration. It became effective on 1 Jan. 1974 and replaces former aid to the aged, blind and disabled, administered by the state with state and federal funds. SSI is supplemented by Medicaid for nursing home patients or hospital patients. State payments for SSI recipients for Aug. 1978 totalled $564,274, covering 22,875 cases. Aid to families with dependent children is granted where one or both parents are disabled or absent and income is insufficient; aid was being granted in Aug. 1978 to 18,984 families (39,124 children) with an average payment per family of $212.94 per month. Total aid under the programme, Aug. 1978, $4m. Payments under Medical Assistance programme Aug. 1978 totalled $8,590,964. There is a programme of assistance for catastrophic illness. Child welfare services include basic child protective services, enforcing child support, establishing paternity and finding missing parents, foster home placements, adoptions; services in divorce cases and licensing of foster homes, day care and residential treatment services, and public guardianship. There are also protective services for adults.

The Work Incentive Programme served about 5,510 persons through the Employment Security Commission and the Bureau of Social Welfare. Of these, 2,180 entered unsubsidized employment.

Books of Reference

Maine Register, State Year-Book and Legislative Manual. Tower Publishing, Portland. Annual
Federal Writers' Project. *Maine, a Guide 'Down East'.* Courier Gazette, 1970
Banks, R., ed., *A History of Maine: a Collection of Readings on the History of Maine 1600–1970.* Kendall/Hunt, 1969
Banks, R., *Maine Becomes A State.* Wesleyan U.P., 1970
Day, C. A., *Farming in Maine, 1060–1940.* Univ. Maine Press, 1963
Rowe, W. H., *Maritime History of Maine.* Norton, New York, 1948

MARYLAND

HISTORY. Maryland, first settled in 1634, was one of the 13 original states.

AREA AND POPULATION. Maryland is bounded north by Pennsylvania, east by Delaware and the Atlantic, south by Virginia and West Virginia, with the Potomac River forming most of the boundary, and west by West Virginia. Chesapeake Bay almost cuts off the eastern end of the state from the rest. Area, 12,303 sq. miles, of which 703 sq. miles are inland water; in addition, water area under Maryland jurisdiction in Chesapeake Bay amounts to 1,726 sq. miles. Census population, 1 April 1980, 4,216,446, an increase since 1970 of 294,047 or 7·5%. In 1978 births were 47,987 (11·6 per 1,000 population); deaths, 32,390 (7·8); infant deaths, 693 (14·4 per 1,000 live births); marriages, 44,376 (10·7); divorces, 15,711 (3·8).

Population for 5 federal censuses (with distribution by sex, 1970) was:

	White	Negro	Indian	Asiatic	Total	Per sq. mile
1920	1,204,737	244,479	32	413	1,449,661	145·8
1930	1,354,226	276,379	50	871	1,631,526	165·0
1950	1,954,975	385,972	314	1,084	2,343,001	237·1
1960	2,573,919	518,410	1,538	5,700	3,100,689	314·0
			All others			
1970	3,194,888	499,479	28,032		3,922,399	396·6
Male	1,565,481	336,950	13,890		1,916,321	—
Female	1,629,407	362,529	14,142		2,006,078	—

Of the total population in 1970, 3,003,935 persons (76·6%) were urban (72·7% in 1960); those 21 years old or older numbered 2,342,854; foreign-born whites, 89,977 in 1960.

The largest city in the state (containing 19·1% of the population of the state) is Baltimore, with 783,320 in 1980; population of metropolitan areas around Baltimore and Washington, D.C., was 3·45m in 1978. Maryland residents in the Washington, D.C., metropolitan area total more than 1m.; other cities (1978) are Dundalk (85,377); Towson (77,799); Silver Spring (77,496); Bethesda (71,621), Bome (37,323 in 1975), Hagerstown (37,233 in 1975), Annapolis (capital), 29,592. Incorporated places: Cumberland, 26,775; Cambridge, 11,476; Frederick, 25,464; Daithersburg, 25,930; Rockville, 43,441.

CONSTITUTION AND GOVERNMENT. The present constitution dates from 1867; it has had 125 amendments. The General Assembly consists of a Senate of 47, and a House of Delegates of 141 members, both elected for 4 years. Voters are citizens who have the usual residential qualifications.

At the 1980 presidential election Carter polled 726,161 votes, Reagan 680,606 and Anderson 119,537.

Maryland sends to Congress 2 senators and 8 representatives.

The state capital is Annapolis. The state is divided into 23 counties and Baltimore City.

Governor: Harry R. Hughes (D.) 1979 ($60,000).
Secretary of State: Fred Wineland ($30,000).

BUDGET. For the fiscal year ending 30 June 1979 general revenues were $3,883,262,000 ($2,633,114,000 from taxation). General expenditures, $4,006,429,000, including $740,997,000 for education and $1,032,662,000 for public welfare and health; $678,421,000 for highways.

Total authorized long-term state debt, 30 June 1979 was $3,068,382,000. (Issued and outstanding, $2,154,075,000; authorized but not issued, $914,307,000.)

Per capita personal income (1979) was $9,150.

ENERGY AND NATURAL RESOURCES

Minerals. Value of mineral production, 1978, was $164·6m. Sand and gravel (13·3m. short tons) and stone (19·5m. short tons) account for over 59% of the total value. Coal is the leading mineral commodity by value followed by Portland cement, sand and gravel and stone. Output of coal was 2·9m. short tons, valued at $58m. Natural gas is produced from 2 fields in Garrett County; 88m. cu. ft in 1978. A third gas field in the same county is used for natural gas storage.

Agriculture. Agriculture is an important industry in the state. In 1980 there were approximately 16,400 farms with an area of 2·8m. acres (35% of the land area).

Farm animals, 1 Jan. 1980, were: Milch cows, 130,000; all cattle, 380,000; swine, 235,000 (1979); sheep and lambs, 20,000; chickens (not broilers), 2·15m. (1979). The most important crops, 1979, were: corn for grain, 58·9m. bu.; soybeans, 11·5m. bu.; tobacco, 26·4m. lb., and hay, 606,000 tons.

Cash receipts from farm marketings, 1978, were $777·5m.; from livestock and livestock products, $511·4m., and crops, $259·2m. Dairy products and broilers accounted for 59·1% of cash receipts in 1978.

INDUSTRY. In 1972 manufactories had 161,800 production workers earning $1,958m.; value added by manufacture, $7,108·7m. Chief industries are food and kindred products, primary metal products, transport equipment, electrical and other machinery, chemicals and products, printing and publishing.

TOURISM. Tourism is one of the state's leading industries. In 1980 tourists spent over $2,000m.

COMMUNICATIONS

Roads. The state highway department maintained, 1 Jan. 1980, 5,239 miles of highways, of which 79 miles were toll roads. The 23 counties maintained 16,902 miles of highways, and the 159 municipalities (including the city of Baltimore) maintained 3,877 miles of streets and alleys. Total mileage, 1 Jan. 1980, of public highways, streets and alleys, 26,018 miles. In 1979, 2·2m. automobiles were registered.

Railways. Railways, in 1980, had 1,192 miles of line.

Aviation. There were, 1979, 39 commercially licensed airports.

Shipping. In 1979 Baltimore was the fourth largest US seaport in value of trade, eighth in tonnage handled.

JUSTICE, RELIGION, EDUCATION AND WELFARE

Justice. Prisons on 20 Oct. 1980 had 7,147 men and 214 women; the total equalled 177 per 100,000 population, a high rate, which may be explained by the fact that Maryland incarcerates domestic relations law violators in state prisons; state prisons also receive a considerable number of persons committed for misdemeanours by magistrates' courts of the counties as well as from Baltimore's court system.

Since 1930 there have been 68 executions (by lethal gas since 1957; earlier by hanging)—7 whites and 37 Negroes for murder, and 6 whites and 18 Negroes for rape. Last execution was June 1961.

Maryland's prison system has conducted a work-release programme for selected prisoners since 1963. All institutions have academic and vocational training programmes.

In accordance with the 1950 Supreme Court decisions declaring segregation unconstitutional, the University of Maryland and other public and private colleges admitted Negro students in Sept. 1956. Elementary and secondary schools accept the ruling, and gradual integration is under way in all counties under different methods.

Religion. Maryland was the first US state to give religious freedom to all who came within its borders. Present religious affiliations of the population are approximately: Protestant, 32%; Roman Catholic, 24%; Jewish, 10%; remaining 34% is non-related and other faiths.

Education. Education is compulsory from 6 to 16 years of age. In Sept. 1979 the public elementary schools (including kindergartens and secondary schools) had 777,725 pupils. Teachers and principals in the elementary and secondary schools numbered 44,648. Average salary of principals and teachers in elementary and secondary schools (1978–79) was $16,941. Current expenditure by local school boards on education, 1978–79, was $1,694·8m., of which the state's contribution was $600m.

In 1979 there were 31 degree-granting 4-year institutions and 19 2-year colleges. The largest two were the University of Maryland system, with 60,536 students (Sept. 1979) and Towson State College with 15,283 students (Sept. 1979).

Health. In Oct. 1979, 79 hospitals (22,047 beds) were licensed by the State Department of Health and Mental Hygiene.

The Maryland State Department of Health, organized in 1874, was in 1969 made part of the Department of Health and Mental Hygiene which performs its functions through its central office, 23 county health departments and the Baltimore City Health Department. For the financial year 1979 the department's budget was $739,367,064, of which $517,036,275 were general funds and $16,181,295 special funds appropriated by the General Assembly. The balance of the budget, $206,149,494, derives from federal funds.

During financial year 1979 Maryland's programme of medical care for indigent and medically indigent patients covered an average of 365,854 persons. The programme, which covers inpatient and outpatient hospital services, laboratory services, skilled nursing home care, physician services, pharmacy services, dental services and home health services, cost approximately $326·3m.

Social Security. Under the supervision of the Department of Employment and Human Resources, local social service departments administer public assistance for needy persons. In June 1980 families with dependent children received $15,204,233 (206,397 recipients, average actual monthly payment $72.17); general public assistance payments were $2,360,460 (21,628 recipients, average actual monthly payments $107.58); foster care of children cost $1,481,930 (7,731 recipients, average actual payment $193.77).

Books of Reference

Statistical Information: Maryland Department of Economic and Community Development, Annapolis, 21401.

Maryland Manual: A Compendium of Legal, Historical and Statistical Information Relating to the State of Maryland. Annapolis. Biennial

State Library: Maryland State Library, Annapolis. *Director:* Michael S. Miller.

MASSACHUSETTS

HISTORY. The first permanent settlement within the borders of the present state was made at Plymouth in Dec. 1620, by the Pilgrims from Holland, who were separatists from the English Church, and formed the nucleus of the Plymouth Colony. In 1628 another company of Puritans settled at Salem, forming eventually the Massachusetts Bay Colony. In 1630 Boston was settled. In the struggle which ended in the separation of the American colonies from the mother country, Massachusetts took the foremost part, and on 6 Feb. 1788 became the sixth state to ratify the US constitution.

AREA AND POPULATION. Massachusetts is bounded north by Vermont and New Hampshire, east by the Atlantic, south by Connecticut and Rhode Island and west by New York. Area, 8,257 sq. miles, 190 sq. miles being inland water (the state government puts the area at 8,093 sq. miles, including 254 sq. miles of water). The census population 1 April 1980 (preliminary), was 5,737,037, an increase of 47,867 or 0·8% since 1970. Births, 1978 were 69,078 (12 per 1,000 population); deaths, 53,860 (9·3 per 1,000); infant deaths, 688 (9·7 per 1,000 live births); marriages, 46,290 (8·0); divorces, 17,777 (3·1).

Population at 4 federal census years (with distribution by sex, 1970):

	White	Negro	Other	Total	Per sq. mile
1940	4,257,596	55,391	3,734	4,316,721	550·7
1950	4,611,503	73,171	5,840	4,690,514	598·4
1960	5,023,144	111,842	13,592	5,148,578	656·8
1970	5,477,624	175,817	35,729	5,689,170	725·8
Male	2,618,930	82,573	17,895	2,719,398	—
Female	2,858,694	93,244	17,834	2,969,772	—

Of the total population in 1970, 4,810,449 persons (84·6%) were urban (83·6% in 1960); those 18 years old or older numbered 3,813,406.

In 1980 the population of the principal towns and cities was:

Boston	562,118	Fall River	92,240	Lawrence	62,770
Worcester	161,384	Lowell	92,160	Medford	58,303
Springfield	152,212	Quincy	83,904	Waltham	58,298
New Bedford	98,397	Newton	83,586	Chicopee	55,048
Cambridge	95,351	Lynn	78,299		
Brockton	94,990	Somerville	77,393		

The largest of 10 standard metropolitan statistical areas, 1970 census were: Boston, 2,753,700; Springfield–Chicopee–Holyoke, 529,922; Worcester, 344,320.

CONSTITUTION AND GOVERNMENT. The constitution dates from 1780 and has had 106 amendments. The legislative body, styled the General Court of the Commonwealth of Massachusetts, meets annually, and consists of the Senate with 40 members, elected biennially, and the House of Representatives of 240 (160 from 1979) members, elected for 2 years. The Governor and Lieut.-Governor are elected for 4 years. The state sends 2 senators and 11 representatives to Congress.

At the 1980 presidential election Reagan polled 1,056,223 votes, Carter 1,053,800. Electors are all citizens 18 years of age or older.

The capital is Boston. The state has 14 counties, 39 cities and 312 towns.

Governor: Edward King (D.), 1979–82 ($40,000).
Lieut.-Governor: Thomas P. O'Neill.
Secretary of the Commonwealth: Michael J. Connelly (D.) ($30,000).

BUDGET. For the fiscal year ending 30 June 1976 the total revenue of the state was $5,459,703,540, ($2,652·5m.) from taxes and $1,316·2m. from federal aid); general expenditures, $4,693,615,522 ($1,243m. for education, $347·5m. for highway and transport construction and $1,260·3m. for public welfare).

The net long-term debt on 30 June 1976 amounted to $2,852·7m.
Per capita personal income (1976) was $6,588.

NATURAL RESOURCES

Minerals. There is little mining within the state. Total mineral output in 1974 was valued at $62m., of which most came from sand, gravel and stone.

Agriculture. On 1 Jan. 1975 there were 5,800 farms (11,179 in 1959) with an area of 710,000 acres. Commercial farms (1974) numbered 4,970, of which 4,347 had gross sales of over $10,000.

Cash income, 1975, totalled $202·2m.; dairy, $58·8m.; greenhouse and nursery, $35·1m.; poultry, $34·4m.; vegetables, $19·7m.; tobacco, $12·8m.; cranberries, $8·7m.; other fruit, $11·2m.; potatoes, $4·2m.; all other, $17·6m.

Principal 1975 crops include cranberries, 810,000 bbls; apples, 2·1m. (42-lb. units); potatoes, 718,000 cwt, and tobacco, 2m. lb. On 1 Jan. 1975 farms in the state had 55,000 milch cows, 107,000 all cattle, 55,000 swine (Dec. 1975), 125,000 turkeys and 2·8m. chickens.

Forestry. State forests cover about 270,000 acres. Commercially important hardwoods are sugar maple, northern red oak and white ash; softwoods are white pine and hemlock. About 100m. bd ft of timber are cut annually.

Fisheries. The 1975 catch amounted to 245·6m. lb. of finfish valued at $51m.; 12·4m. lb. of shellfish ($14·8m.); 1·9m. lb (lobster ($3·3m.).

INDUSTRY. In 1976, 10,043 manufacturing establishments employed an average of 595,425 workers, who earned an annual $7,035·8m.; value added by manufacture (1973) was $11,717·6m. The 5 most important manufacturing groups, based on employment, were electric and electronic equipment, machinery (except electrical), fabricated metal products, instruments and related products, apparel and finished goods.

LABOUR. In July 1977 the work force was 2,751,900. Local unions numbered 2,279 with a combined membership of 583,886; city and state employees forming the largest group. Changes in the industrial pattern have caused the loss of jobs in the shoe and textile industries. In 1976 there were 129 work stoppages involving 61,200 workers which resulted in 741,600 man-days idle.

COMMUNICATIONS

Roads. In Sept. 1977 the state had 32,867 miles of roads and streets and in 1976 registered 3·4m. motor vehicles.

Railways. In 1977 there were 1,874 miles of mainline railway.

Aviation. There were, in 1977, 54 aircraft landing areas for commercial operation, of which 25 were publicly owned.

Shipping. The state had 3 deep-water harbours, the largest of which is Boston (port trade (1976), 26,172,442 short tons). Other ports are Fall River and New Bedford.

JUSTICE, RELIGION, EDUCATION AND WELFARE

Justice. On 13 Sept. 1977 state penal institutions held 3,487 inmates. There have been no executions since 1947.

Religion. The principal religious bodies are the Roman Catholics with 2,864,332 members in 1966; Jewish Congregations, 226,000; Methodists, 94,810; Episcopalians, 102,822; Unitarians, 35,931. Total membership, all denominations, was 3,639,198.

Education. A regulation effective from 1 Sept. 1972 makes school attendance compulsory for ages 6–16. In 1976–77 expenditure by cities and towns on public schools was $2,300m., including $220m. debt retirement and service payments. In 1975–76 there were 61,439 classroom teachers (of whom 2,277 were part-time) and 1,189,160 pupils.

Within the state there were (1976–77) 125 degree-granting institutions of higher learning (including 87 colleges and universities) with about 22,000 full-time staff members and 380,938 students. Some leading institutions are:

Year opened	Name and location of universities and colleges	Students 1976
1636	Harvard University, Cambridge [1]	20,498
1793	Williams College, Williamstown [1]	1,932
1821	Amherst College, Amherst [1]	1,320
1837	Mount Holyoke College, South Hadley [2]	1,964
1843	College of the Holy Cross, Worcester [1]	2,680
1852	Tufts University, Medford [1, 3]	6,232
1861	Mass. Institute of Technology, Cambridge [1]	8,474
1863	University of Massachussetts, Amherst [1]	26,116
1863	Boston College (RC), Chestnut Hill [1]	13,544
1865	Worcester Polytechnic Institute, Worcester [1]	2,831
1869	Boston University, Boston [1]	24,292
1870	Wellesley College, Wellesley [2]	2,045
1875	Smith College, Northampton [1]	2,559
1879	Radcliffe College, Cambridge [1]	...
1885	Springfield College, Springfield [1]	2,842
1887	Clark University, Worcester [1]	2,983
1894	University of Lowell [1]	11,536
1898	Northeastern University, Boston [1, 4]	35,970
1899	Simmons College, Boston [2]	2,625
1948	Brandeis University, Waltham [1]	3,537

[1] Co-educational. [3] Includes Jackson College for women.
[2] For women only. [4] Includes Forsyth Dental Center School.

Health. In 1975 the state had 197 hospitals (with 49,171 beds); average daily census, 40,066, of which 11,712 patients were in public and private mental hospitals and 9,742 patients were in institutions for the mentally retarded.

Social Security. The Department of Public Welfare had an appropriation of $1,379m. in 1976 and paid $422m. in aid to families with dependent children (average 111,000 families per month); other main items were general relief (average 28,805 cases), Supplemental Security Income (average 127,000 cases) and Medical Assistance (average 349,000 cases).

Books of Reference

Annual Reports. Massachusetts and US Boards, Commissions, Departments and Divisions, Boston, 1977
Manual for the General Court. By Clerk of the Senate and Clerk of the House of Representatives, Boston, Mass. Biennial
Mariner, E. C., and Levitan, D., *Your Massachusetts Government.* Arlington, Mass., 1977
New England Board of Higher Education. *Facts.* Wellesley, Mass., 1976–77

MICHIGAN

HISTORY. Michigan, first settled by Marquette at Sault Ste Marie in 1668, became the Territory of Michigan in 1805, with its boundaries greatly enlarged in 1818 and 1834; it was admitted into the Union with its present boundaries on 26 Jan. 1837.

AREA AND POPULATION. Michigan is divided into two by Lake Michigan. The northern part is bounded south by the lake and by Wisconsin, west and north by Lake Superior, east by the North Channel of Lake Huron; between the two latter lakes the Canadian border runs through straits at Sault Ste Marie. The southern part is bounded west and north by Lake Michigan, east by Lake Huron, Ontario and Lake Erie, south by Ohio and Indiana. Area, 58,216 sq. miles, of which 56,818 sq. miles are land area, 1,398 sq. miles are inland water; in addition the Great Lakes area amounts to 38,459 sq. miles. Census population, 1 April 1980, 9,236,891 (preliminary), an increase of 361,808 or 4% since 1970. In 1979 births were 144,452; deaths, 70,533; infant deaths, 1,861; marriages, 89,450; divorces, 44,242.

Population of 5 federal census years (with distribution by sex, 1970):

	White	Negro	Indian	Asiatic	Total	Per sq. mile
1910	2,785,247	17,115	7,519	292	2,810,173	48·9
1930	4,663,507	169,453	7,080	2,285	4,842,325	84·9
1950	5,917,825	442,296	7,000	4,645	6,371,766	111·7
1960	7,085,865	717,581	9,701	10,047	7,823,194	137·2
			All others			
1970	7,833,474	991,066	50,543		8,875,083	156·2
Male	3,520,422	352,142	4,898	5,406	3,882,868	—
Female	3,565,443	365,439	4,803	4,641	3,940,326	—

Of the total population in 1970, 6,553,773 persons (73·8%) were urban (73·4% in 1960). Those 21 years old or older numbered 5,090,126.

Population of the chief cities (census of 1 April 1970) was:

Detroit	1,192,222	Westland	84,621	Wyoming	59,589
Grand Rapids	181,602	Kalamazoo	79,802	Roseville	54,376
Warren	161,173	Saginaw	77,529		
Flint	159,576	Taylor	77,454		
Lansing (capital)	130,208	Pontiac	76,270		
Sterling Heights	108,998	St Clair Shores	76,227		
Livonia	104,660	Southfield	75,492		
Ann Arbor	103,583	Royal Oak	70,795		
Dearborn	90,589	Dearborn Heights	67,680		

Larger standard metropolitan areas, 1970 census: Detroit, 4,163,517; Grand Rapids, 535,702; Flint, 493,402; Lansing, 373,474.

CONSTITUTION AND GOVERNMENT. The present constitution was adopted in April 1963 and became effective on 1 Jan. 1964. The Senate consists of 38 members, elected for 4 years, and the House of Representatives of 110 members, elected for 2 years. The Governor and Lieut.-Governor are elected for 4 years. Electors are all citizens over 18 years of age meeting the usual residential requirements. The state sends to Congress 2 senators and 18 representatives.

At the 1980 presidential election Reagan polled 1,915,225 votes, Carter 1,661,532 and Anderson 275,223.

The capital is Lansing. The state is organized in 83 counties.

Governor: William G. Milliken (R.), 1979–82 ($61,500).
Lieut.-Governor: James H. Brickley (R.), 1979–82 ($40,000).
Secretary of State: Richard H. Austin (D.), ($45,000).

BUDGET. Because of the recession and state constitutional limits on deficit spending the financial year beginning on 1 July 1975 was extended to a fifteen-month period ending on 30 Sept. 1976; subsequent fiscal years run from 1 Oct. to 30 Sept. For the year ending 30 Sept. 1979, the general revenue was $6,419,529m. (taxation, $4,331,188m., and federal aid, $1,844,822m.); total revenue, $9,798,730m.; special revenue funds, $2,538,390m.; general expenditures, $9,442,455m.

Per capita personal income (1979 estimate) was $9,285.

ENERGY AND NATURAL RESOURCES

Minerals. Most important minerals by value of production are iron ore, petroleum and cement. Output (1979, preliminary): Iron ore, 17m. long tons ($607·2m.); Portland cement, 5,003,000 short tons ($205·97m.); petroleum, 35,428,000 bbls ($614·2m.); copper, 44,000 short tons ($79m.); sand and gravel, 50,500 short tons ($125m.); stone, 37·4m. short tons ($97·9m.); lime, 1,018,000 short tons ($42·3m.); natural gas, 161·7m. cu. ft ($270·6m.). Total value of natural salines, $169·3m. Mineral output in 1978 was valued at $2,346·7m.

Agriculture. The state, formerly agricultural, is now chiefly industrial. In 1979 it contained 63,000 farms with a total area of 10·5m. acres; the average farm was 167 acres. Cash income, 1978, from crops, $1,129m.; from livestock and products, $997·6m. Principal crops are maize (production, 1979, 237·5m. bu.), oats (16·5m. bu.), wheat (33·8m. bu.), sugar-beet (1·6m. tons); soybeans (14·3m. bu.), hay (3·8m. tons). On 1 Jan. 1980 there were in the state 132,000 sheep, 400,000 milch cows, 1·31m. all cattle, 960,000 swine, 8m. chickens and 40m. turkey breeder hens. In 1979 the wool clip yielded 934,000 lb. of wool from 118,000 sheep.

Forestry. The forests of Michigan consist of 19,373,400 acres, about 52% of total state land area. About 18·9m. acres of this total is commercial forest, 67% of which is privately owned, 19% state forest, 13% national forest and 1% in various public ownerships. Three-fourths of the timber volume is hardwoods, principally hard and soft maples, aspen, oak and elm. Christmas trees are another important forest crop.

Michigan leads in the number of state parks and public campsites. There are 83 state parks and recreation areas, 6 state forests, 5 national forests and 3 national parks. There are 180 state forest campgrounds and 66 state game and wildlife areas.

INDUSTRY. Transport equipment and non-electrical machinery are the most important manufactures. The state ranks first in 19 manufacturing categories; among principal products are motor vehicles and trucks, cement, chemicals, furniture, paper, cereal, baby food and pharmaceuticals. Total labour force, 1979, 4,370,000, of which 1,090,900 are in manufacturing.

COMMUNICATIONS

Roads. State trunk-line mileage (31 July 1979) totalled, 9,472, all hard surfaced. Passenger car registrations, 13 Oct. 1980, 5,162,138.

Railways. On 1 Jan. 1979 there were 6,150 miles of railway.

Aviation. Airports (1979) numbered 210 licensed airports, 106 emergency airports, 6 licensed seaplane bases and 6 licensed heliports.

JUSTICE, RELIGION, EDUCATION AND WELFARE

Justice. The 1963 Constitution provides that no person shall be denied the equal protection of the law; nor shall any person be denied the enjoyment of his civil or political rights or be discriminated against in the exercise thereof because of religion, race, colour or national origin. A Civil Rights Commission was established, and its powers and duties were implemented by legislation in the extra session of 1963. Earlier statutory enactments guaranteeing civil rights in specific areas are as follows. An Act of 1885, last amended in 1956, orders all places of public accommodation and resort, etc., to furnish equal accommodations without discrimination. An Act of 1941, as last amended, forbids the Civil Service in counties with population exceeding 1m. to discriminate against employees or applicants on the ground of political, racial or religious opinions or affiliations. An Act of 1881 incorporated into the school code of 1955 forbids any discrimination in school facilities. An Act of 1893 incorporated in the insurance code of 1956 prohibits insurance companies from discriminating between white and coloured persons.

In 1951 the legislature restored the unique one-man grand jury system abandoned in 1949.

Religion. There were 2,004,288 Roman Catholics in 1979; largest Protestant denominations, Lutherans, 500,000; United Methodists, 278,245; United Presbyterians, 155,864; Episcopalians, 63,873.

Education. Education is compulsory for children from 6 to 16 years of age. The operating expenditure for graded and ungraded public schools for the fiscal year ending 30 June 1979, was $3,658,491,673; total, including capital and debt expenditures, $4,115,996,605. In 1979 there were 576 school districts (elementary and secondary schools) with 1,965,685 pupils and 88,652 teachers. Teachers' salaries in 1979 averaged $18,016.

In the autumn of 1978 the 13 public 4-year institutions reported 236,035 students and the 54 non-public institutions reported 486,494 students. During fiscal year 1976–77 the public colleges had operating budgets financed by tuition and

$484·8m. by state appropriations. The community colleges had an autumn enrolment (1978) of 187,649 students.

Universities and students (1978):

Founded	Name	Students
1817	University of Michigan	36,577
1849	Eastern Michigan University	18,655
1855	Michigan State University	46,567
1884	Ferris State College	10,208
1885	Michigan Technological University	7,130
1868	Wayne State University	33,423
1892	Central Michigan University	17,802
1889	Northern Michigan University	8,995
1903	Western Michigan University	22,447
1946	Lake Superior State College	2,401
1959	Oakland University	11,220
1960	Grand Valley State College	7,065
1965	Saginaw Valley College	3,706

Social Welfare. Old-age assistance is provided for persons 65 years of age or older who have resided in Michigan for one year before application; assets must not exceed various limits. In 1974 federal Supplementary Security Income (SSI) replaced the adults' programme. In 1979 aid was supplied to a monthly average of 425,616 dependent children in 200,097 families at $319·13 per family.

Health. In 1980 the state had 219 hospitals (40,287 beds) licensed by the state and 21 psychiatric hospitals.

In 1957 a programme came into force which provided for free medical care and hospital treatment for certain categories of persons. On 1 Oct. 1966 this programme was superseded by a more comprehensive programme called 'Medicaid' which, with federal support, disbursed in 1978–79, $1,036·4m. to an estimated 897,666 persons.

Books of Reference

Michigan Department of Economic Development. *Publications*. Lansing
Michigan Manual. Dept of State. Lansing. Biennial
Bureau of Business and Economic Research, Michigan State University. *Michigan Statistical Abstract*. East Lansing, 1980
Bald, F. C., *Michigan in Four Centuries*. 2nd ed. New York, 1961
Catton. B., *Michigan—a Bicentennial History*. Norton, New York, 1976
Lewis, F. E., *State and Local Government in Michigan*. Lansing, 1979
Davis, C. M. (ed.), *Readings in the Geography of Michigan*. Ann Arbor, 1964
Dunbar, W. F., and May, G. S., *Michigan: A History of the Wolverine State*. Grand Rapids, 1980
Milliken, W. G., *Economic Report of the Governor 1980*. Lansing, 1980
Sommers, L. (ed.), *Atlas of Michigan*. East Lansing, 1977

State Library Services: Michigan Department of Education, Lansing 48909. *State Librarian:* Francis X. Scannell.

MINNESOTA

HISTORY. Minnesota, first explored in the 17th century and first settled in the 20 years following the establishment of Fort Snelling (1819), was made a Territory in 1849 (with parts of North and South Dakota), and was admitted into the Union, with its present boundaries, on 11 May 1858.

AREA AND POPULATION. Minnesota is bounded north by Canada, east by Lake Superior and Wisconsin, with the Mississippi River forming the boundary in the south-east, south by Iowa, west by South and North Dakota, with the Red River forming the boundary in the north-west. Area, 84,068 sq. miles, of which 4,059 sq. miles are inland water. Census population, 1 April 1980, 4,077,148 (preliminary), an increase of 6·7% since 1970. Births in 1978, 62,356 (15·6 per 1,000 population); deaths, 33,956 (8·5); infant deaths, 768 (12·3 per 1,000 live births); marriages, 33,832 (8·4); divorces, 14,127 (3·5).

Population in 5 census years (with distribution by sex, 1970) was:

	White	Negro	Indian	Asiatic	Total	Per sq. mile
1910	2,059,227	7,084	9,053	344	2,075,708	25·7
1930	2,542,599	9,445	11,077	832	2,563,953	32·0
1950	2,953,697	14,022	12,533	2,231	2,982,483	37·3
1960	3,371,603	22,263	15,496	3,642	3,413,864	42·7
			All others			
1970	3,805,069	34,868	34,065		3,805,069	47·6
Male	1,863,810	17,641	—		1,863,810	—
Female	1,941,161	17,227	—		1,941,161	—

Of the 1970 population, 2,527,308 persons (64·4%) were urban (62·2% in 1960); those 21 years of age or older numbered 2,219,785; foreign-born whites, 141,655 in 1960.

The largest cities are Minneapolis, 370,091; St Paul (capital), 268,248 (Minneapolis–St Paul standard metropolitan statistical area, 1,972,208 in 1970); Duluth, 92,789; Bloomington, 81,640; Rochester, 54,287.

CONSTITUTION AND GOVERNMENT.

The present constitution dates from 1858; it has had 94 amendments. The Legislature consists of a Senate of 67 members, elected for 4 years, and a House of Representatives of 134 members, elected for 2 years. The Governor and Lieut.-Governor are elected for 4 years. The state sends to Congress 2 senators and 8 representatives.

In the 1980 presidential election Carter polled 954,173 votes, Reagan 873,268.

The capital is St Paul. There are 87 counties, few containing less than 400 sq. miles, the largest being 6,092 sq. miles.

Governor: Albert H. Quie (R), 1979–83 ($58,000).
Lieut.-Governor: Lou Wangberg (R), 1979–83 ($36,000).
Secretary of State: Joan Anderson Growe (DFL), 1979–83 ($30,000).

BUDGET. The general fund budget for the 1979–81 2-year period was $7,900m.; tax relief $760m., education $2,848m., public welfare $1,112m., transport $683m.

Net long-term debt, 30 June 1980, was $881m.

Per capita personal income (1979) was $8,865.

NATURAL RESOURCES

Minerals. The mining of iron ores on the Mesabi, Vermilion and Cuyuna ranges has changed dramatically since the passage of a Taconite Amendment in 1964. Since then new capital investment in taconite facilities has reached approximately $1,751m., bringing the total investment in the taconite industry to over $2,251m. Taconite made up nearly 90·4% of iron-ore shipments in 1978. Shipments of usable iron ore from mines in 1979 was valued at $1,960m. Total mineral output in 1979 was valued at $2,062·5m.

Agriculture. Agriculture, including processing, is the leading industry. In 1980 there were 104,000 farms with a total area of 30·3m. acres (63% of the land area); the average farm was of 291 acres. Average value of land and buildings (1980) $293,700. Commercial farms in 1974 numbered 98,537; 9·9% of the farms were operated by tenant-farmers. Cash income, 1978, from crops, $2,260·86m.; from livestock, $2,591·1m. In 1978 Minnesota ranked first in sweetcorn for processing, turkeys and timothy seed, and second in spring wheat, oats, hay, sugar-beet, red clover seed, creamery butter, non-fat dry milk, cheese and sunflower seed. Other important products are flaxseed, milch cows, milk, corn, barley, swine, cattle for market, rye, soybeans, honey, potatoes, wheat, Italian cheese, lambs, chickens, dry edible beans, and green peas for processing. Of livestock, cattle represents 15·3% of total farm income, swine 13·6% and milk 18·1%. Of crops, corn represents 12·2% and soybeans 16·2%. On 1 Jan. 1980 the farm animals included 2·75m. all cattle, 860,000 milch cows, 264,000 sheep and lambs, 4·9m. swine, 12·5m. chickens and 633,000 breeder hen turkeys. Turkey production, 1979, 24·67m. In 1979 the wool clip amounted to 1,933,000 lb. of wool from 252,000 sheep.

Honey production (1979), 14·7m. lb; beeswax, 266,000 lb. About 95% of US commercial wild rice paddies are in Minnesota. Production from 14,000 acres (1979), 2,150,000 lb. of processed wild rice; production from natural stands, 400,000 lb.

Forestry. Forests of commercial timber cover 14·87m. acres, of which 1,179,000 acres are in a productive reserve classification. In 1977, the acreage available for commercial harvest was 1,715,000 in national forest lands, 2,065,000 in state forest lands, 2,341,000 in county and municipal lands, 772 in forest industry and 5,594,000 in non-industrial private lands. The value of forest products was $1,463,703,565; $659,325,930 of this was from primary forest products harvesting and $804,377,635 from secondary manufacturing.

INDUSTRY. In 1977 there were 6,635 manufacturing establishments; they employed 330,300 production workers who earned $4,677m.; value added by manufacture was (1977), $9,245·3m.

TOURISM. Estimates for 1979 give approximately 8·2m. tourists (55% from outside the state), with a total expenditure of $1,802m.

COMMUNICATIONS

Roads. The state highway system covered 13,169 miles state rural trunk highways in 1977; total highway mileage, 127,393. In 1977, 2,813,327 passenger automobiles were registered.

Railways. There are 8 Class I railroads operating, with mainline mileage of 7,229 (total track miles, 7,510).

Aviation. Airports in 1980 numbered 593 (141 municipal, 27 privately owned for public use, 387 personal use, 11 public seaplane bases, 14 private, 74 for personal use).

JUSTICE, RELIGION, EDUCATION AND WELFARE

Justice. A Civil Rights Act (1927) forbids places of public resort to exclude persons 'on account of race or colour' and another section forbids insurance companies to discriminate 'between persons of the same class on account of race'. Contractors on public works may have their contracts cancelled if 'in the hiring of common or skilled labour' they are found to have discriminated on the grounds of 'race, creed or colour'. The state's penal reformatory system on 31 June 1971 held 2,144 men and women. There is no death penalty in Minnesota.

Religion. The chief religious bodies are: Lutheran with 1,112,495 members in 1970; Roman Catholic, 1,061,614; Methodist, 213,084. Total membership of all denominations, 3,044,055.

Education. In 1979, 1,056 public elementary schools had 24,753 teachers and 1,600 administrative or pupil staff for 390,109 students; 387 non-public elementary schools had 3,779 teachers and 69,150 pupils. The 610 public secondary schools had 20,527 classroom teachers and 4,800 administrative or pupil staff for 416,272 students; 48 non-public secondary schools had 1,532 teachers and 21,769 pupils. In 1979 the 44,021 teachers had an average salary of $17,865. The total public school expenditure (1978–79) was $1,860,321,549, of which $991,678,852 came from state funds. The University of Minnesota at Minneapolis–St Paul, chartered in 1851 and opened in 1869, had a total enrolment in 1979 of 56,290 students and 11,183 academic staff. The 18 public community colleges had a total enrolment of 30,346. Four private junior colleges had 1,686 students. Seven state universities (4-year) had a 1979 enrolment of 39,171. State universities are at Bemidji, Mankato, Marshall, Moorhead, St Cloud, Winona, Minneapolis and St Paul.

Health. In 1980 the state had 165 general acute hospitals with 17,601 beds. Patients resident (average daily census) in institutions under the Department of Public Welfare included 1,520 mentally ill, 2,692 mentally retarded and 637 chemically dependent. There are 2 state nursing homes with (1979–80) a 753-bed capacity.

Social Security. On 1 Jan. 1974 the state administered programmes of old age assistance, aid to the disabled, and aid to the blind were given over to federal administration under the Supplemental Security Income (SSI) Programme. For some states, the new maintenance grants were less than under the state administered programmes. These states could establish a supplemental programme to correct the deficiency. The Minnesota Supplemental Aid (MSA) programme was later expanded to cover individuals who were not receiving SSI and to provide one-time payment for certain special needs such as major home repair, replacement of essential basic furniture or appliances, moving expenses and fuel and utility adjustments.

Books of Reference

Statistical Information: Current information is obtainable from the Department of Economic Development (480 Cedar Street, St Paul 55101); non-current material from the Reference Library, Minnesota Historical Society, St Paul 55101. Demographic information (current) is available on request from the Office of State Demographer, State Planning Agency, 101 Capitol Square Building, 550 Cedar Street, St Paul 55101.

Legislative Manual. Secretary of State. St Paul. Biennial
Minnesota Statistical Profile. Dept of Econ. Dev., Biennial
Blegen, T. C., *Minnesota: A History of the State.* Minnesota Univ. Press, 1963
Minnesota Agriculture Statistics. Dept. of Agric., St Paul. Annual
Manufacturers' Directory. Dept. of Econ. Dev., Biennial

MISSISSIPPI

HISTORY. Mississippi, settled in 1716, was organized as a Territory in 1798 and admitted into the Union on 10 Dec. 1817. In 1804 and in 1812 its boundaries were extended, but in March 1817 a part was taken to form the new Territory of Alabama, leaving the boundaries substantially as at present.

AREA AND POPULATION. Mississippi is bounded north by Tennessee, east by Alabama, south by the Gulf of Mexico and Louisiana, west by the Mississippi River forming the boundary with Louisiana and Arkansas. Area, 47,716 sq. miles, 493 sq. miles being inland water. Census population, 1 April 1980 (preliminary), 2,520,638, an increase of 13·6% since 1970. Births occurring in the state, 1977, were 45,318; births to residents, 45,532; deaths, 22,627; infant deaths, 789; marriages, 26,843; divorces, 12,759.

Population of 5 federal census years (with distribution by sex, 1970):

	White	Negro	Indian	Asiatic	Total	Per sq. mile
1910	786,111	1,009,487	1,253	263	1,797,114	38·8
1930	998,077	1,009,718	1,458	568	2,009,821	42·4
1950	1,188,632	986,494	2,502	1,286	2,178,914	46·1
1960	1,257,546	915,743	3,119	1,481	2,178,141	46·1
			All others			
1970	1,393,283	815,770	7,859		2,216,912	46·9
Male	683,747	386,580	3,890		1,074,217	—
Female	709,536	429,190	3,069		1,142,695	—

Of the population in 1970, 986,642 persons (49·3%) were urban (10·8% in 1940). Those 21 years old or older numbered 1,242,965; foreign-born whites, 6,741. In 1960 in 31 of the 82 counties Negroes constituted 49% or more of the population; Tunica County, with 79% Negro, had the highest percentage of any county in the US.

The largest city (1980) is Jackson, 200,338. Others, 1970: Biloxi, 48,486; Meridian, 45,083; Gulfport, 40,791; Greenville, 39,648; Hattiesburg, 38,277; Columbus, 25,795; Vicksburg, 25,478; Laurel, 24,145; Natchez, 19,704.

CONSTITUTION AND GOVERNMENT. The present constitution was adopted in 1890 without ratification by the electorate; it has since had 48 amendments.

The Legislature consists of a Senate (52 members) and a House of Representatives (122 members), both elected for 4 years, as are also the Governor and Lieut.-Governor. Electors are all citizens who have resided in the state 1 year, in the county 1 year, in the election district 6 months next before the election and have been registered according to law. In the 1980 presidential election Reagan polled 441,089 votes, Carter 429,281 and Anderson 12,036.

The state is represented in Congress by 2 senators and 5 representatives.

The capital is Jackson; there are 82 counties.

Governor: William Forrest Winter (D.), 1980–84 ($53,000).
Lieut.-Governor: Bradford Johnson Dye (D.) ($34,000).
Secretary of State: Edwin Lloyd Pittman (D.) ($34,000).

BUDGET. For the fiscal year ending 30 June 1980 the general revenues were $2,323,247,820 (taxation, $1,239,677,939; federal aid, $849,636,668; other state resources, $233,933,213), and general expenditures were $2,531,284,433 ($902,408,736 for education, $330,855,967 for highways and $601,438,910 for public welfare).

On 30 June 1980 the total net long-term debt was $1,230,222,000.

Per capita personal income (1970) was $2,575 (lowest in US).

ENERGY AND NATURAL RESOURCES

Minerals. Petroleum and natural gas account for about 90% (by value) of mineral production. Output of petroleum, 1979, was 37,326,772 bbls and of natural gas 188,599,472m. cu. ft. There are 7 oil refineries. Value of oil and gas products sold 1979 was $676,207,082.

Agriculture. Agriculture is the leading industry of the state because of the semitropical climate and a rich productive soil. In 1980 farms with annual sales of $1,000 or more numbered 48,000 with an area of 14·5m. acres. Average size of farm was 302 acres (valued at $190,000). This compares with an average farm size of 138 acres (valued at $13,597) in 1960.

Cash income from all crops and livestock during 1979, including government payments, was $2,096·4m. Cash income from crops was $1,191·8m. and from livestock and products, $891·6m. The chief product is soybeans, cash income $654·3m. from 4·2m. acres. In cotton, 1·44m. bales (480 lb.) were produced. As a source of farm income, rice, corn, hay, wheat, oats, sorghum, peanuts, pecans, sweet potatoes, peaches, other vegetables, nursery and forest products continue to contribute.

On 1 Jan. 1980 there were 1·81m. head of cattle and calves on Mississippi farms (twenty-third nationally). Milch cows and heifers which had calved totalled 99,000, beef cows and heifers that had calved, 901,000 (fourteenth nationally); hogs and pigs, 440,000 head, chickens (excluding broilers), 10·5m. In 1979 cash income from livestock and products was 42·8% of total cash receipts. Of this total, $318·8m. was credited to cattle and calves. Cash income from poultry and eggs totalled $386·3m.; dairy products, $101·3m.; swine, $43·2m.

In 1980 there were 82 soil-conservation districts covering 26,342,406 acres.

Forestry. In 1979 income from forestry amounted to $550m.; output of logs, lumber, etc., was 1,670m. bd ft; pulpwood, 4·65m. cords; distillate wood, 14,281 tons; turpentine gum, 505 bbls. There are about 16·5m. acres of forest (55% of the state's area). National forests area, 1979, 1·1m. acres.

INDUSTRY. In 1979 the 3,395 manufacturing establishments employed 236,181 workers, earning $2,646,143,863.

COMMUNICATIONS

Roads. The state in 1980 maintained 10,147 miles of highways, of which 9,984 miles were paved. In 1979, 1,584,056 cars were registered.

Railways. The state in 1979 had 3,444·91 miles of railway.

Aviation. There were 77 public airports in 1980, 67 of them general. There were also 5 privately owned airports.

JUSTICE, RELIGION, EDUCATION AND WELFARE

Justice. In 1977 there were no executions; from 1955 to 1976 executions (by gas-chamber) totalled 31 (7 whites and 14 Negroes for murder, 9 Negroes for rape and 1 Negro for armed robbery). On 30 Sept. 1976 the state prisons had 1,757 inmates.

Religion. Southern Baptists in Mississippi (1979), 612,773 members; Methodists 201,710; Roman Catholics (1980), 96,556; Negro Baptists about 450,000.

The number of churches relative to the population is the highest in the US (one church per 289 persons; national average, 814).

Education. Attendance at school was compulsory until this was repealed by the Legislature in 1956. The public elementary and secondary schools in 1979–80 had 484,784 pupils and 25,815 classroom teachers; private elementary and high schools had 52,772 pupils (1976).

In 1979–80, teachers' average salary was $11,851. The expenditure per pupil in average daily attendance, 1979–80, was $1,603.

There are 17 universities and senior colleges, of which 8 are state-supported. The University of Mississippi, at Oxford (1844), had, 1980–81, 420 instructors and 9,607 students; Mississippi State University, Starkville, 532 instructors and 11,409 students; Mississippi University for Women, at Columbus, 155 instructors and 2,070 students; University of Southern Mississippi, Hattiesburg, 541 instructors and 10,222 students; Jackson State University, Jackson, 323 instructors and 7,359 students; Delta State University, Cleveland, 185 instructors and 3,011 students; Alcorn State University, Lorman, 148 instructors and 2,340 students; Mississippi Valley State University, Itta Bena, 143 instructors and 2,574 students. State allocation, 1980–81, for higher education was $122·9m.

Junior colleges had (1979–80) 47,928 students and 2,005 instructors. The state appropriation for junior colleges, 1979–80, was $31m.

Health. In 1980 the state had 118 acute general hospitals (12,558 beds) listed by the Mississippi Commission on Hospital Care. In 1980, 3 hospitals with facilities for care of the mentally ill had 2,384 beds.

Social Security. Department of Public Welfare figures show (June 1980) 440 persons receiving State Mandatory Supplementation payments amounting to $5,886·9 or an average of $13.38 per case. The state Medicaid commission paid (1979–80) $213·7m. for medical services, including $25m. for drugs, $52·58m. for skilled nursing home care, $59·57m. for hospital services. There was a monthly average of 136,794 persons eligible for benefits in the Aid to Dependent Children's programme. There were 74,378 persons eligible for Aged Medicaid, 1,520 persons eligible for Blind Medicaid and 28,867 persons eligible for Disabled Medicaid benefits (monthly average 1979–80).

Books of Reference

Mississippi Official and Statistical Register. Secretary of State. Jackson. Biennial
Bettersworth, J. K., *Mississippi: A History.* Rev. ed. Austin, Tex., 1964
Wilber, G. L., and Bryant, E. S., *Illustrative Projections of Mississippi Population, 1960 to 1985.* State College, 1964

Mississippi Library Commission: PO Box 3260 Jackson, Ms. 39207. *Head of Information Services:* Sharman B. Smith.

MISSOURI

HISTORY. Missouri, first settled in 1735 at Ste Genevieve, was made a Territory on 1 Oct. 1812, and admitted to the Union on 10 Aug. 1821. In 1837 its boundaries were extended to their present limits.

AREA AND POPULATION. Missouri is bounded north by Iowa, east by the Mississippi River forming the boundary with Illinois and Kentucky, south by Arkansas, south-west by Oklahoma, west by Kansas and Nebraska, with the Missouri River forming the boundary in the north-west. Area, 69,686 sq. miles, 640 sq. miles being water.

Census population, 1 April 1980 (preliminary), 4,906,480, an increase since 1970 of 4·9%. Births, 1979, were 73,757 (15·2 per 1,000 population); deaths, 48,044 (9·9); infant deaths, 1,064 (14·4 per 1,000 live births); marriages, 53,616 (11·0); divorces (1978), 26,076 (5·2).

Population of 5 federal census years (with distribution by sex, 1970):

	White	Negro	Indian	Asiatic	Total	Per sq. mile
1910	3,134,932	157,452	313	638	3,293,335	47·9
1930	3,403,876	223,840	578	1,073	3,629,367	52·4
1950	3,655,593	297,088	547	1,046	3,954,653	57·1
1960	3,922,967	390,853	1,723	3,146	4,319,813	62·5
			All others			
1970	4,177,495	480,172	18,834		4,677,399	67·0
Male	2,029,656	226,296	—		2,255,952	—
Female	2,167,672	253,871	—		2,421,549	—

Of the total population in 1970, 3,278,857 persons (70·1%) were urban (66·6% in 1960). Those 21 years of age or older numbered 2,880,159.

Cities with 50,000 or more people (1980 census) are:

St Louis	448,640	*Other cities, 1970:*			
Kansas City	446,562	University City	46,309	Cape Girardeau	31,282
Springfield	132,014	Joplin	39,256	Ferguson	28,915
Independence	111,760	Raytown	33,632	Webster Groves	26,995
St Joseph	76,555	Jefferson City	32,407	Overland	24,949
Columbia	62,492	Kirkwood	31,890	Gladstone	23,128
Florissant	55,384	St Charles	31,834	Sedalia	22,847

Metropolitan areas, 1980 estimate: St Louis, 2,418,879; Kansas City, 1,313,700.

CONSTITUTION AND GOVERNMENT. A new constitution, the fourth, was adopted on 27 Feb. 1945; it has been amended 26 times. The General Assembly consists of a Senate of 34 members elected for 4 years (half for re-election every 2 years), and a House of Representatives of 163 members elected for 2 years. The Governor and Lieut.-Governor are elected for 4 years. Missouri sends to Congress 2 senators and 9 representatives.

Voters (with the usual exceptions) are all citizens and those adult aliens who, within a prescribed period, have applied for citizenship. In the 1980 presidential election Reagan polled 1,074,181, Carter, 931,182 and Anderson 77,920.

Jefferson City is the state capital. The state is divided into 114 counties and the city of St Louis.

Governor: Christopher Bond (R.), 1981–85 ($37,500).
Lieut.-Governor: Kenneth Rothman (D.), 1981–85 ($16,000).
Secretary of State: James C. Kirkpatrick (D.) 1981–85 ($25,000).

BUDGET. For the year 1977 the total general revenues were $4,870m. (federal revenue, $1,919m., state revenue, $2,951m.); general expenditures were $4,524m.

Total outstanding debt, 1977, was $3,093m.

Per capita personal income (1980) was $9,106.

NATURAL RESOURCES

Minerals. Principal minerals are lead (ranks first in USA), zinc (ranks second), clays, coal, iron ore, and stone for cement and lime manufacture. Value of production (1977) $883m.

Agriculture. In 1980 there were 117,000 farms in Missouri covering 32·3m. acres. The average size of farms is 276 acres. Production of principal crops, 1979: Corn,

228·7m. bu.; soybeans, 186·8m. bu.; wheat, 70·4m. bu.; sorghum grain, 59m. bu.; oats, 2m. bu.; hay, 6m. tons; cotton, 157,000 bales. Cash receipts from farming, 1979, $4,200m. Export value of farm produce, $1,143m., to which soybeans contributed $632·3m.

Forestry. Forest land area, 1974, 12·9m. acres. Timber resources (sawtimber), 128,108·5m. bd ft.

INDUSTRY. The largest employer in 1973 was the transport equipment industry employing 75,450 workers. Other large industries are food and kindred products, electrical equipment and supplies, apparel and related products and non-electrical machinery, leather products, chemicals, paper, metal industries, stone, clay and glass. In 1979 the labour force was 2,326,000, of which 2·24m. were employed; the unemployment rate was 3·7%.

LABOUR. The State Board of Mediation has jurisdiction in labour disputes involving only public utilities. The Prevailing Wage Law (1959) provides that no less than the local hourly rate of wages for work of a similar character shall be paid to any workmen engaged in public works. The Industrial Commission has authority to inspect records and to institute actions for penalties described in the Act. There is a state programme for industrial safety in hand, under the Federal Occupational and Health Act. In 1980–81 the labour force numbered 2,288,000, of which 128,000 were unemployed. The largest employer was the transport equipment industry, with 68,560 workers.

COMMUNICATIONS

Roads. Federal and state highways, Jan. 1980, totalled 32,181 miles. In 1978 there were 3·1m. vehicles licensed in the state. In 1974 there were 31 bus companies and about 1,200 internal truck lines.

Railways. The state has 16 Class I railroads, operating approximately 3,820 miles of main-line track and 1,810 miles of branch-line track.

Aviation. In 1978 there were 116 public airports and 255 private airports.

Shipping. Ten carrier barge lines operate on 1,900 miles of navigable waterways, including the Missouri and Mississippi Rivers. Boat shipping seasons: Missouri River, March–end Nov.; Mississippi River, early March–mid-Dec.

Post and Broadcasting. There were 188 commercial radio stations and 23 TV stations in 1978. The number of telephones in 1978 was 3·53m.

Newspapers. There were (1980) 52 daily and 245 weekly newspapers.

JUSTICE, RELIGION, EDUCATION AND WELFARE

Justice. State prisons in 1979 had an average of 5,260 inmates. Of those committed, 70% are aged 17–29. There have been no executions since 1965 although the death penalty was reinstated in 1978; since 1930 executions (by lethal gas) have totalled 40, including 31 for murder, 6 for rape and 3 for kidnapping. There are about 7,470 law enforcement officers. The Missouri Law Enforcement Assistance Council was created in 1969 for law reform.

Religion. Chief religious bodies are Catholic, with 759,503 members, Southern Baptists (515,383), United Methodists (253,627), Christian Churches (121,827), Lutheran (107,763), Presbyterian (100,056). Total membership, all denominations, about 2·2m. in 1970.

Education. School attendance is compulsory for children from 7 to 16 years for the full term. In the 1979–80 school year, public schools (kindergarten through grade 12) had 953,501 pupils. Total expenditure for public schools in 1978–79, $1,345m. Salaries for teachers (kindergarten through grade 12), 1978–79, averaged $12,881. Institutions for higher education include the University of Missouri, founded in 1839 with campuses at Columbia, Rolla, St Louis and Kansas City, with 2,847 accredited teachers and 47,640 students in 1976. Washington University at St Louis, founded in 1857, and St Louis University (1818), are both private universities. Nine state colleges had 42,879 students in 1975. Two of these are former junior colleges now 4-year colleges with the local junior college district financing the first 2 years and the state financing the third and fourth years. Private liberal arts colleges had (1975) 25,602 students. Public junior colleges had 58,426 students. There are about 60 vocational, professional and technical schools. There were 222,264 students in higher education in autumn 1978.

Health. The state department of Mental Health has 22 hospitals and other centres; costs of operation (together with related community programmes) amount to about $100m.

Social Security. In June 1979 the state was providing medical benefits and welfare payments to 234,190 persons. The largest programme was in aid to dependent children, average monthly receipt, $61.65. In June 1979,187,000 persons received payments which averaged $183.44 per family.

Books of Reference

Official Manual, Secretary of State, Jefferson City. Biennial
Annual Survey of Manufactures, U.S. Dept of Commerce, Bureau of the Census
General Population Characteristics, Office of Comptroller and Budget Director, Jefferson City
Missouri Final Production Count, Office of Comptroller and Budget Director, Jefferson City
Missouri Corporate Planner, Division of Commerce and Industrial Development, Jefferson City

MONTANA

HISTORY. Montana, first settled in 1809, was made a Territory (out of portions of Idaho and Dakota Territories) in 1864 and was admitted into the Union on 8 Nov. 1889.

AREA AND POPULATION. Montana is bounded north by Canada, east by North and South Dakota, south by Wyoming and west by Idaho and the Bitterroot Range of the Rocky Mountains. Area, 147,138 sq. miles, including 1,551 sq. miles of water, of which the federal government, 1977, owned 27,628,000 acres or 29·6%. US Bureau of Indian Affairs administered 5·28m. acres, of which 2,173,000 were allotted to tribes. Census population, 1 April 1980 (preliminary), 786,690, an increase of 13·3% since 1970. Births, 1977, were 13,304 (17·5 per 1,000 population); deaths, 6,397 (8·4); infant deaths, 183 (13·8 per 1,000 live births); marriages, 7,547 (9·9); divorces 4,813 (6·3).

Population in 5 census years (with distribution by sex, 1970) was:

	White	Negro	Indian	Asiatic	Total	Per sq. mile
1910	360,580	1,834	10,745	2,870	376,053	2·6
1930	519,898	1,256	14,798	1,239	537,606	3·7
1950	572,038	1,232	16,606	—	591,024	4·1
1960	650,738	1,467	21,181	1,082	674,767	4·6
1970	663,043	1,995	27,130	1,099	694,409	4·7

			All others			
Male	331,211	1,254	14,540		347,005	—
Female	331,832	741	14,831		347,404	—

Of the total population in 1970, 370,676 persons (53·4%) were urban (50·2% in 1960). There were 347,005 male and 347,404 females (national average, 95·2 males to every 100 females). Persons 18 years of age or older numbered 441,284. Households, 1970, 217,304.

The largest cities (1980) are Billings, 68,317; Great Falls, 56,568. Others, 1970: Missoula, 29,497; Butte, 23,368; Helena (capital), 22,730; Bozeman, 18,670; Havre, 10,558; Kalispell, 10,526; Anaconda, 9,771.

CONSTITUTION AND GOVERNMENT. A new constitution was ratified by the voters on 6 June 1972, and fully implemented on 1 July 1973; the Senate to consist of 50 senators, elected for 4 years, one half at each biennial election. The 100 members of the House of Representatives are elected for 2 years.

The Governor and Lieut.-Governor are elected for 4 years. Montana sends to Congress 2 senators and 2 representatives.

In the 1980 presidential election Reagan polled 206,814 votes, Carter 118,032. The capital is Helena. The state is divided into 56 counties.

Governor: Ted Schwinden (D.), 1981–85 ($37,500).
Secretary of State: Frank Murray (D.), 1977–81 ($24,500).

BUDGET. Total state revenues for the year ending 30 June 1976 were $850,823,000 ($312·3m. from taxes); total expenditures were $783,421,000 ($248·3m. for education, $161·4m. for highways and $69·76m. for public welfare).

Total net long-term debt on 30 June 1977 was $101,392,000.

Per capita personal income (1977) was $5,688.

ENERGY AND NATURAL RESOURCES

Electricity. Electric power generated in Dec. 1978 was 1,767,362 mwh., of which 1,231,158 was hydro-electric and 510,010 from coal-fired plants.

Minerals (1977). Output of crude petroleum, 32·68m. bbls; copper, 86,203 short tons; sand and gravel, 4,867,000 short tons; phosphate rock, undisclosed; silver, 3,367,000 troy oz.; gold, 22,348 troy oz.; zinc, 79 short tons; natural gas, 46,819m. cu. ft; coal, 27,402,400m. short tons. Value of total mineral production (1977), $689,387,000, with petroleum ($280·47m.) the first, coal ($159,756,000) the second and copper ($115,167,000) the third most important commodity.

Agriculture. In 1978 there were 22,900 farms and ranches (50,564 in 1935) with an area of 62·1m. acres (47,511,868 acres in 1935). Large-scale farming predominates; in 1978 the average size per farm was 2,712 acres. Income from all farm marketings was $957,152,000 in 1977 (crops, $443·4m.; livestock, $513·78m.). Irrigated area of total crop land harvested in 1977 was 1,640,400 acres or 18%; value of irrigated crops, $227·78m.

The chief crops are wheat, amounting in 1977 to 130·92m. bu., ranking fifth in US; barley, 55·48m. bu.; oats, 5·6m. bu.; sugar-beet, hay, potatoes, alfalfa, dry beans, flax and cherries. In 1978 there were 27,700 milch cows, 2·57m. all cattle; 211,000 swine.

The wool clip in 1977 was 4,462,000 lb. from 530,000 head of sheep.

Forestry. Total forest area (1974), 28m. acres. In 1977 there were 16·7m. acres within 11 national forests.

INDUSTRY. In 1976 manufacturing establishments numbering 774 had 17,403 production workers; value added by manufacture was (1973) $515·2m.

LABOUR (Aug. 1979). Work force, 396,800; total employed, 380,100; total non-agricultural workers, 334,100; agricultural workers, 46,000. Workers employed by major industry group: Mining, 8,300 (average net weekly earnings, $447.66); contract construction, 19,000 ($356.48); manufacturing, 28,800 ($353.56); transport and public utilities, 24,200 ($329.02; wholesale/retail trade, 81,100 ($188.65); finance/insurance/real estate, 14,300 ($148.48); services, 54,900 ($144.20); government, 69,500 (no income figures available). Average weekly earnings for all workers in private non-agricultural industries $232.13. Total unemployed 16,700 (4·2% of the work force in Aug. 1979 as compared to 5·9% nationally for that month).

There were 23 work stoppages in 1976 involving 2,900 workers, with a total of 14,800 man days idle during the year.

COMMUNICATIONS

Roads. In Jan. 1978 the state had 69,448 miles of public roads and streets including 11,345 miles of federally-aided highway. There were 511,238 passenger vehicles registered, 303,532 trucks and 54,592 motor cycles in Dec. 1978.

Railways. In 1977 there were 4,862 miles of railway in the state.

Aviation. There were 118 airports open for public use in 1979, of which 111 were publicly owned.

JUSTICE, RELIGION, EDUCATION AND WELFARE

Justice. On 31 Oct. 1979 the Montana state prison held 665 inmates. Since 1943 there have been no executions; total since 1930 (all by hanging) was 6; 4 whites and 2 Negroes, for murder.

Religion. The leading religious bodies are (1978): Roman Catholic with 130,000 active members; Lutheran, 62,000; Methodist, 21,000 (church estimates).

Education. On 1 Oct. 1978 public elementary and secondary schools had 164,326 pupils. Pupils of at least one quarter Indian blood, in 1970, numbered 7,943. In autumn 1978 public elementary and secondary school teachers (9,486) had an average salary of $13,541; Total expenditure on public school education (1977–78) was $350m.; expenditure per pupil was $2,130. The Montana University system consists of the Montana State University, at Bozeman (autumn 1979: 10,109 students), the University of Montana, at Missoula, founded in 1895 (8,376), the College of Mineral Science and Technology at Butte (1,386 students), Northern Montana College at Havre (1,209), Eastern Montana College at Billings (3,610) and Western Montana College at Dillon (824).

Social Security. In June 1979, 4,987 persons over age 65 were receiving in medical assistance an average of $463.72 per month; 211 blind persons, $195.58; 3,979 totally disabled, $472.14; 6,058 families (12,052 dependent children) receiving in aid-to-dependent children assistance an average of $196.88 per month. Aid was from state and federal sources.

Health. In Feb. 1979 the state had 63 hospitals (3,548 beds) listed by the Montana Board of Health. Four centres for mental disease and development disorders had 1,093 beds and 867 patients.

Books of Reference

Montana Agricultural Statistics. Dept. of Agriculture, Labor and Industry, Helena. Biennial from 1946
Montana Employment and Labor Force. Montana Dept. of Labor and Industry. Monthly from 1971
Montana Federal-Aid Road Log. Montana Dept. of Highways and US Dept. of Transportation, Federal Highway Administration. Annual from 1938
Montana Vital Statistics. Montana Dept. of Health and Environmental Sciences. Annually from 1954
Statistical Report. Montana Dept. of Social and Rehabilitation Services. Monthly from 1947
Hamilton, J. M., *History of Montana from Wilderness to Statehood.* 2nd. ed. Portland., Oregon, 1970
Lang, W, L., and Myers, R. C., *Montana, Our Land and People.* 1979
Malone, M. P., and Roeder, R. B., *Montana, A History of Two Centuries.* Univ. of Washington Press, 1976
Toole, K. R., *Twentieth Century Montana, A State of Extremes.* Univ. of Oklahoma Press, 1972

NEBRASKA

HISTORY. The Nebraska region was first reached by white men from Mexico under the Spanish general Coronado in 1541. It was ceded by France to Spain in 1763, retroceded to France in 1801, and sold by Napoleon to the US as part of the Louisiana Purchase in 1803. Its first settlement was in 1847, and on 30 May 1854 it became a Territory and on 1 March 1867 a state. In 1882 it annexed a small part of Dakota Territory, and in 1908 it received another small tract from South Dakota.

AREA AND POPULATION. Nebraska is bounded north by South Dakota, with the Missouri River forming the boundary in the north-east and the boundary with Iowa and Missouri to the east; south by Kansas, south-west by Colorado and west by Wyoming. Area, 77,227 sq. miles, of which 744 sq. miles are water. Preliminary census population, 1980: 1,538,788, an increase of 3% since 1970. Births, 1979, were 26,199 (16·6 per 1,000 population); deaths, 14,228 (9·0); infant deaths, 304 (11·6 per 1,000 live births); marriages, 14,074 (8·9): divorces, 6,220 (4).

Population in 5 census years (with distribution by sex, 1970) was:

	White	Negro	Indian	Asiatic	Total	Per sq. mile
1910	1,180,293	7,689	3,502	730	1,192,214	15·5
1920	1,279,219	13,242	2,888	1,023	1,296,372	16·9
1950	1,301,328	19,234	3,954	821	1,325,510	17·3
1960	1,374,764	29,262	5,545	1,195	1,411,330	18·3
1970	1,432,867	39,911	6,624	4,091	1,483,791	19·4
Male	699,842	19,291	3,322	2,000	724,455	—
Female	733,025	20,620	3,302	2,091	759,038	—

Of the total population in 1970, 914,139 persons (61·6%) were urban (53·6% in 1960); 894,145 were 21 years of age or older. The largest cities in the state are: Omaha, with a census population, 1970, of 346,929; Lincoln (capital), 149,518; Grand Island, 31,269; Hastings, 23,580; Fremont, 22,962; Bellevue, 21,953; North Platte, 19,447; Kearney, 19,181; Norfolk, 16,607.

The Bureau of Indian Affairs, as of 30 June 1978, administered 65,000 acres, of which 22,000 acres were allotted to tribal control.

CONSTITUTION AND GOVERNMENT. The present constitution was adopted in 1875; it has been amended 173 times. By an amendment adopted in Nov. 1934 Nebraska has a single-chambered legislature (elected for 4 years) of 49 members—the only state in the Union to have one. The Governor and Lieut.-Governor are elected for 4 years. Amendments adopted in 1912 and 1920 provide for legislation through the initiative and referendum and permit cities of more than 5,000 inhabitants to frame their own charters. A 'right-to-work' amendment adopted 5 Nov. 1946 makes illegal the 'closed shop' demands of trade unions. Nebraska is represented in Congress by 2 senators and 3 representatives.

In the 1980 presidential election Reagan polled 413,338 votes, Carter 164,270 and Anderson 44,024.

The capital is Lincoln. The state has 93 counties.

Governor: Charles Thone (R.), 1979–82 ($40,000).
Lieut.-Governor: Roland A. Luedke (R.) $32,000).
Secretary of State: Allen Beerman (R.) ($32,000).

BUDGET. For the fiscal year ending 30 June 1978 (US Census Bureau figures) the state's revenues were $1,231·6m. (taxation, $680·2m. and federal aid, $305·9m.); general expenditures were $1,144·8m. ($353·8m. for education, $206·1m. for highways and $157·7m. for public welfare).

The state has a bonded indebtedness limit of $100,000.

Per capita personal income (1979) was $8,684.

ENERGY AND NATURAL RESOURCES

Minerals. The total output of minerals, 1979, was valued at $203·5m., petroleum (6m. bbls) and sand and gravel (17m. tons) being the most important.

Agriculture. Nebraska is one of the most important agricultural states. In 1980 it contained approximately 63,000 farms, with a total area of 48m. acres. The average farm was 759 acres.

In 1979, 7m. acres were irrigated and 63,821 irrigation wells were registered.

Cash income from crops (1979), $2,031·5m., and from livestock, $3,526·1m. Principal crops, with estimated 1979 yield: Maize, 793·5m. bu. (ranking third in US); wheat, 86·7m. bu.; sorghums for grain, 144·6m. bu.; oats, 20·1m. bu.; soybeans, 54·7m. bu. About 955 farms grow sugar-beet for 6 factories; output, 1979, 1·5m. short tons. On 1 Jan. 1980 the state contained 6·4m. all cattle (ranking third in US), 120,000 milch cows, 210,000 sheep and 4·2m. swine.

Forestry. The area of national forest, 1976, was 352,000 acres.

INDUSTRY. In 1977, 1,969 manufacturing establishments had 61,400 production workers, earning $665m.; value added by manufacturing (1977), $2,821·8m. The chief industry is meat-packing, employing (1977), 6,600 (5,400 production workers) and value added was $240·2m.

COMMUNICATIONS

Roads. The state-maintained highway system embraced 9,875 miles in 1979; local roads, 86,583 miles. In 1978, 840,579 automobiles were registered.

Railways. In 1979 there were 7,326 miles of railway.

Aviation. Airports (1978) numbered 383, of which 110 were publicly owned.

JUSTICE, RELIGION, EDUCATION AND WELFARE

Justice. A 'Civil Rights Act' revised in 1969 provides that all people are entitled to a 'full and equal enjoyment of the accommodations, advantages, facilities and privileges' of hotels, restaurants, public conveyances, amusement places and other places. The state university is forbidden to discriminate between students 'because of age, sex, color or nationality'. An Act of 1941 declares it to be 'the policy of this state' that no trade union should discriminate, in collective bargaining, 'against any person because of his race or color'.

The state's prisons had, 30 Sept, 1979, 1,964 inmates (78 per 100,000 population). From 1930 to 1962 there were 4 executions (electrocution), 3 white men and 1 American Indian, all for murder, and none since.

Religion. The Roman Catholics had 328,000 members in 1978; Protestant Churches, 489,000; Jews, 7,500 members. Total, all denominations, 824,500 (unofficial figures).

Education. School attendance is compulsory for children from 7 to 16 years of age. Public elementary schools, autumn 1978, had 158,420 enrolled pupils; secondary schools, 139,376 pupils. Teachers' salaries, 1979–80, averaged $13,519. Estimated public school expenditure for year ending 30 June 1979 was $521·4m. Total enrolment in 30 institutions of higher education, autumn 1979, was 86,385 students. The largest institutions were (1979):

Opened	Institution	Students
1869	Univ. of Nebraska, Lincoln (State)	26,120
1878	Creighton Univ., Omaha (RC)	5,420
1887	Nebraska Wesleyan Univ. (Methodist)	1,165
1891	Union College, Lincoln (Seventh Day Adventist)	825
1894	Concordia Teachers' College, Seward (Lutheran)	1,162
1905	Kearney State College, Kearney (State)	6,478
1908	Univ. of Nebraska, Omaha (State)	13,546
1910	Wayne State College, Wayne (State)	2,364
1911	Chadron State College, Chadron (State)	1,913
1966	Bellevue College, Bellevue (Private)	2,272

The state holds 1·52m. acres of land as a permanent endowment of her schools; permanent public school endowment fund in Sept. 1980 was $62·1m.

Health. In 1979 the state had 114 hospitals and 612 patients (1980) in mental hospitals.

Social Security. The administration of public welfare is the responsibility of the County Divisions of Welfare with policy-forming, regulatory, advisory and supervisory functions performed by the State Department of Public Welfare. In 1979 public welfare provided financial aid and/or services as follows: for 6,933 individuals who were aged, blind or disabled, with an average state supplement of $57.66; for 12,467 families with dependent children, with an average payment of $258.24 per family; for 70,206 individuals who had medical needs, $1,346.67 per individual; for 1,252 children in need of child welfare services; for 4,454 children who were in need of crippled children's services and medical care. The amount of aid is based on need in accordance with State assistance standards; the programme of aid to families with dependent children is limited to a maximum maintenance payment of $293 for 1 child plus $71 for each additional child.

Books of Reference

Agricultural Atlas of Nebraska. Univ. of Nebraska Press, 1977
Climatic Atlas of Nebraska. Univ. of Nebraska Press, 1977
Economic Atlas of Nebraska. Univ. of Nebraska Pres, 1977
Nebraska. A Guide to the Cornhusker State. Univ. of Nebraska Press, 1979
Nebraska Statistical Handbook, 1980–81. Nebraska Dept. of Econ. Development, Lincoln
Nebraska Blue-Book. Legislative Council. Lincoln. Biennial
Olson, J. C., *History of Nebraska.* Univ. of Nebraska Press, 1955

State Library: State Law Library, State House, Lincoln. *Librarian:* Larry D. Donelson.

NEVADA

HISTORY. Nevada, first settled in 1851, when it was a part of the Territory of Utah (created 1850), was made a Territory in 1861, enlarged in 1862 by an addition from Utah Territory and admitted into the Union on 31 Oct. 1864 as the 36th state. In 1866 and 1867 the area of the state was significantly enlarged at the expense of the Territories of Utah and Arizona.

AREA AND POPULATION. Nevada is bounded north by Oregon and Idaho, east by Utah, south-east by Arizona, with the Colorado River forming most of the boundary, south and west by California. Area 110,540 sq. miles, 752 sq. miles being water. The federal government in 1973 owned 60,908,872 acres, or 86.5% of the land area. Vacant public lands, 48,340,876 acres. The Bureau of Indian Affairs controlled 1·35m. acres in 1975, of which 1,062,047 acres have been assigned to Indian tribes.

Census population on 1 April 1980 (preliminary), 742,582, an increase of 253,844 or 51.9% since 1970. Births, 1978, were 10,868 (16·5 per 1,000 population); deaths, 5,245 (7·9); infant deaths, 123 (11·3 per 1,000 live births); marriages, 114,156 (173 per 1,000 population, largest of any state); divorces, 9,989 (15·1).

Population in 5 census years (with distribution by sex, 1970) was:

	White	Negro	Indian	Asiatic and all others	Total	Per sq. mile
1910	74,276	513	5,240	1,846	81,875	0·7
1930	84,515	516	4,871	1,156	91,058	0·8
1950	149,908	4,302	5,025	848	160,083	1·5
1960	263,443	13,484	6,681	1,670	285,278	2·6
1970	449,850	27,579	7,329	3,980	488,738	4·4
Male	228,416	13,754	3,516	1,948	247,697	—
Female	221,371	13,825	3,813	2,032	241,041	—

Of the total population in 1970, 395,336 persons (80.9%) were urban (70.4% in 1960). In 1970 native born numbered 470,559; foreign-born, 18,179; those 18 years of age or older, 318,151.

The largest cities are Las Vegas, with population (1980 census, preliminary) of 153,668 (urbanized area 1970, 236,681); Reno, 82,220 (99,687); North Las Vegas, 39,196; Sparks, 38,114; Carson City, 30,807, and Henderson, 20,905. Clark County (Las Vegas, North Las Vegas and Henderson) and Washoe County (Reno and Sparks) together had 81% of the total state population in 1980.

CONSTITUTION AND GOVERNMENT. The constitution adopted in 1864 is still in force, with over 60 amendments. The Legislature meets biennially (and in special sessions) and consists of a Senate of 20 members elected for 4 years, half their number retiring every 2 years, and an Assembly of 40 members elected for 2 years. The Governor, Lieut.-Governor and Attorney-General are elected for 4 years. Qualified electors are all citizens with the usual residential qualification.

Nevada is represented in Congress by 2 senators and 2 representatives. A Supreme Court of 5 members is elected for 4 years on a non-partisan ballot.

In the 1980 presidential election Reagan polled 155,017 votes, Carter 66,466 and Anderson 17,651.

The state capital is Carson City (population, 30,807 in 1980). There are 16 counties, 17 incorporated cities and towns, 44 unincorporated towns and 1 city-county (Carson City).

Governor: Bob List (R.), 1979–82 ($40,000).
Lieut.-Governor: Martin Leavitt (D.) ($6,000).
Secretary of State: William D. Swackhammer (D.) ($25,000).

BUDGET. For the fiscal year ending 30 June 1980 estimated state general fund revenues were $322·4m., including federal receipts; general expenditures were $310m. Education followed by human resources and public safety received the largest appropriations.

State bonded indebtedness on 30 June 1980, was $17·7m. The state has no franchise tax, capital stock tax, special intangibles tax, chain stores tax, stock transfer tax, admissions tax, estate tax, gift tax, income taxes or inheritance tax. The sales and use tax and gaming taxes are the largest revenue producers.

Per capita personal income (1979) was $10,521.

ENERGY AND NATURAL RESOURCES

Electricity. Electricity power stations supplied 8,463m. mwh. in 1978. There were about 316,484 private and commercial customers in 1979. There are 8 suppliers of natural gas producing 51,696,121 m.cu.ft. in 1978.

Minerals. Production, 1979, in order of value was gold, barite, sand and gravel, petroleum. Other minerals are gypsum, iron ore, mercury, lime, lithium, silver, gemstones, lead, molybdenum, fluorspar, perlite, pumice, clays, talc, salt, tungsten, magnesite, diatonite and zinc. Value of mineral output for 1979, $246m.

Agriculture. In 1980, 2,000 farms had a farm area of 9m. acres (9·2m. in 1960). Farms averaged (1978) 4,500 acres. Area under irrigation (1979) was 1·3m. acres compared with 542,976 acres in 1959.

Gross income, 1978, from crops, livestock and government payments, $188m. Cattle, dairy products, hay, potatoes and sheep are the principal commodities in order of cash receipts. Average income per farm, $12,700 (estimate, 1978). Total value of crops produced, $42m., of which hay accounted for 14·4%. On 1 Jan. 1979 there were 15,000 milch cows, 280,000 beef cattle, 114,000 sheep and 8,000 swine.

Forestry. The area of national forests (1975) under US Forest Service administration was 5,051,938 acres.

INDUSTRY. The principal industries are the service industry, especially tourism and legalized gambling, mining and smelting, livestock and irrigated agriculture, chemical manufacturing, and lumber processing. In 1977 there were 731 manufacturing establishments with 15,200 employees, earning $218m.; value added by manufacture (1977) was $498m.; value of shipments, about $800m.

Gaming industry gross revenue for financial year ending 30 June 1980, $2,275·4m. There were at the same time 1,250 licences in force.

LABOUR. In Sept. 1979 unemployment was at 4·9% of the work force. All industries, employed 335,200 workers. Main industries and employees, 1979: Mining, 4,100; contract construction, 27,500; manufacturing, 19,700; transport (except railways), public works and utilities, 22,200; interstate railways, 1,500; hotels, gaming and recreation, 110,000; other service industries, 49,600; retail trade, 65,200; government, 54,700.

COMMUNICATIONS

Roads. Highway mileage (federal, state and local) totalled 49,659 in 1973, of which 16,464 miles were surfaced; motor vehicle registrations at 1 Jan. 1979 numbered 709,643.

Railways. In 1973 there were 1,553 miles of main-line railway. Nevada is served by Southern Pacific, Union Pacific and Western Pacific railways, and Amtrac passenger service for Carlin, Elko, Reno and Sparks.

Aviation. There were (1974) 114 civil airports and heliports (1,307 civil aircraft registered); 16 scheduled airlines operated. During 1978 McCarren International Airport handled 9·1m. passengers and Cannon International Airport handled 2·1m. passengers.

Post. In 1976 there were 11 telephone exchanges with (1978), 627,027 telephones in service.

JUSTICE, RELIGION, EDUCATION AND WELFARE

Justice. Prohibition of marriage between persons of different race was repealed by statute in 1959.

A 1965 Civil Rights Act makes it illegal for persons operating public accommodations, employers of 15 or more employees, labour unions, and employment agencies to discriminate on the basis of race, colour, religion or national origin; a 1971 law makes racial discrimination in the sale or renting of houses illegal. A Commission on Equal Rights of Citizens is charged with enforcing these laws.

Between 1924 and 1967 executions (by lethal gas—the first state to adopt this method, in 1921), numbered 31. Capital punishment was abolished in 1972 and later re-introduced; there was 1 execution (by lethal gas) in 1979.

Prison population, 1976, was 953; men 902, women 51.

Religion. Roman Catholics are the most numerous religious group, followed by members of the Church of Jesus Christ of Latter-day Saints (Mormons) and various Protestant churches.

Education. School attendance is compulsory for children from 7 to 17 years of age. In Oct. 1979 the 184 public elementary schools, including kindergartens, had 93,516 pupils; there were 83 secondary public schools, including junior and high schools, with 45,997. Special schools for handicapped pupils had 8,221. There were 2,879 elementary teachers (average salary $15,283), 2,700 secondary teachers with an average salary of $15,392. There were 36 parochial and private schools. The University of Nevada, Reno, had, in 1979, 390 full-time instructors and 9,447 students (regular, non-degree and correspondent), and University of Nevada, Las Vegas, 300 instructors and 8,742 students. Two-year community colleges operate as part of the University of Nevada system in Carson City, Elko and Las Vegas. There were (1979) 19,175 students.

Health. In 1976 the state had 24 hospitals (3,064 beds) and 19 skilled nursing units (1,158 beds).

Social Security. Old-age assistance is granted to all 65 years of age or older who are in need, and have assets not over $750 ($1,500 for married couples); end of fiscal year 1974–75, total expenditure was $6,179,040 at an average of $140 each person per month, for 3,678 people. Families with dependent children received $7,613,458 at $45.52 monthly average per person. The blind received $328,440 at $170 for 161 people. Nevada is the only state without aid to the permanently and totally disabled.

Books of Reference

Information: Bureau of Business and Economic Research (Univ. of Nevada).

Handbook of the Nevada Legislature, 55th Session, 1969. Legislative Counsel Bureau. Carson City

Legislative Manual, State of Nevada, 55th Cession, 1969. Legislative Counsel Bureau. Carson City

Political History of Nevada. Secretary of State. Carson City, 1965

Financing State and Local Government in Nevada. Legislative Counsel Bureau. Carson City, 1960

Study of General Fund Revenues of the State of Nevada. Legislative Counsel Bureau. Carson City, 1966

Education, Manpower and Economic Data for Nevada. Nevada Employment Security Dept., Carson City, 1971

Bushnell, E., *The Nevada Constitution: Origin and Growth.* Univ. of Nevada Press, 2nd ed., 1968

Hulse, James W., *The Nevada Adventure, A History.* Univ. of Nevada Press, 2nd ed., 1969

Mack, E. M., and Sawyer, B. W., *Here is Nevada: A History of the State.* Sparks, Nevada, 1965

State Library: Nevada State Library, Carson City. *State Librarian:* Mildred J. Heyer.

NEW HAMPSHIRE

HISTORY. New Hampshire, first settled in 1623, is one of the 13 original states of the Union.

AREA AND POPULATION. New Hampshire is bounded north by Canada, east by Maine and the Atlantic, south by Massachusetts and west by Vermont. Area, 9,304 sq. miles, of which 312 sq. miles are inland water. Census population, 1 April 1980, 918,827, an increase of 24·6% since 1970. Births, 1980, were 12,330; deaths, 7,190; infant deaths, 101; marriages, 9,049; divorces, 4,471.

Population at 5 federal censuses (with distribution by sex, 1970) was:

	White	Negro	Indian	Asiatic	Total	Per sq. mile
1910	429,906	564	34	68	430,572	47·7
1930	464,351	790	64	88	465,293	51·6
1950	532,275	731	74	162	533,242	59·1
1960	604,334	1,903	135	549	606,921	65·2
			All others			
1970	733,106	2,505	2,070		737,681	81·7
Male	358,261	1,418	993		360,672	—
Female	374,845	1,087	1,007		377,009	—

Native whites, 1970, were 697,396; foreign-born whites, 36,422. 416,040 (60·1%) were urban (58·3% in 1960); those 21 years of age or older numbered 443,312.

The largest city of the state is Manchester, with a 1980 census population of 90,757. Other cities are: Nashua, 67,817; Concord (capital), 30,360; Portsmouth, 26,214; Dover, 22,265; Keene, 21,385; Rochester, 21,579; Berlin, 13,090; Laconia, 15,579; Claremont, 14,575; Lebanon, 11,052; Somersworth, 10,313.

CONSTITUTION AND GOVERNMENT. While the present constitution dates from 1784, it was extensively revised in 1792 when the state joined the Union. Since 1775 there have been 16 state conventions with 49 amendments adopted to amend the constitution.

The Legislature consists of a Senate of 30 members, elected for 2 years, and a House of Representatives, restricted to between 375 and 400 members, elected for 2 years. The Governor and 5 administrative officers called 'Councillors' are also elected for 2 years.

Electors must be adult citizens, able to read and write, duly registered and not paupers or under sentence for crime. New Hampshire sends to the Federal Congress 2 senators and 2 representatives.

In the 1980 presidential election Reagan polled 221,705 votes, Carter 108,864 and Anderson 49,693.

The capital is Concord. The state is divided into 10 counties.

Governor: Hugh Gallen (D.), 1979–81 ($30,000).
Secretary of State: Robert L. Stark (R.).

BUDGET. The state government's general revenue for the fiscal year ending 30 June 1975 (US Census Bureau figures) was $170m.; general expenditures, $140·3m. ($48·3m. for education and $29·9m. for public welfare).

Net long-term debt of state, 30 June 1975, was $138·6m.
Per capita personal income (1977) was $5,353.

NATURAL RESOURCES

Minerals. Minerals are little worked; they consist mainly of sand and gravel, stone, and clay for building and highway construction.

Agriculture. In 1975, 2,600 farms had a total acreage of 540,000 acres; average farm was 211 acres with average land value at $261 per acre. Commercial farms in 1968 numbered about 1,500 with 600,000 acres of crop land. The US Soil Survey estimates that the state has 164,167 acres of excellent soil, 486,615 acres of fair soil, 530,630 of poor soil and 3,843,798 of non-arable soil. Only 636,195 acres (11% of the total area) show moderate erosion.

Cash income, 1978, from crops and livestock, $86·7m. The chief field crops are hay and vegetables; the chief fruit crop is apples. On 1 Jan. 1975 animals on farms were 40,000 milch cows, 69,000 all cattle, 4,800 sheep, 8,700 swine, 1·8m. poultry, 28,000 turkeys and about 36,225 horses.

Forestry. In 1975 commercial forest land totalled 4,907,400 acres; national forest, 591,909 acres; state forests and parks, 72,353 acres; forest industry ownership, 793,400 acres.

INDUSTRY. In 1975, manufacturing establishments employed 84,900 persons; average weekly wage (1976), $190.30; 54% of manufacturing employment is accounted for in durable goods.

Principal industries are, electrical machinery, non-electrical machinery, metal products, textiles and shoes.

COMMUNICATIONS

Roads. On 1 Jan. 1975 the length of state highways was 4,373 miles, of which the state maintained 4,155 miles and municipalities 218 miles. The length of town roads, urban and rural, totalled 7,918 miles. Motor vehicles registered, 1975, numbered 558,252.

Railways. In 1975 the length of railway in the state was 826 miles.

Aviation. There were 47 airports of which 14 were public.

JUSTICE, RELIGION, EDUCATION AND WELFARE

Justice. The state prison held 262 persons on 1 Aug. 1975. Since 1930 there has been only one execution (by hanging)—a white man, for murder, in 1939.

Religion. The Roman Catholic Church is the largest single body. The largest Protestant churches are Congregational, Episcopal, Methodist and United Baptist Convention of N.H.

Education. School attendance is compulsory for children from 6 to 14 years of age during the whole school term, or to 16 if their district provides a high school. Employed illiterate minors between 16 and 21 years of age must attend evening or special classes, if provided by the district.

In 1975 the 362 public elementary schools enrolled 102,760 pupils and the 97 public secondary schools 69,353 pupils. In 1975, 70 private and parochial elementary schools had 11,817 registered pupils and 20 secondary schools, 6,057. Public school salaries, 1973–74, averaged $9,841. Total expenditure on public schools in 1973–74 was estimated at $195,924,155.

Total enrolment, 1973–74, in 29 institutions of higher education was 27,415 students. Dartmouth College, at Hanover, founded in 1769, had 292 instructors and 3,370 students; the University of New Hampshire, at Durham, founded in 1866, had 615 instructors and 10,297 students.

Health. In 1975 the state had 28 hospitals (3,246 beds). In 1975 mental hospitals had 1,260 patients, and there were 724 persons in institutions for the mentally retarded.

Social Security. The Division of Welfare handles public assistance for (1) aged citizens 65 years or over, (2) needy aged aliens, (3) needy blind persons, (4) needy citizens between 18 and 64 years inclusive, who are permanently and totally disabled, (5) needy children under 21 years, (6) Medicaid and the medically needy not eligible for a monthly grant.

In Sept. 1975, 1,804 persons were receiving old-age assistance of an average $394 per month; 143 blind, $627 annually; 937 permanently and totally disabled, $725 annually; 455 mentally disabled, $850 annually.

Books of Reference

Morrison, L. S., *The Government of New Hampshire*. Concord, 1952
N.H. Register. State Year Book and Legislative Manual. Portland, Maine, 1965
Squires, J. D., *Granite State of the United States*. New York, 1956

NEW JERSEY

HISTORY. New Jersey, first settled in the early 1600s, is one of the 13 original states in the Union.

AREA AND POPULATION. New Jersey is bounded north by New York, east by the Atlantic with Long Island and New York City to the north-east, south by Delaware Bay and west by Pennsylvania. Area (US Bureau of Census), 7,836 sq. miles (304 sq. miles being inland water). Census population, 1 April 1980 (preliminary), 7,364,158, an increase of 2·3% since 1970. Births, 1978, were 93,356 (12·7 per 1,000 population); deaths, 65,161 (8·9); infant deaths, 1,145 (12·3 per 1,000 live births); marriages, 52,993 (7·2); divorces, (1979) 23,611.

Population at 5 federal censuses (with distribution by sex, 1970) was:

	White	Negro	Indian	Asiatic	All others	Total	Per sq. mile
1910	2,445,894	89,760	168	1,345	—	2,537,167	337·7
1930	3,829,663	208,828	213	2,630	122	4,041,334	537·3
1950	4,511,585	318,565	621	3,601	956	4,835,329	642·8
1960	5,539,003	514,875	1,699	8,778	2,427	6,066,782	739·5
1970	6,349,908	770,292	4,706	20,537	22,721	7,168,164	953·1
Male	3,080,215	363,756	2,163	9,831	11,408	3,467,373	—
Female	3,269,693	406,536	2,543	10,706	11,313	3,700,791	—

Of the population in 1970, 6,373,405 persons (88·9%, the highest percentage of any state) were urban (88·6% in 1960); 4,564,050 were 20 years of age or older.

Census population of the larger cities and towns in 1980 was:

Newark	329,498	Irvington	60,792	Parsippany-	
Jersey City	222,764	Union City	55,360	Troy Hills	55,112
Paterson	138,025	Vineland	53,050	Middleton	54,623
Elizabeth	105,384	Passaic	52,260	Union	53,077
Trenton (capital)	90,699	*Census 1970*		Bloomfield	52,029
Camden	84,763	Woodbridge	98,944	Atlantic City	47,859
Clifton	74,417	Hamilton	79,609	Plainfield	46,862
East Orange	76,306	Edison	67,120	Hoboken	45,380
Bayonne	64,982	Cherry Hill	64,395	Montclair	44,043

Largest urbanized areas (1970) were: New York NY–NE New Jersey, 16,206,841 (including Newark, Jersey City, Paterson, Clifton and Passaic); Philadelphia (Pa.–NJ), 744,045; Trenton (NJ–Pa.), 242,673. State population estimates for several of the larger cities and towns in 1979 were: Newark, 307,207; Jersey City, 220,857; Paterson, 144,978; Elizabeth, 102,139; Woodbridge, 94,390; Trenton, 94,030; Camden, 84,871; Hamilton, 83,969.

CONSTITUTION AND GOVERNMENT. The legislative power is vested in a Senate and a General Assembly, the members of which are chosen by the people, all citizens (with necessary exceptions) 18 years of age, with the usual residential qualifications, having the right of suffrage. The present constitution, ratified by the registered voters on 4 Nov. 1947, has been amended 27 times. In 1966 the

Constitutional Convention proposed, and the people adopted, a new plan providing for a 40-member Senate and an 80-member General Assembly. This plan, as certified by the Apportionment Commission and modified by the courts, provides for 40 legislative districts, with 1 senator and 2 assemblymen elected for each. Assemblymen serve 2 years, senators 4 years, except those elected at the election following each census, who serve for 2 years. The Governor is elected for 4 years.

The state sends to Congress 2 senators and 14 representatives.

In the 1980 presidential election Reagan polled 1,546,557 votes, Carter 1,147,364 and Anderson 234,632.

The capital is Trenton. The state is divided into 21 counties, which are subdivided into 567 municipalities—cities, towns, boroughs, villages and townships.

Governor: Brendan T. Byrne (D.), 1978–81 ($65,000).
Secretary of State: Donald Lan ($49,000).

BUDGET. For the year ending 30 June 1978 (US Census Bureau figures) general revenues were $5,833·31m. (taxation, $3,439·86m. and federal aid, $1,459·69m.; general expenditures were $5,773·07m. (education, $1,901·4m.; highways, $315·9m., and public welfare, $1,254·7m.).

Total net long-term debt, 30 June 1978, was $3,087,296,000.

Per capita personal income (1977) was $7,994.

NATURAL RESOURCES

Minerals. The chief minerals are stone ($39m. 1976) and sand and gravel ($39·4m.); others are zinc ($24·9m.), clay products ($331,000), peat and gemstones. New Jersey is a leading producer of glass sand, moulding sand, trap rock and of green sand, used in water-softening. Total value of mineral products, 1976, was $119·8m.

Agriculture. Livestock raising, market-gardening, fruit-growing, horticulture and forestry are pursued. In 1979 (preliminary), 7,600 farms had a total area of 990,000 acres; average farm had 130 acres valued (1978) at $2,057 per acre. In 1974 full owners had 5,593 farms; part-owners 1,672; tenant-farmers, 790.

Cash income, 1978, from crops, $230m., and livestock, $103·5m.

Leading crops are tomatoes (value, $16·4m., 1978), all corn ($30·7m.), peaches ($16·5m.), hay ($23·25m.), blueberries ($15·5m.), soybeans ($42·3m.).

Farm animals on 1 Jan. 1979 included 45,000 milch cows, 108,000 all cattle, 9,600 sheep and lambs and 67,000 swine.

INDUSTRY. In 1976 manufacturing establishments employed 458,400 production workers, receiving $4,851·1m. in wages; value added by manufacture, $20,287·5m. The principal industries by value (1976) are: Chemicals and allied products, $5,626m.; drugs, $2,130m.; food and kindred products, $2,118·4m.; electrical equipment and supplies, $1,601m.; machinery (except electrical), $1,484·9m.

COMMUNICATIONS

Roads. In 1978 there were 33,077 miles of roads (municipal, 23,173 miles; state, 2,217 miles; county, 6,803 miles; others, 884 miles).

Railways. In 1978, the state had 1,619 route miles of railway.

Aviation. There were (1977) 254 airports, of which 34 were publicly owned.

JUSTICE, RELIGION, EDUCATION AND WELFARE

Justice. State prisons in May 1980 had 6,311 inmates. Since 1930 executions (by electrocution) have totalled 74, including 47 whites, 25 Negroes and 2 other races, all for murder. There have been none since 1966.

The constitution of New Jersey forbids discrimination against any person on account of 'religious principles, race, color, ancestry or national origin'. The state has had, since 1945, a 'fair employment act', *i.e.*, a Civil Rights statute forbidding any employer, public or private (with 6 or more employees), to discriminate against any applicant for work (or to discharge any employee) on the grounds of 'race, creed, color, national origin or ancestry'. Trade unions may not bar Negroes from membership.

Religion. The Roman Catholic population of New Jersey in 1979 was 2,885,940. No official Protestant figures are available; estimates place Jewish population at 440,915 (1979).

Education. Elementary instruction is compulsory for all from 6 to 16 years of age and free to all from 5 to 20 years of age. In autumn 1978 public elementary schools had 827,978 and secondary schools had 509,349 enrolled pupils; public colleges in autumn 1979 had 141,405 students, community colleges 104,257 and independent colleges 65,991. The total cost of public schools, 1977–78, $3,115·75m. Average salary of all elementary and secondary classroom teachers in public schools 1979–80 was $17,159.

Rutgers, the State University (founded as Queen's College in 1766) had, in 1979, an opening autumn enrolment of 49,113 full- and part-time students. Princeton (founded in 1746) had 6,058 students. Fairleigh Dickinson (1941), had 18,838; Kean College, 13,533; Montclair State College, 14,805; Glassboro State College, 10,510; Trenton State College, 10,529.

Health. In 1979 the state had 139 hospitals (44,157 beds), listed by the American Hospital Association.

Social Security. In the financial year 1979 gross expenditure for all public assistance programmes was $594,779,763. Average monthly total of cases cost $248,552 with an average grant per case of $199.

Books of Reference

Legislative District Data Book. Bureau of Government Research. Annual
Manual of the Legislature of New Jersey. Trenton. Annual
Boyd, J. P. (ed.), *Fundamentals and Constitutions of New Jersey, 1664–1954*. Princeton, 1964
Cunningham, J. T., *New Jersey: America's Main Road*. Rev. ed. New York, 1976
League of Women Voters of New Jersey. *New Jersey: Spotlight on Government*. Rutgers Univ. Press, 3rd ed., 1978
Lehne, R., and Rosenthal, A. (eds.), *Politics in New Jersey*. Rev. ed., Rutgers Univ. Press, 1979

State Library: 185 W. State Street, Trenton, N.J. 08625. *State Librarian:* Barbara F. Weaver.

NEW MEXICO

HISTORY. The first settlement was established in 1598. Until 1771 New Mexico was the Spanish kings' 'Kingdom of New Mexico'. In 1771 it was annexed to the northern provinces of New Spain. When New Spain won its independence in 1821, it took the name of Republic of Mexico and established New Mexico as its northernmost department. When the war between the US and Mexico was concluded on 2 Feb. 1848 New Mexico was recognized as belonging to the US, and on 9 Sept. 1850 it was made a Territory. Part of the Territory was assigned to Texas; later Utah was formed into a separate Territory; in 1861 another part was transferred to Colorado, and in 1863 Arizona was disjoined, leaving to New Mexico its present area. New Mexico became a state in Jan. 1912.

AREA AND POPULATION. New Mexico is bounded north by Colorado, north-east by Oklahoma, east by Texas, south by Texas and Mexico and west by Arizona. Land area 121,412 sq. miles (221 sq. miles water). Public lands, administered by federal agencies (1975) amounted to 26·7m. acres or 34% of the total area. The Bureau of Indian Affairs held 7·3m. acres; the State of New Mexico held 9·4m. acres; 34·4m. acres were privately owned.

Census population, 1 April 1980 (preliminary), 1,299,968, an increase of 283,968 or 28% since 1970. Vital statistics, 1977: Births, 23,066 (18·1 per 1,000 population); deaths, 8,073 (6·8); infant deaths, 319 (14·5 per 1,000 live births); marriages, 16,385 (13·8); divorces, 9,143 (7·7).

The population in 5 census years (with distribution by sex, 1970) was:

	White	Negro	Indian	Asiatic	Total	Per sq. mile
1910	304,594	1,628	20,573	506	327,301	2·7
1940	492,312	4,672	34,510	324	531,818	4·4
1950	630,211	8,408	41,901	667	681,187	5·6
1960	875,763	17,063	56,255	1,942	951,023	7·8
1970	915,815	19,555	72,788	7,842[1]	1,016,000	8·4
Male	452,120	9,833	35,035	3,836	500,824	—
Female	463,695	9,722	37,753	4,006	515,176	—

[1] Includes unspecified races, 1970.

Native whites, 1970, were 901,740; foreign-born whites, 21,512. Of the 1970 total, 711,334 persons (70%) were urban (65·6% in 1960); 609,784 were 18 years of age or older.

Before 1930 New Mexico was largely a Spanish-speaking state, but since 1945 an influx of population from other states has reduced the percentage of white persons of Spanish origin or descent to an estimated 40%.

The largest cities are Albuquerque, with population (Census, 1980) 328,892. others (1977): Santa Fé (capital), 46,855; Las Cruces, 41,172; Roswell, 39,130; Clovis, 30,257.

CONSTITUTION AND GOVERNMENT. The constitution of 1912 is still in force with 73 amendments. The state Legislature, which meets annually, consists of 42 members of the Senate, elected for 4 years, and 70 members of the House of Representatives, elected for 2 years. The Governor and Lieut.-Governor are elected for 4 years. The state sends to Congress 2 senators and 3 representatives.

In the 1980 presidential election Reagan polled 250,779 votes, Carter 167,826.

The state capital is Santa Fé. For local government the state is divided into 32 counties.

Governor: Bruce King (D.), 1978 ($35,000).
Lieut.-Governor: Robert Mondragon (D.), 1978 ($14.42 hourly rate).
Secretary of State: Shirley Hooper (D.), 1978 ($30,000).

BUDGET. For the year ending 30 June 1977 (US Census Bureau figures) general revenues were $1,560·1m. ($743·2m. from taxation and $427·3m. from federal government); general expenditures, $1,400·3m. (education, $642·9m.; highways, $149·7m., and public welfare, $109m.).

Long-term debt on 30 June 1977 was $879·9m.
Per capita personal income (1978) was $6,574.

ENERGY AND NATURAL RESOURCES

Minerals. New Mexico is the country's largest domestic source of uranium, perlite and potassium salts. Production of recoverable U_3O_8 was 13·2m. lb. in 1977; perlite, 478,000 short tons; potassium salts, 2,137,000 short tons; petroleum, 86,815,000 bbls (of 42 gallons); natural gas, 1,191,535m. cu. ft; natural gas liquids, 9·6m bbls (of 42 gallons); copper, 167,100 short tons; coal, 11·65m. short tons. The value of the total mineral output was $2,906m. An average of 24,500 persons were employed monthly in the mining industry in 1978.

Agriculture. New Mexico produces cereals, vegetables, fruit, livestock and cotton. Dry farming and irrigation have proved profitable in periods of high prices. There were 11,400 farms and ranches covering 46·8m. acres in 1978, average farm (or ranch) was valued (land and buildings) at $168,336 in the 1969 US Census of Agriculture; 3,584 farms and ranches were of 1,000 acres and over.

Cash income, 1978, from crops, $193·3m., and from livestock products, $740·5m. Principal crops are cotton (101,000 bales from 137,000 acres), hay (1·1m. tons from 301,000 acres) and grain sorghums (12·3m. bu. from 267,000 acres). Farm animals on 1 Jan. 1978 included 33,000 milch cows, 1·7m. all cattle, 604,000 sheep and 50,000 swine. National forest area (1978) covered 9·1m. acres.

INDUSTRY. Average monthly non-agricultural employment during 1978 was

444,700: 33,300 were employed in manufacturing, 116,200 in government. In 1972, 17,200 production workers earned $98·7m. during the year; value added by manufacture was $366·2m.

COMMUNICATIONS

Roads. The state, 1977, had 70,858 miles of road, of which the state maintained 12,718 miles. Motor vehicle registrations, 1978, 1,096,939.

Railways. In 1977 there were 2,057 miles of railway.

Aviation. There were 139 airports in March 1978.

JUSTICE, RELIGION, EDUCATION AND WELFARE

Justice. The number of state penitentiary prisoners, average population 1978–79, was 1,619. The death penalty (by electrocution) has been imposed on 8 persons since 1933, 6 whites and 2 Negroes, all for murder. The last execution was in 1960.

Since 1949 the denial of employment by reason of race, colour, religion, national origin or ancestry has been forbidden. A law of 1955 prohibits discrimination in public places because of race or colour.

Religion. There were (1975) approximately 356,530 Protestant Church members and 315,470 Roman Catholics.

Education. Elementary education is free, and compulsory between 6 and 17 years or high-school graduation age. In 1977–78 the 88 school districts had an estimated enrolment of 272,808 students in public elementary and secondary schools. Private and parochial schools had 18,899 pupils. There were 13,271 teachers receiving an average salary of $12,840. Public education expenditure (excluding inter-government transfers) for 1977–78 was $642·9m.

The state-supported 4-year institutes of higher education are (1979):

	Faculty	Students
University of New Mexico, Albuquerque	738	22,033
New Mexico State University, Las Cruces	600	11,864
Eastern New Mexico University, Portales	146	3,707
New Mexico Highlands University, Las Vegas	121	2,219
Western New Mexico University, Silver City	62	1,650
New Mexico Institute of Mining and Technology, Sorocco	75	1,205

Health. In 1978 the state had 51 hospitals (4,781 beds).

Social Security. In March 1979, 14,172 persons were receiving aid to the disabled (average $141.55 per month); 11,104 persons were receiving old-age assistance (average $90.51 per month); 441 persons were receiving aid to the blind (average $142.86 per month); 51,468 people received aid to families with dependent children (average $53.93 per month).

Books of Reference

Writers' Program. *New Mexico: A Guide to the Colorful State.* Rev. ed. New York, 1953
New Mexico Business (monthly; annual review in Jan.–Feb. issue). Bureau of Business and Economic Research, University of N.M., Albuquerque
New Mexico Statistical Abstract: 1975. Bureau of Business and Economic Research, Univ. of N.M., Albuquerque, 1975
Donnelly, T. C., *The Government of New Mexico.* Univ. of N.M. Press, Albuquerque, 1953
Holmes, Jack, *Politics in New Mexico,* Univ. of N.M. Press, Albuquerque, 1966
Muench, D., and Hillerman, T., *New Mexico.* Belding, Portland, Oregon, 1974

NEW YORK STATE

HISTORY. From 1609 to 1664 the region now called New York was claimed by the Dutch; then it came under the rule of the English, who governed the country until the outbreak of the War of Independence. On 20 April 1777 New York adopted a constitution which transformed the colony into an independent state; on 26 July 1788 it ratified the constitution of the US, becoming one of the 13 original states. New York dropped its claim to Vermont after the latter was admitted to the Union in 1791. With the annexation of a small area from Massachusetts in 1853, New York assumed its present boundaries.

AREA AND POPULATION. New York is bounded west and north by Canada with Lake Erie, Lake Ontario and the St Lawrence River forming the boundary; east by Vermont, Massachusetts and Connecticut, south-east by the Atlantic, south by New Jersey and Pennsylvania. Area, 49,576 sq. miles (1,745 sq. miles being water). Census population, 1 April 1980 (preliminary), 17,557,288, a decrease of 3·7% since 1970. Births in 1979 were 234,867; deaths, 162,966; infant deaths, 3,177; marriages, 115,912; divorces, 64,420 (includes all dissolutions).

Population in 5 census years (with distribution by sex, 1970) was:

	White	Negro	Indian	Asiatic	Total	Per sq. mile
1910	8,966,845	134,191	6,046	6,532	9,113,614	191·2
1930	12,143,191	412,814	6,973	15,088	12,588,066	262·6
1950	13,872,095	918,191	10,640	29,266	14,830,192	309·3
1960	15,287,071	1,417,511	16,491	51,678	16,782,304	350·1
			All others			
1970	15,834,090	2,168,949	233,828		18,236,967	380·3
Male	—	1,001,996	—	—	8,715,339	—
Female	—	1,166,953	—	—	9,521,628	—

Of the Asiatics in 1970, 81,378 were Chinese and 20,351 Japanese. 15,602,486 or 85·6% were urban (85·4% in 1960); those 21 years of age or older numbered 11,510,452; foreign-born whites numbered 1,847,926 in 1970. Aliens registered in Jan. 1980 numbered 801,411.

The population of New York City, by boroughs, census of 1 April 1970 (and estimate, 1976) was: Manhattan, 1,539,233 (1,365,300); Bronx, 1,471,701 (1,255,500); Brooklyn, 2,602,012 (2,313,200); Queens, 1,987,174 (1,962,700); Richmond, 295,443 (337,600); total, 7,895,563 (7,234,300). The New York metropolitan statistical area had, in 1970 11,571,899 while the larger New York–NE New Jersey urbanized area had 16,206,841.

Population of other large cities and incorporated places, census, April 1980, was:

Buffalo	357,002	Binghampton	55,745	*Unincorporated towns*	
Rochester	241,509				
Yonkers	194,557	*Other cities, 1976*		Watertown	29,056
Syracuse	170,292			Newburgh	27,327
Albany (capital)	101,767	Rome	48,343	Hempstead	39,395
Utica	75,435	White Plains	47,736	Freeport	39,336
Niagara Falls	71,344	N. Tonawanda	39,881	Valley Stream	39,015
New Rochelle	70,345	Jamestown	37,161	Lindenhurst	29,851
Schenectady	67,877	Elmira	36,691	Rockville Center	26,973
Mount Vernon	66,023	Auburn	32,392	Garden City	26,476
Troy	56,614	Poughkeepsie	31,403	Massapequa Park	20,594

Other large urbanized areas, July 1977; Buffalo, 1·3m.; Rochester, 969,800; Albany–Schenectady–Troy, 792,300.

CONSTITUTION AND GOVERNMENT. The present constitution dates from 1894; a later constitutional convention, 1938, is now legally considered merely to have amended the 1894 constitution, which has now had 93 amendments. The Constitutional Convention of 1967 (4 April through 26 Sept.) was composed of 186 delegates who proposed a new state constitution; however this was rejected by the registered voters on 7 Nov. 1967. The Senate consists of 60 members, and the Assembly of 150 members, both elected every 2 years. The Governor and Lieut.-Governor are elected for 4 years. The right of suffrage resides in every adult who has been a citizen for 90 days, and has the usual residential qualifications; new voters must establish, by certificates or test, that they have had at least an elementary education.

The state is represented in Congress by 2 senators and 34 representatives.

In the 1980 presidential election Reagan polled 2,893,831 votes, Carter 2,728,372 and Anderson 467,801.

The state capital is Albany. For local government the state is divided into 62 counties, 5 of which constitute the city of New York. New York leads in state parks and recreation areas, covering 252,984 acres in 1979.

Cities are in 3 classes, the first class having each 175,000 or more inhabitants and the third under 50,000. Each is incorporated by charter, under special legislation. The government of New York City is vested in the mayor (Edward Koch), elected for 4 years, and a city council, whose president and members are elected for 4 years. The council has a President and 37 members, each elected from a state senatorial district wholly within the city. The mayor appoints all the heads of departments, except the comptroller, who is elected. Each of the 5 city boroughs (Manhattan, Bronx, Brooklyn, Queens and Richmond) has a president, elected for 4 years. Each borough is also a county bearing the same name except Manhattan borough, which, as a county, is called New York, and Brooklyn, which is Kings County.

Governor: Hugh Carey (D.), 1975 ($85,000).
Lieut.-Governor: Mario Cuomo (D.) ($60,000).
Secretary of State: Basil A. Patterson (D.) ($54,500).

BUDGET. The state's general revenues for the financial year ending 31 March 1980 were $13,107m. ($12,729m. from taxes, $254m. from federal revenue sharing); general expenditures were $13,107m. ($5,726m. for education, $2,397m. for social development, $1,598m. for health, $1,332m. for transport.

Per capita personal income was $7,660 in 1978.

The assessed valuation in 1979 of taxable real property in New York City was $39,707m. The assessed valuation of the state was $84,519m.

ENERGY AND NATURAL RESOURCES

Minerals. Production of principal minerals: Sand and gravel (30,000 short tons in 1978), salt (5,928 short tons in 1978), zinc (29,000 short tons in 1978), petroleum (855,000 bbls in 1979), natural gas (15,500m. cu. ft in 1979). The state is a leading producer of titanium concentrate, talc, abrasive garnet, wollastonite and emery. Quarry products include trap rock, slate, marble, limestone and sandstone. Value of mineral output in 1977 $461·8m.

Agriculture. New York has large agricultural interests. On 1 Jan. 1980 it had 44,000 farms, with a total area of 9·8m. acres; average farm was 223 acres.

Cash income, 1979, from crops and livestock, $2,240m. Dairying, with 19,500 farms, 1979, is an important type of farming with produce at a market value of $1,317m. Field crops comprise maize, winter wheat, oats and hay. New York (1979) ranks second in US in the production of apples, and maple syrup. Other products are grapes, tart cherries, peaches, pears, plums, strawberries, raspberries, cabbages, onions, potatoes, maple sugar. Estimated farm animals, 1980, included 1·78m. all cattle, 912,000 milch cows, 65,000 sheep, 139,000 swine (1979) and 10·2m. chickens (1979).

INDUSTRY. In 1979 manufacturing establishments numbering 33,148 employed 1,497,612 workers whose average weekly earnings were $321. Leading industries were clothing, non-electrical machinery, printing and publishing, electrical equipment, instruments, food and allied products and fabricated metals.

COMMUNICATIONS

Roads. There were (1979) 109,199 miles of municipal and rural roads. The New York State Thruway extends 559 miles from New York City to Buffalo; in 1979 receipts from tolls amounted to $146,751,552. The Northway, a 176-mile toll-free highway, is a connecting road from the Thruway at Albany to the Canadian border at Champlain, Quebec.

Motor vehicle registrations in 1979 were 8·5m., most of which (6,903,874) were private passenger vehicles.

Railways. There were in 1980, 5,215 miles of Class I railways.

Aviation. There were 473 airports and other landing areas in 1980.

Shipping. The canals of the state, combined in 1918 in what is called the Improved Canal System, have a length of 524 miles, of which the Erie or Barge canal has 340 miles. In 1978 the canals carried over 1·5m. tons of freight.

JUSTICE, RELIGION, EDUCATION AND WELFARE

Justice. The State Human Rights Law was approved 12 March 1945, effective 1 July, 1945. The State Division of Human Rights is charged with the responsibility of enforcing this law. The division may request and utilize the services of all governmental departments and agencies; adopt and promulgate suitable rules and regulations; test, investigate and pass upon complaints alleging discrimination in employment, in places of public accommodation, resort or amusement, education, and in housing, land and commercial space; hold hearings, subpoena witnesses and require the production for examination of papers relating to matters under investigation; grant compensatory damages and require repayment of profits in certain housing cases among other provisions; apply for court injunctions to prevent frustration of orders of the Commissioner.

On 19 Dec. 1980, 20,895 persons were in state prisons.

In 1963–80 there were no executions. Total executions (by electrocution) from 1930 to 1962 were 329 (234 whites, 90 Negroes, 5 other races; all for murder except 2 for kidnapping).

In 1978 murders reported in New York were 1,823; total violent crimes, 149,218. Police strength (sworn officers) in 1978 was 57,537 (29,629 New York City).

Religion. The chief churches are Roman Catholic, with 6,571,635 members in 1979, Jewish congregations (2,141,745 in 1978) and Protestant Episcopal (305,551 in 1978).

Education. Education is compulsory between the ages of 7 and 16. In autumn 1979 the public elementary schools (grades kindergarten to 6) enrolled 1,498,744 children, public secondary schools (grades 7 to 12) had 1,562,137 pupils; classroom teachers numbered 170,616 in public schools. Total expenditure on public schools in 1978–79 was $8,424,500,000. Teachers' salaries, 1979–80, averaged $19,801.

The state's educational system, including public and private schools and secondary institutions, universities, colleges, libraries, museums, etc., constitutes (by legislative act) the 'University of the State of New York', which is governed by a Board of Regents consisting of 15 members appointed by the Legislature. Within the framework of this 'University' was established in 1948 a 'State University' which controls 64 colleges and educational centres, 30 of which are locally operated community colleges. The 'State University' is governed by a board of 16 Trustees, appointed by the Governor with the consent and advice of the Senate.

Higher education in the state is conducted in 248 institutions (604,832 full-time students), of which 163 are under private control and 85 under public control.

In autumn 1979 the 248 institutions of higher education in the state had a total of 1,049,068 degree and non-degree credit students. Among them were:

Founded	Name and place	Teachers	Students
1754	Columbia University, New York	3,800	16,457
1795	Union University, Schenectady and Albany	236	2,705
1824	Rensselaer Polytechnic Institute, Troy	356	5,708
1831	New York University, New York	2,615	40,000
1846	Colgate University, New York	204	2,399
1846	Fordham University, New York	936	14,906
1847	University of the City of New York, New York	11,442	176,850
1848	University of Rochester, Rochester	1,587	7,881
1854	Polytechnic Institute of New York	242	4,583
1856	St Lawrence University, Canton	165	2,200
1857	Cooper Union Institute of Technology, New York	138	131
1861	Vassar College, Poughkeepsie	231	2,339
1863	Manhattan College, New York	310	4,776
1865	Cornell University, Ithaca	1,700	16,604
1870	Syracuse University, Syracuse	900	14,000
1948	State University of New York	21,280	356,708

The Saratoga Performing Arts Centre (5,100 seats), a non-profit, tax-exempt organization, which opened in 1966, is the summer residence of the New York City Ballet and the Philadelphia Orchestra—two groups which present special educational programmes for students and teachers.

Health. In 1980 the state had 293 hospitals (72,926 beds), 539 skilled nursing homes (69,146 beds) and 248 other institutions (29,918 beds). On 23 Nov. 1978 mental health facilities had 26,473 patients and institutions for the mentally retarded had 15,874 patients.

Social Security. The federal Supplemental Security Income programme covered aid to the needy aged, blind and disabled from 1 Jan. 1975. In the state programme there were 1·35m. welfare recipients in 1978 (monthly average); average benefit, $125.43 per month; medical assistance went to 1,014,753 persons, average $230.80; aid to dependent children in 1978 went to 1,184,511 recipients, average benefits $121.77 per month.

Books of Reference

New York Red Book. Albany, 1979–80
Legislative Manual. Department of State, 1977–79
New York State Statistical Yearbook, 1979–80. Albany
Caldwell, L. K., *The Government and Administration of New York.* New York, 1954
Connery, R. and G. B., *Governing New York State: The Rockefeller Years.* Academy of Political Science, New York, 1974
DePauw, L. G., *The Eleventh Pillar; New York State and the Federal Constitution.* Cornell Univ. Press, 1966
Ellis, D. M., *History of New York State.* Cornell Univ. Press, 1967
Flick, A. (ed.), *History of the State of New York.* Columbia University Press, 1933–37
Kass, A., *Politics in New York State.* Syracuse Univ. Press, 1965
Lincoln, C., *Constitutional History of New York 1809–1877.* Rochester, 1906
Roseberry, C. R., *Capitol Story.* Albany, 1964
Rosenwhike, I., *Population History of New York City.* Syracuse Univ. Press, 1972
Thompson, J. H. (ed.), *Geography of New York State.* Syracuse Univ. Press, 1966
Wolfe, G. R., *New York: A Guide to the Metropolis.* New York Univ. Press, 1975

State Library: The New York State Library, Albany 12230. *State Librarian and Assistant Commissioner for Libraries:* Joseph Shubert.

NORTH CAROLINA

HISTORY. North Carolina, first settled in 1585 by Sir Walter Raleigh and permanently settled in 1663, was one of the 13 original states of the Union.

AREA AND POPULATION. North Carolina is bounded north by Virginia, east by the Atlantic, south by South Carolina, south-west by Georgia and west by Tennessee. Area, 52,712 sq. miles, of which 3,645 sq. miles are inland water. Census population, 1 April 1980 (preliminary), 5,737,140, an increase of 12·8% since 1970.

Births, 1979, were 83,782 (14·9 per 1,000 population); marriages, 45,064 (8); deaths, 46,640 (8·3); infant deaths, 1,270 (15·2 per 1,000 live births); divorces and annulments, 27,445 (4·9).

Population in 5 census years (with distribution by sex, 1980):

	White	Negro	Indian	Asiatic	Total	Per sq. mile
1910	1,500,511	697,843	7,851	82	2,206,287	45·3
1930	2,234,958	918,647	16,579	92	3,170,276	64·5
1950	2,983,121	1,047,353	3,742	—	4,061,929	82·7
1960	3,399,285	1,116,021	38,129	2,012	4,556,155	92·2
			All others			
1970	3,901,767	1,126,478	53,814		5,082,059	104·1
			Non-white			
1980	4,405,514		1,331,626		5,737,140	108·83
Male	2,149,551		629,775		2,779,326	—
Female	2,255,963		701,951		2,957,914	—

Of the total population in 1979, 2,538,900 persons (44·3%) were urban (44·9% in 1970); 67·9% were 20 years old or older; 14·8% were non-white.

Cities (with census population in 1980) are: Charlotte, 310,799; Greensboro, 154,763; Winston-Salem, 131,211; Raleigh (capital), 148,299; Durham (1970), 95,438; High Point, 63,169; Asheville, 57,708; Fayetteville, 59,476.

CONSTITUTION AND GOVERNMENT. The present constitution dates from 1971 (previous constitution, 1776 and 1868/76); it has had 12 amendments. The General Assembly consists of a Senate of 50 members and a House of Representatives of 120 members; all are elected by districts for 2 years. The Governor and Lieut.-Governor are elected for 4 years. The Governor may succeed himself but has no veto. There are 17 other executive heads of department, 8 elected by the people and 7 appointed by the Governor. All registered citizens with the usual residential qualifications have a vote.

The state is represented in Congress by 2 senators and 11 representatives.

In the presidential election of 1980 Reagan polled 915,018 votes, Carter 875,635 and Anderson 52,800.

The capital is Raleigh, established in 1792.

Governor: James B. Hunt, Jr (D.) 1977–85 ($55,104).
Lieut.-Governor: James C. Greene (D.) ($45,636).
Secretary of State: Thad Eure (D.) ($45,636).

BUDGET. General revenue for the year ending 30 June 1980 was $2,842m. ($2,639·2m. from taxation). General expenditure was $2,744·6m. (education, $1,807·8m.; highways, $478m.; human resources, $429·8m.).

On 30 June 1980 the net total long-term debt amounted to $753·7m.

Per capita personal income (1979) was $7,385.

NATURAL RESOURCES

Minerals. Mining production in 1979 was valued at $295·9m. Principal minerals were stone, sand and gravel, phosphate rock, feldspar, clay, mica, lithium minerals, olivine, kaolin and talc. North Carolina ranked first in the production of mica, feldspar, olivine and lithium minerals. It is also the leading producer of bricks. In 1979 North Carolina manufactured 1,030m. bricks valued at over $103m. or 14% of the total US production.

Agriculture. In 1980 there were 98,000 farms in North Carolina covering 12·3m. acres; average size of farms was 126 acres and average value (1 Feb. 1980), $110,100.

Income is primarily from tobacco, poultry, cattle, swine, maize, peanuts and soybeans. Cash income, 1979, from crops, was $1,973·5m. and from livestock, dairy and poultry and products, $1,423·8m.

North Carolina leads in production of tobacco (621·4m. lb., 1979). Production of maize, 1979, was 128,440 bu.; cotton, 43,000 lb.; peanuts, 378·5m. lb.; soybeans, 45m. bu. Also grown extensively are wheat, oats, barley, sweet potatoes, blueberries, hay, peaches and apples. On 1 Jan. 1980 farms had 145,000 milch cows, 1·08m. all cattle, 2·6m. swine and 7,500 sheep. Production of commercial broilers amounted to 377m. in 1979 (fourth highest in US).

Forestry. North Carolina is the largest lumber-producing state in the South and the fifth largest in the US. Timber, covering 21m. acres in 1974 (66% of land area), provided approximately $5,453m. income in forest industries and products. The area of forest lands in public ownership in 1974 was 1·7m. acres.

Fisheries. Fish catch, 1979, amounted to 390m. lb.; value approximately $58·5m.

INDUSTRY. North Carolina's 9,000 industrial establishments in 1979 had 805,000 production workers. Value added (1977 estimate) was $18,105m. The leading industries are textile goods (leading all states), manufacture of cigarettes (about 55% of the US production, leading all states), chemicals, electronics and electrical machinery, processing of food crops and the manufacture of furniture and bricks (leading all states in both). Total receipts of the travel industry, $2,200m. in 1979. In 1979 new industrial investment was $1,330·7m. creating 16,792 new jobs; investment in expansion was $1,095·9m., creating 20,282.

COMMUNICATIONS

Roads. The state was the first to undertake the maintenance of all highways, and maintained, 1974, nearly 75,000 miles of highways, more than any other state. In 1974, 2,752,313 automobiles and 718,957 trucks were registered.

Railways. The state in 1974 contained 4,336 miles of railway, almost wholly diesel-powered.

Aviation. Airports in 1974 numbered 186, of which 58 are publicly owned, and are served by 5 airlines.

Shipping. There are 2 ocean ports, Wilmington and Morehead City.

JUSTICE, RELIGION, EDUCATION AND WELFARE

Justice. Total executions 1910–62, 362. Prison population at 28 Oct. 1980, 15,593.

Religion. Leading denominations are the Baptists (48·9% of church membership in 1974), Methodists (20·7%), Presbyterians (7·7%), Lutherans (3%) and Roman Catholics (2·7%). Total estimate of all denominations in 1974 was 2·58m.

Education. School attendance is compulsory between 6 and 16.

Public school enrolment, 1979–80, was 1,191,342; elementary and secondary schools numbered 2,035. Instructional staff consisted of 67,586 classroom teachers and administrators. Estimated total current expenditure for public schools, 1978–79, $1,706·9m., including $1,080·9m. from state, $403·4m. from local and $222·6m. from federal sources.

In autumn 1979 state-supported colleges and universities included 58 two-year community colleges with 95,670 students; 16 four-year colleges with 112,746 students. The 16 senior universities are all part of the University of North Carolina system, the largest campus being the University of North Carolina at Chapel Hill. This university was founded in 1789 and first opened in 1792. Its 1979–80 enrolment was 20,784 with a faculty of 1,736. The next three largest campuses are North Carolina State University in Raleigh (1887) with an enrolment of 19,516 and a faculty of 1,171, East Carolina University in Greenville (1907) with an enrolment of 12,874 and a faculty of 639; and the University of North Carolina at Greensboro (1891) with an enrolment of 9,925 and a faculty of 516. The total enrolment of public institutions of higher learning in 1979–80 was 254,859.

In addition to the state-supported institutions there were 8 private junior colleges with an enrolment of 4,866 and 30 private senior institutions with a total enrolment of 41,577. The largest of these are Duke University (1924) in Durham, a Methodist affiliated school with 8,140 students, and Wake Forest University (1834) in Winston-Salem, a Baptist school with 3,801 students. The total enrolment in private institutions for 1979–80 was 46,443.

Health. In Dec. 1979 the state had 158 hospitals (30,809 beds).

Social Security. In Dec. 1979 there were 881,381 persons receiving an average of $231.41 a month in social security benefits. Of that number 447,314 were retired, receiving an average of $265.70 a month; 89,380 were disabled ($294.39); 15,717 children of retired persons received $110.71 monthly; 39,678 children of disabled persons received $92.82 monthly; 84,934 widows and widowers received $191.34 monthly.

Books of Reference

North Carolina Manual. Secretary of State. Raleigh. Biennial
North Carolina: A Guide to the Old North State. Univ. of N.C., Chapel Hill, 1955
Corbitt, D. L., *The Formation of the North Carolina Counties.* Raleigh, 1969
Hobbs, S. H., *North Carolina: An Economic and Social Profile.* Univ. of N.C., Chapel Hill, 1958
Lefler, H. T., and Newsome, A. R., *North Carolina: The History of a Southern State.* Univ. of N.C., Chapel Hill, 1963

Powell, W. S., *The North Carolina Gazetteer.* Univ. of N.C., Chapel Hill, 1968
Thornton, M. L., *Bibliography of North Carolina, 1589–1956.* Univ. of N.C., Chapel Hill, 1958
Lonsdale, R. E., *Atlas of North Carolina.* Univ. of N.C., Chapel Hill and OUP, 1967

State Library: North Carolina State Library, Raleigh. *State Librarian:* Philip S. Ogilvie.

NORTH DAKOTA

HISTORY. North Dakota was admitted into the Union, with boundaries as at present, on 2 Nov. 1889; previously it had formed part of the Dakota Territory, established 2 March 1861.

AREA AND POPULATION. North Dakota is bounded north by Canada, east by the Red River (forming a boundary with Minnesota), south by South Dakota and west by Montana. Land area, 69,457 sq. miles, and 1,208 sq. miles of water. The Federal Bureau of Indian Affairs administered (1971) 850,000 acres, of which 153,000 acres were assigned to tribes. Census population, 1 April 1980, (preliminary) 652,437, an increase of 34,676 or 5·6% since 1970. Births in 1979 were 11,882 (18·2 per 1,000 population); deaths, 5,361 (8·2); infant deaths, 159; marriages, 5,668; divorces, 1,944.

Population at 5 census years (with distribution by sex, 1970) was:

	White	Negro	Indian	Asiatic	Total	Per sq. mile
1910	569,855	617	6,486	98	577,056	8·2
1930	671,851	377	8,617	194	680,845	9·7
1950	608,448	257	10,766	143	619,636	8·8
1960	619,538	777	11,736	274	632,446	9·1
			All others			
1970	599,485	2,494	15,782		617,761	8·9
Male	302,338	1,536	7,725		311,609	—
Female	297,147	958	8,047		306,152	—

Of the total population in 1980, 314,013 (48·2%) were urban (44·3% in 1970); those 21 years old or older (1970) numbered 355,763. Estimated outward migration, 1970–80, 17,478.

The largest cities are Fargo with population (census), 1980, of 61,281; Grand Forks, 43,760; Bismarck (capital), 44,502, and Minot, 32,886.

CONSTITUTION AND GOVERNMENT. The present constitution dates from 1889; it has had 95 amendments. The Legislative Assembly consists of a Senate of 50 members elected for 4 years, and a House of Representatives of 100 members elected for 2 years. The Governor and Lieut.-Governor are elected for 4 years. Qualified electors are (with necessary exceptions) all citizens and civilized Indians. The state sends to Congress 2 senators elected by the voters of the entire state and 1 representative.

In the 1980 presidential election Reagan polled 193,695 votes, Carter 79,189 and Anderson 23,640.

The capital is Bismarck. The state has 53 organized counties.

Governor: Arthur A. Link (D.), 1977–81 ($18,000 plus $4,000 expenses).
Lieut.-Governor: Wayne Sanstad (D.), 1977–81 ($2,000 plus $2,000 expenses).
Secretary of State: Ben Meier (R.), 1977–81 ($11,000 plus $3,000 expenses).

FINANCE. General revenue of state and local government year ending 30 June 1977, was $924m.; general expenditures, $854m., taxation provided $445m. and federal aid, $239m.; education took $323m.; highways, $150m., and public welfare, $68m.

Total net long-term debt (local government) on 30 June 1977, $418m.

Per capita personal income (1978) was $7,714.

ENERGY AND NATURAL RESOURCES

Minerals. The mineral resources of North Dakota consist chiefly of oil which was discovered in 1951. Production of crude petroleum in 1979 was 30·8m. bbls; of natural gas, 40,000m. cu. ft. Output (1977) of lignite coal was 14·2m. short tons. Total value of mineral output, 1976, $277·3m.

Agriculture. Agriculture is the chief pursuit of the North Dakota population. In 1980 there were 41,690 farms (61,963 in 1954) with an area of 42m. acres (41,876,924 in 1954); the average farm was of 1,042 acres. The greater number of farms are cash-grain or livestock farms with annual sales of $20,000–$39,999.

Cash income, 1979, from crops, $1,622·2m., and from livestock, $612·5m. North Dakota leads in the production of barley, sunflowers, flaxseed, durum, spring wheat. Other important products are sugar-beet, beans, potatoes, hay, oats, rye and maize.

The state has also an active livestock industry, chiefly cattle raising. On 1 Jan. 1980 the farm animals were: 93,000 milch cows, 2m. all cattle, 236,000 sheep and 370,000 swine. The wool clip yielded (1979), 1·7m. lb. of wool from 175,000 sheep.

Forestry. National forest area, 1977, 422,000 acres, of which 115,000 acres are federally owned or managed.

INDUSTRY. From 1970 to 1979 agricultural employment rose from 51,920 to 52,450; non-agricultural jobs rose from 148,910 to 258,890. Between 1970 and 1979, employment in manufacturing rose from 9,910 to 16,580, in trade from 43,890 to 67,700 and in government from 49,240 to 60,690.

COMMUNICATIONS

Roads. The state highway department maintained, in 1979, 7,127 miles of highway; local authorities, 96,353 miles, and municipal, 3,140 miles.

Car and truck registrations in 1979 numbered 590,793.

Railways. In 1978 there were 5,262 miles of railway.

Aviation. Airports in 1978 numbered 262, of which 107 were publicly owned.

JUSTICE, RELIGION, EDUCATION AND WELFARE

Justice. The state penitentiary, on 1 Oct. 1980, held 294 inmates. Of these, 56 were incarcerated at the North Dakota State Farm. There is no death penalty.

Religion. The leading religious denominations are the Roman Catholics, with 171,185 members in 1975; Combined Lutherans, 216,579; Methodists, 28,880; Presbyterians, 18,636.

Education. School attendance is compulsory between the ages of 7 and 16, or until the 17th birthday if the eighth grade has not been completed. In Sept. 1978 the public elementary schools had 4,358 classroom teachers and 77,212 pupils; secondary schools, 3,032 teachers and 44,477 pupils. Average salary of teachers, 1970, was $6,375 in elementary and $7,263 in secondary schools. State expenditure on public schools, 1970, $122·7m. Private schools had 10,032 elementary pupils, 3,942 secondary pupils and 1,425 teachers in 1978.

The university at Grand Forks, founded in 1883, had 19,217 students in 1980; the state university of agriculture and applied science, at Fargo, 8,317 students plus 362 at Bottineau. Total enrolment in the 8 public institutions of higher education, 1980, 27,774.

Health. In 1977 the state had 53 hospitals (4,051 beds), 53 nursing homes (3,908) and 27 institutions for intermediate care (1,680).

Social Security. In 1974 aid to the aged, blind and disabled was taken out of state programmes and included in federal programmes as Supplemental Security Income (SSI). In 1978 grants were made to 13,300 cases, including 9,400 families with dependent children, 8,000 cases for medical aid. At Dec. 1978, 6,900 people received SSI assistance.

Books of Reference

North Dakota Growth Indicators, 1980. 17th ed. Business and Industrial Development Dept., Bismarck, 1978
North Dakota Industrial Location Facts. Business and Industrial Development Dept., Bismarck, 1979
North Dakota Blue Book. Secretary of State, Bismarck, 1973
Federal Writers' Project. *North Dakota: A Guide to the Northern State*. 2nd ed. OUP, New York, 1950
Goodey, R. B. (ed.), *Readings in the Geography of North Dakota*. North Dakota Studies, 1968
Robinson, E. B., *History of North Dakota*. Univ. of Nebraska Press, 1966

OHIO

HISTORY. Ohio, first settled in 1788, unofficially entered the Union on 19 Feb. 1803; entrance was made official, retroactive to 1 March 1803, on 8 Aug. 1953.

AREA AND POPULATION. Ohio is bounded north by Michigan and Lake Erie, east by Pennsylvania, south-east and south by the Ohio River (forming a boundary with West Virginia and Kentucky) and west by Indiana. Area, 40,975 sq. miles, of which 204 sq. miles are inland water. Census population, 1 April 1980 (preliminary), 10,797,419, an increase of 145,402 or 1·4% since 1970. In 1978 births numbered 161,813 (15·1 per 1,000 population); deaths, 97,928; infant deaths, 2,099 (13 per 1,000 live births); marriages, 104,340 (9·7); divorces and annulments, 58,149 (5·4).

Population at 5 census years (with distribution by sex, 1970) was:

	White	Negro	Indian	Asiatic	Total	Per sq. mile
1910	4,654,897	111,452	127	645	4,767,121	117·0
1930	6,335,173	309,304	435	1,785	6,646,697	161·6
1950	7,428,222	513,072	1,146	3,528	7,946,627	193·8
1960	8,909,698	786,097	1,910	8,692	9,706,397	236·9
			All others			
1970	9,646,997	970,477	34,543		10,652,017	260·0
Male	4,685,685	461,274	3,144	13,265	5,163,373	—
Female	4,961,312	509,203	3,505	14,624	5,488,644	—

Of the total population in 1970, 8,025,697 persons (75·3%) lived in urban areas (73·4% in 1960). Those 21 years old or older numbered 6,431,709; 65 years or over, 998,094.

Census population of chief cities on 1 April 1980 was:

Cleveland	572,532	Hamilton	62,845	Cuyahoga Falls	46,249
Columbus	561,943	Lakewood	61,921	Mentor	40,510
Cincinnati	383,058	Kettering	61,223	Marion	39,222
Toledo	354,265	Euclid	59,896	Newark	38,609
Akron	236,820	Elyria	57,039	Lancaster	38,450
Dayton	193,319	Cleveland Heights	55,563	Upper Arlington	38,279
Youngstown	115,429	Warren	55,456	North Olmsted	37,844
Canton	94,632	Mansfield	53,907	East Cleveland	37,771
Parma	92,578	*Others, 1976:*		Garfield Heights	37,531
Lorain	75,339	Lima	50,982	Zanesville	36,967
Springfield	72,098	Middletown	47,725		

Urbanized areas, 1970 census: Cleveland, 2,064,194; Cincinnati, 1,104,668; Columbus (the capital), 916,228; Dayton, 850,266; Akron, 679,239; Toledo, 574,092; Youngstown-Warren, 536,003; Canton, 372,210.

CONSTITUTION AND GOVERNMENT. The question of a general revision of the constitution drafted by an elected convention is submitted to the people every 20 years. The constitution of 1851 had 105 amendments by 1978.

In the 112th General Assembly the Senate consisted of 33 members and the House of Representatives of 99 members. The Senate is elected for 4 years, half each 2 years; the House is elected for 2 years; the Governor, Lieut.-Governor and Secretary of State for 4 years. Qualified as electors are (with necessary exceptions) all citizens 18 years of age who have the usual residential qualifications. Ohio sends 2 senators and 21 representatives to Congress.

In the 1980 presidential election Reagan polled 2,206,545 votes, Carter, 1,752,414. The capital (since 1816) is Columbus. Ohio is divided into 88 counties.

Governor: James A. Rhodes (R.), 1979–83 ($50,000).
Lieut.-Governor: George V. Voinovich (R.), 1979–83 ($30,000).
Secretary of State: Anthony J. Celebrezze (D.), 1979–83 ($38,000).

BUDGET. For the 2 years ending 30 June 1977 (Budget of the State of Ohio) total general revenue was $5,831·8m. and general expenditure was $5,925·6m.

The net long-term debt of the state on 30 June 1977 was $2,109·3m.

Per capita personal income (1976) was $6,432.

ENERGY AND NATURAL RESOURCES

Minerals. Ohio has extensive mineral resources, of which coal is the most important by value: output (1977) 46·6m. short tons, value $784·2m. Production of other minerals, 1977: Sand and gravel, 41·1m. short tons ($81·7m.); lime, 3·2m. short tons ($112·7m.); crude petroleum, 11·59m. bbls ($143·7m.); natural gas, 84·45m. cu. ft ($107·2m.); clay, 4·36m. short tons ($15·23m.); salt, 3·6m. short tons ($61·8m.); stone, 44·5m. short tons ($114m.).

Agriculture. Ohio is extensively devoted to agriculture. In 1977, 115,000 farms covered 17·2m. acres; average farm was valued at $169,000. Commercial farms (1974 census) with over $2,500 gross sales numbered 70,283. Owners operated 55·2%, part-owners 31·6%, tenant-farmers 13·2% of these farms.

Cash income 1977, from crop and livestock and products, $2,794m. The most important crops in 1977 were: Maize (380·1m. bu., sales value $539·5m.), wheat (72·4m. bu., $143·8m.), oats (24·8m. bu., $14·1m.), soybeans (116·6m. bu., $621·9m.). The wool clip in 1976 yielded 3·35m. lb from 423,000 sheep. On 1 Jan. 1977 there were 1m. swine and 11m. chickens, 2·25m. all cattle and 445,000 sheep.

Forestry. State forest area, 1978, 170,000 acres including reclamation area.

INDUSTRY. In 1977, 16,119 manufacturing employers employed an average of 1·34m. workers. The value added by manufacture in 1973 was $31,174m. The largest industry was manufacturing of non-electrical machinery with an average of 212,282 workers.

COMMUNICATIONS

Roads. The state (1977) maintained 19,458 miles of highway, including 1,303 miles of interstate highways and 241 miles on the Ohio Turnpike; there were 91,511 miles of country, township, city, park and forest development roads. Total miles of highway maintained by all government agencies (1977) 110,969.

Railways. The railroads had 7,400 route miles of track in 1978.

Aviation. Ohio had (1978) 719 airports and airfields, of which 212 are commercial and 527 private, 130 heliports and 2 seaplane bases. There were 6,600 licensed aeroplanes.

JUSTICE, RELIGION, EDUCATION AND WELFARE

Justice. A Civil Rights Act (1933) forbids inns, restaurants, theatres, retail stores and all other places of public resort to discriminate against citizens on grounds of 'colour or race'; none may be denied the right to serve on juries on the grounds of 'colour or race'; insurance companies are forbidden to discriminate between 'white persons and coloured, wholly or partially of African descent'.

A state Civil Rights Commission (created 1959) has general administrative powers to prevent discrimination because of race, colour, religion, national origin or ancestry in employment, labour organization membership, use of public accommodations and in obtaining 'commercial housing' or 'personal residence'. Ohio has no *de jure* segregation in the public schools.

The state's adult correctional institutions, 30 Oct. 1978, held 8,285 inmates (average daily count). Total executions (by electrocution) since 1930 were 170, all for murder. There have been no executions since 1963. The Department of Rehabilitation and Correction was created in July 1972, and has established probation services in 51 counties where services would otherwise be inadequate or non-existent.

Religion. Many religious faiths are represented, including (but not limited to) the Baptist, Jewish, Lutheran, Methodist, Presbyterian and Roman Catholic.

Education. School attendance during full term is compulsory for children from 6 to 18 years of age. In 1977–78, public schools had 2,177,221 enrolled pupils; elementary schools had 49,029 teachers and 1,278,689 enrolled pupils; secondary schools had 45,496 teachers and 898,532 pupils. There were 7,082 special education teachers. Teachers' salaries averaged $13,306. Operating expenditure on elementary and secondary schools for 1976–77 was $2,934m. The state's universities and colleges had a total enrolment (1977) of 436,056 students; the following had 7,000 or more students, autumn 1977:

Founded	Institutions	Enrolments
1804	Ohio University, Athens (State)	13,021
1809	Miami University, Oxford (State)	14,759
1826	Case Western Reserve University, Cleveland	8,108
1850	University of Dayton (R.C.)	9,620
1870	University of Akron (State)	23,121
1872	Ohio State University, Columbus (State)	51,003
1872	University of Toledo (State)	16,933
1874	University of Cincinnati (State-affiliated)	32,952
1887	Sinclair Community College, Dayton	13,752
1908	Youngstown University (State)	15,696
1910	Bowling Green State University (State)	16,439
1912	Kent State University (State)	19,396
1962	Cuyahoga Community College (Municipal)	27,250
1964	Cleveland State University (State)	17,627
1964	Wright State University (State)	13,067

Health. In Oct. 1978 the state had 209 hospitals (49,055 beds) listed by the American Hospital Association. State hospitals for mental diseases and retardation had 6,062 patients on 18 Oct. 1978, and the state psychiatric hospitals had 375 patients.

Social Security. Public assistance is administered through 4 basic programmes: aid to dependent children, emergency assistance, Medicaid and general relief. Total public assistance expenditures during the year ending 30 June 1978 were $1,322·4m. In 1976–77 the number of persons receiving public assistance averaged 626,100 per month. Under the aid to dependent children programme $429·9m. provided assistance to an average of 526,434 recipients per month. Payments for Medicaid were $603·5m.; for social services, $189m.; for general relief, $78·4m., and emergency assistance, $21·6m. Recipients of general relief averaged 47,923 per month, emergency assistance, 30,585. Recipients of Medicaid during the year, 799,915.

Books of Reference

Official Roster: Federal State, County Officers and Department Information. Secretary of State, Columbus. Biennial

Statistical Abstract of Ohio, 1960. Dept. of Industrial and Economic Development. Columbus, 1960

Aumann, F. R., and Walker, H., *The Government and Administration of Ohio.* New York, 1956

Rose, A. H., *Ohio Government, State and Local.* Saint Louis, 1953

Rosebloom, E. H., and Weisenburger, F. P., *A History of Ohio.* State Arch. and Hist. Soc., Columbus, 1953

OKLAHOMA

HISTORY. An unorganized area in the centre of the present state was thrown open to white settlers on 22 April 1889. The Territory of Oklahoma, organized in 1890 to include this area and other sections, was opened to white settlements by runs or lotteries during the next decade. In 1893 the Territory was enlarged by the addition of the Cherokee Outlet, which fixed part of the present northern boundary. On 16 Nov. 1907 Oklahoma was combined with the remaining part of the Indian Territory and admitted as a state with boundaries substantially as now.

AREA AND POPULATION. Oklahoma is bounded north by Kansas, northeast by Missouri, east by Arkansas, south by Texas (the Red River forming part of the boundary) and, at the western extremity of the 'panhandle', by New Mexico and Colorado. Area 69,919 sq. miles, of which 1,137 sq. miles are water. Census population, 1 April 1980 (preliminary), 3,025,266, an increase of 465,803 or 18% since 1970. Births, 1979, were 49,007; deaths, 27,802; infant deaths 611; marriages, 44,452; divorces, including annulments, 22,823.

The population at 5 federal censuses (with distribution by sex, 1970) was:

	White	Negro	Indian	Asiatic	Total	Per sq. mile
1910	1,444,531	137,612	74,825	187	1,657,155	23·9
1930	2,130,778	172,198	92,725	339	2,396,040	34·6
1950	2,032,526	145,503	53,769	534	2,233,351	32·4
1960	2,107,900	153,084	68,689	1,414	2,328,284	33·8
			All others			
1970	2,275,104	177,907	106,218		2,559,253	37·2
Male	1,113,345	81,299	51,711		1,246,355	—
Female	1,167,017	90,593	55,264		1,312,874	—

In 1970, 1,740,137 (68%) were urban (62·9% in 1960). Those 21 years of age or older numbered 1,584,292; 65 years or older, 299,756. Foreign-born whites numbered 20,160. In 1978 the US Bureau of Indian Affairs administered 1,062,858·05 acres, of which 86,433·27 acres were allotted to tribes.

The most important cities with population, 1980 are Oklahoma City (capital), 401,002, Tulsa, 355,500; Lawton, 79,725; Norman, 67,777; Midwest City, 59,100 (1979 estimate).

CONSTITUTION AND GOVERNMENT. The present constitution, dating from 1907, provides for amendment by initiative petition and legislative referendum; it has had 105 amendments.

The Legislature consists of a Senate of 48 members, who are elected for 4 years, and a House of Representatives elected for 2 years and consisting of 101 members. The Governor and Lieut.-Governor are elected for 4-year terms; the Governor can only be elected for two terms in succession. Electors are (with necessary exceptions) all citizens 18 years or older, with the usual qualifications.

The state is represented in Congress by 2 senators and 6 representatives.

In the 1980 presidential election Reagan polled 695,570 votes, Carter 402,026, Anderson 38,284 and Clark 13,828.

The capital is Oklahoma City. The state has 77 counties.

Governor: George Nigh (D.), 1979–83 ($48,000).
Lieut.-Governor: Spencer Bernard (D.) 1979–83 ($27,500).
Secretary of State: Jeanette B. Edmondson (D.) 1979–83 ($24,000).

BUDGET. Total revenue for the year ending 30 June 1980 (State Budget Office figures) was $3,317m. General revenue was $1,014·6m.

Bonded indebtedness for the year ending 30 June 1980, $1,184m.

Per capita personal income (1979) was $8,226.

ENERGY AND NATURAL RESOURCES

Minerals. Resources include petroleum, helium, natural gas, coal (bituminous), copper and silver. Production for the year ending 30 June 1980 was: Petroleum,

145,382,109 bbls; natural gas, 1,889,335,639m. cu. ft. In 1980 there were 78,062 oilwells and 15,024 natural gaswells in production.

Agriculture. In 1979 the state had 71,000 farms with annual sales of $1,000 or more with a total area of 34·5m. acres; average farm was 486 acres with a value, land and buildings, of $256,692. In 1979, there were 38,449 full-time farmers or ranchers, 22,847 part-owners and 8,423 tenants. Large-scale commercial farming is predominant.

Soil erosion is serious. The conservation and development of the renewable natural resources of the state has received close attention by local, county and state governments during the past 40 years. All of the land in the state is within the boundaries of one of the 88 conservation districts. Of the total surface (44m. acres), 30·6m. acres are being operated under a basic conservation plan prepared by the conservation district with assistance from the Soil Conservation Service. There were (1975–76) 99,037 district co-operators. In May 1978, 121,510 acres had suffered damage from wind erosion, during the year compared with 206,840 in 1976–77. The Oklahoma Conservation Commission reported that good conservation measures by farmers, such as minimum tillage and crop residue management, are helping to conserve the moisture and protect crops from wind erosion. Through June 1976, 60 work plans had been approved for the important Washita River Watershed, which was established in 1946 to aid flood control. In addition, 1,007 flood-prevention dams and 20 multi-purpose dams have been built or contracted under this project. In 1978, 16,816,620 acres were within the boundaries of the 185 watersheds in Oklahoma, including 52,450 acres which made up the 6 planned or completed Resource Conservation and Development Projects.

The largest change in land use has been the conversion of 170,284 acres of cropland to grass. This is a continuation of a trend of the last 40 years; cattle and calves rank first in agricultural products, valued, 1979, at $1,462m., winter wheat is second, at $845m.

Cash income from crops and livestock products 1979, $3,162m. The most valuable crop is winter wheat. Other crops (production, 1978) included hay (3·2m. tons), cotton (355,000 bales of 480 lb.), grain sorghums (17·5m. bu.) and peanuts (207m. lb.). On 1 Jan. 1980 the stock included 110,000 milch cows, 5·5m. all cattle, 93,000 sheep and lambs and 370,000 swine.

Forestry. National forest lands, 1980, 218,800 acres; other public forest lands, 343,800 acres. Commercial timber lands, 4·3m. acres. The forest products industry, concentrated in the southeastern counties, employs approximately 7,000 in over 100 manufacturing plants with an estimated combined annual payroll of $75m. Value of shipments of lumber and forest products in 1979 was estimated at $500m.

INDUSTRY. The wholesale and retail trade industry is the largest employer (non-agricultural) followed by service industries. Among manufacturing industries the most important by payroll employment (1979) were: Machinery, 35,700 employees; fabricated metal products, 22,000; food and kindred products, 16,600; electric and electronic equipment, 13,500; transport equipment, 18,500. In 1979 the civilian labour force averaged 1·27m.

COMMUNICATIONS

Roads. In 1980 there were 636 miles of inter-state highway open, 86,468 miles of county roads, 12,178 miles of state-maintained roads, 10,256 miles of city streets, 478 miles of turnpike and 289 miles of park and forest roads. Motor vehicle registrations, 1979, 2,901,991.

Railways. In 1980 Oklahoma had 4,750 miles of railway.

Aviation. Airports, 1980, numbered 279, of which 140 were municipally owned. Seven cities were served by CAB-certificated airlines.

Shipping. The McClellan-Kerr Arkansas Navigation System provides access from east central Oklahoma to New Orleans through the Verdigris, Arkansas and Mississippi rivers. The main ports are Catoosa and Muskogee.

JUSTICE, RELIGION, EDUCATION AND WELFARE

Justice. Penal institutions, Oct. 1980, held 4,803 inmates. There are 10 prisons and 9 community treatment centres.

The death penalty was suspended in 1966 and re-imposed in 1974. Since 1915 there have been 83 (52 whites, 27 Negroes, 4 other races) executions by electrocution replaced (1977) by lethal injection.

Religion. The chief religious bodies in 1979 were Southern Baptists, 659,152; United Methodists, 250,878; Churches of Christ, 80,000; Roman Catholics, 117,563; Disciples of Christ, 46,198; Presbyterian, 39,644; Episcopal, 21,500; Assembly of God, 60,596; Lutheran, 30,536; Nazarene, 21,985.

Education. In 1979–80 there were 583,458 pupils enrolled in elementary and secondary schools, 37,751 teachers at elementary schools and secondary schools had average salaries of $13,668. Total expenditure on public schools (1978–79), $1,100m.

Approximately 75,000 of the 623,000 school age children are handicapped and in need of special education. In 1979–80, there were 3,156 special education units with 60,997 students in class.

The University of Oklahoma (founded at Norman in 1890) had 608 full-time faculty and 19,810 enrolled students in spring 1980; Oklahoma State University of Agriculture and Applied Science (founded in 1890 at Stillwater) had 696 full-time faculty and 20,088 students; Central State University (founded at Edmond in 1890) had 306 full-time faculty and 10,333 students. There are 10 other institutions of higher learning in the state system at the senior level and 14 junior colleges. Total enrolment in institutions of higher education, spring 1980, 146,118.

Health. In 1980 there were 133 hospitals (13,302 beds). In 1980 institutions for mentally retarded had 1,909 inmates; the schools for deaf and blind had 259 children, 3 schools for delinquents, 833 children, 2 children's homes, 711 children and 1 diagnostic and evaluation centre, 546 children.

Social Security. Public assistance, financial year 1980 was being drawn by 146,203 persons, receiving an average monthly payment of $919. This includes old age assistance, aid to families with dependent children, AFDC emergency, AFDC foster home care, aid to the blind and aid to the disabled. Medical payments were made for 223,733 persons, totalled $281·7m. and averaged $1,259.10 per person. Nursing-home service was provided for 26,534 persons at an average of $5,374.54 per person. Non-technical medical care was provided for 10,569 persons at an average of $1,636.49 per person. A total of $25,709,790 was spent for vocational rehabilitation.

Books of Reference

Directory, of Oklahoma. State Election Board, Oklahoma City
Chronicles of Oklahoma. State Historical Society, Oklahoma City (from 1921)
Statistical Abstract of Oklahoma, 1978. Centres for Economic and Management Research, Univ. of Oklahoma, Norman, 1978
Dale, E. E., and Aldrich, G., *History of Oklahoma.* New York, 1969
Debo, Angie, *Oklahoma.* Norman, 1949
McReynolds, Edwin C., *Oklahoma: A History of the Sooner State.* Rev. ed. Univ. of Oklahoma, Norman, 1964
Morgan, H. W., and Morgan, A. H., *Oklahoma: A Bicentennial History.* New York, 1977
Ruth, K., et al., eds., *Oklahoma: A Guide to the Sooner State.* Rev. ed. Univ. of Oklahoma, Norman, 1957
Strain, J. W., *Outline of Oklahoma Government.* Central State Univ., Edmond, 1978

State Library: Oklahoma Dept. of Libraries, 200 N.E. 18th Street, Oklahoma City 73105. *State Librarian and State Archivist:* Robert L. Clark, Jr.

OREGON

HISTORY. Oregon was first settled in 1811 by the Pacific Fur Co. at Astoria, a provisional government was formed on 5 July 1834; a Territorial government was organized, 14 Aug. 1848, and on 14 Feb. 1859 Oregon was admitted to the Union.

AREA AND POPULATION. Oregon is bounded north by Washington, with the Columbia River forming most of the boundary, east by Idaho, with the Snake River forming most of the boundary, south by Nevada and California and west by the Pacific. Area, 96,981 sq. miles, 797 sq. miles being inland water. The federal government owned (1976) 32,370,216 acres (52·55% of the state area). Census population, 1 April 1980 (preliminary), 2,632,663, an increase of 541,278 or 26% since 1970. In 1977 resident births numbered 37,467 (15·6 per 1,000 population); deaths, 20,457 (8·5); infant deaths (deaths within the first year of life), 453 (12·1 per 1,000 live births); marriages, 20,303 (8·5), and divorces, 16,372 (6·8). Five maternal deaths took place in 1977.

Population at 5 federal censuses (with distribution by sex, 1970) was:

	White	Negro	Indian	Asiatic	Total	Per sq. mile
1910	655,090	1,492	5,090	11,093	672,765	7·0
1930	938,598	2,234	4,776	8,179	953,786	9·9
1950	1,497,128	11,529	5,820	6,864	1,521,341	15·8
1960	1,732,037	18,133	8,026	9,120	1,768,687	18·4
1970	2,032,079	26,308	13,510	13,290	2,091,385	—
Male	994,500	13,188	6,576	6,581	1,023,952	—
Female	1,037,579	13,120	6,934	6,709	1,067,433	—

Of the total population in 1970, 1,402,704 persons (67·1%) were urban (62·2% in 1960). Those 21 years and older numbered 1,284,174; 65 years and older, 226,799.

The US Bureau of Indian Affairs (area headquarters in Portland) administers (1976) 742,151·74 acres, of which 597,222·94 acres are held by the US in trust for Indian tribes, and 144,928·8 acres for individual Indians.

The largest towns, according to 1980 census figures (and 1979 estimates), are: Portland, 364,246; Eugene, 104,673; Salem (the capital), 89,161; Corvallis, (41,750); Medford, (38,550); Springfield, (40,950); Beaverton, (28,100); Albany, (26,200).

CONSTITUTION AND GOVERNMENT. The present constitution dates from 1859; some 80 items in it have been amended. The Legislative Assembly consists of a Senate of 30 members, elected for 4 years (half their number retiring every 2 years), and a House of 60 representatives, elected for 2 years. The Governor is elected for 4 years. The constitution reserves to the voters the rights of initiative and referendum and recall. In Nov. 1912 suffrage was extended to women.

The state sends to Congress 2 senators and 5 representatives.

In the 1980 presidential election Reagan polled 571,044 votes, Carter 456,890 and Anderson 112,389.

The capital is Salem. There are 36 counties in the state.

Governor: Victor Atiyeh (R.), 1979–83 ($53,394 plus $1,000 monthly for expenses).

Secretary of State: Norma Paulus (R.), 1977–81 ($43,949).

BUDGET. Oregon has 2-year financial periods. General revenues for the biennium 1979–81 were $13,700,529,247 (federal funds, $1,216m.); general expenditures, $10,092,696,424 (education, $2,150·43m.; economic development and consumer services, $3,414m.; human resources, $2,195m.).

On 14 Oct. 1980 the outstanding bonded debt was $4,856,136,000.

Per capita personal income (1979) was $8,938.

ENERGY AND NATURAL RESOURCES

Electricity. Four privately owned utilities, 11 municipally owned utilities, 16 co-operatives and 4 utility districts provide electricity in the state. The privately owned companies serve 73·45% of the electricity. Private utilities sold 25,014,195,957 kwh. of electric power in 1979.

A federal agency, the Bonneville Power Administration, also markets electric power from 30 federal dams in the Pacific Northwest to 160 public and private utilities and large industrial plants. The dams, which are operated by the Army

Corps of Engineers or the Bureau of Reclamation, had on 31 Dec. 1979 a total generating capacity of 17,926,788 kw. The Bonneville transmission network now covers the states of Oregon, Washington, Idaho, Western Montana, and parts of California, Nevada, Utah and Wyoming.

Minerals. Oregon's mineral resources include gold, silver, copper, lead, mercury, chromite, sand and gravel, stone, clays, lime, silica, diatomite, expansible shale, scoria, pumice and uranium. There is geothermal potential. Oregon is the only state producing nickel in the US. Value of mineral products, 1978, was $123m.

Agriculture. Oregon, which has an area of 61,557,184 acres, is divided by the Cascade Range into two distinct zones as to climate. West of the Cascade Range there is a good rainfall and almost every variety of crop common to the temperate zone is grown; east of the Range stock-raising and wheat-growing are the principal industries and irrigation is needed for row crops and fruits. In 1975 there were 2·18m. acres under irrigation

There were, in 1979, 30,000 farms with an acreage of 18·6m. (30·29% of the land area), including (1974) 5·3m. acres of total crop land; average farm size in 1979 was 622 acres; most are family-owned corporate farms.

Cash receipts from crops in 1978 amounted to $812·7m., and from livestock and livestock products, $455·6m. Principal crops are hay, wheat, potatoes, peppermint, ryegrass seed, pears, onions, snap beans, sweet corn and barley.

Livestock, 1 July 1980: Milch cows, 93,000; cattle and calves, 1·5m.; sheep and lambs, 350,000; swine, 100,000.

In 1979 the wool clip yielded 3·8m. lb.

Forestry. About 29·8m. acres is forested, almost half of the state. Of this amount, 24·2m. is commercial forest land suitable for timber production; ownership is as follows (million acres): US Forestry service, 11·6 (48%); Forest Industry, 5 (22·8%); Small non-industrial landowners, 3·6 (14·7%); US Bureau of Land Management, 2·2 (9%); State of Oregon, 820,000 acres (3·4%) and other owners (city, county, Indian), 496,000 acres (2·1%). Oregon's commercial forest lands provide an annual harvest of 7,800m. board feet of logs, as well as the benefits of recreation, water, grazing, wildlife and fish. Trees vary from the coastal forest of hemlock and spruce to the state's primary species, Douglas-fir, throughout much of western Oregon. In eastern Oregon, ponderosa pine, lodgepole pine and true firs are found. Here, forestry is often combined with livestock grazing to provide an economic operation. Along the Cascade summit and in the mountains of northeast Oregon, alpine species are found. Forest products manufacturing is Oregon's leading industry, and provides for 20% of the country's softwood lumber needs, 40% of its plywood and more than 25% of the hardboard. More than one-third of the economy depends directly or indirectly on timber industries; about 85,000 (1980) people are employed, the annual value of primary production is $4,420m., the payroll is $1,500m.

Fisheries. All food and shellfish landings in the calendar year 1978 amounted to 135,043,614 lb., valued at $55·5m., including salmon, 8,704,892 lb. ($11·62m.); tuna, 18·4m. lb. ($10·3m.); crabs, 12,502,137 lb. ($9·6m.); bottom fish, 37,056,208 lb. ($8m.); shrimp, 57m. lb. ($14·9m.).

INDUSTRY. During 1978, 5,696 manufacturing establishments reported to the Employment Division, average annual employment, 1978, 219,600 with pay of $3,359m.; value added by manufacture (1976), $5,392m.

TOURISM. In 1979, 13,520,033 out-of-state cars visited Oregon; the total 1979 income from tourism was estimated to be $1,082m.

COMMUNICATIONS

Roads. The state maintains (1980) 7,562 miles of primary and secondary highways, almost all surfaced; counties maintain 29,004 miles, and cities 7,391 miles; there were 79,436 miles in national parks and federal reservations. Registered motor vehicles, 31 Dec. 1979, totalled 2·5m.

Railways. The state had (1980) 19 common carrier railways with a total mileage of 4,428.

Aviation. In Oct. 1980 there were 5 public-use and 71 personal-use heliports; 4 public-use seaplane bases; 205 personal-use airports; 108 public-use airports including 37 state-owned airports.

Shipping. Portland is a major seaport for large ocean-going vessels and is 101 miles inland from the mouth of the Columbia River.

Post and Broadcasting. In Dec. 1980 there were 129 commercial radio stations and 13 educational radio stations. There were 12 commercial television stations and 6 educational television stations. There were also 5 campus limited radio stations and 1 subscription radio station.

Newspapers. In 1980 there were 21 daily newspapers with a circulation of 699,713 and 89 non-daily newspapers with a circulation of 349,849.

JUSTICE, RELIGION, EDUCATION AND WELFARE

Justice. There are 3 correctional institutions in Oregon, all in Salem. The Oregon State Penitentiary, on 1 Nov. 1980, held 1,682 males; the Women's Correctional Center had a resident population of 62; and the Oregon Correctional Institution, which is for first offenders, had a population of 747. The Oregon Correctional Division's Release Center in Salem held 190 inmates, 112 inmates were held in Oregon State Hospital wards and 329 inmates were on temporary leave or work release.

The sterilization law, originally passed in 1917, was amended in 1967. The amendments changed the number of persons on the Board of Social Protection from 15 to 7 and provided that the Public Defender would automatically represent all persons examined. The bases on which a person would be subject to examination by the Board are: (a) if such person would be likely to procreate children having an inherited tendency to mental retardation or mental illness, or (b) if such person would be likely to procreate children who would become neglected or dependent because of the person's inability by reason of mental illness or mental retardation to provide adequate care. Up to 1 July 1979, 941 men and 1,741 women have been sterilized.

Religion. The chief religious bodies are Catholic, Baptist, Lutheran, Methodists, Presbyterian and Mormon. Total membership, all denominations, 691,085 in 1971.

Education. School attendance is compulsory from 7 to 18 years of age if the twelfth year of school has not been completed; those between the ages of 16 and 18 years, if legally employed, may attend part-time or evening schools. Others may be excused under certain circumstances. On 30 June 1980 the 965 public elementary schools, 79 junior high schools and 232 standard senior high schools had 30,481 administrators and teachers; net enrolment was 494,635 (excluding transfers between districts), of whom 157,726 were high school pupils. Average salary for all classroom teachers, 1979–80, was $16,266. Total expenditure on elementary and secondary education (1979–80) was $1,380m.

Leading state-supported institutions of higher education (1980–81) included:

	Teachers	Students
University of Oregon, Eugene	878	17,488
University of Oregon Health Sciences Center:		
Medical School, Portland	364	1,502
Dental School, Portland		
Oregon State University, Corvallis	888	17,707
Portland State University, Portland	567	16,854
Oregon College of Education, Monmouth	163	3,150
Southern Oregon College, Ashland	216	4,760
Eastern Oregon College, La Grande	82	1,804
Oregon Institute of Technology, Klamath Falls	143	2,700

Largest of the privately endowed universities are Lewis and Clark College, Portland, with 1980–81, 3,188 students; University of Portland, 2,746 students; Willamette University, Salem, 1,886 students; Reed College, Portland, 1,132 students, and

Linfield College, McMinnville, 1,242 students. There are 13 community colleges and 1 area education district with an estimated enrolment of 275,000 students in 1980–81.

Health. In Oct. 1979 there were 97 licensed hospitals (11,496 beds) and 190 nursing homes with 16,147 beds. In Oct. 1979 there were 4 state hospitals for mentally ill and mentally retarded (2 for mentally ill, 1 for mentally retarded and 1 with both programmes). The average for the mentally ill in Oct. 1979 was 1,151 and for the mentally retarded 1,738.

Social Security. Old-age assistance is provided for all needy persons 65 years or older who meet certain eligibility requirements. In financial year 1979–80, 3,598 cases per month received average payments of $5.36 cash and $87.54 services. For the same period 98,278 persons in 36,166 families with dependent children received an average $279.74 per month; 552 blind recipients $38.56 cash and $62.52 services; 7,009 disabled $15.94 cash and $41.86 services; 4,501 general assistance cases $134.73 cash and $5.45 services.

Medical assistance and mental health costs averaged $14,494,000 per month.

A system of unemployment benefit payments, financed by employers, with administrative allotments made through a federal agency, started 2 Jan. 1938, and covers about 66,500 employers with average employment in 1979 of 1,024,535. By June 1980, $1,717m. in taxes had been paid into the trust fund plus $297·3m. in interest and reimbursed benefits. About $1,691m. has been paid in benefits which from July 1980 range from $38 to $138 weekly and up to $3,588 per year. About 38,406 state employees, 48,060 school employees, 5,507 community college employees and 18,879 political subdivision employees are participants in the public employees retirement programme. The same employees are covered under the federal old-age, survivors and disability insurance programme. Approximately 31,016 retired employees are receiving monthly benefit cheques.

Books of Reference

Oregon Blue Book. Issued by the Secretary of State. Salem. Biennial
Federal Writers' Project. *Oregon: End of the Trail.* Rev. ed. Portland, 1972
Atkeson, R., *Oregon.* Portland, 1968.—*Oregon Coast.* Portland, 1972
Baldwin, E. M. *Geology of Oregon.* Rev. ed. Dubuque, Iowa, 1976
Berry, J., *Profile of Oregon Churches.* Portland, 1963
Carey, C. H. *General History of Oregon, prior to 1861.* 2 vol. (1 vol. reprint, 1971) Portland, 1935
Corning, H. M. (ed.), *Dictionary of Oregon History.* New York, 1956
Dicken, S. N., *Oregon Geography.* 5th ed. Eugene, 1973.—with Dicken, E. F., *Making of Oregon: a Study in Historical Geography.* Portland, 1979
Dodds, G. B. *Oregon: A Bicentennial History.* New York, 1977
Friedman, R., *Oregon for the Curious.* 3rd ed. Portland, 1972
Highsmith, R. M. Jr. (ed.), *Atlas of the Pacific Northwest.* 5th ed. Corvallis, 1973
McArthur, L. A., *Oregon Geographic Names.* 4th ed., rev. and enlarged. Portland, 1974
Patton, Clyde P., *Atlas of Oregon.* Univ. Oregon Press, Eugene, 1976

State Library: The Oregon State Library, Salem. *Librarian:* Marcia Lowell.

PENNSYLVANIA

HISTORY. Pennsylvania, first settled in 1682, is one of the 13 original states in the Union.

AREA AND POPULATION. Pennsylvania is bounded north by New York, east by New Jersey, south by Delaware and Maryland, south-west by West Virginia, west by Ohio and north-west by Lake Erie. Area, 45,333 sq. miles, of which 399 sq. miles are inland water. Census population, 1 April 1980 preliminary, 11,824,561, an increase of 23,795 or 0·2% since 1970. Births, 1978, 151,438; deaths, 119,279; infant deaths, 2,031; marriages, 92,682; divorces, 38,261.

Population at 5 census years (with distribution by sex, 1970) was:

	White	Negro	Indian	All others	Total	Per sq. mile
1910	7,467,713	193,919	1,503	1,976	7,665,111	171·0
1930	9,196,007	431,257	523	3,563	9,631,350	213·8
1950	9,853,848	638,485	1,141	4,538	10,498,012	233·1
1960	10,454,004	852,750	2,122	10,490	11,319,366	251·5

			All others		
1970	10,744,515	1,016,561	32,843	11,793,909	262·3
Male	5,172,655	475,986	15,405	5,664,046	—
Female	5,591,860	540,565	17,438	6,129,863	—

Of the total population in 1970, 8,430,410 persons (71·5%) were urban (71·6% in 1960); 7,358,942 were 21 years of age or older.

The population of the larger cities and townships, 1980 census, was:

Philadelphia	1,680,235	Reading	78,582	Harrisburg	53,113
Pittsburgh	423,962	Bethlehem	70,389	Wilkes-Barre	51,117
Erie	103,634	Altoona	57,000	York	44,464
Scranton	87,378	Lancaster	54,632		

Larger urbanized areas, 1980 census: Philadelphia (in Pennsylvania), 3,665,034; Pittsburgh, 2,260,669; Northeast, 629,979, Allentown–Bethlehem–Easton (in Pennsylvania), 549,700; Harrisburg, 447,265.

CONSTITUTION AND GOVERNMENT. The present constitution dates from 1968. The General Assembly consists of a Senate of 50 members chosen for 4 years, one-half being elected biennially, and a House of Representatives of 203 members chosen for 2 years. The Governor and Lieut.-Governor are elected for 4 years. Every citizen 18 years of age, with the usual residential qualifications, may vote. The state sends to Congress 2 senators and 23 representatives.

In the 1980 presidential election Reagan polled 2,261,872 votes, Carter 1,937,540 and Anderson 292,921.

The state capital is Harrisburg. The state is organized in counties (numbering 67), cities, boroughs, townships and school districts.

Governor: Richard Thornburgh (R.), 1979–83 ($66,000).
Lieut.-Governor: William W. Scranton (R.) ($49,500).

BUDGET. Total revenues for the year ending 30 June 1980 were $6,391·3m.; general fund expenditure, $6,357·4m. (education, $2,975·0m.; transport, $163·7m.; public welfare, $2,155·6m.; environment, $84m.).

On 30 June 1980 total net direct long-term debt amounted to $4,642m.

Per capita personal income (1979) was $8,558.

ENERGY AND NATURAL RESOURCES

Minerals. Pennsylvania is almost the sole producer of anthracite coal; its output reached a peak of 100,445,299 short tons in 1917 with a labour-force of 156,148 men. Production in 1979: Anthracite, 5·0m. tons, with 3,472 men; bituminous coal, 80·3m. tons, with 39,230 men; crude petroleum (1979), 2·6m. bbls; natural gas (1978), 97,763m. cu. ft. Total value of other minerals produced (1978), $590·4m., including $261m. for cement.

Agriculture. Agriculture, market-gardening, fruit-growing, horticulture and forestry are pursued within the state. In 1979 there were 61,000 farms with a total farm area of 9m. acres (4·5m. acres in crops); the average farm was 148 acres with average value per acre of $1,267. Cash income, 1979, from crops, $747m., and from livestock, $1,800m.

Pennsylvania ranks high in the production of tobacco (17·7m. lb., 1979) value $12·7m. and leads in mushrooms (213·8m. lb., value $159·2m.). Other crops are winter wheat (8·12m. bu.), oats (18·4m. bu.), maize (115·4m. bu.), barley (5·4m. bu.) and potatoes (6·0m. cwt). On 1 Jan. 1980 there were on farms: 1·9m. cattle and calves, including 712,000 milch cows, 85,000 sheep, 870,000 swine. Milk production,

1979, was 8,080m. lb. valued at $1,040m., and eggs numbered 3,840m. valued at $178·1m. Pennsylvania is also a major fruit producing state; in 1979 apples totalled 505m. lb.; peaches, 90m. lb.; tart cherries, 6·3m. lbs., and grapes, 55,500 tons. Other important items are soybeans (2m. bu.), vegetables for processing (97,900 tons), fresh vegetables (1·4m. cwt) and broiler-chickens (109·2m.).

Forestry. In 1979 national forest lands totalled 508,480 acres; state forests, 2,047,410 acres; state parks, 296,119 acres; state game land, 1,222,773 acres; game land leased but not owned by the state, 2,102,927 acres (co-operative and safety-zone pro-grammes).

INDUSTRY. Pennsylvania leads in the production of iron and steel. Output of steel, 1978, 28·1m. net tons and of pig-iron, 18·2m. net tons.

In 1978, 16,269 manufacturing establishments employed 1,246,027 workers (wages, $16,180m.); value added by manufacture was $34,402m.

COMMUNICATIONS

Roads. Highways and roads in the state (federal, local and state combined) totalled (1979) 118,495 miles. Registered motor vehicles for 1979 numbered 7,387,590 (includ-ing 5,620,785 passenger cars, 1,408,984 trucks, truck-tractors and trailers).

Railways. In Jan. 1978, 29 railways operated within the state with a line mileage of 7,788.

Aviation. There were (1979) 161 commercial airports, 3 public landing strips, 211 heliports and 370 airports for personal use.

Shipping. Trade at Delaware River ports (1978, short tons) imports, 69·4m., exports, 5·3m. Trade at Erie ports (1979): imports 130,630 tons, exports 25,257 tons.

Post and Broadcasting. Broadcasting stations comprised (1978) 37 television stations and 285 radio stations.

Newspapers. There were (1978) 116 daily and 322 weekly newspapers.

JUSTICE, RELIGION, EDUCATION AND WELFARE

Justice. No executions took place in 1963–80; since 1930 there have been 149 execu-tions (electrocution), all for murder.

State prison population, on 31 Dec. 1979, was 8,203.

Religion. The chief religious bodies in 1977 were the Roman Catholic, with 3,717,667 members; Protestant, 3,150,920 (1971); and Jewish, 469,078. The 5 largest Protestant denominations (by communicants) were: Lutheran Church in America, 766,276; United Methodist, 728,915 (1971), United Presbyterian Church in the USA, 573,905 (1971); United Church of Christ, 257,138; Episcopal, 193,399 (1971).

Education. School attendance is compulsory for children 8–17 years of age. In 1979–80 the public kindergartens and elementary schools had 968,325 pupils; secondary schools had 1,000,476 pupils. Non-public schools had 285,514 elementary pupils and 114,441 secondary pupils. Average salary, public school professional personnel, men $18,529; women $16,244; for classroom teachers, men $17,235, women $16,002.

Leading senior academic institutions (autumn, 1979) included:

Founded	Institutions	Faculty [1]	Students [2]
1740	University of Pennsylvania (non-sect.)	964	22,006
1787	University of Pittsburgh	1,508	34,010
1832	Lafayette College, Easton (Presbyterian)	156	2,348
1842	Villanova University (R.C.)	398	9,978
1846	Bucknell University (Baptist)	205	3,255
1851	St Joseph's College, Philadelphia (RC)	123	5,471
1852	California State College	307	4,387
1855	Pennsylvania State University	2,369	59,803
1855	Millersville State College	303	6,195
1863	LaSalle College, Philadelphia (R.C.)	184	6,777
1866	Lehigh University, Bethlehem (non-sect.)	321	6,291
1871	West Chester State College	468	8,599

Founded	Institutions	Faculty[1]	Students[2]
1875	Indiana University of Pennsylvania	554	12,145
1878	Duquesne University, Pittsburgh (R.C.)	279	6,752
1884	Temple University, Philadelphia	1,363	33,593
1885	Bryn Mawr College	125	1,712
1888	University of Scranton (R.C.)	144	4,434
1891	Drexel University, Philadelphia	292	11,153
1900	Carnegie–Mellon University, Pittsburgh	423	5,515

[1] Full-time instructional.　　　[2] Total enrolments.

Health. In 1979 the state had 231 hospitals (52,310 beds) listed by the State Health Department, excluding federal hospitals and mental institutions. In 1978 the 32 mental hospitals had 11,079 patients (94 per 100,000 population); 60 institutions for the mentally retarded, 10,934 (93).

Social Security. During the year ending 30 June 1979 the monthly average number of cases receiving public assistance was: aid to families with dependent children, 631,510; blind persons, 5,474; general assistance, 154,333.

Payments for medical assistance for the year ending 30 June 1979 totalled $1,189·8m. Under the medical assistance programme payments are made for inpatient hospital care ($398·2m.); nursing care in home ($2m.); care in public institutions (nursing homes, mental institutions and geriatric centres) ($454·9m.); private nursing home care ($105·7m.); other medical care ($229m.).

Books of Reference

Pennsylvania Manual. Dept. of Property and Supplies, Division of Documents. Harrisburg. Biennial
Pennsylvania's Regions, A Survey of the Commonwealth. State Planning Board. Harrisburg, 1967
Pennsylvania Statistical Abstract. Dept. of Commerce, Harrisburg. Annual
Pennsylvania State Industrial Directory. New York. Annual
Carstens, A. H., *What to See in Pennsylvania.* 2nd ed. Cresco, 1965
Klein, P. S., and Hoogenboom, A., *A History of Pennsylvania.* New York, 1973
League of Women Voters of Pennsylvania, *Key to the Keystone State.* Philadelphia, 1972
Pennsylvania Chamber of Commerce, *Pennsylvania Government Today.* State College, Pa., 1973
Stevens, S. K., *Pennsylvania: Birthplace of a Nation.* New York, 1964.—*Exploring Pennsylvania: Geography History, Civics.* 3rd ed. New York, 1968
Wallace, P. A. W., *Pennsylvania: Seed of a Nation.* New York, 1962
Wilkinson, N. B., *Bibliography of Pennsylvania History.* Pa. Historical & Museum Commission. Harrisburg, 1957

RHODE ISLAND

HISTORY. The earliest settlers in the region which now forms the state of Rhode Island were colonists from Massachusetts who had been driven forth on account of their non-acceptance of the prevailing religious beliefs. The first of the settlements was made in 1636, settlers of every creed being welcomed. In 1647 a patent was granted for the government of the settlements, and on 8 July 1663 a charter was executed recognizing the settlers as forming a body corporate and politic by the name of the 'English Colony of Rhode Island and Providence Plantations, in New England, in America'. On 29 May 1790 the state accepted the federal constitution and entered the Union as the last of the 13 original states.

AREA AND POPULATION. Rhode Island is bounded north and east by Massachusetts, south by the Atlantic and west by Connecticut. Area, 1,214 sq. miles, of which 165 sq. miles are inland water. Census population, 1 April 1980 (preliminary), 947,154 a decrease of 0·26% since 1970.

Births, 1978, were 11,515; deaths (excluding foetal deaths), 8,847; infant deaths 158; marriages 7,277; divorces 3,475.

Population of 5 census years was:

	White	Negro	Indian	Asiatic	Total	Per sq. mile
1910	532,492	9,529	284	305	542,610	508·5
1930	677,026	9,913	318	240	687,497	649·3
1950	777,015	13,903		978	791,896	748·5
1960	838,712	18,332	932	1,190	859,488	812·4
1970	914,757	25,338	1,390	5,240	949,723 [1]	905·0

[1] Through tabulation errors there were 2,998 people unaccounted for, as to race and sex, in 1970.

Of the total population in 1970, 824,930 persons (86·9%) were urban (86·4% in 1960); 590,876 were 21 years of age or older.

The chief cities and their population (census, 1980) are Providence, 156,421; Warwick, 87,064; Cranston, 72,034; Pawtucket, 71,033; East Providence, 50,960. Others (1970); Woonsocket, 46,820; Newport, 34,562; North Kingstown (town), 29,793; Middletown (town), 29,290. The Providence–Pawtucket–Warwick Standard Metropolitan Statistical Area had a population of 914,110 in 1970.

CONSTITUTION AND GOVERNMENT. The present constitution dates from 1843; it has had 36 amendments. The General Assembly consists (1978) of a Senate of 50 members and a House of Representatives of 100 members, both elected for 2 years, as are also the Governor and Lieut.-Governor. Every citizen, 18 years of age, who has resided in the state for 30 days, and is duly registered, is qualified to vote.

Rhode Island sends to Congress 2 senators and 2 representatives.

At the 1980 presidential election Carter polled 198,342 votes, Reagan, 154,793.

The capital is Providence. The state has 5 counties (unique in having no political functions) and 39 cities and towns.

Governor: J. Joseph Garrahy (D.), 1979–81 ($42,500).
Lieut.-Governor: Thomas R. Diluglio (D.) 1979–81 ($25,500).
Secretary of State: Robert F. Burns (D.), 1979–81 ($25,500).

BUDGET. For the fiscal year ending 30 June 1979 (Office of the State Controller) general revenues were $881·4m. (taxation, $528·2m., and federal aid, $234·8m.); general expenditures were $864·7m. (education, $238·1m.; highways, $51·6m.; and public welfare, $264·5m.).

Total net long-term debt on 30 June 1978 was $235·6m.

Per capita personal income (1978) was $7,526.

NATURAL RESOURCES

Minerals. The small mineral output, mostly stone, sand and gravel, was valued (1978) at $6m.

Agriculture. While Rhode Island is predominantly a manufacturing state, agriculture contributed $26m. to the general cash income in 1977. In 1969 it had 700 farms with an area of 68,720 acres (10·2% of the total land area), of which 31,840 acres were crop land; the average farm was 98·1 acres, valued (land and buildings) at $72,033.

Fisheries. The number of commercial fishermen in the state in 1970 (US census) was 310; value of all fish landed in 1978, $29·3m.

INDUSTRY. Total civilian employment in 1979 was 406,500, of which 136,400 were manufacturing, 270,100 non-manufacturing. Manufacturing firms totalled 3,344; average weekly earnings for production workers in manufacturing, $183.22; value added by manufacture (1976), $2,295m. Principal industries are metals and machinery, textiles and jewellery–silverware.

COMMUNICATIONS

Roads. The state had (1 Jan. 1978) 5,758 miles of road, of which 1,313 were state-owned. In 1978, 605,000 motor vehicles were registered.

Railways. In 1977, 6 railways operated 135 line-miles.

Aviation. Of the 12 airports in 1979, 7 were state-owned and 5 privately owned. Theodore Francis Green airport at Warwick, near Providence, is served by 5 airlines, and handled 999,594 passengers and 16m. lb. of freight in 1978.

Shipping. Waterborne freight through the Port of Providence (1979) totalled 7·8m. tons.

Broadcasting. There are 22 radio stations and 4 television stations in the state.

JUSTICE, RELIGION, EDUCATION AND WELFARE

Justice. The state's penal institutions, Nov. 1979, had 675 inmates (70 per 100,000 population).

The death penalty is illegal, except that it is mandatory in the case of murder committed by a prisoner serving a life sentence.

Religion. Chief religious bodies are (estimated figures Sept. 1975): Roman Catholic with 597,000 members; Protestant Episcopal (baptized persons), 50,000; Baptist, 22,500; Congregational, 12,000; Methodist, 10,000; Jewish, 24,000.

Education. The school census of 1974 showed 302,155 persons under 20 years of age; at the 1970 US census approximately 70% were attending school. In 1977–78 the 277 public elementary schools had 4,798 teachers and total enrolment of 82,119 pupils; about 15,000 pupils were enrolled in private and parochial schools. The 73 senior and vocational high schools had 4,343 teachers and 74,885 pupils. Teachers' salaries (1977–78) averaged $13,660. Local expenditure, for schools (including evening schools) in 1977–78 totalled $279·8m.

There are 11 institutions of higher learning in the state, including 1 junior college. The state maintains Rhode Island College, at Providence, with 800 faculty members, and 8,800 full-time students (1977), and the University of Rhode Island, at South Kingstown, with over 850 faculty members and over 14,000 students (including graduate students). Brown University, at Providence, founded in 1764, is now non-sectarian; in 1977 it had over 500 full-time faculty members and 6,700 full-time students. Providence College, at Providence, founded in 1917 by the Order of Preachers (Dominican), had (1977) 218 professors and 3,800 students. The largest of the other colleges are Bryant College, at Smithfield, with 125 faculty and over 4,800 students, and the Rhode Island School of Design, in Providence, with about 100 faculty and 1,400 students.

Health. In 1978 the state had 24 hospitals (over 7,000 beds), including 4 mental hospitals.

Social Security. In Oct. 1978 aid to dependent children was being granted to 35,373 children in 17,186 families (52,559 persons), $264.06 per month, and general assistance to 7,119 persons at an average of $187.48 per month. (All other aid programmes were taken over by the federal government.)

Books of Reference

Rhode Island Manual. Prepared by the Secretary of State. Providence
An Introduction to the Economy of Rhode Island. Issue by the Rhode Island Development Council. Providence, 1953
Providence Journal Almanac: A Reference Book for Rhode Islanders. Providence. Annual
Rhode Island Basic Economic Statistics. Rhode Island Dept. of Economic Development. Providence, 1972

State Library: Rhode Island State Library, State House, Providence 02908. *State Librarian:* Elliott E. Andrews.

SOUTH CAROLINA

HISTORY. South Carolina, first settled permanently in 1670, was one of the 13 original states of the Union.

AREA AND POPULATION. South Carolina is bounded in the north by North Carolina, east and south-east by the Atlantic, south-west and west by Georgia. Area, 31,055 sq. miles. Census population, 1 April 1980 preliminary, 3,068,000, an increase of 18·4% since 1970. Births, 1978, were 49,548 (16·9 per 1,000 population); deaths, 24,058 (8·4); infant deaths, 919 (18·5 per 1,000 live births); marriages, 52,969 (17·8); divorces and annulments, 11,901 (3·7).

The population in 5 census years (with distribution by sex, 1970) was:

	White	Negro	Indian	Asiatic	Total	Per sq. mile
1910	679,161	835,843	331	65	1,515,400	49·7
1930	944,049	793,681	959	76	1,738,765	56·8
1950	1,293,405	822,077	554	—	2,117,927	69·9
1960	1,551,022	829,291	1,098	946	2,382,594	78·7

	White	Negro	All others	Total	
1970	1,794,430	789,040	3,588	2,590,516	85·7
Male	891,573	376,912	3,602	1,272,087	—
Female	775,268	412,129	3,443	1,318,429	—

Of the total population in 1970, 1,232,195 persons (47·6%) were urban (41·2% in 1960); those 21 years old or older numbered 1,467,299.

Populations of large towns at the 1970 census (with those of associated metropolitan areas): Columbia (capital), 113,542 (322,880); Charleston, 66,945 (303,849); Greenville, 61,208 (299,502); Spartanburg, 44,546; Rock Hill, 33,846; Anderson, 27,556. Estimated population of the metropolitan areas, 1980: Greenville–Spartanburg, 562,179; Charleston, 415,552; Columbia, 394,849.

CONSTITUTION AND GOVERNMENT. The present constitution dates from 1895, when it went into force without ratification by the electorate. The General Assembly consists of a Senate of 46 members, elected for 4 years (half retiring biennially), and a House of Representatives of 124 members, elected for 2 years. The Governor and Lieut.-Governor are elected for 4 years. Only registered citizens have the right to vote. South Carolina sends to Congress 2 senators and 6 representatives.

At the 1980 presidential election Reagan polled 441,841 votes, Carter 430,385 and Anderson 14,153.

The capital is Columbia.

Governor: Richard Riley (D.), 1979–83 ($60,000).
Secretary of State: John Tucker Campbell (D.) 1979–83 ($45,000).

BUDGET. For the fiscal year ending 30 June 1979 general revenues were $1,404m.; general expenditures were $1,360m.

On 30 June 1979 the total bonded debt was $561m.

Per capita personal income (1979) was $7,027.

NATURAL RESOURCES

Minerals. Non-metallic minerals are of chief importance: value of mineral output in 1978 was $176·4m., chiefly from cement, kaolin, clay, stone, sand and gravel, and vermiculite. South Carolina ranks second nationally in the production of kaolin and vermiculite. Commodities of minor importance produced include scrap mica, lime, feldspar, dimension stone and peat. Potentially economic reserves of phosphate and heavy minerals exist.

Agriculture. In 1978 there were 35,000 farms covering a farm area of 6·5m. acres. The average farm was of 186 acres. Of the 29,275 commercial farms of the 1974 census, there were 1,059 of 1,000 acres or more, average farm 211 acres; owners operated 18,589 farms; tenants 2,802. There were 1,502 farms with $100,000 or more in value of sales.

Cash receipts from farm marketing in 1979 amounted to $680m. for crops and $378m. for livestock. Chief crops are tobacco ($173m.), soybeans ($245m.), and corn ($62m.). Production, 1978: Cotton 115,000 lb.; peaches, 315,000 lb.; soybeans, 32m. bu.; tobacco, 150·5m. lb.; corn, 30·3m. bu. Value of production, 1978, $670m. Livestock on farms, 1978: 690,000 all cattle, 575,000 swine, 7·6m. poultry.

Forestry. The forest industry is important; state and private forest land (1978), 12·4m. acres. National forests amounted to 592,319 acres.

INDUSTRY. A monthly average of 400,931 workers were employed in manufacturing in 1979, earning $1,292m.; value added by manufacture (1977) was $8,095m.
Tourism is the second largest industry; tourists spend annually an estimated $1,700m.

COMMUNICATIONS

Roads. Total highway mileage in the combined highway system in 1979 was 39,116 miles. Motor vehicle registration numbered 2m. in 1979.

Railways. In 1979 the length of railway in the state was 3,003 miles.

Aviation. There were, 1979, 72 major airports and numerous others. There were 1,700 registered aircraft.

Shipping. The state has 3 deep-water ports.

JUSTICE, RELIGION, EDUCATION AND WELFARE

Justice. In June 1980 penal institutions held 8,176 inmates of whom 7,469 were in state prisons.

Education. In 1978–79 the total public-school enrolment was 627,446; there were 376,245 white pupils and 266,834 non-white pupils. The total number of teachers was 26,752; average salary was $11,526.
For higher education the state operates the University of South Carolina, founded at Columbia in 1801, with, 1980, 33,129 enrolled students; Clemson University, founded in 1889, with 11,327 students; The Citadel, at Charleston, with 3,353 students; Winthrop College, Rock Hill, with 4,640 students; Medical University of S. Carolina, at Charleston, with 2,489 students; S. Carolina State College, at Orangeburg, with 3,437 students, and Francis Marion College, at Florence, with 2,703 students; the College of Charleston has 5,164 students and Lander College, Greenwood, 1,694.
There are also 428 private kindergartens, elementary and high schools with total enrolment of 54,047 pupils, and 25 private and denominational colleges and junior colleges with enrolment of 25,514 students.

Health. In 1980 the state had 181 hospitals and nursing homes and 102 intermediate care institutions licensed by the South Carolina Department of Health and Environmental Control.

Social Security. In 1979 Social Security benefits totalling $1,155,981,000 were paid to 434,659 persons. In May 1980, supplemental social security benefits were paid to 83,215 blind, disabled and aged persons (total $9,660,701).

Books of Reference

Reports of the South Carolina State Development Board. Columbia. Annual
South Carolina Legislative Manual. Columbia. Annual
South Carolina Statistical Abstract, 1979. South Carolina Budget and Control Board, Columbia, 1979

State Library: South Carolina State Library, Columbia.

SOUTH DAKOTA

HISTORY. South Dakota was first visited by Europeans in 1743 when Verendrye planted a lead plate (discovered in 1913) on the site of Fort Pierre, claiming the region for the French crown. Beginning with a trading post in 1794, it was settled from 1857 to 1861 when Dakota Territory was organized. It was admitted into the Union on 2 Nov. 1889.

AREA AND POPULATION. South Dakota is bounded north by North Dakota, east by Minnesota, south-east by the Big Sioux River (forming the boundary with Iowa), south by Nebraska (with the Missouri River forming part of the boundary) and west by Wyoming and Montana. Area, 77,047 sq. miles, of which 1,092 sq. miles are water. Area administered by the Bureau of Indian Affairs, 1972, covered 4·96m. acres (10% of the state), of which 2,085,000 acres were held by tribes. The federal government, 1975, owned 3,296,012 acres or 6·743% of the total.

Census population, 1 April 1980 (preliminary), 690,178, an increase of 3·5% since 1970. Provisional estimate, July 1976, 685,993. Births, 1978, were 12,203 (17·7 per 1,000 population); deaths, 6,408 (9·4); infant deaths, 163 (13 per 1,000 live births); marriages, 10,638 (15·4); divorces, 2,449 (3·6).

Population in 5 federal censuses (with distribution by sex, 1970) was:

	White	Negro	Indian	Asiatic	Total	Per sq. mile
1910	563,771	817	19,137	163	583,888	7·6
1930	669,453	646	21,833	101	692,849	9·0
1950	628,504	727	23,344	165	652,720	8·5
1960	653,098	1,114	25,794	336	680,514	8·9
			All others			
1970	630,333	1,627	33,547		666,257	8·8
Male	312,588	994	16,801		330,383	—
Female	317,745	633	17,496		335,874	—

Of the total population in 1970, 297,030 persons (43·4%) were urban (39·3% in 1960); 386,371 were 21 years of age or older; foreign-born whites numbered 18,333, in 1960.

Population of the chief cities (census of 1980) was: Sioux Falls, 81,071; Rapid City, 46,340; Aberdeen, 25,973; Watertown, 15,632, Mitchell, 13,917; Brookings, 14,915; Huron, 13,000.

CONSTITUTION AND GOVERNMENT. Voters are all citizens 18 years of age or older who have complied with certain residential qualifications. The people reserve the right of the initiative and referendum. The Senate has 35 members, and the House of Representatives 70 members, all elected for 2 years; the Governor and Lieut.-Governor are elected for 4 years. The state sends 2 senators and 1 representative to Congress.

In the 1980 presidential election Reagan polled 198,343 votes, Carter 103,855 and Anderson 21,431.

The capital is Pierre (population, 1970, 9,700). The state is divided into 66 organized counties (and 2 whose status was under review in Sept. 1980).

Governor: William Janklow (R.), 1979–83 ($45,000).
Lieut.-Governor: Lowell Hansen, 1979–83 ($5,000–$8,000).
Secretary of State: Alice Kundert, 1979–83 ($30,000).

The salary of the Lieut.-Governor is $5,000 for 30-day legislative sessions (even years) and $8,000 for 45-day sessions (odd years).

BUDGET. For the fiscal year ending 30 June 1980 general revenues were $895·7m. and expenditures, $818·1m. Taxes and fees from state sources furnished $681·2m. and federal receipts $235m.

Per capita personal income (1977) was $5,957.

NATURAL RESOURCES

Minerals. The mineral products include gold (285,512 troy oz. in 1978, largest yield of all states), sand and gravel (6·2m. short tons), silver (54,000 troy oz.). Mineral products, 1978, were valued at $117·6m., of which gold accounts for $55·3m.

Agriculture. In 1974, 42,825 farms had an acreage of 46m.; the average farm had 1,074 acres. Farm units are large; at the 1974 census there were only 3,329 farms of 50 acres or less, compared with 10,533 exceeding 1,000 acres. 12,384 farms sold produce valued at $40,000 or over.

South Dakota ranks first in the US as producer of rye, second in flaxseed and fourth in durum wheat. The leading crops (1979) are oats (98·5m. bu.), maize (210·9m. bu.), wheat (60m. bu.) and barley (20m. bu.). The farm livestock on 1 Jan. 1980 included 4·0m. cattle, 783,000 sheep, 1·7m. swine (1975). There are 148,000 bee colonies.

Forestry. National forest area, 1975, 1,995,000 acres.

INDUSTRY. Food processing is by far the largest industry with an annual value of $116·9m., dairy, lumber and wood products, printing and publishing and non-electrical machinery are other major industries with the electronic components industry rapidly growing. In 1979, manufacturing establishments numbered 916 and had 27,124 workers who earned $342·3m.

COMMUNICATIONS

Roads. Total public road mileage was 72,627 in 1979. Registered passenger cars numbered 365,415, trucks, 197,622.

Railways. In 1979 the railways were 2,725 miles in length.

Aviation. Approved airports, 1979, numbered 84; approved private landing strips, 12.

JUSTICE, RELIGION, EDUCATION AND WELFARE

Justice. State prisons had, in 1980, 1096 inmates. The death penalty was illegal from 1915 to 1938; since 1938, one person has been executed, in 1949 (by electrocution), for murder.

Religion. The chief religious bodies are (1970): Lutherans with 162,243 members, Roman Catholics (138,250), Methodist (45,795), Disciples of Christ (22,374), Presbyterian (19,494), Baptist (16,055) and Episcopal (17,268).

Education. Elementary and secondary education are free from 6 to 21 years of age. Between the ages of 8 and 16, attendance is compulsory. In 1979 147,115 pupils were attending elementary and high (including parochial) schools (11,142 full-time equivalent classroom teachers).

Teachers' salaries (1978–79) averaged an estimated $11,418. Total expenditure on public schools (1978–79), $245·8m.

The School of Mines at Rapid City, established 1885, had, autumn 1980, 105 instructors and 2,393 students; the State University at Brookings, 374 instructors and 6,848 students; the University of South Dakota, founded at Vermillion in 1882, 327 instructors and 5,968 students; Northern State College, 122 instructors and 2,603 students; Black Hills State College, 111 instructors and 2,099 students; Dakota State College, 46 instructors and 1,000 students; University of South Dakota, Springfield, 58 instructors and 852 students. Seven public colleges had 1,142 instructors and 21,763 students. The Government maintains Indian schools on its reservations and 2 outside at Flandreau and Pierre.

Health. In 1979 the state Health Department listed 70 licensed hospitals (5,978 beds).

Social Security. In financial year 1980, a monthly average of 3,864 persons received as old-age assistance $3,586,572 in Supplemental Security Income; 129 blind persons received $232,278; 3,796 disabled, $5,512,746; 20,104 recipients, $18,277,803 in aid for dependent children.

State supplements to federal SSI payments were $19,942 to 65 aged; $3,052 to 6 blind; $27,455 to 77 disabled. Medical payments to the aged were $18,000,779; to the blind $139,480; to the disabled, $18,226,814. Food stamps (federal funds) were sold to 14,030 households monthly: total value, $16,557,754.

Books of Reference

Digest of Annual Reports, 1970–71 et seq. South Dakota Department of Administration. Annual

Governor's Budget Report. South Dakota Bureau of Finance and Management. Annual

South Dakota Facts: An Abstract of Statistics and Graphics Concerning the People and Resources of South Dakota. South Dakota State Planning Bureau, 1977

South Dakota Historical Collections. 1902–72

South Dakota Economic and Business Abstract, 1972. Business Research Bureau, University of S. Dakota. Vermillion, 1972

South Dakota Legislative Manual. Department of Finance, Pierre, S.D. Biennial

Karolevitz, Robert F., *Challenge: the South Dakota Story.* Sioux Falls, 1975

Milton, John R. *South Dakota; a Bicentennial History.* New York, W. W. Norton, 1977

Schell, H. S., *History of South Dakota.* 3rd ed. Lincoln, Neb., 1975

White, H. L. and B., *Who's Who for South Dakota.* Pierre, S.D., 1961

State Library: South Dakota State Library, State Library Building, Pierre, S.D., 57501. *State Librarian:* Clarence L. Coffindaffer.

TENNESSEE

HISTORY. Tennessee, first settled in 1757, was admitted into the Union on 1 June 1796.

AREA AND POPULATION. Tennessee is bounded north by Kentucky and Virginia, east by North Carolina, south by Georgia, Alabama and Mississippi and west by the Mississippi River (forming the boundary with Arkansas and Missouri). Area, 42,244 sq. miles (482 sq. miles water). Census population, 1 April 1980, 4,590,750, an increase of 667,063 or 17% since 1970. Vital statistics, 1978 (provisional): Births, 70,431 (16·2 per 1,000 population); deaths, 41,289 (9·5); infant deaths 1,134 (16·1 per 1,000 live births); marriages, 57,733 (13·3); divorces, 28,816 (6·6).

Population in 5 census years (with distribution by sex, 1970) was:

	White	Negro	Indian	Asiatic	Total	Per sq. mile
1910	1,711,432	473,088	216	53	2,184,789	52·4
1930	2,138,644	477,646	161	105	2,616,556	62·4
1950	2,760,257	530,603	339	334	3,291,718	78·8
1960	2,977,753	586,876	638	1,243	3,567,089	85·4

	White	Negro	All others		Total	Per sq. mile
1970	3,283,432	631,696	8,559		3,923,687	95·0
Male	1,596,572	296,221	4,142		1,896,935	—
Female	1,686,860	335,475	4,417		2,026,752	—

Of the population in 1970, 2,305,181 persons (58·7%) were urban (52·3% in 1960); those 20 years of age or older numbered 2,446,770.

The cities, with population, 1980, are Memphis, 644,838; Nashville (capital), 439,599; Jackson, 200,338; Knoxville, 182,161; Chattanooga, 165,328. Others, 1970: Kingsport, 31,938 (31,916); Oak Ridge, 28,319 (27,742). Standard metropolitan areas (1970): Memphis, 750,112 (1976 estimate, 773,200); Nashville, 699,271 (758,800); Knoxville, 409,409 (443,100); Chattanooga, 281,985 (295,500).

CONSTITUTION AND GOVERNMENT. The state has operated under 3 constitutions, the last of which was adopted in 1870 and has been since amended 22 times (first in 1953). Voters at an election may authorize the calling of a convention limited to altering or abolishing one or more specified sections of the constitution. The General Assembly consists of a Senate of 33 members and a House of Representatives of 99 members, senators elected for 4 years and representatives for 2 years. Qualified as electors are all citizens (with the usual residential and age (18) qualifications). Tennessee sends to Congress 2 senators and 9 representatives.

In the 1980 presidential election Reagan polled 787,761 votes, Carter 783,051 and Anderson 35,991.

For the Tennessee Valley Authority *see* pp. 1408.

The capital is Nashville. The state is divided into 95 counties.

Governor: Andrew Lamar Alexander (R.) 1979–83 ($30,000).
Secretary of State: Gentry Crowell (D.), ($20,000).

BUDGET. For 1976–77 total revenue was $4,295·2m. (taxation, $2,425m. general expenditure, $4,266·1m., included education, $1,027·8.; highways, $490·4m.; public welfare, $430·9m.; health and hospitals, $470·4m.

Total net long-term debt on 30 June 1974 amounted to $522·9m.

Per capita personal income (1977) was $5,785.

ENERGY AND NATURAL RESOURCES

Minerals. Coalfields cover about 5,000 sq. miles; output in 1975 was 8·2m. short tons valued at $140·3m. In 1975 Tennessee led the states in the production of clay (1·3m. short tons valued at $9m.), zinc (83,293 short tons) and pyrite and was an important producer of phosphate rock (2·3m. short tons). Other mineral products are copper, mica, cement, sand and gravel, limestone. Total value of mineral products in 1975 was $424·7m.

Agriculture. In 1978, 110,000 farms coverd 14·6m. acres. The average farm (1969) was of 124 acres (only a few states had a smaller average) valued land and buildings, at $24,178.

Cash income (1977) from crops was $757m.; from livestock, $868m. Main crops were cotton and tobacco.

On 1 Jan. 1976 the domestic animals included 212,000 milch cows, 2·7m. all cattle (1978), 17,000 sheep, 1·1m. swine (1978).

Forestry. Forests occupy 13,695,000 acres (52% of total land area). The forest industry and industries dependent on it employ about 40,000 workers, earning $150m. per year. Wood products are valued at over $500m. per year. National forest system land (1976) 620,000 acres.

INDUSTRY. The manufacturing industries include iron and steel working, but the most important products are chemicals, including synthetic fibres and allied products, electrical equipment and food. In 1977, manufacturing establishments employed 479,000 workers, who received wages of $4,686,000; value added by manufactures in 1977 was $10,724,000.

TOURISM. 48m. out-of-state tourists spent $1,327m. in 1978. 90m. people travelled through the state in 1977. 8·6% of retail business is generated by tourists and travellers. There are 21,260 retail sales and service enterprises based on the tourist business. There are 146,180 people employed in industries directly connected with tourism.

COMMUNICATIONS

Roads. In 1977 there were 81,932 miles of municipal and rural roads, 38,312 miles of surfaced rural roads and 30,639 miles of unsurfaced rural roads. The state is served by 115 intrastate bus companies and 31 privately owned internal bus services.

Motor-vehicle registrations, 1977, totalled 2,586,807.

Railways. The state had (1975) 3,500 miles of track on 11 railways.

Aviation. The state is served by 11 major airlines. Airports, 1970, numbered 78 public airports and 72 private.

JUSTICE, RELIGION, EDUCATION AND WELFARE

Justice. There has been no execution since 1960; since 1930 there have been 22 whites and 44 Negroes executed (by electrocution) for murder and 5 whites and 22 Negroes for rape. A US Supreme Court ruling prohibits the use of capital punishment under present Tennessee law, except for first degree murder.

Prison population, 30 June 1975, 4,561.

The law prohibiting the inter-marriage of white and Negro was declared unconstitutional by the US Supreme Court in June 1967.

Religion. The leading religious bodies are the Southern Baptists, Methodists and Negro Baptists.

Education. School attendance has been compulsory since 1925 and the employment of children under 16 years of age in workshops, factories or mines is illegal.

In 1976–77 there were 1,711 public schools with a net enrolment of 950,855 pupils. In 1977 47,569 teachers earned an average salary of $11,338·4. Total expenditure for operating county and city public schools (kindergarten to Grade 12) in 1976–77 $875·7m. Tennessee has 49 accredited colleges and universities, 18 2-year colleges and 28 vocational schools. The universities include the University of Tennessee, Knoxville (founded 1794), with 29,270 students in 1979; Vanderbilt University, Nashville (1873) with 7,373, Tennessee State University (1912) with 5,396, the University of Tennessee at Chattanooga (1886) with 7,106 and Fisk University (1866) with 1,154.

Health. In 1975 the state had 158 hospitals. In 1975 4,417 patients were in mental hospitals. There were 205 nursing homes in 1977.

Social Security. Old-age assistance was granted (1977) to 69,061 persons, who received an average of $78.4 per person; 1,824 blind persons, $137.54 per person; 63,772 disabled persons, $125.05 per person; 59,803 families with dependent children, $106.65 per family. Unemployment insurance, 69,288 persons receiving $65.76 each.

Books of Reference

Tennessee Dept. of Finance and Administration, Annual Report, 1971
Dept. of Education Annual Report for Tennessee, 1972
Survey of Current Business, 1972
Tennessee Blue Book. Secretary of State, Nashville
Tennessee Statistical Abstract, 1971. Knoxville, 1971

State Library: State Library and Archives, Nashville. *Librarian:* Miss K. Culbertson. *State Historian:* Dr S. Horn.
Statistics: Tennessee Dept. of Public Welfare, 1972.

TEXAS

HISTORY. In 1836 Texas declared its independence of Mexico, and after maintaining an independent existence, as the Republic of Texas, for 10 years, it was on 29 Dec. 1845 received as a state into the American Union. The state's first settlement dates from 1686.

AREA AND POPULATION. Texas is bounded north by Oklahoma, northeast by Arkansas, east by Louisiana, south-east by the Gulf of Mexico, south by Mexico and west by New Mexico. Area, 267,339 sq. miles (including 4,369 sq. miles of inland water). Census population, 1 April 1980 (provisional), 14,228,383, an increase of 27% since 1970. Vital statistics for 1977: Births, 235,791 (18·4 per 1,000 population); deaths, 102,182 (8); infant deaths, 3,470 (14·7 per 1,000 live births); marriages, 161,331 (12·6); divorces, 83,215 (6·5).

Population for 5 census years (with distribution by sex, 1970) was:

	White	Negro	Indian	Asiatic	Total	Per sq. mile
1910	3,204,848	690,049	702	943	3,896,542	14·8
1930	4,967,172	854,964	1,001	1,578	5,824,715	22·1
1950	6,726,534	977,458	2,736	3,392	7,711,194	29·3
1960	8,374,831	1,187,125	5,750	9,848	9,579,677	36·5
			All others			
1970	9,717,128	1,399,005	80,597		11,196,730	42·7
Male	4,767,630	672,901	40,638		5,481,169	—
Female	4,949,498	726,104	39,959		5,715,561	—

Of the population in 1970, 8,921,000 persons (79·7%) were urban (75% in 1960); households numbered 3,432,000. Those 21 years old and older were 6,567,000. A census report, 1970, showed, 1,723,531 persons with Spanish surnames, of whom 1,533,460 were natives of the state.

The largest cities, with census population in 1980, are:

Houston	1,554,992	Amarillo	149,167	Odessa	89,797
Dallas	901,450	Beaumont	118,031	Garland	138,749
San Antonio	783,296	Wichita Falls	93,543	Laredo	91,229
Fort Worth	382,349	Irving	109,575	San Angelo	72,655
El Paso	424,522	Waco	101,267	Galveston	61,601
Austin (capital)	343,390	Arlington	159,117	Midland	70,291
Corpus Christi	230,715	Abilene	98,231	Tyler	70,720
Lubbock	174,157	Pasadena	111,884	Port Arthur	61,106

Larger urbanized areas, 1970: Houston, 1·98m.; Dallas, 1·55m.; San Antonio, 864,014; Fort Worth, 762,086.

CONSTITUTION AND GOVERNMENT. The present constitution dates from 1876; it has been amended 233 times. The Legislature consists of a Senate of 31 members elected for 4 years (half their number retiring every 2 years), and a House of Representatives of 150 members elected for 2 years.

The Governor and Lieut.-Governor are elected for 4 years. Qualified electors are all citizens with the usual residential qualifications. Texas sends to Congress 2 senators and 27 representatives.

In the 1980 presidential election Reagan polled 2,510,705 votes, Carter, 1,881,147. The capital is Austin. The state has 254 counties.

Governor: William P. Clements, Jr (R.), 1979–81 ($71,400).
Lieut.-Governor: William P. Hobby (D.), 1979–81 ($7,200).
Secretary of State: George Strake (R.)

BUDGET. In the fiscal year ending 31 Aug. 1974 general revenues were $5,014,755,658; general expenditures, $4,492,958,989 (education, $1,951,567,413; welfare, $859,672,000; highways, $649,448,272). Texas is unique in the large revenue derived from the severance tax (*i.e.*, tax on the removal of oil, natural gas and sulphur from the soil or waters of the state) which in the 1973–74 fiscal year yielded $526,368,768.

Net long-term debt, 31 Aug. 1974, was $869,060,042.
Per capita personal income (1976) was $6,201.

ENERGY AND NATURAL RESOURCES

Minerals. Texas leads all states by a wide margin in the production of crude petroleum and related minerals. In 1975 Texas had 31% of proved US crude oil reserves. Production, 1976: Crude petroleum, 1,192,053,000 bbls; natural gas, 7,156,518m. cu. ft; natural gasoline, 80,576,000 bbls; butane and propane gases, 208,908,000 bbls. Other minerals include helium, crude gypsum, granite and sandstone, salt and cement. Total value of mineral products in 1976, $17,541,847,000, leading all states.

Agriculture. Texas is one of the most important agricultural states of the Union. In

1969 (census) it had 213,550 farms covering 142,567,000 acres; average farm was of 668 acres valued, land and buildings, at $99,000. Large-scale commercial farms, highly mechanized, dominate in Texas; farms of 1,000 acres or more numbered 23,005, a number far exceeding that of any other state; 29,601 farms sold produce valued at $20,000 or more. But small-scale farming persists; 38,105 farms were under 50 acres.

Soil erosion is serious in some parts. For some 97,297,000 acres drastic curative treatment has been indicated and for 51,164,000 acres, preventive treatment. In 1970 there were 188 soil-conservation districts embracing an area of 166·57m. acres, of which 144,366,000 acres were in farms and ranches.

Production, 1977: Cotton, 5,465,000 bales from 5·2m. acres; yield was 407 lb. per acre compared with the average of 461 lb. for all cotton states; pecans, 32m. lb.; grain sorghum, 230m. bu. Other important crops were maize (73m. bu.), wheat (117m. bu.), oats and barley (27m. bu.), rough rice (23·4m. cwt), peanuts (394m. lb.), oranges (6·9m. boxes), grapefruit (12·4m. boxes), and peaches, potatoes, sweet potatoes.

Cash income, 1978, from crops was $2,901m.; from livestock, $4,646m.

The state has a very great livestock industry, leading in the number of all cattle, 14·5m. on 1 Jan. 1977, and sheep, 2·46m.; it also had 314,000 milch cows, and 890,000 swine. The wool clip in 1977 amounted to 21·5m. lb.; mohair, 8·5m. lb.

Forestry. National forests area under forest service administration (1974) 1,755,028 acres (gross area).

INDUSTRY. The 1976 survey of manufactures showed manufacturing establishments numbering 13,559 employing 837,511 production workers earning $9,571m. Chemical industries along the Gulf Coast, such as the production of synthetic rubber and of primary magnesium (from sea-water), are increasingly important.

COMMUNICATIONS

Roads. The state maintained (31 Aug. 1976) 69,685 miles of roads. Motor registration in 1976, 9·9m.

Railways. The railways (1974) had a total mileage of 19,134 miles, of which 13,303 miles were main lines.

Aviation. Public airports, 1975, numbered 496, in addition, there were 725 private airports.

Shipping. The port of Houston, connected by the Houston Ship Channel (50 miles long) with the Gulf of Mexico, is the largest inland cotton market in the world.

JUSTICE, RELIGION, EDUCATION AND WELFARE

Justice. The prison system, Dec. 1976, held 20,000 men and women. Since 1968 there have been no executions. Total executions from 1930 through 1968 have been 297, of which 210 were for murder, 84 (including 71 Negroes) for rape and 3 for armed robbery.

Texas has adopted 11 laws governing the activities of trade unions. An Act of 1955 forbids the state's payment of unemployment compensation to workers engaged in certain types of strikes.

Religion. The largest religious bodies are Roman Catholics, Baptists, Methodists, Churches of Christ, Lutherans, Presbyterians and Episcopalians.

Education. In 1970 persons 25 years of age or older who reported no school years completed numbered 176,675 (3% of that age group), of whom 154,147 were whites and 21,079 were non-whites; of persons between 5 and 24, 3,101,020 (70·8%) were attending school. School attendance is compulsory from 7 to 17 years of age. In 1965–66 all public schools had completed or begun desegregation. The estimated total enrolment in 1976 was 2,944,925.

In autumn 1976 public elementary schools (kindergarten through grade 6) had 1,562,580 enrolled pupils and 79,400 classroom teachers; secondary schools, 1,370,140 enrolled pupils and 72,100 classroom teachers. Teachers' salaries, 1976, estimate, averaged $11,318. Total public school expenditure, 1976, $2,852m.

The state maintains 127 institutions of higher learning with an estimated enrolment, Sept. 1977, of 725,016 students. The largest institutions, with faculty numbers and student enrolment, were:

Founded	Institutions	Control	Students
1845	Baylor University, Waco	Baptist	9,108
1852	St Mary's University, San Antonio	R.C.	3,286
1869	Trinity University, San Antonio	Presb.	3,538
1873	Texas Christian University, Fort Worth	Christian	6,159
1876	Texas A. and M. Univ., College Station	State	28,848
1876	Prairie View Agr. and Mech. Coll., Prairie View	State	5,146
1879	Sam Houston State University	State	10,749
1883	University of Texas, Austin	State	41,660
1890	North Texas State University	State	17,151
1891	Hardin-Simmons University, Abilene	Baptist	1,649
1895	University of Texas, Arlington	State	17,201
1899	East Texas State University	State	9,586
1899	South West Texas State University	State	14,670
1901	North Texas State University, Denton	State	17,151
1903	Texas Woman's University, Denton	State	8,915
1906	Abilene Christian College, Abilene	Church of Christ	4,220
1911	Southern Methodist University, Dallas	Methodist	8,678
1912	William Marsh Rice University, Houston	—	3,686
1913	University of Texas, El Paso	State	15,885
1923	Stephen F. Austin State University	State	10,446
1923	Texas Technical University, Lubbock	State	22,358
1924	College of Arts and Industries, Kingsville	State	6,600
1934	University of Houston, Houston	State	29,297
1947	Texas Southern University, Houston	State	9,510
1951	Lamar University	State	11,128

Health. In 1975, the state had 571 hospitals (78,609 beds) listed by the American Hospital Association; on 31 Dec. 1975 mental hospitals had 6,100 resident patients and institutions for the mentally retarded, 13,309 resident patients (1974).

Social Security. Aid is from state and federal sources. Old-age assistance was being granted in Dec. 1977 to 183,000 persons, who received an average of $54.44 per month; aid was given to 233,218 dependent children (total, financial year 1977, $121·3m.).

Books of Reference

Texas Almanac. Dallas. Biennial
MacCorkle, S. A., and Smith, D., *Texas Government.* 7th ed. New York, 1974
Richardson, R. N., *Texas, the Lone Star State.* 3rd ed. New York, 1970
Webb, W. P. (ed.), *The Handbook of Texas.* State Hist. Ass., Austin, 1952

Legislative Reference Library: Box 12488, Capitol Station, Austin, Texas 78811. *Director:* James R. Sanders.

UTAH

HISTORY. Utah, which had been acquired by the US during the Mexican war, was settled by Mormons in 1847, and organized as a Territory on 9 Sept. 1850. It was admitted as a state into the Union on 4 Jan. 1896 with boundaries as at present.

AREA AND POPULATION. Utah is bounded north by Idaho and Wyoming, east by Colorado, south by Arizona and west by Nevada. Area, 82,096 sq. miles, of which 2,577 sq. miles are water. The federal government (1967) owned 35,397,274 acres or 67·1% of the area of the state. The area of unappropriated and unreserved lands was 23,268,250 acres in 1974. The Bureau of Indian Affairs in 1974 administered 3,035,190 acres, all of which were allotted to Indian tribes.

Census population, 1 April 1980 (preliminary), 1,461,037, an increase of 38% since 1970. Births in 1977 were 38,237 (30·2 per 1,000 population); deaths, 7,976 (6·3); infant deaths, 453 (11·8 per 1,000 live births); marriages, 15,188 (12); divorces, 6,901 (5·4).

Population at 5 federal censuses (with distribution by sex, 1970) was:

	White	Negro	Indian	Asiatic	Total	Per sq. mile
1910	366,583	1,144	3,123	2,501	373,851	4·5
1930	499,967	1,108	2,869	3,903	507,847	6·2
1950	676,909	2,729	4,201	—	688,862	8·4
1960	873,828	4,148	6,961	5,207	890,627	10·8
1970	1,031,926	6,617	11,273	6,230	1,059,273	12·9
Male	508,997	3,987	5,492	3,089	523,265	6·4
Female	522,929	2,630	5,781	3,141	536,008	6·5

Of the total in 1970, 851,472 persons (80·4%) were urban (74·9% in 1960); 570,349 were 21 years of age or older.

The largest cities are Salt Lake City (capital), with a population (census, 1980) of 162,960; Provo, 74,007; Ogden, 64,444. Others, 1970: Bountiful, 27,853; Orem, 25,729; and Logan, 22,333.

CONSTITUTION AND GOVERNMENT. Utah adopted its present constitution in 1896 (now with 61 amendments). It sends to Congress 2 senators and 2 representatives.

The Legislature consists of a Senate (in part renewed every 2 years) of 30 members, elected for 4 years, and of a House of Representatives of 75 members elected for 2 years. The Governor is elected for 4 years. The constitution provides for the initiative and referendum. Electors are all citizens, who, not being insane or criminal, have the usual residential qualifications.

The capital is Salt Lake City. There are 29 counties in the state.

In the 1980 presidential election Reagan polled 439,687 votes, Carter 124,266.

Governor: Scott Matheson (D.), 1977–81 ($40,000).
Lieut.-Governor: David S. Monson (R.), 1977–81 ($26,500).
Attorney-General: Robert B. Hansen (R.), 1977–81 ($30,000).

BUDGET. For the year ending 30 June 1974 general revenue was $654·1m. while general expenditures were $638·9m. ($289·3m. for education, $113m. for highways and $236m. for social services).

The net long-term debt on 30 June 1974 was about $30m.

Per capita personal income (1976) was $5,923.

ENERGY AND NATURAL RESOURCES

Minerals (1975). Production of principal minerals: Copper, 177,155 short tons; gold, 189,620 troy oz.; petroleum 42·3m. bbls; lead, 12,679 short tons; silver, 2,822,000 troy oz.; zinc, 19,640 short tons. The state also has natural gas, clays, tungsten, molybdenum, uranium and phosphate rock. Total value of mineral production, 1975, $966·4m.

Agriculture. In 1975 Utah had 12,600 farms with a total area of 13m. acres (25% of the total land area), of which about 2m. acres were crop land and about 300,000 acres pasture. About 1m. acres had irrigation; the average farm was of 1,030 acres.

Of the total surface area (52,721,500 acres, including 2,577 sq. miles of water), 9% is severely eroded and only 9·4% is free from erosion; the balance is moderately eroded.

Cash income, 1978, from crops, $104·5m. and from livestock, $352·2m. The principal crops are: Barley (threshed), 7·3m. bu.; wheat (spring and winter, threshed),

5·6m. bu.; oats (threshed), 576,000 bu.; potatoes, 1·1m. cwt.; sugar-beet, 250,000 tons; hay (alfalfa, sweet clover and lespedeza), 1·88m. tons; alfalfa seed, 4·3m. lb.; corn, 1·44m. tons; apples, 35m. lb.; vegetables for processing, 17,350 tons. In 1975 there were 660,000 sheep; 79,000 milch cows; 900,000 all cattle; 41,000 swine. The 1978 wool clip yielded 4·7m. lb. of wool; 936m. lb. of milk were produced; and 1·46m. chickens produced 335m. eggs.

Forestry. Area of national forests, 1970, was 9,088,986 acres, of which 8·01m. acres were under forest service administration.

INDUSTRY. In 1973 the 1,469 manufacturing establishments had 64,128 workers, who earned $549m.; value added by manufacture was (1970) $783·5m. Leading manufactures by value added (1970): primary metals, ordinances and transport, food, fabricated metals and machinery, petroleum products.

COMMUNICATIONS

Roads. The state has about 58,000 miles of highway. In 1974 there were 861,690 motor vehicles registered.

Railways. On 1 July 1974 the state had 1,734 miles of railways.

Aviation. There were (1971) 89 airports (51 municipal, 32 private, 6 commercial).

JUSTICE, RELIGION, EDUCATION AND WELFARE

Justice. The number of inmates of the state prison on 13 Oct. 1975 was 659. Since 1930 total executions have been 14 (13 by shooting, 1 by hanging—the condemned man has choice), all whites, and all for murder.

Religion. Latter-day Saints (Mormons) form about 73% of the church membership of the state, with approximately 829,990 members in 1974; their church is a substantial property-owner. There were (1970) about 50,483 Catholics. Most Protestant denominations are represented.

Education. School attendance is compulsory for children from 6 to 18 years of age. There are 40 school districts. Teachers' salaries, 1973, averaged $9,150. There were (autumn 1974) 316,592 pupils in public elementary and secondary schools. In 1970–71 estimated public school expenditure was $137·2m.

The University of Utah (1850) (21,487 students in 1978) is in Salt Lake City; the Utah State University (1890) (9,436 students) is in Logan. The Mormon Church maintains the Brigham Young University at Provo (1875) with 28,580 students. Other colleges include: Westminster College, Salt Lake City, 1,464 students; Weber State College, Ogden, 8,741; Southern Utah State College, Cedar City, 1,811; College of Eastern Utah, Price, 626; Snow College, Ephraim, 842; Dixie College, St George, 1,203; Utah Technical College, Salt Lake City, 5,644; Utah Technical College, Provo, 3,138; L.D.S. Business College, Salt Lake City, 1,035. Total college students, June 1975, 80,490. A state bond of $70m. was approved in July 1975 for the University of Utah medical centre.

Health. In 1974, the state had 43 hospitals (5,061 beds) listed by the Utah Department of Social Services.

Social Security. The state department of public welfare provided assistance to an average of 44,987 persons per month during the financial year 1974; 34,124 persons received aid to dependent children at an average $74.57 per month; aid to the aged, the blind and disabled is provided from federal funds. Total expenditure of the department for assistance, welfare and administration, 1974–75, was $70,417,582 (state and federal aid).

Books of Reference

Compiled Digest of Administrative Reports. Secretary of State, Salt Lake City. Annual
Statistical Abstract of Government in Utah. Utah Foundation, Salt Lake City. Annual
A Statistical Abstract of Utah's Economy. Bureau of Economic and Business Research, Univ. of Utah, 1964

Utah Agricultural Statistics. Dept. of Agriculture, Salt Lake City. Annual
Utah: Facts. Bureau of Economic and Business Research, Univ. of Utah, 1975
Writers' Program. *A Guide to the State.* New York, 1954
Arrington, L., *Great Basin Kingdom: An Economic History of the Latter-Day Saints, 1830–1900.* Cambridge, Mass., 1958
Nelson, E., *Utah's Economic Patterns.* Salt Lake City, 1956

VERMONT

HISTORY. Vermont, first settled in 1724, was admitted into the Union as the fourteenth state on 4 March 1791. The first constitution was adopted by convention at Windsor, 2 July 1777, and established an independent state government.

AREA AND POPULATION. Vermont is bounded north by Canada, east by New Hampshire, south by Massachusetts and west by New York. Area, 9,267 sq. miles, of which 333 sq. miles are inland water. Census population, 1 April 1980 (preliminary), 511,456, an increase of 15% since 1970. Births, 1977, were 6,413 (13·3 per 1,000 population); deaths, 4,345 (9); infant deaths, 64 (10 per 1,000 live births); marriages, 4,825 (10); divorces, 1,938 (4).

Population at 5 census years (with distribution by sex, 1970) was:

	White	Negro	Indian	Asiatic	Total	Per sq. mile
1910	354,298	1,621	26	11	355,956	39·0
1930	358,966	568	36	41	359,611	38·8
1950	377,188	443	30	48	377,747	40·7
1960	389,092	519	57	172	389,881	42·0
1970	442,553	761	229	787	444,732	48·0
Male	216,230	443	112	381	217,166	—
Female	226,323	318	117	406	227,164	—

Of the population in 1970, 142,889 persons (32·2%) were urban (38·5% in 1960); those 21 years of age or older (1970), 252,809; there were (1960) 23,218 foreign-born whites. Households (1973) numbered 145,000. The largest cities are Burlington, with a population in 1970 of 38,633; Rutland, 19,293; Barre, 10,209.

CONSTITUTION AND GOVERNMENT. The constitution was adopted in 1793 and has since been amended. Amendments are proposed by two-thirds vote of the Senate every 4 years, and must be accepted by two sessions of the legislature; they are then submitted to popular vote. The state Legislature, consisting of a Senate of 30 members and a House of Representatives of 150 members (both elected for 2 years), meets in Jan. in odd-numbered years. The Governor and Lieut.-Governor are elected for 2 years. Electors are all citizens who possess certain residential qualifications and have taken the freeman's oath set forth in the constitution.

The state is divided into 14 counties; there are 251 towns and cities and other minor civil divisions. The state sends to Congress 2 senators and 1 representative, who are elected by the voters of the entire state.

In the 1980 presidential election Reagan polled 94,628 votes, Carter 81,952.

The capital is Montpelier (8,609, census of 1970).

Governor: Richard Snelling (R.) 1979–81 ($36,100).
Lieut.-Governor: Madeline Kurin (D.) ($15,500).
Secretary of State: James Guest (R.) ($19,600).

BUDGET. The general revenue for the year ending 30 June 1974 was $143·5m. (excluding federal aid); highway fund revenue, $70·3m.; general expenditure was $145·9m. (education, $62·8m.; highways, $73·4m., and public welfare, $45·6m.).

Total net long-term debt, 1 July 1974, was $339,035,275.
Per capita personal income (1973) was $4,011.

NATURAL RESOURCES

Minerals. Stone, chiefly granite, marble and slate, is the leading mineral produced in Vermont, contributing about 60% of the total value of mineral products. Other products include asbestos, talc, peat, sand and gravel. Total value of mineral products, 1974, $31·2m.

Agriculture. Agriculture is the most important industry. In 1973 the state had about 6,600 farms with a total area of 1·86m. acres, of which 566,000 acres were crop land; the average farm was of 282 acres valued, land and buildings, at $110,200. Cash income, 1978, from livestock and products, $287m.; from crops, $21m. The 3,385 dairy farms produce 1,958m. lb. of milk annually. The chief agricultural crops are hay, apples and maple syrup. In 1974 Vermont had 293,884 milch cows, 5,364 sheep, 3,595 swine, 342,310 laying hens and 10,220 horses.

Forestry. In 1973 there was cut 98m. bd ft hardwood and 87m. bd ft softwood. In addition, 142,139 cords of pulpwood and boltwood and 185m. bd ft of logs were produced.

National forests area (1972), 242,309 acres. In 1975 there were 34 state forests, and 41 state parks; total acreage 132,329.

INDUSTRY. In 1972, 850 manufacturing establishments employed 37,900 production workers who earned $320·9m.; value added by manufacture was $578·9m.

COMMUNICATIONS

Roads. The state maintained (1974) 2,551 miles of paved and gravelled highways. Total highways, 13,594 miles. Motor vehicle registrations, 1974, 307,045.

Railways. There were, in 1973, 724 miles of main line railway, 277 of which was leased by the state to private operators.

Aviation. There were 23 airports, of which 10 were state operated, 3 municipally owned and 10 privately owned but open to public use.

Post and Broadcasting. In 1978 there were 329,812 telephones in use. There were (1975) 2 commercial television stations, 35 cable television companies franchised to serve 96 communities and 35 radio broadcasting stations.

JUSTICE, RELIGION, EDUCATION AND WELFARE

Justice. During 1972–73 there was an average of 2,444 people under the supervision or in the custody of the Department of Corrections. There is no capital punishment in Vermont. The Vermont State Prison was closed in Aug. 1975 and prisoners transferred to federal prisons and community correction centres.

Religion. The principal denominations (1975) are Roman Catholic (with about 50,000 adult confirmed and 130,000 baptized), United Church of Christ (22,748), United Methodist (about 22,000), Protestant Episcopal (about 7,500), Baptist (about 7,000) and Unitarian-Universalist (2,054 in 1970).

Education. School attendance during the full school term is compulsory for children from 7 to 16 years of age, or to have completed the 10th grade. In 1973–74 the 346 public elementary schools had 64,608 enrolled pupils; the 71 public secondary schools had 41,628 pupils; the 64 private schools had 10,125 pupils. Full-time teachers for public elementary and secondary schools numbered 6,537. Teachers' salaries for 1973–74 averaged $8,573 (elementary) and $9,202 (secondary). The University of Vermont (1791) had 8,500 full-time students in 1973–74; Middlebury College (1800), 1,941 students; Norwich University (1834), 997 students; St Michael's College, 1,543 students; the 4 state colleges, 3,585 students. Total expenditure for education, 1971–72, was an estimated $104m., exclusive of capital outlay.

Health. In July 1972 the state had 18 general hospitals (2,252 beds), 2 mental hospitals (1,474 beds) and 1 T.B. hospital (50 beds). There was 1 federal general hospital with 175 beds.

Social Security. Old-age assistance was being granted in 1974 to 3,423 persons, drawing an average of $64.19 per month; aid to dependent children was being granted to 22,014 persons, drawing an average of $71.64 per month; aid to the blind was being granted to 74 persons, drawing an average of $92.20; and aid to the permanently and totally disabled was being granted to 2,505 persons, drawing an average of $96.43.

Books of Reference

Legislative Directory. Secretary of State, Montpelier. Biennial
Vermont Facts and Figures. Office of Statistical Co-ordination, Montpelier. 3rd ed. 1975
Vermont Year-Book, formerly *Walton's Register.* Chester. Annual

State Library: Vermont Dept. of Libraries, Montpelier. *State Librarian:* John A. McCrossan.

VIRGINIA

HISTORY. The first English Charter for settlements in America was that granted by James I in 1606 for the planting of colonies in Virginia. The state was one of the 13 original states in the Union. Virginia lost just over one-third of its area when West Virginia was admitted into the Union (1863).

AREA AND POPULATION. Virginia is bounded north-west by West Virginia, north-east by Maryland, east by the Atlantic, south by North Carolina and Tennessee and west by Kentucky. Area, 40,817 sq. miles, including 1,037 sq. miles of inland water. Census population, 1 April 1980 (preliminary), 5,346,279, an increase of 697,795 or 15% since 1970. In 1978 there were 73,349 births (14·2 per 1,000 population); 40,649 deaths (7·9); 989 infant deaths (13·5 per 1,000 live births); 58,967 marriages and 22,654 divorces.

Population for 5 federal census years (with distribution by sex, 1970) was:

	White	Negro	Indian	Asiatic	Total	Per sq. mile
1910	1,389,809	671,096	539	168	2,061,612	51·2
1930	1,770,441	650,165	779	466	2,421,851	60·7
1950	2,581,555	734,211	1,056	758	3,318,680	83·2
1960	3,142,443	816,258	2,155	4,725	3,966,949	99·3
			All others			
1970	3,761,514	861,368	25,612		4,648,484	116·9
Male	1,864,716	419,248	13,157		2,297,121	—
Female	1,896,798	442,120	12,455		2,351,373	—

Of the total population in 1970, 2,934,841 persons (63·1%) were urban (55·6% in 1960); those 21 years of age or older numbered 2·79m.

The population (census of 1980) of the principal cities was: Norfolk, 262,803; Richmond, 219,429; Newport News, 144,795; Hampton, 122,383; Portsmouth, 104,068; Alexandria, 102,494; Roanoke, 99,552; Lynchburg, 67,867.

CONSTITUTION AND GOVERNMENT. The present constitution dates from 1971.

The General Assembly consists of a Senate of 40 members, elected for 4 years, and a House of Delegates of 100 members, elected for 2 years. The Governor and Lieut.-Governor are elected for 4 years. Qualified as electors are (with few exceptions) all citizens 18 years of age, fulfilling certain residential qualifications, who have registered. The state sends to Congress 2 senators and 10 representatives.

In the 1980 presidential election Reagan polled 989,609 votes, Carter 752,174 and Anderson 95,418.

The state capital is Richmond; the state contains 95 counties and 41 independent cities.

Governor: John N. Dalton (R.), 1978–82 ($60,000).
Lieut.-Governor: Charles S. Robb (D.), $16,000.
Secretary of the Commonwealth: Frederick T. Gray, Jr. (R.) ($21,400).

BUDGET. General revenue for the year ending 30 June 1979 was $4,732,900,000 (taxation, $2,508,000,000, and federal aid, $2,224,900,000); general expenditures, $4,770·5m. ($1,602,500,000 for education, $923,500,000 for transport and $260,261,111 for public welfare).

Total net long-term debt, 30 June 1979, amounted to $290,527,279.

Per capita personal income (1978) was $7,624.

ENERGY AND NATURAL RESOURCES

Minerals (1979). Coal is the most important mineral, with output of 37,038,148 short tons. Lead and zinc ores, stone, sand and gravel, lime and titanium ore are also produced. Total mineral output was 72m. tons.

Agriculture. In 1974 there were 53,000 farms with an area of 9·67m. acres; average farm had 184 acres and was valued at $102,000.

Income, 1978, from crops, $524m., and from livestock and livestock products, $707m. The chief crops (1978) are corn, hay and peanuts (319m. lb), tobacco (135m. lb.).

Animals on farms on 1 Jan. 1979 included 172,000 milch cows, 1·55m. all cattle, 160,000 sheep and 670,000 swine.

Forestry. National forests, 1978, covered 1,610,000 acres.

INDUSTRY. The manufacture of cigars and cigarettes and of rayon and allied products and the building of ships lead in value of products. In 1976, 4,837 manufacturing establishments employed 375,000 workers; valued added by manufacture was $9,368m.

COMMUNICATIONS

Roads. The state highways system, 31 Dec. 1979, had 60,678 miles of highways, of which 8,888 miles were primary roads. Motor registrations, 1978, 3·33m.

Railways. In 1980 there were 4,021 miles of railways.

Aviation. There were, in 1978, 255 airports, of which 57 were publicly owned.

JUSTICE, RELIGION, EDUCATION AND WELFARE

Justice. Executions (by electrocution) since 1930 totalled 95, including 17 whites and 58 Negroes for murder and 20 Negroes for rape. Prison population, 31 Dec. 1977, 7,143 in federal and state prisons.

Religion. The principal churches are the Baptist, Methodist, Protestant-Episcopal and Presbyterian.

Education. Elementary and secondary instruction is free, and for ages 6–17 attendance is compulsory. No child under 12 may be employed in any mining or manufacturing work.

In 1980 the 141 school districts had, in primary schools, 663,466 pupils and 35,387 teachers and in public high schools, 432,787 pupils and 26,422 teachers. Teachers' salaries (1978–79) averaged $13,288. Total expenditure on education, 1978–79, was $2,105m. The more important institutions for higher education (1979) were:

Founded	Name and place of college	Staff	Students
1693	William and Mary College, Williamsburg (State)	400	6,300
1749	Washington and Lee University, Lexington	145	1,742
1776	Hampden-Sydney College, Hampden-Sydney (Pres.)	53	735
1819	University of Virginia, Charlottesville (State)	1,279	15,900
1832	Randolph-Macon College, Ashland (Methodist)	70	888
1832	University of Richmond, Richmond (Baptist)	193	3,004
1838	Virginia Commonwealth University, Richmond	1,449	19,113
1839	Virginia Military Institute Lexington (State)	92	1,317
1865	Virginia Union University, Richmond	85	1,178
1868	Hampton Institute	205	2,809
1872	Virginia Polytechnic Institute and State University	1,505	19,648
1882	Virginia State College, Petersburg	236	4,310
1910	Radford College (State)	285	5,622
1930	Old Dominion University, Norfolk	580	13,935
1956	George Mason University (State)	315	...

Health. In 1978 the state had 135 hospitals (32,138 beds) listed by the American Hospital Association.

Social Security. In 1938 Virginia established a system of old-age assistance under the Federal Security Act; in March 1979 persons in 1,288 cases were drawing an average grant of \$159.94; aid to permanently and totally disabled, 1,025 cases, average grant \$171.26; aid to dependent children, 160,602 persons, average grant \$72.41; general relief, 11,289 persons, average grant \$123.59.

Books of Reference

Statistical Abstract of Virginia. 2 vols. Charlottesville, 1967–70
Dabney, V., *Virginia, the new Dominion.* 1971
Gottmann, J., *Virginia in our Century.* Charlottesville, 1969

State Library: Virginia State Library, Richmond 23219. *State Librarian:* Donald Haynes.

WASHINGTON

HISTORY. Washington, formerly part of Oregon, was created a Territory in 1853, and was admitted into the Union as a state on 11 Nov. 1889. Its settlement dates from 1811.

AREA AND POPULATION. Washington is bounded north by Canada, east by Idaho, south by Oregon with the Columbia River forming most of the boundary, and west by the Pacific. Area, 68,192 sq. miles, of which 1,622 sq. miles are inland water. Lands owned by the federal government, 1977, were 12·4m. acres or 29·1% of the total area. Census population, 1 April 1980 (preliminary), 4,130,163, an increase of 730,994 or 21·4% since 1970. Births, 1978 were 58,725; deaths, 30,469; infant deaths, 737; marriages, 45,109; divorces and annulments, 26,365.

Population in 5 federal census years (with distribution by sex, 1970) was:

	White	Negro	Indian	Asiatic and others	Total	Per sq. mile
1910	1,109,111	6,058	10,997	15,824	1,141,990	17·1
1930	1,521,661	6,840	11,253	23,642	1,563,396	23·3
1950	2,316,496	30,691	13,816	17,960	2,378,963	35·6
1960	2,751,675	48,738	21,076	31,725	2,853,214	42·8
1970	2,351,055	71,308	33,386	53,420	3,409,169	51·2
Male	1,612,802	37,837	16,678	26,430	1,693,747	—
Female	1,638,253	33,471	16,708	26,990	1,715,422	—

Of the total population in 1970, 2,476,468 persons (72·6%) were urban (68·1% in 1960); 2,057,714 were 21 years of age or older; foreign-born, 156,020.

There are 22 Indian reservations, the largest being held by the Yakima tribe. Indian reservations in Sept. 1978 covered 2,511,400 acres, of which 1,999,725 acres

WASHINGTON 1549

were tribal lands and 508,475 acres were held by individuals. Total Indian population, 1978, 34,001.

Leading cities are Seattle, with a population (1980 census) of 491,897; Spokane, 170,993; Tacoma, 158,101; Bellevue, 73,711. Others (1979 estimate): Yakima, 52,700; Everett, 54,600; Vancouver, 47,400; Bellingham, 44,400; Bremerton, 36,850; Richland, 33,550; Longview, 31,100; Renton, 30,700; Edmonds, 28,750; Walla Walla, 24,750. Urbanized areas (1970 census): Seattle–Everett, 1,238,107; Tacoma, 332,521; Spokane, 229,620.

CONSTITUTION AND GOVERNMENT. The constitution, adopted in 1889, has had 63 amendments. The Legislature consists of a Senate of 49 members elected for 4 years, half their number retiring every 2 years, and a House of Representatives of 98 members, elected for 2 years. The Governor and Lieut.-Governor are elected for 4 years. The state sends 2 senators and 7 representatives to Congress.

Qualified as voters are (with some exceptions) all citizens 18 years of age, having the usual residential qualifications.

In the 1980 presidential election Reagan polled 865,244 votes, Carter 650,193 and Anderson, 185,073.

The capital is Olympia (population, 1970, 23,111; estimate, 1979, 26,900). The state contains 39 counties.

Governor: James McDermott (D.), 1981–85 ($58,900).
Lieut.-Governor: John A. Cherberg (D.), 1977–81 ($26,800).
Secretary of State: Bruce Chapman (R.), 1977–81 ($28,900).

BUDGET. For the 2-year budget period 1979–81 the state's total revenue is (projected) $10,528·9m.; general expenditure is (projected) $7,125·8m. (education, $3,425·1m.; transportation, $764·8m., and human resources, $1,295·9m.). State revenue in the period 1977–79 was $8,344·3m. and expenditure $5,373·3m.

Total net long-term debt on 30 June 1978 was $1,219,982,000.
Per capita personal income (1978) was $8,449.

ENERGY AND NATURAL RESOURCES

Minerals (1977, preliminary). Production of principal minerals: Sand and gravel, 18·5m. short tons; cement, 1·5m. bbls; stone, 12·2m. short tons; coal (1978), 4·7m. short tons; clays, 320,223 short tons. Uranium ore is also mined but production figures are not disclosed. Total mineral output in 1976 was valued at $176·56m.

Agriculture. Agriculture is constantly growing in value because of more intensive and diversified farming and because of the 1m.-acre Columbia Basin Irrigation Project. Irrigated land in farms (1974) amounted to 1,286,412 acres.

In 1978 there were 36,500 farms with an acreage of 16·2m.; average farm was of 444 acres. Realized net income per farm in 1977 was $12,449.

Value of farm production, 1978, was $2,335·4m. (from field crops, $123·4m.; from speciality products, including flowers, bulbs, Christmas trees, $2,335·4m., fruit and vegetables, $548·3m., and from livestock, $558·8m.). Wheat, the leading farm commodity, was valued at $455·5m. Cattle and calves were valued at $175·8m. Other major commodities are milk ($283·8m.), apples ($305·9m.). Washington was the leading state in production of apples, hops and sweet cherries in 1977, and second in Irish potatoes, pears, green peas, asparagus, grapes, dry peas and mint oil.

On 1 Jan. 1978 animals on farms included 176,100 milch cows, 1·27m. all cattle, 62,000 sheep and 68,000 swine. The wool clip in 1977 amounted to 616,000 lb.

Forestry. Forests cover about 23m. acres, of which 9m. acres are national forest. In 1977, 6,590,985m. bd ft of timber was harvested; lumber production (1978) was 4,030m. bd ft; plywood, 10,188m. bd ft, and pulp wood (1977) 3,576,000 short tons. In 1978, 2,241·9m. bd ft of logs were shipped overseas from state ports.

Fisheries. Washington ranks second only to Alaska in the catch of salmon and halibut, and in the production of canned salmon. Value of food fish in 1977 was $193,099,000 processed value. Total weight of food fish caught, 170,911,039 lb., including salmon, 52·4m. lb.; shellfish, 45·4m. lb.; other marine fish, 71·8m. lb.

INDUSTRY. In 1976, 244,000 workers earned $3,594m.; value added by manufacture was $7,297m. Aircraft and aerospace manufacture, lumber and wood products, pulp and paper, plywood, food processing, machinery, metals, shipbuilding and chemicals are the major manufacturing industries.

With about 20% of potential water-power resources of US, the state is first in developed and potential hydro-electricity. Abundance of electric power has made Washington the leading producer of primary aluminium.

COMMUNICATIONS

Roads. The state (1978) maintained 6,917 miles of highway; the counties, 40,481 miles; municipalities, 9,875 miles. Motor vehicle registrations (1978), 3,464,618.

Railways. The railways had, in 1974, 4,676 miles.

Aviation. There were in 1977, 350 airports, 116 publicly owned. In 1977 Seattle–Tacoma Airport traffic was 7·3m. passengers, 46,154 tons of mail and 191,603 tons of freight and express.

JUSTICE, RELIGION, EDUCATION AND WELFARE

Justice. The average daily adult population in state prisons in Nov. 1979 was 3,876. Since 1963 there have been no executions; total 1930–63 (by hanging) was 47, including 40 whites, 5 Negroes and 2 other races, all for murder, except 1 white for kidnapping.

Religion. Chief religious bodies (1971) are the Roman Catholic (366,087), United Methodist (116,723), Lutheran (98,815), Presbyterian (75,818), Latter-day Saints (66,109), Episcopalian (56,319).

Education. Education is given free to all children between the ages of 5 and 21 years, and is compulsory for children from 8 to 15 years of age. In Oct. 1978 the 1,016 elementary schools had 17,257 classroom teachers and 395,560 pupils, 184 junior high schools, 72 middle schools and 276 high schools had 15,009 classroom teachers and 373,686 pupils. In 1978–79 the average salary of teaching staff was $17,357. There were 2,629 teachers of handicapped children. The total expenditure on public elementary and secondary schools for the school year 1977–78 was $1,359·6m. In Oct. 1978 an estimated 300 private and parochial elementary and secondary schools had 52,058 elementary and high school pupils.

The University of Washington, founded 1861, at Seattle, had, autumn 1979, 37,547 students, and Washington State University at Pullman, founded 1890, for science and agriculture, had 16,992 students. Twenty-seven community colleges had (1978) a total enrolment of 180,922 students (88,671 full-time equivalent).

Health. In 1978 the 2 state hospitals for mental illness had a daily average of 1,183 patients; schools for handicapped children, 2,336 residents in Jan. 1979.

In 1979 the state had 110 licensed general hospitals (13,256 beds) and 6 licensed psychiatric hospitals (346 beds).

Social Security. Old-age assistance is provided for persons 65 years of age or older without adequate resources (and not in need of continuing home care) who are residents of the state. In May 1978, 17,737 old people were drawing an average of $97.21 per month; aid to 89,611 children in 48,247 families averaged $265.90 per family monthly; to 519 blind persons, $164.27 per person monthly; to 30,764 totally disabled, $159.91 monthly. 7,089 persons, under foster care, received payments of $255.56 per person. Total unemployment in 1978 averaged 120,000 (6·8% of the labour force). In financial year 1978 the unemployment insurance system covered 90·5% of employers (91,987). Benefits to 132,400 beneficiaries ranged from $17 to $128 per week and averaged (1979) $95.26.

Books of Reference

Washington State Research Council. *Handbook: A Compendium of Statistical and Explanatory Information about State and Local Government in Washington.* 4th ed. Olympia, 1973.—*The Book of Numbers: A Statistical Handbook on Washington State Government.* Olympia, 1977
Washington (State) Office of Financial Management. *Pocket Data Book 1978*

Avery, M. W., Washington, a History of the Evergreen State. Univ. of Wash. Press, 1965.—
Government of Washington State. Univ. of Wash. Press, revised ed. 1973
Ogden, Jr, D. M., and Bone, H. A., *Washington Politics.* New York Univ. Press, 1960
Webster, D. H., and others, *Washington State Government: Administrative Organization and Functions.* Univ. of Wash. Press, 1962.—Supplement No. 1, by Barbara B. Howard, 1968

State Library: Washington State Library, Olympia. *State Librarian:* Roderick Swartz.

WEST VIRGINIA

HISTORY. In 1862, after the state of Virginia had seceded from the Union, the electors of the western portion ratified an ordinance providing for the formation of a new state, which was admitted into the Union by presidential proclamation on 20 June 1863, under the name of West Virginia. Its constitution was adopted by the voters almost unanimously on 26 March 1863.

AREA AND POPULATION. West Virginia is bounded north by Pennsylvania and Maryland, east and south by Virginia, southwest by the Sandy River (forming the boundary with Kentucky) and west by the Ohio River (forming the boundary with Ohio). Area, 24,282 sq. miles, of which 102 sq. miles are water. Census population, 1 April 1980 (preliminary), 1,949,644, an increase of 12·7% since 1970. Births, 1979, 29,726; deaths, 18,871; infant deaths, 408; marriages, 17,738; divorces, 10,048.

Population in 5 federal census years (with distribution by sex, 1970) was:

	White	Negro	Indian	Asiatic	Total	Per sq. mile
1910	1,156,817	64,173	36	93	1,221,119	50·8
1940	1,614,191	114,893	18	103	1,729,205	71·8
1950	1,890,282	114,867	160	243	2,005,552	83·3
1960	1,770,133	89,378	181	419	1,860,421	77·3
1970	673,480	67,342	751	1,463	1,744,237	71·8
Male	811,409	31,634	338	707	844,669	—
Female	862,071	35,705	413	766	899,568	—

Of the total population in 1970, 679,491 (39%) were urban (38·2% in 1960); those 21 years of age or older numbered 1,069,033. Foreign-born whites, 1960, were 23,483.

The 1980 census population of the principal cities was: Huntington, 62,112; Charleston, 61,531. Others, 1970: Wheeling, 48,188; Parkersburg, 44,208; Morgantown, 29,431; Weirton, 27,131; Fairmont, 26,093; Clarksburg, 24,864.

CONSTITUTION AND GOVERNMENT. The present constitution was adopted in 1872; it has had 51 amendments.

The Legislature consists of the Senate of 34 members elected for a term of 4 years, one-half being elected biennially, and the House of Delegates of 100 members, elected biennially. The Governor is elected for 4 years and may succeed himself once. Voters are all citizens (with the usual exceptions) 18 years of age and meeting certain residential requirements. The state sends to Congress 2 senators and 4 representatives.

In the 1980 presidential election Carter polled 367,462 votes, Reagan 334,206 and Anderson 31,691.

The state capital is Charleston. There are 55 counties.

Governor: John D. Rockefeller IV (D.), 1981–85 ($50,000).
Secretary of State: A. James Manchin (D.) ($30,000).

FINANCE. Total revenues for the year ending 30 June 1979 were $3,296,280,427 ($951·2 from general revenue fund, $597·5m. from federal funds, $362·4m. from state road fund, $189·1m. from special revenue fund); general expenditures were $3,271,229,549 (education, $692·8m.; highways, $574·5m.; public welfare, $407·2m.; other governmental costs, $401·3m.).

Bonds outstanding were $1,143,968,000 on 30 June 1979.
Estimated *per capita* personal income (1979) was $7,372.

ENERGY AND NATURAL RESOURCES

Minerals. 55% of the state is underlain with mineable coal; 91,239,618 short tons of coal were produced in 1979; coke (oven and bee-hive), 79,518,753 short tons. Petroleum output, 2,329m. bbls; natural gas production was 146,541m. cu. ft. Salt, sand and gravel, sandstone and limestone are also produced. The total value of mineral output in 1979 was $4,631,339,000.

Agriculture. In 1979 the state had 19,600 farms with an area of 4·18m. acres; average size of farm was 213 acres and valued at $550 per acre. Livestock farming predominates.

Cash income, 1979, from crops was $62·8m.; from government payments, $3m., and from livestock and products, $168·4m. Total area of major crops harvested was 722,000 acres, chief crop being hay (585,000 acres); all corn, 98,000 acres. Apples (260m. lb.) and peaches (25m. lb.) are important fruit crops. Livestock on farms, 1 Jan. 1979, included 545,000 cattle, of which 37,000 were milch cows; sheep, 113,000; hogs, 56,000; chickens, 940,000 excluding broilers. Production, 1979, included 18·7m. broilers, 178m. eggs; 2·6m. turkeys.

Forestry. State forests, 1979, covered 79,258 acres; national forests, 1,647,146 gross acres; 75% of the state is woodland.

INDUSTRY. In 1979, 1,765 manufactories had 126,970 production workers who earned $5,810m. Value added by manufacture (estimate) was $3,660m. Leading industries are primary and fabricated metals, glass, chemicals, wood products, textiles and apparel, and machinery.

In 1979 average state employment was 702,900 who earned an average wage of $293·77 per week.

The first commercial coal liquefaction plant in the USA is being built near Morgantown with the co-operation of the governments of Fed. Rep. of Germany and Japan and the Gulf Oil Co.

COMMUNICATIONS

Roads. Total highways in 1979, 37,394 miles (state maintained, 33,299 miles; interstate, 374 miles; national parks and other roads, 4,095 miles; West Virginia Turnpike, 87 miles). Registered motor vehicles, financial year ending 30 June 1979, numbered 1,153,286.

Railways. In 1979 the state had 3,931 miles of railway, all operated by diesel or electric trains.

Aviation. There were 55 licensed airports in 1979.

Post and Broadcasting. There are 65 AM radio stations, 37 FM radio stations. Television stations number 9 VHF and 3 UHF.

Newspapers. Daily newspapers number 25; weekly newspapers 72.

JUSTICE, RELIGION, EDUCATION AND WELFARE

Justice. The state court system consists of a Supreme Court and 31 circuit courts. The Supreme Court of Appeals, exercising original and appellate jurisdiction, has 5 members elected by the people for 12-year terms. Each circuit court has from 1 to 7 judges (as determined by the Legislature on the basis of population and case-load) chosen by the voters within each circuit for 8-year terms.

Effective on 1 July 1967, the West Virginia Human Rights Act prohibits discrimination in employment and places of public accommodations based on race, religion, colour, national origin or ancestry.

There are 8 penal and correctional institutions which had, on 30 June 1980, 1,590 inmates. In 1965 the State Legislature abolished capital punishment.

Religion. Chief denominations in 1979 were United Methodist (175,000 members, estimated), Baptists (141,000) and Roman Catholics (102,600).

Education. Public school education is free for all from 5 to 21 years of age, and school attendance is compulsory for all between the ages of 7 and 16 (school term, 200 days—180–185 days of actual teaching). The public schools are non-sectarian. During school year 1978–79 elementary schools had 13,049 instructional personnel and 230,647 pupils enrolled; secondary schools, 10,757 and 154,041 respectively. Average minimum salary of instructional personnel (1979–80) was $13,642. Total 1978–79 expenditures for public schools, $700,002,735.

Leading institutions of higher education in 1977:

Founded		Full-time students
1837	Marshall University, Huntington	11,884
	School of Medicine	116
1837	West Liberty State College, West Liberty	2,667
1867	Fairmont State College, Fairmont	5,253
1868	West Virginia University, Morgantown	21,200
	School of Medicine	586
1872	Concord College, Athens	2,174
1872	Glenville State College, Glenville	1,916
1872	Shepherd College, Shepherdstown	3,001
1891	West Virginia State College	4,367
1895	West Virginia Institute of Technology, Montgomery	3,343
1895	Bluefield State College, Bluefield	2,338
1901	Potomac State College of West Virginia Univ., Keyser	1,104
1972	West Virginia College of Graduate Studies	3,323
1976	School of Osteopathic Medicine, Lewisburg	231

In addition to the universities and state-supported schools, there are 3 community colleges (9,329 students in 1980), 10 denominational and private institutions of higher education (10,748 students in 1980) and 20 business colleges.

Health. In 1978–79 the state had 66 hospitals and 56 intermediate-care facilities, 24 skilled-nursing homes and 6 mental hospitals.

Social Security. The Department of Welfare, originating in the 1930s as the Department of Public Assistance, is both state and federally financed. In the year ending 30 June 1980 day care for 5,557 children per month was provided; aid was given to 23,210 families with dependent children (average award, $173.87 per month); handicapped children's services conducted 11,220 examinations; 65,526 families per month received food stamps.

On 1 Jan. 1974 all blind, aged and disabled services were converted to the Federal Supplemental Security Income Programme.

Books of Reference

West Virginia Blue Book. Legislature, Charleston. Annual, since 1916
West Virginia Statistical Handbook, 1974. Bureau of Business Research, W. Va. Univ., Morgantown, 1974
Bibliography of West Virginia. 2 parts. Dept. of Archives and History, Charleston, 1939
West Virginia History. Dept. of Archives and History. Charleston. Quarterly, from 1939
Writers' Program. *West Virginia: A Guide to the Mountain State.* New York, 1948
Ambler, Charles H., and Summers, F. P., *West Virginia: the Mountain State*, Prentice-Hall, 1958
Cometti, Elizabeth, and Summers, F. P., *The Thirty-Fifth State.* Morgantown, 1966
Conley, P., and Doherty, W. T., *West Virginia History.* Charleston, 1974
Davis, C. J., and others, *West Virginia State and Local Government.* West Virginia Univ. Bureau for Government Research, 1963
Munn, Robert F., *Index to West Virginiana.* Education Foundation, Charleston, 1960
Shetler, C., *Guide to the Study of West Virginia History.* Morgantown, 1960; *West Virginia Civil War Literature.* Morgantown, 1963
Williams, J. A., *West Virginia: A Bicentennial History.* New York, 1976

State Library: Division of Archives and History, Dept. of Culture and History, Charleston.

WISCONSIN

HISTORY. Wisconsin was settled in 1670 by French traders and missionaries. Originally a part of New France, it was surrendered to the British in 1763 and in 1783, when ceded to the US, became part of the North-west Territory. It was then contained successively in the Territories of Indiana, Illinois and Michigan. In 1836 it became part of the Territory of Wisconsin, which also included the present states of Iowa, Minnesota and parts of the Dakotas. It was admitted into the Union with its present boundaries on 29 May 1848.

AREA AND POPULATION. Wisconsin is bounded north by Lake Superior and Michigan, east by Lake Michigan, south by Illinois, west by Iowa and Minnesota, with the Mississippi River forming most of the boundary. Area, 56,154 sq. miles, including 1,439 sq. miles of inland water, but excluding any part of the Great Lakes. Preliminary census population, 1 April 1980, 4,705,335, an increase of 6·5% since 1970. Births in 1979 (provisional) were 72,900 (15·4 per 1,000 population); deaths, 39,000 (8·2); infant deaths, 760 (16·1 per 1,000 live births); marriages, 40,424 (8·5); divorces and annulments 17,317 (3·6).

Population in 5 census years (with distribution by sex, 1970) was:

	White	Negro	Indian	Asiatic	Total	Per sq. mile
1910	2,320,555	2,900	10,142	263	2,333,860	42·2
1930	2,916,255	10,739	11,548	464	2,939,006	53·7
1950	3,392,690	28,182	12,196	1,507	3,434,575	62·8
1960	3,858,903	74,546	14,297	4,031	3,951,777	72·2
1970	4,258,959	128,224	18,924	11,624	4,417,933	80·8

	White	Negro	All others	Total	
Male	2,090,226	62,116	15,031	2,167,373	—
Female	2,168,733	66,108	15,517	2,250,358	—

Of the total population in 1970, 2,910,877 persons (65·9%) were urban (63·8% in 1960); 2,593,018 were 21 years old or older. Foreign-born whites (1970) numbered 125,662.

Population of the larger cities, 1980 census, was as follows:

Milwaukee	632,989	Appleton	58,738	Waukesha	40,274
Madison	170,669	Oshkosh	49,608	Beloit	35,729
Racine	85,598	*Others, 1970:*		Fond du Lac	35,515
Green Bay	87,929	La Crosse	51,153	Manitowoc	33,430
Kenosha	77,811	Sheboygan	48,484	Wausau	32,806
West Allis	63,678	Janesville	46,426	Superior	32,237
Wauwatosa	51,173	Eau Claire	44,619	Brookfield	32,140

Population of larger urbanized areas, 1970 census: Milwaukee, 1,403,688; Madison, 290,272; Duluth–Superior (Minn.–Wis.), 265,350; Racine, 170,838; Green Bay, 158,244.

CONSTITUTION AND GOVERNMENT. The constitution, which dates from 1848, has 117 amendments. The legislative power is vested in a Senate of 33 members (1979 term: 20 Democrats, 12 Republicans, 1 vacancy), elected for 4 years, one-half elected alternately, and an Assembly of 99 members (1979 term: 59 Democrats, 39 Republicans, 1 vacancy) all elected simultaneously for 2 years. The Governor and Lieut.-Governor are elected for 4 years. All 6 constitutional officers serve 4-year terms.

Wisconsin has universal suffrage for all citizens over 18 years of age; but, as there is no official list of voters, the size of the electorate is unknown; 1,500,996 voted for Governor in 1978.

Wisconsin is represented in Congress by 2 senators and 9 representatives.

In the 1980 presidential election Reagan polled 1,088,845 votes, Carter 981,584 and Anderson 160,657.

The capital is Madison. The state has 72 counties.

Governor: Lee S. Dreyfus (R.), 1979–83 ($65,801).

Lieut.-Governor: Russell A. Olson (R.), 1979–83 ($36,151).

Secretary of State: Vel R. Phillips (D.), 1979–83 ($32,608).

BUDGET. For the year ending 30 June 1980 (Wisconsin Bureau of Financial Operations figures) total revenue for all funds was $7,381,599,086 ($3,200,669,305 from taxation and $1,541,182,109 from federal aid). General expenditure from all funds was $6,836,970,173 ($2,010,176,419 for education, $445,367,478 for highways).

Per capita personal income (1979) was $8,484.

ENERGY AND NATURAL RESOURCES

Electricity. There were, Dec. 1979, 88 hydro-electric power plants (15 of them municipal, 58 private in Wisconsin; 15 private outside the state) operated by public utilities with a total installed capacity of 439,869 kw.; output, 1979, was 2,267,497m. kwh.

Fossil fuel and nuclear plants numbered 25 (4 municipal); the former had a total installed capacity of 5,720,654 kw.; total output (1979), 21,579,086m. kwh; the 2 nuclear plants had an installed capacity of 1,540,682 kw. and a total output (1979) of 10,202,173m. kwh.

There were also 34 internal combustion reciprocating plants, with a total installed capacity of 107,946 kw. and a total output of (1979) 43,152m. kwh., and 16 internal combustion turbine plants with a total installed capacity of 1,279,700 kw.; total output was (1979) 784,632m. kwh.

There was a total of 165 plants, with a total installed capacity of 9,088,851 kw. and a total output of (1979) 34,876,540m. kwh.

Minerals. Sand and gravel, crushed stone and dimension stone, lime and taconite are the chief mineral products. Mineral production in 1979 was valued at $168m. This value included $60m. for sand and gravel, $46m. for crushed stone and about $18·3m. for lime. Value of all other minerals including lead, zinc, taconite, natural abrasives, peat, cement, gemstones, dimension stone and clay, over $44m.

The large Forest County sulphide deposit (5,000 ft long, about 200 ft wide and over 1,500 ft deep and almost vertical) south of Crandon is estimated at over 80m. tons, averaging 5% zinc, 1% copper and lesser amounts of lead, silver and gold. The Rusk County deposit (6m. tons at 4% copper) and the Oneida County deposit (2·3m. tons at 4·5% zinc and 1% copper) are not currently under development. In 1979, north east Wisconsin was explored for uranium, but no deposits have been found.

Agriculture. The total number of farms has declined in the last 45 years, but farms have become larger and more productive. There were 94,000 farms with a total acreage of 18·6m. acres and an average size of 198 acres in 1980, compared with 142,000 farms with a total acreage of 22·4m. acres and an average of 158 acres in 1959.

Cash income from products sold by Wisconsin farms in 1979 of $4,200m. was the highest on record, and included $3,500m. from livestock and livestock products and $760m. from crops.

Wisconsin ranked first among the states in 1979 in the number of milch cows, milk and butter production, output of American, both Brick and Munster, Italian and Blue Mold Cheese. Production of all cheese accounted for 37·7% of the nation's total. The state also ranked first in bulk sweetened whole condensed milk and bulk sweetened skim condensed milk. In crops the state ranked first for snap beans for processing, green peas for processing, all hay and beets for canning. Production of the principal field crops in 1979 included: Corn for grain, 306m. bu.; corn for silage, 10·8m. tons; oats, 55·8m. bu.; all hay, 12·5m. tons. Other crops of importance 17m. cwt of potatoes, 25·6m. lb. of tobacco, 900,000 bbls of cranberries, 2m. cwt of cabbage, 1·8m. cwt of carrots and the processing crops of 556,000 tons of sweet corn, 104,170 tons of beets for canning, 177,550 tons of green peas and 212,520 tons of snap beans.

Forestry. In Oct. 1980 national forests comprised 1·5m. acres; state forests, 385,000 acres; the county forests, 2·25m. acres. Wisconsin has an estimated 14·6m. acres of forest land (about 43% of land area). The production and remanufacture of wood and products is one of the state's most important industries.

INDUSTRY. Wisconsin has much heavy industry, particularly in the Milwaukee area. In 1980 the state ranked twelfth in manufactured exports; non-electrical machinery was the major industrial group (23% of all manufacturing employment), followed by food processing, fabricated metals, electrical machinery, transport equipment, paper and products, primary metals and printing. Manufacturing establishments in 1978 provided 25·4% of all employment, 35% of all earnings; exports (1978) $2,640m. The total number of establishments was 8,477 in 1980; the biggest concentration is in the south-east.

TOURISM. The tourist-vacation industry ranks among the first three in economic importance. Approximately $5,480m. was spent in 1979 by tourists, more than half of this amount by non-residents. The decline of lumbering and mining in the northern section of the state has increased dependency on the recreation industry. The Division of Tourism of the Department of Development spends $600,000 annually to promote tourism; in financial year 1979–80 about $324,000 was spent on tourist information centres.

COMMUNICATIONS

Roads. The state had on 1 Jan 1980, 107,320 miles of highway. 72% of all roads in the state have a bituminous (or similar) surface. There are 11,936 miles of state trunk roads and 19,602 miles of county trunk roads.

In the year ending 30 June 1980 Wisconsin registered 2,512,202 private motor cars.

Railways. On 1 Jan. 1980 the state had 5,269 road-miles of railway.

Aviation. There were, in 1980, 102 publicly operated airports. Eleven airports were served by 10 certificated air carriers and 12 by commuter air carriers.

Shipping. With the opening of the St Lawrence Seaway in 1959, 14 Wisconsin ports became accessible to ocean-going vessels. Green Bay, Kenosha, Manitowoc, Marinette, Milwaukee, Sheboygan and Superior (one of the world's largest iron-ore and grain ports) have developed foreign waterborne commerce. Cargo is also carried by barge on the river Mississippi. Other ports handle mainly Great Lakes traffic.

JUSTICE, RELIGION, EDUCATION AND WELFARE

Justice. The state's penal, reformatory and correctional system on 31 Aug. 1980 held 4,021 men and 168 women in the 10 institutions for adult and juvenile offenders; the probation and parole system was supervising 16,842 men and 3,091 women. Wisconsin does not impose the death penalty.

Religion. Wisconsin church affiliation, as a percentage of the 1979 population, was estimated at 32·9% Catholic, 20·18% Lutheran, 3·82% Methodist, 10·07% unaffiliated and others.

Education. All children between the ages of 7 and 16 are required to attend school full-time to the end of the school term in which they become 16 years of age. Children living in a district with a vocational school must attend until 18. In 1979–80 the school grades kindergarten–8 had 485,893 pupils and 29,900 (full-time equivalent) teachers; school grades 9–12 had 312,936 pupils and 24,552 teachers. Grade kindergarten–8 teachers' salaries, 1979–80, averaged $15,663; grade 9–12 teachers, $16,395. Total cost per pupil was $2,284 in 1979–80.

In 1978–79 vocational, technical and adult schools had an enrolment of 453,371, and there were 7,879 faculty members. There is a school for the visually handicapped and a school for the deaf.

The University of Wisconsin, established in 1848, was joined by law in 1971 with the Wisconsin State Universities System to become the University of Wisconsin System with 13 degree granting campuses, 14 two-year campuses in the Center System, and the University Extension. The 27 campuses had, in 1979–80, 6,671 full-time professors and instructors, 680 part-time teachers, and 2,283 (full-time equivalent) teaching and research graduate assistants. In autumn 1979, 150,349 students enrolled (10,622 at Eau Claire, 3,799 at Green Bay, 8,860 at La Crosse, 40,233 at Madison, 25,078 at Milwaukee, 10,055 at Oshkosh, 5,292 at Parkside, 4,652 at Platteville, 5,128 at River Falls, 8,942 at Stevens Point, 7,154 at Stout, 2,149 at Superior, 9,678 at Whitewater and 8,707 in the Center System freshman-sophomore centres).

There are also several independent institutions of higher education. These (with 1979–80 enrolment) include 2 universities (12,325), 21 liberal arts colleges (15,713), 5 technical and professional schools (3,816), and 4 theological seminaries (540).

The total expenditure, 1978–79, for all public education (except capital outlay and debt service) was $3,779m.

The state maintains an educational broadcasting and television service.

Health. In Sept. 1980 the state had 148 general and allied special hospitals (22,820 beds), 24 mental hospitals (2,698 beds), 7 treatment centres for alcoholism (161 beds), 1 rehabilitation centre (72 beds). Patients in state and county mental hospitals and institutions for the mentally retarded in July 1980 averaged 2,812.

Social Security. On 1 Jan. 1974 the US Social Security administration assumed responsibility for financial aid (Supplemental Security Income) to persons 65 years old and over, blind persons and totally disabled persons, who satisfy requirements as to need. Recipients receive a federal payment plus a federally administered state supplementary payment, except for those who reside in a medical institution. In June 1979, there were 68,683 SSI recipients in the state. In Oct. 1980 payment levels increased to $337.70 for a single individual, $387.40 for an eligible individual with an ineligible spouse, and $518.00 for an eligible couple. A special payment level of $435.20 may be paid with special approval for an SSI recipient who is developmentally disabled or chronically mentally ill, living in a non-medical living arrangement not his own home. All SSI recipients receive state medical assistance coverage.

Under the Aid to Families with Dependent Children programme, 74,698 families constituting 211,695 persons received an average of $347.56 per family in Oct. 1979; 3,111 children in about 2,732 foster homes received an average of $385.70. Medicaid in financial year 1979 cost $579·6m.

Books of Reference

Wisconsin Statistical Abstract. Wis. Dept. of Administration, State Bureau of Planning and Budget, Madison, 1979
Dictionary of Wisconsin Biography. Wis. Historical Society, Madison, 1960
Wisconsin Blue Book. Wis. Legislative Reference Bureau, Madison. Biennial
Current, R. N., *The History of Wisconsin*, Vol. II. State Historical Society of Wisconsin, Madison, 1976
Nesbit, R. C., *Wisconsin, A History.* State Historical Society of Wisconsin, Madison, 1973
Smith, Alice E., *The History of Wisconsin*, Vol. 1. State Historical Society of Wisconsin, Madison, 1973

State Information Agency: Legislative Reference Bureau, State Capitol, Madison, Wis. 53702. *Chief:* Dr H. Rupert Theobald.

WYOMING

HISTORY. Wyoming, first settled in 1834, was admitted into the Union on 10 July 1890. The name originated with the Delaware Indians.

AREA AND POPULATION. Wyoming is bounded north by Montana, east by South Dakota and Nebraska, south by Colorado, south-west by Utah and west by Idaho. Area 97,914 sq. miles, of which 711 sq. miles are water. The Yellowstone National Park occupies about 2,221,733 acres; the Grand Teton National Park has 310,350 acres. The federal government in 1979 owned 28,888,546 acres (46·1% of the total area of the state). The Federal Bureau of Land Management administers 17,546,188 acres.

Census population, 1 April 1980 (preliminary), 468,909, an increase of 41·1% since 1970. Births in 1979 were 8,668 (18 per 1,000 population); deaths, 2,827 (6); infant deaths, 56 (7 per 1,000 live births); marriages, 5,910 (12·6); divorces, 3,227 (6·9).

Population in 5 census years (with distribution by sex, 1980) was:

	White	Negro	Indian	Asiatic	Total	Per sq. mile
1910	140,318	2,235	1,486	1,926	145,965	1·5
1930	221,241	1,250	1,845	1,229	225,565	2·3
1950	284,009	2,557	3,237	726	290,529	3·0
1960	322,922	2,183	4,020	805	330,066	3·4
			All others			
1970	323,024	2,568	6,824		332,416	3·4
1980	455,780	3,751	9,378		468,909	4·8
Male	228,619	1,992	4,727		235,338	—
Female	227,161	1,759	4,651		233,571	—

Of the total population in 1970, 201,111 persons (60·5%) were urban (56·8% in 1960). Persons over 21 years of age numbered 195,077; foreign-born, 9,896.

The largest towns are Cheyenne (capital), with preliminary census population in 1980 of 47,207; Casper, 50,704; Laramie, 24,339; Rock Springs, 19,411.

CONSTITUTION AND GOVERNMENT. The constitution, drafted in 1890, has since had 43 amendments. The Legislature consists of a Senate of 30 members elected for 4 years, and a House of Representatives of 62 members elected for 2 years. The Governor is elected for 4 years.

The state sends to Congress 2 senators and 1 representative, elected by the voters of the entire state. The suffrage extends to all citizens, male and female, who have the usual residential qualifications.

In the 1980 presidential election Reagan polled 110,700 votes, Carter 49,427, and Anderson 12,072.

The capital is Cheyenne. The state contains 23 counties.

Governor: Ed Herschler (D.), 1979–83 ($54,996).
Secretary of State: Mrs Thyra Thomson (R.), 1979–83 ($37,500).

BUDGET. In the fiscal year ending 1 July 1980 (State Treasurer's figures) general revenues were $971,823,445; general expenditures were $814,851,645. Revenue Sharing Funds from federal government, $4·4m.

Total net long-term debt, 30 June 1979, was $93·76m.
Per capita personal income (1977) was $7,517.

ENERGY AND NATURAL RESOURCES

Minerals. Wyoming is largely an oil-producing state. In 1979 the output of petroleum was valued at $1,099m.; natural gas, $264m. Other mining (1979): Coal, $409m.; trona, $80m.; uranium, $73m.; other minerals mined include iron ore, feldspar, gypsum, limestone, phosphate, sand, gravel and marble, taconite, bentonite and hematite.

Value of mineral products in 1979 was $1,961m.

Agriculture. Wyoming is semi-arid, and agriculture is carried on by irrigation and by dry farming. In 1979 there were 7,200 farms and ranches; total land area 35·1m. acres.

Cash receipts, 1979, from crops, $225·7m.; from livestock and products, $387·6m. Principal commodities are wheat, cattle and calves, lambs and sheep, sugar-beet, barley, hay and wool. Animals on farms on 1 Jan. 1979 included 11,000 milch cows, 1·3m. all cattle, 1·1m. sheep and lambs and 30,000 swine (1978).

INDUSTRY AND TRADE

Industry. In 1978 there were 751 manufacturing establishments. There were 439 mining establishments. A large portion of the manufacturing in the state is based on natural resources, mainly oil and farm products. Leading industries are food, wood products (except furniture) and machinery (except electrical). Casper is the most industrialized city, with 119 manufacturers and 129 mining companies. There were 1,272 new business incorporations in 1979. The Wyoming Industrial Development Corporation assists in the development of small industries by providing credit. Available capital, $3m.

Labour. Retail trade is the largest employer in the state with 41,563 workers in

1980. The total civilian labour force for June 1980 (estimate) was 226,300; non-agricultural, 212,062. The average unemployment rate was 3·2% and average weekly earnings were $275.35 for manufacturing production workers.

Tourism. There are over 5m. tourists annually, mainly sportsmen. The state has the largest elk and pronghorn antelope herds in the world, 11 fish hatcheries and numerous wild game. Receipts from hunters and fishermen in 1979, $10,645,187.

COMMUNICATIONS

Roads. The roads in 1978 comprised 2,867 miles of primary roads, 2,738 miles of secondary roads and 920 miles of inter-state highway. There were (1978) 491,906 registered motor vehicles and 25 bus companies, 12 regular route and 13 charter.

Railways. The railways, 1978, had a length of 2,551 mainline miles (Union Pacific, 1,198).

Aviation. There were 9 towns with regular scheduled services and 5 towns on jet routes in 1979.

JUSTICE, RELIGION, EDUCATION AND WELFARE

Justice. The state penitentiary in July 1979 held 437 male inmates. There are 2 other state correctional institutions. There have been 14 executions in Wyoming, 8 by hanging and 6 by lethal gas.

Religion. Chief religious bodies are the Roman Catholic (with 45,917 members in 1974), Mormon (28,954 in 1971) and Protestant churches (83,327 in 1974). There were 5,000 members of the Eastern Orthodox Church in 1972.

Education. In 1978–79 public elementary and secondary schools had 85,518 pupils. Enrolment in the parochial elementary and secondary schools (1978–79) was 2,663. Approximately 5,262 public school teachers earned an average of $14,497. The average total expenditure per pupil for 1976–77 was $1,558.

The University of Wyoming, founded at Laramie in 1887, had in autumn 1978, 8,921 students. There are 2-year colleges at Casper, Riverton, Torrington, Cheyenne, Powell, Rock Springs and Sheridan with 19,059 students.

Social Welfare. In Jan. 1974 the federal government assumed many of the previous state programmes including old age assistance, aid to the blind and disabled. The state continues to administer over $5m. annually in emergency aid and aid to families with dependent children. In 1979, $3,618,986 was distributed in food stamps. Total state expenditure on public assistance and social services programmes, financial year 1979, $21,607,453.

Health. In 1979 the state had 28 hospitals. There are 32 registered nursing homes.

Books of Reference

News of Big Wyoming. Cheyenne, 1975
Official Directory. Secretary of State. Cheyenne. Biennial
1977 Wyoming Data Handbook. Dept. of Administration and Fiscal Control. Division of Research and Statistics, Cheyenne, 1977
Davis, T. S., *A Study of Wyoming People*. Laramie, 1965
Larsen, T. A., *History of Wyoming*. Rev. ed. Univ. of Nebraska, 1979
Trachsel, H. H., and Wase, R. M., *The Government and Administration of Wyoming*. New York, 1953

OUTLYING TERRITORIES

Non-Self-Governing Territories: Summaries of Information Transmitted to the Secretary-General of the United Nations. Annual
Coulter, J. W., *The Pacific Dependencies of the United States*. New York, 1957
Perkins, W. T., *The United States and its Dependencies*. Leiden, 1962
Wiens, H. J., *Pacific Island Bastions of the US*. New York and London, 1962

GUAM

HISTORY. Magellan is said to have discovered the island in 1521; it was ceded by Spain to the US by the Treaty of Paris (10 Dec. 1898). The island was captured by the Japanese on 10 Dec. 1941, and retaken by American forces from 21 July 1944. Guam is of great strategic importance; substantial numbers of naval and air force personnel occupy about one-third of the usable land.

AREA AND POPULATION. Guam is the largest and most southern island of the Marianas Archipelago, in 13° 26′ N. lat., 144° 43′ E. long. The length is 30 miles, the breadth from 4 to 10 miles, and there are about 210 sq. miles (450 sq. km). Agaña, the seat of government is about 8 miles from the anchorage in Apra Harbour. The census on 1 April 1970 showed a population of 84,996, an increase of 17,952 or 26·8% since 1960; those of Guamanian ancestry numbered about 52,000; foreign-born, 13,484; density was 321 per sq. mile. On 1 Jan. 1970 transient residents connected with the military were estimated at 19,307. Estimated population, 1975, 105,400. The Malay strain is predominant. The native language is Chamorro; English is the official language and is taught in all schools.

CONSTITUTION AND GOVERNMENT. Guam's constitutional status is that of an 'unincorporated territory' of the US. Entry of US citizens is unrestricted; foreign nationals are subject to normal regulations. In 1949 the President transferred the administration of the island from the Navy Department (who held it from 1899) to the Interior Department. The transfer was completed by 1 Aug. 1950, on the passage of the Organic Act, which conferred full citizenship on the Guamanians, who had previously been 'nationals' of the US.

The Governor and his staff constitute the executive arm of the government. He is advised by a Cabinet, and a Sub-Cabinet composed of elected representatives of the 19 municipalities. The Legislature is unicameral; its powers are similar to those of an American state legislature. At the general election of Nov. 1980, the Democratic Party won 10 seats and the Republicans 11. All adults 18 years of age or over are enfranchised. Guam returns one non-voting delegate to the House of Representatives.

Governor: Paul MacDonald Calvo (R.), 1978–82
Lieut.-Governor: Joseph F. Ada (R.)

ECONOMY

Budget. At 30 June 1976 total assets were $43m.; federal grants-in-aid, $23·4m., taxes, $15m.: total liabilities were $45m.

Banking. Recent changes in banking law make it possible for foreign banks to operate in Guam; the first to obtain a licence was the First Commercial Bank of Taiwan.

ENERGY AND NATURAL RESOURCES

Water. Supplies are from springs, reservoirs and groundwater; 65% comes from water-bearing limestone in the north. The Navy and Air Force conserve water in reservoirs. The Water Resources Research Centre is at Guam University.

Agriculture. The major products of the island are maize, sweet potatoes, taro, cassava, bananas, and citrus and truck crops, including breadfruit, coconuts and sugar-cane. In 1970–71, 569 full-time and part-time farmers each held 500 acres under cultivation. Livestock (1978) included 2,000 cattle, 9,000 hogs, and 118,000 poultry. Commercial production (1976) amounted to 1·19m. lb. of fruit and vegetables ($329,835), 2m. doz. eggs ($1·97m.), 513,000 lb. of pork ($428,098), 120,600 lb. of chicken meat ($57,406), 78,795 lb. of beef ($61,775). There is an agricultural experimental station at Inarajan.

Fisheries. Fresh fish caught in 1976 was valued at $187,318. About 16,000 people are active in inshore fishing, with a catch of 208,131 lb. Off-shore fishing produced 26,224 lb., including 16,200 lb. of mackerel. Shrimp farming is being developed.

INDUSTRY AND TRADE

Industry. Guam Economic Development Authority controls three industrial estates: Cabras Island (32 acres); Calvo estate at Tamuning (26 acres); Harmon estate (16 acres). Industries include textile manufacture, cement and petroleum distribution, warehousing, printing, plastics and ship-repair.

Labour. In May 1978 the labour force was 30,000, of which 3,000 were unemployed.

Trade. Guam is the only American territory which has complete 'free trade'; excise duties are levied only upon imports of tobacco, liquid fuel and liquor. In the year ending 30 June 1976 imports were valued at $266·3m. and accounted for 91% of trade.

Tourism. Tourism is developing; there were 1,900 visitors in 1964 and 272,681 in 1979, 190,810 of them from Japan.

COMMUNICATIONS

Roads. There are 183 miles of paved and 63 miles of improved roads.

In 1976 there were 54,156 motor vehicles registered.

Aviation. Four commercial airlines (PANAM, Air Nauru, Island Air and Continental Air Micronesia) serve Guam.

Post and Broadcasting. Overseas telephone and radio dispatch facilities are available. On 1 Jan. 1978. there were 32,689 telephones.

There are 3 commercial radio stations, a commercial television station, a public broadcasting station and a cable television station with 6 channels.

Newspapers. There is 1 daily newspaper and 4 weekly publications (all of which are of military or religious interest only).

JUSTICE, RELIGION, EDUCATION AND WELFARE

Justice. The Organic Act established a District Court with jurisdiction in matters arising under both federal and territorial law; the judge is appointed by the President subject to Senate approval. There is also a Supreme Court and a Superior Court; all judges are locally appointed except the Federal District judge. Misdemeanours are under the jurisdiction of the police court. The Spanish law was superseded in 1933 by 5 civil codes based upon California law.

Religion. About 96% of the Guamanians are Roman Catholics; others are Baptists, Episcopalians, Bahais, Lutherans, Mormons, Presbyterians, Jehovah's Witnesses and members of the Church of Christ and Seventh Day Adventists.

Education. Elementary education is compulsory. There are Chamorro Studies courses and bi-lingual teaching programmes to integrate the Chamorro language and culture into elementary and secondary school courses. There were, 1976–77, 15,888 elementary school pupils, 6,142 junior high and 5,242 senior high school pupils. Department of Education staff, 2,416, including 1,107 teachers. The Catholic schools system also operates 3 senior high schools, 3 junior high and 5 elementary schools. The Seventh Day Adventist Guam Mission Academy operates a school from grades 1 through 12, serving over 100 students. St John's Episcopal Preparatory School provides education for 200 students between kindergarten and the 9th grade. The University of Guam (an accredited institution) had 10,285 students, 1975–76. There is a vocational technical school for high school pupils and adults.

Health. There is a hospital, 8 nutrition centres, a school health programme and an extensive immunization programme. Emphasis is on disease prevention, health education and nutrition.

Books of Reference

Report (Annual) of the Governor of Guam to the US Department of Interior
Beardsley, C., *Guam past and present.* Rutland, Vt, 1964
Carano, P., and Sanchez, P. C., *Complete history of Guam.* Rutland, Vt, 1964

COMMONWEALTH OF PUERTO RICO

HISTORY. Puerto Rico, by the treaty of 10 Dec. 1898 (ratified 11 April 1899), was ceded by Spain to the US. The name was changed from Porto Rico to Puerto Rico by an Act of Congress approved 17 May 1932. Its territorial constitution was determined by the 'Organic Act' of Congress (2 March 1917) known as the 'Jones Act', which ruled until 25 July 1952, when the present constitution of the Commonwealth of Puerto Rico was proclaimed.

AREA AND POPULATION. Puerto Rico is the most easterly of the Greater Antilles and lies between the Dominican Republic and the U.S. Virgin Islands. The island has a land area of 3,435 sq. miles (8,891 sq. km) and a population, according to the census of 1980, of 3,187,566, an increase of 475,533 or 17·5% over 1970. Of the population in 1970 about 529,000 were bilingual, Spanish being the mother tongue and (with English) one of the two official languages. Rural population (1970), 1,180,391 (43·6%).

Vital statistics (1978): Births, 75,066 (23·5 per 1,000 population); deaths, 19,876 (6%); deaths under 1 year, 1,390 (18·5 per 1,000 live births).

Chief towns (1980) are: San Juan, 432,973; Bayamón, 195,965; Ponce, 188,219; Carolina, 165,207; Caguas, 118,020; Mayaguez, 95,886.

The Puerto Rican island of Vieques, 10 miles to the east, has an area of 51·7 sq. miles and 7,628 inhabitants. The island of Culebra, with 1,265 inhabitants, between Puerto Rico and St Thomas, has a good harbour.

CONSTITUTION AND GOVERNMENT. Puerto Rico has representative government, the franchise being restricted to citizens 18 years of age or over, residence (1 year) and such additional qualifications as may be prescribed by the Legislature of Puerto Rico, but no property qualification may be imposed. Women were enfranchised in 1932 (with a literacy test) and fully in 1936. Puerto Ricans do not vote in the US presidential elections, though individuals living on the mainland are free to do so subject to the local electoral laws. The executive power resides in a Governor, elected directly by the people every 4 years. Fourteen heads of departments form the Governor's advisory council, also designated as his Council of Secretaries. The legislative functions are vested in a Senate, composed of 27 members (2 from each of the 8 senatorial districts and 11 senators at large), and the House of Representatives, composed of 51 members (1 from each of the 40 representative districts and 11 elected at large). Puerto Rico sends to Congress a Resident Commissioner to the US, elected by the people for a term of 4 years, but he has no vote in Congress. Puerto Rican men are subject to conscription in US services.

On 27 Nov. 1953 President Eisenhower sent a message to the General Assembly of the UN stating 'if at any time the Legislative Assembly of Puerto Rico adopts a resolution in favour of more complete or even absolute independence' he 'will immediately thereafter recommend to Congress that such independence be granted'.

For an account of the constitutional developments prior to 1952, *see* THE STATESMAN'S YEAR-BOOK, 1952, p. 742. The new constitution was drafted by a Puerto Rican Constituent Assembly and approved by the electorate at a referendum on 3 March 1952. It was then submitted to Congress, which struck out Section 20 of Article 11 covering the 'right to work' and the 'right to an adequate standard of living'; the remainder was passed and proclaimed by the Governor on 25 July 1952.

At the election on 7 Nov. 1976 the New Progressive Party (advocates of statehood), headed by Carlos Romero Barceló, polled 682,607 votes (46·6% of the total); the Popular Democratic Party, headed by Rafael Hernández Colon, polled 634,941 votes (43·3% of the total); the Independence Party (full independence by constitutional means), 58,556 (4% of the total); Partido Socialista Puertorriqueño (full independence), 9,761 votes (0·7% of the total).

Governor: Carlos Romero Barceló (New Progressive Party), 1977–80 ($35,000).

ECONOMY

Budget. Receipts and disbursements (US$) in central government fund for the year ending 30 June 1979 were:

Balance, 1 July 1979	4,568,220	Disbursements	2,884,461,765
Receipts	3,060,838,542	Balance,1 July 1979	180,944,997
Total	3,065,406,762		

Assessed value of property, 30 June 1979, was $6,882·6m., and bonded indebtedness, $1,239·9m.

The US administers and finances the postal service and maintains air and naval bases. US payments in Puerto Rico, including direct expenditures (mainly military), grants-in-aid and other payments to individuals and to business totalled: 1972–73, $854·9m.; 1973–74, $908·1m.; 1974–75, $1,414·3m.; 1975–76, $2,054·9m.; 1976–77, $2,176·1m.; 1977–78, $2,563·4m.; 1978–79, $2,815·8m.

Banking. Nineteen banks on 30 June 1980 had total deposits of $8,652m. and debits of $13,399m. Bank loans were $5,976m.

NATURAL RESOURCES

Minerals. Production (1980): Cement, 1·4m. short tons; stone, 12·2m. short tons, value $44·3m. Total value of mineral production in 1977 was $137·1m.

Agriculture. In 1974 there were 47 'proportional profit' farms of 22,051 cords (about 22,704 acres) (mostly sugar-cane). The land had been bought from the big corporations by the Land Authority.

Production of raw sugar, 96 degrees basis, 1980 crop year, was 174,708 tons.

Livestock (1979): Cattle, 524,000; pigs, 232,000; goats, 23,492; poultry, 6·8m.

COMMERCE. In 1979–80 imports amounted to $8,638·2m., of which $5,134·8m. came from US; exports were valued at $6,941·7m., of which $5,874·1m. went to US.

In 1978–79 the US took: Sugar, 6,048 short tons); tobacco and products, 7,420,258 lb.; rum, 20,226,230 proof gallons ($100m.).

Puerto Rico is not permitted to levy taxes on imports.

Total trade between Puerto Rico and UK (British Department of Trade returns, in £1,000 sterling):

	1976	1977	1978	1979	1980
Imports to UK	14,704	36,369	29,266	40,807	33,002
Exports and re-exports from UK	14,686	17,994	23,291	18,332	16,970

COMMUNICATIONS

Roads. The Department of Public Works had under maintenance in June 1979, 6,864 miles of paved road. Motor vehicles registered 30 June 1979, 1,035,200.

Shipping. In fiscal year 1979–80, 9,106 American and foreign vessels of 51,444,745 gross tons entered and cleared Puerto Rico.

Post and Broadcasting. In 1980 there were 95 broadcasting stations and 10 television companies. There were (1979) 628,123 telephones.

Cinemas (1979). Cinemas numbered 161, with annual attendance of 9·9m.

Newspapers (1980). There are 4 main newspapers; 3 have a circulation of over 125,000.

JUSTICE AND EDUCATION

Justice. The Commonwealth judiciary system is headed by a Supreme Court of 7 members, appointed by the Governor, and consists of a Superior Tribunal with 11 sections and 89 superior judges, a District Tribunal with 38 sections and 98 district judges, and 37 municipal judges all appointed by the Governor. The police force (1980) consisted of 9,032 men and women.

Education. Education was made compulsory in 1899, but in 1975–76, 3% of the children still had no access to schooling. The percentage of illiteracy in 1976 was 8·7% of those 10 years of age or older. Total enrolment in public schools, 1980, was 716,138. Accredited private schools had 96,784 pupils. All instruction below senior high school standard is given in Spanish only.

The University of Puerto Rico, in Río Piedras, 7 miles from San Juan, had 50,248 students in 1978–79 and 9,417 in 5 Regional Colleges. Higher education is also available in the Inter-American University of Puerto Rico (28,749 students in 1978–79), the Catholic University of Puerto Rico (11,138), the Sacred Heart College (5,929) and the Puerto Rico Junior College (13,093). These and other private colleges and universities had 71,224 students in 1978–79.

Books of Reference

Statistical Information: The area of Economic Research and Evaluation of the Puerto Rico Planning Board publishes: (*a*) annual *Economic Report to the Governor*; (*b*) *Statistical Yearbook* (since 1940–41); (*c*) *External Trade Statistics* (annual report); (*d*) *Economic Bulletin* (monthly); (*e*) Reports on national income and balance of payments; (*f*) Socio-Economic Statistics (since 1940). In addition there are annual reports by various Departments.

Annual Reports. Governor of Puerto Rico. Washington
Bird, A., *Bibliografia Puertorriqueña, 1930–45*. Social Science Research Centre, Univ. of Puerto Rico. 2 vols. 1946–47
Crampsey, R. A., *Puerto Rico*. Newton Abbot, 1973
Hill, R. (ed.), *Family and Population Control: A Puerto Rican Experiment*. Univ. of N. Carolina Press, 1959
Jones, C. F., and Pico, R. (ed.), *Symposium on the Geography of Puerto Rico*. Univ. of P.R. Press, 1955
Tumin, M. M., and Feldman, A. S., *Social Class and Social Change in Puerto Rico*. Princeton Univ. Press, 1961

Commonwealth Library: Univ. of Puerto Rico Library, Rio Piedras. *Librarian:* José Lázaro.

AMERICAN SAMOA

HISTORY. The Samoan Islands were first visited by Europeans in the 18th century; the first recorded visit was in 1722. On 14 July 1889 a treaty between the USA, Germany and Great Britain proclaimed the Samoan islands neutral territory, under a 4-power government consisting of the 3 treaty powers and the local native government. By the Tripartite Treaty of 7 Nov. 1899, ratified 19 Feb. 1900, Great Britain and Germany renounced in favour of the US all rights over the islands of the Samoan group east of 171° long. west of Greenwich, the islands to the west of that meridian being assigned to Germany (now the Independent State of Western Samoa, *see* p. 1593). The islands of Tutuila and Aunu'u were ceded to the US by their High Chiefs on 17 April 1900, and the islands of the Manu'a group on 16 July 1904. Congress accepted the islands under a Joint Resolution approved 20 Feb. 1929. Swain's Island, 210 miles north-north-west of the Samoan Islands, was annexed in 1925 and is administered as an integral part of American Samoa.

AREA AND POPULATION. The islands are approximately 650 miles north-east of Fiji. The total area of American Samoa is 76·1 sq. miles (197 sq. km); population, 1970, 27,159, nearly all Polynesians or part-Polynesians. 1977 population estimate, 30,600. The Island of Tutuila, 80 miles from Apia, has an area of 53 sq. miles, with a population (1970) of 24,973 (28,669 in 1977) (including the island of Aunu'u). Ta'u has an area of 17 sq. miles, and the other islands (Ofu and Olosega) of the Manu'a group have an area of about 5 sq. miles with a population of 2,112 in 1970 (1,700 in 1976). Swain's Island, circular in shape, has an area of 1·9 sq. miles and a population, 1970, of 74 (31 in 1977). Rose Island (uninhabited) is 0·4 sq. mile in area. In 1975 there were 1,154 births and 160 deaths.

CONSTITUTION AND GOVERNMENT. American Samoa is constitutionally an unorganized unincorporated territory of the US administered under the Department of the Interior. Its indigenous inhabitants are US nationals and are classified locally as citizens of American Samoa with certain privileges under local laws not granted to non-indigenous persons. Polynesian customs (not inconsistent with US laws) are respected.

Fagatogo is the seat of the Government.

The islands are organized in 14 counties grouped in 3 districts; these counties and districts correspond to the traditional political units. On 25 Feb. 1948 a bicameral legislature was established, at the request of the Samoans, to have advisory legislative functions. With the adoption of the Revised Constitution of American Samoa, effective 1 July 1967, the legislature was vested with limited law-making authority. The lower house, or House of Representatives, is composed of 20 members elected by universal adult suffrage and 1 non-voting member for Swain's Island. The upper house, or Senate, is composed of 18 members elected, in the traditional Samoan manner, in meetings of the chiefs.

Governor: Peter Tali Coleman.
Lieut.-Governor: High Chief Tufele Lia.

ECONOMY

Planning. The first formal Economic Development and Planning Office completed its first year in 1971. Much has been done to promote economic expansion within the Territory and a large amount of outside investment interest has been stimulated.

The Office initiated the first Territorial Comprehensive Plan. This plan when completed will, with periodic updating, provide a guideline to territorial development for the next 20 years. The planning programme was made possible under a Housing and Urban Development '701' grant programme.

The focus will be on physical development and the problems of a rapidly increasing population with severely limited land resources.

Budget. The chief sources of revenue are annual federal grants from the US, and local revenues from individual and corporate income taxes, import duties, sale of utilities, rents and leases and liquor sales. During the fiscal year 1976 the Government had a revenue of $45·4m. including local appropriation of $3·9m. and federal appropriations of $41m.

Banking. The American Samoa branch of the Bank of Hawaii offers all commercial banking services. The Development Bank of American Samoa, government owned, is concerned primarily through loans and guarantees with the economic advancement of the Territory. The American Savings and Loan Bank has a branch in American Samoa.

ENERGY AND NATURAL RESOURCES

Electricity. Net power generated (1976) was 62·6m. kwh., of which 31·6m. kwh. was supplied to large power users and 16m. kwh. to householders. All the Manu'a islands have electricity.

Agriculture. There are virtually no public lands in American Samoa. Nearly all the land is owned by Samoans and, with a few exceptions, cannot be sold except to persons having at least one-half Samoan blood. Of the 48,640 acres of land area, 11,000 acres are suitable for tropical crops, 1,000 acres for most temperate vegetables, 8,000 acres only to such crops as coconut and cacao with good conservation practice, 5,000 acres to controlled forestation and about 22,500 to indigenous and introduced forest with strict conservation measures; 1,000 acres are roads, building sites and villages. Principal crops are taro, bread-fruit, yams, bananas, coconuts, arrowroot and papayas.

Livestock (1978): Pigs, 8,000; goats, 9,000; poultry, 39,000.

INDUSTRY AND TRADE

Industry. Fish canning is important, employing the second largest number of people (after government). Attempts are being made to provide a variety of light industries. Tuna fishing and local inshore fishing are both expanding.

Commerce. In 1977 American Samoa exported goods valued at $81,232,067 and imported goods valued at $54,941,048. Chief exports are canned tuna, watches, pet foods and handicrafts. Chief imports are cement, lumber, rice, flour, fish, meat, fuel oil, sugar.

COMMUNICATIONS

Roads. There are about 45·2 miles of paved roads, 30·8 miles of unpaved and 5·4 miles of secondary roads. There are 12·7 miles of secondary unpaved roads maintained mainly on Tutuila. Motor vehicles registered, 1977, 4,127.

Aviation. PANAM operates between Western America, Honolulu, New Zealand, American Samoa and Tahiti. South Pacific Island Airways and Polynesian Airlines operate daily services between American Samoa and Western Samoa. The islands are also served by Air New Zealand and UTA. Total landings at Pago Pago, 1977, 11,992.

Shipping. The harbour at Pago Pago, which nearly bisects the island of Tutuila, is the only good harbour for large vessels in Samoa. By sea, there is a twice-monthly service between Western America, New Zealand and Australia and regular service between US, South Pacific ports and Japan. In 1977, 779 vessels entered and 737 cleared Pago Pago harbour.

Post and Broadcasting. A commercial radiogram service is available to all parts of the world through 3 principal trunks, Hawaii, Fiji and Western Samoa. Commercial phone services are operated to all parts of the world on a 24-hour service. Number of telephones (June 1978), 4,570.

JUSTICE, EDUCATION AND WELFARE

Justice. Judicial power is vested in a High Court. Fifty-nine district courts, traffic courts and small claims courts are heard without record and appeals therefrom are tried, *de novo*, in the trial division of the High Court. The trial division also has original jurisdiction of all criminal and civil cases. The probate division has jurisdiction of estates, guardianships, trusts and other matters. The land and title division decides cases relating to disputes involving communal land and Matai title court rules on questions and controversy over family titles. The appellate division hears appeals from trial, land and title and probate divisions as well as having original jurisdiction in selected matters. The appellate court is the court of last resort. Two American judges sit with 5 Samoan judges permanently. In addition there are 8 temporary judges or assessors who sit occasionally on cases involving Samoan customs.

Education. Education is compulsory between the ages of 6 and 18. The Government (1978) maintains 24 consolidated elementary schools, 4 senior high schools with technical departments, 1 community college, special education classes for the handicapped and 100 Early Childhood Education Centres for pre-school children. Total elementary and secondary enrolment (1978), 7,492; in ECE schools,1,505; classes for the handicapped, 102; total elementary and secondary classroom teachers, 435. Eight private schools had 1,820 students. Learning is by a variety of media including television.

Health. The Department of Health provides the only medical and dental care in American Samoa. It operates a general hospital (181 beds including 31 bassinets), 2 dispensaries on Tutuila, 4 dispensaries in the Manu'a group, 1 on Aunu'u and 1 on Swain's Island. A $3·5m. tropical medical centre was completed and placed in service in 1968. This now embraces the general hospital as well as out-patient clinics for surgery, obstetrics, gynaecology, emergencies, family practice, internal medicine, paediatrics; there are clinics for treatment of the eye, ear, nose and throat, dental and public health departments.

VIRGIN ISLANDS OF THE UNITED STATES

HISTORY. The Virgin Islands of the United States, formerly known as the Danish West Indies, were named and claimed for Spain by Columbus in 1493. They were later settled by Dutch and English planters, invaded by France in the mid-17th century and abandoned by the French *c*. 1700, by which time Danish influence had been established. St Croix was held by the Knights of Malta between two periods of French rule.

They were purchased by the United States from Denmark for $25m. in a treaty ratified by both nations and proclaimed 31 March 1917. Their value was wholly strategic, inasmuch as they commanded the Anegada Passage from the Atlantic Ocean to the Caribbean Sea and the approach to the Panama Canal. Although the inhabitants were made US citizens in 1927, the islands are, constitutionally, an 'unincorporated territory'.

AREA AND POPULATION. The Virgin Islands group, lying about 40 miles due east of Puerto Rico, comprises the islands of St Thomas (28 sq. miles), St Croix (84 sq. miles), St John (20 sq. miles) and about 50 small islets or cays, mostly uninhabited. The total area of the 3 principal islands is 132 sq. miles, of which the US Government owns 9,599 acres as National Park.

The population, according to the census of 1 April 1970, was 62,800, an increase of 30,701 or 96% since 1960. This figure was afterwards revised to 75,151. Population had slowly declined since 1835, when it stood at 43,000, but began to recover in the 1940s. Estimated population, 1980, was 118,960: St Croix, 60,830; St Thomas, 55,560; St John, 2,570. About 20–25% are native-born, 35–40% from other Caribbean islands, 10% from mainland USA and 5% from Europe. St Croix has over 40% of Puerto Rican origin or extraction, Spanish speaking. In 1979–80 financial year births were 2,512 and deaths, 532.

The capital and only city, Charlotte Amalie, on St Thomas, had a population (1976) of 15,041; there are two towns on St Croix. Christiansted with 3,579 and Frederiksted with 1,939.

CONSTITUTION AND GOVERNMENT The Organic Act of 22 July 1954 gives the US Department of the Interior full jurisdiction; some limited legislative powers are given to a single-chambered legislature, composed of 15 senators elected for 2 years representing the two legislative districts of St Croix and St Thomas St John.

The Governor is elected by the islanders. A new Constitution was under consideration in March 1979, but was rejected by the electorate; a further constitutional convention was held in 1980. A new document was submitted to the President of the United States and to Congress; if approved, it will be submitted to the Virgin Islands electorate in a referendum during 1981. A Status Commission was appointed to advise on and guide towards greater self-determination; government and community are represented.

For administration, there are 13 executive departments, 12 of which are under commissioners and the other, the Department of Law, under an Attorney-General. The US Department of the Interior appoints a Federal Comptroller of government revenue and expenditure.

The franchise is vested in residents who are citizens of the United States, 18 years of age or over. In 1978 there were 27,954 voters, of whom 21,610 participated in the local elections that year.

They do not participate in the US presidential election but they have a non-voting representative in Congress.

The capital is Charlotte Amalie, on St Thomas Island.

Governor: Juan Luis ($45,000).
Lieut.-Governor: Henry A. Millin ($44,000).

ECONOMY

Budget. Under the 1954 Organic Act finances are provided partly from local revenues—customs, federal income tax, real and personal property tax, trade tax, excise tax, pilotage fees, etc.—and partly from Federal Matching Funds, being the excise taxes collected by the federal government on such Virgin Islands products transported to the mainland as are liable.

Revenue for fiscal year ending 30 Sept. 1980, $189·2m., and expenditure $161·7m. with another $27m. committed.

Currency and Banking. United States currency became legal tender on 1 July 1934. Banks are the Chase Manhattan Bank; the Bank of Nova Scotia; the First Federal Savings and Loan Association of Puerto Rico; Barclays Bank International; Bank of America; Citibank; Deposit Insurance National Bank; First Pennsylvania Bank, and the Royal Bank of Canada.

ENERGY AND NATURAL RESOURCES

Electricity. The Virgin Islands Water and Power Authority provides electric power from generating plants on St Croix and St Thomas; St John is served by power cable and emergency generator.

Water. There is a shortage of pure water, of which rain-water is the most reliable source. Every building must have a cistern to provide rain-water for drinking, even in areas served by mains (10 gallons capacity per sq. ft of roof for a single-storey house). There are 6 desalinization plants with a maximum capacity of 8·7m. gallons of fresh water per day. Three others have been obtained and will be put into operation during 1981.

Agriculture. With the phasing out of the sugar-cane industry in St Croix, and the accelerated construction activities carried on in all three islands, the number of farms decreased, but there has recently been a revival of interest in food crops.

Land for fruit, vegetables and animal feed is available on St Croix, and there are tax incentives for development. Sugar has been terminated as a commercial crop and over 4,000 acres of prime land could be utilized for food crops.

Livestock (1980): Cattle, 6,678; goats, 5,346; pigs, 1,739; sheep, 1,562.

Fisheries. There is a fishermen's co-operative with a market at Christiansted. There is a shellfish-farming project at Rust-op-Twist, St Croix.

INDUSTRY AND TRADE

Industry. The main occupations on St Thomas are tourism and government service; on St Croix manufacturing is more important. Manufactures include watches, textiles, pharmaceuticals, rum and fragrances. The Martin Marietta Alumina plant processes bauxite from Africa for refining in mainland USA. The Amerada Hess oil refinery has a capacity of 700,000 bbls per day.

The Virgin Islands offer liberal tax exemptions to persons, firms or companies prepared to invest $50,000 in new industries or in the promotion of tourism.

Commerce. Exports, calendar year 1979, totalled $3,092·6m. and imports $3,766m.

Total trade between the US Virgin Islands and UK (financial years, British Department of Trade returns, in £1,000 sterling):

	1976	1977	1978	1979	1980
Imports to UK	15	11	127	851	39
Exports and re-exports from UK	3,010	3,155	3,255	3,273	18,518

Tourism. Tourism is the most important business. There were about 1·2m. visitors in 1979 spending $333m.

About 602,000 tourists came on cruise ships which made more than 821 calls, mainly at St Thomas which has a good, natural deepwater harbour.

COMMUNICATIONS

Roads. The Virgin Islands have 531·6 miles of roads, and 35,070 motor vehicles were registered in 1979.

Aviation. There is a daily cargo and passenger service between St Thomas and St Croix. Hamilton Airport on St Croix can take all aircraft except Concorde. Harry S. Truman Airport on St Thomas takes 727-class aircraft. There are air connexions to mainland USA, other Caribbean islands, Latin America and Europe.

Shipping. The whole territory has free port status. There is an hourly boat service between St Thomas and St John.

Post and Broadcasting. All three Virgin Islands have a dial telephone system. In Nov. 1980 there were 40,690 telephones. Direct dialling to Puerto Rico and the mainland is now possible. Worldwide radio telegraph service is also available.

The islands are served by 7 radio stations, 4 television stations and 5 newspapers, 2 of them dailies.

RELIGION AND EDUCATION

Religion. There are churches of the Protestant, Roman Catholic and Jewish faiths in St Thomas and St Croix and Protestant and Roman Catholic churches in St John.

Education. Education is compulsory between the ages of 5½ and 16 years, inclusive. In 1980–81 there were 35 public schools (ranging from kindergarten to high schools); enrolment was 25,201; other schools had 7,010 pupils; the public school budget was $42·7m. In 1980 the College of the Virgin Islands had 2,203 registered students: 561 full-time undergraduates, 1,423 part-time undergraduates and 219 graduate students. The College is part of the United States land-grant network of higher education.

Books of Reference

Evans, L. H., *The Virgin Islands: From Naval Base to New Deal*. Ann Arbor, Mich., 1945
Jarvis, J. A., *The Virgin Islands and Their People*. Philadelphia, 1944
McGuire, J. W., *Geographic Dictionary of the Virgin Islands of the United States*. US Coast and Geodetic Survey. Special Publication No. 103. Washington, 1925
Reid, C. F., *Bibliography of the Virgin Islands of the United States*. New York, 1941

TRUST TERRITORY OF THE PACIFIC ISLANDS

HISTORY. Under the Treaty of Versailles (1919) Japan was appointed mandatory to the former German possessions north of the Equator. In 1946 the US agreed to administer the former Japanese-mandated islands of the Caroline, Marshall and Mariana groups (except Guam) as a Trusteeship for the United Nations; the trusteeship agreement was approved by the Security Council 27 April 1947 and came into effect on 18 July 1947. The Trust Territory was administered by the US Navy until 1951, when all the islands except Tinian and Saipan in the Marianas were transferred to the Secretary of the Interior. In 1962 the Interior Department assumed responsibility for them also. On 17 June 1975 the voters of the Northern Mariana Islands, in a plebiscite observed by the UN, adopted the covenant to establish a Commonwealth of the Northern Mariana Islands in Union with the USA. In April 1976 the covenant was approved by the US government and the administration of the Northern Marianas was separated from that of the rest of the Trust Territory; the group has a constitution and a constitutional government, installed 9 Jan. 1978. The rest of the Trust Territory is divided into 3 entities, each with its own constitution. The Marshall Islands, the Federated States of Micronesia (Yap, Kosrae, Truk and Ponape) and the Republic of Belau are all negotiating a status of free association with the US government. Free association will grant the USA the authority to control military and defence activities in return for federal government assistance and budget supports to the autonomous constitutional governments. Termination of the UN Trusteeship Agreement is contingent upon establishing a political status, either free association or independence, for the islands. Negotiations were proceeding in 1981.

AREA AND POPULATION. The Trust Territory extends from 1° to 22° N. lat. and from 142° to 172° E. long. The area is generally known as Micronesia, or 'land of the small islands' (Guam, Kiribati and Nauru not part of the Trust Territory, are also ethnically and geographically Micronesian); total land area 708 sq. miles; population (1979 estimate), 133,500.

The estimated population of the 6 administrative districts as of Oct. 1977 was: Truk, 35,220; Ponape, 21,187; Marshall Islands, 27,096; Belau, 13,519; Yap, 8,482; Kosrae, 4,471. Nine different languages are spoken, each with variations; English is used in the schools and is the official language.

CONSTITUTION AND GOVERNMENT. Constitutional governments are functioning in the Mariana Islands (1978), the Marshall Islands (1979), the Federated States of Micronesia (1979) and the Republic of Belau (1981). Each of the 4 entities is autonomous from the other 3 but all are still legally under the single Trust Territory system. The citizens are Trust Territory citizens until the termination of the Trusteeship. Majuro is the capital of the Marshall Islands. Kolonia, Ponape, is the capital of the Federated States, Koror is the headquarters of Palau and Saipan is the capital of the Commonwealth of the Northern Marianas, as well as the US administrative headquarters.

High Commissioner: Adrian P. Winkel.

INDUSTRY. Tourism is the main source of income from overseas; industrial development is limited. There is some commercial fishing and agriculture, a coconut-processing plant and a tuna-packing plant.

COMMUNICATIONS

Aviation. The island groups are served by Continental Air Micronesia via Honolulu. Internal commuter airlines operate in Ponape, Yap, Marshalls, Belau and the Marianas. There are connexions to international routes at Guam and Hawaii.

JUSTICE, RELIGION, EDUCATION AND WELFARE

Justice. The Trust Territory Code, local constitutions and the Trusteeship Agreement are the foundations for law. Local police are responsible for enforcement. There is a Trust Territory High Court, constitutional courts and lesser courts. Local customs are recognized and protected in legal practice, when not in conflict with higher law.

Religion. Freedom of religion is guaranteed in the Trust Territory Code and all constitutions.

Education. Education is free and compulsory through elementary school (grades 1–8). There are public and private elementary and secondary schools and government post-secondary education.

Health. The public health system, which includes 6 district hospitals as well as other hospitals and clinics in outlying areas, is carried on by a staff consisting chiefly of trained Micronesian medical and dental officers and assistants under senior US doctors.

Books of Reference

Report to the United Nations Trusteeship Council, 1979. Dept. of State, Washington, D.C., 1980
Basic Information. High Commissioner's Office, Saipan

UNINCORPORATED TERRITORIES

Johnston Atoll. Two small islands 1,150 km south-west of Hawaii, administered by the US Air Force. Area, under 1 sq. mile; population, 1970 census, 1,007.

Midway Islands. Two small islands at the western end of the Hawaiian chain, administered by the US Navy. Area, 2 sq. miles; population, 1970 census, 2,220.

Wake Island. Three small islands 3,700 km west of Hawaii, administered by the US Air Force. Area, 3 sq. miles; population, 1970 census, 1,647.

UPPER VOLTA

République de Haute-Volta

Capital: Ouagadougou
Population: 6·6m. (1979)
GNP per capita: US$160 (1978)

HISTORY. A separate colony of Upper Volta was in 1919 carved out of the colony of Upper Senegal and Niger, which had been established in 1904. It was suppressed in 1932 and its territory divided between Ivory Coast, Sudan and Niger. On 4 Sept. 1947 the Territory of Upper Volta was re-established, comprising the area of the old colony of Upper Volta as at 5 Sept. 1932. The Republic of Upper Volta became independent on 5 Aug. 1960 and was admitted to the UN in 1960. On 3 Jan. 1966 the government of Maurice Yameogo was overthrown by a military *coup* led by Leut.-Col. Sangoulé Lamizana, who assumed the Presidency. Constitutional rule was resumed on 21 June 1970 but suspended from 8 Feb. 1974 until May 1978 and again from Nov. 1980.

AREA AND POPULATION. Upper Volta is bounded north and west by Mali, east by Niger, south by Dahomey, Togo, Ghana and the Ivory Coast. The republic covers an area of 274,122 sq. km; population (census, 1975) 5,638,203. Estimate (1979) 6,617,000. Ouagadougou, the capital (172,661 inhabitants), Bobo-Dioulasso (115,063), Koudougou (36,838), Ouahigouya (25,690), Banfora (12,358), Goucoy, Réo, Fada N'Ngourma, Tenkodogo and Kaya are *communes de plein exercice.* The principal autochthonous tribes are the Mossi (48%), Peulh (10%), Lobi-Dagari (7%), Mande (7%), Bobo (7%), Sénoufo (6%), Gourounsi (5%), Bissa (5%), Gourmantché (5%).

CONSTITUTION AND GOVERNMENT. Following the *coup* of 25 Nov. 1980, the 1977 Constitution was suspended and the 57-member National Assembly dissolved. Power is held by the Military Committee for National Recovery and Progress (CMRPN), ruling through an appointed Cabinet composed as follows:

President, Chairman of CMRPN, Prime Minister and Minister of Defence: Col. Saye Zerbo.

Foreign Affairs: Lieut.-Col. Felix Tientarboum. *Interior and Security:* Lieut.-Col. Nezien Badembie. *Justice:* Ouattara Bena. *Finance:* Edmund Ki. *Economy and Planning:* Mamadou Sanfo. *Development:* Maj. Contomparirock. *Commerce, Industrial Development and Mining:* Barry Djibrina. *Public Works, Transport and Urban Planning:* Capt. Gondumou Kani Gaston. *Education and Culture:* Ouegraogo Patoin Albert. *Higher Education and Scientific Research:* Sib Sie Faustain. *Health and Population:* Jean-Marie Kyelen. *Civil Service and Labour:* Alexandre Zoungrana. *Information and Telecommunications:* Lieut.-Col. Hounsouho Bambara Charles. *Youth and Sports:* Lieut. Moussa Georges Boni. *Environment and Tourism:* Ouedraogo Bandre Sylvestre. *Social and Women's Affairs:* Marie-Madeleine Kone Sanou.

National flag: Three horizontal stripes of black, white, red.

DEFENCE

Army. The Army consists of 3 infantry regiments, 1 reconnaisance squadron and support units; total strength (1980), 3,700.

Air Force. Creation of a small air arm to support the land forces began, with French assistance, in 1964. Equipment now comprises 1 HS.748 twin-turboprop freighter, 2

C-47s, 2 twin-turboprop Frégates, an Aero Commander 500, 3 Broussards and 2 Riems/Cessna Super Skymasters for transport and liaison duties. Personnel total about 75.

INTERNATIONAL RELATIONS

Membership. Upper Volta is a member of UN, OAU and is an ACP state of the EEC.

ECONOMY

Planning. The Third Development Plan 1977–81 aimed at an 8·4% average annual real growth in GDP.

Budget. Government revenue and expenditure balanced in 1980 at 40,223m. francs CFA.

Currency. The unit of currency is the *franc*. CFA. £1 = 552·6 *francs* in March 1981.

Banking. The *Banque Centrale des Etats de l'Afrique de l'Ouest* is the bank of issue. The main commercial bank is the *Banque Internationale des Voltas*. In 1976 the savings banks had 668,146 depositors with 26,683,701 *francs* CFA to their credit.

ENERGY AND NATURAL RESOURCES

Electricity. Production of electricity (1976) was 59m. kwh.

Minerals. There are deposits of manganese but exploitation is limited by existing transport facilities. Magnetite, bauxite, zinc, lead, nickel and phosphates have been found in the same area.

Agriculture. Production (1977, in tonnes): Sorghum, 634,812; millet, 354,673; maize, 73,748; groundnuts, 57,073; rice (paddy), 48,328; cotton, 44,675; sesame, 9,382. Rice and groundnuts are of increasing importance.

Livestock (1979): 2·7m. cattle, 1·8m. sheep, 2·7m. goats, 90,000 horses, 180,000 donkeys.

INDUSTRY AND TRADE

Industry. In 1978 gross manufacturing output (including energy) was 21,638 francs CFA, of which foodstuffs (7·17m. francs CFA), textiles (2·36m. francs CFA) and metal products (516m. francs CFA). In 1972 there were 91 industrial units.

Labour. At the end of 1972 the labour force was 2,856,739; some 87% are engaged in agriculture, forestry and fishing. There were (1981) 4 trade unions.

Commerce. In 1977 imports totalled 51,354m. francs CFA and exports 13,614m. francs CFA. The principal export was cotton (5,400m. francs CFA).

Total trade between Upper Volta and UK (British Department of Trade returns, in £1,000 sterling):

	1976	1977	1978	1979	1980
Imports to UK	5,855	2,970	4,496	338	2,819
Exports and re-exports from UK	536	3,687	914	1,234	1,039

COMMUNICATIONS

Roads. The road system comprises 16,462 km, of which 4,460 km are national, 1,920 km departmental, 2,322 km regional and 7,760 km unclassified roads. There were 9,500 private cars and 10,100 commercial vehicles in 1975.

Railway. Ouagadougou is the terminus of the Abidjan–Niger railway. An extension to Tambao is proposed.

Aviation. Ouagadougou and Bobo-Dioulasso are regularly served by UTA and Air Afrique and in 1977 dealt with 63,221 passengers and 3,802 tonnes of freight.

Post. There were, in 1978, some 66 post offices and 3,564 telephones.

JUSTICE, RELIGION, EDUCATION AND WELFARE

Justice. There are courts of first instance at Ouagadougou, Bobo-Dioulasso, Ouahigouya and Fada N'Gourma. The Supreme Court, High Court of Justice and Court of Appeal are all in Ouagadougou.

Religion. The majority of the population (53%) follow animinst religions; 36% are Moslem and 11% Christian (mainly Roman Catholic).

Education. There were, in 1979, 171,000 pupils in 865 primary schools, 15,271 in secondary schools, 1,852 in technical schools and 495 students in teacher-training establishments. The Université d' Ouagadougou had 1,281 students.

Health (1976). There were 5 hospitals, 119 dispensaries with maternity units and 24 maternity units alone with a total of 3,623 beds. There were 107 doctors, 7 dentists, 11 pharmacists, 98 midwives and 1,193 nursing personnel.

DIPLOMATIC REPRESENTATIVES

OF UPPER VOLTA IN GREAT BRITAIN

Ambassador: Victor Kaboré (resides in Paris).

OF GREAT BRITAIN IN UPPER VOLTA

Ambassador: Michael Francis Daly (resides in Abidjan).

OF UPPER VOLTA IN THE USA (5500 16th St., NW, Washington, D.C., 20011)

Ambassador: Telesphore Yaguibou.

OF THE USA IN UPPER VOLTA (PO Box 35, Ouagadougou)

Ambassador: (Vacant).

OF UPPER VOLTA TO THE UNITED NATIONS

Ambassador: Aissé Mensah.

URUGUAY

República Oriental del Uruguay

Capital: Montevideo
Population: 2·9m. (1978)
GNP per capita: US$1,610 (1978)

HISTORY. The Republic of Uruguay, formerly a part of the Spanish Vice-royalty of Río de la Plata and subsequently a province of Brazil, declared its independence 25 Aug. 1825 which was recognized by the treaty between Argentina and Brazil signed at Rio de Janeiro 27 Aug. 1828. The first constitution was adopted 18 July 1830.

AREA AND POPULATION. Uruguay is bounded on the north-east by Brazil, on the south-east by the Atlantic, on the south by the Río de la Plata and on the west by Argentina. The area is 186,926 sq. km (72,172 sq. miles). The following table shows the area and the population of the 19 departments (capitals in brackets) as estimated in May 1975:

Departments	Area, sq. km	Population	Pop. per sq. km
Artigas (Artigas)	11,378	57,528	4·6
Canelones (Canelones)	4,752	313,858	54·3
Cerro-Largo (Melo)	14,929	73,204	4·8
Colonia (Colonia) ·	5,682	110,820	18·5
Durazno (Durazno)	14,315	54,990	3·7
Flores (Trinidad)	4,519	24,684	5·2
Florida (Florida)	12,107	66,092	5·3
Lavalleja (Minas)	12,485	65,240	5·3
Maldonado (Maldonado)	4,111	75,607	14·9
Montevideo (Montevideo City)	664	1,229,748	2,072·6
Paysandú (Paysandú)	13,252	98,735	6·6
Río Negro (Fray Bentos)	8,471	49,816	5·5
Rivera (Rivera)	9,829	79,330	7·8
Rocha (Rocha)	11,089	59,952	5·0
Salto (Salto)	12,603	100,407	7·3
San José (San José)	6,963	88,281	11·4
Soriano (Mercedes)	9,223	80,114	8·4
Tacuarembó (Tacuarembó)	21,015	84,829	3·7
Treinta y Tres (Treinta y Tres)	9,539	45,680	4·5
Total	186,926	2,763,964	14·7

Estimated population in 1978 was 2,886,000. In 1975 Montevideo (the capital) had an estimated population of 1,229,748. Other cities (1975): Salto, 80,000; Paysandú, 80,000; Mercedes, 53,000.

CONSTITUTION AND GOVERNMENT. Since 1900 Uruguay has been unique in her constitutional innovations, all designed to protect her from the emergence of a dictatorship. The favourite device of the group known as the 'Batllistas' (a *Colorado* faction) which, until defeated at the 1958 elections, held the majority for over 90 years, has been the collegiate system of government, in which the two largest political parties were represented.

One such pattern lasted from 1917 to 1933, when it was abolished by a dictator who re-established the system of an individual President. Until 1951 Presidents were elected every 4 years and they selected their own Cabinet Ministers (*see* list of Presidents in THE STATESMAN'S YEAR-BOOK, 1956, p. 1493). In 1951, on the initiative of the 'Batllistas', the Constitution was amended: the individual presidency was abolished and the executive power vested in a National Council of Government of 9 members (6 from the majority and 3 from the minority parties).

1575

As a result of a referendum held on 27 Nov. 1966, Uruguay returned to the presidential system. The President appoints a council of 11 Ministers; the Vice-President presides over the Senate and the General Assembly when this takes place. A new Constitution was rejected by referendum in Dec. 1980.

President: Dr Aparicio Méndez (sworn in for a 5-year term on 1 Sept. 1976).

The Cabinet in April 1980 was as follows:

Interior: Gen. Manuel J. Nuñez. *Foreign Affairs:* Adolfo Folle Martinez. *Justice:* Dr Fernando Bayardo Bengoa. *Economy and Finance:* Dr Valentín Arismendi. *Transport and Public Works:* Eduardo Sampson. *Public Health:* Dr Antonio Cañellas. *Industry and Energy:* Ing. Francisco Tourreilles. *National Defence:* Dr Walter Ravenna. *Agriculture and Fisheries:* Juan Cassou. *Education:* Daniel Darracq. *Labour and Social Security:* Dr Carlos Alberto Maeso. *Secretary to Presidency:* Luis Vargas Garmendia.

Parliament was dissolved by Presidential decree on 27 June 1973 but a return to democratic government has been promised by 1981. A new Constitution was prepared during 1980.

The electorate in 1971 numbered 1·7m.; women constituted 50%.

The Colorado party favours 'statism' and social-welfare legislation. Most banking and all forms of insurance are government monopolies, as are also the railways and all the public utilities. The Government controls cement, fuel, petroleum and alcohol, including the manufacture of *caña.*

National flag: Nine horizontal stripes of white and blue, a white canton with the 'Sun of May' in gold.

National anthem: Orientales, la patria ó la tumba (words by Francisco Acuña de Figueroa; music by Francisco José Deballi).

DEFENCE

Army. The Army is composed of the active army and its reserves. The active army is formed of volunteers, who contract for 1 year or 2 years' service. In 1980 there were 2 regiments of cavalry, 4 artillery and 13 infantry battalions, 5 engineer battalions and 1 air defence battalion. Peace-time strength, 22,000 men.

The reserve is formed by elements who, for some reason or other, retire from the active army. It is reckoned that about 120,000 men could be mobilized in case of war.

Navy. The Navy consists of 3 frigates (*ex-*US old destroyer escorts), 2 escorts (*ex-*US fleet minesweepers), 1 patrol vessel (*ex-*coastal minesweeper), 6 patrol craft, 2 survey ships, 1 salvage vessel, 2 minor amphibious craft, 3 oilers and 3 tenders. Personnel in 1981: 3,500 officers and ratings including naval infantry.

There is a small US-equipped naval air service of 18 aircraft and helicopters with 3 bases on the river Plate estuary.

Air Force. Organized with US aid, the Air Force has about 3,000 personnel and 110 aircraft, including 1 fighter-bomber squadron with 5 AT-33 armed jet trainers, 8 A-37B light strike aircraft, 2 transport squadrons with 4 turboprop FH-227/F.27 Friendships, 6 Brazilian-built EMB-110 Bandeirantes (1 equipped for photographic duties), 10 C-47s and 7 Queen Airs, a search and rescue squadron with light helicopters, and a number of Cessna U-17A/182 and Super Cub aircraft for liaison and reconnaissance duties. Basic training types are the T-41 and T-34.

INTERNATIONAL RELATIONS

Membership. Uruguay is a member of UN, OAS and LAIA (formerly LAFTA).

ECONOMY

Budget. The receipts and expenditure of the national accounts as approved by the National Council of Government (UR$1m.):

	1974	1975	1976	1977	1978	1979
Revenue	587,909	985,501	1,721,679	2,937,583	4,349,819	8,423,600
Expenditure	789,502	1,348,779	2,047,354	3,178,197	4,750,533	8,300,700

Now covering a 5-year period the budget is presented during the year following election of each new government; differences in actual annual income and expenditure and amendments to the budget (including new taxes) must be approved by Parliament each year-end; these usually come forward in July each year.

Expenditures in 1975 (in 1m. nuevo pesos) included 19,463 for education and welfare, 219,237 for defence, 82,757 for health, 152,632 for interior, 43,608 for finance and public works, 7,991 for agriculture and 22,497 for transport and tourism. Expenditure on public works is separately financed from specific revenues (*e.g.*, fuel tax). A law inaugurating income tax came into operation on 1 July 1961, but was repealed on 1 March 1974.

Foreign debt outstanding on 31 Dec. 1979 was US$1,492m. Total reserves of the Banco Central on 31 March 1980 were US$635·2m.

Currency. There is no gold in circulation, but the monetary standard is gold, the theoretical gold coin being the *peso oro*, gold content of which was fixed, Dec. 1964, at 0·05924 gramme. It is equal to 100 *pesos*. The unit of currency is the *Nuevo Peso* (1,000 old pesos) of 100 *centésimos*. The actual circulating medium consists of paper notes issued by the Central Bank in denominations of 10,000, 5,000 and 1,000 old *pesos*. (Some notes have been restamped N$5 and N$10.) New notes in *Nuevo Peso* denominations of 50, 100, 500 and 1,000 are also in circulation, as is a *Nuevo Peso* 5 coin. There are bronze and aluminium coins of 50, 20 and 10 old *pesos*.

In March 1981 there were N$10·27 to the US$; N$22·36 = £1.

Banking. The Bank of the Republic (founded 1896), whose president and directors are appointed by the Government, has a paid-up capital of UR$1,852m. The Banco Central was inaugurated on 16 May 1967. Note circulation on 31 March 1980 was UR$488,500m.

A state-owned National Insurance Bank (*Banco de Seguros del Estado*) has a monopoly of new insurance business of all kinds. The Bank re-insures much of its business in London.

Of the 36 banks in Uruguay the Bank of London and South America (British) has a main office and 12 branch agencies.

Weights and Measures. The metric system was adopted in 1862.

ENERGY AND NATURAL RESOURCES

Electricity. The supply of electricity for light, power and traction has been a State monopoly since 1897. In Jan. 1949 the first hydro-electric plant at the site of the dam of Rincón del Bonete was completed with an installed capacity of 128 megawatts. Another plant at Rincón de Baygorria on the Río Negro came into operation in 1960, with a capacity of 108 megawatts. Five turbines of the Salto Grande hydroelectric dam were operating by Oct. 1980. Power output in Dec. 1979 was 2,749m. kwh.

Oil. An extension of the ANCAP refining plant, opened at Montevideo on 6 Dec. 1961, gives a capacity of 7,500 cu. metres daily of high-octane petrol and high-grade gas for domestic and industrial use.

Agriculture. Uruguay is primarily a pastoral country. Of the total land area of 46m. acres some 41m. are devoted to farming, of which 90% to livestock and 10% to crops. Some large *estancias* have been divided up into family farms; rural landlordism is much less than elsewhere. Uruguay is said to be the only Latin American country in which agricultural workers have the protection of a minimum-wage law. Animals and animal products constituted 43% of the exports in 1977. The 1966 census reported on 79,101 farms of all kinds, totalling 16·5m. hectares.

There were (1979) 10m. cattle, 18·7m. sheep, 525,000 horses, 400,000 pigs, 12,000 goats and 7·6m. poultry.

Wool production in 1979 exceeded 61,000 tonnes.

Agricultural products are raised chiefly in the departments of Paysandú, Río Negro, Colonia, San José, Soriano and Florida. The average farm is about 250 acres. The principal crops and their estimated yield (in tonnes) in 2 crop years were as follows:

	1978	1979		1978	1979
Wheat	173,200	174,200	Barley	38,000	57,400
Linseed	39,800	31,200	Maize	171,700	70,900
Oats	17,300	23,000	Rice	225,600	248,000

Uruguay is self-sufficient in rice, with a surplus for export. Three sugar refineries handle cane and (mainly) beet, their total production being approximately 90,000 tonnes, and approaching self-sufficiency.

Wine is produced chiefly in the departments of Montevideo, Canelones and Colonia, about enough for domestic consumption. The country has some 6m. fruit trees, principally peaches, oranges, tangerines and pears.

Forestry. In 1974 roundwood removals were 1,077,000 cu. metres, of which 1,001,000 cu. metres was softwood.

Fisheries. In 1979, the total catch was 108,000 tonnes. Exports amounted to 47,000 tonnes valued at US$36·2m.

INDUSTRY AND TRADE

Industry. In 1978 there were nearly 77,000 registered enterprises with 405,000 employees. These cover activities such as meat packing, oil refining, cement manufacture, foodstuffs, beverages, leather and textile maufacture, chemicals, light engineering and transport equipment. There are about 100 textile mills, but with the exception of half a dozen large plants, these are on the whole small.

The development of industry is an important economic policy objective and there is a liberal attitude to foreign investment for industrial promotion.

There are a number of public works programmes including airport modernization, port of Montevideo modernization, highways improvements, Montevideo sewage disposal, power production and transmission and telecommunications.

Trade Unions. Trade unions number about 150,000 members. About 1,036,000 (40%) of the population are classed as gainfully occupied.

Commerce. The foreign trade (officially stated in US$, with the figure for imports based on the clearance permits granted and that for exports on export licences utilized) was as follows (in US$1,000):

	1973	1974	1975	1976	1977	1978	1979
Imports	284·8	486·7	516·9	587·2	721·0	757	1,206
Exports	321·5	382·2	381·2	546·5	607·5	694	787

Of the imports in 1979 (in US$1m.) Argentina furnished 197·4; Brazil, 180·8; Middle East, 160; USA and Canada, 123·6, Federal Republic of Germany, 95·1 and UK, 46·1; of the exports in 1979 Brazil took 182·4; Federal Republic of Germany, 128·3; Argentina, 97·1; USA and Canada, 92·1; Netherlands, 57·2; Italy 27·8; UK, 21·7.

Principal imports and exports (in US$1,000):

Imports	1978	1979	Exports	1978	1979
Raw materials	150,500	296,500	Meat and meat products	109,104	141,108
Transport materials	52,200	77,500	Hides, furs and leather		
Fuel and lubricants	158,700	200,300	manufactures	100,100	101,400
Machinery and			Wool	87,819	106,459
accessories	78,900	98,258	Textiles	90,500	76,200

Total trade between Uruguay and UK (British Department of Trade returns, in £1,000 sterling):

	1976	1977	1978	1979	3980
Imports to UK	13,200	16,956	24,256	13,416	16,884
Exports and re-exports from UK	10,525	19,242	17,446	24,735	26,619

Tourism. There were 1,103,857 tourists in 1979 spending an estimated US$268m.

COMMUNICATIONS

Roads. The main highways, linking Montevideo with the interior, have a total length of 9,899 km, of which about 5,000 km are paved. Other roads, unpaved, are about 4,726 km. Considerable improvements, financed both internally and by international loans, have been carried out in the last few years.

Registered motor vehicles, 31 Dec. 1978, are estimated at 220,000 passenger cars and 92,150 trucks and buses.

Railways. The 4 principal railway systems, embracing 2,987 km, were all built by British capital amounting to £14,513,000. The Uruguayan Government in 1948 bought these railways for £7·15m., assuming control in that year. The East Coast Railway (125·5 km) and 3 minor lines were already controlled by the State under a separate administration. In Oct. 1952 the railways were brought under a single administration and a major programme of track upgrading and rolling stock rehabilitation was in progress in 1977. The total railway system open for traffic was (1980) 3,004 km of 1,435 mm gauge. In 1978 it carried 494m. passengers-km, 303m. tonne-km of freight. In 1979 the 27 km line between Mercedes and Ombucito was opened, providing a direct route from Montevideo to Fray Bentos.

Aviation. Carrasco, 22·5 km from Montevideo, is the most important airport. US, Argentine, Brazilian, Chilean, Dutch, French, Fed. German, Italian, Scandinavian and Paraguayan airlines fly to and from Uruguay. The state-operated civil airline PLUNA runs services in the interior of the country and to Brazil, Paraguay and Argentina.

Shipping. On 31 Dec. 1978 the 8 merchant vessels and 4 tankers under the Uruguayan flag had a GRT of 103,336. In 1979, 1,461 vessels cleared Montevideo, 50 being British. River transport (1,270 km) is extensive, its main importance being to link Montevideo with Paysandú and Salto.

Post and Broadcasting. The telegraph lines in operation have a total length of 12,083 km. The telephone system in Montevideo is controlled by the State; small companies operate in the interior. Telephone instruments, 1978, numbered 268,026. There are 1,277 post offices. Uruguay has 54 long-wave and 17 short-wave broadcasting stations. There are about 1m. wireless sets and 200,000 television receivers. There are 4 television stations. The State itself operates one of the most powerful sound broadcasting stations in South America. Two cable companies connect Montevideo with the US and Europe.

Cinemas (1979). Cinemas numbered 85 with seating capacity of 47,000.

Newspapers (1977). There were 5 daily newspapers in Montevideo with aggregate daily circulation of about 210,000; most of the 25–30 provincial newspapers appear bi-weekly.

JUSTICE, RELIGION, EDUCATION AND WELFARE

Justice. The Ministry of Justice was created in 1977 to be responsible for relations between the Executive Power and the Judiciary and other jurisdictional entities. The Court of Justice is made up by 5 members appointed by the Council of the Nation at the suggestion of the Executive Power, for a period of 5 years. This court has original jurisdiction in constitutional, international and admiralty cases, and hears appeals from the appellate courts, of which there are 4, each with 3 judges.

In Montevideo there are also 8 courts for ordinary civil cases, 3 for government (*Juzgado de Hacienda*), as well as criminal and correctional courts. Each departmental capital has a departmental court; each of the 224 judicial divisions has a justice of peace court. In Sept. 1907 the death penalty was abolished, replaced by penal servitude for a period of 30–40 years.

Religion. State and Church are separated, and there is complete religious liberty. The faith professed by the majority of the inhabitants is Roman Catholic. The archbishopric of Montevideo has 9 suffragan bishops in Salto, Melo, Florida, Minas, San José, Canelones, Tacuarembó, Mercedes and Maldonado.

Protestants numbered about 10,500 in 1957.

Education. Primary education is obligatory; both primary and superior education are free.

In 1979 there were 1,050 primary public schools with 364,910 pupils and approximately 10,300 teachers; in 1979, 249 secondary schools had 196,462 pupils. There are also evening courses for adults. Illiteracy is now confined largely to the older age groups.

The University of the Republic at Montevideo, inaugurated in 1849, has about 16,200 students; tuition is free to both native-born and foreign students; there are 10 faculties. There are 43 normal schools for males and females, and a college of arts and trades with about 33,000 students. There are also many religious seminaries throughout the Republic with a considerable number of pupils, a school for the blind, 2 for deaf and dumb and a school of domestic science.

Health. Hospital beds, 1978, numbered (estimate) 17,500; physicians numbered 4,434.

DIPLOMATIC REPRESENTATIVES

OF URUGUAY IN GREAT BRITAIN (48 Lennox Gdns., London, SW1X 0DL)
Ambassador: Dr Osvaldo R. Soriano Mesiá.

OF GREAT BRITAIN IN URUGUAY (Calle Marco Bruto 1073, Montevideo)
Ambassador: Patricia M. Hutchinson.

OF URUGUAY IN THE USA (1918 F St., NW,
Washington, D.C., 20006)
Ambassador: José Perez Caldas.

OF THE USA IN URUGUAY (Calle Lauro Muller 1776, Montevideo)
Ambassador: (Vacant).

OF URUGUAY TO THE UNITED NATIONS
Ambassador: Edmundo Narancío.

Books of Reference

The official gazette is the *Diario Oficial*
Statistical Reports of the Government. Montevideo. Annual and biennial
Anales de Instruccion Primaria. Montevideo. Quarterly

Arcas, J. A., *Historia del siglo XX uruguayo, 1897–1943.* Montevideo, 1950
De Carlos, M., *La escuela púplica uruguaya.* Montevideo, 1949
Fernández Saldaña, J. M., *Diccionario Uruguayo de Biografías.* Montevideo, 1945
Fitzgibbon, R. H., *Uruguay, Portrait of a Democracy.* New Brunswick, NJ, 1954; London, 1956
Montañés, M. T., *Desarrollo de la agricultura en el Uruguay.* Montevideo, 1948
Pendle, G., *Uruguay.* 3rd ed. R. Inst. of Int. Affairs, 1963
Porzecanski, A. C., *Uruguay's Tupamaros.* London and New York, 1973
Salgado, José, *Historia de la Republica O. del Uruguay.* 8 vols. Montevideo, 1943

National Library: Biblioteca Nacional del Uruguay, Guayabo 1793, Montevideo. It publishes *Anuario Bibliográfico Uruguayo.*

VANUATU

Republic of Vanuatu

Capital: Vila
Population: 112,596 (1979)
GNP per capita: US$540 (1978)

HISTORY. The group was administered for some purposes jointly, for others unilaterally, as provided for by Anglo-French Convention of 27 Feb. 1906, ratified 20 Oct. 1906, and a protocol signed at London on 6 Aug. 1911 and ratified on 18 March 1922. On 30 July 1980 the Condominium of the New Hebrides achieved independence and became the Republic of Vanuatu.

AREA AND POPULATION. The Vanuatu group lies roughly 500 miles west of Fiji and 250 miles north-east of New Caledonia. The estimated land area is 5,700 sq. miles (14,760 sq. km). The larger islands of the group are: Espiritu Santo, Male-kula, Epi, Pentecost, Aoba, Maewa, Paama, Ambrym, Efate, Erromanga, Tanna and Aneityum.

There are 3 active volcanoes, on Tanna, Ambrym and Lopevi, respectively. Earth tremors are of common occurrence. Rainfall at Vila (the capital, population (1979) 14,000) averages 90 in. per annum.

The first complete census was taken in 1967. The total population was found to be 77,988, of whom 72,243 were Vanuatuans. Census, Jan. 1979, 112,596.

CONSTITUTION AND GOVERNMENT. General elections took place in Nov. 1975 to elect a 42-member Representative Assembly, replacing the former advisory council. Further general elections took place in Nov. 1979. A committee system was instituted and the Assembly chose its own President from its own mem-bers in 1977. The President replaced the Co-Presidents, who were the Resident Commissioners.

Prime Minister: Walter Hadye Lini, CBE.
Home Affairs and Deputy Prime Minister: F. Timakata. *Education:* D. Kalpokas. *Finance:* K. Kalsakau. *Primary Industry:* T. Reuben Seru. *Health:* G. Worek. *Transport, Communications and Public Works:* J. Naupa. *Land:* S. Regenvanu. *Social Affairs:* W. Korisa.

Flag: Red over green, with a black triangle in the hoist, the three parts being divided by fimbriations of black and yellow, and in the centre of the black triangle a boar's tusk overlaid by two crossed fern leaves.

Language: The national language is Bislama; English and French are also official languages.

ECONOMY

Budget. The budget for 1980 (estimate): Revenue, 1,520m. NH francs; expenditure, 2,682m. NH francs. The main sources of revenue were import and export duties.

Currency. In Sept. 1979, 100 NH francs = $A1.35. Australian decimal currency was introduced in 1966. It and the New Hebrides *franc* are the currencies in use.

Banking. Because of the absence of direct taxation, with the exception of an added value tax on sales of sub-divided land, there has been growing interest in Vanuatu as a finance centre and 500 overseas companies are using Vila and have contributed 450m. NH francs in invisible export earnings. There were 8 banks in Vila in 1980 and there has been a corresponding growth in other professions associated with the finance industry. There is a National Development Bank operated by the govern-ment and branches of the Bank of Indochine et de Suez at Vila and Santo. Barclays Bank International has a branch in Santo.

NATURAL RESOURCES

Minerals. The manganese mine, established at Forari on Efate by the Compagnie Française de Phosphates de l'Océanie, closed in 1968 but was reopened in 1970 by Southland Mining of Australia. Manganese exports, 1979, 25m. NH francs.

Agriculture. The main commercial crops are copra, cocoa and coffee. Yams, taro, manioc and bananas are grown for local consumption. A large number of cattle are reared on plantations, and an up-grading programme using pure-bred Charolais, Limousins and Illawarras has begun. A beef industry is developing.

Livestock (1979): Cattle, 97,000; goats, 7,000; pigs, 65,000; poultry, 140,000.

Forestry. An active forestry development programme is in progress and more than 26 plantations of South American hardwoods have been established.

Fisheries. The principal catch is tuna (1980, 10,000 tonnes) mainly exported to USA.

INDUSTRY AND TRADE

Industry. There is no heavy industry but there is increasing activity in light industry. Industries include a saw-mill, a soft drinks factory, meat canneries and a modern abattoir, and a fish-freezing plant. A few indigenous crafts, such as basketry, canoe-building and pottery, are practised. Subsistence fishing is done by the Vanuatuan, and a plant for freezing of tuna and bonito commenced operation in 1957. This plant, which is sited on Santo, freezes and packages for export to Japan and elsewhere, fish caught by Taiwanese and other vessels under contract to the British company running the plant. There are over 300 co-operative societies handling 85% of the distribution of goods in the islands.

Commerce. Imports and exports were (in 1m. NH francs):

	1977	1978	1979
Imports	3,145	3,691	4,150
Exports	2,535	2,682	2,850

In 1979 the main exports were: Copra, 39,821 tonnes, 1,505m. NH francs; fish, 7,623 tonnes, 831m. NH francs; beef, 750 tonnes, 135m. NH francs. Australia, France and Japan were the major sources of imports and principal imports were food and drink, manufactured goods and petroleum products.

Tourism. Tourism is a growing industry and 1979 there were 30,454 visitors to Vanuatu.

COMMUNICATIONS

Roads. There are approximately 1,000 km of roads in Vanuatu, of these about 35 km are sealed, mostly on Efate Island. There are 7,000 registered motor vehicles in Vanuatu (1980).

Aviation. External air services are provided by Air Pacific, UTA (Unions de Transports Aériens) and Air Nauru. Air Pacific has two services a week Nandi—Vila—Honiara—Brisbane, and one Nandi—Vila—Noumea—Brisbane. UTA has daily flights from Noumea, and a weekly flight to Wallis. Air Nauru gives a weekly service Vila—Nauru. Inter-island flights are provided by Air Melanesiae. The principal airports are Bauer Field (for Vila) and Pekoa (for Santo). Seventeen smaller airfields provide an internal network. In 1977 there were 1,001 overseas aircraft arrivals in Vila, carrying 59,141 passengers.

Shipping. Several international shipping lines serve Vanuatu, linking the country with Australia, New Zealand, other Pacific territories notably Hong Kong, Japan, North America and Europe. The chief ports are Vila and Santo. In 1977, 394 vessels arrived including 48 cruise ships carrying 40,412 visitors. 92,340 tons of cargo were exported and 102,867 tons discharged. Small vessels provide frequent inter-island services.

Telecommunications. Internal telephone and telegram services are provided by the Posts and Telecommunications and Radio Departments. There are automatic telephone exchanges at Vila and Santo; rural areas are served by a network of tele-radio stations. In 1978 there were 2,409 telephones.

External telephone, telegram and telex services are provided by HEBRITEL, through their satellite earth station at Vila. There are direct circuits to Noumea, Sydney, Hong Kong and Paris and high quality communications are available on a 24-hour basis to most countries in the world. Air radio facilities are provided. Marine coast station facilities are available at Vila and Santo. Radio New Hebrides operates a broadcasting service 7 days a week in 3 languages, French, English and Pidgin. A new station is under construction.

JUSTICE, EDUCATION AND WELFARE

Justice. A study was being made in 1980 which could lead to unification of the judicial system.

Education. Primary and secondary education facilities are provided in both English and French. There is one technical training facility in Vila and students undergo higher (university) education either at the University of the South Pacific in Fiji, or University of Papau New Guinea or in France. Teacher training for both English and French language teachers is conducted in Vanuatu.

There were (1980) 115 French language primary and 3 secondary schools and 161 English language primary and 5 secondary schools.

Health. Medical care is provided through a network of 106 hospitals, health centres, clinics and dispensaries administered by the Government with the help of a number of voluntary agencies, and WHO. Public health measures and the control of communicable diseases are the responsibility of the public health administration. Local training schemes are devoted to basic community nurse training at hospitals in Vila, to rural health training and refresher courses at a special training health centre in North Efate, or by attachment to other suitable clinics and health centres, and to training of village sanitarians or health orderlies.

Malaria is still the most serious of the major endemic diseases which also include tuberculosis, leprosy, filariasis and venereal disease. During 1975–76 yaws recurred on some islands and there were epidemic outbreaks of dengue, influenza and gastroenteritis.

For professional and technical education in medicine, nursing, X-ray, dentistry, laboratory work, health inspection, selected students or suitable in-service staff are awarded scholarships and fellowships for overseas training in Solomon Islands, Papua New Guinea, Fiji, New Zealand, Australia, New Caledonia and other countries.

Book of Reference

Annual Report 1968–69. HMSO

VATICAN CITY STATE

Stato della Città del Vaticano

HISTORY. For many centuries the Popes bore temporal sway over a territory stretching across mid-Italy from sea to sea and comprising some 17,000 sq. miles, with a population finally of over 3m. In 1859–60 and 1870 the Papal States were incorporated with the Italian Kingdom. The consequent dispute between Italy and successive Popes was only settled on 11 Feb. 1929 by three treaties between the Italian Government and the Vatican: (1) A Political Treaty, which recognized the full and independent sovereignty of the Holy See in the city of the Vatican; (2) a Concordat, to regulate the condition of religion and of the Church in Italy; and (3) a Financial Convention, in accordance with which the Holy See received 750m. lire in cash and 1,000m. lire in Italian 5% state bonds. This sum was to be a definitive settlement of all the financial claims of the Holy See against Italy in consequence of the loss of its temporal power in 1870. The treaty and concordat were ratified on 7 June 1929. The treaty has been embodied in the Constitution of the Italian Republic of 1947.

The Vatican City State is governed by a Commission appointed by the Pope. The reason for its existence is to provide an extra-territorial, independent base for the Holy See, the government of the Roman Catholic Church.

In 1930 the issue of Papal coinage was resumed, after a lapse of 60 years. In virtue of a special convention between the Vatican City and the Italian Government (last renewed in 1962), each state allows the currency of the other to circulate in its territory. The Vatican City has, however, given an undertaking that the total value of its coins issued in ordinary years will not exceed 100m. lire, 200m. lire in years of 'Sede vacante' or holy years, or 300m. in the year of the opening of a Council.

AREA AND POPULATION. The area of the Vatican City is 44 hectares (108·7 acres). It includes the Piazza di San Pietro (St Peter's Square), which is to remain normally open to the public and subject to the powers of the Italian police. It has its own railway station (opened Nov. 1932), postal facilities, coins and radio. Twelve buildings in and outside Rome enjoy extra-territorial rights, including the Basilicas of St John Lateran, St Mary Major, St Paul without the Walls and the Pope's summer villa at Castel Gandolfo. On 8 Oct. 1951 extra-territorial rights were also granted to a new Vatican radio station on Italian soil. *Radio Vaticana* is broadcasting an extensive service in 31 languages from transmitters in the Vatican City and in Italy.

The Vatican City has about 1,000 inhabitants.

CONSTITUTION. The Pope exercises the sovereignty and has absolute legislative, executive and judicial powers. The judicial power is delegated to a tribunal in the first instance, to the Sacred Roman Rota in appeal and to the Supreme Tribunal of the Signature in final appeal.

The Pope is elected by the College of Cardinals, meeting in secret conclave. The election is by scrutiny and requires a two-thirds majority.

Name and family	Election	Name and family	Election
Benedict XIV (*Lambertini*)	1740	Pius VI (*Braschi*)	1775
Clement XIII (*Rezzonico*)	1758	Pius VII (*Chiaramonti*)	1800
Clement XIV (*Ganganelli*)	1769	Leo XII (*della Genga*)	1823

Name and family	Election	Name and family	Election
Pius VIII (*Castiglioni*)	1829	Pius XI (*Ratti*)	1922
Gregory XVI (*Cappellari*)	1831	Pius XII (*Pacelli*)	1939
Pius IX (*Mastai-Ferretti*)	1846	John XXIII (*Roncalli*)	1958
Leo XIII (*Pecci*)	1878	Paul VI (*Montini*)	1963
Pius X (*Sarto*)	1903	John Paul I (*Luciani*)	1978
Benedict XV (*della Chiesa*)	1914	John Paul II (*Wojtyla*)	1978

Supreme Pontiff: **John Paul II** (Karol Wojtyla), born at Wadowice near Cracow, Poland, 18 May 1920. Archbishop of Cracow 1964–78, created Cardinal in 1967, elected Pope 16 Oct. 1978, inaugurated 22 Oct. 1978.

Pope John Paul II was the first non-Italian to be elected since Pope Adrian VI (a Dutchman) in 1522.

Secretary of State: Cardinal Agostino Casaroli (appointed May 1979).

Flag: Vertically yellow and white, with on the white the crossed keys and tiara of the Papacy.

ROMAN CATHOLIC CHURCH. The Roman Pontiff (in orders a Bishop, but in jurisdiction held to be by divine right the centre of all Catholic unity, and consequently Pastor and Teacher of all Christians) has for advisers and coadjutors the Sacred College of Cardinals, consisting in Jan. 1981 of 126 Cardinals appointed by him from senior ecclesiastics who are either the bishops of important Sees or the heads of departments at the Holy See. In addition to the College of Cardinals, the Pope has created a 'Synod of Bishops'. This consists of the Patriarchs and certain Metropolitans of the Catholic Church of Oriental Rite, of elected representatives of the national episcopal conferences and religious orders of the world, of the Cardinals in charge of the Roman Congregations and of other persons nominated by the Pope. The Synod meets as and when decided by the Pope; its first session was held in the autumn of 1967 and its third session in Oct. 1974.

The central administration of the Roman Catholic Church is carried on by a number of permanent committees called Sacred Congregations, each composed of a number of Cardinals and diocesan bishops (both appointed for 5-year periods), with Consultors and Officials. Besides the Secretariat of State and the Council for Public Affairs of the Church (which deals with external relations) there are now 9 Sacred Congregations, viz.: Doctrine, Oriental Churches, Bishops, the Sacraments and Divine Worship, Clergy, Religious, Catholic Education, Evangelization of the Peoples and Causes of the Saints. There are also 3 Secretariats: for Christian Unity, Non-Christians and Non-Believers; a Prefecture of Economic Affairs, a Prefecture of the Pontifical Household and a Statistical Office. Furthermore, the Roman Curia contains 3 tribunals, the Apostolic Penitentiary, the Supreme Tribunal of the Apostolic Signature and the Sacred Roman Rota; and, lastly, various other councils and commissions dealing with the Laity, Justice and Peace, Women, the Family, the Revision of Canon Law, Social Communications, Migration and Tourism. The Pontifical Academy of Sciences was revived by Pius XI in 1936 with 70 members.

More than 2,500 Roman Catholic prelates and 99 observer-delegates from 27 other Christian Churches attended the Second Vatican Council which met 11 Oct. 1962 and 8 Dec. 1965. Sixteen Constitutions and Decrees were approved at the Council, and 7 commissions were set up to implement these decisions.

DIPLOMATIC REPRESENTATIVES

In its diplomatic relations with foreign countries the Holy See is represented by the Council for Public Affairs of the Church. It maintains permanent observers to the UN in New York and Geneva and to UNESCO and FAO. The Holy See is a member of IAEA and the Vatican City State is a member of UPU and ITU. It therefore attends as a member those international conferences open to State members of the UN and specialized agencies.

Envoy and Minister to the Holy See: Sir Mark Heath KCVO, CMG. *First Secretary:* J. H. Callan, MVO, OBE.

Apostolic Delegate [1] *for Great Britain, Bermuda and Gibraltar:* Mgr Bruno Heim, Titular Archbishop of Xanto.

[1] Apostolic delegate is a representative of the Holy See without diplomatic status or privileges.

Books of Reference

Acta Apostolicæ Sedis Romanæ. Rome
Annuario Pontificio. Rome. Annual
L'Attività della Santa Sede. Rome. Annual
The Catholic Directory. London. Annual
Codex Juris Canonici. Latest ed., 1948
Atlas Missionum. Vatican City, 1958
Bilan du Monde: Encyclopédie catholique du monde chrétien. Tournai, 1964
Cardinale, Mgr. Igino, *Le Saint-Siège et la diplomatie.* Paris and Rome, 1962
Hales, E. E., *The Catholic Church and the Modern World.* London, 1958
Mayer, F. *et al The Vatican: Portrait of a State and a Community.* Dublin, 1980
Nichols, P. *The Politics of the Vatican.* London, 1968
Pallenborg, C., *Vatican Finances.* Harmondsworth, 1971

VENEZUELA

Capital: Caracas
Population: 14·54m. (1979)
GNP per capita: US$2,910 (1978)

Republica de Venezuela

HISTORY. Venezuela formed part of the Spanish colony of New Granada until 1821 when it became independent in union with Colombia. A separate, independent republic was formed in 1830.

AREA AND POPULATION. Venezuela is bounded north by the Caribbean, east by Guyana, south by Brazil, south-west and west by Colombia. The official estimate of the area is 912,050 sq. km (352,143 sq. miles); the frontiers with Colombia, Brazil and Guyana extend for 2,972 miles and its Atlantic coastline stretches for some 2,000 miles. Over half the population live in the valleys of Caracas and Valencia (once the capital). There are 20 states, 2 territories, the federal district and the federal dependencies (*i.e.*, 72 islands in the Antilles); further states may be created from the territories. Bolívar, the largest state, has an area of 91,868 sq. miles; the other states are far smaller. The federal district embraces 745 sq. miles.

The language of the country is Spanish.

Population according to the 1971 census (estimate (1979) 14,539,000):

State	Capital	Population	State	Capital	Population
Anzoátegui	Barcelona	506,297	Portuguesa	Guanare	297,044
Apure	San Fernando	164,705	Sucre	Cumaná	469,006
Aragua	Maracay	543,170	Táchira	San Cristóbal	511,344
Barinas	Barinas	231,046	Trujillo	Trujillo	381,335
Bolívar	Ciudad Bolívar	391,665	Yaracuy	San Felipe	223,540
Carabobo	Valencia	659,339	Zulia	Maracaibo	1,229,037
Cojedes	San Carlos	94,351	Ter. Amazonas	Puerto Ayacucho	21,696
Falcón	Coro	407,957	Ter. Delta		
Guárico	San Juan	318,905	Amacuro	Tucupita	48,139
Lara	Barquisimeto	671,410	Federal District	Caracas	1,860,637
Mérida	Mérida	347,095	Federal Depen-		
Miranda	Los Teques	856,272	dencies	—	463
Monagas	Maturín	298,239			
Nueva Esparta	La Asunción	118,830	Total		10,721,522

The 1971 census excluded tribal Indians estimated at 31,800, of whom 20,000 are in Ter. Amazonas and 4,000 in Zulia. Excluding illegal immigrants, estimated (1979) at about 3m.

Of the working population of 3·2m. more than 82,000 were between 10 and 14 years and 429,000 were between 15 and 19 years.

The 1971 population of Caracas was 1,035,499; Maracaibo, 651,574; Barquisimeto, 330,815; Valencia, 367,154; Maracay, 255,134; San Cristóbal, 152,239; Ciudad Guyana, 143,540; Cabimas, 122,239; Maturín, 121,662; Baruta, 121,066; Cumaná, 119,751; Ciudad Bolívar, 103,728.

Vital statistics, 1979 (estimate): 484,700 births, 74,950 deaths. Life expectancy (1978) 66 years with 53% of population under 18 years.

CONSTITUTION AND GOVERNMENT. The constitution of 1958 provides for popular election for a term of 5 years of a President, a National Congress, and State and Municipal legislative assemblies, and guarantees the freedom of labour, industry and commerce. Aliens are assured of treatment equal to that extended to nationals.

Congress consists of a Senate and a Chamber of Deputies. At least 2 Senators are elected for each State and for the Federal District. Senators must be Venezuelans by birth and over 30 years of age. Deputies must be native Venezuelans over 21 years of age; there is 1 for every 50,000 inhabitants. The territories, on reaching the population fixed by law, also elect deputies. Voting (by proportional representation) is compulsory for men and women over 18. Owing to the high rate of illiteracy, voting is by coloured ballot cards.

The President must be a Venezuelan by birth and over 30 years of age; he has a qualified power of veto.

The following is a list of presidents since 1941:

	Took Office		Took Office
Gen. Isaias Medina Angarita	6 May 1941	Dr Edgard Sanabria	14 Nov. 1958[3]
Rómulo Betancourt	20 Oct. 1945	Rómulo Betancourt	13 Feb. 1959
Rómulo Gallegos	15 Feb. 1948	Raul Leoni	11 March 1964
Lieut.-Col. Carlos Delgado		Rafael Caldera	11 March 1969
Chalbaud	24 Nov. 1948[4]	Carlos Andrés Pérez	12 March 1974
Dr G. Suárez Flamerich	27 Nov. 1950[2]	Rodríguez	
Col. Marcos Pérez Jiménez.	3 Dec. 1952[1]	Dr Luis Herrera Campíns	12 March 1979
Rear-Adm. Wolfgang			
Larrazábal Ugueto	23 Jan. 1958[2, 3]		

[1] Deposed.   [2] Resigned.   [3] Provisional.   [4] Assassinated 13 Nov. 1950.

President: Luis Herrera Campíns, elected 3 Dec. 1978 with 2,469,042 out of 5,412,673 votes, assumed office on 12 March 1979.

Foreign Minister: José Alberto Zambrano Velasco.

At the Congressional elections held in Dec. 1978, 102 of the 187 seats in the Chamber of Deputies were won by Acción Democrática, 64 by COPEI (the Social Christians) and 21 by other parties.

The city of Caracas is the capital. The 20 states, autonomous and politically equal, have each a legislative assembly and an elected governor. The states are divided into 156 districts and 613 municipalities. There are also 2 federal territories with 7 departments, and a federal district with 2 departments and 2 parishes. Each district has a municipal council, and each municipio a communal junta. The federal district and the 2 territories are administered by the President of the Republic.

National flag: Three horizontal stripes of yellow, blue, red, with an arc of 7 white stars in the centre, and the national arms in the canton.

National anthem: Gloria al bravo pueblo (1811; words by Vicente Salias, tune by Juan Landaeta).

DEFENCE. In 1958 a Joint Staff Organization was established under the Minister of Defence for the closer integration of defence policy and administration of the three Services and the National Guard.

Army. All Venezuelans on reaching 18 years of age are liable for 2 years in the Armed Forces. They can opt for the Air Force or the Navy instead of the Army, but their allocation is finally dependent upon current requirements. The Army's established strength of approximately 27,000 all ranks furnishes 1 cavalry battalion, 11 infantry and 2 mechanized battalions, 3 ranger battalions, 3 tank battalions and supporting engineering, artillery, anti-aircraft and supply services. There is a military academy for cadets, a school for staff studies and other technical training schools. Women can also be conscripted, as nurses, clerks, etc.

Navy. Strength includes 3 diesel-powered patrol submarines (2 new built in Federal Republic of Germany and 1 old *ex*-US submarine), 2 old destroyers (*ex*-US), 6 frigates built in Italy (4 new and 2 old), 6 fast missile-armed patrol craft built in Britain in 1974–75, 3 landing ships, 1 transport landing ship (*ex*-repair ship), 1 survey ship, 2 survey launches, 2 transports and 13 tugs. Coastal patrol boats operated by the National Guard now number 43.

New construction includes 2 more frigates, armed with guided missiles and equipped with helicopter, hangar and flight deck, ordered from Italy, and 2 more submarines from the Federal Republic of Germany.

There is a naval academy for the training of officer cadets and a school of staff studies and various technical training schools. Personnel in 1981 exceeded: 7,500 officers and men including 4,000 of the Marine Corps.

Air Force. Formed in 1920, the Air Force of some 4,500 officers and men is a small, but well-equipped service with a total of about 250 aircraft. There are 5 combat squadrons. One is equipped with 9 Mirage IIIE and 4 Mirage 5 supersonic fighters and 2 Mirage 5D trainers. Two others have a total of 15 Canadair CF-5A fighter-bombers and 2 two-seat CF-5Bs. Two bomber squadrons are equipped respectively with 23 modernized Canberra jet-bombers and 20 F-86K Sabre interceptors, 15 OV-10E Bronco twin-turboprop counter-insurgency aircraft, supported by 2 Canberra reconnaissance aircraft. A helicopter force consists of more than 35 Bell JetRangers and 212s, UH-1B/D/H Iroquois and Alouette IIIs. Transport units are equipped with 12 C-123 Providers, 6 C-130H Hercules, 2 HS.748 and 15 C-47s. Communications aircraft are Queen Airs and other types. T-34 Mentors are used for training, together with 24 T-2D Buckeye advanced jet trainers, which have a secondary attack role. A battalion of paratroops comes within Air Force responsibility. There is a staff college and a cadet academy.

National Guard, a volunteer force of some 15,000 under the Ministry of Defence, is broadly responsible for internal security. It includes customs and forestry duties among its tasks.

INTERNATIONAL RELATIONS

Membership. Venezuela is a member of UN, OAS, LAIA (formerly LAFTA), OPEC and the Andean Group.

Aid. Venezuela has lent about US$500m. to the World Bank, SDR 650m. to the IMF and US$100m. to the UN Emergency Fund. A trust fund administered by the Inter-American Development Bank is to distribute US$500m. during 1975–80, and there are separate agreements with a number of Central and Southern American states.

ECONOMY

Planning. The sixth 5-year plan (1981–85) aims to achieve economic growth but with a reorientation of priorities towards social programmes: Education, housing and public services. There are 5 major projects: Caracas metro, Guri hydro-electric scheme, INOS water supply, major housing schemes and the Corpozulia coal and steel complex. These will cost Bs. 67,000m. over 5 years. Oil production will continue at current target levels of 2·2m. bbls. per day but prices are projected to double over the period, resulting in increased earnings, despite growing domestic consumption. GDP is forecast to grow 6% in 1981–85, this is below the 5th plan target of 8·2% but above 5·6% which was actually achieved 1976–80.

Budget. The revenue and expenditure for calendar years were, in Bs.1m., as follows:

	1974	1975	1976	1977	1978	1979
Revenue	42,799	41,270	43,143	51,179	44,480	50,588
Expenditure	40,059	40,266	44,571	50,694	44,273	51,236

The heavy investment required to develop the oil, steel and aluminium industries has created substantial debts, the debt service in 1979 being Bs.8,071m. (9·4% of GDP and 16% of exports) and by 1981 it is forecast to be Bs.16,587m. (18·1% of GDP and 27% of exports). In 1978 the petroleum industry accounted for 49·6% of total government revenues; in 1981 oil revenues are projected at Bs.39,300m.

Currency. The official monetary unit is the *bolivar*. As a result of exchange reforms of Jan. 1964 the selling rate to the public was changed to Bs.4·50 = US$1. The selling rate applicable to iron and petroleum companies is Bs.4·30 = US$1. Cocoa and coffee exporters may sell exchange to the Central Bank at Bs.4·485. Importers of wheat and powdered milk are eligible for subsidies amounting to the difference between the previous selling rate of Bs.3·35 and the current sellers' Bs.4·30 = US$1. In March 1981, £ = Bs.9·34; US$1 = 4·29.

The *bolívar* (Bs.) is divided into 100 *céntimos*. Gold coins, 100 (*pachanos*), 20 and 10 *bolívars* have been minted but are no longer in circulation; silver coins are 5 (*fuerte*), 2, 1 *bolívars*; nickel, 50 (*real*), 25 (*medio*) and 12·5 *céntimos* (*locha*), copper-nickel, 5 *céntimos* (*puya*).

The bank-notes in circulation are 500, 100, 50, 20 and 10 bolívars. The circulation of foreign bank-notes is forbidden.

Banking. The ten major banks are (1980):

	Assets Bs. 1m.	%	Deposits Bs. 1m.	%
Banco Industrial de Venezuela	9,413	6·36	5,091	5·85
Banco de Venezuela	8,822	5·96	6,358	7·31
Banco nacional de Descuento	8,675	5·86	5,632	6·47
Banco Unión	8,555	5·78	6,958	8·00
Banco Mercantil y Agrícola	8,286	5·60	6,390	7·34
Banco de los Trabajadores de Venezuela	7,272	4·92	3,853	4·43
Banco Provincial SAICA	4,845	3·27	4,022	4·62
Banco Latino	4,559	3·08	3,664	4·21
Banco de Maracaibo	4,023	2·72	2,291	3·78
Banco Unido	3,717	2·51	352	0·40

The 5 largest banks attract 30% of all deposits, the largest 2 banks are state controlled and the third largest is run by the government.

ENERGY AND NATURAL RESOURCES

Oil. (1979) Venezuela is the sixth largest petroleum exporting country in the world and the seventh largest producer; production began in 1917 with 18,000 cu. metres. The oil-producing region around Maracaibo, covering some 30,000 sq. miles, produces about three-quarters of Venezuelan petroleum, and the country is likely to remain a major producer of oil well into 21st century. Deposits in the Orinoco region are likely to prove one of the largest heavy oil reserves in the world. Nationalization of the privately owned oil sector in 1976 has proved successful. New distribution channels have been established, with the result that the major transnational companies which took 80% of Venezuela's oil in 1976 handled only 50% in 1980.

Oil production peaked at 3·7m. bbls per day in 1970, but a conservation policy plus reduced export demand has resulted in output dropping to 2·1m. bbls per day in the first half of 1980.

Proven reserves in mid-1979 stood at 18,500m. bbls, probable reserves at 15,000m. and possible at 102,000m. However, these are considered conservative estimates and new fields off-shore have estimated reserves of 6,000–40,000m. bbls. The massive Orinoco tar sands belt has reserves variously estimated at between 700,000m. bbls. and 3,000,000m. bbls. Orinoco is expected to produce 300,000 bbls. per day by 1988.

Minerals. Bauxite is being exploited in the Guayana region by Bauxien, a state agency.There are important goldmines in the region south-east of Bolívar State, and new deposits have been discovered near El Callao (1959) and Sosa Méndez (1961) in the Guayana region. Output, 1977, amounted to 541 kg. Imports of 7,000 kg per annum are necessary for industrial purposes. Diamond output, from Amazonas territory, was 687,000 carats in 1977. Manganese deposits, estimated at several million tons, were discovered in 1954. Phosphate-rock deposits (yielding from 64 to 82% tricalcium phosphate) are found in the state of Falcón; reserves of 15m. tons of high-quality rock have been established. The state of Sucre has large sulphur deposits. Coal is worked in the states of Táchira, Aragua and Anzoátegui, production in 1977 being 115,000 tonnes. Coal proven reserves in Zulia (160m. ton) are to be developed to service a new thermal power station in the Maracaibo area. An important nickel deposit (at Loma de Hierro near Tejerías) is estimated to equal 600,000 tons of pure nickel. Saltmines are now worked by the Government on the Araya peninsula; output, 1964, 202,000 tonnes. Asbestos and copper pyrite are being exploited.

Iron ore is exploited in Bolívar State by the Orinoco Mining Co. and Iron Mines of Venezuela, subsidiaries respectively of the US Steel Corp. and the Bethlehem Steel Co. Proven reserves at the end of 1963 were 1,513m. tonnes. National output of iron ore, 1977, 14·4m. tonnes.

Agriculture. Venezuela is divided into 3 distinct zones—the agricultural, the pastoral and the forest zone. In the first are grown coffee, cocoa, sugar-cane, maize, rice, wheat (grown in the Andes), tobacco, cotton, beans, sisal, etc.; the second affords grazing for more than 6m. cattle and numerous horses; and in the third, which covers a very large portion of the country, tropical products, such as caoutchouc, balatá (a gum resembling rubber), tonka beans, dividivi, copaiba, vanilla, growing wild, are worked by the inhabitants. The 1979 livestock estimate showed cattle, 10m.; pigs, 2·1m.; goats, 1·4m.; sheep, 314,000; poultry, 34m. Area under cultivation is 5,530,898 acres. Agriculture is the weakest sector of the economy, accounting for only 6% of GDP and employing 16·3% of the national workforce. Over 50% of all farmers are engaged in subsistence agriculture and growth rates in agricultural production have not kept pace with the high population increase. Government has introduced a programme of price support, tax incentives and price increases but cattle farming is at present the only profit opportunity.

Production in tonnes in 1978: Coffee, 72,000; maize, 740,000; rice, 600,000, sugar-cane, 5·15m.

The coffee plantations number 62,673, covering 543,400 acres with 135m. bushes. The Venezuelan cocoa, from 13,000 plantations, is considered to be of high quality; it is grown chiefly in the states of Sucre and Miranda. The sugar industry has 6 government and 20 privately owned mills.

Forestry. Resources have been barely tapped; 600 species of wood have been identified. Output of roundwood timber, 1977, broadleaved 8m. cu. metres.

Fisheries. The fishing industry is to be developed by the provision of port and processing facilities, research and training.

Total catch (1977) was 152·2m. tonnes.

INDUSTRY AND TRADE

Industry. Under the 5th National Plan, ending in 1980, a programme has been undertaken to establish the Guayana integrated industrial complex: by mid-1980, Bs.25,000m. had been invested. Plans involved expanding the capacity of the Guri dam to 9,000 mw as a power supply, raising steel capacity at the Sidor mill from 1·2m. to 4·8m. tonnes per annum (a new steel complex is also to be built in Zulia region) and establishing an integrated aluminium industry in the region.

Aluminio del Caroni (Alcasa) is to increase output from 54,000 to 120,000 tonnes per year, and a new facility, Venezolana de Aluminio (Venalum) is to be installed with a capacity of 280,000 tonnes per year, the largest in Latin America. An alumina factory, Interalumina, is to be built.

The shipbuilding industry is being developed and will become the largest in South America. Venezuela is the biggest and most advanced motor vehicle producer within the Andean Pact, with General Motors, Ford, Jeep, Rover, FIAV (Fiat) and Pegaso all having plants in the country.

Industrial development is concentrated in capital intensive areas where it can have a competitive advantage within the Andean Group, whereas in more labour intensive industries, the low labour costs of other member countries gives them an advantage. However, Venezuela currently produces 90% of its requirements of processed food, beverages, tobacco, clothing and textiles.

Labour. The labour force in 1979 was 4·2m. (including 1·25m. legal immigrants), some 32% of the total population (the low percentage is due to 55% of the population being under 20). 17% of the working population is in the primary sector, 27% in secondary and 56% in tertiary.

Job creation is a high priority in the 6th National Plan, with an aim of 200,000 new jobs per year. Unemployment increased from 4·8% to 6% in 1979. However, official statistics exclude the 3m. *indocumentados* (illegal immigrants) who find work on major construction projects such as the Guri dam.

Wages are the highest in Latin America, there is a high turnover of labour and a corresponding rate of absenteeism.

45% of the labour force is unionized. The most powerful confederation is the CTV (*Confederacion de Trabajadores de Venezuela*, formed 1947), which is dominated by the Accion Democratica party. Estimated membership, 1·1m., claims 2m. Comprises 68 regional and industrial federations with over 6,000 unions, including: FCV (peasants), 700,000; FETRACONS (construction workers), 1000,000; FETRASALUD (health workers), 45,000; FETRAMETAL (metal workers and miners), 32,000; the very important FEDEPETROL (oil workers), 6,000; Federacion Venezolana de Maestros (teachers).

Other confederations are CUTV (*Confederacion Unitaria de Trabajadores Venezolanos*, formed 1963). Estimated membership, 40,000, claims 100,000. Comprises 8 regional and 5 industrial federations in 185 local unions; and, CODESA (*Confederacion de Sindicatos Autonomos de Venezuela*, formed 1964). Estimated membership, 10,000, claims 35,000. Dominated by COPEI party. Comprises 120 local unions, including textile, petrol distribution, public health and education workers federations.

Commerce. Venezuela's exports and imports (in US$1m.):

	1976	1977	1978	1979
Exports	9,149	9,661	9,174	13,615
Imports	6,086	10,339	11,022	10,691

Main export markets in 1978 were USA (Bs.13,949m.), Netherlands Antilles (Bs.8,699m.) because of its oil refining and transhipment facilities, Canada (Bs.4,244m.), Puerto Rico (Bs.2,238m.), Italy (Bs.888m.) and Spain (Bs.715m.).

Principal imports are machinery and equipment, manufactured goods, chemical products, foodstuffs.

The USA supplied imports valued at Bs.17,940m. (40% of all imports) in 1978, followed by Federal Republic of Germany (Bs.4,785m), Japan (Bs.4,004m.), Italy (Bs.2,507m.) and the UK (Bs.1,677m.).

Total trade between UK and Venezuela (British Department of Trade returns, in £1,000 sterling):

	1976	1977	1978	1979	1980
Imports to UK	117,636	67,017	71,684	100,823	117,614
Exports and re-exports from UK	128,794	175,035	188,904	137,722	131,684

Tourism. 652,000 tourists visited Venezuela in 1977.

COMMUNICATIONS

Roads. There were, 1977, 58,560 km of road fit for traffic the year round; of these 20,000 km are paved. There are 10,097 km of high-speed 4-lane motorway type. The motorway system runs from Caracas to Puerto Cabello *via* Valencia and will shortly be linked direct with one from La Guaira to Caracas. Venezuela has received two World Bank loans for US$45m. and 30m. in connexion with this programme, for improvements of the express-ways in Caracas and for 2 roads in the south-west of the country. Motor vehicles, 1975, totalled 1,324,600 and included 955,200 passenger cars and 369,400 commercial vehicles. The 1,678-metre Angostura bridge linking the Orinoco cities of Ciudad Bolívar and Soledad was opened in Jan. 1967.

Railways. Plans have existed since 1950 for large scale railway construction but only the Puerto Cabello to Barquisimeto line (175 km–1,435 mm gauge) has been completed. A metro is under construction in Caracas.

Aviation. The chief Venezuelan airlines are LAV (Líneas Aéreas Venezolanas), a government-owned concern, and AVENSA (Aerovías Venezolanas). Both operate numerous internal services. VIASA operates international routes in conjunction with KLM. There are also 3 specialist air freight companies. In all there are over 100 commercial aircraft in operation. In addition to Venezuelan international services, a number of US and Latin American and European lines operate services to Venezuela. British Caledonian operates twice-weekly flights between London and Caracas.

Shipping. Foreign vessels are not permitted to engage in the coasting trade, except by special concessions or by contract with the Government. La Guaira, Maracaibo, Puerto Cabello, Puerto Ordaz and Guanta are the chief ports. In Dec. 1978 the merchant fleet had an aggregate gross tonnage of 824,000; this included tankers of 368,000 gross tons.

The principal navigable rivers are the Orinoco and its tributaries Apure and Arauca, from San Fernando to Tucupita through Ciudad Bolívar, Puerto Ordaz and San Félix; San Juan from Carípito to the Gulf of Paria; and Esculante in Lake Maracaibo.

Post and Broadcasting. The telegraph system had a network, 1975, of 45,000 km with 600 telegraph offices. It is supplemented by wireless telegraphy, with 72 stations, and by wireless telephony. There are telephone systems in the principal towns (nationalized in 1954). There were 847,318 instruments in 1978; 98,192 were in Caracas. The telephone network is to be extended by 100,000 additional lines over the next 3 years. An international telex service operates in the Caracas metropolitan zone. There is a submarine telephone link with USA.

There are 77 radio stations at Caracas, Maracaibo, Maracay and other towns. There are 3 television stations in Caracas (two privately owned), of which 2 cover, with relays, most of the country. In 1979 there were about 1·9m. homes with TV receivers.

Cinemas (1977). There were 563 cinemas and 25 drive-ins.

Newspapers (1976). There were 47 daily newspapers, 32 weeklies and 134 magazines.

JUSTICE, RELIGION AND EDUCATION

Justice. The Supreme Court, which operates in Divisions, each with 5 members, is elected by Congress for 5 years. The country is divided into 20 legal districts. They select their own President and Vice-President. The Federal Procurator-General is appointed for 5 years. There are lower federal courts.

Each state has a Supreme Court with 3 members, a superior court, or superior tribunal, courts of first instance, district courts and municipal courts. In the territories there are civil and military judges of first instance, and also judges in the municipios. Finally, there is an income-tax claims tribunal.

Religion. The Roman Catholic is the prevailing religion, but there is toleration of all others. There are 4 archbishops, 1 at Caracas, who is Primate of Venezuela, 2 at Mérida and 1 at Ciudad Bolívar. There are 19 bishops. In the state primary schools instruction is given only to those children whose parents expressly request it. Protestants number about 20,000.

Education. Elementary instruction is free and, from the age of 7 to 13 (the completion of the primary grade), compulsory. In 1974–75 Venezuela had 11,098 primary schools with (1976–77) 63,198 teachers and a total enrolment of 2,204,000 pupils. In 1976–77 there were 720,000 pupils in secondary schools and the number of students in higher education was 248,000 with 15,972 teaching staff. There were 14 universities. The education budget for 1978–79 was Bs. 7,212,000m.

DIPLOMATIC REPRESENTATIVES

OF VENEZUELA IN GREAT BRITAIN
(1 Cromwell Rd., London SW7)

Ambassador: Vice-Adm. Felix Mendoza-Acosta.

OF GREAT BRITAIN IN VENEZUELA (Edificio La Estancia,
Avenida La Estancia 10, Caracas)

Ambassador: R. L. Secondé, CMG, CVO.

OF VENEZUELA IN THE USA (2445 Massachusetts Ave., NW,
Washington, D.C., 20008)

Ambassador: Marcial Perez-Chiriboga.

OF THE USA IN VENEZUELA (Avenida Francisco de Miranda and Avenida Principal de la Floresta, Caracas)

Ambassador: William H. Luers.

OF VENEZUELA TO THE UNITED NATIONS

Ambassador: Dr Germán Nava-Carrillo.

Books of Reference

Statistical Information: The following are some of the principal publications:
Dirección General de Estadística, Ministerio de Fomento, *Boletín Mensual de Estadística.—Anuario Estadístico de Venezuela, 1978.* Caracas, 1979
Banco Central, *Memoria Annual* and *Boletín Mensual*
Ministerio de Sanidad y Asistencia Social, Dirreción de Salud Pública, *Anuario de Epidemiología y Asistencia Social*

Betancourt, R., *Venezuela's Oil.* London, 1978
Buitrón, A., *Causas y Efectos del Exodo Rural en Venezuela.—Efectos Económicos y Sociales de las Inmigraciones en Venezuela.—Las Inmigraciones en Venezuela.* Pan American Union, Washington, D.C., 1956
Lieuwen, E., *Venezuela.* Rev. ed. OUP, 1969
Lombard, J., *Venezuelan History: A Comprehensive Working Bibliography.* Boston, 1977
Morón, G., *A History of Venezuela* (ed. J. Street). London, 1964
Perales, P., *Manual de Geografía Económica de Venezuela.* Caracas, 1955
Salazar-Carrillo, J., *Oil in the Economic Developmant of Venezuela.* New York, 1976
Tugwell, F., *The Politics of Oil in Venezuela.* Stanford Univ. Press, 1975

VIETNAM

Công Hòa Xã Hôi Chu Nghĩa
Viêt Nam—The Socialist
Republic of Vietnam

Capital: Hanoi
Population: 54m. (1981)
GNP per capita: US$170 (1978)

HISTORY. The recorded history of Vietnam can be traced to Tonkin (now known as the northern part of Vietnam) at the beginning of the Christian era. Conquered by the Chinese (Han dynasty) in B.C. 111, the kingdom of Nam-Viet, as it was then called, broke free of Chinese domination in 939, though at many subsequent periods it again became a nominal vassal of the Chinese emperors.

By the end of the 15th century the Vietnamese had conquered most of the kingdom of Champa (in Annam, now known as the central part of Vietnam) and by the end of the 18th had acquired Cochin-China (now known as the southern part of Vietnam), formerly Cambodian territory.

French interest in Vietnam started in the late 16th century with the arrival of French and Portuguese missionaries. The most notable of these was Alexander of Rhodes, who, in the following century, romanized Vietnamese writing. At the end of the 18th century a French bishop and several soldiers of fortune helped to establish the Emperor Gia-Long (with whom Louis XVI had signed a treaty in 1787) as ruler of a unified Vietnam, known then as the Empire of Annam.

An expedition sent by Napoleon III in 1858 to avenge the death of some French missionaries led in 1862 to the cession to France of part of Cochin-China, and thence, by a series of treaties between 1874 and 1884, to the establishment of French protectorates over Tonkin and Annam, and to the formation of the French colony of Cochin-China. By a Sino-French treaty of 1885 the Empire of Annam (including Tonkin) ceased to be tributary to China. Cambodia had become a French protectorate in 1863, and in 1899, after the extension of French protection to Laos in 1893, the Indo-Chinese Union was proclaimed.

In 1940 Vietnam was occupied by the Japanese and used as a military base for the invasion of Malaya. During the occupation there was considerable underground activity among nationalist, revolutionary and Communist organizations. In 1941 a nominally nationalist coalition of such organizations, known as the Vietminh League, was founded by the Communists.

On 9 March 1945 the Japanese interned the French authorities and proclaimed the 'independence' of Indo-China. In Aug. 1945 they allowed the Vietminh movement to seize power, dethrone Bao Dai, the Emperor of Annam, and establish a republic known as Vietnam, including Tonkin, Annam and Cochin-China, with Hanoi as capital. In Sept. 1945 the French re-established themselves in Cochin-China and on 6 March 1946, after a cease-fire in the sporadic fighting between the French forces and the Vietminh had been arranged, a preliminary convention was signed in Hanoi between the French High Commissioner and President Ho Chi Minh by which France recognized 'the Democratic Republic of Vietnam' as a 'Free State within the Indo-Chinese Federation'. Subsequent conferences convened in the same year at Dalat and Fontainebleau to draft a definitive agreement broke down chiefly over the question of whether or not Cochin-China should be included in the new republic. On 19 Dec. 1946 Vietminh forces made a surprise attack on Hanoi, the signal for hostilities which were to last for nearly 8 years.

An agreement signed by the Emperor Bao Dai on behalf of Vietnam on 8 March 1949 recognized the independence of Vietnam within the French Union, and certain sovereign powers were forthwith transferred to Vietnam. The Paris agreements of 29 Dec. 1954 completed the transfer of sovereignty to Vietnam. Supreme authority in the military field remained with the French until the departure of the last French

C.-in-C. in April 1956. Treaties of independence and association were initialled by representatives of the French and Vietnamese governments on 4 June 1954.

An agreement on the cessation of hostilities in Vietnam was reached on 20 July 1954 at the Geneva conference. The agreement was signed on behalf of the C.-in-C. of the French Forces in Indo-China and on behalf of the C.-in-C. of the People's Army of Vietnam. The Government of Vietnam did not sign the agreement.

The final declaration of the Geneva conference (21 July 1954) declared that general elections should take place in July 1956. These did not take place, and Vietnam remained divided until 1976.

In Paris on 27 Jan. 1973 an agreement was signed ending the war in Vietnam. After the US withdrawal, however, hostilities continued between the North and the South until 1975, when North Vietnamese forces brought about the defeat of the South Vietnamese forces. President Thieu resigned on 21 April. He was replaced by the Vice-President, Tran Van Huong, who was in turn replaced by Gen. Duong Van Minh who surrendered to the Communist forces on 30 April. 150,000–200,000 South Vietnamese fled the country, including the former President Thieu. By 30 April Saigon had fallen.

For details of the former Republic of Vietnam (South Vietnam), *see* THE STATESMAN'S YEAR-BOOK, 1975–76. After the collapse of President Thieu's regime the Provisional Revolutionary Government established an administration in Saigon on 6 June 1975 under the presidency of Huynh Tan Phat. A North–South conference on reunification of Nov. 1975 announced that agreement on 'the basic problems' had been reached. A general election was held on 25 April 1976 for a National Assembly representing the whole country. Voting was by universal suffrage of all citizens of 18 or over, except former functionaries of South Vietnam undergoing 're-education'. The unification of North and South Vietnam into the Socialist Republic of Vietnam took place formally on 2 July 1976. After previous US vetoes the new administration of President Carter indicated that it was not opposed to Vietnam's application to join the UN, and Vietnam was admitted unanimously and without a vote on 20 Sept. 1977. In June 1978 Vietnam was admitted to Comecon and in Nov. 1978 signed a 25-year treaty of friendship and co-operation with the USSR. Relations with China correspondingly deteriorated, an especially exacerbating factor being the successful Vietnamese military intervention in Kampuchea. On 17 Feb. 1979 China invaded North Vietnam, but claimed that its troops had all withdrawn by 19 March. Peace negotiations were commenced on 18 April 1979 but broken off by the Chinese on 6 March 1980.

AREA AND POPULATION. The country has a total area of 329,566 sq. km and is divided administratively into 35 provinces and 3 cities. Areas and populations (in 1,000) at the census of 5 Feb. 1976 were as follows:

Province	Sq. km	Population	Province	Sq. km	Population
Lai Chau	17,408	265·6	Phu Khanh	9,620	1,066·2
Son La	14,656	410·1	Lam Dong	10,000	343·1
Hoang Lien Son	14,125	677·2	Thuan Hai	11,000	836·9
Ha Tuyen	13,519	686·4	Dong Nai	12,130	1,260·3
Cao Bang	13,731	843·9	Song Be	9,500	561·4
Bac Thai	8,615	752·9	Tay Ninh	4,100	625·9
Quang Ninh	7,076	701·8	Long An	5,100	828·8
Vinh Phu	5,187	1,579·5	Dong Thap	3,120	991·3
Ha Bac	4,708	1,466·2	Tien Giang	2,350	1,137·2
Ha Son Binh	6,860	2,041·6	Ben Tre	2,400	932·0
Hai Hung	2,526	1,929·9	Cuu Long	4,200	1,319·1
Thai Binh	1,344	1,416·2	An Giang	4,140	1,361·7
Ha Nam Ninh	3,522	2,574·6	Hau Giang	5,100	1,870·4
Thanh Hoa	11,138	2,262·1	Kien Giang	6,000	834·0
Nghe Tinh	22,380	2,704·6	Minh Hai	8,000	981·1
Binh Tri Thien	19,048	1,751·8	Hanoi [1]	597	1,443·5
Quang Nam – Da Nang	11,376	1,414·4	Ho Chi Minh [1]	1,845	3,460·5
Nghia Binh	14,700	1,789·1	Haiphong [1]	1,515	1,190·9
Gia Lai – Kontum	18,480	465·0			
Dac Lac	18,300	372·7		329,466	47,150·0

[1] Cities.

Population (1981), 54m. (Ho Chi Minh 3·5m.; Hanoi, 2m. (1979)); growth rate (1980) 2·9% per annum.

84% of the population are Vietnamese (Kinh). There are also over 60 minority groups thinly spread in the extensive mountainous regions. The largest minorities are (1976 figures in 1,000): Tay (742); Khmer (651); Thai (631); Muong (618); Nung (472); Meo (349); Dao (294). In 1981 0·5m. Vietnamese were living abroad, mainly in USA.

During 1975–79 some 750,000 refugees ('boat people') left Vietnam, of whom about 70% were of Chinese origin. On 2 June 1979 Vietnam signed a treaty with the UN High Commission for Refugees regulating this exodus, and agreed to halt it altogether in July 1979. In Dec. 1979 an agreement was reached between Vietnam and the UN on behalf of the USA for the settlement of further refugees in the West.

CONSTITUTION AND GOVERNMENT. A new Constitution was adopted in Dec. 1980. It states that Vietnam is a state of proletarian dictatorship and is developing according to Marxism-Leninism. The former, second, North Vietnamese Constitution dated from 1960 (the first was promulgated in 1946).

At the elections for the new National Assembly held on 25 April 1976 turnout was 98·77%. 605 candidates stood and 492 were elected (243 from the South), including 132 women, 67 representatives of ethnic minorities and 13 representatives of religious organizations. New elections were due to be held on 26 Apr. 1981.

Local government authorities are the people's councils, which appoint executive committees. Local elections were held in Ho Chi Minh City and the 38 provinces of the former South Vietnam on 5 May 1977. A special form of autonomous administration has been established in the regions inhabited by the ethnic minorities.

President: Nguyen Huu Tho (*ad interim*).
Chairman of the Standing Committee of the National Assembly: Truong Chinh.

All political power stems from the Communist Party of Vietnam (until Dec. 1976 known as the Workers' Party of Vietnam), founded in 1930; it had 1m. members in Dec. 1979 (8·8% workers; 17% women). In April 1981 the Politburo consisted of Le Duan (*First Secretary*); Truong Chinh (*Chairman of the National Assembly*); Pham Van Dong (*Prime Minister*); Pham Hung (*Deputy Prime Minister and Minister of the Interior*); Le Duc Tho; Vo Nguyen Giap (*Deputy Prime Minister*); Nguyen Duy Trinh (*Deputy Prime Minister*); Le Thanh Nghi (*Deputy Prime Minister*); Gen. Van Tien Dung (*Minister of Defence*); Le Van Luong; Nguyen Van Linh; Vo Chi Cong (*Deputy Prime Minister*); Gen. Chu Huy Man; (alternate): To Huu (*Deputy Prime Minister*); Vo Van Kiet; Do Muoi (*Deputy Prime Minister*). Ministers not in the Politburo include: Nguyen Lam (*Deputy Prime Minister and Chairman, State Planning Commission*); Nguyen Co Thach (*Foreign Minister*); Huynh Tan Phat (*Deputy Prime Minister*); Hoang Anh (*Finance*); Le Khac (*Foreign Trade*); Tran Phuong (*Home Trade*); Dinh Duc Thien (*Transport*); Nguyen Thi Binh (*Education*); Nguyen Ngoc Trieu (*Agriculture*). Tranh Quynh (*Deputy Prime Minister*).

There are 2 puppet parties, the Democratic (founded 1944) and the Socialist (1946), which are unified with the trade and youth unions in the Fatherland Front.

National flag: Red, with a yellow 5-pointed star in the centre.
National anthem: 'Tien quan ca' ('The troops are advancing').

DEFENCE. Conscription is for 3 years at age 18.

Army. Estimated strength in 1980, 1m. organized in 38 infantry divisions (plus 2 training divisions), 2 artillery divisions, 1 armoured regiment, 1 AA division, about 15 independent infantry regiments and 35 independent artillery regiments. There are also 25 SAM regiments and 50 independent AA artillery regiments.

Navy. Before the North Vietnamese victory in 1975 the Navy comprised 3 old coastal escorts, 2 fast missile boats, 28 fast torpedo boats, 22 fast motor gunboats, 34 small patrol boats, 24 landing craft, 4 minesweeping boats, 10 tenders, 100 auxiliaries and 200 armed junks. It also had 10 Mi-4 SAR helicopters.

At least 1 frigate, several other major warships and a considerable number of auxiliaries were captured after the South Vietnamese surrender.

The fleet reportedly includes 2 old frigates, 3 corvettes, 3 old patrol chasers, 2 fast missile boats, 14 fast torpedo boats, 22 fast gunboats, 14 patrol craft, 10 landing ships, 7 landing craft, 15 riverine craft, 24 minesweeping launches, 15 auxiliaries and many armed junks; but it is difficult to accurately assess the operational availability, fitness for sea or steaming capacity of this heterogeneous collection or the availability of trained personnel.

Air Force. The Air Force, built up with Soviet and Chinese assistance, has about 25,000 personal and 500 combat aircraft, including modern US types captured in war. There are reported to be 2 squadrons of variable-geometry MiG-23s, 7 squadrons of MiG-17s, 4 squadrons of Su-7s and Su-20s, and at least 6 squadrons of Northrop F-5A/Es and Cessna A-37s for attack duties; about 120 MiG-21 and 60 F-6 (Chinese-built MiG-19) interceptors; up to 70 C-130 Hercules, An-12, Li-2, An-24, and Il-14 transports; and a strong helicopter force with CH-47 Chinook, UH-1 Iroquois, Mi-4, Mi-6 and Mi-8 helicopters. Fighter pilots are trained in the USSR. 'Guideline', 'Goa' and 'Gainful' missiles are operational in large numbers.

INTERNATIONAL RELATIONS

Membership. Vietnam is a member of UN and Comecon.

ECONOMY

Planning. Long-term forward planning envisages the creation of local industry geared to agriculture manned by surplus peasant labour as a first step towards the development of a heavy industrial base. Targets for the second 5-year plan (1976–80) were not met. Growth in agriculture, 18·7%; industry, 17·3%. The third 5-year plan covers 1981–85.

Curtailment of imports, floods and resistance to new economic measures have contributed to a serious shortage of consumer goods, which it is hoped to correct by stimulating regional industry and utilizing the expertise of former businessmen. (For previous plans *see* THE STATESMAN'S YEAR-BOOK, 1976–77, p. 1473.)

Currency. The monetary unit is the *dong* = 100 *hao*. There are coins of 1, 2 and 5 *hao*, and notes of 1, 2, 5 and 10 *dong*. In March 1981, £1 = 4·75 *dong*; US$1 = 2·18 *dong*. In May 1978 the currency system was unified. The northern *dong* and the southern *piastre* were replaced by a unified *dong* which has the same exchange rate as the old northern *dong*.

Banking. The bank of issue is the National Bank of Vietnam (founded in 1951). There is also a Bank for Foreign Trade (Vietcombank). In 1980 this bank ceased all transactions with US banks.

NATURAL RESOURCES

Electricity. In 1979, 365m. kwh. of electricity were produced. A hydro-electric power station with a capacity of 2m. kw. is being built at Hoa-Binh with Soviet assistance.

Minerals. North Vietnam is rich in anthracite, lignite and hard coal: total reserves are estimated at 20,000m. tonnes. Anthracite production in 1975 was 5m. tonnes. Coal production is estimated at 5m. tonnes per year. There are deposits of iron ore, manganese, titanium, chromite, bauxite and a little gold. Chromite production in 1962 was 35,000 tons. Reserves of apatite are some of the biggest in the world. Estimated production of phosphates in 1971, 1·1m. tonnes; salt, 150,000 tonnes. In 1973 and 1974 the former Vietnamese Government awarded concessions for offshore oil exploration. Oil and natural gas have been found. There are large limestone deposits in Kien Giang, Chau Doc and Thua Thien provinces. A recent geological survey reported on the prospects of valuable bauxite deposits. There is a small coal-bearing region at Nong-Son.

Agriculture. In 1977, 90% of the population was engaged in agriculture. Cereal production was 13·5m. tonnes in 1979. In the North in 1975 agricultural co-operatives were reorganized into larger units. (Previously there had been about 18,000 co-operatives, each comprising 200–400 households and averaging 200 hectares of land each.) In 1977 there were 15,200 co-operatives in the North averaging 300–500 hectares (less than 100 hectares in mountain regions) and a workforce of 1,000–2,000. There were 105 state farms employing in all 70,000 workers and with 55,000 hectares arable and 50,000 hectares of pasture. Other crops include maize, sugarcane, sweet potatoes and cotton. The cultivated area in 1973 was 3·4m. hectares; in 1964, 2·4m. hectares were irrigated.

In the South to redress the disproportionate urbanization of the southern population during the war (40% of the population were living in Ho Chi Minh City by April 1975) resettlement of family units in rural areas began after the Communist take-over. Each family was allotted an average of 5,000 sq. metres of land, a dwelling and agricultural equipment. 1,000 sq. metres of this total are for private plots. Families are grouped by twenties in 'mutual aid and labour cells'. Rice is the main crop cultivated. In 1972, 83,300 hectares produced 20,000 tonnes of rubber. In 1977 there were 74 state farms and a few experimental co-operatives.

The production figures of other crops, 1979, were as follows: Maize (520,000 tonnes from 460,000 hectares), sugar-cane (2·9m. tonnes from 72,000 hectares), tobacco (28,000 tonnes from 32,000 hectares), sweet potatoes (2·4m. tonnes from 380,000 hectares), sorghum (35,000 tonnes from 30,000 hectares), beans (45,000 tonnes from 93,000 hectares), tea (21,000 tonnes), coffee (15,000 tonnes), soybeans (26,000 tonnes). Serious losses to the rice harvest were sustained through typhoons and flooding in 1978 and 1980. Production was some 14m. tonnes in 1980, 4·4m. tonnes short of requirements.

Livestock (1979): Cattle 1·6m.; pigs, 9·3m.; goats, 200,000; poultry, 57·1m.

Forestry. 50% of the North is forested; 3·5m. cu. metres of timber are produced annually.

Fisheries. Fishing is important, especially in Halong Bay. In 1976, 6m. tonnes of sea fish and 180,000 tonnes of freshwater fish were caught (representing only 83% of the planned target.)

INDUSTRY AND TRADE

Industry. In the North next to mining, food processing and textiles are the most important industries; there is also some machine building. Older industries include cement, cotton and silk manufacture. Local industries and handicrafts account for 50% of production.

Production in 1964 (in 1,000 tonnes): Steel, 50; cement, 595; paper, 19·4; sugar, 26·7; mineral fertilizers, 177; cotton fabrics, 105·2m. metres; irrigation pumps, 2,064 units.

Private businesses were taken over in 1978. Foreign firms, principally French, are continuing to function, but all US property has been nationalized. There is little heavy industry. Most industry is concentrated in the Ho-Chi-Minh area.

The following are some figures of production in 1972: Beer, 143·1m. litres; soft drinks, 115·6m. litres; rice alcohol, 12·3m. litres; ice, 309,000 tonnes; acetylene gas, 211,000 cu. metres; carbon dioxide, 102 tonnes.

Production (1979, in 1,000 tonnes): Coal, 6,000; (1980) cement, 729; fertilizer, 700. Kenaf yarn production was 1,615 tons in 1972.

Total production of paper products reached 46,376 tons in 1972.

Labour. Average wage (1980) 40–60 dong per month. In 1967 trade unions had 1·1m. members.

Commerce. USSR and Japan are Vietnam's main trading partners; others are Singapore and Hong Kong. Main exports are coal, farm produce, sea produce and livestock. Imports: technical equipment, industrial raw materials, foodstuffs and medical supplies. The Vietnamese Government recognizes a need for foreign aid and credit for the development of an industrial base. The USSR has given substantial aid, but the amount is declining: 1·4m. tonnes of food in 1975 as against 0·6m. in 1980. (Total aid was 0·8m. tonnes in 1980). There are aid agreements with Japan and France. In 1977 the UN ratified a recommendation of its Economic Commission that international aid should be given for the reconstruction of Vietnam's economy and in 1978 the World Bank approved a virtually interest-free loan of US$90m. repayable over 50 years. Foreign investments are encouraged and guaranteed for 15 years. Profits may be transferred and indemnities paid in the event of nationalization. In the case of foreign firms installed in Vietnam all capital may remain in foreign hands if goods are produced for export only; otherwise the Vietnamese Government will retain 51% of shares.

Trade between Vietnam and UK (British Department of Trade returns, in £1,000 sterling):

	1977	1978	1979	1980
Imports to UK	4,859	152	140	70
Exports and re-exports from UK	261	2,209	5,889	15,203

COMMUNICATIONS

Roads. In 1973 there were about 9,500 km of roads in the North. In 1970 there were 20,905 km of roads in the South. Of these, 5,908 km were asphalted.

Railways. 'Project Reunification', the rebuilding of the Hanoi–Ho Chi Minh City railway, is a major part of the new authorities' programme to repair and extend all communications systems and link them with the North. The Da Nang–Hue railway was reopened in 1975. Important sections of railway have been reconstructed rapidly since the cessation of hostilities in 1975, and through trains commenced running again between Hanoi and Ho Chi Minh City in Jan. 1977. The systems total, 2,600 km.

Aviation. Civil Aviation of Vietnam operates internal services from Hanoi to Ho Chi Minh City, Cao Bang, Na Son and Dien Bien, Vinh and Hue, and from Ho Chi Minh City to Ban Me Thuot and Da Nang, Can Tho, Con Son Island and Quan Long.

Aeroflot (USSR) operate regular services from Ho Chi Minh City to Moscow and from Hanoi to Moscow, Rangoon and Vientiane, Interflug (German Dem. Rep.) to Berlin, Moscow and Dacca and Air France to Paris.

Shipping. The major ports are Haiphong, which can handle ships of 10,000 tons, Ho Chi Minh City and Da Nang, and there are ports at Hong Gai and Haiphong Ben Thuy. There are regular services to Hong Kong, Singapore, Kampuchea and Japan. In 1953 there were 830 km of navigable waterways in the North and, in 1971, 4,783 km in the South.

Cargo is handled by the Vietnam Ocean Shipping Agency; other matters by the Vietnam Foreign Trade Transport Corporation.

Post and Broadcasting. In 1966 there were 1·4m. radios. There were 46,509 telephones in the South in 1974. There were 2m. TV sets in 1980.

Cinemas. There were 41 cinemas in North Vietnam in 1961.

Newspapers. The Party daily is *Nhan Dan* ('The People') circulation, 1981: 200,000. The official daily in the South is *Giai Phong*. Two unofficial dailies, *Cong Giao Va Dan Toc* (Catholic) and *Tin Sang* (independent) are also published.

JUSTICE, RELIGION, EDUCATION AND WELFARE

Justice. There are the Supreme People's Court, local people's courts and military courts. The president of the Supreme Court is responsible to the National Assembly, as is the Procurator-General, who heads the Supreme People's Office of Supervision and Control.

Religion. Taoism is the traditional religion but Buddhism is widespread. The Hoa Hao sect, associated with Buddhism, claimed 1·5m. adherents in 1976. Caodaism, a synthesis of Christianity, Buddhism and Confucianism founded in 1926, has some 2m. followers. There are some 5·3m. Roman Catholics headed by Cardinal Trinh Van Can, Archbishop of Hanoi and 13 bishops.

Education. Primary education consists of a 10-year course divided into 3 levels of 4,

3 and 3 years respectively. In 1977–78 in Vietnam as a whole there were 13m. pupils and students including 1m. at kindergartens and 1m. attending part-time instruction. In North Vietnam in 1973–74 there were 11,563 general education schools, and 237 colleges and vocational middle schools. In 1974–75 there were 161,200 all-level general education teachers.

In the South the former education system is being reorganized and all private and church schools have been placed under state control. At the start of the academic year 1975–76 there were 10,360 schools. There are also 're-education' programmes (*hoc tap*) for adults and anti-illiteracy drives.

In 1977–78 there were 47 institutions of higher education (including 3 universities with 130,000 students (Hanoi, Ho Chi Minh City, Central Highlands University at Ban Me Thuot), 13 industrial colleges, 7 agricultural colleges, 5 economics colleges, 9 teacher-training colleges, 7 medical schools and 3 art schools. In 1981 there were 5,000 Vietnamese studying in the USSR.

Health. In 1965 there were about 480 hospitals. There were some 23,500 doctors in 1979.

DIPLOMATIC REPRESENTATIVES

OF VIETNAM IN GREAT BRITAIN (12–14 Victoria Rd, London, W8)
Ambassador: Tran Hoan (accredited 19 May 1978).

OF GREAT BRITAIN IN VIETNAM (16 Pho Ly Thuong Kiet, Hanoi)
Ambassador: J. W. D. Margetson, CMG.

OF VIETNAM TO THE UNITED NATIONS
Ambassador: Ha Van Lau.

Books of Reference

Buttinger, J., *Vietnam: A Political History*. London, 1969
Chen, J. H.-M., *Vietnam: A Comprehensive Bibliography*. London, 1973
Féray, P.-R., *Le Vietnam au Vingtième Siècle*. Paris, 1979
Goodman, A. E., *The Lost Peace: America's Search for a Negotiated Settlement of the Vietnam War*. Stanford Univ. Press, 1978
Ho Chi Minh, *On Revolution: Selected Writings, 1920–66*. London, 1967
Le Thanh Khoi, *Socialisme et Développement au Vietnam*. Paris, 1978
Le Van Hung, *Vietnamese–English Dictionary*. Paris, 1955
Lewy, G., *America in Vietnam*. OUP, 1979
Nguyen Tien Hung, C., *Economic Developments of Socialist Vietnam, 1955–80*. New York, 1977
Phan Thien Chau, *Vietnamese Communism: A Research Bibliography*. Westport (Conn.), 1975
Pike, D., *History of Vietnamese Communism, 1925–1976*. Stanford Univ. Press, 1978
Popkin, S. L., *The Rational Peasant: The Political Economy of Rural Society in Vietnam*. Berkeley, 1979
Viet Tran, *J'ai Choisi l'Exil*. Paris, 1979

BRITISH VIRGIN ISLANDS

Capital: Road Town
Population: 11,500 (1980)

HISTORY. The Virgin Islands were discovered by Colombus on his second voyage in 1493. The British Virgin Islands were first settled by the Dutch in 1648 and taken over in 1666 by a group of English planters.

AREA AND POPULATION. The British Virgin Islands form the eastern extremity of the Greater Antilles and, exclusive of small rocks and reefs, number 36, of which 16 are inhabited. The largest are Tortola (1970 population, 8,866), Virgin Gorda (904), Anegada (269) and Jost Van Dyke (123). Other islands in the group have a total population of 68. Total area about 59 sq. miles (130 sq. km); population (1980), 11,500. Road Town, on the south-east of Tortola, is a port of entry; population, approximately 3,500.

CONSTITUTION AND GOVERNMENT. The Governor is responsible for defence and internal security, external affairs, the public service, and the courts. The Executive Council consists of the Governor, 1 *ex-officio* member and 4 ministers from the Legislature. The Legislative Council consists of 1 *ex-officio* member, as the Financial Secretary has been replaced by the Minister of Finance who is the Chief Minister, and 9 elected members; the Speaker is elected from outside the Council.

Governor: J. A. Davidson, OBE.
Flag: The British Blue Ensign with the arms of the Colony in the fly.

ECONOMY

Planning. The Government's capital programme in 1978–80 continues to concentrate on improvements to roads, further primary school rebuilding; the first phase of the new hospital as an extension to the present building was already in progress in 1977.

Budget. In 1980 revenue was US$11·5m. Capital expenditure was (1979) US$ 1,760,900, most of it provided by Development Aid Grants but the search for minerals and oil has resulted in US$217,000 being paid to the government in exploration fees.

Currency. The unit of currency is the US dollar.

Banking. Barclays Bank International, the First Pennsylvania Bank, the Bank of Nova Scotia and the Chase Manhattan Bank have branches in the islands. There are also a large number of Trust Companies.

INDUSTRY AND TRADE

Industry. Agricultural production is now very limited with the chief products being livestock (including poultry) fish, fruit and vegetables. The export trade is carried on almost entirely with the Virgin Islands of the USA. The main industry is tourism and related activities, notably construction.

Livestock (1979): Cattle, 2,000; pigs, 3,000; sheep, 7,000; goats, 12,000.

Trade. In 1978 imports were US$14·3m. and exports US$100,000.

COMMUNICATIONS. Number of telephones (1978) 2,495.

EDUCATION AND WELFARE

Education. Primary education is provided in 16 government schools and 9 private schools. Total number of pupils (Dec. 1979) 2,272.

Secondary education to the GCE level is provided at the B.V.I. High School. Total pupils in Dec. 1979, 833.

In 1979 the total number of teachers in all the schools was 182.

Health. In 1979 there were 6 doctors and 34 hospital beds.

Books of Reference

Biennial Report 1971. HMSO
Report of Constitutional Commissioner, 1965. HMSO, 1965
Dookhan, I., *A History of the British Virgin Islands.* Epping, 1975
Elkan, W., and Morley, R., *Employment in a Tourist Economy, British Virgin Islands*
Harrigan, N., and Varlack, P., *British Virgin Islands: A Chronology*

Library: Public Library, Road Town. *Librarian:* Miss Verna Penn, ALA.

WESTERN SAMOA

Capital: Apia
Population: 157,000 (1978)
GNP per capita: US$350 (1976)

Samoa i Sisifo

HISTORY. Western Samoa, a former German protectorate (1900 to the First World War), was administered by New Zealand from 1920 to 1961, at first under a League of Nations Mandate and since 1946 under a United Nations Trusteeship Agreement. In May 1961 a plebiscite held under the supervision of the United Nations on the basis of universal adult suffrage voted overwhelmingly in favour of independence as from 1 Jan. 1962, on the basis of the Constitution, which a Constitutional Convention had adopted in Aug. 1960. In Oct. 1961 the General Assembly of the United Nations passed a resolution to terminate the trusteeship agreement as from 1 Jan. 1962, on which date Western Samoa became an independent sovereign state.

Under a treaty of friendship signed on 1 Aug. 1962 New Zealand acts, at the request of Western Samoa, as the official channel of communication between the Samoan Government and other governments and international organizations outside the Pacific islands area. Liaison is maintained by the New Zealand High Commissioner in Apia, who is the only diplomatic representative accredited to the Government of Western Samoa.

AREA AND POPULATION. Western Samoa lies between 13° and 15° S. lat. and 171° and 173° W. long. It comprises the two large islands of Savai'i and Upolu, the small islands of Manono and Apolima, and several uninhabited islets lying off the coast. The total land area is 1,093 sq. miles (2,830·8 sq. km), of which 659·4 sq. miles (1,707·8 sq. km) are in Savai'i, and 431·5 sq. miles (1,117·6 sq. km) in Upolu; other islands, 2·1 sq. miles (5·4 sq. km). The islands are of volcanic origin, and the coasts are surrounded by coral reefs. Rugged mountain ranges form the core of both main islands and rise to 3,608 ft in Upolu and 6,094 ft in Savai'i. The large area laid waste by lava-flows in Savai'i is a primary cause of that island supporting less than one-third of the population of the islands despite its greater size than Upolu.

The population at the 1976 census was 151,983, of whom 109,765 were in Upolu (including Manono and Apolima) and 42,218 in Savai'i. The capital and chief port is Apia in Upolu (population 32,099 in 1976).

CONSTITUTION AND GOVERNMENT. The Constitution provides for a Head of State known as 'Ao o le Malo', which position from 1 Jan. 1962 was held jointly by the representatives of the two royal lines of Tuiaana/Tuiatua and Malietoa. On the death of HH Tupua Tamasese Mea'ole, CBE, on 5 April 1963, HH Malietoa Tanumafili II, CBE, became, as provided by the constitution, the sole Head of State for life. Future Heads of State will be elected by the Legislative Assembly and hold office for 5-year terms.

The executive power is vested in the Head of State, who appoints the Prime Minister and, on the Prime Minister's advice, the 8 Ministers to form the Cabinet which has general direction and control of the executive Government.

Parliament comprises the Head of State and the Legislative Assembly. The Legislative Assembly has 45 members elected from territorial constituencies on a franchise confined to matais or chiefs (of whom there are about 11,000) and 2 members elected on universal adult suffrage from the individual voters roll, which has replaced the old European roll (approximately 1,350 in 1971).

The Constitution also provides for a Council of Deputies. It may have 3 members.

The only present member is the Hon. Tupua Tamasese Lealofi IV, who assumed the position in 1976.

The official languages are English and Samoan.

Head of State: HH Malietoa Tanumafili II, CBE.
Prime Minister: Tupuola Efi.
National flag: Red with a blue quarter bearing 5 white stars of the Southern Cross.

INTERNATIONAL RELATIONS

Membership. Western Samoa is a member of UN, the Commonwealth and is an ACP state of EEC.

ECONOMY

Budget. In 1980 budgeted revenue was $WS31·4m.; expenditure, $WS22·7m.; statutory expenditure, $WS3·1.

Currency. On 10 July 1966 Western Samoa changed over to decimal currency. The Western Samoa *talà* (dollar) is at parity with the NZ dollar, equally £0·50. Currency in circulation consists of Samoan Treasury notes and coins.

Banking. In 1959 the Bank of Western Samoa was established with a capital of $WS500,000, of which $WS275,000 was subscribed by the Bank of New Zealand and $WS225,000 by the Government of Western Samoa. In 1977 the Pacific Commercial Bank was established jointly by Australia's Bank of New South Wales and the Bank of Hawaii.

NATURAL RESOURCES

Agriculture. The main products are coconuts, cacao and bananas.

Fisheries. The total catch (1977) was 1,270 tonnes.

INDUSTRY AND TRADE

Industry. Some industrial activity is being developed associated with agricultural products and forestry.

Commerce. In 1979, imports were valued at $WS52,794,811 and exports at $WS15,027,494. Principal exports were copra (18,517 tons; $WS8,728,038), cocoa (1,588 tons; $WS3,644,144), taro 126,030 cases; $WS1,186,543), timber (1,498,857 bd ft; $WS265,700), and bananas (33,454 cases; $WS151,919). Chief imports in 1979 included meat ($WS3,166,300), petroleum ($WS5,739,100) and machinery and transport equipment ($WS21,918,200).

Total trade between Western Samoa and UK (British Department of Trade returns, in £1,000 sterling):

	1975	1976	1977	1978	1979	1980
Imports to UK	911	201	776	567	837	572
Exports and re-exports from UK	507	449	609	719	619	710

Tourism. There were 26,114 visitors in 1977.

COMMUNICATIONS

Roads (1979). Western Samoa has over 246 miles of main roads, 251 miles of municipal secondary and village roads and 772 miles of plantation roads fit for light traffic.

A major road development programme has been under way including an all-weather coastal road and a cross-island road, both for Upolu. A rural access roads programme to improve access to plantations is also underway. In 1979 there were 1,573 passenger cars and 2,203 commercial vehicles.

Aviation. Western Samoa is linked by daily air service with American Samoa, which is on the route of the weekly New Zealand–Tahiti and New Zealand–Honolulu air services, with connexions to Fiji, Australia, USA and Europe. There are also services throughout the week to and from Tonga, Fiji, Nauru, the Cook Islands and New Zealand. Internal services link Upolu and Savai'i.

Shipping. Western Samoa is linked to Japan, USA, Europe, Fiji, Australia and New Zealand by regular shipping services. The newly established Pacific Forum Shipping Line has its headquarters in Apia.

Post and Broadcasting. There is a radio communication station at Apia. Radio telephone service connects Western Samoa with American Samoa, Fiji, New Zealand, Australia, Canada, USA and UK. Telephone subscribers numbered 3,260 in 1979.

Cinemas. In 1977 there were 10 cinemas with a seating capacity of 7,168.

Newspapers. In 1979, there was 1 weekly, circulation 20,500, 1 fortnightly (12,000) and 1 monthly (7,890); all were in Samoan and English.

EDUCATION AND WELFARE

Education. In 1979 there were 153 primary, 150 intermediate and 39 secondary schools with a total of 51,792 pupils. There is also a trades training institute, a teacher-training college, a broadcasting training centre and a college of agriculture.

Health. In 1979 there were 30 hospitals (674 beds) and 65 doctors.

DIPLOMATIC REPRESENTATIVES

OF GREAT BRITAIN IN WESTERN SAMOA

High Commissioner: Sir Harold Smedley, KCMG, MBE (resides in Wellington, New Zealand).

OF WESTERN SAMOA IN THE USA
AND ALSO TO THE UNITED NATIONS

Ambassador: Maiava Iulai Toma.

Books of Reference

Statistical Year-Book. 1976
Economic Prospects 1978
The Economy of Western Samoa. 1968
Clare, B. L., *A Review of Social, Labour and Economic Conditions in Western Samoa.* Apia, 1962, reprinted 1963.—*The Parliament of Western Samoa.* Rev. ed. Apia, 1964
Fox, J. W. (ed.), *Western Samoa.* Univ. of Auckland, 1963
Milner, G. B., *Samoan–English, English–Samoan Dictionary.* OUP, 1965

WEST INDIES

HISTORY. The West Indies Federation, established on 3 Jan. 1958, was dissolved in Feb. 1962 after Jamaica and Trinidad had opted out of it.

In 1967 new constitutional arrangements were made for the 'West Indies Associated States', Antigua, St Kitts–Nevis–Anguilla (on 27 Feb.), Dominica, St Lucia (on 1 March), Grenada (on 3 March) and St Vincent (on 1 June) were given self-government in association with Britain which retains powers and responsibilities for defence and external affairs. Grenada became independent in Feb. 1974; Dominica, 3 Nov. 1978; St Lucia, 22 Feb. 1979, and St Vincent on 27 Oct. 1979.

DEFENCE. The responsibility for defence rests with the British Government. International relationships and defence policy are conducted in close consultation with the Associated States by the British Government Representative (J. S. Arthur, CMG).

CURRENCY. After Trinidad and British Guiana had withdrawn from the British Caribbean Currency Board, Barbados, the Leeward Islands (Antigua, St Kitts–Nevis–Anguilla, Montserrat), and the Windward Islands (St Vincent, St Lucia, Dominica) united under the East Caribbean Currency Authority to issue new currency notes of $1, 5, 20 and 100, with effect from 6 Oct. 1965. Barbados subsequently withdrew from ECCA and has established its own central bank.

TRADE. The Caribbean Free Trade Area (CARIFTA now CARICOM) was established on 1 May 1968. *See* International Organizations section in this edition.

SHIPPING. The West Indies Shipping Corporation continues to provide a regular shipping service for passengers and cargo, the West Indies Shipping Corporation Act 1961 continuing with adaptation to be part of the law of the territories, including Jamaica and Trinidad and Tobago.

The West Indies Meteorological Service continues on a completely reorganized basis. It also serves Guyana, British Honduras and British Virgin Islands.

TELECOMMUNICATIONS. The territories are linked by cable, radio-telegraph and radio-telephone. Cable & Wireless (W.I.) Ltd have installed a multi-channel tropospheric scatter-link between Trinidad and Barbados and a network of VHF circuits covering the other territories.

JUSTICE. The Supreme Court of Grenada and the West Indies Associated States has replaced the West Indies Associated States Court of Appeal. In each of the independent countries there is a Court of Appeal.

EDUCATION. The University College of the West Indies, situated at Mona, Jamaica, was affiliated to London University, but became independent in April 1962. It received a Royal Charter in 1949 and has faculties of Medicine, Arts, Natural Sciences and a Department of Education. The former Imperial College of Tropical Agriculture in Trinidad is the faculty of Agriculture and Engineering; a College of Arts and Science has been added. Barbados also has a campus of the University of the West Indies where training is offered in Arts, Natural Science, the Social Sciences, and Law.

Books of Reference

A Survey of Economic Potential and Capital Needs of the Leeward Islands, Windward Islands and Barbados. HMSO, 1963
The West Indies and Caribbean Year Book. London, annual

Burns, Sir Alan, *History of the British West Indies.* 2nd ed. London, 1965
Phillips, Sir F., *Freedom in the Caribbean.* New York, 1977
Proudfoot, M., *Britain and the United States in the Caribbean.* London, 1954

ANTIGUA

History. Antigua was discovered by Colombus in 1493 and named by him after a church in Seville (Spain). It was first colonized by English settlers in 1632.

Area and population, 108 sq. miles (280 sq. km); the islands of Barbuda (62 sq. miles, 160 sq. km) and Redonda (1 sq. mile) are dependencies; population in 1977 was 72,000. Chief town, St John's, 23,500 (1974). In 1974 the birth rate per 1,000 was 18·3, the death rate 7·1; there were (1963) 203 marriages.

In Nov. 1940 sites near Parham were leased to the USA as military and naval bases; in Dec. 1960, 900 acres including Coolidge airfield were released; 300 acres are being retained for 17 years.

Governor: Sir Wilfred Ebenezer Jacobs, KCVO, OBE, QC.
Premier: Hon. Vere C. Bird, Sen.
Flag: Red, with a triangle based on the top edge, divided horizontally black, blue, white, with a rising sun in gold on the black portion.

Industry. Cotton and fruits are grown. Tourism is a thriving industry. There were 67,412 tourists (excluding cruise ship visitors) in 1978.

Finance and Trade. The budget for 1976 was EC$52,052,526. Imports (1974), EC$143,749,504; exports, EC$66,468,288. The chief product is cotton, 178,804 lb. in 1976.

Total trade of Antigua, St Christopher and Montserrat with UK (British Department of Trade returns, in £1,000 sterling):

	1976	1977	1978	1979	1980 [1]
Imports to UK	3,286	4,547	5,606	5,333	1,029
Exports and re-exports from UK	19,004	14,152	16,261	15,065	10,931

[1] Antigua only

Banking. In government savings bank, 4,917 depositors on 31 Dec. 1971, $432,277 deposits. Barclays Bank International, Royal Bank of Canada, Canadian Imperial Bank of Commerce, the Virgin Islands National Bank, the Antilles International Trust Co. and the Bank of Nova Scotia have branches at St John's. The Antigua Co-operative Bank was opened in Jan. 1965.

Roads. There are 600 miles of roads (150 miles main road).

Shipping. The main harbour is the St John's deep water harbour. There are 2 tugs for the berthing of ships and all modern and efficient general cargo handling equipment. The harbour can also accommodate 3 large cruise ships simultaneously.

Post. Telephone lines, 720 miles; 3,104 telephones. There are air-mail service connexions with the rest of the world.

Education. In 1974 there were 67 schools with 484 teachers and 22,000 pupils.

Library: Public Library, St John's. *Librarian:* Mrs Phyllis Meyers.

ST CHRISTOPHER (ST KITTS) AND NEVIS

Area and Population. The area is 101 sq. miles (262 sq. km): St Kitts, 65; Nevis, 36. Population, 1980: St Kitts, 35,104; Nevis, 9,300. Chief town of St Kitts, Basseterre (population, 14,725); of Nevis, Charlestown (population, 1,771).

Constitution and Government. In Feb. 1967 the colonial status was replaced by an 'association' with Britain, giving the islands full internal self-government, while Britain remains responsible for defence and foreign affairs. There is an elected House of Assembly and a Cabinet system of Government. The Premier is the head of the Government and presides at Cabinet meetings.

Governor: Sir Probyn Inniss, MBE.
Prime Minister: Dr Kennedy Alphonse Simmonds.

Flag: Three vertical stripes of green (for agriculture), yellow (for sunshine), blue (for the sky), with a black palm tree in the centre of the flag.

Finance. The 1980 budget balanced at EC\$29·6m. Grant for airport improvement from UK in 1974–75, £1·1m. (1973–74, £1·1m.). Grant aid from UK, 1974–75, £400,000.

Banking. There is a branch of Barclays Bank International, of the Royal Bank of Canada and of the Bank of America at Basseterre, a sub-branch of Barclays Bank International at Charlestown. Local banks are the St Kitts–Nevis–Anguilla National Bank in Basseterre and the Nevis Co-operative Banking Co. Ltd in Nevis.

Trade. Imports, 1979, EC\$86·65m.; exports, EC\$45·47m. Chief exports were sugar (3,683 tons) and molasses (1·4m. gallons).

Tourism. In 1979, there were 28,067 tourists.

Post. There were 2,939 telephones on 1 Oct. 1980 in St Kitts and Nevis.

Education (1977). There were 29 government primary and senior schools and 6 denominational; 6 government and 2 private secondary schools. A teachers' college prepares approximately 30 teachers annually in a 2-year course.

Library: Public Library, Basseterre. *Librarian:* Miss V. Archibald.

Sombrero is a small island in the Leeward Islands group, attached to St Kitts–Nevis–Anguilla; area, 2 sq. miles. Phosphate of lime exists in limited quantities. There is a Board of Trade lighthouse.

ANGUILLA

Area and Population. (35 sq. miles). Population (1977) 6,500.

Constitution and Government. An Act of the UK Parliament, the Anguilla Act (which came into effect on 19 Sept. 1980), formally separated Anguilla from Associated State of St Christopher-Nevis-Anguilla. Anguilla therefore obtained *de jure* the status of a separate dependency which it has enjoyed *de facto* since 1969. Provision is made in the Constitution for a Legislative Assembly, comprising 7 elected members, 2 nominated members and 3 *ex-officio* members, and for an Executive Council comprising the Chief Minister, 2 other Ministers and 2 *ex-officio* members. The Constitution provides for the Executive authority of Anguilla to be exercised by HM Commissioner.

British Commissioner: C. H. Godden.

YEMEN ARAB REPUBLIC

Capital: San'a
Population: 6·5m. (1975)
GNP per capita: US$580 (1978)

al Jamhuriya al Arabiya al Yamaniya

HISTORY. On the death of the Iman Ahmad on 18 Sept. 1962, army officers seized power on 26–27 Sept., declared his son, Saif Al-Islam Al-Badr (Iman Mansur Billah Muhammad), deposed and proclaimed a republic. The republican regime was supported by Egyptian troops, whereas the royalist tribes received aid from Saudi Arabia. On 24 Aug. 1965 President Nasser and King Faisal signed an agreement according to which the two powers are to support a plebiscite to determine the future of the Yemen; a conference of republican and royalist delegates met at Haradh on 23 Nov. 1965, but no plebiscite was agreed upon. At a meeting of the Arab heads of state in Aug. 1967 the President and the King agreed upon disengaging themselves from the civil war in Yemen. At the time there were still about 50,000 Egyptian troops in the country, holding San'a, Ta'iz, Hodeida and the plains, whereas the mountains are in the hands of the royalist tribes. By the end of 1967 the Egyptians had withdrawn.

AREA AND POPULATION. In the north the boundary between the Yemen and Saudi Arabia has been defined by the Treaty of Taif concluded in June 1934. This frontier starts from the sea at a point some 5 or 10 miles north of Maidi and runs due east inland until it reaches the hills some 30 miles from the coast, whence it runs northwards for approximately 50 miles so as to leave the Sa'da Basin within the Yemen. Thence it runs in an easterly and south-easterly direction until it reaches the desert area near Nejran. The area is about 73,300 sq. miles (195,000 sq. km) with a population of 6,471,893, census 1975. There were 1·23m. citizens working abroad mainly in Saudi Arabia and the United Arab Emirates not included in the census total. The capital is San'a with a population of 447,898.

The most important towns are the port of Hodeida (population, 147,982), and Ta'iz (320,323); other towns are Ibb, Yerim, Dhamar and the ports of Mokha and Loheiya.

CONSTITUTION AND GOVERNMENT. On 31 Oct. 1962, 13 April 1963, 17 April 1964, 9 May 1965 the revolutionary council issued 'interim' constitutions and on 28 Dec. 1970 a first permanent constitution was announced with provision for a Council of 179 members (20 members would be chosen by the President and the remainder by general franchise).

In Feb. 1979 fighting started between Yemen Arab Republic and the People's Democratic Republic of Yemen. A ceasefire was established in March and an agreement to unite the 2 countries was reached on 31 March 1979.

On 6 Feb. 1978 a 99-man People's Constituent Assembly was established.

President: Lieut.-Col. Ali Abdullah Saleh.
Prime Minister: Dr Abdel Karim Ali al-Iryani.
National flag: Three horizontal stripes of red, white, black, with a green star in the centre.

DEFENCE

Army. The Army consists of 10 infantry, 2 armoured, 1 parachute and 2 commando brigades, 7 artillery battalions and supports. Strength (1980): 30,000.

Navy. The Navy consists of 2 fast attack craft, 4 patrol craft and 4 fast torpedo-boats. Personnel in 1981 numbered 300 officers and men.

Air Force. Built up with aid from both the USA and USSR, as well as Saudi Arabia, the Air Force is believed to be receiving many new Soviet aircraft, including 20 Su-22 fighter-bombers, 40 MiG-21 fighters, and 4 two-seat F-5Bs, 12 MiG-17s, 4 Il-28 light jet bombers, Il-14, C-47, An-24, 2 C-130 Hercules and 2 Skyvan transports, Mi-4, Mi-8 and Agusta-Bell 204B helicopters and Yak-11 armed trainers. Personnel (1981) about 1,500.

INTERNATIONAL RELATIONS

Membership. The Yemen Arab Republic is a member of UN and the Arab League.

ECONOMY

Planning. A development plan (1976–81) envisages expenditure of 16,500m. riyals. The largest allocations are for infrastructure development.

Budget. The budget for 1978–79 had estimated revenue, 3,013m. riyal; estimated expenditure, 4,384m. riyal.

Currency. The currency is the paper *riyal* of 100 *rial*. In March 1981, 9·82 *riyal* = £1 and 4·57 *riyal* = US$1.

ENERGY AND NATURAL RESOURCES

Oil. In 1977 there were plans to build a refinery.

Minerals. The only commercial mineral being exploited is salt and (1974) production was 1m. tonnes. Reserves (estimate) 25m. tonnes.

Agriculture. Wherever water-supply allows, and in general throughout the south-western part of the country, millet (*dhurra*) is grown as a subsistence crop. The traditional cultivation of coffee (no longer exported through Mokha) continues but is giving place to that of *qat* (*cathula edulis*), a narcotic shrub. Cotton (production, 1979 1,000 tonnes) is grown in the Tihama, the coastal belt, round Bait al Faqih and Zabid (seat of a medieval university). Fruit is plentiful, especially fine grapes from the San'a district.

Livestock (1979): Cattle, 950,000; camels, 106,000; sheep, 3·7m.; goats, 7·8m.; poultry, 3·4m.

INDUSTRY AND TRADE

Industry. There is very little industry. In 1970 there were over 60 industrial enterprises employing 4,750. The largest is a textile factory at San'a. A cement factory with a capacity of 100,000 tonnes a year exists.

Commerce. Imports totalled 6,195m. riyals in 1977–78, the largest items being food and live animals. Exports totalled 35m. in 1977–78.

Total trade between Yemen Arab Republic and UK (British Department of Trade returns, in £1,000 sterling):

	1976	1977	1978	1979	1980
Imports to UK	1,465	455	7,331	2,305	469
Exports and re-exports from UK	19,661	28,356	48,498	49,169	36,428

COMMUNICATIONS

Roads. There were (1974) 1,650 km of roads. An Anglo-Federal German consortium completed the surfacing of the San'a–Ta'iz road in 1975 and the same consortium was working on the Ta'iz–Mokha stretch in 1977.

Aviation. There are 3 international airports: San'a, Ta'iz (under construction) and Hodeida (which is to be extended).

Shipping. Hodeida, Mokha, Salif and Loheiya are the 4 main ports.

Post. There were about 20,000 telephones in 1978.

EDUCATION. There were (1976–77) 221,482 pupils at primary schools, 17,676 at intermediate, and 7,500 at higher secondary schools, and 1,650 at teacher-training establishments. In 1977–78 the University of San'a (founded in 1974) had 3,139 students.

DIPLOMATIC REPRESENTATIVES

OF YEMEN ARAB REPUBLIC IN GREAT BRITAIN
(41 South St., London, W1Y 5PD)

Ambassador: Mohamed A. Alerhani.

OF GREAT BRITAIN IN YEMEN ARAB REPUBLIC
(11/13 Qasr al Jumhuri St., San'a)

Ambassador: J. F. Walker, MBE.

OF YEMEN ARAB REPUBLIC IN THE USA
(600 New Hampshire Ave., NW, Washington, D.C., 20037)

Ambassador: Yahya M. Al-Mutawakel.

OF THE USA IN YEMEN ARAB REPUBLIC (P.O. Box 33, San'a)

Ambassador: George M. Lane.

OF YEMEN ARAB REPUBLIC TO THE UNITED NATIONS

Ambassador: Mohsin Ahmed Alaini.

Books of Reference

Heyworth-Dunne, G. E., *Al-Yemen. Social, Political and Economic Survey.* Cairo, 1952
Ingrams, H., *The Yemen.* London, 1963
Macro, E., *Yemen and the Western World, 1571–1964.* London, 1967
Stookey, R. W., *Yemen: The Politics of the Yemen Arab Republic.* Boulder, 1978

THE PEOPLE'S DEMOCRATIC REPUBLIC OF YEMEN

Capital: Aden
Population: 2m. (1980)
GNP per capita: US$420 (1978)

Jumhurijah al-Yemen
al Dimuqratiyah
al Sha'abijah—
Southern Yemen

HISTORY. Between Aug. and Oct. 1967 the 17 sultanates of the Federation of South Arabia (*see* map in the STATESMAN'S YEAR-BOOK, 1965–66) were overrun by the forces of the National Liberation Front (NLF). The rulers were deposed, resigned or fled. At the same time the rival organization of FLOSY (Front for the Liberation of Occupied South Yemen) fought a civil war against NLF and harassed the British forces and civilians in Aden. In Nov. the UAR withdrew its support from FLOSY, and with the backing of the Army the NLF took over throughout the country.

The last British troops left Aden on 29 Nov., and on 30 Nov. the Southern Yemen People's Republic was proclaimed and the name subsequently changed to the People's Democratic Republic of Yemen.

AREA AND POPULATION. The People's Democratic Republic of Yemen is bounded north by Saudi Arabia, east by Oman, south by the Gulf of Aden and west by the Yemeni Arab Republic. The Republic covers an area of approximately 61,890 sq. miles (160,300 sq. km). The population was (estimate, 1980) 2m. The main towns are Aden (capital) (population, 264,326), including Shaikh Othman (30,000), Mukalla, (100,000) and Mulla (44,626).

The island of **Kamaran** in the Red Sea (area 70 sq. miles) was in British occupation from 1915 to 1967, when the inhabitants opted in favour of remaining with the Republic but Yemen Arab Republic occupied it in 1972.

The island of **Perim** was first occupied by the French in 1738. In 1799 the British took formal possession but evacuated the island the same year. It was re-occupied by the British in Jan. 1851 and was later used as a coaling station. In Nov. 1967 the inhabitants opted in favour of remaining with the Republic.

The island of **Socotra** lying to the east of the Horn of Africa in the Arabian sea (area 1,400 sq. miles) was formerly part of the Sultanate of Qishn and Socotra and became part of the Republic in 1967.

CONSTITUTION AND GOVERNMENT

An amended Constitution was approved by the Supreme People's Council on 31 Oct. 1978.

Secretary General of the Yemen Socialist Party, Chairman of the Presidium of the Supreme People's Council and Prime Minister: Ali Nasser Mohammed.
Deputy Prime Minister: Ali Salim Albaydh. *Deputy Prime Minister and Minister of Fisheries:* Anis Hassan Yayha. *Deputy Prime Minister:* Ali Abdul Ar-razzaq Ba Dhib. *Defence:* Ali Ahmed Nasser Antar. *Chairman of the State Security Committee:* Salih Munassar As-Siyayli. *Foreign Affairs:* Salim Saleh Mohammed. *Interior:* Saleh

Musleh Qassam. *Minister of State for the Council of Ministers:* Abdu Aziz Abdul Wali. *Finance:* Mahmood Said Madhi. *Health:* Dr Abdul Aziz Addali. *Constructions:* Haidar Abubaker Al Attas. *Labour and Civil Service:* Nasr Nasser Ali. *Culture and Tourism:* Rashid Mohammed Thabit. *Education:* Hassan Ahmed Asalami. *Communications:* Abdulla Mohammed Aziz. *Agriculture:* Mohammed Suleiman Nasser. *Industry:* Abdul Kader Bagamal. *Justice:* Khaled Fadhal Mansour. *Trade and Supply:* Ahmed Obeid Al Fadhli. *Planning:* Dr Farag Bin Ghanem. *Housing:* Ahmed Mohammed Alqaatbi.

National flag. Three horizontal stripes of red, white, black, with a blue triangle based on the hoist bearing a red star.

DEFENCE

Army. The Army, about 22,000 strong, consists of 10 infantry brigades, 1 mechanized and 1 marine brigade, and 1 surface-to-air missile regiment.

Navy. The Navy comprises 2 fast missile craft, 2 fast torpedo-boats, 2 fast attack craft, 2 anti-submarine patrol vessels, 9 patrol craft, 1 fleet minesweeper, 3 inshore minesweepers, 3 medium landing ships and 3 minor landing craft, nearly all transferred from the Soviet Navy. Personnel in 1981 totalled 450 officers and men.

Air Force. Formed in 1967, the Air Force is now equipped mainly with aircraft of Soviet design. It has received about 50 MiG-21 fighters, 35 MiG-17 fighter-bombers, a few Il-28 twin-jet bombers, 12 Su-7 and 30 Su-22 attack aircraft, 6 Mi-24 gunship helicopters, 3 An-24 twin-turboprop transports, and about 15 Mi-8 and 6 Mi-4 helicopters. Personnel about 1,300.

INTERNATIONAL RELATIONS

Membership. The People's Democratic Republic of Yemen is a member of UN and the Arab League.

ECONOMY

Budget. The budget of the Republic (in £ sterling) for financial years ending 31 Dec. was as follows:

	1971–72	1972–73	1973–74	1974–75	1975–76
Revenue	14,519,230	13,890,502	13,545,295	18,130,000	13,860,000
Expenditure	22,557,152	25,060,255	23,524,154	27,450,000	25,550,000

Currency. The currency is the South Yemen *dinar* and is divided into 1,000 *fils*. Coins: 50, 25, 5, 1 *fils*; notes: 10, 5 and 1 *dinar*, 500 and 250 *fils*.

Banking. The leading bank is the National Bank of Yemen. All foreign banks have been nationalized.

NATURAL RESOURCES

Agriculture. Agriculture is the main occupation of the people. This is largely of a subsistence nature, sorghum, sesame and millet being the chief crops, and wheat and barley widely grown at the higher elevations. Of increasing importance, however, are the cash crops which have been developed since the Second World War, by far the most important of which is the Abyan long-staple cotton, now the country's major export.

Owing to paucity of rainfall, cultivation is largely confined to fertile valleys and flood plains on silt, built up and irrigated in the traditional manner. These traditional methods are being augmented and replaced by the use of modern earth-moving machinery and pumps. Irrigation schemes with permanent installations are in progress. Production (1979 in 1,000 tonnes): Millet, 70; wheat, 25; cotton lint and seed, 15; sesame, 4; barley, 2.

Livestock (1979): Cattle, 110,000; sheep, 970,000; goats, 1·3m.; poultry, 1·5m.

Fisheries. There is a thriving fisheries industry, fish being the Republic's major export after cotton.

INDUSTRY AND TRADE

Industry. Light industry is being established and paint, match and textile factories in production.

Commerce. Trade is mainly transhipment and entrepôt, Aden serving as a centre of distribution to and from neighbouring territories. Transit trade is mainly in cotton piece-goods, grains, coffee, hides and skins, and cheap consumer goods.

In 1976 imports totalled 116m. dinar; exports and re-exports, 61·2m. dinar.

Total trade between Republic of Yemen and UK (British Department of Trade returns, in £1,000 sterling):

	1976	1977	1978	1979	1980
Imports to UK	781	187	208	2,713	5,685
Exports and re-exports from UK	12,325	22,613	29,030	18,920	25,425

COMMUNICATIONS

Roads. There are 1,150 miles of roads. Registered motor vehicles in 1972 numbered 19,373.

Aviation. Twelve airlines operate scheduled services: Alyemda, Air-India, Ethiopian Airlines, Middle East Airlines, Sudan Airways, Yemen Airlines, Aeroflot, Somali Air, Saudi Airlines, Kuwait Airways, East Africa Airlines and Air Jibuti.

Shipping. Because of its favourable geographical position and its efficient service to ships, Aden used to be one of the busiest oil-bunkering ports in the world, handling some 550 ships a month.

Post. The automatic telephone system provided service to about 9,876 subscribers in 1973.

Radio telephone services are available with London (with extensions to Europe and America), Kenya (with extensions to Tanzania and Uganda), Bombay, Jibuti, Bahrain and Addis Ababa.

Cinemas (1971). There were 19 cinemas with a seating capacity of about 20,000.

EDUCATION. There were (1975) 196,466 primary school pupils, 38,389 secondary school pupils and 2,241 students in technical and higher education.

DIPLOMATIC REPRESENTATIVES

OF THE PEOPLE'S DEMOCRATIC REPUBLIC OF YEMEN IN
GREAT BRITAIN (57 Cromwell Rd., London, SW7 2ED)

Ambassador: (Vacant).

OF GREAT BRITAIN IN THE PEOPLE'S DEMOCRATIC REPUBLIC OF
YEMEN (28 Shara Ho Chi Minh, Khormaksar, Aden)

Chargé d'Affaires: M. T. McKernan.

OF THE PEOPLE'S DEMOCRATIC REPUBLIC OF YEMEN
TO THE UNITED NATIONS

Ambassador: Abdalla Saleh Ashtal.

The US Embassy in Aden was closed on 26 Oct. 1969 and UK acts as the protective power.

Books of Reference

Hickinbotham, Sir T., *Aden*. London, 1959
Ingrams, H., *Arabia and the Isles*. London
Thesiger, W., *Arabian Sands*. London, 1959
Trevaskis, K., *Shades of Amber*. London

YUGOSLAVIA

Capital: Belgrade
Population: 22·3m. (1980)
GNP per capita: US$2,390 (1978)

Socijalistička Federativna
Republika Jugoslavija—
Socialist Federal
Republic of Yugoslavia

HISTORY. On 29 Nov. 1945 Yugoslavia was proclaimed a republic. On 8 March 1947 King Peter II and the other members of the dynasty were deprived of their nationality and their property was confiscated.

The peace treaty with Italy, signed in Paris on 10 Feb. 1947, stipulated the cession to Yugoslavia of the greater part of the Italian province of Venezia Giulia, the commune of Zara and the island of Pelagosa and the adjacent islets.

By an agreement of 10 Nov. 1975 the city of Trieste ('Zone A') was recognized as Italian and the Adriatic coastal portion of the former Free Territory of Trieste ('Zone B') as Yugoslav. A free industrial zone was set up in the Fernetici–Sezana region on both sides of the frontier.

EVENTS. In April 1979 a severe earthquake hit the southern coast killing 200 and making 80,000 homeless.

AREA AND POPULATION. Yugoslavia is bounded in the north by Austria and Hungary, north-east by Romania, east by Bulgaria, south by Greece and west by Albania, the Adriatic Sea and Italy. According to the census taken 31 March 1971 the area and population of Yugoslavia are shown as follows:

Federal units	Area in sq. km	Population	Pop. per sq.km
Bosnia and Herzegovina	51,129	3,746,000	73
Montenegro (Crna Gora)	13,812	530,000	38
Croatia	56,538	4,426,000	78
Macedonia	25,713	1,647,000	64
Slovenia	20,251	1,727,000	85
Serbia with Vojvodina and Kosovo	88,361	8,447,000 [1]	96
	255,804 [2]	20,523,000	80

[1] Serbia proper, 5·25m.; Vojvodina, 1,953,000; Kosovo, 1,244,000.   [2] 98,725 sq. miles.

Population (estimate) 1980: 22·3m.

The federal capital is Belgrade (Beograd).

The population of the principal towns and their conurbations (census, 31 March 1971) are as follows:

	Town	Con- urbation		Town	Con- urbation
Serbia			*Vojvodina* (contd.)		
Belgrade (capital)	755,000	1,209,360	Kikinda	38,000	68,800
Niš	95,000	193,320	Vršac	34,231	50,503
Kragujevac	71,180	130,396	Senta	24,714	31,407
Leskovac	50,000	147,248	Bečej	27,000	44,571
Vojvodina			*Kosovo*		
Novi Sad (capital)	165,000	214,048	Priština (capital)	71,000	152,733
Subotica	97,000	146,755	*Croatia*		
Zrenjanin	72,000	129,846	Zagreb (capital)	562,000	667,687
Pančevo	61,000	110,433	Rijeka-Sušak	129,000	160,630
Sombor	43,971	97,905	Split	151,000	185,047

	Town	Con-urbation		Town	Con-urbation
Croatia (contd.)			Boznia and Herzego-		
Osijek	95,000	143,109	vina (contd.)		
Karlovac	47,532	73,842	Banja Luka	86,000	157,515
Pula	47,414	69,755	Mostar	62,000	89,405
Slovenia			Macedonia		
Ljubljana (capital)	173,530	257,640	Skopje (capital)	308,000	387,889
Maribor	97,167	172,155	Bitolj	65,851	124,648
Kranj	27,209	56,324	Prilep	51,000	96,521
Bosnia and Herzego-			Montenegro		
vina			Titograd (formerly		
Sarajevo (capital)	244,045	292,241	Podgorica) (capi-		
Tuzla	53,825	107,124	tal)	55,000	98,437

The working population at the 1971 census was (in 1,000) 8,890; broken down as follows: Agriculture and forestry, 3,903; industry and mining, 1,575; building, 398; government and administration, 289; crafts, 434; commerce, 524; transport, 324.

Vital statistics for calendar years:

	Live births	Still-born	Deaths	Infantile deaths	Marriages	Divorces
1976	392,364	2,914	182,965	14,430	174,918	24,431
1977	384,808	2,857	182,803	13,682	177,305	22,990
1978	381,387	2,897	191,087	12,909	179,819	24,180
1979	380,615	...	190,459	12,241	177,305	21,268

The Yugoslav (*i.e.*, South Slav) languages proper are Slovene, Macedonian and Serbo-Croat, the latter having 2 variants (Serbian and Croatian) which are regarded as constituting one language. There are claims, largely politically-motivated, that Croatian is a separate language and Macedonian a dialect of Bulgarian. Macedonian is and Serbian may be written in the Cyrillic alphabet. There are also substantial Albanian and Hungarian-speaking minorities. Art. 246 of the Constitution lays down that 'The languages of the nations and nationalities and their alphabets shall be equal throughout the territory of Yugoslavia'. In practice Serbo-Croat serves as a *lingua franca* throughout the country.

CONSTITUTION AND GOVERNMENT. The Constitution passed on 31 Jan. 1946 declared the Federal Republic to be composed of 6 republics: Serbia, Croatia, Slovenia, Bosnia and Herzegovina, Macedonia and Montenegro.

On 13 Jan. 1953 a new Constitution (Fundamental Law) confirmed the management of all public affairs by the workers and their representatives (which was introduced in 1950) as the basis of the entire social, economic and political system of Yugoslavia.

The Constitution promulgated 7 April 1963 changed the name of the country into the Socialist Federal Republic of Yugoslavia, composed of the socialist republics of Bosnia and Herzegovina, Crna Gora (Montenegro), Croatia, Macedonia, Serbia and Slovenia (*i.e.*, now ranking in alphabetical order), and the 2 socialist autonomous provinces of Kosovo and Vojvodina within the framework of Serbia.

Under this Constitution, social self-government was exercised by the representative bodies of communes, districts, autonomous provinces, republics and the Federation and the rights to self-government and distribution of income proclaimed in 1953 were extended to those employed in public services. The former Council of Producers, in which only workers and employees engaged in economic production were represented, was replaced by Councils of Working Communities representing the working people employed in every field of social activity.

All the means of production and all natural resources are social property. Exceptions are peasants' holdings (up to 10 hectares of arable land) and handicrafts. Citizens may be owners of houses and dwellings for personal and family needs.

A new Constitution was proclaimed on 21 Feb. 1974. The political principle of this Constitution is the direct transfer of economic and political decision making power to the working people through the 'assembly system'. An assembly is defined (Art. 132) as 'a body of social self-management and the supreme organ of power within the framework of the rights and duties of its socio-political community'.

Assemblies are based upon the work-place or community and take various forms depending upon the nature of employment. Art. 133 states, 'Working people in basic self-managing organizations and communities and in socio-political organizations shall form delegations for the purpose of the direct exercise of their rights, duties and responsibilities and of organized participation in the performance of the functions of the assemblies of the socio-political communities', and Art. 135, 'Candidates for members of delegations of basic self-managing organizations and communities shall be proposed and determined by the working people in these organizations and communities in the Socialist Alliance of the Working People . . . or in trade union organizations'. At the apex of the assembly system is the federal legislature, the Assembly of the Socialist Federal Republic of Yugoslavia which has 2 Chambers: the Federal Chamber and the Chamber of Republics and Provinces.

The Federal Chamber consists of 30 delegates of self-managing organizations, communities and socio-political organizations from each Republic, and 20 delegates from each Autonomous Province. The Chamber of Republics and Provinces consists of 12 delegates from each Republican Assembly and of 8 delegates from each Provincial Assembly.

The Federal Executive Council consists of a President, 14 members, 8 Federal Secretaries and 6 Chairmen of Federal Committees. Members of the Federal Executive Council are elected in conformity with the principle of equal representation of the Republics with corresponding representation of Autonomous Provinces.

The President of the Federal Executive Council is elected by the Chambers of the Assembly of the SFRY at the proposal of the Presidency; Members of the Council, at the proposal of the candidate President of the Federal Executive Council.

The Presidency of the Republic is elected every 5 years. It has 8 members representing each of the republics and autonomous regions, and an annual President who is head of state.

Every citizen over the age of 18 has the suffrage (16 if employed). At the general election of March–May 1978 turn-out was over 96% of the electorate.

With the death of Josip Broz Tito on 4 May 1980 his constitutionally unique office of President for an unlimited term lapsed.

The membership of the collective Presidency in April 1981 was as follows:

Bosnia and Herzegovina: Cvijetin Mijatović (*President*); *Croatia:* Vladimir Bakarić; *Macedonia:* Lazar Koliševski; *Montenegro:* Vidoje Zarković; *Serbia:* Petar Stambolić (*Vice-President-Elect as of May 1981*); Slovenia: Sergej Krajger (*Vice-President and President-Elect as of May 1981*); *Kosovo:* Fadilj Hodža; *Vojvodina:* Stevan Doronjski.

President of the Assembly of the SFRY: Dragoslav Marković (elected May 1978).

President of the Federal Executive Council (Prime Minister): Veselin Djuranović. *Vice-Presidents:* Branislav Ikonić, Ivo Margan, Andrej Marinc, Dragoljub Stavrev, Gojko Ubiparip.

Federal Secretary for Foreign Affairs: Josip Vrhovec; *Defence:* Gen. Nikola Ljubičić; *Internal Affairs:* Franjo Herljević; *Finance:* Petar Kostić; *Foreign Trade:* Metod Rotar; *Justice:* Luka Banović; *Information:* Ismailj Bajra.

The Communist League of Yugoslavia had 1,623,612 members in June 1978. It is headed by a Presidium of 24 members led by Lazar Mojsov (elected for 1 year in Oct. 1980).

Executive Secretaries: Milan Daljević; Milojko Drulović; Pavle Gaži; Trpe Jakovlevski; Vlado Janžić; Ferhad Kotorić; Nandor Majorić; Marko Orlandić; Djuro Trbović.

National flag: Three horizontal stripes of blue, red, with a large red, yellow-bordered star in the centre.

National anthem: Hej, Slaveni, jošte živi reč naših dedova—O Slavs, our ancestors' words still live.

DEFENCE

The General People's Defence Law of 1969 bases Yugoslavia's defence on the principle of a nation in arms ready to wage partisan war against any invader.

Army. The Yugoslav Army comprises 8 infantry divisions, 8 armoured, 15 infantry, 1 mountain and 1 airborne brigade. Military service is for 15 months. Peace-time strength, 190,000.

Navy. The Navy comprises 7 submarines, 2 midget submarines, 1 new *ex*-Soviet frigate, 15 fast missile boats, 15 fast torpedo boats, 3 patrol vessels, 4 minehunters, 25 patrol boats, 12 inshore minesweepers, 29 river minesweepers, 24 landing craft, 1 survey ship, 1 salvage vessel, 1 yacht, 2 headquarters ships, 10 transports, 2 training ships, 4 ammunition carriers, 6 oilers, 3 water carriers and 12 tugs. Five larger fast missile boats are under construction, and 2 submarines, 1 tank landing ship and 12 assault landing craft were projected. Personnel in 1981 totalled: 14,000 officers and ratings.

Air Force. The Air Force has about 250 combat aircraft and is organized in 2 Air Corps, with HQ at Zagreb and Zemun. There are 2 fighter divisions equipped primarily with about 100 Russian-built MiG-21s, 2 ground-attack divisions of locally-built Jastreb light jet attack aircraft, and 2 squadrons of RT-33A and Jastreb jet reconnaissance aircraft. Transport units fly Il-14, An-26 and C-47 twin-engined aircraft, 4-turboprop An-12s, and a few other types in small numbers. Training types are the nationally-designed UTVA-75 armed primary trainer, Galeb jet basic trainer and the T-33A jet advanced trainer. A large number of Alouette III, Gazelle, Ka-25, Mi-4 and Mi-8 helicopters are in service. 'Guideline' and 'Goa' surface-to-air missiles have been supplied by the USSR. Personnel numbers 40,000.

INTERNATIONAL RELATIONS

Membership. Yugoslavia is a member of UN and has special relationships with Comecon and OECD.

ECONOMY

Planning. A 5-year plan of economic development for 1981–85 envisages that industrial production should increase by 4·5–5%, and that of agriculture by 4·5%. A Danube–Tisa canal system is under construction.

Budget. Revenue and expenditure (Federal, Republican, Provincial and Communal) for calendar years (in 1m. dinars):

	1973	1974	1975	1976	1977	1978
Revenue	59,314	82,302	107,191	148,824	...	...
Expenditure	58,743	81,492	106,545	148,204	165,832	168,487

The revenue, 1976 (and 1975), was composed of 78,424m. (59,944m.) dinars in the federal budget, 40,385m. (21,590m.) dinars in the republican budgets, 8,205m. in the budgets of the autonomous provinces and 11,809m. (18,446m.) dinars in other budgets.

Main items of distributed resources in 1978 (in 1m. dinars): Defence, 43,380; government, 37,278; investments in economy, 6,707; non-economic investments (1977), 5,526.

Currency. On 26 July 1965 the value of 1 *dinar*, divided into 100 *para*, was fixed at 0·710937 milligrammes of fine gold instead of 2·96224 milligrammes. A new *dinar*, equivalent of 100 old dinars, was introduced on 1 Jan. 1966. There are coins of 0·05, 0·1, 0·2, 0·5 and 1, 2, 5 and 10 *dinars*, and notes of 5, 10, 50, 100, 500 and 1,000 *dinars*. Circulation of notes and coins, as of 31 Dec. 1979, was 91,182m. *dinars*. The *dinar* was devalued by 30% in June 1980. Inflation was 39·2% in 1980. In March 1981, £1 = 70·72 *dinars*; US$1 = 29·37 *dinars*.

Banking. The National Bank is the bank of issue. There are also republican National Banks, 115 (in 1980) 'internal banks', 160 'basic banks' and 9 'associated banks'. At 30 Sept. 1979 total credits for working assets amounted to 457,757m. dinars. Savings deposits totalled 152,310m. dinars in 1979.

Weights and Measures. The metric weights and measures have been in use since 1883. The *wagon* of 10 tonnes is used as a unit of measure for coal, roots and corn. The Gregorian calendar was adopted in 1919.

ENERGY AND NATURAL RESOURCES

Electricity. Generation of electricity in 1979 (and 1978) was 54,966m. kwh. (51,755m.), of which 26,558m. kwh. (25,199m.) was hydro-electric.

Minerals. Yugoslavia has considerable mineral resources, including coal (chiefly brown coal), iron, copper ore, gold, lead, chrome, antimony and cement. The most important iron mines are at Vareš and Ljubija in Bosnia, and there are also considerable siderite and limonite iron ores between Prijedor, Sanski Most and Topusko. Copper ore is exploited chiefly at Bor (Serbia). The principal lead mines are at Trepča and Mežice. Chrome mines are in southern Serbia (Kosovo) and Macedonia (Skopje, Kumanovo). There are 2 antimony mines in western Serbia (Podrinje).

Mining output, in 1,000 tonnes, in 1978 (and 1979): Coal, 471 (434); lignite, 30,359 (32,329); bauxite, 2,566 (3,012); salt, 298 (350); manganese ore, 27 (30); iron ore, 4,564 (4,617); copper ore, 17,098 (16,446); lead and zinc ore, 4,078 (4,155); chrome ore, 2 (0·2); antimony ore, 107 (91); crude petroleum, 4,076 (4,143); pyrite concentrates, 406 (452); magnesite, 333 (293). In 1979, gold output was 4,323 kg; silver, 162,181 kg.

Agriculture. Yugoslavia, with a total area of 25,580,400 hectares, had a cultivated area of 9·9m. hectares in 1979. Agriculture is not collectivized, though private holdings are limited to 10 hectares.

Area (in hectares) and yield (in 1,000 tonnes) in 1979: Maize, 2·25m. (10,084); wheat, 1·5m. (4,512); barley, 0·3m. (631); rye, 59,000 (82); tobacco, 59,000 (67); hemp, 4,000 (35); sunflower, 257,119 (525); potatoes, 296,000 (2,724).

Livestock, Jan. 1980: 617,000 horses, 5·4m cattle, 7·3m. sheep, 7·5m. pigs.

The 1979 yield of fruit was as follows (in 1,000 tonnes): Apples, 428; pears, 95; grapes, 1,313; plums, 517; olives, 13; walnuts, 17; 6·7m. hectolitres of wine were produced.

There were, in 1977, 2,599,552 individual holdings and 856,872 peasant co-operatives. Total agricultural work force, 5·4m.; tractors, 225,524

Forestry. The forest areas of Yugoslavia consist largely of beech, oak and fir. Forest area in 1978: 9,217,000 hectares (2,655,000 in private hands). The gross timber cut in 1979 was 19,943,000 cu. metres.

Fisheries. In 1979 the landings of fish were (in tonnes): salt-water, 33,932; freshwater, 22,536. The number of fishing craft was 227 motor vessels (8,814 GRT) and 1,730 sailing and rowing vessels.

INDUSTRY AND TRADE

Employment. In Dec. 1979 there were 5·5m. employed in the social sector (*i.e.*, excluding armed forces and self-employed) of whom 2·1m. were in manufacturing and mining, and 1·2m. in the social services. There were some 775,000 unemployed. There were (1979) 5m. trade union members.

Industry. The majority of industries are situated in the north-west part of the country.

Industrial output (in 1,000 tonnes) in 1978 (and 1979): Pig-iron, 2,081 (2,360); steel, 3,452 (3,536); cement, 8,697 (9,081); sulphuric acid, 968 (1,047); fertilizers, 2,118 (2,446); plastics, 294 (342). Fabrics (in 1m. sq. metres): Cotton, 410 (418); woollen, 73 (75). Sugar (1,000 tonnes), 693 (783). Motor cars (in 1,000s), 254 (279).

Commerce. Foreign trade, in 1m. dinars, for calendar years:

	1975	1976	1977	1978	1979
Imports	146,238	139,970	183,021	189,673	226,362
Exports	77,372	92,694	99,870	107,687	129,085

Imports to Yugoslavia, 1979, in 1m. dinars, from: Federal Republic of Germany, 54,863; USSR, 34,064; Italy, 21,768; USA, 20,129; Czechoslovakia, 9,199; UK, 7,582. Exports from Yugoslavia, 1979, in 1m. dinars, to: USSR, 26,517; Federal Republic of Germany, 14,132; Italy, 13,312; Czechoslovakia, 6,238; German Democratic Republic, 4,986.

The main imports (by value) in 1979 were (in 1m. dinars): Machinery, electrical goods, transport means and parts, 95,598; fuel and lubricants, 42,712; manufactured goods, 42,610; chemical products, 31,408; crude articles, 22,894; food, 18,057. The main exports: Machinery, electrical goods, transport means and parts, 38,274; miscellaneous manufactured products, 17,566; chemical products, 12,087; crude articles, 11,758; foods, 10,874.

In Apr. 1980 a five-year agreement with the EEC was signed to help Yugoslav exports to the EEC and provide financial aid.

Total trade between Yugoslavia and UK (British Department of Trade returns, in £1,000 sterling):

	1976	1977	1978	1979	1980
Imports to UK	33,502	40,487	37,906	51,331	56,802
Exports and re-exports from UK	128,456	175,011	160,317	173,954	190,503

Tourism. In 1979, 5,966,000 (1978: 6,402,000) tourists visited Yugoslavia.

COMMUNICATIONS

Roads (1979, preliminary). There were 52,084 km of asphalted roads and (1978) 39,199 km of macadamized roads. There were 1,863,155 passenger motor cars and 147,997 trucks and buses. The north–south highway is being converted to 6-lane motorway.

Railways. In 1979 Yugoslavia had 9,400 km of railway, of which 2,968 km are electrified, carrying 108m. passengers and 88m. tonnes of freight. In 1976 the new railway linking Belgrade and the Adriatic coast port of Bar was completed.

Aviation. The national airline, Jugoslovenski Aero Transport (Inex Adria-aviopromet, Panadria and Aviogenex) in 1979 flew on its home and international services, 164·3m. km and carried 2·7m. passengers and 92·1m. ton-km of freight; international services (without Panadria), 41·1m. km, 2·2m. passengers and 67·7m. ton-km of freight. The chief airfields are Belgrade, Zagreb, Ljubljana, Sarajevo, Skopje, Dubrovnik, Split, Titograd, Tivat, Pula and Zadar.

Shipping. In 1979 Yugoslavia possessed a total of 455 vessels of 2·4m. gross tons.

In 1979 vessels of 50·8m. net tons entered the ports of Yugoslavia.

In 1977 Yugoslavia had 1,307 river craft with 2,659 passenger capacity. The length of the navigable rivers amounted to 1,673 km, that of canals to 664 km. There are 2 navigable lakes: Skadar (391 sq. km, of which 243 in Yugoslavia) and Ohrid (348 sq. km, of which 230 in Yugoslavia).

Pipeline. An oil pipeline runs from Krk to Belgrade.

Post and Broadcasting. There were 3,721 post offices and 1,913,000 telephone subscribers in 1979. *Jugoslovenska Radiotelevizija* consists of almost 250 main, relay and local stations operating on medium-waves and FM. *Radio Koper* also broadcasts commercial programmes in Italian for northern parts of Italy. National and regional TV programmes are broadcast. Advertisements are broadcast for maximum 170 minutes each week. Number of receivers in 1979: radio, 4·6m.; television, 4·2m.

Cinemas (1979). 1,297, seating 429,000

Theatres (1978–79). 274, seating (professional only), 24,350.

Newspapers (1979). There were 27 dailies, 2,991 other newspapers and 1,408 journals. There are no party newspapers but *Borba* and *Politika* enjoy semi-official status.

JUSTICE, RELIGION, EDUCATION AND WELFARE

Justice. There are county tribunals, district courts, supreme courts of the constituent republics and a Supreme Court. There are also self-management courts, including courts of associated labour. In county tribunals and district courts the judicial functions are exercised by professional judges and by lay assessors constituted into collegia. There are no assessors at the supreme courts.

All judges are elected by the socio-political communities in their jurisdiction. The judges exercise their functions in accordance with the legal provisions enacted since the liberation of the country.

The constituent republics enact their own criminal legislation, but offences concerning state security and the administration are dealt with at federal level.

Religion. Religious communities are separate from the State and are free to perform religious affairs. All religious communities recognized by law enjoy the same rights.

Serbia has been traditionally Orthodox and Croatia Roman Catholic. Moslems are found in the south as a result of the Turkish occupation. The 1953 percentage of the denominations was: Orthodox, 41·2%; Roman Catholic, 31·7%; Moslems, 12·3%; Protestants, 0·9%; without religion, 12·6%.

The Serbian Orthodox Church with its seat in Belgrade has 20 bishoprics within the country and 4 abroad, 3 in US and Canada and 1 in Hungary. The Serbian Orthodox Church numbers about 2,000 priests.

The Macedonian Orthodox Church with the Archbishop of Ohrid and Macedonia as its head in Skopje, has 4 bishoprics in the country and 1 abroad (American–Canadian–Australian). The Macedonian Orthodox Church numbers about 300 priests.

The Roman Catholic Church is divided into two provinces: Zagreb with 4 suffragan sees, and Sarajevo with 2 suffragan sees. In addition, the Roman Catholic Church has 4 archbishoprics, 10 independent bishoprics directly connected with the Vatican and 3 Apostolic Administrators. There is a National Conference of Bishops with the Archbishop of Zagreb, at its head. The Roman Catholic Church has about 4,000 priests.

The Moslem Religious Union has 4 republic Superiorates in Sarajevo, Skopje, Titograd and Priština. The highest authority is the supreme synod of the Islamic Religious Community, which elects the Reis-ul-Ulema and the Supreme Islamic Superiorate.

The Moslem religious community has about 2,000 priests.

The Protestant churches covering 4 independent Lutheran Churches, numbering about 150,000 believers, the Reformed Christian Church, numbering about 60,000 believers, include also several much smaller churches of Baptists, Methodists, Adventists, Nazarenes, etc., numbering together about 100,000 believers. The Protestant churches have about 450 priests.

Also there are independent Old Catholic Churches with Synodal Council at Zagreb.

The Jewish religious community has about 35 communities making up a common league of Jewish Communities with its seat in Belgrade.

Education. Compulsory general education lasts 8 years, secondary 3–4 years. In 1978–9 there were 13,072 primary schools with 130,276 teachers and 2,824,762 pupils, 1,391 secondary schools (not including those covered by the reform programme) with 59,931 teachers and 952,568 pupils, 421 primary schools for adults with 51,474 pupils, 585 secondary schools for adults with 53,779 pupils, 172 technical schools for adults with 17,131 pupils, 20 teacher training schools with 6,007 students.

Primary and secondary schools of ethnic minorities (1978–9): Albanian, 1,636; Hungarian, 970; Bulgarian, 68; Czech, 13; Slovak, 22; Italian, 40; Romanian, 39; Turkish, 95; Ukrainian, 19.

For higher and specialized education there were (1979–80) 351 faculties, academies and high schools with 23,969 professors and instructors and 447,270 students.

Social Welfare. In 1978 there were 30,426 doctors and dentists, and 130,363 hospital beds (10,993 psychiatric).

Health insurance benefits totalled 46,203m. dinars and pensions 88,580m. dinars in 1979.

DIPLOMATIC REPRESENTATIVES

OF YUGOSLAVIA IN GREAT BRITAIN
(5 Lexham Gdns., London, W8 5JJ)

Ambassador: Živan Berisavljevič (accredited 18 March 1977).

OF GREAT BRITAIN IN YUGOSLAVIA (46 Generala Ždanova,
Belgrade)

Ambassador: E. Bolland, CMG.

OF YUGOSLAVIA IN THE USA (2410 California St., NW, Washington, D.C., 20008)

Ambassador: Dimce Belovski.

OF THE USA IN YUGOSLAVIA (50 Kneza Miloša, Belgrade)
Ambassador: Lawrence S. Eagleburger.

OF YUGOSLAVIA TO THE UNITED NATIONS
Ambassador: Miljan Komatina.

Books of Reference

Statistical Information: The Federal Statistical Office (Savezni Zavod za Statistiku; Kneza Miloša 20, Belgrade) was founded in Dec. 1944. *Director:* Ibrahim Latifić. It publishes: *Indeks* (from April 1952, with English and French translations); *Statistički bilten* (1950 ff., with English or French translations); *Statistical Yearbook* (from 1954, with English, Russian and French translations); *Statistics of Foreign Trade of the SFR Yugoslavia* (annual, from 1946; half-yearly, from 1951); *Statistical Pocket-book* (from 1955; in 5 eds.: Yugoslav, English, French, Russian, German).

The Assembly of the SFR of Yugoslavia. Belgrade, 1974
The Constitution of the Socialist Federal Republic of Yugoslavia. Belgrade, 1974
Alexander, S., *Church and State in Yugoslavia since 1945.* CUP, 1979
Auty, P., *Yugoslavia.* New York, 1965.—*Tito: A Biography.* London, 1970
Bogadek, F. A., *English–Croatian, Croatian–English Dictionary.* London, 1950
Borowiec, A., *Yugoslavia after Tito.* New York, 1977
Clissold, S., *A Short History of Yugoslavia.* CUP, 1966
Dedijer, V., *et al., History of Yugoslavia.* New York, 1974
Denitch, B. D., *The Legitimation of a Revolution: The Yugoslav Case.* Yale Univ. Press, 1976
Djilas, M., *Memoir of a Revolutionary.* New York, 1973
Doder, D. *The Yugoslavs.* New York, 1978
Horton, J. J., *Yugoslavia.* Oxford, 1977
Horvat, B., *The Yugoslav Economic System.* White Plains, 1976
Hunter, B., *Soviet–Yugoslav Relations, 1948–72: A Bibliography.* New York, 1976
Jambrek, P., *Development and Social Change in Yugoslavia.* Farnborough, Hants., 1975
Kotnik, J., *Slovensko–angleski slovar.* 4th ed. Ljubljana, 1959
Nord, L., *Nonalignment and Socialism: Yugoslavia's Foreign Policy in Theory and Practice.* Uppsala, 1974
Pavlowitch, S. K., *Yugoslavia.* New York, 1971
Rusinow, D. I., *The Yugoslav Experiment, 1948–1974.* London, 1977
Ristić, Simić, Popović: *An English–Serbocroatian Dictionary.* 2 vols. Belgrade, 1956
Singleton, F., *Twentieth Century Yugoslavia.* London, 1976
Skerlj, R., *English–Slovene Dictionary.* 4th ed. Ljubljana, 1957
Tito, J. B., *The Essential Tito.* New York, 1970
Wilson, D., *Tito's Yugoslavia.* CUP, 1979

National Library: Narodna biblioteka, 56 Kneza Mihailova, Belgrade. *Director:* Svetislav Djurić.

ZAÏRE

Capital: Kinshasa
Population: 29·27. (1979)
GNP per capita: US$210 (1978)

République du Zaïre

HISTORY. Until the middle of the 19th century the territory drained by the Congo River was practically unknown. When Stanley reached the mouth of the Congo in 1877, King Leopold II of the Belgians recognized the immense possibilities of the Congo Basin and took the lead in exploring and exploiting it. The Berlin Conference of 1884–85 recognized King Leopold II as the sovereign head of the Congo Free State.

The annexation of the state to Belgium was provided for by treaty of 28 Nov. 1907, which was approved by the chambers of the Belgian Legislature in Aug. and Sept. and by the King on 18 Oct. 1908. The law of 18 Oct. 1908, called the Colonial Charter (last amended in 1959), provided for the government of the Belgian Congo, until the country became independent on 30 June 1960. For subsequent history to 1977 *see* The STATESMAN'S YEAR-BOOK, 1980–81, p. 1613.

AREA AND POPULATION. Zaïre is bounded north by the Central African Republic, north-east by Sudan, east by Uganda, Rwanda, Burundi and Lake Tanganyika, south by Zambia, south-west by Angola, north-west by Congo. There is a short Atlantic coastline between the two last-named.

The area of the republic is estimated at 2,345,409 sq. km (895,348 sq. miles). The population is composed of 3 ethnical groups: Negroes (Bantu, Sudanese, Nilotics), Pygmies and Hamites (in the east). In the census (1970) the population was 21,637,876. Estimate (1979) 29·27m.

The area (in sq. km) and populations (estimate) at 1 July 1976 of the regions are as follows, together with their capitals:

Region	Sq. km	Population 1976	Chief town	Population 1976
Bandundu	295,658	2,977,918	Bandundu (Banningville)	74,467[1]
Bas-Zaïre	53,920	1,741,080	Matadi	162,396
Equateur	403,293	2,733,171	Mbandaka (Coquilhatville)	149,118
Haut-Zaïre	503,239	3,629,348	Kisangani (Stanleyville)	339,210
Kasai Occidental	156,967	2,817,717	Kananga (Luluabourg)	704,211
Kasai Oriental	168,216	2,078,403	Mbuji-Mayi (Bakwanga)	382,632
Kinshasa City	9,965	2,443,876	Kinshasa (Leopoldville)	2,443,876
Kivu	256,662	3,906,160	Bukavu (Costermansville)	209,051
Shaba	496,965	3,239,431	Lumumbashi (Elizabethville)	451,332
Total	2,344,885	25,567,104		

[1] 1970

Other large towns: Kikwit, 172,450 in 1976; Likasi (Jadotville), 146,394 in 1970. The country and the river were named 'Zaïre' in 1971.

The most important languages are: Kiswahili in the east, Tshiluba in the south, Kikongo in the area between Kinshasa and the coast, while Lingala is spoken widely in and around Kinshasa and along the river; Lingala has become the *lingua franca* after French.

CONSTITUTION AND GOVERNMENT. Following amendments in 1971, 1974 and 1977, a new Constitution was promulgated in Feb. 1978. It established a single-chamber Parliament, the Legislative Council, directly elected with 268 deputies, 1 for every 100,000 inhabitants; a President directly elected for 7 years. The supreme institution is the sole political party, the *Mouvement Populaire de la*

Révolution (MPR); its President is President of the Republic; its chief organ is the Congress which meets once every 5 years and in special session when necessary. It is summoned by the President. A 120-man Central Committee ranks next in importance and all members are appointed by the President. The *Bureau Politique* of the MPR, which directs the Congress, consists of 36 Political Commissioners, 18 nominated by the President and 18 elected members. The Executive Council (or Cabinet) is composed of State Commissioners; led by a First State Commissioner (or Prime Minister); all are appointed by the President.

Regional Commissioners, also appointed by the President, administer the Regions.

President: Mobutu Sese Seko (elected for a third term on 5 Dec. 1977).
Prime Minister: Nguza Karl I Bond.
Deputy Prime Minister, Foreign Affairs: Bomboko Lokumba.
National flag: Green, with a yellow disc bearing an arm holding a flaming torch.

DEFENCE

Army. The country is divided in 9 military regions. Total strength (1980) approximately 18,500. Major units comprise 4 infantry brigades, 1 armoured brigade, 2 parachute battalions and 1 special force brigade. Supporting units include engineer, signal, transport and military police companies.

The *Gendarmerie Nationale* is a separate service with responsibility for security. Estimated strength (1980) 35,000.

Navy. The Navy consists of 3 flotillas, 1 coastal, 1 river and 1 lake, comprise 4 fast gunboats (*ex*-Chinese), 7 fast torpedo boats (4 *ex*-Chinese and 3 *ex*-North Korean), and 29 coastal patrol boats including 10 US-built and 10 French-built. Personnel in 1981 numbered 900 officers and men and 600 marines.

Air Force. The Air Force has been built up with training assistance from Italy. In 1980 it had a squadron of Mirage 5 supersonic fighters, 20 Reims-Cessna Milirole observation and light attack aircraft, 13 Aermacchi MB.326GB, 6 MB.326K armed jet trainers, 7 C-130 Hercules and 3 DHC-5 Buffalo turboprop transports, 10 C-47 and 2 Caribou transports, 29 Bell 47, Alouette and Puma helicopters, 23 SIAI-Marchetti SF.260MC basic trainers and a variety of other transport and training aircraft. Personnel, approximately 1,000.

INTERNATIONAL RELATIONS

Membership. Zaïre is a member of UN, OAU and is an ACP state of EEC.

ECONOMY

Budget. Estimated revenue and expenditure (in 1m. zaïres) for calendar years:

	1970	1971	1972	1973	1974	1975	1976[1]
Revenue	215	289	299	383	447	556	615
Expenditure	300	273	274	364	650	...	471

[1] Provisional.

Currency. The currency unit, is the *zaïre*, divided into 100 *makuta*. Each *likuta* (plural *makuta*) is divided into 100 *sengi*. Bank-notes are issued in the following denominations: 10, 5 and 1 *zaïre*, 50, 20, 10 *makuta*. In March 1981, £1 sterling = 6·87 *zaïre*; US$1 = 3·46 *zaïre*.

Banking. The national bank is Banque du Zaïre. A development bank with state backing is the Société pour Finance et Développement (SOFIDE). Commercial banks operating in Zaïre are Banque de Paris et des Pays-Bas, Banque de Kinshasa, National & Grindlays Bank, Barclays Bank SZPRL, First National City Bank, Union Zaïroise de Banques, Banque Commerciale Zaïroise, Bank du Peuple, Caisse Nationale d'Epargne et de Crédit Immobilier and Banque Internationale pour L'Afrique au Zaïre.

Weights and Measures. The metric system was introduced by law on 17 Aug. 1910.

ENERGY AND NATURAL RESOURCES

Electricity. The installed generating capacity (1974) was hydro, 1,054 mw; thermal, 79 mw.

Minerals. In 1979 most of Zaïre's foreign exchange was derived from mining of copper (450,000 tonnes), zinc concentrates (1975, 141,490), zinc (1975, 79,238), gold (1975, 2,439 kg), cobalt (13,000), cadmium (1975, 264), silver (1975, 84,487). The most important mining area is in the region of Shaba (formerly Katanga). The principal mining companies are the State-owned Gecamines which took over the interests of Union Minière du Haut Katanga in 1967; the Belgian Société Générale des Minerais; the Zaïre-Japanese Sodimiza; the international Société Minière de Tenke-Fungurume which started production in 1976; and 2 diamond companies, MIBA and British Zaïre Diamond Distributors. Offshore oil production began in Nov. 1975.

Agriculture. A new Ministry of Rural Development was established in 1977 to stimulate output. Six projects have been inaugurated, using overseas aid, with the aim of increasing production of palm-oil, cocoa, tea, tobacco, cotton and sugar, and there are also continuing efforts towards improving strains and yields of maize, rice and manioc. Production (1979, in tonnes): Palm-oil, 170,000; coffee, 87,000; rubber, 27,000; cocoa beans, 5,000; tea, 5,000; rice (paddy), 230,000; sugar-cane, 700,000; onions, 10,000; bananas, 310,000; plantains, 1·4m.; mangoes, 172,000. Chief imports (1973) were maize (125,000), rice (52,000), wheat (129,300), meats (16,000). Chief exports (1975) were palm-oil (53,000), coffee (59,000), rubber (24,000), tea (4,600) and timber (49,000 cu. metres).

Livestock (1979): Cattle, 1·1m.; sheep, 779,000; goats, 2·8m.; pigs, 753,000; poultry, 12·4m.

Fisheries. The catch for 1975 was 106,500 tonnes, of which 100,000 tonnes was from inland waters.

INDUSTRY AND TRADE

Commerce. Imports in 1977 totalled 522·7m. zaïres, exports totalled 846·9m. zaïres. In 1975, 65% of the exports (by value) consisted of copper.

Total trade between Zaïre and UK (British Department of Trade returns, in £1,000 sterling):

	1975	1976	1977	1978	1979	1980
Imports to UK	29,933	38,393	59,246	98,471	67,006	52,585
Exports and re-exports from UK	23,609	16,853	18,234	20,658	22,246	27,629

Tourism. There were 40,948 visitors in 1975 spending US$5m.

COMMUNICATIONS

Roads. Of 150,000 km of roads only 20,600 km are of national importance and all roads are earth-surfaced. There were 177,931 motor vehicles registered in Dec. 1975. Of these, 95,978 were cars, 33,505 trucks, 2,989 buses, 9,153 motor cycles, and other types, 36,306.

Railways. The total length of public railways in 1978 was 5,169 km on 4 gauges, 858 km being electrified.

Aviation. There are 2 international and 40 principal airports, and over 150 other landing strips.

Ten international airlines, including British Caledonian Airways, operate in and out of Kinshasa from Europe, Africa and the USA. The national airline Air Zaïre, with a fleet of 25 planes (Nov. 1975), operates on all the main internal routes as well as on international routes to Europe and other African cities. Internal feeder services are assured by the private charter company AMAZ. PANAM act as technical and managerial advisers to Air Zaïre.

Shipping. The Zaïre River and its tributaries are navigable for about 14,000 km. Regular traffic has been established between Kinshasa and Kisangani as well as Ilebo, on the Lualaba (i.e., the river above Kisangani), on some tributaries and on the lakes. Zaïre has only 30 km. of sea coast.

At the port of Matadi, the most important harbour, the imports in 1974 amounted to 655,000 tonnes and the exports to 540,000 tonnes.

Post and Broadcasting. In 1970 there were 351 post offices. Zaïre is included in the Universal Postal Union and in the African Postal Union. Length of telegraph lines, 2,459 km. There were 15 broadcasting stations, 161 stations of wireless telegraphy and 206 telegraph offices; telephones numbered 33,802 in 1978. There is a ground satellite communications station outside Kinshasa.

Cinemas (1974): 91 cinemas had a seating capacity of 23,300.

JUSTICE, RELIGION AND EDUCATION

Justice. In 1976 there was a Supreme Court in Kinshasa, 2 courts of appeal (Kinshasa and Lubumbashi) and 8 courts of first instance. An Appeal Court sits in Kisangani.

Religion. There were, on 31 Dec. 1975, 2,637 foreign Catholic missionaries and 3,375 Catholic nuns. Numerous missionaries were massacred in 1964.

Roman Catholics in 1975 numbered 9m.; Protestants, 1·1m.; Moslems, about 115,000, and Jews, 1,520.

Education. In the state and state-inspected primary schools in 1973–74 there were 3,538,257 pupils while the secondary schools, including technical and teacher-training colleges, numbered 335,203 and 14,483 staff. In 1971 all Institutes of Higher Education combined to form the National University of Zaïre. In the 1976 academic year there was a total of 26,000 students attending the National University.

DIPLOMATIC REPRESENTATIVES

OF ZAÏRE IN GREAT BRITAIN (26 Chesham Place, London, SW1X 8HH)

Ambassador: Lieut.-Gen. Peter Zuze.

OF GREAT BRITAIN IN ZAÏRE (Ave. de l'Equateur, Kinshasa)

Ambassador: A. E. Donald, CMG.

OF ZAÏRE IN THE USA (1800 New Hampshire Ave., NW, Washington, D.C., 20009)

Ambassador: Kasongo Mutuale.

OF THE USA IN ZAÏRE (310 Ave. des Aviateurs, Kinshasa)

Ambassador: Robert B. Oakley.

OF ZAÏRE TO THE UNITED NATIONS

Ambassador: Kabeya wa Mukeba.

Books of Reference

Anstey, R., *King Leopold's Legacy: The Congo Under Belgian Rule 1908–1960.* OUP, 1960
Area Handbook for the Democratic Republic of the Congo (Kinshasa). US Government Printing Office, Washington, 1971
Atlas Général du Congo. Académie Royale, Brussels
Cornevin, R., *Histoire de Congo.* Paris, 1963
Ganshof van de Meersch, W. J., *Fin de la souveraineté Belge au Congo.* Brussels and The Hague, 1965
Gran, G., *Zaire: The Political Economy of Underdevelopment.* New York, 1979
Lefever, Ernest W., *Uncertain Mandate: Politics of the UN Congo Operation.* Johns Hopkins Press, 1967
Martelli, G., *Experiment in World Government: The UN Operation in the Congo 1960–64.* London, 1967
Slade, R. M., *King Leopold's Congo: Aspects of the Development of Race Relations in the Congo's Independent State.* OUP, 1962
Young, C., *Politics in the Congo: Decolonization and Independence.* Princeton UP and OUP, 1965

ZAMBIA

Capital: Lusaka
Population: 5·6m. (1979)
GNP per capita: US$480 (1978)

HISTORY. The independent Republic of Zambia (formerly Northern Rhodesia) came into being on 24 Oct. 1964 after 9 months of internal self-government following the dissolution of the Federation of Rhodesia and Nyasaland on 31 Dec. 1963.

By an Order in Council dated 4 May 1911 the two provinces of North-eastern and North-western Rhodesia were amalgamated under the name of Northern Rhodesia, with effect from 17 Aug. 1911.

By an Order in Council dated 20 Feb. 1924, the office of Governor was created, an executive council constituted and provision made for the institution of a legislative council which, since 1945, had an unofficial majority. On 1 April 1924 the British South Africa Company was relieved of the administration of the territory by the Crown.

AREA AND POPULATION. Zambia is bounded by Tanzania in the north, Malawi in the east, Mozambique in the south-east and by Zimbabwe and South West Africa (Namibia) in the south. The area is 290,586 sq. miles (752,620 sq. km).

The republic is divided into 9 provinces. Their names, headquarters, area (in sq. km) and estimated population in 1978 were as follows:

Province	Headquarters	Area	Population	Province	Headquarters	Area	Population
Lusaka	Lusaka	360	555,000	Eastern	Chipata	69,106	636,000
Copperbelt	Ndola	31,328	1,303,000	Southern	Livingstone	85,283	591,000
Luapula	Mansa	50,567	356,000	N.-Western	Solwezi	125,827	285,000
Northern	Kasama	147,826	628,000	Western	Mongu	126,386	522,000
Central	Kabwe	115,930	1,151,000				

The seat of Government is at Lusaka. The other important centres are Livingstone, the old capital, Ndola, Luanshya, Mufulira, Kitwe, Chililabombwe, Kalulushi and Chingola on the Copperbelt; Kabwe, the oldest mining township; Chipata, centre of a tobacco farming area.

CONSTITUTION AND GOVERNMENT. The Constitution provides for a President, elected in the first instance by the Legislative Assembly, but subsequently at each general election by the electorate. On 13 Dec. 1972 President Kaunda signed a new Constitution based on one-party rule.

The single political party is the United National Independence Party. Its full-time executive organ (headed by a Secretary-General) is the Central Committee, whose 24 members are elected by the National Council of the Party. The Central Committee has precedence over the legislative body, the National Assembly, which is led by the Prime Minister and consists of 125 elected members and up to 10 nominated members, including a cabinet of 18 ministers.

Presidential elections were held in Dec. 1978 and on 16 Dec. President Kaunda was sworn in for a further 5-year term.

The Cabinet, as in Feb. 1981, was composed as follows:

President: Dr Kenneth David Kaunda.
Prime Minister: Nalumino Mundia. *Home Affairs:* Wilted J. Phiri. *Foreign Affairs:* Wilson M. Chakulya. *Legal Affairs and Attorney-General:* F. Chomba. *Education and Culture:* Lameck Goma. *Health:* Rajah Kunda. *Finance:* Kebby Musokotwane. *Commerce and Industry:* Remy Chisupa. *Mines:* Mufuya Mumbuna. *Power, Transport and Communications:* G. Kingsley Chinkuli. *Works and Shipping:* Haswell Y. Mwale. *Labour and Social Services:* Joshua Lumina. *Tourism:* Roger C. Sakuhuka.

Information and Broadcasting: Mark Tambatamba. *Youth and Sports:* Ben Kakoma. *Agriculture and Water Development:* Unia Mwila. *Land and Natural Resources:* Clement M. Mwananskiku. *National Guidance:* Arnold Simuchimba.

Flag: Green, with in the fly a panel of 3 vertical strips of dark red, black and orange, and above these a soaring eagle in gold.

The provinces are administered by Central Committee Members for the provinces who are responsible for the overall government and Party administration of their respective areas. The Members are assisted by a Political Secretary and a Permanent Secretary. Each district in all provinces is headed by a District Governor, and these are directly responsible to their respective provincial Political Secretaries.

DEFENCE

Army. The Army consists of 1 armed regiment, 1 armed reconnaissance battalion, 4 infantry battalions, 1 armoured car squadron, 1 artillery battery and supporting units. Strength, (1980) 12,800.

Air Force. Creation of the Zambian Air Force was assisted initially by an RAF mission. Equipment acquired in this period and still in use includes 5 twin-engined Caribou and 4 single-engined Beaver transports built in Canada. Training and expansion of the Air Force was next taken over by Italy, with the purchase of 20 Aermacchi M.B.326G armed jet basic trainers (of which 13 remain in service), 8 SIAI-Marchetti SF.260M piston-engined trainers and 28 Agusta-Bell 47G/205/212 helicopters. Twelve F-6 (MiG-19) jet fighter-bombers and some BT-6 primary trainers have since been acquired from China, 6 SOKO Jastreb jet light attack aircraft and 6 Galeb jet trainers from Yugoslavia, 7 DHC-5 Buffalo twin-turboprop transports from Canada, 10 C-47s and 2 DC-6Bs built in the USA. 10 Do 28D Skyservant light transports from Germany, 20 Supporter armed light trainers from Sweden, 2 Yak-40 light jet transports and 6 Mi-8 helicopters from the Soviet Union. There is also a squadron of MiG-21s.

INTERNATIONAL RELATIONS

Membership. Zambia is a member of UN, the Commonwealth, OAU and is an ACP state of EEC.

ECONOMY

Planning. A second 5-year development plan (1972–76) envisaged investment of K2,609m. and an economic growth rate of 6·8% per annum. The emphasis has been on rural development and an important goal is to achieve self-sufficiency in staple foodstuffs, particularly maize. The third development plan has been postponed from Jan. 1977 to Jan. 1980.

To promote industrial growth and to ensure greater Zambian participation in the economy the Government has, since 1968, taken a controlling interest in several companies, including the mines. Government's control of those companies in which it has a majority shareholding is exercised *via* the Zambian Industrial and Mining Corporation (ZIMCO) the holding company for the Industrial Development Corporation (INDECO) which controls all industrial and distributive concerns; the Mining Development Corporation (MINDECO) which holds the Government's 51% share in the mines.

Budget. Revenue and expenditure for calendar years (in K1,000):

	1975	1976	1977	1978
Revenue: Current	448,338	443,018	499,017	547,327
Capital fund	169,792	303,729	138,535	135,943
Expenditure: Current	580,991	608,889	660,695	643,296
Capital fund	245,560	327,415	160,282	164,874

Currency. Decimal currency was introduced on 16 Jan. 1968. The *Kwacha* (K) is divided into 100 *ngwee* (n). Notes of K20, K10, K5, K2 and K1 are in use. In March 1981, £1 = 1·82 *Kwacha*; US$1 = 0·84 *Kwacha*.

Banking. Barclays Bank International has 25 branches, 6 sub-branches and 17 agencies; Standard Bank has 18 branches and 17 agencies; National & Grindlays, 10 branches and 1 sub-branch; Zambia National Commercial Bank, 10 branches and 1 in London; the post office saving bank has branches throughout the republic.

The Finance Development Corporation (FINDECO) controls the building societies, all insurance companies, one commercial bank and has shares in a second one. The Agricultural Finance Corporation provides loans to farmers, co-operatives, farmers' associations, agricultural societies and such bodies as will further the agricultural industry.

ENERGY AND NATURAL RESOURCES

Electricity. The total installed capacity of hydro and thermal power stations, excluding Zambia's share of Kariba South, amounts to 855 mw and the energy consumption during 1978 amounted to some 5,626·3m. kwh., including imports from Zaïre.

The hydro stations are located at Mbala, Mansa, Kasama, Mulungushi, Lunsemfwa and Victoria Falls, Lusiwasi and Kafue Gorge. Work has started on the Kariba North Project. The thermal stations are located on the Copperbelt. A number of diesel power stations have been installed, mostly in the North-Western and Northern Provinces.

Minerals. The total value of minerals produced in 1978 was:

	Output (1,000 tonnes)	Value (K1,000)		Output (1,000 tonnes)	Value (K1,000)
Copper (blister)	26·6	23,292	Lead	12·7	4,734
Copper (electrolytic)	629·2	533,766	Coal	615·0	15,902
Zinc	34·4	16,360	Cobalt	1·6	35,342

Agriculture. Although 70% of the population is dependent on agriculture only 10% of GDP is provided by the industry. Principal agricultural products (1977) were maize, 693,000 tonnes; sugar, 71,203 tonnes; cotton, 8,929 tonnes; groundnuts, 7,229 tonnes; tobacco, 5,900 tonnes.

Livestock (1979): 1·8m. cattle; 180,000 pigs; 51,000 sheep; 300,000 goats, and 14m. poultry.

INDUSTRY AND TRADE

Industry. In Dec. 1976 there were 32,500 persons employed in agriculture, forestry and fisheries; 64,360 in mining and quarrying; 43,080 in manufacturing; 50,270 in construction and 20,540 in transport and communications.

Commerce. In 1977 imports totalled K550m., exports K402·5m. The principal imports (1976) were electricity and mineral fuels (K726m.), machinery and transport equipment (K166·9m.), manufactured articles (K96·8m.), chemicals (K77,292,528). Principal exports (1976) were metals (K731·1m.) and tobacco (K5·1m.).

Principal trade areas in 1976 were: Other African countries: imports K800,000, exports K7·9m.; EEC (excluding UK): imports K86·2m., exports K253·3m.; EFTA: imports K25m., exports K35·3m.; other European countries: imports K10·5m., exports K29·5m.; Soviet bloc: imports K1·7m., exports K1·2m.; dollar area: imports K57·1m., exports K116·4m.; sterling area: imports K188·6m., exports K157·4m.; Middle East countries: imports K65·4m., exports K300,000; other Asian countries: imports K33·3m., exports K150·7m.

Total trade between Zambia and UK (British Department of Trade returns, in £1,000 sterling):

	1977	1978	1979	1980
Imports to UK	93,254	68,031	103,570	94,610
Exports and re-exports from UK	80,175	69,770	85,458	103,941

COMMUNICATIONS

Roads. There were (1978) over 4,588 km of tarred roads.

Railways. Zambia Railways are that part of the old Rhodesia Railways north of the Victoria Falls. In 1980 the total route-km was 1,297 km (1,067 mm gauge). The

Tan–Zam railway, giving Zambia access to Dar es Salaam, was opened in 1975, comprising 892 km of route in Zambia.

The line, connecting with Zambia Railways at Kapiri Mposhi, was opened for traffic in Oct. 1975.

Aviation. There were (1978) 130 airports in Zambia (51 government owned). Lusaka is the principal international airport. Seven foreign airlines use Lusaka.

Post. There were (1978) 13 head post offices and 219 other post offices. On 1 Jan. 1978 there were 54,475 telephones.

Cinemas. In 1971 there were 28 cinemas with a seating capacity of 13,400.

Newspapers. There are 2 national daily papers: *The Times of Zambia* (circulation, 65,000) and *Zambia Daily Mail* (45,000).

JUSTICE, RELIGION, EDUCATION AND WELFARE

Justice. The Judiciary consists of the Supreme Court, the High Court and 4 classes of magistrates' courts; all have civil and criminal jurisdiction.

The Supreme Court hears and determines appeals from the High Court. Its seat is at Lusaka.

The High Court exercises the powers vested in the High Court in England, subject to the High Court ordinance of Zambia. Its sessions are held where occasion requires, mostly at Lusaka and Ndola.

All criminal cases tried by subordinate courts are subject to revision by the High Court.

Religion. Freedom of worship is one of the constitutional rights of Zambian citizens. Minority groups, such as the Asian community, are free to practise the religions of Hinduism and Islam, and the views of the leaders of these communities are respected by the Government. The Lumpa Church was banned in 1965 for security reasons, following considerable loss of life, but the Jehovah's Witnesses are allowed to continue their way of life despite the conflict of authority in their views and the views of politicians.

The Christian faith has largely replaced traditional African religion, and the Christian Churches number about 500,000 members and adherents. The Churches, founded mainly from the Western world, are slowly finding their autonomy—as illustrated by the United Church of Zambia (formerly British and French missions) and the Reformed Church of Zambia (formerly South African mission).

There is close co-operation between Catholic and Protestant churches, and the Protestant churches themselves work in the fields of radio, television, education, medicine, refugee aid, etc., through the Christian Council of Zambia. The United Church and the Anglican Church are holding union discussions, and Roman Catholic, Anglican and United Church leaders meet together for consultation, and together they discuss matters of common concern with the President of Zambia, Dr Kaunda.

Education. In 1977 the primary school enrolments were 936,817, secondary school enrolments were 83,757 and 3,752 students were enrolled for teacher-training. In 1977 the University of Zambia had 3,111 full-time students. Government expenditure on education in 1974 was K91·36m.

Health. In 1978 there were 82 hospitals and over 1,000 children's clinics served by 423 doctors.

DIPLOMATIC REPRESENTATIVES

OF ZAMBIA IN GREAT BRITAIN (7–11 Cavendish Pl.,
London, W1N 0HB)

High Commissioner: Lombe Phyllis Chibesakunda (accredited 11 Oct. 1977).

OF GREAT BRITAIN IN ZAMBIA (Independence Ave., Lusaka)

High Commissioner: John R. Johnson, CMG.

OF ZAMBIA IN THE USA (2419 Massachusetts Ave., NW,
Washington, D.C., 20008)

Ambassador: Putteho M. Ngonda.

OF THE USA IN ZAMBIA (PO Box 1617, Lusaka)

Ambassador: Frank G. Wisner.

OF ZAMBIA TO THE UNITED NATIONS

Ambassador: Paul Lusaka.

Books of Reference

General Information: The Director, Zambia Information Services, PO Box 50020, Lusaka.

Office of National Development and Planning, *First National Development Plan 1966–70*
Central Statistical Office, Lusaka, *Statistical Year-Book, 1973*
Laws of Zambia. 13 vols. Govt. Printer, Lusaka
Bond, G. C., *The Politics of Change in a Zambian Community.* Univ. of Chicago Press, 1976
Gann, L. H., *History of Northern Rhodesia to 1953.* London, 1964
Hall, R., *Kaunda, Founder of Zambia.* London, 1964
Kaunda, Kenneth D., *Zambia Shall be Free.* London, 1962.—*Humanism in Zambia.* Lusaka. 2
  vols. 1967 and 1974.—*Zambia's Economic Revolution.* Lusaka, 1968.—*Zambia's Guidelines
  for the Next Decade.* Lusaka, 1968.—*Letter to my Children.* Lusaka, 1973
Kay, G., *A Social Geography of Zambia.* London, 1967
Legum, C., *Zambia Independence and Beyond.* London, 1966
Mebeelo, H., *Reaction to Colonialism.* London, 1971
Mulford, D. C., *The Northern Rhodesia General Election 1962.* OUP, 1964.—*Zambia, the
  Politics of Independence 1957–64.* OUP, 1968
Mwanakatwe, J., *The Growth of Education in Zambia.* London, 1968
Roberts, A., *A History of Zambia.* London, 1977
Sklar, R. L., *Corporate Power in an African State.* Univ. of California Press, 1976
Schultz, J., *Land Use in Zambia.* Munich, 1976
Tordoff, W., *Politics in Zambia.* Manchester Univ. Press, 1974

ZIMBABWE

Capital: Salisbury (Harare)
Population: 7·4m. (1980)
GNP per capita: US$532 (1979)

HISTORY. Prior to Oct. 1923 Southern Rhodesia, like Northern Rhodesia, was under the administration of the British South Africa Co. In Oct. 1922 Southern Rhodesia voted in favour of responsible government. On 12 Sept. 1923 the country was formally annexed to His Majesty's Dominions, and on 1 Oct. 1923 government was established under a governor, assisted by an executive council, and a legislature, with the status of a self-governing colony. For the history of the period 1961–1979 including the period of unilateral declaration of independence *see* THE STATESMAN'S YEAR-BOOK, 1980–81, pp. 1623–25.

AREA AND POPULATION. Zimbabwe is situated between the northern border of the Transvaal and the Zambezi River and is bordered on the east by Mozambique and on the west by the republic of Botswana. The area is 150,699 sq. miles (390,308 sq. km). The capital is Salisbury (Harare). The growth of the population is given in the following table:

	European (census)			*Asiatic and Coloured*	*African total (estimated)*	*Total population (estimated)*
	Males	*Females*	*Total*			
1911	15,580	8,026	23,606	2,912	745,000	772,000
1931	27,280	27,630	49,910	4,102	1,076,000	1,130,000
1941	36,615	32,339	68,954	6,521	1,404,000	1,479,000
1951	71,307	64,289	135,596	10,283	2,170,000	2,320,000
1961	111,720	109,784	221,504	17,812	3,618,150[1]	3,857,466
1969	114,791	113,505	228,296	24,118	4,846,930[2]	5,099,340[2]
1979	—	—	232,000	35,300	6,860,000	7,130,000
1980	—	—	223,000	36,800	7,100,000	7,360,000

[1] Actual Census, April–May 1962.   [2] Actual Census, March–April 1969

Population of main urban areas (1979 estimate):

	Europeans		*Africans*	*Asiatic*	*Coloured*	*Total*
	1978	*1979*				
Salisbury	113,400	103,900	510,000	4,900	8,400	627,000
Bulawayo	54,800	51,100	300,000	2,900	9,200	363,000
Gwelo	8,300	7,600	61,000	400	1,100	70,000
Umtali	8,800	8,100	54,000	600	700	63,000
Que Que	3,900	3,500	47,000	300	300	51,000
Gatooma	2,300	2,100	31,000	200	300	33,000
Wankie	2,600	2,500	30,000	—	—	33,000
Sinoia	1,700	1,400	25,000	300	100	27,000
Fort Victoria	2,500	2,300	21,000	200	300	24,000
Marandellas	2,100	1,900	21,000	—	—	23,000

Vital statistics (European):

	1973	*1974*	*1975*	*1976*	*1977*	*1978*	*1979*
Births	4,401	4,528	4,347	4,079	3,458	3,118	2,695
Deaths	2,042	2,122	2,016	2,085	2,188	2,249	2,224
Immigrants	9,433	9,649	12,425	7,782	5,730	4,360	3,416

In 1979 the European birth rate was 11 per 1,000; the crude death rate, 9·1 per 1,000, and infant mortality, 14 per 1,000. Figures for Africans were estimated as follows (1969): Births, 52 per 1,000; deaths, 16 per 1,000.

CONSTITUTION AND GOVERNMENT. At the Commonwealth Conference held in Lusaka in Aug. 1979 agreement was reached for a new Constitutional Conference to he held in London and this took place between 10 Sept. and 15 Dec.

1979 at Lancaster House. It was attended by the various factions in Zimbabwe-Rhodesia, including Abel Muzorewa, Robert Mugabe and Joshua Nkomo, and was chaired by Lord Carrington. It achieved 3 objectives: (*i*) the terms of the Constitution for an independent Zimbabwe; (*ii*) terms for a return to legality: and (*iii*) a ceasefire. Lord Soames became Governor-General of Southern Rhodesia in Dec. and elections took place in March 1980.

Zimbabwe African National Union (ZANU) won 57 of the 80 black seats, Zimbabwe African People's Party (ZAPU), 20 and United National Council (UANC), 3.

Southern Rhodesia became the Republic of Zimbabwe on 18 April 1980.

President: Canaan Banana.

The Cabinet in March 1981 was composed as follows:

The Prime Minister, Minister of Defence and Minister of the Public Service: Robert Gabriel Mugabe.

Deputy Prime Minister: Simon Muzenda. *Without Portfolio:* Joshua Nkomo. *Finance:* Enos Nkala. *Mines:* Maurice Nyagumbo. *Economic Planning and Development:* Dr Bernard Chidzero. *Home Affairs:* Richard Hove. *Foreign Affairs:* Dr Witness Mangwende. *Labour and Social Services:* Kumbirai Kangai. *Natural Resources and Water Development:* Joseph Msika. *Transport:* Josiah Chinamano. *Justice and Constitutional Affairs:* Simbi Mubako. *Works:* Clement Muchachi. *Minister of State in the Prime Ministers Office:* Emmerson Mnangagwa. *Education and Culture:* Dzingai Mutumbuka. *Youth, Sport and Recreation:* Ernest Kadungure. *Lands, Resettlement and Rural Development:* Dr Sydney Sekeramayi. *Agriculture:* Senator Denis Norman. *Information and Tourism:* Dr Nathan Shamuyarira. *Roads and Road Traffic, Posts and Telecommunications:* Tarcicius Silundika. *Manpower Planning and Development:* Frederick Shava. *Trade and Commerce:* David Smith. *Local Government and Housing:* Dr Eddison Zvobgo. *Health:* Herbert Ushewokunze. *Community Development and Women's Affairs:* Teurai Nhongo. *Industry and Energy Development:* Dr Simba Makoni.

National flag: Seven horizontal stripes of green, yellow, red, black, red, yellow and green; on a white black-edged triangle in the hoist a red star surmounted by the Zimbabwe Bird in yellow.

Some municipal elections were held in Nov. 1980.

DEFENCE

Army. The National Army of Zimbabwe was being formed in 1980–81 and at the time of going to press its exact strength was not known.

Air Force. The Zimbabwe Air Force (regular) has a strength of about 1,500 personnel and 162 aircraft in 8 squadrons, of which 2 are intended primarily for a training role. Headquarters ZAF and New Sarum ZAF station are in Salisbury; the second main base is at Thornhill, Gwelo, with many secondary airfields throughout the country. Equipment includes 1 squadron of Canberra bombers with added underfuselage rocket racks; 1 squadron of Hunter FGA.9 and Vampire FB.9 fighter-bombers, supported by a squadron of Vampire two-seater trainers used also in a strike role; a transport squadron with 4 twin-engined Islanders, a Cessna 402, 13 C-47s and a DC-7C; a squadron with 6 AL.60F5 Trojans for forward air control and 17 Reims/Cessna 337 Lynx attack aircraft; a squadron with 14 SIAI-Marchetti SF.260W Genet light attack aircraft and 17 SF.260C Genet trainers; a helicopter liaison/transport squadron with 49 Allouette II/IIIs and 10 Bell 205s; and a squadron of 6 Cessna 185 light utility aircraft.

INTERNATIONAL RELATIONS
Membership. Zimbabwe is a member of VN and is an ACP state of EEC.

ECONOMY
Budget. Revenue and expenditure (in Z$1,000) for years ending 30 June:

	1976–77	1977–78	1978–79	1979–80	1980–81[1]
Revenue	530,871	610,280	580,193	674,363	863,211
Ordinary expenditure: From revenue and loan funds	683,190	821,276	922,963	1,125,244	1,366,886

[1] Estimate.

Receipts during the year ended 30 June 1979 were (in Z$1,000): Income and profits tax, 315,864; taxes on goods and services, 600,506; transfers (including pensions), 371,776.

The gross amount of the public debt outstanding in June 1980 was Z$1,666,606,316.

Currency. On 17 Feb. 1970 decimal currency was adopted. The unit of currency is the Zimbabwe *dollar* divided into 100 *cents*. In Sept. 1981, £1 = Z$1·41; US$1 = Z$0·65.

Banking. The Reserve Bank of Zimbabwe is the country's central bank; it became operative when the Bank of Rhodesia and Nyasaland ceased operations on 1 June 1965. It acts as banker to the Government and to the commercial banks and as agent of the Government for important financial operations. It is also the central note-issuing authority and co-ordinates the application of the Government's monetary policy.

The post office savings bank had Z$70·8m. fixed deposits at 30 June 1980.

The commercial banks are Barclays Bank International Ltd, Grindlays Bank Ltd, Rhobank Ltd, Standard Bank Ltd, Bank of Credit and Commerce (Zimbabwe) Ltd.

Weights and Measures. The metric system is in use but the US short ton is also used.

ENERGY AND NATURAL RESOURCES

Minerals. The total value of all minerals produced in 1979 was Z$314,804,000. Output (in 1,000 tonnes) and value (in Z$1,000):

	Output			Value		
	1977	1978	1979	1977	1978	1979
Asbestos	273·2	248·9	259·6	67,032	67,007	65,864
Gold (1,000 oz.)	402·0	399·0	386·0	37,214	51,855	80,912
Chrome ore	677·3	477·8	541·8	19,917	13,452	16,139
Coal	3,029·0	3,065·0	3,188·0	21,051	23,708	25,843
Copper	34·8	33·8	29·6	21,964	23,044	35,149
Nickel	16·7	15·7	14·6	42,826	39,456	45,077
Iron Ore	1,176·0	1,123·0	1,201·0	6,833	7,851	7,387
Silver (1,000 oz.)	207·0	1,190·0	977·0	599	4,043	7,259

Agriculture. The most important single food crop in Zimbabwe is maize, the staple food of a large proportion of the population; production in 1977–78 was 1,102,000 tonnes. The livestock industry is second to tobacco as regards its export potential. The country is self-sufficient in dairy production and sales of milk to the Dairy Marketing Board in 1977–78 were 149·8m. kg.

The citrus estates of the British South Africa Company, the state-owned deciduous orchards at Inyanga and a scheme for large-scale citrus growing at Hippo Valley form the basis of the citrus fruit industry in Zimbabwe. However, many parts of the country between 2,500 and 4,000 ft above sea-level are suitable for citrus culture, and large numbers of deciduous fruit trees planted in the Melsetter and Inyanga areas are coming into production.

In 1977–78 seed cotton production was 147,000 tonnes and irrigated wheat production (1978) was 203,000 tonnes.

Zimbabwe has 7 large tea plantations, 2 of which are in the Inyanga district and 5 in Chipinga; production in 1979 was 3,000 tonnes. Coffee growing is of increasing importance. Other crops grown in substantial quantities include small grains (sorghums and millet), soya beans, groundnuts and vegetables. These crops form the basis of much subsistence farming undertaken by the African population.

Tobacco is the most important single product, amounting to about half the total agricultural output (by value). In 1965 tobacco accounted for Z$65m. out of a total of agricultural output of Z$136m.; 1978, Z$84m. out of a total of Z$418m.

Livestock (1979): Cattle, 5m.; asses, 97,000; pigs, 218,000; sheep, 754,000; goats, 2m.; poultry, 8·7m.

INDUSTRY AND TRADE

Industry. Manufacturing industries are becoming increasingly important and have been stimulated by the abrogation of the Customs Convention with the Union in 1955 and the substitution of a trade agreement. In 1973 agriculture formed 10·4% and manufacturing 23·4% of the total economy.

Labour. In 1979 the monthly average number of persons in employment was 989,000. Largest employers of labour were agriculture (333,900), manufacturing (145,100), construction (41,300), mining (59,600), hotels and restaurants (67,700) and domestic service (114,300).

There is a system of national employment bureaux, including youth employment and careers advisory services.

The conditions of service for all workers in industry are negotiated through the 21 Industrial Councils and the 69 Industrial Boards established under the Industrial Conciliation Act. The training, including full-time technical training, and conditions of employment for apprentices are determined by Apprenticeship Committees established in terms of the Apprenticeship Training and Skilled Manpower Development Act.

Workmen's compensation is by compulsory insurance through a government established fund. Health and safety in industry is safeguarded through the Factories and Works Act.

Commerce. Imports and exports (in Z$1,000):

	1975	1976	1977	1978	1979
Imports	461,761	380,518	388,157	404,239	550,908
Exports	517,144	551,583	540,750	612,364	702,302

Principal imports in 1978: Petroleum products, Z$79,016,000; machinery and equipment, Z$72,448,000; transport and equipment, Z$29·67m.; textiles, Z$19,963,000; steel products, Z$17,099,000; chemicals, Z$15·44m.; insecticides, fungicides etc, Z$10,921,000; medicines and drugs, Z$9·66m.

Principal exports in 1978: Unmanufactured tobacco, Z$116,519,000; asbestos, Z$57,344,000; gold, Z$49·8m.; cotton lint, Z$40,063,000; steel, Z$38,945,000; nickel and nickel alloys, Z$36,542,000; meat, Z$34,556,000; ferrochrome, Z$31·6m.; copper, Z$26,857,000; maize, Z$25,433,000; clothing, Z$11,878,000.

Total trade between Rhodesia and UK (British Department of Trade returns, in £1,000 sterling):

	1976	1977	1978	1979	1980
Imports to UK	211	208	234	325	28,632
Exports and re-exports from UK	1,205	1,057	1,146	1,497	16,209

Tourism. In 1979, 79,400 tourists visited Zimbabwe.

COMMUNICATIONS. The Minister of Transport and Power is responsible for the Government's relations with the Zimbabwe Railways and with Air Zimbabwe.

Roads. The Ministry of Roads and Road Traffic is responsible for the construction and maintenance of all main roads and bridges in the country, and assists and supervises junior road authorities who look after the secondary roads. Main roads connect all the main centres of the country with one another and with adjacent territories, and secondary roads serve rural areas. The total length of main roads is 10,000 km and of secondary roads, 73,000 km.

Number of motor vehicles excluding military (Oct. 1966) in Rhodesia: Private cars, 109,408; commercial vehicles (excluding farm tractors), 32,515.

Railways. Zimbabwe is served by the National Railways of Zimbabwe, which connect with the South African Railways to give access to the South African ports; with the Mozambique Railways to give access to the ports of Beira and Maputo; and with the Zambia railway system. In Sept. 1974 another branch of Zimbabwe Railways was opened, which connects with South African Railways at Beitbridge. There were 3,470 km in 1980. In 1978–79 Zimbabwe Railways carried 11·6m. tons of freight and 1·8m. passengers.

Aviation. Air Zimbabwe, in association with Central African Airways, South Africa Airways, Air Malawi and DETA, operates regular scheduled services to Malawi, Mauritius, Mozambique, the Republic of South Africa, and UK. In 1972–73 the Corporation flew 202,146 passenger-miles.

Shipping. Zimbabwe outlets to the sea are the South African ports.

Post and Broadcasting. In 1979 there were 144 post offices and 42 postal agencies. At 1 Jan. 1978 there were 196,750 telephones in Zimbabwe served by 96 exchanges. Zimbabwe Broadcasting Corporation is an independent statutory body broadcasting general service in English and African service in English, Shona, N'debele and Nyanja and 3 regional commercial services in English on medium- and short-waves. Zimbabwe Television Ltd broadcasts one programme 42 hours a week *via* 3 transmitters. In June 1980 there were 74,308 television and 131,379 radio licences.

JUSTICE, RELIGION, EDUCATION AND WELFARE

Justice. The High Court consists of an appellate division and a general division. The appellate division consists of the Chief Justice, the Judge President and at least one other judge of appeal. The general division consists of a number of puisne judges. The appellate division considers appeals from the general division and the lower courts; the general division has full jurisdiction, civil and criminal, over all persons and matters within Zimbabwe. The Chief Justice is the head of the judiciary of Zimbabwe. The Judge President presides over the appellate division in the absence of the Chief Justice. The Courts sit at Salisbury and Bulawayo, and sittings of the general division are held at 3 other principal towns three times a year.

Regional Courts, established in Salisbury and Bulawayo, are intermediate in jurisdiction between the magistrates courts and the High Court, but have no civil jurisdiction. There are 19 principal courts of magistrates and 64 periodical courts presided over by magistrates.

African Courts have jurisdiction over African persons in civil matters which are decided in accordance with African law and custom.

Religion. The largest religious groups are the Anglicans with 86,000 members (36% of the non-African populations), the Presbyterians with 29,000 members (12%) and the Roman Catholics with 35,500 (15%). There are no accurate figures for Africans.

Education. Education is non-racial at all levels and not compulsory.

Government primary schools offer free tuition; government secondary schools charge from Z$8–Z$36 per term. All instruction is given in English. There are also over 3,000 private primary schools and over 140 private secondary schools, all of which must be registered by the Ministry of Education and Culture.

A number of community schools have been established throughout the country, the teachers for which are provided by the government.

There are 8 teacher's training colleges, 4 of which are in association with the University of Zimbabwe.

The University of Zimbabwe provides facilities for higher education. In 1979 the total enrolment of full- and part-time students in the 6 Faculties of Arts, Education, Engineering, Medicine, Science and Social Studies, was 1,931. Of the 1,481 full-time students, 966 were Africans.

Health. In 1977 there were 114 hospitals, clinics and health centres operated by the Ministry of Health; 63 hospitals and clinics were operated by medical missions with government grants-in-aid and 46 without government grants. There was one medical practitioner for every 7,174 inhabitants in Zimbabwe and there was 1 hospital bed for every 347 inhabitants.

Social Welfare. The Children's Protection and Adoption Act provides for the establishment of juvenile courts, the protection, welfare and supervision of children and juveniles; the establishment of corrective institutions and the treatment therein; the recognition, registration and inspection of certified institutions for the reception and custody of juveniles; for the adoption of minors and other matters. Administrative procedures make provision for public assistance and certain grants-in-aid.

DIPLOMATIC REPRESENTATIVE

OF ZIMBABWE IN GREAT BRITAIN
(Zimbabwe Hse., 429 Strand, London, WC2R OSA)

High Commissioner: R. T. Zwinoira.

OF GREAT BRITAIN IN ZIMBABWE
(Stanley Hse., Stanley Ave., Salisbury)

High Commissioner: Ronald Archer Campbell Byatt, CMG.

OF THE USA IN ZIMBABWE
Ambassador: Robert V. Keely.

Books of Reference

Statistical Information: The Central Statistical Office, PO Box 8063, Causeway, Salisbury, Zimbabwe, originated in 1927 as the Southern Rhodesian Government Statistical Bureau. Ten years later its name was changed to Department of Statistics, and in 1948 it assumed its present title when it took over responsibility for certain Northern Rhodesian and Nyasaland statistics (which it relinquished in Dec. 1963 on the dissolution of the Federation). It publishes *Monthly Digest of Statistics.*

Akers, M., *Encyclopaedia Rhodesia.* Salisbury, 1973
Blake, R., *A History of Rhodesia.* London, 1977
Bowman, L. W., *Politics in Rhodesia: White Power in an African State.* OUP, 1974
Cann, L. H., *A History of Southern Rhodesia to 1934.* London, 1965
Davies, D. K., *Race Relations in Rhodesia.* London, 1975
Good, R. C., *U.D.I.: The International Politics of the Rhodesian Rebellion.* London, 1973
Gray, R., and Gelfand, L. H., *Huggins of Rhodesia.* London, 1964
Hanna, A. I., *The Story of the Rhodesias and Nyasaland.* 2nd ed. London, 1965
Howarth, D., *The Shadow of the Dam: The Story of Lake Kariba.* London, 1961
Lardner-Burke, D., *Rhodesia: The Story of the Crisis.* London, 1966
Meredith, M., *The Past is Another Century: Rhodesia 1890–1979.* London, 1979
Morris-Jones, W. H., (ed.) *From Rhodesia to Zimbabwe.* London, 1980
Murphee, M. W. (ed.), *Education, Race and Employment.* Lichfield, 1975
O'Meara, P., *Rhodesia: Racial Conflict or Co-Existence.* Cornell Univ. Press, 1975
Palley, C., *The Constitutional History and Law of Southern Rhodesia, 1888–1965.* OUP, 1966
Palmer, R., *Land and Racial Domination in Rhodesia.* London, 1977
Rayner W., *The Tribe and its Successors: An Account of Traditional Life and European Settlement in Southern Rhodesia.* London, 1962
Sithole, N., *Roots of a Revolution.* OUP, 1977
Vambe, L., *From Rhodesia to Zimbabwe,* London, 1976
Windrich, E., *The Rhodesian Problem: A Documentary Record 1923–73.* London, 1975.—*Britain and the Politics of Rhodesian Independence.* London, 1978

Reference Library: National Archives of Zimbabwe, PO Box 8043, Causeway, Salisbury.

INDEX

PLACE AND INTERNATIONAL ORGANIZATIONS INDEX

PRODUCT INDEX